ROTHMANS
FOOTBALL
YEARBOOK
1997-98

D1341569

EDITOR: GLENDA ROLLIN
EXECUTIVE EDITOR: JACK ROLLIN

HEADLINE

First published in 1997
by HEADLINE BOOK PUBLISHING

10 9 8 7 6 5 4 3 2 1

Front cover photographs: (top left) Wayne Collins (Sheffield W), Alan Shearer (Newcastle U), Scott Oakes (Sheffield W) – *Action Images*; (centre left) Peter Schmeichel (Manchester U) – *Colorsport*; (bottom left) Steve McManaman, Robbie Fowler (Liverpool), Mark Hughes (Chelsea) – *Colorsport*; (right) Ian Wright (Arsenal) – *Action Images*.

Back cover photographs: (left) Juninho (Middlesbrough), Kenny Cunningham (Wimbledon) – *Colorsport*; (right) Sasa Curcic, Dwight Yorke (Aston Villa), Carlton Palmer, Richard Jobson (Leeds U) – *Colorsport*.

British Library Cataloguing in Publication Data
Rothmans Football Yearbook.—1997–98
1. Association Football—Serials
796.334'05

ISBN 0 7472 1930 3 (hardback)
ISBN 0 7472 7738 9 (softback)

Typeset by Wearset, Boldon, Tyne and Wear

Printed and bound in Great Britain by
Mackays of Chatham PLC,
Chatham, Kent

HEADLINE BOOK PUBLISHING
A division of Hodder Headline PLC
338 Euston Road
London NW1 3BH

CONTENTS

INTERNATIONAL FOOTBALL

NON-LEAGUE FOOTBALL

INFORMATION AND RECORDS

INTRODUCTION

The 28th edition of Rothmans Football Yearbook features several innovations including the listing of goal times for domestic matches, articles on the League Managers Association, the National Federation of Supporters clubs, women's football, world transfer records and discipline.

Detailed and varied coverage involves the FA Premier League, Football League, Scottish, Welsh and Irish football, foreign internationals, amateur, schools, university, reserve team, extensive non-league information, awards, records and international directory, the Football Trust, Football and the Law, referees and the work of chaplains. There is also up-to-date data on the 1998 World Cup qualifying tournament.

Transfer fees are given where known. When two clubs have differed as to the amount of a record move, the lower figure has been quoted in both instances. Also the date when a player is signed often varies from one given as his registration.

The Editor would also like to thank Alan Elliott for the Scottish section, Norman Barrett for the Milestones Diary and Ian Vosper for the Obituaries. Thanks are also due to John English and Christine Forrest who provided their usual painstaking and conscientious reading of the proofs.

The Editor would like to pay tribute to the various organisations who have helped to make this edition complete, especially Sheila Andrew of the Football League, Mike Foster of the FA Premier League and the secretaries of all the FA Premier, Football League and Scottish League clubs for their kind co-operation. The ready availability of Football League secretary David Dent and his staff to answer queries was as usual most appreciated especially Chris Hull and thanks are due in equal measure to the Scottish Football League as well as Adrian Cook and Mike Kelleher of the FA Premier League.

ACKNOWLEDGEMENTS

The Editor would also like to express her appreciation of the following individuals and organisations for their co-operation: Glynis Firth, Sandra Whiteside, Lorna Parnell, Debbie Birch, Jonathan Hargreaves (all from the Football League), David C. Thompson of the Scottish League, Alan Dick, Malcolm Brodie, Bob Hennessy, Peter Hughes (English Schools FA), W.P. Goss (AFA), Ken Scott for Vauxhall Conference information, Rev. Nigel Sands, Edward Grayson, Ken Goldman, Grahame Lloyd, Steven Meeson and John Pericich.

Special thanks are due to Lorraine Jerram of Headline Book Publishing Ltd for her expertise, constant support, unflagging patience, sincerity, understanding, perspicacity and appreciation not to mention her unfailing humour.

Finally sincere thanks to John Anderson, Simon Dunnington and Geoff Turner and the production staff at Wearset for their efforts in the production of this book which was much appreciated throughout the year.

Tony Pullein

In September 1996 Tony Pullein, who had been one of the original members of Rothmans Football Yearbook Advisory Panel in 1970, died at the age of 62. He was editor of Football Monthly for ten years and a contributor to the magazine for more than 20.

EDITORIAL

In 1995–96 all eight FA Cup quarter-finalists came from the top division, the first time this had occurred since the competition was re-organised in 1925–26. It seemed that the gulf between the Premier League and the rest of football was widening to a chasm.

Last season, only two clubs from the Third Division survived to enter the third round stage, the first time the lowest division had had such poor representation since 1958; further evidence of the extent of the developing gap? No, quite to the contrary.

Events in 1996–97 changed the situation. Not one of the top four teams in the Premiership at the time of the fifth round had survived to the last 16. And you have to search back 64 years to find its equal.

Last season, five Premier League teams were eliminated by lower opposition, others given a fright. It might have been the continuing glorious uncertainty of the world's oldest competition, but the outcome was just as dramatic in the Coca-Cola Cup. There, though the five European entries were given byes to the third round, the final head count of Premier victims against lesser opposition was nine.

The cost of allowing Arsenal, Aston Villa, Liverpool, Manchester United and Newcastle United to enter late also contributed to the loss of almost a quarter of a million attendances in the Coca-Cola Cup. With one more game played in 1996–97, the comparative figures were 1,529,321 as against 1,776,060.

Of our quintet of contestants, Manchester United reached the Champions Cup semi-final despite suffering their first home defeat in a European tie in 40 years. Yet, not only did Fenerbahce win at Old Trafford, Juventus and Borussia Dortmund followed suit, the Germans completing a rare double over United, despite having six internationals unavailable.

On our international front, England remain on course to reach the World Cup finals in France next year. Expectations will be considerable after Euro '96 and encouraging performances in Le Tournoi during the summer, in spite of the defeat against Brazil.

The Under-21 team is progressing in its European Championship group, but there was disappointment that a weakened under-20 squad did not do better in Malaysia, where the Republic of Ireland performed above themselves to finish third with fewer choices at their disposal.

Less satisfactory was the failure of both the England Under-18's and Under-16's to qualify from their respective European Championship tournaments. However, England schoolboys remained unbeaten during the season and included a 2-1 win over Germany at Wembley, always a memorable occasion at this level.

Overall, interest in the game remains on a high. Aggregate attendances for the four English divisions totalled 22,783,163 almost one million up on 1995–96 and the highest since 1979–80. The competitive spirit which exists throughout our football, as previously described, can be effectively used to the greatest advantage as long as confidence remains at a premium.

Ability, attitude and application are the key words to success. But actually proving yourself better than the opposition is not always as easy as merely predicting it.

COMING NEXT YEAR! ... COMING NEXT YEAR! ...

ROTHMANS FOOTBALL RECORDS

to be published by Headline in October 1998

The most comprehensive football record book ever produced will include:

- All-time, season-by-season, English and Scottish League tables

- Division-by-division leading goalscorers for every League season

- Average League attendances for English clubs since 1888–89

- Record sequences of wins, defeats, unbeaten runs and drawn games

- Full results of top derby matches in England and Scotland

- Milestones reflecting main events in the game's history

- Every British club's result and goalscorer in European competition

- Full line-ups for every UK international played

- Details of all matches in the World Cup and European Championship finals

- Transfer records covering the world's most expensive players

- Year-by-year champions of all European and South American countries

- Stories behind the record-breaking teams and individuals

- Laws of the Game

AND MUCH MORE!

The FOOTBALL TRUST
Helping the game

NEW SOURCE OF FUNDING

Following the dramatic decline in the Trust's income from a pre-lottery level of £37m to an estimated income of some £9m a year, the Football Trust will now receive a major new funding package from the English Sports Council, the Football Association and the FA Premier League to secure their future and enable them to lift the moratorium imposed in December 1996 on the offer of new grants.

The announcement was made at a press conference at Brentford FC in June where the new Minister for Sport, Tony Banks MP reaffirmed the Government's policy commitment of ensuring that the Trust would receive lottery money so that it may continue its essential work for football at all levels throughout the UK.

Under the arrangement:

- The Trust will receive £5m from the FA Premier League for each of the next four years and a £5m contribution from the English Sports Council for the next three years to complete the Taylor task.
- The English Sports Council will make lottery money available on an annual basis including £2.5m for each of the next four years to enable the Trust to continue its ground redevelopment work at all levels of the game.
- The Football Association will provide £10m over the next four years—and intends to continue to make annual donations to the Trust for many years to come.

The football pools, the game's most generous benefactor over the last 30 years, can no longer contribute to the Trust in the way they would wish or have done in the past. But in addition to the package the Trust will continue to benefit from its pools-derived income—the proceeds of a 3% reduction in pool betting duty. This is presently producing some £10m a year for Trust funds.

Lord Aberdare, the Chairman of the Football Trust, which uniquely brings together all the interested parties in football, commented: "The Minister's announcement is tremendous news for British football and will have the support of everyone who cares about the future of our national game.

"This new source of funding to be added to our pools-derived income will enable the Trust to complete its Taylor work, carry on its essential safety work and continue to offer much needed help outside the professional game."

Lord Aberdare also stated that the moratorium on grant offers which they were forced to impose last December, would now be lifted. "We are grateful to the new Labour Government for honouring its pre-election promises and to the Football Association, the FA Premier League and the English Sports Council for providing this essential source of funding."

The Trust assists Training Facilities and Youth Development projects, Safety and Improvement schemes and supports heavily the non-professional grass roots scene. It will now take in discussions in Scotland, Wales and Northern Ireland with a view to reaching similar agreements for lottery cash from the sports councils.

BOB HENNESSY

Major Project Grants Season 1996–97

Club	£s Total project cost (£)	£s Trust grant (£)	Major project
Bury	489,875	306,000	New East and West Stands
Carlisle United	2,138,380	250,000 (increased offer)	Additional works to East Stand
Clyde	1,368,548	250,000	New North and South Stands
Colchester United	126,000	94,500	Redevelopment of Terrace 5
Livingston	6,000,000	500,000	New Almondvale Stadium
Plymouth Argyle	2,300,000	716,000	Mayflower Stand and Eastern End
Ross County	581,756	407,925	New Grandstand and Terracing
Scarborough	612,828	362,778	Redevelopment of West Stand
Southend United	530,250	333,431	Extensions to the West Stand
Stranraer	479,029	327,000	New Grandstand

ROTHMANS FOOTBALL HONOURS

Once again, the Rothmans Football Honours are presented to the team of the 1996–97 season, chosen by the members of the Football Writers' Association. Players eligible had to have appeared in FA Carling Premiership matches during the season. Compared to the previous season when there were no fewer than 50 different players nominated, this year only 34 received votes. While in 1995–96, the favoured formation was 4-4-2, this time the most popular system was 3-5-2.

The player receiving the highest number of votes was David Beckham (Manchester United), who was the only unanimous choice. The other two who came close to gaining the maximum recognition were Alan Shearer (Newcastle United) and Gianfranco Zola (Chelsea), who had been chosen as the FWA's Footballer of the Year.

While Manchester United's players had dominated the previous selection with Peter Schmeichel, Gary Neville, Steve Bruce, Denis Irwin, Eric Cantona, Roy Keane and Ryan Giggs all included in the Rothmans Team of the Season, this year there was a remarkable drop in the number of United players making the final count. In fact, only Neville, Beckham and Keane survived; Alan Shearer (Newcastle U) being the only other player from last season to reappear.

The previous season Ruud Gullit was the only nominee with a London club to make the final selection, this time Chris Perry (Wimbledon), Tony Adams (Arsenal), Sol Campbell (Tottenham H) and Zola (Chelsea) all gained places in the team with the three substitutes Frank Leboeuf (Chelsea), Patrick Vieira (Arsenal) and Mark Hughes (Chelsea), underlining the shift of emphasis to the capital. In fact eight different Arsenal players received votes: David Seaman, Lee Dixon, Martin Keown, Tony Adams, Steve Bould, Dennis Bergkamp, Ian Wright and Vieira.

Even Alex Ferguson's position as Manager of the Season was lost to Wimbledon's Joe Kinnear, while other managers to receive nominations were Martin O'Neill of Leicester City and Kevin Keegan, who left Newcastle United during the season.

Foreign imports figured noticeably. Apart from those making the final selection, Schmeichel, Bergkamp, Dan Petrescu (Chelsea), Roberto Di Matteo (Chelsea) and Oyvind Leonhardsen (Wimbledon) were nominated for the team, while Slaven Bilic (West Ham U, now with Everton) and Fabrizio Ravanelli (Middlesbrough) had support on the substitutes bench.

Rothmans Team of the Season

Nigel Martyn
(Leeds U)

Chris Perry   Tony Adams   Sol Campbell
(Wimbledon)   *(Arsenal)*   *(Tottenham H)*

Gary Neville   David Beckham   Roy Keane   Juninho   Stig-Inge Bjornebye
(Manchester U)   *(Manchester U)*   *(Manchester U)*   *(Middlesbrough)*   *(Liverpool)*

Alan Shearer   Gianfranco Zola
(Newcastle U)   *(Chelsea)*

Manager:
Joe Kinnear *(Wimbledon)*

Substitutes:
Frank Leboeuf *(Chelsea)*
Patrick Vieira *(Arsenal)*
Mark Hughes *(Chelsea)*

MILESTONES DIARY 1996–97

June 1996

England win UEFA's fair play award ... Germany win Euro 96

13   In Euro 96, Holland surge ahead of England and Scotland in Group A with a 2-0 win over Switzerland at Villa Park.

14   The Czech Republic beat Italy 2-1 to split Group C of Euro 96 wide open. Ajax midfielder Edgar Davids is sent home for making disparaging comments about Holland coach Gus Hiddink. Southampton sack manager Dave Merrington.

15   England go top of their group after beating Scotland 2-0 in a thriller at Wembley, Paul Gascoigne scoring a spectacular clinching goal after David Seaman saves a penalty from Scottish captain Gary McAllister.

16   Goals from class strikers are the features of Euro 96 today, two each from Jürgen Klinsmann in Germany's 3-0 defeat of Russia and Davor Suker in the 3-0 win over Denmark which makes Croatia the first country guaranteed a place in the last eight.

17   Chelsea player-manager Ruud Gullit signs a new contract with the club taking him to 1998, with a further two-year option.

18   England storm into the last eight of Euro 96 as Alan Shearer and Teddy Sheringham share 4 goals against Holland at Wembley, but a late goal from Patrick Kluivert is enough to slip the Dutch through at the expense of Scotland, whose 1-0 win over Switzerland at Villa Park is not quite enough. Wins for France and Spain in Group B see them through to the quarter-finals.

19   A dramatic last-ditch equaliser at Anfield gives the Czech Republic a 3-3 draw with Russia and takes them through to the last eight of Euro 96 at the expense of Italy. The Italians are left to rue a Gianfranco Zola spot-kick miss in the goalless draw against 10-man Germany, whose keeper Andreas Köpke, many feel, should have been sent off for the foul that conceded the early penalty. Portugal qualify, too, their 3-0 win over a much-changed Croatia eliminating holders Denmark, whose 3-0 victory against Turkey is academic.

22   Both quarter-finals go to penalties after 0-0 draws despite the 'golden goal' rule. England's heroes are Stuart Pearce, who puts the nightmare of World Cup 90 behind him to take – and score – one of their penalties, and David Seaman, who clinches victory by saving one of Spain's, from Miguel Nadal. At Anfield, Bernard Lama makes the vital save from Clarence Seedorf to give France a 5-4 margin over Holland.

23   In two more closely fought quarter-finals, Germany, who lose Jürgen Klinsmann with a first-half calf injury, struggle to beat Croatia 2-1 despite playing against 10 men for the last quarter, and the Czechs need an outstanding solo goal from midfielder Karel Poborsky to oust Portugal 1-0.

24   Chelsea player-manager Ruud Gullit agrees a club record fee of £2.5m to capture current France international defender Frank Leboeuf from Racing Club Strasbourg.

26   The dream is over for England in Euro 96 as Paul Gascoigne misses a sitter in extra time and hapless Gareth Southgate has his kick saved in the penalty decider – so Germany go through to the final to meet the Czech Republic, who also win 6-5 on penalties, over France. Later the first serious outbreaks of hooliganism of Euro 96 occur in central London, where 200 arrests are made in what the police describe as orchestrated attempts by known soccer hooligans to cause trouble. Some MPs blame the "jingoistic gutter journalism" of the tabloids for sparking the violence.

27   England win UEFA's Fair Play Award for Euro 96.

28   UEFA's decision to bend the rules and allow injury-hit Germany to draft in two new players to their squad for tomorrow's final meets with strong criticism from many quarters.

30   Germany win the European Championships for the third time, coming back from a goal down to beat the Czech Republic 2-1 thanks to an equaliser and then an extra time 'golden goal' from substitute Oliver Bierhoff, a controversial winner in that the referee chooses to ignore a linesman flagging for interference by another German player.

July
England to bid for World Cup 2006 ... Middlesbrough sign Ravanelli for £7m ... Keith Wiseman new FA chairman ... Man U capture Poborsky ... Alan Shearer goes to Newcastle for world record £15m

1   The FA inform UEFA that England will be bidding for the 2006 World Cup finals.

2   Huddersfield sign Bristol Rovers striker Marcus Stewart for a club-record £1.2m.

3   Graeme Souness signs a 3-year contract to manage Southampton. Leeds sign Charlton midfielder Lee Bowyer for £2.6m, a British record for a teenager. Wimbledon sign Millwall defender Ben Thatcher for £2m.

4   Bryan Robson completes another spectacular coup for Middlesbrough with the £7m signing of Italian international striker Fabrizio Ravanelli from Juventus, while West Ham sign Romanian striker Florin Raducioiu from Spanish club Espanol for £2.4m.

5   The influx into Britain of foreign stars continues with Chelsea's signing of Italian midfielder Roberto Di Matteo from Lazio for £4.9m, Man United's double signing of Norwegian striker Ole Gunnar Solskjaer from Molde for £1.5m and central defender Ronny Johnsen from Besiktas (Turkey) for £1.2m, and Rangers' capture of Swede Joachim Bjorklund from Vicenza (Italy) for £2.6m.

9   Transfer rumours fly when a member of the Travel Management staff, Man United's travel company, mischievously adds Alan Shearer's name to an airline passenger list for the club's pre-season friendly in Milan.

11 Solicitor Keith Wiseman, the Southampton vice-chairman, is elected chairman of the FA in succession to Bert Millichip, who stands down after 15 years. Barcelona sign 19-year-old Brazilian striker Ronaldo from PSV for £13.25m.

12 Umbro bow to public reaction and announce they will be phasing out England's much despised indigo blue change strip over the next 18 months for the traditional red.

16 Div 1 Birmingham pay a club record £1.5m for Chelsea striker Paul Furlong. Spanish club Valencia sign Brazilian striker Romario for £5m on a £1m-a-year contract.

17 Without a formal agreement since Nov 1994, when he took over as Spurs manager, Gerry Francis finally signs a two-year contract. Having fought off persistent Man Utd bids for England striker Alan Shearer, the latest of which was for £12m, Blackburn 'counterattack' with an offer of £4m for Eric Cantona. An FA rule change will now enable them to suspend players pending disciplinary hearings.

20 Man Utd sign Czech Euro 96 midfield star Karel Poborsky from Slavia Prague for £3.5m.

22 Southampton defender and former England U-21 skipper Richard Hall joins West Ham for £1.4m (plus up to £0.5m related to appearances).

23 Leeds agree to sell Scotland captain Gary McAllister to Coventry for £3m. Spurs sign Danish international midfielder Allan Nielsen from Brondby for £1.65m. Barry Town beat Dinaburg 2-1 in Latvia, having been held 0-0 at home, in the preliminary round of the UEFA Cup to reach the qualifying round and become the first League of Wales club to progress beyond the opening round of a European competition.

24 Man Utd make a high-profile signing for a low fee – Johan Cruyff's son Jordi from Barcelona for £0.8m, after the Dutch international winger forced the Spanish club to drop their asking price. England coach Glenn Hoddle appoints former Spurs colleague Peter Taylor as the first full-time manager of the U-21s. Former Rangers manager Jock Wallace dies aged 60.

25 As the High Court rubber-stamps a £16m takeover of Leeds by the Caspian Group, manager Howard Wilkinson spends £2.25m of the £12m made available for new players by signing Palace keeper Nigel Martyn.

27 Man City cut short their tour of China as heavy flooding causes chaos.

29 In a remarkable transfer coup, Newcastle manager Kevin Keegan beats Man Utd to the signature of Alan Shearer, signing the Geordie England striker from Blackburn for a world record £15m. Everton sell Nigerian striker Daniel Amokachi to Besiktas (Turkey) for £1.75m.

30 England achieve a 3-2 sudden-death victory over Belgium in France in the European U-18 Championships to gain 3rd place and qualify for the World U-19 Cup in Malaysia next year.

31 Nigeria come back from 3-1 down and beat Brazil 4-3 with a 'golden goal' in the Olympic semifinals.

August
Nigeria win Olympic gold ... Music man buys QPR for £10m ... Lee Sharpe signs for Leeds ... Man U slam Newcastle in Charity Shield ... Arsenal sack Bruce Rioch and appoint Frenchman manager ... Beckham's wonder goal ... Dalglish leaves Rovers

1 Liverpool finalise the signing of Czech midfielder Patrik Berger from Borussia Dortmund for £3.25m pending a medical. After 14 months in the job, Bruce Rioch announces that he has finally signed a contract as Arsenal manager and is waiting for the club to countersign it, while Liam Brady is returning to Highbury as head of youth development.

2 Man Utd striker Andy Cole will miss at least a month of the season after contracting pneumonia.

3 Twice Nigeria come back from a goal down against Argentina in the Olympic final and an 89th-minute winner from Emmanuel Ammunike gives them a 3-2 win and the gold medals. Demonstrating against club chairman Martin Gregory, about 150 Portsmouth fans invade the pitch at half-time during a friendly in Le Havre, France, sit down in the centre circle and force the game's abandonment.

5 The 7-year dynasty of the Thompsons at QPR is ended when music entrepreneur Chris Wright buys the club for £10m.

6 Alan Shearer returns to Tyneside to a rapturous welcome from some 20,000 fans at St James' Park. PFA chief executive Gordon Taylor warns that a players' strike in the Nationwide League (Divs 1, 2 and 3) over their share of TV cash "seems inevitable". Aberdeen make a bright start to their UEFA Cup campaign with a 4-1 victory over Zalgris Vilnius in Lithuania in the 1st leg of the qualifying round, while Celtic hold FC Kosice 0-0 in Slovakia despite having Simon Donnelly sent off after 53min. But League of Wales champions Barry Town have their keeper Mark Ovendale dismissed and lose 3-1 to Budapest Vasutas.

7 Rangers beat Russian champions Alania Vladikavkaz 3-1 at Ibrox in the first leg of their preliminary round European Cup tie.

8 Welsh part-timers Llansantffraid (pop. under 1,000) make an astonishing début in European competition, holding Poland's Ruch Chorzow 1-1 at Wrexham in their Cup-Winners Cup qualifying round 1st-leg tie, while Hearts draw 0-0 with Red Star in Belgrade, but both Irish sides go down at home.

9 Bruce Grobbelaar, who faces court proceedings next January over match-fixing allegations, signs a one-year contract with Plymouth. Leeds' Ghanaian striker Tony Yeboah is to have an exploratory knee operation and will miss the start of the season. The FA fine Liverpool central defender Neil Ruddock £2,000 for exceeding 45 disciplinary points last season.

10 The Scottish Premier campaign opens with a win for Rangers, going after their 9th straight title to equal the record of Celtic, who have Alan Stubbs sent off in their draw at Aberdeen. Leeds sign England international Lee Sharpe from Man Utd for £4.5m. Coventry sign Belgian international defenderer Reggie Genaux from Standard Liège for £1m. Terry Venables agrees to become

Director of Football at financially strapped First Division club Portsmouth. Bookmakers William Hill have stopped taking wagers that Bruce Rioch will not survive the season as Arsenal manager after heavy betting on the event.

11 Double-winning Man United's 4-0 demolition of Newcastle in the FA Charity Shield at Wembley sends tremors through the Premiership.

12 Arsenal confirm the rumours by sacking Bruce Rioch, whose 61 weeks in charge was the briefest ever by a Highbury manager; the club announce they have identified a successor who, widely tipped to be Johan Cruyff, will be revealed shortly, and in the meantime first-team coaches Stewart Houston and Pat Rice take charge.

13 With Cruyff insisting he will not be moving to Highbury, the new front runner for the Arsenal job is Frenchman Arsène Wenger, currently coaching Grampus Eight in Japan. At Old Trafford, Man Utd lose 1-0 in a friendly against Inter-Milan.

14 Arsenal still decline to announce the name of their new manager, but the worst-kept secret in the Premiership is further exposed with the signings of two French midfielders, U-21 star Patrick Vieira from AC Milan for £3.5m and, on a free transfer under the Bosman ruling, Rémi Garde, 30, from Strasbourg, who says he is delighted to have the opportunity to work with Arsène Wenger! Villa sign Yugoslav international Sasa Curcic from Bolton for a reported £4m.

15 The Premiership announce a payout of £22.2m for the end of the season, with the champions to get over £2m and the top 11 finishers at least £1m each. Ray Clemence resigns as manager of Barnet to take up the post of England goalkeeper coach. Sunderland sign striker Niall Quinn from Man City for £1.3m.

16 The new League season is launched on a Friday night by a solitary fixture in the Nationwide Division 1, Man City beating Ipswich 1-0 at Maine Road with a header from Steve Lomas. Arsenal announce that Stewart Houston will be in charge for the next few weeks as Arsène Wenger will not be released from his Japanese club until the end of September. Brighton's punishment for the crowd trouble last season that forced the game against York to be abandoned is to play a match behind closed doors and to have 3pts deducted, both penalties suspended till the end of the season, to be enforced if there is further crowd misbehaviour.

17 Fabrizio Ravanelli hits a hat-trick on his Premiership début for Middlesbrough, who nevertheless are held 3-3 at the Riverside Stadium by Liverpool. Another opening-day hat-trick is chalked up by Kevin Campbell as Forest win 3-0 at Coventry, and Man Utd match this win at Wimbledon, where David Beckham lobs the keeper from just inside his own half. Spurs' 2-0 win at Blackburn is marred by an injury to skipper Gary Mabbutt, who breaks a leg. In all, 27 goals are scored in 9 Premiership matches, including 5 in the last 19min of the 3-3 draw between Derby and Leeds. Turning up for the home game against Carlisle in Div 3, Doncaster manager Sammy Chung finds he's been sacked and that former England striker Kerry Dixon has been appointed in his place. Another Div 3 manager to suffer is Swansea's Jan Molby, who misses a penalty for the first time in 10 years and is sent off for the first time in 14. In Scotland, Rangers, helped by an Ally McCoist hat-trick, win 5-2 at Dunfermline and Celtic beat Raith 4-1.

19 Late goals by Steve McManaman give Liverpool a 2-0 win over Arsenal at Anfield,

20 Barry Town make history, overturning a 3-1 deficit in the UEFA Cup qualifying tie against Budapest Vasutas to win 4-2 on penalties and become the first League of Wales side to reach the first round proper of a major European competition. The two Scottish clubs involved also get through, Celtic with a very late goal by Jorge Cadete against 10-man FC Kosice for a 1-0 aggregate win, and Aberdeen, who almost blow a 4-1 advantage at Pittodrie but beat Zalgris Vilnius 5-4 on aggregate. Sheff Wed's 2-0 win at Leeds is their second victory in five days and takes them to the top of the Premiership.

21 An awesome 7-2 away win over Russian champions Alania Vladikvkaz gives Rangers a 10-3 aggregate win and qualification for the Champions League. The Premiership sees action for the fifth day running and Sheff Wed are the only 100% team left after two completed rounds of matches. Man Utd, trailing to two Duncan Ferguson goals at half-time, rescue their 30-match unbeaten home record with 2 goals in the last 20min against Everton. Kenny Dalglish, Blackburn's director of football, parts with the club by mutual consent.

22 Arsenal admit they approached Arsène Wenger before sacking Bruce Rioch, and confirm that Wenger is their next manager. England coach Glenn Hoddle names Matt Le Tissier, David Beckham and keeper David James in his squad of 22 for the first World Cup qualifier on 1 Sept, and Craig Brown recalls Duncan Ferguson to Scotland's squad. Hearts, held 1-1 at home by Red Star Belgrade, go out of the European Cup-Winners Cup on away goals, while Llansantffraid's fairy-tale is over after their 5-0 defeat by Ruch Chorzow. Glentoran are demolished 8-0 by Sparta Prague.

23 Man City sign Arsenal striker Paul Dickov for £1m. Darren Anderton of Spurs has another groin injury and has to pull out of the England squad.

24 The Premiership have to take Sheff Wed seriously after they maintain their 100% record with a 2-1 win over Newcastle at St James' Park. Rangers scrape a 1-0 win over Dundee Utd at Ibrox to remain the only 100% club in the Scottish Premier.

25 Blackburn win their first point of the season, holding champions Man Utd 2-2 at Old Trafford.

26 Man City fans have their way and manager Alan Ball resigns. Wimbledon, beaten 1-0 at Leeds, remain the only pointless Premiership club after 3 games.

29 Man City are shocked when George Graham declines their offer to take charge at Maine Road. Coventry assistant manager Gordon Strachan causes the temporary abandonment of their reserve match at West Brom when he refuses to leave the field after being red-carded for foul and abusive language.

30 With Tony Adams out through injury, Glenn Hoddle appoints Alan Shearer England captain, apparently for the World Cup qualifying campaign.

31 In World Cup qualifiers, Wales beat San Marino 6-0, Ireland win 5-0 in Liechtenstein and Scotland draw 0-0 in Austria, but N. Ireland go down 1-0 at home to Ukraine. As a prelude to tomorrow's big match, England win the U-21 clash in Moldova 2-0.

September

Fine start for Hoddle ... Ray Wilkins resigns QPR job ... Leeds sack Howard Wilkinson and George Graham takes over ... Tony Adams admits to alcoholism ... Hearts have 4 sent off ... Newcastle go five for five

1   Glenn Hoddle makes an encouraging start in charge as England open their World Cup 98 campaign with an 3-0 win in Moldova in the first fixture between the two countries. FA chief exec Graham Kelly announces an FA initiative to look into the prospects of technical aid for refs, possible off-pitch timing and video evidence.
2   Sheff Wed retain their 100% record, albeit with an unconvincing 2-1 victory over Leicester at Hillsborough, to go 5pts clear in the Premiership after 4 matches, one more than the chasing clubs.
3   The biggest upset in the 2nd round of the Coca-Cola Cup is the 3-1 home defeat of Div 1's West Brom by Colchester, 3rd from bottom of Div 3, who take the tie 5-4 on aggregate. In an extraordinary 3rd round Coca-Cola Cup tie in Scotland, 1st Div Morton, at home to Aberdeen, come back from 2-0 down with 13min to go to lead 3-2, only for Billy Dodds to complete his hat-trick with a minute left and for Aberdeen to run riot with 4 goals in extra time, including a hat-trick from Dean Windass – final score, 3-7.
4   QPR are stunned by player-manager Ray Wilkins's sudden resignation. Villa win 1-0 at Everton to cut Sheff Wed's Premiership lead to 3pts. Wimbledon register their first points with a 1-0 win over Spurs despite having Vinnie Jones sent off for the 12th time in his career. The Glasgow giants move into the last 8 of the Scottish Coca-Cola Cup, Celtic smoothly by 5-1 at Alloa helped by a Jorge Cadete hat-trick, Rangers with some difficulty, 2 goals in the last 7min giving them 3-1 victory over 2nd Div Ayr at Ibrox.
5   Matthew Harding, multi-millionaire vice-chairman of Chelsea, prime minister John Major's favourite club, publicly backs opposition leader Tony Blair and gives £1m to the Labour party.
6   Spurs chairman Alan Sugar unexpectedly drops his libel case against Terry Venables after being repeatedly subpoenaed by his former manager's lawyers for documents related to the action.
7   England midfielder Steve Stone will probably be out of the game for the rest of the season after rupturing a knee tendon in Forest's goalless home draw with Leicester. Sheff Wed lose their first points and their Premiership lead is cut to 1pt by Chelsea, who beat them 2-0 at Hillsborough, while Liverpool go 3rd behind Chelsea on goal difference. Man Utd go 5th with an ominous 4-0 win at Leeds. The only English club left with a 100% record is Barnsley, whose injury-time winner at Man City takes them top of Div 1 with 4 wins, on goal difference above Norwich, who have played a game more. Rangers retain their 100% record in Scotland with a 1-0 victory at Motherwell and lead Celtic by 2pts after 4 games.
9   Leeds manager of 8 years Howard Wilkinson, having lost the confidence of the fans, is sacked by a board who finally lose their patience.
10 George Graham returns to management with Leeds after 19 months in the wilderness. Only Newcastle take advantage of a home tie against foreign opposition in the 1st leg of the UEFA Cup first round, beating Swedish club Halmstad 4-0. Arsenal go down 3-2 to Mönchengladbach, Celtic 2-0 to Hamburg, while Villa are held 1-1 by Helsingborg of Sweden. Barry acquit themselves well in Aberdeen but finish with a 3-1 deficit. Barnsley maintain their 100% record, beating 3rd-placed Stoke 3-0 to go 2pts clear in the Nationwide Div 1. Dundee Utd chairman Jim McLean appoints his brother Tommy manager after sacking Billy Kirkwood, Tommy resigning from Raith a week after being appointed. Iain Munro takes over at St Mirren, replacing Jimmy Bone, who resigned a fortnight ago.
11 Both British teams lose their away ties as the UEFA Champions League gets under way, Man Utd by 1-0 to Juventus and Rangers by a humiliating 3-0 to Grasshoppers.
12 Liverpool beat MyPa-47 1-0 in the 1st-round 1st-leg Cup-Winners Cup tie in Finland.
13 Arsenal stagger from crisis to crisis as first Stewart Houston, holding the fort while manager-elect Arsène Wenger fulfils his contract in Japan, quits to take over as manager of QPR, leaving youth team coach Pat Rice in charge, and then it is revealed that captain Tony Adams has admitted to being an alcoholic. Two old England internationals cross the border, former QPR player-manager Ray Wilkins signing for Hibs and Sheff Wed's Chris Waddle joining Falkirk.
14 Champions Man Utd beat Forest 4-1 to take over at the top of the Premiership on goal difference from Sheff Wed, who play tomorrow, and Newcastle, who beat Blackburn 2-1, Alan Shearer scoring against his old club, who are now bottom. New Leeds manager George Graham sees his side score in the first minute at Coventry, but they lose 2-1. In Div 1, Barnsley lose the last remaining 100% record in England, beaten 3-1 at home by QPR, whose caretaker boss Frank Sibley will make way for new manager Stewart Houston tomorrow. Bolton take over at the top. After the Brentford–Blackpool 1-1 draw in Div 2, a Blackpool player (named by witnesses as Gary Brabin) is arrested by the police in the team coach following an attack on Brentford captain Jamie Bates. In Scotland, Rangers maintain their 100% record and 2pt lead over Celtic with a 3-0 win at Ibrox over Hearts, who finish with 7 men, having had a record-equalling 4 players sent off.
15 With Chelsea held 1-1 by Villa, Liverpool go top of the Premiership by 2pts as the result of their 3-0 victory at Leicester, sub Patrik Berger scoring 2.
16 The FA are to introduce random alcohol tests for players, a move they stressed was planned before the confession of Arsenal skipper Tony Adams. Without the still-injured Adams, Arsenal show tremendous spirit in beating Sheff Wed 4-1 after going a goal down, Ian Wright completing

his hat-trick to notch his 100th League goal for Arsenal and his 150th for the club in 226 League and Cup matches; Wednesday have Des Walker sent off and miss their chance to return to the top of the Premiership. Arsenal officially name Arsène Wenger as their new manager. George Graham appoints former Arsenal and Ireland stopper David O'Leary his assistant at Leeds. Uruguayan-born Danny Bergara is the new Rotherham boss, taking over from Archie Gemmill and John McGovern, who leave by mutual consent. There are more managerial changes in Scotland, with Iain Munro taking over at Raith and Steve Archibald losing his job at East Fife.

17 Man City hit a new low as they crash 4-1 to 3rd Div Lincoln in the 1st leg of the Coca-Cola Cup 2nd round. Derby go down 1-0 at Luton and Spurs are held 1-1 at Preston. In the Scottish Coca-Cola Cup quarter-finals Aberdeen suffer a shock exit, beaten 2-1 at Dundee, while an even bigger surprise is Celtic's 1-0 defeat after extra time at troubled Hearts. Glasgow Rangers announce record trading profits of £7m for 1995-96.

18 Fabrizio Ravanelli scores 4 as Middlesbrough slam Hereford 7-0 in the Coca-Cola Cup 2nd round 1st leg, and Chelsea account for Blackpool 4-1 at Bloomfield Road after conceding a goal in the first minute. But other Premier clubs fare less well against opposition from the Nationwide League, Coventry, Everton, Leeds and Sheff Wed all being held at home, by Birmingham, York, Darlington and Oxford, respectively, while West Ham leave it late to equalise at Barnet. Rangers ease into the Scottish semi-finals with a 4-0 win over Hibs.

19 The PFA inform the League that players will be balloted next week regarding a proposed strike that would affect Nationwide matches scheduled to be televised live, and that the players have until mid-October to reply.

20 In an extraordinary role reversal, Bruce Rioch joins QPR as assistant to Stewart Houston, his former No.2 at Arsenal. There is more trouble at Highbury as left-back Nigel Winterburn is hit with an FA disrepute charge following crowd incidents at the match with Sheff Wed this week.

21 Patrik Berger scores another double as Liverpool slam Chelsea 5-1 and stay 2pts clear of Newcastle. With Man Utd held 0-0 at Villa, Arsenal go 3rd after winning 2-0 at Middlesbrough, Tony Adams coming on as a first-half substitute for the injured Lee Dixon and giving a polished performance. In Div 1, Palace win 6-1 at Reading. In Scotland, Glasgow stay 2pts ahead with a 4-1 win at Kilmarnock as Celtic hammer Dunfermline 5-1.

22 Arsène Wenger makes his first appearance at Highbury and confirms caretaker-manager Pat Rice as his No.2.

23 Wimbledon, who lost their first 3 Premiership matches, beat Southampton 3-1 to chalk up their 4th win on the trot and reach 6th place in the Premiership from bottom 19 days ago. Birmingham back Gary Poole is suspended with immediate effect by the FA, who have received a faxed report from Richard Poulain, referee in Saturday's defeat by Man City, alleging he was pushed by the player. The behaviour of Birmingham fans is also likely to get the club in trouble.

24 In UEFA Cup 2nd leg ties, Newcastle cruise through 5-2 on aggregate despite giving away two late goals at Halmstad, and Aberdeen scrape a 3-3 draw at Barry to prevail 6-4. But Villa are held 0-0 at Helsingborg and go out on away goals, while Celtic, who finish with 9 men, are again beaten 2-0 by Hamburg, who finish with 10. Two Premiership clubs go out of the Coca-Cola Cup to teams from lower divisions after drawing their home leg, Everton losing 3-2 at York and Sheff Wed 1-0 at Oxford. But Leeds win 2-0 at Darlington and Coventry 1-0 at Birmingham. Forest are taken to extra time at Wycombe but score the winning goal, and Gillingham beat Barnsley, also in extra time. Lincoln rub it in at Maine Road with a 1-0 victory to give them a 5-1 winning aggregate. But the performance of the night belongs to lowly 2nd Div club Stockport – defending a 2-1 advantage at Bramall Lane, they slaughter 1st Div Sheff Utd 5-2.

25 In the Champions League, Man Utd beat Rapid Vienna 2-0 at Old Trafford, but Rangers are still pointless after losing 2-1 at home to Auxerre. Arsenal put up a brave showing in the UEFA Cup, levelling on aggregate in Germany after going two down, but two late goals from Mönchengladbach put them through 6-4 on aggregate. In the Coca-Cola Cup, Blackpool, 4-1 down from their home tie, give Chelsea a fright at Stamford Bridge but eventually lose 5-4. Derby are held at home to Luton and lose 3-2. Swindon, starting a goal down at QPR, emerge 4-3 winners after extra time. Coventry's managerial duo Ron Atkinson and Gordon Strachan will face a second FA disrepute charge after an incident at Chelsea last month.

26 Liverpool reach the 2nd round of the Cup-Winners' Cup, beating MyPa-47 3-1 (agg 4-1) at Anfield, while their young central defender Dominic Matteo is called up with the England senior squad for the first time. Arsenal's Paul Merson, nearly two years after his traumatic confessions, is recalled by Glenn Hoddle.

27 Rangers fail to prevent the transmission of a controversial TV documentary in which their England star Paul Gascoigne alleges that clubs encourage players to drink.

28 With Liverpool not playing, Arsenal move up to their shoulders on goal difference in the Premiership after beating Sunderland 2-0, albeit after referee Paul Danson dismisses two Sunderland players and orders their manager Peter Reid from the dug-out. Wimbledon go 3rd after registering their 5th victory on the trot, 2-0 at Derby. Southampton record their first win of the season, a 4-0 drubbing of high-riding Middlesbrough. Palace trounce Southend 6-1 to notch their 16th goal in their last 3 Div 1 matches. Rangers go 5pts clear of Celtic in the Scottish Premier after winning the Old Firm game 2-0 with 2 second-half goals against 10 men, stretching their unbeaten run against their rivals to 7 games although surprisingly recording only their first League win over them at Ibrox for 4 years and inflicting Celtic's first Premier League defeat for 38 games.

29 Liverpool go 3pts clear in the Premiership with a 2-1 win at West Ham, and Man United's 2-0 defeat of Spurs takes them into 3rd place, both their goals scored by their "Baby-faced killer" Ole Gunnar Solskjaer.

30 Dwight Yorke hits a hat-trick for Villa at St James' Park, but it is not enough to stop Newcastle

recording their 5th Premier win out of 5 in September, a 4-3 thriller which propels them into 2nd place, 2pts behind Liverpool. Two more mangers part company with their clubs, Alan Smith sacked by Wycombe after only 15 months and Alex Miller who resigns from Hibs after 10 years, both recent targets of the boo-boys. While Brentford captain Jamie Bates has decided not to press charges against Gary Brabin with the police, the FA have charged the Blackpool defender with misconduct.

October
Extra European Cup place for England team ... Steve Coppell takes hot seat at Maine Road ... Scotland present, Estonia absent ... Gascoigne sent off in Amsterdam, wife battered in hotel ... Guatemala City disaster ... Wimbledon's 7 straight wins ... Newcastle give Man U 5-0 hiding ... Stockport knock Blackburn out of Coca-Cola Cup ... Chelsea director Matthew Harding killed in 'copter crash ... Ray Harford leaves Rovers ... Soton slam Man U 6-3 ... First home defeat for United in Europe

1   Brighton are in trouble with the FA after three pitch invasions at the Goldstone Ground during their 3rd Div defeat by Lincoln by fans anxious about the club's future when they lose the ground at the end of the season. The League alter their rules to allow clubs with players on Under-21 duty to postpone their matches (with 3 or more players on international duty). Arsène Wenger officially takes charge at Arsenal.

3   UEFA announce an extra automatic European Cup place for clubs from England and 7 other countries (Italy, France, Spain, Germany, Portugal, Holland and Belgium). Leeds and England left-back Tony Dorigo begins his comeback with half a reserve match after 7 months out. Birmingham and MD Karren Brady are ordered to appear in court on charges of advertising mis-leading ticket prices. East Fife appoint former St Mirren boss Jimmy Bone as their new manager.

5   In World Cup qualifying matches, Scotland win 2-0 in Latvia, but, but despite a brilliant perfor-mance from veteran keeper Neville Southall, Wales lose 3-1 at home to Holland, the Dutch goals coming in 8min late in the 2nd half, 2 of them from Celtic striker Pierre van Hooijdonk. But N. Ireland's 1-1 draw with Armenia leaves them with a single point from two home matches and already little chance of qualifying. In England's group, Italy win 3-1 in Moldova, with Middlesbrough's Fabrizio Ravanelli scoring 2. In Nationwide Div 2, Paul Barnes scores 5 goals in Burnley's 5-2 defeat of Stockport. There is crowd trouble at Hull where the home side go down 2-0 to late goals from Scunthorpe and lose their unbeaten record in Div 3. Man Utd striker Andy Cole fractures an ankle during a reserve match at Anfield in a collision with Liverpool stopper Neil Ruddock and will be out for nearly 2 months.

7   Man City end their embarrassing 6-week search for a new manager with the appointment of for-mer England winger Steve Coppell, 41, currently technical director at Palace.

8   A suspect package that turns out to be a sandwich delays England U-21s 0-0 draw with Poland by 2hr at Molineux.

9   England beat Poland 2-1 at Wembley, despite going behind in 7min, with an Alan Shearer double before half-time. Italy beat Georgia 1-0 with a header from Middlesbrough striker Fabrizio Ravanelli to share top spot with England in Gp 2. Ireland score an impressive 3-0 victory over Macedonia with 2 goals from Tony Cascarino to share top place in Gp 8 with Romania. But there is farce in Tallinn, where a dispute about the floodlights in what is supposed to be an evening match results in the Scots turning up by themselves for a 3pm kick-off and the match with Estonia being abandoned and initially awarded to Scotland pending a ruling from FIFA.

10   £4.5m Swedish international Tomas Brolin, 26, on loan in Switzerland where he wants to remain, is persuaded to meet with new Leeds manager George Graham, but threatens to retire rather than return to England.

12   A David Beckham goal is enough for Man Utd to beat Premiership leaders Liverpool, who are the only club of the top 6 not to win, leaving them a point 3rd behind Newcastle and on goal difference behind Arsenal, with Man Utd 4th and Wimbledon, whose 4-2 victory over Sheff Wed is their 6th on the trot, 5th. Villa keeper Mark Bosnich, booed by Spurs fans at White Hart Lane who remem-ber last season's dreadful foul on Jürgen Klinsmann, gives the crowd a mock Hitler/Basil Fawlty salute which causes a furore and he later apologises on the radio. Brentford lose the last unbeaten record in the Nationwide League when they go down 2-0 at Crewe, but they still lead Div 2 by 2pts. In Scotland, Celtic, who beat Motherwell 1-0 thanks to a goal from Pierre van Hooijdonk in the 3rd minute of injury time and despite having keeper Gordon Marshall dismissed 6min from the end, move to within 2pts of leaders Rangers, who lose 2-1 at Hibs.

14   The FA charge Mark Bosnich with misconduct after his "Fawlty" impersonation and the police might yet bring criminal charges because of the number of complaints received, while the Villa keeper explains he was not aware of Spurs traditional Jewish following. Sheff Wed break their transfer record with the signing of Benito Carbone from Inter Milan for £3m.

15   British survivors in the UEFA Cup make a shaky start to the 2nd round, Newcastle losing 3-2 to Ferencvaros in Budapest and Aberdeen going down 2-0 at home to Brondby of Denmark. Arsenal's conquerors Mönchengladbach are upset 4-3 at home by Monaco.

16   Man Utd beat Fenerbahce 2-0 away in the Champions League and move to within a point of Juventus, who lose their first points in a 1-1 draw with Rapid in Vienna. Rangers have a bad night in Amsterdam, losing 4-1 to Ajax and having Paul Gascoigne sent off, a needless dismissal for kicking an opponent. AC Milan go down for the 2nd time in 3 matches, 2-1 at Gothenburg. Arsenal's hothead Welsh striker John Hartson, the first player this season to reach 21 disciplinary points, is banned for 3 Premiership games. Southampton break their transfer record, paying Turkish club Galatasaray £1.3 for Dutch international defender Ulrich van Gobbel.

17   Sent off in a European tie last night, Paul Gascoigne wakes up to front-page headlines in the

Daily Mirror alleging he beat up his wife Sheryl in a hotel on Sunday and accompanied by a picture of his bruised and battered bride of 14 weeks – an image that threatens to turn the media and the fans against a hero, the victim of whose escapades and pranks has always been himself: now the knives are out and the debate about whether he should be dropped from the England squad begins. Serious as the Gascoigne situation is, it is put in perspective by a tragedy in Guatemala City, where more than 80 football fans are killed at the World Cup qualifier between Guatemala and Costa Rica: caused possibly by overcrowding due to forged tickets, the disaster is on the scale of Hillsborough in 1989. In Switzerland, Liverpool win the 1st leg of their Cup-Winners Cup 2nd round tie with FC Sion 2-1. Meanwhile, in the courts, another battle in the war between Spurs chairman Alan Sugar and former manager Terry Venables is resolved, with Sugar awarded £100,000 libel damages arising from passages from Venables' autobiography, but Sugar is immediately served with a writ by Venables alleging libel in a Channel 4 documentary.

18   Paul Gascoigne makes a public apology for his sending-off in Amsterdam and for allowing his domestic problems to affect his actions on the pitch, but makes no direct reference to the wife-beating allegations.

19   With Newcastle, Liverpool and Man Utd playing tomorrow, Arsenal go top of the Premiership despite being held to a 0-0 draw at Highbury by 2nd-from-bottom Coventry: they lead on goal difference from Wimbledon, whose wonderful 4-2 win at Chelsea is their 7th on the trot, and Newcastle. Div 3 leaders Fulham's 3-0 victory at Hull is their 6th successive away win, a club record. In the Scottish Premier, Rangers are held to a 2-2 draw at Ibrox by Aberdeen, who come from 2-0 down and equalise with a minute to go, leaving the Gers 3pts above Celtic, who play tomorrow; Paul Gascoigne plays – and scores Rangers' first.

20   Newcastle give champions Man Utd their biggest hiding in 12 years and their first Premiership defeat of the season, 5-0 at St James' Park, taking them 3pts clear of Arsenal and Wimbledon as Liverpool's derby with Everton at Anfield is called off because of a waterlogged pitch. Hearts come back from 2-0 down against Celtic, an injury-time equaliser denying the visitors top spot in the Scottish Premier and leaving Rangers 2pts in the lead. Washington DC United win the inaugural Major League Soccer Cup (the league championship), beating Los Angeles 3-2 in the Boston title game with a sudden-death goal in 'overtime'.

21   The FA and the League give Wembley their support over Manchester in the campaign for England's national sports stadium.

22   Ray Harford's tenure at Ewood Park slips further tonight as Blackburn are knocked out of the Coca-Cola Cup by 2nd Div Stockport with an own goal by Tim Sherwood, the ball going in-off his head from keeper Tim Flowers' attempted punch out. Chelsea are another Premiership club to go out in the 3rd round, beaten 2-1 at Bolton, and Wimbledon fail to live up to their League form and are held 1-1 at home by Luton. Coventry can only draw at Gillingham after taking a 2-0 lead in under half an hour. Rangers return to form in the 1st semi of the Scottish Coca-Cola Cup, slaughtering Premier opponents Dunfermline 6-1 at Parkhead. Villa first-team coach John Gregory takes over the vacant manager's job at Wycombe.

23   In the early hours of the morning, news filters through of a helicopter crash late last night in which popular Chelsea director Matthew Harding was killed along with the pilot and the three other passengers. During the day tributes come in from all sides for this 'man of the people', one of the richest men in the country, who had pumped £26.5m into his beloved club. Premiership sides walk the tightrope in this evening's Coca-Cola Cup ties, Southampton held 2-2 at home by 3rd Div Lincoln, Liverpool clinging on to equity in the last few minutes at Charlton, and Arsenal leaving it late to equalise at Stoke, while Newcastle and a makeshift Man Utd each win their home ties with Div 1 Oldham and Swindon, respectively, by just a single goal. In all-Premier clashes, Villa win 2-1 at Leeds in a repeat of last season's final, Spurs beat Sunderland 2-1 and West Ham, inspired by on-loan Portuguese international Hugo Porfirio, brush Forest aside 4-1. Highest scorers of the night are Middlesbrough, who beat Huddersfield 5-1. Hearts beat Dundee 3-1 in the 2nd semi of the Scottish Coca-Cola Cup.

24   England captain Alan Shearer has a groin operation that will sideline him for some 6-8wks and keep him out of England's World Cup match in Georgia. Coventry's management duo get off with relatively small fines – Strachan £2,000, Atkinson £750 – for misconduct, the former for his refusal to leave the field when sent off in a reserve match on 29 Aug, and the commission decided to take no further action on an earlier incident involving comments made to officials in the game at Chelsea. Palace sign Southampton striker Neil Shipperley for £1m. Newcastle bring in former Irish international stopper Mark Lawrenson to coach their defence on a full-time job.

25   Ray Harford, as expected, parts company with Blackburn, ignominiously dispatched from the Coca-Cola Cup by Stockport and still without a win in the Premiership, his resignation accepted this time by the board: Tony Parkes takes over as caretaker-manager.

26   In an extraordinary Premiership match at the Dell, Southampton shock Man Utd 6-3, goals from Norwegian Egil Ostenstad (3), Israeli Eyal Berkovic (2) and Matt Le Tissier making it 11 conceded by the champions in 2 matches, although they played with 10 men for three-quarters of the game after Roy Keane was dismissed. Their tormentors of 6 days ago, Newcastle, however, without Alan Shearer, go down 2-0 at Leicester, allowing Arsenal to go top on goal difference after their 3-0 defeat of Leeds. Wimbledon's winning run of 7 games comes to an end with a 0-0 draw at Middlesbrough, but they retain 3rd place as Liverpool, now 4pts behind the leaders with 2 games in hand, play tomorrow. It is an emotional time at Stamford Bridge where Chelsea and Spurs fans alike pay tribute to Matthew Harding, and the Chelsea players lay wreaths in front of the newly named Matthew Harding Stand before a minute's silence and a 3-1 Chelsea victory in which player-manager Ruud Gullit appropriately scores his first goal of the season. Bottom League club Brighton manage to hold Div 3 leaders Fulham 0-0 at the Goldstone Ground, but

they could be in more trouble with the FA after fans spill onto the pitch and police advise belea-guered chief exec David Bellotti to leave with his wife 30min before the end. It's as you were in Scotland as Celtic's 4-0 win at Hibs is more than matched by Rangers' 5-0 demolition of Motherwell, with 3 goals from Paul Gascoigne and 2 from Brian Laudrup all scored in the last 40min.

27 Liverpool beat Derby 2-1 to go 3rd in the Premiership, a point behind Arsenal and Newcastle with a game in hand.

29 Inspired by 2-goal Faustino Asprilla, Newcastle beat Ferencvaros 4-0 at St James' Park (6-3 agg) to reach the 3rd round of the UEFA Cup, but a 0-0 draw at Brondby means Aberdeen go out 2-0 on aggregate. Everton sign Nick Barmby from Middlesbrough for £5.75m.

30 More woe for Man Utd as they lose their 40-year unbeaten home record in Europe, beaten 1-0 by Fenerbahce, who can now pinch what should have been an automatic 2nd place for United in their group of the Champions League. Juventus's 5-0 demolition of Rapid Vienna makes them certain quarter-final qualifiers. Rangers lose 1-0 at home to Ajax and cannot now proceed any farther.

31 After early scares when they were twice behind on aggregate, Liverpool beat Sion 6-3 at Anfield (8-4 agg) to reach the quarter-finals of the Cup-Winners Cup, although the Swiss side become the first European visitors to score 3 at Anfield. In test cases at the Court of Appeal, four police offi-cers involved in the 1989 Hillsborough disaster have their right to seek compensation for post-traumatic stress disorder upheld.

November

Gascoigne reprieve ... Man U suffer 3rd Premiership defeat on trot, Blackburn win their 1st ... Tommy Lawton dies ... Too hot for Coppell at Maine Road ... Chelsea sign Zola ... Gascoigne gets 4-match Euro ban ... Wales slaughtered in Holland ... N. Ireland hold Germans ... Venables to coach Roos ... Gazza goals win Rangers Coke final ... Juve World Club champs ... Duane Darby hits 6 ...Bolton shred Spurs 6-1 ... Arsenal top Premiership

1 Glenn Hoddle's decision to include Paul Gascoigne in the squad for next Saturday's World Cup match with Georgia meets with considerable criticism, especially from women's organisations, but the England coach stresses that he has met with his errant star three times in the last fortnight, including sitting in on one of his counselling sessions, and he emphasises the need for counselling rather than cautioning. Div 1 Grimsby sack manager Brian Laws.

2 While Arsenal remain top of the Premiership, a point in front of Newcastle who play tomorrow, after a turbulent 2-2 draw with Wimbledon at Selhurst Park, Chelsea are inflicting on Man Utd their 3rd successive League defeat, their first at Old Trafford since Christmas 1994, by 2-1. Celtic beat Aberdeen 1-0 to go top of the Scottish Premier on goal difference from Rangers, who are held 2-2 at bottom club Raith and relinquish 1st place for the first time in 13 months.

3 Two goals from Peter Beardsley help Newcastle to a 3-1 win over Middlesbrough and a 2pt advantage over Arsenal at the top of the Premiership. Liverpool, kicking off earlier, were expected to go top at least for an hour or so with victory at Ewood Park, but Blackburn, with Chris Sutton scoring 2 on his return from injury, shock them 3-0 to record their first Premiership win of the season. North of the border, Stranraer beat St Johnstone 1-0 in the final of the Scottish League Challenge Cup to win their first major trophy in their 126 years history.

4 Hartlepool, 2nd from bottom of Nationwide Div 3, who were beaten at home on Saturday by bot-tom club Brighton, sack manager Keith Houchen.

5 The reins at Coventry are passed from Ron Atkinson to Gordon Strachan now instead of at the end of the season, and although the manager had agreed to the premature handing-over he is upset by the manner of its execution. Cambridge manager Tommy Taylor resigns to take over at Orient. Keeper David Seaman (Arsenal) is awarded the England Footballer of the Year trophy. FIFA's referees committee proposes that keepers should not be allowed to handle *any* deliberate passes from team-mates, including headers.

6 Former England international Tommy Lawton, arguably the most complete centre-forward of all time, dies at 77.

7 FIFA decide that Scotland must replay their World Cup match with Estonia rather than be awarded a 3-0 win because of its original abandonment. Liverpool striker Stan Collymore faces a big fine after refusing to play for the reserves last night. Coventry defender David Busst, who suffered a horrific leg injury against Man Utd last season, is told his professional career is over.

8 Steve Coppell quits as Man City manager after only 33 days, citing stress-related illness as his rea-son, leaving assistant Phil Neal to take over as caretaker. Chelsea sign Italian star Gianfranco Zola, 30, from Parma for £4.5m. Glenn Hoddle demonstrates his faith in the rehabilitation of self-confessed alcoholic Tony Adams by restoring the captaincy to the Arsenal stopper in Alan Shearer's enforced absence. In place of the injured Barry Horne, Wimbledon's Vinnie Jones is chosen to captain his adopted country in a secret ballot of the Welsh players. UEFA slap a 4-match European ban on Paul Gascoigne for his latest dismissal, taking into consideration his poor recent disciplinary record.

9 Hoddle gets it right in Georgia, using David Batty instead of Steve McManaman, and England come away with a 2-0 win, their 3rd out of 3. But Wales suffer their worst ever World Cup defeat, going down 7-1 to Holland in Eindhoven, where Dennis Bergkamp hits a hat-trick. The perfor-mance of the night, however, belongs to N. Ireland and their keeper Tommy Wright for a 1-1 draw in Nüremberg with Germany, to extend their extraordinary unbeaten run against the European champions to 5 matches. In Gp 8, Macedonia beat Liechtenstein 11-1

10 Scotland beat Sweden 1-0 at Ibrox, thanks to veteran keeper Jim Leighton to lead Gp 4 of the

World Cup qualifiers from Austria, but in Gp 8 Ireland are held to a 0-0 draw by Iceland in Dublin and are only 2nd to Macedonia on goal difference.

11 Troubled Man City announce an annual loss of £3.1m taking their debts to a frightening £26m.

12 Two Premiership clubs involved in tricky Coca-Cola Cup 3rd round replays away from home survive after going a goal down, Southampton beating plucky Div 3 side Lincoln 3-1, their 3 goals coming in the last 16min, and Wimbledon equalising in stoppage time before beating Luton 2-1 after extra time. Tranmere player-manager John Aldridge announces his retirement from international football, leaving himself one short of Frank Stapleton's Irish goalscoring record of 20. Two Div 3 sides appoint new managers, Russell Osman at Cardiff and David Hodgson at Darlington for the second time.

13 In Coca-Cola Cup replays, Premier sides Arsenal beat Stoke 5-2 and Liverpool beat Charlton 4-1, but Coventry, under Gordon Strachan for the first time, go down 1-0 at home to 2nd Div Gillingham. The knives are out at Maine Road for chairman Francis Lee and his board as Man City succumb 3-2 to Oxford in Div 1.

14 An early goal by Brian Laudrup gives Rangers a 1-0 win at Celtic Park, where penalties are missed by Paul Gascoigne for Rangers and Pierre van Hooijdonk for Celtic, quickly restoring Rangers' lead in the Premier League by 3pts. The League finally agree terms for a new deal with the PFA over TV money in which the PFA will get £0.75m at the start of each season with another £0.6m allocated for projects agreed between union and clubs. At the same meeting, League president Gordon McKeag is served notice to resign, but this must be confirmed by a 75% vote at an Emergency General Meeting scheduled for next month.

15 Villa keeper Mark Bosnich gets off with a £1,000 fine and a warning as the FA sensibly accept that his Nazi-style salute at Spurs was just a prank that misfired. Scottish FA chief exec Jim Farry is reported to FIFA's disciplinary committee, no reason given but presumably for remarks he might have made about UEFA chief Lennart Johansson's part in FIFA's decision to replay Scotland's World Cup match with Estonia (Johansson's country Sweden is in the same group).

16 Man Utd halt their recent bad run with a hard-fought 1-0 victory over Arsenal at Old Trafford, enabling Newcastle to stay top despite being held at home 1-1 by West Ham. Liverpool go 2nd with a 2-0 win at Leeds, whose former star Gary Speed scores 3 in Everton's 7-1 drubbing of Southampton. There are no big shocks in the FA Cup, although Cheltenham draw 0-0 at Farnborough. Peterborough and Barnet have to come back from 2-0 down to draw at Farnborough.

17 Former England manager Terry Venables takes up a 19-month £200,000 a year post as Australia's head coach and reveals he will combine it with his also-new role as chairman of 1st Div Portsmouth, spending 40% of his time 'Down Under'. Newcastle draw 1-1 in Metz in the 1st leg of their UEFA Cup 3rd round tie. The upshot of talks between Middlesbrough boss Bryan Robson and midfielder Emerson on his late return from international duty is that the wayward Brazilian will stay.

18 Man United's 1-0 defeat by Juventus at Old Trafford leaves them a point behind 2nd-placed Fenerbahce in their group and with an anxious wait until the last match, in Vienna. With goals from Ally McCoist, Rangers beat Grasshoppers 2-1 at Ibrox to record their first points in Gp A, in which Ajax's home defeat by Auxerre leaves Rangers' three rivals all on 9pts. While Juventus clinch their place in the last 8, AC Milan are still not through for sure, and their Liberian striker George Weah is accused of a serious after-match assault on Porto defender Jorge Costa. Gary Speed scores a late equaliser for Everton at Anfield to prevent Liverpool going top of the Premiership. Arsenal keeper David Seaman could be out for 6 weeks because of broken ribs sustained in their defeat at Old Trafford on Saturday.

21 QPR sign Scottish international striker John Spencer from Chelsea for £2.5m and take midfielder Gavin Peacock on loan.

22 FIFA slap a worldwide ban on Dutch striker Regi Blinker, who joined Sheff Wed from Feyenoord in March, because of claims by Italian club Udinese that they had prior claims on him. The FA fine Blackpool's Gary Brabin £500 and suspend him for 2 games for the incident with Brentford's Jamie Bates after the match at Griffin Park for which Brabin was originally arrested.

23 Newcastle hard man David Batty is sent off for, surprisingly, the first time in his career for clattering Mark Hughes, but the Magpies hold on to a 1-1 draw for the last 30min and stay top as Liverpool are held 1-1 at Anfield by Wimbledon.

24 Arsenal beat Spurs 3-1 at Highbury with 2 goals in the last 3min and move up to 2nd in the Premiership, above Liverpool on goal difference and a point behind Newcastle. In an exciting Coca-Cola Cup final at Celtic Park, Rangers beat Hearts 4-3 after losing a 2-0 lead gained through Ally McCoist, thanks to 2 second-half goals from Paul Gascoigne that put the issue beyond doubt before a last-minute consolation goal for the losers.

25 While bottom Premier club Forest are held 2-2 at home by Blackburn and fail to overtake their opponents, their board finally give their backing to the offer for the club made by the Nottinghamshire Consortium, led by Scottish millionaire Sandy Anderson.

26 Alessandro Del Piero scores the only goal as Juventus beat River Plate of Argentina to win the World Club Championship in Tokyo. Aston Villa, Coca-Cola Cup holders, are knocked out in the 4th round, beaten 1-0 by Wimbledon at Selhurst Park. There are two fine non-League performances in FA Cup 1st round replays, Sudbury beating beleaguered Brighton on penalties at the Goldstone Ground and Woking beating Millwall 1-0 at the New Den with a goal from ex-Chelsea veteran Clive Walker. Whitby go pretty close, too, at Hull, leading 4-3 thanks to a Paul Pitman hat-trick until a minute from time, when Duane Darby equalises and Hull go on to win 8-4 after extra time, Darby scoring 6.

27 All 5 of tonight's 4th-round Coca-Cola Cup ties produce outstanding action, 4 of them home wins and 1 a draw. Div 1 leaders Bolton rip Spurs apart 6-1, John McGinlay striking a hat-trick. Man

Utd, controversially putting out a virtual reserve side, go down 2-0 at Leicester. Premiership 3rd Liverpool beat 2nd-placed Arsenal 4-2 in a match of 3 penalties (Wright 2 Fowler 1) and a sending-off (Bould of Arsenal), while leaders Newcastle go down 3-1 to lowly neighbours Middlesbrough. And 2nd Div Stockport hold West Ham 1-1 at Upton Park. In the FA Cup 1st round replay, non-League Cheltenham hold Peterborough 0-0 for 90min, but go down 3-1 after extra time.

28 TV cook Delia Smith joins the Norwich board. Arsenal's £2.3m Dutch winger Glenn Helder joins Benfica on loan for the rest of the season. UEFA ban AC Milan striker George Weah pending a full inquiry into the alleged head-butting incident in the players' tunnel after their Champions League game with Porto. Peter Shilton joins Orient from West Ham in an attempt to register 4 more League games and reach 1,000.

30 Arsenal beat Newcastle 2-1 in the top-of-the-table clash at St James' Park and take over 1st place by 2pts despite having Tony Adams controversially sent off after a clash with Alan Shearer on 22min when the score was 1-1. Man Utd make 8 changes to the side that lost midweek at Leicester in the Coca-Cola Cup and beat them 3-1 at Old Trafford. Peter Beadle scores a 10min hat-trick in Bristol Rovers' 4-3 Div 2 win over Bury. With Rangers playing tomorrow, Celtic miss their chance to go top, being held 2-2 at home by Hearts. Div 3 side Arbroath sack manager John Brogan after losing 4-3 at home to Inverness. Porto drop their complaint of assault against Milan's George Weah after UEFA announce at least a 1-match suspension.

December

Premier's Parry to join Liverpool ... Man U reach Euro quarters ... Brighton docked 2 points ... Fowler poaches Rush record ... 'Fair-play' Weah banned for 6 ... No-win record for Forest ... Stockport in Coke quarters ... Frank Clark quits Forest ... Wimbledon's unbeaten run ended ... Shilton's millennium ... Magpies maul Cockerels 7-1 ... Liverpool lead Premiership by 5 ... Clark out of Forest into fire

1 Rick Parry, chief exec of the Premier League, is to resign and take up a similar post with Liverpool. Skipper Ian Rush scores his first goal for Leeds in their 2-0 win over Chelsea after 15 barren matches. Rangers ease 5pts clear of Celtic in the Scottish Premier with a 3-0 victory at 3rd-placed club Aberdeen.

2 Liverpool win 2-0 at Spurs to go 2nd in the Premiership behind Arsenal on goal difference. Middlesbrough's £4m midfield star Emerson is back in Brazil, ostensibly to escort his wife back to Teesside, but with an important match with Leicester tomorrow Bryan Robson's injury-depleted side needs him at the Riverside Stadium.

3 Faustino Asprilla scores 2 late goals to put Newcastle into the UEFA Cup quarter-finals with a 2-0 win over Metz (3-1 agg), but gets booked for celebrating the first and is carried off with a hamstring injury that could keep him out for 6 weeks. Danish club Brondby also reach the last 8 with an extraordinary performance at Karlsruhe, slamming the Germans 5-0 to overturn a 3-1 deficit from their home leg. Middlesbrough's win famine continues with a 2-0 home defeat by Leicester.

4 Man Utd beat Rapid 2-0 in Vienna to reach the last 8 of the UEFA Champions League as Fenerbahce fail to beat Juventus. AC Milan make a shock exit, losing 2-1 at the San Siro to Rosenborg, who go through with Porto. Rangers lose 2-1 at Auxerre, who qualify along with Ajax, 1-0 winners over Grasshoppers in Zurich. Arsenal take a 3pt lead in the Premiership after beating Southampton 3-1. Desperate Brighton, bottom of the League, sack manager Jimmy Case and appoint his assistant George Petchey as caretaker.

5 A powerful and moving film is shown on TV, a 'faction' drama with actors, chronicling the Hillsborough disaster through the eyes of some of those who were there and who lost relatives and accusing the Establishment and the police still of a cover-up. UEFA give the go-ahead for a trial scheme to use two referees and possibly external time-keeping. Even though Rosenborg are still in the Champions League, striker Steffen Iversen, a key performer in their defeat of AC Milan last night, moves to Spurs for £2.7m.

6 Leeds £3.5m teenager Lee Bowyer is fined £4,500 in court for incidents in a McDonald's last September. FIFA fine Sheff Wed winger Regi Blinker £36,000 for contractual irregularities but clear him to play again. Arsenal's Ian Wright and Nigel Winterburn are cleared on misconduct charges by the FA disciplinary commission.

7 Arsenal slip up at home and it is only a last-minute strike by Patrick Vieira that earns them a 2-2 draw against Derby, yet Liverpool's shock 1-0 home defeat by Sheff Wed allows the Gunners to open up a 4pt lead. Wimbledon, 3-1 winners at Sunderland, take 2nd spot on goal difference from Liverpool, both with a game in hand. Non-League sides perform their usual deeds of giant-killing in the 2nd round of the FA Cup as 2nd Div sides Blackpool and Cambridge Utd go down at home to Hednesford (0-1) and Woking (0-2), respectively. Enfield draw 1-1 at home to Peterborough and Luton have to come back from a goal down after an hour at Kenilworth Road before beating Boreham Wood 2-1. A fifth side from Div 2, Bristol City, save the League's blushes with their 9-2 drubbing of St Albans, Australian international Paul Agostino notching 4, but Div 3 Orient, with Peter Shilton in goal, lose 2-1 to Stevenage at Brisbane Road. Crewe register an impressive 5-1 win at Hull. In Scotland Rangers twice come from behind to beat Hibs 4-3 at Ibrox and stretch their lead to 8 over Celtic, who lose 2-1 at Motherwell.

8 Liverpool central defender John Scales is all set to join Leeds at lunchtime but come the evening he is a Spurs player, for the same £2.6m fee. A late rally enables West Ham to claw back a 2-goal deficit and draw 2-2 at Upton Park with Man Utd, who stay 6th, 8pts behind leaders Arsenal.

9 Newcastle are held 0-0 at Forest, their first goalless draw in 73 games, but they rise a place to 4th on goal difference, while Forest climb off the bottom above Coventry on goals scored. The

Premier League agree an extension of their Bass/Carling deal, and will receive £36m over 4 years, a 300% increase on their current arrangement. As a result of two pitch invasions at the Goldstone Ground in the match against Lincoln in October, Brighton are docked 2pts by the FA, leaving them 11pts adrift at the bottom of the League.

10 Rangers miss their chance to go 11pts clear in the Scottish Premier, losing 1-0 at Dundee Utd. West Ham's Portuguese international striker Paulo Futre retires from the game owing to persistent knee problems.

11 Spurs striker Chris Armstrong has an ankle operation next week and is expected to be out of action for 6 weeks. Aberdeen's 2-1 victory at Hearts takes them into 2nd spot in the Scottish Premier, above Celtic who now have 2 games in hand. John McCarthy, a half-brother of a victim of the Hillsborough disaster, who was at the match and watched fans being crushed to death, is awarded damages of £200,000 against the South Yorkshire Police for post-traumatic stress disorder, but relatives of victims who watched the tragedy on TV are still ineligible to sue.

12 Southampton win approval to build a new £35m stadium at Stoneham, on the outskirts of the city, and are to set about raising the funds for the project. Brazilian striker Ronaldo (Barcelona) is voted *World Soccer* World Player of the Year, ahead of Alan Shearer (Newcastle).

14 A double from Ian Dowie gives N. Ireland their first victory in Gp 9 of Europe's World Cup qualifying competition, 2-0 over Albania. Wales are held 0-0 at home to Turkey and lose the leadership of Gp 7 to Holland, whose Dennis Bergkamp-inspired 3-0 victory in Belgium takes them 2pts clear with 2 games in hand. Premiership activity is limited by this World Cup action, but Liverpool and Wimbledon move to within a point of leaders Arsenal, Liverpool with a splendid 5-1 victory over Middlesbrough in which Robbie Fowler hits 4, taking them ahead of Wimbledon, who manage only a late 1-0 win over Blackburn. Fowler's 2nd goal is his 100th for the club, achieved in 165 games, one fewer than the record of Ian Rush. Rangers beat Dunfermline 3-1 to lead the Scottish Premier by 9pts from Aberdeen, who are held 0-0 at home by Motherwell, while Celtic's game is postponed because of players on World Cup duty.

15 Serious crowd trouble scars the Bristol derby at Ashton Gate as Rovers score a late equaliser, their celebrating fans spilling on to the pitch are confronted by some 200 City fans and some Rovers players are hurt: the FA are to hold an inquiry.

16 Blackburn confirm what has been an ill-kept secret, that the Swede Sven Goran Eriksson will take over as manager in June, when his contract with Italian club Genoa expires. UEFA extend AC Milan striker George Weah's 1-match ban to 6, having considered the evidence of his after-match clash with Porto's Jorge Costa; Weah, holder of FIFA's fair play award, has cited persistent racial abuse from Costa and may still appeal. Six players are sent off in the two Scottish Cup replays tonight, 3 from each of the losing sides, Albion, who go down 4-0 at Forfar, and Highland League side Huntly, beaten 3-2 by Clyde after extra time, whose culprits include player-manager Doug Rougvie.

17 The Football Trust, whose funding by pools companies has been hit by the success of the National Lottery, is to put on hold its contributions earmarked for stadium work in the lower divisions to implement the Taylor Report. In top v bottom clashes, Liverpool beat Forest 4-2 to take over the Premiership lead by 2pts from Arsenal who now have a game in hand, while Newcastle slip up at Coventry, losing 2-1. Forest's 16th match without a win beats the previous Premiership worst of 15 by Swindon. In the one Scottish Premier fixture Rangers beat Kilmarnock 4-2 to lead by 12pts from Aberdeen, 14 from Celtic who now have 3 games in hand.

18 Div 2 Stockport come back from a goal down to beat West Ham 2-1 in their Coca-Cola Cup replay and will be at home in their first ever quarter-finals to Southampton, who just edge Oxford 3-2. Man Utd draw 1-1 with Sheff Wed at Hillsborough, so remain in 6th place in the Premiership.

19 Frank Clark resigns as manager of Forest, and Stuart Pearce is asked to take over as caretaker-manager of the struggling club. In a landmark case, former Stockport player Brian McCord is awarded interim damages of £50,000 from an opponent, Swansea's John Cornforth, whose tackle during a match in 1993 ended his career, and the balance to which he is entitled will be determined at a later hearing. Newcastle chairman Sir John Hall announces plans for a new 55,000-seat stadium to be built on land next to St James' Park and a stock market flotation to help raise the estimated £100m costs, but there is strong local opposition to the project from some quarters. The Scottish League fine 1st Div Falkirk £25,000 for fielding an ineligible player.

20 Middlesbrough cancel their game with Blackburn on Sunday as manager Bryan Robson claims he is without 23 players through illness or injury, but the club will face a Premier League inquiry. Forest captain Stuart Pearce accepts the additional role of caretaker-manager. The FA charge Liverpool's Neil Ruddock with bringing the game into disrepute over his newspaper piece criticising Alan Sugar, his chairman at former club Spurs. Falkirk sack manager Eamonn Bannon.

21 Stuart Pearce makes a triumphant début as caretaker-manager, leading Forest to their first victory in 17 Premiership games, 2-1 over Arsenal after being a goal down, Arsenal's chances of returning to the top being sabotaged by their striker Ian Wright who contrives to get himself sent off shortly after scoring in the 63rd minute. Man Utd hammer Sunderland 5-0 after a slow start and go 4th. Celtic regain 2nd place in the Scottish Premier beating Dundee Utd 1-0 as Aberdeen lose, but they make no impression on 14pt leaders Rangers, 4-1 winners at Hearts. Alex Totten, dismissed by Kilmarnock a fortnight ago, is appointed Falkirk's new boss.

22 Third-placed Wimbledon's 19-match unbeaten run is upset at Villa, who slam them 5-0 and move up to 4th. The trumpets blare and the red carpet is rolled out at Brisbane Road for Peter Shilton, who makes his historic 1,000th League appearance, in goal for Leyton Orient as they beat 3rd Div bottom club Brighton 2-0.

23 Liverpool draw 1-1 with Newcastle at St James' Park and move 3pts clear of Arsenal, who have a game in hand. Middlesbrough's Fabrizio Ravanelli criticises the club and English football on

Italian TV. Notts County sack managerial duo Colin Murphy and Steve Thompson, putting players Gary Strodder and Tony Agana in temporary charge.

26 Champions Man Utd get into gear for the New Year with a 4-0 win at bottom club Forest, heartened particularly by Andy Cole's goal soon after he returns from injury as a sub, and they go into 3rd place 5pts behind leaders Liverpool with a game in hand. The leaders can only draw 1-1 at home to Leicester to maintain their 3pt lead over Arsenal, held 0-0 at Sheff Wed, while Newcastle crash 1-0 at Blackburn. Middlesbrough wheel out the walking wounded and halt their alarming decline with a stirring 4-2 win over Everton, Juninho scoring twice in the second half. Rangers beat Raith 4-0 but Celtic maintain their position 14pts behind them with 3 games in hand by winning 2-1 at Aberdeen after going a goal down.

28 Shearer, Ferdinand and Lee score 2 apiece as Newcastle take Spurs apart 7-1 at St James' Park to move into 5th place, 5 pts behind Liverpool. Thanks to an early Cantona penalty against his old club Man Utd edge Leeds 1-0 and go 2nd, 2pts behind Liverpool and above Arsenal on goals scored, the Gunners having been held to a 2-2 draw at Highbury by Villa. Wimbledon, after winning 3-1 at Everton, are now the best-placed challengers, 4th on goal difference and 2pts behind the leaders, but with a game in hand of the others. The weather hits the Nationwide programme and a dozen games are postponed. Rangers' game in Scotland is postponed, allowing Celtic, 4-2 winners over Dunfermline, to cut the gap to 11pts with 2 games in hand still.

29 Thanks to an extraordinary blunder by Southampton keeper Dave Beasant and a flash of inspiration from Liverpool captain John Barnes, who steers the misguided clearance in from over 40 yards, the Premiership leaders come away from the Dell with a 1-0 victory and extend their advantage to 5pts. Frank Clark, who quit the Forest job earlier this month, is named as Man City's 5th manager of the season when caretaker Phil Neal stands down after defeat at Barnsley leaves them 4th from bottom of Div 1, their worst position this century.

31 Freezing conditions hit the New Year programme, causing the postponement of 23 games in England and 8 in Scotland already, with pitch inspections planned at several other grounds tomorrow. The icy spell is already threatening Saturday's 3rd round of the Cup.

January 1997

Howard Wilkinson is FA's first Technical Director ... Keegan leaves Newcastle, Dalglish takes his place ... Boro docked 3pts ... Ronaldo voted FIFA Player of Year ...Upton Park pitch invasion after Wrexham Cup shock ... Chelsea vanquish Liverpool in Cup thriller

1 With Liverpool losing 1-0 at Stamford Bridge and Man Utd being held 0-0 at Old Trafford by Villa, Arsenal, 2-0 victors over Middlesbrough, go 2nd, 2pts behind Liverpool with a game in hand, and Ian Wright's goal is his 200th in the League, but John Hartson is the 4th Arsenal player to be sent off in their last 8 matches. Only 3 Premiership games are postponed as a result of the big freeze, but the Nationwide League loses all but 9 of its 36 fixtures and the Scottish League all but 9 of 39.

2 Rangers' Danish striker Erik Bo Andersen comes on as sub for the last 15min at Ibrox and hits 2 goals to inflict Celtic's 3rd Old Firm defeat of the season and leave them struggling 14pts behind Rangers.

4 Only 14 of today's 27 scheduled 3rd round FA Cup ties take place, and Southampton are one Premiership club who wish theirs hadn't, going down 3-1 to 1st Div strugglers Reading at Elm Park, where they have two players sent off, and manager Graeme Souness vents his anger on the referee for ruling the pitch fit for play. Grimsby, however, crash 7-1 at Sheff Wed and 3rd Div Chester are brushed aside 6-0 at Middlesbrough. All but one of the 13 scheduled Nationwide Divs 2 and 3 matches are postponed. The Scottish Premier programme is unaffected, Celtic beating Motherwell 5-0 but making no headway on Rangers, 2-1 winners at Hibs.

5 In the 3rd round of the Cup, a depleted Spurs hold out for 50min at Old Trafford before succumbing 2-0 to Man Utd, Newcastle are held 1-1 at Charlton, and Cup history is created at Goodison Park, where Swindon's Ian Culverhouse is red-carded in a record 52sec for a penalty-box handling offence that sets Everton on the way to 3-0 victory.

6 Former Leeds manager Howard Wilkinson is officially appointed on a 4-year contract as the FA's first Technical Director.

7 Spurs sign Swiss defender Ramon Vega from Cagliari for £3.7m. Tonight's two Coca-Cola quarter-finals, at Ipswich and Stockport, are called off.

8 The much-revered Kevin Keegan causes consternation on Tyneside with his sudden, sensational resignation as Newcastle manager after 5 years. Assistant Terry McDermott takes over as joint caretaker with coach Arthur Cox, the former manager. There is some joy in the North-East, however, with Middlesbrough's shock 2-1 defeat of Liverpool in the Coca-Cola Cup at the Riverside Stadium, and they will be joined in the semi-finals by new favourites Wimbledon, 2-0 victors at Bolton. In Scotland, Jorge Cadete hits 3 in Celtic's 6-0 drubbing of Kilmarnock. Kenny Swain, caretaker of 1st Div Grimsby, is promoted to manager. Referee Richard Poulain, after studying video evidence, admits he was wrong to dismiss Reading's Andy Bernal against West Brom on Boxing Day, and saves the Australian defender from a 5-match ban.

9 Former England manager Bobby Robson, now with Barcelona, turns down the Newcastle job. Ipswich chairman David Sheepshanks is the first chairman of the newly reconstituted 9-man Football League board. Leeds sign Dutch defender Robert Molenaar from FC Volendam for £1m. West Ham transfer Romanian midfielder Ilie Dumitrescu to Clube de Futbol (Mexico) for £1m.

10   Middlesbrough player-manager Bryan Robson retires as a player on his 40th birthday. Liverpool sign £2m-rated Norwegian defender Bjorn Tore Kvarme from Rosenborg on a free transfer under the Bosman ruling. Former Rangers and Scotland captain George Young dies.

11   Premiership leaders Liverpool are held 0-0 at Anfield by lowly West Ham, but stay top, now by 3pts, as Arsenal not only go down 1-0 at Sunderland but have Dennis Bergkamp of all people sent off, their 5th dismissal of the season. Newcastle quickly go 2 up at Villa Park, but are eventually happy with a 2-2 draw, Shaka Hislop saving a penalty from fellow-Trinidadian Dwight Yorke. Dion Dublin is sent off for the second match running as Coventry crash 4-0 to Blackburn. With the cold spell continuing, 13 matches are lost in the Nationwide League, another 6 in Scotland, where Celtic's 2-1 win at Hearts in the Premier takes them to within 8pts of Rangers, who play tomorrow.

12   Man Utd win 2-1 at Spurs to go above Arsenal into 2nd spot in the Premiership, 2pts behind Liverpool but with a game in hand. Rangers cruise past Aberdeen 4-0 to restore their 11pt Premier lead over Celtic.

13   York go down 1-0 at non-League Hednesford in their rearranged 3rd round FA Cup tie.

14   Newcastle have a new messiah, appointing as manager on a 3½-year contract Kenny Dalglish in the hope that he will once again replace the 'irreplaceable' Keegan, as he did as a Liverpool player nearly 20 years ago. There is consternation down the road in Middlesbrough, however, as the club are docked 3pts and fined £50,000 for illegally calling off their game at Blackburn on 21 Dec, leaving them trailing by 4pts at the bottom of the Premiership, not a happy welcome for today's new £2.7m signing, Gianluca Festa, from Inter Milan. Three of the 10 rearranged FA Cup ties are again postponed. Tranmere player-manager John Aldridge is sent off in their 1-0 defeat at 3rd Div high-flyers Carlisle. In Scotland, Celtic come back with late goals to win 2-1 at Raith and close the gap behind Rangers to 8pts, both having played 22 games.

15   In 3rd round Cup replays, Newcastle need an extra-time goal by Alan Shearer to beat Charlton 2-1 in front of new boss Kenny Dalglish at St James' Park, while Dennis Bergkamp atones for his week-end misdemeanour and makes it Sunderland's last-ever Cup tie at Roker Park with an inspired display in Arsenal's 2-0 victory. The performance of the night, perhaps, belongs to 2nd Div Stockport, for a 2-0 win at 1st Div Stoke. Rangers' failure to win at lowly Kilmarnock will encourage their rivals Celtic. Juventus record an amazing 6-1 victory in the 1st leg of the European Super Cup, away to Paris SG, who dropped their exciting 17-year-old striker Nicolas Anelka after his controversial signing for next season by Arsenal earlier in the day. West Ham are returning unsettled and unsatisfactory Romanian striker Florin Raducioiu to Spanish club Espanyol after 6 months and hope to get their money back. The Southampton board reveal that the value of their shares has increased by more than 400-fold following their takeover by aptly named quoted company Secure Retirement.

16   Newcastle announce plans for a spring flotation on the stock market that will raise £40-50m. Leicester pay a club record £1.6m for Oxford defender Matt Elliott. Sam Allardyce becomes the new Notts County manager.

17   Chelsea defender and former England U-21 captain Michael Duberry is out for the rest of the season after having an op for a snapped Achilles tendon.

18   Liverpool beat Villa 3-0 to retain their 2pt lead over Man Utd, who win 2-0 at Coventry, while Newcastle's progress is halted as they concede 2 goals in the last 3min at the Dell as Southampton scramble an unlikely draw and deny Kenny Dalglish a winning start. Middlesbrough put their troubles behind them in brilliant style with a thrilling 4-2 victory over Sheff Wed, hitherto unbeaten in 14 games, all their goals scored by imports, one of whom, Fabrizio Ravanelli, is later sent off for a double-dose of dissent, but they stay bottom. Scottish Premier leaders Rangers bring on their new £4m striker Sebastian Rozental, 20, for the last 15min at Motherwell just 48hr after his arrival from Chile, and win 3-1 to retain their 9pt lead over Celtic, who beat Hibs 4-1.

19   Dennis Bergkamp scores another brilliant goal before starting his 3-game ban as Arsenal beat Everton 3-1 to keep the Premiership leaders in their sights. In Div 1, QPR make the comeback of the decade at Port Vale, after going in at half-time 4-0 down, scoring 3 times in the last 6min to earn an incredible 4-4 draw.

20   Barcelona striker Ronaldo (Brazil) is voted FIFA world player of the year with 329 points. Kenny Dalglish makes his first signing at Newcastle, capturing £2m-rated Portuguese defender Raul on a free transfer as his contract with Farense has been invalidated through the Bosman ruling. Celtic manager Tommy Burns is banned from the touchline for a year and fined £2,000 for remarks made to officials in the match against Rangers at Parkhead in November. Shadow sports minister Tom Pendry, citing a crowd-pressure monitoring system developed by nuclear scientists at Warrington, says standing areas could return to football grounds if Labour win the General Election.

21   Leicester reach the semi-finals of the Coca-Cola Cup with a 1-0 victory at Ipswich. Millwall's share dealings are suspended owing to pressure from creditors, but the club will go into administration to raise fresh capital.

22   In the last Coca-Cola quarter-final, a late equaliser enables Southampton to force a 2-2 draw at Stockport. West Brom sack manager Alan Buckley after more than 2 years in charge, assistant Arthur Mann stepping in as caretaker. Bahamas-based businessman Joe Lewis buys a 25% stake in Rangers with a £40m investment, diluting chairman David Murray's 82% stake in the club. Bristol C are handed a suspended (until 31 Dec) punishment of a 2pt deduction for failing to control spectators at Ashton Gate at the Bristol derby last month.

23   Pizza millionaire Peter Boizot forks out over £1m to buy 97% of 2nd Div Peterborough's shares, halving the club's debts.

24 More clubs are in financial trouble: Bournemouth, with debts of over £3.5m, are put into receivership by their bank, and Darlington make a voluntary arrangement with their creditors. Former Arsenal manager and England coach Don Howe has been appointed right-hand man under the FA's new technical director Howard Wilkinson. Former Port Vale player and manager Roy Sproson dies at 66.

25 It's giant-killing time again in the FA Cup, at all three stages played today: Steve Thompson scores an 89th-min equaliser to give non-League Woking a 1-1 draw at Coventry in their rearranged 3rd round tie, Kevin Russell scores a last-minute winner as 2nd Div Wrexham dump West Ham 1-0 at Upton Park in a replay, sparking a pitch invasion by some 200 distraught and disgusted home fans, and lowly 1st Div Bradford score a remarkable 3-2 win over Everton at Goodison Park in the 4th round aided by a spectacular 40-yard goal from 36-year-old Chris Waddle. In another replay, Leeds edge Palace 1-0 and Bolton slam Luton 6-2. The goals in Wimbledon's splendid draw at Old Trafford both come in the last 2min, Robbie Earle equalising Paul Scholes' goal for Man Utd.

26 In arguably the match of the season so far, in the Cup 4th round, sub Mark Hughes comes on for the 2nd half for Chelsea at Stamford Bridge to spark a remarkable recovery from 2-0 down against Liverpool to magnificent 4-2 victory, Gianluca Vialli scoring the last 2 goals on his return to favour. In the other 4th round tie Ian Woan scores twice as Forest come from behind to beat Newcastle 2-1 at St James'.

28 Two months after walking out at Maine Road, Steve Coppell returns to Selhurst Park to assist Palace manager Dave Bassett part-time.

29 Man Utd beat Wimbledon 2-1 at Old Trafford with 2 goals in the last 15min and go top of the Premiership by a point from Arsenal, 2-1 victors at Upton Park, and now ahead of Liverpool on goals, all three having played 24 games. The heroes of the night are 2nd Div Stockport, who beat Southampton 2-1 at the Dell in their Coca-Cola Cup replay and reach a major semi-final for the first time in their history. Meanwhile Coca-Cola sign a £6m deal that will take their sponsorship of the competition to the end of the millennium. Celtic win 2-0 at Dunfermline and reduce Rangers' lead in the Scottish Premier to 6pts. Everton's unsettled Ukrainian winger Andrei Kanchelskis agrees to join Fiorentina in an £8m deal, making a £2.5m profit for Everton after 18 months since he signed from Man Utd.

30 Millwall chairman Peter Mead and two banks guarantee £850,000 to keep the club playing at least for the rest of the season. Coventry sign Birmingham defender Gary Breen for £2.5m.

31 The FA learn by fax that UEFA have backed a German bid to stage the 2006 World Cup. Man City sign N.Ireland defender Kevin Horlock from Swindon for £1.25m.

February
Wimbledon ko Cup-holders Man Utd in 4th … England's first World Cup defeat at Wembley … Venables buys Bournemouth for £1 … Wright-Schmeichel feud … Penalty furore at Bridge

1 The FA fax a strong protest to UEFA over the apparent fait accompli of their covert backing for Germany's World Cup bid. Man Utd stay top of the Premiership, coming back from a goal down to beat Southampton with a late Eric Cantona strike and stay 1pt ahead of Liverpool, 1-0 winners at Derby. Arsenal are held 0-0 at Leeds and drop back to 3rd. It's the old problem at the New Den as Millwall fans try to attack the referee during their 2-0 defeat by Bristol C and hundreds invade the pitch at the end to demonstrate against manager and board. Celtic lose a great chance to make up ground in Scotland, losing 1-0 at Dundee Utd while Rangers are held 0-0 at home by Hearts.

2 Another heart-stopper for Newcastle boss Kenny Dalglish at St James' Park as he watches Alan Shearer hit a hat-trick in the last 14min for a 4-3 victory over Leicester. It is revealed that 3 years ago UEFA's executive committee (of which Sir Bert Millichip, then FA chairman, was a member) presented a document to FIFA stating that they were in favour of one country per continent candidature for the World Cup; although UEFA concede there was no minuted decision that they favoured Germany, they assert that Sir Bert has been aware of their standpoint for 3 years.

3 The row over the 2006 World Cup gathers pace, with PM John Major and Opposition leader Tony Blair reaffirming their support for England's bid. Newly promoted Plymouth sack manager Neil Warnock.

4 Man Utd suffer their first defeat in the FA Cup, other than in the final, for 4 years, going down 1-0 at Wimbledon in their 4th round replay, while in the 3rd round brave Woking are beaten 2-1 at home by Coventry, giant-killers Bolton, runaway leaders in Div 1, are themselves killed off at home 3-2 by 2nd Div Chesterfield thanks to a hat-trick by teenage striker Kevin Davies, and Peterborough, despite twice taking the lead, lose 4-2 at home to Wrexham.

5 Bradford start legal action against Huddersfield's Kevin Gray for the tackle on Saturday that left new record signing Gordon Watson with a double fracture of his right leg and an estimated 6 months out. Ryan Giggs pulls out of a Wales friendly again.

6 WBA appoint Ray Harford manager. West Ham complete the £2.3m signing of Newcastle striker Paul Kitson. Celtic beat Raith 2-0 to cut Rangers' Premier lead to 4pts.

7 The FA meet with UEFA and earn the right to make a bid for the 2006 World Cup.`

8 Rangers' 3-0 win at Dunfermline restores their 7pt lead in the Scottish Premier.

10 As accountants Coopers & Lybrand warn that football shares, rated at £2-2.5 billion, are overvalued by about £1 billion, Millwall announce £1.5m cuts that call for 20 staff sackings, including manager Jimmy Nicholl, and 12 transfer-listings as well as across-the-board 10% pay cuts; John Docherty takes over as manager. Southend suspend Ronnie Whelan from team-manager duties and sack assistant Theo Foley after an incident with match officials on Saturday.

11 Scotland are held 0-0 by Estonia in their World Cup rematch in Monte Carlo. In friendlies, N.Ireland beat Belgium 3-0, while Ireland draw 0-0 in Wales. Citing lack of financial backing needed to save ailing Oldham, manager Graeme Sharp resigns along with assistant Colin Harvey.

12 A goal by Gianfranco Zola is enough to give Italy a 1-0 win over England at Wembley and bring them level on points in the World Cup group with a game in hand; it is England's first-ever World Cup defeat at Wembley. Terry Venables takes out his option to 'buy' Portsmouth for a nominal £1, enough to give him 51% ownership.

14 West Ham sign Arsenal's Welsh international striker John Hartson for £3.2m.

15 Leeds make a shock exit in the 5th round of the FA Cup, beaten 3-2 at home by Portsmouth, while Forest go down 1-0 at Chesterfield of Div 2 to a penalty conceded by their subsequently red-carded keeper Mark Crossley. Another Div 2 side, regular giant-killers Wrexham, win 3-1 at Birmingham, who were reduced to 10 men after 57min. Arsenal, held 0-0 at Spurs, miss their chance to top the Premiership. In the 4th round of the Scottish Cup, Premier team Dunfermline lose 2-1 at Falkirk and Motherwell are held 1-1 at home by Hamilton of Div 2.

16 Leicester earn a 5th-round Cup replay at Stamford Bridge when a late Eddie Newton own goal gives them a draw after Chelsea had taken a 2-0 lead; the game has to be stopped for 5min after Chelsea's first goal for police to separate rival supporters.

18 Wimbledon hold Leicester 0-0 in the 1st leg of their Coca-Cola Cup semi-final at Filbert St, where Vinnie Jones is the victim of a hand-held laser, the latest weapon of the hooligan.

19 Arsenal not only suffer their first Premiership home defeat of the season, going down 2-1 to Man Utd and leaving themselves 5pts adrift with one game more played, but striker Ian Wright causes more controversy with a reckless, though unpunished, two-footed challenge on Peter Schmeichel and continues his long-running feud with the United keeper as the teams leave the field. But Liverpool stay within a point of United with a comprehensive 4-0 thrashing of Leeds. Newcastle's game at West Ham is postponed because of torrential rain, as is the Stockport-Middlesbrough Coca-Cola semi-final tie.

20 The Wright-Schmeichel confrontation explodes into the headlines, with counter-accusations of violence and racism, and both players likely to suffer repercussions. The FA warn Everton manager Joe Royle for remarks made to referee David Elleray last September. Blackburn complete the signing of Danish striker Per Pedersen from Odense for £2.5m.

21 Sampdoria's Swedish coach Sven Goran Eriksson apologises to Blackburn fans for the long-drawn-out affair (he signed a 3-year contract in December), but he will not be joining the club as manager, having decided to stay in Italy, probably with Lazio.

22 Man Utd retain their 1pt lead despite drawing 1-1 at Chelsea, as Liverpool are held 0-0 at Anfield by lowly Blackburn. Newcastle's 1-0 win at Middlesbrough takes them ahead of gameless Arsenal. Arsenal complete the signing of 17-year-old French forward Nicolas Anelka from PSG, with the Paris club receiving a confidential sum for his immediate transfer. Celtic win 1-0 at Motherwell to cut Rangers' lead temporarily to 4pts.

23 Arsenal appear to blow their title chances completely with their second home defeat in a week, 1-0 to Wimbledon. In Scotland, Rangers restore their 7pt lead with a 3-1 win over Hibs.

24 Forest shareholders vote overwhelmingly to accept the £19m bid of a consortium led by Saracens rugby club owner Nigel Wray and former Spurs chairman Irving Scholar. Inspired by 2-goal Julian Dicks and with goals from Paul Kitson and John Hartson on their home débuts, West Ham win a 4-3 rainswept thriller with Spurs to move out of the Premiership relegation zone.

25 Two key England players will be out of action, Newcastle striker Alan Shearer for at least 6 club matches because he needs a third groin op, and Arsenal keeper David Seaman, who has already missed 3 matches plus an international and is to undergo an exploratory knee op.

26 Chelsea beat Leicester 1-0 in their 5th-round Cup replay thanks to a hotly disputed penalty given by referee Mike Reed in the 117th minute for what seemed an innocent collision and converted by Frank Leboeuf. Middlesbrough win the 1st leg of their Coca-Cola Cup semi 2-0 at Stockport. Blackburn announce their new manager will be Roy Hodgson, currently with Inter-Milan.

27 The Premier League announce that Peter Leaver, QC, a former Spurs director, has been appointed to succeed Rick Parry as chief executive by the end of the season. Palace manager Dave Bassett leaves the club shattered by his decision to join ailing Forest as general manager, relieving caretaker player-manager Stuart Pearce of administrative duties.

28 Steve Coppell returns to Palace as caretaker manager until the end of the season.

March
New Laws ... Match-fixing case stalemate ... Man Utd hammer Porto ... Chesterfield reach Cup semis ... Boro reach first final ... Rangers complete first Old Firm 'quadruple' ... Robbie Fowler saint and sinner ... Joe Royle quits Everton ...

1 New laws for next season promulgated at the International Board meeting in Belfast include: keepers will have their time holding the ball restricted (to 5-6sec), and they may not handle the ball direct from their own team's throw-ins; a player bleeding from a wound must leave the field for treatment. FIFA president João Havelange makes it clear that there will be no one country per continent restrictions on applications to host the 2006 World Cup. In the Premiership, Man Utd beat Coventry 3-1 to go 4pts clear of gameless Liverpool. Forest celebrate the new regime and welcome Dave Bassett with a 1-0 win at Spurs that takes them out of the relegation zone. Derby come back twice from a goal down to beat Chelsea 3-2, Scott Minto scoring for both sides at the Baseball Ground, where Chelsea's Frank Leboeuf is sent off for handball and manager Ruud Gullit, having come on as sub, sustains an ankle injury that will probably keep him off the field for the rest of the season. In Div 1, Palace give Steve Coppell a great start with 4-1 victory at

Oxford Grimsby. In Scotland, 8 of 19 matches are postponed, but Celtic beat Hearts 2-0 and close the Premier League gap to 5pts behind Rangers, held 2-2 at Aberdeen.

2 Liverpool concede their first Premiership goal since New Year's Day, Ian Taylor's strike being enough to leave them pointless at Villa Park and still 4pts behind Man Utd.

3 Len Millard, 78, Cup-winning captain of WBA in 1954, dies.

4 The corruption jury fail to reach a verdict, leaving footballers Bruce Grobbelaar, John Fashanu and Hans Segers and their co-defendants to face a probable retrial. Newcastle are beaten 1-0 in the home leg of their UEFA quarter-final by Monaco. Steffen Iversen hits 3 in Spurs' 4-0 Premiership win at Sunderland.

5 Man Utd virtually assure their passage to the European Cup semi-finals with an awesome 4-0 victory over FC Porto at Old Trafford. Fabrizio Ravanelli hits 3 in Middlesbrough's 6-1 thrashing of Derby, but they are still bottom of the Premiership, 3pts adrift.

6 Liverpool gain an encouraging 1-1 draw from their Cup-Winners' Cup quarter-final 1st leg with Brann Bergen in Norway. After 9 matches and 2 years, Celtic finally beat Rangers, their 2-0 victory at Parkhead putting them in the Cup semi-finals.

7 As a result of their onfield brawl at Carrow Road last December, both Norwich and Palace are fined £10,000, with another £30,000 suspended until June 1998.

8 Middlesbrough win 2-0 at Derby to reach the Cup semi-finals. Arsenal put themselves back in the title chase with a 2-0 win over Forest, as Man Utd lose 2-1 at Sunderland to lead the Gunners by only 3pts with a game in hand. Runaway Div 1 leaders Bolton hammer Swindon 7-0, scoring 4 times in the last 8min. The League's bottom club Brighton could be in trouble after more crowd disturbance at the Goldstone Ground, where fans invade the pitch to attack Orient players during the 4-4 draw.

9 In the three Cup quarter-finals, played at staggered times during the day, Chesterfield win the battle of the mid-table Div 2 clubs with a 1-0 victory over Wrexham, Wimbledon win 2-0 at Sheff Wed, and Chelsea come away from Portsmouth with a convincing 4-1 scoreline. Forest sign Celtic's Dutch striker Pierre van Hooijdonk for £3m rising to a possible club record £4.5m.

10 Lightning strikes Newcastle for the second successive season at Anfield as they are involved in another 4-3 thriller, coming back to parity from 3-0 down before a last-minute header from Robbie Fowler takes Liverpool to within a point of Man Utd.

11 Favourites Wimbledon lose their first chance of reaching Wembley when they are held 1-1 at home to Leicester in the second leg of the Coca-Cola Cup semi-finals and go out on away goals. The Crown Prosecution Service decide not to take action against Man Utd keeper Peter Schmeichel for alleged racist remarks made to Ian Wright in November, and the Arsenal striker endorses an FA League move to effect a reconciliation between the feuding players.

12 In the Coca-Cola Cup, Stockport shock Middlesbrough at the Riverside Stadium with a 6th-minute goal from Sean Connelly and another splendid, gritty performance despite the controversial dismissal of central defender Tony Dinning after 75min, but their 1-0 second-leg victory is not enough and Middlesbrough reach the first final in their 121-year history. Lincoln's Terry Fleming, who gave a team-mate's name to the referee last month to avoid being sent off in the match with Wigan, is banned for three matches.

13 Arsenal's faint title hopes take a knock as a hernia op will keep Paul Merson out for up to 6 weeks. Bradford striker Gordon Watson decides not to pursue GBH proceedings against Huddersfield defender Kevin Gray, but a High Court writ is served against player and club.

15 Liverpool lose ground in the title chase, held to a draw at Forest while Man Utd, Arsenal and Newcastle all win. Plymouth keeper Bruce Grobbelaar's complaint to the police at Shrewsbury regarding racist remarks being made by visiting fans about three opposing players leads to the arrest of a Plymouth follower.

16 Rangers win 1-0 at Parkhead to go 8pts clear of Celtic and complete the first ever League 'quadruple' in the history of Old Firm rivalry. In the Premiership, Chelsea score 6 League goals for the first time in over six years, outclassing Sunderland 6-2.

17 QPR striker Daniele Dichio signs a 3-year contract with Sampdoria for next season, taking advantage of the Bosman ruling to move on a free transfer. Chris Waddle joins Sunderland for the rest of the season.

18 Newcastle are outclassed 3-0 in Monaco, who win their UEFA Cup quarter-final tie 4-0 on aggregate.

19 Man Utd stand fast in Porto for a 0-0 draw to cruise into the European Cup semi-finals 4-0 on aggregate.

20 Liverpool reach the semi-finals of the Cup-Winners Cup, beating Brann Bergen 3-0 (4-1 agg) at Anfield. The Foreign Office demand a report into alleged injuries inflicted on Man Utd fans by Portuguese police after the game with Porto. Bournemouth, making their fifth court appearance in their efforts to avoid being wound-up, are given a final chance as the petition put forward by the Inland Revenue is adjourned until the end of the season.

22 The only top-three team with a Saturday game, Man Utd steal a march on their rivals with a 2-0 victory at Everton to go 6pts ahead. Rangers slip up at home, losing 2-1 to Kilmarnock, but Celtic can only scrape a 2-2 draw at Dunfermline and are still 7pts behind.

24 Refereeing controversy erupts at Highbury, where Gerald Ashby awards Liverpool a penalty despite protests from Robbie Fowler that he wasn't fouled by Arsenal keeper David Seaman, who paradoxically is not even booked; Seaman parries Fowler's spot-kick, but Jason McAteer follows up to score and Liverpool's 2-1 win takes them 3pts clear of Arsenal and to within 3pts of leaders Man Utd. Manager Joe Jordan parts company with Bristol City by mutual consent, leaving assistant Gerry Sweeney in temporary charge.

25   Liverpool striker Robbie Fowler receives plaudits from all sides (except some of his team-mates) for his sporting action against Arsenal yesterday, including a personal fax from FIFA secretary Sepp Blatter.

26   The FA turn down Middlesbrough's appeal against their 3pt deduction. FIFA rule that players of all nationalities may move on free transfers under the Bosman ruling so long as they play in EU countries.

27   After clashes with chairman Peter Johnson over transfer deals, manager Joe Royle quits Everton by mutual consent. John Ward, former Bristol Rov manager and recently No.2 at Burnley, is appointed manager of Bristol City. Saint becomes sinner as Robbie Fowler is fined £900 by UEFA for exposing a T-shirt in a Cup-Winners' Cup tie backing Liverpool dockers, deemed to be a politically motivated action. A new transfer-deadline day record of £8m is set, including West Ham's £1.6m (rising to a possible £2m) for Man City's N.Ireland international Steve Lomas and Newcastle's £1.5m (plus up to £800,000 over 3 years at £8,000 per game) for Bradford midfielder Des Hamilton. Swiss referee Kurt Röthlisburger, accused 3 years ago by Eric Cantona of 'taking a bung', is banned for life by FIFA and UEFA for attempted bribery.

28   Celtic sign Villa striker Tommy Johnson for £2.4m.

29   Mixed fortunes for Britain in World Cup qualifiers: Scotland beat Estonia 2-0 to go top of Gp 4 by 4pts and N.Ireland draw 0-0 at home to Gp 9 leaders Portugal, but Wales blow their chances as they lose 2-1 to Belgium in the last ever match at Cardiff Arms Park, prompting keeper Neville Southall to retire from international football one cap short of his century. Italy beat Moldova 3-0 to take a 3pt lead in Gp 2 over England, whose 2-0 victory over Mexico in a friendly at Wembley features Robbie Fowler's first goal at senior international level.

31   In an almost full Nationwide programmes, Wolves' draw at QPR hands Bolton promotion to the Premiership barring a mathematical disaster.

April
Scotland stretch World Cup lead ... No fixture relief for Ferguson ... Bolton clinch Div 1 title ... James's blunders floor Liverpool ... No-goal decision thwarts Chesterfield ...Claridge strike brings Leicester Coca-Cola glory ... Man Utd meet their match in Euro Cup ... Celtic shocked by Falkirk in Scottish semis ... Barnsley reach top flight at last ... Elton John returns to Watford

1   The FA of Wales is to launch an inquiry into claims made by black Bolton player Nathan Blake that Wales manager Bobby Gould made racist remarks (about black Dutch striker Pierre van Hooijdonk in a post-match discussion last year). Dave Watson is appointed temporary player-manager of Everton.

2   In World Cup qualifiers, Scotland, who have now played 2 more games than the others in their group, take a comfortable 7pt lead after beating Austria 2-0 thanks to goals from Blackburn striker Kevin Gallacher; but Ireland suffer an embarrassing 3-2 defeat in Macedonia and N.Ireland's 2-1 reverse in Ukraine virtually seals their fate. Italy's 0-0 draw in Poland boosts England's chances in Gp.2.

3   Sheff Wed manager David Pleat signs a new 3-year contract.

4   The FA fine last season's Vauxhall Conference champions Stevenage Borough £25,000 (suspended for 2 years) for approaching Torquay in March last year with a proposed deal that would help the 3rd Division's bottom club retain their league status, namely to be paid £30,000 not to sell leading scorer Barry Hayles! The reason for this Machiavellian scheme was that Stevenage's ground was deemed unfit for promotion, unlike that of 2nd-placed Woking's; Stevenage must pay costs of £10,000. Arsenal manager Arsène Wenger describes Man Utd's bid to have the season extended as ridiculous.

5   Man Utd go down 3-2 at home to Derby, giving Arsenal, 3-0 victors at Stamford Bridge, fresh title hopes. Rangers beat Dunfermline 4-0 to open up a 9pt lead in the Scottish premier over Celtic, held to a draw at bottom club Raith.

6   A dramatic equaliser from Leicester's Emile Heskey 2min from the end of extra time in the Coca-Cola Cup final at Wembley forces a replay with Middlesbrough. Liverpool blow their chances of topping the Premiership, losing 2-1 to bottom club Coventry in only their second home defeat of the season.

8   Wigan and Fulham both clinch promotion to Div 2.

9   In the 1st leg of the European Cup semi-finals, Man Utd are unlucky to come away from Dortmund with a 1-0 deficit against Borussia. Bolton clinch the 1st Div title with a 2-1 win at Man City which takes them an uncatchable 20pts clear of closest rivals Barnsley.

10   Liverpool are outplayed in Paris in the 1st leg of their Cup-Winners' Cup semi-final, keeper David James's blunders contributing to PSG's 3-0 victory. The FA decide not to take disciplinary action against Ian Wright and Peter Schmeichel for their public feuding, but warn the players as to their future conduct.

11   Man Utd, faced with playing 4 matches in the last 9 days of the season, draft an appeal to the FA over the Premier League's refusal to extend it beyond 11 May. Carlisle clinch the third automatic promotion spot in Div 3.

12   Man Utd win 3-2 at Blackburn to maintain their 3pt lead over Arsenal, who beat Leicester 2-0. Falkirk of Div 1 score a late equaliser in the Scottish Cup semi-final at Ibrox to take Celtic to a replay. In the Premier, Motherwell beat Raith 5-0 to condemn the losers to Div 1 (barring a series of miracles) and enhance their own hopes of survival.

13   In the FA Cup semi-finals, Chesterfield dig out a late extra-time equaliser against 10-man Middlesbrough in the 3-3 thriller at Old Trafford, but were deprived of a 3-1 lead when the officials fail to see a Jonathan Howard shot rebound over the Middlesbrough line, and Chelsea crush

Wimbledon 3-0 at Highbury. Liverpool return to form with a 2-1 win at Sunderland to keep up the Premiership heat on Man Utd.

14 The second Scottish Cup semi-final ends in another draw, Kilmarnock and Dundee Utd finishing 0-0 at Easter Road. Raith sack manager Iain Munro.

15 Rangers' 6-0 win at Raith confirms the latter's relegation, and now Celtic, 12pts behind their rivals with only 4 games left, must concede that Rangers have equalled their record 9 consecutive titles.

16 A Steve Claridge strike after 10min of extra time gives Leicester a 1-0 win over Middlesbrough in the Coca-Cola Cup final replay at Hillsborough. Liverpool miss another chance to top the Premiership as they are held to a 1-1 draw by Everton at Goodison, and their title hopes are further dashed by the dismissal for fighting, along with Everton's David Unsworth, of leading scorer Robbie Fowler, who will now probably miss their last 3 fixtures. The FA of Wales clear Bobby Gould of racist charges and back him to carry on as team manager.

17 At a meeting in Geneva, the FA win the right to go ahead with their bid to host the 2006 World Cup as UEFA in effect admit that the 'gentleman's agreement' to back Germany for the tournament never existed.

19 Man Utd overpower Liverpool 3-1 at Anfield in the morning thanks to two headed goals from Gary Pallister and another couple of blunders by hapless keeper David James, and have the Premiership title virtually handed to them in the afternoon when Arsenal are held 1-1 at home by Blackburn, leaving United 5pts ahead with a game in hand. Blackburn's Chris Sutton is slammed for a piece of bad sportsmanship that led to their late equaliser at Highbury.

20 Celtic delay Rangers' celebrations by beating Aberdeen 3-0.

21 Arsenal's 1-1 draw at Coventry provides encouragement for Liverpool and Newcastle in the race for 2nd spot and a place in the European Cup. Glenn Hoddle drops David James from the England squad.

22 Middlesbrough reach their first ever FA Cup final with a fluent 3-0 win over brave Chesterfield in the replay at Hillsborough. Kilmarnock reach their first Scottish Cup final for 37 years thanks to a dramatic late goal from Jim McIntyre against Dundee Utd at Easter Road. Brighton's long-term future appears to have been secured with a restructuring involving Bill Archer and a consortium led by lifelong fan Dick Knight, who takes over the chairmanship from Archer.

23 Man Utd fail to take their chances and go down 1-0 (2-0 agg) at Old Trafford to B.Dortmund, who will meet Juventus, awesome conquerors of Ajax 4-1 (6-2), in the European Cup final. Div 1 Falkirk shock favourites Celtic 1-0 at Ibrox in the replayed Scottish Cup semi-final to reach their first final in 40 years.

24 Liverpool, dropping John Barnes for the first time in his career, beat Paris SG 2-0 at Anfield but go out of the Cup-Winners' Cup 3-2 on aggregate. UEFA declare that Leicester will be England's last representatives in the UEFA Cup via the League Cup because of the Premier League's refusal to reduce their number to 18 clubs.

25 England manager Glenn Hoddle warns Paul Gascoigne that unless he puts his life in order his England days are numbered. In their last game at Burnden Park, Bolton are presented with the Div 1 trophy and proceed to beat Charlton 4-1.

26 With no Premiership action because of international commitments, Barnsley take centre stage, beating Bradford 2-0 to clinch promotion to the top flight for the first time in their 110-year history. Elton John is back as chairman of Watford after 7 years, head of a consortium that has taken over the club and plan to share Vicarage Road with Saracens RC. In their last match at the Goldstone Ground, Brighton beat Doncaster 1-0 and move off the bottom of the League for the first time in 29 weeks, tempering the fans' fury at their eviction after 95 years.

28 In a clash of cup giant-killers, Stockport, playing their 66th match, win 1-0 at Chesterfield to clinch promotion to Div 1.

29 UEFA clear Man Utd fans of blame following trouble in Portugal last month and fine Porto for serious lack of organisation at the European Cup tie.

30 A goal each from the Shearer-Sheringham strike force is enough for England to beat Georgia 2-0 at Wembley, but Italy beat Poland 3-0 to maintain their 4pt lead in Gp.2 of the World Cup, although England have a game in hand. Scotland lose 2-1 in Sweden, who, with Austria, have two games in hand and are now snapping at Scotland's heels in Gp.4. Despite losing 1-0 in Romania in Gp.8, Ireland are still in the running for the runners-up spot, but N.Ireland's 0-0 draw in Armenia leaves them virtually out of contention in Gp.9.

May
Zola Footballer of the Year ... Celtic sack Tommy Burns ... Forest relegated ... Brighton survive as Hereford drop out ... Man Utd win 4th Premiership in 5 seasons ... Rangers' 9th title on trot equals Celtic record ... Sun]derland and Boro go down as Newcastle win place in Euro Cup ... Collymore signs for Villa ... Quick-fire Di Matteo inspires Chelsea Wembley triumph ... Au revoir Cantona ... Kilmarnock win Scottish Cup ... Souness quits Saints ... Euro Cup shock for Juventus ... England win crucial qualifier in Katowice

2 Chelsea's Gianfranco Zola is voted Footballer of the Year by a wide margin, completing a hat-trick for overseas players (after Klinsmann and Cantona). Without a trophy for the second consecutive season, Celtic sack manager Tommy Burns.

3 Man Utd manage a 2-2 draw at Leicester after going 2-0 down, and are 3pts ahead of Liverpool, 2-1 victors over Spurs, with a game in hand. Newcastle put themselves into contention for the runners-up spot, continuing their fine surge with a 1-0 victory at Highbury over Arsenal, who will probably have to settle now for a UEFA Cup place. Forest can only draw at home to Wimbledon and are relegated, but Middlesbrough's 3-2 defeat of Villa, thanks to a last-minute Ravanelli

penalty, keeps their hopes of survival alive. West Ham climb nearer to safety with a splendid 5-1 win over Sheff Wed, Paul Kitson hitting 3. Sunderland sign off in style after 99 years at Roker Park with a 3-0 win over Everton. Bury and Wigan clinch the championships of Divs 2 and 3, respectively, and the play-off and relegation places are settled. Brighton's 1-1 draw at Hereford keeps them in the League at the expense of their opponents, who drop out after 25 years. Their place will be taken by Macclesfield, who clinch the Vauxhall Conference title with a 4-1 win at Kettering.

4 The Div 1 programme is completed, with Bradford surviving at the expense of Grimsby. Champions Bolton chalk up 100 goals, but are denied their 100pts by an injury-time equaliser at Tranmere. Celtic cling onto their hopes of a miracle with a 3-1 win at Hibs, leaving them with 6pt and 12-goal deficits behind Rangers to be overhauled in 2 Celtic and 3 Rangers matches.

5 Middlesbrough take a 3-1 lead at Old Trafford, but then have to withstand a siege after Man Utd equalise in the 67th minute, the draw leaving United to win one of their last two matches to retain the title and Boro still a lot to do to stay up, especially with Ravanelli stretchered off after 35min with a hamstring injury. Rangers blow another chance to clinch the Scottish title, losing 2-0 at home to Motherwell.

6 Man Utd retain their Premiership title without playing as Liverpool lose 2-1 at Wimbledon and Newcastle are held 0-0 at West Ham. The Football League consultants, accountants Deloitte Touche, recommend a complete overhaul to include all 22 Vauxhall Conference clubs in regionalised 3rd Divisions, and warn that the League will wither without drastic change.

7 At last the fat lady sings in Scotland - Rangers are crowned champions for the 9th season running to equal Celtic's record, their 1-0 win at Dundee Utd making Celtic's failure to beat Kilmarnock purely academic.

8 Middlesbrough's 0-0 draw at Blackburn, in the fixture that has already cost them 3 deducted points, leaves them still 2pts adrift in 18th place. The Football League chairmen reject regional proposals.

9 Glenn Hoddle calls Man Utd reserve Paul Scholes into the England squad. Arsenal take a £1m plus gamble on Luton youth team captain Matthew Upson, who has made just one substitute appearance for the club, signing him on a long-term contract. Joint managers Jimmy Quinn and Mick Gooding part company with Reading after failing to agree new terms.

10 Palace, leading 1-0 with 2min left of their home-leg Div 1 play-off against Wolves, finish 3-1 winners thanks to a brace from sub Dougie Freedman.

11 The final Premiership programme sees drama at both ends of the table. Liverpool's failure to win at Sheff Wed lets Newcastle, 5-0 conquerors of doomed Forest, into 2nd spot and the European Cup. It's a disastrous day for Newcastle's neighbours at the other end - Sunderland, defeated 1-0 at Wimbledon, and Cup-finalists Middlesbrough, drawing 1-1 at Leeds, are both relegated as Coventry perform their habitual Houdini act with a 2-1 win at Spurs.

13 Striker Stan Collymore signs for Villa for £7m - £1.5m less than Liverpool paid Forest for him 2 years ago.

14 Barcelona, managed by Bobby Robson, beat Paris SG 1-0 in the Cup-Winners' Cup final. A late David Hopkin goal at Molineux puts Palace through 4-3 on aggregate over Wolves to the Div 1 play-off final against Sheff Utd, away-goals winners over Ipswich. Managerless Everton break the Premiership transfer record for a defender, signing Croatian Slaven Bilic from West Ham for £4.25m.

16 Norwich striker Darren Eadie is called into the England squad to replace the injured Paul Merson. Celtic midfielder Paul McStay, 32, announces his retirement after a series of ankle injuries.

17 Inspired by a 43-second goal blasted by midfielder Roberto Di Matteo, Chelsea power to a 2-0 FA Cup victory over luckless Middlesbrough; Ruud Gullit is the first foreign manager to win an FA Cup final and Mark Hughes the first 4-time winner this century.

18 Eric Cantona shatters Man Utd fans by announcing his retirement from football 6 days before his 31st birthday.

19 FA Technical Director Howard Wilkinson publishes his blueprint, the 'Charter for Quality', for the sustained and high-quality development of the country's youngsters. Man Utd's Andy Cole is drafted into the England squad for the injured Les Ferdinand. Channel 5 win exclusive rights to televise Chelsea's European home games next season.

20 England coach Glenn Hoddle is upset with the timing of Liverpool's decision to withdraw Robbie Fowler from the squad to have a nose op. Derby snap up Milan's Italy international wing-back Stefano Eranio, 30, on a free transfer.

21 Watford's David Connolly, 19, becomes the youngest player to score a hat-trick for Ireland as they beat Liechtenstein 5-0 to go 2nd in World Cup Gp.8. Schalke win the UEFA Cup on penalties after losing their away tie 1-0 to Inter at the San Siro. Bolton sign Middlesbrough right-back Neil Cox for £1.5m. Walsall manager Chris Nicholl resigns. Shrewsbury appoint former captain Jake King manager.

23 Jimmy Hill steps down as Fulham chairman after 10 years, and will be replaced by vice-chairman Bill Muddyman. Glenn Hoddle threatens to hammer the reinstated Paul Gascoigne if he disgraces himself with England.

24 England beat S.Africa 2-1 in a friendly at Old Trafford thanks to a controversial winner from Ian Wright, who appeared to handle the ball first, and Gascoigne is carried off after a violent tackle near the end. Kilmarnock beat Falkirk 1-0 in the Scottish Cup final. Northampton beat Swansea 1-0 with a last-minute goal in the Div 3 play-off final. Manager Graeme Souness shocks Southampton with his resignation allegedly after a disagreement with new chairman Rupert Lowe about money for new players, and Lawrie McMenemy stands down as director of football.

25 Crewe beat Brentford 1-0 to win promotion to Div 1, their first time in the next-to-top division since 1896.
26 Skipper David Hopkin hits a spectacular and dramatic winner in the last seconds of normal time to give Palace a 1-0 victory over Sheff Utd and a place in the Premiership.
27 Tony Adams loses his battle with his ankle injury and is out of England's squad, along with new boy Darren Eadie who has strained tendons.
28 Borussia Dortmund produce one of the biggest shocks in European Cup history, beating hot favourites Juventus 3-1. Ian Wright turns to counselling in an attempt to curb his wild side.
29 Mohammed Al Fayed, Egyptian-born owner of Harrods, buys a controlling interest in Fulham with an initial investment of £30m. Rangers sign defenders Lorenzo Amoruso from Fiorentina for £3.95m and Staale Stensaas from Rosenborg for £1.75m.
31 Alan Shearer misses a penalty and Paul Gascoigne is stretchered off again, but goals from Shearer and Teddy Sheringham give England a 2-0 win over Poland in Katowice in their crucial World Cup qualifier, and they are now only a point behind Gp.2 leaders Italy.

June 97
World Cup scoring record ... Roberto's rocket ... England win French tournament

1 Scotland scrape a 3-2 win over Malta in a friendly in Valletta.
2 Liverpool sign Norwegian midfield star Oyvind Leonhardsen for £3.5m. Newcastle midfielder Lee Clark is called into the England squad and signs for Sunderland in a £2.5m deal, a record for the relegated club. West Ham sign Andy Impey from QPR for £1.2m and Israeli international Eyal Berkovic from Southampton for £1.75m. Out-of-contract Scott Booth walks out of Aberdeen after 9 years to join European champions Borussia Dortmund. Iran beat the Maldives 17-0 in an Asian Zone Gp.2 match to set a World Cup scoring record.
3 The 4-team Le Tournoi opens in Lyon with France and Brazil drawing 1-1, the talking point an unforgettable free-kick from Roberto Carlos, a 35-yard bender that goes past the French keeper like a guided missile. Spurs agree a transfer request from England striker Teddy Sheringham, who claims he has been forced out by chairman Alan Sugar and the club's lack of ambition. Sheff Wed keeper Matt Clarke, sent off against Liverpool for handling outside his area, has his 1-match ban lifted when referee David Elleray admits his mistake after watching the incident on video.
4 England beat Italy 2-0 for the first time in 20 years with goals from Ian Wright and Paul Scholes to go top of Le Tournoi. Arsenal sign two more French players, midfielder Emmanuel Petit for £3m and central defender Gilles Grimandi for £2m, both from Monaco, to bring their French contingent up to five. Germany manager Berti Vogts challenges England to a match to determine who bids for the 2006 World Cup. Leicester give manager Martin O'Neill a new 3-year contract, with a £1m compensation clause to deter potential poachers.
7 A late Shearer strike gives England a 1-0 win over hosts France in Le Tournoi. In England's World Cup group, their next opponents Georgia beat Moldova 2-0, and Nigeria are the first country to qualify for the finals after beating Kenya 3-0 in their African Zone group.
8 In a cracking match at Lyon, Brazil come back from 3-1 down to draw with Italy, but the result hands Le Tournoi de France to England whatever their result against the Brazilians. In World Cup activity, Scotland win 1-0 in Belarus to stay 4pts clear in Gp.4, but Austria and Sweden also win away to keep up the pressure.
10 Romario finishes off a superb Brazilian move to give Brazil a 1-0 victory over England, who nevertheless collect the French Tournoi trophy. Rangers sign Juventus defender Sergio Porrini for £3m.
11 Wimbledon chairman Sam Hammam sells his 80% interest to two Norwegian businessmen in a £30m deal that will enable the club to build a new stadium, but insists he will still be running the club. Chelsea sign Feyenoord's Dutch international keeper Ed de Goey, 30, for £2.5m.
12 Graeme Souness signs a 3-year contract to manage Italian Serie B club Torino. Leeds sign Surinam-born Jimmy Floyd Hasselbaink from Boavista for £2m and Norwegian international Alf-Inge Haaland from Forest (tribunal to determine fee). Palace sign Watford keeper Kevin Miller for £1.55m. WBA sign Preston winger Kevin Kilbane for a club record £1.25m. Paul Gascoigne's Rangers contract is extended to the year 2000.

NORMAN BARRETT

ENGLISH LEAGUE TABLES 1996–97

FA CARLING PREMIERSHIP

			Home			Goals		Away			Goals			
		P	W	D	L	F	A	W	D	L	F	A	GD	Pts
1	Manchester U	38	12	5	2	38	17	9	7	3	38	27	+32	75
2	Newcastle U	38	13	3	3	54	20	6	8	5	19	20	+33	68
3	Arsenal	38	10	5	4	36	18	9	6	4	26	14	+30	68
4	Liverpool	38	10	6	3	38	19	9	5	5	24	18	+25	68
5	Aston Villa	38	11	5	3	27	13	6	5	8	20	21	+13	61
6	Chelsea	38	9	8	2	33	22	7	3	9	25	33	+3	59
7	Sheffield W	38	8	10	1	25	16	6	5	8	25	35	−1	57
8	Wimbledon	38	9	6	4	28	21	6	5	8	21	25	+3	56
9	Leicester C	38	7	5	7	22	26	5	6	8	24	28	−8	47
10	Tottenham H	38	8	4	7	19	17	5	3	11	25	34	−7	46
11	Leeds U	38	7	7	5	15	13	4	6	9	13	25	−10	46
12	Derby Co	38	8	6	5	25	22	3	7	9	20	36	−13	46
13	Blackburn R	38	8	4	7	28	23	1	11	7	14	20	−1	42
14	West Ham U	38	7	6	6	27	25	3	6	10	12	23	−9	42
15	Everton	38	7	4	8	24	22	3	8	8	20	35	−13	42
16	Southampton	38	6	7	6	32	24	4	4	11	18	32	−6	41
17	Coventry C	38	4	8	7	19	23	5	6	8	19	31	−16	41
18	Sunderland	38	7	6	6	20	18	3	4	12	15	35	−18	40
19	Middlesbrough	38	8	5	6	34	25	2	7	10	17	35	−9	39*
20	Nottingham F	38	3	9	7	15	27	3	7	9	16	32	−28	34

*Middlesbrough deducted 3 points

NATIONWIDE FOOTBALL LEAGUE DIVISION 1

			Home			Goals		Away			Goals			
		P	W	D	L	F	A	W	D	L	F	A	GLS	Pts
1	Bolton W	46	18	4	1	60	20	10	10	3	40	33	100	98
2	Barnsley	46	14	4	5	43	19	8	10	5	33	36	76	80
3	Wolverhampton W	46	10	5	8	31	24	12	5	6	37	27	68	76
4	Ipswich T	46	13	7	3	44	23	7	7	9	24	27	68	74
5	Sheffield U	46	13	5	5	46	23	7	8	8	29	29	75	73
6	Crystal Palace	46	10	7	6	39	22	9	7	7	39	26	78	71
7	Portsmouth	46	12	4	7	32	24	8	4	11	27	29	59	68
8	Port Vale	46	9	9	5	36	28	8	7	8	22	27	58	67
9	QPR	46	10	5	8	33	25	8	7	8	31	35	64	66
10	Birmingham C	46	11	7	5	30	18	6	8	9	22	30	52	66
11	Tranmere R	46	10	9	4	42	27	7	5	11	21	29	63	65
12	Stoke C	46	15	3	5	34	22	3	7	13	17	35	51	64
13	Norwich C	46	9	10	4	28	18	8	2	13	35	50	63	63
14	Manchester C	46	12	4	7	34	25	5	6	12	25	35	59	61
15	Charlton Ath	46	11	8	4	36	28	5	3	15	16	38	52	59
16	WBA	46	7	7	9	37	33	7	8	8	31	39	68	57
17	Oxford U	46	14	3	6	44	26	2	6	15	20	42	64	57
18	Reading	46	13	7	3	37	24	2	5	16	21	43	58	57
19	Swindon T	46	11	6	6	36	27	4	3	16	16	44	52	54
20	Huddersfield T	46	10	7	6	28	20	3	8	12	20	41	48	54
21	Bradford C	46	10	5	8	29	32	2	7	14	18	40	47	48
22	Grimsby T	46	7	7	9	31	34	4	6	13	29	47	60	46
23	Oldham Ath	46	6	8	9	30	30	4	5	14	21	36	51	43
24	Southend U	46	7	9	7	32	32	1	6	16	10	54	42	39

NATIONWIDE FOOTBALL LEAGUE DIVISION 2

			Home			Goals		Away			Goals			
		P	W	D	L	F	A	W	D	L	F	A	GLS	Pts
1	Bury	46	18	5	0	39	7	6	7	10	23	31	62	84
2	Stockport Co	46	15	5	3	31	14	8	8	7	28	27	59	82
3	Luton T	46	13	7	3	38	14	8	8	7	33	31	71	78
4	Brentford	46	8	11	4	26	22	12	3	8	30	21	56	74
5	Bristol C	46	14	4	5	43	18	7	6	10	26	33	69	73
6	Crewe Alex	46	15	4	4	38	15	7	3	13	18	32	56	73
7	Blackpool	46	13	7	3	41	21	5	8	10	19	26	60	69
8	Wrexham	46	11	9	3	37	28	6	9	8	17	22	54	69
9	Burnley	46	14	3	6	48	27	5	8	10	23	28	71	68
10	Chesterfield	46	10	9	4	25	18	8	5	10	17	21	42	68
11	Gillingham	46	13	3	7	37	25	6	7	10	23	34	60	67
12	Walsall	46	12	8	3	35	21	7	2	14	19	32	54	67
13	Watford	46	10	8	5	24	14	6	11	6	21	24	45	67
14	Millwall	46	12	4	7	27	22	4	9	10	23	33	50	61
15	Preston NE	46	14	5	4	33	19	4	2	17	16	36	49	61
16	Bournemouth	46	8	9	6	24	20	7	6	10	19	25	43	60
17	Bristol R	46	13	4	6	34	22	2	7	14	13	28	47	56
18	Wycombe W	46	13	4	6	31	14	2	6	15	20	42	51	55
19	Plymouth Arg	46	7	11	5	19	18	5	7	11	28	40	47	54
20	York C	46	8	6	9	27	31	5	7	11	20	37	47	52
21	Peterborough U	46	7	7	9	38	34	4	7	12	17	39	55	47
22	Shrewsbury T	46	8	6	9	27	32	3	7	13	22	42	49	46
23	Rotherham U	46	4	7	12	17	29	3	7	13	22	41	39	35
24	Notts Co	46	4	9	10	20	25	3	5	15	13	34	33	35

NATIONWIDE FOOTBALL LEAGUE DIVISION 3

			Home			Goals		Away			Goals			
		P	W	D	L	F	A	W	D	L	F	A	GLS	Pts
1	Wigan Ath	46	17	3	3	53	21	9	6	8	31	30	84	87
2	Fulham	46	13	5	5	41	20	12	7	4	31	18	72	87
3	Carlisle U	46	16	3	4	41	21	8	9	6	26	23	67	84
4	Northampton T	46	14	4	5	43	17	6	8	9	24	27	67	72
5	Swansea C	46	13	5	5	37	20	8	3	12	25	38	62	71
6	Chester C	46	11	8	4	30	16	7	8	8	25	27	55	70
7	Cardiff C	46	11	4	8	30	23	9	5	9	26	31	56	69
8	Colchester U	46	11	9	3	36	23	6	8	9	26	28	62	68
9	Lincoln C	46	10	8	5	35	25	8	4	11	35	44	70	66
10	Cambridge U	46	11	5	7	30	27	7	6	10	23	32	53	65
11	Mansfield T	46	9	8	6	21	17	7	8	8	26	28	47	64
12	Scarborough	46	9	9	5	36	31	7	6	10	29	37	65	63
13	Scunthorpe U	46	11	3	9	36	33	7	6	10	23	29	59	63
14	Rochdale	46	10	6	7	34	24	4	10	9	24	34	58	58
15	Barnet	46	9	9	5	32	23	5	7	11	14	28	46	58
16	Leyton Orient	46	11	6	6	28	20	4	6	13	22	38	50	57
17	Hull C	46	9	8	6	29	26	4	10	9	15	24	44	57
18	Darlington	46	11	5	7	37	28	3	5	15	27	50	64	52
19	Doncaster R	46	9	7	7	29	23	5	3	15	23	43	52	52
20	Hartlepool U	46	8	6	9	33	32	6	3	14	20	34	53	51
21	Torquay U	46	9	4	10	24	24	4	7	12	22	38	46	50
22	Exeter C	46	6	9	8	25	30	6	3	14	23	43	48	48
23	Brighton & HA	46	12	6	5	41	27	1	4	18	12	43	53	47*
24	Hereford U	46	6	8	9	26	25	5	6	12	24	40	50	47

Brighton & HA deducted 2 points.
In the Nationwide Football League, goals scored determine League positions where clubs are level on points.
If teams still cannot be separated, the team that has conceded fewer goals is placed higher.

FOOTBALL LEAGUE PLAY-OFFS 1996–97

SEMI FINALS FIRST LEG

10 MAY

DIVISION 1

Crystal Palace (0) 3 *(Shipperley 68, Freedman 89, 90)*
Wolverhampton W (0) 1 *(Smith 90)*   21,053
Crystal Palace: Nash; Edworthy, Gordon, Roberts, Davies, Linighan, Hopkin, Houghton (Veart), Shipperley, Dyer (Freedman), Rodger.
Wolverhampton W: Stowell; Smith, Thompson, Atkins, Williams, Curle, Osborn, Ferguson, Bull (Foley), Roberts, Thomas.

Sheffield U (1) 1 *(Fjortoft 41)*
Ipswich T (0) 1 *(Stockwell 78)*   22,312
Sheffield U: Kelly; Ward, Nilsen, Hutchison, Tiler, Holdsworth, White (Short), Henry, Fjortoft, Katchuro (Taylor), Whitehouse.
Ipswich T: Wright; Stockwell, Taricco, Sedgley, Swailes, Williams, Uhlenbeek, Vaughan, Gregory (Gudmundsson), Scowcroft, Dyer.

11 MAY

DIVISION 2

Bristol C (1) 1 *(Owers 28)*
Brentford (2) 2 *(Smith 13, Taylor 30)*   15,581
Bristol C: Welch; Owers, Barnard, Shail, Paterson, Edwards, Hewlett (Tinnion), Kuhl (Carey), Nugent (Agostino), Goater, Allen.
Brentford: Dearden; Hurdle, Anderson, Statham, Bates, McGhee, Asaba, Smith, Bent, Hutchings, Taylor.

Crewe Alex (0) 2 *(Rivers 53, Little 68)*
Luton T (1) 1 *(Oldfield 3)*   5467
Crewe Alex: Kearton; Unsworth, Smith S, Westwood, Macauley, Charnock, Whalley, Little (Johnson), Rivers (Tierney), Murphy, Adebola.
Luton T: Feuer; James, Thomas, Waddock (Marshall), Davis S, Patterson, McLaren, Alexander, Oldfield, Thorpe, Fotiadis (Grant).

DIVISION 3

Cardiff C (0) 0
Northampton T (0) 1 *(Parrish 77)*   11,369
Cardiff C: Williams; Jarman, Lloyd, Perry, Young, Fowler, Eckhardt (White), Stoker (Rollo), Dale, Haworth, Middleton.
Northampton T: Woodman; Clarkson, Frain, Sampson, Warburton, Rennie, Parrish, Grayson (Lee), Gayle (Peer), Cooper, Hunter.

Chester C (0) 0
Swansea C (0) 0   5104
Chester C: Sinclair; Davidson, Jenkins, Reid, Woods, Alsford, Flitcroft, Priest, McDonald, Milner, Aiston.
Swansea C: Freestone; Thomas (Heggs), Moreira, Walker, Edwards, Jones, Appleby, Penney, Torpey, Ampadu, Coates.

SEMI FINALS SECOND LEG

14 MAY

DIVISION 1

Ipswich T (1) 2 *(Scowcroft 32, Gudmundsson 33)*
Sheffield U (1) 2 *(Katchuro 9, Walker 77)*   21,467
Ipswich T: Wright; Stockwell, Taricco, Sedgley, Swailes (Dyer), Williams, Uhlenbeek, Vaughan, Gudmundsson (Gregory), Scowcroft, Mason.
Sheffield U: Kelly; Short, Sandford, Henry, Tiler, Holdsworth, White (Hutchison), Ward, Fjortoft, Katchuro (Walker) (Nilsen), Whitehouse.
aet; Sheffield U won on away goals.

Wolverhampton W (1) 2 *(Atkins 30, Williams 85)*
Crystal Palace (0) 1 *(Hopkin 66)*   26,403
Wolverhampton W: Stowell; Smith, Thomas, Atkins, Williams, Curle, Goodman, Ferguson, Bull, Roberts, Osborn (Foley).
Crystal Palace: Nash; Edworthy, Gordon, Roberts, Tuttle, Linighan, Hopkin, Muscat, Shipperley, Dyer (Freedman), Rodger.
Crystal Palace won 4-3 on aggregate.

David Hopkin celebrates his goal for Crystal Palace as they overcome Sheffield United in the play-off final at Wembley. (Action Images)

Crewe players congratulate Shaun Smith after his goal ensured promotion from the play-offs against Brentford. (Action Images)

DIVISION 2

Luton T (2) 2 *(Oldfield 20, 31)*
Crewe Alex (1) 2 *(Little 32, Smith 62)*   8168
Luton T: Feuer; Patterson, Thomas, Waddock (Fotiadis), Davis S, Johnson, McLaren, Alexander, Oldfield, Thorpe, Showler (Marshall).
Crewe Alex: Kearton; Unsworth (Johnson), Smith S, Westwood, Macauley, Charnock, Whalley, Little, Rivers (Garvey), Murphy (Lightfoot), Adebola.
Crewe Alex won 4-3 on aggregate.

Brentford (0) 2 *(Taylor 67, Bent 79)*
Bristol C (0) 1 *(Barnard 49)*   9496
Brentford: Dearden; Hurdle, Anderson, Hutchings, Bates, McGhee, Dennis (Canham), Smith, Bent, Statham, Taylor.
Bristol C: Welch; Owers, Barnard, Shail (Carey) (Bent), Taylor, Edwards, Hewlett, Allen, Nugent, Goater, Tinnion (Goodridge).
Brentford won 4-2 on aggregate.

DIVISION 3

Northampton T (1) 3 *(Sampson 23, Warburton 68, Gayle 77)*
Cardiff C (1) 2 *(Fowler 36, Haworth 90)*   7302
Northampton T: Woodman; Clarkson, Frain, Sampson, Warburton, Rennie, Parrish, Grayson (Gibb), Gayle (Peer), White (Lee), Hunter.
Cardiff C: Williams; Jarman, Lloyd (Gardner), Perry, Young (Philliskirk), Fowler, Eckhardt, White, Dale, Haworth, Middleton (Stoker).
Northampton T won 4-2 on aggregate.

Swansea C (2) 3 *(Thomas 39, Torpey 43, Heggs 64)*
Chester C (0) 0   10,027
Swansea C: Freestone; Thomas, Moreira, Walker, Edwards, Jones (Chapple), Heggs, Penney, Torpey (Brown), Ampadu, Coates.
Chester C: Sinclair; Davidson (Woods), Jenkins, Reid, Whelan, Alsford, Flitcroft, Priest, McDonald (Rimmer), Milner (Jones), Aiston.
Swansea C won 3-0 on aggregate.

FINALS (at Wembley)

24 MAY

DIVISION 3

Northampton T (0) 1 *(Frain 90)*
Swansea C (0) 0   46,804
Northampton T: Woodman; Clarkson, Frain, Sampson, Warburton, Rennie (Peer), Parrish, Lee, Gayle (White), Grayson, Hunter.
Swansea C: Freestone; Thomas (Brown), Moreira, Walker, Edwards, Ampadu, Heggs, Penney, Torpey, Molby, Coates.

25 MAY

DIVISION 2

Brentford (0) 0
Crewe Alex (1) 1 *(Smith S 34)*   34,149
Brentford: Dearden; Hurdle (Ashby), Anderson, Hutchings, Bates, McGhee, Asaba, Smith, Bent (Canham), Statham, Taylor.
Crewe Alex: Kearton; Unsworth, Smith S, Westwood, Macauley, Charnock (Lightfoot), Whalley, Little, Adebola, Murphy (Johnson), Rivers (Garvey).

26 MAY

DIVISION 1

Crystal Palace (0) 1 *(Hopkin 90)*
Sheffield U (0) 0   64,383
Crystal Palace: Nash; Edworthy, Gordon, Roberts, Tuttle, Linighan, Hopkin, Muscat, Shipperley, Dyer, Rodger.
Sheffield U: Tracey; Ward, Nilsen, Spackman (Walker), Tiler, Holdsworth, White, Hutchison (Sandford), Fjortoft, Katchuro (Taylor), Whitehouse.

LEADING GOALSCORERS

LEADING GOALSCORERS 1996–97

	League	FA Cup	Coca-Cola Cup	Other Cups	Total
FA CARLING PREMIERSHIP					
Alan Shearer *(Newcastle U)*	25	1	1	1	28
Ian Wright *(Arsenal)*	23	0	5	2	30
Robbie Fowler *(Liverpool)*	18	1	5	7	31
Ole Gunnar Solskjaer *(Manchester U)*	18	0	0	1	19
Dwight Yorke *(Aston Villa)*	17	2	1	0	20
Fabrizio Ravanelli *(Middlesbrough)*	16	6	9	0	31
Les Ferdinand *(Newcastle U)*	16	1	0	4	21
Mike Evans *(Southampton)*	16	3	0	0	19
(All except 4 League goals for Plymouth Arg)					
Matthew Le Tissier *(Southampton)*	13	0	3	0	16
Dion Dublin *(Coventry C)*	13	0	0	0	13
Stan Collymore *(Liverpool)*	12	2	0	2	16
Juninho *(Middlesbrough)*	12	2	1	0	15
Dennis Bergkamp *(Arsenal)*	12	1	1	0	14
Dean Sturridge *(Derby Co)*	11	2	1	0	14
Steve Claridge *(Leicester C)*	11	1	2	0	14
Eric Cantona *(Manchester U)*	11	0	0	3	14
Chris Sutton *(Blackburn R)*	11	0	1	0	12
Efan Ekoku *(Wimbledon)*	11	0	1	0	12
NATIONWIDE INSURANCE DIVISION 1					
John McGinlay *(Bolton W)*	24	1	5	0	30
Steve Bull *(Wolverhampton W)*	23	0	0	0	23
Trevor Morley *(Reading)*	22	1	0	0	23
Nathan Blake *(Bolton W)*	19	2	3	0	24
Mike Sheron *(Stoke C)*	19	0	5	0	24
Clive Mendonca *(Grimsby T)*	19	0	1	0	20
Nigel Jemson *(Oxford U)*	18	0	5	0	23
John Aldridge *(Tranmere R)*	18	0	2	0	20
Tony Naylor *(Port Vale)*	17	0	3	0	20
John Spencer *(QPR)*	17	1	2	0	20
(Includes 2 Coca-Cola goals for Chelsea)					
Andy Payton *(Huddersfield T)*	17	0	2	0	19
Nigel Pepper *(Bradford C)*	17	1	1	0	19
(All except 5 League goals for York C)					
Neil Redfearn *(Barnsley)*	17	1	1	0	19
Bruce Dyer *(Crystal Palace)*	17	1	0	0	18
Darren Eadie *(Norwich C)*	17	0	0	0	17
Paul Devlin *(Birmingham C)*	16	2	1	0	19
DIVISION 2					
Tony Thorpe *(Luton T)*	28	1	2	0	31
Paul Barnes *(Burnley)*	24	1	0	0	25
Shaun Goater *(Bristol C)*	23	0	1	1	25
Carl Asaba *(Brentford)*	23	0	0	1	24
Iffy Onuora *(Gillingham)*	21	1	1	0	23
Kyle Lightbourne *(Walsall)*	20	4	1	0	25
Philip Clarkson *(Blackpool)*	18	2	1	0	21
(All except 5 League goals for Scunthorpe U)					
Ian Stevens *(Shrewsbury T)*	17	1	0	1	19
Dele Adebola *(Crewe Alex)*	16	1	1	0	18
Brett Angell *(Stockport Co)*	15	1	3	1	20
Tony Ellis *(Blackpool)*	15	0	3	2	20
David Reeves *(Preston NE)*	14	3	1	0	18
(Includes 3 League & 1 Coca-Cola goal for Carlisle U)					
Karl Connolly *(Wrexham)*	14	1	0	0	15
James Quinn *(Blackpool)*	13	1	3	0	17
Andy Cooke *(Burnley)*	13	0	1	0	14
Tommy Mooney *(Watford)*	13	0	0	0	13
DIVISION 3					
Graeme Jones *(Wigan Ath)*	31	0	1	1	33
Gareth Ainsworth *(Lincoln C)*	22	0	2	0	24
Mike Conroy *(Fulham)*	21	0	2	0	23
Colin Cramb *(Doncaster R)*	18	1	1	1	21
Phil Stant *(Lincoln C)*	18	0	0	0	18
(Includes 1 League goal for Bury, 2 for Northampton T)					
Darren Roberts *(Darlington)*	16	0	2	0	18
Adrian Foster *(Hereford U)*	16	0	1	0	17
Paul Baker *(Hartlepool U)*	15	5	3	0	23
(Includes 4 League, 3 Coca-Cola goals for Torquay U; 9 League & 5 FA Cup for Scunthorpe U)					
Craig Maskell *(Brighton & HA)*	14	1	0	1	16
Scott McGleish *(Leyton Orient)*	14	0	0	0	14
(Includes 7 League goals for Cambridge U)					
Duane Darby *(Hull C)*	13	6	0	1	20
Steve White *(Cardiff C)*	13	1	0	0	14
Ian Baird *(Brighton & HA)*	13	0	0	0	13
David Penney *(Swansea C)*	13	0	0	0	13
Andy Milner *(Chester C)*	12	2	0	0	14
Neil Grayson *(Northampton T)*	12	0	0	0	12

REVIEW OF THE SEASON

A disastrous seven days in October seemed to have written off Manchester United's hopes of retaining the FA Carling Premiership title. On Sunday October 20, they crashed 5-0 at Newcastle and on the following Saturday, were beaten 6-3 at Southampton. No aspiring championship team had suffered defeats conceding as many as five and six goals and still gone on to win the title.

And to say that they made this small piece of history by courtesy of the failure of their main rivals, does them scant justice. It took United another week to recover, but 16 matches later they had established an unbeaten run to take them to the top of the division; a position they secured.

Although there was an anti-climatic end to the season when Liverpool's defeat at Wimbledon handed United the Championship, they had lost fewer matches over the same period of the season than all their rivals except Newcastle.

Yet it was a curious season on Tyneside which had seemed likely to end successfully after that trouncing of United. There followed nine games in which only maximum points were taken on one occasion. Though Tottenham were beaten 7-1, manager Kevin Keegan was feeling the pressure and eventually quit to be replaced by Kenny Dalglish. While the team's inconsistencies were being sorted out, particularly in defence, the chance of them overhauling United was always more in theory than practice. But they conceded only five goals in the last ten games. Alan Shearer with 25 League goals was as reliable a marksman as ever.

Arsenal in third place were top in late November and early December after only two defeats in 17. The sequence included a 2-1 win at Newcastle, but the defeats were at Liverpool and Manchester United. They were never able to sustain similar momentum in the second half of the season.

For Liverpool, leaders in January, they continually failed to take advantage of the slips by Manchester United, who also took six points off them. They were involved in another classic 4-3 win over Newcastle in March, but uncharacteristically, the defence often committed elementary errors. Unusually, United's three main rivals all finished on the same number of points.

Aston Villa were never higher than fourth and their best run was five successive wins from the middle of November. Chelsea were unbeaten in their first six matches, but were never able to improve upon that. Their consolation came in a deserved FA Cup Final victory over Middlesbrough.

It was a staccato time at Sheffield Wednesday. It began with four wins, then eight without one. Seven games without defeat from the end of January provided some encouragement, but the season tailed off badly for them.

Eighth place for Wimbledon seemed uncharitable for a team which recovered splendidly after losing

There was disapointment for England in World Cup defeat against Italy but Alan Shearer *(left)* maintained his form at club and international level. He is seen here with Italy's Fabio Cannavaro. (Action Images)

its first three matches, winning the next seven. They ended the year in fourth place, but appeared to be handicapped by their involvement in cup competitions.

Newly-promoted Leicester's pre-occupation with the Coca-Cola Cup, which they won at the second attempt against Middlesbrough, almost cost them their Premiership place during a run of nine games without a win. But they recovered to win their last two matches.

Tottenham suffered a 7-1 defeat at Newcastle at the end of December and also lost 6-1 in the Coca-Cola Cup to Bolton. This, plus failure to beat any of the top four teams said everything for their season. The return to management of George Graham at Leeds United had a noticeable effect on their style of play. They scored only 28 goals, but finished 11th, despite failing to win any of their last nine games.

December was the start of a bleak period for Derby County, during which they fell four places and scored only five goals in nine games. Blackburn Rovers wretched start: four points from a possible 33 and only seven goals, had the alarm bells ringing at Ewood Park. But six games without defeat from February hauled them to safety.

A perilous position of 18th after just one win in 14 matches to mid-February provided a worrying time at West Ham, but the arrival of John Hartson from Arsenal and Paul Kitson from Newcastle gave them the necessary lift. Between them, these two scored 13 of the team's last 19 goals.

Just three wins in the last half of the season pushed Everton dangerously close to the relegation area and cost manager Joe Royle his job, but Southampton capable of defeating anyone – and just as likely to fail – ended confidently, losing only one of their last eight matches to preserve their status.

However it was Coventry who, once again, provided the excitement of leaving their escape until it was almost too late. All this, after just one win from their first 16 matches. Not such good fortune for Sunderland, relegated after one season in the Premier League, following a bright opening when they were sixth after three matches. Scoring goals was a continual problem. Their opening 13 matches produced a mere nine goals, including two penalties. One of their three wins was a 4-1 victory over Nottingham Forest. In the New Year, one goal came from six matches.

Middlesbrough, who were sixth in the middle of September, then endured 12 matches without a win. Cup runs in both major competitions congested their League programme and the deduction of three points for their failure to fulfil a fixture against Blackburn cost them dearly. In bottom place was Nottingham Forest who, after beating Coventry 3-0 on the opening day, failed to win a match in the next 16 or in the last 11.

For First Division champions Bolton Wanderers, they came close to a double century of goals and points, but a draw in their last match cost them two points. They were never headed in the table from Boxing Day, failed to score in only two goalless matches and incredibly suffered only one heavy defeat, 5-2 at bottom club Southend United.

John Barnes *(left)* attempts to match David Beckham stride for stride as Liverpool and Manchester United dispute Premier League points. (Action Images)

Eddie Newton's second goal for Chelsea in the FA Cup Final, killed off any hope of Middlesbrough equalising.
(Colorsport)

The other automatic promotion place went to Barnsley, who began with the flier of five wins. Only a spell of three defeats in four games from Boxing Day spoiled their general consistency.

Wolverhampton Wanderers' poor home record certainly cost them automatic promotion as they were beaten eight times at Molineux. They failed in the play-offs as did Ipswich, who seemed to have timed their play-off push to perfection when they won five games in a row in April. Sheffield United had twice lost to Ipswich in the League but beat them in the play-offs, before losing in turn to Crystal Palace. United were second on 18 January, but then failed to win any of the next five. Thus Palace in sixth place achieved what had always appeared likely: a place in the play-offs, though they had dropped to 10th after losing to Sheffield United in mid-April. Revenge came at the right moment.

Portsmouth's fine eight match unbeaten run to mid-March was their best all season, but not quite good enough for the play-offs. And Port Vale failed to win any of their last three after four successive wins had revived expectations. Standing sixth on Boxing Day after five consecutive victories seemed to be a useful position for Queens Park Rangers, but they were handicapped by poor early New Year form.

Birmingham were seventh at the end of November before five successive reverses plunged them to 20th. Tranmere were unable to win more than two matches in succession and a lack of consistency always troubled Stoke, who were as high as fifth on 18 January. Following only one defeat in their opening 12 matches, Norwich City soon afterwards had another run of ten without a win.

Though the best supported team outside the Premier League, Manchester City were unable to move out of mid-table, despite taking 16 points from a possible 18 to early March. For Charlton Athletic, an inconsistent season resulted from an indifferent start while 16th position at the halfway stage and 16th at the end of the season was the wrong kind of consistency for West Bromwich Albion.

As highly placed as fifth in mid-December, Oxford United chiselled out only seven more wins and Reading hovered above the relegation zone most of the season before improvement in February and March.

Only one goal and two points out of a possible 24 dramatically changed Swindon's season while Huddersfield never fully recovered from a run of nine matches and only three goals all scored in one match.

Bradford City won their last two matches to escape the drop, following a beginning in which they won only three of their first 17 games, scoring just 11 goals. The relegated trio consisted of Grimsby Town, Oldham Athletic and Southend United. Grimsby had two lengthy periods without a win of eight and seven matches; setbacks which proved decisive. Oldham had a poor start, their first win coming in the 11th match and again, this led to their downfall. Southend's one brief moment came in victory over champions Bolton, but they won only one of their last 14 matches.

Second Division champions Bury timed their run to perfection, winning nine of their last 13. This produced some economical scoring – 15 goals, but they conceded only four. Stockport County were not too distracted, despite a fine Coca-Cola Cup run and having to endure 10 games in April. This, after being in 22nd place after seven matches.

Luton also began badly, in third place from the bottom in the first table, rose to second by Boxing Day but still missed out on automatic promotion and eventually during the play-offs. Goals for Brentford dried up when Nicky Forster was sold to Birmingham, only 11 of them coming in the last 20 matches and there was failure for them as well in the play-offs.

Joe Jordan lost his job at Bristol City when the play-offs seemed unlikely, but John Ward revived fortunes which were to be dashed at the last stage. So it was left to sixth placed Crewe Alexandra, who always seemed likely to figure in them to make it up a division, despite briefly stalling in March.

For Blackpool, steady if unspectacular progress in the second half of the season, lifted them to seventh but it was a disappointing similar period for Wrexham and winning only two of their last eight cost Burnley a possible play-off position.

Chesterfield's excellent FA Cup run proved too much for them in the League where they were forced to play nine games in April. Gillingham's New Year revival was not maintained, neither were Walsall able to build upon six consecutive wins from Boxing Day.

A club record of 22 matches without defeat including 15 draws was all Watford could show for their efforts, because only one win and six goals came from their last ten outings.

Despite financial dramas off the field, Millwall were third on 8 March, then scored just four goals in their last 11 games. Preston North End defeated Brentford 1-0 on 8 March, but subsequently were unable to shake off their middle-of-the-table appearance. There were fiscal worries for Bournemouth, too, but there was a revival in the second half of the season.

Ninth place was the highest Bristol Rovers achieved all season and they failed to score in 18 matches. Wycombe Wanderers had just two wins in their first 17 but gradually pulled themselves out of danger. Plymouth Argyle had several long spells without a win and York City were only just off the relegation zone in the second half of the season.

Down went Peterborough United, who used 43 players including one 15 year old schoolboy. They were accompanied by Shrewsbury Town, with only one win from their last 15, Rotherham United who never recovered from failing to win any of their first eight matches and Notts County, who had a disasterous spell of 20 games without victory, a club record.

Wigan Athletic made it a four-time championship success story for Lancashire in 1996–97, by winning the Third Division. They pipped Fulham for the title, chiefly because their attack was invariably smarter than the opposition.

Fulham had held on to top place for long periods, but crucially scored only six goals in their last eight matches. Joining these two in automatic promotion were Carlisle United, the Auto Windscreens Shield winners, whose best run was 11 games without defeat to the beginning of February. They were joined from the play-offs by Northampton Town, who were struggling as low as 21st early in October. Swansea City, beaten by Northampton at Wembley, had one run of six successive wins, while Chester's 12 match unbeaten run to late March kept them in line for the play-offs. Fellow Welsh club Cardiff City were always hovering around a play-off place, but Colchester faltered badly after a run of 18 games without defeat.

Lincoln improved after only one win in their first six matches, but Cambridge won only one of their last 10. Mid-table was probably all that Mansfield could expect after no win in their opening seven matches. Scarborough were as high as fourth in early November then failed and Scunthorpe United were unable to capitalize on a mid-February spurt of five wins in six undefeated games.

Rochdale made an inauspicious start without a win in their first six games and found progress elusive thereafter and a similar sequence of 12 matches for Barnet into the New Year ruined what had been a promising first half of the season.

Leyton Orient's worst run came from mid-January with only one win in 13 matches, while Hull won only one of their last nine. Improved form in the New Year helped Darlington and a run of six games without defeat from mid-February aided Doncaster's situation. Two wins and a draw in the last three games hauled Hartlepool clear, but Torquay had only one win in their last 18. Neighbours Exeter fared slightly better with two successes in their last 11 matches.

Brighton, bottom from 5 October and minus two points, hauled themselves off the foot of the table a week before the end of the season, then dramatically drew 1-1 at Hereford to send their opponents into the Vauxhall Conference, Hereford having managed only five wins from the end of October.

INTRODUCTION TO THE CLUB SECTION

For this year's Rothmans Football Yearbook the players again appear under the club with whom they finished the season and in an A–Z form for easy reference (see pages 410–536). The names of Trainees and Associated Schoolboys are also included under each club's name.

The club section again comprises four pages, the first features the team photograph depicting those players and officials taken at the commencement of the 1996–97 season. On the second page which gives historical and record details for each club there are new entries in the 'Did you know?' series. Record Transfer fees are usually left to the discretion of the club concerned.

The third and fourth pages of this section present a complete record of the League season, including date, venue, opponents, results, half-time score, League position, goalscorers, attendances and complete line-ups including substitutes where used, for every League game in the 1996–97 season. This season goal times have been added, though not official they give an indication of when goals were scored. These appear as superior figures [10, 20, 30].

Squad numbers in the Premier League have been ignored; those used are the familiar ones, 1–11 while the introduction of a third outfield substitute has been recognised as follows:- the first substitute No. 12, the second No. 13 and the third No. 14. However, if there is a substitute goalkeeper he is represented by No. 15 but *only* if he replaces the first choice goalkeeper. Otherwise he adopts one of the other three substitute numbers, as there have been several instances where a goalkeeper has been used as an outfield player because of injuries during the game. Players replaced are respectively noted with superior figures [1], [2], [3] and [g] for goalkeeper. These third and fourth pages also include consolidated lists of goalscorers for the club in League, Coca-Cola Cup and FA Cup matches plus a summary of results in these two main domestic competitions.

The continued increase in the number of matches played on Sundays has resulted in the League positions shown after every League result being taken on that day. Full holiday programmes are also recorded, but the position after mid-week fixtures will not normally have been updated. Attendance figures quoted for the Nationwide Football League are those which appeared in the Press at the time. But those in the FA Carling Premiership are official. The attendance statistics published on pages 573–575 are those officially issued by the FA Premier League and the Football League at the end of the season.

In the totals at the top of each column on page 4, substitute appearances are listed separately by the '+', but have been amalgamated in the totals which feature in the players historical section in the directory mentioned above. Thus these appearances include those as substitute. In fact the directory again features those names appearing on the FA Premier League and Football League's Retained list, which is published at the end of May. Each player's height and weight where known, plus birth place, birth date and source together with total League goals and appearances for each club he has represented, can be found as in previous editions. The player's details remain under the club which retained him at the end of the season. An asterisk '*' by a player's name indicates that he was given a free transfer at the end of the 1996–97 season, a dagger '†' against a name means that he is a non-contract player, a double dagger '‡' indicates that the player's registration was cancelled during the season and a section mark '§' shows the player to be a trainee or associated schoolboy who has made League appearances. Appearances by players in the play-offs are not included in their career totals.

There is also a directory of all League club managers to be found on pages 553–562.

ARSENAL 1996–97   *Back row (left to right):* Gavin McGown, Lee Dixon, Patrick Viera, Steve Bould, John Hartson, Paul Merson, Scott Marshall, Stephen Hughes.
Middle row: Bobby Armitt (Kit Manager), Gary Lewin (Physio), Colin Lewin (Reserve Team Physio), Ray Parlour, David Seaman, John Lukic, Lee Harper, Vince Bartram, Nigel Winterburn,
Matthew Rose, George Armstrong (Reserve Team Coach), Mark James (Masseur).
Front row: Ian Wright, David Platt, Dennis Bergkamp, Glenn Helder, Andy Linighan, Martin Keown, Arsène Wenger (Manager), Tony Adams, Steve Morrow, Adrian Clarke, Ian Selley, Paul Shaw,
Remi Garde.
(Photograph: Kenneth Prater Photography)

FA Premiership   ARSENAL

Arsenal Stadium, Highbury, London N5 1BU. Telephone: (0171) 704 4000. Fax: (0171) 704 4001. Box Office: (0171) 413 3366. Commercial and Marketing: (0171) 704 4100. Recorded information on (0171) 704 4242. Clubline: 0891 202021.

Ground capacity: 38,500 all seated.

Record attendance: 73,295 v Sunderland, Div 1, 9 March 1935.

Record receipts: £392,726.50 v Sampdoria, European Cup-Winners' Cup, semi-final first leg, 6 April 1995.

Pitch measurements: 110yd × 73yd.

Life President: Sir Robert Bellinger GBE, D.SC.

Chairman: P. D. Hill-Wood. *Vice-Chairman:* D. Dein.

Directors: R. G. Gibbs, C. E. B. L. Carr, R. C. L. Carr, D. D. Fiszman.

Managing Director: K. J. Friar.

Manager: Arséne Wenger. *Assistant Manager/Coach:* Pat Rice. *Head Youth Coach:* Don Howe. *Head of Youth Development:* Liam Brady.

Physio: Gary Lewin. *Reserve Coach:* George Armstrong. *Youth Coach:* Don Givens.

Secretary: K. J. Friar. *Assistant Secretary:* David Miles. *Commercial Manager:* John Hazell.

Stadium Manager: J. Beattie.

Year Formed: 1886. *Turned Professional:* 1891. *Ltd Co.:* 1893.

Previous Names: 1886, Dial Square; 1886–91, Royal Arsenal; 1891–1914, Woolwich Arsenal.

Club Nickname: 'Gunners'.

Previous Grounds: 1886–87, Plumstead Common; 1887–88, Sportsman Ground; 1888–90, Manor Ground; 1890–93, Invicta Ground; 1893–1913, Manor Ground; 1913, Highbury.

Foundation: Formed by workers at the Royal Arsenal, Woolwich in 1886 they began as Dial Square (name of one of the workshops) and included two former Nottingham Forest players Fred Beardsley and Morris Bates. Beardsley wrote to his old club seeking help and they provided the new club with a full set of red jerseys and a ball. The club became known as the "Woolwich Reds" although their official title soon after formation was Woolwich Arsenal.

First Football League game: 2 September 1893, Division 2, v Newcastle U (h) D 2-2 – Williams; Powell, Jeffrey; Devine, Buist, Howat; Gemmell, Henderson, Shaw (1), Elliott (1), Booth.

Record League Victory: 12–0 v Loughborough T, Division 2, 12 March 1900 – Orr; McNichol, Jackson; Moir, Dick (2), Anderson (1); Hunt, Cottrell (2), Main (2), Gaudie (3), Tennant (2).

Record Cup Victory: 11–1 v Darwen, FA Cup 3rd rd, 9 January 1932 – Moss; Parker, Hapgood; Jones, Roberts, John; Hulme (2), Jack (3), Lambert (2), James, Bastin (4).

Record Defeat: 0–8 v Loughborough T, Division 2, 12 December 1896.

Most League Points (2 for a win): 66, Division 1, 1930–31.

Most League Points (3 for a win): 83, Division 1, 1990–91.

Most League Goals: 127, Division 1, 1930–31.

Highest League Scorer in Season: Ted Drake, 42, 1934–35.

Most League Goals in Total Aggregate: Cliff Bastin, 150, 1930–47.

Most Capped Player: Kenny Sansom, 77 (86), England.

Most League Appearances: David O'Leary, 558, 1975–93.

Record Transfer Fee Received: £2,800,000 from Nottingham F for Kevin Campbell, July 1995.

Record Transfer Fee Paid: £7,500,000 to Internazionale for Dennis Bergkamp, June 1995.

Football League Record: 1893 Elected to Division 2; 1904–13 Division 1; 1913–19 Division 2; 1919–92 Division 1; 1992– FA Premier League.

Honours: Football League: Division 1 – Champions 1930–31, 1932–33, 1933–34, 1934–35, 1937–38, 1947–48, 1952–53, 1970–71, 1988–89, 1990–91; Runners-up 1925–26, 1931–32, 1972–73; Division 2 – Runners-up 1903–04. *FA Cup:* Winners 1930, 1936, 1950, 1971, 1979, 1993; Runners-up 1927, 1932, 1952, 1972, 1978, 1980. *Double performed:* 1970–71. *Football League Cup:* Winners 1987, 1993; Runners-up 1968, 1969, 1988. *European Competitions: Fairs Cup:* 1963–64, 1969–70 (winners), 1970–71; *European Cup:* 1971–72, 1991–92; *UEFA Cup:* 1978–79, 1981–82, 1982–83, 1996–97; *European Cup-Winners' Cup:* 1979–80 (runners-up), 1993–94 (winners), 1994–95 (runners-up).

Colours: Red shirts with white sleeves, white shorts, red and white hooped stockings. *Change colours:* Yellow with navy band, navy shorts, navy stockings with yellow band.

Did you know?
When Arsenal signed Charlie Buchan from Sunderland in 1925 for £2000 they agreed to pay a further £100 for each goal he scored that season. It cost them an extra £2000.

ARSENAL 1996–97 LEAGUE RECORD

Match No.	Date		Venue	Opponents	Result		H/T Score	Lg. Pos.	Goalscorers	Attendance
1	Aug	17	H	West Ham U	W	2-0	2-0	—	Hartson [27], Bergkamp (pen) [40]	38,056
2		19	A	Liverpool	L	0-2	0-0	—		38,103
3		24	A	Leicester C	W	2-0	1-0	3	Bergkamp (pen) [27], Wright [90]	20,429
4	Sept	4	A	Chelsea	D	3-3	1-2	—	Merson [44], Keown [64], Wright [77]	38,132
5		7	A	Aston Villa	D	2-2	0-1	8	Merson [70], Linighan [90]	37,944
6		16	H	Sheffield W	W	4-1	0-1	—	Platt [57], Wright 3 (1 pen) [61 (p), 78, 89]	33,461
7		21	A	Middlesbrough	W	2-0	2-0	3	Hartson [3], Wright [27]	29,629
8		28	A	Sunderland	W	2-0	0-0	2	Hartson [73], Parlour [88]	38,016
9	Oct	12	H	Blackburn R	W	2-0	1-0	2	Wright 2 [3, 51]	24,303
10		19	H	Coventry C	D	0-0	0-0	2		38,141
11		26	H	Leeds U	W	3-0	2-0	1	Dixon [1], Bergkamp [5], Wright [55]	38,076
12	Nov	2	A	Wimbledon	D	2-2	1-1	2	Wright [6], Merson [64]	25,521
13		16	A	Manchester U	L	0-1	0-0	3		55,210
14		24	H	Tottenham H	W	3-1	1-0	2	Wright (pen) [28], Adams [88], Bergkamp [90]	38,264
15		30	A	Newcastle U	W	2-1	1-1	1	Dixon [11], Wright [60]	36,565
16	Dec	4	H	Southampton	W	3-1	1-0	—	Merson [43], Wright (pen) [57], Shaw [89]	38,033
17		7	H	Derby Co	D	2-2	1-0	1	Adams [45], Vieira [90]	38,018
18		21	A	Nottingham F	L	1-2	0-0	2	Wright [63]	27,384
19		26	A	Sheffield W	D	0-0	0-0	2		23,245
20		28	H	Aston Villa	D	2-2	1-0	3	Wright [12], Merson [73]	38,130
21	Jan	1	H	Middlesbrough	W	2-0	2-0	2	Bergkamp [15], Wright [44]	37,573
22		11	A	Sunderland	L	0-1	0-0	3		21,074
23		19	H	Everton	W	3-1	0-0	3	Bergkamp [55], Vieira [57], Merson [69]	38,095
24		29	A	West Ham U	W	2-1	1-0	—	Parlour [8], Wright [67]	24,382
25	Feb	1	A	Leeds U	D	0-0	0-0	3		35,596
26		15	H	Tottenham H	D	0-0	0-0	3		33,039
27		19	H	Manchester U	L	1-2	0-2	—	Bergkamp [69]	38,172
28		23	H	Wimbledon	L	0-1	0-1	4		37,854
29	Mar	1	A	Everton	W	2-0	2-0	3	Bergkamp [21], Wright [27]	36,980
30		8	H	Nottingham F	W	2-0	0-0	2	Bergkamp 2 (1 pen) [50, 79 (p)]	38,206
31		15	A	Southampton	W	2-0	1-0	3	Hughes [41], Shaw [72]	15,144
32		24	H	Liverpool	L	1-2	0-0	—	Wright [78]	38,068
33	Apr	5	A	Chelsea	W	3-0	1-0	2	Wright [22], Platt [53], Bergkamp [80]	26,923
34		12	A	Leicester C	W	2-0	1-0	2	Adams [35], Platt [66]	38,044
35		19	H	Blackburn R	D	1-1	1-0	2	Platt [18]	38,086
36		21	A	Coventry C	D	1-1	1-1	—	Wright (pen) [19]	20,004
37	May	3	H	Newcastle U	L	0-1	0-1	3		38,179
38		11	A	Derby Co	W	3-1	0-1	3	Wright 2 [55, 90], Bergkamp [82]	18,287

Final League Position: 3

GOALSCORERS

League (62): Wright 23 (4 pens), Bergkamp 12 (3 pens), Merson 6, Platt 4, Adams 3, Hartson 3, Dixon 2, Parlour 2, Shaw 2, Vieira 2, Hughes 1, Keown 1, Linighan 1.
Coca-Cola Cup (8): Wright 5 (3 pens), Bergkamp 1, Merson 1, Platt 1.
FA Cup (3): Bergkamp 1, Hartson 1, Hughes 1.

Seaman D 22	Dixon L 31+1	Winterburn N 38	Keown M 33	Bould S 33	Linighan A 10+1	Parlour R 17+13	Hartson J 14+5	Merson P 32	Bergkamp D 28+1	Morrow S 5+9	Wright I 30+5	Dickov P —+1	Hillier D —+2	Helder G —+2	Lukic J 15	Platt D 27+1	Vieira P 30+1	Adams T 27+1	Shaw P 1+7	Garde R 7+4	McGowan G 1	Marshall S 6+2	Hughes S 9+5	Rose M 1	Harper L 1	Selley I —+1	Anelka N —+4	Match No.
1	2	3	4	5	6	7	8²	9	10¹	11	12	13																1
1	2	3	4	5	6	7	8¹	9	10³	11²	12		13	14														2
1	2	3	4	5	6	7	8¹	9	10²	11	12		13															3
	2	3	4	5¹	6	7	8	9	10	11²	12				1	13												4
	2	3		5	6	11	12	9	10²	4¹	8			13	1	7												5
1	2	3	4	5	6	11¹	10	9			8					7	12											6
1	2¹	3	4	5	6		10	9			8					7	11	12										7
1	2	3²	4	5		12	10	9			8					7	11¹	6		13								8
1	2	3	4	5		12	10¹	9			8					7	11	6										9
1	2	3	4	5			10¹	9	12		8					7	11	6										10
1	2	3¹	4	5			9	10	12		8²					7	11	6		13								11
1	2	3	4	5			9	10¹			8					7	11	6		12								12
1	2	3	4	5			9	10			8					7	11	6										13
	2	3	4	5	12	13	9		10¹		8				1	7²	11	6										14
	2	3	4³	5	12	13	10¹	9²		14	8				1	7	11	6										15
	2	3		5	4	12	10²	9			8				1	7¹	11	6		13								16
	2	3		5	4¹		10	9			8				1	7	11	6		12								17
		3	4	5	6	12	13	9	10²	14	8				1	7	11³				2¹							18
		3	4²	5		2	9	10			8				1	7¹		6	12	11			13					19
		3	4	5		2	9	10	12		8				1		11	6		7¹								20
		3	4	5		2	12	9³	10¹	13	8				1		11	6	14	7²								21
1		3¹	4	5		2	8	9	10							7	11	6				12						22
1	12	3	4	5		2	9	10			8¹					7²	11	6				13						23
1	2	3		5		7	12	9		13	8¹						11	6		14		10²	4³					24
1	2	3		5		7	8¹	9			12						11	6				4	10					25
1	2	3	4	5		7		9¹	10		8				1		11	6				12						26
1	2	3	4	5		7		9	10		8				1		11	6¹				12						27
	2	3		5¹		7³		9	10	12	8				1		11	6	13	4²		14						28
	2	3		5				10	12		8				1	7	11			4¹		6	9					29
	2	3	4				9	10	12						1	7	11	6				5	8¹					30
		3	4			2		10								7	11	6	9¹	12		5	8	1				31
1	2¹	3	4			12		10			8					7	11	6	13	14		5¹	9²					32
1	2	3	4	5		12			10		8³					7	11²	6					9¹			13	14	33
1	2	3	4	5		12			10		8					7	11	6					9¹					34
1	2	3	4	5		12			10		8					7	11	6					9¹					35
1	2¹	3	4	5		12		9²	10		8					7	11	6								13		36
1	2	3	4	5		12		9	10		8					7²	11	6¹								13		37
1	2	3	4	5		12		9²	10		8					7	11¹	6								13		38

Coca-Cola Cup

Third Round	Stoke C	(a)	1-1
		(h)	5-2
Fourth Round	Liverpool	(a)	2-4

FA Cup

Third Round	Sunderland	(h)	1-1
		(a)	2-0
Fourth Round	Leeds U	(h)	0-1

ASTON VILLA 1996–97 *Back row (left to right):* Scott Murray, Phil King, Neil Davis, Gareth Farrelly, Carl Tiler, Riccardo Scimeca, Darren Byfield, Lee Hendrie, Fernando Nelson.
Middle row: Paul Barron (Fitness Coach), Paul McGrath, Gareth Southgate, Ugo Ehiogu, Michael Oakes, Mark Bosnich, Ian Taylor, Gary Charles, Tommy Johnson, Jim Walker (Physio).
Front row: Julian Joachim, Steve Staunton, Franz Carr, Mark Draper, Alan Evans (Assistant Manager), Brian Little (Manager), John Gregory (Coach), Savo Milosevic, Dwight Yorke, Andy Townsend, Alan Wright.

FA Premiership ASTON VILLA

Villa Park, Trinity Rd, Birmingham B6 6HE. Telephone: (0121) 327 2299. Fax: (0121) 322 2107. Commercial Dept: (0121) 327 5399. Commercial Fax: (0121) 328 2099. Clubcall: 0891 121148. Ticketline: 0891 121848. Ticket information: (0121) 327 5353. Club shop: (0121) 327 2800.

Ground capacity: 39,339.

Record attendance: 76,588 v Derby Co, FA Cup 6th rd, 2 March 1946.

Record receipts: £1,196,712 Portugal v Czech Republic, Euro '96, 23 June 1996.

Pitch measurements: 115yd × 72yd.

President: J. A. Alderson. *Chairman:* H. D. Ellis.

Directors: P. D. Ellis, S. M. Stride, M. J. Ansell, D. M. Owen, A. Hales, Dr D. H. Targett.

Manager: Brian Little. *Assistant Manager:* Allan Evans. *First Team Coach:* Kevin MacDonald.

Secretary: Steven Stride. *Director of Youth:* Bryan Jones.

Physio: Jim Walker. *Reserve Team Coach:* Malcolm Beard. *Youth Coach:* Tony McAndrew. *Chief Scout:* Peter Withe. *Fitness Consultant:* Paul Barron.

Commercial Manager: Abdul Rashid. *Stadium Manager:* E. Small.

Year Formed: 1874. *Turned Professional:* 1885. *Ltd Co.:* 1896.

Previous Grounds: 1874–76, Aston Park; 1876–97, Perry Barr; 1897, Villa Park.

Club Nickname: 'The Villans'.

Foundation: Cricketing enthusiasts of Villa Cross Wesleyan Chapel, Aston, Birmingham decided to form a football club during the winter of 1873–74. Football clubs were few and far between in the Birmingham area and in their first game against Aston Brook St. Mary's Rugby team they played one half rugby and the other soccer. In 1876 they were joined by a Scottish soccer enthusiast George Ramsay who was immediately appointed captain and went on to lead Aston Villa from obscurity to one of the country's top clubs in a period of less than 10 years.

First Football League game: 8 September 1888, Football League, v Wolverhampton W, (a) D 1-1 – Warner; Cox, Coulton; Yates, H. Devey, Dawson; A. Brown, Green (1), Allen, Garvey, Hodgetts.

Record League Victory: 12–2 v Accrington S, Division 1, 12 March 1892 – Warner; Evans, Cox; Harry Devey, Jimmy Cowan, Baird; Athersmith (1), Dickson (2), John Devey (4), L. Campbell (4), Hodgetts (1).

Record Cup Victory: 13–0 v Wednesbury Old Ath, FA Cup 1st rd, 30 October 1886 – Warner; Coulton, Simmonds; Yates, Robertson, Burton (2); R. Davis (1), A. Brown (3), Hunter (3), Loach (2), Hodgetts (2).

Record Defeat: 1–8 v Blackburn R, FA Cup 3rd rd, 16 February 1889.

Most League Points (2 for a win): 70, Division 3, 1971–72.

Most League Points (3 for a win): 78, Division 2, 1987–88.

Most League Goals: 128, Division 1, 1930–31.

Highest League Scorer in Season: 'Pongo' Waring, 49, Division 1, 1930–31.

Most League Goals in Total Aggregate: Harry Hampton, 215, 1904–15.

Most Capped Player: Paul McGrath, 51 (83), Republic of Ireland.

Most League Appearances: Charlie Aitken, 561, 1961–76.

Record Transfer Fee Received: £5,500,000 from Bari for David Platt, July 1991.

Record Transfer Fee Paid: £7,000,000 to Liverpool for Stan Collymore, May 1997.

Football League Record: 1888 Founder Member of the League; 1936–38 Division 2; 1938–59 Division 1; 1959–60 Division 2; 1960–67 Division 1; 1967–70 Division 2; 1970–72 Division 3; 1972–75 Division 2; 1975–87 Division 1; 1987–88 Division 2; 1988–92 Division 1; 1992– FA Premier League.

Honours: FA Premier League: – Runners-up 1992–93. *Football League:* Division 1 – Champions 1893–94, 1895–96, 1896–97, 1898–99, 1899–1900, 1909–10, 1980–81; Runners-up 1888–89, 1902–03, 1907–08, 1910–11, 1912–13, 1913–14, 1930–31, 1932–33, 1989–90; Division 2 – Champions 1937–38, 1959–60; Runners-up 1974–75, 1987–88; Division 3 – Champions 1971–72. *FA Cup:* Winners 1887, 1895, 1897, 1905, 1913, 1920, 1957; Runners-up 1892, 1924. *Double Performed:* 1896–97. *Football League Cup:* Winners 1961, 1975, 1977, 1994, 1996; Runners-up 1963, 1971. **European Competitions:** *European Cup:* 1981–82 (winners), 1982–83; *UEFA Cup:* 1975–76, 1977–78, 1983–84, 1990–91, 1993–94, 1994–95, 1996–97. *World Club Championship:* 1982; European Super Cup: 1982–83 (winners).

Colours: Claret and blue shirt, white shorts, claret and blue hooped socks. *Change colours:* Sky blue/claret with white sections shirt, white socks and shorts.

Did you know?
Billy Walker converted three penalty kicks for Aston Villa against Bradford City on 12 November 1921 in a 7–1 win in the First Division.

ASTON VILLA 1996–97 LEAGUE RECORD

Match No.	Date	Venue	Opponents	Result	H/T Score	Lg. Pos.	Goalscorers	Attendance
1	Aug 17	A	Sheffield W	L 1-2	0-0	—	Johnson [88]	26,861
2	21	H	Blackburn R	W 1-0	0-0	—	Southgate [64]	32,457
3	24	H	Derby Co	W 2-0	1-0	4	Joachim [19], Johnson (pen) [47]	34,646
4	Sept 4	A	Everton	W 1-0	0-0	—	Ehiogu [62]	39,115
5	7	H	Arsenal	D 2-2	1-0	4	Milosevic 2 [39, 63]	37,944
6	15	A	Chelsea	D 1-1	1-1	7	Townsend [18]	27,729
7	21	H	Manchester U	D 0-0	0-0	6		39,339
8	30	A	Newcastle U	L 3-4	1-3	—	Yorke 3 [4, 59, 69]	36,400
9	Oct 12	A	Tottenham H	L 0-1	0-0	8		32,840
10	19	H	Leeds U	W 2-0	0-0	7	Yorke [58], Johnson [65]	39,051
11	26	A	Sunderland	L 0-1	0-1	7		21,032
12	Nov 2	H	Nottingham F	W 2-0	1-0	7	Tiler [20], Yorke [64]	35,310
13	16	H	Leicester C	L 1-3	1-2	9	Yorke [15]	36,193
14	23	A	Coventry C	W 2-1	1-0	8	Joachim [29], Staunton [85]	21,335
15	30	H	Middlesbrough	W 1-0	1-0	7	Yorke (pen) [39]	39,053
16	Dec 4	A	West Ham U	W 2-0	1-0	—	Ehiogu [38], Yorke [74]	19,105
17	7	A	Southampton	W 1-0	1-0	4	Townsend [34]	15,232
18	22	H	Wimbledon	W 5-0	2-0	4	Yorke 2 [38, 86], Milosevic [42], Taylor [61], Blackwell (og) [75]	28,875
19	26	H	Chelsea	L 0-2	0-0	5		39,339
20	28	A	Arsenal	D 2-2	0-1	6	Milosevic [68], Yorke [74]	38,130
21	Jan 1	A	Manchester U	D 0-0	0-0	6		55,133
22	11	H	Newcastle U	D 2-2	1-2	6	Yorke [39], Milosevic [52]	39,339
23	18	A	Liverpool	L 0-3	0-0	7		40,489
24	29	H	Sheffield W	L 0-1	0-0	—	—	26,726
25	Feb 1	H	Sunderland	W 1-0	1-0	7	Milosevic [37]	32,491
26	19	H	Coventry C	W 2-1	1-0	—	Yorke 2 [43, 75]	30,409
27	22	A	Nottingham F	D 0-0	0-0	5		25,239
28	Mar 2	H	Liverpool	W 1-0	0-0	5	Taylor [83]	39,339
29	5	A	Leicester C	L 0-1	0-0	—		20,626
30	15	H	West Ham U	D 0-0	0-0	6		35,992
31	22	A	Blackburn R	W 2-0	0-0	5	Johnson [64], Yorke [79]	24,274
32	Apr 5	H	Everton	W 3-1	1-1	5	Milosevic [41], Staunton [50], Yorke [54]	39,339
33	9	A	Wimbledon	W 2-0	1-0	—	Milosevic [26], Wright [78]	9015
34	12	A	Derby Co	L 1-2	0-2	4	Joachim [84]	18,071
35	19	H	Tottenham H	D 1-1	0-0	5	Yorke [81]	39,339
36	22	H	Leeds U	D 0-0	0-0	—		26,884
37	May 3	A	Middlesbrough	L 2-3	0-2	5	Ehiogu [58], Milosevic [77]	30,012
38	11	H	Southampton	W 1-0	1-0	5	Dryden (og) [12]	39,339

Final League Position: 5

GOALSCORERS

League (47): Yorke 17 (1 pen), Milosevic 9, Johnson 4 (1 pen), Ehiogu 3, Joachim 3, Staunton 2, Taylor 2, Townsend 2, Southgate 1, Tiler 1, Wright 1, own goals 2.
Coca-Cola Cup (2): Taylor 1, Yorke 1 (pen).
FA Cup (4): Yorke 2, Curcic 1, Ehiogu 1.

Oakes M 18 + 2	Murray S 1	Staunton S 30	Southgate G 28	Ehiogu U 38	Townsend A 34	Taylor I 29 + 5	Draper M 28 + 1	Yorke D 37	Johnson T 10 + 10	Wright A 38	Joachim J 3 + 12	Scimeca R 11 + 6	Curcic S 17 + 5	Nelson F 33 + 1	Milosevic S 29 + 1	Bosnich M 20	Tiler C 9 + 2	Hendrie L — + 4	Hughes D 4 + 3	Farrelly G 1 + 2	Match No.
1	2^1	3	4	5	6	7	8	9	10	11	12										1
1		3	4	5	6	2	8	9	10^1	11	7	12									2
1		3	4	5	6	2	8	9^1	10	11	12			7^2	13						3
1	6	4	5	7	12	8	11	13	3			14	10^1	2^3	9^1						4
1	6	4	5	7	13	8	11	12	3				10	2^2	9^1						5
1	6	4	5	7	12	8	11	13	3				10^1	2	9^1						6
1	6	4	5	7	12	8	11		3				10^1	2	9						7
1	6	4	5		7	8	11		3				10	2	9						8
	6		5	10		7	8^1	11	13	3	12		4	2	9^2	1	14				9
	6^2		5	11		7		9	10^1	3	12	13	8	2		1	4				10
15		4	5	11	2	8^2	9	10	3		12			7^1		1^6	6	13			11
1		4	5	11		7		9	10	3			8	2			6				12
1		4	5	11		7	12	9	10	3		13	8^2	2^1			6				13
1	6	4	5	11	12	8^3		10	3	9^2	13	7^1	2	14							14
1	6		5	10		7	8	11		3			4	2	9						15
1	6		5	10		7	8	11		3			4	2	9						16
1	6		5	10		7	8	11^1		3	12		4	2	9						17
	6^2		5	10		7	8^1	11		3		12	4	2	9	1		13			18
	6		5	10		7	8^2	11	12	3		13	4	2	9^1	1					19
	6		5	10		7	8^1	11	12	3			4	2	9	1					20
	6		5	10		7^1	8	11	12	3				2	9	1	4				21
	6	8	5			7	11^1	10	3		12	13		2^2	9	1	4				22
		4	5			7	11	10	3				8	2	9	1	6				23
11		4	5			7			3	12	10	8^2		2	9	1	6^1	13			24
11	10		5			7			3			8^1	4	2	9	1	6	12			25
	6	4	5	10		7	8	11	3					2	9	1					26
	6^1	4	5	10		7	8	11	3			12		2	9	1					27
	6^1	4	5	10		7	8	11	3					2	9	1	12				28
		4	5	10		7	8^2	11	12	3		13		2	9^1	1		6			29
		4	5	10		7	8^2	11	12	3	9^1			2		1		13	6		30
	6		5	10		7	8	11	12	3			4	2	9^1	1					31
1	6^2	4	5			7^1	8	11	3		12			2	9			13	10		32
1		4	5	10		7	8	11	3					2	9				6		33
1		4	5	10		7	8^1	11	3	13		12		2	9				6^2		34
1	6	4^2	5	10		7	8^1	11	3		12			2	9			13			35
	6	4	5	10^1		7		11	3				8	2	9	1	12				36
15	6	4	5	10		7		11	3	12		8^1		2	9^2	1^6		13			37
	11	4	5	10		7		8	3				6	2	9	1					38

Coca-Cola Cup

Third Round	Leeds U	(a)	2-1
Fourth Round	Wimbledon	(a)	0-1

FA Cup

Third Round	Notts Co	(a)	0-0
		(h)	3-0
Fourth Round	Derby Co	(a)	1-3

BARNET 1996–97 *Back row (left to right):* Gary Gilbert-Anderson (Physio), Lee Howarth, Shaun Gale, Linvoy Primus, Dean Samuels, Jamie Campbell, Lee Harrison, Lee Hodges, Sam Stockley, Kieren Adams, Jamie Ndah, Jon Ford, Laird Budge (Kit Manager), Terry Harvey (Reserve Team Coach).
Front row: Terry Bullivant (First Team Coach), Sean Devine, Warren Goodhind, Paul Wilson, Phil Simpson, Phil Simpson, Neil Thompson, Matt Brady, Micky Tomlinson, Alan Pardew.

Division 3

BARNET

Underhill Stadium, Barnet Lane, Barnet, Herts EN5 2BE. Telephone: (0181) 441 6932. Fax: (0181) 447 0655.
Ground capacity: 4057.

Record attendance: 11,026 v Wycombe Wanderers. FA Amateur Cup 4th Round 1951–52.

Record Receipts: £31,202 v Portsmouth, FA Cup 3rd Round, 5 January 1991.

Pitch measurements: 112yd × 72yd.

Chairman: A. Kleanthous. *Vice-Chairman:* D. J. Buchler FCA.

Directors: S. Glynne, F. Higgins FCA, J. Barnett.

Manager: John Still. *Physio:* G. Gilbert-Anderson MSF, MAB Phys.

Coach: Mick Halsall. *Secretary:* David Stanley. *Sales and Commercial Manager:* Colin Leggett.

Year Formed: 1888. *Turned Professional:* 1965. *Ltd Co:*

Club Nickname: The Bees.

Previous Names: 1906–19 Barnet Alston FC.

Previous Grounds: 1888-1901, Queens Road; 1901-07, Totteridge Lane.

Foundation: Barnet Football Club was formed in 1888, disbanded in 1901. A club known as Alston Works FC was then formed and in 1906 changed its name to Barnet Alston FC. In 1912 it combined with The Avenue to become Barnet and Alston.

First Football League game: 17 August 1991, Division 4, v Crewe Alex (h) L 4-7 – Phillips; Blackford, Cooper (Murphy), Horton, Bodley (Stein), Johnson, Showler, Carter (2), Bull (2), Lowe, Evans.

Record League Victory: 6–0 v Lincoln C (away), Division 4, 4 September 1991 – Pape; Poole, Naylor, Bodley, Howell, Evans (1), Willis (1), Murphy (1), Bull (2), Lowe, Showler (1 og).

Record Cup Victory: 6–1 v Newport Co, FA Cup 1st rd, 21 November 1970 – McClelland; Lye, Jenkins, Ward, Enbery, King, Powell (1), Ferry, Adams (1), Gray, George (3) (1 og).

Record Defeat: 0–6 v Port Vale, Division 2, 21 August 1993.

Most League Points (3 for a win): 79, Division 3, 1992–93.

Most League Goals: 81, Division 4, 1991–92.

Highest League Scorer in Season: Gary Bull, 20, Division 4, 1991–92.

Most League Goals in Total Aggregate: Gary Bull 37, 1991–96.

Most Capped Player: None

Most League Appearances: Paul Wilson, 174, 1991–97.

Record Transfer Fee Received: £800,000 from Crystal Palace for Dougie Freedman, September 1995.

Record Transfer Fee Paid: £40,000 to Barrow for Kenny Lowe, January 1991 and £40,000 to Runcorn for Mark Carter, February 1991.

Football League Record: Promoted to Division 4 from GMVC 1991; 1991–92 Division 4; 1992–93 Division 3; 1993–94 Division 2; 1994– Division 3.

Honours: Football League: best season 24th, Division 2, 1993–94. *FA Amateur Cup:* Winners 1946. *GM Vauxhall Conference:* Winners 1990–91. *FA Cup:* best season; never past 3rd rd. *League Cup:* never past 2nd rd.

Colours: Amber and black striped shirts, black shorts, black stockings. *Change colours:* Green and white striped shirts, green shorts, green stockings.

Did you know?
By 1946, Barnet could claim to have won at least once every competition for which they had entered, except for the FA Cup.

BARNET 1996–97 LEAGUE RECORD

Match No.	Date	Venue	Opponents	Result	H/T Score	Lg. Pos.	Goalscorers	Attendance
1	Aug 17	A	Cambridge U	L 0-1	0-0	—		2809
2	24	H	Wigan Ath	D 1-1	0-1	19	Hardyman [61]	1905
3	27	A	Brighton & HA	W 3-0	0-0	—	Wilson (pen) [48], Gale [70], Tomlinson [84]	2513
4	31	A	Hull C	D 0-0	0-0	12		4605
5	Sept 7	H	Northampton T	D 1-1	0-1	14	Devine [55]	2982
6	10	A	Mansfield T	D 0-0	0-0	—		1505
7	14	A	Lincoln C	L 0-1	0-0	18		2484
8	21	H	Exeter C	W 3-0	1-0	13	Devine 3 [22, 47, 76]	2020
9	28	A	Scunthorpe U	W 2-1	0-0	10	Wilson (pen) [68], Devine [88]	1942
10	Oct 1	H	Scarborough	L 1-3	0-2	—	Hodges [79]	1606
11	5	H	Torquay U	D 0-0	0-0	12		2456
12	12	A	Cardiff C	W 2-1	1-1	9	Brazil [17], Devine [86]	2879
13	15	A	Colchester U	L 0-1	0-0	—		2732
14	19	H	Hartlepool U	W 1-0	0-0	9	Devine [69]	2265
15	26	H	Carlisle U	D 0-0	0-0	11		2422
16	29	A	Darlington	W 1-0	1-0	—	Codner [32]	1759
17	Nov 2	A	Hereford U	D 1-1	1-0	9	Devine [7]	2655
18	9	H	Rochdale	W 3-2	1-1	8	Devine [37], Hardyman [67], Wilson (pen) [78]	2405
19	19	A	Fulham	L 0-2	0-1	—		4423
20	23	H	Doncaster R	W 3-0	2-0	6	Devine 2 [23, 70], Simpson [31]	2098
21	30	A	Carlisle U	L 1-2	0-0	6	Hodges [84]	4472
22	Dec 3	H	Leyton Orient	D 0-0	0-0	—		2549
23	21	H	Chester C	L 1-2	0-1	12	Campbell [54]	1581
24	26	A	Mansfield T	D 1-1	0-1	14	Brazil [84]	1778
25	28	A	Northampton T	L 0-2	0-1	14		5060
26	Jan 14	A	Swansea C	L 0-3	0-1	—		3570
27	18	A	Scarborough	D 1-1	0-1	17	Hodges [86]	1835
28	25	H	Darlington	D 0-0	0-0	16		1956
29	Feb 1	A	Rochdale	D 1-1	0-0	17	Simpson [58]	1623
30	8	H	Hereford U	L 2-3	1-1	18	Primus [24], Wilson (pen) [73]	2439
31	15	A	Doncaster R	D 1-1	0-1	19	Ndah [47]	2199
32	22	H	Fulham	D 2-2	1-1	18	Hodges [13], Wilson (pen) [61]	3316
33	25	H	Lincoln C	W 1-0	1-0	—	Ndah [16]	1194
34	Mar 1	A	Leyton Orient	W 1-0	1-0	15	Primus [9]	4621
35	4	A	Exeter C	D 1-1	1-0	—	Ford [18]	2394
36	8	H	Chester C	L 0-1	0-0	16		2291
37	15	H	Swansea C	L 0-1	0-1	17		1881
38	22	A	Wigan Ath	L 0-2	0-0	17		3286
39	29	H	Cambridge U	W 2-1	1-1	17	Ndah [45], Primus [81]	2409
40	Apr 1	A	Brighton & HA	L 0-1	0-1	—		9525
41	5	H	Hull C	W 1-0	0-0	15	Ndah [68]	1668
42	8	H	Scunthorpe U	D 1-1	1-0	—	Campbell [44]	1395
43	12	A	Torquay U	W 2-1	0-1	14	Campbell [54], Howarth [75]	1959
44	19	H	Cardiff C	W 3-1	1-0	14	Samuels [24], Gale [59], Middleton (og) [69]	2497
45	26	A	Hartlepool U	L 0-4	0-1	14		3070
46	May 3	H	Colchester U	L 2-4	1-2	15	Campbell [6], Hodges [58]	1909

Final League Position: 15

GOALSCORERS

League (46): Devine 11, Hodges 5, Wilson 5 (5 pens), Campbell 4, Ndah 4, Primus 3, Brazil 2, Gale 2, Hardyman 2, Simpson 2, Codner 1, Ford 1, Howarth 1, Samuels 1, Tomlinson 1, own goal 1.
Coca-Cola Cup (7): Simpson 2, Campbell 1, Codner 1, Devine 1, Tomlinson 1, Wilson 1.
FA Cup (8): Devine 4, Hodges 2, Campbell 1, Simpson 1.

Taylor M 25	Gale S 40 + 3	Primus L 46	Hardyman P 13 + 3	Codner R 20 + 4	Howarth L 37 + 1	Tomlinson M 19 + 11	Simpson P 29 + 3	Dunwell R 1	Devine S 30 + 1	Pardew A 23 + 3	Campbell J 36 + 7	Brady M 1 + 6	Wilson P 37	Mills D — + 2	McDonald D 10 + 8	Brazil G 15 + 4	Adams K 1 + 2	Rattray K 9	Thompson N 1	Goodhind W 1 + 2	Hodges L 28 + 3	Constantinou C 1	Samuels D 13 + 4	Harrison L 21	Stockley S 21	Patterson G 3	Ndah J 12 + 2	Ford J 13	Match No.
1	2	5	3	4	6	7¹	8	9²	10	11	12	13																	1
1	2	5	3	4	6	7²	8¹		10	11	12		9		13														2
1	2	5¹	3	4	6	7	8		10	11			9		12														3
1	2¹	5	3	4	6	7²	8³		10	11		13	9	14	12														4
1	2	5	3¹	4	6	7			10	11			9			8	12												5
1	2	5		4	6	7	8		10	11			9		3¹	12													6
1	2	5		4	6	12	8		10	11		3¹	9								7								7
1	2¹	5		4	6	13	12		10²	11	14		9		3	8		7³											8
1		5	4¹		6				10	11	3		9		2	8		7			12								9
1	2	5	4¹		6		12	13	10	11	4		9		3	8²		7³			14								10
1	2	5			6	12	8		10	11	4		9¹		3	13					7²								11
1	2	5	12		6	13			10	11		14	9		3³	8					7²	4¹							12
1	2	5	12		6				10	11	4		9		3	8¹					7								13
1	2	5	12	13	6				10	11¹	4		9		3	8					7²								14
1	2	5	12	4	6				10	11	7		9		3¹	8													15
1	2	5	3	4¹	6	12			10	11	7		9			8													16
1	2	5¹	3	4	6	13			10	11	7		9²	12	8														17
1	2	5	3	12	4	6¹			10	11²	7		9		13	8³		14											18
1	2	5	3	4	12	8			10	7¹			9		6						11								19
1	2	5¹	3	4	6	7	8²		10	13			9	12	14						11³								20
1	2	5	3	4	6	7¹	8		10				9		12						11								21
1	2	5	3	4	6	7	8		10				9								11								22
1	2	5	3²	4¹	6	7	8³		12	10			9	13	14						11								23
1	2	5	4¹		6	7	8		10				9			11		3			12								24
1	2	5	4		6	7			10				9			11		3			8								25
		5			6		8		10	11	3							7			9			1	2		4		26
	12	5			6	13	8			11	3							7		9	10¹			1	2²		4		27
	12	5			6	13			10	11	3¹							7		9²	8			1	2		4		28
	13	5			6	12	4		10	11	3		9¹					8			7²			1	2				29
		5			6	12	4		10	11¹	3		9					8			7			1	2				30
	3	5			6	11	4			12			9					8			7¹			1	2		10		31
	3	5	12			7	4			11¹			9					8						1	2		10	6	32
	3	5				7	4			11			9					8			12			1	2		10¹	6	33
	3	5				7	4		10	11			9											1	2		8	6	34
	3	5	12				4		10	11¹			9					7						1	2		8	6	35
	3	5				7¹			10	11			9		4			12						1	2		8	6	36
	3	5				7			10	11¹			9		4			12						1	2		8	6	37
	3	5			6	12				11	7³		9		13			8						1	2		10¹	4	38
	3	5			6	8				11²	13		9	12				7						1	2		10¹	4	39
	3	5			6	8				11			9					7						1	2		10	4	40
	3	5			6	12	8¹			11								7		9				1	2		10	4	41
	3	5			6	12	8			11²	13							7		9				1	2		10¹	4	42
	3²	5			6		8¹		12	11			9					7		10				1	2		13	4	43
	3	5			6		8²	12	4	11¹			9	13				7		10				1	2				44
	3	5					8		4	11¹			9					7		10				1	2		12	6	45
	3	5			6	12				11	13		9		8²			4		7¹	10			1	2				46

Coca-Cola Cup

First Round	Exeter C	(a)	4-0	
		(h)	2-0	
Second Round	West Ham U	(h)	1-1	
		(a)	0-1	

FA Cup

First Round	Farnborough T	(a)	2-2	
		(h)	1-0	
Second Round	Wycombe W	(h)	3-3	
		(a)	2-3	

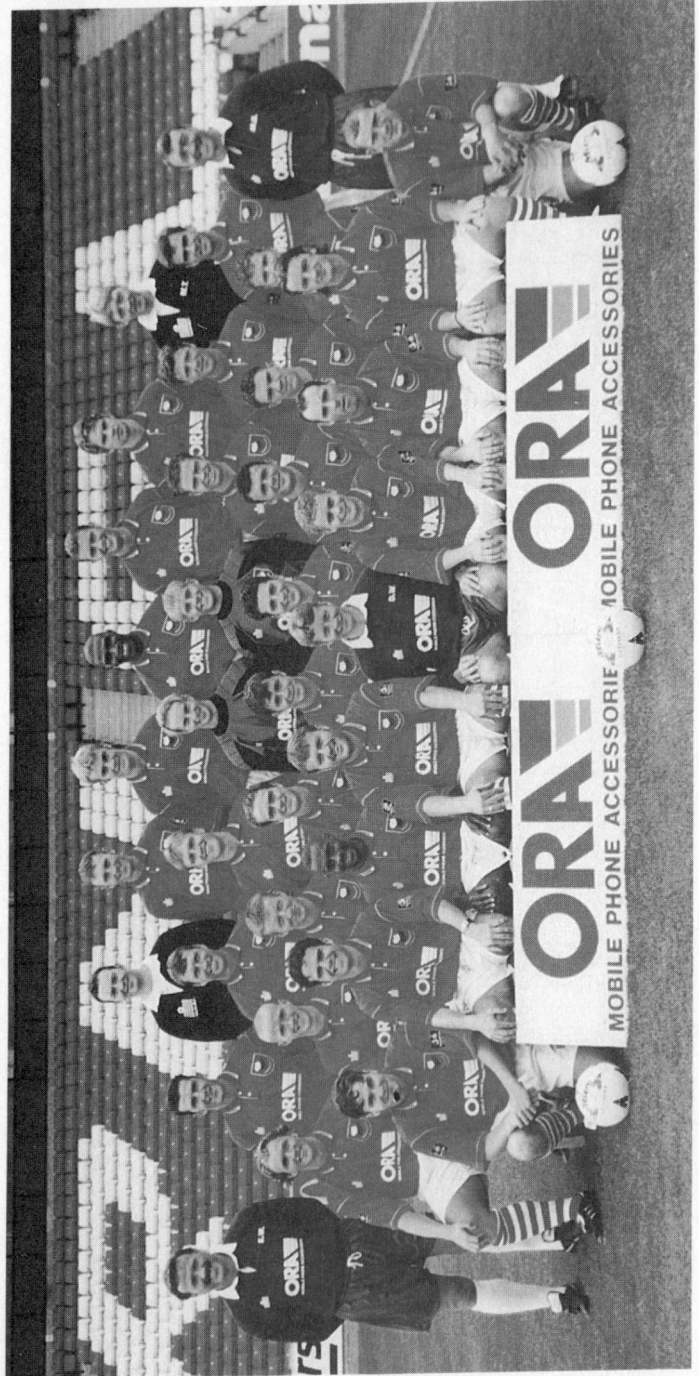

BARNSLEY 1996–97 *Back row (left to right):* Paul Smith (Physio), Dean Jones, Mark Hume, Dave Regis, Darron Clyde, Jonathan Perry, Mick Tarmey (Physio).
Third row: Eric Winstanley (First Team Coach), Paul Wilkinson, Peter Shirtliff, Steve Davis, Adam Sollitt, David Watson, Adrian Moses, Arjan de Zeeuw, Neil Thompson, Malcolm Shotton (Reserve Team Coach).
Second row: Carel van der Velden, Glynn Hurst, Luke Beckett, Laurens Ten-Heuvel, Troy Bennett, Nicky Eaden, Jovo Bosancic, Chris Morgan, Scott Jones.
Front row: Sean McClare, Andrew Liddell, Clint Marcelle, Neil Redfearn, Danny Wilson (Manager), Martin Bullock, Darren Sheridan, Matt Appleby, Andrew Gregory.

FA Premiership
BARNSLEY

Oakwell Ground, Grove St, Barnsley, South Yorkshire S71 1ET. Telephone: (01226) 211211. Fax: (01226) 211444. Clubcall: 0891 121152.

Ground capacity: 18,806.

Record attendance: 40,255 v Stoke C, FA Cup 5th rd, 15 February 1936.

Record receipts: Not disclosed.

Pitch measurements: 110yd × 75yd.

President: Arthur Raynor. *Chairman:* J. A. Dennis.

Directors: C. B. Taylor (Vice-Chairman), C. H. Harrison, M. R. Hayselden, J. N. Kelly, S. M. Hall, I. D. Potter.

Player-Manager: Danny Wilson.

First Team Coach: Eric Winstanley. *Physios:* Michael Tarmey, Paul Smith.

General Manager/Secretary: Michael Spinks. *Lotteries Manager:* Gerry Whewall. *Sales and Marketing Manager:* Graham Barlow.

Year Formed: 1887. *Turned Professional:* 1888. *Ltd Co.:* 1899.

Previous Name: Barnsley St Peter's, 1887–97.

Club Nickname: 'The Tykes', 'Reds' or 'Colliers'.

Foundation: Many clubs owe their inception to the church and Barnsley are among them, for they were formed in 1887 by the Rev. T. T. Preedy, curate of Barnsley St. Peter's and went under that name until it was dropped in 1897 a year before being admitted to the Second Division of the Football League.

First Football League game: 1 September 1898, Division 2, v Lincoln C (a) L 0-1 – Fawcett; McArtney, Nixon; King, Burleigh, Porteous; Davis, Lees, Murray, McCullough, McGee.

Record League Victory: 9–0 v Loughborough T, Division 2, 28 January 1899 – Greaves; McArtney, Nixon; Porteous, Burleigh, Howard; Davis (4), Hepworth (1), Lees (1), McCullough (1), Jones (2). 9–0 v Accrington S, Division 3 (N), 3 February 1934 – Ellis; Cookson, Shotton; Harper, Henderson, Whitworth; Spence (2), Smith (1), Blight (4), Andrews (1), Ashton (1).

Record Cup Victory: 6–0 v Blackpool, FA Cup 1st rd replay, 20 January 1910 – Mearns; Downs, Ness; Glendinning, Boyle (1), Utley; Bartrop, Gadsby (1), Lillycrop (2), Tufnell (2), Forman. 6–0 v Peterborough U, League Cup 1st rd, 2nd leg, 15 September 1981 – Horn; Joyce, Chambers, Glavin (2), Banks, McCarthy, Evans, Parker (2), Aylott (1), McHale, Barrowclough (1).

Record Defeat: 0–9 v Notts Co, Division 2, 19 November 1927.

Most League Points (2 for a win): 67, Division 3 (N), 1938–39.

Most League Points (3 for a win): 80, Division 1, 1996–97.

Most League Goals: 118, Division 3 (N), 1933–34.

Highest League Scorer in Season: Cecil McCormack, 33, Division 2, 1950–51.

Most League Goals in Total Aggregate: Ernest Hine, 123, 1921–26 and 1934–38.

Most Capped Player: Gerry Taggart, 35 (42), Northern Ireland.

Most League Appearances: Barry Murphy, 514, 1962–78.

Record Transfer Fee Received: £1,500,000 from Nottingham F for Carl Tiler, May 1991.

Record Transfer Fee Paid: £310,000 to Celtic for Andy Payton, November 1993.

Football League Record: 1898 Elected to Division 2; 1932–34 Division 3 (N); 1934–38 Division 2; 1938–39 Division 3 (N); 1946–53 Division 2; 1953–55 Division 3 (N); 1955–59 Division 2; 1959–65 Division 3; 1965–68 Division 4; 1968–72 Division 3; 1972–79 Division 4; 1979–81 Division 3; 1981–92 Division 2; 1992–97 Division 1; 1997– FA Premier League.

Honours: Football League: Division 1 – Runners-up 1996–97; Division 3 (N) – Champions 1933–34, 1938–39, 1954–55; Runners-up 1953–54; Division 3 – Runners-up 1980–81; Division 4 – Runners-up 1967–68; Promoted 1978–79. *FA Cup:* Winners 1912; Runners-up 1910. *Football League Cup:* best season: 5th rd, 1982.

Colours: Red shirts, white shorts, red stockings. *Change colours:* Royal blue and black striped shirts, black shorts, black stockings.

Did you know?
The omen of a fine season for Barnsley might have been predicted when they began the 1996–97 season with five wins in a row, their best opening spell for 18 years.

BARNSLEY 1996–97 LEAGUE RECORD

Match No.	Date	Venue	Opponents	Result	H/T Score	Lg. Pos.	Goalscorers	Attendance
1	Aug 17	A	WBA	W 2-1	1-1	—	Marcelle [23], Liddell [55]	18,561
2	25	H	Huddersfield T	W 3-1	1-1	2	Wilkinson [28], Redfearn [73], Marcelle [78]	9787
3	28	H	Reading	W 3-0	2-0	—	Sheridan [24], Liddell 2 [37, 82]	7523
4	Sept 7	A	Manchester C	W 2-1	0-0	1	Marcelle 2 [67, 90]	26,464
5	10	H	Stoke C	W 3-0	1-0	—	Davis [17], Thompson [88], Liddell [90]	11,696
6	14	H	QPR	L 1-3	0-2	2	Wilkinson [69]	13,003
7	21	A	Oldham Ath	W 1-0	1-0	2	Redfearn (pen) [41]	7043
8	28	H	Grimsby T	L 1-3	0-1	2	Liddell [65]	8833
9	Oct 1	A	Ipswich T	D 1-1	1-0	—	Redfearn (pen) [26]	9041
10	12	H	Crystal Palace	D 0-0	0-0	3		9183
11	15	H	Oxford U	D 0-0	0-0	—		6337
12	19	A	Bradford C	D 2-2	1-1	3	Liddell [36], Davis [89]	11,477
13	25	H	Bolton W	D 2-2	0-1	—	Redfearn 2 (1 pen) [57, 67 (p)]	9413
14	29	A	Port Vale	W 3-1	1-0	—	Hendrie [45], De Zeeuw [62], Marcelle [88]	5231
15	Nov 2	A	Wolverhampton W	D 3-3	3-1	4	De Zeeuw [31], Redfearn (pen) [35], Eaden [44]	22,840
16	12	H	Norwich C	W 3-1	0-0	—	Moses [55], Wilkinson [61], Hendrie [71]	9697
17	16	A	Swindon T	L 0-3	0-0	4		10,837
18	23	H	Portsmouth	W 3-2	2-0	3	Wilkinson [17], Hendrie [41], Davis [84]	7449
19	30	A	Bolton W	D 2-2	1-1	3	Redfearn 2 (1 pen) [25 (p), 79]	16,852
20	Dec 3	A	Birmingham C	D 0-0	0-0	—		24,004
21	7	H	Southend U	W 3-0	0-0	3	Hendrie [72], Wilkinson 2 [75, 89]	7483
22	14	H	Tranmere R	W 3-0	1-0	2	Hendrie [17], Wilkinson [65], Redfearn (pen) [89]	8513
23	21	A	Sheffield U	W 1-0	0-0	1	Hendrie [85]	24,384
24	26	A	Stoke C	L 0-1	0-0	3		19,025
25	28	H	Manchester C	W 2-0	2-0	2	Bosancic (pen) [20], Moses [32]	17,159
26	Jan 11	A	QPR	L 1-3	1-1	2	Redfearn [39]	12,058
27	18	H	Ipswich T	L 1-2	0-0	3	Liddell [82]	9872
28	28	A	Grimsby T	W 3-2	2-1	—	Hendrie 3 [31, 38, 77]	6323
29	Feb 1	A	Norwich C	D 1-1	1-0	3	Eaden [18]	17,001
30	8	H	Port Vale	W 1-0	1-0	3	Hendrie [26]	12,246
31	15	A	Charlton Ath	D 2-2	0-1	2	Hendrie 2 [48, 90]	9104
32	22	H	Wolverhampton W	L 1-3	0-2	3	Sheridan [53]	18,024
33	Mar 1	A	Southend U	W 2-1	1-1	3	Redfearn 2 [8, 54]	4855
34	4	H	Swindon T	D 1-1	1-1	—	Redfearn [35]	8518
35	7	H	Sheffield U	W 2-0	1-0	—	Hendrie [36], Eaden [83]	14,668
36	15	A	Tranmere R	D 1-1	0-1	3	Wilkinson [46]	7347
37	22	A	Huddersfield T	D 0-0	0-0	3		14,754
38	28	H	WBA	W 2-0	2-0	—	Redfearn [34], Thompson (pen) [40]	12,087
39	31	A	Reading	W 2-1	2-1	2	Holsgrove (og) [2], Liddell [16]	10,244
40	Apr 5	H	Birmingham C	L 0-1	0-1	2		13,092
41	12	H	Charlton Ath	W 4-0	2-0	2	Marcelle [32], Thompson 2 [36, 81], Hendrie [86]	11,701
42	15	H	Oldham Ath	W 2-0	1-0	—	Hendrie [44], Marcelle [59]	17,476
43	19	A	Crystal Palace	D 1-1	0-1	2	Thompson (pen) [47]	20,006
44	22	A	Portsmouth	L 2-4	0-2	—	Redfearn 2 [62, 73]	8328
45	26	A	Bradford C	W 2-0	1-0	2	Wilkinson [21], Marcelle [87]	18,605
46	May 4	A	Oxford U	L 1-5	0-3	2	Redfearn [59]	8693

Final League Position: 2

GOALSCORERS

League (76): Redfearn 17 (6 pens), Hendrie 15, Wilkinson 9, Liddell 8, Marcelle 8, Thompson 5 (2 pens), Davis 3, Eaden 3, De Zeeuw 2, Moses 2, Sheridan 2, Bosancic 1 (pen), own goal 1.
Coca-Cola Cup (4): Wilkinson 2, Redfearn 1, own goal 1.
FA Cup (4): Bullock 1, Hendrie 1, Marcelle 1, Redfearn 1.

Watson D 46	Eaden N 46	Appleby M 35	Bosancic J 17 + 8	Davis S 24	De Zeeuw A 43	Marcelle C 26 + 14	Redfearn N 43	Wilkinson P 45	Liddell A 25 + 13	Thompson N 24	Sheridan D 39 + 2	Moses A 25 + 3	Regis D — + 4	Bullock M 7 + 21	Van der Velden C 1 + 1	Shirtliff P 12 + 1	Ten-Heuvel L — + 3	Hurst G — + 1	Hendrie J 36	Jones S 12 + 6	Match No.
1	2	3	4¹	5	6	7²	8	9	10	11	12	13									1
1	2	3	4¹	5	6	7	8	9	10	11	12										2
1	2	3	4	5	6		8	9	10	11	7										3
1	2	3		5	6	7	8	9¹	10	11	4		12								4
1	2	3	12	5	6	7	8	9²	10	11	4¹	13									5
1	2	3		5	6	7	8	9	10²	11	4¹	13	12								6
1	2	3	4	5	6	7	8	9	10¹	11	12										7
1	2	3	4³	5	6	7¹	8	9	10	11²		13	12	14							8
1	2	3		5	6		8	9	10	11³	12	13	14	4²					7¹		9
1	2	3		5	6		8	9	10		4	11				12			7¹		10
1	2	3		5	6		8	9	10		4				12				7¹	11	11
1	2²	3		5	6	12	8	9	10¹		4	13							7	11	12
1	2	3		5	6	12	8	9	10		4								7	11¹	13
1	2	3	12	5	6	13	8	9	10¹		4²								7	11	14
1	2	3		5	6	12²	8	9¹	10		4	13							7	11	15
1	2	3	12		6		8	9	10		4	5							7¹	11	16
1	2¹	3			6	13	8	9	10²		4	5				12			7	11	17
1	2	3	13	5	6	12	8	9	10¹	11²	4								7		18
1	2	3	4	5	6	10¹	8	9		11	12								7		19
1	2	3	4¹	5	6	10	8	9		11									7	12	20
1	2	3¹	4²	5	6	10	8	9		11						12			7	13	21
1	2		4	5	6	10¹	8	9	12		3	13		11²					7		22
1	2		4	5	6	10	8¹	9		11	3								7	12	23
1	2	3	4³	5	6	10¹		9	12	11		14		13					7	8²	24
1	2	3	4	5	6	10		9	12	11		8							7¹		25
1	2		4	5¹	6	10	8	9²	13	11	12			3					7		26
1	2	12			6	10³	8	9	7	5²	4	3	11¹	14					13		27
1	2	3²				8	9¹	10¹	11	4	5	12	6	14					7	13	28
1	2	3	12			8	9	10¹	11	4	5		6						7		29
1	2	11			6	12	8	9¹	10	4	5		3						7		30
1	2	11²			6	12	8	9	10¹	4	5		3						7	13	31
1	2²	4¹			6	12	8	9	13	11	5	14	3²						7	10	32
1	2	3			6	12	8	9		4	5	11¹							7	10	33
1	2	3¹			6	12	8	9	13	4	5	11							7²	10	34
1	2	3			6	10	8	9		11	4	5							7		35
1	2	12			6	10	8	9²	13	4¹	5	14	3						7	11³	36
1	2	6				10	8	9	12	3	4	5	11						7¹		37
1	2	3			6	10²	8	9¹	12	11	4	5	13						7		38
1	2	3¹	12		6	10	8	9		11	4	5							7		39
1	2	3¹			6	10²	8	9	12	11	4	5	13						7		40
1	2	3			6	10²	8	9¹	12	11	4	5	13						7		41
1	2	3	8¹		6	10		9	12	11	5	4							7		42
1	2	3¹			6	10	8	9		11	4	5	12						7		43
1	2				6	10¹	8	9	12	11	4	5	13	3²					7		44
1	2				6	12	8	9	10²	3	4	5	11¹	13					7		45
1	2	12			6	13	8	9		11	4¹	5	10	3²					7		46

Coca-Cola Cup

First Round	Rochdale	(a)	1-2
		(h)	2-0
Second Round	Gillingham	(h)	1-1
		(a)	0-1

FA Cup

Third Round	Oldham Ath	(h)	2-0
Fourth Round	QPR	(a)	2-3

BIRMINGHAM CITY 1996–97   *Back row (left to right):* Martin Grainger, Gary Poole, Gary Breen, Kevin Francis, Andy Edwards, Dave Barnett, Gary Ablett, Michael Johnson, Andy Legg.

Middle row: Frank Barlow (Assistant Manager), Arvel Lowe (Fitness Coach), Jason Bowen, John Frain, Ricky Otto, Paul Tait, John Cornforth, Mike Newell, Jonathan Hunt, Mick Mills (Assistant Manager), Neil McDiarmid (Physio). Paul Furlong.

Front row: Steve Finnan, Steve Castle, Bart Griemink, Steve Bruce, Trevor Francis (Manager), Barry Horne, Ian Bennett, Paul Devlin, Paul Barnes.

Division 1   **BIRMINGHAM CITY**

St Andrews, Birmingham B9 4NH. Telephone: (0121) 772 0101. Fax: (0121) 766 7866. Lottery Office/Souvenir Shop: (0121) 772 1245. Clubcall: 0891 121188. Club Soccer Shop: (0121) 766 8274.

Ground capacity: 25,812.

Record attendance: 66,844 v Everton, FA Cup 5th rd, 11 February 1939.

Record receipts: £230,000 v Aston Villa, Coca-Cola Cup 2nd rd 1st leg, 21 September 1993.

Pitch measurements: 115yd × 75yd.

Directors: J. F. Wiseman (Chairman), K. R. Brady (Managing Director), D. Sullivan, D. Gold, R. Gold, B. Gold, H. Brandman, A. G. Jones.

Manager: Trevor Francis. *Coach:* Mick Mills. *Physio:* N. McDiarmid.

Commercial Manager: Allan Robson. *Stadium Manager:* Brian Tew.

Secretary: A. G. Jones BA, MBA.

Year Formed: 1875. *Turned Professional:* 1885. *Ltd Co.:* 1888.

Previous Names: 1875–88, Small Heath Alliance; 1888, dropped 'Alliance'; became Birmingham 1905; became Birmingham City 1945.

Club Nickname: 'Blues'.

Previous Grounds: 1875, waste ground near Arthur St; 1877, Muntz St, Small Heath; 1906, St Andrews.

Foundation: In 1875 cricketing enthusiasts who were largely members of Trinity Church, Bordesley, determined to continue their sporting relationships throughout the year by forming a football club which they called Small Heath Alliance. For their earliest games played on waste land in Arthur Street, the team included three Edden brothers and two James brothers.

First Football League game: 3 September 1892, Division 2, v Burslem Port Vale (h) W 5-1 – Charsley; Bayley, Speller; Ollis, Jenkyns, Devey; Hallam (1), Edwards (1), Short (1), Wheldon (2), Hands.

Record League Victory: 12–0 v Walsall T Swifts, Division 2, 17 December 1892 – Charsley; Bayley, Jones; Ollis, Jenkyns, Devey; Hallam (2), Walton (3), Mobley (3), Wheldon (2), Hands (2). 12–0 v Doncaster R, Division 2, 11 April 1903 – Dorrington; Goldie, Wassell; Beer, Dougherty (1), Howard; Athersmith (1), Leonard (3), McRoberts (1), Wilcox (4), Field (1). Aston. (1 og).

Record Cup Victory: 9–2 v Burton W, FA Cup 1st rd, 31 October 1885 – Hedges; Jones, Evetts (1); F. James, Felton, A. James (1); Davenport (2), Stanley (4), Simms, Figures, Morris (1).

Record Defeat: 1–9 v Sheffield W, Division 1, 13 December 1930 and v Blackburn R, Division 1, 5 January 1895.

Most League Points (2 for a win): 59, Division 2, 1947–48.

Most League Points (3 for a win): 89, Division 2, 1994–95.

Most League Goals: 103, Division 2, 1893–94 (only 28 games).

Highest League Scorer in Season: Joe Bradford, 29, Division 1, 1927–28.

Most League Goals in Total Aggregate: Joe Bradford, 249, 1920–35.

Most Capped Player: Malcolm Page, 28, Wales.

Most League Appearances: Frank Womack, 491, 1908–28.

Record Transfer Fee Received: £2,500,000 from Coventry C for Gary Breen, January 1997.

Record Transfer Fee Paid: £1,500,000 to Chelsea for Paul Furlong, July 1996.

Football League Record: 1892 elected to Division 2; 1894–96 Division 1; 1896–1901 Division 2; 1901–02 Division 1; 1902–03 Division 2; 1903–08 Division 1; 1908–21 Division 2; 1921–39 Division 1; 1946–48 Division 2; 1948–50 Division 1; 1950–1955 Division 2; 1955–65 Division 1; 1965–72 Division 2; 1972–79 Division 1; 1979–80 Division 2; 1980–84 Division 1; 1984–85 Division 2; 1985–86 Division 1; 1986–89 Division 2; 1989–92 Division 3; 1992–94 Division 1; 1994–95 Division 2; 1995– Division 1.

Honours: Football League: Division 1 best season: 6th, 1955–56; Division 2 – Champions 1892–93, 1920–21, 1947–48, 1954–55, 1994–95; Runners-up 1893–94, 1900–01, 1902–03, 1971–72, 1984–85. Division 3 Runners-up 1991–92. *FA Cup:* Runners-up 1931, 1956. *Football League Cup:* Winners 1963. *Leyland Daf Cup:* Winners 1991. *Auto Windscreens Shield:* Winners 1995. **European Competitions:** *European Fairs Cup:* 1955–58, 1958–60 (runners-up), 1960–61 (runners-up), 1961–62.

Colours: Blue shirts, white shorts, blue and white hooped stockings. *Change colours:* Yellow shirts, black shorts.

Did you know?
When Birmingham City won the Second Division Championship in 1947–48, they conceded only 24 goals and had the unusual distinction of finishing with more points (59) than goals scored (55), in the days of two points for a win.

BIRMINGHAM CITY 1996–97 LEAGUE RECORD

Match No.	Date	Venue	Opponents	Result	H/T Score	Lg. Pos.	Goalscorers	Attendance
1	Aug 18	H	Crystal Palace	W 1-0	1-0	—	Devlin 25	18,765
2	24	A	Sheffield U	D 4-4	2-1	6	Furlong 9, Newell 37, Devlin (pen) 75, Hunt 83	16,332
3	Sept 7	A	Tranmere R	L 0-1	0-0	21		8548
4	10	H	Oldham Ath	D 0-0	0-0	—		17,228
5	14	H	Stoke C	W 3-1	2-0	15	Furlong 2 2, 65, Legg 32	18,612
6	21	A	Manchester C	L 0-1	0-0	17		26,757
7	28	H	QPR	D 0-0	0-0	18		17,430
8	Oct 8	A	Huddersfield T	L 0-3	0-3	—		10,904
9	12	H	Bradford C	W 3-0	1-0	19	Devlin 2 1, 50, Hunt 88	25,157
10	15	H	Ipswich T	W 1-0	0-0	—	Bowen 50	15,664
11	18	A	Oxford U	D 0-0	0-0	—		7594
12	26	H	Norwich C	L 2-3	1-1	15	Devlin 2 40, 86	18,869
13	29	A	Portsmouth	D 1-1	1-0	—	Furlong 22	6334
14	Nov 2	A	Port Vale	L 0-3	0-2	20		8388
15	13	H	Bolton W	W 3-1	0-0	—	Furlong 55, Bowen 56, Todd (og) 81	17,033
16	17	A	Wolverhampton W	W 2-1	1-1	14	Breen 8, Legg 58	22,627
17	20	A	Charlton Ath	L 1-2	1-1	—	Legg 13	8574
18	23	H	Swindon T	W 1-0	0-0	10	Furlong 29	16,559
19	26	A	Reading	D 0-0	0-0	—		8407
20	30	A	Norwich C	W 1-0	0-0	7	O'Connor 62	12,764
21	Dec 3	H	Barnsley	D 0-0	0-0	—		24,004
22	7	H	Grimsby T	D 0-0	0-0	8		17,001
23	20	A	Southend U	D 1-1	0-0	—	Devlin 88	5100
24	Jan 10	A	Stoke C	L 0-1	0-1	—		10,049
25	18	H	Reading	W 4-1	1-0	15	Furlong 33, Devlin 2 (1 pen) 56 (p), 75, Gilkes (og) 89	15,363
26	29	A	QPR	D 1-1	1-0	—	Devlin 36	12,138
27	Feb 1	A	Bolton W	L 1-2	0-1	16	Devlin 56	16,737
28	4	H	WBA	L 2-3	1-1	—	O'Connor 14, Devlin (pen) 55	21,600
29	8	H	Portsmouth	L 0-3	0-1	18		15,897
30	23	H	Port Vale	L 1-2	1-1	20	Devlin (pen) 8	13,192
31	26	A	Swindon T	L 1-3	1-2	—	Ablett 22	7428
32	Mar 1	A	Grimsby T	W 2-1	0-1	20	O'Connor 60, Forster 61	5166
33	4	H	Wolverhampton W	L 1-2	0-2	—	Forster 70	19,838
34	8	H	Southend U	W 2-1	2-0	20	Forster 6, O'Connor (pen) 37	13,189
35	11	A	Manchester C	W 2-0	0-0	—	Furlong (pen) 51, Francis 69	20,084
36	16	A	WBA	L 0-2	0-1	19		16,125
37	22	H	Sheffield U	D 1-1	0-0	19	Legg 53	14,969
38	29	A	Crystal Palace	W 1-0	1-0	18	Grainger 40	16,331
39	31	A	Charlton Ath	D 0-0	0-0	16		14,525
40	Apr 5	A	Barnsley	W 1-0	1-0	13	Grainger 12	13,092
41	8	A	Oldham Ath	D 2-2	2-1	—	Furlong 17, Grainger 30	5942
42	12	H	Huddersfield T	W 1-0	0-0	12	Jenkins (og) 90	14,394
43	15	H	Tranmere R	D 0-0	0-0	—		22,364
44	19	A	Bradford C	W 2-0	1-0	12	Devlin 22, Furlong 66	15,123
45	26	H	Oxford U	W 2-0	0-0	10	Devlin 54, Bowen 87	16,109
46	May 4	A	Ipswich T	D 1-1	0-0	10	Devlin 81	20,570

Final League Position: 10

GOALSCORERS

League (52): Devlin 16 (4 pens), Furlong 10 (1 pen), O'Connor 4 (1 pen), Legg 4, Bowen 3, Forster 3, Grainger 3, Hunt 2, Ablett 1, Breen 1, Francis 1, Newell 1, own goals 3.
Coca-Cola Cup (4): Newell 2, Devlin 1 (pen), Furlong 1.
FA Cup (6): Devlin 2 (1 pen), Francis 2, Bruce 1, Furlong 1.

Bennett I 40	Poole G 9+1	Ablett G 39+3	Bruce S 30+2	Breen G 20+2	Tait P 17+9	Devlin P 32+6	Newell M 11+4	Furlong P 37+6	Horne B 33	Legg A 22+11	Hunt J 6+6	Otto R 1+3	Castle S 4+4	Johnson M 28+7	Holland C 28+4	Donowa L —+4	Bowen J 19+6	Finnan S 3	Edwards A 1+2	Gabbiadini M —+2	Frain J 1	Jackson M 10	Sutton S 6	O'Connor M 24	Cooke T 1+3	Francis K 4+15	Brown K 11	Grainger M 21+2	Bass J 11+2	Limpar A 3+1	Forster N 4+3	Barnett D 6	Robinson S 6+3	Hughes B 10+1	Wassall D 8	Match No.
1	2	3	4	5	6¹	7	8	9	10	11²	12	13																								1
1	2	3	4	5		7	8¹	9	10	11²	12			6	13																					2
1	2	3	4	5		7	8	9	10	11²	12		6¹	13																					3
1	2	3	4	5		7²	8	9	10	12	11¹			6	13																				4
1	2	3	4	5		12	8¹	9²	10	11			13	6	14	7²																			5
1	2	3	4	5			8	9	10	11²			12	13	6		7¹																		6
1			4	5	7		9	10	11¹	12			3	6	13		8		2²																7
1		3	4		7		8¹	9	10	11²	6		14	5³	13		12		2																8
1		3	4	5		7		9	10	11	8			6			12		2¹																9
1	12	3	4	5		7³		9	10	11	8²			6	13	2¹	14																		10
1	2	3	4	5	8²	7¹		9	10	11				6	12	13																			11
1	2	3¹	4	5	13	7	12	9	10²	14			8³	6	11																				12
1	2	3	4	5	12	7		9					8	6	11¹					10																13
1		3²	4	5		7		9	10	11¹			12	13	6	8						2													14
1		4		5	7	8	12	9¹	10	13				3	6	11²	14					2³													15
1	12	4	5	8	13	14	9¹	10	7²				3	6	11³							2													16
		4	5	8²	12	13	9	10	7¹				3	6	11							2	1												17
	12	4¹	5	8	7²		9	10	13				3	6	11							2	1												18
		4	5	8¹	13	9³	10	7	14				3	6	11²	12						2	1												19
		4	5	12		9²	10	7	13³				3	6	11							2	1	8¹	14										20
		4	12	5	13	10	7²	9³					3	6	11							2¹	1	8	14										21
		5	4	12	13		9	10					3	6¹	11³							2	1	8	7²	14									22
1		5	4	12	8	13	9	10³					3¹	6	11							2²		7	14										23
1		4			8	7		12	10	9¹				5	11²									6				2	3	13						24
1		5	4			7		9	10		11¹			12	6									8	13			3	2²							25
1		5	4			7		9²	10	11				12	6¹									8	13			2	3							26
1		5				7		9¹	10	11				4	6²									8	12			2	3	13						27
1		5				7		9	10	6	11¹			5	12									8	13			2	3	11¹	14					28
1		4				7		9	10	10¹				5			12							8				2²	3	13						29
1		5	4			7		9¹	12	10	11²	13		3										8				2	3²	11³	14					30
1		5	4			7		9¹	12	10	11²	13		3										8				2	14	6³						31
1		5	4					9²	12	10		13		6	8									11				2³	3¹	14	7					32
1		5	4	8²				9³	12	10				6	13									11	14			3¹	2	7						33
1		5	4	8²				12	10					3³	13			7						6	9			14	2	11¹	7					34
1		5	4	8				10²						12				7						11	9	2	3					6	12			35
1		5	4¹	8	13			10²						12				11						7	9	2³	3					6		14		36
1		5		8	7			9	4															11	12	3	2					6		10¹		37
1		5		12	7¹			9³						4	13									11	14	3	2					8	10²	6		38
1		5		8	7			9¹		12				4³										11	13	3	2				6	14	10²			39
1				12	7²			9						4										11	13	3	2				6	8	10¹	5	40
1		12		13	7³			9						4										11	14	3	2				6¹	8²	10	5	41
1		5		8³	7¹			9		12				4²	11										13	3	2		14				10	6	42
1		5		8	7			9		12				4¹	11²										13	3	2						10	6	43
1		5		12	7¹			9		13				4²	11³										14	3	2				8		10	6	44
1		5	12		7					13				4³		14								11	9²	3	2¹				8		10	6	45
1		5	4		7					12				6¹	11²									9	13	3					8		10	2	46

Coca-Cola Cup

First Round	Brighton & HA	(a)	1-0
		(h)	2-0
Second Round	Coventry C	(a)	1-1
		(h)	0-1

FA Cup

Third Round	Stevenage B	(a)	2-0
	(at Birmingham)		
Fourth Round	Stockport Co	(h)	3-1
Fifth Round	Wrexham	(h)	1-3

BLACKBURN ROVERS 1996–97   *Back row (left to right):* Steve Foster (Physio), Paul Warhurst, Garry Flitcroft, Colin Hendry, Shay Given, Tim Flowers, Nicky Marker, Adam Reed, Stuart Ripley, Terry Darracott (Reserve Team Manager).

Middle Row: Derek Fazackerley (First Team Coach), Niklas Gudmundsson, Jason Wilcox, Henning Berg, Tim Sherwood, Chris Coleman, Chris Sutton, Ian Pearce, Lars Bohinen, Georgios Donis, Tony Parkes (Caretaker Manager).

Front row: Wayne Gill, Tony Whealing, Matty Holmes, Kevin Gallacher, Graeme Le Saux, Jeff Kenna, Ray Harford, Graham Fenton, Gary Croft, Damien Duff, Billy McKinlay, Steve Hitchen.
(Photograph: Action Images)

FA Premiership   **BLACKBURN ROVERS**

Ewood Park, Blackburn BB2 4JF. Telephone: (01254) 698888. Fax: (01254) 671042. Ticket Office: (01254) 671666. Clubcall: 0891 121014. Club Shop-Mail Order: (01254) 672137.

Ground capacity: 31,367.

Record attendance: 61,783 v Bolton W, FA Cup 6th rd, 2 March 1929.

Record receipts: £333,067 v Liverpool, Coca-Cola Cup 4th rd, 30 November 1994.

Pitch measurements: 115yd × 72yd.

Chairman: R. D. Coar BSC. *Vice-Chairman:* R. L. Matthewman. *Directors:* K. C. Lee, I. R. Stanners, G. R. Root FCMA.

Director of Football: Roy Hodgson. *Physio:* Steve Foster. *First Team Coach:* Tony Parkes. *Coach:* Derek Fazackerley.

Commercial Manager: Ken Beamish.

Secretary: Tom Finn. *Stadium Manager:* M. Highmore.

Year Formed: 1875. *Turned Professional:* 1880. *Ltd Co.:* 1897.

Club Nickname: Rovers.

Previous Grounds: 1875-76, all matches played away; 1876, Oozehead Ground; 1877, Pleasington Cricket Ground; 1878, Alexandra Meadows; 1881, Leamington Road; 1890, Ewood Park.

Foundation: It was in 1875 that some Public School old boys called a meeting at which the Blackburn Rovers club was formed and the colours blue and white adopted. The leading light was John Lewis, later to become a founder of the Lancashire FA, a famous referee who was in charge of two FA Cup Finals, and a vice-president of both the FA and the Football League.

First Football League game: 15 September 1888, Football League, v Accrington (h) D 5-5 – Arthur; Beverley, James Southworth; Douglas, Almond, Forrest; Beresford (1), Walton, John Southworth (1), Fecitt (1), Townley (2).

Record League Victory: 9–0 v Middlesbrough, Division 2, 6 November 1954 – Elvy; Suart, Eckersley; Clayton, Kelly, Bell; Mooney (3), Crossan (2), Briggs, Quigley (3), Langton (1).

Record Cup Victory: 11–0 v Rossendale, FA Cup 1st rd, 13 October 1884 – Arthur; Hopwood, McIntyre; Forrest, Blenkhorn, Lofthouse; Sowerbutts (2), J. Brown (1), Fecitt (4), Barton (3), Birtwistle (1).

Record Defeat: 0–8 v Arsenal, Division 1, 25 February 1933.

Most League Points (2 for a win): 60, Division 3, 1974–75.

Most League Points (3 for a win): 89, FA Premier League, 1994–95.

Most League Goals: 114, Division 2, 1954–55.

Highest League Scorer in Season: Ted Harper, 43, Division 1, 1925–26.

Most League Goals in Total Aggregate: Simon Garner, 168, 1978–92.

Most Capped Player: Bob Crompton, 41, England.

Most League Appearances: Derek Fazackerley, 596, 1970–86.

Record Transfer Fee Received: £15,000,000 from Newcastle U for Alan Shearer, July 1996.

Record Transfer Fee Paid: £5,000,000 to Norwich C for Chris Sutton, July 1994.

Football League Record: 1888 Founder Member of the League; 1936–39 Division 2; 1946–48 Division 1; 1948–58 Division 2; 1958–66 Division 1; 1966–71 Division 2; 1971–75 Division 3; 1975–79 Division 2; 1979–80 Division 3; 1980–92 Division 2; 1992– FA Premier League.

Honours: FA Premier League: – Champions 1994–95; Runners-up 1993–94. *Football League:* Division 1 – Champions 1911–12, 1913–14; Division 2 – Champions 1938–39; Runners-up 1957–58; Division 3 – Champions 1974–75; Runners-up 1979–80. *FA Cup:* Winners 1884, 1885, 1886, 1890, 1891, 1928; Runners-up 1882, 1960. *Football League Cup:* Semi-final 1962, 1993. *Full Members' Cup:* Winners 1987. **European Competitions:** *European Cup:* 1995–96. *UEFA Cup:* 1994–95.

Colours: Blue and white halved shirts, white shorts with blue trim, white stockings with blue trim. *Change colours:* Yellow and navy.

Did you know?
Centre-forward Jimmy Brown, 5ft 5ins and under 10 stone, scored 28 goals in 32 FA Cup ties for Blackburn Rovers between 1879 and 1886 including four goals on two occasions against Blackpool and Staveley.

BLACKBURN ROVERS 1996–97 LEAGUE RECORD

Match No.	Date	Venue	Opponents	Result	H/T Score	Lg. Pos.	Goalscorers	Attendance
1	Aug 17	H	Tottenham H	L	0-2	0-1	—	26,960
2	21	A	Aston Villa	L	0-1	0-0	—	32,457
3	25	A	Manchester U	D	2-2	1-1	18	Warhurst [34], Bohinen [51]	54,178
4	Sept 4	H	Leeds U	L	0-1	0-1	—	23,226
5	9	H	Derby Co	L	1-2	1-1	—	Sutton [11]	19,214
6	14	A	Newcastle U	L	1-2	0-1	20	Sutton [85]	36,424
7	21	H	Everton	D	1-1	1-1	20	Donis [32]	27,091
8	28	A	Coventry C	D	0-0	0-0	20		17,032
9	Oct 12	H	Arsenal	L	0-2	0-1	20		24,303
10	19	A	Sheffield W	D	1-1	0-1	20	Bohinen [74]	22,226
11	26	A	West Ham U	L	1-2	1-0	20	Berg [9]	23,947
12	Nov 3	H	Liverpool	W	3-0	2-0	20	Sutton 2 (1 pen) [3 (p), 55], Wilcox [24]	29,598
13	16	H	Chelsea	D	1-1	0-0	19	Gallacher [56]	27,229
14	25	A	Nottingham F	D	2-2	0-1	—	Gallacher [54], Wilcox [57]	17,525
15	30	H	Southampton	W	2-1	1-0	18	Sherwood [27], Sutton [87]	23,018
16	Dec 7	A	Leicester C	D	1-1	1-0	17	Sutton [33]	19,306
17	14	A	Wimbledon	L	0-1	0-0	17		13,246
18	26	H	Newcastle U	W	1-0	0-0	18	Gallacher [75]	30,398
19	28	H	Derby Co	D	0-0	0-0	18		17,847
20	Jan 1	A	Everton	W	2-0	2-0	17	Sherwood [18], Sutton [32]	30,427
21	11	H	Coventry C	W	4-0	3-0	14	Sutton 2 [17, 34], Gallacher [30], Donis [76]	24,055
22	18	A	Sunderland	D	0-0	0-0	14		20,794
23	29	A	Tottenham H	L	1-2	0-1	—	Hendry [57]	22,943
24	Feb 1	H	West Ham U	W	2-1	2-0	13	Gallacher [36], Sutton [39]	21,994
25	22	A	Liverpool	D	0-0	0-0	15		40,747
26	Mar 1	H	Sunderland	W	1-0	0-0	14	Gallacher [84]	24,208
27	5	A	Chelsea	D	1-1	0-0	—	Pedersen [62]	25,784
28	11	H	Nottingham F	D	1-1	0-1	—	Gallacher [64]	20,485
29	15	H	Wimbledon	W	3-1	2-1	12	Gallacher 3 [7, 26, 58]	23,333
30	Mar 19	A	Middlesbrough	L	1-2	0-1	—	Sutton [68]	29,891
31	22	H	Aston Villa	L	0-2	0-0	12		24,274
32	Apr 7	A	Leeds U	D	0-0	0-0	—		27,322
33	12	H	Manchester U	L	2-3	1-2	14	McKinlay [34], Warhurst [86]	30,476
34	19	A	Arsenal	D	1-1	0-1	14	Flitcroft [89]	38,086
35	22	H	Sheffield W	W	4-1	3-0	—	Berg [5], Sherwood [23], Le Saux [39], Flitcroft [58]	20,845
36	May 3	A	Southampton	L	0-2	0-1	13		15,247
37	8	A	Middlesbrough	D	0-0	0-0	—		27,411
38	11	H	Leicester C	L	2-4	1-1	13	Flitcroft [25], Fenton [66]	25,881

Final League Position: 13

GOALSCORERS

League (42): Sutton 11 (1 pen), Gallacher 10, Flitcroft 3, Sherwood 3, Berg 2, Bohinen 2, Donis 2, Warhurst 2, Wilcox 2, Fenton 1, Hendry 1, Le Saux 1, McKinlay 1, Pedersen 1.
Coca-Cola Cup (4): Flitcroft 1, Gallacher 1, Sherwood 1, Sutton 1.
FA Cup (2): Bohinen 1, Sherwood 1.

Flowers T 36	Berg H 36	Kenna J 37	Sherwood T 37	Hendry C 35	Coleman C 8	Ripley S 5+8	Gallacher K 34	Fenton G 5+8	Filtcroft G 27+1	Donis G 11+11	Warhurst P 5+6	Pearce I 7+5	Bohinen L 17+6	Sutton C 24+1	Gudmundsson N —+2	McKinlay B 23+2	Wilcox J 26+2	Marker N 5+2	Croft G 4+1	Beattie J 1	Le Saux G 26	Given S 2	Pedersen P 6+5	Duff D 1	Match No.
1	2	3	4	5	6	7²	8	9	10¹	11	12	13													1
1	2	3	4	5	6	12	7²	13	8¹	11	9		10												2
1	2	3	4	5	6	7	8¹	12		11	9²	13	10												3
1	2	3	4	5	6	7		9	12²	11		8¹	13	10											4
1	2	3	4	5	6¹	7²		8		11			12	10	9	13									5
1	2	3	4²	5	6	12	7	13	8³	11¹			10	9		14									6
1	2	3	4	5	6		11¹	12	8²	7			10	9			13								7
1			4	5	6¹	12	8²	13		7			10	9		14	11³	2	3						8
	1	6	2	4		12				7¹			10	9	13		11²	5	3	8					9
	1	6	2	4		7¹	8		10	12		5	13	9			11²		3						10
	1	6	2	4		12		9	10	7¹					8	11	5	13	3²						11
	1	6	2	4	5		10¹	8				12	9		7	11			3						12
	1	6	2	4	5		10	8					9		7	11	3								13
	1	6	2	4	5		8	10					9		7	11			3						14
	1	6	2	4	5		8²	10	13			12	9		7¹	11			3						15
	1	6	2	4	5		8	10¹	13			12	9		7	11²			3						16
		6	2	4	5		8						10	9		7	11			3	1				17
	1	6	2	4	5		8						10	9		7	11			3					18
		6	2	4	5		8						10	9		7	11			3	1				19
	1	6	2	4	5		8						10	9		7	11			3					20
	1	6	2	4²	5		7¹	13	8	12			10	9			11			3					21
	1	6	2	4	5		7		8				10	9			11			3					22
	1	6	2	4¹	5		7		8	12			10	9			11			3					23
	1	6	2	4	5		10	8	12				9		7	11¹			3					24
	1	6	2	4	5		10	8					9¹		7	11			3			12			25
	1	6	2	4	5		8			7¹	12	10				11	13			3		9²			26
	1	6	2	4	5¹		8	10		13	12					11	7			3		9²			27
	1	6	2	4	5		8	10	12						7	11			3		9¹			28
	1	6	2	4	5		8¹	10	12	13					7	11			3		9²			29
	1	6	2	4	5		8	10	12			13			7¹	11			3		9²			30
	1	6	2	4	5		8	10¹	14			12	9²		7	11			3		13³			31
	1	6	2		5		8					4	10	9		7	11			3					32
	1	6	2	4	5²		8³		10¹	12	9	13				7	11			3		14			33
	1	6	2¹	4	5		8	10				3		9		7	11					12			34
	1	6	2	8	5		10¹	14	7	12		4		9²	11					3		13³			35
	1	6	2¹	4	5		12	8		10		13	3³		7	14			11		9²			36
	1	6	2²	8	5		12	11	13	10		9¹	4		7				3					37
	1		2	4	5²		12	8	9	10			6		7¹		13			3		11			38

Coca-Cola Cup

Second Round	Brentford	(a)	2-1
		(h)	2-0
Third Round	Stockport Co	(h)	0-1

FA Cup

| Third Round | Port Vale | (h) | 1-0 |
| Fourth Round | Coventry C | (h) | 1-2 |

BLACKPOOL 1996-97 *Back row (left to right):* Paul Carden, Mike Davies (Coach), Paul Symons, Lee Thorpe, Andy Watson, Marvin Bryan, John Hooks, Mark Howard, Lee Philpott, Gary Brabin, Mark Taylor (Physio), Lee Shockledge.

Middle row: Matt Greer, Paul Ashcroft, Jamie Cross, Fred O'Donoghue (Youth Liaison), Tony Butler, Ben Dixon, Darren Bradshaw, James Quinn, Henry Heighton, Steve Banks, Craig Allardyce, Scott Darton, Jason Lydiate, Harry McNally (Chief Scout), Jason Jarrett, Clark Carlisle, Steve Longworth, Gary Hall.

Front row: Paul Haddow, Chris Best, Paul Mairs, Alan Crawford (YTS Manager), Andy Barlow, Andy Preece, Tony Ellis, Gary Megson (Manager), Bill Bingham (Director of Football), Dave Linighan, Mark Bonner, Mickey Mellon, Michael Phelan (Assistant Manager), Robbie Talbot, Jamie Skeach, Carl Pepper (on ground).

Division 2 **BLACKPOOL**

Bloomfield Rd Ground, Blackpool FYI 6JJ. Telephone: (01253) 404331 (Ticket/Credit Bookings), (01253) 405331 (Shop/General Enquiries). Fax: (01253) 405011. Clubcall: 0891 121648.

Ground capacity: 11,047.

Record attendance: 38,098 v Wolverhampton W, Division 1, 17 September 1955.

Record receipts: £73,046 v Chelsea, Coca-Cola Cup 2nd rd 1st leg, 18 September 1996.

Pitch measurements: 112yd × 74yd.

Chairman: Mrs V. Oyston. *Deputy Chairman:* K. Chadwick.

Managing Director: Mrs G. Bridge.

Directors: D. Hatton, C. Muir OBE, O. J. Oyston, G. Warburton, J. Wilde MBE, R. Oakley, M. Joyce.

Manager: Nigel Worthington.

Secretary: Carol Banks.

Commercial Manager: Geoffrey Warburton.

Physio: Mark Taylor MCSP. *Stadium Manager:* John Turner.

Year Formed: 1887. *Turned Professional:* 1887. *Ltd Co.:* 1896.

Previous Name: 'South Shore' combined with Blackpool in 1899, twelve years after the latter had been formed on the breaking up of the old 'Blackpool St John's' club.

Club Nickname: 'The Seasiders'.

Previous Grounds: 1887, Raikes Hall Gardens; 1897, Athletic Grounds; 1899, Raikes Hall Gardens; 1899, Bloomfield Road.

Foundation: Old boys of St. John's School who had formed themselves into a football club decided to establish a club bearing the name of their town and Blackpool FC came into being at a meeting at the Stanley Arms Hotel in the summer of 1887. In their first season playing at Raikes Hall Gardens, the club won both the Lancashire Junior Cup and the Fylde Cup.

First Football League game: 5 September 1896, Division 2, v Lincoln C (a) L 1-3 – Douglas; Parr, Bowman; Stuart, Stirzaker, Norris; Clarkin, Donnelly, R. Parkinson, Mount (1), J. Parkinson.

Record League Victory: 7–0 v Preston NE (away), Division 1, 1 May 1948 – Robinson; Shimwell, Crosland; Buchan, Hayward, Kelly; Hobson, Munro (1), McIntosh (5), McCall, Rickett (1).

Record Cup Victory: 7–1 v Charlton Ath, League Cup 2nd rd, 25 September 1963 – Harvey; Armfield, Martin; Crawford, Gratrix, Cranston; Lea, Ball (1), Charnley (4), Durie (1), Oates (1).

Record Defeat: 1–10 v Small Heath, Division 2, 2 March 1901 and v Huddersfield T, Division 1, 13 December 1930.

Most League Points (2 for a win): 58, Division 2, 1929–30.

Most League Points (3 for a win): 86, Division 4, 1984–85.

Most League Goals: 98, Division 2, 1929–30.

Highest League Scorer in Season: Jimmy Hampson, 45, Division 2, 1929–30.

Most League Goals in Total Aggregate: Jimmy Hampson, 247, 1927–38.

Most Capped Player: Jimmy Armfield, 43, England.

Most League Appearances: Jimmy Armfield, 568, 1952–71.

Record Transfer Fee Received: £750,000 from QPR for Trevor Sinclair, August 1993.

Record Transfer Fee Paid: £275,000 to Millwall for Chris Malkin, October 1996.

Football League Record: 1896 Elected to Division 2; 1899 Failed re-election; 1900 Re-elected; 1900–30 Division 2; 1930–33 Division 1; 1933–37 Division 2; 1937–67 Division 1; 1967–70 Division 2; 1970–71 Division 1; 1971–78 Division 2; 1978–81 Division 3; 1981–85 Division 4; 1985–90 Division 3; 1990–92 Division 4; 1992– Division 2.

Honours: Football League: Division 1 – Runners-up 1955–56; Division 2 – Champions 1929–30; Runners-up 1936–37, 1969–70; Division 4 – Runners-up 1984–85. *FA Cup:* Winners 1953; Runners-up 1948, 1951. *Football League Cup:* Semi-final 1962. *Anglo-Italian Cup:* Winners 1971; Runners-up 1972.

Colours: All tangerine. *Change colours:* All royal blue.

Did you know?
Lee Philpott, man-of-the-match for Blackpool against Scunthorpe United in the Coca-Cola Cup on 2 September 1996, donated his mountain bike prize to a local children's charity.

BLACKPOOL 1996–97 LEAGUE RECORD

Match No.	Date	Venue	Opponents	Result		H/T Score	Lg. Pos.	Goalscorers	Attendance
1	Aug 17	H	Chesterfield	L	0-1	0-0	—		6014
2	24	A	Bristol C	W	1-0	1-0	14	Ellis 21	9387
3	27	A	Rotherham U	W	2-1	0-1	—	Philpott 47, Preece 79	2914
4	31	H	Wycombe W	D	0-0	0-0	7		4856
5	Sept 7	H	Walsall	W	2-1	1-0	5	Philpott 14, Quinn (pen) 49	5176
6	10	A	Burnley	L	0-2	0-0	—		13,599
7	14	A	Brentford	D	1-1	0-1	10	Quinn (pen) 83	5908
8	21	H	Shrewsbury T	D	1-1	0-0	10	Ellis 76	4452
9	28	A	Luton T	L	0-1	0-1	13		5303
10	Oct 1	A	Crewe Alex	L	2-3	1-0	—	Brabin 43, Quinn 69	4314
11	5	A	Bury	L	0-1	0-0	17		5317
12	12	H	Gillingham	W	2-0	0-0	16	Ellis 65, Mellon 82	4320
13	15	H	Wrexham	D	3-3	3-0	—	Preece 2 20, 22, Mellon 30	4014
14	19	A	Bristol R	D	0-0	0-0	15		5823
15	26	H	Watford	D	1-1	1-0	14	Quinn 31	6072
16	30	H	Millwall	L	1-2	1-0	—	Malkin 13	7179
17	Nov 2	A	Peterborough U	D	0-0	0-0	17		7011
18	9	H	Bournemouth	D	1-1	1-0	16	Quinn 18	3744
19	19	A	Stockport Co	L	0-1	0-0	—		4572
20	23	H	Notts Co	W	1-0	0-0	15	Quinn (pen) 77	3598
21	30	A	Watford	D	2-2	1-0	16	Malkin 11, Brabin 73	12,017
22	Dec 3	H	Plymouth Arg	D	2-2	1-2	—	Philpott 40, Malkin 56	2690
23	13	A	Preston NE	L	0-3	0-0	—		14,626
24	21	H	York C	W	3-0	1-0	16	Ellis 4, Quinn 2 (1 pen) 62, 72 (p)	3432
25	Jan 1	A	Shrewsbury T	W	3-1	3-0	—	Preece 2 8, 28, Mellon 44	2787
26	18	H	Crewe Alex	L	1-2	1-1	15	Ellis 19	4760
27	25	H	Millwall	W	3-0	2-0	14	Ellis 4, Quinn 26, Darton 58	4523
28	Feb 1	A	Bournemouth	D	0-0	0-0	14		8201
29	8	A	Peterborough U	W	5-1	1-0	16	Ellis 3 13, 48, 61, Preece 49, Bryan 77	4001
30	15	A	Notts Co	D	1-1	1-1	15	Quinn 4	5281
31	22	H	Stockport Co	W	2-1	0-0	13	Quinn 59, Ellis 73	5772
32	25	H	Burnley	L	1-3	1-2	—	Quinn 15	7331
33	Mar 1	A	Plymouth Arg	W	1-0	1-0	13	Ellis 45	5585
34	8	A	York C	L	0-1	0-1	13		3639
35	15	H	Preston NE	W	2-1	1-1	14	Clarkson 2 26, 61	8017
36	18	A	Walsall	D	1-1	0-0	—	Clarkson 48	3459
37	22	A	Bristol C	W	1-0	0-0	12	Preece 53	4518
38	29	A	Chesterfield	D	0-0	0-0	12		4974
39	31	H	Rotherham U	W	4-1	2-0	11	Linighan 11, Clarkson 39, Ellis 64, Barlow 77	5524
40	Apr 5	A	Wycombe W	L	0-1	0-0	11		5619
41	12	H	Bury	W	2-0	0-0	12	Ellis 2 56, 74	6812
42	15	H	Luton T	D	0-0	0-0	—		4382
43	19	A	Gillingham	W	3-2	1-2	11	Quinn 36, Mellon 65, Clarkson 76	5151
44	22	H	Brentford	W	1-0	0-0	—	Preece 57	4030
45	26	H	Bristol R	W	3-2	2-1	7	Preece 2 28, 66, Bonner 36	6673
46	May 3	A	Wrexham	L	1-2	1-1	7	Ellis 14	5664

Final League Position: 7

GOALSCORERS

League (60): Ellis 15, Quinn 13 (4 pens), Preece 10, Clarkson 5, Mellon 4, Malkin 3, Philpott 3, Brabin 2, Barlow 1, Bonner 1, Bryan 1, Darton 1, Linighan 1.
Coca-Cola Cup (7): Ellis 3, Quinn 3, Philpott 1.
FA Cup (1): Quinn 1 (pen).

Banks S 46	Bryan M 34	Barlow A 43+3	Butler T 41+1	Lingham D 42	Thorpe L 2+7	Bonner M 25+4	Mellon M 43	Quinn J 37+1	Ellis T 41+4	Philpott L 20+6	Preece A 35+6	Dixon B 3+8	Brabin G 30+2	Lydiate J 18+2	Darton S 8+7	Onwere U 5+4	Woods B 3	Malkin C 8+7	Bradshaw D 4+6	Brightwell D 1+1	Carden P —+1	Clarkson P 17	Ormerod B —+4	Russell K —+1	Match No.
1	2	3	4	5	6^2	7	8	9	10	11^1	12	13													1
1	2	3	4	5	14	7	8	9^1	10^1	11^2	12	13	6												2
1	2	3	4	5		7	8	9^1	10	11^2	12	13	6												3
1	2	3	4	5^2	12	7^1	8		10	11	9		6	13											4
1	2	3	4			7		9^2	10	11^1	8	12	6	5	13										5
1	2	3^2	4			12	8	9	10	11^1	7	13	6	5											6
1	2	3	4	5^1		12	8	9	10	11^2	7	13	6												7
1	2	3^1	4	5		7^3	8	9	10	11^2	12	13	6	14											8
1	2^2	12	13	5		7	8	9^1	10		14	3	6	4				11^3							9
1	12		4	5		7	8	9	10			3^1	6		2			11							10
1	12		4	5	13	7^1	8	9^3	10^2		14	3	6		2			11							11
1		3	4	5			8	9	10	12	11		6		2			7^1							12
1		3	4	5	12		8	9^1	10		11	13	6		2			7^2							13
1		3	4	5				9	10		11		6		2	7		8^1	12						14
1		3	4	5			8	9^2	10	12	11		6		2		13	7^1							15
1		3	4	5	12		8	9^2	10^3	13	11		6^1		2			7	14						16
1		3	4	5			8	9	12		10^1	11	6		2			7							17
1		3	4	5			8	9	12		10^2	11^1	6^3		2		13	7	14						18
1	2	3	4	5		7	8	9	12	11	6							10^1							19
1	2	3	4	5		7	8	9	12	11	6							10^1							20
1	2	3	4			7	8	9	10		6^1					12		11		5					21
1	2	3	4	12		7			10	11^1								5	8	9	6				22
1		3	5^1	2		7	8	9	10	11										4	6	12			23
1	2	3	4	5		7	8	9	10		6							11							24
1	2	3	4	5		7	8	9	10^2		6^1							11	12			13			25
1	2	3	4	5^1			8	9	10	7^2	11		6					12	13						26
1	2	3	4	5			8	9^1	10	11	6					7		12							27
1	2	3	4	5			8	9	10	11	6					7^1		12							28
1	2	3	4	5			8	9	10	11	6					7									29
1	2	3	4	5			8	9	10	11	7											6			30
1	2	3	4	5			8	9	10	7^1	11^2							12	13			6			31
1	2^2	3^1	4	5			8	9	10	7	11							12	13			6			32
1	2	3	4	5			8	9	10	7^1	11							12				6			33
1		3	4	5	12		8	9	10	11					2			7^1				6			34
1		3	4	5		7	8	9	10	11^1					2				12			6			35
1	2	3	4	5		7^2	8	9^1	10	11								12	13			6			36
1	2	3	4	5		7	8	9	10^1	11								12				6			37
1	2	3	4	5		7	8		10	11	9^1											6	12		38
1	2	3	4	5^1	13	7	8		10	11	9^2								12			6			39
1	2	3^3		5		7^1	8		10	11	12	9^2		4								6	13	14	40
1	2	3		5		9^1	8		10	11			6	4					12			7			41
1	2	3		5		9^2	8		10	12	11^1		6	4								7	13		42
1	2	3	9	5	12		8	13	10	11			6^1	4^2								7			43
1	2	3	4	5			8	9	10^1	13	11^3		6^2						12			7	14		44
1	2	3	4	5	10		8	9			11		6									7			45
1	2	3^1	4	5			8	9	10	12	11		6^2						13			7			46

Coca-Cola Cup

First Round	Scunthorpe U	(a)	1-2
		(h)	2-0
Second Round	Chelsea	(h)	1-4
		(a)	3-1

FA Cup

First Round	Wigan Ath	(h)	1-0
Second Round	Hednesford T	(h)	0-1

BOLTON WANDERERS 1996–97 *Back row (left to right):* Hasney Aljofree, Nathan Blake, Alan Thompson, Jimmy Phillips, Gerry Taggart, Mark Westhead, Aidan Davison, Gudni Bergsson, Mixu Paatelainen, Simon Coleman, Chris Fairclough, Scott Taylor.

Middle row: Steve Carroll (Reserve Team Manager), Phil Brown (First Team Coach), Ewan Simpson (Physio), Nicky Spooner, Stuart Whitehead, Per Frandsen, Greg Strong, Gavin Ward, Keith Branagan, Fabian DeFreitas, Wayne Burnett, Neil Marsh, Steve Quinn, Colin Dyson (Kit Man), Dean Crombie (Youth Team Coach), Jimmy Dewsnip (Assistant Youth Development Officer).

Front row: Colin Todd (Manager), David Lee, Michael Johansen, Bryan Small, John McGinlay, Andy Todd, Scott Green, Sasa Curcic, Steve McAnespie, Scott Sellars, Stuart Whittaker, Martin Dobson (Youth Development Officer), Ian McNeill (Chief Scout).

FA Premiership   **BOLTON WANDERERS**

Burnden Park, Bolton BL3 2QR. (NB Moving to new ground at Horwich). Telephone: (01204) 389200. Fax: (01204) 382334. Ticket Office: (01204) 521101. Ticket Office Fax: (01204) 392474. Commercial Dept: (01204) 24518.

Ground capacity: 20,500.

Record attendance: 69,912 v Manchester C, FA Cup 5th rd, 18 February 1933.

Record receipts: £202,031 v Tottenham H, Coca-Cola Cup 4th rd, 27 November 1996.

Pitch measurements: 113yd × 76yd.

President: Nat Lofthouse.

Chairman: G. Hargreaves.

Directors: P. A. Gartside, G. Ball, G. Seymour, G. Warburton, W. B. Warburton, B. Scowcroft.

Team Manager: Colin Todd. *Physio:* E. Simpson.

Chief Executive & Secretary: Des McBain. *Commercial Manager:* T. Holland.

Year Formed: 1874. *Turned Professional:* 1880. *Ltd Co.:* 1895.

Previous Name: 1874–77, Christ Church FC; 1877 became Bolton Wanderers.

Club Nickname: 'The Trotters'.

Previous Grounds: Park Recreation Ground and Cockle's Field before moving to Pike's Lane ground 1881; 1895, Burnden Park.

Foundation: In 1874 boys of Christ Church Sunday School, Blackburn Street, led by their master Thomas Ogden, established a football club which went under the name of the school and whose president was Vicar of Christ Church. Membership was 6d (two and a half pence). When their president began to lay down too many rules about the use of church premises, the club broke away and formed Bolton Wanderers in 1877, holding their earliest meetings at the Gladstone Hotel.

First Football League game: 8 September 1888, Football League, v Derby Co (h), L 3-6 – Harrison; Robinson, Mitchell; Roberts, Weir, Bullough, Davenport (2), Milne, Coupar, Barbour, Brogan (1).

Record League Victory: 8–0 v Barnsley, Division 2, 6 October 1934 – Jones; Smith, Finney; Goslin, Atkinson, George Taylor; George T. Taylor (2), Eastham, Milsom (1), Westwood (4), Cook. (1 og).

Record Cup Victory: 13–0 v Sheffield U, FA Cup 2nd rd, 1 February 1890 – Parkinson; Robinson (1), Jones; Bullough, Davenport, Roberts; Rushton, Brogan (3), Cassidy (5), McNee, Weir (4).

Record Defeat: 1–9 v Preston NE, FA Cup 2nd rd, 10 December 1887.

Most League Points (2 for a win): 61, Division 3, 1972–73.

Most League Points (3 for a win): 98, Division 1, 1996–97.

Most League Goals: 100, Division 1, 1996–97.

Highest League Scorer in Season: Joe Smith, 38, Division 1, 1920–21.

Most League Goals in Total Aggregate: Nat Lofthouse, 255, 1946–61.

Most Capped Player: Nat Lofthouse, 33, England.

Most League Appearances: Eddie Hopkinson, 519, 1956–70.

Record Transfer Fee Received: £4,500,000 from Liverpool for Jason McAteer, September 1995.

Record Transfer Fee Paid: £1,500,000 to Partizan Belgrade for Sasa Curcic, October 1995 and £1,500,000 to Barnsley for Gerry Taggart, August 1995.

Football League Record: 1888 Founder Member of the League; 1899–1900 Division 2; 1900–03 Division 1; 1903–05 Division 2; 1905–08 Division 1; 1908–09 Division 2; 1909–10 Division 1; 1910–11 Division 2; 1911–33 Division 1; 1933–35 Division 1; 1935–64 Division 1; 1964–71 Division 2; 1971–73 Division 3; 1973–78 Division 2; 1978–80 Division 1; 1980–83 Division 2; 1983–87 Division 3; 1987–88 Division 4; 1988–92 Division 3; 1992–93 Division 2; 1993–95 Division 1; 1995–96 FA Premier League; 1996–97 Division 1; 1997– FA Premier League.

Honours: Football League: Division 1 – Champions 1996–97; Division 2 – Champions 1908–09, 1977–78; Runners-up 1899–1900, 1904–05, 1910–11, 1934–35, 1992–93; Division 3 – Champions 1972–73. *FA Cup:* Winners 1923, 1926, 1929, 1958; Runners-up 1894, 1904, 1953. *Football League Cup:* Runners-up 1995. *Freight Rover Trophy:* Runners-up 1986. *Sherpa Van Trophy:* Winners 1989.

Colours: White shirts, navy blue shorts, blue stockings. *Change colours:* Dark/sky blue shirts, navy blue shorts, blue stockings.

Did you know?
On 29 October 1996, John McGinlay of Bolton Wanderers scored what proved to be the winning goal against Reading at 2-1. Five minutes later, he took over between the posts after the goalkeeper was sent off and kept a clean sheet.

BOLTON WANDERERS 1996–97 LEAGUE RECORD

Match No.	Date	Venue	Opponents	Result	H/T Score	Lg. Pos.	Goalscorers	Attendance
1	Aug 17	A	Port Vale	D	1-1	1-0	—	Thompson [23]	10,057
2	20	H	Manchester C	W	1-0	0-0	—	Frandsen [49]	18,257
3	24	H	Norwich C	W	3-1	1-0	1	Blake 2 [27, 77], Johansen [46]	13,507
4	Sept 1	A	QPR	W	2-1	1-0	1	McGinlay [28], Thompson [90]	11,225
5	7	A	Southend U	L	2-5	2-2	4	Blake [23], McGinlay [31]	4475
6	10	H	Grimsby T	W	6-1	2-1	—	Johansen 2 [9, 80], Blake [19], Fairclough [54], Lee [78], Taylor [90]	12,448
7	14	H	Portsmouth	W	2-0	0-0	1	Blake [49], Fairclough [96]	14,248
8	21	A	Bradford C	W	4-2	2-2	1	Thompson [1], Blake 2 [20, 84], Frandsen [55]	12,034
9	28	H	Stoke C	D	1-1	1-0	1	Blake [42]	16,195
10	Oct 2	A	Wolverhampton W	W	2-1	0-1	1	McGinlay 2 [46, 86]	26,540
11	12	H	Oldham Ath	W	3-1	3-0	1	Johansen [7], McGinlay 2 [20, 31]	14,813
12	15	H	Tranmere R	W	1-0	0-0	—	Sellars [51]	14,136
13	19	A	Charlton Ath	D	3-3	1-3	1	McGinlay 2 (1 pen) [23, 61 (p)], Blake [73]	11,091
14	25	A	Barnsley	D	2-2	1-0	—	McGinlay (pen) [1], De Zeeuw (og) [49]	9413
15	29	H	Reading	W	2-1	1-0	—	Sellars [40], McGinlay [58]	12,677
16	Nov 2	H	Huddersfield T	W	2-0	1-0	1	Thompson [20], McGinlay [72]	15,865
17	13	A	Birmingham C	L	1-3	0-0	—	Sheridan [75]	17,033
18	16	H	Crystal Palace	D	2-2	2-2	1	Sheridan [11], McGinlay (pen) [21]	16,892
19	19	A	Oxford U	D	0-0	0-0	—		7517
20	22	A	Sheffield U	D	1-1	1-1	—	Blake [10]	17,069
21	30	H	Barnsley	D	2-2	1-1	1	Blake [20], Thompson [88]	16,852
22	Dec 8	A	WBA	D	2-2	1-0	1	Frandsen [37], Fairclough [62]	13,082
23	14	H	Ipswich T	L	1-2	0-1	1	Bergsson [70]	13,314
24	22	A	Swindon T	D	2-2	0-1	2	Green [58], McGinlay [84]	8948
25	26	A	Grimsby T	W	2-1	1-0	1	Taggart [26], Blake [72]	8185
26	28	H	Southend U	W	3-1	2-1	1	Sellars 2 [30, 33], McGinlay (pen) [76]	16,357
27	Jan 1	H	Bradford C	W	2-1	0-0	1	Lee [64], Sellars [84]	16,192
28	11	A	Portsmouth	W	3-0	0-0	1	Blake 2 [55, 89], Johansen [74]	10,467
29	18	H	Wolverhampton W	W	3-0	1-0	1	McGinlay [21], Curle (og) [58], Blake [62]	18,980
30	29	A	Stoke C	W	2-1	1-0	—	Pollock [28], McGinlay [54]	15,645
31	Feb 1	H	Birmingham C	W	2-1	1-0	1	Pollock [29], McGinlay (pen) [78]	16,737
32	8	A	Reading	L	2-3	0-0	1	Thompson [61], McGinlay [64]	10,739
33	15	H	Sheffield U	D	2-2	2-1	1	Paatelainen [4], Fairclough [20]	17,922
34	22	A	Huddersfield T	W	2-1	1-1	1	Fairclough [22], Taggart [47]	16,061
35	Mar 2	H	WBA	W	1-0	1-0	1	Blake [34]	13,258
36	4	A	Crystal Palace	D	1-1	0-0	—	Fairclough [90]	16,035
37	8	H	Swindon T	W	7-0	2-0	1	Thompson [30], Frandsen [36], Pollock [53], Bergsson 2 [82, 89], McGinlay [85], Blake [87]	13,981
38	15	A	Ipswich T	W	1-0	1-0	1	McGinlay [26]	16,187
39	18	H	Port Vale	W	4-2	2-1	1	Frandsen [9], Glover (og) [38], Fairclough [81], Blake [83]	14,150
40	22	A	Norwich C	W	1-0	1-0	1	Sellars [24]	17,585
41	Apr 5	H	QPR	W	2-1	1-1	1	Fairclough [44], McGinlay [49]	19,198
42	9	A	Manchester C	W	2-1	1-1	—	Paatelainen [38], Sellars [58]	28,026
43	12	H	Oxford U	W	4-0	2-0	1	Thompson 2 [32, 48], Sellars [40], Blake [61]	15,994
44	19	A	Oldham Ath	D	0-0	0-0	1		10,702
45	25	H	Charlton Ath	W	4-1	0-1	—	Thompson [46], Taggart [65], McGinlay 2 (1 pen) [89 (p), 90]	22,024
46	May 4	A	Tranmere R	D	2-2	1-0	1	McGinlay [27], Pollock [77]	14,309

Final League Position: 1

GOALSCORERS

League (100): McGinlay 24 (6 pens), Blake 19, Thompson 10, Fairclough 8, Sellars 8, Frandsen 5, Johansen 5, Pollock 4, Bergsson 3, Taggart 3, Lee 2, Paatelainen 2, Sheridan 2, Green 1, Taylor 1, own goals 3.
Coca-Cola Cup (11): McGinlay 5 (1 pen), Blake 3, Taggart 1, Taylor 1, Thompson 1.
FA Cup (9): Blake 2, Green 2, Pollock 2, McGinlay 1, Taylor 1, Thompson 1.

Branagan K 36	Green S 7 + 5	Phillips J 36	Frandsen P 40 + 1	Taggart G 43	Fairclough C 46	Johansen M 24 + 9	Sellars S 40 + 2	Blake N 42	McGinlay J 43	Thompson A 34	Lee D 13 + 12	Burnett W — + 1	McAnespie S 11 + 2	Todd A 6 + 9	Bergsson G 30 + 3	Taylor S 2 + 9	Ward G 10 + 1	Sheridan J 12 + 8	Pollock J 18 + 2	Small B 10 + 1	Paatelainen M 3 + 7	Match No.
1	2	3	4	5	6	7	8^1	9	10	11	12											1
1	2	3	4	5	6	7	8^1	9	10	11	12											2
1	2^1	3	4	5	6	7		9	10	11	8	12										3
1		3	4	5	6	7^1	12	9	10	11	8		2									4
1		3	4	5	6	7^2		9	10	11	8^3		2^1	12	13	14						5
1		3	4^1	5	6	7		9	10	11	8^2		2^3	12	14	13						6
1		3	4	5	6	7^1		9	10	11	8^3		2^2	12	13	14						7
1		3	4	5	6	7^2	12	9	10^3	11	8^1			13	2	14						8
1		3	4	5	6	7^2	8^1	9	10^3	11	12			13	2	14						9
1		3	4		6	7	8	9	10	11			2	5								10
1		3	4	5	6	7^1	8	9^3	10	11^2	12			13	2	14						11
1		3	4	5	6	7	8	9	10	11					2							12
1		3	4	5	6	7	8^1	9	10	11	12				2							13
1		3	4	5	6	7	8	9	10	11					2							14
1		3	4	5	6	7^1	8		10	11	12			13	2^2	9						15
1		3	4	5	6	7	8	9^1	10	11					2	12						16
		3	4^1	5	6	7	8	9	10		12				2		1	11				17
1	12	3		5	6	7	8^1	9	10						2			11	4			18
1		3		5	6	7^1	8	9	10		12				2			11	4			19
1		3		5	6		8	9	10					4	2			11	7			20
1	3^2	12			6	13	8	9	10					4	5			11^1	7			21
1		3	4	5	6	12	8	9	10	11	7^1				2							22
1	2	3	4		6	7	8		10		12			5	9			11^1				23
12		3	4	5	6	7^1	8	9	10						2		1	11				24
	7		4	5	6		8	9	10^1						2		1	11	12	3		25
	7^1		4^2	5	6		8	9	10		12	13			2		1	11^3	14	3		26
	7^1		4	5	6		8	9	10		12	13			2^2		1	11		3		27
12			5	6	10	8	9			7					2^1		1	11	4	3		28
12			5	6		8	9	10^1		7					2		1	11	4	3		29
		7	5	6		8	9	10	11						2		1		4	3		30
		7	5	6	12	8^1	9	10	11						2		1		4	3		31
		7^1	5	6		8		10	9			13			2	12	1	11	4	3^2		32
1			7	5	6		8		10	11	12				2			4^1	3	9		33
1		3	7	5	6		8	9^1	10		11				2			4		12		34
1		3	7	5	6	12	8	9	10		11^1				2			4				35
1		3	7^2	5	6	12	8^1	9	10^3	11				13	2			4		14		36
1		3	7^2	5	6	12	8^1	9	10	11^3				13	2			4		14		37
1		3	7	5	6		8	9	10	11					2^1			12	4			38
1		3	7	5	6	4	8	9^1	10	11			2							12		39
1		3	7	5	6		8	9	10	11			2					4				40
1		7^2	5	6	12	8	9^3	10	11						2			13	4^1	3	14	41
1		3	7	5	6		8	9	10^1	11			2					4		12		42
1	12	3	7^2	5	6	14	8	9		11^3			2				13	4		13	10^3	43
1		3^4	7^1	5	6		8	9		11			2			12	14	4	13	10^3		44
1		3	7	5	6	4^2	8	9^3	10	11			12		2^1			13		14		45
1^6		3	7	5	6^2	$6^2$12	8	9^1	10	11					2	15	13	4				46

Coca-Cola Cup

Second Round	Bristol C	(a)	0-0	
		(h)	3-1	
Third Round	Chelsea	(h)	2-1	
Fourth Round	Tottenham H	(h)	6-1	
Fifth Round	Wimbledon	(h)	0-2	

FA Cup

Third Round	Luton T	(a)	1-1	
		(h)	6-2	
Fourth Round	Chesterfield	(h)	2-3	

AFC BOURNEMOUTH 1996–97   *Back row (left to right):* Neil Young, Eddie Howe, Steve Strong, Mike Dean, Jon O'Neill, Dale Gordon (Player/Coach), Leo Cotterell, Owen Coll.
Middle row: Larry Clay (Youth Development Officer), Michael McElhatton, Rob Murray, Mark Watson, Jimmy Glass, Dave Wells, Mark Morris, Steve Fletcher, Ian Cox, John Williams (Assistant Manager).
Front row: Sean O'Driscoll (Youth Team Manager), David Town, Marcus Oldbury, John Bailey, Jason Brissett, Mel Machin (Manager), Matt Holland (Manager), Steve Robinson, Russell Beardsmore, Mark Rawlinson, Steve Hardwick (Physio).

Division 2　　　　　　AFC BOURNEMOUTH

Dean Court Ground, Bournemouth, Dorset BH7 7AF. Telephone: (01202) 395381. Fax: (01202) 309797.

Ground capacity: 10,440.

Record attendance: 28,799 v Manchester U, FA Cup 6th rd, 2 March 1957.

Record receipts: £33,723 v Manchester U, FA Cup 3rd rd, 7 January 1984.

Pitch measurements: 112yd × 75yd.

Chairman: .

Directors: B. E. Willis (Acting-Chairman), N. Hayward.

Secretary: K. R. J. MacAlister.

Manager: Mel Machin. *Assistant Manager:* John Williams. *Youth Team Coach:* Sean O'Driscoll. *Physio:* Steve Hardwick. *Commercial Manager:* . *Stadium Manager:* S. Baker.

Year Formed: 1899. *Turned Professional:* 1912. *Ltd Co.:* 1914.

Previous Names: Boscombe St Johns, 1890–99; Boscombe FC, 1899–1923; Bournemouth & Boscombe Ath FC, 1923–71.

Club Nickname: 'Cherries'.

Previous Grounds: 1899–1910, Castlemain Road, Pokesdown; 1910, Dean Court.

Foundation: There was a Bournemouth FC as early as 1875, but the present club arose out of the remnants of the Boscombe St John's club (formed 1890). The meeting at which Boscombe FC came into being was held at a house in Gladstone Road in 1899. They began by playing in the Boscombe and District Junior League.

First Football League game: 25 August 1923, Division 3 (S), v Swindon T (a), L 1-3 – Heron; Wingham, Lamb; Butt, C. Smith, Voisey; Miller, Lister (1), Davey, Simpson, Robinson.

Record League Victory: 7–0 v Swindon T, Division 3 (S), 22 September 1956 – Godwin; Cunningham, Keetley; Clayton, Crosland, Rushworth; Siddall (1), Norris (2), Arnott (1), Newsham (2), Cutler (1). 10–0 win v Northampton T at start of 1939–40 expunged from the records on outbreak of war.

Record Cup Victory: 11–0 v Margate, FA Cup 1st rd, 20 November 1971 – Davies; Machin (1), Kitchener, Benson, Jones, Powell, Cave (1), Boyer, MacDougall (9 incl. 1p), Miller, Scott (De Garis).

Record Defeat: 0–9 v Lincoln C, Division 3, 18 December 1982.

Most League Points (2 for a win): 62, Division 3, 1971–72.

Most League Points (3 for a win): 97, Division 3, 1986–87.

Most League Goals: 88, Division 3 (S), 1956–57.

Highest League Scorer in Season: Ted MacDougall, 42, 1970–71.

Most League Goals in Total Aggregate: Ron Eyre, 202, 1924–33.

Most Capped Player: Gerry Peyton, 7 (33), Republic of Ireland.

Most League Appearances: Sean O'Driscoll, 423, 1984–95.

Record Transfer Fee Received: £800,000 from Everton for Joe Parkinson, March 1994.

Record Transfer Fee Paid: £210,000 to Gillingham for Gavin Peacock, August 1989.

Football League Record: 1923 Elected to Division 3 (S). Remained a Third Division club for record number of years until 1970; 1970–71 Division 4; 1971–75 Division 3; 1975–82 Division 4; 1982–87 Division 3; 1987–90 Division 2; 1990–92 Division 3; 1992– Division 2.

Honours: Football League: Division 3 – Champions 1986–87; Division 3 (S) – Runners-up 1947–48. Promotion from Division 4 1970–71 (2nd), 1981–82 (4th). *FA Cup:* best season: 6th rd, 1957. *Football League Cup:* best season: 4th rd, 1962, 1964. *Associate Members' Cup:* Winners 1984.

Colours: Red shirts with black 3" stripe and white pinstripe, white shorts, white stockings. *Change colours:* Blue/yellow halved shirts, blue shorts, yellow stockings.

Did you know?
Outside-left Jack Russell scored four goals for Bournemouth in each of two League matches in January 1933 against Clapton Orient and Bristol City.

AFC BOURNEMOUTH 1996–97 LEAGUE RECORD

Match No.	Date	Venue	Opponents	Result	H/T Score	Lg. Pos.	Goalscorers	Attendance
1	Aug 17	H	Watford	L	1-2	0-0	—	Brissett [76]	7672
2	24	A	York C	W	2-1	0-0	11	Brissett [46], Fletcher [75]	2804
3	27	A	Stockport Co	W	1-0	1-0	—	Brissett [30]	3446
4	31	H	Peterborough U	L	1-2	0-1	10	Fletcher [64]	4587
5	Sept 7	H	Crewe Alex	L	0-1	0-1	14		3218
6	10	A	Bristol R	L	2-3	1-0	—	Fletcher [21], Murray [75]	4170
7	14	A	Preston NE	W	1-0	1-0	11	Fletcher [29]	8268
8	21	H	Notts Co	L	0-1	0-1	16		3402
9	28	A	Rotherham U	L	0-1	0-0	20		2648
10	Oct 1	H	Walsall	L	0-1	0-1	—		2747
11	5	A	Gillingham	D	1-1	1-0	22	Holland [23]	6162
12	12	H	Wycombe W	W	2-1	2-0	18	Holland [5], Watson [27]	3984
13	15	H	Plymouth Arg	W	1-0	1-0	—	Fletcher [17]	3818
14	19	A	Wrexham	L	0-2	0-1	18		3945
15	26	A	Luton T	L	0-2	0-1	19		5635
16	29	H	Bristol C	L	0-2	0-0	—		4197
17	Nov 2	H	Bury	D	1-1	1-1	20	Holland [15]	3946
18	9	A	Blackpool	D	1-1	0-1	19	Cox [61]	3744
19	19	H	Brentford	W	2-1	1-1	—	Robinson 2 (1 pen) [29, 64 (p)]	3464
20	23	A	Burnley	L	0-1	0-1	20		8564
21	30	H	Luton T	W	3-2	1-2	17	Robinson 2 [17, 80], Cox [78]	4322
22	Dec 3	A	Shrewsbury T	D	1-1	0-1	—	Holland [49]	1610
23	14	H	Millwall	D	1-1	1-1	18	Holland [25]	4494
24	21	A	Chesterfield	D	1-1	0-1	20	Cox [77]	4174
25	26	H	Bristol R	W	1-0	1-0	13	Watson [25]	5036
26	28	A	Crewe Alex	L	0-2	0-0	14		3585
27	Jan 11	H	Rotherham U	D	1-1	0-0	14	Cox [66]	3161
28	18	A	Walsall	L	1-2	0-1	16	Fletcher [65]	3037
29	25	A	Bristol C	W	1-0	1-0	15	Cox [42]	10,434
30	Feb 1	H	Blackpool	D	0-0	0-0	15		8201
31	4	A	Notts Co	W	2-0	1-0	—	Cox [42], Town [89]	2757
32	8	A	Bury	L	1-2	1-1	13	Robinson (pen) [45]	3559
33	11	H	Preston NE	W	2-0	1-0	—	Brissett [19], Cox [63]	4769
34	15	H	Burnley	D	0-0	0-0	13		6021
35	22	A	Brentford	L	0-1	0-1	14		6071
36	Mar 1	H	Shrewsbury T	D	0-0	0-0	14		5810
37	11	A	Chesterfield	W	3-0	1-0	—	Fletcher [40], Robinson [68], Rawlinson [81]	3368
38	15	A	Millwall	W	1-0	0-0	13	Bailey [78]	8992
39	22	H	York C	D	1-1	1-0	14	Town [8]	4367
40	29	H	Watford	W	1-0	1-0	14	Cox [25]	10,019
41	Apr 1	A	Stockport Co	D	0-0	0-0	—		5476
42	5	A	Peterborough U	L	1-3	0-0	15	Rawlinson [70]	4221
43	12	H	Gillingham	D	2-2	1-1	15	Murray [27], Robinson [89]	5008
44	19	A	Wycombe W	D	1-1	0-0	16	Holland [48]	6043
45	26	H	Wrexham	W	2-1	1-0	15	O'Neill [26], Holland [67]	4805
46	May 3	A	Plymouth Arg	D	0-0	0-0	16		6507

Final League Position: 16

GOALSCORERS

League (43): Cox 8, Fletcher 7, Holland 7, Robinson 7 (2 pens), Brissett 4, Murray 2, Rawlinson 2, Town 2, Watson 2, Bailey 1, O'Neill 1.
Coca-Cola Cup (1): Fletcher 1.
FA Cup (0).

Glass J 35	Young N 44	Beardsmore R 37 + 1	Coll O 16	Murray R 20 + 12	Bailey J 40	Holland M 45	Cox I 44	O'Neill J 7 + 11	Fletcher S 33 + 2	Gordon D 14 + 2	Brissett J 16 + 9	Robinson S 34 + 6	Vincent J 28 + 1	Morris M — + 1	Marshall A 11	Cotterill S 2 + 7	Watson M 6 + 9	Town D 16 + 10	Howe E 7 + 6	Omoyinmi E 5 + 2	Dean M 10 + 2	O'Brien R 1	Rawlinson M 22 + 3	Ferdinand R 10	Christie J 3 + 1	Hayter J — + 2	Match No
1	2	3	4	5	6	7	8	9^1	10	11	12																1
1	2	3	4	5	6	7	8		10	9^1	11	12															2
1	2	3	4	5	6^1	7	8	12	10	9	11^2	13															3
1	2	3^2	4	5^3		7	8	12	10	9	11^1	13	6	14													4
1	2	3	4	5	6	7	8	12	10	9^1		11															5
	2	3	4^1	5	6^2	7	8^3	14	10	11		9	12		1	13											6
	2		4	5	6	7		11	10	9			3		1	8											7
	2	12	4	5	6	7		11	10	9^1		13	3^2		1	8^3	14										8
	2		4	5^1	6^3	7	8	13	10	9^2		12	3		1		14	11									9
	2^2		4			7	5		9	10^1		8			1	13	12	14	3^3	6	11						10
1	2	3		10		7	5	12	9			8					13	14	6^1	11^1	4^3						11
	2	3	4		6^1	7	5		9	13		8				10^3		12	14	11^2							12
	2	3	4	12			5^3		9	6		8				10^1		13	7^2	11		14					13
	2	3	4		6^1	7	5		9	12		8				13		10	11^2								14
	2		4^3		6^1	7	5	12	9			8				13	14	11	10^2								15
	2	3	4^2		6	7	5		9		12	8				10^1	13	11									16
	2	3	4	12	6	7	5		9	10^1		8			1			11									17
1	2			12	6	7	5	9^1	10			8	3				11						4				18
1	2			12	6	7	5	11	9^1		13	8	3^2				14						4	10^3			19
1	2			12	6	7	5	11	9^2		13	8	3^1				14						4	10^3			20
1	2			12		7	5	11^3		9^1	10	8	3						6^2		13		4	14			21
1	2			12	6	7	5					10	8	3							9		4	11^1			22
1	2	11		12	6	7	5					10^1	8^2	3			13^1	14					9	4			23
1	2	11		10	6	7	5						3				8	12					9^1	4			24
1	2	11		8	6	7	5	12					3				10^1						9	4			25
1	2	11		8^1	6^2	7	5	12		13			3				10	14					9^1	4			26
1	2	11			6^3	7	5	10^2		12		8	3				13	14					9^1	4			27
	2^1	4		12	6	7	5	10		11^2		8	3^1				13						9				28
1	2	4			6	7	5	10		11		8^1	3				12						9				29
1	2	4			6	7	5	10		11^1		8	3				12						9				30
1	2	4			6	7	5	10		11		8^1	3				12						9				31
1	2	4		12	6^3	7	5	10		11^2		8	3^1			13							9	14			32
1	2	4			6	7	5	10		11		8	3				9										33
1	2	4	3		6	7	5	10		11^1		8					9								12		34
1		4	3			7	5^1	13	10	11^3		8				14		9	2^2	12					6		35
1		4	2			7	5	10		11		8	3				9								6		36
1	2	4			6	7	5	10				8	3				9							11			37
1	2	4			6	7	5	10^1		12		8	3				9							11			38
1	2	4	10^1		6	7	5					8	3			12	9	13						11^2			39
1	2	4	12^2		6	7	5	10^1				8^3	14	3		13	9							11			40
1	2	4	10		6	7	5					12	8	3			9							11^1			41
1	2	4	10^3		6	7	5					12	8^2			13	9	3^1						11		14	42
1	2	4	10		6	7	5	12				8					9^2	3						11^1		13	43
1	2	4	10		6	7	5	12				8					9^1	3						11			44
1	2	4			6	7	5	10^1					3				9	8		12				11			45
1	2	4^2		12	6	7	5	13				8	3				9^1	10						11			46

Coca-Cola Cup
First Round   Ipswich T   (a) 1-2
                                      (h) 0-3

FA Cup
First Round   Brentford   (a) 0-2

BRADFORD CITY 1996–97 *Back row (left to right):* Wayne Jacobs, Andrew O'Brien, Graham Mitchell, Nicky Mohan, Ian Ormondroyd, David Brightwell, Marco Sas, Carl Shutt.
Middle row: Peter Williams (Goalkeeping Coach), Steve Redmond (Physio), Christian Sansam, Mark Stallard, Des Hamilton, Jonathan Gould, Andy Kiwomya, Richard Huxford, Wayne Bullimore, Bryan Edwards (Kit Manager), Paul Jewell (Reserve Team Manager).
Front row: Gordon Cowans, Craig Midgley, Erik Regtop, Chris Kamara (Manager), Martin Hunter (First Team Coach), Shaun Murray, Tommy Wright, Lee Duxbury.

Division 1 **BRADFORD CITY**

The Pulse Stadium at Valley Parade, Bradford BD8 7DY. Telephone: (01274) 773355 (Office). Fax: (01274) 773356. e-mail: bradfordcityfc@compuserve.com

Ground capacity: 18,018.

Record attendance: 39,146 v Burnley, FA Cup 4th rd, 11 March 1911.

Record receipts: £164,567 v Sheffield Wednesday, FA Cup 5th rd, 16 February 1997.

Pitch measurements: 110yd × 73yd.

Chairman: Geoffrey Richmond. *Vice-Chairman:* David Thompson FCA.

Directors: David Richmond, Elizabeth Richmond, Terry Goddard. *Managing Director:* Shaun Harvey.

Manager: Chris Kamara. *Assistant Manager:* Martin Hunter. *Coach:* Paul Jewell.

Youth Coach: Steve Smith. *Physio:* Steve Redmond.

Secretary: Jon Pollard. *Stadium Manager:* Allan Gilliver.

Year Formed: 1903. *Turned Professional:* 1903. *Ltd Co.:* 1908.

Club Nickname: 'The Bantams'.

Foundation: Bradford was a rugby stronghold around the turn of the century but after Manningham RFC held an archery contest to help them out of financial difficulties in 1903, they were persuaded to give up the handling code and turn to soccer. So they formed Bradford City and continued at Valley Parade. Recognising this as an opportunity of spreading the dribbling code in this part of Yorkshire, the Football League immediately accepted the new club's first application for membership of the Second Division.

First Football League game: 1 September 1903, Division 2, v Grimsby T (a), L 0-2 – Seymour; Wilson, Halliday; Robinson, Millar, Farnall; Guy, Beckram, Forrest, McMillan, Graham.

Record League Victory: 11–1 v Rotherham U, Division 3 (N), 25 August 1928 – Sherlaw; Russell, Watson; Burkinshaw (1), Summers, Bauld; Harvey (2), Edmunds (3), White (3), Cairns, Scriven (2).

Record Cup Victory: 11–3 v Walker Celtic, FA Cup 1st rd (replay), 1 December 1937 – Parker; Rookes, McDermott; Murphy, Mackie, Moore; Bagley (1), Whittingham (1), Deakin (4 incl. 1p), Cooke (1), Bartholomew (4).

Record Defeat: 1–9 v Colchester U, Division 4, 30 December 1961.

Most League Points (2 for a win): 63, Division 3 (N), 1928–29.

Most League Points (3 for a win): 94, Division 3, 1984–85.

Most League Goals: 128, Division 3 (N), 1928–29.

Highest League Scorer in Season: David Layne, 34, Division 4, 1961–62.

Most League Goals in Total Aggregate: Bobby Campbell, 121, 1981–84, 1984–86.

Most Capped Player: Harry Hampton, 9, Northern Ireland.

Most League Appearances: Cec Podd, 502, 1970–84.

Record Transfer Fee Received: £2,000,000 from Newcastle U for Des Hamilton, March 1997.

Record Transfer Fee Paid: £550,000 to Southampton for Gordon Watson, January 1997.

Football League Record: 1903 Elected to Division 2; 1908–22 Division 1; 1922–27 Division 2; 1927–29 Division 3 (N); 1929–37 Division 2; 1937–61 Division 3; 1961–69 Division 4; 1969–72 Division 3; 1972–77 Division 4; 1977–78 Division 3; 1978–82 Division 4; 1982–85 Division 3; 1985–90 Division 2; 1990–92 Division 3; 1992–96 Division 2; 1996– Division 1.

Honours: Football League: Division 1 best season: 5th, 1910–11; Division 2 – Champions 1907–08; Promoted from Division 2 1995–96 (play-offs); Division 3 – Champions 1984–85; Division 3 (N) – Champions 1928–29; Division 4 – Runners-up 1981–82. *FA Cup:* Winners 1911. *Football League Cup:* best season: 5th rd, 1965, 1989.

Colours: Claret and amber shirts, black shorts, black stockings. *Change colours:* Light blue shirts and shorts, blue stockings.

Did you know?
Bradford City recorded two 8–0 wins in consecutive home matches during the 1928–29 season, defeating Tranmere Rovers and Barrow.

BRADFORD CITY 1996–97 LEAGUE RECORD

Match No.	Date	Venue	Opponents	Result		H/T Score	Lg. Pos.	Goalscorers	Attendance
1	Aug 17	H	Portsmouth	W	3-1	0-1	—	Regtop (pen) 62, Duxbury 76, Stallard 88	10,007
2	24	A	Wolverhampton W	L	0-1	0-0	10		24,171
3	28	A	Stoke C	L	0-1	0-0	—		11,918
4	31	H	Tranmere R	W	1-0	0-0	9	Duxbury 73	10,080
5	Sept 7	H	Norwich C	L	0-2	0-2	15		10,054
6	10	A	Sheffield U	L	0-3	0-2	—		12,591
7	14	A	Oxford U	L	0-2	0-0	21		6334
8	21	H	Bolton W	L	2-4	2-2	22	Liburd 35, Sas 39	12,034
9	29	A	Port Vale	D	1-1	0-1	22	Jacobs 83	4706
10	Oct 2	H	Swindon T	W	2-1	1-1	—	Sas (pen) 44, Shutt 47	9249
11	5	H	Southend U	D	0-0	0-0	19		10,156
12	12	A	Birmingham C	L	0-3	0-1	22		25,157
13	16	A	QPR	L	0-1	0-0	—		7776
14	19	H	Barnsley	D	2-2	1-1	22	Waddle 26, Kiwomya 67	11,477
15	26	A	WBA	D	0-0	0-0	23		14,249
16	29	H	Crystal Palace	L	0-4	0-2	—		10,091
17	Nov 2	H	Oldham Ath	L	0-3	0-1	24		10,855
18	8	A	Huddersfield T	D	3-3	3-2	—	Waddle 6, Dreyer 13, Steiner 38	14,126
19	16	H	Ipswich T	W	2-1	1-0	22	Sundgot 2 32, 75	10,504
20	23	A	Charlton Ath	W	2-0	1-0	22	Steiner 44, Waddle 77	12,256
21	30	H	WBA	D	1-1	1-1	22	Sas 31	12,003
22	Dec 7	A	Manchester C	L	2-3	1-2	23	Steiner 2 21, 52	25,035
23	17	H	Reading	D	0-0	0-0	—		10,077
24	21	A	Grimsby T	D	1-1	1-0	23	Duxbury 45	5766
25	26	H	Sheffield U	L	1-2	1-1	23	Jacobs 37	17,475
26	28	A	Norwich C	L	0-2	0-1	23		13,473
27	Jan 1	A	Bolton W	L	1-2	0-0	23	Shutt 87	16,192
28	11	H	Oxford U	W	2-0	1-0	22	O'Brien 14, Shutt 60	13,275
29	18	A	Swindon T	D	1-1	1-0	22	Jacobs 15	7851
30	28	H	Port Vale	W	1-0	1-0	—	Watson 20	15,186
31	Feb 1	H	Huddersfield T	D	1-1	1-1	21	Waddle 40	17,373
32	8	A	Crystal Palace	L	1-3	1-0	21	Waddle 5	14,844
33	22	A	Oldham Ath	W	2-1	0-1	21	Sundgot 48, Edinho 59	9524
34	Mar 1	H	Manchester C	L	1-3	0-0	21	Edinho (pen) 84	17,609
35	4	A	Ipswich T	L	2-3	0-1	—	Sundgot 2 64, 74	9367
36	8	H	Grimsby T	L	3-4	2-3	22	Sundgot 28, Edinho 37, O'Brien 90	15,219
37	15	A	Reading	D	0-0	0-0	22		8435
38	22	H	Wolverhampton W	W	2-1	1-0	21	Edinho 45, Pepper 51	15,351
39	29	A	Portsmouth	L	1-3	1-3	21	Murray 17	12,340
40	31	H	Stoke C	W	1-0	0-0	21	Pepper 49	13,579
41	Apr 4	A	Tranmere R	L	0-3	0-1	—		8531
42	12	A	Southend U	D	1-1	0-1	21	Edinho 67	6697
43	19	H	Birmingham C	L	0-2	0-1	22		15,123
44	26	A	Barnsley	L	0-2	0-1	22		18,605
45	May 1	A	Charlton Ath	W	1-0	1-0	—	Pepper 37	15,780
46	4	H	QPR	W	3-0	2-0	21	Pepper 2 23, 52, Wright 39	14,723

Final League Position: 21

GOALSCORERS

League (47): Sundgot 6, Edinho 5 (1 pen), Pepper 5, Waddle 5, Steiner 4, Duxbury 3, Jacobs 3, Sas 3 (1 pen), Shutt 3, O'Brien 2, Dreyer 1, Kiwomya 1, Liburd 1, Murray 1, Regtop 1 (pen), Stallard 1, Watson 1, Wright 1.
Coca-Cola Cup (1): Stallard 1.
FA Cup (5): Dreyer 3, Steiner 1, Waddle 1.

Gould J 9	Liburd R 33+3	Mitchell G 6	Cowans G 23+1	Mohan N 44	Sas M 31	Hamilton D 24+8	Duxbury L 33	Regtop E 5+3	Stallard M 13+9	Kiwomya A 20+7	Wright T 2+9	Shutt C 10+12	Jacobs W 37+2	Newell M 7	Roberts B 2	Ormondroyd I —+1	Wilder C 4+3	Huxford R 1+1	Sansam C —+1	Blake R 3+2	Nixon E 12	Moore I 6	Midgley C —+1	Brightwell D 2	Pinto S 7+11	Smithard M —+1	Waddle C 25	Murray S 13+4	O'Brien A 18+4	Pehrsson M 1	Sundgot O 11+9	Steiner R 14+1	Dreyer J 27+1	Schwarzer M 13	Vanhala J —+1	Watson G 3	Edinho 15	Pepper N 11	Kulcsar G 9	Davison A 10	Oliveira R 2	Match No.
1	2¹	3	4	5	6	7²	8	9	10	11	12	13																														1
1²	2	3¹	4	5	6	13	8	9¹	10	11	12	7	14																													2
	2	3	4	5	6	7	8		10	11		9			1																											3
	2		4	5	6	7	8	9²	10	11¹	12	13	3		1																											4
1	2		4	5	6	7²	8¹	9³	10	11	12	13	3				14																									5
1	2		4	5	6	7¹	8³	9	10²	11	14		3								12	13																				6
			4¹	5	6	13	8	12	10³	11²	14		3		2						1	9		7																		7
	2	11³	4	5	6	7	8²	12	10¹	13	14		3								1	9																				8
	2	11¹	4	5	6	7²	8	12	10³	13	14		3								1	9																				9
	2		4	5	6	12	8		10	11			3								1	9			7¹																	10
	2		4	5	6	11	8²	12	10				3								1	9			7¹	13																11
	2		4²	5	6	12	8	13	10¹	11			3								1	9³		14	7																	12
	2		4	5		8		12	10¹	11			3								1	9²		13	7		6															13
	2		4¹	5	6	8			10	11			3								1	9²		12	7	13																14
	2		4²	5	6	12	8		10	11			3								1	9¹			7	13																15
	2			5	6²	9	8		10¹	11	12		3								1			14	7	13	4³															16
	2			5	12	8		13	11				14								1		3		7		4³	6¹	9²	10												17
	2		4	5	6	12	8		13				14	3¹							1				7			9²	10³	11												18
1	2		4	5	6	12	8					3¹													7			9	10	11												19
	2		4	5	6	3	8	12																	7			9¹	10	11	1											20
	2		4	5	6	3	8																		7			9	10	11	1											21
12			4³	5	6¹	3	8	13					2											14	7			9²	10	11	1											22
			4	5	6	3	8¹		12				2												7			9²	10	11	1	13										23
			4	5	6	3	8	9¹				12	2												7				10	11	1											24
				5	6²	3	8	4¹	9			12	2								13				7				10	11	1											25
				5		3	8	4				12	2								13				7		6¹	9²	10	11	1											26
	2		4³	5		3	8		12			13	9								14				7		6¹		10²	11	1											27
				5	2	11	8		12				9	3							4				7		6	10¹		1												28
				5	2	11	8					9²	3								4¹				7		6	13	12	1	10											29
6				5	2		8	12	13				3								9³				7²	14		10¹	4	1	11											30
	2			5		9	8	12²	13				3												7		6	10	4	1	11¹											31
	2	12		5	11³	10	8		13				3											14	7		6¹		4	1	9²											32
1	12			5		10	8			11			3								2¹				7		6²	13	4		9											33
1	12			5	6¹	10			13	14			3								2²				7		8³		4		9	11										34
1	2			5		10	8			11¹															7	13	6²		4		9	3										35
1	2³			5	6¹				11												14				7	13	12		4		9	3²	8									36
	2			5						12			3								13				7		6		10		4					9¹	11	8²		1		37
	2												3	9						2¹			8²				7		6				4			10		8	1	5	38
	2²								13				3	9			13		14								7		6		12		4				10³	11	8	1	5¹	39
	2¹			5									3	9			12										7		6				4				10	11	8	1		40
	2			5¹									3	9			13		14								7		6		12		4				10	11³	8²	1		41
				5¹	11								3				2					9					7		6		12		4				10		8	1		42
				5	10								3				2					8					7		6¹		12		4				9	11		1		43
6				5									3	9			2¹		8²				13				7		12				4				10	11	8	1		44
	2			5							8		3	9													7		12				4				10¹	11	6	1		45
	2¹			5							8		3	9			6										7	12	13				4				10²	11		1		46

Coca-Cola Cup

First Round	Sheffield U	(a)	0-3
		(h)	1-2

FA Cup

Third Round	Wycombe W	(a)	2-0
Fourth Round	Everton	(a)	3-2
Fifth Round	Sheffield W	(h)	0-1

BRENTFORD 1996-97 *Back row (left to right):* Joe Omigie, Marcus Bent, Robert Taylor, Barry Ashby, Richard Goddard, Jamie Bates, Malcolm McPherson, Carl Asaba. *Middle row:* Bob Booker (Youth Team Manager), Gus Hurdle, David McGhee, Paul Smith, Tamer Fernandes, Kevin Dearden, Stuart Myall, Carl Hutchings, Roy Johnson (Physio). *Front row:* Paul Abrahams, Ijah Anderson, Lee Harvey, David Webb (Manager), Kevin Lock (Assistant Manager), Nick Forster, Kevin Dennis, Kevin Rapley. (Photograph: Lee Doyle)

Division 2   **BRENTFORD**

Griffin Park, Braemar Rd, Brentford, Middlesex TW8 0NT. Telephone: (0181) 847 2511. Fax: (0181) 568 9940. Commercial Dept: (0181) 560 6062. Press Office: (0181) 847 2511. Clubcall: 0891 121108.

Ground capacity: 12,763.

Record attendance: 38,678 v Leicester C, FA Cup 6th rd, 20 February 1949.

Record receipts: £111,804 v Manchester C, FA Cup 3rd rd, 25 January 1997.

Pitch measurements: 111yd × 74yd.

Chairman: M. M. Lange.

Directors: J. Herting, E. J. Radley-Smith MS, FRCS, LRCP, D. Tana.

Manager: David Webb. *Assistant Manager:* Kevin Lock.

Youth Team Manager: Bob Booker.

Community Officer: Lee Doyle.

Secretary: Polly Kates. *Physio:* R. Johnson.

Safety Officer: Jill Dawson. *Marketing Manager:* Peter Gilham.

Year Formed: 1889. *Turned Professional:* 1899. *Ltd Co.:* 1901.

Club Nickname: 'The Bees'.

Previous Grounds: 1889–91, Clifden Road; 1891–95, Benns Fields, Little Ealing; 1895–98, Shotters Field; 1898–1900, Cross Road, S. Ealing; 1900–04, Boston Park; 1904, Griffin Park.

Foundation: Formed as a small amateur concern in 1889 they were very successful in local circles. They won the championship of the West London Alliance in 1893 and a year later the West Middlesex Junior Cup before carrying off the Senior Cup in 1895. After winning both the London Senior Amateur Cup and the Middlesex Senior Cup in 1898 they were admitted to the Second Division of the Southern League.

First Football League game: 28 August 1920, Division 3, v Exeter C (a), L 0-3 – Young; Hodson, Rosier, Elliott J, Levitt, Amos, Smith, Thompson, Spreadbury, Morley, Henery.

Record League Victory: 9–0 v Wrexham, Division 3, 15 October 1963 – Cakebread; Coote, Jones; Slater, Scott, Higginson; Summers (1), Brooks (2), McAdams (2), Ward (2), Hales (1). (1 og).

Record Cup Victory: 7–0 v Windsor & Eton (away), FA Cup 1st rd, 20 November 1982 – Roche; Rowe, Harris (Booker), McNichol (1), Whitehead, Hurlock (2), Kamara, Joseph (1), Mahoney (3), Bowles, Roberts.

Record Defeat: 0–7 v Swansea T, Division 3 (S), 8 November 1924 and v Walsall, Division 3 (S), 19 January 1957.

Most League Points (2 for a win): 62, Division 3 (S), 1932–33 and Division 4, 1962–63.

Most League Points (3 for a win): 85, Division 2, 1994–95.

Most League Goals: 98, Division 4, 1962–63.

Highest League Scorer in Season: Jack Holliday, 38, Division 3 (S), 1932–33.

Most League Goals in Total Aggregate: Jim Towers, 153, 1954–61.

Most Capped Player: John Buttigieg, (63), Malta.

Most League Appearances: Ken Coote, 514, 1949–64.

Record Transfer Fee Received: £720,000 from Wimbledon for Dean Holdsworth, August 1992.

Record Transfer Fee Paid: £275,000 to Chelsea for Joe Allon, November 1992.

Football League Record: 1920 Original Member of Division 3; 1921–33 Division 3 (S); 1933–35 Division 2; 1935–47 Division 1; 1947–54 Division 2; 1954–62 Division 3 (S); 1962–63 Division 4; 1963–66 Division 3; 1966–72 Division 4; 1972–73 Division 3; 1973–78 Division 4; 1978–92 Division 3; 1992–93 Division 1; 1993– Division 2.

Honours: Football League: Division 1 best season: 5th, 1935–36; Division 2 – Champions 1934–35; Division 3 – Champions 1991–92; Division 3 (S) – Champions 1932–33; Runners-up 1929–30, 1957–58; Division 4 – Champions 1962–63. *FA Cup:* best season: 6th rd, 1938, 1946, 1949, 1989. *Football League Cup:* best season: 4th rd, 1983. *Freight Rover Trophy;* Runners-up 1985.

Colours: Red and white vertical striped shirts, red shorts, red stockings. *Change colours:* Black and white vertical stripes, white shorts, white stockings.

Did you know?
On 18 January 1997, Brentford established a club record with their 25th unbeaten home game, a run stretching back to Boxing Day 1995.

BRENTFORD 1996–97 LEAGUE RECORD

Match No.	Date	Venue	Opponents	Result	H/T Score	Lg. Pos.	Goalscorers	Attendance
1	Aug 17	A	Bury	D	1-1	1-0	—	Taylor 17	3373
2	24	H	Luton T	W	3-2	0-1	3	Asaba 66, Bates 80, Taylor 88	5404
3	27	H	Gillingham	W	2-0	0-0	—	Abrahams 2 63, 74	5384
4	31	A	Shrewsbury T	W	3-0	3-0	2	Asaba 3 14, 18, 21	3530
5	Sept 7	A	Chesterfield	W	2-0	2-0	1	Bates 13, Forster 45	3643
6	10	H	Plymouth Arg	W	3-2	1-1	—	Smith 31, Asaba 71, Bent 84	5377
7	14	H	Blackpool	D	1-1	1-0	1	Asaba 3	5908
8	21	A	Wycombe W	W	1-0	1-0	1	Bent 4	5330
9	28	H	York C	D	3-3	0-1	1	Taylor 53, Asaba 2 83, 89	5243
10	Oct 1	A	Bristol C	W	2-1	1-1	—	Asaba 12, Forster 72	9520
11	5	H	Rotherham U	W	4-2	2-1	1	Asaba 2 24, 59, Taylor 42, Forster 86	6137
12	12	A	Crewe Alex	L	0-2	0-0	1		4313
13	15	A	Peterborough U	W	1-0	0-0	—	Taylor 56	5037
14	19	H	Walsall	D	1-1	1-1	1	Hutchings 28	5419
15	26	H	Millwall	D	0-0	0-0	1		7691
16	29	A	Bristol R	L	1-2	0-1	—	Hutchings 68	5163
17	Nov 2	A	Watford	L	0-2	0-1	2		11,448
18	9	H	Stockport Co	D	2-2	0-0	2	Canham 53, Forster 74	5076
19	19	A	Bournemouth	L	1-2	1-1	—	Anderson 33	3464
20	23	H	Wrexham	W	2-0	1-0	2	Forster 11, Asaba 60	4885
21	29	A	Millwall	D	0-0	0-0	—		7845
22	Dec 3	H	Notts Co	W	2-0	1-0	—	Bent 39, Asaba 74	3675
23	14	A	Burnley	W	2-1	1-0	1	Asaba 15, Forster 54	10,575
24	21	H	Preston NE	D	0-0	0-0	1		5365
25	26	A	Plymouth Arg	W	4-1	1-0	1	Forster 2 7, 87, Asaba 71, Omigie 77	9525
26	Jan 11	A	York C	W	4-2	2-1	1	Asaba 2 7, 40, Forster 2 53, 73	3085
27	18	H	Bristol C	D	0-0	0-0	1		7606
28	21	H	Bristol R	D	0-0	0-0	—		4191
29	Feb 1	A	Stockport Co	W	2-1	0-0	1	McGhee 56, Taylor 76	8650
30	8	H	Watford	D	1-1	1-1	1	Asaba 2	8679
31	22	H	Bournemouth	W	1-0	1-0	1	Asaba 10	6071
32	Mar 1	A	Notts Co	D	1-1	0-1	1	Ashby 86	4323
33	4	H	Wycombe W	D	0-0	0-0	—		5375
34	8	A	Preston NE	L	0-1	0-0	1		9489
35	15	H	Burnley	L	0-3	0-3	1		6624
36	21	A	Luton T	L	0-1	0-0	—		8164
37	25	A	Wrexham	W	2-0	2-0	—	Asaba 2 (1 pen) 29, 44 (p)	4053
38	29	H	Bury	L	0-2	0-2	3		7823
39	31	A	Gillingham	W	2-1	1-1	2	Janney 36, Asaba 50	7361
40	Apr 5	H	Shrewsbury T	D	0-0	0-0	3		5355
41	11	A	Rotherham U	W	1-0	0-0	—	Taylor 76	1797
42	15	H	Chesterfield	W	1-0	1-0	—	Asaba 23	5216
43	19	H	Crewe Alex	L	0-2	0-0	2		6183
44	22	A	Blackpool	L	0-1	0-0	—		4030
45	26	A	Walsall	L	0-1	0-1	4		5359
46	May 3	H	Peterborough U	L	0-1	0-0	4		5274

Final League Position: 4

GOALSCORERS

League (56): Asaba 23 (1 pen), Forster 10, Taylor 7, Bent 3, Abrahams 2, Bates 2, Hutchings 2, Anderson 1, Ashby 1, Canham 1, Janney 1, McGhee 1, Omigie 1, Smith 1.
Coca-Cola Cup (2): Forster 1, Taylor 1.
FA Cup (5): Taylor 2, Forster 1, McGhee 1, Smith 1.

Dearden K 44	Hurdle G 28 + 3	Anderson I 46	Ashby B 40	Bates J 37	McGhee D 44 + 1	Asaba C 44	Smith P 46	Forster N 25	Bent M 29 + 5	Taylor R 43	Abrahams P 5 + 3	Hutchings C 23 + 5	Harvey L 2 + 12	Canham S 13	Dennis K 9 + 3	Omigie J 7 + 6	Statham B 11 + 8	McPherson M 2 + 1	Slade S 4	Fernandes T 2	Janney M 1 + 1	Rapley K 1 + 1	Goddard-Crawley R — + 1	Match No.
1	2	3	4	5	6	7	8	9	10	11														1
1	2	3	4	5	6	7	8[1]		10	11	9[2]	12	13											2
1	2	3	4	5	6	7	8		10	11	9													3
1	2	3	4	5	6	7[1]	8		10	11	9[2]	12	13											4
1	2	3	4	5	6[1]	7	8	9	10	11		12												5
1	2	3	4	5	6[1]	7	8	9	10	11		12												6
1	2	3	4	5		7	8	9[1]	10	11	12				6									7
1	2	3	4	5	12	7	8	9	10[2]	11	13				6[1]									8
1	2	3	4		5	7	8	9	10[1]	11	12		13		6[2]									9
1	2	3	4		5	7[2]	8	9	12	11	10[1]				6	13								10
1	2	3	4		5	7[2]	8	9	12	11	10[1]				6	13								11
1	2	3	4		5	7[2]	8	9	10[1]	11					6	12	13							12
1	2	3	4		5	7	8	9	10	11					6									13
1	2	3	4		5	7	8	9	10[1]	11					6	12								14
1	2	3	4		5	7	8	9		11					6		10							15
1	2	3	4		5	7	8	9	12	11					6		10[1]							16
1	2	3	4		5	7[1]	8	9	10	11					6		12							17
1	2	3[1]	5	4			8	9	10	11		12			6	7								18
1	2	3	4	5	6	7	8	9		11						12	10[1]							19
1	2	3	4	5	6	7	8	9		11						12	10[1]							20
1	2	3	4	5	6	7[1]	8	9		11						12	10							21
1	2	3	4	5	6	7	8	9	10[1]	11						12								22
1	2	3	4	5	6	7	8	9	12	11[1]							10							23
1	2	3	4	5	6	7	8	9	12	11							10							24
1	2	3	4	5	6	7[1]	8	9		11						12	10	•						25
1	2	3	4	5	6	7	8	9	10[1]	11						12								26
1	2	3	4	5	6	7	8	9		11							10							27
1	2[2]	3	4	5	6	7	8	9		11					12	13	10[1]							28
1		3	4	5	6	7	8	9		11		2					10							29
1		3	4	5	6	7	8[2]	9		11		2				12	10[1]	13						30
1		3	4	5	6	7	8	9		11		2				12	10[1]							31
		3	4	5	6	7	8	9[1]		11		2				12	10			1				32
		3	4	5	6	7	8	9		11		2					10			1				33
1	12	3	4	5	6		8	9[2]		11		2		13		7[1]	10							34
1		3	4	5	6	7	8	9[1]		11		2				12	10							35
1		3	4	5	6	7	8	9[1]		11		2				12	10							36
1		3		5	6	7	8	9		11		2		4			10							37
1		3		5	6	7	8	9[1]		11		2		4		12	10							38
1		3	4	5[1]	6	7	8			11		2				9	10				12			39
1		3	4	5	6	7	8			11		2				12	10					9[1]		40
1		3	4	5	9	7	8	12		11		2[1]				6	10							41
1	12	3	4	5[2]	6	7	8	9[1]		11		2				13	10							42
1	12	3	4[2]	5	6	7	8	9[1]		11		2				13	10							43
1		3		5	6	7	8			11		4				9	10	2						44
1		3		5	6	7	8			11		4				9[1]	10	2			12			45
1		3		5	6	7	8			11[2]		4				12	10	2				9[1]	13	46

Coca-Cola Cup

First Round	Plymouth Arg	(h)	1-0
		(a)	0-0
Second Round	Blackburn R	(h)	1-2
		(a)	0-2

FA Cup

First Round	Bournemouth	(h)	2-0
Second Round	Sudbury T	(a)	3-1
Third Round	Manchester C	(h)	0-1

BRIGHTON & HOVE ALBION 1996-97 *Back row (left to right)* Kerry Mayo, Stuart Storer, Philip Andrews, Nicky Rust, Mark Ormerod, Simon Fox, James Virgo, Stuart Tuck.
Middle row: John Jackson (Youth Development Officer), Peter Smith, Denny Mundee, Jason Peake, Gary Hobson, Ian Baird, Mark Fox, Kevin McGarrigle, Malcolm Stuart (Physio).
Front row: Craig Maskell, Paul McDonald, Derek Allan, Jimmy Case (Manager), George Parris, George Petchey (Coach), Ross Johnson, Jeff Minton.
(Photograph: M. Pelling)

Division 3 BRIGHTON & HOVE ALBION

Offices: Hanover House, 118 Queens Road, Brighton BN1 3XG. Telephone: (01634) 851854. Recorded information (team & ticket news etc): Albion Clubline: 0891 440066.

Ground capacity: 10,952.

Record attendance: 36,747 v Fulham, Division 2, 27 December 1958.

Record receipts: £109,615.65 v Crawley T, FA Cup 3rd rd, 4 January 1992.

Pitch measurements: 114yd × 75yd.

President: G. A. Stanley.

Directors: G. A. Stanley, W. E. Archer (Chairman), D. Stanley.

Manager: Steve Gritt. *Assistant Manager:* Jeff Wood.

Secretary: Derek Allan. *Chief Executive/Deputy Chairman:* David Bellotti.

Physio: Malcolm Stuart. *Youth Development Officer:* John Jackson. *Stadium Manager:* Brian Harwood.

Year Formed: 1901. *Turned Professional:* 1901. *Ltd Co.:* 1904.

Previous Grounds: 1901, County Ground; 1902, Goldstone Ground.

Club Nickname: 'The Seagulls'.

Foundation: A professional club Brighton United was formed in November 1897 at the Imperial Hotel, Queen's Road, but folded in March 1900 after less than two seasons in the Southern League at the County Ground. An amateur team, Brighton & Hove Rangers was then formed by some prominent United supporters and after one season at Withdean, decided to turn semi-professional and play at the County Ground. Rangers were accepted into the Southern League but then also folded June 1901. John Jackson the former United manager organised a meeting at the Seven Stars public house, Ship Street on 24 June 1901 at which a new third club Brighton & Hove United was formed. They took over Rangers' place in the Southern League and pitch at County Ground. The name was changed to Brighton & Hove Albion before a match was played because of objections by Hove FC.

First Football League game: 28 August 1920, Division 3, v Southend U (a), L 0-2 – Hayes; Woodhouse, Little; Hall, Comber, Bentley; Longstaff, Ritchie, Doran, Rodgerson, March.

Record League Victory: 9–1 v Newport Co, Division 3 (S), 18 April 1951 – Ball; Tennant (1p), Mansell (1p); Willard, McCoy, Wilson; Reed, McNichol (4), Garbutt, Bennett (2), Keene (1). 9–1 v Southend U, Division 3, 27 November 1965 – Powney; Magill, Baxter; Leck, Gall, Turner; Gould (1), Collins (1), Livesey (2), Smith (3), Goodchild (2).

Record Cup Victory: 10–1 v Wisbech, FA Cup 1st rd, 13 November 1965 – Powney; Magill, Baxter; Collins (1), Gall, Turner; Gould, Smith (2), Livesey (3), Cassidy (2), Goodchild (1). (1 og).

Record Defeat: 0–9 v Middlesbrough, Division 2, 23 August 1958.

Most League Points (2 for a win): 65, Division 3 (S), 1955–56 and Division 3, 1971–72.

Most League Points (3 for a win): 84, Division 3, 1987–88.

Most League Goals: 112, Division 3 (S), 1955–56.

Highest League Scorer in Season: Peter Ward, 32, Division 3, 1976–77.

Most League Goals in Total Aggregate: Tommy Cook, 114, 1922–29.

Most Capped Player: Steve Penney, 17, Northern Ireland.

Most League Appearances: 'Tug' Wilson, 509, 1922–36.

Record Transfer Fee Received: £900,000 from Liverpool for Mark Lawrenson, August 1981.

Record Transfer Fee Paid: £500,000 to Manchester U for Andy Ritchie, October 1980.

Football League Record: 1920 Original Member of Division 3; 1921–58 Division 3 (S); 1958–62 Division 2; 1962–63 Division 3; 1963–65 Division 4; 1965–72 Division 3; 1972–73 Division 2; 1973–77 Division 3; 1977–79 Division 2; 1979–83 Division 1; 1983–87 Division 2; 1987–88 Division 3; 1988–96 Division 2; 1996– Division 3.

Honours: Football League: Division 1 best season: 13th, 1981–82; Division 2 – Runners-up 1978–79; Division 3 (S) – Champions 1957–58; Runners-up 1953–54, 1955–56; Division 3 – Runners-up 1971–72, 1976–77, 1987–88; Division 4 – Champions 1964–65. *FA Cup:* Runners-up 1983. *Football League Cup:* best season: 5th rd, 1979.

Colours: Blue and white striped shirts, blue shorts, white stockings. *Change colours:* All red.

Did you know?
Brighton & Hove Albion defeated Athletique Parisien 9–1 on Boxing Day 1904 in their first match against foreign opposition.

BRIGHTON & HOVE ALBION 1996–97 LEAGUE RECORD

Match No.	Date		Venue	Opponents	Result		H/T Score	Lg. Pos.	Goalscorers	Attendance
1	Aug	17	H	Chester C	W	2-1	0-1	—	Baird [70], Parris [80]	5263
2		24	A	Cardiff C	L	0-1	0-1	12		3463
3		27	A	Barnet	L	0-3	0-0	—		2513
4		31	H	Scunthorpe U	D	1-1	0-0	19	Baird [71]	4365
5	Sept	7	H	Scarborough	W	3-2	1-0	10	Storer [11], Maskell 2 [53, 60]	4008
6		10	A	Colchester U	L	0-2	0-1	—		2540
7		14	A	Exeter C	L	1-2	0-1	16	McDonald [47]	2886
8		21	H	Torquay U	D	2-2	1-2	16	Baird [14], Minton [61]	4889
9		28	A	Northampton T	L	0-3	0-2	21		4402
10	Oct	1	H	Lincoln C	L	1-3	1-1	—	Smith [35]	4411
11		5	A	Wigan Ath	L	0-1	0-1	24		3744
12		12	H	Cambridge U	L	1-2	0-2	24	Storer [50]	4564
13		15	H	Hereford U	L	0-1	0-0	—		3444
14		19	A	Doncaster R	L	0-3	0-0	24		1787
15		26	H	Fulham	D	0-0	0-0	24		8387
16		29	A	Rochdale	L	0-3	0-1	—		1913
17	Nov	2	A	Hartlepool U	W	3-2	2-1	24	Mundee (pen) [21], Minton [36], Morris [65]	1683
18		9	H	Mansfield T	D	1-1	0-1	24	Mundee (pen) [77]	1933
19		19	A	Swansea C	L	0-1	0-1	—		2692
20		23	H	Carlisle U	L	1-3	1-2	24	Baird [9]	4155
21		30	A	Fulham	L	0-2	0-0	24		8279
22	Dec	3	H	Darlington	L	2-3	1-0	—	Maskell [12], Baird [53]	2709
23		14	H	Hull C	W	3-0	1-0	24	McDonald [2], Storer [49], Maskell [76]	3762
24		22	A	Leyton Orient	L	0-2	0-0	24		7944
25		26	H	Colchester U	D	1-1	1-1	24	Mundee (pen) [34]	4830
26		28	A	Scarborough	D	1-1	1-0	24	Storer [34]	2252
27	Jan	1	A	Torquay U	L	1-2	1-1	24	Andrews [34]	2588
28		18	A	Lincoln C	L	1-2	0-0	24	Storer [66]	3056
29		25	H	Rochdale	W	3-0	1-0	24	Maskell 2 [30, 67], Baird [72]	4468
30	Feb	1	A	Mansfield T	D	1-1	1-1	24	Mundee [33]	2456
31		8	H	Hartlepool U	W	5-0	3-0	24	Baird [8], Maskell 3 [22, 45, 56], Hobson [48]	8412
32		11	H	Exeter C	W	1-0	1-0	—	Baird [25]	5835
33		15	A	Carlisle U	L	1-2	1-2	24	Maskell [43]	5465
34		22	H	Swansea C	W	3-2	1-0	24	Baird 2 [34, 54], Maskell [79]	6645
35	Mar	1	A	Darlington	L	0-2	0-2	24		2998
36		4	H	Northampton T	W	2-1	1-0	—	Reinelt [23], Peake [81]	4943
37		8	H	Leyton Orient	D	4-4	2-0	24	Maskell 2 [5, 7], Baird [74], McDonald (pen) [85]	9298
38		15	A	Hull C	L	0-3	0-1	24		3373
39		22	H	Cardiff C	W	2-0	2-0	24	McDonald (pen) [16], Baird [44]	9293
40		29	A	Chester C	L	1-2	1-0	24	Minton [13]	3613
41	Apr	1	H	Barnet	W	1-0	1-0	—	Baird [42]	9525
42		5	A	Scunthorpe U	L	0-1	0-1	24		2925
43		12	H	Wigan Ath	W	1-0	0-0	24	Maskell [64]	8703
44		19	A	Cambridge U	D	1-1	1-1	24	Reinelt [28]	6032
45		26	H	Doncaster R	W	1-0	0-0	23	Storer [67]	11,341
46	May	3	A	Hereford U	D	1-1	0-1	23	Reinelt [62]	8532

Final League Position: 23

GOALSCORERS
League (53): Maskell 14, Baird 13, Storer 6, McDonald 4 (2 pens), Mundee 4 (3 pens), Minton 3, Reinelt 3, Andrews 1, Hobson 1, Morris 1, Parris 1, Peake 1, Smith 1.
Coca-Cola Cup (0).
FA Cup (1): Maskell 1.

Rust N 25	Smith P 26+4	Tuck S 27	Parris G 17+1	Allan D 31	Hobson G 35+2	Mundee D 27+2	Peake J 27+3	Baird J 34+1	Maskell C 37	McDonald P 40+5	Storer S 37+5	McGarrigle K 9+4	Minton J 22+3	Johnson R 21+8	Ormerod M 21	Fox S 5+7	Neal A 8	Warren C 3	Adekola D 1	Andrews P 1+6	Morris M 11+1	Mayo K 22+2	Fox M —+2	Reinelt R 7+5	Humphrey J 11	Martin D 1	Match No.
1	2	3¹	4	5	6	7²	8	9	10	11	12	13															1
1	2	3		5	6²	12	8	9	10	11¹	7		4	13													2
1	2	3	4	5	6	7¹	8²	9	10	13	12		11														3
1	2¹		4	5	6		8	9	10	11	12		7	3													4
			4¹	5	6		8	9	10	11	3	12	7	2	1												5
1	12		4	5	6		8	9	10	11¹	3		7	2													6
1			4	5¹	6	2	8	9	10	11	3		7	12													7
	2				6	10	8	9		11	3¹	4	7	5	1	12											8
1	10			5	6	2	8	9		11	3		7				4										9
1	2			5	6	4	8	9		11			7				10	3									10
1	2¹		4	5	6	10	8	9		11	12		7					3									11
1	2		4	5	6	12	8			11	13		7²			3	10			9¹							12
1			4	5¹	6²	2	8			11	7	12		9	3	10				13							13
1			4		3	2	8	10		11	7	5			6	9											14
1			4	2	6		8	10		11¹	7	9		5	12	3											15
1	12		4	2²	3		8	10		11	7	9¹	13	5		6											16
1	2			3	4		8	10		11	7	6	9								5						17
1	2	8		3¹	4			10		11	7	6	9							12	5						18
		2²		3	4		8	9	10¹	12	7	6	11		1					13	5						19
	3	2²			4		8	9	10	11¹	7	6			1					12	5	13					20
1	2	3¹	4				9	10²	12	7	6	11								13	5	8					21
1	2³	3		4	12	11²		9	10	13	7		14	6								5¹	8				22
1	2	3	4¹	5	6		9		10	11	7		12									8					23
1	2	3	4¹	5	6³	9²	12	13	10	11	7		14									8					24
1	2	3		5		4	8²	9		11	7			6		10¹					12	13					25
1	2	3		5		4	8	9		11	7	12		6		10¹											26
1	2	3	12	5		4	8¹			11	7			6		10				9							27
	2				6	4	8	9	10	11	7			5	1						3						28
	2				6	4	8	9	10	11	7			5	1						3						29
	2				6	4	8²	9	10¹	11	7				1	12					3	13					30
	2	3		5	6	4²		9	10¹	11	7				1	12						8	13				31
	2	3		5	6	4¹		9	10²	11	7			12	1						13	8					32
	2	3		5	6			9	10	11	7			12	1							8	4¹				33
	2	3		5	6	4¹		9	10	11	7			12	1							8					34
	2	3		5	6	4¹	12	9	10	11²					1					13		8		7			35
		3		5	6	4		9	10	11					1						12	8		7¹	2		36
1		3		5	6		8	9	10	11	7			12										4	2¹		37
1		3		5¹	6	12		9	10	11	7			13								8		4¹	2		38
		3			6			9	10	11	7		4	5	1							8			2		39
12		3			6			9	10	11	7		4	5	1							8¹		13	2²		40
		3			6²			9	10	11	7¹		4	5	1						13	8		12	2		41
12		3¹			6			9	10	13			4	5	1							7	8	14	2²	11³	42
		3							10	11	7		4	5	1						6	8		9	2		43
		3							10	11	7		4	5	1						6	8		9	2		44
		3						9	10	11¹	7		4	5	1						6	8		12	2		45
		3	12					9	10	11²	7¹		4	5	1						6	8		13	2		46

Coca-Cola Cup
First Round — Birmingham C — (h) 0-1 / (a) 0-2

FA Cup
First Round — Sudbury T — (a) 0-0 / (h) 1-1

BRISTOL CITY 1996–97 *Back row (left to right):* Junior Bent, Martin Kuhl, Dominic Barclay, Shaun Goater, Keith Welch, Rob Edwards, David Seal, James Brennen, Louis Carey.
Middle row: Buster Footman (Physio), Gerry Sweeney (Assistant Manager), Paul Agostino, Kevin Nugent, Mark Shail, Scott Alderman, Stuart Naylor, Mommainais Bokoto, Richard Perry, Kevin Langan, Dr S. Dasgupta (Club Doctor), Mike Gibson (Coach).
Front row: Dave Bell (Youth Team Coach), Matthew Hewlett, Brian Tinnion, Dwayne Plummer, Garath Lloyden, Joe Jordan (Manager), Alan McLeary, Gary Owers, Darren Barnard, Scott Partridge, Tony Fawthrope (Chief Scout).

Division 2   **BRISTOL CITY**

Ashton Gate, Bristol BS3 2EJ. Telephone: (0117) 9630630 (5 lines). Fax: (0117) 9630400. Commercial: (0117) 9630600. Shop: (0117) 9538566. Clubcall: 0891 121176. Supporters Club: (0117) 9665554. Community Dept: (0117) 9664685.

Ground capacity: 21,479.

Record attendance: 43,335 v Preston NE, FA Cup 5th rd, 16 February 1935.

Record receipts: £148,282 v Everton, FA Cup 4th rd, 29 January 1995.

Pitch measurements: 115yd × 75yd.

Chairman: S. Davidson.

Directors: J. Laycock, J. Clapp, R. Neale, S. Lansdowne, K. Dawe. *Sales Manager:* Shaun Parker.

General Manager: Ian Wilson. *Safety Officer:* Keith Draisey.

Manager: John Ward. *Assistant Manager:* John Gorman.

Physio: H. Footman. *Secretary:* Eddie Harrison. *Stadium Manager:* D. Lewis.

Year Formed: 1894. *Turned Professional:* 1897. *Ltd Co.:* 1897. BCFC (1982) Plc.

Previous Name: Bristol South End 1894–97.

Club Nickname: 'Robins'.

Previous Grounds: 1894, St John's Lane; 1904, Ashton Gate.

Foundation: The name Bristol City came into being in 1897 when the Bristol South End club, formed three years earlier, decided to adopt professionalism and apply for admission to the Southern League after competing in the Western League. The historic meeting was held at The Albert Hall, Bedminster. Bristol City employed Sam Hollis from Woolwich Arsenal as manager and gave him £40 to buy players. In 1901 they merged with Bedminster, another leading Bristol club.

First Football League game: 7 September 1901, Division 2, v Blackpool (a) W 2-0 – Moles; Tuft, Davies; Jones, McLean, Chambers; Bradbury, Connor, Boucher, O'Brien (2), Flynn.

Record League Victory: 9–0 v Aldershot, Division 3 (S), 28 December 1946 – Eddols; Morgan, Fox; Peacock, Roberts, Jones (1); Chilcott, Thomas, Clark (4 incl. 1p), Cyril Williams (1), Hargreaves (3).

Record Cup Victory: 11–0 v Chichester C, FA Cup 1st rd, 5 November 1960 – Cook; Collinson, Thresher; Connor, Alan Williams, Etheridge; Tait (1), Bobby Williams (1), Atyeo (5), Adrian Williams (3), Derrick. (1 og).

Record Defeat: 0–9 v Coventry C, Division 3 (S), 28 April 1934.

Most League Points (2 for a win): 70, Division 3 (S), 1954–55.

Most League Points (3 for a win): 91, Division 3, 1989–90.

Most League Goals: 104, Division 3 (S), 1926–27.

Highest League Scorer in Season: Don Clark, 36, Division 3 (S), 1946–47.

Most League Goals in Total Aggregate: John Atyeo, 314, 1951–66.

Most Capped Player: Billy Wedlock, 26, England.

Most League Appearances: John Atyeo, 597, 1951–66.

Record Transfer Fee Received: £1,750,000 from Newcastle U for Andy Cole, March 1993.

Record Transfer Fee Paid: £500,000 to Arsenal for Andy Cole, July 1992.

Football League Record: 1901 Elected to Division 2; 1906–11 Division 1; 1911–22 Division 2; 1922–23 Division 3 (S); 1923–24 Division 2; 1924–27 Division 3 (S); 1927–32 Division 2; 1932–55 Division 3 (S); 1955–60 Division 2; 1960–65 Division 3; 1965–76 Division 2; 1976–80 Division 1; 1980–81 Division 2; 1981–82 Division 3; 1982–84 Division 4; 1984–90 Division 3; 1990–92 Division 2; 1992– Division 1.

Honours: Football League: Division 1 – Runners-up 1906–07; Division 2 – Champions 1905–06; Runners-up 1975–76; Division 3 (S) – Champions 1922–23, 1926–27, 1954–55; Runners-up 1937–38; Division 3 – Runners-up 1964–65, 1989–90. *FA Cup:* Runners-up 1909. *Football League Cup:* Semi-final 1971, 1989. *Welsh Cup:* Winners 1934. *Anglo-Scottish Cup:* Winners 1978. *Freight Rover Trophy:* Winners 1986; Runners-up 1987.

Colours: Red shirts, white shorts, red and white stockings. *Change colours:* White shirts, black shorts, black and white stockings.

Did you know?
Paul Agostino scored after only 17 seconds for Bristol City in their FA Cup first round replay against Swansea City on 26 November 1996.

1897　**1997**

BRISTOL CITY 1996–97 LEAGUE RECORD

Match No.	Date	Venue	Opponents	Result	H/T Score	Lg. Pos.	Goalscorers	Atten-dance
1	Aug 17	A	Gillingham	L 2-3	0-1	—	Goater [59], Bent [79]	7217
2	24	H	Blackpool	L 0-1	0-1	23		9387
3	27	H	Luton T	W 5-0	2-0	—	Goodridge 2 [11, 50], Nugent [41], Goater [46], Cundy [63]	7028
4	31	A	Bury	L 0-4	0-1	18		4160
5	Sept 7	H	Preston NE	W 2-1	1-0	12	Nugent 2 [16, 79]	8016
6	10	A	Shrewsbury T	L 0-1	0-0	—		2502
7	14	A	Rotherham U	D 2-2	0-0	15	Owers 2 [65, 80]	2546
8	21	H	Walsall	W 4-1	2-1	13	Goater 2 [29, 44], Hewlett [73], Goodridge [90]	7412
9	28	A	Burnley	W 3-2	1-1	10	Goater 2 [12, 62], Taylor [79]	9538
10	Oct 1	H	Brentford	L 1-2	1-1	—	Goodridge [38]	9520
11	5	A	Chesterfield	D 1-1	0-1	13	Owers [90]	4438
12	11	H	York C	W 2-0	1-0	—	Nugent [3], Goodridge [47]	9308
13	15	H	Wycombe W	W 3-0	1-0	—	Agostino [18], Barnard [59], Tinnion [74]	7325
14	19	A	Plymouth Arg	D 0-0	0-0	9		9645
15	26	H	Notts Co	W 4-0	4-0	9	Goater 3 [7, 23, 45], Agostino [17]	9540
16	29	A	Bournemouth	W 2-0	0-0	—	Barnard (pen) [77], Agostino [79]	4197
17	Nov 2	A	Stockport Co	D 1-1	1-0	7	Blackmore [44]	6654
18	9	H	Millwall	D 1-1	0-0	9	Barnard [82]	12,326
19	23	H	Peterborough U	W 2-0	1-0	8	Goater [35], Goodridge [87]	12,312
20	30	A	Notts Co	L 0-2	0-0	11		4693
21	Dec 3	H	Watford	D 1-1	0-0	—	Barnard (pen) [71]	9097
22	15	H	Bristol R	D 1-1	1-0	10	Agostino [16]	18,674
23	21	A	Wrexham	L 1-2	0-1	11	Hewlett [79]	4488
24	26	H	Shrewsbury T	W 3-2	1-2	9	Agostino [18], Barnard (pen) [57], Owers [87]	9803
25	28	A	Preston NE	W 2-0	1-0	6	Agostino [17], Goater [66]	10,905
26	Jan 11	H	Burnley	W 2-1	1-1	4	Bent [19], Goater [68]	10,013
27	18	A	Brentford	D 0-0	0-0	3		7606
28	25	H	Bournemouth	L 0-1	0-1	4		10,434
29	Feb 1	A	Millwall	W 2-0	1-0	3	Goater 2 (1 pen) [15 (p), 63]	9158
30	7	H	Stockport Co	D 1-1	0-1	—	Goater [46]	13,186
31	15	H	Peterborough U	L 1-3	0-1	4	Barnard (pen) [82]	4221
32	22	H	Crewe Alex	W 3-0	0-0	3	Goater [59], Agostino [86], Westwood (og) [88]	11,306
33	Mar 1	A	Watford	L 0-3	0-2	7		8539
34	4	A	Walsall	L 0-2	0-1	—		4322
35	16	A	Bristol R	W 2-1	1-0	9	Agostino [31], Goater [72]	8078
36	18	H	Rotherham U	L 0-2	0-0	—		10,646
37	22	A	Blackpool	L 0-1	0-0	10		4518
38	25	A	Crewe Alex	W 2-1	1-0	—	Bent [36], Goater [72]	3687
39	29	H	Gillingham	L 0-1	0-0	9		11,276
40	Apr 1	A	Luton T	D 2-2	2-1	—	Goater [4], Agostino [40]	7105
41	5	H	Bury	W 1-0	0-0	8	Barnard [66]	10,274
42	15	H	Wrexham	W 2-1	1-0	—	Barnard (pen) [30], Goater [88]	9817
43	19	A	York C	W 3-0	1-0	6	Goater 2 [6, 53], Nugent [47]	3344
44	26	H	Plymouth Arg	W 3-1	1-1	6	Barnard 2 (1 pen) [35, 61 (p)], Nugent [75]	15,368
45	30	H	Chesterfield	W 2-0	2-0	—	Goater [7], Barnard (pen) [38]	16,195
46	May 3	A	Wycombe W	L 0-2	0-2	5		7240

Final League Position: 5

GOALSCORERS

League (69): Goater 23 (1 pen), Barnard 11 (7 pens), Agostino 9, Goodridge 6, Nugent 6, Owers 4, Bent 3, Hewlett 2, Blackmore 1, Cundy 1, Taylor 1, Tinnion 1, own goal 1.
Coca-Cola Cup (5): Agostino 1, Barnard 1, Goater 1, Owers 1, Partridge 1.
FA Cup (11): Agostino 5, Hewlett 2, Kuhl 2, Goodridge 1, Nugent 1.

Naylor S 35	Owers G 46	Barnard D 44	McLeary A 1 + 2	Edwards R 31	Kuhl M 22 + 9	Bent J 17 + 5	Hewlett M 33 + 3	Nugent K 19 + 17	Goater S 39 + 3	Tinnion B 30 + 2	Agostino P 34 + 10	Partridge S — + 6	Welch K 11	Cundy J 6	Shail M 10 + 1	Carey L 40 + 2	Goodridge G 19 + 9	Seal D — + 12	Taylor S 29	Plummer D — + 2	Brennan J 7 + 1	Blackmore C 5	Paterson S 15 + 4	Allen P 13 + 1	Match No.
1	2	3	4	5	6	7[2]	8	9[1]	10	11	12	13													1
	2	3			6	7[2]	8[3]	12	10	11	9[1]	13	1	4	5	14									2
	2	3			6			9	10[2]	11	12		1	4	5	8	7[1]	13							3
	2	3			6			9	10	11	12		1	4	5	8	7[1]								4
1	2	3		5	6	12		9	10[2]	11					4	8	7[1]	13							5
1	2	3		5[2]		7		9[1]	10	11	12				4	8		13	6						6
1	2	3			6			9[1]	10	11	12				4	8	7		5						7
1	2	3		5	12		8	13	10	11	9[2]				4	6[1]	7								8
1	2	3		4	6	12	13		10	11	9[2]					8	7[1]		5						9
1	2	3		4	6	12	13		10	11	9[2]					8[1]	7		5						10
1	2	3		4	6	7[2]		12	10	11	9[1]					8		13	5						11
1	2	3		4	6	12		9	10	11						8[1]	7[2]	13	5						12
1	2	3		4	6				10	11	9					8	7		5						13
1	2	3	12	4	6[1]		13		10[3]	11	9					8	7[2]	14	5						14
1	2	3		4	6[2]			12	10[3]	11	9[1]					8	7	14	5	13					15
1	2	3	12	4	6[1]		13		10		9[3]					8	7	14	5	11[2]					16
1	2	3		4				12	10[2]		9					8	7	13	5	11[1]	6				17
1	2	3		4				12	10[2]	11	9					8	7[1]	13	5[3]	14	6				18
1	2	3		4	6[2]			12	10	11	9[1]					8	7	13	5						19
1	2	3		4[1]	6		13	12	10	11	9[3]					8	7[2]	14	5						20
1	2	3		4				12	10	11	9[1]					8	7		5		6				21
1	2	3		4	6			12	10	11	9[1]						7[2]	13	5					8	22
1	2	3			6			12	10[2]	11	9					8	7[1]	13	5			4			23
1	2	3		4[1]	6	12	13	14	10[3]	11	9					8	7[2]		5						24
1	2	3		4	6	7		12	10[1]	11	9					8			5						25
1	2	3		4	6	7		12	10[1]	11	9					8			5				12		26
1	2	3			6	7		12	10[1]	11	9					8[2]			5			4	13		27
1	2	3			6	7[1]		12	10[2]	11	9								5	13		4		8	28
1	2	3			6	7			10	11	9								5			4		8	29
1	2	3		4	6	7		12	10	11	9								5					8[1]	30
1	2	3		4	6	7		12	10		9[1]								5	11[2]			13	8	31
1	2	3			6	7[2]		12	10	11	9[1]					4		13	5					8	32
1	2	3			6	7		9	10	11[1]						4		12	5					8	33
1	2	3			6	7	13	12	10[2]		9					4			5	11				8[1]	34
1	2	3		4[2]	6	7		12	10[1]		9					8			5	11			13		35
1	2	3			6[1]	7		12	10		9					8		13	5[3]	11[2]	14	4			36
1	2	3		4	6[2]	7		12	10	11	9[1]					8			5				13		37
1	2	3		4	6	7		12	10	11	9[1]					8							5		38
	2	3		4	6	7		12	10[2]		9		1			8		13		11[1]			5		39
	2	3			6	7		12	10[2]		9[1]		1	4		8		13		11			5		40
	2	3		5		7[2]		12	10		9[1]		1	4		8		13		11			6		41
	2	3		5		12			10	11[2]	9[1]		1	4		8	14	13					6	7[3]	42
	2	3			6	7		12	10[1]	11	9[2]		1	4		8		13					5		43
	2	3			6	7		12	10[2]	11[1]	9		1	4		8		13					5		44
	2	3			6[1]	7		12	10	11	9[2]		1	4		8		13					5		45
	2	3			6	7		12	10[1]	11[2]	9		1	4		8		13					5		46

Coca-Cola Cup

First Round	Torquay U	(a)	3-3	
		(h)	1-0	
Second Round	Bolton W	(h)	0-0	
		(a)	1-3	

FA Cup

First Round	Swansea C	(a)	1-1	
		(h)	1-0	
Second Round	St Albans C	(h)	9-2	
Third Round	Chesterfield	(a)	0-2	

BRISTOL ROVERS 1996–97   *Back row (left to right):* Peter Beadle, Billy Clark, Andy Collett, Andy Tillson, Shane Higgs, Paul Miller, Justin Skinner, Lee Martin.
Middle row: Johnathan French, Andy Gurney, Matthew Hayfield, Marcus Browning, Steve Parmenter, Tom Ramasut, Graeme Power, Dave Pritchard, Lee Archer, Steve Bowey, Tom White.
Front row: Roy Dolling (Youth Development Manager), Stuart Harte, Tony Gill (Youth Team Manager/Centre of Excellence Director), Terry Connor (Reserve Team Manager/Assistant Centre of Excellence Director), Ian Holloway (Player/Manager), Geoff Twentyman (Assistant Manager), Phil Kite (Physio), Jamie Cureton, Ray Kendall (Kit Manager), Matthew Lockwood.

Division 2   **BRISTOL ROVERS**

Registered Offices: The Beeches, Broomhill Road, Brislington, Bristol BS4 5BF. (0117) 9772000. *Ground:* The Memorial Ground, Filton Avenue, Horfield, Bristol, BS7 0AQ. Training Ground: (0117) 9772000. Matchday Ticket Office: (0117) 9098848. Pirates Hotline: 0891 664422. Fax: (0117) 9773888. Community Office: (0117) 9773111.

Ground capacity: 8475.

Record attendance: 8078 v Bristol C, 16 March 1997 (Memorial Ground). 9464 v Liverpool, FA Cup 4th rd, 8 February 1992 (Twerton Park). 38,472 v Preston NE, FA Cup 4th rd, 30 January 1960 (Eastville).

Record receipts: £62,480 v Liverpool, FA Cup 4th rd, 8 February 1992.

Pitch measurements: 101m × 68m.

President: Marquis of Worcester.

Vice-Presidents: Dr W. T. Cussen, A. I. Seager, H. E. L. Brown, R. Redmond.

Chairman: D. H. A. Dunford. *Vice-Chairman:* G. M. H. Dunford.

Directors: R. Craig, B. Andrews, V. Stokes, B. Bradshaw, C. Jelf.

Player/Manager: Ian Holloway. *Assistant Manager:* Geoff Twentyman.

Reserve Team Manager: Geoff Twentyman. *Physio:* Phil Kite. *Director of Youth:* Rod Wesson. *Community Scheme Organiser:* Alan Walsh.

Chief Administrator/Club Secretary: Roger Brinsford. *Office Manager:* Mrs Angela Mann.

Year Formed: 1883. *Turned Professional:* 1897. *Ltd Co.:* 1896.

Previous Names: 1883, The Purdown Poachers; 1883, Black Arabs; 1884, Eastville Rovers; 1897, Bristol Eastville Rovers; 1898, Bristol Rovers.

Club Nickname: 'Pirates'.

Previous Grounds: 1883, Purdown; Three Acres, Ashley Hill; Rudgeway, Fishponds; 1894 Eastville; 1986 Twerton Park.

Foundation: Bristol Rovers were formed at a meeting in Stapleton Road, Eastville, in 1883. However, they first went under the name of the Black Arabs (wearing black shirts). Changing their name to Eastville Rovers in their second season, they won the Gloucestershire Senior Cup in 1888–89. Original members of the Bristol & District League in 1892, this eventually became the Western League and Eastville Rovers adopted professionalism in 1897.

First Football League game: 28 August 1920, Division 3, v Millwall (a) L 0-2 – Stansfield; Bethune, Panes; Boxley, Kenny, Steele; Chance, Bird, Sims, Bell, Palmer.

Record League Victory: 7–0 v Brighton & HA, Division 3 (S), 29 November 1952 – Hoyle; Bamford, Geoff Fox; Pitt, Warren, Sampson; McIlvenny, Roost (2), Lambden (1), Bradford (1), Petherbridge (2). (1 og). 7–0 v Swansea T, Division 2, 2 October 1954 – Radford; Bamford, Watkins; Pitt, Muir, Anderson; Petherbridge, Bradford (2), Meyer, Roost (1), Hooper (2). (2 og). 7–0 v Shrewsbury T, Division 3, 21 March 1964 – Hall; Hillard, Gwyn Jones; Oldfield, Stone (1), Mabbutt; Jarman (2), Brown (1), Biggs (1p), Hamilton, Bobby Jones (2).

Record Cup Victory: 6–0 v Merthyr Tydfil, FA Cup 1st rd, 14 November 1987 – Martyn; Alexander (Dryden), Tanner, Hibbitt, Twentyman, Jones, Holloway, Meacham (1), White (2), Penrice (3) (Reece), Purnell.

Record Defeat: 0–12 v Luton T, Division 3 (S), 13 April 1936.

Most League Points (2 for a win): 64, Division 3 (S), 1952–53.

Most League Points (3 for a win): 93, Division 3, 1989–90.

Most League Goals: 92, Division 3 (S), 1952–53.

Highest League Scorer in Season: Geoff Bradford, 33, Division 3 (S), 1952–53.

Most League Goals in Total Aggregate: Geoff Bradford, 242, 1949–64.

Most Capped Player: Neil Slatter, 10 (22), Wales.

Most League Appearances: Stuart Taylor, 546, 1966–80.

Record Transfer Fee Received: £1,200,000 from Huddersfield T for Marcus Stewart, July 1996.

Record Transfer Fee Paid: £370,000 to QPR for Andy Tillson, November 1992.

Football League Record: 1920 Original Member of Division 3; 1921–53 Division 3 (S); 1953–62 Division 2; 1962–74 Division 3; 1974–81 Division 2; 1981–90 Division 3; 1990–92 Division 2. 1992–93 Division 1; 1993– Division 2.

Honours: Football League: Division 2 best season: 4th, 1994–95; Division 3 (S) – Champions 1952–53; Division 3 – Champions 1989–90; Runners-up 1973–74. *FA Cup:* best season: 6th rd, 1951, 1958. *Football League Cup:* best season: 5th rd, 1971, 1972.

Colours: Blue and white quartered shirts, white shorts, blue stockings. *Change colours:* Yellow shirts, black shorts, black stockings.

Did you know?
Matt Lockwood and Lee Martin became the 599th and 600th players to appear in League football for Bristol Rovers on the opening day of the 1996–97 season.

BRISTOL ROVERS 1996–97 LEAGUE RECORD

Match No.	Date	Venue	Opponents	Result	H/T Score	Lg. Pos.	Goalscorers	Attendance
1	Aug 17	H	Peterborough U	W 1-0	1-0	—	Gurney [11]	6232
2	24	A	Preston NE	D 0-0	0-0	10		9752
3	31	H	Stockport Co	D 1-1	1-0	12	Archer [12]	6380
4	Sept 7	A	Millwall	L 0-2	0-0	18		7881
5	10	H	Bournemouth	W 3-2	0-1	—	Tillson [57], Parmenter [66], Beadle [78]	4170
6	14	H	Watford	L 0-1	0-1	14		6276
7	17	A	Wrexham	L 0-1	0-1	—		2401
8	21	A	Plymouth Arg	W 1-0	0-0	12	Archer [78]	8879
9	28	H	Chesterfield	W 2-0	0-0	9	Cureton 2 [59, 70]	5008
10	Oct 1	A	York C	D 2-2	1-2	—	Cureton [18], Beadle [34]	3714
11	4	H	Crewe Alex	W 2-0	0-0	—	Cureton [59], Gurney [81]	6211
12	12	A	Notts Co	D 1-1	0-1	9	Beadle [62]	4558
13	15	A	Rotherham U	D 0-0	0-0	—		2490
14	19	H	Blackpool	D 0-0	0-0	11		5823
15	26	A	Bury	L 1-2	0-1	12	Miller [84]	4082
16	29	H	Brentford	W 2-1	1-0	—	Cureton [9], Browning [47]	5163
17	Nov 2	H	Gillingham	D 0-0	0-0	11		5530
18	12	A	Shrewsbury T	L 0-2	0-1	—		2331
19	19	H	Burnley	L 1-2	0-1	—	Beadle [48]	4123
20	23	A	Luton T	L 1-2	0-1	14	Harris [80]	5315
21	30	H	Bury	W 4-3	3-2	12	Beadle 3 [30, 39, 40], Clark [46]	4496
22	Dec 3	A	Walsall	L 0-1	0-1	—		4084
23	15	A	Bristol C	D 1-1	0-1	13	Beadle [90]	18,674
24	21	H	Wycombe W	L 3-4	1-1	13	Cureton [44], Harris [52], Lockwood [60]	4465
25	26	A	Bournemouth	L 0-1	0-1	15		5036
26	Jan 11	A	Chesterfield	L 0-1	0-1	17		3305
27	18	H	York C	D 1-1	0-1	17	Beadle [79]	4470
28	21	A	Brentford	D 0-0	0-0	—		4191
29	Feb 1	H	Shrewsbury T	W 2-0	0-0	16	Browning [60], Beadle [75]	4924
30	8	A	Gillingham	L 0-1	0-1	16		6900
31	15	H	Luton T	W 3-2	1-1	18	Miller [22], Tillson [47], Holloway [54]	5612
32	22	A	Burnley	D 2-2	1-1	19	Cureton [13], Alsop [80]	8847
33	25	H	Plymouth Arg	W 2-0	2-0	—	Cureton 2 [22, 33]	6005
34	Mar 1	H	Walsall	L 0-1	0-0	18		5891
35	8	A	Wycombe W	L 0-2	0-0	20		5386
36	16	H	Bristol C	L 1-2	0-1	20	Alsop [81]	8078
37	18	A	Watford	L 0-1	0-1	—		6139
38	23	H	Preston NE	W 1-0	0-0	18	Cureton [46]	6405
39	29	A	Peterborough U	W 2-1	0-1	17	Alsop [71], Beadle [78]	6132
40	31	H	Wrexham	W 2-0	1-0	17	Skinner [15], Beadle [80]	6225
41	Apr 5	A	Stockport Co	L 0-1	0-0	17		5689
42	8	H	Millwall	W 1-0	0-0	—	Skinner [60]	5324
43	12	A	Crewe Alex	L 0-1	0-1	16		4281
44	20	H	Notts Co	W 1-0	0-0	15	Bennett [49]	6309
45	26	A	Blackpool	L 2-3	1-2	17	Cureton [26], Parmenter [65]	6673
46	May 3	H	Rotherham U	L 1-2	1-1	17	Monington (og) [35]	5950

Final League Position: 17

GOALSCORERS

League (47): Beadle 12, Cureton 11, Alsop 3, Archer 2, Browning 2, Gurney 2, Harris 2, Miller 2, Parmenter 2, Skinner 2, Tillson 2, Bennett 1, Clark 1, Holloway 1, Lockwood 1, own goal 1.
Coca-Cola Cup (2): Archer 1, Gurney 1.
FA Cup (1): Parmenter 1.

Collett A 44	Martin L 25	Clark B 26 + 1	Tillson A 38	Lockwood M 36 + 3	Holloway I 29 + 2	Browning M 24 + 2	Gurney A 21 + 3	Archer L 18 + 3	Miller P 22 + 3	Beadle P 36 + 6	French J 3 + 1	Parmenter S 10 + 4	Low J — + 3	Skinner J 29 + 5	Power G 16	Cureton J 33 + 5	Ramasut T 5 + 6	White T 18 + 3	Higgs S 2	Hayfield M 12 + 5	Harris J 5 + 1	Pritchard D 26	Bennett F 6 + 5	Alsop J 10 + 6	Morgan R 1	Gayle B 7	Clapham J 4 + 1	Zabek L — + 1	Match No.
1	2	5	6	3	7	4	8	10	9	11																			1
1	2	5	6	3	7		8	10	9^1	11^2				4	12	13													2
1	2	5	6	3	7	4	8	10	9^1	11					12														3
1	2	5	6	3	7	4	8^2	9	10^1	11					12	13													4
1	2	5	6	3	7	4	8^2	9	12	11				10^1	13														5
1	2	5	6	3	7^1	4	8	10		11^2		13	9	12															6
1	2	5		3	7	4	8	10				12		11	6	9^1													7
1	2	5	6	12	7		8		9^1	11				4	3	10													8
1	2	5	6	3	7		8		12	11^1				10	4	9													9
1	2	5	6	12	7		3	9^1	10					8	4	11													10
1	2	5	6		12	4	8	10^2		11	13			7	3	9^1													11
1	2	5	6	10	7	12	8		13	11^2				4	3	9^1													12
1	2	5	6	10	7	12	8			11				4	3	9^1													13
1		5	6	10^1	7	2	8		11	12				4^2	3	9	13												14
1		5	6	12	7	4	2		8	11					3	9	10^1												15
1		5	6		7	4	2	10		11					3	9	8												16
1		5	6		7	4		8		11			9		3		10	2											17
		5		3	7^1	4				11		10^2	12	13	6	9		8^3	1	14		2							18
1		5		3		4	8	10		11					6	9^1				7	12	2							19
1	3	5	6			4		8		11					12		10			7		2	9^1						20
1	3	5	6			4		10^1		11					12	9				7		2	8						21
1	3	5^1	6	10^2	7	4		13		11					12	9		8^3		14		2							22
1		5	6	3		4		12		11				8		9	10			7^1		2							23
1		5	6	3		4		12		11				8		9	13			7^1		2	10^2						24
1	3	5	6	10^1		4	7		9	11				8^2	13		12					2							25
1		4	9		8	6^2	12	10		11				7	5^1	13						2	3						26
1			6	3		4		10	7	11				8	9	5						2							27
1			6	3		4		10	7	11				8	9	5						2							28
1			6	3	12	4		10^1	7	11				8	9	5						2							29
1			6	3	7			10	8	11^3				4	9^1	5				12		2		13					30
1	3		6	11	7			12	8					4	9^2	5		10^1				2		13					31
1	3		6	10	7			8^1	11^2					4	9	5		12				2		13					32
1	3		6	10^1	7		8^2		11					4	9	5		12				2		13					33
1	3		6^1	10^2	7		12	8	11						9	5	4					2		13					34
1	10		6		7			8^1	11					4^3	3^2	9	5			12		2		13	14				35
1	3	12	6		7				13					9	14	5	4					2	8^1	10^2		11^3			36
1			6	3	7			11						4	9	8	5					2	10						37
1			6	3	7			11	10					4^1	9			12				2	10						38
1			6	3	7			11	8^1		4	9						2		12	10			5					39
1		6^1	3^2		7			11	10^3	4	9	12	7				2	13		8			5					14	40
1		7						11	10^1	4^2	9	12	5				2	13		8			6	3					41
1		7						11	10^1	4	9	12	6				2	13		8^2			5	3					42
1		7							10^1	4	9	12	6			2	11	8					5	3					43
1	5	7^1						12	10	13	4	9	6			2^1	11	8					5	3					44
		7^2						12	8^1	13	4^3	3	9	6	1	2	11	10					5	14					45
																													46

Coca-Cola Cup
First Round   Luton T   (a)   0-3
                                                 (h)   2-1

FA Cup
First Round   Exeter C   (h)   1-2

BURNLEY 1996-97 *Back row (left to right):* Ian Duerden, Paul Barnes, Steve Thompson, Mark Winstanley, Peter Swan, Gareth West, Kurt Nogan, Gerry Harrison, Paul Smith.
Middle row: Andy Jones (Physio), Harry Wilson (Reserve Team Coach), Phil Eastwood, Nigel Gleghorn, Vince Overson, Wayne Russell, Marlon Beresford, David Eyres, Jamie Hoyland, Andy Cooke, Terry Pashley (B Team Coach), Alan Harper (A Team Coach).
Front row: Gary Parkinson, Chris Brass, Chris Vinnicombe, Tom Mutton, John Ward (Assistant Manager), Mr F. J. Teasdale (Chairman), Adrian Heath (Manager), Liam Robinson, Damian Matthew, Paul Weller, James Webster.

Division 2

BURNLEY

Turf Moor, Burnley BB10 4BX. Telephone: (01282) 700000. Fax: (01282) 700014. Clubcall: 0891 121153. Credit Card Ticket Sales: (0645) 101010. Ticket Office: (01282) 70010. Community Programme: (01282) 70011. Commercial Department: (01282) 70007.

Ground capacity: 22,546.

Record attendance: 54,775 v Huddersfield T, FA Cup 3rd rd, 23 February 1924.

Record receipts; £150,000 v Liverpool, FA Cup 4th rd, 28 January 1995.

Pitch measurements: 114yd × 72yd.

Chairman: F. J. Teasdale.

Vice-Chairman: Dr R. D. Iven MRCS (Eng), LRCP (Lond), MRCGP.

Directors: B. Rothwell JP, C. Holt, R. Blakeborough.

Manager: Chris Waddle. *Assistant Manager:* Glenn Roeder.

Coaches: Harry Wilson, Terry Pashley, Alan Harper.

Marketing and Sales Co-ordinator: Mandy Speak. *Physio:* Andy Jones.

Year Formed: 1882. *Turned Professional:* 1883. *Ltd Co.:* 1897.

Previous Name: 1881–82, Burnley Rovers.

Club Nickname: 'The Clarets'.

Previous Grounds: 1881, Calder Vale; 1882, Turf Moor.

Foundation: The majority of those responsible for the formation of the Burnley club in 1881 were from the defunct rugby club Burnley Rovers. Indeed, they continued to play rugby for a year before changing to soccer and dropping "Rovers" from their name. The changes were decided at a meeting held in May 1882 at the Bull Hotel.

First Football League game: 8 September 1888, Football League, v Preston NE (a), L 2-5 – Smith; Lang, Bury, Abrams, Friel, Keenan, Brady, Tait, Poland (1), Gallocher (1), Yates.

Record League Victory: 9–0 v Darwen, Division 1, 9 January 1892 – Hillman; Walker, McFettridge, Lang, Matthews, Keenan, Nicol (3), Bowes, Espie (1), McLardie (3), Hill (2).

Record Cup Victory: 9–0 v Crystal Palace, FA Cup 2nd rd (replay), 10 February 1909 – Dawson; Barron, McLean; Cretney (2), Leake, Moffat; Morley, Ogden, Smith (3), Abbott (2), Smethams (1). 9–0 v New Brighton, FA Cup 4th rd, 26 January 1957 – Blacklaw; Angus, Winton; Seith, Adamson, Miller; Newlands (1), McIlroy (3), Lawson (3), Cheesebrough (1), Pilkington (1). 9–0 v Penrith, FA Cup 1st rd, 17 November 1984 – Hansbury; Miller, Hampton, Phelan, Overson (Kennedy), Hird (3 incl. 1p), Grewcock (1), Powell (2), Taylor (3), Biggins, Hutchison.

Record Defeat: 0–10 v Aston Villa, Division 1, 29 August 1925 and v Sheffield U, Division 1, 19 January 1929.

Most League Points (2 for a win): 62, Division 2, 1972–73.

Most League Points (3 for a win): 83, Division 4, 1991–92.

Most League Goals: 102, Division 1, 1960–61.

Highest League Scorer in Season: George Beel, 35, Division 1, 1927–28.

Most League Goals in Total Aggregate: George Beel, 178, 1923–32.

Most Capped Player: Jimmy McIlroy, 51 (55), Northern Ireland.

Most League Appearances: Jerry Dawson, 522, 1907–28.

Record Transfer Fee Received: £750,000 from Luton T for Steve Davis, August 1995.

Record Transfer Fee Paid: £350,000 to Birmingham C for Paul Barnes, September 1996.

Football League Record: 1888 Original Member of the Football League; 1897–98 Division 2; 1898–1900 Division 1; 1900–13 Division 2; 1913–30 Division 1; 1930–47 Division 2; 1947–71 Division 1; 1971–73 Division 2; 1973–76 Division 1; 1976–80 Division 2; 1980–82 Division 3; 1982–83 Division 2; 1983–85 Division 3; 1985–92 Division 4; 1992–94 Division 2; 1994–95 Division 1; 1995– Division 2.

Honours: Football League: Division 1 – Champions 1920–21, 1959–60; Runners-up 1919–20, 1961–62; Division 2 – Champions 1897–98, 1972–73; Runners-up 1912–13, 1946–47; Promoted from Division 2, 1993–94 (play-offs); Division 3 – Champions 1981–82; Division 4 – Champions 1991–92. Record 30 consecutive Division 1 games without defeat 1920–21. *FA Cup:* Winners 1914; Runners-up 1962. *Football League Cup:* semi-final 1961, 1969, 1983. *Anglo–Scottish Cup:* Winners 1979. *Sherpa Van Trophy:* Runners-up 1988. **European Competitions;** *European Cup:* 1960–61. *European Fairs Cup:* 1966–67.

Colours: Claret and blue quartered shirts, white shorts and stockings. *Change colours:* Yellow body with three claret stripes and claret sleeves, claret with 3 yellow stripes shorts, yellow with 3 claret stripes socks.

Did you know?
On 5 October 1996, Paul Barnes scored all five goals for Burnley in their 5–2 win over Stockport County. It was the club's first such feat since Andy Lochhead hit five in the 6–2 win over Chelsea on 24 April 1965.

BURNLEY 1996–97 LEAGUE RECORD

Match No.	Date	Venue	Opponents	Result	H/T Score	Lg. Pos.	Goalscorers	Attendance
1	Aug 17	A	Luton T	W 2-1	2-1	—	Thompson 24, Nogan 32	6484
2	24	H	Walsall	W 2-1	1-1	1	Eyres 21, Nogan 48	10,322
3	27	H	Shrewsbury T	L 1-3	0-1	—	Cooke 49	9072
4	31	A	Millwall	L 1-2	0-0	9	Nogan 75	9281
5	Sept 7	A	Gillingham	L 0-1	0-0	13		6116
6	10	H	Blackpool	W 2-0	0-0	—	Gleghorn 60, Nogan 76	13,599
7	14	H	Wycombe W	W 2-1	2-1	7	Nogan 2 23, 35	9379
8	21	A	Chesterfield	D 0-0	0-0	6		5529
9	28	H	Bristol C	L 2-3	1-1	11	Gleghorn 45, Weller 55	9538
10	Oct 1	A	Bury	L 0-1	0-1	—		7557
11	5	H	Stockport Co	W 5-2	2-0	8	Barnes 5 32, 45, 61, 71, 78	10,332
12	12	A	Rotherham U	L 0-1	0-1	12		4562
13	15	A	Watford	D 2-2	1-1	—	Gleghorn 28, Smith 76	6450
14	19	H	Notts Co	W 1-0	0-0	12	Barnes 80	9372
15	26	A	Plymouth Arg	W 2-1	1-0	10	Nogan 28, Eyres (pen) 47	9602
16	29	A	Preston NE	D 1-1	0-1	—	Nogan 52	12,652
17	Nov 2	A	York C	L 0-1	0-0	12		5958
18	9	H	Crewe Alex	W 2-0	1-0	10	Nogan 31, Matthew 69	9459
19	19	A	Bristol R	W 2-1	1-0	—	Barnes 2 33, 46	4123
20	23	H	Bournemouth	W 1-0	1-0	6	Barnes 6	8564
21	30	A	Plymouth Arg	D 0-0	0-0	8		6289
22	Dec 3	H	Wrexham	W 2-0	2-0	—	Cooke 32, Nogan 40	8587
23	14	H	Brentford	L 1-2	0-1	5	Swan 85	10,575
24	20	A	Peterborough U	L 2-3	1-2	—	Barnes 6, Matthew 83	5283
25	28	H	Gillingham	W 5-1	1-1	7	Cooke 2 21, 86, Smith 62, Barnes 2 (1 pen) 82 (p), 88	10,004
26	Jan 11	A	Bristol C	L 1-2	1-1	8	Smith 36	10,013
27	17	H	Bury	W 3-1	3-1	—	Swan 19, Smith 26, Eyres 29	10,526
28	25	H	Preston NE	L 1-2	1-1	7	Barnes 10	16,186
29	28	H	Chesterfield	D 0-0	0-0	—		7903
30	Feb 1	A	Crewe Alex	D 1-1	0-0	5	Barnes 88	4734
31	8	H	York C	L 1-2	1-1	5	Gleghorn 13	8961
32	15	A	Bournemouth	D 0-0	0-0	8		6021
33	22	H	Bristol R	D 2-2	1-1	8	Matthew 38, Barnes 90	8847
34	25	A	Blackpool	W 3-1	2-1	—	Barnes 3 6, 42, 47	7331
35	Mar 1	A	Wrexham	D 0-0	0-0	8		6947
36	8	H	Peterborough U	W 5-0	3-0	6	Barnes 3 8, 30, 33, Cooke 56, Matthew 85	8646
37	15	A	Brentford	W 3-0	3-0	4	Hoyland 9, Cooke 34, Matthew 45	6624
38	22	A	Walsall	W 3-1	1-0	5	Cooke 2 26, 55, Barnes 85	6306
39	29	H	Luton T	L 0-2	0-2	6		15,490
40	Apr 1	A	Shrewsbury T	L 1-2	0-0	—	Barnes 74	4462
41	5	H	Millwall	W 1-0	1-0	6	Weller 14	9840
42	12	A	Stockport Co	L 0-1	0-0	8		9187
43	15	A	Wycombe W	L 0-5	0-4	—		5786
44	19	H	Rotherham U	D 3-3	1-1	9	Cooke 2 13, 58, Barnes 60	7875
45	26	A	Notts Co	D 1-1	0-0	11	Matthew 90	4591
46	May 3	H	Watford	W 4-1	0-0	9	Cooke 3 (1 pen) 50, 51, 83 (p), Parkinson 66	8269

Final League Position: 9

GOALSCORERS

League (71): Barnes 24 (1 pen), Cooke 13 (1 pen), Nogan 10, Matthew 6, Gleghorn 4, Smith 4, Eyres 3 (1 pen), Swan 2, Weller 2, Hoyland 1, Parkinson 1, Thompson 1.
Coca-Cola Cup (7): Eyres 3, Nogan 2, Cooke 1, Matthew 1.
FA Cup (4): Barnes 1, Eyres 1, Gleghorn 1, Matthew 1.

Beresford M 40	Parkinson G 43	Eyres D 36	Harrison G 32 + 3	Winstanley M 34 + 1	Hoyland J 24 + 1	Matthew D 29 + 3	Thompson S 14 + 5	Nogan K 30 + 1	Cooke A 19 + 12	Gleghorn N 32 + 1	Robinson L 3 + 5	Weller P 22 + 9	Brass C 37 + 2	Barnes P 39 + 1	Smith P 30 + 7	Russell W 6	Swan P 16 + 1	Overson V 6 + 2	Vinnicombe C 6 + 2	Heath A — + 2	Hodgson D 1	Little G 5 + 4	Huxford R 2 + 7	Guinan S — + 6	Match No
1	2	3	4	5	6	7	8	9	10^1	11	12														1
1	2	3	4	5	6			9	10^1	11	12	7	8												2
1	2	3	4	5	6^1		8	9	10	11	12	7													3
1	2	3	4^2	5	6	7	8^1	9	12	11	10		13												4
1	2	3	4	5	6	7		9	12	11					8^1	10									5
1	2	3	4^2	5	6	7		9	12	11					8	10^1	13								6
1	2	3	4	5	6	7		9	12	11					8	10^1									7
	2	3	4^1	5	6				9^2	11				10	8	7	1					13			8
1	2^1			5	6			9	12	11		7	4	10	8				3						9
1	2			5	6			9	10^1	11		7	4	8					3	12					10
1	2	3	4	5				9	12	11		7		10^1	8			6							11
1	2	3	4	5			12	9^2	13	11		7^1		10	8			6							12
1	2	3	4	5		7		9^1	12	11		13		10^3	8^2			6	14						13
1	2	3	4		12	7		9		11				10	8	6	5^1								14
1	2	3	4	5		7		9		11				10	8			6							15
1	2	3	4	5		7		9		11				10	8			6							16
1	2	3	4			7^2		9	12	11		13	6	10^1	8		5								17
1	2	3	4			7		9	12	11			6	10^1	8		5								18
1	2	3	4			7^1		9		11	12		6	10	8		5								19
1	2	3^1	4				12	9	13	11^1		7	6	10^2	8		5		14						20
1	2	3	4					9	10	11		7	6		8		5								21
1	2	3	4					9	10	11		7	6		8		5								22
1	2	3	4^1				13	9	10	11^2		7	6	12	8		5								23
1	2	3	4		6^1	7		9		11			5	10	8								12		24
	2	3^1	4		6	7^2	12	9		11		13	5	10	8		1								25
	2^2		4				12	9		11		13	6	10	8		1	5	3				7^1		26
	2	3	4^1				12	9^2	13	11		14	6	10	8		1	5					7^3		27
1	2^2	3	4				12	9		11^1		13	6	10	8		5						7		28
1		3	4			7	12	9		11^1			6	10	8		5						2		29
1		3	4			7	12	9		11^1		13	6	10	8		5						2^2		30
1	2	3	4^2			7^1		9		11	12		6	10	8		5					13			31
1	2	3	4	5		7^2	13	9		11^3	12		6	10	8^1				14						32
1	2^1	3	5			7		9		11			6	10	8^2			4				12	13		33
1	2	3			6	7		9^1		11	12		4	10^1	8^2		5		14			13			34
1	2		4	5	6	7		9		11				10	8^1				3				12		35
1	2		4	5	6	7	12	9^2		11				10^1	8				3^3	14		13			36
1	2		4	5	6	7	12	9		11				10	8^1				3						37
1	2		4	5	6	7	12	9		11^1				10	8				3						38
1	2		4		6	7		9		11^2				10	8		5^1					12	13		39
1	2		4		6	7		9^3		11^2				10	8		5^1			12		13	14		40
1	2		4		6	7		9^1		11				10	8		5		3				12		41
	2		4		6	7	9			11^2	12			10	8^1		5^3		3		1	13	14		42
	2		4		6	7	9			11^1	12			10	8^3		5^2		3		1	13	14		43
1	2	3	4		6	7		9		11				10	8		5^1						12		44
1	2	3	4		6	7^1		9		11				10	8		5^2						13		45
1	2	3	4		6	7^1	12	9^2		11				10	8		5						13		46

Coca-Cola Cup

First Round	Mansfield T	(a)	3-0
		(h)	2-0
Second Round	Charlton Ath	(a)	1-4
		(h)	1-2

FA Cup

First Round	Lincoln C	(h)	2-1
		(a)	1-1
Second Round	Walsall	(h)	1-1
Third Round	Liverpool	(a)	0-1

BURY 1996-97   *Back row (left to right):* Andy Woodward, Michael Jackson, Steve Jones, Ian Brunskill, Ronnie Jepson, Gordon Armstrong, Paul Butler, Matthew Hurst, Dave Thomson.
Middle row: Cliff Roberts (Coach), Ian Hughes, Lenny Johnrose, Nick Daws, Chris Lucketti, Dean Kiely, Gary Kelly, Lee Bracey, Rob Matthews, Nicky Reid, Winnie Steele, Dave Johnson, Alan Raw (Physio).
Front row: Phil Stant, Tony Rigby, David Pugh, Shaun Reid, Stan Ternent (Manager), Terry Robinson (Chairman), Sam Ellis (Assistant Manager), Stuart Bimson, Dean West, Mark Carter, Barry Shuttleworth.

Division 1   **BURY**

Gigg Lane, Bury BL9 9HR. Telephone: (0161) 764 4881. Fax: (0161) 764 5521. Commercial Dept: (0161) 705 2144. Fax: (0161) 763 3103. Clubcall: 0891 121197. Community Programme: (0161) 797 5423. Social Club: (0161) 764 6771.

Ground capacity: 11,841.

Record attendance: 35,000 v Bolton W, FA Cup 3rd rd, 9 January 1960.

Record receipts: £37,000 v Bolton W, Division 3 play-off, 19 May 1991.

Pitch measurements: 112yd × 72yd.

Chairman: T. Robinson. *Vice-Chairman:* Canon J. R. Smith MA.

Directors: C. H. Eaves, J. Smith, F. Mason.

Manager: Stan Ternent. *Assistant Manager:* Sam Ellis. *Coach:* Cliff Roberts. *Physio:* John Dawson.

Youth Development: W. Joyce. *Stadium Manager:* Wilf Linton.

Assistant Secretary: J. Neville. *Commercial Manager:* Neville Neville.

Year Formed: 1885. *Turned professional:* 1885. *Ltd Co.:* 1897. *Club Nickname:* 'Shakers'.

Club Sponsors: Birthdays.

Foundation: A meeting at the Waggon & Horses Hotel, attended largely by members of Bury Wesleyans and Bury Unitarians football clubs, decided to form a new Bury club. This was officially formed at a subsequent gathering at the Old White Horse Hotel, Fleet Street, Bury on 24 April 1885.

First Football League game: 1 September 1894, Division 2, v Manchester C (h) W 4-2 – Lowe; Gillespie, Davies; White, Clegg, Ross; Wylie, Barbour (2), Millar (1), Ostler (1), Plant.

Record League Victory: 8–0 v Tranmere R, Division 3, 10 January 1970 – Forrest; Tinney, Saile; Anderson, Turner, McDermott; Hince (1), Arrowsmith (1), Jones (4), Kerr (1), Grundy. (1 og).

Record Cup Victory: 12–1 v Stockton, FA Cup 1st rd (replay), 2 February 1897 – Montgomery; Darroch, Barbour; Hendry (1), Clegg, Ross (1); Wylie (3), Pangbourn, Millar (4), Henderson (2), Plant. (1 og).

Record Defeat: 0–10 v Blackburn R, FA Cup preliminary round, 1 October 1887 and v West Ham U, Milk Cup 2nd rd 2nd leg, 25 October 1983.

Most League Points (2 for a win): 68, Division 3, 1960–61.

Most League Points (3 for a win): 84, Division 4, 1984–85 and Division 2, 1996–97.

Most League Goals: 108, Division 3, 1960–61.

Highest League Scorer in Season: Craig Madden, 35, Division 4, 1981–82.

Most League Goals in Total Aggregate: Craig Madden, 129, 1978–86.

Most Capped Player: Bill Gorman, 11 (13), Republic of Ireland and (4), Northern Ireland.

Most League Appearances: Norman Bullock, 506, 1920–35.

Record Transfer Fee Received: £375,000 from Southampton for David Lee, October 1991.

Record Transfer Fee Paid: £175,000 to Shrewsbury T for John McGinlay, July 1990.

Football League Record: 1894 Elected to Division 2; 1895–1912 Division 1; 1912–24 Division 2; 1924–29 Division 1; 1929–57 Division 2; 1957–61 Division 3; 1961–67 Division 2; 1967–68 Division 3; 1968–69 Division 2; 1969–71 Division 3; 1971–74 Division 4; 1974–80 Division 3; 1980–85 Division 4; 1985–96 Division 3; 1996–97 Division 2; 1997– Division 1.

Honours: Football League: Division 1 best season: 4th, 1925–26; Division 2 – Champions 1894–95, 1996–97; Runners-up 1923–24; Division 3 – Champions 1960–61; Runners-up 1967–68; Promoted from Division 3 (3rd) 1995–96. *FA Cup:* Winners 1900, 1903. *Football League Cup:* Semi-final 1963.

Colours: White shirts, royal blue shorts, royal blue stockings. *Change colours:* Black/red check shirts, white shorts, black stockings.

Did you know?
During the 1925–26 season, Bury had a run of eight unbeaten League games which included a 1–0 win at Liverpool, a Christmas double over Manchester City and an 8–1 victory against Burnley.

BURY 1996–97 LEAGUE RECORD

Match No.	Date	Venue	Opponents	Result	H/T Score	Lg. Pos.	Goalscorers	Atten-dance
1	Aug 17	H	Brentford	D 1-1	0-1	—	Jepson [61]	3373
2	24	A	Chesterfield	W 2-1	1-1	6	West [24], Carter [80]	3763
3	27	A	Wycombe W	W 1-0	1-0	—	Jepson [27]	3563
4	31	H	Bristol C	W 4-0	1-0	3	Johnson [34], Carter [48], Jackson [50], Johnrose [88]	4160
5	Sept 7	H	Rotherham U	W 3-1	1-0	2	Carter 2 (1 pen) [26, 47 (p)], Jackson [76]	3523
6	10	A	Crewe Alex	L 0-2	0-1	—		3627
7	14	A	Shrewsbury T	D 1-1	1-1	5	Armstrong [44]	3238
8	21	H	Luton T	D 0-0	0-0	5		3588
9	28	A	Walsall	L 1-3	1-1	8	Carter (pen) [45]	3254
10	Oct 1	H	Burnley	W 1-0	1-0	—	Jepson [14]	7557
11	5	H	Blackpool	W 1-0	0-0	3	Armstrong [87]	5317
12	12	H	Peterborough U	W 2-1	0-0	2	Matthews [53], Johnson [83]	6003
13	16	A	Millwall	L 0-1	0-1	—		6447
14	19	H	Watford	D 1-1	1-1	3	Carter [44]	4092
15	26	H	Bristol R	W 2-1	1-0	3	Stant [37], O'Kane [89]	4082
16	29	A	Wrexham	D 1-1	0-0	—	West [89]	3895
17	Nov 2	A	Bournemouth	D 1-1	1-1	4	Carter [11]	3946
18	9	H	York C	W 4-1	2-1	3	West 2 [18, 20], Pugh [50], O'Kane [85]	4021
19	23	H	Plymouth Arg	W 1-0	1-0	3	Carter [6]	3582
20	30	A	Bristol R	L 3-4	2-3	3	Pugh [44], Johnson [45], Carter (pen) [83]	4496
21	Dec 3	H	Preston NE	W 3-0	1-0	—	Johnrose [14], Johnson [77], Carter [86]	5447
22	14	A	Gillingham	D 2-2	1-1	4	Matthews [21], Randall [47]	5542
23	21	H	Stockport Co	D 0-0	0-0	3		5069
24	28	A	Rotherham U	D 1-1	1-0	3	Matthews [18]	3263
25	Jan 17	A	Burnley	L 1-3	1-3	—	Matthews [32]	10,526
26	Feb 1	A	York C	W 2-0	1-0	6	Jackson [18], Jepson [75]	3423
27	8	H	Bournemouth	W 2-1	1-1	6	Carter (pen) [21], Matthews [59]	3559
28	15	A	Plymouth Arg	L 0-2	0-0	6		5486
29	22	H	Notts Co	W 2-0	0-0	4	Randall [71], Jepson [80]	3430
30	25	H	Wrexham	D 0-0	0-0	—		3419
31	Mar 1	A	Preston NE	L 1-3	1-0	5	O'Kane [14]	8749
32	4	H	Shrewsbury T	W 2-0	2-0	—	Randall [33], Johnson [45]	2690
33	8	A	Stockport Co	L 1-2	0-1	5	Butler [54]	8170
34	15	H	Gillingham	W 3-0	2-0	3	Johnrose [7], Battersby [20], Johnson [90]	3492
35	22	H	Chesterfield	W 1-0	0-0	2	Johnson [74]	4162
36	25	A	Notts Co	W 1-0	1-0	—	Jepson [8]	3306
37	29	H	Brentford	W 2-0	2-0	1	Daws [33], Carter (pen) [41]	7823
38	31	H	Wycombe W	W 2-0	0-0	1	Daws [58], Butler [82]	5714
39	Apr 5	A	Bristol C	L 0-1	0-0	1		10,274
40	8	H	Walsall	W 2-1	1-0	—	Jepson [34], Battersby [74]	4082
41	12	A	Blackpool	L 0-2	0-0	1		6812
42	15	A	Crewe Alex	W 1-0	1-0	—	Jepson [4]	4725
43	19	H	Peterborough U	W 1-0	0-0	1	Johnson [61]	4631
44	22	A	Luton T	D 0-0	0-0	—		7769
45	26	A	Watford	D 0-0	0-0	1		9017
46	May 3	H	Millwall	W 2-0	0-0	1	Jepson [67], Johnrose [76]	9785

Final League Position: 1

GOALSCORERS

League (62): Carter 12 (5 pens), Jepson 9, Johnson 8, Matthews 5, Johnrose 4, West 4, Jackson 3, O'Kane 3, Randall 3, Armstrong 2, Battersby 2, Butler 2, Daws 2, Pugh 2, Stant 1.
Coca-Cola Cup (3): Carter 1, Jackson 1, Pugh 1.
FA Cup (0).

Kiely D 46	West D 46	Hughes I 14 + 8	Daws N 46	Lucketti C 38	Jackson M 31	Armstrong G 16 + 16	Johnson D 34 + 10	Jepson R 24 + 7	Johnrose L 43	Pugh D 16 + 2	Carter M 28 + 12	Rigby T — + 15	Matthews R 22 + 5	Butler P 40 + 1	Reid N 6 + 1	Woodward A 16 + 7	Stant P 3 + 5	Bimson S 1	O'Kane J 11 + 2	Randall A 14 + 5	Battersby T 9 + 2	Scott A 2 + 6	Match No.
1	2	3	4	5[2]	6	7	8[3]	9	10[1]	11	12	13	14										1
1	2	7	4		6	3[1]	8	9	10	11	12			5									2
1	2	7	4		6		8[3]	9[1]	10		11[2]	12	13	5	3	14							3
1	2	7	4		6		8	9[1]	10	11	12[2]	13		5	3								4
1	2	7	4		6[2]	12	8[1]	9	10	11[3]		13	14	5	3								5
1	2	7[1]	4		6	13	8[3]	9	10	11	12		14	5	3[2]								6
1	2	7	4		6	3	8	9	10	11[1]				5		12							7
1	2	7	4		6	3	8[2]	9	10	11[1]		13		5		12							8
1	2		4		6		8	9	10	11	12	13		5	3[1]	7[2]							9
1	2		4	5	6		8	9	10	11[1]	12				3	7							10
1	2		4	5	6		8[2]	9[1]	10[1]	11	12	13	14		3	7							11
1	2		4	5	6[1]		8	9	10	11	12[2]	13			3	7							12
1	2		4	5	6		8[1]	9	10	11[2]	12	13			3	7							13
1	2	12	4	5	6		8	9	10	11[1]		13			3	7							14
1	2	11[2]	4	5	6[1]		8	9	10		12	13			3	7							15
1	2		4	5	6		8	9[1]	10	11	12				3	7							16
1	2		4	5	6		8[2]	9	10	11[1]		13			3	7							17
1	2		4	5	6		8	9[2]	10	11[1]	12	13			3	7							18
1	2		4	5	6[2]		8	9[1]	10	11	12	13			3	7							19
1	2		4	5	6		8	9[2]	10	11	12	13			3[1]	7							20
1	2		4	5	6		8[3]	9[1]	10	11[2]	12	13			3	7				14			21
1	2		4	5	6		8[1]	9[3]	10	11[2]	12	13			3	7				14			22
1	2		4	5	6		8	9[1]	10	11[3]	12	13			3	7[2]				14			23
1	2		4	5	6		8[3]	9	10[2]		12	13	14			7			3[1]	11			24
1	2		4	5	6		8	9[1]	10	11[2]	12	13				7				3			25
1	2		4	5	6		8[1]	9[2]	10	11	12	13				7				3			26
1	2		4	5	6[1]		8	9	10	11	12					7				3			27
1	2		4	5	6[1]		8[2]	9	10	11	12	13	14			7				3[3]			28
1	2		4	5	6		8	9[3]	10[1]	11[2]	12	13	14			7				3			29
1	2	12	4	5	6[3]		8	9	10[1]	11		13	14			7				3			30
1	2	12	4[1]	5	6		8[3]	9[2]	10			13	14			7			11	3			31
1	2		4	5		11	8	9	10[2]		12	13			6	7			3[1]				32
1	2[2]	12	4	5		3[1]	8[3]	9	10			13	14		6	7				11			33
1	2		4	5		3[2]	8[1]	9	10		12	13			6	7				11			34
1	2	12	4	5		3	8[2]	9[1]	10	11		13			6	7							35
1	2	12	4	5		3	8[1]	9	10	11[2]		13	14		6	7							36
1	2	12	4	5[1]		3	8[2]	9[3]	10			13	14		6	7				11			37
1	2[1]		4	5		3[2]	8	9	10	11	12	13			6	7							38
1	2	10	4	5			8[1]	9			12	13			6	7				11		3[2]	39
1	2	12	4	5			8	9	10[1]	11		13	14		6	7[2]						3[3]	40
1	2	8	4	5		3		9[1]	10		12	13			6	7					11[2]		41
1	2	7	4	5		3	8[2]	9	10		12	13			6						11[1]		42
1	2	7	4	5		3	8[1]	9	10		12	13			6						11[2]		43
1	2		4	5		3	8	9	10		12				6	7[1]					11		44
1	2	7[1]	4	5		3	8	9	10		12				6[2]						11[3]		45
1	2	7[1]	4	5		3	8	9	10		12	13	14		6[2]						11[3]		46

Coca-Cola Cup

First Round	Notts Co	(a)	1-1
		(h)	1-0
Second Round	Crystal Palace	(h)	1-3
		(a)	0-4

FA Cup

| First Round | Chesterfield | (a) | 0-1 |

CAMBRIDGE UNITED 1996-97   *Back row (left to right):* Colin Vowden, Marc Joseph, Robbie Turner, Dave Thompson, Paul Wanless, Jody Craddock.
Middle row: Micah Hyde, Adi Hayes, Tony Richards, Scott Barrett, Danny Granville, Jamie Barnwell, Lenny Pack.
Front row: Davey Williamson, Shaun Howes, Paul Raynor, Billy Beall, Matthew Joseph, Keith Oliver.

Division 3 **CAMBRIDGE UNITED**

Abbey Stadium, Newmarket Rd, Cambridge, CB5 8LN. Telephone: (01223) 566500. Fax: (01223) 566502. Abbey Update: 0891 555885.

Ground capacity: 9667.

Record attendance: 14,000 v Chelsea, Friendly, 1 May 1970.

Record receipts: £86,308 v Manchester U, Rumbelows Cup 2nd rd 2nd leg, 9 October 1991.

Pitch measurements: 110yd × 74yd.

Chairman: R. H. Smart. *Vice-Chairman:* R. F. Hunt. *Directors:* G. Harwood, J. Howard, R. Hunt, G. Lowe, R. Summerfield.

Manager: Roy McFarland. *Player/coach:* David Preece. *Youth Manager:* David Batch.

Physio: Ken Steggles.

Secretary: Steve Greenall. *Commercial Manager:* David Smith. *Stadium Manager:* Ian Darler.

Year Formed: 1919. *Turned Professional:* 1946. *Ltd Co.:* 1948.

Club Nickname: The 'U's'.

Previous Name: Abbey United until 1949.

Foundation: The football revival in Cambridge began soon after World War II when the Abbey United club (formed 1919) decided to turn professional and in 1949 changed their name to Cambridge United. They were competing in the United Counties League before graduating to the Eastern Counties League in 1951 and the Southern League in 1958.

First Football League game: 15 August 1970, Division 4, v Lincoln C (h) D 1-1 – Roberts; Thompson, Meldrum (1), Slack, Eades, Hardy, Leggett, Cassidy, Lindsey, McKinven, Harris.

Record League Victory: 6–0 v Darlington, Division 4, 18 September 1971 – Roberts; Thompson, Akers, Guild, Eades, Foote, Collins (1p), Horrey, Hollett, Greenhalgh (4), Phillips. (1 og). 6–0 v Hartlepool U, Division 4, 11 February 1989 – Vaughan; Beck, Kimble, Turner, Chapple (1), Daish, Clayton, Holmes, Taylor (3 incl. 1p), Bull (1), Leadbitter (1).

Record Cup Victory: 5–1 v Bristol C, FA Cup 5th rd second replay, 27 February 1990 – Vaughan; Fensome, Kimble, Bailie (O'Shea), Chapple, Daish, Cheetham (Robinson), Leadbitter (1), Dublin (2), Taylor (1), Philpott (1).

Record Defeat: 0–6 v Aldershot, Division 3, 13 April 1974; v Darlington, Division 4, 28 September 1974; v Chelsea, Division 2, 15 January 1983 and v Brentford, Division 2, 28 January 1995.

Most League Points (2 for a win): 65, Division 4, 1976–77.

Most League Points (3 for a win): 86, Division 3, 1990–91.

Most League Goals: 87, Division 4, 1976–77.

Highest League Scorer in Season: David Crown, 24, Division 4, 1985–86.

Most League Goals in Total Aggregate: Alan Biley, 74, 1975–80.

Most Capped Player: Tom Finney, 7 (15), Northern Ireland.

Most League Appearances: Steve Spriggs, 416, 1975–87.

Record Transfer Fee Received: £1,000,000 from Manchester U for Dion Dublin, August 1992.

Record Transfer Fee Paid: £190,000 to Luton T for Steve Claridge, November 1992.

Football League Record: 1970 Elected to Division 4; 1973–74 Division 3; 1974–77 Division 4; 1977–78 Division 3; 1978–84 Division 2; 1984–85 Division 3; 1985–90 Division 4; 1990–91 Division 3; 1991–92 Division 2; 1992–93 Division 1; 1993–95 Division 2; 1995– Division 3.

Honours: *Football League:* Division 2 best season: 5th, 1991–92; Division 3 – Champions 1990–91; Runners-up 1977–78; Division 4 – Champions 1976–77; Promoted from Division 4 1989–90 (play-offs). *FA Cup:* best season: 6th rd, 1990 (shared record for Fourth Division club), 1991. *Football League Cup:* 5th rd, 1993.

Colours: Amber and black quartered shirts, black shorts, black and amber hooped stockings. *Change colours:* Blue and green halved shirts, blue shorts, blue and green hooped stockings.

Did you know?
The Cambridge United mascot, *Martin The Moose*, was first adopted by fans after John Taylor made a gesture to their supporters after shooting high over the bar during a pre-match warm-up last season.

CAMBRIDGE UNITED 1996–97 LEAGUE RECORD

Match No.	Date	Venue	Opponents	Result		H/T Score	Lg. Pos.	Goalscorers	Attendance
1	Aug 17	H	Barnet	W	1-0	0-0	—	Brazil [71]	2809
2	24	A	Chester C	D	1-1	1-1	6	Hyde [32]	1923
3	27	A	Lincoln C	D	1-1	1-0	—	Turner [7]	2407
4	31	H	Cardiff C	L	0-2	0-2	14		2478
5	Sept 7	H	Torquay U	W	2-1	2-0	7	McGleish 2 [5, 31]	2165
6	10	A	Scunthorpe U	L	2-3	2-1	—	Thompson [23], Housham (og) [38]	1643
7	14	A	Northampton T	W	2-1	1-0	9	Hyde [32], Richards [58]	4584
8	21	H	Scarborough	W	2-1	0-1	6	Richards [78], Benjamin [82]	2387
9	28	A	Exeter C	W	1-0	1-0	4	McGleish [45]	2572
10	Oct 1	H	Darlington	W	5-2	2-1	—	Hyde (pen) [38], Richards [45], McGleish [55], Thompson [73], Shaw (og) [82]	2509
11	5	H	Hartlepool U	W	1-0	1-0	4	Raynor [37]	3406
12	12	A	Brighton & HA	W	2-1	2-0	2	Kyd [21], Richards [43]	4564
13	15	A	Fulham	L	0-3	0-3	—		5791
14	19	H	Rochdale	D	2-2	1-1	3	Hyde [43], McGleish [88]	3163
15	25	H	Doncaster R	L	0-1	0-0	—		3457
16	29	A	Hereford U	W	1-0	0-0	—	Hyde [77]	2371
17	Nov 2	H	Hull C	W	3-1	2-0	2	McGleish [4], Hyde 2 (1 pen) [26 (p), 74]	3563
18	9	H	Swansea C	W	2-1	2-1	2	Raynor [31], McGleish [45]	3178
19	19	A	Carlisle U	L	0-3	0-0	—		3839
20	23	H	Leyton Orient	W	2-0	0-0	2	Barnwell-Edinboro [73], Kyd [76]	4360
21	30	A	Doncaster R	L	1-2	1-0	3	Beall [40]	1608
22	Dec 3	H	Mansfield T	W	2-1	0-0	—	Barnwell-Edinboro [55], Kyd [65]	2716
23	14	A	Wigan Ath	D	1-1	0-0	3	Barnwell-Edinboro [58]	2784
24	20	A	Colchester U	D	2-2	1-0	—	Beall [39], Raynor [63]	3707
25	28	H	Torquay U	W	1-0	1-0	3	Barnwell-Edinboro [32]	2700
26	Jan 14	A	Scarborough	L	0-1	0-0	—		1573
27	18	A	Darlington	L	0-2	0-0	4		2087
28	21	H	Exeter C	W	3-2	3-1	—	Kyd 2 [1, 44], Taylor [24]	2108
29	25	H	Hereford U	L	0-1	0-1	4		3018
30	31	A	Swansea C	L	1-3	0-2	—	Taylor [90]	5772
31	Feb 8	H	Hull C	W	1-0	1-0	5	Raynor [44]	3029
32	15	A	Leyton Orient	D	1-1	1-0	5	Taylor [21]	4418
33	21	H	Carlisle U	L	1-3	1-1	—	Taylor [37]	4294
34	25	H	Scunthorpe U	L	0-2	0-0	—		2033
35	Mar 1	A	Mansfield T	L	0-1	0-1	5		2163
36	7	H	Colchester U	W	1-0	1-0	—	Wanless [5]	3485
37	15	A	Wigan Ath	D	1-1	0-0	6	Wanless [82]	3867
38	22	H	Chester C	D	2-2	2-2	6	Sinclair (og) [5], Barnwell-Edinboro [7]	3044
39	29	A	Barnet	L	1-2	1-1	6	Barnwell-Edinboro [23]	2409
40	31	H	Lincoln C	L	1-3	0-0	8	Kyd [52]	3656
41	Apr 5	A	Cardiff C	D	0-0	0-0	8		3410
42	8	H	Northampton T	D	0-0	0-0	—		4412
43	12	A	Hartlepool U	W	2-0	1-0	7	Kyd [25], Craddock [83]	3186
44	19	H	Brighton & HA	D	1-1	1-1	8	Wanless [14]	6032
45	26	A	Rochdale	L	0-3	0-3	10		1810
46	May 3	H	Fulham	L	0-1	0-1	10		7218

Final League Position: 10

GOALSCORERS

League (53): Hyde 7 (2 pens), Kyd 7, McGleish 7, Barnwell-Edinboro 6, Raynor 4, Richards 4, Taylor 4, Wanless 3, Beall 2, Thompson 2, Benjamin 1, Brazil 1, Craddock 1, Turner 1, own goals 3.
Coca-Cola Cup (1): Thompson 1.
FA Cup (3): Barnwell-Edinboro 1, Beall 1, Kyd 1.

Barrett S 45	Joseph M 44	Vowden C 5 + 1	Granville D 37	Thompson D 15 + 7	Joseph M 5 + 3	Raynor P 43 + 1	Hyde M 38	Brazil G 1	Barnwell-Edinboro J 35 + 5	Beall B 33 + 3	Hayes A 19 + 6	Pack L — + 1	Wanless P 27 + 3	Turner R 2 + 5	Richards T 14 + 9	Wilde A — + 1	McGleish S 10	Preece D 19 + 6	Craddock J 41	Benjamin T 1 + 6	San Miguel X — + 1	Kyd M 22 + 6	Palmer L — + 1	Marshall S 1	Hay D — + 4	Ashbee I 16 + 2	Taylor J 19 + 2	Wilson P 7	Foster C 7	Match No.
1	2	5	3	4	6	7¹	8	9²	10	11	12	13																		1
1	2	5	3	4	6	7	8		10	11¹			9	12																2
1	2		3	4	6	7	8		10				5	9	11															3
1	2		3	4	6	7	8		10	12			5¹	9	11²	13														4
1	2		3	4		7	8		11	6	12			13	5		9²		10¹											5
1	2		3	4²		7¹	8		10	11	12		6	13			9		5											6
1	2	12	3²	4	13	7¹	8		10	11			6				9		5											7
1	2		3	4	6¹		8		10²	11			7				9		5	13		12								8
1	2		3	4	12		8		10	11			7		6		9¹		5											9
1	2²		3	4	6		8		10	11	12		7				9¹		5			13								10
1	2		3	4	6¹		8		10	11	12		7				9²		5			13								11
1	2		3	4	6		8²		10³	11	13		7				9¹	14	5			12								12
1	2		3	4	6		8		12	11	10		7				9¹		5											13
	2		3	4²	6		8		11	10¹			7				9	13	5			12		1						14
1	2		3	4²	6¹		8		10	11			7				9	13	5			12								15
1	2		3		6		8		10	11			7		4		9		5											16
1	2		3	12	6		8		10	11			7¹		4²		9³	13	5			14								17
1¹	2		3		6		8		10	11			7		4		9	12	5											18
1	2		3		6		8		10	11²			7		4		12	13	5			9¹								19
1	2¹		3	12	6		8		10	11			7					4	5			9								20
1	2		3		6		8		10	11			7		12			4¹	5			9								21
1	2		3		6		8		10	11			7					4	5			9								22
1	2		3¹	12	6		8		10	11			7		13			4	5			9²								23
1	2		3		6		8		10	11			7		12			4	5			9¹								24
1	2		3	12			8		10	11¹			7		13			4	5			9²				6				25
1	2		3				8		10²	11			7		12			4¹	5			13				6	9			26
1	2		3	12	6		8¹			11					13			4	5			10²				7	9			27
1	2		3		6		8			11			12		4				5			10¹				7	9			28
1	2		3		6		8		12	11					4¹			13	5			10				7²	9			29
1	2¹		3		6				10	11²	12				13			4	5			8				7	9			30
1	2		3		6		8¹			11					12			4	5			10				7	9			31
1	2		3	12	6		8²			11			14		13			4³	5			10¹				7	9			32
1	2		3	12	6		8			11								4	5			10				7¹	9			33
1	2		3	7	6³		8		12	11	13							4	5			10²				14	9¹			34
1	2		3	12	6¹		8		10	11²								4	5			13				7	9			35
1	2		3		6		8		10	11	12		7					4¹	5								9			36
1	2		3		6		8		10	11			7						5							4	9			37
1	2	3			6		8		10¹	11			7						5			12				4	9			38
1	2				6		8¹		10				7					12	5			13				4	9²	3	11	39
1	2				6		8		10				7					12	5			9				4¹	13	3²	11	40
1	2				6		8		10				7					12	5							4¹	9	3	11	41
1	2				6		8		10¹				7					4	5			12					9	3	11	42
1	2				6		8		12				7					4	5			10¹					9	3	11	43
1	2¹				6		8						7					4	5	13		10²			12		9	3	11	44
1				12	6		8		3				7					4	5	13		10²				2	9		11¹	45
1	2				6		8		11		12		7		4				5			9²				10¹	13	3		46

Coca-Cola Cup

First Round	Hereford U	(a)	0-3	
		(h)	1-1	

FA Cup

First Round	Welling U	(h)	3-0
Second Round	Woking	(h)	0-2

CARDIFF CITY 1996–97 *Back row (left to right):* Steve White, Pat Mountain, Tony Elliott, Steve Williams, Craig Middleton.
Middle row: Gavin Tait (Youth Team Manager), Jason Fowler, Lee Jarman, Simon Haworth, Jimmy Gardner, Jeff Eckhardt, Jimmy Goodfellow (Physio).
Front row: Hayden Flemming, Ian Rodgerson, Jason Perry, Russell Osman (Manager), Kenny Hibbitt (Director of Football), Carl Dale, Tony Philliskirk, Kevin Lloyd.

Division 3 **CARDIFF CITY**

Ninian Park, Cardiff CF1 8SX. Telephone: (01222) 398636. Fax: (01222) 341148. Newsline: 0891 888603.
Ground capacity: 14,980.
Record attendance: 61,566, Wales v England, 14 October 1961.
Club record: 57,893 v Arsenal, Division 1, 22 April 1953.
Record receipts: £141,756 v Manchester C, FA Cup 4th rd, 29 January 1994.
Pitch measurements: 114yd × 78yd.
Directors: S. Kumar (Chairman), R. East, J. Hill, P. Guy, R. Phillips.
Director of Football: Kenny Hibbitt.
Chief Executive Director: Joan Hill.
Secretary: Ceri Whitehead.
Manager: Russell Osman.
Physio: Jimmy Goodfellow.
Year Formed: 1899. *Turned Professional:* 1910. *Ltd Co.:* 1910.
Previous Names: 1899–1902, Riverside; 1902–08, Riverside Albion; 1908, Cardiff City.
Club Nickname: 'Bluebirds'.
Previous Grounds: Riverside, Sophia Gardens, Old Park and Fir Gardens. Moved to Ninian Park, 1910.

Foundation: Credit for the establishment of a first class professional football club in such a rugby stronghold as Cardiff, is due to members of the Riverside club formed in 1899 out of a cricket club of that name. Cardiff became a city in 1905 and in 1908 the local FA granted Riverside permission to call themselves Cardiff City.

First Football League game: 28 August 1920, Division 2, v Stockport Co (a) W 5-2 – Kneeshaw; Brittain, Leyton; Keenor (1), Smith, Hardy; Grimshaw (1), Gill (2), Cashmore, West, Evans (1).

Record League Victory: 9–2 v Thames, Division 3 (S), 6 February 1932 – Farquharson; E. L. Morris, Roberts; Galbraith, Harris, Ronan; Emmerson (1), Keating (1), Jones (1), McCambridge (1), Robbins (5).

Record Cup Victory: 8–0 v Enfield, FA Cup 1st rd, 28 November 1931 – Farquharson; Smith, Roberts; Harris (1), Galbraith, Ronan; Emmerson (2), Keating (3); O'Neill (2), Robbins, McCambridge.

Record Defeat: 2–11 v Sheffield U, Division 1, 1 January 1926.
Most League Points (2 for a win): 66, Division 3 (S), 1946–47.
Most League Points (3 for a win): 86, Division 3, 1982–83.
Most League Goals: 93, Division 3 (S), 1946–47.
Highest League Scorer in Season: Stan Richards, 30, Division 3 (S), 1946–47.
Most League Goals in Total Aggregate: Len Davies, 128, 1920–31.
Most Capped Player: Alf Sherwood, 39 (41), Wales.
Most League Appearances: Phil Dwyer, 471, 1972–85.
Record Transfer Fee Received: £300,000 from Sheffield U for Nathan Blake, February 1994.
Record Transfer Fee Paid: £180,000 to San Jose Earthquakes for Godfrey Ingram, September 1982.

Football League Record: 1920 Elected to Division 2; 1921–29 Division 1; 1929–31 Division 2; 1931–47 Division 3 (S); 1947–52 Division 2; 1952–57 Division 1; 1957–60 Division 2; 1960–62 Division 1; 1962–75 Division 2; 1975–76 Division 3; 1976–82 Division 2; 1982–83 Division 3; 1983–85 Division 2; 1985–86 Division 3; 1986–88 Division 4; 1988–90 Division 3; 1990–92 Division 4; 1992–93 Division 3; 1993–95 Division 2; 1995– Division 3.

Honours: Football League: Division 1 – Runners-up 1923–24; Division 2 – Runners-up 1920–21, 1951–52, 1959–60; Division 3 (S) – Champions 1946–47; Division 3 – Champions 1992–93. Runners-up 1975–76, 1982–83; Division 4 – Runners-up 1987–88. *FA Cup:* Winners 1927 (only occasion the Cup has been won by a club outside England); Runners-up 1925. *Football League Cup:* Semi-final 1966. *Welsh Cup:* Winners 21 times. *Charity Shield:* 1927. **European Competitions:** *European Cup-Winners' Cup:* 1964–65, 1965–66, 1967–68, 1968–69, 1969–70, 1970–71, 1971–72, 1973–74, 1974–75, 1976–77, 1977–78, 1988–89, 1991–92, 1992–93, 1993–94.

Colours: Blue shirts, white shorts, white stockings. *Change colours:* Yellow shirts, black shorts, yellow stockings.

Did you know?
On 28 February 1925, Cardiff City beat Newcastle United 3–0, despite having seven of their players away on international duty that day.

CARDIFF CITY 1996–97 LEAGUE RECORD

Match No.	Date	Venue	Opponents	Result	H/T Score	Lg. Pos.	Goalscorers	Attendance
1	Aug 17	A	Scarborough	D 0-0	0-0	—		2455
2	24	H	Brighton & HA	W 1-0	1-0	7	Eckhardt [43]	3463
3	27	H	Wigan Ath	L 0-2	0-1	—		3354
4	31	A	Cambridge U	W 2-0	2-0	6	White 2 [9, 37]	2478
5	Sept 7	H	Exeter C	W 2-1	1-1	5	White 2 [13, 68]	3659
6	10	A	Torquay U	L 0-2	0-2	—		2041
7	14	A	Scunthorpe U	W 1-0	0-0	5	Middleton [47]	2121
8	21	H	Northampton T	D 2-2	1-0	7	Philliskirk [18], Middleton [83]	4124
9	28	A	Lincoln C	L 0-2	0-1	8		2925
10	Oct 12	H	Barnet	L 1-2	1-1	15	Middleton [26]	2879
11	15	H	Darlington	W 2-0	2-0	—	Dale [3], White [41]	1667
12	19	A	Carlisle U	W 2-0	0-0	10	Dale [49], Fowler [81]	4972
13	26	H	Leyton Orient	W 3-0	3-0	7	White (pen) [22], Gardner [28], Dale [36]	3647
14	29	A	Hull C	D 1-1	1-0	—	Middleton [15]	2775
15	Nov 2	A	Colchester U	D 1-1	0-1	8	White (pen) [57]	3226
16	5	H	Rochdale	W 2-1	1-0	—	Bennett [45], Eckhardt [67]	2834
17	9	H	Fulham	L 1-2	0-2	7	White [89]	6144
18	23	H	Hereford U	W 2-0	0-0	5	White 2 [55, 75]	3900
19	26	A	Chester C	W 1-0	0-0	—	Young [85]	1540
20	30	A	Leyton Orient	L 0-3	0-1	5		4503
21	Dec 3	A	Swansea C	L 1-3	1-2	—	White [45]	3721
22	21	H	Mansfield T	L 1-2	1-0	9	Eckhardt [25]	2238
23	26	H	Torquay U	W 2-0	1-0	6	Burton 2 [38, 77]	3753
24	28	A	Exeter C	L 0-2	0-1	7		3585
25	Jan 1	A	Northampton T	L 0-4	0-2	—		4416
26	11	H	Lincoln C	L 1-3	1-1	7	Fowler [11]	2033
27	18	A	Rochdale	L 0-1	0-1	13		1704
28	25	H	Hull C	W 2-0	1-0	11	Haworth [34], Eckhardt [75]	2328
29	31	A	Fulham	W 4-1	1-0	—	Fowler [29], White 2 [46, 85], Haworth [51]	6459
30	Feb 8	H	Colchester U	L 1-2	0-2	8	Haworth [90]	3912
31	11	A	Hartlepool U	W 3-2	1-0	—	Fowler [32], Eckhardt [67], Stoker [78]	1120
32	16	A	Hereford U	D 1-1	1-0	9	Stoker [36]	4967
33	22	H	Hartlepool U	W 2-0	2-0	9	Haworth [21], Davies [35]	2971
34	Mar 2	A	Swansea C	W 1-0	1-0	7	Haworth [18]	4443
35	8	A	Mansfield T	W 3-1	1-0	7	Haworth [28], Stoker [64], Dale [76]	2569
36	14	H	Doncaster R	L 0-2	0-1	—		5347
37	18	H	Scarborough	D 1-1	0-0	—	Davies [57]	2823
38	22	A	Brighton & HA	L 0-2	0-2	8		9293
39	31	A	Wigan Ath	W 1-0	0-0	6	Haworth [56]	4634
40	Apr 5	H	Cambridge U	D 0-0	0-0	7		3410
41	8	A	Doncaster R	D 3-3	1-0	—	Haworth 2 [32, 88], Fowler [60]	1989
42	12	H	Chester C	W 1-0	1-0	6	Dale [34]	4079
43	15	H	Scunthorpe U	D 0-0	0-0	—		4490
44	19	A	Barnet	L 1-3	0-1	7	Dale [85]	2497
45	26	A	Carlisle U	W 2-0	2-0	7	Dale (pen) [20], Lloyd [37]	5178
46	May 3	A	Darlington	L 1-2	0-0	7	Dale [77]	3686

Final League Position: 7

GOALSCORERS

League (56): White 13 (2 pens), Haworth 9, Dale 8 (1 pen), Eckhardt 5, Fowler 5, Middleton 4, Stoker 3, Burton 2, Davies 2, Bennett 1, Gardner 1, Lloyd 1, Philliskirk 1, Young 1.
Coca-Cola Cup (1): Dale 1.
FA Cup (2): Middleton 1, White 1.

Elliott T 36	Rodgerson I 15 + 6	Lloyd K 27 + 4	Perry J 35	Jarman L 27 + 5	Young S 32	Bennett M 5 + 9	Fowler J 37	White S 32 + 9	Dale C 28 + 5	Phillskirk T 27 + 6	Eckhardt J 34 + 1	Scott A 1 + 1	Gardner J 19 + 9	Baddeley L 4 + 5	Coldicott S 6	Middleton C 40 + 1	Flack S 1	Fleming H 9 + 1	O'Halloran K 8	Haworth S 20 + 4	Mountain P 5	McStay R 1	Michaels J — + 1	Burton D 5	Stoker D 5	Ware P 5	Rollo J 3 + 7	Phillips L 2 + 1	Partridge S 14 + 1	Davies G 6	Williams S 5	Match No.
1	2	3	4	5	6	7	8	9	10	11																						1
1	2	3	4	5	6	7	8^2	9		11	10^1	12	13																			2
1	2	3	4			7	8	9	10^2	11^1	6	5	12	13																		3
1	2	3	4	12	5	7^2	8^1	9		11	6		13		10																	4
1	2	3	4	5	6			9		11	10					8		7														5
1	2	3		5	6			9	12	11^2	4		13			8		7	10^1													6
1	2	3		5	12	6		9	10^2	11^1	4		13			8		7														7
1	2	3		5	6	12		9	10	11^1	4					8		7														8
1	2	3		5^1	6	13		9	10	11	4		12			8^2		7														9
1	2	12	5	11^1	6	13	8^2	9	10	4	3					7																10
1			5	11	6		8	9	10	4	3					7			2													11
1	12	5^1		11	6^3	13	8	9	10	14	4		3			7^1			2													12
1	12	5			6	13	8	9	10	11^2	4		3^1			7			2													13
1		3		5^1	6	13	8^2	9	10	11	4		12			7			2													14
1				5^2	6	12	8^1	9	10	11	4	3	13			7			2													15
1	12			5			8	9	10^1	11	4		3		6	7			2													16
1			5	12			8	9	10	11	4		3^1		6	7			2													17
1	7	2		5	6		9	10	3	4	11					8																18
1	7	2		5	6		9	10	3	4	11					8																19
1		2		5	12	6	9	10	3	4	11^1					8		7														20
1		2		5	6		9	10	3	4	11					8^1		7		12												21
	7	2	3^1		6		9	10		4	11^2					8					12	1		5	13							22
	7	2	12	5			9		3	4	11					8				6		1		10								23
	7^1	2		5			9		3^2	4	11					8			12	6	13	1		10								24
		2	3				9			4	11		5			8		7		6	12	1		10								25
		2		12	7	13	9		3	4	11^2					8	5^1			6		1		10								26
1	12	3	2		6^1					11^2	4		5	13		7								8	9	10						27
1	12	3	2		6^2		5^1	9		4	11			13		7								8	10							28
1	12	3	2		6		5	9			13		4			7^1			10^2					8		11^3	14					29
1	12	3			2		6^1	5	9				4		13	7^2			10					8		11						30
1		3			2			5			9		4			7			10					8		11		6				31
1	12	3			2			5^1			9^2		4			7			10					8		11		6	13			32
1	12	3			2					13	9^2		4			7^1			10					8		11		14	6	5^1		33
1		3			2			6		9^1	12	11^2	4			7			10						13	8	5					34
1		3		12				6		9^2	13	11	4^1			7			10					2		14		8^3	5			35
1		3	4		2			6		9	12					7			10					11				8^1	5			36
1		3	4		2			6		9			12			7^1			10					8				11	5			37
1			4		3^2			6		11^3	9		12		14	13			10					8^1		2		7	5			38
1		3			2			5		6	9		4						10					8				11	7			39
1		3			2			5		6	12		9		11^1	4			10					8					7			40
1		3	4		2			5		6^1			9			11			10					8			12		7			41
		3	4		2			5		6			9			11			10^1					8			12		7		1	42
		3	4		2			5		6^2			9		12	11			10					8			13		7^1		1	43
		3^2	4		2			5					12		9	13			11					10				8^1	7	6	1	44
		3^1	4		2			5		6^2	14		9		12	11			10^3					8			13		7		1	45
		3^1	4		2			5		6^3	14		9		12	13			11					10					7^2		1	46

Coca-Cola Cup
First Round   Northampton T   (h)   1-0
                                              (a)   0-2

FA Cup
First Round   Hendon   (h)   2-0
Second Round   Gillingham   (h)   0-2

CARLISLE UNITED 1996-97 *Back row (left to right):* Kevin Sandwith, Jeff Thorpe, Tony Hopper, Richard Day, George Dixon, Lee Taylor, Lee Dixon, Michael Hodgson.
Third row: Neil Dalton (Assistant Physio), Peter Hampton (Physio), Will Varty, Dean Walling, Lee Peacock, Paul Conway, Paul Pettinger, Tony Caig, Jamie Robinson, Darren Edmondson, Rory Delap, Stephen Heath, John Halpin (Community Officer), David Wilkes (Youth Coach).
Second row: Gareth McAlindon, Steve Hayward, Kona Hislop, David Currie, Owen Archdeacon, Joe Joyce (Coach), Michael Knighton (Chairman & Chief Executive), Mervyn Day (Manager), David Reeves, Rod Thomas, Warren Aspinall, Richard Prokas, Matt Jansen.
Front row: Chris Barton, Craig Thompson, Lee Burton, Scott Dobie, Andrew Douglas, David Moore, Kevin Swanson, Marc Mellon, Liam Bell, Paul Boertien, Mark Jones, Edward Harrison, Mark Elliott.

Division 2

CARLISLE UNITED

Brunton Park, Carlisle CA1 1LL. Telephone: (01228) 26237. Fax: (01228) 30138. Commercial Dept: (01228) 24014. Information Line: 0891 230011.

Record attendance: 27,500 v Birmingham C, FA Cup 3rd rd, 5 January 1957 and v Middlesbrough, FA Cup 5th rd, 7 February 1970.

Record receipts: £125,000 v Sheffield W, FA Cup 4th rd, 25 January 1997.

Ground capacity: 16,651.

Pitch measurements: 117yd × 72yd.

Directors: M Knighton (Chairman), B. Chaytow, R. McKnight, A. Doweck, A. Jenkins.

Dirctor of Coaching: Mervyn Day. *Player-Coach:* Joe Joyce.

Physio: Peter Hampton.

Commercial Manager: Martin Hudson.

Secretary: A. Ritchie.

Year Formed: 1903. *Ltd Co.:* 1921.

Previous Grounds: 1903–05, Milholme Bank; 1905–09, Devonshire Park; 1909– Brunton Park.

Previous Name: Shaddongate United.

Club Nickname: 'Cumbrians' or 'The Blues'.

Foundation: Carlisle United came into being in 1903 through the amalgamation of Shaddongate United and Carlisle Red Rose. The new club was admitted to the Second Division of the Lancashire Combination in 1905–06, winning promotion the following season.

First Football League game: 25 August 1928, Division 3 (N), v Accrington S (a) W 3-2 – Prout; Coulthard, Cook; Harrison, Ross, Pigg; Agar, Hutchison, McConnell (1), Ward (1), Watson (1) o.g.

Record League Victory: 8–0 v Hartlepool U, Division 3 (N), 1 September 1928 – Prout; Smiles, Cook; Robinson (1) Ross, Pigg; Agar (1), Hutchison (1), McConnell (4), Ward (1), Watson. 8–0 v Scunthorpe U, Division 3 (N), 25 December 1952 – MacLaren; Hill, Scott; Stokoe, Twentyman, Waters; Harrison (1), Whitehouse (5), Ashman (2), Duffett, Bond.

Record Cup Victory: 6–0 v Shepshed Dynamo, FA Cup 1st rd, 16 November 1996 – Caig; Hopper, Archdeacon (pen), Walling, Robinson, Pounewatchy, Peacock (1), Conway (1) (Jansen), Smart (McAlindon (1)), Hayward, Aspinall (Thorpe) (2og).

Record Defeat: 1–11 v Hull C, Division 3 (N), 14 January 1939.

Most League Points (2 for a win): 62, Division 3 (N), 1950–51.

Most League Points (3 for a win): 91, Division 3, 1994–95.

Most League Goals: 113, Division 4, 1963–64.

Highest League Scorer in Season: Jimmy McConnell, 42, Division 3 (N), 1928–29.

Most League Goals in Total Aggregate: Jimmy McConnell, 126, 1928–32.

Most Capped Player: Eric Welsh, 4, Northern Ireland.

Most League Appearances: Alan Ross, 466, 1963–79.

Record Transfer Fee Received: £550,000 from QPR for Paul Murray, May 1996.

Record Transfer Fee Paid: £121,000 to Notts Co for David Reeves, December 1993.

Football League Record: 1928 Elected to Division 3 (N); 1958–62 Division 4; 1962–63 Division 3; 1963–64 Division 4; 1964–65 Division 3; 1965–74 Division 2; 1974–75 Division 1; 1975–77 Division 2; 1977–82 Division 3; 1982–86 Division 2; 1986–87 Division 3; 1987–92 Division 4; 1992–95 Division 3; 1995–96 Division 2; 1996–97 Division 3; 1997– Division 2.

Honours: Football League: Division 1 best season: 22nd, 1974–75; Promoted from Division 2 (3rd) 1973–74; Division 3 – Champions 1964–65, 1994–95; Runners-up 1981–82; Promoted from Division 3 1996–97 (play-offs); Division 4 – Runners-up 1963–64. *FA Cup:* 6th rd 1975. *Football League Cup:* Semi-final 1970. *Auto Windscreens Shield:* Winners 1997, Runners-up 1995.

Colours: Blue shirts, white shorts, white stockings. *Change colours:* Green, red, yellow and white shirts, green shorts, green stockings.

Did you know?
Carlisle United appointed Ivor Broadis as player-manager in August 1946, at 23, the youngest ever in the Football League. In February 1949, he transferred himself to Sunderland.

CARLISLE UNITED

CARLISLE UNITED 1996–97 LEAGUE RECORD

Match No.	Date	Venue	Opponents	Result	H/T Score	Lg. Pos.	Goalscorers	Attendance
1	Aug 17	A	Doncaster R	W 1-0	0-0	—	Delap [54]	3003
2	24	H	Hull C	D 0-0	0-0	8		5407
3	27	H	Leyton Orient	W 1-0	0-0	—	Hayward [76]	4973
4	31	A	Fulham	L 0-1	0-1	8		5860
5	Sept 7	H	Swansea C	W 4-1	3-1	4	Hayward [17], Conway [32], Aspinall [38], Archdeacon [86]	5114
6	10	A	Hartlepool U	W 2-1	0-1	—	Hayward [83], Reeves [89]	3077
7	14	A	Scarborough	D 1-1	0-0	3	Edmondson [73]	3524
8	21	H	Darlington	W 1-0	1-0	3	Conway [9]	5701
9	28	A	Torquay U	W 2-1	0-0	2	Reeves [79], Hayward [81]	2435
10	Oct 1	H	Colchester U	W 3-0	1-0	—	Currie [43], Reeves [57], Archdeacon [58]	4089
11	5	H	Mansfield T	D 1-1	0-0	1	Aspinall (pen) [80]	5509
12	12	A	Rochdale	D 2-2	1-1	3	Smart [27], Peacock [54]	3320
13	15	A	Exeter C	L 1-2	1-0	—	Smart [14]	2155
14	19	H	Cardiff C	L 0-2	0-0	4		4972
15	26	A	Barnet	D 0-0	0-0	4		2422
16	29	H	Chester C	W 3-1	0-1	—	Peacock 2 [59, 69], Smart [82]	4187
17	Nov 2	H	Wigan Ath	L 0-3	0-1	5		6235
18	9	A	Northampton T	D 1-1	0-0	4	Conway [59]	4682
19	19	H	Cambridge U	W 3-0	0-0	—	Peacock [73], Smart [80], Aspinall [82]	3839
20	23	A	Brighton & HA	W 3-1	2-1	4	Pounewatchy [27], Aspinall [41], Smart [68]	4155
21	30	H	Barnet	W 2-1	0-0	2	Archdeacon [49], Conway [77]	4472
22	Dec 3	A	Lincoln C	D 1-1	1-1	—	Hayward [32]	2033
23	14	A	Hereford U	W 3-2	2-1	2	Conway [3], Archdeacon [39], Aspinall [90]	1855
24	21	H	Scunthorpe U	W 3-2	2-1	2	Walling 2 [27, 33], Hayward [66]	5646
25	26	H	Hartlepool U	W 1-0	0-0	2	Peacock [82]	6947
26	28	A	Swansea C	W 1-0	0-0	2	Prokas [90]	7340
27	Jan 18	A	Colchester U	D 1-1	1-1	2	Archdeacon [34]	3588
28	Feb 1	H	Northampton T	W 2-1	0-0	2	Conway 2 [47, 60]	5271
29	8	A	Wigan Ath	L 0-1	0-1	3		6195
30	11	A	Scarborough	W 1-0	0-0	—	Peacock [77]	4936
31	15	H	Brighton & HA	W 2-1	2-1	2	Smart [24], Walling [35]	5465
32	21	A	Cambridge U	W 3-1	1-1	—	Peacock [5], Smart 2 [47, 62]	4294
33	25	A	Chester C	D 1-1	0-1	—	McAlindon [81]	2750
34	Mar 1	H	Lincoln C	W 1-0	0-0	1	Smart [48]	4958
35	4	H	Torquay U	W 5-1	2-0	—	Conway [13], Peacock [24], Smart [53], Freestone [81], Delap [85]	4680
36	8	A	Scunthorpe U	D 0-0	0-0	1		3470
37	15	H	Hereford U	L 2-3	2-2	1	Conway [4], Freestone [16]	5063
38	22	A	Hull C	W 1-0	0-0	1	Jansen [90]	3847
39	29	H	Doncaster R	D 0-0	0-0	2		6551
40	31	A	Leyton Orient	L 1-2	1-2	2	Hopper [43]	4604
41	Apr 5	H	Fulham	L 1-2	1-0	3	Delap [20]	9171
42	8	A	Darlington	L 1-2	1-0	—	Delap [8]	4184
43	11	A	Mansfield T	D 0-0	0-0	—		4375
44	26	A	Cardiff C	L 0-2	0-2	3		5178
45	29	H	Rochdale	W 3-2	0-1	—	Hayward [73], Archdeacon [76], Dobie [79]	4882
46	May 3	A	Exeter C	W 2-0	2-0	3	Peacock [35], McAlindon [43]	6170

Final League Position: 3

GOALSCORERS

League (67): Smart 10, Conway 9, Peacock 9, Hayward 7, Archdeacon 6, Aspinall 5 (1 pen), Delap 4, Reeves 3, Walling 3, Freestone 2, McAlindon 2, Currie 1, Dobie 1, Edmondson 1, Hopper 1, Jansen 1, Pounewatchy 1, Prokas 1.
Coca-Cola Cup (6): Thomas 2, Archdeacon 1, Aspinall 1, Hayward 1, Reeves 1.
FA Cup (8): Archdeacon 2 (1 pen), Conway 1, Edmondson 1, McAlindon 1, Peacock 1, own goals 2.

Caig T 46	Edmondson D 19 + 1	Archdeacon O 46	Walling D 46	Pounewatchy S 42	Varty W 31 + 1	Thomas R 23 + 13	Delap R 25 + 7	Peacock L 37 + 7	Hayward S 43	Conway P 22 + 3	Currie D 5 + 4	Aspinall W 39 + 1	Reeves D 8	Kerr D — + 1	Prokas R 10 + 3	Robinson J 6 + 1	McAlindon G 3 + 9	Heath S — + 1	Jansen M 4 + 15	Bass J 3	Smart A 25 + 3	Shirtliff P 5	Hopper T 13 + 7	Freestone C 3 + 2	Thorpe J 2 + 3	Dobie S — + 2	Match No.
1	2	3	4	5	6	7	8[1]	9	10	11	12																1
1	2	3	4	5	6	7	12	9	10	11[2]	8[1]	13															2
1	2	3	4	5	6	7	12	9	10		8[1]	11															3
1	2	3	4	5	6[1]	7[2]	14	8[3]	10	13	12	11	9														4
1	2	3	4	5	6	7		12	10	8[1]		11	9														5
1	2	3	4	5	6	7[1]	13	12	10	8		11[2]	9														6
1	2	3	4	5	6	7[1]	12		10	8		11	9														7
1	2	3	4	5	6	7[3]	12	13	10[2]	8	11[1]		9	14													8
1		3	4	5	6[1]	7[2]	2	11	10				9		8	12	13										9
1		3	4	5		7[3]	2[1]	8	10	12	11[2]		9		13	6	14										10
1		3	4	5		7	2		10	8[1]		11	9		12												11
1		3	4		6	7		8	10			11			5		12		2		9[1]						12
1		3	4		6	7[1]		8	10			11			5[2]		13		12	2	9						13
1		3	4		6			12	10	8		11			5		13		7	2[1]	9[2]						14
1		3	4		6	7	2	12	10			11[2]					13		8[1]		9	5					15
1		3	4		6	7[3]	2	8	10	12	13	11[1]							14		9[2]	5					16
1		3	4		6	7	2	8	10	12		11[1]					13				9[2]	5					17
1		3	4		6	7			10	8		11							12		9[1]	5	2				18
1		3	4		6	12	7[3]		10[2]	8		11			14		13				9	5	2[1]				19
1		3	4	10[1]	6	7		8		12		11[2]			5		13				9		2				20
1		3	4	5	6	7	12	8	10			11									9[1]		2				21
1		3	4	5	6	7		8	10			11									9		2				22
1		3	4	5	6	7		8	10	12	2	11									9[1]						23
1		3	4	5	6	7	2	8[2]	10	12	13	11									9[1]						24
1		3	4	5	6	7[1]	2	8	10	12		11									9						25
1		3	4	5	6	7	2	8	10			11									9						26
1	2	3	4	5	6	7		8	10	12	13	11[1]									9[2]						27
1	2	3	4	5	6	7[1]		8	10			11[2]									9		12		13		28
1	2[2]	3	4	5	6	7	9	8[1]	10[3]			11			12		13		14								29
1		3	4	5	6	7		8	10[2]	12		11			14		13				9[3]		2[1]				30
1		3	4	5	6	7[2]	2	8	10	12		11[1]					13				9						31
1	12	3	4	5	6	7[1]	2	8	10			11									9						32
1	6	3	4	5		7[2]	2	8	10			11			13						9[1]				12		33
1	6	3	4	5		7	2	8	10			11									9						34
1		3	4	5	6	7	2	8[3]	10	12		11[2]									9[1]		13	14			35
1		3	4	5	6	7	2	8[2]	10	12		11									9[1]		13				36
1		3	4	5	6		2	8	10	12	13	11[3]									9[1]		7				37
1		3	4	5	6	7	2	8[1]	10			11					13				9[2]		12				38
1		3	4	5	6	7			10	12		11[1]			8[3]		13				9[2]		2	14			39
1		3	4	5	6	7[2]	9	8	10			11[1]						12			13		2				40
1		3	4	5	6	7[2]	9		10	12		11					13				8[1]		2				41
1		3	4	5	6	7	2[3]	8	10			11[1]			12		13				9[2]		14				42
1		3	4	5	6	7[1]	9	8	10	12		11											2				43
1		3	4	5	6	7	12	8	10			11					13				9[2]		2[1]				44
1		3	4	5	6	7			10			11									9[2]		2		12	13	45
1		3	4	5	6	7[1]	2		10			11									9[2]		12		8	13	46

Coca-Cola Cup

First Round	Chester C	(h)	1-0
		(a)	3-1
Second Round	Port Vale	(a)	0-1
		(h)	2-2

FA Cup

First Round	Shepshed D	(h)	6-0
Second Round	Darlington	(h)	1-0
Third Round	Tranmere R	(h)	1-0
Fourth Round	Sheffield W	(h)	0-2

CHARLTON ATHLETIC 1996–97   *Back row (left to right):* Steve Brown, Jay Notley, Phil Chapple, Andy Petterson, Mike Salmon, Robert Wright, Carl Leaburn, Dean Chandler, Kevin Nicholls.
Middle row: Steve Watts (Youth Development Officer), Terry Westley (Youth Team Coach), Wes Foley, Kevin Lisbie, Bradley Allen, Paul Sturgess, Dean Kearley, Jamie Stuart, Brendan O'Connell, Anthony Barness, Jason Tindall, Shaun Newton, Gary Moss (Assistant Physio), Jimmy Hendry (Physio).
Front row: Paul Linger, David Whyte, Paul Mortimer, Stuart Balmer, Keith Peacock (Reserve Team Coach), Alan Curbishley (Manager), Les Reed (First Team Coach), Richard Rufus, Keith Jones, John Robinson, Mark Robson.
(Photograph: Tom Morris)

Division 1   **CHARLTON ATHLETIC**

The Valley, Floyd Road, Charlton, London SE7 8BL. Telephone: (0181) 333 4000. Fax: (0181) 333 4001. Box Office: (0181) 33 4010. Clubcall 0891 121146.

Ground capacity: 16,000.

Record attendance: 75,031 v Aston Villa, FA Cup 5th rd, 12 February 1938 (at The Valley).

Record receipts: £163,864 v Newcastle United, FA Cup 3rd rd, 5 January 1997.

Pitch measurements: 111yd × 73yd.

President: R. D. Collins.

Chairman: M. A. Simons. *Vice-Chairman:* R. A. Murray.

Directors: R. N. Alwen, G. P. Bone, R. D. Collins, D. J. Hughes, R. D. King, M. C. Stevens, D. G. Ufton, R. C. Whitehand.

Manager: Alan Curbishley.

Reserve Team Manager: Keith Peacock. *Youth Team Manager:* Terry Westley.

Youth Development Officer: Steve Watts. *Physio:* Jimmy Hendry. *Coach:* Les Reed.

Secretary: Chris Parkes.

Marketing Manager: Steve Dixon. *Stadium Manager:* Roy King.

Year Formed: 1905. *Turned Professional:* 1920. *Ltd Co.:* 1919.

Club Nickname: 'Addicks'.

Previous Grounds: 1906, Siemen's Meadow; 1907, Woolwich Common; 1909, Pound Park; 1913, Horn Lane; 1920, The Valley; 1923, Catford (The Mount); 1924, The Valley; 1985 Selhurst Park; 1991 Upton Park; 1992 The Valley.

Foundation: The club was formed on 9 June 1905, by a group of 14 and 15-year-old youths living in streets by the Thames in the area which now borders the Thames Barrier. The club's progress through local leagues was so rapid that after the First World War they joined the Kent League where they spent a season before turning professional and joining the Southern League in 1920. A year later they were elected to the Football League's Division 3 (South).

First Football League game: 27 August 1921, Division 3 (S), v Exeter C (h) W 1-0 – Hughes; Mitchell, Goodman; Dowling (1), Hampson, Dunn; Castle, Bailey, Halse, Green, Wilson.

Record League Victory: 8–1 v Middlesbrough, Division 1, 12 September 1953 – Bartram; Campbell, Ellis; Fenton, Ufton, Hammond; Hurst (2), O'Linn (2), Leary (1), Firmani (3), Kiernan.

Record Cup Victory: 7–0 v Burton A, FA Cup 3rd rd, 7 January 1956 – Bartram; Campbell, Townsend; Hewie, Ufton, Hammond; Hurst (1), Gauld (1), Leary (3), White, Kiernan (2).

Record Defeat: 1–11 v Aston Villa, Division 2, 14 November 1959.

Most League Points (2 for a win): 61, Division 3 (S), 1934–35.

Most League Points (3 for a win): 77, Division 2, 1985–86.

Most League Goals: 107, Division 2, 1957–58.

Highest League Scorer in Season: Ralph Allen, 32, Division 3 (S), 1934–35.

Most League Goals in Total Aggregate: Stuart Leary, 153, 1953–62.

Most Capped Player: John Hewie, 19, Scotland.

Most League Appearances: Sam Bartram, 583, 1934–56.

Record Transfer Fee Received: £2,800,00 from Leeds United for Lee Bowyer, July 1996.

Record Transfer Fee Paid: £600,000 to Chelsea for Joe McLaughlin, August 1989.

Football League Record: 1921 Elected to Division 3 (S); 1929–33 Division 2; 1933–35 Division 3 (S); 1935–36 Division 2; 1936–57 Division 1; 1957–72 Division 2; 1972–75 Division 3; 1975–80 Division 2; 1980–81 Division 3; 1981–86 Division 2; 1986–90 Division 1; 1990–92 Division 2; 1992– Division 1.

Honours: Football League: Division 1 – Runners-up 1936–37; Division 2 – Runners-up 1935–36, 1985–86; Division 3 (S) – Champions 1928–29, 1934–35; Promoted from Division 3 (3rd) 1974–75, 1980–81. *FA Cup:* Winners 1947; Runners-up 1946. *Football League Cup:* best season: 4th rd, 1963, 1966, 1979. *Full Members Cup:* Runners-up 1987.

Colours: Red shirts, white shorts, red stockings. *Change colours:* White shirts, green shorts, white stockings.

Did you know?

In 1922–23 Charlton Athletic, in only their second season in the Football League, eliminated three First Division clubs from the FA Cup: – Manchester City (away) 2–1, Preston North End (home) 2–0 and West Bromwich Albion (home) 1–0.

CHARLTON ATHLETIC 1996–97 LEAGUE RECORD

Match No.	Date	Venue	Opponents	Result	H/T Score	Lg. Pos.	Goalscorers	Attendance
1	Aug 17	A	Huddersfield T	L	0-2	0-1	—	11,858
2	24	H	WBA	D	1-1	0-1	19	Leaburn [70]	9642
3	Sept 3	A	Manchester C	L	1-2	1-0	—	Newton [27]	25,963
4	6	A	Wolverhampton W	L	0-1	0-1	—		21,072
5	10	H	Southend U	W	2-0	2-0	—	Stuart [17], Mortimer [28]	8497
6	14	H	Reading	W	1-0	1-0	20	Leaburn [6]	10,831
7	20	A	Ipswich T	L	1-2	1-0	—	Allen [34]	10,558
8	28	H	Oldham Ath	W	1-0	0-0	16	Whyte [86]	12,178
9	Oct 12	A	Portsmouth	L	0-2	0-0	23		6641
10	15	A	Sheffield U	L	0-3	0-0	—		14,080
11	19	H	Bolton W	D	3-3	3-1	23	Whyte 2 [20, 38], Chapple [29]	11,091
12	26	H	Oxford U	W	2-0	2-0	21	Kinsella [29], Leaburn [31]	10,626
13	29	A	Tranmere R	L	0-4	0-2	—		5527
14	Nov 2	A	Norwich C	W	2-1	0-0	21	Allen [64], Kinsella [82]	14,145
15	16	A	QPR	W	2-1	1-1	18	Poole [19], Allen [70]	12,360
16	20	H	Birmingham C	W	2-1	1-1	—	Allen [39], O'Connell [46]	8574
17	23	H	Bradford C	L	0-2	0-1	18		12,256
18	26	H	Grimsby T	L	1-3	1-1	—	Whyte [19]	9435
19	30	A	Oxford U	W	2-0	0-0	12	Barness [47], Whyte [50]	7080
20	Dec 4	A	Stoke C	L	0-1	0-0	—		7456
21	7	H	Swindon T	W	2-0	0-0	12	Leaburn [58], Whyte [79]	10,565
22	14	H	Port Vale	L	1-3	1-1	16	Chapple [21]	10,003
23	21	A	Crystal Palace	L	0-1	0-0	17		16,279
24	26	A	Southend U	W	2-0	1-0	15	Kinsella [43], Robinson [65]	7508
25	28	H	Wolverhampton W	D	0-0	0-0	16		12,259
26	Jan 1	H	Ipswich T	D	1-1	0-1	14	Robson [78]	10,186
27	11	A	Reading	D	2-2	0-1	13	Lisbie [68], Whyte [81]	7614
28	18	H	Stoke C	L	1-2	0-2	16	Barness [49]	9901
29	Feb 1	A	Grimsby T	L	0-2	0-1	18		4139
30	7	H	Tranmere R	W	3-1	2-1	—	Kinsella [6], Leaburn [42], Robson (pen) [89]	11,283
31	15	H	Barnsley	D	2-2	1-0	17	Nicholls [1], Lee [88]	9104
32	22	H	Norwich C	D	4-4	2-2	18	Kinsella [31], Robson [36], Lee [87], Leaburn [88]	12,405
33	Mar 1	A	Swindon T	L	0-1	0-0	19		9256
34	4	H	QPR	W	2-1	2-1	—	Leaburn [4], Balmer [26]	10,610
35	8	H	Crystal Palace	W	2-1	0-0	15	Lee [55], Robinson [70]	15,000
36	15	A	Port Vale	L	0-2	0-0	18		5905
37	18	A	Oldham Ath	D	1-1	0-0	—	O'Connell [89]	4969
38	22	A	WBA	W	2-1	1-1	17	Robinson [17], Balmer [58]	14,312
39	31	A	Birmingham C	D	0-0	0-0	15		14,525
40	Apr 5	H	Manchester C	D	1-1	1-0	15	Leaburn [43]	15,000
41	9	H	Huddersfield T	W	2-1	0-0	—	Newton 2 [61, 90]	11,032
42	12	A	Barnsley	L	0-4	0-2	14		11,701
43	19	H	Portsmouth	W	2-1	1-1	14	Bright 2 [10, 65]	12,342
44	25	A	Bolton W	L	1-4	1-0	—	Kinsella [14]	22,024
45	May 1	A	Bradford C	L	0-1	0-1	—		15,780
46	4	H	Sheffield U	D	0-0	0-0	15		12,589

Final League Position: 15

GOALSCORERS

League (52): Leaburn 8, Whyte 7, Kinsella 6, Allen 4, Lee 3, Newton 3, Robinson 3, Robson 3 (1 pen), Balmer 2, Barness 2, Bright 2, Chapple 2, O'Connell 2, Lisbie 1, Mortimer 1, Nicholls 1, Poole 1, Stuart 1.
Coca-Cola Cup (8): Allen 2, Robinson 2, Whyte 2, Leaburn 1, Newton 1.
FA Cup (2): Kinsella 1, Robson 1.

Salmon M 25	Barness A 45	Stuart J 10	Jones K 14 + 5	Rufus R 33 + 1	Balmer S 28 + 4	Newton S 39 + 4	Leaburn C 40 + 4	Robinson J 41 + 1	Whyte D 18 + 4	Mortimer P 10 + 1	O'Connell B 33 + 5	Allen B 13 + 5	Chapple P 25 + 1	Brown S 22 + 5	Otto R 5 + 2	Sturgess P 1 + 2	Nicholls K 3 + 3	Kinsella M 37	Lisbie K 4 + 21	Poole G 14 + 2	Robson M 8 + 7	Scott K 4	Petterson A 21	Lee J 7 + 1	Jones S 2	Bright M 4 + 2	Match No.
1	2	3	4	5	6	7[1]	8	9	10[2]	11	12	13															1
1	2	3	4	5	6	7	8	9	10	11[1]	12																2
1	2	3	4		6	7	8	9	10[1]	11		12	5														3
1	2	3[2]	4		6	7	8	9	10	11[1]	12	13	5														4
1	2	3	4		6	7[1]	8	9		11		10	5	12													5
1	2	3	4[1]		6	7	8	9		11	12[2]	10	5	13													6
1	2	3			6	7[3]	8		12	11		10	5	4[7]	9[1]	13	14										7
1	2	3			6	7[3]	8	9	12			10[1]	5	4[7]		13		11									8
1	2		14		6	7	8	9	12		4	10[1]	5		3[2]	13[3]		11									9
1	2			5	6	7[2]	8[1]	9	12		4[3]	10			3	13	14	11									10
1		3[3]		5	12		8	9	10[2]		4	13		6	2			7[1]	11	14							11
1		3			6	2[2]	8	9	10[2]		4		5	12				7	11	13							12
1		3			6	2[2]	8	9	10[1]		4	12	5	13				7[3]	11	14							13
1		3			6	7	8	9	10		4						2	11		5							14
1		3			6	7	8	9	10		4						2	11		5							15
1		3			6	7	8	9[1]	10		4						2	11	12	5							16
1		3[1]			6	7	8	9	10		4						2	11	12	5							17
1		3[1]			6	7	8[2]	9	10		4						2	11	12	5	13						18
1		3		5		7	8	9	10		4			6			2	11									19
1		3		5		7[1]	8	9[2]	10		4			6			2	11	12		13						20
1		3		5		7	8	9	10		4			6			2	11									21
1		3		5		7	8	9	10		4[1]			6	2	12		11									22
1		3[1]				7	8	9[2]	10		4			6	2			11	12		13	5					23
1		3	12			7	8	9[3]	10[3]		4[1]			6	2			11	14		13	5					24
1[1]		3	12			7	8	9	10		4			6	2			11				5					25
	3		12			7[3]	8	9[1]	10		4		2[1]	6				11	13	5			1	14			26
	3			5		7	8		10		4		2	6				11	12		9[1]		1				27
	3		12	5		7[3]	8	9	10[2]		4	13	2[1]	6				11	14				1				28
	3[1]		12	5		7[2]	8	9	10[3]		4	13	2	6			14	11					1				29
	3			5		7	8	9	10[1]		4		2	6				11	12				1				30
	3		4	5		7[2]	8[3]	9	10				2[1]	6			14	11	13				1				31
	3		4	5		7[1]	8[3]	9	10[2]				2	6			14	11	13				1				32
	3			5	6	7[1]	8	9	10[2]		4		2[3]				14	11	13	12			1				33
	3			5	6	7	8	9	10[1]		4		2					11	12				1				34
	3			5	6	7	8	9	10		4		2			6		11					1				35
	3[3]			5	6[1]	7	8[2]	9	10		4		2				14	11	13	12			1				36
	3[3]			5	6[1]	7	8	9	10[2]		4		2				14	11	13	12			1				37
	3		10	5[1]	6	7	8	9			4		2					11	12				1				38
	3		10	5	6	7[1]	8	9			4		2					11	12				1				39
	3		10	5	6	7	8	9			4[1]		2					11	12				1				40
	3		10	5	6	7	8[1]	9			4		2					11[2]	12				1	13			41
	3		10	5	6	7	8	9			4		2[1]					11					1	12			42
	3			5	6	7	12	9			4		2[1]					11	10				1			8	43
	3			5	6	7[2]	12	9			4		2	13				11	10[1]				1			8	44
	3			5	6	7	12	9			4[1]		2					11	10				1			8	45
	3			5	6	7	12	9	10		4[7]		2[1]	13				11					1			8	46

Coca-Cola Cup
Second Round   Burnley   (h) 4-1
                                (a) 2-1
Third Round   Liverpool   (h) 1-1
                                (a) 1-4

FA Cup
Third Round   Newcastle U   (h) 1-1
                                (a) 1-2

CHELSEA 1996–97 *Back row (left to right):* Dave Collyer (Youth Development Officer), Bernie Dixson (Youth Development Officer), Chris McCann, Paul Hughes, Neil Clement, Jakob Kjeldbjerg, Nick Colgan, Michael Duberry, Erland Johnsen, Scott Minto, Mark Nicholls, Bob Orsborn (Kit Manager), Ted Dale (Youth Team Manager).
Middle row: George Price (Reserve Team Physio), Mick McGiven (Reserve Team Manager), Mark Stein, Andy Myers, Craig Burley, David Lee, Dmitri Kharine, Kevin Hitchcock, Frank Leboeuf, Steve Clarke, Frank Sinclair, David Rocastle, Mike Banks (Physio), Terry Byrne (Assistant Physio).
Front row: Eddie Niedzwiecki (Goalkeeping Coach), Gavin Peacock, Dan Petrescu, Eddie Newton, Gianluca Vialli, Dennis Wise, Gwyn Williams (Assistant Manager), Ruud Gullit (Player/Manager), Graham Rix (First Team Coach), Roberto Di Matteo, Mark Hughes, Terry Phelan, John Spencer, Jody Morris, Ade Mafe (Fitness/Conditioning Coach).
(Photograph: Action Images)

FA Premiership

CHELSEA

Stamford Bridge, London SW6 1HS. Telephone: (0171) 385 5545. Fax: (0171) 381 4831. Clubcall: 0891 121159. Ticket News and Promotions: 0891 121011. Ticket Credit Card Service: (0171) 386 7799.

Ground capacity: 31,791 (during ground development); 41,000 (eventually).

Record attendance: 82,905 v Arsenal, Division 1, 12 October 1935.

Record receipts: £488,960 v Liverpool, FA Premier League, 30 December 1995.

Pitch measurements: 113yd × 74yd.

President: G. M. Thomson.

Chairman: K. W. Bates.

Directors: C. Hutchinson (Managing), Ms Y. S. Todd.

Team Manager: Ruud Gullit. *Coach:* Graham Rix.

Physio: Michael Banks. *Reserve Team Manager:* Mick McGiven.

Company Secretary/Director: Yvonne Todd. *Match Secretary and Safety Officer:* Keith Lacy.

Commercial Manager: Carole Phair. *Stadium Manager:* D. Johnson.

Year Formed: 1905. *Turned Professional:* 1905. *Ltd Co.:* 1905.

Club Nickname: 'The Blues'.

Foundation: Chelsea may never have existed but for the fact that Fulham rejected an offer to rent the Stamford Bridge ground from Mr. H. A. Mears who had owned it since 1904. Fortunately he was determined to develop it as a football stadium rather than sell it to the Great Western Railway and got together with Frederick Parker, who persuaded Mears of the financial advantages of developing a major sporting venue. Chelsea FC was formed in 1905, and when admission to the Southern League was denied, they immediately gained admission to the Second Division of the Football League.

First Football League game: 2 September 1905, Division 2, v Stockport Co (a) L 0-1 – Foulke; Mackie, McEwan; Key, Harris, Miller; Moran, J.T. Robertson, Copeland, Windridge, Kirwan.

Record League Victory: 9–2 v Glossop N E, Division 2, 1 September 1906 – Byrne; Walton, Miller; Key (1), McRoberts, Henderson; Moran, McDermott (1), Hilsdon (5), Copeland (1), Kirwan (1).

Record Cup Victory: 13–0 v Jeunesse Hautcharage, ECWC, 1st rd 2nd leg, 29 September 1971 – Bonetti; Boyle, Harris (1), Hollins (1p), Webb (1), Hinton, Cooke, Baldwin (3), Osgood (5), Hudson (1), Houseman (1).

Record Defeat: 1–8 v Wolverhampton W, Division 1, 26 September 1953.

Most League Points (2 for a win): 57, Division 2, 1906–07.

Most League Points (3 for a win): 99, Division 2, 1988–89.

Most League Goals: 98, Division 1, 1960–61.

Highest League Scorer in Season: Jimmy Greaves, 41, 1960–61.

Most League Goals in Total Aggregate: Bobby Tambling, 164, 1958–70.

Most Capped Player: Ray Wilkins, 24 (84), England.

Most League Appearances: Ron Harris, 655, 1962–80.

Record Transfer Fee Received: £2,200,000 from Tottenham H for Gordon Durie, July 1991.

Record Transfer Fee Paid: £4,000,000 to Lazio for Roberto Di Matteo.

Football League Record: 1905 Elected to Division 2; 1907–10 Division 1; 1910–12 Division 2; 1912–24 Division 1; 1924–30 Division 2; 1930–62 Division 1; 1962–63 Division 2; 1963–75 Division 1; 1975–77 Division 2; 1977–79 Division 1; 1979–84 Division 2; 1984–88 Division 1; 1988–89 Division 2; 1989–92 Division 1; 1992– FA Premier League.

Honours: Football League: Division 1 – Champions 1954–55; Division 2 – Champions 1983–84, 1988–89; Runners-up 1906–07, 1911–12, 1929–30, 1962–63, 1976–77. *FA Cup:* Winners 1970, 1997; Runners-up 1915, 1967, 1994. *Football League Cup:* Winners 1965; Runners-up 1972. *Full Members' Cup:* Winners 1986. *Zenith Data Systems Cup:* Winners 1990. **European Competitions:** *European Fairs Cup:* 1958–60, 1965–66, 1968–69; *European Cup-Winners' Cup:* 1970–71 (winners), 1971–72, 1994–95.

Colours: Royal blue with white and amber trim shirts and shorts, white stockings with royal blue and amber trim. *Change colours:* Yellow with sky blue/royal blue trim shirts and shorts, yellow stockings with sky blue trim.

Did you know?
After winning the Football League Championship in 1954–55, Chelsea played the full Dutch national team in Amsterdam and drew 2–2 before a crowd of 55,000, Derek Saunders and Roy Bentley scoring.

CHELSEA 1996–97 LEAGUE RECORD

Match No.	Date	Venue	Opponents	Result	H/T Score	Lg. Pos.	Goalscorers	Attendance
1	Aug 18	A	Southampton	D	0-0	0-0	—	15,186
2	21	H	Middlesbrough	W	1-0	0-0	—	Di Matteo [86]	28,272
3	24	H	Coventry C	W	2-0	1-0	Leboeuf [29], Vialli [74]	25,024
4	Sept 4	A	Arsenal	D	3-3	2-1	—	Leboeuf (pen) [6], Vialli [30], Wise [90]	38,132
5	7	A	Sheffield W	W	2-0	1-0	2	Burley [28], Myers [83]	30,983
6	15	H	Aston Villa	D	1-1	1-1	3	Leboeuf [45]	27,729
7	21	A	Liverpool	L	1-5	0-3	7	Leboeuf (pen) [85]	40,739
8	28	H	Nottingham F	D	1-1	0-0	6	Vialli [51]	26,996
9	Oct 12	A	Leicester C	W	3-1	0-1	6	Vialli [48], Di Matteo [64], Hughes M [80]	20,766
10	19	H	Wimbledon	L	2-4	1-2	6	Minto [9], Vialli (pen) [84]	27,589
11	26	H	Tottenham H	W	3-1	1-1	6	Gullit [27], Lee (pen) [52], Di Matteo [89]	28,318
12	Nov 2	A	Manchester U	W	2-1	1-0	5	Duberry [31], Vialli [61]	55,198
13	16	A	Blackburn R	D	1-1	0-0	5	Petrescu [82]	27,229
14	23	H	Newcastle U	D	1-1	1-1	5	Vialli [24]	29,056
15	Dec 1	A	Leeds U	L	0-2	0-2	7		32,596
16	7	H	Everton	D	2-2	1-2	7	Zola [12], Vialli [55]	27,920
17	15	A	Sunderland	L	0-3	0-1	7		19,617
18	21	H	West Ham U	W	3-1	3-1	8	Hughes M 2 [6, 35], Zola [10]	27,012
19	26	A	Aston Villa	W	2-0	0-0	7	Zola 2 [66, 70]	39,339
20	28	H	Sheffield W	D	2-2	2-1	7	Zola [9], Hughes M [23]	26,608
21	Jan 1	H	Liverpool	W	1-0	1-0	7	Di Matteo [43]	27,291
22	11	A	Nottingham F	L	0-2	0-1	7		28,358
23	18	H	Derby Co	W	3-1	2-1	6	Wise [36], Leboeuf (pen) [44], Hughes P [85]	27,639
24	Feb 1	A	Tottenham H	W	2-1	1-0	5	Campbell (og) [1], Di Matteo [53]	33,027
25	22	H	Manchester U	D	1-1	1-0	7	Zola [2]	28,324
26	Mar 1	A	Derby Co	L	2-3	1-0	7	Minto [16], Leboeuf [54]	18,039
27	5	H	Blackburn R	D	1-1	0-0	—	Minto [63]	25,784
28	12	A	West Ham U	L	2-3	1-0	—	Vialli [26], Hughes M [87]	24,502
29	16	H	Sunderland	W	6-2	2-0	7	Zola [38], Sinclair [43], Petrescu [51], Hughes M 2 [78, 89], Di Matteo [90]	22,762
30	19	H	Southampton	W	1-0	1-0	—	Zola [22]	26,235
31	22	A	Middlesbrough	L	0-1	0-0	6		29,811
32	Apr 5	H	Arsenal	L	0-3	0-1	6		26,923
33	9	A	Coventry C	L	1-3	1-0	—	Hughes P [43]	19,889
34	16	A	Newcastle U	L	1-3	0-3	—	Burley [62]	36,320
35	19	H	Leicester C	W	2-1	1-0	7	Minto [13], Hughes M [73]	26,400
36	22	A	Wimbledon	W	1-0	1-0	—	Petrescu [14]	14,601
37	May 3	H	Leeds U	D	0-0	0-0	6		27,135
38	11	A	Everton	W	2-1	2-0	6	Wise [14], Di Matteo [36]	38,321

Final League Position: 6

GOALSCORERS

League (58): Vialli 9 (1 pen), Hughes M 8, Zola 8, Di Matteo 7, Leboeuf 6 (3 pens), Minto 4, Petrescu 3, Wise 3, Burley 2, Hughes P 2, Duberry 1, Gullit 1, Lee 1 (pen), Myers 1, Sinclair 1, own goal 1.
Coca-Cola Cup (6): Spencer 2, Hughes M 1, Minto 1, Morris 1, Petrescu 1.
FA Cup (17): Hughes M 5, Zola 4, Wise 3, Vialli 2, Burley 1, Di Matteo 1, Leboeuf 1 (pen).

Kharine D 5	Petrescu D 34	Myers A 15+3	Johnsen E 14+4	Leboeuf F 26	Clarke S 31	Burley C 26+5	Di Matteo R 33+1	Vialli G 23+5	Hughes M 32+3	Wise D 27+4	Morris J 6+6	Minto S 24+1	Duberry M 13+2	Spencer J —+4	Hitchcock K 10+2	Nicholls M 3+5	Newton E 13+2	Gullit R 6+6	Lee D 1	Phelan T 1+2	Grodas F 20+1	Zola G 22+1	Sinclair F 17+3	Clement N 1	Hughes P 8+4	Colgan N 1	Parker P 1+3	Granville D 3+2	Forrest C 2+1	Sheerin J —+1	Match No.
1	2	3	4	5	6	7^{1}	8	9	10	11	12																				1
1	2			4	5	6	8	9	10	11	7	3																			2
1	2	3^{2}	4	5	6	12	8	9	10	11	7^{1}	13																			3
1	2	3	4	5^{1}	6	7^{2}	8	9	10	11		12	13																		4
1^{6}	2	3	4	5	6	7	8	9	10	11				15																	5
	2	3	4^{1}	5	6	7^{2}	8	9	10	11	12		13		1																6
	2	3^{2}		5	6	7	8	9	10	11	4^{1}	13	12		1																7
	2			5	6	7	8	9	10	11		3	4		1																8
	2	3	4	5	6	7	8	12	10	11^{2}			13		1			9^{1}													9
	2		4	5	6	7^{2}	8	9	10	12		3^{2}	13		1	14	11^{1}														10
	2		12	6^{1}	13	8	9	10	11			3	4		1	14					7^{2}	5^{3}									11
	2			5	6	7	8	9	10	11		3	4		1																12
	2			6	5	8	9	10	11^{1}			3	4	12	1	7															13
	2			5	6	8^{1}	9	10	11			3	4	12	1	7															14
	2			5	6	8^{1}	9	10^{3}	11^{2}			3	4	13	1	12	14						7								15
	2			5	6	12	9^{2}		11			3^{1}	4		10	8					1	13	7								16
	11^{3}			2	6^{1}	12		13	10			3	4		8	9					1	5	7								17
	2	12			6	7^{2}	8		10				4		9	5					1	13	11			3^{1}					18
	2	3^{1}			6	7	8		10				4		9	5	12				1		11								19
	2				6	7	8		10	12			4		9^{1}	5	3				1		11								20
	2			5	6	7	8		10	12		3^{1}	4		9						1		11								21
	2	3^{1}		5		7^{2}	8	12	10	13			4		9	6					1		11								22
	2	3	12	5		4^{1}	8		10	11^{2}					1	6	13				9		7								23
	2		12	5	6		8		10	11		3			1		7^{1}				9		4								24
	2^{2}		12	5	6		8		10	11		3^{1}			1^{6}		9	13			15		7		4						25
	2			5	6		8	9^{2}	10	11	12	3					14	13^{3}			1		4		7^{1}						26
	2^{1}	6		5		12	8	13	10	11	14	3									1	7^{2}	4		9^{5}						27
	2^{1}		5		6	8		9	12	11		3									1	7	4		10	1					28
	2	5^{2}			6	7	8	12	10	11		3									1	9^{1}	4					13			29
	2		5		6	3	8		10	11											1	7	4		9^{1}		12				30
	2^{3}		5^{1}		6	7	8^{2}	9	12	11		3									1	10	4		13	14					31
	2	12	4^{3}		6	7		9			8	3^{2}			13						1	11	10			5^{1}	14				32
				5	6	2		8	12	10^{2}		3				7					1	11	4		9^{1}		13				33
	12	6	5		2	8			10^{2}	7		3^{3}			13						1^{6}	11	4		9^{1}				15		34
	2			5		11	8	9	10^{2}	7^{1}		3^{3}			13						12	4	14		6	1					35
	2	3		5		7		9			12	8										11^{2}	4	10^{1}		6	1	13			36
	2			5			8^{2}	9	10	11	12	3	7^{1}									1	4		13	6					37
	2			5	6	12	8^{1}	9^{6}	10^{2}	11		3	15	13	7						1		4								38

Coca-Cola Cup

Second Round	Blackpool	(a)	4-1
		(h)	1-3
Third Round	Bolton W	(a)	1-2

FA Cup

Third Round	WBA	(h)	3-0
Fourth Round	Liverpool	(h)	4-2
Fifth Round	Leicester C	(a)	2-2
		(h)	1-0
Sixth Round	Portsmouth	(a)	4-1
Semi Final	Wimbledon (at Highbury)		3-0
Final	Middlesbrough (at Wembley)		2-0

CHESTER CITY 1996–97 *Back row (left to right):* Kevin Noteman, Andy Milner, Chris Knowles, Nick Richardson, Ronnie Sinclair, Roger Preece, Dave Rogers. *Middle row:* Dave Fogg (Youth Team Coach), Greg Brown, Julian Alsford, Dave Flitcroft, Mattie Woods, Spencer Whelan, John Murphy, Stuart Walker (Physio). *Front row:* Iain Jenkins, Stuart Rimmer, Peter Jackson, Gary Shelton (Assistant Manager), Kevin Ratcliffe (Manager), Chris Priest, Ross Davidson, Neil Fisher. (Photograph: Dale Miles)

Division 3   **CHESTER CITY**

The Deva Stadium, Bumpers Lane, Chester CH1 4LT. Telephone: (01244) 371376, 371809. Fax: (01244) 390265. Commercial: (01244) 390243.

Ground capacity: 6000.

Record attendance: 20,500 v Chelsea, FA Cup 3rd rd (replay), 16 January 1952 (at Sealand Road).

Record receipts: £30,609 v Sheffield W, FA Cup 4th rd, 31 January 1987.

Pitch measurements: 115yd×75yd.

Club Patron: Duke of Westminster. *Honorary President:* C. Thompson.

Chairman: M. S. Guterman. *Manager:* Kevin Ratcliffe.

General Manager: Bill Wingrove. *Honorary Vice-Presidents:* J. F. Kane, L. Lloyd, Dr. M. D. Swallow.

Secretary: Derek Barber JP, AMIPD. *Physio:* Stuart Walker.

Year Formed: 1884. *Turned Professional:* 1902. *Ltd Co.:* 1909.

Previous Name: Chester until 1983.

Club Nickname: 'Blues' and 'City'.

Previous Grounds: Faulkner Street; Old Showground; 1904, Whipcord Lane; 1906, Sealand Road; 1990, Moss Rose Ground, Macclesfield; 1992, The Stadium, Bumpers Lane.

Foundation: All students of soccer history have read about the medieval games of football in Chester, but the present club was not formed until 1884 through the amalgamation of King's School Old Boys with Chester Rovers. For many years Chester were overshadowed in Cheshire by Northwich Victoria and Crewe Alexandra who had both won the Senior Cup several times before Chester's first success in 1894–95.

First Football League game: 2 September 1931, Division 3 (N), v Wrexham (a) D 1-1 – Johnson; Herod, Jones; Keeley, Skitt, Reilly; Thompson, Ranson, Jennings (1), Cresswell, Hedley.

Record League Victory: 12–0 v York C, Division 3 (N), 1 February 1936 – Middleton; Common, Hall; Wharton, Wilson, Howarth; Horsman (2), Hughes, Wrightson (4), Cresswell (2), Sargeant (4).

Record Cup Victory: 6–1 v Darlington, FA Cup 1st rd, 25 November 1933 – Burke; Bennett, Little; Pitcairn, Skitt, Duckworth; Armes (3), Whittam, Mantle (2), Cresswell (1), McLachlan.

Record Defeat: 2–11 v Oldham Ath, Division 3 (N), 19 January 1952.

Most League Points (2 for a win): 56, Division 3 (N), 1946–47 and Division 4, 1964–65.

Most League Points (3 for a win): 84, Division 4, 1985–86.

Most League Goals: 119, Division 4, 1964–65.

Highest League Scorer in Season: Dick Yates, 36, Division 3 (N), 1946–47.

Most League Goals in Total Aggregate: Stuart Rimmer, 125, 1985–88, 1991–97.

Most Capped Player: Bill Lewis, 7 (30), Wales.

Most League Appearances: Ray Gill, 408, 1951–62.

Record Transfer Fee Received: £300,000 from Liverpool for Ian Rush, May 1980.

Record Transfer Fee Paid: £94,000 to Barnsley for Stuart Rimmer, August 1991.

Football League Record: 1931 Elected Division 3 (N); 1958–75 Division 4; 1975–82 Division 3; 1982–86 Division 4; 1986–92 Division 3; 1992–93 Division 2; 1993–94 Division 3; 1994–95 Division 2; 1995– Division 3.

Honours: Football League: Division 3 – Runners-up 1993–94; Division 3 (N) – Runners-up 1935–36; Division 4 – Runners-up 1985–86. *FA Cup:* best season: 5th rd, 1977, 1980. *Football League Cup:* Semi-final 1975. *Welsh Cup:* Winners 1908, 1933, 1947. *Debenhams Cup:* Winners 1977.

Colours: Blue and white striped shirts, blue shorts, blue stockings. *Change colours:* Green and black check.

Did you know?
Although Stuart Rimmer is Chester City's all-time leading goalscorer, he did not achieve his first goal in the FA Cup until 16 November 1996 when he scored twice against Stalybridge Celtic.

CHESTER CITY 1996–97 LEAGUE RECORD

Match No.	Date	Venue	Opponents	Result	H/T Score	Lg. Pos.	Goalscorers	Attendance
1	Aug 17	A	Brighton & HA	L 1-2	1-0	—	Murphy [23]	5263
2	24	H	Cambridge U	D 1-1	1-1	17	Shelton [6]	1923
3	27	H	Swansea C	W 2-0	1-0	—	Shelton [36], Milner [78]	1946
4	31	A	Wigan Ath	L 2-4	1-1	16	Milner [13], Noteman [80]	3854
5	Sept 7	H	Lincoln C	W 4-1	2-1	8	Rimmer 2 [2, 79], Davidson [44], Noteman (pen) [58]	1802
6	10	H	Rochdale	W 1-0	0-0	—	Shelton [74]	1774
7	14	A	Torquay U	D 0-0	0-0	7		2341
8	21	H	Scunthorpe U	W 1-0	0-0	5	Fisher [87]	1901
9	28	A	Hartlepool U	L 0-2	0-2	6		2042
10	Oct 1	H	Northampton T	W 2-1	0-0	—	Flitcroft [55], Noteman [79]	1791
11	12	A	Scarborough	D 0-0	0-0	8		2352
12	15	A	Leyton Orient	D 0-0	0-0	—		3115
13	19	H	Exeter C	W 2-1	1-0	7	Helliwell [10], Milner [89]	1941
14	26	H	Hereford U	L 1-3	1-2	8	Noteman [14]	2301
15	29	A	Carlisle U	L 1-3	1-0	—	Noteman [37]	4187
16	Nov 2	A	Doncaster R	W 1-0	0-0	7	Jackson [77]	1534
17	9	H	Hull C	D 0-0	0-0	10		2085
18	22	H	Colchester U	L 1-2	0-2	—	Whelan [53]	2028
19	26	H	Cardiff C	L 0-1	0-0	—		1540
20	30	A	Hereford U	W 2-1	1-0	10	Norton (og) [30], Flitcroft [90]	2210
21	Dec 3	H	Fulham	D 1-1	0-0	—	Reid (pen) [68]	1762
22	14	H	Darlington	W 2-1	1-0	7	McDonald 2 [21, 53]	2073
23	21	A	Barnet	W 2-1	1-0	5	Noteman (pen) [40], McDonald [88]	1581
24	Jan 11	H	Hartlepool U	D 0-0	0-0	9		1885
25	14	H	Rochdale	D 0-0	0-0	—		1679
26	18	A	Northampton T	L 1-5	1-3	10	Noteman [28]	4434
27	28	A	Lincoln C	D 0-0	0-0	—		2330
28	Feb 1	A	Hull C	L 0-1	0-0	14		2513
29	4	A	Mansfield T	W 2-0	1-0	—	Flitcroft [24], McDonald [66]	1688
30	8	H	Doncaster R	W 6-0	2-0	10	Milner 4 [7, 34, 50, 73], Alsford [47], Jones (pen) [83]	2347
31	14	A	Colchester U	D 0-0	0-0	—		3855
32	18	A	Scunthorpe U	W 2-0	1-0	—	Flitcroft [10], Priest [59]	1524
33	22	H	Mansfield T	W 1-0	1-0	7	Noteman [31]	2385
34	25	H	Carlisle U	D 1-1	1-0	—	Noteman [34]	2750
35	Mar 1	A	Fulham	D 1-1	1-0	6	Priest [29]	5780
36	8	H	Barnet	W 1-0	0-0	6	Campbell (og) [65]	2291
37	11	H	Torquay U	D 0-0	0-0	—		2064
38	15	A	Darlington	D 1-1	1-1	5	Milner [44]	2348
39	22	A	Cambridge U	D 2-2	2-2	5	Rimmer [9], Milner [45]	3044
40	29	H	Brighton & HA	W 2-1	0-1	5	Woods [55], Milner [77]	3613
41	31	A	Swansea C	L 1-2	0-1	5	Alsford [59]	6284
42	Apr 5	H	Wigan Ath	D 1-1	1-0	5	Flitcroft [34]	4005
43	12	A	Cardiff C	L 0-1	0-1	8		4079
44	19	A	Scarborough	W 1-0	1-0	6	Milner [14]	2311
45	26	A	Exeter C	W 5-1	0-1	5	Davidson [53], McDonald 2 [57, 63], Milner [80], Flitcroft [86]	4300
46	May 3	H	Leyton Orient	L 0-1	0-1	6		3622

Final League Position: 6

GOALSCORERS

League (55): Milner 12, Noteman 9 (2 pens), Flitcroft 6, McDonald 6, Rimmer 3, Shelton 3, Alsford 2, Davidson 2, Priest 2, Fisher 1, Helliwell 1, Jackson 1, Jones 1 (pen), Murphy 1, Reid 1 (pen), Whelan 1, Woods 1, own goals 2.
Coca-Cola Cup (1): Noteman 1.
FA Cup (4): Milner 2, Rimmer 2.

Sinclair R 37	Davidson R 40	Rogers D 4 + 1	Fisher N 19 + 10	Jackson P 32	Alsford J 43	Richardson N 9	Priest C 30 + 2	Murphy J 4 + 7	Milner A 38 + 8	Noteman K 30 + 5	Rimmer S 22 + 3	Shelton G 18 + 4	Jenkins I 39	Knowles C 2	Cutler N 5	Woods M 9 + 12	Flitcroft D 30 + 2	Brown G — + 1	Helliwell I 8 + 1	Whelan S 18 + 7	Reid S 27	McDonald R 22	Jones J 3 + 14	Aiston S 14	Tallon G 1	Brown W 2	Match No.
1	2²	3	4	5	6	7	8	9	10	11¹	12	13															1
1		3	4	5	6	7		9	10	11			8	2													2
		3	4	5	6	7		9	10	12	11		8¹	2	1												3
		3	13	5	6	7	8	9¹	10	12	11		4²	2	1												4
	2		12	5	6		8	13	10²	11	9		4¹	3	1	14	7³										5
	2		12	5	6		8	13	10²	11	9		4¹	3	1		7										6
	2		12	5	6		8	13	10	11¹	9		4	3²	1		7										7
	2	12	3	5	6	4	8	13	10²	11	9³	14			1		7¹										8
	2		12	5	6	8¹			10	11	9		4	3	1		7										9
1	2		4	5	6				10	11	9	8¹	3			12	7										10
1	2		4				8		10¹	11			3			12	7			5		9					11
1	2		4¹	5	6		8		10	11			3			12	7					9					12
1	2		4	5	6		8¹		10	11			3			12	7					9					13
1	2		4	5³	6				10¹	11	12	8	3			13	7					9²	14				14
1	2		4²		6				10¹	11	12	8	3			13	7					9	5				15
1	2		12	5	6		13		10²	11		8¹	3				7				4	9³	14				16
1	2		12	5	6		13		10	11		8¹	3				7				4	9²					17
1	2	3	12	5			8		10	11							7				4¹	9	6				18
	2	3		5	6		8		10	11	12						7			13	4²	9¹				1	19
1	2		11	5	6		8		10¹		12		3				7			13	4	9²					20
1	2		11	5	6		8		10¹		12		3				7				4	9¹					21
1	2		11	5	6		8		10		12		3				7				4	9¹					22
1	2		8		6				10	11¹	12		3				7			5	4	9					23
1			11²	5	6	7¹	8		10		12		3							13	4	9	2				24
1			11	5	6¹	7	8		10		12		3								4	9	2				25
1	2		7¹	5	6		8		10	11	12		3								4	9					26
1	2			5	6		8		10¹	11			3			12	7				4	9					27
1	2²		12	5	6		8		10	11¹			3				7			13	4	9					28
1			12	5	6		8		10	11¹			3				7			13	2	4	9²				29
1	2			5²	6		8¹		10	11			3			12	7			13	4	9¹	14				30
1	2			5	6		8		10¹	11			3			12	7				4	9					31
1	2¹			5	6		8		10	11			3			12	7³			13	4	9²	14				32
1	2			5	6		8		10	11	12		3							13	4	9¹	7²				33
1	2			5	6		8		10	11			3			12	7				4	9¹					34
1	2			5	6		8		10	11			3			12	7			5	4	9¹					35
1	2			5	6		8		10	11	12		3				7			13	4¹	9²					36
1	2			5	6		8		10	11¹			3			12	7			13	4	9²					37
1	2			5	6		8	9¹	10²	11			3			12	7			13	4						38
1	2²			5	6		8	9³	10		12		3			13	7				4	14	11¹				39
1					6		8	9¹	10				3			2	7				4	12	11	5			40
1	2			5	6		8		10		12		3				7				4	9¹	11				41
1	2				6		8		10				3		4					5		9	11				42
1	2			5	6		8		10				3			12	7				4	9¹	11				43
1	2			5	6		8		10²		12	13	3				7				4	9¹	11				44
1	2	12		5	6		8		10²			13	3				7				4	9³	14	11¹			45
	2			5	6		8		10		12		3				7¹			13	4	9²	11			1	46

Coca-Cola Cup
First Round   Carlisle U   (a)   0-1
                                        (h)   1-3

FA Cup
First Round   Stalybridge C   (h)   3-0
Second Round   Boston U   (h)   1-0
Third Round   Middlesbrough   (a)   0-6

CHESTERFIELD 1996–97 *Back row (left to right):* Tony Lormor, James Lomas, Mark Jules, Lee Rogers, Chris Beaumont, Gary Lund. *Middle row:* Mark Williams, Kevin Davies, Andrew Morris, Andy Beasley, Billy Mercer, Sean Dyche, Darren Carr, Nicky Law. *Front row:* Tom Curtis, Chris Perkins, Phil Robinson, Dave Rushbury (Physio), John Duncan (Manager), Kevin Randall (Assistant Manager), Jonathan Howard, Paul Holland, Jamie Jewitt.

Division 2   **CHESTERFIELD**

Recreation Ground, Chesterfield S40 4SX. Telephone: (01246) 209765. Fax: (01246) 556799. Commercial Dept: (01246) 231535. Spireites Hotline: (0891) 555818.

Ground capacity: 8880.

Record attendance: 30,968 v Newcastle U, Division 2, 7 April 1939.

Record receipts: £45,000 v Mansfield T, Division 3 play-off semi-final, 17 May 1995.

Pitch measurements: 113yd × 71yd.

President: His Grace the Duke of Devonshire MC, DL, JP.

Chairman: J. Norton Lea. *Vice-Chairman:* B. W. Hubbard.

Directors: R. F. Pepper, M. L. Warner.

Manager: John Duncan.

Physio: Dave Rushbury. *Assistant Manager:* Kevin Randall.

Secretary: Nicola Bellamy. *Commercial Manager:* Jim Brown. *Stadium Manager:* W. W. Kenworthy.

Year Formed: 1866. *Turned Professional:* 1891. *Ltd Co:* 1871.

Previous Names: Chesterfield Town.

Club Nickname: 'Blues' or 'Spireites'.

Foundation: Chesterfield are fourth only to Stoke, Notts County and Nottingham Forest in age for they can trace their existence as far back as 1866, although it is fair to say that they were somewhat casual in the first few years of their history playing only a few friendlies a year. However, their rules of 1871 are still in existence showing an annual membership of 2s (10p), but it was not until 1891 that they won a trophy (the Barnes Cup) and followed this a year later by winning the Sheffield Cup, Barnes Cup and the Derbyshire Junior Cup.

First Football League game: 2 September 1899, Division 2, v Sheffield W (a) L 1-5 – Hancock; Pilgrim, Fletcher; Ballantyne, Bell, Downie; Morley, Thacker, Gooing, Munday (1), Geary.

Record League Victory: 10–0 v Glossop NE, Division 2, 17 January 1903 – Clutterbuck; Thorpe, Lerper; Haig, Banner, Thacker; Tomlinson (2), Newton (1), Milward (3), Munday (2), Steel (2).

Record Cup Victory: 5–0 v Wath Ath (away), FA Cup 1st rd, 28 November 1925 – Birch; Saxby, Dennis; Wass, Abbott, Thompson; Fisher (1), Roseboom (1), Cookson (2), Whitfield (1), Hopkinson.

Record Defeat: 0–10 v Gillingham, Division 3, 5 September 1987.

Most League Points (2 for a win): 64, Division 4, 1969–70.

Most League Points (3 for a win): 91, Division 4, 1984–85.

Most League Goals: 102, Division 3 (N), 1930–31.

Highest League Scorer in Season: Jimmy Cookson, 44, Division 3 (N), 1925–26.

Most League Goals in Total Aggregate: Ernie Moss, 161, 1969–76, 1979–81 and 1984–86.

Most Capped Player: Walter McMillen, 4 (7), Northern Ireland.

Most League Appearances: Dave Blakey, 613, 1948–67.

Record Transfer Fee Received: £200,000 from Wolverhampton W for Alan Birch, August 1981.

Record Transfer Fee Paid: £150,000 to Carlisle U for Phil Bonnyman, March 1980.

Football League Record: 1899 Elected to Division 2; 1909 failed re-election; 1921–31 Division 3 (N); 1931–33 Division 2; 1933–36 Division 3 (N); 1936–51 Division 2; 1951–58 Division 3 (N); 1958–61 Division 3; 1961–70 Division 4; 1970–83 Division 3; 1983–85 Division 4; 1985–89 Division 3; 1989–92 Division 4; 1992–95 Division 3; 1995– Division 2.

Honours: Football League: Division 2 best season: 4th, 1946–47; Division 3 (N) – Champions 1930–31, 1935–36; Runners-up 1933–34; Division 4 – Champions 1969–70, 1984–85. *FA Cup:* Semi-final 1997. *Football League Cup:* best season: 4th rd, 1965. *Anglo-Scottish Cup:* Winners 1981.

Colours: Blue shirts, white shorts, blue stockings. *Change colours:* White shirts, blue shorts, white stockings.

Did you know?
Kevin Davies' hat-trick for Chesterfield in their 3-2 FA Cup victory against Bolton Wanderers on 4 February 1997 was the first such treble in the club's history and put them into the fifth round for the first time.

CHESTERFIELD 1996–97 LEAGUE RECORD

Match No.	Date	Venue	Opponents	Result		H/T Score	Lg. Pos.	Goalscorers	Attendance
1	Aug 17	A	Blackpool	W	1-0	0-0	—	Holland [55]	6014
2	24	H	Bury	L	1-2	1-1	12	Law (pen) [14]	3763
3	27	H	Walsall	W	1-0	0-0	—	Howard [77]	3561
4	31	A	Gillingham	W	1-0	0-0	4	Howard [90]	5934
5	Sept 7	H	Brentford	L	0-2	0-2	7		3643
6	10	A	Rotherham U	W	1-0	1-0	—	Howard [39]	2940
7	14	A	Luton T	W	1-0	1-0	3	Curtis (pen) [26]	4763
8	21	H	Burnley	D	0-0	0-0	4		5529
9	28	A	Bristol R	L	0-2	0-0	7		5008
10	Oct 1	H	Shrewsbury T	W	2-1	0-1	—	Williams [71], Lormor [84]	3299
11	5	H	Bristol C	D	1-1	1-1	4	Lormor [22]	4438
12	12	A	Millwall	L	1-2	1-2	7	Beaumont [25]	7765
13	15	A	Notts Co	D	0-0	0-0	—		4265
14	19	H	Crewe Alex	W	1-0	0-0	6	Scott [87]	4030
15	26	H	York C	W	2-0	0-0	4	Scott 2 [46, 73]	4009
16	29	A	Stockport Co	L	0-1	0-0	—		4831
17	Nov 2	H	Wrexham	L	2-3	1-2	9	Curtis (pen) [25], Lormor [85]	4160
18	9	H	Preston NE	W	2-1	0-1	8	Lormor (pen) [79], Williams [81]	4759
19	19	A	Plymouth Arg	W	3-0	1-0	—	Lormor [7], Davies [57], Holland [78]	4237
20	30	A	York C	D	0-0	0-0	9		3328
21	Dec 3	H	Peterborough U	W	2-1	1-1	—	Holland [34], Howard [88]	2805
22	14	A	Wycombe W	L	0-1	0-0	8		4610
23	21	H	Bournemouth	D	1-1	1-0	8	Lormor [14]	4174
24	Jan 11	A	Bristol R	W	1-0	1-0	7	Lormor [11]	3305
25	18	A	Shrewsbury T	L	0-2	0-1	9		2659
26	28	A	Burnley	D	0-0	0-0	—		7903
27	Feb 1	A	Preston NE	W	1-0	0-0	7	Morris [78]	8681
28	8	H	Wrexham	D	0-0	0-0	8		6738
29	18	H	Rotherham U	D	1-1	0-0	—	Lormor [50]	5195
30	22	H	Plymouth Arg	L	1-2	0-0	9	Howard [85]	5833
31	Mar 1	A	Peterborough U	D	1-1	0-1	12	Howard [83]	4458
32	4	H	Luton T	D	1-1	1-1	—	Davies [16]	3731
33	11	A	Bournemouth	L	0-3	0-1	—		3368
34	15	H	Wycombe W	W	4-2	2-2	12	Howard 2 [2, 85], Hewitt [45], Hanson [54]	4354
35	22	A	Bury	L	0-1	0-0	13		4162
36	29	H	Blackpool	D	0-0	0-0	15		4974
37	Apr 1	A	Walsall	D	1-1	1-0	—	Morris [7]	3784
38	5	H	Gillingham	D	2-2	1-0	13	Morris [34], Howard [90]	3926
39	8	H	Watford	D	0-0	0-0	—		4258
40	15	A	Brentford	L	0-1	0-1	—		5216
41	19	H	Millwall	W	1-0	1-0	13	Curtis [38]	5935
42	24	A	Watford	W	2-0	0-0	—	Davies [55], Page (og) [66]	6411
43	26	A	Crewe Alex	W	2-1	1-1	12	Morris [35], Ebdon [67]	4858
44	28	H	Stockport Co	L	0-1	0-1	—		8690
45	30	A	Bristol C	L	0-2	0-2	—		16,195
46	May 3	H	Notts Co	W	1-0	0-0	10	Williams [56]	5736

Final League Position: 10

GOALSCORERS

League (42): Howard 8, Lormor 8 (1 pen), Holland 4, Morris 4, Curtis 3 (2 pens), Davies 3, Scott 3, Williams 3, Beaumont 1, Ebdon 1, Hanson 1, Hewitt 1, Law 1 (pen), own goal 1.
Coca-Cola Cup (2): Gaughan 1, Lormor 1 (pen).
FA Cup (13): Davies 4, Howard 2, Beaumont 1, Curtis 1 (pen), Dyche 1 (pen), Hewitt 1, Lormor 1, Morris 1, Williams 1.

Mercer B 35	Rogers L 14+3	Jules M 41+1	Curtis T 40	Williams M 42	Dyche S 36	Beaumont C 29+4	Hewitt J 36+1	Lormor T 25+11	Holland P 24+1	Howard J 26+9	Davies K 28+6	Law N 4+3	Morris A 19+8	Gaughan S 14+4	Perkins C 26+4	Leaning A 9	Mitchell A 1+1	Morgan P 2	Scott A 4+1	Lund G 7+3	Carr D 12	Patterson G 7+2	Dunn I 10+1	Hanson D 3	Lomas J —+2	Bowater J —+1	Ebdon M 11+1	Mason A 1+1	Allison N —+2	Match No.
1	2	3	4	5	6	7	8	9	10	11^1	12																			1
1		3	4	5	6	7^1		9^2	10	13	8	2	11	12																2
1		3	4	5	6	7		9	10	11	8	2																		3
1		3	4	5	6	7		9^1	10	11	8	2	12																	4
1	3^1	11	4	5	6	7^2	2	12	10	8	13		9																	5
1	3	11	4	5	6		2	12	10	7^1	8		9																	6
1	3	11	4	5	6		2	12	10		8		9^1	7																7
1	3	11	4	5	6		2	9^1		10	8	12		7																8
1^2	3	11^3	4	5	6	12	2	9		10	8	13		7^1	14															9
	3	11	4		6	7^1	2	9		10		12		8		1														10
	3	11	4		6	7	2	9	12	10^2		5		8^1	13	1														11
	3	5	4		6	7	2^1	9	10					8	11	1	12													12
	3	5	4		6	7	2	12	8^1				10	9	11	1														13
	3		4	5	6	7^2	2	12	8				10	9^1	11	1	13													14
1	3		4	5	6	7	2	9	8				10				11													15
1	3		4	5	6	7^1	2	12	8				10^2		9					11	13									16
1	3^1		4	5	6	7^2	2	12	8	13			14		10					11	9^2									17
1	3		4	5	6		2	9	8	12^2	14		13	7						11^1	10^3									18
1	3		4	5	6		2	9	8	12	7^2		13	10^1	11															19
1	3		4	5	6		2	9	8	12	7		13		11					10^1										20
1	12	3	4^1	5	6		2	9	8	10	7		13		11^2															21
1	7	3	4	5	6		2	9			12		10^1	8	11															22
1	12	3	4	5	6		2	9	8	10^1	7		13		11^2															23
1	3		4	5	6	11^1	2	9	8	10	7		12																	24
1	3		4	5	6	11^1	2	9^2	8	10	7		13		12															25
1	3		4	5	6		2		8	10	9				11							7								26
1	3		4	5	6	12	2		8^1	10^2	9		13		11							7								27
1	3		4	5	6^1	8	2	12		10			9		11							7								28
1			4			7	2	9	6	10	8		11^1		3					5	12									29
1			4	5		7^1	2	9		10	8		11^2		3					12	6	13								30
1	12		4	5		7^1	2			13	8		14		3					9^3	6	10	11^2							31
1	3		5			7	2			12	8		9^1		4						6	10	11							32
1	3		4	5			2			10^1			8^2		11^3					12		6	7	9	13	14				33
1	3		4	5	6		2			10			9	8						11			7							34
1	3^3		5	6		7^1	2			10	8		12									4	11	13	9^2		14			35
1	3		5	6	11		2			10^1	8		9										4				7	12		36
1	3		5	6	11		2			10	8		9										4				7			37
1^2	3		5	6	11^1	2	12			10	8		9	13									4				7			38
	3		4	5			2	9	6		12				7^1	1				10			11				8			39
1	3		5		4	12	9						2^3		10^1	6				11		13					7	8^2	14	40
1^3	2	3	4^1	5				12		9			13	8^2	10					6			11				7		14	41
	3		4	5		7		9							8			2	1			6					11		10	42
	3		4	5	6	7				8			9					2	1								11		10	43
	3		4	5	6	7^2		12		13	8		9					2	1								11^1		10	44
	12	3	4	5	6	7^1		9		13			11				8	2	1	10^2										45
	3		4	5				12		9			10	13			8	2	1			6					11^2		7^1	46

Coca-Cola Cup

First Round	Stockport Co	(a)	1-2
		(h)	1-2

FA Cup

First Round	Bury	(h)	1-0
Second Round	Scarborough	(h)	2-0
Third Round	Bristol C	(h)	2-0
Fourth Round	Bolton W	(a)	3-2
Fifth Round	Nottingham F	(h)	1-0
Sixth Round	Wrexham	(h)	1-0
Semi Final	Middlesbrough		3-3
	(at Old Trafford)		
	(at Hillsborough)		0-3

COLCHESTER UNITED 1996–97   *Back row (left to right):* Chris Fry, David Gregory, Tony Adcock, Robbie Reinelt, Adam Locke, Garrett Caldwell, Peter Cawley, Carl Emberson, Tony McCarthy, Richard Wilkins, Ben Lewis, David Barnes, Tony Lock.

Front row: Brian Owen (Physio), Joe Dunne, Nicky Haydon, Simon Betts, Micky Cook (YTS Coach), Steve Wignall (Manager), Matthew Newman (Groundman's Assistant), Steve Whitton (Assistant Manager), Karl Duguid, David Greene, Paul Gibbs, Paul Dyer (Reserves Manager/Chief Scout).

Division 3   **COLCHESTER UNITED**

Layer Rd Ground, Colchester, Essex CO2 7JJ. Telephone: (01206) 508800. Fax: (01206) 508803. Club Shop: (01206) 561180. Soccer Centre: (01206) 571581. Lottery: (01206) 508820.

Ground capacity: 7190.

Record attendance: 19,072 v Reading, FA Cup 1st rd, 27 November 1948.

Record receipts: £26,330 v Barrow, GM Vauxhall Conference, 2 May 1992.

Pitch measurements: 110yd × 71yd.

Patron: The Mayor of Colchester.

Directors: Gordon Parker (Chairman), Peter Heard (Vice-Chairman), John Worsp, Peter Powell.

Managing Director: Stephen Gage.

Manager: Steve Wignall. *Assistant Manager/Coach:* Steve Whitton. *Youth Coach:* Micky Cook.

Physio: Brian Owen. *Consultant Physio:* Ray Cole.

Secretary: Mrs Marie Partner. *Marketing Manager:* John Schultz.

Commercial Manager: Brian Wheeler. *Lottery Manager:* John Cross. *Stadium Manager:* David Blacknall.

Year Formed: 1937. *Turned Professional:* 1937. *Ltd Co.:* 1937.

Club Nickname: 'The U's'.

Foundation: Colchester United was formed in 1937 when a number of enthusiasts of the much older Colchester Town club decided to establish a professional concern as a limited liability company. The new club continued at Layer Road which had been the amateur club's home since 1909.

First Football League game: 19 August 1950, Division 3 (S), v Gillingham (a) D 0-0 – Wright; Kettle, Allen; Bearryman, Stewart, Elder; Jones, Curry, Turner, McKim, Church.

Record League Victory: 9–1 v Bradford C, Division 4, 30 December 1961 – Ames; Millar, Fowler; Harris, Abrey, Ron Hunt; Foster, Bobby Hunt (4), King (4), Hill (1), Wright.

Record Cup Victory: 7–1 v Yeovil T (away), FA Cup 2nd rd (replay), 11 December 1958 – Ames; Fisher, Fowler; Parker, Milligan, Hammond; Williams (1), McLeod (2), Langman (4), Evans, Wright and 7–1 v Yeading, FA Cup 1st rd (replay), 22 November 1994 – Cheesewright; Betts, English, Cawley, Caesar, Locke (Dennis), Fry, Brown (2), Whitton (2) (Thompson), Kinsella (1), Abrahams (2).

Record Defeat: 0–8 v Leyton Orient, Division 4, 15 October 1989.

Most League Points (2 for a win): 60, Division 4, 1973–74.

Most League Points (3 for a win): 81, Division 4, 1982–83.

Most League Goals: 104, Division 4, 1961–62.

Highest League Scorer in Season: Bobby Hunt, 38, Division 4, 1961–62.

Most League Goals in Total Aggregate: Martyn King, 130, 1956–64.

Most Capped Player: None.

Most League Appearances: Micky Cook, 613, 1969–84.

Record Transfer Fee Received: £100,000 from Birmingham C for Steve McGavin, January 1994.

Record Transfer Fee Paid: £40,000 to Lokeren for Dale Tempest, August 1987.

Football League Record: 1950 Elected to Division 3 (S); 1958–61 Division 3; 1961–62 Division 4; 1962–65 Division 3; 1965–66 Division 4; 1966–68 Division 3; 1968–74 Division 4; 1974–76 Division 3, 1976–77 Division 4; 1977–81 Division 3; 1981–90 Division 4; 1990–92 GM Vauxhall Conference; 1992– Division 3.

Honours: Football League: Division 3 (S) best season: 3rd , 1956–57; Division 4 – Runners-up 1961–62. *FA Cup:* best season: 1971, 6th rd (shared record for a Fourth Division club shared with Oxford United and Bradford City). *Football League Cup:* best season: 5th rd, 1975. *Auto Windscreens Shield:* Runners-up: 1997. *GM Vauxhall Conference:* Winners: 1991–92. *FA Trophy:* Winners: 1992.

Colours: Blue and white striped shirts, white shorts, white stockings. *Change colours:* Black/red shirts, black shorts, black stockings with red trim.

Did you know?
On 20 December 1996, Tony Adcock, an 81st minute substitute for Colchester United against Cambridge United, equalised in the last minute at 2–2 for his 200th career goal.

COLCHESTER UNITED 1996–97 LEAGUE RECORD

Match No.	Date	Venue	Opponents	Result	H/T Score	Lg. Pos.	Goalscorers	Attendance
1	Aug 17	H	Hartlepool U	L 0-2	0-0	—		2942
2	24	A	Rochdale	D 0-0	0-0	22		1816
3	27	A	Darlington	D 1-1	1-1	—	Locke [44]	2906
4	31	H	Hereford U	D 1-1	0-0	22	Reinelt [79]	2723
5	Sept 7	A	Fulham	L 1-3	0-1	23	Whitton [67]	5189
6	10	A	Brighton & HA	W 2-0	1-0	—	Kinsella [24], Reinelt [53]	2540
7	14	H	Hull C	D 1-1	0-0	17	Kinsella [50]	3073
8	21	A	Leyton Orient	D 1-1	0-0	17	Fry [51]	5254
9	28	H	Doncaster R	D 2-2	2-2	19	Cawley [26], Adcock [40]	2672
10	Oct 1	A	Carlisle U	L 0-3	0-1	—		4089
11	4	A	Swansea C	D 1-1	1-1	—	Greene [4]	2531
12	12	H	Wigan Ath	W 3-1	0-1	17	Adcock [69], Gregory [76], Duguid [80]	2700
13	15	H	Barnet	W 1-0	0-0	—	Fry [81]	2732
14	19	A	Northampton T	L 1-2	1-1	15	Fry [41]	4119
15	26	A	Lincoln C	L 2-3	2-1	18	Betts (pen) [25], Duguid (pen) [44]	2768
16	29	H	Exeter C	W 1-0	0-0	—	Myers (og) [61]	2384
17	Nov 2	H	Cardiff C	D 1-1	1-0	16	Duguid [18]	3226
18	9	A	Torquay U	W 2-0	0-0	13	Reinelt [62], Abrahams [90]	2251
19	19	H	Scunthorpe U	D 1-1	0-0	—	Sertori (og) [71]	1842
20	22	A	Chester C	W 2-1	2-0	—	Taylor 2 [8, 10]	2028
21	30	H	Lincoln C	W 7-1	3-0	7	Abrahams [19], Taylor 2 (2 pens) [42, 45], Whitton [62], Adcock [83], Fry 2 [87, 90]	2738
22	Dec 3	A	Scarborough	D 1-1	1-0	—	Locke [24]	1605
23	14	A	Mansfield T	D 1-1	0-0	8	Abrahams [73]	1653
24	20	H	Cambridge U	D 2-2	0-1	—	Taylor [60], Adcock [90]	3707
25	26	A	Brighton & HA	D 1-1	1-1	9	Whitton [16]	4830
26	Jan 11	A	Doncaster R	D 0-0	0-0	11		1458
27	14	H	Fulham	W 2-1	1-0	—	Abrahams [42], Fry [71]	3820
28	18	H	Carlisle U	D 1-1	1-1	8	Adcock (pen) [4]	3588
29	25	A	Exeter C	W 3-0	2-0	7	Abrahams [16], Locke 2 [27, 56]	2666
30	31	H	Torquay U	W 2-0	1-0	—	Adcock 2 [44, 56]	3895
31	Feb 4	H	Leyton Orient	W 2-1	1-1	—	Wilkins 2 [11, 76]	3689
32	8	A	Cardiff C	W 2-1	2-0	6	Adcock [6], Whitton [21]	3912
33	14	H	Chester C	D 0-0	0-0	—		3855
34	22	A	Scunthorpe U	L 1-2	0-0	6	Whitton [89]	2738
35	28	H	Scarborough	L 1-3	1-1	—	Adcock [24]	3719
36	Mar 7	A	Cambridge U	L 0-1	0-1	—		3485
37	14	H	Mansfield T	W 2-1	2-0	—	Greene [37], Adcock [43]	3064
38	21	H	Rochdale	W 1-0	0-0	—	Abrahams [59]	3211
39	29	A	Hartlepool U	L 0-1	0-0	7		2725
40	31	H	Darlington	L 0-3	0-2	10		3604
41	Apr 5	A	Hereford U	L 0-1	0-1	12		2535
42	8	A	Wigan Ath	L 0-1	0-1	—		4571
43	11	H	Swansea C	W 3-1	1-0	—	Whitton [22], Sale [56], Abrahams [66]	3162
44	15	A	Hull C	W 2-1	2-1	—	Adcock [21], Sale [26]	2035
45	26	H	Northampton T	D 0-0	0-0	9		5956
46	May 3	A	Barnet	W 4-2	2-1	8	Lock [14], Sale [34], Forbes [56], Haydon [86]	1909

Final League Position: 8

GOALSCORERS

League (62): Adcock 11 (1 pen), Abrahams 7, Fry 6, Whitton 6, Taylor 5 (2 pens), Locke 4, Duguid 3 (1 pen), Reinelt 3, Sale 3, Greene 2, Kinsella 2, Wilkins 2, Betts 1 (pen), Cawley 1, Forbes 1, Gregory 1, Haydon 1, Lock 1, own goals 2.
Coca-Cola Cup (6): Reinelt 2, Adcock 1, Dunne 1, Fry 1, Kinsella 1.
FA Cup (1): Wilkins 1.

Caldwell G 6	Betts S 10	Barnes D 11	McCarthy T 34 + 1	Greene D 44	Cawley P 28	Kinsella M 7	Locke A 22 + 10	Whitton S 36 + 3	Adcock T 26 + 10	Fry C 31 + 11	Reinelt R 8 + 13	Dunne J 23 + 12	Wilkins R 40	Gregory D 32 + 6	Emberson C 35	Duguid K 10 + 10	Kelly T 2 + 1	Abrahams P 27 + 2	Gibbs P 18 + 2	Taylor J 8	Buckle P 24	Lock T 1 + 5	Vaughan J 5	Sale M 10	Pitcher G — + 1	Stamps S 7 + 1	Haydon N — + 1	Forbes S 1	Match No.
1	2	3	4	5	6	7	8	9	10	11^1	12																		1
1		3	4	5	6	7	8	9	10	12	11^1	2																	2
1		3	4	5	6	7	8	9	10^1		12	2	11																3
1		3		5	6	7	8^2	9	10^1	13	12	2	11	4															4
		3		5	6	7	8^1	9^1	12	13	10	2	11	4^2	1	14													5
		3	4	5	6	7		10	9	8		2	11		1														6
		3	4	5^1	6	7		10	9	8		2	11		1	12													7
		3	4	5	6	7		10^2	9	8^1		2	11	13	1	12													8
		3^2	4	5	6	7	12	10	9^4	8		2	11^1	13	1	14													9
		3^2	4	5	6	7	12	10^3	9	8^1		2	11	13	1	14													10
		3		5	6	7		9		8^1	12	2	11	4	1	10													11
		3	4	5		7		9	12	13	14	2^1	11	6	1	10^3	8^1												12
		3	4	5	6			9	12	13		2	11	7	1	10^1	8^2												13
		3	4^2	5	6			9	12	8^3	13	2	11	7	1	10^1	14												14
		3^1	4	5^2			12	9		7	13	2	8	6	1	10		11											15
			4	5	6			9		7		2	8		1	10		11	3										16
			4^3	5	6			9^2	12	7	13	2	8	14	1			11^1	3										17
				5	6	4		7	9	8		2			1			11	3	10									18
		3		5	6				10^1	13	12	2	8	4	1			11^2		7	9								19
		3		5	6	4		9		7	8	2			1			11^1	12	10									20
		3		5	6	4		9^1	12	7	8	2			1			11		10									21
		3		5	6	4		9		7^1	12	2	8		1			11		10									22
		3		5^1	6			9		7	12	2	8		1			11		10		4							23
				5	6^2			9^1	12	7	13	2	8	14	1			11^3	3	10		4							24
			4	5				9	12	7	13	2	8	14	1			11^2	3^1	10^1		6							25
			4	5			12	9	10	7	13	2	8		1			11^1	3^2		6								26
			4	5			12	9	10	7		2	8^1		1			11	3		6								27
			4	5			12	9^2	10	7	13	2	8		1			11^1	3		6								28
			4	5				9	10^2	7	12	2	8		1			11^1	3		6	13							29
1			4	5^1			7	9^1	10	13	12	2	8					11	3		6								30
			4	5			7^1	9	10	12		2	8		1			11	3		6		1						31
			4	5			12	9	10^2	7		2	8		1			11^1	3		6	13	1						32
			4	5			12	9	10^2	7^1		2	8		1			11	3		6	13	1						33
			4	5				9	12	7	13	2	8		1	10^3		11^1	3^2		6	14	1						34
			4	5			12	9	10	7		2	8^1		1		13	11^2	3		6		1						35
			4	5			8	9	10	7^1		2			1		12	11	3		6								36
			4	5			12	9	10	7^2	13	2^1	8		1			11			6^1	14							37
			4	5				9^2	10^3	7^1	13	2	8	14	1		12	11	3		6								38
			4	5				9	12	7^1	13	2	8		1			11^2	3^3		6	14		10					39
			4	5				9^2	10	7		2	8		1	13	12	11	3^1		6								40
			4	5	6^3			9	12^2	13	14	2	8		1			11	3	7				10^1					41
			4	5	6			9	12	13		2		14	1		8^2	11^1	3	7				10^3					42
			4	5	6			9	10^1	12		2			1		13	11^2	3	7	8								43
				5	6		12	9	10^1	13		2		4	1			11^2	3	7	8								44
			4^1	5	6		12	9		7	13	2^2			1			11^3	3		8	10	14						45
			4^1	5	6		12	9^2		7		2			1			11^3	3	11	8	10				13			46

Coca-Cola Cup

First Round	WBA	(h)	2-3
		(a)	3-1
Second Round	Huddersfield T	(a)	1-1
		(h)	0-2

FA Cup

First Round	Wycombe W	(h)	1-2

COVENTRY 1996–97 *Back row (left to right):* Isaias, Michael O'Neill, John Filan, Liam Daish, Steve Ogrizovic, Marcus Hall, Willie Boland.
Middle row: George Dalton (Physio), Iyseden Christie, Paul Telfer, Noel Whelan, Gary McAllister, Paul Williams, Richard Shaw, David Busst, Gary Pendrey (Reserve Team Coach).
Front row: Brian Borrows, Kevin Richardson, Peter Ndlovu, Gordon Strachan (Assistant Manager), Dion Dublin, Ron Atkinson (Manager), Eoin Jess, David Burrows, John Salako.
(Photograph: Action Images)

FA Premiership COVENTRY CITY

Highfield Road Stadium, King Richard Street, Coventry CV2 4FW. Telephone: (01203) 234000. Fax: (01203) 234099. Ticket Office: (01203) 234020. Ticket Office Fax: (01203) 234023. Sales & Marketing: (01203) 234010. Clubcall: 0891 121166. Internet: http://www.ccfc.co.uk.

Ground capacity: 23,662.

Record attendance: 51,455 v Wolverhampton W, Division 2, 29 April 1967.

Record receipts: £272,134 v Tottenham H, Coca-Cola Cup 3rd Rd, 25 October 1995.

Pitch measurements: 110yd × 75yd.

President: E. W. Grove.

Chairman: B. A. Richardson. *Deputy Chairman:* M. C. McGinnity.

Directors: A. M. Jepson, J. F. W Reason, G. Robinson MP. D. A. Higgs.

Secretary: Graham Hover.

Manager: Gordon Strachan. *Assistant Manager:* Alec Miller. *Coach:* Gary Pendrey.

Physio: George Dalton.

Director of Sales & Marketing : Mark Jones. *Stadium Manager:* Don Blair.

Club Statistician: Jim Brown.

Year Formed: 1883. *Turned Professional:* 1893. *Ltd Co.:* 1907.

Previous Names: 1883–98, Singers FC; 1898, Coventry City FC.

Club Nickname: 'Sky Blues'.

Previous Grounds: Binley Road, 1883–87; Stoke Road, 1887–99; Highfield Road, 1899–.

Foundation: Workers at Singers' cycle factory formed a club in 1883. The first success of Singers' FC was to win the Birmingham Junior Cup in 1891 and this led in 1894 to their election to the Birmingham and District League. Four years later they changed their name to Coventry City and joined the Southern League in 1908 at which time they were playing in blue and white quarters.

First Football League game: 30 August 1919, Division 2, v Tottenham H (h) L 0-5 – Lindon; Roberts, Chaplin, Allan, Hawley, Clarke, Sheldon, Mercer, Sambrooke, Lowes, Gibson.

Record League Victory: 9–0 v Bristol C, Division 3 (S), 28 April 1934 – Pearson; Brown, Bisby; Perry, Davidson, Frith; White (2), Lauderdale, Bourton (5), Jones (2), Lake.

Record Cup Victory: 7–0 v Scunthorpe U, FA Cup 1st rd, 24 November 1934 – Pearson; Brown, Bisby; Mason, Davidson, Boileau; Birtley (2), Lauderdale (2), Bourton (1), Jones (1), Liddle (1).

Record Defeat: 2–10 v Norwich C, Division 3 (S), 15 March 1930.

Most League Points (2 for a win): 60, Division 4, 1958–59 and Division 3, 1963–64.

Most League Points (3 for a win): 63, Division 1, 1986–87.

Most League Goals: 108, Division 3 (S), 1931–32.

Highest League Scorer in Season: Clarrie Bourton, 49, Division 3 (S), 1931–32.

Most League Goals in Total Aggregate: Clarrie Bourton, 171, 1931–37.

Most Capped Player: Peter Ndlovu 26 (37) Zimbabwe.

Most League Appearances: George Curtis, 486, 1956–70.

Record Transfer Fee Received: £3,750,000 from Liverpool for Phil Babb, September 1994.

Record Transfer Fee Paid: £3,000,000 to Leeds U for Gary McAllister, July, 1996.

Football League Record: 1919 Elected to Division 2; 1925–26 Division 3 (N); 1926–36 Division 3 (S); 1936–52 Division 2; 1952–58 Division 3 (S); 1958–59 Division 4; 1959–64 Division 3; 1964–67 Division 2; 1967–92 Division 1; 1992– FA Premier League.

Honours: Football League: Division 1 best season: 6th, 1969–70; Division 2 – Champions 1966–67; Division 3 – Champions 1963–64; Division 3 (S) – Champions 1935–36; Runners-up 1933–34; Division 4 – Runners-up 1958–59. *FA Cup:* Winners 1987. *Football League Cup:* best season: Semi-final 1981, 1990. **European Competitions:** *European Fairs Cup:* 1970–71.

Colours: Sky blue and navy stripes, navy shorts, navy stockings. *Change colours:* Red and navy check, navy shorts, red stockings.

Did you know?
Steve Ogrizovic overhauled George Curtis' record for Coventry City of 537 League and Cup appearances during the 1996-97 season.

COVENTRY CITY 1996–97 LEAGUE RECORD

Match No.	Date		Venue	Opponents	Result		H/T Score	Lg. Pos.	Goalscorers	Attendance
1	Aug 17	H		Nottingham F	L	0-3	0-2	—		19,459
2		21	A	West Ham U	D	1-1	1-0	—	McAllister [12]	21,580
3		24	A	Chelsea	L	0-2	0-1	19		25,024
4	Sept 4	H		Liverpool	L	0-1	0-0	—		22,949
5		7	A	Middlesbrough	L	0-4	0-2	20		29,811
6		14	H	Leeds U	W	2-1	0-1	18	Salako [57], Whelan [65]	17,298
7		21	A	Sunderland	L	0-1	0-0	18		19,340
8		28	H	Blackburn R	D	0-0	0-0	19		17,032
9	Oct 13	H		Southampton	D	1-1	0-1	19	Dublin [90]	15,477
10		19	A	Arsenal	D	0-0	0-0	19		38,141
11		26	H	Sheffield W	D	0-0	0-0	19		17,269
12	Nov 4	A		Everton	D	1-1	0-1	—	McAllister [68]	31,477
13		16	A	Wimbledon	D	2-2	0-1	18	Whelan [56], Dublin [70]	10,307
14		23	H	Aston Villa	L	1-2	0-1	18	Dublin [75]	21,335
15		30	A	Derby Co	L	1-2	1-1	19	Dublin [43]	18,042
16	Dec 7	H		Tottenham H	L	1-2	0-1	19	Whelan [60]	19,656
17		17	H	Newcastle U	W	2-1	2-0	—	Huckerby [6], McAllister [31]	22,092
18		21	A	Leicester C	W	2-0	1-0	17	Dublin 2 [11, 72]	20,038
19		26	A	Leeds U	W	3-1	3-1	15	Huckerby [30], Dublin [38], McAllister (pen) [40]	36,465
20		28	H	Middlesbrough	W	3-0	1-0	14	Huckerby [29], McAllister (pen) [64], Liddle (og) [85]	20,605
21	Jan 1	H		Sunderland	D	2-2	2-2	12	Dublin [10], Daish [28]	17,671
22		11	A	Blackburn R	L	0-4	0-3	15		24,055
23		18	H	Manchester U	L	0-2	0-0	16		23,080
24		29	A	Nottingham F	W	1-0	0-0	—	Huckerby [51]	22,619
25	Feb 1	A		Sheffield W	D	0-0	0-0	15		21,793
26		19	A	Aston Villa	L	1-2	0-1	—	Staunton (og) [78]	30,409
27		22	H	Everton	D	0-0	0-0	16		19,452
28	Mar 1	A		Manchester U	L	1-3	0-2	16	Huckerby [86]	55,230
29		3	H	Wimbledon	D	1-1	1-1	—	Dublin [37]	15,266
30		8	H	Leicester C	D	0-0	0-0	16		19,199
31		15	A	Newcastle U	L	0-4	0-2	16		36,571
32		22	H	West Ham U	L	1-3	1-2	18	Rieper (og) [9]	22,290
33	Apr 6	A		Liverpool	W	2-1	0-0	17	Whelan [65], Dublin [90]	40,079
34		9	H	Chelsea	W	3-1	0-1	—	Dublin [49], Williams [51], Whelan [58]	19,889
35		19	A	Southampton	D	2-2	0-1	15	Ndlovu [62], Whelan [74]	15,251
36		21	H	Arsenal	D	1-1	1-1	—	Dublin [2]	20,004
37	May 3	H		Derby Co	L	1-2	0-0	18	McAllister (pen) [59]	22,854
38		11	A	Tottenham H	W	2-1	2-1	17	Dublin [13], Williams [39]	33,029

Final League Position: 17

GOALSCORERS

League (38): Dublin 13, McAllister 6 (3 pens), Whelan 6, Huckerby 5, Williams 2, Daish 1, Ndlovu 1, Salako 1, own goals 3.
Coca-Cola Cup (4): Telfer 2, Daish 1, McAllister 1.
FA Cup (7): Huckerby 2, Jess 2, Whelan 2, own goal 1.

Ogrizovic S 38	Borrows B 16+7	Burrows D 17+1	Richardson K 25+3	Williams P 29+3	Daish L 20	O'Neill M 1	Whelan N 34+1	Dublin D 33+1	McAllister G 38	Salako J 23+1	Jess E 19+8	Ducros A 1+4	Genaux R 3+1	Shaw R 35	Telfer P 31+3	Isaias —+1	Strachan G 3+6	Hall M 10+3	Ndlovu P 10+10	Filan J —+1	Huckerby D 21+4	Breen G 8+1	Evtushok A 3	Boland W —+1	Match No.
1	2	3	4	5	6	7^1	8^2	9	10	11	12	13													1
1	12	3		13	6		9	10	11	4^3	8		2^1	5	7										2
1		3		12	6		8^2	9	10	11	4^1	13	2	5	7										3
1	4	3			6^1		8^2	9	10	11	7	12	2	5			13								4
1	2	3		6			8^1	9	10	11	4^2	12		5	7		13								5
1	2	6	4				8	9	10	11				5	7			3							6
1	2	3	4		6^2		8	9	10	11	12			5^1	7			13							7
1	2	5	4		6		8	9	10	11					7			3							8
1	2^3	5^1	4	12	6		8	13	10	11	9^2				7			3	14						9
1^d	12		2	3^2	6		8	9	10	11	4^1			5	7				13	15					10
1		7	4	6			8	9	10	11				5	2				3						11
1	2^2		4	3	6		8^1	9	10	11				5	7		12		13						12
1		2		3	6		8	9	10	11	4			5					7						13
1	12	3^1		4	6		8	9	10	11	7			5^2	13				2^3		14				14
1		3		6			8	9	10	11^1	4			5	2		12		7						15
1		2^1		3	6		8	9	10	11	4^7	12		5	13				7						16
1	12		8	3	6		9^2	4	10	11	13			5	2						7^1				17
1			8	3	6		9	4	10	11	12			5	2^1						7				18
1			8	3	6		9	4	10	11	12			5	2						7^1				19
1			8	3	6		9	4	10	11				5	2						7				20
1	12		8	3	6		9^1	4	10	11				5	2						7				21
1	3		8	4	6		9	10	11^1	12				5	2						7				22
1	3		4	6			9	10	11	7^1				5	2		12				8				23
1	4		8	6			9	10	11					5	2		3	12			7^1				24
1			8	6			9^1	10	11					5	2		3	12			7	4			25
1		8^1		6			9	10	7^2					5	2	12	3	13			11	4			26
1			8	6			12	9	10					5	2		3	11^1			7	4			27
1				6			8	9	10	7				5	12		3^1	13			11	4	2^2		28
1		8	3				9	4	10	7				5	2						11	6			29
1	12	8					9	4	10	13^3	7^1			5	2^2			14			11	6	3		30
1	12	8^3						4	10	7				2	11		3	13	9^2		6		5^1	14	31
1		12	8	6			9^1	4	10					2	7		3^1	13			11	5			32
1		3	5	6			9	4	10	7^1				2			13	12	8		11^2				33
1	2	3	12	6			8	9	10					5	7		4^1		11^2		13				34
1	2	3^1	12	6			8	9	10					5	4		13		11		7^2				35
1	2	3	12	4			8	9^2	10					5	7		6^1		11		13				36
1	2^1	3		6			8	9	10		13			5	7		4^7		11^3		14	12			37
1		3	4	6			8^1	9	10		12			5	2				11		7				38

Coca-Cola Cup

Second Round	Birmingham C	(h)	1-1
		(a)	1-1
Third Round	Gillingham	(a)	2-2

FA Cup

Third Round	Woking	(h)	1-1
		(a)	2-1
Fourth Round	Blackburn R	(a)	2-1
Fifth Round	Derby Co	(a)	2-3

CREWE ALEXANDRA 1996-97 *Back row (left to right):* Lee Ellison, Steven Pope, Chris Coffey, Brian Launders, Neil Cutler, Mark Gayle, Jake Leberl, Kevin Street, James Collins, Billy Barr.
Middle row: Francis Tierney, Dele Adebola, Rob Savage, Gareth Whalley, Steve Garvey, Ashley Westwood, Shaun Smith, Lee Unsworth, Chris Lightfoot, Jamie Moralee.
Front row: Steve Macauley, Danny Murphy, John Fleet (Kit Man), Steve Holland (Youth Coach), Neil Baker (Assistant Manager), Dario Gradi (Manager), Colin Little, Mark Rivers.
(Photograph: Steve Finch L.R.P.S.)

Division 1 **CREWE ALEXANDRA**

Football Ground, Gresty Rd, Crewe CW2 6EB. Telephone: (01270) 213014.

Ground capacity: 6000.

Record attendance: 20,000 v Tottenham H, FA Cup 4th rd, 30 January 1960.

Record receipts: £41,093 v Liverpool, FA Cup 3rd rd, 6 January 1992.

Pitch measurements: 112yd × 74yd.

President: N. Rowlinson.

Chairman: J. Bowler. *Vice-Chairman:* N. Hassall.

Directors: K. Potts, D. Rowlinson, R. Clayton, J. McMillan, D. Gradi.

Manager: Dario Gradi.

Secretary: Mrs Gill Palin. *Marketing Manager:* Alison Bowler.

Year Formed: 1877. *Turned Professional:* 1893. *Ltd Co.:* 1892.

Club Nickname: 'Railwaymen'.

Foundation: Crewe Alexandra played cricket before they decided to form a football club in 1877. They took the name "Alexandra" after Princess Alexandra. Crewe's first trophy was the Crewe and District Cup in 1887 and it is worth noting that they reached the semi-finals of the FA Cup the following year.

First Football League game: 3 September 1892, Division 2, v Burton Swifts (a) L 1-7 – Hickton; Moore, Cope; Linnell, Johnson, Osborne; Bennett, Pearson (1), Bailey, Barnett, Roberts.

Record League Victory: 8–0 v Rotherham U, Division 3 (N), 1 October 1932 – Foster; Pringle, Dawson; Ward, Keenor (1), Turner (1); Gillespie, Swindells (1), McConnell (2), Deacon (2), Weale (1).

Record Cup Victory: 8–0 v Hartlepool U, Auto Windscreens Shield 1st rd, 17 October 1995 – Gayle; Collins (1), Booty, Westwood (Unsworth), Macauley (1), Whalley (1), Garvey (1), Murphy (1), Savage (1) (Rivers (pen)), Lennon, Edwards (1 og).

Record Defeat: 2–13 v Tottenham H, FA Cup 4th rd replay, 3 February 1960.

Most League Points (2 for a win): 59, Division 4, 1962–63.

Most League Points (3 for a win): 83, Division 2, 1994–95.

Most League Goals: 95, Division 3 (N), 1931–32.

Highest League Scorer in Season: Terry Harkin, 35, Division 4, 1964–65.

Most League Goals in Total Aggregate: Bert Swindells, 126, 1928–37.

Most Capped Player: Bill Lewis, 12 (30), Wales.

Most League Appearances: Tommy Lowry, 436, 1966–78.

Record Transfer Fee Received: £600,000 from Liverpool for Rob Jones, October 1991.

Record Transfer Fee Paid: £80,000 to Barnsley for Darren Foreman, March 1990.

Football League Record: 1892 Original Member of Division 2; 1896 Failed re-election; 1921 Re-entered Division 3 (N); 1958–63 Division 4; 1963–64 Division 3; 1964–68 Division 4; 1968–69 Division 3; 1969–89 Division 4; 1989–91 Division 3; 1991–92 Division 4; 1992–94 Division 3; 1994–97 Division 2; 1997– Division 1.

Honours: Football League: Promoted from Division 2 1996–97 (play-offs). *FA Cup:* best season: semi-final 1888. *Football League Cup:* best season: 3rd rd, 1975, 1976, 1979, 1993. *Welsh Cup:* Winners 1936, 1937.

Colours: Red shirts, red shorts, white stockings. *Change colours:* Navy shirts with sky blue trim, sky blue shorts, navy blue stockings.

Did you know?

When Crewe Alexandra beat Billingham Synthonia 5–0 in the FA Cup first round on 27 November 1948, Jock Basford scored four goals.

CREWE ALEXANDRA 1996–97 LEAGUE RECORD

Match No.	Date	Venue	Opponents	Result	H/T Score	Lg. Pos.	Goalscorers	Attendance
1	Aug 17	H	Stockport Co	W 1-0	0-0	—	Tierney [89]	4310
2	24	A	Peterborough U	D 2-2	1-1	7	Ellison 2 [3, 61]	6357
3	27	A	Preston NE	L 1-2	0-1	—	Murphy [68]	9498
4	31	H	Watford	L 0-2	0-2	15		3655
5	Sept 7	A	Bournemouth	W 1-0	1-0	10	Savage [31]	3218
6	10	H	Bury	W 2-0	1-0	—	Tierney [43], Barr [83]	3627
7	14	H	Wrexham	W 3-1	2-1	6	Adebola 2 [24, 39], Tierney [75]	4469
8	21	A	Millwall	L 0-2	0-0	7		9320
9	28	H	Plymouth Arg	W 3-0	1-0	3	Barr [14], Adebola [61], Murphy [85]	3797
10	Oct 1	H	Blackpool	W 3-2	0-1	—	Rivers [52], Adebola [56], Macauley [69]	4314
11	4	A	Bristol R	L 0-2	0-0	—		6211
12	12	H	Brentford	W 2-0	0-0	4	Rivers [51], Smiths S (pen) [55]	4313
13	15	H	York C	L 0-1	0-0	—		3463
14	19	A	Chesterfield	L 0-1	0-0	8		4030
15	26	A	Shrewsbury T	W 1-0	0-0	8	Murphy [54]	3878
16	29	H	Rotherham U	W 1-0	1-0	—	Barr [44]	3162
17	Nov 2	H	Wycombe W	W 3-0	0-0	3	Adebola [49], Whalley [56], Murphy [60]	3636
18	9	A	Burnley	L 0-2	0-1	6		9459
19	23	H	Walsall	L 0-1	0-1	10		3653
20	30	H	Shrewsbury T	W 5-1	2-1	7	Murphy [33], Smith S [36], Rivers 2 [56, 59], Whalley [78]	4035
21	Dec 3	A	Gillingham	L 1-2	0-2	—	Rivers [71]	3575
22	14	A	Luton T	L 0-6	0-3	11		5455
23	20	H	Notts Co	W 3-0	0-0	—	Adebola 2 [53, 83], Charnock [76]	3125
24	28	H	Bournemouth	W 2-0	0-0	8	Adebola 2 [52, 56]	3585
25	Jan 11	A	Plymouth Arg	L 0-1	0-0	9		4767
26	18	A	Blackpool	W 2-1	1-1	7	Murphy [36], Adebola [80]	4760
27	25	A	Rotherham U	W 4-1	2-0	3	Adebola 2 [31, 67], Murphy [32], Smith S [49]	2832
28	Feb 1	H	Burnley	D 1-1	0-0	4	Macauley [50]	4734
29	8	A	Wycombe W	L 0-2	0-1	4		4902
30	15	H	Walsall	W 1-0	0-0	3	Murphy [47]	4648
31	22	A	Bristol C	L 0-3	0-0	5		11,306
32	Mar 1	H	Gillingham	W 3-2	3-0	4	Barr 2 [14, 26], Murphy [35]	3555
33	8	A	Notts Co	W 1-0	0-0	4	Rivers [87]	4047
34	15	H	Luton T	D 0-0	0-0	5		4475
35	18	H	Millwall	D 0-0	0-0	—		3695
36	22	H	Peterborough U	D 1-1	0-0	6	Murphy [85]	3565
37	25	H	Bristol C	L 1-2	0-1	—	Westwood [47]	3687
38	29	A	Stockport Co	L 0-1	0-1	8		7411
39	31	H	Preston NE	W 1-0	1-0	5	Adebola [41]	4407
40	Apr 5	A	Watford	W 1-0	0-0	5	Whalley [68]	12,441
41	12	H	Bristol R	W 1-0	1-0	5	Adebola [42]	4281
42	15	A	Bury	L 0-1	0-1	—		4725
43	19	A	Brentford	W 2-0	0-0	5	Adebola [59], Smith S [78]	6183
44	22	A	Wrexham	D 1-1	0-0	—	Johnson [62]	4643
45	26	H	Chesterfield	L 1-2	1-1	5	Adebola [4]	4858
46	May 3	A	York C	D 1-1	0-1	6	Westwood [54]	4366

Final League Position: 6

GOALSCORERS
League (56): Adebola 16, Murphy 10, Rivers 6, Barr 5, Smith S 4 (1 pen), Tierney 3, Whalley 3, Ellison 2, Macauley 2, Westwood 2, Charnock 1, Johnson 1, Savage 1.
Coca-Cola Cup (1): Adebola 1.
FA Cup (10): Murphy 3, Adebola 1, Garvey 1, Lightfoot 1, Macauley 1, Smith S 1, Westwood 1, own goal 1.

Gayle M 4	Unsworth L 28+1	Smith S 34+4	Westwood A 43+1	Macauley S 40+2	Whalley G 38	Little C 3+14	Savage R 41	Moralee J 7	Murphy D 44+1	Rivers M 23+4	Tierney F 18+14	Barr B 29+5	Ellison L 3	Adebola D 27+5	Launders B 6+3	Billing P 9+6	Mautone S 3	Lightfoot C 16+9	Garvey S 9+7	Taylor M 6	Johnson S 8+3	Charnock P 24+8	Kearton J 30	Smith P —+1	Anthrobus S 10	Bankole A 3	Match No.
1	2	3	4	5	6	7¹	8	9	10	11²	12	13															1
1	2	3	4	5	6		8³		10	11¹	7			9²	12	13	14										2
1	2	3	4	5	6				10	11¹	7	8		9	12												3
1	2	3	4	5	6				10	11	7	8²		9¹	12		13										4
	2	3	4	5	6	12	8		10	11¹	7²	13		9³			1	14									5
	2	3	4	5	6		8¹			7	13			9	11²	12	1										6
	2	3	4	5	6		8		10		7	13		9	11¹		1	12²									7
	2	3	4	5	6	12	8²		10	7		11¹		9					1	13							8
	2	3	4	5	6²	12	8		10	7¹		11		9					1	13							9
	2	3	4	5		12			10	7		11		9	8¹				1	6							10
	2¹	3	4	5		12			10	7		11		9	8				1	6							11
	2	3	4	5	6		8		10	7	12			9					1	11¹							12
	2	3	4	5			8¹		10	7	12	6		9					1	11							13
	2	3	4	5			8¹		10	7	12	6		9						11	1						14
		3	4	5	6		8³		10	7	9¹	2		12	13			14			11²	1					15
		3	4	5	6		8		10	7	9	2		12	11¹							1					16
		3	4	5	6²		8³		10¹	7	11	2		9	12			13			14	1					17
		3	4	5	6		8²		10	7³	11	2		9¹		13		12			14	1					18
		3	4	5	6		8		10	7	11¹	2				9					12	1					19
		3	4	5	6		8	9²	10³	7¹	11	2				13	12				14	1					20
		3	4	5	6		8¹	9	10	7	11²	2				12					13	1					21
12		3	4	5	13			9³	10			2¹		11	6	14		7²			8	1					22
	12		5	6	13		8	9²	10		2			11	3	4¹					7	1					23
			5	6			8	9¹	10		12	2		11	3	4					7	1					24
	12		4	5	6	13	8	9¹	10		14	2		11²	3¹						7	1					25
		3	4	5	6	11¹	8		10		12			9	13			2²	14		7³	1					26
		3	4	5	6	11	8		10¹		12	13		9	2						7²	1					27
3			4	5	6		8		10			11		9¹	2			12			7	1					28
3			4	5	6³		8		10	12	9²	11			2			14	13		7¹	1					29
3			4	5	6		8		10	7¹	9	11			2²			13	12			1					30
3			4	5	6		8		10			9		11	2			2	7			1					31
3	12		4		6		8		10	13		11			2			5	7²		9¹	1					32
3	4				6		8		10	12		11			2¹			5	7		9	1					33
3	2		4		6		8		10	9¹	12	11²						5	7					1	13		34
3	2		4	12	6		8		10	9		11						5¹	7					1			35
3	2		4	12	6³		8		10	9¹	13	11²						5	7			14	1				36
3	2		4		12		8		10	13	11¹							5	7			6²	1		9		37
	3¹		4		6		8		10		7	2²						5	12		13	11	1		9		38
12			4		6	13	8		10		14	11¹						5	7³		3	2	1		9²		39
12			4		6	7¹	8		10		13	11						5			3	2	1		9		40
	11		5		6	12	7	9	13			10						4			3	2¹	1		8¹		41
			4		6	7	12	8	10		13			11				5¹			3	2	1		9²		42
10	5		4	6	7		8					11									3	2	1		9		43
10	5		4	6	7		8¹	12				11									3	2			9	1	44
	2³	3	4	5	7	12	8		10			11							13			6²	14		9¹	1	45
	2	3	4	5	7	12	8¹		10			11										6	13		9³	1	46

Coca-Cola Cup
First Round   Port Vale   (a)   0-1
                                                   (h)   1-5

FA Cup
First Round   Kidderminster H   (h)   4-1
Second Round   Hull C   (a)   5-1
Third Round   Wimbledon   (h)   1-1
                                    (a)   0-2

CRYSTAL PALACE 1996-97   *Back row (left to right):* David Parry, Steven Thomson, Anthony Folan, Danny Wales, Rory Ginty, Bjorn Enqvist.
Third row: Vic Bettenelli (Kit Manager), Leon McKenzie, Danny Boxall, Anthony Scully, Carlo Nash, Chris Day, Tom Evans, Sagi Burton, David Hopkin, Andy Cyrus, Steve Kember (Reserve Team Coach).
Second row: Ray Lewington (First Team Coach), Darren Pitcher, Carl Veart, Andy Roberts, David Tuttle, Robert Quinn, Jason Harris, George Ndah, Dougie Freedman, Peter Nicholas (Youth Team Manager), Geoff Taylor (Youth Development Officer).
Front Row: Gareth Davies, Dean Gordon, Marc Edworthy, Leif Andersen, Dave Bassett (Manager), Ray Houghton, Bruce Dyer, Jamie Vincent, Simon Rodger.

FA Premiership   **CRYSTAL PALACE**

Selhurst Park, London SE25 6PU. Telephone: (0181) 768 6000. Fax: (0181) 771 5311. Lottery Office: (0181) 768 6094. Club Shop: (0181) 768 6100. Dial-A-Seat Ticketline: (0181) 771 8841. Palace Publications: (0181) 768 6093. Fax: (0181) 653 6312. Palace Clubline: 0891 400 333. Palace Ticket Line: 0891 400 334 (normal 0891 charges apply for these services). Press Office: (0181) 768 6020. Fax: (0181) 768 6114.

Ground capacity: 26,400.

Record attendance: 51,482 v Burnley, Division 2, 11 May 1979.

Record receipts: £327,124 v Manchester U, FA Premier League, 21 April 1993 (League); £336,583 v Chelsea, Coca-Cola Cup 5th rd, 6 January 1993.

Pitch measurements: 110yd × 74yd.

Directors: R. G. Noades (Chairman and Managing), B. Coleman OBE, A. S. C. De Souza, M. E. Lee, S. Hume-Kendall, P. H. J. Norman, R. E. Anderson, V. E. Murphy, S. R. Ebbs MS, FRCS, D. A. Miller, P. L. Morley CBE, JP.

Manager: Steve Coppell. **First Team Coach:** Ray Lewington.

Physio: Gary Sadler. **Stadium Manager:** Vic Worrall.

Company Secretary: Doug Miller. **Club Secretary:** Mike Hurst. **PR and Community Affairs:** Terry Byfield.

Year Formed: 1905. **Turned Professional:** 1905. **Ltd Co.:** 1905.

Club Nickname: 'The Eagles'.

Club Sponsor: TDK.

Previous Grounds: 1905, Crystal Palace; 1915, Herne Hill; 1918, The Nest; 1924, Selhurst Park.

Foundation: There was a Crystal Palace club as early as 1861 but the present organisation was born in 1905 after the formation of a club by the company that controlled the Crystal Palace (building), had been rejected by the FA who did not like the idea of the Cup Final hosts running their own club. A separate company had to be formed and they had their home on the old Cup Final ground until 1915.

First Football League game: 28 August 1920, Division 3, v Merthyr T (a) L 1-2 – Alderson; Little, Rhodes; McCracken, Jones, Feebury; Bateman, Conner, Smith, Milligan (1), Whibley.

Record League Victory: 9–0 v Barrow, Division 4, 10 October 1959 – Rouse; Long, Noakes; Truett, Evans, McNichol; Gavin (1), Summersby (4 incl. 1p), Sexton, Byrne (2), Colfar (2).

Record Cup Victory: 8–0 v Southend U, Rumbelows League Cup 2nd rd (1st leg), 25 September 1990 – Martyn; Humphrey (Thompson (1)), Shaw, Pardew, Young, Thorn, McGoldrick, Thomas, Bright (3), Wright (3), Barber (Hodges (1)).

Record Defeat: 0–9 v Burnley, FA Cup 2nd rd replay, 10 February 1909 and 0–9 v Liverpool, Division 1, 12 September 1990.

Most League Points (2 for a win): 64, Division 4, 1960–61.

Most League Points (3 for a win): 90, Division 1, 1993–94.

Most League Goals: 110, Division 4, 1960–61.

Highest League Scorer in Season: Peter Simpson, 46, Division 3 (S), 1930–31.

Most League Goals in Total Aggregate: Peter Simpson, 153, 1930–36.

Most Capped Player: Eric Young, 19 (21), Wales.

Most League Appearances: Jim Cannon, 571, 1973–88.

Record Transfer Fee Received: £4,500,000 from Tottenham H for Chris Armstrong, June 1995.

Record Transfer Fee Paid: £2,250,000 to Millwall for Andy Roberts, July 1995.

Football League Record: 1920 Original Members of Division 3; 1921–25 Division 2; 1925–58 Division 3 (S); 1958–61 Division 4; 1961–64 Division 3; 1964–69 Division 2; 1969–73 Division 1; 1973–74 Division 2; 1974–77 Division 3; 1977–79 Division 2; 1979–81 Division 1; 1981–89 Division 2; 1989–92 Division 1; 1992–93 FA Premier League; 1993–94 Division 1; 1994–95 FA Premier League; 1995–97 Division 1; 1997– FA Premier League.

Honours: *Football League:* Division 1 – Champions 1993–94; 3rd 1990–91; Promoted from Division 1, 1996–97 (play-offs); Division 2 – Champions 1978–79; Runners-up 1968–69; Division 3 – Runners-up 1963–64; Division 3 (S) – Champions 1920–21; Runners-up 1928–29, 1930–31, 1938–39; Division 4 – Runners-up 1960–61. *FA Cup:* best season: Runners-up 1990. *Football League Cup:* best season; semi-final 1993, 1995. *Zenith Data Systems Cup:* Winners: 1991.

Colours: Red and blue shirts, white shorts, white stockings. **Change colours:** Yellow shirts, blue shorts, yellow stockings.

Did you know?
Despite losing their opening match in the Southern League in 1905–06, Crystal Palace remained unbeaten thereafter and won its Second Division Championship.

CRYSTAL PALACE 1996–97 LEAGUE RECORD

Match No.	Date	Venue	Opponents	Result	H/T Score	Lg. Pos.	Goalscorers	Attendance
1	Aug 18	A	Birmingham C	L 0-1	0-1	—		18,765
2	24	H	Oldham Ath	W 3-1	3-0	11	Hopkin 2 [11, 23], Dyer [44]	12,822
3	27	H	WBA	D 0-0	0-0	—		13,849
4	31	A	Huddersfield T	D 1-1	0-1	12	Freedman [69]	11,166
5	Sept 7	A	Stoke C	D 2-2	2-2	12	Hopkin [13], Freedman [22]	13,540
6	10	H	Ipswich T	D 0-0	0-0	—		12,520
7	14	H	Manchester C	W 3-1	2-0	9	Hopkin 2 [12, 49], Andersen [31]	17,638
8	21	A	Reading	W 6-1	2-0	6	Tuttle [27], Freedman [37], Muscat [50], Dyer (pen) [56], Veart [58], Ndah [77]	9675
9	28	H	Southend U	W 6-1	2-0	5	Muscat [2], Houghton [38], Hopkin [49], Veart [53], Dyer [72], Freedman [79]	14,858
10	Oct 1	A	Portsmouth	D 2-2	1-1	—	Veart [28], Freedman [63]	7212
11	12	A	Barnsley	D 0-0	0-0	5		9183
12	16	A	Port Vale	W 2-0	2-0	—	Dyer [2], Roberts [15]	4522
13	19	H	Swindon T	L 1-2	1-1	4	Dyer (pen) [23]	15,088
14	26	H	Grimsby T	W 3-0	1-0	3	Dyer [44], Veart [55], Freedman [79]	13,665
15	29	H	Bradford C	W 4-0	2-0	—	Shipperley 2 [36, 38], Freedman [58], Hopkin [83]	10,091
16	Nov 2	A	Tranmere R	W 3-1	1-1	3	Dyer [15], Freedman [48], Hopkin [85]	8613
17	10	H	QPR	W 3-0	1-0	2	Dyer [40], Shipperley [71], Hopkin [90]	15,324
18	16	A	Bolton W	D 2-2	2-2	2	Hopkin [39], Freedman [41]	16,892
19	23	H	Wolverhampton W	L 2-3	0-2	2	Veart [51], Dyer [55]	20,655
20	30	A	Grimsby T	L 1-2	1-1	2	Shipperley [5]	5115
21	Dec 7	H	Oxford U	D 2-2	1-0	4	Dyer 2 [16, 80]	17,879
22	14	A	Norwich C	D 1-1	1-0	4	Shipperley [3]	16,395
23	17	H	Sheffield U	L 0-1	0-1	—		12,801
24	21	H	Charlton Ath	W 1-0	0-0	4	Shipperley [87]	16,279
25	26	A	Ipswich T	L 1-3	0-1	4	Gordon (pen) [65]	16,020
26	Jan 11	A	Manchester C	D 1-1	0-0	5	Ndah [83]	27,395
27	18	H	Portsmouth	L 1-2	1-0	8	Quinn [30]	15,498
28	28	A	Southend U	L 1-2	0-1	—	Freedman [68]	5061
29	Feb 1	A	QPR	W 1-0	1-0	6	Hopkin [22]	16,467
30	8	H	Bradford C	W 3-1	0-1	7	Shipperley [61], Ndah [65], Freedman [74]	14,844
31	15	A	Wolverhampton W	W 3-0	1-0	5	Tuttle [17], Veart [72], Dyer [73]	25,919
32	22	H	Tranmere R	L 0-1	0-0	6		15,396
33	Mar 1	A	Oxford U	W 4-1	1-0	6	Gordon [37], Dyer 2 [50, 82], Hopkin [63]	8572
34	4	H	Bolton W	D 1-1	0-0	—	Linighan [50]	16,035
35	8	A	Charlton Ath	L 1-2	0-0	7	Dyer [60]	15,000
36	15	H	Norwich C	W 2-0	2-0	5	Gordon (pen) [30], McKenzie [35]	17,378
37	23	A	Oldham Ath	W 1-0	1-0	5	McKenzie [3]	5282
38	29	H	Birmingham C	L 0-1	0-1	5		16,331
39	Apr 5	A	Huddersfield T	D 1-1	0-0	8	Shipperley [52]	13,541
40	9	A	WBA	L 0-1	0-0	—		12,866
41	12	A	Sheffield U	L 0-3	0-2	10		20,051
42	15	H	Stoke C	W 2-0	2-0	—	Dyer 2 [6, 21]	11,382
43	19	H	Barnsley	D 1-1	1-0	7	Shipperley [30]	20,006
44	23	A	Reading	W 3-2	1-0	—	Linighan [13], Hopkin [49], Shipperley [69]	12,552
45	26	A	Swindon T	W 2-0	1-0	6	Shipperley 2 [44, 89]	10,447
46	May 4	H	Port Vale	D 1-1	1-0	6	Roberts [12]	16,401

Final League Position: 6

GOALSCORERS

League (78): Dyer 17 (2 pens), Hopkin 13, Shipperley 12, Freedman 11, Veart 6, Gordon 3 (2 pens), Ndah 3, Linighan 2, McKenzie 2, Muscat 2, Roberts 2, Tuttle 2, Andersen 1, Houghton 1, Quinn 1.
Coca-Cola Cup (8): Hopkin 2, Veart 2, Edworthy 1, Freedman 1, Muscat 1, Quinn 1.
FA Cup (2): Dyer 1 (pen), Veart 1.

Day C 24	Boxall D 4+2	Muscat K 42+2	Roberts A 45	Tuttle D 39	Edworthy M 42+3	Quinn R 17+4	Houghton R 18+3	Freedman D 33+11	Dyer B 39+4	Veart C 35+4	Hopkin D 38+3	Andersen L 7+7	Ndah G 5+21	Pitcher D 3	McKenzie L 4+17	Mimms B 1	Nash C 21	Harris J —+2	Rodger S 9+2	Trollope P —+9	Scully T —+1	Shipperley N 29+3	Gordon D 26+4	Davies G 5+1	Cyrus A 1	Linighan A 19	Match No.
1	2^1	3	4	5	6	7^2	8	9	10	11^3	12	13	14														1
1	8	3	4	5	2	12	13	9^2	10	11^3	6		14			7^1											2
1		3	4	5	2	8		9	10^1	12	6		11^2	7	13												3
12		3	4	5	2	8		9		11	6		13	7^1	10^2	1											4
1	7^2	3	4	5	2		8	9^1	10	11	6	13	12				13										5
1	7^3	3	4	5	2		8	9	10^2	11^1	6	14	12														6
1	12	3	4	5	2^1		8	9	10^2	11	6	7	13														7
		3	4	5	2	12	8^1	9^3	10^2	11	6	7	13				1	14									8
		3	4	5^1	2	6	8^2	9	10^3	11	12	7	13				1	14									9
		3	4	5^2	2	8		9	10^1	11	6	7	12				1		13								10
1		3		5	2	4		9^3		11	6	7^2	10^1	12					8	13	14						11
1		3	4	5	2	7		9	10^1	11	6			12					8^2	13							12
1		3	4	5	2	7^2		9	10	11^3	6	13		12					8^1	14							13
1		3	4	5	2	7^1		9	10^3	11	6	12		13						14		8^2					14
1		3	4	5	2	7		9	10^1	11	6^1	12		13						14		8^3					15
1		3	4	5	2	7		9^2	10^1	11	6			12						13		8					16
1		3	4	5	2	7^3		9^2	10^1	11	6			12						13		8	14				17
1		3	4	5	2	7^2		9	10	11	6									12		8	13				18
1		3	4	5	2^1			9	10	11	6	7^2	12									8	13				19
1		3	4	5	2^1		12	9^2	10	11	6		13									8^1	7				20
1		3	4	5	2	7^2	8	12	10^2	11												9	6	13			21
1		3	4	5	2	7	9	10^2	11^2					12	13							8	6^1				22
1		3	4	5	2	6	8^3	13	10^2	11^2		7	13	12								9	14				23
1	7		4	5	2^1	6^2	13	10^2	11	12		8	14									9	3				24
1			4	5	2				10^2	11	6^2	12	8	13								9	3		7^1		25
1	7		4	5	2	6		12	10^2	11		8^1	13									9	3				26
1	7^2		4	5	2		10	12	11^1	8		13										9	3			6	27
	7		4	5	2		9^1	10^2	11	8	12						1			13			3			6	28
	7		4	5^2	2			10^1	12	11	8	13					1					9	3			6	29
	7		4	5	2		9^1	12	11	8	13						1					10^2	3			6	30
	7^2		4	5	2		10	12	11^1	8	13						1					9	3			6	31
	7		4	5^1	2	12		10	11	8							1					9	3			6	32
	7		4	5	2			10	11	8	12						1					9^1	3			6	33
	7		4	5^2	2	13		10^1	11	12	8	14					1					9^3	3			6	34
	7		4		2	12		10^1	11	5	8				9	1							3			6	35
	7		4		2	8	12	10^2	11			9^1		1			5		13			3				6	36
	7^3		4		2	8	12	10	5^2	11		9^1		1			14			13		3				6	37
	12		4	5	2^1	8	11^2	10		7		13		1								9	3			6	38
	2^1		4	5^2	13	8	12	10^1		7				1			11					9	3			6	39
	2^1		4		13	8	12	10^1		7				1			11					9	3			6	40
	12		4		2	8	13	10^2		7^1		14		1			11					9^3	3	5		6	41
			4		2	8^1	12	10		7				1			11					9	3	5		6	42
	2		4	5		8		10^2	12	7		13		1			11^1					9	3			6	43
	2		4	5	12	13		10^2	11	7				1								9	3^1	8		6	44
	2		4		11	8	10		12	7^1		13		1								9	3	5^2		6	45

Coca-Cola Cup

Second Round	Bury	(a)	3-1	
		(h)	4-0	
Third Round	Ipswich T	(a)	1-4	

FA Cup

Third Round	Leeds U	(h)	2-2	
		(a)	0-1	

DARLINGTON 1996–97 *Back row (left to right):* Simon Alderson, Sean Gregan, Paul Newell, Frank Johnson, Gary Twynham, David Faulkner, Andy Crosby, Steve Gaughan.
Middle row: Brian Atkinson, Lee Brydon, Simon Shaw, Darren Roberts, Mark Barnard, Robbie Painter, Mark Riley (Physio).
Front row: Paul Olsson, Michael Oliver, Phil Brumwell, Anthony Carrs, Jim Platt (Director of Coaching), Danny Bergara (Assistant Director of Coaching), Danny Key, Robbie Blake.

Division 3   **DARLINGTON**

Feethams Ground, Darlington DL1 5JB. Telephone: (01325) 465097. Fax: (01325) 381377.

Ground capacity: 7046.

Record attendance: 21,023 v Bolton W, League Cup 3rd rd, 14 November 1960.

Record receipts: £32,300 v Rochdale, Division 4, 11 May 1991.

Pitch measurements: 110yd × 74yd.

President: A. Noble.

Chairman: B. Lowery. *Vice-Chairman:* G. Hodgson.

Manager: David Hodgson. *Coach:* Gary Bannister.

Chief Executive/Secretary: K. J. Lavery.

Year Formed: 1883. *Turned Professional:* 1908. *Ltd Co.:* 1891.

Club Nickname: 'The Quakers'.

Foundation: A football club was formed in Darlington as early as 1861 but the present club began in 1883 and reached the final of the Durham Senior Cup in their first season, losing to Sunderland in a replay after complaining that they had suffered from intimidation in the first. The following season Darlington won this trophy and for many years were one of the leading amateur clubs in their area.

First Football League game: 27 August 1921, Division 3 (N), v Halifax T (h) W 2-0 – Ward; Greaves, Barbour; Dickson (1), Sutcliffe, Malcolm; Dolphin, Hooper (1), Edmunds, Wolstenholme, Winship.

Record League Victory: 9–2 v Lincoln C, Division 3 (N), 7 January 1928 – Archibald; Brooks, Mellen; Kelly, Waugh, McKinnell; Cochrane (1), Gregg (1), Ruddy (3), Lees (3), McGiffen (1).

Record Cup Victory: 7–2 v Evenwood T, FA Cup 1st rd, 17 November 1956 – Ward; Devlin, Henderson; Bell (1p), Greener, Furphy; Forster (1), Morton (3), Tulip (2), Davis, Moran.

Record Defeat: 0–10 v Doncaster R, Division 4, 25 January 1964.

Most League Points (2 for a win): 59, Division 4, 1965–66.

Most League Points (3 for a win): 85, Division 4, 1984–85.

Most League Goals: 108, Division 3 (N), 1929–30.

Highest League Scorer in Season: David Brown, 39, Division 3 (N), 1924–25.

Most League Goals in Total Aggregate: Alan Walsh, 90, 1978–84.

Most Capped Player: None.

Most League Appearances: Ron Greener, 442, 1955–68.

Record Transfer Fee Received: £200,000 from Leicester C for Jim Willis, December 1991.

Record Transfer Fee Paid: £95,000 to Motherwell for Nick Cusack, January 1992.

Football League Record: 1921 Original Member Division 3 (N); 1925–27 Division 2; 1927–58 Division 3 (N); 1958–66 Division 4; 1966–67 Division 3; 1967–85 Division 4; 1985–87 Division 3; 1987–89 Division 4; 1989–90 GM Vauxhall Conference; 1990–91 Division 4; 1991– Division 3.

Honours: Football League: Division 2 best season: 15th, 1925–26; Division 3 (N) – Champions 1924–25; Runners-up 1921–22; Division 4 – Champions 1990–91; Runners-up 1965–66. *FA Cup:* best season: 3rd rd, 1911, 5th rd, 1958. *Football League Cup:* best season: 5th rd, 1968. *GM Vauxhall Conference:* Champions 1989–90.

Colours: Black and white. *Change colours:* All tangerine.

Did you know?
Ron Harbertson scored seven goals in five successive FA Cup matches for Darlington in 1957–58.

DARLINGTON 1996–97 LEAGUE RECORD

Match No.	Date		Venue	Opponents	Result	H/T Score	Lg. Pos.	Goalscorers	Attendance
1	Aug	17	A	Hull C	L 2-3	1-1	—	Blake [2], Roberts [65]	4224
2		24	H	Swansea C	W 4-1	2-0	9	Roberts 2 [19, 53], Clode (og) [40], Oliver [66]	2752
3		27	H	Colchester U	D 1-1	1-1	—	Atkinson B (pen) [1]	2906
4		31	A	Doncaster R	L 2-3	1-2	15	Oliver [15], Blake [79]	2185
5	Sept	7	A	Leyton Orient	D 0-0	0-0	15		3856
6		10	H	Wigan Ath	W 3-1	1-0	—	Roberts [32], Oliver [63], Blake [81]	2601
7		14	H	Hereford U	W 1-0	1-0	6	Roberts [45]	3271
8		21	A	Carlisle U	L 0-1	0-1	10		5701
9		28	H	Fulham	L 0-2	0-1	13		3269
10	Oct	1	A	Cambridge U	L 2-5	1-2	—	Naylor [28], Roberts [84]	2509
11		5	H	Rochdale	D 1-1	0-0	15	Kelly [69]	3071
12		12	A	Hartlepool U	W 2-1	1-0	12	Naylor [35], Oliver [78]	3799
13		15	A	Cardiff C	L 0-2	0-2	—		1667
14		19	H	Mansfield T	L 2-4	1-2	17	Roberts [45], Oliver [53]	2532
15		26	A	Northampton T	L 1-3	1-0	21	Naylor [15]	4123
16		29	H	Barnet	L 0-1	0-1	—		1759
17	Nov	2	A	Scarborough	D 1-1	1-0	22	Shaw [28]	2859
18		9	A	Lincoln C	L 0-2	0-1	23		3259
19		19	H	Exeter C	L 0-1	0-0	—		1563
20		23	A	Scunthorpe U	L 2-3	0-3	23	Shaw [64], Blake (pen) [71]	2366
21		30	A	Northampton T	W 3-1	0-1	23	Shaw [46], Roberts 2 [73, 77]	2266
22	Dec	3	A	Brighton & HA	W 3-2	0-1	—	Blake [47], Naylor 2 [62, 87]	2709
23		14	A	Chester C	L 1-2	0-1	23	Atkinson B [68]	2073
24		21	H	Torquay U	L 2-3	1-1	23	Oliver [24], Naylor [86]	2971
25		28	H	Leyton Orient	D 1-1	1-1	22	Atkinson B [13]	2700
26	Jan	11	A	Fulham	L 0-6	0-1	22		5735
27		18	H	Cambridge U	W 2-0	0-0	22	Naylor [86], Blake [89]	2087
28		25	A	Barnet	D 0-0	0-0	22		1956
29	Feb	1	H	Lincoln C	W 5-2	3-0	21	Oliver [24], Kelly [26], Roberts 2 [29, 75], Brumwell [88]	2265
30		4	A	Hereford U	D 1-1	1-1	—	Blake [37]	2003
31		8	A	Scarborough	L 1-4	0-3	20	Oliver [76]	2585
32		15	H	Scunthorpe U	W 2-0	1-0	20	Naylor [3], Twynham [86]	2245
33		22	A	Exeter C	L 2-3	2-2	22	Atkinson B [21], Barbara [25]	2986
34		25	A	Wigan Ath	L 2-3	0-1	—	Twynham [77], Blake (pen) [83]	3667
35	Mar	1	H	Brighton & HA	W 2-0	2-0	20	Blake [4], Twynham [25]	2998
36		8	A	Torquay U	D 1-1	0-1	20	Roberts [51]	1762
37		15	H	Chester C	D 1-1	1-1	19	Crosby [27]	2348
38		22	H	Swansea C	D 1-1	0-1	20	Blake [64]	4176
39		29	H	Hull C	W 1-0	1-0	20	Roberts [39]	3024
40		31	A	Colchester U	W 3-0	2-0	19	Naylor 3 (1 pen) [2, 12, 73 (p)]	3604
41	Apr	5	H	Doncaster R	L 0-3	0-1	21		3071
42		8	H	Carlisle U	W 2-1	0-1	—	Roberts [57], Oliver [85]	4184
43		12	A	Rochdale	L 0-2	0-2	18		1638
44		19	H	Hartlepool U	L 1-2	1-1	19	Roberts [45]	4662
45		26	A	Mansfield T	L 1-2	1-0	20	Shutt [34]	2431
46	May	3	H	Cardiff C	W 2-1	0-0	18	Shutt [47], Roberts [78]	3686

Final League Position: 18

GOALSCORERS

League (64): Roberts 16, Naylor 11 (1 pen), Blake 10 (2 pens), Oliver 9, Atkinson 4 (1 pen), Shaw 3, Twynham 3, Kelly 2, Shutt 2, Barbara 1, Brumwell 1, Crosby 1, own goal 1.
Coca-Cola Cup (4): Roberts 2, Blake 1, Painter 1.
FA Cup (4): Brumwell 1, Crosby 1, Naylor 1, Shaw 1.

Newell P 20	Shaw S 34+4	Barnard M 35+2	Brumwell P 31+7	Crosby A 42	Gregan S 16	Twynham G 21+8	Oliver M 34+5	Roberts D 42+2	Blake R 28+2	Atkinson B 25+5	Carss A 20+9	Innes G 1+14	Brydon L 17+8	Painter R 2+4	Kelly R 13+10	Naylor G 30+7	Faulkner D 2+2	Lucas D 7	McClelland J 1	Key D —+3	Collins M —+1	Laws B 10	Robinson P —+3	Devos J 7+1	Byrne W 1+1	Barbara D 1+5	Hope M 1	Moilanen T 16	Hope R 20	Reed A 14	Hunt D —+1	Lowe K 5+2	Atkinson J 2+3	Shutt C 5+1	Speare J 3	Match No.
1	2	3	4	5	6	7	8^1	9	10^2	11	12	13																								1
1	2	3	4^3	5	6	7	8	9	10^2	11	12	13	14																							2
1	2	3	4	5	6	11^1	7^2	9	10	8	12	13																							3
1	2	3	4^2	5^1	6	11	7	9	10	8	12	13		14																						4
1		2	5	6	4	7^2	9^1	12		10	13	3	8	11																						5
1	3	2	5	6	4	7	9	10^2	8^1	11		13	12																							6
1	3	2	5	6	4	7^1	9	10^2	8	11		12	13																							7
1	3	2	5	6		7	9	10	8	11	12		4^1	13																						8
1	3	2	5^2			4	7	9^1	10^3	8	11	12	6		13	14																				9
1	12	3	2^1			4	7	9		8	11^2		6		13	10	5																			10
12	3	2	5			7	9		8	11^2	4^1		6^3	14	13	10		1																		11
	3^1		2	5	6		7	9		8		13			11	10^2	14	1	4^3																	12
	3		2	5	6	4^2	7	9		8^3		12	13		11	10	4	1	13																	13
	3		2	5	6		7	9		8^3		12	13		11^1	10		1	14																	14
12	3	2^2	5	6		7	9		8			4^1		11	10		1		13																	15
	2	3	8	5	6	4	12	9	13	7^1				11	10^2		1																			16
	7	3	2	5	6	4		9	10^1	8				11	12		1																			17
1	7	3	2	5		4^2	8^3			10^1	12	6		11	9	13			14																	18
1	2	3	8	5	6		9		10^1	7				11								4	12													19
1	2	3^1	7^2	5	6		8	9	10		12		13		11^3							4	14													20
1	2	3	7^1	6			8	9	10			12		11								4	5													21
1	2	3^1	7^2	5			8	9	10	13	12			11								4	6													22
1	2	3	7	5			8^2	9	10	12			13	11^1								4	6													23
1	2		9^1	5			7	13	10	8	3^2		12	11								4	6													24
1	2	12	7			13	8	9	10		14			4								7^3		6^1	13	14										25
1	2	12	7			13	8	9	10		14			11^2								6		3^1		5^3										26
	2	3	12	5			11	9^2	10				8		13							7	4					1	6^1							27
	2	3	12	5			11^2	9	10				8	13	14							7^3	4^1					1	6							28
	2	3	8^3	5		12	7	9	10				4	11^2	13											14		1	6							29
	2	3	8	5			7	9	10				4	11^1	12													1	6							30
	2	3	8	5			7	9^1	10^2	12			4	11^1	13											14		1	6							31
	2	3^1	7	5		12		9	10^3	13			4^2		8	11										14		1	6							32
2^3						12		9	10	7			4	3	8^1									13		11^2		1	5	6	14					33
2			5			12		9^2	10	7	3^3	13	8^1	14	11													1	6	4						34
2			5			7		9^1	10	8^3	3	12		13	11													1	6	4						35
1	2		12	5		7^3		9^2	10	8^1	3	13			11											14			6	4						36
	2	12	13	5		7	14	9^1	10	8^2	3^3				11													1	6	4						37
	2	3	12	5		7^1	13	14	10	8^3	11^2				9													1	6	4						38
	2	3	12	5		7^2	13	9					11		10^3													1	6	4		8^1	14			39
	2	3	8^1	5		7		9^2				11		12	10													1	6	4			13			40
	2	3	12	5		7	13	9^2				11^2			10													1	6	4		8^1		14		41
	2	3	8^1	5			7	9					11															1	6	4		12		10		42
	2	3		5			7	9	12	13			11															1	6^1	4		8^3	14	10^2		43
	3			12		2^1	9	7		4			11															5	6		8		10	1	44
			5^1	2		7	9			3^2	12	13														14		6	4		8	11	10^3	1	45
2	3		5	12		7^1	9		13				8^2															6	4		14	11^3	10	1	46

Coca-Cola Cup

First Round	Rotherham U	(h)	1-0	
		(a)	1-0	
Second Round	Leeds U	(a)	2-2	
		(h)	0-2	

FA Cup

First Round	Runcorn	(a)	4-1
Second Round	Carlisle U	(a)	0-1

DERBY COUNTY 1996–97   *Back row (left to right):* Gordon Guthrie (Assistant Physio), Jason Kavanagh, Gary Rowett, Matt Carbon, Dean Yates, Darryll Powell, Ashley Ward, Christian Dailly, Eric Steele (Goalkeeping Coach), Billy McEwan (Reserve Coach).
Middle row: Steve McClaren (Coach), Chris Boden, Lee Carsley, Darren Wassall, Russell Hoult, Martin Taylor, Ron Willems, Aljosa Asanovic, Paul Trollope, Peter Melville (Physio).
Front row: Kevin Cooper, Chris Powell, Marco Gabbiadini, Igor Stimac, Jim Smith (Manager), Robin van der Laan, Paul Simpson, Dean Sturridge, Sean Flynn.
(Photograph: Raymonds Press Agency)

FA Premiership

DERBY COUNTY

Pride Park Stadium, Derby DE24 8XL. Telephone: (01332) 667503. Fax: (01332) 667519. Clubcall: 0891 121187.

Ground capacity: 30,000.

Record attendance: 41,826 v Tottenham H, Division 1, 20 September 1969.

Record receipts: £265,162 v Coventry C, FA Cup 5th rd, 26 February 1997.

Pitch measurements: 115yd × 75yd.

Chairman: L. V. Pickering. *Vice-Chairman:* P. J. Gadsby.

Directors: J. N. Kirkland, A. S. Webb.

Manager: Jim Smith. *Chief Scout:* Bobby Roberts.

First Team Coach: Steve McClaren. *Physio:* Peter Melville. *Stadium Manager:* David Hollands.

Secretary: Keith Pearson ACIS. *Chief Executive:* Keith Loring. *Commercial Consultant:* Colin Tunnicliffe.

Year Formed: 1884. *Turned Professional:* 1884. *Ltd Co.:* 1896.

Club Nickname: 'The Rams'.

Previous Grounds: 1884–95, Racecourse Ground; 1895–1997, Baseball Ground.

Foundation: Derby County was formed by members of the Derbyshire County Cricket Club in 1884, when football was booming in the area and the cricketers thought that a football club would help boost finances for the summer game. To begin with, they sported the cricket club's colours of amber, chocolate and pale blue, and went into the game at the top immediately entering the FA Cup.

First Football League game: 8 September 1888, Football League, v Bolton W (a) W 6-3 – Marshall; Latham, Ferguson, Williamson; Monks, W. Roulstone; Bakewell (2), Cooper (2), Higgins, H. Plackett, L. Plackett (2).

Record League Victory: 9–0 v Wolverhampton W, Division 1, 10 January 1891 – Bunyan; Archie Goodall, Roberts; Walker, Chalmers, Roulston (1); Bakewell, McLachlan, Johnny Goodall (1), Holmes (2), McMillan (5). 9–0 v Sheffield W, Division 1, 21 January 1899 – Fryer; Methven, Staley; Cox, Archie Goodall, May; Oakden (1), Bloomer (6), Boag, McDonald (1), Allen. (1 og).

Record Cup Victory: 12–0 v Finn Harps, UEFA Cup 1st rd 1st leg, 15 September 1976 – Moseley; Thomas, Nish, Rioch (1); McFarland, Todd (King), Macken, Gemmill, Hector (5), George (3), James (3).

Record Defeat: 2–11 v Everton, FA Cup 1st rd, 1889–90.

Most League Points (2 for a win): 63, Division 2, 1968–69 and Division 3 (N), 1955–56 and 1956–57.

Most League Points (3 for a win): 84, Division 3, 1985–86 and Division 3, 1986–87.

Most League Goals: 111, Division 3 (N), 1956–57.

Highest League Scorer in Season: Jack Bowers, 37, Division 1, 1930–31 and Ray Straw, 37 Division 3 (N), 1956–57.

Most League Goals in Total Aggregate: Steve Bloomer, 292, 1892–1906 and 1910–14.

Most Capped Player: Peter Shilton, 34 (125), England.

Most League Appearances: Kevin Hector, 486, 1966–78 and 1980–82.

Record Transfer Fee Received: £2,900,000 from Liverpool for Dean Saunders, July 1991.

Record Transfer Fee Paid: £2,500,000 to Notts Co for Craig Short, September 1992.

Football League Record: 1888 Founder Member of the Football League; 1907–12 Division 2; 1912–14 Division 1; 1914–15 Division 2; 1915–21 Division 1; 1921–26 Division 2; 1926–53 Division 1; 1953–55 Division 2; 1955–57 Division 3 (N); 1957–69 Division 2; 1969–80 Division 1; 1980–84 Division 2; 1984–86 Division 3; 1986–87 Division 2; 1987–91 Division 1; 1991–92 Division 2; 1992–96 Division 1; 1996– FA Premier League.

Honours: Football League: Division 1 – Champions 1971–72, 1974–75; Runners-up 1895–96, 1929–30, 1935–36, 1995–96; Division 2 – Champions 1911–12, 1914–15, 1968–69, 1986–87; Runners-up 1925–26; Division 3 (N) Champions 1956–57; Runners-up 1955–56. *FA Cup:* Winners 1946; Runners-up 1898, 1899, 1903. *Football League Cup:* Semi-final 1968. *Texaco Cup:* 1972. **European Competitions:** *European Cup:* 1972–73, 1975–76; *UEFA Cup:* 1974–75, 1976–77. *Anglo-Italian Cup:* Runners-up 1993.

Colours: Black shirts with white trim, black shorts with white stripes, white stockings. *Change colours:* Yellow shirts, blue trim on sleeves, royal blue shorts with white trim, yellow stockings with blue and white trim turnover.

Did you know?
When Derby County won the Second Division Championship in 1911–12, they conceded just 28 goals and only one of them in their last eleven matches.

DERBY COUNTY 1996–97 LEAGUE RECORD

Match No.	Date	Venue	Opponents	Result	H/T Score	Lg. Pos.	Goalscorers	Attendance
1	Aug 17	H	Leeds U	D 3-3	0-1	—	Sturridge 2 [77, 88], Simpson [78]	17,925
2	21	A	Tottenham H	D 1-1	0-1	—	Dailly [90]	28,219
3	24	A	Aston Villa	L 0-2	0-1	15		34,646
4	Sept 4	H	Manchester U	D 1-1	1-1	—	Laursen [25]	18,025
5	9	A	Blackburn R	W 2-1	1-1	—	Willems [1], Flynn [85]	19,214
6	14	H	Sunderland	W 1-0	0-0	9	Asanovic (pen) [84]	17,692
7	21	A	Sheffield W	D 0-0	0-0	9		23,487
8	28	H	Wimbledon	L 0-2	0-0	11		17,022
9	Oct 12	H	Newcastle U	L 0-1	0-0	13		18,092
10	19	A	Nottingham F	D 1-1	0-1	12	Dailly [64]	27,771
11	27	A	Liverpool	L 1-2	0-0	16	Ward [89]	39,515
12	Nov 2	H	Leicester C	W 2-0	0-0	11	Ward [56], Whitlow (og) [89]	18,010
13	17	H	Middlesbrough	W 2-1	1-0	10	Asanovic [15], Vickers (og) [47]	17,350
14	23	A	West Ham U	D 1-1	1-1	11	Sturridge [43]	24,576
15	30	H	Coventry C	W 2-1	1-1	9	Asanovic (pen) [12], Ward [79]	18,042
16	Dec 7	A	Arsenal	D 2-2	0-1	11	Sturridge [62], Powell D [71]	38,018
17	16	H	Everton	L 0-1	0-0	—		17,252
18	21	A	Southampton	L 1-3	1-2	11	Dailly [8]	14,901
19	26	A	Sunderland	L 0-2	0-0	12		22,512
20	28	H	Blackburn R	D 0-0	0-0	11		17,847
21	Jan 11	A	Wimbledon	D 1-1	0-0	13	Willems [84]	11,467
22	18	A	Chelsea	L 1-3	1-2	15	Asanovic [25]	27,639
23	29	A	Leeds U	D 0-0	0-0	—		27,523
24	Feb 1	H	Liverpool	L 0-1	0-0	16		18,102
25	15	H	West Ham U	W 1-0	0-0	13	Asanovic (pen) [53]	18,057
26	19	H	Sheffield W	D 2-2	1-1	—	Sturridge [34], Stimac [71]	18,060
27	22	A	Leicester C	L 2-4	1-3	13	Sturridge 2 [2, 47]	20,323
28	Mar 1	H	Chelsea	W 3-2	0-1	12	Minto (og) [51], Asanovic (pen) [62], Ward [90]	18,039
29	5	A	Middlesbrough	L 1-6	0-1	—	Simpson [90]	29,739
30	15	A	Everton	L 0-1	0-0	14		32,140
31	22	H	Tottenham H	W 4-2	2-1	14	Van der Laan [10], Trollope [22], Sturridge [68], Ward [69]	18,083
32	Apr 5	A	Manchester U	W 3-2	2-0	12	Ward [29], Wanchope [35], Sturridge [75]	55,243
33	9	H	Southampton	D 1-1	0-0	—	Ward [66]	17,839
34	12	H	Aston Villa	W 2-1	2-0	11	Rowett [21], Van der Laan [36]	18,071
35	19	A	Newcastle U	L 1-3	1-1	12	Sturridge [1]	36,550
36	23	H	Nottingham F	D 0-0	0-0	—		18,087
37	May 3	A	Coventry C	W 2-1	0-0	10	Burrows (og) [49], Sturridge [67]	22,854
38	11	H	Arsenal	L 1-3	1-0	12	Ward [9]	18,287

Final League Position: 12

GOALSCORERS

League (45): Sturridge 11, Ward 8, Asanovic 6 (4 pens), Dailly 3, Simpson 2, Van der Laan 2, Willems 2, Flynn 1, Laursen 1, Powell D 1, Rowett 1, Stimac 1, Trollope 1, Wanchope 1, own goals 4.
Coca-Cola Cup (2): Simpson 1, Sturridge 1.
FA Cup (8): Van der Laan 3, Sturridge 2, Willems 2, Ward 1.

Hoult R 31 + 1	Parker P 4	Powell C 35	Laursen J 35 + 1	Yates D 8 + 2	Rowett G 35	Asanovic A 34	Sturridge D 29 + 1	Powell D 27 + 6	Gabbiadini M 5 + 9	Dailly C 31 + 5	Flynn S 10 + 7	Simpson P — + 19	Willems R 7 + 9	Shimac I 21	Van der Laan R 15 + 1	Carbon M 6 + 4	Ward A 25 + 5	Carsley L 15 + 9	McGrath P 23 + 1	Trollope P 13 + 1	Rahmberg M — + 1	Taylor M 3	Poom M 4	Wanchope P 2 + 3	Solis M — + 2	Match No.
1	2	3	4¹	5	6	7	8	9²	10³	11	12	13	14													1
1	2¹	3	4		6	7	8³	9	10²	11	12	14	13	5												2
1	2	3	4		6¹	7		9	14	11	8	13	10²	5	12³											3
1		3	2		6	7¹	8³	10	12	11	13	14	9²	5		4										4
1		3	2		4	7	8	10	12	11²	13		9¹	5	6											5
1		3	4		2	7		9	10	11		12		5	8¹	6²	13									6
1	2	3	4		6		8¹	9	10²	11		12		5		13	7									7
1		3	4		2³	7²	8	9¹	13	11		12		5		6	10	14								8
1		3¹	2²		6	7	8³	9	14	11	13	12		5					4							9
1		3	2²		6	7		9		11		12	10¹	4		14	8³	13	5							10
1		3	2		6	7		9²		11¹	14	12	10³	4			8	13	5							11
1		3	2	4	6	7¹	13	9		11²	8	12					10		5							12
1		3	2	6	4	7¹	9²		11³	8	12	13					10	14	5							13
1		3	2¹	6	4	7	9	8		11							10	12	5							14
1			3	4	2	7²	8	9		12	11			6			10	13	5¹							15
1		3	2		4	7¹	8	9		12	11²			6		13	10		5							16
1		3	2		4	7²	8	9¹	13	12	11			6			10		5							17
1		3	2¹	5²	6	7³		9	12	11	8		14	4			10	13								18
1		3	2	12	4		8	9	13	11	7³			6¹			10²	14	5							19
1		3	2	5	4	7	8	12	13	11¹				6			10²	9								20
1		3	2	4¹	6	7	8	12		13	10²		14				9³	11	5							21
1		3	2		4	7	8	9		12				13			6¹	10²	11	5						22
1		3	4			7		12	10²	6		13	9¹	8				2	5	11						23
1		3¹	4²		6	7	8	9		12	14			10	13³			2	5	11						24
1		3			4	7	9			11				6	8			2	5	10						25
1		3			4	7	9			11				6	8¹		12	2	5	10						26
1		3¹	12		4	7	8			11³	13			6			9	2	5²	10	14					27
1		3			4	7	8	5		11				6	10		9	2								28
1		2³			4	7²	8	5		3		12	13	6	11		9	10¹	14							29
		3	4		6	7		9		11	12				13	10	2¹	5²	8		1					30
		3	2			7	8	12		11				10	9²	13	4	5	6¹		1					31
		3	2				8	6		4	12			10		9		5	11			1		7¹		32
15		3	2		6	7²	8	4		5		12		10¹		9			11			1⁰	13			33
1		3	2		4	7³	8	12		6				10¹		9²		5	11					13	14	34
1		3¹	2		4	7	8	12		6				10⁰		9²		5	11					13	14	35
		3	4		5	7	9			6				8		12	2		10		1			11¹		36
		3	4	12	5		8	7		6		13		10²		9	2¹		11		1					37
		3	4		2	7		11²		6		12	8¹	10		9	14	5³	13		1					38

Coca-Cola Cup
Second Round   Luton T   (a)   0-1
                                                (h)   2-2

FA Cup
Third Round   Gillingham   (a)   2-0
Fourth Round   Aston Villa   (h)   3-1
Fifth Round   Coventry C   (h)   3-2
Sixth Round   Middlesbrough   (h)   0-2

DONCASTER ROVERS 1996–97 *Back row (left to right):* Martyn Speight, Simon Black, Martin Paul, Gavin Leech, Gary O'Connor, Steve Pearce, Dean Williams, Adam Wheeler, Ian Clark, Jamie Murphy, Darren Utley.

Middle row: Jim Golze (Youth Team Coach), Dave Dew, David Burns, Paul Robertson, David Larmour, Steve Walker, Earl Robinson, Paul Marquis, Darren Moore, Ian Gore, Martin McDonald, Michael Smith, Dave Cowling.

Front row: Phil McLoughlin (Physio), Scott Colcombe, Lee Warren, Colin Cramb, John Schofield, Kerry Dixon (Player/Manager), Alan Gray, Jim Ryan, Stuart Doling, Paul Birch, Pete Schofield.

Division 3   **DONCASTER ROVERS**

Belle Vue Ground, Doncaster DN4 5HT. Telephone: (01302) 539441. Fax: (01302) 539679. Commercial: (01302) 531000.

Ground capacity: 8608.

Record attendance: 37,149 v Hull C, Division 3 (N), 2 October 1948.

Record receipts: £22,000 v QPR, FA Cup 3rd rd, 5 January 1985.

Pitch measurements: 110yd × 76yd.

Chairman: K. Haran. *Directors:* L. Mabbett, J. Richardson, R. Ashworth.

Manager: Kerry Dixon. *Assistant Manager:* John Schofield. *Coaches:* John Schofield, D. Cowling.

Secretary: Mrs K. J. Oldale. *Physio:* Phil McLoughlin. *Youth Team Coach:* Jim Golze.

Commercial Executive: Terry Burdass. *Stadium Manager:* Peter White.

Year Formed: 1879. *Turned Professional:* 1885. *Ltd Co.:* 1905 and 1920.

Club Nickname: 'Rovers'.

Previous Grounds: 1880–1916, Intake Ground; 1920–22, Benetthorpe Ground; 1922, Low Pasture, Belle Vue.

Foundation: In 1879 Mr. Albert Jenkins got together a team to play a game against the Yorkshire Institution for the Deaf. The players stuck together as Doncaster Rovers joining the Midland Alliance in 1889 and the Midland Counties League in 1891.

First Football League game: 7 September 1901, Division 2, v Burslem Port Vale (h) D 3-3 – Eggett; Simpson, Layton; Longden, Jones, Wright; Langham, Murphy, Price, Goodson (2), Bailey (1).

Record League Victory: 10–0 v Darlington, Division 4, 25 January 1964 – Potter; Raine, Meadows; Windross (1), White, Ripley (2); Robinson, Book (2), Hale (4), Jeffrey, Broadbent (1).

Record Cup Victory: 7–0 v Blyth Spartans, FA Cup 1st rd, 27 November 1937 – Imrie; Shaw, Rodgers; McFarlane, Bycroft, Cyril Smith; Burton (1), Kilourhy (4), Morgan (2), Malam, Dutton.

Record Defeat: 0–12 v Small Heath, Division 2, 11 April 1903.

Most League Points (2 for a win): 72, Division 3 (N), 1946–47.

Most League Points (3 for a win): 85, Division 4, 1983–84.

Most League Goals: 123, Division 3 (N), 1946–47.

Highest League Scorer in Season: Clarrie Jordan, 42, Division 3 (N), 1946–47.

Most League Goals in Total Aggregate: Tom Keetley, 180, 1923–29.

Most Capped Player: Len Graham, 14, Northern Ireland.

Most League Appearances: Fred Emery, 417, 1925–36.

Record Transfer Fee Received: £250,000 from QPR for Rufus Brevett, February 1991.

Record Transfer Fee Paid: £62,500 to Torquay U for Darren Moore, July 1995.

Football League Record: 1901 Elected to Division 2; 1903 Failed re-election; 1904 Re-elected; 1905 Failed re-election; 1923 Re-elected to Division 3 (N); 1935–37 Division 2; 1937–47 Division 3 (N); 1947–48 Division 2; 1948–50 Division 3 (N); 1950–58 Division 2; 1958–59 Division 3; 1959–66 Division 4; 1966–67 Division 3; 1967–69 Division 4; 1969–71 Division 3; 1971–81 Division 4; 1981–83 Division 3; 1983–84 Division 4; 1984–88 Division 3; 1988–92 Division 4; 1992– Division 3.

Honours: Football League: Division 2 best season: 7th, 1901–02; Division 3 (N) Champions 1934–35, 1946–47, 1949–50; Runners-up 1937–38, 1938–39; Division 4 – Champions 1965–66, 1968–69; Runners-up 1983–84. Promoted 1980–81 (3rd). *FA Cup:* best season: 5th rd, 1952, 1954, 1955, 1956. *Football League Cup:* best season: 5th rd, 1976.

Colours: All red. *Change colours:* Yellow shirts, pale blue shorts.

Did you know?
On 8 February 1997, striker Colin Cramb of Doncaster Rovers donned the goalkeeper's shirt following a sending-off in the last two minutes of the match with Chester City and saved a penalty.

**Doncaster Rovers
Football Club Ltd.**
(Founded 1879)

DONCASTER ROVERS 1996–97 LEAGUE RECORD

Match No.	Date	Venue	Opponents	Result	H/T Score	Lg. Pos.	Goalscorers	Attendance
1	Aug 17	H	Carlisle U	L	0-1	0-0	—	3003
2	24	A	Hereford U	L	0-1	0-1	23	2880
3	27	A	Exeter C	D	1-1	0-1	—	Birch [69]	2667
4	31	H	Darlington	W	3-2	2-1	17	Dixon [4], Cramb [46], Schofield [77]	2185
5	Sept 7	H	Mansfield T	D	0-0	0-0	18		1814
6	10	A	Scarborough	L	1-2	0-2	—	Dixon [63]	1959
7	14	A	Rochdale	L	1-2	0-0	22	Clark [69]	1811
8	21	H	Swansea C	L	0-1	0-1	24		1391
9	28	A	Colchester U	D	2-2	2-2	24	Colcombe [20], Schofield (pen) [39]	2672
10	Oct 1	H	Hartlepool U	W	2-1	1-0	—	Moore [35], Cramb (pen) [52]	1471
11	5	H	Leyton Orient	W	2-1	1-0	16	Cramb [14], Lester [82]	1840
12	12	A	Fulham	L	1-3	0-0	19	Birch [82]	5516
13	15	A	Torquay U	L	0-1	0-1	—		1843
14	19	H	Brighton & HA	W	3-0	0-0	18	Cramb [54], Smith [69], McDonald [87]	1787
15	25	A	Cambridge U	W	1-0	0-0	—	Schofield [67]	3457
16	29	H	Lincoln C	L	1-3	1-0	—	Smith [44]	1913
17	Nov 2	H	Chester C	L	0-1	0-0	20		1534
18	9	A	Scunthorpe U	W	2-1	1-0	15	Cramb 2 (1 pen) [8, 70 (p)]	3270
19	19	H	Northampton T	L	1-2	0-0	—	Schofield [54]	1030
20	23	A	Barnet	L	0-3	0-2	20		2098
21	30	H	Cambridge U	W	2-1	0-1	17	Cramb (pen) [58], Ireland [88]	1608
22	Dec 3	A	Wigan Ath	L	1-4	1-3	—	Clark [40]	2606
23	21	A	Hull C	L	1-3	1-0	21	Cramb [18]	2830
24	26	H	Scarborough	L	1-2	1-1	21	Dixon [26]	1745
25	Jan 11	H	Colchester U	D	0-0	0-0	21		1458
26	18	A	Hartlepool U	W	4-2	2-2	21	Cramb 3 [23, 53, 68], Schofield [26]	1708
27	21	A	Mansfield T	L	0-2	0-1	—		2093
28	25	A	Lincoln C	L	2-3	0-1	21	Pearce [47], Moore [72]	3262
29	28	A	Swansea C	L	0-2	0-1	—		3464
30	Feb 1	H	Scunthorpe U	D	1-1	0-0	22	Cramb [79]	3022
31	8	A	Chester C	L	0-6	0-2	23		2347
32	15	H	Barnet	D	1-1	0-0	23	Moore [28]	2199
33	22	A	Northampton T	L	0-2	0-2	23		4577
34	28	H	Wigan Ath	W	2-0	1-0	—	Cramb [25], Mike [46]	2948
35	Mar 8	A	Hull C	D	0-0	0-0	23		3274
36	14	A	Cardiff C	W	2-0	1-0	—	Moore [7], Utley [62]	5347
37	21	H	Hereford U	W	1-0	0-0	—	Cramb [54]	2483
38	25	H	Rochdale	W	3-0	2-0	—	Hill (og) [23], Cramb (pen) [28], Esdaille [82]	2201
39	29	A	Carlisle U	D	0-0	0-0	19		6551
40	31	H	Exeter C	L	1-2	1-0	21	Schofield [40]	2457
41	Apr 5	A	Darlington	W	3-0	1-0	19	Pemberton [30], Cramb 2 [48, 70]	3071
42	8	H	Cardiff C	D	3-3	0-1	—	Moore [75], Schofield [80], Gore [89]	1989
43	12	A	Leyton Orient	L	1-2	0-1	20	Cramb (pen) [87]	3698
44	19	H	Fulham	D	0-0	0-0	20		2920
45	26	A	Brighton & HA	L	0-1	0-0	21		11,341
46	May 3	A	Torquay U	W	2-1	2-0	19	Ireland [8], McDonald [12]	1748

Final League Position: 19

GOALSCORERS

League (52): Cramb 18 (5 pens), Schofield 7 (1 pen), Moore 5, Dixon 3, Birch 2, Clark 2, Ireland 2, McDonald 2, Smith 2, Colcombe 1, Esdaille 1, Gore 1, Lester 1, Mike 1, Pemberton 1, Pearce 1, Utley 1, own goal 1.
Coca-Cola Cup (1): Cramb 1.
FA Cup (1): Cramb 1.

Williams D 27	Murphy J 30+1	Robertson P 3+1	Moore D 41	Gore I 35+1	Birch P 26+1	Schofield J 42	McDonald M 33	Pearce S 8+11	Colcombe S 9+3	Clark I 8+12	Cramb C 40+1	Larmour D 3+17	Dixon K 13+3	Ryan T 22+6	Marquis P 3	Utley D 19+4	Smith M 12+6	Walker S 1	Donnelly M —+2	Bullimore W 4	Lester J 5+6	Ireland S 27	O'Connor G 18	Gray A 1	Warren L 21+4	Doling S 3+2	Esdaille D 16+2	Messer G —+1	Weaver S 2	Mike A 5	Cunningham H 11	Beirne M 1	Wheeler A 1	Ohandjanian D —+1	Pemberton M 9	Coady L 1	Anderson L 6	Fahy A —+5	Match No.
1	2	3	4	5	6	7	8	9	10²	11¹	12	13																											1
1	2	3¹	4	5	6	7	8		10	11²	12					9	13																						2
1	2	12	4	5	11	7	8					3		6¹		10	9																						3
1	2	8³	4¹	5	11	7			10²		12	3	13	14		9							6																4
1	2		4	5²	11	7	8¹		10		12	3	13			9							6																5
1	2		4	5	11	7	8¹		10²		12	3³	13	14		9							6																6
1	2		4	5	11	7			10		12	3	13			9	8²						6¹																7
1	12		4	5	11	7	8		10			3¹	13			2²	9						6																8
1	2		4	5	11	7	12				8	3					10						6		9¹														9
1	2		4	5	11	7	8		9¹			3					10						6		12														10
1	2		4	5	11	7	8		9			3					10¹						6		12														11
1	2		4	5		8	12	9	6²			3¹					10						13																12
1	2		4	5	11	7	6		9¹			3	13	12			10						8²																13
1	2		4	5²	11	7	8		10³		12	3	13	14			9¹						6																14
	2		4		11	7	8		10			3		9	5						6	1																	15
	2		4		11	7	8	12	10²			3	13	9¹	5						6	1																	16
	2				11	7	8		10			3	13	9²	5						6	1	4¹																17
	2		4¹	5	11	7	8		10			3	13	9²			12				6	1																	18
	2			5		7		12		13	10		9	14	4²	3³					11¹	6	1		8														19
	2			5	6	7		12		13	8²		9¹	14	4	3³					10	1			11														20
	2			5	11	7		12	10	13				3	4						6	1	8²		9¹														21
	2			5		7		11²		12	10		13	9	3						6	1	8		4¹														22
	2		4		11¹	7		12	5		6¹	10	13	3		9						1	8																23
	2		4		11			12	13	10	6		9¹	3	5	7²						1	8																24
	2		4	5	11¹	7	6		10					9	3							1	8			12													25
	2		4	5	11²	7		9		13	10¹	12			3		6					1	8³		14														26
	2		4	5		7	8³	9	12	10	13				3¹	6	11²					1	14																27
	2		4	5		7		9	12	10	13				3	6	11¹					1	8																28
	2		4			7	9¹	12	10	13			3²	5	14					11		1	8³	6															29
1	2		4			7	9¹		3²	10		13		6	12					11			8	5																30
1	2		4	5		7¹	12	10	3			9²								11			8	6	13														31
1			4	12		7	3													11			8	6			5	9	2	10¹									32
			4	5		7	3	12												11			8	6¹			2	9	10²		1		13						33
1			4	5	6¹	7	8		10											11			12	3			9	2											34
1			4	5	6	7	8		10¹	12										11			13	3			9	2²											35
1			4	5		7	8		10¹	12			3							11			6	9			2												36
1			4	5		7	8	12²	10				3							11			13	2			9	6¹								9	6¹	37
1			4	5		7	8	6³	10¹	12			3							11			13	14			2⁴	9								9		38
1			4			7	8		10	12										11			5	13	6			2⁴								9	3¹	39
1			4	5		7	8		10	12	13									11			2	6¹			9	3²								9	3²	40
1			4	5		7	8		10	12										11			2	6²			9¹	3	13							9¹	3 13	41
1			4	5		7	8		10											11			2	6¹			9	3	12							9	3 12	42
1			4	5²		7	8		10	12										11			2	6			9	3¹	13							9	3¹ 13	43
			4	5		7	8		10											11	1		2	6			3¹	9									12	44
			4			7			10					6					13	11	1		2	8	5		9¹	3²									12	45
			4	12		7	8		10	13		9²		6¹					14	11	1		2³	3	5														46

Coca-Cola Cup
First Round   York C   (h)   1-1
                                  (a)   0-2

FA Cup
First Round   Stockport Co   (a)   1-2

EVERTON 1996–97   *Back row (left to right):* John Ebbrell, Tony Grant, Vinny Samways, Paul Gerrard, Neville Southall, Andy Hinchcliffe, Matt Jackson, Joe Parkinson.
Middle row: Jim Martin (Kit Manager), Jim Gabriel (Reserve Team Coach), Craig Short, Earl Barrett, Graham Allen, Jonathan O'Connor, Willie Donachie (First Team Coach), Les Helm (Physio).
Front row: Graham Stuart, Michael Branch, Gary Speed, Andrei Kanchelskis, Joe Royle, Dave Watson, Marc Hottiger, Duncan Ferguson, David Unsworth.

FA Premiership   EVERTON

Goodison Park, Liverpool L4 4EL. Telephone: (0151) 330 2200. Fax: (0151) 286 9112. Ticket Infoline: 0891 121599. Clubcall 0891 121199. Dial-A-Seat Service: (0151) 471 8000.

Ground capacity: 40,200.

Record attendance: 78,299 v Liverpool, Division 1, 18 September 1948.

Record receipts: £450,000 v Liverpool, FA Premier League, 16 April 1996.

Pitch measurements: 112yd × 78yd.

Chairman: Peter R. Johnson.

Directors: Sir Desmond Pitcher, Clifford Finch, Richard Hughes, Sir Philip Carter CBE, Dr. David M. Marsh, Keith Tamlin, Bill Kenwright, Arthur Abercromby, Lord Grantchester.

Manager: Howard Kendall. *First Team Coach:* Adrian Heath.

Physio: Les Helm.

Secretary: Michael J. Dunford.

Commercial Manager: Andrew Watson. *Sales Promotion Manager:* Graham Cass.

Stadium Manager: A. Bowen. *Media and Public Relations Executive:* Alan Myers.

Year Formed: 1878. *Turned Professional:* 1885. *Ltd Co.:* 1892.

Previous Name: St Domingo FC, 1878–79.

Club Nickname: 'The Toffees'.

Previous Grounds: 1878, Stanley Park; 1882, Priory Road; 1884, Anfield Road; 1892, Goodison Park.

Foundation: St. Domingo Church Sunday School formed a football club in 1878 which played at Stanley Park. Enthusiasm was so great that in November 1879 they decided to expand membership and changed the name to Everton playing in black shirts with a white sash and nicknamed the "Black Watch". After wearing several other colours, royal blue was adopted in 1901.

First Football League game: 8 September 1888, Football League, v Accrington (h) W 2-1 – Smalley; Dick, Ross; Holt, Jones, Dobson; Fleming (2), Waugh, Lewis, E. Chadwick, Milward.

Record League Victory: 9–1 v Manchester C, Division 1, 3 September 1906 – Scott; Balmer, Crelley; Booth, Taylor (1), Abbott (1); Sharp, Bolton (1), Young (4), Settle (2), George Wilson. 9–1 v Plymouth Arg, Division 2, 27 December 1930 – Coggins; Williams, Cresswell; McPherson, Griffiths, Thomson; Critchley, Dunn, Dean (4), Johnson (1), Stein (4).

Record Cup Victory: 11–2 v Derby Co, FA Cup 1st rd, 18 January 1890 – Smalley; Hannah, Doyle (1); Kirkwood, Holt (1), Parry; Latta, Brady (3), Geary (3), Chadwick, Millward (3).

Record Defeat: 4–10 v Tottenham H, Division 1, 11 October 1958.

Most League Points (2 for a win): 66, Division 1, 1969–70.

Most League Points (3 for a win): 90, Division 1, 1984–85.

Most League Goals: 121, Division 2, 1930–31.

Highest League Scorer in Season: William Ralph 'Dixie' Dean, 60, Division 1, 1927–28 (All-time League record).

Most League Goals in Total Aggregate: William Ralph 'Dixie' Dean, 349, 1925–37.

Most Capped Player: Neville Southall, 91, Wales.

Most League Appearances: Neville Southall, 566, 1981–97.

Record Transfer Fee Received: £8,000,000 from Fiorentina for Andrei Kanchelskis, February 1997.

Record Transfer Fee Paid: £5,750,000 to Middlesbrough for Nick Barmby, October 1996.

Football League Record: 1888 Founder Member of the Football League; 1930–31 Division 2; 1931–51 Division 1; 1951–54 Division 2; 1954–92 Division 1; 1992– FA Premier League.

Honours: *Football League:* Division 1 – Champions 1890–91, 1914–15, 1927–28, 1931–32, 1938–39, 1962–63, 1969–70, 1984–85, 1986–87; Runners-up 1889–90, 1894–95, 1901–02, 1904–05, 1908–09, 1911–12, 1985–86; Division 2 – Champions 1930–31; Runners-up 1953–54. *FA Cup:* Winners 1906, 1933, 1966, 1984, 1995; Runners-up 1893, 1897, 1907, 1968, 1985, 1986, 1989. *Football League Cup:* Runners-up 1977, 1984. *League Super Cup:* Runners-up 1986. *Simod Cup:* Runners-up 1989. *Zenith Data Systems Cup:* Runners-up 1991. **European Competitions:** *European Cup:* 1963–64, 1970–71. *European Cup-Winners' Cup:* 1966–67, 1984–85 (winners), 1995–96. *European Fairs Cup:* 1962–63, 1964–65, 1965–66. *UEFA Cup:* 1975–76, 1978–79, 1979–80.

Colours: Royal blue shirts with white and black trim, white shorts with blue and black trim, blue stockings with black rings. *Change colours:* Amber shirts with black stripes, black shorts, amber stockings.

Did you know?
When Everton's Peter Farrell scored for the Republic of Ireland v England at Goodison Park on 21 September 1949, he became the first international to score an away goal on his home ground.

EVERTON 1996–97 LEAGUE RECORD

Match No.	Date	Venue	Opponents	Result	H/T Score	Lg. Pos.	Goalscorers	Attendance
1	Aug 17	H	Newcastle U	W 2-0	2-0	—	Unsworth (pen) 29, Speed 40	40,117
2	21	A	Manchester U	D 2-2	2-0	—	Ferguson 2 35, 41	54,943
3	24	A	Tottenham H	D 0-0	0-0	8		29,669
4	Sept 4	H	Aston Villa	L 0-1	0-0	—		39,115
5	7	A	Wimbledon	L 0-4	0-1	15		13,684
6	14	H	Middlesbrough	L 1-2	1-0	—	Short 8	39,250
7	21	A	Blackburn R	D 1-1	1-1	16	Unsworth 37	27,091
8	28	H	Sheffield W	W 2-0	1-0	13	Kanchelskis 16, Stuart 60	34,160
9	Oct 12	H	West Ham U	W 2-1	1-0	9	Stuart 14, Speed 78	36,541
10	28	A	Nottingham F	W 1-0	1-0	—	Short 5	19,892
11	Nov 4	H	Coventry C	D 1-1	1-0	—	Stuart (pen) 45	31,477
12	16	H	Southampton	W 7-1	5-1	8	Stuart 12, Kanchelskis 2 22, 35, Speed 3 30, 32, 72, Barmby 57	35,669
13	20	A	Liverpool	D 1-1	0-1	—	Speed 82	40,751
14	23	A	Leicester C	W 2-1	1-0	6	Hinchcliffe 12, Unsworth 52	20,975
15	30	H	Sunderland	L 1-3	0-0	8	Ferguson 64	40,087
16	Dec 7	A	Chelsea	D 2-2	2-1	8	Branch 17, Kanchelskis 28	27,920
17	16	A	Derby Co	W 1-0	0-0	—	Barmby 86	17,252
18	21	H	Leeds U	D 0-0	0-0	7		36,954
19	26	A	Middlesbrough	L 2-4	2-2	8	Unsworth (pen) 31, Ferguson 45	29,673
20	28	H	Wimbledon	L 1-3	1-0	8	Stuart 23	36,733
21	Jan 1	H	Blackburn R	L 0-2	0-2	8		30,427
22	11	A	Sheffield W	L 1-2	0-1	9	Ferguson 63	24,175
23	19	A	Arsenal	L 1-3	0-0	9	Ferguson 90	38,095
24	29	A	Newcastle U	L 1-4	1-0	—	Speed 3	36,143
25	Feb 1	H	Nottingham F	W 2-0	0-0	9	Ferguson 48, Barmby 67	32,567
26	22	A	Coventry C	D 0-0	0-0	10		19,452
27	Mar 1	H	Arsenal	L 0-2	0-2	11		36,980
28	5	A	Southampton	D 2-2	2-0	—	Ferguson 11, Speed 27	15,134
29	8	A	Leeds U	L 0-1	0-1	12		32,055
30	15	H	Derby Co	W 1-0	0-0	13	Watson 79	32,140
31	22	H	Manchester U	L 0-2	0-1	13		40,079
32	Apr 5	A	Aston Villa	L 1-3	1-1	14	Unsworth 14	39,339
33	9	H	Leicester C	D 1-1	1-0	—	Branch 17	30,368
34	12	H	Tottenham H	W 1-0	1-0	12	Speed 11	36,380
35	16	H	Liverpool	D 1-1	0-1	—	Ferguson 65	40,177
36	19	A	West Ham U	D 2-2	0-2	11	Branch 78, Ferguson 90	24,525
37	May 3	A	Sunderland	L 0-3	0-1	12		22,052
38	11	H	Chelsea	L 1-2	0-2	15	Barmby 77	38,321

Final League Position: 15

GOALSCORERS

League (44): Ferguson 10, Speed 9, Stuart 5 (1 pen), Unsworth 5 (2 pens), Barmby 4, Kanchelskis 4, Branch 3, Short 2, Hinchcliffe 1, Watson 1.
Coca-Cola Cup (3): Kanchelskis 1, Rideout 1, Speed 1.
FA Cup (5): Barmby 1, Ferguson 1, Kanchelskis 1 (pen), Speed 1, own goal 1.

Southall N 34	Barrett E 36	Hinchcliffe A 18	Unsworth D 32 + 2	Watson D 29	Parkinson J 28	Kanchelskis A 20	Stuart G 29 + 6	Ferguson D 31 + 2	Ebbrell J 7	Speed G 37	Short C 19 + 4	Grant T 11 + 7	Rideout P 4 + 6	Branch M 13 + 12	Limpar A 1 + 1	Hottiger M 4 + 4	Barmby N 22 + 3	Gerrard P 4 + 1	Allen G — + 1	Hills J 1 + 2	Phelan T 15	Dunne R 6 + 1	Thomsen C 15 + 1	Ball M 2 + 3	Cadamarteri D — + 1	Match No.
1	2	3	4	5¹	6	7	8	9	10	11	12															1
1	2	3	4		6	7¹	8	9	10	11	5	12														2
1	2	3	4		6	7	8¹	9		11	5		10	12												3
1	2	3	4		6	7	8	9		11	5		10¹	12												4
1	2	3	4		6	7	12	9	8	11	5		10¹													5
1	2	3	4		6	7	12	9	8	11	5		10													6
1	2	3	4		6	7	8	9	10		5				11¹											7
1	2	3	4		6¹	7	8²	9		11	5	12	10	13												8
1	2	3	4	5	8	7		9		11	6	12	10¹													9
1	2	3	4¹	5	6²	7	8		10	11	13	12				9										10
1ᵈ	2	3	4	5	6	7	8		10	11						9	15									11
1	2	3	4	5	6	7¹	8	12		11						9										12
1	2	3	4	5	6		8	9		11	12	10¹				7										13
1	2	3²	4	5	6	7³	8	12		11	13	10¹	14			9										14
1	2	3	4	5	6	7	12	9		11	10			8¹												15
1	2	3	4	5	6	7	12	9		11	10¹			8												16
1	2	3²	12	5	6	7		9	4¹	11	10	13					8									17
1	2		4	5²	6		8	9	3	10	12	11¹				14	7				13³					18
1	5		4			6²	8	9	3	11	10¹	12			2		7				13					19
1	4		5		7¹	6	10	9		11	13	12			2	8²	3									20
1	2	12	5		7	10²	9			11		13	4	14		8					3	6¹				21
1	2		4	5	7¹	10	9			11				12		8					3	6				22
	2		4	5	8	7	9			11	6¹	12²	13				1				3	10			23
	2		4	5	6	7	9			11						8	1				3	10			24
	2		4	5		7	9			11	6					8	1				3	10			25
1	2	4¹	5	6		7	9			11	12			13		8²					3	10			26
1	2	4	5	8		12	9			11	6			13		7²					3	10¹			27
1	2	4	5	8¹		12	9			11	6³	14	13			7²					3	10			28
1	2	4	5	8		12	9				6			11¹	13	7					3	10²			29
	2	4	5	6			8	9		11		12				7	1				3	10¹			30
1		4²	5	8		7	9			11	6			12	2¹					3	13	10			31
1		4	5	6²		7	9			11	2		10		12	8¹				3		13			32
1	2		5			7	9			11		4	8¹	12						3²		6	10	13	33
1	2	3	5			7	9			11	4²		8	12						6		10¹	13		34
1	2	3	5			7	9			11			8	12						6		10	4¹		35
1	2		5			7²	9			11			10	8			12		3¹	6		4	13		36
1	2		5				9			11				4	8			7			6	10¹	3	12	37
																										38

EXETER CITY 1996-97   *Back row (left to right):* Marcus Dailly, Leon Braithwaite, Sufyan Ghazghazi, Darren Hughes, Mark Chamberlain.
Middle row: George Kent (Scout), Mike Chapman (Physio), Eamonn Dolan (Community Officer), Jon Richardson, Ashley Bayes, Richard Pears, Matthew Hare, Mike Radford (Youth Development Officer), Noel Blake (Assistant Manager).
Front row: Nicky Medlin, Danny Bailey, Tim Steele, Peter Fox (Manager), Barry McConnell, Chris Myers, Gary Rice.
(Photograph: Mike Drew)

Division 3 **EXETER CITY**

St James Park, Exeter EX4 6PX. Telephone: (01392) 254073. Fax: (01392) 425885. Training Ground: (01395) 232784.

Ground capacity: 10,570.

Record attendance: 20,984 v Sunderland, FA Cup 6th rd (replay), 4 March 1931.

Record receipts: £59,862.98 v Aston Villa, FA Cup 3rd rd, 8 January 1994.

Pitch measurements: 114yd × 73yd.

Honorary President: W. C. Hill.

Chairman: A. I. Doble.

Directors: P. Carter, I. M. Couch, S. W. Dawe, L. G. Vallance, M. Shelbourne.

Manager: Peter Fox. *Assistant Manager/Coach:* Noel Blake. *Physio:* Mike Chapman MCSP.

Chief Executive: Bernard Frowd OBE.

Secretary: Margaret Bond. *Company Secretary:* P. Carter.

Commercial Manager: David Bird.

Year Formed: 1904. *Turned Professional:* 1908. *Ltd Co.:* 1908.

Club Nickname: 'The Grecians'.

Foundation: Exeter City was formed in 1904 by the amalgamation of St. Sidwell's United and Exeter United. The club first played in the East Devon League and then the Plymouth & District League. After an exhibition match between West Bromwich Albion and Woolwich Arsenal was held to test interest as Exeter was then a rugby stronghold, Exeter City decided at a meeting at the Red Lion Hotel to turn professional in 1908.

First Football League game: 28 August 1920, Division 3, v Brentford (h) W 3-0 – Pym; Coleburne, Feebury (1p); Crawshaw, Carrick, Mitton; Appleton, Wright (1), Vowles (1), Dockray.

Record League Victory: 8–1 v Coventry C, Division 3 (S), 4 December 1926 – Bailey; Pollard, Charlton; Pullen, Pool, Garrett; Purcell (2), McDevitt, Blackmore (2), Dent (2), Compton (2). 8–1 v Aldershot, Division 3 (S), 4 May 1935 – Chesters; Gray, Miller; Risdon, Webb, Angus; Jack Scott (1), Wrightson (1), Poulter (3), McArthur (1), Dryden (1). (1 og).

Record Cup Victory: 9–1 v Aberdare, FA Cup 1st rd, 26 November 1927 – Holland; Pollard, Charlton; Phoenix, Pool, Gee; Purcell (2), McDevitt, Dent (4), Vaughan (2), Compton (1).

Record Defeat: 0–9 v Notts Co, Division 3 (S), 16 October 1948 and v Northampton T, Division 3 (S), 12 April 1958.

Most League Points (2 for a win): 62, Division 4, 1976–77.

Most League Points (3 for a win): 89, Division 4, 1989–90.

Most League Goals: 88, Division 3 (S), 1932–33.

Highest League Scorer in Season: Fred Whitlow, 33, Division 3 (S), 1932–33.

Most League Goals in Total Aggregate: Tony Kellow, 129, 1976–78, 1980–83, 1985–88.

Most Capped Player: Dermot Curtis, 1 (17), Eire.

Most League Appearances: Arnold Mitchell, 495, 1952–66.

Record Transfer Fee Received: £500,000 from Rangers for Chris Vinnicombe, November 1989 and £500,000 from Manchester C for Martin Phillips, November 1995.

Record Transfer Fee Paid: £65,000 to Blackpool for Tony Kellow, March 1980.

Football League Record: 1920 Elected Division 3; 1921–58 Division 3 (S); 1958–64 Division 4; 1964–66 Division 3; 1966–77 Division 4; 1977–84 Division 3; 1984–90 Division 4; 1990–92 Division 3; 1992–94 Division 2; 1994– Division 3.

Honours: Football League: Division 3 best season: 8th, 1979–80; Division 3 (S) – Runners-up 1932–33; Division 4 – Champions 1989–90; Runners-up 1976–77. *FA Cup:* best season: 6th rd replay, 1931, 6th rd 1981. *Football League Cup:* never beyond 4th rd. *Division 3 (S) Cup:* Winners 1934.

Colours: Red and white striped shirts, black shorts, red stockings. *Change colours:* Blue and white striped shirts, blue shorts, blue stockings.

Did you know?
Exeter City's first competitive match was against the 110th Royal Artillery Battery in the East Devon Senior League on 10 September 1904. City won 2–1.

EXETER CITY 1996–97 LEAGUE RECORD

Match No.	Date	Venue	Opponents	Result	H/T Score	Lg. Pos.	Goalscorers	Attendance
1	Aug 17	A	Mansfield T	W 1-0	1-0	—	Braithwaite [2]	2149
2	24	H	Scarborough	D 2-2	2-0	3	Braithwaite [24], Sharpe [34]	2816
3	27	H	Doncaster R	D 1-1	1-0	—	Pears [34]	2667
4	31	A	Torquay U	L 0-2	0-2	13		4021
5	Sept 7	A	Cardiff C	L 1-2	1-1	17	Chamberlain (pen) [21]	3659
6	10	H	Fulham	L 0-1	0-1	—		2388
7	14	H	Brighton & HA	W 2-1	1-0	14	Braithwaite [43], Steele [86]	2886
8	21	A	Barnet	L 0-3	0-1	19		2020
9	28	H	Cambridge U	L 0-1	0-1	22		2572
10	Oct 1	A	Wigan Ath	L 0-2	0-0	—		2788
11	5	A	Lincoln C	W 3-2	1-0	20	Flack [42], Braithwaite [46], Blake [73]	3115
12	12	H	Northampton T	L 0-1	0-1	22		3002
13	15	H	Carlisle U	W 2-1	0-1	—	Myers [79], Chamberlain [87]	2155
14	19	A	Chester C	L 1-2	0-1	23	Chamberlain (pen) [46]	1941
15	26	H	Hartlepool U	W 2-0	0-0	16	Rowbotham [57], Myers [86]	3043
16	29	H	Colchester U	L 0-1	0-0	—		2384
17	Nov 2	A	Rochdale	L 0-2	0-2	21		2134
18	9	H	Leyton Orient	W 3-2	1-1	20	Bailey [35], Flack [50], Braithwaite [85]	3171
19	19	A	Darlington	W 1-0	0-0	—	Rowbotham [47]	1563
20	23	H	Hull C	D 0-0	0-0	16		3423
21	30	A	Hartlepool U	D 1-1	1-1	16	Blake [41]	1419
22	Dec 3	H	Hereford U	D 1-1	1-0	—	Blake [11]	2189
23	14	A	Scunthorpe U	L 1-4	1-3	17	Flack [23]	2000
24	21	H	Swansea C	L 1-2	1-1	20	Walker (og) [15]	2801
25	26	A	Fulham	D 1-1	1-1	20	Angus (og) [26]	7892
26	28	H	Cardiff C	W 2-0	1-0	18	Blake [39], Rowbotham [55]	3585
27	Jan 18	H	Wigan Ath	L 0-1	0-1	20		3067
28	21	A	Cambridge U	L 2-3	1-3	—	Blake [35], Flack [56]	2108
29	25	H	Colchester U	L 0-3	0-2	20		2666
30	Feb 1	A	Leyton Orient	D 1-1	0-0	20	Rowbotham [49]	3686
31	8	H	Rochdale	D 0-0	0-0	21		2849
32	11	A	Brighton & HA	L 0-1	0-1	—		5835
33	15	A	Hull C	L 0-2	0-2	22		2668
34	22	H	Darlington	W 3-2	2-2	21	Bailey [5], Rowbotham [35], Crowe [50]	2986
35	Mar 1	A	Hereford U	W 2-1	0-1	19	Blake [52], Crowe [73]	2735
36	4	H	Barnet	D 1-1	0-1	—	Hughes [46]	2394
37	8	A	Swansea C	L 1-3	0-1	19	Rowbotham [56]	3115
38	15	H	Scunthorpe U	L 0-1	0-0	21		3378
39	22	A	Scarborough	W 4-3	3-1	18	Rowbotham [10], Steele [21], Hicks (og) [27], Crowe [54]	2125
40	29	H	Mansfield T	D 0-0	0-0	21		3181
41	31	A	Doncaster R	W 2-1	0-1	20	Crowe 2 [66, 76]	2457
42	Apr 5	A	Torquay U	D 1-1	0-1	20	Steele [49]	4991
43	12	H	Lincoln C	D 3-3	1-1	21	Hare [31], Rowbotham [50], Medlin [58]	2818
44	19	A	Northampton T	L 1-4	0-1	21	Rowbotham (pen) [90]	6400
45	26	H	Chester C	L 1-5	1-0	22	Richardson [8]	4300
46	May 3	A	Carlisle U	L 0-2	0-2	22		6170

Final League Position: 22

GOALSCORERS

League (48): Rowbotham 9 (1 pen), Blake 6, Braithwaite 5, Crowe 5, Flack 4, Chamberlain 3 (2 pens), Steele 3, Bailey 2, Myers 2, Hare 1, Hughes 1, Medlin 1, Pears 1, Richardson J 1, Sharpe 1, own goals 3.
Coca-Cola Cup (0).
FA Cup (3): Flack 1, Rowbotham 1, Sharpe 1.

Bayes A 41	Richardson J 42 + 1	Hughes D 33 + 3	Myers C 31 + 2	Blake N 46	Gayle B 10	Chamberlain M 22 + 4	Bailey D 32 + 3	Braithwaite L 26 + 12	Sharpe J 19 + 2	Steele T 14 + 14	Pears R 6 + 2	McConnell B 20 + 14	Dailly M 8 + 9	Rice G 9 + 6	Hare M 16 + 9	Fox P 5	Flack S 20 + 7	Hodges L 16 + 1	Ghazghazi S 1 + 5	Rowbotham D 25	Richardson N 14	McKeown G 3	Minett J 13	Medlin N 7 + 4	Rees J 7	Baddeley L 8 + 3	Crowe G 10	Birch P 2	Match No.
1	2	3	4	5	6	7	8	9¹	10	11²	12	13																	1
1	2²	3	4	5	6		8	9	10	11¹		7³	12	13	14														2
1	2	3	4	5	6	7	8	9¹		11²	12			13															3
	2		4	5	6	7	8³	10²	9¹	11		3	12	13	14	1													4
1	2	3	4	5	6	7	8²	9	10	11¹		12		13															5
1		3	4	5	6	7	8	9	10	11¹		2		12															6
1		3	4	5	6	7	8²	9	10	12		2¹			11	13													7
1	12	3	4	5	6	7¹		9	10³	14		2¹	13		11	8													8
1	2		4	5	6			9²	10	12		7	3¹		11	8	13												9
1	2	3	4	5				10	11	7²			13	12	6		9	8¹											10
1	2	3	4	5				10		11²			13	12	6		9	8											11
1	2	3	4	5		7			10	11¹				12	6		9	8											12
1	2	3	4	5		7			10	11¹			12		6		9	8											13
1	2	3	4	5		7			11	10			12		6		9	8¹											14
1	2	3¹	4	5				12	10	13	14		11¹		6		9	8		7²									15
1	2	3	4	5				10	11	9	12			6²			13	8¹		7									16
1	2	3	4	5					10	12		13		11²			9¹	8		7	6								17
1	2	3	4	5				10		12			13	11²			9¹	8		7	6								18
1	2	3		5				8		12		11		4	9		10¹			7	6								19
1	2	3¹		5				10		13		12	11	4	14		9³	8²		7	6								20
1	2			5				10		7		3¹	13	11	4		12	9		8²	6								21
1	2			5				10		9		3¹	11	4²	12		13	8		7	6								22
1	2	4¹		5				10		7		3	11	12			9²	8		13	6								23
1	2	4¹		5				10		7		3	12	13	11		14	9²		6	8²								24
	2	4²		5				12	10			9	3	11³	13	14	8			7¹	6		1						25
	2¹			5²				10		9		4	12	3	11		13	8		7	6		1						26
	8		2	5				10²		9		12	11	3¹	4		13			7	6		1						27
	8	12	2	5				10		13	14	4	3²	11¹			9³			7	6		1						28
1	8	12	2	5				10²		9		11³	3		13					7	6			4¹	14				29
1	8	2		5						10		12	3							9¹	7		10	6	4	11			30
1	8	3	2¹	5				10		7²		12								9³	6		13	4	11	14			31
1	8	3	2¹	5				10		7³	14	12								9	6¹		13		4	11			32
1	8	3		5				10		12		2¹		6						9²	7		13		4	11			33
1	8	3	12	5				10				2		6²						9¹	7		13		4	11			34
1	8¹	3	12	5				10		13		2²		6						9	7				4	11			35
1	8	3	12	5				4		10¹		13	2		14					9	7²			6					36
1	8	3	11³	5				4		10		12	2¹							6²	7		13		14	9			37
1	8	3¹	11	5				12		10		13	2¹							9²	7			6		4	14		38
1	8		11	5				12		13		2	3							9	7²		10¹	6	4				39
1	8	12	11	5				2²		13		3¹		6	14					9³	7		10				4		40
1	8	6	11	5				12		13		2	3							9	7		10³				4¹		41
1	8	3	11	5				4		12		2¹		6						9²	7		10						42
1	8	3	11	5						12		2¹		6						9	7		10		4				43
1	8	3	11	5				9				2		6¹							7		10		4		12		44
1	8	3²	11	5				10³		12		2								9¹	7		13	6	4		14		45
1	8	3¹	11³	5				12		13		2		14						9²	7		10	6					46

Coca-Cola Cup
First Round   Barnet   (h)   0-4
                                                (a)   0-2

FA Cup
First Round   Bristol R   (a)   2-1
Second Round   Plymouth Arg   (a)   1-4

FULHAM 1996-97 *Back row (left to right):* Terry Angus, Mark Walton, Danny Cullip, Tony Lange, Simon Stewart, Michael Mison.
Middle row: Chris Smith (Physio), Darren Freeman, Martin Thomas, Rod McAree, Lea Barkus, Chris Honor, Rory Hamill, Paul Watson, John Hamsher, Robbie Herrera, Rob Scott, John Marshall (Youth Team Coach).
Front row: Adam Grover, Glenn Cockerill, Nick Cusack, Len Walker (Assistant Manager), Micky Adams (Player/Manager), Alan Cork (Reserve Team Coach), Simon Morgan, Mike Conroy, Paul Brooker.
(Photograph: Ken Coton)

Division 2 **FULHAM**

Craven Cottage, Stevenage Rd, Fulham, London SW6 6HH. Telephone: (0171) 736 6561. Fax: (0171) 731 7047. Call Line: 0891 440044.

Ground capacity: 14,969.

Record attendance: 49,335 v Millwall, Division 2, 8 October 1938.

Record receipts: £80,247 v Chelsea, Division 2, 8 October 1983.

Pitch measurements: 110yd × 75yd.

General Manager: Ian G. Branfoot.

Chairman: M. Al Fayed.

Directors: W. F. Muddyman (Vice-Chairman), C. A. Swain, S. H. Benson, I. G. Branfoot, J. M. Griffiths.

Team Manager: Micky Adams. *Assistant Manager:* Alan Cork. *Player-Coach:* Micky Adams. *Reserve Team Coach:* Alan Cork. *Youth Team Coach:* John Marshall. *Physio:* Chris Smith, Grad. Dip. Phys. MCSP. *Community Officer:* Gary Mulcahey (0171) 384 3552.

Club Secretary: Mrs Janice O'Doherty. *Corporate Affairs Manager:* Mrs Annie Bassett.

Club Safety Officer: Kevin Moore.

Year Formed: 1879. *Turned Professional:* 1898. *Ltd Co.:* 1903. *Reformed:* 1987.

Club Nickname: 'Cottagers'.

Previous Name: 1879–88, Fulham St Andrew's.

Previous Grounds: 1879 Star Road, Fulham; c.1883 Eel Brook Common, 1884 Lillie Road; 1885 Putney Lower Common; 1886 Ranelagh House, Fulham; 1888 Barn Elms, Castelnau; 1889 Purser's Cross (Roskell's Field), Parsons Green Lane; 1891 Eel Brook Common; 1891 Half Moon, Putney; 1895 Captain James Field, West Brompton; 1896 Craven Cottage.

Foundation: Churchgoers were responsible for the foundation of Fulham, which first saw the light of day as Fulham St. Andrew's Church Sunday School FC in 1879. They won the West London Amateur Cup in 1887 and the championship of the West London League in its initial season of 1892–93. The name Fulham had been adopted in 1888.

First Football League game: 3 September 1907, Division 2, v Hull C (h) L 0-1 – Skene; Ross, Lindsay; Collins, Morrison, Goldie; Dalrymple, Freeman, Bevan, Hubbard, Threlfall.

Record League Victory: 10–1 v Ipswich T, Division 1, 26 December 1963 – Macedo; Cohen, Langley; Mullery (1), Keetch, Robson (1); Key, Cook (1), Leggat (4), Haynes, Howfield (3).

Record Cup Victory: 7–0 v Swansea C, FA Cup 1st rd, 11 November 1995 – Lange; Jupp (1), Herrera, Barkus (Brooker (1)), Moore, Angus, Thomas (1), Morgan, Brazil (Hamill), Conroy (3) (Bolt), Cusack (1).

Record Defeat: 0–10 v Liverpool, League Cup 2nd rd 1st leg, 23 September 1986.

Most League Points (2 for a win): 60, Division 2, 1958–59 and Division 3, 1970–71.

Most League Points (3 for a win): 87, Division 3, 1996–97.

Most League Goals: 111, Division 3 (S), 1931–32.

Highest League Scorer in Season: Frank Newton, 43, Division 3 (S), 1931–32.

Most League Goals in Total Aggregate: Gordon Davies, 159, 1978–84, 1986–91.

Most Capped Player: Johnny Haynes, 56, England.

Most League Appearances: Johnny Haynes, 594, 1952–70.

Record Transfer Fee Received: £333,333 from Liverpool for Richard Money, May 1980.

Record Transfer Fee Paid: £150,000 to Orient for Peter Kitchen, February 1979, and to Brighton & HA for Teddy Maybank, December 1979.

Football League Record: 1907 Elected to Division 2; 1928–32 Division 3 (S); 1932–49 Division 2; 1949–52 Division 1; 1952–59 Division 2; 1959–68 Division 1; 1968–69 Division 2; 1969–71 Division 3; 1971–80 Division 2; 1980–82 Division 3; 1982–86 Division 2; 1986–92 Division 2; 1992–94 Division 2; 1994–97 Division 3; 1997– Division 2.

Honours: Football League: Division 1 best season: 10th, 1959–60; Division 2 – Champions 1948–49; Runners-up 1958–59; Division 3 (S) – Champions 1931–32; Division 3 – Runners-up 1970–71, 1996–97. *FA Cup:* Runners-up 1975. *Football League Cup:* best season: 5th rd, 1968, 1971.

Colours: White shirts, red and black trim, black shorts, white stockings red and black trim. *Change colours:* Red and black halved shirts, white shorts, black stockings with red trim.

Did you know?
In 1953-54, Fulham called upon the services of only 18 players in all League games, finishing 8th in Division Two. There were four ever present players and two who were absent for just one game.

FULHAM F.C.

FULHAM 1996–97 LEAGUE RECORD

Match No.	Date	Venue	Opponents	Result	H/T Score	Lg. Pos.	Goalscorers	Attendance
1	Aug 17	H	Hereford U	W 1-0	0-0	—	Conroy [55]	5277
2	24	A	Hartlepool U	L 1-2	0-0	13	Scott [69]	2457
3	27	A	Rochdale	W 2-1	1-0	—	Cusack [1], Conroy [69]	1689
4	31	H	Carlisle U	W 1-0	1-0	2	Conroy [9]	5860
5	Sept 7	H	Colchester U	W 3-1	1-0	2	Conroy 2 [5, 51], Morgan [79]	5189
6	10	A	Exeter C	W 1-0	1-0	—	Freeman [23]	2388
7	14	A	Swansea C	W 2-1	0-1	1	Conroy [67], Morgan [79]	3791
8	21	H	Mansfield T	L 1-2	0-1	1	Morgan [89]	5740
9	28	A	Darlington	W 2-0	1-0	1	Watson [32], Carpenter [90]	3269
10	Oct 1	H	Torquay U	L 1-2	1-0	—	Scott [17]	4459
11	5	A	Northampton T	W 1-0	0-0	2	Conroy [54]	6171
12	12	H	Doncaster R	W 3-1	0-0	1	Conroy [51], Herrera [64], Carpenter [70]	5516
13	15	H	Cambridge U	W 3-0	3-0	—	Conroy 2 [4, 33], Blake (pen) [44]	5791
14	19	A	Hull C	W 3-0	1-0	1	Freeman [41], Watson [54], Conroy [70]	3986
15	26	A	Brighton & HA	D 0-0	0-0	1		8387
16	29	H	Scunthorpe U	W 2-1	1-1	—	Conroy [25], Freeman [68]	4566
17	Nov 2	H	Lincoln C	L 1-2	1-1	1	Carpenter [31]	6945
18	9	A	Cardiff C	W 2-1	2-0	1	Conroy [1], Blake (pen) [34]	6144
19	19	H	Barnet	W 2-0	1-0	—	Conroy [13], Morgan [82]	4423
20	23	A	Wigan Ath	D 1-1	0-0	1	Scott [80]	5039
21	30	H	Brighton & HA	W 2-0	0-0	1	Conroy [61], Blake (pen) [73]	8279
22	Dec 3	A	Chester C	D 1-1	0-0	—	Freeman [73]	1762
23	14	H	Leyton Orient	D 1-1	0-0	1	Watson [55]	7355
24	21	A	Scarborough	W 2-0	2-0	1	Conroy [16], Scott [43]	2015
25	26	H	Exeter C	D 1-1	1-1	1	Angus [40]	7892
26	Jan 11	H	Darlington	W 6-0	1-0	1	Scott [18], Carpenter [60], Cullip [63], Freeman [82], Brooker [88], Conroy [89]	5735
27	14	A	Colchester U	L 1-2	0-1	—	Morgan [65]	3820
28	18	A	Torquay U	L 1-3	1-0	1	Scott [38]	3386
29	25	A	Scunthorpe U	W 4-1	3-0	1	Cusack [4], Conroy [32], Blake (pen) [40], Scott [82]	3259
30	31	H	Cardiff C	L 1-4	0-1	—	Eckhardt (og) [55]	6459
31	Feb 8	H	Lincoln C	L 0-2	0-1	2		3948
32	11	H	Swansea C	W 2-1	0-0	—	Freeman [64], Brooker [86]	4836
33	15	H	Wigan Ath	D 1-1	0-0	1	Blake (pen) [82]	9448
34	22	A	Barnet	D 2-2	1-1	2	Conroy [29], Scott [67]	3316
35	Mar 1	A	Chester C	D 1-1	0-1	3	Morgan [58]	5780
36	8	H	Scarborough	W 4-0	2-0	2	Cockerill [5], Freeman [7], Blake (pen) [61], Warren [78]	6080
37	16	A	Leyton Orient	W 2-0	0-0	3	Blake (pen) [73], Carpenter [88]	7125
38	22	H	Hartlepool U	W 1-0	1-0	3	Freeman [29]	7222
39	29	H	Hereford U	D 0-0	0-0	3		4473
40	31	H	Rochdale	D 1-1	1-1	3	Conroy [12]	7866
41	Apr 5	A	Carlisle U	W 2-1	0-1	1	Conroy [51], McAree [55]	9171
42	8	A	Mansfield T	D 0-0	0-0	—		3912
43	12	H	Northampton T	L 0-1	0-1	2		11,479
44	19	A	Doncaster R	D 0-0	0-0	2		2920
45	26	H	Hull C	W 2-0	1-0	2	Morgan 2 [30, 49]	10,588
46	May 3	A	Cambridge U	W 1-0	1-0	2	Freeman [14]	7218

Final League Position: 2

GOALSCORERS

League (72): Conroy 21, Freeman 9, Morgan 8, Scott 8, Blake 7 (7 pens), Carpenter 5, Watson 3, Brooker 2, Cusack 2, Angus 1, Cockerill 1, Cullip 1, Herrera 1, McAree 1, Warren 1, own goal 1.
Coca-Cola Cup (6): Conroy 2, Brooker 1, Morgan 1, Watson 1, own goal 1.
FA Cup (0).

Watton M 28	Watson P 44	Herrera R 26	Cullip D 23 + 6	Cusack N 44 + 1	Blake M 40 + 1	McAree R 5 + 4	Mison M 1 + 3	Conroy M 40 + 3	Morgan S 44	Scott R 36 + 7	Thomas M 6 + 20	Brooker P — + 26	Cockerill G 27 + 5	Freeman D 32 + 7	Lange T 18	Angus T 28 + 4	Carpenter R 34	Adams M 2 + 1	Davis S — + 1	Soloman J 1 + 3	Parker P 3	Lawrence M 13 + 2	Stewart D 2 + 1	Hartfield C 1 + 1	Warren C 8 + 3	Match No.
1	2	3	4	5	6	7	8¹	9	10	11²	12	13														1
1	2	3	4¹	5	6	7²		9	10	11	12		8	13												2
	2²	3³	4	5	6	7¹		9	10	11	12		8	13	1	14										3
	2	3	4	5	6		13	9	10	11¹	12		8	7²	1											4
	2	3	4	5	6			9	10	11				7	1	8										5
	2	3	4	5	6		12	9	10	11¹				7	1	8										6
	2	3	4²	5	6			9	10	11¹		13	12	7	1	8										7
1	2	3	4²	5	6		13	9	10	12			14	8¹	7²	11										8
1	2	3	4		6		12	9¹	10		7²	13	14			11²	5	8								9
1	2	3			4	6		9	10		7²	12	13			11¹	5	8								10
1	2	3	12	4	6			9	10		7¹					11	5	8								11
1	2	3		4	6			9	10		7¹					11	5	8	12							12
1	2	3		4	6			9	10		7¹					11	5	8		12						13
1	2	3		4	6		12	9	10		7²	13	14			11³	5¹	8								14
1	2	3		4	6			9	10		7¹	13		12	11		5²	8								15
1	2	3	5	4	6			9	10	11			12	7¹			8									16
1	2	3	5	4				9	10	11			12	7		6¹	8									17
	2	3	5	4	6			9	10²	11¹		12	8			1	13	7								18
	2	3	12	4	6			9	10	11	13		8²			1	5	7¹								19
	2	3	9	4	6				10	11		12	8¹			1	5	7								20
	2	3		4	6			9	10	11			8²	12		1	5	7¹			13					21
	2	3¹		4	6			9	10	11²			8	12		1	5	7			13					22
	2	3	12	4	6¹			9	10	13			8²	11		1	5	7								23
	2		12	4	6	13		9	10	11²			8¹	7	1	5		3¹	14							24
	2			4	6			9	10	11		12	8	7	1	5		3¹								25
	2	3	6					9	10	11¹	13	14	8³	12	1	5	7				4²					26
	2²	3	6	12				9	10	11		14	8³	13	1	5	7¹				4					27
	2³	3¹	12	4	6			9	10	11²		14	13	7	1	5	8									28
	2		5	4	6			9	10	11	12		8¹	7	1		3									29
		5³	4	6	13			9	10	11	12	14		7		8²	3			2¹						30
1			4³	6¹				9	10	11	3	13	8	12		5²						2	14	7		31
1	3		4	6				9	10	11¹	2³	12	8	7		5						13				32
1	3		4	6				9	10	11²	2	12	8¹	7		5						2		13		33
1	3		4	6				9¹	10	12	2	13	8³	7²		5						14	11			34
1	3		4	6					10	12	2	13	8²	7¹		5						9	11			35
1	3		4	6					10	11	13	14	8²	7³		5						2			9¹	36
1	3		8	4	6			12	10	11¹	13	14		7³		5						2			9²	37
1	3			4	6			12	10	11³	13	14		7¹	5	8²						2			9	38
1	3			4	6			12	10	11¹		13		7²	5	8						2			9	39
1	3			4	6			9	10	12		13		7¹	5	8						2			11²	40
1	3		6	4		7		9¹	10	12	13		8			5						2			11²	41
1	3		6	4		7²		9¹	10	12	13	14	8			5						2			11³	42
1	3		6	4	12			9			7³	13	14	8		5¹	10					2²			11	43
1	3		5	4	6			9			11¹	12	8	7²			10					2			13	44
1	3		5	4	6			9	10²			12	8³	7¹		13	11					2			14	45
1	3		5	4	6			9³	10			12	8¹	7²		13	11					2			14	46

Coca-Cola Cup

First Round	Southend U	(a)	2-0
		(h)	1-2
Second Round	Ipswich T	(h)	1-1
		(a)	2-4

FA Cup

First Round	Plymouth Arg	(a)	0-5

GILLINGHAM 1996-97   *Back row (left to right):* Wayne Jones (Physio), Richard Carpenter, Richard Green, Glen Thomas, Steve Butler, Jim Stannard, Mark Harris, Dennis Bailey, Leo Fortune-West, Matt Bryant, Simon Ratcliffe, Kevin Bremner (Youth Team Manager).
Front row: Billy Manuel, Neil Smith, David Puttnam, Andy Hessenthaler, Tony Pulis (Manager), Paul Scally (Chairman), Paul Parsons (Assistant Manager), Mark O'Connor, Ian Chapman, Kevin Rattray, Lennie Piper.

Division 2   GILLINGHAM

Priestfield Stadium, Gillingham, ME7 4DD. Telephone: (01634) 851854/576828. Fax: (01634) 850986.
Ground capacity: 10,600.

Record attendance: 23,002 v QPR, FA Cup 3rd rd, 10 January 1948.

Record receipts: £80,184 v Sheffield W, FA Cup 3rd rd, 7 January 1995.

Pitch measurements: 114yd × 75yd.

Chairman/Chief Executive: P. D. P. Scally.

Director: P. A. Stokes. *Associate Director:* Yvonne Paulley.

Manager: Tony Pulis. *Assistant Manager:* Lindsay Parsons.

Physio: W. Jones.

Secretary: Mrs G. E. Poynter. *Sales and Marketing Manager:* M. Ling.

Year Formed: 1893. *Turned Professional:* 1894. *Ltd Co.:* 1893.

Club Nickname: 'The Gills'.

Previous Name: New Brompton, 1893–1913.

Foundation: The success of the pioneering Royal Engineers of Chatham excited the interest of the residents of the Medway Towns and led to the formation of many clubs including Excelsior. After winning the Kent Junior Cup and the Chatham District League in 1893, Excelsior decided to go for bigger things and it was at a meeting in the Napier Arms, Brompton, in 1893 that New Brompton FC came into being, buying and developing the ground which is now Priestfield Stadium.

First Football League game: 28 August 1920, Division 3, v Southampton (h) D 1-1 – Branfield; Robertson, Sissons; Battiste, Baxter, Wigmore; Holt, Hall, Gilbey (1), Roe, Gore.

Record League Victory: 10–0 v Chesterfield, Division 3, 5 September 1987 – Kite; Haylock, Pearce, Shipley (2) (Lillis), West, Greenall (1), Pritchard (2), Shearer (2), Lovell, Elsey (2), David Smith (1).

Record Cup Victory: 10–1 v Gorleston, FA Cup 1st rd, 16 November 1957 – Brodie; Parry, Hannaway; Riggs, Boswell, Laing; Payne, Fletcher (2), Saunders (5), Morgan (1), Clark (2).

Record Defeat: 2–9 v Nottingham F, Division 3 (S), 18 November 1950.

Most League Points (2 for a win): 62, Division 4, 1973–74.

Most League Points (3 for a win): 83, Division 3, 1984–85 and Division 3, 1995–96.

Most League Goals: 90, Division 4, 1973–74.

Highest League Scorer in Season: Ernie Morgan, 31, Division 3 (S), 1954–55 and Brian Yeo, 31, Division 4, 1973–74.

Most League Goals in Total Aggregate: Brian Yeo, 135, 1963–75.

Most Capped Player: Tony Cascarino, 3 (70), Republic of Ireland.

Most League Appearances: John Simpson, 571, 1957–72.

Record Transfer Fee Received: £350,000 from Tottenham H for Peter Beadle, June 1992.

Record Transfer Fee Paid: £250,000 to Norwich C for Ade Akinbiyi, January 1997.

Football League Record: 1920 Original Member of Division 3; 1921 Division 3 (S); 1938 Failed re-election; Southern League 1938–44; Kent League 1944–46; Southern League 1946–50; 1950 Re-elected to Division 3 (S); 1958–64 Division 4; 1964–71 Division 3; 1971–74 Division 4; 1974–89 Division 3; 1989–92 Division 4; 1992–96; Division 3; 1996– Division 2.

Honours: Football League: Division 3 best season: Runners-up 1995-96; Division 4 – Champions 1963–64; Runners-up 1973–74. *FA Cup:* best season: 5th rd, 1970. *Football League Cup:* best season: 4th rd, 1964, 1997.

Colours: Blue shirts, blue shorts, white stockings. *Change colours:* Red shirts, red shorts, red stockings.

Did you know?
Gillingham conceded only 20 League goals in 1995–96 – a Football League record for 46 games – and goalkeeper Jim Stannard equalled the record of 29 clean sheets in a season.

GILLINGHAM 1996–97 LEAGUE RECORD

Match No.	Date	Venue	Opponents	Result		H/T Score	Lg. Pos.	Goalscorers	Attendance
1	Aug 17	H	Bristol C	W	3-2	1-0	—	Fortune-West [13], Harris [82], Piper [90]	7217
2	24	A	Wycombe W	D	1-1	1-1	4	Ratcliffe [34]	4582
3	27	A	Brentford	L	0-2	0-0	—		5384
4	31	H	Chesterfield	L	0-1	0-0	16		5934
5	Sept 7	H	Burnley	W	1-0	0-0	11	Fortune-West [80]	6116
6	10	A	Luton T	L	1-2	0-1	—	Chapman [81]	4604
7	14	A	Walsall	L	0-1	0-0	18		3419
8	21	H	Rotherham U	W	3-1	3-1	14	Onuora 3 [13, 30, 36]	4920
9	28	A	Stockport Co	L	1-2	0-1	17	Onuora [88]	6049
10	Oct 1	H	Notts Co	W	1-0	0-0	—	Onuora [75]	5482
11	5	H	Bournemouth	D	1-1	0-1	15	Onuora [78]	6162
12	12	A	Blackpool	L	0-2	0-0	17		4320
13	15	A	Shrewsbury T	W	2-1	0-0	—	Onuora [65], Bailey [87]	2042
14	19	H	Millwall	L	2-3	0-1	13	Butler 2 (2 pens) [54, 84]	9305
15	26	H	Preston NE	D	1-1	1-1	13	Onuora [11]	6256
16	29	A	Plymouth Arg	L	0-2	0-0	—		4787
17	Nov 2	A	Bristol R	D	0-0	0-0	16		5530
18	9	H	Wrexham	L	1-2	1-1	18	Ratcliffe [31]	5094
19	19	A	Peterborough U	W	1-0	0-0	—	Onuora [65]	4136
20	23	H	York C	L	0-1	0-1	18		5048
21	30	A	Preston NE	L	0-1	0-0	20		9616
22	Dec 3	H	Crewe Alex	W	2-1	2-0	—	Pennock [19], Smith [38]	3575
23	14	H	Bury	D	2-2	1-1	16	Butler [32], Ratcliffe [51]	5542
24	21	A	Watford	D	0-0	0-0	19		7809
25	26	H	Luton T	L	1-2	1-1	21	Onuora [25]	8598
26	28	A	Burnley	L	1-5	1-1	21	Bailey [14]	10,004
27	Jan 18	A	Notts Co	D	1-1	0-0	21	Puttnam [64]	5008
28	25	H	Plymouth Arg	W	4-1	3-0	18	Curran (og) [5], Green [9], Ratcliffe [26], Akinbiyi [61]	5465
29	Feb 1	A	Wrexham	D	1-1	0-1	18	Akinbiyi [60]	3193
30	8	H	Bristol R	W	1-0	0-0	18	Hessenthaler [57]	6900
31	15	A	York C	W	3-2	1-1	17	Onuora [4], Ratcliffe [67], Akinbiyi [84]	2748
32	22	H	Peterborough U	W	2-1	1-0	15	Onuora 2 [12, 84]	6552
33	Mar 1	A	Crewe Alex	L	2-3	0-3	17	Green [53], Akinbiyi [90]	3555
34	8	H	Watford	W	3-1	0-1	15	Hessenthaler [49], Onuora (pen) [61], Butler [90]	7385
35	15	A	Bury	L	0-3	0-2	17		3492
36	22	H	Wycombe W	W	1-0	0-0	16	Onuora [86]	5932
37	25	A	Rotherham U	W	2-1	1-0	—	Onuora [13], Ratcliffe [57]	2664
38	29	A	Bristol C	W	1-0	0-0	13	Onuora (pen) [74]	11,276
39	31	H	Brentford	L	1-2	1-1	13	Onuora [22]	7361
40	Apr 5	A	Chesterfield	D	2-2	0-1	14	Butler [59], Onuora [77]	3926
41	12	A	Bournemouth	D	2-2	1-1	14	Butler [15], Pennock [83]	5008
42	16	H	Stockport Co	W	1-0	1-0	—	Butler [30]	4485
43	19	H	Blackpool	L	2-3	2-1	14	Galloway [2], Butler [4]	5151
44	26	A	Millwall	W	2-0	1-0	13	Akinbiyi [29], Onuora [85]	8946
45	29	H	Walsall	W	2-0	1-0	—	Onuora [9], Butler [79]	4095
46	May 3	H	Shrewsbury T	W	2-0	0-0	10	Akinbiyi 2 [56, 82]	6183

Final League Position: 10

GOALSCORERS

League (60): Onuora 21 (2 pens), Butler 9 (2 pens), Akinbiyi 7, Ratcliffe 6, Bailey 2, Fortune-West 2, Green 2, Hessenthaler 2, Pennock 2, Chapman 1, Galloway 1, Harris 1, Piper 1, Puttnam 1, Smith 1, own goal 1.
Coca-Cola Cup (8): Ratcliffe 2, Butler 1, Fortune-West 1, Onuora 1, Puttnam 1, Smith 1, own goal 1.
FA Cup (3): Butler 1, Hessenthaler 1, Onuora 1.

Stannard J 38	Humphrey J 9	Ford J 2 + 2	Hessenthaler A 38	Harris M 19 + 2	Bryant M 38 + 1	Chapman I 20 + 3	Ratcliffe S 43	Fortune-West L 7	Butler S 29 + 9	Onuora J 37 + 3	Puttnam D 5 + 9	Bailey D 16 + 14	Piper L 4 + 15	Smith N 42	Carpenter R 1	Morris M 6	O'Connor M 18 + 4	Thomas G 4 + 6	Manuel B 3 + 8	Armstrong C 10	Butters G 30	Green R 28 + 1	Gould J 3	Marshall A 5	Pennock A 26	Akinbiyi A 19	Galloway M 6 + 3	Pinnock J — + 2	Sambrook A — + 1	Match No.
1	2	3	4	5	6	7¹	8	9	10³	11²	12	13	14																	1
1	2	13	4	5	6²	3	8	9³	12	11		10¹	14	7																2
1	2		4	5	6	3	8	9¹	10	11²		12	13	7																3
1	2¹		4	5	6	3	8	9	10	11²	12		13	7																4
1	2		4	5	6	3	8	9	10¹			12		7	11															5
1	2²		4	5	6	3	8	9	10¹	13		12	11	7																6
1	2		4	5	6	3²	8	9¹	12	10		11	13	7																7
1	2	12	4	5¹	6	3	8		10²	9	11³	13	14	7																8
1	2³	3¹	4	5²	6	11	8		9	13	12		14	7		10														9
1			4	5	6	11	8		9	7	12	10¹		2		3														10
1			4	5²	6	11	8		9	13	12	10¹		2		3	7³	14												11
1				5	6	11	8		9	12	13	10²		2			3	7	4¹											12
1				5	6		8		9			7¹	10	2		3	4	12	11											13
1				5	6		8		9			7¹	10	2		3	4¹		11											14
			4		6		8		7			9	10	2			11				3	5								15
					6		8		12	9			10				7²	5¹	13	11	3	2	1							16
				5	6		8		7	9			10	2			11				3	4	1							17
			4		6		8		7	9		10²	12				11			13	3	5¹	1							18
1¹			4	12	6		8		10	9		11²		2			13	7	3	5										19
					6		8		9			7	10¹	12			4	13	11		3	5²		1						20
			6		12		8		10			7²	9	13			2	14	11¹		3	5		1	4³					21
			6		12			10²	9			13		2			4	7¹	11		3	5		1	8					22
			7				8		10	9				2			2	6	12	11¹	3	5		1	4					23
			7		6		8²		10¹	9				12			11		13		3	5		1	4					24
1			7		6		8²		10	9				12			11¹		13		3	5			4					25
1				5	4				12	9		10		8			11¹	6²	13		3	2			7					26
1			7		6		8		10		12			2			11¹				3	5			4	9				27
1			7		6	12	8		10¹					2			11				3	5			4	9				28
1			7		6		8		10			11		2			3				5				4	9				29
1			7	5	6		8			9		11		2			3¹	12							4	10				30
1			7	3	6		8		9	12		11¹		2			13				5²				4	10				31
1					6	11	8		9					2			12				3	5			4	10¹				32
1			7	6²			8		12	9		13		2²			11¹	14			3	5			4	10				33
1			7		6		10		9¹	13		12		2			11³	14			3	5			4	8²				34
1			7	2¹	6		8		9			12		11							3	5			4	10				35
1			7	11	6		8¹		9			12		2							3	5			4	10				36
1			7		6	11	8		12	9¹				2			13				3	5			4	10²				37
1			7		6	11	8		12	9¹		13									3	5			4	10²	2			38
1			7	12	6	11¹	8		13	9				14							3	5¹			2	10	4³			39
1			7		6	11	8		12	9				2							3	5			4	10	8¹			40
1			7		6		4		8²	9¹				2			11				3	12			5	10	13			41
1			7	12	11¹		8		9³	14				13	2						3	5			4	10²	6			42
1			7	5			8		9	12				2			11¹				3				4	10	6			43
1				5					11	9				2							3	4			7	10	6			44
1			7		6		8¹		10	9		11²		2							3	5			4³		12	13	14	45
1			7		6		8		11³	9¹				12	2						3	5²			4	10	13	14		46

Coca-Cola Cup

First Round	Swansea C	(a)	1-0	
		(h)	2-0	
Second Round	Barnsley	(a)	1-1	
		(h)	1-0	
Third Round	Coventry C	(h)	2-2	
		(a)	1-0	
Fourth Round	Ipswich T	(a)	0-1	

FA Cup

First Round	Hereford U	(h)	1-0
Second Round	Cardiff C	(a)	2-0
Third Round	Derby Co	(h)	0-2

GRIMSBY TOWN 1996-97   *Back row (left to right):* Nicky Southall, Tony Gallimore, Andrew Love, Jason Pearcey, Paul Crichton, Peter Handyside, Neil Woods.
Middle row: Mike Bielby (Kit Manager), Daryl Clare, Ashley Fickling, Richard Smith, Steve Livingstone, Mark Lever, Graham Rodger, Jack Lester, Joby Gowshall, James Neil, Paul Harsley, John Oster, Gerry Delahunt (Physio).
Front row: Jamie Forrester, Kevin Jobling, Clive Mendonca, Craig Shakespeare, John Walker, Kenny Swain (Team Manager), Brian Laws, John Cockerill (Youth Coach), John McDermott, Kingsley Black, Darren Wrack, Tommy Widdrington, Gary Childs.

Division 2 GRIMSBY TOWN

Blundell Park, Cleethorpes, North East Lincolnshire DN35 7PY. Telephone: (01472) 697111. Fax: (01472) 693665. Mariners Hotline: 0891 555 855.

Ground capacity: 8870.

Record attendance: 31,657 v Wolverhampton W, FA Cup 5th rd, 20 February 1937.

Record receipts: £119,799 v Aston Villa, FA Cup 4th rd, 29 January 1994.

Pitch measurements: 111yd × 75yd.

President: T. J. Lindley.

Chairman: W. H. Carr. *Vice-Chairman:* T. Aspinall.

Directors: G. Lamming, J. Mager, J. Teanby, C. Aspinall, T. Smith.

Manager: Alan Buckley.

Assistant Manager: John Cockerill.

Chief Executive/Company Secretary: Ian Fleming. *Commercial Manager:* Tony Richardson.

Assistant Commercial Manager/Lottery Manager: T. E. Harvey.

Physio: Gerry Delahunt, FA Treatment of Injuries, MCSP, FSMT, RST.

Year Formed. 1878. *Turned Professional:* 1890. *Ltd Co.:* 1890.

Previous Name: Grimsby Pelham.

Club Nickname: 'The Mariners'.

Previous Grounds: Clee Park; Abbey Park.

Foundation: Grimsby Pelham FC as they were first known, came into being at a meeting held at the Wellington Arms in September 1878. Pelham is the family name of big landowners in the area, the Earls of Yarborough. The receipts for their first game amounted to 6s. 9d. (approx. 39p). After a year, the club name was changed to Grimsby Town.

First Football League game: 3 September 1892, Division 2, v Northwich Victoria (h) W 2-1 – Whitehouse; Lundie, T. Frith; C. Frith, Walker, Murrell; Higgins, Henderson, Brayshaw, Riddoch (2), Ackroyd.

Record League Victory: 9–2 v Darwen, Division 2, 15 April 1899 – Bagshaw; Lockie, Nidd; Griffiths, Bell (1), Nelmes; Jenkinson (3), Richards (1), Cockshutt (3), Robinson, Chadburn (1).

Record Cup Victory: 8–0 v Darlington, FA Cup 2nd rd, 21 November 1885 – G. Atkinson; J. H. Taylor, H. Taylor; Hall, Kimpson, Hopewell; H. Atkinson (1), Garnham, Seal (3), Sharman, Monument (4).

Record Defeat: 1–9 v Arsenal, Division 1, 28 January 1931.

Most League Points (2 for a win): 68, Division 3 (N), 1955–56.

Most League Points (3 for a win): 83, Division 3, 1990–91.

Most League Goals: 103, Division 2, 1933–34.

Highest League Scorer in Season: Pat Glover, 42, Division 2, 1933–34.

Most League Goals in Total Aggregate: Pat Glover, 180, 1930–39.

Most Capped Player: Pat Glover, 7, Wales.

Most League Appearances: Keith Jobling, 448, 1953–69.

Record Transfer Fee Received: £1,000,000 from Blackburn R for Gary Croft, March 1996.

Record Transfer Fee Paid: £300,000 to Southampton for Tommy Widdrington, July 1996.

Football League Record: 1892 Original Member Division 2; 1901–03 Division 1; 1903 Division 2; 1910 Failed re-election; 1911 re-elected Division 2; 1920–21 Division 3; 1921–26 Division 3 (N); 1926–29 Division 2; 1929–32 Division 1; 1932–34 Division 2; 1934–48 Division 1; 1948–51 Division 2; 1951–56 Division 3 (N); 1956–59 Division 2; 1959–62 Division 3; 1962–64 Division 2; 1964–68 Division 3; 1968–72 Division 4; 1972–77 Division 3; 1977–79 Division 4; 1979–80 Division 3; 1980–87 Division 2; 1987–88 Division 3; 1988–90 Division 4; 1990–91 Division 3; 1991–92 Division 2; 1992–97 Division 1; 1997– Division 2.

Honours: Football League: Division 1 best season: 5th, 1934–35; Division 2 – Champions 1900–01, 1933–34; Runners-up 1928–29; Division 3 (N) – Champions 1925–26, 1955–56; Runners-up 1951–52; Division 3 – Champions 1979–80; Runners-up 1961–62; Division 4 – Champions 1971–72; Runners-up 1978–79; 1989–90. *FA Cup:* Semi-finals, 1936, 1939. *Football League Cup:* best season: 5th rd, 1980, 1985. *League Group Cup:* Winners 1982.

Colours: Black and white striped shirts, black shorts, white stockings. *Change colours:* All blue.

Did you know?
Jimmy Carmichael, who scored 137 League goals in 227 appearances for Grimsby Town between 1920 and 1927, achieved a memorable strike to clinch the Third Division (North) Championship on 1 May 1926 against New Brighton.

GRIMSBY TOWN 1996–97 LEAGUE RECORD

Match No.	Date	Venue	Opponents		Result	H/T Score	Lg. Pos.	Goalscorers	Attendance
1	Aug 17	H	Wolverhampton W	L	1-3	0-2	—	Mendonca [62]	7910
2	23	A	Tranmere R	L	2-3	2-1	—	Mendonca (pen) [8], Handyside [45]	6800
3	27	A	Ipswich T	D	1-1	1-1	—	Mendonca [10]	9762
4	31	H	Portsmouth	L	0-1	0-1	22		4747
5	Sept 7	H	Swindon T	W	2-1	2-0	20	Mendonca 2 (1 pen) [8, 32 (p)]	4089
6	10	A	Bolton W	L	1-6	1-2	—	Trollope [27]	12,448
7	14	A	Port Vale	D	1-1	1-1	22	Southall [27]	4892
8	21	H	Oxford U	L	0-2	0-2	23		4120
9	28	A	Barnsley	W	3-1	1-0	20	Shakespeare [15], Forrester [84], McDermott [90]	8833
10	Oct 1	H	Norwich C	L	1-4	1-3	—	Fickling [6]	5266
11	5	H	QPR	W	2-0	2-0	16	Mendonca [12], Widdrington [26]	5472
12	12	A	Reading	D	1-1	0-0	18	Wrack [83]	6656
13	16	A	Southend U	L	0-1	0-0	—		3305
14	19	H	WBA	D	1-1	1-0	21	Fickling [33]	7187
15	26	A	Crystal Palace	L	0-3	0-1	22		13,665
16	29	H	Oldham Ath	L	0-3	0-1	—		3532
17	Nov 3	H	Sheffield U	L	2-4	1-2	23	Livingstone 2 [33, 50]	5935
18	16	H	Stoke C	D	1-1	1-1	24	Mendonca (pen) [20]	5601
19	23	A	Huddersfield T	L	0-2	0-2	24		10,590
20	26	A	Charlton Ath	W	3-1	1-1	—	Mendonca 2 [13, 47], Livingstone [68]	9435
21	30	H	Crystal Palace	W	2-1	1-1	23	Livingstone [10], Rodger [81]	5115
22	Dec 7	A	Birmingham C	D	0-0	0-0	22		17,001
23	21	H	Bradford C	D	1-1	0-1	24	Lester [49]	5766
24	26	H	Bolton W	L	1-2	0-1	24	Childs [69]	8185
25	Jan 11	H	Port Vale	D	1-1	0-0	24	Mendonca [54]	3863
26	18	A	Norwich C	L	1-2	1-2	24	Lester [20]	16,687
27	25	A	Swindon T	D	3-3	2-0	24	Gallimore [5], Appleton [44], Mendonca [87]	9127
28	28	H	Barnsley	L	2-3	1-2	—	Oster [3], Appleton [75]	6323
29	Feb 1	H	Charlton Ath	W	2-0	1-0	24	Mendonca (pen) [25], Lester [52]	4139
30	8	A	Oldham Ath	W	3-0	2-0	24	Oster [12], Woods [19], Mendonca [90]	6549
31	15	H	Huddersfield T	D	2-2	1-1	22	Widdrington [5], Lester [57]	6197
32	22	A	Sheffield U	L	1-3	1-1	23	Lester [42]	17,502
33	Mar 1	H	Birmingham C	L	1-2	1-0	23	Southall [8]	5166
34	5	A	Stoke C	L	1-3	1-0	—	Livingstone [25]	8621
35	8	A	Bradford C	W	4-3	3-2	21	Mendonca 2 [4, 16], Rodger [43], Livingstone [75]	15,219
36	15	H	Manchester C	D	1-1	1-1	21	Appleton [17]	8732
37	18	A	Oxford U	L	2-3	1-0	—	Mendonca [31], Widdrington [80]	6421
38	22	H	Tranmere R	D	0-0	0-0	22		4353
39	31	H	Ipswich T	W	2-1	1-1	22	Mendonca [14], Lee [74]	6268
40	Apr 5	A	Portsmouth	L	0-1	0-0	22		9854
41	12	A	QPR	L	0-3	0-1	22		10,765
42	16	A	Manchester C	L	1-3	1-0	—	Shakespeare [22]	23,334
43	19	H	Reading	W	2-0	1-0	21	Southall [15], Widdrington [71]	4392
44	23	A	Wolverhampton W	D	1-1	1-1	—	Oster [45]	25,474
45	26	A	WBA	L	0-2	0-0	21		15,574
46	May 4	H	Southend U	W	4-0	1-0	22	Southall [44], Mendonca 2 (1 pen) [67, 83 (p)], Lee [85]	7367

Final League Position: 22

GOALSCORERS

League (60): Mendonca 19 (5 pens), Livingstone 6, Lester 5, Southall 4, Widdrington 4, Appleton 3, Oster 3, Fickling 2, Lee 2, Rodger 2, Shakespeare 2, Childs 1, Forrester 1, Gallimore 1, Handyside 1, McDermott 1, Trollope 1, Woods 1, Wrack 1.
Coca-Cola Cup (1): Mendonca 1.
FA Cup (1): Oster 1.

Pearcey J 40	Laws B 3	Gallimore T 36 + 6	Handyside P 8 + 1	Smith R 12 + 2	Widdrington T 41 + 1	Shakespeare C 23 + 3	Webb N 3 + 1	Woods N 21 + 3	Mendonca C 45	Black K 19 + 5	Southall N 23 + 11	Wrack D 5 + 7	McDermott J 29	Livingstone S 23 + 9	Childs G 19 + 8	Forrester J 4 + 9	Walker J — + 1	Fickling A 20 + 7	Trollope P 6 + 1	Jobling K 24 + 4	Lever M 20 + 1	Rodger G 27 + 1	Oster J 21 + 3	Lester J 16 + 6	Appleton M 10	Miller A 3	Love A 3	Neil J — + 1	Lee J 2 + 5	Match No.
1	2¹	3	4	5	6	7	8	9²	10	11	12	13																		1
1		3	4		6	8	9²		10	11	12			2	5	7¹	13													2
1		3	4	6²	5	8			10	11¹	12			2	9	7³	13	14												3
1		3	4	5	6				10	11¹		7		2	9	12		8												4
1			4		6			9	10	11	12			2	5	7¹		8	3											5
1			4		6		12	9	10		11¹	7		2	5⁴			8	3	13										6
1	12		4		6			9	10		11	7		2				8	3¹	5										7
1	12		4¹		6		13	9²	10	11			14	2		7		8²	3	5										8
1	12				6	5			10	11¹		13		2	9	7³	14	4	8	3²										9
1	12			6²	5		13		10	11				2	9	7	8³	4	14	3¹										10
1		3			6	5	12		10	11		13		2	9	7²	8¹	4												11
1	5¹	3			6				10	11	8	13		2	9	7²	12	4												12
1	5³	3			6				10	11¹	8	7		2	9²		12	4			14		13							13
1		3			6				10	11	8	7		2		12	9¹	4			5									14
1		3	12	6	7			9	10	11²	8			2¹		13		4			5									15
1		3	12	6	8			9		11			13	7	10²			4¹		2	5									16
1		3	4		10			6	9²	11			12	8	7¹	13		2³	14		5									17
1		3	4	6	10			9	11					8	7²	13		12	2¹		5									18
1		3¹	4	6	10²			13	9	11				8	7³	14		12	2		5									19
1		3	4	6				11³	9		12			8	7	14		13	2²		5	10¹								20
1		3	4	6				11	9	12	13			8	7¹			2			5	10²								21
1		3	4	6				11	9					8	7			2			5	10								22
1		3	4	6				11	9	12		13		7²				2			5	10¹	8							23
1		3	4	6	12			11	10				7					2¹			5	9	8							24
1		3			6¹			9	10	11²	12	13	2					4		5		7	8							25
1		3						9²	10	12	11			2				4		6¹	5		13	8	7					26
1		3						9	10		11²			2	12	13		4		6³	5		14	8¹	7					27
		3						9³	10		11			2	13	12²		4		14	5		6	8¹	7	1				28
		3			6			9	10					2		12		2			5	4	11	8¹	7	1				29
		3			6			9	10					2		12							5	4	11	8	7	1		30
1		3³		5	6			9¹	10		12			2	13			14						4	11	8²	7			31
1		3		5	6			9	10		12			2	13									4	11	8²	7¹			32
		3²			6	12		9³	10		7			2¹	13		14	5						4	11	8		1		33
			6	3				9	10	5				8²	12			2						4	11¹	13	7	1		34
			6	3				10		11				8				2					9	5	4		7	1		35
1	12		6	3¹				10		11²				8				2			9	5	4	13		7				36
1	12		6	3				10		11²				8³	13			2			9	5¹	4	7	14					37
		3		6	9			10			12			7²				2		5	4	11¹	8					13		38
		3		6	9			10		7				8¹	12			2		5	4		11²					13		39
		3		6³	9			10		7			12	11²			13	2		5	4		14					8¹		40
		3	12	13	9			10		7			2¹					6³		5	4	11	14					8²		41
1		3¹		6	9				7				2	10²				4		8	5		11	12				13		42
1		3		6	9			10		7			2					4			5		11	8						43
1		3		6	9			10	12	7			2							5	4	11²	8¹					13		44
1		3		6	9¹			10	12	7			2			13				5²	4	11	8³					14		45
1		3		6				10	9²	7			2	8³				12			5¹	4	11	13				14		46

Coca-Cola Cup
First Round — Oldham Ath — (a) 1-0 / (h) 0-1

FA Cup
Third Round — Sheffield W — (a) 1-7

HARTLEPOOL UNITED 1996–97   *Back row (left to right):* Chris Horner, Ian Gallagher, Graeme Lee, Denny Ingram, Sean McAuley.
Middle row: Joe Allon, Jamie Allinson, Stephen Howard, Paul O'Connor, Glen Davies, Stephen Pears, Ian McGuckin, Chris McDonald, Billy Horner (Youth Team Coach).
Front row: Gary Hinchley (Physio), Chris Beech, Stephen Halliday, Mick Tait (Assistant Manager), Keith Houchen (Manager), Mark Cooper, David Clegg, Brian Honour (Reserve Team Coach).
(Photograph: Graeme Rowatt Photography)

Division 3   **HARTLEPOOL UNITED**

Victoria Park, Clarence Road, Hartlepool, Cleveland TS24 8B2. Telephone: (01429) 272584. Commercial Dept: (01429) 222077. Fax: (01429) 863007. Football in the Community: (01429) 862595.

Ground capacity: 7229.

Record attendance: 17,426 v Manchester U, FA Cup 3rd rd, 5 January 1957.

Record receipts: £42,300 v Tottenham H, Rumbelows Cup 2nd rd 2nd leg, 9 October 1990.

Pitch measurements: 110yd × 75yd.

Chairman: H. Hornsey.

Directors: A. Bamford, D. Jukes.

Manager: Mick Tait. *Player/Coach:* Paul Baker.

Youth Coach: Billy Horner. *Physio:* Gary Hinchley. *Commercial Manager:* Frank Baggs.

Secretary: Maureen Smith. *Football in the Community Officer:* Brian Honour. *Safety Officer:* Maurice Russell.

Year Formed: 1908. *Turned Professional:* 1908. *Ltd Co.:* 1908.

Club Nickname: 'The Pool'.

Previous Names: Hartlepools United until 1968; Hartlepool until 1977.

Foundation: The inspiration for the launching of Hartlepool United was the West Hartlepool club which won the FA Amateur Cup in 1904–05. They had been in existence since 1881 and their Cup success led in 1908 to the formation of the new professional concern which first joined the North-Eastern League. In those days they were Hartlepools United and won the Durham Senior Cup in their first two seasons.

First Football League game: 27 August 1921, Division 3 (N), v Wrexham (a) W 2-0 – Gill; Thomas, Crilly; Dougherty, Hopkins, Short; Kessler, Mulholland (1), Lister (1), Robertson, Donald.

Record League Victory: 10–1 v Barrow, Division 4, 4 April 1959 – Oakley; Cameron, Waugh; Johnson, Moore, Anderson; Scott (1), Langland (1), Smith (3), Clark (2), Luke (2). (1 og).

Record Cup Victory: 6–0 v North Shields, FA Cup 1st rd, 30 November 1946 – Heywood; Brown, Gregory; Spelman, Lambert, Jones; Price, Scott (2), Sloan (4), Moses, McMahon.

Record Defeat: 1–10 v Wrexham, Division 4, 3 March 1962.

Most League Points (2 for a win): 60, Division 4, 1967–68.

Most League Points (3 for a win): 82, Division 4, 1990–91.

Most League Goals: 90, Division 3 (N), 1956–57.

Highest League Scorer in Season: William Robinson, 28, Division 3 (N), 1927–28 and Joe Allon, 28, Division 4, 1990–91.

Most League Goals in Total Aggregate: Ken Johnson, 98, 1949–64.

Most Capped Player: Ambrose Fogarty, 1 (11), Republic of Ireland.

Most League Appearances: Wattie Moore, 447, 1948–64.

Record Transfer Fee Received: £300,000 from Chelsea for Joe Allon, August 1991.

Record Transfer Fee Paid: £60,000 to Barnsley for Andy Saville, March 1992.

Football League Record: 1921 Original Member of Division 3 (N); 1958–68 Division 4; 1968–69 Division 3; 1969–91 Division 4; 1991–92 Division 3; 1992–94 Division 2; 1994– Division 3.

Honours: Football League: Division 3 best season: 22nd, 1968–69; Division 3 (N) – Runners-up 1956–57. *FA Cup:* best season: 4th rd, 1955, 1978, 1989, 1993. *Football League Cup,* best season: 4th rd, 1975.

Colours: Blue and white striped shirts. *Change colours:* Red shirts with white trim.

Did you know?
Mick Tait became the oldest player since Jack Carr in 1931, to appear for Hartlepool United on 28 September 1996, two days before his 40th birthday.

HARTLEPOOL UNITED 1996–97 LEAGUE RECORD

Match No.	Date	Venue	Opponents	Result	H/T Score	Lg. Pos.	Goalscorers	Attendance
1	Aug 17	A	Colchester U	W 2-0	0-0	—	Allon [52], McAuley [60]	2942
2	24	H	Fulham	W 2-1	0-0	1	Cooper [58], Davies [82]	2457
3	27	H	Mansfield T	D 2-2	1-1	—	Cooper [26], Ingram [89]	2750
4	31	A	Leyton Orient	L 0-2	0-1	4		4342
5	Sept 7	A	Hereford U	W 1-0	0-0	3	Halliday [85]	2735
6	10	H	Carlisle U	L 1-2	1-0	—	Cooper [4]	3077
7	14	A	Wigan Ath	D 1-1	0-0	8	Cooper [90]	2433
8	21	A	Hull C	L 0-1	0-1	11		3886
9	28	H	Chester C	W 2-0	2-0	7	Allon [6], Cooper (pen) [45]	2042
10	Oct 1	A	Doncaster R	L 1-2	0-1	—	Beech [84]	1471
11	5	A	Cambridge U	L 0-1	0-1	11		3406
12	12	H	Darlington	L 1-2	0-1	14	Halliday [61]	3799
13	15	H	Swansea C	D 1-1	1-0	—	Halliday [29]	1310
14	19	A	Barnet	L 0-1	0-0	20		2265
15	26	A	Exeter C	L 0-2	0-0	22		3043
16	29	H	Northampton T	L 0-2	0-2	—		1254
17	Nov 2	H	Brighton & HA	L 2-3	1-2	23	Mike [9], Cooper [86]	1683
18	9	A	Scarborough	W 4-2	1-2	22	Howard [35], Clegg [58], Halliday 2 [66, 72]	3157
19	23	A	Torquay U	W 1-0	0-0	19	Allon [90]	1856
20	30	H	Exeter C	D 1-1	1-1	21	Irvine [31]	1419
21	Dec 3	A	Scunthorpe U	L 1-2	1-1	—	Clegg [20]	1778
22	14	A	Rochdale	W 3-1	2-0	18	Beech [41], Howard [42], Allon [70]	1618
23	21	H	Lincoln C	W 2-1	0-1	17	Cooper (pen) [65], Sunderland [67]	1344
24	26	A	Carlisle U	L 0-1	0-0	19		6947
25	28	H	Hereford U	W 2-1	1-0	17	Allon [4], Howard [73]	1923
26	Jan 1	H	Hull C	D 1-1	0-1	15	Howard [74]	1944
27	11	A	Chester C	D 0-0	0-0	16		1885
28	18	H	Doncaster R	L 2-4	2-2	18	Howard [27], Cooper (pen) [44]	1708
29	25	A	Northampton T	L 0-3	0-2	18		5039
30	Feb 1	H	Scarborough	W 1-0	1-0	16	Cooper [11]	1843
31	8	A	Brighton & HA	L 0-5	0-3	16		8412
32	11	H	Cardiff C	L 2-3	0-1	—	Beech 2 [51, 57]	1120
33	15	H	Torquay U	D 1-1	1-0	17	Beech [38]	1548
34	22	A	Cardiff C	L 0-2	0-2	19		2971
35	Mar 1	H	Scunthorpe U	L 0-1	0-1	21		1300
36	4	A	Wigan Ath	D 2-2	1-1	—	Halliday [54], Howard [76]	3229
37	8	A	Lincoln C	L 1-2	0-1	21	Allon [59]	2915
38	15	H	Rochdale	L 1-2	0-1	22	Beech [59]	1448
39	22	A	Fulham	L 0-1	0-1	23		7222
40	29	H	Colchester U	W 1-0	0-0	22	Beech [78]	2725
41	31	A	Mansfield T	L 0-1	0-1	23		2229
42	Apr 5	A	Leyton Orient	W 3-1	1-1	23	Bradley [41], Baker [57], Halliday [89]	2576
43	12	H	Cambridge U	L 0-2	0-1	23		3186
44	19	A	Darlington	W 2-1	1-1	22	Brown [8], Allon [90]	4662
45	26	H	Barnet	W 4-0	1-0	18	Allon 2 [26, 85], Baker [46], Halliday [64]	3070
46	May 3	A	Swansea C	D 2-2	1-1	20	Howard 2 [17, 63]	5423

Final League Position: 20

GOALSCORERS
League (53): Allon 9, Cooper 9 (3 pens), Halliday 8, Howard 8, Beech 7, Baker 2, Clegg 2, Bradley 1, Brown 1, Davies 1, Ingram 1, Irvine 1, McAuley 1, Mike 1, Sunderland 1.
Coca-Cola Cup (4): Allon 2, Beech 1, Davies 1.
FA Cup (0).

Pears S 16	Ingram D 34 + 3	McAuley S 38	Beech C 42	Davies G 30 + 2	McDonald C 9	Allon J 27 + 3	Cooper M 33	Howard S 26 + 6	Halliday S 28 + 3	Clegg D 24 + 11	Tait M 16 + 3	McGuckin I 21 + 1	Houchen K 2 + 3	Barron M 16	Hislop K 23 + 4	Lee G 23 + 1	Mike A 7	Horace A — + 1	O'Connor P 30	Irvine S 2 + 2	Homer C — + 1	Sunderland J 6 + 7	Walton P 2 + 2	Winstanley C — + 1	Bradley R 12	Elliott A 2 + 2	Proctor M 6	Knowles D 7	Lucas R 7	Cullen J 5 + 1	Baker P 6	Brown M 6	Match No.
1	2	3	4	5	6	7	8	9	10	11[1]	12																						1
1	2	3	7	4	6[1]		8		10	12	11			5	9																		2
1	2	3	6	4		7	8	9[1]	10	11	12			5																			3
1	2	3	11	4	6[2]	7	8	9	10[1]		12	13		5																			4
1	2	3	11	4[1]	6	7	8	9	10		12			5																			5
1	2	3	11	4	6	7[2]	8	9[1]	10		12	13		5																			6
1	2	3	11	4[1]	6	7	8	9	10		12			5																			7
1	2	3	11	4	6[1]	7[2]	8	9	10		12	13		5																			8
1		3	6	4		7	8	9	10	11[1]	12		2	5																			9
1	12	3	6	4		7[2]	8	9	10	11		13	2[1]	5																			10
1	2	3	7		6		8		10					5	11	4	9																11
1	2	3	7		6		8		10		12	13		5	11[1]	4[2]	9																12
1	2	3	7[1]	4	6		8		10		12	13		5	11		9[2]																13
1	12	3	4		6	7[1]	8		10				2	5	11		9																14
1	2	3	4		6	7	8		10					5	11		9																15
1	2[2]	3	4		6	7[3]	8[1]		10		12	13	14	5	11		9																16
1	2	3	4[2]		6	7	8		10		12	13		5	11		9[1]																17
1	2	3	4		6	7	8	9	10					5	11																		18
	2	3	4		6	7	8	9	10[1]		12				11	5			1														19
	2	3	4		6	7	8	9[1]	10		12				11	5			1														20
	2	3	4	5	6	7	8	9	10						11				1														21
	2	3	4		6	7	8	9	10						11	5			1														22
	2	3	4		6	7	8	9	10[1]		12				11	5			1														23
	2	3	4		6	7[1]	8	9	10		12				11	5			1														24
	2	3[1]	4		6	7	8	9	10[2]		12	13			11	5			1														25
	2	3	4		6	7	8	9	10						11	5			1														26
	2	3	4		6	7	8	9	10[1]		12				11	5			1														27
	2	3	4		6	7	8	9	10							5			1						11								28
	2	3	4		6	7	8	9[1]	10[2]		12	13				5			1						11								29
	2	3	4		6	7	8	9	10							5			1						11								30
	2	3	4		6	7	8	9	10[1]		12					5			1						11								31
	2	3	4	5	6		8	9	10										1			7			11								32
	2	3	4		6		8	9[1]	10		12	13			11[2]	5			1			7											33
	2	3	4		6	7[1]	8	9[2]	10		12	13			11	5			1														34
	2	3	4		6[1]	7	8	9	10		12				11	5			1														35
	2	3	4		6	7	8	9	10							5			1						11								36
	2	3	4		6	7	8[2]	9	10		12	13				5			1						11[1]								37
	2	3	4		6[2]	7[1]	8	9	10		12	13			11	5			1														38
	2	3	4[1]		6		8	9[2]	10[3]		12	13	14		11	5			1			7											39
			4		6					11	12	13							1						5	8	2[2]	3	7[1]	9	10		40
			4		6					11	12	13							1						5	8[2]	2	3	7	9[1]	10		41
			4		6	7	8		10[1]		12								1						5		2	3		9	11		42
			4		6	7[1]	8		10		12	13							1						5		2	3[2]		9	11		43
			4		6	7		9[2]	10		12	13							1						5[1]	8	2	3	14		11[3]		44
			4	5	6	7			10										1							8	2	3		9	11		45
			4[1]	5	6				10	11	12								1							8	2	3	7	9			46

Coca-Cola Cup
First Round   Lincoln C   (h) 2-2   (a) 2-3

FA Cup
First Round   York C   (h) 0-0   (a) 0-3

HEREFORD UNITED 1996-97   *Back row (left to right):* Quentin Townsend, Dean Smith, Chris MacKenzie, Nicky Law, Andy Debont, Trevor Mathewson, Gavin Mahon.
Middle row: Simon Shakeshaft (Physio), Neil Bartlett, Gareth Stoker, Chris Hargreaves, John Brough, Gary Cook, Adrian Foster, Phil Preedy, Rob Warner, Dick Bate (Assistant Manager).
Front row: Mark Hibbard, Jamie Pitman, Keith Downing, Graham Turner (Manager), David Norton, Murray Fishlock, Ian Foster.

Vauxhall Conference **HEREFORD UNITED**

Edgar Street, Hereford HR4 9JU. Telephone: (01432) 276666. Fax: (01432) 341359.

Ground capacity: 8843.

Record attendance: 18,114 v Sheffield W, FA Cup 3rd rd, 4 January 1958.

Record receipts: £103,224 v Tottenham H, FA Cup 3rd rd, 6 January 1996.

Pitch measurements: 110yd × 74yd.

Chairman: P. S. Hill FRICS.

Directors: D. H. Vaughan, R. A. Fry, J. Simmons, K. Benjamin (Assoc).

Manager: Graham Turner. *Assistant Manager:* Dick Bate.

Physio: S. Shakeshaft BSC, BA. *Coach:* S. Ritchie.

Secretary: Joan Fennessy. *Commercial Manager:* J. Pulling. *Stadium Manager:* C. Oliver.

Year Formed: 1924. *Turned Professional:* 1924. *Ltd Co.:* 1939.

Club Nickname: 'United'.

Foundation: A number of local teams amalgamated in 1924 under the chairmanship of Dr. E. W. Maples to form Hereford United and joined the Birmingham Combination. They graduated to the Birmingham League four years later.

First Football League game: 12 August 1972, Division 4, v Colchester U (a) L 0-1 – Potter; Mallender, Naylor; Jones, McLaughlin, Tucker; Slattery, Hollett, Owen, Radford, Wallace.

Record League Victory: 6–0 v Burnley (away), Division 4, 24 January 1987 – Rose; Rodgerson, Devine, Halliday, Pejic, Dalziel, Harvey (1p), Wells, Phillips (3), Kearns (2), Spooner.

Record Cup Victory: 6–1 v QPR, FA Cup 2nd rd, 7 December 1957 – Sewell; Tomkins, Wade; Masters, Niblett, Horton (2p); Reg Bowen (1), Clayton (1), Fidler, Williams (1), Cyril Beech (1).

Record Defeat: 0–7 v Middlesbrough, Coca-Cola Cup 2nd rd, 1st leg, 18 September 1996.

Most League Points (2 for a win): 63, Division 3, 1975–76.

Most League Points (3 for a win): 77, Division 4, 1984–85.

Most League Goals: 86, Division 3, 1975–76.

Highest League Scorer in Season: Dixie McNeil, 35, 1975–76.

Most League Goals in Total Aggregate: Stewart Phillips, 93, 1980–88, 1990–91.

Most Capped Player: Brian Evans, 1 (7), Wales.

Most League Appearances: Mel Pejic, 412, 1980–92.

Record Transfer Fee Received: £440,000 from QPR for Darren Peacock, December 1990.

Record Transfer Fee Paid: £80,000 to Walsall for Dean Smith, June 1994.

Football League Record: 1972 Elected to Division 4; 1973–76 Division 3; 1976–77 Division 2; 1977–78 Division 3; 1978–92 Division 4; 1992–97 Division 3; 1997– Vauxhall Conference.

Honours: Football League: Division 2 best season: 22nd, 1976–77; Division 3 – Champions 1975–76; Division 4 – Runners-up 1972–73. *FA Cup:* best season: 4th rd, 1972, 1974, 1977, 1982, 1990, 1992. *Football League Cup:* best season: 3rd rd, 1975. *Welsh Cup:* Winners 1990.

Colours: White and black shirts, black shorts, white stockings. *Change colours:* White and blue striped shirts, blue shorts, blue stockings.

Did you know?
Hereford United won the First Division Championship of the Southern League in 1964–65, finishing 11 points ahead of runners-up Wimbledon.

HEREFORD UNITED 1996–97 LEAGUE RECORD

Match No.	Date	Venue	Opponents	Result	H/T Score	Lg. Pos.	Goalscorers	Attendance
1	Aug 17	A	Fulham	L	0-1	0-0	—	5277
2	24	H	Doncaster R	W	1-0	1-0	15	Stoker [2]	2880
3	27	H	Hull C	L	0-1	0-0	—	2814
4	31	A	Colchester U	D	1-1	0-0	20	Smith [63]	2723
5	Sept 7	H	Hartlepool U	L	0-1	0-0	20		2735
6	10	A	Swansea C	L	0-4	0-3	—	2479
7	14	A	Darlington	L	0-1	0-1	24		3271
8	21	H	Rochdale	W	3-0	1-0	21	Mahon [28], Hargreaves [53], Foster A [84]	2135
9	28	A	Mansfield T	L	1-3	0-1	23	Preedy [70]	1889
10	Oct 1	H	Scunthorpe U	W	3-2	1-0	—	Smith (pen) [37], Hibbard [52], Foster A [75]	1785
11	5	H	Scarborough	D	2-2	1-1	19	Smith [28], Foster A [73]	2506
12	12	A	Torquay U	L	1-2	1-1	21	Hargreaves [2]	2073
13	15	A	Brighton & HA	W	1-0	0-0	—	Foster A [56]	3444
14	19	H	Leyton Orient	W	2-0	0-0	12	Stoker [61], Smith [83]	2625
15	26	A	Chester C	W	3-1	2-1	12	Foster A 2 [22, 76], Brough [32]	2301
16	29	H	Cambridge U	L	0-1	0-0	—		2371
17	Nov 2	H	Barnet	D	1-1	0-1	14	Foster A [56]	2655
18	9	A	Wigan Ath	L	1-4	0-2	16	Preedy [69]	3414
19	19	H	Lincoln C	D	1-1	1-0	—	Stoker [32]	1363
20	23	A	Cardiff C	L	0-2	0-0	18		3900
21	30	H	Chester C	L	1-2	0-1	22	Smith (pen) [55]	2210
22	Dec 3	A	Exeter C	D	1-1	0-1	—	Cross [58]	2189
23	14	A	Carlisle U	L	2-3	1-2	22	Matthewson [45], Smith (pen) [86]	1855
24	20	A	Northampton T	L	0-1	0-0	—		4238
25	26	H	Swansea C	L	0-1	0-1	22		4204
26	28	A	Hartlepool U	L	1-2	0-1	23	Smith [46]	1923
27	Jan 11	H	Mansfield T	L	0-1	0-0	23		1872
28	18	A	Scunthorpe U	L	1-5	1-2	23	Foster A [7]	1986
29	25	A	Cambridge U	W	1-0	1-0	23	Hargreaves [11]	3018
30	Feb 1	H	Wigan Ath	W	3-1	2-1	23	Foster A [23], Beeston [43], Fishlock [48]	2532
31	4	H	Darlington	D	1-1	1-1	—	Beeston [21]	2003
32	8	A	Barnet	W	3-2	1-1	22	Kottila [12], Hargreaves [56], Foster A [70]	2439
33	16	H	Cardiff C	D	1-1	0-1	21	Foster A [53]	4967
34	18	A	Rochdale	D	0-0	0-0	—		1074
35	22	H	Lincoln C	D	3-3	1-1	20	Matthewson [38], Smith [57], Williams [90]	2957
36	Mar 1	A	Exeter C	L	1-2	1-0	22	Williams [41]	2735
37	8	H	Northampton T	L	1-2	0-2	22	Foster A [90]	3043
38	15	A	Carlisle U	W	3-2	2-2	20	Foster A 3 [17, 38, 51]	5063
39	21	A	Doncaster R	L	0-1	0-0	—		2483
40	29	H	Fulham	D	0-0	0-0	23		4473
41	31	H	Hull C	D	1-1	0-1	22	Foster A [50]	2818
42	Apr 5	H	Colchester U	W	1-0	1-0	22	McGorry [45]	2535
43	12	A	Scarborough	D	1-1	1-0	22	Williams [37]	2332
44	19	H	Torquay U	D	1-1	0-1	23	Agana [59]	2852
45	26	A	Leyton Orient	L	1-2	0-0	24	Agana [79]	5599
46	May 3	H	Brighton & HA	D	1-1	1-0	24	Mayo (og) [21]	8532

Final League Position: 24

GOALSCORERS

League (50): Foster A 16, Smith 8 (3 pens), Hargreaves 4, Stoker 3, Williams 3, Agana 2, Beeston 2, Matthewson 2, Preedy 2, Brough 1, Cross 1, Fishlock 1, Hibbard 1, Kottila 1, McGorry 1, Mahon 1, own goal 1.
Coca-Cola Cup (4): Smith 2 (1 pen), Foster A 1, Norton 1.
FA Cup (0).

Debont A 27	Norton D 45	Fishlock M 29+1	Smith D 42	Brough J 32+7	Townsend Q 6+1	Pitman J 4+4	Downing K 16	Foster A 42+1	Foster I 4+15	Mahon G 10+1	Stoker G 25+2	Hargreaves C 42+2	Sutton W 4	Cook G 17+3	Hibbard M 5+2	Preedy P 2+7	Bartlett N —+3	Forsyth M 12	Warner R 16+5	Matthewson T 35	Law N 14	Ellison L —+1	Kottila M 11+2	O'Toole G 1	Cross J 5	Wood T 19	Beeston C 9	Williams J 8+3	Jordan R 1	Sandeman B 7	McGorry B 7	Agana T 3+2	Turner M 6	Match No.
1	2	3	4	5	6	7[1]	8[2]	9	10	11	12	13																						1
1	2	3	4	5	6		8	9			11	7	10																					2
1	2	3	4	5	6		8[1]	9		12	11	7	10																					3
1	2	3	4	5	6		8	9			11	7	10																					4
1	2	3	4	5	6	12	8	9		13	11[2]	7[1]	10																					5
1	2	3	4	5	6[2]	7[1]	8	9	10[3]	14	12	13	11																					6
1	2	3	4	5				9	10[1]	11	7	8	6	12																				7
1			4	5	12	7[1]	2	9		11[2]	8[3]	10	6	3	13	14																		8
1	2		5			11[2]	8	10	6[1]	9		3	12	13				4	7															9
1	2		4	5				9	12		8	10	7					3	11[1]		6													10
1	2		4	5				9			8	10	7					3	11[1]	12	6													11
1	2		4	12				9	11[3]		8	10	7[1]	13					6[2]	3	5	14												12
1	2		4	11				9			8	10	7						6	3	5													13
1	2		4	11[1]				9			8	10	7					12	6	3	5													14
1	2		4	11				9			8	10	7						6	3	5													15
1	2		4	11				9			8	10	7					12	6[1]	3	5													16
1	2		4	11				9			8	10	7						6	3	5													17
1	2		4	11[2]				9			8	10	7[1]					12	6	3	5		13											18
1	2		4	11				9			8	10	7						6	3	5													19
1	2		4	11[1]				9			8	10	12						6	3	5				7									20
1	2		4	11[1]				9		12	7[2]	8	10					13	5	3	6													21
1	2		4	11				9			8	10	7						5	3	6													22
1	2	12	4	11				9		13	8[2]		7[1]						5	3	6	14	10[3]											23
1	2	3	4	11				9		12	8		7[2]					13	5		6		10[1]											24
1	2	3	4	11[1]						12	8		7						5		6				9	10								25
1	2	3	4	5						12	8		7						11[1]		6				9	10								26
	2	3	4	5				9[1]		12	8		7					13		6			11[2]		10	1								27
	2	3	4	5[1]				9	11	12	8		7							6					10	1								28
	2[2]	3	4		12		11	9			8		7					13		6			10[1]			1		5						29
	2	3	4		12		11	9[2]	13			7								8	6		10[1]			1		5						30
	2	3	4		12		11	9[2]	13			7								8	6		10[1]			1		5						31
	2	3	4		12		11	9				7								8	6		10[1]			1		5						32
	2	3	4				11	9				7								8	6		10[1]			1		5	12					33
	2	3	4					9		11		7								8	6		10[1]			1		5	12					34
	2	3	4	7			12	11	9											8[1]	6		10[2]			1		5	13					35
	2	3	4		12		11[2]	9	13											8[1]	6					1		5	10	7				36
	2	3	4	11				9				7								8	6					1		5	10					37
	2	3	4	5[2]	13			9[1]	12			7				11				8	6					1			10					38
	2	3	4	5[1]				9	12			7				11[2]	13			8	6					1			10					39
	2	3	4					9				7									6					1				5	8	10	11	40
	2	3	4					9				7		12							6					1				5	8	10[1]	11	41
	2	3		4[1]	12			9[2]	13			7								10	6					1				5	8		11	42
	2	3	4					9[1]	12			7		13							6					1		10		5	8		11[2]	43
	2	3		4[1]	12			9				7									6					1		10		5	8	13	11[2]	44
	2	3[1]	4					9				7		12							6					1		10		5	8	13	11[2]	45
1	2		4					9				7								3	6							10		5	8		11	46

Coca-Cola Cup

First Round	Cambridge U	(h)	3-0
		(a)	1-1
Second Round	Middlesbrough	(a)	0-7
		(h)	0-3

FA Cup

| First Round | Gillingham | (a) | 0-1 |

HUDDERSFIELD TOWN 1996–97 *Back row (left to right):* Rodney Rowe, Iain Dunn, Jonathan Dyson, Sam Collins, Simon Collins, Simon Baldry, Robbie Ryan.
Middle row: Dennis Booth (First Team Coach), Rob Edwards, Andy Payton, Derek O'Connor, Steve Francis, Tony Norman, Steve Jenkins, Paul Dalton, David Moss (Reserve Team Coach).
Front row: Paul Reid, Darren Bullock, Marcus Stewart, Andy Morrison, Brian Horton (Manager), Lee Sinnott, Kevin Gray, Tom Cowan, Lee Makel.

Division 1   **HUDDERSFIELD TOWN**

The Alfred McAlpine Stadium, Leeds Rd, Huddersfield HD1 6PX. Telephone: (01484) 420335. Fax: (01484) 515122. Ticket Office: (01484) 424444. Club Shop: (01484) 534867. Recorded Information: 0891 121635.

Ground capacity: 19,600.

Record attendance: 67,037 v Arsenal, FA Cup 6th rd, 27 February 1932 (at old ground): 18,775 v Birmingham C, Division 2, 6 May 1995 (at new ground).

Record receipts: £155,149 v Wimbledon, FA Cup 5th rd, 17 February 1996.

Pitch measurements: 115yd × 76yd.

President: Lawrence Batley OBE. *Chairman:* J. M. Asquith.

Directors: D. A. Taylor, E. R. Whiteley, D. G. Headey.

Associate Director: T. J. Cherry.

Manager: Brian Horton. *First Team Coach:* Dennis Booth. *Coach:* David Moss.

Secretary: Alan D. Sykes. *Assistant Secretary:* Ann Hough. *Commercial Manager:* Alan Stevenson.

Physio: John Dickens. *Stadium Manager:* Brian Buckley.

Year Formed: 1908. *Turned Professional:* 1908. *Ltd Co.:* 1908.

Club Nickname: 'The Terriers'.

Foundation: A meeting, attended largely by members of the Huddersfield & District FA, was held at the Imperial Hotel in 1906 to discuss the feasibility of establishing a football club in this rugby stronghold. However, it was not until a man with both the enthusiasm and the money to back the scheme came on the scene, that real progress was made. This benefactor was Mr. Hilton Crowther and it was at a meeting at the Albert Hotel in 1908, that the club formally came into existence with a capital of £2,000 and joined the North-Eastern League.

First Football League game: 3 September 1910, Division 2, v Bradford PA (a) W 1-0 – Mutch; Taylor, Morris; Beaton, Hall, Bartlett; Blackburn, Wood, Hamilton (1), McCubbin, Jee.

Record League Victory: 10–1 v Blackpool, Division 1, 13 December 1930 – Turner; Goodall, Spencer; Redfern, Wilson, Campbell; Bob Kelly (1), McLean (4), Robson (3), Davies (1), Smailes (1).

Record Cup Victory: 7–0 v Lincoln U, FA Cup 1st rd, 16 November 1991 – Clarke; Trevitt, Charlton, Donovan (2), Mitchell, Doherty, O'Regan (1), Stapleton (1) (Wright), Roberts (2), Onuora (1), Barnett (Ireland).

Record Defeat: 1–10 v Manchester C, Division 2, 7 November 1987.

Most League Points (2 for a win): 66, Division 4, 1979–80.

Most League Points (3 for a win): 82, Division 3, 1982–83.

Most League Goals: 101, Division 4, 1979–80.

Highest League Scorer in Season: Sam Taylor, 35, Division 2, 1919–20; George Brown, 35, Division 1, 1925–26.

Most League Goals in Total Aggregate: George Brown, 142, 1921–29 and Jimmy Glazzard, 142, 1946–56.

Most Capped Player: Jimmy Nicholson, 31 (41), Northern Ireland.

Most League Appearances: Billy Smith, 520, 1914–34.

Record Transfer Fee Received: £2,700,000 from Sheffield W for Andy Booth, July 1996.

Record Transfer Fee Paid: £1,200,000 to Bristol R for Marcus Stewart, July 1996.

Football League Record: 1910 Elected to Division 2; 1920–52 Division 1; 1952–53 Division 2; 1953–56 Division 1; 1956–70 Division 2; 1970–72 Division 1; 1972–73 Division 2; 1973–75 Division 3; 1975–80 Division 4; 1980–83 Division 3; 1983–88 Division 2; 1988–92 Division 3; 1992–95 Division 2; 1995– Division 1.

Honours: Football League: Division 1 – Champions 1923–24, 1924–25, 1925–26; Runners-up 1926–27, 1927–28, 1933–34; Division 2 – Champions 1969–70; Runners-up 1919–20, 1952–53; Promoted from Division 2 1994–95 (play-offs); Division 4 – Champions 1979–80. *FA Cup:* Winners 1922; Runners-up 1920, 1928, 1930, 1938. *Football League Cup:* Semi-final 1968. *Autoglass Trophy:* Runners-up 1994.

Colours: Blue and white striped shirts, white shorts, white stockings with single navy hoop. *Change colours:* Ecru shirt with single jade and navy band and jade and navy sleeves, ecru shorts with jade and navy trim, ecru, jade and navy hooped stockings.

Did you know?
Huddersfield Town provided five players for the England v Scotland game at Wembley on 31 March 1928 – the famous Wembley Wizards occasion –– but still managed to beat Bury 3–2 away in the League on the same day.

HUDDERSFIELD TOWN 1996–97 LEAGUE RECORD

Match No.	Date	Venue	Opponents	Result	H/T Score	Lg. Pos.	Goalscorers	Attendance
1	Aug 17	H	Charlton Ath	W 2-0	1-0	—	Bullock [15], Morrison [86]	11,858
2	25	A	Barnsley	L 1-3	1-1	12	Cowan [44]	9787
3	31	H	Crystal Palace	D 1-1	1-0	16	Payton [33]	11,166
4	Sept 7	A	Ipswich T	W 3-1	0-0	7	Payton 2 [47, 57], Stewart [51]	10,661
5	10	H	Tranmere R	L 0-1	0-1	—		10,181
6	13	H	Oldham Ath	W 3-2	1-1	—	Stewart 2 [15, 85], Gray [90]	10,296
7	22	A	Stoke C	L 2-3	2-1	14	Worthington (og) [7], Stewart [36]	9147
8	28	H	Reading	W 1-0	1-0	11	Payton [34]	10,330
9	Oct 8	H	Birmingham C	W 3-0	3-0	—	Edwards [17], Stewart [23], Dalton [45]	10,904
10	12	A	WBA	D 1-1	0-0	7	Cowan [54]	14,960
11	16	A	Swindon T	L 0-6	0-4	—		7724
12	19	H	Southend U	D 0-0	0-0	11		9578
13	26	H	Port Vale	L 0-1	0-0	12		11,017
14	30	A	Wolverhampton W	D 0-0	0-0	—		22,376
15	Nov 2	A	Bolton W	L 0-2	0-1	15		15,865
16	8	H	Bradford C	D 3-3	2-3	—	Dalton [42], Lawson [45], Crosby [48]	14,126
17	16	A	Oxford U	L 0-1	0-0	16		7460
18	19	A	Manchester C	D 0-0	0-0	—		23,314
19	23	H	Grimsby T	W 2-0	2-0	13	Payton 2 [24, 27]	10,590
20	30	A	Port Vale	D 0-0	0-0	15		6026
21	Dec 3	A	Sheffield U	L 1-3	1-2	—	Payton [14]	14,700
22	7	H	Norwich C	W 2-0	1-0	13	Payton 2 [34, 56]	10,749
23	14	A	Portsmouth	L 1-3	0-3	17	Makel [51]	6954
24	21	H	QPR	L 1-2	0-1	18	Payton [51]	10,718
25	26	A	Tranmere R	D 1-1	1-0	18	Payton [21]	10,134
26	28	H	Ipswich T	W 2-0	0-0	18	Lawson [50], Payton [85]	11,467
27	Jan 1	H	Stoke C	W 2-1	1-1	12	Makel [6], Edwards [63]	12,019
28	18	H	Manchester C	D 1-1	0-1	13	Lawson [78]	18,358
29	25	A	Oldham Ath	W 2-1	0-0	13	Payton 2 [71, 83]	8566
30	28	A	Reading	L 1-4	1-3	—	Payton [9]	5710
31	Feb 1	A	Bradford C	D 1-1	1-1	14	Crosby [1]	17,373
32	8	H	Wolverhampton W	L 0-2	0-1	14		15,267
33	15	A	Grimsby T	D 2-2	1-1	16	Stewart [44], Edwards [48]	6197
34	22	H	Bolton W	L 1-2	1-1	16	Cowan [16]	16,061
35	Mar 1	A	Norwich C	L 0-2	0-1	17		13,001
36	4	H	Oxford U	W 1-0	1-0	—	Makel [27]	11,276
37	8	A	QPR	L 0-2	0-1	18		9789
38	15	H	Portsmouth	L 1-3	1-0	20	Stewart [35]	10,512
39	22	H	Barnsley	D 0-0	0-0	20		14,754
40	31	H	Sheffield U	W 2-1	2-1	19	Dalton [1], Cowan [18]	14,551
41	Apr 5	A	Crystal Palace	D 1-1	0-0	20	Payton [61]	13,541
42	9	A	Charlton Ath	L 1-2	0-0	—	Dalton [77]	11,032
43	12	A	Birmingham C	L 0-1	0-0	20		14,394
44	19	H	WBA	D 0-0	0-0	20		12,748
45	26	A	Southend U	W 2-1	1-0	20	Payton [23], Beresford [67]	4762
46	May 4	H	Swindon T	D 0-0	0-0	20		11,506

Final League Position: 20

GOALSCORERS

League (48): Payton 17, Stewart 7, Cowan 4, Dalton 4, Edwards 3, Lawson 3, Makel 3, Crosby 2, Beresford 1, Bullock 1, Gray 1, Morrison 1, own goal 1.
Coca-Cola Cup (9): Stewart 4, Payton 2, Collins 1, Cowan 1, Edwards 1.
FA Cup (2): Crosby 1, Edwards 1.

Francis S 42	Jenkins S 33	Cowan T 42	Bullock D 26+1	Morrison A 9+1	Gray K 36+3	Collins S 10+6	Makel L 19	Stewart M 19+1	Payton A 38	Edwards R 24+9	Sinnott L 29+1	Dalton P 17+12	Reid P 20+2	Dyson J 18+5	Baldry S 2+5	Burnett W 33+2	Ryan R 2+3	Collins S 3+1	Lawson I 8+10	Heary T 2+3	Rowe R 1+6	Crosby G 19+5	Williams M 2	Davies S 3	Tisdale P 1+1	Norman T 4	Dunn I 1+4	Illingworth J 2+1	Browning M 13	Edmondson D 10	Glover L 11	Facey D 1+2	Beresford D 6	Kaye P —+1	Match No.
1	2	3	4	5	6^1	7	8	9	10	11	12																								1
1	2	3	4	5	6	12	8^2	9	10	11^3	7^1	13	14																						2
1		3	4	5	6	2^1		9	10	11		7^2	8	12	13																				3
1	2^1	3	4	5	6	12		9^2	10	11		7				8	13																		4
1		3	4	5^1	6	2		9	10	11		7^2				8			12	13															5
1	2	3	4		6	12		9	10	11^2		7^1				8		5	13																6
1	2	3	4		6	12	7^2	9	10	13	5^1	14				8		11^3																	7
1	2	3	4		6		11	9	10			7				8		5^1	12																8
1	2	3	4		6		7	9^1	10	11	5	12				8																			9
1	2	3	4		6	12	7^1		9^2	10	5	11				8			13																10
1	2	3			6	4				11^3	5	9	7^1	8^2					13	12	10	14													11
1	2	3			6	10^1				11^3	5	7				8			9	12	13	4													12
1	2	3	4^1		6		7		10^2	9	5	12				8			13	14	11^3														13
		3	4		6	2		9			5					8			10^1	12	11		7												14
		3	4^2		6	2			9^2	5		12	13			8			10	14	11		7^1												15
1	2	3	12		6				10	13	5	11				8		9			7^2	4^1													16
1	2	3	4		6			9^2	10	12	5	11^1				8		13			7														17
1	2	3	4	5^1		12		9	10			6	11^2	7		8			13																18
1	2	3	4		6				10	11	5	7			12	8		9^1																	19
1	2	3			6		4^2		10	11^1	5	7			9	8						12		13											20
1	2	3	4		6		7		10		5	12			9	8^1						11													21
1	2	3	4		6		7		10	12	5	8^1			9							11													22
		3	4		6		7		10	12	5				9	8^2						11			2^1	1	13								23
1	2	3			6		7		10	8^1	5			4	9							11				12									24
		3	4		6	2	7		10	8^1	5				9							11				1	12								25
	2	3	4		6^2		8^3	7^1	10	11	5			12	13		14					9				1									26
	2	3	4				7		10	11	5^1			12			9	6				8				1									27
1	2				6		7^3	9	10^1	11^2	12	3	5		4		13					8					14								28
1	2	3	4		6				10	12	7	5	11			9^1						8													29
1	2		4^3		6				10	9^2	7	5	3			13	12					8						11^1	14						30
1	2	3	4		6				10	9	7	5	11									8													31
1		3	4		6	12			10	11^2	9^1	7	5		2					13		8													32
1		3			6	4		9	10^1	11		7	5		2				12			8													33
1	2^1	3			6^2		7	9	10	14		11				5	12		13^3			8							4						34
1		3			6		7	9	10	2^1		12	11		13	5^3	14					8^2							4						35
1		3			6		7	9	10			12	11			5													4	2	8^1				36
1		3			6			9	7^1			11			12	5	10												4	2	8				37
1	2				6			9		12	11		8^2	7^3	3^1				13										4	5	10	14			38
1	2	3^1				12						13	6	11		8	14												4	5	10	12			39
1	2	3							10	12		6	11			8^1													4	5	10^2	9^2	7		40
1	2	3								12		10	6		13	8^2						11							4	5	9		7^1		41
1	2	3	12									10	6		13	8^2						11							4	5	9		7		42
1	2	3^2	8	12								10	13	6^1	7							11							4	5	9		7		43
1	2	3									5	12	10	6	11^1							8							4		9		7		44
1									10		6	12	8			5		11										3	4	2	9^1		7		45
1		3	5						10		6					12^2	13	8^1				11^3							4	2	9		7	14	46

Coca-Cola Cup

First Round	Wrexham	(h)	3-0
		(a)	2-1
Second Round	Colchester U	(h)	1-1
		(a)	2-0
Third Round	Middlesbrough	(a)	1-5

FA Cup

Third Round	QPR	(a)	1-1
		(h)	1-2

HULL CITY 1996–97 *Back row (left to right)*: Paul Wharton, Scott Maxfield, Simon Trevitt, Andy Mason, Steve Wilson, Roy Carroll, Jamie Marks, Duane Darby, Michael Quigley, Kenny Gilbert. *Middle row*: Rod Arnold (Youth Coach), Antonio Doncel, Mark Greaves, Ian Wilkinson, Andy Brown, Neil Allison, Gavin Gordon, Ian Wright, Paul Fewings, Jeff Radcliffe (Physio), Billy Legg (U16 Manager). *Front row*: Gregor Rioch, Adam Lowthorpe, Warren Joyce, Terry Dolan (Manager), Martin Fish (Chairman), Jeff Lee (Assistant Manager), Tony Brien, Neil Mann, Richard Peacock.

Division 3   HULL CITY

Boothferry Park, Hull HU4 6EU. Telephone: (01482) 351119. Fax: (01482) 565752. Commercial Manager: (01482) 566050. Football in the Community Office: (01482) 565088. Club Shop: 01482 328297.

Ground capacity: 12,996.

Record attendance: 55,019 v Manchester U, FA Cup 6th rd, 26 February 1949.

Record receipts: £79,604 v Liverpool, FA Cup 5th rd, 18 February 1989.

Pitch measurements: 115yd × 75yd.

Honorary Vice-President: H. Bermitz.

Vice-Presidents: R. Booth, A. Fetiveau, W. Law.

Chairman: M. W. Fish MCA.

Directors: G. H. C. Needler MA, FCA.

Manager: Mark Hateley. *Assistant Manager:* Jeff Lee.

Secretary: M. W. Fish. *Physio:* Jeff Radcliffe MCSP, SRP.

Commercial Manager: Simon Cawkill. *Stadium Manager:* John Cooper.

Ticket Office/Gate Manager: Wilf Rogerson. *Hon. Medical Officers:* Mr F. R. Howell MA, FRCS, Dr. B. Kell MBBS.

Year Formed: 1904. *Turned Professional:* 1905. *Ltd Co.:* 1905.

Club Nickname: 'The Tigers'.

Previous Grounds: 1904, Boulevard Ground (Hull RFC); 1905, Anlaby Road (Hull CC); 1944–45 Boulevard Ground; 1946, Boothferry Park.

Foundation: The enthusiasts who formed Hull City in 1904 were brave men indeed. More than that they were audacious for they immediately put the club on the map in this Rugby League fortress by obtaining a three-year agreement with the Hull Rugby League club to rent their ground! They had obtained quite a number of conversions to the dribbling code, before the Rugby League forbade the use of any of their club grounds by Association Football clubs. By that time, Hull City were well away having entered the FA Cup in their initial season and the Football League, Second Division after only a year.

First Football League game: 2 September 1905, Division 2, v Barnsley (h) W 4-1 – Spendiff; Langley, Jones; Martin, Robinson, Gordon (2); Rushton, Spence (1), Wilson (1), Howe, Raisbeck.

Record League Victory: 11–1 v Carlisle U, Division 3 (N), 14 January 1939 – Ellis; Woodhead, Dowen; Robinson (1), Blyth, Hardy; Hubbard (2), Richardson (2), Dickinson (2), Davies (2), Cunliffe (2).

Record Cup Victory: 8–2 v Stalybridge Celtic (away), FA Cup 1st rd, 26 November 1932 – Maddison; Goldsmith, Woodhead; Gardner, Hill (1), Denby; Forward (1), Duncan, McNaughton (1), Wainscoat (4), Sargeant (1).

Record Defeat: 0–8 v Wolverhampton W, Division 2, 4 November 1911.

Most League Points (2 for a win): 69, Division 3, 1965–66.

Most League Points (3 for a win): 90, Division 4, 1982–83.

Most League Goals: 109, Division 3, 1965–66.

Highest League Scorer in Season: Bill McNaughton, 39, Division 3 (N), 1932–33.

Most League Goals in Total Aggregate: Chris Chilton, 195, 1960–71.

Most Capped Player: Terry Neill, 15 (59), Northern Ireland.

Most League Appearances: Andy Davidson, 520, 1952–67.

Record Transfer Fee Received: £750,000 from Middlesbrough for Andy Payton, November 1991.

Record Transfer Fee Paid: £200,000 to Leeds U for Peter Swan, March 1989.

Football League Record: 1905 Elected to Division 2; 1930–33 Division 3 (N); 1933–36 Division 2; 1936–49 Division 3 (N); 1949–56 Division 2; 1956–58 Division 3 (N); 1958–59 Division 3; 1959–60 Division 2; 1960–66 Division 3; 1966–78 Division 2; 1978–81 Division 3; 1981–83 Division 4; 1983–85 Division 3; 1985–91 Division 2; 1991–92 Division 3; 1992–96 Division 2; 1996– Division 3.

Honours: Football League: Division 2 best season: 3rd, 1909–10; Division 3 (N) – Champions 1932–33, 1948–49; Division 3 – Champions 1965–66; Runners-up 1958–59; Division 4 – Runners-up 1982–83. *FA Cup:* best season: Semi-final 1930. *Football League Cup:* best season: 4th, 1974, 1976, 1978. *Associate Members' Cup:* Runners-up 1984.

Colours: Amber shirts, black shorts, amber stockings. *Change colours:* All white.

Did you know?
Duane Darby scored a Hull City club record six goals in the FA Cup first round replay against Whitby Town on 26 November 1996. He had almost been omitted from the team because of a knee injury and a touch of influenza.

HULL CITY 1996–97 LEAGUE RECORD

Match No.	Date	Venue	Opponents	Result	H/T Score	Lg. Pos.	Goalscorers	Attendance
1	Aug 17	H	Darlington	W 3-2	1-1	—	Darby 3 [34, 63, 89]	4224
2	24	A	Carlisle U	D 0-0	0-0	4		5407
3	27	A	Hereford U	W 1-0	0-0	—	Darby [50]	2814
4	31	H	Barnet	D 0-0	0-0	3		4605
5	Sept 7	H	Rochdale	D 1-1	0-1	6	Doncel [53]	3451
6	10	A	Lincoln C	W 1-0	1-0	—	Peacock [7]	3069
7	14	A	Colchester U	D 1-1	0-0	4	Gordon [52]	3073
8	21	H	Hartlepool U	W 1-0	1-0	4	Darby [5]	3886
9	28	A	Swansea C	D 0-0	0-0	5		2961
10	Oct 1	H	Mansfield T	D 1-1	0-0	—	Gordon [66]	3579
11	5	H	Scunthorpe U	L 0-2	0-0	5		5414
12	12	A	Leyton Orient	D 1-1	0-0	6	Brien [57]	4490
13	15	A	Scarborough	L 2-3	0-1	—	Turner 2 [55, 76]	3425
14	19	H	Fulham	L 0-3	0-1	11		3986
15	26	A	Wigan Ath	W 2-1	1-0	9	Peacock [11], Trevitt [54]	3887
16	29	H	Cardiff C	D 1-1	0-1	—	Gilbert [79]	2775
17	Nov 2	H	Cambridge U	L 1-3	0-2	11	Brown [79]	3563
18	9	A	Chester C	D 0-0	0-0	11		2085
19	20	H	Torquay U	W 2-0	1-0	—	Darby [39], Peacock [55]	1775
20	23	A	Exeter C	D 0-0	0-0	10		3423
21	30	H	Wigan Ath	D 1-1	0-0	12	Doncel [77]	3537
22	Dec 3	A	Northampton T	L 1-2	0-2	—	Darby [57]	3519
23	14	A	Brighton & HA	L 0-3	0-1	15		3762
24	21	H	Doncaster R	W 3-1	0-1	13	Mason 2 [62, 88], Darby [68]	2830
25	26	H	Lincoln C	W 2-1	2-1	8	Darby [26], Mann [32]	4892
26	Jan 1	A	Hartlepool U	D 1-1	1-0	10	Joyce [13]	1944
27	11	H	Swansea C	D 1-1	0-0	10	Mann [83]	2810
28	18	A	Mansfield T	L 0-1	0-0	14		2286
29	25	A	Cardiff C	L 0-2	0-1	15		2328
30	Feb 1	H	Chester C	W 1-0	0-0	12	Gordon [77]	2513
31	8	A	Cambridge U	L 0-1	0-1	13		3029
32	15	H	Exeter C	W 2-0	2-0	13	Joyce [7], Gordon [22]	2668
33	22	A	Torquay U	D 1-1	0-1	13	Greaves [82]	2072
34	25	A	Rochdale	W 2-1	1-1	—	Joyce [12], Darby [71]	1349
35	Mar 1	H	Northampton T	D 1-1	1-0	12	Darby [24]	3495
36	8	A	Doncaster R	D 0-0	0-0	13		3274
37	15	H	Brighton & HA	W 3-0	1-0	11	Joyce 2 [33, 58], Darby [90]	3373
38	22	H	Carlisle U	L 0-1	0-0	14		3847
39	29	A	Darlington	L 0-1	0-1	14		3024
40	31	H	Hereford U	D 1-1	1-0	14	Greaves [6]	2818
41	Apr 5	A	Barnet	L 0-1	0-0	14		1668
42	12	A	Scunthorpe U	D 2-2	2-1	15	Quigley [16], Lowthorpe [30]	4257
43	15	H	Colchester U	L 1-2	1-2	—	Darby [19]	2035
44	19	H	Leyton Orient	W 3-2	2-1	15	Peacock [24], Mann [31], Rioch (pen) [49]	2647
45	26	A	Fulham	L 0-2	0-1	15		10,588
46	May 3	H	Scarborough	L 0-2	0-1	17		3774

Final League Position: 17

GOALSCORERS

League (44): Darby 13, Joyce 5, Gordon 4, Peacock 4, Mann 3, Doncel 2, Greaves 2, Mason 2, Turner 2, Brien 1, Brown 1, Gilbert 1, Lowthorpe 1, Quigley 1, Rioch 1 (pen), Trevitt 1.
Coca-Cola Cup (4): Rioch 2 (1 pen), Gordon 1, Quigley 1.
FA Cup (9): Darby 6, Joyce 1, Mann 1, Peacock 1.

Carroll R 23	Trevitt S 21 + 1	Rioch G 38 + 1	Wright I 40	Doncel A 22 + 4	Brien T 29 + 3	Joyce W 45	Gilbert K 15 + 4	Darby D 40 + 1	Mann N 24 + 8	Gordon G 19 + 1	Brown A 7 + 19	Maxfield S 10 + 7	Quigley M 23 + 6	Peacock R 34 + 6	Allison N 11	Wilson S 14 + 1	Greaves M 23 + 7	Fewings P 3 + 9	Wharton P — + 1	Marks J 7 + 3	Turner R 5	Dewhurst R 20 + 2	Sansam C 2 + 1	Davison A 9	Ellington L — + 2	Mason A 4 + 2	Lowthorpe A 13 + 1	Elliott S 3	Dickinson P — + 1	Sharman S 2 + 2	Match No.
1	2	3	4	5	6	7	8	9	10²	11¹	12	13																			1
1	2	3	4	5	6	7	8²	9	10³	11¹	12		13	14																	2
1	2	3	4	5	6	7		9	10	11¹			13	8²	12																3
1	2	3	4	5	6	7		9	10²	11¹	12	13	8³	14																	4
1	2	3	4	5	6	7		9	12	10	13	8¹		11²																	5
1¹	2	3	5	8	6	7		9	11	12			10			4															6
1	2	3	5	8	6	7		9¹		11²	13	12		10		4															7
1	2	3²	6	8	5	7		9			12	13	11	10¹		4															8
1	2	3	5	8¹	6	7		9	13	10	12		11²			4															9
	2	3	5		6	7		9	10	11¹			8	12	4	1															10
	2	3¹	5²		6	7	12	9	10			8³	11	4	1	13	14														11
1	2	3	5²		6	7		9	8	12			10¹	4		11³	13	14													12
1	2	3		5	6	12	10	8¹			9	7	4		11																13
1	2	3		6	7²	8	9	10			11	4	5¹	12		13															14
1	2	3		6	7	10¹	9²		13		12	11	4		8	5															15
1	2¹	3	6		7	11	9				12	10	4²	13		8	5														16
1	12	3	6		7	10	9		13			2¹	11³		4	14	8²	5													17
1		3	6	4	7	2²	9		12			10	11		13	8¹	5														18
1		3	6	8	7	9¹			10	11		4		2	5	12															19
1⁶		3¹	6	8	7	9		12	13	10¹	11		15	4²		2	5														20
		6	2	4	7	8²		12		13	3	10¹	11							5	9	1									21
		6	2	4	7	8¹	12	10			3		11			13				5	9²	1									22
		3	6	5	4²	7		9	10			12	11		8			2¹					1	13							23
		6²		4	7	2	9	10			3¹	8	11		5					1			12	13							24
		6		4	7	12	9	10			3¹	8			5					1			11	2							25
		3	6	12	4	7	8	9¹					11		5					1			10	2							26
	2¹	3	6	4		7	10²	9	13			8	12		5					1			11								27
		3	6	4²		7	10	9	13			8	12		5			2					11¹								28
		6	4³	11²	7	12	9	3				8	10		5			2¹	13		1	14									29
1		3	6	4	12		7	9	10¹	11			8		5			2													30
	3	6			8¹	7	9	10	11	12			1	5		2	4														31
1	3	6	12		7		9		8²	13	11		10		4¹		5						2								32
1	3	6			7¹			8	9	11			10		4		5				12		2								33
1	3¹	6			7		9	12	8²	13	11		10		4		5						2								34
1²	12	6			7		9	11¹	8	13	3⁴		10		14		5						2	4							35
	3	6			7		9			11²			10		1	8¹	12			5			2	4	13						36
	3	6	4		7		9	11		12			10		1		8¹			5			2								37
		6	4		7		9	11¹		8			10		1		12			5			2			3					38
		6	4²		7		9	11	12	8¹		14	10		1	13				5³			2			3					39
	3	6	12		7		9	11²	8²			13	10		1	5¹	14						2	4							40
	3	6	4¹	12	7		9		8	11²		10³			1	5	13						2				14				41
	3	6	4	12	7		9	13	8			10	11		1	5¹							2²								42
	2	3	6³	4¹	5	7		9	12	8²			10	11	1	14	13														43
	2	3			5	7		9	11³		12		4²	10	1	13	8¹			6									14		44
	2	3			6	7		11		9			4	10	1	8¹	12			5											45
	2	3	12	6	7			11		9			4	10	1	13	8¹			5²											46

Coca-Cola Cup
First Round   Scarborough   (h) 2-2   (a) 2-3

FA Cup
First Round   Whitby T   (a) 0-0   (h) 8-4
Second Round   Crewe Alex   (h) 1-5

IPSWICH TOWN 1996-97   *Back row (left to right):* Bobby Petta, Gus Uhlenbeek, Danny Sonner, Claus Thomsen, Dave Williams (Physio), James Scowcroft, Kevin Gaughan, Leon Bell.
Middle row: Bryan Klug (Reserve Coach), Geraint Williams, Simon Milton, Kevin Ellis, Wayne Brown, James Holman, Craig Forrest, Richard Wright, Richard Naylor, Chris Swailes, Tony Vaughan,
Adam Tanner, Dale Roberts (First Team Coach).
Front row: Mauricio Taricco, Stuart Slater, Ian Marshall, Paul Mason, Alex Mathie, George Burley (Manager), Tony Mowbray, Steve Sedgley, John Wark, Neil Gregory, Nick Stockwell,
Lee Norfolk.
(Photograph: Allsport)

Division 1

IPSWICH TOWN

Portman Road, Ipswich, Suffolk IP1 2DA. Telephone: (01473) 400500 (4 lines). Fax: (01473) 400040. Ticket Office: (01473) 400555. Sales & Marketing Dept: (01473) 400523.

Ground capacity: 22,675.

Record attendance: 38,010 v Leeds U, FA Cup 6th rd, 8 March 1975.

Record receipts: £105,950 v AZ 67 Alkmaar, UEFA Cup Final 1st leg, 6 May 1981.

Pitch measurements: 112yd × 82yd.

Chairman: David Sheepshanks.

Vice-Presidents: Kenneth H. Brightwell, Harold R. Smith.

Directors: P. Hope-Cobbold, J. Kerridge, R. Moore, John Kerr MBE, R. J. Finbow.

Manager: George Burley. *Assistant Manager:* Dale Roberts. *Reserve Team Coach:* Bryan Klug.

Youth Team Coach: Paul Goddard. *Chief Scout:* Charlie Woods. *Director of Coaching:* Colin Suggett.

Physio: Dave Williams.

Secretary: David C. Rose.

Sales & Promotions Manager: Mike Noye.

Year Formed: 1878. *Turned Professional:* 1936. *Ltd Co.:* 1936.

Club Nickname: 'Blues' or 'Town'.

Foundation: Considering that Ipswich Town only reached the Football League in 1938, many people outside of East Anglia may be surprised to learn that this club was formed at a meeting held in the Town Hall as far back as 1878 when Mr. T. C. Cobbold, MP, was voted president. Originally it was the Ipswich Association FC to distinguish it from the older Ipswich Football Club which played rugby. These two amalgamated in 1888 and the handling game was dropped in 1893.

First Football League game: 27 August 1938, Division 3 (S), v Southend U (h) W 4-2 – Burns; Dale, Parry; Perrett, Fillingham, McLuckie; Williams, Davies (1), Jones (2), Alsop (1), Little.

Record League Victory: 7–0 v Portsmouth, Division 2, 7 November 1964 – Thorburn; Smith, McNeil; Baxter, Bolton, Thompson; Broadfoot (1), Hegan (2), Baker (1), Leadbetter, Brogan (3). 7–0 v Southampton, Division 1, 2 February 1974 – Sivell; Burley, Mills (1), Morris, Hunter, Beattie (1), Hamilton (2), Viljoen, Johnson, Whymark (2), Lambert (1) (Woods). 7–0 v WBA, Division 1, 6 November 1976 – Sivell; Burley, Mills, Talbot, Hunter, Beattie (1), Osborne, Wark (1), Mariner (1) (Bertschin), Whymark (4), Woods.

Record Cup Victory: 10–0 v Floriana, European Cup Prel. rd, 25 September 1962 – Bailey; Malcolm, Compton; Baxter, Laurel, Elsworthy (1); Stephenson, Moran (2), Crawford (5), Phillips (2), Blackwood.

Record Defeat: 1–10 v Fulham, Division 1, 26 December 1963.

Most League Points (2 for a win): 64, Division 3 (S), 1953–54 and 1955–56.

Most League Points (3 for a win): 84, Division 1, 1991–92.

Most League Goals: 106, Division 3 (S), 1955–56.

Highest League Scorer in Season: Ted Phillips, 41, Division 3 (S), 1956–57.

Most League Goals in Total Aggregate: Ray Crawford, 203, 1958–63 and 1966–69.

Most Capped Player: Allan Hunter, 47 (53), Northern Ireland.

Most League Appearances: Mick Mills, 591, 1966–82.

Record Transfer Fee Received: £1,900,000 from Tottenham H for Jason Dozzell, August 1993.

Record Transfer Fee Paid: £1,000,000 to Tottenham H for Steve Sedgley, June 1994.

Football League Record: 1938 Elected to Division 3 (S); 1954–55 Division 2; 1955–57 Division 3 (S); 1957–61 Division 2; 1961–64 Division 1; 1964–68 Division 2; 1968–86 Division 1; 1986–92 Division 2; 1992–95 FA Premier League; 1995– Division 1.

Honours: Football League: Division 1 – Champions 1961–62; Runners-up 1980–81, 1981–82; Division 2 – Champions 1960–61, 1967–68, 1991–92; Division 3 (S) – Champions 1953–54, 1956–57. *FA Cup:* Winners 1978. *Football League Cup:* best season: Semi-final 1982, 1985. *Texaco Cup:* 1973. **European Competitions:** *European Cup:* 1962–63. *European Cup-Winners' Cup:* 1978–79. *UEFA Cup:* 1973–74, 1974–75, 1975–76, 1977–78, 1979–80, 1980–81 (winners), 1981–82, 1982–83.

Colours: Blue shirts, white shorts, blue stockings. *Change colours:* Black and cream striped shirts with red piping, black shorts, cream stockings with a red and black hoop, or jade shirts with maroon sleeves, maroon shorts with jade stripe, maroon stockings with jade hoop.

Did you know?
When Ipswich Town entered the Third Division (South) in 1938–39, their final finishing position of 7th was the highest of any of the newcomers admitted to this division since 1920–21.

IPSWICH TOWN 1996–97 LEAGUE RECORD

Match No.	Date	Venue	Opponents	Result	H/T Score	Lg. Pos.	Goalscorers	Attendance
1	Aug 16	A	Manchester C	L	0-1	0-1	—	29,126
2	24	H	Reading	W	5-2	2-1	9	Vaughan 2 [13, 69], Sedgley (pen) [45], Taricco [72], Scowcroft [87]	9767
3	27	H	Grimsby T	D	1-1	1-1	—	Mason [22]	9762
4	31	A	Oldham Ath	D	3-3	2-2	11	Mathie 2 [13, 75], Stockwell [23]	5339
5	Sept 7	H	Huddersfield T	L	1-3	0-0	16	Mason [76]	10,661
6	10	A	Crystal Palace	D	0-0	0-0	—		12,520
7	14	A	Sheffield U	W	3-1	0-1	12	Sedgley [63], Scowcroft 2 [77, 81]	14,261
8	20	H	Charlton Ath	W	2-1	0-1	—	Sedgley [56], Mathie [72]	10,558
9	28	A	WBA	D	0-0	0-0	8		15,606
10	Oct 1	H	Barnsley	D	1-1	0-1	—	Mathie [63]	9041
11	11	A	Norwich C	L	1-3	0-2	—	Sonner [46]	20,256
12	15	A	Birmingham C	L	0-1	0-0	—		15,664
13	19	H	Portsmouth	D	1-1	1-1	16	Mason [34]	10,514
14	26	H	Tranmere R	L	0-2	0-1	19		11,003
15	30	A	QPR	W	1-0	0-0	—	Mason [66]	10,562
16	Nov 2	A	Oxford U	L	1-3	1-3	18	Tanner [45]	7903
17	9	H	Southend U	D	1-1	1-0	17	Stockwell [7]	10,146
18	16	A	Bradford C	L	1-2	1-1	19	Cundy [37]	10,504
19	19	H	Swindon T	W	3-2	1-0	—	Scowcroft [1], Creaney [52], Sedgley (pen) [61]	7086
20	23	H	Port Vale	W	2-1	1-1	11	Tanner [34], Mason [77]	9491
21	30	A	Tranmere R	L	0-3	0-1	13		10,127
22	Dec 7	A	Wolverhampton W	D	0-0	0-0	16		12,048
23	14	H	Bolton W	W	2-1	1-0	14	Scowcroft 2 [39, 88]	13,314
24	21	H	Stoke C	D	1-1	1-1	14	Mason [46]	10,159
25	26	H	Crystal Palace	W	3-1	1-0	11	Tanner (pen) [45], Mason [52], Naylor [79]	16,020
26	28	A	Huddersfield T	L	0-2	0-0	13		11,467
27	Jan 1	A	Charlton Ath	D	1-1	1-0	13	Tanner (pen) [43]	10,186
28	18	A	Barnsley	W	2-1	0-0	12	Mason [54], Cundy [67]	9872
29	25	H	WBA	W	5-0	4-0	10	Holmes (og) [7], Scowcroft [32], Stockwell [36], Naylor [45], Mason [69]	9381
30	Feb 1	A	Southend U	D	0-0	0-0	12		7232
31	8	H	QPR	W	2-0	1-0	12	Naylor [6], Gregory [82]	12,983
32	15	A	Port Vale	D	2-2	1-2	8	Mason [9], Stockwell [69]	6115
33	22	H	Oxford U	W	2-1	1-0	7	Naylor [45], Stockwell [89]	11,483
34	Mar 1	A	Wolverhampton W	D	0-0	0-0	8		26,700
35	4	H	Bradford C	W	3-2	1-0	—	Sedgley (pen) [18], Sonner [87], Gregory [90]	9367
36	8	A	Stoke C	W	1-0	1-0	6	Taricco [7]	11,933
37	15	H	Bolton W	L	0-1	0-1	7		16,187
38	18	H	Sheffield U	W	3-1	3-1	—	Gregory 3 [1, 11, 37]	10,374
39	22	A	Reading	L	0-1	0-0	6		10,058
40	31	A	Grimsby T	L	1-2	1-1	9	Mason [10]	6268
41	Apr 5	H	Oldham Ath	W	4-0	3-0	7	Scowcroft [3], Williams [35], Stockwell [45], Gregory [52]	11,730
42	12	A	Swindon T	W	4-0	1-0	6	Swailes [38], Stockwell [49], Sedgley (pen) [70], Gudmundsson [86]	8591
43	18	H	Norwich C	W	2-0	2-0	—	Taricco [32], Mason [42]	22,397
44	22	H	Manchester C	W	1-0	1-0	—	Sedgley (pen) [41]	15,824
45	25	A	Portsmouth	W	1-0	1-0	—	Scowcroft [36]	12,101
46	May 4	H	Birmingham C	D	1-1	0-0	4	Gudmundsson [52]	20,570

Final League Position: 4

GOALSCORERS

League (68): Mason 12, Scowcroft 9, Sedgley 7 (5 pens), Stockwell 7, Gregory 6, Mathie 4, Naylor 4, Tanner 4 (2 pens), Taricco 3, Cundy 2, Gudmundsson 2, Sonner 2, Vaughan 2, Creaney 1, Swailes 1, Williams 1, own goal 1.
Coca-Cola Cup (15): Mathie 5, Mason 3, Marshall 1, Milton 1, Naylor 1, Sedgley 1 (pen), Scowcroft 1, Sonner 1, Stockwell 1.
FA Cup (0).

Match No.	Wright R 40	Stockwell M 42+1	Taricco M 41	Thomsen C 10+1	Vaughan T 27+5	Sedgley S 39	Uhlenbeek G 34+4	Williams G 43	Mason P 41+2	Marshall I 2	Petta B 1+5	Mathie A 11+1	Tanner D 10+6	Sonner D 22+7	Scowcroft J 40+1	Milton S 8+15	Gregory N 10+7	Forrest C 6	Naylor R 19+8	Niven S 2	Swailes C 23	Mowbray T 8	Creaney G 6	Wark J 2	Cundy J 13	Jean E —+1	Dyer K 2+11	Howe S 2+1	Gudmundsson N 2+6
1	1	2²	3	4		5¹	6	7	8	9	10	11	12	13															
2	1	2	3	4		8	5		6	11¹	10²	12	9		7	13													
3	1	2¹	3	4		8	5		6	11		12	9		7	10													
4	1	2	3			8	5	12	6	11			9	4¹	7²	10	13												
5	1²	2	3	4	8¹	5			6	11			9		7	10	12		13										
6		3¹	4	12	5	2	6	11					9		7	10	8	1											
7		2	3	4		5	7		6						9¹	10	11	1	12		8								
8		2		4	3	5	7					9²			12	10	11	1	13	6¹	8								
9		2		4	3	5		6	12				9		7	10	11¹	1			8								
10		2		4	3	5		6	11¹				9		7	10	12	1	13		8²								
11	1	7	2			3	5		6				9		8	10	11¹		12		4								
12	1	2²	3			6	5	7							8	10	13		9		11	4¹							
13	1	2	3¹			5	7		6	11		12			9	8	10				4								
14	1	12	3		7¹	5	2		6	11					8	10			13		4		9²						
15	1	2	3					12	6	11			7		8¹	10					4		9	5					
16	1	2	3			5	8¹		6	11					7	10	13		12		4²		9						
17	1	2¹	3			5	7	6	11						8	12	10		9¹		4								
18	1	2	3			5		6	11						8	10	7		12		4		9¹						
19	1	2	3			5		6	12	11					8	10¹	7		4				9						
20	1	2	3			5		6	12	11					8¹	10	7		9		4								
21	1	2	3		12	5	7	6	11						8¹	13	10		9			4²							
22	1	2¹	3			5	7	6	11						12	8	10		9		4								
23	1	2	3			5	7	6	11¹						12	8	10		9		4								
24	1	2¹	3			5	7	6	11						12	8	10		9²		4		13						
25	1	2²	3			5¹	7	6	11						12	8	10		9		4		13						
26	1	2²	3	12			7	6	11						5	8	10		9¹		4		13						
27	1	2	3	4			7		11						5	8	10		9					6					
28	1	2²	3				7	6	11						8	10			12		5				4		13	9¹	
29	1	2	3		12		7	6²	11¹						8	10			9		5				4		13		
30	1	2	3		4		7	6	11						8	10¹	12		9		5								
31	1	2	3		8	4	7	6	11¹							12	13		9		5								10²
32	1	2	3	12	8		7	6	11²						10³	13	14		9		5¹				4				
33		2	3	12	8		7	6²	11						10³	13	14	1	9		5¹				4				
34	1	2	3		4	8	7	6	11¹						10²	12	13		9		5								
35	1	2¹	3		4	8	7²	6	11					12	10³	13	14		9		5								
36	1	3		4				6	11¹						8	10	12		13		5	2	9²				7		
37	1	2	3		4		7¹	6	11						12	10			9		5	8²			13				
38	1	2	3		4	8	7	6	11¹						10³	12			9		5				13				
39	1	2	3		4	8	7	6	11²	12									9		5				13				10¹
40	1	2			4	8	7	6²	11¹	12					13	10			9³		5				3				14
41	1	2	3		8	4	7	6	11¹						10²				9		5						12	13	
42	1	2	3		8	4	7	6¹	11²						12	10			9³		5							13	14
43	1	2	3		8	4	7	6	11¹										9		5						12	10	
44	1	2	3		8	4	7	6	11¹						10				9²		5						12	13	
45	1	2²	3		8	4	7	6	11¹						10	12			9³		5							13	14
46	1	2	3²		8	4	7	6	11³						12	13	10		9¹		5								14

Coca-Cola Cup

First Round	Bournemouth	(h)	2-1	(a)	3-0
Second Round	Fulham	(a)	1-1	(h)	4-2
Third Round	Crystal Palace			(h)	4-1
Fourth Round	Gillingham			(h)	1-0
Fifth Round	Leicester C			(h)	0-1

FA Cup

Third Round	Nottingham F	(a)	0-3

LEEDS UNITED 1996–97 *Back row (left to right):* Mark Jackson, Richard Jobson, Brian Deane, Mark Beeney, Tony Yeboah, Nigel Martyn, Robert Bowman, Paul Beesley, Andy Couzens. *Middle row:* Geoff Ladley (Physio), Mick Hennigan (Assistant Manager), Rod Wallace, Mark Tinkler, Ian Harte, John Pemberton, Mark Ford, Jason Blunt, Lucas Radebe, Harry Kewell, David Williams (Coach).

Front row: Gary Kelly, Tony Dorigo, Carlton Palmer, W.J. Fotherby (Chairman), Howard Wilkinson (Manager), Ian Rush, Andy Gray, Lee Bowyer. (Photograph: Ross-Parry Picture Agency)

FA Premiership

LEEDS UNITED

Elland Road, Leeds LS11 0ES. Telephone: (0113) 2716037 (4 lines). Fax: (0113) 2720370. Ticket Information: 0891 121680. Clubcall: 0891 121180.

Ground capacity: 40,000.

Record attendance: 57,892 v Sunderland, FA Cup 5th rd (replay), 15 March 1967.

Record receipts: £314,063 v Oldham Ath, FA Cup 4th rd, 28 January 1995.

Pitch measurements: 110yd × 72yd.

President: The Right Hon The Earl of Harewood LLD.

Chairman: W. J. Fotherby.

Directors: R. Barker, A. Hudson, J. W. G. Marjason, P. D. G. McCormick, P. Ridsdale, L. H. Silver OBE.

Chief Executive: R. P. Launders.

Manager: George Graham. *Assistant Manager:* David O'Leary.

Company/Club Secretary: Nigel Pleasants.

General Manager: Alan Roberts.

Coach: David Williams.

Physio: David Swift.

Commercial Manager: Bob Baldwin. *Stadium Manager:* William Butterworth.

Year Formed: 1919, as Leeds United after disbandment (by FA order) of Leeds City (formed in 1904).

Turned Professional: 1920. *Ltd Co.:* 1920.

Club Nickname: 'United'.

Foundation: Immediately the Leeds City club (founded in 1904) was wound up by the FA in October 1919, following allegations of illegal payments to players, a meeting was called by a Leeds solicitor, Mr. Alf Masser, at which Leeds United was formed. They joined the Midland League playing their first game in that competition in November 1919. It was in this same month that the new club had discussions with the directors of a virtually bankrupt Huddersfield Town who wanted to move to Leeds in an amalgamation. But Huddersfield survived even that crisis.

First Football League game: 28 August 1920, Division 2, v Port Vale (a) L 0-2 – Down; Duffield, Tillotson; Musgrove, Baker, Walton; Mason, Goldthorpe, Thompson, Lyon, Best.

Record League Victory: 8–0 v Leicester C, Division 1, 7 April 1934 – Moore; George Milburn, Jack Milburn; Edwards, Hart, Copping; Mahon (2), Firth (2), Duggan (2), Furness (2), Cochrane.

Record Cup Victory: 10–0 v Lyn (Oslo), European Cup 1st rd 1st leg, 17 September 1969 – Sprake; Reaney, Cooper, Bremner (2), Charlton, Hunter, Madeley, Clarke (2), Jones (3), Giles (2) (Bates), O'Grady (1).

Record Defeat: 1–8 v Stoke C, Division 1, 27 August 1934.

Most League Points (2 for a win): 67, Division 1, 1968–69.

Most League Points (3 for a win): 85, Division 2, 1989–90.

Most League Goals: 98, Division 2, 1927–28.

Highest League Scorer in Season: John Charles, 42, Division 2, 1953–54.

Most League Goals in Total Aggregate: Peter Lorimer, 168, 1965–79 and 1983–86.

Most Capped Player: Billy Bremner, 54, Scotland.

Most League Appearances: Jack Charlton, 629, 1953–73.

Record Transfer Fee Received: £3,500,000 from Everton for Gary Speed, June 1996.

Record Transfer Fee Paid: £4,500,000 to Parma for Tomas Brolin, 23 November 1995.

Football League Record: 1920 Elected to Division 2; 1924–27 Division 1; 1927–28 Division 2; 1928–31 Division 1; 1931–32 Division 2; 1932–47 Division 1; 1947–56 Division 2; 1956–60 Division 1; 1960–64 Division 2; 1964–82 Division 1; 1982–90 Division 2; 1990–92 Division 1; 1992– FA Premier League.

Honours: Football League: Division 1 – Champions 1968–69, 1973–74, 1991–92; Runners-up 1964–65, 1965–66, 1969–70, 1970–71, 1971–72; Division 2 – Champions 1923–24, 1963–64, 1989–90; Runners-up 1927–28, 1931–32, 1955–56. *FA Cup:* Winners 1972; Runners-up 1965, 1970, 1973. *Football League Cup:* Winners 1968; Runners-up 1996. **European Competitions:** *European Cup:* 1969–70, 1974–75 (runners-up), 1992–93. *European Cup-Winners' Cup:* 1972–73 (runners-up). *European Fairs Cup:* 1965–66, 1966–67 (runners-up), 1967–68 (winners), 1968–69, 1970–71 (winners). *UEFA Cup:* 1971–72, 1973–74, 1979–80, 1995–96.

Colours: White with yellow and blue trim. *Change colours:* Yellow with white and blue trim.

Did you know?

In 1996–97, Leeds United fielded an Uncle and Nephew in the first team, Ian Harte being the nephew of Gary Kelly.

LEEDS UNITED 1996–97 LEAGUE RECORD

Match No.	Date	Venue	Opponents	Result	H/T Score	Lg. Pos.	Goalscorers	Attendance
1	Aug 17	A	Derby Co	D 3-3	1-0	—	Laursen (og) [19], Harte [72], Bowyer [85]	17,925
2	20	H	Sheffield W	L 0-2	0-1	—		31,008
3	26	H	Wimbledon	W 1-0	0-0	—	Sharpe [58]	25,860
4	Sept 4	A	Blackburn R	W 1-0	1-0	—	Harte [40]	23,226
5	7	H	Manchester U	L 0-4	0-1	9		39,694
6	14	A	Coventry C	L 1-2	1-0	12	Couzens [1]	17,298
7	21	H	Newcastle U	L 0-1	0-0	15		36,070
8	28	A	Leicester C	L 0-1	0-0	17		20,359
9	Oct 12	H	Nottingham F	W 2-0	0-0	14	Wallace 2 [46, 90]	29,255
10	19	A	Aston Villa	L 0-2	0-0	16		39,051
11	26	A	Arsenal	L 0-3	0-2	17		38,076
12	Nov 2	H	Sunderland	W 3-0	1-0	16	Ford [27], Sharpe [62], Deane [68]	31,450
13	16	H	Liverpool	L 0-2	0-1	17		39,981
14	23	A	Southampton	W 2-0	0-0	14	Kelly [82], Sharpe [89]	15,241
15	Dec 1	H	Chelsea	W 2-0	2-0	12	Deane [8], Rush [10]	32,596
16	7	A	Middlesbrough	D 0-0	0-0	13		30,018
17	14	H	Tottenham H	D 0-0	0-0	13		33,783
18	21	A	Everton	D 0-0	0-0	12		36,954
19	26	H	Coventry C	L 1-3	1-3	14	Deane [9]	36,465
20	28	A	Manchester U	L 0-1	0-1	15		55,256
21	Jan 1	A	Newcastle U	L 0-3	0-1	15		36,489
22	11	H	Leicester C	W 3-0	2-0	12	Bowyer [40], Rush 2 [45, 69]	29,480
23	20	A	West Ham U	W 2-0	0-0	—	Kelly [53], Bowyer [70]	19,441
24	29	H	Derby Co	D 0-0	0-0	—		27,523
25	Feb 1	H	Arsenal	D 0-0	0-0	11		35,596
26	19	A	Liverpool	L 0-4	0-3	—		38,957
27	22	A	Sunderland	W 1-0	0-0	9	Bowyer [49]	21,846
28	Mar 1	H	West Ham U	W 1-0	0-0	9	Sharpe [47]	30,575
29	8	H	Everton	W 1-0	1-0	9	Molenaar [28]	32,055
30	12	H	Southampton	D 0-0	0-0	—		25,913
31	15	A	Tottenham H	L 0-1	0-1	9		33,040
32	22	A	Sheffield W	D 2-2	2-1	9	Sharpe [17], Wallace [21]	30,373
33	Apr 7	H	Blackburn R	D 0-0	0-0	—		27,322
34	16	A	Wimbledon	L 0-2	0-1	—		7979
35	19	A	Nottingham F	D 1-1	0-1	10	Deane [66]	25,565
36	22	H	Aston Villa	D 0-0	0-0	—		26,884
37	May 3	A	Chelsea	D 0-0	0-0	11		27,135
38	11	H	Middlesbrough	D 1-1	0-0	11	Deane [77]	38,569

Final League Position: 11

GOALSCORERS

League (28): Deane 5, Sharpe 5, Bowyer 4, Rush 3, Wallace 3, Harte 2, Kelly 2, Couzens 1, Ford 1, Molenaar 1, own goal 1.
Coca-Cola Cup (5): Wallace 3, Harte 1, Sharpe 1.
FA Cup (6): Bowyer 2, Wallace 2, Deane 1, own goal 1.

Martyn N 37	Kelly G 34+2	Sharpe L 26	Palmer C 26+2	Radebe L 28+4	Jobson R 10	Ford M 15+1	Couzens A 7+3	Rush I 34+2	Deane B 27+1	Bowyer L 32	Wetherall D 25+4	Tinkler M 1+2	Harte I 10+4	Hateley M 5+1	Gray A 1+6	Wallace R 17+5	Blunt J —+1	Jackson M 11+6	Boyle W —+1	Dorigo T 15+3	Beesley P 11+1	Shepherd P 1	Halle G 20	Kewell H —+1	Yeboah T 6+1	Molenaar R 12	Beeney M 1	Lilley D 4+2	Laurent P 2+2	Match No.
1	2	3	4	5¹	6	7	8²	9	10³	11	12	13	14																	1
1	2	3	4	5¹	6	7³		9		11	12	13	8	10²	14															2
1	12	3	4	13	6		2¹	9		11	5	7²	8	10																3
1	2	10	4	12	6	7²	13	9		11¹	5		3	14	8²															4
1	2	10	4	12	6	7³		9		11¹	5	3	13	14	8²															5
1	2		4	6	12	7¹		9	10	11²	5	3	8		13															6
1	2	11	4		6	7		9²	10¹		5	3	8	12	13															7
1	2	11	4	12	6	7		9	10¹		5	3	8																	8
1	2	3	4		6	7		9¹	10	11²	5		8	12	13															9
1	2	3	4¹	11	6	7	12	9	10		5²		8							13										10
1	2	3	4		6	7	8¹	9	12	11	5		10																	11
1	2		4	3		7	12	9	10	11¹	5		8										6							12
1	2	5	4	3		7		9	10	11						8¹		12					6							13
1	2	3	4	5		7¹		9	10	11						12		8					6							14
1	2	3	4	8		7		9	10	11						5							6							15
1	2	3	4	8		7¹		9	10	11						5		12					6							16
1	2		4	5		7¹		9	10	11						8²		12					6	3	13					17
1	2	11	4	8¹				9	10	7						5		12					6	3						18
1	2		4	8				9	10	11	5²					7		12	6¹				3	13						19
1	2		4	5				9	10	7			12			8		3					6	11¹						20
1	2¹		4	8¹				9²	10	11	5		12	13		7				3	6									21
1	2							9	10	11	5					8		7		3	6							4		22
1	2		4	8				9	10	11	5					7				3			6							23
	2		4	8				12	10	11						9¹		7		3			6		5		1			24
1	2		4					9	10¹	11						12		8		7			3	6		5				25
1	2		4					10	12	9			13			11		8¹		7²			3	6		5				26
1	2	11	4					9	10	7						12				3¹			6	8²		5				27
1		3	12	8				9	10	7¹	6		4							2				11		5				28
1		3	4					9	10	7	6		8							2				11		5				29
1	2	3¹	4					9	10	7	6					12				3			8	11		5				30
1	2	11	4					9	10	7	12									3			6	8¹	5					31
1	2¹	11	4					9	10	7	12					8				3			6		5					32
1	2	11²						9	10	7	5		8¹				4			3			6					12	13	33
1	12	11²	4					9	10³	7	5¹		8							3			6		2			13	14	34
1	2	11¹	12	4					10²	7	5		13							3			6			9		8		35
1	2		4	8				9		11	5		12							3			6			7		10¹		36
1	2		4	8				9	10	11	5									3			6			7				37
1	6	11		4				9¹	10	7	5		12							3			2					8		38

Coca-Cola Cup

Second Round	Darlington	(h)	2-2	
		(a)	2-0	
Third Round	Aston Villa	(h)	1-2	

FA Cup

Third Round	Crystal Palace	(a)	2-2	
		(h)	1-0	
Fourth Round	Arsenal	(a)	1-0	
Fifth Round	Portsmouth	(h)	2-3	

LEICESTER CITY 1996–97　　*Back row (left to right):* Craig Hallam, Emile Heskey, Simon Grayson, Franck Rolling, Steve Walsh, Kevin Poole, Paul Hyde, Julian Watts, Jimmy Willis, Mike Whitlow, Colin Hill.

Middle row: Steve Walford (Coach), Paul Franklin (Coach), John Robertson (Assistant Manager), Steve Wenlock, Stuart Wilson, Kevin Skeldon, Lee Quincey, Stuart Campbell, Andrew Dodds, Alan Smith (Physio), Mick Yeoman (Physio), Paul McAndrew (Kit Manager).

Front row: Neil Lewis, Sam McMahon, Pontus Kaamark, Steve Claridge, Mustafa Izzet, Tom Smeaton (Chairman), Martin O'Neill (Manager), Neil Lennon (Manager), Scott Taylor, Mark Robins, Justin Harrington, Jamie Lawrence.

FA Premiership

LEICESTER CITY

City Stadium, Filbert St, Leicester LE2 7FL. Telephone: (0116) 2915000. Fax: (0116) 2470585. Ticket Office: (0116) 2915232. Clubcall: 0891 121185.

Ground capacity: 22,517.

Record attendance: 47,298 v Tottenham H, FA Cup 5th rd, 18 February 1928.

Record receipts: £268,672 v Manchester U, Coca-Cola Cup 4th rd, 27 November 1996.

Pitch measurements: 110yd × 76yd.

President: K. R. Brigstock.

Chairman: T. Smeaton. *Vice-Chairman:* John Elsom FCA.

Chief Executive: Barrie Pierpoint.

Directors: R. W. Parker, J. E. Sharp, T. W. Shipman, M. F. George.

Manager: Martin O'Neill. *Assistant Manager:* John Robertson. *First Team Coach:* Steve Walford.

Youth Team Coach: David Nish. *Football Secretary:* Ian Silvester. *Company Secretary:* Steve Kind.

Head of Publicity/Press Officer: Paul Mace.

Physio: Alan Smith. *Deputy Chief Executive:* Charles Rayner. *Stadium Manager:* John Petherick.

Year Formed: 1884.

Club Nickname: 'Filberts' or 'Foxes'.

Previous Grounds: 1884, Victoria Park; 1887, Belgrave Road; 1888, Victoria Park; 1891, Filbert Street.

Previous Name: 1884–1919, Leicester Fosse.

Foundation: In 1884 a number of young footballers who were mostly old boys of Wyggeston School, held a meeting at a house on the Roman Fosse Way and formed Leicester Fosse FC. They collected 9d (less than 4p) towards the cost of a ball, plus the same amount for membership. Their first professional, Harry Webb from Stafford Rangers, was signed in 1888 for 2s 6d (12p) per week, plus travelling expenses.

First Football League game: 1 September 1894, Division 2, v Grimsby T (a) L 3-4 – Thraves; Smith, Bailey; Seymour, Brown, Henrys; Hill, Hughes, McArthur (1), Skea (2), Priestman.

Record League Victory: 10–0 v Portsmouth, Division 1, 20 October 1928 – McLaren; Black, Brown; Findlay, Carr, Watson; Adcock, Hine (3), Chandler (6), Lochhead, Barry (1).

Record Cup Victory: 8–1 v Coventry C (away), League Cup 5th rd, 1 December 1964 – Banks; Sjoberg, Norman (2); Roberts, King, McDerment; Hodgson (2), Cross, Goodfellow, Gibson (1), Stringfellow (2). (1 og).

Record Defeat: 0–12 (as Leicester Fosse) v Nottingham F, Division 1, 21 April 1909.

Most League Points (2 for a win): 61, Division 2, 1956–57.

Most League Points (3 for a win): 77, Division 2, 1991–92.

Most League Goals: 109, Division 2, 1956–57.

Highest League Scorer in Season: Arthur Rowley, 44, Division 2, 1956–57.

Most League Goals in Total Aggregate: Arthur Chandler, 259, 1923–35.

Most Capped Player: John O'Neill, 39, Northern Ireland.

Most League Appearances: Adam Black, 528, 1920–35.

Record Transfer Fee Received: £3,250,000 from Aston Villa for Mark Draper, July 1995.

Record Transfer Fee Paid: £1,600,000 to Oxford U for Matt Elliott, 16 Janury 1997.

Football League Record: 1894 Elected to Division 2; 1908–09 Division 1; 1909–25 Division 2; 1925–35 Division 1; 1935–37 Division 2; 1937–39 Division 1; 1946–54 Division 2; 1954–55 Division 1; 1955–57 Division 2; 1957–69 Division 1; 1969–71 Division 2; 1971–78 Division 1; 1978–80 Division 2; 1980–81 Division 1; 1981–83 Division 2; 1983–87 Division 1; 1987–92 Division 2; 1992–94 Division 1; 1994–95 FA Premier League; 1995–96 Division 1; 1996– FA Premier League.

Honours: Football League: Division 1 – Runners-up 1928–29; Promoted from Division 1 1993–94 (play-offs) and 1995–96 (play-offs) Division 2 – Champions 1924–25, 1936–37, 1953–54, 1956–57, 1970–71, 1979–80; Runners-up 1907–08. *FA Cup:* Runners-up 1949, 1961, 1963, 1969. *Football League Cup:* Winners 1964, 1997; Runners-up 1965. **European Competitions:** *European Cup-Winners' Cup:* 1961–62.

Colours: Royal blue shirts, white shorts, blue stockings. *Change colours:* White shirts, royal blue shorts, white stockings.

Did you know?
Leicester City's first ever-present player was Jack Lord, right-half in the club's inaugural season in the Midland League 1891–92. He appeared in 20 League and one FA Cup tie.

LEICESTER CITY 1996–97 LEAGUE RECORD

Match No.	Date		Venue	Opponents	Result		H/T Score	Lg. Pos.	Goalscorers	Attendance
1	Aug	17	A	Sunderland	D	0-0	0-0	—		19,291
2		21	H	Southampton	W	2-1	2-0	—	Heskey 2 [6, 42]	17,562
3		24	H	Arsenal	L	0-2	0-1	12		20,429
4	Sept	2	A	Sheffield W	L	1-2	1-1	—	Claridge [28]	17,657
5		7	A	Nottingham F	D	0-0	0-0	14		24,105
6		15	H	Liverpool	L	0-3	0-0	16		20,987
7		22	A	Tottenham H	W	2-1	1-0	14	Claridge [22], Marshall [86]	24,159
8		28	H	Leeds U	W	1-0	0-0	10	Heskey [60]	20,359
9	Oct	12	H	Chelsea	L	1-3	1-0	12	Watts [44]	20,766
10		19	A	West Ham U	L	0-1	0-0	14		22,285
11		26	H	Newcastle U	W	2-0	1-0	11	Claridge [17], Heskey [79]	21,134
12	Nov	2	A	Derby Co	L	0-2	0-0	13		18,010
13		16	A	Aston Villa	W	3-1	2-1	11	Claridge [8], Parker (pen) [43], Izzet [85]	36,193
14		23	H	Everton	L	1-2	0-1	12	Walsh [83]	20,975
15		30	A	Manchester U	L	1-3	0-0	14	Lennon [90]	55,196
16	Dec	3	A	Middlesbrough	W	2-0	1-0	—	Claridge [45], Izzet [46]	29,709
17		7	H	Blackburn R	D	1-1	0-1	12	Marshall [78]	19,306
18		21	H	Coventry C	L	0-2	0-1	13		20,038
19		26	A	Liverpool	D	1-1	0-0	13	Claridge [76]	40,786
20		28	H	Nottingham F	D	2-2	1-1	12	Heskey [10], Izzet [63]	20,833
21	Jan	11	A	Leeds U	L	0-3	0-2	16		29,480
22		18	H	Wimbledon	W	1-0	0-0	12	Heskey [73]	18,927
23		29	H	Sunderland	D	1-1	1-1	—	Parker (pen) [32]	17,883
24	Feb	2	A	Newcastle U	L	3-4	0-1	14	Elliott [55], Claridge [60], Heskey [68]	36,396
25		22	H	Derby Co	W	4-2	3-1	12	Marshall 3 [7, 24, 27], Claridge [59]	20,323
26	Mar	1	A	Wimbledon	W	3-1	3-0	10	Elliott 2 [17, 27], Robins [32]	11,487
27		5	H	Aston Villa	W	1-0	0-0	—	Claridge [66]	20,626
28		8	A	Coventry C	D	0-0	0-0	10		19,199
29		15	H	Middlesbrough	L	1-3	0-3	11	Marshall [47]	20,561
30		19	H	Tottenham H	D	1-1	0-0	—	Claridge [74]	20,593
31		22	A	Southampton	D	2-2	0-1	11	Heskey [46], Dryden (og) [70]	15,044
32	Apr	9	A	Everton	D	1-1	0-1	—	Marshall [70]	30,368
33		12	A	Arsenal	L	0-2	0-1	13		38,044
34		19	A	Chelsea	L	1-2	0-1	13	Sinclair (og) [47]	26,400
35		23	H	West Ham U	L	0-1	0-0	—		20,327
36	May	3	H	Manchester U	D	2-2	2-1	16	Walsh [16], Marshall [20]	21,068
37		7	H	Sheffield W	W	1-0	0-0	—	Elliott [86]	20,793
38		11	A	Blackburn R	W	4-2	1-1	9	Heskey 2 [13, 56], Claridge [55], Wilson [81]	25,881

Final League Position: 9

GOALSCORERS

League (46): Claridge 11, Heskey 10, Marshall 8, Elliott 4, Izzet 3, Parker 2 (2 pens), Walsh 2, Lennon 1, Robins 1, Watts 1, Wilson 1, own goals 2.
Coca-Cola Cup (12): Claridge 2, Grayson 2, Heskey 2, Lawrence 2, Izzet 1, Lennon 1, Parker 1 (pen), Robins 1.
FA Cup (6): Marshall 2, Claridge 1, Parker 1 (pen), Walsh 1, own goal 1.

Keller K 31	Grayson S 36	Whitlow M 14+3	Watts J 22+4	Walsh S 22	Prior S 33+1	Lennon N 35	Taylor S 20+5	Robins M 5+3	Izzet M 34+1	Heskey E 35	Lawrence J 2+13	Claridge S 29+3	Parker G 22+9	Marshall I 19+9	Lewis N 4+2	Poole K 7	Hill C 6+1	Campbell S 4+6	Kamark P 9+1	Elliott M 16	Wilson S —+2	Guppy S 12+1	Rolling F 1	Match No.
1	2	3	4	5	6	7	8	9¹	10	11	12													1
1	2	3	4	5	6	7	8		10¹	11	12	9												2
1	2	3¹	4	5	6	7	8		10	11		9	12											3
1	2	3	4²	5	6	7	8¹		10	11		9	12	13										4
1	2	3	4	5	6	7	8¹		10	11		9²	12	13										5
1	2	3	4²	5	6¹	7	8		10	11		9	12	13										6
1	2		4	5	6	7	8		10	11		9²	12	13	3¹									7
1	2	3	4	5	6	7	8		10	11	12	9¹												8
1	2	3	4	5	6	7			10	11		8	9											9
1	2	3	4	5	6	7	8¹		10	11	12	9²		13										10
	2	3	4		6¹	7	8³		10	11	12	9	13	14		1	5²							11
1	2	3	4	5	6	7			10	11		9	8											12
	2	3	4²	5	6	7	12		10	11		9	8¹	13		1								13
1	2		4		6	7	8¹		3	11		9	10	5	12									14
1	2		4¹		6	7	8²		3	11³	13	9	10	5	12		14							15
1	2		4		6	7	8		3	11		9	10¹	5				12						16
1	2				6	7	8		3	11		9	12	10	5¹		4							17
1	2				6	7	12		10	11		9		5	13	4	8¹	3²						18
1	2				6		8		3	11	12	9	10	5	7¹	4								19
1	2				6		8	12	10¹	11	13	9	7	5	3²	4³	14							20
1	2				6	7			10	11		9	8	5				3	4					21
1	2	12			6	7	13		4	11		9	8	10²	3¹					5				22
1	2	4			6	7	8¹		3	11	12	9	10							5				23
1	2	4	5		6		8¹					3	9	7	10		11					12		24
	2		5		6	7	8¹	9	10	11	12					1				4		3		25
1	2	12	5		6¹	7	13	9³	10	11²		14	8							4		3		26
1	2		4	5		7	12	9²	10	11¹	13		8							6		3		27
	2		4		6	7		12	11			9¹	8	10		1				5		3		28
	2	12			6	7		13	4	11¹		9	8	10²		1			6¹	4		3		29
	2	12	5			7			10	11	13	9	8²			1			6¹	4		3		30
1					5	6	7		10	11		8	9					2	4			3		31
1		3	4			7	8³	9¹	13		2	12	10			6²	14			5		11		32
	2				6	7			10²	11	13	9¹	8	12		1				4	5	3		33
1	2		5		6	7			10²	11		9	8	12			13			4		3¹		34
1	2	12	5			7			6²	11		9³	8¹	10			13		3	4		14		35
1	2	12	5			7			13	11		9²	8¹	10			14	6²	4			3		36
1	2	12	5	13		7				11		9²	8¹	10			14	6²	4			3		37
1	2²	12			6¹	7				11	13	9	8	10	5		14	3					4³	38

Coca-Cola Cup

Second Round	Scarborough	(a)	2-0
		(h)	2-1
Third Round	York C	(a)	2-0
Fourth Round	Manchester U	(h)	2-0
Fifth Round	Ipswich T	(a)	1-0
Semi-Final	Wimbledon	(h)	0-0
		(a)	1-1
Final	Middlesbrough		1-1
	(at Wembley)		
	(at Hillsborough)		1-0

FA Cup

Third Round	Southend U	(h)	2-0
Fourth Round	Norwich C	(h)	2-1
Fifth Round	Chelsea	(h)	2-2
		(a)	0-1

LEYTON ORIENT 1996-97   *Back row (left to right):* Danny Chapman, Ian Hendon, Mark Warren, Alan McCarthy, Dave Hanson, Alex Inglethorpe, Peter Garland.
Middle row: Steve Shorey (Chief Scout), Terry Spurgeon (Kit Man), Dave Martin, Colin West, Peter Caldwell, Luke Weaver, Les Sealey, Lee Shearer, Andy Arnott, Paul Brush (Director of Coaching/Youth Team Manager), Tony Flynn (Physio).
Front row: Dominic Naylor, Martin Ling, Justin Channing, Alvin Martin, Tommy Cunningham (Reserve Team Manager), Pat Holland (Manager), Tony Kelly, Joe Baker, Sammy Winston, Sammy Ayorinde.

Division 3

LEYTON ORIENT

Leyton Stadium, Brisbane Road, Leyton, London E10 5NE. Telephone: (0181) 539 2223. Fax: (0181) 539 4390. Clubcall: 0891 121150.

Ground capacity: 13,842.

Record attendance: 34,345 v West Ham U, FA Cup 4th rd, 25 January 1964.

Record receipts: £87,867.92 v West Ham U, FA Cup 3rd rd, 10 January 1987.

Pitch measurements: 110yd × 80yd.

Chairman: Barry Hearn.

Chief Executive: Bernard Goodall. *Financial Director:* Steve Dawson.

Directors: Tony Wood OBE, John Goldsmith FRIBA, Rod Cousens, David Dodd, Steve Davis.

Team Manager: Tommy Taylor. *First Team Coach:* Paul Clark. *Physio:* Tony Flynn.

Secretary: David Burton. *Commercial Manager:* Frank Woolf.

Stadium Manager: Janet Hasler.

Year Formed: 1881. *Turned Professional:* 1903. *Ltd Co.:* 1906.

Club Nickname: 'The O's'.

Previous Names: 1881–86, Glyn Cricket and Football Club; 1886–88, Eagle Football Club; 1888–98, Orient Football Club; 1898–1946, Clapton Orient; 1946–66, Leyton Orient; 1966–87, Orient.

Previous Grounds: Glyn Road, 1884–96; Whittles Athletic Ground, 1896–1900; Millfields Road, 1900–30; Lea Bridge Road, 1930–37.

Foundation: There is some doubt about the foundation of Leyton Orient, and, indeed, some confusion with clubs like Leyton and Clapton over their early history. As regards the foundation, the most favoured version is that Leyton Orient was formed originally by members of Homerton Theological College who established Glyn Cricket Club in 1881 and then carried on through the following winter playing football. Eventually many employees of the Orient Shipping Line became involved and so the name Orient was chosen in 1888.

First Football League game: 2 September 1905, Division 2, v Leicester Fosse (a) L 1-2 – Butler; Holmes, Codling; Lamberton, Boden, Boyle; Kingaby (1), Wootten, Leigh, Evenson, Bourne.

Record League Victory: 8–0 v Crystal Palace, Division 3 (S), 12 November 1955 – Welton; Lee, Earl; Blizzard, Aldous, McKnight; White (1), Facey (3), Burgess (2), Heckman, Hartburn (2). 8–0 v Rochdale, Division 4, 20 October 1987 – Wells; Howard, Dickenson (1), Smalley (1), Day, Hull, Hales (2), Castle (Sussex), Shinners (2), Godfrey (Harvey), Comfort (2). 8–0 v Colchester U, Division 4, 15 October 1988 – Wells; Howard, Dickenson, Hales (1p), Day (1). Sitton (1), Baker (1), Ward, Hull (3). Juryeff, Comfort (1).

Record Cup Victory: 9–2 v Chester, League Cup 3rd rd, 15 October 1962 – Robertson; Charlton, Taylor; Gibbs, Bishop, Lea; Deeley (1), Waites (3), Dunmore (2), Graham (3), Wedge.

Record Defeat: 0–8 v Aston Villa, FA Cup 4th rd, 30 January 1929.

Most League Points (2 for a win): 66, Division 3 (S), 1955–56.

Most League Points (3 for a win): 75, Division 4, 1988–89.

Most League Goals: 106, Division 3 (S), 1955–56.

Highest League Scorer in Season: Tom Johnston, 35, Division 2, 1957–58.

Most League Goals in Total Aggregate: Tom Johnston, 121, 1956–58, 1959–61.

Most Capped Player: John Chiedozie, 8 (10), Nigeria.

Most League Appearances: Peter Allen, 432, 1965–78.

Record Transfer Fee Received: £600,000 from Notts Co for John Chiedozie, August 1981.

Record Transfer Fee Paid: £175,000 to Wigan Ath for Paul Beesley, October 1989.

Football League Record: 1905 Elected to Division 2; 1929–56 Division 3 (S); 1956–62 Division 2; 1962–63 Division 1; 1963–66 Division 2; 1966–70 Division 3; 1970–82 Division 2; 1982–85 Division 3; 1985–89 Division 4; 1989–92 Division 3; 1992–95 Division 2; 1995– Division 3.

Honours: Football League: Division 1 best season: 22nd, 1962–63; Division 2 – Runners-up 1961–62; Division 3 – Champions 1969–70; Division 3 (S) – Champions 1955–56; Runners-up 1954–55; Promoted from Division 4 1988–89 (play-offs). *FA Cup:* Semi-final 1978. *Football League Cup:* best season: 5th rd, 1963.

Colours: White shirts with red V, black shorts, red stockings. *Change colours:* Blue and yellow.

Did you know?
Johnny Hartburn scored three goals in three minutes for Leyton Orient against Shrewsbury Town on 22 January 1955.

LEYTON ORIENT 1996–97 LEAGUE RECORD

Match No.	Date	Venue	Opponents	Result	H/T Score	Lg. Pos.	Goalscorers	Attendance
1	Aug 17	H	Scunthorpe U	L	0-1	0-0	—	4430
2	24	A	Lincoln C	D	1-1	0-1	20	Hendon [90]	3067
3	27	A	Carlisle U	L	0-1	0-0	—	4973
4	31	H	Hartlepool U	W	2-0	1-0	18	West [33], Kelly [53]	4342
5	Sept 7	H	Darlington	D	0-0	0-0	19		3856
6	10	A	Northampton T	W	1-0	0-0	—	Chapman [90]	3994
7	14	A	Mansfield T	W	2-0	1-0	11	Hanson 2 [11, 70]	1839
8	21	H	Colchester U	D	1-1	0-0	9	Channing [69]	5254
9	28	A	Rochdale	L	0-1	0-0	12		1994
10	Oct 1	H	Swansea C	W	1-0	0-0	—	Hanson [81]	3536
11	5	A	Doncaster R	L	1-2	0-1	9	Ayorinde [86]	1840
12	12	H	Hull C	D	1-1	0-0	11	Naylor (pen) [71]	4490
13	15	H	Chester C	D	0-0	0-0	—		3115
14	19	A	Hereford U	L	0-2	0-0	13		2625
15	26	A	Cardiff C	L	0-3	0-3	17		3647
16	29	A	Scarborough	L	0-1	0-0	—		2693
17	Nov 2	H	Torquay U	W	1-0	1-0	18	Griffiths [43]	3891
18	9	A	Exeter C	L	2-3	1-1	21	Griffiths [36], Ayorinde [52]	3171
19	23	A	Cambridge U	L	0-2	0-0	22		4360
20	30	H	Cardiff C	W	3-0	1-0	20	Griffiths [34], McGleish [57], Arnott [64]	4503
21	Dec 3	H	Barnet	D	0-0	0-0	—		2549
22	14	A	Fulham	D	1-1	0-0	20	Warren [89]	7355
23	22	H	Brighton & HA	W	2-0	0-0	19	Naylor 2 (1 pen) [57, 65 (p)]	7944
24	26	H	Northampton T	W	2-1	1-1	16	Channing [6], Inglethorpe [79]	4492
25	28	A	Darlington	D	1-1	1-1	15	West [31]	2700
26	Jan 4	H	Mansfield T	W	2-1	1-1	—	McGleish [30], West [88]	3418
27	18	A	Swansea C	L	0-1	0-0	16		3435
28	21	H	Wigan Ath	L	1-2	1-0	—	McGleish [33]	3014
29	25	A	Scarborough	L	1-2	0-0	17	Chapman [90]	2184
30	Feb 1	H	Exeter C	D	1-1	0-0	18	Winston [65]	3686
31	4	A	Colchester U	L	1-2	1-1	—	Channing [33]	3689
32	8	A	Torquay U	D	0-0	0-0	17		2608
33	11	H	Rochdale	W	2-1	1-1	—	Inglethorpe [39], Castle [55]	2406
34	15	H	Cambridge U	D	1-1	0-1	15	McGleish [59]	4418
35	22	A	Wigan Ath	L	1-5	1-1	16	Inglethorpe [8]	3783
36	Mar 1	H	Barnet	L	0-1	0-1	18		4621
37	8	H	Brighton & HA	D	4-4	0-2	18	Griffiths 2 [47, 57], Inglethorpe [50], McGleish [75]	9298
38	16	H	Fulham	L	0-2	0-0	18		7125
39	22	H	Lincoln C	L	2-3	0-1	19	Arnott [53], Timons [81]	4121
40	29	A	Scunthorpe U	W	2-1	0-1	18	Timons [71], Channing [75]	3365
41	31	H	Carlisle U	W	2-1	2-1	16	McGleish 2 [3, 11]	4604
42	Apr 5	A	Hartlepool U	L	1-3	1-1	18	Channing [29]	2576
43	12	H	Doncaster R	W	2-1	1-0	17	Inglethorpe [38], Arnott [62]	3698
44	19	A	Hull C	L	2-3	1-2	17	Inglethorpe [40], Griffiths [66]	2647
45	26	H	Hereford U	W	2-1	0-0	17	Inglethorpe [54], Ling [64]	5599
46	May 3	A	Chester C	W	1-0	1-0	16	Inglethorpe [45]	3622

Final League Position: 16

GOALSCORERS

League (50): Inglethorpe 8, McGleish 7, Griffiths 6, Channing 5, Arnott 3, Hanson 3, Naylor 3 (2 pens), West 3, Ayorinde 2, Chapman 2, Timons 2, Castle 1, Hendon 1, Kelly 1, Ling 1, Warren 1, Winston 1.
Coca-Cola Cup (1): West 1.
FA Cup (3): Channing 1, West 1, Winson 1.

Sealey L 12	Hendon I 28	Naylor D 44	Garland P 13+8	Martin A 16+1	Arnott A 28+3	Martin D 8	Ling M 39+5	Ayorinde S 6+6	West C 22+1	Baker J 15+5	Hanson D 15+10	Chapman D 31+9	Caldwell P 3	Kelly T 6+3	Channing J 40	Riches S 2+3	McCarthy A 3+1	Warren M 25+2	Shearer L 7+1	Weaver L 9	Griffiths C 13	McGleish S 28	Winston S 3+8	Joseph R 15	Morrison D 8	Shilton P 9	Howes S 3+2	Fortune-West L 1+4	Inglethorpe A 10+6	Heidenstrom B 3+1	Ansah A —+2	Clapham J 6	Whyte C 1	Hyde P 13	Castle S 4	Wilkins R 3	Hodges L 3	Atkin P 5	Timons C 6	Match No.
1	2	3	4	5	6	7	8	9	10¹	11²	12	13																												1
	2	3	4	5	6	7	8	9¹	10	11²	12			1	13																									2
1	2	3	4³	5	6	7	8	9¹	10¹			12	13		14	11																								3
1	2	3		5	6	7	8		10			9	12		11	4¹																								4
1	2	3		5	6	7	8	12	10			9¹	13		11	4²																								5
1	2	3	12	5	6	7	8²		10	13	9	4			11¹																									6
1	2	3		5	6	7	8		10	11	9	4																												7
1	2	3		5	6	7¹	8		10		9	4		12	11																									8
1	2	3		5	6		8	12	10		9	4			7²	11	13																							9
1	2	3	12	5	6		8		10		9	4			7²	11¹	13																							10
1	2	3	5¹	6²			8	13	10	11	9	4			7																									11
1	2	3	7				8		10	12	9	4			11		6	5¹																						12
1	2	3	7				8		10	12	9	4					6²	13	5																					13
	2	3	6¹				8		10	7	9	4	1	11	12			5																						14
	2	3	6	5			8	12		7	9	4	1	11	10¹																									15
	2	3	12	6²			8³	13		7	9	4		14	5	1		10	11¹																					16
	2	3	7		6		8	11				4	10	5	1	9																								17
	2	3	12	5²	6		8	13	11			4¹	7	1	9																									18
		3			6		8	11		5¹	7		2	1	10	9	12	4																						19
	2	3	12		6		8	11¹			7			5	10	9¹	13	4	1																					20
	2	3	11		6		8	12			7			5	10¹	9		4	1																					21
		3		12	6¹		8	11²			4			7	5			9	10	1	2	13																		22
	2	3	4				8	9²		12				7	5			10		6	1	13	11¹																	23
	2	3					8	10¹			4			7	5			9²	14	6	1	12	13	11³																24
	2	3					8	10²			4			7	5			9		6	1	12	13	11¹																25
		3	11¹				8	10			4			7	5			9		6	1	11³	7	14																26
		3	2¹	12			8	9²		13	4			5				10		6	1			13																27
	2	3	11¹				8	9²			4			7	5			10	12	6	1	13																		28
	2	3					8	10			4			7	5		1				6		11	12																29
		2		12			8			11	13			7	5		1¹	10	9	6									3	4²										30
		3					8			12	4			7	5			10	9¹	2									3		1	6								31
		3					8			12	4			7	5			10	13										11		1	6								32
	2¹	3		9³			8²			4	12			7	5			10	13					14					11		1	6								33
	2	3		8¹				9¹	12	4				7	5		5¹	1	10	13				4					11		1	6								34
		3					8		11	12	4			7	5			1	10		6				2	9			2											35
		3						12		11	13	4		4			1	10						2	9										6	7			36
		3		12						11¹	13	4		2³	14	5	1	8²	10					9											6¹	7	7²			37
		3		12	7		8²					4¹		2		12		9	10	13	11				13		1				5	6			39
		3	12	7		13						4¹		2		5		9³	10			9¹ 10		11²	14					14		1				8	6			40
		3	12	7		13						4²		2		5		9	10			9¹ 10		11¹	14					14		1				8	6			41
		3	6	7										2		5		9	10			11¹	14			4					1					8				42
		3	6	7										2		5		9	10			11				4					1					8				43
		3	6¹	7							12	8²		2		5		9	10			11	13			4					1									44
		3	6¹	7		8			13	9	12			2				10		11²			4					1									5			45
		3		7		8¹			13	12				2		6		10		11			9²	4					1								5			46

Coca-Cola Cup
First Round   Portsmouth   (a) 0-2
                            (h) 1-0

FA Cup
First Round   Merthyr T   (h) 2-1
Second Round   Stevenage B (h) 1-2

LINCOLN CITY 1996–97 *Back row (left to right):* Steve Holmes, Brett Storey, Jon Whitney, Barry Richardson, John Vaughan, Neil Davies, Steve Fraser, Kevin Austin.
Middle row: Michael Cain (Kit Manager), Glenn Bonnell (Scout), Colin Alcide, Carl Lawrence, John Robertson, Gijsbert Bos, Mark Hone, Grant Brown, Paul Challinor, Roger Cleary (Physio), Ian Whyte (Youth Development Officer).
Front row: Worrell Sterling, Terry Fleming, Gareth Ainsworth, Steve Brown, John Beck (Manager), Shane Westley (Reserve Team Manager), Jason Minett, Tony Dennis, Jason Barnett, Lee Gibson.

Division 3 **LINCOLN CITY**

Sincil Bank, Lincoln LN5 8LD. Telephone: (01522) 880011. Fax: (01522) 880020.

Ground capacity: 10,918.

Record attendance: 23,196 v Derby Co, League Cup 4th rd, 15 November 1967.

Record receipts: £44,184.46 v Everton, Coca-Cola Cup 2nd rd 1st leg, 21 September 1993.

Pitch measurements: 110yd × 75yd.

Hon. Life Presidents: V. C. Withers, D. W. L. Bocock.

Chairman: K. J. Reames. *Vice-Chairman:* H. C. Sills.

Directors: J. Hicks, N. Woolsey, P. Jackson.

Hon. Consultant Surgeon: Mr Brian Smith. *Hon. Club Doctor:* Chris Batty.

Company Secretary: H. C. Sills.

Team Manager: John Beck. *Assistant Manager:* Shane Westley. *Physio:* Keith Oakes.

Commercial Manager: Stuart Donnelly. *Stadium Manager:* Nigel Dennis.

Year Formed: 1883. *Turned Professional:* 1892. *Ltd Co.:* 1892.

Club Nickname: 'The Red Imps'.

Previous Grounds: 1883, John O'Gaunt's; 1894, Sincil Bank.

Foundation: Although there was a Lincoln club as far back as 1861, the present organisation was formed in 1883 winning the Lincolnshire Senior Cup in only their fourth season. They were founder members of the Midland League in 1889 and that competition's first champions.

First Football League game: 3 September 1892, Division 2, v Sheffield U (a) L 2-4 – W. Gresham; Coulton, Neill; Shaw, Mettam, Moore; Smallman, Irving (1), Cameron (1), Kelly, J. Gresham.

Record League Victory: 11–1 v Crewe Alex, Division 3 (N), 29 September 1951 – Jones; Green (1p), Varney; Wright, Emery, Grummett (1); Troops (1), Garvey, Graver (6), Whittle (1), Johnson (1).

Record Cup Victory: 8–1 v Bromley, FA Cup 2nd rd, 10 December 1938 – McPhail; Hartshorne, Corbett; Bean, Leach, Whyte (1); Hancock, Wilson (1), Ponting (3), Deacon (1), Clare (2).

Record Defeat: 3–11 v Manchester C, Division 2, 23 March 1895.

Most League Points (2 for a win): 74, Division 4, 1975–76.

Most League Points (3 for a win): 77, Division 3, 1981–82.

Most League Goals: 121, Division 3 (N), 1951–52.

Highest League Scorer in Season: Allan Hall, 42, Division 3 (N), 1931–32.

Most League Goals in Total Aggregate: Andy Graver, 144, 1950–55 and 1958–61.

Most Capped Player: David Pugh, 3 (7), Wales and George Moulson, 3, Republic of Ireland.

Most League Appearances: Tony Emery, 402, 1946–59.

Record Transfer Fee Received: £400,000 plus increments from Newcastle U for Darren Huckerby, November 1995.

Record Transfer Fee Paid: £63,000 to Leicester C for Grant Brown, January 1990.

Football League Record: 1892 Founder member of Division 2. Remained in Division 2 until 1920 when they failed re-election but also missed seasons 1908–09 and 1911–12 when not re-elected. 1921–32 Division 3 (N); 1932–34 Division 2; 1934–48 Division 3 (N); 1948–49 Division 2; 1949–52 Division 3 (N); 1952–61 Division 2; 1961–62 Division 3; 1962–76 Division 4; 1976–79 Division 3; 1979–81 Division 4; 1981–86 Division 3; 1986–87 Division 4; 1987–88 GM Vauxhall Conference; 1988–92 Division 4; 1992– Division 3.

Honours: *Football League:* Division 2 best season: 5th, 1901–02; Division 3 (N) – Champions 1931–32, 1947–48, 1951–52; Runners-up 1927–28, 1930–31, 1936–37; Division 4 – Champions 1975–76; Runners-up 1980–81. *FA Cup:* best season: 1st rd of Second Series (5th rd equivalent), 1887, 2nd rd (5th rd equivalent), 1890, 1902. *Football League Cup:* best season: 4th rd, 1968. *GM Vauxhall Conference:* Champions 1987–88.

Colours: Red and white striped shirts, white shorts, white stockings with red trim. *Change colours:* All blue.

Did you know?

Lincoln City's first FA Cup tie on 1 November 1884 resulted in a 5–1 win over the long since defunct Hull Town.

LINCOLN CITY 1996–97 LEAGUE RECORD

Match No.	Date	Venue	Opponents	Result	H/T Score	Lg. Pos.	Goalscorers	Attendance
1	Aug 17	A	Torquay U	L	1-2	0-1	—	Ainsworth [71]	2645
2	24	H	Leyton Orient	D	1-1	1-0	18	Ainsworth [32]	3067
3	27	H	Cambridge U	D	1-1	0-1	—	Dennis (pen) [57]	2407
4	30	A	Swansea C	W	2-1	0-1	—	Ainsworth 2 [50, 57]	3111
5	Sept 7	A	Chester C	L	1-4	1-2	16	Holmes [39]	1802
6	10	H	Hull C	L	0-1	0-1	—		3069
7	14	H	Barnet	W	1-0	0-0	15	Martin [76]	2484
8	21	A	Wigan Ath	L	0-1	0-0	18		3394
9	28	H	Cardiff C	W	2-0	1-0	14	Alcide [18], Taylor [87]	2925
10	Oct 1	A	Brighton & HA	W	3-1	1-1	—	Ainsworth [25], Austin [65], Brown G [75]	4411
11	5	H	Exeter C	L	2-3	0-1	10	Ainsworth [90], Dennis [90]	3115
12	12	A	Scunthorpe U	L	0-2	0-1	13		3274
13	15	A	Rochdale	L	0-2	0-2	—		1411
14	19	H	Scarborough	D	1-1	1-0	19	Taylor [25]	2611
15	26	H	Colchester U	W	3-2	1-2	14	Ainsworth [33], Martin [59], Greene (og) [62]	2768
16	29	A	Doncaster R	W	3-1	0-1	—	Alcide 2 [56, 86], Ainsworth [83]	1913
17	Nov 2	A	Fulham	W	2-1	1-1	10	Ainsworth [5], Whitney [77]	6945
18	9	H	Darlington	W	2-0	1-0	9	Whitney 2 [7, 70]	3259
19	19	A	Hereford U	D	1-1	0-1	—	Ainsworth [72]	1363
20	23	H	Mansfield T	D	0-0	0-0	8		3548
21	30	A	Colchester U	L	1-7	0-3	9	Martin [64]	2738
22	Dec 3	A	Carlisle U	D	1-1	1-1	—	Alcide [38]	2033
23	14	H	Northampton T	D	1-1	0-1	12	Ainsworth [67]	2702
24	21	A	Hartlepool U	L	1-2	1-0	14	Bos [16]	1344
25	26	A	Hull C	L	1-2	1-2	15	Stant [21]	4892
26	Jan 11	A	Cardiff C	W	3-1	1-1	14	Stant [18], Perry (og) [51], Ainsworth [67]	2033
27	18	H	Brighton & HA	W	2-1	0-0	12	Stant [57], Ainsworth [89]	3056
28	25	H	Doncaster R	W	3-2	1-0	9	Stant 2 [23, 63], Martin [88]	3262
29	28	A	Chester C	D	0-0	0-0	—		2330
30	Feb 1	A	Darlington	L	2-5	0-3	9	Ainsworth 2 [80, 83]	2265
31	4	H	Wigan Ath	L	1-3	1-2	—	Cort [36]	2241
32	8	H	Fulham	W	2-0	1-0	11	Ainsworth [22], Stant [72]	3948
33	15	A	Mansfield T	D	2-2	0-2	11	Ainsworth [73], Stant [75]	3037
34	22	H	Hereford U	D	3-3	1-1	11	Holmes [11], Bimson [61], Alcide [75]	2957
35	25	A	Barnet	L	0-1	0-1	—		1194
36	Mar 1	A	Carlisle U	L	0-1	0-0	14		4958
37	8	H	Hartlepool U	W	2-1	1-0	11	Ainsworth 2 (1 pen) [28, 67 (p)]	2915
38	15	A	Northampton T	D	1-1	0-0	13	Holmes [65]	5266
39	22	A	Leyton Orient	W	3-2	1-0	12	Ainsworth (pen) [3], Brown S [71], Stant [85]	4121
40	29	H	Torquay U	L	1-2	0-0	12	Alcide [79]	3455
41	31	A	Cambridge U	W	3-1	0-0	11	Robertson [65], Craddock (og) [73], Stant [86]	3656
42	Apr 5	H	Swansea C	W	4-0	1-0	9	Alcide [18], Ainsworth (pen) [56], Stant 2 [62, 74]	3348
43	12	A	Exeter C	D	3-3	1-1	11	Brown S [1], Stant [77], Holmes [88]	2818
44	19	H	Scunthorpe U	W	2-0	2-0	10	Ainsworth [31], Stant [34]	4755
45	26	A	Scarborough	W	2-0	1-0	8	Stant 2 [23, 57]	3607
46	May 3	H	Rochdale	L	0-2	0-0	9		6495

Final League Position: 9

GOALSCORERS

League (70): Ainsworth 22 (3 pens), Stant 15, Alcide 7, Holmes 4, Martin 4, Whitney 3, Brown S 2, Dennis 2 (1 pen), Taylor 2, Austin 1, Bimson 1, Bos 1, Brown G 1, Cort 1, Robertson 1, own goals 3.
Coca-Cola Cup (13): Bos 3, Ainsworth 2, Alcide 2, Holmes 2, Fleming 1, Hone 1, Martin 1, Whitney 1.
FA Cup (1): Bos 1.

Richardson B 36	Holmes S 27 + 1	Whitney J 18	Dennis T 23 + 5	Robertson J 15 + 1	Austin K 44	Ainsworth G 46	Barnett J 33 + 3	Bos G 18 + 5	Brown S 9 + 6	Sterling W 15 + 6	Alcide C 38 + 4	Hone M 26 + 3	Fleming T 37	Martin J 29 + 5	Vaughan J 10	Brown G 34	Minett J 2 + 2	Taylor J 5	Bimson S 13 + 2	Stant P 22	Foran M 1 + 1	Cort C 5 + 1	Stones C — + 2	Match No.
1	2	3	4	5	6	7	8²	9	10¹	11	12	13												1
1	2	3	4	5	6	7		9		10¹	11		8	12										2
	2	3	4	5	6	7	12	9			11		8	10¹	1									3
	2	3	4²	5	6	7		9¹			11	12	13	8	10	1								4
	2	3			5	6	7	13³	14	12	11¹	9		4	8	10²		1						5
1	2	3			6	7		9	10	11			4	8		5								6
1	2	3			6	7		9¹	10²	11	12		4	8	13	5								7
1	2	3	12		6	7		9¹			11		4	8	10²	5	13							8
1	2	3			6	7		12		11			4	8	10¹	5		9						9
1	2	3			6	7				11			4	8	10	5		9						10
1	2	3	4		6	7		9²		12	11		8	10¹	5	13								11
1	2¹	3	12		6	7		13			11		4	8	10²	5		9						12
1		3		5	6	7	12			11	10	4	8		2¹			9						13
1		3	12		6	7	2			11	4	8	10¹	5				9						14
1		3			6	7	2	9		11	4	8	10	5										15
1		3			6	7	2	9		11	4	8	10	5										16
1		3			6	7	2	9		11	4	8	10	5										17
1		3	12		6	7	2	13		11¹	9	4	8	10²	5									18
1			6			7	2	9	12	11	4	3	10¹	5	8									19
1			6			7	2	9	12	11	4	3	10¹	5	8									20
1		8	6	3	7	2	9			11	4		10	5										21
1		8	6	7	2	9			11	4		10	5		3									22
1		8	6	7	2		9	11	4		10	5		3										23
1		8	6	7	2	9	11		4		10	5		3										24
1		12	6	7	2	13		11²	4¹	8	10	5		3	9									25
1		4	6	7	2	12	13	11¹		8	10²	5		3	9									26
1		4	6	7	2	10¹	11		8	12	5		3	9										27
1		4	6	7	2	11		8	10	5		3	9											28
1		4	6	7	2	12	11¹		8	10	5		3	9										29
1	12²	4	6	7	2	11	14		8	10¹	5		3³	9	13									30
1		4	3	7	2		8	12	6	11¹	9	5	10											31
1	3	4	6	7	2	12	11	8	5		9	10¹												32
1	3	4¹	6	7	2	11	8	5	12	9	10													33
1	3		6	7	2	11	8	5	4	9	10													34
1	3		6	7	2	11	12	8	13	5	4¹	9	10²											35
1	3	12	6	7	2	11	4	8	10²	5¹	9	13												36
1	3		6	7	2	12	11	4	8	10	5¹	9												37
1	3	4	6	7	12	2	11	8	10¹	5	9													38
1	3	4	6	7	2	12	10	11¹	8	5	9													39
	3	4	6	7	2	12	8	11	10¹	1	5	9												40
	3	4	5	6	7	2	10	8	11	1	9													41
	3	4	5	6	7	2	10	8¹	11	1	9	12												42
	3	4¹	5	6	7	2	10	11	8	1	9	12												43
	3		5	6	7	2	10	11	8	4	1	9												44
	3		5	6	7	2	10	11	8	4	1	9												45
	3		5	6	7	2	10	11	8¹	4	1	12	9											46

Coca-Cola Cup

First Round	Hartlepool U	(a)	2-2
		(h)	3-2
Second Round	Manchester C	(h)	4-1
		(a)	1-0
Third Round	Southampton	(a)	2-2
		(h)	1-3

FA Cup

First Round	Burnley	(a)	1-2

LIVERPOOL 1996-97 *Back row (left to right):* Ronnie Moran (Chief Coach), Dominic Matteo, Mark Wright, David James, Tony Warner, John Scales, Lee Jones, Doug Livermore (Assistant Manager).

Middle row: Joe Corrigan (Goalkeeping Coach), Rob Jones, Steve Harkness, Jason McAteer, Phil Babb, Mark Leather (Physio), Sammy Lee (Reserve Team Coach), Stig Inge Bjornebye, John Barnes, Jamie Redknapp, Steve McManaman, Robbie Fowler.

Front row: Michael Thomas, Mark Kennedy, Neil Ruddock, Stan Collymore, Roy Evans (Manager), John Barnes (Manager), Jamie Redknapp, Steve McManaman, Robbie Fowler.

FA Premiership   **LIVERPOOL**

Anfield Road, Liverpool L4 0TH. Telephone: (0151) 263 2361. Fax: (0151) 260 8813. Clubcall: 0891 121184. Ticket and Match Information: (0151) 260 9999 (24-hour service) or (0151) 260 8680 (office hours) Credit Card Bookings: 0151–263 5727.

Ground Capacity: 35,000 August 1997 rising to 45,000 February 1998

Record attendance: 61,905 v Wolverhampton W, FA Cup 4th rd, 2 February 1952.

Record receipts: £496,000 v Newcastle U, Coca-Cola Cup 4th rd, 29 November 1995.

Pitch measurements: 111yd × 74yd.

Chairman: D. R. Moores.

Directors: D. M. A. Chestnutt FCA, R. N. Parry BSC, FCA, J. T. Cross, N. White FSCA, T. D. Smith, T. W. Saunders, P. B. Robinson, K. E. B. Clayton FCA.

Vice-President: H. E. Roberts.

Team Manager: Roy Evans. *Assistant Manager:* Doug Livermore. *Coach:* Ronnie Moran. *Physio:* Mark Leather.

Chief Executive/Vice-Chairman: Peter B. Robinson. *Secretary:* Bryce Morrison.

Year Formed: 1892. *Turned Professional:* 1892. *Ltd Co.:* 1892.

Club Nickname: 'Reds' or 'Pool'.

Foundation: But for a dispute between Everton FC and their landlord at Anfield in 1892, there may never have been a Liverpool club. This dispute persuaded the majority of Evertonians to quit Anfield for Goodison Park, leaving the landlord, Mr. John Houlding, to form a new club. He originally tried to retain the name "Everton" but when this failed, he founded Liverpool Association FC on 15 March 1892.

First Football League game: 2 September 1893, Division 2, v Middlesbrough Ironopolis (a) W 2-0 – McOwen; Hannah, McLean; Henderson, McQue (1), McBride; Gordon, McVean (1), M. McQueen, Stott, H. McQueen.

Record League Victory: 10–1 v Rotherham T, Division 2, 18 February 1896 – Storer; Goldie, Wilkie; McCarthy, McQueen, Holmes; McVean (3), Ross (2), Allan (4), Becton (1), Bradshaw.

Record Cup Victory: 11–0 v Stromsgodset Drammen, ECWC 1st rd 1st leg, 17 September 1974 – Clemence; Smith (1), Lindsay (1p), Thompson (2), Cormack (1), Hughes (1), Boersma (2), Hall, Heighway (1), Kennedy (1), Callaghan (1).

Record Defeat: 1–9 v Birmingham C, Division 2, 11 December 1954.

Most League Points (2 for a win): 68, Division 1, 1978–79.

Most League Points (3 for a win): 90, Division 1, 1987–88.

Most League Goals: 106, Division 2, 1895–96.

Highest League Scorer in Season: Roger Hunt, 41, Division 2, 1961–62.

Most League Goals in Total Aggregate: Roger Hunt, 245, 1959–69.

Most Capped Player: Ian Rush, 67 (73), Wales.

Most League Appearances: Ian Callaghan, 640, 1960–78.

Record Transfer Fee Received: £7,000,000 from Aston Villa for Stan Collymore, May 1997.

Record Transfer Fee Paid: £8,500,000 to Nottingham F for Stan Collymore, June 1995.

Football League Record: 1893 Elected to Division 2; 1894–95 Division 1; 1895–96 Division 2; 1896–1904 Division 1; 1904–05 Division 2; 1905–54 Division 1; 1954–62 Division 2; 1962–92 Division 1; 1992– FA Premier League.

Honours: Football League: Division 1 – Champions 1900–01, 1905–06, 1921–22, 1922–23, 1946–47, 1963–64, 1965–66, 1972–73, 1975–76, 1976–77, 1978–79, 1979–80, 1981–82, 1982–83, 1983–84, 1985–86, 1987–88, 1989–90 (Liverpool have a record number of 18 League Championship wins); Runners-up 1898–99, 1909–10, 1968–69, 1973–74, 1974–75, 1977–78, 1984–85, 1986–87, 1988–89, 1990–91; Division 2 – Champions 1893–94, 1895–96, 1904–05, 1961–62. *FA Cup:* Winners 1965, 1974, 1986, 1989, 1992; Runners-up 1914, 1950, 1971, 1977, 1988, 1996; *Football League Cup:* Winners 1981, 1982, 1983, 1984, 1995; Runners-up 1978, 1987. *League Super Cup:* Winners 1986. **European Competitions:** *European Cup:* 1964–65, 1966–67, 1973–74, 1976–77 (winners), 1977–78 (winners), 1978–79, 1979–80, 1980–81 (winners), 1981–82, 1982–83, 1983–84 (winners), 1984–85 (runners-up); *European Cup-Winners' Cup:* 1965–66 (runners-up), 1971–72, 1974–75, 1992–93, 1996–97 (sf); *European Fairs Cup:* 1967–68, 1968–69, 1969–70, 1970–71; *UEFA Cup:* 1972–73 (winners), 1975–76 (winners), 1991–92, 1995–96; *Super Cup:* 1977 (winners), 1978, 1984; *World Club Championship:* 1981 (runners-up).

Colours: All red. *Change colours:* All yellow.

Did you know?
Between the two World Wars, Liverpool included at various times Elisha Scott (an Irishman), Robert Ireland (a Scot), Sam English (an Irishman) and George Poland (a Welshman).

LIVERPOOL 1996–97 LEAGUE RECORD

Match No.	Date	Venue	Opponents	Result	H/T Score	Lg. Pos.	Goalscorers	Atten-dance
1	Aug 17	A	Middlesbrough	D	3-3	2-2	—	Bjornebye [4], Barnes [29], Fowler [65]	30,039
2	19	H	Arsenal	W	2-0	0-0	—	McManaman 2 [68, 74]	38,103
3	24	H	Sunderland	D	0-0	0-0	7		40,503
4	Sept 4	A	Coventry C	W	1-0	0-0	—	Babb [68]	22,949
5	7	H	Southampton	W	2-1	1-0	3	Collymore [39], McManaman [89]	39,189
6	15	A	Leicester C	W	3-0	0-0	1	Berger 2 [58, 77], Thomas [61]	20,987
7	21	H	Chelsea	W	5-1	3-0	1	Fowler [15], Berger 2 [42, 49], Myers (og) [45], Barnes [57]	40,739
8	29	A	West Ham U	W	2-1	1-1	1	Collymore [3], Thomas [55]	25,064
9	Oct 12	A	Manchester U	L	0-1	0-1	3		55,128
10	27	H	Derby Co	W	2-1	0-0	3	Fowler 2 [47, 51]	39,515
11	Nov 3	A	Blackburn R	L	0-3	0-2	4		29,598
12	16	A	Leeds U	W	2-0	1-0	2	Ruddock [13], McManaman [90]	39,981
13	20	H	Everton	D	1-1	1-0	—	Fowler [30]	40,751
14	23	H	Wimbledon	D	1-1	1-0	3	Collymore [1]	39,027
15	Dec 2	H	Tottenham H	W	2-0	1-0	—	Thomas [45], McManaman [49]	32,899
16	7	H	Sheffield W	L	0-1	0-1	3		39,507
17	14	A	Middlesbrough	W	5-1	3-0	2	Fowler 4 [1, 28, 77, 85], Bjornebye [45]	39,491
18	17	H	Nottingham F	W	4-2	2-1	—	Collymore 2 [6, 63], Fowler [27], Lyttle (og) [51]	36,126
19	23	A	Newcastle U	D	1-1	1-1	—	Fowler [45]	36,570
20	26	H	Leicester C	D	1-1	0-0	1	Collymore [80]	40,786
21	29	A	Southampton	W	1-0	0-0	1	Barnes [76]	15,222
22	Jan 1	A	Chelsea	L	0-1	0-1	1		27,291
23	11	H	West Ham U	D	0-0	0-0	1		40,102
24	18	H	Aston Villa	W	3-0	0-0	1	Carragher [50], Collymore [58], Fowler [63]	40,489
25	Feb 1	A	Derby Co	W	1-0	0-0	2	Collymore [75]	18,102
26	19	H	Leeds U	W	4-0	3-0	—	Fowler [21], Collymore 2 [36, 37], Redknapp [87]	38,957
27	22	H	Blackburn R	D	0-0	0-0	2		40,747
28	Mar 2	A	Aston Villa	L	0-1	0-0	2		39,339
29	10	H	Newcastle U	W	4-3	3-0	—	McManaman [29], Berger [30], Fowler 2 [42, 90]	40,751
30	15	A	Nottingham F	D	1-1	1-1	2	Fowler [4]	29,181
31	24	A	Arsenal	W	2-1	0-0	—	Collymore [50], McAteer [65]	38,068
32	Apr 6	A	Coventry C	L	1-2	0-0	3	Fowler [52]	40,079
33	13	A	Sunderland	W	2-1	1-0	3	Fowler [33], McManaman [47]	21,889
34	16	A	Everton	D	1-1	1-0	—	Thomsen (og) [26]	40,177
35	19	H	Manchester U	L	1-3	1-2	3	Barnes [19]	40,892
36	May 3	H	Tottenham H	W	2-1	1-0	2	Collymore [15], Berger [43]	40,003
37	6	A	Wimbledon	L	1-2	0-1	—	Owen [74]	20,194
38	11	A	Sheffield W	D	1-1	0-0	4	Redknapp [83]	38,943

Final League Position: 4

GOALSCORERS

League (62): Fowler 18, Collymore 12, McManaman 7, Berger 6, Barnes 4, Thomas 3, Bjornebye 2, Redknapp 2, Babb 1, Carragher 1, McAteer 1, Owen 1, Ruddock 1, own goals 3.
Coca-Cola Cup (10): Fowler 5 (1 pen), McManaman 2, Berger 1, Redknapp 1, Wright 1.
FA Cup (3): Collymore 2, Fowler 1

James D 38	McAteer J 36 + 1	Bjornebye S 38	Matteo D 22 + 4	Wright M 33	Babb P 21 + 1	McManaman S 37	Collymore S 25 + 5	Fowler R 32	Barnes J 34 + 1	Thomas M 29 + 2	Jones L — + 2	Thompson D — + 2	Berger P 13 + 10	Redknapp J 18 + 5	Ruddock N 15 + 2	Scales J 3	Kennedy M — + 5	Carragher J 1 + 1	Kvarme B 15	Harkness S 5 + 2	Jones R 2	Owen M 1 + 1	Match No
1	2	3	4	5	6	7	8	9	10	11													1
1	2	3	4	5	6	7	8^1	9^2	10	11	12	13											2
1	2	3	4	5	6^1	7	8	9	10	11		12											3
1	2	3	4	5	6	7	8	9	10	11													4
1	2	3	4	5^1	6	7	8^1	9	10	11^2			12	13	14								5
1	2	3	4	5	6	7	8^1	9	10	11			12										6
1	2	3	4	5	6	7		9	10	11			8^1	12									7
1	2	3	4		6	7	8^2		10	11	12		9^1	13	14	5^3							8
1	2	3	4		6	7	8		10	11			9	12		5^1							9
1	2	3	4		6	7		9	10	11			8			5							10
1	2	3^2	4	5	6	7	12	9	10	11			8^1	13									11
1	2	3	4	5		7		9	10	11				8	6								12
1	2	3	4	5		7^1	12	9	10	11				8	6								13
1	2	3	4^1	5	12	7		9	10	11^2			13	8	6								14
1	2	3		5	4	7		9	10	11				8	6								15
1	2	3		5	4^1	7		9	10	11				8	6		12						16
1	2	3		5	4	7	8	9	10	11					6								17
1	2	3	12	5^1	4	7	8	9^2	10	11			13		6								18
1	2	3		5	4	7	8	9	10	11					6								19
1	2	3^2	12	5	4^1	7	8		10	11			9		6		13						20
1	2	3		5	4	7	8^1	9	10	11			12		6								21
1	2	3	12	5^2	4	7	8	9	10	11			13		6^1								22
1	2	3	4	5^1		7	12	9	10^2	11				8	6^3		13	14					23
1	2	3	4	5		7	8^1	9	10	11					6		12						24
1	2	3		5	6	7	8	9	10	11							12		4^1				25
1	2	3	4	5		7	8^1	9^2	10	11					6		12	13					26
1	2	3	4	5		7	8	9	10	11					6								27
1	2	3		5	6	7	8^1	9	10	11							12		4				28
1	2	3		5	6	7		9	10	11			8						4				29
1	2^2	3		5	6	7	12	9	10	11			8^1					13	4				30
1	2	3		5		7	8	9^1	10	11					6		12		4				31
1	2	3^1	4			7	8	9	10	11					6		12			5			32
1		3		5		7		9	10	11			8		6				4		2		33
1	12	3		5		7		9	10	11			8		6				4		2^1		34
1	2^1	3		5		7	12	9	10^2	11			13	8	6				4				35
1	2	3		5		7	8	9	10	11					6				4				36
1	2	3		5		7	8	9^1	10	11					6				4	12			37
1	2	3	12	5		7	8^2		10	11			13		6^3			14	4^1			9	38

Coca-Cola Cup

Third Round	Charlton Ath	(a)	1-1
		(h)	4-1
Fourth Round	Arsenal	(h)	4-2
Fifth Round	Middlesbrough	(a)	1-2

FA Cup

Third Round	Burnley	(h)	1-0
Fourth Round	Chelsea	(a)	2-4

LUTON TOWN 1996-97   *Back row (left to right):* Stuart Douglas, Jamie Woodsford, Sean Evers, Kim Grant, Paul McLaren, Darren Patterson, Gary Simpson, John Taylor, Ben Chenery, Bontcho Guentchev, Graham Alexander, Matthew Upson, Robert Kean, Chris Willmott.

Third row: Cherry Newbery (Club Secretary), Clive Goodyear (Physio), Wayne Turner (First Team Coach), David Oldfield, Des Linton, Marvin Johnson, Nathan Abbey, Ian Feuer, Kelvin Davis, Mitchell Thomas, Aaron Skelton, Andrew Fotiadis, John Moore (Youth Team Coach), Trevor Peake (Reserve Team Coach), Les Shannon (Chief Scout).

Second row: Julian James, Tony Thorpe, Steve Davis, Nigel Terry (Director), David Kohler (Chairman), Lennie Lawrence (Manager), Cliff Bassett (Director), Chris Green (Director), Gary Waddock, Dwight Marshall, Richard Harvey.

Front row: Liam George, Gary Doherty, Jimmy Cox, Steve Augustine, Andrew Barr, Nick Webb, Russell Lawes, Terry Sweeney, Matthew Spring, Andre Scarlett, Andrew Smith, Ian Jones.

Division 2

LUTON TOWN

Kenilworth Road Stadium, 1 Maple Rd, Luton, Beds LU4 8AW. Telephone: (01582) 411622. Ticket Office: (01582) 416976. Credit Hotline: (01582) 30748 (24 hrs). Clubcall: 0891 121123.

Ground capacity: 9975.

Record attendance: 30,069 v Blackpool, FA Cup 6th rd replay, 4 March 1959.

Record receipts: £115,541.20 v West Ham U, FA Cup 6th rd, 23 March 1994.

Pitch measurements: 110yd × 72yd.

Chairman & Managing Director: D. A. Kohler BSC (HONS), ARICS.

Directors: C. S. Bassett, C. T. F. Green, N. S. Terry.

Secretary: Cherry Newbery.

Commercial Manager: Kathy Leather.

Stadium Manager: Geoff Lovell.

Manager: Lennie Lawrence. *First Team Coach:* Wayne Turner. *Coaches:* Trevor Peake, John Moore.

Physio: Clive Goodyear.

Year Formed: 1885. *Turned Professional:* 1890. *Ltd Co.:* 1897.

Club Nickname: 'The Hatters'.

Previous Grounds: 1885, Excelsior, Dallow Lane; 1897, Dunstable Road; 1905, Kenilworth Road.

Foundation: Formed by an amalgamation of two leading local clubs, Wanderers and Excelsior a works team, at a meeting in Luton Town Hall in April 1885. The Wanderers had three months earlier changed their name to Luton Town Wanderers and did not take too kindly to the formation of another Town club but were talked around at this meeting. Wanderers had already appeared in the FA Cup and the new club entered in its inaugural season.

First Football League game: 4 September 1897, Division 2, v Leicester Fosse (a) D 1–1 – Williams; McCartney, McEwen; Davies, Stewart, Docherty; Gallacher, Coupar, Birch, McInnes, Ekins (1).

Record League Victory: 12–0 v Bristol R, Division 3 (S), 13 April 1936 – Dolman; Mackey, Smith; Finlayson, Nelson, Godfrey; Rich, Martin (1), Payne (10), Roberts (1), Stephenson.

Record Cup Victory: 9–0 v Clapton, FA Cup 1st rd (replay after abandoned game), 30 November 1927 – Abbott; Kingham, Graham; Black, Rennie, Fraser; Pointon, Yardley (4), Reid (2), Woods (1), Dennis (2).

Record Defeat: 0–9 v Small Heath, Division 2, 12 November 1898.

Most League Points (2 for a win): 66, Division 4, 1967–68.

Most League Points (3 for a win): 88, Division 2, 1981–82.

Most League Goals: 103, Division 3 (S), 1936–37.

Highest League Scorer in Season: Joe Payne, 55, Division 3 (S), 1936–37.

Most League Goals in Total Aggregate: Gordon Turner, 243, 1949–64.

Most Capped Player: Mal Donaghy, 58 (91), Northern Ireland.

Most League Appearances: Bob Morton, 494, 1948–64.

Record Transfer Fee Received: £2,500,000 from Arsenal for John Hartson, January 1995.

Record Transfer Fee Paid: £850,000 to Odense for Lars Elstrup, August 1989.

Football League Record: 1897 Elected to Division 2; 1900 Failed re-election; 1920 Division 3; 1921–37 Division 3 (S); 1937–55 Division 2; 1955–60 Division 1; 1960–63 Division 2; 1963–65 Division 3; 1965–68 Division 4; 1968–70 Division 3; 1970–74 Division 2; 1974–75 Division 1; 1975–82 Division 2; 1982–96 Division 1; 1996– Division 2.

Honours: Football League: Division 1 best season: 7th, 1986–87; Division 2 – Champions 1981–82; Runners-up 1954–55, 1973–74; Division 3 – Runners-up 1969–70; Division 4 – Champions 1967–68; Division 3 (S) – Champions 1936–37; Runners-up 1935–36. *FA Cup:* Runners-up 1959. *Football League Cup:* Winners 1988; Runners-up 1989. *Simod Cup:* Runners-up 1988.

Colours: White shirts with blue shoulder bar, blue shorts with white trim, blue stockings with orange and white trim. *Change colours:* Yellow shirts with blue trim, yellow shorts with blue trim, yellow stockings.

Did you know?
Joe Payne's famous ten goals for Luton Town were achieved against Bristol Rovers from six shots and four headed goals.

LUTON TOWN 1996–97 LEAGUE RECORD

Match No.	Date	Venue	Opponents	Result		H/T Score	Lg. Pos.	Goalscorers	Attendance
1	Aug 17	H	Burnley	L	1-2	1-2	—	Thorpe [36]	6484
2	24	A	Brentford	L	2-3	1-0	22	Thorpe (pen) [44], Hughes [69]	5404
3	27	A	Bristol C	L	0-5	0-2	—		7028
4	31	H	Rotherham U	W	1-0	0-0	19	Thomas [58]	4547
5	Sept 7	A	Wycombe W	W	1-0	0-0	15	Oldfield [52]	6471
6	10	H	Gillingham	W	2-1	1-0	—	Guentchev [14], Oldfield [52]	4604
7	14	H	Chesterfield	L	0-1	0-1	12		4763
8	21	A	Bury	D	0-0	0-0	15		3588
9	28	H	Blackpool	W	1-0	1-0	12	Grant [17]	5303
10	Oct 5	H	Walsall	W	3-1	1-0	11	Thorpe [45], Showler [60], Fotiadis [69]	5002
11	12	A	Shrewsbury T	W	3-0	1-0	8	Showler [4], Thomas [58], Grant [90]	3357
12	15	A	Stockport Co	D	1-1	1-0	—	Davis [27]	5352
13	19	H	Peterborough U	W	3-0	2-0	7	Davis [11], Showler 2 [25, 55]	5964
14	26	A	Bournemouth	W	2-0	0-0	5	Thorpe 2 (1 pen) [58 (pl, 60]	5635
15	29	A	Watford	D	1-1	0-0	—	Showler [75]	14,109
16	Nov 2	A	Plymouth Arg	D	3-3	1-1	8	Thorpe 3 [10, 64, 86]	7134
17	9	H	Notts Co	W	2-0	2-0	5	Thorpe [21], Hughes [23]	5664
18	19	A	Preston NE	L	2-3	1-2	—	Davis 2 [45, 90]	7004
19	23	H	Bristol R	W	2-1	1-0	4	Marshall [29], Thorpe (pen) [90]	5315
20	30	A	Bournemouth	L	2-3	2-1	6	James [24], Marshall [44]	4322
21	Dec 3	H	York C	W	2-0	0-0	—	Marshall [47], Thorpe [70]	4401
22	14	H	Crewe Alex	W	6-0	3-0	3	Alexander [3], Thorpe 3 (1 pen) [21, 30 (pl, 61], Showler [65], Oldfield [90]	5455
23	18	A	Millwall	W	1-0	0-0	—	Hughes [89]	7077
24	26	A	Gillingham	W	2-1	1-1	2	Thorpe 2 [23, 51]	8598
25	Jan 18	H	Wrexham	D	0-0	0-0	2		5734
26	27	H	Watford	D	0-0	0-0	—		7428
27	Feb 1	A	Notts Co	W	2-1	0-0	2	Hughes [66], Alexander [88]	5025
28	8	H	Plymouth Arg	D	2-2	0-0	2	Thorpe 2 [57, 61]	6439
29	15	A	Bristol R	L	2-3	1-1	2	Thorpe (pen) [10], Waddock [64]	5612
30	22	H	Preston NE	W	5-1	4-0	2	Oldfield 3 [23, 32, 38], Waddock [45], Thomas [73]	6454
31	Mar 1	A	York C	D	1-1	1-0	2	Davis [12]	3788
32	4	A	Chesterfield	D	1-1	1-1	—	Thorpe (pen) [41]	3731
33	8	H	Millwall	L	0-2	0-0	2		8585
34	12	A	Wrexham	L	1-2	1-1	—	Davis [23]	3342
35	15	A	Crewe Alex	D	0-0	0-0	2		4475
36	21	H	Brentford	W	1-0	0-0	—	Thorpe [66]	8164
37	29	A	Burnley	W	2-0	2-0	2	Thorpe 2 [13, 49]	15,490
38	Apr 1	A	Bristol C	D	2-2	1-2	—	Davis [45], Thorpe [74]	7105
39	5	A	Rotherham U	W	3-0	2-0	2	Thorpe 3 [6, 42, 80]	2609
40	8	H	Wycombe W	D	0-0	0-0	—		7626
41	12	A	Walsall	L	2-3	0-1	3	Kiwomya [54], Davis [56]	5415
42	15	A	Blackpool	D	0-0	0-0	—		4382
43	19	H	Shrewsbury T	W	2-0	1-0	3	Thorpe (pen) [45], Marshall [75]	6968
44	22	H	Bury	D	0-0	0-0	—		7769
45	26	A	Peterborough U	W	1-0	0-0	3	Fotiadis [55]	9499
46	May 3	H	Stockport Co	D	1-1	1-1	3	Fotiadis [38]	9347

Final League Position: 3

GOALSCORERS

League (71): Thorpe 28 (7 pens), Davis S 8, Oldfield 6, Showler 6, Hughes 4, Marshall 4, Fotiadis 3, Thomas 3, Alexander 2, Grant 2, Waddock 2, Guentchev 1, James 1, Kiwomya 1.
Coca-Cola Cup (9): Grant 2, Oldfield 2, Thorpe 2 (1 pen), Hughes 1, James 1, own goal 1.
FA Cup (6): Marshall 3, Hughes 1, Johnson 1, Thorpe 1.

Feuer I 46	James J 44	Thomas M 42	Waddock G 38+1	Patterson D 8+2	Johnson M 44	Guentchev B 15+12	Alexander G 44+1	Oldfield D 31+7	Grant K 8+17	Thorpe T 39+2	Fotiadis A 9+8	Linton D 3+4	Davis S 43+1	Hughes C 36	Showler P 21+2	Upson M —+1	Douglas S 2+7	McLaren P 13+11	Skelton A 2+1	Marshall D 9+15	Evers S 1	McGowan G 2	Kiwomya A 5	Harvey R 1+1	Match No.
1	2	3	4	5³	6	7	8	9¹	10²	11	12	13	14												1
1	2	3	4		6	12	8	9	10¹	11			5	7											2
1	2	3	4		6	12	13	9¹	10³	11	14		5	8	7²										3
1	2³	3	4		6	12	8	9²	10¹	13			5	7	11	14									4
1	2	3	4		6	11	8	9		12	10¹		5	7											5
1	2	3	4		6	11	8	9	12		10¹		5	7											6
1	2	3	4		6	11	8	9²	12		10¹		5	7	13										7
1	2	3	4		6	11	8	9			10¹		5	7		12									8
1	2	3	4		6	11	8	9²	10¹	7	12		5		13										9
1	2	3	4		6	11¹	8			7	9²		5	10³	12		13	14							10
1	2³	3	4		6	13	8	10	9¹				5	7	11	12²	14								11
1	2	3	4		6		8	12	10	9¹			5	7	11										12
1	2	3	4		6	12	8	9²		10¹	13		5	7³	11	14									13
1	2	3	4	5		12	8³	9²	7					10	11¹	13	14	6							14
1	2	3	4		6		8	9¹	10				5	7	11	12									15
1	2	3	4		6	12	8		13	10			5	7	11¹	9²									16
1	2	3	4		6	11	8	9	10¹				5	7	12										17
1	2	3	4¹		6	10²	8						5	7	11	9³	12	13	14						18
1	2	3			6	12	8	13	10				5	7	11¹			4		9²					19
1	2	3			6	12	8	13	10²			14	5	7	9¹			4³		11					20
1	2	3			6		8	12	10				5	7	9			4		11¹					21
1	2	3	4		6		8	12	13	10¹			5	9	7					11²					22
1	2	3	4		6	11	8	12		10			5	7				9¹							23
1	2	3	4		6	9	8	12		10			5	7				11¹							24
1	2	3			6	12	8	13	10			14	5	7	9¹			4³		11²					25
1	2	3			6		8	12	10			4	5	7	9					11¹					26
1	2	3			6	11	8	9	12	10¹		4²	5	7				13							27
1	2	3			6	7	8	9	10	12	13		5					11¹		4²					28
1	2	3³	12		6	7	8	9²	10			13	5		11¹			4		14					29
1	2	3	4		6		8	9³	12	10¹			5	7¹	11		13	14							30
1	2	3¹	4		6		8	9¹	10				5	7	11	12	13								31
1	2		4	3	6		8	9¹		12		10	5	7	11										32
1	2		4²	3	6		8	9¹		12		10	5	7³	11			13		14					33
1	2		4²	3	6		8	9¹		12		10¹	5	7	11			13		14					34
1	2		4	3	6		8	9				10	5	7	11										35
1	2	3	4		6		8	9	12	10¹			5	7	11²		13								36
1		3	4		6	12	8	9	10				5	7			13					2¹	11²		37
1		3	4		6	11³	8	9¹	12	10			5	7			13	14				2²			38
1	2	3	4	12	6¹		8	9	10³		13		5	7	11²		14								39
1	2	3	4		6		8	9²	12	10			5	7	11¹		13								40
1	2	3	4²	12	6¹	13	8	9³	10			14	5	7									11		41
1	2	3	4		6	9		10	8				5	7			12						11¹		42
1	2	3	4		6		8	9	10	11²			5	7¹			12							13	43
1	2	3	4		6		8²	12	10	9			5	7			13						11¹		44
1	2	3	4		6		8	9	10	12			5	7									11¹		45
1	2	3	4	5	6		8	9	12	10²				7			13						11¹		46

Coca-Cola Cup

First Round	Bristol R	(h)	3-0
		(a)	1-2
Second Round	Derby Co	(h)	1-0
		(a)	2-2
Third Round	Wimbledon	(a)	1-1
		(h)	1-2

FA Cup

First Round	Torquay U	(a)	1-0
Second Round	Boreham Wood	(h)	2-1
Third Round	Bolton W	(h)	1-1
		(a)	2-6

MACCLESFIELD TOWN 1996–97 *Back row (left to right)*: Neil Mitchell, Peter Davenport, Steve Payne, Mark Bradshaw, Neil Sorvel, Cec Edey.
Middle row: Carwyn Williams, Mark Gardiner, Nathan Peel, Ryan Price, Darren Tinson, Demis Ohandjanian, John Askey.
Front row: Eric Campbell (Physio), Phil Power, Neil Howarth, Sammy McIlroy (Manager), Steve Wood, Andy Levendis, George Prescott (Assistant Manager).
(Photograph: J. Rooney)

Division 3   **MACCLESFIELD TOWN**

The Moss Rose Ground, London Road, Macclesfield, Cheshire SK11 7SP. Telephone: (01625) 264686. Fax: (01625) 264692. Commercial Office: (01625) 264693. Social Club: (01625) 424324. Press Box: (01625) 264690/1. Club Call Line: (0891) 884482.

Ground Capacity: 6028 (seated 1053, standing 4975).

Record attendance: 9008 v Winsford U, Cheshire Senior Cup 2nd rd, 4 February 1948.

Pitch measurements: 100m × 66m.

Chairman: Alan Cash.

Directors: Harry Armstrong, John Brooks, Alan Cash, Reg Flowers, Colin Garlick, Roy Higginbotham, Andy Thomas.

Manager: Sammy McIlroy.

Secretary: Colin Garlick.

Administration Manager: Dianne Hehir.

Commercial Manager: Jackie Birks.

Club Doctor: Dr. Mike Whiteside.

Year formed: 1874.

Club Nickname: 'The Silkmen'.

Foundation: From the mid-19th Century until 1874, Macclesfield Town FC played under rugby rules. In 1891 they moved to the Moss Rose and finished champions of the Manchester & District League in 1906 and 1908. By 1911, they had carried off the Cheshire Senior Cup five times. Macclesfield were founder members of the Cheshire County League in 1919.

Record Win: 15-0 v Chester St Marys, Cheshire Senior Cup, 2nd rd, 16 February 1886.

Record Defeat: 1-13 v Tranmere R reserves, 3 May 1929.

Highest League Scorer in Season: Albert Valentine, 84, 1933–34.

Most Appearances: John Askey, 436, 1987–97.

Record Transfer Fee Received: £40,000 from Sheffield U for Mike Lake, 1988.

Record Transfer Fee Paid: £15,000 to Birmingham C for Ryan Price, November 1995.

Honours: Vauxhall Conference: Champions 1994–95, 1996–97. *FA Trophy:* Winners 1969–70, 1995–96; Runners-up 1988–89. *Bob Lord Trophy:* Winners 1993–94; Runners-up 1995–96, 1996–97. *Vauxhall Conference Championship Shield:* Winners 1996, 1997. *Northern Premier League:* Winners 1968–69, 1969–70, 1986–87; Runners-up 1984–85. *Northern Premier League Challenge Cup:* Winners 1986–87; Runners-up 1969–70, 1970–71, 1982–83. *Northern Premier League Presidents Cup:* Winners 1986–87; Runners-up 1984–85. *Cheshire Senior Cup:* Winners 18 times; Runners-up 11.

Colours: Royal blue shirts, white shorts, blue stockings. *Change Colours:* White shirts, royal blue shorts, white stockings.

Did you know?
Macclesfield Town's ground was used by Chester City for two years from 1990 for Football League matches.

MANCHESTER CITY 1996–97   *Back row (left to right):* Asa Hartford (First Team Coach), Richard Money (First Team Coach), Ronnie Evans (Assistant Physio), Uwe Rosler, Eddie McGoldrick, Steve Lomas, Alan Kernaghan, Tommy Wright, Martyn Margetson, Lee Crooks, Paul Beesley, Chris Greenacre, Nick Summerbee, Rae Ingram, Roy Bailey (Physio), Alex Stepney (Goalkeeping Coach).

Front row: Ian Brightwell, Peter Beagrie, Richard Edghill, Georgi Kinkladze, Scott Hiley, Paul Dickov, Frank Clark (Manager), Kit Symons, Alan Hill (Assistant Manager), Neil Heaney, Kevin Horlock, Jeff Whitley, John Foster, Michael Brown, Martin Phillips.

Division 1   **MANCHESTER CITY**

Maine Road, Moss Side, Manchester M14 7WN. Telephone: (0161) 224 5000. Fax: (0161) 248 8449. Ticket Office: (0161) 226 2224. Dial-A-Seat: (0161) 227 9229. Development Office: (0161) 226 3143. Clubcall: 0891 121191. Ticketcall: 0891 121591.

Ground capacity: 31,458.

Record attendance: 84,569 v Stoke C, FA Cup 6th rd, 3 March 1934 (British record for any game outside London or Glasgow).

Record receipts: £512,235 Manchester U v Oldham Ath, FA Cup semi-final replay, 13 April 1994.

Pitch measurements: 117yd × 78yd.

Chairman: F. H. Lee. *Chief Executive:* M. Turner.

Directors: C. J. Barlow, D. Bernstein, J. Dunkerley, D. Holt, A. Lewis, A. Thomas, M. Turner.

General Secretary: J. B. Halford. *Commercial Manager:* Geoff Durbin.

Manager: Frank Clark. *Assistant Manager:* Alan Hill. *First Team Coaches:* Richard Money, Asa Hartford. *Physio:* Roy Bailey. *Youth Team Coach:* Neil McNab.

Year Formed: 1887 as Ardwick FC; 1894 as Manchester City.

Turned Professional: 1887 as Ardwick FC. *Ltd Co.:* 1894. *Club Nickname:* 'Blues' The Citizens.

Previous Names: 1887–94, Ardwick FC (formed through the amalgamation of West Gorton and Gorton Athletic, the latter having been formed in 1880).

Previous Grounds: 1880–81, Clowes Street; 1881–82, Kirkmanshulme Cricket Ground; 1882–84, Queens Road; 1884–87, Pink Bank Lane; 1887–1923, Hyde Road (1894–1923, as City); 1923, Maine Road.

Foundation: Manchester City was formed as a Limited Company in 1894 after their predecessors Ardwick had been forced into bankruptcy. However, many historians like to trace the club's lineage as far back as 1880 when St. Mark's Church, West Gorton added a football section to their cricket club. They amalgamated with Gorton Athletic in 1884 as Gorton FC. Because of a change of ground they became Ardwick in 1887.

First Football League game: 3 September 1892, Division 2, v Bootle (h) W 7-0 – Douglas; McVickers, Robson; Middleton, Russell, Hopkins; Davies (3), Morris (2), Angus (1), Weir (1), Milarvie.

Record League Victory: 10–1 v Huddersfield T, Division 2, 7 November 1987 – Nixon; Gidman, Hinchcliffe, Clements, Lake, Redmond, White (3), Stewart (3), Adcock (3), McNab (1) Simpson.

Record Cup Victory: 10–1 v Swindon T, FA Cup 4th rd, 29 January 1930 – Barber; Felton, McCloy; Barrass, Cowan, Heinemann; Toseland, Marshall (5), Tait (3), Johnson (1), Brook (1).

Record Defeat: 1–9 v Everton, Division 1, 3 September 1906.

Most League Points (2 for a win): 62, Division 2, 1946–47.

Most League Points (3 for a win): 82, Division 2, 1988–89.

Most League Goals: 108, Division 2, 1926–27.

Highest League Scorer in Season: Tommy Johnson, 38, Division 1, 1928–29.

Most League Goals in Total Aggregate: Tommy Johnson, 158, 1919–30.

Most Capped Player: Colin Bell, 48, England.

Most League Appearances: Alan Oakes, 565, 1959–76.

Record Transfer Fee Received: £3,200,000 from Blackburn R for Garry Flitcroft, March 1996.

Record Transfer Fee Paid: £2,500,000 to Wimbledon for Keith Curle, August 1991 and £2,500,000 to Wimbledon for Terry Phelan, August 1992.

Football League Record: 1892 Ardwick elected founder member of Division 2; 1894 Newly-formed Manchester C elected to Division 2; Division 1 1899–1902, 1903–09, 1910–26, 1928–38, 1947–50, 1951–63, 1966–83, 1985–87, 1989–92; Division 2 1902–03, 1909–10, 1926–28, 1938–47, 1950–51, 1963–66, 1983–85, 1987–89; 1992–96 FA Premier League; 1996– Division 1.

Honours: Football League: Division 1 – Champions 1936–37, 1967–68; Runners-up 1903–04, 1920–21, 1976–77; Division 2 – Champions 1898–99, 1902–03, 1909–10, 1927–28, 1946–47, 1965–66; Runners-up 1895–96, 1950–51, 1987–88. *FA Cup:* Winners 1904, 1934, 1956, 1969; Runners-up 1926, 1933, 1955, 1981. *Football League Cup:* Winners 1970, 1976; Runners-up 1974. **European Competitions:** *European Cup:* 1968–69. *European Cup-Winners' Cup:* 1969–70 (winners), 1970–71. *UEFA Cup:* 1972–73, 1976–77, 1977–78, 1978–79.

Colours: Light blue shirts, white shorts, navy stockings. *Change colours:* White/navy shirts, burgundy trim, navy shorts, white stockings.

Did you know?
Manchester City ended the 1926–27 season with an 8–0 home win and began the following one with a 7–4 win also at Maine Road.

MANCHESTER CITY 1996–97 LEAGUE RECORD

Match No.	Date	Venue	Opponents	Result	H/T Score	Lg. Pos.	Goalscorers	Attendance
1	Aug 16	H	Ipswich T	W 1-0	1-0	—	Lomas [25]	29,126
2	20	A	Bolton W	L 0-1	0-0	—		18,257
3	24	A	Stoke C	L 1-2	0-2	15	Rosler [58]	21,116
4	Sept 3	H	Charlton Ath	W 2-1	0-1	—	Rosler (pen) [83], Creaney [87]	25,963
5	7	H	Barnsley	L 1-2	0-0	14	Clough [74]	26,464
6	10	A	Port Vale	W 2-0	1-0	—	Rosler [10], Dickov [68]	10,770
7	14	A	Crystal Palace	L 1-3	0-2	13	Kavelashvili [79]	17,638
8	21	H	Birmingham C	W 1-0	0-0	10	Kinkladze (pen) [89]	26,757
9	28	A	Sheffield U	L 0-2	0-1	14		20,867
10	Oct 12	A	QPR	D 2-2	1-2	16	Brightwell [31], Kinkladze (pen) [81]	16,265
11	15	A	Reading	L 0-2	0-1	—		11,724
12	19	H	Norwich C	W 2-1	1-0	13	Clough [31], Dickov [54]	28,269
13	27	H	Wolverhampton W	L 0-1	0-0	17		27,296
14	29	A	Southend U	W 3-2	1-0	—	Rosler [44], Kinkladze 2 (1 pen) [59,72 (p)]	8707
15	Nov 2	A	Swindon T	L 0-2	0-0	17		14,374
16	13	H	Oxford U	L 2-3	2-2	—	Dickov [14], Brightwell [16]	23,079
17	16	A	Portsmouth	L 1-2	1-2	21	Rodger [16]	12,841
18	19	H	Huddersfield T	D 0-0	0-0	—		23,314
19	23	H	Tranmere R	L 1-2	0-0	21	Summerbee [53]	26,531
20	27	H	WBA	W 3-2	3-1	—	Rosler [8], Kinkladze 2 (2 pens) [21, 37]	24,200
21	Dec 1	A	Wolverhampton W	L 0-3	0-0	21		23,911
22	7	A	Bradford C	W 3-2	2-1	17	Kinkladze (pen) [3], Dickov [12], Whitley [60]	25,035
23	21	A	Oldham Ath	L 1-2	1-0	20	Kinkladze [37]	12,992
24	26	H	Port Vale	L 0-1	0-1	20		30,344
25	28	A	Barnsley	L 0-2	0-2	21		17,159
26	Jan 11	H	Crystal Palace	D 1-1	0-0	21	Tuttle (og) [64]	27,395
27	18	A	Huddersfield T	D 1-1	1-0	21	Lomas [43]	18,358
28	29	H	Sheffield U	D 0-0	0-0	—		26,551
29	Feb 2	A	Oxford U	W 4-1	2-0	20	Gilchrist (og) [28], Kinkladze 2 [33, 65], Rosler [88]	8824
30	8	H	Southend U	W 3-0	0-0	20	Rosler 2 [49, 70], Kinkladze [57]	26,261
31	22	H	Swindon T	W 3-0	1-0	19	Horlock [16], Summerbee [66], Rosler [69]	27,262
32	Mar 1	A	Bradford C	W 3-1	0-0	16	Rosler 2 (1 pen) [50 (p), 69], Horlock [52]	17,609
33	5	H	Portsmouth	D 1-1	0-0	—	Horlock [47]	26,051
34	8	A	Oldham Ath	W 1-0	0-0	16	Rosler [58]	30,729
35	11	A	Birmingham C	L 0-2	0-0	—		20,084
36	15	A	Grimsby T	D 1-1	1-1	17	Kavelashvili [32]	8732
37	18	A	Tranmere R	D 1-1	0-0	—	O'Brien (og) [86]	12,019
38	22	H	Stoke C	W 2-0	0-0	15	Atkinson [65], Lomas [68]	28,497
39	Apr 5	A	Charlton Ath	D 1-1	0-1	18	Brannan [74]	15,000
40	9	H	Bolton W	L 1-2	1-1	—	Kinkladze [24]	28,026
41	12	A	WBA	W 3-1	3-1	15	Rosler 2 [3, 35], Horlock [23]	20,087
42	16	H	Grimsby T	W 3-1	0-1	—	Atkinson [52], Summerbee 2 [76, 84]	23,334
43	19	H	QPR	L 0-3	0-0	15		27,580
44	22	A	Ipswich T	L 0-1	0-1	—		15,824
45	25	A	Norwich C	D 0-0	0-0	—		14,080
46	May 3	H	Reading	W 3-2	1-2	14	Dickov [34], Rosler [66], Heaney [78]	27,260

Final League Position: 14

GOALSCORERS
League (59): Rosler 15 (2 pens), Kinkladze 12 (6 pens), Dickov 5, Horlock 4, Summerbee 4, Lomas 3, Atkinson 2, Brightwell 2, Clough 2, Kavelashvili 2, Brannan 1, Creaney 1, Heaney 1, Rodger 1, Whitley 1, own goals 3.
Coca-Cola Cup (1): Rosler 1.
FA Cup (4): Summerbee 2, Heaney 1, Rosler 1.

Immel E 4	Brightwell I 36+1	Frontzeck M 8+3	Lomas S 35	Symons K 44	Brown M 7+4	Summerbee N 43+1	Phillips M 1+3	Kavelashvili M 6+18	Kinkladze G 39	Rosler U 43+1	Hiley S 2+1	Creaney G 1+4	Clough N 18+5	Kernaghan A 9+1	Dickov P 25+4	Foster J 3	Dibble A 12+1	Whitley J 12+11	Ingram R 13+5	Crooks L 8+7	Wassall D 14+1	McGoldrick E 33	Rodger S 8	Margetson M 17	Heaney N 10+5	Wright T 13	Beagrie P —+1	Beesley P 6	Horlock K 18	Greenacre C —+4	Brannan G 11	Atkinson D 7+1	Match No.
1	2	3	4	5	6	7	8¹	9²	10	11	12	13																					1
1	2	3¹	4	5	6	12	13	9	10	11	7		8²																				2
1	2		4	5	6¹	7	12	9²	10	11			8	3	13																		3
1			4	5	6	7			10	11		3¹	13	8	12²	9	2																4
		3¹	4	5		7	12		10	11			13	6	9²	2³	1	8	14														5
	3		4	5	2²			12	10	11¹			7		9		1	8	6	13													6
12²	3¹		4	5	2¹			13	10	11			7		9		1	8	6		14												7
	3		4	5		7			10	11			8		9¹		1	12				6	2										8
			4		12	7		13	10	11			8¹		9²	5	1		3			6	2										9
	2		4	5		7		12	10	11			8		9¹		1					6	3										10
	2	12	4	5		7¹		13	10	11			8		9²		1					6	3										11
	2		4	5		7			10¹	11			8		9		1	12				6	3										12
	3²		4	5		2		12	10	11			8		9		1	7¹	13			6											13
	3			5	12	7			10¹	11			8		9		1	2	13			6	4²										14
	12			5		7		13	10	11²			8		9		1				4¹	6	2	3									15
			4	5		7		12	10	11			8		9²		1		13			6	2¹	3									16
	3		4	5		7		12	10	11³			8¹	13				14				6	2⁸	1	9								17
	3		4	5		7		9¹	10	11³			12	13				14				6	2	1	8²								18
	3	12	4³	5		7		11²	10	13			14		9			8				6	2¹	1									19
	3		4	5		7			10	11					9¹			12				2	6	1	8								20
	3		4	5		7			10	11			12		9¹	15	8					2	6		1⁶								21
	6		4	5		7		12	10	11²					9¹			14				2	3	1	8³								22
	6		4	5		7¹		12	10	11			8²		9			13				2	3	1									23
	6		4	5	8	7²		12	10	11¹				13	9			14				2	3³	1									24
	6		4	5	12	7			10	11			8									2¹	3	1	9								25
	6		4	5		7		12	10	11			8²					14	13			2	3³	1	9¹								26
	6		4	5		7			10	11			12		8¹							2	3	1	9								27
	2		4	5		7			10	11			6		9¹							3		1	8		12						28
	2¹		4	5		7			10	11			6									3		1	8	12	9						29
			4	5		7			10	11			12		8¹							2	3	1		6	9						30
	2		4	5		7			10	11			9¹											1	8			6	3	12			31
	2		4	5		7				11			9²					12							8	1	10¹	6	3	13			32
	2		4	5	12	7			10¹	11			9²												8	1		6	3	13			33
	2		4	5		7			10¹	11			9					12							8	1		6	3				34
	2		4	5		7	12		10	11			9¹					13							8	1		6²	3				35
	2		4			7		9¹	10	11		5													8	1		3	12	6			36
	2		4	5		7			10	11			9¹					12							8	1		3		6			37
	2		4	5		7		12	10	11								3						1	9		6		8¹				38
	2			5		7			10	11			4					3						1	9		6		8¹				39
	2			5		7			10	11			9					4¹						1	8		3		6	12			40
	2			5		7		12	10	11³			13		9			14			4²	1					3		6	8¹			41
	2			5		7			10	11²	4		9¹					12				1	13				3		6	8			42
	2			5		7			10	11¹	9		4					1				12					3		6	8			43
	2			5		7		12	10		4							1				9¹					3		6	8			44
	2			5		7			9¹	12	10	11	4					1									3		6	8			45
	2			5		7			11	12			8²		9¹		10	4				1	13				3		6				46

Coca-Cola Cup
Second Round   Lincoln C   (a) 1-4
                                    (h) 0-1

FA Cup
Third Round   Brenford   (a) 1-0
Fourth Round   Watford   (h) 3-1
Fifth Round   Middlesbrough (h) 0-1

MANCHESTER UNITED 1996–97 *Back row (left to right):* Phil Neville, Brian McClair, John O'Kane, Andy Cole, Chris Casper, David May, David Beckham, Ryan Giggs, Roy Keane, Gary Neville. *Middle row:* Albert Morgan (Kit Manager), Jordi Cruyff, Pat McGibbon, Gary Pallister, Raimond van der Gouw, Peter Schmeichel, Kevin Pilkington, Ronny Johnsen, Simon Davies, Lee Sharpe, David Fevre (Physio).

Front row: Terry Cooke, Karel Poborsky, Ole Gunnar Solskjaer, Eric Cantona, Alex Ferguson (Manager), Brian Kidd (Assistant Manager), Nicky Butt, Denis Irwin, Ben Thornley, Paul Scholes.
(Photograph: Action Images)

FA Premiership   **MANCHESTER UNITED**

Sir Matt Busby Way, Old Trafford, Manchester M16 0RA. Telephone: (0161) 872 1661, (0161) 930 1968. Fax: (0161) 876 5502. Ticket and Match Information: (0161) 872 0199. Membership Enquiries and Supporters Club: (0161) 872 5208. Clubcall: 0891 121161.

Ground capacity: 56,387.

Record attendance: 76,962 Wolverhampton W v Grimsby T, FA Cup semi-final, 25 March 1939.

Club record: 70,504 v Aston Villa, Division 1, 27 December 1920.

Record receipts: £739,841 v Borussia Dortmund, European Cup (Champions League), semi-final 2nd leg, 23 April 1997.

Pitch measurements: 116yd × 76yd.

Chairman/Chief Executive: C. M. Edwards.

Directors: J. M. Edelson, Sir Bobby Charlton CBE, E. M. Watkins LL.M., R. L. Olive.

Manager: Alex Ferguson CBE. *Assistant Manager:* Brian Kidd. *Physio:* D. Fevre MCSP, SRP.

Secretary: Kenneth Merrett. *Commercial Manager:* Danny McGregor. *Stadium Manager:* E. Cassin.

Year Formed: 1878 as Newton Heath LYR; 1902, Manchester United.

Turned Professional: 1885. *Ltd Co.:* 1907.

Previous Name: Newton Heath, 1880–1902. *Club Nickname:* 'Red Devils'.

Previous Grounds: 1880–93, North Road, Monsall Road; 1893, Bank Street; 1910, Old Trafford (played at Maine Road 1941–49).

Foundation: Manchester United was formed as comparatively recently as 1902 after their predecessors, Newton Heath, went bankrupt. However, it is usual to give the date of the club's foundation as 1878 when employees of the Lancashire and Yorkshire Railway Company formed Newton Heath L and YR Cricket and Football Club. They won the Manchester Cup in 1886 and as Newton Heath FC were admitted to the Second Division in 1892.

First Football League game: 3 September 1892, Division 1, v Blackburn R (a) L 3-4 – Warner; Clements, Brown; Perrins, Stewart, Erentz; Farman (1), Coupar (1), Donaldson (1), Carson, Mathieson.

Record League Victory (as Newton Heath): 10–1 v Wolverhampton W, Division 1, 15 October 1892 – Warner; Mitchell, Clements; Perrins, Stewart (3), Erentz; Farman (1), Hood (1), Donaldson (3), Carson (1), Hendry (1).

Record League Victory (as Manchester U): 9–0 v Ipswich T, FA Premier League, 4 March 1995 – Schmeichel; Keane (1) (Sharpe), Irwin, Bruce (Butt), Kanchelskis, Pallister, Cole (5), Ince (1), McClair, Hughes (2), Giggs.

Record Cup Victory: 10–0 v RSC Anderlecht, European Cup Prel. rd (2nd leg), 26 September 1956 – Wood; Foulkes, Byrne; Colman, Jones, Edwards; Berry (1), Whelan (2), Taylor (3), Viollet (4), Pegg.

Record Defeat: 0–7 v Blackburn R, Division 1, 10 April 1926 and v Aston Villa, Division 1, 27 December 1930 and v Wolverhampton W, Division 2, 26 December 1931.

Most League Points (2 for a win): 64, Division 1, 1956–57.

Most League Points (3 for a win): 92, FA Premier League, 1993–94.

Most League Goals: 103, Division 1, 1956–57 and 1958–59.

Highest League Scorer in Season: Dennis Viollet, 32, 1959–60.

Most League Goals in Total Aggregate: Bobby Charlton, 199, 1956–73.

Most Capped Player: Bobby Charlton, 106, England.

Most League Appearances: Bobby Charlton, 606, 1956–73.

Record Transfer Fee Received: £7,000,000 from Internazionale for Paul Ince, June 1995.

Record Transfer Fee Paid: £6,250,000 to Newcastle U for Andy Cole, January 1995.

Football League Record: 1892 Newton Heath elected to Division 1; 1894–1906 Division 2; 1906–22 Division 1; 1922–25 Division 2; 1925–31 Division 1; 1931–36 Division 2; 1936–37 Division 1; 1937–38 Division 2; 1938–74 Division 1; 1974–75 Division 2; 1975–92 Division 1; 1992– FA Premier League.

Honours: FA Premier League: – Champions 1992–93, 1993–94, 1995–96, 1996–97; Runners-up 1994–95. *Football League:* Division 1 – Champions 1907–08, 1910–11, 1951–52, 1955–56, 1956–57, 1964–65, 1966–67; Runners-up 1946–47, 1947–48, 1948–49, 1950–51, 1958–59, 1963–64, 1967–68, 1979–80, 1987–88, 1991–92. Division 2 – Champions 1935–36, 1974–75; Runners-up 1896–97, 1905–06, 1924–25, 1937–38. *FA Cup:* Winners 1909, 1948, 1963, 1977, 1983, 1985, 1990, 1994, 1996; Runners-up 1957, 1958, 1976, 1979, 1995. *Football League Cup:* Winners 1992, 1983 (Runners-up), 1991 (Runners-up), 1994 (Runners-up). **European Competitions:** *European Cup:* 1956–57 (s-f), 1957–58 (s-f), 1965–66 (s-f), 1967–68 (winners), 1968–69 (s-f), 1993–94, 1996–97 (s-f). *European Cup-Winners' Cup:* 1963–64, 1977–78, 1983–84, 1990–91 (winners). 1991–92. *European Fairs Cup:* 1964–65. *UEFA Cup:* 1976–77, 1980–81, 1982–83, 1984–85, 1992–93, 1995–96. *World Club Championship:* 1968. *Super Cup:* 1991 (winners).

Colours: Red shirts, white shorts, black stockings. *Change colours:* All white.

Did you know?
Manchester United's Premier League match against Liverpool on 12 October 1996 attracted a crowd of 55,128, the highest at Old Trafford for twelve years.

MANCHESTER UNITED 1996–97 LEAGUE RECORD

Match No.	Date		Venue	Opponents	Result	H/T Score	Lg. Pos.	Goalscorers	Attendance
1	Aug 17	A		Wimbledon	W 3-0	1-0	—	Cantona [25], Irwin [58], Beckham [90]	25,786
2	21	H		Everton	D 2-2	0-2	—	Cruyff [70], Unsworth (og) [82]	54,943
3	25	H		Blackburn R	D 2-2	1-1	5	Cruyff [39], Solskjaer [70]	54,178
4	Sept 4	A		Derby Co	D 1-1	1-1	—	Beckham [38]	18,025
5	7	A		Leeds U	W 4-0	1-0	5	Martyn (og) [3], Butt [49], Poborsky [77], Cantona [90]	39,694
6	14	H		Nottingham F	W 4-1	2-1	2	Solskjaer [22], Giggs [43], Cantona 2 (1 pen) [82, 90 (p)]	54,984
7	21	A		Aston Villa	D 0-0	0-0	4		39,339
8	29	H		Tottenham H	W 2-0	1-0	3	Solskjaer 2 [38, 58]	54,943
9	Oct 12	H		Liverpool	W 1-0	1-0	4	Beckham [23]	55,128
10	20	A		Newcastle U	L 0-5	0-2	5		36,579
11	26	A		Southampton	L 3-6	1-3	5	Beckham [41], May [56], Scholes [89]	15,256
12	Nov 2	H		Chelsea	L 1-2	0-1	6	May [81]	55,198
13	16	H		Arsenal	W 1-0	0-0	6	Winterburn (og) [63]	55,210
14	23	A		Middlesbrough	D 2-2	1-1	7	Keane [17], May [72]	30,063
15	30	H		Leicester C	W 3-1	0-0	5	Butt 2 [75, 87], Solskjaer [85]	55,196
16	Dec 8	A		West Ham U	D 2-2	0-0	6	Solskjaer [54], Beckham [75]	25,045
17	18	A		Sheffield W	D 1-1	0-0	—	Scholes [61]	37,671
18	21	H		Sunderland	W 5-0	2-0	5	Solskjaer 2 [35, 48], Cantona 2 (1 pen) [43 (p), 80], Butt [59]	55,081
19	26	A		Nottingham F	W 4-0	2-0	3	Beckham [25], Butt [44], Solskjaer [67], Cole [76]	29,032
20	28	H		Leeds U	W 1-0	1-0	2	Cantona (pen) [9]	55,256
21	Jan 1	H		Aston Villa	D 0-0	0-0	3		55,133
22	12	A		Tottenham H	W 2-1	1-1	2	Solskjaer [23], Beckham [76]	33,026
23	18	A		Coventry C	W 2-0	0-0	2	Giggs [60], Solskjaer [79]	23,080
24	29	H		Wimbledon	W 2-1	0-0	—	Giggs [76], Cole [83]	55,314
25	Feb 1	H		Southampton	W 2-1	1-1	1	Pallister [19], Cantona [80]	55,269
26	19	A		Arsenal	W 2-1	2-0	—	Cole [18], Solskjaer [32]	38,172
27	22	A		Chelsea	D 1-1	0-1	1	Beckham [68]	28,324
28	Mar 1	H		Coventry C	W 3-1	2-0	1	Breen (og) [4], Cole [5], Poborsky [47]	55,230
29	8	A		Sunderland	L 1-2	0-0	1	Melville (og) [78]	22,204
30	15	H		Sheffield W	W 2-0	1-0	1	Cole [19], Poborsky [61]	55,267
31	22	A		Everton	W 2-0	1-0	1	Solskjaer [35], Cantona [79]	40,079
32	Apr 5	A		Derby Co	L 2-3	0-2	1	Cantona [47], Solskjaer [76]	55,243
33	12	A		Blackburn R	W 3-2	2-1	1	Cole [32], Scholes [43], Cantona [80]	30,476
34	19	H		Liverpool	W 3-1	2-1	1	Pallister 2 [13, 42], Cole [63]	40,892
35	May 3	A		Leicester C	D 2-2	1-2	1	Solskjaer 2 [45, 51]	21,068
36	5	H		Middlesbrough	D 3-3	2-3	—	Keane [34], Neville G [42], Solskjaer [67]	54,489
37	8	H		Newcastle U	D 0-0	0-0	—		55,236
38	11	H		West Ham U	W 2-0	1-0	1	Solskjaer [11], Cruyff [84]	55,249

Final League Position: 1

GOALSCORERS

League (76): Solskjaer 18, Cantona 11 (3 pens), Beckham 8, Cole 7, Butt 5, Cruyff 3, Giggs 3, May 3, Pallister 3, Poborsky 3, Scholes 3, Keane 2, Irwin 1, Neville G 1, own goals 5.
Coca-Cola Cup (2): Poborsky 1, Scholes 1.
FA Cup (3): Scholes 2, Beckham 1.

Schmeichel P 36	Irwin D 29 + 2	Neville P 15 + 3	May D 28 + 1	Keane R 21	Pallister G 27	Cantona E 36	Butt N 24 + 2	Scholes P 16 + 8	Beckham D 33 + 3	Cruyff J 11 + 5	Johnsen R 26 + 5	McClair B 4 + 15	Poborsky K 15 + 7	Giggs R 25 + 1	Neville G 30 + 1	Solskjaer O 25 + 8	Cole A 10 + 10	Van der Gouw R 2	Clegg M 3 + 1	O'Kane J 1	Thornley B 1 + 1	Casper C — + 2	Match No.
1	2	3	4	5	6	7¹	8¹	9	10	11	12	13											1
1	2	3	4		6	7	8		10	9		12	5¹	11									2
1	2	3¹	4²		6	7			10	9	5	8		11	12	13							3
1	3		4²		6	7	8	12	10	9¹	5			11	2	13							4
1	3		4			7	8		10¹	9³	6	12	5²	11	2	13	14						5
1	3				6	7	8¹		10		4	12	5	11	2	9²	13						6
	3			5	6	7			10	9¹	4		12	11	2	8¹	13	1					7
1	3		4		6	7	8	12	10	13			5¹	11¹²	2	9							8
1	3		4			7	8	12	10	11	6		5¹	13	2	9²							9
1	3		4		6	7	8	12	10	13	5¹	14	11³		2	9²							10
1	12	3	4	5	6¹	7	8³	9	10	11²		14			2	13							11
1	2	3	4	5		7	8	9¹	10		6		12			11							12
1		3	4			7	8		10		6		5	11	2	9							13
1			4	5		7	8	9	10	12	6	13			2	3²	11¹						14
1	3		4	5	6	7	8		10	9¹		13	11²		2	12							15
1	3	12	4		6	7			10		2	5	8¹	11		9							16
1	3	12	4		6	7	8	9	13		5¹		11		2²	10							17
1	5	3	4		6²	7	8		10		13	12	11³		2	9¹					14		18
1	3		4			7	8²	5	10		6	13	12	11¹	2	9²	14						19
1	3		4	5		7	12	8¹	10		6			11	2	9²	13						20
1	3		4	5		7	8¹	12	10		6			11	2	9²	13						21
1			4	5	6	7		8¹	10		3³		12	11	2	9²	13				14		22
1	3			5	6	7		8			4¹		10	11	2	9					12		23
1	3			5	6	7		8¹	10					11	4	9	12		2				24
1	3			5	6	7			10		12	8²	11	4	9	13			2¹				25
1	3		5	6		12²			10	13	4¹	8	11		2	7	9						26
1	3	12	5	6					10	13	4¹	8	11²		2	7	9						27
1	3¹	12	4		6	7			10³	8	13	14	5	11²	2		9						28
1	3	5	4			7			10	11¹²	6	9	8¹		2	12	13						29
1	3		4		6	7	5	12	10		13	11			2	8¹	9²						30
1	2	3	4	5	6¹	7	8		10²		12	13		11		9							31
1	12	3		5	6²	7	8¹	13	10		4			11	2¹	14	9						32
	3			5	6	7	8	10¹	12		4				2	11	9	1					33
1		3		5	6	7	8	11¹	10		4	12			2	9							34
1		3	4	5	6	7	8¹	11	12	13					2	10¹	9						35
1	3		4	8	6	7		12	10		5¹				2	11	9						36
1		3	4	5²		7		11	10		6	13	8		2	12	9¹						37
1	2³	3	4			7	8	11¹	10	12	6	13	5²			9			14				38

Coca-Cola Cup

Third Round	Swindon T	(h)	2-1
Fourth Round	Leicester C	(a)	0-2

FA Cup

Third Round	Tottenham H	(h)	2-0
Fourth Round	Wimbledon	(h)	1-1
		(a)	0-1

MANSFIELD TOWN 1996–97 *Back row (left to right):* Darrel Clarke, Iffy Onuora, Nicky Weaver, Mark Sale, Scott Eustace, Ian Robinson.
Middle row: John Doolan, Paul Sherlock, Stewart Hadley, Warren Hackett, Stuart Watkiss, Mark Clifford, Simon Wood.
Front row: Steve Harper, Simon Ireland, Barry Statham (Physio), Keith Haslam (Chairman), Andy King (Manager), Steve Parkin (Coach), Brian Kilcline, David Kerr.

Division 3   **MANSFIELD TOWN**

Field Mill Ground, Quarry Lane, Mansfield NG18 5DA. Telephone: (01623) 23567. Fax: (01623) 25014. Marketing: (01623) 658070. Football in the Community: (01623) 25197.

Ground capacity: 6905.

Record attendance: 24,467 v Nottingham F, FA Cup 3rd rd, 10 January 1953.

Record receipts: £46,915 v Sheffield W, FA Cup 3rd rd, 5 January 1991.

Pitch measurements: 115yd × 70yd.

Chairman/Chief Executive: Keith Haslam.

Director: Mrs M. Haslam. *Associate Directors:* T. Hewson, D. Wardman, K. Woodcock, S. Whetton.

Manager: Steve Parkin.

Physio: Barry Statham.

Community Scheme Organiser: D. Bentley Tel: (01623) 25197.

Secretary: Christine Reynolds. *Marketing:* Nicola Wilcockson.

Year Formed: 1910. *Turned Professional:* 1910. *Ltd Co.:* 1921.

Previous Name: Mansfield Wesleyans 1891–1910.

Club Nickname: 'The Stags'.

Foundation: Many records give the date of Mansfield Town's formation as 1905. But the present club did not come into being until 1910 when the Mansfield Wesleyans (formed 1891) and playing in the Notts and District League, decided to spread their wings and changed their name to Mansfield Town, joining the new Central Alliance in 1911.

First Football League game: 29 August 1931, Division 3 (S), v Swindon T (h) W 3-2 – Wilson; Clifford, England; Wake, Davis, Blackburn; Gilhespy, Readman (1), Johnson, Broom (2), Baxter.

Record League Victory: 9–2 v Rotherham U, Division 3 (N), 27 December 1932 – Wilson; Anthony, England; Davies, S. Robinson, Slack; Prior, Broom, Readman (3), Hoyland (3), Bowater (3).

Record Cup Victory: 8–0 v Scarborough (away), FA Cup 1st rd, 22 November 1952 – Bramley; Chessell, Bradley; Field, Plummer, Lewis; Scott, Fox (3), Marron (2), Sid Watson (1), Adam (2).

Record Defeat: 1–8 v Walsall, Division 3 (N), 19 January 1933.

Most League Points (2 for a win): 68, Division 4, 1974–75.

Most League Points (3 for a win): 81, Division 4, 1985–86.

Most League Goals: 108, Division 4, 1962–63.

Highest League Scorer in Season: Ted Harston, 55, Division 3 (N), 1936–37.

Most League Goals in Total Aggregate: Harry Johnson, 104, 1931–36.

Most Capped Player: John McClelland, 6 (53), Northern Ireland.

Most League Appearances: Rod Arnold, 440, 1970–83.

Record Transfer Fee Received: £500,000 from Middlesbrough for Simon Coleman, September 1989.

Record Transfer Fee Paid: £80,000 to Leicester C for Steve Wilkinson, September 1989.

Football League Record: 1931 Elected to Division 3 (S); 1932–37 Division 3 (N); 1937–47 Division 3 (S); 1947–58 Division 3 (N); 1958–60 Division 3; 1960–63 Division 4; 1963–72 Division 3; 1972–75 Division 4; 1975–77 Division 3; 1977–78 Division 2; 1978–80 Division 3; 1980–86 Division 4; 1986–91 Division 3; 1991–92 Division 4; 1992–93 Division 2; 1993– Division 3.

Honours: Football League: Division 2 best season: 21st, 1977–78; Division 3 – Champions 1976–77; Division 4 – Champions 1974–75; Division 3 (N) – Runners-up 1950–51. *FA Cup:* best season: 6th rd, 1969. *Football League Cup:* best season: 5th rd, 1976. *Freight Rover Trophy:* Winners 1987.

Colours: Amber shirts with royal blue stripe down side, royal blue collar, amber shorts with royal blue stripe down sides, royal blue stockings with amber trim. *Change colours:* White shirts and shorts with thin blue stripe, white stockings with blue stripe.

Did you know?
On 17 September 1910, Mansfield Town achieved their first FA Cup tie victory, beating Market Harborough 5–0 away.

MANSFIELD TOWN 1996–97 LEAGUE RECORD

Match No.	Date	Venue	Opponents	Result		H/T Score	Lg. Pos.	Goalscorers	Atten-dance
1	Aug 17	H	Exeter C	L	0-1	0-1	—		2149
2	24	A	Northampton T	L	0-3	0-1	24		4162
3	27	A	Hartlepool U	D	2-2	1-1	—	Hadley [19], Sale [66]	2750
4	31	H	Rochdale	D	0-0	0-0	24		1861
5	Sept 7	A	Doncaster R	D	0-0	0-0	24		1814
6	10	H	Barnet	D	0-0	0-0	—		1505
7	14	H	Leyton Orient	L	0-2	0-1	23		1839
8	21	H	Fulham	W	2-1	1-0	22	Hadley [39], Harper [88]	5740
9	28	H	Hereford U	W	3-1	1-0	17	Sedgemore [9], Doolan (pen) [55], Walker [90]	1889
10	Oct 1	A	Hull C	D	1-1	0-0	—	Eustace [84]	3579
11	5	A	Carlisle U	D	1-1	0-0	17	Helliwell [76]	5509
12	12	H	Swansea C	D	0-0	0-0	18		2003
13	15	H	Wigan Ath	L	0-1	0-0	—		1942
14	19	A	Darlington	W	4-2	2-1	16	Hadley 2 [6, 77], Watkiss [39], Sale [59]	2532
15	26	A	Scarborough	L	1-2	1-1	20	Kay (og) [44]	2521
16	29	H	Torquay U	L	1-2	0-1	—	Wood [52]	1632
17	Nov 2	H	Scunthorpe U	W	2-0	1-0	19	Sedgemore [8], Kilcline [67]	2210
18	9	A	Brighton & HA	D	1-1	1-0	18	Harper [26]	1933
19	23	A	Lincoln C	D	0-0	0-0	21		3548
20	30	A	Scarborough	W	2-0	0-0	18	Wood 2 [82, 86]	1981
21	Dec 3	A	Cambridge U	L	1-2	0-0	—	Kilcline [56]	2716
22	14	H	Colchester U	D	1-1	0-0	19	Sale [90]	1653
23	21	A	Cardiff C	W	2-1	0-1	18	Sale 2 [49, 58]	2238
24	26	A	Barnet	D	1-1	1-0	18	Primus (og) [27]	1778
25	Jan 4	A	Leyton Orient	L	1-2	1-1	—	Doolan (pen) [17]	3418
26	11	A	Hereford U	W	1-0	0-0	18	Walker [80]	1872
27	18	H	Hull C	W	1-0	0-0	15	Kilcline [83]	2286
28	21	H	Doncaster R	W	2-0	1-0	—	Eustace [23], Clarke [56]	2093
29	Feb 1	A	Brighton & HA	D	1-1	1-1	13	Doolan [38]	2456
30	4	H	Chester C	L	0-2	0-1	—		1688
31	8	A	Scunthorpe U	W	2-0	1-0	14	Doolan [4], Martindale [48]	2600
32	15	H	Lincoln C	D	2-2	2-0	12	Martindale [6], Sedgemore [42]	3037
33	18	A	Torquay U	W	2-1	1-1	—	Clarke [2], Walker (pen) [49]	2071
34	22	A	Chester C	L	0-1	0-1	12		2385
35	Mar 1	H	Cambridge U	W	1-0	1-0	11	Doolan (pen) [6]	2163
36	8	H	Cardiff C	L	1-3	0-1	12	Hackett [54]	2569
37	14	A	Colchester U	L	1-2	0-2	—	Gunn (og) [82]	3064
38	22	H	Northampton T	W	1-0	1-0	13	Eustace [83]	2596
39	29	A	Exeter C	D	0-0	0-0	13		3181
40	31	H	Hartlepool U	W	1-0	1-0	12	Sedgemore [40]	2229
41	Apr 5	A	Rochdale	W	1-0	0-0	11	Cresswell [59]	1620
42	8	H	Fulham	D	0-0	0-0	—		3912
43	11	H	Carlisle U	D	0-0	0-0	—		4375
44	19	A	Swansea C	L	2-3	1-1	11	Ford [18], Eustace [47]	4868
45	26	H	Darlington	W	2-1	0-1	11	Doolan (pen) [49], Ford [56]	2431
46	May 3	A	Wigan Ath	L	0-2	0-0	11		7106

Final League Position: 11

GOALSCORERS

League (47): Doolan 6 (4 pens), Sale 5, Eustace 4, Hadley 4, Sedgemore 4, Kilcline 3, Walker 3 (1 pen), Wood 3, Clarke 2, Ford 2, Harper 2, Martindale 2, Cresswell 1, Hackett 1, Helliwell 1, Watkiss 1, own goals 3.
Coca-Cola Cup (0).
FA Cup (4): Doolan 1, Eustace 1, Ford 1, Wood 1.

Bowling I 46	Eustace S 41+1	Hackett W 35+1	Doolan J 41	Kilcline B 30+1	Watkiss S 30+1	Ireland S 5+1	Hadley S 31+5	Harper S 37+3	Sale M 12+6	Kerr D 9	Williams R 4+12	Wood S 23+8	Robinson I 3+5	Clifford M 3	Sedgemore B 37+2	Walker J 33+3	Helliwell I 4+1	Sherlock P 14+5	Ford T 25+2	Hurst G 5+1	Clarke D 17+2	Martindale G 5	Christie I 8	Williams L 3+3	Cresswell R 5	Young C —+1	Holbrook L —+1	Match No.
1	2	3	4³	5	6²	7	8	9	10¹	11	12	13	14															1
1	6	3¹	4	5	2	7	8	9	10	11		12																2
1	4	3	8	5	6	7	10	9	11			2																3
1	4	3	8	5¹	6	7	10	9	11			2	12															4
1	4	3		5	6		12				10¹	11			2	7	8	9										5
1	4	3		5	6		10¹	12				11²			2	7	8	9	13									6
1	4	3		5	6		12			11¹	10		13		2	7	8	9¹										7
1	4	3		5	6		10	12	9	11¹						7	8		2									8
1	4	3		5	6		10		9	11						7	8		2									9
1	4¹	3³	5	12	6		10	13	11	14						7	8	9²	2									10
1	4	.	5		6		10¹	3	11²		9	13			7	8	12		2									11
1	5	4	6				10	3	12	9¹	11				7	8			2									12
1	5	4	6				10	3	9		11				7	8			2									13
1	5	4	6				10	3	9		11				7	8			2									14
1	12	5	4		6		10	3	9³	13	11				7²	8		14	2¹									15
1	5	4	6				10	3	12		9				7	8		11¹	2									16
1	5	11	4		6		10	3	9						7	8			2									17
1	5	11	4		6		10	3	12		9¹				7	8			2									18
1	5	11	4		6		10	3	12		9¹				7	8			2									19
1	5	11	4		6		10¹	3	12		9				7	8			2									20
1	5	12	11	4	6		10	3	14		9¹				7²	8		13³	2									21
1	5	6	11¹	4			10²	3	12		9				7	8			2		13							22
1	5	6	4		3				9		11				7²	8		12	2¹	10	13							23
1	5	6	4				12	3	9		11				7	8			2	10¹								24
1	5	6	11	4			12	3	9						7	8²		13	2	10¹								25
1	5	6	11	4			12	3	9						7	8			2	10¹								26
1	5	6	11	4			12	3	9²						7	8		13	2	10¹								27
1	5	6	11	4			10	3	12		9¹				7	8			2	7								28
1	5	6	11	4	3		10		9						7¹	8		12	2	7¹								29
1	5	6	11	4	3		10		9²						7	8¹		12	2	13								30
1	5	6	11	4	3										7	8		12	2¹				9	10				31
1	5	6	11	4	3										7	8			2				9	10				32
1	5	6	4		3		12								7¹	8			2		11		9	10				33
1	5	6	4		3		12								7¹	8		13	2²		11		9	10				34
1	5	6	11	4			12	3							7	8			2				9	10¹				35
1	5	6	11	4			9¹	3	12						7²	8		13	2					10				36
1	5	6	11	4			12	9							7	8¹			2					10				37
1	5	6	11	4			9	3	12						7	8²		13	2					10¹				38
1	5	6	4²				10		12		11				7	8			2		3			13	9¹			39
1	5	6	11	4			10¹	3²	12						7	8			2		13		9					40
1	5	6	11	4			10	3							7	8			2						9			41
1	5	6	11	4			10	3	12						7	8			2						9¹			42
1	5	6	11²	4			10	3	12						7	8³		13	2				14		9¹			43
1	5	6	11	4			10²	3	12						7	8			2					9		13		44
1	5	6	11	4			10¹	3	12						7	8			2					9				45
1	5	6	11	4			10¹	3	13		12				7³	8			2					9²			14	46

Coca-Cola Cup
First Round   Burnley   (h) 0-3
    (a) 0-2

FA Cup
First Round   Consett   (h) 4-0
Second Round   Stockport Co   (h) 0-3

MIDDLESBROUGH 1996-97   *Back row (left to right):* Chris Freestone, Craig Liddle, Graham Kavanagh, Jan Fjortoft, Phil Whelan, Derek Whyte, Fabrizio Ravanelli, Phil Stamp, Alan Moore.
Middle row: Bob Ward (Senior Physio), Gordon McQueen (Reserve Team Coach), Chris Morris, Steve Vickers, Juninho, Alan Miller, Ben Roberts, Gary Walsh, Robbie Mustoe, Mikkel Beck, John Hendrie, Mike Kelly (Goalkeeper Coach), Kenny Wharton (A Team Coach).
Front row: John Pickering (First Team Coach), David Geddis (Youth Team Coach), Craig Hignett, Nick Barmby, Craig Hignett, Curtis Fleming, Viv Anderson (Assistant Manager), Nigel Pearson, Bryan Robson (Manager), Branco, Emerson, Clayton Blackmore, Neil Cox, Gary Henderson (Physio), Stuart Fellows.

Division 1 MIDDLESBROUGH

Cellnet Riverside Stadium, Middlesbrough, Cleveland TS3 6RS. Telephone: (01642) 877700. Fax: (01642) 877840. Boro Livewire: 0891 424200. Ticket Office: (01642) 877745. Tour Booking Line: (01642) 877730.

Ground capacity: 30,500.

Record attendance: 53,596 v Newcastle U, Division 1, 27 December 1949. (Cellnet Riverside Stadium): 30,215 v Tottenham H, FA Premier League, 19 October 1996.

Record receipts: £353,549 v Newcastle U, Coca-Cola Cup 4th rd, 27 November 1996.

Pitch measurements: 115yd × 74yd.

Chairman: Steve Gibson.

Director: George Cooke.

Chief Executive: Keith Lamb. ***Secretary:*** Karen Nelson.

Manager: Bryan Robson. ***Assistant Manager:*** Viv Anderson.

Physio: Bob Ward. ***Coach:*** John Pickering. ***Reserve Team Coach:*** Gordon McQueen. ***Youth Team Coach:*** David Geddis. ***Head of Marketing and Commercial:*** John Knox.

Youth Development Officer: Ron Bone. ***Public Relations Manager:*** Dave Allan.

Stadium Manager: Terry Tasker.

Year Formed: 1876; re-formed 1986. ***Turned Professional:*** 1889; became amateur 1892, and professional again, 1899. ***Ltd Co:*** 1892.

Club Nickname: 'Boro'.

Previous Grounds: 1877, Old Archery Ground, Albert Park; 1879, Breckon Hill; 1882, Linthorpe Road Ground; 1903, Ayresome Park; 1995, Cellnet Riverside Stadium.

Foundation: A previous belief that Middlesbrough Football Club was founded at a tripe supper at the Corporation Hotel has proved to be erroneous. In fact, members of Middlesbrough Cricket Club were responsible for forming it at a meeting in the gymnasium of the Albert Park Hotel in 1875.

First Football League game: 2 September 1899, Division 2, v Lincoln C (a) L 0-3 – Smith; Shaw, Ramsey; Allport, McNally, McCracken; Wanless, Longstaffe, Gettins, Page, Pugh.

Record League Victory: 9–0 v Brighton & HA, Division 2, 23 August 1958 – Taylor; Bilcliff, Robinson; Harris (2 p), Phillips, Walley; Day, McLean, Clough (5), Peacock (2), Holliday.

Record Cup Victory: 7–0 v Hereford U, Coca-Cola Cup 2nd rd, 1st leg, 18 September 1996 – Miller; Fleming (1), Branco (1), Whyte, Vickers, Whelan, Emerson (1), Mustoe, Stamp, Juninho, Ravanelli (4).

Record Defeat: 0–9 v Blackburn R, Division 2, 6 November 1954.

Most League Points (2 for a win): 65, Division 2, 1973–74.

Most League Points (3 for a win): 94, Division 3, 1986–87.

Most League Goals: 122, Division 2, 1926–27.

Highest League Scorer in Season: George Camsell, 59, Division 2, 1926–27 (Second Division record).

Most League Goals in Total Aggregate: George Camsell, 326, 1925–39.

Most Capped Player: Wilf Mannion, 26, England.

Most League Appearances: Tim Williamson, 563, 1902–23.

Record Transfer Fee Received: £5,750,000 from Everton for Nick Barmby, November 1996.

Record Transfer Fee Paid: £7,000,000 to Juventus for Fabrizio Ravanelli, August 1996.

Football League Record: 1899 Elected to Division 2; 1902–24 Division 1; 1924–27 Division 2; 1927–28 Division 1; 1928–29 Division 2; 1929–54 Division 1; 1954–66 Division 2; 1966–67 Division 3; 1967–74 Division 2; 1974–82 Division 1; 1982–86 Division 2; 1986–87 Division 3; 1987–88 Division 2; 1988–89 Division 1; 1989–92 Division 2; 1992–93 FA Premier League; 1993–95 Division 1; 1995–97 FA Premier League; 1997– Division 1.

Honours: *Football League:* Division 1 – Champions 1994–95. Division 2 – Champions 1926–27, 1928–29, 1973–74; Runners-up 1901–02, 1991–92. Division 3 – Runners-up 1966–67, 1986–87. *FA Cup:* Runners-up 1997. *Football League Cup:* Runners-up 1997. *Amateur Cup:* Winners 1895, 1898, *Anglo-Scottish Cup:* Winners 1976.

Colours: Red and white. ***Change colours:*** White and royal blue.

Did you know?
Middlesbrough became the first British team to field three Brazilians when Juninho, Emerson and Branco played in the 7–0 win against Hereford United in the Coca-Cola Cup second round first leg on 18 September 1996.

MIDDLESBROUGH 1996–97 LEAGUE RECORD

Match No.	Date	Venue	Opponents	Result	H/T Score	Lg. Pos.	Goalscorers	Attendance
1	Aug 17	H	Liverpool	D 3-3	2-2	—	Ravanelli 3 (1 pen) [26 (p),36,81]	30,039
2	21	A	Chelsea	L 0-1	0-0	—		28,272
3	24	A	Nottingham F	D 1-1	0-0	14	Juninho [49]	24,705
4	Sept 4	H	West Ham U	W 4-1	2-0	—	Emerson [12], Mustoe [28], Ravanelli [51], Stamp [81]	30,061
5	7	H	Coventry C	W 4-0	2-0	7	Ravanelli 2 [3, 73], Juninho 2 [28, 80]	29,811
6	14	A	Everton	W 2-1	0-1	6	Barmby [61], Juninho [81]	39,250
7	21	H	Arsenal	L 0-2	0-2	8		29,629
8	28	A	Southampton	L 0-4	0-2	9		15,230
9	Oct 14	A	Sunderland	D 2-2	1-1	—	Emerson [18], Ravanelli [53]	20,841
10	19	H	Tottenham H	L 0-3	0-2	11		30,215
11	26	H	Wimbledon	D 0-0	0-0	12		29,758
12	Nov 3	A	Newcastle U	L 1-3	0-1	15	Beck [88]	36,577
13	17	A	Derby Co	L 1-2	0-1	15	Ravanelli [73]	17,350
14	23	H	Manchester U	D 2-2	1-1	15	Ravanelli [27], Hignett (pen) [83]	30,063
15	30	A	Aston Villa	L 0-1	0-1	16		39,053
16	Dec 3	H	Leicester C	L 0-2	0-1	—		29,709
17	7	H	Leeds U	D 0-0	0-0	16		30,018
18	14	A	Liverpool	L 1-5	0-3	16	Thomas (og) [75]	39,491
19	26	H	Everton	W 4-2	2-2	17	Hignett [22], Blackmore [37], Juninho 2 [58, 74]	29,673
20	28	A	Coventry C	L 0-3	0-1	17		20,605
21	Jan 1	A	Arsenal	L 0-2	0-2	18		37,573
22	11	H	Southampton	L 0-1	0-0	20		29,509
23	18	H	Sheffield W	W 4-2	2-1	20	Ravanelli (pen) [14], Festa [23], Emerson (pen) [72], Juninho [90]	29,484
24	Feb 1	A	Wimbledon	D 1-1	0-1	20	Mustoe [75]	15,046
25	22	H	Newcastle U	L 0-1	0-1	20		30,063
26	Mar 1	A	Sheffield W	L 1-3	0-2	20	Mustoe [72]	28,206
27	5	H	Derby Co	W 6-1	1-0	—	Kinder [24], Ravanelli 3 [54, 82, 86], Hignett [70], Beck [81]	29,739
28	15	A	Leicester C	W 3-1	3-0	20	Blackmore [9], Juninho [27], Beck [36]	20,561
29	19	A	Blackburn R	W 2-1	1-0	—	Juninho [44], Ravanelli [61]	29,891
30	22	H	Chelsea	W 1-0	0-0	17	Juninho [53]	29,811
31	24	H	Nottingham F	D 1-1	0-1	—	Beck [56]	29,888
32	Apr 9	A	West Ham U	D 0-0	0-0	—		23,988
33	19	H	Sunderland	L 0-1	0-1	19		30,106
34	24	A	Tottenham H	L 0-1	0-0	—		29,940
35	May 3	H	Aston Villa	W 3-2	2-0	19	Ravanelli 2 (1 pen) [20, 90 (p)], Beck [34]	30,012
36	5	A	Manchester U	D 3-3	3-2	—	Juninho [15], Emerson [37], Hignett [40]	54,489
37	8	A	Blackburn R	D 0-0	0-0	—		27,411
38	11	A	Leeds U	D 1-1	0-0	19	Juninho [79]	38,569

Final League Position: 19

GOALSCORERS

League (51): Ravanelli 16 (3 pens), Juninho 12, Beck 5, Emerson 4 (1 pen), Hignett 4 (1 pen), Mustoe 3, Blackmore 2, Barmby 1, Festa 1, Kinder 1, Stamp 1, own goal 1.
Coca-Cola Cup (23): Ravanelli 9 (1 pen), Beck 4, Branco 2, Emerson 2, Fleming 1, Hignett 1, Juninho 1, Stamp 1, Vickers 1, Whyte 1.
FA Cup (18): Ravanelli 6, Beck 2, Hignett 2 (1 pen), Juninho 2, Cox 1, Emerson 1, Festa 1, Fjortoft 1, Stamp 1, own goal 1.

Miller A 10	Cox N 29 + 2	Fleming C 30	Vickers S 26 + 3	Pearson N 17 + 1	Whyte D 20 + 1	Emerson2	Mustoe R 31	Barmby N 10	Juninho34 + 1	Ravanelli F 33	Moore A 10 + 7	Whelan P 9	Stamp P 15 + 9	Brancol + 1	Walsh G 12	Beck M 22 + 3	Hignett C 19 + 3	Summerbell M —+ 2	Morris C 3 + 1	Campbell A —+ 3	Liddle C 5	Fjortoft J 2 + 3	Blackmore C 14 + 2	Robson B 1	Roberts B 9 + 1	Festa G 13	Schwarzer M 7	Kinder V 4 + 2	Freestone C —+ 3	Match No.
1	2	3	4	5	6	7	8	9	10^1	11	12																			1
1	2	3	4	5	6	7	8	9	10	11																				2
1	2	3	4	5		7	8	9	10	11			6																	3
1	2	3	4		5	7	8	9^1	10^2	11	12		6	13																4
1	2	3	4		5	7	8	9	10	11			6																	5
1	2	3	4		5	7	8	9	10	11			6																	6
1	2	3	4^2		5	7^1	8^3	9	10	11	12		6	13	14															7
1	12	2	4^1		5	7		9	10	11	13		6^2	8	3															8
1	2	3	4	5		7	8	9	10	11			6																	9
1	2	3	4	5	6^1	7	8	9	10	11			12																	10
	2	3	4	5^1	12	7	8		10	11			6		1	9														11
	2	3	4		6	7	8		10	11			5		1	9														12
	2	3	4		5		6		10	11	7^1				1	9	8	12												13
	2	3	4		5		6		10	11^1	7		12		1	9	8													14
	5	2			6		8		10^1	11		4			1	9	7		3	12										15
	2	3		5		4			11	7^1			6		1	9	8	12	10^2		13									16
	5	3			6		8			11		4	2		1		7			10	9									17
	5			6	7	10			11			4	2^1		1		8	12		3	9									18
	5		4	6^1	7				10	11					1	9	8^1	12		2		3								19
	5		4		7				10	11					1	9	8^1	3^2	12	2	13		6							20
	5		4			7	8		10^1	11					1	9	12					3	6							21
	2	3	4		5	7^1	8		10	11				13	1	12	9^2						6							22
	3	4	5			8	6		10	11	7					9^1		12						1	2					23
	2	3	4			7	8		10				11			6	9								1	5				24
	2	3	4^1	12			6		10	11	7^3		13			9	8^2						14		1	5				25
	2		4		6^2	7	8		10	9	11^1		13			12							14		5	1	3			26
12	2		5^3		7^2	4			10	11			13			9	8						14		6	1	3^1			27
	2	3	4	5		7^1			10	11	12					9	8						6			1				28
	2			5		7			10	11^1	12		4			9	8						3		6	1				
	2	3	13	5		7			10		12^2		4^1			9	8						11		6	1				
	2	3		5		7			10	11			9	8									6		4	1				
	2		4			7	8		10	9	11^1		12										6	15	1^6	3			
	2		4	5	3	7	8	13	10	11^1			6			9	12^2						1						
		4	5		7	8			10	11^1			2^2			9	12						6		1			3	13
	2		5		7	4			10	11			12			9^1	8						3		1	6			
	2	12	5		7^3	8			10	9^3			4				11^1						3		1	6		13	14
	2		5		7	8			10				4			9	11						3		1	6		13	
	2	12	5		7^3	8			10				4			9	11^2						3^1		1	6		13	14

Coca-Cola Cup

Second Round	Hereford U	(h)	7-0
		(a)	3-0
Third Round	Huddersfield T	(h)	5-1
Fourth Round	Newcastle U	(h)	3-1
Fifth Round	Liverpool	(h)	2-1
Semi-Final	Stockport Co	(a)	2-0
		(h)	0-1
Final	Leicester C		1-1
	(at Wembley)		
	(at Hillsborough)		0-1

FA Cup

Third Round	Chester C	
Fourth Round	Hednesfo…	
Fifth Round	Manche…	
Sixth Round	Derby …	
Semi Final	Chest…	
	(at C…	
	(at '	
Final	Ch…	
	('	

MILLWALL 1996-97   *Back row (left to right):* Tony Dolby, Anton Rogan, Jason Van Blerk, Damian Webber, Dave Savage, Tony Witter, Chris Malkin, Ricky Newman.
Middle row: Keith Johnstone (Physio), Brendan Markey, Keith Stevens, James Connor, Kasey Keller, David Nurse, Tim Carter, Bobby Bowry, Maurice Doyle, Richard Cadette, Ken Barry (Kit Man).
Front row: Ian McDonald (Youth/Reserve Coach), Jason Dair, Paul Hartley, Gerard Lavin, Jimmy Nicholl (Manager), Martin Harvey (Assistant Manager), Lucas Neill, Steve Crawford, David Sinclair, Ron Howard (Chief Scout).

Division 2 **MILLWALL**

Millwall Football & Athletic Company (1985) plc, The Den, Zampa Road, Bermondsey SE16 3LN.
Telephone: (0171) 232 1222. Ticket Office: (0171) 231 9999. Club Shop: (0171) 231 5881. Fax: (0171) 231 3663.

Ground capacity: 20,146 (all-seater).

Record Attendance: 20,093 v Arsenal, FA Cup 3rd rd, 10 January 1994.

Pitch measurements: 100 metres × 68m.

President: Lord Mellish of Bermondsey.

Chairman: Theo Paphitis. *Directors:* To be advised.

Secretary: Yvonne Haines.

Manager: Billy Bonds. *Assistant Manager:* Pat Holland. *Reserve Team Coach:* Keith Stevens.

Youth Team Coach: Kevin O'Callaghan. *Chief Scout:* Bob Pearson. *Youth Development Officer:* Mick Beard.
Physio: Gerry Docherty. *Hon. Medical Officer:* Dr. Charlotte Cowie.

Commercial Manager: Billy Neil. *Stadium Manager:* Colin Sayer. *Marketing Manager:* Mark Cole.

Year Formed: 1885. *Turned Professional:* 1893. *Ltd Co.:* 1894.

Previous Names: 1885, Millwall Rovers; 1889, Millwall Athletic.

Club Nickname: 'The Lions'.

Previous Grounds: 1885, Glengall Road, Millwall; 1886, Back of 'Lord Nelson'; 1890, East Ferry Road; 1901,
North Greenwich; 1910, The Den, Cold Blow Lane; 1993, The Den, Bermondsey.

Foundation: Formed in 1885 as Millwall Rovers by employees of Morton & Co, a jam and marmalade factory
in West Ferry Road. The founders were predominantly Scotsmen. Their first headquarters was The Islanders
pub in Tooke Street, Millwall. Their first trophy was the East End Cup in 1887.

First Football League game: 28 August 1920, Division 3, v Bristol R (h) W 2-0 – Lansdale; Fort, Hodge;
Voisey (1), Riddell, McAlpine; Waterall, Travers, Broad (1), Sutherland, Dempsey.

Record League Victory: 9–1 v Torquay U, Division 3 (S), 29 August 1927 – Lansdale; Tilling, Hill; Amos,
Bryant (3), Graham; Chance, Hawkins (3), Landells (1), Phillips (2), Black. 9–1 v Coventry C, Division 3 (S),
19 November 1927 – Lansdale; Fort, Hill; Amos, Collins (1), Graham; Chance, Landells (4), Cock (2), Phillips
(2), Black.

Record Cup Victory: 7–0 v Gateshead, FA Cup 2nd rd, 12 December 1936 – Yuill; Ted Smith, Inns; Brolly,
Hancock, Forsyth; Thomas (1), Mangnall (1), Ken Burditt (2), McCartney (2), Thorogood (1).

Record Defeat: 1–9 v Aston Villa, FA Cup 4th rd, 28 January 1946.

Most League Points (2 for a win): 65, Division 3 (S), 1927–28 and Division 3, 1965–66.

Most League Points (3 for a win): 90, Division 3, 1984–85.

Most League Goals: 127, Division 3 (S), 1927–28.

Highest League Scorer in Season: Richard Parker, 37, Division 3 (S), 1926–27.

Most League Goals in Total Aggregate: Teddy Sheringham, 93, 1984–91.

Most Capped Player: Eamonn Dunphy, 22 (23), Republic of Ireland.

Most League Appearances: Barry Kitchener, 523, 1967–82.

Record Transfer Fee Received: £2,300,000 from Liverpool for Mark Kennedy, March 1995.

Record Transfer Fee Paid: £800,000 to Derby Co for Paul Goddard, December 1989.

Football League Record: 1920 Original Members of Division 3; 1921 Division 3 (S); 1928–34 Division 2;
1934–38 Division 3 (S); 1938–48 Division 2; 1948–58 Division 3 (S); 1958–62 Division 4; 1962–64 Division 3;
1964–65 Division 4; 1965–66 Division 3; 1966–75 Division 2; 1975–76 Division 3; 1976–79 Division 2; 1979–85
Division 3; 1985–88 Division 2; 1988–90 Division 1; 1990–92 Division 2; 1992–96 Division 1; 1996– Division 2.

Honours: *Football League:* Division 1 best season: 7th 1992–93; Division 2 – Champions 1987–88; Division 3 (S)
– Champions 1927–28, 1937–38; Runners-up 1952–53; Division 3 – Runners-up 1965–66, 1984–85; Division 4 –
Champions 1961–62; Runners-up 1964–65. *FA Cup:* Semi-final 1900, 1903, 1937 (first Division 3 side to reach
semi-final). *Football League Cup:* best season: 5th rd, 1974, 1977, 1995. *Football League Trophy:* Winners 1983.

Colours: Blue shirts, white shorts, blue stockings. *Change colours:* White shirts, black shorts.

Did you know?
Before the Second World War, Millwall were reported to have offered £50,000 for the five Raith Rovers for-
wards. The deal never materialised, but in the summer of 1996 they signed four players from the same club.

MILLWALL 1996–97 LEAGUE RECORD

Match No.	Date	Venue	Opponents	Result	H/T Score	Lg. Pos.	Goalscorers	Attendance
1	Aug 17	H	Wrexham	D 1-1	0-1	—	Crawford (pen) [82]	9371
2	24	A	Watford	W 2-0	1-0	5	Harle [45], Crawford [49]	9495
3	27	A	York C	L 2-3	2-0	—	Savage [7], Malkin [28]	3108
4	31	H	Burnley	W 2-1	0-0	5	Newman [70], Neill [79]	9281
5	Sept 7	H	Bristol R	W 2-0	0-0	4	Rogan [50], Huckerby [60]	7881
6	10	A	Peterborough U	D 3-3	0-1	—	Huckerby [53], Malkin 2 [73, 90]	4442
7	14	A	Notts Co	W 2-1	0-0	4	Neill [61], Robinson (og) [88]	4473
8	21	H	Crewe Alex	W 2-0	0-0	2	Huckerby [66], Dair [89]	9320
9	28	A	Preston NE	L 1-2	0-1	2	Newman [64]	9400
10	Oct 2	H	Stockport Co	L 3-4	1-1	—	Rogan 2 [28, 71], Hartley [74]	7537
11	5	A	Plymouth Arg	D 0-0	0-0	6		7507
12	12	H	Chesterfield	W 2-1	2-1	5	Neill [31], Rogan [36]	7765
13	16	H	Bury	W 1-0	1-0	—	Rogan [22]	6447
14	19	A	Gillingham	W 3-2	1-0	2	Crawford 2 [22, 70], Hartley [72]	9305
15	26	A	Brentford	D 0-0	0-0	2		7691
16	30	H	Blackpool	W 2-1	0-1	—	Rogan 2 (2 pens) [56, 81]	7179
17	Nov 2	H	Walsall	W 1-0	1-0	1	Crawford [3]	9176
18	9	A	Bristol C	D 1-1	0-0	1	Crawford [77]	12,326
19	20	A	Shrewsbury T	W 2-1	1-1	—	Crawford 2 [3, 64]	5770
20	23	A	Rotherham U	D 0-0	0-0	1		3286
21	29	H	Brentford	D 0-0	0-0	—		7845
22	Dec 3	A	Wycombe W	L 0-1	0-0	—		4550
23	14	A	Bournemouth	D 1-1	1-1	2	Bright [11]	4494
24	18	H	Luton T	L 0-1	0-0	—		7077
25	26	H	Peterborough U	L 0-2	0-2	4		8118
26	Jan 11	H	Preston NE	W 3-2	1-2	3	Cadette [23], Crawford [56], Savage [68]	7096
27	18	A	Stockport Co	L 1-5	1-3	5	Webber [28]	7502
28	25	A	Blackpool	L 0-3	0-2	6		4523
29	Feb 1	H	Bristol C	L 0-2	0-1	9		9158
30	8	A	Walsall	L 1-2	1-2	9	Bowry [12]	3833
31	15	H	Rotherham U	W 2-0	0-0	7	Crawford [81], Gayle (og) [90]	7043
32	22	A	Shrewsbury T	D 1-1	0-1	7	Doyle [90]	2968
33	25	H	Notts Co	W 1-0	0-0	—	Savage [85]	5202
34	Mar 1	H	Wycombe W	W 2-1	1-1	3	Hartley [15], Dolby [67]	7539
35	8	A	Luton T	W 2-0	0-0	3	Dolby [79], Hartley [88]	8585
36	15	H	Bournemouth	L 0-1	0-0	6		8992
37	18	A	Crewe Alex	D 0-0	0-0	—		3695
38	22	H	Watford	L 0-1	0-1	8		8713
39	28	A	Wrexham	D 3-3	1-3	—	Crawford [34], Newman [58], Rogan (pen) [80]	4684
40	Apr 2	H	York C	D 1-1	0-0	—	Webber [90]	6161
41	5	A	Burnley	L 0-1	0-1	10		9840
42	8	A	Bristol R	L 0-1	0-0	—		5324
43	12	H	Plymouth Arg	D 0-0	0-0	11		5702
44	19	A	Chesterfield	L 0-1	0-1	12		5935
45	26	H	Gillingham	L 0-2	0-1	14		8946
46	May 3	A	Bury	L 0-2	0-0	14		9785

Final League Position: 14

GOALSCORERS
League (50): Crawford 11 (1 pen), Rogan 8 (3 pens), Hartley 4, Huckerby 3, Malkin 3, Neill 3, Newman 3, Savage 3, Dolby 2, Webber 2, Bowry 1, Bright 1, Cadette 1, Dair 1, Doyle 1, Harle 1, own goals 2.
Coca-Cola Cup (1): Malkin 1.
FA Cup (2): Crawford 1, Savage 1.

Goal-scorer markers are shown in brackets after the shirt number (e.g. 4[1] = shirt 4, 1 goal).

Carter T 46	Doyle M 19+9	Newman R 39+2	Sinclar D 6+2	Witter T 33	Stevens K 6	Bowry B 26+2	Savage D 32+3	Malkin C 7+2	Crawford S 40+2	Dair J 21+3	Neill L 35+4	Hartley P 35+9	Harle M 12+9	Webber D 25+1	Dolby T 15+6	Rogan A 26+2	Huckerby D 6	Hockton D —+2	Robertson G —+1	Fitzgerald S 7	Lavin G 7+2	Van Blerk J 2+2	Bright M 3	Iga A —+1	Bircham M 6	Roche S 4+3	Wilkins R 3	Cadette R 7	Sadlier R 7+3	McRobert L 3+1	Berry G 13+1	McLeary A 15	Canoville D —+2	Match No.
1	2	3	4[1]	5	6	7	8	9	10	11	12	13																						1
1		2		5	6	7	8[1]	9	10[2]	11	12	13	3	4																				2
1	14	2		5	6	7	8[1]	10	11	9[2]	12	13	3[3]	4																				3
1	12	2		5	6	7	8[1]	9	10[3]	11[2]	3	13	4	14																				4
1	12	2		5	6[3]	7[2]		14	10	8	11[1]	13	4			3	9																	5
1	6	2		5		7		9	12	11[1]	8	13	4[2]			3	10																	6
1	4	2		5		7		9	12	11	8[2]	13	6			3	10[1]																	7
1	2	4		5		7		12	9[1]	11	8	13	6			3[2]	10																	8
1	2[3]	4	14	5		7		12	9	8[2]	11[1]	13	6			3	10																	9
1	2	4[1]		5		7	11		9		8[2]	12	6			3	10	13																10
1	2	12			7	6		11[2]	8	9	5	4[2]	10			3[1]		13	14															11
1	12	2		5		7	4[1]		9		8	11			10	3				6														12
1		2		5		7	4[1]		9	12	8	10	13	11[2]		3				6														13
1		2		5		7	4		9[1]		8	10	12	11		3				6														14
1		2		5		7	4		9	12	8	10		11[1]		3				6														15
1		2		5		7	4[1]		9	12	8	10		11		3				6														16
1		2		5		7			9	4	8	11		10[1]		3				6	12													17
1		2		5		7		4	9	10	8	11	3			6[1]					12													18
1	12	6			7	4[2]		9	10	8[1]	11		5	13		3					2													19
1		6			7	4		9	10	8	11		5			3					2													20
1		4	6		7			9	10	8	11		5			3					2													21
1	12		6		7[1]	4		9	10[2]	8	11		5			3					2	13												22
1	7	6				4		9	11	8	12	5[1]									2	3	10											23
1	4	5			12			9	11[3]	8[2]	7[1]	13		14	6						2	3	10											24
1[6]	8	4			9		11[1]		7	6	5	12	3								2[2]	13	10	15										25
1	4	12			7		9[1]		11	6	5			2	3										8	10								26
1	4	12	13		7		9		11	6	5			2	3[1]										8	10[2]								27
1	2[3]	5	6[2]	8	4[1]		9	10	7	12	13	11	3													10[1]								28
1	7		4[3]	6			9	11	2	8	12[2]	5	10	3[1]													14							29
1	4		6			8	9	2	7		5													10	11	3								30
1	12	4	6		8[1]	9	2	7																10		11	3							31
1	12	4	6		8[1]	9	2	7	13															10		11[2]	3	5						32
1	8	4	6		9[1]	2	7	11																10		11[2]	3	5						33
1	8		6	4	9	2	7	11															12	10		3	5							34
1	8		6	4	9	2	7	11															10[1]	12		3	5							35
1	8		6		9	2	7	11															12	10[1]		3	5							36
1	8	4	6		9	2	7	11																10		3	5							37
1	8	4	6		9	2	7	11[1]	12														10[1]			3	5	12						38
1	8			4	9	7	6	11															2	12		10	3	5						39
1	8		6	4	9	11	7	3															2			10[1]	3[1]	5	12					40
1	11	4	6	8	9	2	7	3															2			10		5	12					41
1	8	4	6	12	9[1]	7	3	13																		10[2]	11	5						43
1	8	12	6	9	2	7	3[1]	10															2			13	5							44
1	12	3	6[2]	9	8	2	7	13	10																	11	5							45
1	12	3	6[2]	9	8	2	7	13	10																	11[1]	5							46

Coca-Cola Cup
First Round   Peterborough U   (h)   1-0
                                                       (a)   0-2

FA Cup
First Round   Woking   (a)   2-2
                                                      (h)   0-1

NEWCASTLE UNITED 1996-97   *Back row (left to right):* Ray Thompson (Kit Manager), Chris McMenemy (First Team Coach), Keith Gillespie, Jimmy Crawford, John Beresford, Pavel Srnicek, Shaka Hislop, Robbie Elliott, Chris Holland, Darren Huckerby, Steven Howey, Darren Peacock, Paul Kitson.
Middle row: Lee Clark, Faustino Asprilla, Philippe Albert, Steve Watson, Warren Barton, Steven Howey, Darren Peacock, Paul Kitson.
Front row: David Batty, Alan Shearer, David Ginola, Terry McDermott (Assistant Manager), Kevin Keegan (Manager), Peter Beardsley, Les Ferdinand, Robert Lee.

FA Premiership   NEWCASTLE UNITED

St James' Park, Newcastle-upon-Tyne NE1 4ST. Telephone: (0191) 201 8400. Club Fax: (0191) 201 8600. Lottery Office: (0191) 201 8502. Commercial Dept: (0191) 201 8422. Ticket Office Hotline: (0191) 261 1571. Club Shop: (0191) 201 8426. Club Shop Mail Order Answering Service: (0191) 263 4330. Football in the Community Scheme: (0191) 261 9715. Conference and Banqueting: (0191) 201 8525. Clubcall: 0891 121590. Clubcall Main Line: 0891 121190. Ticket Line: 0891 121590. Club Shop numbers: St James' Park Club Shop: (0191) 201 8426. Metro Centre Club Shop: (0191) 461 0000; (Russell Way): (0191) 460 3509; Within Asda, Metro Centre (0191) 460 3974; Asda, Gosforth (0191) 213 0638; Asda, Blyth (01670) 351653; Newcastle Airport: (0191) 271 2631. Monument Mall: (0191) 232 4488. Eldon Square Club Shop: (0191) 230 0808. Travel Club: (0191) 201 8550. Junior Magpies: (0191) 461 0044. Corporate Hospitality: (0191) 201 8424. Photographic Dept: (0191) 201 8467.

Ground capacity: 36,610.

Record attendance: 68,386 v Chelsea, Division 1, 3 September 1930.

Record receipts: £744,544 v Monaco, UEFA Cup quarter-final, 4 March 1997.

Pitch measurements: 105m × 68m.

President: T. L. Bennett.

Chairman: Sir John Hall.

Vice-Chairman: W. F. Shepherd. *Chief Executive:* A. O. Fletcher.

Directors: D. S. Hall, R. Jones.

Manager: Kenny Dalglish. *Assistant Manager:* Terry McDermott.

Coaches: Alan Irvine, John Carver, Tommy Burns, Terry Gennoe and Chris McMenemy. *Physios:* Derek Wright, Paul Ferris.

Director of Football Administration: Russell Cushing. *Director of Marketing:* Alec King. *Operations Manager:* P. W. Stevens.

Assistant Secretary: Tony Toward. *Youth Development Officer:* John Murray.

Year Formed: 1881. *Turned Professional:* 1889. *Ltd Co.:* 1890.

Club Nickname: 'Magpies'.

Previous Names: Stanley 1881; Newcastle East End 1882–92.

Previous Grounds: South Byker, 1881; Chillingham Road, Heaton, 1886–92.

Foundation: It stemmed from a newly formed club called Stanley in 1881. In October 1882 they changed their name to Newcastle East End to avoid confusion with two other local clubs, Stanley Nops and Stanley Albion. Shortly afterwards another club Rosewood merged with them. Newcastle West End had been formed in August 1882 and they played on a pitch which was part of the Town Moor. Moved to Brandling Park 1885 and St James' Park 1886 (home of Newcastle Rangers). West End went out of existence after a bad run and the remaining committee men invited East End to move to St James' Park. They accepted and, at a meeting in Bath Lane Hall in 1892, changed their name to Newcastle United.

First Football League game: 2 September 1893, Division 2, v Royal Arsenal (a) D 2-2 – Ramsay; Jeffery, Miller; Crielly, Graham, McKane; Bowman, Crate (1), Thompson, Sorley (1), Wallace. Graham and not Crate scored according to some reports.

Record League Victory: 13–0 v Newport Co, Division 2, 5 October 1946 – Garbutt; Cowell, Graham; Harvey, Brennan, Wright; Milburn (2), Bentley (1), Wayman (4), Shackleton (6), Pearson.

Record Cup Victory: 9–0 v Southport (at Hillsborough) FA Cup 4th rd, 1 February 1932 – McInroy; Nelson, Fairhurst; McKenzie, Davidson, Weaver (1); Boyd (1), Jimmy Richardson (3), Cape (2), McMenemy (1), Lang (1).

Record Defeat: 0–9 v Burton Wanderers, Division 2, 15 April 1895.

Most League Points (2 for a win): 57, Division 2, 1964–65.

Most League Points (3 for a win): 96, Division 1, 1992–93.

Most League Goals: 98, Division 1, 1951–52.

Highest League Scorer in Season: Hughie Gallacher, 36, Division 1, 1926–27.

Most League Goals in Total Aggregate: Jackie Milburn, 177, 1946–57.

Most Capped Player: Alf McMichael, 40, Northern Ireland.

Most League Appearances: Jim Lawrence, 432, 1904–22.

Record Transfer Fee Received: £6,250,000 from Manchester U for Andy Cole, January 1995.

Record Transfer Fee Paid: £15,000,000 to Blackburn R for Alan Shearer, July 1996.

Football League Record: 1893 Elected to Division 2; 1898–1934 Division 1; 1934–48 Division 2; 1948–61 Division 1; 1961–65 Division 2; 1965–78 Division 1; 1978–84 Division 2; 1984–89 Division 1; 1989–92 Division 2; 1992–93 Division 1; 1993– FA Premier League.

Honours: *FA Premier League:* Runners-up 1995–96, 1996–97. *Football League:* Division 1 – Champions 1904–05, 1906–07, 1908–09, 1926–27, 1992–93; Division 2 – Champions 1964–65; Runners-up 1897–98, 1947–48. *FA Cup:* Winners 1910, 1924, 1932, 1951, 1952, 1955; Runners-up 1905, 1906, 1908, 1911, 1974. *Football League Cup:* Runners-up 1976. *Texaco Cup:* Winners 1974, 1975. **European Competitions:** *European Fairs Cup:* 1968–69 (winners), 1969–70, 1970–71. *UEFA Cup:* 1977–78, 1994–95, 1996–97. *Anglo-Italian Cup:* Winners 1972–73.

Colours: Black and white striped shirts, black shorts, black stockings. *Change colours:* Dark blue, green and orange.

Did you know?
When Newcastle United beat Liverpool 9–2 on 1 January 1947, seven of United's goals came in the last 30 minutes. The half-time score was 2–2.

NEWCASTLE UNITED 1996–97 LEAGUE RECORD

Match No.	Date	Venue	Opponents	Result	H/T Score	Lg. Pos.	Goalscorers	Attendance
1	Aug 17	A	Everton	L 0-2	0-2	—		40,117
2	21	H	Wimbledon	W 2-0	1-0	—	Batty [3], Shearer [88]	36,385
3	24	H	Sheffield W	L 1-2	1-1	13	Shearer (pen) [13]	36,452
4	Sept 4	A	Sunderland	W 2-1	0-1	—	Beardsley [52], Ferdinand [62]	20,943
5	7	H	Tottenham H	W 2-1	1-1	6	Ferdinand 2 [37, 61]	32,594
6	14	H	Blackburn R	W 2-1	1-0	5	Shearer (pen) [45], Ferdinand [61]	36,424
7	21	A	Leeds U	W 1-0	0-0	2	Shearer [59]	36,070
8	30	H	Aston Villa	W 4-3	3-1	—	Ferdinand 2 [5, 22], Shearer [38], Howey [67]	36,400
9	Oct 12	H	Derby Co	W 1-0	0-0	1	Shearer [76]	18,092
10	20	H	Manchester U	W 5-0	2-0	1	Peacock [12], Ginola [30], Ferdinand [63], Shearer [75], Albert [83]	36,579
11	26	A	Leicester C	L 0-2	0-1	2		21,134
12	Nov 3	H	Middlesbrough	W 3-1	1-0	1	Beardsley 2 (1 pen) [40 (p), 69], Lee [74]	36,577
13	16	H	West Ham U	D 1-1	0-1	1	Beardsley [83]	36,552
14	23	A	Chelsea	D 1-1	1-1	1	Shearer [41]	29,056
15	30	H	Arsenal	L 1-2	1-1	2	Shearer [21]	36,565
16	Dec 9	A	Nottingham F	D 0-0	0-0	—		25,762
17	17	H	Coventry C	L 1-2	0-2	—	Shearer [61]	22,092
18	23	H	Liverpool	D 1-1	1-1	—	Shearer [28]	36,570
19	26	A	Blackburn R	L 0-1	0-0	6		30,398
20	28	H	Tottenham H	W 7-1	2-0	5	Shearer 2 [20, 82], Ferdinand 2 [22, 59], Lee 2 [61, 88], Albert [79]	36,308
21	Jan 1	H	Leeds U	W 3-0	1-0	4	Shearer 2 [4, 77], Ferdinand [87]	36,489
22	11	A	Aston Villa	D 2-2	2-1	4	Shearer [16], Clark [21]	39,339
23	18	A	Southampton	D 2-2	1-0	4	Ferdinand [14], Clark [82]	15,251
24	29	H	Everton	W 4-1	0-1	—	Ferdinand [74], Lee [79], Shearer (pen) [83], Elliott [90]	36,143
25	Feb 2	H	Leicester C	W 4-3	1-0	4	Elliott [3], Shearer 3 [77, 83, 90]	36,396
26	22	A	Middlesbrough	W 1-0	1-0	3	Ferdinand [8]	30,063
27	Mar 1	H	Southampton	L 0-1	0-0	4		36,446
28	10	A	Liverpool	L 3-4	0-3	—	Gillespie [71], Asprilla [87], Barton [88]	40,751
29	15	H	Coventry C	W 4-0	2-0	4	Watson [12], Lee [45], Beardsley (pen) [76], Elliott [87]	36,571
30	23	A	Wimbledon	D 1-1	0-1	4	Asprilla [53]	23,343
31	Apr 5	H	Sunderland	D 1-1	0-1	4	Shearer [77]	36,582
32	13	A	Sheffield W	D 1-1	1-0	5	Elliott [35]	33,798
33	16	H	Chelsea	W 3-1	3-0	—	Shearer 2 [12, 35], Asprilla [30]	36,320
34	19	H	Derby Co	W 3-1	1-1	4	Elliott [12], Ferdinand [52], Shearer [75]	36,550
35	May 3	A	Arsenal	W 1-0	1-0	4	Elliott [44]	38,179
36	6	A	West Ham U	D 0-0	0-0	—		24,617
37	8	A	Manchester U	D 0-0	0-0	—		55,236
38	11	H	Nottingham F	W 5-0	4-0	2	Asprilla [20], Ferdinand 2 [23, 26], Shearer [36], Elliott [77]	36,544

Final League Position: 2

GOALSCORERS

League (73): Shearer 25 (3 pens), Ferdinand 16, Elliott 7, Beardsley 5 (2 pens), Lee 5, Asprilla 4, Albert 2, Clark 2, Barton 1, Batty 1, Gillespie 1, Ginola 1, Howey 1, Peacock 1, Watson 1.
Coca-Cola Cup (2): Beardsley 1 (pen), Shearer 1.
FA Cup (4): Clark 1, Ferdinand 1, Lee 1, Shearer 1.

Hislop S 16	Watson S 33 + 3	Beresford J 18 + 1	Batty D 32	Howey S 8	Albert P 27	Lee R 32 + 1	Gillespie K 23 + 9	Shearer A 31	Ferdinand L 30 + 1	Ginola D 20 + 4	Beardsley P 22 + 3	Elliott R 29	Asprilla F 17 + 7	Clark L 9 + 16	Smicek P 22	Peacock D 35	Barton W 14 + 4	Kitson P — + 3	Crawford J — + 2	Match No.
1	2	3	4	5	6	7	8		9	10	11^1	12								1
	2		4	5	6	7			9	10	11	3	8^1	12	1					2
	2		4	5	6	7^2	12	9	10	11		3	8^1	13	1					3
	2		4		6	7		9	10^1	11	8	3		12	1	5				4
	2				6	7		9	10	11	8	3		4	1	5				5
	2	3	4		6	7^1	12	9	10^3	11	8^2		14	13	1	5				6
	2	3	4		6	7	12	9		11^1	8^2		10	13	1	5				7
	2	3	4		6	7	8	9	10	11^1			12		1	5				8
	2	3	4		6	7	11	9	10		8				1	5				9
	2^2	3	4		6	7^1		9	10	11	8			12	1	5	13			10
	2^2	3	4		6	7		9		11	8		12	10^1	1	5		13		11
			4		6	7	2^1	9		11	8	3	10		1	5	12			12
12	13		4		6	7	2^1	9^3		11	8	3^2	10	14	1	5				13
12			4		6	7	2	9		11^1	8	3	10^2	13	1	5				14
12			4		6	7^1	2	9		11	8	3	10^2		1	5	13			15
	2				6	7	4	9	10	11	8	3			1	5				16
	2				6	7	4	9	10	11	8	3			1	5				17
	2				6	7	4^2	9	10^3	11^1	8	3		12	1	5	13	14		18
	2		4		6	7	11	9	10		8	3			1	5				19
1	2	3	4		6	7	11^1	9	10		8		12			5				20
1	2	3	4		6	7		9	10		8		11			5				21
1	2	3	4		6		7	9				8	11	10		5				22
1		3	4			12	7^1	9	10		8		11	6		5	2			23
1	2		4		6	7	11^2	9	10		8^1	3	12			5	13			24
1	2		4		6	7	11^1	9	10	12		3	8^2	13		5				25
1	4				6	7	8	9	10			3		11		5	2			26
1	4				6	7	11		10^1	12	13	3	9	8^2		5	2			27
1	2		4		6	7			13^3	12	8^2	3	9	10^1		5	11	14		28
1	2		4		6	7^2	12			11^3	8	3	9^1	13		5	10	14		29
1	2		4		6	7	8			11		3	9			5	10			30
1	6		4			7^1	8	9	10^2	11		3	13	12		5	2			31
1	6	3	4			7	8	9^1	10	11				12		5	2			32
1	6	3	4			7	12	9	10^3	13	11		8^1	14		5	2			33
1	6	3	4			7	12	9	10	11			8^1			5	2			34
	6	3	4			7^2	12	9	10	11			8^1	13	1	5	2			35
	2	3	4	6			12	9		11	10^1	7			1	5	8			36
	2	3	4		6		7	9	10^1	11	12				1	5	8			37
	2	3	4^2	6^1			12	9	10			13	11	7^3	1	5	8	14		38

Coca-Cola Cup

Third Round	Oldham Ath		(h)	1-0
Fourth Round	Middlesbrough		(a)	1-3

FA Cup

Third Round	Charlton Ath		(a)	1-1
			(h)	2-1
Fourth Round	Nottingham F		(h)	1-2

NORTHAMPTON TOWN 1996–97   *Back row (left to right):* Michael Whittaker, Ali Gibb, Sean Parrish, Chris Lee, Garry Thompson, Lee Maddison, Claudio Devito, Jason White, Michael Warner.
Middle row: Denis Casey (Physio), Dean Peer, Mark Cooper, Andy Woodman, Ian Sampson, Billy Turley, Chris Burns, David Rennie, Paul Curtis (Youth Team Coach).
Front row: Ian Clarkson, Roy Hunter, Neil Grayson, Ian Atkins (Manager), Ray Warburton, Lee Colkin, Danny O'Shea.
(Photograph: Pete Norton)

Division 2 **NORTHAMPTON TOWN**

Sixfields Stadium, Upton Way, Northampton NN5 5QA. Telephone: (01604) 757773. Fax: (01604) 751613/754960. Ticket Office: (01604) 588338. Soccer Line: 0839 664477.

Ground capacity: 7653 (all seating).

Record attendance (at County Ground): 24,523 v Fulham, Division 1, 23 April 1966. (Sixfields Stadium): 7461 v Barnet, Division 3, 15 October 1994.

Record receipts (at Sixfields): £58,569.70 v Watford, FA Cup 1st rd, 17 November 1996.

Pitch measurements: 116yd × 72yd.

Chairman: B. J. Ward.

Directors: B. Stonhill, B. Hancock, M. Church, D. Kerr, B. Collins, B. Lomax, C. Smith.

Secretary: Mrs Rebecca Kerr. *Company Secretary:* Barry W. Collins.

Manager: Ian Atkins. *Coach:* Danny O'Shea.

Physio: Dennis Casey. *Commercial Manager:* Bob Gorrill. *Stadium Manager:* Martin Girvan (Pall Mall Services).

Year Formed: 1897. *Turned Professional:* 1901. *Ltd Co.:* 1901.

Previous Ground: County Ground.

Club Nickname: 'The Cobblers'.

Foundation: Formed in 1897 by school teachers connected with the Northampton and District Elementary Schools' Association, they survived a financial crisis at the end of their first year when they were £675 in the red and became members of the Midland League – a fast move indeed for a new club. They achieved Southern League membership in 1901.

First Football League game: 28 August 1920, Division 3, v Grimsby T (a) L 0-2 – Thorpe; Sproston, Hewison; Jobey, Tomkins, Pease; Whitworth, Lockett, Thomas, Freeman, MacKechnie.

Record League Victory: 10–0 v Walsall, Division 3 (S), 5 November 1927 – Hammond; Watson, Jeffs; Allen, Brett, Odell; Daley, Smith (3), Loasby (3), Hoten (1), Wells (3).

Record Cup Victory: 10–0 v Sutton T, FA Cup Prel rd, 7 December 1907 – Cooch; Drennan, Lloyd Davies, Tirrell (1), McCartney, Hickleton, Badenock (3), Platt (3), Lowe (1), Chapman (2), McDiarmid.

Record Defeat: 0–11 v Southampton, Southern League, 28 December 1901.

Most League Points (2 for a win): 68, Division 4, 1975–76.

Most League Points (3 for a win): 99, Division 4, 1986–87.

Most League Goals: 109, Division 3, 1962–63 and Division 3 (S), 1952–53.

Highest League Scorer in Season: Cliff Holton, 36, Division 3, 1961–62.

Most League Goals in Total Aggregate: Jack English, 135, 1947–60.

Most Capped Player: E. Lloyd Davies, 12 (16), Wales.

Most League Appearances: Tommy Fowler, 521, 1946–61.

Record Transfer Fee Received: £265,000 from Watford for Richard Hill, July 1987.

Record Transfer Fee Paid: £85,000 to Manchester C for Tony Adcock, January 1988.

Football League Record: 1920 Original Member of Division 3; 1921 Division 3 (S); 1958–61 Division 4; 1961–63 Division 3; 1963–65 Division 2; 1965–66 Division 1; 1966–67 Division 2; 1967–69 Division 3; 1969–76 Division 4; 1976–77 Division 3; 1977–87 Division 4; 1987–90 Division 3; 1990–92 Division 4; 1992–97 Division 3; 1997– Division 2.

Honours: Football League: Division 1 best season: 21st, 1965–66; Division 2 – Runners-up 1964–65; Division 3 – Champions 1962–63; Promoted from Division 3 1996–97 (play-offs); Division 3 (S) – Runners-up 1927–28, 1949–50; Division 4 – Champions 1986–87; Runners-up 1975–76. *FA Cup:* best season: 5th rd, 1934, 1950, 1970. *Football League Cup:* best season: 5th rd, 1965, 1967.

Colours: Claret with white shirts, yellow shoulder panel (Lotto logo), white shorts, claret stockings. *Change colours:* Reverse of (home) first choice.

Did you know?
Harry Loasby scored 28 League and Cup goals in only 30 appearances for Northampton Town between 1927 and 1929 before being transferred to Gillingham.

NORTHAMPTON TOWN 1996–97 LEAGUE RECORD

Match No.	Date	Venue	Opponents	Result	H/T Score	Lg. Pos.	Goalscorers	Attendance
1	Aug 17	A	Wigan Ath	L	1-2	1-0	—	Cooper [28]	3449
2	24	H	Mansfield T	W	3-0	1-0	10	Rennie [36], Hunter [53], Cooper [85]	4162
3	27	H	Torquay U	D	1-1	0-1	—	Rennie [85]	4128
4	31	A	Scarborough	D	1-1	0-0	10	Lee [85]	2520
5	Sept 7	A	Barnet	D	1-1	1-0	12	Lee [6]	2982
6	10	H	Leyton Orient	L	0-1	0-0	—		3994
7	14	H	Cambridge U	L	1-2	0-1	20	Sampson [63]	4584
8	21	A	Cardiff C	D	2-2	0-1	20	Cooper [87], Hunter (pen) [89]	4124
9	28	H	Brighton & HA	W	3-0	2-0	15	Hunter (pen) [27], Lee [30], Gibb [54]	4402
10	Oct 1	A	Chester C	L	1-2	0-0	—	Grayson [72]	1791
11	5	H	Fulham	L	0-1	0-0	21		6171
12	12	A	Exeter C	W	1-0	1-0	16	Lee [29]	3002
13	15	A	Scunthorpe U	L	1-2	1-0	—	Sampson [16]	2079
14	19	H	Colchester U	W	2-1	1-1	14	Parrish [45], Grayson [55]	4119
15	26	H	Darlington	W	3-1	0-1	13	Grayson [52], Warburton [61], Parrish [90]	4123
16	29	A	Hartlepool U	W	2-0	2-0	—	Grayson [1], Parrish [22]	1254
17	Nov 2	A	Swansea C	L	0-1	0-0	12		3335
18	9	H	Carlisle U	D	1-1	0-0	12	Parrish [52]	4682
19	19	A	Doncaster R	W	2-1	1-0	—	Warburton [1], Rush [61]	1030
20	23	H	Rochdale	D	2-2	1-0	11	Hunter [2], White [69]	3836
21	30	A	Darlington	L	1-3	1-0	15	Cooper [39]	2266
22	Dec 3	H	Hull C	W	2-1	2-0	—	Stant 2 (1 pen) [7, 23 (p)]	3519
23	14	A	Lincoln C	D	1-1	1-0	11	Rennie [33]	2702
24	20	H	Hereford U	W	1-0	0-0	—	Grayson [77]	4238
25	26	A	Leyton Orient	L	1-2	1-1	10	Grayson [22]	4492
26	28	H	Barnet	W	2-0	1-0	6	Sampson [40], Cooper [81]	5060
27	Jan 1	H	Cardiff C	W	4-0	2-0	—	Warburton [16], Jarman (og) [42], Cooper [54], Grayson [69]	4416
28	18	H	Chester C	W	5-1	3-1	6	Rush [21], Cooper [24], Warburton [45], Sampson [48], Grayson [82]	4434
29	25	H	Hartlepool U	W	3-0	2-0	5	Grayson 3 [44, 45, 48]	5039
30	Feb 1	A	Carlisle U	L	1-2	0-0	6	Lee [77]	5271
31	8	H	Swansea C	L	1-2	0-1	7	Lee [59]	6178
32	15	A	Rochdale	D	1-1	1-1	8	Rush [9]	1988
33	22	H	Doncaster R	W	2-0	2-0	8	Cooper [12], Grayson [41]	4577
34	Mar 1	A	Hull C	L	0-1	0-1	10	Dewhurst (og) [74]	3495
35	4	A	Brighton & HA	L	1-2	0-1	—	Peer [89]	4943
36	8	A	Hereford U	W	2-1	2-0	8	Parrish [9], Lee [13]	3043
37	15	H	Lincoln C	D	1-1	0-0	8	Hunter (pen) [90]	5266
38	22	H	Mansfield T	L	0-1	0-0	10		2596
39	29	H	Wigan Ath	L	0-1	0-0	10		5914
40	31	A	Torquay U	W	2-1	2-1	9	Parrish [17], Sampson [19]	2335
41	Apr 5	H	Scarborough	W	1-0	0-0	6	Hunter (pen) [54]	4854
42	8	A	Cambridge U	D	0-0	0-0	—		4412
43	12	A	Fulham	W	1-0	1-0	5	White [7]	11,479
44	19	H	Exeter C	W	4-1	1-0	5	Parrish [44], Cooper 2 [47, 53], Gayle [71]	6400
45	26	A	Colchester U	D	0-0	0-0	6		5956
46	May 3	H	Scunthorpe U	W	1-0	0-0	4	Parrish [74]	6828

Final League Position: 4

GOALSCORERS

League (67): Grayson 12, Cooper 10, Parrish 8, Lee 7, Hunter 6 (4 pens), Sampson 5, Warburton 4, Rennie 3, Rush 3, Stant 2 (1 pen), White 2, Gayle 1, Gibb 1, Peer 1, own goals 2.
Coca-Cola Cup (3): Lee 2, own goal 1.
FA Cup (0).

Woodman A 45	Clarkson I 45	Maddison L 34	Sampson I 43	Rennie D 42 + 1	O'Shea D 29 + 6	Burns C 6	Peer D 7 + 14	Cooper M 37 + 4	Grayson N 32 + 8	Hunter R 26 + 10	White J 15 + 17	Gibb A 6 + 12	Lee C 12 + 17	Parrish S 37 + 2	Colkin L 1 + 5	Warner M 1 + 8	Lyne N 1	Thompson G — + 1	Smart A 1	Warburton R 35	Kirby R — + 1	Rush M 14	Stant P 4 + 1	Martin D 10 + 2	Frain J 13	Gayle J 9 + 4	Turley B 1	Match No.
1	2	3	4	5	6	7	8	9^3	10^3	11^1	12	13	14															1
1	2	3	4	5	6	7	8^1	9	11	12	10^2			13														2
1	2	3	4	5	6	7^1		9	11^2	8^3		12	13	10	14													3
1	2	3	4	5		7^2		9	12	6	10^1	11^3	13	8		14												4
1	2	3	4	5	6			9	7^2	11	12	13	8^1	10														5
1	2		4	5	6	9	12	3			11	10	13		8^2		7^3	14										6
1	2	3	4	5	6	8^1		11	13	10	7^3			12	14			9^2										7
1	2		4	5	6		7^1	9	11^2	3	10	12		8	13													8
1	2	3	4	5	6^1			9	12	11	13	7^3	8^2	10		14												9
1	2	3	4	5			10	9	12	11	13	7^1	8^2	6														10
1	2	3^1	4	5	6		13	9	12	11	14	7^2	8^3	10														11
1	2	3	4		6	11		7	12	9^1		13		8^2	10					5								12
1	2	3	4		6	11		7		9^2		12		8^1	10					5	13							13
1	2	3	4		6	11		9	12		8^1	10^2		13	7					5								14
1	2	3	4		6	11^3		9^2	10	12	8^1			13	7	14				5								15
1	2	3	4		6	11		9	10^1			12		13	7	13				5		8^2						16
1	2	3^2	4		6	11^1		9^3	10	12	14			13	7					5		8						17
1	2	3	4		6^1	11		9	10^2	12	13			7						5		8						18
1	2	3	4			11		12	9^2	10^1	6	13		14	7					5		8^3						19
1	2	3^1	4	12	11			13	10	6	14			7						5		8^3	9^2					20
1	2	3	4			11^3		9	10	6^2	8^1			7		12				5			13	14				21
1	2	3	4	6				9	12		8^1	13		7		11				5		10^1	8					22
1	2	3			6	11		13	9	12				7^2						5		10	4					23
1	2	3			6	11		9	8		12			14	7					5		8^2	10^3	4^1				24
1	2	3			6	11		9	8^1					12	7					5		10^1	4^2					25
1	2	3	4		6	11		9	8^1					12	7					5		10^2	13					26
1	2	3				11		9^1	8^2	14	12			13	7					5		10	6^3					27
1	2	3	4		6	11	12	9^2	8			13			7^1					5		10						28
1	2	3^1	4		6	11	12	9^3	8^2	13	14			7						5		10		7				29
1	2		4		6	11^2	12	9^3	8	13				14						5		10	3^1	7				30
1	2^2		4		6	13	12	9^3	8					14						5		10^3	7^1	11				31
1				4	3^1	11	12				6	13			2^2		14			5		8^3	7	10		9		32
1	2	3	4	6				9^3	10	12				7^2	11^1		13			5				8		14		33
1	2	3	4	6				9	10	8		12^2		7			13			5				11^1		13		34
1	2	3	4	6		12		9^2	10	8				7		13				5^1				11^3		14		35
	2	3	4	6		12		9^3	10	8^1			13	11^2	7					5						14	1	36
1	2	3^2	4	6	12			9		8	10			11^3	7^1	13	14			5								37
1	2		4	6	8^1		10	9		12	13	11^2	7	3						5								38
1	2		4	6		12	8	11	10^2	13		7								5					3	9^1		39
1	2		4	6	12		8^2	11	10		13	7								5					3	9^1		40
1	2		4	6		12	10	8^1	11		13^3	14	7							5					3	9^2		41
1	2		4	6	12		13		11	10		8^1	7							5					3	9^2		42
1	2		4	6	12		8^1		11	10^2	13	7								5					3	9		43
1	2		4	6	12		8		11	10		7								5					3	9^1		44
1	2	3	4	6			8	12	11	10^2	13									5					7	9^1		45
1	2		4	6		12	10	8^2	11		13			7						5					3	9^1		46

Coca-Cola Cup

First Round	Cardiff C	(a)	0-1
		(h)	2-0
Second Round	Stoke C	(a)	0-1
		(h)	1-2

FA Cup

First Round	Watford	(h)	0-1

NORWICH CITY 1996-97 *Back row (left to right):* Andrew Brownrigg, Ade Akinbiyi, Rob Newman, Keith Scott, Spencer Prior, Damian Hilton, Keith O'Neill, Andy Johnson.
Middle row: Tim Sheppard (Physio), Carl Bradshaw, Danny Mills, Daryl Sutch, Paul Barber, Bryan Gunn, Andy Marshall, John Polston, Karl Simpson, Johnny Wright, Steve Foley (Reserve Team Coach).
Front row: Jamie Cureton, Shaun Carey, Neil Adams, Robert Fleck, Mike Walker (Manager), John Faulkner (Assistant Manager), Ian Crook, Mike Milligan, Darren Eadie, Matthew Rush.

Division 1 NORWICH CITY

Carrow Road, Norwich NR1 1JE. Telephone: (01603) 760760. Fax: (01603) 613886. Box Office: (01603) 761661. Clubcall: 0891 121144.

Ground capacity: 21,994.

Record attendance: 43,984 v Leicester C, FA Cup 6th rd, 30 March 1963.

Record receipts: £261,918 v Internazionale, UEFA Cup 3rd rd 1st leg, 24 November 1993.

Pitch measurements: 114yd × 74yd.

President: G. C. Watling.

Chairman: Barry Lockwood. *Joint Vice-Chairmen:* R. J. Munby, M. L. Armstrong. *Company Secretary:* T. Nicholls.

Directors: M. M. Foulger, B. J. Skipper, M. Wynn Jones, Delia Smith, G. A. Paterson.

Manager: Mike Walker.

Assistant Manager: John Faulkner.

Youth Team Coach: Keith Webb.

Physio: Tim Sheppard MCSP, SRP.

Secretary: A. R. W. Neville.

Year Formed: 1902. *Turned Professional:* 1905. *Ltd Co.:* 1905.

Club Nickname: 'The Canaries'.

Previous Grounds: 1902, Newmarket Road; 1908–35, The Nest, Rosary Road.

Foundation: Formed in 1902, largely through the initiative of two local schoolmasters who called a meeting at the Criterion Cafe, they were shocked by an FA Commission which in 1904 declared the club professional and ejected them from the FA Amateur Cup. However, this only served to strengthen their determination. New officials were appointed and a professional club established at a meeting in the Agricultural Hall in March 1905.

First Football League game: 28 August 1920, Division 3, v Plymouth Arg (a) D 1-1 – Skermer; Gray, Gadsden; Wilkinson, Addy, Martin; Laxton, Kidger, Parker, Whitham (1), Dobson.

Record League Victory: 10–2 v Coventry C, Division 3 (S), 15 March 1930 – Jarvie; Hannah, Graham; Brown, O'Brien, Lochhead (1); Porter (1), Anderson, Hunt (5), Scott (2), Slicer (1).

Record Cup Victory: 8–0 v Sutton U, FA Cup 4th rd, 28 January 1989 – Gunn; Culverhouse, Bowen, Butterworth, Linighan, Townsend (Crook), Gordon, Fleck (3), Allen (4), Phelan, Putney (1).

Record Defeat: 2–10 v Swindon T, Southern League, 5 September 1908.

Most League Points (2 for a win): 64, Division 3 (S), 1950–51.

Most League Points (3 for a win): 84, Division 2, 1985–86.

Most League Goals: 99, Division 3 (S), 1952–53.

Highest League Scorer in Season: Ralph Hunt, 31. Division 3 (S), 1955–56.

Most League Goals in Total Aggregate: Johnny Gavin, 122, 1945–54, 1955–58.

Most Capped Player: Mark Bowen, 35 (41), Wales.

Most League Appearances: Ron Ashman, 592, 1947–64.

Record Transfer Fee Received: £5,000,000 from Blackburn R for Chris Sutton, July 1994.

Record Transfer Fee Paid: £1,000,000 to Leeds U for Jon Newsome, June 1994.

Football League Record: 1920 Original Member of Division 3; 1921 Division 3 (S): 1934–39 Division 2; 1946–58 Division 3 (S); 1958–60 Division 3; 1960–72 Division 2; 1972–74 Division 1; 1974–75 Division 2; 1975–81 Division 1; 1981–82 Division 2; 1982–85 Division 1; 1985–86 Division 2; 1986–92 Division 1; 1992–95 FA Premier League; 1995– Division 1.

Honours: FA Premier League: best season: 3rd 1992–93. *Football League:* Division 2 – Champions 1971–72, 1985–86. Division 3 (S) – Champions 1933–34; Division 3 – Runners-up 1959–60. *FA Cup:* Semi-finals 1959, 1989, 1992. *Football League Cup:* Winners 1962, 1985; Runners-up 1973, 1975. **European Competitions:** *UEFA Cup:* 1993–94.

Colours: Yellow shirts, yellow shorts, yellow stockings. *Change colours:* All green.

Did you know?
Keith O'Neill's ten-second goal for Norwich City against Stoke City on 12 April 1997 was the fastest in the club's history.

NORWICH CITY FC

NORWICH CITY 1996–97 LEAGUE RECORD

Match No.	Date	Venue	Opponents	Result	H/T Score	Lg. Pos.	Goalscorers	Attendance
1	Aug 17	H	Swindon T	W 2-0	2-0	—	Johnson [26], Fleck [37]	15,165
2	24	A	Bolton W	L 1-3	0-1	13	Eadie [54]	13,507
3	27	A	Oxford U	W 1-0	1-0	—	Adams [12]	7436
4	31	H	Wolverhampton W	W 1-0	1-0	4	Adams (pen) [21]	14,456
5	Sept 7	A	Bradford C	W 2-0	2-0	2	Sutch [9], Eadie [31]	10,054
6	11	H	QPR	D 1-1	1-0	—	Adams [16]	14,000
7	14	H	Southend U	D 0-0	0-0	4		12,461
8	21	A	Portsmouth	W 1-0	1-0	3	Crook [36]	7511
9	28	H	Tranmere R	D 1-1	0-1	3	Fleck [46]	14,511
10	Oct 1	A	Grimsby T	W 4-1	3-1	—	Eadie 2 [2,8], McDermott (og) [29], O'Neill [81]	5266
11	11	H	Ipswich T	W 3-1	2-0	—	Johnson 2 [19,34], Polston [67]	20,256
12	16	H	Oldham Ath	W 2-0	0-0	—	Eadie [71], Adams [74]	12,271
13	19	A	Manchester C	L 1-2	0-1	2	Keith Scott [88]	28,269
14	26	A	Birmingham C	W 3-2	1-1	2	Johnson [19], Adams (pen) [49], Keith Scott [54]	18,869
15	30	H	Sheffield U	D 1-1	0-1	—	Adams [71]	14,534
16	Nov 2	H	Charlton Ath	L 1-2	0-0	2	Milligan [70]	14,145
17	12	A	Barnsley	L 1-3	0-0	—	Newman [73]	9697
18	16	H	Reading	D 1-1	0-0	3	Keith Scott [79]	14,412
19	30	H	Birmingham C	L 0-1	0-0	6		12,764
20	Dec 7	A	Huddersfield T	L 0-2	0-1	7		10,749
21	14	H	Crystal Palace	D 1-1	0-1	8	Adams [71]	16,395
22	18	H	WBA	L 1-5	0-2	—	O'Neill [89]	12,620
23	21	A	Port Vale	L 1-6	0-2	10	Fleck [90]	6278
24	26	A	QPR	L 2-3	1-2	13	Crook [39], Eadie [74]	15,699
25	28	H	Bradford C	W 2-0	1-0	10	Adams (pen) [35], O'Neill [60]	13,473
26	Jan 1	H	Portsmouth	W 1-0	0-0	6	Jackson [77]	11,946
27	18	H	Grimsby T	W 2-1	2-1	6	Polston [27], Sutch [45]	16,687
28	22	A	Stoke C	W 2-1	2-1	—	O'Neill [4], Eadie [11]	10,179
29	28	A	Tranmere R	L 1-3	1-2	—	Eadie [2]	5891
30	Feb 1	H	Barnsley	D 1-1	0-1	5	Eadie [89]	17,001
31	9	A	Sheffield U	W 3-2	0-0	5	Johnson [55], Ottosson [74], Holdsworth (og) [83]	15,301
32	15	H	WBA	L 2-4	0-1	6	Sutch [65], Adams (pen) [78]	14,845
33	22	A	Charlton Ath	D 4-4	2-2	5	Adams 2 (1 pen) [29,64 (p)], Eadie 2 [45,84]	12,405
34	25	A	Southend U	D 1-1	0-0	—	Fleck [87]	5169
35	Mar 1	H	Huddersfield T	W 2-0	1-0	5	Eadie 2 [32,53]	13,001
36	4	A	Reading	L 1-2	1-1	—	Adams (pen) [27]	8174
37	8	H	Port Vale	D 1-1	1-1	5	Jackson [11]	16,101
38	15	A	Crystal Palace	L 0-2	0-2	6		17,378
39	22	H	Bolton W	L 0-1	0-1	8		17,585
40	29	A	Swindon T	W 3-0	1-0	7	Eadie 2 [12,75], O'Neill [48]	10,249
41	31	H	Oxford U	D 1-1	1-1	7	Eadie [9]	14,644
42	Apr 5	A	Wolverhampton W	L 2-3	2-2	9	Broughton [43], Adams (pen) [45]	26,938
43	12	A	Stoke C	W 2-0	1-0	7	O'Neill [1], Eadie [53]	13,805
44	18	A	Ipswich T	L 0-2	0-2	—		22,397
45	25	H	Manchester C	D 0-0	0-0	—		14,080
46	May 4	A	Oldham Ath	L 0-3	0-2	13		5562

Final League Position: 13

GOALSCORERS

League (63): Eadie 17, Adams 13 (7 pens), O'Neill 6, Johnson 5, Fleck 4, Keith Scott 3, Sutch 3, Crook 2, Jackson 2, Polston 2, Broughton 1, Milligan 1, Newman 1, Ottosson 1, own goals 2.
Coca-Cola Cup (3): Adams 2 (1 pen), Johnson 1.
FA Cup (2): Adams 1 (pen), Polston 1.

Gunn B 39	Mills D 27 + 5	Newman R 44	Eadie D 42	Polston J 27 + 4	Crook I 33 + 4	Adams N 45	Fleck R 33 + 3	Milligan M 37	Johnson A 24 + 3	O'Neill K 23 + 3	Akinbiyi A 3 + 9	Sutch D 43 + 1	Bradshaw C 11 + 6	Carey S 8 + 6	Forbes A 3 + 7	Wright J 3 + 1	Rush M — + 2	Scott Keith 5 + 8	Jackson M 19	Ottosson U 4 + 3	Rocastle D 11	Scott Kevin 9	Marshall A 7	Bellamy C — + 3	Broughton D 3 + 5	Simpson K 1 + 2	Moore N 2	Match No.
1	2	3	4	5	6	7	8[1]	9[2]	10	11	12	13																1
1	2	3	4	5	6	7	8[1]	9	10	11	12																	2
1	2	3	11	5	6	7	8[1]	9	10		12		4															3
1	2	3		5	6	7	8[1]	9	10[2]		12	11[3]	4	13	14													4
1	2	3	4	5	6	7	8[1]	9		11[2]	12	10		13														5
1	2	3	11	5	6	7			10		9	8		4														6
1	2	3	11	5	6	7			10		9	8		4														7
1	2	3	4	5	6[1]	7			10	11	9	8		12														8
1		2	4	5		7	8	10	12	11		9	6[1]		3													9
1	2	3[2]	4[3]	5		7	8[1]	9	10	11	12		6	13	14													10
1	2	3	4	5	12	7	8[2]	9	10[1]	11		13	6															11
1	2	3	4	5	10	7	8[1]	9		11			6		12													12
1	2[2]	3	4	5	10	7	8[1]	9	12	11			6		13													13
1	2	3	11	5	6[1]	7		9	8	12			4		10													14
1	3	2	4	5	12	7	13	9	8[1]	11			6		10[2]													15
1	2	3	11	5	6	7	8[1]	9		12	4		10[2]		13													16
1	3	2	11	5	4[2]	7	8	9	10[1]				6	12	13													17
1		2	4	5		7	8	9	10	11			6	3[1]		12												18
1	12	2	4	5	13	7[3]	8	9	10[2]	11			6	3[1]		14												19
1	2	3	4	5		7	8	9	10	11[1]			6		12													20
1	2	3	4	5	6	7	8[1]		10	12			11		9													21
1	5	2	11		9	7	8		10	12			4	13				3[2]	6[1]									22
1	2	3	11		6	7	12		10	9			4	8[1]				5										23
1		2	9	5	6	7		8	10	11			4						3									24
1	12	2	4[3]	5		7	8[2]	9	10[1]	11			6		14			13	3									25
1		2	4	5[1]		7	8	9	10	11	12		6						3									26
1	7	2	4	5[1]	8			11					6		10				3	12	9							27
1	2	4		8[2]	7			11[1]					6		10			12	3	13	9	5						28
1	2	4			7	8[1]	11						6		10[2]	12		3	13	9	5							29
1		2	11		4	7	8	10	12				6					3		9[1]	5							30
1	2			4	7	8	11	10					3	12					9[1]	6	5							31
1	2	11		4	7		8	10					3	12	13				9[1]	6[2]	5							32
1	5	2[1]	4		8	7		11	10				3	12					9	6								33
1		2	4		7	12	11	10					6	13				3	9[1]	8[2]	5							34
	2	4		7	8	11	10						6						3	9	5	1						35
	2	4	12	7	8	11	10[1]						6						3	9	5	1						36
	2	4	10[2]	7	8	11							6	13	12			3	9[1]		5	1						37
1	2		4[1]	7	8							6	5	9[2]	11			12	10[3]	3				13	14			38
1	2	10	4[2]	7	8	9		11[1]				6	5		12				3					13				39
1	12	2	10	13	4[3]	7	8	9		11[1]			6	5[2]					3					14				40
1		2	11	12	4	7	8	10				6	5[1]	13					3							9[2]		41
1	12	2	11		4[1]	7	8[2]	10				6	5	13					3							9		42
12	2	10	13	4	7	8[2]	9[1]	11[3]				6	5					3					1	14				43
10	2	9	12	4	7	8		11[2]				6	5[1]					3					1			13		44
8	5		6	10	7					3			11[1]						3				1	12	9	2	4	45
10	2	11	6[2]	4[1]	7	8[3]			9										3				1	12	13	14	5	46

Coca-Cola Cup

First Round	Oxford U		(a)	1-1
			(h)	2-3

FA Cup

Third Round	Sheffield U	(h)	1-0
Fourth Round	Leicester C	(a)	1-2

NOTTINGHAM FOREST 1996-97   *Back row (left to right):* Steve Stone, Chris Allen, Chris Bart-Williams, Alan Fettis, Alf Inge Haaland, Dean Saunders, Des Lyttle.
Middle row: Richard Money (Coach), Liam O'Kane (Coach), Jason Lee, Nikola Jerkan, Tommy Wright, Mark Crossley, Steve Chettle, Andrea Silenzi, Paul McGregor, John Haselden (Physio), Pete Edwards (Fitness Consultant).
Front row: Scot Gemmill, Kevin Campbell, Bryan Roy, Frank Clark (Manager), Stuart Pearce, Alan Hill (Assistant Manager), David Phillips, Ian Woan, Colin Cooper.
(Photograph: J.M.S. Photography)

Division 1   NOTTINGHAM FOREST

City Ground, Nottingham NG2 5FJ. Telephone: (0115) 9526000. Fax: (0115) 9526003. Information Desk: (0115) 9526016. Commercial Office: (0115) 9526006. Commercial Office Fax: (0115) 9526007. Ticket Office: (0115) 9526002. Souvenir Shop: (0115) 9526026. Junior Reds: (0115) 9526001. Lottery Office: (0115) 9526005. Clubcall: 0891 121174.

Ground capacity: 30,602.

Record attendance: 49,946 v Manchester U, Division 1, 28 October 1967.

Record receipts: £499,099 v Bayern Munich, UEFA Cup quarter-final 2nd leg, 19 March 1996.

Pitch measurements: 116yd × 77yd.

Chairman: I. I. Korn. *Deputy Chairman:* P. W. Soar.

Directors: R. W. Dove, R. A. Fairhall, P. R. Markham, T. H. Farr, K. J. Eggleston.

Manager: Dave Bassett.

Secretary: Paul White. *Commercial Manager:* David Pullan.

Coach: Liam O'Kane. *Physio:* John Haselden.

Year Formed: 1865. *Turned Professional:* 1889. *Ltd Co.:* 1982.

Club Nickname: 'Reds'.

Previous Grounds: 1865, Forest Racecourse; 1879, The Meadows; 1880, Trent Bridge Cricket Ground; 1882, Parkside, Lenton; 1885, Gregory, Lenton; 1890, Town Ground; 1898, City Ground.

Foundation: One of the oldest football clubs in the world, Nottingham Forest was formed at a meeting in the Clinton Arms in 1865. Known originally as the Forest Football Club, the game which first drew the founders together was "shinney" a form of hockey. When they determined to change to football in 1865, one of their first moves was to buy a set of red caps to wear on the field.

First Football League game: 3 September 1892, Division 1, v Everton (a) D 2-2 – Brown; Earp, Scott; Hamilton, A. Smith, McCracken; McCallum, W. Smith, Higgins (2), Pike, McInnes.

Record League Victory: 12–0 v Leicester Fosse, Division 1, 12 April 1909 – Iremonger; Dudley, Maltby; Hughes (1), Needham, Armstrong; Hooper (3), Marrison, West (3), Morris (2), Spouncer (3 incl. 1p).

Record Cup Victory: 14–0 v Clapton (away), FA Cup 1st rd, 17 January 1891 – Brown; Earp, Scott; A. Smith, Russell, Jeacock; McCallum (2), 'Tich' Smith (1), Higgins (5), Lindley (4), Shaw (2).

Record Defeat: 1–9 v Blackburn R, Division 2, 10 April 1937.

Most League Points (2 for a win): 70, Division 3 (S), 1950–51.

Most League Points (3 for a win): 83, Division 1, 1993–94.

Most League Goals: 110, Division 3 (S), 1950–51.

Highest League Scorer in Season: Wally Ardron, 36, Division 3 (S), 1950–51.

Most League Goals in Total Aggregate: Grenville Morris, 199, 1898–1913.

Most Capped Player: Stuart Pearce, 76, England.

Most League Appearances: Bob McKinlay, 614, 1951–70.

Record Transfer Fee Received: £8,500,000 from Liverpool for Stan Collymore, June 1995.

Record Transfer Fee Paid: £2,900,000 to Foggia for Bryan Roy, August 1994.

Football League Record: 1892 Elected to Division 1; 1906–07 Division 2; 1907–11 Division 1; 1911–22 Division 2; 1922–25 Division 1; 1925–49 Division 2; 1949–51 Division 3 (S); 1951–57 Division 2; 1957–72 Division 1; 1972–77 Division 2; 1977–92 Division 1; 1992–93 FA Premier League; 1993–94 Division 1; 1994–97 FA Premier League; 1997– Division 1.

Honours: Football League: Division 1 – Champions 1977–78; Runners-up 1966–67, 1978–79; Division 2 – Champions 1906–07, 1921–22; Runners-up 1956–57; Division 3 (S) – Champions 1950–51. *FA Cup:* Winners 1898, 1959; Runners-up 1991. *Anglo-Scottish Cup:* Winners 1977; *Football League Cup:* Winners 1978, 1979, 1989, 1990; Runners-up 1980, 1992. *Simod Cup:* Winners 1989. *Zenith Data Systems Cup:* Winners: 1992. **European Competitions:** *Fairs Cup:* 1961–62, 1967–68. *European Cup:* 1978–79 (winners), 1979–80 (winners), 1980–81. *Super Cup:* 1979–80 (winners), 1980–81 (runners-up). *World Club Championship:* 1980. *UEFA Cup:* 1983–84, 1984–85, 1995–96.

Colours: Red shirts with black shoulders, white shorts, red stockings. *Change colours:* Yellow and navy.

Did you know?
Nottingham Forest fielded the same 11 players in every FA Cup round during the 1958–59 season, though they finished the final with only ten men after Roy Dwight broke his leg.

NOTTINGHAM FOREST 1996–97 LEAGUE RECORD

Match No.	Date	Venue	Opponents	Result		H/T Score	Lg. Pos.	Goalscorers	Attendance
1	Aug 17	A	Coventry C	W	3-0	2-0	—	Campbell 3 [13, 36, 47]	19,459
2	21	H	Sunderland	L	1-4	1-4	—	Haaland [27]	22,874
3	24	H	Middlesbrough	D	1-1	0-0	10	Pearce [68]	24,705
4	Sept 4	A	Southampton	D	2-2	2-0	—	Campbell [4], Saunders [23]	14,450
5	7	H	Leicester C	D	0-0	0-0	11		24,105
6	14	A	Manchester U	L	1-4	1-2	14	Haaland [4]	54,984
7	21	H	West Ham U	L	0-2	0-1	17		23,352
8	28	A	Chelsea	D	1-1	0-0	16	Lee [90]	26,996
9	Oct 12	A	Leeds U	L	0-2	0-0	17		29,255
10	19	H	Derby Co	D	1-1	1-0	18	Saunders [2]	27,771
11	28	L	Everton	L	0-1	0-1	—		19,892
12	Nov 2	A	Aston Villa	L	0-2	0-1	18		35,310
13	18	A	Sheffield W	L	0-2	0-0	—		16,390
14	25	H	Blackburn R	D	2-2	1-0	—	Pearce (pen) [45], Cooper [90]	17,525
15	30	A	Wimbledon	L	0-1	0-1	20		12,608
16	Dec 9	H	Newcastle U	D	0-0	0-0	—		25,762
17	17	A	Liverpool	L	2-4	1-2	—	Campbell [34], Pearce [60]	36,126
18	21	H	Arsenal	W	2-1	0-0	20	Haaland 2 [67, 89]	27,384
19	26	A	Manchester U	L	0-4	0-2	20		29,032
20	28	A	Leicester C	D	2-2	1-1	20	Clough [37], Cooper [87]	20,833
21	Jan 1	A	West Ham U	W	1-0	1-0	19	Campbell [38]	22,358
22	11	H	Chelsea	W	2-0	1-0	18	Pearce [40], Bart-Williams [53]	28,358
23	19	H	Tottenham H	W	2-1	0-1	17	Roy 2 [47, 62]	27,303
24	29	A	Coventry C	L	0-1	0-0	—		22,619
25	Feb 1	A	Everton	L	0-2	0-0	17		32,567
26	22	H	Aston Villa	D	0-0	0-0	17		25,239
27	Mar 1	A	Tottenham H	W	1-0	1-0	17	Saunders [18]	32,805
28	5	H	Sheffield W	L	0-3	0-0	—		21,485
29	8	A	Arsenal	L	0-2	0-0	17		38,206
30	11	A	Blackburn R	D	1-1	1-0	—	Haaland [18]	20,485
31	15	H	Liverpool	D	1-1	1-1	18	Woan [30]	29,181
32	22	A	Sunderland	D	1-1	0-0	19	Lyttle [86]	21,988
33	24	A	Middlesbrough	D	1-1	1-0	—	Haaland [4]	29,888
34	Apr 5	H	Southampton	L	1-3	0-1	19	Pearce (pen) [88]	25,134
35	19	H	Leeds U	D	1-1	1-0	20	Van Hooijdonk [6]	25,565
36	23	A	Derby Co	D	0-0	0-0	—		18,087
37	May 3	H	Wimbledon	D	1-1	0-1	20	Roy [59]	19,865
38	11	A	Newcastle U	L	0-5	0-4	20		36,544

Final League Position: 20

GOALSCORERS

League (31): Campbell 6, Haaland 6, Pearce 5 (2 pens), Roy 3, Saunders 3, Cooper 2, Bart-Williams 1, Clough 1, Lee 1, Lyttle 1, Van Hooijdonk 1, Woan 1.
Coca-Cola Cup (3): Cooper 1, Lee 1, Roy 1.
FA Cup (5): Saunders 2, Woan 2, Allen 1.

Crossley M 33	Cooper C 36	Pearce S 33	Jerkan N 14	Chettle S 31 +1	Stone S 5	Bart-Williams C 16	Campbell K 16 +1	Saunders D 33 +1	Haaland A 33 +2	Woan I 29 +3	Gemmill S 18 +6	McGregor P — +5	Allen C 16 +8	Roy B 8 +12	Silenzi A 1 +1	Lee J 5 +8	Lyttle D 30 +2	Phillips D 24 +3	Blatherwick S 7	Warner V 2 +1	Howe S — +1	Clough N 10 +3	Guinan S — +2	Wright T 1	Van Hooijdonk P 8	Moore I 1 +4	O'Neil B 4 +1	Fettis A 4	Match No.
1	2	3	4	5	6[1]	7	8	9[2]	10	11	12	13																	1
1	2	3	4	5	6	7	8	9	10	11[1]			12																2
1	2	3		5	6	10	8	9	4	11				7[1]	12														3
1	2	3	4	5	6	7	8[1]	9	10	11						12													4
1	2	3	4	5	6[1]	7		9	10	11	12					8[2]	13												5
1	4	3		5		7	8	9[1]	10	11[2]	12	13					2	6											6
1	4	3		5[1]				9	10	11		7	8	12			2	6											7
1	4	3		5		7[1]		9	10	11	12	13	8[3]	14			2[2]	6											8
1	4	3			6			9		11	12		8[2]	7	13	5	10	2[1]											9
1	4	3[1]			6			9		11	12		8[2]	7	13	5	10	2[1]											10
1	4	3		5			8	9		11	12			7[1]		10	2	6											11
1	4	3		5			8	9		11	12			7		10	2	6[1]											12
1	4	3	6[1]			8		9	10	11[2]	12	13					2	7	5										13
1	4	3		5		8[1]		9	10	11	12	13					2	7	6[2]										14
1	4	3		5		8		9	10	11	7						2[1]	6											15
1	4	3		5		8		9[1]	10	11	7						2	6											16
1	2	3	4[1]	5		8	9	6	11		7	10[2]	12				13												17
1	2	3	4	5		8	9[1]	6	11	12	7	13					10[2]												18
1	2	3		5		8	9	6	11[1]	7[2]	12		13				4	10											19
1	4	3		5		8[2]	9	7	11	13						2	12	6[1]	10										20
1	4	3		5		7		9[1]	10	11	12						2	6				8							21
1	4	3		5		6		10	11	12		9[2]	13				2	7[1]				8							22
1	4	3		5		6	9	10	11	12							2	7[2]				8[1]	13						23
1	4	3		5		8	9	10	11		12	7[1]					2	6											24
1	4			5		6		9	3	12	8		11[1]				2	7				10							25
	4	3	6	5				9[2]	10	8		13	11[1]				2	12		7	1								26
1	4	3	6	5				9	10	8		11[1]	12				2	7						1					27
1	4	3	6[2]	5				9	10	8		12					2	11				7[1]	13						28
1	4	3		5				9[2]	10[1]	12	8	13		7[3]			2	6						11					29
1		3	4	5				9	10	11	8			2[1]	6		14			12			7						30
1	4	3		5				9[2]	10	11[1]	8			12			2	6					7	13					31
1	4	3		5				9[1]	10[1]	11[2]	8			12			2	6					7	13	14				32
1	4	3		5				9	10	11[1]	8			12			2	6					7						33
	4[3]		5		7[1]			12	8	11	10[2]			2	3	14							9	13	6	1			34
			5					9	12	11[1]	8[2]	7		2	3	4							10	13	6	1			35
	4	3[3]	5		12			9[1]	10[2]	8	11	13		2	14		7								6	1			36
	4		5		7[2]	9	12		11	8	13		2	6	10										3[1]	1			37
				5		7																							38

Coca-Cola Cup

Second Round	Wycombe W	(h)	1-0
Third Round	West Ham U	(a)	1-1
		(a)	1-4

FA Cup

Third Round	Ipswich T	(h)	3-0
Fourth Round	Newcastle U	(a)	2-1
Fifth Round	Chesterfield	(a)	0-1

NOTTS COUNTY 1996–97   *Back row (left to right):* Jamie Eaton, Shaun Farrell, Darren Ward, Matthew Redmile, Michael Pollitt, Graeme Hogg, Chris Wilder.
Middle row: Phil Robinson, Shaun Derry, Tony Battersby, Gary Martindale, Gary Strodder, Ian Richardson, Ian Baraclough, Tony Agana, Tim Wilkes, Tommy Gallagher, Dennis Pettit (Physio).
Front row: Gary Jones, Steve Finnan, Richard Walker, Michael Galloway, Sam Allardyce (Manager), Derek Pavis (Chairman), Mark Smith (Assistant Manager), Peter Kennedy, James Hunt, Vinny Arkins, Ian Ridgway.

Division 3

NOTTS COUNTY

County Ground, Meadow Lane, Nottingham NG2 3HJ. Telephone: (0115) 9529000. Fax: (0115) 9553994. Ticket Office: (0115) 9557210. Clubline: 0891 888684. Football in the Community: (0115) 955 7215. Supporters Club: (0115) 9557255.

Ground capacity: 20,300.

Record attendance: 47,310 v York C, FA Cup 6th rd, 12 March 1955.

Record receipts: £124,539.10 v Manchester C, FA Cup 6th rd, 16 February 1991.

Pitch measurements: 114yd × 74yd.

Chairman: D. C. Pavis. *Vice-Chairman:* J. Mounteney.

Directors: W. Barrowcliffe, Mrs V. Pavis, M. Youdell MBE, G. Davey (Managing).

Manager: Sam Allardyce. *Assistant Manager:* Mark Smith. *Youth Coach:* Alan Young.

Secretary: Ian Moat.

Commercial Manager: Gary Hodder. *Conference & Banqueting Manager:* Matthew Foote.

Physio: Roger Clearey. *Stadium Manager:* Bob Davy.

Year Formed: 1862 *(see Foundation).* **Turned Professional:** 1885. *Ltd Co.:* 1888.

Club Nickname: 'Magpies'.

Previous Grounds: 1862, The Park; 1864, The Meadows; 1877, Beeston Cricket Ground; 1880, Castle Ground; 1883, Trent Bridge; 1910, Meadow Lane.

Foundation: For many years the foundation date of the Football League's oldest club was given as 1862 and the club celebrated its centenary in 1962. However, the researches of Keith Warsop have since shown that the club was on a very haphazard basis at that time, playing little more than practice matches. The meeting which put it on a firm footing was held at the George IV Hotel in December 1864, when they became known as the Notts Football Club.

First Football League game: 15 September 1888, Football League, v Everton (a) L 1-2 – Holland; Guttridge, McLean; Brown, Warburton, Shelton; Hodder, Harker, Jardine, Moore (1), Wardle.

Record League Victory: 11–1 v Newport Co, Division 3 (S), 15 January 1949 – Smith; Southwell, Purvis; Gannon, Baxter, Adamson; Houghton (1), Sewell (4), Lawton (4), Pimbley, Johnston (2).

Record Cup Victory: 15–0 v Rotherham T (at Trent Bridge), FA Cup 1st rd, 24 October 1885 – Sherwin; Snook, H. T. Moore; Dobson (1), Emmett (1), Chapman; Gunn (1), Albert Moore (2), Jackson (3), Daft (2), Cursham (4). (1 og).

Record Defeat: 1–9 v Blackburn R, Division 1, 16 November 1889 and v Aston Villa, Division 1, 29 September 1888 and v Portsmouth, Division 2, 9 April 1927.

Most League Points (2 for a win): 69, Division 4, 1970–71.

Most League Points (3 for a win): 87, Division 3, 1989–90.

Most League Goals: 107, Division 4, 1959–60.

Highest League Scorer in Season: Tom Keetley, 39, Division 3 (S), 1930–31.

Most League Goals in Total Aggregate: Les Bradd, 124, 1967–78.

Most Capped Player: Kevin Wilson, 15 (42), Northern Ireland.

Most League Appearances: Albert Iremonger, 564, 1904–26.

Record Transfer Fee Received: £2,500,000 from Derby Co for Craig Short, September 1992.

Record Transfer Fee Paid: £685,000 to Sheffield U for Tony Agana, November 1991.

Football League Record: 1888 Founder Member of the Football League; 1893–97 Division 2; 1897–1913 Division 1; 1913–14 Division 2; 1914–20 Division 1; 1920–23 Division 2; 1923–26 Division 1; 1926–30 Division 2; 1930–31 Division 3 (S); 1931–35 Division 2; 1935–50 Division 3 (S); 1950–58 Division 2; 1958–59 Division 3; 1959–60 Division 4; 1960–64 Division 3; 1964–71 Division 4; 1971–73 Division 3; 1973–81 Division 2; 1981–84 Division 1; 1984–85 Division 2; 1985–90 Division 3; 1990–91 Division 2; 1991–95 Division 1; 1995–97 Division 2; 1997– Division 3.

Honours: Football League: Division 1 best season: 3rd, 1890–91, 1900–01; Division 2 – Champions 1896–97, 1913–14, 1922–23; Runners-up 1894–95, 1980–81; Promoted from Division 2 1990–91 (play-offs); Division 3 (S) – Champions 1930–31, 1949–50; Runners-up 1936–37; Division 3 – Runners-up 1972–73; Promoted from Division 3 1989–90 (play-offs); Division 4 – Champions 1970–71; Runners-up 1959–60. *FA Cup:* Winners 1894; 1995; Runners-up 1994. *Football League Cup:* best season: 5th rd, 1964, 1973, 1976. *Anglo-Italian Cup:* Winners 1995; Runners-up 1891.

Colours: Black and white striped shirts, white shorts, black stockings. *Change colours:* Tartan shirts, black shorts, tartan stockings.

Did you know?

When Notts County beat Port Vale 1–0 in an FA Cup first round tie on 21 November 1970, it ended a 12 year spell in which they had failed to beat a Football League team in the competition.

NOTTS COUNTY 1996–97 LEAGUE RECORD

Match No.	Date	Venue	Opponents	Result	H/T Score	Lg. Pos.	Goalscorers	Attendance
1	Aug 17	H	Preston NE	W 2-1	0-1	—	Jones 50, Martindale 60	6879
2	24	A	Stockport Co	D 0-0	0-0	9		5271
3	31	H	York C	L 0-1	0-1	17		4600
4	Sept 7	A	Plymouth Arg	D 0-0	0-0	17		8109
5	10	H	Watford	L 2-3	0-2	—	Martindale (pen) 83, Robinson 86	3660
6	14	H	Millwall	L 1-2	0-0	21	Baraclough 72	4473
7	21	A	Bournemouth	W 1-0	1-0	19	Jones 40	3402
8	28	H	Wrexham	D 0-0	0-0	21		4216
9	Oct 1	A	Gillingham	L 0-1	0-0	—		5482
10	5	A	Wycombe W	L 0-1	0-1	23		4506
11	8	A	Peterborough U	W 3-1	1-0	—	Agana 15, Heald (og) 50, Martindale 86	5456
12	12	H	Bristol R	D 1-1	1-0	19	Agana 21	4558
13	15	H	Chesterfield	D 0-0	0-0	—		4265
14	19	A	Burnley	L 0-1	0-0	21		9372
15	26	A	Bristol C	L 0-4	0-4	22		9540
16	29	H	Walsall	W 2-0	1-0	—	Strodder 37, Agana 63	3127
17	Nov 2	H	Shrewsbury T	L 1-2	0-1	19	Derry 62	4363
18	9	A	Luton T	L 0-2	0-2	21		5664
19	23	A	Blackpool	L 0-1	0-0	22		3598
20	30	H	Bristol C	W 2-0	1-0	22	Arkins 65, Robinson 75	4693
21	Dec 3	A	Brentford	L 0-2	0-1	—		3675
22	14	H	Rotherham U	D 0-0	0-0	22		3954
23	20	A	Crewe Alex	L 0-3	0-0	—		3125
24	26	H	Watford	D 0-0	0-0	23		9065
25	Jan 11	A	Wrexham	D 3-3	2-1	23	Farrell 28, Martindale 2 (1 pen) 35 (p), 54	3267
26	18	H	Gillingham	D 1-1	0-0	22	Martindale (pen) 56	5008
27	25	A	Walsall	L 1-3	0-1	23	Battersby 76	3261
28	Feb 1	H	Luton T	L 1-2	0-0	23	Richardson 62	5025
29	4	H	Bournemouth	L 0-2	0-1	—		2757
30	8	A	Shrewsbury T	L 1-2	0-0	23	Regis 46	2692
31	15	H	Blackpool	D 1-1	1-1	23	Butler (og) 28	5281
32	22	A	Bury	L 0-2	0-0	23		3430
33	25	A	Millwall	L 0-1	0-0	—		5202
34	Mar 1	H	Brentford	D 1-1	1-0	23	Strodder 18	4323
35	8	H	Crewe Alex	L 0-1	0-0	23		4047
36	15	A	Rotherham U	D 2-2	1-0	23	Regis 37, Redmile 69	2605
37	22	H	Stockport Co	L 1-2	0-1	24	Baraclough 58	4238
38	25	H	Bury	L 0-1	0-1	—		3306
39	29	A	Preston NE	L 0-2	0-1	24		9472
40	31	H	Peterborough U	D 0-0	0-0	24		3848
41	Apr 5	A	York C	W 2-1	1-0	24	Dudley 22, Redmile 88	3115
42	12	A	Wycombe W	L 1-2	1-2	24	Derry 3	4290
43	15	H	Plymouth Arg	W 2-1	0-0	—	Heathcote (og) 66, Jones 86	2423
44	20	A	Bristol R	L 0-1	0-0	23		6309
45	26	H	Burnley	D 1-1	0-0	23	Dudley 64	4591
46	May 3	A	Chesterfield	L 0-1	0-0	24		5736

Final League Position: 24

GOALSCORERS

League (33): Martindale 6 (3 pens), Agana 3, Jones 3, Baraclough 2, Derry 2, Dudley 2, Redmile 2, Regis 2, Robinson 2, Strodder 2, Arkins 1, Battersby 1, Farrell 1, Richardson 1, own goals 3.
Coca-Cola Cup (1): Jones 1.
FA Cup (5): Agana 1, Arkins 1, Jones 1, Kennedy 1, Robinson 1.

Ward D 38	Derry S 37 + 2	Baraclough I 36 + 2	Wilder C 37	Strodder G 28	Hogg G 35	Simpson M 1	Robinson P 33 + 4	Martindale G 16 + 12	Arkins V 13 + 2	Jones G 21 + 6	Hunt J 5 + 4	Battersby T 6 + 12	Murphy S 16	Richardson I 16 + 3	Kennedy P 20 + 2	Wilkes T 3	Agana T 17 + 6	Walker R 13 + 3	Farrell S 10 + 4	Ludlam C 1	Gallagher T 1	Finnan S 18 + 5	Redmile M 23	Ridgway I 3 + 3	Galloway M 4 + 1	Regis D 7 + 3	Nogan L 6	Pollitt M 8	Hendon I 12	Rogers P — + 1	White D 7 + 2	Cunnington S 6 + 2	Dudley C 6 + 4	Mendez G 2 + 1	Mitchell P 1	Diuk W — + 1	Match No.
1	2	3	4	5	6	7	8¹	9	10²	11	12	13																									1
1		3	2	5	6		8	9	10¹	11		12	4	7																							2
1		3	2	5	6¹		8	9	10²	11		12	4	7	13																						3
1	4	3	2		6		8	12		10				5	7		9¹	11																			4
1	4	3	2		6		8	12		11²		13		5	7		9¹	10																			5
1	4	3	2		6		8	9¹	10			12		5	7			11																			6
1	4	3	2		6		8	12	9	10²				5	7		11¹	13																			7
1	4	3	2		6		8	12	9¹	10³		13		5	7			11																			8
1	4¹	3	2		6		8	11	13	10³				5	9		7	12																			9
1	4¹	3	2		6		8	12		9				5	10		7	11²	13																		10
1	4	3	2		6		8	10	9¹			12		5	7			11																			11
1	4		2		6		8	10	9²		13	12		5	7			11¹	3																		12
1	4		2		6		8²			10¹	12	13		5	7		9	11	3																		13
1	4	12	11		6		8		13	10				5	7	3¹	9					2²															14
1	4	3	2		6		8	9¹	10			12		5	7			11																			15
1	8		2	5	6			9		10			4		7			11				3															16
1	8	4	2		6					10¹		12		5	7		9	11²				3	13														17
1	6	4	2	5			8			10					7		9	11				3															18
1	2		4	5			8	9		10		12		6¹	7²			11				3	13														19
1	6	3	2	5			8	9		10		12	4		7¹			11																			20
1	6	3	2	5			8	9		10¹		12	4		7			11																			21
1	6	3	2	5			8	9		10¹		12	4		7			11																			22
1	6¹	3	2				8	9				12	4	5				11				10	7														23
1	3		2				8	9¹		10		12	4	5	7			11				6															24
1	6	3	2	5				9²				13			12		11¹	10				7	4			8											25
1	6	3	2	5			8	9				12		13			11¹	10²				7	4														26
1	6	3	2	5			8	9		10¹				13	12			11				7²	4														27
1	7	3	2	5	6²		8²	9		11					10¹							13	4	14													28
1	2²	3	7	5	6		8	12		10					9¹			11³				13	4		14												29
1	3		2	5	6		8	12							10¹		9²	11				13	4			7											30
1	12	3	2	5	6		8¹	9²										11				13	4			7	10										31
	12	3	2	5	6		8		9	11							9					13				7²	10¹	1									32
	7	12	3¹	5	6												9²	11				13	8			4	10	1	2								33
	7		3	5	6					11												12	8		9²	4	10¹	1	2			13					34
	7		3	5	6												11¹					12	13		9	8	10²	1	2			4					35
	7		3	5	6					11													4		9²	10¹		1	2			8	12	13			36
			3	5	6		8															7¹	4		11	9		1	2			10	12				37
			3	5	8					12				6³			11²					7	4		10			1	2			9¹	13	12	14		38
1			3	5	8		8			12				6²			13					7	2		4	14						9³	10	11¹			39
1	6		3	5			12															7	2		4	13						9²	8	10	11¹		40
1	6			5			11¹															12	2		4	7			3			9²	8	10			41
1	6		3	5			11	12									7¹					2		13	4	9³						14	8²	10			42
1	9		3	5			12	11		13							6					7	4			2							10²	8¹			43
1	9²		3	5			12	10³		11							6¹					7	4			2						13	8	14			44
1	8		3¹	5				9²		10							7					12	4	14		13³			2				11			6	45
	11		3	5	6			12		9							13					7	4³			2		1				8²	10¹			14	46

Coca-Cola Cup

First Round	Bury	(h)	1-1
		(a)	0-1

FA Cup

First Round	Newcastle T	(a)	2-0
Second Round	Rochdale	(h)	3-1
Third Round	Aston Villa	(h)	0-0
		(a)	0-3

OLDHAM ATHLETIC 1996–97   *Back row (left to right):* John Bowden (Kit Manager), Barrie Hart, Andrew Hughes, Lloyd Richardson, Andy Holt, Paul Rickers, Gavin Ramsden, Mark Allott, Lee Randall, Jim Cassell (Chief Scout).
Middle row: Alexis Moreno (Physio), John Gannon, David McNiven, Carl Serrant, Martin Pemberton, Jon Hallworth, Richard Graham, Lee Darnbrough, Darren Lonergan, Lee Richardson, Scott McNiven, Billy Urmson (Youth Coach).
Front row: Andy Holden (Reserve Team Coach), Sean McCarthy, Stuart Barlow, David Beresford, Craig Fleming, Nick Henry, Graeme Sharp (Manager), Nicky Banger, Ian Snodin, Gunnar Halle, Toddy Orlygsson, Steve Redmond, Colin Harvey (First Team Coach).
(Photograph: Action Images)

Division 2   **OLDHAM ATHLETIC**

Boundary Park, Oldham OL1 2PA. Telephone: (0161) 624 4972. Fax: (0161) 627 5915. Ticket Call: 0891 121582. Commercial Office: (0161) 627 1802 Fax: (0161) 652 6501. Clubcall: 0891 121142.

Ground capacity: 13,700.

Record attendance: 47,671 v Sheffield W, FA Cup 4th rd, 25 January 1930.

Record receipts: £138,680 v Manchester U, FA Premier League, 29 December 1993.

Pitch measurements: 110yd × 74yd.

President: R. Schofield.

Chairman & Managing Director: I. H. Stott, *Vice-Chairman:* D. A. Brierley.

Directors: G. T. Butterworth, D. R. Taylor, P. Chadwick, J. Slevin, N. Holden.

Manager: Neil Warnock. *Assistant Manager:* Andy Ritchie.

Secretary: Terry Cale. *Commercial Manager:* Alan Hardy. *Public Relations Office:* Gordon A. Lawton.

Stadium Manager: Stuart Oddy.

Coach: Bill Urmson. *Physio:* Alex Moreno MCSP SRP.

Year Formed: 1895. *Turned Professional:* 1899. *Ltd Co.:* 1906.

Previous Name: 1895, Pine Villa; 1899, Oldham Athletic.

Club Nickname: 'The Latics'.

Previous Ground: Sheepfoot Lane; 1905, Boundary Park.

Foundation: It was in 1895 that John Garland, the landlord of the Featherstall and Junction Hotel, decided to form a football club. As Pine Villa they played in the Oldham Junior League. In 1899 the local professional club Oldham County, went out of existence and one of the liquidators persuaded Pine Villa to take over their ground at Sheepfoot Lane and change their name to Oldham Athletic.

First Football League game: 9 September 1907, Division 2, v Stoke (a) W 3-1 – Hewitson; Hodson, Hamilton; Fay, Walders, Wilson; Ward, W. Dodds (1), Newton (1), Hancock, Swarbrick (1).

Record League Victory: 11–0 v Southport, Division 4, 26 December 1962 – Hollands; Branagan, Marshall; McCall, Williams, Scott; Ledger (1), Johnstone, Lister (6), Colquhoun (1), Whitaker (3).

Record Cup Victory: 10–1 v Lytham, FA Cup 1st rd, 28 November 1925 – Gray; Wynne, Grundy; Adlam, Heaton, Naylor (1), Douglas, Pynegar (2), Ormston (2), Barnes (3), Watson (2).

Record Defeat: 4–13 v Tranmere R, Division 3 (N), 26 December 1935.

Most League Points (2 for a win): 62, Division 3, 1973–74.

Most League Points (3 for a win): 88, Division 2, 1990–91.

Most League Goals: 95, Division 4, 1962–63.

Highest League Scorer in Season: Tom Davis, 33, Division 3 (N), 1936–37.

Most League Goals in Total Aggregate: Roger Palmer, 141, 1980–94.

Most Capped Player: Gunnar Halle, (54), Norway.

Most League Appearances: Ian Wood, 525, 1966–80.

Record Transfer Fee Received: £1,700,000 from Aston Villa for Earl Barrett, February 1992.

Record Transfer Fee Paid: £750,000 to Aston Villa for Ian Olney, June 1992.

Football League Record: 1907 Elected to Division 2; 1910–23 Division 1; 1923–35 Division 2; 1935–53 Division 3 (N); 1953–54 Division 2; 1954–58 Division 3 (N); 1958–63 Division 4; 1963–69 Division 3; 1969–71 Division 4; 1971–74 Division 3; 1974–91 Division 2; 1991–92 Division 1; 1992–94 FA Premier League; 1994–97 Division 1; 1997– Division 2.

Honours: Football League: Division 1 – Runners-up 1914–15; Division 2 – Champions 1990–91; Runners-up 1909–10; Division 3 (N) – Champions 1952–53; Division 3 – Champions 1973–74; Division 4 – Runners-up 1962–63. *FA Cup:* Semi-final 1913, 1990, 1994. *Football League Cup:* Runners-up 1990.

Colours: Blue and red hooped shirts, white shorts, blue and red hooped stockings. *Change colours:* Green and navy shirts, navy shorts, green stockings.

Did you know?
In the season before they were elected to the Second Division of the Football League in 1907 – when Burslem Port Vale resigned at a late hour – Oldham Athletic had finished champions of the Lancashire Combination A Division.

OLDHAM ATHLETIC 1996–97 LEAGUE RECORD

Match No.	Date	Venue	Opponents	Result		H/T Score	Lg. Pos.	Goalscorers	Attendance
1	Aug 17	H	Stoke C	L	1-2	0-2	—	Redmond [76]	8021
2	24	A	Crystal Palace	L	1-3	0-3	23	McCarthy [57]	12,822
3	28	A	Swindon T	L	0-1	0-0	—		8025
4	31	H	Ipswich T	D	3-3	2-2	20	Rickers [1], Redmond [29], Banger [70]	5339
5	Sept 7	H	Sheffield U	L	0-2	0-1	23		7323
6	10	A	Birmingham C	D	0-0	0-0	—		17,228
7	13	A	Huddersfield T	L	2-3	1-1	—	McCarthy 2 [28, 66]	10,296
8	21	H	Barnsley	L	0-1	0-1	24		7043
9	28	A	Charlton Ath	L	0-1	0-0	24		12,178
10	Oct 1	H	WBA	D	1-1	1-0	—	Ormondroyd [8]	5817
11	5	H	Port Vale	W	3-0	3-0	24	Ormondroyd 2 [15, 38], Banger [42]	6051
12	12	A	Bolton W	L	1-3	0-3	24	Allott [84]	14,813
13	16	A	Norwich C	L	0-2	0-0	—		12,271
14	19	H	Reading	D	1-1	0-0	24	Orlygsson (pen) [65]	7171
15	26	A	Southend U	D	0-0	0-0	24		6606
16	29	A	Grimsby T	W	3-0	1-0	—	Ormondroyd [9], Halle 2 [66, 89]	3532
17	Nov 2	A	Bradford C	W	3-0	1-0	22	Barlow 3 [35, 57, 78]	10,855
18	9	H	Portsmouth	D	0-0	0-0	22		7639
19	15	A	Tranmere R	D	1-1	0-1	—	Ormondroyd [72]	8327
20	23	H	Oxford U	W	2-1	1-1	23	Barlow [17], Halle [75]	4851
21	30	A	Southend U	D	1-1	0-1	24	Richardson Lee J (pen) [54]	5001
22	Dec 7	H	QPR	L	0-2	0-0	24		5590
23	14	A	Wolverhampton W	W	1-0	1-0	22	Ormondroyd [15]	22,528
24	21	H	Manchester C	W	2-1	0-1	21	Ormondroyd [63], Banger [72]	12,992
25	28	A	Sheffield U	D	2-2	1-1	20	Henry [35], Rickers [80]	16,130
26	Jan 18	A	WBA	D	1-1	0-1	20	Barlow [66]	12,103
27	25	H	Huddersfield T	L	1-2	0-0	20	Richardson Lee J [77]	8566
28	Feb 1	A	Portsmouth	L	0-1	0-1	23		9135
29	8	H	Grimsby T	L	0-3	0-2	23		6549
30	15	A	Oxford U	L	1-3	0-2	24	Graham [72]	6868
31	22	H	Bradford C	L	1-2	1-0	24	Ormondroyd [41]	9524
32	Mar 1	A	QPR	W	1-0	1-0	24	Banger [33]	10,180
33	4	H	Tranmere R	L	1-2	1-1	—	Banger [39]	5417
34	8	A	Manchester C	L	0-1	0-0	24		30,729
35	15	H	Wolverhampton W	W	3-2	1-1	23	Rickers 2 [2, 87], Barlow [56]	9661
36	18	H	Charlton Ath	D	1-1	0-0	—	Barlow [65]	4969
37	23	H	Crystal Palace	L	0-1	0-1	23		5282
38	29	A	Stoke C	L	1-2	0-2	23	Barlow [87]	11,755
39	31	H	Swindon T	W	5-1	2-0	23	Richardson Lee J (pen) [12], Barlow 3 [22, 71, 75], Rush [80]	5699
40	Apr 5	A	Ipswich T	L	0-4	0-3	23		11,730
41	8	A	Birmingham C	D	2-2	1-2	—	Richardson Lee J (pen) [29], Reid [51]	5942
42	12	A	Port Vale	L	2-3	1-1	23	Garnett [45], Duxbury [82]	8114
43	15	A	Barnsley	L	0-2	0-1	—		17,476
44	19	H	Bolton W	D	0-0	0-0	23		10,702
45	26	A	Reading	L	0-2	0-1	23		8301
46	May 4	H	Norwich C	W	3-0	2-0	23	Moore (og) [27], Rush [29], Barlow [74]	5562

Final League Position: 23

GOALSCORERS

League (51): Barlow 12, Ormondroyd 8, Banger 5, Lee Richardson 4 (3 pens), Rickers 4, Halle 3, McCarthy 3, Redmond 2, Rush 2, Allott 1, Duxbury 1, Garnett 1, Graham 1, Henry 1, Orlygsson 1 (pen), Reid 1, own goal 1.
Coca-Cola Cup (4): Banger 1, McCarthy 1, Redmond 1, Lee Richardson 1.
FA Cup (0).

Hallworth J 4	Halle G 18 + 2	Serrant C 34 + 6	Fleming C 44	Graham R 16 + 3	Redmond S 24	Orlygsson T 23 + 4	Richardson Lee J 27 + 4	McCarthy S 17 + 4	Barlow S 26 + 9	Rickers P 45 + 1	Beresford D 24 + 9	Morrow J 1 + 1	Henry N 21 + 1	Pemberton M — + 3	Banger N 16 + 7	Kelly G 42	Garnett S 22 + 1	McNiven D 2 + 6	Ormondroyd J 26 + 4	Hughes A 7 + 1	Alliott M — + 5	McNiven S 11 + 1	Snodin I 14	Richardson Lloyd M — + 1	Ritchie A 4 + 6	Hodgson D 11 + 1	Duxbury L 11 + 1	Gannon J 1	Foran M — + 1	Rush M 6 + 2	Reid P 9	Holt A — + 1	Match No.
1	2	3	4¹	5	6	7²	8	9	10	11	12	13																					1
1	2	3	5		6		8	9	10²	11	12	7¹	4		13																		2
1	2	3	5		6	7²	8	9		11	10¹		4	12	13																		3
1	2	3	5		6	7	8	9		11			4		10																		4
	3	2	5		6	11¹	8	9		4	7		12	10		1																	5
12	3	2	5		6		8	9	13	11	7¹		4		10²	1																	6
12	3	2	5¹		6		8	9		11	7		4		10	1																	7
	3	12	2		6	7¹	8		13	11³	14		4		10	1	5		9²														8
	3		2		6	7	8			11	12		4¹		10²	1	5	13	9														9
	3	12	2		6	7¹	8			4	11				10	1	5		9														10
	3		2		6	7	8		12	4	11		10¹			1	5		9														11
	3	12	2		6	7¹				4	11					1	5	10²	9	8	13												12
	3	10	2		6	7				4	11¹					1	5	12	9²	8	13												13
	3		2		6	7				4	11		10¹			1	5		9	8	12												14
	3	4²	2		6	7			10		8	11	12			1	5		9¹	13													15
	3	13	2		6	7			10	4	11²		12			1	5		9¹	8													16
	3	12	2		6	7			10	4²	11¹		13			1	5		9	8													17
		3	2	5	6	7¹			10		8	11	4	12		1			9														18
	3	11	2	5	6	7			10¹		8	12	4			1			9														19
	3		2		6	7¹	12		10²		8	11	4	13		1	5		9														20
	3		2		6	7	12		10		8¹	11	4			1	5		9														21
	3		2		6	7	11		10¹		8	12	4			1	5		9														22
	3	2	12		6¹		11		10²		8		4	13		1	5		9			7											23
	3	2	6			11	12	13	8		4		10¹			1	5		9²			7											24
	3	2	6			12	11	13	8		4¹		10²			1	5		9			7											25
	3	2	6				7	11	9¹		8²	13	4			1			10			5											26
	3	2	6				11		8¹	12	13		4			1			9			7²	5										27
	3	2	6				8		12	7	10		4			1			9¹	11²		2	5	13									28
	3	5	6				8		12	7	11³		4			10¹	1		9			13	2²		14								29
	3	6				11			10	7			8	1			9			2	4				5								30
	3	6				11¹			12	10	7		8	1			9			2			13	5³		4²	14						31
	3	6				12	8		13	11	7¹		10²	1			9			2			5	4									32
	3	6				12	8	9	10²	11	7¹			1			13			4	14	5	2³										33
	3	6	2				8	9	10	11	7			1						4		5											34
	3	6	2¹			12	8	9	10	11	7²			1						4	13	5³	14										35
	3	6	12			13	9¹	10	8¹					1						4	14	5	2		7²	11							36
	3	6	12				9	10	5					1			4¹			8		2			7	11							37
	3	6				9²		12	10	5				1			4			8¹	13	2			7	11							38
	3	6				9	12	10	4					1	13						8¹	5²	2		7	11							39
	3	6				9¹	10²	8						1		4	13	12	7³			5	2		14	11							40
	12	6				9¹	10	8						1	4	14	13	7³			3	5¹	2			11							41
	3		6			9	10²	8						1	4	13	12					5	2		7¹	11							42
	3	6				9	10³	8						1	5			7¹	12			4²	2		13	11	14						43
	3	6				9³	10²	8						1	5	12			13	2		14	4		7¹	11							44
																																	45
																																	46

Coca-Cola Cup

First Round	Grimsby T	(h)	0-1
		(a)	1-0
Second Round	Tranmere R	(h)	2-2
		(a)	1-0
Third Round	Newcastle U	(a)	0-1

FA Cup

Third Round	Barnsley	(a)	0-2

OXFORD UNITED 1996–97   *Back row (left to right):* Bobby Ford, Martin Gray, Nigel Jemson, Marc McGregor, David Rush, Mark Angel, Joey Beauchamp, David Smith, Les Robinson, Paul Powell.

Middle row: Elliott Jackson, Mark Harrison (Reserve Team Manager), Maurice Evans (General Manager), Malcolm Elias (Youth Development Officer), Simon Marsh, Phil Gilchrist, Martin Aldridge, Stuart Massey, Malcolm Crosby (Assistant Manager), Mickey Lewis (Youth Team Manager), John Clinkard (Physio), Phil Whitehead.

Front row: Mark Druce, Matt Murphy, Darren Purse, Matt Elliott, Denis Smith (Manager), Mark Stevens, Paul Moody, Todd Lumsden, Mike Ford.

Division 1 **OXFORD UNITED**

Manor Ground, Headington, Oxford OX3 7RS. Telephone: (01865) 761503. Fax: (01865) 741820. Supporters Club: (01865) 763063. Clubline: 0891 440055.

Ground capacity: 9572.

Record attendance: 22,750 v Preston NE, FA Cup 6th rd, 29 February 1964.

Record receipts: £103,411 v Leeds U, FA Cup 4th rd, 29 January 1994.

Pitch measurements: 110yd × 75yd.

President: The Duke of Marlborough.

Directors: G. E. Coppock, K. A. Cox, N. J. W. Harris, D. Smith.

Chairman: R. J. Herd CBE.

Manager: Denis Smith. *Assistant Manager:* Malcolm Crosby. *Coach:* Mark Harrison. *Physio:* John Clinkard.

Secretary: Mick Brown. *Commercial Manager:* Trevor Baxter. *Stadium Manager:* Mick Moore.

Year Formed: 1893. *Turned Professional:* 1949. *Ltd Co.:* 1949.

Club Nickname: 'The U's'.

Previous Names: 1893, Headington; 1894, Headington United; 1960, Oxford United.

Previous Grounds: 1893–94 Headington Quarry; 1894–98 Wootten's Field; 1898–1902 Sandy Lane Ground; 1902–09 Britannia Field; 1909–10 Sandy Lane; 1910–14 Quarry Recreation Ground; 1914–22 Sandy Lane; 1922–25 The Paddock Manor Road; 1925– Manor Ground.

Foundation: There had been an Oxford United club around the time of World War I but only in the Oxfordshire Thursday League and there is no connection with the modern club which began as Headington in 1893, adding "United" a year later. Playing first on Quarry Fields and subsequently Wootten's Fields, they owe much to a Dr. Hitchings for their early development.

First Football League game: 18 August 1962, Division 4, v Barrow (a) L 2-3 – Medlock; Beavon, Quartermain; R. Atkinson, Kyle, Jones; Knight, G. Atkinson (1), Houghton (1), Cornwell, Colfar.

Record League Victory: 7–0 v Barrow, Division 4, 19 December 1964 – Fearnley; Beavon, Quartermain; R. Atkinson (1), Kyle, Jones; Morris, Booth (3), Willey (1), G. Atkinson (1), Harrington (1).

Record Cup Victory: 9–1 v Dorchester T, FA Cup 1st rd, 11 November 1995 – Whitehead; Wood (2), Ford M (1), Smith, Elliott, Gilchrist, Rush (1), Massey (Murphy), Moody (3), Ford R (1), Angel (Beauchamp (1)).

Record Defeat: 0–6 v Liverpool, Division 1, 22 March 1986.

Most League Points (2 for a win): 61, Division 4, 1964–65.

Most League Points (3 for a win): 95, Division 3, 1983–84.

Most League Goals: 91, Division 3, 1983–84.

Highest League Scorer in Season: John Aldridge, 30, Division 2, 1984–85.

Most League Goals in Total Aggregate: Graham Atkinson, 77, 1962–73.

Most Capped Player: Jim Magilton, 18 (36), Northern Ireland.

Most League Appearances: John Shuker, 478, 1962–77.

Record Transfer Fee Received: £1,600,000 from Leicester C for Matt Elliott, January 1997.

Record Transfer Fee Paid: £285,000 to Gillingham for Colin Greenall, February 1988.

Football League Record: 1962 Elected to Division 4; 1965–68 Division 3; 1968–76 Division 2; 1976–84 Division 3; 1984–85 Division 2; 1985–88 Division 1; 1988–92 Division 2; 1992–94 Division 1; 1994–96 Division 2; 1996– Division 1.

Honours: Football League: Division 1 best season: 18th, 1985–86, 1986–87; Division 2 – Champions 1984–85; Runners-up 1995–96; Division 3 – Champions 1967–68, 1983–84; Division 4 – Promoted 1964–65 (4th). *FA Cup:* best season: 6th rd, 1964 (shared record for 4th Division club). *Football League Cup:* Winners 1986.

Colours: Gold shirts with blue sleeves, blue shorts, blue stockings. *Change colours:* Red and black striped shirts, black shorts, black stockings.

Did you know?
Oxford United's last two goalscorers in the Southern League 1961–62 were Graham Atkinson (2) and Bud Houghton. In their opening Football League fixture the following season, Atkinson and Houghton each scored one goal.

OXFORD UNITED F.C.

OXFORD UNITED 1996–97 LEAGUE RECORD

Match No.	Date	Venue	Opponents	Result	H/T Score	Lg. Pos.	Goalscorers	Attendance
1	Aug 17	A	QPR	L	1-2	1-0	—	Jemson [16]	14,703
2	24	H	Southend U	W	5-0	3-0	8	Beauchamp 2 [21,45], Jemson 2 [37,51], Rush [85]	6382
3	27	H	Norwich C	L	0-1	0-1	—		7436
4	31	A	Port Vale	L	0-2	0-1	17		6016
5	Sept 8	A	Reading	L	0-2	0-1	22		8099
6	10	H	Wolverhampton W	D	1-1	1-0	—	Ford M [39]	7468
7	14	H	Bradford C	W	2-0	0-0	17	Jemson [57], Moody [81]	6334
8	21	A	Grimsby T	W	2-0	2-0	15	Jemson (pen) [3], Handyside (og) [10]	4120
9	28	H	Portsmouth	W	2-0	2-0	10	Beauchamp [18], Ford M [38]	7626
10	Oct 1	A	Tranmere R	D	0-0	0-0	—		4577
11	12	A	Swindon T	L	1-1	0-0	13		10,811
12	15	A	Barnsley	D	0-0	0-0	—		6337
13	18	H	Birmingham C	D	0-0	0-0	—		7594
14	26	A	Charlton Ath	L	0-2	0-2	16		10,626
15	29	H	Stoke C	W	4-1	2-0	—	Gray [5], Angel [27], Jemson [78], Aldridge [90]	6381
16	Nov 2	H	Ipswich T	W	3-1	3-1	10	Mowbray (og) [13], Jemson [40], Elliott [44]	7903
17	13	A	Manchester C	W	3-2	2-2	—	Beauchamp [7], Jemson [30], Elliott [87]	23,079
18	16	H	Huddersfield T	W	1-0	0-0	6	Elliott [73]	7460
19	19	H	Bolton W	D	0-0	0-0	—		7517
20	23	A	Oldham Ath	L	1-2	1-1	8	Jemson [8]	4851
21	30	H	Charlton Ath	L	0-2	0-0	10		7080
22	Dec 7	A	Crystal Palace	D	2-2	0-1	9	Jemson [64], Massey [85]	17,879
23	14	H	Sheffield U	W	4-1	3-0	5	Aldridge 3 [13,21,33], Jemson [82]	7737
24	21	A	WBA	D	3-3	1-2	6	Jemson [32], Murphy [78], Elliott [83]	13,782
25	26	A	Wolverhampton W	L	1-3	1-1	9	Gray [33]	26,511
26	28	H	Reading	W	2-1	1-0	6	Beauchamp [7], Murphy [81]	9223
27	Jan 11	A	Bradford C	L	0-2	0-1	11		13,275
28	18	H	Tranmere R	W	2-1	2-1	9	Aldridge [8], Jemson (pen) [35]	7072
29	28	H	Portsmouth	L	1-2	1-1	—	Angel [28]	7301
30	Feb 2	H	Manchester C	L	1-4	0-2	13	Moody [80]	8824
31	7	A	Stoke C	L	1-2	0-2	—	Moody [88]	8609
32	15	A	Oldham Ath	W	3-1	2-0	11	Graham (og) [34], Purse [42], Jemson [89]	6868
33	22	H	Ipswich T	L	1-2	0-1	13	Gabbiadini [59]	11,483
34	Mar 1	H	Crystal Palace	L	1-4	0-1	14	Marsh [85]	8572
35	4	A	Huddersfield T	L	0-1	0-1	—		11,276
36	8	H	WBA	W	1-0	0-0	14	Murphy [88]	8502
37	15	A	Sheffield U	L	1-3	1-3	16	Gilchrist [40]	16,226
38	18	H	Grimsby T	W	3-2	0-1	—	Ford M [62], Gilchrist [66], Aldridge [90]	6421
39	22	A	Southend U	D	2-2	0-1	14	Jemson [82], Aldridge [88]	4102
40	29	H	QPR	L	2-3	2-3	14	Jemson (pen) [10], Moody [23]	8365
41	31	A	Norwich C	D	1-1	1-1	14	Massey [31]	14,644
42	Apr 5	A	Port Vale	L	0-2	0-1	16		7370
43	12	A	Bolton W	L	0-4	0-2	19		15,994
44	19	H	Swindon T	W	2-0	2-0	17	Aldridge [19], Massey [30]	8167
45	26	A	Birmingham C	L	0-2	0-0	18		16,109
46	May 4	H	Barnsley	W	5-1	3-0	17	Beauchamp 2 [18,43], Jemson 2 (1 pen) [26,48(p)], Ford M [70]	8693

Final League Position: 17

GOALSCORERS

League (64): Jemson 18 (4 pens), Aldridge 8, Beauchamp 7, Elliott 4, Ford M 4, Moody 4, Massey 3, Murphy 3, Angel 2, Gilchrist 2, Gray 2, Gabbiadini 1, Marsh 1, Purse 1, Rush 1, own goals 3.
Coca-Cola Cup (11): Jemson 5, Moody 2, Aldridge 1, Elliott 1, Ford M 1, Ford R 1.
FA Cup (0).

Whitehead P 43	Robinson L 36 + 2	Ford M 42	Smith D 45	Elliott M 26	Gilchrist P 38	Rush D 4 + 11	Ford B 29 + 4	Aldridge M 18 + 12	Jemson N 44	Beauchamp J 36 + 9	Moody P 19 + 19	Angel M 15 + 9	Murphy M 5 + 25	Massey S 15 + 14	Gray M 41 + 2	Purse D 25 + 6	Jackson E 3	Marsh S 6 + 2	Gabbiadini M 5	Wilsterman B 1	Whyte C 10	Phillips M — + 1	Weatherstone S — + 1	Match No.
1	2	3	4	5	6	7³	8	9¹	10²	11	12	13	14											1
1	2	3	4	5	6	12	7	13	10¹	11	9²				8³	14								2
1	2	3	4³	5	6	12	7	14	10¹	11	9				8³	13								3
1	2	3	4¹	5	6	10³	7	14		11		9²	12		13	8								4
1	2	3	4²	5	6		7	12		11¹	9	13	14		10³	8								5
1	2	3	4	5	6		7²	9	10¹	11³	12	14	13		8									6
1	2	3	4³	5	6		7	9¹	10	13	12	11²			8	14								7
1	2¹	3	4	5	6		7³	13	10	11	9²	12			8	14								8
		3	4	5	6		7		10¹	11	9	12			8	2	1							9
1	2	3	4¹		6	12	7²		10³	11	9	13	14	8	5									10
1	2	3	4	5	6	9¹			10	11	12			7	8									11
1	2	3	4	5		12			10	11	9¹		13	7²	8	6								12
1	2	3	4	5		12			10²	11³	9¹	13	14	7	8	6								13
1	2	3	4	5		12		9²	10	11	13	7¹			8	6								14
1	2	3	4	5		12		9¹	10²	11	13	7³		14	8	6								15
1	2²	3	4	5	6	12		9¹	10	11		7³		14	8	13								16
1		3	4	5	6	12		9¹	10²	11³	13	7		14	8	2								17
1		3	4	5	6	12		9¹	10²	11	13	7³		14	8	2								18
1		3	4	5	6		12	9²	10	11³	13	7¹		14	8	2								19
1		3	4	5	6	9²			10	11	13	7¹	12	14	8	2³								20
1		3	4¹	5	6	8²	9¹		10	11	13		12	14	7	2								21
1	2	3	4¹	5		13	9	7²	10	11		12			8	6								22
1	2	3	4²	5		9³	7¹	10	11	13		12	14		8	6								23
1	2	3	4	5		9		10	11	7¹	12	13			8	6²								24
1	2	3	4	5		9		10	11	7¹	12				8		6							25
1	2	3	4	5	6	9		10	11	7¹		12	13	8³	14									26
1	2	3	4		6	9	7²	10	11	13		12			8	5¹								27
1	3¹	4			6	9²		10	11	12	7		2	13	8	5								28
1	2	3	4		6	12			10	11	13	7²	14	8³				5¹	9					29
1	2	3	4		6	12	13	10¹	11	14	7			8	5¹				9²					30
1	2		4		6	12			10	11²	14	13	7¹	8	5			3	9³					31
1	2		4		6¹			11	10³	12		13	14	7	8	5		3	9²					32
1	2¹	3²	4		6			11		10	12			13	8	5		14	9²	7				33
1	12	3²	4¹		6			11		10		7	9³	8	5		13				2	14		34
1			4		6			11	9²	10	12		7¹	13	8	5		3			2			35
1	12		4		6			11	9	10	13		7²	14	8	5¹		3³			2			36
1	2	3	4		6			11	12	10	7	9¹		13	8²						5			37
	2	3	4		6			12	10	7²	9		13	11	8	14	1				5³			38
	2	3	4		6			12	10	7	9		13	11¹	8²		1				5			39
1	2	3	4		6			12	10	13	9¹		7²	11	8	5								40
1	2	3³	4²		6			9	10	12		7	13	11¹	8	5								41
1	2	3			6			9	10	12		7	13	11¹	8	5							14	42
1	2	3			6	7			10	12	9²	13	4	11	8¹	14					5³			43
1	2	3	4		6	7		9	10¹	11	12			13	8²						5			44
1	2	3	4		6	7		9	10	12	13				8²	11¹					5			45
1	2	3	4		6	7		12	10	11	9¹				8						5			46

Coca-Cola Cup

First Round	Norwich C	(h)	1-1
		(a)	3-2
Second Round	Sheffield W	(a)	1-1
		(h)	1-0
Third Round	Port Vale	(a)	0-0
		(h)	2-0
Fourth Round	Southampton	(h)	1-1
		(a)	2-3

FA Cup

Third Round	Watford	(a)	0-2

PETERBOROUGH UNITED 1996-97   *Back row (left to right):* Ken Charlery, David Morrison, Lee Power, Mike Basham, Jon Sheffield, Mick Bodley, Mark Tyler, Greg Heald, Sean Farrell, Simon Clark, Roger Willis.

Middle row: Keith Oakes (Physio), Adrian Boothroyd, Tony Spearing, Ben Sedgemore, Danny Carter, Carl Griffiths, Giuliano Grazioli, Scott McGleish, Steve Welsh, Tom Meredith, Gordon Ogbourne (Kit Manager).

Front row: Marcus Ebdon, Niall Inman, Scott Houghton, Zeke Rowe, Lil Fucillo (Assistant Manager), Barry Fry (Director of Football), Mick Halsall (First Team Coach), Martin O'Connor, Derek Payne, Neil Le Bihan, Adam Drury.

Division 3 **PETERBOROUGH UNITED**

London Road Ground, Peterborough PE2 8AL. Telephone: (01733) 63947. Fax: (01733) 557210.

Ground capacity: 15,500.

Record attendance: 30,096 v Swansea T, FA Cup 5th rd, 20 February 1965.

Record receipts: £51,315 v Brighton & HA, FA Cup 5th rd, 15 February 1986.

Pitch measurements: 112yd × 75yd.

Chairman: Peter Boizot MBE. *Vice-Chairman:* Roger Terrell.

Directors: A. Hand, N. Hards, P. Sagar. *Company Secretary:* Timothy Warren. *Club Secretary:* Caroline Hand.

Chief Executive: Richard Maxwell.

First Team Manager: Barry Fry. *Assistant Manager:* Phil Neal. *Youth Team Manager:* Paul Ashworth.

Physio: Roy Johnson.

Year Formed: 1934. *Turned Professional:* 1934. *Ltd Co.:* 1934.

Club Nickname: 'The Posh'.

Foundation: The old Peterborough & Fletton club, founded in 1923, was suspended by the FA during season 1932–33 and disbanded. Local enthusiasts determined to carry on and in 1934 a new professional club Peterborough United was formed and entered the Midland League the following year.

First Football League game: 20 August 1960, Division 4, v Wrexham (h) W 3-0 – Walls; Stafford, Walker; Rayner, Rigby, Norris; Hails, Emery (1), Bly (1), Smith, McNamee (1).

Record League Victory: 8–1 v Oldham Ath, Division 4, 26 November 1969 – Drewery; Potts, Noble; Conmy, Wile, Wright; Moss (1), Price (3), Hall (4), Halliday, Robson.

Record Cup Victory: 7–0 v Harlow T, FA Cup 1st rd, 16 November 1991 – Barber; Luke, Johnson, Halsall (1), Robinson D, Welsh, Sterling (1) (Butterworth), Cooper G (2 (1 pen)), Riley (1) (Culpin (1)), Charlery (1), Kimble.

Record Defeat: 1–8 v Northampton T, FA Cup 2nd rd (2nd replay), 18 December 1946.

Most League Points (2 for a win): 66, Division 4, 1960–61.

Most League Points (3 for a win): 82, Division 4, 1981–82.

Most League Goals: 134, Division 4, 1960–61.

Highest League Scorer in Season: Terry Bly, 52, Division 4, 1960–61.

Most League Goals in Total Aggregate: Jim Hall, 122, 1967–75.

Most Capped Player: Tony Millington, 8 (21), Wales.

Most League Appearances: Tommy Robson, 482, 1968–81.

Record Transfer Fee Received: £350,000 from Walsall for Martin O'Connor, July 1996.

Record Transfer Fee Paid: £450,000 to Birmingham C for Martin O'Connor, November 1996.

Football League Record: 1960 Elected to Division 4; 1961–68 Division 3, when they were demoted for financial irregularities; 1968–74 Division 4; 1974–79 Division 3; 1979–91 Division 4; 1991–92 Division 3; 1992–94 Division 1; 1994–97 Division 2; 1997– Division 3.

Honours: Football League: Division 1 best season: 10th Division 1 1992–93; Division 4 – Champions 1960–61, 1973–74. *FA Cup:* best season: 6th rd, 1965. *Football League Cup:* Semi-final 1966.

Colours: Royal blue shirts, white shorts, white stockings. *Change colours:* All red.

Did you know?
On 24 March 1938, Peterborough United transferred centre-forward Cec Wyles to Everton for £350, a record Midland League fee at the time and made the first profit on the season in their history.

PETERBOROUGH UNITED 1996–97 LEAGUE RECORD

Match No.	Date	Venue	Opponents	Result	H/T Score	Lg. Pos.	Goalscorers	Attendance
1	Aug 17	A	Bristol R	L 0-1	0-1	—		6232
2	24	H	Crewe Alex	D 2-2	1-1	17	Houghton [13], O'Connor (pen) [90]	6357
3	31	A	Bournemouth	W 2-1	1-0	13	Willis [29], Griffiths [87]	4587
4	Sept 7	A	Wrexham	D 1-1	0-1	16	O'Connor [62]	3222
5	10	H	Millwall	D 3-3	1-0	—	Rowe [43], Charlery [65], O'Connor [85]	4442
6	14	H	York C	D 2-2	0-0	16	Rowe [55], Payne [76]	5613
7	21	A	Watford	D 0-0	0-0	17		12,007
8	28	H	Wycombe W	W 6-3	3-3	14	Heald [6], Charlery [41], Payne [42], Clark [48], Farrell 2 [61, 77]	5580
9	Oct 1	A	Plymouth Arg	D 1-1	1-1	—	Regis [28]	4929
10	5	A	Preston NE	W 4-3	1-0	12	Clark [36], Houghton [72], Charlery [82], Rowe [86]	8874
11	8	H	Notts Co	L 1-3	0-1	—	Farrell [65]	5456
12	12	H	Bury	L 1-2	0-0	15	Heald [66]	6003
13	15	H	Brentford	L 0-1	0-0	—		5037
14	19	A	Luton T	L 0-3	0-2	19		5964
15	26	A	Rotherham U	L 0-2	0-1	20		2854
16	29	H	Shrewsbury T	D 2-2	1-0	—	Houghton 2 (1 pen) [32,74 (p)]	5400
17	Nov 2	H	Blackpool	D 0-0	0-0	18		7011
18	9	A	Walsall	L 0-4	0-2	20		3921
19	19	H	Gillingham	L 0-1	0-0	—		4136
20	23	A	Bristol C	L 0-2	0-1	21		12,312
21	30	H	Rotherham U	W 6-2	3-2	21	Carruthers 2 [20, 69], Willis 2 [44, 48], Houghton (pen) [45], Monington (og) [60]	4690
22	Dec 3	A	Chesterfield	L 1-2	1-1	—	Ebdon [13]	2805
23	14	A	Stockport Co	D 0-0	0-0	21		5748
24	20	H	Burnley	W 3-2	2-1	—	Carruthers 2 [20, 27], Morrison [60]	5283
25	26	A	Millwall	W 2-0	2-0	19	Houghton 2 [4, 26]	8118
26	Jan 18	H	Plymouth Arg	D 0-0	0-0	20		6288
27	25	A	Shrewsbury T	D 2-2	1-1	21	Houghton [41], Donowa [50]	2695
28	Feb 1	H	Walsall	L 0-1	0-0	21		4940
29	8	A	Blackpool	L 1-5	0-1	21	Cleaver [90]	4001
30	11	H	Wrexham	L 0-1	0-1	—		2975
31	15	H	Bristol C	W 3-1	1-0	21	Willis 2 [16, 85], Otto [90]	4221
32	22	A	Gillingham	L 1-2	0-1	21	Morrison [80]	6552
33	25	A	Wycombe W	L 0-2	0-1	—		4001
34	Mar 1	H	Chesterfield	D 1-1	1-1	22	Otto [16]	4458
35	4	A	Watford	W 2-1	1-1	—	Charlery [31], Boothroyd (pen) [57]	4200
36	8	A	Burnley	L 0-5	0-3	22		8646
37	15	H	Stockport Co	L 0-2	0-0	22		4857
38	22	A	Crewe Alex	D 1-1	0-0	22	Charlery [62]	3565
39	29	H	Bristol R	L 1-2	1-0	22	Otto [21]	6132
40	31	A	Notts Co	D 0-0	0-0	22		3848
41	Apr 5	H	Bournemouth	W 3-1	0-0	22	Clark [47], De Souza [72], Otto [81]	4221
42	8	A	York C	L 0-1	0-1	—		2790
43	12	A	Preston NE	W 2-0	0-0	22	Willis [50], De Souza [80]	5040
44	19	A	Bury	L 0-1	0-0	22		4631
45	26	H	Luton T	L 0-1	0-0	22		9499
46	May 3	A	Brentford	W 1-0	0-0	21	Drury [88]	5274

Final League Position: 21

GOALSCORERS

League (55): Houghton 8 (2 pens), Willis 6, Charlery 5, Carruthers 4, Otto 4, Clark 3, Farrell 3, O'Connor 3 (1 pen), Rowe 3, De Souza 2, Heald 2, Morrison 2, Payne 2, Boothroyd 1 (pen), Cleaver 1, Donowa 1, Drury 1, Ebdon 1, Griffiths 1, Regis 1, own goal 1.
Coca-Cola Cup (3): Charlery 1, Farrell 1, Griffiths 1.
FA Cup (11): Charlery 6, Carruthers 2, Grazioli 1, Griffiths 1, Houghton 1.

Sheffield J 16	Boothroyd A 24 + 2	Heald G 34 + 2	Welsh S 6	Clark S 30 + 4	Willis R 34 + 6	O'Connor M 18	Williams M 6	Ebdon M 12 + 8	Houghton S 26 + 6	De Souza M 8	Farrell S 4 + 3	Basham M 4 + 1	Bullimore W 2 + 4	Charlery K 36 + 1	Grazioli G — + 4	McGleish S — + 1	Bodley M 31	Inman N — + 3	Spearing T 11 + 2	Payne D 36	Rowe Z 10 + 12	Griffiths C 2 + 10	Carter D 3 + 5	McKeever M 2 + 1	Neal A 4	Drury A 5	Billington D 2 + 3	Tyler M 3	Regis D 4 + 3	Etherington M 1	Huxford R 7	Griemink B 27	Cleaver C 6 + 7	Foran M 2 + 2	Carruthers M 13 + 1	Edwards A 25	Donowa L 16 + 6	Morrison D 4 + 7	Otto R 15	Ramage C 7	Le Bihan N 2	Linton D 8	Match No.
1	2¹	3	4	5	6	7	8	9²	10		11²	12	13	14																													1
1	12	5		3	7	4	8³	11	10	9²				2¹	13		6	14																									2
1	2	5		7	4		12	11¹	10								6		3	8²	9	13																					3
1	2	5		7	4		8¹	11	10								6		3	9	12																						4
1	2	5		7	4		8²	11	10								6		3	9¹	13	12																					5
1	2	5	3	7³	4¹		12	11²	10								6			8	9	13		14																			6
1	2¹	5	6		4	7		12	10											8	9	13			3	11²																	7
1		5	6	12	7	4		2²	13	10³	9		14							8					11		3¹																8
	12	5	6	3	7	4		13	11³		9²									8	14						2¹			1	10												9
	5	3²	11	7³	4			13	10	12							6			8	14								1	9¹	2												10
1		5		3	7²	4			11¹	10	12						6			8	13									9	2												11
	5		3	12	4				11	10¹	13						6			8	7²		14							9²	2	1											12
	2¹	5		3	7³	4		12	11	10	9²						6			8	9		13								14	1											13
1		5		3	12	4		7	11	10²										8¹	9³	13			6						14	2											14
1		5		3	12	4			11	10							6	13	7¹		9²	8³									14	2											15
1		5			4				11	10							6				3	8	9²		7¹			12			2	13											16
1				7				12	11	10²		4					6				13				3	8¹		2		9	5												17
	2¹		3	7²	8	12	11³	10			4						6				14	13					1				2	9	5										18
1	2	5		3	12	4		7¹	11²	10				13			6			8																9							19
1	2	5		3	12	7		4¹	11²	10							6			8	13														9							20
	5		3	2			7	11	10								6			8											1				9	4						21
1		5		3	2			7	11	10							6			8														9	4							22
	2¹	5		3	6³				10										12	8	13										1		14	9	4	7²	11					23
	2	5		3	6			7¹	10							12			8												1			9	4		11					24
	2	5		3	6			7	10										8	12											1			9¹	4	13	11²					25
	5		3	2			7	10						6			8													1			9	4	11¹	12					26
	2			5				7²	10							6		3	8	12										1			9¹	4	11	13						27
	2			3	5			7	10							6			8	12										1			9¹	4	11							28
	2³	12		3	5¹		13		10							6²			8	9										1	14			4	7		11					29
	5		12	2				13		3						6¹			8	14										1	11²			4	7		10	9³				30
	2	5		3	9				10										8											1				4	7		11	6				31
	2	5		3	9				10²										8											1	13			4	7¹	12	11	6				32
	2²	5		3	9				10³										8											1	12	13		4	7	14	11	6¹				33
	2	5		3	9²	12	10											8											1				4	7	13	11	6¹				34
	2	5		3	9²	8	10											12											1				4¹	7	13	11		6			35
	2	5		9			10²						4	3		12									14		1				7²	13	11	8	6¹			36
	2		12			14	10						5	3¹	8	13³		11		12							1	9			4	7	9²		6					37
	2¹	5		6			10						3	8			11	12									1	9			4	7								38
	5³			6	12	9	14						3	8												1	11²		13	4	7¹		10			2				39
	2²			7	12	11						5	3	8												1				9¹	4	13		10			6				40
		3		7	6²	11						5	8													1	12			9¹	4	13		10			2				41
		3		7	6²	11	14						5	8												1	13			9¹	4³	12		10			2				42
		3	12	11²		7	14						5	8										2		1	9¹			4	13		10³			6				43
		3	9	11¹		7	14						5	8³	12								2		1				4	13		10			6²				44
	12	3	9			7¹	8						5	13		14							2						4	11²		10³			6				45
		12	9²			8³	10						5	7	14				3		2	11¹	1	13				4						6				46

Coca-Cola Cup

First Round	Millwall	(a)	0-1
		(h)	2-0
Second Round	Southampton	(a)	0-2
		(h)	1-4

FA Cup

First Round	Cheltenham T	(h)	0-0
		(a)	3-1
Second Round	Enfield	(a)	1-1
		(h)	4-1
Third Round	Plymouth Arg	(a)	1-0
Fourth Round	Wrexham	(h)	2-4

PLYMOUTH ARGYLE 1996–97   *Back row (left to right):* Chris Curran, Tony James, Mick Heathcote, Kevin Blackwell, Bruce Grobbelaar, Richard Logan, Paul Wotton, Danny O'Hagan.
Middle row: Mick Jones (Assistant Manager), Michael Evans, Chris Billy, Gary Clayton, James Dungey, Mark Patterson, Ronnie Mauge, Mark Saunders, Norman Medhurst (Physio).
Front row: Carlo Corrazin, Paul Williams, Chris Leadbitter, Neil Warnock (Manager), Dan McCauley (Chairman), Martin Barlow, Adrian Littlejohn, Neil Illman.

Division 2   PLYMOUTH ARGYLE

Home Park, Plymouth, Devon PL2 3DQ. Telephone: (01752) 562561. Fax: (01752) 606167. Marketing Department: (01752) 569597. Pilgrim Shop: (01752) 558292.

Ground capacity: 19,630.

Record attendance: 43,596 v Aston Villa, Division 2, 10 October 1936.

Record receipts: £128,000 v Burnley, Division 2 play-off, 18 May 1994.

Pitch measurements: 110yd × 72yd.

President: S. J. Rendell.

Chairman: D. McCauley. *Vice-Chairman:* P. Bloom.

Director: Roy Griggs.

Manager: Mick Jones. *Assistant Manager:* Kevin Blackwell. *Physio:* Norman Medhurst.

Secretary/Chief Executive: Roger Matthews.

Year Formed: 1886. *Turned Professional:* 1903. *Ltd Co.:* 1903.

Club Nickname: 'The Pilgrims'.

Previous Name: 1886–1903, Argyle Athletic Club.

Foundation: The club was formed in September 1886 as the Argyle Football Club by former public and private school pupils who wanted to continue playing the game. The meeting was held in a room above the Borough Arms (a Coffee House), Bedford Street, Plymouth. It was common then to choose a local street/terrace as a club name and Argyle or Argyll was a fashionable name throughout the land due to Queen Victoria's great interest in Scotland.

First Football League game: 28 August 1920, Division 3, v Norwich C (h) D 1-1 – Craig; Russell, Atterbury; Logan, Dickinson, Forbes; Kirkpatrick, Jack, Bowler, Heeps (1), Dixon.

Record League Victory: 8–1 v Millwall, Division 2, 16 January 1932 – Harper; Roberts, Titmuss; Mackay, Pullan, Reed; Grozier, Bowden (2), Vidler (3), Leslie (1), Black (1). (1 og). 8–1 v Hartlepool U (a), Division 2, 7 May 1994 – Nicholls; Patterson (Naylor), Hill, Burrows, Comyn, McCall (1), Barlow, Castle (1), Landon (3), Marshall (1), Dalton (2).

Record Cup Victory: 6–0 v Corby T, FA Cup 3rd rd, 22 January 1966 – Leiper; Book, Baird; Williams, Nelson, Newman; Jones (1), Jackson (1), Bickle (3), Piper (1), Jennings.

Record Defeat: 0–9 v Stoke C, Division 2, 17 December 1960.

Most League Points (2 for a win): 68, Division 3 (S), 1929–30.

Most League Points (3 for a win): 87, Division 3, 1985–86.

Most League Goals: 107, Division 3 (S), 1925–26 and 1951–52.

Highest League Scorer in Season: Jack Cock, 32, Division 3 (S), 1925–26.

Most League Goals in Total Aggregate: Sammy Black, 180, 1924–38.

Most Capped Player: Moses Russell, 20 (23), Wales.

Most League Appearances: Kevin Hodges, 530, 1978–92.

Record Transfer Fee Received: £750,000 from Southampton for Mickey Evans, March 1997.

Record Transfer Fee Paid: £250,000 to Hartlepool U for Paul Dalton, June 1992.

Football League Record: 1920 Original Member of Division 3; 1921–30 Division 3 (S); 1930–50 Division 2; 1950–52 Division 3 (S); 1952–56 Division 2; 1956–58 Division 3 (S); 1958–59 Division 3; 1959–68 Division 2; 1968–75 Division 3; 1975–77 Division 2; 1977–86 Division 3; 1986–95 Division 2; 1995–96 Division 3; 1996–Division 2.

Honours: Football League: Division 2 best season: 4th, 1931–32, 1952–53; Division 3 (S) – Champions 1929–30, 1951–52; Runners-up 1921–22, 1922–23, 1923–24, 1924–25, 1925–26, 1926–27 (record of six consecutive years); Division 3 – Champions 1958–59; Runners-up 1974–75, 1985–86, Promoted 1995–96 (play-offs). *FA Cup:* best season: Semi-final 1984. *Football League Cup:* Semi-final 1965, 1974.

Colours: Green and black striped shirts, black shorts, black stockings. *Change colours:* All white.

Did you know?
Lee Phillips, an 89th minute substitute for Plymouth Argyle, became the club's youngest debutant at 16 years 43 days against Gillingham on 29 October 1996.

PLYMOUTH ARGYLE 1996–97 LEAGUE RECORD

Match No.	Date	Venue	Opponents	Result	H/T Score	Lg. Pos.	Goalscorers	Attendance
1	Aug 17	H	York C	W	2-1	0-0	—	Corazzin [61], Heathcote [65]	9035
2	24	A	Wrexham	D	4-4	2-1	2	Evans [10], Littlejohn 2 [25, 63], Logan [66]	3920
3	27	A	Watford	W	2-0	1-0	—	Billy [32], Littlejohn [79]	7349
4	30	H	Preston NE	W	2-1	1-1	—	Evans [3], Logan [66]	9209
5	Sept 7	H	Notts Co	D	0-0	0-0	3		8109
6	10	A	Brentford	L	2-3	1-1	—	Mauge [44], Corazzin [83]	5377
7	14	A	Stockport Co	L	1-3	1-2	9	Evans (pen) [27]	5087
8	21	H	Bristol R	L	0-1	0-0	11		8879
9	28	A	Crewe Alex	L	0-3	0-1	15		3797
10	Oct 1	H	Peterborough U	D	1-1	1-1	—	James [13]	4929
11	5	H	Millwall	D	0-0	0-0	16		7507
12	12	A	Walsall	W	1-0	1-0	13	Littlejohn [15]	3720
13	15	A	Bournemouth	L	0-1	0-1	—		3818
14	19	A	Bristol C	D	0-0	0-0	14		9645
15	26	A	Burnley	L	1-2	0-1	15	Evans [73]	9602
16	29	H	Gillingham	W	2-0	0-0	—	Evans [59], Illman [66]	4787
17	Nov 2	H	Luton T	D	3-3	1-1	14	Mauge [32], Evans 2 (1 pen) [71 (p), 74]	7134
18	9	A	Wycombe W	L	1-2	1-1	14	Williams [39]	5456
19	19	H	Chesterfield	L	0-3	0-1	—		4237
20	23	A	Bury	L	0-1	0-1	19		3582
21	30	H	Burnley	D	0-0	0-0	18		6289
22	Dec 3	A	Blackpool	D	2-2	2-1	—	Wotton [10], Littlejohn [24]	2690
23	14	H	Shrewsbury T	D	2-2	0-1	20	Mauge [58], Evans [80]	5075
24	21	A	Rotherham U	W	2-1	2-1	17	Illman [9], Evans [10]	2269
25	26	H	Brentford	L	1-4	0-1	20	Illman [59]	9525
26	Jan 11	H	Crewe Alex	W	1-0	0-0	15	Logan [90]	4767
27	18	A	Peterborough U	D	0-0	0-0	14		6288
28	25	A	Gillingham	L	1-4	0-3	17	Evans [70]	5465
29	Feb 1	H	Wycombe W	D	0-0	0-0	19		5024
30	8	A	Luton T	D	2-2	0-0	19	Littlejohn [59], Evans [68]	6439
31	15	H	Bury	W	2-0	0-0	19	Logan [63], Corazzin [66]	5486
32	22	A	Chesterfield	W	2-1	0-0	17	Evans [63], Saunders [72]	5833
33	25	A	Bristol R	L	0-2	0-2	—		6005
34	Mar 1	A	Blackpool	L	0-1	0-1	19		5585
35	8	H	Rotherham U	W	1-0	1-0	18	Corazzin (pen) [25]	4717
36	15	A	Shrewsbury T	W	3-2	0-0	15	Billy 2 [52, 60], Illman [87]	3414
37	22	H	Wrexham	L	0-1	0-1	17		5468
38	29	A	York C	D	1-1	0-0	18	Corazzin [54]	3917
39	31	H	Watford	D	0-0	0-0	18		6836
40	Apr 5	A	Preston NE	D	1-1	1-1	18	Saunders [36]	8503
41	8	H	Stockport Co	D	0-0	0-0	—		5089
42	12	A	Millwall	D	0-0	0-0	18		5702
43	15	A	Notts Co	L	1-2	0-0	—	Collins [71]	2423
44	19	H	Walsall	W	2-0	0-0	18	Saunders [75], Barlow [81]	5535
45	26	A	Bristol C	L	1-3	1-1	18	Williams [18]	15,368
46	May 3	H	Bournemouth	D	0-0	0-0	19		6507

Final League Position: 19

GOALSCORERS

League (47): Evans 12 (2 pens), Littlejohn 6, Corazzin 5 (1 pen), Illman 4, Logan 4, Billy 3, Mauge 3, Saunders 3, Williams 2, Barlow 1, Collins 1, Heathcote 1, James 1, Wotton 1.
Coca-Cola Cup (0):
FA Cup (9): Evans 3 (1 pen), Littlejohn 2, Mauge 2, Billy 1, Corazzin 1.

Grobbelaar B 36	Billy C 44 + 1	Williams P 46	Mauge R 29 + 6	Heathcote M 41 + 1	Curran C 20 + 2	Leadbitter C 17 + 2	Logan R 19 + 9	Littlejohn A 33 + 4	Evans M 33	Corazzin C 22 + 8	James T 34	Saunders M 22 + 3	Barlow M 38 + 2	Blackwell K 4	Wotton P 5 + 4	Simpson M 10 + 2	Rowbotham J 12 + 3	Illman N 12 + 13	Phillips L — + 2	Dungey J 6	Patterson M 11 + 1	Collins S 11 + 1	Perkins S 1 + 3	Clayton G — + 1	Match No.
1	2	3	4	5	6	7	8	9	10	11															1
1	2	3	4	5	6	7	8	9	10	11															2
1	2	3	4	5		7	8	9	10		6		11												3
1	2	3	4	5		7	8	9	10		6	12	11^1												4
1	2	3	4	5		7	8	9	10	12	6		11^1												5
1	2	3	4		5	7	8	9	10	11	6														6
1	2	3	4	12	5	7^3	8^1	9	10	11^2	6	14	13												7
1	2	3	4		5	7	8^1	9	10	12	6		11												8
	2	3		5		7	12	9	10	8^2	6	4^1	11	1	13										9
1	2	3		5	4	7^1	12	9	10	8	6		11												10
	2	3		5	4		8	9	10^1	7	6		11	1		12									11
1	2	3	4	5	8		12		9^1	10	6		11		7										12
1	2	3	4	5	8		12		10	9^3	6^1		11		7^2	13	14								13
1	2	3	4	5	8				10	9^1	6		11		7		12								14
1	2	3	4	5^1	8		12		10		6		11^2		7	13	9								15
1	2	3	4	5	8				10		6		11		7		9^1	12							16
1	2^2	3	4^1	5	8	12			10		6		11		7	13	9^1	14							17
	2	3	4^1	5	8	12			10	13	6		11		7^2		9			1					18
1	2	3	4^3	5	8^2	7		12	10	13	6		11		14		9								19
1	2	3		5		8^1		9	10	12	6		11												20
1	2	3		5		8		9	10^1	12	6	13	11			4	7^2								21
1	2	3		5		8		9	10^3	12	6	13	11^1			4	7^2	14							22
1	2	3	4	5		8^2	12	9	10		6		11		7^1		13								23
1	2	3	4	5^1		8	12	13	11		6		10		7		9^2								24
1	2	3	4	5		8^1	12	13	10	14	6		11		7^2		9^1								25
	2	3		5	4		12	9	10		7^2	6	8^1		11		13			1					26
	2	3		5	4		7	9	10			6	8		11					1					27
	2	3	12	5	4^1		8	9	10		6		7^2		11		13			1					28
1	2	3	12	5		8^1	9^2	10	7	6	4		11				13								29
1	2	3	12	5		8	9	10	7	6	4^1		11												30
	2	3	4	5		8	9	10	7	6		11		1											31
1	2	3	4		5	8		10	7	6	11			12			9^1								32
1	2	3	4		5	8	9	10^1	6	7	11			12											33
1	2	3	4	5		8^1	9		6	7^2	11		12			10		13							34
1	2	3		5		9		7		4	11						8				6	10			35
1	2	3		5		9			4	11^1							8	7			6	10	12		36
1	2	3		5		9^1	7		4	11							8	12^2			6	10	13		37
1	2	3	12	5		9	7			6			11^1				8				4	10			38
1	2	3^1	12	5		9	7			4			11				8				6	10			39
	2	3		5		9			4	11				1			8	7			6	10			40
1	2	3	12	5		13		7		4	11						8	9^2			6	10^1			41
1		3	11	5		9		7^1	2	4	10						8				6	12			42
1	12	3	10	5				7^2	2^1	4	11						8	13			6	9			43
1	2	3^1	7	5	12			10^2		4	11						8	13			6	9			44
	2	3	11	5	12	8	9^2		4^3			7	13							1	10	6^1	14		45
	2	3^4	4	5		7^3	10			11		13	8			12				1	6	9^1		14	46

Coca-Cola Cup
First Round   Brentford   (a) 0-1
                                  (h) 0-0

FA Cup
First Round   Fulham   (h) 5-0
Second Round   Exeter C   (h) 4-1
Third Round   Peterborough U   (h) 0-1

PORTSMOUTH 1996–97   *Back row (left to right):* Jason Rees, Deon Burton, Jimmy Carter, Danny Barker, Mark Thompson, Andy Thomson, Scott Bundy, Tony Dobson, Alan McLoughlin, Fitzroy Simpson.

Middle row: Gordon Neave (Kit Man), Neil Sillett (Physio), Danny Hinshelwood, Clinton More, Jon Hawley, Aaron Flahavan, Keith Waldon (First Team Coach), Alan Knight, Russell Perrett, John Durnin, Paul Walsh, Larry May (Youth Team Manager), Martin Hinshelwood (Reserve Team Manager).

Front row: Sammy Igoe, Jason Ahmet, Paul Hall, Robbie Pethick, David Waterman, Martin Allen, Terry Fenwick (Manager), Guy Butters, Lee Bradbury, Lee Russell, Paul Wood, Andy Awford, Anthony Tilley.

Division 1 **PORTSMOUTH**

Fratton Park, Frogmore Rd, Portsmouth PO4 8RA. Telephone: (01705) 731204. Fax: (01705) 734129. Commercial Dept: (01705) 731204. Ticket Office: (01705) 618777. Membership Office: (01705) 825016. Clubcall: 0891 121182.

Ground capacity: 16,061.

Record attendance: 51,385 v Derby Co, FA Cup 6th rd, 26 February 1949.

Record receipts: £233,000 v Chelsea, FA Cup 6th rd, 9 March 1997.

Pitch measurements: 114yd × 72yd.

Chairman: Terry Venables.

Directors: F. Dinenage, J. Hutchison, B. A. V. Henson FCA.

Manager: Terry Fenwick. *First Team Coach:* Keith Waldon.

Secretary: Paul Weld. *Marketing Manager:* Julie Baker.

Reserve Team Coach: Ian McDonald. *Youth Team Coach:* Martin Hinshelwood.

Physio: Neil Sillett.

Year Formed: 1898. *Turned Professional:* 1898. *Ltd Co.:* 1898.

Club Nickname: 'Pompey'.

Foundation: At a meeting held in his High Street, Portsmouth offices in 1898, solicitor Alderman J. E. Pink and five other business and professional men agreed to buy some ground close to Goldsmith Avenue for £4,950 which they developed into Fratton Park in record breaking time. A team of professionals was signed up by manager Frank Brettell and entry to the Southern League obtained for the new club's September 1899 kick-off.

First Football League game: 28 August 1920, Division 3, v Swansea T (h) W 3-0 – Robson; Probert, Potts; Abbott, Harwood, Turner; Thompson, Stringfellow (1), Reid (1), James (1), Beedie.

Record League Victory: 9–1 v Notts Co, Division 2, 9 April 1927 – McPhail; Clifford, Ted Smith; Reg Davies (1), Foxall, Moffat; Forward (1), Mackie (2), Haines (3), Watson, Cook (2).

Record Cup Victory: 7–0 v Stockport Co, FA Cup 3rd rd, 8 January 1949 – Butler; Rookes, Ferrier; Scoular, Flewin, Dickinson; Harris (3), Barlow, Clarke (2), Phillips (2), Froggatt.

Record Defeat: 0–10 v Leicester C, Division 1, 20 October 1928.

Most League Points (2 for a win): 65, Division 3, 1961–62.

Most League Points (3 for a win): 91, Division 3, 1982–83.

Most League Goals: 91, Division 4, 1979–80.

Highest League Scorer in Season: Guy Whittingham, 42, Division 1, 1992–93.

Most League Goals in Total Aggregate: Peter Harris, 194, 1946–60.

Most Capped Player: Jimmy Dickinson, 48, England.

Most League Appearances: Jimmy Dickinson, 764, 1946–65.

Record Transfer Fee Received: £2,000,000 from Tottenham H for Darren Anderton, May 1992.

Record Transfer Fee Paid: £650,000 to Celtic for Gerry Creaney, January 1994.

Football League Record: 1920 Original Member of Division 3; 1921 Division 3 (S); 1924–27 Division 2; 1927–59 Division 1; 1959–61 Division 2; 1961–62 Division 3; 1962–76 Division 2; 1976–78 Division 3; 1978–80 Division 4; 1980–83 Division 3; 1983–87 Division 2; 1987–88 Division 1; 1988–92 Division 2; 1992– Division 1.

Honours: Football League: Division 1 – Champions 1948–49, 1949–50; Division 2 – Runners-up 1926–27, 1986–87; Division 3 (S) – Champions 1923–24; Division 3 – Champions 1961–62, 1982–83. *FA Cup:* Winners 1939; Runners-up 1929, 1934. *Football League Cup:* best season: 5th rd, 1961, 1986.

Colours: Blue shirts, white shorts, red stockings. *Change colours:* Red and black shirts, black shorts, red stockings.

Did you know?
Portsmouth became the first club to rise from the Third Division to win the Football League Championship, a feat they achieved in 1948–49.

PORTSMOUTH 1996–97 LEAGUE RECORD

Match No.	Date	Venue	Opponents	Result	H/T Score	Lg. Pos.	Goalscorers	Attendance
1	Aug 17	A	Bradford C	L	1-3	1-0	—	Hall [26]	10,007
2	23	H	QPR	L	1-2	0-1	—	Igoe [76]	7501
3	27	H	Southend U	W	1-0	0-0	—	Russell [67]	5579
4	31	A	Grimsby T	W	1-0	1-0	10	Rees [45]	4747
5	Sept 7	H	Port Vale	D	1-1	1-0	11	Russell [23]	6448
6	11	A	Swindon T	W	1-0	0-0	—	McLoughlin [73]	8685
7	14	A	Bolton W	L	0-2	0-0	11		14,248
8	21	H	Norwich C	L	0-1	0-1	16		7511
9	28	A	Oxford U	L	0-2	0-2	17		7626
10	Oct 1	H	Crystal Palace	D	2-2	1-1	—	Hall [43], Bradbury [86]	7212
11	4	A	Tranmere R	L	3-4	1-2	—	Bradbury [43], McLoughlin (pen) [78], Perrett [86]	5001
12	12	H	Charlton Ath	W	2-0	0-0	14	Durnin [78], Bradbury [85]	6641
13	15	H	Wolverhampton W	L	0-2	0-1	—		7411
14	19	A	Ipswich T	D	1-1	1-1	19	McLoughlin (pen) [40]	10,514
15	26	A	Stoke C	L	1-3	1-0	20	Bradbury [37]	10,259
16	29	H	Birmingham C	D	1-1	0-1	—	Bradbury [70]	6334
17	Nov 2	H	WBA	W	4-0	4-0	13	Bradbury [9], Simpson [20], Durnin [36], Turner [44]	7354
18	9	A	Oldham Ath	D	0-0	0-0	14		7639
19	16	H	Manchester C	W	2-1	2-1	13	Bradbury [24], Simpson [40]	12,841
20	23	A	Barnsley	L	2-3	0-2	15	Durnin (pen) [65], Bradbury [72]	7449
21	30	H	Stoke C	W	1-0	1-0	11	Turner [4]	7749
22	Dec 7	A	Sheffield U	L	0-1	0-1	18		16,333
23	14	H	Huddersfield T	W	3-1	3-0	15	Simpson (pen) [21], Svensson 2 [41, 44]	6954
24	21	A	Reading	D	0-0	0-0	15		8520
25	26	H	Swindon T	L	0-1	0-0	17		10,605
26	28	A	Port Vale	W	2-0	1-0	15	Hall [11], Svensson [47]	7382
27	Jan 1	A	Norwich C	L	0-1	0-0	17		11,946
28	11	H	Bolton W	L	0-3	0-0	17		10,467
29	18	A	Crystal Palace	W	2-1	0-1	14	Bradbury [55], Thomson [62]	15,498
30	28	H	Oxford U	W	2-1	1-1	—	Hall [37], Svensson [67]	7301
31	Feb 1	H	Oldham Ath	W	1-0	1-0	11	Hall [7]	9135
32	8	A	Birmingham C	W	3-0	1-0	11	Svensson [3], Bradbury [78], McLoughlin (pen) [83]	15,897
33	22	A	WBA	W	2-0	2-0	8	Hillier [27], Burton [45]	15,800
34	Mar 1	H	Sheffield U	D	1-1	1-0	9	Hall [19]	12,715
35	5	A	Manchester C	D	1-1	0-0	—	Simpson [86]	26,051
36	15	A	Huddersfield T	W	3-1	0-1	9	Igoe [58], Hall 2 [61, 62]	10,512
37	22	A	QPR	L	1-2	1-1	12	Bradbury [18]	15,746
38	25	H	Reading	W	1-0	0-0	—	Hall [84]	9248
39	29	H	Bradford C	W	3-1	3-1	6	Bradbury [30], Hall [39], Svensson [43]	12,340
40	31	A	Southend U	L	1-2	0-2	8	Hall [54]	6107
41	Apr 5	H	Grimsby T	W	1-0	0-0	6	Carter [55]	9854
42	12	H	Tranmere R	L	1-3	0-2	9	Hillier [89]	12,004
43	19	A	Charlton Ath	L	1-2	1-1	11	Hall [11]	12,342
44	22	A	Barnsley	W	4-2	2-0	—	McLoughlin (pen) [28], Bradbury 3 [37, 49, 89]	8328
45	25	H	Ipswich T	L	0-1	0-1	—		12,101
46	May 4	A	Wolverhampton W	W	1-0	0-0	7	Hall [80]	26,031

Final League Position: 7

GOALSCORERS

League (59): Bradbury 15, Hall 13, Svensson 6, McLoughlin 5 (4 pens), Simpson 4 (1 pen), Durnin 3 (1 pen), Hillier 2, Igoe 2, Russell 2, Turner 2, Burton 1, Carter 1, Perrett 1, Rees 1, Thomson 1.
Coca-Cola Cup (3): Burton 2, Carter 1.
FA Cup (9): Bradbury 2, Hall 2, McLoughlin 2, Burton 1, Hillier 1, Svensson 1.

Flahavan A 24	Pethick R 27 + 8	Russell L 18 + 2	McLoughlin A 33 + 3	Butters G 7	Awford A 37 + 2	Carter J 23 + 4	Simpson F 40 + 1	Burton D 12 + 9	Hall P 36 + 6	Igoe S 22 + 18	Rees J 1 + 2	Bradbury L 38 + 4	Thomson A 22 + 6	Allen M 3 + 1	Durnin J 16 + 18	Knight A 22	Waterman D — + 4	Dobson T 4 + 2	Turner A 22 + 2	Perrett R 31 + 1	Whitbread A 24	Hillier D 21	Svensson M 17 + 2	Cook A 6 + 2	Match No.
1	2	3	4	5	6	7¹	8	9²	10	11³	12	13	14												1
1	2	3	4	5	6	7¹	8	9	10	12				11											2
1	2	3		5	6	7¹	8	9	10	11	12				4										3
	2	3		5		7²	8	9¹	10	11	6	12			4	1	13								4
1	2	3	4		6	7¹	8	9	10	12									5	11					5
1	2	3	4		6	7	8¹	9²	10	12		13							5	11					6
1	2	3	4		6	7	8	9¹	10		12								5	11					7
1	2	3	4		6	7	8²		10¹	5		9			12					11	13				8
1	2¹	3	4	5	6²	7	8			13	12	9	14							11³	10				9
1		3	4	5	6	7	8		10	12		9					2			11¹					10
1	12	3	4	5¹	6	7	8³		10	13		9	14							11²	2				11
1	2¹	3	4		6	7	8		10²	12		9	13							11	5				12
1			3	4	6¹	7	8			12	2	9	10							11	5				13
1	2	3	4		6	7²	8			12	13	9	14	10						11¹	5³				14
1		3³	4		6	7¹	8			12	13	9	14	10						11²	5	2			15
1		3³	4		6	7¹	8	12			13	9	14	10						11²	5	2			16
1	12		4		6	7	8				13	9	3	10						11²	5	2¹			17
1	12				6	7¹		13		8		9²	3	10						11	5	2	4		18
1	12		4		6	7³	8²	14		13		9	3	10						11¹	5	2			19
1	12		4¹		6	7²		14	13	8		9	3	10						11³	5	2			20
1			4			7¹	8		12	6		9	3	10						11	5	2			21
1	4¹	12			13	8		7²	6			9	3	10					5	11³		2	14		22
1	12				6		8		7	3¹		9		13						11	5	2	4	10²	23
1	6					8		7				9	3							11¹	5	2	4	10	24
1	12		4²			8		7				9	3	13						11³	5	2	6¹	10	25
		3			6	12	8		7			9			4	1			5	2			10¹	11	26
		3		4	6	12	8		7			13	9	1	14				5²	2			10¹	11³	27
		3			6	12	8		7²	13		9	14	5	1				11¹	2³	4	10			28
	2		4		6		8		7			9¹	3	10	1			12		5	11				29
	2		4		6		8		7	12		9	3	13		1				5	11¹	10²			30
	2		4		6		8		7¹	12		9	3			1				5	11	10			31
	2		4¹		6		8		7	12		9	3	13		1				5	11	10²			32
	2				6		8¹	10	7	4		9	3			1	12			5	11				33
			4²		6		8	12	7	2		9	3	13		1				5	11	10¹			34
		12			6		8		7	2		9	3	13		1				5	11	10²	4¹		35
	2		4		6		8		7	12		9	3			1				5	11	10¹			36
	2	12				13	10³	7	4			9	3¹	14		1			5	6	11		8²		37
	2¹		4		6		8		7	12		9		13		1			5	3	11	10²			38
	2	12		6		8¹	13	7	11			9	4³	14		1			5	3		10²			39
	2	12		6			13	7	11			9	4³	14		1			5	3		10²	8¹		40
		5	4	6	8²	12	7	2				9¹	14	1	13				3	11	10³				41
12		4	6	8		7	2					9	3		1				5	11	10¹				42
	2¹		4	12	8²	13	7	10				9	3³	14	1				5	6	11				43
		4	12		8	10³	7	2				9	3	13	1		14	5¹	6	11²					44
		4	6		8	10¹	7	2				9	3²	12	1	13			5	11					45
	6	4			8¹	10³	7²	2				9	3	12	1	13			5	11	14				46

Coca-Cola Cup
First Round   Leyton Orient   (h)   2-0
                                        (a)   0-1
Second Round   Wimbledon   (a)   0-1
                                        (h)   1-1

FA Cup
Third Round   Wolverhampton W   (a)   2-1
Fourth Round   Reading   (h)   3-0
Fifth Round   Leeds U   (a)   3-2
Sixth Round   Chelsea   (h)   1-4

PORT VALE 1996–97 *Back row (left to right):* Stewart Talbot, Dean Glover, Neil Aspin, Matthew Boswell, Lee Mills, Arjan van Heusden, Gareth Griffiths, Paul Musselwhite, Jermaine Holwyn, Justin O'Reilly, Andy Hill.

Middle row: Stan Nicholls (Kit Man), Allen Tankard, Steve Guppy, Martin Foyle, Wayne Corden, Ray Walker, Richard Eyre, Lee Glover, Jim Cooper (Community Officer), Rick Carter (Physio).

Front row: Bill Dearden (Coach), Jon McCarthy, Tony Naylor, Andy Porter, John Rudge (Manager), Dean Stokes, Ian Bogie, Dean Cunningham, Mark Grew (Youth Team Coach).

Division 1 **PORT VALE**

Vale Park, Burslem, Stoke-on-Trent ST6 1AW. Telephone: (01782) 814134. Fax: (01782) 834981. Marketing Dept: (01782) 835524. Clubcall: 0891 121636. Marketing Fax: (01782) 836875. Valiant Leisure Shop: (01782) 818718. Community: (01782) 575594

Ground capacity: 22,356.

Record attendance: 49,768 v Aston Villa, FA Cup 5th rd, 20 February 1960.

Record receipts: £170,349 v Everton, FA Cup 4th rd, 14 February 1996.

Pitch measurements: 114yd × 77yd.

President: J. Burgess.

Chairman: W. T. Bell LAE, TECH. ENG, MIMI.

Directors: A. Belfield, I. McPherson, S. Plant (Associate Director).

Manager: John Rudge. *Secretary:* F. W. Lodey.

Coach: Bill Dearden. *Physio:* Rick Carter. *Medical Officer:* Dr. D. Phillips. *General Manager:* Neil Hughes. *Safety Officer:* W. Stevenson. *Groundsman:* R. Fairbanks. *Community Scheme Officer:* Jim Cooper (01782 575594).

Year Formed: 1876. *Turned Professional:* 1885. *Ltd Co.:* 1911.

Club Nickname: 'Valiants'.

Previous Name: Burslem Port Vale; became Port Vale, 1909.

Previous Grounds: 1876, Limekin Lane, Longport; 1881, Westport; 1884, Moorland Road, Burslem; 1886, Athletic Ground, Cobridge; 1913, Recreation Ground, Hanley; 1950, Vale Park.

Foundation: Formed in 1876 as Port Vale, adopting the prefix 'Burslem' in 1884 upon moving to that part of the city. It was dropped in 1909.

First Football League game: 3 September 1892, Division 2, v Small Heath (a) L 1-5 – Frail; Clutton, Elson; Farrington, McCrindle, Delves; Walker, Scarratt, Bliss (1), Jones. (Only 10 men).

Record League Victory: 9–1 v Chesterfield, Division 2, 24 September 1932 – Leckie; Shenton, Poyser; Sherlock, Round, Jones; McGrath, Mills, Littlewood (6), Kirkham (2), Morton (1).

Record Cup Victory: 7–1 v Irthlingborough, FA Cup 1st rd, 12 January 1907 – Matthews; Dunn, Hamilton; Eardley, Baddeley, Holyhead; Carter, Dodds (2), Beats, Mountford (2), Coxon (3).

Record Defeat: 0–10 v Sheffield U, Division 2, 10 December 1892 and v Notts Co, Division 2, 26 February 1895.

Most League Points (2 for a win): 69, Division 3 (N), 1953–54.

Most League Points (3 for a win): 89, Division 2, 1992–93.

Most League Goals: 110, Division 4, 1958–59.

Highest League Scorer in Season: Wilf Kirkham 38, Division 2, 1926–27.

Most League Goals in Total Aggregate: Wilf Kirkham, 154, 1923–29, 1931–33.

Most Capped Player: Sammy Morgan, 7 (18), Northern Ireland.

Most League Appearances: Roy Sproson, 761, 1950–72.

Record Transfer Fee Received: £1,000,000 from Sheffield W for Ian Taylor, August 1994.

Record Transfer Fee Paid: £450,000 to York C for Jon McCarthy, July 1995.

Football League Record: 1892 Original Member of Division 2. Failed re-election in 1896; Re-elected 1898; Resigned 1907; Returned in Oct, 1919, when they took over the fixtures of Leeds City; 1929–30 Division 3 (N); 1930–36 Division 2; 1936–38 Division 3 (N); 1938–52 Division 3 (S); 1952–54 Division 3 (N); 1954–57 Division 2; 1957–58 Division 3 (S); 1958–59 Division 4; 1959–65 Division 3; 1965–70 Division 4; 1970–78 Division 3; 1978–83 Division 4; 1983–84 Division 3; 1984–86 Division 4; 1986–89 Division 3; 1989–94 Division 2; 1994– Division 1.

Honours: Football League: Division 2 – Runners-up 1993–94; *Division 3 (N)* – Champions 1929–30, 1953–54; Runners-up 1952–53; *Division 4* – Champions 1958–59; Promoted 1969–70 (4th). *FA Cup:* Semi-final 1954, when in Division 3. *Football League Cup:* 3rd rd 1992, 1997. *Autoglass Trophy:* Winners: 1993. *Anglo-Italian Cup:* Runners-up: 1996.

Colours: White shirts, black shorts, black and white stockings. *Change colours:* All yellow.

Did you know?
Stewart Littlewood scored six goals for Port Vale in the first 57 minutes of a 9–1 win over Chesterfield on 24 September 1932.

PORT VALE 1996–97 LEAGUE RECORD

Match No.	Date	Venue	Opponents	Result	H/T Score	Lg. Pos.	Goalscorers	Attendance
1	Aug 17	H	Bolton W	D	1-1	0-1	—	Naylor [72]	10,057
2	24	A	Swindon T	D	1-1	1-0	16	McCarthy [32]	8706
3	27	A	Tranmere R	L	0-2	0-2	—		6123
4	31	H	Oxford U	W	2-0	1-0	13	Naylor [41], Mills [62]	6016
5	Sept 7	A	Portsmouth	D	1-1	0-1	13	Porter [58]	6448
6	10	H	Manchester C	L	0-2	0-1	—		10,770
7	14	H	Grimsby T	D	1-1	1-1	19	Hill [12]	4892
8	21	A	Southend U	D	0-0	0-0	18		4025
9	29	H	Bradford C	D	1-1	1-0	19	Guppy [37]	4706
10	Oct 2	H	QPR	W	2-1	0-1	—	Guppy [70], Naylor [77]	8727
11	5	A	Oldham Ath	L	0-3	0-3	15		6051
12	13	H	Stoke C	D	1-1	0-0	17	Mills [90]	14,396
13	16	H	Crystal Palace	L	0-2	0-2	—		4522
14	19	A	Wolverhampton W	W	1-0	0-0	15	Naylor [66]	22,755
15	26	A	Huddersfield T	W	1-0	0-0	11	McCarthy [54]	11,017
16	29	H	Barnsley	L	1-3	0-1	—	Guppy [52]	5231
17	Nov 2	H	Birmingham C	W	3-0	2-0	12	Naylor 2 [22, 41], Guppy [68]	8388
18	9	A	WBA	D	1-1	1-1	10	Guppy [17]	13,975
19	16	H	Sheffield U	D	0-0	0-0	11		8352
20	23	A	Ipswich T	L	1-2	1-1	14	Naylor [2]	9491
21	30	H	Huddersfield T	D	0-0	0-0	16		6026
22	Dec 7	A	Reading	W	1-0	0-0	15	Talbot [73]	6445
23	14	A	Charlton Ath	W	3-1	1-1	12	Naylor 3 [34, 46, 49]	10,003
24	21	H	Norwich C	W	6-1	2-0	9	Porter [7], Talbot 2 [43, 62], Foyle 2 [47, 90], Mills [69]	6278
25	26	H	Manchester C	W	1-0	1-0	8	Foyle [42]	30,344
26	28	H	Portsmouth	L	0-2	0-1	9		7382
27	Jan 11	A	Grimsby T	D	1-1	0-0	10	Tankard [62]	3863
28	19	H	QPR	D	4-4	4-0	11	Glover [24], Mills [35], Jansson [41], Brazier (og) [45]	5736
29	25	A	Southend U	W	2-1	0-1	7	Guppy [56], McCarthy [84]	5588
30	28	A	Bradford C	L	0-1	0-1	—		15,186
31	Feb 1	H	WBA	D	2-2	1-1	8	Naylor 2 [23, 82]	8093
32	8	A	Barnsley	L	0-1	0-1	10		12,246
33	15	H	Ipswich T	D	2-2	2-1	10	Mills [40], Porter (pen) [43]	6115
34	23	A	Birmingham C	W	2-1	1-1	9	Porter [16], Glover [54]	13,192
35	Mar 1	H	Reading	W	1-0	1-0	7	Naylor [45]	6057
36	4	A	Sheffield U	L	0-3	0-0	—		14,950
37	8	H	Norwich C	D	1-1	1-1	8	McCarthy [26]	16,101
38	15	H	Charlton Ath	W	2-0	0-0	8	Mills 2 [54, 62]	5905
39	18	A	Bolton W	L	2-4	1-2	—	Bogie [3], Talbot [50]	14,150
40	22	H	Swindon T	W	1-0	0-0	7	Mills [52]	6142
41	31	H	Tranmere R	W	2-1	1-1	5	Mills 2 [36, 52]	7469
42	Apr 5	A	Oxford U	W	2-0	1-0	5	Mills [31], Naylor [87]	7370
43	12	H	Oldham Ath	W	3-2	1-1	5	Naylor 2 [32, 85], Mills [76]	8114
44	20	A	Stoke C	L	0-2	0-1	6		16,246
45	27	H	Wolverhampton W	L	1-2	1-2	8	Naylor [40]	13,615
46	May 4	A	Crystal Palace	D	1-1	0-1	8	Mills [61]	16,401

Final League Position: 8

GOALSCORERS

League (58): Naylor 17, Mills 13, Guppy 6, McCarthy 4, Porter 4 (1 pen), Talbot 4, Foyle 3, Glover 2, Bogie 1, Hill 1, Jansson 1, Tankard 1, own goal 1.
Coca-Cola Cup (9): Naylor 3, McCarthy 2, Mills 2, Bogie 1, Foyle 1.
FA Cup (0).

Van Heusden A 13	Hill A 36 + 2	Tankard A 37	Bogie I 28 + 3	Griffiths G 24 + 2	Aspin N 32 + 1	McCarthy J 45	Porter A 44	Foyle M 9 + 28	Naylor T 40 + 3	Guppy S 34	Mills L 22 + 13	Talbot S 25 + 9	Glover D 40 + 2	Walker R 9 + 8	Stokes D 8 + 2	Musselwhite P 33	Corden W 5 + 7	Jansson J 10 + 1	Holwyn J 5 + 2	Koordes R 7 + 6	Match No.
1	2	3	4	5	6	7	8	9^1	10	11	12										1
1	2	3	4	5	6	7	8	12	10^1	11			9								2
1	2^2	3	4^3	5	6	7	8	12	10	11			9^1	13	14						3
1		3	4	5	2	7	8	9	10	11	12		6								4
1	12		4	5^1	2	7	8	9		11	10^2	13	6			3					5
1	2		4	12	5	7	8		10	11		9	6^1	13		3^2					6
1	2	3	4	5^2	6	7	8	9	10	11^1	12	13									7
1	2	3	4^1		5	7	8	9		11	10	12	6								8
1	2	3^2	4^3		5	7	8	12	10	11		9^1	13	6	14						9
1	2	3	12		5	7	8	13	10^2	11		9	6	4							10
1	2^3	3	12	14	5	7		9^2	10	11	13	8	6	4^1							11
1	2^1	3	8^2	5	6^3	7	4	12	10	11	13		9	14							12
	2			5		7^2	8	12	10	11		9^1	3	6	4	1	13				13
	2	3		5		7	8	12	10^1	11			9	6	4	1					14
	2	3		5		7	8	12	10^1	11			9	6	4	1					15
	2	3^2		5		7	8	12	10^1	11		13	9	6	4	1					16
	2	3		5		7	8	12	10^1	11		9	6			1		4			17
	2	3		5		7	8	12	10^1	11		9	6	13		1		4^2			18
	2	3		5		7	8		10	11	12	9	6			1		4^1			19
	2^2	3		5	13	7	8	12	10	11		9^1	14	6	4^3	1					20
		3^2		5	2	7	8	12	10^1	11		9	6			1		4			21
		3		5	2	7	8		10	11		9	6			1		4			22
		3		5	2	7	8	12	10^1	11		9	6		4^2	1	13				23
		3		5	2	7	8		10^1	11	12	9	6			1		4			24
		3		5^1	2	7	8	9	10	11			6		4	1	12				25
12		3	9^2	5	2^1	7	8	13	10	11			6			1		4			26
	2	3		5^1		7	8		10	11		9	6			1		4	12		27
	5	3	12			7	8	13	10	11		9^2	6			1		4^1	2		28
	2	3		10^2		7	8	9	12	11		13	6^1			1		4		5	29
	2	3	4^2			7	8	12	10	11		9^1	6	13		1				5	30
	2		9		6	7	8	12	10^3	11	13		3	4^1		1	14	5^2			31
	2		4^2	5		7	8	12	10^1	11^3		9	13	6	3	1	14				32
	2			5		7	8	12	10^1	11		9^2	6	13	3	1					33
			4	5		7	8	12	10^1		13	9^2	6		3	1	11^3		2	14	34
	2		4^2	5		7	8	12	10^1		13	9	6		3^3	1	14			11	35
	2	3	4	5		7	8		10^1	12		9	6			1				11	36
	2	3	4	5		7	8		10		9		6			1	11^1			12	37
	2	3	4	5		7	8^2		12	10		9	6			1	13			11^1	38
	2	3	4			7	8	12	10^1		9	5	6			1	11^2			13	39
	2	3	4^2	5			8	12	10^1		9	7	6	13		1				11	40
	2	3	4	5		7	8	12	13		9^1	10^2	6			1	14			11^3	41
	2	3	4	5		7^1	8	10		9	12		6			1	13			11^2	42
	2	3	4	5		7^2	8	10		9	12		6			1	13			11^1	43
	2	3	4^2	5		7	8^3	12	10		9	13	6			1	11^1			14	44
1		3^3	8	5^2	2	7		12	10		9	4^1	6				11	13	14		45

Coca-Cola Cup

First Round	Crewe Alex	(h)	1-0	
		(a)	5-1	
Second Round	Carlisle U	(h)	1-0	
		(a)	2-2	
Third Round	Oxford U	(h)	0-0	

FA Cup

Third Round	Blackburn R	(a)	0-1

PRESTON NORTH END 1996–97 *Back row (left to right):* Steve Wilkinson, Russ Wilcox, Andy Saville, Neil McDonald, David Lucas, Teuvo Moilanen, Jamie Squires, Kevin Kilbane, Ryan Kidd, Paul Sparrow.

Middle row: Brian Hickson (Kit Manager), Alan Fogarty (Chief Scout), Gil Brooks, Raymond Sharp, Michael Holt, Mick Rathbone (Physio), Gary Bennett, Tony Grant, Allan Smart, Paul Compton (Youth Coach), Geoff McDougle (Youth Development Officer).

Front row: Mickey Brown, Kevin Gage, Lee Cartwright, Simon Davey, Steve Harrison (First Team Coach), Gary Peters (Manager), David Moyes (Assistant Manager), Ian Bryson, Dean Barrick, Graeme Atkinson, Paul McKenna.

(Photograph: K. Pearson and S. Gifford)

Division 2   **PRESTON NORTH END**

Deepdale, Preston PR1 6RU. Telephone: (01772) 902020. Fax: (01772) 653266. Ticket Enquiries: (01772) 902000. Commercial: (01772) 902001. Shop (01772) 902040.

Ground capacity: 15,295.

Record attendance: 42,684 v Arsenal, Division 1, 23 April 1938.

Record receipts: £68,650 v Sheffield W, FA Cup 3rd rd, 4 January 1992.

Pitch measurements: 110yd × 77yd.

President: Tom Finney OBE, JP.

Chairman: Bryan M. Gray.

Directors: K. W. Leeming, M. J. Woodhouse (snr), D. Shaw (Managing), T. Scholes (Finance Director/Company Secretary).

Manager: Gary Peters. *Assistant Manager:* David Moyes. *Coach:* Steve Harrison.

Secretary: Mrs Audrey Shaw.

Year Formed: 1881. *Turned Professional:* 1885. *Ltd Co.:* 1893.

Club Nicknames: 'The Lilywhites' or 'North End'.

Foundation: North End Cricket and Rugby Club which was formed in 1863, indulged in most sports before taking up soccer in about 1879. In 1881 they decided to stick to football to the exclusion of other sports and even a 16–0 drubbing by Blackburn Rovers in an invitation game at Deepdale, a few weeks after taking this decision, did not deter them for they immediately became affiliated to the Lancashire FA.

First Football League game: 8 September 1888, Football League, v Burnley (h) W 5-2 – Trainer; Howarth, Holmes; Robertson, W. Graham, J. Graham; Gordon (1), Ross (2), Goodall, Dewhurst (2), Drummond.

Record League Victory: 10–0 v Stoke, Division 1, 14 September 1889 – Trainer; Howarth, Holmes; Kelso, Russell (1), Graham; Gordon, Jimmy Ross (2), Nick Ross (3), Thomson (2), Drummond (2).

Record Cup Victory: 26–0 v Hyde, FA Cup 1st rd, 15 October 1887 – Addison; Howarth, Nick Ross; Russell (1), Thomson (5), Graham (1); Gordon (5), Jimmy Ross (8), John Goodall (1), Dewhurst (3), Drummond (2).

Record Defeat: 0–7 v Blackpool, Division 1, 1 May 1948.

Most League Points (2 for a win): 61, Division 3, 1970–71.

Most League Points (3 for a win): 90, Division 4, 1986–87.

Most League Goals: 100, Division 2, 1927–28 and Division 1, 1957–58.

Highest League Scorer in Season: Ted Harper, 37, Division 2, 1932–33.

Most League Goals in Total Aggregate: Tom Finney, 187, 1946–60.

Most Capped Player: Tom Finney, 76, England.

Most League Appearances: Alan Kelly, 447, 1961–75.

Record Transfer Fee Received: £765,000 from Manchester C for Michael Robinson, June 1979.

Record Transfer Fee Paid: £300,000 to Darlington for Sean Gregan, November 1996.

Football League Record: 1888 Founder Member of League; 1901–04 Division 2; 1904–12 Division 1; 1912–13 Division 2; 1913–14 Division 1; 1914–15 Division 2; 1919–25 Division 1; 1925–34 Division 2; 1934–49 Division 1; 1949–51 Division 2; 1951–61 Division 1; 1961–70 Division 2; 1970–71 Division 3; 1971–74 Division 2; 1974–78 Division 3; 1978–81 Division 2; 1981–85 Division 3; 1985–87 Division 4; 1987–92 Division 3; 1992–93 Division 2; 1993–96 Division 3; 1996– Division 2.

Honours: Football League: Division 1 – Champions 1888–89 (first champions), 1889–90; Runners-up 1890–91, 1891–92, 1892–93, 1905–06, 1952–53, 1957–58; Division 2 – Champions 1903–04, 1912–13, 1950–51; Runners-up 1914–15, 1933–34; Division 3 – Champions 1970–71, 1995–96; Division 4 – Runners-up 1986–87. *FA Cup:* Winners 1889, 1938; Runners-up 1888, 1922, 1937, 1954, 1964. *Double Performed:* 1888–89. *Football League Cup:* best season: 4th rd, 1963, 1966, 1972, 1981.

Colours: White and navy shirts, navy shorts, navy stockings. *Change colours:* Red/navy.

Did you know?

In the season before the foundation of the Football League in 1888, Preston North End enjoyed a run of 43 games without defeat before losing to West Bromwich Albion.

**PRESTON
NORTH
END
FC**

PRESTON NORTH END 1996–97 LEAGUE RECORD

Match No.	Date	Venue	Opponents	Result	H/T Score	Lg. Pos.	Goalscorers	Attendance
1	Aug 17	A	Notts Co	L	1-2	1-0	—	Bryson [25]	6879
2	24	H	Bristol R	D	0-0	0-0	20		9752
3	27	H	Crewe Alex	W	2-1	1-0	—	Wilkinson 2 [19, 90]	9498
4	30	A	Plymouth Arg	L	1-2	1-1	—	Wilkinson [41]	9209
5	Sept 7	A	Bristol C	L	1-2	0-1	19	Kilbane [47]	8016
6	10	H	York C	W	1-0	0-0	—	Ashcroft [46]	7608
7	14	H	Bournemouth	L	0-1	0-0	17		8268
8	21	A	Wrexham	L	0-1	0-0	21		5299
9	28	H	Millwall	W	2-1	1-0	18	Holt [4], Saville [46]	9400
10	Oct 1	A	Watford	L	0-1	0-0	—		6434
11	5	H	Peterborough U	L	3-4	0-1	21	Ashcroft 2 [50, 52], Holt [56]	8874
12	12	A	Stockport Co	L	0-1	0-1	23		8405
13	15	A	Walsall	L	0-1	0-0	—		3224
14	19	H	Shrewsbury T	W	2-1	0-0	22	Seabury (og) [47], Reeves [74]	8333
15	26	A	Gillingham	D	1-1	1-1	21	Kilbane [15]	6256
16	29	H	Burnley	D	1-1	1-0	—	Reeves [26]	12,652
17	Nov 2	H	Rotherham U	D	0-0	0-0	21		8997
18	9	A	Chesterfield	L	1-2	1-0	22	Reeves [31]	4759
19	19	H	Luton T	W	3-2	2-1	—	Moyes 2 [35, 40], Ashcroft [88]	7004
20	23	A	Wycombe W	W	1-0	0-0	17	Ashcroft (pen) [52]	4920
21	30	A	Gillingham	W	1-0	0-0	15	Davey [88]	9616
22	Dec 3	A	Bury	L	0-3	0-1	—		5447
23	13	H	Blackpool	W	3-0	0-0	—	Bennett 2 [71, 78], Reeves [74]	14,626
24	21	A	Brentford	D	0-0	0-0	14		5365
25	28	H	Bristol C	L	0-2	0-1	16		10,905
26	Jan 11	A	Millwall	L	2-3	2-1	18	Davey 2 (1 pen) [24, 36 (p)]	7096
27	18	H	Watford	D	1-1	1-1	18	Bennett [13]	8735
28	25	A	Burnley	W	2-1	1-1	16	Ashcroft 2 [6, 69]	16,186
29	Feb 1	H	Chesterfield	L	0-1	0-0	17		8681
30	8	A	Rotherham U	W	1-0	1-0	17	Reeves [35]	3556
31	11	A	Bournemouth	L	0-2	0-1	—		4769
32	15	H	Wycombe W	W	2-1	1-1	16	McKenna [15], Davey [82]	7923
33	22	A	Luton T	L	1-5	0-4	18	Reeves [47]	6454
34	25	A	York C	L	1-3	0-0	—	Cartwright [54]	2515
35	Mar 1	H	Bury	W	3-1	0-1	15	Moyes [52], Reeves [66], Stallard [76]	8749
36	8	H	Brentford	W	1-0	0-0	14	Bryson [69]	9489
37	15	A	Blackpool	L	1-2	1-0	16	Davey [44]	8017
38	18	H	Wrexham	W	2-1	1-1	—	Reeves [21], Ashcroft [60]	8271
39	23	A	Bristol R	L	0-1	0-0	15		6405
40	29	H	Notts Co	W	2-0	1-0	16	Reeves [33], Moyes [65]	9472
41	31	A	Crewe Alex	L	0-1	0-1	16		4407
42	Apr 5	H	Plymouth Arg	D	1-1	1-1	16	Reeves [18]	8503
43	12	A	Peterborough U	L	0-2	0-0	17		5040
44	19	H	Stockport Co	W	1-0	0-0	17	Bryson [79]	10,298
45	26	A	Shrewsbury T	W	2-0	0-0	16	Gregan [67], Davey [90]	5341
46	May 3	H	Walsall	W	2-0	1-0	15	Holt [2], Reeves [72]	10,800

Final League Position: 15

GOALSCORERS

League (49): Reeves 11, Ashcroft 8 (1 pen), Davey 6 (1 pen), Moyes 4, Bennett 3, Bryson 3, Holt 3, Wilkinson 3, Kilbane 2, Cartwright 1, Gregan 1, McKenna 1, Saville 1, Stallard 1, own goal 1.
Coca-Cola Cup (8): Wilkinson 4, Atkinson 1, Davey 1, Holt 1, McDonald 1.
FA Cup (6): Ashcroft 3 (1 pen), Reeves 3.

Rothmans Football Yearbook 1997–98 — page 293

Moilanen T 4	Gage K 16	Barrick D 30+6	Atkinson G 12+5	Wilcox R 35	Kidd R 33+2	Davey S 30+7	Bryson I 32+9	Saville A 12	Wilkinson S 8+2	Kilbane K 32+4	Squires J 6+3	Holt M 8+11	Kay J 7	Moyes D 26	Brown M 5+1	McDonald N 12+10	Mimms B 27	Ashcroft L 26+1	Rankine M 19+4	Bennett G 10+6	Patterson D 2	Reeves D 33+1	Sparrow P 6	Gregan S 21	Beckford D —+2	McKenna P 4+1	O'Hanlon K 13	Cartwright L 14	Teale S 5	Stallard M 4	Nogan K 5+2	Jackson M 7	Lucas D 2	Match No.
1	2¹	3	4	5	6	7	8	9	10	11¹²	12	13																						1
1		3	4²	5		7	8	9	10	11¹				2	6	12	13																	2
1		3	4¹	5		7	8	9	10	11				2	6	12																		3
1		3	4¹	5		7	8	9	10	11				2	6	12																		4
		3	12	5²	13	7	14	9	10	11³				2	6		1	4¹		8														5
		3	10	5		7	12	9		11				2	6		1	4¹		8														6
		3	10¹	5		7	12	9		11		13		2	6		1	4²		8														7
		3	12	5	6	7		9		11		10		2			1	4¹		8														8
		3	12	5	6	7	8	9		11				2		10¹	1	4																9
		3	12	5	6	7	8	9		11¹				2		10²	1	4	13															10
		3	12	5	6	7	8	9				13		2²			1	4	11¹	10														11
	2	3		5	6¹	7	12	9		11²							1	4	13	8		10												12
	2	3		5	6		8			11						7	1	4	10			9												13
	2	3		5	6	12	8			11		13				7¹	1	4	10²			9												14
	2	3		5	6		8			11	12					7	1	4	10¹			9												15
	2	3		5	6		8¹			11	12	13				7	1	4	10²			9												16
	2	3		5	6		8			11	12	13	14			7³	1	4	10²			9												17
		3²	12	5	6		8		10	11		13				7	1	4¹				9	2											18
		3	12	5	6		8		10¹	11						7	1	4				9	2											19
		3	12	5¹	6		8		10²	11		13				7	1	4				9	2											20
		3²	12	5	6		8		10³	11		13	14			7	1	4¹				9	2											21
		3¹	12	5	6		8		10³	11		13	14			7	1	4²				9	2											22
	2	3	10¹	5			8			11	12				6	7	1	4				9												23
		3	12	5			8			11		13			6	7¹	1	4		10²		9	2											24
	2¹	3²	12	5			8			11		13			6	7	1	4		10		9												25
		3²	12	5		7	8			11¹		13	14		6		1	4		10³		9	2											26
	2	3		5		7	8			11²					6		1	4	10¹			9		12	13									27
		3		5		7	8		10	11					6		1	4				9¹	2	12										28
		3²		5		7	8¹		10	11	12				6		1	4				9	2		13									29
		3	12	5		7²	8			11		13	14				1	4	10²			9		6			1	2¹						30
		3¹	12			7	8			11		13							10²			9		6		5	1	2				4		31
		3¹	12			7	8			11²		13										9		6		5	1	2			10	4		32
		3²	12			7	8					13										9		6		5¹	1	2	11		10	4		33
	2	3	12			7	8											4				9		6		5	1		11	10¹		4		34
	2	3				7	8											4				9		6		5	1		11		10	4		35
	2	3				7	8											4				9		6		5	1		11		10	4		36
	2	3	12			7	8											4				9		6	13	5¹	1		11²		10	4		37
	2	3	12			7	8¹											4				9		6		5	1		11		10	4		38
	2¹	3	12			7	8											4				9		6		5	1		11		10	4		39
	2	3				7²	8															9		6		5	1		11¹	7	10	4		40
	2	3	12			7²	8															9		6	13	5	1		11¹		10	4		41
		3	12			7	8															9		6		5	1	2	11		10¹	4		42
		3	12			7³	8					13										9		6	14	5¹	1	2	11²		10	4		43
		3				7¹	8²															9		6	13	5	1	2	11		10	4		44
		3	12			7²	8¹															9		6	13	5		2	11		10	4	1	45
		3	12			7	8															9		6		5		2	11		10¹	4	1	46

Coca-Cola Cup

First Round	Wigan Ath	(a)	3-2
		(h)	4-4
Second Round	Tottenham H	(h)	1-1
		(a)	0-3

FA Cup

First Round	Altrincham	(h)	4-1
Second Round	York C	(h)	2-3

QUEENS PARK RANGERS 1996-97   Back row (left to right): Paul Murray, Trevor Challis, Andrew McDermott, Chris Plummer, Mark Hateley, Karl Ready, Daniele Dichio, Mark Perry, Nigel Quashie, Steve Slade.

Middle row: John Nolan (Kit Man), Danny Maddix, Michael Mahoney-Johnson, David Bardsley, Richard Hurst, Juergen Sommer, Tony Roberts, Steve Yates, Lee Charles, Kevin Gallen, Brian Morris (Physio).

Front row: John Hollins (Reserve Team Manager), Mark Graham, Paul Bruce, Andrew Impey, Matthew Brazier, Bruce Rioch (Assistant Manager), Alan McDonald, Stewart Houston (Manager), Simon Barker, Trevor Sinclair, John Spencer, Rufus Brevett, Warren Neill (Youth Team Manager).

(Photograph: Action Images)

Division 1   **QUEENS PARK RANGERS**

South Africa Road, London W12 7PA. Telephone: (0181) 743 0262. Fax: (0181) 749 0994. Box office: (0181) 740 0503. Supporters Club: (0181) 740 2534. Club Shop: (0181) 749 6862. Marketing: (0181) 740 2514. Ticket Master: (0171) 344 9494.

Ground capacity: 19,148.

Record attendance: 35,353 v Leeds U, Division 1, 27 April 1974.

Record receipts: £218,475 v Manchester U, FA Premier League, 5 February 1994.

Pitch measurements: 112yd × 72yd.

Chairman: Chris Wright. *Chief Executive:* Clive Berlin.

Executive Directors: Alan Hedges, Paul Hart. *Non-Executive Directors:* Nick Blackburn, Sir Terence Burns GCB, Peter Ellis (club).

Manager: Stewart Houston. *Assistant Manager:* Bruce Rioch.

Secretary: Sheila Marson. *Sales and Marketing Executive:* Brian Rowe.

Reserve Team Manager: John Hollins MBE.

Physio: Brian Morris.

Year Formed: 1885 *(see Foundation).* **Turned Professional:** 1898. *Ltd Co.:* 1899.

Club Nicknames: 'Rangers' or 'Rs'. *Previous Name:* 1885–87, St Jude's.

Previous Grounds: 1885 *(see Foundation),* Welford's Fields; 1888–99; London Scottish Ground, Brondesbury, Home Farm, Kensal Rise Green, Gun Club Wormwood Scrubs, Kilburn Cricket Ground; 1899, Kensal Rise Athletic Ground; 1901, Latimer Road, Notting Hill; 1904, Agricultural Society, Park Royal; 1907, Park Royal Ground; 1917, Loftus Road; 1931, White City; 1933, Loftus Road; 1962, White City; 1963, Loftus Road.

Foundation: There is an element of doubt about the date of the foundation of this club, but it is believed that in either 1885 or 1886 it was formed through the amalgamation of Christchurch Rangers and St. Jude's Institute FC. The leading light was George Wodehouse, whose family maintained a connection with the club until comparatively recent times. Most of the players came from the Queen's Park district so this name was adopted after a year as St. Jude's Institute.

First Football League game: 28 August 1920, Division 3, v Watford (h) L 1-2 – Price; Blackman, Wingrove; McGovern, Grant, O'Brien; Faulkner, Birch (1), Smith, Gregory, Middlemiss.

Record League Victory: 9–2 v Tranmere R, Division 3, 3 December 1960 – Drinkwater; Woods, Ingham; Keen, Rutter, Angell; Lazarus (2), Bedford (2), Evans (2), Andrews (1), Clark (2).

Record Cup Victory: 8–1 v Bristol R (away), FA Cup 1st rd, 27 November 1937 – Gilfillan; Smith, Jefferson; Lowe, James, March; Cape, Mallett, Cheetham (3), Fitzgerald (3) Bott (2). 8–1 v Crewe Alex, Milk Cup 1st rd, 3 October 1983 – Hucker; Neill, Dawes, Waddock (1), McDonald (1), Fenwick, Micklewhite (1), Stewart (1), Allen (1), Stainrod (3), Gregory.

Record Defeat: 1–8 v Mansfield T, Division 3, 15 March 1965 and v Manchester U, Division 1, 19 March 1969.

Most League Points (2 for a win): 67, Division 3, 1966–67.

Most League Points (3 for a win): 85, Division 2, 1982–83.

Most League Goals: 111, Division 3, 1961–62.

Highest League Scorer in Season: George Goddard, 37, Division 3 (S), 1929–30.

Most League Goals in Total Aggregate: George Goddard, 172, 1926–34.

Most Capped Player: Alan McDonald, 52, Northern Ireland.

Most League Appearances: Tony Ingham, 519, 1950–63.

Record Transfer Fee Received: £6,000,000 from Newcastle U for Les Ferdinand, June 1995.

Record Transfer Fee Paid: £2,350,000 to Chelsea for John Spencer, November 1996.

Football League Record: 1920 Original Members of Division 3; 1921–48 Division 3 (S); 1948–52 Division 2; 1952–58 Division 3 (S); 1958–67 Division 3; 1967–68 Division 2; 1968–69 Division 1; 1969–73 Division 2; 1973–79 Division 1; 1979–83 Division 2; 1983–92 Division 1; 1992–96 FA Premier League; 1996– Division 1.

Honours: Football League: Division 1 – Runners-up 1975–76; Division 2 – Champions 1982–83; Runners-up 1967–68, 1972–73; Division 3 (S) – Champions 1947–48; Runners-up 1946–47; Division 3 – Champions 1966–67. *FA Cup:* Runners-up 1982. *Football League Cup:* Winners 1967; Runners-up 1986. (In 1966–67 won Division 3 and Football League Cup). **European Competitions:** *UEFA Cup:* 1976–77, 1984–85.

Colours: Blue and white hooped shirts, white shorts, white stockings. *Change colours:* All red with black trim.

Did you know?
Brian Bedford, a £750 signing from Bournemouth, was top scorer for Queens Park Rangers in each of six consecutive seasons from 1959–60 to 1964–65.

QUEENS PARK RANGERS 1996–97 LEAGUE RECORD

Match No.	Date	Venue	Opponents	Result	H/T Score	Lg. Pos.	Goalscorers	Attendance
1	Aug 17	H	Oxford U	W 2-1	0-1	—	Gallen [60], Dichio [79]	14,703
2	23	A	Portsmouth	W 2-1	1-0	—	Gallen 2 [7, 77]	7501
3	28	A	Wolverhampton W	D 1-1	1-1	—	Dichio [41]	25,767
4	Sept 1	H	Bolton W	L 1-2	0-1	6	McDonald [79]	11,225
5	7	H	WBA	L 0-2	0-1	10		12,886
6	11	A	Norwich C	D 1-1	0-1	—	Impey [81]	14,000
7	14	A	Barnsley	W 3-1	2-0	6	Barker [6], Perry [41], Dichio [50]	13,003
8	21	H	Swindon T	D 1-1	1-1	9	Murray [27]	13,662
9	28	A	Birmingham C	D 0-0	0-0	12		17,430
10	Oct 2	A	Port Vale	L 1-2	0-0	—	Barker [79]	8727
11	5	A	Grimsby T	L 0-2	0-2	13		5472
12	12	H	Manchester C	D 2-2	2-1	12	Sinclair [22], Murray [30]	16,265
13	16	H	Bradford C	W 1-0	0-0	—	Brazier [90]	7776
14	20	A	Tranmere R	W 3-2	1-1	8	Slade [9], McDonald [67], Charles [85]	7025
15	26	A	Sheffield U	D 1-1	1-0	9	Slade [18]	17,096
16	30	H	Ipswich T	L 0-1	0-0	—		10,562
17	Nov 2	A	Stoke C	D 1-1	0-1	11	Sinclair [65]	7354
18	10	A	Crystal Palace	L 0-3	0-1	12		15,324
19	16	H	Charlton Ath	L 1-2	1-1	15	Sinclair [12]	12,360
20	23	A	Reading	L 1-2	0-0	19	Spencer [49]	12,847
21	30	A	Sheffield U	W 1-0	1-0	14	Barker (pen) [36]	11,891
22	Dec 7	A	Oldham Ath	W 2-0	0-0	14	Peacock [80], Spencer [89]	5590
23	14	H	Southend U	W 4-0	2-0	11	Barker (pen) [40], Harris (og) [44], Spencer [50], Peacock [68]	11,117
24	21	A	Huddersfield T	W 2-1	1-0	7	Dichio [45], Brazier [50]	10,718
25	26	H	Norwich C	W 3-2	2-1	6	Peacock [22], Dichio [40], McDermott [85]	15,699
26	28	A	WBA	L 1-4	0-1	7	Spencer [65]	19,061
27	Jan 11	H	Barnsley	W 3-1	1-1	6	Spencer 3 [45, 55, 90]	12,058
28	19	A	Port Vale	D 4-4	0-4	7	Holwyn (og) [66], Impey [85], Murray [88], Spencer [90]	5736
29	29	H	Birmingham C	D 1-1	0-1	—	Spencer [59]	12,138
30	Feb 1	H	Crystal Palace	L 0-1	0-1	10		16,467
31	5	A	Swindon T	D 1-1	1-1	—	Hateley [40]	10,830
32	8	A	Ipswich T	L 0-2	0-1	8		12,983
33	22	A	Stoke C	D 0-0	0-0	12		13,121
34	Mar 1	H	Oldham Ath	L 0-1	0-1	13		10,180
35	4	A	Charlton Ath	L 1-2	1-2	—	Dichio [3]	10,610
36	8	H	Huddersfield T	W 2-0	1-0	13	McDermott [4], Spencer [47]	9789
37	12	H	Reading	L 0-2	0-1	—		10,316
38	15	A	Southend U	W 1-0	0-0	13	Roget (og) [82]	6747
39	22	A	Portsmouth	W 2-1	1-1	11	Murray [45], Spencer [77]	15,746
40	29	A	Oxford U	W 3-2	3-2	12	Yates [21], Spencer [28], Peacock [41]	8365
41	31	H	Wolverhampton W	D 2-2	2-1	10	Spencer [13], Peacock [27]	17,376
42	Apr 5	A	Bolton W	L 1-2	1-1	12	Morrow [13]	19,198
43	12	H	Grimsby T	W 3-0	1-0	11	Spencer [45], Murray [79], Slade [90]	10,765
44	19	A	Manchester C	W 3-0	0-0	9	Spencer 2 [49, 53], Slade [76]	27,580
45	26	H	Tranmere R	W 2-0	0-0	7	Dichio [55], Spencer [77]	14,859
46	May 4	A	Bradford C	L 0-3	0-2	9		14,723

Final League Position: 9

GOALSCORERS

League (64): Spencer 17, Dichio 7, Murray 5, Peacock 5, Barker 4 (2 pens), Slade 4, Gallen 3, Sinclair 3, Brazier 2, Impey 2, McDermott 2, McDonald 2, Charles 1, Hateley 1, Morrow 1, Perry 1, Yates 1, own goals 3.
Coca-Cola Cup (3): Brazier 1, Dichio 1, Impey 1.
FA Cup (7): Hateley 2, Peacock 2, McDonald 1, Sinclair 1, Spencer 1.

Sommer J 33	Ready K 28+1	Brevett R 44	Barker S 38	McDonald A 38+1	Yates S 16	Brazier M 22+5	Wilkins R 4	Hateley M 8+5	Gallen K 2	Sinclair T 39	Dichio D 31+6	Jackson M 7	Impey A 26+6	Murray P 26+6	Maddix D 18+7	Slade S 11+6	Quashie N 9+4	Challis T 2	Charles L 6+6	Perry M 2	Plummer C 4+1	Graham M 16+2	Mahoney-Johnson M —+2	Roberts T 13	Spencer J 25	Peacock G 27	McDermott A 6	Morrow S 5	Match No.
1	2	3	4	5	6	7	8	9¹	10	11	12																		1
1		3	4	5	6		8		10²	11	9	2	7¹	12	13														2
1		3	4	5	6		8¹			11	9	2	7	12	10														3
1		3		5	6	10	8¹			11	9	2	7		12	4													4
1		3		5¹	6					11	9	2	4²	12	10	8	7	13											5
1		3	4	5	6					11	9	2	10	12		8	7¹												6
1		3	4	5	6¹	13				11	9	2	10	7	12²							8							7
1		3	4	5		7				11	9	2	10	8							6¹	12							8
1		3	4	5		7				11	9		8			10					6	2							9
1		3	4	5		7				11	9					10		8¹	6	2	12								10
1	2	3	4	5		7				11	9	10²		12						6¹	8	13							11
1	2	3	4	5		12				11		10	6		9²	7¹	13		8										12
1	6	3	4	5		7				11		8	10		9		2												13
1	6	3	4	5		7				11	9²	8	10¹	12	13	2													14
1	6	3	4	5		7	12	11	9¹		8	10²			13	2													15
1	6	3	4	5		7	9	11		12	8	10¹			2														16
1	6	3	4	5		7¹		11	9	12	8	10			2														17
1	6	3	4	5				11	9	7	8	10¹			2														18
1	6	3	4¹	5		12		11	9²	7	8	10			13	2													19
	6	3	4	5				11	12	10	2			9¹							1	7	8		20				20
	6	3	4¹	5				11	13	10	12			9²		2				1	7	8		21					21
	6	3	4	5	10			11	12					9¹		2				1	7	8		22					22
	6	3	4	5	10	12		11	9											1	7¹	8	2	23					23
	6	3	4	5	10			11	9											1	7	8	2	24					24
	6	3	4	5²	10¹			11	9	12		13								1	7	8	2	25					25
	6	3	4		10			11¹	9	12	5									1	7	8	2	26					26
	6	3		5	10	9¹		11²	12	13	4³	14					2			1	7	8		27					27
	6	3		5	10²	9¹		11	12	13	4	14					2³			1	7	8		28					28
1		3		5	10			11	9		2	4	6									7	8	29					29
1		3	7	5	10	12		11	9¹		2	4	6										8	30					30
1	6	3	10	5				9			2		4									7	8	31					31
1	6	3¹⁰	10	5	4	12		9													2	7	8	32					32
1	6	3	4	5	2			9	11	10¹		7					12					8	33						33
1	6	3	4¹	5		12		9	11			10	2									8	7	34					34
1	6	3²	4	5				12	11	9¹	10	13	2									7	8	35					35
1	6		4		3			11	10	5			9									7	8	2	36					36
1	6		4	12	3¹	13		11	10	5			9²									7	8	2	37					37
1	6	3	4	5				11	9	10	2											7	8	38					38
1	6	3	4	5				11¹	9	10	12	2										7	8	39					39
1		3	4	5	6			9	10	11	2											7	8	40					40
1		3	4²	5	6			9¹	10	11	2	13	12									7	8	41					41
1		3	4¹	5				9²	10	11	2	13	12									7	8		6	42				42
		3	4²	5				9³	10	11	2	12	13				14		1	7	8¹		6	43					43
		3		5				9¹	10	11	2	12	4						1	7	8		6	44					44
		3		5				9¹	10	11	2	12	4						1	7	8		6	45					45
	12	3		5¹					10	11	2	9	4						1	7	8		6	46					46

Coca-Cola Cup

Second Round	Swindon T	(a)	2-1
		(h)	1-3

FA Cup

Third Round	Huddersfield T	(h)	1-1
		(a)	2-1
Fourth Round	Barnsley	(h)	3-2
Fifth Round	Wimbledon	(a)	1-2

READING 1996–97 *Back row (left to right)*: Ron Grant (Kit Man), Trevor Morley, Phil Parkinson, Michael Thorp, Paul Holsgrove, Stuart Lovell, Jimmy Garrity, Jeff Hopkins, Andrew Robertson, Lee Nogan, Richard Hill (Coach).

Middle row: Paul Turner (Physio), Martin Williams, Andy Bernal, Paul Bodin, Dariusz Wdowczyk, Salvatore Bibbo, Bobby Mihailov, Michael Meaker, David Bass, Keith McPherson, Guy Sanders, Steve Kean (Youth Team Coach).

Front row: Darren Caskey, Michael Gilkes, Martyn Booty, Steven Swales, Mick Gooding (Joint Player/Manager), Barry Hunter, Jimmy Quinn (Joint Player/Manager), Derek Simpson, Andrew Freeman, Alan Carey, James Lambert.

Division 1 READING

Elm Park, Norfolk Road, Reading RG30 2EF. Telephone: (01189) 507878. Fax: (01189) 566628. Community Office: (01189) 560898. Promotions Office: (01189) 464008.

Ground capacity: 15,000.

Record attendance: 33,042 v Brentford, FA Cup 5th rd, 19 February 1927.

Record receipts: £110,741 v Manchester U, FA Cup 4th rd, 27 January 1996.

Pitch measurements: 112yd × 77yd.

President: F. Orton.

Chairman: John Madejski.

Director: I. Wood-Smith.

Manager: Terry Bullivant.

Chief Executive: Nigel Howe.

Youth Coach: Steve Kean.

Scout: Kevin Dillon.

Physio: Paul Turner.

Commercial Manager: Kevin Girdler.

Secretary: Ms Andrea Barker.

Year Formed: 1871. *Turned Professional:* 1895. *Ltd Co.:* 1895.

Club Nickname: 'The Royals'.

Previous Grounds: 1871, Reading Recreation; Reading Cricket Ground; 1882, Coley Park; 1889, Caversham Cricket Ground; 1896, Elm Park.

Foundation: Reading was formed as far back as 1871 at a public meeting held at the Bridge Street Rooms. They first entered the FA Cup as early as 1877 when they amalgamated with the Reading Hornets. The club was further strengthened in 1889 when Earley FC joined them. They were the first winners of the Berks and Bucks Cup in 1878–79.

First Football League game: 28 August 1920, Division 3, v Newport Co (a) W 1-0 – Crawford; Smith, Horler; Christie, Mavin, Getgood; Spence, Weston, Yarnell, Bailey (1), Andrews.

Record League Victory: 10–2 v Crystal Palace, Division 3 (S), 4 September 1946 – Groves; Glidden, Gulliver; McKenna, Ratcliffe, Young; Chitty, Maurice Edelston (3), McPhee (4), Barney (1), Deverell (2).

Record Cup Victory: 6–0 v Leyton, FA Cup 2nd rd, 12 December 1925 – Duckworth; Eggo, McConnell; Wilson, Messer, Evans; Smith (2), Braithwaite (1), Davey (1), Tinsley, Robson (2).

Record Defeat: 0–18 v Preston NE, FA Cup 1st rd, 1893–94.

Most League Points (2 for a win): 65, Division 4, 1978–79.

Most League Points (3 for a win): 94, Division 3, 1985–86.

Most League Goals: 112, Division 3 (S), 1951–52.

Highest League Scorer in Season: Ronnie Blackman, 39, Division 3 (S), 1951–52.

Most League Goals in Total Aggregate: Ronnie Blackman, 158, 1947–54.

Most Capped Player: Jimmy Quinn, 17 (46), Northern Ireland.

Most League Appearances: Martin Hicks, 500, 1978–91.

Record Transfer Fee Received: £1,575,000 from Newcastle U for Shaka Hislop, August 1995.

Record Transfer Fee Paid: £700,000 to Tottenham H for Darren Caskey, February 1996.

Football League Record: 1920 Original Member of Division 3; 1921–26 Division 3 (S); 1926–31 Division 2; 1931–58 Division 3 (S); 1958–71 Division 3; 1971–76 Division 4; 1976–77 Division 3; 1977–79 Division 4; 1979–83 Division 3; 1983–84 Division 4; 1984–86 Division 3; 1986–88 Division 2; 1988–92 Division 3; 1992–94 Division 2; 1994– Division 1.

Honours: Football League: Division 1 – Runners-up 1994–95; Division 2 – Champions 1993–94; Division 3 – Champions 1985–86. Division 3 (S) – Champions 1925–26; Runners-up 1931–32, 1934–35, 1948–49, 1951–52; Division 4 – Champions 1978–79. *FA Cup:* Semi-final 1927. *Football League Cup:* best season: 5th rd. 1996. *Simod Cup:* Winners 1988.

Colours: Royal blue and white hooped shirts, white shorts, white and blue hooped stockings.
Change colours: Toro red and white shirts, Toro red shorts, Toro red/white stockings.

Did you know?
Reading completed 55 consecutive home League games without suffering a defeat between April 1933 and January 1936.

READING 1996–97 LEAGUE RECORD

Match No.	Date	Venue	Opponents	Result	H/T Score	Lg. Pos.	Goalscorers	Attendance
1	Aug 17	H	Sheffield U	W 1-0	0-0	—	Quinn [82]	11,081
2	24	A	Ipswich T	L 2-5	1-2	14	Nogan [28], Hunter [62]	9767
3	28	A	Barnsley	L 0-3	0-2	—		7523
4	31	H	Stoke C	D 2-2	1-1	15	Morley (pen) [7], Holsgrove [79]	8414
5	Sept 8	H	Oxford U	W 2-0	1-0	8	Williams [14], Morley [83]	8099
6	10	A	WBA	L 2-3	1-2	—	Morley (pen) [4], Parkinson [75]	13,096
7	14	A	Charlton Ath	L 0-1	0-1	18		10,831
8	21	H	Crystal Palace	L 1-6	0-2	19	Morley (pen) [69]	9675
9	28	A	Huddersfield T	L 0-1	0-1	21		10,330
10	Oct 5	A	Wolverhampton W	W 1-0	0-0	20	Lambert [69]	23,193
11	12	H	Grimsby T	D 1-1	0-0	20	Morley (pen) [57]	6656
12	15	H	Manchester C	W 2-0	1-0	—	Nogan 2 [35, 67]	11,724
13	19	A	Oldham Ath	D 1-1	0-0	18	Quinn (pen) [75]	7171
14	26	H	Swindon T	W 2-0	0-0	13	Morley 2 (1 pen) [51 (p), 60]	11,018
15	29	A	Bolton W	L 1-2	0-1	—	Lambert [51]	12,677
16	Nov 2	A	Southend U	L 1-2	0-0	19	Nogan [50]	5002
17	16	A	Norwich C	D 1-1	0-0	20	Morley [56]	14,412
18	23	H	QPR	W 2-1	0-0	20	Morley [73], Nogan [80]	12,847
19	26	H	Birmingham C	D 0-0	0-0	—		8407
20	30	A	Swindon T	L 1-3	1-2	21	Morley [13]	10,874
21	Dec 3	H	Tranmere R	W 2-0	2-0	—	Lambert [10], Morley [33]	5513
22	7	L	Port Vale	L 0-1	0-0	19		6445
23	17	A	Bradford C	D 0-0	0-0	—		10,077
24	21	H	Portsmouth	D 0-0	0-0	19		8520
25	26	H	WBA	D 2-2	1-2	19	Nogan [8], Quinn [73]	10,583
26	28	A	Oxford U	L 1-2	0-1	19	Morley [89]	9223
27	Jan 11	H	Charlton Ath	D 2-2	1-0	19	Williams [26], Lambert [74]	7614
28	18	H	Birmingham C	L 1-4	0-1	19	Holsgrove [51]	15,363
29	28	H	Huddersfield T	W 4-1	3-1	—	Morley [13], McPherson [15], Hunter [30], Lovell [82]	5710
30	Feb 1	A	Tranmere R	D 2-2	1-1	19	Morley 2 [21, 47]	6019
31	8	H	Bolton W	W 3-2	0-0	19	Morley 3 (1 pen) [56, 62 (p), 70]	10,739
32	22	H	Southend U	W 3-2	1-0	17	McPherson [33], Gilkes [60], Morley [76]	7683
33	Mar 1	A	Port Vale	L 0-1	0-1	18		6057
34	4	H	Norwich C	W 2-1	1-1	—	Morley [20], Adams (og) [86]	8174
35	12	A	QPR	W 2-0	1-0	—	Morley [2], Maddix (og) [76]	10,316
36	15	H	Bradford C	D 0-0	0-0	15		8435
37	22	H	Ipswich T	W 1-0	0-0	16	Lovell [90]	10,058
38	25	A	Portsmouth	L 0-1	0-0	—		9248
39	29	A	Sheffield U	L 0-2	0-1	16		15,153
40	31	H	Barnsley	L 1-2	1-2	17	Morley (pen) [27]	10,244
41	Apr 5	A	Stoke C	D 1-1	1-0	17	Lambert [1]	9961
42	12	H	Wolverhampton W	W 2-1	0-0	16	Lovell 2 [90, 90]	14,853
43	19	A	Grimsby T	L 0-2	0-1	18		4392
44	23	A	Crystal Palace	L 2-3	0-1	—	Bodin [57], Williams [82]	12,552
45	26	H	Oldham Ath	W 2-0	1-0	17	Roach [28], Lovell [81]	8301
46	May 3	A	Manchester C	L 2-3	2-1	18	Meaker 2 [2], Symons (og) [33]	27,260

Final League Position: 18

GOALSCORERS

League (58): Morley 22 (7 pens), Nogan 6, Lambert 5, Lovell 5, Quinn 3 (1 pen), Williams 3, Holsgrove 2, Hunter 2, McPherson 2, Bodin 1, Gilkes 1, Meaker 1, Parkinson 1, Roach 1, own goals 3.
Coca-Cola Cup (1): Quinn 1.
FA Cup (3): Caskey 1, Lambert 1, Morley 1 (pen).

Mikhailov B 8	Booty M 14	Bodin P 37	Bernal A 41	Hunter B 26 + 1	Wdowczyk D 8	Williams M 21 + 8	Caskey D 26 + 9	Quinn J 10 + 14	Lovell S 17 + 9	Gooding M 40 + 3	Gilkes M 27 + 5	Nogan L 21 + 11	Parkinson P 15 + 9	Meaker M 15 + 10	Bibbo S 5	Hopkins J 17 + 1	Morley T 36 + 1	Holsgrove P 12 + 2	Hammond N 1	Brown K 5	McPherson K 39	Lambert J 20 + 11	Wright T 17	Swales S 3	Bass D — + 2	Mautone S 15	Blatherwick S 6 + 1	Glasgow B 2 + 2	Roach N 2 + 1	Smith B — + 1	Match No
1	2	3	4	5	6	7[1]	8[3]	9	10[2]	11	12	13	14																		1
1	2	3[1]	4	5	6		8[3]	9	13	11	12	10[2]	7	14																	2
	2[2]	3[1]	4		6		8	9		11		10	7	12	1	5	13														3
	2	3			6		8			11	12	13	10[1]	7[2]	1	5	9	4													4
		3	2		6		8[2]	13	12	11[3]	7	10	14		1	5	9[1]	4													5
		3	2		6[1]		8[2]	7	12	10	9[2]	14	13	11				4	1	5											6
1		3		5			12	10	7	13	8[1]	11		9[2]			4				2	6									7
1		3		5			10	12	7[1]	13	8[2]	11[3]		9			4				2	6	14								8
1		3	4	5	6	7[2]			13	11		10[1]		12			9				2	8									9
		3	4		6[1]	10[2]	12		11	7	14		13			9					2	5	8[3]	1							10
	2[1]	3		5		12	10		11	7					6	9					4	8	1								11
		3	2[1]	5				11	7	10	12				6	9					4	8	1								12
		3	2	5			12	11	7	10	13				6	9[2]					4	8[1]	1								13
		3	2	5		12		11	7	10					6	9					4	8[1]	1								14
		3	2	5			9[2]	13	11	7	10[1]	12	14		6						4[3]	8	1								15
		3	2	5		12	13	11	7	10					6	9					4[1]	8[2]	1								16
		3	2	5		12	8	11	7	10[2]	6	13			9[1]						4		1								17
		3	2[1]	5		8[2]		11	7	10	12	6			9						4	13	1								18
		3	2	5		8	12	11[2]	7[3]	10	13	6			9[1]						4	14	1								19
		3	2			8	12	13	7[1]	10[2]	6[3]	11		5	9						4	14	1								20
		3	4	5		8			10	11						9					6	7	1	2							21
		3	4[2]	5		8			10[1]	11	12					9					6	7	1	2	13						22
		3[1]	2	5		8			10	11	7					9					6	12	1	2							23
		3	4	5		2			10[1]	11	7	12				9					6	8[2]	1		13						24
		3[1]	2	5		8	4	12		11	7	10				9					6		1								25
	2	3	7			8	4	12		11	13	10[1]				9	5[2]				6		1								26
1	2		7			8	4			11	3					9					5	6	10								27
1	2		7	12		8[3]	4	13	14	11	3					9					5	6[1]	10[2]								28
	2	3	4[2]	5		12	13			10	8	7			1	9					6	11[1]									29
	2	3	4	5		12	11	13	10[2]	8			7[1]	1		9					6										30
1[2]	2	3[1]	4	5			11	13	10	12	14		7			9					6	8[3]									31
	2[1]	3	4	5			11		10[2]	12	7		8			9					6	13					1				32
			2	5			11	12	10[1]	4	7[3]		3[2]	8	13	9					6	14				1					33
		3[1]	2	5		13	11	10[2]		4	7	12		8		9					6					1					34
			2	5			11	10		4	7		3	8[1]		9					6	12				1					35
			2				11	10[1]	12	4	7		3	8[2]	5	9					6	13				1					36
			2			12	11[3]		10	4	7[2]	13	14	5		9	3				6	8[1]				1					37
			2			8[1]	11[2]		10	4	7	12	3		5	9	13				6					1					38
	11		2			8[1]			12	4			10	3	5	9	7				6					1					39
	11		2			8[1]	13	12	14	4		10	3[2]		9[3]	7					6					1	5				40
		3	2			8[1]		9[2]	14	11	10[2]	4	12	13		6	7									1	5				41
			2			12	13	9[3]	10	11	4[2]	8		3		6	7[1]									1	5	14			42
	2					9	4	10	11[3]	12	8[2]	3		6	7[1]											1	5	13	14		43
	2[1]	7	5			12	4	10	11	9[3]	3	8[2]		6	13											1	14				44
		3	5			7	12	10	11[1]	13	14	6	8[3]										1	2	4[2]	9					45
		3	2			8	11	10[1]	12	7[2]	6	13			1	5	4[3]	9	14												46

Coca-Cola Cup
First Round   Wycombe W   (h) 1-1   (a) 0-2

FA Cup
Third Round   Southampton   (h) 3-1
Fourth Round   Portsmouth   (a) 0-3

ROCHDALE 1996-97   *Back row (left to right):* Mark Stuart, Mark Leonard, Mike Cerere, Ian Gray, Dave Lancaster, Kevin Gray, David Bayliss, Andy Farrell.
Middle row: Jimmy Robson (Youth Team Manager), Alex Russell, Kevin Formby, Dean Martin, Steve Whitehall, Dave Thompson, John Deary, Andy Gouck, Andy Thackeray, Dave Bywater (Centre of Excellence Coach).
Front row: Keith Hicks (Centre of Excellence Director), Andy Fensome, Jamie Taylor, James Price, Graham Barrow (Manager), Wayne Dowell, Keith Hill, Neil Barlow, Paul Lyons, Joe Hinnighan (First Team Coach/Physio).

Division 3 **ROCHDALE**

Spotland, Sandy Lane, Rochdale OL11 5DS. Telephone: (01706) 44648. Fax: (01706) 48466. Commercial: (01706) 47521.

Ground capacity: 6448.

Record attendance: 24,231 v Notts Co, FA Cup 2nd rd, 10 December 1949.

Record receipts: £46,000 v Burnley, Division 4, 5 May 1992.

Pitch measurements: 114yd × 76yd.

President: Mrs L. Stoney.

Chairman: D. F. Kilpatrick.

Directors: G. R. Brierley, T. Butterworth, C. Dunphy, M. Mace, J. Marsh, G. Morris, K. Clegg.

Manager: Graham Barrow.

Secretary: Mrs Karen Jagger. *Coach:* Jimmy Robson. *Commercial Manager:* S. Walmsley.

Advertising & Sponsorship Manager: L. Duckworth. *Stadium Manager:* Ronnie Cowgill.

Physio: J. Hinnigan.

Year Formed: 1907. *Turned Professional:* 1907. *Ltd Co.:* 1910.

Club Nickname: 'The Dale'.

Foundation: Considering the love of rugby in their area, it is not surprising that Rochdale had difficulty in establishing an Association Football club. The earlier Rochdale Town club formed in 1900 went out of existence in 1907 when the present club was immediately established and joined the Manchester League, before graduating to the Lancashire Combination in 1908.

First Football League game: 27 August 1921, Division 3 (N), v Accrington Stanley (h) W 6-3 – Crabtree; Nuttall, Sheehan; Hill, Farrer, Yarwood; Hoad, Sandiford, Dennison (2), Owens (3), Carney (1).

Record League Victory: 8–1 v Chesterfield, Division 3 (N), 18 December 1926 – Hill; Brown, Ward; Hillhouse, Parkes, Braidwood; Hughes, Bertram, Whitehurst (5), Schofield (2), Martin (1).

Record Cup Victory: 8–2 v Crook T, FA Cup 1st rd, 26 November 1927 – Moody; Hopkins, Ward; Braidwood, Parkes, Barker; Tompkinson, Clennell (3) Whitehurst (4), Hall, Martin (1).

Record Defeat: 1–9 v Tranmere R, Division 3 (N), 25 December 1931.

Most League Points (2 for a win): 62, Division 3 (N), 1923–24.

Most League Points (3 for a win): 67, Division 4, 1991–92.

Most League Goals: 105, Division 3 (N), 1926–27.

Highest League Scorer in Season: Albert Whitehurst, 44, Division 3 (N), 1926–27.

Most League Goals in Total Aggregate: Reg Jenkins, 119, 1964–73.

Most Capped Player: None.

Most League Appearances: Graham Smith, 317, 1966–74.

Record Transfer Fee Received: £300,000 from Wimbledon for Alan Reeves, September 1994.

Record Transfer Fee Paid: £80,000 to Scunthorpe U for Andy Flounders, August 1991.

Football League Record: 1921 Elected to Division 3 (N); 1958–59 Division 3; 1959–69 Division 4; 1969–74 Division 3; 1974–92 Division 4; 1992– Division 3.

Football League: Division 3 best season: 9th, 1969–70; Division 3 (N) – Runners-up 1923–24, 1926–27. *FA Cup:* best season: 5th rd, 1990. *Football League Cup:* Runners-up 1962 (record for 4th Division club).

Colours: Blue shirts with jade trim, white shorts, blue stockings with jade and white hoop on turnover. *Change colours:* White shirt with jade trim, jade shorts, white stockings with jade and blue trim.

Did you know?
On 14 September 1996, Rochdale had one player sent off after 14 minutes against Doncaster Rovers and another dismissed a minute before half-time, but still managed to win 2–1.

ROCHDALE 1996–97 LEAGUE RECORD

Match No.	Date	Venue	Opponents	Result	H/T Score	Lg. Pos.	Goalscorers	Attendance
1	Aug 17	A	Swansea C	L 1-2	0-2	—	Cecere [87]	4272
2	24	H	Colchester U	D 0-0	0-0	21		1816
3	27	H	Fulham	L 1-2	0-1	—	Whitehall [80]	1689
4	31	A	Mansfield T	D 0-0	0-0	23		1861
5	Sept 7	A	Hull C	D 1-1	1-0	22	Deary [43]	3451
6	10	H	Chester C	L 0-1	0-0	—		1774
7	14	H	Doncaster R	W 2-1	0-0	21	Deary (pen) [78], Gouck [81]	1811
8	21	A	Hereford U	L 0-3	0-1	23		2135
9	28	H	Leyton Orient	W 1-0	0-0	20	Whitehall (pen) [76]	1994
10	Oct 5	A	Darlington	D 1-1	0-0	23	Stuart [67]	3071
11	12	H	Carlisle U	D 2-2	1-1	23	Painter [7], Thompson [81]	3320
12	15	H	Lincoln C	W 2-0	2-0	—	Whitehall [44], Painter [45]	1411
13	19	A	Cambridge U	D 2-2	1-1	21	Stuart [26], Painter [72]	3163
14	26	A	Scunthorpe U	D 2-2	1-2	19	Stuart [45], Whitehall [49]	2628
15	29	H	Brighton & HA	W 3-0	1-0	—	Whitehall 2 [31, 56], Painter [50]	1913
16	Nov 2	H	Exeter C	W 2-0	2-0	13	Hill [13], Johnson [37]	2134
17	5	A	Cardiff C	L 1-2	0-1	—	Whitehall [52]	2834
18	9	A	Barnet	L 2-3	1-1	14	Pardew (og) [42], Deary [64]	2405
19	23	A	Northampton T	D 2-2	0-1	17	Farrell 2 [66, 68]	3836
20	30	H	Scunthorpe U	L 1-2	0-1	19	Painter [75]	1969
21	Dec 3	A	Torquay U	W 1-0	0-0	—	Johnson [73]	1087
22	14	H	Hartlepool U	L 1-3	0-2	16	Whitehall [77]	1618
23	21	A	Wigan Ath	W 1-0	1-0	16	Whitehall (pen) [4]	3311
24	Jan 14	A	Chester C	D 0-0	0-0	—		1679
25	18	H	Cardiff C	W 1-0	1-0	19	Leonard [7]	1704
26	25	A	Brighton & HA	L 0-3	0-1	19		4468
27	Feb 1	H	Barnet	D 1-1	0-0	19	Russell [90]	1623
28	4	H	Scarborough	D 3-3	1-1	—	Painter [40], Hill [47], Russell [62]	1166
29	8	A	Exeter C	D 0-0	0-0	19		2849
30	11	A	Leyton Orient	L 1-2	1-1	—	Painter [33]	2406
31	15	H	Northampton T	D 1-1	1-1	18	Deary [44]	1988
32	18	H	Hereford U	D 0-0	0-0	—		1074
33	22	A	Scarborough	D 2-2	2-1	17	Russell [22], Sutherland (og) [44]	2384
34	25	H	Hull C	L 1-2	1-1	—	Russell [5]	1349
35	Mar 1	H	Torquay U	W 2-1	1-1	17	Leonard [6], Gouck [89]	1469
36	8	H	Wigan Ath	W 3-1	3-1	15	Deary [15], Johnson [39], Russell [45]	3254
37	15	A	Hartlepool U	W 2-1	1-0	15	Russell [29], Formby [50]	1448
38	21	A	Colchester U	L 0-1	0-0	—		3211
39	25	A	Doncaster R	L 0-3	0-2	—		2201
40	29	H	Swansea C	L 2-3	2-1	15	Russell 2 [24, 36]	1884
41	31	H	Fulham	D 1-1	1-1	15	Gouck [36]	7866
42	Apr 5	H	Mansfield T	L 0-1	0-0	16		1620
43	12	H	Darlington	W 2-0	2-0	16	Leonard [11], Johnson [18]	1638
44	26	H	Cambridge U	W 3-0	3-0	16	Stuart 2 [16, 39], Russell [43]	1810
45	29	A	Carlisle U	L 2-3	1-0	—	Leonard [25], Stuart [90]	4882
46	May 3	A	Lincoln C	W 2-0	0-0	14	Hill [77], Stuart [82]	6495

Final League Position: 14

GOALSCORERS

League (58): Russell 9, Whitehall 9 (2 pens), Painter 7, Stuart 7, Deary 5 (1 pen), Johnson 4, Leonard 4, Gouck 3, Hill 3, Farrell 2, Cecere 1, Formby 1, Thompson 1, own goals 2.
Coca-Cola Cup (2): Deary 1, Whitehall 1.
FA Cup (3): Deary 1, Johnson 1, Thackeray 1.

Gray I 46	Fensome A 38 + 2	Formby K 12 + 4	Johnson A 46	Hill K 43	Farrell A 37 + 3	Russell A 35 + 4	Deary J 37 + 1	Leonard M 39	Whitehall S 27 + 8	Stuart M 28 + 3	Cecere M 2 + 2	Martin D — + 1	Thompson D 9 + 19	Bayliss D 22 + 2	Lancaster D 1 + 5	Gouck A 22 + 6	Brown M 5	Painter R 21 + 6	Bailey M 13 + 2	Thackeray A 17	Dowell W 6 + 1	Robson G — + 3	Taylor J — + 1	Match No.
1	2	3^2	4	5	6	7^3	8	9	10	11^1	12	13	14											1
1	2	3^1	4	5	6	7^3	8	9	10	11^2			12	13	14									2
1	2	3^2	4	5	6	7	8	9	10	11^1			12		13									3
1	2		4	5	6	11	8	9	10^2	12			7^1	3	13									4
1	2		4	5	6	7^1	8	9	10	11^2			12	3		13								5
1	2		4	5	6	12	8	9	10^2	13			7^1	3	14	11^3								6
1	2		4	5	6	10	8	9		11^1			12	3		13		7^2						7
1	2		4^1	5	6^2	10	8	9	13	11			12	3		7								8
1	2		4		5	8		10	11				12	3	9	6		7^1						9
1	2		4	5	6	10	8^1		9	11				3	13	12		7^2						10
1	2		4	5	6^1	8		9	11				13	3		12		7^2	10					11
1	2		4	5		7		9	10	11				3		6		8						12
1	2		4^1	5	12	7		9	10	11				3		6		8						13
1	2		4	5		7		9	10	11				3		6		8						14
1	2		4	5	12	7		9	10	11				3^1		6		8						15
1	2		4	5	3	7^1		9	10	11			12			6		8						16
1	2		4	5	3	7^1		9	10	11			12			6		8						17
1	2^1		4	5	3	7	12	9	10	11						6		8						18
1	2		4	5	3		8	9	10	11			12	13		6^2		7^1						19
1	2^1		4	5	6^2	13	8	9	10				12			7		3		11				20
1	2		4	5	6		8		10				9^1	12		3		11	7					21
1	2		4	5		8		10					9^1	12		3		11	7^2	6	13			22
1			4	5		8	9	10					2			11		7	6	3				23
1			4	5		8	9	10					12	2		11^1		7	6	3				24
1			4	5		8	9	10^1	12				13	2		11^2		7	6	3				25
1			4	5	12	13	8	9^1		11			14	2		10^2		7	6	3^3				26
1	2		4	5	6	12	8	9	10^3				7	3^1		13		14	11^2					27
1	2		4	5	6	7	8	9	12				13	3		10^1		11^2						28
1	2		4	5	6	7	8		10					9		11	3							29
1	2	12	4	5	6^1	7^2	8		10				14			13	9	11	3^3					30
1	2	12	4		5	7	8	9	13				14	3^1		6	10^2	11^3						31
1	2	11	4		5	10	8	9	12				7^1			6		3						32
1		11^2	4	5	2	10	8	9	12				7^1			6	13	3						33
1	12	11	4	5	2	7^2	8	9	10^3				6	13		3^1		14						34
1	2	10	4	5^1	3	7	8	9	12	11				6										35
1	2	10^1	4	5	3	7	8	9	12	11				6										36
1	2	10	4	5	3	7	8	9		11				6										37
1	2^2	10^1	4	5	3	7	8	9		11				6				12		13				38
1	2^1	10^2	4	5	3	7	8	9		11				6				12		13				39
1	2^1	12	4	5	3	7	8^2	9		11				6	13	10								40
1	2	11^1	4	5	3	7	8	9						6	12	10								41
1	2^1	12	4	5	3	7	8	9						6	11^2	10				13				42
1	2		4	5	6	7	8	9^1		11						12	10	3						43
1			4	5	6	10	8	9		11			7					2	3					44
1	12		4	5	6	10	8	9^2	13	11			7					2^1	3					45
1	2		4	5	6		8	9		11			7					10	3					46

Coca-Cola Cup

First Round	Barnsley	(h)	2-1
		(a)	0-2

FA Cup

First Round	Macclesfield T	(a)	2-0
Second Round	Notts Co	(a)	1-3

ROTHERHAM UNITED 1996–97   *Back row (left to right):* Neil Richardson, Steve Slawson, Dean Fearon, Craig Davis, Steve Farrelly, John McGlashan, Nathan Peel, Ian Breckin.
Middle row: Andy Hayward, Gary Bowyer, Martin James, Darren Garner, Junior McDougald, Andy Roscoe, Bradley Sandeman, Mark Monington, Ian Bailey (Physio).
Front row: Billy Russell (Youth Team Coach), Trevor Berry, Scott Smith, Paul Hurst, Jim Dobbin, Danny Bergara (Chief Coach), Brian Gayle, Shaun Goodwin, Paul Blades, Lee Glover,
John Breckin (Youth Development Officer).

Division 3   **ROTHERHAM UNITED**

Millmoor Ground, Rotherham S60 1HR. Telephone: (01709) 512434. Fax: (01709) 512762. Commercial Dept: (01709) 512760. Fax: (01709) 512763. Football in the Community: (01709) 512761.

Ground Capacity: 11,514.

Record attendance: 25,170 v Sheffield U, Division 2, 13 December 1952 and v Sheffield W, Division 2, 26 January 1952.

Record receipts: £79,155 v Newcastle U, FA Cup 4th rd, 23 January 1993.

Pitch measurements. 115yd × 75yd.

Chairman: K. F. Booth.

Directors: R. Hull (Vice-Chairman), C. A. Luckock, J. A. Webb, N. Freeman. *Chief Executive:* Phil Henson.

Manager: Ronnie Moore. *Youth Development Officer:* John Breckin. *Physio:* Ian Bailey. *Coach:* Billy Russell.

Stadium Manager/Safety Officer: David Sumner.

Commercial Manager: D. Nicholls.

Year Formed: 1870. *Turned Professional:* 1905. *Ltd Co.:* 1920.

Club Nickname: 'The Merry Millers'.

Previous Names: 1877, Thornhill United; 1905, Rotherham County; 1925, amalgamated with Rotherham Town under Rotherham United.

Previous Ground: Red House Ground; 1907, Millmoor.

Foundation: Rotherham were formed in 1870 before becoming Town in the late 1880s. Thornhill United were founded in 1877 and changed their name to Rotherham County in 1905. The Town amalgamated with Rotherham County to form Rotherham United in 1925.

First Football League game: 2 September 1893, Division 2, Rotherham T v Lincoln C (a) D 1-1 – McKay; Thickett, Watson; Barr, Brown, Broadhead; Longden, Cutts, Leatherbarrow, McCormick, Pickering. (1 og) 30 August 1919, Division 2, Rotherham Co v Nottingham F (h) W 2-0 – Branston; Alton, Baines; Bailey, Coe, Stanton; Lee (1), Cawley (1), Glennon, Lees, Lamb.

Record League Victory: 8–0 v Oldham Ath, Division 3 (N), 26 May 1947 – Warnes; Selkirk, Ibbotson; Edwards, Horace Williams, Danny Williams; Wilson (2), Shaw (1), Ardron (3), Guest (1), Hainsworth (1).

Record Cup Victory: 6–0 v Spennymoor U, FA Cup 2nd rd, 17 December 1977 – McAlister; Forrest, Breckin, Womble, Stancliffe, Green, Finney, Phillips (3), Gwyther (2) (Smith), Goodfellow, Crawford (1). 6–0 v Wolverhampton W, FA Cup 1st rd, 16 November 1985 – O'Hanlon; Forrest, Dungworth, Gooding (1), Smith (1), Pickering, Birch (2), Emerson, Tynan (1), Simmons (1), Pugh.

Record Defeat: 1–11 v Bradford C, Division 3 (N), 25 August 1928.

Most League Points (2 for a win): 71, Division 3 (N), 1950–51.

Most League Points (3 for a win): 82, Division 4, 1988–89.

Most League Goals: 114, Division 3 (N), 1946–47.

Highest League Scorer in Season: Wally Ardron, 38, Division 3 (N), 1946–47.

Most League Goals in Total Aggregate: Gladstone Guest, 130, 1946–56.

Most Capped Player: Shaun Goater, 18, Bermuda.

Most League Appearances: Danny Williams, 459, 1946–62.

Record Transfer Fee Received: £255,000 from Fortuna Sittard for Mike Jeffrey, January 1996.

Record Transfer Fee Paid: £150,000 to Millwall for Tony Towner, August 1980.

Football League Record: 1893 Rotherham Town elected to Division 2; 1896 Failed re-election; 1919 Rotherham County elected to Division 2; 1923–51 Division 3 (N); 1951–68 Division 2; 1968–73 Division 3; 1973–75 Division 4; 1975–81 Division 3; 1981–83 Division 2; 1983–88 Division 3; 1988–89 Division 4; 1989–91 Division 3; 1991–92 Division 4; 1992–97 Division 2; 1997– Division 3.

Honours: Football League: Division 2 best season: 3rd, 1954–55 (equal points with champions and runners-up); Division 3 – Champions 1980–81; Division 3 (N) – Champions 1950–51; Runners-up 1946–47, 1947–48, 1948–49; Division 4 – Champions 1988–89; Runners-up 1991–92. *FA Cup:* best season: 5th rd, 1953, 1968. *Football League Cup:* Runners-up 1961. *Auto Windscreens Shield:* Winners 1996.

Colours: Red and white. *Change colours:* Navy and silver shirts, navy shorts with trim, navy stockings.

Did you know?
On 5 November 1927 Tommy Hall, making his debut for Rotherham United against Wigan Borough, scored four times in a 6–0 win.

ROTHERHAM UNITED 1996–97 LEAGUE RECORD

Match No.	Date	Venue	Opponents	Result	H/T Score	Lg. Pos.	Goalscorers	Attendance
1	Aug 17	A	Walsall	D 1-1	1-0	—	Goodwin [43]	4040
2	24	H	Shrewsbury T	L 1-2	1-1	18	McDougald [42]	3037
3	27	H	Blackpool	L 1-2	1-0	—	Hayward [46]	2914
4	31	A	Luton T	L 0-1	0-0	23		4547
5	Sept 7	A	Bury	L 1-3	0-1	23	Hurst [52]	3523
6	10	H	Chesterfield	L 0-1	0-1	—		2940
7	14	H	Bristol C	D 2-2	0-0	24	Berry [48], Richardson (pen) [56]	2546
8	21	A	Gillingham	L 1-3	1-3	24	Bowyer [19]	4920
9	28	H	Bournemouth	W 1-0	0-0	23	Druce [56]	2648
10	Oct 1	A	Wycombe W	L 2-4	2-1	—	Druce [18], Hayward [42]	3438
11	5	A	Brentford	L 2-4	1-2	24	Berry [31], Druce [62]	6137
12	12	H	Burnley	W 1-0	1-0	24	Druce [42]	4562
13	15	H	Bristol R	D 0-0	0-0	—		2490
14	19	A	York C	L 1-2	0-0	24	Sandeman [87]	3410
15	26	H	Peterborough U	W 2-0	1-0	23	Breckin [14], Berry [83]	2854
16	29	A	Crewe Alex	L 0-1	0-1	—		3162
17	Nov 2	A	Preston NE	D 0-0	0-0	23		8997
18	9	H	Watford	D 0-0	0-0	23		3619
19	23	H	Millwall	D 0-0	0-0	23		3286
20	30	A	Peterborough U	L 2-6	2-3	23	Blades [9], Sandeman [30]	4690
21	Dec 3	H	Stockport Co	L 0-1	0-1	—		2133
22	14	A	Notts Co	D 0-0	0-0	24		3954
23	21	H	Plymouth Arg	L 1-2	1-2	24	Breckin [31]	2269
24	28	A	Bury	D 1-1	0-1	24	Goodwin (pen) [87]	3263
25	Jan 11	A	Bournemouth	D 1-1	0-0	24	Hurst [49]	3161
26	18	H	Wycombe W	W 2-1	1-0	24	Goodwin (pen) [17], Glover [66]	2692
27	25	H	Crewe Alex	L 1-4	0-2	24	Jean [80]	2832
28	Feb 1	A	Watford	L 0-2	0-0	24		10,657
29	8	H	Preston NE	L 0-1	0-1	24		3556
30	15	A	Millwall	L 0-2	0-0	24		7043
31	18	A	Chesterfield	D 1-1	0-0	—	Hayward [90]	5195
32	22	H	Wrexham	D 0-0	0-0	24		2539
33	Mar 1	A	Stockport Co	D 0-0	0-0	24		6147
34	8	A	Plymouth Arg	L 0-1	0-1	24		4717
35	15	H	Notts Co	D 2-2	0-1	24	Jean [73], Bowyer [80]	2605
36	18	A	Bristol C	W 2-0	0-0	—	Garner [68], Jean [72]	10,646
37	22	A	Shrewsbury T	W 2-0	1-0	23	McDougald (pen) [22], Hurst [56]	2893
38	25	H	Gillingham	L 1-2	0-1	—	Dillon [51]	2664
39	29	H	Walsall	L 1-2	0-2	23	Hayward [89]	2428
40	31	A	Blackpool	L 1-4	0-2	23	Breckin [88]	5524
41	Apr 5	H	Luton T	L 0-3	0-2	23		2609
42	8	A	Wrexham	L 0-1	0-0	—		2002
43	11	H	Brentford	L 0-1	0-0	—		1797
44	19	A	Burnley	D 3-3	1-1	24	Jean 3 [25, 55, 57]	7875
45	26	A	York C	L 0-2	0-1	24		3122
46	May 3	A	Bristol R	W 2-1	1-1	23	Berry [21], Garner [87]	5950

Final League Position: 23

GOALSCORERS

League (39): Jean 6, Berry 4, Druce 4, Hayward 4, Breckin 3, Goodwin 3 (2 pens), Hurst 3, Bowyer 2, Garner 2, McDougald 2 (1 pen), Sandeman 2, Blades 1, Dillon 1, Glover 1, Richardson 1 (pen).
Coca-Cola Cup (0).
FA Cup (1): McGlashan 1.

Cherry S 20	Sandeman B 20+1	Roscoe A 39+4	Garner D 30	Monington M 28	Breckin I 42	Smith S 9+2	Goodwin S 7+1	Glover L 16+6	Hayward A 32+2	McGlashan J 28+3	Slawson S 2+3	Hurst P 25+5	McDougald J 14+4	Berry T 19+11	Richardson N 10+4	Dobbin J 17+2	Bowyer G 10+1	James M —+3	Crawford J 11	Druce M 16+4	Farrelly S 7	Gayle B 19+1	Blades P 9	Clarke A 1+1	Jean E 7+11	Pilkington K 17	Dillon P 11+2	Bowman R 13	McKenzie R 6+5	Landon R 7+1	Bain K 10+2	Pell R 2	Barnes P 2	Match No.
1	2²	3	4	5	6	7	8	9	10¹	11	12	13																						1
1	2	3	4	5	6	7	8		10	11²	12			9¹	13																			2
1	2	3	4	5	6		8		10	9	11			7																				3
1	2²		4	5	6	3	8	9	10		12	13		7²	11	14																		4
1	11		4	5¹	6	2			10	12		9	3	7¹	13		8																	5
1	11		4		6	2			10			9	3	7	5		8																	6
1	11		4	9	6	2			10	12			3	7¹	5		8																	7
1	2	11	4		6		7		10				3	9	5		8¹		12															8
1	2				6		12		10	11			3	7²	5	4				13	8	9¹												9
1	2				6				10	11			3	7¹	5	4				12	8	9												10
	2	12			6			13	10	11			3	7¹	5	4²					8	9	1											11
1	7	3		5		2			10	11						4				8		9	6											12
1	7	3		5		2			10	11¹						4				8		9	6											13
1	7	3		5		2			10	11²	12		13			4				8		9¹	6											14
	7	3		5		2		9¹	10	11	12					4				8		1	6											15
	7	3		5		2		9	10²	11¹	12					4				8	13	1	6											16
	7	3		5		2			10	11	12					4				8	9¹	1	6											17
	7	3		5		2			10	11	12					4				8	9¹	1	6											18
	7	3		5		2			10	11	12	9²	13			4				8¹		1	6											19
	7	3		5		2			10	11	12	9¹				4				8		1	6											20
1		3		5		7¹		13	10	12	11					4				9²			6	2	8									21
1	12	3	4	5		7¹	8	9²	10	11³		13											6	2	14									22
1		3	4	5	6	7	8	9	10¹	11	12								2															23
1	7	3	4	5	6		8	9	10¹	11	12								2															24
1	7	3	4	5	6		8		10	11	12								2						9¹									25
1	7¹	3	4	5	6		8	9	10	11	12								2															26
1		3	4¹	5	6	7	8²	9	10	11	12								2						13									27
		3¹	4	5		2	8	9	10	11									12	6					7	1								28
		3	4	5		7¹		9	10	11	12								2²	6					8	1	13							29
		3	4	5		2		9	10¹	11	12									7					8	1	6							30
	12		4	5		2		9	10¹	11³		13								7			6		8²	1	3							31
		3²	4	5		7		9	10	11	12	13											6		8	1								32
		3	4	5		7¹	8	9	10	11²									12				6			1	13	2						33
	12		4	5		7²			10³			13								8			6		13	1	3¹	2	11	9	14			34
		3	11¹	5				9	10²	12										8					13	1	6	2	7	4				35
			4	5	6		8	9	10	11	12														7¹	1	4	5	9	3				36
		3	11²	5				9³	10	12										8					13	1	6	2	14	7¹	4			37
		3	11	5		7¹		9²	10											8					13	1	6	2	12	4				38
		3	11¹	5		7		9³	10		12									8²					13	1	6	2	14	4				39
		3	11	5		7¹			10		12									8					13	1	6	2³	14	9²	4			40
		3¹	11	5		7			10		12	13								8						1	6³	2	14	9²	4			41
		3²	11	5		7			10		12									8						1	2	13	9¹	4	6			42
		3	11	5		7			10¹		12									8						1	2		9	4	6			43
		3¹	11	5	6	7			10		12									8						1	12	2	9	4				44
		3¹	11	5	6	7			10³		12	13								8							4	2	14	9²		1		45
	12	11		5	6	7		9	10²											8³					13		3¹	2	14	4		1		46

SCARBOROUGH 1996–97   *Back row (left to right):* David Brooke, Simon Bochenski, Jon Sunderland, Kevin Martin, Dean Macauley, Ian Ironside, Richard Lucas, Matthew Russell, Darren Knowles.
Middle row: Alex Willgrass, Darren Mowbray, Gareth Williams, Ian Thompstone, Garry Bennett, Ray McHale, Stuart Hicks, Jason Rockett, Mark Wells, Andy Ritchie, Tony Daws.
Front row: John Murray, Jamie Mitchell, Rob Hanby, Mick Wadsworth (Manager), John Birley (President), John Russell (Chairman), Gillian Russell (Director/Club Secretary), Chris Hooper, Ben Worrall, Jon Kerr.

Division 3 SCARBOROUGH

The McCain Stadium, Seamer Road, Scarborough YO12 4HF. Telephone: (01723) 375094. Fax: (01723) 378733.

Ground capacity: 6899.

Record Attendance: 11,130 v Luton T, FA Cup 3rd rd, 8 January 1938. Football League: 7314 v Wolverhampton W, Division 4, 15 August 1987.

Record receipts: £37,609.50 v Arsenal, Coca-Cola Cup 4th rd, 6 January 1993.

Pitch measurements: 114yd × 74yd.

President and Chief Executive: John Birley.

Chairman: J. Russell.

Director: Mrs G. Russell.

Manager: Mick Wadsworth. *Assistant Manager:* Ray McHale.

Secretary: Mrs Gillian Russell. *Physio:* J. Murray.

Year Formed: 1879. *Turned Professional:* 1926. *Ltd Co.:* 1933.

Club Nickname: 'The Boro'.

Previous Grounds: 1879–87, Scarborough Cricket Ground; 1887–98, Recreation Ground; 1898– Athletic Ground.

Foundation: Scarborough came into being as early as 1879 when they were formed by members of the town's cricket club and went under the name of Scarborough Cricketers' FC with home games played on the North Marine Road Cricket Ground.

First Football League game: 15 August 1987, Division 4, v Wolverhampton W (h) D 2-2 – Blackwell; McJannet, Thompson, Bennyworth, Richards, Kendall, Hamill, Moss, McHale, Mell (1), Graham.

Record League Victory: 4–0 v Bolton W, Division 4, 29 August 1987 – Blackwell; McJannet, Thompson, Bennyworth (Walker), Richards (1) (Cook), Kendall, Hamill (1), Moss, McHale, Mell (1), Graham. (1 og). 4–0 v Newport Co (away), Division 4, 12 April 1988 – Ironside; McJannet, Thompson, Kamara, Richards (1), Short (1), Adams (Cook 1), Brook, Outhart (1), Russell, Graham.

Record Cup Victory: 6–0 v Rhyl Ath, FA Cup 1st rd, 29 November 1930 – Turner; Severn, Belton; Maskell, Robinson, Wallis; Small (1), Rand (2), Palfreman (2), A. D. Hill (1), Mickman.

Record Defeat: 1–7 v Wigan Ath, Division 3, 11 March 1997.

Most League Points (3 for a win): 77, Division 4, 1988–89.

Most League Goals: 69, Division 4, 1990–91.

Highest League Scorer in Season: Darren Foreman, 27, Division 4, 1992–93.

Most League Goals in Total Aggregate: Darren Foreman, 35, 1991–95.

Most Capped Player: None.

Most League Appearances: Ian Ironside, 183, 1988–91, 1992, 1994–97.

Record Transfer Fee Received: £240,000 from Notts Co for Chris Short, September 1990.

Record Transfer Fee Paid: £102,000 to Leicester C for Martin Russell, March 1989.

Football League Record: Promoted to Division 4 1987; 1992– Division 3.

Honours: Football League: Division 4 best season: 5th, 1988–89. *FA Cup:* best seasons: 3rd rd, 1931, 1938, 1976, 1978, 1995. *Football League Cup:* best season: 4th rd 1993. *FA Trophy:* Winners 1973, 1976, 1977. *GM Vauxhall Conference:* Winners 1986–87.

Colours: White shirts and shorts with red and white hoops. *Change colours:* Black shirts and shorts with green hoops.

Did you know?
Scarborough beat York City 3–1 away in a first round FA Cup tie on 26 November 1932 watched by a local derby crowd of 8,958.

SCARBOROUGH 1996–97 LEAGUE RECORD

Match No.	Date	Venue	Opponents	Result	H/T Score	Lg. Pos.	Goalscorers	Attendance
1	Aug 17	H	Cardiff C	D 0-0	0-0	—		2455
2	24	A	Exeter C	D 2-2	0-2	16	Ritchie [70], Worrall [86]	2816
3	27	A	Scunthorpe U	W 2-0	2-0	—	Williams G [13], Ritchie [45]	2512
4	31	H	Northampton T	D 1-1	0-0	9	Bennett G [75]	2520
5	Sept 7	A	Brighton & HA	L 2-3	0-1	13	Bochenski [84], Ritchie [88]	4008
6	10	H	Doncaster R	W 2-1	2-0	—	Bennett G [33], Williams G [36]	1959
7	14	H	Carlisle U	D 1-1	0-0	12	Rockett [90]	3524
8	21	A	Cambridge U	L 1-2	1-0	12	Mitchell [39]	2387
9	28	H	Wigan Ath	W 3-1	1-1	9	Ritchie 2 [1, 52], Bennett G [77]	2570
10	Oct 1	A	Barnet	W 3-1	2-0	—	Mitchell 2 [11, 62], Ritchie (pen) [21]	1606
11	5	A	Hereford U	D 2-2	1-1	6	Brooke [39], Ritchie [75]	2506
12	12	H	Chester C	D 0-0	0-0	7		2352
13	15	H	Hull C	W 3-2	1-0	—	Williams G [45], Mann (og) [48], Ritchie [65]	3425
14	19	A	Lincoln C	D 1-1	0-1	5	Hicks [76]	2611
15	26	H	Mansfield T	W 2-1	1-1	5	Rockett [13], Williams G [75]	2521
16	29	A	Leyton Orient	W 1-0	0-0	—	Thompstone [70]	2693
17	Nov 2	A	Darlington	D 1-1	0-1	4	Thompstone [90]	2859
18	9	H	Hartlepool U	L 2-4	2-1	5	Bennett G [20], Ritchie [27]	3157
19	23	H	Swansea C	L 0-1	0-0	7		2005
20	30	A	Mansfield T	L 0-2	0-0	8		1981
21	Dec 3	H	Colchester U	D 1-1	0-1	—	Mitchell [52]	1605
22	14	A	Torquay U	L 0-1	0-1	14		1567
23	21	H	Fulham	L 0-2	0-2	15		2015
24	26	A	Doncaster R	W 2-1	1-1	13	Mitchell 2 [15, 74]	1745
25	28	H	Brighton & HA	D 1-1	0-1	12	Brodie [57]	2252
26	Jan 14	H	Cambridge U	W 1-0	0-0	—	Brodie [86]	1573
27	18	H	Barnet	D 1-1	1-0	9	Rockett [29]	1835
28	25	H	Leyton Orient	W 2-1	0-0	8	Currie [47], Brodie [74]	2184
29	Feb 1	A	Hartlepool U	L 0-1	0-1	10		1843
30	4	A	Rochdale	D 3-3	1-1	—	Brooke [26], Rockett [64], Bennett G [80]	1166
31	8	H	Darlington	W 4-1	3-0	9	Currie 3 [21, 25, 48], McElhatton [23]	2585
32	11	A	Carlisle U	L 0-1	0-0	—		4936
33	15	A	Swansea C	W 2-1	0-1	7	Bennett G [48], Williams G [86]	3312
34	22	H	Rochdale	D 2-2	1-2	10	Bennett G [35], Currie (pen) [49]	2384
35	28	A	Colchester U	W 3-1	1-1	—	Williams G 2 [36, 70], Rigby [74]	3719
36	Mar 8	A	Fulham	L 0-4	0-2	9		6080
37	11	A	Wigan Ath	L 1-7	0-4	—	Rockett [82]	3094
38	15	H	Torquay U	W 3-1	1-0	9	Mitchell [35], Bennett G 2 [71, 86]	2257
39	18	A	Cardiff C	D 1-1	0-0	—	Midgley [60]	2823
40	22	H	Exeter C	L 3-4	1-3	9	Currie (pen) [17], Williams G 2 [52, 75]	2125
41	31	H	Scunthorpe U	W 3-2	2-0	7	Midgley [3], Brodie 2 [43, 53]	3212
42	Apr 5	A	Northampton T	L 0-1	0-0	10		4854
43	12	H	Hereford U	D 1-1	0-1	12	Williams G [70]	2332
44	19	A	Chester C	L 0-1	0-1	12		2311
45	26	H	Lincoln C	L 0-2	0-1	13		3607
46	May 3	A	Hull C	W 2-0	1-0	12	Bennett T [13], Wells [86]	3774

Final League Position: 12

GOALSCORERS

League (65): Williams G 10, Bennett G 9, Ritchie 9 (1 pen), Mitchell 7, Currie 6 (2 pens), Brodie 5, Rockett 5, Brooke 2, Midgley 2, Thompstone 2, Bennett T 1, Bochenski 1, Hicks 1, McElhatton 1, Rigby 1, Wells 1, Worrall 1, own goal 1.
Coca-Cola Cup (6): Bennett G 2, Ritchie 2, Daws 1, Williams G 1.
FA Cup (2): Kay 1, Ritchie 1.

Ironside I 39	Knowles D 12 + 5	Lucas R 19 + 9	Bennett G 46	Hicks S 36 + 2	Rockett J 40	Williams A 1	Brooke D 28 + 6	Daws T 4 + 2	Ritchie A 26 + 5	Mitchell J 23 + 20	Williams G 45	Worrall B 6 + 9	Wells M 22 + 8	Bochenski S 5 + 14	Hanby R 1 + 3	Mowbray D 2 + 1	Thompstone I 12 + 7	Sunderland J — + 2	McElhatton M 26 + 2	Kay J 34	Moilanen T 4	Brodie S 23 + 1	Sutherland C 17 + 4	Currie D 16	Rigby T 5	Martin K 3	Midgley C 6	Russell M 1 + 4	Bennett T 4 + 1	Match No.
1	2	3	4[2]	5	6	7	8	9[1]	10	11	12	13																		1
1	2	7	4	5	6		8[3]		10	11	12	13	3[1]	9[2]	14															2
1	2	3	4	5	6		8	9[1]	10[2]	11	12	7	13																	3
1	2	3	4	5			8[2]	9[1]	10	11	12	7	13			6														4
1	2[2]	3	4	5			8[1]		10	11	9[3]	12	14	13	6	7														5
1	2	3	4	5	6[2]		8		10[1]	11	9[3]	13	12				7	14												6
1	2	3	4	5	6		8		11	10	12[2]		9				7[1]	13												7
1	2	3	4	5	6		8		11	9	10						7													8
1			4	5	6		8		10	11	9[1]		3				12		7	2										9
1		12	4[3]	5	6		8[1]		10	11	9[2]		3	13			14		7	2										10
1		12	4	5	6		8		10	11[1]	9[2]		3				13		7	2										11
1			4	5	6		8		10	11[1]	9		3				12		7	2										12
1		12	4	5	6		8[1]		10	11	9[2]		3				13		7	2										13
1		12	4	5	6		8		10	11	13		3[1]				9[2]		7	2										14
1			4	5	6		8[2]		10[1]	11	9		3	12			13		7	2										15
1		12	4	5	6		8[3]		10	11	9[2]		3	13			14		7[1]	2										16
1		12	4	5	6		13		10	11[1]	9[2]		3[3]	14			8		7	2										17
1		3[1]	4	5			8		10	11	9		12	13		6[2]			7	2										18
1		3	4	5			8[1]	13	10	11	9[2]					6	12		7	2										19
1		6	4	5			8		10	11	9[1]		3				12		7	2										20
1		6	4	5			12	13	10	11[2]	9		3				8		7[1]	2										21
	2[1]	3	4	5	6		8	9[2]	10	11	14	12					13		7[3]		1									22
		3	4[1]	5	6		8		10	11	12						7			2	1	9								23
		3	4		6		8		12	11[1]	10	13					7			2	1	9[2]	5							24
		3[1]	4	12	6		8		10		9						7[2]		13	2	1	11	5							25
1		12	4	5[1]	6		13		10[2]	8	9						14		7[3]	2		11	3							26
1		5	4		6		12		10	8	9[2]						13		7[1]	2		11	3							27
1	12		4	5	6		8		10[2]	7[1]	13						14			2		11	3[3]	9						28
1	12		4		6		8[1]		10[2]	7	13		3				14			2		11	5[3]	9						29
1	12	5[1]	4		6		8		13	10	14		3				7[3]			2		11		9[2]						30
1			4	5[2]	6		8		12	10	14						13		7[3]	2[1]		11	3	9						31
1	12		4	5[1]	6		8[2]		14	9[3]	13		3						7	2		11	10							32
1	2		4	12	6				13	10			3				7					11	5[1]	9[2]	8					33
1[2]	2	13	4	5	6				10	12			3				7					11	3[1]	9	8					34
	12		4[3]	5	6				10	13			3				7			2		11[1]	14	9[2]	8	1				35
1		12	4		6				10	13			3[2]				7[1]			2		11	5	9	8					36
1	3[1]	5	4		6				10	12			13				7[3]			2		11	14	9	8[2]					37
1			4	5	6		8		10[1]	13	12									2		11[2]	3[3]	9			7	14		38
1			4	5	6				10	12	8		13							2		11[2]	3	9[1]			7			39
1			4	5	6				10	12	8		13							2		11[1]	3[2]	9[3]			7	14		40
1			4	5	6		8[1]		10	13			3				12			2		11[2]		9[3]			7	14		41
1			4	5	6				10	8[2]			3				12			2		11	13	9[1]			7[3]	14		42
1			4	5	6		8[1]		10	12			3							2		11	13	9[3]			7[2]	14	5	43
1			4		6				10	12							8			2		11	3	9[1]			7		5	44
			4	5	6		8	9			10						12			2	1	11[1]	3				7			45
			4	5	6		8[1]	9[2]	12	13	11[3]						14			2	1		3				7			46

Coca-Cola Cup

First Round	Hull C	(a)	2-2
		(h)	3-2
Second Round	Leicester C	(h)	0-2
		(a)	1-2

FA Cup

First Round	Shrewsbury T	(a)	1-1
		(h)	1-0
Second Round	Chesterfield	(a)	0-2

SCUNTHORPE UNITED 1996-97 *Back row (left to right):* Paul A. Wilson, Kirk Jackson, Mark Samways, Lee Turnbull, Mario Ziccardi, Russell Bradley, Chris Hope.
Middle row: Paul D. Wilson (Youth Development Officer), Mark Sertori, Andy McFarlane, Alan Knill, David Moss, Michael Walsh, Nigel Adkins (Physio).
Front row: Jamie Paterson, David D'Auria, Phil Clarkson, Mick Buxton (Manager), Don Rowing (Chief Executive), John Eyre, Steve Housham, Andrew Murfin.
(Photograph: I. A. Hewitt Photography)

Division 3   **SCUNTHORPE UNITED**

Glanford Park, Scunthorpe, South Humberside DN15 8TD. Telephone: (01724) 848077. Fax: (01724) 857986. *Ground capacity:* 9183.

Record attendance: Old Showground: 23,935 v Portsmouth, FA Cup 4th rd, 30 January 1954. Glanford Park: 8775 v Rotherham U, Division 4, 1 May 1989.

Record receipts: £44,481.50 v Leeds U, Rumbelows Cup 2nd rd lst leg, 24 September 1991.

Pitch measurements: 110yd × 71yd.

Vice-Presidents: I. T. Botham, G. Johnson, A. Harvey, R. Ashman, K. Waters, J. Brownsword, B. Heywood, Dr. J. Zacarias.

Chairman: K. Wagstaff.

Vice-Chairman: R. Garton.

Directors: J. B. Borrill, C. Plumtree, S. Wharton, B. Collen, J. A. C. Godfrey.

Team Manager: Brian Laws.

Chief Executive/Secretary: A. D. Rowing. *Commercial Manager:* A. D. Rowing.

*Year Formed:*1899. *Turned Professional:* 1912. *Ltd Co.:* 1912.

Club Nickname: 'The Iron'.

Previous Names: Amalgamated first with Brumby Hall then North Lindsey United to become Scunthorpe & Lindsey United, 1910; dropped '& Lindsey' in 1958.

Previous ground: Old Showground to 1988.

Foundation: The year of foundation for Scunthorpe United has often been quoted as 1910, but the club can trace its history back to 1899 when Brumby Hall FC, who played on the Old Showground, consolidated their position by amalgamating with some other clubs and changing their name to Scunthorpe United. The year 1910 was when that club amalgamated with North Lindsey United as Scunthorpe and Lindsey United. The link is Mr. W. T. Lockwood whose chairmanship covers both years.

First Football League game: 19 August 1950, Division 3 (N), v Shrewsbury T (h) D 0-0 – Thompson; Barker, Brownsword; Allen, Taylor, McCormick; Mosby, Payne, Gorin, Rees, Boyes.

Record League Victory: 8–1 v Luton T, Division 3, 24 April 1965 – Sidebottom; Horstead, Hemstead; Smith, Neale, Lindsey; Bramley (1), Scott, Thomas (5), Mahy (1), Wilson (1) and 8–1 v Torquay U (away), Division 3, 28 October 1995 – Samways; Housham, Wilson, Ford (1), Knill (1), Hope (Nicholson), Thornber, Bullimore (Walsh), McFarlane (4) (Young), Eyre (2), Paterson.

Record Cup Victory: 9–0 v Boston U, FA Cup 1st rd, 21 November 1953 – Malan; Hubbard, Brownsword; Sharpe, White, Bushby; Mosby (1), Haigh (3), Whitfield (2), Gregory (1), Mervyn Jones (2).

Record Defeat: 0–8 v Carlisle U, Division 3 (N), 25 December 1952.

Most League Points (2 for a win): 66, Division 3 (N), 1956–57, 1957–58.

Most League Points (3 for a win): 83, Division 4, 1982–83.

Most League Goals: 88, Division 3 (N), 1957–58.

Highest League Scorer in Season: Barrie Thomas, 31, Division 2, 1961–62.

Most League Goals in Total Aggregate: Steve Cammack, 110, 1979–81, 1981–86.

Most Capped Player: None.

Most League Appearances: Jack Brownsword, 595, 1950–65.

Record Transfer Fee Received: £350,000 from Aston Villa for Neil Cox, February 1991.

Record Transfer Fee Paid: £80,000 to York C for Ian Helliwell, August 1991.

Football League Record: 1950 Elected to Division 3 (N); 1958–64 Division 2; 1964–68 Division 3; 1968–72 Division 4; 1972–73 Division 3; 1973–84 Division 4; 1984–92 Division 4; 1992– Division 3.

Honours: Football League: Division 2 best season: 4th, 1961–62; Division 3 (N) – Champions 1957–58. *FA Cup:* best season: 5th rd, 1958, 1970. *Football League Cup:* never past 3rd rd.

Colours: Sky blue shirt with three vertical claret stripes, sky blue shorts, claret trim, sky blue stockings, claret trim. *Change colours:* Navy and yellow quarters, navy shorts, navy and yellow hooped stockings.

Did you know?
At the age of 36 years 151 days, Scunthorpe United's Youth Team Coach Paul Wilson, became the oldest Football League debutant without any previous first class experience (Andy Cunningham, a Newcastle United debutant at 38 years 2 days in 1929 was already an established Scottish International with Rangers).

SCUNTHORPE UNITED 1996–97 LEAGUE RECORD

Match No.	Date		Venue	Opponents	Result		H/T Score	Lg. Pos.	Goalscorers	Attendance
1	Aug	17	A	Leyton Orient	W	1-0	0-0	—	Clarkson [69]	4430
2		24	H	Torquay U	W	1-0	0-0	14	Clarkson [70]	2236
3		27	H	Scarborough	L	0-2	0-2	—		2512
4		31	A	Brighton & HA	D	1-1	0-0	7	Eyre [66]	4365
5	Sept	7	A	Wigan Ath	L	0-3	0-1	11		3321
6		10	H	Cambridge U	W	3-2	1-2	—	McFarlane [44], Clarkson [53], Wilson [80]	1643
7		14	H	Cardiff C	L	0-1	0-0	13		2121
8		21	A	Chester C	L	0-1	0-0	14		1901
9		28	H	Barnet	L	1-2	0-0	18	Clarkson [80]	1942
10	Oct	1	A	Hereford U	L	2-3	0-1	—	Bradley [67], Jackson [85]	1785
11		5	A	Hull C	W	2-0	0-0	14	Clarkson [89], Baker [90]	5414
12		12	H	Lincoln C	W	2-0	1-0	10	Housham [27], D'Auria [63]	3274
13		15	H	Northampton T	W	2-1	0-1	—	D'Auria [80], Hope [90]	2079
14		19	A	Swansea C	D	1-1	0-1	8	Eyre [72]	2373
15		26	H	Rochdale	D	2-2	2-1	10	Baker [6], Eyre (pen) [32]	2628
16		29	A	Fulham	L	1-2	1-1	—	Hope [5]	4566
17	Nov	2	A	Mansfield T	L	0-2	0-1	15		2210
18		9	H	Doncaster R	L	1-2	0-1	17	Clarkson [61]	3270
19		19	A	Colchester U	D	1-1	0-0	—	Clarkson [59]	1842
20		23	H	Darlington	W	3-2	3-0	15	Clarkson [14], Baker 2 [28, 43]	2366
21		30	A	Rochdale	W	2-1	1-0	13	Baker [18], Eyre [83]	1969
22	Dec	3	H	Hartlepool U	W	2-1	1-1	—	Baker [11], Clarkson [69]	1778
23		14	A	Exeter C	W	4-1	3-1	5	Calvo-Garcia [22], Sertori [30], Clarkson 2 [45, 74]	2000
24		21	A	Carlisle U	L	2-3	1-2	7	Clarkson [15], McFarlane [73]	5646
25		28	H	Wigan Ath	L	2-3	0-1	11	Eyre (pen) [56], McFarlane [62]	2833
26	Jan	18	H	Hereford U	W	5-1	2-1	11	Housham [1], Clarkson [8], Eyre (pen) [59], Baker 2 [75, 90]	1986
27		25	A	Fulham	L	1-4	0-3	14	Turnbull [79]	3259
28	Feb	1	A	Doncaster R	D	1-1	0-0	15	Baker [75]	3022
29		8	H	Mansfield T	L	0-2	0-1	15		2600
30		15	A	Darlington	L	0-2	0-1	16		2245
31		18	H	Chester C	L	0-2	0-1	—		1524
32		22	H	Colchester U	W	2-1	0-0	15	D'Auria [50], Jones [61]	2738
33		25	A	Cambridge U	W	2-0	0-0	—	Eyre [60], Housham [67]	2033
34	Mar	1	A	Hartlepool U	W	1-0	1-0	13	Eyre [13]	1300
35		8	H	Carlisle U	D	0-0	0-0	14		3470
36		15	A	Exeter C	W	1-0	0-0	12	Jones [64]	3378
37		22	A	Torquay U	W	2-1	2-1	11	Forrester [10], Jones [35]	1761
38		29	H	Leyton Orient	L	1-2	1-0	11	Forrester [24]	3365
39		31	A	Scarborough	L	2-3	0-2	13	Jones [68], Forrester [85]	3212
40	Apr	5	H	Brighton & HA	W	1-0	1-0	13	Hope [27]	2925
41		8	A	Barnet	D	1-1	0-1	—	Jones [79]	1395
42		12	H	Hull C	D	2-2	1-2	13	Forrester 2 [34, 51]	4257
43		15	A	Cardiff C	D	0-0	0-0	—		4490
44		19	A	Lincoln C	L	0-2	0-2	13		4755
45		26	H	Swansea C	W	1-0	0-0	12	Forrester [75]	3130
46	May	3	A	Northampton T	L	0-1	0-0	13		6828

Final League Position: 13

GOALSCORERS

League (59): Clarkson 13, Baker 9, Eyre 8 (3 pens), Forrester 6, Jones 5, D'Auria 3, Hope 3, Housham 3, McFarlane 3, Bradley 1, Calvo-Garcia 1, Jackson 1, Sertori 1, Turnbull 1, Wilson 1.
Coca-Cola Cup (2): Clarkson 1, Moss 1.
FA Cup (8): Baker 5 (1 pen), Clarkson 2, D'Auria 1.

Samways M 25	Hope C 46	Wilson P A 37	Sertori M 42	Knill A 29	Bradley R 22	D'Auria D 39	Moss D 4	McFarlane A 7+7	Eyre J 41+1	Clarkson P 28	Francis J 1+4	Walsh M 32+4	Paterson J 11+18	Gavin M 10+1	Housham S 31+3	Borland J —+2	Dunn I 3	Jackson K —+4	Baker P 21	Calvo-Garcia A 7+6	Turnbull L 11+3	Lucas D 6	Laws B 2+2	Clarke T 15	Jones G 9+2	Forrester J 10	McAuley S 9	Walker J 8+1	Wilson P D —+1	Match No.
1	2	3	4	5	6	7	8	9	10^1	11	12																			1
1	2	3^2	4	5	6	7	8	9	10^1	11	12	13																		2
1	2	3	4	5^1	6	7	8^2	9	10	11	12		13																	3
1	2	3	4	5	6	7	8	9^1	10	11	12																			4
1	2	3	4	5^1	6	7			10	11		9		8	12															5
1	2	3	4		6			9	10	11		5		8	7															6
1	2	3	4		6			9	10	11		5^1	12	8^2	7		13													7
1	2	3	4	5^1	6				10	11		12	8		7^2			13		9										8
1	2^1	3	4		6	5			10	11		12	8		7					9										9
1	2	3^2	4		6	10^3		12		11		5	13	8	7^1			14		9										10
1	2	3	4		6	10				11		5^1	12	8^2	7			14		9	13^3									11
1	2	3	4		6	8		12	10^1	11		5			7					9										12
1	2	3	4		6^2	8		12	10^1	11		5	13		7					9										13
1	2	3	4		6^1	8			10	11		5	12		7					9										14
1	2	3	4		6^1	8		12	10^3	11		5^2	13		7			14		9										15
1	2	3^2	4	5	6	8			10	11		13	12		7^1					9										16
1	2	3	4	5	6^2	8		12	10	11		13			7^1					9										17
1	2^1	3	4	5		8			10	11		12	6		7^2		13			9										18
1	5	3	4			8		12	10^1	11		2	6		7					9										19
1	5	3	4			8				11		2	6		7	12				9	10^1									20
1	5	3	4		6	8^1			10	11		2		9	7	12														21
1	5	3	4		6	8			10	11		2		9	7															22
1	5	3	4		6	8^3			10	11		2		9	7	12														23
1	5	3	4		6^3	8		12	10	11		2	13		7^2			14		9^1										24
	5	3				8			10	11		2	6		7^1	12		4	9			1								25
	6	3		5		8			10	11		2			7			4	9			1								26
	6	3		5		8^1			10^2	11		2	13		7	12		4	9			1								27
	6	3		5		8			10	11		2			7			4	9			1								28
	6	3	4	5^1		8			10	11		2			7				9			1	12							29
	6	3	4	5		10				11		2			7				9			1	12							30
1	6	3	4	5		8^1			10	11		2			7				9		12									31
	6	3	4	5		8				11		2			7				9^1		12			1		10				32
	6	3	4	5		8				11		2			7				9					1		10				33
	6	3	4	5		8				11		2			7				9^1		12			1		10				34
	6	3	4	5		8				11		2			7				9					1		10				35
	6	3	4	5		8				11		2^1			7				9		12			1		10				36
	6	3	4	5		8				11		2			7				9					1		10				37
	6		4	5		8				11					7^1				9					1	2	10	3	12		38
	6		4	5		8				11^1									9		12			1		10	7	3	2	39
	6		4	5		8				11									9		12			1		10^1	7	3	2	40
	5		4		6	8				11		2^1							9		12			1	13	10^2	3	7		41
	5^1		4		6	8				11		2							9					1	12	10	3	7		42
	5		4		6	8				11		2							9^1					1		10	3	7	12	43
	5		4		6^1	8				11		2							9				12	1		10	3	7		44
	5		4		6	8				11^1		2				12			9					1	14	10	3	7		45
	5		4		6^1	8				11^3		2				12^2		13	9					1	14	10	3	7		46

Coca-Cola Cup
First Round   Blackpool   (h) 2-1
                                       (a) 0-2

FA Cup
First Round   Rotherham U   (h) 4-1
Second Round   Wrexham   (a) 2-2
                                         (h) 2-3

SHEFFIELD UNITED 1996-97 *Back row (left to right):* Andy Scott, Charlie Hartfield, Doug Hodgson, Michael Vonk, Alan Kelly, Gareth Taylor, Paul Heritage, Lee Sandford, Don Hutchison, Roger Nilsen, Matt Hocking.

Middle row: John Bailey (Coach), Viv Busby (First Team Coach), Mark Beard, Chris Short, Liam Dyer, Nigel Spackman (Player/Assistant Manager), David White, Phil Starbuck, Petr Katchuro, John Greaves (Kit Man), Denis Circuit (Physio).

Front row: Paul Wood, Steve Hawes, Andy Walker, John Reed, Dane Whitehouse, Howard Kendall (Manager), Mitch Ward, Mark Patterson, Graham Anthony, Wayne Quinn, Chris Bettney.

Division 1   **SHEFFIELD UNITED**

Bramall Lane Ground, Sheffield S2 4SU. Telephone: (0114) 221 5757. Fax: (0114) 272 3030. Ticket Office: (0114) 221 1889. Pools Office: (0114) 221 3131. Club Shop: (0114) 221 3132. Executive Suite: (0114) 221 3133. Football in the Community: (0114) 221 3134. Ticket info line: (0891) 332 950. Clubcall: (0891) 888 650.

Ground capacity: 30,370.

Record attendance: 68,287 v Leeds U, FA Cup 5th rd, 15 February 1936.

Record receipts: £261,758 v Manchester U, FA Cup 5th rd, 14 February 1993.

Pitch measurements: 112yd × 72yd.

Chairman: A. M. McDonald. *Vice-Chairman:* F. Pye.

Directors: A. H. Laver, B. Proctor, K. C. McCabe, S. White.

Manager: . *Assistant Manager:* Nigel Spackman.

Coach: Viv Busby. *Youth Team Managers:* Russell Slade, John Dungworth.

Physio: Denis Circuit. *Secretary:* D. Capper AFA.

Commercial Manager: Andy R. Daykin. *Stadium Manager:* Roy Mitchell.

Community Programme Organiser: Tony Currie, Tel: (0114) 2769314.

Year Formed: 1889. *Turned Professional:* 1889. *Ltd Co.:* 1899.

Club Nickname: 'The Blades'.

Foundation: In March 1889, Yorkshire County Cricket Club formed Sheffield United six days after an FA Cup semi-final between Preston North End and West Bromwich Albion had finally convinced Charles Stokes, a member of the cricket club, that the formation of a professional football club would prove successful at Bramall Lane. The United's first secretary, Mr. J. B. Wostinholm was also secretary of the cricket club.

First Football League game: 3 September 1892, Division 2, v Lincoln C (h) W 4-2 – Lilley; Witham, Cain; Howell, Hendry, Needham (1); Wallace, Dobson, Hammond (3), Davies, Drummond.

Record League Victory: 10–0 v Burslem Port Vale (away), Division 2, 10 December 1892 – Howlett; Witham, Lilley; Howell, Hendry, Needham; Drummond (1), Wallace (1), Hammond (4), Davies (2), Watson (2).

Record Cup Victory: 5–0 v Newcastle U (away), FA Cup 1st rd, 10 January 1914 – Gough; Cook, English; Brelsford, Howley, Sturgess; Simmons (2), Gillespie (1), Kitchen (1), Fazackerley, Revill (1). 5–0 v Corinthians, FA Cup 1st rd, 10 January 1925 – Sutcliffe; Cook, Milton; Longworth, King, Green; Partridge, Boyle (1), Johnson (4), Gillespie, Tunstall. 5–0 v Barrow, FA Cup 3rd rd, 7 January 1956 – Burgin; Coldwell, Mason; Fountain, Johnson, Iley; Hawksworth (1), Hoyland (2), Howitt, Wragg (1), Grainger (1).

Record Defeat: 0–13 v Bolton W, FA Cup 2nd rd, 1 February 1890.

Most League Points (2 for a win): 60, Division 2, 1952–53.

Most League Points (3 for a win): 96, Division 4, 1981–82.

Most League Goals: 102, Division 1, 1925–26.

Highest League Scorer in Season: Jimmy Dunne, 41, Division 1, 1930–31.

Most League Goals in Total Aggregate: Harry Johnson, 205, 1919–30.

Most Capped Player: Billy Gillespie, 25, Northern Ireland.

Most League Appearances: Joe Shaw, 629, 1948–66.

Record Transfer Fee Received: £2,700,000 from Leeds U for Brian Deane, July 1993.

Record Transfer Fee Paid: £1,200,000 to West Ham U for Don Hutchison, January 1996.

Football League Record: 1892 Elected to Division 2; 1893–1934 Division 1; 1934–39 Division 2; 1946–49 Division 1; 1949–53 Division 2; 1953–56 Division 1; 1956–61 Division 2; 1961–68 Division 1; 1968–71 Division 2; 1971–76 Division 1; 1976–79 Division 2; 1979–81 Division 3; 1981–82 Division 4; 1982–84 Division 3; 1984–88 Division 2; 1988–89 Division 3; 1989–90 Division 2; 1990–92 Division 1; 1992–94 FA Premier League; 1994– Division 1.

Honours: Football League: Division 1 – Champions 1897–98; Runners-up 1896–97, 1899–1900; Division 2 – Champions 1952–53; Runners-up 1892–93, 1938–39, 1960–61, 1970–71, 1989–90; Division 4 – Champions 1981–82. *FA Cup:* Winners 1899, 1902, 1915, 1925; Runners-up 1901, 1936. *Football League Cup:* best season: 5th rd, 1962, 1967, 1972.

Colours: Red and white striped shirts with black trim, black shorts and stockings with red trim.
Change colours: All white with black trim.

Did you know?
Centre-forward Arthur Brown of Sheffield United was only 18 years 10 months old when he played for England against Wales on 29 February 1904.

SHEFFIELD UNITED 1996–97 LEAGUE RECORD

Match No.	Date	Venue	Opponents	Result	H/T Score	Lg. Pos.	Goalscorers	Attendance
1	Aug 17	A	Reading	L	0-1	0-0	—	11,081
2	24	H	Birmingham C	D	4-4	1-2	17	Taylor 2 [45, 70], Walker 2 [67, 72]	16,332
3	Sept 7	A	Oldham Ath	W	2-0	1-0	19	Hutchison [27], Sandford [87]	7323
4	10	H	Bradford C	W	3-0	2-0	—	Taylor [27], Whitehouse 2 [45, 58]	12,591
5	14	H	Ipswich T	L	1-3	1-0	16	Ward (pen) [28]	14,261
6	21	H	Wolverhampton W	W	2-1	0-0	13	White [76], Katchuro [90]	25,170
7	28	H	Manchester C	W	2-0	1-0	9	Ward (pen) [45], Taylor [49]	20,867
8	Oct 1	A	Southend U	L	2-3	2-1	—	Walker 2 [7, 34]	3716
9	12	H	Tranmere R	D	0-0	0-0	10		15,059
10	15	H	Charlton Ath	W	3-0	0-0	—	Katchuro 2 [52, 54], Walker [89]	14,080
11	19	A	Stoke C	W	4-0	3-0	6	Vonk 2 [8, 19], Walker [16], Taylor [77]	13,581
12	26	H	QPR	D	1-1	0-1	8	Taylor [83]	17,096
13	30	A	Norwich C	D	1-1	1-0	—	Katchuro [24]	14,534
14	Nov 3	A	Grimsby T	W	4-2	2-1	6	Hutchison [27], Whitehouse 2 [44, 82], Katchuro [80]	5935
15	13	H	WBA	W	2-1	0-0	—	Walker [57], Hutchison [60]	12,167
16	16	A	Port Vale	D	0-0	0-0	5		8352
17	22	H	Bolton W	D	1-1	1-1	—	Taylor [41]	17,069
18	26	H	Swindon T	W	2-0	1-0	—	Taylor [6], Katchuro [61]	12,301
19	30	A	QPR	L	0-1	0-1	4		11,891
20	Dec 3	H	Huddersfield T	W	3-1	2-1	—	Sandford [34], Patterson [38], White [61]	14,700
21	7	H	Portsmouth	W	1-0	1-0	2	Katchuro [14]	16,333
22	14	A	Oxford U	L	1-4	0-3	3	Walker [88]	7737
23	17	A	Crystal Palace	W	1-0	1-0	—	Walker [44]	12,801
24	21	H	Barnsley	L	0-1	0-0	3		24,384
25	26	A	Bradford C	W	2-1	1-1	2	Taylor [26], Scott [47]	17,475
26	28	H	Oldham Ath	D	2-2	1-1	3	Taylor [8], Katchuro [70]	16,130
27	Jan 18	A	Southend U	W	3-0	1-0	2	Katchuro [15], White [50], Taylor [61]	15,049
28	24	H	Wolverhampton W	L	2-3	1-2	—	White 2 [24, 82]	17,490
29	29	A	Manchester C	D	0-0	0-0	—		26,551
30	Feb 1	A	Swindon T	L	1-2	0-0	4	Holdsworth [80]	8811
31	9	H	Norwich C	L	2-3	0-0	4	Katchuro [46], Walker [79]	15,301
32	15	A	Bolton W	D	2-2	1-2	4	Fjortoft [7], Katchuro [55]	17,922
33	22	H	Grimsby T	W	3-1	1-1	4	Fjortoft 3 [45, 62, 68]	17,502
34	Mar 1	A	Portsmouth	D	1-1	0-1	4	Fjortoft [54]	12,715
35	4	H	Port Vale	W	3-0	0-0	—	Ward (pen) [62], Taylor [79], Fjortoft [82]	14,950
36	7	A	Barnsley	L	0-2	0-1	—		14,668
37	15	H	Oxford U	W	3-1	3-1	4	Whitehouse [11], Fjortoft [35], Walker [43]	16,226
38	18	A	Ipswich T	L	1-3	1-3	—	Fjortoft [21]	10,374
39	22	A	Birmingham C	D	1-1	0-0	4	Katchuro [64]	14,969
40	29	H	Reading	W	2-0	1-0	3	Bodin (og) [11], Walker [49]	15,153
41	31	A	Huddersfield T	L	1-2	1-2	4	Sinnott (og) [16]	14,551
42	Apr 5	H	WBA	L	1-2	0-1	4	Fjortoft [69]	15,004
43	12	H	Crystal Palace	W	3-0	2-0	4	Ward (pen) [2], Fjortoft [19], White [89]	20,051
44	19	A	Tranmere R	D	1-1	0-1	4	Whitehouse [50]	10,027
45	25	H	Stoke C	W	1-0	0-0	—	Tiler [66]	25,596
46	May 4	A	Charlton Ath	D	0-0	0-0	5		12,589

Final League Position: 5

GOALSCORERS

League (75): Katchuro 12, Taylor 12, Walker 12, Fjortoft 10, White 6, Whitehouse 6, Ward 4 (4 pens), Hutchison 3, Sandford 2, Vonk 2, Holdsworth 1, Patterson 1, Scott 1, Tiler 1, own goals 2.
Coca-Cola Cup (8): Vonk 2, Walker 2 (1 pen), Katchuro 1, Taylor 1, Ward 1, White 1.
FA Cup (0).

Kelly A 39	Ward M 34	Sandford L 25 + 5	Spackman N 19 + 4	Vonk M 17	Nilsen R 32 + 1	Hutchison D 38 + 3	Patterson M 34 + 1	Taylor G 26 + 8	Walker A 20 + 17	Whitehouse D 30	Katchuro P 28 + 12	White D 31 + 6	Short C 22 + 2	Hodgson D 12 + 1	Starbuck P 1 + 1	Scott A 4 + 4	Holdsworth D 37	Hawes S — + 2	Hartfield C 1 + 1	Parker P 7 + 3	Beard M 9 + 7	Simpson P 2 + 4	Anthony G — + 2	Fjortoft J 15 + 2	Tracey S 7	Henry N 9	Ebbrell J 1	Tiler C 6	Bettney C — + 1	Match No.
1	2	3	4	5	6	7²	8	9¹	10	11	12	13																		1
1		6	4	5	3	8	11	9	10		12²	7		2¹	13															2
1	7	3	13	5	6	4	8	9¹	10²	11	12		2																	3
1	7	3	12	4	5	6	8¹	9	10²	11	13		2																	4
1	7	3		5	6	4	8	9	10¹	11	12²	13	2																	5
1	2		6	5		4	8	9		11	12	7		3	10¹															6
1	2	3			6	4	8	9	10¹	11	12	7		5																7
1	2	3		5		4¹	8		10	11		7	12	6	13	9²														8
1	4		5	3	12	8		10¹	11	9	7	2²			13		6													9
1	2		5	3	4	8	12	10	11	9¹	7						6													10
1	2	3		5		4²	8	12	10	11	9¹	7					6	13												11
1	2	3¹		5	12	4	8	13	10	11	9²	7					6													12
1	7			5	3	4	8	9¹	13	11	10²	12	2				6													13
1	2			5	3	4	8	9¹	12	11	10	7²	13				6													14
1	7²	12		5	3	4	8	9	13	11	10¹		2				6													15
1				5	3	4	8	9	12	11	10²		2				6		7¹	13										16
1	3			5		4²	8	9	10¹	11	12	7	2				6			13										17
1	3			5¹		4	8	9	12	11	10	7	2²				6			13										18
1	3	5				4	8	9	12	11²	10¹	13					6				2	7								19
1	3	5¹			8	4	11	9			10	7					6				2	12								20
1	3	7			6	4²	8	9	12		10¹						5				2	13	11							21
1	5	4²	3		8		9¹		12		10	7	13				6				2	11								22
1		4			8			9			10	7		5		11¹	6				2	3²	12	13						23
1		4				7	8	9			10			5		11¹	6				3	2	12							24
1	12	7				4	8	9			10²			5		11	6				3¹	2	13							25
1		7¹	3			4	8	9	12	11²	10			5			6				2	13								26
1	2²	3	8		6	4	11	9¹	12		10	7		5								13								27
1	2²	3	8¹	5		4	11	9	12		10	7					6					13								28
1	11	3				4	8	9²	10¹			7		5			6	12	13		2									29
1	11		3			4	8				10	7		5			6				2¹		12	9						30
1¹	11		3		8	4³		13	12		10	7	2	5²			6				14			9						31
	11		3		8			12²	13		10¹	7	2	5			6				4			9	1					32
	11	12	4		3		8¹				10	7	2	5			6							9	1					33
1	11			5	3	4	8		12		10¹	7	2				6							9						34
1	11	3		5		4	8	12	13		10	7					6				2¹			9²						35
1	3			5		4	10			11¹	12	7	2				6							9		8				36
	3	12		5		4	13	14	10	11¹		7	2²				6							9¹	1	8				37
	7	5²	3			4			12	11	10¹	13	2				6							9	1	8				38
	7	5	3	12		4	10	13	11²	14			2				6							9¹	1	8¹				39
	3	5		12				9³	10²	11	13	7	2				6							14	1	8	4¹			40
	2	3³	12			4¹		9²	10	11	13	7					6							14	1	8		5		41
1	8	6	12²		3	4	13			11	10	7¹	2				6							9				5		42
1	7	12			3	4¹				11	10¹	13	2				6							9		8		5		43
1	10²	3			8¹	4				11		7	2				6			12				9				5	13	44
1	2	3				4				11	10¹	7		12			6							9		8		5		45
1	2	4¹	3							11	10²	7		13			6			12				9		8		5		46

Coca-Cola Cup				FA Cup			
First Round	Bradford C	(h)	3-0	Third Round	Norwich C	(a)	0-1
		(a)	2-1				
Second Round	Stockport Co	(a)	1-2				
		(h)	2-5				

SHEFFIELD WEDNESDAY 1996-97 *Back row (left to right):* Mark Bright, Dejan Stefanovic, Ryan Jones, Kevin Pressman, Jon Newsome, Matt Clarke, Brian Linighan, Andy Booth, Chris Waddle. *Middle row:* Peter Shreeves (Assistant Manager), Ian Nolan, Guy Whittingham, Michael Williams, Lee Briscoe, Wayne Collins, O'Neill Donaldson, John Sheridan, Richie Humphreys, Dave Galley (Physio). *Front row:* Mark Pembridge, Scott Oakes, Regi Blinker, Des Walker, David Pleat (Manager), Peter Atherton, Graham Hyde, Steve Nicol, David Hirst.

FA Premiership   **SHEFFIELD WEDNESDAY**

Hillsborough, Sheffield S6 1SW. Telephone: (0114) 2212121. Fax: (0114) 2212122. Ticket Office: (0114) 2212400. Clubcall: 0891 121186.

Ground capacity: 39,859.

Record attendance: 72,841 v Manchester C, FA Cup 5th rd, 17 February 1934.

Record receipts: £533,918 Sunderland v Norwich C, FA Cup semi-final, 5 April 1992.

Pitch measurements: 115yd × 74yd.

President: K. T. Addy.

Chairman: D. G. Richards. *Vice-Chairman:* K. T. Addy.

Directors: G. K. Hulley, R. M. Grierson FCA, J. Ashton MP, G. A. Thorpe, H. E. Culley.

Manager: David Pleat. *Assistant Manager:* Peter Shreeves.

Physio: David Galley.

Secretary: Graham Mackrell FCCA. *Commercial Manager:* Sean O'Toole. *Stadium Manager:* T. Grayson.

Year Formed: 1867 (fifth oldest League club).

Turned Professional: 1887. *Ltd Co.:* 1899.

Former Names: The Wednesday until 1929.

Club Nickname: 'The Owls'.

Previous Grounds: 1867, Highfield; 1869, Myrtle Road; 1877, Sheaf House; 1887, Olive Grove; 1899, Owlerton (since 1912 known as Hillsborough). Some games were played at Endcliffe in the 1880s. Until 1895 Bramall Lane was used for some games.

Foundation: Sheffield, being one of the principal centres of early Association Football, this club was formed as long ago as 1867 by the Sheffield Wednesday Cricket Club (formed 1825) and their colours from the start were blue and white. The inaugural meeting was held at the Adelphi Hotel and the original committee included Charles Stokes who was subsequently a founder member of Sheffield United.

First Football League game: 3 September 1892, Division 1, v Notts Co (a) W 1-0 – Allan; Tom Brandon (1), Mumford; Hall, Betts, Harry Brandon; Spiksley, Brady, Davis, R.N. Brown, Dunlop.

Record League Victory: 9–1 v Birmingham, Division 1, 13 December 1930 – Brown; Walker, Blenkinsop; Strange, Leach, Wilson; Hooper (3), Seed (2), Ball (2), Burgess (1), Rimmer (1).

Record Cup Victory: 12–0 v Halliwell, FA Cup 1st rd, 17 January 1891 – Smith; Thompson, Brayshaw; Harry Brandon (1), Betts, Cawley (2); Winterbottom, Mumford (2), Bob Brandon (1), Woolhouse (5), Ingram (1).

Record Defeat: 0–10 v Aston Villa, Division 1, 5 October 1912.

Most League Points (2 for a win): 62, Division 2, 1958–59.

Most League Points (3 for a win): 88, Division 2, 1983–84.

Most League Goals: 106, Division 2, 1958–59.

Highest League Scorer in Season: Derek Dooley, 46, Division 2, 1951–52.

Most League Goals in Total Aggregate: Andy Wilson, 199, 1900–20.

Most Capped Player: Nigel Worthington, 50 (66), Northern Ireland.

Most League Appearances: Andy Wilson, 502, 1900–20.

Record Transfer Fee Received: £2,650,000 from Blackburn R for Paul Warhurst, September 1993.

Record Transfer Fee Paid: £3,000,000 to Internazionale for Benito Carbone, October 1996.

Football League Record: 1892 Elected to Division 1; 1899–1900 Division 2; 1900–20 Division 1; 1920–26 Division 2; 1926–37 Division 1; 1937–50 Division 2; 1950–51 Division 1; 1951–52 Division 2; 1952–55 Division 1; 1955–56 Division 2; 1956–58 Division 1; 1958–59 Division 2; 1959–70 Division 1; 1970–75 Division 2; 1975–80 Division 3; 1980–84 Division 2; 1984–90 Division 1; 1990–91 Division 2; 1991–92 Division 1; 1992– FA Premier League.

Honours: Football League: Division 1 – Champions 1902–03, 1903–04, 1928–29, 1929–30; Runners-up 1960–61; Division 2 – Champions 1899–1900, 1925–26, 1951–52, 1955–56, 1958–59; Runners-up 1949–50, 1983–84. *FA Cup:* Winners 1896, 1907, 1935; Runners-up 1890, 1966, 1993. *Football League Cup:* Winners 1991; Runners-up 1993. **European Competitions:** *Fairs Cup:* 1961–62, 1963–64, 1992–93.

Colours: Blue and white striped shirts, black shorts, black stockings. *Change colours:* Orange shirts, white shorts, white stockings.

Did you know?
Sheffield Wednesday reached the last eight in the FA Cup in nine successive seasons from 1887–88 to 1895–96.

SHEFFIELD WEDNESDAY 1996–97 LEAGUE RECORD

Match No.	Date	Venue	Opponents	Result		H/T Score	Lg. Pos.	Goalscorers	Attendance
1	Aug 17	H	Aston Villa	W	2-1	0-0	—	Humphreys [56], Whittingham [84]	26,861
2	20	A	Leeds U	W	2-0	1-0	—	Humphreys [14], Booth [90]	31,008
3	24	A	Newcastle U	W	2-1	1-1	1	Atherton [15], Whittingham [80]	36,452
4	Sept 2	H	Leicester C	W	2-1	1-1	—	Humphreys [25], Booth [51]	17,657
5	7	H	Chelsea	L	0-2	0-1	1		30,983
6	16	A	Arsenal	L	1-4	1-0	—	Booth [25]	33,461
7	21	H	Derby Co	D	0-0	0-0	5		23,487
8	28	A	Everton	L	0-2	0-1	7		34,160
9	Oct 12	A	Wimbledon	L	2-4	1-2	7	Booth [3], Hyde [72]	10,512
10	19	H	Blackburn R	D	1-1	1-0	9	Booth [3]	22,226
11	26	A	Coventry C	D	0-0	0-0	8		17,269
12	Nov 2	H	Southampton	D	1-1	1-0	9	Newsome [14]	20,106
13	18	H	Nottingham F	W	2-0	0-0	—	Trustfull [63], Carbone [85]	16,390
14	23	A	Sunderland	D	1-1	0-0	10	Oakes [66]	20,617
15	30	H	West Ham U	D	0-0	0-0	10		22,321
16	Dec 7	A	Liverpool	W	1-0	1-0	9	Whittingham [22]	39,507
17	18	H	Manchester U	D	1-1	0-0	—	Carbone [57]	37,671
18	21	H	Tottenham H	D	1-1	1-1	9	Nolan [16]	30,996
19	26	H	Arsenal	D	0-0	0-0	10		23,245
20	28	A	Chelsea	D	2-2	1-2	9	Pembridge [24], Stefanovic [90]	26,608
21	Jan 11	H	Everton	W	2-1	1-0	8	Pembridge [22], Hirst [50]	24,175
22	18	A	Middlesbrough	L	2-4	1-2	8	Pembridge 2 [29, 80]	29,484
23	29	A	Aston Villa	W	1-0	0-0	—	Booth [69]	26,726
24	Feb 1	H	Coventry C	D	0-0	0-0	8		21,793
25	19	A	Derby Co	D	2-2	1-1	—	Collins [9], Hirst [76]	18,060
26	22	H	Southampton	W	3-2	0-2	8	Hirst 2 [49, 55], Booth [78]	15,062
27	Mar 1	H	Middlesbrough	W	3-1	2-0	8	Booth [21], Hyde [43], Pembridge (pen) [90]	28,206
28	5	A	Nottingham F	W	3-0	0-0	—	Carbone 2 [52, 87], Blinker [58]	21,485
29	12	H	Sunderland	W	2-1	1-1	—	Hirst [42], Stefanovic [63]	20,296
30	15	A	Manchester U	L	0-2	0-1	5		55,267
31	22	H	Leeds U	D	2-2	1-2	7	Hirst [20], Booth [51]	30,373
32	Apr 9	H	Tottenham H	W	2-1	1-1	—	Atherton [18], Booth [70]	22,671
33	13	H	Newcastle U	D	1-1	0-1	6	Pembridge [57]	33,798
34	19	H	Wimbledon	W	3-1	1-0	6	Donaldson [42], Trustfull 2 [78, 83]	26,957
35	22	A	Blackburn R	L	1-4	0-3	—	Carbone (pen) [83]	20,845
36	May 3	A	West Ham U	L	1-5	0-3	7	Carbone [82]	24,960
37	7	A	Leicester C	L	0-1	0-0	—		20,793
38	11	H	Liverpool	D	1-1	0-0	7	Donaldson [75]	38,943

Final League Position: 7

GOALSCORERS

League (50): Booth 10, Carbone 6 (1 pen), Hirst 6, Pembridge 6 (1 pen), Humphreys 3, Trustfull 3, Whittingham 3, Atherton 2, Donaldson 2, Hyde 2, Stefanovic 2, Blinker 1, Collins 1, Newsome 1, Nolan 1, Oakes 1.
Coca-Cola Cup (1): Whittingham 1.
FA Cup (10): Booth 3, Humphreys 3, Hyde 1, Pembridge 1, Whittingham 1, own goal 1.

Pressman K 38	Atherton P 37	Nolan I 38	Pembridge M 33 + 1	Stefanovic D 27 + 2	Walker D 36	Collins W 8 + 4	Blinker R 15 + 18	Booth A 32 + 3	Humphreys R 14 + 15	Whittingham G 29 + 4	Hyde G 15 + 4	Oakes S 7 + 12	Nicol S 19 + 4	Trustfull O 9 + 10	Hirst D 20 + 5	Sheridan J — + 2	Bright M — + 1	Williams M — + 1	Newsome J 10	Carbone B 24 + 1	Briscoe L 5 + 1	Donaldson O 2 + 3	Clarke M — + 1	Match No.
1	2	3	4^1	5	6	7	8	9	10^2	11	12	13												1
1	2	3	4	5	6	7^2	8	9	10^1	11	12	13												2
1	2	3	4	5	6	7	8		10^2	11	12	9^1			13									3
1	2	3		5	6	7	4	10	8^1	11				9^2	12	13								4
1	2	3		5	6	7^1	4	10	8^2	11^3			14	12	9	13								5
1	2	3	4	5^1	6	7	8^1	10		11^3				12	13	14	9							6
1	2	3	4^3	5	6		7^2	10^1	12	11		8	13	14	9									7
1	2	3		5	6		8	10	12	11^3	13		4^2	7	9^1	14								8
1	2^1	3	4	5^2		7		10	11^3	8	13	12	14		9				6					9
1	2	3	12		6	7	10	13	14	8				11^1	9^3				5	4^2				10
1	2	3	4		6	8^2	9	12	14	10	13			11^1					5	7^3				11
1	2	3	4		6	12	9	13	14	8	10^2			11^1					5	7^2				12
1	2	3	4	12	6	8	9^2	13		10^1	14			11^3					5	7				13
1	2	3	4		6	9	12	13	8	7^1				11^2					5	10				14
1	5	2^2	4		6	9	12	10	8	14	13			11^1						7		3^2		15
1	2	3	4	5	6	12	9		11	8				10						7^1				16
1	2	3	4	5	6	12	9^2		11	8^3				10	14	13				7^1				17
1	2	3	4	5	6	12	9^3	13	11^2					10	8^1	14				7				18
1	4	3	7	5	6	12	13		11					10^1	2	9^2				8				19
1	2	3	4	5	6	12	9	8^3	11					13	10^2					7^1		14		20
1	4	3	7	5	6	9^1	10	11	8						2					12				21
1	4	3	7	5	6	12	13	9	10^1	11^3	8				2^2					14				22
1	4	3	7	5	6	12	10		11	8					2					9^1				23
1	4	3	7	5	6	12	10		11^1	8					2	13				9^2				24
1	4	3	7		6	8	12	9	10^2						2^1	13			5	11^3		14		25
1	4	3	7	5		8^1	12	13	10^2					14	2	9			6	11^3				26
1	4	3	7	14	6	12	10	13		8^3					2	9^2			5	11^1				27
1	4	2	7		6	8	10^1	12		11^2				13	9^3				5	14	3			28
1	4	2	7	5	6		10	12	11						9					8^1	3			29
1	4	3		5	6	8^1	12	10^2	11					2^3	13	9				7		14		30
1		2	4	5	6	13	12	10	8^2	11					9					7^3	3			31
1	4	2	7		6	12	10	13	11^3					5	9^2					8	3			32
1	4	3	7	5	6^3	14	12	9^2	13	11				8	2^1					10				33
1	4	3	7	5	6	8^1			11					2	12					10	9			34
1	4	3	7		6	12	13		14	11^2				2	5^1	10^3				8	9			35
1	4	3	7	5	6	12	10		11^1					13	2^2	9				8				36
1	2	3	4	5	6	12	10	8	11						9^1					7				37
1^6	2	3	4	5	6		10	8^1	11					12	9^2					7		13	15	38

Coca-Cola Cup
Second Round   Oxford U   (h) 1-1   (a) 0-1

FA Cup
Third Round   Grimsby T   (h) 7-1
Fourth Round   Carlisle U   (a) 2-0
Fifth Round   Bradford C   (a) 1-0
Sixth Round   Wimbledon   (h) 0-2

SHREWSBURY TOWN 1996-97 *Back row (left to right):* Richard Pratley (Coach), Steve Anthrobus, Shaun Wray, Richard Scott, Mark Taylor, Paul Edwards, Peter Whiston, Dean Spink, Darren Rowbotham, Dave Walton, Mark Dempsey, Kevin Summerfield (Coach).
Front row: Ian Reed, Darren Currie, Paul Evans, Fred Davies (Manager), Malcolm Musgrove (Physio), Austin Berkley, James Cope, Ian Stevens, Kevin Seabury.

Division 3   **SHREWSBURY TOWN**

Gay Meadow, Shrewsbury SY2 6AB. Telephone: (01743) 360111. Fax: (01743) 236384. Commercial Dept: (01743) 356316. Clubcall: 0891 121194. Community Officer: Derek Mann (01743) 356623.

Ground capacity: 8000.

Record attendance: 18,917 v Walsall, Division 3, 26 April 1961.

Record receipts: £80,610 v Arsenal, FA Cup 5th rd, 27 February 1991.

Pitch measurements: 114yd × 74yd.

President: F. C. G. Fry. *Vice-President:* Dr J. Millard Bryson.

Chairman: R. Wycherley.

Directors: R. Bailey, A. Hopkins, M. J. Starkey, K. R. Woodhouse.

Associate Directors: M. R. Ashton, H. J. Wilson, K. J. Sayfritz.

Manager: Jake King. *Commercial Manager:* M. Thomas.

Physio: Malcolm Musgrove. *Coaches:* Kevin Summerfield, Richard Pratley.

Secretary: M. J. Starkey. *Operations Manager:* M. R. Ashton.

Club Nickname: 'Town' or 'Blues'.

Year Formed: 1886. *Turned Professional:* 1896. *Ltd Co.:* 1936.

Previous Ground: Old Shrewsbury Racecourse.

Foundation: Shrewsbury School having provided a number of the early England and Wales international players it is not surprising that there was a Town club as early as 1876 which won the Birmingham Senior Cup in 1879. However, the present Shrewsbury Town club was formed in 1886 and won the Welsh FA Cup as early as 1891.

First Football League game: 19 August 1950, Division 3 (N), v Scunthorpe U (a) D 0-0 – Egglestone; Fisher, Lewis; Wheatley, Depear, Robinson; Griffin, Hope, Jackson, Brown, Barker.

Record League Victory: 7–0 v Swindon T, Division 3 (S), 6 May 1955 – McBride; Bannister, Skeech; Wallace, Maloney, Candlin; Price, O'Donnell (1), Weigh (4), Russell, McCue (2).

Record Cup Victory: 11–2 v Marine, FA Cup 1st rd, 11 November 1995 – Edwards, Seabury (Dempsey (1)), Withe (1), Evans (1), Whiston (2), Scott (1), Woods, Stevens (1), Spink (3) (Anthrobus), Walton, Berkley (1 og).

Record Defeat: 1–8 v Norwich C, Division 3 (S), 13 September 1952 and v Coventry C, Division 3, 22 October 1963.

Most League Points (2 for a win): 62, Division 4, 1974–75.

Most League Points (3 for a win): 79, Division 3, 1993–94.

Most League Goals: 101, Division 4, 1958–59.

Highest League Scorer in Season: Arthur Rowley, 38, Division 4, 1958–59.

Most League Goals in Total Aggregate: Arthur Rowley, 152, 1958–65 (thus completing his League record of 434 goals).

Most Capped Player: Jimmy McLaughlin, 5 (12), Northern Ireland and Bernard McNally, 5, Northern Ireland.

Most League Appearances: Colin Griffin, 406, 1975–89.

Record Transfer Fee Received: £385,000 from WBA for Bernard McNally, July 1989.

Record Transfer Fee Paid: £100,000 to Aldershot for John Dungworth, November 1979 and £100,000 to Southampton for Mark Blake, August 1990.

Football League Record: 1950 Elected to Division 3 (N); 1951–58 Division 3 (S); 1958–59 Division 4; 1959–74 Division 3; 1974–75 Division 4; 1975–79 Division 3; 1979–89 Division 2; 1989–94 Division 3; 1994– Division 2.

Honours: Football League: Division 2 best season: 8th, 1983–84, 1984–85; Division 3 – Champions 1978–79, 1993–94; Division 3 – Runners-up 1974–75. *FA Cup:* best season: 6th rd, 1979, 1982. *Football League Cup:* Semi-final 1961. *Welsh Cup:* Winners 1891, 1938, 1977, 1979, 1984, 1985; Runners-up 1931, 1948, 1980. *Auto Windscreens Shield:* Runners-up 1996.

Colours: Blue shirts, white trim, blue shorts, blue stockings, white trim. *Change colours:* Yellow shirts, navy blue sleeves, yellow shorts, yellow stockings, navy blue tops.

Did you know?
On 1 February 1997, Shrewsbury Town's 14-man squad at Bristol Rovers had earned the Club more money than the players actually cost. Mickey Brown's two transfers to Bolton Wanderers and Preston North End had generated a profit of £120,000, whilst only Mark Dempsey (£25,000), Darren Currie (£25,000), Dave Walton (£25,000) and Ian Stevens (£20,000) had required transfer fees.

SHREWSBURY TOWN 1996–97 LEAGUE RECORD

Match No.	Date	Venue	Opponents	Result	H/T Score	Lg. Pos.	Goalscorers	Attendance
1	Aug 18	H	Wycombe W	D 1-1	1-0	—	Stevens [4]	3440
2	24	A	Rotherham U	W 2-1	1-1	8	Stevens 2 [24, 71]	3037
3	27	A	Burnley	W 3-1	1-0	—	Taylor M [20], Scott [48], Stevens [84]	9072
4	31	H	Brentford	L 0-3	0-3	6		3530
5	Sept 7	A	York C	D 0-0	0-0	8		2911
6	10	H	Bristol C	W 1-0	0-0	—	Stevens [76]	2502
7	14	H	Bury	D 1-1	1-1	8	Rowbotham [9]	3238
8	21	A	Blackpool	D 1-1	0-0	8	Stevens [71]	4452
9	28	H	Watford	W 1-0	0-0	5	Evans [78]	3655
10	Oct 1	A	Chesterfield	L 1-2	1-0	—	Dyche (og) [34]	3299
11	8	A	Wrexham	L 1-2	1-1	—	Evans [43]	5031
12	12	H	Luton T	L 0-3	0-1	14		3357
13	15	H	Gillingham	L 1-2	0-0	—	Currie [79]	2042
14	19	A	Preston NE	L 1-2	0-0	17	Stevens [76]	8333
15	26	H	Crewe Alex	L 0-1	0-0	18		3878
16	29	A	Peterborough U	D 2-2	0-1	—	Bennett 2 [49, 90]	5400
17	Nov 2	A	Notts Co	W 2-1	1-0	15	Stevens [22], Bennett [88]	4363
18	12	H	Bristol R	W 2-0	1-0	—	Stevens [29], Spink [75]	2331
19	20	A	Millwall	L 1-2	1-1	—	Stevens [36]	5770
20	23	H	Stockport Co	W 3-2	0-1	12	Stevens [64], Anthrobus [79], Evans [87]	2865
21	30	A	Crewe Alex	L 1-5	1-2	13	Stevens [17]	4035
22	Dec 3	H	Bournemouth	D 1-1	1-0	—	Anthrobus [40]	1610
23	14	A	Plymouth Arg	D 2-2	1-0	14	Spink [45], Evans [47]	5075
24	20	H	Walsall	D 2-2	2-1	—	Anthrobus [11], Stevens [26]	3007
25	26	A	Bristol C	L 2-3	2-1	14	Stevens [32], Nielsen [45]	9803
26	28	H	York C	W 2-0	1-0	12	Evans [32], Stevens [63]	3189
27	Jan 1	H	Blackpool	L 1-3	0-3	—	Ward [77]	2787
28	18	H	Chesterfield	W 2-0	1-0	12	Brown [2], Evans (pen) [50]	2659
29	25	H	Peterborough U	D 2-2	1-1	12	Bodley (og) [25], Anthrobus [61]	2695
30	Feb 1	A	Bristol R	L 0-2	0-0	13		4924
31	8	H	Notts Co	W 2-1	0-0	14	Spink [60], Stevens [80]	2692
32	15	A	Stockport Co	L 1-3	0-0	14	Whiston [60]	6712
33	22	H	Millwall	D 1-1	1-0	16	Anthrobus [40]	2968
34	25	A	Watford	L 0-2	0-1	—		6378
35	Mar 1	A	Bournemouth	D 0-0	0-0	16		5810
36	4	A	Bury	L 0-2	0-2	—		2690
37	8	A	Walsall	D 2-2	0-2	17	Currie [55], Walton [66]	4819
38	15	H	Plymouth Arg	L 2-3	0-0	18	Anthrobus [53], Stevens [72]	3414
39	22	H	Rotherham U	L 0-2	0-1	20		2893
40	29	A	Wycombe W	L 0-3	0-1	20		6562
41	Apr 1	H	Burnley	W 2-1	0-0	—	Brass (og) [80], Spink [86]	4462
42	5	A	Brentford	D 0-0	0-0	19		5355
43	12	H	Wrexham	L 0-1	0-0	21		4553
44	19	A	Luton T	L 0-2	0-1	21		6968
45	26	H	Preston NE	L 0-2	0-0	21		5341
46	May 3	A	Gillingham	L 0-2	0-0	22		6183

Final League Position: 22

GOALSCORERS

League (49): Stevens 17, Anthrobus 6, Evans 6 (1 pen), Spink 4, Bennett 3, Currie 2, Brown 1, Nielsen 1, Rowbotham 1, Scott 1, Taylor M 1, Walton 1, Ward 1, Whiston 1, own goals 3.
Coca-Cola Cup (1): Rowbotham 1.
FA Cup (1): Stevens 1.

Gall B 23	Whiston P 26+1	Spink D 39+2	Watson D 23+1	Taylor L 13+3	Taylor M 33+4	Scott R 20+7	Currie D 25+12	Stevens I 41	Anthrobus S 33	Berkley A 20+4	Seabury K 34+4	Rowbotham D 11+3	Nielsen T 19+3	Evans P 42	Dempsey M 37+3	Edwards P 23	Ward N 5+9	Wray S 1	Bent J 6	Bennett F 2+2	Brown M 17+2	Cope J 3	Nwadike C 1+1	Briscoe A —+1	Wrack D 3+1	Reed I —+3	Blamey N 6	Tate C —+1	Match No.
1	3	5	10	2	4	6	7²	8	9	11¹	12	13																	1
1		5		2	4¹	6		8	9	11	7	12	3	10															2
1		5	4		6		12	8	9	11	2	7	3	10															3
1	12		4	5	6			8	9	11	2	7	3¹	10															4
1		5	3		4	6¹	12	8	9	11	2	7²		10	13														5
1	4			5¹		6	7	8	9	11	2	12	3	10															6
1	4			5			6¹	8	9	11	2	7	3	10	12														7
1		5			4¹	6		8	9	11	2	7	3	10	12														8
1		5				6	7	8	9	11	2			10	3	4													9
1		5	12			6	13	8	9	11¹	2	7	3	10²	4														10
1		5	4			6	12	8	9¹	11	2	7	3	10															11
1		5	10	13	4¹	6		8	9	12²	2	7	3	11															12
		5	3		4	6²	12	8	9		2	7	11	10¹		1	13												13
	12	5	4	13				8	9¹		2	7	3	10	11	1	6²												14
	2		4	5		6	12	8					3¹	10	11	1	9²			7	13								15
	2	5	4			6	12	8					3¹	10	11	1	9²			7	13								16
	2	5	4			6	12	8		11				10	3	1					7¹		9						17
	2	5	4¹			6	12	8		11				10	3	1					7		9						18
		5	4			6		8	9	11	2			10	3	1	7												19
		5	4			6		8	9	11	2			10	3	1	7												20
	6	5	4				12	8	9	11¹	2	7²		10	3	1	13												21
	6¹	5	4				12	8	9	11²	2	7		10	3	1	13												22
	6	5	4						9	11	2			10	3	1					7	8							23
	6	5					12	8	9	11¹	2	13		10	3	1					7²	4							24
	6		4	5				8	9	11	2			10	3	1					7								25
	6		4	5¹			12	8	9	11	2			10	3	1					7								26
	6		4¹	5			12	8	9³	11²	2	13		10	3	1	14				7								27
1		5	4			6	12	8	9	11	2			10	3						7¹								28
1		5	4²			6	12	8	9	11	2	13		10³	3		14				7¹								29
1		4	5					8	9		2			10	3¹			11²			7	6	12	13					30
1		4	9	5		6	12	8		11¹	2			10	3						7								31
1	2¹	5	6		4		12	8	9	11				10	3						7								32
1	2		4	5		6	12		9	11				10	3		13				7²				8¹				33
1	2³	5	6		4¹		12		9	11			13	10	3		14				7				8²				34
1	2	5	6		4			8	9	11				10	3						7								35
1	2	5	6		4			8	9	11				10	3						7								36
1	2	5	6		4²		12	8³	9	11				10	3						7¹					13		14	37
1	2	5	6		4			8	9	11				10¹	3						7	12							38
		5	6		4²		12	8	9	11	2			10	3	1	13				7¹								39
		5	9	6	4¹		12	8		11	2			10	3	1					7²					13			40
		5¹	9	6	4		12	8		11				10	3	1					7					13	2²		41
		5	9	6	4¹		12	8²		11				10	3	1					7					13	2		42
		5	9	6	4			8¹		11				10	3	1					7	12					2		43
	6¹	5	9	6	4			8		11				10	3	1					7	12					2		44
	6		4¹	5²				8	9	11				10	3	1					7	12				13	2		45
			4	5	6		12	8³	9	11²				10	3	1					7					13	2¹	14	46

Coca-Cola Cup
First Round　　　　Tranmere R　　　　(h)　0-2
　　　　　　　　　　　　　　　　　　(a)　1-1

FA Cup
First Round　　　　Scarborough　　　　(h)　1-1
　　　　　　　　　　　　　　　　　　(a)　0-1

SOUTHAMPTON 1996-97 *Back row (left to right):* Paul Tisdale, Neil Heaney, Matthew Oakley, David Hughes, Frankie Bennett, Christer Warren, Neil Maddison.
Middle row: John Mortimore (Assistant Manager), Jim Magilton, Graham Potter, Neil Shipperley, Dave Beasant, Neil Moss, Ken Monkou, Richard Dryden, Alan Neilson, Jim Joyce (Physio).
Front row: Terry Cooper (Assistant Manager), Simon Charlton, Jason Dodd, Matthew Le Tissier, Lawrie McMenemy (Director of Football), Graeme Souness (Manager), Barry Venison, Francis Benali, Gordon Watson, Phil Boersma (Coach).

FA Premiership SOUTHAMPTON

The Dell, Milton Road, Southampton SO15 2XH. Telephone: (01703) 220505. Fax: (01703) 330360. Recorded Ticket Information: (01703) 228575. Clubcall: 0891 121178.

Ground capacity: 15,000.

Record attendance: 31,044 v Manchester U, Division 1, 8 October 1969.

Record receipts: £215,450 v Portsmouth, FA Cup 3rd rd, 7 January 1996.

Pitch measurements: 110yd × 72yd.

Chairman: R. J. G. Lowe.

Vice-Chairman: B. H. D. Hunt.

Directors: I. L. Gordon, K. St. J. Wiseman, M. R. Richards FCA, A. Cowen.

President: J. Corbett. *Vice-President:* E. T. Bates. *Manager:* Dave Jones

Joint Assistant Managers: John Sainty, John Mortimore, Terry Cooper.

Physios: Don Taylor, Jim Joyce.

Secretary: Brian Truscott.

Year Formed: 1885. *Turned Professional:* 1894. *Ltd Co.:* 1897.

Club Nickname: 'The Saints'.

Previous Name: Southampton St Mary's until 1885.

Previous Grounds: 1885, Antelope Ground; 1897, County Cricket Ground; 1898, The Dell.

Foundation: Formed largely by players from the Deanery FC, which had been established by school teachers in 1880. Most of the founders were connected with the young men's association of St. Mary's Church. At the inaugural meeting held in November 1885 the club was named Southampton St. Mary's and the church's curate was elected president.

First Football League game: 28 August 1920, Division 3, v Gillingham (a) D 1-1 – Allen; Parker, Titmuss; Shelley, Campbell, Turner; Barratt, Dominy (1), Rawlings, Moore, Foxall.

Record League Victory: 9–3 v Wolverhampton W, Division 2, 18 September 1965 – Godfrey; Jones, Williams; Walker, Knapp, Huxford; Paine (2), O'Brien (1), Melia, Chivers (4), Sydenham (2).

Record Cup Victory: 7–1 v Ipswich T, FA Cup 3rd rd, 7 January 1961 – Reynolds; Davies, Traynor; Conner, Page, Huxford; Paine (1), O'Brien (3 incl. 1p), Reeves, Mulgrew (2), Penk (1).

Record Defeat: 0–8 v Tottenham H, Division 2, 28 March 1936 and v Everton, Division 1, 20 November 1971.

Most League Points (2 for a win): 61, Division 3 (S), 1921–22 and Division 3, 1959–60.

Most League Points (3 for a win): 77, Division 1, 1983–84.

Most League Goals: 112, Division 3 (S), 1957–58.

Highest League Scorer in Season: Derek Reeves, 39, Division 3, 1959–60.

Most League Goals in Total Aggregate: Mike Channon, 185, 1966–77, 1979–82.

Most Capped Player: Peter Shilton, 49 (125), England.

Most League Appearances: Terry Paine, 713, 1956–74.

Record Transfer Fee Received: £3,300,000 from Blackburn R for Alan Shearer, July 1992.

Record Transfer Fee Paid: £1,400,000 to Galatasaray for Ulrich van Gobbel, October 1996.

Football League Record: 1920 Original Member of Division 3; 1921–22 Division 3 (S); 1922–53 Division 2; 1953–58 Division 3 (S); 1958–60 Division 3; 1960–66 Division 2; 1966–74 Division 1; 1974–78 Division 2; 1978–92 Division 1; 1992– FA Premier League.

Honours: Football League: Division 1 – Runners-up 1983–84; Division 2 – Runners-up 1965–66, 1977–78; Division 3 (S) – Champions 1921–22; Runners-up 1920–21; Division 3 – Champions 1959–60. *FA Cup:* Winners 1976; Runners-up 1900, 1902. *Football League Cup:* Runners-up 1979. *Zenith Data Systems Cup:* Runners-up 1992. **European Competitions:** *European Fairs Cup:* 1969–70. *UEFA Cup:* 1971–72, 1981–82, 1982–83, 1984–85. *European Cup-Winners' Cup:* 1976–77.

Colours: Red and white striped shirts, black shorts, red and white hooped stockings. *Change colours:* White shirts, white shorts, blue stockings.

Did you know?
On 9 March 1901 in the only full international played at The Dell when England met Ireland, Southampton provided three home players:– Jack Robinson, C.B. Fry and Arthur Turner.

SOUTHAMPTON 1996–97 LEAGUE RECORD

Match No.	Date	Venue	Opponents	Result	H/T Score	Lg. Pos.	Goalscorers	Attendance
1	Aug 18	H	Chelsea	D 0-0	0-0	—		15,186
2	21	A	Leicester C	L 1-2	0-2	—	Le Tissier (pen) [68]	17,562
3	24	A	West Ham U	L 1-2	1-0	17	Heaney [19]	21,227
4	Sept 4	H	Nottingham F	D 2-2	0-2	—	Dryden [53], Le Tissier [89]	14,450
5	7	A	Liverpool	L 1-2	0-1	18	Magilton [58]	39,189
6	14	H	Tottenham H	L 0-1	0-0	19		15,251
7	23	A	Wimbledon	L 1-3	0-2	—	Oakley [77]	8572
8	28	H	Middlesbrough	W 4-0	2-0	18	Oakley [11], Le Tissier 2 [28, 48], Watson [82]	15,230
9	Oct 13	A	Coventry C	D 1-1	1-0	18	Le Tissier [17]	15,477
10	19	H	Sunderland	W 3-0	1-0	17	Dodd [38], Le Tissier (pen) [53], Shipperley [89]	15,225
11	26	H	Manchester U	W 6-3	3-1	14	Berkovic 2 [6, 83], Le Tissier [34], Ostenstad 2 [45, 85], Neville G (og) [89]	15,256
12	Nov 2	A	Sheffield W	D 1-1	0-1	14	Le Tissier (pen) [50]	20,106
13	16	A	Everton	L 1-7	1-5	14	Ostenstad [39]	35,669
14	23	H	Leeds U	L 0-2	0-0	17		15,241
15	30	A	Blackburn R	L 1-2	0-1	17	Ostenstad [61]	23,018
16	Dec 4	A	Arsenal	L 1-3	0-1	—	Berkovic [81]	38,033
17	7	H	Aston Villa	L 0-1	0-1	18		15,232
18	21	H	Derby Co	W 3-1	2-1	16	Watson [9], Oakley [13], Magilton (pen) [89]	14,901
19	26	A	Tottenham H	L 1-3	1-2	19	Le Tissier [40]	30,549
20	29	H	Liverpool	L 0-1	0-0	19		15,222
21	Jan 11	A	Middlesbrough	W 1-0	0-0	19	Magilton (pen) [59]	29,509
22	18	H	Newcastle U	D 2-2	0-1	19	Maddison [88], Le Tissier [89]	15,251
23	Feb 1	A	Manchester U	L 1-2	1-1	19	Ostenstad [11]	55,269
24	22	H	Sheffield W	L 2-3	2-0	19	Ostenstad [28], Le Tissier (pen) [33]	15,062
25	26	H	Wimbledon	D 0-0	0-0	—		14,318
26	Mar 1	A	Newcastle U	W 1-0	0-0	19	Le Tissier [56]	36,446
27	5	H	Everton	D 2-2	0-2	—	Slater [59], Short (og) [61]	15,134
28	12	H	Leeds U	D 0-0	0-0	—		25,913
29	15	H	Arsenal	L 0-2	0-1	19		15,144
30	19	A	Chelsea	L 0-1	0-1	—		26,235
31	22	A	Leicester C	D 2-2	1-0	20	Ostenstad [32], Van Gobbel [48]	15,044
32	Apr 5	A	Nottingham F	W 3-1	1-0	20	Magilton [8], Evans 2 [87, 89]	25,134
33	9	A	Derby Co	D 1-1	0-0	—	Powell D (og) [89]	17,839
34	12	H	West Ham U	W 2-0	2-0	16	Evans [13], Berkovic [36]	15,245
35	19	A	Coventry C	D 2-2	1-0	17	Evans [27], Ostenstad [47]	15,251
36	22	A	Sunderland	W 1-0	1-0	—	Ostenstad [22]	21,477
37	May 3	H	Blackburn R	W 2-0	1-0	14	Slater [22], Le Tissier [74]	15,247
38	11	A	Aston Villa	L 0-1	0-1	16		39,339

Final League Position: 16

GOALSCORERS

League (50): Le Tissier 13 (5 pens), Ostenstad 9, Berkovic 4, Evans 4, Magilton 4 (2 pens), Oakley 3, Slater 2, Watson 2, Dodd 1, Dryden 1, Heaney 1, Maddison 1, Shipperley 1, Van Gobbel 1, own goals 3.
Coca-Cola Cup (18): Dryden 3, Le Tissier 3, Ostenstad 3, Watson 3, Berkovic 2, Magilton 2 (1 pen), Charlton 1, Van Gobbel 1.
FA Cup (1): Ostenstad 1.

Beassant D 13 + 1	Dodd J 23	Charlton S 24 + 3	Magilton J 31 + 6	Dryden R 28 + 1	Neilson A 24 + 5	Oakley M 23 + 5	Le Tissier M 25 + 6	Shipperley N 9 + 1	Venison B 2	Heaney N 4 + 4	Basham S 1 + 5	Benali F 14 + 4	Watson G 7 + 8	Potter G 2 + 6	Maddison N 14 + 4	Moss N 3	Lundekvam C 28 + 1	Slater R 22 + 8	Monkou K 8 + 5	Watkinson R — + 2	Ostenstad E 29 + 1	Berkovic E 26 + 2	Van Gobbel U 24 + 1	Woods C 4	Dia A — + 1	Robinson M 3 + 4	Hughes D 1 + 5	Taylor M 18	Warren C — + 1	Evans M 8 + 4	Match No.
1	2	3	4^2	5	6	7^1	8	9	10	11	12	13																			1
1	2	3^3	4	5	11	7	8	9	10	13			6^2	12	14																2
1	2	3	4	5	6	7	8	9^2		11^1			14	12	13	10^3															3
	2	3^3	10^1	5	6	13	8	9		11^2			12	14		1	4	7													4
1	2^1	3	12	5	6	7	8^2	9		14			13		10^3		4	11													5
1		3	10^2	5	2	12	8	9		11^1							4	7	6	13											6
1		3	10^1	5	2	12	7	9^2				8^3	13	14			4	11	6												7
		3	6	5	2	7	9			12^2		8	10			1	4	11^1	13												8
	2	3	10^2	5	6	12	7	9^2				8^3				1	4	11			13	14									9
1	2	3	12	5	8	7^3	14						13				4	11			9^2	10	6^1								10
1	2	3^2	12	5	8^1	11	7^3						14	13			4				9	10	6								11
	2	3	12	5^2	11	7^3	8						13				4^1	14			9	10	6	1							12
	2	3^1	8		13	7^3				12^2			14				4	11	6		9	10	5	1							13
	2		11	6		7^1	8^2					3					4	12	14		9	10	5	1	13^3						14
15	2	3	8^2	5		7							10				12		6		9	11^1	4	1^6	13						15
1	2^1	3	8	5		7^3							14		10^2		4	13	12		9	11	6								16
1	2		12	5		7						8^3	3^2		10^1		4	13	14		9	11	6								17
1		3	12	5^1	2^3						13	6	8^2		7		4	11			9	10				14					18
1			6		2						12	3	8^1		11^2		4	7^3			9	10	5			13	14				19
1			6								12	3	8^1		2		4	7			9	10	5^2			11	13				20
			12	8	2	7					13	3					14	6			9^3	10^2	5			11^1	4	1			21
			12	7^3	5	3	8				13				2			6			9	10^2	4			11^1	14	1			22
		3	4	5	2	7						11	8					6			9	10^2				12	13	1			23
	2	3^2	4			7							8		10		12	6			9	11	5^1			13		1			24
	2	6	8	5		7						3					4	11^1			9	10				12		1			25
		11^2	8	5	6	7^3						3	12				4	13			9	10^1				2		1		14	26
		2^1	12	8	5	11	7					3^2					4	13			9	10^1	6					1		14	27
		3	6	5	2	11^1	7					13	8				4	12			9^2							1		10	28
		3	6	5	8^2	7						2					4^1	11	12		9	13						1		10	29
		3^2	4	5	6	11^1	12					13						7			9	10				2		1		8	30
		3	4	5	6	11	8					12						7			9^1	10				2		1		13	31
		5	6	12		7^1	8^3					3	13				4	11			9	10^2				2		1		14	32
		5	6			7	8^1					3					4	11			9	10				2		1		12	33
		5	6	12	13	7^1						3					4	11			9	10^2				2		1		8	34
		5	6	12		7						3					4	11			9	10^1				2		1		8	35
		5	6	3^1		7	13						14		12		4^3	11			9	10^2				2		1		8	36
			6	5	12	7^1	13					3					4	11			9	10^2				2		1		8	37
			6	8	5	7	12					3					4	11			9^1					2		1		10	38

Coca-Cola Cup

Second Round	Peterborough U	(h)	2-0
		(a)	4-1
Third Round	Lincoln C	(h)	2-2
		(a)	3-1
Fourth Round	Oxford U	(a)	1-1
		(h)	3-2
Fifth Round	Stockport Co	(a)	2-2
		(h)	1-2

FA Cup

Third Round	Reading	(a)	1-3

SOUTHEND UNITED 1996–97 *Back row (left to right):* Keith Dublin, Mark McNally, Andy Sussex, Paul Sansome, Andy Rammell, Simon Royce, Jeroen Boere, Ritchie Hanlon, Leo Roget.
Middle row: Peter Johnson, Peter Trevelian (Coach), Mark Stimson, Andy Harris, Mike Lapper, Phil Gridelet, Steve Tilson, John Gowens (Physio).
Front row: John Nielson, Andy Thomson, Theo Foley (Assistant Manager), Mike Marsh, Ronnie Whelan (Manager), Julian Hails, Paul Byrne.

Division 2 **SOUTHEND UNITED**

Roots Hall Football Ground, Victoria Avenue, Southend-on-Sea SS2 6NQ. Telephone: (01702) 304050. Fax: (01702) 330164. Commercial: (01702) 304050. Soccerline: 0839 664444. Ticket Office: (01702) 304090. Infoline: 0839 664443.

Ground capacity: 12,306.

Record attendance: 31,090 v Liverpool, FA Cup 3rd rd, 10 January 1979.

Record receipts: £83,999 v West Ham U, Division 1, 7 April 1993.

Pitch measurements: 110yd × 74yd.

President: N. J. Woodcock.

Chairman and Managing Director: V. T. Jobson. *Vice-Chairman and Chief Executive:* J. W. Adams.

Secretary: J. W. Adams.

Directors: J. A. Bridge, B. R. Gunner, W. R. Kelleway, D. M. Markscheffel, R. J. Osborne.

Associate Directors: A. W. Jobson, W. E. Parsons.

Manager: . *Assistant Manager:* Peter Trevivian.

Physio: John Gowens. *Commercial Manager:* Jacqueline Parker. *Stadium Manager:* Peter Jones.

Club Nickname: 'The Blues' or 'The Shrimpers'.

Year Formed: 1906. *Turned Professional:* 1906. *Ltd Co.:* 1919.

Previous Grounds: 1906, Roots Hall, Prittlewell; 1920, Kursaal; 1934, Southend Stadium; 1955, Roots Hall Football Ground.

Foundation: The leading club in Southend around the turn of the century was Southend Athletic, but they were an amateur concern. Southend United was a more ambitious professional club when they were founded in 1906, employing Bob Jack as secretary-manager and immediately joining the Second Division of the Southern League.

First Football League game: 28 August 1920, Division 3, v Brighton & HA (a) W 2-0 – Capper; Reid, Newton; Wileman, Henderson, Martin; Nicholls, Nuttall, Fairclough (2), Myers, Dorsett.

Record League Victory: 9–2 v Newport Co, Division 3 (S), 5 September 1936 – McKenzie; Nelson, Everest (1); Deacon, Turner, Carr; Bolan, Lane (1), Goddard (4), Dickinson (2), Oswald (1).

Record Cup Victory: 10–1 v Golders Green, FA Cup 1st rd, 24 November 1934 – Moore; Morfitt, Kelly; Mackay, Joe Wilson, Carr (1); Lane (1), Johnson (5), Cheesmuir (2), Deacon (1), Oswald. 10–1 v Brentwood, FA Cup 2nd rd, 7 December 1968 – Roberts; Bentley, Birks; McMillan (1) Beesley, Kurila; Clayton, Chisnall, Moore (4), Best (5), Hamilton. 10–1 v Aldershot, Leyland Daf Cup Prel rd, 6 November 1990 – Sansome; Austin, Powell, Cornwell, Prior (1), Tilson (3), Cawley, Butler, Ansah (1), Benjamin (1), Angell (4).

Record Defeat: 1–9 v Brighton & HA, Division 3, 27 November 1965.

Most League Points (2 for a win): 67, Division 4, 1980–81.

Most League Points (3 for a win): 85, Division 3, 1990–91.

Most League Goals: 92, Division 3 (S), 1950–51.

Highest League Scorer in Season: Jim Shankly, 31, 1928–29 and Sammy McCrory, 1957–58, both in Division 3 (S).

Most League Goals in Total Aggregate: Roy Hollis, 122, 1953–60.

Most Capped Player: George Mackenzie, 9, Eire.

Most League Appearances: Sandy Anderson, 451, 1950–63.

Record Transfer Fee Received: £2,000,000 from Nottingham F for Stan Collymore, June 1993.

Record Transfer Fee Paid: £400,000 to Galatasaray for Mike Marsh, August 1995.

Football League Record: 1920 Original Member of Division 3; 1921–58 Division 3 (S); 1958–66 Division 3; 1966–72 Division 4; 1972–76 Division 3; 1976–78 Division 4; 1978–80 Division 3; 1980–81 Division 4; 1981–84 Division 3; 1984–87 Division 4; 1987–89 Division 3; 1989–90 Division 4; 1990–91 Division 3; 1991–92 Division 2; 1992–97 Division 1; 1997– Division 2.

Honours: Football League: Best season: 13th, Division 1, 1994–95. Division 3 – Runners-up 1990–91; Division 4 – Champions 1980–81; Runners-up 1971–72, 1977–78. *FA Cup:* best season: old 3rd rd, 1921, 5th rd, 1926, 1952, 1976, 1993. *Football League Cup:* never past 3rd rd.

Colours: Royal blue/yellow. *Change colours:* All red.

Did you know?
When Southend United beat Sheffield United 3–2 on 1 October 1996, it was their 500th League win at the Roots Hall ground.

SOUTHEND UNITED 1996–97 LEAGUE RECORD

Match No.	Date	Venue	Opponents	Result	H/T Score	Lg. Pos.	Goalscorers	Attendance
1	Aug 17	H	Tranmere R	D	1-1	1-1	—	Rammell [1]	4264
2	24	A	Oxford U	L	0-5	0-3	21		6382
3	27	A	Portsmouth	L	0-1	0-0	—		5579
4	31	H	Swindon T	L	1-3	0-1	23	Byrne [87]	4011
5	Sept 7	H	Bolton W	W	5-2	2-2	18	Boere 2 [5, 66], Nielsen [25], Williams [69], Marsh (pen) [90]	4475
6	10	A	Charlton Ath	L	0-2	0-2	—		8497
7	14	A	Norwich C	D	0-0	0-0	23		12,461
8	21	H	Port Vale	D	0-0	0-0	21		4025
9	28	A	Crystal Palace	L	1-6	0-2	23	Williams [82]	14,858
10	Oct 1	H	Sheffield U	W	3-2	1-2	—	Boere 2 [33, 71], Marsh (pen) [54]	3716
11	5	A	Bradford C	D	0-0	0-0	21		10,156
12	13	H	Wolverhampton W	D	1-1	1-0	21	Marsh [38]	5550
13	16	H	Grimsby T	W	1-0	0-0	—	Tilson [79]	3305
14	19	A	Huddersfield T	D	0-0	0-0	20		9578
15	26	A	Oldham Ath	D	0-0	0-0	18		6606
16	29	H	Manchester C	L	2-3	0-1	—	Williams [73], Rammell [84]	8707
17	Nov 2	H	Reading	W	2-1	0-0	16	Nielsen [63], Marsh (pen) [70]	5002
18	9	A	Ipswich T	D	1-1	0-1	16	Rammell [60]	10,146
19	16	H	WBA	L	2-3	2-2	17	Rammell [10], Williams [22]	5120
20	23	A	Stoke C	W	2-1	1-0	17	Williams [37], Sigurdsson (og) [51]	12,821
21	30	H	Oldham Ath	D	1-1	1-0	19	Nielsen [10]	5001
22	Dec 7	A	Barnsley	L	0-3	0-0	21		7483
23	14	A	QPR	L	0-4	0-2	21		11,117
24	20	H	Birmingham C	D	1-1	0-0	—	Williams [63]	5100
25	26	H	Charlton Ath	L	0-2	0-1	22		7508
26	28	A	Bolton W	L	1-3	1-2	22	Rammell [40]	16,357
27	Jan 18	A	Sheffield U	L	0-3	0-1	23		15,049
28	25	A	Port Vale	L	1-2	1-0	23	Thomson [37]	5588
29	28	H	Crystal Palace	W	2-1	1-0	—	Thomson [6], Boere [86]	5061
30	Feb 1	H	Ipswich T	D	0-0	0-0	22		7232
31	8	A	Manchester C	L	0-3	0-0	22		26,261
32	15	H	Stoke C	W	2-1	1-0	21	Thomson [34], Rammell [89]	4625
33	22	A	Reading	L	2-3	0-1	22	Boere 2 [54, 71]	7683
34	25	A	Norwich C	D	1-1	0-0	—	Thomson [51]	5169
35	Mar 1	H	Barnsley	L	1-2	1-1	22	Thomson [12]	4855
36	5	A	WBA	L	0-4	0-2	—		11,792
37	8	A	Birmingham C	L	1-2	0-2	23	Marsh [69]	13,189
38	15	H	QPR	L	0-1	0-0	24		6747
39	22	H	Oxford U	D	2-2	1-0	24	Boere [34], Lapper [47]	4102
40	28	A	Tranmere R	L	0-3	0-3	—		7563
41	31	H	Portsmouth	W	2-1	2-0	24	Gridelet [27], Rammell [45]	6107
42	Apr 5	A	Swindon T	D	0-0	0-0	24		6730
43	12	H	Bradford C	D	1-1	1-0	24	Rammell [40]	6697
44	19	A	Wolverhampton W	L	1-4	1-4	24	Rammell [30]	25,095
45	26	H	Huddersfield T	L	1-2	0-1	24	Boere [82]	4762
46	May 4	A	Grimsby T	L	0-4	0-1	24		7367

Final League Position: 24

GOALSCORERS

League (42): Boere 9, Rammell 9, Williams 6, Marsh 5 (3 pens), Thomson 5, Nielsen 3, Byrne 1, Gridelet 1, Lapper 1, Tilson 1, own goal 1.
Coca-Cola Cup (2): Nielsen 1, Rammell 1.
FA Cup (0).

Royce S 43	Dublin K 46	Stinson M 7+2	Lapper M 23+5	McNally M 32+2	Gridelet P 34+7	Marsh M 35	Hails J 32+5	Byrne P 23+9	Rammell A 26+10	Tilson S 27+1	Boere J 27+9	Harris A 43+1	Roget L 25	Sansome P 3	Williams P 24+9	Nielsen J 17+7	Selley 13+1	Dursun P —+1	Thomson A 14+3	Hanlon R 1+1	Poric A 7	Clarke A 7	Patterson M 4	Codner R 3+1	Jones M —+1	Match No.
1	2	3^1	4	5	6	7	8	9	10	11	12															1
1	2	3^1	4	5	6	7	11	8	10		9	12														2
1	2		4	5	6	7	11^1	12	10		9	3	8													3
	2		4^1	5	6^2	7	11	12	10^3	13	9	3	8	1	14											4
	5			4	6	7	2		3		9	8		1	10	11										5
	5			4	6	7	2	12	3		9	8		1	10	11^1										6
1	3	12	4	6	7	2	8^1	11	9	5		10														7
1	3	12	4	6^3	7	2	8	13	11	9^2	5^1	10	14													8
1	3	2	4	6	7^1	8		11	9	5		10	12													9
1	3	12	4		7		8	11	9	2	5^1	10	6													10
1	3		5	4	12	7		8	11	9	2	10	6^1													11
1	3		5	4	12	7		8	13	11	9^2	2	10	6^1												12
1	3		5	4	12	7		8^2	13	11	9	2	10	6^1												13
1	3		5			7	4	8		11	9	2	10	6												14
1	3		5		12	7	4	8^2	13	11	9	2	10	6^1												15
1	3		5		12	7	4	8	13	11	9^2	2	10	6^1												16
1	3		5	4	12	7	8		9	11		2	10	6^1												17
1	3		5	4	7		8		9	11		2	10	6												18
1	3		5	4	7		8		9	11		2	10	6												19
1	3	12	5^1	4	7		8^2	13^3	9	11	14	2	10	6												20
1	2	3		4	7		8		9	11^1	12	5	10	6												21
1	2	3		4	7		8		9	11	12	5	10^1	6^2	13											22
1	2	3		4	7		8^2		9	11^1		5	10	12	6	13										23
1	4	9^1		3	6			10	8		5	2	11	12	7											24
1	2	3^2		4	7	12		9	11		8	5	10^1	14	6^3		13									25
1	3			4	7	6	8	9	11		2	5	10^1				12									26
1	4		12	6	7			9^2	3	10^1	2	5	13				8	11								27
1	4		12	7	6	11^2	8	9	3^1	13	2	5			10											28
1	3		4^2	7	6	11	8	9^1		12	2	5		13			10^3	14								29
1	4			7	6	3	8	9		12	2	5			11		10^1									30
1	4			7		3	8	9^1		12	2	5			11		10	6								31
1	3		4	7		11^2	8	12		9^1	2	5	14	13			10^3	6								32
1	3		4	7		8	13^3	11^2	12	9	2	5	14				10^1	6								33
1	3		4	7		8	11	12	13	9^2	2	5			10			6^1								34
1	3		4	7		8	11^3	12	13	9	2	5	14				10^2	6^1								35
1	3	12	4	7		8	11^3	14	13	9^2	2	5			10			6^1								36
1	3		4		7	11	8	9		2	5		12				10^1	6								37
1	3	6	4		7	11^1	8	9		2	5		12				10									38
1	3	12	4	2	6	7	11^1	8		9		5					10									39
1	3		4		6	7		8^1	9	12	2	5	13				10^2		11							40
1	3		4		6	7			9	10^1	2	5			12				11		8					41
1	3		4		6	7			9	10	2	5							11	8						42
1	3		4		6^1	7	12	13	9		2	5	10^2						11	8						43
1	5		4			7	6		9^1	3	10	2^2			12				11	8	13					44
1	4		12			8	7	13	14	3^1	10	2	5		9^3				11		6^2					45
1	3		4			12	7	13	9		10^1	2	5^2						11^3	8	6	14				46

Coca-Cola Cup
First Round   Fulham   (h)   0-2   **FA Cup**
                                    (a)   2-1   Third Round   Leicester C   (a)   0-2

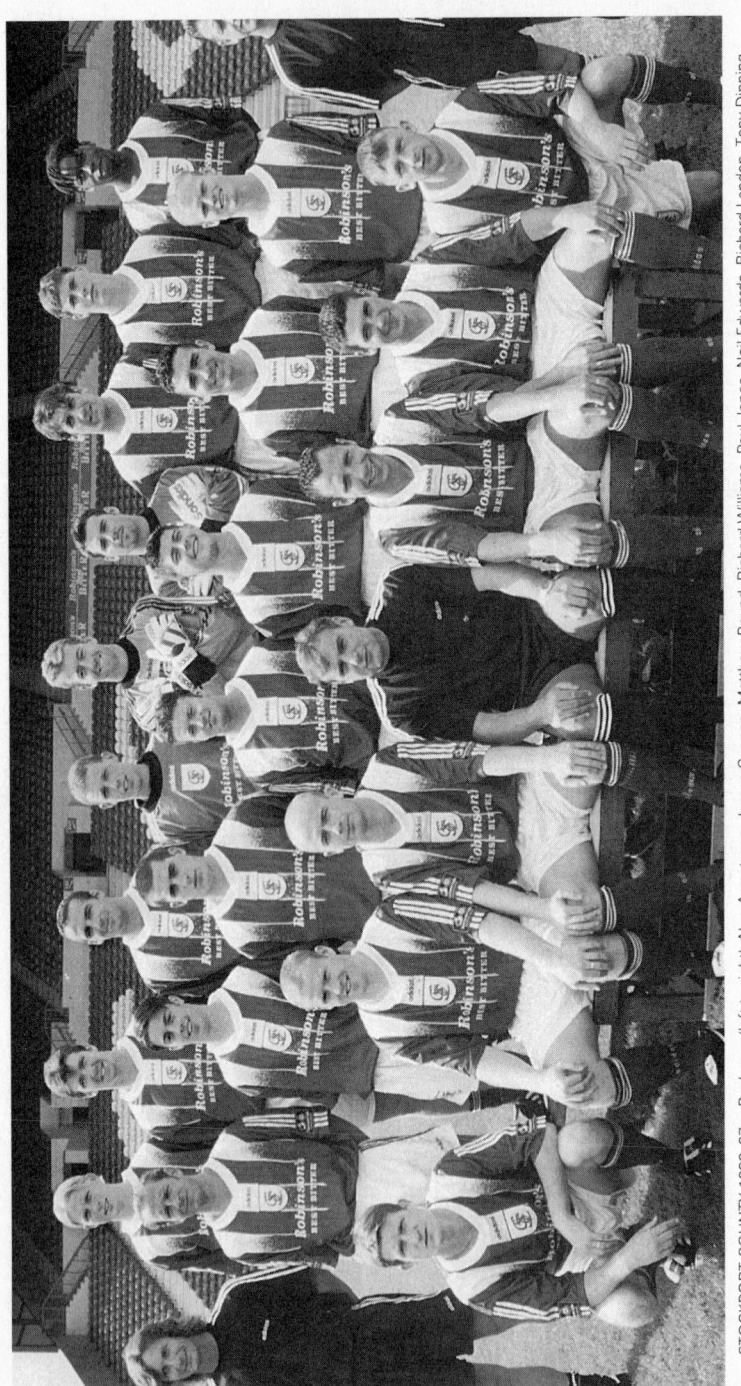

STOCKPORT COUNTY 1996–97   *Back row (left to right):* Alun Armstrong, James Gannon, Matthew Bound, Richard Williams, Paul Jones, Neil Edwards, Richard Landon, Tony Dinning, Adie Mike.

Middle row: Rodger Wylde (Physio), Jeff Eckhardt, Paul Jones, Lea Jones, Damon Searle, Tom Bennett, John Jeffers, Sean Connelly, Joe Jakub (Youth Development Manager).

Front row: Andy Mutch, Kieron Durkan, Chris Marsden, Dave Jones (Manager), Mike Flynn, Paul Ware, Lee Todd.

Division 1 STOCKPORT COUNTY

Edgeley Park, Hardcastle Road, Stockport, Cheshire SK3 9DD. Telephone: (0161) 286 8888. Fax: (0161) 286 8900. Club Shop: (0161) 286 8899. Clubcall: 0891 121638.

Ground capacity: 12,086

Record attendance: 27,833 v Liverpool, FA Cup 5th rd, 11 February 1950.

Record receipts: £181,449 v Middlesbrough, Coca-Cola Cup Semi-final 1st leg, 26 February 1997.

Pitch measurements: 111yd × 72yd.

Hon. Vice-Presidents: Mike Yarwood OBE, Freddie Pye, Andrew Barlow.

Chairman: Brendan Elwood. *Vice-Chairman:* Grahame White.

Directors: Mike Baker, Michael Rains, Brian Taylor, David Jolley.

Secretary: Gary Glendenning BA (HONS), ACCA.

Manager: Gary Megson. *Assistant Manager:* Mike Phelan.

Physio: Rodger Wylde.

Assistant Secretary: Andrea Dawson. *Commercial Manager:* John Rutter.

Marketing Manager and Programme Editor: Steve Bellis.

Year Formed: 1883. *Turned Professional:* 1891. *Ltd Co.:* 1908.

Club Nicknames: 'County' or 'Hatters'.

Previous Names: Heaton Norris Rovers, 1883–88; Heaton Norris, 1888–90.

Previous Grounds: 1883 Heaton Norris Recreation Ground; 1884 Heaton Norris Wanderers Cricket Ground; 1885 Chorlton's Farm, Chorlton's Lane; 1886 Heaton Norris Cricket Ground; 1887 Wilkes' Field, Belmont Street; 1889 Nursery Inn, Green Lane; 1902 Edgeley Park.

Foundation: Formed at a meeting held at Wellington Road South by members of Wycliffe Congregational Chapel in 1883, they called themselves Heaton Norris Rovers until changing to Stockport County in 1890, a year before joining the Football Combination.

First Football League game: 1 September 1900, Division 2, v Leicester Fosse (a) D 2-2 – Moores; Earp, Wainwright; Pickford, Limond, Harvey; Stansfield, Smith (1), Patterson, Foster, Betteley (1).

Record League Victory: 13–0 v Halifax T, Division 3 (N), 6 January 1934 – McGann; Vincent (1p), Jenkinson; Robinson, Stevens, Len Jones; Foulkes (1), Hill (3), Lythgoe (2), Stevenson (2), Downes (4).

Record Cup Victory: 5–0 v Lincoln C, FA Cup 1st rd, 11 November 1995 – Edwards; Connelly, Todd, Bennett, Flynn, Gannon (Dinning), Beaumont, Oliver, Ware, Eckhardt (3), Armstrong (1) (Mike), Chalk (1 og).

Record Defeat: 1–8 v Chesterfield, Division 2, 19 April 1902.

Most League Points (2 for a win): 64, Division 4, 1966–67.

Most League Points (3 for a win): 85, Division 2, 1993–94.

Most League Goals: 115, Division 3 (N), 1933–34.

Highest League Scorer in Season: Alf Lythgoe, 46, Division 3 (N), 1933–34.

Most League Goals in Total Aggregate: Jack Connor, 132, 1951–56.

Most Capped Player: Martin Nash, 2, Canada.

Most League Appearances: Andy Thorpe, 489, 1978–86, 1988–92.

Record Transfer Fee Received: £800,000 from Birmingham C for Kevin Francis, January 1995.

Record Transfer Fee Paid: £150,000 to Preston NE for Mike Flynn, March 1993.

Football League Record: 1900 Elected to Division 2; 1904 Failed re-election; 1905–21 Division 2; 1921–22 Division 3 (N); 1922–26 Division 2; 1926–37 Division 3 (N); 1937–38 Division 2; 1938–58 Division 3 (N); 1958–59 Division 3; 1959–67 Division 4; 1967–70 Division 3; 1970–91 Division 4; 1991–92 Division 3; 1992–97 Division 2; 1997– Division 1.

Honours: Football League: Division 2 – Runners-up 1996–97; Division 3 (N) – Champions 1921–22, 1936–37; Runners-up 1928–29, 1929-30; Division 4 – Champions 1966–67; Runners-up 1990–91. *FA Cup:* best season: 5th rd, 1935, 1950. *Football League Cup:* Semi-final 1997. *Autoglass Trophy:* Runners-up 1992, 1993.

Colours: Royal blue shirts, white shorts, blue stockings. *Change colours:* Black and white quartered shirts, black and white halved shorts, black stockings.

Did you know?
Stockport County's famous 13–0 victory over Halifax Town produced goals at the following times: 8, 14, 50, 51, 53, 57, 59, 61, 65, 66, 80, 86, 88.

STOCKPORT COUNTY 1996–97 LEAGUE RECORD

Match No.	Date	Venue	Opponents	Result	H/T Score	Lg. Pos.	Goalscorers	Attendance
1	Aug 17	A	Crewe Alex	L	0-1	0-0	—		4310
2	24	H	Notts Co	D	0-0	0-0	21		5271
3	27	H	Bournemouth	L	0-1	0-1	—		3446
4	31	A	Bristol R	D	1-1	0-1	22	Jeffers [73]	6380
5	Sept 7	A	Watford	L	0-1	0-0	22		7208
6	10	H	Wrexham	L	0-2	0-1	—		4244
7	14	H	Plymouth Arg	W	3-1	2-1	22	Gannon 2 [1, 10], Armstrong [51]	5087
8	21	A	York C	W	2-1	0-0	20	Angell 2 [48, 51]	3061
9	28	H	Gillingham	W	2-1	1-0	16	Armstrong [11], Morris (og) [51]	6049
10	Oct 2	A	Millwall	W	4-3	1-1	—	Durkan [24], Armstrong 2 [61, 90], Gannon [63]	7537
11	5	A	Burnley	L	2-5	0-2	14	Angell [56], Mutch [75]	10,332
12	12	H	Preston NE	W	1-0	1-0	11	Angell [2]	8405
13	15	A	Luton T	D	1-1	0-1	—	Angell [58]	5352
14	19	A	Wycombe W	W	2-0	1-0	10	Angell 2 [8, 86]	4017
15	26	A	Walsall	D	1-1	0-1	11	Durkan [90]	3767
16	29	H	Chesterfield	W	1-0	0-0	—	Dinning [88]	4831
17	Nov 2	H	Bristol C	D	1-1	0-1	10	Bennett [83]	6654
18	9	A	Brentford	D	2-2	0-0	11	Angell [78], Cavaco [84]	5076
19	19	H	Blackpool	W	1-0	0-0	—	Bennett [69]	4572
20	23	A	Shrewsbury T	L	2-3	1-0	11	Angell [7], Marsden [83]	2865
21	30	H	Walsall	W	2-0	1-0	10	Angell 2 [35, 51]	5333
22	Dec 3	A	Rotherham U	W	1-0	1-0	—	Durkan [35]	2133
23	14	H	Peterborough U	D	0-0	0-0	6		5748
24	21	A	Bury	D	0-0	0-0	6		5069
25	26	A	Wrexham	W	3-2	1-2	5	Armstrong [17], Gannon [62], Dinning (pen) [65]	6736
26	Jan 18	H	Millwall	W	5-1	3-1	4	Mutch [12], Armstrong (pen) [31], Flynn [35], Cavaco 2 [46, 52]	7502
27	Feb 1	H	Brentford	L	1-2	0-0	8	Cavaco [47]	8650
28	7	A	Bristol C	D	1-1	1-0	—	Armstrong [26]	13,186
29	15	A	Shrewsbury T	W	3-1	0-0	5	Angell 2 [75, 76], Armstrong [87]	6712
30	22	A	Blackpool	L	1-2	0-0	6	Linighan (og) [90]	5772
31	Mar 1	H	Rotherham U	D	0-0	0-0	9		6147
32	8	H	Bury	W	2-1	1-0	8	Mutch [2], Jeffers [46]	8170
33	15	A	Peterborough U	W	2-0	0-0	7	Cavaco [46], Marsden [84]	4857
34	22	A	Notts Co	W	2-1	1-0	7	Flynn [29], Hogg (og) [90]	4238
35	29	H	Crewe Alex	W	1-0	1-0	4	Cooper [43]	7411
36	Apr 1	A	Bournemouth	D	0-0	0-0	—		5476
37	5	H	Bristol R	W	1-0	0-0	4	Cooper (pen) [86]	5689
38	8	A	Plymouth Arg	D	0-0	0-0	—		5089
39	12	H	Burnley	W	1-0	0-0	4	Mutch [86]	9187
40	14	H	Watford	W	1-0	0-0	—	Jeffers [52]	7164
41	16	A	Gillingham	L	0-1	0-1	—		4485
42	19	A	Preston NE	L	0-1	0-0	4		10,298
43	22	H	York C	W	2-1	1-1	—	Bennett [27], Angell [74]	6654
44	26	H	Wycombe W	W	2-1	2-0	2	Armstrong [4], Forsyth (og) [31]	9463
45	28	A	Chesterfield	W	1-0	1-0	—	Angell [5]	8690
46	May 3	A	Luton T	D	1-1	1-1	2	Cooper (pen) [8]	9347

Final League Position: 2

GOALSCORERS

League (59): Angell 15, Armstrong 9 (1 pen), Cavaco 5, Gannon 4, Mutch 4, Bennett 3, Cooper 3 (2 pens), Durkan 3, Jeffers 3, Dinning 2 (1 pen), Flynn 2, Marsden 2, own goals 4.
Coca-Cola Cup (20): Mutch 4, Angell 3, Armstrong 3, Bennett 2, Cavaco 2, Connelly 1, Flynn 1, Gannon 1, Ware 1, own goals 2.
FA Cup (8): Durkan 3, Angell 1, Armstrong 1, Flynn 1, Mutch 1, own goal 1.

Jones P 46	Connelly S 45	Searle D 7 + 3	Bennett T 43	Flynn M 46	Bound M 4	Durkan K 36 + 5	Marsden C 34 + 1	Mutch A 15 + 18	Armstrong A 38 + 1	Jeffers J 25 + 9	Ware P 4 + 4	Angell B 30 + 4	Gannon J 38 + 2	Cavaco L 19 + 8	Todd L 39 + 2	Dinning T 12 + 8	Landon R — + 2	Kiko M — + 3	Nash M — + 3	Charlery K 8 + 2	Cooper K 11 + 1	Cowans G 6 + 1	Mike A — + 1	Match No.
1	2	3	4	5	6	7^1	8	9	10	11	12													1
1	2	3	4	5	6	7	8	9^1	10	11			12											2
1	2	3	4	5	6	7^3	8^2	12	10^1	11	13			9	14									3
1	2	3	4	5	6^2			9	12	13		8	11^1	7	10^3	14								4
1	2	3	4	5				9^1	10	11		8	12	6	7^2	13								5
1		3	4^2	5		13	8	9^1	10	11	7	12	6^3	2	14									6
1	2		4	5		7	8		10	11		9	6		3									7
1	2		4	5		7	8		10	11		9	6		3									8
1	2		4	5		7			10	11	8^1	9	6		3	12								9
1	2		4	5		7	8	12	10	11		9^1	6		3									10
1	2		4	5		7	8	12	10	11		9^1	6		3									11
1	2		4	5		7	8	12	10^1	11		9	6		3									12
1	2		4	5		7^1	8		10	11		9	6	12	3									13
1	2	12	4	5		7	8		10	11^1		9	6		3									14
1	2		4^1	5		7	8		10^2	11	12	9	6		13									15
1	2		4	5		7	8		10^1	11		9		12	3	6								16
1	2	12	4	5		7^1	8		13	11		9		10^3	3	6								17
1	2		4	5		7^2	8		10^1	11		9		12	3	6	13							18
1	2		4	5		7^1	8		10	11		9	6	12	3									19
1	2		4	5		7^1	8		10	11		9	6	12	3									20
1	2	12	4	5		7^1	8		10			9	6	11	3									21
1	2		4	5		7	8		10		12	9	6	11^1	3									22
1	2		4	5		7^1	8		10^2		12	9	6	11	3		13							23
1	2			5		7	8		10			9	6	11^1	3	4	12							24
1	2			5		7	8		10		12	9	6	11	3^1	4								25
1	2^2		4	5		7^1	8	9^3	10		12		6	11	3	13	14							26
1	2		4	5			13	12	10		7^1	9^2	6	11	3	8								27
1	2		4	5		7^1			10			9	6	11	3	8	12							28
1	2		4	5		7			10		12	9	6	11^1	3	8								29
1	2		4	5		7	8	12	10		13	9^1	6	11^2	3									30
1	2	3	4	5		7	8	12	10			9^1	6	11^2					13					31
1	2		4	5			8	9	10^1	11	12			7^2	3	6	13							32
1	2		4	5			8	9	10	11				7^1	3	6	12							33
1	2		4	5		7	8	12	10^1	11^2		9	6	13	3									34
1	2		4	5		7^3	8	12	10^1	13			6		3					9	11^2	14		35
1	2		4	5		7		9^1	10				6		3						11	8	12	36
1	2		4	5		7^2		12	10^1				6	13	3					9	11	8		37
1	2			5			13	12	10^2				6	7^1	3	4				9	11	8		38
1	2		4	5			13	12	10^2				6	7	3	14				9	11^1	8^2		39
1	2		4	5			13	12	10^1				6	7^2	3	14				9	11	8^2		40
1	2		4	5			13	12	10	11^1			6		3					9	7	8^2		41
1	2		4	5		7^1	8	12	10	11^2			6		3					9	13			42
1	2		4	5		7^1	8	12	10	13			6^3		3	14				9^2	11			43
1	2		4	5		7^3	8	12	10	13		9^1	6		3	14					11^2			44
1	2		4^1	5		7	8		10			9^2	6		3	12		13		11				45
1	2		4	5		7^1	8	12	10			9^2	6		3			13		11				46

Coca-Cola Cup

First Round	Chesterfield	(h)	2-1	(a)	2-1
Second Round	Sheffield U	(h)	2-1	(a)	5-2
Third Round	Blackburn R			(a)	1-0
Fourth Round	West Ham U	(a)	1-1	(h)	2-1
Fifth Round	Southampton	(h)	2-2	(a)	2-1
Semi-Final	Middlesbrough	(h)	0-2	(a)	1-0

FA Cup

First Round	Doncaster R	(h)	2-1
Second Round	Mansfield T	(a)	3-0
Third Round	Stoke C	(a)	2-0
Fourth Round	Birmingham C	(a)	1-3

STOKE CITY 1996–97   *Back row (left to right):* Stephen Woods, Nigel Worthington, Philip Morgan, Ian Cranson, Carl Muggleton, John Gayle, Mark Prudhoe, Justin Whittle, Aidan Callan.
Middle row: Ashley Grimes, Mike Macari, Mark Birch, Stephen Jagielka, Martin Carruthers, Kevin Keen, John Dreyer, Mike Sheron, Richard Forsyth, Larus Sigurdsson, Paul Macari, Ian Liversedge (Physio).
Front row: Graham Stokoe, Mike Pejic (Coach), Mark Devlin, Simon Sturridge, Lou Macari (Manager), Ray Wallace, Carl Beeston, Chic Bates (Assistant Manager), Neil Mackenzie.

Division 1   **STOKE CITY**

Victoria Ground, Stoke-on-Trent ST4 4EG. Telephone: (01782) 413511. Fax: (01782) 745340. Commercial Dept: (01782) 45840. Soccerline Information: 0891 700278. Football in the Community: (01782) 744347.

Ground capacity: 24,054.

Record attendance: 51,380 v Arsenal, Division 1, 29 March 1937.

Record receipts: £160,000 v Newcastle U, Coca-Cola Cup 3rd rd, 25 October 1995.

Pitch measurements: 116yd × 75yd.

Vice-President: J. A. M. Humphries.

Chairman: P. Coates. *Vice-Chairman:* K. A. Humphreys.

Directors: D. J. Edwards, P. E. Doona BA, FCA.

Manager: Chic Bates. *Coach:* Mike Pejic.

Physio: I. Liversedge MCSP, SRP.

Secretary: M. J. Potts. *Stadium Manager/Safety Officer:* J. Alcock.

Chief Executive: Jez Moxey F. INST SMM.

Year Formed: 1863 *(see Foundation).*

Turned Professional: 1885. *Ltd Co.:* 1908.

Club Nickname: 'The Potters'.

Previous Name: Stoke.

Previous Grounds: 1875, Sweeting's Field; 1878, Victoria Ground (previously known as the Athletic Club Ground).

Foundation: The date of the formation of this club has long been in doubt. The year 1863 was claimed, but more recent research by Wade Martin has uncovered nothing earlier than 1868, when a couple of Old Carthusians, who were apprentices at the local works of the old North Staffordshire Railway Company, met with some others from that works, to form Stoke Ramblers. It should also be noted that the old Stoke club went bankrupt in 1908 when a new club was formed.

First Football League game: 8 September 1888, Football League, v WBA (h) L 0-2 – Rowley; Clare, Underwood; Ramsey, Shutt, Smith; Sayer, McSkimming, Staton, Edge, Tunnicliffe.

Record League Victory: 10–3 v WBA, Division 1, 4 February 1937 – Doug Westland; Brigham, Harbot; Tutin, Turner (1p), Kirton; Matthews, Antonio (2), Freddie Steele (5), Jimmy Westland, Johnson (2).

Record Cup Victory: 7–1 v Burnley, FA Cup 2nd rd (replay), 20 February 1896 – Clawley; Clare, Eccles; Turner, Grewe, Robertson; Willie Maxwell, Dickson, A. Maxwell (3), Hyslop (4), Schofield.

Record Defeat: 0–10 v Preston NE, Division 1, 14 September 1889.

Most League Points (2 for a win): 63, Division 3 (N), 1926–27.

Most League Points (3 for a win): 93, Division 2, 1992–93.

Most League Goals: 92, Division 3 (N), 1926–27.

Highest League Scorer in Season: Freddie Steele, 33, Division 1, 1936–37.

Most League Goals in Total Aggregate: Freddie Steele, 142, 1934–49.

Most Capped Player: Gordon Banks, 36 (73), England.

Most League Appearances: Eric Skeels, 506, 1958–76.

Record Transfer Fee Received: £1,500,000 from Chelsea for Mark Stein, October 1993.

Record Transfer Fee Paid: £580,000 to Birmingham C for Paul Peschisolido, July 1994.

Football League Record: 1888 Founder Member of Football League; 1890 Not re-elected; 1891 Re-elected; relegated in 1907, and after one year in Division 2, resigned for financial reasons; 1919 re-elected to Division 2; 1922–23 Division 1; 1923–26 Division 2; 1926–27 Division 3 (N); 1927–33 Division 2; 1933–53 Division 1; 1953–63 Division 2; 1963–77 Division 1; 1977–79 Division 2; 1979–85 Division 1; 1985–90 Division 2; 1990–92 Division 3; 1992–93 Division 2; 1993– Division 1.

Honours: Football League: Division 1 best season: 4th, 1935–36, 1946–47; Division 2 – Champions 1932–33, 1962–63, 1992–93; Runners-up 1921–22; Promoted 1978–79 (3rd); Division 3 (N) – Champions 1926–27. *FA Cup:* Semi-finals 1899, 1971, 1972. *Football League Cup:* Winners 1972. *Autoglass Trophy:* Winners: 1992. **European Competitions:** *UEFA Cup:* 1972–73, 1974–75.

Colours: Red and white striped shirts, white shorts, white stockings with a red and black band at top. *Change colours:* Green and black striped shirts, black shorts, black stockings.

Did you know?
In 1946–47 when Stoke City finished fourth in the First Division, they were only two points behind champions Liverpool and the 55 points obtained were their highest in the top flight.

STOKE CITY 1996–97 LEAGUE RECORD

Match No.	Date		Venue	Opponents	Result	H/T Score	Lg. Pos.	Goalscorers	Attendance
1	Aug	17	A	Oldham Ath	W 2-1	2-0	—	Sheron 2 [22,43]	8021
2		24	H	Manchester C	W 2-1	2-0	5	Forsyth [27], Sheron [32]	21,116
3		28	H	Bradford C	W 1-0	0-0	—	Sheron (pen) [90]	11,918
4		31	A	Reading	D 2-2	1-1	2	Sheron [25], Forsyth [76]	8414
5	Sept	7	H	Crystal Palace	D 2-2	2-2	3	Sheron [20], Dreyer [32]	13,540
6		10	A	Barnsley	L 0-3	0-1	—		11,696
7		14	A	Birmingham C	L 1-3	0-2	7	Forsyth [66]	18,612
8		22	H	Huddersfield T	W 3-2	1-2	4	Gayle [41], Sheron 2 [77,85]	9147
9		28	A	Bolton W	D 1-1	0-1	6	Kavanagh [90]	16,195
10	Oct	13	A	Port Vale	D 1-1	0-0	8	Keen [65]	14,396
11		16	A	WBA	W 2-0	1-0	—	Wallace [33], Forsyth [72]	16,501
12		19	H	Sheffield U	L 0-4	0-3	10		13,581
13		26	H	Portsmouth	W 3-1	0-1	7	McMahon 2 [59,75], Sheron [71]	10,259
14		29	A	Oxford U	L 1-4	0-2	—	Sheron [59]	6381
15	Nov	2	A	QPR	D 1-1	1-0	9	Kavanagh [4]	7354
16		16	A	Grimsby T	D 1-1	1-1	10	Forsyth [30]	5601
17		23	H	Southend U	L 1-2	0-1	12	Forsyth [52]	12,821
18		30	A	Portsmouth	L 0-1	0-1	18		7749
19	Dec	4	H	Charlton Ath	W 1-0	0-0	—	Sheron [49]	7456
20		7	H	Tranmere R	W 2-0	1-0	10	Sheron [27], Higgins (og) [82]	9931
21		14	H	Swindon T	W 2-0	1-0	7	Stein 2 [44,64]	10,102
22		21	A	Ipswich T	D 1-1	1-1	8	Sheron [23]	10,159
23		26	H	Barnsley	W 1-0	0-0	7	Sheron [72]	19,025
24	Jan	1	A	Huddersfield T	L 1-2	1-1	9	Stein [18]	12,019
25		10	H	Birmingham C	W 1-0	1-0	—	Wallace [18]	10,049
26		18	A	Charlton Ath	W 2-1	2-0	5	Sheron 2 [42,43]	9901
27		22	H	Norwich C	L 1-2	1-2	—	Stein [14]	10,179
28		29	H	Bolton W	L 1-2	0-1	—	Macari [84]	15,645
29	Feb	1	A	Wolverhampton W	L 0-2	0-1	9		27,408
30		7	H	Oxford U	W 2-1	2-0	—	Mackenzie [9], Macari [37]	8609
31		15	A	Southend U	L 1-2	0-1	7	Harris (og) [70]	4625
32		22	H	QPR	D 0-0	0-0	10		13,121
33		28	A	Tranmere R	D 0-0	0-0	—		9127
34	Mar	5	H	Grimsby T	W 3-1	0-1	—	Southall (og) [48], Kavanagh [50], Griffin [78]	8621
35		8	H	Ipswich T	L 0-1	0-1	9		11,933
36		15	A	Swindon T	L 0-1	0-1	12		8878
37		18	H	Wolverhampton W	W 1-0	0-0	—	Forsyth [47]	15,683
38		22	A	Manchester C	L 0-2	0-0	9		28,497
39		29	H	Oldham Ath	W 2-1	2-0	10	Sheron (pen) [17], Macari [40]	11,755
40		31	A	Bradford C	L 0-1	0-0	11		13,579
41	Apr	5	H	Reading	D 1-1	0-1	11	Forsyth [65]	9961
42		12	A	Norwich C	L 0-2	0-1	13		13,805
43		15	A	Crystal Palace	L 0-2	0-2	—		11,382
44		20	H	Port Vale	W 2-0	1-0	13	Sheron 2 [44,85]	16,246
45		25	A	Sheffield U	L 0-1	0-0	—		25,596
46	May	4	H	WBA	W 2-1	1-0	12	McMahon [33], Kavanagh [69]	22,500

Final League Position: 12

GOALSCORERS

League (51): Sheron 19 (2 pens), Forsyth 8, Kavanagh 4, Stein 4, McMahon 3, Macari 3, Wallace 2, Dreyer 1, Gayle 1, Griffin 1, Keen 1, Mackenzie 1, own goals 3.
Coca-Cola Cup (6): Sheron 5, Worthington 1.
FA Cup (0).

Prudhoe M 13	Pickering A 39 + 1	Dreyer J 12	Sigurdsson L 45	Cranson I 6	Forsyth R 40	Worthington N 12	Wallace R 45	Gayle J 8 + 4	Sheron M 41	Beeston C 17 + 1	Devlin M 13 + 8	Keen K 5 + 11	Muggleton C 33	Sturridge S 5	Macari M 15 + 15	Da Costa H 1 + 1	Kavanagh G 32 + 6	McMahon G 31 + 4	Whittle J 35 + 2	Griffin A 29 + 5	Mackenzie N 5 + 17	Carruthers M — + 1	Stein M 11	Stokoe G — + 2	Nyamah K — + 7	Rodger S 5	Flynn S 5	McNally M 3	Match No.
1^1	2	3	4	5	6	7	8	9	10	11	12^2	13																	1
	2	3	4	5	6	7	8	12	10^2	11			1	9^1	13														2
	2	3	4	5	6		8	9	10	11		12	1		7^1														3
	2	3	4	5	6		8	7^2	10	11^1		12	1	9	13														4
	2	3	4	5	6	7	8	12	10	11			1	9^1															5
	2	3	4	5	6	7^2	8	12	10	11			1	9^1	13														6
	2	3	4		6	7^1	8	9	10	11^2		12	1				5	13											7
	2	5	4		3		8	9	10	6^1		12	1				11	7											8
	2	5	4	6	3		8	9^1	10	7^2		12	1				11	13											9
1	2	5	4	6	3		8		10^2	7^3		12			13		11	9^1	14										10
	2	5	4	6	3		8	9^3	10^2	7^2		12	1		13		11		14										11
	2	5	4	6			8	9^1	10	7^2		12	1				11	13		3									12
			4		6	3	8^2		10^1		2	9^3	1		12		11	7	5		13	14							13
			4		6	3^2	8		10		2	9^1	1		12		11	7	5		13								14
	2		4		6	3^2	8		10		12	9^1	1				11	7	5		13								15
	2		4		6		8		10		3	9^1	1		12		11^2	7^3	5		13	14							16
1	2^1		4		6		8		10		3^3	9^2			12		11	7	5		13		14						17
1	2		4		6		8	12	10^1		3^3				13		11	7	5		9^2			14					18
1	2		4		6		8		10						12		11^2	7	5	3	13	9^1							19
1	2		4		6^1		8		10						12		11^2	7	5	3	13	9							20
1	2		4		6		8		10						7^1		11		5	3	12	9							21
1	2		4		6		8		10						12		11^2	7	5	3	13	9^1							22
1	2		4		6^1		8		10						12		11	7	5	3	9								23
1	2^1		4		6		8		10^3						12	13	11^2	7	5	3	9			14					24
1	2		4		6		8		10								11	7	5	3	9								25
1	2		4		6		8		10^1						12		11	7	5	3	9								26
1	2^2		4		6^1		8		10						12		11	7	5	3	13	9							27
	2^1		4		6		8		10				1		12		11	7	5	3	9								28
	2^1		4		6		8		10^1			12	1		9		11	7	5	3									29
			4		6		8		10^1				1		9		11	7	5	3			2	12					30
			4				8^1		10		2		1		9		11	7	5	3			12	13	6^2				31
			4		6				10				1		9		11	7	5	3			2	12	8^1			32
	2		4				8		10				1		9		11	7^2	5	3			12	13				6^1	33
	2		4				8		10				1		9		11	7^2	5	3			12	13				6^1	34
	2		4				8		10				1		9		11	7^2	5	3			12	13				6^1	35
	2		4		6		8		10	8		12	1		9		11^2	7^1	5	3	13								36
	2		4		6		8		10	11			1		9		12	7^1	5	3									37
	2^1		4		6		9		10	8		12	1				11	7^2	5	3	13								38
	2		4		6		11		10	8^1			1		9		12		5	3						7			39
			4		6		2		10	8			1		9				5	3			12			11^1	7		40
			4		6		8		10	11	2^2		1		9		12		5	3			13			7^1			41
12			4		6		8		10	13		14	1		9		11	7^1	5^2	3^2			2						42
			4		6		8		10^3	7^2		13	1		9		12		5	3			2			11^1	14		43
	2		4		6		8		10	11^2			1		9		12		5	3	13					7^1			44
	2		4		6		8		10	11^1			1		9		12		5	3	13							7^2	45
	2		4		6		8		10^1	11			1		9			7	5	3	12								46

Coca-Cola Cup

Second Round	Northampton T	(h)	1-0
		(a)	2-1
Third Round	Arsenal	(h)	1-1
		(a)	2-5

FA Cup

Third Round	Stockport Co	(h)	0-2

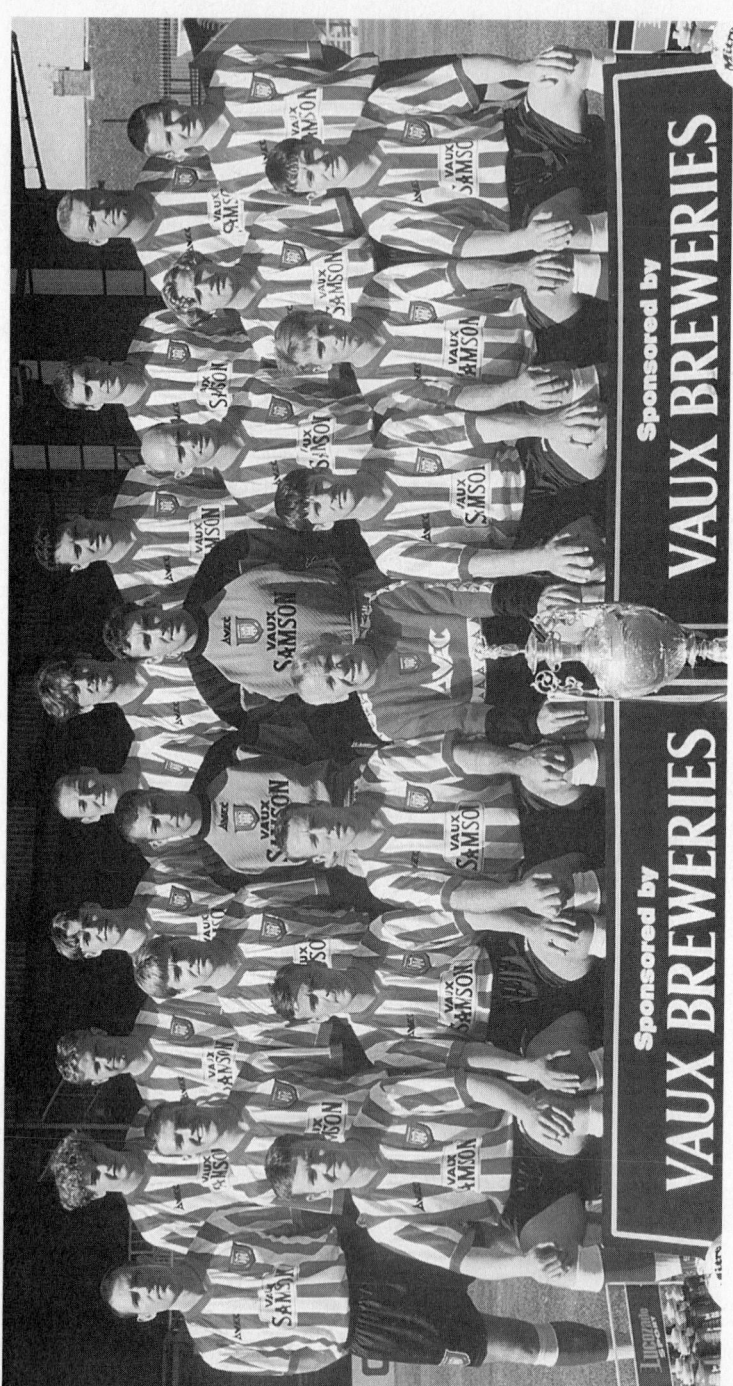

SUNDERLAND 1996–97 *Back row (left to right):* Sam Aiston, Martin Smith, Darren Holloway, John Mullin, Richard Ord, Brett Angell, Andy Melville, Paul Stewart. *Middle row:* Lee Howey, Alex Rae, Gareth Hall, David Preece, Tony Coton, Steve Agnew, Michael Gray, Michael Bridges. *Front row:* Craig Russell, Dariusz Kubicki, Kevin Ball, Peter Reid (Manager), Paul Bracewell, David Kelly, Martin Scott.

Division 1 **SUNDERLAND**

Stadium Park, Sunderland, Tyne and Wear SR5 1BT. Telephone: (0191) 551 5000. Fax: (0191) 567 3986.

Ground capacity: 42,000.

Record attendance: 75,118 v Derby Co, FA Cup 6th rd replay, 8 March 1933.

Record receipts: £187,000 v Manchester U, FA Cup 3rd rd replay, 16 January 1996.

Pitch measurements: 115yd × 75yd.

Chairman: R. S. Murray.

Director: John Fickling (Chief Executive). *Associate Directors:* J. R. Featherstone, G. S. Wood, J. G. Wood.

Manager: Peter Reid. *Assistant Manager:* Paul Bracewell. *General Manager/Secretary:* Mark Blackbourne.

Chief Coach: Bobby Saxton. *Physio:* Gordon Ellis. *Youth Team Coach:* Ricky Sbragia.

Director of Youth: Bob Oates.

Commercial Director: Grahame McDonnell. *Stadium Manager:* Dave Nicholson.

Year Formed: 1879. *Turned Professional:* 1886. *Ltd Co.:* 1906.

Previous Name: 1879–80, Sunderland and District Teacher's AFC.

Previous Grounds: 1879, Blue House Field, Hendon; 1882, Groves Field, Ashbrooke; 1883, Horatio Street; 1884, Abbs Field, Fulwell; 1886, Newcastle Road; 1898–1997, Roker Park.

Foundation: A Scottish schoolmaster named James Allan, working at Hendon Boarding School, took the initiative in the foundation of Sunderland in 1879 when they were formed as The Sunderland and District Teachers' Association FC at a meeting in the Adults School, Norfolk Street. Due to financial difficulties, they quickly allowed members from outside the teaching profession and so became Sunderland AFC in October 1880.

First Football League game: 13 September 1890, Football League, v Burnley (h) L 2-3 – Kirtley; Porteous, Oliver; Wilson, Auld, Gibson; Spence (1), Miller, Campbell (1), Scott, D. Hannah.

Record League Victory: 9–1 v Newcastle U (away), Division 1, 5 December 1908 – Roose; Forster, Melton; Daykin, Thomson, Low; Mordue, Hogg (4), Brown, Holley (3), Bridgett (2).

Record Cup Victory: 11–1 v Fairfield, FA Cup 1st rd, 2 February 1895 – Doig; McNeill, Johnston; Dunlop, McCreadie (1), Wilson; Gillespie (1), Millar (5), Campbell, Hannah (3), Scott (1).

Record Defeat: 0–8 v West Ham U, Division 1, 19 October 1968 and v Watford, Division 1, 25 September 1982.

Most League Points (2 for a win): 61, Division 2, 1963–64.

Most League Points (3 for a win): 93, Division 3, 1987–88.

Most League Goals: 109, Division 1, 1935–36.

Highest League Scorer in Season: Dave Halliday, 43, Division 1, 1928–29.

Most League Goals in Total Aggregate: Charlie Buchan, 209, 1911–25.

Most Capped Player: Charlie Hurley, 38 (40), Republic of Ireland.

Most League Appearances: Jim Montgomery, 537, 1962–77.

Record Transfer Fee Received: £1,500,000 from Crystal Palace for Marco Gabbiadini, September 1991.

Record Transfer Fee Paid: £2,500,000 to Newcastle U for Lee Clark, June 1997.

Football League Record: 1890 Elected to Division 1; 1958–64 Division 2; 1964–70 Division 1; 1970–76 Division 2; 1976–77 Division 1; 1977–80 Division 2; 1980–85 Division 1; 1985–87 Division 2; 1987–88 Division 3; 1988–90 Division 2; 1990–91 Division 1; 1991–92 Division 2; 1992–96 Division 1; 1996–97 FA Premier League; 1997– Division 1.

Honours: Football League: Division 1 – Champions 1891–92, 1892–93, 1894–95, 1901–02, 1912–13, 1935–36, 1995–96; Runners-up 1893–94; 1897–98, 1900–01, 1922–23, 1934–35; Division 2 – Champions 1975–76; Runners-up 1963–64, 1979–80; Division 3 – Champions 1987–88. *FA Cup:* Winners 1937, 1973; Runners-up 1913, 1992. *Football League Cup:* Runners-up 1985. **European Competitions:** *Cup-Winners' Cup:* 1973–74.

Colours: Red and white striped shirts, black shorts, black stockings, red turnover. *Change colours:* Gold shirts with navy trim, gold shorts, gold stockings, navy turnover.

Did you know?
Sunderland scored eight goals in 28 minutes including the last five in eight minutes at Newcastle United on 5 December 1908 during a 9–1 win.

SUNDERLAND 1996–97 LEAGUE RECORD

Match No.	Date	Venue	Opponents	Result	H/T Score	Lg. Pos.	Goalscorers	Attendance
1	Aug 17	H	Leicester C	D 0-0	0-0	—		19,291
2	21	A	Nottingham F	W 4-1	4-1	—	Gray [8], Quinn 2 [17, 31], Ord [43]	22,874
3	24	A	Liverpool	D 0-0	0-0	6		40,503
4	Sept 4	H	Newcastle U	L 1-2	1-0	—	Scott (pen) [19]	20,943
5	8	H	West Ham U	D 0-0	0-0	10		18,581
6	14	A	Derby Co	L 0-1	0-0	13		17,692
7	21	A	Coventry C	W 1-0	0-0	10	Agnew [51]	19,340
8	28	A	Arsenal	L 0-2	0-0	12		38,016
9	Oct 14	H	Middlesbrough	D 2-2	1-1	—	Rae (pen) [21], Russell [61]	20,841
10	19	A	Southampton	L 0-3	0-1	15		15,225
11	26	H	Aston Villa	W 1-0	1-0	13	Stewart [25]	21,032
12	Nov 2	A	Leeds U	L 0-3	0-1	17		31,450
13	16	A	Tottenham H	L 0-2	0-1	16		31,867
14	23	H	Sheffield W	D 1-1	0-0	16	Melville [68]	20,617
15	30	A	Everton	W 3-1	0-0	12	Russell [54], Bridges 2 [74, 87]	40,087
16	Dec 7	H	Wimbledon	L 1-3	0-2	15	Melville [83]	19,617
17	15	H	Chelsea	W 3-0	1-0	14	Duberry (og) [30], Ball [47], Russell [67]	19,617
18	21	A	Manchester U	L 0-5	0-2	14		55,081
19	26	H	Derby Co	W 2-0	0-0	11	Ord [73], Russell [87]	22,512
20	28	A	West Ham U	L 0-2	0-1	13		24,077
21	Jan 1	A	Coventry C	D 2-2	2-2	11	Bridges [6], Agnew (pen) [18]	17,671
22	11	H	Arsenal	W 1-0	0-0	11	Adams (og) [66]	21,074
23	18	H	Blackburn R	D 0-0	0-0	11		20,794
24	29	A	Leicester C	D 1-1	1-1	—	Williams [18]	17,883
25	Feb 1	A	Aston Villa	L 0-1	0-1	12		32,491
26	22	H	Leeds U	L 0-1	0-0	14		21,846
27	Mar 1	A	Blackburn R	L 0-1	0-0	15		24,208
28	4	H	Tottenham H	L 0-4	0-3	—		20,729
29	8	H	Manchester U	W 2-1	0-0	15	Gray [52], Mullin [76]	22,204
30	12	A	Sheffield W	L 1-2	1-1	—	Ball [28]	20,296
31	16	A	Chelsea	L 2-6	0-2	15	Stewart [58], Rae [60]	22,762
32	22	H	Nottingham F	D 1-1	0-0	16	Ball [61]	21,988
33	Apr 5	A	Newcastle U	D 1-1	1-0	15	Gray [32]	36,582
34	13	H	Liverpool	L 1-2	0-1	18	Stewart [53]	21,889
35	19	A	Middlesbrough	W 1-0	1-0	16	Williams [45]	30,106
36	22	H	Southampton	L 0-1	0-1	—		21,477
37	May 3	H	Everton	W 3-0	1-0	17	Stewart (pen) [36], Waddle [57], Johnston [68]	22,052
38	11	A	Wimbledon	L 0-1	0-0	18		21,516

Final League Position: 18

GOALSCORERS

League (35): Russell 4, Stewart 4 (1 pen), Ball 3, Bridges 3, Gray 3, Agnew 2 (1 pen), Melville 2, Ord 2, Quinn 2, Rae 2 (1 pen), Williams 2, Johnston 1, Mullin 1, Scott 1 (pen), Waddle 1, own goals 2.
Coca-Cola Cup (4): Ball 1, Quinn 1, Rae 1, Scott 1.
FA Cup (1): Gray 1.

Coton T 10	Kubicki D 28+1	Scott M 15	Bracewell P 38	Ball K 32	Melville A 30	Gray M 31+3	Ord R 33	Stewart P 20+4	Agnew S 11+4	Kelly D 23+1	Quinn N 8+4	Aiston S —+2	Bridges M 10+15	Russell C 10+19	Rae A 13+10	Hall G 32	Howey L 9+3	Perez L 28+1	Mullin J 9+1	Smith M 6+5	Williams D 10+1	Eriksson J 1	Waddle C 7	Johnston A 4+2	Match No.
1	2	3	4	5	6	7^2	8	9	10^3	11^1	12	13	14												
1	2	3	4	5	6	7	8	9^2	10	11^1			12	13											1
1	2	3	4	5	6	7	8	9	10^1	11			12												2
1	2	3	4	5	6	7	8	9	10^2	11			12												3
1	2	3	4	5	6	7	8	9	10^1	11			12												4
1		3	4^3	5	6	7	8	9^2	10	11^1			12		13	2	14								5
1		3	4	5	6	7	8	9	10	11^1				12		2									6
1	12	3	4^2	5	6	7^3		9	10			13	14	11^1		2	8								7
1	2		4	5	6	7	8	9	10^1				12	11	3										8
1^6		3	4	5	6	7	8	9		11^2			12	10^1	13	2	15								9
	2		4	5	6	7	8	9		11			10^1	12	3			1							10
		3	4	5	6	7		9^3		11			10^1	12	13	2	8^2	1	14						11
	2	3	4	5	6	7^9		9		11			10^1	12	13	2		1		14					12
	2	3	4	5^2	6			9		11			10^1	12	13	7		1		8					13
	2	3	4	5	6	12				13	11		14	9^2	7^2	8		1		10^1					14
	2	3	4	5	6	12	8			11^2			13	9	7^1			1		10					15
		3		4	5	6	7^1	8		12	11		13	9	10^2	2		1							16
		3		4^2	5	6	7^3	8	12	13	11		14	9	10^1	2		1							17
		3		4	5^2	6	12	8		13	11			9	7	2^1		1		10					18
		3		4		6		8		5	11	12	13	9^2	7	2		1		10^1					19
		3		4		6	7	8		5	11		9			2		1	10						20
		3		4		6	7	8		11			9^1	12		2		1	10	5					21
		3		4		6		8		11			12	7	2			1	9	10^1	5				22
		3		4		6	7	8		11			9	10	2			1		5					23
		3^2		4			7^1	8		11			12	10	2			1	9	13	5	6			24
	3	4	5	6	7^1	8		11				12	13	2			1	9^2	14	10^3					25
	3		4^2	5	6	7^3	8		11			12	13	2			1	9^1	14	10					26
	3^2		4	5	6		8		11			12	9^1	7	2			1	10^1	13					27
	3		4^2	5	6	7^1	8		11			10^1	12		2			1	9	13					28
	3		4	5	6	7^2	8	12		11			10^1	9		2	13	1							29
	3		4	5	6	7	8	13		11			10^3		12	2^2	14	1	9^1						30
	3		4	5		7	8	12					9^1		10	2	6	1				11			31
	3		4	5		7^3	8	9^2		12	13		14			2	6	1				11	10^1		32
	3^1		4	5		7	8	9^2		12			13			2	6	1				11	10		33
			4	5		3	8	9					12	13		2	6	1			7		11^1	10^2	34
			4	5		3	8	9		12				13		2^2	6	1			7		11	10^1	35
			4	5		3	8	9		10						2^1	6	1			11		7	12	36
			4^1	5		3	8	9		10^2			13	12		2	6	1			11		7^3	14	37
																									38

Coca-Cola Cup

Second Round	Watford	(a)	2-0
		(h)	1-0
Third Round	Tottenham H	(a)	1-2

FA Cup

Third Round	Arsenal	(a)	1-1
		(h)	0-2

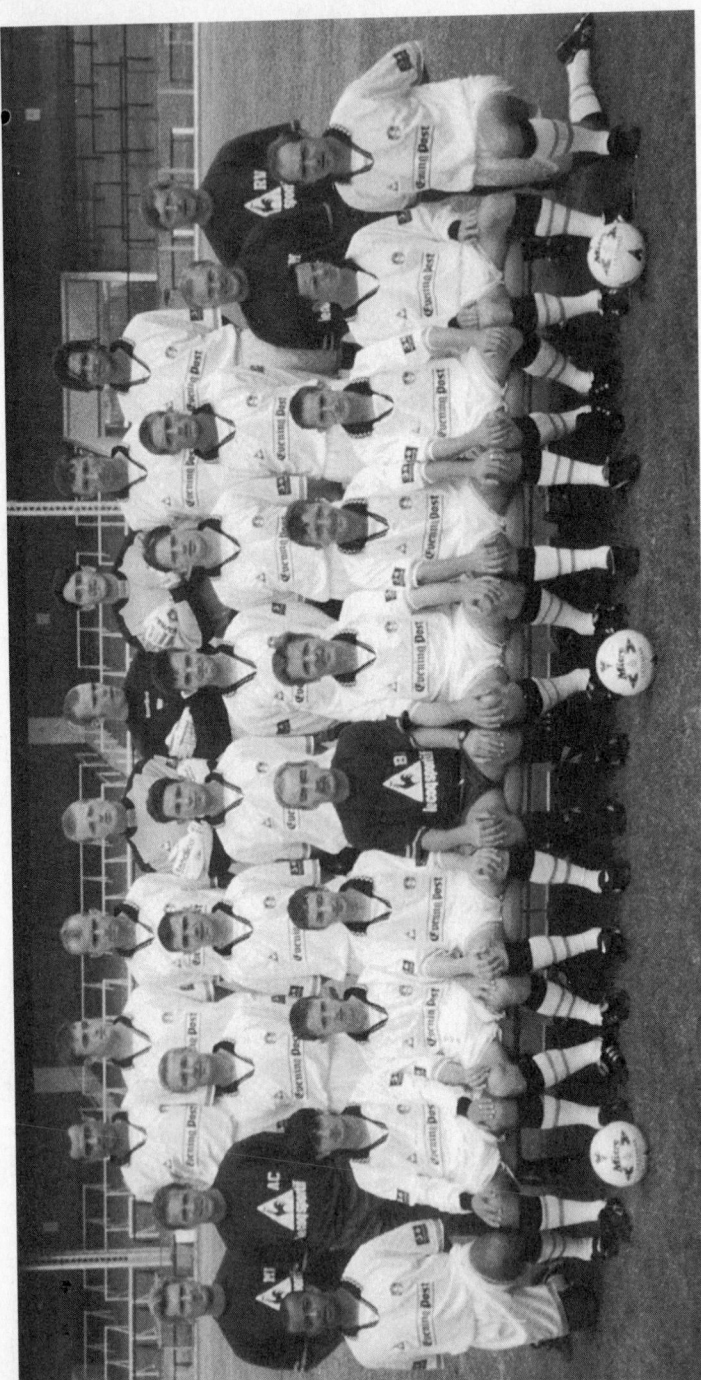

SWANSEA CITY 1996–97   *Back row (left to right):* Joao Moreira, Christian Edwards, Shaun Garnett, Roger Freestone, Ben Miles, Lee Jones, Steve Torpey, Jason Price.
Middle row: Mike Davenport (Physio), Alan Curtis (Youth Team Coach), Linton Brown, David Thomas, Steve Jones, Jonny Grey, Kristian O'Leary, Carl Heggs, Paul Morgan (Kit Man), Ron Walton (Youth Development Officer).
Front row: Kwame Ampadu, Colin McDonald, Robert King, Damien Lacey, Billy Ayre (Assistant Manager), Jan Molby (Player/Manager), David Penney, Mark Clode, Richard Appleby, Shaun Chapple.

Division 3   **SWANSEA CITY**

Vetch Field, Swansea SA1 3SU. Telephone: (01792) 474114. Fax: (01792) 646120. Club Shop: 33 William St, Swansea SA1 3QS. Telephone: (01792) 462584.

Ground capacity: 11,477.

Record attendance: 32,796 v Arsenal, FA Cup 4th rd, 17 February 1968.

Record receipts: £36,477.42 v Liverpool, Division 1, 18 September 1982.

Pitch measurements: 112yd × 74yd.

President: I. C. Pursey MBE.

Chairman: D. J. Sharpe.

Directors: D. G. Hammond FCA, MBIM (Vice-Chairman), M. Griffiths.

Chief Executive: Robin Sharpe.

Manager: Jan Molby. *Assistant Manager:* Billy Ayre. *Coach:* Ronnie Walton.

Youth Team Manager: Alan Curtis. *Physio:* Mike Davenport. *Stadium Manager:* David Healey.

Programme Editor: Major Reg Pike (01792) 474114.

Year Formed: 1912. *Turned Professional:* 1912. *Ltd Co.:* 1912.

Previous Name: Swansea Town until February 1970.

Club Nickname: 'The Swans'.

Foundation: The earliest Association Football in Wales was played in the Northern part of the country and no international took place in the South until 1894, when a local paper still thought it necessary to publish an outline of the rules and an illustration of the pitch markings. There had been an earlier Swansea club, but this has no connection with Swansea Town (now City) formed at a public meeting in June 1912.

First Football League game: 28 August 1920, Division 3, v Portsmouth (a) L 0-3 – Crumley; Robson, Evans; Smith, Holdsworth, Williams; Hole, I. Jones, Edmundson, Rigsby, Spottiswood.

Record League Victory: 8–0 v Hartlepool U, Division 4, 1 April 1978 – Barber; Evans, Bartley, Lally (1) (Morris), May, Bruton, Kevin Moore, Robbie James (3 incl. 1p), Curtis (3), Toshack (1), Chappell.

Record Cup Victory: 12–0 v Sliema W (Malta), ECWC 1st rd 1st leg, 15 September 1982 – Davies; Marustik, Hadziabdic (1), Irwin (1), Kennedy, Rajkovic (1), Loveridge (2) (Leighton James), Robbie James, Charles (2), Stevenson (1), Latchford (1) (Walsh (3)).

Record Defeat: 0–8 v Liverpool, FA Cup 3rd rd, 9 January 1990.

Most League Points (2 for a win): 62, Division 3 (S), 1948–49.

Most League Points (3 for a win): 73, Division 2, 1992–93.

Most League Goals: 90, Division 2, 1956–57.

Highest League Scorer in Season: Cyril Pearce, 35, Division 2, 1931–32.

Most League Goals in Total Aggregate: Ivor Allchurch, 166, 1949–58, 1965–68.

Most Capped Player: Ivor Allchurch, 42 (68), Wales.

Most League Appearances: Wilfred Milne, 585, 1919–37.

Record Transfer Fee Received: £375,000 from Nottingham F for Des Lyttle, July 1993.

Record Transfer Fee Paid: £340,000 to Liverpool for Colin Irwin, August 1981.

Football League Record: 1920 Original Member of Division 3; 1921–25 Division 3 (S); 1925–47 Division 2; 1947–49 Division 3 (S); 1949–65 Division 2; 1965–67 Division 3; 1967–70 Division 4; 1970–73 Division 3; 1973–78 Division 4; 1978–79 Division 3; 1979–81 Division 2; 1981–83 Division 1; 1983–84 Division 2; 1984–86 Division 3; 1986–88 Division 4; 1988–92 Division 3; 1992–96 Division 2; 1996– Division 3.

Honours: Football League: Division 1 best season: 6th, 1981–82; Division 2 – Promoted 1980–81 (3rd); Division 3 (S) – Champions 1924–25, 1948–49; Division 3 – Promoted 1978–79 (3rd); Division 4 – Promoted 1969–70 (3rd), 1977–78 (3rd), 1987–88 (play-offs). *FA Cup:* Semi-finals 1926, 1964. *Football League Cup:* best season: 4th rd, 1965, 1977. *Welsh Cup:* Winners 9 times; Runners-up 8 times. *Autoglass Trophy:* Winners 1994. **European Competitions:** *European Cup-Winners' Cup:* 1961–62, 1966–67, 1981–82, 1982–83, 1983–84, 1989–90, 1991–92.

Colours: White shirts with black double pin stripes, black sleeve with red, white shorts with red trim, white stockings with black top. *Change colours:* Black shirts with red stripes, black shorts with red trim, red stockings with black/white hooped tops.

Did you know?
Swansea City equalled a club record at Hereford United on 26 December 1996, recording their fourth successive away victory.

SWANSEA CITY 1996–97 LEAGUE RECORD

Match No.	Date	Venue	Opponents	Result	H/T Score	Lg. Pos.	Goalscorers	Attendance
1	Aug 17	H	Rochdale	W 2-1	2-0	—	Thomas 13, Penney 43	4272
2	24	A	Darlington	L 1-4	0-2	11	Brown 81	2752
3	27	A	Chester C	L 0-2	0-1	—		1946
4	30	H	Lincoln C	L 1-2	1-0	—	Penney (pen) 35	3111
5	Sept 7	A	Carlisle U	L 1-4	1-3	21	Thomas 9	5114
6	10	H	Hereford U	W 4-0	3-0	—	Thomas 17, Torpey 20, Penney (pen) 31, Jenkins 59	2479
7	14	H	Fulham	L 1-2	1-0	19	Thomas 30	3791
8	21	A	Doncaster R	W 1-0	1-0	15	Penney 45	1391
9	28	H	Hull C	D 0-0	0-0	16		2961
10	Oct 1	A	Leyton Orient	L 0-1	0-0	—		3536
11	4	H	Colchester U	D 1-1	1-1	—	Torpey 38	2531
12	12	A	Mansfield T	D 0-0	0-0	20		2003
13	15	A	Hartlepool U	D 1-1	0-1	—	Torpey 57	1310
14	19	H	Scunthorpe U	D 1-1	1-0	22	Torpey 21	2373
15	26	A	Torquay U	L 0-2	0-0	23		2755
16	29	H	Wigan Ath	W 2-1	2-0	—	Clode 6, Torpey 29	2227
17	Nov 2	H	Northampton T	W 1-0	0-0	17	Torpey 67	3335
18	9	A	Cambridge U	L 1-2	1-2	19	Coates 43	3178
19	19	A	Brighton & HA	W 1-0	1-0	—	Penney 14	2692
20	23	H	Scarborough	W 1-0	0-0	14	Jenkins 59	2005
21	30	H	Torquay U	W 2-0	1-0	11	O'Leary 14, Torpey 50	2889
22	Dec 3	A	Cardiff C	W 3-1	2-1	—	Ampadu 11, Jones 37, Thomas 86	3721
23	21	A	Exeter C	W 2-1	1-1	6	Penney 2 (1 pen) 23 (p), 55	2801
24	26	A	Hereford U	W 1-0	1-0	5	Penney 24	4204
25	28	H	Carlisle U	L 0-1	0-0	5		7340
26	Jan 11	A	Hull C	D 1-1	0-0	6	Brown 87	2810
27	14	H	Barnet	W 3-0	1-0	—	Brown 28, Ampadu 67, Penney (pen) 90	3570
28	18	H	Leyton Orient	W 1-0	0-0	5	Molby 75	3435
29	25	A	Wigan Ath	L 2-3	0-1	6	Torpey 48, Pender (og) 60	4058
30	28	H	Doncaster R	W 2-0	1-0	—	Ampadu 12, Coates 82	3464
31	31	H	Cambridge U	W 3-1	2-0	—	Penney 2 12, 15, Brayson 79	5772
32	Feb 8	A	Northampton T	W 2-1	1-0	4	Brayson 23, Penney (pen) 85	6178
33	11	A	Fulham	L 1-2	0-0	—	Coates 54	4836
34	15	H	Scarborough	L 1-2	1-0	4	Penney (pen) 4	3312
35	22	A	Brighton & HA	L 2-3	0-1	4	Brayson 72, Walker 89	6645
36	Mar 2	H	Cardiff C	L 0-1	0-0	4		4443
37	8	H	Exeter C	W 3-1	1-0	4	Brayson 34, Thomas 2 67, 75	3115
38	15	A	Barnet	W 1-0	1-0	4	Ampadu 14	1881
39	22	H	Darlington	D 1-1	1-0	4	Molby (pen) 5	4176
40	29	A	Rochdale	W 3-2	1-2	4	Molby 2 (1 pen) 31, 59 (p), Brayson 53	1884
41	31	H	Chester C	W 2-1	1-0	4	Molby (pen) 9, Torpey 51	6284
42	Apr 5	A	Lincoln C	L 0-4	0-1	4		3348
43	11	A	Colchester U	L 1-3	0-1	—	Molby 58	3162
44	19	H	Mansfield T	W 3-2	1-1	4	Thomas 19, Heggs 2 67, 72	4868
45	26	A	Scunthorpe U	L 0-1	0-0	4		3130
46	May 3	H	Hartlepool U	D 2-2	1-1	5	Thomas 19, Appleby 58	5423

Final League Position: 5

GOALSCORERS
League (62): Penney 13 (6 pens), Thomas 9, Torpey 9, Molby 6 (3 pens), Brayson 5, Ampadu 4, Brown 3, Coates 3, Heggs 2, Jenkins 2, Appleby 1, Clode 1, Jones 1, O'Leary 1, Walker 1, own goal 1.
Coca-Cola Cup (0).
FA Cup (1): Torpey 1.

Freestone R 45	Appleby R 8 + 3	Clode M 16 + 2	Molby J 26 + 2	Garnett S 6	Jones S 46	Lacey D 9 + 1	Penney D 44	Torpey S 37 + 2	Ampadu K 25 + 4	Thomas D 31 + 5	Chapple S 10 + 8	Brown L 13 + 8	McDonald C 3 + 7	O'Leary K 9 + 3	Heggs C 5 + 9	Coates J 38 + 2	Edwards C 36	Walker K 31	Jenkins L 21 + 2	McGibbon P 1	Casey R 3 + 7	King R 2	Phillips G — + 1	Moreira J 10	Price J 1 + 1	Hills J 11	Brayson P 11	Willer T 7	Jones L 1	Match No.
1	2	3	4	5	6	7	8	9²	10	11¹	12	13																		1
1	2¹	3³	4	5	6	7	8	9	10	11²	12	13	14																	2
1	2¹	3	4	5	6	7²	8	9	10¹	11	12	13	14																	3
1			4	5	6	14	8	12	10	11	2	7²	9¹	3³	13															4
1	7				6		4	8	12	5	11¹	2		13	3	9²	10													5
1	12		5²		6		8	9		11	2	13	14			10	3¹	4	7³											6
1	12		5		6		8	9		11	2¹	13				10	3	4	7²											7
1			5		6	7	8			11	2				9¹	12	10	3	4											8
1	12			5	6		8				2¹	11		4	9	10		3	7											9
1	13		10		6		3	8		11¹	2	12	14	5	9			4	7²											10
1	10				6		3	8		11	2				9	11	5	4	7											11
1	7				6		3	8		11¹	2	12			9	10²	5	4	13											12
1	7				6		3	8			2¹	13			9	12	5	4	11											13
1	2²		10		6		3	8				13			9	12	5¹	4	7											14
1	2²	3			6		8	9		11¹	12	13				10	5	4	7											15
1	3		10		6		8	9			2¹	12				11	5	4	7											16
1	3		10²		6		8	9			2¹	13				12	11	5	4	7										17
1	3				6		8	9	10		2	13				11	5	4¹	7					12²						18
1	3				6		8	9	10		2					11	5	4	7											19
1	3				6		8	9	10		2					11	5	4	7											20
1	12				6		8	9	10²		2	13				11	5	4	7					3¹						21
1	3				6		8	9	10¹		2	12				11	5	4	7											22
1	3		10		6		8	9			2					11	5	4	7											23
1	3		10		6		8	9			2					11	5	4	7											24
1	10				6		8	9			2					11	5	4	7					3						25
1	10				6		8	9			2					11	5	4	7					3						26
1	12		10¹		6		8	9		11³	2	13	14				5	4	7²					3						27
1	10				6		8	9		11¹	2	12					5	4	7					3						28
1	3		10¹		6		8	9			2	12				11	5	4	7											29
1	3¹				6		8	9	10		12		13			11²		4	7³	5			14	2						30
1	10				6		8	9			2	12				11¹	5	4								3	7			31
1	10¹				6		8				2	12				11	5	4			13					3	7²			32
1					6		8	9	10¹		2					11	5	4			12					3	7			33
1					6		8	9¹	10		2	12				11	5	4								3	7			34
1	10²		12		6		8	9			2¹	13				11	5³	4			14					3	7			35
1					6		8	9	10¹		2	12	4			11²	5				13					3	7			36
1					6		8	9	10¹		2	12				11	5									3	7	4		37
1	10				6		8	9			2					11	5									3	7	4		38
1	10				6		8	9			2¹	12				11	5									3	7	4		39
1	10				6		8	9			2	12				11	5									3	7	4¹		40
1	10				6		8	7			2		4¹			11	5				12			3			9			41
1	10				6		8	9			2					12	11	5									7¹			42
1	10				6		8	9			2¹	13				13	11	5								3	7	4²		43
1	10¹				6		8	9			2					12	11	5	4							3	7	4²		44
1	10¹				6		8	9			2					12	11	5	4	7						3		4²		45
7¹	10				6		8	9			2						11		4							3		5	1	46

Coca-Cola Cup
First Round   Gillingham   (h) 0-1   (a) 0-2

FA Cup
First Round   Bristol C   (h) 1-1   (a) 0-1

SWINDON TOWN 1996-97   *Back row (left to right):* Peter Thorne, Wayne Allison, Fraser Digby, Steve Mildenhall, Frank Talia, Shaun Taylor, Kevin Watson, Kevin Horlock.
Middle row: Jonathan Trigg (Physio), Lee Collins, Mark Robinson, Edwin Murray, Steve Finney, Mark Seagraves, Mark Walters, Ty Gooden, Frederic Darras, Dean Hooper, Steve Cowe, Ross MacLaren (Reserve Team Coach).
Front row: Scott Leitch, Ian Culverhouse, Jason Drysdale, Andy Rowland (First Team Coach), Steve McMahon (Manager), Paul Allen, Alex Smith, Wayne O'Sullivan.

Division 1

SWINDON TOWN

County Ground, Swindon, Wiltshire SN1 2ED. Telephone: (01793) 430430. Fax: (01793) 536170. Marketing: (01793) 532121. Marketing Fax: (01793) 423771. Superstore: (01793) 423030. Community Office: (01793) 421303. Clubcall: 0891 121640.

Ground capacity: 15,728.

Record attendance: 32,000 v Arsenal, FA Cup 3rd rd, 15 January 1972.

Record receipts: £149,371 v Bolton W, Coca-Cola Cup semi-final 1st leg, 12 February 1995.

Pitch measurements: 110yd × 70yd.

President: C. J. Green.

Chairman: J. M. Spearman. *Vice-Chairman:* P. T. Archer.

Directors: Sir Seton Wills Bt, C. J. Puffett, J. R. Hunt (Associate), P. R. Godwin CBE, W. Carson OBE (Associate).

Manager: Steve McMahon. *Assistant Manager:* Mike Walsh.

Coach: Ross MacLaren. *Physio:* Jonathan Trigg.

Chief Executive/Secretary: Steve Jones. *Assistant Club Secretary:* Michelle McDonald.

Youth Team Manager: Thomas Wheeldon.

Marketing Manager: Martin Stevens. *Retail Sales and Marketing Manager:* Julian Wetherall.

Community Officers: Clive Maguire and John Holloway.

Year Formed: 1881 *(see Foundation).* *Turned Professional:* 1894. *Ltd Co.:* 1894.

Club Nickname: 'Robins'.

Previous Ground: 1881–96, The Croft.

Foundation: It is generally accepted that Swindon Town came into being in 1881, although there is no firm evidence that the club's founder, Rev. William Pitt, captain of the Spartans (an offshoot of a cricket club) changed his club's name to Swindon Town before 1883, when the Spartans amalgamated with St. Mark's Young Men's Friendly Society.

First Football League game: 28 August 1920, Division 3, v Luton T (h) W 9-1 – Nash; Kay, Macconachie; Langford, Hawley, Wareing; Jefferson (1), Fleming (4), Rogers, Batty (2), Davies (1). (1 og).

Record League Victory: 9–1 v Luton T, Division 3 (S), 28 August 1920 – Nash; Kay, Macconachie; Langford, Hawley, Wareing; Jefferson (1), Fleming (4), Rogers, Batty (2), Davies (1). (1 og).

Record Cup Victory: 10–1 v Farnham U Breweries (away), FA Cup 1st rd (replay), 28 November 1925 – Nash; Dickenson, Weston, Archer, Bew, Adey; Denyer (2), Wall (1), Richardson (4), Johnson (3), Davies.

Record Defeat: 1–10 v Manchester C, FA Cup 4th rd (replay), 25 January 1930.

Most League Points (2 for a win): 64, Division 3, 1968–69.

Most League Points (3 for a win): 102, Division 4, 1985–86 (League record).

Most League Goals: 100, Division 3 (S), 1926–27.

Highest League Scorer in Season: Harry Morris, 47, Division 3 (S), 1926–27.

Most League Goals in Total Aggregate: Harry Morris, 216, 1926–33.

Most Capped Player: Rod Thomas, 30 (50), Wales.

Most League Appearances: John Trollope, 770, 1960–80.

Record Transfer Fee Received: £1,500,000 from Manchester C for Kevin Horlock, January 1997.

Record Transfer Fee Paid: £800,000 to West Ham U for Joey Beauchamp, August 1994.

Football League Record: 1920 Original Member of Division 3; 1921–58 Division 3 (S); 1958–63 Division 3; 1963–65 Division 2; 1965–69 Division 3; 1969–74 Division 2; 1974–82 Division 3; 1982–86 Division 4; 1986–87 Division 3; 1987–92 Division 2; 1992–93 Division 1; 1993–94 FA Premier League; 1994–95 Division 1; 1995–96 Division 2; 1996– Division 1.

Honours: *FA Premier League:* best season: 22nd 1993–94; *Football League:* Division 2 – Champions 1995–96. Division 3 – Runners-up 1962–63, 1968–69; Division 4 – Champions 1985–86 (with record 102 points). *FA Cup:* Semi-finals 1910, 1912. *Football League Cup:* Winners 1969. *Anglo-Italian Cup:* Winners 1970.

Colours: All red. *Change colours:* Black/blue shirts, blue shorts, blue stockings.

Did you know?

On 25 September 1996, Peter Thorne, a 78th-minute substitute for Swindon Town, scored an extra-time Coca-Cola Cup goal at Queens Park Rangers in a 2–1 win. Earlier that afternoon, he had scored for the reserves.

SWINDON TOWN FC

SWINDON TOWN 1996–97 LEAGUE RECORD

Match No.	Date	Venue	Opponents	Result	H/T Score	Lg. Pos.	Goalscorers	Attendance
1	Aug 17	A	Norwich C	L 0-2	0-2	—		15,165
2	24	H	Port Vale	D 1-1	0-1	20	Robinson 62	8706
3	28	H	Oldham Ath	W 1-0	0-0	—	Allison 59	8025
4	31	A	Southend U	W 3-1	1-0	8	Watson 12, Cowe 77, Finney 89	4011
5	Sept 7	A	Grimsby T	L 1-2	0-2	9	Cowe 51	4089
6	11	H	Portsmouth	L 0-1	0-0	—		8685
7	14	H	Tranmere R	W 2-1	1-0	10	Walters (pen) 25, Horlock 76	8430
8	21	A	QPR	D 1-1	1-1	12	Cowe 25	13,662
9	27	H	Wolverhampton W	L 1-2	0-1	—	Horlock 65	8572
10	Oct 2	A	Bradford C	L 1-2	1-1	—	Walters (pen) 25	9249
11	12	H	Oxford U	W 1-0	0-0	15	Horlock 50	10,811
12	16	H	Huddersfield T	W 6-0	4-0	—	Walters 29, Thorne 3 32, 47, 49, Allison 33, Horlock 40	7724
13	19	A	Crystal Palace	W 2-1	1-1	7	Allison 33, Thorne 48	15,088
14	26	A	Reading	L 0-2	0-0	10		11,018
15	30	H	WBA	L 2-3	1-0	—	Allen 36, Thorne 89	8909
16	Nov 2	H	Manchester C	W 2-0	0-0	8	Allison 2 51, 83	14,374
17	16	H	Barnsley	W 3-0	0-0	7	Walters 51, Gooden 66, Finney 68	10,837
18	19	A	Ipswich T	L 2-3	0-1	—	Thorne 76, Allison 90	7086
19	23	A	Birmingham C	L 0-1	0-1	9		16,559
20	26	A	Sheffield U	L 0-2	0-1	—		12,301
21	30	H	Reading	W 3-1	2-1	8	Horlock 5, Allison 25, Walters 87	10,874
22	Dec 7	A	Charlton Ath	L 0-2	0-0	11		10,565
23	14	A	Stoke C	L 0-2	0-1	13		10,102
24	22	H	Bolton W	D 2-2	1-0	13	Walters 33, Allison 73	8948
25	26	A	Portsmouth	W 1-0	0-0	10	Cowe 57	10,605
26	Jan 10	A	Tranmere R	L 1-2	0-1	18	Horlock 64	8763
27	18	H	Bradford C	D 1-1	0-1	18	Horlock 47	7851
28	25	H	Grimsby T	D 3-3	0-2	16	Horlock 52, Allison 63, Walters 69	9127
29	29	A	Wolverhampton W	L 0-1	0-1	—		23,003
30	Feb 1	H	Sheffield U	W 2-1	0-0	15	Elkins 57, Holdsworth (og) 70	8811
31	5	H	QPR	D 1-1	1-1	—	Brevett (og) 38	10,830
32	8	A	WBA	W 2-1	1-0	15	Allison 42, Smith 76	16,219
33	22	A	Manchester C	L 0-3	0-1	14		27,262
34	26	H	Birmingham C	W 3-1	2-1	—	Bullock 12, Broomes 38, Cowe 61	7428
35	Mar 1	A	Charlton Ath	W 1-0	0-0	10	Allison 69	9256
36	4	A	Barnsley	D 1-1	1-1	—	Thorne 41	8518
37	8	A	Bolton W	L 0-7	0-2	12		13,981
38	15	H	Stoke C	W 1-0	1-0	10	Thorne 26	8878
39	22	A	Port Vale	L 0-1	0-0	13		6142
40	29	H	Norwich C	L 0-3	0-1	13		10,249
41	31	A	Oldham Ath	L 1-5	0-2	13	Cowe 87	5699
42	Apr 5	H	Southend U	D 0-0	0-0	14		6730
43	12	H	Ipswich T	L 0-4	0-1	18		8591
44	19	A	Oxford U	L 0-2	0-2	19		8167
45	26	H	Crystal Palace	L 0-2	0-1	19		10,447
46	May 4	A	Huddersfield T	D 0-0	0-0	19		11,506

Final League Position: 19

GOALSCORERS

League (52): Allison 11, Horlock 8, Thorne 8, Walters 7 (2 pens), Cowe 6, Finney 2, Allen 1, Broomes 1, Bullock 1, Elkins 1, Gooden 1, Robinson 1, Smith 1, Watson 1, own goals 2.
Coca-Cola Cup (7): Allison 2, Thorne 2, Leitch 1, O'Sullivan 1, Walters 1.
FA Cup (0).

Talia F 15	Darras F 30 + 5	Drysdale J 13 + 1	Leitch S 36	Allen P 5 + 5	Taylor S 2	Robinson M 43	Walters M 24 + 3	Finney S 8 + 12	Allison W 39 + 2	Horlock K 28	Thorne P 24 + 7	Watson K 17 + 10	Seagraves M 27 + 1	Culverhouse I 31	Cowe S 28 + 10	O'Sullivan W 16 + 9	Smith A 13 + 5	Elkins G 19 + 4	Gooden T 7 + 6	Digby F 31	Collins L 3 + 1	Holcroft P 2 + 1	Kerslake D 8	McMahon S 2 + 1	Mildenhall S — + 1	Broomes M 12	Bullock D 12 + 1	Pattimore M — + 1	Coughlan G 3	King P 5	Anthony G 3	Match No.
1	2	3	4	5	6^3	7	8	9^1	10	11^2	12	13	14																			1
1	2	3	4	5	6	7	8^1	9^2	10	11	12	13																				2
1	2	3	4			7			10	11				8	5	6	9															3
1	2	3	4^2	14		7		12	11	10		8^3	5	6	9^1	13																4
1	2		4	14		7	13	12	11	10^3	8^2	5	6	9		3^1																5
1	2		4	8^2		3^2	7	13	12	11	10	8^1	5	6	9																	6
1	2^1		4	12		7			10	11			5	6	9	8		3														7
1			4			2^2	7	12	10	11	13		5	6	9	8^1		3														8
1	12		4			2^1	7		10	11	13	14	5	6^3	9	8^2		3														9
1	12		4^1			2	7		10	11	13		5	6	9^2	8		3														10
1	8		4^1	13		2^2	7		10^3	11	9		5	6	14	12		3														11
1	8		4^1			2	7		10	11	9		5	6		12		3														12
1	8^3		4^1	5^1		2	7		10	11	9	14	6	13	12		3															13
1	8			5		2	7		10	11	9	4		6^1	12		3^2	13														14
8			11			2		9	10	6			5	7			3	1	4													15
8			4			2	11^1	9	10	6		5		7			3	1	12													16
8			4			2	11	9^1	10	6	12	5^2		13	7^3	14	3	1			2											17
8			4			7	11^1	12	10	6	9	5^2		13		3		1			2											18
			4			5	11		10	6	9	12		7		3^2	13	1	8^1		2											19
			4			5	11^2	12	10	6	9^1	8		7		3	13	1			2											20
			4	12		5	11	9^3	10	6		8		7		2^1	13	3^2	14	1												21
6^1						5	11^3	10		8			7	9	4^2	13	3		1	12		2	14									22
6^1						5	11^2	10	3	8			7	9	4	13	12		1			2										23
			4			5		10	3	8			7	9		6			1	11		2										24
	3		4			6^1		10	11		8^2	5	7	9	12				1			2		13								25
	3		4			6		10	11		12	5^1	7^3	9	13		14		1			2	8^2									26
	3		4			2	7	10	11		8	5	5	9					1							6						27
3^1			4			2	12	10	11		8^2	5	7	9		13			1							6						28
2	3						11^1	10			13		7	9	12	8	5		1			4^2				6						29
12			4			2	11	10				5	7	9	12	8	3^1		1							6						30
3			4			2	11^1	10				5	7	9	12	8			1							6						31
3^1	12					2		11^2	10		13	8	5	7^1		9			1		4					6						32
3			4			2		12	10		9^1		5	7	11^2	13			1							6	8					33
3^2			4			2	12		10			9	5	7	11^1		13		1							6	8					34
3			4			2			10			9	5	7		11			1							6	8					35
		4				2			10			9		7	12	5	11	3	1							6	8					36
	3^2					2		12	10		9^1	5		7	8^3		11	13	1							6	4	14				37
	3					2^1		12	10		9	8^2	5	7	13		11		1							6	4					38
12						2^2		10			9	13	5	7	8^3		11	14	1							4			6^1	3		39
6						2		12			9		5	7^1	10		11		13	1						4				3^2	8	40
6			4			2		12			9			10^1			11	1								8		5	3	7	41
6^2			4			2		12	10		9	13		7^1			11	1								8		5	3		42
12	11		4			2		10			9	5		13	6^1			1	7^2							8		5	3		43
6	3					2		10			9		12	4^1	7	5	11	1								14		3	8^3		44
6	3		4			2		10			9			12		7^1	5	11	1							8					45
6	3	4				2		10			9			12		7^1	5	11	1							8					46

Coca-Cola Cup

First Round	Wolverhampton W	(h)	2-0
		(a)	0-1
Second Round	QPR	(h)	1-2
		(a)	3-1
Third Round	Manchester U	(a)	1-2

FA Cup

| Third Round | Everton | (a) | 0-3 |

TORQUAY UNITED 1996-97 *Back row (left to right)*: Tony Bedeau, Lee Barrow, Alex Watson, Ellis Laight, Jamie Ndah, Matthew Wright, Paul Baker, Wayne Thomas.
Middle row: Paul Maxwell (Assistant Physio), Damien Davey (Physio), Scott Stamps, Ray Newland, Matthew Gregg, Rhys Wilmot, Richard Hancox, Peter Distin (Youth Co-ordinator), Steve McCall (Player/Youth Development Officer/Coach).
Front row: Rodney Jack, Mark Hawthorne, Steve Winter, Garry Nelson (Player/Assistant Coach), Michael Bateson (Chairman), Kevin Hodges (Player/Head Coach), 'Charlie' Oatway, Ian Hathaway, Michael Preston.

Division 3

TORQUAY UNITED

Plainmoor Ground, Torquay, Devon TQ1 3PS. Telephone: (01803) 328666. Fax: (01803) 323976. Clubcall: 0891 121641.

Ground capacity: 6000.

Record attendance: 21,908 v Huddersfield T, FA Cup 4th rd, 29 January 1955.

Record receipts: £26,205 v Exeter C, Division 3, 1 January 1992.

Pitch measurements: 112yd × 74yd.

Chairman/Managing Director: M. Bateson. *Directors:* Mrs S. Bateson, M. Beer, M. Benney, I. Hayman, Miss H. Kindeleit, T. Lilley, B. Palk, W. Rogers.

Manager: Kevin Hodges. *Physio:* D. Davey.

Company Secretary: Miss H. Kindeleit.

Secretary: M. Bateson.

Year Formed: 1899. *Turned Professional:* 1921. *Ltd Co.:* 1921.

Previous Name: 1910, Torquay Town; 1921, Torquay United.

Nickname: 'The Gulls'.

Previous Grounds: 1899, Teignmouth Road; 1900, Torquay Recreation Ground; 1904, Cricket Field Road; 1906–10, Torquay Cricket Ground.

Foundation: The idea of establishing a Torquay club was agreed by old boys of Torquay College and Torbay College, while sitting in Princess Gardens listening to the band. A proper meeting was subsequently held at Tor Abbey Hotel at which officers were elected. This was in 1898 and the club's first competition was the Eastern League (later known as the East Devon League).

First Football League game: 27 August 1927, Division 3 (S), v Exeter C (h) D 1-1 – Millsom; Cook, Smith; Wellock, Wragg, Connor, Mackey, Turner (1), Jones, McGovern, Thomson.

Record League Victory: 9–0 v Swindon T, Division 3 (S), 8 March 1952 – George Webber; Topping, Ralph Calland; Brown, Eric Webber, Towers; Shaw (1), Marchant (1), Northcott (2), Collins (3), Edds (2).

Record Cup Victory: 7–1 v Northampton T, FA Cup 1st rd, 14 November 1959 – Gill; Penford, Downs; Bettany, George Northcott, Rawson; Baxter, Cox, Tommy Northcott (1), Bond (3), Pym (3).

Record Defeat: 2–10 v Fulham, Division 3 (S), 7 September 1931 and v Luton T, Division 3 (S), 2 September 1933.

Most League Points (2 for a win): 60, Division 4, 1959–60.

Most League Points (3 for a win): 77, Division 4, 1987–88.

Most League Goals: 89, Division 3 (S), 1956–57.

Highest League Scorer in Season: Sammy Collins, 40, Division 3 (S), 1955–56.

Most League Goals in Total Aggregate: Sammy Collins, 204, 1948–58.

Most Capped Player: Rodney Jack, St Vincent.

Most League Appearances: Dennis Lewis, 443, 1947–59.

Record Transfer Fee Received: £180,000 from Manchester U for Lee Sharpe, May 1988.

Record Transfer Fee Paid: £60,000 to Dundee for Wes Saunders, July 1990.

Football League Record: 1927 Elected to Division 3 (S); 1958–60 Division 4; 1960–62 Division 3; 1962–66 Division 4; 1966–72 Division 3; 1972–91 Division 4; 1991– Division 3.

Honours: Football League: Division 3 best season: 4th, 1967–68; Division 3 (S) – Runners-up 1956–57; Division 4 – Promoted 1959–60 (3rd), 1965–66 (3rd), 1990–91 (play-offs). *FA Cup:* best season: 4th rd, 1949, 1955, 1971, 1983, 1990. *Football League Cup:* never past 3rd rd. *Sherpa Van Trophy:* Runners-up 1989.

Colours: Yellow and navy striped shirts, navy shorts, yellow stockings. *Change colours:* White shirts, white shorts, white stockings.

Did you know?
Torquay United played a Division 3 (South) Cup semi-final against Norwich City at Highbury on 11 April 1934 and won 4–1 before a crowd of 3727.

TORQUAY UNITED 1996–97 LEAGUE RECORD

Match No.	Date	Venue	Opponents	Result		H/T Score	Lg. Pos.	Goalscorers	Attendance
1	Aug 17	H	Lincoln C	W	2-1	1-0	—	Gittens [24], Jack [90]	2645
2	24	A	Scunthorpe U	L	0-1	0-0	14		2236
3	27	A	Northampton T	D	1-1	1-0	—	Jack [4]	4128
4	31	H	Exeter C	W	2-0	2-0	5	Jack [2], Baker [34]	4021
5	Sept 7	A	Cambridge U	L	1-2	0-2	9	Baker [71]	2165
6	10	H	Cardiff C	W	2-0	2-0	—	Gittens [24], Ndah [45]	2041
7	14	H	Chester C	D	0-0	0-0	10		2341
8	21	A	Brighton & HA	D	2-2	2-1	8	Baker [20], McCall [27]	4889
9	28	H	Carlisle U	L	1-2	0-0	11	Baker [90]	2435
10	Oct 1	A	Fulham	W	2-1	0-1	—	Nelson 2 [78, 83]	4459
11	5	A	Barnet	D	0-0	0-0	8		2456
12	12	H	Hereford U	W	2-1	1-1	5	Watson [45], Winter [60]	2073
13	15	H	Doncaster R	W	1-0	1-0	—	Winter [45]	1843
14	19	A	Wigan Ath	L	2-3	2-2	6	Jack [26], Laight [45]	3374
15	26	H	Swansea C	W	2-0	0-0	6	Oatway [68], Jack [88]	2755
16	29	H	Mansfield T	W	2-1	1-0	—	Hathaway [8], Nelson [79]	1632
17	Nov 2	A	Leyton Orient	L	0-1	0-1	6		3891
18	9	H	Colchester U	L	0-2	0-0	6		2251
19	20	A	Hull C	L	0-2	0-1	—		1775
20	23	H	Hartlepool U	L	0-1	0-0	9		1856
21	30	A	Swansea C	L	0-2	0-1	14		2889
22	Dec 3	H	Rochdale	L	0-1	0-0	—		1087
23	14	H	Scarborough	W	1-0	1-0	13	Stamps [16]	1567
24	21	A	Darlington	W	3-2	1-1	10	Winter [30], Hawthorne 2 [49, 82]	2971
25	26	A	Cardiff C	L	0-2	0-1	12		3753
26	28	H	Cambridge U	L	0-1	0-1	13		2700
27	Jan 1	H	Brighton & HA	W	2-1	1-1	8	Stamps [36], Nelson [87]	2588
28	18	H	Fulham	W	3-1	0-1	7	Gittens [72], Winter (pen) [75], Nelson [81]	3386
29	31	A	Colchester U	L	0-2	0-1	—		3895
30	Feb 8	H	Leyton Orient	D	0-0	0-0	12		2608
31	15	A	Hartlepool U	D	1-1	0-1	14	Jack [64]	1548
32	18	H	Mansfield T	L	1-2	1-1	—	Nelson [18]	2071
33	22	H	Hull C	D	1-1	1-0	14	Jack [8]	2072
34	Mar 1	A	Rochdale	L	1-2	1-1	16	Nelson [11]	1469
35	4	A	Carlisle U	L	1-5	0-2	—	Nelson [49]	4680
36	8	H	Darlington	D	1-1	1-0	17	McFarlane [4]	1762
37	11	A	Chester C	D	0-0	0-0	—		2064
38	15	A	Scarborough	L	1-3	0-1	16	Stamps [53]	2257
39	22	H	Scunthorpe U	L	1-2	1-2	16	Winter (pen) [4]	1761
40	29	A	Lincoln C	W	2-1	0-0	16	Jack [51], McFarlane [59]	3455
41	31	H	Northampton T	L	1-2	1-2	17	Jack [28]	2335
42	Apr 5	A	Exeter C	D	1-1	1-0	17	McFarlane [41]	4991
43	12	H	Barnet	L	1-2	1-0	19	Jack [10]	1959
44	19	A	Hereford U	D	1-1	1-0	18	Winter [45]	2852
45	26	H	Wigan Ath	L	0-3	0-2	19		2481
46	May 3	A	Doncaster R	L	1-2	0-2	21	Bedeau [71]	1748

Final League Position: 21

GOALSCORERS

League (46): Jack 10, Nelson 8, Winter 6 (2 pens), Baker 4, Gittens 3, McFarlane 3, Stamps 3, Hawthorne 2, Bedeau 1, Hathaway 1, Laight 1, McCall 1, Ndah 1, Oatway 1, Watson 1.
Coca-Cola Cup (3): Baker 3 (1 pen).
FA Cup (0).

Newland R 11	Mitchell P 22+2	Barrow L 45+1	McCall S 23+1	Gittens J 33	Watson A 46	Oatway C 39+2	Nelson G 30+4	Baker P 10	Hawthorne M 25+9	Hancox R 6+5	Jack R 30+3	Adcock P —+1	Winter S 36+1	Hathaway I 21+14	Wilmot R 34	Ndah J 9+3	Stamps S 30	Thomas W 1+11	Laight E 6+4	Wright M 7+2	Bedeau A 3+5	Gregory N 5	Hodges K —+1	Preston M —+2	Crane S —+2	McFarlane A 19	Thirlby A 1+2	Hinshelwood D 7+2	Hockley W —+2	Chandler D 4	Howell J 2+2	Tucker L —+1	Hapgood L —+1	Gregg M 1	Match No.
1	2	3	4	5	6	7	8[1]	9	10	11	12																								1
1	2	3	4	5	6	7[2]	8[1]	9	10	11	12	13																							2
1	2	3	4[2]	5	6	7	12	9[1]	13	11	10[1]		8[2]																						3
	2[2]	3	4	5	6	7	12	9		11[1]	10		8	13	1																				4
1	12	3	4	5	6	7[2]	9[3]	8	13				2	14		10	11[1]																		5
1		3	4	5	6	7	8	9					2	12		10	11[1]																		6
1	2	3	4[1]	5	6	7	8	9	12[2]	14				13		10[3]	11																		7
		3	4	5	6	7	8	9	12	13			2[1]		1	10[3]	11[2]	14																	8
		3	4[1]	5	6	7	8[2]	9			12		2	10	1		11		9[1]	11															9
		3		5	6	7	8		4				2	10	1		11		9[1]	11	13														10
		3	4	5	6	7	8				12		2	10	1		11		9[1]	11															11
		3	4	5	6	7[1]	8		12	13	9[3]		2	10	1		11[2]	14																	12
		3	4	5	6	7					9		2	10	1		11	8																	13
		3	4	5	6	7			12		9		2	10[1]	1		11	13	8[2]																14
		3		5	6	7	12		4		11		2	9	1		10	8[1]																	15
		3		5	6	7	8		4		9		2	10[1]	1		11	12																	16
		3	4		6	7	8			12			2	10[1]	1		11		9	5															17
12		3		5	6	7			4[1]	10[4]			2	13	1	14	11		9[2]		8														18
8		3		5	6	7			4		9		2		1		11				12	10[1]													19
	2	3		5	6	7[1]			12		9		4		1	13	14	8[2]			13	10[3]													20
	2	3		5	6	7					9		4		1	8	11[2]	12			13	10[1]													21
	2	3			6				8		9		7	4[2]	1		11	12		5	10[1]	13													22
	2	3	4[2]		6				8		9[1]		7	12	1	13	11			5	10														23
	2	3	4[2]		6				8[1]		10		7	12	1	9	11			5					13										24
	2[1]	3	4		6				12		8		5		1	7[2]	10[3]	9	11						13	14									25
	2	3		5	6		10		8		4		9[1]			7		1	11						13	14									26
	2	3	4	5	6				8[1]		11		9			7		1	12							10									27
	2[2]	3[1]		5	6	13	8		4		9		7[1]	12	1		11									10									28
		3		5	6	7	8		4		9		2[1]	12	1		11									10									29
	2	3		5	6	7	8		4		11		10	1												9									30
	2	3		5[2]	6	7	8		4[1]		11		12	10	1		13									9									31
	2	3	4[1]		6	7	8				11			1		10		5								9	12								32
	2	3	4[2]	5	6[3]	7	8		11[1]		12		10	13												9	14								33
		3	4[1]	5	6	7	8							1			11	12								9	10	2							34
		3		5	6	7	8		4				10[1]	12	1		11	13								9[2]		2							35
		3		5	6	7	8		4		11		10		1											9		2							36
		3	12	5	6	7			4[3]		11		10	13	1		8									9[1]		2[2]	14						37
	12		4[2]	5	6	7	8				11		10	13	1		3									9		2[1]							38
	2[3]	3			6	7	8		12		11[2]		4	10	1		9									9	14		5[1]						39
		3			6	7	8		4		11		2	10[1]	1		13									9	14		5[1]						40
1		3			6	7	8		4		11		2									5				9									41
1		3			6	7	8		4		11		2									5				9	10								42
1		3			6	7			4		11		2[1]	8[2]											12	9	10		5	13					43
1	4[2]	3			6	7	8				11		2[1]	10												9	12		5	13					44
1		3			6				4		11[2]		2	10			13			12	7					9			5[1]	8[3]	14				45
		3			6	7			4[1]				2	10			5		12	11						9[2]		13		8[3]	14			1	46

Coca-Cola Cup
First Round Bristol C (h) 3-3
(a) 0-1

FA Cup
First Round Luton T (h) 0-1

TOTTENHAM HOTSPUR 1996–97   *Back row (left to right):* Chris Hughton (Reserve Team Manager), Andy Turner, Sol Campbell, Darren Anderton, Ronny Rosenthal, Jason Cundy, Jason Dozzell, Stuart Nethercott, Colin Calderwood, Pat Jennings (Goalkeeping Coach).

Middle row: Tony Lenaghan (Physio), Paul Mahorn, Gerry McMahon, Danny Hill, Espen Baardsen, Ian Walker, David Howells, Stephen Carr, Jamie Clapham, Roy Reyland (Kit Manager).

Front row: Ruel Fox, David Kerslake, Justin Edinburgh, Chris Armstrong, Roger Cross (Assistant Manager), Gary Mabbutt, Gerry Francis (Manager), Teddy Sheringham, Dean Austin, Andy Sinton, Clive Wilson.

(Photograph: Action Images)

FA Premiership   **TOTTENHAM HOTSPUR**

748 High Rd, Tottenham, London N17 0AP. Telephone: (0181) 365 5000. Fax: (0181) 365 5005. Commercial Dept: (0181) 365 5010. Ticketline: 0891 335566. Telephone Bookings: (0171) 396 4567. Ticket Office: (0181) 365 5050. Spurs Line: 0891 335555. Members Ticketline: (0181) 365 5100.

Ground capacity: 33,208 (subject to ground closure and redevelopment 1997–98).

Record attendance: 75,038 v Sunderland, FA Cup 6th rd, 5 March 1938.

Record receipts: £336,702 v Manchester U, Division 1, 28 September 1991.

Pitch measurements: 110yd × 73yd.

Directors: A. M. Sugar (Chairman), C. M. Littner (Chief Executive), J. Sedgwick (Finance Director).
Non-Executive: A. G. Berry (Deputy Chairman), D. A. Alexiou, I. Yawetz, C. T. Sandy, J. Ireland (Company Secretary).

President: W. E. Nicholson OBE. *Vice-President:* N. Solomon.

Manager: Gerry Francis. *Assistant Manager:* Roger Cross. *Reserve Team Manager:* Chris Hughton.
Physio: Tony Lenaghan. *Club Secretary:* Peter Barnes. *Commercial Manager:* Mike Rollo. *PRO:* John Fennelly.

Year Formed: 1882. *Turned Professional:* 1895. *Ltd Co.:* 1898.

Club Nickname: 'Spurs'.

Previous Name: 1882–85, Hotspur Football Club.

Previous Grounds: 1882, Tottenham Marshes; 1885, Northumberland Park; 1898, White Hart Lane.

Foundation: The Hotspur Football Club was formed from an older cricket club in 1882. Most of the founders were old boys of St. John's Presbyterian School and Tottenham Grammar School. The Casey brothers were well to the fore as the family provided the club's first goalposts (painted blue and white) and their first ball. They soon adopted the local YMCA as their meeting place, but after a couple of moves settled at the Red House, which is still their headquarters, although now known simply as 748 High Road.

First Football League game: 1 September 1908, Division 2, v Wolverhampton W (h) W 3-0 – Hewitson; Coquet, Burton; Morris (1), D. Steel, Darnell; Walton, Woodward (2), Macfarlane, R. Steel, Middlemiss.

Record League Victory: 9–0 v Bristol R, Division 2, 22 October 1977 – Daines; Naylor, Holmes, Hoddle (1), McAllister, Perryman, Pratt, McNab, Moores (3), Lee (4), Taylor (1).

Record Cup Victory: 13–2 v Crewe Alex, FA Cup 4th rd (replay), 3 February 1960 – Brown; Hills, Henry; Blanchflower, Norman, Mackay; White, Harmer (1), Smith (4), Allen (5), Jones (3 incl. 1p).

Record Defeat: 0–8 v Cologne, UEFA Inter Toto Cup, 22 July 1995.

Most League Points (2 for a win): 70, Division 2, 1919–20.

Most League Points (3 for a win): 77, Division 1, 1984–85.

Most League Goals: 115, Division 1, 1960–61.

Highest League Scorer in Season: Jimmy Greaves, 37, Division 1, 1962–63.

Most League Goals in Total Aggregate: Jimmy Greaves, 220, 1961–70.

Most Capped Player: Pat Jennings, 74 (119), Northern Ireland.

Most League Appearances: Steve Perryman, 655, 1969–86.

Record Transfer Fee Received: £5,500,000 from Lazio for Paul Gascoigne, May 1992.

Record Transfer Fee Paid: £4,500,000 to Crystal Palace for Chris Armstrong, June 1995.

Football League Record: 1908 Elected to Division 2; 1909–15 Division 1; 1919–20 Division 2; 1920–28 Division 1; 1928–33 Division 2; 1933–35 Division 1; 1935–50 Division 2; 1950–77 Division 1; 1977–78 Division 2; 1978–92 Division 1; 1992– FA Premier League.

Honours: Football League: Division 1 – Champions 1950–51, 1960–61; Runners-up 1921–22, 1951–52, 1956–57, 1962–63; Division 2 – Champions 1919–20, 1949–50; Runners-up 1908–09, 1932–33; Promoted 1977–78 (3rd). *FA Cup:* Winners 1901 (as non-League club), 1921, 1961, 1962, 1967, 1981, 1982, 1991; Runners-up 1987. *Football League Cup:* Winners 1971, 1973; Runners-up 1982. **European Competitions:** *European Cup:* 1961–62. *European Cup-Winners' Cup:* 1962–63 (winners), 1963–64, 1967–68, 1981–82, 1982–83, 1991–92. *UEFA Cup:* 1971–72 (winners), 1972–73, 1973–74 (runners-up), 1983–84 (winners), 1984–85.

Colours: White shirts, navy blue shorts, white stockings. *Change colours:* French navy shirts, ecru shorts, French navy stockings.

Did you know?
Willie Evans, a Welshman born in Waunllwyd, scored 96 goals in 203 League and Cup appearances for Tottenham Hotspur in the 1930s. He was capped six times for England.

TOTTENHAM HOTSPUR 1996–97 LEAGUE RECORD

Match No.	Date		Venue	Opponents	Result		H/T Score	Lg. Pos.	Goalscorers	Attendance
1	Aug	17	A	Blackburn R	W	2-0	1-0	—	Armstrong 2 [33, 67]	26,960
2		21	H	Derby Co	D	1-1	1-0	—	Sheringham [34]	28,219
3		24	H	Everton	D	0-0	0-0	9		29,669
4	Sept	4	A	Wimbledon	L	0-1	0-1	—		17,306
5		7	H	Newcastle U	L	1-2	1-1	13	Allen [28]	32,594
6		14	A	Southampton	W	1-0	0-0	11	Armstrong (pen) [66]	15,251
7		22	H	Leicester C	L	1-2	0-1	12	Wilson (pen) [64]	24,159
8		29	A	Manchester U	L	0-2	0-1	14		54,943
9	Oct	12	A	Aston Villa	W	1-0	0-0	11	Nielsen [61]	32,840
10		19	A	Middlesbrough	W	3-0	2-0	8	Sheringham 2 [21, 90], Fox [23]	30,215
11		26	A	Chelsea	L	1-3	1-1	9	Armstrong [41]	28,318
12	Nov	2	H	West Ham U	W	1-0	0-0	8	Armstrong [67]	32,975
13		16	H	Sunderland	W	2-0	1-0	7	Sinton [13], Sheringham [82]	31,867
14		24	A	Arsenal	L	1-3	0-1	9	Sinton [57]	38,264
15	Dec	2	H	Liverpool	L	0-2	0-1	—		32,899
16		7	A	Coventry C	W	2-1	1-0	10	Sheringham [27], Sinton [75]	19,656
17		14	A	Leeds U	D	0-0	0-0	9		33,783
18		21	H	Sheffield W	D	1-1	1-1	10	Nielsen [29]	30,996
19		26	H	Southampton	W	3-1	2-1	9	Iversen 2 [1, 30], Nielsen [64]	30,549
20		28	H	Newcastle U	L	1-7	0-2	10	Nielsen [89]	36,308
21	Jan	12	H	Manchester U	L	1-2	1-1	10	Allen [44]	33,026
22		19	A	Nottingham F	L	1-2	1-0	10	Sinton [2]	27,303
23		29	H	Blackburn R	W	2-1	1-0	—	Iversen [41], Sinton [83]	22,943
24	Feb	1	H	Chelsea	L	1-2	0-1	10	Howells [83]	33,027
25		15	H	Arsenal	D	0-0	0-0	9		33,039
26		24	A	West Ham U	L	3-4	2-3	—	Sheringham [8], Anderton [29], Howells [53]	23,998
27	Mar	1	A	Nottingham F	L	0-1	0-1	13		32,805
28		4	A	Sunderland	W	4-0	3-0	—	Iversen 3 [2, 9, 62], Nielsen [26]	20,729
29		15	H	Leeds U	W	1-0	1-0	10	Anderton [26]	33,040
30		19	A	Leicester C	D	1-1	0-0	—	Sheringham [90]	20,593
31		22	A	Derby Co	L	2-4	1-2	10	Rosenthal [29], Dozzell [50]	18,083
32	Apr	5	H	Wimbledon	W	1-0	0-0	9	Dozzell [81]	32,654
33		9	A	Sheffield W	L	1-2	1-1	—	Nielsen [43]	22,671
34		12	A	Everton	L	0-1	0-1	9		36,380
35		19	H	Aston Villa	D	1-1	0-0	9	Vega [54]	39,339
36		24	H	Middlesbrough	W	1-0	0-0	—	Sinton [71]	29,940
37	May	3	A	Liverpool	L	1-2	1-2	9	Anderton [5]	40,003
38		11	H	Coventry C	L	1-2	1-2	10	McVeigh [44]	33,029

Final League Position: 10

GOALSCORERS

League (44): Sheringham 7, Iversen 6, Nielsen 6, Sinton 6, Armstrong 5 (1 pen), Anderton 3, Allen 2, Dozzell 2, Howells 2, Fox 1, McVeigh 1, Rosenthal 1, Vega 1, Wilson 1 (pen).
Coca-Cola Cup (7): Allen 2, Anderton 2, Armstrong 1, Campbell 1, Sheringham 1.
FA Cup (0).

Walker I 37	Campbell S 38	Edinburgh J 21+3	Howells D 32	Calderwood C 33+1	Mabbutt G 1	Anderton D 14+2	Fox R 19+6	Armstrong C 12	Sheringham T 29	Sinton A 32+1	Nethercott S 2+7	Wilson C 23+3	Dozzell J 10+7	Rosenthal R 4+16	Nielsen A 28+1	Allen R 9+3	Carr S 24+2	Iversen S 16	Scales J 10+2	Vega R 8	Austin D 13+2	Fenn N —+4	McVeigh P 2+1	Baardsen E 1+1	Clapham J —+1	Match No.
1	2	3	4	5	6[1]	7[3]	8	9	10	11	12[2]	13	14													1
1	6	2	4	5		7[2]	8[1]	9	10	11		3	12	13												2
1	6	2	4	5		7		9	10	11		3	8	12												3
1	6	2	4	5		7[1]	10		11	12		3	9[2]	13	8[3]	14										4
1	6	2	4	5		7[1]	12	9		11		3		13	8	10[2]										5
1	6	2	4	5		7[2]	12	9		11[1]	14	3		13	8[3]	10										6
1	9	2[1]	4	5		7			11	12	6	3		13	8	10										7
1	6	12	4[1]	5		7[2]			10	11		3		13	8	9	2									8
1	6	12	4	5		7		9	10	11[1]		3		13	8[2]		2									9
1	6	3	4	5		7		9	10	11					8		2									10
1	6	3	4	5		7[1]		9	10	11	12				8[2]	13	2									11
1	6	3	4	5				9	10	11	12				8	7[1]	2									12
1	6		4	5		7[1]		9	10	11		3	12		8		2									13
1	6		4	5		7		9	10	11		3			8		2									14
1	6	12	4	5		7		9[2]	10	11[1]		3			8	13	2									15
1	6		4	5		7			10	11		3		12	8[1]		2	9								16
1	6		4	5		7			10	11		3			8		2	9								17
1	6[1]		4	5		7			10	11		3			8		2	9	12							18
1	6		4	5		7[1]			10	11		3			8		2	9	12							19
1	6		4	5		7			10	11[1]		3	12[2]	13	8		2	9								20
1	6	3	8	5			12		7	11	10						2[1]	9	4[2]		13					21
1	6	3	8	5[1]					11[2]	12	14			13	10	7[3]	2	9	4							22
1	6	3	4	12		7[1]				11				13	8	10	2	9	5[1]							23
1	5	3[3]	4	12			14			11	6[2]			13	8	10	7[1]	9			2					24
1	6	3	8	5		7			10	11							2	9	4							25
1	6	8[2]		5		7			10	11[1]		3	13	12			2	9	4							26
1	6	8		5					10	11[2]		3	13	12	7			9	4		2[1]					27
1	6	8		5		7			10	11		3[1]		12				9	4		2					28
1	6			5		7			10	11					8	12	2	9[1]	4		3					29
1	6	8[1]		5					10	11			12	13	7		2	9	4		3[2]					30
1	6			5					10	11[1]				8	12	7	2	9	4		3					31
1	6	3				7			10	11					8			9	4	5	2					32
1	5[1]	3	12			7	8[1]		10	11				13				9	4	6[2]	2	14				33
1	11	3		5			12		10						8		7[2]	9	4[3]	6	2[1]	13	14			34
1	6	3	7[1]	5					10	11			12		8		2	9[2]	4				13			35
1	6	3	7	5					10	11					8		2	9	4							36
1[8]	3	9[1]		5		7[2]	12		10	11					8				4	6	2		13	15		37
	6	3				7			10	11[2]					8		2	9[1]	4	5	12			1	13	38

Coca-Cola Cup

Second Round	Preston NE	(a)	1-1
		(h)	3-0
Third Round	Sunderland	(h)	2-1
Fourth Round	Bolton W	(a)	1-6

FA Cup

Third Round	Manchester U	(a)	0-2

TRANMERE ROVERS 1996–97 *Back row (left to right):* Alan Morgan, Gary Scott, Dave Challinor, Graham Branch, Jamie Jardine, Gary Jones, Dave Higgins, Paul Jones, Kenny Irons, John Morrissey.

Middle row: Warwick Rimmer (Youth Development Officer), Alan Rogers, Tommy Marsden, Jon Kenworthy, Ian Moore, Danny Coyne, Eric Nixon, Steve Simonsen, Ged Brannan, Robbie Walker, Greg Blundell, Ray Mathias (Assistant Manager), Les Parry (Physio).

Front row: Kevin Sheedy (Reserve Manager), Pat Nevin, Paul Cook, Liam O'Brien, John McGreal, John Aldridge (Player/Manager), Steve Mungall, Shaun Teale, Gary Stevens, Billy Woods, Keith Crawford, Dave Philpotts (Chief Scout).

(Photograph: Focus Photography)

Division 1　　　**TRANMERE ROVERS**

Prenton Park, Prenton Road West, Birkenhead L42 9PN. Telephone: (0151) 608 4194. Fax: (0151) 608 4385. Commercial: (0151) 608 0371. Shop: (0151) 608 0438. Ticket Office: (0151) 609 0137.

Ground capacity: 16,789 (all seated).

Record attendance: 24,424 v Stoke C, FA Cup 4th rd, 5 February 1972.

Record receipts: £114,150 v Aston Villa, Coca-Cola Cup semi-final, 16 February 1994.

Pitch measurements: 110yd × 70yd.

President: H. B. Thomas.

Chairman and Chief Executive: F. D. Corfe.

Directors: Norman Wilson FAAI, A. J. Adams BDS, G. E. H. Jones LLB, F. J. Williams, J. J. Holsgrove FCA.

Secretary: Mick Horton. *General Manager:* Janet Ratcliffe.

Player-Manager: John Aldridge. *Trainer:* Steve Mungall.

Youth Development Officer: Warwick Rimmer.

Coach: Ray Mathias. *Physio:* Les Parry.

Year Formed: 1884. *Turned Professional:* 1912. *Ltd Co.:* 1920.

Previous Name: Belmont AFC, 1884–85.

Club Nickname: 'The Rovers'.

Previous Grounds: 1884, Steeles Field; 1887, Ravenshaws Field/Old Prenton Park; 1912, Prenton Park.

Foundation: Formed in 1884 as Belmont they adopted their present title the following year and eventually joined their first league, the West Lancashire League in 1889–90, the same year as their first success in the Wirral Challenge Cup. The club almost folded in 1899–1900 when all the players left en bloc to join a rival club, but they survived the crisis and went from strength to strength winning the 'Combination' title in 1907–08 and the Lancashire Combination in 1913–14. They joined the Football League in 1921 from the Central League.

First Football League game: 27 August 1921, Division 3 (N), v Crewe Alex (h) W 4-1 – Bradshaw; Grainger, Stuart (1); Campbell, Milnes (1), Heslop; Moreton, Groves (1), Hyam, Ford (1), Hughes.

Record League Victory: 13–4 v Oldham Ath, Division 3 (N), 26 December 1935 – Gray; Platt, Fairhurst; McLaren, Newton, Spencer; Eden, MacDonald (1), Bell (9), Woodward (2), Urmson (1).

Record Cup Victory: 13–0 v Oswestry U, FA Cup 2nd prel rd, 10 October 1914 – Ashcroft; Stevenson, Bullough, Hancock, Taylor, Holden (1), Moreton (1), Cunningham (2), Smith (5), Leck (3), Gould (1).

Record Defeat: 1–9 v Tottenham H, FA Cup 3rd rd (replay), 14 January 1953.

Most League Points (2 for a win): 60, Division 4, 1964–65.

Most League Points (3 for a win): 80, Division 4, 1988–89 and Division 3, 1989–90.

Most League Goals: 111, Division 3 (N), 1930–31.

Highest League Scorer in Season: Bunny Bell, 35, Division 3 (N), 1933–34.

Most League Goals in Total Aggregate: Ian Muir, 141, 1985–95.

Most Capped Player: John Aldridge, 30 (69), Republic of Ireland.

Most League Appearances: Harold Bell, 595, 1946–64 (incl. League record 401 consecutive appearances).

Record Transfer Fee Received: £1,500,000 from Sheffield W for Ian Nolan, August 1994.

Record Transfer Fee Paid: £450,000 to Aston Villa for Shaun Teale, August 1995.

Football League Record: 1921 Original Member of Division 3 (N): 1938–39 Division 2; 1946–58 Division 3 (N); 1958–61 Division 3; 1961–67 Division 4; 1967–75 Division 3; 1975–76 Division 4; 1976–79 Division 3; 1979–89 Division 4; 1989–91 Division 3; 1991–92 Division 2; 1992– Division 1.

Honours: Football League Division 1 best season: 4th, 1992–93; Promoted from Division 3 1990–91 (play-offs); Division 3 (N) – Champions 1937–38; Promotion to 3rd Division: 1966–67, 1975–76; Division 4 – Runners-up 1988–89. *FA Cup:* best season: 5th rd, 1968. *Football League Cup:* semi-final 1994. *Welsh Cup:* Winners 1935; Runners-up 1934. *Leyland Daf Cup:* Winners 1990; Runners-up 1991.

Colours: White shirts, blue shorts. *Change colours:* Claret/sky blue shirts and shorts.

Did you know?
On 30 November 1996, Tranmere Rovers attracted their best attendance of the season at that time when 10,127 spectators saw them defeat Ipswich Town 3–0. The club had reduced admission prices for the occasion.

TRANMERE ROVERS 1996–97 LEAGUE RECORD

Match No.	Date		Venue	Opponents	Result	H/T Score	Lg. Pos.	Goalscorers	Attendance
1	Aug 17	A	Southend U		D 1-1	1-1	—	Morrissey [22]	4264
2	23	H	Grimsby T		W 3-2	0-2	—	Aldridge 2 (1 pen) [24, 61 (p)], Irons [51]	6800
3	27	H	Port Vale		W 2-0	2-0	—	Mahon [15], Branch [44]	6123
4	31	A	Bradford C		L 0-1	0-0	5		10,080
5	Sept 7	H	Birmingham C		W 1-0	0-0	5	Aldridge [60]	8548
6	10	A	Huddersfield T		W 1-0	1-0	—	Aldridge [36]	10,181
7	14	A	Swindon T		L 1-2	0-1	5	Aldridge [89]	8430
8	21	H	WBA		L 2-3	1-2	7	Aldridge [31], Branch [75]	7848
9	28	A	Norwich C		D 1-1	1-0	7	Aldridge [19]	14,511
10	Oct 1	H	Oxford U		D 0-0	0-0	—		4577
11	4	H	Portsmouth		W 4-3	2-1	—	Branch 2 [1, 31], Jones G [62], Bonetti [90]	5001
12	12	A	Sheffield U		D 0-0	0-0	4		15,059
13	15	A	Bolton W		L 0-1	0-0	—		14,136
14	20	H	QPR		L 2-3	1-1	9	Aldridge (pen) [41], Brannan [87]	7025
15	26	A	Ipswich T		W 2-0	1-0	6	Brannan [32], Vaughan (og) [61]	11,003
16	29	H	Charlton Ath		W 4-0	2-0	—	Moore [16], Jones G [24], Mahon [62], Aldridge [85]	5527
17	Nov 2	H	Crystal Palace		L 1-3	1-1	7	Thorn [3]	8613
18	15	H	Oldham Ath		D 1-1	1-0	—	Aldridge [7]	8327
19	23	A	Manchester C		W 2-1	0-0	6	Higgins [49], Brightwell (og) [67]	26,531
20	30	H	Ipswich T		W 3-0	1-0	5	Brannan [43], Aldridge 2 [76, 80]	10,127
21	Dec 3	A	Reading		L 0-2	0-2	—		5513
22	7	A	Stoke C		L 0-2	0-1	6		9931
23	14	A	Barnsley		L 0-3	0-1	9		8513
24	21	H	Wolverhampton W		L 0-2	0-1	12		9674
25	26	H	Huddersfield T		D 1-1	0-1	12	Brannan [90]	10,134
26	Jan 1	A	WBA		W 2-1	1-1	11	Aldridge 2 [17, 85]	14,770
27	10	H	Swindon T		W 2-1	1-0	—	Nevin 2 [21, 50]	8763
28	18	A	Oxford U		L 1-2	1-2	10	Aldridge [4]	7072
29	28	H	Norwich C		W 3-1	2-1	—	Cook 2 [9, 65], Moore [45]	5891
30	Feb 1	H	Reading		D 2-2	1-1	7	Branch [14], Moore [72]	6019
31	7	A	Charlton Ath		L 1-3	1-2	—	Irons [35]	11,283
32	22	A	Crystal Palace		W 1-0	0-0	11	O'Brien [71]	15,396
33	28	H	Stoke C		D 0-0	0-0	—		9127
34	Mar 4	A	Oldham Ath		W 2-1	1-1	—	Brannan 2 [4, 58]	5417
35	8	A	Wolverhampton W		L 2-3	0-2	10	Irons [55], Aldridge [57]	26,192
36	15	H	Barnsley		D 1-1	1-0	11	Higgins [36]	7347
37	18	H	Manchester C		D 1-1	0-0	—	Jones G [64]	12,019
38	22	A	Grimsby T		D 0-0	0-0	10		4353
39	28	H	Southend U		W 3-0	3-0	—	Irons [6], Jones L [23], Aldridge [35]	7563
40	31	A	Port Vale		L 1-2	1-1	12	Irons [23]	7469
41	Apr 4	H	Bradford C		W 3-0	1-0	—	Jones G 2 [32, 87], Jones L [80]	8531
42	12	A	Portsmouth		W 3-1	2-0	8	Cook [16], Jones G [23], Jones L [83]	12,004
43	15	A	Birmingham C		D 0-0	0-0	—		22,364
44	19	H	Sheffield U		D 1-1	1-0	8	Jones L [26]	10,027
45	26	A	QPR		L 0-2	0-0	11		14,859
46	May 4	H	Bolton W		D 2-2	0-1	11	Aldridge (pen) [60], Jones L [90]	14,309

Final League Position: 11

GOALSCORERS

League (63): Aldridge 18 (3 pens), Brannan 6, Jones G 6, Branch 5, Irons 5, Jones L 5, Cook 3, Moore 3, Higgins 2, Mahon 2, Nevin 2, Bonetti 1, Morrissey 1, O'Brien 1, Thorn 1, own goals 2.
Coca-Cola Cup (5): Aldridge 2 (1 pen), Bonetti 1, Branch 1, Morrissey 1.
FA Cup (0).

Coyne D 21	Stevens G 31	Rogers A 28+3	McGreal J 24	Teale S 25	O'Brien L 41	Morrissey J 21+10	Aldridge J 32+11	Cook P 30+6	Irons K 34+7	Bonetti I 9+4	Branman G 31+3	Moore I 14+7	Nevin P 10+11	Branch G 22+13	Higgins D 21+1	Mahon A 14+11	Morgan A —+1	Thomas T 28+2	Jones G 13+17	Thorn A 19	Nixon E 25	Challinor D 4+1	Jones L 8	Woods B 1	Match No.
1	2	3	4	5	6	7^3	8^2	9	10^1	11	12	13	14												1
1	2	3^1	4^2	5	6	7	8	9	10	11^3	12	13			14										2
1	2			5		7^1	8	9	10			3		12	11	4		6^2	13						3
1	2^2			5		7^1	8	9	10^2			3		12	11	4		6	13						4
1	2			5	6	7	8^1	9	10^2			3		12	11	4			13						5
1	2			5	6	7^1	8^2	9	10			3		13	11	4		12							6
1	2			5	6^1	7	8	9^2	10	12		3			11	4		13							7
1	2			5	6^1	7	8	9		11	3		10		4	12									8
1	2			5	6	12	8^2	9	7	11	3		10^1					13	4						9
1	2			5	6^2	12	8	9	7	11	3		10^1					13	4						10
1	2	3		5	6		8		7	11	9		10					12	4^1						11
1	2	3^2		5	6	12	8	14	7^3	11	9		10^1					13	4						12
1	2			5	6	12	8	9^1	7	11	3		10^2	13				14	4^3						13
1	2			5	6	7^2	8	13	9^3	11^1	3		12	10	4	14									14
1	2	3		5	6		12	10		7	8		11					9^1	4						15
1	2	3		5	6		12	10	13	7	8		11^2					9^1	4						16
1	2	3		5	6^2		12	10	13	7	8^1		14	11				9	4^3						17
1	2	3		5	6		8		12	7		13		4	11^1	10^2	9								18
	2	3		5	6	8^3	11	12	7^1	10^2	13		4					9	14		1				19
	2	3^1		5	6	8	11^3	12	7	10^2	13		4	14				9			1				20
	2	3^1		5	6	8	13	12	7	10^3			4	11				9	14		1				21
	2			5	6	12	8	11	3^1	7			10^2	4				9	13		1				22
	2		4	5	6	7^1	8		10^3	9		13	11^2	12				3	14		1				23
1	2	3	4	5	6^1	12	13		14	7	10		8^2	11				9^3							24
1^1	2	3	4	5	6^1	12	8	9		7	10^3	13	14	11^2											25
1^1	2		4		6^3	7	8^2	9		3	13	10	14	5	12	11									26
	2		4		6^1	10^3	8^2	9	12	7	13	11	14	5		3						1			27
	2	12	4		6^2	10^3	8	9	13	7	14	11^1		5		3						1			28
	2	12	4		9	6	13		7^3	8	11^1	10^2		3	14	5					1				29
	2^1	12	4		9	6			8	11^2	10		7	3	13	5					1				30
	2^1	11	4		9^3	6^2	13	8	12	10			7	3	14	5					1				31
		3	4		6^2	12		10		7	8	11^3	9^1	5	13			2	14		1				32
		3			6	12		10^1		7	8	11	9^3	5	13			2			1		4		33
		3			6	8^2		10		7	9	11^1	12	4				2	13	5	1				34
		3	4		6	8^1	12	10		7	9^2		13	11				2	14	5^3	1				35
		3	4		6	13	8	9	10		12^2	7^1	5	11				2			1				36
		3	4		6	12	13	9	10		7^2	5^3	11^1					2	8		1	14			37
		3	4		6	7^2	8	11^1	10		13		12					2	9		1	5			38
		3	4		6	7	8^1	12	10		13							2	9		1	5	11^2		39
			4		6	7^2	12	8	10^1		13							2	9		1	5	11	3	40
		3	4		6	7^1	8^3	12	10^2		14	13						2	9	5	1		11		41
		3	4		6	7^3	12	8	10		14	13						2^2	9	5^1	1		11		42
		3	4		6	7^1	12	8	10									2	9	5	1		11		43
		3	4		6^2	7^1	12	8	10		13							2	9	5	1		11		44
		3	4		6	7^1	8		10		12							2	9	5	1		11		45
		3	4		6	12	8		10		7			9^1				2		5	1		11		46

Coca-Cola Cup

First Round	Shrewsbury T	(a)	2-0	
		(h)	1-1	
Second Round	Oldham Ath	(a)	2-2	
		(h)	0-1	

FA Cup

Third Round	Carlisle U	(a)	0-1

WALSALL 1996–97 *Back row (left to right):* Tom Bradley (Physio), Dean Keates, David Baldwin, Steve Rowland, Clive Platt, Ian Roper, Trevor Wood, James Walker, Kyle Lightbourne, Adrian Viveash, Paul Mountford, Wayne Thomas, John Keister, Eric McManus (Youth Team Manager).
Front row: Wayne Evans, Darren Rogers, Darren Bradley, Derek Mountfield, Chris Marsh, Chris Nicholl (Manager), Kevin Wilson (Manager), Ray Daniel, Charlie Ntamark, Martin Butler, Stuart Ryder.

Division 2　　　　　　　　　　　　**WALSALL**

Bescot Stadium, Bescot Crescent, Walsall WS1 4SA. Telephone: (01922) 22791. Fax: (01922) 613202. Commercial Dept: (01922) 30696. Saddlers Hotline: 0891 555800.

Ground capacity: 9000.

Record attendance: 10,628 B International, England v Switzerland, 20 May 1991.

Record receipts: £98,828 v Leeds U, FA Cup 3rd rd, 7 January 1995.

Pitch measurements: 110yd × 73yd.

Chairman: J. W. Bonsor.

Directors: M. N. Lloyd, K. R. Whalley, C. Welch, R. M. Tisdale, S. A. Joesbury.

Manager: Jan Sorensen. *General Manager:* Paul Taylor. *Physio:* Tom Bradley.

Secretary/Commercial Manager: Roy Whalley.

Year Formed: 1888. *Turned Professional:* 1888. *Ltd Co.:* 1921.

Club Nickname: 'The Saddlers'.

Previous Names: Walsall Swifts (founded 1877) and Walsall Town (founded 1879) amalgamated in 1888 and were known as Walsall Town Swifts until 1895.

Previous Grounds: Fellows Park to 1990.

Foundation: Two of the leading clubs around Walsall in the 1880s were Walsall Swifts (formed 1877) and Walsall Town (formed 1879). The Swifts were winners of the Birmingham Senior Cup in 1881, while the Town reached the 4th round (5th round modern equivalent) of the FA Cup in 1883. These clubs amalgamated as Walsall Town Swifts in 1888, becoming simply Walsall in 1895.

First Football League game: 3 September 1892, Division 2, v Darwen (h) L 1-2 – Hawkins; Withington, Pinches; Robinson, Whitrick, Forsyth; Marshall, Holmes, Turner, Gray (1), Pangbourn.

Record League Victory: 10–0 v Darwen, Division 2, 4 March 1899 – Tennent; E. Peers (1), Davies; Hickinbotham, Jenkyns, Taggart; Dean (3), Vail (2), Aston (4), Martin, Griffin.

Record Cup Victory: 6–1 v Leytonstone (away), FA Cup 1st rd, 30 November 1946 – Lewis; Netley, Skidmore; Crutchley, Foulkes, Newman; Maund (1), Talbot, Darby (1), Wilshaw (2), Davies (2). 6–1 v Margate, FA Cup 1st rd (replay), 24 November 1955 – Davies; Haddington, Vinall; Dorman, McPherson, Crook; Morris, Walsh (3), Richards (2), McLaren (1), Moore.

Record Defeat: 0–12 v Small Heath, 17 December 1892 and v Darwen, 26 December 1896, both Division 2.

Most League Points (2 for a win): 65, Division 4, 1959–60.

Most League Points (3 for a win): 83, Division 3, 1994–95.

Most League Goals: 102, Division 4, 1959–60.

Highest League Scorer in Season: Gilbert Alsop, 40, Division 3 (N), 1933–34 and 1934–35.

Most League Goals in Total Aggregate: Tony Richards, 184, 1954–63, and Colin Taylor, 184, 1958–63, 1964–68, 1969–73.

Most Capped Player: Mick Kearns, 15 (18), Republic of Ireland.

Most League Appearances: Colin Harrison, 467, 1964–82.

Record Transfer Fee Received: £600,000 from West Ham U for David Kelly, July 1988.

Record Transfer Fee Paid: £175,000 to Birmingham C for Alan Buckley, June 1979.

Football League Record: 1892 Elected to Division 2; 1895 Failed re-election; 1896–1901 Division 2; 1901 Failed re-election; 1921 Original Member of Division 3 (N); 1927–31 Division 3 (S); 1931–36 Division 3 (N); 1936–58 Division 3 (S); 1958–60 Division 4; 1960–61 Division 3; 1961–63 Division 2; 1963–79 Division 3; 1979–80 Division 4; 1980–88 Division 3; 1988–89 Division 2; 1989–90 Division 3; 1990–92 Division 4; 1992–95 Division 3; 1995– Division 2.

Honours: Football League: Division 2 best season: 6th, 1898–99; Division 3 – Runners-up 1960–61, 1994–95; Division 4 – Champions 1959–60; Runners-up 1979–80. *FA Cup:* best season: 5th rd, 1939, 1975, 1978, 1987 and last 16 1889. *Football League Cup:* Semi-final 1984.

Colours: Red and black check shirts, black shorts, white stockings. *Change colours:* Navy blue shirts, navy blue shorts, white stockings.

Did you know?
Between December and mid-February last season, Walsall equalled a club record with six successive League wins.

WALSALL 1996–97 LEAGUE RECORD

Match No.	Date	Venue	Opponents	Result	H/T Score	Lg. Pos.	Goalscorers	Attendance
1	Aug 17	H	Rotherham U	D 1-1	0-1	—	Butler 76	4040
2	24	A	Burnley	L 1-2	1-1	19	Wilson 43	10,322
3	27	A	Chesterfield	L 0-1	0-0	—		3561
4	Sept 7	A	Blackpool	L 1-2	0-1	24	Blake 56	5176
5	10	H	Wycombe W	D 2-2	2-2	—	Wilson 12, Watson 25	2659
6	14	H	Gillingham	W 1-0	0-0	20	Viveash 54	3419
7	21	A	Bristol C	L 1-4	1-2	22	Lightbourne 16	7412
8	24	H	Wrexham	L 0-1	0-0	—		2832
9	28	H	Bury	W 3-1	1-1	22	Viveash 11, Lightbourne 49, Blake 74	3254
10	Oct 1	A	Bournemouth	W 1-0	1-0	—	Hodge 7	2747
11	5	A	Luton T	L 1-3	0-1	18	Lightbourne 70	5002
12	12	H	Plymouth Arg	L 0-1	0-1	20		3720
13	15	H	Preston NE	W 1-0	0-0	—	Wilson 46	3224
14	19	A	Brentford	D 1-1	1-1	20	Lightbourne 17	5419
15	26	H	Stockport Co	D 1-1	1-0	17	Wilson (pen) 23	3767
16	29	A	Notts Co	L 0-2	0-1	—		3127
17	Nov 2	A	Millwall	L 0-1	0-1	22		9176
18	9	H	Peterborough U	W 4-0	2-0	17	Lightbourne 2 25, 87, Wilson (pen) 45, Donowa 76	3921
19	23	H	Crewe Alex	W 1-0	1-0	16	Wilson 29	3653
20	30	A	Stockport Co	L 0-2	0-1	19		5333
21	Dec 3	H	Bristol R	W 1-0	1-0	—	Viveash 15	4084
22	14	H	Watford	D 1-1	1-1	17	Keister 36	3674
23	20	A	Shrewsbury T	D 2-2	1-2	—	Viveash 27, Wilson 76	3007
24	26	A	Wycombe W	W 2-0	0-0	12	Blake 67, Lightbourne 90	5073
25	Jan 18	H	Bournemouth	W 2-1	1-0	13	Viveash 27, Lightbourne 47	3037
26	25	H	Notts Co	W 3-1	1-0	13	Viveash 41, Ntamark 59, Hodge 86	3261
27	Feb 1	A	Peterborough U	W 1-0	0-0	12	Watson 90	4940
28	8	H	Millwall	W 2-1	2-1	12	Watson 20, Viveash 24	3833
29	11	A	York C	W 2-0	0-0	—	Lightbourne 75, Viveash 82	2136
30	15	A	Crewe Alex	L 0-1	0-0	11		4648
31	22	H	York C	D 1-1	0-1	10	Lightbourne 77	3664
32	Mar 1	A	Bristol R	W 1-0	0-0	10	Watson 62	5891
33	4	H	Bristol C	W 2-0	1-0	—	Lightbourne 2 35, 76	4322
34	8	H	Shrewsbury T	D 2-2	2-0	7	Lightbourne 34, Ricketts 39	4819
35	15	A	Watford	L 0-1	0-1	10		7818
36	18	H	Blackpool	D 1-1	0-0	—	Hodge 90	3459
37	22	H	Burnley	L 1-3	0-1	11	Lightbourne 90	6306
38	29	A	Rotherham U	W 2-1	2-0	10	Lightbourne 24, Viveash 33	2428
39	Apr 1	A	Chesterfield	D 1-1	0-1	—	Blake 72	3784
40	5	A	Wrexham	W 2-1	1-0	9	Lightbourne 15, Watson 75	3266
41	8	A	Bury	L 1-2	0-1	—	Lightbourne 71	4082
42	12	H	Luton T	W 3-2	1-0	7	Lightbourne 2 19, 60, Hodge 77	5415
43	19	A	Plymouth Arg	L 0-2	0-0	10		5535
44	26	H	Brentford	W 1-0	1-0	8	Lightbourne 44	5359
45	29	A	Gillingham	L 0-2	0-1	—		4095
46	May 3	A	Preston NE	L 0-2	0-1	12		10,800

Final League Position: 12

GOALSCORERS

League (54): Lightbourne 20, Viveash 9, Wilson 7 (2 pens), Watson 5, Blake 4, Hodge 4, Butler 1, Donowa 1, Keister 1, Ntamark 1, Ricketts 1.
Coca-Cola Cup (1): Lightbourne 1.
FA Cup (7): Lightbourne 4, Wilson 2 (1 pen), Viveash 1.

Walker J 36	Evans W 27+1	Daniel R 8+2	Viveash A 46	Marsh C 28+2	Mountfield D 42	Ntamark C 36+2	Bradley D 21+5	Lightbourne K 45	Wilson K 36+1	Butler M 20+3	Rogers D 1+1	Keister J 30+6	Ricketts M 2+9	Blake M 35+3	Platt C —+1	Watson A 22+14	Wood T 10	Hodge J 32+5	Thomas W 14+6	Keates D 1+1	Donowa L 6	Roper I 5+6	Beckford D 3+5	Ryder S —+1	Match No.
1	2	3[1]	4	5[2]	6	7[3]	8	9	10	11	12	13	14												1
1	2	3	4	5[1]	6	7[3]	8	9	10[2]	11		13	14	12											2
1	2[2]	3	4	5	6		8[1]	9	10	11		12		7		13									3
1			4		6	2	8[1]	9	10	11		3	12	7		5									4
	3	6	12	5		2	8	9	10	13		4		7[1]		11[2]	1								5
1			4	3	6	2	8	9	10	5				7		11									6
1			3	5	6	2	8	9	10	11				7		4									7
			4	3	6	2	12	9	10	5[2]		8		7[1]		13	1	11							8
			4	3	6	2	12	9	10	5		8		7			1	11[1]							9
			4	3	6	2		9	10	5		8		7			1	11							10
	12[2]		4	3	6	2	13	9	10	5[3]		8		7		14	1	11[1]							11
			4	3	6	2	8[2]	9	10					7		12	1	11[1]	5		13				12
			4	3	6	2		9	10					7		12	1	11	5			8[1]			13
			4	3	6	2		9	10					7			1	11	5			8			14
			4	3	6	2		9	10					7			1	11	5			8			15
	12		4	3	6	2[1]		9	10					7		13	1	11	5			8[2]			16
1			4	3	6	2		9	10			12		7		13		11[1]	5[2]			8			17
1	3		4	11	6	2		9	10[2]				12	7		13			5[1]			8			18
1	3		4	5[1]	6	2		9	10			8		7		12		11							19
1	3		4	5	6	2	12	9	10[2]			8		7[1]		13		11							20
1	3		4	5		2	7[1]	9	10[2]	12		8				13		11			6				21
1	3		4	5[1]	6	2	7	9	10			8				12		11							22
1	3		4	5[1]	6	2	7	9	10			8[2]				12		11	13						23
1	3		4	5	6	2		9	10			8		7		12		11[1]							24
1	12	3	4	5[1]	6	2	7	9	10			8				13		11[2]							25
1	5		4		6	2	7[1]	9	10[2]			8				13		11	12			3			26
1	5		4		6[2]	2	7	9	3[1]			8				10		11	12			13			27
1	2		4	3	6		7	9	10	5		8[2]				12		11[1]				13			28
1	3		4	5[3]	6[2]	2	7	9	10[1]			8				12		11	14			13			29
1	5		4	3	6	2	7[2]	9	10			8[3]				12		11[1]	14			13			30
1	5		4	3	6	2	7	9	10[1]			8[2]				12		11	13						31
1	3		4	5	6	2	7[1]	9	10			8				12		11							32
1	3		4	5	6	2		9	10[1]			8		7		12		11							33
1	3		4	5	6	2		9	10[1]			8		7		12		11							34
1	3		4	5[2]	6	2		9	10[1]			8	12	7		13		11							35
1	3		4	5[1]	6	2		9	10			8		7		12		11							36
1	3		4	12	6	2		9	10[1]			8		7		13		11	5[2]						37
1	3		4	5	6[1]	2		9	10[2]			8		7				11				12	13		38
1	3[1]		4	5		2		9	10			8		7				11				6	12		39
1	3		4	5		2		9	10[1]			8		7				11				6	12		40
1	3		4	5	6	2		9	10			8		7				11				3			41
1	3		4	5	6	2	12	9	10[2]			8		7				11[1]					13		42
1	3		4	5	6	2	12	9	10[2]			8		7[1]				11					13		43
1	3		4	5	6	2	8[1]	9						7		12		11				10			44
1	3		4	5	6[1]	2	8	9				13		7		14		11				10[2]	12[2]		45
1	3		4	5		2	12	9				13		7[2]		14		11[2]				6	10		46

Coca-Cola Cup
First Round   Watford   (h)   1-0
                                  (a)   0-2

FA Cup
First Round   Northwich V   (a)   2-2
                                      (h)   3-1
Second Round   Burnley   (h)   1-1
                                      (a)   1-1

WATFORD 1996–97 *Back row (left to right):* Kirk Wheeler (Football in the Community Officer), Kevin Belgrave, Dominic Ludden, Richard Johnson, Colin Simpson, Devon White, Colin Foster, Keith Millen, Steve Palmer, Clint Easton, Wayne Andrews, Roy Clare (Kit Manager).

Middle row: Phil Edwards (Physio), Jimmy Gilligan (Youth Development Officer), Kevin Miller, Nigel Gibbs, Richard Flash, Tommy Mooney, Robert Page, Kerry Dixon, Craig Ramage, David Connolly, Alec Chamberlain, Bobby Downes (Director of Youth Football), Robert Kelly (Youth Team Manager).

Front row: Mark Rooney, Gary Porter, Steve Talboys, Kevin Phillips, Kenny Jackett (Manager), Luther Blissett (Assistant Manager), Gary Penrice, Darren Bazeley, David Holdsworth, Nathan Lowndes.

Division 2 **WATFORD**

Vicarage Road Stadium, Watford WD1 8ER. Telephone: (01923) 496000. Fax: (01923) 496001. Hornet Hotline: 0891 104104. Ticket Office: (01923) 496010. Club Shop: (01923) 496005. Catering: (01923) 221457. Football in the Community: (01923) 440449. Junior Hornets Club: (01923) 496000. Marketing: (01923) 496006.

Ground capacity: 22,000.

Record attendance: 34,099 v Manchester U, FA Cup 4th rd (replay), 3 February 1969.

Record receipts: £181,968.50 v Tottenham Hotspur, Coca-Cola Cup 2nd rd 1st leg, 21 September 1994.

Pitch measurements: 115yd × 75yd.

Life Presidents: Elton John CBE, Geoff Smith.

Chairman: Elton John CBE.

Directors: Rumi Verjee (Vice-Chairman). B. Anderson, C. Lissack, D. Meller, H. Oundjian, T. Rosenberg.

Secretary: John Alexander.

General Manager: Graham Taylor. *First Team Coach:* Kenny Jackett.

Youth Development Officer: Jimmy Gilligan.

Head of Sales and Marketing: Mark Devlin.

Communications Officer: Mike Hayes.

Safety Officer/Stadium Manager: Mick Buttle.

Year Formed: 1891*(see Foundation).* *Turned Professional:* 1897. *Ltd Co.:* 1909.

Club Nickname: 'The Hornets'.

Previous Name: West Herts.

Previous Ground: 1899, Cassio Road; 1922, Vicarage Road.

Foundation: Tracing this club's foundation proves difficult. Nowadays it is suggested that Watford was formed as Watford Rovers in 1891. Another version is that Watford Rovers were not forerunners of the present club whose history began in 1898 with the amalgamation of West Herts and Watford St. Mary's.

First Football League game: 28 August 1920, Division 3, v QPR (a) W 2-1 – Williams; Horseman, F. Gregory; Bacon, Toone, Wilkinson; Bassett, Ronald (1), Hoddinott, White (1), Waterall.

Record League Victory: 8–0 v Sunderland, Division 1, 25 September 1982 – Sherwood; Rice, Rostron, Taylor, Terry, Bolton, Callaghan (2), Blissett (4), Jenkins (2), Jackett, Barnes.

Record Cup Victory: 10–1 v Lowestoft T, FA Cup 1st rd, 27 November 1926 – Yates; Prior, Fletcher (1); F. Smith, 'Bert' Smith, Strain; Stephenson, Warner (3), Edmonds (2), Swan (2), Daniels (1). (1 og).

Record Defeat: 0–10 v Wolverhampton W, FA Cup 1st rd (replay), 13 January 1912.

Most League Points (2 for a win): 71, Division 4, 1977–78.

Most League Points (3 for a win): 80, Division 2, 1981–82.

Most League Goals: 92, Division 4, 1959–60.

Highest League Scorer in Season: Cliff Holton, 42, Division 4, 1959–60.

Most League Goals in Total Aggregate: Luther Blissett, 158, 1976–83, 1984–88, 1991–92.

Most Capped Player: John Barnes, 31 (79), England and Kenny Jackett, 31, Wales.

Most League Appearances: Luther Blissett, 415, 1976–83, 1984–88, 1991–92.

Record Transfer Fee Received: £2,300,000 from Chelsea for Paul Furlong, May 1994.

Record Transfer Fee Paid: £550,000 to AC Milan for Luther Blissett, August 1984.

Football League Record: 1920 Original Member of Division 3; 1921–58 Division 3 (S); 1958–60 Division 4; 1960–69 Division 3; 1969–72 Division 2; 1972–75 Division 3; 1975–78 Division 4; 1978–79 Division 3; 1979–82 Division 2; 1982–88 Division 1; 1988–92 Division 2; 1992–96 Division 1; 1996– Division 2.

Honours: Football League: Division 1 – Runners-up 1982–83; Division 2 – Runners-up 1981–82; Division 3 – Champions 1968–69; Runners-up 1978–79; Division 4 – Champions 1977–78; Promoted 1959–60 (4th). *FA Cup:* Runners-up 1984. *Football League Cup:* Semi- final 1979. **European Competitions:** *UEFA Cup:* 1983–84.

Colours: Yellow shirts, red shorts, red stockings. *Change colours:* Red/black shirts, black shorts, black stockings.

Did you know?
Gifton Noel-Williams scored for Watford against Blackpool on 30 November 1996 aged 16 years 314 days. His 69th minute goal broke a 69-year old club record for the youngest scorer.

Watford

WATFORD 1996–97 LEAGUE RECORD

Match No.	Date	Venue	Opponents	Result	H/T Score	Lg. Pos.	Goalscorers	Attendance
1	Aug 17	A	Bournemouth	W 2-1	0-0	—	Connolly [58], White [73]	7672
2	24	H	Millwall	L 0-2	0-1	13		9495
3	27	H	Plymouth Arg	L 0-2	0-1	—		7349
4	31	A	Crewe Alex	W 2-0	2-0	11	Palmer [2], Mooney [42]	3655
5	Sept 7	H	Stockport Co	W 1-0	1-0	6	Mooney (pen) [50]	7208
6	10	A	Notts Co	W 3-2	2-0	—	Mooney 2 [11, 17], Andrews [90]	3660
7	14	A	Bristol R	W 1-0	1-0	2	White [17]	6276
8	21	H	Peterborough U	D 0-0	0-0	3		12,007
9	28	A	Shrewsbury T	L 0-1	0-0	6		3655
10	Oct 1	H	Preston NE	W 1-0	0-0	—	Palmer [90]	6434
11	5	A	York C	W 2-1	2-0	2	Andrews [2], Penrice [36]	5232
12	12	H	Wrexham	D 1-1	0-1	3	Mooney (pen) [59]	8441
13	15	H	Burnley	D 2-2	1-1	—	Andrews [39], Johnson R [78]	6450
14	19	A	Bury	D 1-1	1-1	4	Andrews [32]	4092
15	26	A	Blackpool	D 1-1	0-1	6	Mooney [54]	6072
16	29	H	Luton T	D 1-1	0-0	—	Bazeley [90]	14,109
17	Nov 2	H	Brentford	W 2-0	1-0	5	Gibbs [25], Mooney [60]	11,448
18	9	A	Rotherham U	D 0-0	0-0	7		3619
19	19	H	Wycombe W	W 1-0	0-0	—	Connolly [89]	7657
20	30	H	Blackpool	D 2-2	0-1	5	Millen [62], Noel-Williams [69]	12,017
21	Dec 3	A	Bristol C	D 1-1	0-0	—	Noel-Williams [56]	9097
22	14	A	Walsall	D 1-1	1-1	7	Johnson R [27]	3674
23	21	H	Gillingham	D 0-0	0-0	7		7809
24	26	H	Notts Co	D 0-0	0-0	6		9065
25	Jan 18	A	Preston NE	D 1-1	1-1	11	Mooney [45]	8735
26	27	A	Luton T	D 0-0	0-0	—		7428
27	Feb 1	H	Rotherham U	W 2-0	0-0	10	Bazeley [50], Slater [65]	10,657
28	8	A	Brentford	D 1-1	1-1	10	Scott [18]	8679
29	22	A	Wycombe W	D 0-0	0-0	12		8438
30	25	H	Shrewsbury T	W 2-0	1-0	—	Phillips [6], Bazeley [68]	6378
31	Mar 1	H	Bristol C	W 3-0	2-0	6	Phillips 3 [9, 26, 77]	8539
32	4	A	Peterborough U	L 1-2	1-1	—	Mooney [2]	4200
33	8	A	Gillingham	L 1-3	1-0	9	Scott [17]	7385
34	15	H	Walsall	W 1-0	1-0	8	Mooney [20]	7818
35	18	H	Bristol R	W 1-0	1-0	—	Mooney [6]	6139
36	22	H	Millwall	W 1-0	1-0	4	Mooney [28]	8713
37	29	H	Bournemouth	L 0-1	0-1	5		10,019
38	31	A	Plymouth Arg	D 0-0	0-0	4		6836
39	Apr 5	A	Crewe Alex	L 0-1	0-0	7		12,441
40	8	A	Chesterfield	D 0-0	0-0	—		4258
41	12	H	York C	W 4-0	3-0	6	Ramage 2 [20, 43], Mooney [39], Easton [87]	7645
42	14	A	Stockport Co	L 0-1	0-0	—		7164
43	19	A	Wrexham	L 1-3	1-2	7	Ramage [45]	3437
44	24	H	Chesterfield	L 0-2	0-0	—		6411
45	26	H	Bury	D 0-0	0-0	9		9017
46	May 3	A	Burnley	L 1-4	0-0	13	Millen [88]	8269

Final League Position: 13

GOALSCORERS

League (45): Mooney 13 (2 pens), Andrews 4, Phillips 4, Bazeley 3, Ramage 3, Connolly 2, Johnson R 2, Millen 2, Noel-Williams 2, Palmer 2, Scott 2, White 2, Easton 1, Gibbs 1, Penrice 1, Slater 1.
Coca-Cola Cup (2): Andrews 1, Porter 1.
FA Cup (9): Connolly 4, Bazeley 3, Noel-Williams 1, White 1.

Miller K 42	Bazeley D 38+3	Mooney T 33+4	Palmer S 40+1	Millen K 42	Page R 35+1	Talboys S 2+1	Connolly D 12+1	White D 19+3	Ramage C 10+1	Johnson R 35+2	Gibbs N 43+2	Andrews W 16+9	Ludden D 18+2	Penrice G 22+10	Porter G 6	Lowndes N —+3	Johnson C 1	Chamberlain A 4	Noel-Williams G 9+16	Robinson P 8+4	Easton C 17	Slater S 13+3	Ward D 7	Armstrong C 15	Scott K 6	Phillips K 13+3	Flash R —+1	Match No
1	2	3	4	5	6	7	8²	9	10¹	11	12	13																1
1	2	13	4	5	6	7¹	8³	9	10	11	12		3²	14														2
1	7	11	4	5	2			9	10					8¹	3	12	6											3
	7	11	4	5	6			9			2		8¹	3	10	12	1											4
1	7	11	4	5	6			9			2		8¹	3	10	12												5
1	7	11	4	5	6			9			2		8	3	10													6
1	7	11	4	5	6			9	12		2		8²	3	13	10¹												7
1	7	11	4	5	6		9¹	12²	13		2		8²	3	14	10												8
1	7	11	4	5		12	13	9¹		6	2		3	10				8²										9
1	7	11	6	5		8¹	9			4	2	12	3	10														10
1	7	11	6	5	12		9			4	2	8	3	10¹														11
1	7	11	6	5			9			4	2	8¹	3	10	12													12
1	7	11	10	5	6		9¹			4	2	8	3	12														13
1	7	11	10	5	6		9			4	2	8¹	3	12														14
1	7	11	10	5	6		9			4	2		3	8														15
1	7	11	10	5	6		9¹			4	2	8²	3²	12					13	14								16
1	7	11	10	5	6		12			2		8¹	4²						13	3								17
1	7	11	10	5	6		8	12			3	2	4	9¹					9¹									18
1	7	11	6	5			8	10			2	9²	12						13	3	4¹							19
1	7	12	6	5			8¹	9²		4	2		10						13	3	11							20
1	7	11	4	5	6		12				2	13	10	9²					9²	3	8¹							21
1			6	5				9		4	2			12	10				9	3	11¹	7						22
1	12		4	5	6		8				2	13		10¹					9	3	11²	7						23
1	7¹		4	5	6		8²				2	12		10					13	3	11	7						24
1	2	11	4		6		8¹	9						3							10		7	5	11			25
1	2		4		6		8¹							3					9		12		7	5	11			26
1	7		4		6						2	12		3					9¹					5	11	8		27
1	7			5	6						2	12		3							4¹				5	11	8	28
1	7			5							2								12	13	4		6		8	9¹	29
1	7			5	6						2	10²							12	3	4				8¹	9	30
1	7	11	4	5	6						2	10							13	3¹					8²	9	31
1	7	11¹	4	5							2								12	3		6			8	9	32
1	7²	8¹	4	5							2	10							12	13	11		6	3		9	33
1	7	8²	4	5	6						2	10¹							13		11			3		9	34
1	7	8	4	5	6						2	10							12		11			3		9¹	35
1	7	8	4	5							2	10							13		11³	14	6¹	3		9	36
1	12	8²	4¹	5	6			11	10		2		7						13					3		9	37
1	7²	12		5	6		9	11	4		2		10						13					3¹		9	38
1		11	4	5	6			9	10		2	12							7					3		8¹	39
1	12	11	4	5	6			9			2	8²	13						10		7			3¹			40
1		11	4	5	6			9			2	8¹							10		7			3		12	41
1		12	4¹	5	6			9	10		2								11		7			3		8	42
	8	12		5	6			9	4		2			10				1	11		7²			3¹		13	43
	7	8	5		6				4		2			10			1	9¹	11					3		12	44
	7	8²		5	6			9¹	4		2			10			1	12	11					3		13	45

Coca-Cola Cup

First Round	Walsall	(a)	0-1
		(h)	2-0
Second Round	Sunderland	(h)	0-2
		(a)	0-1

FA Cup

First Round	Northampton T	(a)	1-0
Second Round	Ashford T	(h)	5-0
Third Round	Oxford U	(h)	2-0
Fourth Round	Manchester C	(a)	1-3

WEST BROMWICH ALBION 1996–97   *Back row (left to right):* Arthur Mann (Assistant Manager), Lee Knight, Simon Buckley, Michael Rodosthenous, Paul Raven, Shane Nicholson.
Chris Hargreaves, Andy Hunt, Daryl Burgess, Paul Mardon, Ian Hamilton, Dean Bennett, Richard O'Kelly (Youth Team Coach).
Middle row: John Trewick (Coach), Paul Mitchell (Physio), Bob Taylor, Stacey Coldicott, Lee Ashcroft, Paul Agnew, Gary Germaine, Nigel Spink, Shaun Cunnington, Paul Groves, Peter Butler,
James Wills, Ronnie Allen, Mark Ashton (Community Officer).
Front row: Kevin Donovan, Paul Peschisolido, Richard Sneekes, Dave Gilbert, Alan Buckley (Manager), David Smith, Gareth Hamner, Paul Holmes, Julian Darby.

Division 1   **WEST BROMWICH ALBION**

The Hawthorns, West Bromwich B71 4LF. Telephone: (0121) 525 8888 (all Depts). Fax: (0121) 553 6634. Registered Office: 'The Tom Silk Building', Halfords Lane, West Bromwich, West Midlands B71 4BR.

Ground capacity: 25,296 (all seated).

Record attendance: 64,815 v Arsenal, FA Cup 6th rd, 6 March 1937.

Record receipts: £244,501 v Coventry C, FA Cup 3rd rd, 18 January 1995.

Pitch measurements: 115yd × 75yd.

President: Sir F. A. Millichip. *Vice-President:* John G. Silk LL.B (Lond).

Chairman: A. B. Hale. *Vice-Chairman:* C. M. Stapleton.

Directors: P. Thompson, J. W. Brandrick, B. Hurst, R. E. McGing, J. D. Wile (Chief Executive).

Manager: Ray Harford. *First Team Coach:* John Trewick. *Physio:* Paul Mitchell.

Secretary: Dr. John J. Evans BA, PHD. (Wales).

Club Statistician: Tony Matthews. *Commercial Manager:* Tom Cardall. *Stadium Manager:* Andy Williamson.

Year Formed: 1878. *Turned Professional:* 1885. *Ltd Co.:* 1892. *plc:* 1996.

Previous Name: 1878–81, West Bromwich Strollers.

Club Nicknames: 'Throstles', 'Baggies', 'Albion'.

Previous Grounds: 1878, Coopers Hill; 1879, Dartmouth Park; 1881, Bunns Field, Walsall Street; 1882, Four Acres (Dartmouth Cricket Club); 1885, Stoney Lane; 1900, The Hawthorns.

Foundation: There is a well known story that when employees of Salter's Spring Works in West Bromwich decided to form a football club, they had to send someone to the nearby Association Football stronghold of Wednesbury to purchase a football. A weekly subscription of 2d (less than 1p) was imposed and the name of the new club was West Bromwich Strollers.

First Football League game: 8 September 1888, Football League, v Stoke (a) W 2-0 – Roberts; J. Horton, Green; E. Horton, Perry, Bayliss; Bassett, Woodhall (1), Hendry, Pearson, Wilson (1).

Record League Victory: 12–0 v Darwen, Division 1, 4 April 1892 – Reader; J. Horton, McCulloch; Reynolds (2), Perry, Groves; Bassett (3), McLeod, Nicholls (1), Pearson (4), Geddes (1). (1 og).

Record Cup Victory: 10–1 v Chatham (away), FA Cup 3rd rd, 2 March 1889 – Roberts; J. Horton, Green; Timmins (1), Charles Perry, E. Horton; Bassett (2), Perry (1), Bayliss (2), Pearson, Wilson (3). (1 og).

Record Defeat: 3–10 v Stoke C, Division 1, 4 February 1937.

Most League Points (2 for a win): 60, Division 1, 1919–20.

Most League Points (3 for a win): 85, Division 2, 1992–93.

Most League Goals: 105, Division 2, 1929–30.

Highest League Scorer in Season: William 'Ginger' Richardson, 39, Division 1, 1935–36.

Most League Goals in Total Aggregate: Tony Brown, 218, 1963–79.

Most Capped Player: Stuart Williams, 33 (43), Wales.

Most League Appearances: Tony Brown, 574, 1963–80.

Record Transfer Fee Received: £1,500,000 from Manchester U for Bryan Robson, October 1981.

Record Transfer Fee Paid: £1,250,000 to Preston NE for Kevin Kilbane, June 1997.

Football League Record: 1888 Founder Member of Football League; 1901–02 Division 2; 1902–04 Division 1; 1904–11 Division 2; 1911–27 Division 1; 1927–31 Division 2; 1931–38 Division 1; 1938–49 Division 2; 1949–73 Division 1; 1973–76 Division 2; 1976–86 Division 1; 1986–91 Division 2; 1991–92 Division 3; 1992–93 Division 2; 1993– Division 1.

Honours: Football League: Division 1 – Champions 1919–20; Runners-up 1924–25, 1953–54; Division 2 – Champions 1901–02, 1910–11; Runners-up 1930–31, 1948–49; Promoted to Division 1 1975–76 (3rd). *FA Cup:* Winners 1888, 1892, 1931, 1954, 1968; Runners-up 1886, 1887, 1895, 1912, 1935. *Football League Cup:* Winners 1966; Runners-up 1967, 1970. **European Competitions:** *European Cup-Winners' Cup:* 1968–69; *European Fairs Cup:* 1966–67; *UEFA Cup:* 1978–79, 1979–80, 1981–82.

Colours: Navy blue and white striped shirts, white shorts, blue and white stockings. *Change colours:* Red shirts with navy blue sleeves, white shorts with navy blue trim, red and navy blue hooped stockings.

Did you know?
Fixture congestion? In 1911–12, West Bromwich Albion played two FA Cup Finals and five League games in the space of ten days including four matches in consecutive days.

WEST BROMWICH ALBION 1996–97 LEAGUE RECORD

Match No.	Date	Venue	Opponents	Result	H/T Score	Lg. Pos.	Goalscorers	Attendance
1	Aug 17	H	Barnsley	L	1-2	1-1	—	Hunt (pen) [43]	18,561
2	24	A	Charlton Ath	D	1-1	1-0	18	Taylor [11]	9642
3	27	A	Crystal Palace	D	0-0	0-0	—		13,849
4	Sept 7	A	QPR	W	2-0	1-0	17	Peschisolido [9], Taylor [88]	12,886
5	10	H	Reading	W	3-2	2-1	—	Hunt 3 [35, 45, 66]	13,096
6	15	H	Wolverhampton W	L	2-4	1-3	14	Hamilton [42], Taylor [66]	20,711
7	21	A	Tranmere R	W	3-2	2-1	11	Gilbert [7], Peschisolido [12], Groves [59]	7848
8	28	H	Ipswich T	D	0-0	0-0	13		15,606
9	Oct 1	A	Oldham Ath	D	1-1	0-1	—	Groves [88]	5817
10	12	H	Huddersfield T	D	1-1	0-0	11	Hunt [88]	14,960
11	16	H	Stoke C	L	0-2	0-1	—		16,501
12	19	A	Grimsby T	D	1-1	0-1	17	Sneekes [62]	7187
13	26	H	Bradford C	D	0-0	0-0	14		14,249
14	30	A	Swindon T	W	3-2	0-1	—	Holmes [47], Peschisolido [54], Sneekes [82]	8909
15	Nov 2	A	Portsmouth	L	0-4	0-4	14		7354
16	9	H	Port Vale	D	1-1	1-1	15	Taylor [35]	13,975
17	13	H	Sheffield U	L	1-2	0-0	—	Coldicott [80]	12,167
18	16	A	Southend U	W	3-2	2-2	12	Peschisolido [18], Smith [44], Hunt [87]	5120
19	27	A	Manchester C	L	2-3	1-3	—	Peschisolido [34], Hamilton [56]	24,200
20	30	A	Bradford C	D	1-1	1-1	17	Groves [24]	12,003
21	Dec 8	H	Bolton W	D	2-2	0-1	20	Peschisolido [48], Taylor (pen) [80]	13,082
22	18	H	Norwich C	W	5-1	2-0	—	Hamilton 2 [24, 51], Hunt 2 [44, 64], Peschisolido [63]	12,620
23	21	H	Oxford U	D	3-3	2-1	16	Sneekes [43], Hunt (pen) [45], Taylor [90]	13,782
24	26	A	Reading	D	2-2	2-1	16	Peschisolido [3], Groves [39]	10,583
25	28	H	QPR	W	4-1	1-0	11	Sneekes [4], Smith [61], Hunt [72], Peschisolido [77]	19,061
26	Jan 1	H	Tranmere R	L	1-2	1-1	15	Burgess [4]	14,770
27	12	A	Wolverhampton W	L	0-2	0-2	15		27,336
28	18	A	Oldham Ath	D	1-1	1-0	17	Taylor [45]	12,103
29	25	A	Ipswich T	L	0-5	0-4	18		9381
30	Feb 1	A	Port Vale	D	2-2	1-1	17	Peschisolido 2 [7, 61]	8093
31	4	A	Birmingham C	W	3-2	1-1	—	Taylor 2 [33, 90], Sneekes [78]	21,600
32	8	H	Swindon T	L	1-2	0-1	16	Hunt (pen) [71]	16,219
33	15	H	Norwich C	W	4-2	1-0	15	Peschisolido 3 [9, 56, 68], Sneekes [49]	14,845
34	22	H	Portsmouth	L	0-2	0-2	15		15,800
35	Mar 2	A	Bolton W	L	0-1	0-1	15		13,258
36	5	H	Southend U	W	4-0	2-0	—	Sneekes [31], Murphy [34], Hunt [74], Raven [90]	11,792
37	8	A	Oxford U	L	0-1	0-0	17		8502
38	16	A	Birmingham C	W	2-0	1-0	14	Sneekes [16], Hamilton [49]	16,125
39	22	H	Charlton Ath	L	1-2	1-1	18	Hunt [32]	14,312
40	28	A	Barnsley	L	0-2	0-2	—		12,087
41	Apr 5	A	Sheffield U	W	2-1	1-0	19	Coldicott [16], Taylor [72]	15,004
42	9	H	Crystal Palace	W	1-0	0-0	—	Peschisolido [79]	12,866
43	12	H	Manchester C	L	1-3	1-3	17	Murphy [45]	20,087
44	19	A	Huddersfield T	D	0-0	0-0	16		12,748
45	26	H	Grimsby T	W	2-0	0-0	16	Hunt [72], Coldicott [89]	15,574
46	May 4	A	Stoke C	L	1-2	0-1	16	Hunt (pen) [85]	22,500

Final League Position: 16

GOALSCORERS

League (68): Hunt 15 (4 pens), Peschisolido 15, Taylor 10 (1 pen), Sneekes 8, Hamilton 5, Groves 4, Coldicott 3, Murphy 2, Smith 2, Burgess 1, Gilbert 1, Holmes 1, Raven 1.
Coca-Cola Cup (4): Donovan 1, Groves 1, Hamilton 1, Hunt 1.
FA Cup (0).

Spink N 4	Holmes P 37 + 1	Nicholson S 16 + 2	Sneekes R 42 + 3	Burgess D 33	Raven P 33	Hamilton J 39	Mardon P 11 + 3	Taylor B 16 + 16	Hunt A 42 + 3	Groves P 27 + 2	Gilbert D 11 + 7	Cunnington S — + 4	Donovan K 17 + 15	Peschisolido P 30 + 7	Smith D 21 + 3	Crichton P 30	Darby J 13 + 4	Ashcroft L 2 + 3	Agnew P 21 + 1	Coldicott S 13 + 6	Butler P 12 + 5	Murphy S 16 + 1	Potter G 2 + 4	Miller A 12	Rodosthenous M — + 1	Joseph R — + 2	McDermott A 6	Bennett D — + 1	Match No.
1	2	3	4	5	6	7	8¹	9	10²	11	12	13																	1
1	2	3	4	5	6	7		9	10²	11	8¹	12	13																2
1	2	3	4	5	6¹	7	12	9	10²	11	8	13																	3
1	2	3	4	5¹	6	7	8	12	10	11				9¹	13														4
	2	3	4		6³	7	5	12	10¹	11	13		14	9	8²	1													5
	2	3	4	6		7	5²	12	10	11	14		13	9¹	8³	1													6
	2	3	4	6		7	5		10	11	8		12	9¹		1													7
	2	3	4	6		7	5		10	11	8¹			9		1	12												8
	2	3	4	5	6¹	7²	8		10	11	12		13	9		1													9
	2	3	4	6		7	5		10	11	8¹					1	12	9											10
	2¹	3	4	6		7	5	12	10	11	8²		13			1		9											11
	2	3	4³	5	6	7	8²	12	10¹	11	13		14	9		1													12
	2	3	4	5	6				10	11	8¹		7			1	9	12											13
	2	3	4	5	6				10	11				9¹		1	7	12	8										14
	2²	3	4³	5	6			12	10¹	11			13	9		1	7	14	8										15
12	3	4	2	6				9²	13	11		8³		7	10	1				5¹	14								16
2	12	5³	6	4				9²	13	11		8¹		7	10	1				3	14								17
2					6	11			10	5	8¹		7	9	12	1				3	4								18
	2	12		5		11			13	10²		6³	7¹	9	8	1				3	4								19
	2	12		5		11			10				7	9	8	1	6			3	4								20
	2	4²		5		11		12	10¹				7	9	8	1	6			3	13								21
	2	4¹		5		11			10				7	9	8	1	6			3	12								22
	2	4		5		11		12	10				7	9	8	1	6¹			3²									23
	2	4		5		11		12	10¹				7	9	8	1	6			3									24
	2		4	5	6	11			10			12	7¹	9	8	1			3										25
	2		4	5¹	6	11		12	10³			13		9	8	1			3			7²							26
	2		4	5	6²	11			10			13	7	9¹		1			3	8									27
			4	2	6³	11	8		9	10¹		13		7²	12	1			3	14	5								28
	2²		5		6	11	8		9	10¹		13			12	1			3	7	4								29
	2		5		6	11	8	12	10			13		9¹		1			3	7²	4								30
	2		5		6	11	8		9	10					12	1	13		3²	7¹	4								31
	2		5		6	11	8		9¹	10		13		7	12	1			3²		4								32
	2		4	5²	6	11			10³				7	9	8¹	1			3		12	13	14						33
	2		4		6¹	11			10				7	9	8	1	13		3³		12	5²	14						34
	2		4		6	11			9				7		8²				3¹	10	5	12		1	13				35
	2³		4		6	11			9				12	7	10¹				3²	13	5	8		1	14				36
	2		4		6	11		12	9²	10	13			7					3²	8	5			1					37
	2		4		6²	11		12	10					7	8				3¹	12	13	5		1					38
	2		4		6	11		12	10				7¹	9	8				3¹		5			1	13				39
			4		6³	11		12	10	5			7¹	9	8				3²	13	14		2	1					40
			4		6	11			9	10					3					7	8	5		1			2		41
			4³		6²	11	13		9¹	10			14		12				3	7	8	5		1			2		42
			4²		6¹	11		12	9	10	11		14		3					7	8	5	13³	1			2		43
			4		6	11			9¹	10			12		3					7	8	5		1			2		44
12			4²		6				10	11¹				9	3					7	8	5		1			2	13	45
12			4		6				10	11²			13	9	3					7	8¹	5		1			2		46

Coca-Cola Cup
First Round   Colchester U   (a)   3-2   (h)   1-3

FA Cup
Third Round   Chelsea   (a)   0-3

WEST HAM UNITED 1996–97   *Back row (left to right):* Adrian Whitbread, Slaven Bilic, Iain Dowie, Ludek Miklosko, Marc Rieper, Steve Mautone, Richard Hall, Steve Jones, Tim Breacker. *Middle row:* Eddie Gillam (Kit Manager), Florin Raducioiu, Ilie Dumitrescu, Keith Rowland, Stan Lazaridis, Danny Williamson, John Moncur, Kenny Brown, Steve Potts, Michael Hughes, Mark Bowen, Robbie Slater, John Green (Physio).
Front row: Paulo Futre, Tony Cottee, Frank Burrows (Coach), Harry Redknapp (Manager), Frank Lampard (Assistant Manager), Julian Dicks, Ian Bishop.

FA Premiership   **WEST HAM UNITED**

Boleyn Ground, Green Street, Upton Park, London E13 9AZ. Telephone General Office: (0181) 548 2748. Ticket Office: (0181) 548 2700. Merchandise Shop: (0181) 548 2722. Fax: (0181) 548 2758. Membership Office: (0181) 548 2727. Promotions: (0181) 548 2777. Dial-a-seat: (0181) 548 2700. Football in the Community: (0181) 548 2707. Clubcall: 0891 121165.

Ground capacity: 25,985.

Record attendance: 42,322 v Tottenham H, Division 1, 17 October 1970.

Record receipts: £339,420 gross v Liverpool, FA Premier League, 22 November 1995.

Pitch measurements: 112yd × 72yd.

Chairman: T. W. Brown FCIS, AII, FCCA. *Vice-Chairman:* M. W. Cearns ACIB.

Directors: C. J. Warner, P. J. Storrie (Managing).

Manager: Harry Redknapp. *Assistant Manager:* Frank Lampard. *Coaches:* Frank Burrows, Tony Carr. *Physio:* John Green BSC, MCSP, SRP.

Football Secretary: Neil Harrison. *Stadium Manager:* John Ball.

Year Formed: 1895. *Turned Professional:* 1900. *Ltd Co.:* 1900.

Previous Name: Thames Ironworks FC, 1895–1900.

Club Nickname: 'The Hammers'.

Previous Ground: Memorial Recreation Ground, Canning Town: 1904 Boleyn Ground.

Foundation: Thames Ironworks FC was formed by employees of this shipbuilding yard in 1895 and entered the FA Cup in their initial season at Chatham and the London League in their second. Short of funds, the club was wound up in June 1900 and relaunched a month later as West Ham United. Connection with the Ironworks was not finally broken until four years later.

First Football League game: 30 August 1919, Division 2, v Lincoln C (h) D 1-1 – Hufton; Cope, Lee; Lane, Fenwick, McCrae; D. Smith, Moyes (1), Puddefoot, Morris, Bradshaw.

Record League Victory: 8–0 v Rotherham U, Division 2, 8 March 1958 – Gregory; Bond, Wright; Malcolm, Brown, Lansdowne; Grice, Smith (2), Keeble (2), Dick (4), Musgrove. 8–0 v Sunderland, Division 1, 19 October 1968 – Ferguson; Bonds, Charles; Peters, Stephenson, Moore (1); Redknapp, Boyce, Brooking (1), Hurst (6), Sissons.

Record Cup Victory: 10–0 v Bury, League Cup 2nd rd (2nd leg), 25 October 1983 – Parkes; Stewart (1), Walford, Bonds (Orr), Martin (1), Devonshire (2), Allen, Cottee (4), Swindlehurst, Brooking (2), Pike.

Record Defeat: 2–8 v Blackburn R, Division 1, 26 December 1963.

Most League Points (2 for a win): 66, Division 2, 1980–81.

Most League Points (3 for a win): 88, Division 1, 1992–93.

Most League Goals: 101, Division 2, 1957–58.

Highest League Scorer in Season: Vic Watson, 42, Division 1, 1929–30.

Most League Goals in Total Aggregate: Vic Watson, 298, 1920–35.

Most Capped Player: Bobby Moore, 108, England.

Most League Appearances: Billy Bonds, 663, 1967–88.

Record Transfer Fee Received: £4,250,000 from Everton for Slaven Bilic, May 1997.

Record Transfer Fee Paid: £3,200,000 to Arsenal for John Hartson, February 1997.

Football League Record: 1919 Elected to Division 2; 1923–32 Division 1; 1932–58 Division 2; 1958–78 Division 1; 1978–81 Division 2; 1981–89 Division 1; 1989–91 Division 2; 1991–93 Division 1; 1993– FA Premier League.

Honours: Football League: Division 1 best season: 3rd, 1985–86; Division 2 – Champions 1957–58, 1980–81; Runners-up 1922–23, 1990–91. *FA Cup:* Winners 1964, 1975, 1980; Runners-up 1923. *Football League Cup:* Runners-up 1966, 1981. **European Competitions:** *European Cup-Winners' Cup:* 1964–65 (winners), 1965–66, 1975–76 (runners-up), 1980–81.

Colours: Claret shirts with blue sleeves, white shorts, light blue with claret hooped stockings. *Change colours:* All sky blue.

Did you know?
West Ham United scored three times in each of their six winning FA Cup matches during the 1963–64 season.

WEST HAM UNITED 1996–97 LEAGUE RECORD

Match No.	Date	Venue	Opponents	Result	H/T Score	Lg. Pos.	Goalscorers	Attendance
1	Aug 17	A	Arsenal	L 0-2	0-2	—		38,056
2	21	H	Coventry C	D 1-1	0-1	—	Rieper [74]	21,580
3	24	H	Southampton	W 2-1	0-1	11	Hughes [73], Dicks (pen) [81]	21,227
4	Sept 4	A	Middlesbrough	L 1-4	0-2	—	Hughes [57]	30,061
5	8	A	Sunderland	D 0-0	0-0	16		18,581
6	14	H	Wimbledon	L 0-2	0-0	17		21,924
7	21	A	Nottingham F	W 2-0	1-0	13	Bowen [45], Hughes [54]	23,352
8	29	H	Liverpool	L 1-2	1-1	15	Bilic [15]	25,064
9	Oct 12	A	Everton	L 1-2	0-1	16	Dicks (pen) [86]	36,541
10	19	H	Leicester C	W 1-0	0-0	13	Moncur [78]	22,285
11	26	A	Blackburn R	W 2-1	0-1	10	Porfirio [77], Berg (og) [85]	23,947
12	Nov 2	A	Tottenham H	L 0-1	0-0	12		32,975
13	16	A	Newcastle U	D 1-1	1-0	13	Rowland [23]	36,552
14	23	H	Derby Co	D 1-1	1-1	13	Bishop [17]	24,576
15	30	D	Sheffield W	D 0-0	0-0	13		22,321
16	Dec 4	A	Aston Villa	L 0-2	0-1	—		19,105
17	8	H	Manchester U	D 2-2	0-0	14	Raducioiu [78], Dicks (pen) [80]	25,045
18	Dec 21	A	Chelsea	L 1-3	1-3	15	Porfirio [11]	27,012
19	28	H	Sunderland	W 2-0	1-0	16	Bilic [34], Raducioiu [90]	24,077
20	Jan 1	H	Nottingham F	L 0-1	0-1	16		22,358
21	11	A	Liverpool	D 0-0	0-0	17		40,102
22	20	H	Leeds U	L 0-2	0-0	—		19,441
23	29	H	Arsenal	L 1-2	0-1	—	Rose (og) [63]	24,382
24	Feb 1	A	Blackburn R	L 1-2	0-2	18	Ferdinand [64]	21,994
25	15	A	Derby Co	L 0-1	0-0	18		18,057
26	24	H	Tottenham H	W 4-3	3-2	—	Dicks 2 (1 pen) [21, 72 (p)], Kitson [22], Hartson [38]	23,998
27	Mar 1	A	Leeds U	L 0-1	0-0	18		30,575
28	12	H	Chelsea	W 3-2	2-1	—	Dicks (pen) [55], Kitson 2 [68, 90]	24,502
29	15	A	Aston Villa	D 0-0	0-0	17		35,992
30	18	A	Wimbledon	D 1-1	0-1	—	Lazaridis [89]	15,771
31	22	A	Coventry C	W 3-1	2-1	15	Hartson 2 [27, 49], Ferdinand [34]	22,290
32	Apr 9	H	Middlesbrough	D 0-0	0-0	—		23,988
33	12	A	Southampton	L 0-2	0-2	17		15,245
34	19	H	Everton	D 2-2	2-0	18	Kitson 2 [10, 32]	24,525
35	23	A	Leicester C	W 1-0	0-0	—	Moncur [75]	20,327
36	May 3	H	Sheffield W	W 5-1	3-0	15	Kitson 3 [5, 13, 89], Hartson 2 [30, 67]	24,960
37	6	H	Newcastle U	D 0-0	0-0	—		24,617
38	11	A	Manchester U	L 0-2	0-1	14		55,249

Final League Position: 14

GOALSCORERS

League (39): Kitson 8, Dicks 6 (5 pens), Hartson 5, Hughes 3, Bilic 2, Ferdinand 2, Moncur 2, Porfirio 2, Raducioiu 2, Bishop 1, Bowen 1, Lazaridis 1, Rieper 1, Rowland 1, own goals 2.
Coca-Cola Cup (8): Dicks 2 (1 pen), Dowie 2, Bilic 1, Cottee 1, Porfirio 1, Raducioiu 1.
FA Cup (1): Porfirio 1.

Miklosko L 36	Breacker T 22 + 4	Rowland K 11 + 4	Rieper M 26 + 2	Bilic S 35	Dicks J 31	Lampard F 3 + 10	Dowie I 18 + 5	Jones S 5 + 3	Williamson D 13 + 2	Hughes M 31 + 2	Slater R 2 + 1	Lazaridis S 13 + 9	Ferdinand R 11 + 4	Futre P 4 + 5	Bowen M 15 + 2	Raducioiu F 6 + 5	Dumitrescu I 3 + 4	Potts S 17 + 3	Cottee T 2 + 1	Moncur J 26 + 1	Mautone S 1	Bishop I 26 + 3	Porfirio H 15 + 8	Newell M 6 + 1	Sealey L 1 + 1	Hartson J 11	Kitson P 14	Omoyinmi E — + 1	Hall R 7	Lomas S 7	Boylan L — + 1	*Match No.*
1	2	3^2	4	5^1	6	7^1	8	9	10	11	12	13	14																			1
1	2^1		4	5	3		8	9^1	10	11		7	6		12	13																2
1	12		4^2	5	3		8		6	11	7^1	9^2			10	2	13	14														3
1	2			5	3	14	12		8	11		7^2			10	6	9^1	13	4^1													4
1	2	13	4	5	3			12	8	11			14		10^3	6	9^1	7^2														5
1	2^1		4	5	3		8		7	11		12			10^1	6	9^2	14	13													6
	12		4	5	3	13	8			11					10	2				9^1	7	1	6^2									7
1	2		4	5	3		8			11						6^2	12			9^1	7	10	13									8
1		3		5	6		8			11					4	12	13	2^1		10		7^2	9									9
1	12		4	5	3		8			11		13				2^1	9^2			7		6	10									10
1	12		4	5	3	13	8			11		7	14	2^1						10^3		6	9^2									11
1	2		4	5	3		8			11	7	12				10^1	6	9														12
1	2	3		5	6		8			11				12		9^1	4	10	7													13
1	2			5	3		8			11	7^1	12		4	10	6	9															14
1	2	3	4	5	6	7	8			11^1	12			10	9																	15
1	2^1	3^2	4	5	6		8			11	13	12		9	10	7																16
1	11^2		4	5^1	3		8			7			2	13	9	12	10	6														17
1	3^2		4	5	6	12				14	11			2	13	7^3		8^1	9	10												18
1			4	5	3	12				6	11			2	13	7^1		8	9	10^2												19
1			4	5	3	12	13			6	11			2^3	7	14	8^1		9	10^2												20
1	2		4	5	3		8^1			6^2	11	12			13		10	7	9^3	14												21
1	2		4	5	3					9	6	11	7^1				8	12	10													22
1	2	3^2	4	5	6	12				13	8	11					7^1		9	10												23
	2	3^1	4	5	6					9^2	7	11	12	13			8		10	1												24
1	2	3^2	5^1	6	13		8			11				4			7	12				10	9									25
1	2		3		12				11		5	6		4		7		8				10	9^1									26
1	2^1	12		5	3	13	8			11			4	6^1				7	10^3				9	14								27
1	2			5	3	13	8			12^2	11			6^1		4		10	7^3	14			9									28
1	2			5	3		6^1			11	12			4		7		8		10	9											29
1	2		4	5	3		12			8	6^2			7		11^1	13	10	9													30
1	2^1	12	4	5	3		13			8^2				6		7		11^3	14	10	9											31
1		3	5						11	7^1		2				8	12			10	9					6	4					32
1	11^1	3^2	5			13				7		12			2		8^3			14		10	9			6	4					33
1		13	5						11			3			2	7^1	12			8^2		10	9			6	4					34
1		13	5			12				11		3			2	7				8^2		10	9^1			6	4					35
1		12	5^1						11^2	3					2	7	13	8				10	9			6	4^3	14				36
1			5			12			11	3					2	7^2	13	8^1				10	9			6	4					37
1^6			5			8			12	11		3^1			2	7		3^1				10	15			9	6	4				38

Coca-Cola Cup

Second Round	Barnet	(a)	1-1	
		(h)	1-0	
Third Round	Nottingham F	(h)	4-1	
Fourth Round	Stockport Co	(h)	1-1	
		(a)	1-2	

FA Cup

Third Round	Wrexham	(a)	1-1	
		(h)	0-1	

WIGAN ATHLETIC 1996–97   *Back row (left to right):* Tony Black, Jesus Seba, Ian Kilford, Charlie Bishop, Gavin Johnson, John Pender, John Butler, Matthew Carragher, Kevin Sharp. *Middle row:* Steve Morgan, Graeme Jones, David Crompton (Youth Development Officer), Alex Cribley (Coach/Physio), Colin Greenall, Frank Lord, John Benson (Assistant Manager), Michael Love, Wayne Biggins. *Front row:* David Lowe, Roberto Martinez, Simon Farnworth, John Deehan (Manager), Lee Butler, Graham Lancashire, Isidro Diaz.

Division 2 WIGAN ATHLETIC

Springfield Park, Wigan WN6 7BA. Telephone: (01942) 244433. Fax: (01942) 494654. Commercial Dept: (01942) 243067. Latics Clubcall: 0891 121655. Football in the Community: (01942) 824599.

Ground capacity: 7466.

Record attendance: 27,526 v Hereford U, 12 December 1953.

Record receipts: £40,577 v Leeds U, FA Cup 6th rd, 15 March 1987.

Pitch measurements: 114yd × 72yd.

President: T. Hitchen.

Chairman: David Whelan.

Directors: S. Jackson, J. Winstanley, C. Ronnie, D. Sharpe, D. Whelan, P. Williams, B. Ashcroft.

Chief Executive/Secretary: Mrs Brenda Spencer. *Assistant Secretary:* Stuart Hayton.

Football Co-Ordinator: Frank Lord.

Manager: John Deehan. *Assistant Manager:* John Benson. *Physio:* Simon Farnworth. *Coach:* Alex Cribley. *Safety Officer:* David Johnson. *Groundsman:* David Pinch.

Year Formed: 1932.

Club Nickname: 'The Latics'.

Foundation: Following the demise of Wigan Borough and their resignation from the Football League in 1931, a public meeting was called in Wigan at the Queen's Hall in May 1932 at which a new club Wigan Athletic, was founded in the hope of carrying on in the Football League. With this in mind, they bought Springfield Park for £2,250, but failed to gain admission to the Football League until 46 years later.

First Football League game: 19 August 1978, Division 4, v Hereford U (a) D 0-0 – Brown; Hinnigan, Gore, Gillibrand, Ward, Davids, Corrigan, Purdie, Houghton, Wilkie, Wright.

Record League Victory: 7–1 v Scarborough, Division 3, 11 March 1997 – Butler L, Butler J, Sharp (Morgan), Greenall, McGibbon (Biggins (1)), Martinez (1), Diaz (2), Jones (Lancashire (1)), Lowe (2), Rogers, Kilford.

Record Cup Victory: 6–0 v Carlisle U (away), FA Cup 1st rd, 24 November 1934 – Caunce; Robinson, Talbot; Paterson, Watson, Tufnell; Armes (2), Robson (1), Roberts (2), Felton, Scott (1).

Record Defeat: 1–6 v Bristol R, Division 3, 3 March 1990.

Most League Points (2 for a win): 55, Division 4, 1978–79 and 1979–80.

Most League Points (3 for a win): 91, Division 4, 1981–82.

Most League Goals: 84, Division 3, 1996–97.

Highest League Scorer in Season: Graeme Jones, 31, Division 3, 1996–97.

Most League Goals in Total Aggregate: Peter Houghton, 62, 1978–84.

Most Capped Player: Roy Carroll, 1, Northern Ireland.

Most League Appearances: Kevin Langley, 317, 1981–86, 1990–94.

Record Transfer Fee Received: £329,000 from Coventry C for Peter Atherton, August 1991.

Record Transfer Fee Paid: £350,000 to Hull C for Roy Carroll, April 1997.

Football League Record: 1978 Elected to Division 4; 1982–92 Division 3; 1992–93 Division 2; 1993–97 Division 3; 1997– Division 2.

Honours: Football League: Division 3 Champions, 1996–97; Division 4 – Promoted (3rd) 1981–82. *FA Cup:* 6th rd 1987. *Football League Cup:* best season: 4th rd, 1982. *Freight Rover Trophy:* Winners 1985.

Colours: Blue and green striped shirts, blue shorts, blue and white stockings. *Change colours:* Yellow with blue trim.

Did you know?
In winning the Cheshire League in three consecutive seasons 1933–34 to 1935–36, Wigan Athletic lost only one home match.

WIGAN ATHLETIC 1996–97 LEAGUE RECORD

Match No.	Date	Venue	Opponents	Result	H/T Score	Lg. Pos.	Goalscorers	Attendance
1	Aug 17	H	Northampton T	W 2-1	0-1	—	Lancashire [56], Biggins [73]	3449
2	24	A	Barnet	D 1-1	1-0	5	Jones [20]	1905
3	27	A	Cardiff C	W 2-0	1-0	—	Jones [34], Kilford [81]	3354
4	31	H	Chester C	W 4-2	1-1	1	Jones 3 (1 pen) [43 (p), 68, 89], Shelton (og) [53]	3854
5	Sept 7	H	Scunthorpe U	W 3-0	1-0	1	Jones [33], Lancashire 2 [52, 56]	3321
6	10	A	Darlington	L 1-3	0-1	—	Greenall [90]	2601
7	14	A	Hartlepool U	D 1-1	0-0	2	Jones [89]	2433
8	21	H	Lincoln C	W 1-0	0-0	2	Lancashire [52]	3394
9	28	A	Scarborough	L 1-3	1-1	3	Lancashire [30]	2570
10	Oct 1	H	Exeter C	W 2-0	0-0	—	Lancashire [55], Jones [80]	2788
11	5	H	Brighton & HA	W 1-0	1-0	3	Jones [23]	3744
12	12	A	Colchester U	L 1-3	1-0	4	Sharp [41]	2700
13	15	A	Mansfield T	W 1-0	0-0	—	Sharp [81]	1942
14	19	H	Torquay U	W 3-2	2-2	2	Jones 3 [22, 41, 89]	3374
15	26	H	Hull C	L 1-2	0-1	2	Morgan [79]	3887
16	29	A	Swansea C	L 1-2	0-2	—	Diaz [80]	2227
17	Nov 2	A	Carlisle U	W 3-0	1-0	3	Diaz 2 [8, 89], Saville [90]	6235
18	9	H	Hereford U	W 4-1	2-0	3	Martinez [15], Jones [43], Greenall [58], Saville [78]	3414
19	23	H	Fulham	D 1-1	0-0	3	Martinez [55]	5039
20	30	A	Hull C	D 1-1	0-0	4	Jones [53]	3537
21	Dec 3	H	Doncaster R	W 4-1	3-1	—	Biggins [11], Johnson [32], Saville [36], Jones [56]	2606
22	14	A	Cambridge U	D 1-1	0-0	4	Kilford [90]	2784
23	21	H	Rochdale	L 0-1	0-1	4		3311
24	28	A	Scunthorpe U	W 3-2	1-0	4	Saville [23], Rogers [60], Kilford [63]	2833
25	Jan 18	A	Exeter C	W 1-0	1-0	3	Johnson [33]	3067
26	21	A	Leyton Orient	W 2-1	0-1	—	Kilford [62], Jones [77]	3014
27	25	H	Swansea C	W 3-2	1-0	2	Jones 2 [25, 56], Kilford [62]	4058
28	Feb 1	A	Hereford U	L 1-3	1-2	3	Rogers [31]	2532
29	4	A	Lincoln C	W 3-1	2-1	—	Jones 2 [15, 88], Johnson [40]	2241
30	8	H	Carlisle U	W 1-0	1-0	1	Lowe [24]	6195
31	15	A	Fulham	D 1-1	0-0	3	Lowe [52]	9448
32	22	H	Leyton Orient	W 5-1	1-1	3	Jones 3 [6, 48, 52], Lancashire [76], Rogers [86]	3783
33	25	H	Darlington	W 3-2	1-0	—	Jones 3 (1 pen) [21, 55 (p), 69]	3667
34	28	A	Doncaster R	L 0-2	0-1	—		2948
35	Mar 4	H	Hartlepool U	D 2-2	1-0	—	Jones [10], Kilford [61]	3229
36	8	A	Rochdale	L 1-3	1-3	3	Jones (pen) [28]	3254
37	11	H	Scarborough	W 7-1	4-0	—	Martinez [10], Lowe 2 [17, 33], Diaz 2 [35, 69], Lancashire [74], Biggins [88]	3094
38	15	H	Cambridge U	D 1-1	0-0	2	Jones [72]	3867
39	22	H	Barnet	W 2-0	0-0	2	Kilford [63], Martinez [79]	3286
40	29	A	Northampton T	W 1-0	0-0	1	Lowe [90]	5914
41	31	H	Cardiff C	L 0-1	0-0	1		4634
42	Apr 5	A	Chester C	D 1-1	0-1	2	Kilford [46]	4005
43	8	H	Colchester U	W 1-0	1-0	—	McGibbon [44]	4571
44	12	A	Brighton & HA	L 0-1	0-0	1		8703
45	26	A	Torquay U	W 3-0	2-0	1	Jones 2 [24, 35], Diaz [58]	2481
46	May 3	H	Mansfield T	W 2-0	0-0	1	Lancashire [46], Lowe [59]	7106

Final League Position: 1

GOALSCORERS

League (84): Jones 31 (3 pens), Lancashire 9, Kilford 8, Diaz 6, Lowe 6, Martinez 4, Saville 4, Biggins 3, Johnson 3, Rogers 3, Greenall 2, Sharp 2, McGibbon 1, Morgan 1, own goal 1.
Coca-Cola Cup (6): Lancashire 4, Greenall 1, Jones 1.
FA Cup (0).

Butler L 46	Carragher M 12+6	Johnson G 37	Greenall C 46	Pender J 27+2	Martinez R 38+5	Kilford J 24+11	Sharp K 30+5	Lancashire G 15+9	Biggins W 20+13	Bishop C 20+1	Lowe D 31+11	Diaz I 26+13	Morgan S 18+5	Kirby R 5+1	Jones G 39+1	Whittaker S 2+1	Seba J —+1	Butler J 20+4	Ward M 5	Love M —+3	Saville A 17+3	Rogers P 18+2	McGibbon P 10	Match No.
1	2	3	4^1	5	6	7^2	8	9	10^3	11	12	13	14											1
1		3	4	5	6^3	14	11^2	9^1	10		12	13	7	2	8									2
1		3	4	5	6^3	12	11^1	9^2	10		13	14	7	2	8									3
1		3	4	5	6			9^1	10		12	13	7	2	8	11^2								4
1		3	4	5	6		11	9	10^2				7	2	8^1		12	13						5
1		3	4	5	6	10	12	9			13	14	7^3	2^2	8	11^1								6
1	2	3	4	5	6^3	12		9^2			13	11	7^1	14	8			10						7
1	2	3	4	5	6		11	9	10			7^1	12		8									8
1	2	3	4	5		12	11^1	9	10			7^2			8			13			6			9
1	2	3	4	5	6		12	9	10^3	13		7^2			8			14			11^1			10
1	2	3	4	5	6		12	9^2	10	13		7^3			8			14			11^1			11
1	2	3	4	5	6	8	11		10^1		7	12^2			9^3			13	14					12
1		3	4	5		10	11	9					7		8			2			6			13
1		3	4	5	12	10	11	9					7^2		8			2			6^1	13		14
1		3	4	5	10		11^1	9					7	6	8			2			12			15
1	11	3	4	5	12		6		10^1	13		7^2			8			2			9			16
1		3	4	5	10		11					7	6		8			2			9			17
1	12	3	4	5	6	13	11		10^3	14		7^2			8			2^1			9			18
1		3	4	5	6	12	11		10			7			8			2^1			9			19
1		3	4	5	6		11		10			7	12		8			2			9^1			20
1	2	3	4	5	6^1	12	11		10^3	13		7^2	14		8						9			21
1	12	3	4	5^1	6	13	11		10^3	8		7						2^2			9	14		22
1	2	3^1	4^2	5	6	12	11		10	8		7									9	13		23
1		3	4	5	6		11		12			7^1	8					2			9	10		24
1		3	4	5	10	7	12		2	11^1					6			8			9			25
1		3	4	5	10	7	9		2	11					6			8						26
1		3	4	5	10	7	9		12	2	11				6			8^1						27
1	5^1	3	4		11	7	13		14	2	9^3	12	6^2		8						10			28
1		3	4		6^1	13	11		14	2	9^2	7^3	12		8				5		10			29
1		3	4		6^1	12	11			2	9	7^2	13		8				5		10			30
1		3	4		6^1		11		12	2	9		7		8				5		10			31
1	12	3	4				11^2		13	14	2	9	7	6^3	8				5^1		10			32
1	12	3	4				13		9^3	6	2	11	7^2		8				5^1		14	10		33
1	12		4		6^2	7	3	13	10^3	2	11	14			8				5^1		9			34
1			4		12	11	3	13		2	10	7^1	6		8						9^2		5	35
1	3^2		4		12	7	11	13		2^3	9	14	6^1		8							10	5	36
1			4		6	11	3^1	13	14		9	7	12		8^2			2				10	5^3	37
1			4		6		11				12	9	7	3	8			2^1				10	5	38
1	2^1	3	4		6	11		12	13			9	7		8^2							10	5	39
1		3	4		6		11	7^2	2^1	13	5	9	12		8							10		40
1	12		4		6^2	2	3	13	11^1	5	9	7			8							10		41
1			4		6		11		12	13	5	7^2			8			2			9^1	10	3	42
1		3	4		6		11			5	12	7^1			8						9	10	2	43
1			4		6	7	3^1	13	12	5	11				8					14	9^2	10	2^3	44
1			4	12	6^2		3	9^3	13	5^1	11	7			8						14	10	2	45
1			4	12	6		3	9^2	13	5	11	7			8^3						14	10	2^1	46

Coca-Cola Cup
First Round   Preston NE   (h) 2-3
                             (a) 4-4

FA Cup
First Round   Blackpool   (a) 0-1

WIMBLEDON 1996-97 *Back row (left to right):* Scott Fitzgerald, Stewart Castledine, Kenny Cunningham, Duncan Jupp, Efan Ekoku, Brendan Murphy, Paul Heald, Mick Harford, Ben Thatcher, Jon Goodman, Iain Laidlaw, Brian McAllister.
Middle row: Syd Neal (Kit Manager), Joe Dillon (Assistant Kit Manager), Terry Burton (Assistant Manager), Danny Hodges, Andy Pearce, Carl Cort, Gary Blissett, Vinnie Jones, Neil Sullivan, Dean Holdsworth, Dean Blackwell, Marcus Gayle, Alan Reeves, Aidan Newhouse, Steve Allen (Physio), Lawrie Sanchez (Reserve Team Manager), Ron Stuart (Chief Scout).
Front row: Roger Smith (Youth Development Officer), Andy Futcher, Richard O'Connor, Grant Payne, Chris Perry, Peter Fear, Robbie Earle, Joe Kinnear (Manager), Jason Euell, Oyvind Leonhardsen, Neal Ardley, Alan Kimble, Andy Clarke, Gary Elkins, Ernie Tippet (Youth Team Manager).

FA Premiership   WIMBLEDON

Selhurst Park, South Norwood, London SE25 6PY. Telephone: (0181) 771 2233. Fax: (0181) 768 0641. Box Office: (0181) 771 8841.

Ground capacity: 26,309.

Record attendance: 30,115 v Manchester U, FA Premier League, 9 May 1993.

Record receipts: £398,422 v Manchester U, FA Cup 4th rd replay, 4 February 1997.

Pitch measurements: 110yd × 74yd.

Chairman: S. G. Reed. *Deputy Chairman:* J. Lelliott.

Managing Director: S. Hammam.

Directors: P. Cork, P. R. Cooper, N. N. Hammam, P. Miller.

Chief Executive: David Barnard.

Manager: Joe Kinnear. *Assistant Manager:* Terry Burton. *Physio:* Steve Allen. *Stadium Manager:* Vic Worrall.

Secretary: Steve Rooke. *Marketing Manager:* Sharon Sillitoe. *Press Manager:* Reg Davis.

Year Formed: 1889. *Turned Professional:* 1964. *Ltd Co.:* 1964.

Previous Name: Wimbledon Old Centrals, 1899–1905.

Previous Ground: Plough Lane.

Club Nickname: 'The Dons'.

Foundation: Old boys from Central School formed this club as Wimbledon Old Centrals in 1889. Their earliest successes were in the Clapham League before switching to the Southern Suburban League in 1902.

First Football League game: 20 August 1977, Division 4, v Halifax T (h) D 3-3 – Guy; Bryant (1), Galvin, Donaldson, Aitken, Davies, Galliers, Smith, Connell (1), Holmes, Leslie (1).

Record League Victory: 6–0 v Newport Co, Division 3, 3 September 1983 – Beasant; Peters, Winterburn, Galliers, Morris, Hatter, Evans (2), Ketteridge (1), Cork (3 incl. 1p), Downes, Hodges (Driver).

Record Cup Victory: 7–2 v Windsor & Eton, FA Cup 1st rd, 22 November 1980 – Beasant; Jones, Armstrong, Galliers, Mick Smith (2), Cunningham (1), Ketteridge, Hodges, Leslie, Cork (1), Hubbick (3).

Record Defeat: 0–8 v Everton, League Cup 2nd rd, 29 August 1978.

Most League Points (2 for a win): 61, Division 4, 1978–79.

Most League Points (3 for a win): 98, Division 4, 1982–83.

Most League Goals: 97, Division 3, 1983–84.

Highest League Scorer in Season: Alan Cork, 29, 1983–84.

Most League Goals in Total Aggregate: Alan Cork, 145, 1977–92.

Most Capped Player: Kenny Cunningham, 10, Republic of Ireland.

Most League Appearances: Alan Cork, 430, 1977–92.

Record Transfer Fee Received: £4,000,000 from Newcastle U for Warren Barton, June 1995.

Record Transfer Fee Paid: £1,700,000 to Millwall for Ben Thatcher, July 1996.

Football League Record: 1977 Elected to Division 4; 1979–80 Division 3; 1980–81 Division 4; 1981–82 Division 3; 1982–83 Division 4; 1983–84 Division 3; 1984–86 Division 2; 1986–92 Division 1; 1992– FA Premier League.

Honours: FA Premier League : best season: 6th, 1993–94; *Football League:* Division 3 – Runners-up 1983–84; Division 4 – Champions 1982–83. *FA Cup:* Winners 1988. *Football League Cup:* Semi-final 1996–97. *League Group Cup:* Runners-up 1982. *Amateur Cup:* Winners 1963; Runners-up 1935, 1947.

Colours: All navy blue with yellow trim. *Change colours:* Red shirts with black trim, black shorts, red stockings with black trim.

Did you know?
Among Wimbledon's honours over the years are the Guernsey Cup, Bruges Tournament, Oxford Hospital Cup and the Westminster Hospital Cup.

WIMBLEDON 1996–97 LEAGUE RECORD

Match No.	Date	Venue	Opponents	Result	H/T Score	Lg. Pos.	Goalscorers	Attendance
1	Aug 17	H	Manchester U	L 0-3	0-1	—		25,786
2	21	A	Newcastle U	L 0-2	0-1	—		36,385
3	26	A	Leeds U	L 0-1	0-0	—		25,860
4	Sept 4	H	Tottenham H	W 1-0	1-0	—	Earle [3]	17,306
5	7	H	Everton	W 4-0	1-0	12	Ardley [33], Gayle [46], Earle [59], Ekoku [73]	13,684
6	14	A	West Ham U	W 2-0	0-0	8	Clarke [59], Ekoku [86]	21,924
7	23	H	Southampton	W 3-1	2-0	—	Gayle [12], Ekoku 2 [35, 72]	8572
8	28	A	Derby Co	W 2-0	0-0	4	Earle [49], Gayle [70]	17,022
9	Oct 12	H	Sheffield W	W 4-2	2-1	5	Ekoku [2], Earle [31], Leonhardsen [67], Jones [96]	10,512
10	19	A	Chelsea	W 4-2	2-1	3	Earle [4], Ardley [16], Gayle [64], Ekoku [78]	27,589
11	26	A	Middlesbrough	D 0-0	0-0	4		29,758
12	Nov 2	H	Arsenal	D 2-2	1-1	3	Jones [44], Gayle [67]	25,521
13	16	H	Coventry C	D 2-2	1-0	4	Earle [45], Gayle [54]	10,307
14	23	H	Liverpool	D 1-1	0-1	4	Leonhardsen [67]	39,027
15	30	H	Nottingham F	W 1-0	1-0	4	Earle [37]	12,608
16	Dec 7	A	Sunderland	W 3-1	2-0	2	Ekoku 2 [8, 29], Holdsworth [89]	19,617
17	14	H	Blackburn R	W 1-0	0-0	3	Holdsworth [85]	13,246
18	22	A	Aston Villa	L 0-5	0-2	3		28,875
19	28	A	Everton	W 3-1	0-1	4	Ekoku [59], Leonhardsen [70], Gayle [76]	36,733
20	Jan 11	H	Derby Co	D 1-1	0-0	5	Gayle [60]	11,467
21	18	A	Leicester C	L 0-1	0-0	5		18,927
22	29	A	Manchester U	L 1-2	0-0	—	Perry [61]	55,314
23	Feb 1	H	Middlesbrough	D 1-1	1-0	6	Cox (og) [22]	15,046
24	23	A	Arsenal	W 1-0	1-0	6	Jones [21]	37,854
25	Feb 26	A	Southampton	D 0-0	0-0	—		14,318
26	Mar 1	H	Leicester C	L 1-3	0-3	6	Holdsworth [66]	11,487
27	3	A	Coventry C	D 1-1	1-1	—	Ekoku [32]	15,266
28	15	A	Blackburn R	L 1-3	1-2	8	Ekoku [39]	23,333
29	18	H	West Ham U	D 1-1	1-0	—	Harford [19]	15,771
30	23	H	Newcastle U	D 1-1	1-0	8	Leonhardsen [28]	23,343
31	Apr 5	A	Tottenham H	L 0-1	0-0	8		32,654
32	9	H	Aston Villa	L 0-2	0-1	—		9015
33	16	H	Leeds U	W 2-0	1-0	—	Holdsworth [19], Castledine [74]	7979
34	19	A	Sheffield W	L 1-3	0-1	8	Goodman [85]	26,957
35	22	H	Chelsea	L 0-1	0-1	—		14,601
36	May 3	A	Nottingham F	D 1-1	1-0	8	Leonhardsen [16]	19,865
37	6	H	Liverpool	W 2-1	1-0	—	Euell [43], Holdsworth [55]	20,194
38	11	H	Sunderland	W 1-0	0-0	8	Euell [85]	21,516

Final League Position: 8

GOALSCORERS

League (49): Ekoku 11, Gayle 8, Earle 7, Holdsworth 5, Leonhardsen 5, Jones 3, Ardley 2, Euell 2, Castledine 1, Clarke 1, Goodman 1, Harford 1, Perry 1, own goal 1.
Coca-Cola Cup (9): Gayle 3, Holdsworth 2, Castledine 1, Ekoku 1, Fear 1, Leonhardsen 1.
FA Cup (9): Earle 4, Gayle 2, Holdsworth 2, Perry 1.

Sullivan N 36	Cunningham K 36	Thatcher B 9	Jones V 29	McAllister B 19 + 4	Perry C 37	Clarke A 4 + 7	Earle R 32	Gayle M 34 + 2	Holdsworth D 10 + 15	Leonhardsen O 27	Harford M 3 + 10	Ekoku E 28 + 2	Ardley N 33 + 1	Euell J 4 + 3	Blackwell D 22 + 5	Goodman J 6 + 7	Kimble A 28 + 3	Fear P 9 + 9	Jupp D 6	Castledine S 4 + 2	Heald P 2	Cort C — + 1	Reeves A — + 2	Match No.
1	2	3	4^2	5	6	7	8	9^1	10^1	11	12	13	14											1
1	2	3	4	5	6	9	8	12	10^2	11^1			7	13										2
1	2	3	4^1	5	6	11^2	8	10				9	7		12	13								3
1	2	3	4	5	6	12	8	11^1			13	9^1	7			10^3	14							4
1	2	3	4	5	6	12	8	11			13	9^2	7			10^1								5
1	2	3	4	5	6	12	8	11				9^2	7		13	10^1								6
1	2			5	6	12	8	11^1	10^2	4		9	7		13		3							7
1	2		4	5	6		8	11		10^1	13	9^2	7		12		3							8
1	2	3	4	5^1	6		8	11	13	10^2		9^2	7		12	14								9
1	2		4		6		8	11	12	10		9^2	7		5		3	13						10
1	2	3^2	4		6		8^3	11	12	10		9^1	7		5	13	14							11
1	2	3	4		6		8	11		10		9	7		5									12
1	2		4		6		8	11	12	10		9^1	7^2		5		3	13						13
1	2		4^1		6		8	11		10		9	7		5		3	12						14
1	2		4		6	12	8	11^1	13	10^3	14	9^2	7		5		3							15
1	2		4		6		8^1	11^2	13	10	12	9	7		5		3							16
1	2				6		8	11	12	10		9^1	7		5		3	4						17
1	2^2		4	12	6^1		8	11	13	10		9	7		5		3							18
1	8		4	6			11			10		9	7		5		3		2					19
1	2		4	12	6	13	8	11		10^1		9^2	7		5		3							20
1	2		4	3	6		8	11		10^1	12	9	7^2		5	13								21
1	4				6		8	11^2	12	10		9^1			5	13	3	7	2					22
1	4	10			6		8	11^2	12			9^1	7^3		5	13	3	14	2					23
1	2		4^1	12	6		8	11^2	13	10^3		9	7		5		3	14						24
1	2			12	6		8	11^2	13			9^2	7		5	14	3	10	4^1					25
1	2				6	11^1	8		10		12		7		5	9^2	3	4		13				26
	2		4		6		8	11^1	13		12	9^2	7		5		3			10	1			27
1	2		4		6		8	11		10	12	9			5	7^1	3							28
1	2		4		6		8	11	12	7	10	9^1			5		3							29
1	2				6		8	7	12	11	10^1	9			5		3	4						30
1	2		4		6		8	11	9	10			7^1		5	12	3							31
		5	6	12				10		9^2	7^1	11				3	4	2	8	1		13		32
1	2		4^1	5	6		9	10	11			7				3	8		12					33
1	2		5	6^3			9^1	10	11^1			7	12		13	3	4		8				14	34
1	2^2		4	5	6		12	10			7	13			9^1	3	11		8					35
1			4^1	5	6		8	9		10		7	11			3	12	2^2				13		36
1	2		4	5	6		8^1	9	10			7	11			3	12							37
1	2		4^2	5	6			9^1	10	8		12	7	11		3	13							38

Coca-Cola Cup

Second Round	Portsmouth	(h)	1-0	
		(a)	1-1	
Third Round	Luton T	(h)	1-1	
		(a)	2-1	
Fourth Round	Aston Villa	(h)	1-0	
Fifth Round	Bolton W	(a)	2-0	
Semi-Final	Leicester C	(a)	0-0	
		(h)	1-1	

FA Cup

Third Round	Crewe Alex	(a)	1-1
		(h)	2-0
Fourth Round	Manchester U	(a)	1-1
		(h)	1-0
Fifth Round	QPR	(h)	2-1
Sixth Round	Sheffield W	(a)	2-0
Semi Final	Chelsea		0-3
	(at Highbury)		

WOLVERHAMPTON WANDERERS 1996–97   *Back row (left to right):* Andy Thompson, Steve Corica, Robbie Dennison, Jermaine Wright, Mike Stowell, Chris Westwood, Dennis Pearce, Simon Osborn, Jamie Smith.

Middle row: Mark McGhee (Manager), Colin Lee (Assistant Manager), Robert Savvyers, Carl Robinson, Darren Ferguson, Richard Leadbeater, Emeka Nwadike, Steve Froggatt, Dominic Foley, Mark Venus, Neil Masters, Mark Rankine, Chris Turner (Youth Coach), Mike Hickman (Coach).

Front row: Taff Davies (Kit Manager), Dave Hancock (Physio), Eric Young, Tony Popovic, Dean Richards, Brian Law, Geoff Thomas, Steve Bull, Neil Emblen, Adrian Williams, Iwan Roberts, Don Goodman, Mark Atkins, Barry Holmes (Physio), Chris Evans (Youth Development Officer).

(Photograph: Action Images)

Division 1 **WOLVERHAMPTON WANDERERS**

Molineux Grounds, Wolverhampton WV1 4QR. Telephone: (01902) 655000; Fax: (01902) 687006.
Ground capacity: 28,525.
Record attendance: 63,315 v Liverpool, FA Cup 5th rd, 11 February 1939.
Record receipts: £276,168 v Tottenham H, FA Cup 4th rd, 7 February 1996.
Pitch measurements: 110yd × 75yd.
President: Sir Jack Hayward.
Chairman: Jonathan Hayward.
Directors: Jack Harris, John Harris, Nic Stones, John Richards, Michael Blackburn.
Manager: Mark McGhee. *Assistant Manager:* Colin Lee. *Stadium Manager:* Clive Mountford.
Coach: Mike Hickman. *Physios:* Barry Holmes, Dave Hancock.
Secretary: Richard Skirrow.
Year Formed: 1877*(see Foundation).* *Turned Professional:* 1888. *Ltd Co.:* 1982.
Club Nickname: 'Wolves'.
Previous Grounds: 1877, Goldthorn Hill; 1879, John Harper's Field; 1881, Dudley Road; 1889, Molineux.
Previous Names: 1880, St Luke's, Blakenhall combined with Blakenhall Wanderers to become Wolverhampton Wanderers (1923) Ltd until 1982.
Foundation: Another club where precise details of information are confused, due in part to the existence of an earlier Wolverhampton club which played rugby. However, it is now considered likely that it came into being in 1879 when players from St. Luke's (founded 1877) and Goldthorn (founded 1876) broke away to form Wolverhampton Wanderers Association FC.
First Football League game: 8 September 1888, Football League, v Aston Villa (h) D 1-1 – Baynton; Baugh, Mason; Fletcher, Allen, Lowder; Hunter, Cooper, Anderson, White, Cannon. Scorer – Cox (og).
Record League Victory: 10–1 v Leicester C, Division 1, 15 April 1938 – Sidlow; Morris, Dowen; Galley, Cullis, Gardiner; Maguire (1), Horace Wright, Westcott (4), Jones (1), Dorsett (4).
Record Cup Victory: 14–0 v Cresswell's Brewery, FA Cup 2nd rd, 13 November 1886 – I. Griffiths; Baugh, Mason; Pearson, Allen (1), Lowder; Hunter (4), Knight (2), Brodie (4), B. Griffiths (2), Wood. Plus one goal 'scrambled through'.
Record Defeat: 1–10 v Newton Heath, Division 1, 15 October 1892.
Most League Points (2 for a win): 64, Division 1, 1957–58.
Most League Points (3 for a win): 92, Division 4, 1988–89.
Most League Goals: 115, Division 2, 1931–32.
Highest League Scorer in Season: Dennis Westcott, 38, Division 1, 1946–47.
Most League Goals in Total Aggregate: Steve Bull, 240, 1986–97.
Most Capped Player: Billy Wright, 105, England (70 consecutive).
Most League Appearances: Derek Parkin, 501, 1967–82.
Record Transfer Fee Received: £1,150,000 from Manchester C for Steve Daley, September 1979.
Record Transfer Fee Paid: £1,850,000 to Bradford C for Dean Richards, May 1995.
Football League Record: 1888 Founder Member of Football League: 1906–23 Division 2; 1923–24 Division 3 (N); 1924–32 Division 2; 1932–65 Division 1; 1965–67 Division 2; 1967–76 Division 1; 1976–77 Division 2; 1977–82 Division 1; 1982–83 Division 2; 1983–84 Division 1; 1984–85 Division 2; 1985–86 Division 3; 1986–88 Division 4; 1988–89 Division 3; 1989–92 Division 2; 1992– Division 1.
Honours: *Football League:* Division 1 – Champions 1953–54, 1957–58, 1958–59; Runners-up 1937–38, 1938–39, 1949–50, 1954–55, 1959–60; Division 2 – Champions 1931–32, 1976–77; Runners-up 1966–67, 1982–83; Division 3 (N) – Champions 1923–24; Division 3 – Champions 1988–89; Division 4 – Champions 1987–88. *FA Cup:* Winners 1893, 1908, 1949, 1960; Runners-up 1889, 1896, 1921, 1939. *Football League Cup:* Winners 1974, 1980. *Texaco Cup:* Winners: 1971. *Sherpa Van Trophy:* Winners 1988. **European Competitions:** *European Cup:* 1958–59, 1959–60. *European Cup-Winners' Cup:* 1960–61. *UEFA Cup:* 1971–72 (runners-up), 1973–74, 1974–75, 1980–81.
Colours: Gold shirts, black shorts, gold stockings. *Change colours:* All teal.
Did you know?
When Steve Bull scored for Wolverhampton Wanderers at Huddersfield Town on 8 February 1997 in a 2–1 win, it was his 500th appearance for the club.

**Wolverhampton
Wanderers FC**

WOLVERHAMPTON WANDERERS 1996–97 LEAGUE RECORD

Match No.	Date		Venue	Opponents	Result	H/T Score	Lg. Pos.	Goalscorers	Attendance
1	Aug 17		A	Grimsby T	W 3-1	2-0	—	Bull 3 [36,45,69]	7910
2		24	H	Bradford C	W 1-0	0-0	3	Bull [72]	24,171
3		28	H	QPR	D 1-1	1-1	—	Osborn [24]	25,767
4		31	A	Norwich C	L 0-1	0-1	7		14,456
5	Sept 6		H	Charlton Ath	W 1-0	1-0	—	Thompson (pen) [39]	21,072
6		10	A	Oxford U	D 1-1	0-1	—	Roberts [54]	7468
7		15	A	WBA	W 4-2	3-1	3	Roberts 3 [4,27,53], Bull [14]	20,711
8		21	H	Sheffield U	L 1-2	0-0	5	Thompson (pen) [89]	25,170
9		27	A	Swindon T	W 2-1	1-0	—	Ferguson [44], Foley [85]	8572
10	Oct 2		H	Bolton W	L 1-2	1-0	—	Ferguson [12]	26,540
11		5	H	Reading	L 0-1	0-0	6		23,193
12		13	A	Southend U	D 1-1	0-1	6	Bull [73]	5550
13		15	A	Portsmouth	W 2-0	1-0	—	Bull 2 [12,68]	7411
14		19	H	Port Vale	L 0-1	0-0	5		22,755
15		27	A	Manchester C	W 1-0	0-0	4	Bull [77]	27,296
16		30	H	Huddersfield T	D 0-0	0-0	—		22,376
17	Nov 2		H	Barnsley	D 3-3	1-3	5	Goodman [28], Bull [61], Roberts [86]	22,840
18		17	H	Birmingham C	L 1-2	1-1	9	Bull [10]	22,627
19		23	A	Crystal Palace	W 3-2	2-0	7	Corica 2 [9,14], Thomas [61]	20,655
20	Dec 1		H	Manchester C	W 3-0	0-0	6	Roberts 2 [46,54], Dennison [80]	23,911
21		7	A	Ipswich T	D 0-0	0-0	5		12,048
22		14	H	Oldham Ath	L 0-1	0-1	6		22,528
23		21	A	Tranmere R	W 2-0	1-0	5	Osborn (pen) [5], Bull [76]	9674
24		26	H	Oxford U	W 3-1	1-1	5	Osborn 2 [13,67], Goodman [63]	26,511
25		28	A	Charlton Ath	D 0-0	0-0	4		12,259
26	Jan 12		H	WBA	W 2-0	2-0	4	Richards [3], Roberts [37]	27,336
27		18	A	Bolton W	L 0-3	0-1	4		18,980
28		24	A	Sheffield U	W 3-2	2-1	—	Atkins [19], Osborn [25], Bull [88]	17,490
29		29	H	Swindon T	W 1-0	1-0	—	Bull [36]	23,003
30	Feb 1		A	Stoke C	W 2-0	1-0	2	Bull 2 [16,55]	27,408
31		8	A	Huddersfield T	W 2-0	1-0	2	Froggatt [37], Bull [84]	15,267
32		15	H	Crystal Palace	L 0-3	0-1	3		25,919
33		22	A	Barnsley	W 3-1	2-0	2	Bull [2], Roberts [23], Froggatt [59]	18,024
34	Mar 1		H	Ipswich T	D 0-0	0-0	2		26,700
35		4	A	Birmingham C	W 2-1	2-0	—	Bull [1], Goodman [23]	19,838
36		8	H	Tranmere R	W 3-2	2-0	2	Bull 2 [34,41], Roberts [79]	26,192
37		15	A	Oldham Ath	L 2-3	1-1	2	Bull [24], Roberts [76]	9661
38		18	A	Stoke C	L 0-1	0-0	—		15,683
39		22	A	Bradford C	L 1-2	0-1	2	Goodman [55]	15,351
40		31	A	QPR	D 2-2	1-2	3	Goodman [39], Curle (pen) [70]	17,376
41	Apr 5		H	Norwich C	W 3-2	2-2	3	Thomas [19], Curle (pen) [35], Roberts [78]	26,938
42		12	A	Reading	L 1-2	0-0	3	Atkins [75]	14,853
43		19	A	Southend U	W 4-1	4-1	3	Ferguson [7], Bull [9], Atkins [35], Goodman [40]	25,095
44		23	H	Grimsby T	D 1-1	1-1	—	Gilkes [10]	25,474
45		27	A	Port Vale	W 2-1	2-1	3	Thomas [34], Atkins [42]	13,615
46	May 4		H	Portsmouth	L 0-1	0-0	3		26,031

Final League Position: 3

GOALSCORERS
League (68): Bull 23, Roberts 12, Goodman 6, Osborn 5 (1 pen), Atkins 4, Ferguson 3, Thomas 3, Corica 2, Curle 2 (2 pens), Froggatt 2, Thompson 2 (2 pens), Dennison 1, Foley 1, Gilkes 1, Richards 1.
Coca-Cola Cup (1): Osborn 1.
FA Cup (1): Ferguson 1.

Stowell M 46	Romano S 1+3	Froggatt S 27	Atkins M 44+1	Venus M 36+4	Richards D 19+2	Thompson A 26+6	Corica S 33+3	Bull S 43	Roberts I 24+9	Osborn S 33+2	Ferguson D 10+6	Smith J 36+2	Curle K 20+1	Wright J —+3	Emblen N 27+1	Foley D —+5	Crowe G 5+1	Van der Laan R 7	Dowe J 5+3	Pearce D 4	Dennison R 9+5	Leadbeater R —+1	Young E 1	Goodman D 19+8	Thomas G 15+7	Williams A 6	Law B 4+3	Gilkes M 5	Robinson C 1+1	Match No.
1	2[1]	3	4	5	6	7	8	9	10	11	12																			1
1		3	4	5[1]	6	7	8	9	10	11	12	2																		2
1		3	4	5	6	7	8	9	10	11		2																		3
1		3	4	5	6	7	8	9	10	11		2																		4
1		3	4	5	6	7	8[1]	9	10	11	12	2																		5
1		3	4[1]	5	6	7	8[2]	9	10	11		2	12	13																6
1		3	4	5	6	7	8	9	10	11		2																		7
1		3	4	5	6	7	8[1]	9	10	11		2	12																	8
1		3	4	5	6	7	12	9	10	8		2[2]			11[1]	13														9
1		3	4	5	6	7	12	9	10[2]	8		2			11[1]	13														10
1	12	3	4	5	6	7	11[3]	9	10[2]	8		2[1]			13	14														11
1	12	3	4	5	6		8[2]	9				2[1]	13		11[2]		7		10											12
1	12	3[1]	4	5	6		8	9				2	12		11		7		10[2]	3				13	6					13
1			4	5	6			9				2			10	8	7[1]			3	11				12					14
1			4[2]	5	6			9			12	2			8		7		10[1]	3	11				13					15
1			4	5	6			9	12	11		2			10[2]		7[1]			3[3]	3[1]	14		8						16
1			4	5	6	3		9	10	11		2				7[2]			12					8[1]	13					17
1			4	5		2		9	10	11					6			7		3				8[1]	13					18
1			4	5		2		7[1]	9	10	11				6					3					8					19
1			4	5		2		7	9	10	11				6				12	3					8					20
1			4	5	12	2[1]		7	9	10[2]	11	12			6					3				13	8					21
1			4	5	12			7[3]	9	10	11				6[1]				13	3				14	8[2]					22
1			4	5				7	9	11		2			6					3				10	8[1]					23
1			4	5				7	9	11		2			6					3				10	8					24
1	3[1]		4		6	12			9	10	11		2	5	7										8					25
1	3	12		4	6	13			9	10	11[2]		2	5	7[3]									14	8[1]					26
1	3	4			2	7		9		11				6	8									10						27
1	3	4				2	7	9		11					6	8								10		5				28
1	3	4		2	6		7	9		11					6	8								10[1]		5				29
1	3	4		2	7		9	12	11						6	8								10		5				30
1	3	4		2	7		9		11						6	8								10		5				31
1	3	4	12	2[2]	7[3]	9	13	11			6	8												10	14	5[1]				32
1	3	4	5	12	7[1]	9	10[2]	11		2	6	8[3]												13	14					33
1	3	4[3]	5	12	7	9[2]	10	11		2[1]	6	8												13	14					34
1	3[2]	4	5		2	7	9	12	11	13	6	8												10[1]						35
1		4	5	3	7[2]	9	12	11	13	2	6	8												10[1]						36
1		4	5	3	7[3]	9	12	11	13	2[2]	6	8[1]												10	14					37
1		4	3		2	7[1]	9	10	11[2]	12		6	5					14						13	8[3]					38
1		4	5		3	7	9	12	11		2	6	8[2]											10[1]	13					39
1	3	4	5[2]		7[1]		9	11	8	2	6													10	12	13				40
1	3	4					9	11[1]	8	2	5													10	6		7	12		41
1	3[1]	11	13	12			9		8	2	5													10	6		4	7[2]		42
1	3[1]	11		12			9	13	8	2	5		6[3]											10	14		4	7[1]		43
1		11	12			3[1]	13	9	14	8	2	5												10	6[2]		4	7		44
1		4	12					7[2]	9	13	8	2	6					10						11	5[1]		14	3[1]		45
1		4[2]	5		3			9[3]		8[1]	2	12	14	10										13	11	6		7		46

Coca-Cola Cup
First Round   Swindon T   (a)   0-2   (h)   1-0

FA Cup
Third Round   Portsmouth   (h)   1-2

WREXHAM 1996–97 *Back row left to right:* Paul Jones, Craig Skinner, Lewis Coady, Brian Carey, Mark Cartwright, Andy Marriott, Scott Williams, Jonathan Cross, Mark McGregor, Steve Watkin.

Middle row: Steven Futcher, Bryan Hughes, Karl Connolly, Andrew Thomas, Barry Jones, David Ridler, Neil Wainwright, David Brammer, Wayne Phillips, Steve Morris, Martyn Chalk.

Front row: Gareth Owen, Gareth Wilson, Kevin Russell, Neil Roberts, Robert Williams, Tony Humes, Phil Hardy, Deryn Brace, Stephen Carragher.

Division 2   **WREXHAM**

Racecourse Ground, Mold Road, Wrexham LL11 2AH. Telephone: (01978) 262129. Fax: (01978) 357821. Commercial Dept: (01978) 352536. Community Office: (01978) 358545. Clubcall: 0891 121642.

Ground capacity: 9200.

Record attendance: 34,445 v Manchester U, FA Cup 4th rd, 26 January 1957.

Record receipts: £126,012 v West Ham U, FA Cup 4th rd, 4 February 1992.

Pitch measurements: 111yd × 71yd.

Chairman: W. P. Griffiths.

Managing Director: D. L. Rhodes.

Directors: C. Griffiths, S. Mackreth, G. Paletta, B. Williams (Vice-Chairman), P. Griffiths.

Manager: Brian Flynn. *Assistant Manager:* Kevin Reeves.

Secretary: D. L. Rhodes. *Player-Coach:* Joey Jones.

Commercial Manager: Allan Thomas. *Physio:* Mel Pejic.

Year Formed: 1873 (oldest club in Wales).

Turned Professional: 1912. *Ltd Co.:* 1912.

Previous Ground: Acton Park.

Club Nickname: 'Robins'.

Foundation: The oldest club still in existence in Wales, Wrexham was founded in 1873 by a group of local businessmen initially to play a 17-a-side game against the Provincial Insurance team. By 1875 their team formation was reduced to 11 men and a year later they were among the founders of the Welsh FA.

First Football League game: 27 August 1921, Division 3 (N), v Hartlepools U (h) L 0-2 – Godding; Ellis, Simpson; Matthias, Foster, Griffiths; Burton, Goode, Cotton, Edwards, Lloyd.

Record League Victory: 10–1 v Hartlepool U, Division 4, 3 March 1962 – Keelan; Peter Jones, McGavan; Tecwyn Jones, Fox, Ken Barnes; Ron Barnes (3), Bennion (1), Davies (3), Ambler (3), Ron Roberts.

Record Cup Victory: 6–0 v Gateshead, FA Cup 1st rd, 20 November 1976 – Lloyd; Evans, Whittle, Davis, Roberts, Thomas (Hill), Shinton (3 incl. 1p), Sutton, Ashcroft (2), Lee (1), Griffiths. 6–0 v Charlton Ath, FA Cup 3rd rd, 5 January 1980 – Davies; Darracott, Kenworthy, Davis, Jones (Hill), Fox, Vinter (3), Sutton, Edwards (1), McNeil (2), Carrodus.

Record Defeat: 0–9 v Brentford, Division 3, 15 October 1963.

Most League Points (2 for a win): 61, Division 4, 1969–70 and Division 3, 1977–78.

Most League Points (3 for a win): 80, Division 3, 1992–93.

Most League Goals: 106, Division 3 (N), 1932–33.

Highest League Scorer in Season: Tom Bamford, 44, Division 3 (N), 1933–34.

Most League Goals in Total Aggregate: Tom Bamford, 175, 1928–34.

Most Capped Player: Dai Davies, 28 (51), Wales.

Most League Appearances: Arfon Griffiths, 592, 1959–61, 1962–79.

Record Transfer Fee Received: £800,000 from Birmingham C for Bryan Hughes, March 1997.

Record Transfer Fee Paid: £210,000 to Liverpool for Joey Jones, October 1978.

Football League Record: 1921 Original Member of Division 3 (N); 1958–60 Division 3; 1960–62 Division 4; 1962–64 Division 3; 1964–70 Division 4; 1970–78 Division 3; 1978–82 Division 2; 1982–83 Division 3; 1983–92 Division 4; 1992–93 Division 3; 1993– Division 2.

Honours: Football League: Division 2 best season: 15th, 1978–79; Division 3 – Champions 1977–78, Runners-up 1992–93; Division 3 (N) – Runners-up 1932–33; Division 4 – Runners-up 1969–70. *FA Cup:* best season: 6th rd, 1974, 1978, 1997. *Football League Cup:* best season: 5th rd, 1961, 1978. *Welsh Cup:* Winners 23 times (record); Runners-up 22 times (record). **European Competition:** *European Cup-Winners' Cup:* 1972–73, 1975–76, 1978–79, 1979–80, 1984–85, 1986–87, 1990–91, 1995–96.

Colours: Red shirts, white shorts, white stockings. *Change colours:* White shirts, black shorts, white stockings.

Did you know?
Tommy Bamford, with five goals in an 8–1 win over Carlisle United on 17 March 1934, produced the best individual scoring performance by a Wrexham player.

WREXHAM 1996–97 LEAGUE RECORD

Match No.	Date	Venue	Opponents	Result	H/T Score	Lg. Pos.	Goalscorers	Attendance
1	Aug 17	A	Millwall	D	1-1	1-0	—	Watkin 21	9371
2	24	H	Plymouth Arg	D	4-4	1-2	15	Phillips 2 42, 73, Connolly 2 71, 87	3920
3	Sept 7	H	Peterborough U	D	1-1	1-0	20	Connolly 12	3222
4	10	A	Stockport Co	W	2-0	1-0	—	Watkin 27, Skinner 47	4244
5	14	A	Crewe Alex	L	1-3	1-2	19	Ward 45	4469
6	17	H	Bristol R	W	1-0	1-0	—	Cross 45	2401
7	21	H	Preston NE	W	1-0	0-0	9	Phillips 78	5299
8	24	A	Walsall	W	1-0	0-0	—	Cross 64	2832
9	28	A	Notts Co	D	0-0	0-0	4		4216
10	Oct 8	H	Shrewsbury T	W	2-1	1-1	—	Watkin 42, Brace 87	5031
11	12	A	Watford	D	1-1	1-0	6	Humes 32	8441
12	15	A	Blackpool	D	3-3	0-3	—	Brammer 54, Phillips 55, Chalk (pen) 57	4014
13	19	H	Bournemouth	W	2-0	1-0	5	Skinner 15, Connolly 90	3945
14	26	A	Wycombe W	D	0-0	0-0	7		5548
15	29	H	Bury	D	1-1	0-0	—	Hughes 63	3895
16	Nov 2	H	Chesterfield	W	3-2	2-1	6	Connolly 5, Morris 38, Owen 88	4160
17	9	A	Gillingham	W	2-1	1-1	4	Morris 20, Connolly 74	5094
18	23	A	Brentford	L	0-2	0-1	9		4885
19	30	H	Wycombe W	W	1-0	1-0	4	Skinner 1	3280
20	Dec 3	A	Burnley	L	0-2	0-2	—		8587
21	14	A	York C	L	0-1	0-0	9		2600
22	21	H	Bristol C	W	2-1	1-0	5	Watkin (pen) 15, Hughes 67	4488
23	26	H	Stockport Co	L	2-3	2-1	7	Watkin 7, Morris 16	6736
24	Jan 11	H	Notts Co	D	3-3	1-2	10	Connolly 2 37, 77, Watkin 75	3267
25	18	A	Luton T	D	0-0	0-0	10		5734
26	Feb 1	H	Gillingham	D	1-1	1-0	11	Connolly 45	3193
27	8	A	Chesterfield	D	0-0	0-0	11		6738
28	11	A	Peterborough U	W	1-0	1-0	—	Hughes 30	2975
29	22	A	Rotherham U	D	0-0	0-0	11		2539
30	25	A	Bury	D	0-0	0-0	—		3419
31	Mar 1	H	Burnley	D	0-0	0-0	11		6947
32	12	H	Luton T	W	2-1	1-1	—	Bennett 2 (1 pen) 24 (p), 56	3342
33	15	H	York C	D	0-0	0-0	11		3874
34	18	A	Preston NE	L	1-2	1-1	—	Bennett 10	8271
35	22	A	Plymouth Arg	W	1-0	1-0	9	Humes 40	5468
36	25	H	Brentford	L	0-2	0-2	—		4053
37	28	H	Millwall	D	3-3	3-1	—	Humes 22, Phillips 29, Bennett (pen) 40	4684
38	31	A	Bristol R	L	0-2	0-1	12		6225
39	Apr 5	H	Walsall	L	1-2	0-1	12	Connolly (pen) 87	3266
40	8	H	Rotherham U	W	1-0	0-0	—	Connolly 48	2002
41	12	A	Shrewsbury T	W	1-0	0-0	9	Bennett 90	4553
42	15	A	Bristol C	L	1-2	0-1	—	Morris 71	9817
43	19	H	Watford	W	3-1	2-1	8	Connolly 2 (1 pen) 36 (p), 44, Skinner 79	3437
44	22	H	Crewe Alex	D	1-1	0-0	—	McGregor 77	4643
45	26	A	Bournemouth	L	1-2	0-1	10	Connolly 74	4805
46	May 3	H	Blackpool	W	2-1	1-1	8	Watkin 5, Humes 52	5664

Final League Position: 8

GOALSCORERS

League (54): Connolly 14 (2 pens), Watkin 7 (1 pen), Bennett 5 (2 pens), Phillips 5, Humes 4, Morris 4, Skinner 4, Hughes 3, Cross 2, Brace 1, Brammer 1, Chalk 1 (pen), McGregor 1, Owen 1, Ward 1.
Coca-Cola Cup (1): Skinner 1.
FA Cup (17): Hughes 6, Russell 3, Watkin 3 (1 pen), Morris 2, Connolly 1, Humes 1, Ward 1.

Marriott A 43	Brace D 26	Hardy P 13	Phillips W 26	Soloman J 2	Carey B 38	Chalk M 34+9	Russell K 37+4	Connolly K 27+3	Watkin S 24+2	Owen G 12+11	Brammer D 17+4	McGregor M 37+1	Ward P 24	Skinner C 21+6	Humes T 34	Cross J 11+7	Hughes B 20+3	Morris S 10+7	Jones B 14+8	Cartwright M 3	Williams S 3+1	Roberts P —+1	Jones L 2+4	Bennett G 15	Ridler D 7+4	Jones P 6	Match No.
1	2	3	4	5	6	7	8^1	9	10	11	12																1
1	3		4	5	6	7	8^1	9	10^3		12		2	11	13												2
1	3		4		6	7	8^1	9^2	13	12			2	11	10	5											3
1	3		4		6	7	8		9	12			2	11^1	10	5											4
1	3	4^1			6	7	8		9	12			2	11	10^2	5	13										5
1	3	4			6	7	8		9				2	11		5	10										6
1	3	4			6	7^1	8	9		12			2	11		5	10										7
1	3				6	7	8	9		11			2			5	10	4									8
1	3				6	7	8^1		9^3	11	12		2			5	10	4	13								9
1	3				6	7	8		9^2	11			2	12		5	10^1	4	13								10
1	3	4^1			6	7	8		9	11			2	13		5^3	10^2	12	14								11
1	3	4			6	7	8			11			2		9		10	5									12
1	3	4			6	7	8	12					2^2	11	9		13	10^1	5								13
1	2	3	4^3		6	7	8^1	9						11	10^2	5	12	13	14								14
1^2	2	3			6	7	8^1	9		12				11		5	4	10	13								15
	2	3			6	7^2	8^1	9		12				11		5	4	10	13	1							16
	2	3			6		7^1	12	8					11		5	4	10		1							17
	2	3			6		12	8	9					11	7	5^2	4	10^1	13	1							18
1	2^2	3			6			8^1	9	10	12	13		11		7	4		5								19
1	3				6			9^1	8	12	10	13	2	11	7	5	4^2										20
1	3				6			9	8				2	11	7	5	4	10									21
1	3				6		7	12	9	8^1			2	11		5	4	10									22
1	3^1				6		7		9	8^2			2	11		5	4	10			12	13					23
1	3				6		7	12	9	10	8		2	11^1		5	4										24
1	3				6		7		9	10	8		2	11		5	4										25
1	3				6		7^1		9	10	8		2	11		5	4						12				26
1	3				6		7^3	8	9	10	12		2	11		5^2	4^1		13				14				27
1	3				6		7	8	9				2	11		5	4	10									28
1	3				6		7	8	9^1	10			2	11		5	4						12				29
1	3				6		7	8^2		10	12	13	2	11		5	4						9^1				30
1	3				6			9	8^1	10	12		2	11		5	4						13	7^2			31
1	3^1		4		6			9		8	10		2	11		5							12	7			32
1			4		6^3		8^2	9	10^1	12		11	2			5			13		3			7	14		33
1			4				8^3	9	10	12		11	2			5			13		3			7	6		34
1			4		6		8	9^1	10	12		11	2			5					3			7			35
1			4		6		8^1	9	10^2	12		11	2			5			13		3^3			7	14		36
1			4		6		8^2	9	10^1	12		11	2			5			13					7		3	37
1			4		6		8	9	10^2	12		11				5					2^1			7	13	3	38
1			4		6		8^1	9	10	12		11	2			5			13					7^2		3	39
1			4		6		8	9	10	12		11	2											7^1	5	3	40
1			4				8	9^2	10	12		11	2			5^3			13				14	7	6	3^1	41
1			4		6		8	9	10	12		11	2						13					7^2	5	3^1	42
1			4		6		8	9^1	10	12		11	2						13		3			7^2	5		43
1			4		6		8	9^2	10	12			2	11^1					13		3			7	5		44
1			4		6		8^1	9	10	12		11	2						13		3			7^2	5		45
1			4^1		6		8	9	10	12		11	2			5								7^2	13	3	46

Coca-Cola Cup
First Round Huddersfield T (a) 0-3
  (h) 1-2

FA Cup
First Round Colwyn Bay (a) 1-1 (h) 2-0
Second Round Scunthorpe U (h) 2-2 (a) 3-2
Third Round West Ham U (h) 1-1 (a) 1-0
Fourth Round Peterborough U (a) 4-2
Fifth Round Birmingham C (a) 3-1
Sixth Round Chesterfield (a) 0-1

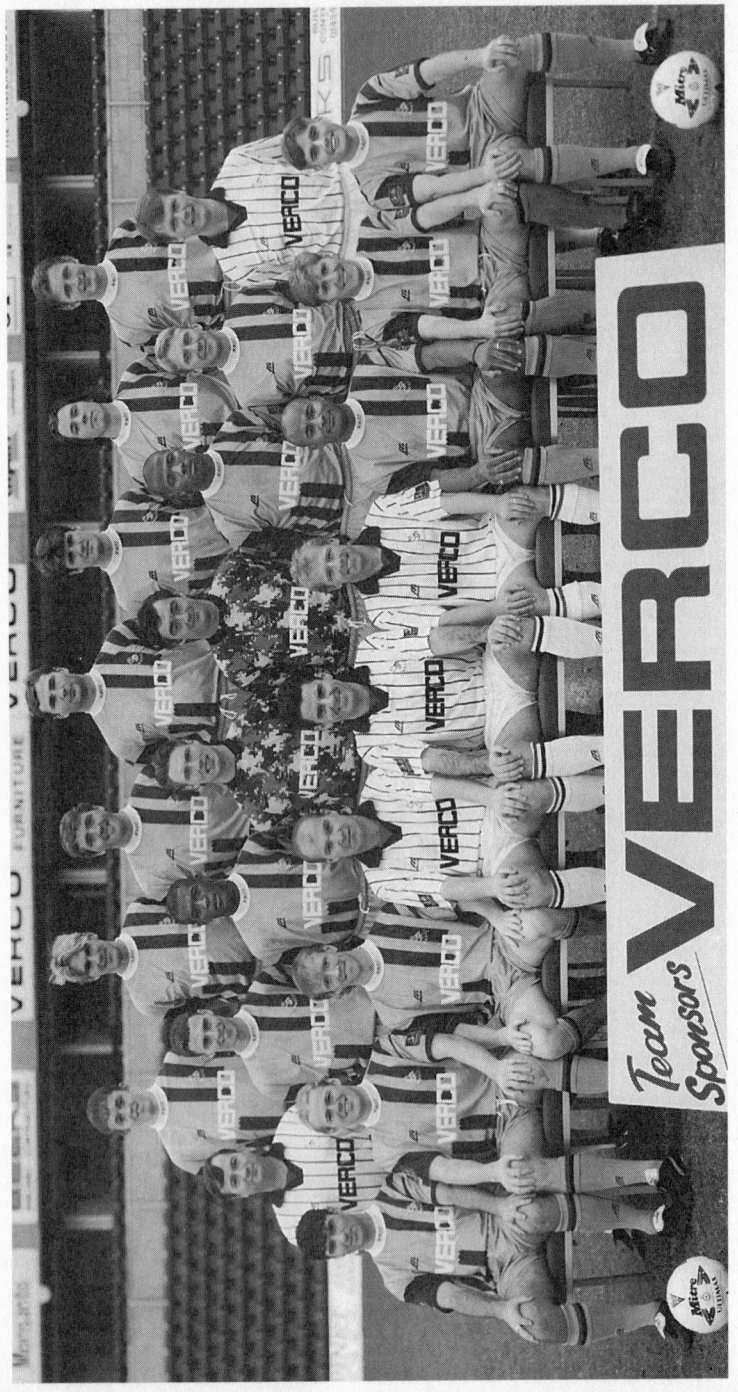

WYCOMBE WANDERERS 1996–97   *Back row (left to right):* Anthony Clark, Matthew Lawrence, Paul McCarthy, Terry Evans, Matt Crossley, Gary Patterson, Terry Skiverton.
Middle row: Adrian Cole (Youth Development Officer), Dave Farrell, Steve Brown, John Cheesewright, Brian Parkin, John Williams, Brian McGorry, David Jones (Physio).
Front row: Jason Cousins, Keith Ryan, Dave Carroll, Richard Hill (Assistant Manager), John Gregory (Manager), Neil Smillie (Youth Team Manager), Miguel De Souza, Steve McGavin, Mickey Bell.

Division 2   WYCOMBE WANDERERS

Adams Park, Hillbottom Road, Sands, High Wycombe HP12 4HJ. Telephone (01494) 472100. Fax: (01494) 527633. Credit Card Hotline: (01494) 441118. Information Line 0891 446855.

Ground Capacity: 10,000 new stand; now seats 7250.

Record attendance: 9007 v West Ham U, FA Cup 3rd rd, 7 January 1995.

Record receipts: £61,221 (net of VAT) v West Ham U, FA Cup 3rd rd, 7 January 1995.

Pitch measurements: 115yd × 75yd.

Patron: J. Adams.

President: M. E. Seymour.

Chairman: I. L. Beeks.

Directors: G. Peart (Financial), G. Richards, B. R. Lee, A. Parry, A. Thibault, G. Cox.

Associate Director: J. Goldsworthy.

Manager: John Gregory. ***Assistant Manager:*** Richard Hill. ***Secretary:*** John Reardon.

Physio: David Jones. ***Marketing Manager:*** Mark Austin. ***Promotions Manager:*** Mike Phillips.

Year Formed: 1884. ***Turned Professional:*** 1974. ***Club Nicknames:*** 'Chairboys' (after High Wycombe's tradition of furniture making), 'The Blues'.

Previous Ground: 1887 The Rye; 1893 Spring Meadow; 1895 Loakes Park, 1899 Daws Hill Park; 1901 Loakes Park; 1990 Adams Park.

Foundation: In 1884 a group of young furniture trade workers started playing together informally under the name of North Town Wanderers, the area of the town where they lived. They decided to better themselves by entering junior football and in 1887 Jim Ray, secretary, and Datchett Webb, captain, called a meeting at the Steam Engine public house. Wycombe Wanderers FC was formed and probably named after the famous FA Cup winners, The Wanderers, who had visited the town in 1877 for a tie with the original High Wycombe club.

First Football League Game: 14 August 1993, Division 3 v Carlisle U (a), D 2-2: Hyde; Cousins, Horton (Langford), Kerr, Crossley, Ryan, Carroll, Stapleton, Thompson, Scott, Guppy (1) (Hutchinson). Wycombe's first goal was an own goal by Chris Curran.

Record League Victory: 4–0 v Scarborough (h), Division 3, 2 November 1993 – Hyde; Cousins, Horton, Crossley (1), Evans T, Ryan, Carroll (1), Hayrettin, Thompson (Hemmings), Scott (2), Guppy.

Record Cup Victory: 5–0 v Hitchin T (away), FA Cup 2nd rd, 3 December 1994 – Hyde; Cousins, Brown, Crossley, Evans, Ryan (1), Carroll, Bell (1), Thompson, Garner (3) (Hemmings), Stapleton (Langford).

Record Defeat: 0–5 v Walsall, Auto Windscreens Shield 1st rd, 7 November 1995.

Most League Points: 70, Division 3, 1993–94.

Most League Goals: 66, Division 3, 1993–94.

Highest League Goalscorer in Season: Miguel De Souza 18, 1995–96.

Most League Goals in Total Aggregate: Miguel de Souza, 29, 1995–97.

Most League Appearances: Dave Carroll, 171, 1993–97.

Record Transfer Fee Received: £375,000 from Swindon T for Keith Scott, November 1993.

Record Transfer Fee Paid: £140,000 to Birmingham C for Steve McGavin, March 1995.

Football League Record: Promoted to Division 3 from GMVC in 1993; 1993–94 Division 3; 1994– Division 2.

Honours: *Football League:* Division 2 best season: 6th, 1994–95; *FA Amateur Cup:* Winners 1931; *FA Trophy:* Winners 1991, 1993; *GM Vauxhall Conference:* Winners 1992–93; *FA Cup:* best season: 3rd rd 1975, 1986, 1994, 1995; *Football League Cup:* never beyond 2nd rd.

Colours: Light & dark blue striped quartered shirts, light blue shorts, light blue stockings. ***Change colours:*** All white.

Did you know?
Miguel De Souza scored for Wycombe Wanderers against Burnley after only 16 seconds on 14 September 1996, the fastest goal in the club's history.

Founded 1884

WYCOMBE WANDERERS 1996–97 LEAGUE RECORD

Match No.	Date	Venue	Opponents	Result	H/T Score	Lg. Pos.	Goalscorers	Attendance
1	Aug 18	A	Shrewsbury T	D	1-1	0-1	—	Brown [66]	3440
2	24	H	Gillingham	D	1-1	1-1	16	Carroll [8]	4582
3	27	H	Bury	L	0-1	0-1	—		3563
4	31	A	Blackpool	D	0-0	0-0	20		4856
5	Sept 7	H	Luton T	L	0-1	0-0	21		6471
6	10	A	Walsall	D	2-2	2-2	—	Evans [14], De Souza [28]	2659
7	14	A	Burnley	L	1-2	1-2	23	De Souza [1]	9379
8	21	H	Brentford	L	0-1	0-1	23		5330
9	28	A	Peterborough U	L	3-6	3-3	24	Mahoney-Johnson 2 [11, 34], Carroll [15]	5580
10	Oct 1	H	Rotherham U	W	4-2	1-2	—	Lawrence [45], McGavin 2 [75, 78], Williams [85]	3438
11	5	H	Notts Co	W	1-0	1-0	20	McGavin [8]	4506
12	12	A	Bournemouth	L	1-2	0-2	22	Farrell [48]	3984
13	15	A	Bristol C	L	0-3	0-1	—		7325
14	19	H	Stockport Co	L	0-2	0-1	23		4017
15	26	H	Wrexham	D	0-0	0-0	24		5548
16	29	A	York C	L	0-2	0-1	—		2254
17	Nov 2	A	Crewe Alex	L	0-3	0-0	24		3636
18	9	H	Plymouth Arg	W	2-1	1-1	24	Brown [23], McGavin [74]	5456
19	19	A	Watford	L	0-1	0-0	—		7657
20	23	H	Preston NE	L	0-1	0-0	24		4920
21	30	A	Wrexham	L	0-1	0-1	24		3280
22	Dec 3	A	Millwall	W	1-0	0-0	—	Bell [77]	4550
23	14	H	Chesterfield	W	1-0	0-0	23	De Souza [80]	4610
24	21	A	Bristol R	W	4-3	1-1	22	Carroll [45], Bell [62], Simpson [69], Evans [86]	4465
25	26	A	Walsall	L	0-2	0-0	22		5073
26	Jan 18	A	Rotherham U	L	1-2	0-1	23	Carroll (pen) [89]	2692
27	25	H	York C	W	3-1	1-0	22	Read 2 [10, 90], Forsyth [54]	4193
28	Feb 1	A	Plymouth Arg	D	0-0	0-0	22		5024
29	8	A	Crewe Alex	W	2-0	1-0	22	Read [35], De Souza [90]	4902
30	15	A	Preston NE	L	1-2	1-1	22	McGavin [25]	7923
31	22	H	Watford	D	0-0	0-0	22		8438
32	25	H	Peterborough U	W	2-0	1-0	—	McGavin [11], De Souza [61]	4001
33	Mar 1	A	Millwall	L	1-2	1-1	21	Forsyth [39]	7539
34	4	A	Brentford	D	0-0	0-0	—		5375
35	8	H	Bristol R	W	2-0	0-0	21	Stallard [50], Brown [64]	5386
36	15	A	Chesterfield	L	2-4	2-2	21	Stallard [5], Brown [23]	4354
37	22	A	Gillingham	L	0-1	0-1	21		5932
38	29	H	Shrewsbury T	W	3-0	1-0	21	Scott [14], Stallard [49], Carroll [67]	6562
39	31	A	Bury	L	0-2	0-0	21		5714
40	Apr 5	H	Blackpool	W	1-0	0-0	21	Scott [65]	5619
41	8	A	Luton T	D	0-0	0-0	—		7626
42	12	A	Notts Co	W	2-1	2-1	20	Brown [1], McGavin [31]	4290
43	15	H	Burnley	W	5-0	4-0	—	Carroll 2 (2 pens) [12, 29], McGavin [33], Stallard [42], Read [82]	5786
44	19	H	Bournemouth	D	1-1	0-0	19	Scott [54]	6043
45	26	A	Stockport Co	L	1-2	0-2	19	Carroll (pen) [71]	9463
46	May 3	A	Bristol C	W	2-0	2-0	18	Carroll [23], McGavin [45]	7240

Final League Position: 18

GOALSCORERS

League (51): Carroll 9 (4 pens), McGavin 9, Brown 5, De Souza 5, Read 4, Stallard 4, Scott 3, Bell 2, Evans 2, Forsyth 2, Mahoney-Johnson 2, Farrell 1, Lawrence 1, Simpson 1, Williams 1.
Coca-Cola Cup (4): Williams 2, Evans 1, McCarthy 1.
FA Cup (8): Williams 4, De Souza 2, Carroll 1, McGavin 1.

Parkin B 24	Lawrence M 12 + 1	Bell M 46	McCarthy P 36 + 4	Evans T 38 + 4	Patterson G 6 + 3	Carroll D 42 + 1	Brown S 28 + 6	De Souza M 29 + 4	Williams J 11 + 8	Farrell D 17 + 10	Markman D — + 2	Mahoney-Johnson M 2 + 2	Cousins J 36 + 1	Wilkins R 1	McGavin S 33 + 2	Crossley M 7 + 2	Skiverton T 2 + 4	Davis N 13	Cheesewright J 18	Kavanagh J 27	Simpson M 16 + 4	Forsyth M 22 + 1	Cornforth J 8 + 2	Read P 7 + 6	Harkin M — + 4	Stallard M 12	Taylor M 4	Scott K 9	Match No.
1	2	3	4	5	6	7	8	9	10[1]	11	12																		1
1	2	3	4	5	6	7	8	9	10	11																			2
1	2	3	4	5	6	7	8	9	10[1]	11	12																		3
1	2	3	4	5	6[2]	7	8	9	10[1]	12		11	13																4
1	6	3	4	5		7		9	10[1]	11		12	2		8														5
1	6	3	4	5	12	7	8[1]	9	10	11			2																6
1	6	3	4	5	12	7[1]	8	9	10	11			2																7
1	6	3	4	5		7	8	9[1]		11	12		2		10														8
1	6	3	4	5[2]		7	8	12		11[1]		9	2		10	13													9
1	6	3	4	5		7	8[1]	9	12	11			2		10														10
1	6	3	4	5		7	12	9[1]	8	11			2		10														11
1		3	4	5	6	7		9	8	11			2		10														12
1		3	4	5	6	7	8	12	10[2]	9[1]			2		11	13													13
1		3	4	5		7	8	9[1]	6	11			2		10	12													14
1		3	4	5		7[1]	8[2]	12		11			2		10	6	13	9											15
		3	4[2]	5			8	12	13	11			2		10	6	7[1]	9	1										16
		3	4	5		7	8	12							10	6	11[1]	9	1	2									17
		3[1]	4	5		7	8	11		12					10	6		9	1	2									18
		3	4	5		7	8	11		12					10	6		9[1]	1	2									19
		3	4	5		7	8	11		12					10	6		9[1]	1	2									20
8[2]		3	4	5[1]		7		11	12	13			2		10			9	1	6									21
		3	4	5		7	8	11					2		10			9	1	6									22
		3	4		12	7[2]		9	13				2		10	5	8[1]		1	6	11								23
		3	4	5		7[1]		12	9				2		10	8			1	11[2]	6	13							24
		3		5				12	9	13			2[2]		10		7		1	6	11	4	8[1]						25
		3		5	12	7							2		10		8		1	4[1]	11	6		9					26
12		3		5[2]	13	7	14						2		10	8[2]			1	4	11	6		9[1]					27
	3		5			7	8						2		10				1	4	11	6		9					28
	3	12	5			7	8						2		10[1]				1	4	11	6		9					29
	3		5			7	8		12				2[2]		10[1]				1	4	11	6		9	13				30
	3	4	5			7	8		12				2[1]		10				1		11	6		9					31
	3	4	5			7	8[2]		12				2		10		14		1		11[3]	6		9[1]	13				32
	3	4	5			7	8		9				2		10[1]				1		11	6	12						33
1	3		5			7	12	8		9[2]			2						4		11	6	10[1]	13					34
1	3	12	5			7	11[1]	8[3]					2			13			4			6	10[2]			14	9		35
1	3		5			7	11	8					2[1]						4			6	10					9	36
1	3	2	5			7		8[1]		12									4		11	6	10					9	37
	3	12	5			7[1]		13					2		14				4		11	6[1]	10[2]			9	1	8	38
	3		5			7							2		12				4		11	6	10[1]			9	1	8	39
	3	12	5			13	14						2		7[1]				4		11[2]	6	10[3]			9	1	8	40
	3		5			7		11					2		10				4			6		12		9[1]	1	8	41
1	3	4	5			7		11							10[3]					2[1]	12	6	14	13		9[2]		8	42
1	3		5			7[2]		11		12					10[3]					2	4	13		14		9		8[1]	43
1	3		5			7		11[1]							10					2	4	12	6	13		9[2]		8	44
1	3		5	12		7		11[2]							10					2	4		6[1]	13		9		8	45
1	3		5	12		7		11[1]							10[3]					2	4	13		14		9		8[2]	46

Coca-Cola Cup

First Round	Reading	(a)	1-1
		(h)	2-0
Second Round	Nottingham F	(a)	0-1
		(h)	1-1

FA Cup

First Round	Colchester U	(a)	2-1
Second Round	Barnet	(a)	3-3
		(h)	3-2
Third Round	Bradford C	(h)	0-2

YORK CITY 1996–97   *Back row (left to right):* Nigel Pepper, Neil Campbell, Paul Atkin, Tony Barras, Neil Tolson, Steve Tutill, John Sharples, Richard Cresswell, Adrian Randall.
Middle row: Jeff Miller (Physio), Glenn Naylor, Andy McMillan, Martin Reed, Andy Warrington, Wayne Osborne, Alan Pouton, Paul Stephenson, Paul Stancliffe (Assistant Manager).
Front row: Darren Williams, Gary Himsworth, Paddy Atkinson, Gary Bull, Alan Little (Manager), Steve Bushell, Scott Jordan, Wayne Hall, Graeme Murty.

Division 2   **YORK CITY**

Bootham Crescent, York YO3 7AQ. Telephone: (01904) 624447. Fax: (01904) 631457.

Ground capacity: 9534.

Record attendance: 28,123 v Huddersfield T, FA Cup 6th rd, 5 March 1938.

Record receipts: £63,680 v Manchester U, Coca-Cola Cup 2nd rd 2nd leg, 3 October 1995.

Pitch measurements: 115yd × 74yd.

Chairman: D. M. Craig OBE, JP, BSC, FICE, FI, MUN E, FCI ARB, M CONS E.

Directors: B. A. Houghton, C. Webb, E. B. Swallow, J. E. H. Quickfall FCA.

Manager: Alan Little. *First Team Coach:* Derek Bell.

Secretary: Keith Usher. *Commercial Manager:* Mrs Maureen Leslie.

Physio: Jeff Miller.

Hon. Orthopaedic Surgeon: Mr Peter De Boer MA, FRCS. *Medical Officer:* Dr R. Porter.

Year Formed: 1922. *Turned Professional:* 1922. *Ltd Co.:* 1922.

Club Nickname: 'Minstermen'.

Previous Ground: 1922, Fulfordgate; 1932, Bootham Crescent.

Foundation: Although there was a York City club formed in 1903 by a soccer enthusiast from Darlington, this has no connection with the modern club because it went out of existence during World War I. Unlike many others of that period who restarted in 1919, York City did not re-form until 1922 and the tendency now is to ignore the modern club's pre-1922 existence.

First Football League game: 31 August 1929, Division 3 (N), v Wigan Borough (a) W 2-0 – Farmery; Archibald, Johnson; Beck, Davis, Thompson; Evans, Gardner, Cowie (1), Smailes, Stockhill (1).

Record League Victory: 9–1 v Southport, Division 3 (N), 2 February 1957 – Forgan; Phillips, Howe; Brown (1), Cairney, Mollatt; Hill, Bottom (4 incl. 1p), Wilkinson (2), Wragg (1), Fenton (1).

Record Cup Victory: 6–0 v South Shields (away), FA Cup 1st rd, 16 November 1968 – Widdowson; Baker (1p), Richardson; Carr, Jackson, Burrows; Taylor, Ross (3), MacDougall (2), Hodgson, Boyer.

Record Defeat: 0–12 v Chester, Division 3 (N), 1 February 1936.

Most League Points (2 for a win): 62, Division 4, 1964–65.

Most League Points (3 for a win): 101, Division 4, 1983–84.

Most League Goals: 96, Division 4, 1983–84.

Highest League Scorer in Season: Bill Fenton, 31, Division 3 (N), 1951–52; Arthur Bottom, 31, Division 3 (N), 1954–55 and 1955–56.

Most League Goals in Total Aggregate: Norman Wilkinson, 125, 1954–66.

Most Capped Player: Peter Scott, 7 (10), Northern Ireland.

Most League Appearances: Barry Jackson, 481, 1958–70.

Record Transfer Fee Received: £450,000 from Port Vale for Jon McCarthy, July 1995.

Record Transfer Fee Paid: £140,000 to Burnley for Adrian Randall, December 1995.

Football League Record: 1929 Elected to Division 3 (N); 1958–59 Division 4; 1959–60 Division 3; 1960–65 Division 4; 1965–66 Division 3; 1966–71 Division 4; 1971–74 Division 3; 1974–76 Division 2; 1976–77 Division 3; 1977–84 Division 3; 1984–88 Division 3; 1988–92 Division 4; 1992–93 Division 3; 1993– Division 2.

Honours: *Football League:* Division 2 best season: 15th, 1974–75; Division 3 – Promoted 1973–74 (3rd); Division 4 – Champions 1983–84. *FA Cup:* Semi-finals 1955, when in Division 3. *Football League Cup:* best season: 5th rd, 1962.

Colours: Red shirts, blue shorts, red stockings. *Change colours:* All blue.

Did you know?
When York City defeated Everton in the Coca-Cola Cup Second Round last season, it was the first meeting between the clubs in any senior competition.

YORK CITY 1996–97 LEAGUE RECORD

Match No.	Date	Venue	Opponents	Result	H/T Score	Lg. Pos.	Goalscorers	Attendance
1	Aug 17	A	Plymouth Arg	L 1-2	0-0	—	Pepper (pen) [79]	9035
2	24	H	Bournemouth	L 1-2	0-0	24	Pepper [81]	2804
3	27	H	Millwall	W 3-2	0-2	—	Pepper 2 (1 pen) [57 (p), 62], Tolson [71]	3108
4	31	A	Notts Co	W 1-0	1-0	8	Tolson [23]	4600
5	Sept 7	H	Shrewsbury T	D 0-0	0-0	9		2911
6	10	A	Preston NE	L 0-1	0-0	—		7608
7	14	A	Peterborough U	D 2-2	0-0	13	Bushell [58], Pepper [85]	5613
8	21	H	Stockport Co	L 1-2	0-0	18	Tolson [47]	3061
9	28	A	Brentford	D 3-3	1-0	19	Tolson [3], Randall [49], Murty [71]	5243
10	Oct 1	H	Bristol R	D 2-2	2-1	—	Tolson [13], Randall [53]	3714
11	5	H	Watford	L 1-2	0-2	19	Pepper (pen) [80]	5232
12	11	A	Bristol C	L 0-2	0-1	—		9308
13	15	A	Crewe Alex	W 1-0	0-0	—	Himsworth [81]	3463
14	19	H	Rotherham U	W 2-1	0-0	16	Stephenson [65], Pepper [90]	3410
15	26	A	Chesterfield	L 0-2	0-0	16		4009
16	29	H	Wycombe W	W 2-0	1-0	—	Pepper (pen) [36], Tolson [53]	2254
17	Nov 2	H	Burnley	W 1-0	0-0	13	Murty [61]	5958
18	9	A	Bury	L 1-4	1-2	13	Himsworth [21]	4021
19	23	A	Gillingham	W 1-0	1-0	13	Tolson [24]	5048
20	30	H	Chesterfield	D 0-0	0-0	14		3328
21	Dec 3	A	Luton T	L 0-2	0-0	—		4401
22	14	H	Wrexham	W 1-0	0-0	12	Humes (og) [89]	2600
23	21	A	Blackpool	L 0-3	0-1	15		3432
24	28	A	Shrewsbury T	L 0-2	0-1	17		3189
25	Jan 11	H	Brentford	L 2-4	1-2	19	Pepper (pen) [45], Pouton [80]	3085
26	18	A	Bristol R	D 1-1	1-0	19	Pepper (pen) [1]	4470
27	25	A	Wycombe W	L 1-3	0-1	20	Campbell [70]	4193
28	Feb 1	H	Bury	L 0-2	0-1	20		3423
29	8	A	Burnley	W 2-1	1-1	20	Tolson [6], Jordan [90]	8961
30	11	H	Walsall	L 0-2	0-0	—		2136
31	15	H	Gillingham	L 2-3	1-1	20	Bushell [23], Barras [79]	2748
32	22	A	Walsall	D 1-1	1-0	20	Pepper (pen) [21]	3664
33	25	H	Preston NE	W 3-1	0-0	—	Bull [57], Pepper [65], Rowe [81]	2515
34	Mar 1	H	Luton T	D 1-1	0-1	20	Tolson [48]	3788
35	8	H	Blackpool	W 1-0	1-0	19	Sharples [19]	3639
36	15	A	Wrexham	D 0-0	0-0	19		3874
37	22	A	Bournemouth	D 1-1	0-1	19	Gilbert [65]	4367
38	29	H	Plymouth Arg	D 1-1	0-0	19	Bushell [77]	3917
39	Apr 2	A	Millwall	D 1-1	0-0	—	Tolson [48]	6161
40	5	H	Notts Co	L 1-2	0-1	20	Rowe [79]	3115
41	8	H	Peterborough U	W 1-0	1-0	—	Bull [42]	2790
42	12	A	Watford	L 0-4	0-3	19		7645
43	19	H	Bristol C	L 0-3	0-1	20		3344
44	22	A	Stockport Co	L 1-2	1-1	—	Tolson [20]	6654
45	26	A	Rotherham U	W 2-0	1-0	20	Rowe [45], Tolson [68]	3122
46	May 3	H	Crewe Alex	D 1-1	1-0	20	Tinkler [25]	4366

Final League Position: 20

GOALSCORERS

League (47): Pepper 12 (7 pens), Tolson 12, Bushell 3, Rowe 3, Bull 2, Himsworth 2, Murty 2, Randall 2, Barras 1, Campbell 1, Gilbert 1, Jordan 1, Pouton 1, Sharples 1, Stephenson 1, Tinkler 1, own goal 1.
Coca-Cola Cup (7): Tolson 3, Bull 1, Bushell 1, Murty 1, Pepper 1.
FA Cup (6): Tolson 2, Barras 1, Himsworth 1, Pepper 1, own goal 1.

Warrington A 27	McMillan A 46	Atkinson P 13 + 1	Randall A 13 + 3	Atkin P 6 + 6	Barras T 46	Hinsworth G 32 + 1	Bushell S 26 + 5	Bull G 33 + 8	Tolson N 39 + 1	Stephenson P 33 + 2	Pepper N 26 + 3	Murty G 25 + 2	Pouton A 18 + 4	Cresswell R 9 + 8	Sharples J 28	Naylor G — + 1	Williams D — + 1	Hall W 12 + 1	Campbell N 5 + 6	Tutill S 13 + 2	Clarke T 17	Jordan S 7 + 8	Rush D 1 + 1	Prudhoe M 2	Harrison T — + 1	Rowe R 9 + 1	Gilbert D 9	Greening J — + 5	Tinkler M 9	Reed M 2	Match No.
1	2	3	4	5	6	7	8^1	9	10	11^2	12	13																			1
1	2		4	5	6	7^2	8^1	9^3	10	11	12	3	13	14																	2
1	2	8			6	3			10	9	4	7		11^1	5		12														3
1	2	8			6	3	13	12	9^1	11^2	4	7		10	5																4
1	2	8			6	3		12	9	11	4	7		10^1	5																5
1	2	8			6	3			10	9	11	4	7		5																6
1	2				6	3	8		10	9	11^1	4	7		5		12														7
1	2	8^1	13		6	3^3	12		10	9	11	4	7	14	5^2																8
1	2	8^1	12		6				10	9^2	11	4	7		5			3	13												9
1	2	8			6				10^1	9	11	4	7		5			3	12												10
1	2	8	5^1		6			13	10^3	9	11^2	4	7		14			3	12												11
	2	3	8^1		6			13	10	9	11	4^2	7						12	5	1										12
	2	8			6		11			9		4	7	10^1				3	12	5	1										13
	2	8			6		11^1	13		9	12	4	7	10^2				3		5	1										14
	2		5		6		11	8	10	9		4	7					3			1										15
	2				6		11	8	10	9		4	7					3		5	1										16
	2				6		11	8	10	9		4	7					3		5	1										17
	2		12		6		11	8	10	9		4^1	7	13				3^2		5	1										18
	2				6		11	8^1	10	9	3	4	7	12						5	1										19
	2		12		6	3			10	9	11	4^1	7	8						5	1										20
	2		12	13	6	3^1			10	9^3	11	4	7	8^2	14					5	1										21
	2		3	12	6	7^2			10	9	11^1	4		8^3	13					5	1	14									22
	2		3		6				10	9	11	4	7^1	12						5	1	8									23
	2		3	8	6				10	9^1	11	4^2	7	12						5	1	13									24
	2		3		6			12	10^2	9	11	4	7^1	8	13					5	1										25
	2		3		6	7		12			11	4		8	9					5	1	10^1									26
	2		3		6	7^2		12			11^1	4	13	8	10^3				14	5	1	9									27
	2		3		6			12	13		11	4^1	7	8	10^3				14	5	1	9^2									28
1	2				6	3	11			9		4	7							5						8	10				29
1	2				6	3	11			9	12	4	7		13					5						10^2	8^1				30
	2^2		3	12	6		11^1		10	9		4	7		13					5			1			8^3	14				31
	2			12	6	3		8	10		11	4	7			11				5			1				9				32
1	2				6	3			10		11	4	7	8						5							9				33
1	2				6	3			10		11	4	7	8						5							9				34
1	2				6	3			10	9		4	7		12					5							8^1	11			35
1	2				6^2	3			10	9		4	7		12					5		13					8^1	11			36
1	2				6	3			10	9		4	7^1		12					5		13					8^3	11			37
1	2				6	3			10^2	9		4	7					12		5		12				13		11^1	8		38
1	2				6				10	9		4	7^1					3		5		12						11	8		39
1	2				6				10			4	7					3		5						9		11	8		40
1	2				6				10	9		4	7					3^1		5		12				13		11^2	8		41
1	2		3		6				10	9		4	7							5		12						11	8^1		42
1	2		3		6				10	9		4	7							5						11^1		12	8		43
1	2		3		6				12	9		4	13							5		10^1				11^2	7	14	8^3		44
1	2		3	12	6			13		9		4	7^1							5		10^2				11			8		45
1	2		3		6	7^1		13		9		4								5		10				11		12^2	8		46

Coca-Cola Cup

First Round	Doncaster R	(a)	1-1
		(h)	2-0
Second Round	Everton	(a)	1-1
		(h)	3-2
Third Round	Leicester C	(h)	0-2

FA Cup

First Round	Hartlepool U	(a)	0-0
		(h)	3-0
Second Round	Preston NE	(a)	3-2
Third Round	Hednesford T	(a)	0-1

ENGLISH LEAGUE PLAYERS DIRECTORY

*Free transfer, †Non-contract, ‡Registration cancelled, §Trainee/Schoolboy

Player	Ht	Wt	Pos	Birth Date	Birth Place	Source	Clubs	League App	Gls
ARSENAL									
Adams Tony	6 3	13 11	D	10 10 66	London	Apprentice	Arsenal	395	27
Anelka Nicolas	6 0	12 00	F	14 3 79	Versailles		Paris St Germain	10	1
							Arsenal	4	—
Bartram Vince	6 2	13 07	G	7 8 68	Birmingham	Local	Wolverhampton W	5	—
							Blackpool (loan)	9	—
							WBA (loan)	—	—
							Bournemouth	132	—
							Arsenal	11	—
							Wolverhampton W (loan)	—	—
Bergkamp Dennis	6 0	12 05	F	18 5 69	Amsterdam		Ajax	185	103
							Internazionale	52	11
							Arsenal	62	23
Black Michael	5 8	11 08	M	6 10 76	Chigwell	Trainee	Arsenal	—	—
Bould Steve	6 4	14 02	D	16 11 62	Stoke	Apprentice	Stoke C	183	6
							Torquay U (loan)	9	—
							Arsenal	244	5
Clarke Adrian*	5 10	11 00	F	28 9 74	Suffolk	Trainee	Arsenal	7	—
							Rotherham U (loan)	2	—
							Southend U (loan)	7	—
Crowe Jason	5 9	10 09	M	30 9 78	Sidcup	Trainee	Arsenal	—	—
Dixon Lee	5 8	11 08	D	17 3 64	Manchester	Local	Burnley	4	—
							Chester C	16	1
							Chester	41	—
							Bury	45	5
							Stoke C	71	5
							Arsenal	324	20
Garde Remi	5 9	11 07	M	3 4 66	L'Arbresle		Lyon	81	13
							Strasbourg	68	3
							Arsenal	11	—
Gislason Valur	6 1	11 12	M	8 9 77	Reykjavik		Fram	30	2
							Arsenal	—	—
Harper Lee	6 1	13 11	G	30 10 71	London	Sittingbourne	Arsenal	1	—
Helder Glenn	5 11	11 07	F	28 10 68	Leiden		Sparta	93	9
							Vitesse	52	12
							Arsenal	39	3
Hughes Stephen	6 0	12 08	M	18 9 76	Wokingham	Trainee	Arsenal	16	1
Keown Martin	6 1	12 04	D	24 7 66	Oxford	Apprentice	Arsenal	22	0
							Brighton & HA (loan)	16	—
							Brighton & HA (loan)	7	1
							Aston Villa	112	3
							Everton	96	—
							Arsenal	147	2
Kiwomya Chris	5 9	10 07	F	2 12 69	Huddersfield	Trainee	Ipswich T	225	51
							Arsenal	14	3
Lukic John	6 4	13 07	G	11 12 60	Chesterfield	Apprentice	Leeds U	146	—
							Arsenal	223	—
							Leeds U	209	—
							Arsenal	15	—
Macdonald James	6 0	12 05	M	21 2 79	Inverness	Trainee	Arsenal	—	—
Marshall Scott	6 1	12 05	D	1 5 73	Edinburgh	Trainee	Arsenal	21	1
							Rotherham U (loan)	10	1
							Oxford U (loan)	—	—
							Sheffield U (loan)	17	—
McGowan Gavin	5 8	11 07	M	16 1 76	Blackheath	Trainee	Arsenal	5	—
							Luton T (loan)	2	—
Merson Paul	6 0	13 02	F	20 3 68	London	Apprentice	Arsenal	327	78
							Brentford (loan)	7	—
Parlour Ray	5 10	11 12	M	7 3 73	Romford	Trainee	Arsenal	136	6
Platt David	5 10	11 12	M	10 6 66	Chadderton	Chadderton	Manchester U	—	—
							Crewe Alex	134	55
							Aston Villa	121	50
							Bari	29	11
							Juventus	16	3
							Sampdoria	55	17
							Arsenal	57	10
Rankin Isiah	5 10	11 00	F	22 5 78	London	Trainee	Arsenal	—	—
Rose Matthew	5 11	11 01	D	24 9 75	Dartford	Trainee	Arsenal	5	—

(Transferrd to QPR, May 1997)

Name	Ht	Wt	Pos	Birth date	Birthplace	Source	Clubs	Apps	Gls
Seaman David	6 4	14 10	G	19 9 63	Rotherham	Apprentice	Leeds U	—	—
							Peterborough U	91	—
							Birmingham C	75	—
							QPR	141	—
							Arsenal	249	—
Selley Ian	5 9	10 01	M	14 6 74	Chertsey	Trainee	Arsenal	41	—
							Southend U (loan)	4	—
Shaw Paul	5 11	12 02	F	4 9 73	Burnham	Trainee	Arsenal	12	2
							Burnley (loan)	9	4
							Cardiff C (loan)	6	—
							Peterborough U (loan)	12	5
Taylor Ross	5 10	11 12	D	14 1 77	Southend	Trainee	Arsenal	—	—
Upson Matthew	6 1	11 05	D	18 4 79	Eye	Trainee	Luton T	1	—
							Arsenal	—	—
Vieira Patrick	6 4	13 00	M	23 6 76	Dakar		Cannes	49	2
							AC Milan	2	—
							Arsenal	31	2
Wicks Matthew	6 2	13 05	D	8 9 78	Reading	Manchester U	Arsenal	—	—
Winterburn Nigel	5 8	11 04	D	11 12 63	Coventry	Local	Birmingham C	—	—
							Oxford U	—	—
							Wimbledon	165	8
							Arsenal	346	7
Woolsey Jeff*	5 11	12 03	D	8 11 77	Upminster	Trainee	Arsenal	—	—
Wright Ian	5 9	11 08	F	3 11 63	Woolwich	Greenwich Bor	Crystal Palace	225	89
							Arsenal	197	118

Trainees
Black, Thomas R; Bowes, Terence D; Clark, Peter J; Day, James R; Doherty, Lee J; Donaldson, David; Douglas, Andrew R; Gislason, Stefan; Gray, Julian R; Lincoln, Greg D; Livermore, David; McLeod, Allan J; Perna, Ferdinando; Richardson, Lee; Riza, Omer K; Thorogood, Marc T; Vernazza, Paulo A P.

Associated Schoolboys
Bothroyd, Jay; Britton, Leon; Brown, Jermaine A; Chilvers, Liam C; Halls, John; Holsgrove, Peter; Itonga, Carlin D; Noble, David J; Palmer, Marc K; Santry, Steven; Sidwell, Steven J; Stack, Graham.

Associated Schoolboys who have accepted the club's offer of a Traineeship/Contract
Boateng, Daniel; Cole, Ashley; Cowell, Clayden; Harper, James A; Taylor, Stuart J; Weston, Rhys D.

ASTON VILLA

Name	Ht	Wt	Pos	Birth date	Birthplace	Source	Clubs	Apps	Gls
Bosnich Mark	6 1	14 07	G	13 1 72	Fairfield	Croatia Sydney	Manchester U	3	—
							Aston Villa	134	1
Burchell Lee‡	5 7	10 11	M	12 11 76	Birmingham	Trainee	Aston Villa	—	—
Burgess Richard‡	5 8	11 00	F	18 8 78	Bromsgrove	Trainee	Aston Villa	—	—
Byfield Darren	5 11	11 11	F	29 9 76	Birmingham	Trainee	Aston Villa	—	—
Carr Franz‡	5 6	11 10	F	24 9 66	Preston	Apprentice	Blackburn R	—	—
							Nottingham F	131	17
							Sheffield W (loan)	12	—
							West Ham U (loan)	3	—
							Newcastle U	25	3
							Sheffield U	18	4
							Leicester C (loan)	13	1
							Aston Villa	3	—
Charles Gary	5 9	11 03	D	13 4 70	London	Trainee	Nottingham F	56	1
							Leicester C (loan)	8	—
							Derby Co	61	3
							Aston Villa	50	1
Collins Lee	6 1	12 06	D	10 9 77	Birmingham	Trainee	Aston Villa	—	—
Collymore Stan	6 3	14 10	F	22 1 71	Stone	Stafford R	Crystal Palace	20	1
							Southend U	30	15
							Nottingham F	65	41
							Liverpool	61	26
							Aston Villa	—	—
Curcic Sasa	5 9	11 00	M	14 2 72	Belgrade		OFK Belgrade	49	5
							Partizan Belgrade	74	16
							Bolton W	28	4
							Aston Villa	22	—
Davis Neil	5 10	11 07	F	15 8 73	Bloxwich	Redditch U	Aston Villa	2	—
							Wycombe W (loan)	13	—
Draper Mark	5 10	12 04	F	11 11 70	Long Eaton	Trainee	Notts Co	222	40
							Leicester C	39	5
							Aston Villa	65	2
Ehiogu Ugo	6 2	14 10	D	3 11 72	London	Trainee	WBA	2	—
							Aston Villa	142	7
Farrelly Gareth	6 0	12 13	M	28 8 75	Dublin	Home Farm	Aston Villa	8	—
							Rotherham U (loan)	10	2
Hazell Reuben			M	24 4 79	Birmingham	Trainee	Aston Villa	—	—
Hendrie Lee	5 10	10 02	F	18 5 77	Birmingham	Trainee	Aston Villa	7	—
Hines Leslie	5 7	9 10	M	7 1 77	Germany	Trainee	Aston Villa	—	—

Name					Birthplace	Source	Clubs	Apps	Gls
Hughes David	6 4	13 06	D	1 2 78	Wrexham	Trainee	Aston Villa	7	—
Jaszczun Tommy	5 10	10 10	D	16 9 77	Kettering	Trainee	Aston Villa	—	—
Joachim Julian	5 6	12 00	F	20 9 74	Peterborough	Trainee	Leicester C	99	25
							Aston Villa	26	4
Johnson Tommy	5 11	12 07	F	15 1 71	Newcastle	Trainee	Notts Co	118	47
(Transferred to Celtic, March 1997)							Derby Co	98	30
							Aston Villa	57	13
Kirby Alan	5 7	10 06	M	8 9 77	Waterford	Trainee	Aston Villa	—	—
Lee Alan	6 2	13 09	F	21 8 78	Galway	Trainee	Aston Villa	—	—
Lescott Aaron	5 8	10 09	M	1 12 78	Birmingham	Trainee	Aston Villa	—	—
Middleton Darren	6 0	11 05	F	28 12 78	Lichfield	Trainee	Aston Villa	—	—
Miley John‡	6 0	10 08	D	5 9 77	Birmingham	Trainee	Aston Villa	—	—
Milosevic Savo	6 1	13 08	F	2 9 73	Bijelina		Partizan Belgrade	98	64
							Aston Villa	67	21
Murray Scott	5 9	10 12	F	26 5 74	Aberdeen	Fraserburgh	Aston Villa	4	—
Nelson Fernando	5 11	11 08	D	5 11 71	Lisbon		Sporting	115	3
							Aston Villa	34	—
Oakes Michael	6 2	14 07	G	30 10 73	Northwich	Trainee	Aston Villa	20	—
							Scarborough (loan)	1	—
							Tranmere R (loan)	—	—
Petty Ben	6 0	12 05	D	22 3 77	Solihull	Trainee	Aston Villa	—	—
Rachel Adam	5 11	12 08	G	10 12 76	Birmingham	Trainee	Aston Villa	—	—
Scimeca Riccardo	6 1	13 03	D	13 6 75	Leamington Spa	Trainee	Aston Villa	34	—
Southgate Gareth	6 0	12 03	M	3 9 70	Watford	Trainee	Crystal Palace	152	15
							Aston Villa	59	2
Staunton Steve	6 1	12 11	D	19 1 69	Drogheda	Dundalk	Liverpool	65	—
							Bradford C (loan)	8	—
							Aston Villa	181	15
Taylor Ian	6 1	12 00	M	4 6 68	Birmingham	Moor Green	Port Vale	83	28
							Sheffield W	14	1
							Aston Villa	81	6
Townsend Andy	5 11	13 06	M	27 7 63	Maidstone	Weymouth	Southampton	83	5
							Norwich C	71	8
							Chelsea	110	12
							Aston Villa	131	8
Walker Richard	6 0	12 00	F	8 11 77	Birmingham	Trainee	Aston Villa	—	—
Wright Alan	5 4	9 09	D	28 9 71	Ashton under Lyme	Trainee	Blackpool	98	0
							Blackburn R	74	1
							Aston Villa	84	3
Yorke Dwight	5 10	12 03	F	3 11 71	Tobago	St Clair's	Aston Villa	200	61

Trainees
Appleby, Mark; Blackburn, Bradley; Blackwood, Michael; Elias, Phillip; George, Matthew; Hadland, Guy W; Hickman, John A; Meredith, Alex D; Pulisciano, Nathan I; Reece, Dominic M A; Ridley, Martin J; Sheridan, Darragh; Tongue, Philip G; Vassell, Darius.

Associated Schoolboys
Bell, Liam M; Berks, David; Bewers, Jonathan; Britton, Jonathan A; Bull, Nikki; Court, David J; Davenport, Calum R; Folds, Liam J; Halliday, James S; Impey, Daniel; Jackson, Ben P; McConnell, Peter M; Myhill, Boaz G 0; Prosser, Owain M; Pulisciano, Ashley L; Reeves, Martin L; Rhule, Jonathan; Roberts, Matthew; Ryan, Jordan C; Stock, Stephen A; Tranter, Martin; Tucker, Matthew; Watson, Anthony C.

Associated Schoolboys who have accepted the club's offer of a Traineeship/Contract
Evans, Stephen G; Ghent, Matthew I; Harding, David M; Melaugh, Gavin M J; Price, Michael; Thornley, Stuart.

BARNET

Name					Birthplace	Source	Clubs	Apps	Gls
Adams Kieran	5 11	11 03	M	20 10 77	St Ives	Trainee	Barnet	8	—
Brady Matthew	5 11	11 01	M	27 10 77	London	Trainee	Barnet	10	—
Brazil Gary‡	5 10	11 03	F	19 9 62	Tunbridge Wells	Crystal Palace	Sheffield U	62	9
							Port Vale (loan)	6	3
							Preston NE	166	58
							Newcastle U	23	2
							Fulham	213	47
							Cambridge U	1	1
							Barnet	19	2
Campbell Jamie	6 2	13 00	M	21 10 72	Birmingham	Trainee	Luton T	36	1
							Mansfield T (loan)	3	1
							Cambridge U (loan)	12	1
							Barnet	67	5
Constantinou Costas‡			D	24 9 68	Limassol		Barnet	1	—
Devine Sean	6 0	13 08	F	6 9 72	Lewisham	Omonia	Barnet	66	30
Dunwell Richard*	6 1	13 02	F	17 6 71	Islington	Collier Row	Barnet	14	1
Ford John	6 0	12 12	D	12 4 68	Birmingham	Cradley T	Swansea C	160	7
							Bradford C	19	—
							Gillingham	4	—
							Barnet	13	1

Name	Ht	Wt	Pos	Date	Birthplace	Source	Clubs	Apps	Gls
Gale Shaun	6 1	12 02	D	8 10 69	Reading	Trainee	Portsmouth	3	—
							Barnet	114	5
Goodhind Warren	5 11	11 02	D	16 8 77	Johannesburg	Trainee	Barnet	3	—
Hamlet Alan‡	6 0	11 03	D	30 9 77	Watford	Trainee	Barnet	3	—
Hardyman Paul	5 7	12 03	D	11 3 64	Portsmouth	Waterford	Portsmouth	117	3
							Sunderland	106	9
							Bristol R	67	5
							Wycombe W	15	—
							Barnet	16	2
Harrison Lee	6 2	12 08	G	12 9 71	Billericay	Trainee	Charlton Ath	—	—
							Fulham (loan)	—	—
							Gillingham (loan)	2	—
							Fulham (loan)	—	—
							Fulham	12	—
							Barnet	21	—
Hodges Lee	6 0	12 00	F	4 9 73	Epping	Trainee	Tottenham H	4	—
							Plymouth Arg (loan)	7	2
							Wycombe W (loan)	4	—
							Barnet	105	26
Howarth Lee	6 3	13 09	D	3 1 68	Bolton	Chorley	Peterborough U	62	—
							Mansfield T	57	2
							Barnet	57	1
McDonald David	5 10	12 11	D	2 1 71	Dublin	Trainee	Tottenham H	2	—
							Gillingham (loan)	10	—
							Bradford C (loan)	7	—
							Reading (loan)	11	—
							Peterborough U	29	—
							Barnet	95	—
Mills Danny	5 11	11 07	M	13 2 75	Sidcup	Trainee	Charlton Ath	—	—
							Barnet	21	—
Ndah Jamie*	6 2	12 07	F	5 8 71	East Dulwich	Kingstonian	Torquay U	28	4
							Barnet	14	4
Pardew Alan*	6 1	12 07	M	18 7 61	Wimbledon	Yeovil T	Crystal Palace	128	8
							Charlton Ath	104	24
							Barnet	67	—
Pearce Lee‡			M	22 11 77	Hammersmith	Trainee	Barnet	—	—
Primus Linvoy	6 0	13 07	D	14 9 73	Stratford	Trainee	Charlton Ath	4	—
							Barnet	127	7
Rattray Kevin	5 11	11 02	M	6 10 68	London	Woking	Gillingham	26	3
							Barnet	9	—
Samuels Dean	5 10	12 06	F	29 3 73	Hackney	Boreham Wood	Barnet	17	1
Simpson Phil	5 9	11 01	M	18 10 69	London	Stevenage Bor	Barnet	56	3
Stockley Sam	5 8	11 00	D	5 9 77	Tiverton	Trainee	Southampton	—	—
							Barnet	21	—
Thompson Neil*	5 9	12 04	D	30 4 78	Hackney	Trainee	Barnet	3	—
Tomlinson Micky	5 8	11 00	M	15 9 72	Lambeth	Trainee	Leyton Orient	14	1
							Barnet	93	4
Wilson Paul	5 10	11 02	M	29 9 64	London	Barking	Barnet	174	16

Trainees
Beverstock, Paul R; Coggon, Simon J; Constantinou, Anthony; Cowen, Benjamin J; Galloway, Neil J; Harvey, Michael J; Jones, Stavros; Keilty, Paul R; McMenemy, Thomas; Osbourne, Dion R; Webb, Adam J.

BARNSLEY

Name	Ht	Wt	Pos	Date	Birthplace	Source	Clubs	Apps	Gls
Appleby Matty	5 7	11 04	D	16 4 72	Middlesbrough	Trainee	Newcastle U	20	—
							Darlington (loan)	10	1
							Darlington	79	7
							Barnsley	35	—
Beckett Duane	5 8	10 11	D	31 1 78	Sheffield	Trainee	Barnsley	—	—
Beckett Luke	5 11	11 02	F	25 11 76	Sheffield	Trainee	Barnsley	—	—
Bennett Troy*	5 9	11 13	M	25 12 75	Barnsley	Trainee	Barnsley	2	—
							Scarborough (loan)	5	1
Bosancic Jovo	5 11	12 04	M	7 8 70	Novi Sad	Uniao Madeira	Barnsley	25	1
Bullock Antony	6 1	13 08	G	18 2 72	Warrington	Leek T	Barnsley	—	—
Bullock Martin	5 4	10 09	M	5 3 75	Derby	Eastwood T	Barnsley	98	1
Clyde Darron‡	6 4	11 13	D	26 3 76	Limavady	Trainee	Barnsley	—	—
Davis Steve	5 11	12 12	D	26 7 65	Birmingham	Stoke C	Crewe Alex	145	1
							Burnley	147	11
							Barnsley	107	10
De Zeeuw Arjan	6 1	13 03	D	16 4 70	Castricum	Vitesse 22	Telstar	102	5
							Barnsley	74	3
Eaden Nicky	5 8	11 09	D	12 12 72	Sheffield	Trainee	Barnsley	176	8

Fleming Gary‡	5 7	11 09	D	17 2 67	Derry	Apprentice	Nottingham F	74	0
							Manchester C	14	—
							Notts Co (loan)	3	—
							Barnsley	239	—
Gregory Andrew	5 8	10 09	M	8 10 76	Barnsley	Trainee	Barnsley	—	—
Hendrie John	5 7	11 12	F	24 10 63	Lennoxtown	Apprentice	Coventry C	21	2
							Hereford U (loan)	6	—
							Bradford C	173	46
							Newcastle U	34	4
							Leeds U	27	5
							Middlesbrough	192	44
							Barnsley	36	15
Hume Mark	6 2	11 11	D	21 5 78	Barnsley	Trainee	Barnsley	—	—
Hurst Glynn‡	5 10	11 06	F	17 1 76	Barnsley	Tottenham H	Barnsley	8	—
							Swansea C (loan)	2	1
							Mansfield T (loan)	6	—
Jackson Chris	5 9	11 06	F	16 1 76	Barnsley	Trainee	Barnsley	23	2
Jones Dean	6 1	12 03	D	12 10 77	Barnsley	Trainee	Barnsley	—	—
Jones Scott	5 10	11 06	D	1 5 75	Sheffield	Trainee	Barnsley	22	—
Liddell Andrew	5 6	10 09	F	28 6 73	Leeds	Trainee	Barnsley	164	33
Marcelle Clint	5 4	10 00	F	9 11 68	Port of Spain		Falgueiras	21	0
							Barnsley	40	8
McClare Sean	5 9	10 13	M	12 1 78	Rotherham	Trainee	Barnsley	—	—
Morgan Chris	5 10	11 11	D	13 2 78	Barnsley	Trainee	Barnsley	—	—
Moses Adrian	5 10	12 08	D	4 5 75	Doncaster	School	Barnsley	56	3
Perry Jonathan	6 0	11 11	D	22 11 76	Hamilton	Trainee	Barnsley	—	—
Prendergast Rory	5 8	12 00	F	6 4 78	Pontefract	Rochdale	Barnsley	—	—
Redfearn Neil	5 8	12 00	M	20 6 65	Dewsbury	Nottingham F	Bolton W	35	1
							Lincoln C (loan)	10	1
							Lincoln C	90	12
							Doncaster R	46	14
							Crystal Palace	57	10
							Watford	24	3
							Oldham Ath	62	16
							Barnsley	255	61
Regis Dave	6 0	13 08	F	3 3 64	Paddington	Barnet	Notts Co	46	15
							Plymouth Arg	31	4
							Bournemouth (loan)	6	2
							Stoke C	63	15
							Birmingham C	6	2
							Southend U	38	9
							Barnsley	16	1
							Peterborough U (loan)	7	1
							Notts Co (loan)	10	2
Rose Karl	5 8	10 08	F	12 10 78	Barnsley		Barnsley	—	—
Sheridan Darren	5 4	10 12	D	8 12 67	Manchester	Winsford U	Barnsley	120	4
Shirtliff Peter*	6 1	12 02	D	6 4 61	Sheffield	Apprentice	Sheffield W	188	4
							Charlton Ath	103	7
							Sheffield W	104	4
							Wolverhampton W	69	—
							Barnsley	45	—
							Carlisle U (loan)	5	—
Sollitt Adam*	6 0	10 09	G	22 6 77	Sheffield	Trainee	Barnsley	—	—
Ten-Heuvel Laurens	6 0	12 01	F	6 6 76	Duivendrecht	Den Bosch	Barnsley	6	—
Thompson Neil	6 0	13 05	D	2 10 63	Beverley	Nottingham F	Hull C	31	—
						Scarborough	Scarborough	87	15
							Ipswich T	206	19
							Barnsley	24	5
Van der Velden Carel	5 11	13 08	M	3 8 72	Arnheim	Den Bosch	Barnsley	9	—
Watson David	5 11	12 03	G	10 11 73	Barnsley	Trainee	Barnsley	142	—
Wilkinson Paul	6 1	11 10	F	30 10 64	Louth	Apprentice	Grimsby T	71	27
							Everton	31	7
							Nottingham F	34	5
							Watford	134	52
							Middlesbrough	166	49
							Oldham Ath (loan)	4	1
							Watford (loan)	4	—
							Luton T (loan)	3	—
							Barnsley	45	9
Wilson Danny‡	5 6	11 00	M	1 1 60	Wigan	Wigan Ath	Bury	90	8
							Chesterfield	100	13
							Nottingham F	10	1
							Scunthorpe U (loan)	6	3
							Brighton & HA	135	33
							Luton T	110	24
							Sheffield W	98	11
							Barnsley	77	2

Trainees
Bagshaw, Paul J; Bassinder, Gavin D; Butler, Ian M; Clyde, Glynn N; Coleano, Rudi A; Cross, Matthew F; Harris, Christopher; Heckingbottom, Marc; Hulson, Shane E; Kennedy, Paul J; Shenton, Daniel R; Smith, Andrew A; Taylor, David J; Wood, James; Young, Mark.

Non-Contract
Shotton, Malcolm.

Associated Schoolboys
Barraclough, Carl; Bird, Martin P; Dixon, Lee; Donoghue, Matthew J; Greensmith, Adam A; Horbury, Russell; Kay, Antony R; Kirby, Jonathan; Marsh, Adam; O'Connor, Kevin; Pressley, Mark; Reece, Gary L; Richards, Duncan; Toone, Leigh S.

Associated Schoolboys who have accepted the club's offer of a Traineeship/Contract
Cataroche, David; Goodyear, Craig; Jackson, Paul S; Sidebottom, Frazer; Wilkinson, Craig.

BIRMINGHAM CITY

Name				DOB	Birthplace	Signed from	Club	Apps	Gls
Ablett Gary	6 0	11 04	D	19 11 65	Liverpool	Apprentice	Liverpool	109	1
							Derby Co (loan)	6	—
							Hull C (loan)	5	—
							Everton	128	5
							Sheffield U (loan)	12	—
							Birmingham C	42	1
Barnes Steve	5 4	10 05	F	5 1 76	Wembley	Welling U	Birmingham C	3	—
Barnett Dave‡	6 0	13 00	D	16 4 67	London	Windsor & Eton	Colchester U	20	0
							WBA	—	—
							Walsall	5	—
					Kidderminster H	Barnet	59	3
							Birmingham C	46	—
Bass Jonathan	6 0	12 02	D	1 1 76	Weston-Super-Mare	Trainee	Birmingham C	18	—
							Carlisle U (loan)	3	—
Bennett Ian	6 0	12 10	G	10 10 71	Worksop	Newcastle U	Peterborough U	72	—
							Birmingham C	132	—
Bowen Jason	5 6	11 00	M	24 8 72	Merthyr	Trainee	Swansea C	124	26
							Birmingham C	48	7
Brown Kenny	5 8	11 06	D	11 7 67	Upminster	Apprentice	Norwich C	25	—
							Plymouth Arg	126	4
							West Ham U	63	5
							Huddersfield T (loan)	5	—
							Reading (loan)	12	1
							Southend U (loan)	6	—
							Crystal Palace (loan)	6	2
							Reading (loan)	5	—
							Birmingham C	11	—
Bruce Steve	6 0	12 06	D	31 12 60	Corbridge	Apprentice	Gillingham	205	29
							Norwich C	141	14
							Manchester U	309	36
							Birmingham C	32	—
Devlin Paul	5 8	11 05	F	14 4 72	Birmingham	Stafford R	Notts Co	141	25
							Birmingham C	54	23
Dukes Lee			M	24 10 79	Walsall	Trainee	Birmingham C	—	—
Dyer Wayne‡	6 0	10 00	F	24 11 77	Birmingham	Trainee	Birmingham C	—	—
Forster Nicky	5 9	11 05	F	8 9 73	Caterham	Horley T	Gillingham	67	24
							Brentford	109	39
							Birmingham C	7	3
Francis Delton‡	5 9	11 04	F	12 3 78	Birmingham	Trainee	Birmingham C	—	—
Francis Kevin	6 7	15 08	F	6 12 67	Moseley	Mile Oak R	Derby Co	10	0
							Stockport Co	152	88
							Birmingham C	53	12
Furlong Paul	6 0	11 00	F	1 10 68	London	Enfield	Coventry C	37	4
							Watford	79	37
							Chelsea	64	13
							Birmingham C	43	10
Grainger Martin	5 10	11 07	D	23 8 72	Enfield	Trainee	Colchester U	46	7
							Brentford	101	12
							Birmingham C	31	3
Hatton Paul	6 0	11 00	F	2 11 78	Kidderminster	Trainee	Birmingham C	—	—
Hinton Craig	5 11	11 00	D	26 11 77	Wolverhampton	Trainee	Birmingham C	—	—
Holland Chris	5 9	11 05	M	11 9 75	Whalley	Trainee	Preston NE	1	—
							Newcastle U	3	—
							Birmingham C	32	—
Horne Barry	5 10	12 03	M	18 5 62	St Asaph	Rhyl	Wrexham	136	17
							Portsmouth	70	7
							Southampton	112	6
							Everton	123	3
							Birmingham C	33	—
Hughes Bryan	5 9	10 00	M	19 6 76	Liverpool	Trainee	Wrexham	94	12
							Birmingham C	11	—

Hunt Jonathan	5 10	11 00	M	2 11 71	London	Slough T	Barnet	33	—
							Southend U	49	6
							Birmingham C	77	18
Johnson Michael	5 11	11 00	D	4 7 73	Nottingham	Trainee	Notts Co	107	—
							Birmingham C	68	—
Legg Andy	6 0	12 10	M	28 7 66	Neath	Briton Ferry	Swansea C	163	29
							Notts Co	89	9
							Birmingham C	45	5
Limpar Anders‡	5 8	11 02	F	24 9 65	Solna		Brommapojkarna	77	12
							Orgryte	47	9
							Young Boys	17	6
							Cremonese	24	3
							Arsenal	96	17
							Everton	66	5
							Birmingham C	4	—
McKenzie Christy‡	5 11	11 07	F	26 2 78	Birmingham	Trainee	Birmingham C	—	—
Muir Ian‡	5 8	11 00	F	5 5 63	Coventry	Apprentice	QPR	2	2
							Burnley (loan)	2	1
							Birmingham C	1	—
							Brighton & HA	4	—
							Swindon T (loan)	2	—
							Tranmere R	314	141
							Birmingham C	1	—
							Darlington (loan)	4	1
Newell Mike	6 0	13 00	F	27 1 65	Liverpool	Liverpool	Crewe Alex	3	—
							Wigan Ath	72	25
							Luton T	63	18
							Leicester C	81	21
							Everton	68	15
							Blackburn R	130	28
							Birmingham C	15	1
							West Ham U (loan)	7	—
							Bradford C (loan)	7	—
O'Connor Martin	5 8	10 08	M	10 12 67	Walsall	Bromsgrove R	Crystal Palace	2	—
							Walsall (loan)	10	1
							Walsall	94	21
							Peterborough U	18	3
							Birmingham C	24	4
Otto Ricky	5 10	11 00	M	9 11 67	Hackney	Dartford	Leyton Orient	56	13
							Southend U	64	17
							Birmingham C	46	6
							Charlton Ath (loan)	7	—
							Peterborough U (loan)	15	4
Rea Simon	6 1	13 00	D	20 9 76	Coventry	Trainee	Birmingham C	1	—
Robinson Steve	5 9	11 00	M	17 10 75	Nottingham	Trainee	Birmingham C	15	—
							Peterborough U (loan)	5	—
Sutton Steve‡	6 1	14 00	G	16 4 61	Hartington	Apprentice	Nottingham F	199	—
							Mansfield T (loan)	8	—
							Derby Co (loan)	14	—
							Coventry C (loan)	1	—
							Luton T (loan)	14	—
							Derby Co	61	—
							Reading (loan)	2	—
							Birmingham C	6	—
Tait Paul	6 1	10 07	M	31 7 71	Sutton	Trainee	Birmingham C	170	14
							Millwall (loan)	—	—
Webb Matthew‡	5 8	9 12	M	24 9 76	Bristol	Trainee	Birmingham C	1	—

Trainees
Burden, Neil S; Butler, Stuart; Crockett, Daniel J; Dodd, Andrew J; Dyson, James G; Higgs, Andrew I; Homer, Paul L; Ingram, Mark A; Jones, Mark A; Lutz, Steven G; Powell, Jason D; Sandland, Paul N; White, Paul.

Associated Schoolboys
Cozens, Leon; Danquah, Kwabena A; Dunn, Matthew J; Feely, Michael D; Hilton, Ashley J; Lloyd, Spencer J; McLinden, Andrew J; Rose, Michael J.

Associated Schoolboys who have accepted the club's offer of a Traineeship/Contract
Bowden, Christopher J; Burns, Robert J; Johnson, Andrew; Lanns, Jason M.

BLACKBURN ROVERS

Beattie James	6 1	12 00	F	27 2 78	Lancaster	Trainee	Blackburn R	1	—
Benson Mark	5 5	10 05	D	7 8 78	Dublin	Trainee	Blackburn R	—	—
Berg Henning	6 0	12 04	D	1 9 68	Eidsvoll	Lillestrom	Blackburn R	159	4
Bohinen Lars	6 1	12 01	M	8 9 69	Vadso		Valerengen	33	5
							Viking	10	—
							Young Boys	58	6
							Nottingham F	64	7
							Blackburn R	42	6
Brewer Ben			D	6 10 78	Pontypool	Trainee	Blackburn R	—	—

Name	Ht	Wt	Pos	Born	Birthplace	Source	Club	Apps	Gls
Broomes Marlon	6 0	12 12	D	28 11 77	Birmingham	Trainee	Blackburn R	—	—
							Swindon T (loan)	12	1
Brown John			D	24 12 79	Edinburgh		Blackburn R	—	—
Cassin Graham	5 10	11 07	F	24 3 78	Dublin	Belvedere	Blackburn R	—	—
Chisholm Craig*	5 11	10 08	M	21 9 77	Glasgow	Trainee	Blackburn R	—	—
Coleman Chris	6 2	14 03	D	10 6 70	Swansea	Apprentice	Swansea C	160	2
							Crystal Palace	154	13
							Blackburn R	28	—
Coughlan Graham	6 2	13 04	D	18 11 74	Dublin	Bray Wanderers	Blackburn R	—	—
							Swindon T (loan)	3	—
Croft Gary	5 9	11 08	D	17 2 74	Stafford	Trainee	Grimsby T	149	3
							Blackburn R	5	—
Donis George	6 0		M	29 10 69	Greece		Yannina	22	3
							Panathinaikos	136	34
							Blackburn R	22	2
Duff Damien	5 10	9 07	F	2 3 79	Ballyboden		Blackburn R	1	—
Fenton Graham	5 10	12 10	F	22 5 74	Wallsend	Trainee	Aston Villa	32	3
							WBA (loan)	7	3
							Blackburn R	27	7
Fitzpatrick Lee			M	31 10 78	Manchester	Trainee	Blackburn R	—	—
Flitcroft Garry	6 0	12 09	M	6 11 72	Bolton	Trainee	Manchester C	115	13
							Bury (loan)	12	—
							Blackburn R	31	3
Flowers Tim	6 3	14 04	G	3 2 67	Kenilworth	Apprentice	Wolverhampton W	63	—
							Southampton (loan)	—	—
							Southampton	192	—
							Swindon T (loan)	2	—
							Swindon T (loan)	5	—
							Blackburn R	141	—
Gallacher Kevin	5 8	11 03	F	23 11 66	Clydebank	Duntocher BC	Dundee U	131	27
							Coventry C	100	28
							Blackburn R	90	25
Gill Wayne	5 10	11 04	M	28 11 75	Chorley	Trainee	Blackburn R	—	—
Given Shay	6 1	12 10	G	20 4 76	Lifford	Celtic	Blackburn R	2	—
							Swindon T (loan)	—	—
							Swindon T (loan)	5	—
							Sunderland (loan)	17	—
Gudmundsson Niklas	5 11	12 01	F	29 2 72	Sweden		Halmstad	141	46
							Blackburn R	6	—
							Ipswich T (loan)	8	2
Hendry Colin	6 1	12 07	D	7 12 65	Keith	Islavale	Dundee	41	2
							Blackburn R	102	22
							Manchester C	63	5
							Blackburn R	200	11
Hitchen Steve*	5 10	11 04	D	28 11 76	Salford	Trainee	Blackburn R	—	—
Holmes Matt	5 7	11 00	F	1 8 69	Luton	Trainee	Bournemouth	114	8
							Cardiff C (loan)	1	—
							West Ham U	76	4
							Blackburn R	9	1
Johnson Damien	5 9	10 00	M	18 11 78	Blackburn	Trainee	Blackburn R	—	—
Kenna Jeff	5 11	12 03	D	28 8 70	Dublin	Trainee	Southampton	114	4
							Blackburn R	78	1
Le Saux Graeme	5 10	12 02	D	17 10 68	Jersey	St Pauls	Chelsea	90	8
							Blackburn R	129	7
Malone Chris‡	5 11	10 02	F	29 12 75	Drogheda		Blackburn R	—	—
Marker Nicky	6 0	13 00	D	3 5 65	Exeter	Apprentice	Exeter C	202	3
							Plymouth Arg	202	13
							Blackburn R	54	1
McCallion Edward			D	25 1 79	Derry		Blackburn R	—	—
McCrone Chris*	6 1	12 07	G	5 2 77	Preston	Trainee	Blackburn R	—	—
McKinlay Billy	5 8	11 04	M	22 4 69	Glasgow	Hamilton Th	Dundee U	222	23
							Blackburn R	44	3
Morgan Thomas*	5 8	10 08	M	30 3 77	Dublin	Belvedere	Blackburn R	—	—
Pearce Ian	6 4	14 04	D	7 5 74	Bury St Edmunds	Schoolboy	Chelsea	4	—
							Blackburn R	57	2
Pedersen Per	5 11	13 05	F	30 3 69	Aalborg		Odense	44	16
							Lyngby	96	38
							Odense	49	27
							Blackburn R	11	1
Reed Adam	6 0	11 00	D	18 2 75	Bishop Auckland	Trainee	Darlington	52	1
							Blackburn R	—	—
							Darlington (loan)	14	—
Ripley Stuart	6 0	13 00	F	20 11 67	Middlesbrough	Apprentice	Middlesbrough	249	26
							Bolton W (loan)	5	1
							Blackburn R	158	11

Name	Ht	Wt	Pos	Birthdate	Birthplace	Source	Club	Apps	Gls
Ryan Ciaran			D	3 9 79	Dublin	Trainee	Blackburn R	—	—
Sherwood Tim	6 1	12 09	M	2 2 69	St Albans	Trainee	Watford	32	2
							Norwich C	71	10
							Blackburn R	196	17
Staton Luke	5 7	9 10	M	10 3 79	Doncaster	Trainee	Blackburn R	—	—
Stewart Gareth			G	3 2 80	Preston	Trainee	Blackburn R	—	—
Sutton Chris	6 3	13 07	F	10 3 73	Nottingham	Trainee	Norwich C	102	35
							Blackburn R	78	26
Thomas James			F	16 1 79	Swansea	Trainee	Blackburn R	—	—
Warhurst Paul	6 0	11 04	D	26 9 69	Stockport	Trainee	Manchester C	—	—
							Oldham Ath	67	2
							Sheffield W	66	6
							Blackburn R	57	4
Whealing Anthony	5 9	10 02	D	3 9 76	Manchester	Trainee	Blackburn R	—	—
Wilcox Jason	6 0	11 00	F	15 7 71	Bolton	Trainee	Blackburn R	188	24
Williams Anthony			G	20 9 77		Trainee	Blackburn R	—	—
Worrell David	5 10	11 08	D	12 1 78	Dublin	Trainee	Blackburn R	—	—

Trainees
Berry, Adam; Connolly, Patrick J; Dunn, David J I; Featherstone, James L; Harding, John M; Lomax, Michael J; McAvoy, Andrew D; Obeng, Junior L; Owler, Lee R; Richards, Ian; Richardson, Leam N; Scates, Garth; Taylor, Martin; Trudgill, Paul C; Watkins, Steven L; Whittle, Christopher T; Woodfield, Craig M.

Associated Schoolboys
Emmerson, Scott; Hardy, Lee; Hevicon, Ryan; Howson, Stuart L; Moore, Gary L; Stainsby, James H; Woodhead, Robert A.

Associated Schoolboys who have accepted the club's offer of a Traineeship/Contract
Baldacchino, Ryan L; Dunning, Darren; Dunning, Richard; Hawe, Steven J; Topley, Jonathan W.

BLACKPOOL

Name	Ht	Wt	Pos	Birthdate	Birthplace	Source	Club	Apps	Gls
Allardyce Craig‡	6 3	13 01	D	9 6 75	Bolton	Trainee	Preston NE	1	—
							Blackpool	1	—
Banks Steve	6 0	13 02	G	9 2 72	Hillingdon	Trainee	West Ham U	—	—
							Gillingham	67	—
							Blackpool	70	—
Barlow Andy*	5 9	11 01	D	24 11 65	Oldham		Oldham Ath	261	5
							Bradford C (loan)	2	—
							Blackpool	80	2
Bonner Mark	5 10	11 00	M	7 6 74	Ormskirk	Trainee	Blackpool	146	11
Brabin Gary	5 11	14 08	M	9 2 70	Liverpool	Trainee Runcorn	Stockport Co	2	—
							Doncaster R	59	11
							Bury	5	—
							Blackpool	32	2
Bradshaw Darren	5 11	11 04	D	19 3 67	Sheffield	Matlock T	Chesterfield	18	—
							York C	59	3
							Newcastle U	38	—
							Peterborough U	73	1
							Plymouth Arg (loan)	6	1
							Blackpool	61	1
Bryan Marvin	6 0	12 02	D	2 8 75	Paddington	Trainee	QPR	—	—
							Doncaster R (loan)	5	1
							Blackpool	80	2
Butler Tony	6 2	12 00	D	28 9 72	Stockport	Trainee	Gillingham	148	5
							Blackpool	42	—
Carden Paul§	5 8	11 10	F	29 3 79	Liverpool	Trainee	Blackpool	1	—
Clarkson Phil	5 10	12 05	M	13 11 68	Hambleton	Fleetwood T	Crewe Alex	98	27
							Scunthorpe U	52	19
							Blackpool	17	5
Darton Scott*	5 11	11 02	M	27 3 75	Ipswich	Trainee	WBA	15	—
							Blackpool	42	1
Dixon Ben	6 1	11 00	D	16 9 74	Lincoln	Trainee	Lincoln C	43	—
							Blackpool	11	—
Ellis Tony	5 11	11 00	F	20 10 64	Salford	Northwich Vic	Oldham Ath	8	—
							Preston NE	86	26
							Stoke C	77	19
							Preston NE	72	48
							Blackpool	128	46
Hooks John‡	5 8	11 07	D	10 2 77	Armagh	Southampton	Blackpool	—	—
Linighan David	6 2	12 06	D	9 1 65	Hartlepool	Local	Hartlepool U	91	5
							Leeds U (loan)	—	—
							Derby Co	—	—
							Shrewsbury T	65	1
							Ipswich T	277	12
							Blackpool	71	5
Lydiate Jason	5 11	12 03	D	29 10 71	Manchester	Trainee	Manchester U	—	—
							Bolton W	30	—
							Blackpool	63	1

Malkin Chris	6 3	12 09	F	4 6 67	Hoylake	Overpool	Tranmere R	232	60
							Millwall	52	14
							Blackpool	15	3
Mellon Micky	5 9	11 03	M	18 3 72	Paisley	Trainee	Bristol C	35	1
							WBA	45	6
							Blackpool	114	14
Onwere Udo*	6 0	11 07	M	9 11 71	Hammersmith	Trainee	Fulham	85	7
							Lincoln C	43	4
							Blackpool	9	—
Ormerod Brett	5 11	11 04	F	18 10 76	Blackburn	Accrington S	Blackpool	4	—
Parks Tony*	5 10	11 05	G	28 1 63	Hackney		Tottenham H	37	0
							Oxford U (loan)	5	—
							Gillingham (loan)	2	—
							Brentford	71	—
							QPR (loan)	—	—
							Fulham	2	—
							West Ham U	6	—
							Stoke C	2	—
							Falkirk	112	—
							Blackpool	—	—
Phelan Mike†	5 11	11 01	D	24 9 62	Nelson	Apprentice	Burnley	168	9
							Norwich C	156	9
							Manchester U	102	2
							WBA	21	—
							Blackpool	—	—
Philpott Lee	5 9	11 08	M	21 2 70	Barnet	Trainee	Peterborough U	4	—
							Cambridge U	134	17
							Leicester C	75	3
							Blackpool	36	3
Preece Andy	6 1	12 00	F	27 3 67	Evesham	Evesham U	Northampton T	1	—
						Worcester C	Wrexham	51	7
							Stockport Co	97	42
							Crystal Palace	20	4
							Blackpool	82	24
Quinn James	6 1	12 10	F	15 12 74	Coventry	Trainee	Birmingham C	4	—
							Blackpool	137	33
							Stockport Co (loan)	1	—
Russell Keith	5 10	12 00	M	31 1 74	Aldridge	Hednesford T	Blackpool	1	—
Symons Paul*	5 10	11 03	F	20 4 76	North Shields	Trainee	Blackpool	1	—
Thorpe Lee*	6 0	11 06	F	14 12 75	Wolverhampton	Trainee	Blackpool	12	—

Trainees
Ashcroft, Paul R; Best, Christopher J; Carden, Paul; Carlisle, Clarke J; Cross, James R; Greer, Matthew J; Haddow, Paul A; Hall, Gary A; Heighton, Henry P; Jarrett, Jason L M; Longworth, Steven P; Pepper, Carl; Seaton, Simon J; Shockledge, Lee S; Skeoch, Jamie A; Talbot, Robert T.

Non-Contract
Phelan, Michael C.

Associated Schoolboys
Blinkhorn, Craig L; Bridges, Simon; Coid, Daniel J; Connell, Darren; Crumblehulme, Daniel J; Ellison, Gavin; Munday, Jason; Nicholson, Kevin J; Porter, Benjamin T; Sidebotham, Paul; Singleton, Richard P; Smith, Robert.

Associated Schoolboys who have accepted the club's offer of a Traineeship/Contract
Bamber, Michael J; Dickinson, Ian J; Ellis, Christopher; Lazenby, Mark; Nowland, Adam C; Robinson, Philip D; Thompson, Philip.

BOLTON WANDERERS

Aljofree Hasney	6 0	12 01	D	11 7 78	Manchester	Trainee	Bolton W	—	—
Bergsson Gudni	6 1	12 03	D	21 7 65	Reykjavik	Valur	Tottenham H	71	2
							Bolton W	75	7
Blake Nathan	5 11	13 12	F	27 1 72	Cardiff	Chelsea	Cardiff C	131	35
							Sheffield U	69	34
							Bolton W	60	20
Branagan Keith	6 0	13 02	G	10 7 66	Fulham		Cambridge U	110	—
							Millwall	46	—
							Brentford (loan)	2	—
							Gillingham (loan)	1	—
							Fulham (loan)	—	—
							Bolton W	166	—
Coleman Simon	6 0	10 08	D	13 6 68	Worksop	Apprentice	Mansfield T	96	7
							Middlesbrough	55	2
							Derby Co	70	2
							Sheffield W	16	1
							Bolton W	34	5
Fairclough Chris	5 11	11 02	D	12 4 64	Nottingham	Apprentice	Nottingham F	107	1
							Tottenham H	60	5
							Leeds U	193	21
							Bolton W	79	8
Feeney Gareth*			M	5 12 78	Manchester	Trainee	Bolton W	—	—

Name			Pos	DOB	Birthplace	Source	Clubs	Apps	Gls
Frandsen Per	6 1	12 06	M	6 2 70	Copenhagen	B 1903	Lille	109	19
							FC Copenhagen	55	19
							Bolton W	41	5
Green Scott	5 10	12 05	M	15 1 70	Walsall	Trainee	Derby Co	—	—
							Bolton W	220	25
Johansen Michael	5 6	10 05	M	22 7 72	Golstrup		KB Copenhagen	15	1
							B 1903	26	1
							FC Copenhagen	114	17
							Bolton W	33	5
Lee David	5 7	11 00	M	5 11 67	Whitefield	Blackburn Schools	Bury	208	35
							Southampton	20	—
							Bolton W	155	17
Marsh Neil*			D	9 9 77	Warrington	Trainee	Bolton W	—	—
McAnespie Steve	5 9	10 07	D	1 2 72	Kilmarnock	Vasterhauringe	Raith R	40	—
							Bolton W	22	—
McGinlay John	5 9	11 04	F	8 4 64	Inverness	Elgin C	Shrewsbury T	60	27
							Bury	25	9
							Millwall	34	10
							Bolton W	185	87
Paatelainen Mixu	6 0	13 11	F	3 2 67	Helsinki	Valkeakosken Haka	Dundee U	133	33
							Aberdeen	75	23
							Bolton W	69	15
Phillips Jimmy	6 0	12 07	D	8 2 66	Bolton	Apprentice	Bolton W	108	2
							Rangers	25	—
							Oxford U	79	8
							Middlesbrough	139	6
							Bolton W	161	1
Pollock Jamie	5 10	14 00	M	16 2 74	Stockton	Trainee	Middlesbrough	155	17
							Osasuna	—	—
							Bolton W	20	4
Quinn Stephen*			M	8 3 78	Manchester	Trainee	Bolton W	—	—
Sellars Scott	5 7	9 10	M	27 11 65	Sheffield	Apprentice	Leeds U	76	12
							Blackburn R	202	35
							Leeds U	7	—
							Newcastle U	61	5
							Bolton W	64	11
Sheridan John	5 10	12 01	M	1 10 64	Stretford	Local	Leeds U	230	47
							Nottingham F	—	—
							Sheffield W	197	25
							Birmingham C (loan)	2	—
							Bolton W	20	2
Small Bryan	5 9	11 09	D	15 11 71	Birmingham	Trainee	Aston Villa	36	—
							Birmingham C (loan)	3	—
							Bolton W	12	—
Spooner Nicky	5 10	11 09	D	5 6 71	Manchester	Trainee	Bolton W	23	2
Strong Greg	6 2	11 12	D	5 9 75	Bolton	Trainee	Wigan Ath	35	3
							Bolton W	1	—
Taggart Gerry	6 1	12 03	D	18 10 70	Belfast	Trainee	Manchester C	12	1
							Barnsley	212	16
							Bolton W	54	4
Taylor Scott	5 10	11 04	F	5 5 76	Chertsey	Staines	Millwall	28	—
							Bolton W	12	1
Thompson Alan	6 0	12 08	M	22 12 73	Newcastle	Trainee	Newcastle U	16	—
							Bolton W	124	24
Todd Andy	5 10	10 11	D	21 9 74	Derby	Trainee	Middlesbrough	8	—
							Swindon T (loan)	13	—
							Bolton W	27	2
Ward Gavin	6 3	14 05	G	30 6 70	Sutton Coldfield	Aston Villa	Shrewsbury T	—	—
							WBA	—	—
							Cardiff C	59	—
							Leicester C	38	—
							Bradford C	36	—
							Bolton W	16	—
Westhead Mark*			G	19 7 75	Blackpool		Bolton W	—	—
Whitehead Stuart	5 11	12 04	M	17 7 76	Bromsgrove	Bromsgrove R	Bolton W	—	—
Whittaker Stuart*	5 7	9 03	M	2 1 75	Liverpool	Liverpool	Bolton W	3	5
							Wigan Ath (loan)	3	—
Xiourouppa Costas			F	11 9 79	Dudley	Trainee	Bolton W	—	—

Trainees

Corrigan, Noel P; Dawson, Christopher J; Doherty, Martin A; Fagan, Steven J; Glennon, Mathew W; Haley, Craig; Hallatt, Christopher; Holden, Dean T J; Marston, Neil J; McCleave, Michael J; McLeod, James; Minchella, Marco; Morrison, Peter A; Potter, Lee; Pryers, Lee M; Truman, Kevin M.

Associated Schoolboys
Astle, Brook M; Bell, Philip S; Bohannon, Paul W; Buggie, Lee D; Derbyshire, Robert W; Dixon, Christopher; Fox, Mathew J; Lindsay, Allistair W; Marshall, Craig L; Newbrook, Dale; O'Malley, Carl; Parkinson, Neil F; Salt, Graeme D; Shinks, Dominic M; Spencer, Steven L; Tagoe, Darrel J; Turner, Daniel R; Whiting, Ashley; Willett, Ryan T.

Associated Schoolboys who have accepted the club's offer of a Traineeship/Contract
Laidlaw, Simon G.

BOURNEMOUTH

Name	Ht	Wt	Pos	Birthdate	Birthplace	Signed from	Clubs	Apps	Gls
Andrews Ian*	6 2	14 01	G	1 12 64	Nottingham	Apprentice	Leicester C Swindon T (loan) Celtic Leeds U (loan) Southampton Bournemouth Leicester C (loan)	126 1 5 1 10 64 —	— — — — — — —
Bailey John	5 8	10 02	M	6 5 69	London	Enfield	Bournemouth	84	5
Beardsmore Russell	5 8	10 04	M	28 9 68	Wigan	Apprentice	Manchester U Blackburn R (loan) Bournemouth	56 2 149	4 — 3
Brissett Jason	5 9	12 00	M	7 9 74	Redbridge	Arsenal	Peterborough U Bournemouth	35 93	— 7
Carberry Garrett‡			M	1 11 75	Glasgow		Bournemouth	—	—
Coll Owen	6 0	11 07	D	9 4 76	Donegal	Amateur	Tottenham H Bournemouth	— 24	— —
Cotterell Leo	5 9	10 00	D	2 9 74	Cambridge	Trainee	Ipswich T Bournemouth	2 9	— —
Cox Ian	6 0	12 00	M	25 3 71	Croydon	Carshalton Ath	Crystal Palace Bournemouth	15 52	— 8
Dean Michael	5 9	11 10	M	9 3 78	Weymouth	Trainee	Bournemouth	17	—
Fletcher Steve	6 2	14 09	F	26 6 72	Hartlepool	Trainee	Hartlepool U Bournemouth	32 149	4 24
Glass Jimmy	6 1	13 04	G	1 8 73	Epsom	Trainee	Crystal Palace Portsmouth (loan) Bournemouth	— 3 48	— — —
Gordon Dale‡	5 10	11 08	F	9 1 67	Gt Yarmouth	Apprentice	Norwich C Rangers West Ham U Peterborough U (loan) Millwall (loan) Bournemouth	206 45 9 6 6 16	31 6 1 1 — —
Hayter James§			F	9 4 79	Newport	Trainee	Bournemouth	2	—
Holland Matthew	5 9	11 12	M	11 4 74	Bury	Trainee	West Ham U Bournemouth	— 104	— 18
Howe Eddie	5 9	11 02	D	29 11 77	Amersham	Trainee	Bournemouth	18	—
Kearn Stewart‡			G	1 12 75	Salisbury		Sheffield W Bournemouth	— —	— —
Murray Robert	5 11	12 07	D	31 10 74	Hammersmith	Trainee	Bournemouth	143	12
O'Brien Roy‡	6 1	12 00	D	27 11 74	Cork	Trainee	Arsenal Wigan Ath Bournemouth	— — —	— — —
O'Neill Jon	5 11	12 00	F	2 1 74	Glasgow	Queen's Park BC	Queen's Park Celtic Bournemouth	91 1 24	30 — 1
Rawlinson Mark	5 10	11 04	M	9 6 75	Bolton	Trainee	Manchester U Bournemouth	— 44	— 2
Robinson Steve	5 9	11 02	F	10 12 74	Lisburn	Trainee	Tottenham H Leyton Orient (loan) Bournemouth	2 — 113	— — 19
Strong Steve‡			F	15 3 78	Watford	Trainee	Bournemouth	2	—
Town David	5 7	11 13	F	9 12 76	Bournemouth	Trainee	Bournemouth	39	2
Vincent Jamie	5 10	11 09	D	18 6 75	London	Trainee	Crystal Palace Bournemouth (loan) Bournemouth	25 8 29	— — —
Watson Mark*	5 9	11 00	F	28 12 73	Birmingham	Sutton U	West Ham U Leyton Orient (loan) Cambridge U (loan) Shrewsbury T (loan) Bournemouth	1 1 4 1 15	— 1 1 — 2
Wells David	6 2	12 07	G	29 12 77	Portsmouth	Trainee	Bournemouth	1	—
Young Neil	5 9	12 00	D	31 8 73	Harlow	Trainee	Tottenham H Bournemouth	— 117	— —

Trainees
Bowers, Tyronne G; Broadhurst, Karl M; Camfield, Adam J; Chavez-Munoz, Adrian M; Coupland, Terry A; Davey, Benjamin A; Dodds, Ishmael J L; Fletcher, Carl N; Fricker, Matthew; Griffin, Antony R; Hayter, James E; Hughes, Daniel R; Jenkins, Jamie; Jenkins, Jody D; Johnson, Robert N; Kemp, Steven; Nash, Adam D; Stone, Nicholas J.

Associated Schoolboys
Ford, James A; Holland, Christopher J; Lattimer, James D; Leach, Graham M; Martin, Jamie G; Trickey, Steven I; Williams, Peter J.

Associated Schoolboys who have accepted the club's offer of a Traineeship/Contract
Birmingham, David P; Saunders, Steele.

BRADFORD CITY

Name	Ht	Wt	Pos	Birthdate	Birthplace	Source	Club	Apps	Gls
Blake Robbie	5 8	11 00	F	4 3 76	Middlesbrough	Trainee	Darlington	68	21
							Bradford C	5	—
Brightwell David*	6 1	13 05	D	7 1 71	Lutterworth	Trainee	Manchester C	43	1
							Chester C (loan)	6	—
							Lincoln C (loan)	5	—
							Stoke C (loan)	1	—
							Bradford C	24	—
							Blackpool (loan)	2	—
Davison Aidan*	6 1	13 12	G	11 5 68	Sedgefield	Billingham Syn	Notts Co	1	—
							Leyton Orient (loan)	—	—
							Bury	—	—
							Chester C (loan)	—	—
							Blackpool (loan)	—	—
							Millwall	34	—
							Bolton W	37	—
							Ipswich T (loan)	—	—
							Hull C (loan)	9	—
							Bradford C	10	—
Dreyer John	6 1	13 02	D	11 6 63	Alnwick	Wallingford T	Oxford U	60	2
							Torquay U (loan)	5	—
							Fulham (loan)	12	2
							Luton T	214	13
							Stoke C	49	3
							Bolton W (loan)	2	—
							Bradford C	28	1
Edinho	5 8	12 12	F	21 2 67	Brazil		Chaves	32	14
							Guimaraes	32	15
							Bradford C	15	5
Gould Jonathan	6 1	12 07	G	18 7 68	Paddington	Clevedon T	Halifax T	32	—
							WBA	—	—
							Coventry C	25	—
							Bradford C (loan)	9	—
							Bradford C	9	—
							Gillingham (loan)	3	—
Jacobs Wayne	5 8	11 02	D	3 2 69	Sheffield	Apprentice	Sheffield W	6	—
							Hull C	129	4
							Rotherham U	42	2
							Bradford C	105	4
Jewell Paul	5 8	12 01	F	28 9 64	Liverpool	Apprentice	Liverpool	—	—
							Wigan Ath	137	35
							Bradford C	269	56
							Grimsby T (loan)	5	1
Kiwomya Andy	5 10	10 10	F	1 10 67	Huddersfield	Trainee	Barnsley	1	—
							Sheffield W	—	—
						Retired injury	Dundee	21	1
							Rotherham U	7	—
						Halifax T	Scunthorpe U	9	3
							Bradford C	43	3
							Luton T (loan)	5	1
Kulcsar George	6 1	13 08	D	12 8 67	Budapest		Antwerp	66	1
							Bradford C	9	—
Liburd Richard	5 10	10 12	D	26 9 73	Nottingham	Forest Ath	Middlesbrough	41	1
							Bradford C	78	3
Midgley Craig	5 7	11 01	F	24 5 76	Bradford	Trainee	Bradford C	9	1
							Scarborough (loan)	16	1
							Scarborough (loan)	6	2
Mitchell Graham‡	6 2	12 13	D	16 2 68	Shipley	Apprentice	Huddersfield T	244	2
							Bournemouth (loan)	4	—
							Bradford C	65	1
Mohan Nicky	6 1	13 01	D	6 10 70	Middlesbrough	Trainee	Middlesbrough	99	4
							Hull C (loan)	5	1
							Leicester C	23	—
							Bradford C	83	4
Murray Shaun	5 7	10 10	M	7 2 70	Newcastle	Trainee	Tottenham H	—	—
							Portsmouth	34	1
							Millwall (loan)	—	—
							Scarborough	29	5
							Bradford C	92	8
O'Brien Andrew	5 10	10 06	D	29 6 79	Harrogate	Trainee	Bradford C	22	2
Oliveira Rault‡	6 1	13 10	D	20 8 72	Portugal	Farense	Bradford C	2	—

Pehrsson Magnus‡			M	25 5 76	Malmo		Djurgaarden	47	3
							Bradford C	1	—
Pepper Nigel	5 10	11 13	M	25 4 68	Rotherham	Apprentice	Rotherham U	45	1
							York C	235	39
							Bradford C	11	5
Pinto Sergio‡	5 7	11 02	M	8 1 73	Escudos	Fatima	Bradford C	18	—
Regtop Erik‡	6 0	13 00	F	16 2 68	Emmen		Ajax	3	—
							Telstar	14	13
							Groningen	24	5
							Ajax	—	—
							Telstar	9	1
							Herrenveen	99	26
							Bradford C	8	1
Sas Marco	6 1	12 05	D	16 2 71	Vlaardingden		Sparta	49	—
							NAC Breda	48	—
							Bradford C	31	3
Smithard Matthew‡	5 9	10 09	F	13 6 76	Leeds	Trainee	Leeds U	—	—
							Bradford C	1	—
Steiner Rob‡			F	20 6 73	Finsprong		Norrkoping	41	14
							Bradford C	15	4
Sundgot Ole	6 1	11 04	F	21 3 72	Olsumd		Molde	69	30
							Oldham Ath	—	—
							Bradford C	20	6
Vanhala Jari†	5 9	11 01	F	29 8 65	Finland		Bradford C	1	—
Watson Gordon	5 10	12 08	F	20 3 71	Sidcup	Trainee	Charlton Ath	31	7
							Sheffield W	66	15
							Southampton	52	8
							Bradford C	3	1
Wilder Chris	5 11	12 08	D	23 9 67	Stocksbridge	Apprentice	Southampton	—	—
							Sheffield U	93	1
							Walsall (loan)	4	—
							Charlton Ath (loan)	1	—
							Charlton Ath (loan)	2	—
							Leyton Orient (loan)	16	1
							Rotherham U	132	11
							Notts Co	46	—
							Bradford C	7	—
Wright Tommy*	5 7	11 05	F	10 1 66	Dunfermline	Apprentice	Leeds U	81	24
							Oldham Ath	112	23
							Leicester C	129	22
							Middlesbrough	53	5
							Bradford C	45	5
Youds Eddie	6 1	13 03	D	3 5 70	Liverpool	Trainee	Everton	8	—
							Cardiff C (loan)	1	—
							Wrexham (loan)	20	2
							Ipswich T	50	1
							Bradford C	47	7

Trainees
Airdrie, Stewart W; Barley, Scott L; Bates, Craig A; Bolland, Paul G; Bower, Mark J; Brown, Paul M; Edwards, Gavin P; Hamilton, James; Langhorn, Richard; Lee, Damien A; Machell, Richard A; McLean, Ian J; Nettleton, James D; Payne, Dean; Shields, Antony J; Stevenson, Matthew J; Verity, Daniel R.

Associated Schoolboys
Clark, Gareth A; Dunnachie, Andrew K; Kerr, Scott A; Kinch, Liam D; Lloyd, Matthew; Spence, Oliver; Tyson, Gary W; Wilson, James D.

Associated Schoolboys who have accepted the club's offer of a Traineeship/Contract
Brown, Liam; Grant, Gareth M; Meehan, Mark; Walker, Lee.

Player who does not hold a current contract but his registration has been retained by the club
Holmes, Richard M; Hutton, Peter; Tomlinson, Paul.

BRENTFORD

Anderson Ijah	5 8	10 03	D	30 12 75	Hackney	Tottenham H	Southend U	—	—
							Brentford	71	3
Asaba Carl	6 1	13 07	F	28 1 73	London	Dulwich Hamlet	Brentford	54	25
							Colchester U (loan)	12	2
Ashby Barry	6 1	13 08	D	21 11 70	London	Trainee	Watford	114	3
							Brentford	121	4
Bates Jamie	6 2	14 00	D	24 2 68	London	Trainee	Brentford	352	16
Bent Marcus	6 2	12 04	F	19 5 78	Hammersmith	Trainee	Brentford	46	4
Canham Scott	5 10	11 08	M	5 11 74	London	Trainee	West Ham U	—	—
							Torquay U (loan)	3	—
							Brentford (loan)	14	—
							Brentford	13	1

								App	Gls
Dearden Kevin	5 11	14 01	G	8 3 70	Luton	Trainee	Tottenham H	1	—
							Cambridge U (loan)	15	—
							Hartlepool U (loan)	10	—
							Oxford U (loan)	—	—
							Swindon T (loan)	1	—
							Peterborough U (loan)	7	—
							Hull C (loan)	3	—
							Rochdale (loan)	2	—
							Birmingham C (loan)	12	—
							Portsmouth (loan)	—	—
							Brentford	163	—
Dennis Kevin	5 10	12 00	F	14 12 76	Islington	Arsenal	Brentford	12	—
Fernandes Tamer	6 2	13 13	G	7 12 74	London	Trainee	Brentford	12	0
Goddard-Crawley Richard	6 3	14 00	M	31 3 78	Burnt Oak	Arsenal	Brentford	1	—
Harvey Lee*	5 10	12 06	M	21 12 66	Harlow	Harrow	Leyton Orient	184	23
							Nottingham F	2	—
							Brentford	105	6
Hurdle Gus	6 0	11 04	D	14 10 73	London	Fulham	Brentford	54	—
Hutchings Carl	6 0	11 06	M	24 9 74	London	Trainee	Brentford	119	2
McGhee David	5 11	12 05	F	19 6 76	Sussex	Trainee	Brentford	88	7
McPherson Malcolm	6 1	12 00	F	19 12 74	Glasgow	Yeovil T	West Ham U	—	—
							Brentford	3	—
Myall Stuart	5 10	13 07	M	12 11 74	Eastbourne	Trainee	Brighton & HA	80	4
							Brentford	—	—
Omigie Joe	6 2	13 00	F	13 6 72	Hammersmith	Donna	Brentford	23	1
Rapley Kevin	5 9	10 08	F	21 9 77	Reading	Trainee	Brentford	2	—
Smith Paul	6 0	13 10	M	18 9 71	Lenham	Trainee	Southend U	20	1
							Brentford	159	11
Statham Brian	5 9	11 12	D	21 5 69	Zimbabwe	Apprentice	Tottenham H	24	—
							Reading (loan)	8	—
							Bournemouth (loan)	2	—
							Brentford (loan)	18	—
							Brentford	148	1
Taylor Robert	6 1	13 06	F	30 4 71	Norwich	Trainee	Norwich C	—	—
							Leyton Orient (loan)	3	1
							Birmingham C	—	—
							Leyton Orient	73	20
							Brentford	133	43

Trainees
Brooks, Leyton C C; Clark, Dean W; Denys, Ryan; Duffy, Gary; Green, Darren J; Mitchell, Terry F; Ryan, Warren R; Tunnell, Lee F.

Associated Schoolboys
Windell, Gavin.

Associated Schoolboys who have accepted the club's offer of a Traineeship/Contract
Dobson, Michael; Muldowney, Jamie J; Patel, Neerav.

BRIGHTON & HOVE ALBION

								App	Gls
Adekola David‡	6 0	12 10	F	19 5 68	Lagos	Bristol C	Bury	35	12
							Exeter C (loan)	3	1
							Bournemouth	—	—
							Wigan Ath	4	—
							Hereford U	—	—
							Cambridge U	5	1
							Brighton & HA	1	—
Allan Derek	6 0	12 01	D	24 12 74	Irving	Ayr U BC	Ayr U	5	—
							Southampton	1	—
							Brighton & HA (loan)	8	—
							Brighton & HA	31	—
Andrews Philip*	5 11	10 07	F	14 9 76	Andover	Trainee	Brighton & HA	25	1
Baird Ian	6 0	12 00	F	1 4 64	Rotherham	Apprentice	Southampton	22	5
							Cardiff C (loan)	12	6
							Newcastle U (loan)	5	1
							Leeds U	85	33
							Portsmouth	20	1
							Leeds U	77	17
							Middlesbrough	63	19
							Hearts	64	15
							Bristol C	57	11
							Plymouth Arg	27	5
							Brighton & HA	35	13
Fox Mark*	5 11	10 06	M	17 11 75	Basingstoke	Trainee	Brighton & HA	25	1
Fox Simon*	5 10	10 04	F	28 8 77	Basingstoke	Trainee	Brighton & HA	21	—
Hobson Gary	6 2	13 04	D	12 11 72	North Ferriby	Trainee	Hull C	142	—
							Brighton & HA	46	1

Name					Birthplace	Source	Club	Apps	Gls
Humphrey John*	5 10	11 11	D	31 1 61	Paddington	Apprentice	Wolverhampton W	149	3
							Charlton Ath	194	3
							Crystal Palace	160	2
							Reading (loan)	8	—
							Charlton Ath	28	—
							Gillingham	9	—
							Brighton & HA	11	—
Johnson Ross	6 0	12 12	D	2 1 76	Brighton	Trainee	Brighton & HA	51	—
Maskell Craig	5 10	11 10	F	10 4 68	Aldershot	Apprentice	Southampton	6	1
							Swindon T (loan)	—	—
							Huddersfield T	87	43
							Reading	72	26
							Swindon T	47	22
							Southampton	17	1
							Bristol C (loan)	5	1
							Brighton & HA	52	18
Mayo Kerry	5 10	12 11	M	21 9 77	Cuckfield	Trainee	Brighton & HA	24	—
McDonald Paul	5 6	10 00	F	20 4 68	Motherwell	Merry Street BC	Hamilton A	215	26
							Southampton	3	—
							Burnley (loan)	9	1
							Brighton & HA	50	4
McGarrigle Kevin*	5 11	11 00	D	9 4 77	Newcastle	Trainee	Brighton & HA	45	1
Minton Jeffrey	5 6	11 00	M	28 12 73	Hackney	Trainee	Tottenham H	2	1
							Brighton & HA	103	16
Morris Mark	6 2	14 00	D	26 9 62	Carshalton	Apprentice	Wimbledon	168	9
							Aldershot (loan)	14	—
							Watford	41	1
							Sheffield U	56	3
							Bournemouth	194	8
							Gillingham (loan)	6	—
							Brighton & HA	12	1
Mundee Denny	5 10	13 00	M	10 10 68	Swindon	Apprentice	QPR	—	—
							Swindon T	—	—
							Bournemouth	100	6
							Torquay U (loan)	9	—
							Brentford	84	16
							Brighton & HA	61	7
Ormerod Mark	6 0	12 11	G	5 2 76	Bournemouth	Trainee	Brighton & HA	21	—
Parris George*	5 9	13 00	M	11 9 64	Barking	Apprentice	West Ham U	239	12
							Birmingham C	39	1
							Brentford (loan)	5	—
							Bristol C (loan)	6	—
							Brighton & HA (loan)	18	2
							Norrkoping	4	—
							Brighton & HA	56	3
Peake Jason	5 10	13 00	M	29 9 71	Leicester	Trainee	Leicester C	8	1
							Hartlepool U (loan)	6	1
							Halifax T	33	1
							Rochdale	95	6
							Brighton & HA	30	1
Reinelt Robbie	5 11	11 11	M	11 3 74	Epping	Trainee	Aldershot	5	—
							Gillingham	52	5
							Colchester U	48	10
							Brighton & HA	12	3
Rust Nicky	6 0	13 02	G	25 9 74	Ely	Arsenal	Brighton & HA	161	—
Smith Peter	6 1	12 02	D	12 7 69	Stone	Alma Swanley	Brighton & HA	99	3
Storer Stuart	5 11	12 12	F	16 1 67	Rugby	Local	Mansfield T	1	—
							Birmingham C	8	—
							Everton	—	—
							Wigan Ath (loan)	12	—
							Bolton W	123	12
							Exeter C	77	8
							Brighton & HA	82	9
Tuck Stuart	5 11	11 00	D	1 10 74	Brighton	Trainee	Brighton & HA	69	—
Virgo James*	5 10	12 10	D	21 12 76	Brighton	Trainee	Brighton & HA	—	—

Trainees
Armstrong, Paul G; Carter, Richard A J; Fox, Terence M; Kennett, Paul J; McNally, Ross J; Rowlands, James S; Ryan, Darragh J; Saul, Eric M; Smith, Grant G; Streeter, Terry S; Westcott, John P J.

Associated Schoolboys
Vanson, Lloyd D.

BRISTOL CITY

Name					Birthplace	Source	Club	Apps	Gls
Agostino Paul	5 11	12 12	F	9 6 75	Woodville		Young Boys	29	3
							Bristol C	84	19

Allen Paul*	5 7	11 03	M	28 8 62	Aveley	Apprentice	West Ham U	152	6
							Tottenham H	292	23
							Southampton	43	1
							Luton T (loan)	4	—
							Stoke C (loan)	17	1
							Swindon T	37	1
							Bristol C	14	—
Barclay Dominic	5 10	11 07	F	5 9 76	Bristol	Trainee	Bristol C	4	—
Barnard Darren	5 10	12 00	D	30 11 71	Rinteln	Wokingham T	Chelsea	29	2
							Reading (loan)	4	—
							Bristol C	78	15
Bent Junior	5 5	10 06	F	1 3 70	Huddersfield	Trainee	Huddersfield T	36	6
							Burnley (loan)	9	3
							Bristol C	181	20
							Stoke C (loan)	1	—
							Shrewsbury T (loan)	6	—
Bokoto Mommainais	5 11	11 13	F	20 10 74	France	Maria Aalter	Bristol C	—	—
Brennan Jim	5 9	11 06	M	8 5 77	Toronto	Sora Lazio	Bristol C	8	—
Carey Louis	5 10	11 05	D	22 1 77	Bristol	Trainee	Bristol C	65	—
Edwards Robert	6 0	11 06	D	1 7 73	Kendal	Trainee	Carlisle U	48	5
							Bristol C	156	3
Goater Shaun	6 1	11 10	F	25 2 70	Bermuda		Manchester U	—	—
							Rotherham U	209	70
							Notts Co (loan)	1	—
							Bristol C	42	23
Goodridge Greg	5 6	10 00	F	10 2 75	Barbados	Lambada	Torquay U	38	4
							QPR	7	1
							Bristol C	28	6
Hewlett Matthew	6 2	10 11	M	25 2 76	Bristol	Trainee	Bristol C	76	4
Kuhl Martin*	5 11	11 13	M	10 1 65	Frimley	Apprentice	Birmingham C	111	5
							Sheffield U	38	4
							Watford	4	—
							Portsmouth	157	27
							Derby Co	68	1
							Notts Co (loan)	2	—
							Bristol C	94	7
Langan Kevin	6 1	11 05	D	7 4 78	Jersey	Trainee	Bristol C	—	—
Loydon Gareth*			M	23 3 78	Hereford	Trainee	Bristol C	—	—
Naylor Stuart	6 4	12 02	G	6 12 62	Wetherby	Yorkshire Amat	Lincoln C	49	—
							Peterborough U (loan)	8	—
							Crewe Alex (loan)	38	—
							Crewe Alex (loan)	17	—
							WBA	355	—
							Bristol C	35	—
Nugent Kevin	6 1	13 03	F	10 4 69	Edmonton	Trainee	Leyton Orient	94	20
							Plymouth Arg	131	32
							Bristol C	70	14
Owers Gary	6 0	12 07	M	3 10 68	Newcastle	Apprentice	Sunderland	268	25
							Bristol C	104	8
Paterson Scott	5 11	12 00	D	13 5 72	Aberdeen	Cove Rangers	Liverpool	—	—
							Bristol C	40	1
Perry Richard*			M	20 8 78	Bristol	Trainee	Bristol C	—	—
Phillips Steve	6 1	11 10	G	6 5 78	Bath	Paulton R	Bristol C	—	—
Plummer Dwayne	5 10	10 09	F	12 10 76	Bristol	Trainee	Bristol C	13	—
Seal David	5 11	12 00	F	26 1 72	Penrith NSW	Aalst	Bristol C	51	10
Shail Mark	6 1	13 03	D	15 10 66	Sweden	Yeovil T	Bristol C	101	4
Taylor Shaun	6 1	13 00	D	26 2 63	Plymouth	Bideford	Exeter C	200	16
							Swindon T	212	30
							Bristol C	29	1
Tinnion Brian	6 1	13 00	D	23 2 68	Stanley	Apprentice	Newcastle U	32	2
							Bradford C	145	22
							Bristol C	149	13
Welch Keith	6 2	12 00	G	3 10 68	Bolton	Trainee	Bolton W	—	—
							Rochdale	205	—
							Bristol C	206	—

Trainees
Badman, Mark; Brown, Aaron W; Doherty, Thomas E; Fowler, Paul M; Garton, Darren K; Hale, Matthew J; Hobbs, Darren J; Jordan, Andrew J; Martinsen, Havard; Morrison, Scott E; Ridge, Neil A; Rutkowski, Alexei J; Sloan, Christopher J; Smith, Dwayne D; Vanes, Michael A; Wilmot, Ellis J.

Associated Schoolboys
Cashman, Daryl; Claridge, Jamie; Clarke, Robert; Coles, Daniel; Farmer, Christopher; Havard, Ryan L; Jordan, Thomas; King, Rohan; Lowe, David J; Lowe, Oliver; McLay, Steven; Poynter, Christopher; Reynolds, Nicholas; Saunders, Mark; Shorey, Adam; Taggart, Damien; Woodman, Craig A.

Associated Schoolboys who have accepted the club's offer of a Traineeship/Contract
Ball, Alex; Burnell, Joseph M; Hill, Matthew C; Sammut, Benjamin; Turner, Daniel J; Whittington, Geoffrey.

Player who does not hold a current contract but his registration has been retained by the club
Stewart, Christopher A.

BRISTOL ROVERS

Alsop Julian	6 4	13 00	F	28 5 73	Nuneaton	Halesowen T	Bristol R	16	3
Archer Lee	5 6	9 06	F	6 11 72	Bristol	Trainee	Bristol R	126	15
Beadle Peter	6 2	13 07	F	13 5 72	London	Trainee	Gillingham	67	14
							Tottenham H	—	—
							Bournemouth (loan)	9	2
							Southend U (loan)	8	1
							Watford	23	1
							Bristol R	69	24
Bennett Frankie	5 7	12 01	F	3 1 69	Birmingham	Halesowen T	Southampton	19	1
							Shrewsbury T (loan)	4	3
							Bristol R	11	1
Bowey Steven‡	5 8	10 09	D	10 7 74	Durham	Forest Green R	Bristol R	—	—
Clark Billy	6 0	12 03	D	19 5 67	Christchurch	Trainee	Bournemouth	4	—
							Bristol R	248	14
Collett Andy	6 0	12 10	G	28 10 73	Middlesbrough	Trainee	Middlesbrough	2	—
							Bristol R	74	—
Cureton Jamie	5 7	10 07	F	28 8 75	Bristol	Trainee	Norwich C	29	6
							Bournemouth (loan)	5	—
							Bristol R	38	11
French Jon	5 10	10 10	M	25 9 76	Bristol	Trainee	Bristol R	14	1
Gurney Andy*	5 9	10 07	M	25 1 74	Bristol	Trainee	Bristol R	108	9
Harte Stuart*	5 9	10 10	D	12 12 77	Basingstoke	Trainee	Bristol R	—	—
Hayfield Matt	5 10	11 07	M	8 8 75	Bristol	Trainee	Bristol R	23	0
Higgs Shane	6 2	12 12	G	13 5 77	Oxford	Trainee	Bristol R	2	—
Holloway Ian	5 7	10 10	M	12 3 63	Kingswood	Apprentice	Bristol R	111	14
							Wimbledon	19	2
							Brentford (loan)	13	2
							Brentford	17	—
							Torquay U (loan)	5	—
							Bristol R	179	26
							QPR	147	4
							Bristol R	31	1
Kite Phil	6 2	15 04	G	26 10 62	Bristol	Apprentice	Bristol R	96	—
							Tottenham H (loan)	—	—
							Southampton	4	—
							Middlesbrough (loan)	2	—
							Gillingham	70	—
							Bournemouth	7	—
							Sheffield U	11	—
							Mansfield T (loan)	11	—
							Plymouth Arg (loan)	2	—
							Rotherham U (loan)	1	—
							Crewe Alex (loan)	5	—
							Stockport Co (loan)	5	—
							Cardiff C	18	—
							Bristol C	6	—
							Bristol R	—	—
Lockwood Matthew	5 9	10 12	M	17 10 76	Rochford	Trainee	QPR	—	—
							Bristol R	39	1
Low Josh	6 0	11 12	M	15 2 79	Bristol	Trainee	Bristol R	4	—
Martin Lee	6 0	12 08	D	5 2 68	Hyde		Manchester U	73	1
							Celtic	19	—
							Bristol R	25	—
Miller Paul	6 0	11 07	F	31 1 68	Bisley	Trainee	Wimbledon	80	10
							Newport Co (loan)	6	2
							Bristol C (loan)	3	—
							Bristol R	105	22
Morgan Ryan	6 1	12 07	M	12 7 78	Bristol	Trainee	Bristol R	1	—
Parmenter Steve	5 9	11 00	F	22 1 77	Chelmsford	Trainee	QPR	—	—
							Bristol R	14	2
Power Graeme	5 11	10 10	D	7 3 77	Northwick Park	Trainee	QPR	—	—
							Bristol R	16	—
Pritchard David	5 7	11 04	D	27 5 72	Wolverhampton	Telford U	WBA	5	—
							Telford U	Bristol R	92	—
Ramasut Tom	5 10	11 00	M	30 8 77	Cardiff		Norwich C	—	—
							Bristol R	11	—
Skinner Justin	6 0	11 03	M	30 1 69	Hounslow	Apprentice	Fulham	135	23
							Bristol R	183	12
Tillson Andy	6 2	12 10	D	30 6 66	Huntingdon	Kettering T	Grimsby T	105	5
							QPR	29	2
							Grimsby T (loan)	4	—
							Bristol R	158	5
White Tom	5 11	12 02	D	26 1 76	Bristol	Trainee	Bristol R	27	—
Zabek Lee§	6 0	12 00	M	13 10 78	Bristol	Trainee	Bristol R	1	—

Trainees
Basford, Luke W B; Brown, Justin C; Claridge, Robert R; Coles, Kevin J; Court, Anthony M; Davey, James A; De-Long, Nicholas M; Edwards, Christian M S; French, James R; Hope, David J; Lloyd, Andrew P; Pritchard, Justin; Smith, Mark J W; Teague, Simon J; Westlake, Tristan M; White, Daniel A J; White, Jonathan W; Zabek, Lee K.

Associated Schoolboys
Bright, Jarrod S; Bryant, Simon; Cleverley, Benjamin R; Cleverley, Daniel J; Cordy, Philip A; French, Steven D; Gilroy, David; Gosling, Jamie J; Hopkins, Craig S; Newell, Michael W; Pope, Mark; Powell, Gary N; Price, Oliver; Scott, Robert T; Shore, Andrew J; Watts, David J; Williamson, Matthew J; Winter, Hadleigh; Zabek, James K.

Associated Schoolboys who have accepted the club's offer of a Traineeship/Contract
Adams, Michael J; Hines, Alistair; Pendry, Dean; Trought, Michael.

BURNLEY

Name					Birthplace	Source	Club	Apps	Gls
Barnes Paul	5 11	12 06	M	16 11 67	Leicester	Apprentice	Notts Co	53	14
							Stoke C	24	3
							Chesterfield (loan)	1	—
							York C	148	76
							Birmingham C	15	7
							Burnley	40	24
Beresford Marlon	6 1	13 05	G	2 9 69	Lincoln	Trainee	Sheffield W	—	—
							Bury (loan)	1	—
							Ipswich T (loan)	—	—
							Northampton T (loan)	13	—
							Crewe Alex (loan)	3	—
							Northampton T (loan)	15	—
							Burnley	206	—
Brass Chris	5 9	12 06	D	24 7 75	Easington	Trainee	Burnley	53	—
							Torquay U (loan)	7	—
Carr-Lawton Colin			M	5 9 78	South Shields	Trainee	Burnley	—	—
Cooke Andy	5 11	12 08	F	20 1 74	Stoke	Newtown	Burnley	54	18
Duerden Ian	5 10	12 07	F	27 3 78	Burnley	Trainee	Burnley	—	—
Eastwood Philip	5 10	12 02	F	6 4 78	Blackburn	Trainee	Burnley	—	—
Eyres David	5 9	11 10	F	26 2 64	Liverpool	Rhyl	Blackpool	158	38
							Burnley	162	36
Gleghorn Nigel	6 0	13 07	M	12 8 62	Seaham	Seaham Red Star	Ipswich T	66	11
							Manchester C	34	7
							Birmingham C	142	33
							Stoke C	166	26
							Burnley	33	4
Harrison Gerry	5 9	12 03	M	15 4 72	Lambeth	Trainee	Watford	9	—
							Bristol C	38	1
							Cardiff C (loan)	10	1
							Hereford U (loan)	6	—
							Huddersfield T	—	—
							Burnley	89	3
Heath Adrian‡	5 6	11 00	F	11 1 61	Newcastle under Lyme	Apprentice	Stoke C	95	16
							Everton	226	71
						Espanol	Aston Villa	9	—
							Manchester C	75	4
							Stoke C	6	—
							Burnley	115	29
							Sheffield U	4	—
							Burnley	5	—
Helliwell Ian	6 4	14 08	F	7 11 62	Rotherham	Matlock T	York C	160	40
							Scunthorpe U	80	22
							Rotherham U	52	4
							Stockport Co	39	13
							Burnley	4	—
							Mansfield T (loan)	5	1
							Chester C (loan)	9	1
Hoyland Jamie	6 0	14 00	D	23 1 66	Sheffield	Apprentice	Manchester C	2	—
							Bury	172	35
							Sheffield U	89	6
							Bristol C (loan)	6	—
							Burnley	78	3
Huxford Richard	5 10	11 06	D	25 7 69	Scunthorpe	Kettering T	Barnet	33	1
							Millwall	32	—
							Birmingham C (loan)	5	—
							Bradford C	61	2
							Peterborough U (loan)	7	—
							Burnley	9	—
Little Glen	6 3	13 00	M	15 10 75	Wimbledon	Trainee	Crystal Palace	—	—
							Glentoran	—	—
							Burnley	9	—

Name	Ht	Wt	Pos	Birth date	Birthplace	Source	Clubs	Apps	Gls
Matthew Damian	5 11	10 10	M	23 9 70	Islington	Trainee	Chelsea	21	—
							Luton T (loan)	5	—
							Crystal Palace	24	1
							Bristol R (loan)	8	—
							Burnley	32	6
Overson Vince	6 2	14 13	D	15 5 62	Kettering	Apprentice	Burnley	211	6
							Birmingham C	182	3
							Stoke C	170	6
							Burnley	8	—
Parkinson Gary	5 11	13 00	D	10 1 68	Thornaby	Everton	Middlesbrough	202	5
							Southend U (loan)	6	—
							Bolton W	3	—
							Burnley	135	4
Robinson Liam*	5 7	12 07	F	20 12 65	Bradford	Nottingham F	Huddersfield T	21	2
							Tranmere R (loan)	4	3
							Bury	262	89
							Bristol C	41	4
							Burnley	63	9
Russell Wayne*	6 2	12 12	G	29 11 67	Cardiff	Ebbw Vale	Burnley	24	—
Seba Jesus‡	5 6	9 13	M	11 4 74	Zaragoza	Zaragoza	Wigan Ath	21	3
							Burnley	—	—
Smith Paul	6 0	13 03	F	22 1 76	Easington	Trainee	Burnley	48	4
Swan Peter	6 3	15 09	D	28 9 66	Leeds	Local	Leeds U	49	11
							Hull C	80	24
							Port Vale	111	5
							Plymouth Arg	27	2
							Burnley	49	7
Thompson Steve*	5 11	13 05	M	2 11 64	Oldham	Apprentice	Bolton W	335	49
							Luton T	5	—
							Leicester C	127	18
							Burnley	49	1
Vinnicombe Chris	5 8	10 12	D	20 10 70	Exeter		Exeter C	39	1
							Rangers	23	1
							Burnley	72	3
Webster James*	5 8	11 03	M	1 8 78	Burnley	Trainee	Burnley	—	—
Weller Paul	5 8	11 02	M	6 3 75	Brighton	Trainee	Burnley	56	3
West Gareth	6 1	11 10	D	1 8 78	Oldham	Trainee	Burnley	—	—
Winstanley Mark	6 1	12 08	D	22 1 68	St Helens	Trainee	Bolton W	220	3
							Burnley	124	5

Trainees
Bowden, Paul A; Cotton, David P; Devenney, Michael P; Fogarty, Richard P; Francis, Martin N; Graham, Paul D; Gray, Adam R; Heffernan, Jason T; Henry, David; Heywood, Matthew S; Mawson, Craig J; McDonald, Christopher N; Murphy, Terence P; O'Leary, Daniel W J; Pates, Bradley J; Pennington, Lee D; Scott, Christopher J; Smith, Carl P.

Non-Contract
Heath, Adrian P.

Associated Schoolboys
Gardiner, Marc.

Associated Schoolboys who have accepted the club's offer of a Traineeship/Contract
Kelly, Eamonn; Maylett, Bradley; McCoy, James J.

BURY

Name	Ht	Wt	Pos	Birth date	Birthplace	Source	Clubs	Apps	Gls
Armstrong Gordon	6 0	12 11	M	15 7 67	Newcastle	Apprentice	Sunderland	349	50
							Bristol C (loan)	6	—
							Northampton T (loan)	4	1
							Bury	32	2
Bracey Lee	6 1	13 07	G	11 9 68	Barking	Trainee	West Ham U	—	—
							Swansea C	99	—
							Halifax T	73	—
							Bury	67	—
							Ipswich T (loan)	—	—
Brunskill Iain*	5 10	12 05	D	5 11 76	Ormskirk	Trainee	Liverpool	—	—
							Bury	—	—
Butler Paul	6 2	13 00	D	2 11 72	Manchester	Trainee	Rochdale	158	10
							Bury	41	2
Buxton Nicholas‡			M	6 9 76	Doncaster		Bury	—	—
Carter Mark*	5 9	12 07	F	17 12 60	Liverpool	Runcorn	Barnet	82	30
							Bury	134	62
Crossland Mark			M	14 12 78	Tameside	Lincoln C	Bury	—	—
Daws Nick	5 11	13 03	M	15 3 70	Manchester	Altrincham	Bury	190	7
Hirst Matthew	6 2	14 04	F	14 11 77	St Albans	Millwall	Bury	—	—
Hughes Ian	5 10	12 08	M	2 8 74	Bangor	Trainee	Bury	162	1

Jepson Ronnie	6 1	13 00	F	12 5 63	Audley	Nantwich T	Port Vale	22	0
							Peterborough U (loan)	18	5
							Preston NE	38	8
							Exeter C	54	21
							Huddersfield T	107	36
							Bury	31	9
Johnrose Lenny	5 10	12 04	M	29 11 69	Preston	Trainee	Blackburn R	42	11
							Preston NE (loan)	3	1
							Hartlepool U	66	11
							Bury	117	14
Johnson David	5 6	12 05	F	15 8 76	Jamaica	Trainee	Manchester U	—	—
							Bury	80	13
Jones Steve*	5 4	10 11	M	25 10 76	Derry		Blackpool	—	—
							Bury	—	—
Kiely Dean	6 0	12 13	G	10 10 70	Salford	WBA	Coventry C	—	—
							Ipswich T (loan)	—	—
							York C (loan)	—	—
							York C	210	—
							Bury	46	—
Lucketti Chris	6 0	13 04	D	21 9 71	Littleborough	Trainee	Rochdale	1	—
							Stockport Co	—	—
							Halifax T	78	2
							Bury	146	5
Matthews Rob	6 0	13 00	F	14 10 70	Slough	Loughborough University	Notts Co	43	11
							Luton T	11	—
							York C	17	1
							Bury	43	9
Pugh David	5 10	13 02	F	19 9 64	Liverpool	Runcorn	Chester C	179	23
							Bury	102	28
Randall Adrian	5 11	12 04	M	10 11 68	Amesbury	Apprentice	Bournemouth	3	—
							Aldershot	107	12
							Burnley	125	8
							York C	32	2
							Bury	19	3
Reid Nicky*	5 10	12 04	D	30 10 60	Urmston	Apprentice	Manchester C	217	2
							Blackburn R	174	9
							Bristol C (loan)	4	—
							WBA	20	—
							Wycombe W	8	—
						Witton A	Bury	25	—
Rigby Tony	5 7	12 12	M	10 8 72	Ormskirk	Barrow	Bury	140	18
							Scarborough (loan)	5	1
Shuttleworth Barry*	5 8	11 00	F	9 7 77	Accrington	Trainee	Bury	—	—
Steele Winnie*	5 8	11 02	M	28 2 77	Basildon	Trainee	Bury	—	—
Thompstone Ian‡	6 0	13 00	F	17 1 71	Manchester	Trainee	Manchester C	1	1
							Oldham Ath	—	—
							Exeter C	15	3
							Halifax T	31	9
							Scunthorpe U	60	8
							Rochdale	25	1
							Scarborough	19	2
							Bury	—	—
Thomson Peter*	6 3	13 04	F	30 6 77	Crumpsall	Stand Ath	Bury	—	—
West Dean	5 10	12 02	D	5 12 72	Morley	Leeds U	Lincoln C	119	20
							Bury	83	5
Woodward Andy	6 0	13 06	D	23 9 73	Stockport	Trainee	Crewe Alex	20	—
							Bury	32	—

Trainees
Andrew, Steven P; Barrass, Matthew R; Denney, Philip M; Forrest, Martyn W; Green, Alexander J; Hines, Rowan J; Horne, Matthew S M; Jones, John D; Joyce, Wayne E; McGaw, Daniel; McPadden, Ian J; Phillips, Paul D; Shaw, James A; Solotti, James P; Swailes, Daniel; Warner, Daniel G; Watson, Richard; Wilkinson, Steven D; Willcox, Robert; Winrow, Brian; Wright, Gary J; Young, Ian T.

Non-Contract
Radcliffe, Matthew S.

Associated Schoolboys
Buckley, Matthew T H; Gaynor, John; Gleaves, Carl M; Hanson, Peter V; Hardiker, John D; Haslam, Adrian M; Hughes, Paul; Jackson, Paul J; Manivannan, Paul; Menzies, Anton M; O'Neill, Paul D; Popiolek, John P; Stenardson, Ashley C; Thompson, Nicholas A; Totterdell, Jamie; Wakes, Jeffrey R A.

Associated Schoolboys who have accepted the club's offer of a Traineeship/Contract
Bury, Daniel J; Connell, Lee A; Halford, Stephen P; Hill, Nicholas D; Hutchinson, Ian P A; Smith, Paul A; Sturtivant, David M; Wardle, Darren C.

CAMBRIDGE UNITED

Ashbee Ian	6 0	13 07	D	6 9 76	Birmingham	Trainee	Derby Co	1	—
							Cambridge U	18	—

Name			Pos	Born	Birthplace	From	Club	Apps	Gls
Barnwell-Edinboro Jamie	5 10	11 05	F	26 12 75	Hull	Trainee	Coventry C	1	—
							Swansea C (loan)	4	—
							Wigan Ath (loan)	10	1
							Cambridge U	47	8
Barrett Scott	6 0	14 03	G	2 4 63	Ilkeston	Ilkeston T	Wolverhampton W	30	—
							Stoke C	51	—
							Colchester U (loan)	13	—
							Stockport Co (loan)	10	—
							Colchester U	—	—
							Gillingham	51	—
							Cambridge U	76	—
Beall Billy	5 7	10 06	M	4 12 77	Enfield	Trainee	Cambridge U	51	6
Benjamin Trevor	6 2	13 06	M	8 2 79	Kettering	Trainee	Cambridge U	12	1
Craddock Jody	6 0	12 00	D	25 7 75	Redditch	Christchurch	Cambridge U	145	4
Davies Martin‡	6 2	13 04	G	28 6 74	Swansea	Trainee	Coventry C	—	—
							Cambridge U	15	—
Hay Darran‡	6 1	13 08	F	17 12 69	Hitchin	Biggleswade	Cambridge U	33	3
Hayes Adie	6 0	11 09	M	22 5 78	Norwich	Trainee	Cambridge U	26	—
Hyde Micah	5 9	11 07	M	10 11 74	Newham	Trainee	Cambridge U	107	13
Joseph Marc	6 1	12 09	D	10 11 76	Leicester	Trainee	Cambridge U	20	0
Joseph Matt	5 7	10 05	D	30 9 72	Bethnal Green	Trainee	Arsenal	—	—
							Gillingham	—	—
							Cambridge U	152	6
Kyd Michael	5 11	12 07	F	21 5 77	Hackney	Trainee	Cambridge U	56	9
Lomas Andrew†			G	26 4 65	Hartlepool	Stevenage Borough	Cambridge U (loan)	2	—
						Rushden & Diamonds	Cambridge U	—	—
Marshall Shaun	6 1	12 12	G	3 10 78	Fakenham	Trainee	Cambridge U	1	—
Pack Lenny*	5 10	13 05	M	27 9 76	Salisbury	Trainee	Cambridge U	15	0
Palmer Lee*	6 0	12 12	D	19 9 70	Croydon	Trainee	Gillingham	120	5
							Cambridge U	31	1
Preece David	5 6	11 02	M	28 5 63	Bridgnorth	Apprentice	Walsall	111	5
							Luton T	336	21
							Derby Co	13	1
							Birmingham C (loan)	6	—
							Swindon T (loan)	7	1
							Cambridge U	25	—
Raynor Paul	5 11	13 03	M	29 4 66	Nottingham	Apprentice	Nottingham F	3	—
							Bristol R (loan)	8	—
							Huddersfield T	50	9
							Swansea C	191	27
							Wrexham (loan)	6	—
							Cambridge U	49	2
							Preston NE	80	9
							Cambridge U	79	7
Richards Tony	5 10	13 06	F	17 9 73	Newham	Sudbury T	Cambridge U	42	5
San Miguel Xavier‡	6 0	11 12	M	7 5 71	Bilbao		Cambridge U	1	—
Statham Mark†	6 2	13 03	G	7 3 76	Daveyhulme	Trainee	Nottingham F	—	—
							Wigan Ath	2	—
							Cambridge U	—	—
Taylor John	6 3	14 03	F	24 10 64	Norwich	Local	Colchester U	—	—
						Sudbury T	Cambridge U	160	46
							Bristol R	95	44
							Bradford C	36	11
							Luton T	37	3
							Lincoln C (loan)	5	2
							Colchester U (loan)	8	5
							Cambridge U	21	4
Thompson David	6 2	12 11	D	20 11 68	Ashington	Trainee	Millwall	92	6
							Bristol C	17	—
							Brentford	10	1
							Blackpool	17	—
							Cambridge U	44	2
Turner Robbie‡	6 3	13 11	F	18 9 66	Easington	Apprentice	Huddersfield T	—	—
							Cardiff C	39	8
							Hartlepool U (loan)	7	1
							Bristol R	26	2
							Wimbledon	10	—
							Bristol C	52	12
							Plymouth Arg	66	17
							Notts Co	8	1
							Shrewsbury T (loan)	9	—
							Exeter C	45	7
							Cambridge U	17	4
							Hull C (loan)	5	2
Vowden Colin*	6 0	12 11	D	13 9 71	Newmarket	Cambridge C	Cambridge U	30	—

Wanless Paul	6 0	13 02	M	14 12 73	Banbury	Trainee	Oxford U	32	0
							Lincoln C	8	—
							Cambridge U (loan)	14	1
							Cambridge U	30	3
Wilde Adam	5 10	11 08	D	22 5 79	Southampton	Trainee	Cambridge U	1	—
Williamson Davey	5 6	10 03	D	15 12 75	Hong Kong	Irvine Vics	Motherwell	—	—
							Cambridge U	—	—

Trainees
Armstrong, Dean P; Brown, Dwight C; Cockrill, Darren P; Dolby, Lee R; Huckstepp, Kris; Kett, Jamie C; King, Stuart; Mason, Terry S; McAvoy, Lawrence D; Newbery, Martin B S; Newby, Keith; Rutter, Aron J; Scales, Jamie; Taylor, Mark J; Webb, Darren L.

Non-Contract
McCammon, Mark J.

Associated Schoolboys
Bridges, David; Chillingworth, Daniel T; Haniver, Matthew G; Lockhart, Duncan; Paynter, Owen; Sandford, Daniel; West, Ross.

Associated Schoolboys who have accepted the club's offer of a Traineeship/Contract
Fox, Karl; Gibson, Mark A; Gill, Matthew J; Hann, Matthew; McNeill, Martin J; Youngs, Thomas A J.

CARDIFF CITY

Bennett Mickey†	5 10	11 11	M	22 7 69	Camberwell	Apprentice	Charlton Ath	35	2
							Wimbledon	18	2
							Brentford	46	4
							Charlton Ath	24	1
							Millwall	2	—
							Cardiff C	14	1
Clark Allan‡	5 7	10 08	F	11 9 77	Islington	Trainee	Cardiff C	—	—
Cross John	5 9	13 00	M	6 4 76	Barking	Trainee	QPR	—	—
							Cardiff C	—	—
Dale Carl	5 9	11 11	F	29 4 66	Colwyn Bay	Bangor C	Chester C	116	41
							Cardiff C	188	67
Eckhardt Jeff	6 0	11 07	D	7 10 65	Sheffield		Sheffield U	74	2
							Fulham	249	25
							Stockport Co	62	7
							Cardiff C	35	5
Elliott Tony	6 1	13 07	G	30 11 69	Nuneaton		Birmingham C	—	—
							Hereford U	75	—
							Huddersfield T	15	—
							Carlisle U	22	—
							Cardiff C	36	—
Fleming Hayden*	5 7	9 11	D	14 3 78	Islington	Trainee	Cardiff C	32	—
Fowler Jason	6 3	11 11	M	20 8 74	Bristol	Trainee	Bristol C	25	0
							Cardiff C	37	5
Gardner Jimmy*	5 11	11 08	F	27 9 67	Dunfermline	Ayresome North	Queen's Park	2	—
							Motherwell	16	—
							St Mirren	41	1
							Scarborough	6	1
							Cardiff C	63	5
Harding Paul‡	5 10	12 05	M	6 3 64	Mitcham	Barnet	Notts Co	54	1
							Southend U (loan)	5	—
							Watford (loan)	2	—
							Birmingham C	22	—
							Cardiff C	36	—
Haworth Simon	6 4	13 01	F	30 3 77	Cardiff	Trainee	Cardiff C	37	9
Jarman Lee	6 3	13 02	D	16 12 77	Cardiff	Trainee	Cardiff C	64	0
Jones Ian‡			D	26 8 76	Germany	Trainee	Cardiff C	3	—
Lloyd Kevin	6 0	11 10	D	26 9 70	Llanidloes	Caersws	Hereford U	51	3
							Cardiff C	31	1
McStay Ray†	5 11	11 00	M	16 5 70	Hamilton	Celtic BC	Celtic	—	—
							Hamilton A	30	5
							Hereford U	—	—
							Cardiff C	1	—
Michael Jamie§			M	28 10 78	Pontypridd	Trainee	Cardiff C	1	—
Middleton Craig	5 10	11 05	M	10 9 70	Nuneaton	Trainee	Coventry C	3	—
							Cambridge U	59	10
							Cardiff C	41	4
Mountain Pat†	6 0	12 01	G	1 8 76	Pontypridd	Barry T	Cardiff C	5	—
Osman Russell†	5 11	12 01	D	14 2 59	Repton	Apprentice	Ipswich T	294	17
							Leicester C	108	8
							Southampton	96	6
							Bristol C	70	3
							Plymouth Arg	—	—
							Brighton & HA	12	—
							Cardiff C	15	—

Name							Club	Apps	Gls
Partridge Scott	5 9	10 09	M	13 10 74	Leicester	Trainee	Bradford C	5	—
							Bristol C	57	7
							Torquay U (loan)	5	2
							Plymouth Arg (loan)	7	2
							Scarborough (loan)	7	—
							Cardiff C	15	—
Perry Jason	5 11	11 12	D	2 4 70	Caerphilly	Trainee	Cardiff C	281	5
Phillips Lee§	6 1	11 09	D	18 3 79	Aberdare	Trainee	Cardiff C	3	—
Philliskirk Tony	6 1	13 00	F	10 2 65	Sunderland	Amateur	Sheffield U	80	20
							Rotherham U (loan)	6	1
							Oldham Ath	10	1
							Preston NE	14	6
							Bolton W	141	51
							Peterborough U	43	15
							Burnley	40	9
							Carlisle U (loan)	3	1
							Cardiff C	61	5
Rodgerson Ian*	5 8	11 07	M	9 4 66	Hereford	Pegasus Jun	Hereford U	100	6
							Cardiff C	99	4
							Birmingham C	95	13
							Sunderland	10	—
							Cardiff C	55	1
Rollo James†	5 11	10 10	M	22 5 76	Wisbech	Trainee	Walsall	—	—
							Cardiff C	10	—
Scott Andy‡	6 1	11 10	D	27 6 75	Manchester	Trainee	Blackburn R	—	—
							Cardiff C	16	1
Stoker Gareth	5 9	10 10	M	22 2 73	Bishop Auckland	Leeds U	Hull C	30	2
							Hereford U	70	6
							Cardiff C	17	3
Vick Leigh*	6 0	12 05	F	8 1 78	Cardiff	Trainee	Cardiff C	4	—
White Steve	5 11	12 08	F	2 1 59	Chipping Sudbury	Mangotsfield U	Bristol R	50	20
							Luton T	72	25
							Charlton Ath	29	12
							Lincoln C (loan)	3	—
							Luton T (loan)	4	—
							Bristol R	101	24
							Swindon T	244	83
							Hereford U	76	44
							Cardiff C	38	13
Wigg Nathan‡	5 9	11 03	M	27 9 74	Newport	Trainee	Cardiff C	58	1
Williams Steven*	6 3	13 11	G	16 10 74	Aberystwyth	Coventry C	Cardiff C	33	0
Young Scott	6 3	12 08	M	14 1 76	Tonypandy	Trainee	Cardiff C	101	1

Trainees
Butler, David M; Cadette, Nathan D; Dennis, Richard O; Hill, John A; Hughes, William D; Hunt, David C; Jeremiah, Jerome; Loveless, Ian C; Michael, James D; Phillips, Lee; Rendell, John D; Roberts, Christian J; Smith, Gavin J; Thomas, Daniel G; Wedgbury, Karl D.

Non-Contract
Osman, Russell C; Rollo, James S; Tait, Gavin P.

Associated Schoolboys
Hicks, Mike; Phillips, Darryl J; Pratt, Leigh; Skelly, Lee; Slade-Jones, Daryl; Vaughan, Daniel; Watts, Leigh T.

Associated Schoolboys who have accepted the club's offer of a Traineeship/Contract
George, Stephen A; Howse, Ian; Kelly, Philip; Owen, Philip; Parnell, Blake.

CARLISLE UNITED

Name							Club	Apps	Gls
Archdeacon Owen	5 9	11 01	M	4 3 66	Glasgow	Gourock U	Celtic	76	7
							Barnsley	233	23
							Carlisle U	46	6
Aspinall Warren	5 9	12 08	F	13 9 67	Wigan	Apprentice	Wigan Ath	10	1
							Everton	7	—
							Wigan Ath (loan)	41	21
							Aston Villa	44	14
							Portsmouth	132	21
							Swansea C (loan)	5	—
							Bournemouth	33	9
							Carlisle U (loan)	7	1
							Carlisle U	82	11
Boertien Paul	5 10	11 00	D	20 1 79	Haltwhistle	Trainee	Carlisle U	—	—
Caig Tony	6 0	13 04	G	11 4 74	Whitehaven	Trainee	Carlisle U	140	—
Conway Paul	6 1	12 12	M	17 4 70	London	Oldham Ath	Carlisle U	89	22
Day Richard	6 2	13 10	G	25 1 79	Chelmsford	Trainee	Carlisle U	—	—
Delap Rory	6 1	12 09	M	6 7 76	Coldfield	Trainee	Carlisle U	56	7
Dixon George	6 0	14 05	G	24 10 78	Whitehaven	Trainee	Carlisle U	—	—
Dixon Lee‡	5 10	10 02	M	30 11 77	Douglas	Trainee	Carlisle U	—	—
Dobie Scott	6 1	11 12	F	10 10 78	Workington	Trainee	Carlisle U	2	1

Hayward Steve	5 11	12 07	M	8 9 71	Walsall	Trainee	Derby Co	26	1
							Carlisle U	90	13
Heath Stephen*	6 0	12 11	D	15 11 77	Hull	Trainee	Leeds U	—	—
							Carlisle U	1	—
Hopper Tony	5 11	12 02	M	31 5 76	Carlisle	Trainee	Carlisle U	31	1
Jansen Matthew	5 10	10 13	F	20 10 77	Carlisle	Trainee	Carlisle U	19	1
Joyce Joe	5 9	11 01	D	18 3 61	Consett	School	Barnsley	334	4
							Scunthorpe U	91	2
							Carlisle U	50	—
							Darlington (loan)	4	—
Kerr Dylan	5 9	11 04	D	14 1 67	Valletta	Arcadia Shepherds	Leeds U	13	—
(Transferred to Kilmarnock, October 1996)							Doncaster R (loan)	7	1
							Blackpool (loan)	12	1
							Reading	89	5
							Carlisle U	1	—
McAlindon Gareth	5 9	11 10	F	6 4 77	Hexham	Newcastle U	Carlisle U	15	2
Peacock Lee	6 0	13 01	F	9 10 76	Paisley	Trainee	Carlisle U	74	11
Pettinger Paul*	6 1	14 00	G	1 10 75	Sheffield	Barnsley	Leeds U	—	—
							Torquay U (loan)	3	—
							Rotherham U (loan)	1	—
							Gillingham	—	—
							Carlisle U	—	—
Pounewatchy Stephane	6 0	15 00	D	10 2 68	Paris		Martigues	44	2
							Gueugnon	30	—
							Carlisle U	42	1
Prokas Richard	5 9	11 05	M	22 1 76	Penrith	Trainee	Carlisle U	72	2
Robinson Jamie‡	6 1	12 04	D	22 2 72	Liverpool	Trainee	Liverpool	—	—
							Barnsley	9	—
							Carlisle U	57	4
Sandwith Kevin	5 11	12 05	M	30 4 78	Workington	Trainee	Carlisle U	—	—
Smart Allan	5 11	13 04	F	8 7 74	Perth		Caledonian Th	4	—
							Preston NE	21	6
							Carlisle U (loan)	4	—
							Northampton T (loan)	1	—
							Carlisle U	28	10
Stevens Ian	5 11	12 04	F	21 10 66	Malta	Trainee	Preston NE	11	2
							Stockport Co	2	—
						Lancaster C	Bolton W	47	7
							Bury	110	38
							Shrewsbury T	111	37
							Carlisle U	—	—
Taylor Lee	6 0	12 13	D	12 9 77	Whitehaven	Trainee	Carlisle U	—	—
Thomas Rod*	5 6	11 02	F	10 10 70	London	Trainee	Watford	84	9
							Gillingham (loan)	8	1
							Carlisle U	146	16
Thorpe Jeff	5 11	12 12	M	17 11 72	Whitehaven	Trainee	Carlisle U	136	6
Varty Will	6 0	12 06	D	1 10 76	Workington	Trainee	Carlisle U	32	0
Walling Dean	5 11	11 13	D	17 4 69	Leeds	Apprentice	Leeds U	—	—
							Rochdale	65	8
						Guiseley	Carlisle U	230	22

Trainees
Barton, Christopher; Bell, Liam R; Burton, Lee R; Douglas, Andrew S; Harrison, Edward W; Howe, Jamie I; Jones, Mark A; Mellon, Marc R; Millar, Stuart J; Moore, David G; Swanson, Kevin; Thompson, Craig.

Non-Contract
Dalton, Neil J; Smith, Simon; Wilkes, David A.

Associated Schoolboys
Antony, Paul M; Brain, Jonathan R; Clark, Barry J; Foster, Craig; Heggie, John A; Hetherington, Philip M; Higginson, Andrew J; Hoolikin, Lee; Hore, John; Jack, Michael L; Johnston, Craig; Jones, Andrew D; Kelleher, Christopher; Lewis, Craig; Reid, Paul M; Rooke, Steven; Skinner, Stephen K; Thurston, Mark R; Thwaites, Adam.

Associated Schoolboys who have accepted the club's offer of a Traineeship/Contract
Benson, Jon K; Hampton, James; Heath, Jamie; Hodgson, Alan; Skelton, Gavin; Swann, Michael.

CHARLTON ATHLETIC

Allen Bradley	5 7	10 07	F	13 9 71	Harold Wood	School	QPR	81	27
							Charlton Ath	28	7
Balmer Stuart	6 1	12 04	D	20 9 69	Falkirk	Celtic BC	Celtic	—	—
							Charlton Ath	211	8
Barness Anthony	5 10	12 01	D	25 2 72	Lewisham	Trainee	Charlton Ath	27	1
							Chelsea	14	—
							Middlesbrough (loan)	—	—
							Southend U (loan)	5	—
							Charlton Ath	45	2

Player	Ht	Wt	Pos	Birth date	Birthplace	Source	Club	Apps	Gls
Bright Mark‡	6 1	13 00	F	6 662	Stoke	Leek T	Port Vale	29	10
							Leicester C	42	6
							Crystal Palace	227	92
							Sheffield W	133	48
							Millwall (loan)	3	1
							Sion	—	—
							Charlton Ath	6	2
Brown Steve	6 1	13 10	D	13 572	Brighton	Trainee	Charlton Ath	108	3
Chandler Dean*	6 1	11 02	D	6 576	Ilford	Trainee	Charlton Ath	2	1
							Torquay U (loan)	4	—
Chapple Phil	6 2	12 07	D	26 1166	Norwich	Apprentice	Norwich C	—	—
							Cambridge U	187	19
							Charlton Ath	107	11
Curbishley Alan	5 10	11 07	M	8 1157	Forest Gate	Apprentice	West Ham U	85	5
							Birmingham C	130	11
							Aston Villa	36	1
							Charlton Ath	63	6
							Brighton & HA	116	13
							Charlton Ath	28	—
Emblen Paul			F	3 476	Bromley	Tonbridge A	Charlton Ath	—	—
Foley Westley‡			M	2 877	Clapton	Trainee	Charlton Ath	—	—
Jones Keith	5 9	10 11	M	14 1065	Dulwich	Apprentice	Chelsea	52	7
							Brentford	169	13
							Southend U	90	11
							Charlton Ath	75	1
Jones Steve	5 11	12 00	F	17 370	Cambridge	Billericay T	West Ham U	16	4
							Bournemouth	74	26
							West Ham U	8	—
							Charlton Ath	2	—
Kearley Dean			D	11 1077	Greenwich	Trainee	Charlton Ath	—	—
Kinsella Mark	5 9	11 05	M	12 872	Dublin	Home Farm	Colchester U	180	27
							Charlton Ath	37	6
Leaburn Carl	6 3	13 00	F	30 369	Lewisham	Apprentice	Charlton Ath	308	50
							Northampton T (loan)	9	—
Linger Paul*	5 6	10 03	M	20 1274	Stepney	Trainee	Charlton Ath	23	1
Lisbie Kevin	5 9	11 00	F	17 1078	Hackney	Trainee	Charlton Ath	25	1
Mortimer Paul	5 11	11 03	M	8 568	Kensington	Fulham	Charlton Ath	113	17
							Aston Villa	12	1
							Crystal Palace	22	2
							Brentford (loan)	6	—
							Charlton Ath	56	10
Newton Shaun	5 8	11 00	M	20 875	Camberwell	Trainee	Charlton Ath	131	10
Nicholls Kevin			M	2 179	Newham	Trainee	Charlton Ath	6	1
Notley Jay*			M	4 1277	London	Trainee	Charlton Ath	—	—
O'Connell Brendan	5 9	12 01	F	12 1166	London		Portsmouth	—	—
							Exeter C	81	19
							Burnley	64	17
							Huddersfield T (loan)	11	1
							Barnsley	240	35
							Charlton Ath	38	2
Petterson Andy	6 2	14 12	G	26 969	Fremantle		Luton T	19	—
							Swindon T (loan)	—	—
							Ipswich T (loan)	—	—
							Ipswich T (loan)	1	—
							Charlton Ath	39	—
							Bradford C (loan)	3	—
							Ipswich T (loan)	1	—
							Plymouth Arg (loan)	6	—
							Colchester U (loan)	5	—
Poole Gary	6 0	11 00	D	11 967	Stratford	Arsenal	Tottenham H	—	—
						Barnet	Cambridge U	43	—
							Barnet	40	2
							Plymouth Arg	39	5
							Southend U	44	2
							Birmingham C	72	—
							Charlton Ath	16	1
Robinson John	5 10	11 02	M	29 871	Bulawayo	Apprentice	Brighton & HA	62	6
							Charlton Ath	149	15
Robson Mark*	5 7	10 02	M	22 569	Newham	Trainee	Exeter C	26	7
							Tottenham H	8	—
							Reading (loan)	7	—
							Watford (loan)	1	—
							Plymouth Arg (loan)	7	—
							Exeter C (loan)	8	1
							West Ham U	47	8
							Charlton Ath	105	9
Rufus Richard	6 1	10 05	D	12 175	Lewisham	Trainee	Charlton Ath	103	—

Salmon Mike	6 2	12 12	G	14 7 64	Leyland	Local	Blackburn R	1	—
							Chester C (loan)	16	—
							Stockport Co	118	—
							Bolton W	26	—
							Wrexham (loan)	17	—
							Wrexham	83	—
							Charlton Ath	139	—
Stuart Jamie	5 10	11 00	D	15 10 76	Southwark	Trainee	Charlton Ath	49	3
Sturgess Paul*	5 11	12 05	D	4 8 75	Dartford	Trainee	Charlton Ath	51	0
Tindall Jason			F	15 11 77	Stepney	Trainee	Charlton Ath	—	—
Whyte David	5 8	10 07	F	20 4 71	Greenwich	Greenwich Bor	Crystal Palace	27	4
							Charlton Ath (loan)	8	2
							Charlton Ath	85	28
Wright Robert*			G	17 9 77	London	QPR	Charlton Ath	—	—

Trainees
Ali, Sharmarke; Cella, Nicholas D; Fortune, Jonathan J; Goldup, Robert J; Hawkins, John A; James, Kevin E; Kessell, Anthony L; Lee, Matthew A; McCann, Lawrence; Minors, Dwayne J; Neufville, Marvin C; Nwanokwu, Uchenna J N; Odum-Jones, Bobby C; Terry, Paul E; Toms, Frazer P.

Associated Schoolboys
Ashman, Kacey P; Bolangi, Pierre; Collis, David J; Defoe, Jermain; Durrant, George; Smith, Richard.

Associated Schoolboys who have accepted the club's offer of a Traineeship/Contract
Allman, Anthony; Beale, Michael; Day, Aaron A; Hockley, David; Izzet, Kemal; Konchesky, Paul; Parker, Scott; Turner, Sam.

CHELSEA

Burley Craig	6 1	12 13	M	24 9 71	Ayr	Trainee	Chelsea	113	7
Clarke Steve	5 10	12 05	D	29 8 63	Saltcoats	Beith Jun	St Mirren	151	6
							Chelsea	304	6
Clement Neil	6 0	12 09	D	3 10 78	Reading	Trainee	Chelsea	1	—
Colgan Nick	6 1	13 06	G	19 9 73	Eire	Drogheda	Chelsea	1	—
							Crewe Alex (loan)	—	—
							Grimsby T (loan)	—	—
							Millwall (loan)	—	—
Di Matteo Roberto	5 10	12 00	M	29 5 70	Sciaffusa		Schaffhausen	50	2
							Zurich	34	6
							Aarau	32	1
							Lazio	57	5
							Chelsea	34	7
Duberry Michael	6 1	13 10	D	14 10 75	Enfield	Trainee	Chelsea	38	1
							Bournemouth (loan)	7	—
Granville Danny	5 11	12 01	D	19 1 75	Islington	Trainee	Cambridge U	99	7
							Chelsea	5	—
Grodas Frode			G	24 10 64	Sogndal		Lillestrom	182	1
							Chelsea	21	—
Gullit Ruud	6 3	13 12	F	1 9 62	Surinam	DWS Amsterdam	Haarlem	91	32
							Feyenoord	85	30
							PSV Eindhoven	68	46
							AC Milan	117	35
							Sampdoria	31	15
							AC Milan	8	3
							Sampdoria	22	9
							Chelsea	43	4
Harley Jon			M	26 9 79	Maidstone	Trainee	Chelsea	—	—
Hitchcock Kevin	6 1	12 12	G	5 10 62	Custom House	Barking	Nottingham F	—	—
							Mansfield T (loan)	14	—
							Mansfield T	168	—
							Chelsea	93	—
							Northampton T (loan)	17	—
							West Ham U (loan)	—	—
Hughes Mark	5 10	13 01	F	1 11 63	Wrexham	Apprentice	Manchester U	89	37
							Barcelona	28	4
							Bayern Munich (loan)	18	6
							Manchester U	256	82
							Chelsea	66	16
Hughes Paul	6 0	12 06	M	19 4 76	Hammersmith	Trainee	Chelsea	12	2
Imber Noel‡			G	4 12 76	London	Trainee	Arsenal	—	—
							Chelsea	—	—
Johnsen Erland	6 1	14 04	D	5 4 67	Fredrikstad	Bayern Munich	Chelsea	145	1
Kharine Dmitri	6 2	13 09	G	16 8 68	Moscow		Torpedo Moscow	63	0
							Dynamo Moscow	40	—
							CSKA Moscow	34	—
							Chelsea	107	—
Kjeldbjerg Jakob‡	6 3	13 08	D	21 10 69	Frederiks	Silkeborg	Chelsea	52	2
Leboeuf Franck	6 0	12 00	D	22 1 68	Paris	Laval	Strasbourg	172	40
							Chelsea	26	6

Lee David	6 3	14 11	D	26 11 69	Kingswood	Trainee	Chelsea	150	11
							Reading (loan)	5	5
							Plymouth Arg (loan)	9	1
							Portsmouth (loan)	5	—
McCann Chris*	5 8	10 08	D	28 11 76	Plaistow	Trainee	Chelsea	—	—
Minto Scott	5 10	12 04	D	6 8 71	Cheshire	Trainee	Charlton Ath	180	7
							Chelsea	54	4
Morris Jody	5 5	10 02	M	22 12 78	London	Trainee	Chelsea	13	—
Myers Andy	5 10	12 11	M	3 11 73	Hounslow	Trainee	Chelsea	71	2
Newton Eddie	6 0	12 08	F	13 12 71	Hammersmith	Trainee	Chelsea	140	8
							Cardiff C (loan)	18	4
Nicholls Mark	5 10	10 01	F	30 5 77	Hillingdon	Trainee	Chelsea	8	—
Parker Paul*	5 7	11 07	D	4 4 64	West Ham	Apprentice	Fulham	153	2
							QPR	125	1
							Manchester U	105	1
							Derby Co	4	—
							Sheffield U	10	—
							Fulham	3	—
							Chelsea	4	—
Petrescu Dan	5 10	11 07	M	22 12 67	Bucharest		Steaua	95	26
							FC Olt (loan)	24	—
							Foggia	55	7
							Genoa	24	1
							Sheffield W	37	3
							Chelsea	58	5
Rix Graham†	5 9	11 00	F	23 10 57	Doncaster	Apprentice	Arsenal	351	41
							Brentford (loan)	6	—
						Caen, Le Havre	Dundee	14	2
							Chelsea	1	—
Rocastle David	5 9	12 07	F	2 5 67	Lewisham	Apprentice	Arsenal	218	24
							Leeds U	25	2
							Manchester C	21	2
							Chelsea	29	—
							Norwich C (loan)	11	—
Sheerin Joe§			F	8 11 77	Hammersmith	Trainee	Chelsea	1	—
Sinclair Frank	5 9	12 09	D	3 12 71	Lambeth	Trainee	Chelsea	147	6
							WBA (loan)	6	1
Stein Mark	5 6	11 07	F	29 1 66	S. Africa		Luton T	54	19
							Aldershot (loan)	2	1
							QPR	33	4
							Oxford U	82	18
							Stoke C	94	50
							Chelsea	50	21
							Stoke C (loan)	11	4
Vialli Gianluca	5 10	13 05	F	9 7 64	Cremona		Cremonese	105	23
							Sampdoria	223	85
							Juventus	72	27
							Chelsea	28	9
Wise Dennis	5 6	10 10	F	16 12 66	Kensington	Southampton	Wimbledon	135	27
							Chelsea	218	43
Zola Gianfranco	5 5	10 02	F	5 7 66	Oliena		Nuorese	31	10
							Torres	88	21
							Napoli	105	32
							Parma	102	49
							Chelsea	23	8

Trainees
Aggrey, James E; Broad, Stephen; Crittenden, Nicholas J; Davies, Stephen T; Hampshire, Steven G; Harrison, Gavin A; Potter, Daniel R J; Quinn, Paul J; Richardson, Jay G; Sheerin, Joseph E; Wolleaston, Robert A.

Non-Contract
Rix, Graham.

Associated Schoolboys
Baines, John J; Barrett, Neil W; Baxter, Darren L; Dolan, Joseph; Evans, Rhys K; Hajgato, Geza; Hammond, Jermaine D; Knight, Leon L; Martin, Paul; Parkes, Lee W; Rattray, John W; Ross, Andrew; Royal, Mark; Strode, Matthew J; Thornton, Paul E; Wolton, Lee.

Associated Schoolboys who have accepted the club's offer of a Traineeship/Contract
Demetrious, Shayne; King, John S; Nichols, Paul D; Osborne, Steven J; Terry, John G.

CHESTER CITY

Alsford Julian	6 2	13 01	D	24 12 72	Poole	Trainee	Watford	13	1
							Chester C	102	2
Brown Greg*	5 10	11 06	M	31 7 78	Manchester	Trainee	Chester C	4	—
Brown Wayne	6 0	11 12	G	14 1 77	Southampton	Trainee	Bristol C	1	—
						Weston-Super-Mare	Chester C	2	—

Name	Ht	Wt	Pos	Born	Birthplace	Source	Club	Apps	Gls
Davidson Ross	5 8	11 06	D	13 11 73	Chertsey	Walton & Hersham	Sheffield U	2	—
							Chester C	59	3
Fisher Neil	5 10	10 09	M	7 11 70	St Helens	Trainee	Bolton W	24	1
							Chester C	73	3
Flitcroft David	5 11	13 05	M	14 1 74	Bolton	Trainee	Preston NE	8	2
							Lincoln C (loan)	2	—
							Chester C	81	8
Jackson Peter*	6 0	13 06	D	6 4 61	Bradford	Apprentice	Bradford C	278	24
							Newcastle U	60	3
							Bradford C	58	5
							Huddersfield T	155	3
							Chester C	100	3
Jenkins Iain	5 9	11 10	D	24 12 72	Whiston	Trainee	Everton	5	—
							Bradford C (loan)	6	—
							Chester C	126	—
Jones Jon	5 11	11 05	F	27 10 78	Wrexham	Trainee	Chester C	17	1
McDonald Rod	5 10	12 06	F	20 3 67	London	Colne D	Walsall	149	41
							Partick T	41	10
							Chester C	22	6
Milner Andy	6 0	11 00	F	10 2 67	Kendal	Netherfield	Manchester C	—	—
							Rochdale	127	25
							Chester C	124	24
Murphy John	6 1	14 00	F	18 10 76	Whiston	Trainee	Chester C	34	4
Noteman Kevin*	5 10	11 12	F	15 10 69	Preston	Trainee	Leeds U	1	—
							Doncaster R	106	20
							Mansfield T	95	15
							Doncaster R	4	1
							Chester C	68	18
Preece Roger‡	5 8	10 11	M	9 6 69	Much Wenlock	Coventry C	Wrexham	110	12
							Chester C	170	4
Priest Chris	5 10	10 10	M	18 10 73	Leigh	Trainee	Everton	—	—
							Chester C	95	16
Ratcliffe Kevin	6 1	13 06	D	12 11 60	Mancot	Apprentice	Everton	359	2
							Dundee	4	—
							Everton	—	—
							Cardiff C	25	1
							Nottingham F	—	—
							Derby Co	6	—
							Chester C	23	—
Regis Cyrille‡	6 0	13 04	F	9 2 58	French Guyana	Molesey, Hayes	WBA	237	82
							Coventry C	238	47
							Aston Villa	52	12
							Wolverhampton W	19	2
							Wycombe W	35	9
							Chester C	29	7
Reid Shaun	5 8	12 10	M	13 10 65	Huyton	Local	Rochdale	133	4
							Preston NE (loan)	3	—
							York C	106	7
							Rochdale	107	10
							Bury	21	1
							Chester C	27	1
Richardson Nick	6 1	12 06	M	11 4 67	Halifax	Local	Halifax T	101	17
							Cardiff C	111	13
							Wrexham (loan)	4	2
							Chester C (loan)	6	1
							Bury	5	—
							Chester C	46	4
Rimmer Stuart	5 7	11 00	F	12 10 64	Southport	Apprentice	Everton	3	—
							Chester C	114	67
							Watford	10	1
							Notts Co	4	2
							Walsall	88	31
							Barnsley	15	1
							Chester C	213	59
							Rochdale (loan)	3	—
							Preston NE (loan)	2	—
Rogers Dave‡	6 1	12 00	D	25 8 75	Liverpool	Trainee	Tranmere R	—	—
							Chester C	25	1

Shelton Gary	5 7	10 12	M	21 3 58	Nottingham	Apprentice	Walsall	24	—
							Aston Villa	24	7
							Notts Co (loan)	8	—
							Sheffield W	198	18
							Oxford U	65	1
							Bristol C	150	24
							Rochdale (loan)	3	—
Sinclair Ronnie	5 11	12 09	G	19 11 64	Stirling	Apprentice	Chester C	66	6
							Nottingham F	—	—
							Wrexham (loan)	11	—
							Derby Co (loan)	—	—
							Sheffield U (loan)	—	—
							Leeds U (loan)	—	—
							Leeds U	8	—
							Halifax T (loan)	4	—
							Halifax T (loan)	10	—
							Bristol C	44	—
							Walsall (loan)	10	—
							Stoke C	80	—
							Bradford C (loan)	—	—
Tallon Gary	5 9	11 10	M	5 9 73	Drogheda	Trainee	Chester C	37	—
(on loan from Kilmarnock)							Blackburn R	—	—
							Kilmarnock	4	—
Whelan Spencer	6 2	11 00	D	17 9 71	Liverpool	Liverpool	Chester C	1	—
Woods Mattie	6 1	12 13	D	9 9 76	Gosport	Trainee	Chester C	180	4
							Everton	—	—
							Chester C	21	1

Trainees
Clench, Philip R; Dobson, Ryan A; Giles, Martin W; Hussaney, James A; Kinsey, Benjamin; Kinsey, Joel; Love, James S; Patterson, Phillip M; Quinn, Philip; Shelton, Andrew M; Smith, Paul; Thompson, Scott R; Warrington, Craig A; Whitehead, Stephen J; Williams, Scott J; Wright, Darren.

Associated Schoolboys
Doughty, Matthew L.

Associated Schoolboys who have accepted the club's offer of a Traineeship/Contract
McKay, Matthew P; Rendell, Carl.

CHESTERFIELD

Allison Neil*	6 2	11 10	D	20 10 73	Hull	Trainee	Hull C	106	3
							Swindon T	—	—
							Chesterfield	2	—
Beasley Andrew‡	6 1	12 10	G	5 2 64	Sedgley	Apprentice	Luton T	—	—
							Mansfield T (loan)	—	—
							Gillingham (loan)	—	—
							Mansfield T	94	—
							Peterborough U (loan)	7	—
							Scarborough (loan)	4	—
							Bristol R (loan)	1	—
							Doncaster R	37	—
							Chesterfield	32	—
Beaumont Chris	5 11	11 12	M	5 12 65	Sheffield	Denaby U	Rochdale	34	7
							Stockport Co	258	39
							Chesterfield	33	1
Bowater Jason§			M	5 4 78	Chesterfield	Trainee	Chesterfield	1	—
Carr Darren	6 2	13 07	D	4 9 68	Bristol	Trainee	Chesterfield	1	—
							Bristol R	30	0
							Newport Co	9	—
							Sheffield U	13	1
							Crewe Alex	104	5
							Chesterfield	76	3
Chambers Leroy†	5 11	12 00	F	25 10 72	Sheffield	Trainee	Sheffield W	—	—
							Chester C	21	1
							Chesterfield	—	—
Curtis Tom	5 8	10 08	M	1 3 73	Exeter	School	Derby Co	—	—
							Chesterfield	162	8
Dunn Iain	5 10	10 07	M	1 4 70	Derwent	School	York C	77	11
							Chesterfield	13	1
						Goole T	Huddersfield T	120	14
							Scunthorpe U (loan)	3	—
							Chesterfield	11	—
Dyche Sean	6 0	11 07	D	28 6 71	Kettering	Trainee	Nottingham F	—	—
							Chesterfield	231	8
Ebdon Marcus	5 10	11 02	M	17 10 70	Pontypool	Trainee	Everton	—	—
							Peterborough U	147	15
							Chesterfield	12	1
Gaughan Steve	6 0	12 04	M	14 4 70	Doncaster	Hatfield Main	Doncaster R	67	3
							Sunderland	—	—
							Darlington	171	15
							Chesterfield	18	—
Hewitt Jamie	5 10	10 08	M	17 5 68	Chesterfield	School	Chesterfield	249	14
							Doncaster R	33	—
							Chesterfield	132	9

Holland Paul	5 11	12 10	M	8 7 73	Lincoln	School	Mansfield T	149	25
							Sheffield U	18	1
							Chesterfield	42	5
Howard Jonathan	5 11	11 07	F	7 10 71	Sheffield	Trainee	Rotherham U	36	5
							Chesterfield	77	12
Jules Mark	5 7	10 09	D	5 9 71	Bradford	Trainee	Bradford C	—	—
							Scarborough	77	16
							Chesterfield	130	3
Lampkin Kevin†	6 0	12 02	M	20 12 72	Liverpool	Trainee	Liverpool	—	—
							Huddersfield T	13	—
							Mansfield T	42	3
							Chesterfield	—	—
Leaning Andy	6 2	13 00	G	18 5 63	York	Rowntree Mackintosh	York C	69	—
							Sheffield U	21	—
							Bristol C	75	—
							Lincoln C	36	—
							Chesterfield	9	—
Lomas James	5 11	10 09	M	18 10 77	Chesterfield	Trainee	Chesterfield	2	—
Lormor Tony	6 0	11 05	F	29 10 70	Ashington	Trainee	Newcastle U	8	3
							Norwich C (loan)	—	—
							Lincoln C	100	30
							Peterborough U	5	—
							Chesterfield	100	31
Lund Gary*	6 1	12 08	F	13 9 64	Grimsby	School	Grimsby T	60	24
							Lincoln C	44	13
							Notts Co	248	62
							Hull C (loan)	11	3
							Hull C (loan)	11	3
							Chesterfield	18	1
Mason Andy*	5 11	11 11	F	22 11 74	Bolton	Trainee	Bolton W	—	—
							Hull C	26	4
							Chesterfield	2	—
Mercer Billy	6 1	11 00	G	22 5 69	Liverpool	Trainee	Liverpool	—	—
							Rotherham U	104	—
							Sheffield U	4	—
							Nottingham F (loan)	—	—
							Chesterfield	69	—
Mitchell Andy*	6 0	12 00	D	12 9 76	Rotherham	Trainee	Aston Villa	—	—
							Chesterfield	2	—
Morris Andy	6 4	14 07	F	17 11 67	Sheffield	School	Rotherham U	7	—
							Chesterfield	261	55
							Exeter C (loan)	7	2
Perkins Chris	5 11	10 09	M	9 1 74	Nottingham	Trainee	Mansfield T	8	—
							Chesterfield	70	—
Rogers Lee	5 11	12 01	D	28 10 66	Doncaster	Doncaster R	Chesterfield	331	1
Williams Mark	6 0	12 04	D	28 9 70	Stalybridge	Newtown	Shrewsbury T	102	3
							Chesterfield	84	6
Wilson Mark†			M	12 5 78	Derby	Derby Co	Chesterfield	—	—

Trainees
Bamford, Paul G; Bowater, Jason; Clark, Damian M; Deakin, Mark; Henshaw, Carl H; Partridge, Paul G; Pearce, Alexander G; Sheppard, Jody; Spencer, Matthew.

COLCHESTER UNITED

Abrahams Paul	5 11	11 02	F	31 10 73	Colchester	Trainee	Colchester U	55	8
							Brentford	35	8
							Colchester U (loan)	8	2
							Colchester U	29	7
Adcock Tony	6 0	11 05	F	27 2 63	Bethnal Green	Apprentice	Colchester U	210	98
							Manchester C	15	5
							Northampton T	72	30
							Bradford C	38	6
							Northampton T	35	10
							Peterborough U	111	35
							Luton T	2	—
							Colchester U	77	23
Barnes David‡	5 10	11 01	D	16 11 61	London	Apprentice	Coventry C	9	—
							Ipswich T	17	—
							Wolverhampton W	88	4
							Aldershot	69	1
							Sheffield U	82	1
							Watford	16	—
							Colchester U	11	—
Betts Simon	5 7	11 00	D	3 3 73	Middlesbrough	Trainee	Ipswich T	—	—
							Scarborough	—	—
							Colchester U	146	9

Name	Ht	Wt	Pos	Born	Birthplace	Previous	Clubs	Apps	Gls
Buckle Paul	5 7	11 03	M	16 12 70	Welwyn	Trainee	Brentford	57	1
							Torquay U	59	9
							Exeter C	22	2
							Northampton T	—	—
							Wycombe W	—	—
							Colchester U	24	—
Caldwell Garrett	6 1	12 12	G	6 11 73	Princeton		Colchester U	6	—
Cawley Peter	6 4	15 07	D	15 9 65	London	Chertsey T	Wimbledon	1	—
							Bristol R (loan)	10	—
							Fulham (loan)	5	—
							Bristol R	3	—
							Southend U	7	1
							Exeter C	7	—
							Barnet	3	—
							Colchester U	153	8
Cook Anthony‡			M	17 9 76	Hemel Hempstead	Trainee	Colchester U	2	—
Duguid Karl	5 11	11 05	F	21 3 78	Hitchin	Trainee	Colchester U	36	4
Dunne Joe	5 9	11 08	D	25 5 73	Dublin	Trainee	Gillingham	115	1
							Colchester U	40	1
Emberson Carl	6 1	12 00	G	13 7 73	Epsom	Trainee	Millwall	—	—
							Colchester U (loan)	13	—
							Colchester U	96	—
Forbes Steve	6 1	11 04	M	24 12 75	London	Sittingbourne	Millwall	5	—
							Colchester U	1	1
Fry Chris	5 10	10 07	F	23 10 69	Cardiff	Trainee	Cardiff C	55	1
							Hereford U	90	10
							Colchester U	130	16
Gibbs Paul‡	5 10	11 09	D	26 10 72	Gorleston	Diss T	Colchester U	53	3
Greene David	6 4	14 04	D	26 10 73	Luton	Trainee	Luton T	19	—
							Colchester U (loan)	14	1
							Brentford (loan)	11	—
							Colchester U	44	2
Gregory David	5 10	12 00	M	23 1 70	Colchester	Trainee	Ipswich T	32	2
							Hereford U (loan)	2	—
							Peterborough U	3	—
							Colchester U	48	1
Haydon Nicky	5 10	11 07	M	10 8 78	Barking	Trainee	Colchester U	1	1
Lewis Ben*	5 10	12 04	D	22 6 77	Chelmsford	Trainee	Colchester U	2	—
Lock Tony	5 11	12 09	F	3 9 76	Harlow	Trainee	Colchester U	9	2
Locke Adam	6 0	12 00	M	20 8 70	Croydon	Trainee	Crystal Palace	—	—
							Southend U	73	4
							Colchester U (loan)	4	—
							Colchester U	79	8
McCarthy Tony	6 1	12 06	D	9 11 69	Dublin	Shelbourne	Millwall	21	1
							Crewe Alex (loan)	2	—
							Colchester U	89	1
Pitcher Geoff‡	5 7	11 05	M	15 8 75	Carshalton	Trainee	Millwall	—	—
							Watford	13	2
						Kingstonian	Colchester U	1	—
Sale Mark	6 3	13 05	F	27 2 72	Burton-on-Trent	Trainee	Stoke C	2	—
							Cambridge U	—	—
							Birmingham C	21	—
							Torquay U	44	8
							Preston NE	13	7
							Mansfield T	45	12
							Colchester U	10	3
Stamps Scott	5 10	11 00	D	20 3 75	Edgbaston	Trainee	Torquay U	86	5
							Colchester U	8	—
Whitton Steve	6 1	12 04	M	4 12 60	East Ham	Apprentice	Coventry C	74	21
							West Ham U	39	6
							Birmingham C (loan)	8	2
							Birmingham C	95	28
							Sheffield W	32	4
							Ipswich T	88	15
							Colchester U	95	20
Wilkins Richard	6 0	12 02	M	28 5 65	Streatham	Haverhill R	Colchester U	152	22
							Cambridge U	81	7
							Hereford U	77	5
							Colchester U	40	2

Trainees
Armitage, Gavin L; Barnes, Ben C P; Cook, Meyrick D; Cooksey, Ernest G; Craft, Daryl J; King, Aaron S; Kingshott, Daryll N; McCormack, Francis P; Newman, Robert D; Palfreyman, Andrew M; Rainford, David J; Rogers, Joel H; Terry, Simon J; Walsh, Marc D; Wiles, Ian R.

Associated Schoolboys
Atkinson, Robert P; Delaney, Paul M; Gyoury, Nicky D; Sinclair, Simon; Slatter, Daniel C; Smith, Nathan; Wheatstone, Jonathan M.

Associated Schoolboys who have accepted the club's offer of a Traineeship/Contract
Taylor, Andrew D; Watkins, John.

COVENTRY CITY

Name	Ht	Wt	Pos	Born	Birthplace	Source	Club	Apps	Gls
Andrews John			D	27 9 78	Cork	Trainee	Coventry C	—	—
Barnett Christopher			M	20 12 78	Derby	Trainee	Coventry C	—	—
Blake Aslam	5 11	11 12	F	19 10 79	Birmingham	Trainee	Coventry C	—	—
Blake Tim‡	6 2	13 00	D	25 9 75	Merthyr	Trainee	Coventry C	—	—
Boland Willie	5 9	11 02	M	6 8 75	Ennis	Trainee	Coventry C	44	—
Borrows Brian	5 10	11 12	D	20 12 60	Liverpool	Amateur	Everton	27	—
							Bolton W	95	—
							Coventry C	409	11
							Bristol C (loan)	6	—
Breen Gary	6 3	11 12	D	12 12 73	London	Charlton Ath	Maidstone U	19	—
							Gillingham	51	—
							Peterborough U	69	1
							Birmingham C	40	2
							Coventry C	9	—
Burrows David	5 10	11 08	D	25 10 68	Dudley	Apprentice	WBA	46	1
							Liverpool	146	3
							West Ham U	29	1
							Everton	19	—
							Coventry C	40	—
Busst David*	6 1	12 10	D	30 6 67	Birmingham	Moor Green	Coventry C	50	4
Christie lyseden	6 0	12 06	F	14 11 76	Coventry	Trainee	Coventry C	1	—
							Bournemouth (loan)	4	—
							Mansfield T (loan)	8	—
Costello Lorcan*	5 9	11 02	D	11 11 76	Dublin	Trainee	Coventry C	—	—
Daish Liam	6 2	13 05	D	23 9 68	Portsmouth	Apprentice	Portsmouth	1	—
							Cambridge U	139	4
							Birmingham C	73	3
							Coventry C	31	2
Dublin Dion	6 2	12 04	F	22 4 69	Leicester		Norwich C	—	—
							Cambridge U	156	52
							Manchester U	12	2
							Coventry C	99	40
Ducros Andrew	5 4	9 08	F	16 9 77	Evesham	Trainee	Coventry C	5	—
Eustace John	5 10	11 12	M	3 11 79	Solihull	Trainee	Coventry C	—	—
Evtushok Alex	6 2	12 10	D	11 1 70	Ukraine		Karpaty Lvov	64	4
							Dnepr	27	2
							Karpaty Lvov	9	—
							Coventry C	3	—
Faulconbridge Craig			F	20 4 78	Nuneaton	Trainee	Coventry C	—	—
Filan John	5 11	13 02	G	8 2 70	Sydney	Budapest St George	Cambridge U	68	0
							Nottingham F (loan)	—	—
							Coventry C	16	—
Genaux Regis	5 11	12 06	D	31 8 73	Belgium		Standard Liege	151	1
							Coventry C	4	—
Gillespie Gary*	6 2	12 07	D	5 7 60	Stirling	School	Falkirk	22	—
							Coventry C	172	6
							Liverpool	156	14
							Celtic	69	2
							Coventry C	3	—
Goodwin Scott	5 9	11 08	D	13 9 78	Hull	Trainee	Coventry C	—	—
Hall Marcus	6 1	12 02	D	24 3 76	Coventry	Trainee	Coventry C	43	0
Hawkins Colin*	6 1	12 06	G	17 8 77	Galway		Coventry C	—	—
Healy Brett*	5 8	10 08	M	6 10 77	Coventry	Trainee	Coventry C	—	—
Huckerby Darren	5 9	11 04	F	23 4 76	Nottingham	Trainee	Lincoln C	28	5
							Newcastle U	1	—
							Millwall (loan)	6	3
							Coventry C	25	5
Isaias *	5 10	12 10	M	17 11 63	Rio	Benfica	Coventry C	12	2
Jess Eoin	5 10	11 07	F	13 12 70	Aberdeen	Rangers	Aberdeen	201	50
							Coventry C	39	1
McAllister Gary	5 10	10 11	M	25 12 64	Motherwell	Fir Park BC	Motherwell	59	6
							Leicester C	201	47
							Leeds U	231	31
							Coventry C	38	6
McMenamin Chris*	5 10	11 10	M	27 12 73	Donegal	Hitchin T	Coventry C	—	—
Mitten Paul‡	5 8	10 12	F	22 12 75	Stockport	Manchester U	Stockport Co	—	—
							Coventry C	—	—
Ndlovu Peter	5 8	10 2	F	25 2 73	Zimbabwe	Highlanders	Coventry C	177	37
Nolan Carl*			D	7 3 78	Coventry	Trainee	Coventry C	—	—

Name	Ht	Wt	Pos	DOB	Birthplace	Source	Club	Apps	Gls
O'Neill Michael	5 11	10 10	F	5 7 69	Portadown	Coleraine	Newcastle U	48	15
							Dundee U	64	11
							Hibernian	98	19
							Coventry C	1	—
O'Toole Gavin*	5 9	11 00	M	19 9 75	Dublin	Trainee	Coventry C	—	—
							Hereford U (loan)	1	—
Ogrizovic Steve	6 5	15 00	G	12 9 57	Mansfield	ONRYC	Chesterfield	16	—
							Liverpool	4	—
							Shrewsbury T	84	—
							Coventry C	478	1
Prenderville Barry	6 0	12 08	D	16 10 76	Dublin	Trainee	Coventry C	—	—
Quinn Barry	6 0	12 02	M	9 5 79	Dublin	Trainee	Coventry C	—	—
Richardson Kevin	5 7	11 07	M	4 12 62	Newcastle	Apprentice	Everton	109	16
							Watford	39	2
							Arsenal	96	5
							Real Sociedad	37	—
							Aston Villa	143	13
							Coventry C	75	—
Salako John	5 9	12 03	F	11 2 69	Nigeria	Trainee	Crystal Palace	215	22
							Swansea C (loan)	13	3
							Coventry C	61	4
Shaw Richard	5 9	12 08	D	11 9 68	Brentford	Apprentice	Crystal Palace	207	3
							Hull C (loan)	4	—
							Coventry C	56	—
Shilton Sam	5 10	11 06	M	21 7 78	Nottingham	Schoolboy	Plymouth Arg	3	—
							Coventry C	—	—
Strachan Gavin	5 10	11 07	M	23 12 78	Aberdeen	Trainee	Coventry C	—	—
Strachan Gordon	5 6	10 06	M	9 2 57	Edinburgh		Dundee	60	13
							Aberdeen	183	55
							Manchester U	160	33
							Leeds U	197	37
							Coventry C	26	—
Telfer Paul	5 9	11 06	M	21 10 71	Edinburgh	Trainee	Luton T	144	19
							Coventry C	65	1
Whelan Noel	6 2	12 03	F	30 12 74	Leeds	Trainee	Leeds U	48	7
							Coventry C	56	14
Williams Jamie‡	5 7	9 06	M	21 2 77	Coventry	Trainee	Coventry C	—	—
Williams Paul	6 0	12 10	D	26 3 71	Burton	Trainee	Derby Co	160	26
							Lincoln C (loan)	3	—
							Coventry C	64	4
Willis Adam	6 1	12 02	M	21 9 76	Nuneaton	Trainee	Coventry C	—	—

Trainees
Beech, Sean P; Bindley, Christopher J; Burrows, Mark; Colwell, Richard P; Devaney, Martin T; Hughes, Craig A; McGregor, Scott C; Morgan, Leon R; Mullen, Nicky R; Sumner, Jed; Vincent, Luke R; Williams, Jamie L.

Associated Schoolboys
Ashby, Jason; Brush, David J; Cook, Matthew; Cudworth, Thomas J S; Dagnan, Kieran; Downing, Roy J; Earl, Peter R; English, Mark M; Gough, Steven; Hall, Daniel; Jesson, Laurence M; Lewis, David M J; McSheffrey, Gary; Messenger, Kevin; Muir, Richard A D; Mullin, Patrick J; Padmore, Stephen R; Pead, Craig G; Shanahan, Aaron; Steane, Ben; Thompson, Nathan.

Associated Schoolboys who have accepted the club's offer of a Traineeship/Contract
Eribenne, Chutwun Y; Kirkland, Christopher E; Pearson, David; Watson, Steven.

CREWE ALEXANDRA

Name	Ht	Wt	Pos	DOB	Birthplace	Source	Club	Apps	Gls
Adebola Dele	6 3	12 06	F	23 6 75	Lagos	Trainee	Crewe Alex	97	32
Anthrobus Steve	6 3	12 13	F	10 11 68	Lewisham		Millwall	21	4
							Southend U (loan)	—	—
							Wimbledon	28	—
							Peterborough U (loan)	2	—
							Chester C (loan)	7	—
							Shrewsbury T	72	16
							Crewe Alex	10	—
Bankole Ademola			G	9 9 69	Nigeria	Leyton Orient	Crewe Alex	3	—
Barr Billy*	5 11	10 08	M	21 1 69	Halifax	Trainee	Halifax T	196	13
						Halifax T	Crewe Alex	85	7
Billing Peter*	6 0	13 02	D	24 10 64	Liverpool	South Liverpool	Everton	1	—
							Crewe Alex	88	1
							Coventry C	58	1
							Port Vale (loan)	12	—
							Port Vale	14	—
							Hartlepool U	36	—
							Crewe Alex	15	—
Bunce Chet‡			M	29 8 75	Auckland	Melville	Crewe Alex	—	—
Charnock Phil	5 10	11 03	M	14 2 75	Southport	Trainee	Liverpool	—	—
							Blackpool (loan)	4	—
							Crewe Alex	32	1

Coffey Chris‡			D	10 10 77	Newry	Arsenal	Crewe Alex	—	—
Collins James			M	28 5 78	Liverpool	Trainee	Crewe Alex	—	—
Cutler Neil	6 4	13 04	G	3 9 76	Birmingham	Trainee	WBA	—	—
							Coventry C (loan)	—	—
							Chester C (loan)	1	—
							Crewe Alex	—	—
							Chester C (loan)	5	—
Garvey Steve	5 9	10 09	F	22 11 73	Tameside	Trainee	Crewe Alex	95	6
Gayle Mark	6 2	12 03	G	21 10 69	Bromsgrove	Trainee	Leicester C	—	—
							Blackpool	—	—
						Worcester C	Walsall	75	—
							Crewe Alex	83	—
							Liverpool (loan)	—	—
							Birmingham C (loan)	—	—
Johnson Seth			D	12 3 79	Birmingham	Trainee	Crewe Alex	11	1
Kearton Jason	6 1	11 10	G	9 7 69	Ipswich (Aus)	Brisbane Lions	Everton	6	—
							Stoke C (loan)	16	—
							Blackpool (loan)	14	—
							Notts Co (loan)	10	—
							Preston NE (loan)	—	—
							Crewe Alex	30	—
Launders Brian*	5 10	11 10	M	8 1 76	Dublin	Trainee	Crystal Palace	4	—
							Oldham Ath (loan)	—	—
							Crewe Alex	9	—
Lightfoot Chris	6 1	12 00	M	1 4 70	Warrington	Trainee	Chester C	277	32
							Wigan Ath	14	1
							Crewe Alex	31	—
Little Colin	5 10	11 00	F	4 11 72	Wythenshaw	Hyde U	Crewe Alex	29	1
Macauley Steve	6 1	12 00	D	4 3 69	Lytham	Fleetwood T	Crewe Alex	165	20
Moralee Jamie	5 11	11 00	F	2 12 71	Wandsworth	Trainee	Crystal Palace	6	—
							Millwall	67	19
							Watford	49	7
							Crewe Alex	7	—
Murphy Danny	5 9	10 08	M	18 3 77	Chester	Trainee	Crewe Alex	134	27
Norris Richard			M	5 1 78	Birkenhead	Marine	Crewe Alex	—	—
Parker Justin‡			D	11 11 76	Stoke	Trainee	Crewe Alex	—	—
Pope Steven	5 11	11 00	D	8 9 76	Mow Cop	Trainee	Crewe Alex	—	—
Rivers Mark	5 10	11 00	F	26 11 75	Crewe	Trainee	Crewe Alex	60	16
Savage Rob	6 0	10 01	F	18 10 74	Wrexham	Trainee	Manchester U	—	—
							Crewe Alex	77	10
Smith Peter			F	18 9 78	Rhuddlan	Trainee	Crewe Alex	1	—
Smith Shaun	5 10	11 00	D	9 4 71	Leeds	Trainee	Halifax T	7	—
							Crewe Alex	195	24
Street Kevin			M	25 11 77	Crewe	Trainee	Crewe Alex	—	—
Tierney Francis	5 10	11 00	M	10 9 75	Liverpool	Trainee	Crewe Alex	83	10
Turpin Simon‡	6 3	11 08	D	11 8 75	Blackburn	Trainee	Crewe Alex	—	—
Unsworth Lee	5 11	11 02	D	25 2 73	Eccles	Ashton U	Crewe Alex	58	—
Westwood Ashley	6 0	11 03	D	31 8 76	Bridgnorth	Trainee	Manchester U	—	—
							Crewe Alex	77	6
Whalley Gareth	5 10	11 06	M	19 12 73	Manchester	Trainee	Crewe Alex	162	8

Trainees
Allen, Christopher D; Brown, Christopher M; Burrows, Benjamin J; Chadwick, Gareth P; Cox, Lee A; Critchley, Neil; Hulse, Robert W; Jones, Andrew J; Knight, Darren P; Lunt, Kenny V; Morse, Peter R; Mottram, Paul G; Richardson, Paul M; Smith, Aaran P; Webster, Colin J L; Welsby, Kevin J; Whittaker, David A; Wright, David.

Associated Schoolboys
Angell, Barry; Baylis, Philip; Blake, Mathew L; Bostock, Andrew M; Edwards, Paul; Griffiths, Thomas P; Harris, Paul J; Jeffs, Ian D; Jones, John P; Jones, Robert A; Liddle, Gareth J C; Lunt, Gary T; Malpass, John; Marrow, James F J; Marsh, Nicholas J; McCready, Christopher J; Morris, Alexander S; Rix, Benjamin; Robinson, James G; Shore, Peter T; Vaughan, David O; Westwood, Lee K; Wilcock, James W.

Associated Schoolboys who have accepted the club's offer of a Traineeship/Contract
Arrowsmith, Paul; Beeston, Mark A; Foster, Stephen J; Grant, John; Hill, Sammy G; Hoult, Stephen R; Laurie, Carl A; Walker, Richard S.

CRYSTAL PALACE

Andersen Leif	6 4	13 00	D	19 4 71	Fredrikstad	Moss	Crystal Palace	30	1
Boxall Danny	5 8	10 05	D	24 8 77	Croydon	Trainee	Crystal Palace	7	—
Burton Sagi	6 2	13 06	D	25 11 77	Birmingham	Trainee	Crystal Palace	—	—
Carlisle Wayne	5 7	10 00	M	9 9 79	Lisburn	Trainee	Crystal Palace	—	—
Cyrus Andrew*	5 8	9 03	D	30 9 76	Lambeth	Trainee	Crystal Palace	1	—
Davies Gareth	6 1	12 00	D	11 12 73	Hereford	Trainee	Hereford U	95	1
							Crystal Palace	26	2
							Cardiff C (loan)	6	2

Name	Ht	Wt	Pos	Birthdate	Birthplace	Source	Club	Apps	Gls
Day Chris	6 2	13 06	G	28 7 75	Whipps Cross	Trainee	Tottenham H	—	—
							Crystal Palace	24	—
Dyer Bruce	5 11	11 03	F	13 4 75	Ilford	Trainee	Watford	31	6
							Crystal Palace	105	31
Edworthy Marc	5 7	9 08	D	24 12 72	Barnstaple	Trainee	Plymouth Arg	69	1
							Crystal Palace	89	—
Enqvist Bjorn‡	5 10	10 09	M	12 10 77	Lund	Malmo	Crystal Palace	—	—
Evans Tom*	6 0	12 00	G	31 12 76	Doncaster	Trainee	Sheffield U	—	—
							Crystal Palace	—	—
							Coventry C (loan)	—	—
Folan Anthony	6 0	11 00	F	18 9 78	Lewisham	Trainee	Crystal Palace	—	—
Freedman Dougie	5 9	11 02	F	21 1 74	Glasgow	Trainee	QPR	—	—
							Barnet	47	27
							Crystal Palace	83	31
Ginty Rory	5 9	11 00	M	23 1 77	Galway	Trainee	Crystal Palace	—	—
Gordon Dean	6 0	13 04	D	10 2 73	Thornton Heath	Trainee	Crystal Palace	164	18
Graham Gareth	5 7	10 07	M	6 12 78	Belfast	Trainee	Crystal Palace	—	—
Harris Jason	6 1	11 10	F	24 11 76	Sutton	Trainee	Crystal Palace	2	—
							Bristol R (loan)	6	2
Hibbert James	5 11	11 07	D	30 10 79	Ashford	Trainee	Crystal Palace	—	—
Hopkin David	5 9	10 03	M	21 8 70	Greenock	Pt Glasgow R BC	Morton	18	0
							Chelsea	40	1
							Crystal Palace	83	21
Houghton Ray	5 7	10 10	M	9 1 62	Glasgow	Amateur	West Ham U	1	—
							Fulham	129	16
							Oxford U	83	10
							Liverpool	153	28
							Aston Villa	95	6
							Crystal Palace	72	7
Kennedy Richard	5 11	11 00	M	28 8 78	Waterford	Trainee	Crystal Palace	—	—
Linighan Andy	6 4	13 10	D	18 6 62	Hartlepool	Smiths BC	Hartlepool U	110	4
							Leeds U	66	3
							Oldham Ath	87	6
							Norwich C	86	8
							Arsenal	118	5
							Crystal Palace	19	2
Martin Andrew	6 0	10 10	F	28 2 80	Cardiff	Trainee	Crystal Palace	—	—
McKenzie Leon	5 11	10 00	F	17 5 78	Croydon	Trainee	Crystal Palace	33	2
Morrison Clinton	5 10	10 00	F	14 5 79	Tooting	Trainee	Crystal Palace	—	—
Mullins Hayden	5 11	10 07	D	27 3 79	Reading	Trainee	Crystal Palace	—	—
Muscat Kevin	5 11	11 07	D	7 8 73	Crawley	South Melbourne	Crystal Palace	44	2
Nash Carlo	6 4	12 07	G	13 9 73	Bolton	Clitheroe	Crystal Palace	21	—
Ndah George	6 1	11 04	M	23 12 74	Camberwell	Trainee	Crystal Palace	75	8
							Bournemouth (loan)	12	2
Ormshaw Gareth	6 0	11 07	G	8 7 79	Durban	Ramblers	Crystal Palace	—	—
Parry David‡	5 10	11 02	M	12 3 78	Belfast	Trainee	Crystal Palace	—	—
Pitcher Darren	5 9	12 02	M	12 10 69	London	Trainee	Charlton Ath	173	8
							Crystal Palace	64	—
Quinn Robert	5 11	11 02	D	8 11 76	Sidcup	Trainee	Crystal Palace	22	1
Roberts Andy	5 10	13 00	M	20 3 74	Dartford	Trainee	Millwall	138	5
							Crystal Palace	83	2
Rodger Simon	5 9	11 09	M	3 10 71	Shoreham	Trainee	Crystal Palace	126	5
							Manchester C (loan)	8	1
							Stoke C (loan)	5	—
Scully Tony	5 7	11 05	M	12 6 76	Dublin	Trainee	Crystal Palace	3	—
							Bournemouth (loan)	10	—
							Cardiff C (loan)	14	—
Shipperley Neil	6 1	13 11	F	30 10 74	Chatham	Trainee	Chelsea	37	7
							Watford (loan)	6	1
							Southampton	66	12
							Crystal Palace	32	12
Stevens David	5 10	11 00	F	29 4 79	Ashford	Trainee	Crystal Palace	—	—
Thomson Steven	5 7	10 00	M	23 1 78	Glasgow	Trainee	Crystal Palace	—	—
Tuttle David	6 2	12 10	D	6 2 72	Reading	Trainee	Tottenham H	13	—
							Peterborough U (loan)	7	—
							Sheffield U	63	1
							Crystal Palace	49	3
Veart Carl	5 10	11 05	F	21 5 70	Whyalla	Adelaide C	Sheffield U	66	15
							Crystal Palace	51	6
Wales Danny‡	6 0	11 00	F	17 11 77	London	Trainee	Crystal Palace	—	—
Wordsworth Dean			F	2 7 72	London	Bromley	Crystal Palace	—	—

Trainees
Clarke, Jonathan; Harney, Michael D; Loughran, Kieran; Sears, Paul M; Small-King, Shane O P; Woozley, David J.

Associated Schoolboys
Bibby, Matthew J; Dimond, Kristian; Fieldwick, Lee P; Gooding, Scott; Hunt, David.

Associated Schoolboys who have accepted the club's offer of a Traineeship/Contract
Boardman, Jonathan G; Dsane, Roscoe; Fowler, Michael D; Hankin, Sean A; Harris, Richard; Kendall, Lee M; Manby, David J; Wilde, Bobby.

DARLINGTON

Name			Pos	Birth date	Birthplace	Prev. club	Club	Apps	Gls
Alderson Simon†	5 11	11 08	D	15 12 77	Darlington	Trainee	Darlington	—	—
Atkinson Brian	5 9	12 02	M	19 1 71	Darlington	Trainee	Sunderland	141	4
							Carlisle U (loan)	2	—
							Darlington	30	3
Atkinson Jon†			M	18 9 72	Ashington	Morpeth T	Darlington	5	—
Barbara Daniel‡			F	12 10 74	France	FC Lourosa	Darlington	6	1
Barnard Mark	5 10	11 07	D	27 11 75	Sheffield	Trainee	Rotherham U	—	—
							Darlington	74	3
Brumwell Phil	5 8	11 00	M	8 8 75	Darlington	Trainee	Sunderland	—	—
							Darlington	66	1
Brydon Lee	5 11	11 00	D	15 11 74	Stockton	Trainee	Liverpool	—	—
							Darlington	25	—
Byrne Wesley†	5 9	11 03	D	9 2 77	Dublin	Trainee	Middlesbrough	—	—
							Darlington	2	—
Carss Anthony*	5 9	11 05	M	31 3 76	Alnwick	Bradford C	Blackburn R	—	—
							Darlington	57	2
Collins Michael‡	5 10	12 00	D	6 9 77	Belfast	Coleraine	Darlington	1	—
Crosby Andy	6 2	13 07	D	3 3 73	Rotherham	Leeds U	Doncaster R	51	0
							Darlington	147	2
Devos Jason			D	2 1 74	Ontario	Montreal Impact	Darlington	8	—
Faulkner David‡	6 1	12 13	D	8 10 75	Sheffield	Trainee	Sheffield W	—	—
							Darlington	4	—
Hope Mark†			D	13 6 70	Isleworth	Porthleven	Darlington	1	—
Hope Richard	6 2	12 06	D	22 6 78	Stockton	Trainee	Blackburn R	—	—
							Darlington	20	—
Hunt David§			D	5 3 80	Durham	Trainee	Darlington	1	—
Innes Gary‡	5 10	11 00	F	7 10 77	Shotley Bridge		Darlington	15	—
Johnson Frank†	6 3	13 00	G	24 2 77	South Shields		Darlington	—	—
Kelly Russell‡	5 10	11 00	M	10 8 76	Ballymoney	Trainee	Leyton Orient (loan)	6	—
							Darlington	23	2
Key Danny‡	5 6	11 00	M	1 1 77	Darlington	Trainee	Darlington	3	—
Lowe Kenny*	6 1	11 13	M	6 11 64	Sedgefield	Apprentice	Hartlepool U	54	3
						Barrow	Scarborough	4	—
							Barnet	72	5
						Barrow	Stoke C	9	—
							Birmingham C	21	3
							Carlisle U (loan)	2	—
							Hartlepool U (loan)	13	3
							Darlington	7	—
McClelland John†	6 2	13 02	D	7 12 55	Belfast	Portadown	Cardiff C	4	1
						Bangor	Mansfield T	125	8
							Rangers	96	4
							Watford	184	3
							Leeds U	24	—
							Watford (loan)	1	—
							Notts Co (loan)	6	—
							St Johnstone	27	—
							Wycombe W	—	—
						Retired	Darlington	1	—
Naylor Glenn	5 11	11 00	F	11 8 72	York	Trainee	York C	111	30
							Darlington (loan)	4	1
							Darlington	37	11
Newell Paul‡	6 2	14 07	G	23 2 69	Greenwich	Trainee	Southend U	15	—
							Leyton Orient	61	—
							Colchester U (loan)	14	—
							Barnet	16	—
							Darlington	41	—
Oliver Michael	5 10	12 04	M	2 8 75	Cleveland	Trainee	Middlesbrough	—	—
							Stockport Co	22	1
							Darlington	39	9
Olsson Paul†	6 0	12 10	M	24 12 65	Hull	Apprentice	Hull C	—	—
							Exeter C (loan)	8	—
							Exeter C	35	2
							Scarborough	48	5
							Hartlepool U	171	13
							Darlington	76	8

Name	Ht	Wt	Pos	Born	Birthplace	Source	Club	Apps	Gls
Roberts Darren	6 0	12 04	F	12 10 69	Birmingham	Burton Alb	Wolverhampton W	21	5
							Hereford U (loan)	6	5
							Doncaster R	—	—
							Chesterfield	25	1
							Darlington	44	16
Robinson Paul§			F	20 11 78	Sunderland	Trainee	Darlington	7	—
Shaw Simon	5 11	11 02	M	21 9 73	Teeside	Trainee	Darlington	145	10
Shutt Carl	5 11	10 10	F	10 10 61	Sheffield	Spalding U	Sheffield W	40	16
							Bristol C	46	10
							Leeds U	79	17
							Birmingham C	26	4
							Manchester C (loan)	6	—
							Bradford C	88	15
							Darlington	6	2
Speare James*	6 1	13 00	G	5 11 76	Liverpool	Trainee	Everton	—	—
							Darlington	3	—
Twynham Gary	5 11	12 07	M	8 2 76	Manchester	Trainee	Manchester U	—	—
							Darlington	31	3

Trainees
Campbell, Paul A; Carfoot, Jamie; Christie, David; Dann, Steven W; Darke, Peter; Gilmore, Paul A; Henwood, Mark D; Hunt, David; Pickersgill, Stephen; Robinson, Paul D; Roxby, John P; Tarrant, Neil K.

Associated Schoolboys
Foster, Stephen M; Gordon, Steven M; Liddle, Graham B; Williamson, Garry.

Associated Schoolboys who have accepted the club's offer of a Traineeship/Contract
Carter, Michael D; Kilty, Mark T; Skelton, Craig E; Stokoe, Dennis M.

DERBY COUNTY

Name	Ht	Wt	Pos	Born	Birthplace	Source	Club	Apps	Gls
Asanovic Aljosa	6 1	11 12	M	14 12 65	Split		Hajduk Split	116	28
							Metz	35	13
							Cannes	28	7
							Montpellier	43	10
							Hajduk Split	33	8
							Derby Co	34	6
Boden Chris	5 9	11 12	D	13 10 73	Wolverhampton	Trainee	Aston Villa	1	—
							Barnsley (loan)	4	—
							Derby Co	10	—
							Shrewsbury T (loan)	5	—
Carbon Matt	6 2	14 00	D	8 6 75	Nottingham	Trainee	Lincoln C	69	10
							Derby Co	16	—
Carsley Lee	5 9	12 00	D	28 2 74	Birmingham	Trainee	Derby Co	82	3
Cooper Kevin	5 7	10 07	M	8 2 75	Derby	Trainee	Derby Co	2	—
							Stockport Co (loan)	12	3
Dailly Christian	6 0	12 06	D	23 10 73	Dundee		Dundee U	141	18
							Derby Co	36	3
Davies Will‡	6 2	13 01	F	27 9 75	Derby	Trainee	Derby Co	2	—
Elliott Steven			M	29 10 78	Derby	Trainee	Derby Co	—	—
Flynn Sean	5 8	12 00	M	13 3 68	Birmingham	Halesowen T	Coventry C	97	9
							Derby Co	59	3
							Stoke C (loan)	5	—
Gabbiadini Marco*	5 10	13 00	F	20 1 68	Nottingham	Apprentice	York C	60	14
							Sunderland	157	74
							Crystal Palace	15	5
							Derby Co	188	50
							Birmingham C (loan)	2	—
							Oxford U (loan)	5	1
Hoult Russell	6 4	14 07	G	22 11 72	Ashby	Trainee	Leicester C	10	—
							Lincoln C (loan)	2	—
							Blackpool (loan)	—	—
							Bolton W (loan)	4	—
							Lincoln C (loan)	15	—
							Derby Co (loan)	15	—
							Derby Co	73	—
Kozluk Robert			M	5 8 77	Mansfield	Trainee	Derby Co	—	—
Laursen Jacob	5 11	12 01	D	6 10 71	Vejle		Silkeborg	125	8
							Derby Co	36	1
McDonald Jamie			M	29 1 80	Luton	Trainee	Derby Co	—	—
McGrath Paul*	6 2	14 03	D	4 12 59	Ealing	St Patrick's Ath	Manchester U	163	12
							Aston Villa	253	9
							Derby Co	24	—
Murphy Shaun*			M	21 12 77	Derby	Trainee	Derby Co	—	—
Poom Mart	6 5	13 05	G	3 2 72	Tallinn	FC Wil Flora Tallinn	Portsmouth	4	—
							Derby Co	4	—
Powell Chris	5 10	11 07	M	8 9 69	Lambeth	Trainee	Crystal Palace	3	—
							Aldershot (loan)	11	—
							Southend U	248	3
							Derby Co	54	—

Name	Ht	Wt	Pos	Birthdate	Birthplace	Source	Club	Apps	Gls
Powell Darryl	6 0	13 00	M	15 1 71	Lambeth	Trainee	Portsmouth	132	16
							Derby Co	70	6
Radzki Lee			M	14 11 78	Mansfield	Trainee	Derby Co	—	—
Rahmberg Marino‡	5 11	11 12	M	7 8 74	Orebro	Degerfors	Lyngby	6	1
							Derby Co	1	—
Rowett Gary	6 0	12 07	D	6 3 74	Bromsgrove	Trainee	Cambridge U	63	9
							Everton	4	—
							Blackpool	17	—
							Derby Co	70	1
Simpson Paul	5 8	11 11	F	26 7 66	Carlisle	Apprentice	Manchester C	121	18
							Oxford U	144	43
							Derby Co	185	48
							Sheffield U (loan)	6	—
Smith Craig	6 1	13 07	M	2 8 76	Mansfield	Trainee	Derby Co	—	—
Solis Mauricio	5 8	12 00	M	13 12 72	Costa Rica	Herediano	Derby Co	2	—
Stimac Igor	6 2	13 00	D	6 9 67	Metkovic	Hajduk Split	Cadiz	62	4
							Hajduk Split	21	2
							Derby Co	48	2
Sturridge Dean	5 8	12 06	F	27 7 73	Birmingham	Trainee	Derby Co	92	32
							Torquay U (loan)	10	5
Sutton Wayne	6 0	13 09	D	1 10 75	Derby	Trainee	Derby Co	7	—
							Hereford U (loan)	4	—
Taylor Martin*	5 11	13 09	G	9 12 66	Tamworth	Mile Oak R	Derby Co	97	—
							Carlisle U (loan)	10	—
							Scunthorpe U (loan)	8	—
							Crewe Alex (loan)	6	—
							Wycombe W (loan)	4	—
Tretton Andrew*	6 0	12 08	D	9 10 76	Derby	Trainee	Derby Co	—	—
Trollope Paul	6 0	12 00	M	3 6 72	Swindon	Trainee	Swindon T	—	—
							Torquay U (loan)	10	—
							Torquay U	96	16
							Derby Co	55	5
							Grimsby T (loan)	7	1
							Crystal Palace (loan)	9	—
Van der Laan Robin	6 0	13 08	M	5 9 68	Schiedam	Wageningen	Port Vale	176	24
							Derby Co	55	8
							Wolverhampton W (loan)	7	—
Wanchope Paulo	6 4	12 05	F	31 1 76	Costa Rica	Herediano	Derby Co	5	1
Ward Ashley	6 1	13 00	F	24 11 70	Manchester	Trainee	Manchester C	1	—
							Wrexham (loan)	4	2
							Leicester C	10	—
							Blackpool (loan)	2	1
							Crewe Alex	61	25
							Norwich C	53	18
							Derby Co	37	9
Wassall Darren‡	6 0	12 07	D	27 6 68	Edgbaston		Nottingham F	27	—
							Hereford U (loan)	5	—
							Bury (loan)	7	1
							Derby Co	98	—
							Manchester C (loan)	15	—
							Birmingham C (loan)	8	—
Wilkinson Mark			M	16 3 79	Coventry	Trainee	Derby Co	—	—
Willems Ron	6 1	12 05	F	20 9 66	Epe		PEC Zwolle	43	7
							Twente	85	16
							Ajax	47	15
							Grasshoppers	56	18
							Derby Co	49	13
Wright Nick	5 9	11 07	F	15 10 75	Derby	Trainee	Derby Co	—	—
Yates Dean	6 1	12 08	D	26 10 67	Leicester	Apprentice	Notts Co	314	33
							Derby Co	59	3

Trainees
Greenhill, Ross F; McBridge, Liam; Messina, Roberto; Murphy, Leroy A; Rattray, Vincent M; Rowntree, Martyn E; Thornhill, Wayne; Wall, James.

Associated Schoolboys
Adams, Wayne A; Alexander, Earl; Archbold, Shaun J; Askey, Richard; Clare, Robert; Evatt, Ian R; Murray, Adam D; Pitter, Dominic J; Rickards, Scott; Robinson, Marvin L S C; Sidhu, Amrit S; Smith, Matthew E; Stanley, Matthew S; Stevens, Paul; Thompson, Mitchell G; Villers, Lee W; Wraith, Paul J.

Associated Schoolboys who have accepted the club's offer of a Traineeship/Contract
Bate, Christopher T; Betteridge, Thomas D; Gummer, Sean M; Hanson, Craig P; Morton, Colin; Phillips, Tom.

DONCASTER ROVERS

Name	Ht	Wt	Pos	Birthdate	Birthplace	Source	Club	Apps	Gls
Anderson Lee†	5 7	10 08	D	4 10 73	Manchester	Trainee	Bury	29	—
							Doncaster R	6	—
Beirne Michael‡			F	21 9 73	Manchester	Manchester C	Doncaster R	1	—

Name	Ht	Wt	Pos	Born	Birthplace	Source	Club	Apps	Gls
Black Simon‡	6 1	11 09	F	9 11 75	Marston Green	Trainee	Birmingham C	2	—
							Doncaster R	—	—
Bunch James‡	5 9	11 05	D	5 12 76	Sandwell	Trainee	Birmingham C	—	—
							Doncaster R	—	—
Byng David‡	6 2	13 12	F	9 7 77	Walsgrave	Trainee	Torquay U	24	3
							Doncaster R	—	—
Clark Ian	5 11	11 02	M	23 10 74	Stockton	Stockton	Doncaster R	43	3
Coady Lewis†	6 1	11 05	F	20 9 76	Liverpool	Trainee	Wrexham	2	—
							Doncaster R	1	—
Colcombe Scott‡	5 6	10 04	F	15 12 71	West Bromwich	Trainee	WBA	—	—
							Torquay U	89	1
							Doncaster R	42	4
Cramb Colin	6 0	13 00	F	23 6 74	Lanark	Hamilton A BC	Hamilton A	48	10
							Southampton	1	—
							Falkirk	8	1
							Hearts	6	—
							Doncaster R	62	25
Cunningham Harvey			D	11 9 68	Manchester	Trafford Barons	Doncaster R	11	—
Dixon Kerry	6 1	13 10	F	24 7 61	Luton	Dunstable	Reading	116	51
							Chelsea	335	147
							Southampton	9	2
							Luton T (loan)	17	3
							Luton T	58	16
							Millwall	31	9
							Watford	11	—
							Doncaster R	16	3
Doling Stuart‡	5 8	12 00	M	28 10 72	Newport, IOW	Trainee	Portsmouth	37	4
							Torquay U	—	—
							Doncaster R	6	—
Donnelly Mark§				22 12 79	Leeds	Trainee	Doncaster R	2	—
Esdaille Darren			D	4 11 74	Manchester	Hyde U	Doncaster R	18	1
Fahy Alan†			M	27 1 72	Liverpool	Barrow	Doncaster R	5	—
Gore Ian	5 11	12 04	D	10 1 68	Whiston		Birmingham C	—	—
						Southport	Blackpool	200	—
							Torquay U	25	2
							Doncaster R	41	1
Gray Alan‡	6 0	12 02	D	26 5 74	Carlisle	US Colleges	Doncaster R	1	—
Hawthorne Mark			M	21 8 79	Sunderland	Trainee	Doncaster R	—	—
Hayrettin Hakan‡	5 9	12 04	M	4 2 70	London	Trainee Barnet	Leyton Orient	—	—
							Barnet	6	—
							Torquay U (loan)	4	—
							Wycombe W	19	1
							Cambridge U	17	—
							Doncaster R	—	—
Ireland Simon	5 10	10 07	M	23 11 71	Barnstaple	School	Huddersfield T	19	—
							Wrexham (loan)	5	—
							Blackburn R	1	—
							Mansfield T (loan)	9	1
							Mansfield T	85	10
							Doncaster R	27	2
Jones Ian‡	5 7	10 02	M	25 10 76	Birmingham	Trainee	Birmingham C	—	—
							Doncaster R	—	—
Knight Jason‡	6 1	11 09	M	16 9 74	Australia	West Ham U	Doncaster R	4	—
Larmour David	5 9	11 00	F	23 8 77	Belfast	Liverpool	Doncaster R	20	0
Leach Gavin‡	6 1	13 06	M	9 8 77	Middlesbrough	Stockton	Doncaster R	—	—
Marquis Paul*	6 2	12 04	D	29 8 72	Enfield	Trainee	West Ham U	1	—
							Doncaster R	29	1
McDonald Martin	6 0	11 07	M	4 12 73	Glasgow	Southport	Doncaster R	33	2
Messer Gary§			F	22 9 79	Consett	Trainee	Doncaster R	1	—
Moore Darren	6 2	15 00	D	22 4 74	Birmingham	Trainee	Torquay U	103	8
							Doncaster R	76	7
Murphy Jamie‡	6 1	13 00	D	25 2 73	Manchester	Trainee	Blackpool	55	1
							Doncaster R	54	—
O'Connor Gary*	6 3	13 00	G	7 4 74	Newtongrange	Dalkeith Th	Hearts	—	—
							Berwick R	39	—
							Hearts	3	—
							Doncaster R	26	—
Paul Martin‡	5 8	9 07	F	2 2 75	Whalley	Trainee	Bristol R	22	1
							Doncaster R	—	—
Pemberton Martin	5 11	10 04	F	1 2 76	Bradford	Trainee	Oldham Ath	5	—
							Doncaster R	9	1
Pearce Stephen	6 0	12 04	F	29 9 74	Sutton Coldfield	Trainee	Wolverhampton W	—	—
							Doncaster R	19	1

Name	Ht	Wt	Pos	Born	Birthplace	Source	Club	Apps	Gls
Robertson Paul‡	5 7	11 08	D	5 2 72	Stockport	York C	Stockport Co	10	—
							Bury	8	—
						Runcorn	Doncaster R	20	—
Robinson Earl‡	6 3	12 05	M	8 10 78	Birmingham		Doncaster R	—	—
Ryan Tim‡	5 11	12 00	D	10 12 74	Stockport	Trainee	Scunthorpe U	2	—
						Buxton	Doncaster R	28	—
Schofield Jon	5 11	11 08	M	16 5 65	Barnsley	Gainsborough T	Lincoln C	231	11
							Doncaster R	110	12
Smith Mike	5 10	11 05	M	28 9 73	Liverpool	Runcorn	Doncaster R	31	2
Speight Martyn‡			D	26 7 78	Stockton	Trainee	Doncaster R	1	—
Utley Darren	6 0	11 07	D	28 9 77	Barnsley	Trainee	Doncaster R	24	1
Walker Steven‡			M	2 11 73	Ashington	Blyth Spartans	Doncaster R	1	—
Warren Lee	6 0	12 00	M	28 2 69	Manchester	Trainee	Leeds U	—	—
							Rochdale	31	1
							Hull C	153	1
							Lincoln C (loan)	3	1
							Doncaster R	81	2
Wheeler Adam*	6 0	13 10	G	29 11 77	Sheffield	Newcastle U	Doncaster R	1	—
Williams Dean	6 1	12 09	G	5 1 72	Lichfield	Tamworth	Brentford	7	—
							Doncaster R	79	—

Trainees
Borg, John C A; Combellack, Brian; Crosby, Marc H R; Debenham, Robert K; Donnelly, Mark P; Hammond, Andrew B; Hilton, Maurice; Hoggeth, Gary D; Horan, Mark A; Messer, Gary M; Ramsay, John W; Robinson, Andrew; Tedaldi, Dominico A.

Associated Schoolboys
Betts, Robert.

Associated Schoolboys who have accepted the club's offer of a Traineeship/Contract
Ball, Nicholas C; Beal, Philip L; McDonald, Anthony; Powell, Richard J; Rackstraw, Anthony E; Reeve, David T; Wild, Robert F.

Player who does not hold a current contract but his registration has been retained by the club
Turnbull, Jonathan; Williams, Philip D.

EVERTON

Name	Ht	Wt	Pos	Born	Birthplace	Source	Club	Apps	Gls
Allen Graham	6 1	12 00	D	8 4 77	Bolton	Trainee	Everton	1	—
Ball Michael			D	2 10 79	Liverpool	Trainee	Everton	5	—
Barmby Nick	5 6	11 00	F	11 2 74	Hull	Trainee	Tottenham H	87	20
							Middlesbrough	42	8
							Everton	25	4
Barrett Earl	5 10	11 02	D	28 4 67	Rochdale	Apprentice	Manchester C	3	—
							Chester C (loan)	12	—
							Oldham Ath	183	7
							Aston Villa	119	1
							Everton	61	—
Bilic Slaven	6 2	13 02	D	11 9 68	Split		Hajduk Split	109	13
							Karlsruhe	54	5
							West Ham U	48	2
Branch Michael	5 9	11 00	F	18 10 78	Liverpool	Trainee	Everton	28	3
Cadamarteri Danny			F	12 10 79	Bradford	Trainee	Everton	1	—
Dunne Richard			D	21 9 79	Dublin	Trainee	Everton	7	—
Ferguson Duncan	6 4	14 06	F	27 12 71	Stirling	Carse T	Dundee U	77	28
							Rangers	14	2
							Everton	74	22
Gerrard Paul	6 2	13 01	G	22 1 73	Heywood	Trainee	Oldham Ath	119	1
							Everton	5	—
Grant Tony	5 10	10 02	M	14 11 74	Liverpool	Trainee	Everton	36	1
							Swindon T (loan)	3	1
Grugel Mark‡	5 8	10 00	M	9 3 76	Liverpool	Local	Everton	—	—
Hills John	5 9	11 00	D	21 4 78	St Annes-on-Sea	Trainee	Blackpool	—	—
							Everton	4	—
							Swansea C (loan)	11	—
Hinchcliffe Andy	5 10	12 10	D	5 2 69	Manchester	Apprentice	Manchester C	112	8
							Everton	165	7
Hottiger Marc	5 9	11 00	D	7 11 67	Lausanne		Lausanne	123	5
							Sion	67	13
							Newcastle U	39	1
							Everton	17	1
Hussin Edward*	5 10	12 00	D	13 12 77	Liverpool	Trainee	Everton	—	—
Jevons Phillip			M	1 8 79	Liverpool	Trainee	Everton	—	—
Kanchelskis Andrei	5 10	12 12	F	23 1 69	Kirovograd		Dynamo Kiev	22	1
(Transferred to Fiorentina, February 1997)							Donetsk	21	3
							Manchester U	123	28
							Everton	52	20
McCann Gavin	5 11	11 00	M	10 1 78	Blackpool	Trainee	Everton	—	—
Moore Richard*	6 2	13 07	G	2 9 77	Scunthorpe	Trainee	Everton	—	—

Name			Pos	DOB	Birthplace	Status	Club	Apps	Gls
O'Connor Jonathan	6 0	11 00	D	29 10 76	Darlington	Trainee	Everton	4	—
O'Toole John			G	23 2 79	Merseyside	Trainee	Everton	—	—
Parkinson Joe	5 11	12 02	M	11 6 71	Eccles	Trainee	Wigan Ath	119	6
							Bournemouth	30	1
							Everton	90	3
Phelan Terry	5 8	10 00	D	16 3 67	Manchester	Trainee	Leeds U	14	—
							Swansea C	45	—
							Wimbledon	159	1
							Manchester C	103	1
							Chelsea	15	—
							Everton	15	—
Price Chris*	5 9	11 09	M	24 10 75	Liverpool	Trainee	Everton	—	—
							Oxford U (loan)	—	—
Quayle Mark*	5 9	10 02	F	2 10 78	Liverpool	Trainee	Everton	—	—
Rideout Paul‡	5 11	12 00	F	14 8 64	Bournemouth	Apprentice	Swindon T	95	38
							Aston Villa	54	19
							Bari	99	23
							Southampton	75	19
							Swindon T (loan)	9	1
							Notts Co	11	3
							Rangers	12	1
							Everton	112	29
Samways Vinny‡	5 8	11 02	M	27 10 68	Bethnal Green	Apprentice	Tottenham H	193	11
							Everton	23	2
							Wolverhampton W (loan)	3	—
							Birmingham C (loan)	12	—
Short Craig	6 0	11 04	D	25 6 68	Bridlington	Pickering T	Scarborough	63	7
							Notts Co	128	6
							Derby Co	118	9
							Everton	46	4
Southall Neville	6 1	12 02	G	16 9 58	Llandudno	Winsford U	Bury	39	—
							Everton	566	—
							Port Vale (loan)	9	—
Speed Gary	5 11	10 12	M	8 9 69	Mancot	Trainee	Leeds U	248	39
							Everton	37	9
Stuart Graham	5 8	11 06	F	24 10 70	Tooting	Trainee	Chelsea	87	14
							Everton	122	20
Thomsen Claus	6 3	11 06	M	31 5 70	Aarhus	Aarhus	Ipswich T	81	7
							Everton	16	—
Townsend Richard*	5 7	11 07	M	5 5 78	Chester	Trainee	Everton	—	—
Tynan Robert‡	5 9	11 00	M	13 1 78	Birkenhead	Trainee	Everton	—	—
Unsworth David	6 0	13 00	D	16 10 73	Chorley	Trainee	Everton	116	11
Watson Dave	5 11	11 12	D	20 11 61	Liverpool	Amateur	Liverpool	—	—
							Norwich C	212	11
							Everton	369	23

Trainees
Davies, Paul; Dempsey, Gary W; Denton, Adam M; Drew, Padraig E; Eaton, Adam P; Farley, Adam J; Gabrielson, Daniel J; Hardman, Christopher S; Holmes, Neil; Lane, Christopher; McDermott, Wayne; Milligan, Jamie; Obrien, Michael G; Poppleton, David J; Regan, Carl A; West, Andrew; Williams, David P.

Associated Schoolboys
Ashton, Stephen D J; Attwell, Jamie W; Barton, Joseph A; Burgess, Benjamin K; Chadwick, Nicholas G; Clarke, Peter M; Curran, Damien M; Dempsey, Paul; Doforo, Liam; Edwards, Anthony S; Fleetwood, Ronnie; Hogan, Barry; Hogg, Craig A; Jagielka, Philip N; Kearney, Thomas J; Leahey, Stephen; Machin, Jonathan P; O'Hanlon, Sean P; Pilkington, George E; Potter, Jack D; Tuft, Dean K; Woodstock, Colin.

Associated Schoolboys who have accepted the club's offer of a Traineeship/Contract
Hibbert, Anthony J; Howarth, Carl J; Jeffers, Francis; Knowles, David J; Logan, Damian G; McLeod, Kevin A; O'Brien, Edward; Osman, Leon; Wright, John George.

EXETER CITY

Name			Pos	DOB	Birthplace	Status	Club	Apps	Gls
Baddeley Lee	6 1	12 07	D	12 7 74	Cardiff	Trainee	Cardiff C	133	1
							Exeter C	11	—
Bailey Danny	5 8	12 11	M	21 5 64	Leyton	Apprentice Dagenham Wealdstone	Bournemouth	2	—
							Torquay U	1	—
							Exeter C	64	2
							Reading	50	2
							Fulham (loan)	3	—
							Exeter C	152	4
Bayes Ashley	6 1	13 05	G	19 4 72	Lincoln	Trainee	Brentford	4	—
							Torquay U	97	—
							Exeter C	41	—
Bellotti Ross†			G	15 5 78	Pembury	Trainee	Exeter C	2	—
Birch Paul	5 6	10 04	M	20 11 62	West Bromwich	Apprentice	Aston Villa	173	16
							Wolverhampton W	142	15
							Preston NE (loan)	11	2
							Doncaster R	27	2
							Exeter C	2	—

Name	Ht	Wt	Pos	Date	Birthplace	Source	Club	Apps	Gls
Blake Noel	6 2	14 02	D	12 1 62	Jamaica	Sutton Coldfield T	Aston Villa	4	—
							Shrewsbury T (loan)	6	—
							Birmingham C	76	5
							Portsmouth	144	10
							Leeds U	51	4
							Stoke C	75	3
							Bradford C (loan)	6	—
							Bradford C	39	3
							Dundee	54	2
							Exeter C	90	8
Braithwaite Leon	6 0	12 00	F	17 12 72	Hackney	Bishops Stortford	Exeter C	61	8
Chamberlain Mark‡	5 9	12 00	M	19 11 61	Stoke	Apprentice	Port Vale	96	17
							Stoke C	112	17
							Sheffield W	66	8
							Portsmouth	167	20
							Brighton & HA	19	2
							Exeter C	59	4
Dailly Marcus‡			M	1 10 75	Dundee	Dundee U	Exeter C	17	—
Flack Steve	6 1	11 04	F	29 5 71	Cambridge	Cambridge C	Cardiff C	11	1
							Exeter C	27	4
Fox Peter	5 11	13 10	G	5 7 57	Scunthorpe	Apprentice	Sheffield W	49	—
							West Ham U (loan)	—	—
							Barnsley (loan)	1	—
							Stoke C	409	—
							Wrexham (loan)	—	—
							Exeter C	108	—
Ghazghazi Sufyan	5 7	11 00	F	24 8 77	Honiton	Trainee	Exeter C	6	—
Hare Matthew	6 2	13 00	D	26 12 76	Barnstaple	Trainee	Exeter C	38	1
Hughes Darren	5 11	13 01	D	6 10 65	Prescot	Apprentice	Everton	3	—
							Shrewsbury T	37	1
							Brighton & HA	26	2
							Port Vale	184	4
							Northampton T	21	—
							Exeter C	62	1
McConnell Barry	5 11	10 03	F	1 1 77	Exeter	Trainee	Exeter C	42	—
McKeown Gary	5 10	11 07	M	19 10 70	Oxford	Trainee	Arsenal	—	—
(On loan from Dundee)							Shrewsbury T (loan)	8	1
							Dundee	76	5
							Exeter C	3	—
Medlin Nicky	5 7	10 01	M	23 11 76	Camborne	Trainee	Exeter C	17	1
Minett Jason	5 9	10 04	M	12 8 71	Peterborough	Trainee	Norwich C	3	—
							Exeter C (loan)	12	—
							Exeter C	76	3
							Lincoln C	46	5
							Exeter C	13	—
Myers Chris*	5 10	11 10	D	1 4 69	Yeovil	Apprentice	Torquay U	105	7
							Dundee	6	—
							Torquay U (loan)	6	—
							Wrexham	—	—
							Scarborough	9	—
							Exeter C	41	2
Pears Richard*	5 10	12 07	F	16 7 76	Exeter	Trainee	Exeter C	60	8
Rice Gary	5 9	11 10	D	29 9 75	Zambia	Trainee	Exeter C	44	0
Richardson Jon	6 1	12 05	D	29 8 75	Nottingham	Trainee	Exeter C	131	3
Rowbotham Darren	5 10	12 13	F	22 10 66	Cardiff	Trainee	Plymouth Arg	46	2
							Exeter C	118	47
							Torquay U	14	3
							Birmingham C	36	6
							Hereford U (loan)	8	2
							Mansfield T (loan)	4	—
							Crewe Alex	61	21
							Shrewsbury T	40	9
							Exeter C	25	9
Sharpe John‡	5 11	11 06	M	9 8 75	Birmingham	Trainee	Manchester C	—	—
							Exeter C (loan)	14	1
							Exeter C	21	1
Steele Tim*	5 10	11 04	F	1 12 67	Coventry	Apprentice	Shrewsbury T	61	5
							Wolverhampton W	75	7
							Stoke C (loan)	7	1
							Bradford C	11	—
							Hereford U	32	2
							Exeter C	28	3

Trainees
Ahearn, Jamie P; Harris, Daniel; Holloway, Christopher D; Holmes, Mark; Rendle, Daniel L; Steer, Richard; Thomas, William N; Vinnicombe, Luke; Vittles, James M S; Walker, Scott; Watts, Andrew M; Whitmore, Jake; Wilkinson, John C.

Associated Schoolboys
Bray, Adam; Clemoes, Joseph G; Conibere, Brett D; Fox, Robert A; Hallam, Robin S; Hayes, Gary J; Hensor, Stephen J; Hughes, Paul M; Jee, Russell; McBain, Ian S; Orchard, Jack F; Pointing, Neil T; Schamroth, Daniel S; Wainwright, Thomas W; Walker, David.

Associated Schoolboys who have accepted the club's offer of a Traineeship/Contract
Hillson, Bradley; Watts, Shaun S.

FULHAM

Name	Ht	Wt	Pos	DOB	Birthplace	Source	Club	Apps	Gls
Adams Micky†	5 8	11 04	M	8 11 61	Sheffield	Apprentice	Gillingham	92	5
							Coventry C	90	9
							Leeds U	73	2
							Southampton	144	7
							Stoke C	10	3
							Fulham	29	9
Angus Terry	6 0	13 10	D	14 1 66	Coventry	VS Rugby	Northampton T	116	6
							Fulham	122	5
Barkus Lea*	5 6	10 10	F	7 12 74	Reading	Trainee	Reading	15	1
							Fulham	9	1
Blake Mark	6 0	12 06	D	17 12 67	Portsmouth	Apprentice	Southampton	18	2
							Colchester U (loan)	4	1
							Shrewsbury T (loan)	10	—
							Shrewsbury T	132	3
							Fulham	114	15
Brooker Paul	5 8	9 13	F	25 11 76	Hammersmith	Trainee	Fulham	46	4
Carpenter Richard	5 11	13 00	M	30 9 72	Sheppey	Trainee	Gillingham	122	4
							Fulham	34	5
Cockerill Glenn*	5 10	12 08	M	25 8 59	Grimsby	Louth U	Lincoln C	71	10
							Swindon T	26	1
							Lincoln C	115	25
							Sheffield U	62	10
							Southampton	287	32
							Leyton Orient	90	7
							Fulham	32	1
Conroy Mike	6 0	13 03	F	31 12 65	Glasgow	Apprentice	Coventry C	—	—
							Clydebank	114	38
							St Mirren	10	1
							Reading	80	7
							Burnley	77	30
							Preston NE	57	22
							Fulham	83	30
Cullip Danny	6 0	12 00	D	17 9 76	Bracknell	Trainee	Oxford U	—	—
							Fulham	29	1
Cusack Nick	6 0	12 08	D	24 12 65	Rotherham	Alvechurch	Leicester C	16	1
							Peterborough U	44	10
							Motherwell	77	17
							Darlington	21	6
							Oxford U	61	10
							Wycombe W (loan)	4	—
							Fulham	114	14
Davis Sean§			M	20 9 79	Clapham	Trainee	Fulham	1	—
Freeman Darren	5 11	13 04	F	22 8 73	Brighton	Horsham T	Gillingham	12	—
							Fulham	39	9
Hamill Rory	5 10	12 02	F	4 5 76	Coleraine	Portstewart	Fulham	48	7
(Transferred to Glentoran, December 1996)									
Hamsher John*	5 10	11 04	D	14 1 78	Lambeth	Trainee	Fulham	3	—
Herrera Robbie	5 6	10 07	D	12 6 70	Torbay	Trainee	QPR	6	—
							Torquay U (loan)	11	—
							Torquay U (loan)	5	—
							Fulham	119	2
Lange Tony*	6 0	14 06	G	10 12 64	London	Apprentice	Charlton Ath	12	—
							Aldershot (loan)	7	—
							Aldershot	125	—
							Wolverhampton W	8	—
							Aldershot (loan)	2	—
							Torquay U (loan)	1	—
							Portsmouth (loan)	—	—
							WBA	48	—
							Fulham	59	—
Lawrence Matthew	6 1	12 12	M	19 6 74	Northampton	Grays Ath	Wycombe W	16	1
							Fulham	15	—
Marshall John*	5 10	12 04	D	18 8 64	Surrey	Apprentice	Fulham	411	28
McAree Rod	5 7	10 10	M	10 8 74	Dungannon	Trainee	Liverpool	—	—
							Bristol C	6	—
							Fulham	26	3
Mison Michael	6 3	14 00	M	8 11 75	London	Trainee	Fulham	55	5
Morgan Simon	5 10	12 05	M	5 9 66	Birmingham	Trainee	Leicester C	160	3
							Fulham	271	42
Scott Rob	6 1	12 02	F	15 8 73	Epsom	Sutton U	Sheffield U	6	1
							Scarborough (loan)	8	3
							Northampton T (loan)	5	—
							Fulham	64	13

Soloman Jason‡	6 1	12 01	D	6 10 70	Welwyn	Trainee	Watford	100	5
							Peterborough U (loan)	4	—
							Wycombe W	13	1
							Wrexham	2	—
							Fulham	4	—
Stewart Simon	6 2	13 08	D	1 11 73	Leeds	Trainee	Sheffield W	6	—
							Shrewsbury T (loan)	4	—
							Fulham	3	—
Thomas Martin	5 8	12 06	M	12 9 73	Lyndhurst	Trainee	Southampton	—	—
							Leyton Orient	5	2
							Fulham	86	8
Walton Mark	6 4	15 00	G	1 6 69	Merthyr	Swansea C	Luton T	—	—
							Colchester U	40	—
							Norwich C	22	—
							Wrexham (loan)	6	—
							Dundee	—	—
							Bolton W	3	—
						Fakenham T	Fulham	28	—
Watson Paul	5 8	10 09	D	4 1 75	Hastings	Trainee	Gillingham	62	2
							Fulham	44	3

Trainees
Bjurstrom, Paul A; Buckley, Jamie J; Cornwall, Lucas C; Davis, Sean; Fitzgerald, Philip J; Gray, Ryan; Henderson, Kevin; Jennings, Gary B; Jones, Lee P; Palmer, Ryan W J; Smith, Kevin A; Smith, Paul I D; Symons, Shaun P; Taylor, Mark P; Wilkinson, James S; Willis, Jonathan M.

GILLINGHAM

Akinbiyi Ade	6 0	12 07	F	10 10 74	Hackney	Trainee	Norwich C	49	3
							Hereford U (loan)	4	2
							Brighton & HA (loan)	7	4
							Gillingham	19	7
Bailey Dennis	5 10	11 00	F	13 11 65	Lambeth	Farnborough T	Crystal Palace	5	1
							Bristol R (loan)	17	9
							Birmingham C	75	23
							Bristol R (loan)	6	1
							QPR	39	10
							Charlton Ath (loan)	4	—
							Watford (loan)	8	4
							Brentford (loan)	6	3
							Gillingham	75	10
Bryant Matthew	6 0	12 04	D	21 9 70	Bristol	Trainee	Bristol C	203	7
							Walsall (loan)	13	—
							Gillingham	39	—
Butler Steve	6 1	12 07	F	27 1 62	Birmingham	Wokingham T	Brentford	21	3
						Maidstone U	Maidstone U	76	41
							Watford	62	9
							Bournemouth (loan)	1	—
							Cambridge U	109	51
							Gillingham	58	14
Butters Guy	6 2	13 03	D	30 10 69	Hillingdon	Trainee	Tottenham H	35	1
							Southend U (loan)	16	3
							Portsmouth	154	6
							Oxford U (loan)	3	1
							Gillingham	30	—
Chapman Ian	5 8	11 12	D	31 5 70	Brighton	Trainee	Brighton & HA	281	14
							Gillingham	23	1
Fortune-West Leo	6 4	13 00	F	9 4 71	Newham	Stevenage Bor	Gillingham	47	14
							Leyton Orient (loan)	5	—
Green Richard	6 0	13 01	D	22 11 67	Wolverhampton	Apprentice	Shrewsbury T	125	5
							Swindon T	—	—
							Gillingham	191	16
Harris Mark*	6 2	13 01	D	15 7 63	Reading	Wokingham T	Crystal Palace	2	—
							Burnley (loan)	4	—
							Swansea C	228	14
							Gillingham	65	3
Hessenthaler Andy	5 7	10 04	M	17 8 65	Gravesend	Redbridge Forest	Watford	195	11
							Gillingham	38	2
Iga Andrew†			G	9 12 77	Kampala	Trainee	Millwall	1	—
							Gillingham	—	—
Manuel Billy*	5 9	11 10	D	28 6 69	Hackney	Apprentice	Tottenham H	—	—
							Gillingham	87	5
							Brentford	94	1
							Cambridge U	10	—
							Peterborough U	27	2
							Gillingham	21	—
Masters Neil	5 10	14 05	D	25 5 72	Lisburn	Trainee	Bournemouth	38	2
							Wolverhampton W	12	—
							Gillingham	—	—

O'Connor Mark   5 8   10 12   M   10 3 63   Rochdale   Apprentice

Club	Apps	Gls
QPR	3	—
Exeter C (loan)	38	1
Bristol R	80	10
Bournemouth	128	12
Gillingham	116	8
Bournemouth	58	3
Gillingham	40	1

Onuora Iffy   6 0   12 07   F   28 7 67   Glasgow   British Univ

Club	Apps	Gls
Huddersfield T	165	30
Mansfield T	28	8
Gillingham	40	21

Pennock Adrian   6 0   12 07   D   27 3 71   Ipswich   Trainee

Club	Apps	Gls
Norwich C	1	—
Bournemouth	131	9
Gillingham	26	2

Pinnock James§   M   1 8 78   Dartford   Trainee   Gillingham   2   —

Piper Len   5 8   11 06   M   8 8 77   London   Trainee

Club	Apps	Gls
Wimbledon	—	—
Gillingham	19	1

Puttnam Dave*   5 10   11 12   M   3 2 67   Leicester   Leicester U

Club	Apps	Gls
Leicester C	7	—
Lincoln C	177	21
Gillingham	40	2

Ratcliffe Simon   6 0   12 10   M   8 2 67   Davyhulme   Apprentice

Club	Apps	Gls
Manchester U	—	—
Norwich C	9	—
Brentford	214	14
Gillingham	84	9

Sambrook Andrew§   M   13 7 79   Chatham   Trainee   Gillingham   1   —

Smith Neil   5 8   11 12   M   30 9 71   London   Trainee

Club	Apps	Gls
Tottenham H	—	—
Gillingham	212	10

Stannard Jim   6 2   16 00   G   6 10 62   London   Local

Club	Apps	Gls
Fulham	41	—
Charlton Ath (loan)	1	—
Southend U (loan)	17	—
Southend U	92	—
Fulham	348	1
Gillingham	84	—

Thomas Glen   6 0   13 02   D   6 10 67   Hackney   Apprentice

Club	Apps	Gls
Fulham	251	6
Peterborough U	8	—
Barnet	23	—
Gillingham	25	—

Trainees
Bovis, Danny S; Cole, Jody; Corbett, James J; Edge, Roland; Eggleton, Russell; Halls, Christopher J; Norman, Steven D; Osborne, Tommy P; Pinnock, James E; Radbourne, Richard J; Saunders, Jay L; Smith, Darren K; Tydeman, Samuel.

Non-Contract
Bremner, Kevin J; Scally, Paul D P.

Associated Schoolboys who have accepted the club's offer of a Traineeship/Contract
Sambrook, Andrew J.

GRIMSBY TOWN

Black Kingsley   5 8   12 03   F   22 6 68   Luton   School

Club	Apps	Gls
Luton T	127	26
Nottingham F	98	14
Sheffield U (loan)	11	2
Millwall (loan)	3	1
Grimsby T	24	—

Childs Gary*   5 7   10 08   F   19 4 64   Birmingham   Apprentice

Club	Apps	Gls
WBA	3	—
Walsall	131	17
Birmingham C	55	2
Grimsby T	233	26

Clare Daryl   5 9   12 00   F   1 8 78   Jersey   Trainee   Grimsby T   1   —

Fickling Ashley   5 10   11 08   D   15 11 72   Sheffield   Trainee

Club	Apps	Gls
Sheffield U	—	—
Darlington (loan)	14	—
Darlington (loan)	1	—
Grimsby T	39	2

Gallimore Tony   5 11   12 05   D   21 2 72   Crewe   Trainee

Club	Apps	Gls
Stoke C	11	—
Carlisle U (loan)	16	—
Carlisle U (loan)	8	1
Carlisle U	116	8
Grimsby T	52	2

Gowshall Joby*   5 10   13 00   D   7 8 75   Louth   Trainee   Grimsby T   —   —

Handyside Peter   6 1   13 07   D   31 7 74   Dumfries   Trainee   Grimsby T   98   1

Harsley Paul*   5 8   11 05   M   29 5 78   Scunthorpe   Trainee   Grimsby T   —   —

Jobling Kevin   5 9   12 02   D   1 1 68   Sunderland   Apprentice

Club	Apps	Gls
Leicester C	9	—
Grimsby T	255	9
Scunthorpe U (loan)	—	—

Lester Jack   5 10   12 00   F   8 10 75   Sheffield   Trainee

Club	Apps	Gls
Grimsby T	34	5
Doncaster R (loan)	11	1

Lever Mark   6 3   13 06   D   29 3 70   Beverley   Trainee   Grimsby T   264   8

Livingstone Steve	6 1	13 07	F	8	9 68	Middlesbrough	Trainee	Coventry C	31	5
								Blackburn R	30	10
								Chelsea	1	—
								Port Vale (loan)	5	—
								Grimsby T	131	28
Love Andrew	6 2	13 10	G	28	3 79	Grimsby	Trainee	Grimsby T	3	—
McDermott John	5 7	10 13	D	3	2 69	Middlesbrough	Trainee	Grimsby T	333	6
Mendonca Clive	5 10	12 07	F	9	9 68	Islington	Apprentice	Sheffield U	13	4
								Doncaster R (loan)	2	—
								Rotherham U	84	27
								Sheffield U	10	1
								Grimsby T (loan)	10	3
								Grimsby T	156	56
Neil Jim	5 8	11 13	D	28	2 76	Bury St Edmunds	Trainee	Grimsby T	2	—
Orie Eric‡			M	25	7 68	Utrecht		Blackpool	—	—
							FK Austria	Grimsby T	—	—
Oster John	5 8	10 08	F	8	12 78	Boston	Trainee	Grimsby T	24	3
Pearcey Jason	6 1	14 00	G	23	7 71	Leamington Spa	Trainee	Mansfield T	77	—
								Grimsby T	45	—
Quy Andy*	6 0	13 04	G	4	7 76	Harlow	Tottenham H	Derby Co	—	—
								Grimsby T	—	—
Rodger Graham	6 2	13 08	D	1	4 67	Glasgow	Apprentice	Wolverhampton W	1	—
								Coventry C	36	2
								Luton T	28	2
								Grimsby T	135	11
Shakespeare Craig*	5 10	13 06	M	26	10 63	Birmingham	Apprentice	Walsall	284	45
								Sheffield W	17	—
								WBA	112	12
								Grimsby T	106	10
Smith Richard	6 0	13 05	D	3	10 70	Lutterworth	Trainee	Leicester C	98	1
								Cambridge U (loan)	4	—
								Grimsby T	32	—
Southall Nicky	5 10	13 00	M	28	1 72	Middlesbrough	Trainee	Hartlepool U	138	24
								Grimsby T	67	5
Webb Neil‡	6 1	13 07	M	30	7 63	Reading	Apprentice	Reading	72	22
								Portsmouth	123	34
								Nottingham F	146	47
								Manchester U	75	8
								Nottingham F	30	3
								Swindon T (loan)	6	—
								Grimsby T	4	—
Widdrington Tommy	5 8	11 01	M	1	10 71	Newcastle	Trainee	Southampton	75	3
								Wigan Ath (loan)	6	—
								Grimsby T	42	4
Woods Neil*	6 0	13 00	F	30	7 66	York	Apprentice	Doncaster R	65	16
								Rangers	3	—
								Ipswich T	27	5
								Bradford C	14	2
								Grimsby T	216	42
Wrack Darren	5 9	12 07	F	5	5 76	Cleethorpes	Trainee	Derby Co	26	1
								Grimsby T	12	1
								Shrewsbury T (loan)	4	—

Trainees
Brown, James K; Butterfield, Daniel P; Chapman, Ben; Croudson, Steven D; Dimech, Mark; Hanslip, Nicholas; Jarvis, Paul W; Melbourne, James; Oakes, Andrew; Osgar, Gareth R; Oswin, Matthew S W; Rockhill, Antony J; Soley, Martin R; Stephenson, Lee; Taylor, Jonathan F; Young, James R.

Associated Schoolboys
Brown, Kevin.

Associated Schoolboys who have accepted the club's offer of a Traineeship/Contract
Bloomer, Matthew B; Crew, Lee N.

HARTLEPOOL UNITED

Allinson Jamie*	6 1	12 05	D	15	6 78	Stockton	Trainee	Hartlepool U	4	—
Allon Joe	5 11	12 12	F	12	11 66	Gateshead	Trainee	Newcastle U	9	2
								Swansea C	34	11
								Hartlepool U	112	50
								Chelsea	14	2
								Port Vale (loan)	6	—
								Brentford	45	19
								Southend U (loan)	3	—
								Port Vale	23	9
								Lincoln C	4	—
								Hartlepool U	52	17

Player	Ht	Wt	Pos	DOB	Birthplace	From	Club	Apps	Goals
Baker Paul	6 0	13 00	F	5 1 63	Newcastle	Bishop Auckland	Southampton	—	11
							Carlisle U	71	11
							Hartlepool U	197	67
							Motherwell	9	1
							Gillingham	62	16
							York C	48	18
							Torquay U	30	8
							Scunthorpe U	21	9
							Hartlepool U	6	2
Beech Chris	5 10	11 12	M	16 9 74	Blackpool	Trainee	Blackpool	82	4
							Hartlepool U	42	7
Clegg David*	5 9	10 04	M	23 10 76	Liverpool	Trainee	Liverpool	—	—
							Hartlepool U	35	2
Cooper Mark	5 10	12 03	M	18 12 68	Wakefield	Trainee	Bristol C	—	—
							Exeter C	50	12
							Southend U (loan)	5	—
							Birmingham C	39	4
							Fulham	14	—
							Huddersfield T (loan)	10	4
							Wycombe W	2	1
							Exeter C	88	20
							Hartlepool U	33	9
Cullen Jon†			D	10 1 73	Durham	Trainee	Doncaster R	9	—
						Morpeth T	Hartlepool U	6	—
Davies Glen	6 1	13 09	D	20 2 76	Brighton	Trainee	Burnley	—	—
							Hartlepool U	32	1
Elliott Andy†			M	2 5 74	Newcastle		Hartlepool U	4	—
Foster Lee‡			F	21 10 77	Bishop Auckland	Trainee	Hartlepool U	1	—
Gallagher Ian*	5 10	11 08	M	30 5 78	Hartlepool	Trainee	Hartlepool U	1	—
Halliday Stephen	5 10	12 11	F	3 5 76	Sunderland	Charlton Ath	Hartlepool U	109	20
Hislop Kona*	5 11	12 01	M	21 12 70	London		Livingston	4	1
							Hartlepool U	27	—
Homer Chris‡	5 9	11 04	M	16 4 77	Stockton	Trainee	Hartlepool U	7	—
Horace Alain‡			M	4 12 71	Madagascar	Mulhouse	Hartlepool U	1	—
Houchen Keith*	6 2	13 04	F	25 7 60	Middlesbrough	Chesterfield	Hartlepool U	170	65
							Orient	76	20
							York C	67	19
							Scunthorpe U	9	3
							Coventry C	54	7
							Hibernian	57	11
							Port Vale	49	10
							Hartlepool U	109	27
Howard Steve	6 1	14 06	M	10 5 76	Durham	Tow Law T	Hartlepool U	71	15
Hutt Stephen§			F	19 2 79	Middlesbrough	Trainee	Hartlepool U	1	—
Ingram Denny	5 10	12 03	D	27 6 76	Sunderland	Trainee	Hartlepool U	118	3
Irvine Stuart§			F	1 3 79	Hartlepool	Trainee	Hartlepool U	4	1
Knowles Darren	5 6	11 01	D	8 10 70	Sheffield	Trainee	Sheffield U	—	—
							Stockport Co	63	—
							Scarborough	144	2
							Hartlepool U	7	—
Lee Graeme	6 2	13 05	D	31 5 78	Middlesbrough	Trainee	Hartlepool U	30	—
Lucas Richard	5 10	12 06	M	22 9 70	Sheffield	Trainee	Sheffield U	10	—
							Preston NE	50	—
							Lincoln C (loan)	4	—
							Scarborough	116	—
							Hartlepool U	7	—
McDonald Chris	6 2	13 00	F	14 10 75	Edinburgh	Trainee	Arsenal	—	—
							Hartlepool U	9	—
McGuckin Ian	6 2	13 11	D	24 4 73	Middlesbrough	Trainee	Hartlepool U	152	8
O'Connor Paul†			G	17 8 71	Easington	Blyth Spartans	Hartlepool U	31	—
Pears Steve	6 0	14 00	G	22 1 62	Brandon	Apprentice	Manchester U	4	—
							Middlesbrough (loan)	12	—
							Middlesbrough	327	—
							Liverpool	—	—
							Hartlepool U	16	—
Proctor Mark†	5 10	11 09	M	30 1 61	Middlesbrough	Apprentice	Middlesbrough	109	12
							Nottingham F	64	5
							Sunderland (loan)	5	—
							Sunderland	112	19
							Sheffield W	59	4
							Middlesbrough	120	6
							Tranmere R (loan)	13	1
							Tranmere R	18	—
						South Shields	Hartlepool U	6	—
Slater Darren§			D	4 1 79	Bishop Auckland	Trainee	Hartlepool U	1	—

Sunderland Jon‡	6 0	11 13	M	2 11 75	Newcastle	Trainee	Blackpool	2	—
							Scarborough	8	—
							Hartlepool U	13	1
Tait Mick	5 11	12 13	D	30 9 56	Wallsend	Apprentice	Oxford U	64	23
							Carlisle U	106	20
							Hull C	33	3
							Portsmouth	240	30
							Reading	99	9
							Darlington	79	2
						Gretna	Hartlepool U	139	3
Walton Paul§			F	2 7 79	Sunderland	Trainee	Hartlepool U	10	—
Winstanley Craig†			F	23 8 78	Hartlepool	Trainee	Hartlepool U	1	—

Trainees
Briggs, John D; Dunwell, Michael; Evans, Nicholas A; Farnaby, Stephen; Forster, Alan C; Goodwin, Marc T; Hutt, Stephen G; Irvine, Stuart C; Lake, Craig R; Maxwell, Richard S; Miller, Thomas W; Moss, Paul W; Slater, Darren; Sullivan, Wayne A; Timmons, Darren; Walton, Paul A.

Non-Contract
Cullen, David J; Elliott, Andrew; O'Connor, Paul D; Proctor, Mark G.

Associated Schoolboys
Walton, Phillip.

Associated Schoolboys who have accepted the club's offer of a Traineeship/Contract
Hay, Andrew J.

HEREFORD UNITED

Agana Tony	5 11	12 05	F	2 10 63	London	Weymouth	Watford	15	1
							Sheffield U	118	42
							Notts Co	145	15
							Leeds U (loan)	2	—
							Hereford U	5	2
Bartlett Neal*	5 9	11 07	M	7 4 75	Southampton	Trainee	Southampton	8	—
						BK Haken	Hereford U	3	—
Brough John*	6 0	12 11	D	8 1 73	Heanor	Trainee	Notts Co	—	—
							Shrewsbury T	16	1
						Telford U	Hereford U	79	3
Cook Garry	6 0	13 00	M	31 3 78	Northampton	Trainee	Hereford U	20	—
Debont Andy	6 0	15 07	G	7 2 74	Wolverhampton	Trainee	Wolverhampton W	—	—
							Hartlepool U (loan)	1	—
							Hereford U (loan)	8	—
							Hereford U	27	—
Downing Keith‡	5 9	11 05	M	23 7 65	Oldbury	Mile Oak R	Notts Co	23	1
							Wolverhampton W	191	8
							Birmingham C	1	—
							Stoke C	16	—
							Cardiff C	4	—
							Hereford U	45	—
Fishlock Murray	5 8	10 09	D	23 9 73	Marlborough	Trowbridge T	Hereford U	71	4
Foster Adrian	5 10	12 01	F	19 3 71	Kidderminster	Trainee	WBA	27	2
							Torquay U	75	24
							Gillingham	40	9
							Exeter C (loan)	7	—
							Hereford U	43	15
Foster Ian	5 7	10 07	F	11 11 76	Merseyside	Liverpool	Hereford U	19	—
Hargreaves Chris	5 11	12 07	F	12 5 72	Cleethorpes	Trainee	Grimsby T	51	5
							Scarborough (loan)	3	—
							Hull C	49	—
							WBA	1	—
							Hereford U (loan)	17	2
							Hereford U	44	4
Hibbard Mark*	5 7	9 08	F	12 8 77	Hereford	Trainee	Hereford U	7	1
Jordan Roy§			M	17 4 78	Plymouth	Trainee	Hereford U	1	—
Kottila Mika‡			F	22 9 74	Helsinki		FinnPa	1	—
							HJK Helsinki	33	6
							Rops	—	—
						Rops	Hereford U	13	1
Law Nicky‡	6 1	13 10	D	8 9 61	London	Apprentice	Arsenal	—	—
							Barnsley	114	1
							Blackpool	66	1
							Plymouth Arg	38	5
							Notts Co	47	4
							Scarborough (loan)	12	—
							Rotherham U	128	4
							Chesterfield	111	11
							Hereford U	14	—
MacKenzie Chris*	6 0	12 06	G	14 5 72	Northampton	Corby T	Hereford U	60	1
Mahon Gavin	5 11	12 07	M	2 1 77	Birmingham	Trainee	Wolverhampton W	—	—
							Hereford U	11	1

Name	Ht	Wt	Pos	Birth date	Birthplace	Source	Clubs	Apps	Gls
Matthewson Trevor*	6 1	13 06	D	12 2 63	Sheffield	Apprentice	Sheffield W	3	—
							Newport Co	75	—
							Stockport Co	80	—
							Lincoln C	43	2
							Birmingham C	168	12
							Preston NE	12	1
							Bury	34	—
						Witton Alb	Hereford U	35	2
McGorry Brian	5 10	12 07	M	16 4 70	Liverpool	Weymouth	Bournemouth	61	11
							Peterborough U	52	6
							Wycombe W	4	—
							Cardiff C (loan)	7	—
							Hereford U	7	1
Norton David	5 10	11 10	M	3 3 65	Cannock	Apprentice	Aston Villa	44	2
							Notts Co	27	1
							Rochdale (loan)	9	—
							Hull C (loan)	15	—
							Hull C	134	5
							Northampton T	82	—
							Hereford U	45	—
Pitman Jamie	5 8	10 12	M	6 1 76	Warminster	Trainee	Swindon T	3	—
							Hereford U	21	—
Preedy Phil*	5 10	11 02	M	20 11 75	Hereford	Trainee	Hereford U	51	4
Sandeman Bradley*	5 11	11 07	D	24 2 70	Northampton	Trainee	Northampton T	58	3
							Maidstone U	57	8
							Port Vale	69	1
							Rotherham U	21	2
							Hereford U	7	—
Smith Dean	6 0	13 00	D	19 3 71	West Bromwich	Trainee	Walsall	142	2
							Hereford U	117	19
Townsend Quentin*	5 11	12 07	D	13 2 77	Worcester	Trainee	Wolverhampton W	—	—
							Hereford U	7	—
Turner Mark*	6 1	13 00	M	4 10 72	Bebbington	Trainee	Wolverhampton W	1	—
							Northampton T	4	—
						Telford U	Hereford U	6	—
Warner Rob	5 10	11 06	D	20 4 77	Stratford	Trainee	Hereford U	37	—
Williams John*	6 1	13 12	M	11 5 68	Birmingham	Cradley T	Swansea C	39	11
							Coventry C	80	11
							Notts Co (loan)	5	2
							Stoke C (loan)	4	—
							Swansea C (loan)	7	2
							Wycombe W	48	9
							Hereford U	11	3
Wood Trevor*	5 11	13 06	G	3 11 68	Jersey	Apprentice	Brighton & HA	—	—
							Port Vale	42	—
							Walsall	69	—
							Hereford U	19	—

Trainees
Brown, Jamie W; Durham, Ryan M; Hill, Jonathan M; Homer, Ian C; Jackson, Scott S; Jones, Dafydd J; Jordan, Roy A; King, Christopher A; Medford, Mark; Ogiesby, Andrew; Smith, Darryl C; Vaughan, Ian D; Williams, Andrew J; Williams, Gavin J.

Non-Contract
West, Charles E.

Associated Schoolboys
Rai, Adam K.

HUDDERSFIELD TOWN

Name	Ht	Wt	Pos	Birth date	Birthplace	Source	Clubs	Apps	Gls
Baldry Simon	5 10	11 06	F	12 2 76	Huddersfield	Trainee	Huddersfield T	42	2
Beresford David	5 7	10 06	M	11 11 76	Middleton	Trainee	Oldham Ath	64	2
							Swansea C (loan)	6	—
							Huddersfield T	6	1
Browning Marcus	6 1	13 00	M	22 4 71	Bristol	Trainee	Bristol R	174	13
							Hereford U (loan)	7	5
							Huddersfield T	13	—
Burnett Wayne	5 10	12 00	M	4 9 71	Lambeth	Trainee	Leyton Orient	40	—
							Blackburn R	—	—
							Plymouth Arg	70	3
							Bolton W	2	—
							Huddersfield T	35	—
Collins Sam	6 2	13 07	D	5 6 77	Pontefract	Trainee	Huddersfield T	4	—
Cowan Tom	5 8	11 10	D	28 8 69	Bellshill	Netherdale BC	Clyde	16	2
							Rangers	12	—
							Sheffield U	45	—
							Stoke C (loan)	14	—
							Huddersfield T (loan)	10	—
							Huddersfield T	122	8

Crosby Gary*	5 8	9 00	F	8 5 64	Sleaford	Lincoln U	Lincoln C	7	—
						Grantham T	Nottingham F	152	12
							Grimsby T (loan)	3	—
							Huddersfield T	44	6
Dalton Paul	5 11	12 06	M	25 4 67	Middlesbrough	Brandon U	Manchester U	—	—
							Hartlepool U	151	37
							Plymouth Arg	98	25
							Huddersfield T	58	9
Dyson Jon	6 1	12 09	D	18 12 71	Mirfield	School	Huddersfield T	105	2
Edmondson Darren	6 0	12 00	D	4 11 71	Coniston	Trainee	Carlisle U	214	9
							Huddersfield T	10	—
Edwards Rob	5 9	12 04	F	23 2 70	Manchester	Trainee	Crewe Alex	155	44
							Huddersfield T	46	10
Facey Delroy	6 0	13 00	F	22 4 80	Huddersfield	Trainee	Huddersfield T	3	—
Francis Steve	6 1	14 00	G	29 5 64	Billericay	Apprentice	Chelsea	71	0
							Reading	216	—
							Huddersfield T	174	—
Gonsalves Ryan*	5 11	12 00	D	22 12 77	Leeds	Trainee	Huddersfield T	—	—
Gray Kevin	6 0	14 00	D	7 1 72	Sheffield	Trainee	Mansfield T	141	3
							Huddersfield T	82	1
Heary Thomas	5 10	11 03	M	14 2 79	Dublin	Trainee	Huddersfield T	5	—
Illingworth Jeremy	5 10	12 07	M	20 5 77	Huddersfield	Trainee	Huddersfield T	3	—
Jenkins Steve	5 11	12 03	D	16 7 72	Merthyr	Trainee	Swansea C	165	1
							Huddersfield T	64	1
Kaye Peter	5 8	11 06	F	4 2 79	Huddersfield	Trainee	Huddersfield T	1	—
Kelly Mark*	6 0	11 10	M	5 10 76	Gibraltar	Trainee	Huddersfield T	—	—
Lawson Ian	6 0	11 08	F	4 11 77	Huddersfield	Trainee	Huddersfield T	18	3
Makel Lee	5 9	11 05	M	11 1 73	Sunderland	Trainee	Newcastle U	12	1
							Blackburn R	6	—
							Huddersfield T	52	5
Morrison Andy	6 1	13 10	D	30 7 70	Inverness	Trainee	Plymouth Arg	113	6
							Blackburn R	5	—
							Blackpool	47	3
							Huddersfield T	10	1
Murphy Stephen	5 11	12 00	D	5 4 78	Dublin	Belvedere	Huddersfield T	—	—
Norman Tony*	6 1	13 08	G	24 2 58	Mancot	Amateur	Burnley	—	—
							Hull C	372	—
							Sunderland	198	—
							Huddersfield T	7	—
O'Connor Derek	5 11	12 01	G	9 3 78	Dublin	Crumplin U	Huddersfield T	—	—
Payton Andy	5 9	11 13	F	23 10 67	Burnley	Apprentice	Hull C	144	55
							Middlesbrough	19	3
							Celtic	36	15
							Barnsley	108	41
							Huddersfield T	38	17
Ryan Robbie	5 10	12 00	D	11 8 76	Dublin	Belvedere	Huddersfield T	5	—
Sanders Steven*	5 10	12 00	D	2 6 78	Halifax	Trainee	Huddersfield T	—	—
Sinnott Lee	6 1	13 00	D	12 7 65	Pelsall	Apprentice	Walsall	40	2
							Watford	78	2
							Bradford C	173	6
							Crystal Palace	55	—
							Bradford C	34	1
							Huddersfield T	87	1
Stewart Marcus	5 10	10 06	F	7 11 72	Bristol	Trainee	Bristol R	171	57
							Huddersfield T	20	7
Stott Michael*	5 11	11 07	M	26 12 77	Huddersfield	Trainee	Huddersfield T	—	—
Sweet Ben*	6 0	12 05	M	21 7 78	Huddersfield	Trainee	Huddersfield T	—	—

Trainees
Bemrose, Daniel S; Crossley, Ryan S; Cuss, Paul M; Greene, Neil T; Scott, Paul; Smith, Steve D; Stansfield, James E; Walker, Richard J; Williams, Adam R.

Associated Schoolboys
Bennett, Ric J; Brown, Christopher; Clarke, Doni J; Fowler, Adam M; Hay, Nathan A; Liversidge, Gareth J; Oleksewycz, Stephen M; Pringle, Andrew; Sanderson, Michael; Sasimowicz, Steven; Senior, Philip A; Stead, Jonathan; Worthington, Jonathan.

Associated Schoolboys who have accepted the club's offer of a Traineeship/Contract
Atkinson, Robert F; Cartwright, Christopher; Gledhill, James; Horsley, Jamie L; Mattis, Dwayne; Senior, Michael G.

HULL CITY

Brien Tony	6 0	13 02	D	10 2 69	Dublin	Apprentice	Leicester C	16	1
							Chesterfield	204	8
							Rotherham U	43	2
							WBA	2	—
							Mansfield T (loan)	4	—
							Chester C (loan)	8	—
							Hull C	32	1

Brown Andrew	6 3	13 10	F	11 10 76	Edinburgh	Trainee	Leeds U	—	—
							Hull C	26	1
Darby Duane	5 11	12 06	F	17 10 73	Birmingham	Trainee	Torquay U	108	26
							Doncaster R	17	4
							Hull C	49	14
Dewhurst Rob	6 3	14 00	D	10 9 71	Keighley	Trainee	Blackburn R	13	—
							Darlington (loan)	11	1
							Huddersfield T (loan)	7	—
							Hull C	106	10
Dickinson Patrick§	5 10	10 08	M	6 5 78	Vancouver	Trainee	Hull C	1	—
Doncel Antonio	6 0	12 01	D	31 1 67	Lugo	Ferrol	Hull C	26	2
Ellington Lee§			D	3 7 80	Bradford	Trainee	Hull C	2	—
Fewings Paul	6 0	12 06	F	18 2 78	Hull	Trainee	Hull C	39	2
Gilbert Kenny‡	5 8	10 07	M	8 3 75	Aberdeen	East End A	Aberdeen	—	—
							Hull C	32	1
Gordon Gavin	6 1	12 00	F	24 6 79	Manchester	Trainee	Hull C	33	7
Greaves Mark	6 1	13 00	D	22 1 75	Hull	Brigg Town	Hull C	30	2
Joyce Warren	5 9	12 00	M	20 1 65	Oldham	School	Bolton W	184	17
							Preston NE	177	34
							Plymouth Arg	30	3
							Burnley	70	9
							Hull C (loan)	9	3
							Hull C	45	5
Laister Jamie§			M	9 2 79	Newport	Trainee	Hull C	—	—
Lowthorpe Adam	5 7	11 03	D	7 8 75	Hull	Trainee	Hull C	58	1
Mann Neil	5 10	12 01	M	19 11 72	Nottingham	Grantham T	Hull C	106	5
Marks Jamie	5 9	10 13	D	18 3 77	Belfast	Trainee	Leeds U	—	—
							Hull C	15	—
Maxfield Scott	5 10	11 05	D	13 7 76	Doncaster	Trainee	Doncaster R	29	1
							Hull C	21	—
Peacock Richard	5 10	11 05	F	29 10 72	Sheffield	Sheffield FC	Hull C	133	17
Quigley Michael	5 7	11 04	M	2 10 70	Manchester	Trainee	Manchester C	12	0
							Wrexham (loan)	4	—
							Hull C	42	2
Rioch Greg	5 11	12 10	D	24 6 75	Sutton	Trainee	Luton T	—	—
							Barnet (loan)	3	—
							Peterborough U	18	—
							Hull C	39	1
Sansam Christian‡	6 0	11 00	F	26 12 75	Hull	Trainee	Scunthorpe U	21	1
							Scarborough	6	—
							Bradford C	1	—
							Hull C	3	—
Sharman Sam	5 10	12 01	D	7 11 77	Hull	Sheffield W	Hull C	4	—
Trevitt Simon	5 11	12 09	D	20 12 67	Dewsbury	Apprentice	Huddersfield T	229	3
							Hull C	47	1
Wharton Paul	5 4	10 00	M	26 6 77	Newcastle	Trainee	Leeds U	—	—
							Hull C	10	—
Wilkinson Ian	6 2	13 00	D	19 9 77	Ferriby	Trainee	Hull C	8	1
Wilson Steve	5 10	10 12	G	24 4 74	Hull	Trainee	Hull C	94	0
Wright Ian	6 1	13 04	D	10 3 72	Lichfield	Trainee	Stoke C	6	—
							Bristol R	54	1
							Hull C	40	—

Trainees
Baker, Matthew C; Bradshaw, Christopher; Capuano, Julian; Dickinson, Patrick J; Edwards, Michael; Ellington, Lee S; Harvey, Jarred; Hennessy, Simon P; Laister, Jamie R; Loughins, Glenn T; O'Brien, Kieron J; Oakes, Gary C; Stock, Nicholas; Sykes, Simon J; Tucker, Dexter C.

Associated Schoolboys
Artymiuk, Michael J; Benson, Philip A; Harrison, Richard C; Leebetter, James E; Macklin, Lee; Marris, Christopher J; Massey, Andrew K; Peat, Nathan N M; Waslin, Daniel.

Associated Schoolboys who have accepted the club's offer of a Traineeship/Contract
Blythe, Michael; Bolder, Adam P; Feeney, John; Thacker, Martin; Wilson, Paul A.

IPSWICH TOWN

Bell Leon	5 8	11 00	M	23 9 77	Ipswich	Trainee	Ipswich T	—	—
Brown Wayne	6 0	12 06	D	20 8 77	Barking	Trainee	Ipswich T	—	—
Cundy Jason	6 1	13 13	D	12 11 69	Wimbledon	Trainee	Chelsea	41	1
							Tottenham H (loan)	10	—
							Tottenham H	16	1
							Crystal Palace (loan)	4	—
							Bristol C (loan)	6	1
							Ipswich T	13	2
Dyer Kieron	5 7	9 07	M	29 12 78	Ipswich	Trainee	Ipswich T	13	—
Ellis Kevin*	6 2	12 07	D	12 5 77	Gt Yarmouth	Trainee	Ipswich T	1	—

Forrest Craig	6 5	14 00	G	20 9 67	Vancouver	Apprentice	Ipswich T	263	—
							Colchester U (loan)	11	—
							Chelsea (loan)	3	—
Gaughan Kevin	6 0	12 05	D	6 3 78	Glasgow		Ipswich T	—	—
Gregory Neil	5 11	11 10	F	7 10 72	Zambia	Trainee	Ipswich T	37	8
							Chesterfield (loan)	3	1
							Scunthorpe U (loan)	10	7
							Torquay U (loan)	5	—
Hollman James*	6 0	12 00	G	22 3 78	Canterbury	Trainee	Ipswich T	—	—
Mason Paul	5 9	12 01	M	3 9 63	Liverpool	Groningen	Aberdeen	158	27
							Ipswich T	112	25
Mathie Alex	5 10	11 07	F	20 12 68	Bathgate	Celtic BC	Celtic	11	—
							Morton	74	31
							Port Vale (loan)	3	—
							Newcastle U	25	4
							Ipswich T	64	24
Milton Simon	5 10	11 05	M	23 8 63	Fulham	Bury St Edmunds	Ipswich T	261	48
							Exeter C (loan)	2	3
							Torquay U (loan)	4	1
Mowbray Tony	6 1	13 00	D	22 11 63	Saltburn	Apprentice	Middlesbrough	348	25
							Celtic	78	6
							Ipswich T	27	2
Naylor Richard	6 1	13 07	F	28 2 77	Leeds	Trainee	Ipswich T	27	4
Niven Stuart	5 11	12 08	M	24 12 78	Glasgow	Trainee	Ipswich T	2	—
Norfolk Lee*	5 10	11 03	M	17 10 75	Dunedin NZ	Trainee	Ipswich T	3	—
Petta Bobby	5 7	11 03	M	6 8 74	Rotterdam	Feyenoord	Ipswich T	6	—
Scowcroft James	6 1	12 02	F	15 11 75	Bury St Edmunds	Trainee	Ipswich T	64	11
Sedgley Steve	6 1	13 13	M	26 5 68	Enfield	Apprentice	Coventry C	84	3
							Tottenham H	164	8
							Ipswich T	105	15
Sonner Danny	5 11	12 08	M	9 1 72	Wigan	Wigan Ath	Burnley	6	—
							Bury (loan)	5	3
						Erzgebirge Aue	Ipswich T	29	2
Stockwell Mick	5 9	11 04	M	14 2 65	Chelmsford	Apprentice	Ipswich T	395	28
Swailes Chris	6 2	12 07	D	19 10 70	Gateshead	Bridlington T	Doncaster R	49	0
							Ipswich T	28	1
Tanner Adam	6 0	12 01	M	25 10 73	Maldon	Trainee	Ipswich T	36	6
Taricco Mauricio	5 8	11 05	D	10 3 73	Buenos Aires	Argentinos Juniors	Ipswich T	80	3
Uhlenbeek Gus	5 10	12 06	M	20 8 70	Paramaribo		Ajax	2	—
							Cambuur	39	—
							TOPS SV	22	3
							Ipswich T	78	4
Vaughan Tony	6 1	11 02	D	11 10 75	Manchester	Trainee	Ipswich T	67	3
Wark John*	5 11	12 12	D	4 8 57	Glasgow	Apprentice	Ipswich T	296	94
							Liverpool	70	28
							Ipswich T	89	23
							Middlesbrough	32	2
							Ipswich T	154	18
Williams Geraint	5 7	12 06	M	5 1 62	Cwmpare	Apprentice	Bristol R	141	8
							Derby Co	277	9
							Ipswich T	194	3
Wright Richard	6 2	13 00	G	5 11 77	Ipswich	Trainee	Ipswich T	66	—

Trainees
Beckham, Michael J; Burgess, Mark P; Coburn, Neil; Fox, Justin A; Keeble, Christopher M; Kennedy, John N; Lowes, Brendan; Midgley, Neil A; Stewart, Colin J; Theobald, David J; White, David W.

Associated Schoolboys
Artun, Erdem K; Barker, Rory; Byrne, Richard A; Colden, Lee J; Haywood, Jamie B; Hulyer, Lee A; Kinsella, Sean I; Logan, Richard J; Miller, Adam E; Riley, Dominic M.

Associated Schoolboys who have accepted the club's offer of a Traineeship/Contract
Dixon, Matthew F; Farrington, Louie M; Supple, Michael J; Wright, Carl A J.

LEEDS UNITED

Beeney Mark	6 4	14 07	G	30 12 67	Pembury		Gillingham	2	—
							Maidstone U	50	—
							Aldershot (loan)	7	—
							Brighton & HA	69	—
							Leeds U	34	—
Blunt Jason	5 9	10 10	M	16 8 77	Penzance	Trainee	Leeds U	4	—
Bowyer Lee	5 9	9 09	M	3 1 77	London	Trainee	Charlton Ath	46	8
							Leeds U	32	4
Boyle Wesley			M	30 3 79	Portadown	Trainee	Leeds U	1	—

Name	Ht	Wt	Pos	DOB	Birthplace	Source	Club	Apps	Gls
Brolin Tomas			M	29 11 69	Hudiksvall		Sundsvall Norrkoping Parma Leeds U Zurich (loan) Parma (loan)	54 11 133 19 3 11	13 7 20 4 — —
Butler John			D	28 10 79	Dublin	Belvedere	Leeds U	—	—
Byrne Nicky*			M	9 10 78	Dublin		Leeds U	—	—
Couzens Andy	5 9	11 06	D	4 6 75	Shipley	Trainee	Leeds U	28	1
Davies Lawrence‡			F	3 9 77	Abergavenny	Trainee	Leeds U	—	—
Deane Brian	6 3	12 07	F	7 2 68	Leeds	Apprentice	Doncaster R Sheffield U Leeds U	66 197 138	12 82 32
Donnelly Paul			M	31 8 79	Dublin	Trainee	Leeds U	—	—
Dorigo Tony	5 10	10 10	D	31 12 65	Melbourne	Apprentice	Aston Villa Chelsea Leeds U	111 146 171	1 11 5
Evans Paul*			G	28 12 73	South Africa	Witts Univ	Leeds U Crystal Palace (loan) Bradford C (loan)	— — —	— — —
Ford Mark	5 7	10 08	M	10 10 75	Pontefract	Trainee	Leeds U	29	1
Foster Martin	5 5	9 10	M	29 10 77	Sheffield	Trainee	Leeds U	—	—
Gray Andy	6 1	12 00	M	15 11 77	Harrogate	Trainee	Leeds U	22	—
Halle Gunnar	5 11	11 00	D	11 8 65	Larvik	Lillestrom	Oldham Ath Leeds U	188 20	17 —
Harte Ian	5 9		D	31 8 77	Drogheda	Trainee	Leeds U	18	2
Jackson Mark	5 11		D	30 9 77	Barnsley	Trainee	Leeds U	18	—
Jobson Richard	6 2	12 10	D	9 5 63	Hull	Burton Alb	Watford Hull C Oldham Ath Leeds U	28 221 189 22	4 17 10 1
Kelly Gary	5 8	13 03	D	9 7 74	Drogheda	Home Farm	Leeds U	156	2
Kewell Harry	5 11		M	22 9 78	Australia	NSW Academy	Leeds U	3	—
Knarvik Tommy			M	1 11 79	Bergen	Skjerjard	Leeds U	—	—
Laurent Pierre	5 8	10 10	F	13 12 70	Tulle	Tulle	Bastia Leeds U	73 4	13 —
Lilley Derek	5 10	12 07	F	9 2 74	Paisley	Everton BC	Morton Leeds U	180 6	57 —
Lynch Damien			D	31 7 79	Dublin		Leeds U	—	—
Martyn Nigel	6 1	14 07	G	11 8 66	St Austell	St Blazey	Bristol R Crystal Palace Leeds U	101 272 37	— — —
Matthews Lee			M	16 1 79	Middlesbrough	Trainee	Leeds U	—	—
Maybury Alan			M	8 8 78	Dublin	Trainee	Leeds U	1	—
McPhail Stephen			M	9 12 79	London	Trainee	Leeds U	—	—
Molenaar Robert	6 2	14 04	D	27 2 69	Holland		Volendam Leeds U	124 12	3 1
Palmer Carlton	6 2	12 04	D	5 12 65	Oldbury	Trainee	WBA Sheffield W Leeds U	121 205 102	4 14 5
Pemberton John*	5 11	12 12	D	18 11 64	Oldham	Chadderton	Rochdale Crewe Alex Crystal Palace Sheffield U Leeds U	1 121 78 68 53	— 1 2 — —
Quinn Andrew			M	1 9 79	Halifax		Leeds U	—	—
Radebe Lucas	6 1	11 09	M	12 4 69	Johannesburg	Kaiser Chiefs	Leeds U	57	0
Robinson Paul			G	15 10 79	Beverley	Trainee	Leeds U	—	—
Rush Ian	6 0	12 06	F	20 10 61	St Asaph	Apprentice	Chester C Liverpool Juventus Liverpool Leeds U	34 224 29 245 36	14 139 7 90 3
Sharpe Lee	6 0	12 06	F	27 5 71	Halesowen	Trainee	Torquay U Manchester U Leeds U	14 193 26	3 21 5
Shepherd Paul			F	17 11 77	Leeds	Trainee	Leeds U	1	—
Wallace Rodney	5 7	11 03	F	2 10 69	Lewisham	Trainee	Southampton Leeds U	128 181	45 43
Wetherall David	6 2	13 12	D	14 3 71	Sheffield	School	Sheffield W Leeds U	— 147	— 9
Woodgate Jonathan			D	22 1 80		Trainee	Leeds U	—	—
Wright Andrew			M	21 10 78	Leeds	Trainee	Leeds U	—	—

Name							Club	Apps	Gls
Yeboah Tony	5 11	13 13	F	6 6 66	Kumasi	Okwawu U	Saarbrucken	65	26
							Eintracht Frankfurt	123	68
							Leeds U	47	24

Trainees
Dixon, Kevin R; Doyle, Kevin; Espey, Keith A; Hackworth, Anthony; Jackson, Daniel M D; Morgan, Simon R; Ray, Mark.

Associated Schoolboys
Crawford, Dale; Froggatt, Jonathan P; Hague, Philip J; Hanley, Michael; Hider, Allan J; Lockwood, Adam B; Manousios, Nicholas G; Porter, Graeme; Price, Jamie B; Singh, Harpal; Walker, Liam J.

Associated Schoolboys who have accepted the club's offer of a Traineeship/Contract
Evans, Gareth J; Evans, Kevin; Jones, Matthew G; Lagan, Brian; Miller, Scott R J; Smith, Alan; Watson, David S.

LEICESTER CITY

Name							Club	Apps	Gls
Campbell Stuart	5 10	10 08	M	9 12 77	Corby	Trainee	Leicester C	10	—
Claridge Steve	5 11	11 08	F	10 4 66	Portsmouth	Fareham T	Bournemouth	7	1
						Weymouth	Crystal Palace	—	—
							Aldershot	62	19
							Cambridge U	79	28
							Luton T	16	2
							Cambridge U	53	18
							Birmingham C	88	35
							Leicester C	46	16
Dodds Andrew*	6 0	10 11	D	15 10 77	Gateshead	Trainee	Leicester C	—	—
Elliott Matt	6 3	14 10	D	1 11 68	Roehampton	Epsom & Ewell	Charlton Ath	—	—
							Torquay U	124	15
							Scunthorpe U (loan)	8	1
							Scunthorpe U	53	7
							Oxford U	148	21
							Leicester C	16	4
Farrell Lee‡			M	12 10 79	Leicester	Lincoln C	Leicester C	—	—
Grayson Simon	6 0	12 06	D	16 12 69	Ripon	Trainee	Leeds U	2	—
							Leicester C	188	4
Guppy Steve	5 11	10 09	M	29 3 69	Winchester	Southampton	Wycombe W	41	8
							Newcastle U	—	—
							Port Vale	105	12
							Leicester C	13	—
Hallam Craig‡	5 10	12 05	F	11 11 76	Leicester	Trainee	Leicester C	—	—
Harrington Justin*	5 9	10 09	F	18 6 75	Truro	Trainee	Norwich C	—	—
							Leicester C	—	—
Heskey Emile	6 2	13 02	M	11 1 78	Leicester	Trainee	Leicester C	66	17
Hill Colin*	6 0	12 07	D	12 11 63	Hillingdon	Apprentice	Arsenal	46	1
							Brighton & HA (loan)	—	—
						Maritimo	Colchester U	69	—
							Sheffield U	82	1
							Leicester C (loan)	10	—
							Leicester C	135	—
Izzet Muzzy	5 10	10 12	M	31 10 74	Mile End	Trainee	Chelsea	—	—
							Leicester C (loan)	9	1
							Leicester C	35	3
Kalac Zeljko‡	6 7	14 03	G	16 12 72	Camperdown	Sydney U	Leicester C	1	—
Kamark Pontus	5 10	12 03	D	5 4 69	Sweden		IFK Gothenburg	126	1
							Leicester C	11	—
Keller Kasey	6 1	12 07	G	27 1 69	Washington	Portland University	Millwall	176	—
							Leicester C	31	—
Lawrence Jamie	6 0	12 06	F	8 3 70	Balham	Cowes	Sunderland	4	—
							Doncaster R	25	3
							Leicester C	47	1
Lenhart Sascha‡			M	16 12 73	Cologne		Leicester C	—	—
Lennon Neil	5 9	12 04	D	25 6 71	Lurgan	Trainee	Manchester C	1	—
							Crewe Alex	147	15
							Leicester C	50	2
Lewis Neil	5 8	10 05	M	28 6 74	Wolverhampton	Trainee	Leicester C	67	1
Marshall Ian	6 1	12 12	F	20 3 66	Liverpool	Apprentice	Everton	15	1
							Oldham Ath	170	36
							Ipswich T	84	32
							Leicester C	28	8
McMahon Sam	5 10	11 06	M	10 2 76	Newark	Trainee	Leicester C	4	1
Parker Garry	6 0	13 02	M	7 9 65	Oxford	Apprentice	Luton T	42	3
							Hull C	84	8
							Nottingham F	103	17
							Aston Villa	95	13
							Leicester C	85	7

Name	Ht	Wt	Pos	DOB	Birthplace	Signed from	Clubs	Apps	Gls
Platnauer Nicky†	5 11	12 10	D	10 6 61	Leicester	Bedford T	Bristol R	24	7
							Coventry C	44	6
							Birmingham C	28	2
							Reading (loan)	7	—
							Cardiff C	115	6
							Notts Co	57	1
							Port Vale (loan)	14	—
							Leicester C	35	—
							Scunthorpe U	14	2
							Mansfield T	25	—
							Lincoln C	27	—
							Leicester C	—	—
Poole Kevin*	5 10	12 06	G	21 7 63	Bromsgrove	Apprentice	Aston Villa	28	—
							Northampton T (loan)	3	—
							Middlesbrough	34	—
							Hartlepool U (loan)	12	—
							Leicester C	163	—
Prior Spencer	6 3	12 12	D	22 4 71	Rochford	Trainee	Southend U	135	3
							Norwich C	74	1
							Leicester C	34	—
Quincey Lee*	5 10	12 07	D	5 10 77	Leicester	Trainee	Leicester C	—	—
Robins Mark	5 8	11 08	F	22 12 69	Ashton under Lyme	Apprentice	Manchester U	48	11
							Norwich C	67	20
							Leicester C	56	12
Rolling Frank*	6 2	13 00	D	23 8 68	Colnar	FC Pau	Ayr U	35	2
							Leicester C	18	—
Skeldon Kevin	5 11	11 03	F	27 4 78	Edinburgh	Trainee	Leicester C	—	—
Taylor Scott	5 9	12 00	M	28 11 70	Portsmouth	Trainee	Reading	207	24
							Leicester C	64	6
Ullathorne Robert	5 8	11 03	M	11 10 71	Wakefield	Trainee	Norwich C	94	7
							Osasuna	18	—
							Leicester C	—	—
Walsh Steve	6 3	14 06	D	3 11 64	Fulwood	Local	Wigan Ath	126	4
							Leicester C	309	47
Watts Julian	6 3	12 01	D	17 3 71	Sheffield	Trainee	Rotherham U	20	1
							Sheffield W	16	1
							Shrewsbury T (loan)	9	—
							Leicester C	35	1
Wenlock Stephen	5 7	11 01	D	11 3 78	Peterborough	Trainee	Leicester C	—	—
Whitlow Mike	6 0	13 03	D	13 1 68	Northwich	Witton Alb	Leeds U	77	4
							Leicester C	147	8
Willis Jimmy‡	6 2	12 04	D	12 7 68	Liverpool	Blackburn R	Halifax T	—	—
							Stockport Co	10	—
							Darlington	90	6
							Leicester C	60	3
							Bradford C (loan)	9	1
Wilson Stuart	5 8	9 12	F	16 9 77	Leicester	Trainee	Leicester C	2	1

Trainees
Arcos-Diaz, Miguel; Branston, Guy; Emerson, Paul G; Fox, Martin R; Goodwin, Thomas N; Heppell, Stuart E; Hodges, John K; Jackson, Matthew; Jaffa, Graeme; Jones, Gareth; Magee, Martyn; McCann, Timothy M; Mitchell, Ross J; Neil, Gary D C; Oakes, Stefan T; Ramm, Daniel A; Wilson, Stevie J.

Associated Schoolboys
Dawson, Craig A; Eastell, Richard J; Harrison, Andrew J; Heath, Matthew P; Maye, Daniel P C; Noble, Karl N; Nurse, Matthew J; Owen, Ben R; Piper, Matthew J; Preston, Niki P; Ratcliffe, David P; Savage, Michael J; Sexton, Sean; White, Christopher I.

Associated Schoolboys who have accepted the club's offer of a Traineeship/Contract
Bacon, Carl R; Noble, Craig P; Orme, Richard P B; Saddington, David; Salter, Alex; Weale, Richard J.

LEYTON ORIENT

Name	Ht	Wt	Pos	DOB	Birthplace	Signed from	Clubs	Apps	Gls
Ansah Andy†	5 9	11 03	F	19 3 69	Lewisham	Crystal Palace	Brentford	8	2
							Southend U	157	33
							Brentford (loan)	3	1
							Brentford (loan)	6	1
							Peterborough U	2	1
							Gillingham	2	—
							Leyton Orient	2	—
Arnott Andy	6 0	12 02	M	18 10 73	Chatham	Trainee	Gillingham	73	12
							Manchester U (loan)	—	—
							Leyton Orient	50	6
Ayorinde Sam	6 0	12 07	F	20 10 74	Lagos	Sturm Graz	Leyton Orient	13	2
Baker Joe	5 8	10 07	F	9 4 77	London	Charlton Ath	Leyton Orient	40	0
Caldwell Peter‡	6 1	13 00	G	5 6 72	Dorchester	Trainee	QPR	—	—
							Leyton Orient	31	—

Name	Ht	Wt	Pos	Born	Birthplace	Source	Club	Apps	Gls
Capleton Mel†	5 11	12 00	G	24 10 73	London	Trainee	Southend U	—	—
							Blackpool	11	—
							Leyton Orient	—	—
Channing Justin	5 11	11 07	D	19 11 68	Reading	Apprentice	QPR	55	5
							Bristol R	130	10
							Leyton Orient	40	5
Chapman Danny*	6 0	12 08	D	21 11 74	Greenwich	Trainee	Millwall	12	—
							Leyton Orient	78	4
Clark Paul†	5 9	13 13	M	14 9 58	Benfleet	Apprentice	Southend U	33	1
							Brighton & HA	79	9
							Reading (loan)	2	—
							Southend U	276	3
							Gillingham	90	1
							Cambridge U	2	—
							Leyton Orient	—	—
Garland Peter*	5 9	12 08	M	20 1 71	Croydon	Trainee	Tottenham H	1	—
							Newcastle U	2	—
							Charlton Ath	53	2
							Wycombe W (loan)	5	—
							Leyton Orient	21	—
Griffiths Carl	5 10	11 05	F	15 7 71	Oswestry	Trainee	Shrewsbury T	143	54
							Manchester C	18	4
							Portsmouth	14	2
							Peterborough U	16	2
							Leyton Orient	13	6
Hanson Dave	6 1	13 01	F	19 11 68	Huddersfield	Farsley Celtic	Bury	1	—
						Hednesford T	Leyton Orient	36	4
							Chesterfield (loan)	3	1
Heidenstrom Bjorn‡			M	15 1 68	Porsgrunn	Odd Grenland	Leyton Orient	4	—
Howes Shaun	5 10	11 07	D	7 11 77	Norwich	Trainee	Cambridge U	1	—
							Leyton Orient	5	—
Hyde Paul	6 1	14 09	G	7 4 63	Hayes	Hayes	Wycombe W	105	—
							Leicester C	—	—
							Leyton Orient	13	—
Inglethorpe Alex	5 11	11 04	M	14 11 71	Epsom	School	Watford	12	2
							Barnet (loan)	6	3
							Leyton Orient	46	17
Kelly Tony‡	5 11	11 08	F	14 2 66	Meridan		Bristol C	6	1
						St Albans C	Stoke C	58	5
							Hull C (loan)	6	1
							Cardiff C (loan)	5	1
							Bury	57	10
							Leyton Orient	43	4
							Colchester U (loan)	3	—
Ling Martin	5 7	10 08	M	15 7 66	West Ham	Apprentice	Exeter C	116	14
							Swindon T	2	—
							Southend U	138	31
							Mansfield T (loan)	3	—
							Swindon T (loan)	1	—
							Swindon T	149	10
							Leyton Orient	44	1
Longden Adam†			M	8 5 71	Rotherham	Cambridge U	Leyton Orient	—	—
Martin Alvin‡	6 1	13 07	D	29 7 58	Bootle	Apprentice	West Ham U	469	27
							Leyton Orient	17	—
McCarthy Alan*	5 11	12 10	D	11 1 72	London	Trainee	QPR	11	—
							Watford (loan)	9	—
							Plymouth Arg (loan)	2	—
							Leyton Orient	47	—
McGleish Scott	5 9	11 00	F	10 2 74	Camden Town	Edgware T	Charlton Ath	6	—
							Leyton Orient (loan)	6	1
							Peterborough U	13	—
							Colchester U (loan)	15	6
							Cambridge U (loan)	10	7
							Leyton Orient	28	7
Morrison Dave	5 11	12 10	M	30 11 74	Waltham Forest	Chelmsford C	Peterborough U	77	12
							Leyton Orient	8	—
Naylor Dominic	5 9	12 01	D	12 8 70	Watford	Trainee	Watford	—	—
							Halifax T	6	1
						Barnet	Barnet	51	—
							Plymouth Arg	85	—
							Gillingham	31	1
							Leyton Orient	44	3
Riches Steve	6 2	12 06	M	6 8 76	Sydney	US Univ	Leyton Orient	5	—
Shearer Lee	6 4	12 01	D	23 10 77	Rochford	Trainee	Leyton Orient	18	1

Name							Club	Apps	Gls
Shilton Peter‡	6 1	14 00	G	18 9 49	Leicester	Apprentice	Leicester C	286	1
							Stoke C	110	—
							Nottingham F	202	—
							Southampton	188	—
							Derby Co	175	—
							Plymouth Arg	34	—
							Wimbledon	—	—
							Bolton W	1	—
							Coventry C	—	—
							West Ham U	—	—
							Leyton Orient	9	—
Timons Chris†	6 1	12 07	D	8 12 74	Longworth	Clipstone Welfare	Mansfield T	39	2
							Chesterfield	—	—
							Leyton Orient	6	2
Warren Mark	6 0	12 02	D	12 11 74	Hackney	Trainee	Leyton Orient	101	5
							West Ham U (loan)	—	—
Weaver Luke			G	26 6 79	Woolwich	Trainee	Leyton Orient	9	—
							West Ham U (loan)	—	—
West Colin	6 1	13 09	F	13 11 62	Wallsend	Apprentice	Sunderland	102	21
							Watford	45	20
							Rangers	10	2
							Sheffield W	45	8
							WBA	73	22
							Port Vale (loan)	5	1
							Swansea C	33	12
							Leyton Orient	135	42
Wilkins Ray†	5 8	11 00	M	14 9 56	Hillingdon	Apprentice	Chelsea	179	30
							Manchester U	160	7
							AC Milan	73	2
							Paris St Germain	10	—
							Rangers	70	2
							QPR	154	7
							Crystal Palace	1	—
							QPR	21	—
							Wycombe W	1	—
							Hibernian	16	—
							Millwall	3	—
							Leyton Orient	3	—
Williams Lee‡			F	13 3 77	Essex		Leyton Orient	3	—
Winston Sam			F	6 8 78	London	Norwich C	Leyton Orient	11	1

Trainees
Barrett, Adam N; Cockerill, David A; Ellerton, Gary J; Everingham, William L; Fairey, Paul; Harrington, Daniel J; Jones, Anthony S; Jones, David; Morris, Jamie B; Philips, Wayne D; Warren, Kevin; Williams, Michael J.

Non-Contract
Timons, Christopher.

Associated Schoolboys
Antoine, Marlon A.

Player who does not hold a current contract but his registration has been retained by the club
Honeyball, Scott R; Brazier, Jeffrey C.

LINCOLN CITY

Name							Club	Apps	Gls
Ainsworth Gareth	5 9	11 09	F	10 5 73	Blackburn	Blackburn R	Preston NE	5	—
							Cambridge U	4	1
							Preston NE	82	12
							Lincoln C	77	34
Alcide Colin	6 2	13 11	M	14 4 72	Huddersfield	Emley	Lincoln C	69	13
Anderson Richard†			M	12 12 72	Hastings		Lincoln C	—	—
Austin Kevin	6 1	14 00	D	12 2 73	Hackney	Saffron Walden	Leyton Orient	109	3
							Lincoln C	44	1
Barnett Jason	5 9	10 10	D	21 4 76	Shrewsbury	Trainee	Wolverhampton W	—	—
							Lincoln C	68	2
Bimson Stuart	5 11	11 08	D	29 9 69	Liverpool	Macclesfield T	Bury	36	—
							Lincoln C	15	1
Bos Gijsbert	6 5	13 07	F	22 3 73	Spakenburg	Ijsselmeervogels	Lincoln C	34	6
Brown Grant	6 0	11 12	D	19 11 69	Sunderland	Trainee	Leicester C	14	0
							Lincoln C	288	12
Brown Steve	6 0	11 06	F	6 12 73	Southend	Trainee	Southend U	10	2
							Scunthorpe U	—	—
							Colchester U	62	17
							Gillingham	9	2
							Lincoln C	41	5
Challinor Paul†	6 1	12 02	D	6 4 76	Newcastle under Lyme	Trainee	Birmingham C	—	—
							Lincoln C	—	—
Davies Neil‡	6 2	14 02	F	9 11 76	Liverpool	Fleetwood T	Lincoln C	—	—

Name	Ht	Wt	Pos	DOB	Birthplace	From	Club	Apps	Gls
Dennis Tony*	5 7	10 11	M	1 12 63	Eton	Apprentice	Plymouth Arg	9	—
							Exeter C	4	—
						Slough T	Cambridge U	111	10
							Chesterfield	10	—
							Colchester U	65	5
							Lincoln C	28	2
Dickins Matt‡	6 4	14 00	G	3 9 70	Sheffield	Trainee	Sheffield U	—	—
							Leyton Orient (loan)	—	—
							Lincoln C	27	—
							Blackburn R	1	—
							Blackpool (loan)	19	—
							Lincoln C (loan)	—	—
							Grimsby T (loan)	—	—
							Rochdale (loan)	4	—
							Stockport Co	13	—
							Lincoln C	—	—
Dobbs Gerald†	5 8	11 07	D	24 1 71	Lambeth	Trainee	Wimbledon	33	1
							Cardiff C (loan)	3	—
							Lincoln C	—	—
Fleming Terry	5 9	10 01	M	5 1 73	Marston Green	Trainee	Coventry C	13	—
							Northampton T	31	1
							Preston NE	32	2
							Lincoln C	59	—
Fraser Steve*	6 3	13 07	D	21 2 78	Nottingham	Grimsby T	Lincoln C	—	—
Gibson Lee*	5 9	11 02	M	3 1 78	Skegness	Trainee	Lincoln C	—	—
Holmes Steve	6 2	13 00	D	13 1 71	Middlesbrough	Guisborough T	Preston NE	13	1
							Hartlepool U (loan)	5	2
							Lincoln C	51	6
Hone Mark	6 1	12 00	M	31 3 68	Croydon	Trainee	Crystal Palace	4	—
						Welling U	Southend U	56	—
							Lincoln C	29	—
Martin Jae	5 11	11 00	F	5 2 76	London	Trainee	Southend U	8	—
							Leyton Orient (loan)	4	—
							Birmingham C	7	—
							Lincoln C	34	4
Richardson Barry	6 1	12 01	G	5 8 69	Wallsend	Trainee	Sunderland	—	—
							Scunthorpe U	—	—
							Scarborough	30	—
							Northampton T	96	—
							Preston NE	20	—
							Lincoln C	70	—
Robertson John	6 2	12 08	D	8 1 74	Liverpool	Trainee	Wigan Ath	112	4
							Lincoln C	38	1
Stant Phil	6 1	12 07	F	13 10 62	Bolton	Camberley Army	Reading	4	2
							Hereford U	89	38
							Notts Co	22	6
							Blackpool (loan)	12	5
							Lincoln C (loan)	4	—
							Huddersfield T (loan)	5	1
							Fulham	19	5
							Mansfield T	57	32
							Cardiff C	79	34
							Mansfield T (loan)	4	1
							Bury	62	23
							Northampton T (loan)	5	2
							Lincoln C	22	15
Sterling Worrell	5 7	10 01	M	8 6 65	Bethnal Green	Apprentice	Watford	94	14
							Peterborough U	193	29
							Bristol R	119	6
							Lincoln C	21	—
Stones Craig§			M	31 5 80	Scunthorpe	Trainee	Lincoln C	2	—
Storey Brett†			M	7 7 77	Sheffield	Trainee	Sheffield U	—	—
							Lincoln C	2	1
Vaughan John	5 10	13 01	G	26 6 64	Isleworth	Apprentice	West Ham U	—	—
							Charlton Ath (loan)	6	—
							Bristol R (loan)	6	—
							Wrexham (loan)	4	—
							Bristol C (loan)	2	—
							Fulham	44	—
							Bristol C (loan)	3	—
							Cambridge U	178	—
							Charlton Ath	6	—
							Preston NE	66	—
							Lincoln C	10	—
							Colchester U (loan)	5	—

Westley Shane	6 2	13 01	D	16 6 65	Canterbury	Apprentice	Charlton Ath	8	—
							Southend U	144	10
							Norwich C (loan)	—	—
							Wolverhampton W	50	2
							Brentford	64	1
							Southend U (loan)	5	—
							Cambridge U	3	—
							Lincoln C	9	1
Whitney Jon	5 11	13 08	D	23 12 70	Nantwich	Winsford U	Huddersfield T	18	—
							Wigan Ath (loan)	12	—
							Lincoln C	44	5

Trainees
Aiken, Christopher A; Davie, Lee T; Hart, Adam J; Heaton, Matthew P; Hewson, Ross; Hubbard, Christopher R; Lawrence, Carl M M; Lynn, Daniel J; McGill, Andrew J; O'Callaghan, Sean; Reeson, Nicholas D; Smith, Matthew P; Stones, Craig; Wilkins, Ian J.

Associated Schoolboys
Burbidge, Matthew M; Fleming, Ross J; Gray, Darren K; Hitchens, Ben N.

LIVERPOOL

Babb Phil	6 0	12 03	D	30 11 70	Lambeth	Trainee	Millwall	—	—
							Bradford C	80	14
							Coventry C	77	3
							Liverpool	84	1
Barnes John	5 11	12 07	M	7 11 63	Jamaica	Sudbury Court	Watford	233	65
							Liverpool	314	84
Berger Patrik	6 2	12 06	M	10 11 73	Prague		Slavia Prague	89	24
							Borussia Dortmund	25	4
							Liverpool	23	6
Bjornebye Stig Inge	5 10	11 09	D	11 12 69	Norway		Strammen	19	—
							Kongsvinger	62	3
							Rosenborg	21	3
							Liverpool	91	2
Brazier Philip			D	3 9 77	Liverpool	Trainee	Liverpool	—	—
Byrne Niall			F	3 9 79	Dublin	Trainee	Liverpool	—	—
Carragher James			D	28 1 78	Bootle	Trainee	Liverpool	2	1
Cassidy Jamie	5 9	10 08	M	21 11 77	Liverpool	Trainee	Liverpool	—	—
Culshaw Thomas	5 10	12 02	M	10 10 78	Liverpool	Trainee	Liverpool	—	—
Dalglish Paul	5 9	10 00	M	18 2 77	Glasgow	X Form	Celtic	—	—
							Liverpool	—	—
Fowler Robbie	5 11	11 10	F	9 4 75	Liverpool	Trainee	Liverpool	140	83
Friars Sean			M	15 5 79	Derry	Trainee	Liverpool	—	—
Harkness Steve	5 10	11 02	M	27 8 71	Carlisle	Trainee	Carlisle U	13	—
							Liverpool	71	2
							Huddersfield T (loan)	5	—
							Southend U (loan)	6	—
James David	6 5	14 02	G	1 8 70	Welwyn	Trainee	Watford	89	—
							Liverpool	161	—
Jones Lee	5 8	10 08	F	29 5 73	Wrexham	Trainee	Wrexham	39	10
							Liverpool	3	—
							Crewe Alex (loan)	8	1
							Wrexham (loan)	20	9
							Wrexham (loan)	6	—
							Tranmere R (loan)	8	5
Jones Rob	5 8	11 00	D	5 11 71	Wrexham	Trainee	Crewe Alex	75	2
							Liverpool	162	—
Kennedy Mark	5 11	11 00	F	15 5 76	Dublin	Belvedere	Millwall	43	9
							Liverpool	15	—
Kvarme Bjorn	6 1	12 04	D	17 7 72	Trondheim		Rosenborg	88	2
							Liverpool	15	—
Matteo Dominic	6 1	11 10	D	24 4 74	Dumfries	Trainee	Liverpool	49	—
							Sunderland (loan)	1	—
McAteer Jason	5 11	11 10	M	18 6 71	Birkenhead	Marine	Bolton W	114	8
							Liverpool	66	1
McManaman Steve	6 0	10 06	F	11 2 72	Liverpool	School	Liverpool	208	31
Nielsen Jorgen			G	6 5 71	Nykobing		Liverpool	—	—
Owen Michael			F	14 12 79	Chester	Trainee	Liverpool	2	1
Prior Lee*			D	30 10 77	Liverpool	Trainee	Liverpool	—	—
Quinn Mark‡			M	7 10 77	Warrington	Trainee	Liverpool	—	—
Quinn Stuart*			M	11 12 77	Whiston	Trainee	Liverpool	—	—
Redknapp Jamie	6 0	12 10	M	25 6 73	Barton on Sea	Trainee	Bournemouth	13	0
							Liverpool	157	15
Rizzo Nicky			M	9 6 79	Sydney	Sydney Olympic	Liverpool	—	—
Roberts Gareth			D	6 2 78	Wrexham	Trainee	Liverpool	—	—

Ruddock Neil	6 2	12 12	D	9 5 68	London	Apprentice	Millwall	—	—
							Tottenham H	9	
							Millwall	2	1
							Southampton	107	9
							Tottenham H	38	3
							Liverpool	113	11
Thomas Michael	5 9	12 06	M	24 8 67	Lambeth	Apprentice	Arsenal	163	24
							Portsmouth (loan)	3	—
							Liverpool	113	8
Thompson David	5 7	10 00	M	12 9 77	Birkenhead	Trainee	Liverpool	2	—
Turkington Edmond			M	15 5 78	Merseyside	Trainee	Liverpool	—	—
Warner Anthony	6 4	13 09	G	11 5 74	Liverpool	School	Liverpool	—	—
Whitehead Russell*	5 8	10 04	D	28 8 76	Liverpool		Liverpool	—	—
Williams Daniel			M	12 7 79	Wrexham	Trainee	Liverpool	—	—
Wright Mark	6 2	13 03	D	1 8 63	Dorchester	Amateur	Oxford U	10	—
							Southampton	170	7
							Derby Co	144	10
							Liverpool	152	5

Trainees
Cass, Matthew; Dunbavin, Ian S; Gerrard, Steven G; Hessey, Sean P; Jones, Jason A W; Maxwell, Layton J; Murphy, Neil A; Naylor, Roy; O'Mara, Paul; Partridge, Richard J; Rigoglioso, Adriano; Wright, Stephen J; Yates, Michael A.

Associated Schoolboys
Armstrong, Ian; Atherton, Michael A; Baker, Carl P; Beck, Lee T; Brownlie, Stuart I; Cavanagh, Peter J; Coupe, Alan E; Crookes, Peter; Culshaw, Paul R; Daniels, David A; Danns, Neil A; De Arostegui, Daniel; Evans, Gareth J; Harrison, Jamie; Kennedy, Michael J; Marsden, Joseph G; McIlroy, Brian P; Miles, John F; Obrien, Christopher T; Olsen, James P; Park, Stephen M; Paxton, Andrew J; Porter, Stephen; Prince, Neil M; Robinson, Craig; Spence, Andrew P; Tamm, Christopher W; Torpey, Stephen R; Veitch, Paul; Walters, Marc A; Warnock, Stephen; Williams, Robert.

Associated Schoolboys who have accepted the club's offer of a Traineeship/Contract
Bishop, David S; Boardman, John S; Boggan, John R; Gregson, Neil R; Harkin, Bryan; Jones, Eifion P; Navarro, Alan; Roberts, John P.

LUTON TOWN

Abbey Nathan	6 1	12 00	G	11 7 78	Islington	Trainee	Luton T	—	—
Alexander Graham	5 10	12 02	M	10 10 71	Coventry	Trainee	Scunthorpe U	159	18
							Luton T	82	3
Chenery Ben‡	6 1	12 05	D	28 1 77	Ipswich	Trainee	Luton T	2	—
Davis Kelvin	6 0	14 00	G	29 9 76	Bedford	Trainee	Luton T	16	0
							Torquay U (loan)	2	—
Davis Steve	6 2	14 07	D	30 10 68	Hexham	Trainee	Southampton	7	—
							Burnley (loan)	9	—
							Notts Co (loan)	2	—
							Burnley	162	22
							Luton T	80	10
Douglas Stuart	5 8	11 05	F	9 4 78	London	Trainee	Luton T	17	1
Evers Sean	5 9	9 11	M	10 10 77	Hitchin	Trainee	Luton T	2	—
Feuer Ian	6 7	15 06	G	20 5 71	Las Vegas	Los Angeles Salsa	West Ham U	—	—
							Peterborough U (loan)	16	—
							Luton T	84	—
Fotiadis Andrew	5 11	11 00	F	6 9 77	Hitchin	School	Luton T	17	3
George Liam			F	2 2 79	Luton	Trainee	Luton T	—	—
Grant Kim	5 10	10 12	F	25 9 72	Ghana	Trainee	Charlton Ath	123	18
							Luton T	35	5
Guentchev Bontcho*	5 10	11 07	M	7 7 64	Bulgaria	Sporting Lisbon	Ipswich T	61	6
							Luton T	62	10
Harvey Richard*	5 10	11 12	D	17 4 69	Letchworth	Apprentice	Luton T	155	4
							Blackpool (loan)	5	—
Hughes Ceri	5 10	12 07	M	26 2 71	Pontypridd	Trainee	Luton T	175	17
James Julian	5 10	12 04	D	22 3 70	Tring	Trainee	Luton T	258	13
							Preston NE (loan)	6	—
Johnson Marvin	6 1	13 06	D	29 10 68	Wembley	Apprentice	Luton T	246	4
Kean Robert			M	3 6 78	Luton	Trainee	Luton T	—	—
Marshall Dwight	5 7	11 02	F	3 10 65	Jamaica	Grays Ath	Plymouth Arg	99	27
							Middlesbrough (loan)	3	—
							Luton T	95	24
McLaren Paul	6 1	13 04	M	17 11 76	High Wycombe	Trainee	Luton T	37	1
Oldfield David	6 0	13 04	F	30 5 68	Perth (Aus)	Apprentice	Luton T	29	4
							Manchester C	26	6
							Leicester C	188	26
							Millwall (loan)	17	6
							Luton T	72	8

Patterson Darren	6 1	12 10	D	15 10 69	Belfast	Trainee	WBA	—	—
							Wigan Ath	97	6
							Crystal Palace	22	1
							Luton T	33	—
							Preston NE (loan)	2	—
Peake Trevor†	6 0	12 09	D	10 2 57	Nuneaton	Nuneaton Bor	Lincoln C	171	7
							Coventry C	278	6
							Luton T	178	—
Showler Paul	5 7	11 00	M	10 10 66	Doncaster	Altrincham	Barnet	71	12
							Bradford C	88	15
							Luton T	23	6
Simpson Gary‡	6 3	13 11	D	14 2 76	Ashford	Trainee	Luton T	—	—
							Fulham (loan)	7	—
Skelton Aaron*	6 0	12 06	D	22 11 74	Welwyn	Trainee	Luton T	8	—
Sweeney Terry			F	26 1 79	Paisley	Trainee	Luton T	—	—
Thomas Mitchell	6 2	13 00	D	2 10 64	Luton	Apprentice	Luton T	107	1
							Tottenham H	157	6
							West Ham U	38	3
							Luton T	125	4
Thorpe Tony	5 9	12 04	F	10 4 74	Leicester	Leicester C	Luton T	92	36
Waddock Gary	5 10	12 05	M	17 3 62	Alperton	Apprentice	QPR	203	8
						Charleroi	Millwall	58	2
							QPR	—	—
							Swindon T (loan)	6	—
							Bristol R	71	1
							Luton T	115	3
Willmott Chris	6 2	11 05	D	30 9 77	Bedford	Trainee	Luton T	—	—
Woodsford Jamie‡	5 10	12 00	F	9 11 76	Ipswich	Trainee	Luton T	10	0

Trainees
Augustine, Steve K; Barr, Andrew R; Boyce, Emmerson O; Clarke, Richard J; Cox, James D; Doherty, Gary M T; Fraser, Stuart T; Jones, Ian; Lawes, Russell I; McIndoe, Michael; Scarlett, Andre P; Spring, Matthew J; Webb, Nicholas M.

Non-Contract
Peake, Trevor.

Associated Schoolboys
Cheek, Neil J; Clarke, Duane; Cumberbatch, Dominic; Deller, Christopher J; Harrington, Joseph; Mansell, Lee R; Mentore, Ezra; Minton, Alex; Moran, Ryan J; Orchard, Lee; Robert, Steven; Thomas, William J.

Associated Schoolboys who have accepted the club's offer of a Traineeship/Contract
Ayres, James M; Howe, Darren; McCormack, Wayne; Tate, Daniel A.

MACCLESFIELD TOWN

Askey John	6 0	12 01	F	4 11 64	Stoke	Port Vale	Macclesfield T	—	—
Bradshaw Mark	5 9	10 03	D	7 9 69	Ashton		Blackpool	42	1
							York C (loan)	1	—
						Stafford R	Macclesfield T	—	—
Byrne Chris	5 9	10 02	M	9 2 75	Hulme		Crewe Alex	—	—
						Droylsden	Macclesfield T	—	—
Davenport Peter	5 10	11 06	F	24 3 61	Birkenhead	Everton	Nottingham F	118	54
							Manchester U	92	22
							Middlesbrough	59	7
							Sunderland	99	15
							Airdrie	38	9
							St Johnstone	22	4
						Southport	Stockport Co	6	1
							Macclesfield T	.	—
Edey Cec	6 1	12 04	D	12 3 65	Manchester	Witton A	Macclesfield T	—	—
Gardiner Mark	5 10	12 07	M	25 12 66	Cirencester		Swindon T	10	—
							Torquay U	49	4
							Crewe Alex	193	33
						Fredrikstad	Chester C (loan)	3	—
							Macclesfield T	—	—
Gee Danny	5 11	12 05	D	6 5 74	Northwich	Barnton	Macclesfield T	—	—
Howarth Neil	6 1	12 12	D	15 11 71	Bolton		Burnley	1	—
							Macclesfield T	—	—
Levendis Andy	5 8	11 06	M	4 1 78	Cheadle	Oldham Ath	Macclesfield T	—	—
Mitchell Neil	5 6	12 12	F	7 11 74	Lytham	Trainee	Blackpool	67	8
							Rochdale (loan)	4	—
Oakes Andy	6 1	11 02	GK	11 1 77	Northwich	Witton A	Bury	—	—
						Barnton	Macclesfield T	—	—
Ohandjanian Dmis†	5 8	10 12	F	1 5 78	Manchester	Curzon Ashton	Doncaster R	1	—
Payne Steve	5 11	12 02	D	1 8 75	Castleford		Huddersfield T	—	—
							Macclesfield T	—	—
Peel Nathan‡	6 1	13 03	F	17 5 72	Blackburn	Trainee	Preston NE	10	1
							Sheffield U	1	—
							Halifax T (loan)	3	—
							Burnley	16	2
							Rotherham U (loan)	9	4
							Mansfield T (loan)	2	—
							Doncaster R (loan)	2	—
							Rotherham U	—	—

Name		Ht	Wt	Pos	DOB	Birthplace	Source	Club	Apps	Gls
Power	Phil	5 7	11 07	F	25 7 67	Salford	Witton A	Crewe Alex	11	2
							Stalybridge C	Macclesfield T	—	—
Price	Ryan	6 5	13 04	GK	13 3 70	Coven	Stafford R	Birmingham C	—	—
								Macclesfield T	—	—
Sorvel	Neil	5 10	11 04	M	2 3 73	Whiston		Crewe Alex	9	—
								Macclesfield T	—	—
Tinson	Darren	5 10	12 12	D	15 11 69	Connah's Quay	Northwich V	Macclesfield T	—	—
Williams	Carwyn	5 9	11 10	F	21 10 74	Pwllheli		Crewe Alex	—	—
							Northwich V	Macclesfield T	—	—
Wood	Steve	5 8	10 12	M	23 6 63	Oldham	Ashton U	Macclesfield T	—	—

MANCHESTER CITY

Name		Ht	Wt	Pos	DOB	Birthplace	Source	Club	Apps	Gls
Atkinson	Dalian*	6 0	13 10	F	21 3 68	Shrewsbury		Ipswich T	1	—
								Ipswich	59	18
								Sheffield W	38	10
								Real Sociedad	26	12
								Aston Villa	87	23
								Fenerbahce	24	10
								Manchester C	8	2
Beagrie	Peter	5 8	12 00	M	28 11 65	Middlesbrough	Local	Middlesbrough	33	2
								Sheffield U	84	11
								Stoke C	54	7
								Everton	114	11
								Sunderland (loan)	5	1
								Manchester C	52	3
Beech	Chris*	5 9	11 00	F	5 11 75	Congleton	Trainee	Manchester C	—	—
Beesley	Paul	6 1	12 07	D	21 9 65	Liverpool	Marine	Wigan Ath	155	3
								Leyton Orient	32	1
								Sheffield U	168	7
								Leeds U	22	—
								Manchester C	6	—
Bentley	Jim*	6 1	13 00	D	11 6 76	Liverpool	Trainee	Manchester C	—	—
Blore	Darren*			D	28 10 77	Oldham	Trainee	Manchester C	—	—
Brannan	Ged	6 0	12 05	D	15 1 72	Liverpool	Trainee	Tranmere R	238	20
								Manchester C	11	1
Brightwell	Ian	5 10	12 05	M	9 4 68	Lutterworth	Congleton T	Manchester C	300	18
Brisco	Neil	6 0	11 05	M	26 1 78	Wigan	Trainee	Manchester C	—	—
Brown	Michael	5 9	10 07	G	6 11 79	Stranraer	Trainee	Manchester C	—	—
Brown	Michael R	5 8	11 08	M	25 1 77	Hartlepool	Trainee	Manchester C	32	—
								Hartlepool U (loan)	6	1
Callaghan	Anthony	5 7	10 00	D	11 1 78	Manchester	Trainee	Manchester C	—	—
Clough	Nigel	5 10	12 03	M	19 3 66	Sunderland	AC Hunters	Nottingham F	311	101
								Liverpool	39	7
								Manchester C	38	4
								Nottingham F (loan)	13	1
Creaney	Gerry	5 11	13 06	F	13 4 70	Coatbridge	Celtic BC	Celtic	113	36
								Portsmouth	60	32
								Manchester C	20	4
								Oldham Ath (loan)	9	2
								Ipswich T (loan)	6	1
Crooks	Lee	5 11	12 01	M	14 1 78	Wakefield	Trainee	Manchester C	15	—
Dibble	Andy	6 2	16 02	G	8 5 65	Cwmbran	Apprentice	Cardiff C	62	—
(Transferred to Rangers, March 1997)								Luton T	30	—
								Sunderland (loan)	12	—
								Huddersfield T (loan)	5	—
								Manchester C	115	—
								Aberdeen (loan)	5	—
								Middlesbrough (loan)	19	—
								Bolton W (loan)	13	—
								WBA (loan)	9	—
								Oldham Ath (loan)	—	—
Dickov	Paul	5 5	11 09	F	1 11 72	Glasgow	Trainee	Arsenal	21	3
								Luton T (loan)	15	1
								Brighton & HA (loan)	8	5
								Manchester C	29	5
Edghill	Richard	5 9	11 03	D	23 9 74	Oldham	Trainee	Manchester C	49	—
Fenton	Anthony	5 10	10 02	D	23 11 79	Preston	Trainee	Manchester C	—	—
Fenton	Nicholas	5 10	10 04	D	23 11 79	Preston	Trainee	Manchester C	—	—
Foster	John	5 11	13 02	D	19 9 73	Blackley	Trainee	Manchester C	19	—
Freeman	Nathan*			G	5 8 77	Portsmouth	Trainee	Manchester C	—	—
								Fulham (loan)	—	—
Frontzeck	Michael	5 11	12 12	D	26 3 64	Moenchen-gladbach	Odenkirchen	Moenchengladbach	190	17
(Transferred to Freiburg, January 1997)								Stuttgart	163	16
								Bochum	28	2
								Moenchengladbach	8	—
								Manchester C	23	—

Greenacre Chris	5 11	12 08	F	23 12 77	Wakefield	Trainee	Manchester C	4	—
Harris Sammy*			D	2 4 78	Stockport	Trainee	Manchester C	—	—
Heaney Neil	5 9	11 07	F	3 11 71	Middlesbrough	Trainee	Arsenal	7	—
							Hartlepool U (loan)	3	—
							Cambridge U (loan)	13	4
							Southampton	61	5
							Manchester C	15	1
Hiley Scott	5 9	11 05	M	27 9 68	Plymouth	Trainee	Exeter C	210	12
							Birmingham C	49	—
							Manchester C	9	—
Horlock Kevin	6 0	12 00	M	1 11 72	Plumstead	Trainee	West Ham U	—	—
							Swindon T	163	22
							Manchester C	18	4
Immel Eike*	6 2	13 05	G	27 11 60	Marburg/Lahn	Stadtallendorf	Borussia Dortmund	247	—
							Stuttgart	287	—
							Manchester C	42	—
Ingram Rae	5 11	12 08	D	6 12 74	Manchester	Trainee	Manchester C	23	—
Kavelashvili Mikhail	5 11	12 01	M	22 7 71	Tbilisi	Spartak Vladikavkaz	Manchester C	28	3
Kelly Ray	5 11	12 00	F	29 12 76	Athlone	Athlone T	Manchester C	—	—
Kernaghan Alan	6 2	14 01	D	25 4 67	Otley	Apprentice	Middlesbrough	212	16
							Charlton Ath (loan)	13	—
							Manchester C	62	1
							Bolton W (loan)	11	—
							Bradford C (loan)	5	—
Kinkladze Georgiou	5 8	10 09	M	6 7 73	Tbilisi	Dynamo Tbilisi	Manchester C	76	16
Margetson Martyn	6 0	14 00	G	8 9 71	West Neath	Trainee	Manchester C	23	0
							Bristol R (loan)	3	—
							Bolton W (loan)	—	—
							Luton T (loan)	—	—
Mason Gary	5 8	10 01	M	15 10 79	Edinburgh	Trainee	Manchester C	—	—
McGlinchey Brian	5 7	10 02	M	26 10 77	Derry	Trainee	Manchester C	—	—
McGoldrick Eddie	5 10	11 07	M	30 4 65	London	Nuneaton Bor, Kettering T	Northampton T	107	9
							Crystal Palace	147	11
							Arsenal	38	—
							Manchester C	33	—
Morley David			D	25 9 77	St Helens	Trainee	Manchester C	—	—
Morley Neil	5 8	10 02	M	16 11 78	Warrington	Trainee	Manchester C	—	—
Phillips Martin	5 9	10 03	F	13 3 76	Exeter	Trainee	Exeter C	52	5
							Manchester C	15	—
Rimmer Stephen	6 3	13 02	D	23 5 79	Liverpool	Trainee	Manchester C	—	—
Rosler Uwe	6 1	12 06	F	15 11 68	Attenburg	Chemie Leipzig	Magdeburg	62	22
							Dynamo Dresden	33	4
							Nuremberg	28	—
							Dynamo Dresden	7	—
							Manchester C	123	44
Rowlands Aled	5 6	10 00	F	9 6 78	Bangor	Trainee	Manchester C	—	—
Summerbee Nicky	5 11	12 08	F	26 8 71	Altrincham	Trainee	Swindon T	112	6
							Manchester C	122	6
Symons Kit	6 1	13 07	D	8 3 71	Basingstoke	Trainee	Portsmouth	161	10
							Manchester C	82	2
Tarpey Ged*	6 0	13 00	D	28 4 77	Manchester	Trainee	Manchester C	—	—
Thomas Scott	5 9	11 02	M	30 10 74	Bury	Trainee	Manchester C	2	—
Weaver Nick	6 3	13 01	G	2 3 79	Sheffield	Trainee	Mansfield T	1	—
							Manchester C	—	—
Whitley Jeffrey			M	14 4 75	Zambia	Trainee	Manchester C	23	1
Whitley Jim	5 9	11 00	M	14 4 75	Zambia	Trainee	Manchester C	—	—
Wills David	5 5	9 04	F	9 3 79	Ashton-u-Lyne	Trainee	Manchester C	—	—
Wright Tommy	6 1	14 05	G	29 8 63	Belfast	Linfield	Newcastle U	73	—
							Hull C (loan)	6	—
							Nottingham F	11	—
							Reading (loan)	17	—
							Manchester C	13	—

Trainees
Acton, Richard F; Bailey, Alan; Burrows, Benjamin A; Doherty, George; Gallagher, Benn S; Maddocks, Marc N; Muir, Alex; Pridham, Christopher; Reilly, Alan; Sailesman, Neil A; Wardley, Andrew.

Associated Schoolboys
Creasy, Neil; Demetriou, Costas M; Higginson, Matthew; Hodgson, Steven G; Jones, Michael J; Kershaw, Christopher P; Long, Gary A; Marshall, James; Mike, Leon J.

Associated Schoolboys who have accepted the club's offer of a Traineeship/Contract
Daly, Lee C; Duff, Greg J; Garfield, Darren; Holmes, Shaun; Laycock, David; McNab, Joe; McNab, Neil; O'Keefe, Gerald J.

MANCHESTER UNITED

Name	Ht	Wt	Pos	Birthdate	Birthplace	Source	Clubs	Apps	Gls
Appleton Michael	5 9	12 04	M	4 12 75	Salford	Trainee	Manchester U	—	—
							Lincoln C (loan)	4	—
							Grimsby T (loan)	10	3
Beckham David	6 0	11 12	M	2 5 75	Leytonstone	Trainee	Manchester U	73	14
							Preston NE (loan)	5	2
Brebner Grant	5 9	10 01	M	6 12 77	Edinburgh	Trainee	Manchester U	—	—
Brightwell Stuart	5 6	10 11	F	31 1 79	Easington	Trainee	Manchester U	—	—
Brown David	5 10	12 07	F	2 10 78	Bolton	Trainee	Manchester U	—	—
Brown Wesley	6 1	12 02	D	13 10 79	Manchester	Trainee	Manchester U	—	—
Butt Nicky	5 10	11 05	M	21 1 75	Manchester	Trainee	Manchester U	82	8
Cantona Eric	6 2	14 01	F	24 5 66	Paris		Auxerre	13	2
							Martigues	—	—
							Auxerre	68	21
							Marseille	22	5
							Bordeaux	11	6
							Montpellier	33	10
							Marseille	18	8
							Nimes	17	2
							Leeds U	28	9
							Manchester U	143	64
Casper Chris	6 0	12 01	D	28 4 75	Burnley	Trainee	Manchester U	2	—
							Bournemouth (loan)	16	1
Clegg Michael	5 8	11 09	D	3 7 77	Tameside	Trainee	Manchester U	4	—
Cole Andy	5 10	12 01	F	15 10 71	Nottingham	Trainee	Arsenal	1	—
							Fulham (loan)	13	3
							Bristol C (loan)	12	8
							Bristol C	29	12
							Newcastle U	70	55
							Manchester U	72	30
Cooke Terry	5 7	10 00	F	5 8 76	Marston Green	Trainee	Manchester U	4	—
							Sunderland (loan)	6	—
							Birmingham C (loan)	4	—
Cruyff Jordi	6 1	11 00	F	9 2 74	Amsterdam	Ajax	Barcelona	41	11
							Manchester U	16	2
Culkin Nick	6 3	13 03	G	6 7 78	York	York C	Manchester U	—	—
Curtis John	5 10	11 07	D	3 9 78	Nuneaton	Trainee	Manchester U	—	—
Davies Simon	6 0	11 06	M	23 4 74	Middlewich	Trainee	Manchester U	11	—
							Exeter C (loan)	6	1
							Huddersfield T (loan)	3	—
Duncan Andrew	6 0	13 05	D	20 10 77	Hexham	Trainee	Manchester U	—	—
Gibson Paul	6 3	13 00	G	1 11 76	Sheffield	Trainee	Manchester U	—	—
Giggs Ryan	5 11	10 12	F	29 11 73	Cardiff	School	Manchester U	207	42
Hilton David‡	5 11	10 10	D	10 11 77	Barnsley	Trainee	Manchester U	—	—
Irwin Denis	5 8	10 10	D	31 10 65	Cork	Apprentice	Leeds U	72	1
							Oldham Ath	167	4
							Manchester U	256	15
Johnsen Ronny	6 3	13 01	D	10 6 69	Sandefjord	Eik	Lyn	31	7
							Lillestrom	23	4
							Besiktas	22	1
							Manchester U	31	—
Keane Roy	5 11	12 02	M	10 8 71	Cork	Cobh Ramb	Nottingham F	114	22
							Manchester U	112	15
Macken Jonathan	5 11	12 04	F	7 9 77	Manchester	Trainee	Manchester U	—	—
May David	6 0	13 03	D	24 6 70	Oldham	Trainee	Blackburn R	123	3
							Manchester U	64	6
McClair Brian	5 10	12 12	F	8 12 63	Airdrie	Apprentice	Aston Villa	—	—
							Motherwell	39	15
							Celtic	145	99
							Manchester U	342	88
McGibbon Patrick	6 2	13 10	D	6 9 73	Lurgan	Portadown	Manchester U	—	—
							Swansea C (loan)	1	—
							Wigan Ath (loan)	10	1
Mulryne Philip	5 7	10 13	M	1 1 78	Belfast	Trainee	Manchester U	—	—
Murdock Colin	6 3	12 13	D	2 7 75	Ballymena	Trainee	Manchester U	—	—
Mustoe Neil	5 8	12 13	F	5 11 76	Gloucester	Trainee	Manchester U	—	—
Neville Gary	5 11	12 04	D	18 2 75	Bury	Trainee	Manchester U	81	1
Neville Philip	5 11	11 10	D	21 1 77	Bury	Trainee	Manchester U	44	0
Notman Alex	5 7	11 05	M	10 12 79	Edinburgh	Trainee	Manchester U	—	—
O'Kane John	5 10	11 11	D	15 11 74	Nottingham	Trainee	Manchester U	2	—
							Wimbledon (loan)	—	—
							Bury (loan)	13	3

Pallister Gary	6 4	15 00	D	30 6 65	Ramsgate	Billingham T	Middlesbrough	156	5
							Darlington (loan)	7	—
							Manchester U	284	12
Pilkington Kevin	6 1	13 01	G	8 3 74	Hitchin	Trainee	Manchester U	4	—
							Rochdale (loan)	6	—
							Rotherham U (loan)	17	—
Poborsky Karel	5 9	11 05	M	30 3 72	Jindinchuv-Hadec		Ceske Budejovice	82	15
							Viktoria Zizkov	28	10
							Slavia Prague	26	11
							Manchester U	22	3
Schmeichel Peter	6 4	15 13	G	18 11 63	Gladsaxe		Hvidovre	88	6
							Brondby	119	2
							Manchester U	226	—
Scholes Paul	5 7	11 08	F	16 11 74	Salford	Trainee	Manchester U	67	18
Smith Tommy	5 10	12 08	M	25 11 77	Northampton	Trainee	Manchester U	—	—
Solskjaer Ole Gunnar	5 10	11 08	F	26 2 73	Kristiansund		Molde	42	31
							Manchester U	33	17
Teather Paul	6 0	11 05	M	26 12 77	Rotherham	Trainee	Manchester U	—	—
Thornley Ben	5 9	11 08	F	21 4 75	Bury	Trainee	Manchester U	4	—
							Stockport Co (loan)	10	1
							Huddersfield T (loan)	12	2
Tomlinson Graeme	5 10	12 07	F	10 12 75	Watford	Trainee	Bradford C	17	6
							Manchester U	—	—
							Luton T (loan)	7	—
Trees Robert*	5 10	11 07	M	18 12 77	Manchester	Trainee	Manchester U	—	—
Twiss Michael	5 11	12 08	F	26 12 77	Salford	Trainee	Manchester U	—	—
Van der Gouw Raimond	6 3	13 07	G	24 3 63	Oldenzaal		Go Ahead	97	—
							Vitesse	258	—
							Manchester U	2	—
Wallwork Ronnie	5 10	12 12	D	10 9 77	Manchester	Trainee	Manchester U	—	—
Wellens Richard	5 9	10 07	M	26 3 80	Manchester	Trainee	Manchester U	—	—
Wilson Mark	6 0	12 02	F	9 2 79	Scunthorpe	Trainee	Manchester U	—	—

Trainees
Bickerton, Gary; Byers, Alexander J; Calderone, Christopher J; Ford, Ryan; Healy, David J; Higginbotham, Daniel J; Millard, Ross J; Mills, Leon J; Naylor, Gavin E; Phillips, Jonathan J; Ryan, Michael S P; Sadler, Adam; Wood, Jamie.

Associated Schoolboys
Albiston, Ryan P; Carter, Nicky M; Clark, Benjamin; Coates, Craig; Davis, James R; Dickman, Jonjo; Dodd, Ashley M; Gardiner, Gareth; Jones, Rhodri G; Kendrick, Scott; Lennon, Anthony C; Parkinson, Simon A; Rose, Michael; Sampson, Gary J F; Strange, Gareth A; Studley, Mark L; Szmid, Marek A; Tate, Alan; Taylor, Andrew J; Tonge, Michael W; Walker, Joshua G; Webber, Daniel V; Wood, Neil A.

Associated Schoolboys who have accepted the club's offer of a Traineeship/Contract
Chadwick, Luke H; Clegg, George G; Evans, Wayne A; Fitzpatrick, Ian M; Gaff, Gerard A; Hickson, Jason M; Newham, Stephen J C; Roche, Lee P; Rose, Stephen D; Studley, Dominic P.

MANSFIELD TOWN

Alexander Keith†	6 4	14 08	F	14 11 58	Nottingham	Barnet	Grimsby T	83	26
							Stockport Co	11	—
							Lincoln C	45	4
							Mansfield T	3	—
Bowling Ian	6 3	14 03	G	27 7 65	Sheffield	Gainsborough T	Lincoln C	59	—
							Hartlepool U (loan)	1	—
							Bradford C (loan)	7	—
							Bradford C	29	—
							Mansfield T	90	—
Clarke Darrell	5 10	10 03	M	16 12 77	Mansfield	Trainee	Mansfield T	22	2
Clifford Mark*	5 10	10 10	D	11 9 77	Nottingham	Trainee	Mansfield T	4	—
Doolan John	6 1	13 01	D	7 5 74	Liverpool	Trainee	Everton	—	—
							Mansfield T	107	9
Ellison Lee‡	5 10	10 00	F	13 1 73	Bishop Auckland	Trainee	Darlington	72	17
							Hartlepool U (loan)	4	1
							Leicester C	—	—
							Crewe Alex	4	2
							Hereford U	1	—
							Mansfield T	—	—
Eustace Scott	6 0	14 01	D	13 6 75	Leicester	Trainee	Leicester C	1	—
							Mansfield T	69	5
Ford Tony	5 9	13 02	D	14 5 59	Grimsby	Apprentice	Grimsby T	354	54
							Sunderland (loan)	9	1
							Stoke C	112	13
							WBA	114	14
							Grimsby T	68	3
							Bradford C (loan)	5	—
							Scunthorpe U	76	9
						Barrow	Mansfield T	27	2

Name	Ht	Wt	Pos	Born	Birthplace	Source	Club	Apps	Gls
Hackett Warren	6 0	13 00	D	16 12 71	Plaistow	Tottenham H	Leyton Orient	72	3
							Doncaster R	46	2
							Mansfield T	68	4
Hadley Stewart	6 0	12 12	F	30 12 72	Dudley	Halesowen T	Derby Co	—	—
							Mansfield T	122	31
Harper Steve	5 10	11 06	D	3 2 69	Newcastle-under-Lyme	Trainee	Port Vale	28	2
							Preston NE	77	10
							Burnley	69	8
							Doncaster R	65	11
							Mansfield T	69	7
Holbrook Leigh§			M	6 8 79	Belper	Trainee	Mansfield T	1	—
Kerr David	5 11	12 09	M	6 9 74	Dumfries	Trainee	Manchester C	6	—
							Mansfield T (loan)	5	—
							Mansfield T	9	—
Kilcline Brian*	6 2	14 13	D	7 5 62	Nottingham	Apprentice	Notts Co	158	9
							Coventry C	173	28
							Oldham Ath	8	—
							Newcastle U	32	—
							Swindon T	17	—
							Mansfield T	50	3
Parkin Steve	5 6	11 01	D	7 11 65	Mansfield	Apprentice	Stoke C	113	5
							WBA	48	2
							Mansfield T	87	3
Peters Mark*	6 0	13 00	D	6 7 72	St Asaph	Trainee	Manchester C	—	—
							Norwich C	—	—
							Peterborough U	19	—
							Mansfield T	47	6
Robinson Ian*	5 9	10 09	M	25 8 78	Nottingham	Trainee	Mansfield T	17	1
Sedgemore Ben	5 10	12 04	M	5 8 75	Wolverhampton	Trainee	Birmingham C	—	—
							Northampton T (loan)	1	—
							Mansfield T (loan)	9	—
							Peterborough U	17	—
							Mansfield T	39	4
Sherlock Paul*	5 10	12 04	M	17 11 73	Wigan	Trainee	Notts Co	12	1
							Mansfield T	39	2
Walker John	5 6	10 04	M	12 12 73	Glasgow	Clydebank BC	Rangers	—	—
							Clydebank	27	2
							Grimsby T	3	1
							Mansfield T	36	3
Watkiss Stuart	6 1	13 00	D	8 5 66	Wolverhampton	Apprentice Rushall Olympic	Wolverhampton W	2	—
							Walsall	62	2
							Hereford U	19	—
							Mansfield T	31	1
Williams Lee†	5 7	11 07	M	3 2 73	Birmingham	Trainee	Aston Villa	—	—
							Shrewsbury T (loan)	3	—
							Peterborough U	91	1
							Tranmere R	—	—
							Mansfield T	6	—
Williams Ryan§	5 4	10 02	D	31 8 78	Mansfield	Trainee	Mansfield T	26	3
Wood Simon*	5 9	12 13	M	24 9 76	Hull	Trainee	Coventry C	—	—
							Mansfield T	41	4
Young Christopher§			F	11 8 79	Manchester		Mansfield T	1	—

Trainees
Cooper, Dale J; Dunkley, Marlon J; Hassell, Robert J F; Holbrook, Leigh W; Hutchinson, James A A; Ingram, Aaron D; Leech, James; Rankin, Darrel A; Reynolds, Curtis P; Roberts, Duncan A; Sedlan, Jason M; Sisson, Michael A; Wiggington, Mark; Wilkins, Christopher J; Williams, Ryan N; Young, Christopher W.

Non-Contract
Williams, Lee.

Associated Schoolboys
Blevins, Shaun; Elliott, Dominic S; Footitt, Nicholas A; Gash, Marc; Gatward, Jon-Joseph; Jervis, David J; Overton, Paul D; Smith, Dale; Smith, Mark J; Stringfellow, Daniel J; Toon, Dominic; Walker, James N; Ward, Ashley.

Associated Schoolboys who have accepted the club's offer of a Traineeship/Contract
Asher, Alistair A; Milner, Jonathan.

MIDDLESBROUGH

Name	Ht	Wt	Pos	Born	Birthplace	Source	Club	Apps	Gls
Anderson Viv*	6 1	13 00	D	29 7 56	Nottingham	Apprentice	Nottingham F	328	15
							Arsenal	120	9
							Manchester U	54	2
							Sheffield W	70	8
							Barnsley	20	3
							Middlesbrough	2	—
Bagayoko Salif‡	6 0	11 10	F	9 5 77	Manosque	Trainee	Middlesbrough	—	—
Barron Michael*	5 11	11 07	D	22 12 74	Chester-le-Street	Trainee	Middlesbrough	3	—
							Hartlepool U (loan)	16	—

Name	Ht	Wt	Pos	Born	Birthplace	Source	Clubs	Apps	Gls
Beck Mikkel	6 2	12 09	F	12 5 73	Aarhus	Kolding	B 1909	13	2
							Fortuna Cologne	79	26
							Middlesbrough	25	5
Blackmore Clayton	5 8	11 13	M	23 9 64	Neath	Apprentice	Manchester U	186	19
							Middlesbrough	51	4
							Bristol C (loan)	5	1
Branco‡			D	4 4 64	Bage	Internacional	Middlesbrough	9	—
Campbell Andrew			F	18 4 79	Middlesbrough	Trainee	Middlesbrough	5	—
Cole Ben*			G	23 10 77	Co Durham	Trainee	Middlesbrough	—	—
Connor Paul			F	12 1 79	Bishop Auckland	Trainee	Middlesbrough	—	—
Cox Neil	6 0	13 07	D	8 10 71	Scunthorpe	Trainee	Scunthorpe U	17	1
							Aston Villa	42	3
							Middlesbrough	106	3
Cummins Michael	6 0	11 12	M	1 6 78	Dublin	Trainee	Middlesbrough	—	—
Emerson	6 0	14 05	M	12 4 72	Rio	Curitiba	Belenenses	55	1
							Porto	60	9
							Middlesbrough	32	4
Festa Gianluca	6 0	13 06	D	15 3 69	Cagliari		Cagliari	156	—
							Fersuicis (loan)	26	2
							Internazionale	66	3
							Roma (loan)	21	1
							Middlesbrough	13	1
Fleming Curtis	5 10	12 08	D	8 10 68	Manchester	St Patrick's Ath	Swindon T	—	—
						St Patrick's Ath	Middlesbrough	156	1
Freestone Chris	5 10	12 01	F	4 9 71	Nottingham	Arnold T	Middlesbrough	7	1
							Carlisle U (loan)	5	2
Gavin Jason			D	14 3 80	Dublin	Trainee	Middlesbrough	—	—
Harrison Craig	6 0	11 13	D	10 11 77	Gateshead	Trainee	Middlesbrough	—	—
Hignett Craig	5 9	11 03	M	12 1 70	Whiston	Liverpool	Crewe Alex	121	42
							Middlesbrough	120	26
Juninho	5 5	10 00	F	22 2 73	Sao Paulo	Sao Paulo	Middlesbrough	56	14
Kinder Vladimir	5 10	13 00	D	9 3 69	Bratislava	Karlovy Vary	Slovan Bratislava	148	19
							Middlesbrough	6	1
Lee Paddy*			M	2 8 77	Dublin	Manchester U	Middlesbrough	—	—
Liddle Craig	5 11	12 05	D	21 10 71	Chester-le-Street	Blyth Spartans	Middlesbrough	19	—
McGargle Stephen*	5 9	10 06	M	24 10 75	Gateshead	Trainee	Middlesbrough	—	—
Moore Alan	5 9	11 02	M	25 11 74	Dublin	Rivermount	Middlesbrough	110	14
Moreira Fabio			M	14 3 72	Rio	Chaves	Middlesbrough	—	—
Morris Chris*	5 11	11 05	D	24 12 63	Newquay		Sheffield W	74	1
							Celtic	163	8
							Middlesbrough	82	3
Mustoe Robbie	5 10	11 10	M	28 8 68	Oxford		Oxford U	91	10
							Middlesbrough	211	16
Ormerod Anthony			M	31 3 79	Middlesbrough	Trainee	Middlesbrough	—	—
Pearson Nigel	6 1	14 03	D	21 8 63	Nottingham	Heanor T	Shrewsbury T	153	5
							Sheffield W	180	14
							Middlesbrough	87	3
Ravanelli Fabrizio	6 1	13 04	F	11 12 68	Perugia		Perugia	90	41
							Avellino	7	—
							Casertana (loan)	27	12
							Reggiana	66	24
							Juventus	111	41
							Middlesbrough	33	16
Richardson Paul*	6 0	11 03	F	22 7 77	Durham	Trainee	Middlesbrough	—	—
Roberts Ben	6 1	13 03	G	22 6 75	Bishop Auckland	Trainee	Middlesbrough	10	0
							Hartlepool U (loan)	4	—
							Wycombe W (loan)	15	—
							Bradford C (loan)	2	—
Robson Bryan	5 9	12 05	M	11 1 57	Witton Gilbert	Apprentice	WBA	197	39
							Manchester U	345	74
							Middlesbrough	25	1
Schwarzer Mark	6 5	13 08	G	6 10 72	Sydney	Dynamo Dresden	Kaiserslautern	4	—
							Bradford C	13	—
							Middlesbrough	7	—
Stamp Philip	5 10	13 05	M	12 12 75	Middlesbrough	Trainee	Middlesbrough	49	3
Summerbell Mark	5 10	10 03	M	30 10 76	Durham	Trainee	Middlesbrough	3	—
Swalwell Andrew			M	29 3 79	Middlesbrough	Trainee	Middlesbrough	—	—
Vickers Steve	6 1	13 02	D	13 10 67	Bishop Auckland	Spennymoor U	Tranmere R	311	11
							Middlesbrough	131	7
Walsh Gary	6 3	14 11	G	21 3 68	Wigan	Apprentice	Manchester U	50	—
							Airdrieonians (loan)	3	—
							Oldham Ath (loan)	6	—
							Middlesbrough	44	—

Whelan Phil	6 4	14 07	D	7 3 72	Stockport		Ipswich T	82	2
							Middlesbrough	22	1
White Alan	6 0	13 04	D	22 3 76	Darlington		Middlesbrough	—	—
White Darren			D	13 1 79	Easington	Trainee	Middlesbrough	—	—
Whyte Derek	5 11	12 13	D	31 8 68	Glasgow	Celtic BC	Celtic	216	7
							Middlesbrough	159	2

Trainees
Baker, David A; Baker, Steven R; Bowes, Martin; Burdock, Gary; Carter, Graeme J; Dunn, Thomas; Graham, Christian J; Jackson, John; Jones, Thomas A M; Kell, Richard; Middleton, James R; Patterson, Mark; Reeve, Christopher J; Stockdale, Robert K; Terrell, Paul A; Trevor, Kris A; Walklate, Steven.

Associated Schoolboys
Beckett, Christopher P; Bell, Steven G; Boase, Leon A; Brackstone, Stephen; Greenwood, David; Hudson, Mark; Jewell, Adam R; Lee, David J; Mawson, Gary K; Moat, David J; Pybus, David A; Rogers, Nicholas G; Russell, Samuel I; Smith, Liam; Taylor, Andrew; Todd, Michael W.

Associated Schoolboys who have accepted the club's offer of a Traineeship/Contract
Allon, Wayne; Booth, Gregory; Hanson, Christian; McStea, Anthony C.

MILLWALL

Aris Steven			D	27 4 78	London		Millwall	—	—
Berry Greg*	5 11	12 00	F	5 3 71	Essex	East Thurrock U	Leyton Orient	80	14
							Wimbledon	7	1
							Millwall	34	1
							Brighton & HA (loan)	6	2
							Leyton Orient (loan)	7	
Bircham Marc			M	11 5 78	Brent	Trainee	Millwall	6	—
Bowry Bobby	5 8	10 08	M	19 5 71	Croydon		Crystal Palace	50	1
							Millwall	66	3
Cadette Richard*	5 7	12 00	F	21 3 65	Hammersmith	Wembley	Orient	21	4
							Southend U	90	48
							Sheffield U	28	7
							Brentford	87	20
							Bournemouth (loan)	8	1
							Falkirk	92	32
							Millwall	24	5
Canoville Dean			M	30 11 78	Perivale	Trainee	Millwall	2	—
Carter Tim	6 2	13 00	G	5 10 67	Bristol	Apprentice	Bristol R	47	0
							Newport Co (loan)	1	—
							Carlisle U (loan)	4	—
							Sunderland	37	—
							Bristol C (loan)	3	—
							Birmingham C (loan)	2	—
							Hartlepool U	18	—
							Millwall	4	—
							Oxford U	12	—
							Millwall	50	—
Connor James	6 0	13 00	D	22 8 74	Twickenham	Trainee	Millwall	9	—
Crawford Steve	5 10	10 07	F	9 1 74	Dunfermline		Raith R	115	22
							Millwall	42	11
Dair Jason	5 11	10 08	F	15 6 74	Dunfermline		Raith R	94	11
							Millwall	24	1
Dolby Tony*	5 11	12 08	F	16 4 74	Greenwich	Trainee	Millwall	66	3
							Barnet (loan)	16	2
Doyle Maurice	5 8	10 07	M	17 10 69	Ellesmere Port	Trainee	Crewe Alex	8	2
							QPR	6	—
							Crewe Alex (loan)	7	2
							Wolverhampton W (loan)	—	—
							Millwall	46	1
Edwards Daniel			M	20 12 79	Greenwich	Trainee	Millwall	—	—
Fuchs Uwe‡	6 2	12 00	F	23 7 66	Germany	Pirmasens	Homburg	60	9
							Stuttgart Kickers	10	2
							Fortuna Cologne	67	36
							Fortuna Dusseldorf	25	7
							Cologne	19	4
							Kaiserslautern	19	3
							Middlesbrough	15	9
							Millwall	32	5
Harle Mike	6 0	12 06	D	31 10 72	Lewisham	Sittingbourne	Millwall	21	1
							Bury (loan)	1	—
Hartley Paul	5 9	10 04	M	19 10 76	Baillieston	Mill United BC	Hamilton A	47	11
							Millwall	44	4
Hockton Danny			F	7 2 79	Barking	Trainee	Millwall	2	—
Holsgrove Lee			D	13 12 79	Halton	Trainee	Millwall	—	—
Keown Darren*	6 1	13 09	F	5 5 78	Chertsey	Trainee	Millwall	—	—
Lavin Gerard	5 10	11 00	D	5 2 74	Corby	Trainee	Watford	126	3
							Millwall	29	—

Markey Brendan			F	19 5 76	Dublin	Bohemians	Millwall	—	—
McLeary Alan	5 10	10 06	D	6 10 64	Lambeth	Apprentice	Millwall	307	5
							Sheffield U (loan)	3	—
							Wimbledon (loan)	4	—
							Charlton Ath	66	3
							Bristol C	34	—
							Millwall	15	—
McRobert Lee	5 9	10 12	M	4 10 72	Bromley	Sittingbourne	Millwall	18	1
Neill Lucas	6 1	12 00	M	9 3 78	Sydney	NSW Academy	Millwall	52	3
Newman Ricky	5 10	12 06	M	5 8 70	Guildford	Trainee	Crystal Palace	48	3
							Maidstone U (loan)	10	1
							Millwall	77	4
Nightingale Lewis*			M	25 3 79	Greenwich	Trainee	Millwall	—	—
Nurse David	6 3	12 06	G	12 10 76	Kings Lynn	Trainee	Manchester C	—	—
							Millwall	—	—
Pitwood Adam			M	24 1 80	Crawley	School	Millwall	—	—
Robertson Graham	5 11	10 10	F	2 11 76	Edinburgh	Balgorie Colts	Raith R	—	—
							Millwall	1	—
Roche Stephen			M	2 10 78	Dublin	Belvedere	Millwall	7	—
Rogan Anton*	5 11	12 06	D	25 3 66	Belfast	Distillery	Celtic	127	4
							Sunderland	46	1
							Oxford U	58	3
							Millwall	36	8
Sadlier Richard	6 2	12 10	F	14 1 79	Dublin	Belvedere	Millwall	10	—
Savage Dave	6 2	12 07	M	30 7 73	Dublin	Longford T	Millwall	99	5
Stevens Keith	6 0	12 12	D	21 6 64	Merton	Apprentice	Millwall	455	9
Van Blerk Jason*	6 1	13 00	D	16 3 68	Sydney	Go Ahead	Millwall	73	2
Webber Damien	6 4	14 00	D	8 10 68	Rustington	Bognor Regis T	Millwall	64	4
Witter Tony	6 2	13 02	D	12 8 65	London	Grays Ath	Crystal Palace	—	—
							QPR	1	—
							Millwall (loan)	—	—
							Plymouth Arg (loan)	3	1
							Reading (loan)	4	—
							Millwall	91	2

Trainees
Field, Lewis M; Jenkins, Stuart M; Poulter, Simon; Smith, Philip A; Stevens, Shaun D; Thompson, Samuel J; Venables, Ross; White, Darren J.

Associated Schoolboys
Bubb, Byron J; Canoville, Lee; Davies, Alex J; Deegan, Darren S; Draper, Craig J E; Kenny, Ciaran M; McDonald, Paul; Rees, Matthew R; Squires, Oliver H; Williams, Leon K.

Associated Schoolboys who have accepted the club's offer of a Traineeship/Contract
Barnard, Richard M; Bull, Ronnie R; Davies, Robert M; Little, Joseph G; Maguire, Stephen J; O'Dunsi, Leke; Powell, Terry M; Reid, Steven J.

Player who does not hold a current contract but his registration has been retained by the club
Fuchs, Uwe.

NEWCASTLE UNITED

Albert Philippe	6 3	13 00	D	10 8 67	Bouillon		Charleroi	65	7
							Mechelen	87	5
							Anderlecht	50	9
							Newcastle U	67	8
Arnison Paul	5 9	10 12	M	18 9 77	Hartlepool	Trainee	Newcastle U	—	—
Asprilla Faustino	5 9	11 03	F	10 11 69	Tulua		Cucuta	15	7
							Nacional	61	25
							Parma	84	25
							Newcastle U	38	7
Barrett Paul	5 9	10 11	M	13 4 78	Newcastle	Trainee	Newcastle U	—	—
Barton Warren	5 11	12 00	D	19 3 69	Stoke Newington	Leytonstone/Ilford	Maidstone U	42	0
							Wimbledon	180	10
							Newcastle U	49	1
Batty David	5 8	12 00	M	2 12 68	Leeds	Trainee	Leeds U	211	4
							Blackburn R	54	1
							Newcastle U	43	2
Beardsley Peter	5 8	11 07	F	18 1 61	Newcastle	Wallsend BC	Carlisle U	104	22
						Vancouver Whitecaps	Manchester U	—	—
						Vancouver Whitecaps	Newcastle U	147	61
							Liverpool	131	46
							Everton	81	25
							Newcastle U	129	46
Beresford John	5 5	10 12	M	4 9 66	Sheffield	Apprentice	Manchester C	—	—
							Barnsley	88	5
							Portsmouth	107	8
							Newcastle U	161	1

Name							Club	Apps	Gls
Brayson Paul	5 4	10 10	F	16 9 77	Newcastle	Trainee	Newcastle U	—	—
							Swansea C (loan)	11	5
Burghall Terence	6 0	11 06	F	25 9 78	Liverpool	Liverpool	Newcastle U	—	—
Clark Lee	5 7	11 07	M	27 10 72	Wallsend	Trainee	Newcastle U	195	23
Crawford Jimmy	6 0	11 06	M	1 5 73	Chicago	Bohemians	Newcastle U	2	—
							Rotherham U (loan)	11	—
Eatock David	5 4	10 05	F	11 11 76	Wigan	Chorley	Newcastle U	—	—
Elliott Robbie	5 10	10 13	D	25 12 73	Gosforth	Trainee	Newcastle U	79	9
Elliott Stuart	5 8	11 05	D	27 8 77	London	Trainee	Newcastle U	—	—
							Hull C (loan)	3	—
Ferdinand Les	5 11	13 05	F	18 12 66	Acton	Hayes	QPR	163	80
							Brentford (loan)	3	—
							Besiktas (loan)	24	14
							Newcastle U	68	41
Gillespie Keith	5 10	11 05	F	18 2 75	Larne	Trainee	Manchester U	9	1
							Wigan Ath (loan)	8	4
							Newcastle U	77	7
Ginola David	5 11	11 10	F	25 1 67	Gassin		Toulon	81	4
							Racing Paris	61	8
							Brest	50	10
							Paris St Germain	115	32
							Newcastle U	58	6
Hamilton Des	5 10	12 13	M	15 8 76	Bradford	Trainee	Bradford C	88	5
							Newcastle U	—	—
Harper Steve	6 0	12 03	G	3 2 70	Easington	Seaham Red Star	Newcastle U	—	—
							Bradford C (loan)	1	—
							Stockport Co (loan)	—	—
Hislop Shaka	6 4	14 04	G	22 2 69	Hackney	Howard Univ	Reading	104	—
							Newcastle U	40	—
Howey Steve	6 2	11 12	M	26 10 71	Sunderland	Trainee	Newcastle U	154	6
Hughes Aaron	6 0	11 02	D	8 11 79	Magherafelt	Trainee	Newcastle U	—	—
Keen Peter	6 0	11 09	G	16 11 76	Middlesbrough	Trainee	Newcastle U	—	—
Lee Robert	5 11	11 13	F	1 2 66	West Ham	Hornchurch	Charlton Ath	298	59
							Newcastle U	181	39
Peacock Darren	6 2	12 12	D	3 2 68	Bristol	Apprentice	Newport Co	28	—
							Hereford U	59	4
							QPR	126	6
							Newcastle U	113	2
Shearer Alan	5 11	12 06	F	13 8 70	Newcastle	Trainee	Southampton	118	23
							Blackburn R	138	112
							Newcastle U	31	25
Srnicek Pavel	6 2	14 07	G	10 3 68	Ostrava	Banik Ostrava	Newcastle U	148	—
Walker Kashka	5 9	10 10	M	10 11 78	Toronto	Canada SA	Newcastle U	—	—
Watson Steve	6 0	12 07	D	1 4 74	North Shields	Trainee	Newcastle U	172	11

Trainees
Asiamah, Anthony; Barrett, Lee C; Beharall, David; Broadbent, David; Gibson, Barry J; Knight, Paul; McClen, James D; Milbourne, Ian; Muir, Karl J; Peterson, Owen; Reed, Matthew W; Scott, Ryan L; Shutt, Matthew J; Tait, Jordan A; Talbot, Paul M; Woodcock, Christopher J.

Non-Contract
Burt, David C.

Associated Schoolboys
Boyd, Mark E; Charlton, Craig D; Collins, Shaun T; Cowan, David R; D'Amore, David R; Hogg, Ryan; Parry, Anthony.

Associated Schoolboys who have accepted the club's offer of a Traineeship/Contract
Green, Stuart; Hogg, Graham; Warwick, Stephen J.

NORTHAMPTON TOWN

Name							Club	Apps	Gls
Beckford Jason	5 9	14 03	F	14 2 70	Manchester	Trainee	Manchester C	20	1
							Blackburn R (loan)	4	—
							Port Vale (loan)	5	1
							Birmingham C	7	2
							Bury (loan)	3	—
							Stoke C	4	—
							Millwall	9	—
							Northampton T	1	—
Boxford Eddie†	5 9	11 00	D	7 12 77	Northampton	Trainee	Northampton T	—	—
Brock Stuart†	6 1	13 03	G	26 9 76	Sandwell	Trainee	Aston Villa	—	—
							Northampton T	—	—
Burns Chris‡	6 1	14 03	M	9 11 67	Manchester	Cheltenham T	Portsmouth	90	9
							Swansea C (loan)	4	—
							Bournemouth (loan)	14	1
							Swansea C	5	—
							Northampton T	66	9
Cahill Ollie‡	5 10	11 01	F	29 9 75	Clonmel	Clonmel	Northampton T	11	1

Name			Pos	DOB	Birthplace	Source	Club	Apps	Goals
Clarkson Ian	5 10	12 03	D	4 12 70	Birmingham	Trainee	Birmingham C	136	—
							Stoke C	75	—
							Northampton T	45	—
Colkin Lee	5 10	12 08	D	15 7 74	Nuneaton	Trainee	Northampton T	99	3
Cooper Mark*	6 3	14 02	F	5 4 67	Cambridge	Apprentice	Cambridge U	71	17
							Tottenham H	—	—
							Shrewsbury T	6	2
							Gillingham	49	11
							Leyton Orient	150	45
							Barnet	67	19
							Northampton T	41	10
Devito Claudio†	6 1	12 02	F	21 7 78	Peterborough	Trainee	Northampton T	—	—
Frain John	5 9	12 00	D	8 10 68	Birmingham	Apprentice	Birmingham C	274	23
							Northampton T	13	—
Gayle John	6 3	15 00	F	30 7 64	Bromsgrove	Burton Alb	Wimbledon	20	2
							Birmingham C	44	10
							Walsall (loan)	4	1
							Coventry C	3	—
							Burnley	14	3
							Stoke C	26	4
							Gillingham (loan)	9	3
							Northampton T	13	1
Gibb Ali	5 9	11 07	M	17 2 76	Salisbury	Trainee	Norwich C	—	—
							Northampton T	41	3
Grayson Neil	5 10	12 09	F	1 11 64	York	Rowntree Mackintosh	Doncaster R	29	6
							York C	1	—
							Chesterfield	15	—
						Boston U	Northampton T	120	31
Hunter Roy	5 10	12 10	M	29 10 73	Cleveland	Trainee	WBA	9	1
							Northampton T	70	6
Kirby Ryan†	6 0	12 00	D	6 9 74	Chingford	Trainee	Arsenal	—	—
							Doncaster R	78	—
							Preston NE	—	—
							Crewe Alex	—	—
							Wigan Ath	6	—
							Northampton T	1	—
Knowles Chris†	5 11	12 00	G	4 2 78	Stone	Peterborough U	Chester C	2	—
							Hereford U	—	—
							Northampton T	—	—
Lee Christian	6 1	11 09	F	8 10 76	Aylesbury	Doncaster R	Northampton T	34	7
Lyne Neil†	6 1	12 09	F	4 4 70	Leicester	Leicester U	Nottingham F	—	—
							Walsall (loan)	7	—
							Shrewsbury T (loan)	16	6
							Shrewsbury T	64	11
							Cambridge U	17	—
							Chesterfield (loan)	6	1
							Hereford U	63	2
							Northampton T	1	—
Maddison Lee*	6 0	12 10	D	5 10 72	Bristol	Trainee	Bristol R	73	—
							Northampton T	55	—
Martin Dave	6 1	13 02	M	25 4 63	East Ham	Apprentice	Millwall	140	6
							Wimbledon	35	3
							Southend U	221	19
							Bristol C	38	1
							Northampton T (loan)	7	1
							Gillingham	31	1
							Leyton Orient	8	—
							Northampton T	12	—
							Brighton & HA (loan)	1	—
O'Shea Danny*	6 0	13 02	D	26 3 63	Kennington	Apprentice	Arsenal	6	—
							Charlton Ath (loan)	9	—
							Exeter C	45	2
							Southend U	118	12
							Cambridge U	203	1
							Northampton T	80	1
Parrish Sean	5 10	11 05	M	14 3 72	Wrexham	Trainee Telford U	Shrewsbury T	3	—
							Doncaster R	66	8
							Northampton T	39	8
Peer Dean	6 2	12 02	M	8 8 69	Dudley	Trainee	Birmingham C	120	8
							Mansfield T (loan)	10	—
							Walsall	45	8
							Northampton T	63	2
Rennie David	6 0	13 00	D	29 8 64	Edinburgh	Apprentice	Leicester C	21	1
							Leeds U	101	5
							Bristol C	104	8
							Birmingham C	35	4
							Coventry C	82	3
							Northampton T	43	3

Sampson Ian	6 2	13 01	D	14 11 68	Wakefield	Goole T	Sunderland	17	1
							Northampton T (loan)	8	—
							Northampton T	118	11
Tallentire Dean†			D	26 1 77	Bedford	Rushden & Diamonds	Northampton T	—	—
Thompson Garry*	6 1	14 07	F	7 10 59	Birmingham	Apprentice	Coventry C	134	38
							WBA	91	39
							Sheffield W	36	7
							Aston Villa	60	17
							Watford	34	8
							Crystal Palace	20	3
							QPR	19	1
							Cardiff C	43	5
							Northampton T	50	6
Turley Billy	6 3	14 13	G	15 7 73	Wolverhampton	Evesham U	Northampton T	3	—
Warburton Ray	6 0	13 00	D	7 10 67	Rotherham	Apprentice	Rotherham U	4	—
							York C	90	9
							Northampton T (loan)	17	1
							Northampton T	118	10
Warner Michael	5 9	10 12	M	17 1 74	Harrogate	Tamworth	Northampton T	9	—
White Jason	5 11	12 11	F	19 10 71	Meriden	Derby Co	Scunthorpe U	68	16
							Darlington (loan)	4	1
							Scarborough	63	20
							Northampton T	77	18
Woodman Andy	6 2	13 06	G	11 8 71	Denmark Hill	Apprentice	Crystal Palace	—	—
							Exeter C	6	—
							Northampton T	99	—

Trainees
Ahern, John P A; Bedford, Grant E; Burden, Anthony P; Coles, Michael; Collins, Adam A; Hibbert, Michael B; Hughes, Garry; Leczynski, Alexander J; Marlow, Daniel J; McCleary, Kevin D; Potter, Daniel; Sutton, Brian; Tucker, Karl G.

Non-Contract
Atkins, Ian L; Brock, Stuart A; De Vito, Claudio G; Tallentire, Dean.

Associated Schoolboys
Binder, Paul M; Brydon, Adam T; Champlovier, Neil M; Dedman, Adam L; Gould, James R; Silvestri, Lorenzo.

Associated Schoolboys who have accepted the club's offer of a Traineeship/Contract
Finlay, Mathew D.

NORWICH CITY

Adams Neil	5 8	10 12	M	23 11 65	Stoke	Local	Stoke C	32	4
							Everton	20	—
							Oldham Ath (loan)	9	—
							Oldham Ath	129	23
							Norwich C	134	18
Allen Alex			D	10 2 80	Doncaster	Trainee	Norwich C	—	—
Barber Paul*	6 3	14 00	G	30 8 77	Burnley	Trainee	Norwich C	—	—
Bellamy Craig	5 9	10 10	M	13 7 79	Cardiff	Trainee	Norwich C	3	—
Bradshaw Carl	5 10	11 11	D	2 10 68	Sheffield	Apprentice	Sheffield W	32	4
							Barnsley (loan)	6	1
							Manchester C	5	—
							Sheffield U	147	8
							Norwich C	64	2
Broughton Drewe			F	25 10 78	Hitchin	Trainee	Norwich C	8	1
Brownrigg Andrew	6 0	11 10	D	2 8 76	Sheffield	Trainee	Hereford U	8	—
							Norwich C	—	—
Carey Shaun	5 9	10 10	M	13 5 76	Kettering	Trainee	Norwich C	23	—
Crook Ian	5 8	10 08	M	18 1 63	Romford	Apprentice	Tottenham H	20	1
							Norwich C	341	18
Eadie Darren	5 8	11 00	F	10 6 75	Chippenham	Trainee	Norwich C	114	28
Fleck Robert	5 8	11 09	F	11 8 65	Glasgow	Possil YM	Partick T	2	1
							Rangers	85	29
							Norwich C	143	40
							Chelsea	40	3
							Bolton W (loan)	7	1
							Bristol C (loan)	10	1
							Norwich C	77	14
Forbes Adrian	5 8	11 04	F	23 1 79	London	Trainee	Norwich C	10	—
Gunn Bryan	6 2	13 08	G	22 12 63	Thurso	Invergordon BC	Aberdeen	15	0
							Norwich C	386	—
Hilton Damien	6 2	12 06	F	6 9 77	Norwich	Trainee	Norwich C	—	—

Name							Club	Apps	Gls
Jackson Matt	6 1	12 07	D	19 10 71	Leeds	School	Luton T	9	—
							Preston NE (loan)	4	—
							Everton	138	4
							Charlton Ath (loan)	8	—
							QPR (loan)	7	—
							Birmingham C (loan)	10	—
							Norwich C	19	2
Johnson Andy	6 1	12 02	M	2 5 74	Bristol	Trainee	Norwich C	66	13
Llewellyn Chris	5 11	11 06	M	29 8 79	Swansea	Trainee	Norwich C	—	—
Marshall Andy	6 2	13 00	G	14 4 75	Bury	Trainee	Norwich C	31	—
							Bournemouth (loan)	11	—
							Gillingham (loan)	5	—
Marshall Lee	6 0	11 11	D	21 1 79	Islington	Enfield	Norwich C	—	—
Milligan Mike	5 8	11 00	M	20 2 67	Manchester	Trainee	Oldham Ath	162	17
							Everton	17	1
							Oldham Ath	117	6
							Norwich C	91	5
Mills Danny	6 0	11 11	D	18 5 77	Norwich	Trainee	Norwich C	46	—
Moore Neil*	6 1	12 07	D	21 9 72	Liverpool	Trainee	Everton	5	—
							Blackpool (loan)	7	—
							Oldham Ath (loan)	5	—
							Carlisle U (loan)	13	—
							Rotherham U (loan)	11	—
							Norwich C	2	—
Newman Rob	6 2	13 00	D	13 12 63	Bradford-on-Avon	Apprentice	Bristol C	394	52
							Norwich C	190	14
O'Neill Keith	6 1	11 09	M	16 2 76	Dublin	Trainee	Norwich C	46	7
Ottosson Ulf‡			F	2 7 68	Sweden		Degerfors	63	20
							Chaves	11	—
							Norwich C	7	1
Polston John	5 11	11 12	D	10 6 68	Walthamstow	Apprentice	Tottenham H	24	1
							Norwich C	203	8
Scott Keith	6 2	13 10	F	9 6 67	London	Leicester U	Lincoln C	16	2
							Wycombe W	Wycombe W	15	10
							Swindon T	51	12
							Stoke C	25	3
							Norwich C	25	5
							Bournemouth (loan)	8	1
							Watford (loan)	6	2
							Wycombe W (loan)	9	3
Scott Kevin	6 2	14 03	D	17 12 66	Easington	Middlesbrough	Newcastle U	227	8
							Tottenham H	18	1
							Port Vale (loan)	17	1
							Charlton Ath (loan)	4	—
							Norwich C	9	—
Shore Jamie	5 9	10 09	M	1 9 77	Bristol	Trainee	Norwich C	—	—
Simpson Karl	5 11	11 06	D	12 10 76	Newmarket	Trainee	Norwich C	4	—
Sutch Daryl	6 0	11 13	M	11 9 71	Lowestoft	Trainee	Norwich C	125	6
Wright Johnny*	5 9	11 05	D	24 11 75	Belfast	Trainee	Norwich C	7	—

Trainees
Alexander, Anthony M T; Andrews, Bradley J; Coote, Adrian; Davis, Kori M; Green, Joseph A; Hardy, Coren P A; Henderson, Tommy S; Kenton, Darren E; Lewis, Craig K; McCullough, Stephen P; Parker, Kevin J; Stuart, Adam J; Tipple, Gaven L; Walker, Trevor W; Way, Darren; Wilson, Che C.

Associated Schoolboys
Bilham, Neil; Blois, Lewis P; Burton, Shane E; Carr, Shaun L; Culbertson, Richard D J; Dore, Jonathan; Elmes, John; Gay, Daniel K; Green, Robert P; Heighway, Greg; Karim, Alexis W; Kirby, Tom; Ngopwani, Pitshou M; Rafis, Daniel; Roberts, Michael A; Thompson, Ian R.

Associated Schoolboys who have accepted the club's offer of a Traineeship/Contract
Belgrave, Barrington; Etunmu, Anayo S; Goreham, Paul M; Joynson, Matthew; Russell, Darel F.

NOTTINGHAM FOREST

Name							Club	Apps	Gls
Allen Chris	5 11	12 04	M	18 11 72	Oxford	Trainee	Oxford U	150	12
							Nottingham F (loan)	3	1
							Nottingham F	24	—
Anderson Dale	5 11	11 12	F	10 11 79	Birmingham	Trainee	Nottingham F	—	—
Archer Paul	5 8	9 07	M	25 4 78	Leicester	Trainee	Nottingham F	—	—
Armstrong Craig	5 11	12 10	M	23 5 75	South Shields	Trainee	Nottingham F	4	—
							Burnley (loan)	4	—
							Bristol R (loan)	14	—
							Gillingham (loan)	10	—
							Watford (loan)	15	—
Atkinson Craig*	6 0	11 02	M	29 9 77	Rotherham	Trainee	Nottingham F	—	—
Barber Andrew‡	5 9	9 08	D	4 2 79	Darlington	Trainee	Nottingham F	—	—

Name					Birthplace	Signed from	Club	Apps	Gls
Bart-Williams Chris	5 11	11 00	M	16 6 74	Freetown	Trainee	Leyton Orient	36	2
							Sheffield W	124	16
							Nottingham F	49	1
Blatherwick Steve	6 1	15 00	D	20 9 73	Nottingham	Notts Co	Nottingham F	10	—
							Wycombe W (loan)	2	—
							Hereford U (loan)	10	1
							Reading (loan)	7	—
Bough Gareth*	5 10	12 01	G	17 10 78	Nottingham	Trainee	Nottingham F	—	—
Burns John	5 10	11 00	M	4 12 77	Dublin	Belvedere	Nottingham F	—	—
Campbell Kevin	6 1	13 08	F	4 2 70	Lambeth	Trainee	Arsenal	166	46
							Leyton Orient (loan)	16	9
							Leicester C (loan)	11	5
							Nottingham F	38	9
Chettle Steve	6 1	13 01	D	27 9 68	Nottingham	Apprentice	Nottingham F	325	7
Clark Richard‡	5 11	13 04	G	6 4 77	Nuneaton	Trainee	Nottingham F	—	—
Cooper Colin	5 9	11 09	D	28 2 67	Sedgefield		Middlesbrough	188	6
							Millwall	77	6
							Nottingham F	145	15
Cooper Richard	5 9	11 00	D	27 9 79	Nottingham	Trainee	Nottingham F	—	—
Cowling Lee	5 9	10 03	M	22 9 77	Doncaster	Trainee	Nottingham F	—	—
Cox Christopher	5 7	10 01	M	17 9 79	Sunderland	Trainee	Nottingham F	—	—
Crossley Mark	6 0	16 00	G	16 6 69	Barnsley	Trainee	Nottingham F	271	—
							Manchester U (loan)	—	—
Dawson Andrew	5 9	10 02	M	20 10 78	Northallerton	Trainee	Nottingham F	—	—
Fettis Alan	6 2	13 00	G	1 2 71	Belfast	Ards	Hull C	135	2
							WBA (loan)	3	—
							Nottingham F	4	—
Finnigan John	5 8	10 11	M	28 3 76	Wakefield	Trainee	Nottingham F	—	—
Fitchett Scott	5 8	9 06	M	20 1 79	Manchester	Trainee	Nottingham F	—	—
Follett Richard	5 9	10 02	D	29 8 79	Leamington Spa	Trainee	Nottingham F	—	—
Freeman David	5 10	10 13	F	25 11 79	Dublin	Cherry Orchard	Nottingham F	—	—
Gemmill Scot	5 11	11 06	M	2 1 71	Paisley	School	Nottingham F	181	19
George Daniel	6 1	12 01	D	22 10 78	Lincoln	Trainee	Nottingham F	—	—
Goodlad Mark	6 0	13 02	G	9 9 79	Barnsley	Trainee	Nottingham F	—	—
Grim Robert	5 11	11 08	M	10 9 78	London	Trainee	Nottingham F	—	—
Guinan Stephen	6 1	13 07	F	24 12 75	Birmingham	Trainee	Nottingham F	4	—
							Darlington (loan)	3	1
							Burnley (loan)	6	—
Haaland Alf-Inge	5 10	12 12	D	23 11 72	Stavanger	Bryne	Nottingham F	75	7
Harewood Marlon	6 1	10 00	D	25 8 79	Hampstead	Trainee	Nottingham F	—	—
Henry David	6 3	14 09	G	12 11 77	Belfast		Nottingham F	—	—
Hodgson Richard	5 10	11 04	M	1 10 79	Sunderland	Trainee	Nottingham F	—	—
Howe Stephen	5 7	10 06	M	6 11 73	Annitsford	Trainee	Nottingham F	14	2
							Ipswich T (loan)	3	—
Irving Richard‡	5 8	10 07	F	10 9 75	Halifax	Trainee	Manchester U	—	—
							Nottingham F	1	—
Jerkan Nikola	6 2	12 07	D	8 12 64	Sinj	Hajduk Split	Oviedo	203	1
							Nottingham F	14	—
Lee Jason	6 3	13 03	F	9 5 71	Newham	Trainee	Charlton Ath	—	—
							Stockport Co (loan)	2	—
							Lincoln C	93	21
							Southend U	24	3
							Nottingham F	76	14
							Charlton Ath (loan)	8	3
							Grimsby T (loan)	7	1
Lyttle Des	5 8	12 13	D	26 9 71	Wolverhampton	Worcester C	Swansea C	46	1
							Nottingham F	140	3
Macari Jon	5 9	11 04	F	15 12 79	Stoke	Trainee	Nottingham F	—	—
McGregor Paul	5 10	11 06	F	17 12 74	Liverpool	Trainee	Nottingham F	30	3
Melton Stephen	5 11	10 11	M	3 10 78	Lincoln	Trainee	Nottingham F	—	—
Moore Ian	5 11	12 02	F	26 8 76	Birkenhead	Trainee	Tranmere R	58	12
							Bradford C (loan)	6	—
							Nottingham F	5	—
Morgan Ian*	6 2	12 10	D	11 10 77	Birmingham	Trainee	Nottingham F	—	—
O'Neill Brian *(on loan from Celtic)*	6 1	12 04	M	6 9 72	Paisley	X Form	Celtic	120	8
							Nottingham F	5	—
O'Neill Shane‡	5 10	12 00	M	20 6 78	Limavady	Trainee	Nottingham F	—	—
Orr Stephen‡	5 7	10 00	F	19 1 78	Belper	Trainee	Nottingham F	—	—
Pearce Stuart	5 10	12 12	D	24 4 62	Shepherds Bush	Wealdstone	Coventry C	51	4
							Nottingham F	401	63

Phillips David	5 9	12 05	M	29 7 63	Wegberg	Apprentice	Plymouth Arg	73	15
							Manchester C	81	13
							Coventry C	100	8
							Norwich C	152	18
							Nottingham F	126	5
Porteous Andrew	5 11	10 11	M	13 9 79	Edinburgh	Trainee	Nottingham F	—	—
Rigby Malcolm‡	6 1	12 03	G	13 3 76	Nottingham	Notts Co	Nottingham F	—	—
Roy Bryan	5 10	10 10	M	12 2 70	Amsterdam		Ajax	126	17
							Foggia	50	14
							Nottingham F	85	24
Saunders Dean	5 8	10 06	F	21 6 64	Swansea	Apprentice	Swansea C	49	12
							Cardiff C (loan)	4	—
							Brighton & HA	72	21
							Oxford U	59	22
							Derby Co	106	42
							Liverpool	42	11
							Aston Villa	112	37
							Galatasaray	27	15
							Nottingham F	34	3
Silenzi Andrea	6 3	11 13	F	10 2 66	Rome		Lodigiani	49	18
							Arezzo	19	—
							Reggiana	67	32
							Napoli	39	6
							Torino	82	24
							Nottingham F	12	—
Smith Paul	5 11	11 07	M	25 1 76	Hastings	Hastings T	Nottingham F	—	—
Stone Steve	5 8	12 05	M	20 8 71	Gateshead	Trainee	Nottingham F	138	18
Stratford Lee‡	5 10	10 09	M	11 11 75	Barnsley	Trainee	Nottingham F	—	—
Thom Stuart	6 2	11 12	D	27 12 76	Dewsbury	Trainee	Nottingham F	—	—
Todd Andrew	6 0	11 03	M	22 2 79	Nottingham	Trainee	Nottingham F	—	—
Turner Barry	5 9	10 01	M	1 12 78	Nottingham	Trainee	Nottingham F	—	—
Van Hooijdonk Pierre	6 4	13 13	F	29 11 69	Steenbergen		RBC	69	33
							NAC	99	71
							Celtic	69	44
							Nottingham F	8	1
Walley Mark‡	5 10	11 01	F	17 9 76	Barnsley	Trainee	Nottingham F	—	—
Warner Vance	6 0	13 02	M	3 9 74	Leeds	Trainee	Nottingham F	5	—
							Grimsby T (loan)	3	—
Whitney Scott‡			D	10 3 79	Northampton	Trainee	Nottingham F	—	—
Winters Kris			M	28 8 79	Dundalk	Trainee	Nottingham F	—	—
Woan Ian	5 10	12 02	M	14 12 67	Wirrall	Runcorn	Nottingham F	187	30
Wood Scott	5 10	11 11	M	16 11 79	Nottingham	Trainee	Nottingham F	—	—

Trainees
Beardshaw, Mark; Browne, Bevan; Gorman, Peter; Toner, Robert.

Associated Schoolboys
Gill, Robert; Glover, Simon D; Kearney, Martin R; Mitchell, Dean J; Robinson, Paul M; Sherwood, Benjamin D; Wright-Phillips, Shaun C.

Associated Schoolboys who have accepted the club's offer of a Traineeship/Contract
Ashley, Neil; Dawson, Kevin; Donlon, Jason A; Higgins, Paul; Howarth, Paul; Rees, Daniel; Thomas, Danny.

NOTTS COUNTY

Arkins Vinny	6 2	11 10	F	18 9 70	Dublin	Home Farm	Dundee U	—	—
(Transferred to Portadown, February 1997)						Shamrock R	St Johnstone	48	11
							Shelbourne	Notts Co	38	8
Baraclough Ian	6 1	12 02	D	4 12 70	Leicester	Trainee	Leicester C	—	—
							Wigan Ath (loan)	9	2
							Grimsby T (loan)	4	—
							Grimsby T	1	—
							Lincoln C	73	10
							Mansfield T	47	5
							Notts Co	73	4
Battersby Tony	6 0	12 07	F	30 8 75	Doncaster	Trainee	Sheffield U	10	1
							Southend U (loan)	8	1
							Notts Co	39	8
							Bury (loan)	11	2
Cunnington Shaun	5 11	11 08	M	4 1 66	Bourne	Bourne T	Wrexham	199	12
							Grimsby T	182	13
							Sunderland	58	8
							WBA	13	—
							Notts Co	8	—
Derry Shaun	5 10	10 13	D	6 12 77	Nottingham	Trainee	Notts Co	51	2
Diuk Wayne§			M	26 5 80	Nottingham	Trainee	Notts Co	1	—
Dudley Craig	5 10	11 04	F	12 9 79	Ollerton	Trainee	Notts Co	10	2
Eaton Jamie*	5 10	10 06	D	27 10 77	Nottingham	Trainee	Notts Co	—	—

Name	Ht	Wt	Pos	Birthdate	Birthplace	Source	Club	Apps	Gls
Farrell Sean	6 1	13 03	F	28 2 69	Watford	Apprentice	Luton T	25	1
							Colchester U (loan)	9	1
							Northampton T (loan)	4	1
							Fulham	94	31
							Peterborough U	66	20
							Notts Co	14	1
Finnan Steve	5 9	10 09	F	20 4 76	Chelmsford	Welling U	Birmingham C	15	1
							Notts Co (loan)	17	2
							Notts Co	23	—
Gallagher Tommy‡	5 10	10 08	D	25 8 74	Nottingham	Trainee	Notts Co	43	2
Galloway Mick	5 11	11 05	M	13 10 74	Nottingham	Trainee	Notts Co	21	0
							Gillingham (loan)	9	1
Hendon Ian	5 11	11 05	D	5 12 71	Ilford	Trainee	Tottenham H	4	—
							Portsmouth (loan)	4	—
							Leyton Orient (loan)	6	—
							Barnsley (loan)	6	—
							Leyton Orient	131	5
							Birmingham C (loan)	4	—
							Notts Co	12	—
Hogg Graeme	6 1	12 04	D	17 6 64	Aberdeen	Apprentice	Manchester U	83	1
							WBA (loan)	7	—
							Portsmouth	100	2
							Hearts	58	3
							Notts Co	62	—
Hunt James*	5 8	10 03	M	17 12 76	Nottingham	Trainee	Notts Co	19	1
Jones Gary	6 1	12 09	F	6 4 69	Huddersfield	Rossington Main	Doncaster R	20	2
						Boston U	Southend U	70	16
							Lincoln C (loan)	4	2
							Notts Co	45	8
							Scunthorpe U (loan)	11	5
Kennedy Peter	5 11	11 11	F	10 9 73	Lurgan	Portadown	Notts Co	22	—
Martindale Gary	6 0	12 00	F	24 6 71	Liverpool	Burscough	Bolton W	—	—
							Peterborough U	31	15
							Notts Co	44	12
							Mansfield T (loan)	5	2
Mendez Gabriel‡	5 8	11 00	M	12 3 73	Buenos Aires	Parramatta E	Notts Co	3	—
Mitchell Paul§			D	8 11 78	Nottingham	Trainee	Notts Co	1	—
Pollitt Michael	6 4	14 00	G	29 2 72	Bolton	Trainee	Manchester U	—	—
							Oldham Ath (loan)	—	—
							Bury	—	—
							Lincoln C	57	—
							Darlington	55	—
							Notts Co	8	—
Redmile Matthew	6 46	12 11	D	12 11 76	Nottingham	Trainee	Notts Co	23	2
Richardson Ian	5 10	11 01	M	22 10 70	Barking	Dagenham & Redbridge	Birmingham C	7	—
							Notts Co	34	1
Ridgway Ian*	5 8	10 06	M	28 12 75	Nottingham	Trainee	Notts Co	7	—
Robinson Phil	5 10	11 07	M	6 1 67	Stafford	Apprentice	Aston Villa	3	1
							Wolverhampton W	71	8
							Notts Co	66	5
							Birmingham C (loan)	9	—
							Huddersfield T	75	5
							Northampton T (loan)	14	—
							Chesterfield	61	17
							Notts Co	37	2
Roddie Andrew‡	5 9	11 00	M		Glasgow		Aberdeen	27	5
							Motherwell	55	—
							Notts Co	—	—
Strodder Gary	6 1	13 03	D	1 4 65	Cleckheaton	Apprentice	Lincoln C	132	6
							West Ham U	65	2
							WBA	140	8
							Notts Co	71	5
Walker Richard*	5 10	11 09	D	9 11 71	Derby	Trainee	Notts Co	67	4
							Mansfield T (loan)	4	—
Ward Darren	5 11	12 09	G	11 5 74	Worksop	Trainee	Mansfield T	81	—
							Notts Co	84	—
White Devon	6 3	14 00	F	2 3 64	Nottingham	Arnold T	Lincoln C	29	4
						Boston U	Bristol R	202	53
							Cambridge U	22	4
							QPR	26	9
							Notts Co	40	15
							Watford	38	7
							Notts Co	9	—
Wilkes Tim‡	6 0	12 00	F	7 11 77	Nottingham	Trainee	Notts Co	3	—

Trainees
Bateman, Neal S; Beckford-Quailey, Damion A; Best, Russell S; Diuk, Wayne J; Gee, Christopher; Henshaw, Terrence R; Hickling, Graham J; Jones, Kevin P; Marshall, Ben; Matthews, Jamie L; Mitchell, Paul; Newton, Richard J; Randall, Dean; Smith, Neil S; Smith, Richard; Williams, Anthony C.

Associated Schoolboys
Abbott, Lennon R; Baum, Adam; Briggs, Andrew; Brodsky, Richard; Davies, Andrew; Green, Martin; Harrad, Kirk; Holmes, Michael J; Holtham, Daniel; Housley, Craig; Johnson, Lewis; Maine, Justin; McCaul, Matthew; Osborne, Calum; Pennant, Jermaine; Poznanski, Lee; Ritchie, Andrew; Rycroft, Symon; Skevington, Matthew.

Associated Schoolboys who have accepted the club's offer of a Traineeship/Contract
Brough, Michael; Cockerill, Colin P; Cooke, Russell; Holmes, Richard; Lindley, James E; Norwood, Andrew M; Osborne, Matthew A; Wigginton, Steven.

OLDHAM ATHLETIC

Allott Mark	6 0	10 12	F	16 3 78	Manchester	Trainee	Oldham Ath	5	1
Banger Nicky*	5 10	11 03	F	25 2 71	Southampton	Trainee	Southampton	55	8
							Oldham Ath	64	10
Barlow Stuart	5 10	11 00	F	16 7 68	Liverpool	School	Everton	71	10
							Rotherham U (loan)	—	—
							Oldham Ath	61	19
Darnbrough Lee*	6 1	12 12	G	15 9 77	Ashton	Trainee	Oldham Ath	—	—
Duxbury Lee	5 10	10 07	D	7 10 69	Keighley	Trainee	Bradford C	209	25
							Rochdale (loan)	10	—
							Huddersfield T	29	2
							Bradford C	63	7
							Oldham Ath	12	1
Fleming Craig	6 0	12 09	D	6 10 71	Calder	Trainee	Halifax T	57	—
							Oldham Ath	164	1
Gannon John‡	5 10	10 09	M	18 12 66	Wimbledon	Apprentice	Wimbledon	16	2
							Crewe Alex (loan)	15	—
							Sheffield U (loan)	16	1
							Sheffield U	158	5
							Middlesbrough (loan)	7	—
							Oldham Ath	6	—
Garnett Shaun	6 2	13 01	D	22 11 69	Wallasey	Trainee	Tranmere R	112	5
							Chester C (loan)	9	—
							Preston NE (loan)	10	2
							Wigan Ath (loan)	13	1
							Swansea C	15	—
							Oldham Ath	23	1
Graham Richard	6 2	12 09	D	28 11 74	Dewsbury	Trainee	Oldham Ath	88	5
Hallworth Jon*	6 2	13 6	G	26 10 65	Stockport	School	Ipswich T	45	0
							Swindon T (loan)	—	—
							Fulham (loan)	—	—
							Bristol R (loan)	2	—
							Oldham Ath	174	—
Hart Barrie	6 1	11 09	D	17 7 77	Oldham	Trainee	Oldham Ath	—	—
Hodgson Doug	6 3	13 05	D	27 2 69	Frankston	Heidelberg	Sheffield U	30	0
							Plymouth Arg (loan)	5	—
							Burnley (loan)	1	—
							Oldham Ath	12	—
Holden Andy*	6 1	13 02	D	14 9 62	Flint	Rhyl	Chester C	100	17
							Wigan Ath	49	4
							Oldham Ath	22	4
Holt Andy	6 1	11 11	D	21 5 78	Manchester	Trainee	Oldham Ath	1	—
Hughes Andy	6 0	11 00	M	2 1 78	Manchester	Trainee	Oldham Ath	23	1
Innes Mark			D	27 9 78	Bellshill	Trainee	Oldham Ath	—	—
Kelly Gary	5 11	12 10	G	3 8 66	Fulwood	Apprentice	Newcastle U	53	0
							Blackpool (loan)	5	—
							Bury	236	—
							West Ham U (loan)	—	—
							Oldham Ath	42	—
Lonergan Darren*	6 0	13 01	D	28 1 74	Waterford	Waterford	Oldham Ath	2	—
McCarthy Sean	6 1	12 10	F	12 9 67	Bridgend	Bridgend	Swansea C	91	25
							Plymouth Arg	70	19
							Bradford C	131	60
							Oldham Ath	115	35
McNiven David	5 10	10 06	F	27 5 78	Leeds	Trainee	Oldham Ath	8	—
McNiven Scott	5 10	10 06	D	27 5 78	Leeds	Trainee	Oldham Ath	28	0
Morrow John‡	5 7	10 00	F	20 11 71	Belfast	Linfield	Rangers	5	—
							Oldham Ath	2	—
Murphy Gerard			M	19 12 78	Manchester	Trainee	Oldham Ath	—	—
Orlygsson Toddy	5 11	10 12	M	2 8 66	Odense	FC Akureyi	Nottingham F	37	2
							Stoke C	90	16
							Oldham Ath	43	1

Ormondroyd Ian	6 4	14 00	F	22 9 64	Bradford	Thackley	Bradford C	87	20
							Oldham Ath (loan)	10	1
							Aston Villa	56	6
							Derby Co	25	8
							Leicester C	77	7
							Hull C (loan)	10	6
							Bradford C	38	6
							Oldham Ath	30	8
Ramplin Jamie			M	14 10 79	Manchester	Trainee	Oldham Ath	—	—
Ramsden Gavin*	5 11	10 08	D	4 11 77	Manchester	Trainee	Oldham Ath	—	—
Randall Lee‡	5 11	11 00	D	12 4 78	Glasgow	Trainee	Oldham Ath	—	—
Redmond Steve	6 0	11 02	D	2 11 67	Liverpool	Apprentice	Manchester C	235	7
							Oldham Ath	171	4
Reid Paul	5 10	10 12	M	19 1 68	Oldbury	Apprentice	Leicester C	162	21
							Bradford C (loan)	7	—
							Bradford C	82	15
							Huddersfield T	77	6
							Oldham Ath	9	1
Richardson Lee J	5 11	10 06	M	12 3 69	Halifax		Halifax T	56	2
							Watford	41	1
							Blackburn R	62	3
							Aberdeen	64	6
							Oldham Ath	88	21
Richardson Lloyd M	6 0	11 02	F	7 10 77	Dewsbury	Trainee	Oldham Ath	1	—
Rickers Paul	5 10	10 07	M	9 5 75	Leeds	Trainee	Oldham Ath	73	5
Ritchie Andy	5 11	11 10	F	28 11 60	Manchester	Apprentice	Manchester U	33	13
							Brighton & HA	89	23
							Leeds U	136	40
							Oldham Ath	217	82
							Scarborough	68	17
							Oldham Ath	10	—
Rush Matthew	5 11	11 02	F	6 8 71	Dalston	Trainee	West Ham U	48	5
							Cambridge U (loan)	10	—
							Swansea C (loan)	13	—
							Norwich C	3	—
							Northampton T (loan)	14	3
							Oldham Ath	8	2
Serrant Carl	6 0	10 02	D	12 9 75	Bradford	Trainee	Oldham Ath	60	1
Sharp Graeme*	6 1	11 06	F	16 10 60	Glasgow	Eastercraigs	Dumbarton	40	17
							Everton	322	111
							Oldham Ath	109	30
Snodin Ian*	5 10	11 03	D	15 8 63	Rotherham	Apprentice	Doncaster R	188	25
							Leeds U	51	6
							Everton	148	3
							Sunderland (loan)	6	—
							Oldham Ath	57	—
Swain Iain			M	16 10 79	Glasgow	Trainee	Oldham Ath	—	—

Trainees
Campbell, Jamie; Clitheroe, Lee; Earnshaw, Mark; Fairhurst, Scott; Hotte, Mark S; Jablonski, Mark P; Jeffries, Paul M; Johnson, Alan; Mather, Gregg R; McKechnie, Ewan; Miskelly, David T; Oldham, Gavin P; Rowlands, Gareth C; Salt, Phillip T; Selfe, Oliver; Tipton, Matthew J; Walsh, Daniel G; Yorke-Robinson, David; Zarac, Neil.

Associated Schoolboys
Boshell, Daniel K; Brough, Austin; Broughton, Matthew R; Clark, Liam; Colton, Thomas; Donnelly, Mark; Doran, Joseph; Heptinstall, Simon; Hodgkinson, Anthony L; Johnston, Patrick; Lush, Simon; McLean, Michael J; Nugent, Robert; Otto, Alastair; Pashley, Adam; Roberts, Glen R; Saunders, John J; Smith, Benjamin; Sutcliffe, Arren; Wharton, Nathan; Wright, Matthew.

OXFORD UNITED

Aldridge Martin	5 11	12 02	F	6 12 74	Northampton	Trainee	Northampton T	70	17
							Oxford U	48	17
Angel Mark	5 10	11 10	F	23 8 75	Newcastle	Trainee	Sunderland	—	—
							Oxford U	51	3
Beauchamp Joey	5 10	12 11	M	13 3 71	Oxford	Trainee	Oxford U	124	20
							Swansea C (loan)	5	2
							West Ham U	—	—
							Swindon T	45	3
							Oxford U	77	14
Ford Bobby	5 8	11 00	M	22 9 74	Bristol	Trainee	Oxford U	98	5
Ford Mike	6 0	12 06	D	9 2 66	Bristol	Apprentice	Leicester C	—	—
							Devizes T	Cardiff C	145	13
							Oxford U	267	16
Gilchrist Phil	6 0	13 12	D	25 8 73	Stockton	Trainee	Nottingham F	—	—
							Middlesbrough	—	—
							Hartlepool U	82	—
							Oxford U	98	6

Name							Club	Apps	Gls
Gray Martin	5 9	11 05	M	17 8 71	Stockton	Trainee	Sunderland	64	1
							Aldershot (loan)	5	—
							Fulham (loan)	6	—
							Oxford U	50	2
Jackson Elliott	6 2	14 06	G	27 8 77	Swindon	Trainee	Oxford U	3	—
Jemson Nigel	5 11	13 03	F	10 8 69	Hutton	Trainee	Preston NE	32	8
							Nottingham F	47	13
							Bolton W (loan)	5	—
							Preston NE (loan)	9	2
							Sheffield W	51	9
							Grimsby T (loan)	6	2
							Notts Co	14	1
							Watford (loan)	4	—
							Coventry C (loan)	—	—
							Rotherham U (loan)	16	5
							Oxford U	44	18
Lewis Mickey	5 9	12 10	M	15 2 65	Birmingham	School	WBA	24	—
							Derby Co	43	1
							Oxford U	300	7
Marsh Simon	5 11	11 04	D	29 1 77	Ealing	Trainee	Oxford U	21	1
Massey Stuart	5 10	12 13	M	17 11 64	Crawley	Sutton U	Crystal Palace	2	—
							Oxford U	86	7
McGregor Marc*	5 9	11 10	M	30 4 78	Southend	Trainee	Oxford U	—	—
Moody Paul	6 3	14 08	F	13 6 67	Portsmouth	Waterlooville	Southampton	12	0
							Reading (loan)	5	1
							Oxford U	136	49
Murphy Matt	6 0	12 06	F	20 8 71	Northampton	Corby T	Oxford U	88	15
Phillips Marcus*	5 11	12 00	M	17 10 73	Bradford-on-Avon	Trainee	Swindon T	—	—
							Utrecht	7	—
						Witney T	Swindon T	—	—
							Oxford U	1	—
Powell Paul	5 8	11 06	D	30 6 78	Wallingford	Trainee	Oxford U	3	—
Purse Darren	6 2	12 10	D	14 2 77	London	Trainee	Leyton Orient	55	3
							Oxford U	31	1
Reeves Steve‡	5 11	13 00	G	24 9 74	Dagenham	Trainee	Everton	—	—
							Chelsea	—	—
							Oxford U	—	—
Robinson Les	5 8	12 10	D	1 3 67	Shirerook	Local	Mansfield T	15	—
							Stockport Co	67	3
							Doncaster R	82	12
							Oxford U	248	2
Smith David	5 8	12 09	M	26 12 70	Liverpool	Trainee	Norwich C	18	—
							Oxford U	132	1
Stevens Mark	6 5	12 07	F	3 12 77	Swindon	School	Oxford U	—	—
Van Eys Frank‡			D	2 11 71	Geleen	RC Mechelen	Oxford U	—	—
Weatherstone Simon	5 9	11 11	F	26 1 80	Reading	Trainee	Oxford U	1	—
Whitehead Phil	6 2	15 11	G	17 12 69	Halifax	Trainee	Halifax T	42	—
							Barnsley	16	—
							Halifax T (loan)	9	—
							Scunthorpe U (loan)	8	—
							Scunthorpe U (loan)	8	—
							Bradford C (loan)	6	—
							Oxford U	154	—
Whyte Chris*	6 3	15 00	D	2 9 61	London	Amateur	Arsenal	90	8
							Crystal Palace (loan)	13	—
						Los Angeles R	WBA	84	7
							Leeds U	113	5
							Birmingham C	68	1
							Coventry C (loan)	1	—
							Charlton Ath	11	—
						Detroit Neon	Leyton Orient	1	—
							Oxford U	10	—
Wilsterman Brian	6 1	13 01	D	19 11 66	Surinam	Beerschot	Oxford U	1	—

Trainees
Best, Gavin; Clarke, Daniel P; Cook, James S; Davies, Gary L; Davis, Paul; Emsden, Nigel G; Evans, David A; Folland, Robert W; Greason, Craig S; Grey, Iain M; Rose, Andrew M; Shepherd, Sam R; Whelan, Paul L; Wright, Anthony A.

Associated Schoolboys
Boyce, Jonathon P; Davies, Mathew; Devonald, Steven E; Gostick, Ryan J; Hackett, Christopher; Holder, Jorden A; Inns, Alan F; Jones, Brynmor R; King, Simon; Meade, Nathan S; Ricketts, Sam D; Silva, Simon; Spence, Brynley J; Townsend, Ben; Whitehead, Dean; Wickens, Gary J.

Associated Schoolboys who have accepted the club's offer of a Traineeship/Contract
Davies, Alex; Richards, Andrew; Shepheard, Jonathan.

PETERBOROUGH UNITED

Name				Birth date	Birthplace	Source	Club	Apps	Gls
Basham Mike*	6 2	13 02	M	27 9 73	Barking	Trainee	West Ham U	—	—
							Colchester U (loan)	1	—
							Swansea C	29	1
							Peterborough U	19	1
Bodley Mike	6 1	13 01	D	14 9 67	Hayes	Apprentice	Chelsea	6	1
							Northampton T	20	—
							Barnet	69	3
							Southend U	67	2
							Gillingham (loan)	7	—
							Birmingham C (loan)	3	—
							Peterborough U	31	—
Boothroyd Aidy	5 9	11 07	D	8 2 71	Bradford	Trainee	Huddersfield T	10	—
							Bristol R	16	—
							Hearts	4	—
							Mansfield T	102	3
							Peterborough U	26	1
Bullimore Wayne	5 9	12 01	M	12 9 70	Mansfield	Trainee	Manchester U	—	—
							Barnsley	35	1
							Stockport Co	—	—
							Scunthorpe U	67	11
							Bradford C	2	—
							Doncaster R (loan)	4	—
							Peterborough U	6	—
Carruthers Martin	5 11	11 07	F	7 8 72	Nottingham	Trainee	Aston Villa	4	—
							Hull C (loan)	13	6
							Stoke C	91	13
							Peterborough U	14	4
Carter Danny*	5 9	12 01	F	29 6 69	Hackney	Billericay T	Leyton Orient	188	22
							Peterborough U	45	1
Castle Steve	5 10	12 07	M	17 5 66	Ilford	Apprentice	Orient	243	55
							Plymouth Arg	101	35
							Birmingham C	23	1
							Gillingham (loan)	6	1
							Leyton Orient (loan)	4	1
							Peterborough U	—	—
Clark Simon	6 0	12 12	D	12 3 67	Boston	Stevenage Bor	Peterborough U	107	4
Cleaver Christopher	5 9	11 07	F	24 3 79	Hitchin	Trainee	Peterborough U	13	1
De Souza Miguel	5 11	13 08	F	11 2 70	Newham	Dagenham	Birmingham C	15	—
							Bury (loan)	3	—
							Wycombe W	83	29
							Peterborough U	8	2
Donowa Lou‡	5 9	11 00	M	24 9 64	Ipswich	Apprentice	Norwich C	62	11
							Stoke C (loan)	4	1
						Coruna, Willem II	Ipswich T	23	1
							Bristol C	24	3
							Birmingham C	116	18
							Crystal Palace (loan)	—	—
							Burnley (loan)	4	—
							Shrewsbury T (loan)	4	—
							Walsall (loan)	6	1
							Peterborough U	22	1
Drury Adam	5 10	11 08	D	29 8 78	Cottenham	Trainee	Peterborough U	6	1
Edwards Andy	6 2	12 00	D	17 9 71	Epping	Trainee	Southend U	147	5
							Birmingham C	40	1
							Peterborough U	25	—
Etherington Matthew§				14 8 81	Truro	School	Peterborough U	1	—
Foran Mark	6 3	13 04	D	30 10 73	Aldershot	Trainee	Millwall	—	—
							Sheffield U	11	1
							Rotherham U (loan)	3	—
							Wycombe W (loan)	5	—
							Peterborough U	21	1
							Lincoln C (loan)	2	—
							Oldham Ath (loan)	1	—
Grazioli Guiliano	5 11	12 00	F	23 3 75	London	Wembley	Peterborough U	7	1
Griemink Bart	6 3	15 04	G	29 3 72	Holland	WKE	Birmingham C	20	0
							Barnsley (loan)	—	—
							Peterborough U	27	—
Heald Greg	6 2	13 01	D	26 9 71	London	Enfield	Peterborough U	105	6
Houghton Scott	5 6	12 01	M	22 10 71	Hitchin	Trainee	Tottenham H	10	2
							Ipswich T (loan)	8	1
							Cambridge U (loan)	—	—
							Gillingham (loan)	3	—
							Charlton Ath (loan)	6	—
							Luton T	16	1
							Walsall	78	14
							Peterborough U	32	8

Name	Ht	Wt	Pos	Born	Birthplace	Source	Club	Apps	Gls
Inman Niall	5 9	11 06	F	6 2 78	Wakefield	Trainee	Peterborough U	4	—
Le Bihan Neil*	6 0	12 03	M	14 3 76	Croydon	Tottenham H	Peterborough U	31	0
Linton Des	6 1	13 10	D	5 9 71	Birmingham	Trainee	Leicester C	11	—
							Luton T	83	1
							Peterborough U	8	—
Meredith Tom†	5 10	11 08	M	27 10 77	Enfield	Trainee	Peterborough U	2	—
Neal Ashley†	6 1	14 10	D	16 12 74	Northampton	Trainee	Liverpool	—	—
							Brighton & HA (loan)	8	—
							Huddersfield T	—	—
							Peterborough U	4	—
Payne Derek	5 6	10 08	M	26 4 67	Edgware	Hayes	Barnet	51	6
							Southend U	35	—
							Watford	36	1
							Peterborough U	36	2
Perkins Declan†	5 11	12 04	F	17 10 75	Ilford	Trainee	Southend U	6	—
							Cambridge U (loan)	2	1
							Peterborough U	—	—
Rowe Zeke	5 10	11 08	M	30 10 73	Stoke Newington	Trainee	Chelsea	—	—
							Barnet (loan)	10	2
							Brighton & HA (loan)	9	3
							Peterborough U	22	3
Sheffield Jon	6 0	12 08	G	1 2 69	Bedworth	Apprentice	Norwich C	1	—
							Aldershot (loan)	11	—
							Ipswich T (loan)	—	—
							Aldershot (loan)	15	—
							Cambridge U (loan)	2	—
							Cambridge U	54	—
							Colchester U (loan)	6	—
							Swindon T (loan)	2	—
							Hereford U (loan)	8	—
							Peterborough U	62	—
							Watford (loan)	—	—
							Oldham Ath (loan)	—	—
Spearing Tony*	5 7	12 00	D	7 10 64	Romford	Apprentice	Norwich C	69	—
							Stoke C (loan)	9	—
							Oxford U (loan)	5	—
							Leicester C	73	1
							Plymouth Arg	35	—
							Peterborough U	111	2
Stanislaus Roger†	5 11	13 02	D	2 11 68	Hammersmith	Trainee	Arsenal	—	—
							Brentford	111	4
							Bury	176	5
							Leyton Orient	21	—
							Peterborough U	—	—
Tyler Mark	5 11	12 00	G	2 4 77	Norwich	Trainee	Peterborough U	8	—
Willis Roger	6 0	12 00	M	17 6 67	Islington		Grimsby T	9	—
						Barnet	Barnet	44	13
							Watford	36	2
							Birmingham C	19	5
							Southend U	31	7
							Peterborough U	40	6

Trainees
Campbell, James R; Costick, Paul; Davies, Simon; French, Daniel J; Haley, Grant R; Hotchkiss, Jonathan E; Kenna, Warren J; Koogi, Anders B; McCafferty, Sean T P; Miller, Neil C; O'Donnell, Noel G; Pendleton, Matthew; Wilson, Simon M.

Non-Contract
Neal, Ashley J.

Associated Schoolboys
Alcraft, Kevin S R; Earey, Oliver C; Ferguson, Scott J; Lang, Adam B; McCormick, Charles; Sturmey, Paul J; Vaughan, Jonathan R.

Associated Schoolboys who have accepted the club's offer of a Traineeship/Contract
Cable, Aaron P; Etherington, Matthew; Jelleyman, Gareth A; Sadler, Christopher J.

PLYMOUTH ARGYLE

Name	Ht	Wt	Pos	Born	Birthplace	Source	Club	Apps	Gls
Barlow Martin	5 7	10 03	M	25 6 71	Barnstable	Trainee	Plymouth Arg	220	15
Beswetherick John*	5 11	11 04	D	15 1 78	Liverpool	Trainee	Plymouth Arg	—	—
Billy Chris	5 11	11 08	M	2 1 73	Huddersfield	Trainee	Huddersfield T	94	4
							Plymouth Arg	77	7
Blackwell Kevin*	5 11	12 10	G	21 11 58	Luton	Barnet	Scarborough	44	—
							Notts Co	—	—
							Torquay U	18	—
							Huddersfield T	5	—
							Plymouth Arg	24	—
Clayton Gary*	5 11	12 08	M	2 2 63	Sheffield	Burton Alb	Doncaster R	35	5
							Cambridge U	179	17
							Peterborough U (loan)	4	—
							Huddersfield T	19	1
							Plymouth Arg	37	2

Collins Simon	6 0	11 02	M	16 12 73	Pontefract	Trainee	Huddersfield T	52	3
							Plymouth Arg	12	1
Corazzin Carlo	5 9	12 05	F	25 12 71	Canada	Vancouver 86ers	Cambridge U	105	39
							Plymouth Arg	36	6
Curran Chris	5 11	11 09	D	17 9 71	Birmingham	Trainee	Torquay U	152	4
							Plymouth Arg	30	—
Dann Craig*	5 6	10 07	M	14 12 77	Luton	Trainee	Plymouth Arg	—	—
Dungey James	5 9	11 08	G	7 2 78	Plymouth	Trainee	Plymouth Arg	10	—
Grobbelaar Bruce*	6 1	13 00	G	6 10 57	Durban	Vancouver Whitecaps	Crewe Alex	24	1
							Liverpool	440	—
							Stoke C (loan)	4	—
							Southampton	32	—
							Plymouth Arg	36	—
Heathcote Mike	6 2	12 08	D	10 9 65	Durham	Spennymoor U	Sunderland	9	—
							Halifax T (loan)	7	1
							York C (loan)	3	—
							Shrewsbury T	44	6
							Cambridge U	128	13
							Plymouth Arg	86	5
Illman Neil	5 7	10 07	F	29 4 75	Doncaster	Trainee Eastwood T	Middlesbrough	1	—
							Plymouth Arg	25	4
							Cambridge U (loan)	5	—
James Tony	6 3	14 02	D	27 6 67	Sheffield	Gainsborough T	Lincoln C	29	—
							Leicester C	107	11
							Hereford U	35	4
							Plymouth Arg	34	1
Leadbitter Chris*	5 9	10 07	M	17 10 67	Middlesbrough	Apprentice	Grimsby T	—	—
							Hereford U	36	1
							Cambridge U	176	18
							Bournemouth	54	3
							Plymouth Arg	52	1
Littlejohn Adrian	5 9	11 00	F	26 9 70	Wolverhampton	WBA	Walsall	44	1
							Sheffield U	69	12
							Plymouth Arg	79	23
Logan Richard	6 0	13 03	D	24 5 69	Barnsley	Gainsborough T	Huddersfield T	45	1
							Plymouth Arg	59	8
Mauge Ron	5 10	10 06	M	10 3 69	Islington	Trainee	Charlton Ath	—	—
							Fulham	50	2
							Bury	108	10
							Manchester C (loan)	—	—
							Plymouth Arg	72	10
O'Hagan Danny‡	6 1	13 08	F	24 4 76	Padstow	Trainee	Plymouth Arg	9	1
Patterson Mark	5 10	11 05	D	13 9 68	Leeds	Trainee	Carlisle U	22	0
							Derby Co	51	3
							Plymouth Arg	134	3
Perkins Steven†	6 2	13 08	D	5 11 75	Southport	Crediton U	Plymouth Arg	4	—
Phillips Lee§			F	16 9 80	Penzance	School	Plymouth Arg	2	—
Richardson Dominic*	5 10	11 02	F	19 3 78	Plymouth	Trainee	Plymouth Arg	—	—
Rowbotham Jason†	5 9	11 09	D	3 1 69	Cardiff	Trainee	Plymouth Arg	9	—
							Shrewsbury T	—	—
							Hereford U	5	1
							Raith R	56	1
							Wycombe W	27	—
							Plymouth Arg	15	—
Saunders Mark	5 10	11 06	M	23 7 71	Reading	Tiverton	Plymouth Arg	35	4
Williams Paul	5 10	11 00	D	11 9 69	Leicester	Trainee	Leicester C	—	—
							Stockport Co	70	4
							Coventry C	14	—
							WBA (loan)	5	—
							Huddersfield T (loan)	9	—
							Plymouth Arg	92	4
Wotton Paul	5 11	11 07	M	17 8 77	Plymouth	Trainee	Plymouth Arg	17	1

Trainees
Ashton, Jon F; Avery, Andrew; Bushby, Ryan; Ford, Liam A; Francis, Kevin; Howell, Peter; Latham, Matthew J; McGovern, Brendan; Parsons, Mathew; Sargent, Andrew D; Smith, Lee M; Taylor, Matthew A; Young, Ryan.

Non-Contract
Perkins, Steven W; Rowbotham, Jason.

Associated Schoolboys
Baker, Paul M; Cook, Matthew A; Cusack, Aaron; Griffiths, Nicholas A; Harling, Christian L; Hill, Andrew J; O'Connor, Ryan L; Parnell, Simon R; Rollerson, Daniel M; Sobey, Billy; South, David; Steadman, Thomas W.

Associated Schoolboys who have accepted the club's offer of a Traineeship/Contract
Adams, Stephen M; Hampton, Andrew J; Jordan, John E; Phillips, Lee P.

PORTSMOUTH

Name	Ht	Wt		Birthdate	Birthplace	Source	Club	Apps	Gls
Ahmet Jason‡			M	4 1 78	Winchester	Trainee	Portsmouth	—	—
Allen Martin	5 11	12 06	M	14 8 65	Reading	School	QPR	136	16
							West Ham U	190	25
							Portsmouth	31	4
Awford Andy	5 9	11 09	D	14 7 72	Worcester	Worcester C	Portsmouth	203	1
Barker Daniel‡			M	13 10 77	Winchester	Trainee	Portsmouth	—	—
Bradbury Lee	6 2	13 10	F	15 7 71	Oswestry	Cowes	Portsmouth	54	15
							Exeter C (loan)	14	5
Bundy Scott	6 1	12 00	F	20 10 77	Southampton	Trainee	Portsmouth	—	—
Burton Deon	5 8	10 09	F	25 10 76	Ashford	Trainee	Portsmouth	62	10
							Cardiff C (loan)	5	2
Carter Jimmy	5 10	11 02	M	9 11 65	London	Apprentice	Crystal Palace	—	—
							QPR	—	—
							Millwall	110	10
							Liverpool	5	—
							Arsenal	25	2
							Oxford U (loan)	5	—
							Oxford U (loan)	4	—
							Portsmouth	62	5
Cook Andy	5 9	12 00	M	10 8 69	Romsey	Apprentice	Southampton	16	1
							Exeter C	70	1
							Swansea C	62	—
							Portsmouth	8	—
Dobson Tony*	6 1	11 09	D	5 2 69	Coventry	Apprentice	Coventry C	54	1
							Blackburn R	41	—
							Portsmouth	53	2
							Oxford U (loan)	5	—
							Peterborough U (loan)	4	—
Durnin John	5 10	11 10	F	18 8 65	Bootle	Waterloo Dock	Liverpool	—	—
							WBA (loan)	5	2
							Oxford U	161	44
							Portsmouth	119	14
Fenwick Terry†	5 10	11 12	D	17 11 59	Co. Durham	Apprentice	Crystal Palace	70	—
							QPR	256	33
							Tottenham H	93	8
							Leicester C (loan)	8	1
							Swindon T	28	—
							Portsmouth	—	—
Flahavan Aaron	6 1	11 12	G	15 12 75	Southampton	Trainee	Portsmouth	24	—
Hall Paul	5 9	10 02	F	3 7 72	Manchester	Trainee	Torquay U	93	1
							Portsmouth	159	32
Hawley Jon	6 0	12 05	D	23 1 78	Lincoln	Trainee	Portsmouth	—	—
Hillier David	5 10	11 12	M	18 12 69	Blackheath	Trainee	Arsenal	104	2
							Portsmouth	21	2
Hinshelwood Danny	5 9	11 00	D	4 12 75	Bromley	Trainee	Nottingham F	—	—
							Portsmouth	5	—
							Torquay U (loan)	9	—
Igoe Sammy	5 6	9 07	M	30 9 75	Spelthorne	Trainee	Portsmouth	63	2
Knight Alan	6 1	13 11	G	3 6 61	Balham	Apprentice	Portsmouth	642	—
McGrath Lloyd‡	5 8	12 05	M	24 2 65	Birmingham	Apprentice	Coventry C	214	4
							Portsmouth	18	—
McLoughlin Alan	5 8	10 10	M	20 4 67	Manchester	Local	Manchester U	—	—
							Swindon T	9	—
							Torquay U	24	4
							Swindon T	97	19
							Southampton	24	1
							Aston Villa (loan)	—	—
							Portsmouth	212	38
More Clinton‡	5 10	11 00	F	20 8 77	High Wycombe	Bognor Regis T	Portsmouth	—	—
Perrett Russell	6 2	13 00	D	18 6 73	Barton-on-Sea	AFC Lymington	Portsmouth	41	1
Pethick Robbie	5 10	11 11	M	8 9 70	Tavistock	Weymouth	Portsmouth	135	1
Rees Jason*	5 5	9 10	F	22 12 69	Pontypridd	Trainee	Luton T	82	—
							Mansfield T (loan)	15	1
							Portsmouth	43	3
							Exeter C (loan)	7	—
Russell Lee	5 10	11 09	D	3 9 69	Southampton	Trainee	Portsmouth	115	3
							Bournemouth (loan)	3	—
Simpson Fitzroy	5 8	12 00	M	26 2 70	Trowbridge	Trainee	Swindon T	105	9
							Manchester C	71	4
							Bristol C (loan)	4	—
							Portsmouth	71	9
Simpson Robert	5 10	11 06	F	3 3 76	Luton	Trainee	Tottenham H	—	—
							Portsmouth	—	—

Svensson Mathias	6 0	12 04	F	24 9 74	Boras		Elfsborg	22	15
							Portsmouth	19	6
Thompson Mark	6 2	11 07	M	17 9 77	Southampton	Trainee	Portsmouth	—	—
Thomson Andy	6 3	14 00	D	28 3 74	Swindon	Trainee	Swindon T	22	0
							Portsmouth	44	1
Tilley Anthony*	5 7	10 06	F	11 2 77	Zambia	Brighton & HA	Portsmouth	—	—
Turner Andy	5 10	11 02	M	23 5 75	Woolwich	Trainee	Tottenham H	20	3
							Wycombe W (loan)	4	—
							Doncaster R (loan)	4	1
							Huddersfield T (loan)	5	1
							Southend U (loan)	6	—
							Portsmouth	24	2
Walsh Paul	5 8	10 04	F	1 10 62	Plumstead	Apprentice	Charlton Ath	87	24
							Luton T	80	24
							Liverpool	77	25
							Tottenham H	128	19
							QPR (loan)	2	—
							Portsmouth	73	14
							Manchester C	53	16
							Portsmouth	21	5
Waterman David	5 10	13 02	D	16 5 77	Guernsey	Trainee	Portsmouth	4	—
Whitbread Adrian	6 0	12 02	D	22 10 71	Epping	Trainee	Leyton Orient	125	2
							Swindon T	36	1
							West Ham U	10	1
							Portsmouth (loan)	13	—
							Portsmouth	24	—
Wood Paul*	5 9	11 06	F	1 11 64	Middlesbrough	Apprentice	Portsmouth	47	6
							Brighton & HA	92	8
							Sheffield U	28	3
							Bournemouth (loan)	21	—
							Bournemouth	78	18
							Portsmouth	32	3

Trainees
Burrows, Marc P; Cook, Aaron; Goodban, Matthew N; Guile, Neil R; Jukes, Nathan B; Karimzadeh, Ashkan; Macdonald, Gary; Nelson, Michael J; Porter, Daniel J; Rees, Gavin R; Sargent, Steven; Tardif, Christopher L; Waterman, Lee; Williams, Adam L; Wright, David S; Wyatt, Nicky.

Associated Schoolboys
Barnett, Phillip; Cooper, Stuart G; Cox, James; Craggs, Christopher R; Davis, Adam R; Dodd, Jonathon; Griffiths, Ben; Hunt, Aaron J; Irwin, Andrew R; Jerman, Tim R; Osborne, Benjamin H; Parodi, Milan; Smith, Luke J; Spencer, Andrew J; Wilson, Michael A.

Associated Schoolboys who have accepted the club's offer of a Traineeship/Contract
Connolly, Gary M; Eastman, Wayne; Fisher, Daniel; Hawkins, David J; Holbrook, Adam P; Hussey, Stuart R; Linpow, Steven J; Nightingale, Luke R; Pettefer, Carl J.

PORT VALE

Aspin Neil	6 0	13 12	D	12 4 65	Gateshead	Apprentice	Leeds U	207	5
							Port Vale	292	3
Bogie Ian	5 9	11 10	M	6 12 67	Newcastle	Apprentice	Newcastle U	14	—
							Preston NE	79	12
							Millwall	51	1
							Leyton Orient	65	5
							Port Vale	72	6
Boswell Matthew	6 2	13 08	G	19 8 77	Shrewsbury		Port Vale	—	—
Corden Wayne	5 10	11 03	M	1 11 75	Leek	Trainee	Port Vale	15	0
Cunningham Dean*	5 7	10 06	F	28 5 77	Burslem	Trainee	Port Vale	—	—
Eyre Richard	5 11	11 06	M	15 9 76	Poynton	Trainee	Port Vale	—	—
Foyle Martin	5 11	12 01	F	2 5 63	Salisbury	Amateur	Southampton	12	1
							Blackburn R (loan)	—	—
							Aldershot	98	35
							Oxford U	126	36
							Port Vale	200	60
Glover Dean	5 11	12 02	D	29 12 63	West Bromwich	Apprentice	Aston Villa	28	—
							Sheffield U (loan)	5	—
							Middlesbrough	50	5
							Port Vale	338	14
Griffiths Gareth	6 4	14 04	D	10 4 70	Winsford	Rhyl	Port Vale	91	4
Hill Andy	6 0	13 08	D	21 1 65	Maltby	Apprentice	Manchester U	—	—
							Bury	264	10
							Manchester C	98	6
							Port Vale	73	1
Holwyn Jermaine	6 2	13 01	D	16 4 73	Amsterdam	Ajax	Port Vale	7	—
Jansson Jan‡	5 10	12 04	M	26 1 68	Kalmar		Norrkoping	73	9
							Port Vale	11	1
Koordes Rogier	6 1	12 11	M	13 6 72	Holland		Telstar	12	—
							Port Vale	13	—

McCarthy Jon	5 10	11 04	M	18 8 70	Middlesbrough		Hartlepool U	1	—
						Shepshed	York C	199	31
							Port Vale	90	11
Mills Lee	6 2	12 09	F	10 7 70	Mexborough	Stocksbridge PS	Wolverhampton W	25	2
							Derby Co	16	7
							Port Vale	67	21
Musselwhite Paul	6 2	14 04	G	22 12 68	Portsmouth		Portsmouth	—	—
							Scunthorpe U	132	—
							Port Vale	203	—
Naylor Tony	5 7	10 06	F	29 3 67	Manchester	Droylsden	Crewe Alex	122	45
							Port Vale	115	37
O'Reilly Justin	6 0	13 08	F	29 6 73	Derby	Gresley R	Port Vale	—	—
Porter Andy	5 9	12 00	M	17 9 68	Holmes Chapel	Trainee	Port Vale	316	21
Ruscoe Scott*	5 10	11 04	M	15 12 77	Shrewsbury	Stoke C	Port Vale	—	—
Stokes Dean	5 8	11 02	D	23 5 70	Birmingham	Halesowen T	Port Vale	52	—
Talbot Stuart	6 0	13 07	M	14 6 73	Birmingham	Moor Green	Port Vale	56	4
Tankard Allen	5 10	12 10	D	21 5 69	Islington	Trainee	Southampton	5	—
							Wigan Ath	209	4
							Port Vale	131	2
Van Heusden Arjan	6 2	13 12	G	11 12 72	Alphen	Noordwijk	Port Vale	22	—
Walker Ray*	5 11	12 03	M	28 9 63	North Shields	Apprentice	Aston Villa	23	0
							Port Vale (loan)	15	1
							Port Vale	351	33
							Cambridge U (loan)	5	—

Trainees
Boyd, Stephen J; Burns, Liam; Commander, Andrew P; Hancock, Darren K; Humphreys, Jonny J J; Jackson, Leon; Male, Andrew S; McShane, Antony M; O'Callaghan, George; Plant, Robert A; Rochester, Daniel D; Smolenski, Andrew W; Stanbrook, Clive; Williams, Stephen J.

Associated Schoolboys
Blount, Ivan G W; Carrigan, Benjamin D; Donnelly, Paul M; Gardner, Anthony; Hancock, Glynn R; Lightfoot, Philip A; Rowland, Stephen J; Simpson, Benjamin J.

PRESTON NORTH END

Ashcroft Lee	5 10	11 02	F	7 9 72	Preston	Trainee	Preston NE	91	13
							WBA	90	17
							Notts Co (loan)	6	—
							Preston NE	27	8
Atkinson Graeme	5 8	11 05	M	11 11 71	Hull	Trainee	Hull C	149	23
							Preston NE	76	6
Barrick Dean	5 8	12 00	D	30 9 69	Hemsworth	Trainee	Sheffield W	11	2
							Rotherham U	99	7
							Cambridge U	91	3
							Preston NE	76	—
Bryson Ian*	5 11	12 12	M	26 11 62	Kilmarnock		Kilmarnock	215	40
							Sheffield U	155	36
							Barnsley	16	3
							Preston NE	151	19
Cartwright Lee	5 9	11 00	M	19 9 72	Rossendale	Trainee	Preston NE	196	14
Davey Simon	5 10	12 00	M	1 10 70	Swansea	Trainee	Swansea C	49	4
							Carlisle U	105	18
							Preston NE	88	19
Gage Kevin	5 10	12 12	D	21 4 64	Chiswick	Apprentice	Wimbledon	168	15
							Aston Villa	115	8
							Sheffield U	112	7
							Preston NE	23	—
Grant Tony	5 9	11 12	D	20 8 76	Louth	Trainee	Leeds U	—	—
(Transferred to Glenavon, January 1997)							Preston NE	1	—
Gregan Sean	6 1	13 09	D	29 3 74	Cleveland	Trainee	Darlington	136	4
							Preston NE	21	1
Holt Michael	5 10	11 06	F	28 7 77	Burnley	Trainee	Blackburn R	—	—
							Preston NE	19	3
Jackson Michael	5 11	13 10	D	4 12 73	Chester	Trainee	Crewe Alex	5	—
							Bury	125	9
							Preston NE	7	—
Jakub Joe†	5 6	9 06	M	7 12 56	Falkirk	Apprentice	Burnley	42	—
							Bury	265	27
						AZ Alkmaar	Chester C	42	1
							Burnley	163	8
							Chester C	36	—
							Wigan Ath	16	—
							Preston NE	—	—
Kidd Ryan	6 1	13 03	D	6 10 71	Radcliffe	Trainee	Port Vale	1	—
							Preston NE	148	4
Kilbane Kevin	6 0	13 00	M	1 2 77	Preston	Trainee	Preston NE	48	3

Name			Pos	DOB	Birthplace	Previous	Club	Apps	Goals
Lucas David	6 1	13 04	G	23 11 77	Preston		Preston NE	3	—
							Darlington (loan)	6	—
							Darlington (loan)	7	—
							Scunthorpe U (loan)	6	—
McDonald Neil	6 0	13 10	D	2 11 65	Wallsend	Wallsend BC	Newcastle U	180	24
							Everton	90	4
							Oldham Ath	24	1
							Bolton W	4	—
							Preston NE	33	—
McKenna Paul	5 7	11 13	M	20 10 77	Chorley	Trainee	Preston NE	5	1
Mimms Bobby	6 4	14 04	G	12 10 63	York	Halifax T	Rotherham U	83	0
							Everton	29	—
							Notts Co (loan)	2	—
							Sunderland (loan)	4	—
							Blackburn R (loan)	6	—
							Manchester C (loan)	3	—
							Tottenham H	37	—
							Aberdeen (loan)	6	—
							Blackburn R	128	—
							Crystal Palace	1	—
							Preston NE	27	—
Moilanen Teuvo	6 5	13 10	G	12 12 73	Oulu		Ilves	63	—
							Jaro	26	—
							Preston NE	6	—
							Scarborough (loan)	4	—
							Darlington (loan)	16	—
Morgan Mark			M	23 10 78	Belfast	Trainee	Preston NE	—	—
Moyes David	6 1	12 12	D	25 4 63	Glasgow	Drumchapel Amat	Celtic	24	—
							Cambridge U	79	1
							Bristol C	83	6
							Shrewsbury T	96	11
							Dunfermline Ath	105	13
							Hamilton A	5	—
							Preston NE	134	15
Nogan Kurt	5 11	11 11	F	9 9 70	Cardiff	Trainee	Luton T	33	3
							Peterborough U	—	—
							Brighton & HA	97	49
							Burnley	92	33
							Preston NE	7	—
O'Hanlon Kelham	6 1	13 12	G	16 5 62	Saltburn		Middlesbrough	87	—
							Rotherham U	248	—
							Carlisle U	83	—
							Preston NE	23	—
							Dundee U	30	—
							Preston NE	13	—
Rankine Mark	5 10	11 01	D	30 9 69	Doncaster	Trainee	Doncaster R	164	20
							Wolverhampton W	132	1
							Preston NE	23	—
Reeves David	6 0	12 06	F	19 11 67	Birkenhead	Heswall	Sheffield W	17	2
							Scunthorpe U (loan)	4	2
							Scunthorpe U (loan)	6	4
							Burnley (loan)	16	8
							Bolton W	134	29
							Notts Co	13	2
							Carlisle U	127	48
							Preston NE	34	11
Sparrow Paul	6 0	11 00	D	24 3 75	London	Trainee	Crystal Palace	1	—
							Preston NE	19	—
Squires Jamie	6 2	13 03	D	15 11 75	Preston	Trainee	Preston NE	31	—
Sulley Christ	5 8	10 00	D	3 12 59	Camberwell	Apprentice	Chelsea	—	—
							Bournemouth	206	3
							Dundee U	7	—
							Blackburn R	134	3
							Port Vale	40	1
							Preston NE	21	1
Wilcox Russ	6 0	12 12	D	25 3 64	Hemsworth	Apprentice	Doncaster R	1	—
						Frickley Ath	Northampton T	138	9
							Hull C	100	7
							Doncaster R	81	6
							Preston NE	62	1
Wilkinson Steve	5 11	11 11	F	1 9 68	Lincoln	Apprentice	Leicester C	9	1
							Rochdale (loan)	—	—
							Crewe Alex (loan)	5	2
							Mansfield T	232	83
							Preston NE	52	13

Trainees
Barnes, Stephen W; Boase, Marc; Bradford, Scott C; Butler, Carl W; Cliff, Stuart J; Harron, Alexander; Heys, Daniel J; Jones, Darren M; Numberson, Kevin R; Old, Andrew B; Ollerton, Neil; Smith, Andrew P; Smith, Gary A; Southworth, Brian J; Sutton, Christopher W; Turner, John.

Non-Contract
Peters, Gary

Associated Schoolboys
Clarkson, Christian; Maguire, Gary J; O'Neil, John M; Parr, Sean K; Roberts, Karl M; Underwood, Jeffrey H; Whitfield, Richard; Wright, Mark S; Wright, Ronnie M.

Associated Schoolboys who have accepted the club's offer of a Traineeship/Contract
Connolly, James M.

QUEENS PARK RANGERS

Bardsley David	5 10	11 07	D	11 9 64	Manchester	Apprentice	Blackpool	45	—
							Watford	100	7
							Oxford U	74	7
							QPR	241	4
Barker Simon	5 9	11 07	M	4 11 64	Farnworth	Apprentice	Blackburn R	182	35
							QPR	292	30
Brazier Matthew	5 8	11 06	M	2 7 76	Whipps Cross	Trainee	QPR	38	2
Brevett Rufus	5 8	11 04	D	24 9 69	Derby	Trainee	Doncaster R	109	3
							QPR	129	1
Bruce Paul	5 11	12 01	F	18 2 78	London	Trainee	QPR	—	—
Challis Trevor	5 8	11 00	D	23 10 75	Paddington	Trainee	QPR	13	—
Charles Lee	5 11	12 04	F	20 8 71	Hillingdon	Chertsey T	QPR	16	1
							Barnet (loan)	5	—
Dichio Daniele	6 3	12 03	F	19 10 74	Hammersmith	Trainee	QPR	75	20
							Barnet (loan)	9	2
Gallen Kevin	5 11	12 10	F	21 9 75	Hammersmith	Trainee	QPR	69	21
Graham Mark	5 7	10 12	M	24 10 74	Newry	Trainee	QPR	18	0
Graham Richard	5 7	10 00	F	5 8 79	Newry	Trainee	QPR	—	—
Hart Paul			G	16 11 78	London	Trainee	QPR	—	—
Hateley Mark	6 4	12 08	F	7 11 61	Liverpool	Apprentice	Coventry C	93	25
(Transferred to Rangers, March 1997)							Portsmouth	38	22
							AC Milan	66	17
							Monaco	59	22
							Rangers	165	85
							QPR	27	3
							Leeds U (loan)	6	—
							Rangers	4	1
Hurst Richard	6 0	13 00	G	23 12 76	Hammersmith	Trainee	QPR	—	—
Impey Andrew	5 8	11 02	M	13 9 71	Hammersmith	Yeading	QPR	187	13
Langley Richard	5 10	11 04	F	27 12 79	London	Trainee	QPR	—	—
Lopez Rik			F	25 12 79	Northwick Park	Arsenal	QPR	—	—
Lusardi Mario			F	27 9 79	Islington	Trainee	QPR	—	—
Maddix Danny	5 11	11 07	D	11 10 67	Ashford	Apprentice	Tottenham H	—	—
							Southend U (loan)	2	—
							QPR	213	7
Mahoney-Johnson Michael	5 10	12 00	F	6 11 76	Paddington	Trainee	QPR	2	—
							Wycombe W (loan)	4	2
McDonald Alan*	6 2	13 11	D	12 10 63	Belfast	Apprentice	QPR	402	13
							Charlton Ath (loan)	9	—
Morrow Steve	6 0	11 03	D	2 7 70	Bangor	Trainee	Arsenal	62	1
							Reading (loan)	10	—
							Watford (loan)	8	—
							Reading (loan)	3	—
							Barnet (loan)	1	—
							QPR	5	1
Murray Frazer	5 8	10 06	M	24 9 79	Paisley	Trainee	QPR	—	—
Murray Paul	5 8	10 05	M	31 8 76	Carlisle	Trainee	Carlisle U	41	1
							QPR	33	5
Owen Karl	5 11	12 06	D	12 10 79	Coventry	Trainee	QPR	—	—
Peacock Gavin	5 8	11 08	M	18 11 67	Eltham	Apprentice	QPR	17	1
							Gillingham	70	11
							Bournemouth	56	8
							Newcastle U	105	35
							Chelsea	103	17
							QPR	27	5
Perry Mark	5 10	11 03	D	19 10 78	Perivale	Trainee	QPR	2	1
Plummer Chris	6 2	12 09	D	12 10 76	Isleworth	Trainee	QPR	6	—
Purser Wayne	5 10	12 00	F	13 4 80	Basildon	Trainee	QPR	—	—
Quashie Nigel	5 9	11 00	M	20 7 78	Nunhead	Trainee	QPR	24	0
Ready Karl	6 1	13 03	D	14 8 72	Neath	Trainee	QPR	90	3
Roberts Tony	6 0	13 11	G	4 8 69	Bangor	Trainee	QPR	112	—

Sharp Lee‡	6 2	14 00	G	18 12 76	Lincoln	Lincoln U	QPR	—	—
Sinclair Trevor	5 10	12 05	F	2 3 73	Dulwich	Trainee	Blackpool	112	15
							QPR	141	13
Slade Steve	6 0	10 13	F	6 10 75	Hackney	Trainee	Tottenham H	5	—
							QPR	17	4
							Brentford (loan)	4	—
Sommer Jurgen	6 5	15 12	G	27 2 69	New York		Luton T	82	—
							Brighton & HA (loan)	1	—
							Torquay U (loan)	10	—
							QPR	66	—
Spencer John	5 7	11 05	F	11 9 70	Glasgow	Rangers BC	Rangers	13	2
							Morton (loan)	4	1
							Chelsea	103	36
							QPR	25	17
Whittle David			D	2 12 78	Waterford	Trainee	QPR	—	—
Yates Steve	5 10	12 02	D	29 1 70	Bristol	Trainee	Bristol R	197	—
							QPR	98	2

Trainees
Ashton, Lee; Currie, Michael J; Franklin, Damien M; Lione, Angelo M; O'Connor, Sean D; Roostan, Benjamin L; Spiller, Richard B.

Associated Schoolboys
Browne, Ricky D; Burgess, Oliver D; Campbell, Dudley J; Cochrane, Justin V; D'Austin, Ryan A; Dick, Alex R; Duncan, Lyndon E; Mills, Christopher M; Pacquette, Richard; Patterson, Simon G; Rustem, Adam R; Shelton, Richard; Sofo-Yarabi, Farouk; White, Liam J C; Wright, Daniel J; Yhdego, Esayes Y.

Associated Schoolboys who have accepted the club's offer of a Traineeship/Contract
Anderson, Peter M; Brown, Carlos D; Bubb, Alvin R; Jeanne, Leon; Norman, Brian P.

READING

Bass David*	5 11	12 07	M	29 11 74	Frimley	Trainee	Reading	11	—
Bernal Andy	5 10	12 05	D	16 7 66	Canberra	Sporting Gijon	Ipswich T	9	—
						Sydney Olympic	Reading	108	2
Bibbo Sal	6 2	14 00	G	24 8 74	Basingstoke	Bournemouth	Sheffield U	—	—
							Chesterfield (loan)	1	—
							Reading	5	—
Bodin Paul	6 0	12 06	D	13 9 64	Cardiff	Chelsea	Newport Co	—	—
							Cardiff C	57	3
						Bath C	Newport Co	6	1
							Swindon T	93	9
							Crystal Palace	9	—
							Newcastle U (loan)	6	—
							Swindon T	146	28
							Reading	37	1
Booty Martyn	5 8	11 02	D	30 5 71	Kirby Muxloe	Trainee	Coventry C	5	—
							Crewe Alex	96	5
							Reading	31	1
Carey Alan‡	5 7	10 10	D	21 8 75	Greenwich	Trainee	Reading	3	—
Caskey Darren	5 8	11 09	M	21 8 74	Basildon	Trainee	Tottenham H	32	4
							Watford (loan)	6	1
							Reading	50	2
Freeman Andy	5 7	9 04	F	8 9 77	Reading	Crystal Palace	Reading	1	—
Garrity James‡			M	7 5 78	Newcastle	Newcastle U	Reading	—	—
Glasgow Byron	5 6	10 11	M	18 2 79	London	Trainee	Reading	4	—
Gooding Mick*	5 7	11 04	M	12 4 59	Newcastle	Bishop Auckland	Rotherham U	102	10
							Chesterfield	12	—
							Rotherham U	156	33
							Peterborough U	47	21
							Wolverhampton W	44	4
							Reading	314	26
Hammond Nicky	6 0	11 13	G	7 9 67	Hornchurch	Apprentice	Arsenal	—	—
							Bristol R (loan)	3	—
							Peterborough U (loan)	—	—
							Aberdeen (loan)	—	—
							Swindon T	67	—
							Plymouth Arg	4	—
							Reading	6	—
Holsgrove Paul	6 2	12 11	F	26 8 69	Wellington	Trainee	Aldershot	3	—
							Wimbledon (loan)	—	—
							WBA (loan)	—	—
						Wokingham T	Luton T	2	—
						Heracles	Millwall	11	—
							Reading	68	6

Name						Birthplace	Source	Club		
Hopkins Jeff*	6 0	12 11	D	14 4 64		Swansea	Apprentice	Fulham	219	4
								Crystal Palace	70	2
								Plymouth Arg (loan)	8	—
								Bristol R	6	—
								Reading	131	3
Hunter Barry	6 3	13 02	D	18 11 68		Coleraine	Crusaders	Wrexham	91	4
								Reading	27	2
Lambert James	5 7	11 02	F	14 9 73		Henley	School	Reading	90	13
Lovell Stuart	5 10	12 03	M	9 1 72		Sydney	Trainee	Reading	212	57
Mautone Steve	6 2	13 03	G	10 8 70		Myrtleford	Canberra Cosmos	West Ham U	1	—
								Crewe Alex (loan)	3	—
								Reading	15	—
McPherson Keith	5 10	12 00	D	11 9 63		Greenwich	Apprentice	West Ham U	1	—
								Cambridge U (loan)	11	1
								Northampton T	182	8
								Reading	232	8
Meaker Michael	5 11	12 00	M	18 8 71		Greenford	Trainee	QPR	34	1
								Plymouth Arg (loan)	4	—
								Reading	46	1
Mikhailov Bobby‡	6 1	12 04	G	12 2 63		Bulgaria	Botev Plovdiv	Reading	24	—
Morley Trevor	5 11	12 01	F	20 3 61		Nottingham	Nuneaton Bor	Northampton T	107	39
								Manchester C	72	18
								West Ham U	81	24
								Brann	8	4
								West Ham U	41	20
								Brann	6	1
								West Ham U	56	13
								Brann	7	4
								Reading	54	26
Nogan Lee	5 8	11 01	F	21 5 69		Cardiff	Apprentice	Oxford U	64	10
								Brentford (loan)	11	2
								Southend U (loan)	6	1
								Watford	105	26
								Southend U (loan)	5	—
								Reading	91	26
								Notts Co (loan)	6	—
Parkinson Phil	6 0	12 09	M	1 12 67		Chorley	Apprentice	Southampton	—	—
								Bury	145	5
								Reading	178	8
Quinn Jimmy*	6 1	13 10	F	18 11 59		Belfast	Oswestry T	Swindon T	49	10
								Blackburn R	71	17
								Swindon T	64	30
								Leicester C	31	6
								Bradford C	35	14
								West Ham U	47	18
								Bournemouth	43	19
								Reading	182	71
Roach Neville	5 10	11 00	F	29 9 78		Reading	Trainee	Reading	3	1
Robertson Andrew*	5 11	11 02	M	7 11 77		Wokingham	Oxford U	Reading	—	—
Sanders Guy*	6 0	11 04	D	18 2 78		Rugby	Trainee	Reading	—	—
Simpson Derek‡	5 10	10 09	M	23 12 78		Lanark	Trainee	Reading	—	—
Smith Ben	5 9	11 09	M	23 11 78		Chelmsford	Arsenal	Reading	1	—
Swales Steve	5 8	10 03	D	26 12 73		Whitby	Trainee	Scarborough	54	1
								Reading	12	—
Thorp Michael	6 0	11 07	D	5 12 75		Wallington	Trainee	Reading	2	—
Wdowczyk Dariusz	5 11	11 11	D	21 9 62		Warsaw	Legia Warsaw	Celtic	116	4
								Reading	76	—
Williams Martin	5 9	11 12	F	12 7 73		Luton	Leicester C	Luton T	40	2
								Colchester U (loan)	3	—
								Reading	44	4

Trainees
Bicknell, Matthew B; Bristow, Jason P; Curtis, Richard S; Dowling, Daniel K; Dowling, Luke J; Fenner, Greg A; Forbes, Andrew J; Green, Stephen J; Harrison, Ross; Holloway, Neil S; Lyttle, Clive A; May, Steven J; Norris, Jordan R; Rooke, Maxwell J M; Woodley, Nathan.

Associated Schoolboys
Allaway, Shaun.

ROCHDALE

Bailey Mark	5 9	10 12	M	12 8 76	Stoke	Trainee	Stoke C	—	—
							Rochdale	15	—
Barlow Neil*	5 11	11 07	D	24 3 78	Bury	Trainee	Rochdale	2	—
Bayliss David	6 0	11 01	D	8 6 76	Liverpool	Trainee	Rochdale	53	0
Cecere Mike‡	6 0	12 07	F	4 1 68	Chester	Apprentice	Oldham Ath	52	8
							Huddersfield T	54	8
							Stockport Co (loan)	1	—
							Walsall	112	32
							Exeter C	43	11
							Rochdale	4	1
Deary John*	5 10	12 07	M	18 10 62	Ormskirk	Apprentice	Blackpool	303	43
							Burnley	215	23
							Rochdale	91	10
Dowell Wayne*	5 10	11 13	D	28 12 73	Co Durham	Trainee	Burnley	6	—
							Carlisle U (loan)	7	—
							Rochdale	7	—
Farrell Andy	5 11	12 00	D	7 10 65	Colchester	School	Colchester U	105	5
							Burnley	257	19
							Wigan Ath	54	1
							Rochdale	40	2
Fensome Andy	5 8	11 09	D	18 2 69	Northampton	Trainee	Norwich C	—	—
							Newcastle U (loan)	—	—
							Cambridge U	126	1
							Preston NE	93	1
							Rochdale	40	—
Formby Kevin*	5 10	11 09	D	22 7 71	Ormskirk	Burscough	Rochdale	67	1
Gouck Andy	5 10	12 12	M	8 6 72	Blackpool	Trainee	Blackpool	148	12
							Rochdale	28	3
Gray Ian	6 2	13 00	G	25 2 75	Manchester	Trainee	Oldham Ath	—	—
							Rochdale (loan)	12	—
							Rochdale	66	—
Gray Kevin†			M	5 4 78	Manchester	Stockport Co	Rochdale	—	—
Hill Keith	6 0	12 04	D	17 5 69	Bolton	Apprentice	Blackburn R	96	3
							Plymouth Arg	123	2
							Rochdale	43	3
Johnson Alan	6 0	14 00	D	19 2 71	Ince	Trainee	Wigan Ath	180	13
							Lincoln C	63	—
							Preston NE (loan)	2	—
							Rochdale	46	4
Lancaster David‡	6 3	14 03	F	8 9 61	Preston	Colne Dynamoes	Blackpool	8	1
							Chesterfield (loan)	12	4
							Chesterfield	69	16
							Rochdale	40	14
							Bury	10	1
							Rochdale (loan)	14	2
							Rochdale	6	—
Leonard Mark	6 1	13 02	F	27 9 62	St Helens	Witton Alb	Everton	—	—
							Tranmere R (loan)	7	—
							Crewe Alex	54	15
							Stockport Co	73	24
							Bradford C	157	29
							Rochdale	9	1
							Preston NE	22	1
							Chester C	32	8
							Wigan Ath	64	12
							Rochdale	39	4
Lyons Paul‡	5 6	9 0	M	24 6 77	Leigh	Manchester U	Rochdale	3	—
Martin Dean‡	5 11	11 00	M	9 9 67	Halifax	Apprentice	Halifax T	153	7
							Scunthorpe U	106	7
							Rochdale	53	—
Martin Lee†	6 0	13 00	G	9 9 68	Huddersfield	Trainee	Huddersfield T	54	—
							Blackpool	98	—
							Bradford C (loan)	—	—
							Rochdale	—	—
Painter Robbie	5 10	12 02	M	26 1 71	Ince	Trainee	Chester C	84	8
							Maidstone U	30	5
							Burnley	26	2
							Darlington	115	28
							Rochdale	27	7
Price James*	5 9	11 00	D	1 2 78	Preston	Trainee	Rochdale	3	—
Robson Glen	5 10	10 10	F	25 9 77	Sunderland	Murton	Rochdale	3	—
Russell Alex	5 10	11 00	M	17 3 73	Crosby	Burscough	Rochdale	71	10

Stuart Mark	5 9	11 09	D	15 12 66	Hammersmith	QPR	Charlton Ath	107	28
							Plymouth Arg	57	11
							Ipswich T (loan)	5	2
							Bradford C	29	5
							Huddersfield T	15	3
							Rochdale	138	35
Taylor Jamie*	5 8	10 07	F	11 1 77	Bury	Trainee	Rochdale	36	4
Thackeray Andy*	5 9	11 00	M	13 2 68	Huddersfield	School	Manchester C	—	—
							Huddersfield T	2	—
							Newport Co	54	4
							Wrexham	152	14
							Rochdale	165	13
Thompson David*	5 10	13 00	D	27 5 62	Manchester	N Withington	Rochdale	155	13
							Manchester U (loan)	—	—
							Notts Co	55	8
							Wigan Ath	108	14
							Preston NE	46	4
							Chester C	80	9
							Rochdale	111	11
Whitehall Steve	5 11	11 07	F	8 12 66	Bromborough	Southport	Rochdale	238	75

Trainees
Attwood, Wayne M; Brannelly, Ashley C; Edghill, Philip A; Gray, David; Hill, Paul S; Lambert, Dale L; Litster, Stuart P; Matthews, Lee A; Ogden, John; Stevens, David G; Swettenham, Andrew B; Taylor, Neil; Thompson, Roy A; Wilkinson, Michael W.

Non-Contract
Irwin, Nicholas J.

Associated Schoolboys
Bell, Colin; Fielding, David P; Gilks, Daniel; O'Reilly, Gareth; Rudd, Paul G; Westmoreland, Darren P.

Associated Schoolboys who have accepted the club's offer of a Traineeship/Contract
Bywater, Stephen M; Hicks, Graham; Loft, Paul; Taylor, Carl D.

ROTHERHAM UNITED

Ashcroft Richard‡			M	3 10 77	Manchester	Trainee	Rotherham U	—	—
Bain Kevin	5 11	12 05	M	19 9 72	Kirkcaldy	Abbey Star	Dundee	74	2
							Rotherham U	12	—
Barnes Phil§			G			Trainee	Rotherham U	2	—
Berry Trevor	5 6	11 00	M	1 8 74	Haslemere	Bournemouth	Aston Villa	—	—
							Rotherham U	66	11
Blades Paul‡	6 0	12 00	D	5 1 65	Peterborough	Apprentice	Derby Co	166	1
							Norwich C	47	—
							Wolverhampton W	107	2
							Rotherham U	43	2
Bowman Rob	6 0	12 04	D	21 11 75	Durham	Trainee	Leeds U	7	—
							Rotherham U	13	—
Bowyer Gary*	6 1	13 04	M	22 6 71	Manchester		Hereford U	14	2
							Nottingham F	—	—
							Rotherham U	38	2
Breckin Ian	5 11	11 07	D	24 2 75	Rotherham	Trainee	Rotherham U	132	6
Cherry Steve‡	6 1	13 00	G	5 8 60	Nottingham	Apprentice	Derby Co	77	0
							Port Vale (loan)	4	—
							Walsall	71	—
							Plymouth Arg	73	—
							Chesterfield (loan)	10	—
							Notts Co	266	—
							Watford	4	—
							Plymouth Arg (loan)	16	—
							Rotherham U	20	—
Davis Craig	6 2	12 00	G	12 10 77	Rotherham	Trainee	Rotherham U	—	—
Dillon Paul	5 9	10 11	D	22 10 78	Limerick	Trainee	Rotherham U	13	1
Dobbin Jim*	5 9	11 00	M	17 9 63	Dunfermline	Whitburn BC	Celtic	2	—
							Motherwell (loan)	2	—
							Doncaster R	64	13
							Barnsley	129	12
							Grimsby T	164	21
							Rotherham U	19	—
Druce Mark	6 0	12 07	F	3 3 74	Oxford	Trainee	Oxford U	52	4
							Rotherham U	20	4
Fearon Dean‡	6 1	13 12	D	9 1 76	Barnsley	Schoolboy	Barnsley	—	—
							Rotherham U	—	—
Garner Darren	5 9	12 07	M	10 12 71	Plymouth	Trainee	Plymouth Arg	27	1
							Dorchester T	Rotherham U	61	3

Gayle Brian*	6 1	13 07	D	6 3 65	Kingston		Wimbledon	83	3
							Manchester C	55	3
							Ipswich T	58	4
							Sheffield U	117	9
							Exeter C	10	—
							Rotherham U	20	—
							Bristol R (loan)	7	—
Glover Lee	5 11	11 09	F	24 4 70	Kettering	Trainee	Nottingham F	76	9
							Leicester C (loan)	5	1
							Barnsley (loan)	8	—
							Luton T (loan)	1	—
							Port Vale	52	7
							Rotherham U	22	1
							Huddersfield T (loan)	11	—
Goodwin Shaun*	5 8	11 04	M	14 4 69	Rotherham	Trainee	Rotherham U	267	37
Hayward Andy	6 0	11 00	M	21 6 70	Barnsley	Frickley Ath	Rotherham U	107	12
Hurst Paul	5 4	9 00	D	25 9 74	Sheffield	Trainee	Rotherham U	87	4
James Martin‡	5 10	11 10	M	18 5 71	Formby	Trainee	Preston NE	98	11
							Stockport Co	32	—
							Rotherham U	44	—
Jean Earl			F	9 10 71	St Lucia	Coimbra	Ipswich T	1	—
							Rotherham U	18	6
McDougald Junior	5 9	11 00	F	12 1 75	Big Spring	Trainee	Tottenham H	—	—
							Brighton & HA	78	14
							Chesterfield (loan)	9	3
							Rotherham U	18	2
McGlashan John*	6 2	13 00	M	3 6 67	Dundee	Dundee Violet	Montrose	68	11
							Millwall	16	—
							Cambridge U (loan)	1	—
							Fulham (loan)	5	1
							Peterborough U	46	3
							Rotherham U	74	5
McIntosh Andrew‡			M	12 5 78	Salford	Trainee	Rotherham U	—	—
McKenzie Robert§	5 9	11 05	M	22 3 79	Hexham	Trainee	Rotherham U	11	0
Monington Mark	6 1	14 02	D	21 10 70	Bilsthorpe	School	Burnley	84	5
							Rotherham U	64	2
Pell Robert§	6 0	13 01	D	5 2 79	Leeds	Trainee	Rotherham U	2	—
Richardson Neil*	6 0	13 00	D	3 3 68	Sunderland	Brandon U	Rotherham U	141	7
							Exeter C (loan)	14	—
Roscoe Andy	5 10	11 08	D	4 6 73	Liverpool	Trainee	Liverpool	—	—
							Bolton W	3	—
							Rotherham U	119	6
Slawson Steve‡	6 2	11 08	M	13 11 72	Hucknall	Trainee	Notts Co	38	4
							Burnley (loan)	5	2
							Shrewsbury T (loan)	6	—
							Mansfield T	29	5
							Rotherham U	5	—
Smith Scott‡	5 8	11 00	D	6 3 75	Christchurch	Trainee	Rotherham U	36	—
Viljoen Nik‡	5 10	12 00	F	3 12 76	New Zealand	Trainee	Rotherham U	8	2

Trainees
Bagshaw, Neil D; Barnes, Philip K; Barton, Warren L; Gordon, James D; Hall, Matthew D; Howard, Daniel R; Hudson, Daniel R; Ingledow, Jamie G; Levers, Roger; McKenzie, Robert A; Otter, Simon A; Pell, Robert A; Sedgwick, Christopher E; Smith, Jamie M; Spiby, Dale K; Trower, Kevin J; Welsh, Ewan J.

Associated Schoolboys
Alabi, Stephen; Ashton, Richard J; Barraclough, Simon D; Beggs, John A; Boyd, Darren; Buck, Antony E D; Capill, Stephen L; Colliver, James L; Cunningham, David G F; Foster, James W; Haythorne, Craig A; Hensman, Matthew D; Hirst, Nicky C; Holmes, Ian; Holyer, Ian D; Johnson, Mark I; Kangley, Philip; Ollivant, Glenn; Phillips, Andrew N; Sandland, Guy; Sherratt, Christopher R; Swallow, Ainsley; Wilkinson, Matthew D; Winder, Nathan J.

Associated Schoolboys who have accepted the club's offer of a Traineeship/Contract
Allen, Paul C; Beesley, Darren; Lax, Ryan A; Merris, David A; Roden, Craig.

SCARBOROUGH

Bazelya Eammon	5 7	9 12	M	25 10 78	Birmingham	Trainee	Scarborough	—	—
Bennett Gary	6 1	13 01	D	4 12 61	Manchester	Amateur	Manchester C	—	—
							Cardiff C	87	11
							Sunderland	369	23
							Carlisle U	26	5
							Scarborough	46	9
Bochenski Simon	5 10	11 13	F	6 12 75	Worksop	Trainee	Barnsley	1	—
							Scarborough	19	1
Brodie Steve	5 8	10 10	F	14 1 73	Sunderland	Trainee	Sunderland	12	—
							Doncaster R (loan)	5	1
							Scarborough	24	5

Name	Ht	Wt	Pos	DOB	Birthplace	Source	Club	Apps	Gls
Brooke David*	5 8	11 02	M	23 11 75	Barnsley	Trainee	Barnsley	—	—
							Scarborough	34	2
Burridge John†	5 11	13 03	G	3 12 51	Workington	Apprentice	Workington	27	—
							Blackpool	134	—
							Aston Villa	65	—
							Southend U (loan)	6	—
							Crystal Palace	88	—
							QPR	39	—
							Wolverhampton W	74	—
							Derby Co (loan)	6	—
							Sheffield U	109	—
							Southampton	62	—
							Newcastle U	67	—
							Hibernian	65	—
							Newcastle U	—	—
							Scarborough	3	—
							Lincoln C	4	—
							Aberdeen	3	—
							Newcastle U	—	—
							Dumbarton	3	—
							Falkirk	3	—
							Manchester C	4	—
							Notts Co	—	—
							Darlington	3	—
							Grimsby T	—	—
							Northampton T	—	—
						Purfleet	Q of S	6	—
							Scarborough	—	—
Currie David‡	5 11	12 10	F	27 11 62	Stockton	Local	Middlesbrough	113	31
							Darlington	76	33
							Barnsley	80	30
							Nottingham F	8	1
							Oldham Ath	31	3
							Barnsley	75	12
							Rotherham U (loan)	5	2
							Huddersfield T (loan)	7	1
							Carlisle U	89	14
							Scarborough	16	6
Daws Tony‡	5 8	11 10	F	10 9 66	Sheffield	Apprentice	Notts Co	8	1
							Sheffield U	11	3
							Scunthorpe U	183	63
							Grimsby T	16	1
							Lincoln C	51	13
							Scarborough	6	—
Hanby Robert‡	5 8	11 09	D	24 12 74	Pontefract	Trainee	Barnsley	—	—
							Scarborough	4	—
Hicks Stuart‡	6 1	13 03	D	30 5 67	Peterborough	Wisbech T	Colchester U	64	—
							Scunthorpe U	67	1
							Doncaster R	36	—
							Huddersfield T	22	1
							Preston NE	12	—
							Scarborough	85	2
Ironside Ian‡	6 2	13 10	G	8 3 64	Sheffield	N Ferriby U	Scarborough	88	—
							Middlesbrough	13	—
							Scarborough (loan)	7	—
							Stockport Co	19	—
							Scarborough	88	—
Kay John	5 10	11 05	D	29 1 64	Sunderland	Apprentice	Arsenal	14	—
							Wimbledon	63	2
							Middlesbrough (loan)	8	—
							Sunderland	199	—
							Shrewsbury T (loan)	7	—
							Preston NE	7	—
							Scarborough	34	—
Macauley Dean*			D	20 4 78	Scarborough	Trainee	Scarborough	—	—
Martin Kevin	6 0	12 08	G	22 6 76	Bromsgrove	Trainee	Scarborough	6	—
McElhatton Mike	6 1	13 00	D	16 4 75	Co. Kerry	Trainee	Bournemouth	42	2
							Scarborough	28	1
Mitchell Jamie	5 7	10 01	M	6 11 76	Glasgow	Trainee	Norwich C	—	—
							Scarborough	43	7
Mowbray Darren‡			D	24 1 78	Middlesbrough	Middlesbrough	Scarborough	3	—
Rimmer Neill†	5 6	10 05	M	13 11 67	Liverpool	Apprentice	Everton	1	—
							Ipswich T	22	3
							Wigan Ath	190	10
							Scarborough	—	—
Rockett Jason	5 11	11 05	D	26 9 69	London		Rotherham U	—	—
							Scarborough	140	9
Russell Matthew	5 11	11 05	M	17 1 78	Dewsbury	Trainee	Scarborough	5	—

							Club	Apps	Gls
Sutherland Colin	6 0	11 05	D	15 3 75	Glasgow	Kilpatrick Juve	Clydebank	35	2
							Scarborough	21	—
Wells Mark*	5 8	11 02	M	17 10 71	Leicester	Trainee	Notts Co	2	—
							Huddersfield T	23	4
							Scarborough	62	3
Williams Andy†	6 0	11 10	M	19 7 62	Birmingham	Solihull Bor	Coventry C	9	—
							Rotherham U	87	13
							Leeds U	46	3
							Port Vale (loan)	5	—
							Notts Co	39	2
							Huddersfield T (loan)	6	—
							Rotherham U	51	2
							Hull C	34	—
							Scarborough	1	—
Williams Gareth	5 10	12 01	F	12 3 67	Isle of Wight	Gosport Bor	Aston Villa	12	—
							Barnsley	34	6
							Hull C (loan)	4	—
							Hull C (loan)	16	2
							Bournemouth	1	—
							Northampton T	50	1
							Scarborough	45	10
Worrall Ben	5 6	9 11	M	7 12 75	Swindon	Trainee	Swindon T	3	—
							Scarborough	15	1

Trainees
Bradley, Paul S; Carr, Graeme; Connor, Joseph P; Gamble, Crawford S; Hopps, Paul M; Jackson, Richard; Lee, Mark; Lowery, Mark; McNaughton, Michael I; Radigan, Neil; Stancliffe, Paul J.

Associated Schoolboys who have accepted the club's offer of a Traineeship/Contract
Grant, Leigh.

SCUNTHORPE UNITED

							Club	Apps	Gls
Borland John*	5 8	11 08	M	28 1 77	Lancaster	Trainee	Burnley	1	—
							Scunthorpe U	2	—
Bradley Russell‡	6 2	13 00	D	28 3 66	Birmingham	Dudley T	Nottingham F	—	—
							Hereford U (loan)	12	1
							Hereford U	77	3
							Halifax T	56	3
							Scunthorpe U	119	5
							Hartlepool U (loan)	12	1
Calvo-Garcia Alexander	5 11	11 08	M	1 1 72	Ordizia	Eibar	Scunthorpe U	13	1
Clarke Tim	6 4	15 07	G	19 9 68	Stourbridge	Halesowen T	Coventry C	—	—
							Huddersfield T	70	—
							Rochdale (loan)	2	—
							Shrewsbury T	31	—
					Witton Alb	York C	17	—
							Scunthorpe U	15	—
D'Auria David	5 8	11 09	M	26 3 70	Swansea	Trainee	Swansea C	45	6
						Barry T	Scarborough	52	8
							Scunthorpe U	66	8
Eyre John	5 11	12 06	F	9 10 74	Humberside	Trainee	Oldham Ath	10	1
							Scunthorpe U (loan)	9	8
							Scunthorpe U	81	18
Farrelly Stephen†	6 5	15 07	G	27 3 65	Liverpool	Macclesfield T	Rotherham U	7	—
							Scunthorpe U	—	—
Forrester Jamie	5 6	10 04	F	1 11 74	Bradford	Auxerre	Leeds U	9	—
							Southend U (loan)	5	—
							Grimsby T (loan)	9	1
							Grimsby T	41	6
							Scunthorpe U	10	6
Francis John‡	5 8	12 13	F	12 11 63	Dewsbury	Emley	Halifax T	4	—
							Sheffield U	42	6
							Burnley	101	26
							Cambridge U	29	3
							Burnley	76	10
							Scunthorpe U	5	—
Gavin Mark	5 9	11 00	M	10 12 63	Bailleston	Apprentice	Leeds U	30	3
							Hartlepool U (loan)	7	—
							Carlisle U	13	1
							Bolton W	49	3
							Rochdale	23	6
							Hearts	9	—
							Bristol C	69	6
							Watford	13	—
							Bristol C	41	2
							Exeter C	77	4
							Scunthorpe U	11	—
Hope Chris	6 1	12 07	D	14 11 72	Sheffield	Darlington	Nottingham F	—	—
							Scunthorpe U	151	6
Housham Steven	5 10	12 07	D	24 2 76	Gainsborough T	Trainee	Scunthorpe U	66	3

Jackson Kirk*	6 0	12 00	F	16 10 76	Barnsley	Trainee	Sheffield W	—	—
							Scunthorpe U	4	1
Knill Alan*	6 3	13 04	D	8 10 64	Slough	Apprentice	Southampton	—	—
							Halifax T	118	6
							Swansea C	89	3
							Bury	144	8
							Cardiff C (loan)	4	—
							Scunthorpe U	131	8
Laws Brian†	5 10	11 00	D	14 10 61	Wallsend	Apprentice	Burnley	125	12
							Huddersfield T	56	1
							Middlesbrough	107	12
							Nottingham F	147	4
							Grimsby T	46	2
							Darlington	10	—
							Scunthorpe U	4	—
McAuley Sean	5 11	11 13	D	23 6 72	Sheffield	Trainee	Manchester U	—	—
							St Johnstone	62	—
							Chesterfield (loan)	1	1
							Hartlepool U	84	1
							Scunthorpe U	9	—
Moss David	6 2	13 03	F	15 11 68	Doncaster	Boston U	Doncaster R	18	5
(Transferred to Partick T, September 1996)							Chesterfield	71	16
							Scunthorpe U	4	—
Murfin Andrew‡	5 10	10 07	D	26 11 77	Doncaster		Scunthorpe U	1	—
Paterson Jamie	5 3	10 02	F	26 4 73	Dumfries	Trainee	Halifax T	86	18
							Falkirk	4	—
							Scunthorpe U	55	2
Samways Mark*	6 2	14 00	G	11 11 68	Doncaster	Trainee	Doncaster R	121	—
							Scunthorpe U (loan)	8	—
							Scunthorpe U	172	—
							York C (loan)	—	—
Sertori Mark	6 1	14 00	M	1 9 67	Manchester		Stockport Co	4	—
							Lincoln C	50	9
							Wrexham	110	3
							Bury	13	1
							Scunthorpe U	42	1
Turnbull Lee‡	6 0	12 09	M	27 9 67	Stockton	Local	Middlesbrough	16	4
							Aston Villa	—	—
							Doncaster R	123	21
							Chesterfield	87	26
							Doncaster R	11	1
							Wycombe W	11	1
							Scunthorpe U (loan)	10	3
							Scunthorpe U	37	4
Walker Justin	5 10	12 12	M	6 9 75	Nottingham	Trainee	Nottingham F	—	—
							Scunthorpe U (loan)	9	—
							Scunthorpe U	9	—
Walsh Michael	5 11	12 09	D	5 8 77	Rotherham	Trainee	Scunthorpe U	64	—
Wilson Paul*	5 10	12 00	D	2 8 68	Bradford	Trainee	Huddersfield T	15	0
							Norwich C	—	—
							Northampton T	141	6
							Halifax T	45	7
							Burnley	31	—
							York C	22	—
							Scunthorpe U	77	2
							Cambridge U (loan)	7	—
Wilson Paul D†			D	16 11 60	Doncaster		Scunthorpe U	1	—
Ziccardi Mario†	6 2	12 02	G	1 12 77	Aylesbury	Trainee	Scunthorpe U	—	—

Trainees
Edmond, Christopher; Handley, Karl G; Hooley, Gareth R; Kitching, Daniel; McCormack, Steven R; Mitchell, Barry S; Nottingham, Steven E; Page, Brian J; Render, Craig; Serrant, Wesley P; Walton, Paul J.

Non-Contract
Adkins, Nigel H; Laws, Brian; Lillis, Mark A; Wilson, Paul D.

Associated Schoolboys
Anderson, Mark J; Doyle, Philip; Sparrow, Matthew.

SHEFFIELD UNITED

Beard Mark	5 10	11 04	D	8 10 74	Roehampton	Trainee	Millwall	45	2
							Sheffield U	36	—
Bettney Chris	5 10	10 10	F	27 10 77	Chesterfield	Trainee	Sheffield U	1	—
Dyer Liam*	5 11	10 03	D	2 5 78	Doncaster	Trainee	Sheffield U	—	—
Ebbrell John	5 10	11 11	M	1 10 69	Bromborough		Everton	217	13
							Sheffield U	1	—

Name							Club	Apps	Gls
Fjortoft Jan-Aage	6 3	14 03	F	10 1 67	Aaesund		Hamar	22	10
							Lillestrom	35	20
							Rapid Vienna	128	62
							Swindon T	72	28
							Middlesbrough	41	9
							Sheffield U	17	10
Hartfield Charlie*	6 0	13 08	M	4 9 71	London	Trainee	Arsenal	—	—
							Sheffield U	56	1
							Fulham (loan)	2	—
Hawes Steve	5 8	11 11	M	17 7 78	High Wycombe	Trainee	Sheffield U	4	—
Henry Nick	5 10	10 12	M	21 2 69	Liverpool	Trainee	Oldham Ath	273	19
							Sheffield U	9	—
Heritage Paul	6 2	12 11	G	17 4 79	Sheffield	Trainee	Sheffield U	—	—
Hocking Matthew	5 11	11 05	D	30 1 78	Boston	Trainee	Sheffield U	—	—
Holdsworth David	6 0	12 10	D	8 11 68	Walthamstow	Trainee	Watford	258	10
							Sheffield U	37	1
Hutchison Don	6 1	11 11	M	9 5 71	Gateshead	Trainee	Hartlepool U	24	2
							Liverpool	45	7
							West Ham U	35	11
							Sheffield U	60	5
Katchuro Petr	6 0	12 06	F	2 8 72	Minsk		Dynamo 93	15	7
							Dynamo Minsk	60	52
							Sheffield U	40	12
Kelly Alan	6 3	14 02	G	11 8 68	Preston	Trainee	Preston NE	142	—
							Sheffield U	175	—
Key Lance*	6 3	15 00	G	13 5 68	Kettering	Histon	Sheffield W	—	—
							York C (loan)	—	—
							Oldham Ath (loan)	2	—
							Portsmouth (loan)	—	—
							Oxford U (loan)	6	—
							Lincoln C (loan)	5	—
							Hartlepool U (loan)	1	—
							Rochdale (loan)	14	—
							Dundee U	4	—
							Sheffield U	—	—
Nilsen Roger	5 11	11 13	D	8 8 69	Tromso	Viking Stavanger	Sheffield U	127	—
Patterson Mark	5 8	11 12	M	24 5 65	Darwen	Apprentice	Blackburn R	101	20
							Preston NE	55	19
							Bury	42	10
							Bolton W	169	11
							Sheffield U	56	3
							Southend U (loan)	4	—
Quinn Wayne	5 10	11 11	M	19 11 76	Truro		Sheffield U	—	—
Reed John*	5 9	12 04	M	27 8 72	Rotherham	Trainee	Sheffield U	15	2
							Scarborough (loan)	14	6
							Scarborough (loan)	6	—
							Darlington (loan)	10	2
							Mansfield T (loan)	13	2
Sandford Lee	6 0	13 07	D	22 4 68	Basingstoke	Apprentice	Portsmouth	72	1
							Stoke C	258	8
							Sheffield U	30	2
Scott Andy	6 1	11 09	F	2 8 72	Epsom	Sutton U	Sheffield U	69	6
							Chesterfield (loan)	5	3
							Bury (loan)	8	—
Short Chris	5 10	12 03	D	9 5 70	Munster	Pickering T	Scarborough	43	1
							Manchester U (loan)	—	—
							Notts Co	94	2
							Huddersfield T (loan)	6	—
							Sheffield U	39	—
Spackman Nigel	6 1	13 03	M	2 12 60	Romsey	Andover	Bournemouth	119	10
							Chelsea	141	12
							Liverpool	51	—
							QPR	29	1
							Rangers	100	1
							Chelsea	67	—
							Sheffield U	23	—
Starbuck Phil*	5 11	13 05	F	24 11 68	Nottingham	Apprentice	Nottingham F	36	2
							Birmingham C (loan)	3	—
							Hereford U (loan)	6	—
							Blackburn R (loan)	6	1
							Huddersfield T	137	36
							Sheffield U	36	2
							Bristol C (loan)	5	1
Taylor Gareth	6 2	13 08	F	25 2 73	Weston-Super-Mare	Southampton	Bristol R	47	16
							Crystal Palace	20	1
							Sheffield U	44	14

Tiler Carl	6 2	13 10	D	11 2 70	Sheffield	Trainee	Barnsley	71	3
							Nottingham F	69	1
							Swindon T (loan)	2	—
							Aston Villa	12	1
							Sheffield U	6	1
Tracey Simon	6 0	13 12	G	9 12 67	Woolwich	Apprentice	Wimbledon	1	—
							Sheffield U	161	—
							Manchester C (loan)	3	—
							Norwich C (loan)	1	—
							Wimbledon (loan)	1	—
Vonk Michael	6 3	13 01	D	28 10 68	Alkmaar		AZ	112	8
							SVV/Dordrecht	29	1
							Manchester C	91	3
							Oldham Ath (loan)	5	1
							Sheffield U	34	2
Walker Andy	5 8	11 05	F	6 4 65	Glasgow	Baillieston Jun	Motherwell	76	17
							Celtic	108	30
							Newcastle U (loan)	2	—
							Bolton W	67	44
							Celtic	42	9
							Sheffield U	51	20
Ward Mitch	5 9	11 07	M	11 6 71	Sheffield	Trainee	Sheffield U	148	10
							Crewe Alex (loan)	4	1
White David	6 1	13 09	M	30 10 67	Manchester		Manchester C	285	79
							Leeds U	42	9
							Sheffield U	65	13
Whitehouse Dane	5 10	12 08	M	14 10 70	Sheffield	Trainee	Sheffield U	214	36
Wood Paul‡	5 8	10 04	M	14 10 77	Sheffield	Trainee	Sheffield U	—	—

Trainees
Bamforth, Liam A; Capper, David A; Davies, Kevin J; Doane, Ben N D C; Eastwood, Mark; James, Owen; Johnson, David S M; Lewin, Karlda D; Ludlam, Ryan; Mays, Ross A; Morris, Lee; Strickland, Robert P; Tracey, Richard S; Woodhouse, Curtis.

Associated Schoolboys
Adams, Carl; Anderson, Michael; Burrows, Robin J; Crutchley, Wayne; Hudson, Jamie R; Parkin, Andrew T; Thornley, Carl; Willey, Edward R.

Associated Schoolboys who have accepted the club's offer of a Traineeship/Contract
Burke, Paul; Burley, Adam; Camm, Liam M; Henderson, Ewan; McAutrie, Craig J; Mosley, Matthew J; Patterson, Jamie; Strickland, Steven J.

SHEFFIELD WEDNESDAY

Agogo Manuel			M	1 8 79	Accra		Sheffield W	—	—
Atherton Peter	5 11	14 00	D	6 4 70	Wigan	Trainee	Wigan Ath	149	1
							Coventry C	114	—
							Sheffield W	114	3
Barker Richard‡	6 1	13 05	F	30 5 75	Sheffield	Trainee	Sheffield W	—	—
							Doncaster R (loan)	6	—
Batty Mark	5 9	10 12	F	30 1 79	Nottingham	Trainee	Sheffield W	—	—
Billington David			D	15 10 80	Oxford	Trainee	Peterborough U	5	—
							Sheffield W	—	—
Blinker Regi	5 8	11 07	F	2 6 69	Surinam		Feyenoord	51	3
							Den Bosch	25	6
							Feyenoord	187	42
							Sheffield W	42	3
Booth Andy	6 1	13 00	F	6 12 73	Huddersfield	Trainee	Huddersfield T	123	54
							Sheffield W	35	10
Briscoe Lee	5 11	11 13	F	30 9 75	Pontefract	Trainee	Sheffield W	39	—
Carbone Benito	5 6	10 10	F	14 8 71	Bagnara Calabra		Torino	8	—
							Reggina	31	5
							Casert	31	4
							Ascoli	28	6
							Torino	28	3
							Napoli	29	5
							Internazionale	32	2
							Sheffield W	25	6
Clarke Matthew	6 4	13 08	G	3 11 73	Sheffield	Trainee	Rotherham U	124	—
							Sheffield W	1	—
Collins Wayne	6 0	12 00	M	4 3 69	Manchester	Winsford U	Crewe Alex	117	14
							Sheffield W	12	1
Daly Matthew*	6 3	14 05	D	8 10 76	Dewsbury		Sheffield W	—	—
Donaldson O'Neill	5 11	12 02	F	24 11 69	Birmingham	Hinckley	Shrewsbury T	28	4
							Doncaster R	9	2
							Mansfield T (loan)	4	6
							Sheffield W	9	3
Haslam Steven			M	6 9 79	Sheffield	Trainee	Sheffield W	—	—
Hercock David	5 7	11 12	M	17 4 77	Peterborough	Cambridge C	Sheffield W	—	—

Hirst David	6 0	14 00	F	7 12 67	Barnsley	Apprentice	Barnsley	28	9
							Sheffield W	288	106
Humphreys Richie	5 11	14 06	F	30 11 77	Sheffield	Trainee	Sheffield W	34	3
Hyde Graham	5 8	12 06	M	10 11 70	Doncaster	Trainee	Sheffield W	149	10
Jones Ryan	6 3	14 00	M	23 7 73	Sheffield	Trainee	Sheffield W	41	6
							Scunthorpe U (loan)	11	3
Kotylo Krystof	5 10	11 02	M	28 9 77	Sheffield	School	Sheffield W	—	—
Linighan Brian*	6 3	12 12	D	2 11 73	Hartlepool	Trainee	Sheffield W	1	—
Ludlam Craig*	5 11	11 05	D	8 11 76	Sheffield	Trainee	Sheffield W	—	—
							Notts Co (loan)	1	—
McKeever Mark			F	16 11 78	Derry	Trainee	Peterborough U	3	—
							Sheffield W	—	—
Newsome Jon	6 3	13 10	D	6 9 70	Sheffield	Trainee	Sheffield W	7	—
							Leeds U	76	3
							Norwich C	62	7
							Sheffield W	18	2
Nicol Steve	5 10	12 06	D	11 12 61	Irvine	Ayr U BC	Ayr U	70	7
							Liverpool	343	36
							Notts Co	32	2
							Sheffield W	42	—
Nolan Ian	5 11	12 00	D	9 7 70	Liverpool	Marine	Tranmere R	88	1
							Sheffield W	109	4
Oakes Scott	5 11	11 11	M	5 8 72	Leicester	Trainee	Leicester C	3	—
							Luton T	173	27
							Sheffield W	19	1
Pembridge Mark	5 7	12 03	M	29 11 70	Merthyr Tydfil	Trainee	Luton T	60	6
							Derby Co	110	28
							Sheffield W	59	7
Platts Mark	5 8	11 12	F	23 5 79	Sheffield	Trainee	Sheffield W	2	—
Poric Adem	5 10	12 06	M	22 4 73	London	St George's Budapest	Sheffield W	10	0
							Southend U (loan)	7	—
Pressman Kevin	6 1	14 13	G	6 11 67	Fareham	Apprentice	Sheffield W	196	—
							Stoke C (loan)	4	—
Pringle Alan*			M	8 3 78	Sunderland	Trainee	Sheffield W	—	—
Scargill Jon*	6 1	14 02	G	9 4 77	Dewsbury	Trainee	Sheffield W	—	—
Smith Gavin	5 10	10 10	F	24 9 77	Sheffield	Trainee	Sheffield W	—	—
Stefanovic Dejan	6 2	13 02	D	28 10 74	Yugoslavia	Red Star Belgrade	Sheffield W	35	2
Stevens Andrew*	5 7	10 07	D	24 9 77	Sheffield	Trainee	Sheffield W	—	—
Thorpe Steven*	5 11	11 08	D	27 9 77	Sheffield	Trainee	Sheffield W	—	—
Trustfull Orlando	5 11	13 00	M	4 8 70	Amsterdam		Haarlem	14	—
							SVV	28	—
							SVV/Dordrecht	22	1
							Twente	9	—
							Feyenoord	78	13
							Sheffield W	19	3
Walker Des	5 11	11 11	D	26 11 65	Hackney	Apprentice	Nottingham F	264	1
							Sampdoria	30	—
							Sheffield W	152	—
Weaver Simon	6 1	10 08	D	20 12 77	Doncaster	Trainee	Sheffield W	—	—
							Doncaster R (loan)	2	—
Whittingham Guy	5 10	12 00	F	10 11 64	Evesham	Yeovil T, Army	Portsmouth	160	88
							Aston Villa	25	5
							Wolverhampton W (loan)	13	8
							Sheffield W	83	18
Williams Michael*	5 11	11 04	F	21 11 69	Bradford	Maltby MW	Sheffield W	23	1
							Halifax T (loan)	9	1
							Huddersfield T (loan)	2	—
							Peterborough U (loan)	6	—

Trainees
Bettney, Scott; Davis, Ryan L; Harkin, Thomas E; Harrison, Mark J; Hibbins, John J; Hiner, Daniel; Hutchinson, Sean A; King, Christopher; Lenagh, Steven M; Powell, Vill W; Siddall, Christopher J; Simpkins, James M; Simpkins, Michael J; Todd, Luke G; Wainwright, Jody; Wood, Scott R; Woodward, Jonathan J.

Associated Schoolboys
Braybrook, Peter R; Fraser, Andrew J; Hamshaw, Matthew T; Heywood, Immanuel; Houlahan, Martin J; Huntley, James A; Jones, Philip; Nelson, Craig M; Parkin, Lee; Rand, Craig; Tevendale, James R; Williams, Oliver.

Associated Schoolboys who have accepted the club's offer of a Traineeship/Contract
Coubrough, James R; Haslam, Nathan L; Higgins, Alex J; Hutton, John; Nicholson, Kevin J.

SHREWSBURY TOWN

Berkley Austin	5 11	11 06	F	28 1 73	Dartford	Trainee	Gillingham	3	—
							Swindon T	1	—
							Shrewsbury T	62	1

Name	Ht	Wt	Pos	Born	Birthplace	Source	Club	Apps	Gls
Blamey Nathan	5 11	11 00	D	10 6 77	Plymouth	Trainee	Southampton	—	—
							Shrewsbury T	6	—
Briscoe Anthony§			F	16 8 78	Birmingham	Trainee	Shrewsbury T	1	—
Brown Mickey	5 9	11 12	F	8 2 68	Birmingham	Apprentice	Shrewsbury T	190	9
							Bolton W	33	3
							Shrewsbury T	67	11
							Preston NE	16	1
							Rochdale (loan)	5	—
							Shrewsbury T	19	1
Cope James	6 1	11 01	M	4 10 77	Birmingham	Trainee	Shrewsbury T	4	—
Currie Darren	5 11	12 07	M	29 11 74	Hampstead	Trainee	West Ham U	—	—
							Shrewsbury T (loan)	17	2
							Leyton Orient (loan)	10	—
							Shrewsbury T	50	4
Dempsey Mark	5 7	12 10	D	10 12 72	Dublin	Trainee	Gillingham	48	2
							Leyton Orient	43	1
							Shrewsbury T	68	2
Edwards Paul	6 2	12 09	G	22 2 65	Liverpool	St. Helens T	Crewe Alex	29	—
							Shrewsbury T	169	—
Evans Paul	5 7	12 01	M	1 9 74	Oswestry	Trainee	Shrewsbury T	127	14
Gall Benny	6 1	13 11	G	14 3 71	Copenhagen	Herfolge	Dordrecht	33	—
							De Graafschap	—	—
							Shrewsbury T	23	—
Hawkes Marc‡	6 0	11 05	F	22 9 76	Stoke	Trainee	Stoke C	—	—
							Shrewsbury T	—	—
Jackson David‡	5 9	11 00	D	22 8 78	Solihull	Trainee	Shrewsbury T	1	—
Lynch Tom‡	6 0	13 03	D	10 10 64	Limerick	Limerick	Sunderland	4	—
							Shrewsbury T	234	14
Nielsen Thomas	6 1	13 07	D	25 3 72	Aarhus	Fremad	Shrewsbury T	22	1
Nwadike Chukwuemeka	6 0	12 07	D	9 8 78	Camberwell	Trainee	Wolverhampton W	—	—
							Shrewsbury T	2	—
Reed Ian	5 8	10 13	M	4 9 75	Lichfield	Trainee	Shrewsbury T	18	2
Scott Richard	5 9	12 13	M	29 9 74	Dudley	Trainee	Birmingham C	12	—
							Shrewsbury T	71	8
Seabury Kevin	5 9	11 05	D	24 11 73	Shrewsbury	Trainee	Shrewsbury T	103	—
Spink Dean	5 11	14 00	D	22 1 67	Birmingham	Halesowen T	Aston Villa	—	—
							Scarborough (loan)	3	2
							Bury (loan)	6	1
							Shrewsbury T	273	52
Summerfield Kevin†	6 0	12 07	M	7 1 59	Walsall	Apprentice	WBA	9	4
							Birmingham C	5	1
							Walsall	54	17
							Cardiff C	10	1
							Plymouth Arg	139	26
							Exeter C (loan)	4	—
							Shrewsbury T	163	22
Tate Craig§			F	16 10 79	South Shields	Trainee	Shrewsbury T	1	—
Taylor Lee	5 11	12 00	D	24 2 76	Hammersmith	Faweh	Shrewsbury T	16	—
Taylor Mark	5 8	12 04	M	22 2 66	Birmingham	Local	Walsall	113	4
							Sheffield W	9	—
							Shrewsbury T (loan)	19	2
							Shrewsbury T	231	13
Walton David	6 2	14 07	D	10 4 73	Bedlingham	Trainee	Sheffield U	—	—
							Shrewsbury T	122	9
Ward Nicholas	5 9	11 09	F	30 11 77	Wrexham	Trainee	Shrewsbury T	14	1
Whiston Peter	6 0	12 02	D	4 1 68	Widnes		Plymouth Arg	10	0
							Torquay U (loan)	8	1
							Torquay U	32	—
							Exeter C	85	7
							Southampton	1	—
							Shrewsbury T	55	3
Wray Shaun	6 1	12 10	F	14 3 78	Dudley	Trainee	Shrewsbury T	4	—

Trainees
Ashton, Anthony J; Bell, Lee J; Briscoe, Anthony M; Corns, Stuart R; Dignam, Michael G; Newman, John; Pountney, Craig F; Rose, Scott; Tate, Craig D.

Associated Schoolboys
Green, Stewart C; Jones, Matthew N; Sidaway, Carl J; Vaughan, Nathan J; Woodley, Frederick R.

Associated Schoolboys who have accepted the club's offer of a Traineeship/Contract
Harman, Jeremy; Neville, Mark.

Player who does not hold a current contract but his registration has been retained by the club
Nielsen, Thomas.

SOUTHAMPTON

Basham Steve	5 10	11 07	F	2 12 77	Southampton	Trainee	Southampton	6	—
Beasant Dave	6 4	14 05	G	20 3 59	Willesden	Edgware T	Wimbledon	340	—
							Newcastle U	20	—
							Chelsea	133	—
							Grimsby T (loan)	6	—
							Wolverhampton W (loan)	4	—
							Southampton	88	—
Benali Francis	5 9	11 00	M	30 12 68	Southampton	Apprentice	Southampton	220	—
Berkovic Eyal	5 7	10 00	M	2 4 72	Haifa		Maccabi Haifa	128	25
							Southampton	28	4
Care Simon‡	5 8	10 00	M	23 12 77	Newbury	Trainee	Southampton	—	—
Charlton Simon	5 8	11 09	D	25 10 71	Huddersfield	Trainee	Huddersfield T	124	1
							Southampton	111	2
Davies Kevin	6 0	13 05	F	26 3 77	Sheffield	Trainee	Chesterfield	129	22
							Southampton	—	—
Dia Ali‡			F	20 8 65	Senegal	Lubeck	Southampton	1	—
Dodd Jason	5 10	12 04	D	2 11 70	Bath	Bath C	Southampton	195	6
Dryden Richard	5 11	13 11	D	14 6 69	Stroud	Trainee	Bristol R	13	—
							Exeter C	51	7
							Manchester C (loan)	—	—
							Notts Co	31	1
							Plymouth Arg (loan)	5	—
							Birmingham C	48	—
							Bristol C	37	2
							Southampton	29	1
Evans Mike	6 1	13 04	F	1 1 73	Plymouth	Trainee	Plymouth Arg	163	38
							Blackburn R (loan)	—	—
							Southampton	12	4
Flahavan Darryl	5 10	12 01	G	28 11 78	Southampton	Trainee	Southampton	—	—
Hughes David	5 10	11 07	M	30 12 72	St Albans	Trainee	Southampton	31	3
Le Tissier Matthew	6 0	14 00	F	14 10 68	Guernsey	Trainee	Southampton	357	140
Lundekvam Claus	6 3	13 03	D	22 2 73	Norway		Brann	53	—
							Southampton	29	—
Maddison Neil	5 10	11 11	M	2 10 69	Darlington	Trainee	Southampton	163	18
Magilton Jim	6 0	14 00	M	6 5 69	Belfast	Apprentice	Liverpool	—	—
							Oxford U	150	34
							Southampton	125	13
Monk Garry§	5 11	11 13	D	6 3 79	Bedford	Trainee	Torquay U	5	—
							Southampton	—	—
Monkou Ken	6 3	14 06	D	29 11 64	Surinam	Feyenoord	Chelsea	94	2
							Southampton	144	8
Moss Neil	6 2	13 09	G	10 5 75	New Milton	Trainee	Bournemouth	22	—
							Southampton	3	—
Neilson Alan	5 11	13 01	D	26 9 72	Wegburg	Trainee	Newcastle U	42	1
							Southampton	47	—
Oakley Matthew	5 10	12 01	M	17 8 77	Peterborough	Trainee	Southampton	39	3
Ostenstad Egil	5 11	13 00	F	2 1 72	Haugesund		Viking	128	54
							Southampton	30	9
Piper David	5 8	10 00	D	31 10 77	Bournemouth	Trainee	Southampton	—	—
Robinson Matthew	5 11	11 07	M	23 12 74	Exeter	Trainee	Southampton	13	0
Sheerin Paul‡	5 10	12 00	M	28 8 74	Edinburgh	Whitehill Welfare	Alloa	9	—
							Southampton	—	—
Slater Robbie	5 10	13 03	M	22 11 64	Ormskirk	Anderlecht	Lens	81	4
							Blackburn R	18	—
							West Ham U	25	2
							Southampton	30	2
Spedding Duncan	6 1	11 01	D	7 9 77	Camberley	Trainee	Southampton	—	—
Taylor Maik	6 3	14 02	G	4 9 71	Germany	Farnborough T	Barnet	70	0
							Southampton	18	—
Tisdale Paul‡	5 9	11 13	M	14 1 73	Malta	School	Southampton	16	1
							Northampton T (loan)	5	—
							Huddersfield T (loan)	2	—
Van Gobbel Ulrich	6 0	15 00	D	16 1 71	Surinam		Willem II	34	3
							Feyenoord	122	2
							Galatasaray	24	2
							Southampton	25	1
Venison Barry	5 10	11 12	M	16 8 64	Consett	Apprentice	Sunderland	173	2
							Liverpool	110	1
							Newcastle U	109	1
							Galatasaray	8	—
							Southampton	24	—

Warren Christer	5 10	11 12	F	10 10 74	Poole	Cheltenham T	Southampton	8	—
							Brighton & HA (loan)	3	—
							Fulham (loan)	11	1
Watkinson Russ	6 0	12 00	F	3 12 77	Epsom	Woking	Southampton	2	—
Williams Andrew	5 10	10 10	F	8 10 77	Bristol	Trainee	Southampton	—	—

Trainees
Batchelor, Adam; Bevan, Scott; Blake, Dean J F; Bradley, Shayne; Bridge, Wayne M; Catley, Andrew; Collins, Christopher P; Davis, Neil; Deegan, Christopher M; Desborough, Daniel; Gibbens, Kevin; James, Kevin S; Jenkins, Stephen M; McCarthy, Craig; Monk, Garry; Sullivan, Andrew; Warner, Philip.

Associated Schoolboys
Ashford, Ryan M; Benfield, Sean R; Blayney, Alan; Bradshaw, Neil S R; Canavan, Michael G; Darbyshire, Jonathan R; Gordon, Scott; Green, Christopher; Grimshaw, Steven; Howard, Brian R W; Huxley, Matthew S; Lewis, Christopher; Madgwick, Benjamin; Marfell, Andrew K; Mitchell, Lloyd G; Wallace, Adam.

Associated Schoolboys who have accepted the club's offer of a Traineeship/Contract
Cleife, Lloyd R; Lashley, Simon D; Liddon, Paul G; Malessa, Antony G; Senda, Daniel L; Sims, Adam D; Waller, Andrew P; Webber, Lloyd E; Wilson, Richard S.

SOUTHEND UNITED

Boere Jeroen	6 3	13 02	F	18 11 67	Arnhem	Go Ahead	West Ham U	25	6
							Portsmouth (loan)	5	—
							WBA (loan)	5	—
							Crystal Palace	8	1
							Southend U	42	11
Byrne Paul	5 11	13 00	M	30 6 72	Dublin	Trainee	Oxford U	6	—
						Bangor	Celtic	28	4
							Brighton & HA (loan)	8	1
							Southend U	73	6
Codner Robert†	5 11	11 08	F	23 1 65	Walthamstow	Barnet	Brighton & HA	266	39
							Reading	4	—
							Peterborough U	2	—
							Barnet	32	1
							Southend U	4	—
Dublin Keith	6 0	12 10	D	29 1 66	Wycombe	Apprentice	Chelsea	51	—
							Brighton & HA	132	5
							Watford	168	2
							Southend U	129	5
Dursun Peter‡	5 11	11 10	F	8 1 75	Aarhus		Southend U	1	—
Gridelet Phil	5 11	13 00	M	30 4 67	Edgware	Barnet	Barnsley	6	—
							Rotherham U (loan)	9	—
							Southend U	139	8
Hails Julian	5 10	11 02	F	20 11 67	Lincoln	Hemel Hempstead	Fulham	109	12
							Southend U	105	6
Hanlon Ritchie*			M	26 5 78	Kenton	Chelsea	Southend U	2	—
Harris Andrew	5 10	11 11	D	26 2 77	Springs	Trainee	Liverpool	—	—
							Southend U	44	—
Henriksen Tony	6 3	13 09	G	25 4 73	Hammel	Randers Freja	Southend U	—	—
Jones Mark§			M	4 8 79	Havering	Trainee	Southend U	1	—
Lapper Mike	6 0	12 02	D	28 8 70	California	USSF	Southend U	52	1
Marsh Mike	5 8	11 00	F	21 7 69	Liverpool	Kirkby T	Liverpool	69	2
							West Ham U	49	1
							Coventry C	15	2
							Galatasaray	3	—
							Southend U	75	10
Nielsen John			M	7 4 72	Aarhus		Ikast	19	—
							Southend U	24	3
Rammell Andy	6 2	13 10	F	10 2 67	Nuneaton	Atherstone U	Manchester U	—	—
							Barnsley	185	44
							Southend U	43	11
Roche David	6 0	13 02	M	13 12 70	Newcastle	Trainee	Newcastle U	36	—
							Peterborough U (loan)	4	—
							Doncaster R	50	8
							Southend U	4	—
Roget Leo	6 1	12 02	D	1 8 77	Ilford	Trainee	Southend U	33	1
Royce Simon	6 2	12 10	G	9 9 71	Forest Gate	Heybridge Swifts	Southend U	112	—
Sansome Paul*	6 0	13 06	G	6 10 61	N Addington	Crystal Palace	Millwall	156	—
							Southend U	308	—
							Birmingham C (loan)	1	—
Stimson Mark	5 10	12 06	D	27 12 67	Plaistow	Trainee	Tottenham H	2	—
							Leyton Orient (loan)	10	—
							Gillingham (loan)	18	—
							Newcastle U	86	2
							Portsmouth (loan)	4	—
							Portsmouth	58	2
							Barnet (loan)	5	—
							Southend U	19	—

Name							Club	Apps	Gls
Sussex Andy*	6 3	13 08	M	23 11 64	Islington	Apprentice	Orient	144	17
							Crewe Alex	102	24
							Southend U	76	14
							Brentford (loan)	3	—
Thomson Andy	5 10	10 12	F	1 4 71	Motherwell	Jerviston BC	Q of S	175	93
							Southend U	89	22
Tilson Steve*	5 11	12 10	M	27 7 66	Wickford	Burnham Ramb	Southend U	239	26
							Brentford (loan)	2	—
Whelan Ronnie*	5 9	12 03	M	25 9 61	Dublin	Home Farm	Liverpool	362	46
							Southend U	34	1
Williams Paul	5 7	10 09	F	16 8 65	London	Woodford T	Charlton Ath	82	23
							Brentford (loan)	7	3
							Sheffield W	93	25
							Crystal Palace	46	7
							Sunderland (loan)	3	—
							Birmingham C (loan)	11	—
							Charlton Ath	9	—
							Torquay U (loan)	9	—
							Southend U	33	6

Trainees
Fitzpatrick, Trevor J J; Jones, Mark; Kinseley, Mark; Leggatt, Philip D; Morrish, Adam; Perkins, Christopher P; Taylor, Paul S; Thurley, Westley S.

Associated Schoolboys
Spittle, Stephen.

Player who does not hold a current contract but his registration has been retained by the club
Roche, David.

STOCKPORT COUNTY

Name							Club	Apps	Gls
Angell Brett	6 2	13 10	F	20 8 68	Marlborough	Cheltenham T	Derby Co	—	—
							Stockport Co	70	28
							Southend U	115	47
							Everton (loan)	1	—
							Everton	19	1
							Sunderland	10	—
							Sheffield U (loan)	6	2
							WBA (loan)	3	—
							Stockport Co	34	15
Armstrong Alun	6 0	10 05	F	22 2 75	Gateshead	School	Newcastle U	—	—
							Stockport Co	130	36
Bennett Tom	5 11	11 08	D	12 12 69	Falkirk	Trainee	Aston Villa	—	—
							Wolverhampton W	115	2
							Stockport Co	67	4
Bound Matthew	6 2	13 09	D	9 11 72	Trowbridge	Trainee	Southampton	5	—
							Hull C (loan)	7	1
							Stockport Co	44	5
							Lincoln C (loan)	4	—
Cavaco Luis	5 9	11 06	F	1 3 72	Portugal	Estoril	Stockport Co	27	5
Charlery Ken	6 0	12 00	F	28 11 64	Stepney	Beckton U	Maidstone U	59	11
							Peterborough U	51	19
							Watford	48	13
							Peterborough U	70	24
							Birmingham C	17	4
							Southend U (loan)	3	—
							Peterborough U	56	12
							Stockport Co	10	—
Connelly Sean	5 10	11 10	D	26 6 70	Sheffield	Hallam	Stockport Co	166	—
Cowans Gordon	5 7	9 07	M	27 10 58	Durham	Apprentice	Aston Villa	286	42
							Bari	94	3
							Aston Villa	117	7
							Blackburn R	50	2
							Aston Villa	11	—
							Derby Co	36	—
							Wolverhampton W	37	—
							Sheffield U	20	—
							Bradford C	24	—
							Stockport Co	7	—
Da Costa Nelson	5 10	12 03	D	8 12 78	Angola	Belenenses	Stockport Co	—	—
Dinning Tony	5 11	12 00	D	12 4 75	Wallsend	Trainee	Newcastle U	—	—
							Stockport Co	70	4
Durkan Kieron	5 10	10 05	M	1 12 73	Chester	Trainee	Wrexham	50	3
							Stockport Co	57	3
Edwards Neil	5 8	11 02	G	5 12 70	Aberdare	Trainee	Leeds U	—	—
							Huddersfield T (loan)	—	—
							Stockport Co	164	—

Flynn Mike	6 0	11 02	D	23 2 69	Oldham	Trainee	Oldham Ath	40	1
							Norwich C	—	—
							Preston NE	136	7
							Stockport Co	191	11
Gannon Jim	6 2	13 00	D	7 9 68	Southwark	Dundalk	Sheffield U	—	—
							Halifax T (loan)	2	—
							Stockport Co	280	51
							Notts Co (loan)	2	—
Hallows Marcus‡	6 1	12 09	M	7 7 75	Bolton	Leigh RMI	Bolton W	—	—
							Stockport Co	—	—
Jeffers John	5 10	11 10	F	5 10 68	Liverpool	Trainee	Liverpool	—	—
							Port Vale	180	10
							Shrewsbury T (loan)	3	1
							Stockport Co	57	6
Jones Lea	6 0	14 06	D	25 9 77	Southport	Trainee	Stockport Co	—	—
Jones Paul	6 3	14 00	G	18 4 67	Chirk	Kidderminster H	Wolverhampton W	33	—
							Stockport Co	46	—
Jones Paul*	5 10	11 00	D	22 5 78	Douglas	Trainee	Stockport Co	—	—
Kiko Manuel	5 10	12 05	F	24 10 76	Portugal	Belenenses	Stockport Co	3	—
Landon Richard	6 3	13 05	F	22 3 70	Worthing	Bedworth U	Plymouth Arg	30	12
							Stockport Co	13	5
							Rotherham U (loan)	8	—
Marsden Chris	6 0	10 12	M	3 1 69	Sheffield	Trainee	Sheffield U	16	1
							Huddersfield T	121	9
							Coventry C (loan)	7	—
							Wolverhampton W	8	—
							Notts Co	10	—
							Stockport Co	55	3
Mike Adie‡	6 0	11 06	F	16 11 73	Manchester	Trainee	Manchester C	16	2
							Bury (loan)	7	1
							Stockport Co	9	—
							Hartlepool U (loan)	7	1
							Doncaster R (loan)	5	1
Mutch Andy	5 10	11 00	F	28 12 63	Liverpool	Southport	Wolverhampton W	289	96
							Swindon T	50	6
							Wigan Ath (loan)	7	1
							Stockport Co	44	8
Nash Martin	5 11	12 03	F	27 12 75	Regina	Vancouver	Stockport Co	3	—
Searle Damon	5 11	10 04	D	26 10 71	Cardiff	Trainee	Cardiff C	234	3
							Stockport Co	10	—
Todd Lee	5 5	10 03	D	7 3 72	Hartlepool	Hartlepool U	Stockport Co	225	2
Ware Paul‡	5 9	11 05	M	7 11 70	Congleton	Trainee	Stoke C	115	10
							Stockport Co	54	4
							Cardiff C (loan)	5	—
Williams Richard*	6 0	13 00	G	31 8 77	Wolverhampton	WBA	Stockport Co	—	—

Trainees
Ansell, Gary S; Baker, Andrew C; Barrow, Paul S; Carden, Simon; Cross, Jonathan R; Cunliffe, Stephen; Fish, David; Flood, James A; Foster, Leroy T; Green, Robert J; Gunn, Martin F; Kilduff, Daniel T; King, John P; Lewis, Gary S; Shearer, Lee C; Taylor, Greg; Vaughan, Francis H; Wilbraham, Aaron T; Yongo, Daniel T T A.

Associated Schoolboys
Briggs, Keith.

STOKE CITY

Beeston Carl*	5 11	12 13	M	30 6 67	Stoke	Apprentice	Stoke C	236	13
							Hereford U (loan)	9	2
Birch Mark	5 11	12 02	D	5 1 77	Stoke	Trainee	Stoke C	—	—
Cairns Kwesi	5 5	10 00	M	5 8 79	Westminster		Stoke C	—	—
Callan Aiden*	5 9	11 04	M	8 10 76	Stoke	Trainee	Stoke C	—	—
Cartwright Jamie	5 6	9 06	M	11 10 79	Lichfield	Trainee	Stoke C	—	—
Clarke Clive	5 11	12 03	D	14 1 80	Dublin	Trainee	Stoke C	—	—
Cranson Ian‡	6 0	13 05	D	2 7 64	Easington	Apprentice	Ipswich T	131	5
							Sheffield W	30	—
							Stoke C	223	9
Crowe Dean	5 5	11 03	F	6 6 79	Stockport	Trainee	Stoke C	—	—
Da Costa Hugo†			D	4 11 73	Tramagal		Amadora	10	—
							Stoke C	2	—
Devlin Mark	5 10	11 13	M	18 1 73	Irvine	Trainee	Stoke C	55	2
Forsyth Richard	5 10	12 13	M	3 10 70	Dudley	Kidderminster H	Birmingham C	26	2
							Stoke C	40	8
Fraser Stuart‡	6 0	12 01	G	1 8 78	Cheltenham		Stoke C	—	—
Godbold Jamie	5 4	9 0	F	10 1 80	Great Yarmouth	Trainee	Stoke C	—	—
Griffin Andrew	5 8	10 10	D	17 3 79	Wigan	Trainee	Stoke C	34	1
Heath Robert	5 8	10 00	M	31 8 78	Stoke		Stoke C	—	—

Jagielka Stephen*	5 8	11 05	F	10 3 78	Manchester	Trainee	Stoke C	—	—
Kavanagh Graham	5 10	12 06	M	2 12 73	Dublin	Home Farm	Middlesbrough	35	3
							Darlington (loan)	5	—
							Stoke C	38	4
Keen Kevin	5 7	10 09	M	25 2 67	Amersham	Apprentice	West Ham U	219	21
							Wolverhampton W	42	7
							Stoke C	70	6
Macari Mike	5 7	11 05	F	4 2 73	Kilwinning	Trainee	West Ham U	—	—
							Stoke C	30	3
Macari Paul	5 8	11 06	F	23 8 76	Manchester	Trainee	Stoke C	—	—
Mackenzie Neil	6 2	12 05	M	15 4 76	Birmingham		Stoke C	22	1
McMahon Gerry	5 11	11 13	F	29 12 73	Belfast	Glenavon	Tottenham H	16	—
							Barnet (loan)	10	2
							Stoke C	35	3
McNally Mark	5 11	12 02	D	10 3 71	Bellshill	Celtic BC	Celtic	123	3
							Southend U	54	2
							Stoke C	3	—
Morgan Phil	6 2	14 01	G	18 12 74	Stoke	Trainee	Ipswich T	1	—
							Stoke C	—	—
							Chesterfield (loan)	2	—
Muggleton Carl	6 2	13 03	G	13 9 68	Leicester	Apprentice	Leicester C	46	—
							Chesterfield (loan)	17	—
							Blackpool (loan)	2	—
							Hartlepool U (loan)	8	—
							Stockport Co (loan)	4	—
							Liverpool (loan)	—	—
							Stoke C (loan)	6	—
							Sheffield U (loan)	—	—
							Celtic	12	—
							Stoke C	63	—
							Rotherham U (loan)	6	—
							Sheffield U (loan)	1	—
Nyamah Kofi	5 10	11 07	F	20 6 75	Islington	Trainee	Cambridge U	23	2
						Kettering T	Stoke C	7	—
O'Connor James	5 7	10 04	M	1 9 79	Dublin	Trainee	Stoke C	—	—
Pickering Ally	5 9	11 04	D	22 6 67	Manchester	Buxton	Rotherham U	88	2
							Coventry C	65	—
							Stoke C	40	—
Prudhoe Mark	6 0	14 00	G	8 11 63	Washington	Apprentice	Sunderland	7	—
							Hartlepool U (loan)	3	—
							Birmingham C	1	—
							Walsall	26	—
							Doncaster R (loan)	5	—
							Sheffield W (loan)	—	—
							Grimsby T (loan)	8	—
							Hartlepool U (loan)	13	—
							Bristol C (loan)	3	—
							Carlisle U	34	—
							Darlington	146	—
							Stoke C	82	—
							Peterborough U (loan)	6	—
							Liverpool (loan)	—	—
							York C (loan)	2	—
Sheron Mike	5 10	11 13	F	11 1 72	Liverpool	Trainee	Manchester C	100	24
							Bury (loan)	5	1
							Norwich C	28	2
							Stoke C	69	34
Sigurdsson Larus	6 0	12 12	D	4 6 73	Akureyri	Thor	Stoke C	114	1
Stokoe Graham	6 1	12 13	M	17 12 75	Newcastle	Birmingham C	Stoke C	2	—
							Hartlepool U (loan)	8	—
Sturridge Simon	5 6	11 05	F	9 12 69	Birmingham	Trainee	Birmingham C	150	30
							Stoke C	67	14
Taaffe Stephen	5 5	9 0	F	10 9 79	Stoke	Trainee	Stoke C	—	—
Wallace Ray	5 7	11 05	D	2 10 69	Lewisham	Trainee	Southampton	35	—
							Leeds U	7	—
							Swansea C (loan)	2	—
							Reading (loan)	3	—
							Stoke C	109	9
							Hull C (loan)	7	—
Whittle Justin	6 1	12 13	D	18 3 71	Derby	Celtic	Stoke C	45	—
Woods Stephen	5 11	11 13	D	15 12 76	Davenham	Trainee	Stoke C	—	—
Wooliscroft Ashley	5 10	11 02	D	28 12 79	Stoke	Trainee	Stoke C	—	—
Worthington Nigel*	5 11	12 05	D	4 11 61	Ballymena	Ballymena U	Notts Co	67	4
							Sheffield W	338	12
							Leeds U	43	1
							Stoke C	12	—

Trainees
Brownsword, Andrew; Simon, Courtney; Simpson, Andrew P; Wade, Robert S.

Associated Schoolboys
Goodfellow, Marc D.
Associated Schoolboys who have accepted the club's offer of a Traineeship/Contract
Bullock, Matthew; Dixon, Calvin G.

SUNDERLAND

Name	Ht	Wt	Pos	DOB	Birthplace	Source	Club	Apps	Gls
Agnew Steve	5 10	11 12	M	9 11 65	Shipley	Apprentice	Barnsley	194	29
							Blackburn R	2	—
							Portsmouth (loan)	5	—
							Leicester C	56	4
							Sunderland	60	9
Aiston Sam	6 1	12 13	F	21 11 76	Newcastle	Newcastle U	Sunderland	16	—
							Chester C (loan)	14	—
Ball Kevin	5 9	12 09	D	12 11 64	Hastings	Apprentice	Portsmouth	105	4
							Sunderland	255	16
Beavers Paul	6 3	13 05	F	2 10 78	Blackpool	Trainee	Sunderland	—	—
Bracewell Paul	5 9	12 04	M	19 7 62	Stoke	Apprentice	Stoke C	129	5
							Sunderland	38	4
							Everton	95	7
							Sunderland	113	2
							Newcastle U	73	3
							Sunderland	76	—
Bridges Michael	6 1	11 02	F	5 8 78	Whitley Bay	Trainee	Sunderland	40	7
Conlon Paul	5 9	11 08	F	5 1 78	Sunderland	Trainee	Hartlepool U	15	4
							Sunderland	—	—
Coton Tony	6 2	16 02	G	19 5 61	Tamworth	Mile Oak R	Birmingham C	94	—
							Hereford U (loan)	—	—
							Watford	233	—
							Manchester C	164	—
							Manchester U	—	—
							Sunderland	10	—
Dickman Elliot	5 9	9 08	D	11 10 78	Hexham	Trainee	Sunderland	—	—
Eriksson Jan	6 0	13 03	D	24 8 67	Sundsvall		AIK	73	2
							Norrkoping	34	3
							Kaiserslautern	37	4
							AIK	7	—
							Helsingborg	23	2
							Sunderland	1	—
Grant Stephen‡	5 10	11 07	F	14 4 77	Birr	Athlone T	Sunderland	—	—
Gray Michael	5 8	10 12	D	3 8 74	Sunderland	Trainee	Sunderland	145	10
Hall Gareth	5 11	13 04	D	12 3 69	Croydon	Apprentice	Chelsea	138	4
							Sunderland	46	—
Heckingbottom Paul	6 0	12 05	D	17 7 77	Barnsley	Manchester U	Sunderland	—	—
Heiselberg Kim	5 11	11 07	D	21 9 77	Tarm	Esbjerg	Sunderland	—	—
Holloway Darren	6 0	12 05	D	3 10 77	Bishop Auckland	Trainee	Sunderland	—	—
Howey Lee	6 3	14 05	F	1 4 69	Sunderland	AC Hemptinne	Sunderland	69	8
Johnston Alan	5 7	9 07	F	14 12 73	Glasgow		Hearts	84	12
							Rennes	23	2
							Sunderland	6	1
Kelly David	5 11	11 11	F	25 11 65	Birmingham	Alvechurch	Walsall	147	63
							West Ham U	41	7
							Leicester C	66	22
							Newcastle U	70	35
							Wolverhampton W	83	26
							Sunderland	34	2
Kubicki Dariusz	5 11	12 02	D	6 6 63	Kozuchow	Legia Warsaw	Aston Villa	25	—
							Sunderland (loan)	15	—
							Sunderland	121	—
Lloyd Gary*			M	25 11 77	Middlesbrough	Trainee	Sunderland	—	—
Mawson David*	5 11	12 05	F	4 3 77	Sunderland	Trainee	Sunderland	—	—
Melville Andy	6 1	13 12	D	29 11 68	Swansea	School	Swansea C	175	22
							Oxford U	135	13
							Sunderland	150	11
Mullin John	6 01	12 05	F	11 8 75	Bury	School	Burnley	18	2
							Sunderland	20	2
Naisbett Philip	6 2	12 05	G	2 1 79	Easington	Trainee	Sunderland	—	—
Ord Richard	6 2	12 12	D	3 3 69	Easington	Trainee	Sunderland	229	7
							York C (loan)	3	—
Perez Lionel	6 0	14 02	G	24 4 67	Bagnols Ceze		Nimes	74	—
							Bordeaux	16	—
							Sunderland	29	—
Pickering Steven*	5 10	9 13	M	25 9 76	Sunderland	Trainee	Sunderland	—	—
Preece David*	6 2	12 03	G	28 8 76	Sunderland	Trainee	Sunderland	—	—
Provan John*			D	10 11 77	Glasgow	Trainee	Sunderland	—	—

Quinn Niall	6 5	15 03	F	6 10 66	Dublin		Arsenal	67	14
							Manchester C	203	66
							Sunderland	12	2
Rae Alex	5 9	11 05	M	30 9 69	Glasgow	Bishopbriggs	Falkirk	83	20
							Millwall	218	63
							Sunderland	23	2
Russell Craig	5 10	12 08	F	4 2 74	Jarrow	Trainee	Sunderland	147	31
Scott Martin	5 9	11 02	M	7 1 68	Sheffield	Apprentice	Rotherham U	94	3
							Nottingham F (loan)	—	—
							Bristol C	171	14
							Sunderland	82	7
Smith Martin	5 11	12 00	F	13 11 74	Sunderland	Trainee	Sunderland	95	20
Stewart Paul	5 11	11 10	M	7 10 64	Manchester	Apprentice	Blackpool	201	56
							Manchester C	51	26
							Tottenham H	131	28
							Liverpool	32	1
							Crystal Palace (loan)	18	3
							Wolverhampton W (loan)	8	2
							Burnley (loan)	6	—
							Sunderland	36	5
Tate Chris*			F	27 12 77	York	York C	Sunderland	—	—
Thirlwell Paul	5 11	11 04	M	13 2 79	Newcastle	Trainee	Sunderland	—	—
Waddle Chris*	6 1	13 03	F	14 12 60	Hedworth	Tow Law T	Newcastle U	170	46
							Tottenham H	138	33
							Marseille	107	22
							Sheffield W	109	10
							Falkirk	4	1
							Bradford C	25	5
							Sunderland	7	1
Williams Darren	5 11	11 02	M	28 4 77	Middlesbrough	Trainee	York C	20	—
							Sunderland	11	2
Woods Chris*	6 2	14 12	G	14 11 59	Boston	Apprentice	Nottingham F	—	—
							QPR	63	—
							Norwich C (loan)	10	—
							Norwich C	206	—
							Rangers	173	—
							Sheffield W	107	—
							Reading (loan)	5	—
						Colorado R	Southampton	4	—
						USSF	Sunderland	—	—

Trainees
Barnes, Liam; Barton, Michael; Dolan, Glen T; Frampton, Kevin W; Gibson, Daniel; Ingram, Stuart P; Jackson, Dennis; Johnston, Michael; Lamb, Kris A; Lumsdon, Christopher; Peters, Stephen; Pitts, Matthew; Porter, Christopher I; Somerville, John F; Wright, Andrew.

Associated Schoolboys
Dowell, Adam; Hope, Shaun; Marchant, Ross; McGhie, Gareth; Rowland, Nicholas; South, Gary; Stewart, Craig M; Taylor, Alan; Turns, Craig; Vickers, Thomas A; Vyse, Brian.

Associated Schoolboys who have accepted the club's offer of a Traineeship/Contract
Convery, Mark; Maley, Mark; Proctor, Michael A.

SWANSEA CITY

Ampadu Kwame	5 10	11 10	M	20 12 70	Bradford	Belvedere	Arsenal	2	—
							Plymouth Arg (loan)	6	1
							WBA (loan)	7	1
							WBA	42	3
							Swansea C	129	12
Appleby Ritchie	5 9	11 04	F	18 9 75	Middlesbrough	Trainee	Newcastle U	—	—
							Darlington (loan)	—	—
							Ipswich T	3	—
							Swansea C	11	1
Brown Linton	5 10	12 07	F	12 4 68	Driffield	Guiseley	Halifax T	3	—
							Hull C	121	23
							Swansea C	25	3
Casey Ryan	6 0	10 02	F	3 1 79	Coventry	Trainee	Swansea C	10	—
Chapple Shaun	5 11	12 03	M	14 2 73	Swansea	Trainee	Swansea C	103	9
Clode Mark	5 10	10 10	D	24 2 73	Plymouth	Trainee	Plymouth Arg	—	—
							Swansea C	109	3
Coates Jonathan	5 8	10 04	F	27 6 75	Swansea	Trainee	Swansea C	67	4
Edwards Christian	6 2	11 09	M	23 11 75	Caerphilly	Trainee	Swansea C	83	2
Freestone Roger	6 3	14 06	G	19 8 68	Newport	Trainee	Newport Co	13	—
							Chelsea	42	—
							Swansea C (loan)	14	—
							Hereford U (loan)	8	—
							Swansea C	269	3
Grey Jonathan*	5 11	11 04	M	2 9 77	Swansea	Trainee	Swansea C	—	—

Heggs Carl	6 1	13 02	F	11 10 70	Leicester	Paget R	WBA	40	3
							Bristol R (loan)	5	1
							Swansea C	46	7
Jenkins Lee	5 9	10 00	F	28 6 79	Pontypool	Trainee	Swansea C	23	2
Jones Lee	6 3	14 04	G	9 8 70	Pontypridd	Porth	Swansea C	4	—
							Crewe Alex (loan)	—	—
Jones Steve	5 10	12 02	D	25 12 70	Bristol	Cheltenham T	Swansea C	63	1
King Robert	5 8	10 06	D	2 9 77	Merthyr	Trainee	Swansea C	2	—
Lacey Damien	5 9	11 03	M	3 8 77	Bridgend	Trainee	Swansea C	10	—
McDonald Colin	5 7	11 04	F	10 4 74	Edinburgh	Musselburgh Wsr	Hibernian	—	—
							Falkirk	56	11
							Swansea C	18	—
Miles Ben	6 1	11 07	G	13 4 76	Middlesex	Trainee	Swansea C	—	—
Molby Jan	6 2	15 10	M	4 7 63	Kolding	Ajax	Liverpool	218	44
							Barnsley (loan)	5	—
							Norwich C (loan)	3	—
							Swansea C	40	8
Moreira Joao	6 3	14 00	D	30 6 70	Oporto	Benfica	Swansea C	10	—
O'Leary Kristian	6 0	13 04	D	30 8 77	Port Talbot	Trainee	Swansea C	13	1
Penney David	5 10	12 00	M	17 8 64	Wakefield	Pontefract	Derby Co	19	—
							Oxford U	110	15
							Swansea C (loan)	12	3
							Swansea C (loan)	11	2
							Swansea C	108	18
Phillips Gareth§	5 8	9 08	M	19 7 79	Porth	Trainee	Swansea C	1	—
Price Jason	6 2	11 05	M	12 4 77	Aberdare	Aberaman Ath	Swansea C	2	—
Thomas David	5 11	12 07	F	26 9 75	Caerphilly	Trainee	Swansea C	56	10
Torpey Steve	6 3	14 03	F	18 12 70	Islington	Trainee	Millwall	7	—
							Bradford C	96	22
							Swansea C	162	44
Walker Keith	6 0	13 03	M	17 4 66	Edinburgh	ICI Juveniles	Stirling Albion	91	17
							St Mirren	43	6
							Swansea C	230	6
Willer Thomas†	6 4	13 04	D	19 9 68	Copenhagen	HIK Copenhagen	Swansea C	7	—

Trainees
Cunningham, Barry L; Davies, Dewi O; Dyer, Steven P; Freeman, Stuart; James, Rhys A; Jones, Christopher J; Jones, Dean; Kissick, Lee P; Mackay, James S; Mainwaring, Carl A; Milsom, Greg H; Munroe, Karl A; Phillips, Gareth R; Roberts, Stuart I; Rosselli, Dean A; Simon, Neil P; Taylor, James J.

Associated Schoolboys
Berry, James; Davies, Ross D; Gregson, Lyndon; Howard, Martin; Jones, Huw R; Jones, Mathew; Kern, Jamie T; Morgan, Ian K; Thomas, Jonathan F; Todd, Christopher.

Associated Schoolboys who have accepted the club's offer of a Traineeship/Contract
Barwood, Daniel D; De-Vulgt, Leigh S; Watkins, David J.

SWINDON TOWN

Allison Wayne	6 1	14 00	F	16 10 68	Huddersfield		Halifax T	84	23
							Watford	7	—
							Bristol C	195	48
							Swindon T	85	28
Anthony Graham*	5 8	10 10	M	9 8 75	South Shields	Trainee	Sheffield U	3	—
							Scarborough (loan)	2	—
							Swindon T	3	—
Bullock Darren	5 9	12 10	M	12 2 69	Worcester	Nuneaton Bor	Huddersfield T	128	16
							Swindon T	13	1
Collins Lee	5 8	10 08	M	3 2 74	Bellshill	Possil U	Albion R	45	1
							Swindon T	9	—
Cowe Steve	5 6	10 10	M	29 9 74	Gloucester	Trainee	Aston Villa	—	—
							Swindon T	49	7
Culverhouse Ian	5 10	11 02	D	22 9 64	Bishop's Stortford	Apprentice	Tottenham H	2	—
							Norwich C	296	—
							Swindon T	86	—
Darras Frederic	6 0	11 06	D	19 8 66	Calais		Auxerre	27	—
							Sochaux	54	—
							Bastia	39	—
							Swindon T	35	—
Digby Fraser	6 2	13 10	G	23 4 67	Sheffield	Apprentice	Manchester U	—	—
							Oldham Ath (loan)	—	—
							Swindon T (loan)	—	—
							Swindon T	379	—
							Manchester U (loan)	—	—
Drysdale Jason	5 10	13 00	D	17 11 70	Bristol	Trainee	Watford	145	11
							Newcastle U	—	—
							Swindon T	28	—

Elkins Gary	5 9	13 00	D	4 5 66	Wallingford	Apprentice	Fulham	104	2
							Exeter C (loan)	5	—
							Wimbledon	110	3
							Swindon T	23	1
Finney Stephen	5 11	13 00	F	31 10 73	Hexham	Trainee	Preston NE	6	1
							Manchester C	—	—
							Swindon T	50	14
Gooden Ty	5 8	12 02	M	23 10 72	Canvey Island	Wycombe W	Swindon T	59	6
Holcroft Peter	5 9	11 05	M	3 1 76	Liverpool	Trainee	Everton	—	—
							Swindon T	3	—
Hooper Dean‡	5 10	12 12	M	13 4 71	Harefield	Hayes	Swindon T	4	—
							Peterborough U (loan)	4	—
King Phil	5 11	12 09	D	28 12 67	Bristol	Apprentice	Exeter C	27	—
							Torquay U	24	3
							Swindon T	116	4
							Sheffield W	129	2
							Notts Co (loan)	6	—
							Aston Villa	16	—
							WBA (loan)	4	—
							Swindon T	5	—
Leitch Scott	5 8	11 10	D	6 10 69	Motherwell	Shettleston Jun	Dunfermline Ath	89	16
							Hearts	55	2
							Swindon T	43	—
Maclaren Ross‡	5 10	12 12	M	14 4 62	Edinburgh	Rangers	Shrewsbury T	161	18
							Derby Co	122	4
							Swindon T	197	9
McMahon Steve†	5 9	11 08	M	20 8 61	Liverpool	Apprentice	Everton	100	11
							Aston Villa	75	7
							Liverpool	204	29
							Manchester C	87	1
							Swindon T	41	—
Mildenhall Steve	6 4	12 10	G	13 5 78	Swindon	Trainee	Swindon T	1	—
Murray Edwin‡	5 11	12 00	D	31 8 73	Redbridge	Trainee	Swindon T	12	1
O'Sullivan Wayne	5 8	10 09	D	25 2 74	Akrotiri	Trainee	Swindon T	89	3
Pattimore Michael§			F	15 3 79	Newport	Trainee	Swindon T	1	—
Robinson Mark	5 10	12 04	D	21 11 68	Rochdale	Trainee	WBA	2	—
							Barnsley	137	6
							Newcastle U	25	—
							Swindon T	129	2
Seagraves Mark	6 0	13 12	D	22 10 66	Bootle	Apprentice	Liverpool	—	—
							Norwich C (loan)	3	—
							Manchester C	42	—
							Bolton W	157	7
							Swindon T	56	—
Smith Alex	5 9	10 06	D	15 2 76	Liverpool	Trainee	Everton	—	—
							Swindon T	26	1
Talia Frank	6 1	13 08	G	20 7 72	Melbourne	Sunshine GC	Blackburn R	—	—
							Hartlepool U (loan)	14	—
							Swindon T	31	—
Taylor Craig			M	24 1 74	Plymouth	Dorchester T	Swindon T	—	—
Thorne Peter	6 0	13 00	F	21 6 73	Manchester	Trainee	Blackburn R	—	—
							Wigan Ath (loan)	11	—
							Swindon T	77	27
Walters Mark	5 10	12 08	M	2 6 64	Birmingham	Apprentice	Aston Villa	181	39
							Rangers	106	32
							Liverpool	94	14
							Stoke C (loan)	9	2
							Wolverhampton W (loan)	11	3
							Southampton	5	—
							Swindon T	27	7
Watson Kevin	5 9	12 09	M	3 1 74	Hackney	Trainee	Tottenham H	5	—
							Brentford (loan)	3	—
							Bristol C (loan)	2	—
							Barnet (loan)	13	—
							Swindon T	27	1

Trainees
Coupe, Matthew W E; Davis, Sol S; Finlayson, Alexander J; Haines, Jonathan J; Hodson, Stuart M; Hulbert, Robin J; Hunt, Daniel J; Macdiarmid, Philip E; Meechan, Alexander T; O'Connell, Christopher W; Organ, Christopher D; Pattimore, Michael R; Thorne, Wayne P; Wheeldon, Thomas V.

Non-Contract
McMahon, Stephen; Trigg, Jonathan M.

Associated Schoolboys
Evans, Keri S.

Associated Schoolboys who have accepted the club's offer of a Traineeship/Contract
Peters, Bradley S.

TORQUAY UNITED

Name	Ht	Wt	Pos	Date	Birthplace	Source	Club	Apps	Gls
Adcock Paul‡	5 8	10 02	F	2 5 72	Ilminster	Trainee	Plymouth Arg	21	2
						Bath C	Torquay U	1	—
Barrow Lee	5 11	12 05	D	1 5 73	Worksworth	Trainee	Notts Co	—	—
							Scarborough	11	—
							Torquay U	162	5
Bedeau Anthony§	5 9	11 01	M	24 3 79	Hammersmith	Trainee	Torquay U	12	1
Crane Steve‡	5 11	12 07	F	3 6 72	Essex		Gillingham	13	1
							Torquay U	2	—
Gittens Jon	6 0	12 07	D	22 1 64	Moseley	Paget R	Southampton	18	—
							Swindon T	126	6
							Southampton	19	—
							Middlesbrough (loan)	12	1
							Middlesbrough	13	—
							Portsmouth	83	2
							Torquay U	33	3
Gregg Matt§			G	30 11 78	Cheltenham	Trainee	Torquay U	2	—
Hancox Richard‡	5 10	13 00	F	4 10 70	Stourbridge	Stourbridge S	Torquay U	82	10
Hapgood Leon§			M	7 8 79	Torbay	Trainee	Torquay U	1	—
Hathaway Ian*	5 6	10 06	M	22 8 68	Wordsley	Bedworth U	Mansfield T	44	2
							Rotherham U	13	1
							Torquay U	140	14
Hawthorne Mark*	5 10	12 02	M	31 10 73	Glasgow	Trainee	Crystal Palace	—	—
							Sheffield U	—	—
							Walsall	—	—
							Torquay U	58	2
Hockley Wayne§			F	6 9 78	Torbay	Trainee	Torquay U	2	—
Hodges Kevin	5 8	11 03	M	12 6 60	Bridport	Apprentice	Plymouth Arg	530	81
							Torquay U (loan)	3	—
							Torquay U	68	4
Howell Jamie†			M	19 2 77	Rustington	Trainee	Arsenal	—	—
							Portsmouth	—	—
							Torquay U	4	—
Jack Rodney	5 7	10 07	F	28 9 72	Kingston, Jamaica	Lambada	Torquay U	47	12
Laight Ellis‡	5 10	11 02	F	30 6 76	Birmingham	Trainee	Torquay U	41	3
McCall Steve	5 11	12 08	M	15 10 60	Carlisle	Apprentice	Ipswich T	257	7
							Sheffield W	29	2
							Carlisle U (loan)	6	—
							Plymouth Arg	100	5
							Torquay U	24	1
McFarlane Andy	6 3	12 06	F	30 11 66	Wolverhampton	Cradley T	Portsmouth	2	—
							Swansea C	55	8
							Scunthorpe U	60	19
							Torquay U	19	3
Mitchell Paul*	5 8	12 00	D	20 10 71	Bournemouth	Trainee	Bournemouth	12	—
							West Ham U	1	—
							Bournemouth	4	—
							Torquay U	24	—
Nelson Garry	5 10	11 13	F	16 1 61	Braintree	Amateur	Southend U	129	17
							Swindon T	79	7
							Plymouth Arg	74	20
							Brighton & HA	144	46
							Notts Co (loan)	2	—
							Charlton Ath	185	37
							Torquay U	34	8
Newland Ray*	6 3	14 00	G	19 7 71	Liverpool	Everton	Plymouth Arg	26	—
							Chester C	10	—
							Torquay U	28	—
Oatway Charlie	5 7	11 00	M	28 11 73	Hammersmith	Yeading	Cardiff C	32	—
							Torquay U	65	1
Preston Michael	5 8	10 07	M	22 11 77	Plymouth	Trainee	Torquay U	10	—
Thirlby Anthony‡	5 8	10 05	M	4 3 76	Germany	Trainee	Exeter C	39	2
						Tiverton	Torquay U	3	—
Thomas Wayne§	5 11	11 10	F	28 8 78	Walsall	Trainee	Torquay U	18	—
Tucker Lee§			F	10 8 78	Plymouth	Trainee	Torquay U	1	—
Watson Alex	6 1	11 09	D	15 4 68	Liverpool	Apprentice	Liverpool	4	—
							Derby Co (loan)	5	—
							Bournemouth	151	5
							Gillingham (loan)	10	1
							Torquay U	75	3

Wilmot Rhys*	6 2	13 05	G	21 2 62	Newport	Apprentice	Arsenal	8	—
							Hereford U (loan)	9	—
							Orient (loan)	46	—
							Swansea C (loan)	16	—
							Plymouth Arg (loan)	17	—
							Plymouth Arg	116	—
							Grimsby T	33	—
							Crystal Palace	6	—
							Torquay U	34	—
Winter Steve*	5 7	11 00	D	26 10 73	Bristol	Trainee	Walsall	18	—
						Taunton T	Torquay U	73	6
Wright Matthew*	6 1	11 07	D	1 6 78	Norwich	Trainee	Torquay U	9	—

Trainees
Bedeau, Anthony C O; Froude, Paul T; Gomm, Richard A; Gregg, Matthew S; Hadley, Shaun L; Hapgood, Leon D; Hockley, Wayne; Hogg, Christopher; Newell, Justin J; Smillie, Duncan; Thomas, Wayne J R; Tucker, Lee A; Tully, Stephen R.

Associated Schoolboys
Grinsill, Justin A.

Associated Schoolboys who have accepted the club's offer of a Traineeship/Contract
Medlin, Daniel L.

TOTTENHAM HOTSPUR

Allen Rory	5 11	11 02	F	17 10 77	Beckenham	Trainee	Tottenham H	12	2
Anderton Darren	6 1	12 05	F	3 3 72	Southampton	Trainee	Portsmouth	62	7
							Tottenham H	132	22
Arber Mark	6 1	11 09	D	9 10 77	South Africa	Trainee	Tottenham H	—	—
Armstrong Chris	6 0	12 10	F	19 6 71	Newcastle	Llay Welfare	Wrexham	60	13
							Millwall	28	5
							Crystal Palace	118	45
							Tottenham H	48	20
Austin Dean	6 0	11 06	D	26 4 70	Hemel Hempstead	St. Albans C	Southend U	96	2
							Tottenham H	124	—
Baardsen Espen	6 5	13 03	G	7 12 77	San Rafael	San Francisco AB	Tottenham H	2	—
Brady Garry	5 10	10 95	M	7 9 76	Glasgow	Trainee	Tottenham H	—	—
Brown Simon	6 2	15 01	G	3 12 76	Chelmsford	Trainee	Tottenham H	—	—
Bunn James			F	12 1 78	Tottenham	Trainee	Tottenham H	—	—
Calderwood Colin	6 0	13 00	D	20 1 65	Glasgow	Amateur	Mansfield T	100	1
							Swindon T	330	20
							Tottenham H	125	2
Campbell Sol	6 21	14 04	D	18 9 74	Newham	Trainee	Tottenham H	134	2
Carr Stephen	5 9	12 04	D	29 8 76	Dublin	Trainee	Tottenham H	27	0
Clapham Jamie	5 9	10 11	M	7 12 75	Lincoln	Trainee	Tottenham H	1	—
							Leyton Orient (loan)	6	—
							Bristol R (loan)	5	—
Clemence Stephen	5 11	11 07	M	31 3 78	Liverpool	Trainee	Tottenham H	—	—
Darcy Ross	6 0	12 02	D	21 3 78	Balbriggan	Trainee	Tottenham H	—	—
Davies Darren	5 8	11 07	D	13 8 78	Port Talbot	Trainee	Tottenham H	—	—
Dozzell Jason	6 2	13 10	M	9 12 67	Ipswich	School	Ipswich T	332	52
							Tottenham H	84	13
Edinburgh Justin	5 10	12 01	D	18 12 69	Basildon	Trainee	Southend U	37	—
							Tottenham H (loan)	—	—
							Tottenham H	173	1
Fenn Neale	5 10	12 08	F	18 1 77	Edmonton	Trainee	Tottenham H	4	—
Fox Ruel	5 6	10 05	F	14 1 68	Ipswich	Apprentice	Norwich C	172	22
							Newcastle U	58	12
							Tottenham H	51	7
Gain Peter	6 1	11 00	M	11 11 76	Hammersmith	Trainee	Tottenham H	—	—
Gower Mark			M	5 10 78	Edmonton	Trainee	Tottenham H	—	—
Hill Danny	5 9	11 12	M	1 10 74	Edmonton	Trainee	Tottenham H	10	—
							Birmingham C (loan)	5	—
							Watford (loan)	1	—
Howells David	6 0	12 07	M	15 12 67	Guildford	Trainee	Tottenham H	257	22
Iversen Steffen	6 1	11 08	F	10 11 76	Oslo		Rosenborg	25	10
							Tottenham H	16	6
Janney Mark*	5 10	12 00	F	2 12 77	Romford	Trainee	Tottenham H	—	—
							Brentford (loan)	2	1
Kerslake David*	5 9	12 03	D	19 6 66	Stepney	Apprentice	QPR	58	6
							Swindon T	135	1
							Leeds U	8	—
							Tottenham H	37	—
							Swindon T (loan)	8	—
Mabbutt Gary	5 10	13 01	D	23 8 61	Bristol	Apprentice	Bristol R	131	10
							Tottenham H	466	27
Maher Kevin	6 0	12 05	D	17 10 76	Ilford	Trainee	Tottenham H	—	—

Mahorn Paul	5 10	13 01	F	13 8 73	Whipps Cross	Trainee	Tottenham H	1	—
							Fulham (loan)	3	—
							Burnley (loan)	8	1
							Brentford (loan)	—	—
Mannix Alan*	5 8	10 09	M	23 10 77	Castle Knock	Trainee	Tottenham H	—	—
McVeigh Paul	5 6	10 05	F	6 12 77	Belfast	Trainee	Tottenham H	3	1
Nethercott Stuart	6 1	14 00	D	21 3 73	Chadwell Heath	Trainee	Tottenham H	54	—
							Maidstone U (loan)	13	1
							Barnet (loan)	3	—
Nielsen Allan	5 8	11 02	M	13 3 71	Esbjerg	Esbjerg	Bayern Munich	1	—
							Sion	—	—
							Odense	55	9
							FC Copenhagen	26	3
							Brondby	42	11
							Tottenham H	29	6
Rosenthal Ronny*	5 11	12 13	F	11 10 63	Haifa	Standard Liege	Luton T (loan)	—	—
							Liverpool (loan)	8	7
							Liverpool	66	14
							Tottenham H	88	4
Scales John	6 2	13 05	D	4 7 66	Harrogate		Leeds U	—	—
							Bristol R	72	2
							Wimbledon	240	11
							Liverpool	65	2
							Tottenham H	12	—
Sheringham Teddy	6 0	12 08	F	2 4 66	Highams Park	Apprentice	Millwall	220	93
							Aldershot (loan)	5	—
							Nottingham F	42	14
							Tottenham H	166	76
Sinton Andy	5 8	11 01	M	19 3 66	Newcastle	Apprentice	Cambridge U	93	13
							Brentford	149	28
							QPR	160	22
							Sheffield W	60	3
							Tottenham H	42	6
Spencer Simon*	5 10	11 04	M	10 9 76	Islington	Trainee	Tottenham H	—	—
Townley Leon	6 2	13 03	D	16 2 76	Loughton	Trainee	Tottenham H	—	—
Vega Ramon	6 3	13 00	D	14 6 71	Olten	Trimbach	Grasshoppers	156	13
							Cagliari	14	—
							Tottenham H	8	1
Walker Ian	6 2	13 01	G	31 10 71	Watford	Trainee	Tottenham H	163	—
							Oxford U (loan)	2	—
							Ipswich T (loan)	—	—
Webb Simon	5 11	12 03	M	19 1 78	Castle Bar	Trainee	Tottenham H	—	—
Wilson Clive	5 7	11 04	D	13 11 61	Manchester	Local	Manchester C	98	9
							Chester (loan)	21	2
							Chelsea	81	5
							Manchester C (loan)	11	—
							QPR	172	12
							Tottenham H	54	1
Wormull Simon*	5 10	12 03	M	1 12 76	Crawley	Trainee	Tottenham H	—	—

Trainees
Bauckham, Luke; Delicata, Julian; Dobson, Stephen G; Dormer, James S; Evans, James M; Hillier, Ian M; Kersey, Lee D; Lee, David J; Marriott, Alan; Marshall, Christopher J; O'Brien, Kevin G; Piercy, John W; Samways, Shane A; Sinclair, Jamie; Southgate, Glenn S; Spencer, Ryan L; Stone, Gavin; Twidell, Daren; Vaughan, Wayne S R; Warrington, Russell C; Young, Luke P.

Associated Schoolboys
Adams, Terry P; Brennan, Martin I; Burke, Andrew J; Burnham, Sean E; Darbo, Roy; Elliott, Anthony R; Jackson, Johnnie; Lovett, Scott C; Mapes, Charles E; McCann, Peter; Morley, Wayne; Saker, Blake M; Shave, Kieron P; Shelley, Christopher T; Tait, Allan D; White, Ross A.

Associated Schoolboys who have accepted the club's offer of a Traineeship/Contract
Bernard, Narada M; Clist, Simon J; Crouch, Peter J; Duffin, Ciaran; Hunt, Nicholas G; King, Ledley; Mills, Stephen J; Poole, Glenn S; Stonebridge, Ian R.

TRANMERE ROVERS

Aldridge John	5 11	12 03	F	18 9 58	Liverpool	South Liverpool	Newport Co	170	69
							Oxford U	114	72
							Liverpool	83	50
							Real Sociedad	63	33
							Tranmere R	228	133
Bonetti Ivano‡	5 10	11 05	F	1 8 64	Brescia	Torino	Grimsby T	19	3
							Tranmere R	13	1
Branch Graham	6 2	12 02	F	12 2 72	Liverpool	Heswall	Tranmere R	77	7
							Bury (loan)	4	1
Challinor Dave	6 2	12 00	D	2 10 75	Chester	Bromborough Pool	Tranmere R	5	—
Connolly Stuart	5 8	10 09	M	8 12 77	Dublin	Stella Maris	Tranmere R	—	—

Name	Ht	Wt	Pos	DOB	Birthplace	Source	Club	Apps	Gls
Cook Paul	5 11	11 00	M	22 6 67	Liverpool	Marine	Wigan Ath	83	14
							Norwich C	6	—
							Wolverhampton W	193	19
							Coventry C	37	3
							Tranmere R	51	4
Coyne Danny	5 11	12 06	G	27 8 73	Prestatyn	Trainee	Tranmere R	78	—
Crawford Keith*	5 11	11 02	F	31 10 78	Dublin	Belvedere	Tranmere R	—	—
Higgins Dave*	6 0	11 00	D	19 8 61	Liverpool	Eagle	Tranmere R	347	12
Hynes Martin*	5 8	10 03	F	10 9 77	Prescot	Trainee	Tranmere R	—	—
Irons Kenny	5 10	11 02	M	4 11 70	Liverpool	Trainee	Tranmere R	265	35
Jardine Jamie*	6 4	12 07	D	1 2 77	Birkenhead		Tranmere R	—	—
Jones Gary	6 3	13 05	F	10 5 75	Chester	Trainee	Tranmere R	78	12
Jones Martin‡	6 1	13 03	G	27 3 75	Liverpool	Trainee	Tranmere R	—	—
Jones Paul*	6 1	11 09	D	3 6 78	Liverpool	Trainee	Tranmere R	—	—
							Blackpool (loan)		
Kenworthy Jon‡	5 8	10 07	M	18 8 74	St Asaph	Trainee	Tranmere R	26	2
							Chester C (loan)	7	1
Mahon Alan	5 10	11 05	M	4 4 78	Dublin	Crumplin U	Tranmere R	27	2
McGreal John	5 11	10 12	D	2 6 72	Birkenhead	Trainee	Tranmere R	117	1
McIntyre Kevin			M	23 12 77	Liverpool	Trainee	Tranmere R	—	—
Morgan Alan	5 10	11 00	D	2 11 73	Aberystwyth	Trainee	Tranmere R	5	1
Morrissey John	5 8	11 09	F	8 3 65	Liverpool	Apprentice	Everton	1	
							Wolverhampton W	10	1
							Tranmere R	409	48
Mungall Steve*	5 8	11 12	D	22 5 58	Bellshill		Motherwell	20	—
							Tranmere R	512	13
Nevin Pat	5 6	11 09	F	6 9 63	Glasgow	Gartcosh U	Clyde	73	17
							Chelsea	193	36
							Everton	109	16
							Tranmere R (loan)	8	—
							Tranmere R	193	30
Nixon Eric	6 4	14 00	G	4 10 62	Manchester	Curzon Ashton	Manchester C	58	—
							Wolverhampton W (loan)	16	—
							Bradford C (loan)	3	—
							Southampton (loan)	4	—
							Carlisle U (loan)	16	—
							Tranmere R (loan)	8	—
							Tranmere R	333	—
							Blackpool (loan)	20	—
							Bradford C (loan)	12	—
O'Brien Liam	6 1	11 10	M	5 9 64	Dublin	Shamrock R	Manchester U	31	2
							Newcastle U	151	19
							Tranmere R	118	7
Parkinson Andrew			M	27 5 79	Liverpool	Liverpool	Tranmere R	—	—
Rogers Alan	5 10	11 08	D	3 1 77	Liverpool	Trainee	Tranmere R	57	2
Scott Gary*	5 8	11 02	D	3 2 78	Liverpool	Trainee	Tranmere R	—	—
Simonsen Steve	6 2	12 08	G	3 4 79	South Shields	Trainee	Tranmere R	—	—
Stevens Gary	5 11	11 02	D	27 3 63	Barrow	Apprentice	Everton	208	8
							Rangers	187	8
							Tranmere R	102	1
Teale Shaun	6 0	12 02	D	10 3 64	Southport	Weymouth	Bournemouth	100	4
							Aston Villa	147	2
							Tranmere R	54	—
							Preston NE (loan)	5	—
Thomas Tony	5 11	12 05	D	12 7 71	Liverpool	Trainee	Tranmere R	257	12
Thorn Andy	6 0	13 02	D	12 11 66	Carshalton	Apprentice	Wimbledon	107	2
							Newcastle U	36	2
							Crystal Palace	128	3
							Wimbledon	37	1
							Hearts	1	—
							Tranmere R	19	1
Woods Billy*	6 0	12 00	M	24 10 73	Cork	Cork C	Tranmere R	1	—
							Blackpool (loan)	3	—

Trainees
Baxter, Brett R; Crowe, Barry E; Edge, Christopher; Gedman, James; Gibbons, Frank; Gibson, Neil D; Graves, Stuart R; Haworth, Martin; Hill, Clinton S; Holmes, Thomas M; Howard, Michael A; Jones, Darren J; Koumas, Jason; Lampkin, Ricky J; Moran, Andrew J; Powell, Gareth F; Sexton, Warren; Small, Glenn J; Taylor, John; Tippett, Ryan; Tynan, Paul S; Waters, Anthony P; Williams, Mark T.

Associated Schoolboys
Douglas, Michael; Dreves, Thomas; Hay, Alexander; Hinds, Richard P; Lovell, Darren B; Taylor, Craig; Taylor, Michael; Wright, Kevin.

Associated Schoolboys who have accepted the club's offer of a Traineeship/Contract
Davies, Kevin M; Sharps, Ian W; Taylor, Perry L.

WALSALL

Name	Ht	Wt	Pos	Birthdate	Birthplace	Source	Club	Apps	Gls
Beckford Darren	6 1	11 01	F	12 5 67	Manchester	Apprentice	Manchester C	11	—
							Bury (loan)	12	5
							Port Vale (loan)	11	4
							Port Vale	167	68
							Norwich C	38	8
							Oldham Ath	52	11
							Hearts	8	—
							Preston NE	2	—
							Fulham	—	—
							Walsall	8	—
Blake Mark	5 11	12 06	M	16 12 70	Nottingham	Trainee	Aston Villa	31	2
							Wolverhampton W (loan)	2	—
							Portsmouth	15	—
							Leicester C	49	4
							Walsall	38	4
Bradley Darren*	5 11	13 03	D	24 11 65	Birmingham	Apprentice	Aston Villa	20	—
							WBA	254	9
							Walsall	71	1
Butler Martin	5 11	11 09	F	15 9 74	Dudley	Trainee	Walsall	74	8
Daniel Ray*	5 8	12 08	D	10 12 64	Luton	Apprentice	Luton T	22	4
							Gillingham (loan)	5	—
							Hull C	58	3
							Cardiff C	56	1
							Portsmouth	100	4
							Notts Co (loan)	5	—
							Walsall	35	—
Evans Wayne	5 10	12 07	D	25 8 71	Abermule	Welshpool	Walsall	129	—
Hodge John	5 7	11 03	F	1 4 69	Ormskirk	Exmouth	Exeter C	65	10
							Swansea C	112	10
							Walsall	37	4
Keates Dean	5 5	10 03	M	30 6 78	Walsall	Trainee	Walsall	2	—
Keister John	5 8	10 09	M	11 11 70	Manchester	Faweh FC	Walsall	90	2
Lightbourne Kyle	6 2	12 04	F	29 9 68	Bermuda		Scarborough	19	3
							Walsall	165	65
Marsh Chris	5 10	13 02	M	14 1 70	Dudley	Trainee	Walsall	266	21
Mountfield Derek*	6 1	13 08	D	2 11 62	Liverpool	Apprentice	Tranmere R	26	1
							Everton	106	19
							Aston Villa	90	9
							Wolverhampton W	83	4
							Carlisle U	31	3
							Northampton T	4	—
							Walsall	70	1
Mountford Paul†	5 9	10 06	M	26 4 78	Wordsley	Trainee	Walsall	—	—
Ntamark Charlie	5 9	11 09	M	22 7 64	Paddington	Boreham Wood	Walsall	276	12
Platt Clive			F	27 10 77	Wolverhampton	Trainee	Walsall	5	2
Ricketts Michael			F	4 12 78	Birmingham	Trainee	Walsall	12	2
Rogers Darren	5 11	13 02	D	9 4 70	Birmingham	Trainee	WBA	14	1
							Birmingham C	18	—
							Wycombe W (loan)	1	—
							Walsall	54	—
Roper Ian	6 3	14 00	D	20 6 77	Nuneaton	Trainee	Walsall	16	—
Rowland Steve†	5 10	11 06	D	11 2 78	Birmingham	Trainee	Walsall	—	—
Ryder Stuart	6 0	12 08	D	6 11 73	Sutton	Trainee	Walsall	88	5
Smith Mark	6 1	13 09	G	2 1 73	Birmingham	Trainee	Nottingham F	—	—
							Crewe Alex	63	—
							Walsall	—	—
Thomas Wayne	5 8	12 02	M	28 8 78	Walsall	Trainee	Walsall	20	—
Viveash Adrian	6 3	12 13	D	30 9 69	Swindon	Trainee	Swindon T	54	2
							Reading (loan)	5	—
							Reading (loan)	6	—
							Barnsley (loan)	2	1
							Walsall	77	9
Walker James	5 11	13 03	G	9 7 73	Sutton-in-Ashfield	Trainee	Notts Co	—	—
							Walsall	97	—
Watson Andy	5 9	11 02	D	1 4 67	Huddersfield	Harrogate T	Halifax T	83	15
							Swansea C	14	1
							Carlisle U	56	22
							Blackpool	115	43
							Walsall	36	5
Wilson Kevin	5 8	11 03	F	18 4 61	Banbury	Banbury U	Derby Co	122	30
							Ipswich T	98	34
							Chelsea	152	42
							Notts Co	69	3
							Bradford C (loan)	5	—
							Walsall	125	38

Trainees
Cooper, Ian A; Danks, Paul R; Davies, Thomas D; Gadsby, Matthew J; Jones, Daniel; Jones, Darren; Langley, James T; Moore, Paul; Naisbitt, Daniel J; Perry, Mark; Southwick, Matthew L; Sutton, Peter A; Ulfig, Steven P; Wood, Richard D.

Non-Contract
Mountford, Paul J.

Associated Schoolboys
Birch, Gary S; Carter, Alfonso; Fogarty, Shane G; Hawley, Carl L; Hodgetts, Andrew J; Scott, Ben.

Associated Schoolboys who have accepted the club's offer of a Traineeship/Contract
Edwards, Gary S; Gozzard, Paul J.

WATFORD

Name	Ht	Wt	Pos	Birthdate	Birthplace	Source	Clubs	Apps	Gls
Andrews Wayne	5 9	11 04	F	25 11 77	Paddington	Trainee	Watford	26	4
Bazeley Darren	5 10	11 02	D	5 10 72	Northampton	Trainee	Watford	184	16
Belgrave Kevin*	5 6	9 02	D	20 4 78	Bedford	Trainee	Watford	—	—
Chamberlain Alec	6 2	13 09	G	20 6 64	March	Ramsey T	Ipswich T	—	—
							Colchester U	184	—
							Everton	—	—
							Tranmere R (loan)	15	—
							Luton T	138	—
							Chelsea (loan)	—	—
							Sunderland	90	—
							Liverpool (loan)	—	—
							Watford	4	—
Connolly David	5 8	10 09	F	6 6 77	Willesden	Trainee	Watford	26	10
Easton Clint	5 11	10 04	M	1 10 77	Barking	Trainee	Watford	17	1
Flash Richard	5 9	11 08	M	8 4 76	Birmingham	Trainee	Manchester U	—	—
							Wolverhampton W	—	—
							Watford	1	—
Flatts Mark‡	5 6	9 08	M	14 10 72	Haringey	Trainee	Arsenal	16	—
							Cambridge U (loan)	5	1
							Brighton & HA (loan)	10	1
							Bristol C (loan)	6	—
							Grimsby T (loan)	5	—
							Watford	—	—
Foster Colin*	6 4	14 01	D	16 7 64	Chislehurst	Apprentice	Orient	174	10
							Nottingham F	72	5
							West Ham U	93	5
							Notts Co (loan)	9	—
							Watford	66	8
							Cambridge U (loan)	7	—
Gibbs Nigel	5 7	11 04	D	20 11 65	St Albans	Apprentice	Watford	336	4
Grieves Daniel	5 9	10 07	M	21 9 78	Watford	Trainee	Watford	—	—
Johnson Andy	5 9	12 01	F	25 1 79	Brighton	Trainee	Watford	—	—
Johnson Chris	5 9	12 03	M	25 1 79	Brighton	Trainee	Watford	1	—
Johnson Richard	5 10	11 13	M	27 4 74	Kurri Kurri	Trainee	Watford	122	6
Lowndes Nathan	5 11	10 04	F	2 6 77	Salford	Trainee	Leeds U	—	—
							Watford	3	—
Ludden Dominic	5 7	10 09	D	30 3 74	Basildon	Trainee	Leyton Orient	58	1
							Watford	33	—
Millen Keith	6 2	12 04	D	26 9 66	Croydon	Juniors	Brentford	305	17
							Watford	116	3
Miller Kevin	6 1	13 00	G	15 3 69	Falmouth	Newquay	Exeter C	163	—
							Birmingham C	24	—
							Watford	128	—
Mooney Tommy	5 11	12 06	F	11 8 71	Teesside North	Trainee	Aston Villa	—	—
							Scarborough	107	30
							Southend U	14	5
							Watford (loan)	10	2
							Watford	108	22
Noel-Williams Gifton	6 1	14 06	F	21 1 80	Islington	Trainee	Watford	25	2
Page Robert	6 0	12 05	D	3 9 74	Llwynpia	Trainee	Watford	64	0
Palmer Steve	6 1	12 13	M	31 3 68	Brighton	Cambridge University	Ipswich T	111	2
							Watford	76	3
Penrice Gary*	5 8	10 06	F	23 3 64	Bristol	Bristol C	Bristol R	188	54
							Watford	43	18
							Aston Villa	20	1
							QPR	82	20
							Watford	39	2
Phillips Kevin	5 7	11 00	F	25 7 73	Hitchin	Baldock T	Watford	59	24
Pluck Colin	6 0	12 10	D	6 9 78	London	Trainee	Watford	—	—
Porter Gary*	5 6	11 00	M	6 3 66	Sunderland	Apprentice	Watford	400	47

Ramage Craig	5 9	11 08	M	30 3 70	Derby	Trainee	Derby Co	42	4
							Wigan Ath (loan)	10	2
							Watford	104	27
							Peterborough U (loan)	7	—
Robinson Paul	5 9	12 11	D	14 12 78	Watford	Trainee	Watford	12	—
Rooney Mark	5 10	10 10	D	19 5 78	Lambeth	Trainee	Watford	—	—
Simpson Colin*	6 1	11 05	F	30 4 76	Oxford	Trainee	Watford	1	—
Slater Stuart	5 8	10 05	M	27 3 69	Sudbury	Apprentice	West Ham U	141	11
							Celtic	43	3
							Ipswich T	72	4
							Leicester C	—	—
							Watford	16	1
Talboys Steve	5 11	11 10	M	18 9 66	Bristol	Gloucester C	Wimbledon	26	1
							Watford	3	—
Ward Darran	6 3	12 10	D	13 9 78	Kenton	Trainee	Watford	8	—

Trainees
Boyce, Mark D; Cave, Vincent K; Cornock, Grant L W; Jones, Mark C; Panayi, Sofroni; Perpetuini, David P; Reid, Lewis I; Rogers, David A; Smith, Thomas W.

Associated Schoolboys
Beadle, Garry P; Brathwaite, Daniel S; Brown, Daniel; Chamberlain, Terry; Clark, Robert A; Deamer, William D; Dickie, James P; Dobson, Michael J; Eldridge, Russell; Ettienne, Leon A; Fisher, Dale; Fisken, Gary S; Gates, Matthew; Lee, Richard A; Lonergan, Sean; Neill, Thomas E; Reynolds, Adam T; Sinclair, Steve; Small, Aaron; Swannell, Sam A; Walker, Benjamin R.

Associated Schoolboys who have accepted the club's offer of a Traineeship/Contract
Farley, Craig; Langston, Matthew J; Marsh, David K; Maynard, Stuart A C; Murphy, Mitchell E.

WEST BROMWICH ALBION

Agnew Paul*	5 9	10 07	D	15 8 65	Lisburn	Cliftonville	Grimsby T	241	3
							WBA	39	1
Bennett Dean‡	5 10	11 00	M	13 12 77	Wolverhampton		WBA	1	—
Buckley Simon‡	5 10	11 00	F	29 2 76	Stafford	Trainee	Grimsby T	—	—
							WBA	—	—
Burgess Daryl	5 11	12 04	D	20 4 71	Birmingham	Trainee	WBA	256	8
Butler Peter	5 9	11 02	M	27 8 66	Halifax	Apprentice	Huddersfield T	5	—
							Cambridge U (loan)	14	1
							Bury	11	—
							Cambridge U	55	9
							Southend U	142	9
							Huddersfield T (loan)	7	—
							West Ham U	70	3
							Notts Co	20	—
							Grimsby T (loan)	3	—
							WBA (loan)	9	—
							WBA	17	—
Coldicott Stacy	5 8	11 04	D	29 4 74	Worcester	Trainee	WBA	82	3
							Cardiff C (loan)	6	—
Crichton Paul	6 1	12 02	G	3 10 68	Pontefract	Apprentice	Nottingham F	—	—
							Notts Co (loan)	5	—
							Darlington (loan)	5	—
							Peterborough U (loan)	4	—
							Darlington (loan)	3	—
							Swindon T (loan)	4	—
							Rotherham U (loan)	6	—
							Torquay U (loan)	13	—
							Peterborough U	47	—
							Doncaster R	77	—
							Grimsby T	133	—
							WBA	30	—
Darby Julian	6 0	11 04	M	3 10 67	Bolton	Trainee	Bolton W	270	36
							Coventry C	55	5
							WBA	39	1
Donovan Kevin	5 8	11 02	F	17 12 71	Halifax	Trainee	Huddersfield T	20	1
							Halifax T (loan)	6	—
							WBA	168	19
Germaine Gary	6 0	13 10	G	2 8 76	Birmingham	Trainee	WBA	—	—
							Scunthorpe U (loan)	11	—
Gilbert Dave	5 4	10 08	M	22 6 63	Lincoln	Apprentice	Lincoln C	30	1
							Scunthorpe U	1	—
						Boston U	Northampton T	120	21
							Grimsby T	259	41
							WBA	58	6
							York C (loan)	9	1
Groves Paul	5 11	11 05	M	28 2 66	Derby	Burton Alb	Leicester C	16	1
							Lincoln C (loan)	8	1
							Blackpool	107	21
							Grimsby T	184	38
							WBA	29	4

							Club	Apps	Gls
Hamilton Ian	5 9	11 03	F	14 12 67	Stevenage	Apprentice	Southampton	—	—
							Cambridge U	24	1
							Scunthorpe U	145	18
							WBA	203	22
Hanmer Gary			D	12 10 73	Shrewsbury	Newtown	WBA	—	—
Herbert Craig*	5 10	11 00	D	9 11 75	Coventry	Torquay U	WBA	8	—
Holmes Paul	5 10	10 13	D	18 2 68	Wortley	Apprentice	Doncaster R	47	1
							Torquay U	138	4
							Birmingham C	12	—
							Everton	21	—
							WBA	56	1
Hunt Andy	6 0	11 12	F	9 6 70	Thurrock	Kettering T	Newcastle U	43	11
							WBA (loan)	10	9
							WBA	164	54
Joseph Roger†	5 11	11 10	D	24 12 65	Paddington	Juniors	Brentford	104	2
							Wimbledon	162	—
							Millwall (loan)	5	—
							Leyton Orient	15	—
							WBA	2	—
Knight Lee‡			M	12 4 78	Birmingham	Trainee	WBA	—	—
Mardon Paul	6 0	11 10	D	14 9 69	Bristol	Trainee	Bristol C	42	—
							Doncaster R (loan)	3	—
							Birmingham C	64	—
							WBA	103	2
McDermott Andrew	5 9	11 03	D	24 3 77	Sydney	Aust Inst of Sport	QPR	6	2
							WBA	6	—
Miller Alan	6 3	14 08	G	29 3 70	Epping	Trainee	Arsenal	8	—
							Plymouth Arg (loan)	13	—
							WBA (loan)	3	—
							Birmingham C (loan)	15	—
							Middlesbrough	57	—
							Huddersfield T (loan)	—	—
							Grimsby T (loan)	3	—
							WBA	12	—
Murphy Shaun	6 1	12 00	D	5 11 70	Sydney	Perth Italia	Notts Co	109	5
							WBA	17	2
Nicholson Shane	5 10	11 00	D	3 6 70	Newark	Trainee	Lincoln C	133	6
							Derby Co	74	1
							WBA	36	—
Peschisolido Paul	5 7	10 06	F	25 5 71	Canada	Toronto Blizzard	Birmingham C	43	16
							Stoke C	66	19
							Birmingham C	9	1
							WBA	37	15
Potter Graham	6 1	11 12	M	20 5 75	Solihull	Trainee	Birmingham C	25	2
							Wycombe W (loan)	3	—
							Stoke C	45	1
							Southampton	8	—
							WBA	6	—
Raven Paul	6 1	12 11	D	28 7 70	Salisbury	School	Doncaster R	52	4
							WBA	212	14
							Doncaster R (loan)	7	—
Rodosthenous Michael	5 11	11 02	F	25 8 76	Islington	Trainee	WBA	1	—
Smith David	5 8	10 08	M	29 3 68	Gloucester		Coventry C	154	19
							Bournemouth (loan)	1	—
							Birmingham C	38	3
							WBA	80	2
Sneekes Richard	5 11	12 03	M	30 10 68	Amsterdam		Ajax	3	—
							Volendam	31	7
							Fortuna Sittard	126	20
						Locarno	Bolton W	55	7
							WBA	58	18
Spink Nigel	6 2	14 06	G	8 8 58	Chelmsford	Chelmsford C	Aston Villa	361	—
							WBA	19	—
Taylor Bob	5 10	12 02	F	3 2 67	Horden	Horden CW	Leeds U	42	9
							Bristol C	106	50
							WBA	223	94
Wills James‡			M	23 6 78	Solihull	Trainee	WBA	—	—

Trainees
Adamson, Christopher; Blake, Marvin A; Bowman, Darren M; Buckley, Adam C; Cooper, James L; Craven, Dean; Cunningham, Darren; Gabbidon, Daniel L; Garrity, Michael; Heath, Dominic; Ince, James; James, Anthony; Lowndes, Jamie A; McNamara, Ricky P; McWilliams, Jamie K; Smith, Benjamin G; Tranter, Carl.

Non-Contract
Joseph, Roger

Associated Schoolboys
Briggs, Mark; Scott, Mark; Withers, Lee T.

Associated Schoolboys who have accepted the club's offer of a Traineeship/Contract
Abercrombie, Garry B; Ball, Richard; Chambers, Adam C; Chambers, James A; Joynson, Dean; Oliver, Adam.

WEST HAM UNITED

Name	Ht	Wt	Pos	DOB	Birthplace	From	Club	Apps	Gls
Bishop Ian	5 9	10 12	M	29 5 65	Liverpool	Apprentice	Everton	1	—
							Crewe Alex (loan)	4	—
							Carlisle U	132	14
							Bournemouth	44	2
							Manchester C	19	2
							West Ham U	251	12
Blaney Steven*	6 0	13 00	D	24 3 77	Orsett	Trainee	West Ham U	—	—
Boogers Marco	6 1	12 00	M	12 1 67	Dordrecht		DS 79	60	18
							Utrecht	60	15
							RKC	33	14
							Fortuna Sittard	29	13
							RKC	71	32
							Sparta	25	11
							West Ham U	4	—
Bowen Mark	5 8	11 11	D	7 12 63	Neath	Apprentice	Tottenham H	17	2
(Transferred to Shimizu, March 1997)							Norwich C	320	24
							West Ham U	17	1
Boylan Lee§			F	2 9 78	Chelmsford	Trainee	West Ham U	1	—
Breacker Tim	5 11	13 00	D	2 7 65	Bicester	Apprentice	Luton T	210	3
							West Ham U	218	8
Cottee Tony	5 7	11 03	F	11 7 65	West Ham	Apprentice	West Ham U	212	92
(Transferred to Selangor, October 1996)							Everton	184	72
							West Ham U	67	23
Coyne Christopher	6 1	13 10	D	20 12 78	Brisbane	Perth SC	West Ham U	—	—
Dicks Julian	5 10	13 00	D	8 8 68	Bristol	Apprentice	Birmingham C	89	1
							West Ham U	159	29
							Liverpool	24	3
							West Ham U	94	21
Dowie Iain	6 1	13 07	F	9 1 65	Hatfield	Hendon	Luton T	66	16
							Fulham (loan)	5	1
							West Ham U	12	4
							Southampton	122	30
							Crystal Palace	19	6
							West Ham U	56	8
Dumitrescu Ilie	5 9	10 07	M	6 1 69	Bucharest		FC Olt	32	1
(Transferred to Club America, December 1996)							Steaua	163	71
							Tottenham H	18	4
							Sevilla (loan)	13	1
							West Ham U	10	—
Ferdinand Rio	6 2	12 00	D	7 11 78	Peckham	Trainee	West Ham U	16	2
							Bournemouth (loan)	10	—
Finn Neil§			G	29 12 78	London	Trainee	West Ham U	1	—
Futre Paulo‡	5 8	11 06	F	28 2 66	Montijo		Sporting Lisbon	21	3
							Porto	81	25
							Atletico Madrid	163	38
							Benfica (loan)	11	3
							Marseille	8	2
							Reggiana (loan)	1	1
							Reggiana	12	4
							AC Milan	—	—
							West Ham U	9	—
Hall Richard	6 2	13 11	D	14 3 72	Ipswich	Trainee	Scunthorpe U	22	3
							Southampton	126	12
							West Ham U	7	—
Hartson John	6 1	14 06	F	5 4 75	Swansea	Trainee	Luton T	54	11
							Arsenal	53	14
							West Ham U	11	5
Hodges Lee	5 5	10 02	F	2 3 78	Newham	Trainee	West Ham U	—	—
							Exeter C (loan)	17	—
							Leyton Orient (loan)	3	—
Hughes Michael	5 6	10 08	F	2 8 71	Larne	Carrick R	Manchester C	26	1
							Strasbourg	83	9
							West Ham U (loan)	17	2
							West Ham U (loan)	28	—
							West Ham U	33	3
Kitson Paul	5 11	10 12	F	9 1 71	Murton	Trainee	Leicester C	50	6
							Derby Co	105	36
							Newcastle U	36	10
							West Ham U	14	8
Lampard Frank	6 0	11 12	M	20 6 78	Romford	Trainee	West Ham U	15	—
							Swansea C (loan)	9	1
Lazaridis Stan	5 9	12 00	M	16 8 72	Perth	West Adelaide	West Ham U	26	1
Lomas Steve	6 0	11 09	M	18 1 74	Hanover	Trainee	Manchester C	111	8
							West Ham U	7	—
Mean Scott	5 11	13 08	M	13 12 73	Crawley	Trainee	Bournemouth	74	8
							West Ham U	—	—

Miklosko Ludek	6 5	14 00	G	9 12 61	Protesov	Banik Ostrava	West Ham U	302	—
Moncur John	5 7	9 10	M	22 9 66	Stepney	Apprentice	Tottenham H	21	1
							Cambridge U (loan)	4	—
							Doncaster R (loan)	4	—
							Portsmouth (loan)	7	—
							Brentford (loan)	5	1
							Ipswich T (loan)	6	—
							Nottingham F (loan)	—	—
							Swindon T	58	5
							West Ham U	77	4
Moore Jason	5 8	11 04	D	16 2 79	Dover	Trainee	West Ham U	—	—
Nieminen Mikko‡			M	25 9 78	Finland		Jazz	4	—
							West Ham U	—	—
Omoyimni Emmanuel	5 6	10 07	M	28 12 77	Nigeria	Trainee	West Ham U	1	—
							Bournemouth (loan)	7	—
Philson Graeme	5 10	11 00	D	24 3 75	Ireland	Coleraine	West Ham U	—	—
Porfirio Hugo‡			F	28 9 73	Lisbon		Sporting	11	—
							Tirsense (loan)	19	—
							Uniao Leiria (loan)	28	8
							West Ham U	23	2
Potts Steve	5 7	10 11	D	7 5 67	Hartford (USA)	Apprentice	West Ham U	332	1
Raducioiu Florin	5 10	11 06	F	17 3 70	Bucharest		Dinamo Bucharest	76	29
(Transferred to Espanyol, January 1997)							Bari	30	5
							Verona (loan)	30	2
							Brescia (loan)	29	13
							AC Milan (loan)	7	2
							Espanyol	46	14
							West Ham U	11	2
Rieper Marc	6 3	13 10	D	5 6 68	Denmark	Aarhus	Brondby	81	3
							West Ham U	85	4
Rowland Keith	5 10	10 00	M	1 9 71	Portadown	Trainee	Bournemouth	72	2
							Coventry C (loan)	2	—
							West Ham U	73	1
Sealey Les	6 1	13 06	G	29 9 57	Bethnal Green	Apprentice	Coventry C	158	—
							Luton T	207	—
							Plymouth Arg (loan)	6	—
							Manchester U (loan)	2	—
							Manchester U	31	—
							Aston Villa	18	—
							Coventry C (loan)	2	—
							Birmingham C (loan)	12	—
							Manchester U	—	—
							Blackpool	7	—
							West Ham U	2	—
							Leyton Orient	12	—
							West Ham U	2	—
Williamson Danny	5 10	11 06	M	5 12 73	West Ham	Trainee	West Ham U	51	5
							Doncaster R (loan)	13	1

Trainees
Alexander, Gary G; Bartley, Daniel R; Bowen, Justin J R; Boylan, Lee M; Etherington, Craig; Fernley, Daniel P; Finn, Neil E; Goodwin, Lee J; Henry, Anthony F; Keith, Joseph R; McCann, Grant S; McFarlane, Anthony Z; Miller, Robert; O'Reilly, Alexander; Partridge, David W; Purches, Stephen R; Richardson, Stuart J; Sains, Christopher F; Wells, Andrew R.

Associated Schoolboys
Abul, Koya; Birch, Francis A; Cleaver, Dean; Cole, Joseph J; Cooper, Ashley D; Iriekpen, Ezomo; Kelly, Adam J R; Kelly, Wayne J E; Lee, Philip C; Manur, Rayif; Mercer, James F; Richards, Lee J; Taylor, Sam A J; Tobolewski, Ross; Unal, Mehmet.

Associated Schoolboys who have accepted the club's offer of a Traineeship/Contract
Angus, Stevland; Briggs, Ryan D; Byrne, Shaun R; Gray, Edward; Newton, Adam L.

WIGAN ATHLETIC

Biggins Wayne*	5 11	11 00	F	20 11 61	Sheffield	Apprentice	Lincoln C	8	1
						King's Lynn	Burnley	78	29
							Norwich C	79	16
							Manchester C	32	9
							Stoke C	122	46
							Barnsley	47	16
							Celtic	9	—
							Stoke C	27	6
							Luton T (loan)	7	1
							Oxford U	10	1
							Wigan Ath	51	5
Bishop Charlie	5 9	13 07	D	16 2 68	Nottingham	Stoke C	Watford	—	—
							Bury	114	6
							Barnsley	130	1
							Preston NE (loan)	4	—
							Burnley (loan)	9	—
							Wigan Ath	21	—
Black Tony	5 8	11 01	F	15 7 69	Barrow	Bamber Bridge	Wigan Ath	30	2

Name	Height	Weight	Pos	Date of Birth	Birthplace	Source	Clubs	Apps	Gls
Butler John*	5 11	12 01	D	7 2 62	Liverpool	Prescot Cables	Wigan Ath	245	15
							Stoke C	262	7
							Wigan Ath	57	1
Butler Lee	6 1	14 04	G	30 5 66	Sheffield	Haworth Colliery	Lincoln C	30	—
							Aston Villa	8	—
							Hull C (loan)	4	—
							Barnsley	120	—
							Scunthorpe U (loan)	2	—
							Wigan Ath	46	—
Carragher Matthew*	5 9	10 07	D	14 1 76	Liverpool	Trainee	Wigan Ath	119	—
Carroll Roy	6 2	11 09	G	30 9 77	Belfast	Trainee	Hull C	46	0
							Wigan Ath	—	—
Diaz Isidro	5 7	9 04	M	15 5 72	Valencia	Balaguer	Wigan Ath	76	16
Farnworth Simon	5 11	13 04	G	28 10 63	Chorley	Apprentice	Bolton W	113	—
							Stockport Co (loan)	10	—
							Tranmere R (loan)	7	—
							Bury	105	—
							Preston NE	81	—
							Wigan Ath	126	—
Fearns Terry*	5 11	10 12	M	24 10 77	Liverpool	Trainee	Wigan Ath	—	—
Greenall Colin	5 11	12 12	D	30 12 63	Billinge	Apprentice	Blackpool	183	9
							Gillingham	62	4
							Oxford U	67	2
							Bury (loan)	3	—
							Bury	68	5
							Preston NE	29	1
							Chester C	42	1
							Lincoln C	43	3
							Wigan Ath	83	4
Johnson Gavin	5 11	11 07	D	10 10 70	Eye	Trainee	Ipswich T	132	11
							Luton T	5	—
							Wigan Ath	64	6
Jones Graeme	6 0	12 12	F	13 3 70	Gateshead	Bridlington T	Doncaster R	92	26
							Wigan Ath	40	31
Kilford Ian	5 10	11 00	M	6 10 73	Bristol	Trainee	Nottingham F	1	—
							Wigan Ath (loan)	8	3
							Wigan Ath	95	16
Lancashire Graham	5 10	11 12	F	19 10 72	Blackpool	Trainee	Burnley	31	8
							Halifax T (loan)	2	—
							Chester C (loan)	11	7
							Preston NE	23	2
							Wigan Ath	29	12
Lowe David	5 10	11 04	F	30 8 65	Liverpool	Apprentice	Wigan Ath	188	40
							Ipswich T	134	37
							Port Vale (loan)	9	2
							Leicester C	94	22
							Port Vale (loan)	19	5
							Wigan Ath	49	9
Martinez Roberto	5 11	11 12	M	13 7 73	Balaguer	Balaguer	Wigan Ath	85	13
Moore Andy‡	5 9	11 12	D	2 5 78	Liverpool	Trainee	Wigan Ath	—	—
Morgan Steve	6 0	11 00	D	19 9 68	Oldham	Apprentice	Blackpool	144	10
							Plymouth Arg	121	6
							Coventry C	68	2
							Bristol R (loan)	5	—
							Wigan Ath	23	1
Pender John	6 0	13 09	D	19 11 63	Luton	Apprentice	Wolverhampton W	117	3
							Charlton Ath	41	—
							Bristol C	83	3
							Burnley	171	8
							Wigan Ath	70	1
Rogers Paul	6 0	11 13	M	21 3 65	Portsmouth	Sutton U	Sheffield U	125	10
							Notts Co	22	2
							Wigan Ath	20	3
Salt Daniel*	5 10	9 10	D	17 11 77	Warrington	Trainee	Wigan Ath	—	—
Saville Andy	6 1	12 11	F	12 12 64	Hull	Local	Hull C	100	18
							Walsall	38	5
							Barnsley	82	21
							Hartlepool U	37	13
							Birmingham C	59	17
							Burnley (loan)	4	1
							Preston NE	56	30
							Wigan Ath	20	4
Sharp Kevin	5 9	10 07	M	19 9 74	Ontario	Auxerre	Leeds U	17	—
							Wigan Ath	55	8
Tyrell Kevin*	5 10	12 05	F	5 10 77	Warrington	Trainee	Wigan Ath	—	—

Ward Mark‡	5 6	10 00	M	10 10 62	Prescot	Northwich Vic	Oldham Ath	84	12
							West Ham U	165	12
							Manchester C	55	14
							Everton	83	6
							Birmingham C (loan)	9	1
							Birmingham C	54	6
							Huddersfield T	8	—
							Wigan Ath	5	—

Trainees
Alexander, Paul M; Baccino, Stephen D; Birch, Christopher J; Crompton, Paul A; Cunliffe, David A; Elwell, Steven P; Fitzhenry, Neil; Foulds, Jason J; Gallagher, Damien J; Hatton, Barry K; Hilton, Darren J; Just, Paul G; Lloyd, Neil E; Lynch, Paul E; McKie, Tony; Seddon, Gareth J; Sing, Stephen.

Associated Schoolboys
Brougham, Kevin; Court, Mark; Donachie, Stuart G; Greenwood, Stephen; Hart, Matthew; Hughes, Benjamin; Jones, Richard; Kay, Stephen B; McMahon, Francis; Morris, Andrew; Newnes, Luke; Oakes, David; Peoples, Victor; Pitts, Douglas J; Sutcliffe, David; Woodyer, Anthony.

Associated Schoolboys who have accepted the club's offer of a Traineeship/Contract
Coyne, John; Dann, John J; Jones, Philip A; Rhead, Michael; Smith, David; Wiswell, Gareth.

WIMBLEDON

Ardley Neal	5 11	11 09	M	1 9 72	Epsom	Trainee	Wimbledon	105	8
Blackwell Dean	6 1	12 10	D	5 12 69	Camden	Trainee	Wimbledon	119	1
							Plymouth Arg (loan)	7	—
Blissett Gary‡	6 0	12 07	F	29 6 64	Manchester	Altrincham	Crewe Alex	122	39
							Brentford	233	79
							Wimbledon	31	3
							Wycombe W (loan)	4	2
							Crewe Alex (loan)	10	1
Castledine Stewart	6 1	12 13	M	22 1 73	Wandsworth	Trainee	Wimbledon	21	4
							Wycombe W (loan)	7	3
Clarke Andy	5 10	11 07	F	22 7 67	Islington	Barnet	Wimbledon	156	17
Cort Carl	6 4	12 07	F	1 11 77	Southwark	Trainee	Wimbledon	1	—
							Lincoln C (loan)	6	1
Cunningham Kenny	5 11	11 02	D	28 6 71	Dublin	Tolka R	Millwall	136	1
							Wimbledon	97	—
Earle Robbie	5 9	10 10	F	27 1 65	Newcastle under Lyme	Stoke C	Port Vale	294	77
							Wimbledon	202	48
Ekoku Efan	6 1	12 00	F	8 6 67	Manchester	Sutton U	Bournemouth	62	21
							Norwich C	37	15
							Wimbledon	85	27
Euell Jason	5 11	11 02	F	6 2 77	South London	Trainee	Wimbledon	16	4
Fear Peter	5 10	11 07	D	10 9 73	London	Trainee	Wimbledon	63	2
Fitzgerald Scott	6 0	12 02	D	13 8 69	London	Trainee	Wimbledon	106	1
							Sheffield U (loan)	6	—
							Millwall (loan)	7	—
Francis Damien	6 1	10 07	M	27 2 79	London	Trainee	Wimbledon	—	—
Futcher Andy	5 7	10 07	D	10 2 78	Enfield	Trainee	Wimbledon	—	—
Gardner James	5 11	10 06	D	26 10 78	Beckenham	Trainee	Wimbledon	—	—
Gayle Marcus	6 1	12 09	M	27 9 70	Hammersmith	Trainee	Brentford	156	22
							Wimbledon	103	15
Goodman Jon	6 0	12 03	F	2 6 71	Walthamstow	Bromley	Millwall	109	35
							Wimbledon	59	11
Harford Mick	6 3	14 05	F	12 2 59	Sunderland	Lambton St BC	Lincoln C	115	41
							Newcastle U	19	4
							Bristol C	30	11
							Birmingham C	92	25
							Luton T	139	57
							Derby Co	58	15
							Luton T	29	12
							Chelsea	28	9
							Sunderland	11	2
							Coventry C	1	1
							Wimbledon	61	9
Hawkins Peter	6 0	11 04	D	18 9 78	Maidstone	Trainee	Wimbledon	—	—
Heald Paul	6 2	12 05	G	20 9 68	Wath-on-Dearne	Trainee	Sheffield U	—	—
							Leyton Orient	176	—
							Coventry C (loan)	2	—
							Crystal Palace (loan)	—	—
							Swindon T (loan)	2	—
							Wimbledon	20	—
Hinds Leigh	5 8	10 07	F	17 8 78	Beckenham	Trainee	Wimbledon	—	—
Hodges Danny	6 0	12 07	D	14 9 76	Greenwich	Trainee	Wimbledon	—	—

Name								Club	Apps	Gls
Holdsworth Dean	5 11	11 13	F	8 11 68	Walthamstow	Trainee		Watford	16	3
								Carlisle U (loan)	4	1
								Port Vale (loan)	6	2
								Swansea C (loan)	5	1
								Brentford (loan)	7	1
								Brentford	110	53
								Wimbledon	164	58
Jennings Patrick	5 9	11 00	G	24 9 79	Herts			Wimbledon	—	—
Jones Vinnie	6 0	11 12	M	5 1 65	Watford	Wealdstone		Wimbledon	77	9
								Leeds U	46	5
								Sheffield U	35	2
								Chelsea	42	4
								Wimbledon	153	12
Jupp Duncan	6 0	12 11	D	25 1 75	Guildford	Trainee		Fulham	105	2
								Wimbledon	6	—
Kimble Alan	5 10	12 04	D	6 8 66	Poole			Charlton Ath	6	—
								Exeter C (loan)	1	—
								Cambridge U	299	24
								Wimbledon	102	—
Laidlaw Iain*	6 2	12 07	D	10 12 76	Newcastle	Trainee		Wimbledon	—	—
Leonhardsen Oyvind	5 10	11 02	M	17 8 70	Norway	Clausenengen		Molde	64	9
								Rosenborg	63	20
								Wimbledon	76	13
McAllister Brian	5 11	12 05	D	30 11 70	Glasgow	Trainee		Wimbledon	78	—
								Plymouth Arg (loan)	8	—
								Crewe Alex (loan)	13	1
Murphy Brendan	5 11	11 12	G	19 8 75	Wexford	Bradford C		Wimbledon	—	—
Newhouse Aidan*	6 2	13 05	M	23 5 72	Wallasey	Trainee		Chester C	44	6
								Wimbledon	23	2
								Tranmere R (loan)	—	—
								Port Vale (loan)	2	—
								Portsmouth (loan)	6	1
								Torquay U (loan)	4	2
O'Connor Richard	5 9	10 07	F	30 8 78	Wandsworth	Trainee		Wimbledon	—	—
Odlum Gary	5 11	11 04	D	19 10 78	Beckenham	Trainee		Wimbledon	—	—
Payne Grant*	5 9	11 04	F	25 12 75	Woking	Trainee		Wimbledon	—	—
Pearce Andy	6 4	14 11	D	20 4 66	Bradford-on-Avon	Halesowen T		Coventry C	71	4
								Sheffield W	69	3
								Wimbledon	7	—
Perry Chris	5 8	10 08	D	26 4 73	London	Trainee		Wimbledon	98	1
Reeves Alan	6 0	12 00	D	19 11 67	Birkenhead	Heswall		Norwich C	—	—
								Gillingham (loan)	18	—
								Chester C	40	2
								Rochdale	121	9
								Wimbledon	57	4
Renner Victor	6 0	11 02	F	18 4 79	Sierra Leone	Trainee		Wimbledon	—	—
Reynolds Paul	6 1	11 04	D	13 9 78	Widnes	Trainee		Wimbledon	—	—
Searle Stuart*	6 2	13 00	G	27 2 79	Wimbledon			Wimbledon	—	—
Sullivan Neil	6 0	12 01	G	24 2 70	Sutton	Trainee		Wimbledon	68	—
								Crystal Palace (loan)	1	—
Thatcher Ben	5 11	12 07	D	30 11 75	Swindon	Trainee		Millwall	90	1
								Wimbledon	9	—

Trainees
Henty, Gary P; Lake, Stuart L; Miller, Paul J; O'Sullivan, Marcus F; Owusu, Ansah O; Petrovic, Timotije; Rothon, John D; Vella, Simon G; Watkins, Drew A; Williamson, Lee A; Williamson, Russell I.

Associated Schoolboys
Cook, Paul T; Hillman, Luke H; Innocent, Anton L; Jones, Mark C; Okikiolu, Kola S; Tapp, Alex; Taylor, Glen J.

Associated Schoolboys who have accepted the club's offer of a Traineeship/Contract
Agyemang, Patrick; Gray, Wayne.

WOLVERHAMPTON WANDERERS

Name								Club	Apps	Gls
Atkins Mark	6 0	13 01	M	14 8 68	Doncaster			Scunthorpe U	48	2
								Blackburn R	257	35
								Wolverhampton W	77	7
Bull Steve	6 0	12 10	F	28 3 65	Tipton	Apprentice		WBA	4	2
								Wolverhampton W	428	240
Corica Steve	5 8	10 10	M	24 3 73	Cairns	Marconi		Leicester C	16	2
								Wolverhampton W	53	2
Crowe Glen	5 10	12 13	F	25 12 77	Dublin	Trainee		Wolverhampton W	12	1
								Exeter C (loan)	10	5

Curle Keith	6 1	12 12	D	14 11 63	Bristol	Apprentice	Bristol R	32	4
							Torquay U	16	5
							Bristol C	121	1
							Reading	40	—
							Wimbledon	93	3
							Manchester C	171	11
							Wolverhampton W	21	2
Daley Tony	5 9	11 00	M	18 11 67	Birmingham	Apprentice	Aston Villa	233	31
							Wolverhampton W	19	3
De Jong Davy‡			M	26 4 75	Rotterdam		Wolverhampton W	—	—
Dennison Robbie*	5 9	12 00	M	30 4 63	Banbridge	Glenavon	WBA	16	1
							Wolverhampton W	293	40
							Swansea C (loan)	9	—
Dixon Alan			M	9 10 79	Dublin	Trainee	Wolverhampton W	0	—
Dowe Jens‡			M	1 6 68	Rostock	Greifswald	Hansa Rostock	146	22
							Munich 1860	51	4
							Hamburg	4	—
							Wolverhampton W	8	—
Emblen Neil	6 0	13 03	D	19 6 71	Bromley	Sittingbourne	Millwall	12	—
							Wolverhampton W	88	9
Ferguson Darren	5 8	12 02	M	9 2 72	Glasgow	Trainee	Manchester U	27	—
							Wolverhampton W	87	4
Foley Dominic	6 1	12 08	F	7 7 76	Cork	St James Gate	Wolverhampton W	10	1
Froggatt Steve	5 10	11 00	M	9 3 73	Lincoln	Trainee	Aston Villa	35	2
							Wolverhampton W	65	5
Gilkes Michael	5 8	11 02	M	20 7 65	Hackney	Leicester C	Reading	393	43
							Chelsea (loan)	1	—
							Southampton (loan)	6	—
							Wolverhampton W	5	1
Goodman Don	5 10	13 03	F	9 5 66	Leeds	School	Bradford C	70	14
							WBA	158	60
							Sunderland	116	40
							Wolverhampton W	95	25
Jones Mark			M	7 9 79	Walsall	Trainee	Wolverhampton W	0	—
Law Brian*	6 2	14 02	D	1 1 70	Merthyr	Apprentice	QPR	20	—
							Wolverhampton W	31	1
Leadbeater Richard	6 0	11 05	F	21 10 77	Dudley	Trainee	Wolverhampton W	1	—
Osborn Simon	5 8	11 03	M	19 1 72	New Addington	Apprentice	Crystal Palace	55	5
							Reading	32	5
							QPR	9	1
							Wolverhampton W	56	7
Pearce Dennis*	5 10	11 02	D	10 9 74	Wolverhampton	Trainee	Aston Villa	—	—
							Wolverhampton W	9	—
Richards Dean	6 2	13 08	D	9 6 74	Bradford	Trainee	Bradford C	86	4
							Wolverhampton W (loan)	10	2
							Wolverhampton W	58	2
Roberts Iwan	6 3	14 04	F	26 6 68	Bangor	Trainee	Watford	63	9
							Huddersfield T	142	50
							Leicester C	100	41
							Wolverhampton W	33	12
Robinson Carl	5 10	11 11	M	13 10 76	Llandrindod Welly	Trainee	Wolverhampton W	2	—
							Shrewsbury T (loan)	4	—
Romano Serge*	5 9	11 09	D	25 5 64	Metz		Metz	71	6
							Toulouse	66	2
							Martigues	59	3
							Wolverhampton W	4	—
Segers Hans†	5 11	12 07	G	30 10 61	Eindhoven	PSV Eindhoven	Nottingham F	58	—
							Stoke C (loan)	1	—
							Sheffield U (loan)	10	—
							Dunfermline Ath (loan)	4	—
							Wimbledon	267	—
							Wolverhampton W	—	—
Smith James	5 8	10 01	D	17 9 74	Birmingham	Trainee	Wolverhampton W	76	—
Stowell Mike	6 3	13 10	G	19 4 65	Portsmouth	Leyland Motors	Preston NE	—	—
							Everton	—	—
							Chester C (loan)	14	—
							York C (loan)	6	—
							Manchester C (loan)	14	—
							Port Vale (loan)	7	—
							Wolverhampton W (loan)	7	—
							Preston NE (loan)	2	—
							Wolverhampton W	278	—
Thomas Geoff*	6 1	13 07	M	5 8 64	Manchester	Local	Rochdale	11	1
							Crewe Alex	125	20
							Crystal Palace	195	26
							Wolverhampton W	46	8
Thompson Andy*	5 7	11 01	D	9 11 67	Cannock	Apprentice	WBA	24	1
							Wolverhampton W	376	43

Name	Ht	Wt	Pos	Birth	Birthplace	Source	Club	Apps	Gls
Venus Mark	6 0	12 09	D	6 4 67	Hartlepool		Hartlepool U	4	—
							Leicester C	61	1
							Wolverhampton W	287	7
Westwood Chris	6 0	12 02	D	13 2 77	Dudley	Trainee	Wolverhampton W	—	—
Williams Adrian	6 1	13 03	D	16 8 71	Reading	Trainee	Reading	196	14
							Wolverhampton W	6	—
Wright Jermaine	5 10	11 09	M	21 10 75	Greenwich	Trainee	Millwall	—	—
							Wolverhampton W	16	—
							Doncaster R (loan)	13	—
Young Eric*	6 3	13 07	D	25 3 60	Singapore	Slough T	Brighton & HA	126	10
							Wimbledon	99	9
							Crystal Palace	161	15
							Wolverhampton W	31	2

Trainees
Andrews, Keith J; Bray, Justin R; Crowe, Seamie M M; Hackett, Stephen A L; Hampton, Richard P; Hill, Daniel F; Hook, Lee; Hughes, Daniel P; Keane, Robert D; Naylor, Lee M; Sawyers, Robert; Stimpson, Ben N; Turpin, Jamie L; Winstone, Alexander T.

Non-Contract
Segers, Johannes C.

Associated Schoolboys
Clegg, Dean R; Dickson, Andrew; Downes, Lee; Easter, Jermaine M; Gilmore, Craig C; Jeffery, James M; Jones, Kenny R; Keith, Daryl G; Morrow, Andrew J; Pierce, Mark; Reeks, Stuart J; Rollins, Mark; Rushbury, Ian D; Tudor, Shane; Webster, Andrew J.

Associated Schoolboys who have accepted the club's offer of a Traineeship/Contract
Clark, David; Denner, Lee A; McCann, Marc.

WREXHAM

Name	Ht	Wt	Pos	Birth	Birthplace	Source	Club	Apps	Gls
Bennett Gary	5 11	12 00	F	20 9 63	Kirby	Kirby T	Wigan Ath	20	3
							Chester C	126	36
							Southend U	42	6
							Chester C	80	15
							Wrexham	121	77
							Tranmere R	29	9
							Preston NE	24	4
							Wrexham	15	5
Brace Deryn	5 7	10 12	D	15 3 75	Haverfordwest	Trainee	Norwich C	—	—
							Wrexham	57	2
Brammer David	5 10	12 00	M	28 2 75	Bromborough	Trainee	Wrexham	70	6
Carey Brian	6 3	13 12	D	31 5 68	Cork	Cork C	Manchester U	—	—
							Wrexham (loan)	3	—
							Wrexham (loan)	13	1
							Leicester C	58	1
							Wrexham	38	—
Cartwright Mark	6 2	13 06	G	13 1 73	Chester	York C	Wrexham	3	—
Chalk Martyn	5 6	10 00	F	30 8 69	Swindon	Louth U	Derby Co	7	1
							Stockport Co	43	6
							Wrexham	62	5
Connolly Karl	5 9	11 00	F	9 2 70	Prescot	Napoli (Liverpool)	Wrexham	238	61
Cross Jonathan	5 10	11 07	M	2 3 75	Wallasey	Trainee	Wrexham	117	12
							Hereford U (loan)	5	1
Futcher Stephen‡			M	24 10 76	Chester	Trainee	Wrexham	—	—
Gardner Dave†	5 9	11 00	M	17 9 76	Salford	Manchester U	Manchester C	—	—
							Wrexham	—	—
Hardy Phil	5 7	11 08	D	9 4 73	Chester	Trainee	Wrexham	231	—
Humes Tony	6 0	12 00	D	19 3 66	Blyth	Apprentice	Ipswich T	120	10
							Wrexham	163	8
Jones Barry	5 11	11 12	D	20 6 70	Prescot	Prescot T	Liverpool	—	—
							Wrexham	181	4
Jones Paul*	5 11	11 08	D	2 10 76	Wirral	Trainee	Wrexham	6	—
Marriott Andy	6 1	12 08	G	11 10 70	Nottingham	Trainee	Arsenal	—	—
							Nottingham F	11	—
							WBA (loan)	3	—
							Blackburn R (loan)	2	—
							Colchester U (loan)	10	—
							Burnley (loan)	15	—
							Wrexham	171	—
McGregor Mark	5 11	11 05	D	16 2 77	Chester	Trainee	Wrexham	71	2
Morris Steve	5 10	12 00	F	13 5 76	Liverpool	Liverpool	Wrexham	42	9
Owen Gareth	5 7	12 00	M	21 10 71	Chester	Trainee	Wrexham	214	21
Phillips Wayne	5 10	11 02	M	15 12 70	Bangor	Trainee	Wrexham	187	15
Ridler Dave	6 1	12 02	D	12 3 76	Liverpool	Prescot T	Wrexham	11	0
Roberts Neil	5 10	11 01	F	7 4 78	Wrexham	Trainee	Wrexham	—	—
Roberts Paul	5 11	11 09	F	29 7 77	Bangor	Porthmadog	Wrexham	1	—

Name	Ht	Wt	Pos	Born	Birthplace	Signed from	Club	Apps	Gls
Russell Kevin	5 9	10 12	F	6 12 66	Portsmouth	Brighton & HA	Portsmouth	4	1
							Wrexham	84	43
							Leicester C	43	10
							Peterborough U (loan)	7	3
							Cardiff C (loan)	3	—
							Hereford U (loan)	3	1
							Stoke C (loan)	5	1
							Stoke C	40	5
							Burnley	28	6
							Bournemouth	30	1
							Notts Co	11	—
							Wrexham	81	7
Skinner Craig	5 10	11 00	F	21 10 70	Bury	Trainee	Blackburn R	16	—
							Plymouth Arg	53	4
							Wrexham	50	7
Thomas Andy*	6 0	11 03	D	14 12 77	Chester	Trainee	Wrexham	—	—
Wainwright Neil	6 0	11 05	F	4 11 77	Warrington	Trainee	Wrexham	—	—
Ward Peter	5 10	11 07	F	15 10 64	Durham	Chester-le-Street	Huddersfield T	37	2
							Rochdale	84	10
							Stockport Co	142	10
							Wrexham	58	6
Watkin Steve	5 10	11 10	F	16 6 71	Wrexham	School	Wrexham	197	54
Williams Rob*	5 10	11 06	M	11 2 78	Hanover	Trainee	Wrexham	—	—
Williams Scott	6 0	12 00	D	7 8 74	Bangor	Trainee	Wrexham	29	—
Wilson Gareth*	5 9	11 01	M	23 5 78	St Asaph	Trainee	Wrexham	—	—
Wright Anthony†	5 11	11 05	F	6 3 78	Liverpool	Trainee	Wrexham	—	—

Trainees
Cooper, Steven D; Davies, Andrew M; Edwards, Leigh; Ellison, Barry J; Gibson, Robin J; Griffiths, Andrew; Hennessey, David J; Hooson, David J; Hopkins, Stephen A; Jones, Craig S; Jones, Phillip B; Mazzarella, Paul; McNeil, Jamie S; Morris, Robert I; Nall, Darren; Pepper, Julian M; Roberts, Stephen W; Shone, Gareth; Swanick, David; Taylor, Paul A; Thomas, Stephen; Walsh, David; Williams, Daniel F.

Associated Schoolboys
Andrews, Carl; Brand, Benjamin J; Campbell, Luke; Graham, Adam; Johnson, Darran M; Jones, Adam; Lee, Kenneth; O'Toole, Dominic; Owen, Adam L; Pejic, Shaun M; Powell, Sean; Renshaw, Jamie L; Rishworth, Stephen P; Taylor, Michael J; Watkin, Daniel T; Whitley, John; Williams, David P; Williams, Gavin P.

WYCOMBE WANDERERS

Name	Ht	Wt	Pos	Born	Birthplace	Signed from	Club	Apps	Gls
Bell Mickey	5 9	11 08	D	15 11 71	Newcastle	Trainee	Northampton T	153	10
							Wycombe W	118	6
Brown Steve	5 11	11 08	D	6 7 66	Northampton		Northampton T	158	19
							Wycombe W	121	8
Carroll Dave	6 0	11 08	F	20 9 66	Paisley	Ruislip Manor	Wycombe W	171	29
Cheesewright John*	5 11	14 03	G	12 1 73	Hornchurch	Tottenham H	Southend U	—	—
							Birmingham C	1	—
						Braintree T	Colchester U	40	—
							Wimbledon	—	—
							Wycombe W	18	—
Clark Anthony*	5 6	11 08	F	7 4 77	London		Wycombe W	4	—
Cornforth John	6 1	12 08	M	7 10 67	Whitley Bay	Apprentice	Sunderland	32	2
							Doncaster R (loan)	7	3
							Shrewsbury T (loan)	3	—
							Lincoln C (loan)	9	1
							Swansea C	149	16
							Birmingham C	8	—
							Wycombe W	10	—
Cousins Jason	5 10	12 06	D	14 10 70	Hayes	Trainee	Brentford	21	—
							Wycombe W	145	3
Crossley Matt*	6 1	13 00	D	18 3 68	Basingstoke	Overton U	Wycombe W	96	3
Evans Terry*	6 4	15 10	D	12 4 65	Hammersmith	Hillingdon Bor	Brentford	229	23
							Wycombe W	136	15
Farrell Dave*	5 9	11 07	F	11 11 71	Birmingham	Redditch U	Aston Villa	6	—
							Scunthorpe U (loan)	5	1
							Wycombe W	60	8
Forsyth Mike	5 11	12 06	D	20 3 66	Liverpool	Apprentice	WBA	29	—
							Northampton T (loan)	—	—
							Derby Co	325	8
							Notts Co	7	—
							Hereford U (loan)	12	—
							Wycombe W	23	2
Harkin Maurice			F	16 8 79	Derry	Trainee	Wycombe W	4	—
Kavanagh Jason	5 9	12 07	D	23 11 71	Birmingham	Birmingham C	Derby Co	99	1
							Wycombe W (loan)	27	—
							Wycombe W	27	—
Love Michael†	5 11	12 04	M	27 11 73	Stockport	Hinckley Ath	Wigan Ath	3	—
							Wycombe W	—	—
Markman Damien‡			F	7 1 78	Ascot		Wycombe W	4	—

McCarthy Paul	5 10	13 05	D	4 8 71	Cork	Trainee	Brighton & HA	181	6
							Wycombe W	40	—
McGavin Steve	5 8	12 03	F	24 1 69	North Walsham	Sudbury T	Colchester U	58	17
							Birmingham C	23	2
							Wycombe W	78	13
Parkin Brian	6 4	14 07	G	12 10 65	Birkenhead	Local	Oldham Ath	6	—
							Crewe Alex (loan)	12	—
							Crewe Alex	86	—
							Crystal Palace (loan)	—	—
							Crystal Palace	20	—
							Bristol R	241	—
							Wycombe W	24	—
Patterson Gary*	6 0	13 00	M	27 11 72	Newcastle	Trainee	Notts Co	—	—
							Shrewsbury T	57	2
							Wycombe W	59	2
							Barnet (loan)	3	—
							Chesterfield (loan)	9	—
Read Paul	5 11	12 06	F	25 9 73	Harlow	Trainee	Arsenal	—	—
							Leyton Orient (loan)	11	—
							Southend U (loan)	4	1
							Wycombe W	13	4
Ryan Keith	5 11	12 07	M	25 6 70	Northampton	Berkhamsted T	Wycombe W	89	9
Simpson Michael	5 9	10 08	M	28 2 74	Derby	Trainee	Notts Co	49	3
							Plymouth Arg (loan)	12	—
							Wycombe W	20	1
Skiverton Terry*	5 11	12 06	D	26 6 75	Mile End	Trainee	Chelsea	—	—
							Wycombe W (loan)	10	—
							Wycombe W	10	1
Stallard Mark	5 11	12 12	F	24 10 74	Derby	Trainee	Derby Co	27	2
							Fulham (loan)	4	3
							Bradford C	43	10
							Preston NE (loan)	4	1
							Wycombe W	12	4

Trainees
Allen, Lee S; Baird, Andrew C; Beeton, Alan M; Brannan, Francis J L; Cowie, Stuart G; Craker, Lewis D; Dee, Richard; Fitzpatrick, Daniel J; Glynn, James A R; Hall, Graham A; Hodson, Matthew J; Keys, Thomas E; Lamb, Jeffrey D; Passmore, Lee M; Patton, Aaron A; Rowlands, Martin C; Sheffield, James E; Teale, Richard J; Wraight, Gary P.

Associated Schoolboys
Colley, Daniel P; Moakes, Daniel G; Nye, Timothy J; Powell, Kevin; Rama-Dominguez, James.

Associated Schoolboys who have accepted the club's offer of a Traineeship/Contract
James, Matthew.

Player who does not hold a current contract but his registration has been retained by the club
Baker, Neil.

YORK CITY

Atkin Paul*	6 0	13 00	D	3 9 69	Nottingham	Trainee	Notts Co	—	—
							Bury	21	1
							York C	153	3
							Leyton Orient (loan)	5	—
Atkinson Paddy	5 9	11 06	D	22 5 70	Singapore	Sheffield U	Hartlepool U	21	3
						Workington	York C	36	—
Barras Tony	6 0	13 00	D	29 3 71	Stockton	Trainee	Hartlepool U	12	—
							Stockport Co	99	5
							Rotherham U (loan)	5	1
							York C	109	5
Bull Gary	5 10	12 02	F	12 6 66	West Bromwich	Swindon T	Southampton	—	—
							Cambridge U	19	4
						Barnet	Barnet	83	37
							Nottingham F	12	1
							Birmingham C (loan)	10	6
							Brighton & HA (loan)	10	2
							Birmingham C (loan)	6	—
							York C	56	10
Bushell Steve	5 9	11 05	M	28 12 72	Manchester	Trainee	York C	134	8
Campbell Neil	5 10	13 00	F	26 1 77	Middlesbrough	Trainee	York C	11	1
Cresswell Richard	5 11	11 07	F	20 9 77	Bridlington	Trainee	York C	33	1
							Mansfield T (loan)	5	1
Greening Jonathan	5 11	11 07	F	2 1 79	Scarborough	Trainee	York C	5	—
Hall Wayne	5 9	10 06	D	25 10 68	Rotherham	Darlington	York C	272	8
Harrison Tom‡	5 9	11 08	M	22 1 74	Edinburgh	Salvesen BC	Hearts	9	1
							Dunfermline Ath	2	—
							Clyde	27	4
							York C	1	—

Name							Club	Apps	Gls
Himsworth Gary	5 7	9 10	F	19 12 69	Appleton	Trainee	York C	88	8
							Scarborough	92	6
							Darlington	94	8
							York C	41	3
Jordan Scott	5 9	11 05	M	19 7 75	Newcastle	Trainee	York C	79	5
McMillan Andy	5 11	11 02	D	22 6 68	Bloemfontein		York C	358	4
Murty Graeme	5 10	11 12	M	13 11 74	Middlesbrough	Trainee	York C	83	6
Osborne Wayne*	5 10	11 07	M	14 1 77	Stockton	Trainee	York C	6	—
Pouton Alan	6 0	12 02	M	1 2 77	Newcastle	Newcastle U	Oxford U	—	—
							York C	22	1
Reed Martin	6 1	11 07	F	10 1 78	Scarborough	Trainee	York C	2	—
Rowe Rodney	5 8	12 00	M	30 7 75	Huddersfield	Trainee	Huddersfield T	34	2
							Scarborough (loan)	14	1
							Bury (loan)	3	—
							York C	10	3
Rush David	5 8	11 04	F	15 1 71	Sunderland	Trainee	Sunderland	59	12
							Hartlepool U (loan)	8	2
							Peterborough U (loan)	4	1
							Cambridge U (loan)	2	—
							Oxford U	92	21
							York C	2	—
Sharples John	6 0	11 03	D	26 1 73	Bury	Manchester U	Hearts	—	—
							Ayr U	53	4
							York C	38	1
Stephenson Paul	5 9	12 05	F	2 1 68	Wallsend	Apprentice	Newcastle U	61	1
							Millwall	98	6
							Gillingham (loan)	12	2
							Brentford	70	2
							York C	62	3
Thornton Mark‡			D	17 11 76	Newcastle	Trainee	Newcastle U	—	—
							York C	—	—
Tinkler Mark	5 11	12 03	M	24 10 74	Bishop Auckland	Trainee	Leeds U	25	—
							York C	9	1
Tolson Neil	6 3	11 05	F	25 10 73	Wordley	Trainee	Walsall	9	1
							Oldham Ath	3	—
							Bradford C	63	12
							Chester C (loan)	4	—
							York C	40	12
Tutill Steve	5 11	12 01	D	1 10 69	Derwent	Trainee	York C	299	6
Warrington Andy	6 3	12 11	G	10 6 76	Sheffield	Trainee	York C	33	0

Trainees
Abblett, Mark P; Boyes, Scott; Cruddas, David A; Dale, Richard B; Dawson, Andrew S; Douglass, Russell B; Foreman, John R; Garratt, Martin B G; Lamb, Stephen C; Lee, Stuart; Massey, Miles G; Middleditch, Stephen J; Norris, Michael; Pledger, Darren A; Render, Patrick J L; Rennison, Graham L; Siddle, James D.

Associated Schoolboys
Fielding, John R; Golding, Alexander C; Hakami, Darren R; Howarth, Russell M; Hubbard, Christopher; Muthana, Paul A; Reece, Paul T; Rennison, Shaun; Wood, Paul A.

Associated Schoolboys who have accepted the club's offer of a Traineeship/Contract
Batchelor, Peter; Bullock, Lee; Dibie, Michael; Farley, Michael C; Fox, Christian; Mohan, John; Urwin, Jonathan G; Walters, Steven K.

THE FOREIGN (INTERNATIONAL) LEGION

The following full international players born outside the UK played in the FA Premier League and Nationwide Football League in 1996–97.

	Player	Club	From	Fee £s
AUSTRALIA	Paul Agostino	Bristol C	Young Boys Berne	50,000
	Andy Bernal	Reading	Sydney Olympic	30,000
	Mark Bosnich	Aston Villa	Croatia Sydney	Free
	Steve Corica	Wolverhampton W	Leicester C	1,100,000
	John Filan	Coventry C	Cambridge U	300,000
	George Kulcsar	Bradford C	Antwerp	100,000
	Stan Lazaridis	West Ham U	West Adelaide	300,000
	Kevin Muscat	Crystal Palace	South Melbourne	75,000
	Robbie Slater	Southampton	West Ham U	250,000
	Mark Schwarzer	Middlesbrough	Bradford C	1,500,000
	Jason Van Blerk	Millwall	Go Ahead	300,000
	Carl Veart	Crystal Palace	Sheffield U	200,000
BARBADOS	Greg Goodridge	Bristol C	QPR	50,000
BELARUS	Petr Katchuro	Sheffield U	Dynamo Minsk	650,000
BELGIUM	Philippe Albert	Newcastle U	Anderlecht	2,650,000
	Regis Genaux	Coventry C	Standard Liege	1,000,000
BERMUDA	Shaun Goater	Bristol C	Rotherham U	175,000
	Kyle Lightbourne	Walsall	Scarborough	Free
BRAZIL	Branco	Middlesbrough	Internacional	Free
	Emerson	Middlesbrough	Porto	4,000,000
	Isaias	Coventry C	Benfica	500,000
	Juninho	Middlesbrough	Sao Paulo	4,750,000
BULGARIA	Boncho Guentchev	Luton T	Ipswich T	Free
	Bobby Mikhailov	Reading	Botev Plovdiv	300,000
CAMEROON	Charlie Ntamark	Walsall	Boreham Wood	Free
CANADA	Carlo Corazzin	Plymouth Arg	Cambridge U	150,000
	Craig Forrest	Ipswich T	Trainee	
	Martin Nash	Stockport Co	Vancouver	undisclosed
	Paul Peschisolido	Birmingham C	Stoke C	400,000
COLOMBIA	Faustino Asprilla	Newcastle U	Parma	7,500,000
COSTA RICA	Mauricio Solis	Derby Co	Heridiano	600,000
	Paulo Wanchope	Derby Co	Heridiano	600,000
CROATIA	Alijosa Asanovic	Derby Co	Hajdk Split	950,000
	Slaven Bilic	West Ham U	Karlsruhe	1,650,000
	Nikola Jerkan	Nottingham F	Oviedo	1,000,000
	Igor Stimac	Derby Co	Hajduk Split	1,500,000
CYPRUS	Costas Constantinou	Barnet	Omonia	60,000
CZECH REPUBLIC	Patrik Berger	Liverpool	Borussia Dortmund	3,250,000
	Ludek Miklosko	West Ham U	Banik Ostrava	300,000
	Karel Poborsky	Manchester U	Slavia Prague	3,500,000
	Pavel Srnicek	Newcastle U	Banik Ostrava	350,000
DENMARK	Mikkel Beck	Middlesbrough	Fortuna Cologne	Free
	Per Frandsen	Bolton W	FC Copenhagen	1,250,000
	Jacob Laursen	Derby Co	Silkeborg	500,000
	Jan Molby	Swansea C	Liverpool	Free
	Allan Nielsen	Tottenham H	Brondby	1,650,000
	Per Pedersen	Blackburn R	Odense	2,500,000
	Marc Rieper	West Ham U	Brondby	1,000,000
	Peter Schmeichel	Manchester U	Brondby	550,000
	Claus Thomsen	Everton	Ipswich T	900,000
ESTONIA	Mart Poom	Derby Co	Flora	500,000
FINLAND	Mixu Paatelainen	Bolton W	Aberdeen	300,000
	Jari Vanhala	Bradford C	Finn Pa	Non-contract
FRANCE	Eric Cantona	Manchester U	Leeds U	1,200,000
	David Ginola	Newcastle U	Paris St Germain	2,500,000
	Frank Leboeuf	Chelsea	Strasbourg	2,500,000
	Patrick Vieira	Arsenal	AC Milan	3,500,000
GEORGIA	Mikhail Kavelashvili	Manchester C	Spartak Vladikavkaz	1,400,000
	Georgi Kinkladze	Manchester C	Dynamo Tbilisi	2,000,000

GERMANY	Michael Frontzeck	Manchester C	Moenchengladbach	350,000
	Eike Immel	Manchester C	Stuttgart	400,000
	Uwe Rosler	Manchester C	Dynamo Dresden	750,000
GHANA	Tony Yeboah	Leeds U	Eintracht Frankfurt	3,400,000
GREECE	George Donis	Blackburn R	Panathinaikos	Free
HOLLAND	Dennis Bergkamp	Arsenal	Inter Milan	7,500,000
	Regi Blinker	Sheffield W	Feyenoord	275,000
	Jordi Cruyff	Manchester U	Barcelona	1,400,000
	Ruud Gullit	Chelsea	Sampdoria	Free
	Glenn Helder	Arsenal	Vitesse	2,300,000
	Bryan Roy	Nottingham F	Foggia	2,500,000
	Orlando Trustfull	Sheffield W	Feyenoord	750,000
	Ulrich Van Gobbel	Southampton	Galatasaray	1,300,000
	Pierre Van Hooijdonk	Nottingham F	Celtic	3,500,000
ICELAND	Gudni Bergsson	Bolton W	Tottenham H	65,000
	Thorvaldur Orlygsson	Oldham Ath	Stoke C	180,000
	Larus Sigurdsson	Stoke C	Thor	undisclosed
ISRAEL	Eyal Berkovic	Southampton	Maccabi Haifa	1,000,000
	Ronny Rosenthal	Tottenham H	Liverpool	250,000
ITALY	Roberto Di Matteo	Chelsea	Lazio	4,900,000
	Fabrizio Ravanelli	Middlesbrough	Juventus	7,000, 000
	Andrea Silenzi	Nottingham F	Torino	1,800,000
	Gianluca Viallia	Chelsea	Juventus	Free
	Gianfranco Zola	Chelsea	Parma	4,500,000
NIGERIA	Efan Ekoku	Wimbledon	Norwich C	900,000
NORWAY	Espen Baardsen	Tottenham H	San Francisco	Free
	Henning Berg	Blackburn R	Lillestrom	400,000
	Stig Inge Bjornebye	Liverpool	Rosenborg	600,000
	Lars Bohinen	Blackburn R	Nottingham F	700,000
	Jan Aage Fjortoft	Sheffield U	Middlesbrough	700,000
	Froda Grodas	Chelsea	Lillestrom	60,000
	Alf Inge Haaland	Nottingham F	Young Boys	250,000
	Gunnar Halle	Leeds U	Oldham Ath	400,000
	Erland Johnsen	Chelsea	Bayern Munich	300,000
	Ronny Johnsen	Manchester U	Besiktas	1,200,000
	Oyvind Leonhardsen	Wimbledon	Rosenborg	400,000
	Claus Lundekvam	Southampton	Brann	400,000
	Roger Nilsen	Sheffield U	Viking Stavanger	550,000
	Egil Ostenstad	Southampton	Viking	800,000
	Ole Gunnar Solskjaer	Manchester U	Molde	1,500,000
POLAND	Dariusz Kubicki	Sunderland	Aston Villa	100,000
	Dariusz Wdowczyk	Reading	Celtic	Free
PORTUGAL	Paulo Futre	West Ham U	AC Milan	Free
	Fernando Nelson	Aston Villa	Sporting Lisbon	1,750,000
	Hugo Porfirio	West Ham U	Sporting Lisbon	Loan
ROMANIA	Illie Dumitrescu	West Ham U	Tottenham H	1,500,000
	Dan Petrescu	Chelsea	Sheffield W	2,300,000
	Florin Raducioiu	West Ham U	Espanyol	2,400,000
RUSSIA	Andrei Kanchelskis	Everton	Manchester U	5,500,000
	Dmitri Kharine	Chelsea	CSKA Moscow	200,000
SLOVAKIA	Vladimir Kinder	Middlesbrough	Slovan Bratislava	1,000,000
SOUTH AFRICA	Lucas Radebe	Leeds U	Kaiser Chiefs	250,000
ST VINCENT	Rodney Jack	Torquay U	Lambada	Free
SWEDEN	Jan Erikson	Sunderland	Helsingborg	250,000
	Niklas Gudmundsson	Blackburn R	Halmstad	Loan
	Pontus Kamark	Leicester C	IFK Gothenburg	840,000
	Anders Limpar	Birmingham C	Everton	100,000
	Marino Rahmberg	Derby Co	Degerfors	undisclosed
	Robert Steiner	Bradford C	Norrkoping	Loan
SWITZERLAND	Marc Hottiger	Everton	Newcastle U	700,000\
	Ramon Vega	Tottenham H	Cagliari	3,750,000
TRINIDAD & TOBAGO	Dwight Yorke	Aston Villa	Signal Hill	120,000
	Clint Marcelle	Barnsley	Felgueiras	Free
USA	Ian Feuer	Luton T	West Ham U	580,000
	Kasey Keller	Leicester C	Millwall	900,000
	Michael Lapper	Southend U	USSF	150,000
	Jurgen Sommer	QPR	Luton T	600,000
UKRAINE	Alex Evtushok	Coventry C	Dnepr	800,000
YUGOSLAVIA	Sasa Curcic	Bolton W	Partizan Belgrade	1,000,000
	Savo Milosevic	Aston Villa	Partizan Belgrade	3,500,000
	Dejan Stefanovic	Sheffield W	Red Star Belgrade	2,000,000
ZIMBABWE	Bruce Grobbelaar	Plymouth Arg	Southampton	Free
	Peter Ndlovu	Coventry C	Highlanders	10,000

TRANSFERS 1996–97

JULY 1996	From	To	Fee in £s
10 Ablett, Gary I.	Everton	Birmingham City	390,000
3 Allen, Christopher A.	Oxford United	Nottingham Forest	450,000
19 Appleby, Matthew W.	Darlington	Barnsley	200,000
12 Archdeacon, Owen D.	Barnsley	Carlisle United	Free
31 Austin, Kevin L.	Leyton Orient	Lincoln City	30,000
31 Baird, Ian J.	Plymouth Argyle	Brighton & Hove Albion	35,000
23 Beaumont, Christopher P.	Stockport County	Chesterfield	30,000
1 Bishop, Darren C.	Barnsley	Wigan Athletic	20,000
16 Black, Kingsley	Nottingham Forest	Grimsby Town	25,000
3 Blackford, Gary	Enfield	Slough Town	undisclosed
8 Booth, Andrew D.	Huddersfield Town	Sheffield Wednesday	2,700,000
5 Bowyer, Lee D.	Charlton Athletic	Leeds United	2,800,000
30 Brabin, Gary	Bury	Blackpool	200,000
22 Bunce, Nathan	Yeading	Hayes	undisclosed
22 Butler, Paul J.	Rochdale	Bury	100,000
30 Butler, Philip A.	Gillingham	Blackpool	225,000
19 Caesar, John	Aylesbury United	Chesham United	undisclosed
9 Campbell, Jason	Ilkeston Town	Lincoln United	undisclosed
19 Carey, Brian P.	Leicester City	Wrexham	100,000
10 Chamberlain, Alec F.R.	Sunderland	Watford	40,000
11 Clarke, Matthew J.	Rotherham United	Sheffield Wednesday	325,000
18 Coton, Anthony P.	Manchester United	Sunderland	600,000
4 Crawford, Stephen	Raith Rovers	Millwall	1,000,000 combined
29 Cotter, Michael A.	Gravesend & Northfleet	Burton Albion	undisclosed
30 Cutler, Neil	West Bromwich Albion	Crewe Alexandra	undisclosed
4 Dair, Jason	Raith Rovers	Millwall	1,000,000 combined
13 Davies, Martin L.	Cambridge United	Rushden & Diamonds	6,000
12 Dixon, Ben	Lincoln City	Blackpool	20,000
25 Dowell, Wayne A.	Burnley	Rochdale	Free
11 Foreman, Darren	Hednesford Town	Gateshead	undisclosed
25 Forsyth, Richard	Birmingham City	Stoke City	200,000
4 Freeman, Darren B.A.	Gillingham	Fulham	15,000
17 Furlong, Paul A.	Chelsea	Birmingham City	1,500,000
17 Goater, Leonardo S.	Rotherham United	Bristol City	175,000
8 Groves, Paul	Grimsby Town	West Bromwich Albion	600,000
19 Hall, Richard A.	Southampton	West Ham United	1,400,000
4 Hartley, Paul	Hamilton Academical	Millwall	400,000
25 Hobbs, Paul	Hendon	Chesham United	undisclosed
19 Horne, Barry	Everton	Birmingham City	250,000
12 Houghton, Scott A.	Walsall	Peterborough United	60,000
12 Hunter, Barry V.	Wrexham	Reading	400,000
8 Izzet, Mustafa K.	Chelsea	Leicester City	650,000
26 Jemson, Nigel B.	Notts County	Oxford United	60,000
27 Jennings, Gareth J.	Hednesford Town	Gresley Rovers	undisclosed
27 Jepson, Ronald F.	Huddersfield Town	Bury	40,000
8 Jones, Graeme A.	Doncaster Rovers	Wigan Athletic	150,000
25 Jones, Paul S.	Wolverhampton Wanderers	Stockport County	60,000
10 Joyce, Warren G.	Burnley	Hull City	Free
31 Kerr, David W.	Manchester City	Mansfield Town	20,000
19 Laker, Barry J.	Banstead Athletic	Sutton United	undisclosed
30 Martin, David	Gillingham	Leyton Orient	Free
26 Martyn, Antony M.	Crystal Palace	Leeds United	2,250,000
23 Matthew, Damien	Crystal Palace	Burnley	65,000
26 McAllister, Gary	Leeds United	Coventry City	3,000,000
5 McCarthy, Paul J.	Brighton & Hove Albion	Wycombe Wanderers	100,000
30 McDougald, David E.J.	Brighton & Hove Albion	Rotherham United	50,000
4 Morrison, Andrew C.	Blackpool	Huddersfield Town	500,000
19 Myers, Martin C.	Telford United	Solihull Borough	undisclosed
16 Nash, Carlo J.	Clitheroe	Crystal Palace	35,000
29 Newell, Michael C.	Blackburn Rovers	Birmingham City	775,000
26 O'Connell, Brendan	Barnsley	Charlton Athletic	125,000
12 O'Connor, Martin J.	Walsall	Peterborough United	350,000
26 O'Neill, Michael A.	Hibernian	Coventry City	500,000
4 Payton, Andrew P.	Barnsley	Huddersfield Town	350,000
30 Peake, Jason W.	Rochdale	Brighton & Hove Albion	80,000
24 Peschisolido, Paolo P.	Birmingham City	West Bromwich Albion	600,000
22 Piper, Leonard H.	Wimbledon	Gillingham	40,000
23 Potter, Graham S.	Stoke City	Southampton	250,000
23 Purse, Darren J.	Leyton Orient	Oxford United	100,000
15 Roberts, Iwan W.	Leicester City	Wolverhampton Wanderers	1,000,000
22 Sandford, Lee R.	Stoke City	Sheffield United	500,000
30 Shearer, Alan	Blackburn Rovers	Newcastle United	15,000,000
17 Sealey, Leslie J.	West Ham United	Leyton Orient	Free
4 Sinclair, David	Raith Rovers	Millwall	1,000,000 combined
12 Slade, Steven A.	Tottenham Hotspur	Queens Park Rangers	350,000

	From	To	Fee in £s
1 Speed, Gary A.	Leeds United	Everton	3,500,000
23 St. Hilaire, Martin	Chesham United	Enfield	undisclosed
2 Stewart, Marcus P.	Bristol Rovers	Huddersfield Town	1,200,000
5 Thatcher, Ben D.	Millwall	Wimbledon	1,700,000
15 Tolson, Neil	Bradford City	York City	60,000
30 Watson, Paul D.	Gillingham	Fulham	13,000
11 Widdrington, Thomas	Southampton	Grimsby Town	300,000
3 Wilkins, Richard J.	Hereford United	Colchester United	30,000
3 Williams, Adrian	Reading	Wolverhampton Wanderers	750,000
19 Wrack, Darren	Derby County	Grimsby Town	100,000

TEMPORARY TRANSFERS

18 Mean, Scott	AFC Bournemouth	West Ham United	

AUGUST 1996

	From	To	Fee in £s
8 Barness, Anthony	Chelsea	Charlton Athletic	165,000
5 Bodley, Michael J.	Southend United	Peterborough United	75,000
16 Bright, David J.	Mangotsfield United	Clevedon Town	undisclosed
8 Bryant, Matthew	Bristol City	Gillingham	65,000
5 Butler, Peter J.	Notts County	West Bromwich Albion	175,000
29 Canham, Scott W.	West Ham United	Brentford	25,000
1 Coates, Daniel	Hednesford Town	Halesowen Town	undisclosed
9 Collins, Wayne A.	Crewe Alexandra	Sheffield Wednesday	600,000
15 Cousins, Robert P.	Bath City	Yeovil Town	undisclosed
23 Curcic, Sasa	Bolton Wanderers	Aston Villa	4,000,000
2 Curle, Keith	Manchester City	Wolverhampton Wanderers	650,000
9 Day, Christopher N.	Tottenham Hotspur	Crystal Palace	225,000
12 Debont, Andrew C.	Wolverhampton Wanderers	Hereford United	Free
23 Dickov, Paul	Arsenal	Manchester City	1,000,000
6 Dryden, Richard A.	Bristol City	Southampton	150,000
22 Eckhardt, Jeffrey E.	Stockport County	Cardiff City	30,000
7 Fergusson, Stephen J.	Worcester City	Gloucester City	undisclosed
16 Ford, Jonathan S.	Bradford City	Gillingham	15,000
16 Gaughan, Steven E.	Darlington	Chesterfield	undisclosed
2 Gerrard, Paul W.	Oldham Athletic	Everton	1,000,000
15 Gill, Jeremy M.	Bath City	Yeovil Town	undisclosed
15 Glover, Edward L.	Port Vale	Rotherham United	150,000
19 Goodridge, Gregory R.S.	Queens Park Rangers	Bristol City	50,000
12 Hargreaves, Christian	West Bromwich Albion	Hereford United	Free
7 Hessenthaler, Andrew	Watford	Gillingham	235,000
17 Jackson, Joseph	Worcester City	Bilston Town	undisclosed
13 James, Anthony C.	Hereford United	Plymouth Argyle	60,000
17 Keller, Kasey C.	Millwall	Leicester City	900,000
15 Kiely, Dean L.	York City	Bury	undisclosed
16 Leitch, Donald S.	Heart of Midlothian	Swindon Town	15,000
31 Marshall, Ian P.	Ipswich Town	Leicester City	800,000
7 Oakes, Scott J.	Luton Town	Sheffield Wednesday	425,000
16 Onuora, Ifem	Mansfield Town	Gillingham	12,500
15 Overson, Vincent D.	Stoke City	Burnley	Free
2 Parrish, Sean	Doncaster Rovers	Northampton Town	35,000
15 Pickering, Albert G.	Coventry City	Stoke City	280,000
17 Prior, Spencer J.	Norwich City	Leicester City	600,000
17 Quinn, Niall J.	Manchester City	Sunderland	1,300,000
13 Rhodes, Jason P.	Burton Albion	Bilston Town	undisclosed
16 Robinson, Philip J.	Chesterfield	Notts County	80,000
15 Rodwell, James	Halesowen Town	Rushden & Diamonds	undisclosed
12 Scott, Ian J.	Kettering Town	Worcester City	undisclosed
14 Sharpe, Lee S.	Manchester United	Leeds United	4,500,000
19 Showler, Paul	Bradford City	Luton Town	50,000
15 Simpkins, John P.	Newport (IW)	Salisbury City	undisclosed
30 Vincent, Jamie R.	Crystal Palace	AFC Bournemouth	25,000
16 Welsh, Stephen	Partick Thistle	Peterborough United	undisclosed
13 Wyatt, Michael J.	Forest Green Rovers	Bath City	undisclosed

TEMPORARY TRANSFERS

23 Adebowale, Andrew	Gloucester City	St Albans City
19 Angell, Brett A.	Sunderland	Stockport County
27 Bass, David	Reading	Basingstoke Town
16 Bochenski, Simon	Barnsley	Scarborough
16 Boyce, David J.	Havant Town	Salisbury City
30 Coldicott, Stacy	West Bromwich Albion	Cardiff City
21 Crookes, Dominic	Dagenham & Redbridge	Northwich Victoria
23 Cundy, Jason V.	Tottenham Hotspur	Bristol City
30 Cutler, Neil A.	Crewe Alexandra	Chester City
16 Dennis, Leonard C.	Sutton United	Welling United
23 Dunwell, Richard K.	Barnet	Walton & Hersham
31 Evans, Thomas	Crystal Palace	Harrow Borough
17 Flaherty, Terence	Yeading	Berkhamsted Town
30 Grant, Anthony J.	Preston North End	Glenavon
17 Green, Christopher M.	Sutton United	Margate

	From	To	Fee in £s
17 Harding, Paul	Cardiff City	Kettering Town	
23 Harrison, Richard	Matlock Town	Alfreton Town	
20 Hateley, Mark W.	Queens Park Rangers	Leeds United	
20 Jackson, Matthew A.	Everton	Queens Park Rangers	
27 Kelly, Gary A.	Bury	Oldham Athletic	
17 Lee, Kevin A.	Forest Green Rovers	Evesham United	
30 Mahoney-Johnsen, Michael	Queens Park Rangers	Wycombe Wanderers	
27 Martin, Jae A.	Birmingham City	Lincoln City	
27 Masters, Paul J.	Salisbury City	Waterlooville	
16 Mee, Edward W.	Hayes	Wembley	
30 Miles, Benjamin D.	Swansea City	Slough Town	
31 Milsom, Paul J.	Gloucester City	Forest Green Rovers	
30 Moore, Chris T.	Bishops Stortford	Billericay Town	
14 O'Hagan, Daniel A.	Plymouth Argyle	Weston-Super-Mare	
30 Pack, Lenny J.	Cambridge United	Baldock Town	
27 Roberts, Ben J.	Middlesbrough	Bradford City	
8 Smith, John U.	Fleet Town	Wokingham Town	
30 Trollope, Paul J.	Derby County	Grimsby Town	
1 Turpin, Simon A.	Crewe Alexandra	Sligo Rovers	
30 Whittaker, Stuart	Bolton Wanderers	Wigan Athletic	
21 Wigg, Nathan M.	Cardiff City	Merthyr Tydfill	
30 Williams, Darren P.	Dagenham & Redbridge	Boreham Wood	

SEPTEMBER 1996

6 Barnes, Paul L.	Birmingham City	Burnley	350,000
20 Boyce, David J.	Havant Town	Salisbury City	undisclosed
17 Burnett, Wayne	Bolton Wanderers	Huddersfield Town	150,000
26 Carpenter, Richard	Gillingham	Fulham	25,000
19 Elkins, Gary	Wimbledon	Swindon Town	100,000
13 Flack, Steven R.	Cardiff City	Exeter City	10,000
19 Garnett, Shaun M.	Swansea City	Oldham Athletic	150,000
5 Hollingdale, Robert	Wembley	Boreham Wood	undisclosed
17 Kelly, Gary A.	Bury	Oldham Athletic	10,000
27 Kinsella, Mark	Colchester United	Charlton Athletic	150,000
18 May, Leroy A.	Kidderminster Harriers	Kettering Town	undisclosed
17 McMahon, Gerard J.	Tottenham Hotspur	Stoke City	450,000
13 Moss, David	Scunthorpe United	Partick Thistle	undisclosed
27 Naylor, Glenn	York City	Darlington	undisclosed
6 O'Hanlon, Kelham G.	Dundee United	Preston North End	12,000
20 Ormondroyd, Ian	Bradford City	Oldham Athletic	Free
6 Parks, Anthony	Falkirk	Blackpool	Free
17 Rankine, Simon M.	Wolverhampton Wanderers	Preston North End	100,000
13 Rattray, Kevin	Gillingham	Barnet	15,000
20 Richardson, John P.	Enfield	Hendon	undisclosed
27 Riley, Andrew	Kingstonian	Sutton United	undisclosed
6 Robertson, Paul	Doncaster Rovers	Witton Albion	undisclosed
6 Sedgemore, Benjamin R.	Peterborough United	Mansfield Town	Free
3 Slater, Robert D.	West Ham United	Southampton	250,000
6 Taylor, Shaun	Swindon Town	Bristol City	50,000
4 Turner, Andrew P.	Tottenham Hotspur	Portsmouth	250,000
6 Warmington, Curtis	Kingstonian	Hendon	undisclosed
5 Watson, Andrew A.	Blackpool	Walsall	60,000
17 Wood, Jeffrey J.	Aldershot Town	Ford United	undisclosed

TEMPORARY TRANSFERS

20 Adams, Kieren	Barnet	Hayes
14 Anderson, Mark R.	Aldershot Town	Wokingham Town
5 Ashcroft, Lee	West Bromwich Albion	Preston North End
6 Barron, Michael J.	Middlesbrough	Hartlepool United
23 Boswell, Matthew H.	Port Vale	Hinckley Town
9 Brown, Kenneth J.	West Ham United	Reading
13 Brown, Michael A.	Preston North End	Rochdale
20 Bullimore, Wayne A.	Bradford City	Doncaster Rovers
6 Burnett, Wayne	Bolton Wanderers	Huddersfield Town
20 Byng, David	Doncaster Rovers	Ilkeston Town
26 Campbell, David A.	Tamworth	Sutton Coldfield Town
30 Charnock, Philip A.	Liverpool	Crewe Alexandra
27 Crawford, James	Newcastle United	Rotherham United
9 Crichton, Paul A.	Grimsby Town	West Bromwich Albion
20 Cureton, Jamie	Norwich City	Bristol Rovers
26 Druce, Mark A.	Oxford United	Rotherham United
20 Dunn, Iain G.W.	Huddersfield Town	Scunthorpe United
27 Forsyth, Michael E.	Notts County	Hereford United
9 Griemink, Bart	Birmingham City	Barnsley
26 Hamill, Rory	Fulham	Glentoran
28 Hannigan, Al J.	Rushden & Diamonds	Enfield
6 Helliwell, Ian	Burnley	Mansfield Town
13 Hodges, Lee L.	West Ham United	Exeter City
20 Hodgson, Stephen	Morecambe	Gretna

	From	To	Fee in £s
5 Holland, Christopher J.	Newcastle United	Birmingham City	
6 Huckerby, Darren C.	Newcastle United	Millwall	
26 Johnstone, Glenn P.	Morecambe	Gretna	
13 Kavanagh, Graham A.	Middlesbrough	Stoke City	
20 Lester, Jack W.	Grimsby Town	Doncaster Rovers	
9 Marshall, Andrew J.	Norwich City	AFC Bournemouth	
6 Mautone, Steve	West Ham United	Crewe Alexandra	
6 McAvoy, Gordon	Farnborough Town	Staines Town	
20 McElhatton, Michael	AFC Bournemouth	Scarborough	
2 McGleish, Scott	Peterborough United	Cambridge United	
20 McGoldrick, Eddie J.	Arsenal	Manchester City	
28 Mitten, Charles H.	Dover Athletic	Margate	
13 Moore, Ian R.	Tranmere Rovers	Bradford City	
23 Morris, Mark J.	AFC Bournemouth	Gillingham	
27 Neal, Ashley J.	Liverpool	Brighton & Hove Albion	
13 Nixon, Eric W.	Tranmere Rovers	Bradford City	
30 Omoyinmi, Emmanuel	West Ham United	AFC Bournemouth	
20 O'Riordan, Donald J.	Gloucester City	Dorchester Town	
19 Otto, Ricky	Birmingham City	Charlton Athletic	
6 Palmer, Lee J.	Cambridge United	Woking	
6 Reeder, Andrew	Chesham United	Uxbridge	
30 Regis, David	Barnsley	Peterborough United	
18 Rigby, Malcolm R.	Nottingham Forest	Ilkeston Town	
21 Scott, Andrew M.	Cardiff City	Merthyr Tydfil	
27 Scott, Ian J.	Worcester City	Hinckley Town	
13 Smart, Allan A.C.	Preston North End	Northampton Town	
2 Sutton, Wayne F.	Derby County	Hereford United	
27 Taylor, John P.	Luton Town	Lincoln City	
20 Taylor, Martin J.	Derby County	Crewe Alexandra	
6 Trigg, Darryl	Enfield	Chesham United	
6 Walker, John	Grimsby Town	Mansfield Town	
11 Wassall, Darren P.	Derby County	Manchester City	
23 Woodsford, Jamie M.	Luton Town	Kettering Town	

OCTOBER 1996

	From	To	Fee in £s
23 Abrahams, Paul	Brentford	Colchester United	20,000
4 Baker, David P.	Torquay United	Scunthorpe United	15,000
31 Bolton, James I.	Kingstonian	Hendon	undisclosed
18 Butters, Guy	Portsmouth	Gillingham	150,000
23 Carter, Reckey	Kettering Town	Solihull Borough	undisclosed
2 Crichton, Paul A.	Grimsby Town	West Bromwich Albion	250,000
18 Cureton, Jamie	Norwich City	Bristol Rovers	200,000
4 Dennis, Leonard C.	Sutton United	Welling United	undisclosed
23 Druce, Mark A.	Oxford United	Rotherham United	50,000
4 Evans, Stuart P.	Gresley Rovers	Halesowen Town	undisclosed
14 Farrell, Sean P.	Peterborough United	Notts County	80,000
31 Finnan, Stephen J.	Birmingham City	Notts County	300,000
15 Foster, Stephen	Telford United	Woking	undisclosed
11 Griemink, Bart	Birmingham City	Peterborough United	25,000
11 Hendrie, John G.	Middlesbrough	Barnsley	250,000
8 Holdsworth, David G.	Watford	Sheffield United	450,000
31 Holland, Christopher J.	Newcastle United	Birmingham City	600,000
12 Johnstone, Glenn P.	Morecambe	Gretna	undisclosed
11 Kavanagh, Graham A.	Middlesbrough	Stoke City	undisclosed
11 Kirkup, Andrew	Rushden & Diamonds	Gloucester City	undisclosed
11 Law, Nicholas	Chesterfield	Hereford United	Free
14 Malkin, Christopher G.	Millwall	Blackpool	275,000
23 McElhatton, Michael T.	AFC Bournemouth	Scarborough	15,000
24 McGoldrick, Eddie J.P.	Arsenal	Manchester City	300,000
12 McGrath, Paul	Aston Villa	Derby County	100,000
31 Morris, Mark J.	AFC Bournemouth	Brighton & Hove Albion	Free
4 Pennock, Adrian B.	AFC Bournemouth	Gillingham	20,000
9 Reeves, David	Carlisle United	Preston North End	300,000
25 Saville, Andrew V.	Preston North End	Wigan Athletic	100,000
25 Scott, Ian J.	Worcester City	Hinckley Town	undisclosed
25 Shipperley, Neil J.	Southampton	Crystal Palace	1,000,000
9 Smart, Allan A.C.	Preston North End	Carlisle United	exch.
31 Sugrue, James S.	Hayes	Aldershot Town	2000
27 Walker, Clive	Stourbridge	Nuneaton Borough	undisclosed
24 Whitbread, Adrian R.	West Ham United	Portsmouth	250,000
18 Williams, Darren	York City	Sunderland	50,000

TEMPORARY TRANSFERS

	From	To	
23 Abbey, Nathanael	Luton Town	Worcester City	
26 Anderson, Mark R.	Aldershot Town	Bracknell Town	
18 Armstrong, Steven C.	Nottingham Forest	Gillingham	
11 Bass, Jonathan D.M.	Birmingham City	Carlisle United	
28 Bennett, Frank	Southampton	Shrewsbury Town	
28 Bent, Junior A.	Bristol City	Shrewsbury Town	

	From	*To*	*Fee in £s*
15 Casey, Paul	Boston United	Lincoln United	
25 Creaney, Gerard	Manchester City	Ipswich Town	
29 Cundy, Jason V.	Tottenham Hotspur	Ipswich Town	
29 Davies, Simon I.	Manchester United	Huddersfield Town	
25 Davis, Neil	Aston Villa	Wycombe Wanderers	
9 Davison, Aidan J.	Bolton Wanderers	Ipswich Town	
14 Donowa, Brian L.	Birmingham City	Walsall	
18 Duerden, Ian	Burnley	Glentoran	
25 Duff, Michael	Cheltenham Town	Cirencester Town	
18 Endersby, Lee A.	Harrow Borough	Stevenage Borough	
11 Fitzgerald, Scott B.	Wimbledon	Millwall	
18 Forman, Darren	Gateshead	Guiseley	
14 Gabbiadini, Marco	Derby County	Birmingham City	
17 Gibson, Paul R.	Manchester United	Halifax Town	
28 Gould, Jonathan A.	Bradford City	Gillingham	
11 Grant, Anthony	Preston North End	Glenavon	
14 Grazioli, Giuliano	Peterborough United	Woking	
31 Griffiths, Carl B.	Peterborough United	Leyton Orient	
4 Grime, Dominic	Stevenage Borough	Berkhamsted Town	
4 Grime, Nicholas	Stevenage Borough	Berkhamsted Town	
28 Hallam, Mark J.	Ilkeston Town	Hinckley Town	
11 Hay, Darren A.	Woking	Cambridge United	
11 Helliwell, Ian	Burnley	Chester City	
25 Heyes, Darren L.	Halifax Town	VS Rugby	
17 Hodgson, Douglas J.	Sheffield United	Burnley	
16 Hulme, Kevin	Macclesfield Town	Halifax Town	
4 Huxford, Richard	Bradford City	Peterborough United	
4 Iga, Andrew	Millwall	Sittingbourne	
18 Ireland, Simon P.	Mansfield Town	Doncaster Rovers	
31 Jackson, Matthew A.	Everton	Birmingham City	
11 Kelly, Anthony O.N.	Leyton Orient	Colchester United	
21 Kilner, Aidan	Woking	Hampton	
25 Lake, Stuart J.	Hednesford Town	Nuneaton Borough	
4 Lock, Anthony	Colchester United	Chelmsford City	
3 Lucas, David A.	Preston North End	Darlington	
18 Ludlum, Craig	Sheffield Wednesday	Notts County	
25 Marchant, Giles R.	Sutton United	Wokingham Town	
8 Martin, Jae A.	Birmingham City	Lincoln City	
30 Midwood, Michael	Halifax Town	Accrington Stanley	
4 Mike, Adrian R.	Stockport County	Hartlepool United	
14 Morgan, Philip J.	Stoke City	Chesterfield	
4 Morrison, David E.	Peterborough United	Rushden & Diamonds	
4 Neil, James	Grimsby Town	Grantham Town	
5 Notley, Jay	Charlton Athletic	Dagenham & Redbridge	
15 Odegbami, Joseph O.	Dulwich Hamlet	Purfleet	
25 O'Kane, John A.	Manchester United	Bury	
4 Pack, Lenny J.	Cambridge United	Baldock Town	
10 Painter, Peter R.	Darlington	Rochdale	
4 Patterson, Darren J.	Luton Town	Preston North End	
14 Payne, Grant	Wimbledon	Woking	
26 Pilkington, Paul	Dover Athletic	Margate	
28 Rodger, Simon L.	Crystal Palace	Manchester City	
24 Rowbotham, Darren	Shrewsbury Town	Exeter City	
11 Rowbotham, Jason	Wycombe Wanderers	Plymouth Argyle	
28 Rush, Matthew J.	Norwich City	Northampton Town	
18 Scott, Andrew	Sheffield United	Chesterfield	
25 Shirtliff, Peter A.	Barnsley	Carlisle United	
4 Simpson, Michael	Notts County	Plymouth Argyle	
1 Smith, Daniel K.	Crawley Town	Worthing	
8 Sowerby, Colin P.	Dover Athletic	Ashford Town	
4 Taylor, Stephen C.	Hednesford Town	Bromsgrove Rovers	
11 Trollope, Paul J.	Derby County	Crystal Palace	
14 Turner, Robert P.	Cambridge United	Hull City	
3 Turpin, Simon A.	Crewe Alexandra	Ashton United	
11 Van der Laan, Robertus P.	Derby County	Wolverhampton Wanderers	
11 Warren, Christer	Southampton	Brighton & Hove Albion	
11 Wells, David P.	AFC Bournemouth	Salisbury City	
14 Wicks, Daniel G.	Slough Town	Egham Town	
1 Williams, Darren P.	Dagenham & Redbridge	Leyton Penant	
25 Williams, Lee	Leyton Orient	Purfleet	
18 Williams, Michael A.	Sheffield Wednesday	Huddersfield Town	
10 Williamson, David F.	Cambridge United	Coleraine	
10 Woods, Billy	Tranmere Rovers	Blackpool	
4 Wright, Thomas J.	Nottingham Forest	Reading	

NOVEMBER 1996

22 Angell, Brett A.	Sunderland	Stockport County	120,000
8 Ashcroft, Lee	West Bromwich Albion	Preston North End	150,000
2 Barmby, Nicholas J.	Middlesbrough	Everton	5,750,000

	From	To	Fee in £s
29 Bennett, Frank	Southampton	Bristol Rovers	15,000
19 Bochenski, Simon	Barnsley	Scarborough	Free
18 Carruthers, Martin G.	Stoke City	Peterborough United	75,000
1 Casey, Paul	Boston United	Lincoln United	undisclosed
2 Culley, Mark	Matlock Town	Eastwood Town	undisclosed
26 Cundy, Jason V.	Tottenham Hotspur	Ipswich Town	200,000
7 Dreyer, John B.	Stoke City	Bradford City	25,000
29 Edwards, Andrew D.	Birmingham City	Peterborough United	exch.
1 Finnan, Stephen	Birmingham City	Notts County	undisclosed
18 Francis, Joseph D.	Enfield	Hayes	undisclosed
29 Gregan, Sean M.	Darlington	Preston North End	300,000
8 Hannigan, Al J.	Rushden & Diamonds	Enfield	undisclosed
27 Heaney, Neil A.	Southampton	Manchester City	500,000
7 Hemmings, Anthony G.	Macclesfield Town	Hednesford Town	undisclosed
4 Hillier, David	Arsenal	Portsmouth	250,000
11 Holcroft, Peter I.	Everton	Swindon Town	Free
23 Huckerby, Darren	Newcastle United	Coventry City	1,000,000
29 Kavanagh, Jason C.	Derby County	Wycombe Wanderers	20,000
29 Little, Glen	Glentoran	Burnley	100,000
5 Martin, Jae A.	Birmingham City	Lincoln City	25,000
22 McGleish, Scott	Peterborough United	Leyton Orient	50,000
11 Mean, Scott	AFC Bournemouth	West Ham United	100,000
27 Norris, Richard	Marine	Crewe Alexandra	undisclosed
29 O'Connor, Martin J.	Peterborough United	Birmingham City	450,000
13 Poole, Gary J.	Birmingham City	Charlton Athletic	250,000
7 Rowbotham, Darren	Shrewsbury Town	Exeter City	Free
29 Sealey, Leslie J.	Leyton Orient	West Ham United	Free
15 Sharp, Raymond	Preston North End	Dunfermline Athletic	undisclosed
22 Sharratt, Christopher	Altrincham	Southport	undisclosed
22 Spencer, John	Chelsea	Queens Park Rangers	2,500,000
19 Taylor, Stephen C.	Hednesford Town	Bromsgrove Rovers	undisclosed
8 Walker, John	Grimsby Town	Mansfield Town	undisclosed
8 Welsh, Steven G.	Peterborough United	Dunfermline Athletic	65,000
6 Wordsworth, Dean	Bromley	Crystal Palace	undisclosed

TEMPORARY TRANSFERS

	From	To
29 Bimson, Stuart J.	Bury	Lincoln City
1 Blackmore, Clayton G.	Middlesbrough	Bristol City
1 Bowder, Stanley R.	Yeading	Maidenhead United
18 Christie, Iyseden	Coventry City	AFC Bournemouth
6 Conlon, Paul R.	Sunderland	Gateshead
29 Cooke, Terence J.	Manchester United	Birmingham City
29 Davison, Aidan J.	Bolton Wanderers	Hull City
1 Davison, Robert	Halifax Town	Guiseley
1 Eastwood, Philip	Burnley	Leek Town
1 Fenwick, Christopher G.	Cheltenham Town	Evesham United
8 Ferdinand, Rio G.	West Ham United	AFC Bournemouth
11 Garner, Simon	Woking	Walton & Hersham
22 Gregory, Neil R.	Ipswich Town	Torquay United
30 Hallam, Mark J.	Ilkeston Town	Witney Town
8 Harper, Stephen	Newcastle United	Gateshead
22 Harris, Jason A.	Crystal Palace	Bristol Rovers
29 Hodgson, Simeon P.	Kidderminster Harriers	Rushden & Diamonds
5 Hooks, John R.	Blackpool	Glentoran
8 Howell, Ian R.	Gloucester City	Cirencester Town
29 Hurst, Glynn	Barnsley	Mansfield Town
29 Jardine, Jamie	Tranmere Rovers	Altrincham
1 Kavanagh, Jason C.	Derby County	Wycombe Wanderers
29 Kerslake, David	Tottenham Hotspur	Swindon Town
15 Le Bihan, Neil E.	Peterborough United	Bishops Stortford
19 Markey, Brendan	Millwall	Dundalk
21 Marshall, Andrew J.	Norwich City	Gillingham
6 Mildenhall, Stephen J.	Swindon Town	Gloucester City
22 Moore, Christian	Forest Green Rovers	Grantham Town
29 Morgan, Alan M.	Tranmere Rovers	Altrincham
22 Morgan, Philip	Stoke City	Macclesfield Town
29 O'Halloran, Keith J.	Middlesbrough	Cardiff City
22 O'Toole, Gavin F.	Coventry City	Hereford United
1 Omoyinmi, Emmanuel	West Ham United	AFC Bournemouth
22 Peacock, Gavin K.	Chelsea	Queens Park Rangers
12 Reeder, Andrew	Chesham United	Uxbridge
25 Reid, Shaun	Bury	Chester City
8 Richardson, Neil T.	Rotherham United	Exeter City
7 Sang, Neil	Morecambe	Gretna
22 Sansome, Paul E.	Southend United	Gravesend & Northfleet
30 Scargill, Jonathan M.	Sheffield Wednesday	Matlock Town
13 Sheridan, John J.	Sheffield Wednesday	Bolton Wanderers
22 Stant, Philip R.	Bury	Northampton Town
22 Stein, Mark E.S.	Chelsea	Stoke City

	From	*To*	*Fee in £s*
22 Stephenson, David	Hendon	Chesham United	
1 Stevens, Neal	Hayes	Harrow Borough	
8 Taylor, John P.	Luton Town	Colchester United	
1 Thomson, Peter	Bury	Witton Albion	
29 Tisdale, Paul R.	Southampton	Huddersfield Town	
29 Trotter, Michael	Halifax Town	VS Rugby	
15 Tyler, Mark R.	Peterborough United	Yeovil Town	
15 Wales, Danny P.	Crystal Palace	Worthing	
2 Young, Jason R.	Bedford Town	Buckingham Town	

DECEMBER 1996

13 Ashbee, Ian	Derby County	Cambridge United	Free
30 Bimson, Stuart J.	Bury	Lincoln City	Free
6 Charnock, Philip A.	Liverpool	Crewe Alexandra	Free
6 Cornforth, John M.	Birmingham City	Wycombe Wanderers	50,000
31 Dicks, Grantley	Bath City	Trowbridge Town	undisclosed
4 Dykstra, Sieb	Queens Park Rangers	Dundee United	100,000
6 Forsyth, Michael E.	Notts County	Wycombe Wanderers	50,000
13 Halle, Gunnar	Oldham Athletic	Leeds United	400,000
10 Hamill, Rory	Fulham	Glentoran	5000
31 Hodson, Simeon P.	Kidderminster Harriers	Rushden & Diamonds	undisclosed
24 Jackson, Matthew A.	Everton	Norwich City	450,000
24 Marginson, Karl K.	Chorley	Barrow	undisclosed
31 Murphy, Shaun P.	Notts County	West Bromwich Albion	500,000
13 Neal, Ashley J.	Liverpool	Huddersfield Town	Free
10 Nwadike, Chukwuemeka I.	Wolverhampton Wanderers	Shrewsbury Town	Free
24 Peacock, Gavin K.	Chelsea	Queens Park Rangers	800,000
12 Randall, Adrian J.	York City	Bury	undisclosed
24 Samuels, Dean	Boreham Wood	Barnet	undisclosed
11 Scales, John R.	Liverpool	Tottenham Hotspur	2,600,000
27 Sheridan, John J.	Sheffield Wednesday	Bolton Wanderers	180,000
26 Stant, Philip R.	Bury	Lincoln City	undisclosed
20 Sutherland, Colin	Clydebank	Scarborough	undisclosed
24 Sutton, David W.	Ashton United	Newcastle Town	undisclosed
31 Taylor, Maik S.	Barnet	Southampton	500,000
20 Venables, David	Stevenage Borough	Kettering Town	undisclosed
24 Williams, Lee	Leyton Orient	Purfleet	undisclosed

TEMPORARY TRANSFERS

13 Abbey, Nathanael	Luton Town	Basingstoke Town	
19 Ayorinde, Samuel T.	Leyton Orient	Rushden & Diamonds	
16 Bartley, Carl A.	Hayes	Carshalton Athletic	
6 Boswell, Matthew H.	Port Vale	Redditch United	
13 Bright, Mark A.	Sheffield Wednesday	Millwall	
12 Brightwell, David J.	Bradford City	Blackpool	
20 Brodie, Stephen E.	Sunderland	Scarborough	
27 Brown, Kenneth J.	West Ham United	Birmingham City	
12 Brown, Michael A.	Preston North End	Shrewsbury Town	
24 Burton, Deon J.	Portsmouth	Cardiff City	
13 Cain, Ian D.	Morecambe	Lancaster City	
2 Charnock, Philip A.	Liverpool	Crewe Alexandra	
2 Clarke, Adrian J.	Arsenal	Rotherham United	
21 Clough, Nigel H.	Manchester City	Nottingham Forest	
6 Coady, Lewis	Wrexham	Sligo Rovers	
20 Cook, Andrew C.	Swansea City	Portsmouth	
3 Costello, Mark B.	Sutton United	Staines Town	
2 Cross, Jonathan N.	Wrexham	Hereford United	
13 Donowa, Brian L.	Birmingham City	Peterborough United	
24 Fitzgerald, Scott B.	Wimbledon	Millwall	
23 Flanagan, Matthew J.	Guiseley	Lancaster City	
5 Ford, Richard J.	Forest Green Rovers	Clevedon Town	
6 Futcher, Stephen A.	Wrexham	Sligo Rovers	
17 Hamlet, Alan	Boreham Wood	Chertsey Town	
6 Hanlon, Ritchie K.	Southend United	Dover Athletic	
14 Harris, Andrew C.	Sutton United	Hendon	
20 Haw, Stephen	Chorley	Witton Albion	
3 Hewitt, Darren P.	Havant Town	Waterlooville	
12 Holmes, David J.	Gloucester City	Hednesford Town	
14 Hooker, Jonathan W.	Bishops Stortford	Billericay Town	
24 Inman, Niall E.	Peterborough United	Cambridge City	
6 Kenworthy, Jonathan R.	Tranmere Rovers	Southport	
24 Lancaster, David	Rochdale	Bamber Bridge	
23 Lucas, David A.	Preston North End	Scunthorpe United	
30 McGregor, Marc	Oxford United	Ards	
20 McKeown, Gary J.	Dundee	Exeter City	
13 Marchant, Giles R.	Sutton United	Wokingham Town	
27 Martin, Dean S.	Rochdale	Halifax Town	
13 Mayers, Kenneth	Chorley	Southport	
12 Moilanen, Teuvo	Preston North End	Scarborough	

	From	To	Fee in £s
19 Myall, Stuart T.	Brentford	Hastings Town	
21 Newell, Michael C.	Birmingham City	West Ham United	
10 O'Reilly, Justin M.	Port Vale	Macclesfield Town	
24 Phillips, Steven J.	Bristol City	Gloucester City	
13 Riches, Steven A.	Leyton Orient	Billericay Town	
24 Roberts, Neil	Wrexham	Bangor City	
24 Rodosthenous, Michael	West Bromwich Albion	Telford United	
13 Rogers, Paul A.	Notts County	Wigan Athletic	
19 Rush, Matthew J.	Norwich City	Northampton Town	
30 Scott, Andrew M.	Cardiff City	Bath City	
20 Scott, Kevin W.	Tottenham Hotspur	Charlton Athletic	
4 Selley, Ian	Arsenal	Southend United	
12 Shearer, Lee	Leyton Orient	Hastings Town	
5 Simpson, Michael	Notts County	Wycombe Wanderers	
6 Simpson, Paul D.	Derby County	Sheffield United	
13 Vansittart, Jonathan	Sutton United	Crawley Town	
18 Walker, Clive	Nuneaton Borough	Bilston Town	
20 Woodsford, Jamie	Luton Town	Hitchin Town	

JANUARY 1997

	From	To	Fee in £s
13 Akinbiyi, Adeola P.	Norwich City	Gillingham	250,000
31 Breen, Gary	Birmingham City	Coventry City	2,500,000
27 Brown, Kenneth J.	West Ham United	Birmingham City	75,000
10 Brown, Michael A.	Preston North End	Shrewsbury Town	20,000
18 Elliott, Matthew S.	Oxford United	Leicester City	1,600,000
24 Endersby, Lee A.	Harrow Borough	Enfield	undisclosed
7 Ferrett, Christopher	Fleet Town	Basingstoke Town	undisclosed
31 Fjortoft, Jan-Aage	Middlesbrough	Sheffield United	700,000
25 Forinton, Howard L.	Oxford City	Yeovil Town	undisclosed
31 Forster, Nicholas M.	Brentford	Birmingham City	700,000
16 Grant, Anthony	Preston North End	Glenavon	undisclosed
17 Hallam, Mark J.	Ilkeston Town	Hinckley Town	undisclosed
31 Horlock, Kevin	Swindon Town	Manchester City	1,500,000
14 Humphrey, John	Gillingham	Brighton & Hove Albion	Free
28 Ireland, Simon P.	Mansfield Town	Doncaster Rovers	50,000
18 Jackson, Justin J.	Morecambe	Woking	undisclosed
24 Leworthy, David J.	Dover Athletic	Rushden & Diamonds	undisclosed
20 Limpar, Anders	Everton	Birmingham City	100,000
27 Linighan, Andrew	Arsenal	Crystal Palace	110,000
10 McFarlane, Andrew A.	Scunthorpe United	Torquay United	20,000
17 Minett, Jason	Lincoln City	Exeter City	Free
1 Phelan, Terrence M.	Chelsea	Everton	850,000
20 Pilkington, Paul	Dover Athletic	Margate	undisclosed
17 Read, Paul	Arsenal	Wycombe Wanderers	35,000
27 Reid, Shaun	Bury	Chester City	30,000
31 Rush, David	Oxford United	York City	80,000
27 Simpson, Michael	Notts County	Wycombe Wanderers	undisclosed
31 Sinclair, David	Millwall	Dundee United	undisclosed
29 Stoker, Gareth	Hereford United	Cardiff City	80,000
20 Stapleton, Simon J.	Slough Town	Rushden & Diamonds	undisclosed
18 Thomsen, Claus	Ipswich Town	Everton	900,000
11 Turner, Lee	Gravesend & Northfleet	Margate	undisclosed
17 Watson, Gordon W.	Southampton	Bradford City	550,000
23 Webster, Kenny	Stevenage Borough	Harrow Borough	undisclosed

TEMPORARY TRANSFERS

	From	To
17 Appleton, Michael A.	Manchester United	Grimsby Town
24 Armstrong, Steven C.	Nottingham Forest	Watford
23 Beeston, Carl F.	Stoke City	Hereford United
31 Bellingham, Mark	Cheltenham Town	Halesowen Town
10 Bignall, Michael G.	Stevenage Borough	Baldock Town
27 Brady, Matthew	Barnet	Sligo Rovers
30 Brayson, Paul	Newcastle United	Swansea City
22 Broomes, Marlon C.	Blackburn Rovers	Swindon Town
31 Callinan, Stephen	Sudbury Town	Cambridge City
29 Clapham, James R.	Tottenham Hotspur	Leyton Orient
24 Currie, David N.	Carlisle United	Scarborough
30 Elsey, David J.	Cheltenham Town	Cirencester Town
22 Foran, Mark J.	Peterborough United	Lincoln City
24 Frain, John W.	Birmingham City	Northampton Town
31 Gabbiadini, Marco	Derby County	Oxford United
30 Hills, John D.	Everton	Swansea City
17 Hope, Richard P.	Blackburn Rovers	Darlington
17 Howe, Stephen R.	Nottingham Forest	Ipswich Town
23 Innes, Gary J.	Darlington	Waterford United
31 Jones, Philip L.	Liverpool	Wrexham
27 Kenworthy, Jonathan	Tranmere Rovers	Portadown
24 Keown, Darren P.	Millwall	Harrow Borough
31 Knight, Keith	Halesowen Town	Cheltenham Town

	From	To	Fee in £s
24 Landon, Richard J.	Stockport County	Macclesfield Town	
24 May, David	Enfield	Bromley	
10 McMahon, Sam K.	Leicester City	Kettering Town	
8 Miller, Alan J.	Middlesbrough	Huddersfield Town	
28 Miller, Alan J.	Middlesbrough	Grimsby Town	
31 Mitchell, Shaun A.	Basingstoke Town	Bognor Regis Town	
17 Moilanen, Teuvo J.	Preston North End	Darlington	
8 Moore, Neil	Everton	Norwich City	
27 Morgan, Alan M.	Tranmere Rovers	Portadown	
25 Moss, Raymond	Marine	Witton Albion	
16 O'Kane, John A.	Manchester United	Bury	
6 Patterson, Gary	Wycombe Wanderers	Barnet	
10 Pemberton, Martin	Oldham Athletic	Ards	
23 Pilkington, Kevin W.	Manchester United	Rotherham United	
31 Rees, Jason M.	Portsmouth	Exeter City	
10 Richefond, Gary	Ilkeston Town	Matlock Town	
9 Rocastle, David C.	Chelsea	Norwich City	
21 Scott, Kevin W.	Tottenham Hotspur	Norwich City	
24 Sheppard, Simon	Boreham Wood	Baldock Town	
24 Street, Kevin	Crewe Alexandra	St Patricks Athletic	
13 Terry, Peter E.	Basingstoke Town	Maidenhead United	
25 Tovey, Paul W.	Bath City	Yate Town	
20 Turley, William L.	Northampton Town	Kettering Town	
17 Wright, Thomas J.	Nottingham Forest	Manchester City	

FEBRUARY 1997

	From	To	Fee in £s
18 Adams, Darren S.	Aldershot Town	Dover Athletic	3000
14 Alsop, Julian M.	Halesowen Town	Bristol Rovers	15,000
4 Arkins, Vincent T.	Notts County	Portadown	undisclosed
6 Baddeley, Lee M.	Cardiff City	Exeter City	Free
7 Beesley, Paul	Leeds United	Manchester City	500,000
28 Bennett, Gary M.	Preston North End	Wrexham	100,000
14 Blamey, Nathan	Southampton	Shrewsbury Town	Free
21 Bowman, Robert A.	Leeds United	Rotherham United	Free
14 Brodie, Stephen E.	Sunderland	Scarborough	Free
18 Browning, Marcus T.	Bristol Rovers	Huddersfield Town	500,000
24 Bullock, Darren J.	Huddersfield Town	Swindon Town	400,000
6 Clarkson, Philip I.	Scunthorpe United	Blackpool	80,000
27 Cook, Andrew C.	Swansea City	Portsmouth	35,000
10 Donowa, Brian L.	Birmingham City	Peterborough United	Free
28 Dunn, Iain G.W.	Huddersfield Town	Chesterfield	30,000
10 Gayle, John	Stoke City	Northampton Town	25,000
28 Guppy, Stephen A.	Port Vale	Leicester City	850,000
14 Hartson, John	Arsenal	West Ham United	3,200,000
24 Hendon, Ian M.	Leyton Orient	Notts County	50,000
28 Henry, Nicholas I.	Oldham Athletic	Sheffield United	500,000
28 Hodgson, Douglas J.H.	Sheffield United	Oldham Athletic	undisclosed
17 Hope, Richard P.	Blackburn Rovers	Darlington	Free
14 Jones, Stephen G.	West Ham United	Charlton Athletic	400,000
10 Kitson, Paul	Newcastle United	West Ham United	2,300,000
7 Lawrence, Matthew J.	Wycombe Wanderers	Fulham	Free
14 Marchant, Giles R.	Sutton United	Wokingham Town	undisclosed
14 Partridge, Scott M.	Bristol City	Cardiff City	50,000
28 Pepper, Colin N.	York City	Bradford City	100,000
14 Potter, Graham S.	Southampton	West Bromwich Albion	150,000
13 Reinelt, Robert S.	Colchester United	Brighton & Hove Albion	15,000
18 Rice, Marc G.	Bognor Regis Town	Havant Town	undisclosed
21 Ritchie, Andrew T.	Scarborough	Oldham Athletic	Free
19 Rowe, Rodney C.	Huddersfield Town	York City	80,000
26 Schwarzer, Mark	Bradford City	Middlesbrough	1,500,000
25 Scott, Kevin W.	Tottenham Hotspur	Norwich City	250,000

TEMPORARY TRANSFERS

	From	To
21 Aiston, Sam J.	Sunderland	Chester City
14 Barclay, Dominic	Bristol City	Slough Town
26 Bartram, Vincent L.	Arsenal	Wolverhampton Wanderers
8 Bayliss, Warren L.	Hampton	Windsor & Eton
21 Benstead, Graham M.	Rushden & Diamonds	Kingstonian
17 Blackstone, Ian K.	Chorley	Guiseley
21 Bos, Gijsbert	Lincoln City	Gateshead
14 Bradley, Russell	Scunthorpe United	Hartlepool United
7 Brown, Stephen R.	Lincoln City	Dover Athletic
19 Campbell, David A.	Tamworth	Paget Rangers
3 Castle, Stephen C.	Birmingham City	Leyton Orient
7 Christie, Iyseden	Coventry City	Mansfield Town
21 Clarke, Timothy J.	York City	Scunthorpe United
3 Cort, Carl E.R.	Wimbledon	Lincoln City
21 Crossley, Matthew	Wycombe Wanderers	Rushden & Diamonds
21 Crowe, Glen M.	Wolverhampton Wanderers	Exeter City

	From	To	Fee in £s
15 Cuggy, Michael S.	Hastings Town	Gateshead	
21 Davies, Gareth M.	Crystal Palace	Cardiff City	
18 Davis, Kelvin G.	Luton Town	Doncaster Rovers	
20 Denton, Edward J.	Abingdon Town	Aylesbury United	
10 Duerden, Ian C.	Burnley	Bamber Bridge	
28 Elliott, Stuart T.	Newcastle United	Hull City	
28 Fleming, Hayden V.	Cardiff City	Inter Cable-Tel	
21 Ford, Jonathan S.	Gillingham	Barnet	
21 Gayle, Mark S.R.	Crewe Alexandra	Birmingham City	
12 Gentle, Justin	Enfield	St Albans City	
21 Gibson, Lee	Lincoln City	Lincoln United	
28 Hardyman, Paul G.T.	Barnet	Slough Town	
9 Harris, Andrew C.	Sutton United	Staines Town	
5 Hartfield, Charles J.	Sheffield United	Fulham	
28 Hodges, Lee L.	West Ham United	Leyton Orient	
21 Howell, Ian R.	Gloucester City	Cirencester Town	
21 Jones, Gary	Notts County	Scunthorpe United	
19 Jones, Paul N.	Tranmere Rovers	Blackpool	
5 Lee, Jason B.	Nottingham Forest	Charlton Athletic	
14 Martin, Dean S.	Rochdale	Halifax Town	
7 Martindale, Gary	Notts County	Mansfield Town	
17 Mautone, Steve	West Ham United	Reading	
22 McDonald, Tony	Witton Albion	Redcliffe Borough	
15 McGargle, Stephen	Middlesbrough	Blyth Spartans	
7 Mee, Edward W.	Hayes	Maidenhead United	
14 Mike, Adrian R.	Stockport County	Doncaster Rovers	
28 Miller, Alan J.	Middlesbrough	West Bromwich Albion	
8 Moore, Christian	Forest Green Rovers	Bedworth United	
14 Nogan, Lee M.	Reading	Notts County	
6 Otto, Ricky	Birmingham City	Peterborough United	
7 Palmer, Lee J.	Cambridge United	Dover Athletic	
7 Patterson, Gary	Wycombe Wanderers	Chesterfield	
7 Poric, Adem	Sheffield Wednesday	Southend United	
14 Price, Christopher	Everton	Oxford United	
19 Prudhoe, Mark	Stoke City	York City	
10 Ramage, Craig D.	Watford	Peterborough United	
21 Reed, Adam M.	Blackburn Rovers	Darlington	
14 Reed, Ian	Shrewsbury Town	Stafford Rangers	
7 Regis, David	Barnsley	Notts County	
14 Rigby, Anthony A.	Bury	Scarborough	
14 Robinson, Ian B.	Mansfield Town	Ilkeston Town	
14 Rodger, Simon L.	Crystal Palace	Stoke City	
7 Scargill, Jonathan M.	Sheffield Wednesday	Boston United	
7 Scott, Keith	Norwich City	Watford	
27 Scully, Anthony D.T.	Crystal Palace	Portadown	
21 Sheffield, Jonathan	Peterborough United	Watford	
14 Shepherd, Mark	Kidderminster Harriers	Moor Green	
13 Slade, Steven A.	Queens Park Rangers	Brentford	
14 Stallard, Mark	Bradford City	Preston North End	
14 Stevens, Mark	Oxford United	Ards	
6 Teale, Shaun	Tranmere Rovers	Preston North End	
20 Thorp, Michael S.	Reading	Fareham Town	
7 Townsend, Quentin	Hereford United	Worcester City	
3 Vaughan, John	Lincoln City	Colchester United	
22 Walker, Clive	Nuneaton Borough	Redditch United	
6 Walton, Byron J.	Slough Town	Hendon	
14 Weaver, Simon D.	Sheffield Wednesday	Doncaster Rovers	
10 Wilkes, Timothy C.	Notts County	Grantham Town	
17 Wrack, Darren	Grimsby Town	Shrewsbury Town	

MARCH 1997

28 Agana, Patrick A.O.	Notts County	Hereford United	Free
26 Anthony, Graham J.	Sheffield United	Swindon Town	Free
24 Anthrobus, Stephen A.	Shrewsbury Town	Crewe Alexandra	75,000
27 Baker, David P.	Scunthorpe United	Hartlepool United	undisclosed
27 Beresford, David	Oldham Athletic	Huddersfield Town	350,000
24 Bignall, Michael G.	Stevenage Borough	Morecambe	undisclosed
27 Birch, Paul	Doncaster Rovers	Exeter City	Free
27 Blake, Robert J.	Darlington	Bradford City	300,000
7 Blondrage, Andrew J.	Sittingbourne	Margate	undisclosed
14 Brannan, Gerard D.	Tranmere Rovers	Manchester City	750,000
26 Charlery, Kenneth L.	Peterborough United	Stockport County	75,000
26 Clarke, Timothy J.	York City	Scunthorpe United	undisclosed
6 Collins, Simon	Huddersfield Town	Plymouth Argyle	60,000
24 Cowans, Gordon S.	Bradford City	Stockport County	Free
14 Cunnington, Shaun G.	West Bromwich Albion	Notts County	undisclosed
14 Davison, Aidan J.	Bolton Wanderers	Bradford City	Free
27 Desouza, Juan M.I.	Wycombe Wanderers	Peterborough United	50,000
21 Devine, Steven B.	Hednesford Town	Gresley Rovers	undisclosed

	From	To	Fee in £s
11 Dibble, Andrew G.	Manchester City	Rangers	undisclosed
7 Duxbury, Lee E.	Bradford City	Oldham Athletic	350,000
4 Ebbrell, John K.	Everton	Sheffield United	1,000,000
21 Ebdon, Marcus	Peterborough United	Chesterfield	100,000
3 Edmondson, Darren S.	Carlisle United	Huddersfield Town	200,000
4 Evans, Michael J.	Plymouth Argyle	Southampton	750,000
17 Forbes, Steven D.	Millwall	Colchester United	Free
27 Ford, Jonathan S.	Gillingham	Barnet	25,000
21 Forrester, Jamie M.	Grimsby Town	Scunthorpe United	50,000
27 Frain, John W.	Birmingham City	Northampton Town	Free
27 Gilkes, Michael E.	Reading	Wolverhampton Wanderers	50,000
21 Granville, Daniel P.	Cambridge United	Chelsea	300,000
7 Griffiths, Carl B.	Peterborough United	Leyton Orient	100,000
27 Hamilton, Derrik V.	Bradford City	Newcastle United	1,500,000
14 Hateley, Mark	Queens Park Rangers	Rangers	300,000
12 Hughes, Bryan	Wrexham	Birmingham City	800,000
26 Jackson, Michael J.	Bury	Preston North End	125,000
4 Kearn, Stewart	AFC Bournemouth	Bashley	undisclosed
26 King, Philip G.	Aston Villa	Swindon Town	Free
27 Linton, Desmond M.	Luton Town	Peterborough United	25,000
27 Marshall, Lee	Enfield	Norwich City	undisclosed
27 Mason, Andrew J.	Hull City	Chesterfield	undisclosed
27 McAuley, Sean	Hartlepool United	Scunthorpe United	undisclosed
27 McDermott, Andrew	Queens Park Rangers	West Bromwich Albion	400,000
27 McGorry, Brian P.	Wycombe Wanderers	Hereford United	Free
27 McNally, Mark	Southend United	Stoke City	120,000
27 Miller, Alan J.	Middlesbrough	West Bromwich Albion	500,000
12 Mitchell, Shaun A.	Basingstoke Town	Hampton	undisclosed
15 Moore, Ian R.	Tranmere Rovers	Nottingham Forest	750,000
21 Morrison, David E.	Peterborough United	Leyton Orient	15,000
13 Nogan, Kurt	Burnley	Preston North End	150,000
20 Pemberton, Martin C.	Oldham Athletic	Doncaster Rovers	Free
27 Reid, Paul R.	Huddersfield Town	Oldham Athletic	100,000
7 Rogers, Paul A.	Notts County	Wigan Athletic	50,000
27 Rush, Matthew J.	Norwich City	Oldham Athletic	165,000
10 Sale, Mark D.	Mansfield Town	Colchester United	20,000
27 Shutt, Carl S.	Bradford City	Darlington	undisclosed
7 Stallard, Mark	Bradford City	Wycombe Wanderers	135,000
27 Stamps, Scott	Torquay United	Colchester United	10,000
26 Tiler, Carl	Aston Villa	Sheffield United	650,000
26 Tinkler, Mark R.	Leeds United	York City	75,000
20 Waddle, Christopher R.	Bradford City	Sunderland	75,000
14 White, Devon W.	Watford	Notts County	undisclosed
27 Wilder, Christopher J.	Notts County	Bradford City	150,000
14 Wilkes, Timothy C.	Notts County	Kettering Town	undisclosed
4 Wright, Thomas J.	Nottingham Forest	Manchester City	450,000

TEMPORARY TRANSFERS

14 Adams, Kieran C.	Barnet	St Albans City
18 Andrews, Ian E.	AFC Bournemouth	Leicester City
14 Armstrong, Steven C.	Nottingham Forest	Watford
21 Atkin, Paul A.	York City	Leyton Orient
27 Ayorinde, Samuel T.	Leyton Orient	Altrincham
21 Bankole, Ademola	Crewe Alexandra	Hyde United
3 Battersby, Anthony	Notts County	Bury
27 Bennett, Troy	Barnsley	Scarborough
27 Blatherwick, Steven S.	Nottingham Forest	Reading
7 Bowder, Stanley R.	Yeading	Chertsey Town
14 Bracey, Lee M.I.	Bury	Ipswich Town
27 Brown, Michael R.	Manchester City	Hartlepool United
7 Bywater, Paul R.	Stafford Rangers	Stourbridge
18 Carr-Lawton, Colin	Burnley	Leek Town
27 Chandler, Dean A.R.	Charlton Athletic	Torquay United
27 Clapham, James R.	Tottenham Hotspur	Bristol Rovers
27 Clarke, Adrian J.	Arsenal	Southend United
7 Clyde, Darron E.J.	Barnsley	Boston United
24 Cooper, Kevin L.	Derby County	Stockport County
25 Coughlan, Graham	Blackburn Rovers	Swindon Town
27 Cresswell, Richard P.W.	York City	Mansfield Town
27 Cutler, Neil A.	Crewe Alexandra	Leek Town
27 Duerden, Ian C.	Burnley	Southport
21 Dunwell, Richard K.	Barnet	Cheltenham Town
3 Elsey, David J.	Cheltenham Town	Cirencester Town
3 Evans, Paul A.	Leeds United	Bradford City
27 Evans, Thomas R.	Crystal Palace	Coventry City
27 Farrell, Sean P.	Notts County	Torquay United
27 Flynn, Sean M.	Derby County	Stoke City
3 Foran, Mark J.	Peterborough United	Oldham Athletic
26 Forrest, Craig L.	Ipswich Town	Chelsea

	From	To	Fee in £s
27 Fortune-West, Leo O.	Gillingham	Leyton Orient	
26 Foster, Colin J.	Watford	Cambridge United	
27 Freeman, Nathan	Manchester City	Fulham	
3 Freestone, Christopher M.	Middlesbrough	Carlisle United	
7 French, Jonathan C.F.	Bristol Rovers	Bath City	
27 Galloway, Michael A.	Notts County	Gillingham	
27 Gayle, Brian W.	Rotherham United	Bristol Rovers	
7 Gentle, Dominic	Enfield	Stevenage Borough	
7 Gilbert, David J.	West Bromwich Albion	York City	
3 Glover, Edward L.	Rotherham United	Huddersfield Town	
21 Gudmundsson, Niklas	Blackburn Rovers	Ipswich Town	
27 Guinan, Stephen	Nottingham Forest	Burnley	
10 Hanson, David P.	Leyton Orient	Chesterfield	
27 Harper, Stephen A.	Newcastle United	Stockport County	
27 Harris, Samuel R.	Manchester City	Altrincham	
27 Harte, Stuart G.	Bristol Rovers	Bath City	
21 Haynes, Junior L.A.	Hayes	Dulwich Hamlet	
3 Hinshelwood, Danny M.	Portsmouth	Torquay United	
10 Howes, Shaun	Leyton Orient	Billericay Town	
27 Janney, Mark	Tottenham Hotspur	Brentford	
27 Jones, Philip L.	Liverpool	Tranmere Rovers	
14 Jones, Stephen G.	Bury	Hyde United	
7 Keown, Darren P.	Millwall	Ashford Town	
27 Kiwomya, Andrew D.	Bradford City	Luton Town	
5 Lancaster, David	Rochdale	Bamber Bridge	
3 Landon, Richard J.	Stockport County	Rotherham United	
27 Lee, Jason B.	Nottingham Forest	Grimsby Town	
6 Lumsden, Todd M.	Oxford United	Ards	
14 Mahorn, Paul G.	Tottenham Hotspur	Brentford	
27 Martin, David	Northampton Town	Brighton & Hove Albion	
3 McGibbon, Patrick C.	Manchester United	Wigan Athletic	
27 McGowan, Gavin G.	Arsenal	Luton Town	
7 McNiven, David J.	Oldham Athletic	Linfield	
14 Midgley, Craig S.	Bradford City	Scarborough	
27 Mildenhall, Stephen J.	Swindon Town	Salisbury City	
27 Miles, Benjamin D.	Swansea City	Slough Town	
27 Mison, Michael	Fulham	Stevenage Borough	
27 Morrow, Stephen J.	Arsenal	Queens Park Rangers	
21 Murray, Edwin J.	Forest Green Rovers	Evesham United	
27 Musgrove, Neil	Aldershot Town	Fleet Town	
17 Newell, Michael C.	Birmingham City	Bradford City	
27 Patterson, Mark A.	Sheffield United	Southend United	
17 Powell, Paul	Oxford United	Ards	
1 Procopi, Carl	Sutton United	Molesey	
31 Puttnam, David P.	Gillingham	Yeovil Town	
24 Rattray, Kevin	Barnet	Welling United	
21 Reilly, James L.	Sudbury Town	Cambridge City	
28 Richardson, Dominic K.	Plymouth Argyle	Weston-Super-Mare	
27 Ryan, Tim J.	Doncaster Rovers	Altrincham	
25 Samways, Mark	Scunthorpe United	York City	
21 Scott, Andrew	Sheffield United	Bury	
27 Scott, Keith	Norwich City	Wycombe Wanderers	
27 Sheffield, Jonathan	Peterborough United	Oldham Athletic	
7 Sheppard, Simon	Boreham Wood	Baldock Town	
26 Tallon, Gerrit T.	Kilmarnock	Chester City	
14 Taylor, David	Ilkeston Town	Grantham Town	
27 Taylor, Martin J.	Derby County	Wycombe Wanderers	
27 Tindall, Jason	Charlton Athletic	Dulwich Hamlet	
27 Turley, William L.	Northampton Town	Kettering Town	
26 Walker, Justin	Nottingham Forest	Scunthorpe United	
7 Warren, Christer	Southampton	Fulham	
26 Wassall, Darren P.	Derby County	Birmingham City	
19 Weaver, Luke D.S.	Leyton Orient	West Ham United	
13 Westhead, Mark	Bolton Wanderers	Stalybridge Celtic	
27 Williams, Michael A.	Sheffield Wednesday	Peterborough United	
3 Williams, Steven D.	Cardiff City	Newport County	
27 Wilson, Paul A.	Scunthorpe United	Cambridge United	

APRIL 1997

	From	To	Fee in £s
16 Carroll, Roy E.	Hull City	Wigan Athletic	350,000
2 Gilkes, Earl G.M.	Reading	Wolverhampton Wanderers	50,000
3 Gray, Andrew R.	Boston United	Lincoln United	undisclosed
1 Lomas, Stephen M.	Manchester City	West Ham United	1,600,000
3 Masters, Neil B.	Wolverhampton Wanderers	Gillingham	undisclosed
11 Mautone, Steve	West Ham United	Reading	250,000
9 Morrow, Stephen J.	Arsenal	Queens Park Rangers	500,000
1 Russell, Keith D.	Hednesford Town	Blackpool	undisclosed
30 Taylor, Craig	Dorchester Town	Swindon Town	undisclosed

MAY 1997

	From	*To*	*Fee in £s*
22 Battersby, Anthony	Notts County	Bury	undisclosed
16 Bilic, Slaven	West Ham	Everton	4,250,000
16 Collymore, Stanley V.	Liverpool	Aston Villa	7,000,000
27 Cox, Neil J.	Middlesbrough	Bolton Wanderers	1,200,000
14 Davies, Kevin C.	Chesterfield	Southampton	750,000
23 Foster, Stephen	Woking	Bristol Rovers	150,000
29 Gentle, Justin	Enfield	St Albans City	undisclosed
29 Hannigan, Al J.	Enfield	Yeovil Town	undisclosed
19 Hughes, Lee	Kidderminster Harriers	West Bromwich Albion	200,000
23 Hunt, Jonathan R.	Birmingham City	Derby County	exch.
23 Mendonca, Clive P.	Grimsby Town	Charlton Athletic	700,000
13 Miller, Barry S.	Wokingham Town	Farnborough Town	undisclosed
23 Murdoch, Colin J.	Manchester United	Preston North End	undisclosed
29 Norbury, Michael S.	Halifax Town	Hednesford Town	undisclosed
30 Parkinson, Gary	Burnley	Preston North End	undisclosed
20 Rose, Matthew	Arsenal	Queens Park Rangers	500,000
13 Stevens, Ian D.	Shrewsbury Town	Carlisle United	100,000
14 Upson, Matthew J.	Luton Town	Arsenal	1,000,000
14 Walker, Justin	Nottingham Forest	Scunthorpe United	undisclosed
17 Wassall, Darren P.	Derby County	Birmingham City	exch.

LEAGUE MANAGERS ASSOCIATION

The League Managers Association, which shares a birthdate with the FA Premier League, has 'How can we help?' as its unofficial motto. The brainchild of Graham Taylor, the then-England manager, the LMA has made great strides in its short lifetime.

Those five years have without doubt been the most eventful in the game's long history. Apart from the advent of the Premier League itself and the consequent escalation in television revenues, the traditional transfer market, domestic as well as international, has been thrown into turmoil by the Bosman judgement.

Taylor's motivation was the belief that club managers possessed a vast store of knowledge and experience which was not being used for the benefit of the game. They lacked a forum through which to express their views to legislators and decision-makers.

Both the Football Association and the Premier League were quick to recognise that the newly-formed LMA could make a useful contribution to the debates which would ultimately reshape the game in England. Today it has a very full programme of meetings with various official committees and working parties.

Perhaps the first significant achievement was the introduction into Premier League regulations of Codes of Conduct regulating the appointment and termination of managers. Its value in preventing cases reaching the High Court has been demonstrated more than once.

Surprisingly the Football League has refused to adopt similar regulations which would undoubtedly have defused several undignified and image-damaging rows as managers changed clubs in recent seasons.

Other LMA initiatives led to major reviews of the structure of reserve-team football and the disciplinary system, both of which had remained unchanged for many years and no longer served the game's best interests.

The FA had already started a major review of the coaching structure which, pre-eminent 30 years ago, had fallen behind most European countries. Invited to join the various working parties, LMA representatives have spent many hours at Lilleshall and Loughborough University and have undoubtedly added impetus to this key operation.

In addition to producing a regular newsletter for members, the LMA has also produced a number of general discussion papers. One, for example, assessed the merits of the European system in which the head coach concentrates on the training and preparation of the senior team while all other playing matters are controlled by a director of football. It suggested this structure as the way forward for many English clubs.

Others examined in depth the youth development organisations of FC Parma in Italy and Holland's Ajax club, and the technical department of the French Federation which has transformed that country's football in the past decade was also examined in detail.

Most of the Committee members who launched the Association are still in place. Although Howard Wilkinson has moved from Leeds United to become the first technical director of the FA, he remains the LMA chairman and Alex Ferguson, Frank Clark, Brian Little, Brian Flynn and David Pleat are still on the Committee along with Dave Bassett and Kenny Hibbitt.

The chief executive throughout the setting-up period was John Camkin, the former chairman of Lunn Poly Ltd, who had extensive football experience as a journalist, broadcaster and director of Coventry City. He is now the secretary.

The new organisation was strongly supported by the fledgling Premier League and also funded by all three television organisations in recognition of the contribution made by managers to matches shown on the screen.

Once established, the Association appointed Frank Clark, managing director of Leyton Orient, as part-time chief executive. When Frank moved to Nottingham Forest, Steve Coppell became the first full-time chief executive, to be followed by Jim Smith and Gordon Milne.

All three followed Clark back into club jobs and, in July 1996, the vastly experienced John Barnwell, late of Peterborough, Wolves, Notts County, Walsall and Northampton Town, took over at the Association's new offices in Leamington Spa.

ENGLISH LEAGUE MANAGERS

GM General Manager,　CC Chief Coach,　HC Head Coach,　DoC Director of Coaching,　DoF Director of Football,
* Secretary-Manager,　MD Managing Director,　TM Team Manager,　TD Technical Director.

ARSENAL
Sam Hollis 1894–97, Tom Mitchell 1897–98, George Elcoat 1898–99, Harry Bradshaw 1899–1904, Phil Kelso 1904–08, George Morrell 1908–15, Leslie Knighton 1919–25, Herbert Chapman 1925–34, George Allison 1934–47, Tom Whittaker 1947–56, Jack Crayston 1956–58, George Swindin 1958–62, Billy Wright 1962–66, Bertie Mee 1966–76, Terry Neill 1976–83, Don Howe 1984–86, George Graham 1986–95, Bruce Rioch 1995–96, Arsene Wenger September 1996– .

ASTON VILLA
George Ramsay 1884–1926*, W. J. Smith 1926–34*, Jimmy McMullan 1934–35, Jimmy Hogan 1936–44, Alex Massie 1945–50, George Martin 1950–53, Eric Houghton 1953–58, Joe Mercer 1958–64, Dick Taylor 1965–67, Tommy Cummings 1967–68, Tommy Docherty 1968–70, Vic Crowe 1970–74, Ron Saunders 1974–82, Tony Barton 1982–84, Graham Turner 1984–86, Billy McNeill 1986–87, Graham Taylor 1987–90, Dr. Jozef Venglos 1990–91, Ron Atkinson 1991–94, Brian Little November 1994– .

BARNET
Lester Finch, George Wheeler, Dexter Adams, Tommy Coleman, Gerry Ward, Gordon Ferry, Brian Kelly, Bill Meadows, Barry Fry, Roger Thompson, Don McAllister, Barry Fry, Edwin Stein, Gary Phillips (player-manager) 1993–94, Ray Clemence 1994–96, Alan Mullery (DoF) 1996–97, Terry Bullivant 1997, John Still June 1997– .

BARNSLEY
Arthur Fairclough 1898–1901*, John McCartney 1901–04*, Arthur Fairclough 1904–12, John Hastie 1912–14, Percy Lewis 1914–19, Peter Sant 1919–26, John Commins 1926–29, Arthur Fairclough 1929–30, Brough Fletcher 1930–37, Angus Seed 1937–53, Tim Ward 1953–60, Johnny Steele 1960–71 (continued as GM), John McSeveney 1971–72, Johnny Steele (GM) 1972–73, Jim Iley 1973–78, Allan Clarke 1978–80, Norman Hunter 1980–84, Bobby Collins 1984–85, Allan Clarke 1985–89, Mel Machin 1989–93, Viv Anderson 1993–94, Danny Wilson June 1994– .

BIRMINGHAM CITY
Alfred Jones 1892–1908*, Alec Watson 1908–10, Bob McRoberts 1910–15, Frank Richards 1915–23, Billy Beer 1923–27, Leslie Knighton 1928–33, George Liddell 1933–39, Harry Storer 1945–48, Bob Brocklebank 1949–54, Arthur Turner 1954–58, Pat Beasley 1959–60, Gil Merrick 1960–64, Joe Mallett 1965, Stan Cullis 1965–70, Fred Goodwin 1970–75, Willie Bell 1975–77, Jim Smith 1978–82, Ron Saunders 1982–86, John Bond 1986–87, Garry Pendrey 1987–89, Dave Mackay 1989–1991, Lou Macari 1991, Terry Cooper 1991–93, Barry Fry 1993–96, Trevor Francis May 1996– .

BLACKBURN ROVERS
Thomas Mitchell 1884–96*, J. Walmsley 1896–1903*, R. B. Middleton 1903–25, Jack Carr 1922–26 (TM under Middleton to 1925), Bob Crompton 1926–30 (Hon. TM), Arthur Barritt 1931–36 (had been Sec. from 1927), Reg Taylor 1936–38, Bob Crompton 1938–41, Eddie Hapgood 1944–47, Will Scott 1947, Jack Bruton 1947–49, Jackie Bestall 1949–53, Johnny Carey 1953–58, Dally Duncan 1958–60, Jack Marshall 1960–67, Eddie Quigley 1967–70, Johnny Carey 1970–71, Ken Furphy 1971–73, Gordon Lee 1974–75, Jim Smith 1975–78, Jim Iley 1978, John Pickering 1978–79, Howard Kendall 1979–81, Bobby Saxton 1981–86, Don Mackay 1987–91, Kenny Dalglish 1991–95, Ray Harford 1995–97, Roy Hodgson June 1997– .

BLACKPOOL
Tom Barcroft 1903–33* (Hon. Sec.), John Cox 1909–11, Bill Norman 1919–23, Maj. Frank Buckley 1923–27, Sid Beaumont 1927–28, Harry Evans 1928–33 (Hon. TM), Alex "Sandy" Macfarlane 1933–35, Joe Smith 1935–58, Ronnie Suart 1958–67, Stan Mortensen 1967–69, Les Shannon 1969–70, Bob Stokoe 1970–72, Harry Potts 1972–76, Allan Brown 1976–78, Bob Stokoe 1978–79, Stan Ternent 1979–80, Alan Ball 1980–81, Allan Brown 1981–82, Sam Ellis 1982–89, Jimmy Mullen 1989–90, Graham Carr 1990, Bill Ayre 1990–94, Sam Allardyce 1994–96, Gary Megson 1996–97, Nigel Worthington July 1997– .

BOLTON WANDERERS
Tom Rawthorne 1874–85*, J. J. Bentley 1885–86*, W. G. Struthers 1886–87*, Fitzroy Norris 1887*, J. J. Bentley 1887–95*, Harry Downs 1895–96*, Frank Brettell 1896–98*, John Somerville 1898–1910, Will Settle 1910–15, Tom Mather 1915–19, Charles Foweraker 1919–44, Walter Rowley 1944–50, Bill Ridding 1951–68, Nat Lofthouse 1968–70, Jimmy McIlroy 1970, Jimmy Meadows 1971, Nat Lofthouse 1971 (then admin. man. to 1972), Jimmy Armfield 1971–74, Ian Greaves 1974–80, Stan Anderson 1980–81, George Mulhall 1981–82, John McGovern 1982–85, Charlie Wright 1985, Phil Neal 1985–92, Bruce Rioch 1992–95, Roy McFarland 1995–96, Colin Todd January 1996– .

AFC BOURNEMOUTH
Vincent Kitcher 1914–23*, Harry Kinghorn 1923–25, Leslie Knighton 1925–28, Frank Richards 1928–30, Billy Birrell 1930–35, Bob Crompton 1935–36, Charlie Bell 1936–39, Harry Kinghorn 1939–47, Harry Lowe 1947–50, Jack Bruton 1950–56, Fred Cox 1956–58, Don Welsh 1958–61, Bill McGarry 1961–63, Reg Flewin 1963–65, Fred Cox 1965–70, John Bond 1970–73, Trevor Hartley 1974–78, John Benson 1975–78, Alec Stock 1979–80, David Webb 1980–82, Don Megson 1983, Harry Redknapp 1983–92, Tony Pulis 1992–94, Mel Machin August 1994– .

BRADFORD CITY
Robert Campbell 1903–05, Peter O'Rourke 1905–21, David Menzies 1921–26, Colin Veitch 1926–28, Peter O'Rourke 1928–30, Jack Peart 1930–35, Dick Ray 1935–37, Fred Westgarth 1938–43, Bob Sharp 1943–46, Jack Barker 1946–47, John Milburn 1947–48, David Steele 1948–52, Albert Harris 1952, Ivor Powell 1952–55, Peter Jackson 1955–61,

Bob Brocklebank 1961–64, Bill Harris 1965–66, Willie Watson 1966–69, Grenville Hair 1967–68, Jimmy Wheeler 1968–71, Bryan Edwards 1971–75, Bobby Kennedy 1975–78, John Napier 1978, George Mulhall 1978–81, Roy McFarland 1981–82, Trevor Cherry 1982–87, Terry Dolan 1987–89, Terry Yorath 1989–90, John Docherty 1990–91, Frank Stapleton 1991–94, Lennie Lawrence 1994–95, Chris Kamara November 1995– .

BRENTFORD
Will Lewis 1900–03*, Dick Molyneux 1903–06, W. G. Brown 1906–08, Fred Halliday 1908–26 (only secretary to 1922), Ephraim Rhodes 1912–15, Archie Mitchell 1921–22, Harry Curtis 1926–49, Jackie Gibbons 1949–52, Jimmy Blain 1952–53, Tommy Lawton 1953, Bill Dodgin Snr 1953–57, Malcolm Macdonald 1957–65, Tommy Cavanagh 1965–66, Billy Gray 1966–67, Jimmy Sirrel 1967–69, Frank Blunstone 1969–73, Mike Everitt 1973–75, John Docherty 1975–76, Bill Dodgin Jnr 1976–80, Fred Callaghan 1980–84, Frank McLintock 1984–87, Steve Perryman 1987–90, Phil Holder 1990–93, David Webb May 1993– .

BRIGHTON & HOVE ALBION
John Jackson 1901–05, Frank Scott-Walford 1905–08, John Robson 1908–14, Charles Webb 1919–47, Tommy Cook 1947, Don Welsh 1947–51, Billy Lane 1951–61, George Curtis 1961–63, Archie Macaulay 1963–68, Fred Goodwin 1968–70, Pat Saward 1970–73, Brian Clough 1973–74, Peter Taylor 1974–76, Alan Mullery 1976–81, Mike Bailey 1981–82, Jimmy Melia 1982–83, Chris Cattlin 1983–86, Alan Mullery 1986–87, Barry Lloyd 1987–93, Liam Brady 1993–95, Jimmy Case 1995–96, Steve Gritt December 1996– .

BRISTOL CITY
Sam Hollis 1897–99, Bob Campbell 1899–1901, Sam Hollis 1901–05, Harry Thickett 1905–10, Sam Hollis 1911–13, George Hedley 1913–15, Jack Hamilton 1915–19, Joe Palmer 1919–21, Alex Raisbeck 1921–29, Joe Bradshaw 1929–32, Bob Hewison 1932–49 (under suspension 1938–39), Bob Wright 1949–50, Pat Beasley 1950–58, Peter Doherty 1958–60, Fred Ford 1960–67, Alan Dicks 1967–80, Bobby Houghton 1980–82, Roy Hodgson 1982, Terry Cooper 1982–88 (Director from 1983), Joe Jordan 1988–90, Jimmy Lumsden 1990–92, Denis Smith 1992–93, Russell Osman 1993–94, Joe Jordan 1994–97, John Ward March 1997– .

BRISTOL ROVERS
Alfred Homer 1899–1920 (continued as secretary to 1928), Ben Hall 1920–21, Andy Wilson 1921–26, Joe Palmer 1926–29, Dave McLean 1929–30, Albert Prince-Cox 1930–36, Percy Smith 1936–37, Brough Fletcher 1938–49, Bert Tann 1950–68 (continued as GM to 1972), Fred Ford 1968–69, Bill Dodgin Snr 1969–72, Don Megson 1972–77, Bobby Campbell 1978–79, Harold Jarman 1979–80, Terry Cooper 1980–81, Bobby Gould 1981–83, David Williams 1983–85, Bobby Gould 1985–87, Gerry Francis 1987–91, Martin Dobson 1991, Dennis Rofe 1992, Malcolm Allison 1992–93, John Ward 1993–96, Ian Holloway May 1996– .

BURNLEY
Arthur F. Sutcliffe 1893–96*, Harry Bradshaw 1896–99*, Ernest Magnall 1899–1903*, Spen Whittaker 1903–10, R. H. Wadge 1910–11*, John Haworth 1911–25, Albert Pickles 1925–32, Tom Bromilow 1932–35, Alf Boland 1935–39*, Cliff Britton 1945–48, Frank Hill 1948–54, Alan Brown 1954–57, Billy Dougall 1957–58, Harry Potts 1958–70 (GM to 1972), Jimmy Adamson 1970–76, Joe Brown 1976–77, Harry Potts 1977–79, Brian Miller 1979–83, John Bond 1983–84, John Benson 1984–85, Martin Buchan 1985, Tommy Cavanagh 1985–86, Brian Miller 1986–89, Frank Casper 1989–91, Jimmy Mullen 1991–96, Adrian Heath 1996–97, Chris Waddle July 1997– .

BURY
T. Hargreaves 1887*, H. S. Hamer 1887–1907*, Archie Montgomery 1907–15, William Cameron 1919–23, James Hunter Thompson 1923–27, Percy Smith 1927–30, Arthur Paine 1930–34, Norman Bullock 1934–38, Jim Porter 1944–45, Norman Bullock 1945–49, John McNeil 1950–53, Dave Russell 1953–61, Bob Stokoe 1961–65, Bert Head 1965–66, Les Shannon 1966–69, Jack Marshall 1969, Les Hart 1970, Tommy McAnearney 1970–72, Alan Brown 1972–73, Bobby Smith 1973–77, Bob Stokoe 1977–78, David Hatton 1978–79, Dave Connor 1979–80, Jim Iley 1980–84, Martin Dobson 1984–89, Sam Ellis 1989–90, Mike Walsh 1990–95, Stan Ternent September 1995– .

CAMBRIDGE UNITED
Bill Whittaker 1949–55, Gerald Williams 1955, Bert Johnson 1955–59, Bill Craig 1959–60, Alan Moore 1960–63, Roy Kirk 1964–66, Bill Leivers 1967–74, Ron Atkinson 1974–78, John Docherty 1978–83, John Ryan 1984–85, Ken Shellito 1985, Chris Turner 1985–90, John Beck 1990–1992, Ian Atkins 1992–93, Gary Johnson 1993–95, Tommy Taylor 1995–96, Roy McFarland November 1996– .

CARDIFF CITY
Davy McDougall 1910–11, Fred Stewart 1911–33, Bartley Wilson 1933–34, B. Watts-Jones 1934–37, Bill Jennings 1937–39, Cyril Spiers 1939–46, Billy McCandless 1946–48, Cyril Spiers 1948–54, Trevor Morris 1954–58, Bill Jones 1958–62, George Swindin 1962–64, Jimmy Scoular 1964–73, Frank O'Farrell 1973–74, Jimmy Andrews 1974–78, Richie Morgan 1978–82, Len Ashurst 1982–84, Jimmy Goodfellow 1984, Alan Durban 1984–86, Frank Burrows 1986–89, Len Ashurst 1989–91, Eddie May 1991–94, Terry Yorath 1994–95, Eddie May 1995, Kenny Hibbitt (CC) 1995, Phil Neal 1996, Russell Osman 1996, Kenny Hibbitt December 1996– .

CARLISLE UNITED
Harry Kirkbride 1904–05*, McCumiskey 1905–06*, Jack Houston 1906–08*, Bert Stansfield 1908–10, Jack Houston 1910–12, Davie Graham 1912–13, George Bristow 1913–30, Billy Hampson 1930–33, Bill Clarke 1933–35, Robert Kelly 1935–36, Fred Westgarth 1936–38, David Taylor 1938–40, Howard Harkness 1940–45, Bill Clark 1945–46*, Ivor Broadis 1946–49, Bill Shankly 1949–51, Fred Emery 1951–58, Andy Beattie 1958–60, Ivor Powell 1960–63, Alan Ashman 1963–67, Tim Ward 1967–68, Bob Stokoe 1968–70, Ian MacFarlane 1970–72, Alan Ashman 1972–75, Dick Young

1975–76, Bobby Moncur 1976–80, Martin Harvey 1980, Bob Stokoe 1980–85, Bryan "Pop" Robson 1985, Bob Stokoe 1985–86, Harry Gregg 1986–87, Cliff Middlemass 1987–91, Aidan McCaffery 1991–92, David McCreery 1992–93, Mick Wadsworth (DoC) 1993–96, Mervyn Day January 1996– .

CHARLTON ATHLETIC
Bill Rayner 1920–25, Alex McFarlane 1925–27, Albert Lindon 1928, Alex McFarlane 1928–32, Jimmy Seed 1933–56, Jimmy Trotter 1956–61, Frank Hill 1961–65, Bob Stokoe 1965–67, Eddie Firmani 1967–70, Theo Foley 1970–74, Andy Nelson 1974–79, Mike Bailey 1979–81, Alan Mullery 1981–82, Ken Craggs 1982, Lennie Lawrence 1982–91, Steve Gritt/Alan Curbishley 1991–95, Alan Curbishley June 1995– .

CHELSEA
John Tait Robertson 1905–07, David Calderhead 1907–33, Leslie Knighton 1933–39, Billy Birrell 1939–52, Ted Drake 1952–61, Tommy Docherty 1962–67, Dave Sexton 1967–74, Ron Suart 1974–75, Eddie McCreadie 1975–77, Ken Shellito 1977–78, Danny Blanchflower 1978–79, Geoff Hurst 1979–81, John Neal 1981–85 (Director to 1986), John Hollins 1985–88, Bobby Campbell 1988–91, Ian Porterfield 1991–93, David Webb 1993, Glenn Hoddle 1993–96, Ruud Gullit May 1996– .

CHESTER CITY
Charlie Hewitt 1930–36, Alex Raisbeck 1936–38, Frank Brown 1938–53, Louis Page 1953–56, John Harris 1956–59, Stan Pearson 1959–61, Bill Lambton 1962–63, Peter Hauser 1963–68, Ken Roberts 1968–76, Alan Oakes 1976–82, Cliff Sear 1982, John Sainty 1982–83, John McGrath 1984, Harry McNally 1985–92, Graham Barrow 1992–94, Mike Pejic 1994–95, Derek Mann 1995, Kevin Ratcliffe April 1995– .

CHESTERFIELD
E. Russell Timmeus 1891–95*, Gilbert Gillies 1895–1901, E. F. Hind 1901–02, Jack Hoskin 1902–06, W. Furness 1906–07, George Swift 1907–10, G. H. Jones 1911–13, R. L. Weston 1913–17, T. Callaghan 1919, J. J. Caffrey 1920–22, Harry Hadley 1922, Harry Parkes 1922–27, Alec Campbell 1927, Ted Davison 1927–32, Bill Harvey 1932–38, Norman Bullock 1938–45, Bob Brocklebank 1945–48, Bobby Marshall 1948–52, Ted Davison 1952–58, Duggie Livingstone 1958–62, Tony McShane 1962–67, Jimmy McGuigan 1967–73, Joe Shaw 1973–76, Arthur Cox 1976–80, Frank Barlow 1980–83, John Duncan 1983–87, Kevin Randall 1987–88, Paul Hart 1988–91, Chris McMenemy 1991–93, John Duncan February 1993– .

COLCHESTER UNITED
Ted Fenton 1946–48, Jimmy Allen 1948–53, Jack Butler 1953–55, Benny Fenton 1955–63, Neil Franklin 1963–68, Dick Graham 1968–72, Jim Smith 1972–75, Bobby Roberts 1975–82, Allan Hunter 1982–83, Cyril Lea 1983–86, Mike Walker 1986–87, Roger Brown 1987–88, Jock Wallace 1989, Mick Mills 1990. Ian Atkins 1990–91, Roy McDonough 1991–94, George Burley 1994, Steve Wignall January 1995– .

COVENTRY CITY
H. R. Buckle 1909–10, Robert Wallace 1910–13*, Frank Scott-Walford 1913–15, William Clayton 1917–19, H. Pollitt 1919–20, Albert Evans 1920–24, Jimmy Kerr 1924–28, James McIntyre 1928–31, Harry Storer 1931–45, Dick Bayliss 1945–47, Billy Frith 1947–48, Harry Storer 1948–53, Jack Fairbrother 1953–54, Charlie Elliott 1954–55, Jesse Carver 1955–56, Harry Warren 1956–57, Billy Frith 1957–61, Jimmy Hill 1961–67, Noel Cantwell 1967–72, Bob Dennison 1972, Joe Mercer 1972–75, Gordon Milne 1972–81, Dave Sexton 1981–83, Bobby Gould 1983–84, Don Mackay 1985–86, George Curtis 1986–87 (became MD), John Sillett 1987–90, Terry Butcher 1990–92, Don Howe 1992, Bobby Gould 1992–93, Phil Neal 1993–95, Ron Atkinson 1995–96 (became DoF), Gordon Strachan (player-manager) November 1996– .

CREWE ALEXANDRA
W. C. McNeill 1892–94*, J. G. Hall 1895–96*, R. Roberts* (1st team sec.) 1897, J. B. Bromerley 1898–1911* (continued as Hon. Sec. to 1925), Tom Bailey 1925–38, George Lillicrop 1938–44, Frank Hill 1944–48, Arthur Turner 1948–51, Harry Catterick 1951–53, Ralph Ward 1953–55, Maurice Lindley 1955–58, Harry Ware 1958–60, Jimmy McGuigan 1960–64, Ernie Tagg 1964–71 (continued as secretary to 1972), Dennis Viollet 1971, Jimmy Melia 1972–73, Ernie Tagg 1974, Harry Gregg 1975–78, Warwick Rimmer 1978–79, Tony Waddington 1979–81, Arfon Griffiths 1981–82, Peter Morris 1982–83, Dario Gradi June 1983– .

CRYSTAL PALACE
John T. Robson 1905–07, Edmund Goodman 1907–25 (had been secretary since 1905 and afterwards continued in this position to 1933). Alec Maley 1925–27, Fred Mavin 1927–30, Jack Tresadern 1930–35, Tom Bromilow 1935–36, R. S. Moyes 1936, Tom Bromilow 1936–39, George Irwin 1939–47, Jack Butler 1947–49, Ronnie Rooke 1949–50, Charlie Slade and Fred Dawes (joint managers) 1950–51, Laurie Scott 1951–54, Cyril Spiers 1954–58, George Smith 1958–60, Arthur Rowe 1960–62, Dick Graham 1962–66, Bert Head 1966–72 (continued as GM to 1973), Malcolm Allison 1973–76, Terry Venables 1976–80, Ernie Walley 1980, Malcolm Allison 1980–81, Dario Gradi 1981, Steve Kember 1981–82, Alan Mullery 1982–84, Steve Coppell 1984–93, Alan Smith 1993–95, Steve Coppell (TD) 1995–96, Dave Bassett 1996–97, Steve Coppell May 1997– (previously Caretaker from February).

DARLINGTON
Tom McIntosh 1902–11, W. L. Lane 1911–12*, Dick Jackson 1912–19, Jack English 1919–28, Jack Fairless 1928–33, George Collins 1933–36, George Brown 1936–38, Jackie Carr 1938–42, Jack Surtees 1942, Jack English 1945–46, Bill Forrest 1946–50, George Irwin 1950–52, Bob Gurney 1952–57, Dick Duckworth 1957–60, Eddie Carr 1960–64, Lol Morgan 1964–66, Jimmy Greenhalgh 1966–68, Ray Yeoman 1968–70, Len Richley 1970–71, Frank Brennan 1971, Ken Hale 1971–72, Allan Jones 1972, Ralph Brand 1972–73, Dave Sexton 1973–74, Billy Horner 1974–76, Peter Madden 1976–78, Len Walker 1978–79, Billy Elliott 1979–83, Cyril Knowles 1983–87, Dave Booth 1987–89, Brian Little 1989–91, Frank Gray 1991–92, Ray Hankin 1992, Billy McEwan 1992–93, Alan Murray 1993–95, Paul Futcher 1995, David Hodgson/ Jim Platt (DoC) 1995, Jim Platt 1995–96, David Hodgson November 1996– .

DERBY COUNTY

Harry Newbould 1896–1906, Jimmy Methven 1906–22, Cecil Potter 1922–25, George Jobey 1925–41, Ted Magner 1944–46, Stuart McMillan 1946–53, Jack Barker 1953–55, Harry Storer 1955–62, Tim Ward 1962–67, Brian Clough 1967–73, Dave Mackay 1973–76, Colin Murphy 1977, Tommy Docherty 1977–79, Colin Addison 1979–82, Johnny Newman 1982, Peter Taylor 1982–84, Roy McFarland 1984, Arthur Cox 1984–93, Roy McFarland 1993–95, Jim Smith June 1995– .

DONCASTER ROVERS

Arthur Porter 1920–21*, Harry Tufnell 1921–22, Arthur Porter 1922–23, Dick Ray 1923–27, David Menzies 1928–36, Fred Emery 1936–40, Bill Marsden 1944–46, Jackie Bestall 1946–49, Peter Doherty 1949–58, Jack Hodgson and Sid Bycroft (joint managers) 1958, Jack Crayston 1958–59 (continued as Sec-Man to 1961), Jackie Bestall (TM) 1959–60, Norman Curtis 1960–61, Danny Malloy 1961–62, Oscar Hold 1962–64, Bill Leivers 1964–66, Keith Kettleborough 1966–67, George Raynor 1967–68, Lawrie McMenemy 1968–71, Maurice Setters 1971–74, Stan Anderson 1975–78, Billy Bremner 1978–85, Dave Cusack 1985–87, Dave Mackay 1987–89, Billy Bremner 1989–91, Steve Beaglehole 1991–93, Ian Atkins 1994, Sammy Chung 1994–96, Kerry Dixon (player-manager) August 1996– .

EVERTON

W. E. Barclay 1888–89*, Dick Molyneux 1889–1901*, William C. Cuff 1901–18*, W. J. Sawyer 1918–19*, Thomas H. McIntosh 1919–35*, Theo Kelly 1936–48, Cliff Britton 1948–56, Ian Buchan 1956–58, Johnny Carey 1958–61, Harry Catterick 1961–73, Billy Bingham 1973–77, Gordon Lee 1977–81, Howard Kendall 1981–87, Colin Harvey 1987–90, Howard Kendall 1990–93, Mike Walker 1994, Joe Royle 1994–97, Howard Kendall June 1997– .

EXETER CITY

Arthur Chadwick 1910–22, Fred Mavin 1923–27, Dave Wilson 1928–29, Billy McDevitt 1929–35, Jack English 1935–39, George Roughton 1945–52, Norman Kirkman 1952–53, Norman Dodgin 1953–57, Bill Thompson 1957–58, Frank Broome 1958–60, Glen Wilson 1960–62, Cyril Spiers 1962–63, Jack Edwards 1963–65, Ellis Stuttard 1965–66, Jock Basford 1966–67, Frank Broome 1967–69, Johnny Newman 1969–76, Bobby Saxton 1977–79, Brian Godfrey 1979–83, Gerry Francis 1983–84, Jim Iley 1984–85, Colin Appleton 1985–87, Terry Cooper 1988–91, Alan Ball 1991–94, Terry Cooper 1994–95, Peter Fox June 1995– .

FULHAM

Harry Bradshaw 1904–09, Phil Kelso 1909–24, Andy Ducat 1924–26, Joe Bradshaw 1926–29, Ned Liddell 1929–31, Jim MacIntyre 1931–34, Jimmy Hogan 1934–35, Jack Peart 1935–48, Frank Osborne 1948–64 (was secretary-manager or GM for most of this period), Bill Dodgin Snr 1949–53, Duggie Livingstone 1956–58, Bedford Jezzard 1958–64 (GM for last two months), Vic Buckingham 1965–68, Bobby Robson 1968, Bill Dodgin Jnr 1969–72, Alec Stock 1972–76, Bobby Campbell 1976–80, Malcolm Macdonald 1980–84, Ray Harford 1984–96, Ray Lewington 1986–90, Alan Dicks 1990–91, Don Mackay 1991–94, Ian Branfoot 1994–96 (continued as GM), Micky Adams February 1996– .

GILLINGHAM

W. Ironside Groombridge 1896–1906* (previously financial secretary), Steve Smith 1906–08, W. I. Groombridge 1908–19*, George Collins 1919–20, John McMillan 1920–23, Harry Curtis 1923–26, Albert Hoskins 1926–29, Dick Hendrie 1929–31, Fred Mavin 1932–37, Alan Ure 1937–38, Bill Harvey 1938–39, Archie Clark 1939–58, Harry Barratt 1958–62, Freddie Cox 1962–65, Basil Hayward 1966–71, Andy Nelson 1971–74, Len Ashurst 1974–75, Gerry Summers 1975–81, Keith Peacock 1981–87, Paul Taylor 1988, Keith Burkinshaw 1988–89, Damien Richardson 1989–93, Mike Flanagan 1993–95, Neil Smillie 1995, Tony Pulis June 1995– .

GRIMSBY TOWN

H. N. Hickson 1902–20*, Haydn Price 1920, George Fraser 1921–24, Wilf Gillow 1924–32, Frank Womack 1932–36, Charles Spencer 1937–51, Bill Shankly 1951–53, Billy Walsh 1954–55, Allenby Chilton 1955–59, Tim Ward 1960–62, Tom Johnston 1962–64, Jimmy McGuigan 1964–67, Don McEvoy 1967–68, Bill Harvey 1968–69, Bobby Kennedy 1969–71, Lawrie McMenemy 1971–73, Ron Ashman 1973–75, Tom Casey 1975–76, Johnny Newman 1976–79, George Kerr 1979–82, David Booth 1982–85, Mike Lyons 1985–87, Bobby Roberts 1987–88, Alan Buckley 1988–94, Brian Laws 1994–96, Kenny Swain 1997, Alan Buckley May 1997– .

HARTLEPOOL UNITED

Alfred Priest 1908–12, Percy Humphreys 1912–13, Jack Manners 1913–20, Cecil Potter 1920–22, David Gordon 1922–24, Jack Manners 1924–27, Bill Norman 1927–31, Jack Carr 1932–35 (had been player-coach since 1931), Jimmy Hamilton 1935–43, Fred Westgarth 1943–57, Ray Middleton 1957–59, Bill Robinson 1959–62, Allenby Chilton 1962–63, Bob Gurney 1963–64, Alvan Williams 1964–65, Geoff Twentyman 1965, Brian Clough 1965–67, Angus McLean 1967–70, John Simpson 1970–71, Len Ashurst 1971–74, Ken Hale 1974–76, Billy Horner 1976–83, Johnny Duncan 1983, Mike Docherty 1983, Billy Horner 1984–86, John Bird 1986–88, Bobby Moncur 1988–89, Cyril Knowles 1989–91, Alan Murray 1991–93, Viv Busby 1993, John MacPhail 1993–94, David McCreery 1994–95, Keith Houchen 1995–96, Mick Tait December 1996– .

HEREFORD UNITED

Eric Keen 1939, George Tranter 1948–49, Alex Massie 1952, George Tranter 1953–55, Joe Wade 1956–62, Ray Daniels 1962–63, Bob Dennison 1963–67, John Charles 1967–71, Colin Addison 1971–74, John Sillett 1974–78, Mike Bailey 1978–79, Frank Lord 1979–82, Tommy Hughes 1982–83, Johnny Newman 1983–87, Ian Bowyer 1987–90, Colin Addison 1990–91, John Sillett 1991–92, Greg Downs 1992–94, John Layton 1994–95, Graham Turner (DoF) August 1995– .

HUDDERSFIELD TOWN

Fred Walker 1908–10, Richard Pudan 1910–12, Arthur Fairclough 1912–19, Ambrose Langley 1919–21, Herbert Chapman 1921–25, Cecil Potter 1925–26, Jack Chaplin 1926–29, Clem Stephenson 1929–42, David Steele 1943–47,

George Stephenson 1947–52, Andy Beattie 1952–56, Bill Shankly 1956–59, Eddie Boot 1960–64, Tom Johnston 1964–68, Ian Greaves 1968–74, Bobby Collins 1974, Tom Johnston 1975–78 (had been GM since 1975), Mike Buxton 1978–86, Steve Smith 1986–87, Malcolm Macdonald 1987–88, Eoin Hand 1988–92, Ian Ross 1992–93, Neil Warnock 1993–95, Brian Horton June 1995– .

HULL CITY
James Ramster 1904–05*, Ambrose Langley 1905–13, Harry Chapman 1913–14, Fred Stringer 1914–16, David Menzies 1916–21, Percy Lewis 1921–23, Bill McCracken 1923–31, Haydn Green 1931–34, John Hill 1934–36, David Menzies 1936, Ernest Blackburn 1936–46, Major Frank Buckley 1946–48, Raich Carter 1948–51, Bob Jackson 1952–55, Bob Brocklebank 1955–61, Cliff Britton 1961–70 (continued as GM to 1971), Terry Neill 1970–74, John Kaye 1974–77, Bobby Collins 1977–78, Ken Houghton 1978–79, Mike Smith 1979–82, Bobby Brown 1982, Colin Appleton 1982–84, Brian Horton 1984–88, Eddie Gray 1988–89, Colin Appleton 1989, Stan Ternent 1989–91, Terry Dolan 1991–97, Mark Hateley July 1997– .

IPSWICH TOWN
Mick O'Brien 1936–37, Scott Duncan 1937–55 (continued as secretary), Alf Ramsey 1955–63, Jackie Milburn 1963–64, Bill McGarry 1964–68, Bobby Robson 1969–82, Bobby Ferguson 1982–87, Johnny Duncan 1987–90, John Lyall 1990–94, George Burley December 1994– .

LEEDS UNITED
Dick Ray 1919–20, Arthur Fairclough 1920–27, Dick Ray 1927–35, Bill Hampson 1935–47, Willis Edwards 1947–48, Major Frank Buckley 1948–53, Raich Carter 1953–58, Bill Lambton 1958–59, Jack Taylor 1959–61, Don Revie 1961–74, Brian Clough 1974, Jimmy Armfield 1974–78, Jock Stein 1978, Jimmy Adamson 1978–80, Allan Clarke 1980–82, Eddie Gray 1982–85, Billy Bremner 1985–88, Howard Wilkinson 1988–96, George Graham September 1996– .

LEICESTER CITY
William Clark 1896–97, George Johnson 1898–1907*, James Blessington 1907–09, Andy Aitken 1909–11, John William Bartlett 1912–14, Peter Hodge 1919–26, William Orr 1926–32, Peter Hodge 1932–34, Andy Lochhead 1934–36, Frank Womack 1936–39, Tom Bromilow 1939–45, Tom Mather 1945–46, Johnny Duncan 1946–49, Norman Bullock 1949–55, David Halliday 1955–58, Matt Gillies 1959–68, Frank O'Farrell 1968–71, Jimmy Bloomfield 1971–77, Frank McLintock 1977–78, Jock Wallace 1978–82, Gordon Milne 1982–86, Bryan Hamilton 1986–87, David Pleat 1987–91, Brian Little 1991–94, Mark McGhee 1994–95, Martin O'Neill December 1995– .

LEYTON ORIENT
Sam Omerod 1905–06, Ike Ivenson 1906, Billy Holmes 1907–22, Peter Proudfoot 1922–29, Arthur Grimsdell 1929–30, Peter Proudfoot 1930–31, Jimmy Seed 1931–33, David Pratt 1933–34, Peter Proudfoot 1935–39, Tom Halsey 1939, Bill Wright 1939–45, Willie Hall 1945, Bill Wright 1945–46, Charlie Hewitt 1946–48, Neil McBain 1948–49, Alec Stock 1949–56, 1956–57, 1958–59, Johnny Carey 1961–63, Benny Fenton 1963–64, Dave Sexton 1965, Dick Graham 1966–68, Jimmy Bloomfield 1968–71, George Petchey 1971–77, Jimmy Bloomfield 1977–81, Paul Went 1981, Ken Knighton 1981, Frank Clark 1982–91 (MD), Peter Eustace 1991–94, Chris Turner/John Sitton 1994–95, Pat Holland 1995–96, Tommy Taylor November 1996– .

LINCOLN CITY
David Calderhead 1900–07, John Henry Strawson 1907–14 (had been secretary), George Fraser 1919–21, David Calderhead Jnr. 1921–24, Horace Henshall 1924–27, Harry Parkes 1927–36, Joe McClelland 1936–46, Bill Anderson 1946–65 (GM to 1966), Roy Chapman 1965–66, Ron Gray 1966–70, Bert Loxley 1970–71, David Herd 1971–72, Graham Taylor 1972–77, George Kerr 1977–78, Willie Bell 1977–78, Colin Murphy 1978–85, John Pickering 1985, George Kerr 1985–87, Peter Daniel 1987, Colin Murphy 1987–90, Allan Clarke 1990, Steve Thompson 1990–93, Keith Alexander 1993–94, Sam Ellis 1994–95, Steve Wicks (HC) 1995, John Beck October 1995– .

LIVERPOOL
W. E. Barclay 1892–96, Tom Watson 1896–1915, David Ashworth 1920–22, Matt McQueen 1923–28, George Patterson 1928–36 (continued as secretary), George Kay 1936–51, Don Welsh 1951–56, Phil Taylor 1956–59, Bill Shankly 1959–74, Bob Paisley 1974–83, Joe Fagan 1983–85, Kenny Dalglish 1985–91, Graeme Souness 1991–94, Roy Evans January 1994– .

LUTON TOWN
Charlie Green 1901–28*, George Thomson 1925, John McCartney 1927–29, George Kay 1929–31, Harold Wightman 1931–35, Ted Liddell 1936–38, Neil McBain 1938–39, George Martin 1939–47, Dally Duncan 1947–58, Syd Owen 1959–60, Sam Bartram 1960–62, Bill Harvey 1962–64, George Martin 1965–66, Allan Brown 1966–68, Alec Stock 1968–72, Harry Haslam 1972–78, David Pleat 1978–86, John Moore 1986–87, Ray Harford 1987–89, Jim Ryan 1900–91, David Pleat 1991–95, Terry Westley 1995, Lennie Lawrence December 1995– .

MANCHESTER CITY
Joshua Parlby 1893–95*, Sam Omerod 1895–1902, Tom Maley 1902–06, Harry Newbould 1906–12, Ernest Magnall 1912–24, David Ashworth 1924–25, Peter Hodge 1926–32, Wilf Wild 1932–46 (continued as secretary to 1950), Sam Cowan 1946–47, John "Jock" Thomson 1947–50, Leslie McDowall 1950–63, George Poyser 1963–65, Joe Mercer 1965–71 (continued as GM to 1972), Malcolm Allison 1972–73, Johnny Hart 1973, Ron Saunders 1973–74, Tony Book 1974–79, Malcolm Allison 1979–80, John Bond 1980–83, John Benson 1983, Billy McNeill 1983–86, Jimmy Frizzell 1986–87 (continued as GM), Mel Machin 1987–89, Howard Kendall 1990, Peter Reid 1990–93, Brian Horton 1993–95, Alan Ball 1995–96, Steve Coppell 1996, Frank Clark December 1996– .

MANCHESTER UNITED
Ernest Magnall 1900–12, John Robson 1914–21, John Chapman 1921–26, Clarence Hildrith 1926–27, Herbert Bamlett 1927–31, Walter Crickmer 1931–32, Scott Duncan 1932–37, Jimmy Porter 1938–44, Walter Crickmer 1944–45*, Matt Busby 1945–69 (continued as GM then Director), Wilf McGuinness 1969–70, Frank O'Farrell 1971–72, Tommy Docherty 1972–77, Dave Sexton 1977–81, Ron Atkinson 1981–86, Alex Ferguson November 1986– .

MANSFIELD TOWN
John Baynes 1922–25, Ted Davison 1926–28, Jack Hickling 1928–33, Henry Martin 1933–35, Charlie Bell 1935, Harold Wightman 1936, Harold Parkes 1936–38, Jack Poole 1938–44, Lloyd Barke 1944–45, Roy Goodall 1945–49, Freddie Steele 1949–51, George Jobey 1952–53, Stan Mercer 1953–55, Charlie Mitten 1956–58, Sam Weaver 1958–60, Raich Carter 1960–63, Tommy Cummings 1963–67, Tommy Eggleston 1967–70, Jock Basford 1970–71, Danny Williams 1971–74, Dave Smith 1974–76, Peter Morris 1976–78, Billy Bingham 1978–79, Mick Jones 1979–81, Stuart Boam 1981–83, Ian Greaves 1983–89, George Foster 1989–93, Andy King 1993–96, Steve Parkin October 1996– .

MIDDLESBROUGH
John Robson 1899–1905, Alex Mackie 1905–06, Andy Aitken 1906–09, J. Gunter 1908–10*, Andy Walker 1910–11, Tom McIntosh 1911–19, Jimmy Howie 1920–23, Herbert Bamlett 1923–26, Peter McWilliam 1927–34, Wilf Gillow 1934–44, David Jack 1944–52, Walter Rowley 1952–54, Bob Dennison 1954–63, Raich Carter 1963–66, Stan Anderson 1966–73, Jack Charlton 1973–77, John Neal 1977–81, Bobby Murdoch 1981–82, Malcolm Allison 1982–84, Willie Maddren 1984–86, Bruce Rioch 1986–90, Colin Todd 1990–91, Lennie Lawrence 1991–94, Bryan Robson May 1994– .

MILLWALL
William Henderson 1894–99*, E. R. Stopher 1899–1900, George Saunders 1900–11, Herbert Lipsham 1911–19, Robert Hunter 1919–33, Bill McCracken 1933–36, Charlie Hewitt 1936–40, Bill Voisey 1940–44, Jack Cock 1944–48, Charlie Hewitt 1948–56, Ron Gray 1956–57, Jimmy Seed 1958–59, Reg Smith 1959–61, Ron Gray 1961–63, Billy Gray 1963–66, Benny Fenton 1966–74, Gordon Jago 1974–77, George Petchey 1978–80, Peter Anderson 1980–82, George Graham 1982–86, John Docherty 1986–90, Bob Pearson 1990, Bruce Rioch 1990–92, Mick McCarthy 1992–96, Jimmy Nicholl 1996–97, John Docherty 1997, Billy Bonds June 1997– .

NEWCASTLE UNITED
Frank Watt 1895–32*, Andy Cunningham 1930–35, Tom Mather 1935–39, Stan Seymour 1939–47 (Hon-manager), George Martin 1947–50, Stan Seymour 1950–54 (Hon-manager), Duggie Livingstone 1954–56, Stan Seymour 1956–58 (Hon-manager), Charlie Mitten 1958–61, Norman Smith 1961–62, Joe Harvey 1962–75, Gordon Lee 1975–77, Richard Dinnis 1977, Bill McGarry 1977–80, Arthur Cox 1980–84, Jack Charlton 1984, Willie McFaul 1985–88, Jim Smith 1988–91, Ossie Ardiles 1991–92, Kevin Keegan 1992–97, Kenny Dalglish January 1997– .

NORTHAMPTON TOWN
Arthur Jones 1897–1907*, Herbert Chapman 1907–12, Walter Bull 1912–13, Fred Lessons 1913–19, Bob Hewison 1920–25, Jack Tresadern 1925–30, Jack English 1931–35, Syd Puddefoot 1935–37, Warney Cresswell 1937–39, Tom Smith 1939–49, Bob Dennison 1949–54, Dave Smith 1954–59, David Bowen 1959–67, Tony Marchi 1967–68, Ron Flowers 1968–69, Dave Bowen 1969–72 (continued as GM and secretary to 1985 when joined the board), Billy Baxter 1972–73, Bill Dodgin Jnr 1973–76, Pat Crerand 1976–77, Bill Dodgin Jnr 1977, John Petts 1977–78, Mike Keen 1978–79, Clive Walker 1979–80, Bill Dodgin Jnr 1980–82, Clive Walker 1982–84, Tony Barton 1984–85, Graham Carr 1985–90, Theo Foley 1990–92, Phil Chard 1992–93, John Barnwell 1993–95, Ian Atkins January 1995– .

NORWICH CITY
John Bowman 1905–07, James McEwen 1907–08, Arthur Turner 1909–10, Bert Stansfield 1910–15, Major Frank Buckley 1919–20, Charles O'Hagan 1920–21, Albert Gosnell 1921–26, Bert Stansfield 1926, Cecil Potter 1926–29, James Kerr 1929–33, Tom Parker 1933–37, Bob Young 1937–39, Jimmy Jewell 1939, Bob Young 1939–45, Cyril Spiers 1946–47, Duggie Lochhead 1947–50, Norman Low 1950–55, Tom Parker 1955–57, Archie Macaulay 1957–61, Willie Reid 1961–62, George Swindin 1962, Ron Ashman 1962–66, Lol Morgan 1966–69, Ron Saunders 1969–73, John Bond 1973–80, Ken Brown 1980–87, Dave Stringer 1987–92, Mike Walker 1992–94, John Deehan 1994–95, Martin O'Neill 1995, Gary Megson 1995–96, Mike Walker June 1996– .

NOTTINGHAM FOREST
Harry Radford 1889–97*, Harry Haslam 1897–1909*, Fred Earp 1909–12, Bob Masters 1912–25, John Baynes 1925–29, Stan Hardy 1930–31, Noel Watson 1931–36, Harold Wightman 1936–39, Billy Walker 1939–60, Andy Beattie 1960–63, Johnny Carey 1963–68, Matt Gillies 1969–72, Dave Mackay 1972, Allan Brown 1973–75, Brian Clough 1975–93, Frank Clark 1993–96, Stuart Pearce 1996–97, Dave Bassett May 1997– (previously GM from February).

NOTTS COUNTY
Edwin Browne 1883–93*, Tom Featherstone 1893*, Tom Harris 1893–1913*, Albert Fisher 1913–27, Horace Henshall 1927–34, Charlie Jones 1934–35, David Pratt 1935, Percy Smith 1935–36, Jimmy McMullan 1936–37, Harry Parkes 1938–39, Tony Towers 1939–42, Frank Womack 1942–43, Major Frank Buckley 1944–46, Arthur Stollery 1946–49, Eric Houghton 1949–53, George Poyser 1953–57, Tommy Lawton 1957–58, Frank Hill 1958–61, Tim Coleman 1961–63, Eddie Lowe 1963–65, Tim Coleman 1965–66, Jack Burkitt 1966–67, Andy Beattie (GM 1967), Billy Gray 1967–68, Jimmy Sirrel 1969–75, Ron Fenton 1975–77, Jimmy Sirrel 1978–82 (continued as GM to 1984), Howard Wilkinson 1982–83, Larry Lloyd 1983–84, Richie Barker 1984–85, Jimmy Sirrel 1985–87, John Barnwell 1987–88, Neil Warnock 1989–93, Mick Walker 1993–94, Russell Slade 1994–95, Howard Kendall 1995, Colin Murphy June 1995 (continued as GM to 1996), Steve Thompson 1996, Sam Allardyce January 1997– .

OLDHAM ATHLETIC
David Ashworth 1906–14, Herbert Bamlett 1914–21, Charlie Roberts 1921–22, David Ashworth 1923–24, Bob Mellor 1924–27, Andy Wilson 1927–32, Jimmy McMullan 1933–34, Bob Mellor 1934–45 (continued as secretary to 1953), Frank Womack 1945–47, Billy Wootton 1947–50, George Hardwick 1950–56, Ted Goodier 1956–58, Norman Dodgin 1958–60, Jack Rowley 1960–63, Les McDowall 1963–65, Gordon Hurst 1965–66, Jimmy McIlroy 1966–68, Jack Rowley 1968–69, Jimmy Frizzell 1970–82, Joe Royle 1982–94, Graeme Sharp 1994–97, Neil Warnock February 1997– .

OXFORD UNITED
Harry Thompson 1949–58 (Player-Manager 1949-51), Arthur Turner 1959–69 (continued as GM to 1972), Ron Saunders 1969, George Summers 1969–75, Mike Brown 1975–79, Bill Asprey 1979–80, Ian Greaves 1980–82, Jim Smith 1982–85, Maurice Evans 1985–88, Mark Lawrenson 1988, Brian Horton 1988–93, Denis Smith September 1993– .

PETERBOROUGH UNITED
Jock Porter 1934–36, Fred Taylor 1936–37, Vic Poulter 1937–38, Sam Madden 1938–48, Jack Blood 1948–50, Bob Gurney 1950–52, Jack Fairbrother 1952–54, George Swindin 1954–58, Jimmy Hagan 1958–62, Jack Fairbrother 1962–64, Gordon Clark 1964–67, Norman Rigby 1967–69, Jim Iley 1969–72, Noel Cantwell 1972–77, John Barnwell 1977–78, Billy Hails 1978–79, Peter Morris 1979–82, Martin Wilkinson 1982–83, John Wile 1983–86, Noel Cantwell 1986–88 (continued as GM), Mick Jones 1988–89, Mark Lawrenson 1989–90, Chris Turner 1991–92, Lil Fuccillo 1992–93, John Still 1994–95, Mick Halsall 1995–96, Barry Fry May 1996– .

PLYMOUTH ARGYLE
Frank Brettell 1903–05, Bob Jack 1905–06, Bill Fullerton 1906–07, Bob Jack 1910–38, Jack Tresadern 1938–47, Jimmy Rae 1948–55, Jack Rowley 1955–60, Neil Dougall 1961, Ellis Stuttard 1961–63, Andy Beattie 1963–64, Malcolm Allison 1964–65, Derek Ufton 1965–68, Billy Bingham 1968–70, Ellis Stuttard 1970–72, Tony Waiters 1972–77, Mike Kelly 1977–78, Malcolm Allison 1978–79, Bobby Saxton 1979–81, Bobby Moncur 1981–83, Johnny Hore 1983–84, Dave Smith 1984–88, Ken Brown 1988–90, David Kemp 1990–92, Peter Shilton 1992–95, Steve McCall 1995, Neil Warnock June 1995–97, Mick Jones May 1997– .

PORTSMOUTH
Frank Brettell 1898–1901, Bob Blyth 1901–04, Richard Bonney 1905–08, Bob Brown 1911–20, John McCartney 1920–27, Jack Tinn 1927–47, Bob Jackson 1947–52, Eddie Lever 1952–58, Freddie Cox 1958–61, George Smith 1961–70, Ron Tindall 1970–73 (GM to 1974), John Mortimore 1973–74, Ian St. John 1974–77, Jimmy Dickinson 1977–79, Frank Burrows 1979–82, Bobby Campbell 1982–84, Alan Ball 1984–89, John Gregory 1989–90, Frank Burrows 1990–1991, Jim Smith 1991–95, Terry Fenwick February 1995– .

PORT VALE
Sam Gleaves 1896–1905*, Tom Clare 1905–11, A. S. Walker 1911–12, H. Myatt 1912–14, Tom Holford 1919–24 (continued as trainer), Joe Schofield 1924–30, Tom Morgan 1930–32, Tom Holford 1932–35, Warney Cresswell 1936–37, Tom Morgan 1937–38, Billy Frith 1945–46, Gordon Hodgson 1946–51, Ivor Powell 1951, Freddie Steele 1951–57, Norman Low 1957–62, Freddie Steele 1962–65, Jackie Mudie 1965–67, Sir Stanley Matthews (GM) 1965–68, Gordon Lee 1968–74, Roy Sproson 1974–77, Colin Harper 1977, Bobby Smith 1977–78, Dennis Butler 1978–79, Alan Bloor 1979, John McGrath 1980–83, John Rudge March 1984– .

PRESTON NORTH END
Charlie Parker 1906–15, Vincent Hayes 1919–23, Jim Lawrence 1923–25, Frank Richards 1925–27, Alex Gibson 1927–31, Lincoln Hayes 1931–1932 (run by committee 1932–36), Tommy Muirhead 1936–37, (run by committee 1937–49), Will Scott 1949–53, Scot Symon 1953–54, Frank Hill 1954–56, Cliff Britton 1956–61, Jimmy Milne 1961–68, Bobby Seith 1968–70, Alan Ball Sr 1970–73, Bobby Charlton 1973–75, Harry Catterick 1975–77, Nobby Stiles 1977–81, Tommy Docherty 1981, Gordon Lee 1981–83, Alan Kelly 1983–85, Tommy Booth 1985–86, Brian Kidd 1986, John McGrath 1986–90, Les Chapman 1990–92, John Beck 1992–94, Gary Peters December 1994– .

QUEENS PARK RANGERS
James Cowan 1906–13, Jimmy Howie 1913–20, Ted Liddell 1920–24, Will Wood 1924–25 (had been secretary since 1903), Bob Hewison 1925–30, John Bowman 1930–31, Archie Mitchell 1931–33, Mick O'Brien 1933–35, Billy Birrell 1935–39, Ted Vizard 1939–44, Dave Mangnall 1944–52, Jack Taylor 1952–59, Alec Stock 1959–65 (GM to 1968), Bill Dodgin Jnr 1968, Tommy Docherty 1968, Les Allen 1968–71, Gordon Jago 1971–74, Dave Sexton 1974–77, Frank Sibley 1977–78, Steve Burtenshaw 1978–79, Tommy Docherty 1979–80, Terry Venables 1980–84, Gordon Jago 1984, Alan Mullery 1984, Frank Sibley 1984–85, Jim Smith 1985–88, Trevor Francis 1988–90, Don Howe 1990–91, Gerry Francis 1991–94, Ray Wilkins 1994–96, Stewart Houston September 1996– .

READING
Thomas Sefton 1897–1901*, James Sharp 1901–02, Harry Matthews 1902–20, Harry Marshall 1920–22, Arthur Chadwick 1923–25, H. S. Bray 1925–26 (secretary only since 1922 and 1926–35), Andrew Wylie 1926–31, Joe Smith 1931–35, Billy Butler 1935–39, John Cochrane 1939, Joe Edelston 1939–47, Ted Drake 1947–52, Jack Smith 1952–55, Harry Johnston 1955–63, Roy Bentley 1963–69, Jack Mansell 1969–71, Charlie Hurley 1972–77, Maurice Evans 1977–84, Ian Branfoot 1984–89, Ian Porterfield 1989–91, Mark McGhee 1991–94, Jimmy Quinn/Mick Gooding 1994–97, Terry Bullivant June 1997– .

ROCHDALE
Billy Bradshaw 1920, (run by committee 1920–22), Tom Wilson 1922–23, Jack Peart 1923–30, Will Cameron 1930–31, Herbert Hopkinson 1932–34, Billy Smith 1934–35, Ernest Nixon 1935–37, Sam Jennings 1937–38, Ted Goodier 1938–52, Jack Warner 1952–53, Harry Catterick 1953–58, Jack Marshall 1958–60, Tony Collins 1960–68, Bob Stokoe 1967–68, Len Richley 1968–70, Dick Conner 1970–73, Walter Joyce 1973–76, Brian Green 1976–77, Mike Ferguson 1977–78,

Doug Collins 1979, Bob Stokoe 1979–80, Peter Madden 1980–83, Jimmy Greenhoff 1983–84, Vic Halom 1984–86, Eddie Gray 1986–88, Danny Bergara 1988–89, Terry Dolan 1989–91, Dave Sutton 1991–94, Mick Docherty 1995–96, Graham Barrow May 1996– .

ROTHERHAM UNITED
Billy Heald 1925–29 (secretary only for long spell), Stanley Davies 1929–30, Billy Heald 1930–33, Reg Freeman 1934–52, Andy Smailes 1952–58, Tom Johnston 1958–62, Danny Williams 1962–65, Jack Mansell 1965–67, Tommy Docherty 1967–68, Jimmy McAnearney 1968–73, Jimmy McGuigan 1973–79, Ian Porterfield 1979–81, Emlyn Hughes 1981–83, George Kerr 1983–85, Norman Hunter 1985–87, Dave Cusack 1987–88, Billy McEwan 1988–91, Phil Henson 1991–94, Archie Gemmill/ John McGovern 1994–96, Danny Bergara 1996–97, Ronnie Moore May 1997– .

SCARBOROUGH
B. Chapman 1945–47*, George Hall 1946–47, Harold Taylor 1947–48, Frank Taylor 1948–50, A. C. Bell (Director & Hon. TM) 1950–53, Reg Halton 1953–54, Charles Robson (Hon. TM) 1954–57, George Higgins 1957–58, Andy Smailes 1959–61, Eddie Brown 1961–64, Albert Franks 1964–65, Stuart Myers 1965–66, Graham Shaw 1968–69, Colin Appleton 1969–73, Ken Houghton 1974–75, Colin Appleton 1975–81, Jimmy McAnearney 1981–82, John Cottam 1982–84, Harry Dunn 1984–86, Neil Warnock 1986–88, Colin Morris 1989, Ray McHale 1989–93, Phil Chambers 1993, Steve Wicks 1993–94, Billy Ayre 1994, Ray McHale 1994–96, Mitch Cook (DoC) 1996, Mick Wadsworth June 1996– .

SCUNTHORPE UNITED
Harry Allcock 1915–53*, Tom Crilly 1936–37, Bernard Harper 1946–48, Leslie Jones 1950–51, Bill Corkhill 1952–56, Ron Suart 1956–58, Tony McShane 1959, Bill Lambton 1959, Frank Soo 1959–60, Dick Duckworth 1960–64, Fred Goodwin 1964–66, Ron Ashman 1967–73, Ron Bradley 1973–74, Dick Rooks 1974–76, Ron Ashman 1976–81, John Duncan 1981–83, Allan Clarke 1983–84, Frank Barlow 1984–87, Mick Buxton 1987–91, Bill Green 1991–93, Richard Money 1993–94, David Moore 1994–96, Mick Buxton 1996–97, Brian Laws February 1997– .

SHEFFIELD UNITED
J. B. Wostinholm 1889–1899*, John Nicholson 1899–1932, Ted Davison 1932–52, Reg Freeman 1952–55, Joe Mercer 1955–58, Johnny Harris 1959–68 (continued as GM to 1970), Arthur Rowley 1968–69, Johnny Harris (GM resumed TM duties) 1969–73, Ken Furphy 1973–75, Jimmy Sirrel 1975–77, Harry Haslam 1978–81, Martin Peters 1981, Ian Porterfield 1981–86, Billy McEwan 1986–88, Dave Bassett 1988–95, Howard Kendall 1995–97.

SHEFFIELD WEDNESDAY
Arthur Dickinson 1891–1920*, Robert Brown 1920–33, Billy Walker 1933–37, Jimmy McMullan 1937–42, Eric Taylor 1942–58 (continued as GM to 1974), Harry Catterick 1958–61, Vic Buckingham 1961–64, Alan Brown 1964–68, Jack Marshall 1968–69, Danny Williams 1969–71, Derek Dooley 1971–73, Steve Burtenshaw 1974–75, Len Ashurst 1975–77, Jackie Charlton 1977–83, Howard Wilkinson 1983–88, Peter Eustace 1988–89, Ron Atkinson 1989–91, Trevor Francis 1991–95, David Pleat June 1995– .

SHREWSBURY TOWN
W. Adams 1905–12*, A. Weston 1912–34*, Jack Roscamp 1934–35, Sam Ramsey 1935–36, Ted Bousted 1936–40, Leslie Knighton 1945–49, Harry Chapman 1949–50, Sammy Crooks 1950–54, Walter Rowley 1955–57, Harry Potts 1957–58, Johnny Spuhler 1958, Arthur Rowley 1958–68, Harry Gregg 1968–72, Maurice Evans 1972–73, Alan Durban 1974–78, Richie Barker 1978, Graham Turner 1978–84, Chic Bates 1984–87, Ian McNeill 1987–90, Asa Hartford 1990–91, John Bond 1991–93, Fred Davies 1994 (previously caretaker-manager from 1993)–97, Jake King May 1997– .

SOUTHAMPTON
Cecil Knight 1894–95*, Charles Robson 1895–97, E. Arnfield 1897–1911* (continued as secretary), George Swift 1911–12, Ernest Arnfield 1912–19, Jimmy McIntyre 1919–24, Arthur Chadwick 1925–31, George Kay 1931–36, George Gross 1936–37, Tom Parker 1937–43, J. R. Sarjantson stepped down from the board to act as secretary-manager 1943–47 with the next two listed being team managers during this period, Arthur Dominy 1943–46, Bill Dodgin Snr 1946–49, Sid Cann 1949–51, George Roughton 1952–55, Ted Bates 1955–73, Lawrie McMenemy 1973–85, Chris Nicholl 1985–91, Ian Branfoot 1991–94, Alan Ball 1994–95, Dave Merrington 1995–96, Graeme Souness 1996–97, Dave Jones June 1997– .

SOUTHEND UNITED
Bob Jack 1906–10, George Molyneux 1910–11, O. M. Howard 1911–12, Joe Bradshaw 1912–19, Ned Liddell 1919–20, Tom Mather 1920–21, Ted Birnie 1921–34, David Jack 1934–40, Harry Warren 1946–56, Eddie Perry 1956–60, Frank Broome 1960, Ted Fenton 1961–65, Alvan Williams 1965–67, Ernie Shepherd 1967–69, Geoff Hudson 1969–70, Arthur Rowley 1970–76, Dave Smith 1976–83, Peter Morris 1983–84, Bobby Moore 1984–86, Dave Webb 1986–87, Dick Bate 1987, Paul Clark 1987–88, Dave Webb (GM) 1988–92, Colin Murphy 1992–93, Barry Fry 1993, Peter Taylor 1993–95, Steve Thompson 1995, Ronnie Whelan 1995–97.

STOCKPORT COUNTY
Fred Stewart 1894–1911, Harry Lewis 1911–14, David Ashworth 1914–19, Albert Williams 1919–24, Fred Scotchbrook 1924–26, Lincoln Hyde 1926–31, Andrew Wilson 1932–33, Fred Westgarth 1934–36, Bob Kelly 1936–38, George Hunt 1938–39, Bob Marshall 1939–49, Andy Beattie 1949–52, Dick Duckworth 1952–56, Billy Moir 1956–60, Reg Flewin 1960–63, Trevor Porteous 1963–65, Bert Trautmann (GM) 1965–66, Eddie Quigley (TM) 1965–66, Jimmy Meadows 1966–69, Wally Galbraith 1969–70, Matt Woods 1970–71, Brian Doyle 1972–74, Jimmy Meadows 1974–75, Roy Chapman 1975–76, Eddie Quigley 1976–77, Alan Thompson 1977–78, Mike Summerbee 1978–79, Jimmy McGuigan 1979–82, Eric Webster 1982–85, Colin Murphy 1985, Les Chapman 1985–86, Jimmy Melia 1986, Colin Murphy 1986–87, Asa Hartford 1987–89, Danny Bergara 1989–95, Dave Jones 1995–97, Gary Megson July 1997– .

STOKE CITY
Tom Slaney 1874–83*, Walter Cox 1883–84*, Harry Lockett 1884–90, Joseph Bradshaw 1890–92, Arthur Reeves 1892–95, William Rowley 1895–97, H. D. Austerberry 1897–1908, A. J. Barker 1908–14, Peter Hodge 1914–15,

Joe Schofield 1915–19, Arthur Shallcross 1919–23, John "Jock" Rutherford 1923, Tom Mather 1923–35, Bob McGrory 1935–52, Frank Taylor 1952–60, Tony Waddington 1960–77, George Eastham 1977–78, Alan A'Court 1978, Alan Durban 1978–81, Richie Barker 1981–83, Bill Asprey 1984–85, Mick Mills 1985–89, Alan Ball 1989–91, Lou Macari 1991–93, Joe Jordan 1993–94, Lou Macari 1994–97, Chic Bates July 1997– .

SUNDERLAND
Tom Watson 1888–96, Bob Campbell 1896–99, Alex Mackie 1899–1905, Bob Kyle 1905–28, Johnny Cochrane 1928–39, Bill Murray 1939–57, Alan Brown 1957–64, George Hardwick 1964–65, Ian McColl 1965–68, Alan Brown 1968–72, Bob Stokoe 1972–76, Jimmy Adamson 1976–78, Ken Knighton 1979–81, Alan Durban 1981–84, Len Ashurst 1984–85, Lawrie McMenemy 1985–87, Denis Smith 1987–91, Malcolm Crosby 1992–93, Terry Butcher 1993, Mick Buxton 1993–95, Peter Reid March 1995– .

SWANSEA CITY
Walter Whittaker 1912–14, William Bartlett 1914–15, Joe Bradshaw 1919–26, Jimmy Thomson 1927–31, Neil Harris 1934–39, Haydn Green 1939–47, Bill McCandless 1947–55, Ron Burgess 1955–58, Trevor Morris 1958–65, Glyn Davies 1965–66, Billy Lucas 1967–69, Roy Bentley 1969–72, Harry Gregg 1972–75, Harry Griffiths 1975–77, John Toshack 1978–83 (resigned October re-appointed in December) 1983–84, Colin Appleton 1984, John Bond 1984–85, Tommy Hutchison 1985–86, Terry Yorath 1986–89, Ian Evans 1989–90, Terry Yorath 1990–91, Frank Burrows 1991–95, Kevin Cullis 1996, Jan Molby February 1996– .

SWINDON TOWN
Sam Allen 1902–33, Ted Vizard 1933–39, Neil Harris 1939–41, Louis Page 1945–53, Maurice Lindley 1953–55, Bert Head 1956–65, Danny Williams 1965–69, Fred Ford 1969–71, Dave Mackay 1971–72, Les Allen 1972–74, Danny Williams 1974–78, Bobby Smith 1978–80, John Trollope 1980–83, Ken Beamish 1983–84, Lou Macari 1984–89, Ossie Ardiles 1989–91, Glenn Hoddle 1991–93, John Gorman 1993–94, Steve McMahon November 1994– .

TORQUAY UNITED
Percy Mackrill 1927–29, A. H. Hoskins 1929*, Frank Womack 1929–32, Frank Brown 1932–38, Alf Steward 1938–40, Billy Butler 1945–46, Jack Butler 1946–47, John McNeil 1947–50, Bob John 1950, Alex Massie 1950–51, Eric Webber 1951–65, Frank O'Farrell 1965–68, Alan Brown 1969–71, Jack Edwards 1971–73, Malcolm Musgrove 1973–76, Mike Green 1977–81, Frank O'Farrell 1981–82 (continued as GM to 1983), Bruce Rioch 1982–84, Dave Webb 1984–85, John Sims 1985, Stuart Morgan 1985–87, Cyril Knowles 1987–89, Dave Smith 1989–91, John Impey 1991–92, Ivan Golac 1992, Paul Compton 1992–93, Don O'Riordan 1993–95, Eddie May 1995–96, Kevin Hodges (HC) June 1996– .

TOTTENHAM HOTSPUR
Frank Brettell 1898–99, John Cameron 1899–1906, Fred Kirkham 1907–08, Peter McWilliam 1912–27, Billy Minter 1927–29, Percy Smith 1930–35, Jack Tresadern 1935–38, Peter McWilliam 1938–42, Arthur Turner 1942–46, Joe Hulme 1946–49, Arthur Rowe 1949–55, Jimmy Anderson 1955–58, Bill Nicholson 1958–74, Terry Neill 1974–76, Keith Burkinshaw 1976–84, Peter Shreeves 1984–86, David Pleat 1986–87, Terry Venables 1987–91, Peter Shreeves 1991–92, Ossie Ardiles 1993–94, Gerry Francis November 1994– .

TRANMERE ROVERS
Bert Cooke 1912–35, Jackie Carr 1935–36, Jim Knowles 1936–39, Bill Ridding 1939–45, Ernie Blackburn 1946–55, Noel Kelly 1955–57, Peter Farrell 1957–60, Walter Galbraith 1961, Dave Russell 1961–69, Jackie Wright 1969–72, Ron Yeats 1972–75, John King 1975–80, Bryan Hamilton 1980–85, Frank Worthington 1985–87, Ronnie Moore 1987, John King 1987–96, John Aldridge April 1996– .

WALSALL
H. Smallwood 1888–91*, A. G. Burton 1891–93, J. H. Robinson 1893–95, C. H. Ailso 1895–96*, A. E. Parsloe 1896–97*, L. Ford 1897–98*, G. Hughes 1898–99*, L. Ford 1899–1901*, J. E. Shutt 1908–13*, Haydn Price 1914–20, Joe Burchell 1920–26, David Ashworth 1926–27, Jack Torrance 1927–28, James Kerr 1928–29, Sid Scholey 1929–30, Peter O'Rourke 1930–32, Bill Slade 1932–34, Andy Wilson 1934–37, Tommy Lowes 1937–44, Harry Hibbs 1944–51, Tony McPhee 1951, Brough Fletcher 1952–53, Major Frank Buckley 1953–55, John Love 1955–57, Billy Moore 1957–64, Alf Wood 1964, Reg Shaw 1964–68, Dick Graham 1968, Ron Lewin 1968–69, Billy Moore 1969–72, John Smith 1972–73, Doug Fraser 1973–77, Dave Mackay 1977–78, Alan Ashman 1978, Frank Sibley 1979, Alan Buckley 1979–86, Neil Martin (joint manager with Buckley) 1981–82, Tommy Coakley 1986–88, John Barnwell 1989–90, Kenny Hibbitt 1990–94, Chris Nicholl 1994–97, Jan Sorensen June 1997– .

WATFORD
John Goodall 1903–10, Harry Kent 1910–26, Fred Pagnam 1926–29, Neil McBain 1929–37, Bill Findlay 1938–47, Jack Bray 1947–48, Eddie Hapgood 1948–50, Ron Gray 1950–51, Haydn Green 1951–52, Len Goulden 1952–55 (GM to 1956), Johnny Paton 1955–56, Neil McBain 1956–59, Ron Burgess 1959–63, Bill McGarry 1963–64, Ken Furphy 1964–71, George Kirby 1971–73, Mike Keen 1973–77, Graham Taylor 1977–87, Dave Bassett 1987–88, Steve Harrison 1988–90, Colin Lee 1990, Steve Perryman 1990–93, Glenn Roeder 1993–96, Kenny Jackett 1996–97, Graham Taylor May 1997– (GM since February 1996).

WEST BROMWICH ALBION
Louis Ford 1890–92*, Henry Jackson 1892–94*, Edward Stephenson 1894–95*, Clement Keys 1895–96*, Frank Heaven 1896–1902*, Fred Everiss 1902–48, Jack Smith 1948–52, Jesse Carver 1952, Vic Buckingham 1953–59, Gordon Clark 1959–61, Archie Macaulay 1961–63, Jimmy Hagan 1963–67, Alan Ashman 1967–71, Don Howe 1971–75, Johnny Giles 1975–77, Ronnie Allen 1977, Ron Atkinson 1978–81, Ronnie Allen 1981–82, Ron Wylie 1982–84, Johnny Giles 1984–85, Ron Saunders 1986–87, Ron Atkinson 1987–88, Brian Talbot 1988–91, Bobby Gould 1991–92, Ossie Ardiles 1992–93, Keith Burkinshaw 1993–94, Alan Buckley 1994–97, Ray Harford February 1997– .

WEST HAM UNITED
Syd King 1902–32, Charlie Paynter 1932–50, Ted Fenton 1950–61, Ron Greenwood 1961–74 (continued as GM to 1977), John Lyall 1974–89, Lou Macari 1989–90, Billy Bonds 1990–94, Harry Redknapp August 1994– .

WIGAN ATHLETIC
Charlie Spencer 1932–37, Jimmy Milne 1946–47, Bob Pryde 1949–52, Ted Goodier 1952–54, Walter Crook 1954–55, Ron Suart 1955–56, Billy Cooke 1956, Sam Barkas 1957, Trevor Hitchen 1957–58, Malcolm Barrass 1958–59, Jimmy Shirley 1959, Pat Murphy 1959–60, Allenby Chilton 1960, Johnny Ball 1961–63, Allan Brown 1963–66, Alf Craig 1966–67, Harry Leyland 1967–68, Alan Saunders 1968, Ian McNeill 1968–70, Gordon Milne 1970–72, Les Rigby 1972–74, Brian Tiler 1974–76, Ian McNeill 1976–81, Larry Lloyd 1981–83, Harry McNally 1983–85, Bryan Hamilton 1985–86, Ray Mathias 1986–89, Bryan Hamilton 1989–93, Dave Philpotts 1993, Kenny Swain 1993–94, Graham Barrow 1994–95, John Deehan November 1995– .

WIMBLEDON
Les Henley 1955–71, Mike Everitt 1971–73, Dick Graham 1973–74, Allen Batsford 1974–78, Dario Gradi 1978–81, Dave Bassett 1981–87, Bobby Gould 1987–90, Ray Harford 1990–91, Peter Withe 1991, Joe Kinnear January 1992– .

WOLVERHAMPTON WANDERERS
George Worrall 1877–85*, John Addenbrooke 1885–1922, George Jobey 1922–24, Albert Hoskins 1924–26 (had been secretary since 1922), Fred Scotchbrook 1926–27, Major Frank Buckley 1927–44, Ted Vizard 1944–48, Stan Cullis 1948–64, Andy Beattie 1964–65, Ronnie Allen 1966–68, Bill McGarry 1968–76, Sammy Chung 1976–78, John Barnwell 1978–81, Ian Greaves 1982, Graham Hawkins 1982–84, Tommy Docherty 1984–85, Bill McGarry 1985, Sammy Chapman 1985–86, Brian Little 1986, Graham Turner 1986–94, Graham Taylor 1994–95, Mark McGhee December 1995 – .

WREXHAM
Ted Robinson 1912–25* (continued as secretary to 1930), Charlie Hewitt 1925–29, Jack Baynes 1929–31, Ernest Blackburn 1932–36, Jimmy Logan 1937–38, Arthur Cowell 1938, Tom Morgan 1938–40, Tom Williams 1940–49, Les McDowall 1949–50, Peter Jackson 1951–54, Cliff Lloyd 1954–57, John Love 1957–59, Billy Morris 1960–61, Ken Barnes 1961–65, Billy Morris 1965, Jack Rowley 1966–67, Alvan Williams 1967–68, John Neal 1968–77, Arfon Griffiths 1977–81, Mel Sutton 1981–82, Bobby Roberts 1982–85, Dixie McNeil 1985–89, Brian Flynn November 1989– .

WYCOMBE WANDERERS
First coach appointed 1951. Prior to Brian Lee's appointment in 1969, the team was selected by a Match Committee which met every Monday evening. James McCormack 1951–52, Sid Cann 1952–61, Graham Adams 1961–62, Don Welsh 1962–64, Brian Darvill 1964–68, Brian Lee 1969–76, Ted Powell 1976–77, John Reardon 1977–78, Andy Williams 1978–80, Mike Keen 1980–84, Paul Bence 1984–86, Alan Gane 1986–87, Peter Suddaby 1987–88, Jim Kelman 1988–90, Martin O'Neill 1990–95, Alan Smith 1995–96, John Gregory October 1996– .

YORK CITY
Bill Sherrington 1924–60 (was secretary for most of this time but virtually secretary-manager for a long pre-war spell), John Collier 1929–36, Tom Mitchell 1936–50, Dick Duckworth 1950–52, Charlie Spencer 1952–53, Jimmy McCormick 1953–54, Sam Bartram 1956–60, Tom Lockie 1960–67, Joe Shaw 1967–68, Tom Johnston 1968–75, Wilf McGuinness 1975–77, Charlie Wright 1977–80, Barry Lyons 1980–81, Denis Smith 1982–87, Bobby Saxton 1987–88, John Bird 1988–91, John Ward 1991–93, Alan Little March 1993– .

The things they said ...

Danish Euro 96 referee Peter Mikkelsen, when asked about the Romanian shot against Bulgaria that was not given as a goal but shown on TV to have crossed the line:
"I did not see whether the ball crossed the line. It is not my problem. Anyway, England won the 1966 World Cup like that."

Former World Cup referee Michel Vautrot in an article in FIFA Magazine:
"In *The Marriage of Figaro*, Beaumarchais – who certainly wasn't thinking about women referees – said: 'The most adventurous woman feels within her a voice which says: be beautiful if you can, be wise if you want, but be respected at all costs'."

ITV commentary on the Rangers v Vladikavkaz European Cup match:
"... and it unfortunately goes right down the keeper's throat" (Ron Atkinson) "... where it hits him on the knees, so to speak" (John Helm).

League referees assessor Keith Cooper on the new rule allowing officials to play an advantage for 2-3 sec:
"I've been playing this rule for years, anyway."

Gary Lineker in a *Radio Times* interview:
"We don't need people like Vinnie Jones who is just a self-hyped personality – fine for him, but he isn't a good player and no benefit to the game."

Round robin letter from Vinnie Jones and his Wimbledon team-mates:
"[Lineker] has the charisma of a jellyfish – a jellyfish without a sting."

Ian Wright on Arsenal team-mate Tony Adams's public confession of alcoholism:
"It takes a lot of bottle."

Arsene Wenger, Arsenal's manager-elect, on Spurs' home defeat by Leicester during his trip to Europe while still contracted to Grampus 8 in Japan:
"I tried to watch the Spurs match on television in my hotel yesterday, but I fell asleep."

Sung by the 800 Scotland supporters in Estonia for the World Cup qualifying tie for which the home side failed to turn up:
"There's only one team in Tallinn."

The *News of the World* headlines above an interview with Terry Venables about Newcastle boss Kevin Keegan on the day (20 Oct) Newcastle shattered Man United 5-0 at St James' Park:
"KEV'S LEARNT NOTHING: His side has soft centre"

Herman Ouseley, chairman of the Campaign for Racial Equality, at the launch in October of a new phase of the 3-year-old 'Let's kick racism out of football' campaign:
"The Football League Management Committee still want to pretend there is no racism in the game and it's all a hooligan problem. If we have to tackle this problem – and it is a serious problem – then we must first be ready to recognise we have a problem."

Chelsea's Gianfranco Zola, asked how he felt about the close marking of Peter Atherton of Sheffield Wed:
"I prefer my wife."

Newcastle manager Kevin Keegan on his sensational mid-season resignation:
"I have taken the club as far as I can."

Sunderland manager Peter Reid, on his French keeper Lionel Perez's display against Arsenal at Highbury in the FA Cup:
"Magnifico, or whatever they say in Paris."

Chelsea manager Ruud Gullit on veteran striker Mark Hughes:
"He's playing better and better, even if he is going grey and looks like a pigeon."

A young Newcastle fan on the news that Kevin Keegan had resigned:
"How can he leave us? He's God around here. He's even bigger than God. He's the life of Newcastle. People name their children after him. There are even dogs named after him."

Middlesbrough star Fabrizio Ravanelli, in an Italian newspaper before the club were docked 3 points for illegally calling off a match:
"I reckon we will be relegated. I'm almost certain of it. I went to the training camp, but everything was locked up.... We are the tail-enders. We have hardly any hopes of salvation, and they give us three days off. The situation, I am very sorry to say, is truly tragic."

Southampton manager Graeme Souness, after they are beaten 2-1 by Stockport at the Dell in the Coca-Cola Cup quarter-finals:
"The hardest job I've got is going home to be a good husband and father. When you get a result like this, it can often affect your home life and I don't want that to happen."

Chelsea's Italian star Gianfranco Zola, on the pitfalls of improving his English at Stamford Bridge:
"I try, but every time I listen some place like Dennis Wise, my English go down."

Palace chairman Ron Noades on Steve Coppell's brief sojourn as Man City manager:
"I don't think his departure was down to ill-health. I think that's just something Manchester City put out."

TV summariser Chris Waddle, analysing a slow-motion replay of a challenge by Newcastle's Steve Watson on a Monaco attacker in the penalty box:
"He's just caught the back of his ankle, I think. It was a fair challenge."

FIFA secretary Sepp Blatter on the question of video help for referees:
"We are anxious television doesn't take over the game by controlling a referee. Football is composed of human beings, human frailties, mistakes and errors [not to mention tautology]. We have to live with that."

FIFA president João Havelange re England's interest in staging the 2006 World Cup:
"The new, refurbished Wembley would be a temple of football capable of staging the opening and final matches."

Bruce Grobbelaar, after the deadlocked match-fixing trial:
"We could try a penalty shoot-out."

Brentford manager David Webb on being barracked by some travelling fans after their 1-0 defeat at Preston:
"We are top of the League, but with people like that there is no point in carrying on. If that is the fans' attitude after our first defeat in 15 games, I will resign."

Bruce Grobbelaar, playing in goal for Plymouth at Shrewsbury, on the arrest of a visiting fan after he had complained about him to police for racial abuse:
"I know this fan and had no problems pointing him out. He follows Plymouth to most of the northern grounds, and abuses our own black players too. It's something I feel very strongly about – there is no room for racism in sport."

Reactions to Robbie Fowler's sporting appeal to referee Gerald Ashby not to award a penalty against Arsenal's David Seaman in the Premiership game at Highbury:
FIFA secretary Sepp Blatter – **"It is the kind of gesture which helps maintain the integrity of the game at a time when there is a disturbing trend towards cheating."**
England coach Glenn Hoddle – **"It was a very honest and human reaction, especially in the light of all the negative human reaction we've seen this season.... Now whether that is the right thing professionally, whether Roy Evans would be happy with that, whether I would be happy with that if he did it playing for me, that's a different kettle of fish."**
PFA chief executive Gordon Taylor – **"I'd like any youngster coming into the game to use Robbie as a role model for what he did. Football is still a sport; it is a welcome return to the old values."**
Liverpool team-mate Steve Harkness – **"We tried to shut his mouth. You've got to take all the luck you can."**
Premier League referees' spokesman David Elleray – **"... there doesn't need to be contact for a penalty to be given if the referee is satisfied the player only went down to avoid a challenge that would have fouled him."**

Brian Clough on Paul Gascoigne:
"It's a talent wasted. He has dissipated his talent and I don't think the image he gives the game is good."

England's Paul Ince, tying himself in knots on being asked which club he will join at the end of the season"
"I'll announce my decision after the final [UEFA Cup]. I know whether or not I'm leaving. I just don't know where I'm going. My decision isn't about football, it's for my family. I'm not leaving because I don't like it at Inter – er, if I leave, that is."

Paul Ince, reacting to the view from Blackburn that he's past his best:
"They haven't snubbed me. Do me a favour! Let's face it, would I want to go there?"

FIFA secretary-general Sepp Blatter:
"In some countries you have a big match on television every day. It is too much and is a threat to the game."

FIFA secretary-general Sepp Blatter, on the size of the English and Spanish top divisions:
"Both of them are too big. The Premiership has 20 teams and the Spanish First Division 22. A much more sensible figure would be 16 teams."

England coach Glenn Hoddle on the controversial withdrawal from the England squad of Liverpool's Robbie Fowler and Steve McManaman:
"As one door shuts, another door opens for players coming in. Robbie and Steve know that."

Hoddle on Paul Gascoigne's return to the England side for the friendly against South Africa at Old Trafford:
"If Gascoigne steps out of line here, I'll hammer him. The alarm has already gone off once."

Southampton manager Graeme Souness on his surprise resignation at the end of the season:
"I came to the club with high hopes and expectations for the future, but it is now clear to me that I am not able to take the club forward in the way that I would have liked."

Souness on the departure of Lawrie McMenemy after his own resignation from Southampton:
"Forget me – managers come and go. But Lawrie is an institution at Southampton. He is what the club is all about, and to let him go is absolute madness."

Hereford manager Graham Turner on the League transfer tribunal's decision to take the Bosman ruling into account for the first time when valuing a footballer, cutting the club's asking price to Orient of £200,000 to £42,500 for defender Dean Smith:
"I'm staggered and gob-smacked. This is going to send shock waves through football."

Southampton chairman Rupert Lowe on ex-manager Graeme Souness's resignation and immediate discussions with another club:
"When he [Souness] left, it was only a matter of days after we held one of the most friendly and productive meetings I've been involved in. I don't wish to speculate about Graeme's reasons for leaving. Only he really knows what happened. But he was seen having lunch with Torino's president in the week before he resigned. What can you say about that?"

FA CHARITY SHIELD WINNERS 1908–96

1908	Manchester U v QPR	4-0 after 1-1 draw
1909	Newcastle U v Northampton T	2-0
1910	Brighton v Aston Villa	1-0
1911	Manchester U v Swindon T	8-4
1912	Blackburn R v QPR	2-1
1913	Professionals v Amateurs	7-2
1920	WBA v Tottenham H	2-0
1921	Tottenham H v Burnley	2-0
1922	Huddersfield T v Liverpool	1-0
1923	Professionals v Amateurs	2-0
1924	Professionals v Amateurs	3-1
1925	Amateurs v Professionals	6-1
1926	Amateurs v Professionals	6-3
1927	Cardiff C v Corinthians	2-1
1928	Everton v Blackburn R	2-1
1929	Professionals v Amateurs	3-0
1930	Arsenal v Sheffield W	2-1
1931	Arsenal v WBA	1-0
1932	Everton v Newcastle U	5-3
1933	Arsenal v Everton	3-0
1934	Arsenal v Manchester C	4-0
1935	Sheffield W v Arsenal	1-0
1936	Sunderland v Arsenal	2-1
1937	Manchester C v Sunderland	2-0
1938	Arsenal v Preston NE	2-1
1948	Arsenal v Manchester U	4-3
1949	Portsmouth v Wolverhampton W	1-1*
1950	World Cup Team v Canadian Touring Team	4-2
1951	Tottenham H v Newcastle U	2-1
1952	Manchester U v Newcastle U	4-2
1953	Arsenal v Blackpool	3-1
1954	Wolverhampton W v WBA	4-4*
1955	Chelsea v Newcastle U	3-0
1956	Manchester U v Manchester C	1-0
1957	Manchester U v Aston Villa	4-0
1958	Bolton W v Wolverhampton W	4-1
1959	Wolverhampton W v Nottingham F	3-1
1960	Burnley v Wolverhampton W	2-2*
1961	Tottenham H v FA XI	3-2
1962	Tottenham H v Ipswich T	5-1
1963	Everton v Manchester U	4-0
1964	Liverpool v West Ham U	2-2*
1965	Manchester U v Liverpool	2-2*
1966	Liverpool v Everton	1-0
1967	Manchester U v Tottenham H	3-3*
1968	Manchester C v WBA	6-1
1969	Leeds U v Manchester C	2-1
1970	Everton v Chelsea	2-1
1971	Leicester C v Liverpool	1-0
1972	Manchester C v Aston Villa	1-0
1973	Burnley v Manchester C	1-0
1974	Liverpool† v Leeds U	1-1
1975	Derby Co v West Ham U	2-0
1976	Liverpool v Southampton	1-0
1977	Liverpool v Manchester U	0-0*
1978	Nottingham F v Ipswich T	5-0
1979	Liverpool v Arsenal	3-1
1980	Liverpool v West Ham U	1-0
1981	Aston Villa v Tottenham H	2-2*
1982	Liverpool v Tottenham H	1-0
1983	Manchester U v Liverpool	2-0
1984	Everton v Liverpool	1-0
1985	Everton v Manchester U	2-0
1986	Everton v Liverpool	1-1*
1987	Everton v Coventry C	1-0
1988	Liverpool v Wimbledon	2-1
1989	Liverpool v Arsenal	1-0
1990	Liverpool v Manchester U	1-1*
1991	Arsenal v Tottenham H	0-0*
1992	Leeds U v Liverpool	4-3
1993	Manchester U† v Arsenal	1-1
1994	Manchester U v Blackburn R	2-0
1995	Everton v Blackburn R	1-0

* Each club retained shield for six months.   † Won on penalties.

FA CHARITY SHIELD 1996

Manchester U (2) 4, Newcastle U (0) 0

At Wembley, 11 August 1996, attendance 73,214

Manchester U: Schmeichel; Irwin (Neville G), Neville P, May, Keane, Pallister, Cantona, Beckham, Scholes (Cruyff), Butt (Poborsky), Giggs.

Scorers: Cantona 25, Butt 30, Beckham 86, Keane 88.

Newcastle U: Srnicek; Watson, Beresford, Batty, Peacock, Albert, Lee, Beardsley (Asprilla), Shearer, Ferdinand, Ginola (Gillespie).

Referee: P. Durkin (Portland).

ENGLISH LEAGUE 1888–89 to 1996–97

FA PREMIER LEAGUE
Maximum points: a 126; b 114.

	First	Pts	Second	Pts	Third	Pts
1992–93a	Manchester U	84	Aston Villa	74	Norwich C	72
1993–94a	Manchester U	92	Blackburn R	84	Newcastle U	77
1994–95a	Blackburn R	89	Manchester U	88	Nottingham F	77
1995–96a	Manchester U	82	Newcastle U	78	Liverpool	71
1996–97b	Manchester U	75	Newcastle U*	68	Arsenal*	68

FIRST DIVISION
Maximum points: 138

1992–93	Newcastle U	96	West Ham U*	88	Portsmouth††	88
1993–94	Crystal Palace	90	Nottingham F	83	Millwall††	74
1994–95	Middlesbrough	82	Reading††	79	Bolton W	77
1995–96	Sunderland	83	Derby Co	79	Crystal Palace††	75
1996–97	Bolton W	98	Barnsley	80	Wolverhampton W	76

SECOND DIVISION
Maximum points: 138

1992–93	Stoke C	93	Bolton W	90	Port Vale††	89
1993–94	Reading	89	Port Vale	88	Plymouth Arg*††	85
1994–95	Birmingham C	89	Brentford††	85	Crewe Alex††	83
1995–96	Swindon T	92	Oxford U	83	Blackpool††	82
1996–97	Bury	84	Stockport Co	82	Luton T	78

THIRD DIVISION
Maximum points: a 126; b 138.

1992–93a	Cardiff C	83	Wrexham	80	Barnet	79
1993–94a	Shrewsbury T	79	Chester C	74	Crewe Alex	73
1994–95a	Carlisle U	91	Walsall	83	Chesterfield	81
1995–96a	Preston NE	86	Gillingham	83	Bury	79
1996–97b	Wigan Ath*	87	Fulham	87	Carlisle U	84

††*Not promoted after play-offs.*

FOOTBALL LEAGUE
Maximum points: a 44; b 60

	First	Pts	Second	Pts	Third	Pts
1888–89a	Preston NE	40	Aston Villa	29	Wolverhampton W	28
1889–90a	Preston NE	33	Everton	31	Blackburn R	27
1890–91a	Everton	29	Preston NE	27	Notts Co	26
1891–92b	Sunderland	42	Preston NE	37	Bolton W	36

FIRST DIVISION to 1991–92
Maximum points: a 44; b 52; c 60; d 68; e 76; f 84; g 126; h 120; k 114.

1892–93c	Sunderland	48	Preston NE	37	Everton	36
1893–94c	Aston Villa	44	Sunderland	38	Derby Co	36
1894–95c	Sunderland	47	Everton	42	Aston Villa	39
1895–96c	Aston Villa	45	Derby Co	41	Everton	39
1896–97c	Aston Villa	47	Sheffield U*	36	Derby Co	36
1897–98c	Sheffield U	42	Sunderland	37	Wolverhampton W*	35
1898–99d	Aston Villa	45	Liverpool	43	Burnley	39
1899–1900d	Aston Villa	50	Sheffield U	48	Sunderland	41
1900–01d	Liverpool	45	Sunderland	43	Notts Co	40
1901–02d	Sunderland	44	Everton	41	Newcastle U	37
1902–03d	The Wednesday	42	Aston Villa*	41	Sunderland	41
1903–04d	The Wednesday	47	Manchester C	44	Everton	43
1904–05d	Newcastle U	48	Everton	47	Manchester C	46
1905–06e	Liverpool	51	Preston NE	47	The Wednesday	44
1906–07e	Newcastle U	51	Bristol C	48	Everton*	45
1907–08e	Manchester U	52	Aston Villa*	43	Manchester C	43
1908–09e	Newcastle U	53	Everton	46	Sunderland	44
1909–10e	Aston Villa	53	Liverpool	48	Blackburn R*	45
1910–11e	Manchester U	52	Aston Villa	51	Sunderland*	45
1911–12e	Blackburn R	49	Everton	46	Newcastle U	44
1912–13e	Sunderland	54	Aston Villa	50	Sheffield W	49
1913–14e	Blackburn R	51	Aston Villa	44	Middlesbrough*	43
1914–15e	Everton	46	Oldham Ath	45	Blackburn R*	43
1919–20f	WBA	60	Burnley	51	Chelsea	49
1920–21f	Burnley	59	Manchester C	54	Bolton W	52
1921–22f	Liverpool	57	Tottenham H	51	Burnley	49
1922–23f	Liverpool	60	Sunderland	54	Huddersfield T	53
1923–24f	Huddersfield T*	57	Cardiff C	57	Sunderland	53
1924–25f	Huddersfield T	58	WBA	56	Bolton W	55
1925–26f	Huddersfield T	57	Arsenal	52	Sunderland	48
1926–27f	Newcastle U	56	Huddersfield T	51	Sunderland	49
1927–28f	Everton	53	Huddersfield T	51	Leicester C	48
1928–29f	Sheffield W	52	Leicester C	51	Aston Villa	50
1929–30f	Sheffield W	60	Derby Co	50	Manchester C*	47
1930–31f	Arsenal	66	Aston Villa	59	Sheffield W	52
1931–32f	Everton	56	Arsenal	54	Sheffield W	50
1932–33f	Arsenal	58	Aston Villa	54	Sheffield W	51

Won or placed on goal average, goal difference or most goals scored.

	First	Pts	Second	Pts	Third	Pts
1933–34f	Arsenal	59	Huddersfield T	56	Tottenham H	49
1934–35f	Arsenal	58	Sunderland	54	Sheffield W	49
1935–36f	Sunderland	56	Derby Co*	48	Huddersfield T	48
1936–37f	Manchester C	57	Charlton Ath	54	Arsenal	52
1937–38f	Arsenal	52	Wolverhampton W	51	Preston NE	49
1938–39f	Everton	59	Wolverhampton W	55	Charlton Ath	50
1946–47f	Liverpool	57	Manchester U*	56	Wolverhampton W	56
1947–48f	Arsenal	59	Manchester U*	52	Burnley	52
1948–49f	Portsmouth	58	Manchester U*	53	Derby Co	53
1949–50f	Portsmouth*	53	Wolverhampton W	53	Sunderland	52
1950–51f	Tottenham H	60	Manchester U	56	Blackpool	50
1951–52f	Manchester U	57	Tottenham H*	53	Arsenal	53
1952–53f	Arsenal*	54	Preston NE	54	Wolverhampton W	51
1953–54f	Wolverhampton W	57	WBA	53	Huddersfield T	51
1954–55f	Chelsea	52	Wolverhampton W*	48	Portsmouth*	48
1955–56f	Manchester U	60	Blackpool*	49	Wolverhampton W	49
1956–57f	Manchester U	64	Tottenham H*	56	Preston NE	56
1957–58f	Wolverhampton W	64	Preston NE	59	Tottenham H	51
1958–59f	Wolverhampton W	61	Manchester U	55	Arsenal*	50
1959–60f	Burnley	55	Wolverhampton W	54	Tottenham H	53
1960–61f	Tottenham H	66	Sheffield W	58	Wolverhampton W	57
1961–62f	Ipswich T	56	Burnley	53	Tottenham H	52
1962–63f	Everton	61	Tottenham H	55	Burnley	54
1963–64f	Liverpool	57	Manchester U	53	Everton	52
1964–65f	Manchester U*	61	Leeds U	61	Chelsea	56
1965–66f	Liverpool	61	Leeds U*	55	Burnley	55
1966–67f	Manchester U	60	Nottingham F*	56	Tottenham H	56
1967–68f	Manchester C	58	Manchester U	56	Liverpool	55
1968–69f	Leeds U	67	Liverpool	61	Everton	57
1969–70f	Everton	66	Leeds U	57	Chelsea	55
1970–71f	Arsenal	65	Leeds U	64	Tottenham H*	52
1971–72f	Derby Co	58	Leeds U*	57	Liverpool*	57
1972–73f	Liverpool	60	Arsenal	57	Leeds U	53
1973–74f	Leeds U	62	Liverpool	57	Derby Co	48
1974–75f	Derby Co	53	Liverpool*	51	Ipswich T	51
1975–76f	Liverpool	60	QPR	59	Manchester U	56
1976–77f	Liverpool	57	Manchester C	56	Ipswich T	52
1977–78f	Nottingham F	64	Liverpool	57	Everton	55
1978–79f	Liverpool	68	Nottingham F	60	WBA	59
1979–80f	Liverpool	60	Manchester U	58	Ipswich T	52
1980–81f	Aston Villa	60	Ipswich T	56	Arsenal	53
1981–82g	Liverpool	87	Ipswich T	83	Manchester U	78
1982–83g	Liverpool	82	Watford	71	Manchester U	70
1983–84g	Liverpool	80	Southampton	77	Nottingham F*	74
1984–85g	Everton	90	Liverpool*	77	Tottenham H	77
1985–86g	Liverpool	88	Everton	86	West Ham U	84
1986–87g	Everton	86	Liverpool	77	Tottenham H	71
1987–88h	Liverpool	90	Manchester U	81	Nottingham F	73
1988–89k	Arsenal*	76	Liverpool	76	Nottingham F	64
1989–90k	Liverpool	79	Aston Villa	70	Tottenham H	63
1990–91k	Arsenal†	83	Liverpool	76	Crystal Palace	69
1991–92g	Leeds U	82	Manchester U	78	Sheffield W	75

No official competition during 1915–19 and 1939–46; Regional Leagues operated.
†2 pts deducted

SECOND DIVISION to 1991–92

Maximum points: a 44; b 56; c 60; d 68; e 76; f 84; g 126; h 132; k 138.

	First	Pts	Second	Pts	Third	Pts
1892–93a	Small Heath	36	Sheffield U	35	Darwen	30
1893–94b	Liverpool	50	Small Heath	42	Notts Co	39
1894–95c	Bury	48	Notts Co	39	Newton Heath*	38
1895–96c	Liverpool*	46	Manchester C	46	Grimsby T*	42
1896–97c	Notts Co	42	Newton Heath	39	Grimsby T	38
1897–98c	Burnley	48	Newcastle U	45	Manchester C	39
1898–99d	Manchester C	52	Glossop NE	46	Leicester Fosse	45
1899–1900d	The Wednesday	54	Bolton W	52	Small Heath	46
1900–01d	Grimsby T	49	Small Heath	48	Burnley	44
1901–02d	WBA	55	Middlesbrough	51	Preston NE*	42
1902–03d	Manchester C	54	Small Heath	51	Woolwich A	48
1903–04d	Preston NE	50	Woolwich A	49	Manchester U	48
1904–05d	Liverpool	58	Bolton W	56	Manchester U	53
1905–06e	Bristol C	66	Manchester U	62	Chelsea	53
1906–07e	Nottingham F	60	Chelsea	57	Leicester Fosse	48
1907–08e	Bradford C	54	Leicester Fosse	52	Oldham Ath	50
1908–09e	Bolton W	52	Tottenham H*	51	WBA	51
1909–10e	Manchester C	54	Oldham Ath*	53	Hull C*	53
1910–11e	WBA	53	Bolton W	51	Chelsea	49
1911–12e	Derby Co*	54	Chelsea	54	Burnley	52
1912–13e	Preston NE	53	Burnley	50	Birmingham	46
1913–14e	Notts Co	53	Bradford PA*	49	Woolwich A	49
1914–15e	Derby Co	53	Preston NE	50	Barnsley	47
1919–20f	Tottenham H	70	Huddersfield T	64	Birmingham	56
1920–21f	Birmingham*	58	Cardiff C	58	Bristol C	51
1921–22f	Nottingham F	56	Stoke C*	52	Barnsley	52

*Won or placed on goal average/goal difference.

	First	Pts	Second	Pts	Third	Pts
1922–23f	Notts Co	53	West Ham U*	51	Leicester C	51
1923–24f	Leeds U	54	Bury*	51	Derby Co	51
1924–25f	Leicester C	59	Manchester U	57	Derby Co	55
1925–26f	Sheffield W	60	Derby Co	57	Chelsea	52
1926–27f	Middlesbrough	62	Portsmouth*	54	Manchester C	54
1927–28f	Manchester C	59	Leeds U	57	Chelsea	54
1928–29f	Middlesbrough	55	Grimsby T	53	Bradford PA*	48
1929–30f	Blackpool	58	Chelsea	55	Oldham Ath	53
1930–31f	Everton	61	WBA	54	Tottenham H	51
1931–32f	Wolverhampton W	56	Leeds U	54	Stoke C	52
1932–33f	Stoke C	56	Tottenham H	55	Fulham	50
1933–34f	Grimsby T	59	Preston NE	52	Bolton W*	51
1934–35f	Brentford	61	Bolton W*	56	West Ham U	56
1935–36f	Manchester U	56	Charlton Ath	55	Sheffield U*	52
1936–37f	Leicester C	56	Blackpool	55	Bury	52
1937–38f	Aston Villa	57	Manchester U*	53	Sheffield U	53
1938–39f	Blackburn R	55	Sheffield U	54	Sheffield W	53
1946–47f	Manchester C	62	Burnley	58	Birmingham C	55
1947–48f	Birmingham C	59	Newcastle U	56	Southampton	52
1948–49f	Fulham	57	WBA	56	Southampton	55
1949–50f	Tottenham H	61	Sheffield W*	52	Sheffield U*	52
1950–51f	Preston NE	57	Manchester C	52	Cardiff C	50
1951–52f	Sheffield W	53	Cardiff C*	51	Birmingham C	51
1952–53f	Sheffield U	60	Huddersfield T	58	Luton T	52
1953–54f	Leicester C*	56	Everton	56	Blackburn R	55
1954–55f	Birmingham C*	54	Luton T*	54	Rotherham U	54
1955–56f	Sheffield W	55	Leeds U	52	Liverpool*	48
1956–57f	Leicester C	61	Nottingham F	54	Liverpool	53
1957–58f	West Ham U	57	Blackburn R	56	Charlton Ath	55
1958–59f	Sheffield W	62	Fulham	60	Sheffield U*	53
1959–60f	Aston Villa	59	Cardiff C	58	Liverpool*	50
1960–61f	Ipswich T	59	Sheffield U	58	Liverpool	52
1961–62f	Liverpool	62	Leyton Orient	54	Sunderland	53
1962–63f	Stoke C	53	Chelsea*	52	Sunderland	52
1963–64f	Leeds U	63	Sunderland	61	Preston NE	56
1964–65f	Newcastle U	57	Northampton T	56	Bolton W	50
1965–66f	Manchester C	59	Southampton	54	Coventry C	53
1966–67f	Coventry C	59	Wolverhampton W	58	Carlisle U	52
1967–68f	Ipswich T	59	QPR*	58	Blackpool	58
1968–69f	Derby Co	63	Crystal Palace	56	Charlton Ath	50
1969–70f	Huddersfield T	60	Blackpool	53	Leicester C	51
1970–71f	Leicester C	59	Sheffield U	56	Cardiff C*	53
1971–72f	Norwich C	57	Birmingham C	56	Millwall	55
1972–73f	Burnley	62	QPR	61	Aston Villa	50
1973–74f	Middlesbrough	65	Luton T	50	Carlisle U	49
1974–75f	Manchester U	61	Aston Villa	58	Norwich C	53
1975–76f	Sunderland	56	Bristol C*	53	WBA	53
1976–77f	Wolverhampton W	57	Chelsea	55	Nottingham F	52
1977–78f	Bolton W	58	Southampton	57	Tottenham H*	56
1978–79f	Crystal Palace	57	Brighton & HA*	56	Stoke C	56
1979–80f	Leicester C	55	Sunderland	54	Birmingham C*	53
1980–81f	West Ham U	66	Notts Co	53	Swansea C*	50
1981–82g	Luton T	88	Watford	80	Norwich C	71
1982–83g	QPR	85	Wolverhampton W	75	Leicester C	70
1983–84g	Chelsea*	88	Sheffield W	88	Newcastle U	80
1984–85g	Oxford U	84	Birmingham C	82	Manchester C	74
1985–86g	Norwich C	84	Charlton Ath	77	Wimbledon	76
1986–87g	Derby Co	84	Portsmouth	78	Oldham Ath††	75
1987–88h	Millwall	82	Aston Villa*	78	Middlesbrough	78
1988–89k	Chelsea	99	Manchester C	82	Crystal Palace	81
1989–90k	Leeds U*	85	Sheffield U	85	Newcastle U††	80
1990–91k	Oldham Ath	88	West Ham U	87	Sheffield W	82
1991–92k	Ipswich T	84	Middlesbrough	80	Derby Co	78

No official competition during 1915–19 and 1939–46; Regional Leagues operated.
††Not promoted after play-offs.

THIRD DIVISION to 1991–92
Maximum points: 92; 138 from 1981–82.

	First	Pts	Second	Pts	Third	Pts
1958–59	Plymouth Arg	62	Hull C	61	Brentford*	57
1959–60	Southampton	61	Norwich C	59	Shrewsbury T*	52
1960–61	Bury	68	Walsall	62	QPR	60
1961–62	Portsmouth	65	Grimsby T	62	Bournemouth*	59
1962–63	Northampton T	62	Swindon T	58	Port Vale	54
1963–64	Coventry C*	60	Crystal Palace	60	Watford	58
1964–65	Carlisle U	60	Bristol C*	59	Mansfield T	59
1965–66	Hull C	69	Millwall	65	QPR	57
1966–67	QPR	67	Middlesbrough	55	Watford	54
1967–68	Oxford U	57	Bury	56	Shrewsbury T	55
1968–69	Watford*	64	Swindon T	64	Luton T	61
1969–70	Orient	62	Luton T	60	Bristol R	56
1970–71	Preston NE	61	Fulham	60	Halifax T	56
1971–72	Aston Villa	70	Brighton & HA	65	Bournemouth*	62
1972–73	Bolton W	61	Notts Co	57	Blackburn R	55

Won or placed on goal average/goal difference.

	First	Pts	Second	Pts	Third	Pts
1973–74	Oldham Ath	62	Bristol R*	61	York C	61
1974–75	Blackburn R	60	Plymouth Arg	59	Charlton Ath	55
1975–76	Hereford U	63	Cardiff C	57	Millwall	56
1976–77	Mansfield T	64	Brighton & HA	61	Crystal Palace*	59
1977–78	Wrexham	61	Cambridge U	58	Preston NE*	56
1978–79	Shrewsbury T	61	Watford*	60	Swansea C	60
1979–80	Grimsby T	62	Blackburn R	59	Sheffield W	58
1980–81	Rotherham U	61	Barnsley*	59	Charlton Ath	59
1981–82	Burnley*	80	Carlisle U	80	Fulham	78
1982–83	Portsmouth	91	Cardiff C	86	Huddersfield T	82
1983–84	Oxford U	95	Wimbledon	87	Sheffield U*	83
1984–85	Bradford C	94	Millwall	90	Hull C	87
1985–86	Reading	94	Plymouth Arg	87	Derby Co	84
1986–87	Bournemouth	97	Middlesbrough	94	Swindon T	87
1987–88	Sunderland	93	Brighton & HA	84	Walsall	82
1988–89	Wolverhampton W	92	Sheffield U*	84	Port Vale	84
1989–90	Bristol R	93	Bristol C	91	Notts Co	87
1990–91	Cambridge U	86	Southend U	85	Grimsby T*	83
1991–92	Brentford	82	Birmingham C	81	Huddersfield T	78

FOURTH DIVISION (1958–1992)
Maximum points: 92; 138 from 1981–82.

	First	Pts	Second	Pts	Third	Pts	Fourth	Pts
1958–59	Port Vale	64	Coventry C*	60	York C	60	Shrewsbury T	58
1959–60	Walsall	65	Notts Co*	60	Torquay U	60	Watford	57
1960–61	Peterborough U	66	Crystal Palace	64	Northampton T*	60	Bradford PA	60
1961–62†	Millwall	56	Colchester U	55	Wrexham	53	Carlisle U	52
1962–63	Brentford	62	Oldham Ath*	59	Crewe Alex	59	Mansfield T*	57
1963–64	Gillingham*	60	Carlisle U	60	Workington	59	Exeter C	58
1964–65	Brighton & HA	63	Millwall*	62	York C	62	Oxford U	61
1965–66	Doncaster R*	59	Darlington	59	Torquay U	58	Colchester U*	56
1966–67	Stockport Co	64	Southport*	59	Barrow	59	Tranmere R	58
1967–68	Luton T	66	Barnsley	61	Hartlepools U	60	Crewe Alex	58
1968–69	Doncaster R	59	Halifax T	57	Rochdale*	56	Bradford C	56
1969–70	Chesterfield	64	Wrexham	61	Swansea C	60	Port Vale	59
1970–71	Notts Co	69	Bournemouth	60	Oldham Ath	59	York C	56
1971–72	Grimsby T	63	Southend U	60	Brentford	59	Scunthorpe U	57
1972–73	Southport	62	Hereford U	58	Cambridge U	57	Aldershot*	56
1973–74	Peterborough U	65	Gillingham	62	Colchester U	60	Bury	59
1974–75	Mansfield T	68	Shrewsbury T	62	Rotherham U	59	Chester*	57
1975–76	Lincoln C	74	Northampton T	68	Reading	60	Tranmere R	58
1976–77	Cambridge U	65	Exeter C	62	Colchester U*	59	Bradford C	59
1977–78	Watford	71	Southend U	60	Swansea C*	56	Brentford	56
1978–79	Reading	65	Grimsby T*	61	Wimbledon*	61	Barnsley	61
1979–80	Huddersfield T	66	Walsall	64	Newport Co	61	Portsmouth*	60
1980–81	Southend U	67	Lincoln C	65	Doncaster R	56	Wimbledon	55
1981–82	Sheffield U	96	Bradford C*	91	Wigan Ath	91	Bournemouth	88
1982–83	Wimbledon	98	Hull C	90	Port Vale	88	Scunthorpe U	83
1983–84	York C	101	Doncaster R	85	Reading*	82	Bristol C	82
1984–85	Chesterfield	91	Blackpool	86	Darlington	85	Bury	84
1985–86	Swindon T	102	Chester C	84	Mansfield T	81	Port Vale	79
1986–87	Northampton T	99	Preston NE	90	Southend U	80	Wolverhampton W††	79
1987–88	Wolverhampton W	90	Cardiff C	85	Bolton W	78	Scunthorpe U††	77
1988–89	Rotherham U	82	Tranmere R	80	Crewe Alex	78	Scunthorpe U††	77
1989–90	Exeter C	89	Grimsby T	79	Southend U	75	Stockport Co††	74
1990–91	Darlington	83	Stockport Co*	82	Hartlepool U	82	Peterborough U	80
1991–92†*	Burnley	83	Rotherham U*	77	Mansfield T	77	Blackpool	76

†*Maximum points:* 88 owing to Accrington Stanley's resignation.   ††*Not promoted after play-offs.*
†**Maximum points:* 126 owing to Aldershot being expelled.

THIRD DIVISION—SOUTH (1920–1958)
Maximum points: a 84; b 92.

	First	Pts	Second	Pts	Third	Pts
1920–21a	Crystal Palace	59	Southampton	54	QPR	53
1921–22a	Southampton*	61	Plymouth Arg	61	Portsmouth	53
1922–23a	Bristol C	59	Plymouth Arg*	53	Swansea T	53
1923–24a	Portsmouth	59	Plymouth Arg	55	Millwall	54
1924–25a	Swansea T	57	Plymouth Arg	56	Bristol C	53
1925–26a	Reading	57	Plymouth Arg	56	Millwall	53
1926–27a	Bristol C	62	Plymouth Arg	60	Millwall	56
1927–28a	Millwall	65	Northampton T	55	Plymouth Arg	53
1928–29a	Charlton Ath*	54	Crystal Palace	54	Northampton T*	52
1929–30a	Plymouth Arg	68	Brentford	61	QPR	51
1930–31a	Notts Co	59	Crystal Palace	51	Brentford	50
1931–32a	Fulham	57	Reading	55	Southend U	53
1932–33a	Brentford	62	Exeter C	58	Norwich C	57
1933–34a	Norwich C	61	Coventry C*	54	Reading*	54
1934–35a	Charlton Ath	61	Reading	53	Coventry C	51
1935–36a	Coventry C	57	Luton T	56	Reading	54
1936–37a	Luton T	58	Notts Co	56	Brighton & HA	53
1937–38a	Millwall	56	Bristol C	55	QPR*	53
1938–39a	Newport Co	55	Crystal Palace	52	Brighton & HA	49

* Won or placed on goal average/goal difference.

	First	Pts	Second	Pts	Third	Pts
1939–46	Competition cancelled owing to war.					
1946–47a	Cardiff C	66	QPR	57	Bristol C	51
1947–48a	QPR	61	Bournemouth	57	Walsall	51
1948–49a	Swansea T	62	Reading	55	Bournemouth	52
1949–50a	Notts Co	58	Northampton T*	51	Southend U	51
1950–51b	Nottingham F	70	Norwich C	64	Reading*	57
1951–52b	Plymouth Arg	66	Reading*	61	Norwich C	61
1952–53b	Bristol R	64	Millwall*	62	Northampton T	62
1953–54b	Ipswich T	64	Brighton & HA	61	Bristol C	56
1954–55b	Bristol C	70	Leyton Orient	61	Southampton	59
1955–56b	Leyton Orient	66	Brighton & HA	65	Ipswich T	64
1956–57b	Ipswich T*	59	Torquay U	59	Colchester U	58
1957–58b	Brighton & HA	60	Brentford*	58	Plymouth Arg	58

THIRD DIVISION—NORTH (1921–1958)
Maximum points: a 76; b 84; c 80; d 92.

	First	Pts	Second	Pts	Third	Pts
1921–22a	Stockport Co	56	Darlington*	50	Grimsby T	50
1922–23a	Nelson	51	Bradford PA	47	Walsall	46
1923–24b	Wolverhampton W	63	Rochdale	62	Chesterfield	54
1924–25b	Darlington	58	Nelson*	53	New Brighton	53
1925–26b	Grimsby T	61	Bradford PA	60	Rochdale	59
1926–27b	Stoke C	63	Rochdale	58	Bradford PA	55
1927–28b	Bradford PA	63	Lincoln C	55	Stockport Co	54
1928–29g	Bradford C	63	Stockport Co	62	Wrexham	52
1929–30b	Port Vale	67	Stockport Co	63	Darlington*	50
1930–31b	Chesterfield	58	Lincoln C	57	Wrexham*	54
1931–32c	Lincoln C*	57	Gateshead	57	Chester	50
1932–33b	Hull C	59	Wrexham	57	Stockport Co	54
1933–34b	Barnsley	62	Chesterfield	61	Stockport Co	59
1934–35b	Doncaster R	57	Halifax T	55	Chester	54
1935–36b	Chesterfield	60	Chester*	55	Tranmere R	55
1936–37b	Stockport Co	60	Lincoln C	57	Chester	53
1937–38b	Tranmere R	56	Doncaster R	54	Hull C	53
1938–39b	Barnsley	67	Doncaster R	56	Bradford C	52
1939–46	Competition cancelled owing to war.					
1946–47b	Doncaster R	72	Rotherham U	60	Chester	56
1947–48b	Lincoln C	60	Rotherham U	59	Wrexham	50
1948–49b	Hull C	65	Rotherham U	62	Doncaster R	50
1949–50b	Doncaster R	55	Gateshead	53	Rochdale*	51
1950–51d	Rotherham U	71	Mansfield T	64	Carlisle U	62
1951–52d	Lincoln C	69	Grimsby T	66	Stockport Co	59
1952–53d	Oldham Ath	59	Port Vale	58	Wrexham	56
1953–54d	Port Vale	69	Barnsley	58	Scunthorpe U	57
1954–55d	Barnsley	65	Accrington S	61	Scunthorpe U*	58
1955–56d	Grimsby T	68	Derby Co	63	Accrington S	59
1956–57d	Derby Co	63	Hartlepools U	59	Accrington S*	58
1957–58d	Scunthorpe U	66	Accrington S	59	Bradford C	57

* Won or placed on goal average.

PROMOTED AFTER PLAY-OFFS
(Not accounted for in previous section)

1986–87	Aldershot to Division 3.
1987–88	Swansea C to Division 3.
1988–89	Leyton Orient to Division 3.
1989–90	Cambridge U to Division 3; Notts Co to Division 2; Sunderland to Division 1.
1990–91	Notts Co to Division 1; Tranmere R to Division 2; Torquay U to Division 3.
1991–92	Blackburn R to Premier League; Peterborough U to Division 1.
1992–93	Swindon T to Premier League; WBA to Division 1; York C to Division 2.
1993–94	Leicester C to Premier League; Burnley to Division 1; Wycombe W to Division 2.
1994–95	Huddersfield T to Division 1.
1995–96	Leicester C to Premier League; Bradford C to Division 1; Plymouth Arg to Division 2.
1996–97	Crystal Palace to Premier League; Crewe Alex to Division 1; Northampton T to Division 2.

LEAGUE TITLE WINS

FA PREMIER LEAGUE – Manchester U 4, Blackburn R 1.

LEAGUE DIVISION 1 – Liverpool 18, Arsenal 10, Everton 9, Manchester U 7, Aston Villa 7, Sunderland 7, Newcastle U 5, Sheffield W 4, Huddersfield T 3, Leeds U 3, Wolverhampton W 3, Blackburn R 2, Portsmouth 2, Preston NE 2, Burnley 2, Manchester C 2, Tottenham H 2, Derby Co 2, Bolton W, Chelsea, Crystal Palace, Sheffield U, WBA, Ipswich T, Nottingham F, Middlesbrough 1 each.

LEAGUE DIVISION 2 – Leicester C 6, Manchester C 6, Sheffield W 5, Birmingham C (one as Small Heath) 5, Derby Co 4, Liverpool 4, Ipswich T 3, Leeds U 3, Notts Co 3, Preston NE 3, Middlesbrough 3, Stoke C 3, Bury 2, Grimsby T 2, Norwich C 2, Nottingham F 2, Tottenham H 2, WBA 2, Aston Villa 2, Burnley 2, Chelsea 2, Manchester U 2, West Ham U 2, Wolverhampton W 2, Bolton W 2, Swindon T, Huddersfield T, Bristol C, Brentford, Bradford C, Everton, Fulham, Sheffield U, Newcastle U, Coventry C, Blackpool, Blackburn R, Sunderland, Crystal Palace, Luton T, QPR, Oxford U, Millwall, Oldham Ath, Reading 1 each.

LEAGUE DIVISION 3 – Portsmouth 2, Oxford U 2, Shrewsbury T 2, Carlisle U 2, Preston NE 2, Plymouth Arg, Southampton, Bury, Northampton T, Coventry C, Hull C, QPR, Watford, Leyton Orient, Aston Villa, Bolton W, Oldham Ath, Blackburn R, Hereford U, Mansfield T, Wrexham, Grimsby T, Rotherham U, Burnley, Bradford C, Bournemouth, Reading, Sunderland, Wolverhampton W, Bristol R, Cambridge U, Brentford, Cardiff C, Wigan Ath 1 each.

LEAGUE DIVISION 4 – Chesterfield 2, Doncaster R 2, Peterborough U 2, Port Vale, Walsall, Millwall, Brentford, Gillingham, Brighton & HA, Stockport Co, Luton T, Notts Co, Grimsby T, Southport, Mansfield T, Lincoln C,

Cambridge U, Watford, Reading, Huddersfield T, Southend U, Sheffield U, Wimbledon, York C, Swindon T, Northampton T, Wolverhampton W, Rotherham U, Exeter C, Darlington, Burnley 1 each.

To 1957–58

DIVISION 3 (South) – Bristol C 3; Charlton Ath, Ipswich T, Millwall, Notts Co, Plymouth Arg, Swansea T 2 each; Brentford, Bristol R, Cardiff C, Crystal Palace, Coventry C, Fulham, Leyton Orient, Luton T, Newport Co, Nottingham F, Norwich C, Portsmouth, QPR, Reading, Southampton, Brighton & HA 1 each.

DIVISION 3 (North) – Barnsley, Doncaster R, Lincoln C 3 each; Chesterfield, Grimsby T, Hull C, Port Vale, Stockport Co 2 each; Bradford PA, Bradford C, Darlington, Derby Co, Nelson, Oldham Ath, Rotherham U, Stoke C, Tranmere R, Wolverhampton W, Scunthorpe U 1 each.

RELEGATED CLUBS

1891–92 League extended. Newton Heath, Sheffield W and Nottingham F admitted. *Second Division formed* including Darwen.
1892–93 In Test matches, Sheffield U and Darwen won promotion in place of Notts Co and Accrington S.
1893–94 In Tests, Liverpool and Small Heath won promotion. Newton Heath and Darwen relegated.
1894–95 After Tests, Bury promoted, Liverpool relegated.
1895–96 After Tests, Liverpool promoted, Small Heath relegated.
1896–97 After Tests, Notts Co promoted, Burnley relegated.
1897–98 Test system abolished after success of Stoke C and Burnley. League extended. Blackburn R and Newcastle U elected to First Division. *Automatic promotion and relegation introduced.*

FA PREMIER LEAGUE TO DIVISION 1

1992–93 Crystal Palace, Middlesbrough, Nottingham F
1993–94 Sheffield U, Oldham Ath, Swindon T
1994–95 Crystal Palace, Norwich C, Leicester C, Ipswich T

1995–96 Manchester C, QPR, Bolton W
1996–97 Sunderland, Middlesbrough, Nottingham F

DIVISION 1 TO DIVISION 2

1898–99 Bolton W and Sheffield W
1899–1900 Burnley and Glossop
1900–01 Preston NE and WBA
1901–02 Small Heath and Manchester C
1902–03 Grimsby T and Bolton W
1903–04 Liverpool and WBA
1904–05 League extended. Bury and Notts Co, two bottom clubs in First Division, re-elected.
1905–06 Nottingham F and Wolverhampton W
1906–07 Derby Co and Stoke C
1907–08 Bolton W and Birmingham C
1908–09 Manchester C and Leicester Fosse
1909–10 Bolton W and Chelsea
1910–11 Bristol C and Nottingham F
1911–12 Preston NE and Bury
1912–13 Notts Co and Woolwich Arsenal
1913–14 Preston NE and Derby Co
1914–15 Tottenham H and Chelsea*
1919–20 Notts Co and Sheffield W
1920–21 Derby Co and Bradford PA
1921–22 Bradford C and Manchester U
1922–23 Stoke C and Oldham Ath
1923–24 Chelsea and Middlesbrough
1924–25 Preston NE and Nottingham F
1925–26 Manchester C and Notts Co
1926–27 Leeds U and WBA
1927–28 Tottenham H and Middlesbrough
1928–29 Bury and Cardiff C
1929–30 Burnley and Everton
1930–31 Leeds U and Manchester U
1931–32 Grimsby T and West Ham U
1932–33 Bolton W and Blackpool
1933–34 Newcastle U and Sheffield U
1934–35 Leicester C and Tottenham H
1935–36 Aston Villa and Blackburn R
1936–37 Manchester U and Sheffield W
1937–38 Manchester C and WBA
1938–39 Birmingham C and Leicester C
1946–47 Brentford and Leeds U
1947–48 Blackburn R and Grimsby T
1948–49 Preston NE and Sheffield U
1949–50 Manchester C and Birmingham C
1950–51 Sheffield W and Everton
1951–52 Huddersfield T and Fulham
1952–53 Stoke C and Derby Co
1953–54 Middlesbrough and Liverpool

1954–55 Leicester C and Sheffield W
1955–56 Huddersfield T and Sheffield U
1956–57 Charlton Ath and Cardiff C
1957–58 Sheffield W and Sunderland
1958–59 Portsmouth and Aston Villa
1959–60 Luton T and Leeds U
1960–61 Preston NE and Newcastle U
1961–62 Chelsea and Cardiff C
1962–63 Manchester C and Leyton Orient
1963–64 Bolton W and Ipswich T
1964–65 Wolverhampton W and Birmingham C
1965–66 Northampton T and Blackburn R
1966–67 Aston Villa and Blackpool
1967–68 Fulham and Sheffield U
1968–69 Leicester C and QPR
1969–70 Sunderland and Sheffield W
1970–71 Burnley and Blackpool
1971–72 Huddersfield T and Nottingham F
1972–73 Crystal Palace and WBA
1973–74 Southampton, Manchester U, Norwich C
1974–75 Luton T, Chelsea, Carlisle U
1975–76 Wolverhampton W, Burnley, Sheffield U
1976–77 Sunderland, Stoke C, Tottenham H
1977–78 West Ham U, Newcastle U, Leicester C
1978–79 QPR, Birmingham C, Chelsea
1979–80 Bristol C, Derby Co, Bolton W
1980–81 Norwich C, Leicester C, Crystal Palace
1981–82 Leeds U, Wolverhampton W, Middlesbrough
1982–83 Manchester C, Swansea C, Brighton & HA
1983–84 Birmingham C, Notts Co, Wolverhampton W
1984–85 Norwich C, Sunderland, Stoke C
1985–86 Ipswich T, Birmingham C, WBA
1986–87 Leicester C, Manchester C, Aston Villa
1987–88 Chelsea**, Portsmouth, Watford, Oxford U
1988–89 Middlesbrough, West Ham U, Newcastle U
1989–90 Sheffield W, Charlton Ath, Millwall
1990–91 Sunderland and Derby Co
1991–92 Luton T, Notts Co, West Ham U
1992–93 Brentford, Cambridge U, Bristol R
1993–94 Birmingham C, Oxford U, Peterborough U
1994–95 Swindon T, Burnley, Bristol C, Notts Co
1995–96 Millwall, Watford, Luton T
1996–97 Grimsby T, Oldham Ath, Southend U
**Relegated after play-offs.*
Subsequently re-elected to Division 1 when League was extended after the War.

DIVISION 2 TO DIVISION 3

1920–21 Stockport Co
1921–22 Bradford PA and Bristol C
1922–23 Rotherham Co and Wolverhampton W
1923–24 Nelson and Bristol C
1924–25 Crystal Palace and Coventry C
1925–26 Stoke C and Stockport Co
1926–27 Darlington and Bradford C
1927–28 Fulham and South Shields
1928–29 Port Vale and Clapton Orient
1929–30 Hull C and Notts Co
1930–31 Reading and Cardiff C

1931–32 Barnsley and Bristol C
1932–33 Chesterfield and Charlton Ath
1933–34 Millwall and Lincoln C
1934–35 Oldham Ath and Notts C
1935–36 Port Vale and Hull C
1936–37 Doncaster R and Bradford C
1937–38 Barnsley and Stockport Co
1938–39 Norwich C and Tranmere R
1946–47 Swansea T and Newport Co
1947–48 Doncaster R and Millwall
1948–49 Nottingham F and Lincoln C

1949–50 Plymouth Arg and Bradford PA	1974–75 Millwall, Cardiff C, Sheffield W
1950–51 Grimsby T and Chesterfield	1975–76 Oxford U, York C, Portsmouth
1951–52 Coventry C and QPR	1976–77 Carlisle U, Plymouth Arg, Hereford U
1952–53 Southampton and Barnsley	1977–78 Blackpool, Mansfield T, Hull C
1953–54 Brentford and Oldham Ath	1978–79 Sheffield U, Millwall, Blackburn R
1954–55 Ipswich T and Derby Co	1979–80 Fulham, Burnley, Charlton Ath
1955–56 Plymouth Arg and Hull C	1980–81 Preston NE, Bristol C, Bristol R
1956–57 Port Vale and Bury	1981–82 Cardiff C, Wrexham, Orient
1957–58 Doncaster R and Notts Co	1982–83 Rotherham U, Burnley, Bolton W
1958–59 Barnsley and Grimsby T	1983–84 Derby Co, Swansea C, Cambridge U
1959–60 Bristol C and Hull C	1984–85 Notts Co, Cardiff C, Wolverhampton W
1960–61 Lincoln C and Portsmouth	1985–86 Carlisle U, Middlesbrough, Fulham
1961–62 Brighton & HA and Bristol R	1986–87 Sunderland**, Grimsby T, Brighton & HA
1962–63 Walsall and Luton T	1987–88 Huddersfield T, Reading, Sheffield U**
1963–64 Grimsby T and Scunthorpe U	1988–89 Shrewsbury T, Birmingham C, Walsall
1964–65 Swindon T and Swansea T	1989–90 Bournemouth, Bradford C, Stoke C
1965–66 Middlesbrough and Leyton Orient	1990–91 WBA and Hull C
1966–67 Northampton T and Bury	1991–92 Plymouth Arg, Brighton & HA, Port Vale
1967–68 Plymouth Arg and Rotherham U	1992–93 Preston NE, Mansfield T, Wigan Ath, Chester C
1968–69 Fulham and Bury	1993–94 Fulham, Exeter C, Hartlepool U, Barnet
1969–70 Preston NE and Aston Villa	1994–95 Cambridge U, Plymouth Arg, Cardiff C, Chester C, Leyton Orient
1970–71 Blackburn R and Bolton W	1995–96 Carlisle U, Swansea C, Brighton & HA, Hull C
1971–72 Charlton Ath and Watford	1996–97 Peterborough U, Shrewsbury T, Rotherham U, Notts Co
1972–73 Huddersfield T and Brighton & HA	
1973–74 Crystal Palace, Preston NE, Swindon T	

DIVISION 3 TO DIVISION 4

1958–59 Rochdale, Notts Co, Doncaster R, Stockport Co	1974–75 Bournemouth, Tranmere R, Watford, Huddersfield T
1959–60 Accrington S, Wrexham, Mansfield T, York C	1975–76 Aldershot, Colchester U, Southend U, Halifax T
1960–61 Chesterfield, Colchester U, Bradford C, Tranmere R	1976–77 Reading, Northampton T, Grimsby T, York C
1961–62 Newport Co, Brentford, Lincoln C, Torquay U	1977–78 Port Vale, Bradford C, Hereford U, Portsmouth
1962–63 Bradford PA, Brighton & HA, Carlisle U, Halifax T	1978–79 Peterborough U, Walsall, Tranmere R, Lincoln C
1963–64 Millwall, Crewe Alex, Wrexham, Notts Co	1979–80 Bury, Southend U, Mansfield T, Wimbledon
1964–65 Luton T, Port Vale, Colchester U, Barnsley	1980–81 Sheffield U, Colchester U, Blackpool, Hull C
1965–66 Southend U, Exeter C, Brentford, York C	1981–82 Wimbledon, Swindon T, Bristol C, Chester
1966–67 Doncaster R, Workington, Darlington, Swansea T	1982–83 Reading, Wrexham, Doncaster R, Chesterfield
1967–68 Scunthorpe U, Colchester U, Grimsby T, Peterborough U (demoted)	1983–84 Scunthorpe U, Southend U, Port Vale, Exeter C
1968–69 Oldham Ath, Crewe Alex, Hartlepool, Northampton T	1984–85 Burnley, Orient, Preston NE, Cambridge U
1969–70 Bournemouth, Southport, Barrow, Stockport Co	1985–86 Lincoln C, Cardiff C, Wolverhampton W, Swansea C
1970–71 Reading, Bury, Doncaster R, Gillingham	1986–87 Bolton W**, Carlisle U, Darlington, Newport Co
1971–72 Mansfield T, Barnsley, Torquay U, Bradford C	1987–88 Doncaster R, York C, Grimsby T, Rotherham U**
1972–73 Rotherham U, Brentford, Swansea C, Scunthorpe U	1988–89 Southend U, Chesterfield, Gillingham, Aldershot
1973–74 Cambridge U, Shrewsbury T, Southport, Rochdale	1989–90 Cardiff C, Northampton T, Blackpool, Walsall
	1990–91 Crewe Alex, Rotherham U, Mansfield T
	1991–92 Bury, Shrewsbury T, Torquay U, Darlington
	** *Relegated after play-offs.*

APPLICATIONS FOR RE-ELECTION
FOURTH DIVISION

Eleven: Hartlepool U.
Seven: Crewe Alex.
Six: Barrow (lost League place to Hereford U 1972), Halifax T, Rochdale, Southport (lost League place to Wigan Ath 1978), York C.
Five: Chester C, Darlington, Lincoln C, Stockport Co, Workington (lost League place to Wimbledon 1977).
Four: Bradford PA (lost League place to Cambridge U 1970), Newport Co, Northampton T.
Three: Doncaster R, Hereford U.
Two: Bradford C, Exeter C, Oldham Ath, Scunthorpe U, Torquay U.
One: Aldershot, Colchester U, Gateshead (lost League place to Peterborough U 1960), Grimsby T, Swansea C, Tranmere R, Wrexham, Blackpool, Cambridge U, Preston NE.
Accrington S resigned and Oxford U were elected 1962.
Port Vale were forced to re-apply following expulsion in 1968.
Aldershot expelled March 1992. Maidstone U resigned August 1992.

THIRD DIVISIONS NORTH & SOUTH

Seven: Walsall.
Six: Exeter C, Halifax T, Newport Co.
Five: Accrington S, Barrow, Gillingham, New Brighton, Southport.
Four: Rochdale, Norwich C.
Three: Crystal Palace, Crewe Alex, Darlington, Hartlepool U, Merthyr T, Swindon T.
Two: Aberdare Ath, Aldershot, Ashington, Bournemouth, Brentford, Chester, Colchester U, Durham C, Millwall, Nelson, QPR, Rotherham U, Southend U, Tranmere R, Watford, Workington.
One: Bradford C, Bradford PA, Brighton & HA, Bristol R, Cardiff C, Carlisle U, Charlton Ath, Gateshead, Grimsby T, Mansfield T, Shrewsbury T, Torquay U, York C.

LEAGUE STATUS FROM 1986–87

RELEGATED FROM LEAGUE		PROMOTED TO LEAGUE
1986–87	Lincoln C	Scarborough
1987–88	Newport Co	Lincoln C
1988–89	Darlington	Maidstone U
1989–90	Colchester U	Darlington
1990–91	—	Barnet
1991–92	—	Colchester U
1992–93	Halifax T	Wycombe W
1993–94	—	—
1994–95	—	—
1995–96	—	—
1996–97	Hereford U	Macclesfield T

LEAGUE ATTENDANCES SINCE 1946–47

Season	Matches	Total	Div. 1	Div. 2	Div. 3 (S)	Div. 3 (N)
1946–47	1848	35,604,606	15,005,316	11,071,572	5,664,004	3,863,714
1947–48	1848	40,259,130	16,732,341	12,286,350	6,653,610	4,586,829
1948–49	1848	41,271,414	17,914,667	11,353,237	6,998,429	5,005,081
1949–50	1848	40,517,865	17,278,625	11,694,158	7,104,155	4,440,927
1950–51	2028	39,584,967	16,679,454	10,780,580	7,367,884	4,757,109
1951–52	2028	39,015,866	16,110,322	11,066,189	6,958,927	4,880,428
1952–53	2028	37,149,966	16,050,278	9,686,654	6,704,299	4,708,735
1953–54	2028	36,174,590	16,154,915	9,510,053	6,311,508	4,198,114
1954–55	2028	34,133,103	15,087,221	8,988,794	5,996,017	4,051,071
1955–56	2028	33,150,809	14,108,961	9,080,002	5,692,479	4,269,367
1956–57	2028	32,744,405	13,803,037	8,718,162	5,622,189	4,601,017
1957–58	2028	33,562,208	14,468,652	8,663,712	6,097,183	4,332,661

Season	Matches	Total	Div. 1	Div. 2	Div. 3	Div. 4
1958–59	2028	33,610,985	14,727,691	8,641,997	5,946,600	4,276,697
1959–60	2028	32,538,611	14,391,227	8,399,627	5,739,707	4,008,050
1960–61	2028	28,619,754	12,926,948	7,033,936	4,784,256	3,874,614
1961–62	2015	27,979,902	12,061,194	7,453,089	5,199,106	3,266,513
1962–63	2028	28,885,852	12,490,239	7,792,770	5,341,362	3,261,481
1963–64	2028	28,535,022	12,486,626	7,594,158	5,419,157	3,035,081
1964–65	2028	27,641,168	12,708,752	6,984,104	4,436,245	3,512,067
1965–66	2028	27,206,980	12,480,644	6,914,757	4,779,150	3,032,429
1966–67	2028	28,902,596	14,242,957	7,253,819	4,421,172	2,984,648
1967–68	2028	30,107,298	15,289,410	7,450,410	4,013,087	3,354,391
1968–69	2028	29,382,172	14,584,851	7,382,390	4,339,656	3,075,275
1969–70	2028	29,600,972	14,868,754	7,581,728	4,223,761	2,926,729
1970–71	2028	28,194,146	13,954,337	7,098,265	4,377,213	2,764,331
1971–72	2028	28,700,729	14,484,603	6,769,308	4,697,392	2,749,426
1972–73	2028	25,448,642	13,998,154	5,631,730	3,737,252	2,081,506
1973–74	2027	24,982,203	13,070,991	6,326,108	3,421,624	2,163,480
1974–75	2028	25,577,977	12,613,178	6,955,970	4,086,145	1,992,684
1975–76	2028	24,896,053	13,089,861	5,798,405	3,948,449	2,059,338
1976–77	2028	26,182,800	13,647,585	6,250,597	4,152,218	2,132,400
1977–78	2028	25,392,872	13,255,677	6,474,763	3,332,042	2,330,390
1978–79	2028	24,540,627	12,704,549	6,153,223	3,374,558	2,308,297
1979–80	2028	24,623,975	12,163,002	6,112,025	3,999,328	2,349,620
1980–81	2028	21,907,569	11,392,894	5,175,442	3,637,854	1,701,379
1981–82	2028	20,006,961	10,420,793	4,750,463	2,836,915	1,998,790
1982–83	2028	18,766,158	9,295,613	4,974,937	2,943,568	1,552,040
1983–84	2028	18,358,631	8,711,448	5,359,757	2,729,942	1,557,484
1984–85	2028	17,849,835	9,761,404	4,030,823	2,667,008	1,390,600
1985–86	2028	16,488,577	9,037,854	3,551,968	2,490,481	1,408,274
1986–87	2028	17,379,218	9,144,676	4,168,131	2,350,970	1,715,441
1987–88	2030	17,959,732	8,094,571	5,341,599	2,751,275	1,772,287
1988–89	2036	18,464,192	7,809,993	5,887,805	3,035,327	1,791,067
1989–90	2036	19,445,442	7,883,039	6,867,674	2,803,551	1,891,178
1990–91	2036	19,508,202	8,618,709	6,285,068	2,835,759	1,768,666
1991–92	2064*	20,487,273	9,989,160	5,809,787	2,993,352	1,694,974

Season	Matches	Total	FA Premier	Div. 1	Div. 2	Div. 3
1992–93	2028	20,657,327	9,759,809	5,874,017	3,483,073	1,540,428
1993–94	2028	21,683,381	10,644,551	6,487,104	2,972,702	1,579,024
1994–95	2028	21,856,020	11,213,168	6,044,293	3,037,752	1,560,807
1995–96	2036	21,844,416	10,469,107	6,566,349	2,843,652	1,965,308
1996–97	2036	22,783,163	10,804,762	6,931,539	3,195,223	1,851,639

Figures include matches played by Aldershot.

LEAGUE ATTENDANCES 1996–97

FA CARLING PREMIERSHIP ATTENDANCES

	Average Gate			Season 1996/97	
	1995/96	1996/97	+/−%	Highest	Lowest
Arsenal	37,568	37,821	+0.7	38,264	33,461
Aston Villa	32,614	36,027	+10.5	39,339	26,726
Blackburn Rovers	27,714	24,947	−10.0	30,476	19,214
Chelsea	25,466	27,001	+6.0	29,056	22,762
Coventry City	18,507	19,625	+6.0	23,080	15,266
Derby County	14,327	17,889	+24.9	18,287	17,022
Everton	35,435	36,186	+2.1	40,177	30,368
Leeds United	32,578	32,109	−1.4	39,981	25,860
Leicester City	16,530	20,184	+22.1	21,134	17,562
Liverpool	39,553	39,777	+0.6	40,892	36,126
Manchester United	41,700	55,081	+32.1	55,314	54,178
Middlesbrough	29,283	29,848	+1.9	30,215	29,484
Newcastle United	36,507	36,466	−0.1	36,579	36,143
Nottingham Forest	25,916	24,587	−5.1	29,181	17,525
Sheffield Wednesday	24,877	25,693	+3.3	38,943	16,390
Southampton	14,820	15,099	+1.9	15,256	14,318
Sunderland	17,482	20,865	+19.4	22,512	18,581
Tottenham Hotspur	30,510	31,067	+1.8	33,040	22,943
West Ham United	22,340	23,242	+4.0	25,064	19,105
Wimbledon	13,246	15,156	+14.4	25,786	8,572

TOTAL ATTENDANCES:	10,804,762 (380 games)
	Average 28,434 (+3.21%)
HIGHEST:	55,314 Manchester United v Wimbledon
LOWEST:	8,572 Wimbledon v Southampton
HIGHEST AVERAGE:	55,081 Manchester United
LOWEST AVERAGE:	15,099 Southampton

NATIONWIDE FOOTBALL LEAGUE: DIVISION ONE ATTENDANCES

	Average Gate			Season 1996/97	
	1995/96	1996/97	+/−%	Highest	Lowest
Barnsley	8,086	11,356	+40.4	18,605	6,307
Birmingham City	18,090	17,751	−1.9	25,157	13,189
Bolton Wanderers	18,822	15,826	−15.9	22,030	12,448
Bradford City	5,708	12,925	+126.4	17,609	9,249
Charlton Athletic	11,185	11,081	−0.9	14,816	8,487
Crystal Palace	15,248	16,085	+5.5	21,410	12,633
Grimsby Town	5,992	5,859	−2.2	9,041	3,927
Huddersfield Town	13,151	12,175	−7.4	18,358	9,578
Ipswich Town	12,604	11,953	−5.2	22,025	7,053
Manchester City	27,869	26,753	−4.0	30,729	23,079
Norwich City	14,581	14,719	+0.9	20,256	11,946
Oldham Athletic	6,634	7,045	+6.2	12,992	4.852
Oxford United	5.876	7,608	+29.5	9,221	6,334
Port Vale	8,227	7,385	−10.2	14,396	4,522
Portsmouth	9,406	8,857	−5.8	12,844	5,579
Queens Park Rangers	15,683	12,554	−20.0	17,376	7,776
Reading	8,918	9,160	+2.7	14,853	5,513
Sheffield United	12,901	16,638	+29.0	25,596	12,301
Southend United	5,898	5,072	−14.0	8,274	3,046
Stoke City	12,275	12,698	+3.4	21,735	7,444
Swindon Town	10,602	9,917	−6.5	14,792	7,452
Tranmere Rovers	7,861	8,127	+3.4	14,309	4,577
West Bromwich Albion	15,061	15,064	0.0	21,179	11,792
Wolverhampton Wanderers	24,786	24,763	−0.1	27,336	21,072

TOTAL ATTENDANCES:	6,931,539 (552 games)
	Average 12,557 (+5.6%)
HIGHEST:	30,729 Manchester City v Oldham Athletic
LOWEST:	3,046 Southend United v Grimsby Town
HIGHEST AVERAGE:	26.753 Manchester City
LOWEST AVERAGE:	5,072 Southend United

NATIONWIDE FOOTBALL LEAGUE: DIVISION TWO ATTENDANCES

	Average Gate			Season 1996/97	
	1995/96	1996/97	+/−%	Highest	Lowest
AFC Bournemouth	4,213	4,581	+8.7	8,201	2,747
Blackpool	5,818	4,987	−14.3	8,017	2,690
Brentford	4,768	5,832	+22.3	8,679	3,675
Bristol City	7,017	10,802	+53.9	18,642	7,028
Bristol Rovers	5,279	5,630	+6.6	8,078	4,123
Burnley	9,064	10,053	+10.9	16,186	7,903
Bury	3,262	4,502	+38.0	9,785	2,690
Chesterfield	4,884	4,639	−5.0	8,690	2,805
Crewe Alexandra	3,974	3,978	+0.1	4,858	3,125
Gillingham	7,198	6,021	−16.3	9,305	3,572
Luton Town	7,223	6,781	−6.1	9,623	4,978
Millwall	9,571	7,743	−19.1	9,371	5,702
Notts County	5,130	4,239	−17.4	6,879	2,423
Peterborough United	4,655	5,295	+13.7	9,499	2,975
Plymouth Argyle	7,120	6,495	−8.8	9,645	4,237
Preston North End	10,012	9,411	−6.0	14,626	7,004
Rotherham United	3,413	2,844	−16.7	4,562	1,797
Shrewsbury Town	3,348	3,177	−5.1	5,341	1,610
Stockport County	5,903	6,424	+8.8	9,187	3,446
Walsall	3,982	3,892	−2.3	6,306	2,659
Watford	9,457	8,894	−5.6	14,109	6,139
Wrexham	3,705	4,112	+11.0	6,864	2,002
Wycombe Wanderers	4,573	5,232	+14.4	8,438	3,438
York City	3,538	3,359	−5.1	5,958	2,136

TOTAL ATTENDANCES: 3,195,223 (552 games)
Average 5,788 (+12.3%)
HIGHEST: 18,642 Bristol City v Bristol Rovers
LOWEST: 1,610 Shrewsbury Town v AFC Bournemouth
HIGHEST AVERAGE: 10,802 Bristol City
LOWEST AVERAGE: 2,844 Rotherham United

NATIONWIDE FOOTBALL LEAGUE: DIVISION THREE ATTENDANCES

	Average Gate			Season 1996/97	
	1995/96	1996/97	+/−%	Highest	Lowest
Barnet	2,282	2,141	−6.2	3,316	1,194
Brighton & Hove Albion	5,448	5,844	+7.3	10,923	1,933
Cambridge United	2,767	3,363	+21.5	6,032	2,033
Cardiff City	3,420	3,594	+5.1	6,144	1,667
Carlisle United	5,704	5,440	−4.6	9,171	3,839
Chester City	2,674	2,263	−15.4	4,005	1,540
Colchester United	3,274	3,245	−0.9	5,920	1,842
Darlington	2,408	2,796	+16.1	4,662	1,563
Doncaster Rovers	2,090	2,091	0.0	3,274	1,030
Exeter City	3,442	3,014	−12.4	4,991	2,155
Fulham	4,191	6,644	+58.5	11,479	4,423
Hartlepool United	2,072	2,107	+1.7	3,799	1,120
Hereford United	2,973	2,931	−1.4	8,350	1,382
Hull City	3,803	3,413	−10.3	5,414	1,775
Leyton Orient	4,478	4,336	−3.3	7,946	2,419
Lincoln City	2,870	3,163	+10.2	6,495	2,033
Mansfield Town	2,415	2,282	−5.5	4,375	1,505
Northampton Town	4,831	4,823	−0.2	6,822	3,519
Rochdale	2,214	1,829	−17.4	3,320	1,074
Scarborough	1,714	2,455	+43.2	3,607	1,573
Scunthorpe United	2,434	2,606	+7.1	4,257	1,524
Swansea City	2,996	3,850	+28.5	7,353	2,227
Torquay United	2,454	2,380	−3.0	4,021	1,087
Wigan Athletic	2,856	3,899	+36.5	7,106	2,606

TOTAL ATTENDANCES: 1,851,639 (552 games)
Average 3,354 (−5.8%)
HIGHEST: 11,479 Fulham v Northampton Town
LOWEST: 1,030 Doncaster Rovers v Northampton Town
HIGHEST AVERAGE: 6,644 Fulham
LOWEST AVERAGE: 1,829 Rochdale

LEAGUE CUP FINALISTS 1961–97

Played as a two-leg final until 1966. All subsequent finals at Wembley.

Year	Winners	Runners-up	Score
1961	Aston Villa	Rotherham U	0-2, 3-0 (aet)
1962	Norwich C	Rochdale	3-0, 1-0
1963	Birmingham C	Aston Villa	3-1, 0-0
1964	Leicester C	Stoke C	1-1, 3-2
1965	Chelsea	Leicester C	3-2, 0-0
1966	WBA	West Ham U	1-2, 4-1
1967	QPR	WBA	3-2
1968	Leeds U	Arsenal	1-0
1969	Swindon T	Arsenal	3-1 (aet)
1970	Manchester C	WBA	2-1 (aet)
1971	Tottenham H	Aston Villa	2-0
1972	Stoke C	Chelsea	2-1
1973	Tottenham H	Norwich C	1-0
1974	Wolverhampton W	Manchester C	2-1
1975	Aston Villa	Norwich C	1-0
1976	Manchester C	Newcastle U	2-1
1977	Aston Villa	Everton	0-0, 1-1 (aet), 3-2 (aet)
1978	Nottingham F	Liverpool	0-0 (aet), 1-0
1979	Nottingham F	Southampton	3-2
1980	Wolverhampton W	Nottingham F	1-0
1981	Liverpool	West Ham U	1-1 (aet), 2-1

MILK CUP

1982	Liverpool	Tottenham H	3-1 (aet)
1983	Liverpool	Manchester U	2-1 (aet)
1984	Liverpool	Everton	0-0 (aet), 1-0
1985	Norwich C	Sunderland	1-0
1986	Oxford U	QPR	3-0

LITTLEWOODS CUP

1987	Arsenal	Liverpool	2-1
1988	Luton T	Arsenal	3-2
1989	Nottingham F	Luton T	3-1
1990	Nottingham F	Oldham Ath	1-0

RUMBELOWS LEAGUE CUP

1991	Sheffield W	Manchester U	1-0
1992	Manchester U	Nottingham F	1-0

COCA-COLA CUP

1993	Arsenal	Sheffield W	2-1
1994	Aston Villa	Manchester U	3-1
1995	Liverpool	Bolton W	2-1
1996	Aston Villa	Leeds U	3-0
1997	Leicester C	Middlesbrough	1-1 (aet), 1-0 (aet)

LEAGUE CUP WINS
Aston Villa 5, Liverpool 5, Nottingham F 4, Arsenal 2, Leicester C 2, Manchester C 2, Norwich C 2, Tottenham H 2, Wolverhampton W 2, Birmingham C 1, Chelsea 1, Leeds U 1, Luton T 1, Manchester U 1, Oxford U 1, QPR 1, Sheffield W 1, Stoke C 1, WBA 1.

APPEARANCES IN FINALS
Aston Villa 7, Liverpool 7, Nottingham F 6, Arsenal 5, Manchester U 4, Norwich C 4, Leicester C 3, Manchester C 3, Tottenham H 3, WBA 3, Chelsea 2, Everton 2, Leeds U 2, Luton T 2, QPR 2, Sheffield W 2, Stoke C 2, West Ham U 2, Wolverhampton W 2, Birmingham C 1, Bolton W 1, Middlesbrough 1, Newcastle U 1, Oldham Ath 1, Oxford U 1, Rochdale 1, Rotherham U 1, Southampton 1, Sunderland 1, Swindon T 1.

APPEARANCES IN SEMI-FINALS
Aston Villa 10, Liverpool 9, Arsenal 8, Tottenham H 8, Manchester U 7, West Ham U 7, Nottingham F 6, Chelsea 5, Leeds U 5, Manchester C 5, Norwich C 5, WBA 4, Birmingham C 3, Burnley 3, Everton 3, Leicester C 3, Middlesbrough 3, QPR 3, Sheffield W 3, Swindon T 3, Wolverhampton W 3, Blackburn R 2, Bolton W 2, Bristol C 2, Coventry C 2, Crystal Palace 2, Ipswich T 2, Luton T 2, Oxford U 2, Plymouth Arg 2, Southampton 2, Stoke C 2, Sunderland 2, Blackpool 1, Bury 1, Cardiff C 1, Carlisle U 1, Chester C 1, Derby Co 1, Huddersfield T 1, Newcastle U 1, Oldham Ath 1, Peterborough U 1, Rochdale 1, Rotherham U 1, Shrewsbury T 1, Stockport Co 1, Tranmere R 1, Walsall 1, Watford 1, Wimbledon 1.

COCA-COLA CUP 1996–97

FIRST ROUND, FIRST LEG

20 AUG

Brentford (0) 1 *(Taylor 63)*
Plymouth Arg (0) 0 3034
Brentford: Dearden; Hurdle, Anderson, Ashby, Bates, McGhee, Asaba (Harvey), Smith, Forster, Bent, Taylor.
Plymouth Arg: Grobbelaar; Billy, Williams, Mauge, Heathcote, Curran, Leadbitter, Logan, Littlejohn, Evans, Corazzin.

Cardiff C (0) 1 *(Dale 54)*
Northampton T (0) 0 2294
Cardiff C: Elliott; Rodgerson, Lloyd, Perry, Jarman, Young, Bennett, Fowler, White, Dale (Scott), Philliskirk.
Northampton T: Woodman; Clarkson, Maddison, Sampson, Rennie, O'Shea, Burns, Gibb (Colkin), Cooper (White), Grayson, Hunter (Peer).

Carlisle U (1) 1 *(Archdeacon 40)*
Chester C (0) 0 4042
Carlisle U: Caig; Edmondson, Archdeacon, Walling, Pounewatchy, Varty, Thomas (Currie), Delap, Peacock, Hayward, Conway.
Chester C: Sinclair; Davidson (Woods), Rogers, Fisher, Jackson, Alsford, Richardson, Shelton, Murphy, Milner, Rimmer.

Colchester U (1) 2 *(Kinsella 1, Fry 77)*
WBA (1) 3 *(Hunt 22, Hamilton 71, Donovan 85)* 3521
Colchester U: Caldwell; Betts (Fry), Barnes, McCarthy, Greene, Cawley, Kinsella, Locke, Whitton, Adcock, Reinelt.
WBA: Spink; Holmes, Nicholson, Sneekes, Mardon, Raven, Hamilton, Gilbert, Taylor, Hunt (Donovan), Groves (Cunnington).

Darlington (1) 1 *(Blake 2)*
Rotherham U (0) 0 2023
Darlington: Newell; Shaw, Barnard, Brumwell, Crosby, Gregan, Oliver, Atkinson, Roberts, Blake (Painter), Twynham.
Rotherham U: Cherry; Sandeman, Roscoe, Garner, Monington, Breckin, Smith, Goodwin, Hayward (Berry), Glover (Slawson), McGlashan.

Doncaster R (1) 1 *(Cramb 42)*
York C (1) 1 *(Tolson 37)* 1852
Doncaster R: Williams; Murphy, Robertson, Moore, Gore, Birch, Schofield, McDonald, Dixon (Larmour), Cramb, Clark (Smith).
York C: Warrington; McMillan, Himsworth, Bushell (Pepper), Atkin, Barras, Murty, Randall, Tolson, Bull (Naylor), Stephenson.

Exeter C (0) 0
Barnet (3) 4 *(Simpson 6, Devine 26, Codner 29,*
Tomlinson 74) 2975
Exeter C: Bayes; Richardson, Hughes, Myers, Blake, Gayle, Chamberlain, Bailey, Braithwaite, Sharpe (McConnell), Steele (Pears).
Barnet: Taylor; Gale, Hardyman, Codner (Campbell), Primus, Howarth, Tomlinson (Dunwell), Simpson, Wilson (McDonald), Devine, Pardew.

Hartlepool U (0) 2 *(Davies 73, Allon 80)*
Lincoln C (1) 2 *(Bos 16, Alcide 58)* 2073
Hartlepool U: Pears; Ingram, McAuley, Beech, Davies, McDonald (Houchen), Allon (Lee), Cooper, Howard, Halliday, Tait (McGuckin).
Lincoln C: Richardson; Holmes, Fleming, Dennis (Hone) (Minett), Austin, Brown G, Ainsworth, Barnett, Bos, Sterling, Alcide.

Hereford U (0) 3 *(Norton 69, Foster A 80, Smith 81)*
Cambridge U (0) 0 1982
Hereford U: Debont; Norton, Fishlock, Smith, Brough, Townsend, Pitman (Stoker), Downing, Foster A, Foster I (Hargreaves), Mahon.

Cambridge U: Barrett; Matt Joseph, Granville, Thompson, Vowden, Marc Joseph, Raynor, Wanless (Hayes), Brazil (Benjamin), Barnwell-Edinboro, Beall.

Huddersfield T (2) 3 *(Stewart 12, 25, 53)*
Wrexham (0) 0 5178
Huddersfield T: Francis; Jenkins, Cowan, Reid, Morrison (Dyson), Sinnott, Simon Collins (Dalton), Makel, Stewart, Payton, Edwards (Lawson).
Wrexham: Marriott; Brace, Hardy, Phillips, Soloman, Carey, Chalk, Owen, Connolly, Watkin (Cross), Ward (Brammer).

Hull C (1) 2 *(Rioch 40, Quigley 60)*
Scarborough (1) 2 *(Daws 12, Ritchie 48)* 2134
Hull C: Carroll; Trevitt (Quigley), Rioch, Wright, Doncel, Brien (Allison), Joyce, Gilbert, Darby, Maxfield, Gordon (Brown).
Scarborough: Ironside; Knowles, Lucas, Thompstone (Wells), Bennett, Rockett, Williams A, Brooke, Daws (Mitchell), Ritchie, Williams G.

Ipswich T (1) 2 *(Marshall 32, Mason 71)*
Bournemouth (0) 1 *(Fletcher 57)* 6163
Ipswich T: Wright; Stockwell (Vaughan), Taricco, Thomsen, Sedgley, Williams, Mason, Sonner, Mathie, Marshall, Petta (Uhlenbeek).
Bournemouth: Glass; Young, Beardsmore, Coll, Murray, Bailey, Holland, Cox, Gordon (O'Neill), Fletcher, Brissett.

Luton T (1) 3 *(Grant 36, Thorpe 45 (pen), Oldfield 57)*
Bristol R (0) 0 2643
Luton T: Feuer; James (Guentchev), Thomas, Waddock, Davis S, Johnson (Patterson), Hughes, Alexander, Oldfield, Grant, Thorpe (Showler).
Bristol R: Collett; Martin, Lockwood, Browning, Clark, Tillson, Holloway, Gurney (Low), Miller (Parmenter), Archer, Beadle.

Mansfield T (0) 0
Burnley (1) 3 *(Cooke 31, Nogan 50, Eyres 74)* 1708
Mansfield T: Bowling; Harper, Hackett, Doolan, Kilcline, Eustace, Ireland, Hadley, Williams (Robinson), Sale, Kerr.
Burnley: Beresford; Parkinson, Eyres, Harrison, Winstanley, Hoyland, Matthew, Thompson (Brass), Nogan, Cooke (Robinson), Gleghorn.

Notts Co (0) 1 *(Jones 64)*
Bury (0) 1 *(Pugh 75)* 2141
Notts Co: Ward; Derry, Baraclough, Wilder, Strodder, Hogg, Richardson, Robinson, Martindale, Arkins, Jones.
Bury: Kiely; West, Pugh (Johnrose), Hughes, Butler, Jackson, Daws, Armstrong, Jepson, Johnson (Matthews), Carter.

Oldham Ath (0) 0
Grimsby T (1) 1 *(Mendonca 21)* 2975
Oldham Ath: Hallworth; Halle, Serrant, Fleming, Graham (Henry), Redmond, Orlygsson, Richardson (Beresford), McCarthy (Pemberton), Barlow, Rickers.
Grimsby T: Pearcey; McDermott, Gallimore, Handyside, Smith (Livingstone), Widdrington, Childs (Fickling), Webb (Southall), Shakespeare, Mendonca, Black.

Oxford U (1) 1 *(Jemson 30)*
Norwich C (1) 1 *(Johnson 29)* 6062
Oxford U: Whitehead; Robinson, Ford M, Smith, Elliott, Gilchrist, Ford R, Massey, Aldridge (Moody), Jemson (Rush), Beauchamp.
Norwich C: Gunn; Mills, Newman, Eadie, Polston, Crook, Adams, Fleck (Akinbiyi), Milligan, Johnson (Bradshaw), O'Neill.

Port Vale (1) 1 *(Naylor 22)*
Crewe Alex (0) 0   5236
Port Vale: Van Heusden; Hill, Tankard, Bogie, Griffiths, Aspin, McCarthy, Porter, Foyle (Mills), Naylor, Guppy.
Crewe Alex: Gayle; Unsworth, Smith, Westwood, Macauley, Launders, Tierney, Savage, Ellison, Murphy, Rivers (Little).

Portsmouth (1) 2 *(Burton 9, 56)*
Leyton Orient (0) 0   3102
Portsmouth: Flahavan; Pethick, Russell, McLaughlin, Butters, Awford, Carter (Bradbury), Simpson, Burton, Hall, Igoe.
Leyton Orient: Sealey; Hendon, Naylor, Garland, Martin A, Arnott, Martin D, Ling (Hanson), Ayorinde (Chapman), West, McCarthy.

Reading (0) 1 *(Quinn 57)*
Wycombe W (0) 1 *(Williams 64)*   6210
Reading: Mikhailov; Booty, Bodin, Bernal, Hunter, Wdowczyk, Williams M (Parkinson), Caskey, Quinn (Nogan), Lovell, Gooding.
Wycombe W: Parkin; Lawrence, Bell, McCarthy, Evans, Patterson, Carroll, Brown, De Souza, Williams, Farrell.

Rochdale (0) 2 *(Deary 61, Whitehall 74)*
Barnsley (1) 1 *(Wilkinson 24)*   2426
Rochdale: Gray; Fensome, Formby (Thompson), Johnson, Hill, Farrell, Russell, Deary, Leonard, Whitehall (Cecere), Stuart.
Barnsley: Watson; Eaden, Appleby, Bosancic (Sheridan), Davis, De Zeeuw, Marcelle (Regis), Redfearn, Wilkinson, Liddell, Thompson.

Scunthorpe U (2) 2 *(Moss 16, Clarkson 18)*
Blackpool (1) 1 *(Quinn 12)*   1880
Scunthorpe U: Samways; Hope, Wilson, Sertori, Knill, Bradley, D'Auria, Moss, McFarlane, Eyre, Clarkson.
Blackpool: Banks; Bryan, Barlow, Butler, Linighan, Orie, Bonner, Mellon, Quinn, Ellis, Philpott (Preece).

Sheffield U (1) 3 *(Vonk 8, White 69, Walker 76)*
Bradford C (0) 0   7575
Sheffield U: Kelly; Short, Ward (Hutchison), Spackman, Vonk, Sandford, White, Patterson, Taylor, Walker (Katchuro), Whitehouse (Starbuck).
Bradford C: Gould; Liburd, Mitchell, Cowans, Mohan, Sas, Shutt, Duxbury, Regtop, Stallard, Kiwomya.

Southend U (0) 0
Fulham (1) 2 *(Conroy 3, Watson 89)*   3084
Southend U: Royce; Harris, Dublin, Lapper, McNally, Nielsen, Marsh, Hails (Boere), Byrne, Rammell, Tilson.
Fulham: Walton; Watson, Herrera, Cullip, Cusack, Blake, McAree, Cockerill, Conroy, Morgan, Scott (Thomas).

Stockport Co (1) 2 *(Mutch 20, 53)*
Chesterfield (0) 1 *(Lormor 64 (pen))*   3088
Stockport Co: Jones; Connelly, Searle, Bennett, Flynn, Bound, Durkan (Gannon), Marsden, Mutch, Armstrong (Angell), Jeffers.
Chesterfield: Mercer; Rogers (Perkins), Jules, Curtis, Williams, Dyche, Beaumont, Hewitt (Davies), Lormor, Holland, Howard.

Swansea C (0) 0
Gillingham (0) 1 *(Torpey 73 (og))*   2711
Swansea C: Freestone; Appleby, Clode, Molby, Garnett, Jones S, Lacey (Chapple), Penney, Torpey, Ampadu, Thomas (Brown).
Gillingham: Stannard; Humphrey, Ford, Hessenthaler, Harris, Bryant, Chapman, Ratcliffe, Bailey (Puttnam), Smith, Onuora.

Swindon T (1) 2 *(Allison 42, Leitch 66)*
Wolverhampton W (0) 0   7451
Swindon T: Talia; Darras, Drysdale, Leitch, Allen (Seagraves), Taylor, Robinson, Walters (Watson), Finney, Allison, Horlock.
Wolverhampton W: Stowell; Romano (Smith), Froggatt, Atkins, Venus, Richards, Thompson (Wright), Corica, Bull, Roberts, Ferguson.

Torquay U (1) 3 *(Baker 44 (pen), 46, 56)*
Bristol C (0) 3 *(Goater 51, Agostino 70,*
Partridge 82)   2824
Torquay U: Newland; Mitchell, Barrow, McCall (Hawthorne), Gittens, Watson, Oatway, Nelson, Baker, Jack (Adcock), Hancox.
Bristol C: Naylor; Owers, Barnard, McLeary, Edwards, Kuhl, Bent (Partridge), Hewlett, Nugent (Agostino), Goater, Tinnion.

Walsall (0) 1 *(Lightbourne 54)*
Watford (0) 0   2659
Walsall: Walker; Evans, Daniel, Viveash, Marsh, Mountfield, Ntamark, Bradley, Lightbourne, Wilson (Ricketts), Butler (Platt).
Watford: Miller; Bazeley, Mooney, Palmer, Millen, Page, Gibbs, Connolly, White, Ramage (Penrice), Johnson.

Wigan Ath (1) 2 *(Lancashire 7, Jones 86)*
Preston NE (3) 3 *(Wilkinson 13, 26, 36)*   3713
Wigan Ath: Butler; Carragher (Greenall), Johnson, Bishop (Jones), Pender, Martinez, Lowe (Kilford), Sharp, Lancashire, Biggins, Morgan.
Preston NE: Moilanen; Squires, Barrick, Atkinson, Wilcox, Kidd, Davey, Bryson, Saville, Wilkinson, Kilbane.

21 AUG

Brighton & HA (0) 0
Birmingham C (0) 1 *(Devlin 49 (pen))*   5132
Brighton & HA: Rust; Smith, Tuck, Parris, Allan, Hobson, Minton (Storer), Peake, Baird, Maskell, McDonald.
Birmingham C: Bennett; Poole, Ablett, Bruce, Breen, Castle, Devlin, Newell (Hunt), Furlong, Horne, Legg (Johnson).

Millwall (1) 1 *(Malkin 9)*
Peterborough U (0) 0   5145
Millwall: Carter; Newman, Harle, Bowry, Witter, Stevens, Hartley (Neill), Savage, Malkin, Crawford, Dair (Dolby).
Peterborough U: Sheffield; Basham, Welsh, O'Connor, Heald, Bodley, Willis, Ebdon, Farrell (Grazioli), Charlery, Inman (Houghton).

Shrewsbury T (0) 0
Tranmere R (1) 2 *(Aldridge 30, Bonetti 56)*   2875
Shrewsbury T: Gall; Whiston (Seabury), Nielsen, Spink, Taylor M, Taylor L, Scott, Stevens, Anthrobus (Rowbotham), Walton, Currie (Berkley).
Tranmere R: Coyne; Stevens, Rogers, McGreal, Teale, O'Brien, Morrissey, Aldridge, Cook, Irons (Brannan), Bonetti (Branch).

FIRST ROUND, SECOND LEG

3 SEPT

Barnet (2) 2 *(Campbell 11, Wilson 36)*
Exeter C (0) 0   1330
Barnet: Taylor; Gale, Hardyman, Codner, Primus, Howarth (Goodhind), Campbell, Simpson (Adams), Wilson, Devine (Mills), Pardew.
Exeter C: Bayes; Richardson, Hughes, Myers, Blake (Hare), Dailly, Chamberlain, Bailey, Braithwaite (McConnell), Sharpe, Pears (Ghazghazi).
Barnet won 6-0 on aggregate.

Barnsley (1) 2 *(Redfearn 17, Wilkinson 74)*
Rochdale (0) 0   5638
Barnsley: Watson; Eaden, Appleby, Bochenski (Marcelle), Davis, De Zeeuw, Sheridan, Redfearn, Wilkinson, Liddell, Thompson.
Rochdale: Gray; Fensome, Bayliss, Johnson, Hill, Farrell, Russell (Thackeray), Deary, Leonard, Lancaster (Thompson), Stuart.
Barnsley won 3-2 on aggregate.

Blackpool (1) 2 *(Ellis 9, Philpott 64)*
Scunthorpe U (0) 0 2560
Blackpool: Banks; Bryan, Barlow, Butler, Lydiate, Brabin, Bonner, Mellon, Preece, Ellis, Philpott.
Scunthorpe U: Samways; Hope, Wilson, Sertori, Knill (Francis), Bradley, D'Auria, Gavin (Housham), McFarlane, Eyre, Clarkson.
Blackpool won 3-2 on aggregate.

Bournemouth (0) 0 4119
Ipswich T (1) 3 *(Scowcroft 12, Mathie 61, Stockwell 66)*
Bournemouth: Glass; Young, Beardsmore (Town), Coll, Murray (Vincent), Bailey, Holland, Cox, Gordon (O'Neill), Fletcher, Robinson.
Ipswich T: Wright; Stockwell, Taricco, Thomsen, Sedgley, Williams, Sonner, Vaughan, Mathie, Scowcroft, Mason (Milton).
Ipswich T won 5-1 on aggregate.

Bradford C (0) 1 *(Stallard 68)*
Sheffield U (0) 2 *(Ward 66, Walker 77 (pen))* 3593
Bradford C: Gould; Mitchell, Jacobs, Cowans (Huxford), Mohan, Sas, Hamilton, Duxbury, Regtop (Wright), Stallard, Ormondroyd (Shutt).
Sheffield U: Kelly; Short, Sandford, Hutchison, Vonk, Nilsen, Ward, Patterson, Taylor (Katchuro), Walker, Whitehouse.
Sheffield U won 5-1 on aggregate.

Bristol C (0) 1 *(Barnard 70)*
Torquay U (0) 0 4513
Bristol C: Naylor; Owers, Barnard, Carey, Edwards, Kuhl (Hewlett), Goodridge, Paterson, Nugent, Goater (Agostino), Tinnion.
Torquay U: Newland; Winter, Barrow (Nelson), McCall, Gittens, Watson, Oatway, Baker, Mitchell (Hathaway), Jack, Hancox.
Bristol C won 4-3 on aggregate.

Burnley (2) 2 *(Matthew 2, Eyres 45)*
Mansfield T (0) 0 2884
Burnley: Russell; Parkinson, Eyres, Brass, Winstanley, Hoyland, Matthew, Thompson, Nogan (Cooke), Robinson, Gleghorn (Weller).
Mansfield T: Bowling; Clifford, Hackett, Wood (Sherlock), Doolan, Watkiss, Ireland, Robinson, Sale, Williams, Harper.
Burnley won 5-0 on aggregate.

Bury (1) 1 *(Carter 25)*
Notts Co (0) 0 2571
Bury: Kiely; West, Reid N, Daws, Butler, Jackson, Hughes, Johnson, Matthews (Woodward), Johnrose, Carter.
Notts Co: Ward; Wilder, Baraclough, Derry, Strodder, Murphy, Richardson (Arkins), Robinson, Martindale, Battersby, Kennedy.
Bury won 2-1 on aggregate.

Cambridge U (0) 1 *(Thompson 52)*
Hereford U (0) 1 *(Smith 50 (pen))* 1164
Cambridge U: Barrett; Matt Joseph, Granville, Thompson, Palmer, San Miguel (Raynor), Richards, Hyde, McGleish, Barnwell-Edinboro, Beall.
Hereford U: Debont; Norton, Fishlock, Smith, Brough, Townsend, Stoker (Sutton), Downing, Foster A, Hargreaves (Foster I), Mahon.
Hereford U won 4-1 on aggregate.

Chester C (0) 1 *(Noteman 90)*
Carlisle U (1) 3 *(Reeves 42, Aspinall 61, Hayward 72)* 1947
Chester C: Knowles; Jenkins, Rogers, Fisher, Jackson, Alsford, Richardson, Shelton (Flitcroft), Murphy (Noteman), Milner, Rimmer.
Carlisle U: Caig; Edmondson, Archdeacon, Walling, Pounewatchy, Varty, Thomas (Delap), Conway (Robinson), Reeves, Hayward, Aspinall (Peacock).
Carlisle U won 4-1 on aggregate.

Chesterfield (0) 1 *(Gaughan 61)*
Stockport Co (0) 2 *(Ware 76, Mutch 84)* 3334
Chesterfield: Mercer; Law, Jules, Gaughan, Williams, Dyche, Beaumont (Morris), Davies, Lormor, Holland, Howard.

Stockport Co: Jones; Connelly, Searle, Bennett, Flynn, Gannon, Cavaco (Todd), Ware, Mutch, Armstrong, Jeffers.
Stockport Co won 4-2 on aggregate.

Crewe Alex (1) 1 *(Adebola 16)*
Port Vale (2) 5 *(Bogie 26, McCarthy 34, Foyle 75, Naylor 84, Mills 85)* 4471
Crewe Alex: Gayle; Unsworth, Smith, Westwood, Macauley, Whalley, Tierney (Garvey), Savage, Adebola, Murphy, Rivers (Launders).
Port Vale: Van Heusden; Aspin, Tankard (Talbot), Bogie, Griffiths, Glover, McCarthy, Porter, Foyle (Mills), Naylor, Guppy.
Port Vale won 6-1 on aggregate.

Fulham (0) 1 *(Conroy 88)*
Southend U (2) 2 *(Nielson 16, Rammell 28)* 4297
Fulham: Lange; Thomas, Herrera (Angus), Cullip, Cusack, Blake, Freeman, Cockerill (Mison), Conroy, Morgan, Scott.
Southend U: Sansome; Hails, Tilson, McNally, Dublin, Gridelet, Marsh, Harris, Boere, Rammell, Nielsen (Williams).
Fulham won 3-2 on aggregate.

Gillingham (1) 2 *(Fortune-West 20, Butler 73)*
Swansea C (0) 0 3633
Gillingham: Stannard; Humphrey, Chapman, Hessenthaler, Harris, Bryant, Puttnam (Smith), Ratcliffe, Fortune-West (Bailey), Butler, Onuora (Piper).
Swansea C: Freestone; Chapple, O'Leary (Moreira), Edwards, Garnett, Jones S, Brown (Torpey), Penney, Appleby, Coates, Thomas.
Gillingham won 3-0 on aggregate.

Grimsby T (0) 0
Oldham Ath (0) 1 *(McCarthy 57)* 2371
Grimsby T: Pearcey; McDermott, Gallimore, Handyside, Shakespeare, Widdrington, Childs (Southall), Livingstone, Woods (Forrester), Mendonca, Black.
Oldham Ath: Hallworth; Halle, Serrant, Henry, Graham, Redmond, Beresford (Orlygsson), Richardson, McCarthy, Banger, Rickers.
aet; Oldham Ath won 5-4 on penalties.

Lincoln C (2) 3 *(Martin 12, Holmes 25, Alcide 77)*
Hartlepool U (0) 2 *(Allon 46, Beech 58)* 2389
Lincoln C: Vaughan; Holmes, Whitney, Hone, Robertson, Austin, Ainsworth, Fleming, Bos (Alcide), Martin (Brown S), Sterling.
Hartlepool U: Pears; Ingram, McAuley, Davies, McGuckin, McDonald (Halliday), Allon, Cooper, Houchen, Beech, Clegg.
Lincoln C won 5-4 on aggregate.

Northampton T (0) 2 *(Lee 62, 78)*
Cardiff C (0) 0 3567
Northampton T: Woodman; Clarkson, Grayson (Maddison), Sampson, Rennie, O'Shea, Gibb (White), Lee (Colkin), Cooper, Parris, Hunter.
Cardiff C: Elliott; Rogerson, Lloyd, Perry, Jarman (Gardner), Young, Bennett (Middleton), Fowler, White, Eckhardt, Philliskirk.
Northampton T won 2-1 on aggregate.

Peterborough U (1) 2 *(Charlery 15, Griffiths 114)*
Millwall (0) 0 4610
Peterborough U: Sheffield; Boothroyd, Spearing, O'Connor, Heald, Bodley, Willis (Griffiths), Payne (Ebdon), Rowe, Charlery, Houghton (Carter).
Millwall: Carter; Neill, Rogan, Webber, Witter, Stevens, Bowry, Newman, Malkin, Dolby (Hartley), Dair (Harle).
aet; Peterborough U won 2-1 on aggregate.

Plymouth Arg (0) 0
Brentford (0) 0 5180
Plymouth Arg: Grobbelaar; Billy, Williams, Saunders (Corazzin), Heathcote (Curran), James, Leadbitter, Logan, Littlejohn, Evans, Barlow.
Brentford: Dearden; Hurdle, Anderson, Ashby, Bates, McGhee, Asaba, Smith, Abrahams (Harvey) (Hutchings), Bent, Taylor.
Brentford won 1-0 on aggregate.

Preston NE (2) 4 *(Davey 18, Wilkinson 34, Atkinson 74, McDonald 120)*
Wigan Ath (1) 4 *(Lancashire 2, 83, 89, Greenall 63)* 5767
Preston NE: Lucas; Kay, Barrick, Atkinson, Wilcox (Kidd), Moyes, Davey (McDonald), Bryson, Saville, Wilkinson, Kilbane (Brown).
Wigan Ath: Butler; Carragher (Seba), Johnson, Greenall, Pender, Martinez, Morgan (Diaz), Jones (Biggins), Lancashire, Lowe, Kilford.
aet; Preston NE won 7-6 on aggregate.

Rotherham U (0) 0
Darlington (0) 1 *(Roberts 57)* 1749
Rotherham U: Cherry; Sandeman, Hurst, Garner (Dobbin), Richardson, Breckin, Berry, Goodwin (Hayward), Smith, Glover (McGlashan), Roscoe.
Darlington: Newell; Brumwell, Barnard, Twynham, Crosby, Gregan, Oliver, Atkinson (Innes), Roberts (Painter), Blake (Brydon), Carss.
Darlington won 2-0 on aggregate.

Scarborough (2) 3 *(Williams G 13, Bennett 20, 51)*
Hull C (0) 2 *(Rioch 63 (pen), Gordon 90)* 2656
Scarborough: Ironside; Knowles, Lucas, Bennett, Hicks, Mowbray, Thompstone (Bochenski), Brooke, Mitchell (Worrall), Ritchie, Williams G.
Hull C: Carroll; Trevitt, Rioch, Wright, Doncel, Brien, Joyce, Quigley (Gordon), Darby, Mann (Maxfield), Peacock.
Scarborough won 5-4 on aggregate.

Tranmere R (0) 1 *(Branch 71)*
Shrewsbury T (0) 1 *(Rowbotham 70)* 3028
Tranmere R: Coyne; Thomas, Brannan, Higgins, Teale, O'Brien (Mahon), Jones, Aldridge, Cook, Irons (Moore), Branch.
Shrewsbury T: Gall; Seabury, Taylor L, Taylor M, Spink, Scott (Neilsen), Rowbotham, Stevens, Anthrobus, Evans (Currie), Berkley (Dempsey).
Tranmere R won 3-1 on aggregate.

WBA (0) 1 *(Groves 84)*
Colchester U (1) 3 *(Reinelt 22, 49, Dunne 54)* 9809
WBA: Spink; Holmes, Nicholson (Donovan), Sneekes (Cunnington), Mardon, Burgess, Hamilton, Gilbert (Ashcroft), Taylor, Peschisolido, Groves.
Colchester U: Caldwell (Adcock); Dunne, Betts, Gregory, Greene, Cawley, Kinsella, Locke, Whitton, Reinelt (Fry), Wilkins.
Colchester U won 5-4 on aggregate.

Watford (1) 2 *(Andrews 16, Porter 69)*
Walsall (0) 0 5325
Watford: Miller; Gibbs, Ludden, Palmer, Millen, Page, Bazeley, Andrews (Lowndes), White, Porter, Mooney.
Walsall: Walker; Ntamark, Daniel, Viveash, Marsh, Mountfield, Blake, Bradley, Lightbourne, Wilson, Butler.
Watford won 2-1 on aggregate.

Wrexham (0) 1 *(Skinner 62)*
Huddersfield T (1) 2 *(Payton 10, Edwards 55)* 1776
Wrexham: Marriott; McGregor, Brace, Phillips, Soloman (Jones B), Carey, Chalk, Russell, Connolly, Watkin (Skinner), Ward.
Huddersfield T: Francis; Jenkins, Cowan, Bullock, Morrison, Gray, Dalton (Dyson), Reid, Stewart (Rowe), Payton, Edwards.
Huddersfield T won 5-1 on aggregate.

Wycombe W (0) 2 *(Evans 65, Williams 75)*
Reading (0) 0 5069
Wycombe W: Parkin; Lawrence, Bell, McCarthy, Evans, Cousins, Carroll, Brown, De Souza, Williams, Farrell.
Reading: Mikhailov; Booty (Bernal), Bodin, Holsgrove, Hopkins, Wdowczyk (Quinn), Parkinson (Gilkes), Williams M, Morley, Gooding.
Wycombe W won 3-1 on aggregate.

York C (1) 2 *(Pepper 30, Bushell 81)*
Doncaster R (0) 0 2757
York C: Warrington; McMillan, Himsworth, Pepper, Sharples, Barras, Murty, Randall (Bushell), Tolson, Cresswell (Bull), Stephenson.

Doncaster R: Williams; Murphy, Colcombe (Ryan), Moore, Gore, Utley, Schofield, McDonald (Larmour), Dixon (Pearce), Cramb, Birch.
York C won 3-1 on aggregate.

4 SEPT

Birmingham C (1) 2 *(Newell 40, 86)*
Brighton & HA (0) 0 20,050
Birmingham C: Bennett; Poole, Ablett, Bruce, Breen (Johnson), Castle, Devlin, Newell, Furlong (Hunt), Horne, Legg.
Brighton & HA: Rust; Smith (Johnson), Storer, Parris, Allan, Hobson, Minton, Peake, Baird, Maskell, McDonald.
Birmingham C won 3-0 on aggregate.

Bristol R (2) 2 *(Gurney 6, Archer 20)*
Luton T (0) 1 *(Oldfield 63)* 2320
Bristol R: Collett; Martin, Lockwood, Browning, Clark, Tillson, Holloway, Gurney (Low), Miller, Archer, Parmenter (French).
Luton T: Feuer; James, Thomas, Hughes, Davis S, Johnson, Linton, Alexander, Oldfield, Guentchev, Showler (Fotiadis).
Luton T won 4-2 on aggregate.

Leyton Orient (0) 1 *(West 59)*
Portsmouth (0) 0 3177
Leyton Orient: Sealey; Hendon, Naylor, Channing, Martin A, Arnott, Martin D (Ayorinde), Ling, Hanson, West, Kelly.
Portsmouth: Flahavan; Pethick, Russell, McLoughlin, Butters, Awford, Carter, Simpson, Burton, Hall, Igoe (Turner).
Portsmouth won 2-1 on aggregate.

Norwich C (1) 2 *(Adams 11 (pen), 116)*
Oxford U (0) 3 *(Elliott 52, Ford M 95, Aldridge 103)* 7301
Norwich C: Gunn; Mills, Newman, Eadie, Polston, Crook (Carey), Adams, Fleck, Milligan, Sutch, O'Neill (Akinbiyi).
Oxford U: Whitehead; Robinson, Ford M, Smith (Angel), Elliott (Purse), Gilchrist, Ford R, Gray, Moody, Massey (Aldridge), Beauchamp.
aet; Oxford U won 4-3 on aggregate.

Wolverhampton W (1) 1 *(Osborn 5)*
Swindon T (0) 0 10,760
Wolverhampton W: Stowell; Smith, Froggatt, Atkins, Venus, Richards, Thompson, Corica (Wright), Bull, Roberts, Osborn.
Swindon T: Talia; Darras, Drysdale (Taylor), Leitch, Seagraves, Culverhouse, Robinson, Watson, Cowe, Thorne, Horlock.
Swindon T won 2-1 on aggregate.

SECOND ROUND, FIRST LEG

17 SEPT

Barnsley (0) 1 *(Onuora 89 (og))*
Gillingham (0) 1 *(Ratcliffe 64)* 4491
Barnsley: Watson; Eaden, Appleby, Bosancic (Bullock), Davis, De Zeeuw, Marcelle, Redfearn, Wilkinson, Liddell (Regis), Thompson.
Gillingham: Stannard; Ford, Chapman, Hessenthaler, Harris, Bryant, Smith, Ratcliffe, Onuora, Piper (Butler), Bailey (Puttnam).

Brentford (1) 1 *(Forster 44)*
Blackburn R (2) 2 *(Flitcroft 17, Sutton 20)* 8938
Brentford: Dearden; Hurdle, Anderson, Ashby, Bates, Canham, Asaba, Smith, Forster, Bent (Abrahams), Taylor.
Blackburn R: Flowers; Berg (Pearce), Kenna, Sherwood, Hendry, Coleman, Donis (Fenton), Flitcroft, Sutton, Bohinen, Gallacher.

Bury (1) 1 *(Jackson 12)*
Crystal Palace (2) 3 *(Edworthy 10, Hopkin 15, 90)* 3472
Bury: Kiely; West, Armstrong, Daws, Butler, Jackson, Hughes, Johnson (Matthews), Jepson, Johnrose (Stant), Carter.
Crystal Palace: Day; Edworthy, Muscat, Roberts, Tuttle, Hopkin, Andersen, Houghton, Quinn, Dyer (Ndah), Veart (Freedman).

Charlton Ath (3) 4 *(Leaburn 5, Robinson 41, 48, Allen 45)*
Burnley (1) 1 *(Eyres 7)* 4874
Charlton Ath: Salmon; Barness, Stuart, Brown, Chapple, Balmer, Newton, Leaburn (Whyte), Robinson (Sturgess), Allen, Mortimer.
Burnley: Beresford; Parkinson, Eyres, Harrison, Winstanley, Hoyland, Matthew (Smith), Brass, Nogan (Cooke), Barnes, Gleghorn.

Fulham (1) 1 *(Morgan 4)*
Ipswich T (0) 1 *(Milton 78)* 6947
Fulham: Walton; Watson, Herrera, Cullip (Scott), Cusack, Blake, Freeman, Cockerill, Conroy, Morgan, Angus.
Ipswich T: Forrest; Stockwell, Tarrico (Vaughan), Thomsen, Sedgley, Williams, Uhlenbeek (Naylor), Wark, Mathie, Scowcroft, Milton.

Huddersfield T (1) 1 *(Cowan 45)*
Colchester U (0) 1 *(Adcock 46)* 5112
Huddersfield T: Francis; Jenkins, Cowan, Bullock, Sam Collins, Gray, Reid (Lawson), Burnett, Stewart, Payton, Edwards (Simon Collins).
Colchester U: Emberson; Dunne, Betts, McCarthy, Greene, Cawley, Kinsella, Reinelt (Duguid), Fry (Locke), Adcock, Wilkins.

Lincoln C (2) 4 *(Fleming 30, Holmes 45, Bos 48, Whitney 79)*
Manchester C (1) 1 *(Rosler 1)* 7599
Lincoln C: Richardson; Holmes, Whitney, Hone, Brown G, Austin, Ainsworth, Fleming, Bos, Martin, Sterling (Alcide).
Manchester C: Dibble; Brown (Crooks), Ingram, Lomas, Symons, Wassall, Summerbee, Whitley, Dickov, Clough, Rosler.

Luton T (1) 1 *(James 26)*
Derby Co (0) 0 4459
Luton T: Feuer; James, Thomas, Waddock, Davis S, Johnson, Hughes, Alexander, Oldfield, Grant (Fotiadis), Guentchev.
Derby Co: Hoult; Rowett, Powell C, Laursen, Stimac, Parker, Asanovic, Van der Laan (Carsley), Ward, Simpson (Cooper), Dailly.

Oldham Ath (1) 2 *(Redmond 31, Richardson 84)*
Tranmere R (2) 2 *(Aldridge 13 (pen), Morrissey 33)* 3094
Oldham Ath: Kelly; Halle, Serrant, Henry, Fleming, Redmond, Orlygsson, Richardson, McCarthy (McNiven D), Banger (Barlow), Rickers.
Tranmere R: Coyne; Stevens, Brannan, Higgins, Teale, O'Brien, Morrissey, Aldridge, Cook, Irons, Branch (McGreal).

Port Vale (0) 1 *(Naylor 49)*
Carlisle U (0) 0 3505
Port Vale: Van Heusden; Hill, Tankard, Bogie, Aspin, Glover, McCarthy, Porter, Foyle, Naylor (Mills), Guppy.
Carlisle U: Caig; Delap, Archdeacon, Walling, Pounewatchy, Varty, Thomas (Peacock), Conway, Reeves, Hayward, Aspinall.

Preston NE (0) 1 *(Holt 90)*
Tottenham H (1) 1 *(Anderton 2)* 16,258
Preston NE: Mimms; Kay, Barrick, Rankine, Wilcox, Kidd, Davey, Bryson, Saville, Holt, Kilbane.
Tottenham H: Walker; Edinburgh, Wilson, Howells, Calderwood, Campbell, Anderton, Nielsen, Armstrong, Allen, Fox.

Scarborough (0) 0
Leicester C (1) 2 *(Izzet 9, Lawrence 81)* 4168
Scarborough: Ironside; Knowles, Hanby, Bennett, Hicks, Rockett, Worrall (Russell), Lucas, Mitchell, Bochenski, Williams G.
Leicester C: Keller; Lewis, Lawrence, Watts, Walsh, Rolling (Campbell), Parker, Taylor, Claridge (Heskey), Robins, Izzet.

Stockport Co (2) 2 *(Flynn 23, Bennett 39)*
Sheffield U (0) 1 *(Vonk 49)* 4004
Stockport Co: Jones; Connelly, Todd, Bennett, Flynn, Gannon, Durkan, Marsden, Angell, Armstrong, Jeffers.
Sheffield U: Kelly; Short, Sandford, Hutchison, Vonk, Nilsen (Hodgson), Ward, Patterson, Taylor, Katchuro (White), Whitehouse.

Watford (0) 0
Sunderland (2) 2 *(Quinn 11, Rae 34)* 9136
Watford: Miller; Gibbs, Ludden, Palmer, Millen, Page, Penrice, Andrews (Ramage), White, Porter, Mooney.
Sunderland: Coton; Scott, Hall, Bracewell, Rae (Ball), Melville, Gray, Ord, Stewart (Russell), Agnew, Quinn.

18 SEPT

Barnet (1) 1 *(Simpson 13)*
West Ham U (0) 1 *(Cottee 77)* 3849
Barnet: Taylor; Gale, McDonald, Codner, Primus, Howarth, Rattray (Campbell), Simpson (Tomlinson), Wilson, Devine, Pardew.
West Ham U: Mautone; Breacker (Lazaridis), Dicks, Rieper, Bilic, Bowen, Moncur (Lampard), Dowie, Cottee, Bishop, Hughes.

Blackpool (1) 1 *(Quinn 1)*
Chelsea (1) 4 *(Morris 16, Petrescu 46, Hughes M 64, Spencer 85)* 9666
Blackpool: Banks; Bryan, Dixon (Barlow), Butler, Linighan, Brabin, Bonner (Lydiate), Mellon, Quinn, Ellis, Preece.
Chelsea: Hitchcock; Petrescu, Clarke (Nicholls), Morris, Duberry, Lee, Burley, Di Matteo, Spencer, Hughes M, Wise.

Bristol C (0) 0
Bolton W (0) 0 6351
Bristol C: Naylor; Owers, Barnard, McLeary, Edwards, Carey (Kuhl), Goodridge, Hewlett, Agostino, Goater (Nugent), Tinnion.
Bolton W: Branagan; McAnespie, Phillips, Fransen, Taggart, Fairclough, Johansen, Lee (Todd), Blake, McGinlay, Thompson.

Coventry C (0) 1 *(Daish 88)*
Birmingham C (1) 1 *(Furlong 37)* 11,828
Coventry C: Ogrizovic; Burrows, Borrows, Richardson, Shaw, Daish, Telfer, Whelan, Dublin, McAllister, Salako.
Birmingham C: Bennett; Poole, Ablett, Bruce, Breen, Castle (Tait), Bowen (Devlin), Horne, Furlong, Newell, Legg.

Everton (0) 1 *(Kanchelskis 58)*
York C (0) 1 *(Tolson 55)* 11,527
Everton: Southall; Barrett, Hinchcliffe, Unsworth, Short, Parkinson, Kanchelskis, Ebbrell, Ferguson, Grant (Rideout), Speed.
York C: Warrington; McMillan, Himsworth, Pepper, Sharples, Barras, Murty, Randall, Tolson, Bull, Stephenson (Cresswell).

Leeds U (1) 2 *(Wallace 15, 50)*
Darlington (1) 2 *(Roberts 40, Painter 73)* 15,711
Leeds U: Martyn; Kelly, Harte, Ford, Wetherall, Jobson, Gray (Blunt), Wallace, Rush, Couzens, Sharpe.
Darlington: Newell; Brumwell, Barnard, Twynham (Brydon), Crosby, Gregan, Atkinson, Oliver, Roberts, Blake (Painter), Carss.

Middlesbrough (3) 7 *(Ravanelli 21, 31, 55, 73 (pen),*
Emerson 32, Branco 57, Fleming 69)
Hereford U (0) 0 17,136
Middlesbrough: Miller; Fleming, Branco, Vickers, Whyte,
Whelan, Emerson, Mustoe (Moore), Stamp, Juninho
(Hendrie), Ravanelli.
Hereford U: Debont; Pitman, Sutton (Cook), Smith,
Brough, Townsend, Stoker, Foster I, Foster A,
Hargreaves, Mahon.

Nottingham F (0) 1 *(Roy 48)*
Wycombe W (0) 0 6482
Nottingham F: Crossley; Lyttle, Pearce, Cooper, Chettle,
Phillips, Bart-Williams, Roy, Saunders, Haaland
(Gemmill), Woan (Lee).
Wycombe W: Parkin; Cousins, Bell, McCarthy, Evans,
Lawrence, Carroll, Brown, De Souza, Patterson, Farrell.

Sheffield W (1) 1 *(Whittingham 13)*
Oxford U (0) 1 *(Moody 85)* 7499
Sheffield W: Pressman; Atherton, Nolan, Pembridge,
Newsome (Nicol), Blinker, Williams, Trustfull
(Humphreys), Hurst, Booth, Whittingham.
Oxford U: Whitehead; Robinson, Ford M, Smith, Elliott,
Gilchrist, Ford R (Murphy), Gray (Massey), Aldridge
(Moody), Jemson, Beauchamp.

Southampton (1) 2 *(Le Tissier 18, Watson 81)*
Peterborough U (0) 0 14,467
Southampton: Moss; Neilson, Charlton, Lundekvam,
Dryden, Monkou, Slater (Shipperley), Le Tissier,
Watson, Magilton, Oakley.
Peterborough U: Sheffield; Boothroyd, Welsh, O'Connor,
Heald, Bodley, Ebdon, Payne (Billington), Rowe
(Griffiths), Charlery, Spearing (Houghton).

Stoke C (0) 1 *(Worthington 60)*
Northampton T (0) 0 6093
Stoke C: Muggleton; Pickering, Dreyer, Sigurdsson,
Devlin, Forsyth (Keen), Worthington, Wallace, Gayle
(Macari M), Sheron, McMahon (Da Costa).
Northampton T: Woodman; Clarkson, Maddison,
Sampson, Rennie, O'Shea, Grayson, Peer (Gibb), White
(Colkin), Parris, Hunter.

Swindon T (0) 1 *(Walters 63)*
QPR (0) 2 *(Dichio 77, Impey 79)* 7843
Swindon T: Talia; Darras, O'Sullivan, Leitch, Seagraves,
Culverhouse, Walters, Allen, Cowe, Allison, Horlock.
QPR: Sommer; Brazier, Brevett, Barker, McDonald,
Plummer, Graham, Murray, Dichio, Impey, Sinclair.

Wimbledon (0) 1 *(Holdsworth 58)*
Portsmouth (0) 0 3811
Wimbledon: Heald; Jupp, Kimble, Jones, Reeves,
Blackwell, Fear, Eueli (Ardley), Clarke, Holdsworth,
Leonhardsen (Harford).
Portsmouth: Flahavan; Pethick, Russell, McLoughlin,
Dobson (Igoe), Awford, Carter, Simpson, Perrett, Hall
(Bradbury), Turner.

SECOND ROUND, SECOND LEG

24 SEPT

Birmingham C (0) 0
Coventry C (0) 1 *(McAllister 63)* 15,281
Birmingham C: Bennett; Edwards (Legg), Ablett, Bruce,
Breen, Castle, Devlin, Newell, Furlong, Horne, Donowa
(Bowen).
Coventry C: Ogrizovic; Borrows, Hall, Richardson,
Burrows, Daish, Telfer, Whelan, Dublin, McAllister,
Salako.
Coventry C won 2-1 on aggregate.

Blackburn R (1) 2 *(Gallacher 43, Sherwood 74)*
Brentford (0) 0 9599
Blackburn R: Flowers (Given); Berg, Kenna, Sherwood,
Hendry, Croft, Donis, Gallacher, Sutton (Fenton),
Bohinen, Wilcox.
Brentford: Dearden; Hurdle, Anderson, Ashby, Bates
(McGhee), Canham, Asaba (Abrahams), Smith, Forster,
Bent, Taylor.
Blackburn R won 4-1 on aggregate.

Bolton W (0) 3 *(McGinlay 47, Blake 92, Thompson 107)*
Bristol C (0) 1 *(Owers 57)* 6367
Bolton W: Branagan; Bergsson, Phillips, Fransen,
Taggart, Fairclough, Johansen (Sellars), Lee (Taylor),
Blake (Todd), McGinlay, Thompson.
Bristol C: Naylor; Owers, Barnard, Edwards, McCleary,
Hewlett, Goodridge, Carey, Agostino (Nugent), Goater
(Seal), Tinnion (Kuhl).
Bolton W won 3-1 on aggregate.

Burnley (1) 1 *(Nogan 45)*
Charlton Ath (1) 2 *(Allen 15, Whyte 90)* 2281
Burnley: Russell; Parkinson, Eyres, Hoyland, Winstanley,
Overson, Weller, Smith, Nogan, Barnes, Gleghorn.
Charlton Ath: Petterson; Barness, Stuart (Whyte),
Nicholls, Chapple, Balmer, Newton, Leaburn, Sturgess
(Lisbie), Allen, Mortimer.
Charlton Ath won 6-2 on aggregate.

Carlisle U (1) 2 *(Thomas 8, 74)*
Port Vale (1) 2 *(McCarthy 41, Mills 78)* 5545
Carlisle U: Caig; Delap, Archdeacon, Robinson (Jansen),
Pounewatchy, Varty, Thomas, Conway (Prokas), Reeves,
Hayward, Peacock.
Port Vale: Van Heusden; Hill, Tankard, Bogie (Walker),
Aspin, Glover, McCarthy, Porter, Foyle, Mills, Guppy
(Talbot).
Port Vale won 3-2 on aggregate.

Colchester U (0) 0
Huddersfield T (0) 2 *(Stewart 98, Simon*
Collins 110) 4095
Colchester U: Emberson; Dunne (Gregory), Betts
(Whitton), McCarthy, Greene, Cawley, Locke, Reinelt,
Fry, Adcock (Duguid), Wilkins.
Huddersfield T: Francis; Jenkins, Cowan (Sam Collins),
Bullock, Makel (Simon Collins), Gray, Reid, Burnett,
Stewart, Payton, Edwards (Lawson).
Huddersfield T won 3-1 on aggregate.

Crystal Palace (3) 4 *(Veart 21, Quinn 30, Muscat 41,*
Freedman 47)
Bury (0) 0 5195
Crystal Palace: Nash; Edworthy, Muscat, Roberts, Tuttle,
Quinn, Andersen (Boxall), Houghton (Harris),
Freedman (Dyer), Ndah, Veart.
Bury: Kiely; West, Bimson, Daws, Butler, Jackson,
Hughes, Rigby (Matthews), Jepson, Johnrose (Johnson),
Carter.
Crystal Palace won 7-1 on aggregate.

Darlington (0) 0
Leeds U (2) 2 *(Wallace 18, Harte 30)* 6298
Darlington: Newell; Brumwell, Barnard, Twynham
(Kelly), Crosby, Gregan, Oliver (Painter), Atkinson,
Roberts, Blake, Carss.
Leeds U: Martyn; Kelly, Harte, Palmer, Wetherall,
Jobson, Ford, Wallace, Sharp, Couzens, Gray.
Leeds U won 4-2 on aggregate.

Gillingham (0) 1 *(Puttnam 97)*
Barnsley (0) 0 5666
Gillingham: Stannard; Humphrey, Ford, Hessenthaler,
Morris, Bryant, Smith, Ratcliffe, Onuora (Bailey), Piper
(Puttnam), Chapman.
Barnsley: Watson; Eaden, Appleby, Van der Velden
(Bosancic), Davis, De Zeeuw, Marcelle (Regis),
Redfearn, Wilkinson, Bullock, Hurst.
Gillingham won 2-1 on aggregate.

Hereford U (0) 0
Middlesbrough (1) 3 *(Beck 24, Stamp 48,*
Branco 51) 4522
Hereford U: Debont; Warner, Hibbard, Smith, Brough,
Sutton, Downing (Cook), Stoker, Foster A, Hargreaves
(Preedy), Mahon.
Middlesbrough: Miller (Roberts); Morris, Branco, Cox,
Vickers, Whelan, Stamp, Fjortoft, Beck, Hendrie, Moore.
Middlesbrough won 10-0 on aggregate.

Ipswich T (1) 4 *(Sonner 28, Sedgley 50 (pen), Mathie 63, 69)*
Fulham (1) 2 *(Sedgley 31 (og), Brooker 72)* 6825
Ipswich T: Forrest; Stockwell (Uhlenbeek), Vaughan, Thomsen, Sedgley, Swailes, Mason, Sonner, Mathie, Scowcroft, Milton.
Fulham: Walton; Watson (Marshall), Herrera, Cullip (Brooker), Cusack, Blake, Scott, Adams (Mison), Conroy, Morgan, Angus.
Ipswich T won 5-3 on aggregate.

Manchester C (0) 0
Lincoln C (1) 1 *(Bos 17)* 14,242
Manchester C: Dibble; McGoldrick (Brown), Frontzeck (Phillips), Lomas, Symons, Wassall, Summerbee, Clough, Dickov (Kavelashvili), Kinkladze, Rosler.
Lincoln C: Richardson; Holmes, Whitney, Hone, Brown G, Austin, Ainsworth, Fleming (Minett), Bos (Dennis), Martin (Brown S), Alcide.
Lincoln C won 5-1 on aggregate.

Northampton T (0) 1 *(Gayle 89 (og))*
Stoke C (0) 2 *(Sheron 100, 108)* 5088
Northampton T: Woodman; Clarkson, Maddison, Sampson, Rennie, O'Shea, Gibb (White), Parrish (Peer), Cooper, Hunter, Colkin (Grayson).
Stoke C: Muggleton (Prudhoe); Pickering, Dreyer, Sigurdsson, Devlin, Da Costa (Macari M), Worthington, Wallace, Gayle, Sheron, McMahon (Keen).
Stoke C won 3-1 on aggregate.

Oxford U (0) 1 *(Jemson 85)*
Sheffield W (0) 0 6863
Oxford U: Whitehead; Robinson, Ford M, Smith, Elliott, Gilchrist, Ford R (Murphy), Gray, Moody (Aldridge), Jemson, Beauchamp.
Sheffield W: Pressman; Atherton (Oakes), Nolan, Blinker, Stefanovic, Walker (Nicol), Trustfull, Hyde, Booth, Humphreys, Whittingham.
Oxford U won 2-1 on aggregate.

Sheffield U (1) 2 *(Taylor 34, Katchuro 65)*
Stockport Co (3) 5 *(Gannon 25, Armstrong 30, 81, Bennett 33, Angell 62)* 6285
Sheffield U: Kelly; Ward, Hodgson (Starbuck), Hutchison, Vonk, Spackman, White, Patterson, Taylor, Katchuro, Whitehouse.
Stockport Co: Jones; Connelly, Todd, Bennett, Flynn, Gannon, Durkan, Marsden, Angell, Armstrong, Jeffers.
Stockport Co won 7-3 on aggregate.

Sunderland (1) 1 *(Scott 6)*
Watford (0) 0 10,659
Sunderland: Coton; Hall, Scott, Rae, Ball, Melville, Smith, Ord, Stewart (Bridges), Agnew (Kelly), Russell.
Watford: Miller; Gibbs, Ludden, Johnson R, Palmer, Page, Bazeley (Talboys), Andrews (Noel-Williams), White, Penrice, Mooney.
Sunderland won 3-0 on aggregate.

Tranmere R (0) 0
Oldham Ath (0) 1 *(Banger 50)* 3711
Tranmere R: Coyne; Stevens, Brannan, Higgins (Mahon), Teale, O'Brien, Morrissey (Irons), Aldridge, Cook (Jones), Branch, Bonetti.
Oldham Ath: Kelly; Halle, Serrant, Henry, Fleming, Redmond, Orlygsson, Richardson, Barlow (Beresford), Banger (McNiven D), Rickers.
Oldham Ath won 3-2 on aggregate.

Wycombe W (1) 1 *(McCarthy 38)*
Nottingham F (0) 1 *(Lee 102)* 6310
Wycombe W: Parkin; Cousins, Bell, McCarthy, Evans, Lawrence, Carroll (Williams), Brown, De Souza, McGavin, Farrell.
Nottingham F: Crossley; Lyttle, Pearce, Cooper, Blatherwick, Phillips, Bart-Williams, Gemmill (Roy), Saunders (Haaland), Lee, Woan.
Nottingham F won 2-1 on aggregate.

York C (1) 3 *(Tolson 35, Bull 57, Murty 86)*
Everton (1) 2 *(Rideout 24, Speed 90)* 7854
York C: Warrington; McMillan, Hall, Pepper, Sharples, Barras, Murty, Randall, Tolson, Bull, Stephenson.
Everton: Southall; Barrett, Hinchcliffe, Unsworth, Hottiger, Parkinson, Kanchelskis, Stuart, Rideout (Branch), Speed, Limpar.
York C won 4-3 on aggregate.

25 SEPT

Chelsea (0) 1 *(Spencer 63)*
Blackpool (1) 3 *(Ellis 35, 61,Quinn 46)* 11,732
Chelsea: Grodas; Petrescu, Minto (Nicholls), Duberry, Leboeuf, Clarke, Burley, Di Matteo, Vialli, Spencer, Morris.
Blackpool: Banks; Bryan, Dixon (Barlow), Lydiate, Linighan, Brabin, Bonner, Mellon, Quinn (Thorpe), Ellis (Preece), Onwere.
Chelsea won 5-4 on aggregate.

Derby Co (2) 2 *(Sturridge 40, Simpson 45)*
Luton T (1) 2 *(Grant 12, Thorpe 68)* 13,569
Derby Co: Hoult; Rowett, Parker (Cooper), Laursen (Van der Laan), Powell D, Carbon, Dailly, Carsley, Sturridge, Gabbiadini (Ward), Simpson.
Luton T: Feuer; James, Thomas, Waddock, Davis S, Johnson, Hughes (Thorpe), Alexander, Oldfield, Grant, Guentchev.
Luton T won 3-2 on aggregate.

Leicester C (1) 2 *(Lawrence 40, Parker 90 (pen))*
Scarborough (0) 1 *(Ritchie 77)* 10,793
Leicester C: Poole; Lawrence (Lenhart), Lewis, Rolling, Walsh (Campbell), Hill, Parker, Lennon, Robins, Izzet, Heskey.
Scarborough: Ironside; Hanby (Knowles), Wells, Bennett, Hicks, Rockett, McIlhatton, Brooke, Lucas (Mitchell), Bochenski (Ritchie), Williams G.
Leicester C won 4-1 on aggregate.

Peterborough U (0) 1 *(Farrell 50)*
Southampton (2) 4 *(Watson 33, Charlton 36, Magilton 56, Dryden 78)* 8220
Peterborough U: Sheffield; Billington (Carter), Drury, O'Connor, Heald, Welsh, Willis, Payne, Houghton (Grazioli), Charlery, McKeever (Farrell).
Southampton: Moss; Neilson (Oakley), Charlton (Potter), Lundekvam, Dryden, Monkou, Le Tissier, Watson (Watkinson), Shipperley, Magilton, Slater.
Southampton won 6-1 on aggregate.

Portsmouth (1) 1 *(Carter 41)*
Wimbledon (0) 1 *(Gayle 47)* 4006
Portsmouth: Flahavan; Pethick, Russell, McLoughlin, Butters, Awford, Carter, Simpson, Bradbury, Perrett, Turner (Hall).
Wimbledon: Sullivan; Cunningham, Kimble, Jones, Blackwell, Perry, Clarke, Earle, Gayle, Holdsworth (Leonhardsen), Fear.
Wimbledon won 2-1 on aggregate.

QPR (0) 1 *(Brazier 55)*
Swindon T (1) 3 *(O'Sullivan 45, Allison 66, Thorne 102)* 6976
QPR: Sommer; Graham, Brevett, Barker, McDonald, Plummer, Brazier, Murray (Quashie), Dichio, Impey (Charles), Sinclair.
Swindon T: Talia; Robinson, Elkins, Leitch (Thorne) (Finney), Seagraves, Culverhouse, Walters, O'Sullivan, Cowe (Hulbert), Allison, Horlock.
Swindon T won 4-3 on aggregate.

Tottenham H (1) 3 *(Anderton 31, Allen 62, 76)*
Preston NE (0) 0 20,080
Tottenham H: Walker; Carr, Wilson, Howells, Calderwood, Campbell, Anderton (Nielsen), Fox, Allen, Sheringham, Sinton.
Preston NE: Mimms; Kay, Barrick, Rankine (McDonald), Wilcox, Kidd, Davey, Atkinson, Saville, Holt, Kilbane.
Tottenham H won 4-1 on aggregate.

West Ham U (0) 1 *(Bilic 48)*
Barnet (0) 0   15,264
West Ham U: Mautone; Breacker, Dicks, Rieper, Bilic, Bishop, Moncur, Dowie, Cottee (Jones), Dumitrescu, Lazaridis (Ferdinand).
Barnet: Taylor; Gale (Campbell), McDonald, Codner, Primus, Howarth, Rattray (Hodges), Hardyman (Tomlinson), Wilson, Devine, Pardew.
West Ham U won 2-1 on aggregate.

THIRD ROUND

22 OCT

Blackburn R (0) 0
Stockport Co (1) 1 *(Sherwood 23 (og))*   14,622
Blackburn R: Flowers; Kenna, Croft, Sherwood (Bohinen), Pearce, Berg, Donis, Flitcroft, Beattie (Marker), Gallacher, Wilcox.
Stockport Co: Jones; Connelly, Todd, Bennett, Flynn, Gannon, Durkan, Marsden, Angell, Armstrong, Cavaco (Searle).

Bolton W (2) 2 *(McGinlay 22, Blake 43)*
Chelsea (1) 1 *(Minto 2)*   16,867
Bolton W: Branagan; Bergsson, Phillips, Fransen, Taggart, Fairclough, Johansen, Sellars, Blake, McGinlay (Taylor), Thompson.
Chelsea: Hitchcock; Gullit, Minto (Phelan), Johnsen, Leboeuf, Clarke, Burley, Di Matteo, Spencer, Hughes, Wise.

Gillingham (0) 2 *(Onuora 58, Ratcliffe 75)*
Coventry C (2) 2 *(Telfer 25, 27)*   10,603
Gillingham: Stannard; Smith, Morris, Hessenthaler, Harris, Bryant, Butler, Ratcliffe, Onuora, Bailey (Puttnam), Chapman.
Coventry C: Ogrizovic; Borrows, Hall, Richardson, Shaw, Williams, Telfer, Whelan, Dublin, McAllister, Salako.

Ipswich T (2) 4 *(Mason 25, 76, Mathie 37, 68)*
Crystal Palace (1) 1 *(Veart 4)*   8390
Ipswich T: Wright; Uhlenbeek, Taricco, Mowbray, Sedgley, Williams, Vaughan, Sonner, Mathie (Naylor), Scowcroft, Mason (Stockwell).
Crystal Palace: Day; Edworthy, Muscat, Roberts, Tuttle, Hopkin, Andersen (Quinn), McKenzie, Freedman (Harris), Dyer, Veart.

Port Vale (0) 0
Oxford U (0) 0   4942
Port Vale: Musselwhite; Hill, Tankard, Walker, Griffiths, Glover, McCarthy, Porter, Mills, Naylor, Guppy.
Oxford U: Whitehead; Robinson, Ford M, Smith, Elliott, Purse, Massey, Gray, Moody, Jemson, Beauchamp.

Wimbledon (1) 1 *(Holdsworth 24)*
Luton T (1) 1 *(Hughes 41)*   5043
Wimbledon: Sullivan; Cunningham, Kimble, Jones, Blackwell, Perry, Gayle, Earle, Fear, Holdsworth (Clarke), Leonhardsen.
Luton T: Feuer; James, Thomas, Waddock, Davis S, Johnson, Thorpe, Alexander, Oldfield, Hughes, Showler.

York C (0) 0
Leicester C (0) 2 *(Lennon 60, Grayson 86)*   8406
York C: Clarke; McMillan, Hall, Pepper, Tutill, Barras, Murty, Randall, Tolson (Cresswell), Bull, Himsworth (Stephenson).
Leicester C: Keller; Grayson, Whitlow, Watts, Walsh, Prior, Lennon, Taylor (Lawrence), Claridge, Parker, Heskey.

23 OCT

Charlton Ath (1) 1 *(Whyte 18)*
Liverpool (1) 1 *(Fowler 21)*   15,000
Charlton Ath: Salmon; Brown, Barness, O'Connell, Chapple, Rufus, Newton, Leaburn, Robinson, Whyte (Lisbie), Otto.
Liverpool: James; McAteer, Bjornebye, Matteo, Scales, Babb, McManaman, Berger, Fowler, Barnes, Thomas.

Leeds U (0) 1 *(Sharpe 69)*
Aston Villa (0) 2 *(Taylor 70, York 77 (pen))*   15,803
Leeds U: Martyn; Kelly, Sharpe, Palmer, Beesley (Harte), Jobson, Ford, Couzens, Rush, Wallace, Radebe (Wetherall).
Aston Villa: Bosnich; Nelson (Draper), Wright, Scimeca, Ehiogu, Tiler, Taylor, Curcic, Yorke, Johnson, Townsend.

Manchester U (1) 2 *(Poborsky 19, Scholes 72)*
Swindon T (0) 1 *(Thorne 52)*   49,305
Manchester U: Van der Gouw; Neville G, Neville P, May, Keane, Casper, Thornley, Appleton (Davies), McClair, Scholes, Poborsky.
Swindon T: Talia; Robinson, Elkins, Leitch, Seagraves, Culverhouse, Walters, Darras, Thorne (Cowe), Allison, Horlock.

Middlesbrough (2) 5 *(Juninho 17, Emerson 42, Ravanelli 72, 76, Beck 85)*
Huddersfield T (0) 1 *(Payton 87)*   26,615
Middlesbrough: Walsh; Cox, Fleming, Vickers, Pearson (Whyte), Stamp (Moore), Emerson, Mustoe, Beck, Juninho, Ravanelli.
Huddersfield T: Francis; Jenkins, Cowan, Bullock, Sinnott, Gray, Makel, Burnett, Lawson (Edwards), Payton, Simon Collins (Dalton).

Newcastle U (1) 1 *(Beardsley 25 (pen))*
Oldham Ath (0) 0   36,314
Newcastle U: Hislop; Barton, Elliott, Batty, Peacock, Albert, Asprilla (Kitson), Beardsley, Ferdinand, Clark, Ginola.
Oldham Ath: Kelly; Fleming, Halle, Rickers, Serrant, Redmond, Orlygsson, McNiven S (Hughes), Banger, Barlow, Beresford.

Southampton (0) 2 *(Le Tissier 46, Van Gobbel 54)*
Lincoln C (1) 2 *(Hone 21, Ainsworth 85)*   14,516
Southampton: Beasant; Dodd, Potter (Charlton), Lundekvam, Dryden, Van Gobbel, Le Tissier (Watson), Neilson, Ostenstad, Berkovic, Oakley (Magilton).
Lincoln C: Richardson; Barnett, Whitney, Hone (Minett), Brown G, Austin, Ainsworth, Fleming (Dennis), Bos, Martin (Sterling), Alcide.

Stoke C (1) 1 *(Sheron 26)*
Arsenal (0) 1 *(Wright 78)*   20,804
Stoke C: Muggleton; Pickering (McMahon), Worthington, Sigurdsson, Dreyer, Forsyth, Whittle, Wallace, Keen, Sheron, Kavanagh.
Arsenal: Seaman; Dixon, Winterburn, Keown, Bould, Adams, Platt, Wright, Merson, Bergkamp (Hartson), Vieira.

Tottenham H (0) 2 *(Armstrong 71, Campbell 90)*
Sunderland (1) 1 *(Ball 31)*   24,867
Tottenham H: Walker; Carr, Edinburgh, Howells, Calderwood, Campbell, Fox, Nielsen (Allen), Armstrong, Sheringham, Wilson.
Sunderland: Perez; Kubicki, Hall, Bracewell, Ball, Melville, Gray, Ord, Stewart, Bridges (Russell), Kelly.

West Ham U (1) 4 *(Dowie 16, 56, Porfirio 67, Dicks 73 (pen))*
Nottingham F (1) 1 *(Cooper 29)*   19,402
West Ham U: Miklosko; Bowen, Dicks, Rieper, Bilic, Bishop, Lazaridis, Dowie, Porfirio, Monkou, Hughes.
Nottingham F: Crossley; Cooper, Haaland, Phillips, Blatherwick, Bart-Williams, Roy, Gemmill, Saunders, Lee, Woan.

THIRD ROUND REPLAY

5 NOV

Oxford U (2) 2 *(Jemson 13, 39)*
Port Vale (0) 0   5279
Oxford U: Whitehead; Robinson, Ford M, Smith, Elliott, Purse, Angel, Gray, Aldridge (Massey), Jemson, Beauchamp (Rush).
Port Vale: Musselwhite; Hill, Tankard, Walker, Griffiths, Glover, McCarthy, Porter, Mills (Foyle), Naylor, Corden (Talbot).

THIRD ROUND REPLAYS

12 NOV

Lincoln C (1) 1 *(Ainsworth 9)*
Southampton (0) 3 *(Magilton 75 (pen), Watson 84,*
Berkovic, 90) 10,523
Lincoln C: Richardson; Barnett, Whitney, Hone
(Minett), Brown G, Austin, Ainsworth, Fleming, Bos,
Alcide, Martin (Brown S).
Southampton: Woods; Dodd, Charlton, Lundekvam, Van
Gobbel, Monkou, Dryden (Slater), Le Tissier (Watson),
Ostenstad, Magilton, Berkovic.

Luton T (1) 1 *(Blackwell 28 (og))*
Wimbledon (0) 2 *(Castledine 90, Fear 98)* 8076
Luton T: Feuer; James, Thomas, Waddock, Davis S,
Johnson, Hughes, Alexander, Grant (McLaren), Thorpe
(Douglas), Showler (Guentchev).
Wimbledon: Sullivan; Cunningham, Kimble, Fear,
Blackwell, Perry, Gayle (Clarke), Castledine, Ekoku
(Reeves), Holdsworth (Harford), Ardley.

13 NOV

Arsenal (1) 5 *(Wright 41 (pen), 63, Platt 46, Bergkamp 68,*
Merson 73)
Stoke C (1) 2 *(Sheron 35, 88)* 33,962
Arsenal: Seaman; Dixon, Winterburn, Keown, Bould,
Adams, Platt, Wright, Merson, Bergkamp (Hartson),
Vieira (Morrow).
Stoke C: Muggleton; Pickering (Griffin), Devlin,
Sigurdsson, Whittle, Forsyth, McMahon (Macari M),
Wallace, Keen (Carruthers), Sheron, Kavanagh.

Coventry C (0) 0
Gillingham (0) 1 *(Smith 71)* 12,639
Coventry C: Ogrizovic; Borrows, Williams, Richardson,
Shaw, Daish, Telfer (Dublin), Jess (Strachan), Whelan,
McAllister, Salako.
Gillingham: Stannard; Smith, Harris, Green, Bryant,
Hessenthaler, Butler, Ratcliffe, Onuora, Bailey,
Armstrong.

Liverpool (2) 4 *(Wright 14, Redknapp 18, Fowler 48, 73)*
Charlton Ath (1) 1 *(Newton 21)* 20,714
Liverpool: James; McAteer, Bjornebye, Matteo, Wright,
Ruddock, McManaman, Redknapp, Fowler, Barnes,
Thomas.
Charlton Ath: Salmon; Stuart (Nicholls), Barness,
O'Connell, Balmer, Rufus, Newton, Leaburn (Lisbie),
Robinson, Allen, Otto.

FOURTH ROUND

26 NOV

Ipswich T (0) 1 *(Naylor 73)*
Gillingham (0) 0 13,537
Ipswich T: Wright; Stockwell, Taricco, Cundy
(Uhlenbeek), Sedgley, Williams, Milton (Sonner),
Tanner, Naylor, Scowcroft, Mason.
Gillingham: Marshall; Smith, Harris, Hessenthaler,
Green, Pennock, O'Connor (Piper), Ratcliffe,
Armstrong, Butler, Bailey (Puttnam).

Oxford U (0) 1 *(Moody 90)*
Southampton (1) 1 *(Dryden 26)* 9473
Oxford U: Whitehead; Purse, Ford M, Smith (Murphy),
Elliott, Gilchrist, Angel (Ford R), Gray, Aldridge
(Moody), Jemson, Beauchamp.
Southampton: Woods; Dodd, Charlton, Lundekvam, Van
Gobbel, Dryden, Oakley, Watson, Ostenstad, Beerkovic
(Magilton), Slater (Maddison).

Wimbledon (1) 1 *(Gayle 44)*
Aston Villa (0) 0 7573
Wimbledon: Sullivan; Cunningham, Kimble, Jones,
Blackwell, Perry, Gayle (Harford), Earle, Ekoku
(Clarke), Leonhardsen, Ardley.
Aston Villa: Oakes; Nelson, Wright, Southgate (Scimeca),
Ehiogu, Staunton, Taylor, Draper, Yorke, Townsend,
Joachim (Milosevic).

27 NOV

Bolton W (2) 6 *(McGinlay 6, 37, 74 (pen), Taggart 60,*
Blake 79, Taylor 86)
Tottenham H (1) 1 *(Sheringham 19)* 18,621
Bolton W: Branagan; Bergsson, Phillips, Thompson
(Frandsen), Taggart, Fairclough, Lee, Sellars, Blake,
McGinlay (Taylor), Sheridan (Todd).
Tottenham H: Walker; Carr, Wilson, Howells,
Calderwood, Campbell, Anderton, Dozzell (Fox),
Armstrong, Sheringham, Sinton.

Leicester C (1) 2 *(Claridge 38, Heskey 77)*
Manchester U (0) 0 20,428
Leicester C: Keller; Grayson, Whitlow (Watts), Izzet,
Walsh, Prior, Lennon, Taylor (Lawrence), Claridge,
Parker, Heskey.
Manchester U: Van der Gouw; O'Kane (Appleton),
Clegg, May, Keane, Casper, Cruyff, McClair, Scholes,
Poborsky (Cooke), Thornley (Davies).

Liverpool (2) 4 *(McManaman 26, Fowler 39 (pen), 52,*
Berger 72)
Arsenal (1) 2 *(Wright 13 (pen), 68 (pen))* 32,814
Liverpool: James; McAteer, Bjornebye, Babb, Wright,
Ruddock, McManaman, Berger, Fowler, Barnes,
Thomas.
Arsenal: Lukic; Dixon, Winterburn (Morrow), Keown,
Bould, Adams, Platt, Wright, Merson (Parlour), Hartson,
Vieira.

Middlesbrough (1) 3 *(Whyte 27, Beck 61, Ravanelli 89)*
Newcastle U (1) 1 *(Shearer 45)* 29,831
Middlesbrough: Walsh; Morris, Fleming, Vickers, Whyte,
Mustoe, Emerson, Hignett (Stamp), Beck, Juninho,
Ravanelli.
Newcastle U: Srnicek; Gillespie (Watson), Elliott, Batty,
Peacock, Albert, Lee, Beardsley, Shearer, Asprilla
(Kitson), Ginola.

West Ham U (1) 1 *(Raducioiu 12)*
Stockport Co (0) 1 *(Cavaco 51)* 20,061
West Ham U: Miklosko; Breacker, Dicks, Potts, Bilic,
Lampard, Lazaridis (Dumitrescu), Dowie, Raducioiu,
Bishop, Hughes.
Stockport Co: Jones; Connelly, Todd, Bennett, Flynn,
Gannon, Durkan (Dinning), Marsden, Angell,
Armstrong, Jeffers (Cavaco).

FOURTH ROUND REPLAY

18 DEC

Southampton (1) 3 *(Berkowitz 21, Dryden 52, Ostenstad*
58)
Oxford U (1) 2 *(Jemson 42, Ford R 59)* 10,737
Southampton: Beasant; Maddison, Van Gobbel (Monkou),
Magilton, Dryden, Lundekvam, Oakley, Watson,
Ostenstad, Berkowitz, Slater.
Oxford U: Whitehead; Robinson, Ford M, Smith, Elliott,
Purse, Gray (Massey), Ford R, Aldridge (Moody),
Jemson, Beauchamp.

Stockport Co (2) 2 *(Dowie 23 (og), Angell 27)*
West Ham U (1) 1 *(Dicks 22)* 9834
Stockport Co: Jones; Connelly, Todd, Bennett, Flynn,
Gannon, Durkan, Marsden, Angell, Armstrong, Cavaco
(Dinning).
West Ham U: Miklosko; Bowen, Dicks, Rieper, Bilic,
Bishop, Moncur, Dowie (Williamson), Porfirio,
Dumitrescu, Hughes.

FIFTH ROUND

8 JAN

Bolton W (0) 0
Wimbledon (2) 2 *(Ekoku 3, Leonhardsen 22)*   16,968
Bolton W: Ward; Todd, Small, Fransen, Taggart, Fairclough, Lee, Sellars, Blake, McGinlay (Green), Sheridan (Pollock).
Wimbledon: Sullivan; Cunningham, Kimble, Jones, Blackwell, Perry, Ardley, Earle, Ekoku (Clarke), Leonhardsen (McAllister), Gayle (Harford).

Middlesbrough (2) 2 *(Hignett 14, Vickers 27)*
Liverpool (0) 1 *(McManaman 65)*   28,670
Middlesbrough: Walsh; Cox, Fleming, Vickers, Whyte, Blackmore, Emerson, Mustoe, Hignett, Juninho (Stamp), Ravanelli.
Liverpool: James; Jones R (Carragher), Bjornebye (Kennedy), Matteo, Wright, Babb, McAteer, Berger, Fowler, Thomas, McManaman.

21 JAN

Ipswich T (0) 0
Leicester C (1) 1 *(Robins 42)*   20,793
Ipswich T: Wright; Stockwell, Vaughan, Cundy, Swailes, Williams, Uhlenbeek, Sonner (Milton), Howe (Naylor), Scowcroft, Mason.
Leicester C: Keller; Grayson (Hill), Kamark, Parker, Watts, Prior, Lennon, Izzet, Claridge, Robins (Taylor), Heskey.

22 JAN

Stockport Co (2) 2 *(Armstrong 25, Cavaco 26)*
Southampton (1) 2 *(Ostenstad 16, 85)*   9840
Stockport Co: Jones; Connelly, Todd, Bennett, Flynn, Gannon, Durkan, Marsden, Angell, Armstrong, Cavaco.
Southampton: Beasant; Maddison (Lundekvam), Charlton (Slater), Magilton, Van Gobbel, Monkou, Oakley, Le Tissier, Ostenstad, Hughes (Berkowitz), Neilson.

FIFTH ROUND REPLAY

29 JAN

Southampton (1) 1 *(Le Tissier 8)*
Stockport Co (0) 2 *(Angell 62, Mutch 83)*   13,428
Southampton: Beasant; Neilson, Oakley (Maddison), Lundekvam, Van Gobbel, Monkou, Le Tissier, Magilton, Ostenstad, Berkowitz, Slater (Hughes).
Stockport Co: Jones; Connelly, Todd, Bennett, Flynn, Gannon, Durkan (Jeffers), Dinning, Angell (Mutch), Armstrong, Cavaco.

SEMI-FINAL FIRST LEG

18 FEB

Leicester C (0) 0
Wimbledon (0) 0   16,021
Leicester C: Keller; Grayson, Ullathorne (Lawrence), Watts, Walsh, Prior, Izzet, Taylor, Claridge, Parker, Heskey.
Wimbledon: Sullivan; Cunningham, Kimble, Jones, Blackwell, Perry, Gayle (Holdsworth), Earle, Ekoku, Goodman, Leonhardsen.

26 FEB

Stockport Co (0) 0
Middlesbrough (0) 2 *(Beck 73, Ravanelli 79)*   11,778
Stockport Co: Jones; Connelly, Todd, Bennett, Flynn, Gannon, Durkan, Marsden, Angell, Armstrong, Cavaco (Jeffers).
Middlesbrough: Schwarzer; Cox, Fleming, Stamp, Pearson, Festa, Emerson, Mustoe, Beck, Hignett, Ravanelli.

SEMI-FINAL SECOND LEG

11 MAR

Wimbledon (1) 1 *(Gayle 23)*
Leicester C (0) 1 *(Grayson 53)*   17,810
Wimbledon: Sullivan; Cunningham, Kimble, Jones, Blackwell, Perry, Ardley (Harford), Earle, Ekoku, Leonhardsen, Gayle.
Leicester C: Keller; Grayson, Izzett, Watts, Walsh, Prior, Lennon, Parker, Claridge (Robins), Lawrence (Taylor), Heskey.
aet.

12 MAR

Middlesbrough (0) 0
Stockport Co (1) 1 *(Connelly 6)*   29,633
Middlesbrough: Schwarzer; Cox, Fleming, Mustoe (Blackmore), Pearson, Festa, Emerson, Hignett, Beck, Juninho, Ravanelli.
Stockport Co: Jones; Connelly, Todd, Bennett, Flynn, Dinning, Cavaco (Gannon), Marsden, Mutch (Angell), Armstrong, Jeffers (Nash).

FINAL (AT WEMBLEY)

6 APR

Leicester C (0) 1 *(Heskey 118)*
Middlesbrough (0) 1 *(Ravanelli 95)*   76,757
Leicester C: Keller; Grayson, Whitlow (Robins), Kamark, Walsh, Prior, Lennon, Parker, Claridge, Izzet (Taylor), Heskey.
Middlesbrough: Schwarzer; Cox, Fleming, Mustoe, Pearson, Festa, Emerson, Hignett, Beck, Juninho, Ravanelli.

FINAL REPLAY (AT HILLSBOROUGH)

16 APR

Leicester C (0) 1 *(Claridge 100)*
Middlesbrough (0) 0   39,428
Leicester C: Keller; Grayson, Whitlow (Lawrence), Kamark, Walsh, Prior, Lennon, Parker, Claridge (Robins), Izzet, Heskey.
Middlesbrough: Roberts; Cox (Moore), Kinder, Festa (Vickers), Pearson, Blackmore, Emerson, Mustoe, Ravanelli, Juninho, Hignett (Beck).
Referee: M. Bodenham (East Looe).

FOOTBALL LEAGUE COMPETITION ATTENDANCES

LEAGUE CUP ATTENDANCES

Season	Attendances	Games	Average
1960/61	1,204,580	112	10,755
1961/62	1,030,534	104	9,909
1962/63	1,029,893	102	10,097
1963/64	945,265	104	9,089
1964/65	962,802	98	9,825
1965/66	1,205,876	106	11,376
1966/67	1,394,553	118	11,818
1967/68	1,671,326	110	15,194
1968/69	2,064,647	118	17,497
1969/70	2,299,819	122	18,851
1970/71	2,035,315	116	17,546
1971/72	2,397,154	123	19,489
1972/73	1,935,474	120	16,129
1973/74	1,722,629	132	13,050
1974/75	1,901,094	127	14,969
1975/76	1,841,735	140	13,155
1976/77	2,236,636	147	15,215
1977/78	2,038,295	148	13,772
1978/79	1,825,643	139	13,134
1979/80	2,322,866	169	13,745
1980/81	2,051,576	161	12,743
1981/82	1,880,682	161	11,681
1982/83	1,679,756	160	10,498
1983/84	1,900,491	168	11,312
1984/85	1,876,429	167	11,236
1985/86	1,579,916	163	9,693
1986/87	1,531,498	157	9,755
1987/88	1,539,253	158	9,742
1988/89	1,552,780	162	9,585
1989/90	1,836,916	168	10,934
1990/91	1,675,496	159	10,538
1991/92	1,622,337	164	9,892
1992/93	1,558,031	161	9,677
1993/94	1,744,120	163	10,700
1994/95	1,530,478	157	9,748
1995/96	1,776,060	162	10,963
1996/97	1,529,321	163	9,382

COCA-COLA CUP 1996–97

Round	Aggregate	Games	Average
One	262,883	66	3,983
Two	429,238	54	7,948
Three	382,371	22	17,381
Four	173,900	10	17,390
Five	89,535	5	17,907
Semi-finals	75,209	4	18,802
Final	116,185	2	58,093
Total	1,529,321	163	9,382

AUTO WINDSCREENS SHIELD 1996–97

Round	Aggregate	Games	Average
One	25,721	16	1,608
Two	37,371	16	2,336
Area Quarter-finals	17,552	8	2,194
Area Semi-finals	14,726	4	3,681
Area finals	24,912	4	6,228
Final	45,077	1	45,077
Total	165,359	49	3,375

Middlesbrough's Juninho moves away from the attention of Neil Lennon (Leicester City) during the Coca-Cola Cup Final. (Action Images)

AUTO WINDSCREENS SHIELD 1996–97

SOUTHERN SECTION FIRST ROUND

7 DEC

Hereford U (0) 0
Millwall (2) 4 *(Dair 4, 48, Crawford 38, 53)* 1701
Hereford U: Debont; Norton, Matthewson, Smith, Warner, Cross (Foster I), Cook, Stoker, Foster A, Hargreaves (Preedy), Brough.
Millwall: Carter; Lavin (Aris), Van Blerk, Newman, Webber, Sinclair, Doyle, Neill (Robertson), Crawford, Dair, Dolby (McRobert).

NORTHERN SECTION FIRST ROUND

9 DEC

Chesterfield (0) 0
Preston NE (0) 2 *(Atkinson 51, Bennett 87)* 1169
Chesterfield: Leaning; Hewitt, Jules, Timons (Lomas), Carr, Mitchell, Beaumont, Gaughan, Lormor, Morris, Perkins.
Preston NE: O'Hanlon; Sparrow, Barrick, McKenna, Squires, Gregan, Atkinson, Davey, Bennett, Wilkinson, Bryson.

10 DEC

Bury (1) 3 *(Johnrose 20, Carter 59, Lucketti 64)*
Darlington (1) 1 *(Barbara 31)* 1436
Bury: Kiely; Woodward, Armstrong (Rigby), Daws, Lucketti, Butler, Jackson, Carter (Jepson), Johnson, Johnrose (Hughes), Matthews.
Darlington: Newell; Shaw, Barnard, Atkinson B (Brumwell), Crosby, Brydon, Twynham (Oliver), Carss, Roberts, Barbara (Blake), Naylor.

Carlisle U (0) 2 *(Walling 66, McAlindon 85)*
Rochdale (0) 0 3622
Carlisle U: Caig; Thomas (Varty), Delap, Walling, Edmondson, Pounewatchy, Peacock, Conway, Jansen (McAlindon), Hayward, Aspinall.
Rochdale: Gray; Fensome (Thackeray), Bayliss, Johnson, Hill, Russell, Bailey, Deary, Cecere (Thompson), Whitehall, Painter.

Doncaster R (1) 1 *(Cramb 27 (pen))*
Stockport Co (0) 2 *(Gray 70 (og), Cavaco 71)* 988
Doncaster R: O'Connor; Gray (Ramsay), Ryan, Moore, Gore (Colcombe), Clark, Schofield, Warren, Dixon, Cramb, Birch.
Stockport Co: Jones; Connelly, Todd, Ware (Dinning), Flynn, Gannon, Durkan, Marsden, Angell, Cavaco (Nash), Jeffers (Kiko).

Hartlepool U (0) 0
Burnley (1) 2 *(Nogan 14, Eyres 55)* 921
Hartlepool U: O'Connor; Ingram (Gallagher), McAuley, Beech (Hutt), Lee, Davies, Allon, Cooper, Howard, Clegg, Hislop (Irvine).
Burnley: Beresford; Parkinson, Eyres, Overson (Harrison), Swan, Brass, Weller (Little), Smith, Nogan, Cooke, Gleghorn (Thompson).

Hull C (2) 3 *(Wright 41, Darby 42, Joyce 68)*
Chester C (1) 1 *(McDonald 29)* 553
Hull C: Davison; Marks, Rioch, Brien, Doncel, Wright, Joyce, Gilbert (Maxfield), Darby, Mann, Sansam (Ellington).
Chester C: Sinclair; Davidson, Jenkins, Woods, Jackson (Whelan), Alsford, Flitcroft, Priest, McDonald (Milner), Rimmer, Fisher (Noteman).

Rotherham U (0) 0
Blackpool (0) 1 *(Preece 90)* 1143
Rotherham U: Cherry; Breckin, Roscoe, Dobbin (Blades), Monington, Gayle, Berry, Goodwin, McDougald, McGlashan, Clarke (Glover).
Blackpool: Banks; Thorpe, Barlow, Dixon, Darton, Bradshaw, Bonner, Haddow, Symons, Carden, Preece.

Scarborough (0) 0
Notts Co (1) 1 *(Martindale 45 (pen))* 952
Scarborough: Burridge; Knowles, Wells, Bennett (Thompstone), Hicks, Lucas, McElhatton (Worrall), Brooke, Daws, Ritchie (Bochenski), Williams G.
Notts Co: Pollitt; Wilder (Gallagher), Baraclough, Redmile, Walker, Rogers, Finnan (Ridgway), Hunt, Martindale, Wilkes, Richardson.

SOUTHERN SECTION FIRST ROUND

10 DEC

Bristol R (0) 1 *(Harris 77)*
Brentford (1) 2 *(Omigie 39, Asaba 48)* 2752
Bristol R: Collett; Martin, Power (Lockwood), Browning, Clark, Tillson, Hayfield, Gurney (Skinner), Harris, Archer (Parmenter), Cureton.
Brentford: Fernandes; Harvey, Statham, Ashby, Bates, McGhee, Asaba, McPherson, Omigie, Dennis, Taylor.

Cambridge U (0) 0
Colchester U (0) 1 *(Whitton 89)* 1108
Cambridge U: Barrett; Matthew Joseph, Granville, Wanless, Craddock, Raynor (Marc Joseph), Hayes, Hyde, Turner, Richards (Barnwell-Edinboro), Beall.
Colchester U: Emberson; Gregory, Barnes, Locke (Dunne), Greene, Cawley, Fry, Wilkins, Whitton, Taylor, Abrahams.

Gillingham (0) 1 *(Piper 50)*
Cardiff C (0) 2 *(Eckhardt 90, Dale 112)* 1193
Gillingham: Marshall; Humphrey, Ford, Chapman, Thomas (Harris), Manuel, Puttnam, Pennock, Piper, Bailey (Pinnock), Armstrong.
Cardiff C: Mountain; Perry, Philliskirk, Eckhardt, Young, O'Halloran (Bennett), Rodgerson, Middleton, White (Jarman), Dale, Gardner.
aet; Cardiff C won on sudden death.

Luton T (0) 2 *(Davis S 51, Grant 85)*
Leyton Orient (1) 1 *(Ling 27)* 1594
Luton T: Davis K; James (Alexander), Skelton, Waddock (Showler), Davis S, Patterson, Hughes, Linton, Guentchev, Grant, Marshall (Oldfield).
Leyton Orient: Weaver; Hendon, Naylor, Chapman, Warren, Arnott (Inglethorpe), Channing, Ling, McGleish, Joseph, West.

Plymouth Arg (1) 2 *(Illman 36, Wotton 68)*
Bournemouth (0) 0 944
Plymouth Arg: Dungey; Billy, Leadbitter, Wotton, Heathcote, Curran, Illman, Logan, Littlejohn (Phillips) (Richardson), Evans, Barlow.
Bournemouth: Glass; Young, Vincent (Beardsmore), Ferdinand, Cox, Bailey, Holland, Robinson, Murray, Brissett (Town), Rawlinson (Watson).

17 DEC

Brighton & HA (1) 3 *(Maskell 45, McDonald 87 (pen), Virgo 92)*
Fulham (1) 2 *(Cusack 31, Scott 76)* 1310
Brighton & HA: Rust; Smith, Virgo, Parris, Allan, Hobson, Fox S (Johnson), Mayo, Mundee (Andrews), Maskell, McDonald.
Fulham: Walton; Watson, Adams, Cusack, Angus, Cullip, Freeman (Scott), Thomas, Conroy, Morgan (Mison), Brooker (Blake).
aet; Brighton & HA won on sudden death.

SOUTHERN SECTION SECOND ROUND

7 JAN

Brentford (1) 2 *(Forster 22, Taylor 91)*
Barnet (0) 1 *(Samuels 84)* 1455
Brentford: Dearden; Hurdle, Anderson, Ashby, Bates, McGhee, Asaba, Smith, Forster, Omigie (Bent), Taylor.
Barnet: Harrison; Stockley, Campbell, Patterson, Primus, Howarth, Rattray, Simpson, Hodges, Samuels, Pardew.
aet; Brentford won on sudden death.

Millwall (1) 2 *(Crawford 10, Savage 76)*
Colchester U (0) 3 *(Adcock 53, 89, Buckle 93)* 2795
Millwall: Iga; Newman, Harle, Savage, Webber, Rogan (Sinclair), Hartley (Doyle), Wilkins, Crawford (Van Blerk), Bright, Dolby.
Colchester U: Emberson; Gregory, Gibbs, McCarthy, Greene, Buckle, Fry (Locke), Wilkins, Whitton, Adcock, Abrahams.
aet; Colchester U won on sudden death.

Watford (1) 2 *(Page 45, Connolly 57 (pen))*
Torquay U (0) 1 *(Watson 88)* 2298
Watford: Miller; Bazeley, Gibbs, Palmer, Millen, Page, Slater, Connolly, White, Penrice, Mooney.
Torquay U: Wilmot; Mitchell, Barrow, McCall, Gittens, Watson, Hawthorne (Wright), Crane (Preston), Jack, Ndah (Thomas), Stamps.

SOUTHERN SECTION FIRST ROUND

8 JAN

Swansea C (0) 1 *(Thomas 66)*
Wycombe W (0) 1 *(McGorry 73)* 1638
Swansea C: Freestone; Thomas, Moreira, Walker, Edwards, Jones, Brown (Molby), Penney, Torpey, Ampadu, Coates (Clode).
Wycombe W: Cheesewright; Cousins (Lawrence), Bell, Kavanagh (Crossley), McCarthy, Forsyth, McGorry, Davis, De Souza, McGavin, Simpson (Brown).
aet; Swansea C won 6-5 on penalties.

NORTHERN SECTION SECOND ROUND

13 JAN

Bury (1) 6 *(Pugh 28, Carter 47, Johnson 71, Jepson 75 (pen), 85, Daws 89)*
Mansfield T (0) 0 1331
Bury: Kiely; Woodward, Pugh (Randall), Daws, Lucketti, Jackson, Butler, Carter (Johnson), Jepson, Johnrose, Matthews (Rigby).
Mansfield T: Bowling; Ford, Harper, Kilcline, Eustace, Hackett, Sedgemore, Walker, Wood (Hurst), Hadley, Doolan (Clarke).

14 JAN

Blackpool (2) 4 *(Mellon 3, Butler 44, Ellis 61, 83)*
Lincoln C (0) 0 1578
Blackpool: Banks; Bryan, Barlow, Butler, Linighan, Brabin, Dixon (Onwere), Mellon, Quinn (Malkin), Ellis, Preece.
Lincoln C: Richardson; Barnett, Bimson, Dennis (Minett), Brown G, Austin, Ainsworth, Fleming, Stant, Bos (Martin) (Sterling), Alcide.

Shrewsbury T (2) 3 *(Anthrobus 1, Stevens 45, Evans 109 (pen))*
Wigan Ath (0) 2 *(Martinez 59, Jones 77)* 1639
Shrewsbury T: Edwards; Seabury, Dempsey, Reed (Scott), Neilsen, Walton, Brown (Ward), Stevens, Anthrobus, Evans, Berkley.
Wigan Ath: Butler L; Bishop, Johnson (Sharp), Greenall, Pender, Morgan (Biggins), Kilford, Jones, Saville, Butler J (Martinez), Lowe.
aet; Shrewsbury won on sudden death.

SOUTHERN SECTION SECOND ROUND

14 JAN

Cardiff C (0) 1 *(Dale 89)*
Exeter C (0) 1 *(Rowbotham 74)* 793
Cardiff C: Mountain; Perry, Lloyd (White), Eckhardt (Middleton), Baddeley, Young, Fowler, O'Halloran, Dale (Philliskirk), Burton, Gardner.
Exeter C: Fox; Chamberlain (Medlin), Rice, Dailly, Blake, Richardson N, Rowbotham, Richardson J, Flack (Braithwaite), Bailey, Hare.
aet; Exeter C won 4-2 on penalties.

Plymouth Arg (1) 1 *(Wotton 33)*
Brighton & HA (0) 0 1295
Plymouth Arg: Dungey; Rowbotham, Williams, Wotton, Heathcote, Saunders, Corazzin (Billy), Logan, Littlejohn, Evans, Barlow.
Brighton & HA: Ormerod; Smith, Tuck (Mayo), Mundee, Johnson, Hobson, Parris (McGarrigle), Peake, Baird, Maskell, McDonald.

NORTHERN SECTION SECOND ROUND

21 JAN

York C (0) 1 *(Himsworth 65)*
Preston NE (0) 0 1428
York C: Clarke; McMillan, Atkinson (Murty), Pepper, Tutill, Barras, Himsworth, Pouton, Campbell, Cresswell, Stephenson.
Preston NE: O'Hanlon; Cartwright, Kidd, Davey, Wilcox, Squires (Moyes), Atkinson, Bryson, Reeves (Ashcroft), Beckford, McKenna.

SOUTHERN SECTION SECOND ROUND

21 JAN

Peterborough U (0) 2 *(Donowa 41, Heald 67)*
Walsall (0) 0 2274
Peterborough U: Griemink; Willis, Clark, Edwards, Heald, Bodley, Donowa, Payne, Carruthers, Charlery, Morrison.
Walsall: Walker; Ntamark, Daniel, Viveash, Evans, Mountfield, Bradley, Blake, Lightbourne, Wilson, Watson (Hodge).

Swansea C (0) 0
Bristol C (1) 1 *(Owers 2)* 5600
Swansea C: Freestone; Thomas, Moreira (King), Walker, Edwards, Jones, Jenkins (Clode), Penney, Torpey, Chapple, Coates.
Bristol C: Welch; Owers, Barnard, Patterson, Taylor, Hewlett, Bent (Goodridge), Langan, Agostino, Goater (Nugent), Tinnion.

NORTHERN SECTION SECOND ROUND

28 JAN

Carlisle U (2) 4 *(Conway 21, 26, 77, Pounewatchy 65)*
Hull C (0) 0 3716
Carlisle U: Caig; Hopper, Archdeacon, Walling, Varty, Pounewatchy, Peacock (Thomas), Conway, Delap (Smart), Hayward, Aspinall (McAlindon).
Hull C: Carroll; Lowthorpe (Gilbert), Mann, Brien (Mason), Dewhurst (Wilson), Wright, Joyce, Quigley, Darby, Greaves, Gordon.

Scunthorpe U (0) 1 *(Hope 54)*
Notts Co (0) 1 *(Hunt 90)* 1076
Scunthorpe U: Lucas; Housham, Wilson, Laws, Knill (Sertori), Hope, Paterson (Jackson), D'Auria, Baker, Calvo-Garcia (Gavin), Clarkson.
Notts Co: Pollitt; Gallagher, Walker, Rogers, Hogg, Hunt, Galloway, Richardson (Ridgway), Farrell (Wilkes), Martindale, Roddie (Kennedy).
aet; Scunthorpe U won 4-2 on penalties.

Wrexham (0) 0
Crewe Alex (0) 1 *(Murphy 77)*   2216
Wrexham: Marriott; Brace, Hardy (Jones B), Owen, Ridler, Carey, Chalk, Russell, Connolly, Morris (Hughes), Brammer (Gardner).
Crewe Alex: Kearton; Billing, Smith, Westwood, Macauley, Whalley, Charnock, Savage, Adebola, Murphy, Little (Garvey) (Tierney).

SOUTHERN SECTION QUARTER-FINALS

28 JAN

Brentford (0) 0
Colchester U (1) 1 *(Abrahams 33)*   2253
Brentford: Dearden; Hutchings, Statham, Ashby, Bates, McGhee, Asaba, Smith (McPherson), Dennis (Omigie), Bent, Taylor.
Colchester U: Emberson; Gregory, Gibbs, McCarthy, Cawley, Buckle, Fry, Wilkins, Locke, Adcock, Abrahams.

Exeter C (0) 0
Peterborough U (0) 1 *(Donowa 88)*   1478
Exeter C: Bayes; Chamberlain (Medlin), Rice, Hughes, Blake, Richardson N, Rowbotham, Richardson J, Flack, Bailey, Braithwaite.
Peterborough U: Griemink; Boothroyd, Clark, Edwards, Willis, Bodley, Morrison (Griffiths), Payne, Carruthers (Rowe), Charlery, Donowa.

NORTHERN SECTION QUARTER-FINALS

4 FEB

Crewe Alex (1) 1 *(Tierney 21)*
Blackpool (0) 0   3033
Crewe Alex: Kearton; Billing, Unsworth, Westwood, Macauley, Whalley, Charnock, Savage, Tierney, Murphy, Barr.
Blackpool: Banks; Bryan, Barlow (Onwere), Butler, Linighan, Brabin, Darton, Mellon, Quinn (Lydiate), Ellis (Malkin), Preece.

York C (0) 0
Carlisle U (2) 2 *(Thomas 13, Archdeacon 32)*   1922
York C: Warrington; McMillan (Stephenson), Atkinson, Bushell, Sharples, Barras, Murty, Jordan, Campbell (Harrison), Rush (Tolson), Himsworth.
Carlisle U: Caig; Edmondson, Archdeacon, Walling, Varty, Pounewatchy, Thomas, Conway (Prokas), Smart (Jansen), Hayward, Delap.

NORTHERN SECTION SECOND ROUND

4 FEB

Burnley (0) 0
Stockport Co (1) 1 *(Nash 18)*   4251
Burnley: Beresford; Huxford, Eyres, Thompson, Swan, Brass, Matthew (Winstanley), Smith, Robinson (Carr-Lawton), Weller, Gleghorn.
Stockport Co: Edwards; Todd, Searle, Dinning, Bound, Gannon, Durkan, Kiko (Bennett), Mike (Connolly), Mutch, Nash (Jones L).

SOUTHERN SECTION SECOND ROUND

4 FEB

Northampton T (0) 1 *(Rush 89)*
Luton T (0) 0   4201
Northampton T: Woodman; Clarkson, Maddison, Sampson (O'Shea), Martin (Peer), Rennie, Frain, Grayson, Lee, Rush, Warner (Colkin).
Luton T: Feuer; Patterson, Thomas, Evers, Davis S, Johnson, Hughes, Alexander, Grant, Marshall (Fotiadis), Guentchev (Oldfield).

NORTHERN SECTION QUARTER-FINAL

11 FEB

Bury (1) 1 *(Butler 32)*
Stockport Co (1) 2 *(Dinning 9 (Pen), Angell 99)*   2497
Bury: Kiely; West, O'Kane, Daws (Randall), Lucketti, Jackson, Butler, Carter, Johnson, Johnrose (Armstrong), Matthews.
Stockport Co: Edwards; Connelly, Todd, Bennett, Flynn, Gannon, Cavaco, Dinning, Angell, Mutch (Mike), Nash (Durkan).
aet; Stockport Co won on sudden death.

Shrewsbury T (1) 2 *(Berkley 14, Evans 100 (pen))*
Scunthorpe U (0) 1 *(Hope 88)*   1728
Shrewsbury T: Gall; Scott, Dempsey, Whiston, Nielsen, Walton, Brown (Taylor M), Stevens, Spink, Evans, Berkley (Anthrobus).
Scunthorpe U: Lucas; Walsh, Wilson, Sertori, Knill, Hope, Housham, Laws (D'Auria), Baker, Eyre, Gavin.
aet; Shrewsbury T won on sudden death.

SOUTHERN SECTION QUARTER-FINAL

11 FEB

Plymouth Arg (0) 0
Northampton T (1) 2 *(Martin 33, Gayle 48)*   1499
Plymouth Arg: Dungey; Billy (Rowbotham), Williams, Mauge, Heathcote, James, Corazzin (Illman), Logan, Littlejohn, Evans, Barlow.
Northampton T: Woodman; Clarkson, Frain, Sampson, Warburton, Martin (Maddison), Peer, Grayson, Gayle, White (Warner), O'Shea.

Watford (1) 2 *(Andrews 36, Bazeley 87 (pen))*
Bristol C (1) 1 *(Goater 23)*   3142
Watford: Miller; Gibbs, Ludden, Easton, Palmer, Page, Bazeley, Scott, Andrews (Phillips), Johnson R, Robinson.
Bristol C: Naylor; Owers, Barnard, Edwards, Taylor, Hewlett, Bent, Allen, Agostino, Goater, Tinnion (Goodridge).

NORTHERN SECTION SEMI-FINALS

18 FEB

Shrewsbury T (0) 1 *(Evans 67)*
Carlisle U (0) 2 *(Walling 60, Archdeacon 65 (pen))*   2774
Shrewsbury T: Gall; Whiston, Dempsey, Taylor M, Spink, Walton, Brown, Wrack, Anthrobus, Evans, Berkley (Ward).
Carlisle U: Caig; Delap, Archdeacon, Walling, Varty, Pounewatchy, Hopper, Peacock, Smart (Thomas), Hayward, Aspinall (Prokas).

SOUTHERN SECTION SEMI-FINALS

18 FEB

Colchester U (0) 2 *(Greene 66, Buckle 75)*
Northampton T (0) 1 *(Martin 67)*   3795
Colchester U: Vaughan; Gregory, Gibbs, McCarthy, Greene, Buckle, Fry (Cawley), Wilkins, Locke, Adcock, Abrahams (Lock).
Northampton T: Woodman; Clarkson, Maddison (Colkin), Hunter, Warburton, Sampson, Martin (White), Rennie, Gayle, Lee, Frain.

Watford (0) 0
Peterborough U (0) 1 *(Otto 49)*   4941
Watford: Miller; Gibbs, Ludden, Easton, Palmer, Page, Bazeley, Scott, Andrews (Phillips), Johnson R, Robinson (Penrice).
Peterborough U: Griemink; Boothroyd, Clark, Edwards, Heald, Le Bihan, Donowa, Payne, Willis, Charlery, Otto.

NORTHERN SECTION SEMI-FINAL

4 MAR

Crewe Alex (1) 1 *(Murphy 24)*
Stockport Co (1) 1 *(Marsden 41)*   3529
Crewe Alex: Kearton; Billing (Smith S), Unsworth, Westwood, Lightfoot, Whalley, Garvey, Savage, Charnock, Murphy, Barr (Rivers).
Stockport Co: Jones; Connelly, Todd, Bennett, Flynn, Dinning, Durkan (Cavaco), Marsden, Angell (Mutch), Armstrong, Jeffers.
aet; Stockport Co won 5-3 on penalties.

SOUTHERN FINAL FIRST LEG

11 MAR

Peterborough U (2) 2 *(Otto 14, Charlery 35)*
Colchester U (0) 0   4556
Peterborough U: Tyler; Boothroyd, Spearing, Edwards, Bodley, Ramage (Le Bihan), Donowa (Morrison), Payne, Willis, Charlery, Otto.
Colchester U: Emberson; Gregory, Dunne, McCarthy, Greene, Buckle, Fry (Sale), Locke, Whitton, Adcock, Duguid (Gibbs).

NORTHERN FINAL FIRST LEG

18 MAR

Carlisle U (0) 2 *(Archdeacon 55, 90 (pen))*
Stockport Co (0) 0   7057
Carlisle U: Caig; Delap, Archdeacon, Walling, Varty, Pounewatchy, Freestone, Conway, Smart (Peacock), Hayward, Aspinall.
Stockport Co: Jones; Connelly, Todd, Bennett, Flynn, Dinning, Cavaco (Durkan), Marsden, Mutch, Armstrong (Angell), Jeffers.

SOUTHERN FINAL SECOND LEG

18 MAR

Colchester U (1) 3 *(Fry 38, Buckle 80, Abrahams 100)*
Peterborough U (0) 0   5000
Colchester U: Emberson; Gregory, Gibbs (Abrahams), McCarthy, Greene, Buckle, Fry, Wilkins, Whitton (Locke), Adcock, Sale.
Peterborough U: Griemink; Boothroyd, Spearing, Edwards, Heald, Bodley, Le Bihan (Donowa), Payne, Willis, Charlery, Cleaver (Houghton).
aet; Colchester U won on sudden death.

NORTHERN FINAL SECOND LEG

25 MAR

Stockport Co (0) 0
Carlisle U (0) 0   8593
Stockport Co: Jones; Connelly, Todd, Bennett, Flynn, Gannon, Durkan (Cavaco), Marsden, Angell (Mutch), Armstrong, Cooper (Cowans).
Carlisle U: Caig; Delap, Archdeacon, Walling, Varty, Pounewatchy, Peacock, Prokas (Hopper), Freestone (Thomas), Hayward, Aspinall (Jansen).

FINAL (AT WEMBLEY)

20 APR

Carlisle U (0) 0
Colchester U (0) 0   45,077
Carlisle U: Caig; Delap, Archdeacon, Whalley, Varty, Pounewatchy, Conway, Peacock, Smart (Thomas) (Jansen), Hayward, Aspinall.
Colchester U: Emberson; Gibbs (Fry), Dunne, Gregory (Locke), Greene, Cawley, Sale, Wilkins, Whitton, Adcock, Abrahams (Duguid).
aet; Carlisle U won 4-3 on penalties.
Referee: J. Kirkby (Sheffield).

FA CUP FINALS 1872–1997

1872 and 1874–92	Kennington Oval	1911	Replay at Old Trafford
1873	Lillie Bridge	1912	Replay at Bramall Lane
1886	Replay at Derby (Racecourse Ground)		
1893	Fallowfield, Manchester	1915	Old Trafford, Manchester
1894	Everton	1920–22	Stamford Bridge
1895–1914	Crystal Palace	1923 to date	Wembley
1901	Replay at Bolton	1970	Replay at Old Trafford
1910	Replay at Everton		

Year	Winners	Runners-up	Score
1872	Wanderers	Royal Engineers	1-0
1873	Wanderers	Oxford University	2-0
1874	Oxford University	Royal Engineers	2-0
1875	Royal Engineers	Old Etonians	2-0 (after 1-1 draw aet)
1876	Wanderers	Old Etonians	3-0 (after 1-1 draw aet)
1877	Wanderers	Oxford University	2-1 (aet)
1878	Wanderers*	Royal Engineers	3-1
1879	Old Etonians	Clapham R	1-0
1880	Clapham R	Oxford University	1-0
1881	Old Carthusians	Old Etonians	3-0
1882	Old Etonians	Blackburn R	1-0
1883	Blackburn Olympic	Old Etonians	2-1 (aet)
1884	Blackburn R	Queen's Park, Glasgow	2-1
1885	Blackburn R	Queen's Park, Glasgow	2-0
1886	Blackburn R†	WBA	2-0 (after 0-0 draw)
1887	Aston Villa	WBA	2-0
1888	WBA	Preston NE	2-1
1889	Preston NE	Wolverhampton W	3-0
1890	Blackburn R	Sheffield W	6-1
1891	Blackburn R	Notts Co	3-1
1892	WBA	Aston Villa	3-0
1893	Wolverhampton W	Everton	1-0
1894	Notts Co	Bolton W	4-1
1895	Aston Villa	WBA	1-0
1896	Sheffield W	Wolverhampton W	2-1
1897	Aston Villa	Everton	3-2
1898	Nottingham F	Derby Co	3-1
1899	Sheffield U	Derby Co	4-1
1900	Bury	Southampton	4-0
1901	Tottenham H	Sheffield U	3-1 (after 2-2 draw)
1902	Sheffield U	Southampton	2-1 (after 1-1 draw)
1903	Bury	Derby Co	6-0
1904	Manchester C	Bolton W	1-0
1905	Aston Villa	Newcastle U	2-0
1906	Everton	Newcastle U	1-0
1907	Sheffield W	Everton	2-1
1908	Wolverhampton W	Newcastle U	3-1
1909	Manchester U	Bristol C	1-0
1910	Newcastle U	Barnsley	2-0 (after 1-1 draw)
1911	Bradford C	Newcastle U	1-0 (after 0-0 draw)
1912	Barnsley	WBA	1-0 (aet, after 0-0 draw)
1913	Aston Villa	Sunderland	1-0
1914	Burnley	Liverpool	1-0
1915	Sheffield U	Chelsea	3-0
1920	Aston Villa	Huddersfield T	1-0 (aet)
1921	Tottenham H	Wolverhampton W	1-0
1922	Huddersfield T	Preston NE	1-0
1923	Bolton W	West Ham U	2-0
1924	Newcastle U	Aston Villa	2-0
1925	Sheffield U	Cardiff C	1-0
1926	Bolton W	Manchester C	1-0
1927	Cardiff C	Arsenal	1-0
1928	Blackburn R	Huddersfield T	3-1
1929	Bolton W	Portsmouth	2-0
1930	Arsenal	Huddersfield T	2-0
1931	WBA	Birmingham	2-1
1932	Newcastle U	Arsenal	2-1
1933	Everton	Manchester C	3-0
1934	Manchester C	Portsmouth	2-1
1935	Sheffield W	WBA	4-2
1936	Arsenal	Sheffield U	1-0
1937	Sunderland	Preston NE	3-1
1938	Preston NE	Huddersfield T	1-0 (aet)
1939	Portsmouth	Wolverhampton W	4-1
1946	Derby Co	Charlton Ath	4-1 (aet)
1947	Charlton Ath	Burnley	1-0 (aet)
1948	Manchester U	Blackpool	4-2
1949	Wolverhampton W	Leicester C	3-1
1950	Arsenal	Liverpool	2-0
1951	Newcastle U	Blackpool	2-0
1952	Newcastle U	Arsenal	1-0

Year	Winners	Runners-up	Score
1953	Blackpool	Bolton W	4-3
1954	WBA	Preston NE	3-2
1955	Newcastle U	Manchester C	3-1
1956	Manchester C	Birmingham C	3-1
1957	Aston Villa	Manchester U	2-1
1958	Bolton W	Manchester U	2-0
1959	Nottingham F	Luton T	2-1
1960	Wolverhampton W	Blackburn R	3-0
1961	Tottenham H	Leicester C	2-0
1962	Tottenham H	Burnley	3-1
1963	Manchester U	Leicester C	3-1
1964	West Ham U	Preston NE	3-2
1965	Liverpool	Leeds U	2-1 (aet)
1966	Everton	Sheffield W	3-2
1967	Tottenham H	Chelsea	2-1
1968	WBA	Everton	1-0 (aet)
1969	Manchester C	Leicester C	1-0
1970	Chelsea	Leeds U	2-1 (aet)
	(after 2-2 draw, after extra time, at Wembley)		
1971	Arsenal	Liverpool	2-1 (aet)
1972	Leeds U	Arsenal	1-0
1973	Sunderland	Leeds U	1-0
1974	Liverpool	Newcastle U	3-0
1975	West Ham U	Fulham	2-0
1976	Southampton	Manchester U	1-0
1977	Manchester U	Liverpool	2-1
1978	Ipswich T	Arsenal	1-0
1979	Arsenal	Manchester U	3-2
1980	West Ham U	Arsenal	1-0
1981	Tottenham H	Manchester C	3-2
	(after 1-1 draw, after extra time, at Wembley)		
1982	Tottenham H	QPR	1-0
	(after 1-1 draw, after extra time, at Wembley)		
1983	Manchester U	Brighton & HA	4-0
	(after 2-2 draw, after extra time, at Wembley)		
1984	Everton	Watford	2-0
1985	Manchester U	Everton	1-0 (aet)
1986	Liverpool	Everton	3-1
1987	Coventry C	Tottenham H	3-2 (aet)
1988	Wimbledon	Liverpool	1-0
1989	Liverpool	Everton	3-2 (aet)
1990	Manchester U	Crystal Palace	1-0
	(after 3-3 draw, after extra time, at Wembley)		
1991	Tottenham H	Nottingham F	2-1 (aet)
1992	Liverpool	Sunderland	2-0
1993	Arsenal	Sheffield W	2-1 (aet)
	(after 1-1 draw, after extra time, at Wembley)		
1994	Manchester U	Chelsea	4-0
1995	Everton	Manchester U	1-0
1996	Manchester U	Liverpool	1-0
1997	Chelsea	Middlesbrough	2-0

* *Won outright, but restored to the Football Association.*
† *A special trophy was awarded for third consecutive win.*

FA CUP WINS

Manchester U 9, Tottenham H 8, Aston Villa 7, Arsenal 6, Blackburn R 6, Newcastle U 6, Everton 5, Liverpool 5, The Wanderers 5, WBA 5, Bolton W 4, Manchester C 4, Sheffield U 4, Wolverhampton W 4, Sheffield W 3, West Ham U 3, Bury 2, Chelsea 2, Nottingham F 2, Old Etonians 2, Preston NE 2, Sunderland 2, Barnsley 1, Blackburn Olympic 1, Blackpool 1, Bradford C 1, Burnley 1, Cardiff C 1, Charlton Ath 1, Clapham R 1, Coventry C 1, Derby Co 1, Huddersfield T 1, Ipswich T 1, Leeds U 1, Notts Co 1, Old Carthusians 1, Oxford University 1, Portsmouth 1, Royal Engineers 1, Southampton 1, Wimbledon 1.

APPEARANCES IN FINALS

Manchester U 14, Arsenal 12, Everton 12, Liverpool 11, Newcastle U 11, WBA 10, Aston Villa 9, Tottenham H 9, Blackburn R 8, Manchester C 8, Wolverhampton W 8, Bolton W 7, Preston NE 7, Old Etonians 6, Sheffield U 6, Sheffield W 6, Chelsea 5, Huddersfield T 5, *The Wanderers 5, Derby Co 4, Leeds U 4, Leicester C 4, Oxford University 4, Royal Engineers 4, Sunderland 4, West Ham U 4, Blackpool 3, Burnley 3, Nottingham F 3, Portsmouth 3, Southampton 3, Barnsley 2, Birmingham C 2, *Bury 2, Cardiff C 2, Charlton Ath 2, Clapham R 2, Notts Co 2, Queen's Park (Glasgow) 2, *Blackburn Olympic 1, *Bradford C 1, Brighton & HA 1, Bristol C 1, *Coventry C 1, Crystal Palace 1, Fulham 1, *Ipswich T 1, Luton T 4, Middlesbrough 1, *Old Carthusians 1, QPR 1, Watford 1, *Wimbledon 1.
 * *Denotes undefeated.*

APPEARANCES IN SEMI-FINALS

Everton 23, Manchester U 21, Liverpool 20, WBA 19, Arsenal 18, Aston Villa 18, Blackburn R 16, Sheffield W 16, Tottenham H 15, Chelsea 13, Derby Co 13, Newcastle U 13, Wolverhampton W 13, Bolton W 12, Nottingham F 12, Sheffield U 11, Sunderland 11, Manchester C 10, Preston NE 10, Southampton 10, Birmingham C 9, Burnley 8, Leeds U 8, Leicester C 8, Huddersfield T 7, Old Etonians 6, Oxford University 5, West Ham U 6, Fulham 5, Notts Co 5, Portsmouth 5, The Wanderers 5, Luton T 4, Queen's Park (Glasgow) 4, Royal Engineers 4, Blackpool 3, Cardiff C 3, Clapham R 3, Crystal Palace (professional club) 3, Ipswich T 3, Millwall 3, Norwich C 3, Old Carthusians 3, Oldham Ath 3, Stoke C 3, The Swifts 3, Watford 3, Barnsley 2, Blackburn Olympic 2, Bristol C 2, Bury 2, Charlton Ath 2, Grimsby T 2, Swansea T 2, Swindon T 2, Wimbledon 2, Bradford C 1, Brighton & HA 1, Cambridge University 1, Chesterfield 1, Coventry C 1, Crewe Alex 1, Crystal Palace (amateur club) 1, Darwen 1, Derby Junction 1, Glasgow R 1, Hull C 1, Marlow 1, Old Harrovians 1, Middlesbrough 1, Orient 1, Plymouth Arg 1, Port Vale 1, QPR 1, Reading 1, Shropshire W 1, York C 1.

FA CUP 1996–97
SPONSORED BY LITTLEWOODS POOLS

PRELIMINARY AND QUALIFYING ROUNDS

Preliminary Round

Workington v Worksop Town	1-0
Ossett Town v Armthorpe Welfare	3-1
Eastwood Hanley v Crook Town	0-1
St Helens Town v Peterlee Newtown	2-2, 2-1
Hebburn v Dunston FB	0-5
Harrogate Town v Whitley Bay	6-0
Pontefract Collieries v Pickering Town	1-2
Alnwick Town v Consett	0-0, 0-2
Esh Winning v Oldham Town	1-3
Northallerton v Morpeth Town	0-1
Flixton v RTM Newcastle	4-1
Blackpool (Wren) Rovers v Hucknall Town	1-2
Bootle v Seaham Red Star	2-0
Brandon United v Tadcaster Albion	3-1
Ryhope CA v Arnold Town	1-2
Netherfield v Shildon	3-0
Ossett Albion v Brigg Town	2-1
Nantwich Town v South Shields	5-0
Ferryhill Athletic v Yorkshire Amateur	1-2
(at Chester-le-Street Town FC)	
Harrogate Railway v Stockton	5-2
Willington v Borrowash Victoria	2-1
Ashington v Ashfield United	4-5
Newcastle Town v Denaby United	1-0
Murton v Congleton Town	1-0
Washington v Bridgnorth Town	0-0, 1-2
Eccleshill United v Hallam	2-1
Trafford v Clitheroe	2-1
Glasshoughton Welfare v Matlock Town	1-2
Shotton Comrades v Garforth Town	0-4
Cheadle Town v Burscough	0-0, 0-2
Whitby Town v Whickham	6-2
Hatfield Main v Farsley Celtic	0-0, 1-2
Droylsden v Stocksbridge Park Steels	1-5
Thackley v Selby Town	0-4
Kidsgrove Athletic v Chester-Le-Street Town	0-3
Rossendale United v Castleton Gabriels	1-1, 4-2
Louth United v Guisborough Town	2-2, 1-4
Heanor Town v Sheffield	3-4
Horden CW v Atherton Collieries	0-4
Shifnal Town v Chadderton	1-2
Belper Town v Leigh RMI	1-1, 1-3
Harworth CI v Blidworth MW	0-0, 2-2, 1-2
Evenwood Town v Darwen	3-1
Stapenhill v Salford City	3-0
Liversedge v Atherton LR	0-0, 2-2, 2-2, 1-3
Kimberley Town v Rossington Main	1-1, 0-3
Prudhoe Town v Maine Road	1-1, 2-1
Blakenall v Glossop North End	3-0
North Ferriby United v Great Harwood Town	4-0
Bedworth United v Paget Rangers	2-2, 2-1
Wellingborough Town v Cogenhoe United	0-3
Banbury United v VS Rugby	0-1
Rocester v Bolehall Swifts	5-1
Halesowen Harriers v Long Buckby	2-2, 1-1, 2-1
Stafford Rangers v Redditch United	1-1, 1-0
Chasetown v Boldmere St Michaels	2-0
Barwell v Bilston Town	0-2
West Midlands Police v Westfields	1-2
Lye Town v Desborough Town	0-4
(at Desborough Town FC)	
Dudley Town v Tamworth	1-3
Rushall Olympic v Pelsall Villa	1-3
Willenhall Town v Hinckley Town	1-0
Newport Pagnell Town v Wednesfield	0-1
Northampton Spencer v Oldbury United	1-0
Stourport Swifts v Pershore Town	0-4
Stratford Town v Shepshed Dynamo	0-2
Knypersley Victoria v Stewarts & Lloyds	4-0
(at Stoke City FC)	
Sutton Coldfield Town v Moor Green	0-0, 2-3
Rothwell Town v Bourne Town	5-1
Watton United v Bedford Town	1-4

Wingate & Finchley v Spalding United	0-1
Fakenham Town v Maldon Town	2-2, 0-2
(at Maldon Town FC)	
Burnham Ramblers v Great Yarmouth Town	1-1, 1-3
Witham Town v Grantham Town	2-5
Tilbury v Diss Town	1-1, 0-1
Lowestoft Town v Boston Town	1-2
Wroxham v Great Wakering Rovers	2-2, 1-0
Haverhill Rovers v Holbeach United	5-1
Wivenhoe Town v Raunds Town	2-2, 0-3
March Town United v Barkingside	2-1
East Thurrock United v Mirrlees Blackstone	4-2
Bury Town v Milton Keynes	4-1
Saffron Walden Town v Newmarket Town	2-2, 0-0
(abandoned at half time 0-0 due to serious injury to a	
Newmarket player)	0-3
Corby Town v Eynesbury Rovers	5-1
Harringey Borough v Hornchurch	0-3
Soham Town Rangers v Stamford AFC	0-2
Cornard United v Gorleston	0-2
Basildon United v Woodbridge Town	0-2
Leyton Pennant v Collier Row & Romford	0-0, 0-1
Tiptree United v Hadleigh United	1-0
Harefield United v Halstead Town	2-4
Arlesey Town v Potton United	3-1
Southend Manor v Braintree Town	0-5
Berkhamsted Town v Chesham United	2-3
Ruislip Manor v Clacton Town	1-1, 2-3
Concord Rangers v Barking	2-2, 0-1
Hoddesdon Town v Stotfold	0-1
(at Ware FC)	
Potters Bar Town v Cheshunt	5-1
Uxbridge v Leighton Town	2-1
Hillingdon Borough v Stowmarket Town	1-4
Felixstowe Port & Town v Clapton	0-1
Langford v Brackley Town	0-4
Royston Town v Southall	1-0
Edgware Town v Flackwell Heath	1-1, 1-1, 3-0
Brimsdown Rovers v Tring Town	1-3
Ford United v Harwich & Parkeston	1-0
Welwyn Garden City v Wootton Blue Cross	2-0
Erith & Belvedere v Kingsbury Town	2-2, 1-0
Hemel Hempstead v Ware	1-0
Bowers United v Hanwell Town	2-1
Stansted v Aveley	2-1
Biggleswade Town v London Colney	0-1
Sheppey United v Harlow Town	1-2
Margate v Banstead Athletic	0-1
Bedfont v Tunbridge Wells	1-2
Peacehaven & Telscombe v Dorking	5-0
Portfield v Three Bridges	1-3
Selsey v Thamesmead Town	3-1
Dartford v Horsham	1-1, 0-1
Ashford Town (Middlesex) v Slade Green	2-0
Shoreham v Wealdstone	0-1
Southwick v Oakwood	0-0, 2-1
Wick v Herne Bay	0-2
Worthing v Fisher 93	0-1
Merstham v Deal Town	3-2
Langney Sports v Chalfont St Peter	1-3
Mile Oak v Lancing	5-1
Croydon Athletic v Lewes	2-0
Tonbridge v Leatherhead	1-0
Raynes Park Vale v Burnham	1-4
Pagham v Northwood	1-4
Ringmer v Steyning Town	7-0
Whitehawk v Whitstable Town	1-6
St Leonards Stamcroft v Metropolitan Police	2-0
Viking Sports v Corinthian	2-0
Arundel v Canterbury City	3-0
Hailsham Town v Redhill	2-2, 1-2
Hassocks v Egham Town	1-3
Whyteleafe v Chatham Town	3-3, 0-2
Corinthian-Casuals v Chipstead	1-1, 4-2

Burgess Hill Town v Epsom & Ewell	4-1
Horsham YMCA v Littlehampton Town	6-1
East Grinstead v Folkestone Invicta	2-3
Wimborne Town v Andover	1-1, 1-0
Eastleigh v Hungerford Town	0-3
Cove v Ash United	1-0
Wokingham Town v Fareham Town	0-0, 1-4
Thatcham Town v Brockenhurst	2-0
Lymington AFC v Windsor & Eton	6-1
(at Brockenhurst FC)	
Bemerton Heath Harlequins v Bicester Town	2-0
Maidenhead United v Havant Town	0-1
Fleet Town v Waterlooville	2-0
Godalming & Guildford v Carterton Town	5-2
Bournemouth v Abingdon Town	1-3
Gosport Borough v Ryde	2-1
Portsmouth Royal Navy v Camberley Town	1-6
Cirencester Town v Yate Town	1-0
Mangotsfield United v Chippenham Town	6-1
Falmouth Town v Barnstaple Town	3-0
Devizes Town v Westbury United	2-0
Melksham Town v Bridgwater Town	2-1
Weston-Super-Mare v Brislington	2-0
Torrington v Paulton Rovers	3-0
Endsleigh v Bristol Manor Farm	0-3
St Blazey v Minehead	2-0
Glastonbury v Calne Town	2-4
Welton Rovers v Saltash United	3-2
Frome Town v Elmore	3-0
Tuffley Rovers v Taunton Town	2-5
Bridport v Clevedon Town	0-1

First Qualifying Round

St Helens Town v Gateshead	0-0, 1-5
Billingham Town v Dunston FB	2-0
Workington v Crook Town	3-1
Buxton v Ossett Town	1-2
Oldham Town v Halifax Town	2-3
Durham City v Morpeth Town	5-1
Harrogate Town v Consett	0-1
Bishop Auckland v Pickering Town	3-1
Brandon United v Morecambe	0-6
Gretna v Arnold Town	1-1, 0-3
Flixton v Bootle	2-0
Guiseley v Hucknall Town	4-0
Yorkshire Amateur v Stalybridge Celtic	0-1
Ashton United v Harrogate Railway	3-0
Netherfield v Nantwich Town	3-1
Accrington Stanley v Ossett Albion	1-1, 1-2
Merton v Frickley Athletic	1-3
Easington Colliery v Winsford United	2-7
Willington v Newcastle Town	1-3
Bradford (Park Avenue) v Ashfield United	1-0
Matlock Town v Leek Town	1-0
Tow Law Town v Gainsborough Trinity	1-1, 0-2
Bridgnorth Town v Trafford	2-1
Eastwood Town v Eccleshill United	1-0
Farsley Celtic v Knowsley United	1-0
Warrington Town v Hyde United	0-1
Garforth Town v Whitby Town	1-3
Mossley v Burscough	3-1
Rossendale United v Southport	0-5
Burton Albion v Guisborough Town	1-0
Stocksbridge Park Steels v Chester-Le-Street Town	4-2
Emley v Selby Town	3-0
Leigh RMI v Alfreton Town	2-0
Radcliffe Borough v Marine	0-2
Sheffield v Chadderton	2-1
Billingham Synthonia v Atherton Collieries	1-0
Atherton LR v Ilkeston Town	1-0
West Auckland Town v Bamber Bridge	1-3
Blidworth MW v Stapenhill	0-1
Curzon Ashton v Evenwood Town	1-0
North Ferriby United v Chorley	4-1
Lincoln United v Lancaster City	2-2, 2-3
Rossington Main v Blakenall	1-2
Bedlington Terriers v Prudhoe Town	4-0
Rocester v Kettering Town	0-3
Hinckley Athletic v Halesowen Harriers	5-1
Bedworth United v VS Rugby	3-3, 3-0
Atherstone United v Cogenhoe United	3-1
Westfields v Rushden & Diamonds	0-4
Leicester United withdrew v Desborough Town w.o.	
Stafford Rangers v Bilston Town	0-1
Gresley Rovers v Chasetown	2-1

Wednesfield v Hednesford Town	0-0, 0-6
Racing Club Warwick v Northampton Spencer	1-1, 2-2, 5-1
Tamworth v Willenhall Town	4-1
Evesham United v Pelsall Villa	4-0
Moor Green v Solihull Borough	1-2
Stourbridge v Halesowen Town	1-0
Pershore Town v Knypersley Victoria	1-2
Sandwell Borough v Shepshed Dynamo	0-0, 2-5
Maldon Town v Boston United	2-7
Sudbury Wanderers v Great Yarmouth Town	1-1, 1-0
Rothwell Town v Spalding United	2-3
Bishops Stortford v Bedford Town	2-0
Wroxham v Kings Lynn	3-2
Canvey Island v Haverhill Rovers	3-1
Grantham Town v Boston Town	2-0
Cambridge City v Diss Town	6-1
Bury Town v Heybridge Swifts	0-0, 0-3
Wisbech Town v Newmarket Town	2-1
Raunds Town v East Thurrock United	2-4
Chelmsford City v March Town United	5-0
Gorleston v Sudbury Town	1-2
Billericay Town v Woodbridge Town	4-0
Corby Town v Stamford AFC	4-1
Purfleet v Hornchurch	5-1
Arlesey Town v Stevenage Borough	0-3
(at Hitchin Town FC)	
Marlow v Braintree Town	0-2
Collier Row & Romford v Halstead Town	1-1, 0-4
Baldock Town v Tiptree United	2-0
Stotfold v Hayes	0-2
Hertford Town v Potters Bar Town	1-2
Chesham United v Barking	3-1
Grays Athletic v Clacton Town	6-0
Brackley Town v Dagenham & Redbridge	1-1, 0-1
Wembley v Royston Town	0-2
Uxbridge v Clapton	5-1
Harrow Borough v Stowmarket Town	4-1
Welwyn Garden City v Aylesbury United	1-4
Barton Rovers v Erith & Belvedere	2-2, 2-1
Edgware Town v Ford United	3-3, 3-2
Boreham Wood v Tring Town	8-1
London Colney v St Albans City	0-0, 1-4
(at St Albans City)	
Hampton v Harlow Town	2-1
Hemel Hempstead v Stansted	0-1
Yeading v Bowers United	6-0
Three Bridges v Farnborough Town	1-6
Bracknell Town v Selsey	4-2
Banstead Athletic v Peacehaven & Telscombe	1-3
Carshalton Athletic v Tunbridge Wells	6-0
Southwick v Welling United	1-2
Walton & Hersham v Herne Bay	1-1, 0-1
Horsham v Wealdstone	1-0
Dulwich Hamlet v Ashford Town (Middlesex)	2-0
Mile Oak v Dover Athletic	0-3
(at Shoreham FC)	
Hendon v Croydon Athletic	2-0
Fisher Athletic v Chalfont St Peter	3-2
Aldershot Town v Merstham	8-1
Ringmer v Chertsey Town	1-2
Molesey v Whitstable Town	3-1
Tonbridge v Northwood	2-0
Hastings Town v Burnham	2-0
Redhill v Crawley Town	0-1
Croydon v Egham Town	3-1
St Leonards Stamcroft v Arundel	4-1
Bromley v Viking Sports	4-0
Horsham YMCA v Sittingbourne	2-3
Staines Town v Folkestone Invicta	2-0
Chatham Town v Burgess Hill Town	1-2
Tooting & Mitcham United v Corinthian-Casuals	5-0
Fareham Town v Worcester City	2-1
Witney Town v Oxford City	1-1, 3-2
Wimborne Town v Cove	5-0
Buckingham Town v Hungerford Town	3-6
Havant Town v Bashley	0-3
Basingstoke Town v Gloucester City	0-3
Thatcham Town v Bemerton Heath Harlequins	1-1, 3-2
Thame United v Lymington AFC	1-1, 1-1, 3-1
Gosport Borough v Cheltenham Town	0-1
Weymouth v Camberley Town	2-0
Fleet Town v Abingdon Town	0-3
Salisbury City v Godalming & Guildford	0-0, 2-0
Devizes Town v Bath City	2-2, 1-3
Bideford v Melksham Town	2-6

596 *Rothmans Football Yearbook 1997–98*

Cirencester Town v Falmouth Town	2-0
Newport AFC v Mangotsfield United	5-2
St Blazey v Merthyr Tydfil	0-7
Trowbridge Town v Calne Town	3-0
Weston-Super-Mare v Bristol Manor Farm	4-0
Forest Green Rovers v Torrington	4-5
Clevedon Town v Dorchester Town	4-1
Backwell United v Yeovil Town	0-6
(at Yeovil Town FC)	
Welton Rovers v Taunton Town	0-6
Tiverton Town v Frome Town	3-0

Second Qualifying Round

Billingham Town v Workington	0-1
Gateshead v Ossett Town	5-1
Durham City v Consett	1-1
(Tie awarded to Consett; Durham City fielded an ineligible player)	
Halifax Town v Bishop Auckland	1-4
Arnold Town v Flixton	0-0, 0-2
Morecambe v Guiseley	4-1
Ashton United v Netherfield	2-0
Stalybridge Celtic v Ossett Albion	4-1
Winsford United v Newcastle Town	0-1
Frickley Athletic v Bradford (Park Avenue)	1-0
Gainsborough Trinity v Bridgnorth Town	2-1
Leek Town v Eastwood Town	1-0
Hyde United v Whitby Town	0-1
Farsley Celtic v Mossley	3-1
Burton Albion v Stocksbridge Park Steels	2-1
Southport v Emley	1-1, 3-2
Marine v Sheffield	1-0
Leigh RMI v Billingham Synthonia	1-1, 3-2
Bamber Bridge v Stapenhill	5-3
Atherton LR v Curzon Ashton	3-2
Lancaster City v Blakenall	6-0
North Ferriby United v Bedlington Terriers	1-0
Hinckley Athletic v Bedworth United	1-1, 1-3
Kettering Town v Atherstone United	0-0, 6-1
Desborough Town v Bilston Town	2-2, 2-5
Rushden & Diamonds v Gresley Rovers	4-0
Racing Club Warwick v Tamworth	0-5
Hednesford Town v Evesham United	6-1
Stourbridge v Knypersley Victoria	0-0, 0-1
Solihull Borough v Shepshed Dynamo	1-1, 0-1
Sudbury Wanderers v Spalding United	3-2
Boston United v Bishops Stortford	3-0
Canvey Island v Grantham Town	1-1, 1-0
Wroxham v Cambridge City	1-1, 0-2
Wisbech Town v East Thurrock United	2-1
Heybridge Swifts v Chelmsford City	1-1, 1-2
Billericay Town v Corby Town	0-0, 1-1, 1-3
Sudbury Town v Purfleet	2-1
Braintree Town v Halstead Town	3-1
Stevenage Borough v Baldock Town	1-1, 2-1
Potters Bar Town v Chesham United	0-4
(at Boreham Wood FC)	
Hayes v Grays Athletic	1-1, 0-0, 2-0
Royston Town v Uxbridge	0-5
Dagenham & Redbridge v Harrow Borough	0-0, 2-0
Barton Rovers v Edgware Town	1-2
Aylesbury United v Boreham Wood	0-3
Hampton v Stansted	2-2, 1-2
St Albans City v Yeading	1-1, 1-0
Bracknell Town v Peacehaven & Telscombe	5-2
Farnborough Town v Carshalton Athletic	3-2
Herne Bay v Horsham	1-0
Welling United v Dulwich Hamlet	2-1
Hendon v Fisher Athletic	0-0, 1-0
Dover Athletic v Aldershot Town	2-0
Molesey v Tonbridge	0-0, 2-1
Chertsey Town v Hastings Town	2-3
Croydon v St Leonards Stamcroft	0-7
Crawley Town v Bromley	0-4
Staines Town v Burgess Hill Town	2-1
(at Bedfont FC)	
Sittingbourne v Tooting & Mitcham United	4-5
Witney Town v Wimborne Town	2-1
Fareham Town v Hungerford Town	4-2
Gloucester City v Thatcham Town	1-3

Bashley v Thame United	4-3
Weymouth v Abingdon Town	1-0
Cheltenham Town v Salisbury City	4-3
Melksham Town v Cirencester Town	0-1
Bath City v Newport AFC	5-2
Trowbridge Town v Weston-Super-Mare	2-1
Merthyr Tydfil v Torrington	3-1
Yeovil Town v Taunton Town	0-0, 5-3
Clevedon Town v Tiverton Town	0-2

Third Qualifying Round

Gateshead v Workington	4-0
Bishop Auckland v Consett	0-1
Morecambe v Flixton	6-2
Stalybridge Celtic v Ashton United	2-1
Frickley Athletic v Newcastle Town	1-1, 1-2
Leek Town v Gainsborough Trinity	2-0
Farsley Celtic v Whitby Town	0-1
Southport v Burton Albion	4-1
Leigh RMI v Marine	2-0
Atherton LR v Bamber Bridge	1-1, 0-2
North Ferriby United v Lancaster City	0-2
Kettering Town v Bedworth United	0-1
Rushden & Diamonds v Bilston Town	1-0
Hednesford Town v Tamworth	4-2
Shepshed Dynamo v Knypersley Victoria	1-0
Boston United v Sudbury Wanderers	10-1
Cambridge City v Canvey Island	0-3
Chelmsford City v Wisbech Town	2-3
Sudbury Town v Corby Town	1-0
Stevenage Borough v Braintree Town	3-1
Hayes v Chesham United	1-0
Dagenham & Redbridge v Uxbridge	3-0
Boreham Wood v Edgware Town	3-2
St Albans City v Stansted	5-0
Farnborough Town v Bracknell Town	3-2
Welling United v Herne Bay	2-0
Dover Athletic v Hendon	0-1
Hastings Town v Molesey	2-1
Bromley v St Leonards Stamcroft	1-1, 5-2
Tooting & Mitcham United v Staines Town	0-1
Fareham Town v Witney Town	0-1
Bashley v Thatcham Town	0-1
Cheltenham Town v Weymouth	1-0
Bath City v Cirencester Town	2-0
Merthyr Tydfil v Trowbridge Town	1-0
Tiverton Town v Yeovil Town	0-2

Fourth Qualifying Round

Witton Albion v Kidderminster Harriers	1-4
Gateshead v Consett	0-1
Stalybridge Celtic v Leek Town	1-0
Bedworth United v Boston United	0-2
Hednesford Town v Telford United	2-0
Newcastle Town v Bamber Bridge	4-0
Colwyn Bay v Nuneaton Borough	1-0
Whitby Town v Blyth Spartans	2-1
Leigh RMI v Runcorn	2-4
Barrow v Altrincham	1-1, 0-4
Spennymoor United v Southport	2-2, 1-2
Lancaster City v Morecambe	1-1, 2-2, 2-4
Shepshed Dynamo v Bromsgrove Rovers	2-0
Merthyr Tydfil v Yeovil Town	2-1
Hitchin Town v Wisbech Town	1-2
Hastings Town v Hendon	1-1, 0-2
Bath City v Cheltenham Town	0-0, 1-4
Bromley v Sutton United	1-0
Staines Town v Welling United	0-1
(at Harrow Borough FC)	
Witney Town v St Albans City	0-4
Rushden & Diamonds v Bognor Regis Town	2-0
Ashford Town v Kingstonian	3-1
Boreham Wood v Thatcham Town	5-0
Hayes v Slough Town	1-0
Gravesend & Northfleet v Stevenage Borough	1-5
Cinderford Town v Farnborough Town	0-4
Canvey Island v Sudbury Town	0-1
Newport (IW) v Dagenham & Redbridge	1-4

FA CUP 1996–97
SPONSORED BY LITTLEWOODS POOLS

COMPETITION PROPER

FIRST ROUND

15 NOV

Woking (1) 2 *(Foster 3, Walker 56 (pen))*
Millwall (2) 2 *(Savage 19, Crawford 28)*   5448
Woking: Batty; Howard, Foster, Brown, Jones, Thompson, Wye S, Taylor, Steele, Hunter (Hay), Walker.
Millwall: Carter; Newman, Rogan (Van Blerk), Savage, Witter, Harle (Lavin), Bowry, Neill, Crawford, Dair, Hartley.

16 NOV

Ashford T (1) 2 *(Warrilow 25, Dent 72)*
Dagenham & Redbridge (1) 2 *(Stimson 14, Creaser 67)*
                                                 1813
Ashford T: Munden; Morris (Chambers), O'Brien, Donn, Warrilow, Wynter, Wheeler, White, Allon, Dent, Ross.
Dagenham & Redbridge: Gothard; Culverhouse, Davidson C, Double, Conner, Creaser, Parratt, Pratt, Rogers, Stimson, Naylor.

Blackpool (1) 1 *(Quinn 32 (pen))*
Wigan Ath (0) 0   5465
Blackpool: Banks; Bryan, Barlow, Butler, Linighan, Brabin, Bonner, Mellon, Quinn, Malkin, Philpott.
Wigan Ath: Butler L; Butler J (Carragher), Johnson, Greenall, Pender, Martinez, Lowe (Diaz), Jones, Saville, Biggins, Sharp.

Boreham Wood (1) 1 *(Robbins 8)*
Rushden & Diamonds (1) 1 *(Hackett 24)*   1567
Boreham Wood: Sheppard; Daly (Fox), Joyce (Hollingdale), Hatchett, Nisbet, Harrigan, Prutton, Heffer, Robbins, Samuels T (Samuels D), Shaw.
Rushden & Diamonds: Davies; Wooding, Tucker, Holden, Rodwell, Wilson, King, Butterworth (Bailey), Alford (Wilkin), Collins, Hackett.

Boston U (1) 3 *(Chambers L 21, 56, Chambers S 85)*
Morecambe (0) 0   2935
Boston U: Bastock; Armstrong (Melson), Withe, Fee, Hardy, Chambers S, Chambers L, Appleby, Brown, Williams, Mason (Munton).
Morecambe: Banks; Knowles, Lavelle, Miller, Hughes, Burns, Cain (Monk), Grimshaw, McCluskie (Ceraolo), Norman (McKearney), Leaver.

Brentford (1) 2 *(Smith 25, Forser 77)*
Bournemouth (0) 0   4509
Brentford: Dearden; Hurdle, Anderson, Ashby, Bates, McGhee, Asaba (Omigie), Smith, Forster (Harvey), Canham, Taylor.
Bournemouth: Glass; Young, Vincent, Cole (Murray), Cox, Bailey, Holland, Robinson, Gordon (Watson), Fletcher, Dean (O'Neill).

Bristol R (0) 1 *(Parmenter 90)*
Exeter C (0) 2 *(Rowbotham 57, Flack 89)*   5841
Bristol R: Collett; Pritchard, Power, Tillson (Skinner), Lockwood (Parmenter), Browning, Holloway, Miller (French), Cureton, Ramasut, Beadle.
Exeter C: Bayes; Richardson J, Hughes, Myers, Blake, Hare, Dailly, Rowbotham, Flack, Bailey, McConnell (Braithwaite).

Bromley (1) 1 *(Kane 9)*
Enfield (2) 3 *(West 16, 24, 68)*   2709
Bromley: Wietecha; Rawlings, Campbell (Hope), Coles, Campfield (Dennington), Adedeji, Sharman, Loveday (Francis), Warden, Thompkins, Kane.
Enfield: Pape; Hannigan, Underwood, Carstairs, Terry, St Hilaire, Moran, Edwards, West, Annon, Gentle J.

Burnley (1) 2 *(Gleghorn 31, Matthew 75)*
Lincoln C (0) 1 *(Bos 47)*   6484
Burnley: Beresford; Parkinson (Weller), Eyres, Harrison, Swan, Brass, Matthew, Smith, Nogan, Barnes (Cooke), Gleghorn.
Lincoln C: Richardson; Barnett, Whitney, Hone, Brown G, Robertson, Ainsworth, Fleming, Bos (Sterling), Martin, Alcide.

Cambridge U (3) 3 *(Beall 2, Kyd 20, Barnwell-Edinboro 34)*
Welling U (0) 0   3187
Cambridge U: Barrett; Matthew Joseph, Granville, Wanless (Thompson), Craddock, Raynor, Hayes, Hyde, Kyd (Turner), Barnwell-Edinboro, Beall (Preece).
Welling U: Knight; Watts, Cooper, Trott, Copley (Farley), Horton, Brown (Lewington), Rutherford, Morah, Dennis, Lakin.

Cardiff C (1) 2 *(White 31, Middleton 88)*
Hendon (0) 0   2592
Cardiff C: Elliott; Jarman, Philliskirk, Eckhardt, Young, Fowler, Rodgerson, Middleton, White, Dale, Bennett.
Hendon: Wagenaar; Whyte, Clarke, Murphy, Warmington, Kelly P, Adams (Kelly T), Price, Darlington (Bolton), Richardson, Lewis.

Carlisle U (3) 6 *(Davidson 16 (og), Corbett 34 (og), Peacock 36, Conway 60, Archdeacon 74 (pen), McAlindon 87)*
Shepshed Dynamo (0) 0   4394
Carlisle U: Caig; Hopper, Archdeacon, Walling, Robinson, Pounewatchy, Peacock, Conway (Jansen), Smart (McAlindon), Hayward, Aspinall (Thomas).
Shepshed Dynamo: Selby; Doughty (Igoe), Bancroft, Knight, Rowe (Chamberlain), Davidson, O'Kane, Corbett, Okeredolu, Riddell (Parkins), Hare.

Chester C (0) 3 *(Rimmer 52, 87, Milner 89)*
Stalybridge C (0) 0   3151
Chester C: Sinclair; Davidson, Jenkins (Whelan), Woods, Jackson, Alsford, Flitcroft, Fisher, Milner, Rimmer, Noteman (Rogers).
Stalybridge C: Williams; Bates, Colthup, Hine, Boardman, Hall, Burke, Jones, Trott, Arnold, Charles.

Chesterfield (1) 1 *(Williams 41)*
Bury (0) 0   5104
Chesterfield: Mercer; Hewitt, Jules, Curtis, Williams, Dyche, Davies, Holland, Lormor, Lund (Morris), Perkins.
Bury: Kiely; West, Pugh, Daws, Lucketti, Jackson (Armstrong), Butler, Carter, Matthews, Johnrose, Johnson (Jepson).

Colchester U (0) 1 *(Wilkins 69)*
Wycombe W (1) 2 *(De Souza 43, Williams 65)* 4378
Colchester U: Emberson; Dunne, Gibbs, Gregory (Adcock), Greene, Cawley, Fry, Wilkins, Reinelt (Duguid), Locke, Abrahams.
Wycombe W: Cheesewright; Cousins, Bell, McCarthy, Evans, Crossley, Carroll, Brown (Patterson), Williams, McGavin, De Souza.

Colwyn Bay (0) 1 *(Roberts G 66)*
Wrexham (0) 1 *(Hughes 76)*   4679
Colwyn Bay: Roberts R; McCosh, Fuller, Harley, Graham, Price, Dulson, Roberts G (Drury), Williams, Donnelly, Rigby.
Wrexham: Cartwright; McGregor, Hardy, Hughes, Humes, Carey, Chalk (Skinner), Owen, Connolly, Morris, Ward.

Crewe Alex (2) 4 *(Macauley 14, Murphy 27, 56, Lightfoot 73)*
Kidderminster H (0) 1 *(Yates 65)*   4651
Crewe Alex: Kearton; Barr, Smith, Westwood, Macauley, Whalley, Rivers, Savage, Moralee (Lightfoot), Murphy, Tierney.
Kidderminster H: Steadman; Bignot, Prindiville, Weir, Grindley, Yates, Webb (Casey), Willett (Olney), Hughes, McCue (Deakin), Doherty.

Farnborough T (2) 2 *(Wingfield 31, Boothe 39)*
Barnet (0) 2 *(Devine 72, 90)*   2566
Farnborough T: MacKenzie; Stemp, Underwood, Day, Williams, Harford (McAvoy), Boothe, Harlow, Gavin, Baker, Wingfield (Mintram).
Barnet: Taylor; Gale, Hardyman, Codner, Primus, McDonald, Campbell, Tomlinson (Simpson), Wilson, Devine, Hodges.

Gillingham (1) 1 *(Butler 25)*
Hereford U (0) 0   5280
Gillingham: Stannard; Smith, Butters, Hessenthaler (Harris), Green, Bryant, Piper (Chapman), Ratcliffe, Onuora, Butler, O'Connor (Puttnam).
Hereford U: Debont; Norton, Matthewson, Smith, Law, Hibbard (Preedy), Cook (Warner), Stoker, Foster A, Hargreaves, Brough.

Hartlepool U (0) 0
York C (0) 0   3011
Hartlepool U: O'Connor; Ingram, McAuley, Beech, Lee, McGuckin, Clegg, Cooper, Howard, Halliday, Hislop.
York C: Clarke; McMillan, Hall, Pepper, Tutill, Barras, Murty, Bushell, Tolson, Bull (Campbell), Himsworth (Randall).

Hednesford T (1) 2 *(Russell 11, O'Connor 68)*
Southport (0) 1 *(Collins 85 (og))*   2060
Hednesford T: Cooksey; Carty, Russell, Simpson, Comyn, Collins, McNally (Devine), Lambert, Hemmings, Street, O'Connor.
Southport: Stewart; Anderson (Morgan), Eyre, Horner, Jones, Butler, Clark, Whittaker (Dove), Preece, Gamble (Davenport), McDonald.

Leyton Orient (0) 2 *(Winston 73, West 88)*
Merthyr Tydfil (0) 1 *(Evans 47)*   4421
Leyton Orient: Weaver; Hendon, Naylor, Chapman, Garland (Baker), Arnott, Warren, Ling, Ayorinde (Winston), West, Channing.
Merthyr Tydfil: Wager; Barnhouse, Downs, Abraham, O'Brien, Wimbleton, Mardenborough (Pascoe), Wigley, Rees (Ramsey), Evans (Summers), Jones.

Macclesfield T (0) 0
Rochdale (2) 2 *(Deary 10, Johnson 32)*   3134
Macclesfield T: Oakes; Tinson, Edey, Payne, Howarth, Sorvel, Circuit (Bradshaw), Wood, Coates (Williams), Power, Mitchell.
Rochdale: Gray; Fensome, Farrell, Johnson, Hill, Gouck, Deary, Painter, Leonard, Whitehall, Stuart.

Mansfield T (3) 4 *(Ford 30, Eustace 42, Doolan 45, Wood 74)*
Consett (0) 0   3183
Mansfield T: Bowling; Ford, Harper (Clarke), Kilcline, Eustace, Watkiss, Sedgemore, Walker, Wood, Hadley (Williams), Doolan (Sherlock).
Consett: Lee; Woodward, Gray (Hagan), Quinn, Sugden, Smith, Rowell, Suddes, McLeod, Outterside, Brown (Clarke).

Northwich V (1) 2 *(Cooke 38, 78)*
Walsall (0) 2 *(Wilson 49, Lightbourne 52)*   3142
Northwich V: Greygoose; Ward, Fairclough, Crookes, Simpson, Bishop, Humphreys, Steele (Tait), Walters, Cooke, Vicary (Duffy).
Walsall: Walker; Ntamark, Daniel, Viveash, Thomas, Mountfield, Keister, Hodge, Lightbourne, Wilson, Marsh.

Peterborough U (0) 0
Cheltenham T (0) 0   5271
Peterborough U: Sheffield; Boothroyd, Clark, O'Connor, Heald, Bodley, Willis (Carter) (Ebdon), Payne, Rowe (Grazioli), Charlery, Houghton.
Cheltenham T: Maloy; Wooton (Bloomer), Wring, Banks, Freeman, Victory, Howells, Wright, Boyle (Eaton), Smith (Chenoweth), Clarke.

Plymouth Arg (1) 5 *(Mauge 38, Evans 54 (pen), 78, Littlejohn 80, Corazzin 88)*
Fulham (0) 0   7104
Plymouth Arg: Grobbelaar; Billy, Williams, Mauge, Heathcote (Saunders), James, Leadbitter (Corazzin), Curran, Illman (Littlejohn), Evans, Barlow.
Fulham: Lange; Watson, Herrera, Cusack, Cullip, Blake, Carpenter, Cockerill (Brooker), Conroy, Morgan, Scott.

Preston NE (3) 4 *(Reeves 17, 30, 37, Ashcroft 79)*
Altrincham (0) 1 *(Shepherd 78 (pen))*   8286
Preston NE: Mimms; Sparrow, Kidd, Rankine, Wilcox, Moyes, Ashcroft (Holt), McDonald, Reeves (Bryson), Wilkinson, Kilbane.
Altrincham: Dickins; Shepherd, Heesom, France, Maddox, Doherty, Hardy (Cain), Harris, Pritchard, Carmody, Rimmer.

Runcorn (1) 1 *(Heavey 29)*
Darlington (2) 4 *(Naylor 8, Shaw 34, Crosby 67, Brumwell 75)*   1268
Runcorn: Morris; O'Shaughnessy, Ashton, Callahan, Finley, Chadwick (Carragher), Whalley, Heavey, Dunne, Randles, Lee.
Darlington: Newell; Shaw, Barnard, Brumwell, Crosby, Gregan, Carss, Key (Brydon), Oliver, Blake (Robinson), Naylor.

Scunthorpe U (2) 4 *(Baker 9, 90, D'Auria 27, Clarkson 70)*
Rotherham U (0) 1 *(McGlashan 14)*   3892
Scunthorpe U: Samways; Walsh, Wilson, Sertori, Knill, Patterson, Housham, D'Auria, Baker, Eyre, Clarkson.
Rotherham U: Farrelly; Breckin, Roscoe (Smith), Dobbin, Monington, Gayle, Sandeman (Berry), Goodwin, McDougald, Glover, McGlashan.

Shrewsbury T (1) 1 *(Stevens 7)*
Scarborough (0) 1 *(Ritchie 61)*   2819
Shrewsbury T: Edwards; Whiston, Dempsey, Spink, Taylor M (Scott), Walton, Seabury, Stevens, Anthrobus, Evans, Currie (Ward).
Scarborough: Ironside; Kay, Wells, Bennett, Hicks, Rockett (Lucas), Thompstone, Brooke, Mitchell, Ritchie (McElhatton), Williams G.

Stevenage B (1) 2 *(Catlin 36, Hayles 74)*
Hayes (2) 2 *(Williams 2, Haynes 40)*   3288
Stevenage B: Gallagher; Webster, Mutchell, Grime (Venables), Smith, Barrowcliff, Beevor, Browne (Crawshaw), Cretton, Catlin, Hayles.
Hayes: Meara; Brady, Goodliffe, Kelly, Cox, Bunce, Hyatt, Hooper, Williams (Roberts), Haynes (Bartley), Wilkinson.

Stockport Co (0) 2 *(Flynn 59, Mutch 62)*
Doncaster R (0) 1 *(Cramb 55)*   4211
Stockport Co: Jones; Connelly, Todd, Bennett, Flynn, Gannon, Durkan, Marsden, Mutch (Landon), Armstrong, Jeffers.
Doncaster R: O'Connor; Murphy, Ryan (Clark), Utley, Gore, Colcombe (Warren), Schofield, McDonald (Pearce), Dixon, Cramb, Birch.

Sudbury T (0) 0
Brighton & HA (0) 0   3112
Sudbury T: Mokler; Girling, Stafford (French), Carter, Tracey, Rolph, Cheetham, Brown, McClean, Smith, Adams (Greaves).
Brighton & HA: Rust; Parrish, Hobson, Mundee (Baird), Morris, McGarrigle, Storer, Peake, Minton, Maskell, McDonald.

Swansea C (0) 1 *(Torpey 70)*
Bristol C (1) 1 *(Kuhl 45)*   5623
Swansea C: Freestone; Brown (O'Leary), Clode, Moreira, Edwards, Jones, Jenkins, Penney, Torpey, Ampadu, Coates (King).
Bristol C: Naylor; Owers, Barnard, Edwards, Taylor, Kuhl, Goodridge, Carey, Agostino, Goater, Tinnion.

Torquay U (0) 0
Luton T (1) 1 *(Hughes 41)*   3450
Torquay U: Wilmot; Winter (Mitchell), Barrow, Hawthorne, Gittens, Watson, Oatway, Nelson, Laight (Ndah), Hancox (Hathaway), Stamps.
Luton T: Feuer; James (Patterson), Skelton, Waddock, Davis S, Johnson, Hughes, Alexander, Douglas (Marshall), Guentchev, Showler.

Wisbech T (0) 1 *(Munns 50)*
St Albans C (0) 2 *(Howell 56, 89)*   2509
Wisbech T: Edmonds; Shelton, Lindsay, Sharman, Moore, Massingham (Topliss), Parrott, Ward, Munns, Williams (Gallagher), Setchell.
St Albans C: Howells; Polston, Omogbehin (Risley), Bashir, Mudd, Coleman, Cobb, Howell, Clark, Evans, Haworth.

17 NOV

Newcastle T (0) 0
Notts Co (0) 2 *(Kennedy 50, Robinson 63)*   3918
Newcastle T: Butler; Beardmore, Williams, Dunn, Johnson, Holmes, Ritchie, Lawton (Wade), Burndred, Poxon, Pestridge.
Notts Co: Ward; Wilder, Walker (Hunt), Hogg, Redmile, Derry, Finnan, Robinson, Jones (Arkins), Farrell, Kennedy.
at Stoke C.

Northampton T (0) 0
Watford (0) 1 *(Bazeley 71)*   7342
Northampton T: Woodman; Clarkson, Maddison (Colkin), Sampson, Warburton, Hunter, Parrish, White (Lee), Cooper, Grayson, O'Shea (Warner).
Watford: Miller; Gibbs, Robinson, Easton, Millen, Page (Johnson C), Bazeley, Connolly (Andrews), White, Palmer, Mooney.

Whitby T (0) 0
Hull C (0) 0   3337
Whitby T: Campbell; Martin (Goodchild), Logan, Goodrick, Pearson, Cooke, Borthewick (Robertson), Hodgson, Robinson, Toman, Pitman.
Hull C: Carroll; Marks, Rioch, Greaves, Wright, Brien, Joyce, Brown, Darby (Mann), Quigley, Peacock (Maxfield).

FIRST ROUND REPLAY

25 NOV

Dagenham & Redbridge (1) 1 *(Rogers 5)*
Ashford T (0) 1 *(White 76)*   2424
Dagenham & Redbridge: Gothard; Culverhouse (Jacques), Davidson, Double, Conner, Creaser, Parratt (John), Pratt, Rogers, Stimson (Johnson), Naylor.
Ashford T: Munden; Morris (Chambers), O'Brien, Allon, Warrilo, Wynter, Wheeler, White, Carruthers (Donn), Dent, Ross.
(aet; Ashford T won 4-3 on penalties).

FIRST ROUND REPLAYS

26 NOV
Barnet (0) 1 *(Devine 72)*
Farnborough T (0) 0   2215
Barnet: Taylor; Gale, Hardyman, Codner, Primus, Howarth, Tomlinson (Campbell), Simpson, Wilson, Devine, Hodges.
Farnborough T: MacKenzie; Stemp (McAvoy), Underwood, Williams, Mintram, Harford, Boothe, Harlow, Gavin, Robson, Wingfield.

Brighton & HA (1) 1 *(Maskell 43)*
Sudbury T (1) 1 *(Brown 23)*   3902
Brighton & HA: Rust; Parris, Hobson, Mundee, Morris, McGarrigle, Storer, Peake (Mayo), Baird, Maskell, McDonald (Andrews).
Sudbury T: Mokler; Girling (Bell), Stafford (Reilly), Adams (Rolph), Tracey, Carter, Cheetham, Brown, McClean, Smith, English.
(aet; Sudbury T won 4-3 on penalties).

Bristol C (1) 1 *(Agostino 1)*
Swansea C (0) 0   8017
Bristol C: Naylor; Owers, Barnard, Edwards, Taylor (Hewlett), Kuhl, Goodridge, Carey, Agostino, Goater (Nugent), Tinnion.
Swansea C: Freestone; O'Leary, Clode (Thomas), Moreira, Edwards, Jones, Heggs, Penney, Torpey, Ampadu, Coates.

Hayes (0) 0
Stevenage B (1) 2 *(Hayles 22, 79)*   2965
Hayes: Meara; Brady (Randall), Goodliffe, Kelly, Cox, Bunce, Hyatt, Hooper, Williams, Haynes, Wilkinson.
Stevenage B: Gallagher; Kirby, Mutchell, Sodje, Smith, Cretton, Beevor, Trebble, Venables (Crawshaw), Catlin, Hayles (Browne).

Hull C (3) 8 *(Darby 9, 30, 45, 89, 98, 107, Peacock 97, Mann 118)*
Whitby T (2) 4 *(Pitman 10, 47 (pen), 50 (pen), Robinson 21)*   2900
Hull C: Wilson; Marks (Gilbert), Maxfield, Brien, Dewhurst, Wright, Joyce, Brown (Mann), Darby, Quigley (Doncel), Peacock.
Whitby T: Campbell; Martin (Robertson), Logan, Goodrick, Pearson, Cook, Borthwick (Goodchild), Hodgson, Robinson (Hall), Toman, Pitman.

Millwall (0) 0
Woking (1) 1 *(Walker 9)*   6084
Millwall: Carter; Lavin, Rogan, Savage, Webber, Newman, Bowry, Neill (Dolby), Crawford, Dair (Sinclair), Hartley.
Woking: Batty; Howard, Taylor, Foster, Brown, Jones, Thompson, Wye S, Steele, Hunter (Hay), Walker.

Rushden & D (1) 2 *(Wilkin 15, Collins 90)*
Boreham Wood (1) 3 *(Heffer 45, Samuels T 72, Samuels D 90)*   2619
Rushden & D: Davies; Wooding (Capone), Tucker, Holden, Rodwell, Smith, King (Bailey), Butterworth, Wilkin, Collins, Hackett (Furnell).
Boreham Wood: Sheppard; Daly, Joyce, Howard, Nisbet, Harrigan, Prutton, Heffer, Robbins (Samuels D), Samuels T, Shaw.

Scarborough (0) 1 *(Kay 47)*
Shrewsbury T (0) 0   2247
Scarborough: Ironside; Kay, Wells, Bennett, Hicks, Lucas, McElhatton, Thompstone, Mitchell (Daws), Ritchie, Williams G.
Shrewsbury T: Edwards; Whiston (Nielsen), Dempsey, Taylor M, Spink, Scott (Berkley), Seabury, Stevens, Anthrobus, Evans, Currie.

Walsall (2) 3 *(Lightbourne 33, 50, Wilson 41 (pen))*
Northwich V (0) 1 *(Tait 69)* 3491
Walsall: Walker; Ntamark, Daniel, Viveash, Marsh, Mountfield, Thomas, Keister, Lightbourne (Watson), Wilson, Hodge.
Northwich V: Greygoose; Reddish, Fairclough, Crookes, Simpson, Bishop, Humphreys, Duffy, Steele, Cooke (Tait), Vickery (Ward).

Wrexham (1) 2 *(Hughes 45, 81)*
Colwyn Bay (0) 0 4106
Wrexham: Marriott; Brace, Hardy, Hughes, Jones, Carey, Skinner, Russell, Connolly, Morris (Watkin), Ward.
Colwyn Bay: Roberts R; McCosh, Fuller, Harley (Caton), Graham, Price, Dulson, Roberts G (Drury), Williams, Donnelly, Rigby.

York C (2) 3 *(Pepper 41, Himsworth 45, Tolson 54)*
Hartlepool U (0) 0 3257
York C: Clarke; Murty, Atkinson, Pepper, Tutill, Barras, Stephenson, Pouton, Tolson (Cresswell), Bull (Campbell), Himsworth.
Hartlepool U: Pears; Ingram, McAuley, Beech, Lee, McGuckin, Allon, Tait, Clegg, Halliday (Irvine), Hislop.

FIRST ROUND REPLAY

27 NOV

Cheltenham T (0) 1 *(Smith 118 (pen))*
Peterborough U (0) 3 *(Charlery 91, 120, Grazioli 115)*
4160
Cheltenham T: Maloy; Wotton, Banks, Freeman, Ring, Victory (Bloomer), Howells, Wright (Chenoweth), Clarke, Smith, Eaton (Boyle).
Peterborough U: Sheffield; Boothroyd, Clark, Ebdon (Willis), Heald, Bodley, O'Connor, Payne (Grazioli), Rowe, Charlery, Houghton (Morrison).

SECOND ROUND

6 DEC

Plymouth Arg (2) 4 *(Evans 30, Mauge 32, Billy 80, Littlejohn 90)*
Exeter C (1) 1 *(Sharpe 45)* 12,911
Plymouth Arg: Grobbelaar; Billy, Williams, Mauge, Heathcote, James, Wotton, Leadbitter, Littlejohn, Evans, Barlow.
Exeter C: Bayes; Richardson J, Sharpe, Myers, Blake, Hare, Rowbotham (Braithwaite), Dailly, Flack, Bailey, Chamberlain (McConnell).

7 DEC

Barnet (2) 3 *(Simpson 7, Hodges 32, Devine 68)*
Wycombe W (0) 3 *(McGavin 59, Williams 60, 77)* 3176
Barnet: Taylor; Gale, Hardyman, Codner, Primus, Howarth, Tomlinson, Simpson, Wilson, Devine, Hodges.
Wycombe W: Cheesewright; Cousins, Bell, McCarthy, Lawrence, Patterson (Harkin), Carroll, Williams, Farrell, McGavin, De Souza (Skiverton).

Blackpool (0) 0
Hednesford T (0) 1 *(O'Connor 87)* 4583
Blackpool: Banks; Thorpe, Barlow, Dixon, Lydiate, Bradshaw, Bonner, Onwere, Malkin (Preece), Ellis, Philpott (Carden).
Hednesford T: Cooksey; Russell, Collins, Simpson, Essex, Comyn, Hemmings, Lambert, Lake, Devine (Harnett), O'Connor.

Bristol C (5) 9 *(Goodridge 13, Agostino 22, 42, 48, 76, Kuhl 25, Hewlett 43, 55, Nugent 81)*
St Albans C (0) 2 *(Clark 54, Daly 66)* 7136
Bristol C: Naylor; Owers, Barnard, Hewlett, Paterson, Kuhl (Doherty), Goodridge, Carey, Agostino, Nugent, Tinnion.
St Albans C: Howells; Mudd, Polston, Coleman (Risley), Daly, Bashir, Evans, Cobb, Howell (Blackman), Haworth (Martin), Clark.

Cambridge U (0) 0
Woking (0) 2 *(Walker 74, Taylor 83)* 5857
Cambridge U: Barrick; Matthew Joseph, Granville, Preece (Turner), Craddock, Raynor, Hayes (Thompson), Hyde, Kyd, Barnwell-Edinboro, Beall.
Woking: Batty; Howard, Taylor, Foster, Brown, Jones, Thompson, Wye S, Steele (Ellis), Hay (Hunter), Walker.

Cardiff C (0) 0
Gillingham (1) 2 *(Onuora 18, Hessenthaler 66)* 3474
Cardiff C: Mountain; Perry, Philliskirk (Haworth), Eckhardt, Young, Fowler (Bennett), Rodgerson, Middleton, White, Dale, Gardner.
Gillingham: Stannard; O'Connor, Butters (Bailey), Manuel (Ford), Green, Parris, Hessenthaler, Pennock, Onuora, Butler, Chapman.

Carlisle U (0) 1 *(Edmondson 89)*
Darlington (0) 0 5625
Carlisle U: Caig; Hopper, Archdeacon, Walling, Edmondson, Pounewatchy, Peacock, Conway (Thomas), Smart (Delap), Hayward, Aspinall (Jansen).
Darlington: Newell; Shaw, Barnard, Laws, Crosby, Devos, Brumwell (Atkinson B), Oliver, Roberts, Blake, Naylor.

Chester C (1) 1 *(Milner 5)*
Boston U (0) 0 3344
Chester C: Sinclair; Davidson, Jenkins, Woods, Jackson, Alsford, Flitcroft, Priest, Milner (Whelan), Rimmer, Fisher (Noteman).
Boston U: Bastock; Armstrong (Melson), Withe, Fee, Hardy, Chambers S, Chambers L, Appleby, Brown, Cook (Smaller), Mason (Munton).

Chesterfield (1) 2 *(Davies 22, Lormor 76)*
Scarborough (0) 0 4475
Chesterfield: Mercer; Hewitt, Jules, Curtis, Williams, Carr, Davies, Holland, Lormor, Howard, Perkins.
Scarborough: Ironside (Martin); Knowles, Daws (Wells), Bennett, Hicks, Lucas, McElhatton, Thompstone (Brooke), Mitchell, Ritchie, Williams G.

Enfield (1) 1 *(Marshall 19)*
Peterborough U (0) 1 *(Charlery 52)* 2847
Enfield: Pape; Hannigan, Underwood, Carstairs, Terry, Fitzgerald, Moran, Edwards (Gentle J), West, Marshall (St Hilaire), Annon.
Peterborough U: Griemink; Willis, Clark, Edwards, Heald, Bodley, Ebdon (Morrison), Payne, Carruthers (Grazioli), Charlery, Houghton (Boothroyd).

Hull C (1) 1 *(Joyce 44)*
Crewe Alex (1) 5 *(Garvey 10, Murphy 46, Adebola 56, Smith 59, Brien 61 (og))* 3756
Hull C: Wilson; Doncel, Rioch, Brien, Dewhurst, Wright, Joyce, Quigley (Sansam), Darby, Mann, Peacock.
Crewe Alex: Kearton; Barr, Smith, Westwood (Billing), Macauley, Whalley, Rivers (Adebola), Savage, Moralee, Murphy, Garvey.

Leyton Orient (1) 1 *(Channing 9)*
Stevenage B (2) 2 *(Brown 1, Catlin 22)* 6980
Leyton Orient: Shilton; Hendon, Naylor, Shearer (Winston), Warren, Arnott (Inglethorpe), Channing, Ling, McGleish, Garland (Chapman), West.
Stevenage B: Gallagher; Kirby, Mutchell, Sodje, Smith, Barrowcliff, Beevor, Browne, Catlin, Cretton, Hayles (Crawshaw).

Luton T (0) 2 *(Marshall 67, 84)*
Boreham Wood (0) 1 *(Robbins 60)*   5332
Luton T: Feuer; James, Skelton (Grant), Waddock, Davis
S, Patterson, Hughes, Alexander (Guentchev), Showler,
Thorpe, Marshall.
Boreham Wood: Sheppard; Howard, Nisbet, Harrigan,
Daly, Joyce (Hollingdale), Heffer, Prutton, Shaw,
Robbins, Samuels T (Samuels D).

Mansfield T (0) 0
Stockport Co (1) 3 *(Ford 45 (og), Durkan 54, 69)*   3354
Mansfield T: Bowling; Ford, Harper, Kilcline, Eustace,
Hackett, Wood, Walker, Sale (Ireland), Hadley, Doolan.
Stockport Co: Jones; Connelly, Todd, Bennett, Flynn,
Gannon, Durkan, Marsden, Angell, Armstrong (Jeffers),
Cavaco (Dinning).

Notts Co (1) 3 *(Jones 41, Arkins 70, Agana 90)*
Rochdale (0) 1 *(Thackeray 83)*   3584
Notts Co: Ward; Wilder, Baraclough, Hogg, Strodder,
Derry, Finnan, Robinson, Arkins (Battersby), Jones,
Kennedy (Agana).
Rochdale: Gray; Fensome, Bayliss, Johnson, Hill, Farrell,
Bailey (Thackeray), Deary, Cecere (Thompson),
Whitehall, Painter.

Preston NE (0) 2 *(Ashcroft 78, 83 (pen))*
York C (2) 3 *(Barras 40, Tolson 74, Moyes 16 (og))*   7893
Preston NE: Mimms; Gage (Squires), Kidd, Rankine
(Davey), Wilcox, Moyes, Ashcroft, McDonald, Reeves,
Holt (Atkinson), Bryson.
York C: Clarke; McMillan, Atkinson (Jordan), Pouton,
Tutill, Barras, Himsworth, Murty, Tolson, Bull,
Stephenson.

Sudbury T (1) 1 *(McClean 23)*
Brentford (0) 3 *(McGhee 51, Taylor 58, 74)*   3973
Sudbury T: Mokler; Girling (French), Stafford (Ball),
Adams (Reilly), Tracey, Carter, Cheetham, Brown,
McClean, Smith, English.
Brentford: Dearden; Hurdle, Anderson, Ashby, Bates,
McGhee, Asaba, Smith, Forster (Harvey), Bent
(Omigie), Taylor.
(at Colchester U).

Walsall (0) 1 *(Lightbourne 90)*
Burnley (0) 1 *(Eyres 66)*   5031
Walsall: Walker; Ntamark, Evans, Viveash, Marsh,
Mountfield, Bradley, Keister (Blake), Lightbourne,
Wilson, Hodge (Watson).
Burnley: Beresford; Parkinson, Eyres, Harrison, Swan,
Brass, Weller, Smith, Nogan, Cooke, Gleghorn.

Watford (0) 5 *(Bazeley 50, 72, Connolly 76, 81, 89)*
Ashford T (0) 0   7590
Watford: Miller; Gibbs, Bazeley, Palmer, Millen, Page,
Mooney (Connolly), Slater (Johnson R), Noel-Williams,
Penrice, Robinson.
Ashford T: Munden; Morris, O'Brien, Allan, Warrilow,
Wynter, Wheeler, White (Chambers), Curruthers, Dent,
Ross.

Wrexham (1) 2 *(Morris 20, Watkin 89)*
Scunthorpe U (1) 2 *(Baker 18, 66 (pen))*   3780
Wrexham: Marriott; McGregor, Hardy, Hughes, Humes,
Carey, Skinner, Russell, Connolly, Morris, Ward
(Watkin).
Scunthorpe U: Samways; Walsh, Wilson, Sertori, Hope,
Bradley, Calvo-Garcia, D'Auria, Baker, Eyre
(McFarlane), Clarkson.

SECOND ROUND REPLAYS

17 DEC
Peterborough U (3) 4 *(Houghton 20, Charlery 21,
Carruthers 36, 53)*
Enfield (1) 1 *(St Hilaire 31)*   3997
Peterborough U: Griemink; Boothroyd (Spearing), Clark,
Edwards, Heald, Willis, Morrison (Rowe), Payne,
Carruthers (Inman), Charlery, Houghton.
Enfield: Pape; Hannigan (Marshall), Underwood,
Carstairs, Terry, Fitzgerald (Gentle J), St Hilaire, Moran,
Edwards, West (Gentle D), Annon.

Scunthorpe U (1) 2 *(Baker 7, Clarkson 72)*
Wrexham (0) 3 *(Hughes 70, Morris 87, Watkin 114 (pen))*
    3976
Scunthorpe U: Samways; Walsh (McFarlane), Wilson,
Sertori, Hope, Housham, Calvo-Garcia (Paterson),
D'Auria, Baker, Eyre, Clarkson.
Wrexham: Marriott; McGregor, Hardy, Hughes, Humes
(Jones L), Carey, Skinner (Brammer), Owen, Connolly
(Watkin), Morris, Ward.
aet

Wycombe W (1) 3 *(Williams 28, Carroll 58, De Souza 76)*
Barnet (1) 2 *(Campbell 26, Hodges 90)*   3851
Wycombe W: Cheesewright; Cousins, Bell (Farrell),
McCarthy, Crossley, Patterson (Brown), Carroll
(Harkin), Williams, De Souza, McGavin, Kavanagh.
Barnet: Taylor; Gale, Hardyman, Codner (Pardew),
Primus, Howarth, Tomlinson, Simpson (Brazil), Wilson,
Campbell, Hodges.

Burnley (0) 0
Walsall (1) 1 *(Lightbourne 8)*   5995
Burnley: Beresford; Parkinson, Eyres, Winstanley, Swan
(Hoyland), Brass, Weller, Smith, Nogan, Barnes,
Gleghorn.
Walsall: Walker; Ntamark, Evans, Viveash, Marsh,
Mountfield, Bradley, Keister, Lightbourne, Wilson,
Hodge.
Match abandoned at half-time; floodlight failure.

SECOND ROUND REPLAY

23 DEC
Burnley (1) 1 *(Barnes 43)*
Walsall (0) 1 *(Viveash 74)*   5799
Burnley: Beresford; Parkinson, Eyres, Hoyland,
Winstanley, Harrison (Brass), Matthew, Smith, Little
(Weller), Barnes, Gleghorn.
Walsall: Walker; Ntamark, Evans, Viveash, Marsh,
Mountfield, Bradley (Blake), Keister, Lightbourne,
Wilson, Hodge.
(aet; Burnley won 4-2 on penalties).

THIRD ROUND

4 JAN
Arsenal (1) 1 *(Hartson 10)*
Sunderland (1) 1 *(Gray 20)*   37,793
Arsenal: Lukic; Parlour, Winterburn, Keown, Bould,
Adams, Morrow (Shaw), Hartson, Merson, Bergkamp,
Vieira.
Sunderland: Perez; Hall, Kubicki, Bracewell, Agnew
(Williams), Melville, Gray, Ord, Bridges (Aiston), Mullin
(Russell), Kelly.

Blackburn R (0) 1 *(Bohinen 68)*
Port Vale (0) 0   19,891
Blackburn R: Flowers; Kenna, Le Saux, Sherwood
(Marker), Hendry, Berg, McKinlay, Gallacher, Sutton,
Bohinen, Wilcox (Fenton).
Port Vale: Musselwhite; Aspin, Tankard, Jansson,
Griffiths, Glover (Bogie), McCarthy, Porter, Stokes
(Foyle), Naylor, Guppy.

Chelsea (1) 3 *(Wise 39, Burley 74, Zola 90)*
WBA (0) 0   27,446
Chelsea: Grodas; Petrescu, Minto (Burley), Duberry, Leboeuf, Clarke, Zola, Di Matteo, Newton, Hughes M (Vialli), Wise.
WBA: Crichton; Holmes, Murphy, Sneekes, Burgess, Raven (Taylor), Groves (Butler), Smith (Agnew), Peschisolido, Hunt, Hamilton.

Liverpool (1) 1 *(Collymore 12)*
Burnley (0) 0   33,252
Liverpool: James; McAteer, Bjornebye, Matteo, Wright, Babb, McManaman, Collymore, Berger, Barnes (Kennedy), Thomas.
Burnley: Beresford; Parkinson, Eyres, Harrison, Winstanley, Hoyland (Cooke), Weller (Little), Smith, Brass, Barnes, Gleghorn.

Middlesbrough (3) 6 *(Ravanelli 21, 50, Hignett 26, Cox 44, Beck 56, Stamp 79)*
Chester C (0) 0   18,684
Middlesbrough: Walsh; Cox (Fleming), Liddle, Vickers, Whyte, Blackmore, Emerson, Hignett, Beck (Fjortoft), Mustoe (Stamp), Ravanelli.
Chester C: Sinclair; Woods, Jenkins, Fisher, Whelan, Alsford, Shelton (Giles), Priest, Milner, Rimmer, Noteman (Brown G).

Norwich C (1) 1 *(Polston 32)*
Sheffield U (0) 0   12,356
Norwich C: Gunn; Newman, Jackson, Eadie, Polston, Sutch, Adams, Crook, Milligan (Scott), Johnson (Carey), O'Neill.
Sheffield U: Kelly; Beard, Sandford, Spackman, Hodgson (Nilsen), Holdsworth, White, Patterson, Walker, Katchuro, Scott (Hartfield).

Nottingham F (2) 3 *(Saunders 19, 74, Allen 28)*
Ipswich T (0) 0   14,681
Nottingham F: Crossley; Lyttle, Pearce, Cooper, Chettle, Phillips, Allen (Gemmill), Campbell (Roy), Saunders, Haaland, Woan.
Ipswich T: Wright; Stockwell, Taricco, Cundy, Tanner, Williams, Uhlenbeek, Sonner, Thomsen, Scowcroft, Dyer (Naylor).

Plymouth Arg (0) 0
Peterborough U (0) 1 *(Charlery 58)*   7299
Plymouth Arg: Grobbelaar; Billy, Williams, Mauge, Heathcote, James, Wotton (Saunders), Leadbitter (Corazzin), Illman, Evans, Barlow (Littlejohn).
Peterborough U: Griemink; Willis, Clark, Edwards, Heald, Bodley, Houghton, Payne, Carruthers (Griffiths), Charlery, Morrison (Basham).

QPR (0) 1 *(Hateley 88)*
Huddersfield T (0) 1 *(Crosby 64)*   11,776
QPR: Roberts; Graham, Brevett, Barker, Maddix, Ready, Spencer, Peacock, Dichio (Hateley), Brazier (Impey), Sinclair.
Huddersfield T: Norman (Simon Collins); Jenkins, Cowan, Bullock, Dyson (Reid), Heary, Makel, Crosby, Lawson (Burnett), Payton, Edwards.

Reading (1) 3 *(Lambert 19, Caskey 55, Morley 76 (pen))*
Southampton (0) 1 *(Ostenstad 49)*   11,537
Reading: Mikhailov; Booty, Gilkes, Caskey, Holsgrove, McPherson, Bernal, Williams (Glasgow), Morley, Lambert, Gooding.
Southampton: Beasant; Maddison, Benali, Lundekvam (Watson), Van Gobbel (Oakley), Magilton, Robinson (Charlton), Le Tissier, Ostenstad, Berkovich, Slater.

Sheffield W (3) 7 *(Humphreys 15, 48, Booth 34, 69, Hyde 54, Pembridge 83, Fickling 45 (og))*
Grimsby T (0) 1 *(Oster 66)*   20,590
Sheffield W: Pressman; Atherton, Nolan, Pembridge, Stefanovic, Walker, Blinker (Trustfull), Hyde (Nicol), Booth, Humphreys, Whittingham.
Grimsby T: Pearcey; Jobling, Gallimore, Fickling, Rodger, Widdrington, Childs (Oster), Lester, Woods, Mendonca, Black.

Stevenage B (0) 0
Birmingham C (1) 2 *(Francis 27, Devlin 64 (pen))* 15,365
Stevenage B: Gallagher; Kirby, Mutchell, Sodje, Smith, Barrowcliff, Beevor, Browne (Crawshaw), Catlin (Trebble), Webster (Adams), Hayles.
Birmingham C: Bennett; Bass, Grainger (Johnson), Bruce, Ablett, Holland (Legg), Devlin, Tait, Francis, Horne, Bowen.
(at Birmingham C).

Wolverhampton W (0) 1 *(Ferguson 68)*
Portsmouth (0) 2 *(McLoughlin 68, Hall 80)*   23,626
Wolverhampton W: Stowell; Smith, Dennison, Atkins, Venus, Emblen, Corica (Ferguson), Thomas, Bull, Goodman (Roberts), Osborn.
Portsmouth: Knight; Whitbread, Pethick, McLoughlin, Perrett (Thomson), Awford, Hall, Simpson, Bradbury, Durnin, Hillier.

Wrexham (1) 1 *(Hughes 6)*
West Ham U (1) 1 *(Porfirio 44)*   9747
Wrexham: Marriott; McGregor, Hardy, Hughes, Humes, Carey, Chalk, Owen (Russell), Watkin, Morris (Roberts), Ward.
West Ham U: Miklosko; Breacker, Dicks, Potts, Rieper, Williamson, Bishop, Jones, Porfirio, Moncur, Hughes.

5 JAN

Charlton Ath (0) 1 *(Kinsella 78)*
Newcastle U (1) 1 *(Lee 33)*   15,000
Charlton Ath: Petterson; Sturgess, Barness, O'Connell (Jones K), Rufus, Chapple, Newton, Leaburn, Robson, Whyte, Kinsella.
Newcastle U: Hislop; Watson, Beresford, Batty, Peacock, Albert, Lee, Beardsley, Shearer, Ferdinand, Clark.

Everton (2) 3 *(Kanchelskis 2 (pen), Barmby 18, Ferguson 50)*
Swindon T (0) 0   20,411
Everton: Southall; Barrett, Speed, Branch, Watson, Dunne, Kanchelskis, Barmby, Ferguson (Grant), Rideout, Stuart.
Swindon T: Digby; Robinson, Elkins, Leitch, Seagraves, Horlock, Culverhouse, Collins (O'Sullivan), Cowe (Watson), Allison, Walters (Drysdale).

Manchester U (0) 2 *(Scholes 51, Beckham 82)*
Tottenham H (0) 0   52,495
Manchester U: Schmeichel; Neville G, Irwin (McClair), May, Keane, Johnsen, Cantona, Scholes, Cole (Solskjaer), Beckham, Giggs.
Tottenham H: Walker; Carr, Edinburgh, Howells, Calderwood, Campbell, Austin, Fenn, Allen, Nielsen, Sinton.

Wycombe W (0) 0
Bradford C (2) 2 *(Dreyer 25, 34)*   5173
Wycombe W: Cheesewright; Cousins, Bell, Kavanagh, McCarthy, Forsyth, Carroll, Williams (Farrell), De Souza, McGavin, Brown (Evans).
Bradford C: Schwarzer; Liburd, Jacobs, Kiwomya (Wright), Mohan, Dreyer, Hamilton (Pinto), Duxbury, Waddle, Shutt, O'Brien.

13 JAN

Hednesford T (1) 1 *(Russell 43 (pen))*

York C (0) 0 3169

Hednesford T: Cooksey; Carty, Russell, Simpson, Comyn, Collins, McNally, Lambert, Lake, Fitzpatrick, O'Connor.
York C: Clarke; McMillan, Atkinson (Tutill), Pepper, Sharples, Barras, Himsworth, Pouton (Murty), Tolson, Bull, Stephenson.

14 JAN

Barnsley (2) 2 *(Bullock 27, Marcelle 30)*

Oldham Ath (0) 0 9936

Barnsley: Watson; Eaden, Moses, Bosancic (Sheridan), Thompson, De Zeeuw, Hendrie (Liddell), Redfearn, Wilkinson, Marcelle (Jones), Bullock.
Oldham Ath: Kelly; Fleming, Serrant, Henry, Garnett, Graham, McNiven S (Beresford), Rickers (Orlygsson), Ormondroyd, Banger (McCarthy), Richardson.

Carlisle U (1) 1 *(Archdeacon 30)*

Tranmere R (0) 0 10,090

Carlisle U: Caig; Edmondson, Archdeacon, Walling, Varty, Pounewatchy, Peacock (Delap), Conway, Smart (Thomas), Hayward, Aspinall.
Tranmere R: Nixon; Stevens, Thomas (Irons), McGreal, Higgins, O'Brien (Moore), Brannan, Aldridge, Cook, Morrissey (Branch), Nevin.

Chesterfield (0) 2 *(Howard 69, 88)*

Bristol C (0) 0 5193

Chesterfield: Mercer; Hewitt, Jules, Curtis, Williams, Dyche, Davies, Holland, Lormor, Howard, Morris.
Bristol C: Naylor; Owers, Barnard, Kuhl (Nugent), Taylor, Hewlett, Bent (Goodridge), Carey, Agostino, Goater (Edwards), Tinnion.

Crewe Alex (1) 1 *(Westwood 12)*

Wimbledon (1) 1 *(Perry 25)* 5011

Crewe Alex: Kearton; Lightfoot, Smith, Westwood, Macauley, Whalley, Charnock, Savage, Adebola, Murphy, Little.
Wimbledon: Sullivan; Cunningham, Kimble, Jones, McAllister, Perry, Ardley, Earle, Ekoku, Leonhardsen, Clarke (Goodman).

Crystal Palace (1) 2 *(Dyer 6 (pen), Veart 69)*

Leeds U (2) 2 *(Deane 3, Andersen 7 (og))* 21,052

Crystal Palace: Day; Edworthy, Gordon, Roberts, Andersen, Hopkin, Muscat, Ndah (McKenzie), Shipperley, Dyer, Veart.
Leeds U: Martyn; Kelly, Dorigo (Sharpe), Radebe, Wetherall, Beesley, Jackson, Wallace, Rush, Deane, Bowyer.

Notts Co (0) 0

Aston Villa (0) 0 13,315

Notts Co: Ward; Wilder, Baraclough, Redmile, Strodder, Derry (Galloway), Finnan, Robinson, Martindale, Farrell (Battersby), Agana (Walker).
Aston Villa: Bosnich; Scimeca, Wright, Southgate, Ehiogu, Tiler, Joachim, Townsend, Milosevic, Johnson, Staunton (Hendrie).

Gillingham (0) 0

Derby Co (0) 0 9529

Abandoned after 66 minutes; frozen pitch.

THIRD ROUND REPLAY

14 JAN

Huddersfield T (1) 1 *(Edwards 7)*

QPR (1) 2 *(Peacock 26, McDonald 89)* 11,814

Huddersfield T: Francis; Jenkins, Reid, Bullock, Dyson, Burnett, Makel, Crosby, Stewart (Lawson), Payton, Edwards (Simon Collins).
QPR: Roberts; Graham, Brevett, Murray, McDonald, Ready, Spencer (Dichio), Peacock, Hateley, Brazier, Sinclair.

THIRD ROUND

15 JAN

Leicester C (1) 2 *(Claridge 40, Marshall 48)*

Southend U (0) 0 13,982

Leicester C: Keller; Grayson, Kamark, Watts, Marshall, Prior, Campbell, Parker, Claridge, Izzet (Wilson), Heskey.
Southend U: Royce; Harris, Dublin, McNally (Hails), Roget, Nielsen, Marsh, Byrne (Thomson), Rammell, Williams (Boere), Tilson.

Stoke C (0) 0

Stockport Co (1) 2 *(Durkan 25, Armstrong 90)* 9961

Stoke C: Prudhoe; Pickering, Griffin, Sigurdsson, Whittle, Forsyth, McMahon, Wallace, Devlin (Macari M), Sheron, Kavanagh (MacKenzie).
Stockport Co: Jones; Connelly, Todd, Bennett, Flynn, Gannon, Durkan (Dinning), Marsden, Angell (Mutch), Armstrong, Cavaco.

THIRD ROUND REPLAYS

15 JAN

Newcastle U (1) 2 *(Clark 33, Shearer 100)*

Charlton Ath (0) 1 *(Robson 55)* 36,398

Newcastle U: Hislop; Watson (Barton), Beresford, Batty, Peacock, Albert (Elliott), Gillespie, Beardsley, Shearer, Clark, Ginola (Ferdinand).
Charlton Ath: Petterson; Brown, Barness, O'Connell, Rufus, Chapple, Newton (Robinson), Leaburn, Robson, Whyte, Jones K (Lisbie).

Sunderland (0) 0

Arsenal (0) 2 *(Bergkamp 46, Hughes 65)* 15,277

Sunderland: Perez; Hall, Kubicki, Mullin (Aiston), Williams, Melville, Gray, Ord, Russell, Bridges (Smith), Kelly.
Arsenal: Seaman; Parlour, Winterburn, Keown, Bould, Adams, Platt, Hughes, Merson, Bergkamp, Vieira.

THIRD ROUND

21 JAN

Gillingham (0) 0

Derby Co (0) 2 *(Willems 53, Van der Laan 89)* 9508

Gillingham: Stannard; Thomas (Chapman), Butters, Pennock, Green, Bryant, Hessenthaler, Ratcliffe, Smith, Butler, O'Connor (Puttnam).
Derby Co: Hoult; Laursen, Powell C, Rowett, McGrath, Flynn, Dailly, Sturridge (Simpson), Willems (Carbon), Powell D (Van der Laan), Carsley.

Luton T (0) 1 *(Johnson 89)*

Bolton W (1) 1 *(Pollock 26)* 7414

Luton T: Feuer; James, Thomas, Linton, Davis S, Johnson, Hughes, Alexander, Showler, Thorpe, Marshall (Grant).
Bolton W: Ward; Bergsson, Small, Pollock, Fairclough, Coleman, Lee, Sellars, Blake, Green (Frandsen), Sheridan.

Watford (0) 2 *(White 71, Connolly 80)*
Oxford U (0) 0　　　　　　　　　　　　9502
Watford: Miller; Bazeley, Gibbs, Palmer, Millen, Page, Slater, Connolly, White, Johnson R, Mooney (Easton).
Oxford U: Whitehead; Robinson, Ford M, Smith (Murphy), Purse, Gilchrist, Aldridge (Moody), Gray, Ford R (Massey), Jemson, Beauchamp.

THIRD ROUND REPLAY

21 JAN

Wimbledon (1) 2 *(Earle 11, Holdsworth 46)*
Crewe Alex (0) 0　　　　　　　　　　　4951
Wimbledon: Sullivan; Cunningham, McAllister, Jones, Blackwell, Perry, Ardley (Jupp), Earle, Holdsworth, Leonhardsen, Gayle (Harford).
Crewe Alex: Billing (Tierney), Smith, Westwood, Macauley, Whalley, Charnock, Savage, Adebola, Murphy, Little (Garvey).

22 JAN

Aston Villa (1) 3 *(Yorke 24, 53, Ehiogu 67)*
Notts Co (0) 0　　　　　　　　　　　25,006
Aston Villa: Bosnich; Scimeca, Wright, Southgate, Ehiogu, Tiler, Townsend, Curcic, Milosevic, Johnson (Hendrie), Yorke.
Notts Co: Ward; Wilder, Baraclough, Redmile, Strodder, Derry (Walker), Finnan, Robinson, Martindale, Farrell, Agana (Galloway).

FOURTH ROUND

25 JAN

Birmingham C (1) 3 *(Furlong 29, Devlin 48, Francis 69)*
Stockport Co (0) 1 *(Angell 82)*　　　18,487
Birmingham C: Bennett; Breen, Grainger (Johnson), Bruce, Ablett, Holland, Devlin (Bowen), Legg, Furlong, Horne, Hunt (Francis).
Stockport Co: Jones; Connelly, Todd, Bennett, Flynn, Gannon, Durkan, Marsden (Dinning), Angell, Armstrong, Cavaco (Mutch).

Carlisle U (0) 0
Sheffield W (1) 2 *(Whittingham 11, Booth 47)*　16,104
Carlisle U: Caig; Edmondson (Thomas), Archdeacon, Walling, Varty, Pounewatchy, Peacock, Conway, Smart (Delap), Hayward, Aspinall (Jansen).
Sheffield W: Pressman; Atherton, Nolan, Pembridge, Newsome, Walker, Collins, Hyde, Booth, Humphreys, Whittingham.

Everton (0) 2 *(O'Brien 54 (og), Speed 90)*
Bradford C (0) 3 *(Dreyer 49, Waddle 51, Steiner 59)*　30,007
Everton: Southall; Barrett, Phelan (Grant), Short, Watson, Parkinson, Kanchelskis, Barmby, Ferguson, Stuart, Speed.
Bradford C: Schwarzer; Sas, Jacobs, Dreyer, Mohan, O'Brien, Waddle, Duxbury, Steiner, Kiwomya (Stallard), Hamilton (Liburd).

Derby Co (2) 3 *(Van der Laan 36, Sturridge 40, Willems 69)*
Aston Villa (0) 1 *(Curcic 76)*　　　17,977
Derby Co: Hoult; Dailly, Powell C, Rowett (Simpson), McGrath, Trollope, Asanovic, Sturridge, Willems, Van der Laan, Carsley.
Aston Villa: Bosnich; Scimeca, Wright, Southgate, Ehiogu, Staunton, Townsend (Nelson), Curcic, Milosevic, Hendrie, Yorke.

Hednesford T (1) 2 *(O'Connor 14, 90)*
Middlesbrough (1) 3 *(Lambert 26 (og), Fjortoft 86, Ravanelli 88)*　　　　　　　　　　　27,511
Hednesford T: Cooksey; Carty, Russell (McNally), Simpson, Essex, Comyn, Collins, Lambert, Lake (Devine), Fitzpatrick, O'Connor.
Middlesbrough: Roberts; Kinder, Whyte, Vickers, Festa, Mustoe, Emerson, Moore, Beck (Fjortoft), Juninho, Ravanelli.
at Middlesbrough.

Leicester C (1) 2 *(Marshall 32, Parker 67 (pen))*
Norwich C (1) 1 *(Adams 39 (pen))*　16,703
Leicester C: Keller; Lawrence (Robins), Kamark (Watts), Parker, Elliott, Prior, Lennon, Izzet, Claridge, Marshall, Heskey.
Norwich C: Gunn; Newman, Jackson, Carey (Keith Scott), Mills, Sutch, Adams, Fleck (Ottosson), Forbes, Milligan, Eadie.

Manchester U (0) 1 *(Scholes 89)*
Wimbledon (0) 1 *(Earle 90)*　　　53,342
Manchester U: Schmeichel; Clegg, Irwin, Casper, Keane, Neville G, Cantona, McClair (Solksjaer), Scholes, Poborsky (Cole), Giggs.
Wimbledon: Sullivan; Cunningham, Kimble, Jones, Blackwell, Perry, Ardley (Jupp), Earle, Ekoku (Holdsworth), Leonhardsen, Gayle.

Portsmouth (0) 3 *(Hall 68, Bradbury 76, Hillier 86)*
Reading (0) 0　　　　　　　　　　　15,003
Portsmouth: Knight; Pethick, Thomson, McLoughlin, Perrett, Awford, Hall, Simpson, Bradbury, Durnin (Svensson), Hillier.
Reading: Bibbo; Booty, Gilkes, Caskey (Lovell), Hunter, Holsgrove, Bernal, Williams, Morley, Lambert, Gooding.

QPR (2) 3 *(Peacock 20, Spencer 26, Sinclair 74)*
Barnsley (1) 2 *(Redfearn 13, Hendrie 86)*　14,317
QPR: Roberts; Maddix, Brevett, Murray, McDonald, Ready, Spencer, Peacock, Dichio (Hateley), Impey, Sinclair.
Barnsley: Watson; Eaden, Appleby (Liddell), Bosancic (Bullock), Moses, De Zeeuw, Hendrie, Redfearn, Wilkinson, Marcelle (Jones), Sheridan.

THIRD ROUND

25 JAN

Brentford (0) 0
Manchester City (0) 1 *(Summerbee 62)*　12,019
Brentford: Dearden; Hutchings, Statham (Omigie), Ashby, Bates, McGhee, Asaba, Smith, Forster, Bent, Taylor.
Manchester City: Margetson; Brightwell, Ingram, Lomas, Symons, Kernaghan, Summerbee, McGoldrick, Heaney, Kinkladze, Rosler.

Coventry C (0) 1 *(Jess 75)*
Woking (0) 1 *(Thompson 89)*　　　16,040
Coventry C: Ogrizovic; Telfer, Borrows, Richardson, Shaw, Williams, Huckerby, Jess, Whelan, McAllister, Salako.
Woking: Batty; Howard, Taylor, Foster, Brown, Jones, Thompson, Wye S, Steele, Hunter (Hay), Walker.

THIRD ROUND REPLAYS

25 JAN

Leeds U (1) 1 *(Wallace 42)*
Crystal Palace (0) 0　　　　　　　　21,903
Leeds U: Martin; Kelly, Dorigo, Palmer, Halle, Radebe, Jackson, Wallace, Rush, Deane, Bowyer.
Crystal Palace: Day; Edworthy, Muscat, Roberts, Tuttle, Hopkin, Gordon, Ndah, Shipperley, Dyer (McKenzie), Veart (Freedman).

Bolton W (1) 6 *(McGinlay 8, Blake 52, 66, Thompson 64, Pollock 83, Green 90)*
Luton T (2) 2 *(Marshall 32, Thorpe 36)* 9713
Bolton W: Ward; Bergsson, Small, Pollock, Taggart, Fairclough, Frandsen, Sellars (Johansen), Blake, McGinlay (Green), Sheridan (Thompson).
Luton T: Feuer; James, Thomas, Linton, Davis S, Johnson, Hughes, Alexander, Showler (Guentchev), Thorpe, Marshall (Fotiadis).

West Ham U (0) 0
Wrexham (0) 1 *(Russell 90)* 16,763
West Ham U: Miklosko; Breacker, Dicks, Ferdinand, Bilic, Williamson, Lazaridis (Porfirio), Bishop, Jones, Lampard, Hughes.
Wrexham: Marriott; McGregor, Hardy, Hughes, Humes, Carey, Chalk, Owen (Russell), Connolly, Watkin, Ward.

FOURTH ROUND

26 JAN

Chelsea (0) 4 *(Hughes 50, Zola 58, Vialli 63, 76)*
Liverpool (2) 2 *(Fowler 10, Collymore 21)* 27,950
Chelsea: Hitchcock; Petrescu, Minto (Hughes M), Sinclair, Leboeuf, Clarke, Zola, Di Matteo, Vialli, Newton, Wise.
Liverpool: James; McAteer, Bjornebye (Berger), Kvarme, Wright, Matteo, McManaman, Collymore, Fowler, Barnes, Redknapp.

Newcastle U (0) 1 *(Ferdinand 60)*
Nottingham F (0) 2 *(Woan 76, 80)* 36,434
Newcastle U: Hislop; Barton (Clark), Beresford (Watson), Batty, Peacock, Elliott, Lee, Beardsley, Shearer, Ferdinand, Ginola (Gillespie).
Nottingham F: Crossley; Lyttle, Pearce, Cooper, Chettle, Phillips, Bart-Williams, Roy (Lee), Campbell, Haaland, Woan.

4 FEB

Arsenal (0) 0
Leeds U (1) 1 *(Wallace 12)* 38,115
Arsenal: Seaman; Dixon, Morrow, Keown, Bould, Adams, Parlour, Wright, Merson, Hughes (Hartson), Vieira.
Leeds U: Martyn; Kelly, Dorigo, Palmer, Molenaar, Halle, Jackson, Wallace (Rush), Harte, Deane, Bowyer (Wetherall).

Bolton W (1) 2 *(Taylor 14, Green 89)*
Chesterfield (1) 3 *(Davies 7, 50, 75)* 10,854
Bolton W: Ward; Green, Small, Pollock, Taggart, Fairclough, Frandsen, Johansen, Blake, Taylor (Lee), Thompson.
Chesterfield: Mercer; Hewitt, Jules, Curtis, Williams, Dyche, Carr, Beaumont, Davies, Howard, Perkins.

Peterborough U (1) 2 *(Charlery 20, Griffiths 47)*
Wrexham (1) 4 *(Ward 23, Watkin 57, Russell 58, 64)* 8734
Peterborough U: Griemink; Boothroyd (Heald), Clark, Edwards, Willis, Bodley, Rowe (Ebdon), Payne, Griffiths, Charlery, Morrison (Cleaver).
Wrexham: Marriott; McGregor, Brace, Hughes, Humes, Carey, Chalk (Owen), Russell, Connolly, Watkin, Ward.

FOURTH ROUND REPLAY

4 FEB

Wimbledon (0) 1 *(Gayle 63)*
Manchester U (0) 0 25,601
Wimbledon: Sullivan; Cunningham, Kimble, Jones, Blackwell, Perry, Gayle (Goodman), Earle, Ekoku, Holdsworth (Harford), Leonhardsen (McAllister).
Manchester U: Schmeichel; Neville G, Irwin (McClair), Johnsen, Keane, Pallister, Cantona, Poborsky (Solskjaer), Cole, Beckham, Giggs.

THIRD ROUND REPLAY

4 FEB

Woking (1) 1 *(Steele 36)*
Coventry C (1) 2 *(Whelan 11, Foster 79 (og))* 6000
Woking: Batty; Howard, Taylor, Foster, Brown, Jones, Thompson, Wye S, Steele, Hay (Hunter), Walker.
Coventry C: Ogrizovic; Hall, Burrows, Richardson, Shaw, Williams, Telfer, Jess (Strachan), Whelan, McAllister, Huckerby (Ndlovu).

FOURTH ROUND

5 FEB

Manchester C (1) 3 *(Heaney 24, Summerbee 61, Rosler 71)*
Watford (0) 1 *(Noel-Williams 58)* 24,031
Manchester C: Margetson; Crooks, Ingram, Lomas, Symons, Kernaghan, Summerbee, McGoldrick, Heaney, Kinkladze, Rosler (Creaney).
Watford: Miller; Gibbs, Ludden, Palmer, Ward, Page, Slater, Bazeley, Noel-Williams (Robinson), Johnson R, Easton (Andrews).

FIFTH ROUND

15 FEB

Birmingham C (1) 1 *(Bruce 37)*
Wrexham (0) 3 *(Hughes 51, Humes 61, Connolly 90)* 21,511
Birmingham C: Bennett; Brown, Johnson, Bruce, Ablett (Bowen), Holland, Devlin, Horne, Furlong, Legg, Limpar (Newell).
Wrexham: Marriott; McGregor, Brace, Hughes, Humes, Carey, Chalk (Brammer), Russell, Connolly, Watkin, Ward.

Chesterfield (0) 1 *(Curtis 54 (pen))*
Nottingham F (0) 0 8890
Chesterfield: Mercer; Hewitt, Jules, Curtis, Carr, Holland, Beaumont, Davies, Morris, Howard, Perkins.
Nottingham F: Crossley; Lyttle, Haaland, Cooper, Chettle, Blatherwick (McGregor), Bart-Williams, Roy (Fettis), Saunders, Campbell, Woan (Gemmill).

Leeds U (0) 2 *(Bowyer 52, 90)*
Portsmouth (1) 3 *(McLoughlin 7, Svensson 67, Bradbury 86)* 35,604
Leeds U: Martyn; Kelly, Dorigo, Palmer, Molenaar, Halle, Jackson (Rush), Wallace, Deane, Radebe, Bowyer.
Portsmouth: Knight; Pethick, Thomson, McLoughlin (Igoe), Perrett, Awford, Hall, Simpson (Dobson), Bradbury, Svensson (Allen), Hillier.

Manchester C (0) 0
Middlesbrough (0) 1 *(Juninho 77)* 30,462
Manchester C: Margetson; McGoldrick, Ingram, Lomas, Symons, Brightwell, Summerbee, Brown (Beagrie), Crooks, Kinkladze (Dickov), Rosler.
Middlesbrough: Roberts; Cox, Fleming, Vickers, Festa, Whyte, Hignett, Mustoe, Stamp, Juninho, Ravanelli.

Wimbledon (1) 2 *(Gayle 44, Earle 55)*
QPR (1) 1 *(Hateley 41)* 22,395
Wimbledon: Sullivan; Cunningham, Kimble, Jones, Blackwell, Perry, Gayle, Earle, Ekoku, Holdsworth (Goodman), Leonhardsen (McAllister).
QPR: Sommer; Yates, Brevett (Dichio), Barker, McDonald, Ready, Spencer, Peacock, Hateley, Murray, Sinclair.

FOURTH ROUND

15 FEB

Blackburn R (1) 1 *(Sherwood 1)*
Coventry C (2) 2 *(Jess 28, Huckerby 44)*   21,123
Blackburn R: Flowers; Kenna, Le Saux, Sherwood, Hendry, Berg, McKinlay, Flitcroft (Warhurst), Sutton (Donis), Gallacher, Wilcox.
Coventry C: Ogrizovic; Telfer, Hall, Borrows, Shaw, Williams, Jess, Richardson, Wheeler, McAllister, Huckerby (Ndlovu).

FIFTH ROUND

16 FEB

Bradford C (0) 0
Sheffield W (0) 1 *(Humphreys 84)*   17,830
Bradford C: Schwarzer; Pinto (Liburd), Jacobs, Dreyer, Mohan, O'Brien, Waddle, Duxbury, Edinho, Hamilton, Kiwomya (Midgley).
Sheffield W: Pressman; Atherton, Nolan, Pembridge, Newsome, Walker, Carbone (Hirst), Hyde, Booth, Humphreys, Nicol.

Leicester C (0) 2 *(Walsh 52, Newton 88 (og))*
Chelsea (2) 2 *(Di Matteo 16, Hughes M 35)*   19,125
Leicester C: Keller; Campbell (Lawrence), Grayson, Watts, Walsh, Prior, Taylor, Robins (Wilson), Claridge, Marshall, Parker.
Chelsea: Hitchcock; Petrescu, Minto, Sinclair, Leboeuf, Clarke, Zola (Vialli), Di Matteo (Gullit), Newton, Hughes M, Wise.

26 FEB

Derby Co (2) 3 *(Ward 16, Van der Laan 40, Sturridge 87)*
Coventry C (2) 2 *(Huckerby 5, Whelan 12)*   18,003
Derby Co: Hoult; Carsley, Dailly, Laursen, Powell D, Rowett, Trollope, Asanovic, Van der Laan, Sturridge, Ward.
Coventry C: Ogrizovic; Telfer, Hall, Richardson, Shaw, Williams, Jess (Ndlovu 79), Whelan, Dublin, McAllister, Huckerby.

FIFTH ROUND REPLAY

26 FEB

Chelsea (0) 1 *(Leboeuf 117 (pen))*
Leicester C (0) 0   26,053
Chelsea: Grodas; Petrescu (Johnsen 106), Clarke, Sinclair, Leboeuf, Minto (Vialli 7), Newton, Di Matteo, Zola, Hughes M, Wise.
Leicester C: Keller; Grayson, Izzet, Elliott, Walsh, Prior, Parker, Lennon, Claridge (Taylor 73), Marshall, Heskey.

SIXTH ROUND

8 MAR

Derby Co (0) 0
Middlesbrough (1) 2 *(Juninho 39, Ravanelli 90)*   17,567
Derby Co: Taylor; Carsley, Powell C, Flynn (Rowett), Powell D (Simpson), Stimac, Asanovic, Trollope, Ward, Willems (Gabbiadini), Dailly.
Middlesbrough: Roberts; Fleming, Blackmore, Mustoe, Pearson, Festa, Stamp, Hignett, Beck, Juninho, Ravanelli.

9 MAR

Chesterfield (0) 1 *(Beaumont 58)*
Wrexham (0) 0   8735
Chesterfield: Mercer; Hewitt, Jules, Curtis, Williams, Dyche, Beaumont (Gaughan), Holland (Dunn), Morris, Howard, Perkins.

Wrexham: Marriott; McGregor, Brace, Hughes, Humes, Carey, Chalk (Bennett), Russell, Connolly, Watkin, Ward (Owen).

Portsmouth (0) 1 *(Burton 82)*
Chelsea (2) 4 *(Hughes M 25, Wise 43, 86, Zola 56)* 15,701
Portsmouth: Knight; Pethick, Thomson, McLoughlin, Perrett, Awford, Hall, Simpson (Igoe), Bradbury, Svensson (Burton), Hillier.
Chelsea: Grodas; Petrescu, Minto, Sinclair, Leboeuf (Johnsen), Clarke, Zola, Di Matteo (Burley), Hughes P, Hughes M, Wise.

Sheffield W (0) 0
Wimbledon (0) 2 *(Earle 74, Holdsworth 90)*   25,032
Sheffield W: Pressman; Nicol, Nolan, Atherton, Newsome (Humphreys), Walker, Pembridge, Hyde (Hirst), Booth, Carbone, Whittingham.
Wimbledon: Sullivan; Cunningham, Kimble, Jones, Blackwell, Perry, Ardley, Earle, Ekoku (McAllister), Leonhardsen, Gayle (Holdsworth).

SEMI-FINALS

13 APR

Middlesbrough (0) 3 *(Ravanelli 64, Hignett 70 (pen), Festa 100)*   (at Old Trafford)
Chesterfield (0) 3 *(Morris 54, Dyche 60 (pen), Hewitt 119)*   49,640
Middlesbrough: Roberts; Fleming, Kinder, Vickers, Festa, Mustoe, Emerson, Hignett (Moore), Beck (Blackmore), Juninho, Ravanelli.
Chesterfield: Mercer; Hewitt, Jules, Curtis, Williams, Dyche, Holland (Beaumont), Davies, Morris, Howard, Perkins (Carr).

Wimbledon (0) 0   (at Highbury)
Chelsea (1) 3 *(Hughes M 43, 90, Zola 64)*   32,674
Wimbledon: Sullivan; Cunningham, Kimble, Jones, Blackwell, Perry, Ardley (Holdsworth), Earle, Ekoku, Leonhardsen, Gayle.
Chelsea: Grodas; Burley, Clarke, Sinclair, Leboeuf, Johnsen, Newton, Di Matteo, Zola, Hughes M, Wise.

SEMI-FINAL REPLAY

22 APR

Chesterfield (0) 0   (at Hillsborough)
Middlesbrough (1) 3 *(Beck 12, Ravanelli 57, Emerson 89)*   30,339
Chesterfield: Mercer; Hewitt, Jules, Curtis, Williams, Dyche, Davies, Holland, Morris, Howard (Carr), Perkins.
Middlesbrough: Roberts; Cox (Whyte), Blackmore, Vickers, Pearson, Mustoe, Emerson, Hignett, Beck, Juninho (Stamp), Ravanelli.

FINAL (AT WEMBLEY)

17 MAY

Chelsea (1) 2 *(Di Matteo 1, Newton 82)*
Middlesbrough (0) 0   79,160
Chelsea: Grodas; Petrescu, Minto, Sinclair, Leboeuf, Clarke, Zola (Vialli 88), Di Matteo, Newton, Hughes M, Wise.
Middlesbrough: Roberts; Blackmore, Fleming, Stamp, Pearson, Festa, Emerson, Mustoe (Vickers 28), Ravanelli (Beck 23), Juninho, Hignett (Kinder 74).
Di Matteo's 43 seconds goal was the fastest in Wembley Cup Final history.
Referee: S. Lodge (Barnsley).

FA CUP ATTENDANCES 1967–97

	1st Round	2nd Round	3rd Round	4th Round	5th Round	6th Round	Semi-Finals & Final	Total	No. of matches	Average per match
1996-97	209,521	122,324	651,139	402,293	199,873	67,035	191,813	1,843,998	151	12,211
1995-96	185,538	115,669	748,997	391,218	274,055	174,142	156,500	2,046,199	167	12,252
1994-95	219,511	125,629	640,017	438,596	257,650	159,787	174,059	2,015,249	161	12,517
1993-94	190,683	118,031	691,064	430,234	172,196	134,705	228,233	1,965,146	159	12,359
1992-93	241,968	174,702	612,494	377,211	198,379	149,675	293,241	2,047,670	161	12,718
1991-92	231,940	117,078	586,014	372,576	270,537	155,603	201,592	1,935,340	160	12,095
1990-91	194,195	121,450	594,592	530,279	276,112	124,826	196,434	2,038,518	162	12,583
1989-90	209,542	133,483	683,047	412,483	351,423	123,065	277,420	2,190,463	170	12,885
1988-89	212,775	121,326	690,199	421,255	206,781	176,629	167,353	1,966,318	164	12,173
1987-88	204,411	104,561	720,121	443,133	281,461	119,313	177,585	2,050,585	155	13,229
1986-87	209,290	146,761	593,520	349,342	263,550	119,396	195,533	1,877,400	165	11,378
1985-86	171,142	130,034	486,838	495,526	311,833	184,262	192,316	1,971,951	168	11,738
1984-85	174,604	137,078	616,229	320,772	269,232	148,690	242,754	1,909,359	157	12,162
1983-84	192,276	151,647	625,965	417,298	181,832	185,382	187,000	1,941,400	166	11,695
1982-83	191,312	150,046	670,503	452,688	260,069	193,845	291,162	2,209,625	154	14,348
1981-82	236,220	127,300	513,185	356,987	203,334	124,308	279,621	1,840,955	160	11,506
1980-81	246,824	194,502	832,578	534,402	320,530	288,714	339,250	2,756,800	169	16,312
1979-80	267,121	204,759	804,701	507,725	364,039	157,530	355,541	2,661,416	163	16,328
1978-79	243,773	185,343	880,345	537,748	243,683	263,213	249,897	2,604,002	166	15,687
1977-78	258,248	178,930	881,406	540,164	400,751	137,059	198,020	2,594,578	160	16,216
1976-77	379,230	192,159	942,523	631,265	373,330	205,379	258,216	2,982,102	174	17,139
1975-76	255,533	178,099	867,880	573,843	471,925	206,851	205,810	2,759,941	161	17,142
1974-75	283,956	170,466	914,994	646,434	393,323	268,361	291,369	2,968,903	172	17,261
1973-74	214,236	125,295	840,142	747,909	346,012	233,307	273,051	2,779,952	167	16,646
1972-73	259,432	169,114	938,741	735,825	357,386	241,934	226,543	2,928,975	160	18,306
1971-72	277,726	236,127	986,094	711,399	486,378	230,292	248,546	3,158,562	160	19,741
1970-71	329,687	230,942	956,683	757,852	360,687	304,937	279,644	3,220,432	162	19,879
1969-70	345,229	195,102	925,930	651,374	319,893	198,537	390,700	3,026,765	170	17,805
1968-69	331,858	252,710	1,094,043	883,675	464,915	188,121	216,232	3,431,554	157	21,857
1967-68	322,121	236,195	1,229,519	771,284	563,779	240,095	223,831	3,586,824	160	22,418

THE SCOTTISH SEASON 1996–97

The Bad News first? Scottish club teams have again not done well in Europe. Our four representatives (Rangers in the Champions Cup, Hearts in the Cup Winners, and Celtic and Aberdeen in the UEFA) made no real mark, though there were good performances – in particular, Hearts losing out to Red Star only on an away goal. But now it is back to the drawing board. However, there is a stir apparent: the Old Firm at least have every intention of attracting attention – for the right reasons. A vast influx of players from overseas has caused comment amongst a public hopefully looking for home-raised players amongst the ranks, and finding increasing difficulty in coping with spelling, pronunciation – and even geographical locations – and bewildered by the variety of comings and goings. Not many are going to grumble if there is success in due course.

At international level, Craig Brown continues to inspire, and fairly moderate teams have achieved success greater than could have been expected. The Scotland manager (and his back-room team) study the opposition, and then manage to invoke a team spirit; this has been missing on other occasions. There have been disappointments: the farce in Estonia, ably abetted by a FIFA committee which either knew not what it was doing, or perhaps knew too well; the subsequent draw in Monaco. Despite an occasional stumble, there have been heroic results, and a visit to France next year is well in the sights. Perhaps Craig Brown will be able to select a team and play it; though it may fairly be said that players called up to replace those injured have played their hearts out.

So to the home scene: A fair pre-season guess might have selected Rangers and Celtic to fill the top two places. So it was, and, as so often in the past, the results of the matches between the two were of paramount importance: Rangers won all four games, and, despite some other poor results, they moved gently and inexorably to their record-equalling ninth successive league win. Celtic, were for much of the time, more or less in the picture; but rather less than more. A strong Celtic is needed: the new team have a difficult task ahead, but good luck to them.

If the top places were looking settled, the rest of the division was much more interesting: the most extraordinary advance came from Dundee United: after six games, they lay at the bottom of the pile, having amassed a total of one point, and a rapid return to the First Division looked probable. Yet by early January they had worked their way up the table to third, a position they held comfortably to the end of the season. From mid-December, a sequence of thirteen undefeated games included only two draws. Managers come – and managers go, usually when the results are poor. They do not always get the credit when results are good, but Mr McLean fully earned the superlatives heaped upon him. Perhaps the other Mr McLean should also share the credit, for a brave appointment. Anyway, Dundee United are back in Europe, where their name is not unknown – especially in Barcelona. Hearts had a good season, with Jim Jefferies bringing on a young team with much enthusiasm; Dunfermline earned a sound mid-table place, but Aberdeen, prominent in the early season, faded. All was not well at Kirkcaldy, and Raith Rovers spent most of the season at the foot of the table: changes, and speculated changes, did not help, and the relegation place looked destined before it became certain. But what of the other three? Motherwell could not find their form; Hibernian, changing managers in mid-season, struggled; but it was Kilmarnock, also with a new manager, who flirted with the bottom places until a run of four wins, starting in early March, and including the scalps of both Celtic and Rangers, saw them rise to a more promising position. Killie, too, were – as we shall see – to find glory elsewhere later. As the last league games came, all three clubs were in the shadow of the dreaded Play-off: as the minutes ticked away, first one, then another of the clubs looked doomed. As the final whistles blew, it was found that all three games were drawn, leaving Hibs in the 9th place.

In the First Division, several teams vied with each other for supremacy. Into November, and St Johnstone showed their class and determination by forging ahead; they soon had a substantial lead. Dundee, Falkirk, Partick and St Mirren all showed signs of challenging, but all were inconsistent when it mattered; it was left to Airdrieonians to slide home in second position. Of the teams who had come up, East Fife were soon lost, but Stirling Albion, taking time to settle, found their form and sped away from the struggling Clydebank who joined the Fifers in the drop.

Then came the Play-off: Hibs v Airdrieonians: the two encounters did little to enhance the image of the game; rugged determination was the order of the day, and it was perhaps significant that the final game, with Hibs defending a precarious 1-0 lead from their home game, included three goals scored from the spot. Large crowds turned out and many enjoyed the competitive jousting; not so the managers, though the relief of one was tempered by his thoughts of the disappointment of the other.

Livingston were away to a flying start in the Second Division, winning their first five games, and establishing a good points lead. They could not keep going at this pace, and were gradually overhauled by Ayr and Hamilton, both determined to regain the upper division. In the end these latter two took top places by some margin, the champions being decided by a drawn game between them at the end of April. Ayr finished only just ahead of Hamilton, but the latter are delighted by their quick and deserved return to the First Division. Livingston finished in third place: well done! Berwick Rangers were the fall guys here, and a tussle between Dumbarton and Stranraer to join them in the Third Division saw the latter gain the necessary win in the last game; so Dumbarton were relegated.

The former Highland League clubs in the Third Division have shown in their brief league experience that they were to be reckoned with: last season Ross County threw away a fine position with a poor run in; this time, they finished strongly, but Forfar Athletic, on the same points and with the better goal difference, also finished in devastating form, and a series of commanding wins blew them back to the Second Division whilst Ross County were left to contemplate what might have been. Meantime, Inverness Caledonian Thistle, in their new and well-placed, well-designed ground, carried all before them, and, if they relaxed for the last games when promotion was assured, none could deny their supremacy: they still finished nine points clear of the rest. Albion Rovers deserve a mention: they have languished at or near the foot of the league for a while, but this time they were away to a brisk start, and a mid-table final position was just reward.

The League Challenge Cup was won by Stranraer amidst scenes of excitement after the final at Broadwood Stadium; their opponents, St Johnstone, who had been the obvious favourites, could, on this occasion, only congratulate a team which had pushed itself to extremes of energy and dedication to register a first major success.

The Coca-Cola Cup, always an enjoyable crowd-puller, had its usual crop of interesting results: Albion Rovers beat Falkirk; Alloa Athletic beat Motherwell on penalties; Hearts only just squeezed home against those well-known cup fighters, Stenhousemuir; and Airdrie beat Raith (they always seem to play each other in every cup). Dundee did well to reach a semi-final against Hearts, who lost in the excellent final at Celtic Park to Rangers by the odd goal in seven.

Finally, the Tennent's Scottish Cup: there were no major shocks early on, though Huntly, subsequently the comfortable winners of the Highland League, took Clyde to a close replay. After this, Clyde disposed of Ayr United and St Mirren, and they then lost to Kilmarnock by the narrowest of margins. Falkirk, meantime, had been struggling against Berwick Rangers; it needed a replay before they could go forward, to meet and defeat Dunfermline in the fourth round. Next they eliminated Raith Rovers, who had just won against Airdrie (what did I say?) in the quarter-finals; whilst at this stage Celtic achieved their lone season's triumph against Rangers. Both semi-finals were drawn. In the replays, Kilmarnock beat Dundee United with a very late goal; whilst Falkirk, scoring early against Celtic, held on grimly. So, with both the 'under dogs' winning, it was a Kilmarnock–Falkirk final, a repeat of the final forty years earlier. In a fitting 'family' game at Ibrox to end the season, Kilmarnock were the winners, by the only goal. Perhaps the best touch came from the Kilmarnock scorer who, at the end of the game, went straight to his former (and defeated) manager to apologise for scoring against him. Isn't this what football ought to be about?

ALAN ELLIOTT

ABERDEEN   Premier Division

Year Formed: 1903. *Ground & Address:* Pittodrie Stadium, Pittodrie St, Aberdeen AB2 1QH. *Telephone:* 01224 632328.
Ground Capacity: all seated: 21,634. All. *Size of Pitch:* 110yd × 72yd.
Chairman: Ian R. Donald. *Secretary:* Ian J. Taggart. *General Manager:* David Johnston.
Manager: Roy Aitken. *Coach:* Tommy Craig. *Physios:* David Wylie, John Sharp.
Managers since 1975: Ally MacLeod; Billy McNeill; Alex Ferguson; Ian Porterfield; Alex Smith and Jocky Scott; Willie
Miller. *Club Nicknames(s):* The Dons. *Previous Grounds:* None.
Record Attendance: 45,061 v Hearts, Scottish Cup 4th rd; 13 Mar, 1954.
Record Transfer Fee received: £1.75 million for Eoin Jess to Coventry City (February 1996).
Record Transfer Fee paid: £1m+ for Paul Bernard from Oldham Athletic (September 1995).
Record Victory: 13-0 v Peterhead, Scottish Cup; 9 Feb, 1923.
Record Defeat: 0-8 v Celtic, Division 1; 30 Jan, 1965.
Most Capped Players: Alex McLeish, 77, Scotland.
Most League Appearances: 556: Willie Miller, 1973-90.
Most League Goals in Season (Individual): 38: Benny Yorston, Division I; 1929-30.
Most Goals Overall (Individual): 199: Joe Harper.

ABERDEEN 1996–97 LEAGUE RECORD

Match No.	Date	Venue	Opponents	Result	H/T Score	Lg. Pos.	Goalscorers	Attendance
1	Aug 10	H	Celtic	D 2-2	0-1	—	Windass (pen) [74], Shearer [80]	18,595
2	17	A	Motherwell	D 2-2	1-1	6	Windass [24], Shearer [72]	6206
3	25	H	Hearts	W 4-0	1-0	—	Miller [44], Dodds [53], Windass [76], Glass [84]	13,515
4	Sept 7	A	Raith R	W 4-1	3-1	3	Windass [11], Dodds 3 [19, 26, 84]	4729
5	14	H	Kilmarnock	W 3-0	0-0	3	Kombouare [47], Dodds 2 [66, 75]	11,826
6	21	H	Hibernian	L 0-2	0-1	3		12,475
7	28	A	Dundee U	L 0-1	0-0	3		10,359
8	Oct 12	H	Dunfermline Ath	W 3-0	2-0	3	Dodds 2 [10, 26], Young [89]	10,404
9	19	A	Rangers	D 2-2	1-2	3	Irvine [44], Dodds [89]	50,076
10	26	H	Raith R	W 1-0	0-0	3	Miller [77]	11,246
11	Nov 2	A	Celtic	L 0-1	0-0	3		50,124
12	16	H	Dundee U	D 3-3	1-1	3	Kiriakov [25], Kombouare [78], Dodds [88]	13,807
13	23	A	Hibernian	W 1-0	1-0	3	Windass [44]	10,931
14	Dec 1	A	Rangers	L 0-3	0-1	—		19,168
15	7	A	Dunfermline Ath	W 3-2	1-1	3	Miller [10], Rowson [55], Windass [78]	5465
16	11	A	Hearts	W 2-1	0-1	—	Shearer [75], Windass [78]	11,477
17	14	H	Motherwell	D 0-0	0-0	2		10,442
18	21	A	Kilmarnock	L 0-3	0-1	3		6114
19	26	H	Celtic	L 1-2	1-1	—	Dodds [13]	16,748
20	28	H	Hibernian	D 1-1	0-1	3	Shearer [90]	9834
21	Jan 1	A	Dundee U	L 0-4	0-1	—		9548
22	4	H	Dunfermline Ath	L 0-2	0-0	5		9137
23	12	A	Rangers	L 0-4	0-2	—		47,509
24	18	A	Raith R	D 2-2	1-1	5	Rowson [25], Miller [46]	3950
25	Feb 1	H	Kilmarnock	W 2-1	2-0	5	Windass 2 [20, 24]	8361
26	8	A	Motherwell	D 2-2	2-0	5	Dodds 2 [12, 33]	5555
27	10	H	Hearts	D 0-0	0-0	—		8642
28	22	A	Dunfermline Ath	L 0-3	0-2	5		5553
29	Mar 1	H	Rangers	D 2-2	1-1	5	Kombouare [34], Goram (og) [57]	16,331
30	15	H	Dundee U	D 1-1	1-0	5	Windass [35]	13,645
31	22	A	Hibernian	L 1-3	0-1	6	Craig [52]	9615
32	Apr 5	H	Motherwell	D 0-0	0-0	5		9317
33	12	A	Hearts	D 0-0	0-0	5		11,186
34	20	A	Celtic	L 0-3	0-1	—		46,989
35	May 3	H	Raith R	W 2-0	2-0	6	Millen (og) [9], Dodds [34]	10,763
36	10	A	Kilmarnock	D 1-1	1-0	6	Dodds [34]	10,027

Final League Position: 6

Honours

League Champions: Division I 1954-55. Premier Division 1979-80, 1983-84, 1984-85; *Runners-up:* Division I 1910-11, 1936-37, 1955-56, 1970-71, 1971-72. Premier Division 1977-78, 1980-81, 1981-82, 1988-89, 1989-90, 1990-91, 1992-93, 1993-94.
Scottish Cup Winners: 1947, 1970, 1982, 1983, 1984, 1986, 1990; *Runners-up:* 1937, 1953, 1954, 1959, 1967, 1978, 1993.
League Cup Winners: 1955-56, 1976-77, 1985-86, 1989-90, (Coca Cola cup) 1995-96; *Runners-up:* 1946-47, 1978-79, 1979-80, 1987-88, 1988-89, 1992-93.
Drybrough Cup Winners: 1971, 1980.

European: *European Cup* 12 matches (1980-81, 1984-85, 1985-86); *Cup Winners Cup Winners:* 1982-83. Semi-finals 1983-84. 37 matches (1967-68, 1970-71, 1978-79, 1982-83, 1983-84, 1986-87, 1990-91, 1993-94); *UEFA Cup* 42 matches (*Fairs Cup:* 1968-69. *UEFA Cup:* 1971-72, 1972-73, 1973-74, 1977-78, 1979-80, 1981-82, 1987-88, 1988-89, 1989-90, 1991-92, 1994-95, 1996–97).
Club colours: Shirt, Shorts, Stockings: Red with white trim.

Goalscorers: *League (45):* Dodds 15, Windass 10 (1 pen), Miller 4, Shearer 4, Kombouare 3, Rowson 2, Craig 1, Glass 1, Irvine 1, Kiriakov 1, Young 1, own goals 2. *Scottish Cup (2):* Booth 1, Dodds 1. *Coca Cola Cup (10):* Windass 5, Dodds 4, Glass 1.

Watt M 9	Buchan J 9+5	Woodthorpe C 14+5	Tzvetanov T 27	Irvine B 24+1	Inglis J 15	Miller J 26+4	Windass D 29	Bernard P 13+1	Kiriakov I 26+1	Glass S 20+4	Shearer D 2+19	Rowson D 30+4	Dodds W 31	Walker N 19	Grant B 2	Young D 22+4	Kombouare A 30	McKimmie S 14	Kpedekpo M —+5	Wyness D 1+6	Craig M 2+3	Booth S 8+11	Ingolfsson H 1+5	Stillie D 8	Anderson R 14	Match No.
1	2	3	4¹	5	6	7²	8	9	10	11	12	13														1
1	2	12²	3	5	6	7	9	4¹	10	11	13			8												2
		3	5	6	7		9		10	11				8	1	2	4									3
	13	3	5			7¹	9		10	11²	12			8	1	2	4	6								4
	13	3	5¹			9³	12	10	11²	14	4		8	1		7	6	2								5
	11	3	5			7¹	10		9	12	8	1		4	6	2²	13									6
	11²	3	5			9	10		12	4¹	8	1		4	6	2	13									7
		3	5	7²		10	9	4	8¹	1	11	6	2	13	12											8
		3	5	7		10	12	4	8	1	11	6	2			9										9
		3	5	7	9²	10		4	8	1	11¹	6	2	13	12											10
		3	5¹	7	9	10		4	8²	1	11	6	2	13	12											11
	12	3	5	7²	9	10	14	4	8	1	11²	6	2¹	13												12
	12	3	5	7²	10	9		4	8¹	1	14	6	2	13	11¹											13
		3	5	12	10²	9		4	8	1	7¹	6	2	11	13											14
		3	5	7	10	9		4	8	1	11¹	6	2	12												15
			5	7	10	3	9	12	13	4	8²	1	11¹	6	2											16
			5	7	10	3	9	12	13	4	8²	1	11¹	6	2											17
		3	5	7¹	10	9	2	11	13	4⁴	8	1		6	12											18
		3	5	7	10	9³	2	11¹	14	4	8²	1	12	6	13											19
		3	5	7	10²	9	2	11¹	13	4⁴	8	1	14	6	12											20
		3	5	7³	10¹	9	4	11²	13	14	8	1		6	2	12										21
		3	5	6	7		10¹	12	13	4	8	11				9²							1	2		22
		3¹	5		7	10		2	11	4	8²			9	6				13	12	1				2	23
1		3	5		7	10	9	13		4	8¹			11²	6					12					2	24
1	13	3		5	7¹	10		11		4	8			9	6			12							2²	25
1	12		3¹	5	13	10		9²	11	4	8			7	6								9²		2	26
1	14	3		5	7¹		12	11	13	4	8			10³	6								9²		2	27
1	5	3³	14		12		10	11		4	8			7¹	6	13							9²		2	28
1	10¹	3		5	7²	8		11		4				6		12	14						9³ 13		2	29
1	8	3		5	7¹	10		11		4				6		12						9			2	30
	7	3		5		10		11		4²				6		12	13	8	9¹		1				2	31
	6		3	5		10	8¹	11	12	4				7²			13	9			1				2	32
	6	11	3	5		10		9	14	4	8³			12		7²	13				1				2¹	33
	4	11	3	5	12	10¹		9³	14	7	8²			6			13				1				2	34
	12	11³	3	5	7	10	9		13	4	8			6							1				2	35
	13	11	3	5	7²	10¹	9		12	4	8			6							1				2	36

AIRDRIEONIANS

First Division

Year Formed: 1878. *Ground & Address:* Broadwood Stadium, Cumbernauld G68 9NE. Address for all correspondence:
32 Stirling Street, Airdrie, ML6 0AH *Telephone:* 01236 762067.
Ground Capacity: all seated: 6300. *Size of Pitch:* 112yd × 76yd.
Chairman and Secretary: George W. Peat CA.
Manager: Alex MacDonald. *Physio:* Ian Constable. *Coach:* John Binnie.
Managers since 1975: I. McMillan; J. Stewart; R. Watson; W. Munro; A. MacLeod; D. Whiteford; G. McQueen; J. Bone.
Club Nickname(s): The Diamonds or The Waysiders. *Previous Grounds:* Mavisbank, Broomfield Park.
Record Attendance: 24,000 v Hearts, Scottish Cup; 8 Mar, 1952.
Record Transfer Fee received: £200,000 for Sandy Clark to West Ham U, May 1982.
Record Transfer Fee paid: £175,000 for Owen Coyle from Clydebank, February 1990.
Record Victory: 15-1 v Dundee Wanderers, Division II; 1 Dec, 1894.
Record Defeat: 1-11 v Hibernian, Division I; 24 Oct, 1959.
Most Capped Player: Jimmy Crapnell, 9, Scotland.
Most League Appearances: 523; Paul Jonquin, 1962-79.
Most League Goals in Season (Individual): 53, Hugh Baird, Division II, 1954-55. *Most Goals Overall (Individual):* —

AIRDRIEONIANS 1996–97 LEAGUE RECORD

Match No.	Date	Venue	Opponents	Result	H/T Score	Lg. Pos.	Goalscorers	Attendance
1	Aug 17	A	Stirling A	W 1-0	0-0	—	Lawrence [67]	1598
2	24	H	East Fife	D 0-0	0-0	3		1334
3	Sept 7	A	Dundee	W 1-0	1-0	3	Davies [17]	2756
4	14	H	Greenock Morton	L 1-2	1-0	4	McPhee [29]	2081
5	21	H	Partick Th	D 4-4	2-3	6	Cooper 2 (1 pen) [10, 73 (p)], McPhee 2 [41, 89]	1997
6	24	A	St Johnstone	D 1-1	1-0	—	Connolly P [4]	2877
7	28	A	Falkirk	D 1-1	1-1	5	Connolly P [5]	3923
8	Oct 12	A	Clydebank	W 4-1	1-0	4	Lovering (og) [44], Davies [66], Lawrence [69], McPhee [89]	604
9	15	H	St Mirren	D 2-2	1-0	—	Smith [14], Cooper [50]	1635
10	19	H	Stirling A	W 3-1	0-0	3	Eadie 2 (1 pen) [58 (p), 66], Black [68]	1303
11	26	A	East Fife	W 4-0	1-0	3	Davies [7], Eadie [55], Lawrence [60], McPhee [80]	885
12	Nov 2	A	Greenock Morton	D 1-1	1-1	1	McPhee [44]	2658
13	9	H	Dundee	D 0-0	0-0	1		2173
14	16	H	Falkirk	L 0-1	0-1	5		2428
15	23	H	Partick Th	D 0-0	0-0	3		3109
16	30	A	St Mirren	W 3-2	1-0	3	Davies [17], McPhee [48], Black [59]	3536
17	Dec 11	H	Clydebank	W 3-1	2-1	—	Davies [8], McPhee [43], Sweeney [68]	975
18	18	A	St Johnstone	L 0-1	0-0	—		2159
19	21	A	Stirling A	W 2-1	2-1	2	Connolly P 2 [4, 34]	1220
20	Jan 11	A	Dundee	L 1-2	0-1	3	Eadie [73]	2469
21	14	A	Greenock Morton	W 1-0	0-0	—	Smith [74]	1416
22	18	H	St Mirren	D 1-1	1-0	4	Stewart [23]	2216
23	22	H	Partick Th	D 1-1	1-1	—	Eadie [1]	2029
24	Feb 1	A	Clydebank	D 1-1	1-1	4	Eadie [9]	459
25	8	A	St Johnstone	D 2-2	0-1	5	Connolly P [46], Stewart [79]	3669
26	22	A	East Fife	D 1-1	1-1	5	Eadie [45]	1138
27	25	A	Falkirk	W 3-0	1-0	—	Cooper 2 (1 pen) [17, 62 (p)], Connolly P [65]	2590
28	Mar 8	A	Partick Th	W 2-1	0-0	3	Sandison [77], Wilson [90]	2723
29	15	H	Falkirk	W 2-0	0-0	2	Cooper 2 [53, 75]	2090
30	22	A	St Mirren	W 2-1	1-1	2	Jack [3], Cooper [79]	4648
31	Apr 5	H	Clydebank	W 4-1	1-0	2	Connolly P [25], Davies [46], Stewart [62], Black (pen) [69]	1424
32	12	H	Dundee	W 2-0	1-0	2	Johnston [20], Black (pen) [49]	2530
33	19	A	Greenock Morton	D 1-1	0-1	2	Connolly P [48]	2073
34	26	H	Stirling A	L 1-2	1-1	2	Mackay [21]	1902
35	May 3	A	East Fife	D 0-0	0-0	2		2010
36	10	H	St Johnstone	L 0-1	0-0	2		1977

Final League Position: 2

Honours
League Champions: Division II 1902-03, 1954-55, 1973-74; *Runners-up:* Division I 1922-23, 1923-24, 1924-25, 1925-26.
First Division 1979-80, 1989-90, 1990-91, 1996–97. Division II 1900-01, 1946-47, 1949-50, 1965-66.
Scottish Cup Winners: 1924; *Runners-up:* 1975, 1992, 1995. *Scottish Spring Cup Winners:* 1976.
League Cup semi-finalists: 1991-92, 1994-95.
B&Q Cup Winners: 1994-95.

European: *UEFA Cup* 2 matches (1992-93).
Club colours: Shirt: White with red diamond. Shorts: White. Stockings: Red.

Goalscorers: *League (56):* Connolly P 8, Cooper 8 (2 pens), McPhee 8, Eadie 7 (1 pen), Davies 6, Black 4 (2 pens), Lawrence 3, Stewart 3, Smith 2, Jack 1, Johnston 1, Mackay 1, Sandison 1, Sweeney 1, Wilson 1, own goal 1. *Scottish Cup (1):* Sandison 1. *Coca Cola Cup (3):* Cooper 1, Eadie 1, Hetherston 1. *League Challenge Cup (0).*

Martin J 27	Jack P 30	Smith A 21 + 7	Sandison S 36	Sweeney S 26	Black K 26 + 2	Johnston F 15 + 6	Davies J 31	Cooper S 18 + 5	Lawrence A 10 + 17	Hetherston P 5	Wilson M 21 + 8	Boyle J 19 + 7	Connolly P 24 + 11	Stewart A 31	McPhee B 24 + 4	McIntyre T 5 + 2	Eadie K 9 + 6	Rhodes A 9	Connolly G 1 + 3	Mackay G 8	Martin A — + 1	Match No.
1	2	3	4	5	6²	7	8	9	10³	11¹	12	13	14									1
1	2	3¹	4	5	6²	7	8	9¹	10	11	13	14	12									2
1	3	11	4	5		12	6	9		8²	13	7	14	2¹	10³							3
1	3	11	4²	5		9	12	8¹	6		7	13	2	10								4
1	3		4³	5	13	11	8	9	14	6¹		7	12	2²	10							5
1	3²		4	5	11		8	9	12		6		2	7	10¹	13						6
1		3	4	5	13	12	6	9	14		8²	7¹	11³	10	2							7
1	3	11	4	5	6		8	9²	12		7¹		2	10	13							8
1		11	4	5	6	2	8	9²	13		12		7¹	10	3							9
1	3	11	4	5	6³	14	8	9²	12		7¹		2	10	13							10
1	3		4	5	6	11	8	7²			12	13	2	10	9¹							11
1	3	11	4	5		8	12	7²		6	13		2	10	9¹							12
	3	11	4	5		8	7			6	12		2	10	9¹			1				13
1	3		4	5		8	12	11²		6	7	13	2	10	9¹							14
1	3		4	5		8	9	11¹		6	7		10	2	12							15
1	3	11¹	4	5	6	12	8	9	13		7		2	10²								16
1	3		4	5	6²	11	8	12			10	13	7¹	2	9							17
1	3	11	4¹	5	6		10	12			8	13	7²	2	9							18
1	3	11	4	5¹	6	13	10		14		8	12	7	2²	9³							19
1	3	11	4	5	6		8	12		10¹		7²	2	9	13							20
1	3	11	4	5	6		8	7¹		10		12	2	9								21
1	3	11¹	4	5	6		8	12		10²	13	7	2	9								22
1	3²	13	4	5	6		8	9		10	7	12	2		11¹							23
1		3	4		6		8	12	13		10	7¹	11	2		5¹	9					24
1	3	11¹	4		6		8	14		10	12	7	2		13	5³	9²					25
1	3	12	4		6		10²			8	7	11	2		13	5¹	9³		14			26
1		3	4	5	6			9¹	13		7	2	11²	8	12		10					27
1		3	4¹	5²	6	12		9	10³		8	7	11	2			13		14			28
	5	12	4		6	3	10	9			7	11²	2					1	13	8¹		29
	3		4		6	5	10	9			7	11¹	2				12	1		8		30
	3		4		6	5	10	12			7	9	2		11¹			1		8		31
	3	13	4		6¹	5	10	12			7²	9	2		11			1		8		32
	3¹	12	4		6	5	10	13			7	9	2		11			1		8²		33
	3¹	12	4		6	5	14	10³			7	9	2		11²		13	1		8		34
	3	14	4		6	5	10	13			7¹	9	2		11¹		12	1		8²		35
	3		4	5		7	8¹	9	12			10	2		11²			1		6	13	36

ALBION ROVERS   Third Division

Year Formed: 1882. *Ground & Address:* Cliftonhill Stadium, Main St, Coatbridge ML5 3RB. *Telephone:* 01236 606334.
Ground capacity: total: 1238, seated: 538. *Size of Pitch:* 110yd × 70yd.
Chairman: Andrew Dick, *Company Secretary:* David Shanks BSc. *General Manager:* John Reynolds.
Commercial Manager: Gordon Dishington.
Manager: Vinnie Moore. *Assistant Manager:* Tom O'Neil. *Youth Development:* Jimmy Lindsay.
Physio: William Cowan. *Managers since 1975:* G. Caldwell; S. Goodwin; H. Hood; J. Baker; D. Whiteford; M. Ferguson;
W. Wilson; B. Rooney; A. Ritchie; T. Gemmell; D. Provan; M. Oliver; B. McLaren; T. Gemmell; T Spence; J. Crease.
Club Nickname(s): The Wee Rovers. *Previous Grounds:* Cowheath Park, Meadow Park, Whifflet.
Record Attendance: 27,381 v Rangers, Scottish Cup 2nd rd; 8 Feb, 1936.
Record Transfer Fee received: £40,000 from Motherwell for Bruce Cleland.
Record Transfer Fee paid: £7000 for Gerry McTeague to Stirling Albion, September 1989.
Record Victory: 12-0 v Airdriehill, Scottish Cup; 3 Sept, 1887.
Record Defeat: 1-11 v Partick T, League Cup, 11 August 1993.
Most Capped Player: Jock White, 1 (2), Scotland.
Most League Appearances: 399, Murdy Walls, 1921-36.
Most League Goals in Season (Individual): 41: Jim Renwick, Division II; 1932-33.
Most Goals Overall (Individual): 105: Bunty Weir, 1928-31.

ALBION ROVERS 1996–97 LEAGUE RECORD

Match No.	Date	Venue	Opponents	Result	H/T Score	Lg. Pos.	Goalscorers	Atten- dance
1	Aug 17	H	Forfar Ath	W 2-0	0-0	—	Cody [50], McGuire [90]	457
2	23	A	East Stirling	W 1-0	0-0	—	McGuire [62]	503
3	31	H	Cowdenbeath	W 2-0	1-0	1	Walker 2 [28, 66]	866
4	Sept 7	H	Inverness CT	D 0-0	0-0	1		845
5	14	A	Arbroath	W 3-1	2-1	1	Dickson [10], Walker [20], McKenzie [70]	524
6	21	H	Alloa	D 1-1	0-0	1	Walker [71]	892
7	28	A	Queen's Park	D 1-1	0-1	1	McKenzie [86]	616
8	Oct 5	H	Montrose	L 1-2	1-1	2	Moore [40]	950
9	12	A	Ross Co	L 2-3	2-1	3	Clark [23], Dickson [24]	1145
10	19	A	Forfar Ath	D 0-0	0-0	4		393
11	27	H	East Stirling	W 4-3	1-2	—	Moore [15], McGuire (pen) [61], Dickson [76], Walker [85]	603
12	Nov 2	H	Arbroath	W 1-0	1-0	2	Walker [31]	591
13	9	A	Inverness CT	D 1-1	0-0	2	McKenzie [70]	3734
14	16	H	Queen's Park	D 1-1	1-0	2	Clark [44]	736
15	30	A	Montrose	L 1-2	0-1	5	McKilligan [78]	534
16	Dec 3	A	Alloa	L 0-2	0-1	—		217
17	21	H	Ross Co	L 0-2	0-1	7		406
18	Jan 18	H	Montrose	W 2-1	1-1	6	Moore [24], Haro (og) [79]	319
19	25	A	Forfar Ath	L 1-3	0-1	6	Martin [88]	423
20	28	A	Queen's Park	D 0-0	0-0	—		432
21	Feb 1	A	Ross Co	L 1-3	1-1	7	Gardner [16]	1136
22	4	A	Cowdenbeath	D 1-1	0-0	—	Gardner [51]	166
23	15	H	Inverness CT	L 0-3	0-0	7		608
24	18	A	Arbroath	W 2-1	0-0	—	Watters 2 [61, 63]	286
25	21	A	East Stirling	W 4-1	3-1	6	McKenzie [9], Gardner [14], Watters [39], Boal [46]	320
26	28	H	Cowdenbeath	W 4-0	3-0	5	McKenzie 2 [16, 39], Watters 2 [33, 65]	502
27	Mar 5	A	Alloa	W 3-0	2-0	—	Watters 2 [32, 44], McKenzie [64]	405
28	8	A	Alloa	L 0-2	0-1	4		464
29	15	H	Queen's Park	W 2-1	1-0	4	Dickson [40], Watters [52]	547
30	22	A	Montrose	W 4-0	1-0	4	Shepherd [37], Watters 2 [61, 85], Gardner [72]	355
31	Apr 5	H	Ross Co	L 1-2	0-1	4	Gardner [89]	704
32	12	A	Inverness CT	L 1-4	1-2	4	Moore [37]	2960
33	19	H	Arbroath	L 1-2	1-1	4	Moore [24]	454
34	26	A	Forfar Ath •	L 1-3	0-1	5	Kelly [49]	438
35	May 2	H	East Stirling	D 1-1	0-0	—	Watters [85]	396
36	10	A	Cowdenbeath	D 0-0	0-0	5		153

Final League Position: 5

Honours
League Champions: Division II 1933-34, Second Division 1988-89; *Runners-up:* Division II 1913-14, 1937-38, 1947-48.
Scottish Cup Runners-up: 1920. *League Cup:* —.
Club Colours: Shirt: Yellow with black trim. Shorts: Black. Stockings: Black.

Goalscorers: *League (50):* Watters 11, McKenzie 7, Walker 6, Gardner 5, Moore 5, Dickson 4, McGuire 3 (1 pen), Clark 2, Boal 1, Cody 1, Kelly 1, McKilligan 1, Martin 1, Shepherd 1, own goal 1. *Scottish Cup (0). Coca Cola Cup (7):* McGuire 3, McKenzie 2, MacFarlane 1, McInally 1. *League Challenge Cup (1):* McKenzie 1.

Ross S 24	Byrne D 29	Pickering M 13	MacFarlane C 10+2	Martin P 25	McInally A 13+3	McKenzie D 17+15	Cody S 8+1	Walker T 20+4	Moore V 27	Gallagher J 7+1	McGuire D 8+8	Reilly R 4+10	Clark M 14+3	Angus J 8	Harty I 4+5	McKenna A —+1	Dickson J 17+4	McKilligan N 28+2	Tannock R 4	McGowan N 16+1	Gardner L 16	Watters W 23+1	Duncan C 10	Brown M 6	Davidson A 1	Mitchell C 11+2	McInnes I 9+3	McGuinness E 1	Boal B 8+6	Leonard M 1+2	Webster D 2+1	Kennedy A 1	Shepherd A 5	Kelly G 4+1	Mitchell A 1	Robertson S 1	Russell R —+1	Match No.
1	2	3	4	5	6	7	8^1	9^2	10	11	12	13																										1
1	2	3	4	5	7	8^2	6^3	9^1	10	11	12	13	14																									2
1	2		4	5	6	12	8	9	10^2		7	11^1	13	3																								3
1	2^1		4	5		7		9	10		6	11^2		8	3	12	13																					4
1	2		4	5		12	13	9^3	10^2	7	11^1	14	6	3		8																					5
1	2^3		4	5	13	12		9		7	11^2	14	6	3	10^1	8																					6
1	2		4	5	8	13		9^2	11^1	7	12	6	3	10																							7
1	2		4	5	13		12	8		7^1	9^2	10	3	11	6																						8
1			5	6	10^2		9	8	12		13	7	3^1		11	2	4																					9
1	2		4	5	6^1	13		9	10	11^3	12	8		7^2	14	3																						10
1^9	2		4	5		9	10	12		6				15	7	3	8^1	11																				11
	2		5	14	11^3	10		12	13	6				8^1	7	3	9^2	1	4																			12
	2		5	13	11^2	10		12	7					8	6	3	9^1	1	4																			13
	2		5	12		9^1	10	14	13	8^2				7	3^3	6		11	4	1																		14
	2	14		8	12			7^2	9^1	6				11^2	13	4	3		10	1	5																	15
	4	12		10	14	9		7^2	13	8				11	6^2	5^1	3			1	5																	16
		7	13		8	10			6	3^1				12	2	4	11^2		9	1	5																	17
		5		12		11	10		13					6	2		3	8	9^1	1		4	7^2															18
		5	13	12		9		10^1	14					6^3	2		3	8	11^2	4	7																	19
	4	5				9					11		12	2			3	8		1	6	7	10^1															20
	4	5				11	10^1				12	13		14	2		3	8	9^2		6	7^3																21
1	4	3	5			9								2				8	12	1		6	7	10	11^1													22
1	4	3		5		12	6	9^1	10					2				7	11			5	8^2	13														23
1	4	3		5		11	6^2	10						7^1	2			8	9		13		12															24
1	4	3		5		11	6	10^1						2				7	9		12		8															25
1	4	3		5		11	6^1	10						2				8	9^3		13		7^2	14	12													26
1	4	3		5		11		10		12				2				7	9				8^1		6													27
1	4	3^1				11	6^3	14	10					2				12	7	9			13	8^2	5													28
1	4	3				11			5					12	10	2		8	9				7^1		6													29
1	4	3				11			6						5			7	9				10			8	2											30
1	4	3		5		11^2	13	10		12				2				8	9				7^1		6													31
1	3^2		5		11^3	13	10							6				8^1	9		4	7	12	14				2										32
1			6	13		10				11			8^2	4	3		9				2	7^1	12				5											33
1			7	10						11			6		3		9				4						5	8	2									34
1	4		7	10						11^2			6^1	5	3		9				2	13	12					8^3	14									35
	2		8^2	11						10^1				5	3		9				4	7	12											1	6	13	36

ALLOA ATHLETIC
Third Division

Year Formed: 1883. *Ground & Address:* Recreation Park, Clackmannan Rd, Alloa FK10 1RR. *Telephone:* 01259 722695.
Ground Capacity: total: 4111, seated: 424. *Size of Pitch:* 110yd × 75yd.
Chairman: Robert Hopkins. *Secretary:* E. G. Cameron. *Commercial Manager:* William McKie.
Manager: Tom Hendrie. *Assistant Manager:* John Coughlin. *Physio:* Alan Anderson.
Managers since 1975: H. Wilson; A. Totten; W. Garner; J. Thomson; D. Sullivan; G. Abel; B. Little; H. McCann; W. Lamont; Pat McAuley. *Club Nickname(s):* The Wasps. *Previous Grounds:* None.
Record Attendance: 13,000 v Dunfermline Athletic, Scottish Cup 3rd rd replay; 26 Feb, 1939.
Record Transfer Fee received: £60,000 for Paul Sheerin to Southampton (1992).
Record Transfer Fee paid: £10,000 for Douglas Lawrie from Stirling Albion.
Record Victory: 9-2 v Forfar Ath, Division II; 18 Mar, 1933.
Record Defeat: 0-10 v Dundee, Division II; 8 Mar, 1947: v Third Lanark, League Cup, 8 Aug, 1953.
Most Capped Player: Jock Hepburn, 1, Scotland.
Most League Appearances: —.
Most League Goals in Season (Individual): 49: William 'Wee' Crilley, Division II; 1921-22.
Most Goals Overall (Individual): —.

ALLOA 1996–97 LEAGUE RECORD

Match No.	Date	Venue	Opponents	Result	H/T Score	Lg. Pos.	Goalscorers	Atten- dance
1	Aug 17	A	Montrose	W 2-1	1-0	—	Dwyer 2 [17, 73]	450
2	24	H	Arbroath	D 1-1	0-0	5	Dwyer [57]	559
3	31	A	Inverness CT	L 0-1	0-0	5		1685
4	Sept 7	A	Ross Co	W 2-1	1-0	2	Dwyer 2 [3, 73]	1192
5	14	H	Cowdenbeath	D 1-1	0-1	2	Nelson [68]	508
6	21	A	Albion R	D 1-1	0-0	3	McCormack [90]	892
7	28	H	East Stirling	W 1-0	1-0	3	Dwyer [44]	501
8	Oct 5	A	Queen's Park	L 1-2	1-2	5	Kane [12]	647
9	12	H	Forfar Ath	L 3-4	3-3	5	Moffat 2 [15, 44], Cowan [18]	395
10	19	A	Montrose	W 3-1	0-1	5	Irvine [47], McAneny P [61], Gilmour [83]	555
11	26	A	Arbroath	W 2-0	0-0	2	Moffat [76], Mackay [87]	480
12	Nov 2	A	Cowdenbeath	L 0-2	0-1	6		504
13	9	H	Ross Co	L 1-3	1-1	7	Dwyer [40]	615
14	16	A	East Stirling	D 2-2	1-1	7	Gilmour [28], McCormack [84]	426
15	30	H	Queen's Park	W 2-1	0-0	7	Irvine [62], McAneny P [78]	449
16	Dec 3	H	Albion R	W 2-0	1-0	—	Irvine [20], Dwyer [71]	217
17	21	A	Montrose	W 3-2	1-1	4	Irvine [36], Dwyer 2 [59, 67]	606
18	Jan 18	H	Queen's Park	W 3-1	1-1	4	Irvine 2 [12, 51], Dwyer [70]	408
19	21	H	East Stirling	D 1-1	0-0	—	McAneny P [86]	435
20	Feb 1	H	Forfar Ath	L 0-3	0-2	4		427
21	8	H	Cowdenbeath	W 1-0	1-0	4	Wilson S [30]	381
22	15	A	Ross Co	L 1-3	0-1	5	Piggott [76]	1546
23	22	H	Arbroath	L 0-2	0-0	5		388
24	25	A	Forfar Ath	D 1-1	0-0	—	Pew [90]	371
25	Mar 1	A	Inverness CT	L 1-3	0-2	6	Cowan [75]	1397
26	5	A	Albion R	L 0-3	0-2	—		405
27	8	H	Queen's Park	W 2-0	1-0	5	Piggott 2 [11, 90]	464
28	11	H	Inverness CT	L 0-2	0-1	—		441
29	15	A	East Stirling	W 3-0	1-0	5	Simpson [20], Cowan [72], Irvine [74]	386
30	22	A	Queen's Park	W 4-0	0-0	5	Pew [57], Irvine [62], Simpson 2 [67, 70]	399
31	Apr 5	A	Forfar Ath	L 0-1	0-0	5		433
32	12	H	Ross Co	D 1-1	1-0	5	Irvine [20]	597
33	19	A	Cowdenbeath	L 1-2	0-2	5	Irvine [84]	183
34	26	H	Montrose	W 1-0	1-0	4	Irvine [15]	308
35	May 3	A	Arbroath	W 2-1	0-0	4	Irvine [65], McAnenay M [85]	364
36	10	H	Inverness CT	W 1-0	1-0	4	Pew [16]	507

Final League Position: 4

Honours
League Champions: Division II 1921-22; *Runners-up:* Division II 1938-39. Second Division 1976-77, 1981-82, 1984-85, 1988-89.
Scottish Cup: —.
League Cup: —.
Club colours: Shirt: Gold with black trim. Shorts: Black. Stockings: Gold.

Goalscorers: *League (50):* Irvine 12, Dwyer 11, Cowan 3, McAneny P 3, Moffat 3, Pew 3, Piggott 3, Simpson 3, Gilmour 2, McCormack 2, Kane 1, McAnenay M 1, Mackay 1, Nelson 1, Wilson S 1. *Scottish Cup (4):* Dwyer 1, Irvine 1, McAneny P 1, Mackay 1. *Coca Cola Cup (4):* Dwyer 1, Irvine 1, McAneny P 1, McAvoy 1. *League Challenge Cup (3):* Irvine 3.

Balfour R 15	Valentine C 35	McAvoy N 4 + 2	Nelson M 21 + 3	Cowan M 30	Kane K 27 + 1	McCormack J 25	Mackay S 10 + 3	Dwyer P 14 + 1	Irvine W 33	Little T 10 + 10	McAneny P 30 + 2	Moffat B 12 + 3	Gilmour J 14 + 16	McAnenay M 10 + 15	Wilson S 22	Johnston N — + 2	Wylie R — + 2	McCulloch K 11 + 4	Monaghan M 19	Pew D 20 + 1	Cadden S — + 1	Tennant S 2	Wilson M 14 + 2	Dick A — + 1	Piggott J 5 + 9	Simpson P 8 + 3	Lamont W 1	Mathieson M 3	Cameron J 1	Match No.
1	2	3³	4	5³	6	7	8	9	10²	11	12	13	14																	1
1	2		4	5	7	3	8	9	10	6¹		11	12																	2
1	2	3	4	5³	7	6	8	9	10		12	11²	13																	3
1	2	6¹	11	5	7³	4	8²	9	10		3	14	12	13																4
1	2		3	5	7	6		9	10	11	4		12	8¹																5
1	2	13	3³	5	7	6	8¹	9	10	11²	4	14	12																	6
1	2	14	12	5	7		8	9³	10	6¹	4	11	3²	13																7
1	2	10	3³	5	7	6²			11¹	4	9	13	12	8	14															8
1	2		3³	5	7	6	9²		10	14	4	11	12	13	8¹															9
1	2		3	5	7¹		6		10	4	9	11	8²		13	12														10
1	2		3	5		6	12		10	13	4	9	11²	8¹	7															11
1	2		3³	5		6		12	10	14	4	9	11¹	8³	7		13													12
1	2		3	5		6		10		12	4	9²	11¹	8	7	13														13
	2		3	5			8		9		4	10³	6¹	12	7		13	1	11											14
	2		3	5			7³		9	10	13	4	11	6²	12				1	8¹	14									15
	2		3	5				8³	9	10	13	4	11¹	6²	14	7			1	12										16
	2		7	5				8	9	10		4		6					1	11		3								17
	2		3	5		7³			9	10		4	11¹	13	8				1	6²			12	14						18
	2			5	11²				9	10		4	13	12	8				1	7		3¹	6							19
	2		3	5	7³		12		10	14	4		11²	8¹					13	1	9		6							20
	2	13			9³	3²			10		4		14	8	7				5	1	11¹		6		12					21
	2			9	3				10	4			8¹	7					5	1	11		6		12					22
	2		5	11	3¹				10	14	4		12	8¹	7				13	1	6				9³					23
	2			11²		13			10	14	4		6	8³	3				5	1	7				9¹	12				24
	7		5	12	3¹				10		4		14		8				2¹	1	11³		6		13	9				25
	2		5	7					10	12	4		11		3					1	8		6¹		13	9²				26
	2		5						10	11¹	3		12		7				4	1	8		6		9					27
1	3		5	11					10		4				7				2		8		6		9¹	12				28
1	2		5	7²	3				10				13	8					4		11¹		6		12	9				29
	2			7	3				10		4			8					5		11		6²		13	12	1	9¹		30
	2			7	3				10		5			8					4	1	6		12			11¹		9		31
	2		3		7	8			10¹		5		12	14					4	1	6				13	11²		9³		32
			5	7	3				10		4		13	12	8				2	1			6²			9¹		11		33
	2	14	5	7	3				10²	9¹	4³		11	13	8					1			6		12					34
	4		3	5	7¹	2			10	6			12							11			8			9			1	35
	4		3	5	7¹	2			10	11³			14	12						1	6			8		13	9²			36

ARBROATH   Third Division

Year Formed: 1878. *Ground & Address:* Gayfield Park, Arbroath DD11 1QB. *Telephone and Fax:* 01241 872157.
Ground Capacity: 6488. seated: 715. *Size of Pitch:* 115yd × 71yd.
President: John D. Christison. *Secretary:* Charles Kinnear. *Commercial Manager:* Sandy Watt.
Manager: David Baikie. *Assistant Manager:* Graeme Irons. *Physio:* William Shearer. *Coaches:* John Martin, Ian
Fairweather.
Managers since 1975: A. Henderson; I. J. Stewart; G. Fleming; J. Bone; J. Young; W. Borthwick; M. Lawson, D.
McGrain MBE, J. Scott, J. Brogan, T. Campbell, G. Mackie.
Club Nickname(s): The Red Lichties. *Previous Grounds:* None.
Record Attendance: 13,510 v Rangers, Scottish Cup 3rd rd; 23 Feb, 1952.
Record Transfer Fee received: £120,000 for Paul Tosh to Dundee (Aug 1993).
Record Transfer Fee paid: £20,000 for Douglas Robb from Montrose (1981).
Record Victory: 36-0 v Bon Accord, Scottish Cup 1st rd; 12 Sept, 1885.
Record Defeat: 1-9 v Celtic, League Cup 3rd rd; 25 Aug 1993.
Most Capped Player: Ned Doig, 2 (5), Scotland.
Most League Appearances: 445: Tom Cargill, 1966-81.
Most League Goals in Season (Individual): 45: Dave Easson, Division II; 1958-59.
Most Goals Overall (Individual): 120: Jimmy Jack; 1966-71.

ARBROATH 1996–97 LEAGUE RECORD

Match No.	Date	Venue	Opponents	Result	H/T Score	Lg. Pos.	Goalscorers	Atten- dance
1	Aug 17	H	Ross Co	W 3-1	2-1	—	Watters 3 [35, 40, 60]	494
2	24	A	Alloa	D 1-1	0-0	3	Watters [65]	559
3	31	H	East Stirling	D 0-0	0-0	4		492
4	Sept 7	A	Montrose	D 0-0	0-0	5		826
5	14	H	Albion R	L 1-3	1-2	7	McCarron [4]	524
6	21	A	Forfar Ath	D 1-1	1-0	7	Pew [1]	605
7	28	H	Cowdenbeath	L 0-1	0-1	6		405
8	Oct 5	A	Inverness CT	L 0-2	0-1	8		2086
9	12	H	Queen's Park	W 1-0	0-0	7	Pew [79]	433
10	19	A	Ross Co	L 0-2	0-0	8		1326
11	26	H	Alloa	L 0-2	0-0	8		480
12	Nov 2	A	Albion R	L 0-1	0-1	8		591
13	9	H	Montrose	L 1-2	0-0	9	Scott [88]	666
14	16	A	Cowdenbeath	D 2-2	0-2	9	Grant [46], Wylie [80]	301
15	23	A	Forfar Ath	D 1-1	1-0	9	McVicar (pen) [14]	533
16	30	H	Inverness CT	L 1-4	0-2	9	Grant [84]	457
17	Dec 14	A	Queen's Park	L 1-3	0-3	10	Grant [88]	403
18	26	H	Ross Co	W 2-1	0-0	—	McCormick [55], McAulay [80]	581
19	Jan 1	H	Cowdenbeath	W 1-0	0-0	—	McWalter [84]	469
20	18	A	Inverness CT	L 1-4	0-2	9	Grant [85]	1742
21	Feb 1	H	Queen's Park	D 0-0	0-0	9		326
22	4	A	Forfar Ath	D 1-1	0-0	—	McAulay [50]	655
23	15	A	Montrose	L 0-1	0-1	9		686
24	18	H	Albion R	L 1-2	0-0	—	McAulay [78]	286
25	22	A	Alloa	W 2-0	0-0	9	McVicar (pen) [55], McCarron [71]	388
26	26	A	East Stirling	D 0-0	0-0	—		144
27	Mar 4	H	East Stirling	L 1-2	1-2	—	McWalter [7]	172
28	8	H	Forfar Ath	D 3-3	1-2	9	McAulay [30], Grant [71], Glennie (og) [84]	521
29	15	A	Cowdenbeath	D 1-1	1-0	9	Reynolds [35]	142
30	22	H	Inverness CT	D 0-0	0-0	9		570
31	Apr 5	A	Queen's Park	L 1-3	0-1	9	McCarron [66]	387
32	12	H	Montrose	D 1-1	0-0	9	Hope [53]	432
33	19	A	Albion R	W 2-1	1-1	9	Gallagher [18], Scott [88]	454
34	26	A	Ross Co	L 0-1	0-0	9		1672
35	May 3	H	Alloa	L 1-2	0-0	9	McWalter [75]	364
36	10	A	East Stirling	L 0-3	0-1	10		258

Final League Position: 10

Honours
League Champions Runners-up: Division II 1934-35, 1958-59, 1967-68, 1971-72.
Scottish Cup: Quarter-finals: 1993.
League Cup: —.
Club colours: Shirt: Maroon with white and sky blue trim. Shorts: White. Stockings: Maroon with white and sky blue hooped tops.

Goalscorers: *League (31):* Grant 5, McAulay 4, Watters W 4, McCarron 3, McWalter 3, McVicar 2 (2 pens), Pew 2, Scott 2, Gallagher 1, Hope 1, McCormick 1, Reynolds 1, Wylie 1, own goal 1. *Scottish Cup (5):* McCormick 2, Grant 1, McCarron 1, Wylie 1. *Coca Cola Cup (0). League Challenge Cup (2):* Peters 1, Welsh 1.

Hinchcliffe C 27	Peters S 17	Florence S 20+7	Waters M 7	Ward J 14+1	McAulay J 36	Pew D 13	Gardner L 10	Watters W 10	McVicar D 20+1	Clark P 3+1	Scott S 11+16	McCarron J 19+5	Roberts P 7+7	McWalter M 23+1	Mackie B 3	Welsh B 1+7	Crawford J 26	Bilsland B 6	Gallagher J 24+1	Moonlight P 1+1	Grant B 15+2	Tennant S 2	Kerr J 1	Wylie R 21	Longmuir K 2+3	McCormick S 2+2	Morrison P 8+2	Arthur G 9	Hope D 10	Balfour G 10	Murray I —+1	Orr J 6+1	Phinn J 2	Dunn G —+1	Reynolds C 9	Valentine S 1	Match No.
1	2	3	4²	5	6	7¹	8	9	10	11	12	13																									1
1	2	3	4¹	5	6	7	8	9	10²	11	12			13																							2
1	2	3		5	6	4	8	9	10²	11	7¹	12	13																								3
1	2	3		5	6	7	8	9	4		12	10¹	11																								4
1	2	3			6	7	8	9¹	12	11	4	10²	5	13																							5
1	2	3		5	6	7	8	9¹	12	4	10²	13	11																								6
1	2²	3	11	5	6	7	8	9			12	4¹	10	13																							7
1	2	3	8	5	6¹	7²	11	9	12	4	10	13																									8
1	2	3¹	8	5	6	7	11	9	12	10	4																										9
1	2²	3	8¹	5	6	7	11	9	13	12	10	4																									10
1	2	3¹		5	6	7			10²	13	8		4	9	11	12																					11
1	4	11		2	6	7					12	9¹		5	3	8	10																				12
1	2			5	6	7	12	8	4²		13			3		10¹	11		9																		13
1	12			6	9		13		4		11¹	7²		10			8	2	3		5																14
1				2	6		11	8	12		4	13		7²			10	9	3¹		5																15
1	11			2	6		9	12	4		3	7¹		10			8		5																		16
1	2¹	11			4		8	12	7		6			3			9		5		10²	13															17
1	2			4	3		12	8	10		6			11			5		9¹		7																18
1	2			6	4		3	12	8		10			11			5		9		7¹																19
		6		4	3		8¹	10			2	12		9			5		13		7²			1			11										20
1	12	8		4	11²		6	3	9		5			13			7		10¹		2			5	13	7		10¹	2								21
1	10	4		3	11		6	8	9		5			13			7²		2¹		12			5	13	7²		2¹	12								22
1	13	4		3	11²	10	12		6		8			9			5		7¹		2			5		7¹				2							23
	11²			8	4		12	7			3			10			5		9¹					5	9¹	13	1			2	6						24
	12			4	3		11²	10			6			8			9		5		13			5	13	7¹	1			2							25
	12			4	3		11¹	10			6			8			9		5		7			5		7	1			2							26
	12			4	7		10		9		6			8¹			11		5		13			5		13	1⁶			2	3²				15		27
1	13			4	7		11	9			6			8			12		5		3			5					3	2¹			10¹				28
1	12			4			13	10			6			8			7²		5					5			11¹	3				9	2				29
1	2			4			7	9¹			6			8			12		5					5			11	3					10				30
1	3			4			12	7			6			8			5¹										10	2					11				31
	2			4	5		12	7			6			8										1		11	3¹						10				32
	2			4	3		12	7	9¹		6			8					5					1		11							10				33
	2			4	3		12	7			6			5										1		11	8						10¹				34
	2			4			12	7	9		6			8			5							1		11	3¹						10				35
1	3¹			4			12	8	9		6			2			5²							11	7		13						10				36

AYR UNITED   First Division

Year Formed: 1910. *Ground & Address:* Somerset Park, Tryfield Place, Ayr KA8 9NB. *Telephone:* 01292 263435.
Ground Capacity: 12,128. seated: 1450. *Size of Pitch:* 110yd × 72yd.
Chairman: W. J. Barr. *Administrator:* Brian Caldwell. *Secretary:* J. E. Eyley. *Sales and Marketing:* Mrs Angela Smith.
Merchandising: Wendy Messenger. *Lottery Manager:* Andrew Davie.
Manager: Gordon Dalziel. *Assistant Manager:* Alistair Dawson.
Managers since 1975: Alex Stuart; Ally MacLeod; Willie McLean; George Caldwell; Ally MacLeod; George Burley;
Simon Stainrod. *Club Nickname(s):* The Honest Men. *Previous Grounds:* None.
Record Attendance: 25,225 v Rangers, Division I; 13 Sept, 1969.
elticRecord *Transfer Fee received:* £300,000 for Steven Nicol to Liverpool (Oct 1981).
Record Transfer Fee paid: £50,000 for Peter Weir from St Mirren, June 1990.
Record Victory: 11-1 v Dumbarton, League Cup; 13 Aug, 1952.
Record Defeat: 0-9 in Division I v Rangers (1929); v Hearts (1931); B Division v Third Lanark (1954).
Most Capped Player: Jim Nisbet, 3, Scotland.
Most League Appearances: 459, John Murphy, 1963–78.
Most League League and Cup Goals in Season (Individual): 66, Jimmy Smith, 1927-28.
Most League and Cup Goals Overall (Individual): 213, Peter Price, 1955–61.

AYR UNITED 1996–97 LEAGUE RECORD

Match No.	Date	Venue	Opponents	Result	H/T Score	Lg. Pos.	Goalscorers	Attendance
1	Aug 17	H	Hamilton A	D 1-1	0-1	—	English [86]	2227
2	24	A	Brechin C	D 1-1	1-0	6	Kerrigan [12]	419
3	31	H	Berwick R	W 6-0	2-0	3	Smith P [25], English [34], Kerrigan 2 [48, 83], George [86], Mercer [88]	1594
4	Sept 7	A	Stenhousemuir	W 2-1	1-0	2	Smith P (pen) [30], Mercer [89]	708
5	14	H	Clyde	L 2-4	0-3	4	Smith P [78], Biggart [81]	1995
6	21	A	Queen of the S	W 2-1	1-0	3	English [15], Kerrigan [48]	1813
7	28	H	Stranraer	W 2-0	1-0	2	Smith P [8], Kerrigan [67]	1915
8	Oct 5	A	Dumbarton	W 3-1	2-1	2	Kinnaird [28], Henderson [37], English [55]	939
9	12	H	Livingston	W 1-0	1-0	1	Connor [10]	2578
10	19	A	Hamilton A	W 2-1	0-1	1	Kerrigan [69], English [85]	1173
11	26	H	Brechin C	W 1-0	1-0	1	Smith T [41]	1973
12	Nov 2	A	Clyde	W 3-2	2-1	1	Kinnaird [14], English [23], Kerrigan [71]	1254
13	9	H	Stenhousemuir	L 1-2	1-1	1	Smith P [14]	2025
14	16	A	Stranraer	W 1-0	0-0	1	Horace [73]	1021
15	23	H	Queen of the S	W 1-0	1-0	1	Kerrigan [18]	1969
16	30	H	Dumbarton	L 1-4	1-0	1	English [24]	1773
17	Dec 14	A	Livingston	L 0-1	0-1	2		3542
18	28	A	Berwick R	W 2-1	1-1	2	Smith P [44], Horace [48]	525
19	Jan 18	A	Dumbarton	D 1-1	1-0	2	Sharp (og) [39]	801
20	21	H	Stranraer	W 2-0	2-0	—	Jamieson [25], Scott [39]	1696
21	28	H	Hamilton A	W 1-0	0-0	—	Scott [51]	1905
22	Feb 1	H	Livingston	W 1-0	0-0	1	Kerrigan [59]	2568
23	5	A	Queen of the S	W 3-1	0-0	—	Smith P [54], Scott [70], Kerrigan [82]	1506
24	8	H	Clyde	W 3-1	2-0	1	Kerrigan 3 [9, 39, 82]	2006
25	15	A	Stenhousemuir	W 2-1	2-1	1	George [40], Scott [45]	833
26	22	A	Brechin C	D 1-1	0-1	1	Smith P [77]	439
27	Mar 1	H	Berwick R	W 2-0	1-0	1	Kerrigan [35], Jamieson [46]	1648
28	8	H	Queen of the S	D 2-2	2-1	1	Smith P [28], Smith T [38]	1942
29	15	A	Stranraer	W 1-0	0-0	1	Horace [76]	847
30	22	A	Dumbarton	D 1-1	1-1	1	Horace [44]	1575
31	Apr 5	A	Livingston	L 1-2	1-0	1	Hood [27]	2512
32	12	H	Stenhousemuir	W 2-1	1-0	1	Smith T [34], Traynor [63]	1743
33	19	A	Clyde	D 1-1	1-0	1	Traynor [10]	1207
34	26	H	Hamilton A	D 1-1	1-0	1	Scott [28]	5156
35	May 3	H	Brechin C	W 2-0	1-0	1	Jamieson [36], Smith T (pen) [67]	3164
36	10	A	Berwick R	W 2-0	2-0	1	Scott [43], Horace [44]	1423

Final League Position: 1

Honours
League Champions: Division II 1911-12, 1912-13, 1927-28, 1936-37, 1958-59, 1965-66. Second Division 1987-88, 1996–97;
Runners-up: Division II 1910-11, 1955-56, 1968-69.
Scottish Cup: —. *League Cup:* —.
*B&Q Cup: Runners-up:*1990-91, 1991-92.
Club colours: Shirt: White with black trim. Shorts: White. Stockings: White.

Goalscorers: *League (61):* Kerrigan 14, Smith P 9 (1 pen), English 7, Scott 6, Horace 5, Smith T 4 (1 pen), Jamieson 3, George 2, Kinnaird 2, Mercer 2, Traynor 2, Biggart 1, Connor 1, Henderson 1, Hood 1, own goal 1. *Scottish Cup (0).* *Coca Cola Cup (7):* English 2, Kerrigan 2, Connor 1, Henderson 1, Hood 1. *League Challenge Cup (4):* Smith P 2, English 1, Jamieson 1.

Smith H 35	Law R 10 + 6	Hood G 20 + 1	Coyle R 29 + 1	Jamieson W 26	Connor R 18	Smith P 27 + 6	English I 17	Kerrigan S 22 + 5	Henderson D 19 + 10	George D 17 + 3	Kinnaird P 13 + 14	Traynor J 30 + 4	Dalziel G — + 1	Mercer J 1 + 12	Biggart K — + 3	Watson P 20 + 6	Ward M 1	Smith C — + 1	Smith T 19 + 2	McStay J 6 + 4	Humphries M 22	Horace A 21 + 1	Clark J — + 1	Castilla D 1	Scott R 17 + 1	Bell R 5 + 1	Match No.
1	2²	3	4	5	6	7	8	9	10¹	11	12	13															1
1	2	3	4¹	5	6	7	8²	9	13	10	11³	12	14														2
1	2¹	4²	13	5	6	7³	8	9	10	12	11	3		14													3
1	2²	3	4		6	7³	8	9	10	12	11	5		14	13												4
1	2	3	4	5¹	6	9	8		10²	7	11³	12		13	14												5
1		5	4		6	10¹	8	9	11	12		2				3			7								6
1		5	4		6	7	8	9	11	10	12	2				3											7
1	12	5¹	4		6	7	8	9²	10	11		2		14	13	3³											8
1	13	5	4		6	7	8	9²	10¹	11	12	2				3											9
1	14	5¹	4		6	7	8	9	13	11¹	12	2		10³		3											10
1		5	4		6	7	8¹	9	13	11²	12	2		10		3											11
1	12	5	4		6²	7¹	8	9³	13	11		2	14	10		3											12
1	13	5	4²		6	7	8	9	12	11¹		2	14	10³		3											13
1	2	5	4			7	8	9	10²	11	12	13				3¹					6						14
1	2¹	5	4			7	8	9²	10	11	12	13				3					6						15
1	2	5	4			7	8	9	10²	11¹	12	13				3					6						16
1	2	5	4			7	8¹	9²	10	11	12	13				3					6						17
1	2	5	4				8	9	10²	11¹	12	13				3					6						18
	2	5	4			7	8		10	11²	12	13				3					6¹			1	9		19
1	2	5³	4			7	8		10	11²	12	13	14			3¹					6				9		20
1	2¹	5	4			7			10	11	12	13	14			3					6	8²			9³		21
1	2	5	4			7			10¹	11	12	13	14			3²					6	8³			9		22
1	2	5	4			7			10	11	12	13				3					6²	8¹			9		23
1	2	5	4			7			10²	11	12	13				3					6	8²			9		24
1	2	5	4			7			10¹	11	12	13				3					6	8²			9		25
1	2	5	4			7²			10	11	12	13				3					6	8¹			9		26
1	2	5	4			7			10	11	12	13				3²					6	8			9¹		27
1	2	5	4¹			7			10	11²	12	13	14			3					6	8			9³		28
1	2	5	4			7			10¹	11	12	13				3					6	8			9²		29
1	2	5	4¹			7			10	11	12	13	14			3					6³	8			9²		30
1	2	5	4			7¹			10		12	13				3					6	8			9²	11	31
1	2	5	4			7			10		12					3					6	8			9¹	11	32
1	2	5	4			7			10	11¹	12	13				3					6	8			9²		33
1	2	5	4			7			10		12	13				3					6	8¹			9²	11	34
1	2	5	4			7			10		12	13				3¹					6	8			9²	11	35
1	2	5	4			7³			10		12	13	14			3					6	8¹			9²	11	36

BERWICK RANGERS Third Division

Year Formed: 1881. *Ground & Address:* Shielfield Park, Tweedmouth, Berwick-upon-Tweed TD15 2EF. *Telephone:* 01289 307424. *Fax (to Secretary):* 01289 307623. Club 24 hour hotline 01891 800697. *Ground Capacity:* 4131. seated: 1366. *Size of Pitch:* 112yd × 76yd.
Chairman: Tom Davidson. *Vice-chairman:* Moray McLaren. *Company Secretary:* Sheila Stoddart. *Club Secretary:* Dennis McCleary.
Manager: Jimmy Thomson. *Physio:* Glynn Jones. *Coaches:* Ian Oliver, Ian Smith
Managers since 1975: H. Melrose; G. Haig; W. Galbraith; D. Smith; F. Connor; J. McSherry; E. Tait; J. Thomson; J. Jefferies; J. Anderson, J. Crease, T. Hendrie, I. Ross.
Club Nickname(s): The Borderers. *Previous Grounds:* Bull Stob Close, Pier Field, Meadow Field, Union Park, Old Shielfield.
Record Attendance: 13,365 v Rangers, Scottish Cup 1st rd; 28 Jan, 1967.
Record Victory: 8-1 v Forfar Ath. Division II; 25 Dec, 1965; v Vale of Leithen, Scottish Cup; Dec, 1966.
Record Defeat: 1-9 v Hamilton A, First Division; 9 Aug, 1980.
Most Capped Player: —.
Most League Appearances: 435;: Eric Tait, 1970-87.
Most League Goals in Season (Individual): 38: Ken Bowron, Division II; 1963-64.
Most Goals Overall (Individual): 115: Eric Tait, 1970-87.

BERWICK RANGERS 1996–97 LEAGUE RECORD

Match No.	Date	Venue	Opponents	Result	H/T Score	Lg. Pos.	Goalscorers	Attendance
1	Aug 17	A	Clyde	L 1-2	1-1	—	McGlynn [45]	805
2	24	H	Stenhousemuir	L 0-6	0-2	10		391
3	31	A	Ayr U	L 0-6	0-2	10		1594
4	Sept 7	H	Queen of the S	D 2-2	1-1	10	Miller [10], McGlynn (pen) [79]	432
5	14	A	Hamilton A	L 2-4	1-1	10	Forrester 2 [21, 81]	579
6	21	H	Dumbarton	W 3-1	1-0	9	Grant [33], Craig [56], Robinson [81]	326
7	28	A	Livingston	L 1-2	0-1	9	Forrester [63]	2398
8	Oct 5	A	Brechin C	L 2-3	1-1	10	Forrester [24], Robinson (pen) [50]	312
9	12	H	Stranraer	L 1-2	1-1	10	Neil [20]	313
10	19	H	Clyde	L 1-5	1-2	10	Craig [23]	397
11	26	A	Stenhousemuir	D 1-1	1-0	10	Robinson [21]	423
12	Nov 2	H	Hamilton A	L 0-2	0-1	10		454
13	9	A	Queen of the S	L 1-2	0-1	10	Walton [85]	946
14	16	H	Livingston	L 1-2	0-2	10	Fraser [77]	564
15	23	A	Dumbarton	L 0-1	0-0	10		601
16	30	H	Brechin C	D 0-0	0-0	10		376
17	Dec 14	A	Stranraer	D 1-1	0-0	10	Neil [81]	671
18	21	A	Clyde	D 0-0	0-0	10		620
19	28	H	Ayr U	L 1-2	1-1	10	Robinson (pen) [5]	525
20	Jan 1	A	Livingston	D 2-2	1-1	—	Forrester [19], Walton [89]	2029
21	11	H	Dumbarton	L 0-3	0-1	10		346
22	18	A	Brechin C	L 1-3	1-2	10	Clegg [29]	265
23	Feb 1	H	Stranraer	W 2-0	2-0	10	Neil (pen) [19], McParland [36]	302
24	8	A	Hamilton A	L 1-4	0-0	10	Little [66]	512
25	15	H	Queen of the S	D 1-1	0-0	10	Manson [88]	381
26	22	H	Stenhousemuir	W 1-0	1-0	10	Clegg [10]	326
27	Mar 1	A	Ayr U	L 0-2	0-1	10		1648
28	8	A	Dumbarton	D 2-2	1-2	10	Manson [24], Reid [81]	446
29	15	H	Livingston	D 1-1	0-0	10	Clegg [80]	453
30	22	H	Brechin C	W 1-0	0-0	10	Neil [88]	337
31	Apr 5	A	Stranraer	D 1-1	1-0	10	Forrester [42]	480
32	12	A	Queen of the S	L 0-2	0-1	10		1019
33	19	H	Hamilton A	L 0-5	0-2	10		520
34	26	H	Clyde	L 0-2	0-0	10		339
35	May 3	A	Stenhousemuir	D 1-1	1-0	10	Little (pen) [14]	302
36	10	H	Ayr U	L 0-2	0-2	10		1423

Final League Position: 10

Honours
League Champions: Second Division 1978-79. *Runners-up* Second Division 1993-94.
Scottish Cup: —.
League Cup: Semi-final 1963-64.
Club colours: Shirt: Black with gold diamonds and gold pinstripe. Shorts: Black, gold trim. Stockings: Black with gold tops.

Goalscorers: *League (32):* Forrester 6, Neil 4 (1 pen), Robinson 4 (2 pens), Clegg 3, Craig 2, Little 2 (1 pen), McGlynn 2 (1 pen), Manson 2, Walton 2, Fraser 1, Grant 1, McParland 1, Miller 1, Reid 1. *Scottish Cup (4):* McParland 2, Neil 1, Walton 1. *Coca Cola Cup (0).League Challenge Cup (0).*

Young N 8	Watkins D 7+4	Graham T 27+3	Coates S 3	Reid A 28+3	Smith S 3	Craig K 18+8	Fraser G 33	Ward B 1+1	Walton K 31+4	McGlynn D 7+5	Clegg N 11+3	Miller G 2+5	Wilson M 4	Forrester P 24+6	Robinson D 14+2	Stewart G 24+2	Grant D 18+4	Smith I —+1	Neil M 21+1	Lamont W 3	Irvine N 24+1	McParland I 8+1	Collier D 16	Paxton G —+3	Garrity J 1+1	Finlayson D 19	Laidler M 15	Burgess M 9	Manson C 8+3	Little G 6+7	Ludlow L 3+3	Match No.
1	2	3	4	5	6	7^2	8	9^1	10	11	12	13																				1
1	7	3	6^2	5	4^1	13	10		12	9				2	8	11																2
1	2	3		5	4	7^2	6		10^2	11		13	8	9		12																3
1	7^1	10		4		12	6		13		11^2	2	8	9	3	5																4
1	3	2^1	4		8		6	10	11	7^2				9	12	5	13															5
1	11			4		7	6		3					8	9	2	5		10													6
	11^2			4		7^1	6		3		13			8	9	2	5		10	1	12											7
	11			4^2		13	6		3		12			10^3	9^1	2	5		8		1	7	14									8
	11	2^1		4			6		12	13				8	9^2	3	5		10		1	7										9
13	11	2^3		4			6		3		12			8^1	9^2		5		10		1	7	14									10
12	11			4			6		3		13	14		10^3	9^2	2^1	5		8		1	7										11
	11			4		12	6		3	7^1				8	9	2	5		10		1											12
	11^2	2		4		12	6		3	7^1	13			8	9		5		10		1											13
	12			4		11^1	6		3					8^2	9	2	5		10		1	7	13									14
	12			4		13	10		6					8^1	9	2^2	5				1	7	11			3						15
	11			4			6				12			8	9^1	2	5		10		1	7	3									16
	11			4			6							8	9	2	5		10		1	7	3									17
	11			4		13	6				12			8	9^1	2	5		10		1	7^2	3									18
13	11			4			6				12			8	9^1	2	5		10		1	7^2	3									19
				4			6		11					8	9	2	3		10		1	7					5					20
	11^1	3		4			6				12			8^2	9	2			10		1	7	13				5					21
	11						6				12			8^1	9	2	4		10		1	7	13				5	3				22
1	11			4			6				12			8	9^2	2			10			7^1	13				5	3				23
1	11			4		13	6							8^1	9	2^2	5		10			7	3							12		24
	11			4			6				12				9^1	2	5		10		1	7	3							8		25
13		3		4		7	6				12			8	9^1	2										1	10	5		11^2		26
		3		4		7	6							8	9	2	12						13			1	10^1	5		11^2		27
		12		4		7^3	6							8	9	2	5						13			1	10^1		3^2	11		28
13		12		4		7	6^2							10^2	9	2	5		8				14			1			3	11^1		29
		14		4		7	6							8^2	9^3	2	5		10				13			1			3	11^1	12	30
		14		4		7	6							10^2	9^1	2	5^2		8				13			1			3	11	12	31
		5		4		7	10							13	9^2	2			8				6			1			3	12	11^1	32
		5		4		7	10^1							11^2	9^3	2			8				6			1	14		3	12	13	33
	11	5		4		7	10								9^2	2			8^1				6			1	14		3	12^2	13	34
	11	5				7^1	10								9	2	4						6			1			3	8	12	35
	11	5					10							12	9^2	2	4						6			1	7		3	13	8^1	36

BRECHIN CITY   Second Division

Year Formed: 1906. *Ground & Address:* Glebe Park, Trinity Rd, Brechin, Angus DD9 6BJ. *Telephone:* 01356 622856.
Fax (to Secretary): 01356 625524.
Ground Capacity: total: 3980. seated: 1518. *Size of Pitch:* 110yd × 67yd.
Chairman: Hugh Campbell Adamson. *Secretary:* Ken Ferguson.
Manager: John Young. *Assistant Manager:* Cammy Evans. *Physio:* Tom Gilmartin.
Managers since 1975: Charlie Dunn; Ian Stewart; Doug Houston; Ian Fleming; John Ritchie, Ian Redford. *Club Nickname(s):* The City. *Previous Grounds:* Nursery Park.
Record Attendance: 8122 v Aberdeen, Scottish Cup 3rd rd: 3 Feb, 1973.
Record Transfer Fee received: £100,000 for Scott Thomson to Aberdeen (1991).
Record Transfer Fee paid: £16,000 for Sandy Ross from Berwick Rangers (1991).
Record Victory: 12-1 v Thornhill, Scottish Cup 1st rd; 28 Jan, 1926.
Record Defeat: 0-10 v Airdrieonians, Albion R and Cowdenbeath, all in Division II; 1937-38.
Most Capped Player: —.
Most League Appearances: 459: David Watt, 1975-89.
Most League Goals in Season (Individual): 26: W. McIntosh, Division II; 1959-60.
Most Goals Overall (Individual): 131: Ian Campbell.

BRECHIN CITY 1996–97 LEAGUE RECORD

Match No.	Date	Venue	Opponents	Result	H/T Score	Lg. Pos.	Goalscorers	Attendance
1	Aug 17	A	Stenhousemuir	D 0-0	0-0	—		381
2	24	H	Ayr U	D 1-1	0-1	7	Farnan [88]	419
3	31	A	Dumbarton	D 1-1	1-0	7	Kerrigan [13]	650
4	Sept 7	A	Livingston	L 1-2	0-1	8	Feroz [69]	1832
5	14	H	Stranraer	L 0-2	0-2	9		285
6	21	H	Hamilton A	L 0-2	0-1	10		356
7	28	A	Clyde	L 0-1	0-0	10		681
8	Oct 5	H	Berwick R	W 3-2	1-1	8	Kerrigan [13], Brand 2 [62, 70]	312
9	12	A	Queen of the S	W 5-1	3-1	8	Kerrigan 2 [9, 29], Brand 2 [12, 54], Sorbie [87]	893
10	19	H	Stenhousemuir	D 0-0	0-0	8		354
11	26	A	Ayr U	L 0-1	0-1	8		1973
12	Nov 9	H	Livingston	D 0-0	0-0	8		400
13	16	H	Clyde	L 1-2	0-1	8	McKellar [87]	356
14	30	A	Berwick R	D 0-0	0-0	9		376
15	Dec 4	A	Hamilton A	L 1-5	1-2	—	Kerrigan [43]	379
16	7	A	Stranraer	W 1-0	0-0	9	Sorbie [86]	778
17	14	H	Queen of the S	D 3-3	2-2	8	Brown [2], Sorbie [28], Ferguson [60]	328
18	21	A	Stenhousemuir	L 1-3	1-1	8	Ferguson [18]	332
19	28	H	Dumbarton	W 2-1	0-0	7	Conway [50], Brand [54]	356
20	Jan 18	H	Berwick R	W 3-1	2-1	7	McKellar 2 [9, 85], Kerrigan [32]	265
21	21	A	Clyde	D 1-1	0-0	—	Kerrigan [46]	557
22	Feb 1	A	Queen of the S	L 1-2	1-0	7	Brown [29]	819
23	8	H	Stranraer	D 0-0	0-0	8		451
24	22	H	Ayr U	D 1-1	1-0	8	Buick [20]	439
25	26	A	Livingston	W 3-2	1-2	—	Feroz 2 [25, 56], Brown [68]	1323
26	Mar 1	A	Dumbarton	W 2-1	1-1	6	McKellar [11], Sorbie [65]	411
27	4	H	Hamilton A	L 0-1	0-1	—		358
28	8	A	Hamilton A	L 0-4	0-2	7		634
29	15	H	Clyde	W 2-1	1-1	6	Christie [30], Conway [49]	337
30	22	A	Berwick R	L 0-1	0-0	7		337
31	Apr 5	H	Queen of the S	L 0-1	0-1	7		388
32	12	H	Livingston	W 1-0	1-0	7	Christie [37]	471
33	19	A	Stranraer	W 1-0	0-0	7	Feroz [48]	416
34	26	H	Stenhousemuir	D 1-1	1-0	7	Brand [39]	306
35	May 3	A	Ayr U	L 0-2	0-1	7		3164
36	10	H	Dumbarton	L 0-3	0-2	7		620

Final League Position: 7

Honours
League Champions: Second Division 1982-83. C Division 1953-54. Second Division 1989-90. *Runners-up:* 1992-93. Third Division Runners-up 1995-96
Scottish Cup: —.
League Cup: —.
Club colours: Shirt, Shorts, Stockings: Red with white trimmings.

Goalscorers: *League (36):* Kerrigan 7, Brand 6, Feroz 4, McKellar 4, Sorbie 4, Brown 3, Christie 2, Conway 2, Ferguson 2, Buick 1, Farnan 1. *Scottish Cup (6):* Brand 2, Sorbie 2, Brown 1, Kerrigan 1. *Coca Cola Cup (3):* Feroz 2, Kerrigan 1. *League Challenge Cup (0).*

Garden S 24 + 1	Christie G 27 + 2	Brown R 34	Cairney H 31	Conway F 35	Scott D 30	Feroz C 16 + 15	Farnan C 35	Brand R 20 + 8	Kerrigan S 25 + 4	Ferguson S 17 + 3	McKellar J 19 + 12	Heddle I 11 + 5	Smith G 8 + 1	Ross A — + 2	McNeill W 1 + 9	Buick G 18 + 2	Sorbie S 22 + 6	Allan R 12	Baillie R 7 + 1	Black R 1 + 2	Dailly M 3	Match No.
1	2	3	4	5	6	7¹	8	9	10²	11	12	13										1
1	2	3³		5	6	7	8	9¹	10	11¹	13	12	4	14								2
1	2¹	3	4	5	6	13	8	9²	7³	11	10				14	12						3
1	2	3	4	5	6	12	8	9¹	7²	11	10					13						4
1	2¹	3	4	5	6	13	8	9²	7³	11	14	10				12						5
1	2		4	5	6²	9	8	14	10	3	7³	11¹				13	12					6
1	14	3	4	5	6	9	2	12	10¹	11³	7²					13	8					7
1	5	3	4		6	7	2	9¹	10²	11					12	8	13					8
	11	3	4³	5	6	7¹	2	9	10²	14	12					8	13	1				9
	11	3	4	5	6	7	2	9¹	10²	13						8	12	1				10
	11	3	4	5	6	7²	2	9¹	10	12						8	13	1				11
	11	3	4	5	6		2	10		7						8	9	1				12
	11³	3	4	5	6	12	2	10	14	7						8²	9¹	1	13			13
	11	3	4	5	6	12	2	10²	13	7						8	9¹	1				14
		3		5	6	12	8	10	11²	7¹			4				9	1	2	13		15
		3	4	5	6	12	8	10¹	11	7²					13		9	1	2			16
		3	4	5	6		8	12	10¹	11	7						9	1	2			17
			4	5	6		8	12	10¹	11	7³	14		3	13		9	1	2²			18
13		3	4	5			8	10¹		11	7²	12				6	9	1	2			19
1		3	4	5	6	12	8	10¹		11	7						9		2			20
1	14	3	4	5	6	12	8	10¹		11	7	13					9²		2³			21
1	2	3	4	5	6	13		12	10¹	11		7²				8	9					22
1	11	3	4	5	6	12	2	9¹	10	7						8						23
1	11	3		5			2	9	10¹			7	6	4		8	12					24
1	11	3		5		10²	2	9²	13			7	6	4		8	12					25
1	11	3	4	5		13	2	12	10¹			7²	6			8	9					26
1	11	3	4	5		7	2	10¹				13	6		12	8	9²					27
1	11	3	4	5	10	7¹	2	12				13	6²			8	9					28
1	11	3	4	5		13	2	10	12			7²	6			8	9¹					29
1		3	4	5	6	7¹	2	10	12						13	8	9²		11			30
1	11²	3	4	5	6	12	2		10¹			7				8	9			13		31
1	11	3	4	5	6	10	8	12				7¹	2				9					32
1	11	3	4	5	6	7	8	10²	13			12	2				9¹					33
1	11	3	4	5	6	7²	2	10¹				12	13				9			8		34
1	11	3		5	6	7	2	10¹				12	4				9			8		35
	11	3	4	5	6	12	2	10¹		7²		13					9	1		8		36

CELTIC   Premier Division

Year Formed: 1888. *Ground & Address:* Celtic Park, 95 Kerrydale St, Glasgow G40 3RE. *Telephone:* 0141 556 2611.
Ground Capacity: all seated: 47,500. *Size of Pitch:* 115yd × 75yd.
Managing Director Fergus McCann. *Secretary:* Dominic Keane.
General Manager: Jock Brown. *Assistant General Manager:* David Hay. *Head Coach:* Wim Jensen. *Reserve Coach:* Murdo MacLeod. *Youth Development:* Willie McStay. *Kit Manager:* John Clark. *Physio:* Brian Scott. *Assistant Physio:* Neil McLeod.
Managers since 1975: Jock Stein, Billy McNeill, David Hay, Billy McNeill, Liam Brady, Lou Macari, Tommy Burns.
Club Nickname(s): The Bhoys. *Previous Grounds:* None.
Record Attendance: 92,000 v Rangers, Division I; 1 Jan, 1938.
Record Transfer Fee received: £1,400,000 for Paul Elliott to Chelsea, July 1991.
Record Transfer Fee paid: £1,750,000 for Phil O'Donnell from Motherwell, September 1994.
Record Victory: 11-0 Dundee, Division I; 26 Oct, 1895.
Record Defeat: 0-8 v Motherwell, Division I; 30 Apr, 1937.
Most Capped Player: Paul McStay, 76, Scotland.
Most League Appearances: 486: Billy McNeill 1957-75.
Most League Goals in Season (Individual): 50: James McGrory, Division I; 1935-36.
Most Goals Overall (Individual): 397: James McGrory; 1922-39.

CELTIC 1996–97 LEAGUE RECORD

Match No.	Date	Venue	Opponents	Result	H/T Score	Lg Pos.	Goalscorers	Atten- dance
1	Aug 10	A	Aberdeen	D 2-2	1-0	—	Van Hooijdonk [24], Thom [90]	18,595
2	17	H	Raith R	W 4-1	2-0	2	Van Hooijdonk [16], Thom 2 [25, 50], Donnelly [87]	46,795
3	24	A	Kilmarnock	W 3-1	0-1	2	Di Canio [61], Thom [64], Cadete [89]	15,970
4	Sept 7	H	Hibernian	W 5-0	3-0	2	McGinlay (og) [4], Cadete 2 [14, 45], O'Neil [51], Van Hooijdonk [72]	47,148
5	14	A	Dundee U	W 2-1	1-0	2	Van Hooijdonk [43], Mackay [89]	12,205
6	21	H	Dunfermline Ath	W 5-1	3-0	2	Cadete [32], Di Canio 2 [35, 45], Van Hooijdonk 2 [72, 89]	49,692
7	28	A	Rangers	L 0-2	0-0	2		50,124
8	Oct 12	H	Motherwell	W 1-0	0-0	2	Van Hooijdonk [90]	49,289
9	20	A	Hearts	D 2-2	1-0	—	Van Hooijdonk 2 [37, 51]	13,352
10	26	A	Hibernian	W 4-0	1-0	2	Thom 2 [31, 74], Van Hooijdonk [61], Donnelly [77]	13,930
11	Nov 2	H	Aberdeen	W 1-0	0-0	1	Di Canio [70]	50,124
12	14	H	Rangers	L 0-1	0-1	—		50,000
13	30	H	Hearts	D 2-2	1-1	2	O'Neil [43], Di Canio (pen) [77]	49,804
14	Dec 7	A	Motherwell	L 1-2	0-1	2	Hay [83]	11,589
15	21	H	Dundee U	W 1-0	1-0	2	O'Donnell [39]	46,483
16	26	A	Aberdeen	W 2-1	1-1	—	Cadete [40], Di Canio [83]	16,748
17	28	H	Dunfermline Ath	W 4-2	2-1	2	Cadete 2 [35, 52], Van Hooijdonk [38], Donnelly [59]	45,751
18	Jan 2	A	Rangers	L 1-3	0-1	—	Di Canio [65]	50,019
19	4	H	Motherwell	W 5-0	2-0	2	Di Canio (pen) [30], Van Hooijdonk [40], Cadete 2 [75, 86], Wieghorst [87]	45,259
20	8	H	Kilmarnock	W 6-0	2-0	—	Cadete 3 [18, 65, 89], McNamara [22], Wieghorst [80], Hay [88]	45,535
21	11	A	Hearts	W 2-1	1-1	2	Cadete 2 [26, 68]	15,424
22	14	A	Raith R	W 2-1	0-1	—	Cadete [73], Hay [90]	8544
23	18	H	Hibernian	W 4-1	2-0	2	Van Hooijdonk 2 [21, 48], McLaughlin [42], Cadete [68]	48,986
24	29	A	Dunfermline Ath	W 2-0	2-0	—	McStay [36], Cadete [40]	17,919
25	Feb 1	A	Dundee U	L 0-1	0-0	2		12,483
26	6	H	Raith R	W 2-0	0-0	—	Cadete [47], Di Canio [79]	44,770
27	22	A	Motherwell	W 1-0	1-0	2	Cadete [10]	12,131
28	Mar 1	H	Hearts	W 2-0	1-0	2	Cadete [28], Di Canio [69]	49,578
29	11	A	Kilmarnock	L 0-2	0-1	—		15,087
30	16	H	Rangers	L 0-1	0-1	—		49,733
31	22	H	Dunfermline Ath	D 2-2	0-2	2	O'Donnell [61], Donnelly [71]	13,092
32	Apr 5	A	Raith R	D 1-1	0-0	2	Di Canio [88]	7914
33	20	H	Aberdeen	W 3-0	1-0	—	Cadete 2 [38, 62], Thom [52]	46,989
34	May 4	A	Hibernian	W 3-1	2-1	—	Cadete 2 [12, 65], Di Canio [43]	10,546
35	7	H	Kilmarnock	D 0-0	0-0	—		42,788
36	10	H	Dundee U	W 3-0	1-0	2	Cadete [11], Hay [85], Johnson [89]	46,742

Final League Position: 2

Honours
League Champions: (35 times) Division I 1892-93, 1893-94, 1895-96, 1897-98, 1904-05, 1905-06, 1906-07, 1907-08, 1908-09, 1909-10, 1913-14, 1914-15, 1915-16, 1916-17, 1918-19, 1921-22, 1925-26, 1935-36, 1937-38, 1953-54, 1965-66, 1966-67, 1967-68, 1968-69, 1969-70, 1970-71, 1971-72, 1972-73, 1973-74. Premier Division 1976-77, 1978-79, 1980-81, 1981-82, 1985-86, 1987-88. *Runners-up:* 24 times.
Scottish Cup Winners: (30 times) 1892, 1899, 1900, 1904, 1907, 1908, 1911, 1912, 1914, 1923, 1925, 1927, 1931, 1933, 1937, 1951, 1954, 1965, 1967, 1969, 1971, 1972, 1974, 1975, 1977, 1980, 1985, 1988, 1989, 1995; *Runners-up:* 16 times.
League Cup Winners: (9 times) 1956-57, 1957-58, 1965-66, 1966-67, 1967-68, 1968-69, 1969-70, 1974-75, 1982-83; *Runners-up:* 10 times.

European: *European Cup Winners:* 1966-67. 78 matches (1966-67 winners, 1967-68, 1968-69, 1969-70 runners-up, 1970-71, 1971-72 semi-finals, 1972-73, 1973-74 semi-finals, 1974-75, 1977-78, 1979-80, 1981-82, 1982-83, 1986-87, 1988-89); *Cup Winners' Cup:* 39 matches (1963-64 semi-finals, 1965-66 semi-finals, 1975-76, 1980-81, 1984-85, 1985-86, 1989-90, 1995-96); *UEFA Cup:* 32 matches (*Fairs Cup:* 1962-63, 1964-65. *UEFA Cup:* 1976-77, 1983-84, 1987-88, 1991-92, 1992-93, 1993-94, 1996-97).
Club colours: Shirt: Green and white hoops. Shorts: White. Stockings: White.

Goalscorers: *League (78):* Cadete 25, Van Hooijdonk 14, Di Canio 12 (1 pen), Thom 7, Donnelly 4, Hay 4, O'Donnell 2, O'Neil 2, Wieghorst 2, Johnson 1, Mackay 1, McLaughlin 1, McNamara 1, McStay 1, own goal 1. *Scottish Cup (11):* Di Canio 3, Cadete 2, Mackay 2, O'Donnell 2, Johnson 1, Van Hooijdonk 1. *Coca Cola Cup (8):* Cadete 5, Thom 2, Van Hooijdonk 1.

Marshall G 11	Boyd T 31	McKinlay T 24+3	McNamara J 30	Stubbs A 20	Grant P 21+2	O'Donnell P 19	McStay P 14+1	Van Hooijdonk P 19+2	Thom A 18+5	Cadete J 30+1	O'Neil B 15+1	Hughes J 5+1	McLaughlin B 8+12	Wieghorst M 11+6	Donnelly S 20+9	McBride J —+2	Di Canio P 25+1	Anthony M —+2	Mackay M 18+2	Gray S 7+4	Kerr S 25+1	Hay C 4+10	Elliot B —+1	Hannah D 14+4	Annoni E 3	Johnson T 3+1	Kelly P 1	Match No.
1	2	3	4	5	6	7	8	9	10	11¹	12																	1
1	2	3	4		6			9	10¹	11²	5	7	8	12	13													2
1	2	3	4					9²	10	11	8	5	7¹	12	13													3
1	2	3		5¹	6			9	10³	11²	4	12	14	8	13		7											4
1	2		4		6			9	10¹	11	8	5		13	12		7²		3									5
1	2		4					9		11	8	5	13	6²	10		7¹	12	3									6
1	2	3	4	8	6				10¹		9²	5	13	12	11		7											7
1	2		4	5	6			9			3		11²	8¹	10		7		12	13								8
	2		4	5	6			9	12		10		13	8²	11¹		7			3	1							9
	2		4	5¹	6			9²	10¹		3		13	8	11		7		14	12	1							10
	2	12	4	5	6						3	10¹	8	11			7				1	9²		13				11
	2	12	4	5	6			9	10²		13	3¹	8	11			7				1							12
	2	3	4	5	6				10¹	11	8			9			7				1	12						13
	2	3	4³		6			10	11	9²			8¹	7	14		5	13	1	12								14
	2	3		5	6	8		10	11	4	12			7			1	9¹										15
	2	3	4	5	6	8		11		10	9¹		7				1	12										16
	2	3		5²		6	8³	9	11	4	14	10¹	7	13			1					12						17
3		2		5²		6	8	12	13	11	4	9¹	7				1					10						18
	2		4		6²		9	10¹	11	14	12	13	7³	5	3	1						8						19
	2		4		6¹	8	9		11	12	13	7³	5	3	1	14	10²											20
	2		4		6	8	9²		11	13	12	7¹	5	3	1	10												21
	2	13	4		6	12	9		11	8¹	7²	5	3²	1	14	10												22
	2	3	4		8	9	10¹	11	12			5	1	7	6													23
	2	3¹	4	12	6	8	9	11²		7	5	1	13	10														24
		3	4	2	6	8	9	11		7	5	1	13	10														25
	2	3	4	2	14	6	8	9¹	11³	10²	7	5	1	13	12													26
	2	3	4		6	10	8	12	11	9¹	7	5	1															27
	3		4		6	13	10¹	11	9	12	7²	5	1				8	2										28
	3	4	9	6¹	7	8	10	11	13	12	5²	1		2														29
	3	4	9¹	6²	10	8		11	12	7	5	1	13	2														30
	2	3	4		6	8	12	11	10	9		1	7¹	5														31
	2	3	4	5	6	8¹	11	10	9²	1	7	13	8	13														32
	2	3	4	5	6²		10	11	12	9	7¹	1	13	8														33
1	2	3	4		6	12	11		7	5	10¹		8	9														34
1	2	3		6	10¹	11	12	7	5	8²	13	4	9															35
1	2	3		6²	10¹	11³	12	7	5	13	8	9	4															36

CLYDE

Second Division

Year Formed: 1878. *Ground & Address:* Broadwood Stadium, Cumbernauld, G68 9NE. *Telephone:* 01236 451511.
Ground Capacity: total: 8200 all seated. *Size of Pitch:* 112yd × 76yd.
Chairman: John F. McBeth FRICS. *Secretary:* John D. Taylor. *Commercial Manager:* John Donnelly.
Manager: Gardner Speirs. *Physio:* J. Watson: *Coaches:* Gordon Wylde, Steven Clark.
Managers since 1975: S. Anderson; C. Brown; J. Clark, A. Smith. *Club Nickname(s):* The Bully Wee. *Previous Grounds:*
Barrowfield & Shawfield Stadium.
Record Attendance: 52,000 v Rangers, Division I; 21 Nov, 1908.
Record Transfer Fee received: £95,000 for Pat Nevin to Chelsea (July 1983).
Record Transfer Fee paid: £14,000 for Harry Hood from Sunderland (1966).
Record Victory: 11-1 v Cowdenbeath, Division II; 6 Oct, 1951.
Record Defeat: 0-11 v Dumbarton, Scottish Cup 4th rd, 22 Nov, 1879; v Rangers, Scottish Cup 4th rd, 13 Nov, 1880.
Most Capped Player: Tommy Ring, 12, Scotland.
Most League Appearances: 428: Brian Ahern.
Most League Goals in Season (Individual): 32: Bill Boyd, 1932-33.
Most Goals Overall (Individual): —.

CLYDE 1996–97 LEAGUE RECORD

Match No.	Date	Venue	Opponents	Result		H/T Score	Lg. Pos.	Goalscorers	Atten- dance
1	Aug 17	H	Berwick R	W	2-1	1-1	—	Annand 2 [42, 67]	805
2	24	A	Hamilton A	L	0-2	0-0	5		917
3	31	H	Queen of the S	L	0-2	0-0	8		951
4	Sept 7	H	Dumbarton	L	0-1	0-0	9		721
5	14	A	Ayr U	W	4-2	3-0	6	Mathieson [20], Annand 2 [37, 69], O'Neill Mart [45]	1995
6	21	A	Stranraer	D	0-0	0-0	6		513
7	28	H	Brechin C	W	1-0	0-0	5	Annand [56]	681
8	Oct 5	A	Livingston	D	0-0	0-0	5		2799
9	12	H	Stenhousemuir	L	0-4	0-3	6		780
10	19	A	Berwick R	W	5-1	2-1	5	Brownlie 2 [10, 58], Annand 3 (1 pen) [43, 73, 89 (p)]	397
11	26	H	Hamilton A	D	1-1	0-0	5	Knox [75]	1103
12	Nov 2	H	Ayr U	L	2-3	1-2	5	Brownlie [38], Annand [54]	1254
13	9	A	Dumbarton	D	2-2	1-1	7	Mathieson [24], Brownlie [68]	724
14	16	A	Brechin C	W	2-1	1-0	4	Annand 2 (1 pen) [26, 65 (p)]	356
15	30	H	Livingston	W	2-0	1-0	4	Mathieson [22], Annand [89]	1053
16	Dec 10	A	Stranraer	W	1-0	1-0	—	Annand [16]	483
17	21	H	Berwick R	D	0-0	0-0	4		620
18	Jan 15	A	Queen of the S	W	2-0	1-0	—	Annand 2 [18, 89]	1117
19	18	A	Livingston	D	0-0	0-0	4		2533
20	21	H	Brechin C	D	1-1	0-0	—	Prunty [84]	557
21	28	A	Stenhousemuir	D	0-0	0-0	—		553
22	Feb 1	H	Stenhousemuir	W	3-0	1-0	4	Annand 2 [33, 52], Gibson A [50]	709
23	5	A	Stranraer	L	0-1	0-1	—		468
24	8	A	Ayr U	L	1-3	0-2	4	Knox [58]	2006
25	22	A	Hamilton A	L	0-4	0-0	4		856
26	Mar 4	H	Dumbarton	W	2-1	1-0	—	Mathieson [33], Annand [68]	480
27	8	H	Stranraer	W	3-0	0-0	4	Annand [48], O'Neill Mart 2 [58, 67]	680
28	11	H	Queen of the S	W	2-1	0-0	—	O'Neill Mart [68], Annand [73]	574
29	15	A	Brechin C	L	1-2	1-1	4	Annand [31]	337
30	22	H	Livingston	L	0-1	0-0	4		841
31	Apr 5	A	Stenhousemuir	D	1-1	0-1	4	Brownlie [89]	500
32	12	A	Dumbarton	L	0-2	0-0	4		554
33	19	H	Ayr U	D	1-1	0-1	4	McCheyne [68]	1207
34	26	A	Berwick R	W	2-0	0-0	4	Carrigan [62], McCheyne [75]	339
35	May 3	H	Hamilton A	L	0-1	0-1	4		1011
36	10	A	Queen of the S	W	1-0	0-0	4	Gibson A [72]	1819

Final League Position: 4

Honours
League Champions: Division II 1904-05, 1951-52, 1956-57, 1961-62, 1972-73. Second Division 1977-78, 1981-82, 1992-93.
Runners-up: Division II 1903-04, 1905-06, 1925-26, 1963-64.
Scottish Cup Winners: 1939, 1955, 1958; *Runners-up:* 1910, 1912, 1949.
League Cup: —
Club colours: Shirt: White with red and black trim. Shorts: Black. Stockings: Black with red and white tops.

Goalscorers: *League (42):* Annand 21 (1 pen), Brownlie 5, Mathieson 4, Martin O'Neill 4, Gibson A 2, Knox 2, McCheyne 2, Carrigan 1, Prunty 1. *Scottish Cup (9):* Annand 2, A Gibson 2, Brownlie 1, McEwan 1, McInulty 1, Mathieson 1, Michael O'Neill 1. *Coca Cola Cup (2):* Annand 1, Brown 1. *League Challenge Cup (4):* Mathieson 2, Annand 1, Knox 1.

McLean M 29	Knox K 36	McInulty S 28 + 3	Ferguson G 20 + 1	McConnell I 8 + 2	Brown J 25 + 1	O'Neill Mart 21 + 8	Gibson A 33 + 2	Annand E 29	Mathieson M 19 + 8	Brownlie P 30 + 3	Harrison T 3 + 5	O'Neill Mich 12 + 10	McEwan C 31 + 3	Gillies K 24 + 2	McLay J — + 1	Parks G — + 2	Prunty J 15 + 2	Campbell P 16 + 8	Carrigan B 5 + 9	Gibson L — + 2	McCheyne G 4 + 4	Balfour R 7	Coleman S — + 1	Robertson G 1	McPhee G — + 1	Match No.
1	2³	3	4	5	6¹	7	8	9	10²	11	12	13	14													1
1	2	3	4	5	6¹	12	8	9	10	11³	14			7³		13										2
1	2	3	4		6	7	8²	9	10	11¹	13	14	5¹			12										3
1	2	3	4	5	14		8¹	9	10	12	11³	7		6²		13										4
1	4	3		5		8	10	9	11¹	7		6²	2	12		13										5
1	4	3	12	5		6	10	9	11	7¹			2	8												6
1	4	3		5		6	10²	9	11	7¹	13		12	2		8										7
1	4	3		5		6	10	9	11	7¹			12	2		8										8
1	4	3		5	13		10	9	11	7¹		6²	12	2		8										9
1	6	3¹	4	5		8³	10	9	11	7²	14	13	2				12									10
1	6	3	4	5		8³	10	9	11¹	7		12	2³	13		14										11
1	6	3¹	4	5			10	9	11	7		12	2	8												12
1	6		4	5			10	9¹	11	7³		12	2	8²				3	13		14					13
1	6	3		5	14		10	9¹	11	7³		12	2	8²			4	13								14
1	6	3		5	12		10	9	11	7			2	8¹			4									15
1	6	3		5	12		10	9		7		11²	2	8¹			4	13								16
1	6			5	13		3	9	11¹			7	2	8²			4	10	12							17
1	6	3		5	12			9	13			11²	2	8			4	10	7¹							18
1	6	3		5			13	9	12	7		11¹	2	8			4	10²								19
1	6	3		5	13	14		9	12	7		11¹	2	8²			4	10³								20
1	6	3		5	10	11		9	13	7²			2	8¹			4	12								21
1	6	3		5	10	11¹		9¹	12	7²	14		2				4	8	13							22
1	6	3		5	10	11		9	12	7²			2				4	8¹	13							23
1	6	3¹	12	5		11		9		7²			2	8			4	10	13							24
1	6			5	2	3		11¹		7		12	8				4	10	9²	13						25
1	6			5		3	9	11	7				2	8			4¹	10	12							26
1	6	13	4	5	12	3		9³	11²	7			2	8¹			10		14							27
1	6	13	4	5	8	3	9	12	7			2³	11²				10¹		14							28
1	6	13	4	5	11	3	9	12	7²				2	8¹			10									29
	6		4	5	8	3	9¹		7	11							10	12	2				1			30
	6	3¹	4²	5	7	10		11		9	2						8	13	12				1			31
	6	3¹	4	5	7	10		11		9	2						8¹	13			1	12				32
	6	3	4	5	7	10		11²		9	2						8¹	12	13			1				33
	6	3	4¹	5³	8¹	10		12		9	2	14					13	7			11	1				34
	6	3		5	4	10		9¹			2	8					12	7			11	1				35
	6	3			4	10		12			9²	2	8				7	11¹				1		5	13	36

CLYDEBANK   Second Division

Year Formed: 1965. *Club Address:* Burnbrae, Milngavie, Glasgow G62 6HX. *Telephone:* 0141 955 9048. *Fax:* 0141 955 9049
Home matches at Boghead Park, Dumbarton in 1996-97. *Ground Capacity:* 5503. *Size of Pitch:* 110yd × 68yd.
Chairman: C.G.Steedman. *Secretary:* A.Steedman. *Commercial Manager:* David Curwood.
Managing Director: I.C.Steedman. *Physio:* Peter Salila.
Managers since 1975: William Munro, J.S.Steedman. *Club Nickname(s):* The Bankies. *Previous Grounds:* None.
Record Attendance: 14,900 v Hibernian, Scottish Cup 1st rd; 10 Feb, 1965.
Record Transfer Fee received: £175,000 for Owen Coyle from Airdrieonians, (Feb 1990).
Record Transfer Fee paid: £50,000 for Gerry McCabe from Clyde.
Record Victory: 8-1 Arbroath, First Division; 3 Jan 1977.
Record Defeat: 1-9 v Gala Fairydean, Scottish Cup qual rd; 15 Sept, 1965.
Most Capped Player: —.
Most League Appearances: 620: Jim Fallon; 1968-86.
Most League Goals in Season (Individual): 29: Ken Eadie, First Division, 1990-91.
Most League Goals Overall (Individual): 138, Ken Eadie 1988-95.

CLYDEBANK 1996–97 LEAGUE RECORD

Match No.	Date	Venue	Opponents	Result	H/T Score	Lg. Pos.	Goalscorers	Attendance
1	Aug 17	A	Greenock Morton	L	0-3	0-2	—		2927
2	24	H	Stirling A	W	1-0	0-0	7	Nicholls [73]	507
3	Sept 3	A	East Fife	D	1-1	1-1	—	McMahon [44]	721
4	7	H	St Mirren	W	2-1	2-1	4	Agnew (pen) [3], Teale [19]	1399
5	14	A	Falkirk	L	0-2	0-0	6		3701
6	21	H	St Johnstone	W	2-1	1-0	5	Teale [30], Grady [70]	850
7	28	A	Partick Th	L	0-1	0-1	6		2192
8	Oct 5	A	Dundee	L	1-2	0-1	6	McMahon [85]	2585
9	12	H	Airdrieonians	L	1-4	0-1	8	Grady [54]	604
10	19	A	Greenock Morton	W	2-1	1-1	8	Agnew 2 (1 pen) [2 (pl), 70]	1417
11	26	A	Stirling A	L	0-2	0-0	8		898
12	Nov 2	H	Falkirk	L	0-1	0-1	8		632
13	9	A	St Mirren	L	0-1	0-0	8		3956
14	16	H	Partick Th	L	1-3	1-0	8	Nicholls [33]	1786
15	23	A	St Johnstone	L	0-2	0-2	8		3760
16	30	H	Dundee	D	0-0	0-0	8		552
17	Dec 11	A	Airdrieonians	L	1-3	1-2	—	Grady [30]	975
18	21	H	East Fife	W	2-0	0-0	8	Brannigan [50], Agnew (pen) [65]	306
19	26	A	Greenock Morton	D	2-2	1-2	—	Grady [10], McMahon [72]	2392
20	Jan 1	A	Partick Th	L	1-3	1-0	—	Connell [5]	1822
21	4	A	Falkirk	D	1-1	0-1	8	Grady [68]	2333
22	18	A	Dundee	L	0-1	0-0	9		1954
23	Feb 1	H	Airdrieonians	D	1-1	1-1	9	Teale [1]	459
24	4	H	St Johnstone	D	1-1	0-0	—	Brown [55]	629
25	8	A	East Fife	W	2-1	1-1	9	Agnew [30], Grady [60]	663
26	15	H	St Mirren	L	0-1	0-0	9		1156
27	22	H	Stirling A	L	1-2	1-1	9	Brown [10]	686
28	Mar 1	A	St Johnstone	L	0-1	0-0	9		2688
29	15	H	Partick Th	W	4-1	0-0	9	Grady 2 [60, 77], Teale [62], Connell [89]	1112
30	22	H	Dundee	D	0-0	0-0	9		622
31	Apr 5	A	Airdrieonians	L	1-4	0-1	9	Miller [60]	1424
32	12	A	St Mirren	L	0-1	0-0	9		2634
33	19	H	Falkirk	L	1-2	0-0	9	Teale [75]	535
34	26	H	Greenock Morton	L	0-1	0-0	9		505
35	May 3	A	Stirling A	L	2-4	0-1	9	Teale [68], Paterson G (og) [83]	1109
36	10	H	East Fife	L	0-4	0-0	9		269

Final League Position: 9

Honours
League Champions: Second Division 1975-76; Runners-up: First Division 1976-77, 1984-85.
Scottish Cup: Semi-finalists 1990. League Cup: —.
Club colours: Shirt: Vertical red and white stripes. Shorts: Black with red and white vertical stripes. Stockings: Black.

Goalscorers: League (31): Grady 8, Teale 6, Agnew 5 (2 pens), McMahon 3, Brown 2, Connell 2, Nicholls 2, Brannigan 1, Miller 1, own goal 1. Scottish Cup (0). Coca Cola Cup (0). League Challenge Cup (0).

Matthews G 11	Agnew P 25 + 3	Sutherland C 9	Irons D 35	Brannigan K 35	Nicholls D 33 + 1	Teale G 32 + 1	Connell G 25 + 3	McMahon S 12 + 8	Grady J 36	Bowman G 22	Robertson J 6 + 19	Barnes D 6	Lovering P 25 + 1	Miller S 11 + 13	Currie T 24 + 4	Templeton R 1	Hardie D — + 1	Murdoch S 13 + 2	McKinstry J 2 + 4	Melvin W 1 + 2	McFarlane I 16	Brown J 12 + 1	Connaghan D 1	Adamson C 1	Robertson S 2	McKelvie D — + 1	Match No.
1	2	3	4	5	6	7	8	9	10	11¹	12																1
	3	4	5	6	7	8	9¹	10³	11	14			1	2	12	13											2
	2		4	5	6	7²	8	10	9¹	11	12		1	3	13												3
1	2	3	4	5	6	7		10¹	9	11			8		12												4
	2	6	4	5²		8	7	13	10¹	9³	11		1	3	12	14											5
1	8	3	4	5	6	7		10	9	11			2														6
1	8²	3	4	5	6	7	12	10³	9	11	14		2¹	13													7
1	10	3	4	5	6		7	12	9	11	13		8²	2¹													8
	8		4	5	6	7²	2	10¹	9	11	12		1	3	13												9
	8		4	5	6	7³	2	12	9	11²	10¹		1	3	13	14											10
1	8		4	5	6	7¹	2	10	9	11				3	12												11
1	8	3	4	5	6	7		12	9¹	11				2	10												12
1	8		4	5	6		10		9	11	7¹			3	12	2											13
1			4	5	6		3	14	9	11	10²			2	7¹			8¹	12	13							14
1	8		4	5	6	7	2		9¹	11	12			3	10												15
1	10²		2	5	6	7¹	8		9	11				3	12	13		4									16
12	3¹		4	5	6	7	8	10³	9	11				2	1	13											17
13	8²		5	6	7		2	10¹	9	11	12			3	1			4									18
	8		4	5	6	7¹	12		9	11				3	1			2				10					19
	4			5	6	7²	8	13	9	11	12			3	1			2				10¹					20
	4			5	6	7¹	8	10²	9	11	12			3	1			13	2								21
8	2		6			7²	13		9	11¹			5	3	1			4	12			10					22
8	11			5	6	7	2		9					3	1			4			4	10					23
8	11			5	6	7			9					3	1			4	2		12	10³					24
8	11			5	6	7²	12		9					3	1			13	2		4	10¹					25
8²	11			5	6	7	13		9¹					3	1				2³		4	10			14		26
8¹	11			5	6	7	13		9					3	1			12	2²		4	10					27
	11²			5	6	7	13		9				8	3	1			12	2		4	10¹					28
	4			5	6	7¹	8		9	11				3	1			12	2			10					29
12	4			5	6	7	8¹		9	11				3	1			13	2			10²					30
8				6²	5	7¹	13		9	11				3	1			12			4	10					31
	4		10	5		7²	8		9	11				3	1			13	2		6¹	12					32
8	10			5	12	6			9	11				3	1			4	2		7¹			1			33
				5	3	7	6		9	13			8	2	1			4	11²	12		10¹					34
8			4	5	3	7	6		9	11¹			10	2	1			12									35
6	10		5²	3	7¹	4			9	11	13		8³	2	1			12							1	14	36

COWDENBEATH Third Division

Year Formed: 1881. *Ground & Address:* Central Park, Cowdenbeath KY4 9EY. *Telephone:* 01383 610166. *Fax:* 01383 512132.
Ground Capacity: total: 5268. seated: 1622. *Size of Pitch:* 107yd × 66yd.
Chairman: Gordon McDougall. *Secretary:* Tom Ogilvie. *Commercial Manager:* Joe McNamara.
Manager: Samuel Conn. *Assistant Manager:* Michael Hendry. *Coaches:* Graham Buckley, Bert Oliver. *Physio:* Brian McNeill
Managers since 1975: D. McLindon; F. Connor; P. Wilson; A. Rolland; H. Wilson; W. McCulloch; J. Clark; J. Craig; R.
Campbell; J. Blackley; J. Brownlie, A. Harrow, J. Reilly, P Dolan, T. Steven. *Previous Grounds:* North End Park,
Cowdenbeath.
Record Attendance: 25,586 v Rangers, League Cup quarter-final; 21 Sept, 1949.
Record Transfer Fee received: £30,000 for Nicky Henderson to Falkirk, (March 1994).
Record Transfer Fee paid: —
Record Victory: 12-0 v Johnstone, Scottish Cup 1st rd; 21 Jan, 1928.
Record Defeat: 1-11 v Clyde, Division II; 6 Oct, 1951.
Most Capped Player: Jim Paterson, 3, Scotland.
Most League and Cup Appearances: 491 Ray Allan 1972-75, 1979-89.
Most League Goals in Season (Individual): 54, Rab Walls, Division II, 1938-39.
Most Goals Overall (Individual): 127, Willie Devlin, 1922-26, 1929-30.

COWDENBEATH 1996–97 LEAGUE RECORD

Match No.	Date		Venue	Opponents	Result		H/T Score	Lg. Pos.	Goalscorers	Attendance
1	Aug	17	A	Inverness CT	W	3-1	1-0	—	Bowmaker [44], Conn [65], Wood [80]	1524
2		24	H	Montrose	W	1-0	0-0	1	Sinclair [77]	266
3		31	A	Albion R	L	0-2	0-1	3		866
4	Sept	7	H	Queen's Park	D	1-1	0-0	3	Conn (pen) [58]	279
5		14	A	Alloa	D	1-1	1-0	3	Bowmaker [18]	508
6		21	H	Ross Co	L	0-1	0-0	4		308
7		28	A	Arbroath	W	1-0	1-0	5	Petrie [41]	405
8	Oct	5	A	Forfar Ath	W	5-2	1-1	3	Stewart [1], Coulston [70], Sinclair [73], Winter [79], Ritchie [84]	363
9		12	H	East Stirling	W	1-0	0-0	2	Malloy [82]	192
10		19	H	Inverness CT	L	3-4	1-1	3	Petrie [17], Winter [49], McMahon [73]	321
11		26	A	Montrose	W	2-0	2-0	1	Winter [22], McMahon [35]	444
12	Nov	2	A	Alloa	W	2-0	1-0	1	Wood 2 [36, 52]	504
13		9	A	Queen's Park	L	0-1	0-1	1		543
14		16	H	Arbroath	D	2-2	2-0	1	McMahon [4], Stewart [25]	301
15		23	A	Ross Co	L	0-1	0-1	4		1382
16	Dec	10	H	Forfar Ath	L	1-3	1-0	—	Stewart [32]	186
17		14	A	East Stirling	L	0-1	0-1	7		286
18		21	A	Inverness CT	L	1-2	0-0	6	Stewart [46]	2188
19	Jan	1	A	Arbroath	L	0-1	0-0	—		469
20		18	A	Forfar Ath	L	0-3	0-2	7		384
21		28	H	Ross Co	D	1-1	0-0	—	Wood [73]	169
22	Feb	1	H	East Stirling	W	2-0	0-0	6	Wood 2 [61, 83]	134
23		4	H	Albion R	D	1-1	0-0	—	Coulston [78]	166
24		8	A	Alloa	L	0-1	0-1	6		381
25		15	H	Queen's Park	L	1-4	0-2	6	Coulston [68]	244
26		22	H	Montrose	L	0-1	0-1	7		175
27		28	A	Albion R	L	0-4	0-3	8		502
28	Mar	8	A	Ross Co	L	0-4	0-1	8		1460
29		15	H	Arbroath	D	1-1	0-1	7	Sinclair [68]	142
30		22	H	Forfar Ath	L	1-2	1-1	7	Scott [10]	196
31	Apr	5	A	East Stirling	D	2-2	0-1	8	Nolan [78], Coulston [82]	258
32		12	A	Queen's Park	L	1-2	0-1	8	Coulston [55]	402
33		19	H	Alloa	W	2-1	2-0	8	Stewart [32], Nolan [34]	183
34		26	H	Inverness CT	W	2-1	2-0	7	Sinclair [13], Scott [17]	282
35	May	3	A	Montrose	D	0-0	0-0	7		279
36		10	H	Albion R	D	0-0	0-0	7		153

Final League Position: 7

Honours
League Champions: Division II 1913-14, 1914-15, 1938-39; *Runners-up:* Division II 1921-22, 1923-24, 1969-70. Second Division 1991-92.
Scottish Cup: Quarter-finals: 1931.
League Cup: Semi-finals: 1959-60, 1970-71.
Club colours: Shirt: Royal blue 1" vertical stripe with red piping on sleeve seam. Shorts: White with blue side stripe. Stockings: Royal blue.

Goalscorers: *League (38):* Wood 6, Coulston 5, Stewart 5, Sinclair 4, McMahon 3, Winter 3, Bowmaker 2, Conn 2, Nolan 2, Petrie 2, Scott 2, Malloy 1, Ritchie 1. *Scottish Cup (1):* Scott 1. *Coca Cola Cup (1):* Sinclair 1. *League Challenge Cup (0).*

Russell N 30	Munro K 32	Baillie R 15+2	Meldrum G 33	Sinclair C 30	Conn S 28	Hamilton A 12+5	Bowmaker K 15+5	Wood G 23	Ritchie A 24+7	Brough G 5+7	Stewart W 22+8	Houston A —+1	Winter C 31+1	McKinnon M —+2	Humphreys M 22+3	Coulston D 12+14	Petrie E 15+2	McMahon B 13	Malloy B 3+5	Lockhart D —+1	Scott M 14+3	Moffat J 2	Miller G 2+1	Nolan T 6	Millar P 2+1	Godfrey R 4	Manson S 1+1	Fairley S —+1	Match No.
1	2	3²	4	5	6	7	8	9	10	11¹	12	13																	1
1	2	3	4	5	6	7	11¹	9	8	12			10																2
1	2		4	5	6	7¹	3	10	8	11²			9	12	13														3
1		3	8	5	6			11	4	10	13		9			2¹	7²	12											4
1	2	3	4	5	6			11	8	10²			9			13	7¹	12											5
1	2		3	5	6	12	8¹		11²				9			13	7	10	4										6
1	2		3	5	6			9	12		7		10			11¹	8	4											7
1	4	3	11	7	6			12			9		10			2¹	13	8²	5										8
1	8	3	11	5	6				4	10¹	7²		9			12	2				13								9
1	7	3	11	8¹	6			9	12				10			2	4	5											10
1		3		6	2		4	10	12		7		9	13		11¹	8²	5											11
1	12	3		6	2	11¹	4	8		10			9				7	5											12
1	6³	12	3		4	7		2	10		11²		9		13	8¹	5	14											13
1	8		3		4	2	13	6	10	11²	7		9						5¹	12									14
1	8		3		6	2		4	10²	13	7¹		9		11			5	12										15
1	7	3	4	8		2	13		11		9		10²			12			6	5¹									16
1	4	6	3	8		2¹		12	11³	9²		13			5	10		7			14								17
1	2	3	4	10		13	12		7²		11		8		6	14		5³					9¹						18
1	2	3¹	6	7		14	11		12		10		8		4	13		5³					9²						19
1	5¹	3	8	6	2	11²	10	12		13	7		4			14							9³						20
1	6	3	11¹	8	2²	13	9		12	10		4			7	,5²					14								21
1	5	3	7	6	8		11		9	10		4	2																22
1	5	3	7	6	8	14		10		9¹	11²		4	12³	2			13											23
	2	4	3	5	8		11¹	9	10²		12		6	13	7								1						24
1		3	4	6²	8		5¹	14			12		10			2	13	7			9³			11					25
1	2		4	8		11³	10	3	14	13		6¹			5	12	7				9²								26
1	2	3	4	8		11²	10		12		6				5	7¹					9	13							27
1	2	3	4	8		10¹	6		13		9				5	7				12	11²								28
1	2²		8	4		6	10	3		11	7		5	12				13			9¹								29
1	2		8	4		6¹		3	12	11	7		5	10				9											30
1	2	11	8	4			3		7¹		6		5	12				9		10									31
	2	11	8²	4¹			3		7		6		5	12				9	1	10	13								32
	2		4				3		11		6		5	10				7		9	8	1							33
	2		4	8			3		11¹		6		5	10				7		9		1	12						34
	2		4	8		12		3	11¹				5	10				7		9		1	6						35
	2		4	8		12	11		3	14	10³			5				7²		9		6¹	1		13				36

DUMBARTON Third Division

Year Formed: 1872. *Ground & Address:* Boghead Park, Miller St, Dumbarton G82 2JA. *Telephone:* 01389 762569/767864. *Fax:* 01389 762629
Ground Capacity: total: 5503. seated: 303. *Size of Pitch:* 110yd × 68yd.
Chairman: D. Dalglish. *Company Secretary:* Colin J. Hosie.
Manager: Ian Wallace. *Assistant Manager:* Jimmy Brown. *Coach:* Ringo Watts. *Physio:* David Stobie.
Managers since 1975: A. Wright; D. Wilson; S. Fallon; W. Lamont; D. Wilson; D. Whiteford; A. Totten; M. Clougherty; R. Auld; J. George; W. Lamont; M. MacLeod, J. Fallon. *Club Nickname(s):* The Sons. *Previous Grounds:* Broadmeadow, Ropework Lane.
Record Attendance: 18,000 v Raith Rovers, Scottish Cup; 2 Mar, 1957.
Record Transfer Fee received: £125,000 for Graeme Sharp to Everton (March 1982).
Record Transfer Fee paid: £50,000 for Charlie Gibson from Stirling Albion (1989).
Record Victory: 13-1 v Kirkintilloch Central. 1st Rd; 1 Sept, 1888.
Record Defeat: 1-11 v Albion Rovers, Division II; 30 Jan, 1926: v Ayr United, League Cup; 13 Aug, 1952.
Most Capped Player: James McAulay, 9, Scotland.
Most League Appearances: 297: Andy Jardine, 1957-67.

DUMBARTON 1996–97 LEAGUE RECORD

Match No.	Date	Venue	Opponents	Result	H/T Score	Lg. Pos.	Goalscorers	Atten-dance
1	Aug 17	H	Stranraer	D 1-1	1-0	—	Dallas [43]	560
2	24	A	Queen of the S	L 1-2	0-0	8	Meechan J [66]	1127
3	31	H	Brechin C	D 1-1	0-1	9	McGivern [57]	650
4	Sept 7	A	Clyde	W 1-0	0-0	5	Ward [87]	721
5	14	H	Livingston	L 2-4	1-3	7	McKinnon [41], Ward [65]	762
6	21	A	Berwick R	L 1-3	0-1	8	Ward [76]	326
7	28	H	Stenhousemuir	D 1-1	0-0	8	Meechan J [67]	524
8	Oct 5	H	Ayr U	L 1-3	1-2	9	Dallas [13]	939
9	12	A	Hamilton A	L 0-2	0-0	9		533
10	19	A	Stranraer	L 0-2	0-1	9		460
11	26	H	Queen of the S	L 1-2	1-0	9	Rowe (og) [31]	562
12	Nov 2	A	Livingston	L 0-5	0-3	9		1941
13	9	H	Clyde	D 2-2	1-1	9	Wilson [5], McKinnon [90]	724
14	16	A	Stenhousemuir	W 1-0	0-0	9	Meechan J [73]	564
15	23	H	Berwick R	W 1-0	0-0	8	Ward [51]	601
16	30	A	Ayr U	W 4-1	0-1	8	McKinnon [49], Glancy 2 [56, 65], Ward [83]	1773
17	Dec 14	H	Hamilton A	L 1-3	0-1	9	Wilson [55]	733
18	26	H	Stranraer	D 2-2	0-1	—	Sharp [63], Meechan J [90]	686
19	28	A	Brechin C	L 1-2	0-0	9	Granger (pen) [89]	356
20	Jan 11	A	Berwick R	W 3-0	1-0	7	Glancy [33], King [54], Ward [82]	346
21	18	H	Ayr U	D 1-1	0-1	9	Sharp [90]	801
22	21	H	Stenhousemuir	L 0-2	0-1	—		470
23	Feb 1	A	Hamilton A	L 0-4	0-3	9		505
24	8	H	Livingston	L 2-3	1-1	9	Mooney [35], McKinnon [62]	503
25	22	A	Queen of the S	L 0-4	0-0	9		908
26	Mar 1	H	Brechin C	L 1-2	1-1	9	Hringsson [16]	411
27	4	A	Clyde	L 1-2	0-1	—	Hringsson [51]	480
28	8	H	Berwick R	D 2-2	2-1	9	Hringsson [18], Sharp [21]	446
29	15	A	Stenhousemuir	W 4-1	1-0	9	Wilson [21], King [48], Glancy [60], Sharp [90]	376
30	22	A	Ayr U	D 1-1	1-1	9	Meechan J [27]	1575
31	Apr 5	H	Hamilton A	L 0-3	0-1	9		718
32	12	H	Clyde	W 2-0	0-0	9	Wilson [54], Ward [61]	554
33	19	A	Livingston	W 2-1	0-1	8	Meechan J [81], Sharp [83]	1579
34	26	H	Stranraer	L 0-1	0-0	9		739
35	May 3	H	Queen of the S	L 0-3	0-1	9		643
36	10	A	Brechin C	W 3-0	2-0	9	Glancy 2 [11, 73], Reilly [39]	620

Final League Position: 9

Rothmans Football Yearbook 1997–98 635

Most Goals in Season (Individual): 38: Kenny Wilson, Division II; 1971-72.
Most Goals Overall (Individual): 169: Hughie Gallacher, 1954-62 (including C Division 1954-55).

Honours
League Champions: Division I 1890-91 (shared with Rangers), 1891-92. Division II 1910-11, 1971-72. Second Division 1991-92; *Runners-up:* First Division 1983-84. Division II 1907-08.
Scottish Cup Winners: 1883; *Runners-up:* 1881, 1882, 1887, 1891, 1897. *League Cup:* —.
Club colours: Shirt: White with yellow horizontal band between two black bands. Shorts: White. Stockings: White with black and gold hooped tops.

Goalscorers: *League (44):* Ward 7, Glancy 6, Meechan J 6, Sharp 5, McKinnon 4, Wilson 4, Hringsson 3, Dallas 2, King 2, Granger 1 (pen), McGivern 1, Mooney 1, Reilly 1, own goal 1. *Scottish Cup (0). Coca Cola Cup (1):* Dallas 1. *League Challenge Cup (0).*

MacFarlane I 9	Gow S 21 + 3	Sharp L 35	Marsland J 30 + 1	Meechan J 36	King T 27	Melvin M 23	McGarvey M 7 + 5	McKinnon C 34	Mooney M 18 + 4	Dallas S 15 + 1	Ward H 26 + 9	Granger A 2 + 4	Glancy M 24 + 8	McGivern S 1 + 1	McGall J — + 6	Goldie J 1 + 3	Davidson W 12 + 4	McCabe G 4	Meechan K 14	McKenzie G 4 + 1	Wilson W 21	Scott J — + 1	Dennison P 2	Barnes D 11	Parks G 4	McCuaig R — + 1	Hringsson H 3	Mellis A 1	Bruce J 9	Reilly R 2 + 6	Reid D — + 1	Match No.
1	2	3	4	5	6	7	8	9	10¹	11²	12	13	14																			1
1	2	3	4	5	6	7	8³	10	14	11¹	12	13			9²																	2
1	2	3	4	5	6	7	8²	9	10¹	11	12			13																		3
1	2	3	4	5	6	7		9²	8	10¹	11	12			13																	4
1	2	3	4	5	6	7		9²	8¹	10³	11		14		13	12																5
1	2	3	4	5	6	7		9¹	12	10²	11		8		13																	6
1	2	3	4	5		7	8	10	12	9	11		6¹																			7
1	2	3		5		4	8²	9	7¹	10	11		6		12	13																8
1⁰	4	3		5		6	8	7	15	9	11		12				2	10¹														9
	4	3	8	5		6			10	9	12		7				2	11¹	1													10
	6	3¹	4	5	8		13		10	9	12		7³	14			2	11²	1													11
	4		6	5			11	8	9²	12	13		7¹	2	10		1	3														12
	3	4	5	8			10	6²	12	9¹	13		2	1	11	7																13
	5	3		4	6		9	8	10²	12	13		2	1	11¹	7																14
	3	5		4	7		11	8	10¹	9²	12		2	1		6	13															15
	4	3		5	8		10	7	11¹	9			2	1	12	6																16
	4	3	13	5	8¹		12	10	7	11	9		2²		6	1																17
	3	5	2	4	8		11	7¹	9	12	10		6	1																		18
	3	5	2	4	8	13	11	7¹	9²	12	10		6	1																		19
	3	4	5	6	13	8	11	7²	9	12			2¹	1	10																	20
	2	3	4		8¹	7	6	9	11	12	5		1	10																		21
	2	3	4	8		7	6	9	11	5			1	10																		22
	7	4	3	2		10	8	12	9¹	11	5	6		1																		23
	5	6	4	3		10	7	9	11	2		1	8																			24
5	3	6	4	2	12	7	11	10²		1	9	8¹	13																			25
5	3	2	8	6	4	7	11	10¹	12	1	9																					26
5	3	2	8	6	4	10¹	12	1	11	9	7																					27
	3	2	8	6	4	10	7¹	12	1	11	9	5																				28
	5	2	7	8	3	10	9¹	11	6	1	4	12																				29
	5	2	7	8	4	10	9¹	11	1	6	3	12																				30
12	3	2	8	6³	4	10²	13	11	1	7	5¹	9	14																			31
	3	2	8	6	4	10	11¹	9	1	7	1	5	12																			32
	3	2	8	6	4	10	11¹	9	7	1	5	12																				33
13	3	2	8	6	4	10²	11¹	9	7	1	5	12																				34
12	3	2	8	6	4¹	10	11	9	7²	1	5	13																				35
	5	2	3	7		10	8¹	9	12	6	1	4	11																			36

DUNDEE

First Division

Year Formed: 1893. *Ground & Address:* Dens Park Stadium, Sandeman St, Dundee DD3 7JY. *Telephone:* 01382 826104.
Fax: 01382 832284.
Ground Capacity: 14,177. seated: 10,877. *Size of Pitch:* 110yd × 72yd.
Chairman: Jim Marr. *Chief Executive:* Peter Marr.
Manager: John McCormack. *Assistant Manager:* Jim McInally. *Coaches:* Harry Hay. *Youth Coach:* Ray Farningham.
Physio: Jim Crosby. *Youth Development:* Kenny Cameron.
Managers since 1975: David White; Tommy Gemmell; Donald Mackay; Archie Knox; Jocky Scott; Dave Smith; Gordon
Wallace; Iain Munro; Simon Stainrod; Jim Duffy. *Club Nickname(s):* The Dark Blues or The Dee. *Previous Grounds:*
Carolina Port 1893-98.
Record Attendance: 43,024 v Rangers, Scottish Cup; 1953.
Record Transfer Fee received: £500,000 for Tommy Coyne to Celtic (March 1989).
Record Transfer Fee paid: £200,000 for Jim Leighton (Feb 1992).
Record Victory: 10-0 Division II v Alloa; 9 Mar, 1947 and v Dunfermline Ath; 22 Mar, 1947.
Record Defeat: 0-11 v Celtic, Division I; 26 Oct, 1895.
Most Capped Player: Alex Hamilton, 24, Scotland.
Most League Appearances: 341: Doug Cowie 1945-61.
Most League Goals in Season (Individual): 52: Alan Gilzean, 1963-64.
Most Goals Overall (Individual): 113: Alan Gilzean.

DUNDEE 1996–97 LEAGUE RECORD

Match No.	Date	Venue	Opponents	Result		H/T Score	Lg. Pos.	Goalscorers	Attendance
1	Aug 17	A	Partick Th	D	0-0	0-0	—		3152
2	24	H	Greenock Morton	W	2-1	2-1	2	Charnley [3], Tosh [27]	3561
3	31	A	Stirling A	D	1-1	0-1	2	Shaw [74]	1772
4	Sept 7	H	Airdrieonians	L	0-1	0-1	5		2756
5	14	A	St Mirren	W	1-0	0-0	3	Ferguson [49]	2391
6	21	H	East Fife	W	2-0	1-0	2	Raeside [41], Hamilton [62]	2511
7	28	A	St Johnstone	W	1-0	1-0	1	Shaw [10]	5112
8	Oct 5	H	Clydebank	W	2-1	1-0	1	Shaw [45], Adamczuk [50]	2585
9	12	A	Falkirk	W	1-0	1-0	1	Raeside [2]	2855
10	19	H	Partick Th	L	0-2	0-1	1		3303
11	26	A	Greenock Morton	D	0-0	0-0	1		3320
12	Nov 2	H	St Mirren	L	0-1	0-0	2		2731
13	9	A	Airdrieonians	D	0-0	0-0	2		2173
14	16	H	St Johnstone	L	1-1	0-0	6		3840
15	30	A	Clydebank	D	0-0	0-0	5		552
16	Dec 7	H	Falkirk	W	2-0	0-0	4	Anderson [62], Rae [84]	2198
17	14	H	Stirling A	D	1-1	0-0	4	O'Driscoll [79]	1828
18	17	A	East Fife	W	7-1	2-0	—	Winnie [8], O'Driscoll [26], Anderson 2 [46, 65], Raeside [51], Tosh [55], Rae [80]	869
19	26	A	Partick Th	D	2-2	1-0	—	Anderson [16], Tosh [84]	2693
20	28	H	East Fife	W	6-0	4-0	2	Tosh [2], Power 2 [28, 45], Charnley [32], O'Driscoll 2 [62, 67]	2282
21	Jan 1	A	St Johnstone	L	2-7	1-1	—	Charnley [32], O'Driscoll (pen) [83]	7087
22	11	H	Airdrieonians	W	2-1	1-0	2	O'Driscoll [24], Power [69]	2469
23	18	A	Clydebank	W	1-0	0-0	2	O'Driscoll [70]	1954
24	28	A	St Mirren	L	2-3	1-1	—	Shaw [33], Robertson [60]	2331
25	Feb 1	A	Falkirk	D	1-1	0-0	2	O'Driscoll [90]	2480
26	8	A	Stirling A	W	1-0	0-0	2	Shaw [67]	1425
27	22	H	Greenock Morton	W	1-0	1-0	2	O'Driscoll [25]	2264
28	Mar 1	A	East Fife	D	1-1	0-0	2	Power [72]	1234
29	15	H	St Johnstone	D	0-0	0-0	3		5634
30	22	A	Clydebank	D	0-0	0-0	3		622
31	Apr 5	H	Falkirk	L	0-2	0-0	3		3454
32	12	A	Airdrieonians	L	0-2	0-1	4		2530
33	19	H	St Mirren	W	2-0	1-0	3	Anderson [6], McKeown [64]	2462
34	26	H	Partick Th	D	1-1	0-0	4	Annand [68]	2416
35	May 3	A	Greenock Morton	D	1-1	1-1	3	Anderson (og) [24]	1617
36	10	H	Stirling A	W	4-2	2-0	3	Annand [18], Raeside [28], O'Driscoll [68], Tait (og) [86]	2089

Final League Position: 3

Honours
League Champions: Division I 1961-62. First Division 1978-79, 1991-92. Division II 1946-47; *Runners-up:* Division I 1902-03, 1906-07, 1908-09, 1948-49, 1980-81.
Scottish Cup Winners: 1910; *Runners-up:* 1925, 1952, 1964.
League Cup Winners: 1951-52, 1952-53, 1973-74; *Runners-up:* 1967-68, 1980-81. *(Coca-Cola Cup):* 1995–96.
B&Q (Centenary) Cup: Winners: 1990-91 *Runners-up:* 1994-95.

European: *European Cup:* 1962-63 (semi-final). *Cup Winners:* 1964-65.
UEFA Cup: (Fairs Cup 1967-68 semi-final), 1971-72, 1973-74, 1974-75.
Club colours: Shirt: Dark blue with red and white trim. Shorts: White. Stockings: Blue and white.

Goalscorers: *League (47):* O'Driscoll 10, Anderson 5, Shaw 5, Power 4, Raeside 4, Tosh 4, Charnley 3, Annand 2, Rae 2, Adamczuk 1, Ferguson 1, Hamilton 1, McKeown 1, Robertson 1, Winnie 1, own goals 2. *Scottish Cup (5):* Anderson 2, Power 2, O'Driscoll 1. *Coca Cola Cup (7):* Hamilton 5, Raeside 1, Tosh 1. *League Challenge Cup (6):* Tosh 2, Farningham 1, Hamilton 1, Magee 1, Shaw 1.

Thomson W 25	Smith B 36	McQueen T 16+1	Duffy J 2	Raeside R 34	Bain K 12	Adamczuk D 30	Charnley J 15	Tosh P 19+5	Hamilton J 12	Magee K 10+15	Anderson I 28+7	Shaw G 18+3	McKeown G 16+3	Winnie D 26	Ferguson I 5+9	Farningham R 3+5	Rae G 11+8	Tully C 16+5	Ward M 1	Croce L 1	Skomard O 1+3	McGlynn D 11	O'Driscoll J 18+2	Power L 9+1	Cargill A —+2	Robertson H 15	Annand E 5	Elliot J 1+3	Bayne G —+2	Match No.
1	2	3	4	5	6	7	8	9	10	11^1	12																			1
1	2	3	4	5	6	7	8^2	9	10		11^1	12	13																	2
1	2	3		5	4^2	11	8			12	10^1	7	14		6	9^3	13													3
1	2^3			5		11	8	9	10	3^2	13		4^1		6	7	12	14												4
1	2			5	4	11		9	10^1		13				6	12	7^2	3	8											5
1	2			5	4		8^3	9	10^2	11^1	12	7	14		6		13	3												6
1	2	3		5	4	11	8^3	9		12	13	7^2	10^1		6		14													7
1	2	3^1		5	4	11	8	9		12	13	7			6	10^2														8
1	2	3		5	4	11	8	9	10^1			6	7		12															9
1	2	3		5	4	11		9	10^2	12	8	7			13	6^1														10
1	2			5	4	11		10		12	9^1	7			3	8		6												11
1	2			5			8^1	9	10	11		7			3	12	13	6		4^2										12
1	2	3		5	6		8			12		11	7^1	10		9		4												13
1	2			5			8			9^1	10	12	7		11		3	13	4		6^2									14
1	2	8		5	6			9	10			7^1			3	11^2	13	4				12								15
	2			5			8	11	12	10^2		7^1			3	14	6^3	4				13	1	9						16
	2	3^1		5			8	11	12			7			6	13		4				10^2	1	9						17
	2	3		5	4	11	8					7^3			6^1	14		12				13	1	9^2	10					18
1	2	3^1		5			8	11	4			7			6			12					9	10						19
1	2			5			8^2	11	6	12		7^1			3	14		4					9	10^3	13					20
1	2			5	4			10		11		7^2			6		3^1	12					8	9	13					21
1	2	3		5^1	4					13		7			6		8	12					9^2	10		11				22
	2	3^1		5	4			14		13		7			6		8	12				1	9^2	10^3		11				23
	2			5	4			6^2		12	8^1	7			3			13				1	9	10		11				24
1	2	3^1		5	4					12	8	7	10		6								9			11				25
1	2			5	4^2			12		14	8	7	6	3				13					9^1	10^3		11				26
	2			5	4					9	8	7	6					3				1	10			11				27
	2			5	4					9^2	13	8	7	6				3				1	10^1	12		11				28
	2			5	4					9	13	7	12	6				3				1	8	10^1		11^2				29
	2			5	4			10				8^1	7	6	12			3				1	9			11				30
	2			5^1	4						8	7		6	13			3				1	10				11^2	9	12	31
1	2			5	4					12	11	7^1	8	6^2				13									10	9		32
1	2							11			8	7^1	6	5	14	4	3						9^2				10^3	12	13	33
1	2							11^1				7	12	6	5	4	3						8^2				10	9	13	34
1	2	10^1		5						12	8	7	6^2	4	13		3										11	9		35
	2	12		5^1	4							7	6	3	8			13				1					11	9^3	10^2	36

DUNDEE UNITED   Premier Division

Year Formed: 1909 (1923). *Ground & Address:* Tannadice Park, Tannadice St, Dundee DD3 7JW. *Telephone:* 01382
833166. *Fax:* 01382 889398. *Ground Capacity:* total: 12,616 all seated: stands: east 2868, west 2104, south 2201, George
Fox 5151, executive boxes 292.
Size of Pitch: 110yd × 74yd.
Chairman: James Y. McLean. *Company Secretary:* Miss Priti Trivedi. *Commercial Manager:* Bill Campbell.
Manager: Thomas McLean. *Coaches:* Maurice Malpas, Gordon Wallace. *Physio:* David Rankine.
Managers since 1975: J. McLean, I.Golac, W. Kirkwood. *Club Nickname(s):* The Terrors. *Previous Grounds:* None.
Record Attendance: 28,000 v Barcelona, Fairs Cup; 16 Nov, 1966.
Record Transfer Fee received: £4,000,000 for Duncan Ferguson from Rangers (July 1993).
Record Transfer Fee paid: £600,000 for Gordon Petric from Partizan Belgrade (Nov 1993).
Record Victory: 14-0 v Nithsdale Wanderers, Scottish Cup 1st rd; 17 Jan, 1931.
Record Defeat: 1-12 v Motherwell, Division II; 23 Jan, 1954.
Most Capped Player: Maurice Malpas, 55, Scotland.
Most League Appearances: 612, Dave Narey; 1973-94.
Most Appearances in European Matches: 76, Dave Narey (record for Scottish player).
Most League Goals in Season (Individual): 41: John Coyle, Division II; 1955-56.
Most Goals Overall (Individual): 158: Peter McKay.

DUNDEE UNITED 1996–97 LEAGUE RECORD

Match No.	Date	Venue	Opponents	Result		H/T Score	Lg. Pos.	Goalscorers	Atten- dance
1	Aug 10	H	Motherwell	D	1-1	1-0	—	McSwegan [7]	8157
2	17	H	Hibernian	L	0-1	0-1	8		8589
3	24	A	Rangers	L	0-1	0-0	8		48,285
4	Sept 7	A	Hearts	L	0-1	0-0	9		11,848
5	14	H	Celtic	L	1-2	0-1	9	McSwegan [87]	12,205
6	21	A	Raith R	L	2-3	2-1	10	McSwegan [2], McLaren [38]	5068
7	28	H	Aberdeen	W	1-0	0-0	8	McSwegan [67]	10,359
8	Oct 12	H	Kilmarnock	D	0-0	0-0	8		7365
9	19	A	Dunfermline Ath	D	1-1	0-0	9	Winters [64]	6982
10	26	H	Hearts	W	1-0	0-0	8	Winters [67]	9393
11	Nov 2	A	Motherwell	W	3-1	0-0	7	Olofsson [55], McKinnon [57], Winters [89]	5814
12	16	A	Aberdeen	D	3-3	1-1	8	McLaren [43], Winters [66], Olofsson [82]	13,807
13	23	H	Raith R	L	1-2	0-1	8	Duffy [85]	8028
14	30	H	Dunfermline Ath	D	1-1	0-0	7	Winters [71]	7646
15	Dec 7	A	Kilmarnock	W	2-0	1-0	6	Olofsson 2 [22, 51]	5814
16	10	H	Rangers	W	1-0	0-0	—	Gough (og) [66]	12,417
17	14	A	Hibernian	D	1-1	1-1	4	McLaren (pen) [44]	8250
18	21	A	Celtic	L	0-1	0-1	6		46,483
19	26	H	Motherwell	W	2-0	1-0	—	McSwegan [36], Hannah [67]	8072
20	28	A	Raith R	W	1-0	1-0	4	Olofsson [2]	5767
21	Jan 1	H	Aberdeen	W	4-0	1-0	—	Winters [40], Pressley 2 [54, 66], Olofsson [68]	9548
22	4	H	Kilmarnock	W	2-0	0-0	3	Malpas [58], McKinnon [61]	8508
23	11	A	Dunfermline Ath	W	3-1	0-0	3	Olofsson 2 [55, 58], McInally [89]	7698
24	18	A	Hearts	W	2-1	1-1	3	Olofsson [16], McKinnon [83]	12,777
25	Feb 1	H	Celtic	W	1-0	0-0	3	McSwegan [88]	12,483
26	8	H	Hibernian	D	0-0	0-0	3		9219
27	22	A	Kilmarnock	W	3-2	1-1	3	McKinnon 3 [45, 66, 75]	6054
28	Mar 1	H	Dunfermline Ath	W	2-1	1-0	3	McLaren [36], Olofsson [90]	8160
29	12	A	Rangers	W	2-0	1-0	—	Winters [27], Olofsson [47]	49,192
30	15	A	Aberdeen	D	1-1	0-1	3	Olofsson [68]	13,645
31	22	H	Raith R	W	2-1	0-0	3	Millar (og) [57], Winters [70]	8367
32	Apr 5	A	Hibernian	L	0-2	0-0	3		10,951
33	19	A	Motherwell	D	1-1	0-1	3	Zetterlund [70]	5382
34	May 3	H	Hearts	W	1-0	0-0	3	McSwegan [72]	7405
35	7	H	Rangers	L	0-1	0-1	—		12,180
36	10	A	Celtic	L	0-3	0-1	3		46,742

Final League Position: 3

Honours
League Champions: Premier Division 1982-83. Division II 1924-25, 1928-29; *Runners-up:* Division II 1930-31, 1959-60. First Division Runners-up 1995-96.
Scottish Cup Winners: 1994; *Runners-up:* 1974, 1981, 1985, 1987, 1988, 1991.
League Cup Winners: 1979-80, 1980-81;*Runners-up:* 1981-82, 1984-85.
Summer Cup Runners-up: 1964-65. *Scottish War Cup Runners-up:* 1939-40.

European: *European Cup:* 8 matches 1983-84 (semi-finals), 1988-89; *Cup Winners Cup:* 4 matches: 1974-75; *UEFA Cup Runners-up:* 1986-87. *Fairs Cup:* 10 matches: 1966-67, 1969-70, 1970-71. *UEFA Cup:* 70 matches:1971-72, 1975-76, 1977-78, 1978-79, 1979-80, 1980-81, 1981-82, 1982-83, 1984-85, 1985-86, 1986-87, 1987-88, 1989-90, 1990-91, 1993-94.
Club colours: Tangerine jersey, Black shorts. Change colours: White with two black hoops with mauve trim, black and white with mauve trim shorts.

Goalscorers: *League (46):* Olofsson 12, Winters 8, McSwegan 7, McKinnon 6, McLaren 4 (1 pen), Pressley 2, Duffy 1, Hannah 1, McInally 1, Malpas 1, Zetterlund 1, own goals 2. *Scottish Cup (8):* Winters 3, McLaren 2, McSwegan 1, Olofsson 1, own goal 1. *Coca Cola Cup (4):* Coyle 2, McSwegan 1, Winters 1.

Maxwell A 10	Shannon R 7+2	McQuilken J 6+3	Pressley S 36	Perry M 33+2	Benneker A 6+1	McKinnon R 17+9	Bowman D 26+2	McSwegan G 15+16	Johnson G 2+5	Coyle O 6+4	Duffy C 6+7	Winters R 27+9	McLaren A 29+5	Hannah D 9+3	Malpas M 26	Robertson A 1+3	McInally J 12+4	Pedersen J 25	Olofsson K 22+3	Key L 4	Zetterlund L 25	Walker P 2+1	Dijkstra S 22	Easton C 1+1	Wirmola J 1+2	Dolan J 11+2	Sinclair D 3+3	McKinnie S 6	Thompson S —+1	Black P —+1	Match No
1	2	3	4	5	6	7^2	8	9	10^1	11	12	13																			1
1	13	3^1	4	2	5		8	9	10	6	12	7	11^2																		2
1	13	3	4	2	5	11^2		9^1	10	8	12	7	6																		3
1	2	3	4	6	5	7	8	9		10	11^1	13	12^2																		4
1	3^1	12	4	5	6	8^2	2	9	13	14		7^3	11	10																	5
1	3	13	4	5	6		2	9	8^1	12		7^2	11	10																	6
1	2	6	5	14			8	9		11^2		7^1	12^3	10	3	13															7
1	2	12	4	5			8	9		11^3		14	7^2	10^1	3	13	6														8
1	2	11^1	4	5			8			13		9	12	10	3	7^2	6														9
1			4	5		8^2	2	12				7^3	11	10	3	14	13	6	9^1												10
			4	5		10	2	9^1				12	11^2	13	3		6	7		1	8										11
			4	5		10^1	2	9				12	11^2		3	13	6	7		1	8										12
			4	5		10^1	2		14	13		9^1	11		3		6	7		1	8			12							13
			4	5		12	2^1			10		9	11		3		6	7^1		1	8										14
			4	5		12	2	13		10		9^1	11		3		6	7^1			8		1								15
			4	5^1		13	2	14		12^2		9^1	11		3	10	6	7			8		1								16
			4	5		13	2	12				9	11		3	10^2	6	7^1			8		1								17
			4	5			2^3	12	13			9	11	10	3		6	7^1			8		1								18
			4	5		10^1	2	9^3				7	11	12	3	13	6	14			8^2		1								19
			4	5		12	2	13				9	11^1		3		6	7			8		1								20
			4	5		12	2^1	13				9^2	11		3	10^3	6	7			8		1		14						21
			4	5^1		2		13	12			9^1	11^2		3	10^1	6	7			8		1		14						22
			4	5		2^2		14				9^3	11^1		3	12		7			8		1			13	10				23
			4	5^2		12		14	13			9^1	11^1		3	2		7			8		1			6	10				24
			4	5				12	13			9^2	11^3		3	2^1	6	7			8		1			10	14				25
			4	5^3				9	14	12		11^1			3	2^2	6	7			8		1			10	13				26
		4	13			11	2^1	12				9	14		3		6	7^3			8		1			10	5^2				27
			4	5		2		7^1		13		9	11		3		6	12			8^2		1			10					28
			4	5		12	2					9	11^1		3		6	7			8		1			10					29
			4	5			2	13	12			9	11		3		6	7			8		1			10^1					30
			4			10^1	2^3	13				9	11^2		3		6	7			8		1			12	14	5			31
			4	5		13	12			14		9	11^1		3		6	12			8^3		1			10^2	2				32
			4	5		11	2	9^2				7	13	14			6	12			8^3		1			10^1	2				33
			4	12		14	2^1	7				9^2			6						8	11^3	1	10		5	3	13			34
			4	5		10		9				13	11^2			2	6	7			8^1		1			12	3				35
			4	5		8		12				13	9	11^1		2					7^3	1				10	6^2	3		14	36

DUNFERMLINE ATHLETIC Premier Division

Year Formed: 1885. *Ground & Address:* East End Park, Halbeath Rd, Dunfermline KY12 7RB. *Telephone:* 01383 724295. *Fax:* 01383 723468.
Ground Capacity: under reconstruction. *Size of Pitch:* 115yd × 68yd.
Chairman: C. R. Woodrow. *Secretary:* P. A. M. D'Mello. *Commercial Manager:* Miss Audrey Bastianelli.
Manager: Bert Paton. *Assistant Manager:* Dick Campbell. *Coach:* Brian Rice.
Physio: Philip Yeates, MCSP.
Managers since 1975: G. Miller; H. Melrose; P. Stanton; T. Forsyth; J. Leishman; I. Munro; J. Scott. *Club Nickname(s):* The Pars. *Previous Grounds:* None.
Record Attendance: 27,816 v Celtic, Division I, 30 April, 1968.
Record Transfer Fee received: £300,000 for Istvan Kozma to Liverpool (Feb 1992).
Record Transfer Fee paid: £540,000 for Istvan Kozma from Bordeaux (Sept 1989).
Record Victory: 11-2 v Stenhousemuir, Division II, 27 Sept, 1930.
Record Defeat: 1-11 v Hibernian, Scottish Cup, 3rd rd replay, 26 Oct, 1889.
Most Capped Player: Istvan Kozma, 13 (29), Hungary.
Most League Appearances: 497: Norrie McCathie; 1981-96.
Most League Goals in Season (Individual): 53: Bobby Skinner, Division II, 1925-26.
Most Goals Overall (Individual): 154: Charles Dickson.

DUNFERMLINE ATHLETIC 1996–97 LEAGUE RECORD

Match No.	Date	Venue	Opponents	Result	H/T Score	Lg. Pos.	Goalscorers	Atten- dance
1	Aug 17	H	Rangers	L	2-5	0-1	—	Moore [79], Den Bieman [85]	16,782
2	24	A	Hibernian	D	0-0	0-0	9		9801
3	Sept 7	A	Kilmarnock	D	2-2	1-1	8	Britton 2 [39, 87]	6623
4	10	H	Hearts	W	2-1	0-1	—	Tod [54], Smith [62]	7787
5	14	H	Motherwell	D	1-1	1-0	6	Clark [5]	5690
6	21	A	Celtic	L	1-5	0-3	7	Britton [65]	49,692
7	28	A	Raith R	W	3-1	1-0	7	Britton [45], French [51], Millar M [90]	8634
8	Oct 12	A	Aberdeen	L	0-3	0-2	7		10,404
9	19	H	Dundee U	D	1-1	0-0	7	Tod [78]	6982
10	26	H	Kilmarnock	W	2-1	1-1	5	Smith [2], Britton [48]	5269
11	Nov 2	A	Hearts	L	0-2	0-2	6		12,517
12	16	A	Raith R	W	2-1	2-0	5	Miller (og) [8], French [24]	6762
13	30	A	Dundee U	D	1-1	0-0	6	Smith [87]	7646
14	Dec 7	H	Aberdeen	L	2-3	1-1	8	Millar M 2 (1 pen) [43 (p), 46]	5465
15	11	H	Hibernian	W	2-1	0-0	—	Millar M [63], Ireland [82]	5295
16	14	H	Rangers	L	1-3	0-1	6	Moore [89]	45,878
17	21	A	Motherwell	W	3-2	1-2	4	Millar M [27], Smith 2 [53, 74]	4529
18	26	H	Hearts	L	2-3	1-0	—	Fleming [20], Moore [60]	9736
19	28	A	Celtic	L	2-4	1-2	7	Britton 2 [65, 68]	45,751
20	Jan 1	H	Raith R	W	2-0	0-0	—	Britton 2 [60, 62]	7236
21	4	A	Aberdeen	W	2-0	0-0	6	Petrie 2 [48, 60]	9137
22	11	H	Dundee U	L	1-3	0-0	6	Welsh [84]	7698
23	18	A	Kilmarnock	L	1-2	0-0	6	Smith [81]	5813
24	29	A	Celtic	L	0-2	0-2	—		17,919
25	Feb 1	H	Motherwell	W	3-1	2-1	6	Millar M [10], Tod [26], Britton [75]	4796
26	8	H	Rangers	L	0-3	0-1	6		16,153
27	22	H	Aberdeen	W	3-0	2-0	6	Petrie [43], Britton [45], Smith [90]	5553
28	Mar 1	A	Dundee U	L	1-2	0-1	6	Fleming [68]	8160
29	8	A	Hibernian	L	0-1	0-1	6		8877
30	15	A	Raith R	W	1-0	1-0	6	Smith [29]	5882
31	22	H	Celtic	D	2-2	2-0	5	Britton [16], Curran [29]	13,092
32	Apr 5	A	Rangers	L	0-4	0-2	6		49,832
33	12	H	Hibernian	D	1-1	1-1	6	Britton [12]	8752
34	19	A	Hearts	D	1-1	1-0	5	Young [27]	10,174
35	May 3	H	Kilmarnock	W	3-1	1-0	5	Tod [36], Smith 2 [48, 90]	5904
36	10	A	Motherwell	D	2-2	1-1	5	French [38], Bingham [59]	9676

Final League Position: 5

Honours
League Champions: First Division 1988-89, 1995-96. Division II 1925-26. Second Division 1985-86; *Runners-up:* First Division 1986-87, 1993-94, 1994-95. Division II 1912-13, 1933-34, 1954-55, 1957-58, 1972-73. Second Division 1978-79.
Scottish Cup Winners: 1961, 1968; *Runners-up:* 1965.
League Cup Runners-up: 1949-50, 1991-92.
European: *European Cup:* —. *Cup Winners Cup:* 1961-62, 1968-69 (semi-finals). *UEFA Cup:* 1962-63, 1964-65, 1965-66, 1966-67, 1969-70 (*Fairs Cup*).
Club colours: Shirt: Black and white vertical stripes, stippled with red dots. Shorts: Black with white side panel. Stockings: White with red chevrons.

Goalscorers: *League (52):* Britton 13, Smith 10, Millar M 6 (1 pen), Tod 4, French 3, Moore 3, Petrie 3, Fleming 2, Bingham 1, Clark 1, Curran 1, Den Bieman 1, Ireland 1, Welsh 1, Young 1, own goal 1. *Scottish Cup (5):* Smith 2, Curran 1, French 1, Petrie 1. *Coca Cola Cup (8):* Bingham 2, Britton 2, French 2, Moore 2.

Westwater I 28 + 1	Den Bieman I 21 + 7	Fleming D 23 + 3	Clark J 8	Tod A 35	Rice B 4 + 4	Moore A 13 + 13	Robertson C 31	Smith A 30 + 5	Britton G 27 + 6	French H 34 + 1	Miller C 19 + 3	Bingham D 5 + 12	McCulloch M 4 + 5	Petrie S 24 + 4	Shaw G — + 3	Millar M 19 + 4	Lemajic Z 8	Curran H 18 + 2	Welsh S 20	Sharp R 14 + 1	Ireland C 7 + 2	Young S 2	Fraser J 2	Match No.
1	2	3	4¹	5	6	7	8	9	10²	11	12	13												1
1	4	3		5	8¹	7²	6	9	10	11	2			12	13									2
1	4	3		5		7¹	6	9	8	10	2			13		11	12							3
1	4	3		5		7	6	9	8¹	10	2	13		11²	12									4
1	4¹	3	6	5	12	7		9	8²		2	14	10	11³	13									5
1	4	3¹	6	5		8	9	10	7²	2	13		11		12									6
	4	3	6	5		8	9	10¹	7	2		11		12	1									7
	4	3	6	5	12	8	9²	10¹	7		13	11	2	1										8
	4	3¹		5		7	8	9	10	6	2		11		1	12								9
	2		5	4		7	8	9	10	6		11	3	1										10
	2		5	4		7	8	9	10	6¹	12	11	3	1										11
			5	4	12	8	9	10²	7	2	11¹	3	1	13	6									12
15			4	12	8	9	10	7	2¹	11	6	1⁶		5	3									13
1			4	13	8	9	10¹	7	2	12	11²	6			3	5								14
1	11		4		8	9²	13	7¹	2	12	6	10			3	5								15
1	2	11	4	13	8	9¹	12	7²	6	10					3	5								16
1	2	11	4	13	8	9³	14	7²	3	12	6¹	10			5									17
1	2	11³	4	8		9¹	12	7	3	13	6	10			5									18
1	2	11¹	4	8		13	9	7²	3	14	10	6²			5	12								19
1	12		4	8	9²	10	7	2¹	13	11		3	6	5										20
1	13		4	7²	8	14	9³	12	2	11	10		6¹	5	3									21
1			4	8	9	10¹	7	12	2	11		6	5	3										22
1	13		4	6²	8	9	7	2³	12	14	11	10	5	3¹										23
1	2³	12	4	14	8	9	7	11	10	6¹	5	13	3²											24
1	14	12	4	6¹	8	9²	13	7	11³	10	3	2	5											25
1	2		4	14	8	9²	12	7	13	10³	11	6	5	3¹										26
1	14	3	4	8	12	9¹	7³	2	13	11²	10	6	5											27
1	3		4	12	8	9	7	11¹	10	6	5	2												28
1	14	3	4	13	8	12	9	7²	10¹	11	6³	5	2											29
1	2	4		13	8	9¹	10²	7	11	12	6	5	3											30
1	2	11¹	4	14	8	9²	10	7	12	13	6²	5	3											31
1	2	11¹	4	12	8	9	10	7²	13	6	5	3												32
1	13	11³	4	12	8	9²	10	7¹	14	6	2	5	3											33
14	3		4	7²	8	13	9	10	2	12	6¹	1	5	11³										34
1	2		4	12	7¹	9	10	11	6		5	3			8									35
1	3		4	12		9	10	7	11		2	5	13	6²	8¹									36

EAST FIFE   Second Division

Year Formed: 1903. *Ground & Address:* Bayview Park, Methil, Fife KY8 3AG (moving during 1998–99). *Telephone:* 01333 426323. *Fax:* 01333 426376.
Ground Capacity: total: 5385. seated: 600. *Size of Pitch:* 110yd × 71yd.
Chairman: Julian Danskin. *Secretary:* J. Derrick Brown. *Commercial Manager:* Patrick McAuley.
Manager: James Bone. *Assistant Manager:* Patrick McAuley. *Physio:* Alex MacQueen. *Coach:* Gordon Rae.
Managers since 1975: Frank Christie; Roy Barry; David Clarke; Gavin Murray, Alex Totten, Steve Archibald.
Club Nickname(s): The Fifers. *Previous Grounds:* None.
Record Attendance: 22,515 v Raith Rovers, Division I; 2 Jan, 1950.
Record Transfer Fee received: £150,000 for Paul Hunter from Hull C (March 1990).
Record Transfer Fee paid: £70,000 for John Sludden from Kilmarnock (July 1991).
Record Victory: 13-2 v Edinburgh City, Division II; 11 Dec, 1937.
Record Defeat: 0-9 v Hearts, Division I; 5 Oct, 1957.
Most Capped Player: George Aitken, 5 (8), Scotland.
Most League Appearances: 517: David Clarke, 1968-86.
Most League Goals in Season (Individual): 41: Jock Wood, Division II; 1926-27 and Henry Morris, Division II; 1947-48.
Most Goals Overall (Individual): 225: Phil Weir (215 in League).

EAST FIFE 1996–97 LEAGUE RECORD

Match No.	Date	Venue	Opponents	Result	H/T Score	Lg. Pos.	Goalscorers	Atten- dance
1	Aug 17	H	St Mirren	L	0-4	0-2	—		1375
2	24	A	Airdrieonians	D	0-0	0-0	9		1334
3	Sept 3	H	Clydebank	D	1-1	1-1	—	Beaton [43]	721
4	7	A	Greenock Morton	D	0-0	0-0	9		2885
5	14	H	St Johnstone	L	1-4	0-2	10	Scott [89]	2090
6	21	A	Dundee	L	0-2	0-1	10		2511
7	28	H	Stirling A	D	2-2	0-1	10	Scott [53], Hutcheon [78]	984
8	Oct 5	H	Falkirk	W	3-1	3-0	9	Andrew [7], Donaghy [25], Berry (og) [40]	1809
9	12	A	Partick Th	L	0-6	0-4	9		1791
10	19	A	St Mirren	L	1-4	1-2	9	Hutcheon [31]	2491
11	26	H	Airdrieonians	L	0-4	0-1	10		885
12	Nov 13	A	St Johnstone	L	0-3	0-2	—		2517
13	16	A	Stirling A	L	1-2	1-1	10	Gibson (og) [44]	895
14	30	A	Falkirk	L	1-2	1-2	10	Allan [38]	2330
15	Dec 11	H	Greenock Morton	L	0-3	0-2	—		645
16	17	H	Dundee	L	1-7	0-2	—	Winiarski [86]	869
17	21	A	Clydebank	L	0-2	0-0	10		306
18	26	H	St Mirren	L	0-3	0-1	—		1199
19	28	A	Dundee	L	0-6	0-4	10		2282
20	Jan 1	H	Stirling A	L	1-3	1-1	—	Moffat [31]	588
21	7	H	Partick Th	L	1-3	1-1	—	Christie [1]	800
22	11	A	Greenock Morton	L	0-2	0-1	10		1754
23	18	A	Falkirk	L	0-2	0-2	10		1025
24	28	H	St Johnstone	D	2-2	2-2	—	Cameron [30], Bailey [36]	1431
25	Feb 1	A	Partick Th	L	1-3	0-2	10	MacFarlane [54]	1833
26	8	H	Clydebank	L	1-2	1-1	10	Irons (og) [3]	663
27	22	A	Airdrieonians	D	1-1	1-1	10	Dyer [19]	1138
28	Mar 1	H	Dundee	D	1-1	0-0	10	Dyer [71]	1234
29	15	A	Stirling A	L	1-4	0-2	10	Ronald [61]	895
30	22	A	Falkirk	L	1-3	1-0	10	MacFarlane [16]	1906
31	Apr 5	H	Partick Th	L	0-2	0-1	10		1002
32	12	H	Greenock Morton	L	1-4	0-3	10	Dyer [62]	728
33	19	A	St Johnstone	L	2-3	0-2	10	Ronald 2 [63, 66]	6454
34	26	A	St Mirren	L	0-1	0-0	10		1537
35	May 3	A	Airdrieonians	D	0-0	0-0	10		2010
36	10	A	Clydebank	W	4-0	0-0	10	Ronald [46], Allan [47], Dyer [87], Cusick [88]	269

Final League Position: 10

Honours

League Champions: Division II 1947-48; *Runners-up:* Division II 1929-30, 1970-71. Second Division 1983-84., 1995-96
Scottish Cup Winners: 1938; *Runners-up:* 1927, 1950.
League Cup Winners: 1947-48, 1949-50, 1953-54.
Club colours: Shirt: Amber with black collar and cuffs. Shorts: Amber with black flashes. Stockings: Amber with 3 black stripes on top.

Goalscorers: *League (28):* Dyer 4, Ronald 4, Allan 2, Hutcheon 2, MacFarlane 2, Scott 2, Andrew 1, Baillie 1, Beaton 1. Cameron 1, Christie 1, Cusick 1, Donaghy 1, Moffat 1, Winiarski 1, own goals 3. *Scottish Cup (3):* Christie 2, Baillie 1. *Coca Cola Cup (1):* Dwarika 1. *League Challenge Cup (2):* Archibald 1, Scott 1.

Hamilton L 30	Dixon A 26+2	Gibb R 30	Cusick J 25+5	Kinnell A —+1	Beaton D 5	McStay J 9	Donaghy M 23	Archibald S 5	Scott R 15	Allan G 30+2	Lewis G 6+10	Dwarika A 12+6	Hutcheon S 18+6	Andrew B 27+4	Demmin C 1+5	Robertson D 5+2	Hope D 5+5	Winiarski S 6+9	Gartshore P 15+8	Mair I —+1	Nicol G 1+4	Yates D 2	Fennell K 1	Stigson O 3	Bogie G 5+3	McPherson G 1+3	Cameron R 13+2	Johnston G 16	Moffat B 7+1	MacFarlane C 9+2	Christie K 9	Ritchie I 13	Rushford C 1	Bailey L 5+5	Dyer M 9+2	Ronald P 8	Carmichael D —+1	Sweeney C —+1	Match No.
1	2	3	4	5	6	7	8	9	10	11¹	12																												1
1	4	3	6	5	2	7	8²	9	12	14		10¹	11³	13																									2
	4	3	6	5	2	7²	8	9¹	12	13		10	11		1																								3
1		3	6	5	2³	7	8²	9¹	4	13	12	10	11	14																									4
1	4¹	3	6		2²	7	8	9	5	14	13	10¹	11	12																									5
1	4	3	6		2				9	5	11	8²	10¹	7	13		12																						6
1	4	3	6		2				9	5	11	8	10	7¹			12																						7
1	4	3	6¹		2		8³		9	5	11		10²	7	12		13	14																					8
1	4¹	3³	6		2				9	5	11²	8	10	7			12	13	14																				9
1	4	3							9	6	10¹	8	11	7			12	5	2²	13																			10
1	2	3	6		11³				9	4¹		8²	10	7	5		12	13	14																				11
1	2	3	6				8		9	5	14	12	11³	7			10²	4¹	13																				12
1	2		6				8		9³	5	13	11	10	7²		14	4	12	3¹																				13
1	2	3	4	5¹			8		9	6	13	7	10²				11	12²			14																		14
1	12	3	6				8		9	4	13	7	10¹				11²	2³	14		5																		15
1	2	3	4				8		6	13	7³	14	9				11¹	12						5²	10														16
1		3	4						6				10	9	14			7¹	8³		13	5			11²	2	12												17
		3					8						10¹	9	1			7	3		12				11	2	5												18
1			4				8			6		7	10	9				11	3			5				2													19
1	11	6								4			7		9		12	3	2¹						8	5	10												20
	11	13								4		12	14	9	1			3			2¹				8	6³	10	5	7										21
1	11									2		8²	14	9³				13			12				4¹	6	10	5	7		3								22
	6	11¹	2²							8		12	10	9				13	3³		14									4	5	1	7						23
	2									8		11		14				10¹							6	5	7²	12	4	3					9¹	13			24
	2		12							8		11		13				3¹							10³	5	7	6		4					9¹	14			25
1	10		14							2		13	12					3							8²	5	7¹	6		4					9³	11			26
1	10²	11	12							8		2						13							5	9²	6¹	4	3		14		7					27
1		11	2							8		14	6³												10²	5		4	3	12	7		9¹	13				28
1	12	11³					8						7								14				6³	5	13	2	4	3				9²	10			29
1	7	11					8										2								12	4²	5	6²		3		13	9	10				30
1	4	11³		14						2		12	7					10							8¹	5	6²		3		9				13		31
1	8	11	4¹							2		13						6²						7³	14	5		12	3			9	10				32
1	8¹	11	12							2		7						13						14	6³	5		4	3			9³	10				33
1	8	11	4							2		7³						9¹						14	12	6²	5	3	13			9	10				34
1	6	11	4				8			2		7						12						5			3					9	10				35
1	6	11	4				8¹			2		7²						12						13	5		3			14		9	10³				36

EAST STIRLINGSHIRE   Third Division

Year Formed: 1880. *Ground & Address:* Firs Park, Firs St, Falkirk FK2 7AY. *Telephone:* 01324 623583. *Fax:* 01324 637 862
Ground Capacity: total: 1880. seated: 200. *Size of Pitch:* 112yd × 72yd.
Chairman/Commercial Manager: Leslie G. Thomson. *Vice Chairman:* Angus Williamson. *Secretary:* Margaret Thomson.
Manager: John Brownlie. *Physio:* Paul Green.
Managers since 1975: I. Ure; D. McLinden; W. P. Lamont; A. Ferguson; W. Little; D. Whiteford; D. Lawson; J. D.
Connell; A. Mackin; Dom Sullivan; Billy McCulley; Billy Little. *Club Nickname(s):* The Shire. *Previous Grounds:*
Burnhouse, Randyford Park, Merchiston Park, New Kilbowie Park.
Record Attendance: 12,000 v Partick T, Scottish Cup 3rd rd; 19 Feb 1921.
Record Transfer Fee received: £35,000 for Jim Docherty to Chelsea (1978).
Record Transfer Fee paid: £6,000 for Colin McKinnon from Falkirk (March 1991).
Record Victory: 11-2 v Vale of Bannock, Scottish Cup 2nd rd; 22 Sept, 1888.
Record Defeat: 1-12 v Dundee United, Division II; 13 Apr, 1936.
Most Capped Player: Humphrey Jones, 5 (14), Wales.
Most League Appearances: 379: Gordon Simpson, 1968-80.
Most League Goals in Season (Individual): 36: Malcolm Morrison, Division II; 1938-39.
Most Goals Overall (Individual): —.

EAST STIRLINGSHIRE 1996–97 LEAGUE RECORD

Match No.	Date	Venue	Opponents	Result	H/T Score	Lg. Pos.	Goalscorers	Attendance
1	Aug 17	A	Queen's Park	D 3-3	2-2	—	Elder (og) [9], Watt [36], Ronald [46]	470
2	23	H	Albion R	L 0-1	0-0	—		503
3	31	A	Arbroath	D 0-0	0-0	9		492
4	Sept 7	H	Forfar Ath	W 2-1	0-0	6	Inglis 2 [55, 87]	331
5	14	A	Inverness CT	L 0-2	0-1	8		1316
6	21	H	Montrose	L 1-3	0-1	10	Abercromby [72]	308
7	28	A	Alloa	L 0-1	0-1	10		501
8	Oct 5	H	Ross Co	L 0-1	0-0	10		398
9	12	A	Cowdenbeath	L 0-1	0-0	10		192
10	19	H	Queen's Park	W 2-1	1-1	10	McBride [28], Inglis [69]	369
11	27	A	Albion R	L 3-4	2-1	—	Inglis [30], McBride 2 [42, 63]	603
12	Nov 2	H	Inverness CT	D 0-0	0-0	10		398
13	9	A	Forfar Ath	L 0-3	0-1	10		325
14	16	H	Alloa	D 2-2	1-1	10	Inglis [30], Ramsay [66]	426
15	26	A	Montrose	L 0-1	0-0	—		334
16	30	A	Ross Co	D 1-1	0-0	10	Sneddon [57]	1261
17	Dec 14	H	Cowdenbeath	W 1-0	1-0	9	Watt [35]	286
18	21	H	Queen's Park	L 0-3	0-1	9		404
19	Jan 18	A	Ross Co	L 2-3	2-2	10	Watt [7], Farrell (og) [12]	343
20	21	A	Alloa	D 1-1	0-0	—	Inglis [64]	435
21	Feb 1	A	Cowdenbeath	L 0-2	0-0	10		134
22	4	H	Montrose	W 4-2	3-0	—	Neill [1], Watt [26], Sneddon 2 [43, 67]	218
23	8	A	Inverness CT	L 2-3	1-2	10	Inglis [45], McBride [46]	1642
24	15	H	Forfar Ath	L 0-3	0-1	10		282
25	21	H	Albion R	L 1-4	1-3	10	Hringsson [37]	320
26	26	H	Arbroath	D 0-0	0-0	—		144
27	Mar 4	A	Arbroath	W 2-1	2-1	—	Inglis [19], McKenzie [37]	172
28	8	A	Montrose	W 2-0	0-0	10	McBride [48], Hunter [65]	392
29	15	H	Alloa	L 0-3	0-1	10		386
30	22	A	Ross Co	L 0-1	0-1	10		1614
31	Apr 5	H	Cowdenbeath	D 2-2	1-0	10	Muirhead [21], Neill [84]	258
32	12	A	Forfar Ath	L 0-1	0-0	10		391
33	19	H	Inverness CT	L 0-3	0-1	10		404
34	26	H	Queen's Park	W 1-0	0-0	10	Watt [63]	318
35	May 2	H	Albion R	D 1-1	0-0	—	Ramsay [46]	396
36	10	H	Arbroath	W 3-0	1-0	9	Neill (pen) [16], Inglis [56], Muirhead [72]	258

Final League Position: 9

Honours
League Champions: Division II 1931-32; C Division 1947-48. *Runners-up:* Division II 1962-63. Second Division 1979-80. Division Three 1923-24.
Scottish Cup: —.
League Cup: —.
Club colours: Shirt: Black and white stripes. Shorts: Black and white. Stockings: Black with 3 tangerine bands on top.

Goalscorers: *League (36):* Inglis 9, McBride 5, Watt 5, Neill 3 (1 pen), Sneddon 3, Muirhead 2, Ramsay 2, Abercromby 1, Hringsson 1, Hunter 1, McKenzie 1, Ronald 1, own goals 2. *Scottish Cup (4):* Stirling 2, Abercromby 1, Inglis 1. *Coca Cola Cup (1):* Ramsay. *League Challenge Cup (1):* Ronald 1.

McDougall G 22	Watt D 25	Russell G 30	Campbell C 22	Neill A 36	Ramsay S 20 + 5	Ronald P 21 + 3	Hunter M 14 + 9	McBride M 31	Cochrane M 7 + 10	Conway V 2 + 1	Scott M — + 8	Inglis G 25 + 3	Sneddon S 26 + 1	Wilson E 10	Hamilton G 20 + 1	Murray N 3 + 3	Abercromby M 15 + 4	Jack A — + 1	Wilson S 1	Muirhead D 12 + 11	McStay R 1	Ross B 13 + 1	Hughes J 1	Stirling A 19 + 4	Kerr R 3	Nisbett I 1	Paterson P 7 + 7	Lamont W 3	MacNamee P 1 + 2	Hringsson H 1	Devine W 1	McKenzie C 1	Farquhar A 2 + 4	Match No.
1	2	3	4	5	6	7¹	8	9	10	11	12																							1
1	2	3	4	5	6	7	8	9	10¹	11²		12	13																					2
	2³	3	4	11	8	12	7²	9	14			10¹	5	1	6	13																		3
	2	3	4	6	10	7		9					11	5	1	8																		4
	2	3	4	6	10	7¹	12	9	13				11	5²	1	8																		5
	2	4	6	3			7²	9	12			11	5	1	10¹		8	13																6
	2	4	6	3³				10	8²		13	12	7	5¹	1	14	9			11														7
		3	4	5	6	11¹	8				2	13	7	1	12		10			9²														8
		3	4	5	6	12	8²	11	13		14		7	1	2³		10			9¹														9
		3	4	5	6			10	9		12	14	7³	1	2	8²	13			11¹														10
			6	11	10	8		9	13			7	5	1	2	3¹	12			4²														11
1	2		6	3				10	13			11	7³	5			8¹			14				4	9²	12								12
1	2		6	3				10	13		9²	12	7¹	5			14			4³				11	8									13
1		3¹		4	6	8		10			9	12	7	5			2							11										14
1		3³		4	6	8		10			9	12	13	7²			5			2¹				14			11							15
1	8	3		4	6			10			9²		12	5			2			13				11			7¹							16
1	8²	3		4	6			10			9		5¹	2			12			13				11			7							17
1	8¹	3		4	6			10			9		5²	2			12			13				11			7							18
	2²	3		4	6	13	10		12			9	7	5	1		8¹							11³			14							19
1	6	2		3	4			10			9		7	5			8							11										20
1	2	3		6	4¹			10³			12	9	7²	5			8					13		11			14							21
		4	3	6				10³	8		9	7¹	5			2²	12			14			1	11			13							22
		4	3	6				8	9		13	7	5			2				10¹		12	1	11²										23
		4	3	6				10²	8¹		9	7	5			2				12			1	11			13							24
1		4	3	6				12	13			11	7			2				8¹				10²			14		5³	9				25
1		3		5				10¹				11	7			2				8		12		6			4		9					26
	2			3	12			4				9	7²			8				10		6		5			13			1		11¹		27
1	8	3		6								7	11			2				10				9			4	5						28
1	8	3		6				10				11	12			2				9				7¹			4	5						29
1				5	7							11	12			4	2			10		8³		3			6¹		9²	14		13		30
1		2		4	3							7	11¹			5				8				6			9		12			10²		31
1		2		4	3	13						7	11			5	8²			10				6			14		9³			12		32
1	8	2		4	3	14			12			7³	11²			5				10¹				6			9					13		33
1	8	2		4	3	10¹			12			7³	14			11²				5				6			9					13		34
1		2		4	3	13			10²			7	5¹			8				6				12			9					11		35
1	8¹	2		4	3				10³			11	5			9²				12				6			14			7		13		36

FALKIRK

First Division

Year Formed: 1876. *Ground & Address:* Brockville Park, Hope St, Falkirk FK1 5AX. *Telephone:* 01324 624121. *Fax:* 01324 612418.
Ground Capacity: total: 9706. seated: 2661. *Size of Pitch:* 110yd × 72yd.
Chairman: G. J. Fulston. *Secretary:* Alex Blackwood. *General Manager:* Jim Hendry. *Commercial Executive:* George Miller.
Manager: Alex Totten. *Assistant Manager:* Walter Kidd. *Physio:* Bob McCallum. *Coach:* Willie Wilson.
Managers since 1975: J. Prentice; G. Miller; W. Little; J. Hagart; A. Totten; G. Abel; W. Lamont; D. Clarke; J. Duffy; W. Lamont; J. Jefferies; J. Lambie E. Bannon; A. Totten. *Club Nickname(s):* The Bairns. *Previous Grounds:* Randyford 1876–81; Blinkbonny Grounds 1881–83; Brockville Park 1883 to present.
Record Attendance: 23,100 v Celtic, Scottish Cup 3rd rd; 21 Feb, 1953.
Record Transfer Fee received: £380,000 for John Hughes to Celtic (Aug 1995).
Record Transfer Fee paid: £225,000 to Chelsea for Kevin McAllister (Aug 1991).
Record Victory: 12-1 v Laurieston, Scottish Cup 2nd rd; 23 Sept, 1893.
Record Defeat: 1-11 v Airdrieonians, Division I; 28 Apr, 1951.
Most Capped Player: Alex Parker, 14 (15), Scotland.
Most League Appearances: (post-war): 353, George Watson, 1975–87.
Most League Goals in Season (Individual): 43: Evelyn Morrison, Division I; 1928-29.
Most Goals Overall (Individual): Dougie Moran, 86, 1957–61 and 1964–67.

FALKIRK 1996–97 LEAGUE RECORD

Match No.	Date	Venue	Opponents	Result	H/T Score	Lg. Pos.	Goalscorers	Attendance
1	Aug 17	A	St Johnstone	D 0-0	0-0	—		4114
2	24	H	Partick Th	W 1-0	0-0	4	McGrillen [47]	3489
3	31	A	Greenock Morton	L 0-1	0-0	6		3584
4	Sept 7	A	Stirling A	L 0-1	0-0	—		1881
5	14	H	Clydebank	W 2-0	0-0	5	Foster [70], Waddle [75]	3701
6	21	A	St Mirren	W 1-0	0-0	4	McGrillen (pen) [90]	3945
7	28	H	Airdrieonians	D 1-1	1-1	4	Hagen [9]	3923
8	Oct 5	A	East Fife	L 1-3	0-3	4	McGraw [75]	1809
9	12	H	Dundee	L 0-1	0-1	5		2855
10	19	H	St Johnstone	W 2-0	2-0	6	Ferguson 2 [19, 27]	3208
11	26	A	Partick Th	L 0-3	0-1	7		3556
12	Nov 2	A	Clydebank	W 1-0	1-0	7	McGraw [20]	632
13	9	H	Stirling A	W 5-2	0-1	5	Mitchell [58], McGraw [83], Gray [86], Elliot [87], Hamilton [89]	2948
14	16	A	Airdrieonians	W 1-0	1-0	3	James [28]	2428
15	30	H	East Fife	W 2-1	2-1	2	McGrillen [4], Ferguson [7]	2330
16	Dec 7	A	Dundee	L 0-2	0-0	2		2198
17	14	H	Greenock Morton	D 0-0	0-0	2		2536
18	26	A	St Johnstone	L 1-3	1-1	—	McGrillen [25]	6331
19	Jan 4	H	Clydebank	D 1-1	1-0	6	McGraw [39]	2333
20	8	H	St Mirren	D 1-1	1-1	—	McGraw [27]	2382
21	11	A	Stirling A	D 0-0	0-0	7		2087
22	14	A	St Mirren	L 0-1	0-1	—		2778
23	18	A	East Fife	W 2-0	2-0	6	McGraw [5], Craig [25]	1025
24	Feb 1	H	Dundee	D 1-1	0-0	6	Ward [48]	2480
25	22	H	Partick Th	W 2-1	2-1	6	McAllister 2 [33, 39]	3181
26	25	H	Airdrieonians	L 0-3	0-1	—		2590
27	Mar 4	A	Greenock Morton	W 2-0	2-0	—	McAllister [28], McGraw [44]	1376
28	11	H	St Mirren	D 1-1	0-1	—	Oliver [75]	2497
29	15	A	Airdrieonians	L 0-2	0-0	6		2090
30	22	H	East Fife	W 3-1	0-1	5	McGrillen [59], James [63], Fellner [81]	1906
31	Apr 5	A	Dundee	W 2-0	0-0	5	McGowan 2 [69, 71]	3454
32	7	H	Stirling A	D 2-2	0-1	—	McKenzie [46], McGrillen [74]	2376
33	19	A	Clydebank	W 2-1	0-0	5	Fellner [63], Craig [75]	535
34	26	H	St Johnstone	L 1-4	1-1	5	Fellner [5]	3686
35	May 3	A	Partick Th	L 1-2	0-0	5	McGraw [49]	1512
36	10	H	Greenock Morton	W 3-0	1-0	5	McGrillen [23], James [46], Fellner [79]	2018

Final League Position: 5

Honours
League Champions: Division II 1935-36, 1969-70, 1974-75. First Division 1990-91, 1993-94. Second Division 1979-80;
Runners-up: Division I 1907-08, 1909-10. First Division 1985-86, 1988-89. Division II 1904-05, 1951-52, 1960-61.
Scottish Cup Winners: 1913, 1957; *Runners-up:* 1997. *League Cup Runners-up:* 1947-48. *B&Q Cup Winners:* 1993-94.
Club colours: Shirt: Navy blue. Shorts: White. Stockings: Navy blue.

Goalscorers: *League (42):* McGraw 8, McGrillen 7, Fellner 4, Ferguson 3, James 3, McAllister 3, Craig 2, McGowan 2,
Elliot 1, Foster 1, Gray 1, Hagen 1, Hamilton 1, McKenzie 1, Mitchell 1, Oliver 1, Waddle 1, Ward 1. *Scottish Cup (9):*
Craig 2, Hagen 2, James 2, McAllister 1, McGraw 1, McGrillen 1. *Coca Cola Cup (2):* Craig 2. *League Challenge Cup
(2):* Hagen 1, McGraw 1.

Mathers P 16	McKenzie S 26+2	Mitchell G 17+3	McGowan J 29	Berry N 9	Hamilton B 18+1	Seaton A 26+3	Craig A 10+3	McGrillen P 24+7	Graham A 5+2	Hagen D 31+3	Elliot D 8+9	Whiteside G —+1	Corrigan M 8+9	McGraw M 20+9	De Massis S —+1	Kidd W 1	Foster W 10+4	Gray A 13+5	Waddle C 4	Ferguson D 13+1	James K 17+1	Nelson C 20	Tortolano J 11+1	Lawrie A 7+5	Huttunen T 2	Kaijasitta P —+1	Olson J —+1	Kelly T —+1	Oliver N 14+1	McAllister K 14+1	Crabbe S 10+2	Ward K 9+1	Fellner G 4+3	Crawford G —+2	Match No.
1	2	3	4	5	6	7	8¹	9²	10	11¹	12	13	14																						1
1	2	3	4	5	6	7	8	9³	10¹	11²			13	12	14																				2
1	8		4	5	6	3		9	12	11³	13							7²		2	10¹	14													3
1	2	3	4²	5	6	7		9	10¹	11	13		12					8																	4
1	2¹	3	4	5	6	7		9	10	11²			13							8	12														5
1	3	4¹	5	6	7			9	10	11	13		12							8²	2														6
1	3		5	6	7	4		9	10	11			12	10						2¹	8														7
1		4	5	6	7	3		9³		11	14		13	10²			8			2	12														8
1		4²	5	6	7	8		9	12	11	13			10¹						2	3														9
			4		6	7¹		9²		11	12		14	13			10²	8		3	1	2	5												10
		12	4		6	7		9		11	13		14	10³			8¹			3	1	2²	5												11
	2	3	5	6			14	11	12	9				10¹			8				1	4³	7²	13											12
	2¹	3	5			8		10		11	12			9			13				6²	1	4	7											13
	2		5	6	4			12		11³	7		14	9²			10¹			13	8	3	1												14
	2¹		5	6		13		9		11²	7		10³	12			8			3	1	4					14								15
	2	3	5	6			14	13		9	11		7	10¹			12			8²	1	4³													16
	2	3	5			7³		9¹		11²	14		12	10			8			6	1	4		13											17
	7	3²	4		12			10		9	11¹		13					6		8	5	1						2							18
1	6		3					10			11		12	9			7²			8¹	5		2	13				4							19
1	8				6			10			11			9						5	3	2						4	7						20
1	8							6²			10¹		9	11			13			12	5		3	2					4	7					21
1	6	2			8		3				13		10	11¹			9²				5		12					4	7						22
14	12	2			8			6³	13		11¹			10²							5	1	3					4	7	9					23
8	5	2					3	13	12		6			10			4					1							7	9¹	11²				24
8	4	2					3	13			10			12			6			5	1								7	9¹	11²				25
8²	4	2					3¹	13			10			12			6			5	1								7	9	11				26
	5	3				6	14			10	13			8			4¹				1		12					2	7²	9³	11			27
6	5	3						11			10		12	8			4				1		2					2	7	9¹				28
12	5	3				8		11			10			6²			9				4	1						2¹	7	13				29
8	4					3	12			6¹			2	9³			5				1	13							7	11²	10	14		30
8			3					11			6			2							5	1						4	7	9	10			31
1	8	5¹				3		6	11		14			2			10³				12							4	9²	7	13			32
1	6²	4¹				3		8	11³	13				2			9				5							12	14	7	10			33
	8	3¹						11			6			9²			4				1						2	5	12	13	7	10		34
1	8	12				3					2			10			6¹				5						4	7	9²	11	13		35
		3						11			10			2	8²		6				5¹	1		12			4	7³	9		13	14	36

FORFAR ATHLETIC   Second Division

Year Formed: 1885. *Ground & Address:* Station Park, Carseview Road, Forfar. *Telephone:* 01307 463576/462259.
Fax: 01307 466956.
Ground Capacity: total: 8732. seated: 739. *Size of Pitch:* 115yd × 69yd.
Chairman and Secretary: David McGregor.
Manager: Ian McPhee. *Assistant Manager:* Billy Bennett. *Physio:* Jim Peacock. *Coaches:* Raymond Lorimer, Malcolm Lowe.
Managers since 1975: Jerry Kerr; Archie Knox; Alex Rae; Doug Houston; Henry Hall; Bobby Glennie; Paul Hegarty; Tommy Campbell. *Club Nickname(s):* Loons. *Previous Grounds:* None.
Record Attendance: 10,780 v Rangers, Scottish Cup 2nd rd; 2 Feb, 1970.
Record Transfer Fee received: £57,000 for Craig Brewster to Raith R (July 1991).
Record Transfer Fee paid: £50,000 for Ian McPhee from Airdrieonians (1991).
Record Victory: 14-1 v Lindertis, Scottish Cup 1st rd; 1 Sept 1988.
Record Defeat: 2-12 v King's Park, Division II; 2 Jan, 1930.
Most Capped Player: —.
Most League Appearances: 480: Ian McPhee, 1978–88 and 1991–97.

FORFAR ATHLETIC 1996–97 LEAGUE RECORD

Match No.	Date	Venue	Opponents	Result	H/T Score	Lg. Pos.	Goalscorers	Attendance
1	Aug 17	A	Albion R	L	0-2	0-0	—	457
2	24	H	Inverness CT	W	3-1	1-0	6	Morgan [16], Higgins 2 [81, 87]	427
3	31	A	Queen's Park	W	4-1	2-0	2	Loney [11], Mann (pen) [13], Morgan [80], Hannigan [81]	590
4	Sept 7	A	East Stirling	L	1-2	0-0	4	Higgins [75]	331
5	14	H	Ross Co	L	0-2	0-0	6		425
6	21	H	Arbroath	D	1-1	0-1	6	Honeyman [79]	605
7	28	A	Montrose	L	1-4	1-2	7	Mann [26]	698
8	Oct 5	H	Cowdenbeath	L	2-5	1-1	9	Mann (pen) [10], Hannigan [78]	363
9	12	A	Alloa	W	4-3	3-3	9	Honeyman 2 [8, 65], Lee [36], Craig [42]	395
10	19	H	Albion R	D	0-0	0-0	7		393
11	26	H	Inverness CT	W	2-0	1-0	6	Morgan [20], Glennie [49]	454
12	Nov 2	A	Ross Co	D	1-1	1-1	7	Honeyman [13]	1669
13	9	H	East Stirling	W	3-0	1-0	6	Morgan (pen) [44], McPhee [73], Lee [88]	325
14	16	H	Montrose	W	3-1	0-0	6	Honeyman [58], Morgan (pen) [61], Bowes [78]	583
15	23	A	Arbroath	D	1-1	0-1	6	Loney [89]	533
16	Dec 10	A	Cowdenbeath	W	3-1	0-1	—	Morgan [71], Honeyman [86], Roberts [89]	186
17	Jan 1	A	Montrose	W	4-0	2-0	—	Hannigan 2 [9, 80], Morgan [35], Loney [76]	802
18	11	H	Queen's Park	D	2-2	1-1	4	Honeyman [42], Roberts [88]	423
19	18	H	Cowdenbeath	W	3-0	2-0	3	Honeyman [7], Mann [33], Roberts [47]	384
20	25	A	Albion R	W	3-1	1-0	2	Hannigan 2 [25, 65], Honeyman [89]	423
21	Feb 1	A	Alloa	W	3-0	2-0	2	Honeyman 2 [20, 28], Loney [80]	427
22	4	H	Arbroath	D	1-1	0-0	—	Lee [81]	655
23	8	H	Ross Co	L	0-1	0-0	3		571
24	15	A	East Stirling	W	3-0	1-0	3	Morgan [39], Cargill [46], Craig [59]	282
25	22	A	Inverness CT	D	1-1	0-0	2	Mann [51]	2507
26	25	H	Alloa	D	1-1	0-0	—	Allison [74]	371
27	Mar 1	A	Queen's Park	L	0-4	0-3	2		466
28	8	A	Arbroath	D	3-3	2-1	3	Cargill [36], Honeyman [42], Roberts [60]	521
29	15	H	Montrose	W	5-3	5-1	3	Honeyman [4], Morgan 2 [23, 24], Mann [43], Roberts [44]	457
30	22	A	Cowdenbeath	W	2-1	1-1	3	Roberts [44], Cargill [49]	196
31	Apr 5	H	Alloa	W	1-0	0-0	3	Honeyman [80]	433
32	12	H	East Stirling	W	1-0	0-0	2	Morgan [65]	391
33	19	A	Ross Co	D	1-1	1-0	2	Morgan [21]	3034
34	26	A	Albion R	W	3-1	1-0	2	Honeyman [14], Allison [72], Mann [73]	438
35	May 3	A	Inverness CT	W	4-0	3-0	2	Morgan 2 [9, 46], Honeyman 2 [26, 29]	3852
36	10	H	Queen's Park	W	4-0	2-0	2	Arbuckle (og) [22, 88], Morgan (pen) [31], Hannigan [60]	1195

Final League Position: 2

Most League Goals in Season (Individual): 45: Dave Kilgour, Division II; 1929–30.
Most Goals Overall (Individual): 124, John Clark.

Honours
League Champions: Second Division 1983–84. Third Division 1994–95; *Runners-up:* 1996–97. C Division 1948–49.
Scottish Cup: Semi-finals 1982.
League Cup: Semi-finals 1977–78.
Club colours: Shirt: Sky Blue with narrow Navy vertical stripe. Shorts: Navy. Stockings: Navy.

Goalscorers: *League (74):* Honeyman 17, Morgan 15 (2 pens), Hannigan 7, Mann 7 (2 pens), Roberts 6, Loney 4, Cargill 3, Higgins 3, Lee 3, Allison 2, Craig 2, Bowes 1, Glennie 1, McPhee1, own goals 2. *Scottish Cup (4):* Allison 1, Honeyman 1, Lee 1, Morgan 1. *Coca Cola Cup (2):* Higgins 1, Inglis 1. *League Challenge Cup (0):*

Donegan J 24+1	Bowes M 30+2	McPhee 16+3	Allison J 34+1	Glennie S 18+2	Craig D 33	Morgan A 36	Hamilton J 31+1	Higgins G 8+1	Inglis G 1	Sexton B 2+1	Honeyman B 29+6	Mann R 31+1	Arthur G 6	Loney J 23+9	Lee J 13+2	Hannigan P 24+10	Farquharson S —+1	Orr J —+2	Roberts P 7+11	Cargill A 15+1	Robertson D 6	Gray A 1	Nairn J —+1	Match No.
1	2	3	4	5	6	7	8^1	9	10	11^2	12	13												1
	8	6^2	5	3		7	2	9			10	4	1	11^1	12	13								2
	8^2	6	5	3		7	2	9			10	4	1	11^1	12	13								3
	8^1	12	6	5	3	7	2	9			10^2	4	1	11		13								4
	2	8	6	5	3	7	9				10	4	1	11^1	12									5
	2	13	6	5	3	7^1	10				12	4	1	11	8^2	9								6
15	2	8	5	3		7	9^2	6			13	4^1	1^6	11	10	12								7
1	4	2	5	3		7	12	10			13	6		11^2	8^1	9								8
1	2	8	5	3		7	4				10	11		6		9								9
1	2^1	8	5	3		7	4	12			10	11		6		9								10
1	2	8	5	3		7	4				10	11^1		6		9			12					11
1	2	8	5	3		7	4				10	11		6		9								12
1	12	11^1	6	5	3	7^2	4				10	2		8		9			13					13
1	12	6	5	3		7	4				10	2		11^2	8	9^1			13					14
1	9^2	12	6^1	5	3	7	4				10	2		11	8				13					15
1		6	5	3		7	4				10	2		11^1	8	9			12					16
1	5	6		3		7	4				10^1	2		11	8	9			12					17
1	5	6		3		7	4				10^2	2		11	8	9^1			13	12				18
1	2^1	8	12	3		7^1	4				11	5		13	10	14			9^2	6				19
1	2	8		3		7	4				11	5		12	10	9^1				6				20
1	2^1	8		3		7^2	4				11	5		12	10	9			13	6				21
1	2	8^1		3		7	4				11	5		9^2	10	12			13	6				22
1	2			3		7	4				11^1	5		9	10	8			12	6				23
1	2	8		3		7	4	13				5		12	10	9^2			11^1	6				24
1	2	8		3		7	4				12	5		13	10	9^2			11^1	6				25
1	2	8		3		7	4				11^1	5		12	10	9				6				26
1	2	8	2	3		7	4				13	5		11^2	10	9^1			12	6				27
1	4	3	8	2		7					11	5		10		9			6					28
1	3	2				7	4				11	5		8		9			10	6				29
1	3	2				7	4				11^1	5		12	8	9			10	6				30
	3	12		2		7	4				11	5		9^1	8	13			10^2	6	1			31
	2	8		3		7	4				11	5		12	10	9^1				6	1			32
	2	8		3		7	4				11^2	5		9^1	10	12			13	6	1			33
	2^3	8		3		7	4				11^2	5		12	10	9			13		1	6^1	14	34
	2	8		3		7	4				11	5		6^1	10	9			12		1			35
	2^2	8	13	3		7	4				11	5		6^1	10	9			12		1			36

GREENOCK MORTON   First Division

Year Formed: 1874. *Ground & Address:* Cappielow Park, Sinclair St, Greenock. *Telephone:* 01475 723571.
Ground Capacity: total: 14,267. seated: 5257. *Size of Pitch:* 110yd × 71yd.
Chairman: John Wilson. *Secretary:* Mrs Jane Rankin.
Manager: Allan McGraw. *Assistant Manager:* Peter Cormack, Sr. *Physio:* John Tierney. *Coach:* John McMaster.
Managers since 1975: Joe Gilroy; Benny Rooney; Alex Miller; Tommy McLean; Willie McLean. *Club Nickname(s):* The
Ton. *Previous Grounds:* Grant Street 1874, Garvel Park 1875, Cappielow Park 1879, Ladyburn Park 1882, (Cappielow
Park 1883).
Record Attendance: 23,500 v Celtic; 1922.
Record Transfer Fee received: £350,000 for Neil Orr to West Ham U.
Record Transfer Fee paid: £150,000 for Allan Mahood from Nottingham Forest.
Record Victory: 11-0 v Carfin Shamrock, Scottish Cup 1st rd; 13 Nov, 1886.
Record Defeat: 1-10 v Port Glasgow Ath, Division II; 5 May, 1894 and v St Bernards, Division II; 14 Oct, 1933.
Most Capped Player: Jimmy Cowan, 25, Scotland.
Most League Appearances: 358: David Hayes, 1969-84.
Most League Goals in Season (Individual): 58: Allan McGraw, Division II; 1963-64.
Most Goals Overall (Individual): —.

GREENOCK MORTON 1996–97 LEAGUE RECORD

Match No.	Date	Venue	Opponents	Result		H/T Score	Lg. Pos.	Goalscorers	Atten- dance
1	Aug 17	H	Clydebank	W	3-0	2-0	—	Lilley 2 [17, 28], Flannery [90]	2927
2	24	A	Dundee	L	1-2	1-2	5	Lilley [17]	3561
3	31	H	Falkirk	W	1-0	0-0	1	Rajamaki [57]	3584
4	Sept 7	H	East Fife	D	0-0	0-0	2		2885
5	14	A	Airdrieonians	W	2-1	0-1	2	Rajamaki [84], Lindberg [86]	2081
6	21	A	Stirling A	W	3-1	1-1	1	Flannery [3], Lilley [54], Lindberg [76]	1924
7	28	A	St Mirren	L	1-3	0-2	2	Hawke [50]	5847
8	Oct 5	H	Partick Th	W	1-0	1-0	2	Reid [37]	3945
9	12	A	St Johnstone	L	0-1	0-1	2		3841
10	19	A	Clydebank	L	1-2	1-1	4	Lilley [11]	1417
11	26	H	Dundee	D	0-0	0-0	4		3320
12	Nov 2	H	Airdrieonians	D	1-1	1-1	5	Lilley (pen) [22]	2658
13	16	A	St Mirren	L	0-1	0-0	7		6336
14	23	H	Stirling A	W	3-2	1-0	7	Lilley 3 [26, 61, 70]	2204
15	30	A	Partick Th	D	0-0	0-0	7		3501
16	Dec 7	H	St Johnstone	L	0-2	0-0	7		2993
17	11	A	East Fife	W	3-0	2-0	—	Rajamaki [24], Anderson [35], Lilley [76]	645
18	14	A	Falkirk	D	0-0	0-0	6		2536
19	26	H	Clydebank	D	2-2	2-1	—	Lilley [43], Anderson [45]	2392
20	Jan 8	A	Stirling A	L	3-4	2-3	—	Blair [28], Lilley [36], Anderson [78]	1005
21	11	H	East Fife	W	2-0	1-0	6	Cormack [15], Flannery [88]	1754
22	14	A	Airdrieonians	L	0-1	0-0	—		1416
23	18	H	Partick Th	L	1-3	1-2	7	Hawke [25]	2437
24	Feb 1	A	St Johnstone	L	0-1	0-0	7		3625
25	4	H	St Mirren	W	2-0	1-0	—	Lilley [32], Mahood [65]	4156
26	22	A	Dundee	L	0-1	0-1	7		2264
27	Mar 1	H	Stirling A	D	1-1	0-1	7	Mahood [46]	1804
28	4	A	Falkirk	L	0-2	0-2	—		1376
29	15	A	St Mirren	L	1-3	1-1	7	Hawke [29]	5024
30	22	A	Partick Th	W	3-0	1-0	7	Lilley 2 [6, 71], Anderson [65]	1873
31	Apr 5	H	St Johnstone	L	0-1	0-0	7		2189
32	12	A	East Fife	W	4-1	3-0	7	Hawke 2 [4, 18], Mahood [13], Rajamaki [72]	728
33	19	H	Airdrieonians	D	1-1	1-0	7	Hawke [9]	2073
34	26	A	Clydebank	W	1-0	0-0	7	Hawke [66]	505
35	May 3	H	Dundee	D	1-1	1-1	8	McPherson [36]	1617
36	10	A	Falkirk	L	0-3	0-1	8		2018

Final League Position: 8

Honours
League Champions: First Division 1977-78, 1983-84, 1986-87. Division II 1949-50, 1963-64, 1966-67. Second Division 1994-95. *Runners-up:* Division 1 1916-17, Division II 1899-1900, 1928-29, 1936-37.
Scottish Cup Winners: 1922; *Runners-up:* 1948. *League Cup Runners-up:* 1963-64.
B&Q Cup: Runners-up: 1992-93.
European: *UEFA Cup (Fairs):* 1968-69.
Club colours: Shirt: Royal blue and white 4" Hoops. Shorts: White with royal blue panel down side. Stockings: Royal blue and white hoops.

Goalscorers: *League (42):* Lilley 15 (1 pen), Hawke 7, Anderson 4, Rajamaki 4, Flannery 3, Mahood 3, Lindberg 2, Blair 1, Cormack 1, McPherson 1, Reid 1. *Scottish Cup (11):* Hawke 3, Lilley 2 (1 pen), Mahood 2, Blair 1, Cormack 1, Mason 1, own goal 1. *Coca Cola Cup (4):* Lilley 2, Anderson 1, Cormack 1. *League Challenge Cup (8):* Lilley 3, Flannery 2, Anderson 1, Matheson 1, Rajamaki 1.

Wylie D 32	Collins D 35	Cormack P 25	Reid B 26	McCahill S 22	Lindberg J 24	Lilley D 25	Mahood A 27	Hawke W 25+7	Anderson J 31	Rajamaki M 23+10	McPherson C 17+12	Flannery P 6+14	Matheson R 8+13	McArthur S 24+3	Johnstone D 11+2	Blair P 11+5	Aitken S 10+3	Blaikie A 4+1	Mason B 2+2	Inglis N 4	Slavin B 1	Hunter J 3	Willoughby J —+1	Match No.
1	2	3	4	5	6³	7	8	9¹	10¹	11	12	13	14											1
1	2	3		6	5		7	8³	9²	4¹	11	10	14	13	12									2
1	2	3		6	5		7	8²	9³	4	11¹	12	14	13	10									3
1	2	3	4	5	6³		8¹	13	10	11²	14	9		12										4
1	2	3	4²	5	6	7		12	8	14	10³	9¹	11	13										5
1	2¹			5	6	7	8³	13	4	11	14	9¹	10	3	12									6
1	2			5	6	7¹	8	12	4	11	13	9	11²	3										7
1	2	3	6	5				9	4		13	11²	12	10		7¹	8							8
1	2	3	6	5		7²		9	4	12		13		10			8	11¹						9
1	2	3	6	5		7	8¹	9²	4	11	13	12				10								10
1	2	3	6	5	10¹	7		9	4	11	12					8								11
1	2	3	6	5	10³	7		9	4²	11	12	14	13			8¹								12
1	2	3	6	5		7	9¹		4	11	10		12			8								13
1	2		6	5		7	9	12	4	11²	10		13	3		8¹								14
1	2		6	5		7¹	8	9		11	10	12¹		3		13	4							15
1	2		4	5	6	7	8	9		11²	10¹			3		13	12							16
1	2		4	5	6¹	7	8²	9	10	11³		14	12	3	13									17
1	2		4		6	7	8	9¹	10	11			12	3	5									18
1	2		4		6	7	8		12	10	11			3	5	9¹								19
1	2		4		6	7¹	8		10	11		12		3	5	9								20
1	2	10		5	6¹		8	9²	4	11	12	13		3		7								21
1	2	10		5			8	9	4	11¹	6²	13	12	3		7								22
1	2	10	6	5			8	9	4²	12	13	11¹	14	3³		7								23
1	2	10	5¹		6	7	8	9²		11³	12		14	3	4	13								24
1	2	10			6	7	8		5	12	11			3	4				9¹					25
1	2	10		5		7	8	12	4	13	11²			3		14		9¹	6³					26
1	2	10		5	6	7	8	9	4	12	11¹			3										27
		5						11¹	6	13	8			7	4	9²	10	1	2	3	12			28
1	2	10	5		6	7	8	9	4	12				3		11¹								29
1	2	10	5		6	7	8	9	4		11¹	3				12								30
1	2	10		6		8	9	4		11¹		3	5	7	12									31
1	2²	10		6		8	9	4	12	11¹	14		3	5	7³		13							32
1	2	10		6		8	9	4	12	11		13	3¹	5	7²									33
	2		5	6		9	4	12	10²	8		3	7¹			13	1		11					34
	2	10	5	6		9	4	11	8		7	3				1								35
	2	10	5	6		9¹		11	8³	14	7		3	13	12²		1		4					36

HAMILTON ACADEMICAL   First Division

Year Formed: 1874. *Ground:* Cliftonville Stadium, Main St, Coatbridge ML5 3RB. *Telephone (match days only):* 01236 606 334. *Club Address:* Tudor Lodge, 51 Burnbank Road, Hamilton ML3 9AQ.
Ground Capacity: 1238, seated: 538. *Size of Pitch:* 104yd × 70yd.
Secretary: Scott A. Struthers BA. *Commercial Manager:* John Queen.
Manager: Sandy Clark. *Physio:* Jim Fallon.
Managers since 1975: J. Eric Smith; Dave McParland; John Blackley; Bertie Auld; John Lambie; Jim Dempsey; John Lambie; Billy McLaren; Iain Munro. *Club Nickname(s):* The Accies. *Previous Grounds:* Bent Farm, South Avenue, South Haugh.
Record Attendance: 28,690 v Hearts, Scottish Cup 3rd rd; 3 Mar, 1937.
Record Transfer Fee received: £380,000 for Paul Hartley to Millwall (July 1996).
Record Transfer Fee paid: £60,000 for Paul Martin from Kilmarnock (Oct 1988) and for John McQuade from Dumbarton (Aug 1993).
Record Victory: 11-1 v Chryston, Lanarkshire Cup; 28 Nov, 1885.
Record Defeat: 1-11 v Hibernian, Division I; 6 Nov, 1965.
Most Capped Player: Colin Miller, 29, Canada, 1988-94.
Most League Appearances: 447: Rikki Ferguson, 1974-88.
Most League Goals in Season (Individual): 34: David Wilson, Division I; 1936-37.
Most Goals Overall (Individual): 246: David Wilson, 1928-39.

HAMILTON ACADEMICAL 1996–97 LEAGUE RECORD

Match No.	Date	Venue	Opponents	Result		H/T Score	Lg. Pos.	Goalscorers	Atten- dance
1	Aug 17	A	Ayr U	D	1-1	1-0	—	Clark [23]	2227
2	24	H	Clyde	W	2-0	0-0	3	McEntegart [77], McFarlane [88]	917
3	31	A	Livingston	L	0-1	0-1	5		2627
4	Sept 7	A	Stranraer	W	3-0	2-0	3	McGill [3], McFarlane [41], McIntosh (pen) [48]	529
5	14	H	Berwick R	W	4-2	1-1	2	Ritchie 2 [23, 89], McFarlane [47], McGill [63]	579
6	21	A	Brechin C	W	2-0	1-0	2	McIntosh [21], McGill [46]	356
7	28	H	Queen of the S	D	2-2	0-1	3	McGill [51], Ritchie [89]	705
8	Oct 5	A	Stenhousemuir	W	1-0	0-0	3	McCulloch [65]	740
9	12	H	Dumbarton	W	2-0	0-0	2	Thomson [65], Ritchie [75]	533
10	19	H	Ayr U	L	1-2	1-0	3	McIntosh [39]	1173
11	26	A	Clyde	D	1-1	0-0	3	McFarlane [53]	1103
12	Nov 2	A	Berwick R	W	2-0	1-0	3	Quitongo [39], McCormick [73]	454
13	9	H	Stranraer	W	4-0	1-0	3	Hillcoat [34], Sherry 2 [59, 66], Ritchie [81]	654
14	16	A	Queen of the S	D	1-1	0-0	3	Sherry [74]	1304
15	Dec 4	H	Brechin C	W	5-1	2-1	—	Ritchie 3 [36, 38, 47], Sherry 2 [65, 77]	379
16	10	H	Stenhousemuir	L	0-2	0-1	—		520
17	14	A	Dumbarton	W	3-1	1-0	3	Fotheringham [40], Ritchie 2 [55, 65]	733
18	Jan 18	A	Stenhousemuir	L	1-3	0-2	3	Fotheringham [48]	550
19	22	A	Queen of the S	W	4-1	1-0	—	McCormick 3 [2, 48, 66], Ritchie [64]	554
20	28	A	Ayr U	L	0-1	0-0	—		1905
21	Feb 1	H	Dumbarton	W	4-0	3-0	3	Ritchie 4 [4, 33, 43, 53]	505
22	5	H	Livingston	D	3-3	0-2	—	McCormick [53], Ritchie 2 [74, 82]	813
23	8	H	Berwick R	W	4-1	0-0	3	Ritchie 3 [48, 67, 70], Clark [55]	512
24	22	H	Clyde	W	4-0	0-0	3	Ritchie 2 [49, 73], McIntosh [51], McFarlane [86]	856
25	Mar 4	A	Brechin C	W	1-0	1-0	—	Ritchie [5]	358
26	8	H	Brechin C	W	4-0	2-0	2	Thomson [27], Ritchie 2 [39, 88], Davidson [70]	634
27	12	A	Stranraer	W	1-0	0-0	—	McFarlane [70]	505
28	15	A	Queen of the S	L	0-1	0-0	2		1318
29	22	H	Stenhousemuir	D	1-1	0-0	2	Quitongo [53]	596
30	30	A	Livingston	W	2-1	2-1	—	McIntosh (pen) [35], Ritchie [41]	3436
31	Apr 5	A	Dumbarton	W	3-0	1-0	2	McCormick 2 [30, 51], Ritchie [90]	718
32	12	H	Stranraer	W	2-1	2-1	2	Quitongo [12], Ritchie [22]	797
33	19	A	Berwick R	W	5-0	2-0	2	McIntosh [7], Ritchie 3 [13, 68, 79], Sherry [88]	520
34	26	A	Ayr U	D	1-1	0-1	2	McIntosh (pen) [73]	5156
35	May 3	A	Clyde	W	1-0	1-0	2	McEntegart [5]	1011
36	10	H	Livingston	D	0-0	0-0	2		825

Final League Position: 2

Honours
League Champions: First Division 1985-86, 1987-88; *Runners-up:* Second Division 1996–97. Division II 1903-04; *Runners-up:* Division II 1952-53, 1964-65.
Scottish Cup Runners-up: 1911, 1935. *League Cup:* Semi-finalists three times.
B&Q Cup Winners: 1991-92 and 1992-93.
Club colours: Shirt: Red and white hoops. Shorts: White. Stockings: White.

Goalscorers: *League (75):* Ritchie 31, McCormick 7, McIntosh 7 (2 pens), McFarlane 6, Sherry 6, McGill 4, Quitongo 3, Clark 2, Fotheringham 2, McEntegart 2, Thomson 2, Davidson 1, Hillcoat C 1, McCulloch 1. *Scottish Cup (6):* Ritchie 3, Clark 2, McEntegart 1. *Coca Cola Cup (1):* Sherry 1. *League Challenge Cup (3):* Quitongo 3.

Scott C 5	Hillcoat C 36	Renicks S 33	McEntegart S 23 + 2	Baptie C 11 + 4	McKenzie P 12 + 7	Quitongo J 31 + 3	Thomson S 32 + 3	Ritchie P 36	Clark G 15 + 17	McBride J 2 + 1	McCormick S 16 + 3	Lorimer D — + 3	Sherry J 24	McFarlane D 10 + 10	McIntosh M 33	McGill D 8	Paris S 2	Hillcoat J 2	McCulloch S 19 + 5	Ferguson A 27	Davidson W 5 + 7	Fotheringham K 6 + 8	McQuade J — + 4	Cunnington E 8	Geraghty M — + 1	Match No.
1	2	3	4	5	6	7[2]	8	9	10	11[1]	12		13													1
1	2	3	4	5	6	7	11	9[1]	10[2]				13	8	12											2
1		3	5	2	7	4		9[1]	10	11[2]	13			8	12	6										3
1	2	3	8	5	4	7[3]	12	9					14	13	10[2]	6	11[1]									4
	2	3	5	8		7	4	9	12					10	6	11[1]	1									5
1	2	3	8	5		7	4	9	12					10[1]	6	11										6
	2	3	8	5		7[1]	4	9	12					10[2]	6	11		1	13							7
	2	3	8[1]	5	13		4	9	12					10	6	11		1	7[2]							8
	2	3		5		7	4	9	12				8	10[1]	6	11[2]				1	13					9
	2	3		5	13	7[1]	4	9	10				8[2]		6	11			12	1						10
	2	3		5	12	7[2]	4	9	13				8	11[1]	6	10				1						11
	2	3	13			7[3]	4	9	10[2]		12		8	11[1]	6				5	1	14					12
	2	3	10			7	4[2]	9	13				8	11[1]	6				5	1	12					13
	2	3	10			7	4	9	12				8	11[1]	6				5	1						14
	2	3	13		10	7[1]	4[2]	9[3]	11				8		6				5	1	14	12				15
	2	3	12		10[1]	7[2]	4	9	11[3]				8		6				5	1	13	14				16
	2	3	10[1]	14	13		4	9[3]	12				8	11	6				5	1		7[2]				17
	2	3	10				4[1]	9	13				8	11[2]	6				5	1	12	7				18
	2	3	4		12			9	13				8[2]	10[1]	6				5	1	7	11				19
	2	3	4		13	7		9	12				8	10[2]	6				5	1	11[1]					20
	2	3	4[1]		12	7	8	9[2]	11				13	10	6				5[3]	1	14					21
	2	3	4			7	11	9	12				8[1]	10	6				5	1						22
	2	3	4			7[1]	8	9	11				12	10[2]	6				5	1	13					23
	2	3	8[2]		12	7	4	9	11				13	10[3]	6				5[1]	1	14					24
	2	3	8			7[1]	4	9	11					10[2]	6				5	1	12	13				25
	2	3	8[1]			7	4	9	11				14	10[3]	6[2]				5	1	13	12				26
	2	3	12			7[2]	4	9	11				13	10[3]	6[1]				5	1	14	8				27
	2	3	14		6		4	9	13				8	11[2]	12				5[1]	1	10	7[2]				28
	2	3				7	4	9					8	10[1]	6					1	11	12		5		29
	2	3	11		12	7[1]	4	9	10				8		6					1				5		30
	2	3	11			7[1]	4	9	13				8	10[2]	6					1		12		5		31
	2	3	11			7	4	9					8	10[1]	6					1		12		5		32
	2	3	11			7[3]	4[1]	9	12				8	10[2]	6					1	14			5	13	33
	2	3	11			7	4[1]	9	13				8	10	6				12	1				5[2]		34
	2	3	4			7[2]	12	9[3]	13				8	10	6				11[1]	1	14			5		35
	2	3	11			7	4[2]	9[3]	13				8	10	6				12	1	14			5[1]		36

HEART OF MIDLOTHIAN   Premier Division

Year Formed: 1874. *Ground & Address:* Tynecastle Park, Gorgie Rd, Edinburgh EH11 2NL. *Telephone:* 0131 337 6132.
Fax: 0131 346 0699.
Ground Capacity: 18,300. *Size of Pitch:* 108yd × 73yd.
Chairman: Leslie Deans. *Chief Executive:* Christopher Robinson. *Secretary:* L. W. Porteous. *Sales and Marketing Manager:* Susan Bonnar. *Commercial Manager:* Tommy Dickson.
Manager: Jim Jefferies. *Assistant Manager:* Billy Brown.
Physio: Alan Rae. *Coaches:* Paul Hegarty, Peter Houston.
Managers since 1975: J. Hagart; W. Ormond; R. Moncur; T. Ford; A. MacDonald; A. MacDonald & W. Jardine; A. MacDonald; J. Jordan, S. Clark, T. McLean.
Club Nickname(s): Hearts. *Previous Grounds:* The Meadows 1874, Powderhall 1878, Old Tynecastle 1881, (Tynecastle Park, 1886).
Record Attendance: 53,396 v Rangers, Scottish Cup 3rd rd; 13 Feb, 1932.
Record Transfer Fee received: £2,100,000 for Alan McLaren from Rangers (October 1994).
Record of Transfer paid: £750,000 for Derek Ferguson to Rangers (July 1990).
Record Victory: 21-0 v Anchor, EFA Cup 30th October 1880.
Record Defeat: 1-8 v Vale of Leven, Scottish Cup, 1888.
Most Capped Player: Bobby Walker, 29, Scotland.
Most League Appearances: 515: Gary Mackay, 1980-97.
Most League Goals in Season (Individual): 44: Barney Battles.
Most Goals Overall (Individual): 208: John Robertson, 1983-97.

HEART OF MIDLOTHIAN 1996–97 LEAGUE RECORD

Match No.	Date		Venue	Opponents	Result	H/T Score	Lg. Pos.	Goalscorers	Attendance
1	Aug	17	H	Kilmarnock	W 3-2	2-1	—	Ritchie 2 [12, 63], Weir [14]	10,854
2		25	A	Aberdeen	L 0-4	0-1	—		13,515
3	Sept	7	H	Dundee U	W 1-0	0-0	4	Robertson (pen) [74]	11,848
4		10	A	Dunfermline Ath	L 1-2	1-0	—	Weir [2]	7787
5		14	A	Rangers	L 0-3	0-1	7		47,240
6		21	H	Motherwell	D 1-1	0-0	6	Weir [58]	10,932
7		28	A	Hibernian	W 3-1	3-0	5	Cameron 2 [19, 30], Robertson [40]	14,217
8	Oct	12	A	Raith R	D 1-1	1-0	5	Robertson [2]	6037
9		20	H	Celtic	D 2-2	0-1	—	Cameron [53], McPherson [89]	13,352
10		26	A	Dundee U	L 0-1	0-0	6		9393
11	Nov	2	H	Dunfermline Ath	W 2-0	2-0	4	Weir [26], Cameron [43]	12,517
12		11	A	Motherwell	W 2-0	0-0	—	Paille [54], Robertson [88]	5441
13		16	H	Hibernian	D 0-0	0-0	4		15,129
14		30	A	Celtic	D 2-2	1-1	4	Cameron [31], McCann [65]	49,804
15	Dec	7	H	Raith R	D 0-0	0-0	4		10,719
16		11	H	Aberdeen	L 1-2	1-0	—	Cameron [7]	11,477
17		14	A	Kilmarnock	L 0-2	0-0	5		5832
18		21	H	Rangers	L 1-4	0-1	7	Robertson [56]	15,139
19		26	A	Dunfermline Ath	W 3-2	0-1	—	Miller C (og) [50], Robertson (pen) [61], Fulton [81]	9736
20		28	A	Motherwell	W 4-1	1-0	5	Robertson 2 [21, 75], Weir [52], Hamilton [63]	11,164
21	Jan	1	A	Hibernian	W 4-0	1-0	—	Robertson [33], Hamilton 2 [62, 87], Cameron [65]	15,826
22		4	A	Raith R	W 2-1	1-1	4	Robertson [5], Hamilton [72]	6460
23		11	A	Celtic	L 1-2	1-1	4	Hamilton [38]	15,424
24		18	H	Dundee U	L 1-2	1-1	4	Robertson [23]	12,777
25	Feb	1	A	Rangers	D 0-0	0-0	4		50,024
26		8	H	Kilmarnock	W 2-0	1-0	4	Ritchie [22], McCann [71]	11,020
27		10	H	Aberdeen	D 0-0	0-0	—		8642
28		22	A	Raith R	W 3-2	3-2	4	Weir [24], McCann 2 [35, 37]	10,341
29	Mar	1	A	Celtic	L 0-2	0-1	4		49,578
30		15	H	Hibernian	W 1-0	0-0	4	McCann [82]	15,136
31		22	H	Motherwell	W 1-0	1-0	4	Paille [12]	6245
32	Apr	5	A	Kilmarnock	L 0-1	0-1	4		7877
33		12	A	Aberdeen	D 0-0	0-0	4		11,186
34		19	H	Dunfermline Ath	D 1-1	0-1	4	Robertson [90]	10,174
35	May	3	A	Dundee U	L 0-1	0-0	4		7405
36		10	H	Rangers	W 3-1	0-0	4	Cameron [80], Robertson 2 (1 pen) [82 (p), 86]	13,097

Final League Position: 4

Honours
League Champions: Division I 1894-95, 1896-97, 1957-58, 1959-60. First Division 1979-80; *Runners-up:* Division I 1893-94, 1898-99, 1903-04, 1905-06, 1914-15, 1937-38, 1953-54, 1956-57, 1958-59, 1964-65. Premier Division 1985-86, 1987-88, 1991-92. First Division 1977-78, 1982-83.
Scottish Cup Winners: 1891, 1896, 1901, 1906, 1956; *Runners-up:* 1903, 1907, 1968, 1976, 1986, 1996.
League Cup Winners: 1954-55, 1958-59, 1959-60, 1962-63; *Runners-up:* 1961-62, 1996–97.

European: *European Cup* 4 matches (1958-59, 1960-61). *Cup Winners Cup:* 6 matches (1976-77, 1996–97). *UEFA Cup:* 34 matches (*Fairs Cup:* 1961-62, 1963-64, 1965-66. *UEFA Cup:* 1984-85, 1986-87, 1988-89, 1990-91, 1992-93, 1993-94).
Club colours: Shirt: Maroon. Shorts: White. Stockings: Maroon with white tops.

Goalscorers: *League (46):* Robertson 14 (2 pens), Cameron 8, Weir 6, Hamilton 5, McCann 5, Ritchie 3, Paille 2, Fulton 1, Mackay 1, McPherson 1. *Scottish Cup (6):* Robertson 2, Cameron 1, Hamilton 1, Pointon 1, Weir 1. *Coca Cola Cup (11):* Robertson 3, Beckford 2, Cameron 2 (1 pen), Fulton 1, McCann 1, Paille 1, Weir 1.

Rousset G 33	Frail S 4+5	Ritchie P 27+1	Weir D 34	Mackay G 20+7	Bruno P 11+2	McCann N 25+5	Cameron C 36	Beckford D 6+2	Fulton S 25+4	Pointon N 24+1	McManus A 10+5	Colquhoun J 4+7	Thomas K 4+9	McPherson D 26	Goss J 7+3	Robertson J 26+2	Salvatori S 12+2	Naysmith G 10	Thorn A 1	Paille S 11+7	Callaghan S 4	Hamilton J 12+6	Burns J —+2	Murray G 2+2	Murie D 6+1	Locke G 11	McKenzie R 3	Horn R 1	Holmes D 1	Match No.
1	2	3	4	5	6³	7²	8	9	10	11¹	12	13	14																	1
1	14	3	4	6¹	12		8		10	11	2³	13		5	7	9²														2
1		3	2	12	6	7	8	4¹	10	11				5		9														3
1		3	2	4³	6¹	7	8²		10	11	12	13	14	5		9														4
1	12	3	2	4³	6	7	8¹		10	11		13	14	5		9²														5
1		3	2	12	6¹	7	8	4	10	11		13		5		9²														6
1	12	3¹	4	6	2	7	8		10	11				5		9														7
1		3	4	6	2		8		10	11¹	12	13		5	7²	9														8
1		3	4	6²	2		8¹		10	11	12	13		5	7	9														9
1		5	4	6	2		8		10	11²	12	13	14		7	9¹		3												10
1		3	4¹	6	2		8		10	11	12	13		5	7	9²														11
1		3	4	6	2		8		10	11	12			5	7¹	9														12
1		3	4	6	2		8²		10	11³	12	13	14	5	7	9														13
1		5	4	6	2		8		10	11					7	9		3												14
1	14	5	4	6	2		8		10	11	12	13			7³	9¹		3												15
1	12		4¹	6	2		8		10	11		13		5	7²	9		3												16
1		5	4³	6	2¹	7²	8		10	11	12	13	14			9		3												17
1		5	4	6	2³		8¹		10	11²			14		7	9	13	3				12								18
1		5	4	6		7	8		10							9		3		11						2				19
1		5	4	6²			8		10		12					9¹	7³	3		11		13		14		2				20
1		5	4	6		7	8		10							9		3		11		12				2				21
1		5	4	6		7	8		10							9		3¹		11		12				2				22
1		5	4	6¹		7	8		10							9		3		11		12				2				23
1		5	4	6		7	8		10							9		3		11		12				2¹				24
1		5	4	6			8		10							9		3		11		12	7¹			2				25
1		5	4	6			8		10							9¹	7²	3		11		13		12		2				26
		5¹	4	6			8		10		12					9³	7	3²				13		14		2		1		27
1		5	4	6		7	8		10¹							9²	13	3		11²		12		14		2				28
1		5	4	6		7	8		10							9¹	13	3		11³	8	12				2				29
1		5	4	6		7	8		10							9		3		11¹		12				2				30
1		5	4	6			8		10²							9¹	13	3		11		12	7			2				31
1		5	4	6			8		10							9¹	13	3		11		12	7²			2				32
1		5	4	6			8²		10							9¹	12	3		11		13³	7	14		2				33
1		5	4	6³		7	8²		10							9	13	3		11		12		14		2¹				34
		5	4	6			8		10							9³		3		11		13	7¹	12		2	1			35
		5	4	6		7	8²		10							9	13	3		11		12				2	1		10¹	36

HIBERNIAN   Premier Division

Year Formed: 1875. *Ground & Address:* Easter Road Stadium, Albion Rd, Edinburgh EH7 5QG. *Telephone:* 0131 661 2159. *Fax:* 0131 659 6488.
Ground Capacity: total: 16,218. *Size of Pitch:* 112yd × 74yd.
Chairman: Lex Gold. *Secretary:* Mary Anne McAdam. *Commercial Manager:* Ian Erskine.
Manager: Jim Duffy. *Assistant Manager:* Jackie McNamara.
Physio: Stuart Collie.
Managers since 1975: Eddie Turnbull; Willie Ormond; Bertie Auld; Pat Stanton; John Blackley, Alex Miller. *Club Nickname(s):* Hibees. *Previous Grounds:* Meadows 1875-78, Powderhall 1878-79, Mayfield 1879-80, First Easter Road 1880-92, Second Easter Road 1892-.
Record Attendance: 65,860 v Hearts, Division I; 2 Jan, 1950.
Record Transfer Fee received: £1,000,000 for Andy Goram to Rangers (June 1991).
Record Transfer Fee paid: £420,000 for Keith Wright from Dundee.
Record Victory: 22-1 v 42nd Highlanders; 3 Sept, 1881.
Record Defeat: 0-10 v Rangers; 24 Dec, 1898.
Most Capped Player: Lawrie Reilly, 38, Scotland.
Most League Appearances: 446: Arthur Duncan.
Most League Goals in Season (Individual): 42: Joe Baker.
Most Goals Overall (Individual): 364: Gordon Smith.

HIBERNIAN 1996–97 LEAGUE RECORD

Match No.	Date	Venue	Opponents	Result	H/T Score	Lg. Pos.	Goalscorers	Attendance
1	Aug 10	H	Kilmarnock	L 1-2	1-2	—	Weir [28]	8734
2	17	A	Dundee U	W 1-0	1-0	5	McAllister [30]	8589
3	24	H	Dunfermline Ath	D 0-0	0-0	4		9801
4	Sept 7	A	Celtic	L 0-5	0-3	7		47,148
5	14	H	Raith R	W 1-0	0-0	4	Kirk (og) [54]	8260
6	21	A	Aberdeen	W 2-0	1-0	4	Jackson D [44], Wright [69]	12,475
7	28	H	Hearts	L 1-3	0-3	6	Jackson D (pen) [55]	14,217
8	Oct 12	H	Rangers	W 2-1	0-1	4	Jackson D (pen) [58], Donald [62]	12,436
9	19	A	Motherwell	D 1-1	1-0	4	Harper [7]	6784
10	26	H	Celtic	L 0-4	0-1	4		13,930
11	Nov 1	A	Kilmarnock	L 2-4	2-2	—	Harper [19], Dow [30]	10,872
12	16	A	Hearts	D 0-0	0-0	6		15,129
13	23	H	Aberdeen	L 0-1	0-1	6		10,931
14	30	H	Motherwell	W 2-0	1-0	5	Jackson D 2 [36, 85]	7390
15	Dec 7	A	Rangers	L 3-4	2-1	5	Wright [20], Jackson D [40], McGinlay [85]	48,053
16	11	A	Dunfermline Ath	L 1-2	0-0	—	Jackson D [73]	5295
17	14	H	Dundee U	D 1-1	1-1	7	Harper [20]	8250
18	21	A	Raith R	W 3-0	0-0	5	Jackson D 2 [61, 79], McGinlay [67]	4229
19	26	H	Kilmarnock	L 0-1	0-1	—		8912
20	28	A	Aberdeen	D 1-1	1-0	6	Jackson D [14]	9834
21	Jan 1	H	Hearts	L 0-4	0-1	—		15,826
22	4	H	Rangers	L 1-2	1-1	7	Harper [8]	12,650
23	11	A	Motherwell	L 1-2	0-2	7	Dow [48]	5855
24	18	A	Celtic	L 1-4	0-2	8	Harper [63]	48,986
25	Feb 1	H	Raith R	D 1-1	1-0	7	Kirkwood (og) [15]	9365
26	8	A	Dundee U	D 0-0	0-0	7		9219
27	23	A	Rangers	L 1-3	0-1	—	Dennis [54]	47,618
28	Mar 1	H	Motherwell	D 1-1	0-0	8	Wright [51]	8190
29	8	H	Dunfermline Ath	W 1-0	1-0	8	Wright [14]	8877
30	15	A	Hearts	L 0-1	0-0	9		15,136
31	22	H	Aberdeen	W 3-1	1-0	8	McGinlay 2 [2, 16], Tosh [72]	9615
32	Apr 5	H	Dundee U	W 2-0	0-0	8	Charnley [73], McGinlay [78]	10,951
33	12	A	Dunfermline Ath	D 1-1	0-0	7	Jackson D [31]	8752
34	19	A	Kilmarnock	D 1-1	1-1	7	Montgomerie (og) [45]	10,886
35	May 4	H	Celtic	L 1-3	1-2	8	Power [34]	10,546
36	10	A	Raith R	D 1-1	1-1	9	McGinlay [26]	6274

Final League Position: 9

Honours
League Champions: Division I 1902-03, 1947-48, 1950-51, 1951-52. First Division 1980-81. Division II 1893-94, 1894-95, 1932-33; *Runners-up:* Division I 1896-97, 1946-47, 1949-50, 1952-53, 1973-74, 1974-75.
Scottish Cup Winners: 1887, 1902; *Runners-up:* 1896, 1914, 1923, 1924, 1947, 1958, 1972, 1979.
League Cup Winners: 1972-73, 1991-92; *Runners-up:* 1950-51, 1968-69, 1974-75, 1993-94.

European: *European Cup:* 6 matches (1955-56 semi-finals). *Cup Winners Cup:* 6 matches (1972-73). *UEFA Cup:* 56 matches (*Fairs Cup:* 1960-61 semi-finals, 1961-62, 1962-63, 1965-66, 1967-68, 1968-69, 1970-71. *UEFA Cup:* 1973-74, 1974-75, 1975-76, 1976-77, 1978-79, 1992-93).
Club colours: Shirt: Green with white sleeves. Shorts: White. Stockings: Green with white trim.

Goalscorers: *League (38):* Jackson D 11 (2 pens), McGinlay 6, Harper 5, Wright 4, Dow 2, Charnley 1, Dennis 1, Donald 1, McAllister 1, Power 1, Tosh 1, Weir 1, own goals 3. *Scottish Cup (3):* Jackson D 1 (pen), McGinlay 1, Miller G 1. *Coca Cola Cup (4):* Dow 1, Lavety 1, McGinlay 1, Wright 1.

Leighton J 35	Miller W 31	Welsh B 17	Millen A 16 + 3	Donald G 8 + 3	Hunter G 16 + 1	Weir M 1 + 7	Cameron I 9 + 8	Wright K 17 + 9	Jackson D 30	McGinlay P 29	McAllister K 10 + 9	Dow A 17 + 5	Lavety B 6 + 4	Harper K 23 + 3	Jackson C 15 + 4	McLaughlin J 9	Renwick M 6 + 3	Wilkins R 15 + 1	Dods D 17 + 3	Schmugge T 1	Reid C 1	Hughes J 4	Shannon R 5	Riipa J 1	Love G 6 + 1	Riley P — + 1	Grant B 9 + 3	Dennis S 4	Miller G 3 + 3	McQuiken J 9	Elliot D 5 + 2	Charnley J 9	Tosh P 6	Power L 6	Match No.
1	2	3	4	5²	6	7¹	8	9	10	11	12	13																							1
1	2	5	4		6	13		9	10	11	8²	3	7¹	12																					2
1	2	5	4		6²			9	10	11	8	3	7¹	12	13																				3
1	2	5	4	13			8²	12	10¹	11		7³		9	3	6	14																		4
1	2	6	4	3			13	9	10²			7³		11		5¹	14	8	12																5
1	2	6	4					9	10²	11		3				13	12	8	5	7¹															6
1	2	6	4					9	10	11	12	3		7				8	5																7
1	2	12	3	6			7²		10	11	13	14		9	4¹			8³	5																8
1	2	4	3	6¹			14	12	10²	11		7³		13	9			8	5																9
	2	6	3				8		10	11		7	12	9			4¹	5			1														10
1	2	4¹	3²				13		10	11	12	8		9		7	6	5				1													11
1	2	12			6		13		10	11		7²		8	9¹								5	3	4										12
1	2	6				13	14	12	10	11		7²		8	9¹			4³	5						3										13
1	2	5			6		12	9	10	11		7¹		8				4²							3		13								14
1	2	5			6		12	9	10¹	11		13		8	7			4²							3										15
1	2	5			6			9	10	11	12			8	7			4	3¹																16
1	2	6					13	9	10	11		7		4	8²			12					5	3¹											17
1		4	12	2²	6¹			9	10	11	13	3		7				8	5																18
1	2	6		13			7	9²	10	12	11			8¹	5								3		4										19
1	6	2					11	9	10	7²	13	12		8	5								3		4¹										20
1	2	4	12	6			7	8¹	10	11		9³		13	14			3					5²												21
1	2¹	5			6		13	10	11	14		7³		9	8			4²	12				3												22
1	2	6¹	4		12		9		11	7		10	8²														3³		13	5	14				23
1	2	5	4		12				11	7	9			13	8												10¹		3²	6					24
1	2		7						11		9	6															4	5	12	3	10¹	8			25
1	2	12							11	9¹	7	6															4	5	10	3		8			26
1			6		12	13	10		9	11		2															4	5	7²	3	8¹			27
1	3	5						11	10	9¹		6		2	4												7	12				8			28
1	3	5						8	10¹	11		12		9	7			2	4													6			29
1	3	5						8	10	11		12		9¹	7			2	4													6			30
1	2	5						13	12			11		9¹		6		14	4										3			8²	7	10²	31
1	2		12						11	10¹		6		5	4												13		3	14		8²	7	9³	32
1	2							13	10	11¹		12		6	5			4											3		11		7	9²	33
1	2							12	10			8²		6	5			4											13		3	11	7	9¹	34
1									10			9		11¹	5	2		4									6				3	12	7	8	35
1	5								13	10	11¹		6	12		4	2														3	9²	7	8	36

INVERNESS CALEDONIAN THISTLE
Second Division

Year Formed: 1994. *Ground & Address:* Caledonian Stadium, East Longman, Inverness. 01463 222880. *Address for Correspondence:* 28 Greig St, Inverness IV3 5PX. *Telephone:* 01463 230274.
Ground Capacity: 5600, seated 2200. *Size of Pitch:* 114yd × 74yd.
President: Dugald McGilvray. *Hon. Life President:* John S.McDonald. *Secretary:* Jim Falconer.
Manager: S.W.Paterson. *Assistant Manager:* Alec Caldwell. *Physio:* Ian Manning. *Coach:* Alex Young.
Record Attendance: 5525 v Ross Co, 15 Mar 1997.
Record Victory: 6-1, v Albion Rovers, 21 October 1995.
Record Defeat: 0-4, v Queen's Park, Third Division, 20 August 1994 and v Montrose, Third Division, 14 February 1995.
Most League Appearances: 91, Michael Noble, 1994-97.
Most League Goals in Season: 27, Ian Stewart, 1996-97.
Most Goals Overall (Individual): 50, Ian Stewart, 1995-97.

INVERNESS CALEDONIAN THISTLE 1996–97 LEAGUE RECORD

Match No.	Date	Venue	Opponents	Result	H/T Score	Lg. Pos.	Goalscorers	Atten-dance
1	Aug 17	H	Cowdenbeath	L 1-3	0-1	—	Thomson (pen) [52]	1524
2	24	A	Forfar Ath	L 1-3	0-1	10	Thomson (pen) [75]	427
3	31	H	Alloa	W 1-0	0-0	8	Teasdale [86]	1685
4	Sept 7	A	Albion R	D 0-0	0-0	9		845
5	14	H	East Stirling	W 2-0	1-0	5	Hercher [35], Noble [46]	1316
6	21	H	Queen's Park	D 2-2	1-0	5	Stewart [21], Christie [75]	1452
7	28	A	Ross Co	W 3-1	1-0	4	Stewart 2 [3, 63], Thomson [89]	3519
8	Oct 5	H	Arbroath	W 2-0	1-0	4	Thomson [25], Stewart [54]	2086
9	12	A	Montrose	D 2-2	0-0	4	Stewart [49], Ross [81]	643
10	19	A	Cowdenbeath	W 4-3	1-1	1	Thomson 2 (1 pen) [4, 89 (p)], Hercher [76], Stewart [90]	321
11	26	A	Forfar Ath	L 0-2	0-1	4		454
12	Nov 2	A	East Stirling	D 0-0	0-0	5		398
13	9	H	Albion R	D 1-1	0-0	5	Stewart [74]	3734
14	16	H	Ross Co	W 2-0	0-0	3	Stewart 2 [49, 88]	4562
15	23	A	Queen's Park	W 3-2	3-1	1	McLean [12], Wilson [16], Christie [22]	786
16	30	A	Arbroath	W 4-1	2-0	1	Wilson [9], Addicoat [43], Stewart [58], Christie [86]	457
17	Dec 14	H	Montrose	W 2-0	2-0	1	Stewart [13], McLean [37]	2477
18	21	H	Cowdenbeath	W 2-1	0-0	1	Stewart 2 [47, 68]	2188
19	Jan 18	A	Arbroath	W 4-1	2-0	1	Hercher 2 [29, 57], McLean [30], Ross [81]	1742
20	22	A	Queen's Park	W 1-0	0-0	—	Stewart [80]	1432
21	Feb 1	A	Montrose	W 2-0	1-0	1	McLean [40], Stewart [88]	520
22	8	H	East Stirling	W 3-2	2-1	1	Stewart [14], Wilson [16], McLean [71]	1642
23	12	A	Ross Co	W 3-0	2-0	—	McLean 2 [35, 61], Wilson [42]	4482
24	15	A	Albion R	W 3-0	0-0	1	Teasdale [54], Tokely [76], Stewart [85]	608
25	22	H	Forfar Ath	D 1-1	0-0	1	Stewart [84]	2507
26	Mar 1	A	Alloa	W 3-1	2-0	1	Stewart 2 [4, 35], Ross [70]	1397
27	8	A	Queen's Park	W 2-1	0-0	1	Stewart [74], Tokely [76]	857
28	11	A	Alloa	W 2-0	1-0	—	McLean [36], Noble [57]	441
29	15	H	Ross Co	W 3-0	1-0	1	Stewart 2 [44, 76], Thomson [74]	5525
30	22	A	Arbroath	D 0-0	0-0	1		570
31	Apr 5	H	Montrose	W 3-2	1-2	1	Stewart 3 [12, 66, 80]	3036
32	12	H	Albion R	W 4-1	2-1	1	Thomson 2 [6, 44], Wilson [74], De Barros [77]	2960
33	19	A	East Stirling	W 3-0	1-0	1	Stewart [45], Ross [70], Thomson [87]	404
34	26	A	Cowdenbeath	L 1-2	0-2	1	Cherry [69]	282
35	May 3	H	Forfar Ath	L 0-4	0-3	1		3852
36	10	A	Alloa	L 0-1	0-1	1		507

Final League Position: 1

Rothmans Football Yearbook 1997–98

659

Honours
Scottish Cup: Quarter-finals 1996.
League Champions: Third Division 1996–97.
Club Colours: Shirts: Blue with white stripes and thin red stripe. Shorts: Blue. Stockings: Blue with red tops.

Goalscorers: *League (70):* Stewart 27, Thomson 10 (3 pens), McLean 8, Wilson 5, Hercher 4, Ross 4, Christie 3, Noble 2, Teasdale 2, Tokely 2, Addicoat 1, Cherry 1, De Barros 1. *Scottish Cup (2):* McLean 1, Stewart 1. *Coca Cola Cup (0).*
League Challenge Cup (3): Cherry 1, Stewart 1, Thomson 1.

Calder J 35	MacArthur I 34	Hastings R 34	Bennett G 3+6	Noble M 34	Cherry P 31	Wilson B 27+2	Teasdale M 36	Stewart I 34+2	Christie C 30+3	Thomson B 21+2	Hercher A 10+3	Ross D 26+5	Sinclair N —+3	Tokely R 13+11	De Barros M 4+17	McLean S 17+3	Addicoat W 6+8	MacMillan N 1	Match No.
1	2	3	4	5	6	7²	8	9¹	10	11	12	13							1
1	2	3	4	5		7	8	9	10	11	6								2
1	4	3		5	6	7	2	12	10	9	8¹	11²	13						3
1	4	3		5	6		2	7	10	9	8	11							4
1	4	3	14	5	6		2	13	10	9²	8³	11¹		7	12				5
1	4	3¹	12	5	6		2	8	10	9		11³		7²	13	14			6
1	4			5	3		2	8	10	9	6	11		7¹	12				7
1	4	3		5	6		2	8	10¹	9	12		13	7²	11				8
1	4	3		5	6		2	8		9	10	11		7					9
1	4	3		5	6	14	2	8	10²	9	12	7¹		13	11³				10
1	4	3	14		5	7	2	8		9	11³	6¹		10²	12	13			11
1	4	3	12	5		7	2	8		9¹	6	11		13	10²				12
1	4	3	12	5		7	2	8	10²	9		6¹	13	11					13
1	4	3		5		7	2	8	10	9¹	14		12	13	11³	6²			14
1	4	3		5	6	7	2	8	10			12		9	11¹				15
1	4	3		5	6	7	2	8	10		12			9	11¹				16
1	4	3		5	6	7	2	8	10		12			9	11¹				17
1	4	3		5	6	7	2	8	10		12			9	11¹				18
1	4	3	14	5	6³	7	2	8	13	10	12	11²		9¹					19
		4	3		5	6	7	2	8	12	11²	10¹		9	13			1	20
1	4	3		5	6	7	2	8	10	9¹	11			12					21
1	4	3		5	6	7	2	8	10	11		9							22
1	4	3		5	6²	7³	2	8	10	11	13	14		9¹	12				23
1	4	3		5		7	2	8	10	11	6	9							24
1	4	3		5	6	7	2	8	10	11¹		12	9						25
1	4¹	3		5	6		2	8²	10	13	11	12	7	9					26
1	4	3¹		5	6	7	2	8	10	11²	12	13	9						27
1	4	3		5	6	7	2	8	10	11		9							28
1	4	3		5	6	7³	2	8	10	12	11²	14	13	9¹					29
1	4	3		5	6	7¹	2	8	10	9²	11²	12	13	14					30
1	4¹	3		5	6	7³	2	8	10	9	11²	12	13	14					31
1		3		5	6	7	2	8	10	9¹	11²	4	12	13					32
1		3		5	6	7¹	2	8	10	9	11²	4	13	12					33
1	4	3		5	6	12	2	8	13	9	10	11²	7¹						34
1	4	3		5	6	7²	2¹	8³	10	9	11	12	13	14					35
1	4		3	6¹	7	2	8³	10	9	11²	14	5	13	12					36

KILMARNOCK
Premier Division

Year Formed: 1869. *Ground & Address:* Rugby Park, Kilmarnock KA1 2DP. *Telephone:* 01563 525184. *Fax:* 01563 522181.
Ground Capacity: total: 18,128 seated. *Size of Pitch:* 114yd × 72yd.
Chairman: R. Hamilton. *Secretary:* Kevin Collins. *Commercial Manager:* Denny Martin. *Stadium Manager:* G. Hollas.
Manager: Bobby Williamson. *Assistant Managers:* Jim Clark, Gerry McCabe. *Physio:* Hugh Allan.
Managers since 1975: W. Fernie; D. Sneddon; J. Clunie; E. Morrison; J. Fleeting; T. Burns; A. Totten. *Club Nickname(s):*
Killie. *Previous Grounds:* Rugby Park (Dundonald Road); The Grange; Holm Quarry; Present ground since 1899.
Record Attendance: 35,995 v Rangers, Scottish Cup; 10 March, 1962.
Record Transfer Fee received: £300,000 for Shaun McSkimming to Motherwell,1995.
Record Transfer Fee paid: £300,000 for Paul Wright from St Johnstone, 1995.
Record Victory: 11-1 v Paisley Academical, Scottish Cup; 18 Jan, 1930 (15-0 v Lanemark, Ayrshire Cup; 15 Nov, 1890).
Record Defeat: 1-9 v Celtic, Division I; 13 Aug, 1938.
Most Capped Player: Joe Nibloe, 11, Scotland.
Most League Appearances: 481: Alan Robertson, 1972-88.
Most League Goals in Season (Individual): 34: Harry 'Peerie' Cunningham 1927-28 and Andy Kerr 1960-61.
Most Goals Overall (Individual): 148: W. Culley; 1912-23.

KILMARNOCK 1996–97 LEAGUE RECORD

Match No.	Date	Venue	Opponents	Result	H/T Score	Lg. Pos.	Goalscorers	Attendance
1	Aug 10	A	Hibernian	W 2-1	2-1	—	Mitchell [20], Henry [26]	8734
2	17	A	Hearts	L 2-3	1-2	4	Wright [43], Lauchlan [88]	10,854
3	24	H	Celtic	L 1-3	1-0	6	Reilly [27]	15,970
4	Sept 7	H	Dunfermline Ath	D 2-2	1-1	6	Wright 2 (1 pen) [44, 56 (p)]	6623
5	14	A	Aberdeen	L 0-3	0-0	8		11,826
6	21	H	Rangers	L 1-4	1-0	8	Reilly [19]	14,812
7	28	A	Motherwell	L 0-1	0-1	9		5700
8	Oct 12	A	Dundee U	D 0-0	0-0	9		7365
9	19	H	Raith R	W 2-1	1-1	8	Brown [37], Wright [58]	5829
10	26	A	Dunfermline Ath	L 1-2	1-1	9	Findlay [22]	5269
11	Nov 1	H	Hibernian	W 4-2	2-2	9	Henry [15], McIntyre [22], Wright [52], McGinlay (og) [58]	10,872
12	16	H	Motherwell	L 2-4	0-1	9	Wright 2 [55, 87]	7087
13	30	A	Raith R	L 0-1	0-0	9		3750
14	Dec 7	H	Dundee U	L 0-2	0-1	10		5814
15	14	H	Hearts	W 2-0	0-0	10	McKee [52], Mitchell [86]	5832
16	17	A	Rangers	L 2-4	1-1	—	Montgomerie [3], Roberts [87]	39,469
17	21	H	Aberdeen	W 3-0	1-0	9	Burke 2 [12, 58], Roberts [90]	6114
18	26	A	Hibernian	W 1-0	1-0	—	McIntyre [42]	8912
19	Jan 4	A	Dundee U	L 0-2	0-0	8		8508
20	8	A	Celtic	L 0-6	0-2	—		45,535
21	11	A	Raith R	L 0-1	0-1	9		5505
22	15	H	Rangers	D 1-1	0-0	—	McKee [46]	15,662
23	18	H	Dunfermline Ath	W 2-1	0-0	7	Wright 2 [55, 87]	5813
24	21	A	Motherwell	L 0-2	0-2	—		5508
25	Feb 1	A	Aberdeen	L 1-2	0-2	8	McIntyre [47]	8361
26	8	A	Hearts	L 0-2	0-1	9		11,020
27	22	H	Dundee U	L 2-3	1-1	9	Malpas (og) [3], Wright [69]	6054
28	Mar 5	A	Raith R	L 1-2	0-1	—	McIntyre [87]	3306
29	11	H	Celtic	W 2-0	1-0	—	Wright [22], Burke [71]	15,087
30	15	H	Motherwell	W 1-0	0-0	7	Wright [77]	7612
31	22	A	Rangers	W 2-1	1-0	7	McIntyre [38], Wright [81]	50,036
32	Apr 5	H	Hearts	W 1-0	1-0	7	Wright [5]	7877
33	19	H	Hibernian	D 1-1	1-1	8	Wright [14]	10,886
34	May 3	A	Dunfermline Ath	L 1-3	0-1	8	McIntyre [50]	5904
35	7	A	Celtic	D 0-0	0-0	—		42,788
36	10	H	Aberdeen	D 1-1	0-1	7	Holt [73]	10,027

Final League Position: 7

Honours

League Champions: Division I 1964-65. Division II 1897-98, 1898-99; *Runners-up:* Division I 1959-60, 1960-61, 1962-63, 1963-64. First Division 1975-76, 1978-79, 1981-82, 1992-93. Division II 1953-54, 1973-74. Second Division 1989-90.
Scottish Cup Winners: 1920, 1929, 1997; *Runners-up:* 1898, 1932, 1938, 1957, 1960.
League Cup Runners-up: 1952-53, 1960-61, 1962-63.

European: *European Cup:* 1965-66. *UEFA Cup (Fairs):* 1964-65 (semi-finals), 1969-70, 1970-71.
Club colours: Shirt: Blue and white vertical stripes. Shorts: Blue. Stockings: Blue.

Goalscorers: *League (41):* Wright 15 (1 pen), McIntyre 6, Burke 3, Henry 2, McKee 2, Mitchell 2, Reilly 2, Roberts 2, Brown 1, Findlay 1, Holt 1, Lauchlan 1, Montgomerie 1, own goals 2. *Scottish Cup (10):* Henry 3, Wright 3 (1 pen), McIntyre 2, Brown 1, McGowne 1. *Coca Cola Cup (0).*

Lekovic D 30	MacPherson A 33	Tallon G 4	Reilly M 31+2	Whitworth N 7	Anderson D 16+1	Mitchell A 23+7	Henry J 18+4	Wright P 29+2	McIntyre J 29+2	McKee C 14+11	Lauchlan J 7+3	Montgomerie R 19+2	Roberts M 2+8	Findlay W 15+5	Brown T 7+17	Holt G 10+2	McGowne K 30+1	Kerr D 27	Meldrum C 6	Bagen D 16+1	Kerr A 2+2	Burke A 14+3	Hamilton S 6	Prytz R 1+2	Match No
1	2	3	4	5¹	6	7	8²	9	10	11³	12	13	14												1
1	2	3²	8	5	6	7		9	10	4			13	11¹	12										2
1	2	3	6	5		7	8¹	9	10	11²			4	13	12										3
1	2	4²	5	3		7	8	9	10			12	13	11¹		6									4
1	2	4	5	3		7	8¹	9	10			12		11		6									5
1	2	4	5	3		7		9	10	11¹		12		8		6									6
1	2	4¹	5	3		7		9	10	11²		12	13	8		6									7
1	2					7	8	9¹	10	12		5	4	13	11¹	6	3								8
1	2					7	8	9	10	11		5	4	12		6	3								9
1	2					7	8	9	10			5	4	11		6	3								10
	2	12		6			8¹	9	10	7		5	4	11			3	1							11
	2	12				13	8	9	10	7		5	4¹	11		6	3²	1							12
	2	8				12	7³	9²	10	11¹	4	5		13	14	6	3	1							13
	2	8				13		9		11	6	4¹	14	12	10²	5	3	1		7³					14
1	2	8				7		9		11	4	5		6			3	10							15
1	2	8				7		9²			4	5¹	13	6		12	3		10³	11	14				16
1	2	8				7			9¹		4	12	6			5	3		10	13	11²				17
1		8				7			9¹		4	12	6			5	3		10	13	11²	2			18
1		8	5			7		12	9	10¹			13	6		4	3				11²	2			19
1	2	4	8			7		9				13		12		5¹	3			6	11³	10			20
1	6	8	4			7		9				13		12		5	3		10		11¹	2²			21
1	2	8	4			7		9¹	10	11²			6			5	3		12	13					22
1	2	8	4			7	12	9	10	11²	13		6¹			5	3								23
1	2	8	4			7¹	12	9	10	11³	13		6			5				14			3²		24
1	2	6	4	13		12		9			10		8¹	5		3			7²	11					25
1	2	6²	4	7		13	12	9		10¹			8	5		3			11						26
1	2	6	13	7¹		8		9	12	14		4		10³		5	3²			11					27
1	2	6	3			8		9	12	13		4	7²	10¹		5				11					28
	2	6				8		9¹	10	13		4		12		5	3	1		7²	11				29
	2	6	13			8³		9	10	12		4		14		5	3	1		7²	11¹				30
1	2	6	13			8		9	10	12		4				5	3			7²	11¹				31
1		6				8³		9	10	12		4	13	14		5	3			7¹	11²	2			32
1	2	6				8¹		9	10²	14		4	13	11		5	3			7³				12	33
1	2	6				8²		9¹	10	13		4		12	11	5	3			7³				14	34
1	2	6	4	13				9¹		14		12		10		5	3			7²	11		8¹		35
1	2	6				8		9²				4		13	12	10	5	3		7¹	11				36

LIVINGSTON
Second Division

Year Formed: 1974. *Ground:* Almondvale Stadium, Almondvale Stadium Road, Livingston EH54 7DN. *Telephone:* 01506 417000. *Fax:* 01506 418888.
Ground Capacity: total: 6100. Main stand only used 7500. *Size of Pitch:* 105yd × 72yd.
Chairman: William P Hunter. *Secretary:* J.R.S.Renton. *Vice-chairman:* Hugh Cowan.
Manager: Jim Leishman. *Club Doctor:* Dr Box. *Physio:* Arthur Duncan. *Coach:* George McNeil.
Managers since 1975: John Bain; Alec Ness; Willie MacFarlane; Terry Christie; Michael Lawson. *Club Nickname:* Livvy Lions. *Previous Grounds:* None.
Record Attendance: 4000 v Albion Rovers, League Cup 1st rd; 9 Sept, 1974.
Record Transfer Fee received: £115,000 for John Inglis to St Johnstone (1990).
Record Transfer Fee paid: £28,000 for Victor Kasule from Albion Rovers (1987).
Record Victory: 6-0 v Raith R, Second Division; 9 Nov, 1985.
Record Defeat: 0-8 v Hamilton A. Division II; 14 Dec, 1974.
Most Capped Player (under 18): I. Little.
Most League Appearances: 446: Walter Boyd, 1979-89.
Most League Goals in Season (Individual): 21: John McGachie, 1986-87. *(Team):* 69; Second Division, 1986-87.
Most Goals Overall (Individual): 64: David Roseburgh, 1986-93.

LIVINGSTON 1996–97 LEAGUE RECORD

Match No.	Date	Venue	Opponents	Result	H/T Score	Lg. Pos.	Goalscorers	Attendance
1	Aug 17	H	Queen of the S	W 3-1	3-0	—	McMartin [19], Duthie [43], Harvey [45]	1453
2	24	A	Stranraer	W 2-1	1-0	1	McLeod [8], Harvey [90]	523
3	31	H	Hamilton A	W 1-0	1-0	1	Harvey [39]	2627
4	Sept 7	H	Brechin C	W 2-1	1-0	1	Williamson [20], Young [72]	1832
5	14	A	Dumbarton	W 4-2	3-1	1	Harvey 2 (1 pen) [9 (pl, 44], Young [30], McLeod [70]	762
6	21	A	Stenhousemuir	D 0-0	0-0	1		683
7	28	H	Berwick R	W 2-1	1-0	1	Harvey 2 (1 pen) [4 (pl, 78]	2398
8	Oct 5	H	Clyde	D 0-0	0-0	1		2799
9	12	A	Ayr U	L 0-1	0-1	3		2578
10	19	A	Queen of the S	D 2-2	1-1	2	Young [17], Duthie [70]	1158
11	26	H	Stranraer	W 2-0	1-0	2	Harvey [11], Tierney [61]	1923
12	Nov 2	H	Dumbarton	W 5-0	3-0	2	Young [16], Harvey 2 [20, 34], Duthie [53], Alleyne [80]	1941
13	9	A	Brechin C	D 0-0	0-0	2		400
14	16	A	Berwick R	W 2-1	2-0	2	Callaghan T 2 [20, 23]	564
15	30	A	Clyde	L 0-2	0-1	2		1053
16	Dec 7	H	Stenhousemuir	W 2-1	0-1	2	Harvey [72], Laidlaw [83]	1500
17	14	A	Ayr U	W 1-0	1-0	1	Harvey [1]	3542
18	21	H	Queen of the S	W 2-1	2-1	1	McMartin [21], Duthie [36]	2178
19	Jan 1	H	Berwick R	D 2-2	1-1	—	Campbell [10], Graham [70]	2029
20	11	A	Stenhousemuir	W 3-1	2-0	1	McLeod [19], Harvey [44], Campbell [75]	631
21	18	H	Clyde	D 0-0	0-0	1		2533
22	Feb 1	A	Ayr U	L 0-1	0-0	2		2568
23	5	A	Hamilton A	D 3-3	2-0	—	Campbell [16], Duthie 2 [26, 79]	813
24	8	A	Dumbarton	W 3-2	1-1	2	Duthie [15], Harvey [74], McLeod [77]	503
25	22	A	Stranraer	D 1-1	0-1	2	Bailey [79]	584
26	26	H	Brechin C	L 2-3	2-1	—	Harvey [15], Bailey [36]	1323
27	Mar 8	H	Stenhousemuir	L 1-3	0-2	3	Bailey [88]	2196
28	15	A	Berwick R	D 1-1	0-0	3	Callaghan W [86]	453
29	22	A	Clyde	W 1-0	0-0	3	Bailey [72]	841
30	30	H	Hamilton A	L 1-2	1-2	—	Bailey [2]	3436
31	Apr 5	H	Ayr U	W 2-1	0-1	3	McMartin [55], Young [89]	2512
32	12	A	Brechin C	L 0-1	0-1	3		471
33	19	H	Dumbarton	L 1-2	1-0	3	McLeod [18]	1579
34	26	A	Queen of the S	W 2-1	0-0	3	Bailey 2 [60, 90]	1511
35	May 3	H	Stranraer	W 3-0	1-0	3	Bailey [30], Laidlaw [55], Forrest [76]	1491
36	10	A	Hamilton A	D 0-0	0-0	3		825

Final League Position: 3

Honours
League Champions: Second Division 1986-87. Third Division 1995-96; *Runners-up:* Second Division 1982-83. First Division 1987-88.
Scottish Cup: —. *League Cup:* Semi-finals 1984-85. *B&Q Cup:* Semi-finals 1992-93, 1993-94.
Club colours: Shirt: Black with yellow trim. Shorts: Black. Stockings: Black.

Goalscorers: *League (56):* Harvey 15 (2 pens), Bailey 8, Duthie 7, McLeod 5, Young 5, Campbell 3, McMartin 3, Callaghan T 2, Laidlaw 2, Alleyne 1, Callaghan W 1, Forrest 1, Graham 1, Tierney 1, Williamson 1. *Scottish Cup (1):* Bailey 1. *Coca Cola Cup (2):* Callaghan T 1, Young 1. *League Challenge Cup (1):* Young 1.

Douglas R 36	Williamson S 32	Campbell S 30	Davidson G 20+1	Tierney G 22	McLeod G 19	McMartin G 33+1	Callaghan T 32	Harvey G 27+2	Bailey L 13+10	Duthie M 32+1	Young J 21+13	Sinclair C 4+8	Alleyne D 14+9	Callaghan W 7+13	Watson D 20+3	Laidlaw S 4+9	Smart C 10+6	Graham T 15	Forrest G 5	Match No.
1	2	3	4	5	6	7	8	9^1	10	11^2	12	13								1
1	2	3	4	5	6	7	8	9		11	10^1	12								2
1	2	3	4	5	6	7	8	9^2		11^1	10	12	13							3
1	2	3	4	5	6	7	8	9^2		11^1	10	12	13							4
1	2	3	4	5	6	7	8	9		11^1	10	12								5
1	2^1	3	4	5	6	7	8	9		11^2	10^3	13		12	14					6
1	2	3	4	5		7	8	9		11	10^2	12		13	6^1					7
1	2	3	4	5	6^1	7^2	8	9		11	10^3	12	13	14						8
1	2	3	4	5		7	8	9		11	10		6							9
1	2	3	4	5		7	8	9		11	10^1		6	12						10
1	2	3	4	5		7	8	9^1		11	10^2		6	12	13					11
1	2	3	4	5		7	8	9	13	11	10^1		6	12^2						12
1	2	3	4	5		7	8	9		11	10		6							13
1	2	3	4	5		7	8	9^2	13	11	10		6^1				12			14
1	2	3	4^2			5		7	10^1		8	11	9	6		13	12			15
1	2	3					7^2	8	9	12	11	10^1	6		5	13		4		16
1	2	3					7	8	9^1	13	11	10^2	6		5	12		4		17
1	2	3					7	8	9	12	11	10^1	6^2		5	13		4		18
1		3^1	4				7		9		11	10	12	6		2		8	5	19
1		3	2	5	6	7		10					9	8		11	4			20
1		3	4			7		8^1	9^2	14	11	13			10^3	2		12	5	21
1		2^1		4		6	7	8	10^3	14	11	13		12	9^2	3			5	22
1	4	11				7	8		14	3	10^3			9^2	2	13	12	5	6^1	23
1	4				6	7	8	12	13	3	10^2	14		9^1	2		11^3	5		24
1	5			4	6	7	8^1	9^2	13	11	10^3	3		14	2		12			25
1	4	3^1		5	6	7^2	8	9	10	11	13		12		2					26
1	4^2				7	8	9	10	11	13	12	6^1		3		2	5			27
1	4	3			6		8	9	10^2	11	13	7		14	2^1		12^3	5		28
1	4	3	12	5	6		8	9^3	10^2	11	14			14	2^1		7			29
1	4	3^1	2	5	7	12	8	9	10^2	11	13		14		6^3					30
1	4			6	7		9^2	3	13		11	12	10		2^1	5				31
1	4			6	7^2	8^1		10^2	11	12		13	9	3	14	2	5			32
1	4	3			6	7		10^2	12	11^1	13	2	9	8	5					33
1	4	3			6	7	8^1	10		12	14	13	2	9^2	5	11^3				34
1	4	3	5^1		7	8^2		9^3	12	13	11	14	2	10	6					35
1	5	3		2^3	13	11^1	8	12	14	6	10	4	9^2		7					36

MONTROSE   Third Division

Year Formed: 1879. *Ground & Address:* Links Park, Wellington St, Montrose DD10 8QD. *Telephone:* 01674 673200.
Ground Capacity: total: 4338. seated: 1338. *Size of Pitch:* 113yd × 70yd.
Chairman: Michael Craig. *Secretary:* Malcolm J. Watters.
Manager: Tommy Campbell. *Physio:* Allan Borthwick.
Managers since 1975: A. Stuart; K. Cameron; R. Livingstone; S. Murray; D. D'Arcy; I. Stewart; C. McLelland; D. Rougvie; J. Leishman, J Holt, A. Dornan, D. Smith.
Club Nickname(s): The Gable Endies. *Previous Grounds:* None.
Record Attendance: 8983 v Dundee, Scottish Cup 3rd rd; 17 Mar, 1973.
Record Transfer Fee received: £50,000 for Gary Murray to Hibernian (Dec 1980).
Record Transfer Fee paid: £17,500 for Jim Smith from Airdrieonians (Feb 1992).
Record Victory: 12-0 v Vale of Leithen, Scottish Cup 2nd rd; 4 Jan, 1975.
Record Defeat: 0-13 v Aberdeen; 17 Mar, 1951.
Most Capped Player: Alexander Keillor, 2 (6), Scotland.
Most League Appearances: 408: David Larter, 1987-97.
Most League Goals in Season (Individual): 28: Brian Third, Division II; 1972-73.
Most Goals Overall (Individual): —.

MONTROSE 1996–97 LEAGUE RECORD

Match No.	Date	Venue	Opponents	Result	H/T Score	Lg. Pos.	Goalscorers	Attendance
1	Aug 17	H	Alloa	L 1-2	0-1	—	Nelson (og) [85]	450
2	24	A	Cowdenbeath	L 0-1	0-0	8		266
3	31	H	Ross Co	W 2-1	2-0	7	McGlashan [1], Smith [5]	532
4	Sept 7	H	Arbroath	D 0-0	0-0	8		826
5	14	A	Queen's Park	W 2-0	1-0	4	Taylor 2 [32, 68]	404
6	21	A	East Stirling	W 3-1	1-0	2	McGlashan [29], Taylor [53], Mailer [86]	308
7	28	H	Forfar Ath	W 4-1	2-1	2	McGlashan (pen) [5], Masson P 2 [38, 72], Taylor [62]	698
8	Oct 5	A	Albion R	W 2-1	1-1	1	Haro [26], Taylor [62]	950
9	12	H	Inverness CT	D 2-2	0-0	1	McGlashan [65], Craib [86]	643
10	19	A	Alloa	L 1-3	1-0	2	McGlashan [12]	555
11	26	H	Cowdenbeath	L 0-2	0-2	5		444
12	Nov 2	H	Queen's Park	W 3-2	0-1	3	Taylor 3 [52, 88, 90]	519
13	9	A	Arbroath	W 2-1	0-0	3	Ingram [54], Cooper [75]	666
14	16	A	Forfar Ath	L 1-3	0-0	4	Ingram [72]	583
15	26	H	East Stirling	W 1-0	0-0	—	Tindal (pen) [65]	334
16	30	H	Albion R	W 2-1	1-0	2	McGlashan 2 [11, 61]	534
17	Dec 7	A	Ross Co	D 4-4	2-2	1	Bird [31], Ingram [40], Tindal [53], Taylor [81]	1346
18	14	A	Inverness CT	L 0-2	0-2	2		2477
19	21	H	Alloa	L 2-3	1-1	3	Ingram [17], Tindal [86]	606
20	Jan 1	H	Forfar Ath	L 0-4	0-2	—		802
21	18	A	Albion R	L 1-2	1-1	5	McGlashan (pen) [9]	319
22	Feb 1	H	Inverness CT	L 0-2	0-1	5		520
23	4	A	East Stirling	L 2-4	0-3	—	Bird [67], Masson C [89]	218
24	8	A	Queen's Park	W 1-0	0-0	5	Fisher [60]	408
25	15	H	Arbroath	W 1-0	1-0	4	Winiarski [44]	686
26	22	A	Cowdenbeath	W 1-0	1-0	4	MacDonald [39]	175
27	Mar 8	H	East Stirling	L 0-2	0-0	6		392
28	11	H	Ross Co	D 0-0	0-0	—		412
29	15	A	Forfar Ath	L 3-5	1-5	6	Masson C [13], McGlashan [68], Smith [73]	457
30	22	H	Albion R	L 0-4	0-1	6		355
31	Apr 5	A	Inverness CT	L 2-3	2-1	6	McGlashan (pen) [23], Smith [42]	3036
32	12	A	Arbroath	D 1-1	0-0	6	Tindal [47]	432
33	19	A	Queen's Park	D 1-1	0-0	6	Haro [51]	388
34	26	A	Alloa	L 0-1	0-1	6		308
35	May 3	H	Cowdenbeath	D 0-0	0-0	6		279
36	10	A	Ross Co	L 1-3	1-0	6	McGlashan [28]	2144

Final League Position: 6

Honours
League Champions: Second Division 1984-85, *Runners-up:* 1990-91. Third Division, *Runners-up:* 1994-95.
Scottish Cup: Quarter-finals 1973, 1976.
League Cup: Semi-finals 1975-76.
B&Q Cup: Semi-finals: 1992-93.
League Challenge Cup: semi-finals: 1996-97.
Club colours: Shirt: Royal blue with white sleeves. Shorts: White. Stockings: Royal blue.

Goalscorers: *League (46):* McGlashan 11, Taylor 9, Ingram 4, Tindal 4 (1 pen), Smith 3, Bird 2, Haro 2, Masson C 2, Masson P 2, Cooper 1, Craib 1, Fisher 1, MacDonald 1, Mailer 1, Winiarski 1, own goal 1. *Scottish Cup (0). Coca Cola Cup (0). League Challenge Cup (9):* McGlashan 4 (1 pen), Glass 1, Ingram 1, Masson P 1, Smith 1, Taylor 1.

Larter D 24	Mailer C 31 + 1	Craib M 26	Tindal K 31	Purves S 13 + 4	Haro M 30	Taylor S 26 + 5	Bird J 24 + 3	McGlashan C 30	Smith S 9 + 4	Glass S 11 + 5	Stephen L 3 + 10	Ingram N 20 + 9	MacDonald i 24 + 2	Masson P 14 + 9	Cooper C 19 + 2	Tosh J 2 + 4	Fisher D 20 + 2	Butter J 12	Thomson N 7 + 3	Winiarski S 10	Masson C 8	Cassioe S — + 1	Slythe M — + 1	Dorward R 2	Match No
1	2	3	4	5	6^1	7	8	9	10	11^2	12	13													1
1	2	5	3		6	7	8	9	10			12	4	11^1											2
1	2	5	3		6	7	8^1	9^2	10^3			12	14	4	11	13									3
1	2	5	3		6	9^2	8	10^1				13	12	4	11		7								4
1	2	5	3		6	9	8	10				4	11	7^1	12										5
1	2	5			6	10	8	9		12	3	4^1	11	7											6
1	2^3	5	3		6	10	8	9^2				12	13	4^1	11	7	14								7
1	2	5	3		6	10	8	9				12	4^1	11	7										8
1	2	5	3		6	10	8^3	9				14	13	4	11^2	7^1	12								9
1	2	5	3		6	10	8^2	9				12	4^1	13	11	7									10
1	2	5	3		6	10	8^1	9				13	12	14	4^3	11^2	7								11
1	2^2	5	11		6	9	8				3	14	10	4	13	7^1	12^3								12
1	2	5	11	13	6	9	8^1				3^2	10	4	12	7										13
1	2	5	3^2	13	6	9	8	10				4	11^1	7	12										14
1		5	11	2	6	9	8				3	10	4	12	7^1										15
1	12	5	11	2^1	6		8	9			3	10	4	13	7^2										16
1	2	5	11		6	13	8^1	9			3	10^2	4	12	7										17
1	2	5	11^2		6	12	13	9			3	10^1	4	8	7										18
1	2	5	11	13	6^2	12		9			3	10	4^1	7											19
1	2	5	11		6^1	13	8	9			3^3	14	10^2	4	12		7								20
	3	5	2		6	10	8	9				12		11			7	1	4^1						21
	3	5					8	9				10				7^1	4	1	11	2	6	12			22
	3	5			13	9	8					12			7	2^1	4^2	1	11^3	10	6		14		23
	2	5	3				8	9				10^1	12		7^2		4	1	13	11	6				24
	2	5	3				8	9				10	12		7^1		4	1		11	6				25
		3	5			12		9				10^1	4	11	7		8	1	2		6				26
		11	3	6			8	9			12	10	4^1				7	1	2	5					27
		11	3	6		10		9				4					7	1	2	8	5				28
	3		11	6		10		9			12	13	4^1				7	1	2^2	8	5				29
	2	5	3		6	10		9			12		4^1		7		8	1	13	11^2					30
	3	5			6	10		9				4	12	11	7^1		8	1	2						31
	3	5		8	6	10		9				4		11	15	7^1	12	1^6	2						32
1	3	5		8	6	10		9				4	13	11	12		7^2		2^1						33
1	2	5		8	6	10	11	9				4	3		12		7^1								34
1	11	2	4	5	10^2	13	9	12				6		8	7^1									3	35
1	10	2	12	5	7		9	11^2				6		8	4^1		13							3	36

MOTHERWELL
Premier Division

Year Formed: 1886. *Ground & Address:* Fir Park, Motherwell ML1 2QN. *Telephone:* 01698 333333. *Fax:* 01698 276333.
Ground Capacity: total: 13,742 all seated. *Size of Pitch:* 110yd × 75yd.
Chairman: John C. Chapman. *Secretary:* Alan C. Dick. *Commercial Manager:* John Swinburne.
Manager: Alex McLeish. *Assistant Manager:* Andy Watson. *Physio:* John Porteous. *Coach:* Jim Griffin.
Managers since 1975: Ian St. John; Willie McLean; Rodger Hynd; Ally MacLeod; David Hay; Jock Wallace; Bobby
Watson, Tommy McLean.
Club Nickname(s): The Well. *Previous Grounds:* Roman Road, Dalziel Park.
Record Attendance: 35,632 v Rangers, Scottish Cup 4th rd replay; 12 Mar, 1952.
Record Transfer Fee received: £1,750,000 for Phil O'Donnell to Celtic, September 1994.
Record Transfer Fee paid: £400,000 for Mitchell Van Der Gaag from PSV Eindhoven, March 1995.
Record Victory: 12-1 v Dundee U, Division II; 23 Jan, 1954.
Record Defeat: 0-8 v Aberdeen, Premier Division; 26 Mar, 1979.
Most Capped Player: George Stevenson, 12, Scotland; Tommy Coyne, 12, Republic of Ireland.
Most League Appearances: 626: Bobby Ferrier, 1918-37.
Most League Goals in Season (Individual): 52: Willie McFadyen, Division I; 1931-32.
Most Goals Overall (Individual): 283: Hugh Ferguson, 1916-25.

MOTHERWELL 1996–97 LEAGUE RECORD

Match No.	Date	Venue	Opponents	Result	H/T Score	Lg. Pos.	Goalscorers	Atten- dance
1	Aug 10	A	Dundee U	D	1-1	0-1	—	Van Der Gaag [75]	8157
2	17	H	Aberdeen	D	2-2	1-1	7	McSkimming 2 (1 pen) [40 (p), 51]	6206
3	24	A	Raith R	W	3-0	2-0	3	Van Der Gaag 2 [23, 58], Arnott [31]	4837
4	Sept 7	H	Rangers	L	0-1	0-1	5		12,288
5	14	A	Dunfermline Ath	D	1-1	0-1	5	May [57]	5690
6	21	A	Hearts	D	1-1	0-0	5	Arnott [48]	10,932
7	28	H	Kilmarnock	W	1-0	1-0	4	Arnott [19]	5700
8	Oct 12	A	Celtic	L	0-1	0-0	6		49,289
9	19	H	Hibernian	D	1-1	0-1	5	McSkimming [73]	6784
10	26	A	Rangers	L	0-5	0-0	7		48,160
11	Nov 2	H	Dundee U	L	1-3	0-0	8	Ross [61]	5814
12	11	H	Hearts	L	0-2	0-0	—		5441
13	16	A	Kilmarnock	W	4-2	1-0	7	Coyne 3 [9, 59, 89], Philliben [49]	7087
14	30	A	Hibernian	L	0-2	0-1	8		7390
15	Dec 7	H	Celtic	W	2-1	1-0	7	Davies [40], Ross [89]	11,589
16	11	H	Raith R	L	0-1	0-0	—		4040
17	14	A	Aberdeen	D	0-0	0-0	8		10,442
18	21	H	Dunfermline Ath	L	2-3	2-1	8	Ireland (og) [12], Coyne [29]	4529
19	26	A	Dundee U	L	0-2	0-1	—		8072
20	28	A	Hearts	L	1-4	1-1	9	Coyne [13]	11,164
21	Jan 4	A	Celtic	L	0-5	0-2	9		45,259
22	11	H	Hibernian	W	2-1	2-0	8	McSkimming [20], Hunter (og) [22]	5855
23	18	H	Rangers	L	1-3	0-1	9	Coyle [71]	13,166
24	21	H	Kilmarnock	W	2-0	2-0	—	Coyle 2 [3, 38]	5508
25	Feb 1	A	Dunfermline Ath	L	1-3	1-2	9	Van Der Gaag [17]	4796
26	8	H	Aberdeen	D	2-2	0-2	8	Falconer [48], Burns [57]	5555
27	18	A	Raith R	W	5-1	2-0	—	Coyle [27], Van Der Gaag [40], Coyne 2 [48, 54], May [81]	3052
28	22	H	Celtic	L	0-1	0-1	7		12,131
29	Mar 1	A	Hibernian	D	1-1	0-0	7	Coyne [64]	8190
30	15	A	Kilmarnock	L	0-1	0-0	8		7612
31	22	H	Hearts	L	0-1	0-1	9		6245
32	Apr 5	A	Aberdeen	D	0-0	0-0	9		9317
33	12	H	Raith R	W	5-0	1-0	9	Falconer [18], Weir [48], Coyne 2 [53, 71], Coyle [79]	4691
34	19	H	Dundee U	D	1-1	1-0	9	Coyne (pen) [36]	5382
35	May 5	A	Rangers	W	2-0	1-0	—	Coyle 2 (1 pen) [10, 85 (p)]	50,059
36	10	H	Dunfermline Ath	D	2-2	1-1	8	Weir [32], Van Der Gaag [73]	9676

Final League Position: 8

Honours

League Champions: Division I 1931-32. First Division 1981-82, 1984-85. Division II 1953-54, 1968-69; *Runners-up:* Premier Division 1994-95. Division I 1926-27, 1929-30, 1932-33, 1933-34. Division II 1894-95, 1902-03. *Scottish Cup:* 1952, 1991; *Runners-up:* 1931, 1933, 1939, 1951.
League Cup: 1950-51. *Runners-up:* 1954-55 *Scottish Summer Cup:* 1944, 1965.
Club colours: Shirt: Amber with claret hoop and trimmings. Shorts: Claret. Stockings: Amber.

European: *UEFA Cup* 2 matches 1995-96

Goalscorers: *League (44):* Coyne 11 (1 pen), Coyle 7 (1 pen), Van Der Gaag 6, McSkimming 4 (1 pen), Arnott 3, Falconer 2, May 2, Ross 2, Weir 2, Burns 1, Davies 1, Philliben 1, own goals 2. *Scottish Cup (6):* Coyle 3, Davies 1, McSkimming 1, Van Der Gaag 1. *Coca Cola Cup (0).*

Howie S 30	May E 34	McSkimming S 23	Van Der Gaag M 26	Martin B 34	Denham G 5 + 4	Hendry J 5 + 1	Dolan J 18	Coyne T 24 + 3	Falconer W 21	Davies W 20 + 5	McMillan S 13 + 3	Burns A 16 + 14	Wishart F 15 + 3	Arnott D 11 + 9	Ross I 21 + 9	Raddie A 8 + 4	McCulloch L 1 + 14	McCart C 16 + 3	Philliben J 11 + 6	Lehtonen J 4 + 2	Woods S 6	Coyle O 15	Valakari S 11	Essandoh R — + 1	Weir M 5	Christie K 3 + 1	Match No.
1	2	3	4	5	6	7^1	8	9^2	10	11	12	13															1
1	2	6	4	5			8		10^1		3	12	7	9	11												2
1	2^2		4	5			8	6	3	10	7	9^1	11	12	13												3
1	2	6	4	5			8	11^1	3^2	10^3	7	9	12	14	13												4
1	2	3	4	5			8		10	11		13	7	9^2	12		6^1										5
1	2	3^1	4	5			8		10	11		12	7	9	6^2		13										6
1	2		4	5	12		8			11	10^1		7	9	3		6										7
1	2	3		5	6		10			11^1		8^2	7	9^1	12	13	14	4									8
1	2	3	4	5			10^2			8		11	7	9	12	13	6^1										9
1	2	3		5			8		10	11		9	7^1		4	12	6										10
1	2	3		5	12		10			11^1		8	7	9	4		6										11
1	2	10		5	3			9		12^3		7		8^2	11^1	14	13	6	4								12
1	7	3		5	4			9		10^2		12^3		8^1	11	14		6	2	13							13
1	7	3		5	4			9		10		12		8^1	11			6	2								14
1^6	7	3		5	4			9		10^1		8^2	13	12	11			6	2		15						15
	7	3		5	4			9		8^2		12		10^1	11	13		6	2	1							16
	7		5	13	4			9		3^1	10			12	11			6	2^2	1	8						17
	7	4	5				8	9		10	3^1	2^2		11	13			6	12	1							18
	7^1	4	5^3				8	9	3	10		13		12	11^2			6	14	2	1						19
	7	3	4	5^3			8	9	11	10^2		14	12	13				6	2^1		1						20
	7	3^2	4		12		5	9		8	10	14		13	11^3			6^1	2		1						21
1	7^1	6	4	5				9		10		12		14	2			3^2	13		8^3	11					22
1	8	6	4	5				9		10			7		2			3				11					23
1	8	6	4	5				9		10		13	7^2		2^1			3	12			11					24
1	8		4	5				9^2		10		7		12	6^1			3	13		2	11					25
1	8	6^1		5	3			9		10		12	7		2							11	4				26
1	2	6^1	4	5				9^2		10		7^3		12	3			13	14			11	8				27
1	7		4	5	12			9				6			2			3^1	10^2			11	8	13			28
1	2		4	5				9		10^2		12		6	7^1			3	13			11	8				29
1	2^1		4	5				9		10		13	7	12	3			14				11^3	6	8^2			30
1			4	5				9^2		13		10	7	14	3^3			6	12			11	8		2^1		31
1			4	5				9^1		13		10		8^2	12			3	6			11	7		2		32
1	2^2	4^3	5	13				9		10		6^1		12				14				11	8		7	12	33
1	2^2		4	5				9		10^1		3		12	13							11	8		7	6	34
1	2	10^2	4	5				9^1				6		13	12			3				11	8		7		35
1	2	10^1	4	5				9^2				6		12	3			13				11	8		7		36

PARTICK THISTLE

First Division

Year Formed: 1876. *Ground & Address:* Firhill Park, 80 Firhill Rd, Glasgow G20 7BA. *Telephone:* 0141 945 4811. *Fax:* 0141 945 1525
Ground Capacity: total: 20,876. seated: 9076. *Size of Pitch:* 110yd × 74yd.
Chairman: James Oliver. *Secretary:* Lorna Howgate. *Commercial Manager:* Lisa Brown.
Head Coach: John McVeigh. *Assistant Head Coach:* Gordon Chisholm. *Physio:* Iain McFadyen.
Managers since 1975: R. Auld; P. Cormack; B. Rooney; R. Auld; D. Johnstone; W. Lamont; S. Clark; J. Lambie, M. MacLeod. *Club Nickname(s):* The Jags. *Previous Grounds:* Jordanvale Park; Muirpark; Inchview; Meadowside Park.
Record Attendance: 49,838 v Rangers, Division I; 18 Feb, 1922.
Record Transfer Fee received: £200,000 for Mo Johnston to Watford.
Record Transfer Fee paid: £85,000 for Andy Murdoch from Celtic (Feb 1991).
Record Victory: 16-0 v Royal Albert, Scottish Cup 1st rd; 17 Jan, 1931.
Record Defeat: 0-10 v Queen's Park, Scottish Cup; 3 Dec, 1881.
Most Capped Player: Alan Rough, 51 (53), Scotland.
Most League Appearances: 410: Alan Rough, 1969-82.
Most League Goals in Season (Individual): 41: Alec Hair, Division I; 1926-27.
Most Goals Overall (Individual): —.

PARTICK THISTLE 1996–97 LEAGUE RECORD

Match No.	Date	Venue	Opponents	Result	H/T Score	Lg. Pos.	Goalscorers	Attendance
1	Aug 17	H	Dundee	D	0-0	0-0	—	3152
2	24	A	Falkirk	L	0-1	0-0	8	3489
3	31	H	St Mirren	D	1-1	1-1	8	Stirling (pen) [26]	3664
4	Sept 7	A	St Johnstone	L	0-2	0-0	10		3707
5	14	H	Stirling A	D	1-1	0-1	9	Henderson [56]	2175
6	21	A	Airdrieonians	D	4-4	3-2	9	Moss 2 [7, 25], Henderson [43], Adams [58]	1997
7	28	H	Clydebank	W	1-0	1-0	8	Evans [11]	2192
8	Oct 5	A	Greenock Morton	L	0-1	0-1	8		3945
9	12	H	East Fife	W	6-0	4-0	6	Dinnie [5], Evans 3 [36, 41, 82], Farrell [43], Maskrey [48]	1791
10	19	A	Dundee	W	2-0	1-0	7	Moss 2 [9, 58]	3303
11	26	H	Falkirk	W	3-0	1-0	5	Adams 2 [11, 76], Moss [53]	3556
12	Nov 2	A	Stirling A	W	2-1	2-1	4	Lyons [9], Macdonald [23]	2189
13	16	A	Clydebank	W	3-1	0-1	4	Adams [46], Evans [65], Stirling [90]	1786
14	19	H	St Johnstone	L	0-4	0-2	—		2721
15	23	H	Airdrieonians	D	0-0	0-0	4		3109
16	30	H	Greenock Morton	D	0-0	0-0	4		3501
17	Dec 14	A	St Mirren	L	2-3	2-0	7	Evans [21], Moss [44]	3306
18	26	H	Dundee	D	2-2	0-1	—	Stirling (pen) [70], Evans [80]	2693
19	Jan 1	H	Clydebank	W	3-1	0-1	—	Farrell [54], Adams [57], Stirling [77]	1822
20	4	H	Stirling A	D	1-1	0-1	5	Stirling (pen) [61]	2585
21	7	A	East Fife	W	3-1	1-1	—	Lyons [2], Moss 2 [60, 88]	800
22	13	A	St Johnstone	D	0-0	0-0	—		7910
23	18	A	Greenock Morton	W	3-1	2-1	3	Stirling [8], Moss [34], Docherty [81]	2437
24	22	A	Airdrieonians	D	1-1	1-1	—	Adams [29]	2029
25	Feb 1	H	East Fife	W	3-1	2-0	3	Maskrey [14], Adams [27], Moss [90]	1833
26	8	H	St Mirren	D	0-0	0-0	3		3347
27	22	A	Falkirk	L	1-2	1-2	4	Stirling [4]	3181
28	Mar 8	H	Airdrieonians	L	1-2	0-0	5	McWilliams [55]	2723
29	15	A	Clydebank	L	1-4	0-0	5	Adams [81]	1112
30	22	A	Greenock Morton	L	0-3	0-1	6		1873
31	Apr 5	A	East Fife	W	2-0	1-0	6	Evans 2 [11, 50]	1002
32	12	H	St Johnstone	L	0-4	0-2	6		2824
33	19	A	Stirling A	L	0-2	0-0	6		1281
34	26	A	Dundee	D	1-1	0-0	6	Lyons [90]	2416
35	May 3	H	Falkirk	W	2-1	0-0	6	Moss [62], McWilliams (pen) [67]	1512
36	10	A	St Mirren	L	0-2	0-2	6		2501

Final League Position: 6

Honours
League Champions: First Division 1975-76. Division II 1896-97, 1899-1900, 1970-71; *Runners-up:* First Division 1991-92. Division II 1901-02.
Scottish Cup Winners: 1921; *Runners-up:* 1930.
League Cup Winners: 1971-72; *Runners-up:* 1953-54, 1956-57, 1958-59.

European: *UEFA Cup:* 6 matches (*Fairs Cup:* 1963-64. *UEFA Cup:* 1972-73).
Club colours: Shirt: Red and yellow broad vertical stripes. Shorts: Black. Stockings: Yellow with red turnover.

Goalscorers: *League (49):* Moss 11, Evans 9, Adams 8, Stirling 7 (3 pens), Lyons 3, Farrell 2, Henderson 2, McWilliams 2 (1 pen), Maskrey 2, Dinnie 1, Docherty 1, Macdonald 1. *Scottish Cup (0). Coca Cola Cup (4):* Evans 3, Stirling 1. *League Challenge Cup (6):* Stirling 2, Evans 1, Henderson 1, McWilliams 1, Maskrey 1 (pen).

Cairns M 10	Milne C 22 + 3	Stirling J 34	Henderson N 12 + 4	Slavin J 17 + 1	Watson G 35	Evans G 29	Farrell D 31	Maskrey S 29 + 2	Turner T 7 + 4	Lyons A 29 + 6	Smith T — + 1	Macdonald W 11 + 5	McWilliams D 18 + 4	Docherty S 8 + 14	Dinnie A 13 + 1	Moss D 31	Adams C 26 + 4	Hillcoat J 26	McCall I 1 + 6	Ayton S 3	Te Jero J — + 1	Hringsson H 1 + 2	Archibald A 2 + 3	Apiliga R 1	McKenzie J — + 2	Ritchie J — + 1	Match No.
1	2	3	4^1	5	6	7	8^2	9	10	11	12	13															1
1	2	3	4^1	5	6	7	8	9	10	11^2			12	13													2
1	2^1	3	13	5	6	7	8	9^3	12	11			10^2	14	4												3
1	14	3	12	5	6^3	7		9	10^2	11		8^1			4	13	2										4
1	2	3	8	5	6	7		9		11					4^1	12	10										5
1		3	8	5	6	7^1	4	11	12	2						10	9										6
1	13	3	8^1	5	6	7	4	11	12	2						10^2	9										7
1	13	3	8	5	6	7	4	11^1	12	2^2						10	9										8
	2	3	8		6	7	4	11^2				14	12	13	5	10^1	9^3	1									9
	2	3	8		6	7	4	11^2			12	13	14		5^1	10^3	9	1									10
	2	3	8^2	5	6	7^3			12	11		4		14		10^1	9	1	13								11
	2	3	13	5	6	7^2	8		12	11					4	10^1	9	1									12
	2	3	12	5	6	7	8^1			11					4	10	9	1									13
		3	8	5	6	7			12	11					4^1	10	9	1	2								14
	2	3	8	5	6^1	7		11^2	12			13		4		10	9	1									15
	2	3	8	5	6	7		11							4	10	9^1	1	12								16
	2	3		5	6	7	9	11^1				8			4	10		1	12								17
	2	3		5	6	7	9	8^1		11				13	4^2	10		1	12								18
	2	3		5	6	7	8	11^1							4	10	9	1	12								19
	2	3		5	6	7	8	11^2					12		4^1	10	9	1	13								20
	2	3		5	6	7	8	11^1					12		4	10	9	1	4								21
	2	3		5	6	7	8	11							4	10	9	1									22
	2	3	14	5	6	7^1	8^2	11^2					12		4	10	9	1	13								23
	2	3		5	6	7^1	8	11					12		4	10	9	1									24
	2	3		5	6^1		8	11					12	13	4	10	9	1					7^2				25
	2	3		5	6	7	8	11							4	10	9	1									26
	2	3		5	6	7	8	11^1					12		4	10	9	1									27
		3		5	6	7^2	8	11				4				10^1	9	1	12	13							28
	2	3		5	6	7	8	11				14	12	13	4^1	10^2	9^3	1									29
	2	3		5	6	7^2	8	11					12		4^1	10	9	1	13								30
1	2	3^1	4	5	6	7		9		11		8				10	12										31
1		3^2	4	5	6	7		9^3		11		8				10	2^1		12			14	13				32
	2			5	6^1	7	8^3	11^2					12	14			9	1					3	4	13		33
		3		5	6	7	8	11				8			4	10	9	1									34
	2	3^2	4	5	6	7^1		11				8	12			10	9	1	13								35
	2	3	4	5	6	7^1	8^2	11							4	10	9	1	13	12							36

QUEEN OF THE SOUTH   Second Division

Year Formed: 1919. *Ground & Address:* Palmerston Park, Dumfries DG2 9BA. *Telephone and Fax:* 01387 254853.
Ground Capacity: total: 8352. seated: 3549. *Size of Pitch:* 112yd × 73yd.
Chairman: Norman Blount. *Secretary:* Richard Shaw MBE. *Commercial Manager:* Robert McKinnel.
Co-managers: Rowan Alexander and Mark Shanks.
Managers since 1975: M. Jackson; W. Hunter; B. Little; G. Herd; H. Hood; A. Busby; R. Clark; M. Jackson; D. Wilson;
W. McLaren; F. McGarvey; A. MacLeod; D. Frye; W. McLaren. *Club Nickname(s):* The Doonhamers. *Previous
Grounds:* None.
Record Attendance: 24,500 v Hearts, Scottish Cup 3rd rd; 23 Feb, 1952.
Record Transfer Fee received: £250,000 for Andy Thomson to Southend U (1994).
Record Transfer Fee paid: £30,000 for Jim Butter from Alloa Athletic (1995).
Record Victory: 11-1 v Stranraer, Scottish Cup 1st rd; 16 Jan, 1932.
Record Defeat: 2-10 v Dundee, Division I; 1 Dec, 1962.
Most Capped Player: Billy Houliston, 3, Scotland.
Most League Appearances: 731: Allan Ball, 1963–82.
Most League Goals in Season (Individual): 37: Jimmy Gray, Division II; 1927-28.
Most Goals in Season: 41: Jimmy Rutherford, 1931–32.
Most Goals Overall (Individual): 250: Jim Patterson, 1949–63.

QUEEN OF THE SOUTH 1996–97 LEAGUE RECORD

Match No.	Date		Venue	Opponents	Result		H/T Score	Lg. Pos.	Goalscorers	Attendance
1	Aug	17	A	Livingston	L	1-3	0-3	—	Flannigan [85]	1453
2		24	H	Dumbarton	W	2-1	0-0	4	Mallan [60], Flannigan [83]	1127
3		31	A	Clyde	W	2-0	0-0	2	Townsley [64], Bryce [88]	951
4	Sept	7	A	Berwick R	D	2-2	1-1	4	Mallan [35], Lilley [59]	432
5		14	H	Stenhousemuir	W	1-0	0-0	3	Flannigan [88]	1123
6		21	H	Ayr U	L	1-2	0-1	4	Flannigan (pen) [60]	1813
7		28	A	Hamilton A	D	2-2	1-0	4	Mallan [23], Flannigan (pen) [70]	705
8	Oct	5	A	Stranraer	L	1-2	0-0	4	Alexander [78]	713
9		12	H	Brechin C	L	1-5	1-3	5	Bryce [1]	893
10		19	H	Livingston	D	2-2	1-1	6	Mallan [23], Flannigan [83]	1158
11		26	A	Dumbarton	W	2-1	0-1	6	McFarlane [68], Mallan [77]	562
12	Nov	2	A	Stenhousemuir	L	1-2	1-0	6	Nesovic [9]	486
13		9	H	Berwick R	W	2-1	1-0	4	Mallan [35], Nesovic [88]	946
14		16	H	Hamilton A	D	1-1	0-0	5	Mallan [48]	1304
15		23	A	Ayr U	L	0-1	0-1	5		1969
16		30	H	Stranraer	W	3-2	1-1	5	Rowe 3 [6, 60, 88]	1284
17	Dec	14	A	Brechin C	D	3-3	2-2	5	Flannigan [12], Mallan [24], Rowe [68]	328
18		21	A	Livingston	L	1-2	1-2	6	Flannigan [44]	2178
19	Jan	15	H	Clyde	L	0-2	0-1	—		1117
20		18	A	Stranraer	L	1-3	1-1	6	Mallan [6]	564
21		22	A	Hamilton A	L	1-4	0-1	—	Alexander [88]	554
22	Feb	1	H	Brechin C	W	2-1	0-1	6	Nesovic [74], Bryce [88]	819
23		5	H	Ayr U	L	1-3	0-0	—	Nesovic [84]	1506
24		8	H	Stenhousemuir	L	2-3	2-1	7	Townsley [8], Flannigan [38]	1011
25		15	A	Berwick R	D	1-1	0-0	7	Flannigan [46]	381
26		22	H	Dumbarton	W	4-0	0-0	6	Bryce 4 [54, 74, 76, 77]	908
27	Mar	8	A	Ayr U	D	2-2	1-2	6	Thomson [42], Flannigan [72]	1942
28		11	A	Clyde	L	1-2	0-0	—	Bryce [83]	574
29		15	H	Hamilton A	W	1-0	0-0	7	Bryce [68]	1318
30		22	H	Stranraer	D	1-1	1-0	6	Rowe [30]	1176
31	Apr	5	A	Brechin C	W	1-0	1-0	6	McKeown B [23]	388
32		12	H	Berwick R	W	2-0	1-0	6	Bryce 2 [41, 83]	1019
33		19	A	Stenhousemuir	W	3-0	0-0	5	Bryce [55], Nesovic [68], Mallan [75]	476
34		26	H	Livingston	L	1-2	0-0	5	Leslie (pen) [56]	1511
35	May	3	A	Dumbarton	W	3-0	1-0	5	Mallan 3 [23, 73, 90]	643
36		10	H	Clyde	L	0-1	0-0	5		1819

Final League Position: 5

Rothmans Football Yearbook 1997–98

Honours

League Champions: Division II 1950-51; *Runners-up:* Division II 1932-33, 1961-62, 1974-75. Second Division 1980-81, 1985-86.
Scottish Cup: semi-finalists 1949–50.
League Cup: semi-finalists 1950–51, 1960–61.
B&Q Cup: semi-finalists 1991–92.
Club colours: Shirt: Royal blue. Shorts: White. Stockings: Royal blue with white tops.

Goalscorers: *League (55):* Mallan 13, Bryce 12, Flannigan 11 (2 pens), Nesovic 5, Rowe 5, Alexander 2, Townsley 2, Leslie 1 (pen), Lilley 1, McFarlane 1, McKeown B 1, Thomson 1. *Scottish Cup (4):* Brown 1, Leslie 1, Mallan 1, Nesovic 1. *Coca Cola Cup (0). League Challenge Cup (4):* Flannigan 2, Mallan 1 (pen), Nesovic 1.

Mathieson D 36	Kennedy D 20+1	McKeown D 27+2	Cochrane G 7+2	Lilley D 20+2	McKeown B 26	Wilson S 1	Bryce T 34+1	Mallan S 28+6	Flannigan C 26+2	Brown J 15	Laing D 5+4	MacLean J 2+5	Rowe G 25+1	Leslie S 17+3	Alexander R 5+6	Nesovic A 26+4	Lancaster I 3+3	Townsley D 29+2	McFarlane A 6	Hughes J 2+2	Irving C —+1	Brydson E —+4	Lee P —+1	McAllister J 4+2	Herriot S —+3	Aitken A 14	Thomson J 16	Doig C 2+2	Cleeland M —+1	Match No.
1	2	3^3	4^2	5	6	7^1	8	9	10	11	12	13	14																	1
1	2	3	13	5	6		8	12	10	11	7^2				4^3	9^1	14													2
1		13		5	6		8	9^2	10	3	7^1				12	2	4	11												3
1	2	3		5	6		8	9	10	11						7		4												4
1	2	3			6^1		8	9	10	11				5	12		7	4												5
1	2^2	3		5			8	9	10	11				6	12	13	7^1	4												6
1	2	3		5			8	9	10^2	11^1				6	12	13	7	4												7
1	2	3		5			8	9	10	11^2	12			6		13	7^1	4												8
1	12	3	14	5			8	9	11	7^3	6^1			2	13	10^2		4												9
1	2	3			6		8	9	10					5	4			11	7											10
1	2	3					8	9	10^1					5	4	6		11	7	12										11
1	2	3			6		8	9						5	7^1	12	10	4	11											12
1	2	3			6		8	9						5	7	10^1		4	11					12						13
1	2^3	3			6		8	9					13	5^2		10	7	4	11^1					14	12					14
1		3	2		6		8	9	12					5		10	7^1	4				11								15
1		3	2		6		8^1	9	7					5		10	12	4				11								16
1		3	2^1		6		8	9	7					5		10	12	4				11								17
1	2	3			6		8	9	7	11				5		10		4												18
1		3	2		6^2		8	9		11^1	13			5^3	4	10	7							12	14					19
1		3	2				8^2	9	11^3			14		5^1	4	10	7	13					6	12						20
1		3	2^2				12							7^1	6	9	10	8						11	13	4	5			21
1		3			6		8	9	12	11	7^1			4	2^2	10	13										5			22
1		3			6		8	9	7	11^1	12			4		10	2										5			23
1	3^2	13			6		8	9	10	11	7^1			4			2							12			5			24
1		2			6		8	13	9					4	11	12	10^1	7^2								3	5			25
1	2				6		8		9					4	11	10	7									3	5			26
1	2^1	12			6		8	13	9	11				4	7	10^2										3	5			27
1	2				6		8	12	9^2					4	11^1	13	10	7								3	5			28
1	2	11			6		8	12	9					4		10^1	7									3	5			29
1	2	12	11		6		8	13	9					4^1		10	7^2									3	5			30
1	2	11	4		6		8	9	10							7										3	5			31
1	2^2	11	4		6^1		8	9^1	10				14	7	12											3	5	13		32
1	2	7^1	4				8	9	10^2	11	13			6												3	5	12		33
1	2	7	4				8^1	12		11	11			10												3	5			34
1	2	4					9	7^2	8	10^3			6		12	14										3	5	11^1	13	35
1	2	4					8	9	13	7			10^1	6			12									3	5	11^2		36

QUEEN'S PARK   Third Division

Year Formed: 1867. **Ground & Address:** Hampden Park, Mount Florida, Glasgow G42 9BA. **Telephone:** 0141 632 1275.
Fax: 0141 636 1612.
Ground Capacity: total: 9222 during reconstruction. **Size of Pitch:** 115yd × 75yd.
President: H. Gordon Wilson. **Secretary:** Alistair Mackay. **Physio:** R.C.Findlay. **Player/Coach:** Graeme J. Elder.
Coaches since 1975: D.McParland, J.Gilroy, E Hunter, H. McGann. **Club Nickname(s):** The Spiders. **Previous Grounds:**
1st Hampden (Recreation Ground); (Titwood Park was used as an interim measure between 1st & 2nd Hampdens); 2nd
Hampden (Cathkin); 3rd Hampden.
Record Attendance: 95,772 v Rangers, Scottish Cup, 18 Jan, 1930.
Record for Ground: 149,547 Scotland v England, 1937.
Record Transfer Fee received: Not applicable due to amateur status.
Record Transfer Fee paid: Not applicable due to amateur status.
Record Victory: 16-0 v St. Peters, Scottish Cup 1st rd; 29 Aug, 1885.
Record Defeat: 0-9 v Motherwell, Division I; 26 Apr, 1930.
Most Capped Player: Walter Arnott, 14, Scotland.
Most League Appearances: 473: J. B. McAlpine.

QUEEN'S PARK 1996–97 LEAGUE RECORD

Match No.	Date	Venue	Opponents	Result	Score	H/T Lg. Pos.	Goalscorers	Atten- dance
1	Aug 17	H	East Stirling	D	3-3	2-2	—	Graham [13], McGoldrick [43], McLauchlan [88]	470
2	24	A	Ross Co	W	2-1	1-0	4	Arbuckle [1], Maxwell [74]	1252
3	31	H	Forfar Ath	L	1-4	0-2	6	Orr [87]	590
4	Sept 7	A	Cowdenbeath	D	1-1	0-0	7	McLauchlan [83]	279
5	14	H	Montrose	L	0-2	0-1	9		404
6	21	A	Inverness CT	D	2-2	0-1	9	Caven [52], Orr [81]	1452
7	28	H	Albion R	D	1-1	1-0	8	Falconer [18]	616
8	Oct 5	H	Alloa	W	2-1	2-1	6	Kennedy 2 [22, 23]	647
9	12	A	Arbroath	L	0-1	0-0	8		433
10	19	A	East Stirling	L	1-2	1-1	9	McGoldrick [11]	369
11	26	H	Ross Co	L	0-3	0-1	9		607
12	Nov 2	A	Montrose	L	2-3	1-0	9	Hardie [39], Falconer [87]	519
13	9	H	Cowdenbeath	W	1-0	1-0	8	Fitzpatrick [8]	543
14	16	A	Albion R	D	1-1	0-1	8	McLauchlan [76]	736
15	23	A	Inverness CT	L	2-3	1-3	8	Maxwell [45], McLauchlan [60]	786
16	30	A	Alloa	L	1-2	0-0	8	Hardie [52]	449
17	Dec 14	H	Arbroath	W	3-1	3-0	8	Kennedy [13], Maxwell [19], McLauchlan [32]	403
18	21	H	East Stirling	W	3-0	1-0	8	Ferry 2 [20, 61], Hardie [82]	404
19	Jan 11	A	Forfar Ath	D	2-2	1-1	8	Ferry [38], Caven [56]	423
20	18	A	Alloa	L	1-3	1-1	8	McGoldrick [42]	408
21	22	A	Inverness CT	L	0-1	0-0	—		1432
22	28	H	Albion R	D	0-0	0-0	—		432
23	Feb 1	A	Arbroath	D	0-0	0-0	8		326
24	8	H	Montrose	L	0-1	0-0	8		408
25	15	A	Cowdenbeath	W	4-1	2-0	8	Edgar [30], Graham [39], McGoldrick [55], Ferry [57]	244
26	Mar 1	H	Forfar Ath	W	4-0	3-0	7	Ferry 2 [1, 82], Hardie [6], Maxwell [17]	466
27	4	A	Ross Co	L	0-2	0-1	—		1014
28	8	H	Inverness CT	L	1-2	0-0	7	Edgar [71]	857
29	15	A	Albion R	L	1-2	0-1	8	Kennedy [59]	547
30	22	H	Alloa	L	0-4	0-0	8		399
31	Apr 5	H	Arbroath	W	3-1	1-0	7	Ferry [39], Graham [46], McGoldrick [82]	387
32	12	H	Cowdenbeath	W	2-1	1-0	7	Edgar [23], Maxwell [84]	402
33	19	A	Montrose	D	1-1	0-0	7	Kennedy [81]	388
34	26	A	East Stirling	L	0-1	0-0	8		318
35	May 3	H	Ross Co	L	1-2	1-0	8	Kennedy [5]	856
36	10	A	Forfar Ath	L	0-4	0-2	8		1195

Final League Position: 8

Most League Goals in Season (Individual): 30: William Martin, Division I; 1937-38.
Most Goals Overall (Individual): 163: J. B. McAlpine.

Honours
League Champions: Division II 1922-23. B Division 1955-56. Second Division 1980-81.
Scottish Cup Winners: 1874, 1875, 1876, 1880, 1881, 1882, 1884, 1886, 1890, 1893; *Runners-up:* 1892, 1900.
League Cup: —.
FA Cup runners-up: 1884, 1885.
Club colours: Shirt: White and black hoops. Shorts: White. Stockings: White with black hoops.

Goalscorers: *League (46):* Ferry 7, Kennedy 6, McGoldrick 5, McLauchlan 5, Maxwell 5, Hardie 4, Edgar 3, Graham 3, Caven 2, Falconer 2, Orr 2, Arbuckle 1, Fitzpatrick 1. *Scottish Cup (3):* Caven 1, Falconer 1, own goal 1. *Coca Cola Cup (3):* Falconer 1, McGoldrick 1, Maxwell 1. *League Challenge Cup (1):* Falconer 1.

Bruce G 31	Wilson D 18+6	Graham D 29	Elder G 24	Caven R 27+2	Maxwell M 33	McLauchlan M 21+8	Arbuckle D 31	Edgar S 16	Orr G 9+1	McGoldrick K 31	Cameron C —+3	Falconer M 8+14	Kennedy K 19+9	Ferry D 21+11	Smith D —+8	King D 9+3	Hardie M 14+9	Smith M 12+6	Callan D 1+1	Fraser R 7+1	Smith J 7+2	Fitzpatrick I 14+2	Reilly R —+1	Ferguson P 9	Starr S 5	Match No.
1	2^2	3^3	4	5	6	7	8	9^1	10	11	12	13	14													1
1	2	3	4	5	6	7^2	8	9^3	10^1	11		13	12	14												2
1	2	3	4	5	6	7^1	8	9^2	10^3	11		14	12	13												3
1	12			5	6	7	3	9	2^1	11		13	8	10^2	4											4
1	2	3	4	5	6	7		9^2		11		10	8^1	13	12											5
1	2	11	4	5	6	13			10^2	3		9^3	12	14		7	8^1									6
1	2	11	4	5	6	14			10	3	13	9^3				8^1	7^2	12								7
1	2		4^1	5	6	14	11^3		10	3		9^2	8	13		12	7									8
1	2		4	5						11	10^1	3	12	9^2	8		6			7		13				9
1	2		4	5					10^2	3	12	11	9^1	8^2	14		6	13		7						10
1	11		4	5		13	8		10^1	3^2		9	12			6	2^3	7				14				11
1	2	3		5	6	7	4			11			12	10^1			8				13	9^2				12
1	2	3^2		5	6	7	8			11			12	10^3			13	14			4	9^1				13
1	2	3	4	5	6	7	8			11			12	13	10^1							9^2				14
1	2^2	3	4	5	6	7	8			11			12	13	10							9^1				15
1	2	3	4	5	6	7^3	8			11			13	14	10	12						9^2				16
1			4^2	5	6	7	3			11	12	2	10	13				8				9^1				17
1			4	5		7	3^1			11	13	2	10	14		6	12				8^3	9^2				18
1	11		4	5		7	3			11	12	2	10			6	13				8^2	9^1				19
1		3	4	5	6	7^2				11			10	13		12	2	8				9^1				20
1	12	2^1	4	5		7^2	3			11			10			6	13	8				9^1	14			21
1		3	4	5	6	7				11		2	10	12		13					8^2	9^1				22
1		3	4	5	6	7		9		11		2^2	10	13		12					8^1					23
1	2		4		6	7^1	3	9		11	12		10	8							5					24
1	13	3	4	5	6	10^1	8	9		11		2^2		12		7										25
1	14	3		5	6		8	9^2		11		2	10^3			7^1	12				4	13				26
1	12	3^1			6		8	9		11		2	10			7					5		4			27
1	12	3			6		8	9		11		2^1	10			7^2	13				5		4			28
1	2	3		13	6		8	9		11		12	10^1			7^2	14				5		4			29
1	2	7			6	12	8	9^2	3	4		13						11^1			5			10		30
1	7	2			6		8^1	9	3	11		13	12	10^2		5								4		31
		3	4	5		13	8	9		11^1			12	10^2						2	7			6	1	32
		3^2	4	5		13	8			11^1		14	12	10						2	7	9^2		6	1	33
		6		7	8			9^1		11		13	14	10^2						2^3	7	12			1	34
	2	3	4	5^1		13	8			10		14		6			12				7^3	9^2	11		1	35
	2^2	3	4	5		13	8			10		6	12	7							9		11^1		1	36

RAITH ROVERS   First Division

Year Formed: 1883. *Ground & Address:* Stark's Park, Pratt St, Kirkcaldy KY1 1SA. *Telephone:* 01592 263514. *Fax:* 01592 642833.
Ground Capacity: total: 10,721 (all seated). *Size of Pitch:* 113yd × 70yd.
Chairman: Alan Kelly. *General Manager:* W.McPhee.
Manager: Jimmy Nicholl. *Assistant Manager:* Alex Smith. *Physio:* John McCreadie. *Coach:* Andy Harrow.
Managers since 1975: R. Paton; A. Matthew; W. McLean; G. Wallace; R. Wilson; F. Connor; J. Nicholl; J. Thomson; T. McLean; I. Munro. *Club Nickname:* Rovers. *Previous Grounds:* Robbie's Park.
Record Attendance: 31,306 v Hearts, Scottish Cup 2nd rd; 7 Feb, 1953.
Record Transfer Fee received: £900,000 for S. McAnespie to Bolton Wanderers (Sept 1995).
Record Transfer Fee paid: £225,000 for Paul Harvey from Airdrieonians (1996).
Record Victory: 10-1 v Coldstream, Scottish Cup 2nd rd; 13 Feb, 1954.
Record Defeat: 2-11 v Morton, Division II; 18 Mar, 1936.
Most Capped Player: David Morris, 6, Scotland.
Most League Appearances: 430: Willie McNaught.
Most League Goals in Season (Individual): 38: Norman Haywood, Division II; 1937-38.
Most Goals Overall (Individual): 154: Gordon Dalziel (League), 1987-94.

RAITH ROVERS 1996–97 LEAGUE RECORD

Match No.	Date	Venue	Opponents	Result	H/T Score	Lg. Pos.	Goalscorers	Attendance
1	Aug 10	A	Rangers	L	0-1	0-1	—	46,221
2	17	A	Celtic	L	1-4	0-2	10	Duffield [67]	46,795
3	24	H	Motherwell	L	0-3	0-2	10		4837
4	Sept 7	H	Aberdeen	L	1-4	1-3	10	Bonar [3]	4729
5	14	A	Hibernian	L	0-1	0-0	10		8260
6	21	H	Dundee U	W	3-2	1-2	9	Taylor 2 [5, 60], Twaddle [86]	5068
7	28	A	Dunfermline Ath	L	1-3	0-1	10	Twaddle [47]	8634
8	Oct 12	H	Hearts	D	1-1	0-1	10	Thomson SM [70]	6037
9	19	A	Kilmarnock	L	1-2	1-1	10	Rougier [3]	5829
10	26	A	Aberdeen	L	0-1	0-0	10		11,246
11	Nov 2	H	Rangers	D	2-2	1-0	10	Twaddle [27], Thomson SM [78]	9722
12	16	H	Dunfermline Ath	L	1-2	0-2	10	Duffield [84]	6762
13	23	A	Dundee U	W	2-1	1-0	10	Bergersen [24], Kirk [52]	8028
14	30	H	Kilmarnock	W	1-0	0-0	10	Lennon [90]	3750
15	Dec 7	A	Hearts	D	0-0	0-0	9		10,719
16	11	A	Motherwell	W	1-0	0-0	—	Lennon [87]	4040
17	21	H	Hibernian	L	0-3	0-0	10		4229
18	26	A	Rangers	L	0-4	0-2	—		48,322
19	28	H	Dundee U	L	0-1	0-1	10		5767
20	Jan 1	A	Dunfermline Ath	L	0-2	0-0	—		7236
21	4	H	Hearts	L	1-2	1-1	10	Lennon [1]	6460
22	11	A	Kilmarnock	W	1-0	1-0	10	Twaddle [31]	5505
23	14	H	Celtic	L	1-2	1-0	—	Andersen S [16]	8544
24	18	A	Aberdeen	D	2-2	1-1	10	Andersen S [15], Lennon [85]	3950
25	Feb 1	A	Hibernian	D	1-1	0-1	10	Lennon [69]	9365
26	6	A	Celtic	L	0-2	0-0	—		44,770
27	18	H	Motherwell	L	1-5	0-2	—	Duffield [79]	3052
28	22	A	Hearts	L	2-3	2-3	10	Craig [5], Makela [40]	10,341
29	Mar 5	A	Kilmarnock	W	2-1	1-0	—	Andersen S [13], Kirkwood [60]	3306
30	15	H	Dunfermline Ath	L	0-1	0-1	10		5882
31	22	A	Dundee U	L	1-2	0-0	10	Duffield [83]	8367
32	Apr 5	H	Celtic	D	1-1	0-0	10	Craig [90]	7914
33	12	A	Motherwell	L	0-5	0-1	10		4691
34	15	H	Rangers	L	0-6	0-4	10		9745
35	May 3	A	Aberdeen	L	0-2	0-2	10		10,763
36	10	H	Hibernian	D	1-1	1-1	10	Duffield [7]	6274

Final League Position: 10

Honours
League Champions: First Division: 1992-93, 1994-95. Division II 1907-08, 1909-10 (shared), 1937-38, 1948-49; *Runners-up:* Division II 1908-09, 1926-27, 1966-67. Second Division 1975-76, 1977-78, 1986-87.
Scottish Cup Runners-up: 1913. *League Cup Winners: (Coca-Cola Cup):* 1994-95. *Runners-up:* 1948-49.
Club colours: Shirt: Navy blue, white trim. Shorts: White. Stockings: White.

European: *UEFA Cup* 6 matches 1995-96

Goalscorers: *League (29):* Duffield 5, Lennon 5, Twaddle 4, Andersen S 3, Craig 2, Taylor 2, Thomson SM 2, Bergersen 1, Bonar 1, Kirk 1, Kirkwood 1, Makela 1, Rougier 1. *Scottish Cup (6):* Andersen S 2, Craig 1, Kirk 1, Kirkwood 1, Rougier 1. *Coca Cola Cup (2):* Rougier 2.

Thomson SY 28	Kirkwood D 13+4	Bonar P 9+7	Browne P 4	Dennis S 16	Craig D 28	Thomson SM 18+4	McInally J 4	Rougier A 27+3	Lennon D 35	Harvey P 10+8	Twaddle K 23+5	Dargo C 1+4	Millar J 25+2	Duffield P 23+10	Krivokapic M 6	Kirk S 18+7	McCulloch G 3+3	Geddes R 3	Taylor A 14+4	Mitchell G 20	Scott C 5	Lorimer D 1+2	Andersen V 18+1	Bergersen K 6	Skonhoff O 1	McGill D 3+6	Millen A 13	Andersen S 7	Hallum C 6	Makela J 8	Stein J —+2	Match No.
1	2	3	4	5	6	7	8	9²	10	11¹	12	13																				1
1	2²	3	4	5	6	7¹	8	9³	10	14	13		11	12																		2
1		3	6	5		12	2	7	10	8¹	11		4	9																		3
1	8²	3	6¹	5		7	2	11	10				12	9³	4	14	13															4
	3²			5	6¹	7³		11	10	14	13		12	9	4	8	2	1														5
	6¹	3		5				11	10		12		8	9	4	2		1	7													6
	3²			5		12		11	10¹	13	6²		8	9	4	2	14	1	7													7
1	13			5	9			11²		8	12		3	10¹	4	2			7	6												8
	14			5	9³			11	10¹	8	7		3	12	4²	13			2	6	1											9
	3²			5	13			11	10	8³	7		4	9		12			2¹	6	1	14										10
	13			5	8			9	10		7¹		3	12					2	6	1		4²	11								11
1				5	2	9		7	10				3	12						6			4	11	8¹							12
1	13			5	9				10		7		3	8¹					2	6	12		4	11²								13
1				5	9			7	10				3	8¹					2	6			4	11			12					14
1				5	9				10	13	7		3	8²					2	6	12		4	11¹								15
1				5	9				10		7		3	8					2¹	6	12		4	11								16
1				5	9				10		7¹		3	8					2	6	12	11²	4				13					17
1				5	3	9²		11	10		7			12					2	6	8		4¹				13					18
1				5	3	9		11	10		7¹			8					2	6			4				12					19
1				5	3	8		12	10	14	11		13						2	6	7¹		4²				9³					20
	12			5	6	7		11	10	13			3	8					2			1	4¹				9²					21
				5	13			11	10		7²		3	14					2¹		12	1	4					6	8	9³		22
1				5	11				10		7		3						2				4					6	8	9		23
1	13			5				11¹	10		7²		3	12					2				4					6	8	9		24
1	2			5				11	10		7¹		3	12									4			13		6	8	9²		25
1				5				11	10		7		3	12	2								4			13		6	8¹	9²		26
1	12	13		5				11	10		7²		3	8					2¹		14		4					6		9³		27
1	9²	12		5				13	10		7		3	8					2¹									6	11	4		28
1	9			5				12	10		7		3	8					2²				13					6	11¹	4		29
1	9¹			5					10	11	7		3	8		12				4								6		2		30
1	9			5				11	10	4	7		3	8		12				6										2¹		31
1	9			5				11	10	4	7¹			8		12	3			6										2		32
1	9	13		5				11	10		7²			8		12	3¹			6			4							2		33
1	12	3		5				9	10	8³	13					2				6			11¹					4		7²	14	34
1	3			5					10	12	7²	13		8		11				6						9¹		4		2		35
1	3²			5					10	13	7³	12	11			8	9¹	2		6								4		14		36

RANGERS
Premier Division

Year Formed: 1873. *Ground & Address:* Ibrox Stadium, Edminston Drive, Glasgow G51 2XD. *Telephone:* 0141 427 8500. *Fax:* 0141 427 2676.
Ground Capacity: total: 50,500. *Size of Pitch:* 115yd × 78yd.
Chairman: David Murray. *Secretary:* R. C. Ogilvie. *Commercial Manager:* Bob Reilly.
Manager: Walter Smith, OBE. *Assistant Manager:* Archie Knox. *Physio:* Grant Downie. *Coach:* Tommy Moller Nielsen.
Reserve team coaches: John McGregor, John Brown.
Managers since 1975: Jock Wallace; John Greig; Jock Wallace; Graeme Souness. *Club Nickname(s):* The Gers. *Previous Grounds:* Burnbank, Kinning Park.
Record Attendance: 118,567 v Celtic, Division I; 2 Jan, 1939.
Record Transfer Fee received: £5,580,000 for Trevor Steven to Marseille (Aug 1991).
Record Transfer Fee paid: £4.3 million for Paul Gascoigne from Lazio (July 1995).
Record Victory: 14-2 v Blairgowrie, Scottish Cup 1st rd; 20 Jan, 1934.
Record Defeat: 2-10 v Airdrieonians; 1886.
Most Capped Player: Ally McCoist, 58, Scotland.
Most League Appearances: 496: John Greig, 1962-78.
Most League Goals in Season (Individual): 44: Sam English, Division I; 1931–32.
Most Goals Overall (Individual): 244: Ally McCoist; 1985–97.

RANGERS 1996–97 LEAGUE RECORD

Match No.	Date	Venue	Opponents	Result		H/T Score	Lg. Pos.	Goalscorers	Attendance
1	Aug 10	H	Raith R	W	1-0	1-0	—	Steven [24]	46,221
2	17	A	Dunfermline Ath	W	5-2	1-0	1	Van Vossen 2 [17, 87], McCoist 3 (1 pen) [46 (p), 80, 83]	16,782
3	24	H	Dundee U	W	1-0	0-0	1	Gascoigne [76]	48,285
4	Sept 7	A	Motherwell	W	1-0	1-0	1	Gough [39]	12,288
5	14	H	Hearts	W	3-0	1-0	1	Durie [40], Gascoigne [48], McCoist [81]	47,240
6	21	A	Kilmarnock	W	4-1	0-1	1	Gascoigne 2 (1 pen) [68 (p), 76], Van Vossen 2 [84, 86]	14,812
7	28	H	Celtic	W	2-0	0-0	1	Gough [51], Gascoigne [89]	50,124
8	Oct 12	A	Hibernian	L	1-2	1-0	1	Albertz [9]	12,436
9	19	H	Aberdeen	D	2-2	2-1	1	Gascoigne [28], Laudrup (pen) [37]	50,076
10	26	H	Motherwell	W	5-0	0-0	1	Laudrup 2 [50, 77], Gascoigne 3 [65, 79, 83]	48,160
11	Nov 2	A	Raith R	D	2-2	0-1	2	Van Vossen [58], McCoist [65]	9722
12	14	A	Celtic	W	1-0	1-0	—	Laudrup [7]	50,009
13	Dec 1	A	Aberdeen	W	3-0	1-0	—	Robertson [38], Laudrup [78], Miller [86]	19,168
14	7	H	Hibernian	W	4-3	1-2	1	Ferguson [34], McCoist 2 [71, 74], Laudrup [83]	48,053
15	10	A	Dundee U	L	0-1	0-0	—		12,417
16	14	H	Dunfermline Ath	W	3-1	1-0	1	McCoist [5], Gough [80], Andersen [82]	45,878
17	17	H	Kilmarnock	W	4-2	1-1	—	Andersen 3 [20, 50, 70], Robertson [60]	39,469
18	21	A	Hearts	W	4-1	1-0	1	Robertson [23], Laudrup [48], Albertz (pen) [67], Gascoigne [84]	15,139
19	26	H	Raith R	W	4-0	2-0	—	Gough [29], Gascoigne [36], Albertz [47], McCoist [80]	48,322
20	Jan 2	H	Celtic	W	3-1	1-0	—	Albertz [11], Andersen 2 [83, 89]	50,019
21	4	A	Hibernian	W	2-1	1-1	1	Andersen [11], Albertz (pen) [72]	12,650
22	12	A	Aberdeen	W	4-0	2-0	—	Andersen 2 [20, 34], Albertz (pen) [59], Laudrup [85]	47,509
23	15	A	Kilmarnock	D	1-1	0-0	—	Gascoigne [77]	15,662
24	18	A	Motherwell	W	3-1	1-0	1	Albertz [20], Laudrup [60], Gascoigne [88]	13,166
25	Feb 1	H	Hearts	D	0-0	0-0	1		50,024
26	8	A	Dunfermline Ath	W	3-0	1-0	1	Durie [35], Albertz [64], Laudrup [70]	16,153
27	23	H	Hibernian	W	3-1	1-0	—	Gough [3], Albertz [49], Laudrup [67]	47,618
28	Mar 1	A	Aberdeen	D	2-2	1-1	1	Laudrup [5], Moore [64]	16,331
29	12	H	Dundee U	L	0-2	0-1	—		49,192
30	16	A	Celtic	W	1-0	1-0	—	Laudrup [44]	49,733
31	22	H	Kilmarnock	L	1-2	0-1	1	Durie [53]	50,036
32	Apr 5	H	Dunfermline Ath	W	4-0	2-0	1	Albertz [8], Petric [19], Laudrup [70], Hateley [80]	49,832
33	15	A	Raith R	W	6-0	4-0	—	Petric [9], Durie 2 [19, 22], Robertson [26], Laudrup [55], McCoist [80]	9745
34	May 5	A	Motherwell	L	0-2	0-1	—		50,059
35	7	A	Dundee U	W	1-0	1-0	1	Laudrup [11]	12,180
36	10	A	Hearts	L	1-3	0-0	1	McInnes [81]	13,097

Final League Position: 1

Honours

League Champions: (46 times) Division I 1890-91 (shared), 1898-99, 1899-1900, 1900-01, 1901-02, 1910-11, 1911-12, 1912-13, 1917-18, 1919-20, 1920-21, 1922-23, 1923-24, 1924-25, 1926-27, 1927-28, 1928-29, 1929-30, 1930-31, 1932-33, 1933-34, 1934-35, 1936-37, 1938-39, 1946-47, 1948-49, 1949-50, 1952-53, 1955-56, 1956-57, 1958-59, 1960-61, 1962-63, 1963-64, 1974-75. Premier Division: 1975-76, 1977-78, 1986-87, 1988-89, 1989-90, 1990-91, 1991-92, 1992-93, 1993-94, 1994-95, 1995-96, 1996–97; *Runners-up:* 23 times.
Scottish Cup Winners: (27 times) 1894, 1897, 1898, 1903, 1928, 1930, 1932, 1934, 1935, 1936, 1948, 1949, 1950, 1953, 1960, 1962, 1963, 1964, 1966, 1973, 1976, 1978, 1979, 1981, 1992, 1993, 1996; *Runners-up:* 16 times.
League Cup Winners: (20 times) 1946-47, 1948-49, 1960-61, 1961-62, 1963-64, 1964-65, 1970-71, 1975-76, 1977-78, 1978-79, 1981-82, 1983-84, 1984-85, 1986-87, 1987-88, 1988-89, 1990-91, 1992-93, 1993-94, 1996–97; *Runners-up:* 7 times.

European: *European Cup:* 87 matches (1956-57, 1957-58, 1959-60 semi-finals, 1961-62, 1963-64, 1964-65, 1975-76, 1976-77, 1978-79, 1987-88, 1989-90, 1990-91, 1991-92, 1992-93 final pool, 1993-94, 1994-95, 1995-96; 1996–97).
Cup Winners Cup Winners: 1971-72. 50 matches (1960-61 runners-up, 1962-63, 1966-67 runners-up, 1969-70, 1971-72 winners, 1973-74, 1977-78, 1979-80, 1981-82, 1983-84). *UEFA Cup:* 38 matches (*Fairs Cup:* 1967-68, 1968-69 semi-finals, 1970-71 *UEFA Cup;* 1982-83, 1984-85, 1985-86, 1986-87, 1988-89).
Club colours: Shirt: Royal blue with red and blue panels. Shorts: White with red and blue panels. Stockings: Red with black tops.

Goalscorers: *League (85):* Laudrup 16, Gascoigne 13 (1 pen), Albertz 10, McCoist 10 (1 pen), Andersen 9, Durie 5, Gough 5, Van Vossen 5, Robertson 4, Petric 2, Ferguson 1, Hateley 1, McInnes 1, Miller 1, Moore 1, Steven 1. *Scottish Cup (5):* Andersen 1, McCoist 1, Robertson 1, Rozental 1, Steven 1. *Coca Cola Cup (20):* Van Vossen 4, Albertz 3, Gascoigne 3, McCoist 3, Andersen 2, Laudrup 2, McInnes 2, Durie 1.

Goram A 25	Steven T 5 + 3	Albertz J 31 + 1	Gough R 27	Petric G 23 + 3	Bjorklund J 28	Durie G 14 + 2	McInnes D 10 + 11	McCoist A 13 + 12	McCall S 7	Laudrup B 33	Durrant I 4 + 4	Van Vossen P 6 + 8	Miller C 7 + 6	Cleland A 32	Gascoigne P 23 + 3	Ferguson J 18 + 6	Moore C 23	Andersen E 6 + 11	Boyack S — + 1	Snelders T 4	Shields G 6	Robertson D 21 + 1	Wilson S 1	McLaren A 17 + 1	Rozental S — + 1	Dibble A 7	Hateley M 4	Fitzgerald D — + 1	Wright S 1	Match No.
1	2	3	4	5	6	7¹	8³	9	10	11²	12	13	14																	1
1		3	4	5¹	6		13	9	10	11		7	8²	2	12															2
1		3	4	5	6	13	14	9²	10	11³		12	7¹	2	8															3
1		3	4	5	6	7	9		10	11				2	8															4
1		3	4	5²	6	10	9¹	14	7	11³		13		2	8	12														5
1		3	4	5¹	6	7			10²	11		12		9	8	13	2													6
1		3	4	5	6				10	11		9		7	8	12	2¹													7
1		3	4	5²	6	13				11		9¹		7	8	10³	2	12	14											8
	3	4		6		12			11	14	7²	9¹	10	8	13³	5				1	2									9
	10	4	5	6		7	13		11²				3	8		2¹	9			1		12								10
	10	4	5	6			9			7	11¹		2	8			12			1		3								11
	10	4	5	6		9¹			11		12		2	8	7							3								12
1	10¹	4	5	6²			9		11³			13		8	12	7	14				2	3								13
1	13	4				7	9		11²					8	10	6	12				2¹	3	5							14
1	12	4	5			7¹	9²		11				2	8	10	6	13					3								15
1	7	12	4	5			9²		11				2	8	10	6¹	13					3								16
1	7¹	10	4	14		12	13		11²				2	8	6		9					3	5²							17
1	7¹	10²	4			13	12		11				2	8	6		9					3	5							18
1		10	4			12	9		11²			7	2	8¹	6		13					3	5							19
1		10		4	6		9³					13	12	2	8¹	11	7²	14				3	5							20
	10		5			7	13		11²			12	2	8	6	9				1	4¹	3								21
1	10	4	12	6		7			11				2	8¹			9					3	5							22
1	10	4	5²	6			9		11		12		2	8	7	3¹							13							23
1	10	4				12			11				2	8	7	6¹	9²					3		5	13					24
1		4		6	7	8²	9¹		11		13		2		10		12					3		5						25
1	10	4		6	7				11				2	8	9							3		5						26
1	7¹	10	4		6	9²	12		11				2	8		13						3		5						27
1		10¹		4²	6	9		13	11				2	8	7	12						3		5						28
1	12	10²		4¹	6	7		13	11			9	2	8	3									5						29
		3	4¹		6			13	11	9²		12	2		8	7								5		1	10			30
	10²		14	6	7³		12		11	9		8¹	2			4			3				5		1		13		31
	8		4	6	9			11¹	12			2			7						3		5		1	10				32
	8¹		4	6	9		14	11³				2	13	12	7						3		5		1	10			33
	8²	4		6	9³		14	11	13			2	12		7¹						3		5		1	10			34
			4	6	9	13	12	11¹				10	2	8²	7						3		5		1				35
	3		5	6	12	13	9¹			11²	10³	14		8	7					2				1			4		36

ROSS COUNTY   Third Division

Year Formed: 1929. *Ground & Address:* Victoria Park, Dingwall IV15 9QW. *Telephone:* 01349 862253. *Fax:* 01349 866277.
Ground Capacity: total 5400, seated 1520. *Size of Ground:* 110×75yd.
Secretary: Donald MacBean. *Office Secretary:* Mrs Cathie Caird. *Commercial Manager:* Brian Campbell.
Manager: Neale Cooper. *Assistant Manager:* Jim Kelly. *Physio:* Douglas Sim. *Record Attendance:* 8000, v Rangers, Scottish Cup, 28 February 1966.
Record Transfer Fee Received: £40,000 for Barry Wilson to Raith R, Sept.1994.
Record Transfer Fee Paid: £25,000 for Barry Wilson from Southampton, Oct.1992.
Record Victory: 11-0 v St Cuthbert Wanderers, Scottish Cup, Dec.1993.
Record Defeat: 1-10 v Inverness Thistle, Highland League.
Most League Appearances: 104: K. Ferries, 1994–97.
Most League Goals in Season: 22: D. Adams, 1996–97.
Most League Goals (Overall): 23: B. Grant, 1994–97.
Club Colours: Shirt: Dark Blue with White trim. Shorts: White. Stockings: Red.

ROSS COUNTY 1996–97 LEAGUE RECORD

Match No.	Date	Venue	Opponents	Result		H/T Score	Lg. Pos.	Goalscorers	Atten- dance
1	Aug 17	A	Arbroath	L	1-3	1-2	—	MacLeod Andy [26]	494
2	24	H	Queen's Park	L	1-2	0-1	9	Golabek [71]	1252
3	31	A	Montrose	L	1-2	0-2	10	MacLeod Andy [47]	532
4	Sept 7	H	Alloa	L	1-2	0-1	10	Ross [47]	1192
5	14	A	Forfar Ath	W	2-0	0-0	10	Connelly [59], Ross [86]	425
6	21	A	Cowdenbeath	W	1-0	0-0	8	Adams (pen) [88]	308
7	28	H	Inverness CT	L	1-3	0-1	9	Adams [62]	3519
8	Oct 5	A	East Stirling	W	1-0	0-0	7	Ross [48]	398
9	12	H	Albion R	W	3-2	1-2	6	Adams 2 [9, 89], Herd [70]	1145
10	19	A	Arbroath	W	2-0	0-0	6	Ross [46], Farrell [90]	1326
11	26	A	Queen's Park	W	3-0	1-0	3	MacLeod Andy [28], Adams 2 (1 pen) [51 (p), 59]	607
12	Nov 2	H	Forfar Ath	D	1-1	1-1	4	Adams [2]	1669
13	9	A	Alloa	W	3-1	1-1	4	Adams 2 [45, 49], Ross [86]	615
14	16	A	Inverness CT	L	0-2	0-0	5		4562
15	23	H	Cowdenbeath	W	1-0	1-0	2	Adams (pen) [21]	1382
16	30	H	East Stirling	D	1-1	0-0	3	Adams [70]	1261
17	Dec 7	H	Montrose	D	4-4	2-2	3	Ferguson [6], McBain 2 [40, 66], Clark [69]	1346
18	21	A	Albion R	W	2-0	1-0	2	Farrell [34], MacLeod Andy [68]	406
19	26	A	Arbroath	L	1-2	0-0	—	MacLeod Andy (pen) [70]	581
20	Jan 18	A	East Stirling	W	3-2	2-2	2	Ferguson 2 [3, 29], Adams [65]	343
21	28	A	Cowdenbeath	D	1-1	0-0	—	Ross [54]	169
22	Feb 1	H	Albion R	W	3-1	1-1	3	Ross 2 [3, 58], Adams [85]	1136
23	8	A	Forfar Ath	W	1-0	0-0	2	Hart [90]	571
24	12	H	Inverness CT	L	0-3	0-2	—		4482
25	15	H	Alloa	W	3-1	1-0	2	McBain [4], Adams 2 [50, 55]	1546
26	Mar 4	H	Queen's Park	W	2-0	1-0	—	Ferries [32], McBain [50]	1014
27	8	A	Cowdenbeath	W	4-0	1-0	2	Ross [37], Adams 2 [57, 87], Gilbert [79]	1460
28	11	A	Montrose	D	0-0	0-0	—		412
29	15	A	Inverness CT	L	0-3	0-1	2		5525
30	22	H	East Stirling	W	1-0	1-0	2	Adams [24]	1614
31	Apr 5	A	Albion R	W	2-1	1-0	2	Wood [40], Golabek [48]	704
32	12	A	Alloa	D	1-1	0-1	3	Adams [69]	597
33	19	H	Forfar Ath	D	1-1	0-1	3	Golabek [56]	3034
34	26	H	Arbroath	W	1-0	0-0	3	Ferries [63]	1672
35	May 3	A	Queen's Park	W	2-1	0-1	3	Hewitt [81], Adams [90]	856
36	10	A	Montrose	W	3-1	0-1	3	Adams 2 [74, 76], MacLeod Andy [79]	2144

Final League Position: 3

Goalscorers: *League (58):* Adams 22 (3 pens), Ross 9, MacLeod 6, McBain 4, Ferguson 3, Golabek 3, Farrell 2, Ferries 2, Clark 1, Connelly 1, Gilbert 1, Hart 1, Herd 1, Hewitt 1, Wood 1. *Scottish Cup (3):* Ross 3. *Coca Cola Cup (1):* Adams 1. *League Challenge Cup (0).*

Hutchison S 25	Herd W 28 + 2	Braddie J 27 + 2	Watt W 1	MacLeod Alex 1	Williamson R 16 + 3	Ferries K 27 + 9	Grant B 1 + 4	MacLeod Andy 16 + 8	Mackay D 24	Golabek S 9 + 7	Milne C — + 2	Somerville C 7 + 1	Cormack D 4	Matheson D 2	Bellshaw J 27 + 3	Bradshaw P 1 + 2	Adams D 31 + 3	Connelly G 13 + 5	Cooper N 4	Fotheringham K 4 + 3	Ross A 22	Farrell G 22 + 1	McBain R 26 + 1	Furphy W 16 + 3	Ferguson S 13 + 3	Clark J 1	Hart R — + 4	Gilbert K 13	Morgan K 7	Wood G 6 + 1	Hewitt J 2 + 5	Match No.
1	2	3	4	5	6	7^2	8	9	10	11^1	12	13																				1
	6^2	3				7^3	13	10	8	12	14	2	1	4	5		9^1	11														2
	4	10				7	13	8	2	11		6^1	1	3^2	5		9	12														3
1	2^3	10			12	7		6^2	3^1	11					5		13	14	4	8	9											4
	3				4	7		12	6			2	1		5		10	8		11^1	9											5
	10^1	3				7	13	12	6		14	2	1		5^3		8		4	11^2	9											6
1		3			8	7	12	10^1	6			2			5		11		4		9											7
1	4	3				7^1		12	6			2			5		8				10	11	9									8
1	12	3			8	7		6				2^1			5		11				10^2	13	9^3	4								9
1	4	3			8^1	7		14	6						5		11	12			13	9^3	2	10^2								10
1	4	3			14	7^2		6							5		8	10			12	9	2^3	11^1	13							11
1	4	3			12	7^1		6							5		8	10			9	2	11									12
1	4	3			12			6	13						5		8	10			9	7^2	11	2^1								13
1	4	3			12	7^2		6	13						5		8	10^1			9	2	11									14
1	4	3			12	7^1		6	14						5		8	10^4				2	11	13	9^2							15
1	4	3			7	13		6	14						5		8	12				2	11^3	10^1	9^2							16
1	4	3			13			12	6								8	10				2^2	11	5	7^1	9						17
1	2	12			5	13		9	6			11^1					8	10				7^3	3	4^2		14						18
1	2	3			5^1	13		9	6						12		8	10^3				7	11^{12}	4	14							19
1	4	3				7		10	6^1						5		12				9	2^3	11	13	8							20
1	4	3^1				7		2							5		10				9	12	11	6	8							21
1	4	3			14	7		10^2	6						5		13				9	2^1	11	8^3	12							22
1	4	3				7		2							5		10				9	11^1	8	6	12							23
1	4	12			14	7		6^1									11^2				9	8	3	5	10		4	13^3				24
1		3			4	7									5		8	12			9	2	11		10			6				25
1	4	3			12	7									5		8	10			9	2	11		6^1							26
1	4	3				7									5		8	10			9	2	11		6							27
1	4	3				7									5		8	12			9	2	11	10^1	6							28
1	4	3^1			12	7									5		8				9	2	11	10	6							29
	4	3			12	7									5		8^2					2	11	10^1	6			6	1	9	13	30
	4	3			10	7		12							5		8					2	11^1	5	6			6	1	9^2	13	31
	4				10	7		3							5		8					2	11	5	6			6	1	9^1	12	32
	4				2	7		12	3						5		8					13	11^1	5	6			6	1	9	10^2	33
	4				2	7^2		12							5^1		8					11^3	10	14	6			6	1	9	13	34
	4^1				2	7		10							12		8					11^2	5	6	14		3	1		9^3	13	35
					2	7		10							5		8				9	13	4	6			3^2	1	12	11^1		36

Rothmans Football Yearbook 1997–98

ST JOHNSTONE   Premier Division

Year Formed: 1884. *Ground & Address:* McDiarmid Park, Crieff Road, Perth PH1 2SJ. *Telephone:* 01738 626961. *Fax:* 01738 625 771. *Clubcall:* 0898 121559.
Ground Capacity: total: 10,673 (all seated). *Size of Pitch:* 115yd × 75yd.
Chairman: G.S.Brown. *Secretary and Managing Director:* Stewart Duff.
Manager: Paul Sturrock. *Sales Executive:* Helen Harcus. *Physio:* David Henderson. *Coach:* John Blackley. *Youth Development Coach:* Alistair Stevenson.
Managers since 1975: J. Stewart; J. Storrie; A. Stuart; A. Rennie; I. Gibson; A. Totten, J. McClelland. *Club Nickname(s):* Saints. *Previous Grounds:* Recreation Grounds, Muirton Park.
Record Attendance: (McDiarmid Park): 10,504 v Rangers, Premier Division; 20 Oct, 1990.
Record Transfer Fee received: £750,000 for Billy Dodds to Aberdeen, 1994.
Record Transfer Fee paid: £300,000 for Billy Dodds from Dundee, 1994.
Record Victory: 9-0 v Albion R, League Cup; 9 March, 1946.
Record Defeat: 1-10 v Third Lanark, Scottish Cup; 24 January, 1903.
Most Capped Player: George O'Boyle, 10, Northern Ireland.
Most League Appearances: 298: Drew Rutherford.
Most League Goals in Season (Individual): 36: Jimmy Benson, Division II; 1931-32.
Most Goals Overall (Individual): 140: John Brogan, 1977-83.

ST JOHNSTONE 1996–97 LEAGUE RECORD

Match No.	Date	Venue	Opponents	Result		H/T Score	Lg. Pos.	Goalscorers	Attendance
1	Aug 17	H	Falkirk	D	0-0	0-0	—		4114
2	24	A	St Mirren	W	3-0	1-0	1	Scott [2], Grant 2 [59, 82]	3493
3	Sept 7	H	Partick Th	W	2-0	0-0	1	Grant [74], Tosh [90]	3707
4	14	A	East Fife	W	4-1	2-0	1	Scott [3], O'Boyle 2 (1 pen) [36 (p), 60], Grant [74]	2090
5	21	H	Clydebank	L	1-2	0-1	3	O'Neil [47]	850
6	24	H	Airdrieonians	D	1-1	0-1	—	Jenkinson [65]	2877
7	28	H	Dundee	L	0-1	0-1	3		5112
8	Oct 12	H	Greenock Morton	W	1-0	1-0	3	Scott [30]	3841
9	15	A	Stirling A	W	3-1	1-0	—	Sekerlioglu [8], Jenkinson [52], Grant (pen) [84]	1432
10	19	A	Falkirk	L	0-2	0-2	2		3208
11	26	H	St Mirren	W	4-0	0-0	2	Sekerlioglu 2 [50, 72], Grant [79], Ferguson [88]	3567
12	Nov 13	H	East Fife	W	3-0	2-0	—	Weir [4], Grant [8], O'Boyle [79]	2517
13	16	A	Dundee	W	1-0	0-0	1	O'Boyle [77]	3840
14	19	A	Partick Th	W	4-0	2-0	1	Davidson [5], Griffin [38], Grant 2 [58, 72]	2721
15	23	H	Clydebank	W	2-0	2-0	1	Grant [21], O'Boyle [39]	3760
16	30	H	Stirling A	W	5-0	2-0	1	Davidson [22], O'Boyle 2 [30, 67], Tosh [54], Grant [66]	3520
17	Dec 7	A	Greenock Morton	W	2-0	0-0	1	Sekerlioglu [75], O'Neil [86]	2993
18	18	A	Airdrieonians	W	1-0	0-0	1	Jenkinson [53]	2159
19	26	H	Falkirk	W	3-1	1-1	—	Grant [32], Weir [47], Scott [64]	6331
20	Jan 1	H	Dundee	W	7-2	1-1	1	Grant 2 [26, 51], Scott [55], Tosh [60], Jenkinson 2 [72, 79], O'Boyle [81]	7087
21	13	H	Partick Th	D	0-0	0-0	—		7910
22	18	A	Stirling A	W	4-1	2-1	1	Weir [6], O'Boyle 2 [21, 67], O'Neil [85]	1810
23	28	A	East Fife	D	2-2	2-2	—	Sekerlioglu [20], O'Boyle [31]	1431
24	Feb 1	H	Greenock Morton	W	1-0	0-0	1	Ferguson [80]	3625
25	4	A	Clydebank	D	1-1	0-0	—	McAnespie [71]	629
26	8	H	Airdrieonians	D	2-2	1-0	1	O'Boyle [37], Preston [96]	3669
27	22	A	St Mirren	L	1-2	1-2	1	McAnespie [38]	4188
28	Mar 1	H	Clydebank	W	1-0	0-0	1	Scott [60]	2688
29	15	A	Dundee	D	0-0	0-0	1		5634
30	22	H	Stirling A	D	1-1	0-0	1	Jenkinson [55]	4500
31	Apr 5	A	Greenock Morton	W	1-0	0-0	1	Grant (pen) [60]	2189
32	12	A	Partick Th	W	4-0	2-0	1	Scott 2 [24, 33], Sekerlioglu [48], Grant [68]	2824
33	19	H	East Fife	W	3-2	2-0	1	Scott 2 [12, 76], Grant [30]	6454
34	26	A	Falkirk	W	4-1	1-1	1	Scott 2 [3, 82], Grant 2 [54, 90]	3686
35	May 3	H	St Mirren	W	1-0	1-0	1	McCluskey [27]	5149
36	10	A	Airdrieonians	W	1-0	0-0	1	Colquhoun [52]	1977

Final League Position: 1

Honours
League Champions: First Division 1982–83, 1989–90, 1996–97. Division II 1923–24, 1959–60, 1962–63; *Runners-up:* Division II 1931–32. Second Division 1987–88.
Scottish Cup: Semi-finals 1934, 1968, 1989, 1991.
League Cup: Runners-up: 1969.
League Challenge Cup: Runners-up: 1996–97.

European: *UEFA Cup:* 1971–72.
Club colours: Shirt: Royal blue with white trim. Shorts: White. Stockings: Royal blue with white hoops.

Goalscorers: *League (74):* Grant 19 (2 pens), O'Boyle 12 (1 pen), Scott 12, Jenkinson 6, Sekerlioglu 6, O'Neil 3, Tosh 3, Weir 3, Davidson 2, Ferguson 2, McAnespie 2, Colquhoun 1, Griffin 1, McCluskey 1, Preston 1. *Scottish Cup (0). Coca Cola Cup (6):* Grant 2, O'Boyle 2, Scott 1. Tosh 1. *League Challenge Cup (15):* Grant 5 (1 pen), Farquhar 2, O'Boyle 2 (1 pen), O'Neil 1, Preston 1, Scott 1, Sekerlioglu 1, Whiteford 1, own goal 1.

Main A 34	McQuillan J 32	Davidson C 18 + 2	Sekerlioglu A 22 + 2	Weir J 32	McGowne K 2	Scott P 24 + 5	O'Neil J 25 + 4	Grant R 31 + 2	O'Boyle G 23 + 2	Tosh S 22 + 5	Preston A 23 + 9	Jenkinson L 22 + 3	Griffin D 26 + 3	Donaldson E 3 + 1	Farquhar G 3 + 2	McCluskey S 7 + 3	King C 2 + 2	Whiteford A 8 + 3	Fyhr P 3 + 1	Ferguson I 3 + 5	Dasovic N 14	Bowman G 4	McAnespie K 1 + 8	Colquhoun J 6	O'Halloran K 4 + 1	Robertson S 2	Brown G — + 1	Match No.
1	2	3	4	5	6	7	8	9	10	11^1	12																	1
1	2	3	4	5^1	6	7	8	9	10		12	11^1	13															2
1	2					7		9	10	8	11		6	3	4	5												3
1	2		5			7	8	9^1	10	11	3				6	4		12										4
1	2	13	5			7	8	9	10	11^1	3		12	6		4^2												5
1	2					7	8	9	10	4	3	11	6			5												6
1	2		5			7	8	9	10	4^1	3	11	6			12												7
1	2	4	5			7	8	9	10^2	14	3	11^3	6^1		12		13											8
1	2	4	5			7	8	9		12	3	11			6		10^1											9
1	2	4	5			7	8	9		12	3	11			6		10^1											10
1	2	4^3	5			8	9		7	3	11	6^1	14		12	10^2	13											11
1	2	3	4^3	5		8^2	9	12	14	13	11	6			10^1					7								12
1	2	3	4	5		13	8	9	10^2		12	11^1	6							7								13
1	2	3	4	5		12		9	10	8^1		11	6							7								14
1	2	3	4^3	5		14	13	9	10	8^2	12	11^1	6							7								15
1	2	3	4^3	5		14	13	9	10	8^2	11		6^1			12				7								16
1	2	3	4	5			12	9	10	8^1	11		6							7								17
1	2	3	4	5		7	12	9		8^1	13	11^2	6							7								18
1	2	3^1		5		10	4	9		8		11	12			6				7								19
1	2	13	5			10^2	4	9	12	8^1	3^3	11	6	14						7								20
1		12	5			4	2	9	10	8	3	11^1	6							7								21
1			4	5		11	2	9	10	8^1	3		6							12	7							22
1	2	12	4	5			8^3	9	10	11^2	3^1	13	6							14	7							23
1	2		4	5		7	9^1	10	8			6	3									13	11^1	12				24
1	2		4	5		7	13	10	8^2			3	14	6		9^3						11^1	12					25
1		3	4^3	5		7	8^1	9	10^2	14	12	6				2		13	11									26
1		3		5			8		10	9	4	11^1	6			13	2^2		7	12								27
1	2	3		5		7	8		10		4	11	6					9^1		12								28
1	2	3^1		5		7	8		10		4	11	6		5	12		9										29
1	2		4			7	8^1	9	10^2		3	11	6	12	5			13										30
1	2	3	4	5		7	8^1	9			11		6											10	12			31
1	2	3	4^1	5		7^3		9		14	12	11	6										13	10^2	8			32
1	2	3		5		7		9			4	11	6											10	8			33
	2		5			7		9		4	11		6										3	12	10^1	8^2	1	34
1	2	3	4^1	5		7		9		8^2	13	11	12	6										10				35
	2		5			12		14			11		6^1			7^3	4			9^2		3	13	10	8	1		36

ST MIRREN   First Division

Year Formed: 1877. *Ground & Address:* St Mirren Park, Love St, Paisley PA3 2EJ. *Telephone:* 0141 889 2558/0141 840 1337. *Fax:* 0141 848 6444.
Ground Capacity: total: 15,410. seated 9395. *Size of Pitch:* 112yd × 73yd.
Managing Director: John F. Paton. *Secretary:* Jack Copland.
Manager: Tony Fitzpatrick. *Physio:* Andrew Binning.
Managers since 1975: Alex Ferguson; Jim Clunie; Rikki MacFarlane; Alex Miller; Alex Smith; Tony Fitzpatrick; David Hay; Jimmy Bone. *Club Nickname(s):* The Buddies. *Previous Grounds:* Short Roods 1877-79, Thistle Park Greenhill 1879-83, Westmarch 1883-94.
Record Attendance: 47,438 v Celtic, League Cup, 20 Aug, 1949.
Record Transfer Fee received: £850,000 for Ian Ferguson to Rangers (1988).
Record Transfer Fee paid: £400,000 for Thomas Stickroth from Bayer Uerdingen (1990).
Record Victory: 15-0 v Glasgow University, Scottish Cup 1st rd; 30 Jan, 1960.
Record Defeat: 0-9 v Rangers, Division I; 4 Dec, 1897.
Most Capped Player: Godmundor Torfason, 29, Iceland.
Most League Appearances: 351: Tony Fitzpatrick, 1973-88.
Most League Goals in Season (Individual): 45: Dunky Walker, Division I; 1921-22.
Most Goals Overall (Individual): 221: David McCrae, 1923-24.

ST MIRREN 1996–97 LEAGUE RECORD

Match No.	Date	Venue	Opponents	Result	H/T Score	Lg. Pos.	Goalscorers	Atten- dance
1	Aug 17	A	East Fife	W 4-0	2-0	—	Gillies 2 [27, 69], Hetherston (pen) [34], Taylor [80]	1375
2	24	H	St Johnstone	L 0-3	0-1	6		3493
3	31	A	Partick Th	D 1-1	1-1	4	Watson [10]	3664
4	Sept 7	A	Clydebank	L 1-2	1-2	6	Fenwick [38]	1399
5	14	H	Dundee	L 0-1	0-0	8		2391
6	21	H	Falkirk	L 0-1	0-0	8		3945
7	28	A	Greenock Morton	W 3-1	2-0	7	Mendes [9], Dick [42], Hetherston [77]	5847
8	Oct 12	A	Stirling A	W 2-1	1-1	7	Gillies [20], Watson [89]	3261
9	15	A	Airdrieonians	D 2-2	0-1	—	Yardley 2 [61, 90]	1635
10	19	H	East Fife	W 4-1	2-1	5	Watson [33], Yardley 3 [45, 79, 83]	2491
11	26	A	St Johnstone	L 0-4	0-0	6		3567
12	Nov 2	A	Dundee	W 1-0	0-0	6	Yardley [77]	2731
13	9	H	Clydebank	W 1-0	0-0	4	Dick [54]	3956
14	16	H	Greenock Morton	W 1-0	0-0	2	Watson [53]	6336
15	30	A	Airdrieonians	L 2-3	0-1	6	Fenwick 2 [71, 78]	3536
16	Dec 10	A	Stirling A	D 1-1	1-0	—	Mendes [6]	1038
17	14	H	Partick Th	W 3-2	0-2	5	Yardley 2 [53, 55], Fenwick [72]	3306
18	26	A	East Fife	W 3-0	1-0	—	Gillies 3 [40, 59, 63]	1199
19	Jan 8	A	Falkirk	D 1-1	1-1	—	Yardley [14]	2382
20	14	H	Falkirk	W 1-0	1-0	—	Yardley (pen) [42]	2778
21	18	A	Airdrieonians	D 1-1	0-1	5	Mendes [60]	2216
22	28	H	Dundee	W 3-2	1-1	—	Fenwick 2 [25, 69], Turner [79]	2331
23	Feb 1	H	Stirling A	L 1-3	1-2	5	Hetherston (pen) [39]	3756
24	4	A	Greenock Morton	L 0-2	0-1	—		4156
25	8	A	Partick Th	D 0-0	0-0	5		3347
26	15	A	Clydebank	W 1-0	0-0	3	Yardley [65]	1156
27	22	H	St Johnstone	W 2-1	2-1	3	Foster [27], Turner [44]	4188
28	Mar 11	A	Falkirk	D 1-1	1-0	—	Yardley [37]	2497
29	15	H	Greenock Morton	W 3-1	1-1	4	Yardley 2 [37, 89], McGarry [51]	5024
30	22	H	Airdrieonians	L 1-2	1-1	4	Foster [21]	4648
31	Apr 5	A	Stirling A	L 0-1	0-1	4		1701
32	12	H	Clydebank	W 1-0	0-0	3	Yardley [65]	2634
33	19	A	Dundee	L 0-2	0-1	4		2462
34	26	H	East Fife	W 1-0	0-0	3	Dick [52]	1537
35	May 3	A	St Johnstone	L 0-1	0-1	4		5149
36	10	H	Partick Th	W 2-0	2-0	4	Watson (og) [11], Munro [25]	2501

Final League Position: 4

Honours
League Champions: First Division 1976-77. Division II 1967-68; *Runners-up:* 1935-36.
Scottish Cup Winners: 1926, 1959, 1987. *Runners-up* 1908, 1934, 1962.
League Cup: Runners-up 1955-56.
B&Q Cup: Runners-up 1993-94. *Victory Cup:* 1919-20. *Summer Cup:* 1943-44. *Anglo-Scottish Cup:* 1979-80.

European: *Cup Winners' Cup:* 1987-88. *UEFA Cup:* 1980-81, 1983-84, 1985-86.
Club colours: Shirt: Black and white vertical stripes. Shorts: Black. Stockings: Black with white trim. Change colours: Predominantly red.

Goalscorers: *League (48):* Yardley 15, Fenwick 6, Gillies 6, Watson 4, Dick 3, Hetherston 3 (2 pens), Mendes 3, Foster 2, Turner 2, McGarry 1, Munro 1, Taylor 1, own goal 1. *Scottish Cup (1):* Gillies 1. *Coca Cola Cup (5):* Gillies 1, Hetherston 1, Iwelumo 1, Taylor 1, Yardley 1. *League Challenge Cup (1):* Hetherston 1.

Combe A 36	Dick J 24 + 1	Baker M 31	McWhirter N 26 + 1	Fenwick P 27	Watson S 26	Hetherston B 20 + 2	Taylor S 11 + 1	Gillies R 29	Mendes J 32 + 4	Yardley M 28 + 2	McLaughlin B 27	Archdeacon P 1 + 5	Iwelumo C 2 + 12	McGarry S 5 + 6	Smith B 20 + 5	McGuire J — + 3	Munro S 25 + 1	McLaren J — + 1	Turner T 17	Foster W 8	Galloway G 1 + 1	Murray H — + 1	Fallon W — + 2	Match No.
1	2	3	4¹	5	6	7	8	9	10	11	12													1
1	2	3		5	6	7¹	8	9	10	11²	4	12	13											2
1	2	3	13	5	6	7²	8		10³	11	4		14	9¹	12									3
1	8	3	4	5	6	7²		9	10¹		2	12	11³		13	14								4
1		3	4		6	7	8		10	11	5		12	9¹	2									5
1	8	3	4		6	7		9	10	11¹	5	12			2									6
1	8¹	3	4		6	7		9	10		5	12			2		11							7
1		3	4		6	7	8²	9	10	12	5		13		2		11							8
1		3	4		6	7¹	8	9	10	12	5				2		11							9
1		3	4	5	6¹	7		9²	10	11³	12	14	13		2		8							10
1		3	4	5	6	7¹	13	9	10	11	12				2		8²							11
1	8	3	4	5		7		9	10	11	2						6							12
1	8	3	4	5		7			10	11	2			9			6							13
1	8	3	4		6			9	10	11	5				2		7							14
1	8	3	4	5	6¹	7			10	11	2			9			12							15
1	8¹	3	4	5	6		12	9	10	11					2		7							16
1	8	3	4²	5	6			9¹	10	11	2		13	12			7							17
1	8	3	4¹	5	6	7		9	10	11	2			12										18
1	8	3	4	5	6			9	10¹	11	2						7	12						19
1	8	3		5	6			9¹	12	11	4				2		7		10					20
1	8¹	3		5	6			9	12	11	4				2		7		10					21
1	8¹	3	4	5	6	7		9	10	12					2		11							22
1	12	3	4	5	6	7		9	10²	11					2	13	8¹							23
1	8¹	3	4	5	6	7²		9	12	11					2	13	10							24
1		3		5	6			9	10	11	4				2		8		7					25
1		3		5	6			9¹	10	11	4		12		2		8		7					26
1		3		5	6			9	12	11	4				2		8		7	10¹				27
1				5	6	7			10	11	4		12		2		3		8	9¹				28
1					6	7			10	11	4		12				5		8	9¹	3			29
1				5	6	7			10¹	11	4		12		2		3		8	9				30
1	2		4		6	7			10	11³	5¹		14			13	3		8	9²			12	31
1	2		4	5	6	7			10	11			12				3		8	9¹				32
1	2	3	4	5		7¹			10	11			12			13	6		8	9²				33
1	6	3	4				8¹		10²	11	5		12		2		7			9		13		34
1	6	3	4	5		7			10				13		2		11²		8	9¹			12	35
1	6	3	4	5		7			10					9¹	2		11		8				12	36

STENHOUSEMUIR   Second Division

Year Formed: 1884. *Ground & Address:* Ochilview Park, Gladstone Rd, Stenhousemuir FK5 5QL. *Telephone:* 01324 562992.
Ground Capacity: total: 3520. seated: 310. *Size of Pitch:* 113yd × 74yd.
Chairman: A Terry Bulloch. *Secretary:* David O.Reid. *Commercial Manager:* John Sharp.
Manager: Terry Christie. *Assistant Manager:* Graeme Armstrong. *Physio:* Lee Campbell. *Coach:* Gordon Buchanan.
Managers since 1975: H. Glasgow; J. Black; A. Rose; W. Henderson; A. Rennie; J. Meakin; D. Lawson. *Club Nickname(s):* The Warriors. *Previous Grounds:* Tryst Ground 1884-86, Goschen Park 1886-90.
Record Attendance: 12,500 v East Fife, Scottish Cup 4th rd; 11 Mar, 1950.
Record Transfer Fee received: £30,000 for David Beaton to Falkirk (June 1989).
Record Transfer Fee paid: £7000 to Meadowbank T for Lee Bullen (Nov 1990).
Record Victory: 9-2 v Dundee U, Division II; 19 Apr, 1937.
Record Defeat: 2-11 v Dunfermline Ath. Division II; 27 Sept, 1930.
Most Capped Player: —.
Most League Appearances: 360: Archie Rose.
Most League Goals in Season (Individual): 32: Robert Taylor, Division II; 1925-26.
Most Goals Overall (Individual): —.

STENHOUSEMUIR 1996–97 LEAGUE RECORD

Match No.	Date	Venue	Opponents	Result	H/T Score	Lg. Pos.	Goalscorers	Atten- dance
1	Aug 17	H	Brechin C	D 0-0	0-0	—		381
2	24	A	Berwick R	W 6-0	2-0	2	Little [27], Hume 2 [32, 52], Sprott [53], Hutchison 2 [57, 60]	391
3	31	H	Stranraer	L 0-1	0-0	4		510
4	Sept 7	H	Ayr U	L 1-2	0-1	6	Hunter [53]	708
5	14	A	Queen of the S	L 0-1	0-0	8		1123
6	21	H	Livingston	D 0-0	0-0	7		683
7	28	A	Dumbarton	D 1-1	0-0	7	Henderson [85]	524
8	Oct 5	H	Hamilton A	L 0-1	0-0	7		740
9	12	A	Clyde	W 4-0	3-0	7	Haddow 3 [15, 20, 35], Fisher [69]	780
10	19	A	Brechin C	D 0-0	0-0	7		354
11	26	H	Berwick R	D 1-1	0-1	7	Little [69]	423
12	Nov 2	H	Queen of the S	W 2-1	0-1	7	Hunter [73], Hutchison [85]	486
13	9	A	Ayr U	W 2-1	1-1	5	Hunter [18], Haddow [89]	2025
14	16	H	Dumbarton	L 0-1	0-0	6		564
15	Dec 7	A	Livingston	L 1-2	1-0	6	Little [32]	1500
16	10	A	Hamilton A	W 2-0	1-0	—	Little [21], Henderson [77]	520
17	21	H	Brechin C	W 3-1	1-1	5	Little [13], Hunter [46], Hutchison [79]	332
18	Jan 11	H	Livingston	L 1-3	0-2	5	Little [65]	631
19	18	A	Hamilton A	W 3-1	2-0	5	Hunter 2 [15, 30], Henderson [52]	550
20	21	A	Dumbarton	W 2-0	1-0	—	Little [20], Fisher [70]	470
21	25	A	Stranraer	D 2-2	1-2	5	Henderson [29], Hume [87]	454
22	28	H	Clyde	D 0-0	0-0	—		553
23	Feb 1	A	Clyde	L 0-3	0-1	5		709
24	8	A	Queen of the S	W 3-2	1-2	5	Haddow 2 (2 pens) [36, 73], Hunter [52]	1011
25	15	H	Ayr U	L 1-2	1-2	5	Innes [16]	833
26	22	A	Berwick R	L 0-1	0-1	5		326
27	Mar 4	H	Stranraer	W 4-0	2-0	—	Haddow 2 [1, 72], Little 2 [30, 56]	267
28	8	A	Livingston	W 3-1	2-0	5	Little 2 [34, 68], Haddow [38]	2196
29	15	H	Dumbarton	L 1-4	0-1	5	Haddow [70]	376
30	22	A	Hamilton A	D 1-1	0-0	5	Little [75]	596
31	Apr 5	H	Clyde	D 1-1	1-0	5	Roseburgh [42]	500
32	12	A	Ayr U	L 1-2	0-1	5	Roseburgh [70]	1743
33	19	H	Queen of the S	L 0-3	0-0	6		476
34	26	A	Brechin C	D 1-1	0-1	6	Little [77]	306
35	May 3	H	Berwick R	D 1-1	0-1	6	Little [47]	302
36	10	A	Stranraer	L 1-2	0-0	6	Stewart [65]	559

Final League Position: 6

Honours
League Champions: —. *Scottish Cup:* Semi-finals 1902-03. Quarter-finals 1994-95 *League Cup:* Quarter-finals 1947-48, 1960-61, 1975-76. *League Challenge Cup:* Winners 1995-96.
Club colours: Shirt: Maroon with silver stripe. Shorts: White with maroon insert. Stockings: White.

Goalscorers: *League (49):* Little 14, Haddow 10 (2 pens), Hunter 7, Henderson 4, Hutchison 4, Hume 3, Fisher 2, Roseburgh 2, Innes 1, Sprott 1, Stewart 1. *Scottish Cup (1):* Hume 1. *Coca Cola Cup (1):*Sprott 1. *League Challenge Cup (0).*

Ellison S 24	Sprott A 23+7	Banks A 16+2	Armstrong G 34	Thomson J 12+1	Henderson J 35+1	Haddow L 27+1	Fisher J 31	Hunter P 29+1	Hutchison G 29+1	Little I 35	Logan P 1+4	Roseburgh D 8+14	McGeachie G 20+5	Hume A 5+18	Stewart I 2+2	Christie M 7+1	Innes C 23+1	McKee K 13	Alexander N 12	Campbell M 7+5	Whiteford S —+1	Brown S 3	Match No.
1	2	3	4	5	6	7¹	8	9²	10	11	12	13											1
1	2¹	3	4	5		7³	8		10	11	12	14	6	9²	13								2
1	2	4²	5³	7	3	8	12	10	11	14		13	6	9¹									3
1	2	4	5	7	3	8	9	10³	11		12	13	6¹										4
1	2	4	5	7	3¹	8	9	11	10				6²			12	13						5
1	2²	3¹	4	5	7	8	9	10³	11	13	12	14	6										6
1	2¹		5	12		8	9		11		13	4	10	6	3		7²						7
1		5¹	2	12		8	9		11	14	13	4	10	6²	3		7³						8
1	2¹		4	10	3	8	9		11	12				5			6	7					9
1	2	12	4	10	3	8	9²		11				5	13			6	7¹					10
1	2	3	4	5	7¹	10	8²	9	12	11	13						6						11
1	12		4	7	3¹	8²	9	10	11	13		5					6	2					12
1			4	7	3	8	9	10¹	11	5	12						6	2					13
1			4	7¹	3	8	9	10	11	5	12						6	2					14
1	2		4	7	3	8	9²	10	11	12		5	13				6¹						15
1	2		4	6	7	3	8	9	10	11		5¹					12						16
	2		4	6	7	3	8	9	10	11		5					1						17
1	12		4	5	7	3	8	9	10	11		6¹					2						18
1	6		4	12	7	3	8	9	10	11		5¹								2			19
1	6		4		7	3	8	9	10¹	11		5								2	12		20
1	12	6	4		7	3	8	9	10	11		5²	13							2¹			21
1	12	6	4		7		8	9²	10	11		5	13							2	3¹		22
1	12	6	4		7	3	8	9	10	11		5²								2¹	13		23
1	2	6	4		7¹	3	8	9	10³	11			12					5²		13	14		24
1	2¹	6	4		7	3	8¹	9	10	11			13					5³		14			25
	2	6²	4		7	3	8	9¹	10			12	13				5	1		14	11²		26
	12	6¹	4		7	3	8	9¹	10	11			13				5	1		2			27
		6	4		7	3	8	9	10	11							5	1		2			28
		6	4		7		9	8	10	11	12	3¹					5	1		2			29
		6	4		7		9	10	11	8	3	12					5	1		2¹			30
	12	6	4		7	3	9	10	11²	8		2¹	13				5	1					31
	13	6	4		7¹	3	9²	10	11	8	12	14					5	1		2³			32
	2		4		7²	3	8	10	11	6	13	12					5	1				9¹	33
	2		4		7		10	11	3	13		9²	12	6			5	1				8¹	34
	2	3¹	4		7		10	11	8	12	13	9²	6				5	1					35
	10		4		7		8		11	3	5	9	6	2			1						36

STIRLING ALBION　　First Division

Year Formed: 1945. *Ground & Address:* Forthbank Stadium, Springkerse Industrial Estate, Stirling FK7 7UJ.
Telephone: 01786 450399. *Fax:* 01786 448592.
Ground Capacity: 3808. seated: 2508. *Size of Pitch:* 110yd × 74yd.
Chairman: Peter McKenzie. *Secretary:* Mrs Marlyn Hallam.
Manager: Kevin Drinkell. *Assistant Manager:* Ray Stewart. *Physio:* George Cameron.
Managers since 1975: A.Smith; G.Peebles; J.Fleeting, J.Brogan. *Club Nickname(s):* The Binos. *Previous Grounds:* Annfield 1945–92.
Record Attendance: 26,400 (at Annfield) v Celtic, Scottish Cup 4th rd; 14 Mar, 1959. 3808 v Aberdeen, Scottish Cup 4th rd, 15 February 1996 (Forthbank).
Record Transfer Fee received: £70,000 for John Philliben to Doncaster R (Mar 1984).
Record Transfer Fee paid: £25,000 for Craig Taggart from Falkirk (Aug 1994).
Record Victory: 20-0 v Selkirk, Scottish Cup 1st rd; 8 Dec, 1984.
Record Defeat: 0-9 v Dundee U, Division I; 30 Dec, 1967.
Most Capped Player: —.
Most League Appearances: 504: Matt McPhee, 1967-81.

STIRLING ALBION 1996–97 LEAGUE RECORD

Match No.	Date	Venue	Opponents	Result	H/T Score	Lg. Pos.	Goalscorers	Attendance
1	Aug 17	H	Airdrieonians	L	0-1	0-0	—	1598
2	24	A	Clydebank	L	0-1	0-0	10	507
3	31	H	Dundee	D	1-1	1-0	9	Wood [26]	1772
4	Sept 7	H	Falkirk	W	1-0	0-0	7	McCormick [60]	1881
5	14	A	Partick Th	D	1-1	1-0	7	McCormick [26]	2175
6	21	H	Greenock Morton	L	1-3	1-1	7	Gibson [37]	1924
7	28	A	East Fife	D	2-2	1-0	9	McCormick [43], Paterson G [82]	984
8	Oct 12	A	St Mirren	L	1-2	1-1	10	Bone (pen) [36]	3261
9	15	H	St Johnstone	L	1-3	0-1	—	Taggart [64]	1432
10	19	A	Airdrieonians	L	1-3	0-0	10	Paterson G [62]	1303
11	26	H	Clydebank	W	2-0	0-0	9	Paterson G [70], McQuilter [80]	898
12	Nov 2	H	Partick Th	L	1-2	1-2	9	Bone [25]	2189
13	9	A	Falkirk	L	2-5	1-0	9	Taggart [4], McCormick [74]	2948
14	16	H	East Fife	W	2-1	1-1	9	Bone [25], McCormick [70]	895
15	23	A	Greenock Morton	L	2-3	0-1	9	Hjarsson [51], McQuilter [68]	2204
16	30	A	St Johnstone	L	0-5	0-2	9		3520
17	Dec 10	H	St Mirren	D	1-1	0-1	—	McCormick [79]	1038
18	14	A	Dundee	D	1-1	0-0	8	Tait [89]	1828
19	21	H	Airdrieonians	L	1-2	1-2	9	Hjarsson [14]	1220
20	Jan 1	A	East Fife	W	3-1	1-1	—	McLaren [12], Bone [48], Tait [89]	588
21	4	A	Partick Th	D	1-1	1-0	9	McLaren [37]	2585
22	8	H	Greenock Morton	W	4-3	3-2	—	Reid (og) [4], Bone [42], McLaren 2 [44, 60]	1005
23	11	H	Falkirk	D	0-0	0-0	8		2087
24	18	A	St Johnstone	L	1-4	1-2	8	Bennett [7]	1810
25	Feb 1	A	St Mirren	W	3-1	2-1	8	Hjartarsson [19], Bone [25], Tait [70]	3756
26	8	H	Dundee	L	0-1	0-0	8		1425
27	22	A	Clydebank	W	2-1	1-1	8	Hjartarsson [22], Paterson A [85]	686
28	Mar 1	A	Greenock Morton	D	1-1	1-0	8	Wylie (og) [10]	1804
29	15	H	East Fife	W	4-1	2-0	8	McCormick [9], Paterson G [30], Bone [62], Bennett [64]	895
30	22	A	St Johnstone	D	1-1	0-0	8	Deas [77]	4500
31	Apr 5	H	St Mirren	W	1-0	1-0	8	Paterson A [25]	1701
32	7	A	Falkirk	D	2-2	1-0	—	Tait [20], McLaren [89]	2376
33	19	H	Partick Th	W	2-0	0-0	8	Bone [58], Bennett [64]	1281
34	26	A	Airdrieonians	W	2-1	1-1	8	McCormick [29], Bone [81]	1902
35	May 3	H	Clydebank	W	4-2	1-0	7	Tait 2 [4, 65], Irons (og) [56], Hjartarsson [66]	1109
36	10	A	Dundee	L	2-4	0-2	7	Bennett 2 (2 pens) [75, 87]	2089

Final League Position: 7

Most League Goals in Season (Individual): 27: Joe Hughes, Division II; 1969-70.
Most Goals Overall (Individual): 129: Billy Steele, 1971-83.

Honours
League Champions: Division II 1952-53, 1957-58, 1960-61, 1964-65. Second Division 1976-77, 1990-91, 1995-96; *Runners-up:* Division II 1948-49, 1950-51.
Scottish Cup: —. *League Cup:* —.
Club colours: Shirt: Red and white halves. Shorts: Red and white halves. Stockings: Red.

Goalscorers: *League (54):* Bone 9 (1 pen), McCormick 8, Tait 6, Bennett 5 (2 pens), Hjartarsson 5, McLaren 5, Paterson G 4, McQuilter 2, Paterson A 2, Taggart 2, Deas 1, Gibson 1, Wood 1, own goals 3. *Scottish Cup (0). Coca Cola Cup (1):* Gibson 1. *League Challenge Cup (4):* Bone 3, Gibson 1.

McGeown M 36	Paterson A 34	Deas P 32	Gibson J 28 + 8	McQuilter R 31	Paterson G 33	Bone A 34	Jack S 7 + 8	McCormick S 29 + 2	Taggart C 22 + 3	McLeod J 5 + 1	Wood D 5 + 8	Bennett N 26 + 7	Watson P — + 1	Tait T 22 + 4	McGrotty G — + 12	Mitchell C 13 + 1	McLaren S 8 + 15	Hjartarsson G 20 + 1	Carberry G 10 + 1	Forrest E 1	Mortimer P — + 1	Match No.
1	2	3	4²	5	6	7	8	9	10	11¹	12	13										1
1	2	3	4³	5	6	7	8	9	10¹	11²	13	12			14							2
1	2	3	4	5	6²	7	8¹	9	10	11³	13	12			14							3
1	2	3	4²	5	6	7	13	9	10	11¹				8	12							4
1	2	3	4²	5	6	7		9	10	11¹	12			8	13							5
1	2	3	4	5	6²	7		9	10	11¹	12			8	13							6
1	2	3	4	5	6	7		9	10	12		11¹		8								7
1	2	3	4³	5	6	7		9	10			11²		8¹	14	13	12					8
1	2	3	4²	5	6	7		9	10			11¹		8	12	13						9
1	2	3	4¹	5	6	7	12	9²	10			11		8		13						10
1	2	3	4¹	5	6	7		9	10			11		8	12							11
1	2	3	4¹	5	6	7		9	10			11²		8		13	12					12
1	2	3	4¹	5	6	7		9	10			11²		8		13						13
1	2	3	4	5	7	6		9¹	10			11		8	12							14
1	2	3	12	5	6	7²		9	10			11		8¹		13	4					15
1	2	3¹	12	5	6	7³	14	9	10			11		8		13	4²					16
1	2	8²	12	5	6	7		9	10			11¹		3		13	4					17
1	2	8	12	5	6	7		9	10³			11¹		3	14	13	4²					18
1	2	10²	12	5	6	7	8	9				11¹		3	14	13	4³					19
1	2	3	12	5	6	7			10			11		8		13	4¹	9²				20
1	2	3³	13	5	6	7			10			11²		8	14	12	4	9¹				21
1	2	3	4	5	6	7			10			11		8				9				22
1	2	3	4¹	5	6	7			10			11		8		13	12	9²				23
1	2¹	3	4	5	6	7²			10			11		8		13	12	9				24
1	2	3	4	5	6	7¹			10²			11		8		13	12	9				25
1	2	3	4²	5	6	7¹			10			11		8		13	12	9				26
1	2	3	4		6	7			10			11		8			12	9	5¹			27
1	2	3	4¹		6	7²			10			11		8		13	12	9	5			28
1	2	3	12	5	6	7			10¹			11		8				9	4			29
1	2	3	12	5	6	7¹			10¹			11		8		13		9	4			30
1	2	3	12	5	6	7			10¹			11		8		13		9²	4			31
1	2	3	12	5	6	7			10¹			11³		8	14	13		9	4²			32
1	3	2		5	6	7			10¹			11		8			12	9	4			33
1	3	2		5	6	7			10¹			11		8²		13	12	9	4			34
1	2	3	11	5	6	7¹			10					8²	14	13	12	9	4³			35
1	2	11	12		6				10			8		3			4¹	9	7²	5	13	36

STRANRAER   Second Division

Year Formed: 1870. *Ground & Address:* Stair Park, London Rd, Stranraer DG9 8BS. *Telephone:* 01776 703271.
Ground Capacity: total: 6100. seated: 1800. *Size of Pitch:* 110yd × 70yd.
Chairman/Secretary: Graham Rodgers. *Commercial Manager:* T. L. Sutherland.
Manager: Campbell Money. *Assistant Manager/Coach:* Jim Denny.
Managers since 1975: J. Hughes; N. Hood; G. Hamilton; D. Sneddon; J. Clark; R. Clark; A. McAnespie. *Club Nickname(s):* The Blues. *Previous Grounds:* None.
Record Attendance: 6500 v Rangers, Scottish Cup 1st rd; 24 Jan, 1948.
Record Transfer Fee received: £30,000 for Duncan George to Ayr Utd.
Record Transfer Fee paid: £15,000 for Colin Harkness from Kilmarnock (Aug 1989).
Record Victory: 7-0 v Brechin C, Division II; 6 Feb, 1965.
Record Defeat: 1-11 v Queen of the South, Scottish Cup 1st rd; 16 Jan, 1932.
Most Capped Player: —.
Most League Appearances: 256: Danny McDonald.
Most League Goals in Season (Individual): 27: Derek Frye, Second Division; 1977-78.
Most Goals Overall (Individual): —.

STRANRAER 1996–97 LEAGUE RECORD

Match No.	Date	Venue	Opponents	Result	H/T Score	Lg. Pos.	Goalscorers	Attendance
1	Aug 17	A	Dumbarton	D 1-1	0-1	—	McIntyre [50]	560
2	24	H	Livingston	L 1-2	0-1	9	Young [68]	523
3	31	A	Stenhousemuir	W 1-0	0-0	6	McCaffrey [77]	510
4	Sept 7	H	Hamilton A	L 0-3	0-2	7		529
5	14	A	Brechin C	W 2-0	2-0	5	Sloan [24], Young [45]	285
6	21	H	Clyde	D 0-0	0-0	5		513
7	28	A	Ayr U	L 0-2	0-1	6		1915
8	Oct 5	H	Queen of the S	W 2-1	0-0	6	Docherty [50], Lansdowne [52]	713
9	12	A	Berwick R	W 2-1	1-1	4	McIntyre [30], Young [78]	313
10	19	H	Dumbarton	W 2-0	1-0	4	Docherty [5], Young [76]	460
11	26	A	Livingston	L 0-2	0-1	4		1923
12	Nov 9	A	Hamilton A	L 0-4	0-1	6		654
13	16	H	Ayr U	L 0-1	0-0	7		1021
14	30	A	Queen of the S	L 2-3	1-1	7	Sloan 2 [35, 51]	1284
15	Dec 7	H	Brechin C	L 0-1	0-0	7		778
16	10	A	Clyde	L 0-1	0-1	—		483
17	14	H	Berwick R	D 1-1	0-0	7	McIntyre [89]	671
18	26	A	Dumbarton	D 2-2	1-0	—	Young [15], McIntyre [86]	686
19	Jan 18	H	Queen of the S	W 3-1	1-1	8	Docherty [26], McAulay [58], McIntyre [61]	564
20	21	A	Ayr U	L 0-2	0-2	—		1696
21	25	H	Stenhousemuir	D 2-2	2-1	7	McIntyre 2 [34, 39]	454
22	Feb 1	A	Berwick R	L 0-2	0-2	8		302
23	5	H	Clyde	W 1-0	1-0	—	Crawford [27]	468
24	8	A	Brechin C	D 0-0	0-0	6		451
25	22	H	Livingston	D 1-1	1-0	7	Higgins [35]	584
26	Mar 4	A	Stenhousemuir	L 0-4	0-2	—		267
27	8	A	Clyde	L 0-3	0-0	8		680
28	12	H	Hamilton A	L 0-1	0-0	—		505
29	15	H	Ayr U	L 0-1	0-0	8		847
30	22	A	Queen of the S	D 1-1	0-1	8	Black [56]	1176
31	Apr 5	H	Berwick R	D 1-1	0-1	8	McMillan [75]	480
32	12	A	Hamilton A	L 1-2	1-2	8	Crawford [34]	797
33	19	H	Brechin C	L 0-1	0-0	9		416
34	26	H	Dumbarton	W 1-0	0-0	8	Higgins [86]	739
35	May 3	A	Livingston	L 0-3	0-1	8		1491
36	10	H	Stenhousemuir	W 2-1	0-0	8	McGeachie (og) [71], McCaffrey [78]	559

Final League Position: 8

Honours
League Champions: Second Division 1993-94.
Scottish Cup: —.
League Cup: —.
Qualifying Cup Winners: 1937.
League Challenge Cup Winners: 1996–97.
Club colours: Shirt: Royal blue and red quarters. Shorts: White. Stockings: Royal blue.

Goalscorers: *League (29):* McIntyre 7, Young 5, Docherty 3, Sloan 3, Crawford 2, Higgins 2, McCaffrey 2, Black 1, Lansdowne 1, McAulay 1, McMillan 1, own goal 1. *Scottish Cup (1):* Young 1. *Coca Cola Cup (3):* Docherty 1, Sloan 1, Young 1. *League Challenge Cup (9):* Sloan 4, Docherty 1 (pen), McAulay 1, McCaffrey 1, McIntyre 1, McMillan 1.

Duffy B 27	Duncan G 9+6	Crawford D 14+6	Millar G 20	Howard N 2+1	McCaffrey J 25	Sloan T 26+5	McIntyre P 28	Young G 24+6	Docherty R 25+6	Lansdowne A 30	Hughes J 22+5	McLaren J —+1	Gallagher A 13	McMillan J 9+17	Black T 26	McAulay J 25+1	Robertson J 20+11	Higgins G 17+4	Gallacher I 14+4	Matthews G 9	McStay R —+1	Duffy J —+1	Jack A —+1	Campbell M 1	McCrindle S —+3	Hay G 9	Friels G 1+5	Match No.
1	2²	3	4	5	6	7	8²	9	10	11	12	13																1
1		3	4		6	7	8	9	10	11¹	2				5	12												2
1	2		4		6		11	9	13	7¹	12				5	10²	3³	8	14									3
1	11		4		6	7²	2	9	10	8					5¹	13	3	12										4
1			4¹		6	7³	2²	9	11	8	12				5	14	3	10	13									5
1	8¹				6	7	2	9	11		4				5²	12	3	10	13									6
1	12				6	7	2	9	11²	8	4				5	13	3	10¹										7
1	12				6	7	2	13	11	8¹	4				5³	9²	3	10	14									8
1	13				6	7	2	12	11	8²	4				5	9¹	3	10³	14									9
1			14		6	7¹	2	12	11	8²	4				5³	9	3	10	13									10
1					6	7¹	2	9	11	8³	4				5²	10	3	14	13	12								11
1	2	3			6	7			11³	8¹	4				5²	9	10	13	12	14								12
1	8	3	4	5³	6	7²								14	11	13	10¹	12	9	2								13
1	13	3	4		6	7	8			11¹	12					10	5	9	2²									14
	6	3				7³	8	13	11		4¹				5	14	10	2	9²	1	12							15
	12	3		5	7¹		8		11²		4				6	13		10	9	2	1							16
7¹		3			6		13	8	12	11	4					5	10	9²	2	1								17
		3			6	7		9	11	8¹	4					10	5		2	1			12					18
1					6	7¹	2	9	11	8	4				12	3	10	5	13									19
1					6		2	9²	11³	8	4¹				7	3	10	5	13	12			14					20
1	12		4			7³			11	8¹					14	3	10	5	9²	2						6	13	21
1	10¹		4²			7			11	8					13	3	5	9	2						12	6		22
1	11		4		10	7		9²							5¹	13	3		2	8						6	12	23
1	11²		4¹		10	6³	7	9	13						5	14	3		2	8					12		5¹	24
1	11				12	7		9¹	13	8	4					3	5	10²	2							6		25
1	11				7			9²	12	8	4				13	3	5	10	2¹							6		26
1	12				7			9	11	8	4²					3¹	2	5	10							6	13	27
	12		4					9	11	8²						3¹	10	5	7	2	1					6	13	28
		14	4			7		9	11¹	8					13	12	3	10	5⁷	2	1					6³		29
	11		4			7	8	12²							13	3	10	5	9	2¹	1					6		30
			4		6	7¹	2²	9		8					13	3	11	12		1						5	10	31
	11				6	13		9		8	4				7	3²	10		2	1			12				5¹	32
1	13		4		6			9	10	8¹			14		7³	3	11²	5	2				12					33
1	13		4		6	7¹	10	9	2²	8						3	5	11							12			34
1	12		4		6	7³	10	9	13	8	2²					3	5	11							14			35
1			4		6	7	13	9	11	8	2¹					3	5	10²							12			36

SCOTTISH LEAGUE 1996–97

Premier Division

	P	Home W	D	L	Goals F	A	Away W	D	L	Goals F	A	Pt	GD
Rangers	36	13	2	3	44	16	12	3	3	41	17	80	+52
Celtic	36	14	2	2	48	9	9	4	5	30	23	75	+46
Dundee U	36	10	4	4	21	10	7	5	6	25	23	60	+13
Hearts	36	8	6	4	27	20	6	4	8	19	23	52	+3
Dunfermline Ath	36	8	4	6	32	30	4	5	9	20	35	45	–13
Aberdeen	36	6	8	4	25	19	4	6	8	20	35	44	–9
Kilmarnock	36	8	4	6	28	26	3	2	13	13	35	39	–20
Motherwell	36	5	5	8	24	25	4	6	8	20	30	38	–11
Hibernian	36	6	4	8	18	25	3	7	8	20	30	38	–17
Raith R	36	3	5	10	18	39	3	2	13	11	34	25	–44

First Division

	P	Home W	D	L	Goals F	A	Away W	D	L	Goals F	A	Pt	GD
St Johnstone	36	12	5	1	37	10	12	3	3	37	13	80	+51
Airdrieonians	36	6	7	5	26	19	9	8	1	30	15	60	+22
Dundee	36	10	3	5	26	14	5	10	3	21	19	58	+14
St Mirren	36	12	0	6	28	21	5	7	6	20	20	58	+7
Falkirk	36	8	7	3	28	20	7	2	9	14	19	54	+3
Partick T	36	6	8	4	24	21	6	4	8	25	27	48	+1
Stirling Albion	36	8	3	7	27	25	4	7	7	27	36	46	–7
Greenock Morton	36	6	7	5	20	19	6	2	10	22	22	45	+1
Clydebank	36	6	4	8	19	24	1	3	14	12	35	28	–28
East Fife	36	1	5	12	15	48	1	3	14	13	44	14	–64

Second Division

	P	Home W	D	L	Goals F	A	Away W	D	L	Goals F	A	Pt	GD
Ayr U	36	12	3	3	32	16	11	5	2	29	17	77	+28
Hamilton A	36	11	5	2	47	17	11	3	4	28	11	74	+47
Livingston	36	11	3	4	32	18	7	7	4	24	20	64	+18
Clyde	36	8	4	6	21	18	6	6	6	21	21	52	+3
Queen of the S	36	8	3	7	27	27	5	5	8	28	30	47	–2
Stenhousemuir	36	4	6	8	19	23	7	5	6	30	20	44	+6
Brechin C	36	5	7	6	18	22	5	4	9	18	27	41	–13
Stranraer	36	6	5	7	17	18	3	4	11	12	33	36	–22
Dumbarton	36	2	7	9	21	35	7	1	10	23	31	35	–22
Berwick R	36	4	4	10	15	36	0	7	11	17	39	23	–43

Third Division

	P	Home W	D	L	Goals F	A	Away W	D	L	Goals F	A	Pt	GD
Inverness CT	36	13	3	2	37	19	10	4	4	33	18	76	+33
Forfar Ath	36	10	5	3	35	19	9	5	4	39	26	67	+29
Ross Co	36	10	4	4	33	22	10	3	5	25	19	67	+17
Alloa	36	9	4	5	24	21	7	3	8	26	26	55	+3
Albion R	36	8	4	6	27	22	5	6	7	23	25	49	+3
Montrose	36	6	5	7	19	27	6	2	10	27	35	43	–16
Cowdenbeath	36	6	6	6	22	23	4	3	11	16	28	39	–13
Queen's Park	36	7	3	8	27	29	2	6	10	19	30	36	–13
East Stirlingshire	36	6	4	8	21	29	2	5	11	15	29	33	–22
Arbroath	36	4	6	8	18	25	2	7	9	13	27	31	–21

PLAY-OFF: Hibernian (9th place, Premier Division) v Airdrieonians (runners-up, First Division)

17 MAY at Easter Road Stadium
Hibernian (1) 1 *(Cooper (og), 13)*
Airdrieonians (0) 0   15,308
Hibernian: Leighton; Renwick, McQuilken, Hunter, Hughes, Welsh, Tosh (Power), Dow, Wright (Lavety), Jackson D, McGinlay.
Airdrieonians: Rhodes; Stewart, Jack (Smith); Sandison, Sweeney, Black, Johnston, Mackay, Cooper, Davies, Connolly P.

22 MAY at Broadwood Stadium
Airdrieonians (1) 2 *(Connolly P 1, Black (pen) 86)*
Hibernian (0) 4 *(Jackson D (pen) 46, (pen) 69, Tosh 72, Wright 83)*   7560
Airdrieonians: Rhodes; Stewart, Jack, Sandison, Sweeney, Black, Johnston, Mackay (McPhee), Cooper, Davies, Connolly P.
Hibernian: Leighton; Renwick, McQuilken, Grant, Hughes, Welsh, Tosh, Dow, Power (Lavety), Jackson D (Harper), McGinlay (Wright).

SCOTTISH LEAGUE 1890–91 to 1996–97

*On goal average/difference. †Held jointly after indecisive play-off. ‡Won on deciding match.
††Held jointly. ¶Two points deducted for fielding ineligible player.
Competition suspended 1940–45 during war; Regional Leagues operating. ‡‡Two points deducted for registration irregularities.

PREMIER DIVISION

Maximum points: 72

	First	Pts	Second	Pts	Third	Pts
1975–76	Rangers	54	Celtic	48	Hibernian	43
1976–77	Celtic	55	Rangers	46	Aberdeen	43
1977–78	Rangers	55	Aberdeen	53	Dundee U	40
1978–79	Celtic	48	Rangers	45	Dundee U	44
1979–80	Aberdeen	48	Celtic	47	St Mirren	42
1980–81	Celtic	56	Aberdeen	49	Rangers*	44
1981–82	Celtic	55	Aberdeen	53	Rangers	43
1982–83	Dundee U	56	Celtic*	55	Aberdeen	55
1983–84	Aberdeen	57	Celtic	50	Dundee U	47
1984–85	Aberdeen	59	Celtic	52	Dundee U	47
1985–86	Celtic*	50	Hearts	50	Dundee U	47

Maximum points: 88

1986–87	Rangers	69	Celtic	63	Dundee U	60
1987–88	Celtic	72	Hearts	62	Rangers	60

Maximum points: 72

1988–89	Rangers	56	Aberdeen	50	Celtic	46
1989–90	Rangers	51	Aberdeen*	44	Hearts	44
1990–91	Rangers	55	Aberdeen	53	Celtic*	41

Maximum points: 88

1991–92	Rangers	72	Hearts	63	Celtic	62
1992–93	Rangers	73	Aberdeen	64	Celtic	60
1993–94	Rangers	58	Aberdeen	55	Motherwell	54

Maximum points: 108

1994–95	Rangers	69	Motherwell	54	Hibernian	53
1995–96	Rangers	87	Celtic	83	Aberdeen*	55
1996–97	Rangers	80	Celtic	75	Dundee U	60

FIRST DIVISION

Maximum points: 52

1975–76	Partick T	41	Kilmarnock	35	Montrose	30

Maximum points: 78

1976–77	St Mirren	62	Clydebank	58	Dundee	51
1977–78	Morton*	58	Hearts	58	Dundee	57
1978–79	Dundee	55	Kilmarnock*	54	Clydebank	54
1979–80	Hearts	53	Airdrieonians	51	Ayr U*	44
1980–81	Hibernian	57	Dundee	52	St Johnstone	51
1981–82	Motherwell	61	Kilmarnock	51	Hearts	50
1982–83	St Johnstone	55	Hearts	54	Clydebank	50
1983–84	Morton	54	Dumbarton	51	Partick T	46
1984–85	Motherwell	50	Clydebank	48	Falkirk	45
1985–86	Hamilton A	56	Falkirk	45	Kilmarnock	44

Maximum points: 88

1986–87	Morton	57	Dunfermline Ath	56	Dumbarton	53
1987–88	Hamilton A	56	Meadowbank T	52	Clydebank	49

Maximum points: 78

1988–89	Dunfermline Ath	54	Falkirk	52	Clydebank	48
1989–90	St Johnstone	58	Airdrieonians	54	Clydebank	44
1990–91	Falkirk	54	Airdrieonians	53	Dundee	52

Maximum points: 88

1991–92	Dundee	58	Partick T*	57	Hamilton A	57
1992–93	Raith R	65	Kilmarnock	54	Dunfermline Ath	52
1993–94	Falkirk	66	Dunfermline Ath	65	Airdrieonians	54

Maximum points: 108

1994–95	Raith R	69	Dunfermline Ath*	68	Dundee	68
1995–96	Dunfermline Ath	71	Dundee U*	67	Morton	67
1996–97	St Johnstone	80	Airdrieonians	60	Dundee*	58

SECOND DIVISION

Maximum points: 52

1975–76	Clydebank*	40	Raith R	40	Alloa	35

Maximum points: 78

1976–77	Stirling A	55	Alloa	51	Dunfermline Ath	50
1977–78	Clyde*	53	Raith R	53	Dunfermline Ath	48

1978–79	Berwick R	54	Dunfermline Ath	52	Falkirk	50
1979–80	Falkirk	50	East Stirling	49	Forfar Ath	46
1980–81	Queen's Park	50	Queen of the S	46	Cowdenbeath	45
1981–82	Clyde	59	Alloa*	50	Arbroath	50
1982–83	Brechin C	55	Meadowbank T	54	Arbroath	49
1983–84	Forfar Ath	63	East Fife	47	Berwick R	43
1984–85	Montrose	53	Alloa	50	Dunfermline Ath	49
1985–86	Dunfermline Ath	57	Queen of the S	55	Meadowbank T	49
1986–87	Meadowbank T	55	Raith R*	52	Stirling A*	52
1987–88	Ayr U	61	St Johnstone	59	Queen's Park	51
1988–89	Albion R	50	Alloa	45	Brechin C	43
1989–90	Brechin C	49	Kilmarnock	48	Stirling A	47
1990–91	Stirling A	54	Montrose	46	Cowdenbeath	45
1991–92	Dumbarton	52	Cowdenbeath	51	Alloa	50
1992–93	Clyde	54	Brechin C*	53	Stranraer	53
1993–94	Stranraer	56	Berwick R	48	Stenhousemuir*	47
			Maximum points: 108			
1994–95	Morton	64	Dumbarton	60	Stirling A	58
1995–96	Stirling A	81	East Fife	67	Berwick R	60
1996–97	Ayr U	77	Hamilton A	74	Livingston	64

THIRD DIVISION
Maximum points: 108

1994–95	Forfar Ath	80	Montrose	67	Ross Co	60
1995–96	Livingston	72	Brechin C	63	Caledonian T	57
1996–97	Inverness CT	76	Forfar Ath*	67	Ross Co	67

FIRST DIVISION to 1974–75
Maximum points: a 36; b 44; c 40; d 52; e 60; f 68; g 76; h 84.

	First	Pts	Second	Pts	Third	Pts
1890–91a	Dumbarton††	29	Rangers††	29	Celtic	21
1891–92b	Dumbarton	37	Celtic	35	Hearts	34
1892–93a	Celtic	29	Rangers	28	St Mirren	20
1893–94a	Celtic	29	Hearts	26	St Bernard's	23
1894–95a	Hearts	31	Celtic	26	Rangers	22
1895–96a	Celtic	30	Rangers	26	Hibernian	24
1896–97a	Hearts	28	Hibernian	26	Rangers	25
1897–98a	Celtic	33	Rangers	29	Hibernian	22
1898–99a	Rangers	36	Hearts	26	Celtic	24
1899–1900a	Rangers	32	Celtic	25	Hibernian	24
1900–01c	Rangers	35	Celtic	29	Hibernian	25
1901–02a	Rangers	28	Celtic	26	Hearts	22
1902–03b	Hibernian	37	Dundee	31	Rangers	29
1903–04d	Third Lanark	43	Hearts	39	Celtic*	38
1904–05d	Celtic‡	41	Rangers	41	Third Lanark	35
1905–06e	Celtic	49	Hearts	43	Airdrieonians	38
1906–07f	Celtic	55	Dundee	48	Rangers	45
1907–08f	Celtic	55	Falkirk	51	Rangers	50
1908–09f	Celtic	51	Dundee	50	Clyde	48
1909–10f	Celtic	54	Falkirk	52	Rangers	46
1910–11f	Rangers	52	Aberdeen	48	Falkirk	44
1911–12f	Rangers	51	Celtic	45	Clyde	42
1912–13f	Rangers	53	Celtic	49	Hearts*	41
1913–14g	Celtic	65	Rangers	59	Hearts*	54
1914–15g	Celtic	65	Hearts	61	Rangers	50
1915–16g	Celtic	67	Rangers	56	Morton	51
1916–17g	Celtic	64	Morton	54	Rangers	53
1917–18f	Rangers	56	Celtic	55	Kilmarnock*	43
1918–19f	Celtic	58	Rangers	57	Morton	47
1919–20h	Rangers	71	Celtic	68	Motherwell	57
1920–21h	Rangers	76	Celtic	66	Hearts	50
1921–22h	Celtic	67	Rangers	66	Raith R	51
1922–23g	Rangers	55	Airdrieonians	50	Celtic	46
1923–24g	Rangers	59	Airdrieonians	50	Celtic	46
1924–25g	Rangers	60	Airdrieonians	57	Hibernian	52
1925–26g	Celtic	58	Airdrieonians*	50	Hearts	50
1926–27g	Rangers	56	Motherwell	51	Celtic	49
1927–28g	Rangers	60	Celtic*	55	Motherwell	55
1928–29g	Rangers	67	Celtic	51	Motherwell	50
1929–30g	Rangers	60	Motherwell	55	Aberdeen	53
1930–31g	Rangers	60	Celtic	58	Motherwell	56
1931–32g	Motherwell	66	Rangers	61	Celtic	48
1932–33g	Rangers	62	Motherwell	59	Hearts	50
1933–34g	Rangers	66	Motherwell	62	Celtic	47

1934–35g	Rangers	55	Celtic	52	Hearts	50
1935–36g	Celtic	66	Rangers*	61	Aberdeen	61
1936–37g	Rangers	61	Aberdeen	54	Celtic	52
1937–38g	Celtic	61	Hearts	58	Rangers	49
1938–39g	Rangers	59	Celtic	48	Aberdeen	46
1946–47e	Rangers	46	Hibernian	44	Aberdeen	39
1947–48e	Hibernian	48	Rangers	46	Partick T	36
1948–49e	Rangers	46	Dundee	45	Hibernian	39
1949–50e	Rangers	50	Hibernian	49	Hearts	43
1950–51e	Hibernian	48	Rangers*	38	Dundee	38
1951–52e	Hibernian	45	Rangers	41	East Fife	37
1952–53e	Rangers*	43	Hibernian	43	East Fife	39
1953–54e	Celtic	43	Hearts	38	Partick T	35
1954–55e	Aberdeen	49	Celtic	46	Rangers	41
1955–56f	Rangers	52	Aberdeen	46	Hearts*	45
1956–57f	Rangers	55	Hearts	53	Kilmarnock	42
1957–58f	Hearts	62	Rangers	49	Celtic	46
1958–59f	Rangers	50	Hearts	48	Motherwell	44
1959–60f	Hearts	54	Kilmarnock	50	Rangers*	42
1960–61f	Rangers	51	Kilmarnock	50	Third Lanark	42
1961–62f	Dundee	54	Rangers	51	Celtic	46
1962–63f	Rangers	57	Kilmarnock	48	Partick T	46
1963–64f	Rangers	55	Kilmarnock	49	Celtic*	47
1964–65f	Kilmarnock*	50	Hearts	50	Dunfermline Ath	49
1965–66f	Celtic	57	Rangers	55	Kilmarnock	45
1966–67f	Celtic	58	Rangers	55	Clyde	46
1967–68f	Celtic	63	Rangers	61	Hibernian	45
1968–69f	Celtic	54	Rangers	49	Dunfermline Ath	45
1969–70f	Celtic	57	Rangers	45	Hibernian	44
1970–71f	Celtic	56	Aberdeen	54	St Johnstone	44
1971–72f	Celtic	60	Aberdeen	50	Rangers	44
1972–73f	Celtic	57	Rangers	56	Hibernian	45
1973–74f	Celtic	53	Hibernian	49	Rangers	48
1974–75f	Rangers	56	Hibernian	49	Celtic	45

SECOND DIVISION to 1974–75

Maximum points: a 76; b 72; c 68; d 52; e 60; f 36; g 44.

1893–94f	Hibernian	29	Cowlairs	27	Clyde	24
1894–95f	Hibernian	30	Motherwell	22	Port Glasgow	20
1895–96f	Abercorn	27	Leith Ath	23	Renton	21
1896–97f	Partick T	31	Leith Ath	27	Kilmarnock*	21
1897–98f	Kilmarnock	29	Port Glasgow	25	Morton	22
1898–99f	Kilmarnock	32	Leith Ath	27	Port Glasgow	25
1899–1900f	Partick T	29	Morton	28	Port Glasgow	20
1900–01f	St Bernard's	25	Airdrieonians	23	Abercorn	21
1901–02g	Port Glasgow	32	Partick T	31	Motherwell	26
1902–03g	Airdrieonians	35	Motherwell	28	Ayr U*	27
1903–04g	Hamilton A	37	Clyde	29	Ayr U	28
1904–05g	Clyde	32	Falkirk	28	Hamilton A	27
1905–06g	Leith Ath	34	Clyde	31	Albion R	27
1906–07g	St Bernard's	32	Vale of Leven*	27	Arthurlie	27
1907–08g	Raith R	30	Dumbarton*‡‡	27	Ayr U	27
1908–09g	Abercorn	31	Raith R*	28	Vale of Leven	28
1909–10g	Leith Ath‡	33	Raith R	33	St Bernard's	27
1910–11g	Dumbarton	31	Ayr U	27	Albion R	25
1911–12g	Ayr U	35	Abercorn	30	Dumbarton	27
1912–13d	Ayr U	34	Dunfermline Ath	33	East Stirling	32
1913–14g	Cowdenbeath	31	Albion R	27	Dunfermline Ath*	26
1914–15d	Cowdenbeath*	37	St Bernard's*	37	Leith Ath	37
1921–22a	Alloa	60	Cowdenbeath	47	Armadale	45
1922–23a	Queen's Park	57	Clydebank¶	50	St Johnstone¶	45
1923–24a	St Johnstone	56	Cowdenbeath	55	Bathgate	44
1924–25a	Dundee U	50	Clydebank	48	Clyde	47
1925–26a	Dunfermline Ath	59	Clyde	53	Ayr U	52
1926–27a	Bo'ness	56	Raith R	49	Clydebank	45
1927–28a	Ayr U	54	Third Lanark	45	King's Park	44
1928–29b	Dundee U	51	Morton	50	Arbroath	47
1929–30a	Leith Ath*	57	East Fife	57	Albion R	54
1930–31a	Third Lanark	61	Dundee U	50	Dunfermline Ath	47
1931–32a	East Stirling*	55	St Johnstone	55	Raith R*	46
1932–33c	Hibernian	54	Queen of the S	49	Dunfermline Ath	47
1933–34c	Albion R	45	Dunfermline Ath*	44	Arbroath	44
1934–35c	Third Lanark	52	Arbroath	50	St Bernard's	47
1935–36c	Falkirk	59	St Mirren	52	Morton	48

1936–37c	Ayr U	54	Morton	51	St Bernard's	48
1937–38c	Raith R	59	Albion R	48	Airdrieonians	47
1938–39c	Cowdenbeath	60	Alloa*	48	East Fife	48
1946–47d	Dundee	45	Airdrieonians	42	East Fife	31
1947–48e	East Fife	53	Albion R	42	Hamilton A	40
1948–49e	Raith R*	42	Stirling A	42	Airdrieonians*	41
1949–50e	Morton	47	Airdrieonians	44	Dunfermline Ath*	36
1950–51e	Queen of the S*	45	Stirling A	45	Ayr U*	36
1951–52e	Clyde	44	Falkirk	43	Ayr U	39
1952–53e	Stirling A	44	Hamilton A	43	Queen's Park	37
1953–54e	Motherwell	45	Kilmarnock	42	Third Lanark*	36
1954–55e	Airdrieonians	46	Dunfermline Ath	42	Hamilton A	39
1955–56b	Queen's Park	54	Ayr U	51	St Johnstone	49
1956–57b	Clyde	64	Third Lanark	51	Cowdenbeath	45
1957–58b	Stirling A	55	Dunfermline Ath	53	Arbroath	47
1958–59b	Ayr U	60	Arbroath	51	Stenhousemuir	46
1959–60b	St Johnstone	53	Dundee U	50	Queen of the S	49
1960–61b	Stirling A	55	Falkirk	54	Stenhousemuir	50
1961–62b	Clyde	54	Queen of the S	53	Morton	44
1962–63b	St Johnstone	55	East Stirling	49	Morton	48
1963–64b	Morton	67	Clyde	53	Arbroath	46
1964–65b	Stirling A	59	Hamilton A	50	Queen of the S	45
1965–66b	Ayr U	53	Airdrieonians	50	Queen of the S	47
1966–67a	Morton	69	Raith R	58	Arbroath	57
1967–68b	St Mirren	62	Arbroath	53	East Fife	49
1968–69b	Motherwell	64	Ayr U	53	East Fife*	48
1969–70b	Falkirk	56	Cowdenbeath	55	Queen of the S	50
1970–71b	Partick T	56	East Fife	51	Arbroath	46
1971–72b	Dumbarton*	52	Arbroath	52	Stirling A	50
1972–73b	Clyde	56	Dumfermline Ath	52	Raith R*	47
1973–74b	Airdrieonians	60	Kilmarnock	58	Hamilton A	55
1974–75a	Falkirk	54	Queen of the S*	53	Montrose	53

Elected to First Division: 1894 Clyde; 1895 Hibernian; 1896 Abercorn; 1897 Partick T; 1899 Kilmarnock; 1900 Morton and Partick T; 1902 Port Glasgow and Partick T; 1903 Airdrieonians and Motherwell; 1905 Falkirk and Aberdeen; 1906 Clyde and Hamilton A; 1910 Raith R; 1913 Ayr U and Dumbarton.

RELEGATED FROM PREMIER DIVISION

1974–75 *No relegation due to League reorganization*
1975–76 Dundee, St Johnstone
1976–77 Hearts, Kilmarnock
1977–78 Ayr U, Clydebank
1978–79 Hearts, Motherwell
1979–80 Dundee, Hibernian
1980–81 Kilmarnock, Hearts
1981–82 Partick T, Airdrieonians
1982–83 Morton, Kilmarnock
1983–84 St Johnstone, Motherwell
1984–85 Dumbarton, Morton
1985–86 *No relegation due to League reorganization*
1986–87 Clydebank, Hamilton A
1987–88 Falkirk, Dunfermline Ath, Morton
1988–89 Hamilton A
1989–90 Dundee
1990–91 *None*
1991–92 St Mirren, Dunfermline Ath
1992–93 Falkirk, Airdrieonians
1993–94 *See footnote*
1994–95 Dundee U
1995–96 Partick T, Falkirk
1996–97 Raith R

RELEGATED FROM DIVISION 1

1974–75 *No relegation due to League reorganization*
1975–76 Dunfermline Ath, Clyde
1976–77 Raith R, Falkirk
1977–78 Alloa Ath, East Fife
1978–79 Montrose, Queen of the S
1979–80 Arbroath, Clyde
1980–81 Stirling A, Berwick R
1981–82 East Stirling, Queen of the S
1982–83 Dunfermline Ath, Queen's Park
1983–84 Raith R, Alloa
1984–85 Meadowbank T, St Johnstone
1985–86 Ayr U, Alloa
1986–87 Brechin C, Montrose
1987–88 East Fife, Dumbarton
1988–89 Kilmarnock, Queen of the S
1989–90 Albion R, Alloa
1990–91 Clyde, Brechin C
1991–92 Montrose, Forfar Ath
1992–93 Meadowbank T, Cowdenbeath
1993–94 *See footnote*
1994–95 Ayr U, Stranraer
1995–96 Hamilton A, Dumbarton
1996–97 Clydebank, East Fife

RELEGATED FROM DIVISION 2

1994–95 Meadowbank T, Brechin C
1995–96 Forfar Ath, Montrose
1996–97 Dumbarton, Berwick R

RELEGATED FROM DIVISION 1 (TO 1973–74)

1921–22 *Queen's Park, Dumbarton, Clydebank
1922–23 Albion R, Alloa Ath
1923–24 Clyde, Clydebank
1924–25 Third Lanark, Ayr U
1925–26 Raith R, Clydebank

1926–27 Morton, Dundee U
1927–28 Dunfermline Ath, Bo'ness
1928–29 Third Lanark, Raith R
1929–30 St Johnstone, Dundee U
1930–31 Hibernian, East Fife

1931–32 Dundee U, Leith Ath	1956–57 Dunfermline Ath, Ayr U
1932–33 Morton, East Stirling	1957–58 East Fife, Queen's Park
1933–34 Third Lanark, Cowdenbeath	1958–59 Queen of the S, Falkirk
1934–35 St Mirren, Falkirk	1959–60 Arbroath, Stirling A
1935–36 Airdrieonians, Ayr U	1960–61 Ayr U, Clyde
1936–37 Dunfermline Ath, Albion R	1961–62 St Johnstone, Stirling A
1937–38 Dundee, Morton	1962–63 Clyde, Raith R
1938–39 Queen's Park, Raith R	1963–64 Queen of the S, East Stirling
1946–47 Kilmarnock, Hamilton A	1964–65 Airdrieonians, Third Lanark
1947–48 Airdrieonians, Queen's Park	1965–66 Morton, Hamilton A
1948–49 Morton, Albion R	1966–67 St Mirren, Ayr U
1949–50 Queen of the S, Stirling A	1967–68 Motherwell, Stirling A
1950–51 Clyde, Falkirk	1968–69 Falkirk, Arbroath
1951–52 Morton, Stirling A	1969–70 Raith R, Partick T
1952–53 Motherwell, Third Lanark	1970–71 St Mirren, Cowdenbeath
1953–54 Airdrieonians, Hamilton A	1971–72 Clyde, Dunfermline Ath
1954–55 *No clubs relegated*	1972–73 Kilmarnock, Airdrieonians
1955–56 Stirling A, Clyde	1973–74 East Fife, Falkirk

*Season 1921–22 – only 1 club promoted, 3 clubs relegated.

Scottish League championship wins: Rangers 47, Celtic 35, Aberdeen 4, Hearts 4, Hibernian 4, Dumbarton 2, Dundee 1, Dundee U 1, Kilmarnock 1, Motherwell 1, Third Lanark 1.

At the end of the 1993–94 season four divisions were created assisted by the admission of two new clubs Ross County and Caledonian Thistle. Only one club was promoted from Division 1 and Division 2. The three relegated from the Premier joined with teams finishing second to seventh in Division 1 to form the new Division 1. Five relegated from Division 1 combined with those who finished second to sixth to form a new Division 2 and the bottom eight in Division 2 linked with the two newcomers to form a new Division 3.

Rangers again succeeded in the Scottish League Championship, but here Paul Gascoigne seems to be getting tied up with Celtic's Paolo Di Canio. (Colorsport)

SCOTTISH LEAGUE CUP FINALS 1946–97

Season	Winners	Runners-up	Score
1946–47	Rangers	Aberdeen	4-0
1947–48	East Fife	Falkirk	4-1 after 0-0 draw
1948–49	Rangers	Raith R	2-0
1949–50	East Fife	Dunfermline Ath	3-0
1950–51	Motherwell	Hibernian	3-0
1951–52	Dundee	Rangers	3-2
1952–53	Dundee	Kilmarnock	2-0
1953–54	East Fife	Partick T	3-2
1954–55	Hearts	Motherwell	4-2
1955–56	Aberdeen	St Mirren	2-1
1956–57	Celtic	Partick T	3-0 after 0-0 draw
1957–58	Celtic	Rangers	7-1
1958–59	Hearts	Partick T	5-1
1959–60	Hearts	Third Lanark	2-1
1960–61	Rangers	Kilmarnock	2-0
1961–62	Rangers	Hearts	3-1 after 1-1 draw
1962–63	Hearts	Kilmarnock	1-0
1963–64	Rangers	Morton	5-0
1964–65	Rangers	Celtic	2-1
1965–66	Celtic	Rangers	2-1
1966–67	Celtic	Rangers	1-0
1967–68	Celtic	Dundee	5-3
1968–69	Celtic	Hibernian	6-2
1969–70	Celtic	St Johnstone	1-0
1970–71	Rangers	Celtic	1-0
1971–72	Partick T	Celtic	4-1
1972–73	Hibernian	Celtic	2-1
1973–74	Dundee	Celtic	1-0
1974–75	Celtic	Hibernian	6-3
1975–76	Rangers	Celtic	1-0
1976–77	Aberdeen	Celtic	2-1
1977–78	Rangers	Celtic	2-1
1978–79	Rangers	Aberdeen	2-1
1979–80	Dundee U	Aberdeen	3-0 after 0-0 draw
1980–81	Dundee U	Dundee	3-0
1981–82	Rangers	Dundee U	2-1
1982–83	Celtic	Rangers	2-1
1983–84	Rangers	Celtic	3-2
1984–85	Rangers	Dundee U	1-0
1985–86	Aberdeen	Hibernian	3-0
1986–87	Rangers	Celtic	2-1
1987–88	Rangers	Aberdeen	3-3
		(Rangers won 5-3 on penalties)	
1988–89	Rangers	Aberdeen	3-2
1989–90	Aberdeen	Rangers	2-1
1990–91	Rangers	Celtic	2-1
1991–92	Hibernian	Dunfermline Ath	2-0
1992–93	Rangers	Aberdeen	2-1
1993–94	Rangers	Hibernian	2-1
1994–95	Raith R	Celtic	2-2
		(Raith R won 6-5 on penalties)	
1995–96	Aberdeen	Dundee	2-0
1996–97	Rangers	Hearts	4-3

SCOTTISH LEAGUE CUP WINS

Rangers 20, Celtic 9, Hearts 4, Aberdeen 5, Dundee 3, East Fife 3, Dundee U 2, Hibernian 2, Motherwell 1, Partick T 1, Raith R 1.

APPEARANCES IN FINALS

Rangers 26, Celtic 21, Aberdeen 11, Hibernian 7, Dundee 6, Hearts 6, Dundee U 4, Partick T 4, East Fife 3, Kilmarnock 3, Dunfermline Ath 2, Motherwell 2, Raith R 2, Falkirk 1, Morton 1, St Johnstone 1, St Mirren 1, Third Lanark 1.

SCOTTISH COCA-COLA CUP 1996–97

FIRST ROUND

4 AUG

Albion R (1) 4 *(McGuire 29, 79, 82, McKenzie 87)*
Arbroath (0) 0 353
Albion R: Ross; Byrne, Pickering, MacFarlane, Martin (Reid), McKenna (McKenzie), Gallagher (Dickson), McInally, Walker, Moore, McGuire.
Arbroath: Hinchcliffe; Florence, McVicar, Waters, Ward, McAulay, Pew, McCarron (McMillan), McWalter, Watters (Scott), Mackie (Roberts).

Ayr U (1) 5 *(Kerrigan 16, 51, English 57, 59, Hood 70)*
Livingston (1) 2 *(Young 15, Callaghan T 80)* 1634
Ayr U: McCulloch (Smith H); Law, Hood, Coyle (Traynor), Jamieson, Connor, Smith P, English, Kerrigan, Henderson, Kinnaird (Smith C).
Livingston: Douglas; Watson, Campbell, Davidson, Tierney, McLeod, McMartin, Callaghan T, Young, Bailey, Duthie (Alleyne).

Brechin C (3) 3 *(Feroz 15, 38, Kerrigan 44)*
Montrose (0) 0 470
Brechin C: Garden; Baillie, Brown, Cairney, Conway, Scott, McNeill, Farnan, Feroz, Kerrigan (McKellar), Christie.
Montrose: Larter; Mailer, Craib, Tindal, Purves, Haro, Taylor, Bird (Ingram), McGlashan, Smith, Glass (Stephen).

Clyde (0) 1 *(Annand 96)*
Inverness CT (0) 0 *aet* 899
Clyde: McLean; McCheyne, McInulty, Ferguson, McConnell, Brown, Harrison (McEwan), Knox, Annand, Mathieson (Michael O'Neill), Brownlie (Prunty).
Inverness CT: Calder; Cherry, Hastings, McArthur, Noble (Bennett), Tokely (Hercher), Wilson (Ross), Teasdale, Stewart, Christie, Thomson.

Cowdenbeath (0) 1 *(Sinclair 86)*
Forfar Ath (1) 2 *(Inglis 7, Higgins 99) aet* 311
Cowdenbeath: Russell; Baillie, Meldrum, Wood, Sinclair, Conn, Hamilton (Munro), Ritchie, Stewart, Brough (Bowmaker), Winter.
Forfar Ath: Donegan; Allison, Craig, Mann, Glennie, Bowes (McPhee), Morgan, Inglis, Higgins, Honeyman, Christie (Loney).

East Stirling (1) 1 *(Ramsay 27)*
Alloa (1) 3 *(McAvoy 29, Irvine 91, Dwyer 94) aet* 465
East Stirling: McDougall; Watt, Russell, Cochrane, Sneddon, Neill, Hunter (Abercromby), Campbell (Farquhar), Ramsay, Lee, McBride.
Alloa: Balfour; Valentine, McAvoy (Gilmour), McCulloch, Cowan, McCormack, Kane, Mackay, Dwyer, Irvine, Moffat.

Queen's Park (0) 3 *(Maxwell 83, Falconer 96, McGoldrick 117)*
Ross Co (0) 1 *(Adams 55) aet* 638
Queen's Park: Bruce; Wilson (Orr), Graham, Elder (Ferguson), Caven, Maxwell, McLauchlan, Arbuckle, Edgar, Cameron (Falconer), McGoldrick.
Ross Co: Cormack; Somerville, Broddle, Cooper (Williamson), Bellshaw, Herd, Ferries, Grant (Andy MacLeod), Adams, Mackay, Golabek.

Stranraer (1) 2 *(Young 13, Sloan 69)*
Queen of the S (0) 0 613
Stranraer: Duffy; Duncan, Hughes, Millar, Howard, McCaffrey, Sloan (McMillan), McIntyre, Young, Docherty (Crawford), Lansdowne.
Queen of the S: Mathieson; Wilson (Laing), McKeown D, Leslie, Lilley, McKeown B, Nicoll (Irving), Bryce, Mallan, Flannigan, Brown.

SECOND ROUND

13 AUG

Airdrieonians (1) 3 *(Cooper 26, Hetherston 73, Eadie 110)*
Raith R (1) 2 *(Rougier 13, 71) aet* 2137
Airdrieonians: Martin; Jack, Smith, Sandison, Johnston, Black (Eadie), Boyle, Davies, Cooper, Connolly P (Lawrence), Hetherston (Wilson).
Raith R: Thomson SY; Kirkwood, Bonar (Millar), Browne, Dennis, Craig, Thomson SM (Twaddle), McInally, Rougier, Lennon, Harvey (Duffield).

Brechin C (0) 0
Hibernian (1) 2 *(Lavety 41, Dow 58)* 1294
Brechin C: Garden; Christie, Brown, Cairney, Conway, Scott, Feroz (McKellar), Farnan, Ross (Brand), McNeill (Kerrigan), Ferguson.
Hibernian: Leighton; Miller W, Dow, Millen, Welsh, Hunter, Lavety, Cameron (McAllister), Wright, Jackson D, McGinlay.

Dundee (0) 2 *(Raeside 75, Hamilton 85)*
Dumbarton (1) 1 *(Dallas 28)* 1872
Dundee: Langfield; Smith, McQueen, Duffy (Farningham), Raeside, Bain, Adamczuk, Charnley, Anderson, Hamilton, Magee (Elliot).
Dumbarton: MacFarlane; Gow, Sharp, Marsland, Meechan J, King, Melvin, McGarvey, McKinnon, Mooney, Dallas.

East Fife (1) 1 *(Dwarika 25)*
St Johnstone (3) 5 *(O'Boyle 15, Scott 23, Tosh 40, Grant 64, 90)* 1724
East Fife: Hamilton; Dixon, Gibb, McStay, Beaton, Cusick (Demmin), Dwarika (Hutcheon), Archibald, Scott, Allan, Lewis.
St Johnstone: Main; McQuillan (McCluskey), Davidson, Sekerlioglu, Weir, Griffin, Scott (Preston), O'Neil, Grant, O'Boyle, Tosh (Farquhar).

Falkirk (1) 2 *(Craig 1, 54)*
Albion R (2) 3 *(MacFarlane 38, McKenzie 42, McInally 65)* 1894
Falkirk: Nelson; McKenzie, Mitchell, McGowan, Berry, Hamilton, Hagen, Craig, McGrillen, Graham (McGraw), Elliot (Corrigan).
Albion R: Ross; Byrne, Pickering, MacFarlane, Martin, Cody (Clark), McInally, Reilly, Walker (McGuire), McKenzie, Gallagher.

Greenock Morton (1) 1 *(Cormack 32)*
Hamilton A (1) 1 *(Sherry 25)* 2405
Greenock Morton: Wylie; Collins, Cormack, Reid, Matheson (McArthur), Anderson, Lilley, Mahood, Hawke (Flannery), McPherson, Rajamaki.
Hamilton A: Ferguson; Hillcoat, Renicks, McEntegart, McKenzie, McIntosh, Quitongo, Sherry, Baptie, Ritchie, McBride (Clark).
aet (Greenock Morton won 4-3 on penalties)

Kilmarnock (0) 0
Ayr U (1) 1 *(Connor 12)* 8543
Kilmarnock: Lekovic; MacPherson, Tallon, Reilly, Whitworth, Anderson, Mitchell, Henry (Montgomerie), Wright, McIntyre, McKee (Roberts).
Ayr U: Smith H; Law, Hood, Coyle, Jamieson, Connor, Smith P, English, Kerrigan (Kinnaird), Henderson, George (Traynor).

Motherwell (0) 0
Alloa (0) 0 3503
Motherwell: Howie; May, McSkimming, Philliben, Martin, Denham, McMillan, Dolan (Wishart), Burns (Arnott), Falconer, Davies.
Alloa: Balfour; Valentine, McAvoy (Gilmour), Nelson, Cowan, McCormack, Kane (Little), Mackay, Dwyer, Irvine, Moffat.
aet (Alloa won 4-2 on penalties)

Partick T (0) 3 *(Stirling 47, Evans 60, 81)*
Forfar Ath (0) 0   1626
Partick T: Cairns; Milne, Stirling, Henderson, Slavin,
Watson, Evans, Farrell (Macdonald), Maskrey
(Docherty), Turner, Lyons.
Forfar Ath: Donegan; Allison, McPhee, Bowes, Glennie,
Craig, Christie, Inglis, Higgins, Morgan, Hannigan
(Sexton).

Queen's Park (0) 0
Aberdeen (1) 2 *(Glass 43, Windass 83)*   2021
Queen's Park: Bruce; Wilson, McGoldrick, Maxwell,
Caven, King, Kennedy (Falconer), Arbuckle, Edgar
(Cameron), McLauchlan (Orr), Graham.
Aberdeen: Watt; McKimmie, Tsvetanov, Rowson (Craig),
Irvine, Inglis, Miller (Young), Windass, Shearer,
Kiriakov, Glass.

St Mirren (1) 4 *(Taylor 44, Gillies 51, Hetherston 62,*
Iwelumo 90)
Berwick R (0) 0   1744
St Mirren: Combe; Dick (McLaughlin), Baker,
McWhirter, Fenwick, Watson, Hetherston, Taylor,
Gillies, Mendes (Archdeacon), Yardley (Iwelumo).
Berwick R: Young; Wilson (Smith), Graham, Coates,
Reid, Walton, Rutherford (Ward), Fraser, McGlynn,
Craig, Miller.

Stirling Albion (1) 1 *(Gibson 28)*
Dundee U (1) 2 *(Winters 1, Coyle 78)*   1673
Stirling Albion: McGeown; Paterson A, Deas, Gibson,
McQuilter, Paterson G, Bone, Jack, McCormick,
Taggart, McLeod (Wood)(Bennett).
Dundee U: Maxwell; Shannon, McQuilken, Pressley,
Benneker, Perry, Winters (Coyle), Bowman, McSwegan,
Johnson (McKinnon), Duffy.

14 AUG

Clyde (0) 1 *(Brown 68)*
Celtic (1) 3 *(Cadete 11, 67, Thom 87)*   7382
Clyde: McLean; McCheyne (Martin O'Neill), McInulty
(McEwan), Ferguson, McConnell, Brown, Gibson, Knox,
Annand, Mathieson, Brownlie (Michael O'Neill).
Celtic: Marshall; Boyd, Wieghorst, McNamara, Hughes,
Grant, Donnelly, McStay (McLaughlin), Van Hooijdonk,
Thom (Anthony), Cadete.

Clydebank (0) 0
Rangers (2) 3 *(Van Vossen 28, 30, McCoist 54)*   6376
Clydebank: Matthews; Agnew, Sutherland, Irons,
Brannigan, Nicholl (McMahon), Teale, Connell (Currie),
Lovering, Grady (Robertson), Bowman.
Rangers: Goram; Wright (McGinty), Albertz, Gough
(McCoist), Petric, Shields, Durrant, McInnes, Miller,
McCall, Van Vossen.

Hearts (0) 1 *(McCann 74)*
Stenhousemuir (1) 1 *(Sprott 35)*   9303
Hearts: Rousset; Frail, Ritchie (McCann), Weir, Mackay,
Bruno, Colquhoun (Beckford), Cameron, Robertson
(Thomas), Fulton, Pointon.
Stenhousemuir: Ellison; Sprott, Banks, Armstrong,
Thomson, Christie, McKee (Logan), Fisher, Hunter
(McGeachie), Hutchison, Henderson.
aet (Hearts won 5-4 on penalties)

Stranraer (0) 1 *(Docherty 70)*
Dunfermline Ath (2) 2 *(French 10, Moore 20)*   613
Stranraer: Duffy B; Duncan, Crawford, Millar, Howard,
McCaffrey, Sloan, Gallagher A (McMillan), Young,
Docherty, Lansdowne(McLaren).
Dunfermline Ath: Westwater; Den Bieman, Fleming,
Clark, Tod, Rice (McCulloch), Moore, Robertson, Smith,
Britton, French (Bingham).

THIRD ROUND
3 SEPT

Albion R (0) 0
Hibernian (1) 2 *(Wright 19, McGinlay 70)*   1202
Albion R: Ross; Byrne, Angus, MacFarlane, Martin,
McInally (Gallagher), McGuire, Cody (Clark), Walker,
Moore, McKenzie (Reilly).
Hibernian: Leighton; Miller, Dow (Cameron), Millen,
Welsh, McLaughlin, McAllister (Jackson C), Harper,
Wright, Jackson D, McGinlay.

Dundee U (1) 2 *(Coyle 20, McSwegan 110)*
Dundee (1) 2 *(Hamilton 40, 97)*   11,902
Dundee U: Maxwell; Perry, McQuilken, Pressley,
Benneker, Duffy, McLaren (McKinnon), Bowman,
McSwegan, Coyle, Winters.
Dundee: Thomson; Smith, McQueen (Magee), Bain
(McKeown), Raeside, Winnie, Shaw (Ferguson),
Charnley, Tosh, Hamilton, Adamczuk.
aet (Dundee won 4-2 on penalties)

Greenock Morton (0) 3 *(Lilley 79, 84, Anderson 80)*
Aberdeen (2) 7 *(Dodds 13, 52, 90, Windass 104, 107, 111,*
118) aet   6324
Greenock Morton: Wylie; Collins, Cormack, Reid,
McCahill, Lindberg (McArthur), Lilley, Mahood, Hawke
(Flannery), Anderson, Rajamaki (McPherson).
Aberdeen: Walker; Grant, Tsvetanov (Woodthorpe),
Young, Inglis, Kombouare, Miller (Shearer), Dodds,
Windass, Kiriakov, Glass.

Partick T (1) 1 *(Evans 35)*
Airdrieonians (0) 0   2679
Partick T: Cairns; Dinnie, Stirling, McWilliams, Slavin,
Watson, Evans (Docherty), Farrell (Macdonald),
Maskrey (Henderson), Turner, Lyons.
Airdrieonians: Martin; Stewart, Smith, Sandison
(Connolly P), Sweeney, Black, Jack, Davies, Cooper,
Eadie (Boyle), Lawrence (McPhee).

St Johnstone (0) 1 *(O'Boyle 51)*
Hearts (1) 3 *(Cameron 15, Beckford 99, Robertson 107)*
aet   6806
St Johnstone: Main; McQuillan, Preston, Sekerlioglu
(Farquhar), Weir (McCluskey), Griffin, Scott, O'Neil,
Grant, O'Boyle, Tosh (Donaldson).
Hearts: Rousset; Mackay, Ritchie, Weir, McPherson,
Bruno (Fulton), McCann, Colquhoun (Robertson),
Beckford (Frail), Cameron, Pointon.

4 SEPT

Alloa (0) 1 *(McAneny P 47)*
Celtic (1) 5 *(Thom 41, Cadete 51, 62, 72, Van Hooijdonk*
53)   12,582
Alloa: Balfour; Valentine, McCormack, McAneny P,
Cowan, McAvoy (Gilmour), Kane, Mackay (McAnenay
M), Dwyer (Moffat), Irvine, Nelson.
Celtic: Marshall; Boyd (Wieghorst), McKinlay,
McNamara, Stubbs, Grant, Di Canio, O'Neil, Van
Hooijdonk, Thom (Donnelly), Cadete (McLaughlin).

Dunfermline Ath (1) 3 *(Britton 30, Bingham 64, French 67)*
St Mirren (1) 1 *(Yardley 37)*   4202
Dunfermline Ath: Westwater; Miller C, Fleming, Den
Bieman, Tod, Robertson, Moore, Britton (Petrie), Smith,
French (Rice), Bingham (Shaw).
St Mirren: Combe; McLaughlin, Baker, McWhirter,
Fenwick, Watson, Hetherston (Smith), Taylor, Gillies
(Iwelumo), Mendes, Yardley.

Rangers (0) 3 *(Albertz 48, Gascoigne 84, McInnes 90)*
Ayr U (0) 1 *(Henderson 59)*   44,732
Rangers: Goram; Cleland, Albertz, Gough, Petric,
Bjorklund, Durie, Gascoigne, Durrant (McKnight),
Miller (McInnes), Van Vossen.
Ayr U: Smith H; Traynor, Law, Coyle, Jamieson, Hood,
George, Connor, Smith P, Henderson (Biggart),
Kinnaird.

QUARTER-FINALS

17 SEPT

Dundee (1) 2 *(Tosh 34, Hamilton 89)*
Aberdeen (0) 1 *(Dodds 71)* 8670
Dundee: Thomson; Smith, Rae, Bain, Raeside, Winnie, Shaw (Ferguson), Charnley, Tosh, Hamilton, Adamczuk (Farningham).
Aberdeen: Walker; McKimmie, Tsvetanov, Rowson (Shearer), Inglis, Kombouare, Bernard, Dodds, Windass, Kiriakov, Glass.

Dunfermline Ath (0) 2 *(Bingham 60, Britton 79)*
Partick T (0) 0 5322
Dunfermline Ath: Westwater; Miller C, Fleming, Den Bieman, Tod, Clark, Bingham (Rice), Britton, Smith, French, Petrie.
Partick T: Cairns; Milne, Stirling, Dinnie, Slavin, Watson, Evans, Henderson, Maskrey (Adams), Moss, Lyons.

Hearts (0) 1 *(Robertson 109)*
Celtic (0) 0 *aet* 14,442
Hearts: Rousset; McManus, Naysmith, Salvatori, McPherson, Thorn, Thomas (Goss), Mackay (Fulton), Robertson, Cameron, McCann.
Celtic: Marshall; Boyd, Mackay, McNamara, Hughes, Grant, Di Canio, Gray (Donnelly), Van Hooijdonk, Thom (Wieghorst), Cadete.

Rangers (1) 4 *(Durie 28, Van Vossen 47, 80, Albertz 88)*
Hibernian (0) 0 45,104
Rangers: Goram; Moore (Ferguson), Albertz, Gough, Petric, Bjorklund, Durie, Gascoigne (McInnes), McCoist (Van Vossen), McCall, Cleland.
Hibernian: Leighton; Miller W, Dow, Millen, Dods, Welsh, McAllister (Harper), Wilkins (Jackson C), Wright, Jackson D, McGinlay.

SEMI-FINALS

22 OCT at Celtic Park

Dunfermline Ath (0) 1 *(Moore 61)*
Rangers (1) 6 *(Laudrup 41, 69, McInnes 56, Andersen 62, 64, Albertz 82)* 16,791
Dunfermline Ath: Lemajic; Miller C, Millar M (Fleming), Den Bieman, Clark, Tod, Moore, Robertson, Smith (Britton), French, Petrie.
Rangers: Snelders; Cleland, Robertson (Shields), Gough, Petric, Bjorklund, McInnes, Gascoigne, Andersen, Albertz, Laudrup (Durrant).

23 OCT at Easter Road Stadium

Hearts (2) 3 *(Beckford 20, Cameron 29 (pen), Paille 60)*
Dundee (0) 1 *(Hamilton 72)* 15,653
Hearts: Rousset; McManus, Pointon, Weir, McPherson (Ritchie), Mackay, Paille (Goss), Bruno, Robertson (Beckford), Cameron, Callaghan.
Dundee: Thomson; Smith, McQueen (Farningham), Bain (Magee), Raeside (Anderson), Tully, Shaw, Charnley, Tosh, Hamilton, Adamczuk.

FINAL

24 NOV at Celtic Park

Rangers (2) 4 *(McCoist 10, 26, Gascoigne 63, 65)*
Hearts (1) 3 *(Fulton 44, Robertson 60, Weir 88)* 48,559
Rangers: Goram; Cleland (Robertson), Moore, Gough, Petric, Bjorklund, Miller, Gascoigne, McCoist, Albertz, Laudrup.
Hearts: Rousset; Weir, Pointon, Mackay, Ritchie, Bruno, Paille (Beckford), Fulton, Robertson, Cameron, McCann.
Referee: H Dallas (Motherwell)

SCOTTISH CUP FINALS 1874–1997

Year	Winners	Runners-up	Score
1874	Queen's Park	Clydesdale	2-0
1875	Queen's Park	Renton	3-0
1876	Queen's Park	Third Lanark	2-0 after 1-1 draw
1877	Vale of Leven	Rangers	3-2 after 0-0 and 1-1 draws
1878	Vale of Leven	Third Lanark	1-0
1879	Vale of Leven*	Rangers	
1880	Queen's Park	Thornlibank	3-0
1881	Queen's Park†	Dumbarton	3-1
1882	Queen's Park	Dumbarton	4-1 after 2-2 draw
1883	Dumbarton	Vale of Leven	2-1 after 2-2 draw
1884	Queen's Park‡	Vale of Leven	
1885	Renton	Vale of Leven	3-1 after 0-0 draw
1886	Queen's Park	Renton	3-1
1887	Hibernian	Dumbarton	2-1
1888	Renton	Cambuslang	6-1
1889	Third Lanark§	Celtic	2-1
1890	Queen's Park	Vale of Leven	2-1 after 1-1 draw
1891	Hearts	Dumbarton	1-0
1892	Celtic¶	Queen's Park	5-1
1893	Queen's Park	Celtic	2-1
1894	Rangers	Celtic	3-1
1895	St Bernard's	Renton	2-1
1896	Hearts	Hibernian	3-1
1897	Rangers	Dumbarton	5-1
1898	Rangers	Kilmarnock	2-0
1899	Celtic	Rangers	2-0
1900	Celtic	Queen's Park	4-3
1901	Hearts	Celtic	4-3
1902	Hibernian	Celtic	1-0
1903	Rangers	Hearts	2-0 after 1-1 and 0-0 draws
1904	Celtic	Rangers	3-2
1905	Third Lanark	Rangers	3-1 after 0-0 draw
1906	Hearts	Third Lanark	1-0
1907	Celtic	Hearts	3-0
1908	Celtic	St Mirren	5-1
1909	••		
1910	Dundee	Clyde	2-1 after 2-2 and 0-0 draws
1911	Celtic	Hamilton A	2-0 after 0-0 draw
1912	Celtic	Clyde	2-0
1913	Falkirk	Raith R	2-0
1914	Celtic	Hibernian	4-1 after 0-0 draw
1920	Kilmarnock	Albion R	3-2
1921	Partick T	Rangers	1-0
1922	Morton	Rangers	1-0
1923	Celtic	Hibernian	1-0
1924	Airdrieonians	Hibernian	2-0
1925	Celtic	Dundee	2-1
1926	St Mirren	Celtic	2-0
1927	Celtic	East Fife	3-1
1928	Rangers	Celtic	4-0
1929	Kilmarnock	Rangers	2-0
1930	Rangers	Partick T	2-1 after 0-0 draw
1931	Celtic	Motherwell	4-2 after 2-2 draw
1932	Rangers	Kilmarnock	3-0 after 1-1 draw
1933	Celtic	Motherwell	1-0
1934	Rangers	St Mirren	5-0
1935	Rangers	Hamilton A	2-1
1936	Rangers	Third Lanark	1-0
1937	Celtic	Aberdeen	2-1
1938	East Fife	Kilmarnock	4-2 after 1-1 draw
1939	Clyde	Motherwell	4-0
1947	Aberdeen	Hibernian	2-1
1948	Rangers	Morton	1-0 after 1-1 draw
1949	Rangers	Clyde	4-1
1950	Rangers	East Fife	3-0
1951	Celtic	Motherwell	1-0
1952	Motherwell	Dundee	4-0
1953	Rangers	Aberdeen	1-0 after 1-1 draw
1954	Celtic	Aberdeen	2-1
1955	Clyde	Celtic	1-0 after 1-1 draw
1956	Hearts	Celtic	3-1
1957	Falkirk	Kilmarnock	2-1 after 1-1 draw
1958	Clyde	Hibernian	1-0
1959	St Mirren	Aberdeen	3-1
1960	Rangers	Kilmarnock	2-0
1961	Dunfermline Ath	Celtic	2-0 after 0-0 draw
1962	Rangers	St Mirren	2-0
1963	Rangers	Celtic	3-0 after 1-1 draw
1964	Rangers	Dundee	3-1

Year	Winners	Runners-up	Score
1965	Celtic	Dunfermline Ath	3-2
1966	Rangers	Celtic	1-0 after 0-0 draw
1967	Celtic	Aberdeen	2-0
1968	Dunfermline Ath	Hearts	3-1
1969	Celtic	Rangers	4-0
1970	Aberdeen	Celtic	3-1
1971	Celtic	Rangers	2-1 after 1-1 draw
1972	Celtic	Hibernian	6-1
1973	Rangers	Celtic	3-2
1974	Celtic	Dundee U	3-0
1975	Celtic	Airdrieonians	3-1
1976	Rangers	Hearts	3-1
1977	Celtic	Rangers	1-0
1978	Rangers	Aberdeen	2-1
1979	Rangers	Hibernian	3-2 after 0-0 and 0-0 draws
1980	Celtic	Rangers	1-0
1981	Rangers	Dundee U	4-1 after 0-0 draw
1982	Aberdeen	Rangers	4-1 (aet)
1983	Aberdeen	Rangers	1-0 (aet)
1984	Aberdeen	Celtic	2-1 (aet)
1985	Celtic	Dundee U	2-1
1986	Aberdeen	Hearts	3-0
1987	St Mirren	Dundee U	1-0 (aet)
1988	Celtic	Dundee U	2-1
1989	Celtic	Rangers	1-0
1990	Aberdeen	Celtic	0-0 (aet)
		(Aberdeen won 9-8 on penalties)	
1991	Motherwell	Dundee U	4-3 (aet)
1992	Rangers	Airdrieonians	2-1
1993	Rangers	Aberdeen	2-1
1994	Dundee U	Rangers	1-0
1995	Celtic	Airdrieonians	1-0
1996	Rangers	Hearts	5-1
1997	Kilmarnock	Falkirk	1-0

*Vale of Leven awarded cup, Rangers failing to appear for replay after 1-1 draw.
†After Dumbarton protested the first game, which Queen's Park won 2-1.
‡Queen's Park awarded cup, Vale of Leven failing to appear.
§Replay by order of Scottish FA because of playing conditions in first match, won 3-0 by Third Lanark.
¶After mutually protested game which Celtic won 1-0.
••Owing to riot, the cup was withheld after two drawn games – between Celtic and Rangers 2-2 and 1-1.

SCOTTISH CUP WINS

Celtic 30, Rangers 27, Queen's Park 10, Aberdeen 7, Hearts 5, Clyde 3, Kilmarnock 3, St Mirren 3, Vale of Leven 3, Dunfermline Ath 2, Falkirk 2, Hibernian 2, Motherwell 2, Renton 2, Third Lanark 2, Airdrieonians 1, Dumbarton 1, Dundee 1, Dundee U 1, East Fife 1, Morton 1, Partick T 1, St Bernard's 1.

APPEARANCES IN FINAL

Celtic 47, Rangers 43, Aberdeen 14, Queen's Park 12, Hearts 11, Hibernian 10, Kilmarnock 8, Vale of Leven 7, Clyde 6, Dumbarton 6, St Mirren 6, Third Lanark 6, Dundee U 7, Motherwell 6, Renton 5, Airdrieonians 4, Dundee 4, Dunfermline Ath 3, East Fife 3, Falkirk 3, Hamilton A 2, Morton 2, Partick T 2, Albion R 1, Cambuslang 1, Clydesdale 1, Raith R 1, St Bernard's 1, Thornlibank 1.

TENNENTS SCOTTISH CUP 1996–97

FIRST ROUND

7 DEC

Alloa (1) 3 *(Dwyer 15, McAneny P 71, Mackay 88)*
Hawick Royal Albert (1) 1 *(Graham 30)*   452
Alloa: Monaghan; Valentine, Nelson, McAneny P,
Cowan, Gilmour, Pew, Mackay, Dwyer, Irvine, Moffat
(McAnenay M).
Hawick Royal Albert: Sinclair; Wharton, Main, Waldie,
Page, Halfpenny (Thompson), Wallace (Copeland),
Potts, Cockburn, Graham, McFarlane (Scott).

Elgin C (0) 0
Whitehill Welfare (3) 3 *(Wood 20, 26, Millar 36)*   1011
Elgin C: Pirie; Dunsire, McLennan, Mone, Moir,
Maguire, Whyte (McHardy R), Ord (Morrison),
Polworth, Green D (McHardy P), Green M.
Whitehill Welfare: Cantley; Neill, Gowrie, McCulloch,
Steel, Millar, Sneddon D (McGarry), Bennett (Richford),
Tulloch, Wood, Thorburn (Middlemist).

14 DEC

Albion R (0) 0
Forfar Ath (0) 0   710
Albion R: Duncan; Byrne, Angus, MacFarlane, Martin,
Clark, McGuire, Dickson, Watters, Walker, McKenzie
(Reilly).
Forfar Ath: Donegan; Mann, Craig, Hamilton, Glennie,
Allison, Morgan, Lee, Hannigan, Honeyman, Loney
(Bowes).

Huntly (1) 1 *(Copland 30)*
Clyde (0) 1 *(Gibson 58)*   944
Huntly: Gardiner; Rougvie, Allan, Copland, Paterson,
Morland, Brown (Gray), Stewart, Selbie, Whyte (Yeats
C), Lennox.
Clyde: McLean; McEwan, McInulty (Carrigan), Prunty,
Brown, Knox, Brownlie, Gillies, Annand, Gibson,
Mathieson (Martin O'Neill).

FIRST ROUND REPLAYS

16 DEC

Clyde (1) 3 *(Annand 28, McEwan 84, Mathieson 95)*
Huntly (1) 2 *(Stewart 25, Copland 85)*   772
Clyde: McLean; McEwan, McInulty (Martin O'Neill),
Prunty, Brown, Knox, Brownlie (Michael O'Neill),
Gillies (Campbell), Annand, Gibson, Mathieson.
Huntly: Gardiner; Yeats T, Allan, Copland, Paterson,
Morland, Rougvie, Stewart (Yeats C)(Brown), Selbie,
Whyte (Gray), Lennox.
aet

Forfar Ath (1) 4 *(Allison 43, Honeyman 74, Lee 78,
Morgan 89)*
Albion R (0) 0   606
Forfar Ath: Donegan; Mann, Craig, Hamilton, Glennie
(Bowes), Allison, Morgan, Lee, Hannigan, Honeyman,
Loney.
Albion R: Duncan; Byrne, Angus, MacFarlane, Martin,
Clark, McGuire, Reilly, Watters (Moore), Walker,
Dickson (Harty).

SECOND ROUND

4 JAN

Berwick R (0) 2 *(McParland 69, 84)*
Peterhead (1) 1 *(Simpson 27 (pen))*   484
Berwick R: Collier; Stewart, Grant, Reid, Finlayson,
Craig (Graham), McParland, Neil, Robinson, Walton,
Watkins (Miller).
Peterhead: Pirie; Watson, Cheyne, King, Simpson,
McCreadie, Yule, Cormack, Milne, Brown, Smith
(McKenzie).

Queen's Park (0) 2 *(Caven 48, Falconer 82)*
Gala Fairydean (1) 1 *(Forrest 41)*   791
Queen's Park: Bruce; Kennedy, Arbuckle, Maxwell,
Caven, King (Wilson), McLauchlan, Fraser, Fitzpatrick
(Falconer), Ferry, McGoldrick.
Gala Fairydean: Massie; Nisbet (Whitehead),
Connachan, Forrest, McNaughton (Neilson), Sneddon,
Manson, Allan, Landells, Findlay, McGinley.

7 JAN

Ayr U (0) 0
Clyde (1) 2 *(Annand 44, Michael O'Neil 51)*   2168
Ayr U: Smith H; Law (George), Humphries
(Henderson), Hood, Jamieson, Traynor, Smith P,
Horace, Kerrigan, Connor, Kinnaird
Clyde: McLean; McEwan, McInulty, Prunty, Brown,
Knox, Brownlie, Gillies, Annand, Campbell, Michael
O'Neill (Mathieson).

11 JAN

East Stirling (2) 4 *(Inglis 1, Stirling 34, 75, Abercromby 82)*
Brora R (1) 3 *(Murray 22, McFee 78, 88)*   446
East Stirling: McDougall; Watt, Russell, Campbell,
Sneddon, Neill, Inglis, Muirhead (Abercromby),
McBride, Ronald, Stirling.
Brora R: Gray; Jack, Cowie, Ross, Allan, Anderson,
McFee (Mailley), Winter, Morris (Farquhar),
MacDougall, Murray (MacDonald).

Spartans (0) 0
Arbroath (0) 0   275
Spartans: Oliver; Ettles, McCall, Findlay, Thomson,
McKeating, Durkin, Knox, Govan (Mitchell), Harley,
Nixon.
Arbroath: Arthur; Peters (Scott), McVicar, McAulay,
Wylie, Ward, Morrison (Florence), McCarron,
McCormick, McWalter, Gallagher.

Whitehill Welfare (1) 2 *(Middlemist 31, Millar 52)*
Queen of the S (1) 3 *(Nesovic 23, Leslie 66, Mallan 78)*
                                                         937
Whitehill Welfare: Cantley; Neill, Gowrie, Cockburn
(Brown), Steel, Millar, Thorburn, Bennett, Tulloch,
Wood (McGarry), Middlemist (Sneddon).
Queen of the S: Mathieson; Kennedy (Alexander),
McKeown D, Leslie, Lilley, McKeown B, Nesovic
(Brown), Bryce, Mallan (Laing), Flannigan, McAllister.

13 JAN

Brechin C (2) 2 *(Sorbie 13, 39)*
Livingston (0) 1 *(Bailey 65)*   405
Brechin C: Garden; Baillie, Brown, Cairney, Conway,
Scott, McKellar, Farnan, Sorbie (Heddle), Brand
(Kerrigan), Ferguson.
Livingston: Douglas; Watson, Campbell, Davidson,
Graham, McLeod, McMartin (Sinclair), Smart, Callaghan
(Harvey), Young, Duthie (Bailey).

Cowdenbeath (0) 1 *(Scott 49)*
Dumbarton (0) 0   294
Cowdenbeath: Russell; Hamilton, Meldrum,
Humphreys,McMahon, Conn, Petrie, Sinclair, Scott,
Winter, Bowmaker.
Dumbarton: Barnes; Davidson, Meechan J, Marsland,
Sharp, McGarvey, King, McKinnon (Granger), Ward,
Glancy, Mooney (Scott).

Forfar Ath (0) 0
Alloa (0) 1 *(Irvine 87)*   618
Forfar Ath: Donegan; Mann, Craig, Hamilton, Bowes,
Allison, Morgan, Lee, Hannigan, Roberts, Loney
(Sexton).
Alloa: Monaghan; Valentine, Nelson, McAneny P,
Cowan, Gilmour (Little), Wilson, Mackay (Kane),
Dwyer, Irvine, Pew.

Ross Co (2) 3 *(Ross 2, 36, 64)*
Montrose (0) 0　　　　　　　　　　　　1193
Ross Co: Hutchison; Farrell (Furphy), Broddle, Herd, Bellshaw, Mackay, Ferries, Ferguson (Connelly), Ross (Adams), Andy MacLeod, McBain.
Montrose: Larter; Mailer, Glass, MacDonald, Craib, Haro, Fisher, Ingram (Purves), McGlashan, Taylor, Tindal.

Stenhousemuir (0) 1 *(Hume 89)*
Hamilton A (0) 2 *(Ritchie 51, Clark 86)*　　641
Stenhousemuir: Ellison; Sprott (Hume), Haddow, Armstrong, Thomson, Banks, Henderson, Fisher, Hunter, Hutchison, Little.
Hamilton A: Ferguson; Hillcoat C, Renicks, Thomson, McCulloch, McIntosh, Fotheringham (Clark), Sherry, Ritchie, McEntegart, McCormick (Quitongo).

Stranraer (0) 1 *(Young 76)*
Inverness CT (0) 1 *(McLean 63)*　　　　577
Stranraer: Matthews; Gallacher I, Crawford, Hughes, Robertson, McCaffrey, McIntyre, Lansdowne, Young, McAulay (Duncan), Docherty (Sloan).
Inverness CT: Calder; Teasdale, Hastings, MacArthur (Bennett), Noble, Cherry, Wilson (Hercher), Stewart, McLean, Christie, Ross (Tokely).

SECOND ROUND REPLAY

13 JAN

Arbroath (1) 3 *(McCarron 23, Wylie 65, Grant 78)*
Spartans (0) 0　　　　　　　　　　　　503
Arbroath: Arthur; Crawford, McVicar, McAulay, Wylie (Florence), Ward, Morrison (Scott), McCarron, Grant, McWalter, Gallagher.
Spartans: Oliver; Ettles (McCann), McCall, Findlay, Thomson, McKeating, Durkin, Knox (Burns), Govan (Harley), Mitchell, Nixon.

15 JAN

Inverness CT (0) 0
Stranraer (0) 0　　　　　　　　　　　　1407
Inverness CT: Calder; Teasdale, Hastings, MacArthur (Bennett), Noble, Cherry, Wilson, Stewart, McLean, Christie, Ross (Tokely).
Stranraer: Duffy B; Gallacher I (Sloan), Crawford (Duncan), Hughes, Robertson, McCaffrey, McIntyre, Lansdowne, Young (McMillan), McAulay, Docherty.
aet (Inverness CT won 4-3 on penalties)

THIRD ROUND

23 JAN

Hibernian (0) 2 *(Miller G 48, McGinlay 77)*
Aberdeen (0) 2 *(Booth 70, Dodds 74)*　　9588
Hibernian: Leighton; Miller W, Love, Grant, Dennis, Hunter, Dow, Harper, Miller G (Cameron), Jackson D, McGinlay.
Aberdeen: Watt; Anderson, Woodthorpe, Rowson (Glass), Inglis, Kombouare, Miller, Kiriakov, Booth (Shearer), Windass (Dodds), Young.

25 JAN

Arbroath (2) 2 *(McCormick 36, 41)*
Greenock Morton (1) 2 *(Hope 20 (og), Hawke 70)*　1410
Arbroath: Arthur; McAulay, Gallagher, McVicar, Wylie, Crawford, Scott, Hope, McCormick, Grant, Florence (Morrison).
Greenock Morton: Wylie; Collins, McArthur, Reid, McCahill (McPherson), Lindberg, Blair (Flannery), Mahood, Hawke, Cormack, Rajamaki.

Clyde (1) 3 *(McInulty 22, Brownlie 67, Gibson 89)*
St Mirren (0) 1 *(Gillies 52)*　　　　　3359
Clyde: McLean; McEwan, McInulty, Prunty, Brown, Knox, Brownlie (Mathieson), Gillies, Annand, Martin O'Neill, Gibson.
St Mirren: Combe; Smith (McWhirter), Baker, McLaughlin, Fenwick, Watson (Iwelumo),Munro (Hetherston), Dick, Gillies, Mendes, Turner.

Dundee (1) 3 *(Power 18, O'Driscoll 65, Anderson 68)*
Queen of the S (1) 1 *(Brown 36)*　　　2391
Dundee: McGlynn; Smith, McQueen (Anderson), Adamczuk, Raeside, Winnie, Shaw, Rae (Tosh), O'Driscoll, Power, Robertson.
Queen of the S: Mathieson; Lilley, McKeown D, Leslie, Rowe, McKeown B, Laing (Flannigan), Bryce, Mallan, Nesovic, Brown.

Dunfermline Ath (3) 4 *(Curran 18, French 42, Smith 44, 76)*
Ross Co (0) 0　　　　　　　　　　　　4786
Dunfermline Ath: Westwater; Den Bieman, McCulloch (Young), Tod, Welsh (Ireland), Rice (Sharp), French, Robertson, Smith, Curran, Bingham.
Ross Co: Hutchison; Farrell, Broddle, Herd, Bellshaw, Ferguson (Williamson), Ferries, Adams (Mackay), Ross, Andy MacLeod, McBain.

Falkirk (0) 1 *(Craig 75)*
Berwick R (1) 1 *(Walton 22)*　　　　　2459
Falkirk: Nelson; McGowan (Foster), Tortolano (Seaton), Gray, Mitchell, Craig, McAllister, Hamilton (McKenzie), McGraw, McGrillen, Hagen.
Berwick R: Collier; Stewart, Laidler, Fraser, Finlayson, Irvine, McParland (Robinson), Craig (Young), Forrester, Walton, Graham.

Hearts (3) 5 *(Cameron 8, Weir 12, Robertson 22,63, Pointon 68)*
Cowdenbeath (0) 0　　　　　　　　　11,485
Hearts: Rousset; Locke, Pointon, Weir, McPherson, Mackay (Frail), McCann (Goss), Fulton, Robertson, Cameron, Hamilton (Paille).
Cowdenbeath: Russell; Hamilton, Meldrum, Conn, McMahon (Munro), Humphreys, Stewart, Winter, Scott (Petrie), Sinclair (Ritchie), Wood.

Inverness CT (1) 1 *(Stewart 12)*
Hamilton A (1) 3 *(McEntegart 16, Ritchie 73, 88)*　3310
Inverness CT: Calder; Teasdale, Hastings, MacArthur, Noble, Cherry, Wilson, Stewart (Tokely), McLean, Christie (Hercher), Ross (Addicoat).
Hamilton A: Ferguson; Hillcoat C, Renicks, McEntegart, McCulloch, McIntosh, Davidson (Thomson), Sherry, Ritchie, McCormick, Fotheringham (Quitongo).

Kilmarnock (1) 2 *(McGowne 44, Brown 48)*
East Stirling (0) 0　　　　　　　　　4783
Kilmarnock: Lekovic; MacPherson, Anderson, Reilly, McGowne, Henry, Bagen, Roberts, McIntyre (Kerr D), Brown, McKee (Burke).
East Stirling: McDougall; Watt, Russell, Ramsay (Hunter), Sneddon, Neill, Inglis, Abercromby, McBride, Ronald, Stirling (Kerr).

Partick T (0) 0
Motherwell (0) 2 *(McSkimming 65, Davies 76)*　5503
Partick T: Hillcoat; Slavin, Stirling, McWilliams, Farrell, Watson, Macdonald (Ayton), Maskrey, Adams, Moss (Docherty), Lyons.
Motherwell: Howie; Philliben, Ross, Van Der Gaag, Martin, McSkimming (Wishart), Burns (Davies), May, Coyne, Falconer, Coyle (McCulloch).

Queen's Park (0) 1 *(Hutcheon 62 (og))*
East Fife (1) 3 *(Christie 39, 69, Baillie 54)*　921
Queen's Park: Bruce; Graham, Arbuckle, Elder, Caven, Maxwell, McLauchlan (Wilson), Fraser, Falconer (Fitzpatrick), Ferry (King), McGoldrick.
East Fife: Hamilton; Dixon, Ritchie, Christie, Johnston, Cameron (Dwarika), Andrew (Gartshore), Donaghy, Baillie (Cusick), Hutcheon, Allan.

Rangers (2) 2 *(Andersen 9, Rozental 30)*
St Johnstone (0) 0 45,037
Rangers: Goram; Cleland, Robertson, Gough, McLaren, Moore, Ferguson, Gascoigne (McCoist), Andersen, Albertz (McInnes), Rozental (Durie).
St Johnstone: Main; McQuillan, Preston, Sekerlioglu, Weir, Griffin, Dasovic, O'Neil, Grant (Ferguson), O'Boyle, Scott (Tosh).

Stirling Albion (0) 0
Dundee U (0) 2 *(Winters 51, McSwegan 82)* 6642
Stirling Albion: McGeown; Paterson A, Deas, Gibson, McQuilter, Paterson G, Bone (Jack), Tait, McCormick, McLaren (Hjartarsson), Bennett.
Dundee U: Dijkstra; McInally (Bowman), Malpas, Pressley, Perry, Pedersen, Olofsson, Zetterlund, Winters (Walker), Dolan, McLaren (McSwegan).

26 JAN at Firhill Stadium

Clydebank (0) 0
Celtic (3) 5 *(Cadete 2, 10, Mackay 29, Van Hooijdonk 56, Di Canio 80)* 16,285
Clydebank: McFarlane; Irons, Connaghan, Murdoch, Currie, Nicholls, Teale, Agnew, Grady, Brown (Connell), Bowman.
Celtic: Kerr; Boyd, McKinlay, McNamara, Mackay, O'Donnell (Hannah), Di Canio, McStay (Hay), Van Hooijdonk, McLaughlin, Cadete.

27 JAN

Airdrieonians (1) 1 *(Sandison 34)*
Raith R (0) 4 *(Craig 49, Kirkwood 58, Rougier 82, Andersen S 89)* 3112
Airdrieonians: Martin; Stewart, Smith, Sandison, Jack, Black, Boyle, Davies, Cooper, Wilson, Connolly P (McPhee).
Raith R: Thomson SY; Kirkwood, Millar, Andersen V, Craig, Millen, Twaddle, Andersen S, Hallum, Lennon, Rougier.

4 FEB

Brechin C (2) 3 *(Brown 34, Brand 41, Kerrigan 76)*
Alloa (0) 0 410
Brechin C: Garden; Farnan, Brown, Cairney, Conway, Scott, McKellar (Feroz), Buick, Brand, Kerrigan, Christie.
Alloa: Monaghan; Valentine, Nelson, McAneny P, Cowan (Little), Gilmour, McAnenay M, Wilson, Kane, Irvine (McCulloch), Pew.

THIRD ROUND REPLAYS
28 JAN

Aberdeen (0) 0
Hibernian (0) 0 15,464
Aberdeen: Watt; Anderson, Woodthorpe, Rowson, Inglis, Kombouare, Miller, Kiriakov (Glass), Booth (Shearer), Windass (Dodds), Young.
Hibernian: Leighton; Miller W, Love, Grant, Dennis, McLaughlin, Cameron, Miller G (Jackson C), Harper, Jackson D (Welsh), McGinlay.
aet (Hibernian won 5-3 on penalties)

Greenock Morton (0) 4 *(Lilley 53, Blair 58, Hawke 66, Cormack 84)*
Arbroath (0) 0 2262
Greenock Morton: Wylie; Collins, McArthur, Johnstone, Reid, Lindberg (McPherson), Lilley (Flannery), Mahood, Hawke (Matheson), Cormack, Blair.
Arbroath: Hinchcliffe; Peters (Longmuir), Gallagher, McVicar, Wylie, Crawford, Scott, Hope, McCormick (Florence), Grant, Morrison.

4 FEB

Berwick R (1) 1 *(Neil 16)*
Falkirk (1) 2 *(Craig 11, McGraw 54)* 1318
Berwick R: Young; Fraser, Stewart, Reid, Finlayson, Irvine (Robinson), Graham (Craig), Neil, Forrester, Walton, Grant.
Falkirk: Nelson; McGowan, Seaton, Mitchell, James, Craig, McAllister, Gray, McGraw, McGrillen, Hagen.

FOURTH ROUND

15 FEB

Brechin C (1) 1 *(Brand 1)*
Raith R (0) 2 *(Kirk 49, Andersen S 66)* 2203
Brechin C: Garden; Farnan, Brown, Cairney, Conway, Heddle, McKellar, Buick, Brand (Feroz), Kerrigan (Smith), Christie.
Raith R: Thomson SY; Kirk (Kirkwood), Millar, Andersen V, Craig, Millen, Twaddle, Andersen S (Hallum), Duffield, Lennon, Rougier.

Clyde (0) 0
Kilmarnock (0) 1 *(Wright 62 (pen))* 4483
Clyde: McLean; McEwan (Carrigan), McCheyne, Prunty, Brown, Knox, Brownliw, Gillies, Annand, Campbell, Mathieson (McConnell).
Kilmarnock: Lekovic; MacPherson, Kerr D, Montgomerie, McGowne, Reilly, Mitchell, Brown, Wright, Bagen, McKee (Burke).

Falkirk (1) 2 *(McAllister 27, Hagen 72)*
Dunfermline Ath (1) 1 *(Petrie 12)* 6090
Falkirk: Nelson; McGowan, Seaton, Mitchell, James, Gray, McAllister, McKenzie, Crabbe (McGraw), Hagen, Ward.
Dunfermline Ath: Westwater; Miller C, Fleming, Tod, Welsh (Moore), Millar M, Bingham, Robertson, Smith (French), Britton, Petrie.

Greenock Morton (1) 2 *(Lilley 4 (pen), Hawke 76)*
Dundee (0) 2 *(Power 51, Anderson 85)* 4195
Greenock Morton: Wylie; Collins, McArthur, Anderson, McCahill, Lindberg, Lilley, Aitken, Hawke, Cormack, McPherson (Rajamaki).
Dundee: Thomson; Tully, McQueen, Adamczuk, Raeside, Rae (McKeown), Shaw, Anderson, Tosh (O'Driscoll), Power (Magee), Robertson.

Motherwell (1) 1 *(Coyle 34)*
Hamilton A (0) 1 *(Clark 69)* 8050
Motherwell: Howie; May, McMillan (McSkimming), Van Der Gaag, Martin, Denham (Ross), Burns, Davies, Coyne, Falconer, Coyle.
Hamilton A: Ferguson; Hillcoat C, Renicks, Thomson, McCulloch, McIntosh, Quitongo, Sherry, Ritchie, McCormick, Clark.

Rangers (3) 3 *(Robertson 12, Steven 27, McCoist 36)*
East Fife (0) 0 41,064
Rangers: Goram; Cleland, Robertson, Gough, Steven, Bjorklund, Durie (Durrant), Ferguson, McCoist, Albertz, Laudrup (Andersen).
East Fife: Hamilton; Allan, Ritchie, Christie, Johnston, Gibb, Dwarika (Baillie), Donaghy, Andrew (Cameron), Dixon (Cusick), Dyer.

16 FEB

Hearts (0) 1 *(Hamilton 81)*
Dundee U (0) 1 *(McManus 67 (og))* 14,833
Hearts: Rousset; Locke (Murray), Pointon (Robertson), Weir, McPherson, McManus, Salvatori (Mackay), Fulton, Hamilton, Cameron, McCann.
Dundee U: Dijkstra; McInally (McKinnon), Malpas, Pressley, Perry, Pedersen, Olofsson, Zetterlund, Winters (McSwegan), Dolan, McLaren.

17 FEB

Hibernian (0) 1 *(Jackson D 83 (pen))*
Celtic (1) 1 *(O'Donnell 16)* 16,000
Hibernian: Leighton; Renwick, McQuilken, Grant, Dennis, Hunter, Jackson C (Miller G), Charnley, Harper, Jackson D, Elliot (Wright).
Celtic: Kerr; Boyd, McKinlay, Mackay, Stubbs, O'Donnell, Di Canio, McStay, Van Hooijdonk, Thom (Hay), Hannah.

FOURTH ROUND REPLAYS
18 FEB

Dundee (0) 0
Greenock Morton (0) 1 *(Mason 106)* 4346
Dundee: Thomson; Smith, Rae (McKeown), Adamczuk, Raeside, Tully, Shaw, Anderson (Magee), Tosh, Power (O'Driscoll), Robertson.
Greenock Morton: Wylie; Collins, McArthur, Anderson, McCahill, Lindberg (Mason), Lilley, Aitken, Hawke (Rajamaki), Cormack, McPherson.
aet

25 FEB

Dundee U (1) 1 *(Winters 4)*
Hearts (0) 0 12,376
Dundee U: Dijkstra; McKinnon (Sinclair), Malpas, Pressley, Perry, Pedersen, Olofsson, Zetterlund, Winters (McSwegan), Dolan, McLaren (McInally).
Hearts: Rousset; Locke (Robertson), Naysmith, Weir, McPherson, Ritchie, Salvatori (Mackay), Fulton, Hamilton, Cameron, McCann.

26 FEB

Celtic (1) 2 *(O'Donnell 33, Di Canio 54)*
Hibernian (0) 0 45,880
Celtic: Kerr; Boyd, McKinlay, McNamara, Mackay, Grant, Di Canio, McStay (McLaughlin), Donnelly (Thom), O'Donnell, Cadete.
Hibernian: Leighton; Renwick, Miller W, Grant (Cameron), Dods, McCaffrey (Miller G), Jackson C, Charnley, Harper, Jackson D, Wright.

Hamilton A (0) 0
Motherwell (1) 2 *(Coyle 1, 76)* 4285
Hamilton A: Ferguson; Hillcoat C, Renicks, Thomson, McKenzie, McIntosh, Quitongo, McEntegart, Ritchie, McCormick (McFarlane), Clark.
Motherwell: Howie; Philliben, Ross, Van Der Gaag, Martin, McMillan, May, Davies (Burns), Coyne, McCulloch, Coyle.

QUARTER-FINALS
6 MAR

Celtic (2) 2 *(Mackay 11, Di Canio 19)*
Rangers (0) 0 49,284
Celtic: Kerr; Annoni, McKinlay, McNamara, Mackay, Grant, Di Canio (Thom), McStay, Stubbs, O'Donnell (Hannah), Cadete.
Rangers: Goram; Cleland (Durrant), Robertson, Petric, McLaren, Bjorklund, Moore, Ferguson, Andersen (McCoist), Albertz (Van Vossen), Laudrup.

8 MAR

Dundee U (0) 4 *(McLaren 46, 65, Winters 62, Olofsson 87)*
Motherwell (0) 1 *(Van Der Gaag 80)* 11,112
Dundee U: Dijkstra; McKinnon (Sinclair), Malpas, Pressley, Perry, Pedersen, Olofsson, Zetterlund, Winters (McSwegan), Dolan (McInally), McLaren.
Motherwell: Howie; McMillan, Ross (Denham), Van Der Gaag, Martin, Valakari (Davies), Burns, McCulloch, Coyne, Falconer, Coyle.

Falkirk (1) 2 *(James 44, Hagen 81)*
Raith R (0) 0 6701
Falkirk: Nelson; Oliver, McGowan, Gray, James, Mitchell (Seaton), McAllister, Craig (McGraw), Crabbe, Hagen, Ward (McGrillen).
Raith R: Thomson SY; Kirk (Rougier), Millar, Mitchell (Harvey), Craig, Millen, Twaddle, Duffield, Kirkwood, Lennon, Andersen S.

Greenock Morton (0) 2 *(Mahood 55, 62)*
Kilmarnock (3) 5 *(Henry 13, 40, 88, Wright 31, McIntyre 66)* 8826
Greenock Morton: Wylie; Collins, McArthur (McPherson), Anderson, McCahill, Lindberg (Aitken), Lilley, Mahood, Hawke, Cormack, Rajamaki (Matheson).
Kilmarnock: Lekovic; MacPherson, Kerr D, Montgomerie, Hamilton, Reilly, Bagen (Findlay), Henry, Wright (Brown), McIntyre, Burke (McKee).

SEMI-FINALS
12 APR at Ibrox Stadium

Celtic (0) 1 *(Johnson 70)*
Falkirk (0) 1 *(James 85)* 45,261
Celtic: Kerr; Boyd, McKinlay, Annoni, Stubbs (McNamara), O'Donnell, Di Canio, Hannah, Johnson, Thom, Cadete.
Falkirk: Nelson; McGowan, Seaton, Oliver, James, Gray, McAllister, McKenzie (Craig), Crabbe (Fellner), Hagen, McGrillen.

14 APR at Easter Road Stadium

Kilmarnock (0) 0
Dundee U (0) 0 12,391
Kilmarnock: Lekovic; MacPherson, Kerr D, Montgomerie, McGowne, Reilly, Bagen, Henry, Wright, McIntyre, McKee (Brown).
Dundee U: Dijkstra; McKimmie, Malpas, Duffy, Perry, Pedersen, Olofsson, Zetterlund, Winters (McSwegan), Dolan, McLaren (Bowman).

SEMI-FINALS REPLAYS
22 APR at Easter Road Stadium

Dundee U (0) 0
Kilmarnock (0) 1 *(McIntyre 86)* 9265
Dundee U: Dijkstra; Duffy, Malpas (Bowman), Pressley, Perry, Pedersen, Olofsson, Zetterlund, McKinnon, Dolan (Winters), McLaren.
Kilmarnock: Lekovic; MacPherson, Kerr D, Montgomerie, McGowne, Reilly, Bagen (McKee), Henry, Wright (Brown), McIntyre, Holt.

23 APR at Ibrox Stadium

Falkirk (1) 1 *(McGrillen 20)*
Celtic (0) 0 35,879
Falkirk: Nelson; McGowan, Seaton, Oliver, James, Gray, McAllister, McKenzie, Crabbe (Fellner), Hagen, McGrillen (Craig).
Celtic: Kerr; Boyd, McKinlay, McNamara, Stubbs, O'Donnell (Johnson), Di Canio, Hannah, Donnelly (McLaughlin), Thom, Cadete.

FINAL
24 MAY at Ibrox Stadium

Kilmarnock (1) 1 *(Wright 20)*
Falkirk (0) 0 48,953
Kilmarnock: Lekovic; MacPherson, Kerr D, Montgomerie, McGowne, Reilly, Bagen (Mitchell), Burke, Wright (Henry), McIntyre (Brown), Holt.
Falkirk: Nelson; McGowan, Seaton, Oliver, James, Gray, McAllister, McKenzie, Crabbe (Craig), Hagen, McGrillen (Fellner).
Referee: H Dallas (Motherwell)

SCOTTISH LEAGUE CHALLENGE CUP 1996–97

FIRST ROUND

8 AUG

Dundee (1) 3 *(Tosh 22, Hamilton 56, Magee 70)*
Stenhousemuir (0) 0   1304
Dundee: Thomson; Smith, McQueen, Duffy, Bain,
Raeside, Adamczuk, Charnley (McKeown), Tosh,
Hamilton, Magee (Anderson).
Stenhousemuir: Ellison; Sprott, Banks, Armstrong,
Thomson, Haddow (Henderson), McKee (Logan),
Fisher, Hunter, Hutchison, Little.

Hamilton A (1) 2 *(Quitongo 23, 89)*
St Mirren (0) 1 *(Hetherston 76)*   898
Hamilton A: Ferguson; Hillcoat C, Renicks, Thomson,
McKenzie, McIntosh, Quitongo, Sherry, Baptie, Ritchie,
Clark.
St Mirren: Combe; Dick, Baker, McWhirter, Fenwick,
Archdeacon (Smith), Hetherston, Taylor, Lavety,
Watson, Yardley (Iwelumo).

10 AUG

Albion R (0) 1 *(McKenzie 80)*
St Johnstone (0) 2 *(Grant 58, O'Boyle 108 (pen))*   856
Albion R: Ross; Byrne (Brown), Pickering, MacFarlane,
Martin, Gallagher, McGuire (Dickson), McInally,
Walker (Harty), Moore, McKenzie.
St Johnstone: Main; McQuillan, Davidson, Griffin, Weir,
McGowne (Tosh), O'Neil, Scott (Farquhar), Grant,
O'Boyle, Preston.
aet

Alloa (0) 3 *(Irvine 53, 64, 81)*
Clyde (3) 3 *(Mathieson 19, 42, Knox 33)*   577
Alloa: Balfour; Valentine, McAvoy (Gilmour),
McCulloch (Nelson), Cowan, McCormack, Kane (Little),
Mackay, Dwyer, Irvine, Moffat.
Clyde: McLean; McCheyne, McInulty, Ferguson,
McConnell, Brown, Martin O'Neill (Harrison), Knox,
Annand (Michael O'Neill), Mathieson, Brownlie
(McEwan).
aet (Clyde won 5-4 on penalties)

Arbroath (0) 2 *(Peters 65, Welsh 115)*
Queen of the S (0) 3 *(Flannigan 67, 105, Mallan 100
(pen))*   386
Arbroath: Hinchcliffe; Peters, Florence, Waters M, Ward,
McAulay, Pew (Elliot), Gardner, Watters W, Scott
(Welsh), Clark.
Queen of the S: Mathieson; Kennedy, McKeown D,
Leslie (Cochrane), Lilley, McKeown B, Wilson (Laing),
Bryce, Mallan, Flannigan, Brown (Rowe).
aet

Berwick R (0) 0
Stranraer (2) 2 *(Docherty 23 (pen), Sloan 32)*   325
Berwick R: Young; Wilson, Walton (Miller), Smith, Reid,
Coates, Rutherford, Forrester (Craig), McGlynn, Fraser,
Graham.
Stranraer: Duffy B; Duncan (Gallacher I), Crawford,
Millar, Howard, McCaffrey, Sloan, Robertson
(McLaren), Young (McMillan), Docherty, Lansdowne.

Brechin C (0) 0
Stirling Albion (0) 0   333
Brechin C: Garden; Christie, Brown, Cairney, Conway,
Scott, Feroz, Farnan, Ross (Brand), McNeill (McKellar),
Ferguson.
Stirling Albion: McGeown, Paterson A, Deas, Gibson
(Jack), McQuilter, Paterson G, Bennett, Tait,
McCormick, Taggart, McLeod (Wood).
aet (Stirling Albion won 3-0 on penalties)

Clydebank (0) 0
East Stirling (0) 0   263
Clydebank: Matthews; Agnew, Sutherland, Irons,
Brannigan, Nicholls, Teale, Connell, Robertson (Miller),
Grady, Bowman.
East Stirling: McDougall; Cochrane, Russell, Campbell,
Sneddon (Abercromby), Neill, McBride, Ronald, Hunter
(Ross), Lee (Scott), Watt.
aet (East Stirling won 3-2 on penalties)

Cowdenbeath (0) 0
Falkirk (0) 2 *(Hagen 94, McGraw 102)*   845
Cowdenbeath: Russell; Munro, Baillie, Meldrum, Sinclair,
Conn, Hamilton, Ritchie, Houston (McGregor), Brough
(Stewart), Winter.
Falkirk: Nelson; McKenzie, Mitchell, McGowan, Berry,
Hamilton, Hagen (Corrigan), Craig, McGrillen, Graham
(McGraw), Elliot.
aet

Forfar Ath (0) 0
Greenock Morton (2) 4 *(Lilley 30, 61, Rajamaki 42,
Flannery 68)*   747
Forfar Ath: Donegan; Allison (Loney), Craig (Hamilton),
Mann, Glennie, Bowes, Morgan, Inglis, Higgins,
Honeyman, McPhee.
Greenock Morton: Wylie; Collins, Cormack, Anderson,
McCahill, Lindberg, Lilley (Flannery), Mahood, Hawke,
McPherson (Matheson), Rajamaki (McArthur).

Livingston (0) 1 *(Young 70)*
Inverness C T (1) 2 *(Thomson 9, Cherry 90)*   1335
Livingston: Douglas; Watson, Duthie, Davidson, Tierney,
McLeod, McMartin, Bailey, Young, Callaghan T,
Sinclair.
Inverness C T: Calder; MacArthur, Hastings, Bennett,
Noble (McAllister), Cherry, Wilson, Teasdale, Stewart,
Christie, Thomson.

Montrose (1) 2 *(Smith 17, Glass 48)*
Dumbarton (0) 0   309
Montrose: Larter; Mailer, Craib, Tindal, Purves, Haro,
Taylor, Bird (Ingram), McGlashan, Smith, Glass.
Dumbarton: MacFarlane; Gow, Sharp, Marsland,
Meechan J, McGarvey, Mooney, King, McKinnon,
Granger (Glancy), Ward (Melvin).

Partick T (0) 3 *(Stirling 55, Henderson 105, Maskrey 113
(pen)*
Queen's Park (0) 1 *(Falconer 53)*   2078
Partick T: Cairns; Milne, Stirling, McWilliams
(Henderson), Slavin, Watson, Evans (Docherty), Farrell
(Macdonald), Maskrey, Turner, Lyons.
Queen's Park: Bruce; Wilson, Graham, Maxwell, Caven,
King, McLauchlan (Orr), Arbuckle, Edgar (Falconer),
Cameron (Kennedy), McGoldrick.
aet

Ross Co (0) 0
Ayr U (1) 4 *(English 35, Smith P 49, 75, Jamieson 73)* 963
Ross Co: Cormack; Matheson, Mackay, Herd (Ruickbie),
Bellshaw, Watt, Ferries, Adams, Milne, Connelly,
Golabek.
Ayr U: Smith H; Law, Hood, Coyle, Jamieson (Traynor),
Connor (George), Smith P, English, Kerrigan (Mercer),
Henderson, Kinnaird.

SECOND ROUND

26 AUG

Ayr U (0) 0
St Johnstone (1) 4 *(Scott 44, O'Neil 53, Law 59 (og),
Sekerlioglu 60)*   1812
Ayr U: Smith H; Law, Traynor, Hood, Jamieson
(Wilson), Connor, Smith P, English, Smith C (Mercer),
Henderson, Kinnaird (Biggart).
St Johnstone: Main; McQuillan (Whiteford), Davidson,
Sekerlioglu, Weir, Griffin, Scott (Farquhar), O'Neil,
Grant (Tosh), O'Boyle, Preston.

27 AUG

Airdrieonians (0) 0
Dundee (1) 2 *(Tosh 10, Shaw 70)* 1313
Airdrieonians: Martin; Jack, Johnston, Sandison, Stewart (McIntyre), Black (Lawrence), Boyle (Connelly G), Davies, Eadie, Wilson, Connolly P.
Dundee: Thomson; Smith, McQueen, Farningham, Raeside, Winnie, Shaw, McKeown, Tosh (Ferguson), Hamilton, Adamczuk.

East Fife (1) 2 *(Archibald 16, Scott 83)*
Falkirk (0) 0 942
East Fife: Hamilton; McStay (Lewis), Gibb, Dixon, Beaton (Allan), Cusick, Donaghy, Archibald (Winiarski), Scott, Hutcheon, Andrew.
Falkirk: Mathers; McKenzie, Corrigan (Kidd), McGowan, Berry, Hamilton, Seaton, McGraw, McGrillen, Gray (Graham), Hagen (Elliot).

Greenock Morton (1) 2 *(Lilley 12, Anderson 48)*
Queen of the S (0) 1 *(Nesovic 80)* 1858
Greenock Morton: Wylie; Collins, Cormack, Johnstone, McCahill, Reid, Lilley (Matheson), Anderson, Flannery (Hawke), McArthur, Rajamaki (McPherson).
Queen of the S: Mathieson; Kennedy (Nesovic), McKeown D, Townsley, Lilley, McKeown B, Laing (Lancaster), Bryce, Mallan, Flannigan, Brown (McFarlane).

Montrose (1) 2 *(McGlashan 20, 52)*
East Stirling (1) 1 *(Ronald 17)* 337
Montrose: Larter; Mailer, Tindal, MacDonald, Craib, Haro, Taylor, Bird, McGlashan, Smith, Masson P.
East Stirling: Wilson; Russell, Conway (Cochrane), Campbell, Neill, Sneddon, Ronald, Ramsay, Scott (Hunter), Murray (Kerr), McBride.

Partick T (0) 2 *(McWilliams 49, Stirling 70)*
Hamilton A (0) 1 *(Quitongo 88)* 1693
Partick T: Cairns; Milne (Macdonald), Stirling, Dinnie, Slavin, Watson, Docherty, Farrell, Maskrey (Henderson), McWilliams, Lyons.
Hamilton A: Scott (Paris); McKenzie, Hillcoat, McEntegart (Lorimer), Baptie, McIntosh, Quitongo, Sherry, McFarlane (McBride), Clark, Thomson.

Stirling Albion (0) 3 *(Gibson 57, Bone 70, 85)*
Inverness C T (0) 1 *(Stewart 81)* 838
Stirling Albion: McGeown; Paterson A, Deas, Gibson, McQuilter, Paterson G, Bone, Jack (McGrotty), McCormick, Taggart, Woods (Bennett).
Inverness C T: Calder; Teasdale, Hastings, MacArthur, Noble, Cherry, Wilson, Hercher, Thomson, Christie, Ross (Stewart).

28 AUG

Stranraer (0) 2 *(McCaffrey 62, Sloan 84)*
Clyde (1) 1 *(Annand 25)* 518
Stranraer: Duffy B; McIntyre (Duncan), Crawford, Millar, Gallagher A, McCaffrey, Sloan, Lansdowne, Young, McMillan, Docherty (McAulay).
Clyde: McLean; Knox, McInulty, Ferguson, Gillies (Harrison), Brown, Martin O'Neill, Gibson (Prunty), Annand, Mathieson (McEwan), Brownlie.

QUARTER-FINALS

10 SEPT

Dundee (0) 1 *(Farningham 66)*
St Johnstone (4) 5 *(Grant 1, Whiteford 27, Preston 38, Farquhar 44, 54)* 2346
Dundee: Thomson; Rae, Duffy (Tully), Farningham, Raeside, Winnie, Anderson, McKeown (Charnley), Tosh, Hamilton, Magee (Ferguson).
St Johnstone: Main; McQuillan, Preston (McAnespie), Farquhar, Whiteford, Griffin, Donaldson, O'Neil (King), Grant, O'Boyle, Tosh.

East Fife (0) 0
Stranraer (0) 1 *(Sloan 63)* 606
East Fife: Hamilton; McStay, Gibb (Gartshore), Dixon, Beaton (Demmin), Cusick, Donaghy, Allan, Andrew, Hutcheon, Winiarski (Mair).
Stranraer: Duffy; McIntyre, Duncan, Millar, Gallagher A, McCaffrey, Sloan, Lansdowne, Young (McMillan), McAulay, Docherty.

Greenock Morton (2) 2 *(Matheson 3, Flannery 14)*
Partick T (1) 1 *(Evans 40)* 2513
Greenock Morton: Wylie; Anderson, Cormack, Reid, McCahill, McPherson, Lilley, Mahood, Flannery (Blair), McArthur, Matheson (Rajamaki).
Partick T: Cairns; Milne, Stirling, McWilliams (Adams), Slavin, Dinnie (Ayton), Evans, Henderson, Docherty, Turner, Lyons.

Stirling Albion (0) 1 *(Bone 65)*
Montrose (1) 3 *(Ingram 6, Masson P 56, Taylor 65)* 616
Stirling Albion: McGeown; Paterson A, Deas, Gibson, McQuilter, Paterson G, Bone, Tait (Mitchell), McCormick, Taggart, Wood (McGrotty).
Montrose: Larter; Mailer, Tindal, MacDonald, Craib, Haro, Cooper (Tosh), Bird, Taylor, Ingram (Stephen), Masson P.

SEMI-FINALS

2 OCT

Stranraer (2) 3 *(McIntyre 7, McAulay 16, McMillan 76)*
Greenock Morton (0) 0 1383
Stranraer: Duffy B; McIntyre, Black, Hughes, Gallagher A (Robertson), McCaffrey, Sloan (Bilsland), Lansdowne, McMillan, McAulay (Crawford), Docherty.
Greenock Morton: Wylie; Collins, Cormack, Anderson, McCahill, McPherson (Blair), Matheson, Mahood, Hawke, McArthur, Rajamaki.

8 OCT

St Johnstone (1) 4 *(Grant 31, 56, 70 (pen), O'Boyle 75)*
Montrose (1) 2 *(McGlashan 41, 87 (pen))* 2675
St Johnstone: Main; McQuillan, Preston, Sekerlioglu (Tosh), Weir, Griffin, Scott, O'Neil, Grant (Fyhr), O'Boyle, Jenkinson.
Montrose: Larter; Mailer (Tosh), Tindal, MacDonald (Ingram), Craib, Haro, Cooper, Bird (Stephen), McGlashan, Taylor, Masson P.

FINAL

3 NOV at Broadwood Stadium

Stranraer (1) 1 *(Sloan 27)*
St Johnstone (0) 0 5522
Stranraer: Duffy B; Duncan, Black (Crawford), Hughes, Gallagher A (Robertson), McCaffrey, Sloan, Lansdowne, Young (McMillan), McAulay, Docherty.
St Johnstone: Main; McQuillan, Preston, Sekerlioglu (Fyhr), Weir, Griffin, Tosh, O'Neil, Grant, Ferguson (Farquhar), Jenkinson.
Referee: K W Clark (Paisley)

WELSH FOOTBALL 1996–97

Welsh football is rapidly starting to resemble the proverbial curate's egg. On the international front, little progress towards reaching that elusive final stage of a major competition was made but at club level, Barry Town created history on the European stage and Wrexham, Cardiff and Swansea all gave their supporters something to smile about. This season, a new televised tournament involving most of the top clubs in Wales will give the game an even higher profile yet the national team's status continues to decline.

Back-to-back defeats by Holland—including a humiliating 7-1 hammering in Eindhoven—did not augur well. Belgium's 2-1 win and a 0-0 draw with Turkey at Cardiff Arms Park finally put paid to Welsh chances of reaching next year's World Cup finals in France. Impending trips to Istanbul and Brussels are likely to provide equally cold comfort.

Sadly, manager Bobby Gould has proved an easy target for his critics. His poor record of just four wins in 13 matches merely underlines the harsh reality of competing in international football with an impoverished squad. In truth, Gould has had little alternative but to build for the future. With the thirtysomethings virtually gone—only Mark Hughes remains first choice for Wales—it was inevitable that youngsters would be blooded.

Perhaps some players were discarded too early, Gould's self-confessed tactical naivety at international level has been cruelly exposed but no one can deny his part in the emergence of young talent. Robert Page of Watford and John Hartson, the West Ham striker—both products of a promising Under-21 squad—have made their mark—although Hartson's elevation to the full national side was long overdue.

Give youth its head—and journalists something to write about—appears to have been Gould's policy. If nothing else, he has added spice to a depressing diet of defeats. After being beaten 3-1 at Cardiff Arms Park by Holland, he wore a wig at the post-match press conference in a light-hearted attempt to lift the gloom. The despondency created by the Belgium defeat was overshadowed by Gould becoming embroiled in an alleged race row with the black Bolton striker Nathan Blake and then a 1-0 win in Scotland resulted in an extraordinary journey through his *curriculum vitae*. When asked by a radio reporter about his future with Wales, Gould quickly catalogued his credentials for becoming the new manager of either Everton, Celtic and Southampton. In hindsight, it proved a shrewd move because he was later offered a two-year extension to his contract.

After threatening to complete a unique domestic treble during the previous season, Barry Town made history by sweeping the board. They retained their League of Wales title by a staggering 21 points before beating Bangor City in a penalty shoot-out to lift the League Cup and finally disposing of a spirited Cwmbran side with a 2-1 win in the Welsh Cup Final. Nobody could begrudge Barry their success. As the only full-time club—partly through local council backing—they were expected to dominate again. Yet it was their UEFA Cup exploits which put them firmly on the football map of Britain and, indeed, of Europe.

Barry became the first League of Wales club to reach the first round of the UEFA Cup after beating Dinaburg from Latvia and Vasutas of Hungary. A 3-1 defeat by Aberdeen at Pittodrie in the first leg of the historic first round tie simply inspired Barry to produce a magnificent display on a wet and windy night at revamped Jenner Park. They scored an early goal, went 2-1 down but recovered to lead 3-2 before Aberdeen's third put the tie beyond them. Barry's adventure was over but their quest for greater European glory will continue this season, courtesy of benefactor Paula O'Halloran, when they take part in the qualifying rounds of the Champions League.

The other Welsh representatives, Mid-Wales clubs Newtown and Llansantffraid, fared less well—being soundly beaten by FC Skonto from Latvia and Poland's Ruch Chorzow respectively. Newtown deserve credit for staging their UEFA Cup tie at an upgraded Latham Park while the village side of Llansantffraid upset the odds by holding the Polish Cup Winners at home before being blown away in the away leg.

Over the summer, Ebbw Vale saw their ambition rewarded by representing Wales in the Intertoto Cup while Inter Cable-Tel will compete in the UEFA Cup this season as league runners-up. Ton Pentre, who resigned, Holywell and Briton Ferry were relegated as the FAW complied with UEFA's recommendations to reduce the size of the League of Wales.

The three Welsh Nationwide League clubs promised much but eventually delivered little. Wrexham maintained their remarkable FA Cup giant-killing tradition by beating West Ham and Birmingham en route to the quarter-finals and then froze in a 1-0 defeat by fellow Second Division side Chesterfield. For the second successive season, the Robins narrowly missed out on a promotion play-off place.

In the Third Division, Cardiff and Swansea both reached the play-offs with Cardiff, as they had all season, flattering to deceive and losing to Northampton. Relegated Swansea, with former Liverpool star Jan Molby at the helm, swept aside Chester in the semi-finals. They appeared to be heading towards extra-time at Wembley when a disputed twice-taken Northampton free-kick in the fourth minute of injury time brought their season to a cruel end. Player/manager Molby has performed a minor miracle in transforming the ugly ducklings into proud Swans. Who would bet against him going one better and securing automatic promotion next time around?

The new FAW Invitation Cup will almost produce the reunification of Welsh football. Wrexham, Cardiff and Swansea will be joined by Barry, Newton and Conwy from the League of Wales and Merthyr, who like the other exiled clubs, Colwyn Bay and Newport, had a disappointing season in the English pyramid. Whether the competition will justify the optimism of its backers—the BBC and the FAW—is another matter. The financial rewards—as much as £100,000 to the winners—have persuaded the clubs to add the new tournament to their already crowded fixture lists. Far away from the riches of the Premiership, money doesn't just talk—it shouts.

GRAHAME LLOYD

LEAGUE OF WALES

		Home			Goals		Away			Goals		
	P	W	D	L	F	A	W	D	L	F	A	Pts
Barry Town	40	18	2	0	78	15	15	4	1	51	11	105
Inter Cable-Tel	40	15	3	2	46	14	11	3	6	34	18	84
Ebbw Vale	40	13	4	3	50	14	10	5	5	37	26	78
Caernarfon Town	40	12	4	4	39	26	11	5	4	42	32	78
Newtown	40	10	5	5	32	22	12	0	8	42	27	71
Llansantffraid	40	10	4	6	40	30	9	8	3	38	24	69
Conwy United	40	11	5	4	33	13	9	3	8	33	31	68
Bangor City	40	12	3	5	41	22	8	2	10	41	40	65
Cwmbran Town	40	9	4	7	39	24	10	4	6	32	27	65
Porthmadog	40	10	4	6	38	27	8	4	8	26	33	62
Connah's Quay Nomads	40	9	3	8	35	34	7	6	7	27	30	57
Cemaes Bay	40	5	5	10	26	33	8	5	7	36	39	49
Aberystwyth Town	40	8	2	10	41	35	5	6	9	26	47	47
Caersws	40	6	4	10	23	39	5	5	10	30	38	42
Flint Town United	40	5	3	12	26	43	6	5	9	22	33	41
Carmarthen Town	40	5	3	12	19	41	6	4	10	22	38	40
Welshpool	40	4	7	9	27	37	6	2	12	23	43	39
Ton Pentre	40	7	3	10	33	45	5	0	15	26	54	39
Rhyl	40	6	5	9	24	23	4	3	13	27	48	38
Holywell Town	40	4	4	12	30	43	3	4	13	22	38	29
Briton Ferry Athletic	40	4	1	15	26	60	1	0	19	13	69	16

Only two clubs relegated because Ton Pentre decided to withdraw from the League. As a result, only Holywell and Briton Ferry Athletic went down.

LEAGUE OF WALES

	Aberystwyth Town	Bangor City	Barry Town	Briton Ferry Athletic	Caernarfon Town	Caersws	Carmarthen Town	Cemaes Bay	Connah's Quay	Conwy United	Cwmbran Town	Ebbw Vale	Flint Town United	Holywell Town	Inter Cable-Tel	Llansantffraid	Newtown	Porthmadog	Rhyl	Ton Pentre	Welshpool
Aberystwyth Town	—	1-2	1-4	3-1	4-5	1-2	2-0	6-2	3-3	0-1	4-1	2-3	2-0	1-2	0-1	1-2	1-0	3-0	2-1	2-3	2-2
Bangor City	5-1	—	0-4	1-0	0-2	2-1	0-0	3-1	1-1	1-2	0-1	4-2	3-1	2-1	2-1	0-2	2-1	0-0	3-0	8-1	4-0
Barry Town	8-1	0-0	—	4-0	5-2	4-0	6-0	4-3	2-0	5-0	3-0	7-3	2-0	1-0	3-0	3-3	3-1	1-0	6-1	7-1	4-0
Briton Ferry Athletic	1-3	3-2	0-4	—	2-5	2-2	0-2	2-1	0-1	2-4	1-4	0-2	3-1	4-3	1-4	1-8	2-5	1-2	0-3	0-2	1-2
Caernarfon Town	2-2	1-4	1-3	6-2	—	3-2	2-1	1-1	3-1	3-3	2-3	1-0	0-0	3-0	0-1	2-1	3-0	2-1	1-0	1-0	2-1
Caersws	0-1	2-0	0-0	3-1	1-2	—	1-4	0-1	0-2	2-6	3-1	0-5	1-5	2-1	1-1	1-1	0-3	2-2	2-0	0-3	2-0
Carmarthen Town	0-4	1-5	1-1	2-0	1-3	2-3	—	2-4	1-0	0-2	2-3	0-2	1-0	1-0	1-1	0-0	0-3	2-1	2-0	0-4	2-3
Cemaes Bay	1-1	3-2	1-2	4-2	1-1	0-1	1-3	—	1-2	1-1	1-0	0-2	1-2	3-3	1-4	0-1	0-1	0-3	1-1	5-1	1-0
Connah's Quay Nomads	4-1	2-4	1-4	2-0	1-0	1-1	3-1	5-3	—	0-3	1-5	0-3	0-1	0-0	0-3	0-1	4-0	3-3	4-1	1-0	3-0
Conwy United	4-0	1-0	0-1	6-0	0-1	2-0	2-0	0-0	3-0	—	1-1	2-2	1-1	0-3	1-0	1-1	2-0	0-1	3-2	2-0	2-0
Cwmbran Town	6-0	1-3	0-4	2-3	1-1	2-1	2-2	2-2	0-1	3-1	—	0-1	1-2	2-1	2-1	3-1	1-3	2-1	4-4	3-1	2-1
Ebbw Vale	4-0	2-2	1-1	4-0	3-1	3-1	4-0	0-0	1-3	1-0	3-0	—	0-1	5-0	3-1	2-2	0-1	4-0	3-1	3-0	4-0
Flint Town United	0-1	3-4	0-8	3-1	0-3	1-1	4-0	1-3	0-2	0-1	2-4	0-1	—	2-1	0-2	1-1	1-3	2-3	3-2	2-1	1-1
Holywell Town	3-3	0-4	0-0	3-1	1-4	3-2	0-1	1-1	3-4	1-4	0-1	1-1	0-1	—	0-3	1-3	5-0	2-3	3-1		2-3
Inter Cable-Tel	1-0	4-1	1-2	7-0	6-1	3-0	1-0	2-1	0-0	3-0	1-1	2-1	2-1	2-0	—	1-1	1-0	1-0	2-1	3-0	3-4
Llansantffraid	3-2	4-1	1-0	3-0	2-3	3-2	3-3	1-2	2-2	3-1	0-1	3-1	2-2	2-1	1-1	—	1-3	0-2	0-1	4-2	2-0
Newtown	2-1	2-0	0-3	3-0	1-1	2-1	2-1	6-2	0-0	1-0	0-1	2-2	5-1	1-1	0-1	0-3	—	3-0	1-1	0-3	1-0
Porthmadog	2-2	2-0	1-4	2-0	0-0	1-3	0-0	2-4	2-0	3-1	2-1	1-1	3-0	4-1	0-2	4-1	0-4	—	6-0	2-1	1-2
Rhyl	0-2	1-2	1-2	4-0	1-1	1-1	4-0	0-1	3-1	1-1	0-0	0-2	1-1	0-2	1-0	1-3	3-1	0-1	—	2-1	0-1
Ton Pentre	1-1	4-3	0-2	3-2	2-3	2-2	0-1	1-2	4-3	1-0	0-3	1-1	3-0	1-0	0-3	1-2	1-7	3-4	1-3	—	4-3
Welshpool	0-0	3-2	1-2	4-0	0-3	0-4	1-3	0-2	1-1	0-2	1-1	0-2	2-2	2-2	1-4	1-1	1-3	1-1	2-1	6-1	—

OFFICE VISIONS WELSH LEAGUE

Division One

	P	W	D	L	F	A	Pts
Haverfordwest	34	25	4	5	111	24	79
Llanelli	34	21	6	7	76	43	69
AFC Rhondda	34	20	8	6	65	30	68
Treowen	34	19	8	7	74	39	66
Goytre United	34	20	5	9	67	43	65
Afan Lido	34	18	9	7	60	31	63
Cardiff Corries	34	16	6	12	44	56	54
Grange Quins*	34	15	5	14	75	58	47
Maesteg Park	34	11	11	12	53	52	44
Port Talbot	34	12	7	15	38	49	43
Cardiff Civil Service	34	12	6	16	50	61	42
Llanwern	34	10	9	15	49	53	39
Aberaman	34	10	8	16	48	53	38
Taffs Well	34	9	8	17	39	60	35
Abergavenny Thursdays	34	10	3	21	39	68	33
Risca	34	8	5	21	32	69	29
Penrhiwceiber	34	6	5	23	31	103	23
Caldicot Town	34	4	7	23	37	86	19

* Three points deducted for fielding ineligible player.

PA ROWLANDS CYMRU ALLIANCE

	P	W	D	L	F	A	Pts
Rhayader Town	34	21	12	1	79	25	75
Rhydymwyn	34	20	8	6	75	48	68
Llandudno	34	19	9	6	84	31	66
Oswestry Town	34	19	9	6	79	31	66
Cefn Druids	34	19	8	7	74	50	65
Knighton Town	34	19	6	9	68	46	63
Llandrindod Wells	34	16	7	11	67	44	55
Penrhyncoch**	34	15	9	10	71	56	48
Brymbo Broughton	34	10	14	10	47	48	44
Lex XI	34	12	4	18	54	72	40
Denbigh Town	34	11	5	18	60	70	38
Mold Alexandre*	34	12	5	17	51	64	38
Buckley Town	34	10	5	19	39	64	35
Llanidloes Town	34	9	7	18	36	77	34
Mostyn	34	8	9	17	46	67	33
Penycae	34	9	3	22	40	99	30
Ruthin Town	34	7	3	24	39	68	24
Rhos Aelwyd	34	7	3	24	42	91	24

** Six points deducted for fielding ineligible player.
* Three points deducted for fielding ineligible player.

WELSH CUP 1996-97

Preliminary Round
Berriew v Carno	2-3
Chirk AAA v British Aerospace	2-2
replay British Aerospace v Chirk AAA	5-4
Corwen Amateurs v Rhostyllen Villa	2-0
Gresford Athletic v Rhos Aelwyd	4-3
Llandyrnog United v Prestatyn Town	2-2
replay Prestatyn Town v Llandyrnog United	2-0
Nantlle Vale v Llangefni Town	5-0
Penparcau v Montgomery Town	2-4
Montgomery Town dismissed from competition for rule infringement	
Penycae v Penley	5-2
Trelewis Welfare v Pontlottyn Blast Furnace	1-4

First Round
Abercynon Athletic v Hoover Sports	2-4
Brecon Corinthians v Newport YMCA	1-5
Caerau United v Abergavenny Thursdays	2-2
replay Abergavenny Thursdays v Caerau United	4-3 *aet*
Caerleon v Panteg	1-0
Caldicot Town v Pontypridd Town	4-0
Cardiff Civil Service v Bridgend Town	1-1
replay Bridgend Town v Cardiff Civil Service	4-2 *aet*
British Aerospace v Cefn Druids	1-2
Ferndale Athletic v Port Talbot Athletic	1-5
Garw v Pontyclun	1-3
Goytre United v Maesteg Park	0-1
Grange Harlequins v Cardiff Corinthians	3-0
Gresford Athletic v Buckley Town	1-3
Haverfordwest County v Penrhiwceiber Rangers	6-2
Knighton Town v Carno	7-0
Lex XI FC Wrexham v Mold Alexandra	6-0
Llandrindod Wells v Denbigh Town	3-1
Llandudno v Mostyn	2-2
replay Mostyn v Llandudno	0-0 *aet*
Mostyn won 10-9 on penalties	
Llanelli v Skewen Athletic	1-1
replay Skewen Athletic v Llanelli	3-4 *aet*
Llanidloes Town v Brymbo Broughton	1-1
replay Brymbo Broughton v Llanidloes Town	4-2
Llanwern v UWI Cardiff	3-0
Nantlle Vale v Penycae	1-4
Oswestry Town v Corwen Amateurs	8-1
CPD Penrhyncoch v Ruthin Town	1-2
Pontardawe Athletic v AFC Rhondda	2-0
Porth Tywyn Suburbs v Afan Lido	2-0
Porthcawl Town v Blaenrhondda	4-2
Rhayader Town v Prestatyn Town	3-1
Rhydymwyn v Penparcau	5-0
South Wales Police v Aberaman Athletic	3-0
Taffs Well v Ammanford	2-0
Tonyrefail Welfare v BP Llandarcy	0-3
Treharris Athletic v Morriston Town	4-0
Pontlottyn Blast Furnace v Treowen Stars	0-5

Second Round
Abergavenny Thursdays v BP Llandarcy	1-2
Aberystwyth Town v Penycae	9-0
Brymbo Broughton v Caersws	0-2
Caldicot Town v Ton Pentre	1-4
Carmarthen Town v Briton Ferry Athletic	1-2
Cefn Druids v Oswestry Town	5-1
Cemaes Bay v Mostyn	3-0
Grange Harlequins v Risca United	2-1

Haverfordwest County v Bridgend Town	1-1
replay Bridgend Town v Haverfordwest County	2-1
Hoover Sports v Maesteg Park	1-2
Holywell Town v Rhydymwyn	0-0
replay Rhydymwyn v Holywell Town	1-2
Knighton Town v Lex XI FC Wrexham	0-1
Llanwern v Newport YMCA	3-0
Pontardawe Athletic v Ebbw Vale	0-0
replay Ebbw Vale v Pontardawe Athletic	2-1 *aet*
Porth Tywyn Suburbs v Caerleon	5-0
Porthcawl Town v Pontyclun	3-2
CPD Porthmadog v Buckley Town	6-1
Rhayader Town v Ruthin Town	1-0
Rhyl v Connah's Quay Nomads	0-1
South Wales Police v Taffs Well	1-5
Treharris Athletic v Llanelli	2-2
replay Llanelli v Treharris Athletic	4-0
Treowen Stars v Port Talbot Athletic	0-1
Welshpool Town v Llandrindod Wells	2-2
replay Llandrindod Wells v Welshpool Town	5-6 *aet*

Third Round
Briton Ferry Athletic v Rhayader Town	1-1
replay Rhayader Town v Briton Ferry Athletic	1-2
Caersws v Bangor City	3-2
BP Llandarcy v Llanwern	3-0
Flint Town United v Cwmbran Town	1-4
Cefn Druids v Ebbw Vale	1-1
replay Ebbw Vale v Cefn Druids	3-0
Caernarfon Town v Ton Pentre	4-0
Conwy United v Inter Cable-Tel	2-0
Newton v Maesteg Park	3-4
Porthcawl Town v Connah's Quay Nomads	3-0
Bridgend Town v Aberystwyth Town	0-1
Port Talbot Athletic v Welshpool Town	4-3
Grange Harlequins v Llanelli	1-0
Holywell Town v Taffs Well	1-0
Porth Tywyn Suburbs v Lex XI FC Wrexham	4-1
Llansantffraid v Barry Town	0-2
Cemaes Bay v CPD Porthmadog	3-2

Fourth Round
Aberystwyth Town v Ebbw Vale	2-2
replay Ebbw Vale v Aberystwyth Town	1-2
Porthcawl Town v Port Talbot Athletic	1-0
Grange Harlequins v Cwmbran Town	1-3
Porth Tywyn Suburbs v Caersws	1-3
(Maesteg Park v Holywell Town 0-1 Abandoned)	
Maesteg Park v Holywell Town	2-2
replay Holywell Town v Maesteg Park	2-0
Barry Town v Cemaes Bay	2-0
Briton Ferry Athletic v BP Llandarcy	1-2
Caernarfon Town v Conwy United	1-1
replay Conwy United v Caernarfon Town	2-0

Quarter-finals
Barry Town v Caersws	3-1
Porthcawl Town v Aberystwyth Town	0-2
BP Llandarcy v Conwy United	0-2
Holywell Town v Cwmbran Town	1-1
replay Cwmbran Town v Holywell Town	2-0

Semi-finals
Aberystwyth Town v Cwmbran Town (at Llanelli)	0-2
Barry Town v Conwy United (at Newtown)	1-0

Final: Barry Town (1) 2 Cwmbran Town (0) 1

(At Ninian Park, Cardiff, 18 May 1997)

Barry Town: Ovendale; Evans T, Knott (Pike, 67), Lloyd, York, Jones, Barnett, Loss, Bird, Griffith, Ryan.
Scorer: Griffith 7, 73
Cwmbran Town: O'Hagan; Walker (Battle, 84), Powell, Gibbins (Payne, 78), Blackie, Parfitt, Carter, Goodridge, Davies (Summers, 55), Dyer, Watkins.
Scorer: Watkins 48
Referee: A. Howells (Port Talbot)
Attendance: 3,000

NORTHERN IRISH FOOTBALL 1996–97

A season of mixed fortunes—a season when Irish League clubs suddenly discovered expenditure had to be cut and it was economic suicide attempting to keep up with the Joneses. A cold douche of reality hit them.

With the advent of promotion and relegation two seasons ago clubs, fearing relegation or desperate for promotion, embarked on signing big name players and offered them exorbitant wages. Consequently, Northern Ireland became an El Dorado for players from England, Scotland and the Republic of Ireland.

The gravy train, however, eventually hit the buffer with clubs finding gate receipts diminishing, debts spiralling and bankruptcy facing many. Costs had to be cut, staffs pruned, air travel from England and Scotland eliminated and strict budgetary controls introduced. Those measures were necessary otherwise some clubs would have died.

The most momentous decision, however, on the domestic front was that by the Irish League Management Committee to increase the number of Premier Division sides from eight to 10 by promoting Ballymena United and Omagh Town, First Division winners and runners-up, and retaining an eight club format for the First Division by admitting Limavady United and Dungannon Swifts.

Ards, Premier Division bottom club, triumphed in a relegation home and away play-off with Bangor, third in the First Division, to maintain their senior status. "That was a nightmare I would never want to experience again. That is what real pressure in football is all about—not going for championships," said manager Roy Coyle who, in 12 seasons with Linfield, won more than 30 trophies.

Coleraine were the Premier Division pace-setters throughout the season but it was Crusaders, consistent and with an ability to grind down opponents, who took the Smirnoff title and a place in Europe. Glenavon, a most progressive club, triumphed in the Bass Irish Cup Final with a 1-0 victory over Cliftonville and their Mourneview Park, Lurgan, stadium, one of the best equipped in Ireland, was the venue for Northern Ireland's B international match with Portugal.

Yet again it was a season horribilis for Linfield and Glentoran. Neither won a major trophy which meant non-European qualification. Improvements must be made over the next nine months as disillusioned fans are becoming somewhat impatient. Irish League football needs a strong vibrant Linfield and Glentoran.

Sponsorship continued at a high level in all competitions apart from the Ulster Cup. Junior, youth, schoolboy and mini-soccer are all commercially backed making the Irish FA development programme the envy of many countries. "Our future looks bright," said general secretary David Bowen.

From an international viewpoint failure to qualify from Group Nine for the World Cup finals in France in 1998 was a major blow. This was due, primarily, to an early 1-0 home defeat by the Ukraine and a scoreless draw with Armenia. From then on it was an uphill battle.

The pattern changed: there were commendable draws with European champions Germany in Nuremberg, and Portugal in Belfast; a 3-0 friendly win over Belgium, an away draw with Armenia and, despite a 2-0 defeat by Italy in Palermo, they again revealed a high degree of skill and promise.

Finally, the scoreless draw against Thailand in the heat and humidity of Bangkok in May underlined the depth of talent available to manager Bryan Hamilton. Most of the established players were unavailable but the youngsters, five under 21, played magnificently in a strange environment.

"I reckon we have now around 35 players all capable of competing for places in the senior side," said Hamilton. "It is essential, however, we continue with their development programme, keep the production line rolling, enter the European Under-21 championship, hope as many players as possible can join Premiership clubs and, most important of all, play regularly."

There have been major developments also at Windsor Park, the international headquarters, where a new multi-million pound stand on the site of the renowned Spion Kop will be opened in August to coincide with the World Cup visit of the Germans.

While, as I stated earlier, some Irish League clubs are finding the going tough generally the overall state of Northern Ireland football is excellent, qualification for the Euro 2000 finals would be the icing on the cake—a fantastic financial boost and launching pad for the new millennium.

MALCOLM BRODIE

WILKINSON SWORD LEAGUE CUP

Semi-finals

Crusaders v Linfield (*at The Oval*)   1-1
  (*aet*) (*Crusaders won 4-1 on penalties*)
Glentoran v Portadown (*Mourneview Park*)   2-1

Final

Crusaders 1 Glentoran 0 (*at Windsor Park*)
Crusaders: McKeown; Mellon, McMullan, Dunlop, Callaghan, Murray, O'Brien, Dwyer (Arthur), Baxter, Dully, Burrows.
Glentoran: Armstrong; Drake, Smyth (Parker), Walker, Devine, May, Finlay, Little, McCourt, Baxter, Hamill.
Scorer: Crusaders—Dully.
Referee: G. Keatley (Bangor).
Attendance: 3000.

SMIRNOFF IRISH LEAGUE

Premier Division

	P	W	D	L	F	A	Pts
Crusaders	28	12	10	6	39	26	46
Coleraine	28	10	13	5	37	31	43
Glentoran	28	10	11	7	36	30	41
Portadown	28	10	8	10	36	32	38
Linfield	28	10	8	10	35	33	38
Glenavon	28	8	11	9	35	34	35
Cliftonville	28	7	9	12	23	38	30
Ards	28	5	10	13	33	50	25

Relegation play-off: First leg: Bangor (third placed in first division) 0 Ards 1; second leg: Ards 1 Bangor 0.

First Division

	P	W	D	L	F	A	Pts
Ballymena United	28	21	2	5	49	17	65
Omagh Town	28	15	5	8	40	39	50
Bangor	28	15	4	9	42	29	49
Ballyclare Comrades	28	11	4	13	44	42	37
Newry Town	28	10	5	13	32	35	35
Distillery	28	10	4	14	31	37	34
Larne	28	9	5	14	34	48	32
Carrick Rangers	28	5	3	20	26	51	18

Promoted: Ballymena United and Omagh Town.

Irish League leading scorers: 28—Garry Haylock (Portadown), Stephen Baxter (Crusaders); 27—Glenn Ferguson (Glenavon); 25—Glenn Hunter (Crusaders); 19—Dean Doherty (Carrick Rangers); 18—Paul Stokes (Cliftonville), Michael McHugh (Omagh Town).

IRISH LEAGUE CHAMPIONSHIP WINNERS

1891	Linfield	1910	Cliftonville	1934	Linfield	1961	Linfield	1981	Glentoran
1892	Linfield	1911	Linfield	1935	Linfield	1962	Linfield	1982	Linfield
1893	Linfield	1912	Glentoran	1936	Belfast Celtic	1963	Distillery	1983	Linfield
1894	Glentoran	1913	Glentoran	1937	Belfast Celtic	1964	Glentoran	1984	Linfield
1895	Linfield	1914	Linfield	1938	Belfast Celtic	1965	Derry City	1985	Linfield
1896	Distillery	1915	Belfast Celtic	1939	Belfast Celtic	1966	Linfield	1986	Linfield
1897	Glentoran	1920	Belfast Celtic	1940	Belfast Celtic	1967	Glentoran	1987	Linfield
1898	Linfield	1921	Glentoran	1948	Belfast Celtic	1968	Glentoran	1988	Glentoran
1899	Distillery	1922	Linfield	1949	Linfield	1969	Linfield	1989	Linfield
1900	Belfast Celtic	1923	Linfield	1950	Linfield	1970	Glentoran	1990	Portadown
1901	Distillery	1924	Queen's Island	1951	Glentoran	1971	Linfield	1991	Portadown
1902	Linfield	1925	Glentoran	1952	Glenavon	1972	Glentoran	1992	Glentoran
1903	Distillery	1926	Belfast Celtic	1953	Glentoran	1973	Crusaders	1993	Linfield
1904	Linfield	1927	Belfast Celtic	1954	Linfield	1974	Coleraine	1994	Linfield
1905	Glentoran	1928	Belfast Celtic	1955	Linfield	1975	Linfield	1995	Crusaders
1906	Cliftonville	1929	Belfast Celtic	1956	Linfield	1976	Crusaders	1996	Portadown
	Distillery	1930	Linfield	1957	Glentoran	1977	Glentoran	1997	Crusaders
1907	Linfield	1931	Glentoran	1958	Ards	1978	Linfield		
1908	Linfield	1932	Linfield	1959	Linfield	1979	Linfield		
1909	Linfield	1933	Belfast Celtic	1960	Glenavon	1980	Linfield		

FIRST DIVISION

1996   Coleraine
1997   Ballymena United

ULSTER CUP

First Round, First Leg

Ballymena United v Crusaders	1-1
Newry Town v Coleraine	2-3
Carrick Rangers v Ards	0-3
Omagh Town v Glenavon	1-1
Larne v Cliftonville	1-4
Distillery v Linfield	1-3
Ballyclare Comrades v Portadown	1-0
Bangor v Glentoran	0-1

Second Leg

Crusaders v Ballymena United	3-2
Coleraine v Newry Town	2-1
Ards v Carrick Rangers	3-0
Glenavon v Omagh Town	3-2
Cliftonville v Larne	0-0
Linfield v Distillery	3-1
Portadown v Ballyclare Comrades	3-2
Glentoran v Bangor	1-1

Quarter-finals

Glenavon v Coleraine	1-3
Ards v Glentoran	3-4 *(aet)*
Linfield v Crusaders	2-3
Cliftonville v Ballyclare Comrades	4-1

Semi-finals

Coleraine v Glentoran *(at Seaview)*	1-0
Cliftonville v Crusaders *(at The Oval)*	0-4

Final

Coleraine 1 Crusaders 1 *(at Windsor Park)*
(aet; Coleraine won 4-3 on penalties)
Crusaders: McKeown; Dornan, McMullan, Dunlop, Callaghan, Murray, O'Brien, Dunne (Dwyer), Baxter, Hunter G (Morgan), Burrows.
Coleraine: Lamont; McAuley, Brunton, Aspinal, Gaston, Doherty, Shiels, O'Dowd (McIver), McCallen, McAllister, Surgeon (Ramage).
Scorers: Coleraine—McAllister; Crusaders—Brunton (o.g.).
Referee: Barr (Belfast).
Attendance: 2500.
Penalty shoot out: Crusaders—*Scored:* McMullan, Baxter, Dwyer. *Missed:* Morgan, McKeown. Coleraine—*Scored:* Brunton, Aspinal, Shiels, Gaston. *Missed:* McAllister.

Winners

1949	Linfield	1959	Glenavon	1969	Coleraine	1979	Linfield	1989	Glentoran
1950	Larne	1960	Linfield	1970	Linfield	1980	Ballymena U	1990	Portadown
1951	Glentoran	1961	Ballymena U	1971	Linfield	1981	Glentoran	1991	Bangor
1952		1962	Linfield	1972	Coleraine	1982	Glentoran	1992	Linfield
1953	Glentoran	1963	Crusaders	1973	Ards	1983	Glentoran	1993	Crusaders
1954	Crusaders	1964	Linfield	1974	Linfield	1984	Linfield	1994	Bangor
1955	Glenavon	1965	Coleraine	1975	Coleraine	1985	Coleraine	1995	Portadown
1956	Linfield	1966	Glentoran	1976	Glentoran	1986	Coleraine	1996	Portadown
1957	Linfield	1967	Linfield	1977	Linfield	1987	Larne	1997	Coleraine
1958	Distillery	1968	Coleraine	1978	Linfield	1988	Glentoran		

CALOR COUNTY ANTRIM SHIELD

First Round

Ballyclare Comrades v Chimney Corner	0-1
Ballymena United v Carrick Rangers	2-0
Bangor v Linfield	0-3
Cliftonville v Ards	1-0
Crusaders v Comber Rec	8-0
Larne v Distillery	0-1
(aet, won on sudden death)	
Newry Town v Glentoran	0-5
Portadown v Glenavon	2-0

Second Round

Crusaders v Distillery	0-0
(Crusaders won 7-6 on penalties)	
Ballymena United v Chimney Corner	2-0
Cliftonville v Glentoran	0-0
(Cliftonville won 5-4 on penalties)	
Portadown v Linfield	3-2

Semi-finals

Cliftonville v Crusaders *(at Windsor Park)*	2-1
Ballymena United v Portadown	2-1
(aet, Ballymena won on sudden death)	

Final

Ballymena United 0 Cliftonville 0 (abandoned) *(at Windsor Park)*
Cliftonville: Rice; Hill, Flynn, Tabb, Small, Shepherd, McCann, O'Neill, O'Connor, Stokes, Donnelly.
Ballymena United: Beck; Carlisle, Stewart, Allen, McConnell, Bustard, Knell, Boyd, Patton, Loughery, Smyth J.
Referee: A. Snoddy (Carryduff).
Note: The match was abandoned in the 66th minute when a linesman was struck by a liquid filled bottle.
Attendance: 3300 (receipts £16,619).

Second Match

Ballymena United 0 Cliftonville 0 *(at Windsor Park)*
(aet; Cliftonville won 5-4 on penalties)
Ballymena United: Beck; Carlisle, Stewart (Murray), Allen, McConnell, Bustard, Knell (Muir), Boyd, Feehan (Patton), Loughery, Smyth J.
Cliftonville: Reece; Hill, Flynn, Tabb, Shepherd, Small, McCaw, O'Neill (Collins), Stokes, Donnelly.
Referee: A. Snoddy (Carryduff).
Penalty shoot out: Cliftonville *scorers*—Stokes, Small, O'Connor, Hill, McCann. Ballymena United *scorers*—Allen, Patton, Smyth, Bustard. Murray's last kick was saved by Reece, signed for one game from West Bromwich Albion. He presented his medal to injured goalkeeper Paul Rice.
Note: Police restricted attendance to 2000—1000 tickets issued to each club.
Actual attendance: 1900 (receipts £6475).

BASS IRISH CUP 1996–97

Fifth Round

Newry Town v Omagh	0-0, 1-3
Carrick Rangers v RUC	0-0, 1-2
Dungannon Swifts v Loughall	1-1, 1-3
British Telecom v Crumlin United	1-1, 1-4
Glentoran v Distillery	4-0
Glenavon v Ards	1-0
Drumaness Mills v Limavady United	1-3
Crusaders v Institute	4-1
Portadown v Dunmurry Rec	3-0
Ballyclare Comrades v Cliftonville	2-3
FC Énkalon v Portstewart	1-1, 1-3
Coleraine v Linfield	2-1
Larne v Coagh United	0-2
Park v Chimney Corner	0-4
Bangor v Ballymena United	3-0
Brantwood v Dundela	0-2

Sixth Round

Crumlin United v Loughgall	1-2
Crusaders v Portadown	1-0
Dundela v Coagh United	1-2
Glenavon v Glentoran	2-0
Limavady United v Bangor	1-1, 2-0
Portstewart v Coleraine	0-1

RUC v Cliftonville	0-3
Omagh Town v Chimney Corner	3-2

Quarter-finals

Loughgall v Coleraine	1-1, 1-0
Cliftonville v Crusaders	3-1
Glenavon v Coagh United	4-0
Omagh Town v Limavady United	2-2, 1-0

Semi-finals

Glenavon v Omagh Town *(The Oval)*	5-0
Loughgall v Cliftonville *(Windsor Park)*	1-3

Final

Glenavon 1 Cliftonville 0 *(at Windsor Park)*
Cliftonville: Reece; Hill (Strang), Flynn, Tabb, Davey, O'Neill, McCann, Collins, Small (Toland), Stokes, Donnelly.
Glenavon: O'Neill; Caffrey, Glendinning, Doherty, Byrne, Smyth, Johnston, McCoy (Murphy), Ferguson, Grant, Gregg (Williamson).
Scorer: Grant.
Referee: H. Barr (Bangor).
Attendance: (restricted by police) 8222.

IRISH CUP FINALS (from 1946–47)

1946–47	Belfast Celtic 1, Glentoran 0	1972–73	Glentoran 3, Linfield 2
1947–48	Linfield 3, Coleraine 0	1973–74	Ards 2, Ballymena U 1
1948–49	Derry City 3, Glentoran 1	1974–75	Coleraine 1:0:1, Linfield 1:0:0
1949–50	Linfield 2, Distillery 1	1975–76	Carrick Rangers 2, Linfield 1
1950–51	Glentoran 3, Ballymena U 1	1976–77	Coleraine 4, Linfield 1
1951–52	Ards 1, Glentoran 0	1977–78	Linfield 3, Ballymena U 1
1952–53	Linfield 5, Coleraine 0	1978–79	Cliftonville 3, Portadown 2
1953–54	Derry City 1, Glentoran 0	1979–80	Linfield 2, Crusaders 0
1954–55	Dundela 3, Glenavon 0	1980–81	Ballymena U 1, Glenavon 0
1955–56	Distillery 1, Glentoran 0	1981–82	Linfield 2, Coleraine 1
1956–57	Glenavon 2, Derry City 0	1982–83	Glentoran 1:2, Linfield 1:1
1957–58	Ballymena U 2, Linfield 0	1983–84	Ballymena U 4, Carrick Rangers 1
1958–59	Glenavon 2, Ballymena U 0	1984–85	Glentoran 1:1, Linfield 1:0
1959–60	Linfield 5, Ards 1	1985–86	Glentoran 2, Coleraine 1
1960–61	Glenavon 5, Linfield 1	1986–87	Glentoran 1, Larne 0
1961–62	Linfield 4, Portadown 1	1987–88	Glentoran 1, Glenavon 0
1962–63	Linfield 2, Distillery 1	1988–89	Ballymena U 1, Larne 0
1963–64	Derry City 2, Glentoran 0	1989–90	Glentoran 3, Portadown 0
1964–65	Coleraine 2, Glenavon 1	1990–91	Portadown 2, Glenavon 1
1965–66	Glentoran 2, Linfield 0	1991–92	Glenavon 2, Linfield 1
1966–67	Crusaders 3, Glentoran 1	1992–93	Bangor 1:1:1, Ards 1:1:0
1967–68	Crusaders 2, Linfield 0	1993–94	Linfield 2, Bangor 0
1968–69	Ards 4, Distillery 2	1994–95	Linfield 3, Carrick Rangers 1
1969–70	Linfield 2, Ballymena U 1	1995–96	Glentoran 1, Glenavon 0
1970–71	Distillery 3, Derry City 0	1996–97	Glenavon 1, Cliftonville 0
1971–72	Coleraine 2, Portadown 1		

SUN-LIFE GOLD CUP
SECTIONAL TABLES

Section A	P	W	D	L	F	A	Pts
Portadown	3	2	1	0	4	1	7
Bangor	3	2	0	1	5	1	6
Coleraine	3	1	1	1	4	1	4
Newry Town	3	0	0	3	1	11	0

Section B	P	W	D	L	F	A	Pts
Crusaders	3	3	0	0	8	2	9
Ballymena United	3	2	0	1	6	3	6
Larne	3	0	1	2	3	7	1
Ards	3	0	1	2	3	8	1

Section C	P	W	D	L	F	A	Pts
Omagh Town	3	2	0	1	3	2	6
Glentoran	3	1	1	1	6	3	4
Cliftonville	3	1	1	1	5	5	4
Carrick Rangers	3	1	0	2	4	8	3

Section D	P	W	D	L	F	A	Pts
Linfield	3	2	1	0	4	1	7
Glenavon	3	2	0	1	11	1	6
Distillery	3	0	2	1	2	9	2
Ballyclare Comrades	3	0	1	2	3	9	1

SUN-LIFE GOLD CUP 1996–97
Quarter-finals

Bangor v Linfield	0-2
Ballymena United v Portadown	0-0
(aet; Ballymena won 3-1 on penalties)	
Omagh Town v Glenavon	2-3
Glentoran v Crusaders	2-3
(aet)	

Semi-finals

Linfield v Ballymena United *(at The Oval)*   2-0
Glenavon v Crusaders *(at New Grosvenor Stadium, Ballyskeagh)*   2-0

Final

Linfield 1 Glenavon 0 *(at The Oval)*
Linfield: Collins; Collier, Easton, McCoosh, Brush, Gorman, Beatty, Douglas (Clelland), Barker, McBride (Millar), Bailie.
Glenavon: O'Neill; McCartan, Glendinning, Murphy, Caffrey, Smyth, Williamson (Evans), Johnston, Ferguson, Grant, Mulholland (Fraser).
Scorer: Linfield—Barker.
Referee: L. Irvine (Limavady).
Attendance: 3523 (receipts £16,875).

WHERE THE TROPHIES WENT

	Winners	Runners-up
Smirnoff Irish League:		
Premier Division	Crusaders	Coleraine
First Division	Ballymena United	Omagh Town
Bass Irish Cup	Glenavon	Cliftonville
Sun-Life Gold Cup	Linfield	Glenavon
Wilkinson Sword League Cup	Crusaders	Glentoran
Ulster Cup	Coleraine	Crusaders
Calor County Antrim Shield	Cliftonville	Ballymena United
Calor Country Antrim Junior Shield	Grove United	Immaculata
Coca Cola League Cup Final	Glenavon	Glentoran
Irish Intermediate Cup	Chimney Corner	Dungannon Swifts
McEwans Mid Ulster Cup	Dungannon	Distillery
Mid Ulster Shield	Hill Street	Derryhirk United
North West Senior Cup	Omagh Town	Coleraine
Bob Radcliffe Memorial Cup	Loughgall	Armagh City
Ormo Irish Junior Cup	Newington YC	Lisbellaw United
Smirnoff Knock Out Cup	Institute	Chimney Corner
Irish News Cup	Derry City	Sligo Rovers
Calor Steel & Sons Cup	Chimney Corner	Comber Rec
George Wilson Cup	Portadown Res	Glenavon Res
Harry Cavan Coca Cola Youth Club	Linfield Rangers	Ballymena United
Wilkinson Sword B Division		
Section 1	Loughgall	Chimney Corner
Section 2	Crusaders Res	Linfield Swifts
Irish Youth League	Glentoran Colts	Glenavon III
Irish Youth League Cup	Glenavon III	Glentoran Colts

EUROPEAN CUP

EUROPEAN CUP FINALS 1956–97

Year	Winners	Runners-up	Venue	Attendance	Referee
1956	Real Madrid 4	Reims 3	Paris	38,000	Ellis (E)
1957	Real Madrid 2	Fiorentina 0	Madrid	124,000	Horn (Ho)
1958	Real Madrid 3	AC Milan 2 *(aet)*	Brussels	67,000	Alsteen (Bel)
1959	Real Madrid 2	Reims 0	Stuttgart	80,000	Dutsch (WG)
1960	Real Madrid 7	Eintracht Frankfurt 3	Glasgow	135,000	Mowat (S)
1961	Benfica 3	Barcelona 2	Berne	28,000	Dienst (Sw)
1962	Benfica 5	Real Madrid 3	Amsterdam	65,000	Horn (Ho)
1963	AC Milan 2	Benfica 1	Wembley	45,000	Holland (E)
1964	Internazionale 3	Real Madrid 1	Vienna	74,000	Stoll (A)
1965	Internazionale 1	Benfica 0	Milan	80,000	Dienst (Sw)
1966	Real Madrid 2	Partizan Belgrade 1	Brussels	55,000	Kreitlein (WG)
1967	Celtic 2	Internazionale 1	Lisbon	56,000	Tschenscher (WG)
1968	Manchester U 4	Benfica 1 *(aet)*	Wembley	100,000	Lo Bello (I)
1969	AC Milan 4	Ajax 1	Madrid	50,000	Ortiz (Sp)
1970	Feyenoord 2	Celtic 1 *(aet)*	Milan	50,000	Lo Bello (I)
1971	Ajax 2	Panathinaikos 0	Wembley	90,000	Taylor (E)
1972	Ajax 2	Internazionale 0	Rotterdam	67,000	Helies (F)
1973	Ajax 1	Juventus 0	Belgrade	93,500	Guglovic (Y)
1974	Bayern Munich 1	Atletico Madrid 1	Brussels	65,000	Loraux (Bel)
Replay	Bayern Munich 4	Atletico Madrid 0	Brussels	65,000	Delcourt (Bel)
1975	Bayern Munich 2	Leeds U 0	Paris	50,000	Kitabdjian (F)
1976	Bayern Munich 1	St Etienne 0	Glasgow	54,864	Palotai (H)
1977	Liverpool 3	Moenchengladbach 1	Rome	57,000	Wurtz (F)
1978	Liverpool 1	FC Brugge 0	Wembley	92,000	Corver (Ho)
1979	Nottingham F 1	Malmo 0	Munich	57,500	Linemayr (A)
1980	Nottingham F 1	Hamburg 0	Madrid	50,000	Garrido (P)
1981	Liverpool 1	Real Madrid 0	Paris	48,360	Palotai (H)
1982	Aston Villa 1	Bayern Munich 0	Rotterdam	46,000	Konrath (F)
1983	Hamburg 1	Juventus 0	Athens	75,000	Rainea (R)
1984	Liverpool 1	Roma 1	Rome	69,693	Fredriksson (Se)
	(aet; Liverpool won 4–2 on penalties)				
1985	Juventus 1	Liverpool 0	Brussels	58,000	Daina (Sw)
1986	Steaua Bucharest 0	Barcelona 0	Seville	70,000	Vautrot (F)
	(aet; Steaua won 2–0 on penalties)				
1987	Porto 2	Bayern Munich 1	Vienna	59,000	Ponnet (Bel)
1988	PSV Eindhoven 0	Benfica 0	Stuttgart	70,000	Agnolin (I)
	(aet; PSV won 6–5 on penalties)				
1989	AC Milan 4	Steaua Bucharest 0	Barcelona	97,000	Tritschler (WG)
1990	AC Milan 1	Benfica 0	Vienna	57,500	Kohl (A)
1991	Red Star Belgrade 0	Marseille 0	Bari	56,000	Lanese (I)
	(aet; Red Star won 5–3 on penalties)				
1992	Barcelona 1	Sampdoria 0 *(aet)*	Wembley	70,827	Schmidhuber (G)
1993	Marseille* 1	AC Milan 0	Munich	64,400	Rothlisberger (Sw)
1994	AC Milan 4	Barcelona 0	Athens	70,000	Don (E)
1995	Ajax 1	AC Milan 0	Vienna	49,730	Craciunescu (Ro)
1996	Juventus 1	Ajax 1	Rome	67,000	Vega (Sp)
	(aet; Juventus won 4–2 on penalties)				
1997	Borussia Dortmund 3	Juventus 1	Munich	59,000	Puhl (H)

Subsequently stripped of title.

EUROPEAN CUP 1996–97

QUALIFYING ROUND, FIRST LEG
FC Brugge (1) 2 *(Nielsen 25, Spehar 55)*, Steaua (1) 2
(*Ilie A 44, 61*)   14,000
IFK Gothenburg (1) 3 *(Blomqvist 37, Pettersson S 50,
Andersson 57)*, Ferencvaros (0) 0   5513
Grasshoppers (2) 5 *(Turkyilmaz 12, 47, Esposito 44,
Moldovan 58, Koller 89)*, Slavia Prague (0) 0   9300
Maccabi Tel Aviv (0) 0, Fenerbahce (1) 1 *(Kemalettin 43)*
                                                                          26,000
Panathinaikos (1) 1 *(Warzycha 19)*, Rosenborg (0) 0
                                                                          35,000
Rangers (0) 3 *(McInnes D 50, McCoist 60, Petric 79)*,
Alania Vladikavkaz (1) 1 *(Yanovski 29)*   44,799
Rapid Vienna (1) 2 *(Stumpf 8, Guggi 89)*, Dynamo Kiev
(0) 0   29,500
Widzew Lodz (1) 2 *(Dembinski 64, Bjur 75)*, Brondby (0)
1 *(Majak 73)*   4500

QUALIFYING ROUND, SECOND LEG
Alania Vladikavkaz (2) 2 *(Yanovski 14, Suleimanov 24
(pen))*, Rangers (4) 7 *(McCoist 1, 13, 18, Van Vossen
40, Laudrup 55, 83, Miller 86)*   32,000
Brondby (2) 3 *(Moller 31, Bjur 44, Vilfort 47)*, Widzew
Lodz (0) 2 *(Citko 56, Wojtala 89)*   10,438
Dynamo Kiev (1) 2 *(Kalitvintsev 6, Maximov 77)*, Rapid
Vienna (3) 4 *(Ivanov 23, 42, Kuhbauer 32,
Khatskevich 62 (og)*   80,000
Fenerbahce (1) 1 *(Okechukwu 18)*, Maccabi Tel
Aviv (0) 1 *(Dricks 75)*   27,000
Ferencvaros (1) 1 *(Horvath 15)*, IFK Gothenburg (0) 1
(Andersson A 87)   12,000
Rosenborg (0) 3 *(Strand 63, Iversen 95, Heggem 98)*,
Panathinaikos (0) 0   18,625
Slavia Prague (0) 0, Grasshoppers (0) 1 *(Turkyilmaz 70)*
                                                                           3000
Steaua (2) 3 *(Ilie A 33 (pen), 45, Nagy 55)*, FC Brugge (0) 0
                                                                          16,000

CHAMPIONS LEAGUE

GROUP A
Auxerre (0) 0, Ajax (1) 1 *(Litmanen 4)*   18,500
Grasshoppers (2) 3 *(Yakin 18, Turkyilmaz 28, 79)*,
Rangers (0) 0   20,030
Ajax (0) 0, Grasshoppers (0) 1 *(Yakin 60)*   48,000
Rangers (0) 1 *(Gascoigne 71)*, Auxerre (0) 2 *(Deniaud 55,
69)*   37,344
Ajax (2) 4 *(Dani 25, 40, Babangida 83, Wooter 89)*,
Rangers (0) 1 *(Durrant 87)*   47,000
Auxerre (1) 1 *(Deniaud 42)*, Grasshoppers (0) 0   19,000
Grasshoppers (2) 3 *(Moldovan 17, 29 (pen), Gren 59)*,
Auxerre (0) 1 *(Gren 47 (og))*   19,200
Rangers (0) 0, Ajax (1) 1 *(Scholten 38)*   42,265
Ajax (1) 1 *(Babangida 44)*, Auxerre (1) 2*(Diomede 11,
Marlet 56)*   49,000
Rangers (0) 2 *(McCoist 66 (pen), 72)*, Grasshoppers (0) 1
(Berger 76)   34,192
Auxerre (2) 2 *(Laslandes 20, Marlet 32)*, Rangers (1) 1
(Gough 36)   21,300
Grasshoppers (0) 0, Ajax (1) 1 *(Kluivert 31)*   20,000

FINAL TABLE

	P	W	D	L	F	A	Pts
Auxerre	6	4	0	2	8	7	12
Ajax	6	4	0	2	8	4	12
Grasshoppers	6	3	0	3	8	5	9
Rangers	6	1	0	5	5	13	3

GROUP B
Atletico Madrid (2) 4 *(Esnaider 32, 45, Simeone 64, 85)*,
Steaua Bucharest (0) 0   47,000
Borussia Dortmund (1) 2 *(Herrlich 45, 68)*, Widzew Lodz
(0) 1 *(Citko 84)*   39,600
Steaua Bucharest (0) 0, Borussia Dortmund (2) 3
(Ricken 7, Heinrich 37, Chapuisat 79)   15,000
Widzew Lodz (1) 1 *(Citko 45)*, Atletico Madrid (2) 4
(Pantic 24, Simeone 32, 60, Kiko 61)   18,000
Atletico Madrid (0) 0, Borussia Dortmund (0) 1 *(Reuter
50)*   47,000
Steaua Bucharest (0) 1 *(Bogusz 82 (og))*, Widzew Lodz
(0) 0   9,000

Borussia Dortmund (1) 1 *(Herrlich 17)*, Atletico Madrid
(2) 2 *(Roberto 37, Pantic 42)*   45,000
Widzew Lodz (1) 2 *(Majak 39, Czerwiec 49)*, Steaua
Bucharest (0) 0   6000
Steaua Bucharest (0) 1 *(Ilie S 51)*, Atletico Madrid (1) 1
(Pantic 23)   8000
Widzew Lodz (2) 2 *(Dembinski 15, 20)*, Borussia
Dortmund (1) 2 *(Lambert 14, Kohler 62)*   18,000
Atletico Madrid (0) 1 *(Pantic 83)*, Widzew Lodz (0) 0
                                                                          40,000
Borussia Dortmund (3) 5 *(Chapuisat 3, 22, Tretschok 43,
Riedle 62, Zorc 64)*, Steaua Bucharest (1) 3 *(Ilie S 17
(pen), Baciu 52, Calin 79)*   40,000

FINAL TABLE

	P	W	D	L	F	A	Pts
Atletico Madrid	6	4	1	1	12	4	13
Borussia Dortmund	6	4	1	1	14	8	13
Widzew Lodz	6	1	1	4	6	10	4
Steaua Bucharest	6	1	1	4	5	15	4

GROUP C
Juventus (1) 1 *(Boksic 34)*, Manchester U (0) 0   50,000
Rapid Vienna (0) 1 *(Stumpf 69)*, Fenerbahce (1) 1
(Bolic 30)   41,500
Fenerbahce (0) 0, Juventus (1) 1 *(Boksic 21)*   28,000
Manchester U (2) 2 *(Solskjaer 20, Beckham 27)*, Rapid
Vienna (0) 0   51,831
Fenerbahce (0) 0, Manchester U (0) 2 *(Beckham 55,
Cantona 59)*   26,200
Rapid Vienna (1) 1 *(Lesiak 20)*, Juventus (1) 1 *(Vieri 9)*
                                                                          48,000
Juventus (3) 5 *(Boksic 4, 59, Montero 27, Del Piero 28,
74)*, Rapid Vienna (0) 0   35,000
Manchester U (0) 0, Fenerbahce (0) 1 *(Bolic 77)*   53,297
Fenerbahce (0) 1 *(Hogh 75)*, Rapid Vienna (0) 0   30,000
Manchester U (0) 0, Juventus (1) 1 *(Del Piero 36 (pen))*
                                                                          53,529
Juventus (1) 2 *(Padovano 41, Amoruso 84)*, Fenerbahce
(0) 0   12,900
Rapid Vienna (0) 0, Manchester U (1) 2 *(Giggs 24,
Cantona 71)*   45,000

FINAL TABLE

	P	W	D	L	F	A	Pts
Juventus	6	5	1	0	11	1	16
Manchester U	6	3	0	3	6	3	9
Fenerbahce	6	2	1	3	3	6	7
Rapid Vienna	6	0	2	4	2	12	2

GROUP D
IFK Gothenburg (1) 2 *(Erlingmark 38, 49)*, Rosenborg
(1) 3 *(Jakobsen 32, Iversen 52, Brattbakk 64)*   23,682
AC Milan (1) 2 *(Simone 14, Weah 68)*, Porto (0) 3 *(Artur
53, Jardel 75, 83)*   24,000
Porto (1) 2 *(Artur 27, 55)*, IFK Gothenburg (0) 1 *(Jorge
Costa 72 (og))*   30,000
Rosenborg (1) 1 *(Soltvedt 15)*, AC Milan (3) 4 *(Simone 6,
23, 55, Weah 55)*   20,849
IFK Gothenburg (0) 2 *(Wahlstedt 74, Alexandersson 84)*,
AC Milan (0) 1 *(Weah 52)*   42,450
Rosenborg (0) 0, Porto (0) 1 *(Jardel 90)*   20,400
AC Milan (3) 4 *(Boban 3, Albertini 13 (pen), Locatelli 43,
Roberto Baggio 90)*, IFK Gothenburg (2) 2
(Blomqvist 26, Andersson A 32)   29,803
Porto (2) 3 *(Zahovic 31, Drulovic 40, Oliveira 70)*,
Rosenborg (0) 0   15,000
Porto (0) 1 *(Edmilson 70)*, AC Milan (0) 1 *(Davids 55)*
                                                                          50,000
Rosenborg (0) 1*(Skammelsrud 66 (pen))*, IFK
Gothenburg (0) 0   19,000
IFK Gothenburg (0) 0, Porto (0) 2 *(Jardel 64, Edmilson
89)*   19,448
AC Milan (1) 1 *(Dugarry 45)*, Rosenborg (1) 2
(Brattbakk 29, Heggem 69)   28,695

FINAL TABLE

	P	W	D	L	F	A	Pts
Porto	6	5	1	0	12	4	16
Rosenborg	6	3	0	3	7	11	9
AC Milan	6	2	1	3	13	11	7
IFK Gothenburg	6	1	0	5	7	13	3

QUARTER-FINALS, FIRST LEG
Ajax (0) 1 *(Kluivert 53)*, Atletico Madrid (1) 1 *(Esnaider 8)*   51,000
Borussia Dortmund (1) 3 *(Riedle 12, Schneider 54, Moller 82)*, Auxerre (0) 1 *(Lamouchi 75)*   47,500
Manchester U (2) 4 *(May 22, Cantona 34, Giggs 61, Cole 80)*, Porto (0) 0   53,415
Rosenborg (0) 1 *(Soltvedt 51)*, Juventus (0) 1 *(Vieri 52)*   20,246

QUARTER-FINALS, SECOND LEG
Atletico Madrid (1) 2 *(Kiko 29, Pantic 109 (pen))*, Ajax (0) 3 *(Ronald De Boer 48, Dani 99, Babangida 119)*   50,000
Auxerre (0) 0, Borussia Dortmund (0) 1 *(Ricken 59)*   21,000

Juventus (1) 2 *(Zidane 29, Amoruso 85 (pen))*, Rosenborg (0) 0   35,371
Porto (0) 0, Manchester U (0) 0   40,000

SEMI-FINALS, FIRST LEG
Ajax (0) 1 *(Litmanen 65)*, Juventus (2) 2 *(Amoruso 14, Vieri 42)*   51,333
Borussia Dortmund (0) 1 *(Tretschok 76)*, Manchester U (0) 0   48,500

SEMI-FINALS, SECOND LEG
Juventus (2) 4 *(Lombardo 34, Vieri 36, Amoruso 79, Zidane 80)*, Ajax (0) 1 *(Melchiot 76)*   69,000
Manchester U (0) 0, Borussia Dortmund (1) 1 *(Ricken 7)*   53,606

FINAL

Borussia Dortmund (2) 3, Juventus (0) 1

(in Munich, 28 May 1997, 59,000)

Borussia Dortmund: Klos; Kohler, Sammer, Kree, Reuter, Lambert, Paulo Sousa, Heinrich, Moller (Zorc 88), Chapuisat (Ricken 70), Riedle (Herrlich 67).
Scorers: Riedle 29, 34, Ricken 71.
Juventus: Peruzzi; Porrini (Del Piero 46), Ferrara, Montero, Juliano, Di Livio, Deschamps, Jugovic, Zidane, Vieri (Amoruso 70), Boksic.
Scorer: Del Piero 64.

Hot favourites Juventus were surprisingly beaten by Borussia Dortmund in the Champions Cup Final. Zinedine Zidane (Juventus) evades Dortmund's Paul Lambert *(right)*. (Colorsport)

EUROPEAN CUP 1996–97 – BRITISH AND IRISH CLUBS

QUALIFYING ROUND, FIRST LEG

7 AUG

Rangers (0) 3(*McInnes D 50, McCoist 60, Petric 79*)
Alania Vladikavkaz (1) 1(*Yanovski 29*)   44,799
Rangers: Goram; Cleland, Petric, Gough, Bjorklund, Albertz, Ferguson I (McInnes D 19), McCall, McCoist (Van Vossen 74), Durie, Laudrup.
Alania Vladikavkaz: Kramarenko; Kornienko, Tetradze, Pagaev, Revishvili (Botsiev), Agaev, Dzhioev, Yanovski, Tedeev, Kasimov (Skysh), Suleimanov (Sergeev).

QUALIFYING ROUND, SECOND LEG

21 AUG

Alania Vladikavkaz (2) 2 (*Yanovski 14, Suleimanov 24 (pen)*)
Rangers (4) 7 (*McCoist 1, 13, 18, Van Vossen 40, Laudrup 55, 83, Miller 86*)   32,000
Alania Vladikavkaz: Khapov; Kornienko (Skysh), Dzhioev, Tetradze, Shelia, Revishvili, Timofeiev, Yanovski, Tedeev (Agaev), Suleimanov (Derkauh), Kaniichtchev.
Rangers: Goram; Cleland, Petric, Gough, Bjorklund, Albertz, McInnes D (Durrant), McCall, McCoist (Durie), Van Vossen (Miller), Laudrup.

GROUP A

11 SEPT

Grasshoppers (2) 3 (*Yakin 18, Turkyilmaz 28, 79*)
Rangers (0) 0   20,030
Grasshoppers: Zuberbuhler; Gamperle, Haas, Gren, Thuler, Magnin (Lombardo), Esposito (Koller), Yakin, Vogel, Moldovan, Turkyilmaz (Rzasa).
Rangers: Goram; Cleland (McInnes), Albertz, Petric, Gough, Bjorklund, Durie (Miller), Gascoigne, McCoist (Van Vossen), McCall, Laudrup.

25 SEPT

Rangers (0) 1 (*Gascoigne 71*)
Auxerre (0) 2 (*Deniaud 55, 69*)   37,344
Rangers: Goram; Moore (Andersen), Cleland, Albertz, Gough, Bjorklund, McInnes, Gascoigne, Van Vossen, Durie (Ferguson I), Laudrup.
Auxerre: Charbonnier; Goma, West, Danjou, Rabarivony, Violeau, Henna, Saib, Lamouchi, Deniaud (Sibierski), Diomede.

16 OCT

Ajax (2) 4 (*Dani 25, 40, Babangida 83, Wooter 89*)
Rangers (0) 1 (*Durrant 87*)   47,000
Ajax: Van der Sar; Santos, Frank De Boer, Bogarde, Veldman, Scholten, Ronald De Boer, Dani (Wooter), Babangida, Reuser (Witschge), Overmars.
Rangers: Snelders; Moore, Cleland, McCall, Gough, Bjorklund, McInnes (Van Vossen), Ferguson I (Durrant), Laudrup (Miller), Gascoigne, Albertz.

30 OCT

Rangers (0) 0
Ajax (1) 1 (*Scholten 38*)   42,265
Rangers: Snelders; Shields, Wilson (Andersen), Robertson, Miller (Van Vossen), Bjorklund, Petric, McInnes (McCoist), Durrant, Laudrup, Albertz.
Ajax: Van der Sar; Melchiot, Santos, Veldman, Frank De Boer (Wooter), Scholten, Witschge, Ronald de Boer, Babangida (Dani), Kluivert, Overmars (Turpijn).

20 NOV

Rangers (0) 2 (*McCoist 66 (pen), 72*)
Grasshoppers (0) 1 (*Berger 76*)   34,192
Rangers: Goram; Cleland, Robertson, Wilson, Gough, Petric, Miller, Moore, McCoist, Van Vossen (Andersen), Albertz.

Grasshoppers: Zuberbuhler; Haas, Gren, Smiljanic, Thuler, Lombardo, Vogel (Subiat), Esposito, Comisetti (Berger), Magnin, Turkyilmaz.

4 DEC

Auxerre (2) 2 (*Laslandes 20, Marlet 32*)
Rangers (1) 1 (*Gough 36*)   21,300
Auxerre: Cool; Goma, Silvestre, Danjou, Rabarivony, Violeau, Assati, Saib, Marlet, Laslandes, Lepaul (Sibierski).
Rangers: Goram; Shields, Petric (McCoist), Gough, Moore, Robertson, Steven, McInnes, Van Vossen (Wilson), Ferguson, Andersen.

GROUP C

Juventus (1) 1 (*Boksic 34*)
Manchester U (0) 0   50,000
Juventus: Peruzzi; Montero, Porrini, Ferrara, Pessotto, Conte, Zidane (Di Livio), Deschamps, Boksic, Vieri (Amoruso), Del Piero (Juliano).
Manchester U: Schmeichel; Neville G, Irwin, Johnsen, Poborsky (Solskjaer), Pallister, Cantona, Butt, Cruyff (Cole), Beckham, Giggs (McClair).

25 SEPT

Manchester U (2) 2 (*Solskjaer 20, Beckham 27*)
Rapid Vienna (0) 0   51,831
Manchester U: Schmeichel; Neville G, Irwin, Johnsen (May), Keane, Pallister, Cantona, Poborsky (Butt), Solskjaer (Cole), Beckham, Giggs.
Rapid Vienna: Konsel; Schottel, Ivanov, Lesiak, Prosenik, Heraf, Kuhbauer, Zingler (Jovanovic), Ratajczyk, Wagner (Stumpf), Stoger (Barisic).

16 OCT

Fenerbahce (0) 0
Manchester U (0) 2 (*Beckham 55, Cantona 59*)   26,200
Fenerbahce: Rustu; Ilker, Okechukwu, Hogh, Ibrahim, Bulent (Erol), Okocha, Kemalettin, Tuncay (Aygun), Bolic, Kostadinov (Tarik).
Manchester U: Schmeichel; Neville G, Irwin, May, Johnsen, Pallister, Cantona, Butt, Solskjaer, Beckham, Cruyff (Poborsky).

30 OCT

Manchester U (0) 0
Fenerbahce (0) 1 (*Bolic 77*)   53,297
Manchester U: Schmeichel; Neville G (Neville P), Irwin, May, Keane, Johnsen, Cantona, Butt, Poborsky (Scholes), Beckham, Cruyff (Solskjaer).
Fenerbahce: Rustu; Ilker, Uche, Kemalettin, Saffet, Hogh (Bulent), Tuncay (Mustafa), Erol, Okocha, Bolic (Tarik), Kostadinov.

20 NOV

Manchester U (0) 0
Juventus (1) 1 (*Del Piero 36 (pen)*)   53,529
Manchester U: Schmeichel; Neville G, Neville P (McClair), May, Keane, Johnsen, Cantona, Butt, Solskjaer (Cruyff), Beckham, Giggs.
Juventus: Peruzzi; Porrini, Ferrara, Montero, Torricelli (Juliano), Di Livio (Tacchinardi), Deschamps, Jugovic, Zidane, Boksic, Del Piero.

4 DEC

Rapid Vienna (0) 0
Manchester U (1) 2 (*Giggs 24, Cantona 71*)   45,000
Rapid Vienna: Konsel; Schottel, Ivanov, Zingler, Prosinik, Heraf, Kuhbauer, Stoger (Mandreko), Ratajczyk, Wagner, Stumpf (Penksa).
Manchester U: Schmeichel; Neville G (Casper), Irwin, May, Keane (McClair), Pallister, Cantona, Butt (Poborsky), Solskjaer, Beckham, Giggs.

QUARTER-FINALS, FIRST LEG

5 MAR

Manchester U (2) 4 *(May 22, Cantona 34, Giggs 61, Cole 80)*
Porto (0) 0 53,415
Manchester U: Schmeichel; Neville G, Irwin, May, Johnsen, Pallister, Cantona, Solskjaer, Cole, Beckham, Giggs.
Porto: Hilario; Conceicao, Jorge Costa, Aloisio, Paulinho Santos, Barroso, Joao Costa (Jardel), Zahovic, Drulovic, Edmilson, Artur (Rui Barros).

QUARTER-FINALS, SECOND LEG

19 MAR

Porto (0) 0
Manchester U (0) 0 40,000
Porto: Wozniak: Joao Pinto I (Zahovic) (Wetl), Jorge Costa, Joao Pinto II, Mendes (Mielcarski), Edmilson, Paulinho Santos, Barroso, Rui Jorge, Drulovic, Jardel.
Manchester U: Schmeichel; Neville G, Irwin (Neville P), May, Keane, Pallister, Cantona, Butt, Solskjaer (Scholes), Beckham (Poborsky), Johnsen.

SEMI-FINALS, FIRST LEG

9 APR

Borussia Dortmund (0) 1 *(Tretschok 76)*
Manchester U (0) 0 48,500
Borussia Dortmund: Klos; Reuter, Kree, Feiersinger, Lambert, Ricken (Freund), Paulo Sousa, Heinrich, Moller, Herrlich (Zorc), Tretschok.
Mancheser U: Van der Gouw; Neville G, Irwin, Johnsen, Keane, Pallister, Cantona, Butt, Solskjaer (Cole), Beckham, Giggs (Scholes).

SEMI-FINALS, SECOND LEG

23 APR

Manchester U (0) 0
Borussia Dortmund (1) 1 *(Ricken 7)* 53,606
Manchester U: Schmeichel; Neville G, Neville P, May (Scholes), Johnsen, Pallister, Cantona, Butt, Cole, Beckham, Solskjaer (Giggs).
Borussia Dortmund: Klos; Kohler, Feiersinger, Kree, Ricken (Zorc), Reuter (Tretschok), Moller, Lambert, Heinrich, Chapuisat, Riedle (Herrlich).

Manchester United's finest performance in European football for many years came in their 4–0 success over Porto. Ole Gunnar Solksjaer tussles with Jorge Costa. (Action Images)

EUROPEAN CUP-WINNERS' CUP

EUROPEAN CUP-WINNERS' CUP FINALS 1961–97

Year	Winners	Runners-up	Venue	Attendance	Referee
1961	Fiorentina 2	Rangers 0 *(1st Leg)*	Glasgow	80,000	Steiner (A)
	Fiorentina 2	Rangers 1 *(2nd Leg)*	Florence	50,000	Hernadi (H)
1962	Atletico Madrid 1	Fiorentina 1	Glasgow	27,389	Wharton (S)
Replay	Atletico Madrid 3	Fiorentina 0	Stuttgart	45,000	Tschenscher (WG)
1963	Tottenham Hotspur 5	Atletico Madrid 1	Rotterdam	25,000	Van Leuwen (Ho)
1964	Sporting Lisbon 3	MTK Budapest 3 *(aet)*	Brussels	9000	Van Nuffel (Bel)
Replay	Sporting Lisbon 1	MTK Budapest 0	Antwerp	18,000	Versyp (Bel)
1965	West Ham U 2	Munich 1860 0	Wembley	100,000	Szolt (H)
1966	Borussia Dortmund 2	Liverpool 1 *(aet)*	Glasgow	41,657	Schwinte (F)
1967	Bayern Munich 1	Rangers 0 *(aet)*	Nuremberg	69,480	Lo Bello (I)
1968	AC Milan 2	Hamburg 0	Rotterdam	60,000	Ortiz (Sp)
1969	Slovan Bratislava 3	Barcelona 2	Basle	40,000	Van Ravens (Ho)
1970	Manchester C 2	Gornik Zabrze 1	Vienna	10,000	Schiller (A)
1971	Chelsea 1	Real Madrid 1 *(aet)*	Athens	42,000	Scheurer (Sw)
Replay	Chelsea 2	Real Madrid 1 *(aet)*	Athens	24,000	Bucheli (Sw)
1972	Rangers 3	Moscow Dynamo 2	Barcelona	35,000	Ortiz (Sp)
1973	AC Milan 1	Leeds U 0	Salonika	45,000	Mihas (Gr)
1974	Magdeburg 2	AC Milan 0	Rotterdam	5000	Van Gemert (Ho)
1975	Dynamo Kiev 3	Ferencvaros 0	Basle	13,000	Davidson (S)
1976	Anderlecht 4	West Ham U 2	Brussels	58,000	Wurtz (F)
1977	Hamburg 2	Anderlecht 0	Amsterdam	65,000	Partridge (E)
1978	Anderlecht 4	Austria/WAC 0	Paris	48,679	Adlinger (WG)
1979	Barcelona 4	Fortuna Dusseldorf 3 *(aet)*	Basle	58,000	Palotai (H)
1980	Valencia 0	Arsenal 0	Brussels	40,000	Christov (Cz)
	(aet; Valencia won 5-4 on penalties)				
1981	Dynamo Tbilisi 2	Carl Zeiss Jena 1	Dusseldorf	9000	Lattanzi (I)
1982	Barcelona 2	Standard Liege 1	Barcelona	100,000	Eschweiler (WG)
1983	Aberdeen 2	Real Madrid 1 *(aet)*	Gothenburg	17,804	Menegali (I)
1984	Juventus 2	Porto 1	Basle	60,000	Prokop (EG)
1985	Everton 3	Rapid Vienna 1	Rotterdam	30,000	Casarin (I)
1986	Dynamo Kiev 3	Atletico Madrid 0	Lyon	39,300	Wohrer (A)
1987	Ajax 1	Lokomotiv Leipzig 0	Athens	35,000	Agnolin (I)
1988	Mechelen 1	Ajax 0	Strasbourg	39,446	Pauly (WG)
1989	Barcelona 2	Sampdoria 0	Berne	45,000	Courtney (E)
1990	Sampdoria 2	Anderlecht 0	Gothenburg	20,103	Galler (Sw)
1991	Manchester U 2	Barcelona 1	Rotterdam	45,000	Karlsson (Se)
1992	Werder Bremen 2	Monaco 0	Lisbon	16,000	D'Elia (I)
1993	Parma 3	Antwerp 1	Wembley	37,393	Assenmacher (G)
1994	Arsenal 1	Parma 0	Copenhagen	33,765	Krondl (Czr)
1995	Zaragoza 2	Arsenal 1	Paris	42,424	Ceccarini (I)
1996	Paris St Germain 1	Rapid Vienna 0	Brussels	37,500	Pairetto (I)
1997	Barcelona 1	Paris St Germain 0	Rotterdam	40,000	Merk (G)

EUROPEAN CUP-WINNERS' CUP 1996–97

QUALIFYING ROUND, FIRST LEG
Chemlon Humenne (0) 1 *(Lubarsky 71)*, Flamurtari (0) 0
  12,000
Constructorul (1) 1 *(Rogachev 20)*, Hapoel Ironi Rishon
  (0) 0   6000
Dynamo Batumi (3) 6 *(Tugushi 11, 23, 55, Ujmajuridze*
  27, 70, 88), HB (0) 0   6400
Glentoran (0) 1 *(Little 53)*, Sparta Prague (0) 2 *(Siegl 49,*
  Lokvenc 90)   2200
Karabach (0) 0, MyPa (0) 1 *(Mahlio 85)*   11,500
Kispest Honved (1) 1 *(Toth 11)*, Sloga (0) 0   5500
Kotaik (0) 1 *(Berberyan 80)*, AEK Larnaca (0) 0   4000
Llansantffraid (0) 1 *(Arwel Jones 83)*, Ruch Chorzow (1)
  1 *(Gesior 6)*   1558
MPKC (0) 2 *(Yaromko 51, Skorobogatko 70)*, KR
  Reykjavik (0) 2 *(Dadasson 88, Jonsson 90)*   7500
Olimpija Ljubljana (0) 1 *(Bozgo 50)*, Levski Sofia (0) 0
  2500
Red Star Belgrade (0) 0, Hearts (0) 0   28,000
Sadam Tallinn (1) 2 *(Krolov 25 (pen), Viikmae 74)*, Niva
  Vinnitsa (0) 1 *(Romanchuk 77)*   700
Shelbourne (1) 1 *(Geoghegan S 43)*, Brann (2) 3 *(Mjelde*
  27, Pedersen J 29, Eftevaag 67 (pen))   3010
Sion (3) 4 *(Chassot 14, Bonvin 27, Pancev 36, Vercruysse*
  90), Kareda (0) 2 *(Baranauskas 73, Dancenka 89)*
  6200
Universitate (0) 1 *(Zareis 43)*, Vaduz (1) 1 *(Perez 38)* 500
Valletta (0) 1 *(Doncic 75)*, Gloria (0) 2 *(Iftodi 52, Dancus*
  67)   2500
Varteks (1) 2 *(Mumlek 41, Maretic 81 (pen))*, Union
  Luxembourg (0) 1 *(Gretinich 87)*   3000

QUALIFYING ROUND, SECOND LEG
AEK Larnaca (2) 5 *(Kudic 28, Alexandrou 41, Kalacevic*
  60, Kapunovic 82, Markou 84), Kotaik (0) 0   5000
Brann (1) 2 *(Mjelde 8, Pedersen J 70)*, Shelbourne (1) 1
  (Rutherford 3)   2188
Flamurtari (0) 0, Chemlon Humenne (0) 2 *(Lubarsky 50,*
  Valkucak 54)   5000
Gloria (1) 2 *(Lazar 32, Voica 84)*, Valletta (1) 1 *(Agius*
  24)   5000
Hapoel Ironi Rishon (2) 3 *(Sabag 10, Kapeta 26, Sibola*
  58), Constructorul (1) 2 *(Rogachev 42, Skiden 87)*
  5000
HB (0) 0, Dynamo Batumi (2) 3 *(Glonti 20, 21,*
  Ujmajuridze 63)   800
Hearts (1) 1 *(McPherson 44)*, Red Star Belgrade (0) 1
  (Marinovic 59)   15,062
Kareda (0) 0, Sion (0) 0   2500
KR Reykjavik (0) 1 *(Danielsson 90)*, MPKC (0) 0   2950
Levski Sofia (0) 1 *(Simeonov 58)*, Olimpija
  Ljubljana (0) 0   25,000
MyPa (0) 1 *(Musaev 27)*, Karabach (1) 1 *(Keskitalo 120)*
  500
Niva Vannitsa (0) 1 *(Romanchuk 66)*, Sadam Tallinn (0) 0
  15,000
Ruch Chorzow (1) 5 *(Bak A 1, 55, Arwel Jones 47 (og),*
  Bak M 62, 63), Llansantffraid (0) 0   6700
Sloga (0) 0, Kispest Honved (0) 1 *(Ghinda 81)*   5000
Sparta Prague (4) 8 *(Gunda 1, 25, Mistr 19, Siegl 24, 48,*
  80, Svoboda Z 78, Gabrel 86), Glentoran (0) 0   7000
Union Luxembourg (0) 0, Varteks (0) 3 *(Besek 63,*
  Mumler 78 (pen), Cvetko 87)   800
Vaduz (0) 1 *(Polverino 49)*, Universitate (0) 1
  (Zarins 49)   700

FIRST ROUND, FIRST LEG
Aarhus (1) 1 *(Bak L 15)*, Olimpija Ljubljana (0) 1
  (Bozgo 57)   5900
AEK Athens (1) 1 *(Batista 45)*, Chemlon Humenne (0) 0
  25,000
Barcelona (1) 2 *(Ronaldo 19, 77)*, AEK Larnaca (0) 0
  30,000
Benfica (3) 5 *(Donizete 24, Joao Pinto 25, Jamir 31,*
  Valdo 68, 89), Ruch Chorzow (0) 1 *(Gesior 73)*17,000
CS Brugge (3) 3 *(Gernso 6, Vanmaele 27, Camerman 32)*,
  Brann (1) 2 *(Flo 38, Eftevaag 90 (pen))*   3500
Constructorul (0) 0, Galatasaray (0) 1 *(Knup 73)*   7000

Dynamo Batumi (1) 1 *(Mujiri 18)*, PSV Eindhoven (0) 1
  (Nilis 39 (pen))   14,000
Gloria (1) 1 *(Lazar 3)*, Fiorentina (0) 1 *(Batistuta 47)*
  12,000
Kaiserslautern (0) 1 *(Wegmann 59)*, Red Star Belgrade
  (0) 0   27,000
Lokomotiv Moscow (1) 1 *(Cherevchenko 12)*,
  Varteks (0) 0   5000
MyPa (0) 0, Liverpool (0) 1 *(Bjornebye 61)*   5500
Nimes (0) 3 *(Jeunechamp 65, Prejet 75, Meilhac 86)*,
  Kispest Honved (0) 1 *(Toth 70)*   9000
KR Reykjavik (0) 0, AIK Stockholm (0) 1 *(Nordin 80)*
  3500
Sion (0) 2 *(Colombo 50, Bonvin 85)*, Niva Vinnitsa (0) 0
  6500
Sturm Graz (1) 2 *(Vastic 8, Mahlich 85)*, Sparta Prague
  (1) 2 *(Repka 57, Lokvenc 72)*   5000
Vaduz (0) 0, Paris St Germain (3) 4 *(Le Guen 12, Dely*
  Valdes 40, Leonardo 44, Allou 73)   1900

FIRST ROUND, SECOND LEG
AIK Stockholm (0) 1 *(Simpson 79)*, KR Reykjavik (0) 1
  (Benediktsson 90)   3267
AEK Larnaca (0) 0, Barcelona (0) 0   7000
Brann (1) 4 *(Mjelde 5, 82, Eftevaag 79, Helland 88)*, CS
  Brugge (0) 0   6104
Chemlon Humenne (1) 1 *(Dina 1)*, AEK Athens (2) 2
  (Nikolaidis 19, Batista 44)   14,700
Fiorentina (1) 1 *(Orlando 22)*, Gloria (0) 0   20,000
Galatasaray (0) 4 *(Hakan Sukur 49, 80, Arif 73, Hagi 75)*,
  Constructorul (0) 0   20,000
Kispest Honved (0) 1 *(Piroska 62)*, Nimes (2) 2 *(Ecker 6,*
  Sabin 38)   5000
Liverpool (1) 3 *(Berger 18, Collymore 59, Barnes 78)*,
  MyPa (0) 1 *(Keskitalo 64)*   39,013
Niva Vinnitsa (0) 0, Sion (2) 4 *(Lukic 2, Vercruysse 9, 63,*
  Milton 49)   12,000
Olympija Ljubljana (0) 0, Aarhus (0) 0   6500
Paris St Germain (2) 3 *(Allou 22, Roche 40, Mboma 50)*,
  Vaduz (0) 0   16,000
PSV Eindhoven (1) 3 *(Nilis 15, Eykelkamp 53, Marcelo*
  83), Dynamo Batumi (0) 0   14,220
Red Star Belgrade (0) 4 *(Stankovic 55, 96, Njegus 107,*
  Pantelic 120), Kaiserslautern (0) 0   70,000
Ruch Chorzow (0) 0, Benfica (0) 0   4547
Sparta Prague (0) 1 *(Hornak 87)*, Sturm Graz (0) 1
  (Novotny 76 (og))   5000
Varteks (0) 2 *(Vugrinec 63, 80)*, Lokomotiv Moscow (1) 1
  (Kossolapov 41)   10,000

SECOND ROUND, FIRST LEG
Barcelona (2) 3 *(Giovanni 34, 36, Figo 54)*, Red Star
  Belgrade (1) 1 *(Zivkovic 21)*   73,000
Benfica (1) 1 *(Joao Pinto 8)*, Lokomotiv Moscow (0) 0
  10,000
Brann (2) 2 *(Mjelde 30, 35 (pen))*, PSV Eindhoven (0) 1
  (Cocu 90)   7811
Fiorentina (1) 2 *(Batistuta 7, Schwarz 57)*, Sparta Prague
  (0) 1 *(Siegl 80)*   22,400
Galatasaray (3) 4 *(Hakan Sukur 5, 31, 49, Tugay 13)*,
  Paris St Germain (2) 2 *(Le Guen 18, Dely Valdes 19)*
  30,000
Nimes (1) 1 *(Fidani 88)*, AIK Stockholm (2) 3 *(Simpson*
  9, Pacha 12, Johansson M 70)   12,000
Olimpija Ljubljana (0) 0, AEK Athens (1) 2 *(Kostis 12,*
  Ketsbaia 49)   3000
Sion (1) 1 *(Bonvin 11)*, Liverpool (1) 2 *(Fowler 24,*
  Barnes 60)   16,500

SECOND ROUND, SECOND LEG
AEK Athens (2) 4 *(Savevski 4 (pen), 83, Batista 20,*
  Maladenis 80), Olimpija Ljubljana (0) 0   25,000
AIK Stockholm (0) 0, Nimes (0) 1 *(Brundin 69 (og))* 5620
Liverpool (1) 6 *(McManaman 28, Bjornebye 54, Barnes*
  65, Fowler 70, 71, Berger 89), Sion (2) 3 *(Chassot 19,*
  64, Bonvin 23)   38,514

Lokomotiv Moscow (1) 2 *(Solomatin 9, Guaras 59)*,
Benfica (0) 3 *(Panduru 48, Donizete 63, Joao Pinto
89)* 6000
Paris St Germain (2) 4 *(Leonardo 9, Dely Valdes 22,
Loko 58, Rai 78)*, Galatasaray (0) 0 34,032
PSV Eindhoven (0) 2 *(Eykelkamp 75, Zenden 82)*, Brann
(1) 2 *(Hasund 35, Flo 60)* 19,000
Red Star Belgrade (0) 1 *(Jovicic 47)*, Barcelona (0) 1
(Giovanni 48) 50,000
Sparta Prague (1) 1 *(Lokvenc 5)*, Fiorentina (0) 1
(Robbiati 63) 16,000

QUARTER-FINALS, FIRST LEG
Barcelona (1) 3 *(Popescu 2, Ronaldo 55, Pizzi 75)*, AIK
Stockholm (1) 1 *(Simpson 1)* 65,000
Benfica (0) 0, Fiorentina (1) 2 *(Baiano 45, Batistuta 90)*
58,000
Brann (0) 1 *(Hasund 47)*, Liverpool (1) 1 *(Fowler 10)*
12,700
Paris St Germain (0) 0, AEK Athens (0) 0 21,952

QUARTER-FINALS, SECOND LEG
AEK Athens (0) 0, Paris St Germain (2) 3 *(Loko 22, 44,
80)* 28,000
AIK Stockholm (0) 1 *(Simpson 75)*, Barcelona (1) 1
(Ronaldo 9) 35,049
Fiorentina (0) 0, Benfica (1) 1 *(Pacheco 22)* 35,071
Liverpool (1) 3 *(Fowler 25 (pen), 77, Collymore 60)*,
Brann (0) 0 40,326

SEMI-FINALS, FIRST LEG
Barcelona (1) 1 *(Nadal 43)*, Fiorentina (0) 1 *(Batistuta
63)* 120,000
Paris St Germain (2) 3 *(Leonardo 11, Cauet 43, Leroy
84)*, Liverpool (0) 0 35,142

SEMI-FINALS, SECOND LEG
Fiorentina (0) 0, Barcelona (2) 2 *(Fernando Couto 30,
Guardiola 35)* 48,000
Liverpool (1) 2 *(Fowler 11, Wright 79)*, Paris St Germain
(0) 0 38,984

FINAL

Barcelona (1) 1, Paris St Germain (0) 0

(in Rotterdam, 14 May 1997, 45,000)

Barcelona: Vitor Baia; Ferrer, Abelardo, Fernando
Couto, Sergi, Figo, Popescu (Amor 46), Guardiola,
De la Pena (Stoichkov 84), Luis Enrique (Pizzi 89),
Ronaldo.
Scorer: Ronaldo 38 (pen).
Paris St Germain: Lama; Domi, Le Guen (Dely Vales
68), N'Gotty, Fournier (Algerino 57), Leroy, Guerin,
Rai, Cauet, Leonardo, Loko (Pouget 78).
Referee: Merk (Germany).

Ronaldo's penalty for Barcelona divided the teams in the Cup-Winner's Cup Final with Paris St. Germain the
beaten holders. (Colorsport)

EUROPEAN CUP-WINNERS' CUP 1996–97 – BRITISH AND IRISH CLUBS

QUALIFYING ROUND, FIRST LEG

8 AUG

Glentoran (0) 1 *(Little 53)*
Sparta Prague (0) 2 *(Siegl 49, Lokvenc 90)* 2200
Glentoran: Armstrong; Mathieson, Smyth M, Parker, Devine, Walker, Finlay, Little, Smith T (Kirk), Batey, McBride (Cook).
Sparta Prague: Caloun; Votava, Mistr, Gabrel, Hornak, Svoboda Z, Svoboda V (Lokvenc), Novotny, Jarosik, Siegl, Frydek (Obajdin).

Llansantffraid (0) 1 *(Arwel Jones 83)*
Ruch Chorzow (1) 1 *(Gesior 6)* 1558
Llansantffraid: Mulliner; Whelan J, Curtiss, Brown, Arwel Jones, Thomas, Adrian Jones, Evans, Morgan (Davies), Edwards (Whelan C), Abercrombie.
Ruch Chorzow: Kolodziejczyk; Fornalak, Pieniazek, Bak M, Jaworski, Bak A, Mosor, Rowicki (Wawrzyciek), Srutwa (Mizia), Grzesik.

Red Star Belgrade (0) 0
Hearts (0) 0 28,000
Red Star Belgrade: Milosevic; Zivkovic, Djorovic, Stankovic P, Marinovic, Ognjenovic, Pantelic (Virievic), Jovicic, Stankovic D (Vanic), Anic.
Hearts: Rousset; Frail (McManus), Weir, McPherson, Ritchie, Pointon, Goss, Bruno, Mackay, Cameron, Colquhoun (Thomas).

Shelbourne (1) 1 *(Geoghegan S 43)*
Brann (2) 3 *(Mjelde 27, Pedersen J 29, Eftevaag 67 (pen))* 3010
Shelbourne: Gough; Costello, Neville, Campbell, Vaudequin, O'Rourke (Golden), Flood, Geoghegan D, Sheridan, Rutherford (Smith), Geoghegan S.
Brann: Christensen; Brendesaether, Lundekvam, Eftevaag, Pedersen M, Pedersen J, Helland, Ludvigsen (Hasund), Bakkerud, Mjelde (Johannessen), Flo (Karlsbakk).

QUALIFYING ROUND, SECOND LEG

22 AUG

Brann (1) 2 *(Mjelde 8, Pedersen J 70)*
Shelbourne (1) 1 *(Rutherford 3)* 2188
Brann: Christensen; Brendesaether, Eftevaag, Lundekvam, Helland, Pedersen J, Bakkerud, Pedersen M, Flo (Karlsbakk), Mjelde, Gylfason.
Shelbourne: Gough; Costello, Geoghegan D, Neville, Rutherford, Vaudequin, Flood, O'Rourke, Sheridan, Geoghegan S, Tilson.

Hearts (1) 1 *(McPherson 44)*
Red Star Belgrade (0) 1 *(Marinovic 59)* 15,062
Hearts: Rousset; Cameron, Colquhoun, Bruno (Thomas), Pointon, Fulton, Mackay (Robertson), McCann, McPherson, Ritchie, Weir.
Red Star Belgrade: Milosevic; Zivkovic, Djorovic, Njegus, Stankovic P, Marinovic, Ognjenovic (Sakic), Anic, Jovicic, Stankovic D (Vanic), Boskovic (Vulevic).

Ruch Chorzow (1) 5 *(Bak A 1, 55, Arwel Jones 47 (og), Bak M 62, 63)*
Llansantffraid (0) 0 6700
Ruch Chorzow: Lech; Gasior, Bak A, Mosor, Gaca (Rowicki), Gesior, Srutwa, Grzesik, Bak M (Wawrzyciek), Pieniazek, Mizia (Zaba).

Llansantffraid: Mulliner; Whelan J (Jones G), Curtiss, Brown (Davies), Arwel Jones, Thomas, Adrian Jones, Evans, Morgan (Whelan C), Edwards, Abercrombie.

Sparta Prague (4) 8 *(Gunda 1, 25, Mistr 19, Siegl 24, 48, 80, Svoboda Z 78, Gabrel 86)*
Glentoran (0) 0 7000
Sparta Prague: Ondruska; Repka, Mistr (Svoboda V), Gabrel, Hornak, Svoboda Z, Gunda, Novotny, Lokvenc (Obajdin), Siegl, Frydek (Jarosik).
Glentoran: Armstrong; Quigley (Elliott), Smyth M, Parker, Devine, Walker (Houston), Finlay, Mathieson (Kirk), Smith T, Batey, McBride.

FIRST ROUND, FIRST LEG

12 SEPT

MyPa (0) 0
Liverpool (0) 1 *(Bjornebye 61)* 5500
MyPa: Jakonen; Huttunen, Koskinen, Hernesniemi, Viljanen, Moore, Mahlio, Pohja, Groenholm (Jalonen), Allen (Kangaskorpi), Keskitalo (Enberg).
Liverpool: James; McAteer, Bjornebye, Matteo, Wright, Babb, McManaman, Collymore, Fowler, Barnes, Thomas.

FIRST ROUND, SECOND LEG

26 SEPT

Liverpool (1) 3 *(Berger 18, Collymore 59, Barnes 78)*
MyPa (0) 1 *(Keskitalo 64)* 39,013
Liverpool: James; McAteer, Bjornebye, Matteo (Ruddock), Wright (Scales), Babb, McManaman, Collymore, Berger (Redknapp), Barnes, Thomas.
MyPa: Jakonen; Moore, Viljanen, Koskinen, Huttunen, Mahlio, Pohja, Allen (Jalonen), Kautonen, Groenholm (Kangaskorpi), Keskitalo (Enberg).

SECOND ROUND, FIRST LEG

17 OCT

Sion (1) 1 *(Bonvin 11)*
Liverpool (1) 2 *(Fowler 24, Barnes 60)* 16,500
Sion: Lehmann; Wicky, Milton, Quentin, Gaspoz, Sylvestre, Vercruysse, Longfat, Zambaz (Chassot), Lukic, Bonvin (Vincze).
Liverpool: James; McAteer, Bjornebye, Matteo, Scales, Babb, McManaman, Berger, Fowler (Redknapp), Barnes, Thomas.

SECOND ROUND, SECOND LEG

31 OCT

Liverpool (1) 6 *(McManaman 28, Bjornebye 54, Barnes 65, Fowler 70, 71, Berger 89)*
Sion (2) 3 *(Chassot 19, 64, Bonvin 23)* 38,514
Liverpool: James; McAteer, Bjornebye, Matteo, Scales (Redknapp), Babb, McManaman, Berger, Fowler, Barnes, Thomas.
Sion: Lehmann; Milton, Wicky, Quentin, Gaspoz (Buhlmann), Longfat (Zambaz), Vercruysse, Sylvestre, Colombo, Chassot, Bonvin (Vincze).

QUARTER-FINALS, FIRST LEG

6 MAR

Brann (0) 1 *(Hasund 47)*
Liverpool (1) 1 *(Fowler 10)*   12,700
Brann: Bahus; Pedersen M, Ludvigsen, Eftevaag, Paldan, Gylfason, Moen (Mjelde), Helland, Hasund, Skjaelaaen, Flo.
Liverpool: James; McAteer, Bjornebye, Matteo, Harkness, Ruddock, McManaman, Berger, Fowler, Barnes, Redknapp.

QUARTER-FINALS, SECOND LEG

20 MAR

Liverpool (1) 3 *(Fowler 25 (pen), 77, Collymore 60)*
Brann (0) 0   40,326
Liverpool: James; McAteer, Bjornebye, Harkness, Wright, Matteo (Babb), McManaman, Berger (Collymore), Fowler, Barnes, Redknapp.
Brann: Bahus; Paldan, Ludvigsen, Eftevaag, Pedersen M, Skjaelaaen (Johannessen), Helland, Moen, Hasund (Gunveit), Mjelde, Flo.

SEMI-FINALS, FIRST LEG

10 APR

Paris St Germain (2) 3 *(Leonardo 11, Cauet 43, Leroy 84)*
Liverpool (0) 0   35,142
Paris St Germain: Lama; N'Gotty, Le Guen, Domi (Algerino), Fournier, Guerin, Cauet, Rai, Leroy (Allou), Loko (Pouget), Leonardo.
Liverpool: James; McAteer, Bjornebye, Matteo, Wright, Harkness, McManaman, Collymore (Thomas), Fowler, Barnes, Redknapp.

SEMI-FINALS, SECOND LEG

24 APR

Liverpool (1) 2 *(Fowler 11, Wright 79)*
Paris St Germain (0) 0   38,984
Liverpool: James; McAteer, Bjornebye, Thomas, Wright, Ruddock, McManaman, Collymore, Fowler, Berger (Kennedy), Redknapp.
Paris St Germain: Lama; Fournier, N'Gotty, Le Guen, Algerino, Leroy, Rai, Guerin, Cauet, Leonardo (Pimental), Loko (Pouget).

EUROPEAN CUP DRAWS 1997–98

EUROPEAN CUP
First Qualifying Round (British and Irish clubs only):
Derry City v Branik Maribor (Slovenia); Crusaders v Dynamo Tbilisi (Georgia); GI Gotu (Faeroes) v Rangers; Dynamo Kiev (Ukraine) v Barry Town.

Second Qualifying Round:
Besiktas (Turkey) v Derry City or Branik Maribor; IFK Gothenburg (Sweden) v GI Gotu or Rangers; Brondby (Denmark) v Dynamo Kiev or Barry Town; Newcastle U v Partizan Belgrade (Yugoslavia) or Croatia Zagreb (Croatia); Bayer Leverkusen (Germany) v Crusaders or Dynamo Tbilisi.

EUROPEAN CUP-WINNERS' CUP
First Qualifying Round (British and Irish clubs only):
Legia Warsaw (Poland) v Glenavon; Cwmbran v Nacional (Romania); Kilmarnock v Shelbourne.

UEFA CUP
First Qualifying Round (British and Irish clubs only):
Inter-Cable Tel v Celtic; Grasshoppers (Switzerland) v Coleraine; Bohemians v Ferencvaros (Hungary); Principat (Andorra) v Dundee U.

INTER-CITIES FAIRS & UEFA CUP

FAIRS CUP FINALS 1958–71
(Winners in italics)

Year	First Leg	Attendance	Second Leg	Attendance
1958	London 2 Barcelona 2	45,466	*Barcelona* 6 London 0	62,000
1960	Birmingham C 0 Barcelona 0	40,500	*Barcelona* 4 Birmingham C 1	70,000
1961	Birmingham C 2 Roma 2	21,005	*Roma* 2 Birmingham C 0	60,000
1962	Valencia 6 Barcelona 2	65,000	Barcelona 1 *Valencia* 1	60,000
1963	Dynamo Zagreb 1 Valencia 2	40,000	*Valencia* 2 Dynamo Zagreb 0	55,000
1964	*Zaragoza* 2 Valencia 1	50,000	(in Barcelona)	
1965	*Ferencvaros* 1 Juventus 0	25,000	(in Turin)	
1966	Barcelona 0 Zaragoza 1	70,000	Zaragoza 2 *Barcelona* 4	70,000
1967	Dynamo Zagreb 2 Leeds U 0	40,000	Leeds U 0 *Dynamo Zagreb* 0	35,604
1968	Leeds U 1 Ferencvaros 0	25,368	Ferencvaros 0 *Leeds U* 0	70,000
1969	Newcastle U 3 Ujpest Dozsa 0	60,000	Ujpest Dozsa 2 *Newcastle U* 3	37,000
1970	Anderlecht 3 Arsenal 1	37,000	*Arsenal* 3 Anderlecht 0	51,612
1971	Juventus 0 Leeds U 0 *(abandoned 51 minutes)*	42,000		
	Juventus 2 Leeds U 2	42,000	*Leeds U* 1* Juventus 1	42,483

UEFA CUP FINALS 1972–97
(Winners in italics)

1972	Wolverhampton W 1 Tottenham H 2	45,000	*Tottenham H* 1 Wolverhampton W 1	48,000
1973	Liverpool 0 Moenchengladbach 0 *(abandoned 27 minutes)*	44,967		
	Liverpool 3 Moenchengladbach 0	41,169	Moenchengladbach 2 *Liverpool* 0	35,000
1974	Tottenham H 2 Feyenoord 2	46,281	*Feyenoord* 2 Tottenham H 0	68,000
1975	Moenchengladbach 0 Twente 0	45,000	Twente 1 *Moenchengladbach* 5	24,500
1976	Liverpool 3 FC Brugge 2	56,000	FC Brugge 1 *Liverpool* 1	32,000
1977	Juventus 1 Athletic Bilbao 0	75,000	Athletic Bilbao 2 *Juventus* 1*	43,000
1978	Bastia 0 PSV Eindhoven 0	15,000	*PSV Eindhoven* 3 Bastia 0	27,000
1979	Red Star Belgrade 1 Moenchengladbach 1	87,500	*Moenchengladbach* 1 Red Star Belgrade 0	45,000
1980	Moenchengladbach 3 Eintracht Frankfurt 2	25,000	*Eintracht Frankfurt* 1* Moenchengladbach 0	60,000
1981	Ipswich T 3 AZ 67 Alkmaar 0	27,532	AZ 67 Alkmaar 4 *Ipswich T* 2	28,500
1982	Gothenburg 1 Hamburg 0	42,548	Hamburg 0 *Gothenburg* 3	60,000
1983	Anderlecht 1 Benfica 0	45,000	Benfica 1 *Anderlecht* 1	80,000
1984	Anderlecht 1 Tottenham H 1	40,000	*Tottenham H* 1[1] Anderlecht 1	46,258
1985	Videoton 0 Real Madrid 3	30,000	*Real Madrid* 0 Videoton 1	98,300
1986	Real Madrid 5 Cologne 1	80,000	Cologne 2 *Real Madrid* 0	15,000
1987	Gothenburg 1 Dundee U 0	50,023	Dundee U 1 *Gothenburg* 1	20,911
1988	Espanol 3 Bayer Leverkusen 0	42,000	*Bayer Leverkusen* 3[2] Espanol 0	22,000
1989	Napoli 2 Stuttgart 1	83,000	Stuttgart 3 *Napoli* 3	67,000
1990	Juventus 3 Fiorentina 1	45,000	Fiorentina 0 *Juventus* 0	32,000
1991	Internazionale 2 Roma 0	68,887	Roma 1 *Internazionale* 0	70,901
1992	Torino 2 Ajax 2	65,377	*Ajax* 0* Torino 0	40,000
1993	Borussia Dortmund 1 Juventus 3	37,000	*Juventus* 3 Borussia Dortmund 0	62,781
1994	Salzburg 0 Internazionale 1	47,500	*Internazionale* 1 Salzburg 0	80,326
1995	Parma 1 Juventus 0	23,000	Juventus 1 *Parma* 1	80,750
1996	Bayern Munich 2 Bordeaux 0	62,000	Bordeaux 1 *Bayern Munich* 3	36,000
1997	Schalke 1 Internazionale 0	56,824	Internazionale 1 *Schalke* 0[3]	81,670

*won on away goals   [1]*Tottenham H won 4-3 on penalties aet*   [2]*Bayer Leverkusen won 3-2 on penalties aet*
[3]*Schalke won 4-1 on penalties aet*

UEFA CUP 1996–97

PRELIMINARY ROUND, FIRST LEG
Akranes (1) 2 *(Gudjonsson 43, Bibercic 72)*, Sileks (0) 0
    1000
Anorthosis (0) 4 *(Michalovic 53, 83, Kokits 60, 72)*,
  Shirak (0) 0   2000
B36 (1) 1 *(Hentze 34 (pen))*, Apoel (4) 5 *(Sotiriou 5, 26,*
  Fasouliotis 11, Alexandrou 36, 68)   297
Barry Town (0) 0, Dinaburg (0) 0   2500
Becej (0) 0, Mura (0) 0   4000
Beitar Jerusalem (3) 3 *(Salloi 17, Harazi 21, Pisont 43)*,
  Floriana (0) 1 *(Veslji 55)*   11,000
Bohemians (1) 1 *(Swan 1)*, Dynamo Minsk (0) 1
  (Matovski 65)   3000
Croatia Zagreb (2) 4 *(Sliskovic 25, Krznar 42, Cvitanovic*
  53, 79 (pen)), SK Tirana (0) 0   12,000
Dynamo 93 Minsk (3) 3 *(Sinkovets 5, 10, Orlovski 7)*,
  Tiligul (0) 1 *(Kosse 87)*   2000
Dynamo Tbilisi (1) 4 *(Iashvili 36, 72, Gogichaishvili 78,*
  Demetradze 87), Grevenmacher (0) 0   15,000
Haka (0) 2 *(Ristila 56, 80)*, Flora Tallinn (1) 2 *(Rooba 22,*
  Leetma 90)   1645
HIT Gorica (0) 0, Vardar (1) 1 *(Trajcev 44)*   3000
Hutnik (2) 9 *(Yahaja 29, Romuzga 37, 67, Wojnecki 65,*
  74, Zajac 70, 73, Shipovski 85 (pen), Jamroz 90),
  Khazri (0) 0   5000
Jazz Pori (1) 3 *(Suikkanen 38, Leivo-Jokimaki 49,*
  Piracaia 77), GI Gotu (0) 1 *(Heinason 89)*   3190
Jeunesse Esch (2) 2 *(Ganser 31, Theis 43)*, Legia Warsaw
  (3) 4 *(Pisz 4, Sokolowski 39, Staniek 41, 60)*   1500
Lantana (0) 2 *(Bragin 60, Gruznov 79)*, IBV (0) 1
  (Gudmundsson 55)   1000
Maccabi Haifa (0) 0, Partizan Belgrade (1) 1 *(Svetlicic 10)*
    6000
Neftchi Baku (0) 2 *(Rzayev 57, Vakhabzade 90)*,
  Lokomotiv Sofia (1) 1 *(Borisov 7)*   20,000
Newtown (0) 1 *(Brown 90)*, Skonto Riga (1) 4 *(Astayev*
  36, 71, Lobanyov 75, 80)   2000
Portadown (0) 0, Vojvodina (1) 1 *(Cilinsek 27)*   1500
Pyunik (1) 3 *(Avetissian A 23, 53, Mikhitarian 74)*, HJK
  Helsinki (1) 1 *(Lechtinen 43)*   4500
St Patrick's Ath (1) 3 *(Glynn 44, O'Flaherty 64,*
  McDonnell 74), Slovan Bratislava (3) 4 *(Nemeth 10,*
  40, Maixner 18, Karasy 77)   4500
Slavia Sofia (2) 4 *(Panayotov 31, 72, Totev 42,*
  Pramatarov 85), Inkaras (2) 3 *(Poderis 5,*
  Maciulevicius 13, 76)   4000
Silema Wanderers (0) 1 *(Turner 65)*, Margveti (1) 3
  (Gongadze 24, Endeladze 77, Ukleba 86)   1000
Teuta (1) 1 *(Begeja 2)*, Kosice (0) 4 *(Sovic 47, 62,*
  Obsiinik 87, Koslej 89)   4000
Zalgiris (0) 2 *(Vencevicius 82, Pukelevicius 86)*, Crusaders
  (0) 0   5000
Zimbru Chisinau (0) 0, Hajduk Split (2) 4 *(Skoko 19, 56,*
  71, Vucko 31)   7000

PRELIMINARY ROUND, SECOND LEG
Apoel (1) 4 *(Ioannou 14, 50, Sotiriou 60, Kozma 74*
  (pen)), B36 (2) 2 *(Hedjen 38, Reinagson 43)*   1000
Crusaders (0) 2 *(Morgan 83, 90)*, Zalgiris (1) 1
  (Razanauskas 18)   1500
Dinaburg (0) 1 *(Tarasov 60)*, Barry Town (1) 2 *(Pike 35,*
  Evans C 85)   500
Dynamo Minsk (0) 0, Bohemians (0) 0   8000
Flora Tallinn (0) 0, Haka (1) 1 *(Popovic 14)*   670
Floriana (0) 1 *(Buhagiar 79)*, Beitar Jerusalem (3) 5
  (Amsalem 17, Ohana 20, Harazi 40, Salloi 71,
  Abuksis 80)   3000
GI Gotu (0) 0, Jazz Pori (0) 1 *(Moraes 86)*   1147
Grevenmacher (1) 2 *(Scholten 37, Lauer 55)*, Dynamo
  Tbilisi (2) 3 *(Kiknadze 48, Kerdzevadze 71)*   500
Hajduk Split (0) 2 *(Skoko 66, Butorovic 82)*, Zimbru
  Chisinau (1) 2 *(Miterev 70)*   8000
HJK Helsinki (1) 5 *(Vasara 32, Lehtola 50, Lehtinen 86,*
  Aniche 97, Hyrylainen 110), Pyunik (1) 2 *(Sanamyan*
  41, Avetissian A 103)   1100
IBV (0) 0, Lantana (0) 0   300
Inkaras (1) 1 *(Matciulevicius 13 (pen)*, Slavia Sofia (0) 1
  (Ivanov 84)   4000
Khazri (2) 2 *(Talov 12, Aliyev 37)*, Hutnik (1) 2
  (Zumkowski 17, Wakhaia 85)   10,000

Kosice (0) 2 *(Rusnak 57, 68)*, Teuta (0) 1 *(Dobi 55)*   2762
Legia Warsaw (1) 3 *(Mieciel 17, 62, Oreshchuk 67)*,
  Jeunesse Esch (0) 0   3000
Lokomotiv Sofia (3) 6 *(Pavlov 18, 29, Mechev 31,*
  Radivojevic 51, Marinov 71, Gerov 89), Neftchi Baku
  (0) 0   6000
Margveti (0) 0, Slima Wanderers (1) 3 *(Galea 14, Muscat*
  50, Turner 89 (pen))   6000
Mura (1) 2 *(Skaper 15, 48)*, Becej (0) 0   4000
Partizan Belgrade (1) 3 *(Trenevski 33, Saveljic 52, Hristov*
  83), Maccabi Haifa (1) 1 *(Revivo 10)*   10,000
Shirak (1) 2 *(Arutyunyan 15, Vardanian 52)*, Anorthosis
  (1) 2 *(Gogic 18 (pen), Mihailovic 47)*   5000
Sileks (1) 1 *(Karanfilovski 41)*, Akranes (0) 0   3000
Skonto Riga (1) 3 *(Astayev 45, Ivanov V 70, Yeliseyev*
  80), Newtown (0) 0   3500
Slovan Bratislava (0) 1 *(Tittel 82)*, St Patrick's Ath (0) 0
    5200
Tiligul (0) 1 *(Pogorelov 49)*, Dynamo 93 Minsk (1) 1
  (Lobanov 10)   4000
SK Tirana (2) 2 *(Fortuzi 23, Gallo 27)*, Croatia Zagreb
  (3) 6 *(Cvitanovic 1, Simic 32, Maric 37, Gaspar 56,*
  Rukavina 60, Saric 82)   1000
Vardar (1) 2 *(Trajcov 3, Jakimovski 77)*, HIT Gorica (1)
  1 *(Demirovic 42)*   7000
Vojvodina (2) 4 *(Lerinc 10, Stojak 15, Milosevski 58,*
  Cilinsek 87), Portadown (0) 1 *(Casey 79)*   8000

QUALIFYING ROUND, FIRST LEG
Akranes (0) 0, CSKA Moscow (2) 2 *(Karsakov 34,*
  Yankauskas 37)   1200
Anorthosis (1) 1 *(Stavrou 17)*, Neuchatel Xamax (1) 2
  (Vernier 29, Lesniak 57)   7000
Aarau (1) 2 *(Georgiev 21, Skrzypczak 55, Pavlicevic 76,*
  86), Lantana (0) 0   3500
Beitar Jerusalem (0) 1 *(Tretiak 46)*, Bodo Glimt (2) 5
  (Johansen 23, 36, Barik 51, 56, Arensson 75)   9000
BVSC (2) 3 *(Bukszegi 5, Egressy 42, Farkas 67 (pen))*,
  Barry Town (1) 1 *(Evans T 14)*   2000
Croatia Zagreb (1) 3 *(Sliskovic 6, Cvitanovic 71 (pen),*
  Saric 79), Spartak Moscow (1) 1 *(Galic 44 (og))*
    21,000
Dynamo Minsk (0) 2 *(Makovsky M 51, Makovsky V 61)*,
  Besiktas (0) 0 *(Topraktepe 60)*   4000
Dynamo Moscow (1) 1 *(Kobelyov 15)*, Jazz Pori (1) 1
  (Laaksonen 30)   2500
Dynamo Tbilisi (2) 2 *(Gogichaishvili 13, Lashvili 19)*,
  Molde (0) 1 *(Stavrum 66)*   19,000
Graz (1) 2 *(Vukovic 45, Muzek 54)*, Vojvodina (0) 0 2000
Hajduk Split (0) 1 *(Skoko 50)*, Torpedo Moscow (0) 0
    16,000
Halmstad (0) 0, Vardar (0) 0   2479
Helsingborg (1) 1 *(Pringle 45)*, Dynamo 93 Minsk (0) 1
  (Orlovski 48)   6007
HJK Helsinki (0) 2 *(Lehkosuo 56, Lehtinen 65)*, Odessa
  (2) 2 *(Mizine 35, Musolitin 44)*   1250
Iraklis (0) 0, Apoel (0) 1 *(Sotiriou 48)*   12,000
Kosice (0) 0, Celtic (0) 0   16,000
Legia Warsaw (0) 0 *(Mosor 9, Staniek 27, Oreshchuk 88)*,
  Haka (0) 0   5000
Lyngby (0) 0, Mura (0) 0   842
Partizan Belgrade (0) 0, National (0) 0   20,000
Rapid Bucharest (0) 1 *(Mironas 75)*, Lokomotiv Sofia (0) 0
    8000
Sigma Olomouc (0) 1 *(Baranek 78)*, Hutnik (0) 0
  Played behind closed doors.
Skonto Riga (0) 0, Malmo (1) 3 *(Andersson 35, Kindvall*
  60, Olsson 80)   7000
Slavia Sofia (0) 1 *(Totev 75)*, Tirol (1) 1 *(Kitzbichler 34)*
    4000
Silema Wanderers (0) 0, Odense (0) 2 *(Schjonberg 81,*
  Pedersen 90)   3500
Slovan Bratislava (1) 2 *(Slovak 25, Kinder 65)*,
  Trabzonspor (1) 1 *(Arveladze S 4)*   8000
Zalgiris (0) 1 *(Razanauskas 49)*, Aberdeen (1) 4 *(Dodds*
  43, 81 (pen), Glass 72, Shearer 90)   1800

QUALIFYING ROUND, SECOND LEG
Aberdeen (0) 1 *(Irvine 85)*, Zalgiris (0) 3 *(Mikulenas 53, 86, Pukelevicius 76 (pen))* 8772
Apoel (1) 2 *(Alexandrou 5, Porbokis 89)*, Iraklis (0) 1 *(Sotiriou 86)* 12,000
Barry Town (1) 3 *(Pike 45 (pen), O'Gorman 46, Evans C 78)*, BVSC (0) 1 *(Egressy 63)* 2500
aet; Barry Town won 4-2 on penalties.
Besiktas (0) 2 *(Oktay 63, Ertugrul 71)*, Dynamo Minsk (0) 0 30,000
Bodo Glimt (1) 2 *(Sorensen 6, Johansen 60)*, Beitar Jerusalem (0) 1 *(Salloi 87)* 1600
Celtic (0) 1 *(Cadete 88)*, Kosice (0) 0 44,448
CSKA Moscow (2) 4 *(Mavsesyan 35, 40, Leonidas 53, Yankauskas 62)*, Akranes (0) 1 *(Hognason 80)* 2500
Dynamo 93 Minsk (0) 0, Helsingborg (2) 3 *(Nilson R 25 (pen), Powell 34, Pringle 77)* 6000
Haka (0) 1 *(Popovits 60)*, Legia Warsaw (1) 1 *(Mieciel 5)* 2100
Hutnik (2) 3 *(Yahaya 29, Stolarz 39, Ramuzga 71)*, Sigma Olomouc (1) 1 *(Kovar 6)* 5000
Jazz Pori (1) 1 *(Leivo-Jokimaki 40)*, Dynamo Moscow (0) 3 *(Kobelev 59 (pen), Artemov 67, 80)* 1500
Lantana (0) 2 *(Lebret 80, Hepner 85)*, Aarau (0) 0 500
Lokomotiv Sofia (0) 0, Rapid Bucharest (0) 1 *(Butoiu 90)* 2500
Malmo (0) 1 *(Kindvall 47)*, Skonto Riga (0) 1 *(Stepanov 80)* 2074
Molde (0) 0, Dynamo Tbilisi (0) 0 1428
Mura (0) 0, Lyngby (1) 2 *(Jonsson 24, 69)* 5000
National (1) 1 *(Ganea 6)*, Partizan Belgrade (0) 0 8000
Neuchatel Xamax (4) 4 *(Sandjak 10, 27, Cyprien 17, Vernier 37)*, Anorthosis (0) 0 4100
Odense (4) 7 *(Schjonberg 22, 59, 82, Jensen 24, Bisgaard 33, 45, Henriksen 57)*, Sliema Wanderers (1) 1 *(Teplov 40)* 3159
Odessa (0) 2 *(Chumachenko 64, Mizin 68)*, HJK Helsinki (0) 0 3500
Spartak Moscow (1) 2 *(Melyashin 28, Alenichev 56)*, Croatia Zagreb (0) 0 25,000
Tirol (3) 4 *(Slivovski 28, Krinner 31, Kitzbichler 44, Sacharjev 73 (og))*, Slavia Sofia (0) 1 *(Sheitanov 48)* 6000
Torpedo Moscow (1) 2 *(Kamaltsev 19, Vostrosablin 82 (pen))*, Hajduk Split (0) 0 6800
Trabzonspor (2) 4 *(Hami 1, Arveladze S 11, Orhan 67, Abdullah 71)*, Slovan Bratislava (0) 1 *(Nemeth 57)* 35,000
Vardar (0) 0, Halmstad (0) 1 *(Nilsson 50)* 10,000
Vojvodina (0) 1 *(Stojak 50)*, Graz (2) 5 *(Ramusch 44, Sabitzer 47, 73, Wieger 52, Anicic 85)* 8000

FIRST ROUND, FIRST LEG
Aberdeen (1) 3 *(Windass 7, Glass 57, Young 65)*, Barry Town (1) 1 *(Jones 13)* 13,400
Alania Vladikavkaz (1) 2 *(Yanovski 21, Shelia 49)*, Anderlecht (1) 1 *(Agayev 5 (og))* 25,000
Apoel (1) 2 *(Alexandrou 26, Sotiriou 55)*, Espanyol (2) 2 *(Benitez 30, Ouedec 45)* 12,000
Arsenal (0) 2 *(Merson 54, Wright 89)*, Moenchengladbach (1) 3 *(Juskowiak 36, Effenberg 45, Passlack 80)* 36,894
Aston Villa (1) 1 *(Johnson 14)*, Helsingborg (0) 1 *(Wibran 81)* 25,818
Bodo Glimt (1) 1 *(Berg 32)*, Trabzonspor (1) 2 *(Arveladze S 3, Unal 74)* 1955
Brondby (2) 5 *(Vilfort 21 (pen), Bjur 56, Moller 66, 88, 89)*, Aarau (0) 0 8976
FC Brugge (1) 1 *(Staelens 2)*, Lyngby (1) 1 *(Bjerre 32)* 6000
Celtic (0) 0, Hamburg (1) 2 *(Baron 3, Schupp 71)* 45,412
CSKA Moscow (0) 0, Feyenoord (0) 1 *(Van Wonderen 85)* 5000
Dynamo Kiev (0) 0, Neuchatel Xamax (0) 0 35,000
Ekeren (0) 3 *(Radzinski 56, Vande Walle 58 (pen), Czerniatynski 81)*, Graz (1) 1 *(Strafner 8)* 4000
Ferencvaros (2) 3 *(Zavadszky 11, Varesanovic 35 (og), Arany 52)*, Olympiakos (1) 1 *(Ivic 30)* 7000
Guingamp (0) 0, Internazionale (1) 3 *(Ganz 25, Djorkaeff 72 (pen), Sforza 87)* 7800
Hutnik (0) 0, Monaco (0) 1 *(Ikpeba 87)* 8000
Lens (0) 0, Lazio (0) 1 *(Chamot 85)* 18,714
Malmo (1) 1 *(Andersson A 83)*, Slavia Prague (0) 2 *(Asanin 70, Vagner 86)* 3961
Montpellier (1) 1 *(Ferhaoui 8)*, Sporting Lisbon (0) 1 *(Hadji 64)* 13,000

Newcastle U (2) 4 *(Ferdinand 6, Asprilla 26, Albert 51, Beardsley 54)*, Halmstad (0) 0 28,124
Odense (2) 2 *(Hemmingsen 43, Pedersen 44)*, Boavista (0) 3 *(Simic 53, Nuno Gomes 75, Tavares 85)* 3789
Odessa (0) 0, National (0) 0 12,000
Panathinaikos (3) 4 *(Lymberopoulos 26, 39, Alexoudis 34, Georgiadis 80)*, Legia Warsaw (2) 2 *(Szykier 3, Kucharski 45)* 25,000
Parma (1) 2 *(Chiesa 40, 83)*, Guimaraes (0) 1 *(Gilmar 77)* 5863
Rapid Bucharest (0) 1 *(Tartau 67)*, Karlsruhe (0) 0 15,000
Roma (3) 3 *(Tommasi 7, Fonseca 18, 42 (pen))*, Dynamo Moscow (0) 0 46,647
RWD Molenbeek (0) 0, Besiktas (0) 0 8000
Schalke (2) 3 *(Wilmots 8, 73, Mulder 14)*, Roda (0) 0 50,061
Spartak Moscow (3) 3 *(Tikhonov 14, 37, Kechinov 20)*, Silkeborg (0) 2 *(Thygesen 53, Reese 72)* 7000
Tenerife (0) 3 *(Vivar Dorado 46, Kodro 56, Pinilla 66)*, Maccabi Tel Aviv (0) 2 *(Mizrahi 60, Nimni 87 (pen))* 18,000
Tirol (0) 0, Metz (0) 0 5000
Torpedo Moscow (0) 0, Dynamo Tbilisi (1) 1 *(Djamarauli 35)* 8000
Valencia (2) 3 *(Engonga 20 (pen), Lopez 27, Moya 47)*, Bayern Munich (0) 0 40,000

FIRST ROUND, SECOND LEG
Aarau (0) 0, Brondby (1) 2 *(Moller 39, Daugaard 90 (pen)* 2010
Anderlecht (2) 4 *(Johnson 28, De Bilde 38, Zetterberg 62, 69)*, Alania Vladikavkaz (0) 0 7000
Barry Town (1) 3 *(O'Gorman 4, Ryan 71 (pen), Bird 82)*, Aberdeen (2) 3 *(Dodds 15, 25, Rowson 83)* 6500
Bayern Munich (1) 1 *(Navarro 2 (og))*, Valencia (0) 0 44,000
Besiktas (1) 3 *(Ertugrul 40, Amokachi 50, Oktay 89)*, RWD Molenbeek (0) 0 30,000
Boavista (1) 1 *(Nuno Gomes 11)*, Odense (0) 2 *(Hjorth 65, Pedersen 68)* 300
Dynamo Moscow (1) 1 *(Tscherischev 19 (pen)*, Roma (1) 3 *(Fonseca 45 (pen), Tommasi 71, Berretta 77)* 16,000
Dynamo Tbilisi (0) 1 *(Djamarauli 50)*, Torpedo Moscow (0) 1 *(Vostrosablin 80)* 55,000
Espanyol (0) 1 *(Cristobal 63)*, Apoel (0) 0 19,000
Feyenoord (0) 1 *(Van Wonderen 78)*, CSKA Moscow (0) 1 *(Minko 63)* 20,000
Graz (0) 2 *(Sabitzer 65, 86 (pen))*, Ekeren (0) 0 3000
Guimaraes (1) 2 *(Vitor Paneira 15, Ricardo 49)*, Parma (0) 0 7847
Halmstad (0) 2 *(Arvidsson 74, Svensson M 81)*, Newcastle U (1) 1 *(Ferdinand 43)* 7847
Hamburg (1) 2 *(Baron 23, Breitenreiter 49)*, Celtic (0) 0 29,639
Helsingborg (0) 0, Aston Villa (0) 0 16,000
Internazionale (1) 1 *(Branca 7)*, Guingamp (0) 1 *(Wreh 74)* 7000
Karlsruhe (0) 4 *(Keller 51, 78, Wuck 57, Dundee 69)*, Rapid Bucharest (0) 1 *(Chirita 70)* 16,200
Lazio (1) 1 *(Fuser 40)*, Lens (0) 1 *(Smicer 68)* 30,000
Legia Warsaw (0) 2 *(Mieciel 52, Kucharski 90)*, Panathinaikos (0) 0 10,000
Lyngby (0) 0, FC Brugge (0) 2 *(Borkelmans 62, Spahar 84)* 3721
Maccabi Tel Aviv (0) 1 *(Gadi Bromer 49)*, Tenerife (1) 1 *(Vivar Dorado 43)* 5000
Metz (1) 1 *(Song 4)*, Tirol (0) 0 11,940
Moenchengladbach (1) 3 *(Juskowiak 23, 90, Effenberg 74)*, Arsenal (1) 2 *(Wright 42, Merson 49)* 34,000
Monaco (1) 3 *(Anderson 37, 83, Martin 81)*, Hutnik (0) 1 *(Adamczyk 64 (pen))* 4500
National (0) 2 *(Moisescu 47, Niculescu 58)*, Odessa (0) 0 7000
Neuchatel Xamax (1) 2 *(Lesniak 25, Isabella 54)*, Dynamo Kiev (0) 1 *(Maximov 60)* 8600
Olympiakos (1) 2 *(Ivic 27, Sabanis 77)*, Ferencvaros (1) 2 *(Miriuta 22, Limperger 47)* 28,000
Roda (1) 2 *(Vurens 25, Dooley 76 (og))*, Schalke (1) 2 *(Wagner 15, Wilmots 73)* 12,000
Silkeborg (1) 1 *(Thygesen 31)*, Spartak Moscow (1) 2 *(Tikhonov 42, Sonksen 51 (og))* 3565
Slavia Prague (2) 3 *(Penicka 13, Vagner 29, Horvath 69 (pen))*, Malmo (0) 1 *(Fjellstrom 56)* 4602
Sporting Lisbon (0) 1 *(Oceano 61 (pen))*, Montpellier (0) 0 18,000

Trabzonspor (3) 3 *(Unal 36, Hami 38, Hasan 43)*, Bodo
Glimt (0) 1 *(Johansen S 88)*   23,000

SECOND ROUND, FIRST LEG
Aberdeen (0) 0, Brondby (1) 2 *(Sand 44, Hansen 89)*
                                                     15,000
FC Brugge (2) 2 *(Verheyen 10, Staelens 36)*, National (0) 0
                                                      7000
Dynamo Tbilisi (1) 1 *(Gogichaishvili 26 (pen)*, Boavista
(0) 0   65,000
Espanyol (0) 0, Feyenoord (1) 3 *(Van Gastel 21, Taument
57, Larsson 89)*   29,000
Ferencvaros (2) 3 *(Horvath 7, Lisztes 17, 57)*, Newcastle
U (2) 2 *(Ferdinand 25, Shearer 35)*   18,000
Guimaraes (1) 1 *(Ricardo 8)*, Anderlecht (0) 1
(Zetterberg 77)   13,000
Hamburg (2) 3 *(Breitenreiter 17, Baron 34, Kovacevic 58)*,
Spartak Moscow (0) 0   17,347
Helsingborg (1) 2 *(Jonsson 14, 60)*, Neuchatel Xamax (0) 0
                                                      7808
Internazionale (0) 1 *(Angloma 81)*, Graz (0) 0   8145
Karlsruhe (1) 3 *(Fink 45, 75, Dundee 58)*, Roma (0) 0
                                                     25,000
Lazio (0) 1 *(Nedved 66)*, Tenerife (0) 0   30,000
Legia Warsaw (1) 1 *(Sokolowski 22)*, Besiktas (0) 1
(Orhan 70)   18,000
Metz (2) 2 *(Traore 5, Lang 13)*, Sporting Lisbon (0) 0
                                                     15,000
Moenchengladbach (0) 2 *(Hochstatter 57, Andersson 72)*,
Monaco (1) 4 *(Collins 12, Ikpeba 58, 90, Henry 78)*
                                                     25,000
Schalke (0) 1 *(Max 77)*, Trabzonspor (0) 0   51,100
Slavia Prague (0) 0, Valencia (0) 1 *(Moya 73)*   10,012

SECOND ROUND, SECOND LEG
Anderlecht (0) 0, Guimaraes (0) 0   12,000
Besiktas (1) 2 *(Amokachi 14, Yankov 76)*, Legia Warsaw
(1) 1 *(Kucharski 37)*   35,000
Boavista (2) 5 *(Latapy 4, 67, Jimmy 27, 55, Tavares 89)*,
Dynamo Tbilisi (0) 0   20,000
Brondby (0) 0, Aberdeen (0) 0   12,005
Feyenoord (0) 0, Espanyol (1) 1 *(Arteaga 9)*   30,000
Graz (1) 1 *(Sabitzer 36 (pen))*, Internazionale (0) 0 10,500
Internazionale won 5-3 on penalties.
Monaco (0) 0, Moenchengladbach (0) 1 *(Klinkert 70)*
                                                     17,000
Newcastle U (1) 4 *(Asprilla 42, 58, Ginola 65, Ferdinand
90)*, Ferencvaros (0) 0   35,740
National (0) 1 *(Niculescu 63)*, FC Brugge (0) 1 *(Verheyen
62)*   18,000
Neuchatel Xamax (0) 1 *(Bonalair 51 (pen))*, Helsingborg
(1) 1 *(Jonsson 43)*   7200
Roma (2) 2 *(Balbo 22, 27)*, Karlsruhe (0) 1 *(Keller 84)*
                                                     47,000
Spartak Moscow (2) 2 *(Meleshine 10, Tikhonov 42 (pen))*,
Hamburg (1) 2 *(Schupp 29, Hartmann 73)*   11,000
Sporting Lisbon (0) 2 *(Sa Pinto 73, 85)*, Metz (1) 1
(Arpinon 18)   30,000
Tenerife (3) 5 *(Nesta 15 (og), Kodro 26, Juanele 38, 61,
Jokanovic 48)*, Lazio (2) 3 *(Nedved 13, Fuser 30,
Casiraghi 46)*   25,000
Trabzonspor (0) 3 *(Arveladze S 55, Hami 66, 70)*, Schalke
(2) 3 *(De Kock 33, 36, Max 73)*   23,000
Valencia (0) 0, Slavia Prague (0) 0   37,000

THIRD ROUND, FIRST LEG
Brondby (0) 1 *(Bagger 90)*, Karlsruhe (2) 3 *(Hassler 42,
44, Dundee 79)*   24,414
FC Brugge (1) 2 *(Stanic 35, Spehar 59)*, Schalke (0) 1
(Buskens 51)   13,000
Helsingborg (0) 0, Anderlecht (0) 0   8304
Internazionale (3) 5 *(Sforza 6, 58, Angloma 13, Ganz 22,
66)*, Boavista (0) 1 *(Hasselbaink 62)*   20,018
Metz (0) 1 *(Traore 67)*, Newcastle U (1) 1 *(Beardsley 31
(pen)*   16,700
Monaco (1) 3 *(Anderson 49, Ikpeba 71, Blondeau 76)*,
Hamburg (0) 0   10,000
Tenerife (0) 0, Feyenoord (0) 0   22,000
Valencia (2) 3 *(Vlaovic 17, Ali Guncar 23 (og), Ferreira
83)*, Besiktas (0) 1 *(Oktay 32)*   25,000

THIRD ROUND, SECOND LEG
Anderlecht (0) 1 *(Walem 68)*, Helsingborg (0) 0   12,000
Besiktas (2) 2 *(Serdar 16, Oktay 45 (pen))*, Valencia (2) 2
(Inaqui 24, Vlaovic 44)   30,000
Boavista (0) 0, Internazionale (1) 2 *(Djorkaeff 12 (pen),
Ince 66)*   15,000
Feyenoord (0) 2 *(Sanchez 82, Bosz 87)*, Tenerife (2) 4
(Felipe 5, Juanele 45, 60, Paz 74)   25,000
Hamburg (0) 0, Monaco (0) 2 *(Ikpeba 63, Benarbia 90
(pen)*   28,634
Karlsruhe (0) 0, Brondby (2) 5 *(Bagger 41, Eggen 43,
Vilfort 58, Moller 74, 81)*   21,000
Newcastle U (0) 2 *(Asprilla 80, 82)*, Metz (0) 0   35,641
Schalke (1) 2 *(Max 10, Mulder 90)*, FC Brugge (0) 0
                                                     46,300

QUARTER-FINALS, FIRST LEG
Anderlecht (1) 1 *(Versavel 27)*, Internazionale (0) 1
(Ganz 75)   25,379
Newcastle U (0) 0, Monaco (0) 1 *(Anderson 59)*   36,215
Schalke (1) 2 *(Linke 44, Wilmots 82)*, Valencia (0) 0
                                                     56,824
Tenerife (0) 0, Brondby (1) 1 *(Sand 29)*   21,000

QUARTER-FINALS, SECOND LEG
Brondby (0) 0, Tenerife (0) 2 *(Pinilla 21, Mata 120)* 39,807
Internazionale (1) 2 *(Ganz 12, 60)*, Anderlecht (1) 1
(Preko 33)   34,221
Monaco (1) 3 *(Legwinski 42, Benarbia 50, 67)*, Newcastle
U (0) 0   18,500
Valencia (1) 1 *(Poyatos 45)*, Schalke (1) 1 *(Mulder 18)*
                                                     45,000

SEMI-FINALS, FIRST LEG
Internazionale (3) 3 *(Ganz 16, 29, Zamorano 39)*,
Monaco (0) 1 *(Ikpeba 72)*   50,000
Tenerife (1) 1 *(Felipe 5 (pen))*, Schalke (0) 0   23,000

SEMI-FINALS, SECOND LEG
Monaco (0) 1 *(Ikpeba 70)*, Internazionale (0) 0   18,500
Schalke (0) 2 *(Linke 68, Wilmots 106)*, Tenerife (0) 0
                                                     58,624

FINAL FIRST LEG

Schalke (0) 1, Internazionale (0) 0

(in Gelsenkirchen, 7 May 1997, 56,824)

Schalke: Lehmann; De Kock, Thon, Linke, Eigenrauch,
Muller, Anderbrugge, Nemec, Buskens (Max 67),
Latal, Wilmots.
Scorer: Wilmots 71.
Internazionale: Pagliuca; Bergomi, Paganin M, Galante,
Pistone, Zanetti, Sforza, Fresi (Berti 61), Winter,
Zamorano.
Referee: Batta (France).

FINAL SECOND LEG

Internazionale (0) 1, Schalke (0) 0

(in Milan, 21 May 1997, 81,670)

Internazionale: Pagliuca; Bergomi (Angloma 70),
Paganin M, Fresi, Pistone, Zanetti (Berti 120), Ince,
Sforza (Winter 81), Djorkaeff, Ganz, Zamorano.
Scorer: Zamorano 84.
Schalke: Lehmann; Latal (Held 111), De Kock, Thon,
Linke, Buskens, Eigenrauch, Nemec, Muller
(Anderbrugge 97), Max, Wilmots.
(aet; Schalke won 4-1 on penalties).
Referee: Aranda (Spain).

UEFA CUP 1996–97 – BRITISH AND IRISH CLUBS

PRELIMINARY ROUND, FIRST LEG

17 JULY

Bohemians (1) 1 *(Swan 1)*
Dynamo Minsk (0) 1 *(Matovski 65)*   3000
Bohemians: Henderson; Prizeman (Ryan), Mullen, Best (Byrne T), O'Driscoll, McGrath, Mooney, O'Connor, Swan, Hanrahan, Parks (Dully).
Dynamo Minsk: Varivonchik; Insrovitch, Ostrovski, Jouravel, Volodenkov (Dovnar), Lavrik, Tcherniavski, Makovski M, Makarenko (Shavrov), Makovski V, Podrez (Ostrikov).

Newtown (0) 1 *(Brown 90)*   2000
Skonto Riga (1) 4 *(Astafyev 36, 71, Lobanyov 75, 80)*
Newtown: Barton; Evans J (Thomas), Evans M, Reynolds, Wilding, Pike, Williams, Roberts, Holmans (Wickham), Brown, Pryce.
Skonto Riga: Laizans; Pindeyev (Pakhar), Astafyev, Zemlinsky (Ivanov K), Shevlyakov, Stepanov, Ivanov V, Blagonadezhdin, Yeliseyev, Babicev, Shtolcers (Lobanyov).

Portadown (0) 0
Vojvodina (1) 1 *(Cilinsek 27)*   1500
Portadown: Keenan; Major, Davidson, Casey, Strain, Stewart, Carlyle, Peebles, Haylock, Russell (Candlish), Kennedy.
Vojvodina: Zilic; Saraba, Grujic, Dundjerski, Milosevic (Stojak), Bjegovic, Ilic, Cilinsek, Racic (Lerinc), Milosevski, Djurkovic (Milicevic).

Zalgiris (0) 2 *(Vencevicius 82, Pukelevicius 86)*
Crusaders (0) 0   5000
Zalgiris: Spetyla; Sorokinas (Karvelis), Skerla, Zvirgzdauskas, Stonkus, Vencevicius, Rimkus, Razanauskas, Darincevas, Mikulenas (Pukelevicius), Morinas.
Crusaders: McKeown; McMullan, Dornan, Dunlop, Callaghan, Murray, Lawlor R, Baxter (Hunter G), Burrows, Livingstone (Dwyer), Lawlor M.

18 JULY

Barry Town (0) 0
Dinaburg (0) 0   2500
Barry Town: Ovendale; Evans T, Lloyd, French, York, Norman, Barnett, Loss (Ryan), Bird, Jones, Evans C (Pike).
Dinaburg: Digulyov; Glazov, Zizilev (Smirnov), Isakov, Pogodin, Burlakov, Fedotov, Shmikov, Karashauskas, Baushev (Zhavoronkov), Tarasov.

St Patrick's Ath (1) 3 *(Glynn 44, O'Flaherty 64, McDonnell 74)*
Slovan Bratislava (3) 4 *(Nemeth 10, 40, Maixner 18, Karasy 77)*   4500
St Patrick's Ath: McKenna; Burke, Reilly (Campbell), McDonnell, Lynch, Gormley, Osam, Crolly, Glynn, Moody (O'Flaherty), Morristoe.
Slovan Bratislava: Molnar; Stupala, Nemeth, Sobona (Juriga), Tinder, Tittel, Pecko (Slovak), Tomaschek, Gomes, Faktor, Maixner (Karasy).

PRELIMINARY ROUND, SECOND LEG

23 JULY

Dinaburg (0) 1 *(Tarasov 60)*
Barry Town (1) 2 *(Pike 35, Evans C 85)*   500
Dinaburg: Digulyov; Glazov, Beraya, Isakov, Pogodin (Smirnov) (Žizilev), Burlakov, Fedotov, Shmikov, Karashauskas, Baushev (Zhavoronkov), Tarasov.
Barry Town: Ovendale; Evans T, Lloyd, French, York, Norman, Barnett, Loss, Bird, Jones, Pike (Evans C).

24 JULY

Crusaders (0) 2 *(Morgan 83, 90)*
Zalgiris (1) 1 *(Razanauskas 18)*   1500
Crusaders: McKeown; McMullan, Dornan, Dunlop, Callaghan, Murray, Baxter, Hunter G (Morgan), Burrows, Lawlor M (Mellon), Hunter K (Dunne).
Zalgiris: Spetyla; Sorokinas, Skerla, Zvirgzdauskas, Stonkus, Vencevicius, Rimkus, Razanauskas, Mikulenas (Karvelis), Pukelevicius (Darincevas), Morinas.

Dynamo Minsk (0) 0
Bohemians (0) 0   8000
Dynamo Minsk: Varivonchik; Ostrovski, Mishchishin, Lavrik, Makovski M, Lourvitch, Jouravel, Ostrikov (Makarenko), Volodenkov, Chavrov (Podrez), Makovski V.
Bohemians: Henderson; O'Connor, O'Driscoll, Mullen, Byrne T, Parkes (Byrne S) (Maher), McGrath, Hanrahan, Prizeman, Swan, Dully (Ryan).

Skonto Riga (1) 3 *(Astafyev 45, Ivanov V 70, Yeliseyev 80)*
Newtown (0) 0   3500
Skonto Riga: Laizans; Ivanov K (Stepanov), Astafyev, Zemlinsky, Shevlyakov, Yeliseyev, Ivanov V, Blagonadezhdin (Pakhar), Pindeyev, Babicev (Lobanyov), Shtolcers.
Newtown: Barton; Evans J, Evans M, Reynolds, Wilding, Pike (Thomas), Williams, Roberts, Holmans, Brown (Wickham), Pryce (Hanmer).

Slovan Bratislava (0) 1 *(Tittel 82)*
St Patrick's Ath (0) 0   5200
Slovan Bratislava: Molnar; Stupala, Tittel, Karasy, Kinder, Juriga (Pecko), Faktor (Demo), Tomaschek, Maixner, Nemeth (Rusnak), Gomes.
St Patrick's Ath: Byrne G; Burke, McDonald, Lynch, Osam, Crolly, Mulraney, Gormley (Campbell P), Reilly (Byrne J), Glynn, Morrisroe (O'Flaherty).

Vojvodina (2) 4 *(Lerinc 10, Stojak 15, Milosevski 58, Cilinsek 87)*
Portadown (0) 1 *(Casey 79)*   8000
Vojvodina: Zilic; Aleksic (Vrantjes), Grujic, Dundjerski, Milosevic, Bjegovic, Lerinc (Josipovic), Cilinsek, Stojak (Milicevic), Milosevski, Djurkovic.
Portadown: Keenan; Major, Davidson, Casey, Byrne, Stewart, Carlyle (Fulton), Peebles, Haylock, Candlish (Evans), Kennedy.

QUALIFYING ROUND, FIRST LEG

6 AUG

Kosice (0) 0
Celtic (0) 0   16,000
Kosice: Juracka; Koziej, Karasek, Sovic (Obsitnik), Zvara, Janocko (Lalik), Kozak, Kral, Prazenica, Hornyak (Semenik), Rusnak.
Celtic: Marshall; Boyd, McKinlay, McNamara, Grant, McStay, Thom, Cadete (Van Hooijdonk), O'Donnell (Weighorst), O'Neil, Donnelly.

BVSC (2) 3 *(Bukszegi 5, Egressy 42, Farkas 67 (pen))*
Barry Town (1) 1 *(Evans T 14)*   2000
BVSC: Vegh; Bondarenko, Djurasovic, Molnar, Farkas, Eros, Bukszegi (Csordas), Stanici, Egressy, Zovath, Fuzi (Javor).
Barry Town: Ovendale; Evans T, Lloyd (Ryan), French, York, Norman, Barnett, Loss, Jones, Evans C (O'Gorman), Pike (Mountain).

Zalgiris (0) 1 *(Razanauskas 49)*
Aberdeen (1) 4 *(Dodds 43, 81 (pen), Glass 72, Shearer
90)*   1800
Zalgiris: Spetyla; Sorokinas, Skerla, Zvirgzdauskas,
Stonkus, Rimkus, Razanauskas, Mikulenas, Pukelevicius,
Morinas, Preiksaitis.
Aberdeen: Watt; McKimmie, Woodthorpe, Bernard,
Irvine, Inglis, Miller (Rowson), Windass (Shearer),
Kiriakov, Glass, Dodds.

QUALIFYING ROUND, SECOND LEG

20 AUG

Aberdeen (0) 1 *(Irvine 85)*
Zalgiris (0) 3 *(Mikulenas 53, 86, Pukelevicius 76 (pen))*
                                                          8772
Aberdeen: Watt; Buchan (Grant), Woodthorpe, Kiriakov,
Irvine, Inglis, Miller, Shearer, Windass, Dodds
(Kpedekpo), Glass.
Zalgiris: Merkelis; Sorokinas, Skerla, Zvirgzdauskas,
Suliauskas (Radzius), Novikovas, Pukelevicius, Morinas,
Preiksaitas, Vencevicius, Mikulenas.

Barry Town (1) 3 *(Pike 45 (pen), O'Gorman 46, Evans C
78)*
BVSC (0) 1 *(Egressy 63)*   2500
Barry Town: Mountain; Johnson, Lloyd, French, York,
O'Gorman (Evans C), Barnett (Misbah), Huggins, Ryan
(Griffith), Pike, Bird.
BVSC: Vegh; Komlosi (Bognar), Molnar, Eros, Bukszegi,
Stanici, Egressy, Zovath (Csordas), Fuzi, Pomper
(Farkas), Feher.
aet; Barry Town won 4-2 on penalties.

Celtic (0) 1 *(Cadete 88)*
Kosice (0) 0   44,448
Celtic: Marshall; Boyd, McKinlay, McNamara, Grant,
Van Hooijdonk, Thom, Cadete, Hughes, Wieghorst,
McLoughlin (Di Canio).
Kosice: Juracka; Koziej (Obsitnik), Sovic, Zvara, Janocko
(Lalik), Kozak, Semenik, Tarzenica, Hornyak, Toth,
Rusnak.

FIRST ROUND, FIRST LEG

10 SEPT

Aberdeen (1) 3 *(Windass 7, Glass 57, Young 65)*
Barry Town (1) 1 *(Jones 13)*   13,400
Aberdeen: Walker; Grant, Tsvetanov, Miller
(Woodthorpe), Inglis, McKimmie, Young (Rowson),
Kiriakov, Dodds (Shearer), Windass, Glass.
Barry Town: Ovendale; Johnson, Lloyd, Barnett, York,
French, Loss, Jones, Pike, Bird, Ryan.

Arsenal (0) 2 *(Merson 54, Wright 89)*
Moenchengladbach (1) 3 *(Juskowiak 36, Effenberg 45,
Passlack 80)*   36,894
Arsenal: Seaman; Dixon, Winterburn, Platt, Keown,
Linighan, Parlour (Bould), Wright, Merson, Bergkamp
(Helder), Hartson.
Moenchengladbach: Kamps; Schneider, Lupescu,
Fournier, Andersson, Neun, Nielsen (Wynhoff),
Passlack, Juskowiak (Kastenmaier), Effenberg,
Hochstatter.

Aston Villa (1) 1 *(Johnson 14)*
Helsingborg (0) 1 *(Wibran 81)*   25,818
Aston Villa: Oakes; Nelson, Southgate, Ehiogu, Staunton,
Wright, Townsend, Draper, Milosevic, Johnson, Yorke.
Helsingborg: Andersson S; Nilsson R, Nilsson O, Jonsson
M, Eriksson, Jacobsson, Ljung, Jansson, Wibran, Powell
(Pringle), Fursth.

Celtic (0) 0
Hamburg (1) 2 *(Baron 3, Schupp 71)*   45,412
Celtic: Marshall; Boyd, McKinlay (Mackay), Wieghorst
(McNamara), Hughes, O'Neil, Grant, Thom, Van
Hooijdonk, Cadete, Di Canio (McLaughlin).

Hamburg: Golz; Henchoz, Hollerbach, Dowe
(Hartmann), Fischer, Friis-Hansen, Kmetsch, Schopp,
Ivanauskas (Schupp), Baron, Sporl.

Newcastle U (2) 4 *(Ferdinand 6, Asprilla 26, Albert 51,
Beardsley 54)*
Halmstad (0) 0   28,124
Newcastle U: Srnicek; Howey (Albert), Watson (Barton),
Clark, Peacock, Lee (Gillespie), Asprilla, Beardsley,
Shearer, Ferdinand, Ginola.
Halmstad: Nordberg; Wiberg, Andersson F, Andersson
T, Mattsson, Karlsson, Smith, Arvidsson, Vougt
(Lennartsson), Andersson R (Ljungberg), Svensson M.

FIRST ROUND, SECOND LEG

24 SEPT

Barry Town (1) 3 *(O'Gorman 4, Ryan 71 (pen), Bird 82)*
Aberdeen (2) 3 *(Dodds 15, 25, Rowson 83)*   6500
Barry Town: Ovendale; Johnson, Lloyd, Barnett, York,
French, O'Gorman (Evans C), Jones, Pike (Griffith),
Ryan (Huggins), Bird.
Aberdeen: Walker; Grant, Tsvetanov, Kiriakov
(Shearer), Irvine, McKimmie, Rowson, Young, Dodds,
Windass, Woodthorpe.

Halmstad (0) 2 *(Arvidsson 74, Svensson M 81)*
Newcastle U (1) 1 *(Ferdinand 43)*   7847
Halmstad: Svensson H; Jonsson, Arvidsson, Andersson
T, Andersson F, Ljungberg (Selakovic), Lennartsson
(Karlsson), Smith, Svensson M, Andersson R, Vougt.
Newcastle U: Srnicek; Barton, Beresford, Batty (Clark),
Peacock, Albert, Lee, Asprilla (Kitson), Shearer,
Ferdinand, Gillespie.

Hamburg (1) 2 *(Baron 23, Breitenreiter 49)*
Celtic (0) 0   29,639
Hamburg: Golz; Henchoz (Kovacevic), Fischer, Schopp,
Friis-Hansen, Kmetsch (Hartmann), Hollerbach, Schupp,
Baron (Salihamidzic), Sporl, Breitenreiter.
Celtic: Marshall; McNamara, Boyd, Hughes, Stubbs,
Mackay, Di Canio (Donnelly), O'Neil, Thom
(Wieghorst), Grant, Cadete (Van Hooijdonk).

Helsingborg (0) 0
Aston Villa (0) 0   16,000
Helsingborg: Andersson S; Nilsson R, Eriksson,
Jacobsson, Nilsson O, Jonsson M, Wibran, Jansson,
Lantz (Jonsson A), Fursth (Ljung), Powell (Pringle).
Aston Villa: Oakes; Nelson (McGrath), Wright,
Southgate, Ehiogu, Staunton, Taylor, Draper, Milosevic
(Johnson), Townsend, Yorke.

25 SEPT

Moenchengladbach (1) 3 *(Juskowiak 23, 90, Effenberg
74)*
Arsenal (1) 2 *(Wright 42, Merson 49)*   34,000
Moenchengladbach: Kamps; Neun, Fournier (Stadler),
Andersson, Passlack, Nielsen (Wynhoff), Lupescu,
Schneider, Effenberg, Juskowiak, Pettersson
(Hochstatter).
Arsenal: Seaman; Keown, Winterburn, Linighan
(Parlour), Bould, Adams (Helder), Platt, Wright,
Merson, Hartson, Vieira.

SECOND ROUND, FIRST LEG

15 OCT

Aberdeen (0) 0
Brondby (1) 2 *(Sand 44, Hansen 89)*   15,000
Aberdeen: Walker; McKimmie, Tsvetanov, Miller, Inglis,
Irvine, Young (Booth), Rowson, Dodds, Windass,
Kiriakov (Shearer).
Brondby: Krogh; Colding, Eggen, Nielsen, Skarbalius,
Vilfort, Jensen, Sand, Ravn (Thogersen), Daugaard
(Bjerregaard), Moller (Hansen).

Ferencvaros (2) 3 *(Horvath 7, Lisztes 17, 57)*
Newcastle U (2) 2 *(Ferdinand 25, Shearer 35)*   18,000
Ferencvaros: Szeiler; Telek, Kuznetsov, Janos, Nyilas, Lisztes (Hollo), Miriuta, Nagy, Szucs, Horvath (Zabavszky), Nichenko.
Newcastle U: Srnicek; Watson, Beresford, Batty, Peacock, Albert, Lee, Beardsley, Shearer, Ferdinand, Gillespie (Ginola).

SECOND ROUND, SECOND LEG

29 OCT
Brondby (0) 0
Aberdeen (0) 0   12,005
Brondby: Krogh; Nielsen, Ravn (Risager), Daugaard, Moller, Vilfort, Sand (Bjur), Hansen (Bagger), Colding, Eggen, Skarbalius.
Aberdeen: Walker; McKimmie, Irvine, Miller (Craig), Kiriakov, Dodds, Rowson, Booth (Woodthorpe), Windass, Young, Tsvetanov.

Newcastle U (1) 4 *(Asprilla 42, 58, Ginola 65, Ferdinand 90)*
Ferencvaros (0) 0   35,740
Newcastle U: Srnicek; Gillespie (Barton), Elliott, Batty, Peacock, Albert, Lee, Beardsley, Ferdinand, Asprilla, Ginola.
Ferencvaros: Szeiler; Hrutka, Telek, Kuznetsov (Arany), Szucs, Horvath (Hollo), Nyilas, Jagodics, Nagy, Miriuta (Zavadszky), Nichenko.

THIRD ROUND, FIRST LEG

19 NOV
Metz (0) 1 *(Traore 67)*
Newcastle U (1) 1 *(Beardsley 31 (pen))*   16,700
Metz: Letizi; Song, Terrier, Kastendeuch, Lang, Pires, Serredszum, Blanchard, Arpinon, Isaias, Traore.
Newcastle U: Srnicek; Barton, Beresford (Elliott), Batty, Peacock, Albert, Lee, Beardsley, Asprilla, Ginola, Gillespie.

THIRD ROUND, SECOND LEG

3 DEC
Newcastle U (0) 2 *(Asprilla 80, 82)*
Metz (0) 0   35,641
Newcastle U: Srnicek; Gillespie, Elliott, Batty, Peacock, Albert, Lee, Beardsley, Shearer, Asprilla (Clark), Ginola (Watson).
Metz: Biancarelli; Song, Kastendeuch, Terrier, Strasser, Lang, Serredszum, Blanchard (Isaias), Arpinon (Oyawole), Pires, Traore.

QUARTER-FINALS, FIRST LEG

4 MAR
Newcastle U (0) 0
Monaco (0) 1 *(Anderson 59)*   36,215
Newcastle U: Hislop; Barton, Elliott, Watson, Peacock, Albert, Lee, Batty, Ginola, Clark, Gillespie.
Monaco: Barthez; Martin, Dumas, Grimandi, Blondeau, Legwinski, Benarbia, Djetou, Collins, Anderson, Henry (Ikpeba).

QUARTER-FINALS, SECOND LEG

18 MAR
Monaco (1) 3 *(Legwinski 42, Benarbia 50, 67)*
Newcastle U (0) 0   18,500
Monaco: Barthez; Blondeau, Grimandi (Martin), Dumas, Petit, Djetou, Benarbia (Scifo), Legwinski, Anderson, Henry (Ikpeba), Collins.
Newcastle U: Hislop; Watson, Elliott, Batty, Peacock (Beresford), Albert, Lee, Beardsley (Gillespie), Asprilla, Barton (Clark), Ginola.

Jubilant Schalke players in festive mood after the German team had defeated much-fancied Internazionale in the UEFA Cup Final. (Colorsport)

Summary of Appearances

EUROPEAN CUP (1955–97)

English clubs
12 Liverpool
8 Manchester U
3 Nottingham F, Leeds U
2 Derby Co, Wolverhampton W, Everton, Aston Villa, Arsenal
1 Burnley, Tottenham H, Ipswich T, Manchester C, Blackburn R

Scottish clubs
18 Rangers
15 Celtic
3 Aberdeen
2 Hearts
1 Dundee, Dundee U, Kilmarnock, Hibernian

Welsh clubs
1 Cwmbran

Northern Ireland clubs
18 Linfield
8 Glentoran
2 Crusaders, Portadown
1 Glenavon, Ards, Distillery, Derry C, Coleraine

Eire clubs
7 Shamrock R, Dundalk
6 Waterford
3 Drumcondra
2 Bohemians, Limerick, Athlone T, Shelbourne
1 Cork Hibs, Cork Celtic, Cork City, Derry C*, Sligo R, St Patrick's Ath

Winners: Celtic 1966–67; Manchester U 1967–68; Liverpool 1976–77, 1977–78, 1980–81, 1983–84; Nottingham F 1978–79, 1979–80; Aston Villa 1981–82

Finalists: Celtic 1969–70; Leeds U 1974–75; Liverpool 1984–85

EUROPEAN CUP-WINNERS' CUP (1960–97)

English clubs
6 Tottenham H
5 Manchester U, Liverpool
4 West Ham U
3 Arsenal, Chelsea, Everton
2 Manchester C
1 Wolverhampton W, Leicester C, WBA, Leeds U, Sunderland, Southampton, Ipswich T

Scottish clubs
10 Rangers
8 Aberdeen, Celtic
3 Dundee U
2 Dunfermline Ath, Hearts
1 Dundee, Hibernian, St Mirren, Motherwell, Airdrieonians

Welsh clubs
14 Cardiff C
8 Wrexham
7 Swansea C
2 Bangor C
1 Borough U, Newport Co, Merthyr Tydfil, Barry T, Llansantfraid

Northern Ireland clubs
8 Glentoran
4 Ballymena U, Coleraine, Glenavon
3 Crusaders, Linfield
2 Ards, Bangor
1 Derry C, Distillery, Portadown, Carrick Rangers, Cliftonville

Eire clubs
6 Shamrock R
3 Limerick, Waterford, Dundalk, Bohemians, Shelbourne
2 Cork Hibs, Galway U, Sligo R, Derry C*
1 Cork Celtic, St Patrick's Ath, Finn Harps, Home Farm, University College Dublin, Cork City, Bray W

Winners: Tottenham H 1962–63; West Ham U 1964–65; Manchester C 1969–70; Chelsea 1970–71; Rangers 1971–72; Aberdeen 1982–83; Everton 1984–85; Manchester U 1990-91; Arsenal 1993–94

Finalists: Rangers 1960–61, 1966–67; Liverpool 1965–66; Leeds U 1972–73; West Ham U 1975–76; Arsenal 1979–80, 1994–95

EUROPEAN FAIRS CUP & UEFA CUP (1955–97)

English clubs
9 Leeds U
8 Ipswich T, Liverpool
7 Manchester U, Aston Villa, Arsenal
6 Everton, Newcastle U
5 Southampton, Tottenham H, Nottingham F
4 Manchester C, Birmingham C, Wolverhampton W, WBA
3 Chelsea, Sheffield W
2 Stoke C, Derby Co, QPR
1 Burnley, Coventry C, Norwich C, London Rep XI, Watford, Blackburn R

Scottish clubs
17 Dundee U
14 Hibernian
12 Aberdeen
10 Celtic,
9 Hearts
8 Rangers
5 Dunfermline Ath
4 Dundee
3 St Mirren, Kilmarnock
2 Partick T, Motherwell
1 Morton, St Johnstone, Raith R

Welsh Clubs
1 Inter Cardiff, Bangor C, Afan Lido, Newtown, Barry T

Northern Ireland clubs

11 Glentoran
6 Coleraine
5 Linfield
4 Glenavon, Portadown
3 Crusaders
2 Bangor
1 Ards, Ballymena U

Eire clubs
9 Bohemians
5 Dundalk
4 Shamrock R
3 Finn Harps, Shelbourne
2 Drumcondra, St Patrick's Ath, Derry C*, Cork City
1 Cork Hibs, Athlone T, Limerick, Drogheda U, Galway U

Winners: Leeds U 1967–68, 1970–71; Newcastle U 1968–69; Arsenal 1969–70; Tottenham H 1971–72, 1983–84; Liverpool 1972–73, 1975–76; Ipswich T 1980–81

Finalists: London 1955–58, Birmingham C 1958–60, 1960–61; Leeds U 1966–67; Wolverhampton W 1971–72; Tottenham H 1973–74; Dundee U 1986–87

* Now play in League of Ireland

INTER-TOTO CUP 1996

Group 1

	P	W	D	L	F	A	Pts
Standard Liege	4	3	1	0	8	2	10
Aalborg	4	3	0	1	7	5	9
Stuttgart	4	2	0	2	8	4	6
Hapoel Haifa	4	0	2	2	7	12	2
Cliftonville	4	0	1	3	2	9	1

Group 2

	P	W	D	L	F	A	Pts
Linz ASK	4	4	0	0	11	1	12
Werder Bremen	4	3	0	1	8	5	9
Djurgaarden	4	2	0	2	15	4	6
Apollon Limassol	4	1	0	3	4	13	3
B68	4	0	0	4	2	15	0

Group 3

	P	W	D	L	F	A	Pts
Orebro	4	3	1	0	12	6	10
FC Copenhagen	4	3	1	0	7	4	10
Maribor	4	1	1	2	4	5	4
FK Austria	4	1	0	3	9	8	3
Keflavik	4	0	1	3	2	11	1

Group 4

	P	W	D	L	F	A	Pts
Silkeborg	4	3	1	0	11	2	10
Zaglebie	4	2	2	0	5	1	8
Charleroi	4	1	2	1	5	5	5
Ried	4	1	0	3	4	9	3
Conwy	4	0	1	3	1	9	1

Group 5

	P	W	D	L	F	A	Pts
Nantes	4	3	1	0	12	0	10
Lillestrom	4	3	0	1	11	4	9
Heerenveen	4	1	1	2	4	5	4
Kaunas	4	1	0	3	4	10	3
Sligo	4	0	2	2	3	8	2

Group 6

	P	W	D	L	F	A	Pts
Segesta	4	3	1	0	7	3	10
Orgryte	4	2	2	0	8	2	8
Lucerne	4	2	0	2	4	5	6
Rennes	4	1	1	2	5	5	4
Hapoel Tel Aviv	4	0	0	4	1	10	0

Group 7

	P	W	D	L	F	A	Pts
Volgograd	4	3	0	1	12	5	9
Basle	4	2	1	1	14	7	7
Antalya	4	2	0	2	7	7	6
Donetsk	4	1	1	2	5	8	4
Ataka-Aura	4	1	0	3	2	13	3

Group 8

	P	W	D	L	F	A	Pts
Kamaz	4	3	1	0	8	3	10
Munich 1860	4	2	0	2	8	3	6
Kaucuk	4	2	0	2	5	4	6
Spartak Varna	4	1	2	1	5	5	5
LKS Lodz	4	0	1	3	1	12	1

Group 9

	P	W	D	L	F	A	Pts
Karlsruhe	4	3	1	0	7	2	10
Uni Craiova	4	3	0	1	7	3	9
Trnava	4	2	1	1	11	3	7
Daugava	4	1	0	3	4	12	3
Cukaricki	4	0	0	3	2	11	0

Group 10

	P	W	D	L	F	A	Pts
Lierse	4	3	0	1	6	3	9
Vasas	4	2	1	1	9	5	7
Groningen	4	1	2	1	7	5	5
Gaziantep	4	1	2	1	4	4	5
Narva Trans	4	0	1	3	2	11	1

Group 11

	P	W	D	L	F	A	Pts
Ekaterinburg	4	3	1	0	7	3	10
CSKA Sofia	4	2	1	1	8	4	7
Strasbourg	4	1	3	0	4	2	6
Kocaeli	4	1	1	2	7	9	4
Hibernians	4	0	0	4	5	13	0

Group 12

	P	W	D	L	F	A	Pts
Guingamp	4	3	1	0	6	2	10
Zemun	4	3	0	1	8	6	9
Jaro	4	2	1	1	6	3	7
Dinamo Bucharest	4	1	0	3	4	6	3
Kolkheti	4	0	0	4	3	10	0

SEMI-FINALS
Standard Liege 2, 1, Nantes 1, 0
Karlsruhe 3, 2, Lierse 2,0
Volgograd 2,5, Linz ASK 2,0
Guingamp 0, 4, Kamaz 2,0
Segesta 4,1, Orebro 0,4
Silkeborg 2,0, Ekaterinburg 1,1

FINALS, FIRST LEG
Standard Liege 1, Karlsruhe 0
Volgograd 2, Guingamp 1
Segesta 1, Silkeborg 2

FINALS, SECOND LEG
Karlsruhe* 3, Standard Liege 1
Guingamp* 1, Volgograd 0
Silkeborg* 0, Segesta 1

*Three successful clubs gain access to the first round of the 1996–97 UEFA Cup.

WORLD CLUB CHAMPIONSHIP

Played annually up to 1974 and intermittently since then between the winners of the European Cup and the winners of the South American Champions Cup — known as the Copa Libertadores. In 1980 the winners were decided by one match arranged in Tokyo in February 1981 and the venue has been the same since. AC Milan replaced Marseille who had been stripped of their European Cup title in 1993.

1960	Real Madrid beat Penarol 0-0, 5-1
1961	Penarol beat Benfica 0-1, 5-0, 2-1
1962	Santos beat Benfica 3-2, 5-2
1963	Santos beat AC Milan 2-4, 4-2, 1-0
1964	Inter-Milan beat Independiente 0-1, 2-0, 1-0
1965	Inter-Milan beat Independiente 3-0, 0-0
1966	Penarol beat Real Madrid 2-0, 2-0
1967	Racing Club beat Celtic 0-1, 2-1, 1-0
1968	Estudiantes beat Manchester United 1-0, 1-1
1969	AC Milan beat Estudiantes 3-0, 1-2
1970	Feyenoord beat Estudiantes 2-2, 1-0
1971	Nacional beat Panathinaikos* 1-1, 2-1
1972	Ajax beat Independiente 1-1, 3-0
1973	Independiente beat Juventus* 1-0
1974	Atlético Madrid* beat Independiente 0-1, 2-0
1975	Independiente and Bayern Munich could not agree dates; no matches.
1976	Bayern Munich beat Cruzeiro 2-0, 0-0
1977	Boca Juniors beat Borussia Moenchengladbach* 2-2, 3-0
1978	Not contested
1979	Olimpia beat Malmö* 1-0, 2-1

1980	Nacional beat Nottingham Forest 1-0
1981	Flamengo beat Liverpool 3-0
1982	Penarol beat Aston Villa 2-0
1983	Gremio Porto Alegre beat SV Hamburg 2-1
1984	Independiente beat Liverpool 1-0
1985	Juventus beat Argentinos Juniors 4-2 on penalties after a 2-2 draw
1986	River Plate beat Steaua Bucharest 1-0
1987	FC Porto beat Penarol 2-1 after extra time
1988	Nacional (Uru) beat PSV Eindhoven 7-6 on penalties after 1-1 draw
1989	AC Milan beat Atletico Nacional (Col) 1-0 after extra time
1990	AC Milan beat Olimpia 3-0
1991	Red Star Belgrade beat Colo Colo 3-0
1992	Sao Paulo beat Barcelona 2-1
1993	Sao Paulo beat AC Milan 3-2
1994	Velez Sarsfield beat AC Milan 2-0
1995	Ajax beat Gremio Porto Alegre 4-3 on penalties after 0-0 draw

*European Cup runners-up; winners declined to take part.

1996

26 November in Tokyo

Juventus (0) 1

River Plate (0) 0 55,000

Juventus: Peruzzi; Ferrara, Porrini, Torricelli, Montero, Di Livio, Deschamps, Jugovic, Zidane (Tacchinardi 86), Del Piero, Boksic.
Scorer: Del Piero 82.
River Plate: Bonano; Diaz, Berizzo, Ayala, Sorin, Astrada, Montserrat, Berti (Gancedo 75), Ortega, Francescoli, Cruz (Salas 84).
Referee: De Freitas (Brazil).

EUROPEAN SUPER CUP

Played annually between the winners of the European Champions' Cup and the European Cup-Winners' Cup. AC Milan replaced Marseille in 1993–94.

Previous Matches

1972	Ajax beat Rangers 3-1, 3-2
1973	Ajax beat AC Milan 0-1, 6-0
1974	Not contested
1975	Dynamo Kiev beat Bayern Munich 1-0, 2-0
1976	Anderlecht beat Bayern Munich 4-1, 1-2
1977	Liverpool beat Hamburg 1-1, 6-0
1978	Anderlecht beat Liverpool 3-1, 1-2
1979	Nottingham F beat Barcelona 1-0, 1-1
1980	Valencia beat Nottingham F 1-0, 1-2
1981	Not contested
1982	Aston Villa beat Barcelona 0-1, 3-0
1983	Aberdeen beat Hamburg 0-0, 2-0
1984	Juventus beat Liverpool 2-0
1985	Juventus v Everton not contested due to UEFA ban on English clubs
1986	Steaua Bucharest beat Dynamo Kiev 1-0
1987	FC Porto beat Ajax 1-0, 1-0
1988	KV Mechelen beat PSV Eindhoven 3-0, 0-1
1989	AC Milan beat Barcelona 1-1, 1-0
1990	AC Milan beat Sampdoria 1-1, 2-0
1991	Manchester U beat Red Star Belgrade 1-0
1992	Barcelona beat Werder Bremen 1-1, 2-1
1993	Parma beat AC Milan 0-1, 2-0
1994	AC Milan beat Arsenal 0-0, 2-0
1995	Ajax beat Zaragoza 1-1, 4-0

1996–97

First Leg, 15 January 1997, Paris

Paris St Germain 0 (1) *(Rai 53 (pen))*　29,519

Juventus (4) 6 *(Porrini 5, Padovano 22, 40, Ferrara 36, Lombardo 83, Amoruso 89)*

Paris St Germain: Lama; Domi (Leonardo 55), Le Guen, N'Gotty, Algerino (Kenedy 34), Fournier, Guerin, Leroy, Rai, Loko, Dely Valdes (Pouget 61).
Juventus: Peruzzi; Torricelli, Ferrara (Iuliano 73), Porrini, Pessotto, Deschamps, Di Livio, Zidane, Tacchinardi (Lombardo 67), Padovano (Amoruso 73), Del Piero.
Referee: Levnikov (Russia).

Second Leg, 5 February 1997, Palermo

Juventus (1) 3 *(Del Piero 36, 70, Vieri 90)*

Paris St Germain (0) 1 *(Rai 64 (pen))*　35,100

Juventus: Peruzzi; Torricelli (Porrini 72), Ferrara, Montero, Pessotto, Di Livio, Tacchinardi (Lombardo 67), Zidane, Jugovic, Del Piero, Padovano (Vieri 67).
Paris St Germain: Lama; Kenedy, Le Guen, Domi, Algerino, Cauet, Leonardo (Allou 80), Guerin (Leroy 75), Rai, Dely Valdes, Loko (Calenda 90).
Referee: Muhmenthaler (Switzerland).

INTERNATIONAL DIRECTORY

The latest available information has been given regarding numbers of clubs and players registered with FIFA, the world governing body. Where known, official colours are listed. With European countries, League tables show a number of signs. * indicates relegated teams, + play-offs, *+ relegated after play-offs, ++ promoted.

There are 197 member associations and one provisional member, Palestine. The four home countries, England, Scotland, Northern Ireland and Wales, are dealt with elsewhere in the Yearbook; but basic details appear in this directory.

EUROPE

ALBANIA

Federation Albanaise De Football, Rruga Dervish Hima Nr. 31, Tirana.
Founded: 1930; *Number of Clubs:* 49; *Number of Players:* 5,192; *National Colours:* Red shirts, black shorts, red stockings.
Telephone: 00–355–42 27 877; *Cable:* ALBSPORT TIRANA; *Telex:* 2228 bfssh ab. *Fax:* 00 355–42 27 877.

International matches 1996
Bosnia (a) 0-0, Greece (a) 1-2, Portugal (h) 0-3, Armenia (h) 1-1, Northern Ireland (a) 0-2.

League Championship wins (1930-37; 1945–96)
Dinamo Tirana 15; Partizani Tirana 15; 17 Nentori 8; SK Tirana 8; Vllaznia 7; Flamurtari 1; Labinoti 1; Skenderbeu 1, Teuta 1.

Cup wins (1948–97)
Partizani Tirana 14; Dinamo Tirana 12; 17 Nentori 6; Vllaznia 5; Flamurtari 2; SK Tirana 2; Labinoti 1; Elbasan 1; Teuta 1.

Final League Table 1996–97

	P	W	D	L	F	A	Pts
Flamurtari	17	12	1	4	34	15	37
SK Tirana	17	10	4	3	34	8	34
Vllaznia	17	11	0	6	24	16	33
Apolonia	17	9	4	4	22	15	31
Partizani	17	9	4	4	19	15	31
Shkumbini	17	8	2	7	26	17	26
Laci	17	7	4	6	19	19	25
Lushnje	17	6	6	5	17	14	24
Bylis	17	6	4	7	18	16	22
Besa	17	6	4	7	15	14	22
Teuta	17	6	3	8	14	13	21
Sopoti	17	7	0	10	11	19	21
Tomori	17	5	5	7	10	18	20
Elbasan	17	6	2	9	16	25	20
Shquiponia	17	5	4	8	13	20	19
Olimpik	17	5	1	11	21	24	16
Albpetrol	17	4	4	9	12	27	16
Skenderbeu	17	4	2	11	12	33	14

Due to civil unrest, competition abandoned in January.

Top scorer: Paco (Flamurtari) 14.
Cup Final: Flamurtari 2, Partizani 2.
Partizani won 4-3 on penalties.

ANDORRA

Federacio Andorrana de Futbol, Camp d'Esports d'Alxovall, Carretera d'Os de Civis, s/n Saint Julia de Loria.
Telephone: 00376 8422224; *Fax:* 00376 84225.

International matches 1996
Estonia (h) 1-6.

Final League Table 1996–97

	P	W	D	L	F	A	Pts
Principat	22	20	1	1	115	12	61
Veterans	22	19	2	1	84	25	59
Encamp	22	12	5	5	66	25	41
Santa Colma	22	10	3	9	57	31	33
Aldosa	22	10	3	9	34	37	22
Sporting	22	8	6	8	51	39	30
Sant Julia	22	9	3	10	38	52	30
Massana	22	6	7	9	32	43	25
Inter	22	7	4	11	31	48	25
Les Bons	22	6	4	12	37	66	22
Gimnastic	22	4	4	14	31	84	16
Spordany	22	0	0	22	23	137	0

Top scorer: Patreceo (Principat) 25.
Cup Final: Principat 7, Sant Julia 0.

ARMENIA

Football Federation of Armenia, 9, Abovian Str. 375001 Erevan, Armenia.
Number of Clubs: 956; *Number of Players:* 12,055.
Telephone: 00374 2/527014; *Telex:* 885–52 3376; *Fax:* 00374 2/151573.

International matches 1996
Morocco (a) 0-6, France (a) 0-2, Peru (a) 0-4, Paraguay (a) 2-1, Ecuador (a) 0-3, Portugal (h) 0-0, Northern Ireland (a) 1-1, Germany (h) 1-5, Albania (a) 1-1.

League Championship wins (1992–97)
Shirak Gyumri 2; Pyunik 2; Ararat Erevan 1; Homenmen 1.

Cup wins (1992–97)
Ararat Erevan 3; Pyunik 1; Kotaik 1.

Final League Table 1996–97

	P	W	D	L	F	A	Pts
Pyunik	22	19	2	1	67	9	59
Ararat	22	17	1	4	54	18	52
FC Erevan	22	16	2	4	58	24	50
Shirak	22	15	2	5	57	11	47
Cement	22	13	3	6	49	26	42
Van	22	11	1	10	41	34	34
Kotaik	22	8	4	10	41	27	28
Karabach	22	7	4	11	23	29	25
Homenmen	22	7	1	14	30	59	22
Arabkir	22	4	0	18	20	89	12
Zanzekour	22	2	3	17	9	77	9
CSKA*	22	1	1	20	10	56	4

Top scorer: Avetissian (Pyunik) 19.
Cup Final: Ararat Erevan 1, Pyunik 0.

AUSTRIA

Oesterreichischer Fussball-Bund, Wiener Stadion, Sektor A/F, Meierestrasse, A-1020 Wien.
Founded: 1904; *Number of Clubs:* 2,081; *Number of Players:* 253,576; *National Colours:* White shirts, black shorts, black stockings.
Telephone: 0043 1 727 18; *Cable:* FOOTBALL WIEN; *Telex:* 111919 oefb a; *Fax:* 0043 1 728 1632.

International matches 1996
Switzerland (h) 1-0, Hungary (a) 2-0, Czech Republic (h) 1-0, Scotland (h) 0-0. Sweden (a) 1-0, Latvia (h) 2-1.

League Championship wins (1912–97)
Rapid Vienna 30; FK Austria 22; Admira-Energie-Wacker 9; First Vienna 6; Tirol-Svarowski-Innsbruck 7; Wiener Sportklub 3; Austria Salzburg 3; FAC 1; Hakoah 1; Linz ASK 1; WAF 1; Voest Linz 1.

Cup wins (1919–97)
FK Austria 25; Rapid Vienna 14; TS Innsbruck (prev. Wacker Innsbruck) 7; Admira-Energie-Wacker (prev. Sportklub Admira & Admira-Energie) 5; First Vienna 3; Sturm Graz 2; Linz ASK 1; Wacker Vienna 1; WAF 1; Wiener Sportklub 1; Graz 1; Stockerau 1.

Final League Table 1996–97

	P	W	D	L	F	A	Pts
Austria Salzburg	36	19	12	5	54	25	69
Rapid	36	18	12	6	68	35	66
Sturm Graz	36	14	13	9	49	30	55
Innsbruck	36	16	7	13	49	40	55
Graz	36	11	14	11	39	42	47
FK Austria	36	12	10	14	51	46	46
Linz ASK	36	9	17	10	38	47	44
Ried	36	12	6	18	43	58	42
FC Linz	36	6	13	17	33	50	31
Admira Wacker+	36	6	10	20	37	73	28

Admira Wacker defeated Steyr; Linz ASK and FC Linz have now merged.

Top scorer: Wagner (Rapid) 21.
Cup Final: Sturm Graz 2, First Vienna 1.

AZERBAIJAN

Association of Football Federations of Azerbaijan, Husu Haciyev kuc., 42, 37009 Baku, Azerbaijan.
Number of Clubs: 2,200. *Number of Players:* 131,000.
Telephone: 00994 12 94 49 16; *Fax:* 00994 12 98 93 93; *Telex:* 142349 affa su.

International matches 1996

Estonia (a) 0-0, Faeroes (h) 3-0, Turkey (h) 0-1, Belarus (a) 2-2, Norway (a) 0-5, Switzerland (h) 1-0, Oman (a) 1-2, Hungary (h) 0-3.

League Championship wins (1992–97)

Neftchi 3; Karabach 1; Kopaz 1; Turan 1.

Cup wins (1992–97)

Karabach 2; Kopaz 2; Neftchi 1; Inshatchi 1.

Final League Table 1996–97

	P	W	D	L	F	A	Pts
Neftchi	30	23	5	2	98	20	74
Agdam	30	23	2	5	61	25	71
Khazri	30	20	6	4	59	23	66
Turan	30	19	7	4	48	13	64
Kopaz	30	18	4	8	59	26	58
Khazar	30	18	4	8	58	30	58
Farid	30	13	8	9	45	31	47
Pambygchi	30	11	5	14	41	47	38
Baky	30	10	7	13	37	41	37
Vilvash	30	9	6	15	38	52	33
OIK	30	7	6	17	26	50	27
Shamkir	30	8	2	20	30	106	26
Kur-Nur	30	7	4	19	30	59	25
PA	30	5	7	18	23	49	22
Neftchala*	30	5	6	19	27	68	21
U-18 Milli*	30	4	1	25	38	78	13

Top scorer: Burbanov (Neftchi) 25.
Cup Final: Kopaz 1, Khazri 0.

BELARUS

Belarus Football Association, 8–2 Kyrov Str. 220600 Minsk, Belarus.
Founded: 1992; *Number of Players:* 120,000.
Telephone: 007 0172 27 29 20; *Telex:*252175 athlet su; *Fax:* 007 0172 27 29 20.

International matches 1996

Turkey (a) 2-3, Slovakia (a) 0-4, Poland (a) 1-1, Azerbaijan (h) 2-2, Sweden (a) 1-5, Lithuania (h) 2-2, Estonia (h) 1-0, Estonia (a) 0-1, Latvia (h) 1-1.

League Championship wins (1992–96)

Dynamo Minsk 5; MPKC Mozyr 1.

Cup wins (1992–96)

Dynamo Minsk 2; Neman 1; Dynamo 93 Minsk 1; MPKC Mozyr 1; Belshina 1.

Final Table 1996

	P	W	D	L	F	A	Pts
MPKC Mozyr	30	24	4	2	64	17	76
Dynamo Minsk	30	23	6	1	83	20	75
Belshina	30	20	3	7	67	32	63
Dynamo 93 Minsk	30	17	5	8	44	30	56
Lokomotiv 96	30	13	10	7	48	27	49
Ataka Aura	30	13	5	12	31	42	44
Naftan	30	13	4	13	43	52	43
Molodechno	30	11	8	11	42	33	41
Dnepr Mogilyov	30	11	6	13	33	36	39
Dynamo Brest	30	7	11	12	39	43	32
Shakhter	30	8	5	17	29	50	29
Torpedo Minsk	30	7	8	15	32	53	29
Neman	30	7	8	15	25	50	29
Torpedo Mogilyov	30	7	6	17	27	64	27
Obuvshchik*	30	6	6	18	26	43	24
Vedrich*	30	4	3	23	14	57	15

Top scorer: Khlebosolov (Belshina) 34.
Cup Final: Belshina 2, Dynamo Minsk 0.

BELGIUM

Union Royale Belge Des Societes De Football; Eturl, Association, Rue De La Loi 43, Boite 1, B-1040 Bruxelles.
Founded: 1895; *Number of Clubs:* 2,120; *Number of*

Players: 390,468; *National Colours:* Red shirts with tricoloured trim, red shorts, red stockings with trim.
Telephone: 0032 2 477 12 11; *Cable:* UBSFA BRUX-ELLES; *Telex:* 23257 bvbfbf b; *Fax:* 0032 2 478 23 91.

International matches 1996

France (h) 0-2, Russia (h) 0-0, Italy (a) 2-2, Turkey (h) 2-1, San Marino (a) 3-0, Holland (h) 0-3.

League Championship wins (1896–1997)

Anderlecht 24; Union St Gilloise 11; FC Brugge 10; Standard Liege 8; Beerschot 7; RC Brussels 6; FC Liege 5; Daring Brussels 5; Antwerp 4; Mechelen 4; Lierse SK 4; SV Brugge 3; Beveren 2; RWD Molenbeek 1.

Cup wins (1954–97)

Anderlecht 8; FC Brugge 7; Standard Liege 5; Beerschot 2; Waterschei 2; Beveren 2; Gent 2; Antwerp 2; Lierse SK 1; Racing Doornik 1; Waregem 1; SV Brugge 1; Mechelen 1; FC Liege 1; Ekeren 1.

Final League Table 1996–97

	P	W	D	L	F	A	Pts
Lierse	34	21	10	3	70	38	73
FC Brugge	34	22	5	7	69	34	71
Mouscron	34	17	10	7	60	38	61
Anderlect	34	16	10	8	59	36	58
Lommel	34	16	9	9	50	48	57
Antwerp	34	16	5	13	50	49	53
Standard Liege	34	16	2	16	55	55	50
Genk	34	13	10	11	50	43	49
Ekeren	34	13	7	14	55	56	46
Harelbeke	34	11	12	11	50	43	45
Lokeren	34	11	7	16	41	56	40
St Truiden	34	10	9	15	46	56	39
Charleroi	34	10	7	17	44	57	37
Gent	34	10	6	18	44	58	36
RWD Molenbeek	34	8	11	15	32	43	35
Aalst	34	8	11	15	43	55	35
Mechelen*	34	7	10	17	33	55	31
CS Brugge*	34	6	9	19	35	66	27

Top scorer: Spehar (FC Brugge) 26.
Cup Final: Ekeren 4, Anderlecht 2.

BOSNIA HERZEGOVINA

Bosnia & Herzegovina Football Federation, D. Ozme 7/III, 71000 Sarajevo.
Telephone: 00387 71664836, 670345; *Satellite Telephone:* 0087 114/46271; *Fax:* 00387 71205554.

International matches 1996

Albania (h) 0-0, Greece (a) 0-3, Croatia (h) 1-4, Italy (h) 2-1, Slovenia (a) 2-1, Brazil (a) 0-1.

BULGARIA

Bulgarian Football Union, Gotcho Gopin 19, 1000 Sofia.
Founded: 1923; *Number of Clubs:* 376; *Number of Players:* 48,240; *National Colours:* White shirts, green shorts, red stockings.
Telephone: 00359 2 87 74 90; *Cable:* BULFUTBOL; *Telex:* 23145 bfs bg; *Fax:* 00359 2 80 32 37.

International matches 1996

England (a) 0-1, Slovakia (a) 0-0, Macedonia (h) 3-0, UAR (h) 4-1, Spain (a) 1-1, Romania (h) 1-0, France (a) 1-3, Israel (a) 1-2, Luxembourg (a) 2-1, Saudi Arabia (a) 0-1, Thailand (a) 4-0, Cyprus (a) 3-1.

League Championship wins (1925–97)

CSKA Sofia 28; Levski Sofia 19; Slavia Sofia 7; Vladislav Varna 3; Lokomotiv Sofia 3; Trakia Plovdiv 2; AC 23 Sofia 1; Botev Plovdiv 1; SC Sofia 1; Sokol Varna 1; Spartak Plovdiv 1; Tichka Varna 1; JSZ Sofia 1; Beroe Stara Zagora 1; Etur 1.

Cup wins (1946–97)

Levski Sofia 18; CSKA Sofia 15; Slavia Sofia 7; Lokomotiv Sofia 4; Botev Plovdiv 1; Spartak Plovdiv 1; Spartak Sofia 1; Marek Stanke 1; Trakia Plovdiv 1; Spartak Varna 1; Sliven 1.

Final League Table 1996–97

	P	W	D	L	F	A	Pts
CSKA Sofia	30	22	5	3	65	19	71
Neftochimik	30	20	7	3	70	20	67
Slavia Sofia	30	14	6	7	61	23	57
Levski Sofia	30	14	11	5	58	30	53
Botev Plovdiv	30	14	3	13	41	41	45
Mineur	30	12	8	10	28	35	44
Lokomotiv Sofia	30	13	4	13	59	47	43
Levski Kustendil	30	13	3	14	51	52	42
Spartak Varna	30	13	3	14	40	41	42
Lokomotiv Plovdiv	30	12	5	13	38	41	41
Dobrudja	30	11	6	13	44	48	39
Spartak Pleven	30	12	3	15	35	46	39
Etur	30	10	5	15	37	53	35
Maritza*	30	8	8	14	38	45	32
Montana*	30	8	4	18	32	54	28
Rakovski*	30	0	1	29	8	110	1

Top scorer: Pramatarov (Slavia Sofia) 26.
Cup Final: CSKA Sofia 3, Levski Sofia 1.

CROATIA

Croatian Football Federation, Illica 21/11, CRO-41000 Zagreb, Croatia.
Telephone: 00385 1/4554100. *Fax:* 00385 41 42 46 39.

International matches 1996

Poland (h) 2-1, South Korea (h) 3-0, Israel (h) 2-0, Hungary (h) 4-1, England (a) 0-0, Eire (a) 2-2, Turkey (h) 1-0, Denmark (h) 3-0, Portugal (a) 0-3, Germany (a) 1-2, Bosnia (a) 4-1, Greece (h) 1-1, Morocco (h) 2-2, Czech Republic (h) 1-1.

League Championship wins (1941-44; 1992–97)
Hajduk Split 3; Croatia Zagreb 3; Gradanski 3; Concordia 1.

Cup wins (1992–97)
Croatia Zagreb 3; Hajduk Split 2; Inker 1.

Final League Table 1996–97

	P	W	D	L	F	A	Pts
Croatia Zagreb	30	26	3	1	90	23	81
Hajduk Split	30	18	6	6	53	22	60
Dragovoljac	30	13	10	7	51	37	49
Rijeka	30	13	7	10	44	32	46
Zagreb	30	13	6	11	43	39	45
Varteks	30	12	6	12	34	35	42
Sibenik	30	11	8	11	35	30	41
Osijek	30	12	5	13	40	38	41
Mladost 127	30	10	10	10	37	36	40
Zadarcommerce	30	11	7	12	39	45	40
Segesta*	30	9	12	9	35	34	39
Marsonia*	30	11	5	14	38	50	38
Vinkovci*	30	11	0	19	35	56	33
Orijent*	30	5	11	14	28	53	26
Istra Pola*	30	6	7	17	25	54	25
Inker*	30	6	3	21	22	65	21

Top scorer: Cvitanovic (Croatia Zagreb) 20.
Cup Final: Croatia Zagreb 2, Zagreb 1.

CYPRUS

Cyprus Football Association, Stasinos Str. 1, Engomi 152, P.O. Box 5071, Nicosia.
Founded: 1934; *Number of Clubs:* 85; *Number of Players:* 6,000; *National Colours:* Sky blue shirts, white shorts, blue and white stockings.
Telephone: 00357 2 44 53 41; *Cable:* FOOTBALL NICOSIA; *Telex:* 3880 football cy; *Fax:* 00357 2 47 25 44.

International matches 1996

Libya (a) 0-1, Estonia (h) 1-0, Georgia (h) 0-2, Iceland (a) 1-2, Poland (a) 2-2, Russia (a) 0-4, Kuwait (h) 0-0, Israel (h) 2-0, Bulgaria (h) 1-3.

League Championship wins (1935–97)
Omonia 17; Apoel 16; Anorthosis 8; AEL 5; EPA 3; Olympiakos 3; Apollon 2; Pezoporikos 2; Chetin Kayal 1; Trast 1.

Cup wins (1935–97)
Apoel 16; Omonia 10; AEL 6; EPA 5; Anorthosis 4; Apollon 4; Trast 3; Chetin Kayal 2; Olympiakos 1; Pezoporikos 1; Salamina 1.

Final League Table 1996–97

	P	W	D	L	F	A	Pts
Anorthosis	26	20	5	1	58	14	65
Apollon	26	16	4	6	43	22	52
Omonia	26	14	4	8	39	31	46
AEK	26	11	8	7	49	37	41
Apoel	26	12	4	10	57	43	40
Ethnikos	26	11	4	11	48	36	37
Paralimni	26	9	8	9	46	46	35
Salamina	26	8	10	8	43	36	34
Anagennisi	26	9	5	12	27	42	32
Apop	26	9	4	13	27	36	31
Alki	26	8	6	12	41	49	30
Aris*	26	7	7	12	30	45	28
Olympiakos*	26	8	3	15	28	47	27
Apep*	26	3	2	21	22	75	11

Top scorer: Kostantinou (Paralimni) 17.
Cup Final: Apoel 2, Omonia 0.

CZECH REPUBLIC

Football Association of Czech Republic, Diskarska 100, 169 00 Prague 6, Czech Republic.
Number of Clubs: 3,562; *Number of Players:* 237,200; *National Colours:* Red shirts, white shorts, blue stockings.
Telephone: (General Secretary) 0042 2 20513575 (International and PR Dept) 0042 2 520156; *Fax:* 0042 2 35 27 84.

International matches 1996

Turkey (h) 3-0, Eire (h) 2-0, Austria (a) 0-1, Switzerland (a) 2-1, Germany (a) 0-2, Italy (h) 2-1, Russia (h) 3-3, Portugal (h) 1-0, France (h) 0-0, Germany (a) 1-2, Iceland (h) 2-1, Malta (h) 6-0, Spain (h) 0-0, Yugoslavia (a) 0-1, Nigeria (h) 2-1, Croatia (a) 1-1.

League Championship wins (1926–93)
Sparta Prague 20; Slavia Prague 12; Dukla Prague (prev. UDA) 11; Slovan Bratislava 7; Spartak Trnava 5; Banik Ostrava 3; Inter-Bratislava 3; Spartak Hradec Kralove 1; Viktoria Zizkov 1; Zbrojovka Brno 1; Bohemians 1; Vitkovice 1.

Cup wins (1961–93)
Dukla Prague 8; Sparta Prague 8; Slovan Bratislava 5; Spartak Trnava 4; Banik Ostrava 3; Lokomotiv Kosice 3; TJ Gottwaldov 1; Dunajska Streda 1.
From 1993–94, there were two separate countries; the Czech Republic and Slovakia.

League Championship wins (1993–97)
Sparta Prague 4; Slavia Prague 1.

Cup wins (1994–97)
Viktoria Zizkov 1; Spartak Hradec Kralove 1; Sparta Prague 1; Slavia Prague 1.

Final League Table 1996–97

	P	W	D	L	F	A	Pts
Sparta Prague	30	19	8	3	61	20	65
Slavia Prague	30	18	7	5	59	24	61
Jablonek	30	17	5	8	40	29	56
Boby Brno	30	14	10	6	44	35	52
Slovan Liberec	30	12	10	8	33	30	46
Ceske Budejovice	30	11	11	8	38	40	44
Petra Drnovice	30	12	7	11	53	44	43
Sigma Olomouc	30	10	10	10	36	30	40
Kaucuk Opava	30	10	10	10	34	35	40
Banik Ostrava	30	8	13	9	33	35	37
Viktoria Plzen	30	7	11	12	33	37	32
Viktoria Zizkov	30	6	11	13	17	33	29
Teplice	30	6	10	14	21	37	28
Hradec Kralove	30	5	13	12	22	39	28
Karvina*	30	6	7	17	25	50	25
Bohemians*	30	4	7	19	22	53	19

Top scorer: Siegl (Sparta Prague) 19.
Cup Final: Slavia Prague 1, Dukla Prague 0.

DENMARK

Dansk Boldspil Union, Ved Amagerbanen 15, DK-2300, Copenhagen S.
Founded: 1889; *Number of Clubs:* 1,555; *Number of Players:* 268,517; *National Colours:* Red shirts, white shorts, red stockings.
Telephone: 0045 31 95 05 11; *Cable:* DANSKBOLDSPIL COPENHAGEN; *Telex:* 15545 dbu dk; *Fax:* 0045 31 95 05 88.

International matches 1996

Romania (h) 2-2, Finland (h) 0-0, Thailand (h) 3-1, Romania (a) 1-2, Germany (a) 0-2, Scotland (h) 2-0, Ghana (h) 1-0, Portugal (a) 1-1, Croatia (a) 0-3, Turkey (h) 3-0, Sweden (a) 1-0, Slovenia (a) 2-0, Greece (h) 2-1, France (h) 1-0.

League Championship wins (1913–97)

KB Copenhagen 15; B 93 Copenhagen 10; AB (Akademisk) 9; B 1903 Copenhagen 7; Brondby 7; Frem 6; Esbjerg BK 5; Vejle BK 5; AGF Aarhus 5; Hvidovre 3; Odense BK 3; B 1909 Odense 2; Koge BK 2; Lyngby 2; FC Copenhagen 1; Silkeborg 1, AaB Aalborg 1.

Cup wins (1955–97)

Aarhus GF 9; Vejle BK 6; Randers Freja 3; Lyngby 3; OB Odense 3; B1909 Odense 2; Aalborg BK 2; Esbjerg BK 2; Frem 2; B 1903 Copenhagen 2; Brondby 2; FC Copenhagen 2; B 93 Copenhagen 1; KB Copenhagen 1; Vanlose 1; Hvidovre 1; B1913 Odense 1.

Final League Table 1996–97

	P	W	D	L	F	A	Pts
Brondby	33	20	8	5	64	39	68
Vejle	33	14	12	7	57	38	54
Aarhus	33	14	10	9	75	51	52
Herfolge	33	15	7	11	46	42	52
Aalborg	33	12	11	10	45	40	47
Silkeborg	33	10	15	8	51	55	45
Odense	33	11	8	14	59	61	41
FC Copenhagen	33	10	11	12	35	43	41
Lyngby	33	10	10	13	50	61	40
AB Copenhagen	33	8	12	13	56	62	36
Viborg*	33	6	11	16	31	58	29
Hvidovre*	33	5	11	17	39	59	25

Top scorer: Molnar (Lyngby) 24.
Cup Final: FC Copenhagen 2, Ikast 0.

ENGLAND

The Football Association, 16 Lancaster Gate, London W2 3LW
Founded: 1863; *Number of Clubs:* 42,000; *Number of Players:* 2,250,000; *National Colours:* White shirts, navy blue shorts, white stockings.
Telephone: 0171 262 4542; *Cable:* FOOTBALL ASSOCIATION LONDON W2; *Telex:* 261110; *Fax:* 0171 402 0486.

ESTONIA

Estonian Football Association, Voidu 16, Tallinn EE 0012.
Number of Clubs: 40; *Number of Players:* 12,000.
Telephone: 00372 6/542715, 542716, 542717; *Telex:* 173236 sport su; *Fax:* 00372 6/542719.

International matches 1996

Azerbaijan (h) 0-0, Cyprus (a) 0-1, Faeroes (h) 2-2, Iceland (h) 0-3, Turkey (h) 0-0, Latvia (h) 1-1, Lithuania (h) 1-1, Belarus (a) 0-1, Belarus (h) 1-0, Finland (a) 2-2, Indonesia (h) 3-0, Andorra (a) 6-1.

League Championship wins (1922-40; 1992–97)

Sport 8; Estonia 5; Norma Tallinn 2; Flora Tallinn 2; Tallinn JK 2; Kalev 2; LFLS 1; Olimpia 1; Lantana 1.

Cup wins (1992–97)

Sadam 2; VMV Tallinn 1; Nikol Tallinn 1; Norma Tallinn 1, Lantana 1.

Qualifying League Table 1996-97

	P	W	D	L	F	A	Pts
Lantana	14	11	2	1	35	10	35
Flora	14	9	2	3	27	9	29
Marlekor	14	6	4	4	20	17	22
Lelle	14	5	6	3	20	16	21
Trans	14	5	5	4	20	19	20
Sadam	14	5	1	8	24	26	16
Johvi*	14	4	1	9	10	20	13
Vall*	14	0	1	13	10	49	1

Final League Table 1996–97

	P	W	D	L	F	A	Pts
Lantana	10	7	2	1	22	6	41
Flora	10	7	2	1	25	7	38
Sadam	10	5	1	4	13	9	24
Lelle	10	3	0	7	7	21	20
Marlekor	10	2	2	6	7	19	19
Trans	10	2	1	7	8	20	14

Half points added from qualifying table.

Top scorer: Bragin (Lantana) 18.
Cup Final: Sadam 3, Lantana 2.

FAEROE ISLANDS

Fotboltssamband Foroya, The Faeroes' Football Assn., Gundalur, P.O. Box 1028, FR-110, Torshavn.
Founded: 1979; *Number of Clubs:* 16; *Number of Players:* 1,014.
Telephone: 00298 16 707; *Telex:* 81332 itrott FA; *Fax:* 00298 19 079.

International matches 1996

Estonia (a) 2-2, Azerbaijan (a) 0-3, Yugoslavia (a) 1-3, Slovakia (h) 1-2, Spain (h) 2-6, Yugoslavia (h) 1-8, Slovakia (a) 0-3.

League Championship wins (1942–96)

KI Klaksvik 15; HB Torshavn 14; TB Tvoroyri 7; GI Gotu 7; B36 Torshavn 5; B68 Toftir 3; SI Sorvag 1; IF Fuglafjordur 1; B71 Sandur 1.

Cup wins (1955–96)

HB Torshavn 24; TB Tvoroyri 4; KI Klaksvik 4; GI Gotu 3; B36 Torshavn 1; VB Vagur 1; NSI Runavik 1; B71 Sandur 1.

Final League Table 1996

	P	W	D	L	F	A	Pts
GI	18	12	3	3	52	13	39
KI	18	11	6	1	47	16	39
HB	18	11	2	5	48	28	35
B36	18	9	5	4	34	21	32
VB	18	7	3	8	19	25	24
IF	18	6	5	7	25	32	23
B68	18	5	3	10	23	34	18
B71	18	4	6	8	20	40	18
FSV	18	3	1	14	19	48	10
TB*	18	3	4	11	21	51	13

Top scorer: K. Mokore (KI) 20.
Cup Final: GI 2, HB 2.
GI won 5-2 on penalties.

FINLAND

Suomen Palloliitto Finlands Bollfoerbund, Kuparitie 1, P.O. Box 29, SF-00441 Helsinki.
Founded: 1907; *Number of Clubs:* 1,135; *Number of Players:* 66,100; *National Colours:* White shirts, blue shorts, white stockings.
Telephone: 00358 0 701 01 01; *Cable:* SUOMIFOTBOLL HELSINKI; *Telex:* 126033 spl sf; *Fax:* 00358 0 701 01 099.

International matches 1996

Thailand (a) 0-1, Denmark (a) 0-0, Romania (a) 1-1, Thailand (a) 2-5, Kuwait (a) 0-1, Kuwait (a) 1-0, France (a) 0-2, Turkey (h) 1-2, Latvia (a) 0-0, Hungary (a) 0-1, Switzerland (h) 2-3, Estonia (h) 2-2.

League Championship wins (1949–96)

Helsinki JK 9; Turun Palloseura 5; Kuopion Palloseura 5; Valkeakosken Haka 5; Kuusysi 4; Lahden Reipas 3; IF Kamraterna 3; Ilves-Kissat 2; Jazz Pori 2; Kotkan TP 2; OPS Oulu 2; Torun Pyrkiva 1; IF Kronohagens 1; Helsinki PS 1; Kokkolan PV 1; Vasa 1; TPV Tampere 1.

Cup wins (1955–96)

Valkeakosken Haka 9; Lahden Reipas 7; HJK Helsinki 5; Kotkan TP 4; Mikkeli 2; Kuusysi 2; Kuopion Palloseura 2; Ilves Tampere 2; TPS Turku 2; ; MyPa 2; IFK Abo 1; Drott 1; Helsinki PS 1; Pallo-Peikot 1; Rovaniemi PS 1.

Final League Table 1996

	P	W	D	L	F	A	Pts
Jazz Pori	27	13	8	6	47	33	47
MyPa	27	14	3	10	43	32	45
TPS Turku	27	13	5	9	40	35	44
FinnPa	27	11	9	7	32	25	42
Jaro	27	11	6	10	34	25	39
Inter	27	11	6	10	28	30	39

Relegation Table 1996

	P	W	D	L	F	A	Pts
VPS	27	12	5	10	33	25	41
RoPS Rovaniemi	27	11	6	10	35	29	39
HJK Helsinki+	27	11	5	11	36	37	38
Ilves*	27	8	6	13	26	43	30
Haka*	27	7	6	14	35	42	27
Mikkeli*	27	5	5	17	18	50	20

Top scorer: Luiz Antonio (Jazz Pori) 17.
Cup Final: HJK Helsinki 0, TPS Turku 0.
HJK Helsinki won 4-3 on penalties.

FRANCE

Federation Francaise De Football, 60 Bis A
venue D'Iena, F-75783 Paris, Cedex 16.
Founded: 1919; *Number of Clubs:* 21,629; *Number of
Players:* 1,692,205; *National Colours:* Blue shirts, white
shorts, red stockings.
Telephone: 0033 1 44 31 73 00; *Cable:* CEFI PARIS 034;
Telex: 640000 fedfoot f; *Fax:* 0033 1 47 20 82 96.

International matches 1996
Portugal (h) 3-2, Greece (h) 3-1, Belgium (a) 2-0, Finland
(h) 2-0, Germany (a) 1-0, Armenia (h) 2-0, Romania (h)
1-0, Spain (h) 1-1, Bulgaria (h) 3-1, Holland (h) 0-0,
Czech Republic (a) 0-0, Mexico (h) 2-0, Turkey (h) 4-0,
Denmark (a) 0-1.

League Championship wins (1933–97)
Saint Etienne 10; Olympique Marseille 8; Nantes 7; Stade
de Reims 6; AS Monaco 6; OGC Nice 4; Girondins
Bordeaux 4; Lille OSC 3; Paris St Germain 2; FC Sete 2;
Sochaux 2; Racing Club Paris 1; Roubaix-Tourcoing 1;
Strasbourg 1; Auxerre 1.

Cup wins (1918–97)
Olympique Marseille 10; Saint Etienne 6; Lille OSC 5;
Racing Club Paris 5; Red Star 5; AS Monaco 5;
Olympique Lyon 4; Girondins Bordeaux 3; Paris St
Germain 3; OGC Nice 3; CAS Genereaux 2; Nancy 2;
Racing Club Strasbourg 2; Sedan 2; FC Sete 2; Stade de
Reims 2; SO Montpellier 2; Stade Rennes 2; Auxerre 2;
AS Cannes 1; Club Français 1; Excelsior Roubaix 1; Le
Havre 1; Olympique de Pantin 1; CA Paris 1; Sochaux 1;
Toulouse 1; Bastia 1; Nantes 1; Metz 1.

Final League Table 1996–97

	P	W	D	L	F	A	Pts
Monaco	38	23	10	5	69	30	79
Paris St Germain	38	18	13	7	57	31	67
Nantes	38	16	16	6	61	32	64
Bordeaux	38	16	15	7	59	42	63
Metz	38	17	11	10	40	30	62
Auxerre	38	17	10	11	49	32	61
Bastia	38	17	10	11	54	47	61
Lyon	38	16	12	10	59	50	60
Strasbourg	38	19	3	16	52	49	60
Montpellier	38	12	15	11	40	40	51
Marseille	38	12	13	13	43	48	49
Guingamp	38	11	13	14	32	36	46
Lens	38	12	9	17	40	52	45
Le Havre	38	10	13	15	34	43	43
Cannes	38	9	14	15	25	41	41
Rennes	38	10	10	18	40	58	40
Caen*	38	7	16	15	35	46	37
Nancy*	38	9	10	19	33	51	37
Lille*	38	8	11	19	32	58	35
Nice*	38	5	8	25	30	68	23

Top scorer: Guivarc'h (Rennes) 22.
Cup Final: Nice 1, Guingamp 1.
Nice won 4-2 on penalties.

GEORGIA

Football Federation of Georgia, 5 Shota Iamanidze Str,
Tbillisi 380012, Georgia.
Founded: 1992; *Number of Clubs:* 4050. *Number of
Players:* 115,000.
Telephone: 007 8832 96 07 10; *Telex:* 340744. *Fax:* 00995
32/001128.

International matches 1996
Cyprus (a) 2-0, Romania (a) 0-5, Greece (a) 1-2, Norway
(a) 0-1, Italy (a) 0-1, England (h) 0-2, Libya (a) 2-4, Libya
(a) 2-3.

League Championship wins (1990–97)
Dynamo Tbilisi 8.

Cup wins (1992–1997)
Dynamo Tbilisi 7.

Final League Table 1996–97

	P	W	D	L	F	A	Pts
Dynamo Tbilisi	30	26	3	1	101	23	81
Kolkheti	30	18	8	4	71	22	62
Dynamo Batumi	30	18	5	7	54	29	59
Merani 91	30	14	4	12	70	58	46
Torpedo Kutaisi	30	13	1	16	51	57	40
Odishi	30	12	2	16	44	66	38
Margveti	30	11	4	15	35	53	37
Samgurali	30	10	7	13	30	39	37
Dila Gori	30	10	6	14	30	39	36
Sioni	30	11	2	17	43	57	35
Gorda	30	11	2	17	43	55	35
TSU	30	8	10	12	37	39	34
Guria	30	10	3	17	34	65	33
Samtredia*	30	9	4	17	31	57	31
Kakheti*	30	10	1	19	29	66	26
Iveria*	30	5	6	19	24	61	21

Top scorers: Udzhmadzhuridze (Dynamo Batumi) 25,
Demetradze (Dynamo Tbilisi) 25, Ashvetya (Torpedo
Kutaisi) 25.
Cup Final: Dynamo Tbilisi 1, Batumi 0.

GERMANY

Deutsche Fussball-Bund, Otto-Fleck-Schneise 6, Postfach
710265, D-6000, Frankfurt (Main) 71.
Founded: 1900; *Number of Clubs:* 26,760; *Number of
Players:* 5,260,320; *National Colours:* White shirts, black
shorts, white stockings.
Telephone: 0049 69 678 80; *Cable:* FUSSBALL FRANK-
FURT; *Telex:* 416815 dfb d; *Fax:* 0049 69 678 82 66.

International matches 1996
Portugal (a) 2-1, Denmark (h) 2-0, Holland (a) 1-0,
Northern Ireland (a) 1-1, France (h) 0-1, Liechtenstein
(h) 9-1, Czech Republic (h) 2-0, Russia (h) 3-0, Italy (h)
0-0, Croatia (h) 2-1, England (h) 1-1, Czech Republic (h)
2-1, Poland (a) 2-0, Armenia (a) 5-1, Northern Ireland
(h) 1-1, Portugal (h) 0-0.

League Championship wins (1903–97)
Bayern Munich 14; IFC Nuremberg 9; Schalke 04 7; SV
Hamburg 6; Borussia Moenchengladbach 5; Borussia
Dortmund 5; VfB Stuttgart 4; VfB Leipzig 3; Sp Vgg
Furth 3; IFC Cologne 3; IFC Kaiserslautern 3; Werder
Bremen 3; Viktoria Berlin 2; Hertha Berlin 2; Hanover
96 2; Dresden SC 2; Munich 1860 1; Union Berlin 1; FC
Freiburg 1; Phoenix Karlsruhe 1; Karlsruher FV 1;
Holsten Kiel 1; Fortuna Dusseldorf 1; Rapid Vienna 1;
VfB Mannheim 1; Rot-Weiss Essen 1; Eintracht
Frankfurt 1; Eintracht Brunswick 1.

Cup wins (1935–97)
Bayern Munich 8; IFC Cologne 4; Eintracht Frankfurt 4;
IFC Nuremberg 3; SV Hamburg 3; Werder Bremen 3;
Moenchengladbach 3; VfB Stuttgart 3; Dresden SC 2;
Fortuna Dusseldorf 2; Karlsruhe SC 2; Munich 1860 2;
Schalke 04 2; Borussia Dortmund 2; Kaiserslautern 2; Fort
Vienna 1; VfB Leipzig 1; Kickers Offenbach 1; Rapid
Vienna 1; Rot-Weiss Essen 1; SW Essen 1; Bayer
Uerdingen 1; Hannover 96 1; Leverkusen 1.

Final League Table 1996–97

	P	W	D	L	F	A	Pts
Bayern Munich	34	20	11	3	68	34	71
Leverkusen	34	21	6	7	69	41	69
Borussia Dortmund	34	19	6	9	63	41	63
Stuttgart	34	18	7	9	78	40	61
Bochum	34	14	11	9	54	51	53
Karlsruhe	34	13	10	11	55	44	49
Munich 1860	34	13	10	11	56	56	49
Werder Bremen	34	14	6	14	53	52	48
Duisburg	34	12	9	13	44	49	45
Cologne	34	13	5	16	62	62	44
Moenchengladbach	34	12	7	15	46	48	43
Schalke	34	11	10	13	35	40	43
Hamburg	34	10	11	13	46	60	41
Bielefeld	34	11	7	16	46	54	40
Hansa Rostock	34	11	7	16	35	46	40
Dusseldorf*	34	9	6	19	26	57	33
Freiburg*	34	8	5	21	43	67	29
St Pauli*	34	7	6	21	32	69	27

Top scorer: Kirsten (Leverkusen) 22.
Cup Final: Stuttgart 2, Cottbus 0.

GREECE

Federation Hellenique De Football, Singrou Avenue 137, Athens.
Founded: 1926; *Number of Clubs:* 4,050; *Number of Players:* 180,000; *National Colours:* White shirts, blue shorts, white stockings.
Telephone: 0030 1 933 88 50; *Cable:* FOOTBALL ATHENES; *Telex:* 215328 epo gr; *Fax:* 0030 1 935 96 66.

International matches 1996
Israel (h) 2-1, France (a) 1-3, Portugal (a) 0-1, Slovenia (h) 2-0, Georgia (h) 2-1, Albania (h) 2-1, Bosnia (h) 3-0, Denmark (a) 1-2, Croatia (a) 1-1.

League Championship wins (1928–97)
Olympiakos 26; Panathinaikos 18; AEK Athens 11; Aris Salonika 3; PAOK Salonika 2; Larissa 1.

Cup wins (1932–97)
Olympiakos 20; Panathinaikos 16; AEK Athens 11; PAOK Salonika 2; Aris Salonika 1; Ethnikos 1; Iraklis 1; Panionios 1; Kastoria 1; Larissa 1; Ofi Crete 1.

Final League Table 1996–97

	P	W	D	L	F	A	Pts
Olympiakos	34	26	6	2	72	14	84
AEK Athens	34	22	6	6	75	28	72
PAOK Salonika	34	19	9	6	53	28	66
Ofi Crete	34	20	6	8	51	28	66
Panathinaikos	34	20	4	10	60	25	64
Kavala	34	16	7	11	42	43	55
Paniliakos	34	13	6	15	39	49	45
Ionikos	34	12	8	14	40	47	44
Apollon	34	12	6	16	39	42	42
Veria	34	11	8	15	33	33	41
Kalamata	34	10	11	13	34	50	41
Xanthi	34	10	9	15	53	59	39
Panachaiki	34	9	12	13	31	38	39
Iraklis	34	11	6	17	41	54	39
Athinaikos	34	11	7	16	41	59	40
Aris Salonika*	34	9	11	14	32	48	35
Edessiakos*	34	7	7	20	38	61	28
Kastoria*	34	1	5	28	13	81	8

Aris 3 points deducted.
Top scorer: Alexandris (Olympiakos) 23.
Cup Final: AEK Athens 0, Panathinaikos 0.
AEK Athens won 5-3 on penalties.

HOLLAND

Koninklijke Nederlandsche Voetbalbond, Woudenbergseweg 56, Postbus 515, NL-3700 AM, Zeist.
Founded: 1889; *Number of Clubs:* 3,097; *Number of Players:* 962,397; *National Colours:* Orange shirts, white shorts, orange stockings.
Telephone: 00343 499211; *Cable:* VOETBAL ZEIST; *Telex:* 40497 knvb nl; *Fax:* 00343 491487.

International matches 1996
Germany (h) 0-1, China (h) 2-0, Eire (h) 3-1, Scotland (h) 0-0, Switzerland (h) 2-0, England (a) 1-4, France (a) 0-0, Brazil (h) 2-2, Wales (a) 3-1, Wales (h) 7-1, Belgium (a) 3-0.

League Championship wins (1898–97)
Ajax Amsterdam 26; Feyenoord 14; PSV Eindhoven 14; HVV The Hague 8; Sparta Rotterdam 6; Go Ahead Deventer 4; HBS The Hague 3; Willem II Tilburg 3; RCH Haarlem 2; RAP 2; Heracles 2; ADO The Hague 2; Quick The Hague 1; BVV Schiedam 1; NAC Breda 1; Eindhoven 1; Enschede 1; Volewijckers Amsterdam 1; Limburgia 1; Rapid JC Haarlem 1; DOS Utrecht 1; DWS Amsterdam 1; Haarlem 1; Be Quick Groningen 1; SVV Schiedam 1; AZ 67 Alkmaar 1.

Cup wins (1899–97)
Ajax Amsterdam 12; Feyenoord 10; PSV Eindhoven 8; Quick The Hague 4; AZ 67 Alkmaar 3; Rotterdam 3; DFC 2; Fortuna Geleen 2; Haarlem 2; HBS The Hague 2; RCH 2; VOC 2; Wageningen 2; Willem II Tilburg 2; FC Den Haag 2; Concordia Rotterdam 1; CVV 1; Eindhoven 1; HVV The Hague 1; Longa 1; Quick Nijmegen 1; RAP 1; Roermond 1; Schoten 1; Velocitas Breda 1; Velocitas Groningen 1; VSV 1; VUC 1; VVV Groningen 1; ZFC 1; NAC Breda 1; Twente Enschede 1; Utrecht 1; Roda 1.

Final League Table 1996–97

	P	W	D	L	F	A	Pts
PSV Eindhoven	34	24	5	5	90	26	77
Feyenoord	34	22	7	5	67	34	73
Twente	34	20	5	9	60	33	65
Ajax	34	17	10	7	55	31	61
Vitesse	34	15	10	9	53	41	55
Roda JC	34	16	7	11	56	47	55
Heerenveen	34	13	11	10	58	47	50
De Graafschap	34	13	6	15	52	55	45
NAC Breda	34	10	10	14	41	54	40
Groningen	34	9	12	13	43	56	39
Fortuna Sittard	34	9	12	13	36	52	39
Utrecht	34	8	14	12	42	52	38
Sparta	34	11	5	18	41	57	38
Volendam	34	9	11	14	36	55	38
Willem II	34	9	8	17	34	50	35
RKC Waalwijk+	34	8	7	18	39	61	34
NEC Nijmegen+	34	7	11	16	35	61	32
AZ*	34	6	7	21	27	52	25

Top scorer: Nilis (PSV Eindhoven) 21.
Cup Final: Roda 4, Heerenveen 2.

HUNGARY

Magyar Labdarugo Szovetseg, Hungarian Football Federation, Nepkoztarsasag Utja 47, H-1061 Budapest VI.
Founded: 1901; *Number of Clubs:* 1944; *Number of Players:* 95,986; *National Colours:* Red shirts, white shorts, green stockings.
Telephone: 0036 1 252 92 96; *Cable:* MLSZ BUDAPEST; *Telex:* 225782 misz h; *Fax:* 0036 1 252 99 86.

International matches 1996
Croatia (h) 1-4, Austria (h) 0-2, England (a) 0-3, Italy (h) 0-2, UAR (h) 3-1, Finland (h) 1-0, Norway (a) 0-3, Azerbaijan (a) 3-0.

League Championship wins (1901–97)
Ferencvaros 26; MTK-VM Budapest 20; Ujpest Dozsa 19; Honved 13; Vasas Budapest 6; Csepel 4; Raba Gyor 3; BTC 2; Nagyvarad 1; Vac 1.

Cup wins (1910–97)
Ferencvaros 17; MTK-VM Budapest 10; Ujpest Dozsa 8; Raba Gyor 4; Kispest Honved 4; Vasas Budapest 3; Diösgyör 2; Bocskai 1; III Ker 1; Kispesti AC 1; Soroksar 1; Szolnoki MAV 1; Siofok Banyasz 1; Bekescsaba 1; Pecs 1.
Cup not regularly held until 1964.

Final League Table 1996–97

	P	W	D	L	F	A	Pts
MTK	34	26	7	1	86	25	85
Ujpest	34	23	7	4	75	35	76
Ferencvaros	34	22	8	4	69	37	74
Vasas	34	20	6	8	50	31	66
Debrecen	34	14	10	10	55	38	52
BVSC	34	14	7	13	43	36	49
Kispest Honved	34	12	9	13	42	44	45
Videoton	34	10	12	12	45	44	42
Gyori	34	10	12	12	44	51	42
Haladas	34	10	10	14	39	42	40
Vac	34	10	10	14	40	47	40
Siofok	34	10	10	14	36	53	40
Zalaegerszeg	34	11	7	16	34	51	40
Bekescsaba	34	10	6	18	37	62	36
Ker	34	8	11	15	45	55	35
Stadler	34	7	7	20	27	50	28
Csepel*	34	5	10	19	43	70	25
Pecs*	34	6	7	21	29	68	25

Stadler relegated for corruption.
Top scorer: Illes (MTK) 23.
Cup Final: MTK 6, 2, BVSC 0, 0.

ICELAND

Knattspyrnusamband Island, P.O. Box 8511, 128 Reykjavik.
Founded: 1929; *Number of Clubs:* 73; *Number of Players:* 23,673; *National Colours;* Blue shirts, white shorts, blue stockings.
Telephone: 00354 1 81 44 44; *Cable* KSI REYKJAVIK; *Telex:* 2314 isi is; *Fax:* 00354 1 68 97 93.

International matches 1996
Slovenia (a) 1-7, Russia (h) 0-3, Malta (a) 4-1, Estonia (h) 3-0, Macedonia (h) 1-1, Cyprus (h) 2-1, Czech Republic (a) 1-2, Lithuania (a) 0-2, Romania (h) 0-4, Eire (a) 0-0.

League Championship wins (1912–96)
KR 20; Valur 19; Fram 18; IA Akranes 17; Vikingur 5; IBK Keflavik 3; IBV Vestmann 2; KA Akureyri 1.

Cup wins (1960–96)
KR 9; Valur 8; Fram 7; IA Akranes 6; IBV Vestmann 3; IBA Akureyri 1; Vikingur 1; IBK Keflavik 1.

Final League Table 1996

	P	W	D	L	F	A	Pts
IA Akranes	18	13	1	4	46	19	40
KR	18	11	4	3	38	16	37
Leiftur	18	8	5	5	33	28	29
IBV	18	8	1	9	29	32	25
Valur	18	7	3	8	23	25	24
Stjarnan	18	6	5	7	25	32	23
Grindavik	18	5	4	9	23	34	19
IBK	18	4	7	7	16	28	19
Fylkir*	18	5	3	10	26	30	18
UBK*	18	3	7	8	19	34	16

Top scorer: Dadason (KR) 14.
Cup Final: IA Akranes 2, IBV 1.

REPUBLIC OF IRELAND

The Football Association of Ireland, (Cumann Peile Na H-Eireann), 80 Merrion Square, South Dublin 2.
Founded: 1921; *Number of Clubs:* 3,190; *Number of Players:* 124,615; *National Colours:* Green shirts, white shorts, green stockings.
Telephone: 00353 1 676 68 64; *Cable:* SOCCER DUBLIN; *Telex:* 91397 fai ei; *Fax:* 00353 1 661 09 31.

League Championship wins (1922–97)
Shamrock Rovers 15; Dundalk 9; Shelbourne 8; Bohemians 7; Waterford 6; Cork United 5; Drumcondra 5; St Patrick's Athletic 5; St James's Gate 2; Cork Athletic 2; Sligo Rovers 2; Limerick 2; Athlone Town 2; Derry City 2; Dolphin 1; Cork Hibernians 1; Cork Celtic 1; Cork City 1.

Cup wins (1922–97)
Shamrock Rovers 24; Dundalk 8; Drumcondra 5; Bohemians 5; Shelbourne 5; Cork Athletic 2; Cork United 2; St James's Gate 2; St Patrick's Athletic 2; Cork Hibernians 2; Limerick 2; Waterford 2; Derry City 2; Athlone Town 2; Sligo 2; Alton United 1; Cork 1; Fordsons 1; Transport 1; Finn Harps 1; Home Farm 1; UCD 1; Bray Wanderers 1; Galway United 1.

Final League Table 1996–97

	P	W	D	L	F	A	Pts
Derry City	33	19	10	4	58	27	67
Bohemians	33	16	9	8	43	32	57
Shelbourne	34	15	9	10	54	39	54
Cork City	33	15	9	9	38	24	54
St Patrick's Ath	33	13	14	6	45	33	53
Sligo Rovers	33	12	11	10	43	43	47
Shamrock Rovers	33	10	13	10	43	46	43
UCD	33	12	7	14	34	39	43
Finn Harps	34	11	9	14	44	45	42
Dundalk	33	9	9	15	32	50	36
Bray Wanderers*	33	5	8	20	30	59	23
Home Farm*	33	3	10	20	26	53	19

Top scorers: Cousins (Shamrock Rovers) 16, Geoghegan (Shelbourne) 16.
Cup Final: Shelbourne 2, Derry City 0.

ISRAEL

Israel Football Association, 12 Carlibach Street, P.O. Box 20188, Tel Aviv 61201.
Founded: 1928; *Number of Clubs:* 544; *Number of Players:* 30,449; *National Colours:* White shirts, blue shorts, white stockings.
Telephone: 00972 3 570 59 99; *Cable:* CADUREGEL TEL AVIV; *Fax:* 00972 3 570 20 44.

International matches 1996
Greece (a) 1-2, Lithuania (h) 4-2, Croatia (a) 0-2, South Korea (h) 4-5, Romania (a) 0-2, Bulgaria (h) 2-1, Russia (h) 1-1, Cyprus (a) 0-2, Luxembourg (h) 1-0.

League Championship wins (1932–97)
Maccabi Tel Aviv 18; Hapoel Tel Aviv 12; Hapoel Petah Tikva 6; Maccabi Haifa 5; Maccabi Netanya 5; Beitar Jerusalem 3; Hakoah Ramat Gan 2; Hapoel Beersheba 2; Bnei Yehouda 1; British Police 1; Hapoel Kfar Sava 1; Hapoel Ramat Gan 1.

Cup wins (1928–97)
Maccabi Tel Aviv 19; Hapoel Tel Aviv 9; Beitar Jerusalem 5; Maccabi Haifa 4; Hapoel Haifa 3; Hapoel Kfar Sava 3; Beitar Tel Aviv 2; Bnei Yehouda 2; Hakoah Ramat Gan 2; Hapoel Petah Tikva 2; Maccabi Petah Tikva 2; British Police 1; Hapoel Jerusalem 1; Hapoel Lod 1; Maccabi Netanya 1; Hapoel Beersheba 1.

Final League Table 1996–97

	P	W	D	L	F	A	Pts
Beitar Jerusalem	30	21	6	3	62	20	69
Hapoel Petah Tikva	30	18	6	6	57	37	60
Hapoel Beersheba	30	19	3	8	44	25	60
Maccabi Petah Tikva	30	14	10	6	39	22	52
Maccabi Haifa	30	13	9	8	48	34	48
Maccabi Tel Aviv	30	13	7	10	47	34	46
Hapoel Haifa	30	12	7	11	34	33	43
Hapoel Kfar Sabah	30	11	7	12	34	39	40
Ironi Rishon	30	11	7	12	35	47	40
Bnei Yehuda	30	10	8	12	32	40	38
Hapoel Beit Shean	30	9	7	14	29	34	34
Hapoel Jerusalem	30	9	7	14	30	41	34
Hapoel Tel Aviv	30	8	9	13	29	32	33
Maccabi Herzliya	30	9	5	16	19	28	32
Zafirim Holon*	30	4	9	17	17	43	21
Hapoel Taibe*	30	4	3	23	19	66	15

Top scorer: Kakoun (Hapoel Petah Tikva) 21.
Cup Final: Hapoel Beersheba 1, Maccabi Tel Aviv 0.

ITALY

Federazione Italiana Giuoco Calcio, Via Gregorio Allegri 14, C.P. 2450, I-00198, Roma.
Founded: 1898; *Number of Clubs:* 20,961; *Number of Players:* 1,420,160; *National Colours:* Blue shirts, white shorts, blue stockings, white trim.
Telephone: 0039 6 849 11 11; *Cable:* FEDERCALCIO ROMA; *Telex:* 611483 calcio i; *Fax:* 0039 6 849 12 526.

International matches 1996
Wales (h) 3-0, Belgium (h) 2-2, Hungary (a) 2-0, Russia (h) 2-1, Czech Republic (a) 1-2, Germany (a) 0-0, Moldova (a) 3-1, Bosnia (a) 1-2, Georgia (h) 1-0.

League Championship wins (1898–1997)
Juventus 24; AC Milan 15; Inter-Milan 13; Genoa 9; Torino 8; Pro Vercelli 7; Bologna 7; Fiorentina 2; Napoli 2; AS Roma 2; Casale 1; Novese 1; Cagliari 1; Lazio 1; Verona 1; Sampdoria 1.

Cup wins (1922–97)
Juventus 9; AS Roma 8; Fiorentina 5; Torino 4; AC Milan 4; Sampdoria 4; Inter-Milan 3; Napoli 3; Bologna 2; Atalanta 1; Genoa 1; Lazio 1; Vado 1; Venezia 1; Parma 1; Vicenza 1.

Final League Table 1996–97

	P	W	D	L	F	A	Pts
Juventus	34	17	14	3	51	24	65
Parma	34	18	9	7	41	26	63
Internazionale	34	15	14	5	51	35	59
Lazio	34	15	10	9	54	37	55
Udinese	34	15	9	10	53	41	54
Sampdoria	34	14	11	9	60	46	53
Bologna	34	13	10	11	50	44	49
Vicenza	34	12	11	11	43	38	47
Fiorentina	34	10	15	9	46	41	45
Atalanta	34	11	11	12	44	46	44
AC Milan	34	11	10	13	43	45	43
Roma	34	10	11	13	46	47	41
Napoli	34	9	14	11	38	45	41
Cagliari+	34	9	10	15	45	55	37
Perugia*	34	10	7	17	48	62	37
Piacenza+	34	7	16	11	29	45	37
Verona*	34	6	9	19	38	64	27
Reggiana*	34	2	13	19	28	67	19

Top scorer: Inzaghi (Atalanta) 24.
Cup Final: Napoli 1, 0, Vicenza 0, 3.

LATVIA

Latvian Football Federation, Augsiela, 1, LV-1009, Riga.
Founded: 1921; *Number of Clubs:* 50; *Number of Players:* 12,000.
National Colours: Carmine red shirts, white shorts, carmine red stockings.
Telephone: 00371 2 29 29 88; *Telex:* 161183 ritm su; *Fax:* 00371 8 82 83 31.
Cable: Augsiela 1, LV–1009, Riga.

International matches 1996
Estonia (a) 1-1, Lithuania (a) 1-2, Finland (h) 0-0, Sweden (h) 1-1, Scotland (h) 0-2, Belarus (a) 1-1, Austria (a) 1-2.

League Championship wins (1922–96)
ASK Riga 9; RFK Riga 8; Olympia Liepaya 7; Sarkanais Metalurgs Liepaya 7; VEF Riga 6; Skonto Riga 6; Energija Riga 4; Elektrons Riga 3; Torpedo Riga 3; Daugava Liepaya 2; ODO Riga 2; Khimikis Daugavpils 2; RAF Yelgava 2; Keisermezhs Riga 2; Dinamo Riga 1; Zhmilyeva Team 1; Darba Rezervi 1; REZ Riga 1; Start Brotseni 1; Venta Ventspils 1; Yurnieks Riga 1; Alfa Riga 1; Gauya Valmiera 1.

Cup wins (1937–96)
Elektrons Riga 7; Sarkanais Metalurgs Liepaya 5; ODO Riga 3; VEF Riga 3; ASK Riga 3; Tseltnieks Riga 3; RAF Yelgava 3; RFK Riga 2; Daugava Liepaya 2; Start Brotseni 2; Selmash Liepaya 2; Yurnieks Riga 2; Khimikis Daugavpils 2; Skonto Riga 2; Rigas Vilki 1; Dinamo Liepaya 1; Dinamo Riga 1; REZ Riga 1; Voulkan Kouldiga 1; Baltija Liepaya 1; Venta Ventspils 1; Pilot Riga 1; Lielupe Yurmala 1; Energija Riga 1; Torpedo Riga 1; Daugava SKIF Riga 1; Tseltnieks Daugavpils 1; Olympia Riga 1.

Final League Table 1996
Group A (for 1-6 places)

	P	W	D	L	F	A	Pts
Skonto Riga	28	23	4	1	98	12	73
Daugava Riga	28	18	7	3	61	18	61
Dinaburg Daugavpils	28	13	8	7	53	31	47
Universitate Riga	28	11	6	11	37	45	39
Baltika Liepaja	28	11	5	12	32	44	38
Starts Brotseni	28	6	5	17	26	69	23

Group B (for 7–10 places)

	P	W	D	L	F	A	Pts
Lokomotive Daugavpils	30	10	9	11	38	45	39
Vairogs Rezekne	30	9	6	15	37	54	33
Skonto/Metals Riga	30	7	6	17	25	53	27
Yurnieks Riga	30	4	8	18	25	61	20

Top scorer: Mikholap (Daugava Riga) 33.
Cup Final: RAF Yelgava 2, Skonto Riga 1
RAF Yelgava now called Universitate Riga.

LIECHTENSTEIN

Liechtensteiner Fussball-Verband, Altenbach 11, Postfach 165, 9490 Vaduz.
Founded: 1933; *Number of Clubs:* 7; *Number of Players:* 1,247; *National Colours:* Blue & red shirts, red shorts, blue stockings.
Telephone: 004175 237 4747; *Cable:* FUSSBALLVERBAND VADUZ; *Fax:* 004175 237 4748.

International matches 1996
Macedonia (a) 0-3, Germany (a) 1-9, Eire (h) 0-5, Lithuania (a) 1-2, Macedonia (h) 1-11.
Liechtenstein has no national league. Teams compete in Swiss regional leagues.

Cup wins (1946–96)
Vaduz 26; Balzers 11; Triesen 8; Eschen/Mauren 4; Schaan 2.
Cup Final: Balzers 3, Vaduz 2.

LITHUANIA

Lithuanian Football Federation, Seimyniskiu str. 15, 2051 Vilnius. Championship of 14 teams.
Number of Clubs: 20; *Number of Players:* 16,600.
Telephone: 00370 2/723654/58; *Telex:* 0539-261518 lsr; *Fax:* 00370 2/723651.

International matches 1996
Israel (a) 2-4, Latvia (h) 2-1, Estonia (a) 1-1, Belarus (a) 2-2, Ukraine (a) 2-5, Romania (a) 0-3, Iceland (h) 2-0, Liechtenstein (h) 2-1, Brazil (a) 1-3, Indonesia (h) 4-0.

League Championship wins (1922–96)
Kovas Kaunas 6; KSS Klaipeda 6; LFLS Kaunas 4; Zalgiris Vilnius 3; LGSF Kaunas 2; MSK Kaunas 1; Ekranas Panevezys 1; Romar Mazeikiai 1; Inkaras Grifas 1.

Cup wins (1992–97)
Zalgiris Vilnius 3; Inkaras 1; Kareda 1.

Final Table 1996–97

	P	W	D	L	F	A	Pts
Kareda	28	19	7	2	61	12	64
Zalgiris	28	17	5	6	56	19	56
Inkarus	28	15	8	5	41	19	53
Kaunas	28	12	5	11	33	31	41
Ekranas	28	8	10	10	28	32	34
Panerys	28	6	8	14	20	40	26
Atlantas	28	4	6	18	21	66	18
Volmeta*	28	3	7	18	19	60	16

Top scorer: Pocius (Kareda) 14

LUXEMBOURG

Federation Luxembourgeoise De Football, (F.L.F.), 50, Rue De Strasbourg, L-2560, Luxembourg.
Founded: 1908; *Number of Clubs:* 126; *Number of Players:* 21,684; *National Colours:* Red shirts, white shorts, blue stockings.
Telephone: 00352 48 86 65; *Cable:* FOOTBALL LUXEMBOURG; *Telex:* 2426 flf lu; *Fax:* 00352 40 02 01.

International matches 1996
Morocco (a) 0-2, Switzerland (h) 1-1, Bulgaria (h) 1-2, Russia (h) 0-4, Israel (a) 0-1.

League Championship wins (1910–97)
Jeunesse Esch 24; Spora Luxembourg 11; Stade Dudelange 10; Avenir Beggen 7; Red Boys Differdange 6; US Hollerich-Bonnevoie 5; Fola Esch 5; US Luxembourg 5; Aris Bonnevoie 3; Progres Niedercorn 3.

Cup wins (1922–97)
Red Boys Differdange 16; US Luxembourg 10; Jeunesse Esch 10; Spora Luxembourg 8; Avenir Beggen 6; Stade Dudelange 4; Progres Niedercorn 4; Fola Esch 3; Alliance Dudelange 2; US Rumelange 2; Aris Bonnevoie 1; US Dudelange 1; Jeunesse Hautcharage 1; National Schiffige 1; Racing Luxembourg 1; SC Tetange 1; Hesperange 1, Grevenmacher 1.

Final Table 1996–97

	P	W	D	L	F	A	Pts
Jeunesse Esch	22	17	5	0	56	11	56
Grevenmacher	22	15	5	2	56	20	50
Union	22	10	8	4	44	23	38
Avenir Beggen	22	11	5	6	45	27	38
FC Wiltz 71	22	11	3	8	32	40	36
Sporting Mertzig	22	8	8	6	45	39	32
Hobscheid	22	7	5	10	23	42	26
Spora	22	6	5	11	33	40	23
F91 Dudelange	22	6	4	12	27	43	22
Rumelange	22	5	3	14	33	59	18
Rodange*	22	4	4	14	25	42	16
Aris*	22	2	5	15	22	55	11

Top scorers: Iovino (FC Wiltz 71) 19, Zaritski (Sporting Mertzig) 19.
Cup Final: Jeunesse Esch 2, Union 0.

MACEDONIA

Football Association of the Former Yugoslav Republic of Macedonia, VIII-ma Udarna Brigada 31A, MAC-91000Skopje.
Telephone: 00389 1 22 90 42; *Fax:* 00389 1 23 54 48.

International matches 1996

Malta (h) 1-0, Liechtenstein (h) 3-0, Bulgaria (a) 0-3, Iceland (a) 1-1, Eire (a) 0-3, Liechtenstein (a) 11-1, Malta (h) 0-2, Romania (h) 0-3.

League Championship wins (1993-97)

Vardar 3; Sileks 2.

Cup wins (1993-97)

Vardar 2; Sileks 1.

Final Table 1996–97

	P	W	D	L	F	A	Pts
Sileks	26	19	5	2	83	23	62
Pobeda	26	17	3	6	55	26	54
Vardar	26	12	10	4	33	12	46
Sloga	26	11	7	8	38	29	40
Makedonia	26	11	4	11	39	28	37
Sasa	26	10	7	9	36	32	37
Belasica	26	9	7	10	32	40	34
Balkan	26	8	9	9	31	26	33
Pelister	26	9	6	11	36	35	33
Bregalnica	26	9	6	11	29	33	33
Tikves	26	8	8	10	33	39	32
Semertanica	26	8	5	13	32	39	29
Skendia	26	8	5	13	27	48	29
Rudar	26	2	2	22	18	110	8

Top scorer: Micevski (Sileks) 18.
Cup Final: Sileks 4, Sloga 1.

MALTA

Malta Football Association, 280 St. Paul Street, Valletta.
Founded: 1900; *Number of Clubs:* 252; *Number of Players:* 5,544; *National Colours:* Red shirts, white shorts, red stockings.
Telephone: 00356 22 26 97; *Cable:* FOOTBALL MALTA VALLETTA; *Telex:* 1752 malfa mw; *Fax:* 00356 24 51 36.

International matches 1996

Russia (a) 0-2, Slovenia (h) 0-0, Iceland (h) 1-4, Macedonia (a) 0-1, Yugoslavia (a) 0-6, Czech Republic (a) 0-6, Slovakia (a) 0-6, UAR (a) 1-1, UAR (a) 0-0, Macedonia (a) 2-0, Spain (h) 0-3.

League Championship wins (1910–97)

Floriana 25; Sliema Wanderers 23; Valletta 15; Hibernians 8; Hamrun Spartans 7; Rabat Ajax 2; St George's 1; KOMR 1.

Cup wins (1935–96)

Floriana 18; Sliema Wanderers 17; Valletta 8; Hamrun Spartans 6; Hibernians 5; Gzira United 1; Melita 1; Zurrieq 1; Rabat Ajax 1.

Final League Table 1996–97

	P	W	D	L	F	A	Pts
Valletta	27	21	4	2	80	22	67
Birkirkara	27	18	6	3	46	21	60
Floriana	27	16	5	6	56	28	63
Silema Wanderers	27	14	4	9	58	30	46
Hamrun Spartans	27	12	3	12	46	40	39
Hibernians	27	10	7	10	39	38	37
Pieta Hotspurs	27	11	3	13	35	41	36
Naxxar Lions	27	5	7	15	18	45	22
Rabat Ajax*	27	5	3	19	32	73	18
Lija Athletic*	27	2	0	25	22	94	6

Top scorer: Doncic (Valletta) 32.
Cup Final: Valletta 2, Hibernians 0.

MOLDOVA

Moldavian Football Federation, Bd Stefan cel Mare 73, 277001 Chisinau, Moldavia.
Number of Clubs: 143; *Number of Players:* 75,000.
Telephone: 00373 2 22 12 95. *Fax:* 00373 2 22 22 44. *Telex:* 64163218.

International matches 1996

Ukraine (h) 2-2, Romania (a) 1-3, Turkey (a) 0-2, England (h) 0-3, Italy (h) 1-3, Indonesia (h) 2-1, Poland (a) 1-2.

League Championship wins (1992–97)

Zimbru Chisinau 5; Constructorul 1.

Cup wins (1992–97)

Tiligul 4; Combat 1; Zimbru Chisinau 1.

Final League Table 1996–97

	P	W	D	L	F	A	Pts
Constructorul	30	26	3	1	82	10	81
Zimbru Chisinau	30	22	4	4	112	21	70
Tiligul	30	20	8	2	73	12	68
Otaci	30	19	6	5	58	21	63
Olimpia	30	18	6	6	75	34	60
Sperante	30	10	9	11	34	36	42
Locomotiva	30	12	5	13	44	58	41
Bender	30	12	5	13	42	45	41
Unisport	30	12	5	13	40	44	41
Codru+	30	12	4	14	43	48	40
Agro+	30	11	3	16	53	47	36
Victoria	30	7	8	15	33	61	29
MHM 93*	30	6	7	17	32	53	25
Ciuhur*	30	6	7	17	20	97	24
Spumante*	30	3	4	23	21	44	13
Attila*	30	1	1	28	10	141	4

Codru three points deducted.

Top scorer: Rogaciov (Olimpia) 35.
Cup Final: Zimbru Chisinau 0, Otaci 0.
Zimbru Chisinau won 7-6 on penalties.

NORTHERN IRELAND

Irish Football Association Ltd, 20 Windsor Avenue, Belfast BT9 6EG.
Founded: 1880; *Number of Clubs:* 1,555; *Number of Players:* 24,558; *National Colours:* Green shirts, white shorts, green stockings.
Telephone: 01232 66 94 58/59; *Cable:* FOOTBALL BELFAST; *Telex:* 747317 ifa ni g; *Fax:* 01232 66 76 20.

NORWAY

Norges Fotballforbund Ullevaal Stadion, Postboks 3823, Ulleval Hageby, 0805 Oslo 8.
Founded: 1902; *Number of Clubs:* 1,810; *Number of Players:* 300,000; *National Colours:* Red shirts, white shorts, blue & white stockings.
Telephone: 0047 22 95 10 00; *Cable* FOTBALLFOR-BUND OSLO; *Telex:* 71722 nff n; *Fax:* 0047 22 95 10 10.
International matches 1996
Spain (a) 0-1, Northern Ireland (a) 2-0, Spain (h) 0-0, Azerbaijan (h) 5-0, Georgia (h) 1-0, Hungary (h) 3-0, Switzerland (a) 1-0.

League Championship wins (1938–96)

Rosenborg Trondheim 10; Fredrikstad 9; Viking Stavanger 8; Lillestroem 6; Valerengen 4; Larvik Turn 3; Brann Bergen 2; Lyn Oslo 2; IK Start 2; Friedig 1; Fram 1; Skeid Oslo 1; Strömsgodset Drammen 1; Moss 1.

Cup wins (1902–96)

Odds Bk Skien 11; Fredrikstad 10; Lyn Oslo 8; Skeid

Oslo 8; Sarpsborg FK 6; Rosenborg Trondheim 6; Brann Bergen 5; Orn F Horten 4; Lillestroem 4; Viking Stavanger 4; Strömsgodset Drammen 4; Frigg 3; Mjondalens F 3; Bodo-Glimt 2; Mercantile 2; Tromso 2; Grane Nordstrand 1; Kvik Halden 1; Sparta 1; Gjovik 1; Valerengen 1; Moss 1; Byrne 1, Molde 1.
(Known as the Norwegian Championship for HM The King's Trophy).

Final League Table 1996

	P	W	D	L	F	A	Pts
Rosenborg	26	18	5	3	82	26	59
Lillestrom	26	13	7	6	54	33	46
Viking	26	12	7	7	50	32	43
Brann	26	11	9	6	64	50	42
Tromso	26	11	8	7	46	41	41
Stabaek	26	9	9	8	47	45	36
Kongsvinger	26	9	7	10	39	49	34
Molde	26	9	6	11	45	38	33
Skeid	26	10	2	14	33	59	32
Bodo-Glimt	26	9	4	13	44	49	31
Stromsgodset	26	8	5	13	40	59	29
Moss*	26	7	8	11	28	47	29
Valerengen*	26	6	10	10	31	41	28
Start*	26	5	3	18	37	71	18

Top scorer: Brattbakk (Rosenborg) 28.
Cup Final: Tromso 2, Bodo-Glimt 1.

POLAND

Federation Polonaise De Foot-Ball, Al. Ujazdowskie 22, 00-478 Warszawa.
Founded: 1923; *Number of Clubs:* 5,881; *Number of Players:* 317,442; *National Colours:* White shirts, red shorts, white & red stockings.
Telephone: 0048 22 6223398, 6211975; *Cable:* PEŻETPEEN WARSZAWA; *Telex:* 815320 pzpn pl; *Fax:* 0048 22 629 24 89.

International matches 1996
Japan (a) 0-5, Croatia (a) 1-2, Slovenia (h) 0-0, Belarus (h) 1-1, Russia (a) 0-2, Cyprus (h) 2-2, Germany (h) 0-2, UAR (h) 1-0, England (a) 1-2, Moldova (h) 2-1.

League Championship wins (1921–97)
Gornik Zabrze 14; Ruch Chorzow 13; Wisla Krakow 6; Legia Warsaw 6; Widzew Lodz 6; Lech Poznan 5; Pogon Lwow 4; Cracovia 3; Warta Poznan 2; Polonia Bytom 2; Stal Mielec 1; Garbarnia Krakow 1; Polonia Warsaw 1; LKS Lodz 1; Slask Wroclaw 1; Szombierki Bytom 1; Zaglebie Lubin 1.

Cup wins (1951–97)
Legia Warsaw 12; Gornik Zabrze 6; Zaglebie Sosnowiec 4; Lech Poznan 3; GKS Katowice 3; Ruch Chorzow 3; Slask Wroclaw 2; Gwardia Warsaw 1; LKS Lodz 1; Polonia Warsaw 1; Wisla Krakow 1; Stal Rzeszow 1; Arka Gdynia 1; Lechia Gdansk 1; Widzew Lodz 1; Miedz Legnica 1.

Final League Table 1996–97

	P	W	D	L	F	A	Pts
Widzew	34	25	6	3	74	21	81
Legia	34	24	5	5	66	27	77
Odra	34	16	7	11	51	44	55
Katowice	34	14	11	9	47	40	53
Amica	34	14	10	10	41	40	52
LKS Lodz	34	13	10	11	55	45	49
Zaglebie Lubin	34	13	10	11	44	38	49
Polonia	34	13	9	12	40	44	48
Stomil	34	12	8	14	45	46	44
Rakow	34	11	11	12	35	39	44
Lech	34	11	11	12	40	40	44
Wisla	34	11	9	13	33	42	42
Gornik Zabrze	34	11	8	15	40	45	41
Ruch	34	9	13	12	41	41	40
GKS*	34	11	7	16	36	43	40
Hutnik*	34	8	11	15	34	46	35
Slask*	34	6	6	22	24	56	24
Sokol*	34	5	6	23	18	67	21

Top scorer: Trzeciak (LKS Lodz) 18.
Cup Final: Legia 2, Katowice 0.

PORTUGAL

Federacao Portuguesa De Futebol, Praca De Alegria N.25, Apartado 21.100, P-1128, Lisboa Codex.
Founded: 1914; *Number of Clubs:* 204; *Number of Players:* 79,235; *National Colours:* Red shirts, white shorts, red stockings.

Telephone: 00351 1 347 59 34; *Cable:* FUTEBOL LIS-BOA; *Telex:* 13489 fpf p; *Fax:* 00351 1 346 72 31.

International matches 1996
France (a) 2-3, Germany (h) 1-2, Greece (h) 1-0, Eire (a) 1-0, Denmark (h) 1-1, Turkey (h) 1-0, Croatia (h) 3-0, Czech Repbulic (a) 0-1, Armenia (a) 0-0, Ukraine (a) 1-2, Albania (a) 3-0, Ukraine (h) 1-0, Germany (h) 0-0.

League Championship wins (1935–97)
Benfica 30; Sporting Lisbon 16; FC Porto 16; Belenenses 1.

Cup wins (1939–97)
Benfica 23; Sporting Lisbon 12; FC Porto 8; Boavista 5; Belenenses 3; Vitoria Setubal 2; Academica Coimbra 1; Leixoes Porto 1; Sporting Braga 1; Amadora 1.

Final League Table 1996–97

	P	W	D	L	F	A	Pts
Porto	34	27	4	3	80	24	85
Sporting Lisbon	34	22	6	6	55	19	72
Benfica	34	17	7	10	49	30	58
Braga	34	15	10	9	39	40	55
Guimaraes	34	15	8	11	51	46	53
Salgueiros	34	14	10	10	49	48	52
Boavista	34	12	13	9	62	39	49
Maritimo	34	13	8	13	39	38	47
Amadora	34	12	11	11	39	38	47
Chaves	34	12	10	12	39	45	46
Farense	34	10	12	12	34	34	42
Setubal	34	10	10	14	38	41	40
Belenenses	34	10	10	14	37	50	40
Leca	34	9	9	16	33	42	36
Rio Ave	34	8	11	15	35	42	35
Espinho*	34	9	6	19	26	56	33
Leiria*	34	8	6	20	25	53	30
Gil Vicente*	34	4	7	23	29	74	19

Top scorer: Jardel (Porto) 30.
Cup Final: Boavista 3, Benfica 2.

ROMANIA

Federatia Romana De Fotbal, Vasile Conta 16, Bucharest 70130.
Founded: 1908; *Number of Clubs:* 414; *Number of Players:* 22,920; *National Colours:* Yellow shirts, blue shorts, red stockings.
Telephone: 0040 1 617 33 43; *Cable:* SPORTROM BUCURESTI-FOTBAL; *Telex:* 10097 frf r; *Fax:* 0040 1 312 83 24

International matches 1996
Qatar (a) 3-2, Denmark (a) 2-2, Thailand (h) 3-0, Finland (h) 1-1, Denmark (h) 2-1, Yugoslavia (a) 0-1, Georgia (h) 5-0, Moldova (h) 3-1, France (a) 0-1, Bulgaria (a) 0-1, UAE (h) 1-2, Israel (h) 2-0, Lithuania (h) 3-0, Iceland (a) 4-0, Macedonia (a) 3-0.

League Championship wins (1910–97)
Steaua Bucharest 19; Dinamo Bucharest 14; Venus Bucharest 8; Chinezul Timisoara 6; UT Arad 6; Ripensia Temesvar 4; Uni Craiova 4; Petrolul Ploesti 3; Olimpia Bucharest 2; Colentina Bucharest 2; Arges Pitesti 2; ICO Oradea 2; Soc RA Bucharest 1; Prahova Ploesti 1; Coltea Brasov 1; Juventus Bucharest 1; Metalochimia Resita 1; Ploesti United 1; Unirea Tricolor 1; Rapid Bucharest 1.

Cup wins (1934–97)
Steaua Bucharest 19; Rapid Bucharest 9; Dinamo Bucharest 7; Uni Craiova 6; UT Arad 2; Ripensia Temesvar 2; Politehnica Timisoara 2; Petrolul Ploesti 2; ICO Oradeo 1; Metalochimia Resita 1; Stinta Cluj 1; CFR Turnu Severin 1; Chimia Ramnicu Vilcea 1; Jiul Petroseni 1; Progresul Bucharest 1; Progresul Oradea 1; Gloria Bistrita 1.

Final League Table 1996–97

	P	W	D	L	F	A	Pts
Steaua	34	23	4	7	86	40	73
National	34	20	5	9	68	37	65
Dinamo	34	18	5	11	56	34	59
Otelul	34	17	6	11	54	39	57
Bacau	34	16	5	13	42	41	53
Ceahlaul	34	15	7	12	51	50	52
Arges	34	14	8	12	46	37	50
Constanta	34	15	4	15	47	50	49
Rapid Bucharest	34	13	9	12	45	41	48
Petrolul	34	13	7	14	48	43	46
Uni Craiova	34	12	7	15	48	52	43
Sportul	34	12	6	16	36	52	42
Gloria	34	11	8	15	38	45	41
Uni Cluj	34	12	5	17	53	67	41
Jiul	34	12	5	17	33	61	41
Tirgoviste	34	11	5	18	32	55	38
Politehnica*	34	10	5	19	45	65	35
Brasov*	34	9	5	20	42	61	32

Top scorer: Ilie S (Steaua) 31.
Cup Final: Steaua 4, National 2.

RUSSIA

Football Union of Russia; Luzhnetskaya Naberezyhnaja, 8. SU-119270 Moscow. *Telephone:* 0070 95 248 08 34; *Telex:* 411287 priz su; *Fax:* 0070 502 220 20 37; *Founded:* 1992; *Number of Clubs:* 43,700; *Number of Players:* 2,170,000.

International matches 1996
Malta (h) 2-0, Iceland (a) 3-0, Slovenia (a) 3-1, Eire (a) 2-0, Belgium (a) 0-0, Qatar (a) 5-2, UAE (h) 1-0, Poland (h) 2-0, Italy (a) 1-2, Germany (a) 0-3, Czech Republic (a) 3-3, Brazil (h) 2-2, Cyprus (h) 4-0, Israel (a) 1-1, Luxembourg (a) 4-0.

League Championship wins (1945–96)
Spartak Moscow 15; Dynamo Kiev 13; Dynamo Moscow 11; CSKA Moscow 7; Torpedo Moscow 3; Dynamo Tbilisi 2; Dnepr Dnepropetrovsk 2; Saria Voroshilovgrad 1; Ararat Erevan 1; Dynamo Minsk 1; Zenit Leningrad 1; Spartak Vladikavkaz 1.

Cup wins (1936–97)
Spartak Moscow 11; Dynamo Kiev 10; Torpedo Moscow 7; Dynamo Moscow 7; CSKA Moscow 5; Donetsk Shaktyor 4; Lokomotiv Moscow 4; Dynamo Tbilisi 2; Ararat Erevan 2; Karpaty Lvov 1; SKA Rostov 1; Zenit Leningrad 1; Metallist Kharkov 1; Dnepr 1.

Final League Table 1996

	P	W	D	L	F	A	Pts
Vladikavkaz	34	22	6	6	64	35	72
Spartak Moscow	34	21	9	4	70	34	72
Volgograd	34	21	7	6	58	27	70
Dynamo Moscow	34	20	7	7	60	35	67
CSKA Moscow	34	20	6	8	58	35	66
Lokomotiv Moscow	34	15	10	9	46	31	55
Baltika	34	12	10	12	44	35	46
Novgorod	34	13	6	15	39	50	45
Krylia Sovekov	34	12	9	13	31	38	45
Zenit	34	13	4	17	32	37	43
Rostov	34	11	8	15	58	60	41
Torpedo Moscow	34	10	11	13	42	51	41
Chernomorets	34	11	6	17	38	51	39
Kamaz	34	10	6	18	43	57	36
Sotchi	34	10	6	18	38	57	36
Ekaterinbourg*	34	8	9	17	38	57	33
Tekstilchik Kamychin*	34	4	12	18	25	48	24
Lada*	34	4	6	24	18	64	18

Play-off for title: Spartak Moscow 2, Vladikavkaz 1.

*Top scorer:*Maslov (Rostov) 23.
Cup Final: Lokomotiv Moscow 2, Dynamo Moscow 0.

SAN MARINO

Federazione Sammarinese Giuoco Calcio, Viale Campo dei Giudei, 14; 47031-Rep. San Marino.
Founded: 1931; *Number of Clubs:* 17; *Number of Players:* 1,033; *Colours:* Blue and white.
Telephone: 0039549 99 05 15; *Cable:* FEDERCALCIO SAN MARINO; *Telex:* 0505284 cogmar; *Fax:* 0039549 99 23 48.

International matches 1996
Wales (a) 0-5, Wales (h) 0-6, Belgium (h) 0-3, Turkey (a) 0-7.

League Championship wins (1986–96)
Tre Fiori 4; Fiorita 2; Faetano 2; Domagnano 1; Montevito 1, Libertas 1.

Cup wins (1986–96)
Domagnano 4; Libertas 3; Faetano 1, Fiorita 1, Tre Fiori 1; Cosmos 1.

SCOTLAND

The Scottish Football Association Ltd, 6 Park Gardens, Glasgow G3 7YF.
Founded: 1873; *Number of Clubs:* 6,148; *Number of Players:* 135,474; *National Colours:* Dark blue shirts, white shorts, red stockings.
Telephone: 0141 332 6372; *Cable:* EXECUTIVE GLASGOW; *Telex:* 778904 sfa g; *Fax:* 0141 332 7559.

SLOVAKIA

Slovak Football Association, Junacka 6, 83280 Bratislava, Slovakia.
Number of Clubs: 2,140; *Number of Players:* 141,000.
Telephone: 0042 7 279 01 51; *Fax:* 0042 7 279 05 54.

International matches 1996
Bolivia (a) 0-2, Belarus (h) 4-0, Bulgaria (h) 0-0, Sweden (a) 1-2, Mexico (a) 2-5, Faeroes (a) 2-1, Malta (h) 6-0, Faeroes (h) 3-0, Spain (a) 1-4.

League Championship wins (1939-44; 1994–97)
Slovan Bratislava 7; Bystrica 1; OAP Bratislava 1; Kosice 1.

Cup wins (1994–97)
Tatran Presov 1; Inter 1; Humenne 1; Slovan Bratislava 1.

Final League Table 1996–97

	P	W	D	L	F	A	Pts
Kosice	30	21	7	2	61	19	70
Spartak Trnava	30	21	6	3	66	24	69
Slovan Bratislava	30	15	5	10	49	33	50
Inter	30	13	9	8	35	35	48
Dukla Bystrica	30	13	5	12	48	37	44
Tatran Presov	30	12	7	11	37	38	43
Bardejov	30	11	7	12	34	36	40
Prievidza	30	10	7	13	41	43	37
Lokomotiv Kosice	30	8	13	9	27	31	37
Petrzalka	30	10	7	13	29	48	37
Zilina	30	11	3	16	29	34	36
Humenne	30	11	3	16	34	44	36
Tauris	30	11	3	16	31	46	36
Dunajska Streda	30	9	7	14	29	45	34
Kerametal	30	8	8	14	29	43	32
Nitra	30	5	5	20	22	48	20

Top scorer: Kozlej (Kosice) 22.
Cup Final: Slovan Bratislava 1, Tatran Presov 0 aet.

SLOVENIA

Football Association of Slovenia, P.P. 3986, 1001 Ljubljana, Slovenia.
Founded: 1992; *Number of Clubs:* 232; *Number of Players:* 15,048.
Telephone: 00386 61 133 40 63; *Fax:* 00386 61 30 23 37.

International matches 1996
Iceland (h) 7-1, Malta (a) 0-0, Russia (h) 1-3, Poland (a) 0-0, Greece (a) 0-2, UAE (h) 2-2, Denmark (h) 0-2, Bosnia (h) 1-2.

League Championship wins (1992–97)
SCT Olimpija 4; Gorica 1; Branik Maribor 1.

Cup wins (1992–97)
Branik Maribor 3; SCT Olimpija 2; Mura 1.

Final League Table 1996–97

	P	W	D	L	F	A	Pts
Branik Maribor	36	21	8	7	71	34	71
Primorje	36	19	9	8	64	25	66
Gorica	36	18	11	7	52	33	65
Publikum	36	12	11	13	55	61	47
Olimpija	36	11	12	13	54	52	45
Korotan	36	12	9	15	32	39	45
Mura	36	9	16	11	36	45	43
Rudar	36	10	12	14	43	53	42
Beltinci+	36	7	11	18	37	69	32
Koper*	36	8	7	21	28	61	31

Top scorer: Kamberovic (Publikum) 21.
Cup Final: Primorje 0, 0, Branik Maribor 0, 3.

SPAIN

Real Federacion Espanola De Futbol, Calle Alberto Bosch 13, Apartado Postal 347, E-28014 Madrid.
Founded: 1913; *Number of Clubs:* 10,240; *Number of Players:* 408,135; *National Colours:* Red shirts, dark blue shorts, black stockings, yellow trim.
Telephone: 0034 1 420 13 62; *Cable:* FUTBOL MADRID; *Telex:* 42420 rfef e; *Fax:* 0034 1 420 20 94.

International matches 1996
Norway (h) 1-0, Norway (a) 0-0, Bulgaria (h) 1-1, France (a) 1-1, Romania (h) 2-1, England (a) 0-0, Faeroes (a) 6-2, Czech Republic (a) 0-0, Slovakia (h) 4-1, Yugoslavia (h) 2-0, Malta (a) 3-0.

League Championship wins (1929-36; 1940–97)
Real Madrid 27; Barcelona 14; Atletico Madrid 9; Athletic Bilbao 8; Valencia 4; Real Sociedad 2; Real Betis 1; Seville 1.

Cup wins (1902–97)
Athletic Bilbao 23; Barcelona 23; Real Madrid 17; Atletico Madrid 9; Valencia 5; Real Zaragoza 4; Real Union de Irun 3; Seville 3; Espanol 2; Arenas 1; Ciclista Sebastian 1; Racing de Irun 1; Vizcaya Bilbao 1; Real Betis 1; Real Sociedad 1, La Coruna 1.

Final League Table 1996–97

	P	W	D	L	F	A	Pts
Real Madrid	42	27	11	4	85	36	92
Barcelona	42	28	6	8	102	48	90
Betis	42	21	14	7	81	46	77
La Coruna	42	21	14	7	57	30	77
Atletico Madrid	42	20	11	11	76	64	71
Athletic Bilbao	42	16	16	10	72	57	64
Valladolid	42	18	10	14	57	46	64
Real Sociedad	42	18	9	15	50	47	63
Tenerife	42	15	11	16	69	57	56
Valencia	42	15	11	16	63	59	56
Compostela	42	13	14	15	52	65	53
Espanyol	42	14	9	19	51	57	51
Santander	42	11	17	14	52	54	50
Zaragoza	42	12	14	16	58	66	50
Sporting Gijon	42	13	11	18	45	63	50
Celta	42	12	13	17	51	54	49
Oviedo	42	12	12	18	49	65	48
Rayo Vallecano+	42	13	6	23	43	62	45
Extremadura*	42	11	11	20	35	64	44
Sevilla*	42	12	7	23	50	69	43
Hercules*	42	12	5	25	40	77	41
Logrones*	42	9	6	27	33	85	33

Top scorer: Ronaldo (Barcelona) 34.
Cup Final: Barcelona 3, Betis 2.

SWEDEN

Svenska Fotbollfoerbundet, Box 1216, S-17123 Solna.
Founded: 1904; *Number of Clubs:* 3,250; *Number of Players:* 485,000; *National Colours:* Yellow shirts, blue shorts, yellow and blue stockings.
Telephone: 0046 8 735 09 00; *Cable:* FOOTBALL-S; *Telex:* 17711 fotboll s; *Fax:* 0046 8 27 51 47.

International matches 1996
Australia (h) 2-0, Japan (h) 1-1, Australia (a) 0-0, Northern Ireland (a) 2-1, Slovakia (h) 2-1, South Korea (a) 2-0, Belarus (h) 5-1, Denmark (h) 0-1, Latvia (a) 2-1, Austria (h) 0-1, Scotland (a) 0-1.

League Championship wins (1896–1996)
IFK Gothenburg 18; Oergryte IS Gothenburg 14; Malmo FF 14; IFK Norrköping 11; AIK Stockholm 9; Djurgaarden 8; GAIS Gothenburg 6; IF Helsingborg 5; Boras IF Elfsborg 4; Oster Vaxjo 4; Halmstad 2; Atvidaberg 2; IFK Ekilstune 1; IF Gavic Brynas 1; IF Gothenburg 1; Fassbergs 1; Norrköping IK Sleipner 1.

Cup wins (1941–96)
Malmo FF 13; IFK Norrköping 6; AIK Stockholm 6; IFK Gothenburg 4; Atvidaberg 2; Kalmar 2; GAIS Gothenburg 1; IF Helsingborg 1; Raa 1; Landskrona 1; Oster Vaxjo 1; Djurgaarden 1; Degerfors 1, Halmstad 1.

Final League Table 1996

	P	W	D	L	F	A	Pts
IFK Gothenburg	26	17	5	4	61	23	56
Malmo	26	13	7	6	33	26	46
Helsingborg	26	13	5	8	39	26	44
AIK	26	12	7	7	36	23	43
Orebro	26	13	3	10	34	29	42
Osters	26	10	6	10	37	39	36
Halmstad	26	9	8	9	34	37	35
Norrköping	26	9	7	10	31	29	34
Degefors	26	9	7	10	34	41	34
Orgryte	26	8	7	11	27	30	31
Umea*+	26	8	6	12	35	45	30
Trelleborg+	26	9	3	14	33	48	30
Djurgaarden*	26	8	3	15	28	43	27
Oddevold*	26	5	4	17	20	43	19

Top scorer: Andersson (IFK Gothenburg) 19.
Cup Final: AIK 2, Elfsborg 1.

SWITZERLAND

Schweizerisher Fussballverband. Haus des Schweizer Fussballs, Worbstrasse 48, 3074 Muri/BE. Mailing Address: PO Box 3000 Bern 15.
Founded: 1895; *Number of Clubs:* 1,473; *Number of Players:* 185,286; *National Colours:* Red shirts, white shorts, red stockings.
Telephone: 0041 31 950 81 11; *Cable:* SWISSFOOT BERNE; *Telex:* 912910 sfv ch; *Fax:* 0041 31 950 81 81.

International matches 1996
Luxembourg (a) 1-1, Austria (a) 0-1, Wales (h) 2-0, Czech Republic (h) 1-2, England (a) 1-1, Holland (a) 0-2, Scotland (a) 0-1, Azerbaijan (a) 0-1, Finland (a) 3-2, Norway (h) 0-1.

League Championship wins (1898–1997)
Grasshoppers 24; Servette 16; Young Boys Berne 11; FC Zurich 9; FC Basle 8; Lausanne 7; La Chaux-de-Fonds 3; FC Lugano 3; Winterthur 3; FX Aarau 3; Neuchatel Xamax 2; Sion 2; FC Anglo-American 1; St Gallen 1; FC Brühl 1; Cantonal-Neuchatel 1; Biel 1; Bellinzona 1; FC Etoile Le Chaux-de-Fonds 1; Lucerne 1.

Cup wins (1926–97)
Grasshoppers 18; FC Sion 9; Lausanne 7; La Chaux-de-Fonds 6; Young Boys Berne 6; Servette 6; FC Basle 5; FC Zurich 5; Lucerne 2; FC Lugano 2; FC Granges 1; St Gallen 1; Urania Geneva 1; Young Fellows Zurich 1; Aarau 1.

Qualifying Table 1996–97

	P	W	D	L	F	A	Pts
Nauchatel Xamax	22	12	8	2	37	21	44
Grasshoppers	22	10	9	3	42	19	39
Sion	22	9	10	3	31	17	37
Aarau	22	9	8	5	21	14	35
Lausanne	22	9	7	6	35	32	34
St Gallen	22	7	9	6	21	26	30
Zurich	22	6	9	7	24	25	27
Basle	22	5	10	7	32	33	25
Servette	22	5	9	8	24	25	24
Lucerne	22	4	11	7	28	33	23
Lugano*	22	2	9	11	14	32	15
Young Boys Berne*	22	3	3	16	17	39	12

Top scorer: Moldovan (Grasshoppers) 17.

Final Table 1996–97

	P	W	D	L	F	A	Pts
Sion	14	9	3	2	18	10	49
Neuchatel Xamax	14	6	6	2	22	14	46
Grasshoppers	14	7	4	3	37	18	45
Lausanne	14	8	2	4	20	16	43
Aarau	14	3	4	7	17	22	31
St Gallen	14	3	4	7	13	26	28
Zurich	14	1	7	6	9	18	24
Basle	14	3	2	9	16	28	24

Teams take half points from qualifying table.
Cup Final: Sion 3, Lucerne 3.
Sion won 5–4 on penalties.

Promotion/Relegation Table 1996–97

	P	W	D	L	F	A	Pts
Servette	14	7	4	3	18	10	25
Etoile Carouge	14	7	3	4	15	13	24
Lucerne	14	6	5	3	16	12	23
Kriens	14	6	4	4	22	16	22
Young Boys Berne	14	5	5	4	19	17	20
Soleure	14	3	5	6	9	17	14
Lugano	14	2	5	7	11	17	11
Schaffhausen	14	2	5	7	13	21	11

Top scorer: Moldovan (Grasshoppers) 10.

TURKEY

Federation Turque De Football, Konur Sokak No. 10, Ankara Kizilay.
Founded: 1923; *Number of Clubs:* 230; *Number of Players:* 64,521; *National Colours:* White shirts, white shorts, red and white stockings.
Telephone: 0090 212 282 70 10; *Cable:* FUTBOLSPOR ANKARA; *Fax:* 0090 212 282 70 15.

International matches 1996
Belarus (h) 3-2, Czech Republic (a) 0-3, Azerbaijan (a) 1-0, Ukraine (h) 3-2, Estonia (a) 0-0, Finland (a) 2-1, Croatia (a) 0-1, Portugal (a) 0-1, Denmark (a) 0-3, Moldova (h) 2-0, Belgium (a) 1-2, France (a) 0-4, San Marino (h) 7-0, Wales (a) 0-0.

League Championship wins (1960–97)
Fenerbahce 13; Galatasaray 11; Besiktas 10; Trabzonspor 6.

Cup wins (1963–97)
Galatasaray 11; Besiktas 5; Trabzonspor 5; Fenerbahce 4; Goztepe Izmir 2; Altay Izmir 2; Ankaragucu 2; Eskisehirspor 1; Bursapor 1; Genclerbirligi 1; Sakaryaspor 1; Kocaeli 1.

Final League Table 1996–97

	P	W	D	L	F	A	Pts
Galatasaray	34	25	7	2	90	29	82
Besiktas	34	22	8	4	88	26	74
Fenerbahce	34	22	7	5	78	25	73
Trabzonspor	34	22	6	6	73	33	72
Bursa	34	17	8	9	54	37	59
Istanbul	34	16	7	11	56	44	55
Kocaeli	34	12	12	10	37	35	48
Gaziantep	34	13	8	13	38	50	47
Samsun	34	12	9	13	49	52	45
Antalya	34	13	6	15	38	49	45
Genclerbirligi	34	11	6	17	37	48	39
Ankaragucu	34	10	8	16	39	52	38
Van	34	10	7	17	31	50	37
Altay	34	9	10	15	30	60	37
Dardanel	34	10	6	18	35	65	36
Sariyer*	34	9	7	18	41	54	34
Denizli*	34	5	5	24	36	81	20
Zeytinburnu*	34	2	5	27	26	86	11

Top scorer: Hakan Sukur (Galatasaray) 28.
Cup Final: Trabzonspor 1, 0, Kocaeli 1, 1.

UKRAINE

Football Federation of Ukraine, Ulianovyh Street 1, P.O. Box 503, 252150 Kiev, Ukraine.
Founded: 1992; *Number of Teams:* 30,460; *Number of Players:* 757,758.
Telephone: 0070 44 264 72 98, 2691793; *Fax:* 0070 44 264 75 64, 269 25 50; *Telex:* 0680 631461 UFF+.

International matches 1996
Moldova (a) 2-2, Turkey (a) 2-3, Lithuania (h) 5-2, Northern Ireland (a) 1-0, Portugal (h) 2-1, Portugal (a) 0-1.

League Championship wins (1992–97)
Dynamo Kiev 4; Tavria Simferopol 1.

Cup wins (1992–97)
Chernomorets 2; Dynamo Kiev 2; Shakhtjor Donetsk 2.

Final League Table 1996–97

	P	W	D	L	F	A	Pts
Dynamo Kiev	30	23	4	3	69	20	73
Donetsk	30	19	5	6	72	28	62
Vorskla	30	17	7	6	50	26	58
Dnepr	30	14	13	3	48	19	55
Karpaty	30	15	7	8	36	23	52
Simferopol	30	13	5	12	36	46	44
Chemomorets	30	12	6	12	36	31	42
Metallurg	30	12	5	13	48	44	41
Ternopol	30	11	6	13	34	37	39
Kirovograd	30	11	3	16	31	55	36
CSKA	30	9	8	13	33	35	35
Krivoj	30	9	6	15	24	48	33
Prekarpate	30	8	7	15	33	49	31
Torpedo	30	8	5	17	25	56	29
Kremen*	30	7	3	20	28	57	24
Vinnitsa*	30	4	6	20	19	48	18

Top scorer: Rebrov (Dynamo Kiev) 17.
Cup Final: Donetsk 1, Dnepr 0.

WALES

The Football Association of Wales Limited, Plymouth Chambers, 3 Westgate Street, Cardiff.
Founded: 1876; *Number of Clubs:* 2,326; *Number of Players:* 53,926; *National Colours:* All red. *Telephone:* 01222 372325; *Telex:* 497 363 faw g; *Fax:* 01222 343961.

YUGOSLAVIA

Yugoslav Football Association, P.O. Box 263, Terazije 35, 11000 Beograd.
Founded: 1919; *Number of Clubs:* 6,532; *Number of Players:* 229,024; *National Colours:* Blue shirts, white shorts, red stockings.
Telephone: 00381 11 323 3447, 323 4253; *Cable:* JUGO-FUDBAL BEOGRAD; *Telex:* 11666 sfj yu; *Fax:* 00381 11 323 3433.

International matches 1996
Romania (h) 1-0, Faeroes (h) 3-1, Mexico (a) 0-0, Japan (a) 0-1, Malta (h) 6-0, Faeroes (a) 8-1, Czech Republic (h) 1-0, Spain (a) 0-2, Argentina (a) 3-2.

League Championship wins (1923–97)
Red Star Belgrade 20; Partizan Belgrade 15; Hajduk Split 9; Gradjanski Zagreb 5; BSK Belgrade 5; Dynamo Zagreb 4; Jugoslavija Belgrade 2; Concordia Zagreb 2; FC Sarajevo 2; Vojvodina Novi Sad 2; HASK Zagreb 1; Zeljeznicar 1.

Cup wins (1947–97)
Red Star Belgrade 16; Hajduk Split 9; Dynamo Zagreb 8; Partizan Belgrade 7; BSK Belgrade 2; OFK Belgrade 2; Rijeka 2; Velez Mostar 2; Vardar Skopje 1; Borac Banjaluka 1.

Final League Table 1996–97
Group A

	P	W	D	L	F	A	Pts
Partizan Belgrade	33	26	6	1	88	17	84
Red Star Belgrade	33	25	3	5	77	30	78
Vojvodina	33	15	8	10	49	35	53
Hajduk	33	12	8	13	34	37	44
Proleter	33	12	6	15	48	49	42
Zemun	33	10	11	12	40	37	41
Cukaricki	33	11	8	14	35	46	41
Mladost L	33	12	5	16	45	59	41
Rad	33	10	10	13	33	38	40
Buducnost	33	11	6	16	26	44	39
Becej*	33	11	5	17	34	48	38
Borac*	33	4	2	27	22	91	14

Group B

	P	W	D	L	F	A	Pts
Obilic	33	25	4	4	65	16	79
Zeleznik	32	20	3	9	53	34	63
Loznica	33	20	1	12	48	25	61
Radnicki Nis	33	16	8	9	66	36	56
OFK Belgrade	33	16	8	9	44	28	56
Rudar	33	14	5	14	45	46	47
Buducnost V	33	12	7	14	42	48	43
Sutjeska	33	12	3	18	42	56	39
Kikinda	33	7	8	18	16	42	29
Spartak	32	8	5	19	26	59	29
Sloboda	33	7	7	19	28	52	28
Mladost BJ	33	5	11	17	23	56	26

Top scorer: Jovicic (Red Star Belgrade) 21.
Cup Final: Vojvodina 0, 0, Red Star 0, 1.

SOUTH AMERICA

ARGENTINA

Asociacion Del Futbol Argentina, Viamonte 1366/76, 1053 Buenos Aires.
Founded: 1893; *Number of Clubs:* 3,035; *Number of Players:* 306,365; *National Colours:* Blue & white shirts, black shorts, white stockings.
Telephone: 00541 404 276; *Cable:* FUTBOL BUENOS AIRES; *Telex:* 17848 AFA AR; *Fax:* 54-1 3754410.
League Champions 1996: Velez Sarsfield.

BOLIVIA

Edificio Federacion Boliviana De Futbol, Av. Libertador Bolivar No. 1148, Casilla de Correo 484, Cochabamba, Bolivia.
Founded: 1925; *Number of Clubs:* 305; *Number of Players:* 15,290; *National Colours:* Green shirts, white shorts, green stockings.
Telephone: 0059142 45889; *Cable:* FEDFUTBOL COCHABAMBA; *Telex:* 6239 FEDBOL; *Fax:* 0059142 82132.
League Champions 1996: Bolivar.

BRAZIL

Confederacao Brasileira De Futebol, Rua Da Alfandega, 70, P.O. Box 1078, 20.070 Rio De Janeiro.
Founded: 1914; *Number of Clubs:* 12,987; *Number of Players:* 551,358; *National Colours:* Yellow shirts, blue shorts, white stockings, green trim.
Telephone: 005521 221 5937; *Cable:* DESPORTOS RIO DE JANEIRO; *Telex:* 2121509 CBDS BR; *Fax:* 005521 252 9294.
League Champions 1996: Gremio.

CHILE

Federacion De Futbol De Chile, Avda. Quillin No. 5635, Casilla postal 3733, Correo Central, Santiago de Chile.
Founded: 1895; *Number of Clubs:* 4,598; *Number of Players:* 609,724; *National Colours:* Red shirts, blue shorts, white stockings.
Telephone: 00562 2849000; *Cable:* FEDFUTBOL SAN-TIAGO DE CHILE; *Telex:* 440474 FEBOL CZ; *Fax:* 00562 2843510.
League Champions 1996: Colo Colo.

COLOMBIA

Federacion Colombiana De Futbol, Avenida 32, No. 16-22 piso 40. Apartado Aereo 17602, Santafe de Bogota.
Founded: 1925; *Number of Clubs:* 3,685; *Number of Players:* 188,050; *National Colours:* Red shirts, blue shorts, tricolour stockings.
Telephone: 00571 2853320, 2853145, 2855220; *Telex:* 45598 COLFU CO; *Fax:* 00571 2854340.
League Champions 1996: Deportivo.

ECUADOR

Federacion Ecuatoriana De Futbol, Calle Jose Mascote 1.103 (Piso 2), Luque, Casilla 7447, Guayaquil.
Founded: 1925; *Number of Clubs:* 170; *Number of Players:* 15,700; *National Colours:* Yellow shirts, blue shorts, red stockings.
Telephone: 005934 371674; *Cable:* ECUAFUTBOL GUAYAQUIL; *Telex:* 42970 FEECFU ED; *Fax:* 005934 373320.
League Champions 1996: Emelec.

PARAGUAY

Liga Paraguaya De Futbol, Estadio De Sajonia, Calles Mayor Martinez Y Alejo Garcia, Asuncion.
Founded: 1906; *Number of Clubs:* 1,500; *Number of Players:* 140,000; *National Colours:* Red & white shirts, blue shorts, blue stockings.
Telephone: 0059521 81743; *Telex:* 627 PY FUTBOL; *Fax:* 0059521 81743.
League Champions 1996: Serro Porteno.

PERU

Federacion Peruana De Futbol, Estadio Nacional, Puerto No. 4, Calle Jose Diaz, Lima.
Founded: 1922; *Number of Clubs:* 10,000; *Number of Players:* 325,650; *National Colours:* White shirts, red trim, white shorts, white stockings.
Telephone: 005114 337070; *Cable* FEPEFUTBOL LIMA; *Fax:* 005114 335552; *Telex:* 20066 FEPEFUT PE.
League Champions 1996: Sporting Cristal.

URUGUAY

Asociacion Uruguaya De Futbol, Guayabo 1531, Montevideo.
Founded: 1900; *Number of Clubs:* 1,091; *Number of Players:* 134,310; *National Colours:* Light blue shirts, black shorts, black stockings.
Telephone: 00598442 407101; *Cable:* FUTBOL MONTE-VIDEO; *Fax:* 00598442 407873; *Telex:* AUF UY 22607.
League Champions 1996: Penarol.

VENEZUELA

Federacion Venezolana De Futbol, Avda Este Estadio Nacional, El Paraiso Apdo. Postal 14160, Candelaria, Caracas.
Founded: 1926; *Number of Clubs:* 1,753; *Number of Players:* 63,175; *National Colours:* Magenta shirts, white shorts, white stockings.
Telephone/Fax: 00582 4618010; *Cable:* FEVEFUTBOL CARACAS; *Telex:* 26140 FVFCS VC.
League Champions 1996: Minerven.

ASIA

AFGHANISTAN

The Football Federation of National Olympic Committee, Kabul.
Founded: 1922; *Number of Clubs:* 30; *Number of Players:* 3,300; *National Colours:* White shirts, white shorts, white stockings.
Telephone: 0093 20579; *Cable:* OLYMPIC KABUL.

BAHRAIN

Bahrain Football Association, P.O. Box 5464, Bahrain.
Founded: 1951; *Number of Clubs:* 25; *Number of Players:* 2,030; *National Colours:* White shirts, red shorts, white stockings.
Telephone: 00973 728218; *Cable:* BAHKORA BAHRAIN; *Telex:* 9040 FAB BN; *Fax:* 00973 729361.

BANGLADESH

Bangladesh Football Federation, Stadium, Dhaka 2.
Founded: 1972; *Number of Clubs:* 1,265; *Number of Players:* 30,385; *National Colours:* Orange shirts, white shorts, green stockings.
Telephone: 008802 236072; *Cable:* FOOTBALFED DHAKA; *Telex:* 642460 BHL BJ. *Fax:* 00880–2 863191.

BRUNEI

Brunei Amateur Football Association, P.O. Box 2010, Bandar Seri Begawan 1920, Brunei Darussalam.
Founded: 1959; *Number of Clubs:* 22; *Number of Players:* 830; *National Colours:* Gold shirts, black shorts, gold stockings.
Telephone: 006732 383883, 858585; *Cable:* BAFA BRUNEI; *Telex:* BU 2575 Attn: BAFA; *Fax:* 006732 382900.

BURMA (now Myanmar)

Myanmar Football Federation, Aung San Memorial Stadium, Kandawgalay Post Office, Yangon.
Founded: 1947; *Number of Clubs:* 600; *Number of Players:* 21,000; *National Colours:* Red shirts, white shorts, red stockings.
Telephone: 00951 75249; *Cable:* YANGON MYANMAR; *Telex:* 21218 BRCROS BRN.

CAMBODIA

Federation Khmere De Football Association, C.P. 101, Complex Sportif National, Phnom-Penh.
Founded: 1933; *Number of Clubs:* 30; *Number of Players:* 650; *National Colours:* Red shirts, white shorts, red stockings.
Telephone: 0085523 22469; *Cable:* FKFA PHNOM-PENH.

CHINA PR

Football Association of The People's Republic of China, 9 Tiyuguan Road, Beijing.
Founded: 1924; *Number of Clubs:* 1,045; *Number of Players:* 2,250,000; *National Colours:* Red shirts, white shorts, red stockings.
Telephone: 00861 07117018/9; *Cable:* SPORTSCHINE BEIJING; *Telex:* 22034 ACSF CN; *Fax:* 00861 07142533.

Final League Table 1996

	P	W	D	L	F	A	Pts
Dalian	22	12	10	0	42	18	46
Shanghai	22	10	9	3	38	18	39
August 1st	22	8	11	3	28	19	35
Beijing	22	9	6	7	30	25	33
Shandong	22	8	7	7	23	24	31
Sichuan	22	7	9	6	22	23	30
Guangzhou	22	7	8	7	26	25	29
Tianjin	22	6	8	8	20	30	26
Guangdong	22	5	10	7	20	25	25
Jilin	22	4	8	10	20	30	20
Shenzhen	22	3	7	12	13	29	16
Guangzhou II	22	2	9	11	10	26	15

Top scorer: Su Maozhen (Shandong) 13.

HONG KONG

The Hong Kong Football Association Ltd, 55 Fat Kwong Street, Homantin, Kowloon, Hong Kong.
Founded: 1914; *Number of Clubs:* 69; *Number of Players:* 3,274; *National Colours:* Red shirts, white shorts, red stockings.
Telephone: 00852 27129122; *Cable:* FOOTBALL HONG KONG; *Telex:* 40518 FAHKG HX; *Fax:* 00852 27604303.

INDIA

All India Football Federation , Netaji Indoor Stadium, Eden Gardens, Calcutta 700 021.
Founded: 1937; *Number of Clubs:* 2,000; *Number of Players:* 56,000; *National Colours:* Light blue shirts, white shorts, dark blue stockings.
Telephone: 0091497 500199; *Cable:* SOCCER CALCUTTA; *Telex:* 212216 MCPL IN; *Fax:* 0091 497500923.

INDONESIA

All Indonesia Football Federation, Main Stadium Senayan, Gate VII, P.O. Box 2305, Jakarta.
Founded: 1930; *Number of Clubs:* 2,880; *Number of Players:* 97,000; *National Colours:* Red shirts, white shorts, red stockings.
Telephone: 006221 581541; *Cable:* PSSI JAKARTA; *Telex:* 65739 as; *Fax:* 006221 584386.

IRAN

IR Iran Football Federation, Shahid Keshvari Sports Complex, Mirdamad Ave., Razan Jonoobi Str., Tehran 15875.
Founded: 1920; *Number of Clubs:* 6,326; *Number of Players:* 306,000; *National Colours:* Green shirts, white shorts, red stockings.
Telephone: 009821 2258151, 2258117, 2258118; *Cable:* FOOTBALL IRAN TEHRAN; *Fax:* 009821 2258123; *Telex:* 212691 nocir.

IRAQ

Iraqi Football Association, Olympic Committee Building, Palestine Street, Baghdad.
Founded: 1948; *Number of Clubs:* 155; *Number of Players:* 4,400; *National Colours:* White shirts, white shorts, white stockings.
Telephone: 009641 774 8261; *Cable:* BALL BAGHDAD; *Telex:* 214074 IRFA IK; *Fax:* 009641 7728424.

JAPAN

The Football Association of Japan, 2nd Floor, Gotoh Ikueikai Bldg, 1-10-7 Dogenzaka, Shibuya-Ku, Tokyo 150, Japan.
Founded: 1921; *Number of Clubs:* 13,047; *Number of Players:* 358,989; *National Colours:* Blue shirts, white shorts, blue stockings.
Telephone: 00813 3476211; *Cable:* SOCCERJAPAN TOKYO; *Telex:* 2422975 FOTJPN J; *Fax:* 00813 34762291.

Final League Table 1996

	P	W	D	L	F	A	Pts
Kashima	30	21	3	6	61	34	66
Grampas 8	30	21	0	9	63	39	63
Flugels	30	21	0	9	58	44	63
Jubilo	30	20	2	8	53	38	62
Kashiwa	30	20	0	10	67	52	60
Urawa	30	19	2	9	51	31	59
Verdy	30	19	0	11	68	42	57
Marinos	30	14	0	16	39	40	42
JEF	30	13	1	15	45	47	40
Shimizu	30	12	1	17	50	60	37
Bellmare	30	12	0	18	47	58	36
Gamba	30	11	0	19	38	59	33
Cerezo	30	10	0	20	38	56	30
Sanfrecce	30	10	0	20	36	60	30
Avispa	30	9	2	19	42	64	29
Kyoto	30	8	0	22	22	54	24

Top scorer: Kazu Miura (Verdy) 23.

JORDAN

Jordan Football Association, P.O. Box 1054, Amman.
Founded: 1949; *Number of Clubs:* 98; *Number of Players:* 4,305; *National Colours:* White shirts, white shorts, white stockings.
Telephone: 009626 624481; *Cable:* JORDAN FOOTBALL ASSOCIATION AM; *Telex:* 22415 FOBALL JO. *Fax:* 009626 624454.

KAZAKHSTAN

Football Association of the Republic of Kazakhstan, 44 Abai Street, 480072 Almaty, Kazakhstan.
Number of Clubs: 5,793; *Number of Players:* 260,000.
Telephone: 0073272 674492; *Fax:* 0073272 671885; *Telex:* 251347 TREK SU.

KOREA, NORTH

Football Association of The Democratic People's Rep. of Korea, Munsin-Dong 2, Dongdaewon Distr, Pyongyang.
Founded: 1928; *Number of Clubs:* 90; *Number of Players:* 3,420; *National Colours:* Red shirts, white shorts, red stockings.
Telephone: 008502 3998; *Cable:* DPR KOREA FOOTBALL PYONGYANG; *Telex:* 5472 KP; *Fax:* 008502 814403.

KOREA, SOUTH

Korea Football Association, 110-39, Kyeonji-Dong, Chongro-Ku, Seoul.
Founded: 1928; *Number of Clubs:* 476; *Number of Players:* 2,047; *National Colours:* Red shirts, red shorts, red stockings.
Telephone: 00822 7336764; *Cable:* FOOTBALLKOREA SEOUL; *Telex:* KFASEL K 25373; *Fax:* 00822 7352755.

KUWAIT

Kuwait Football Association, Udailiyya, BL. 4, Al-Ittihad St, P.O. Box 2029 (Safat), 13021 Safat.
Founded: 1952; *Number of Clubs:* 14 (senior); *Number of Players:* 1,526; *National Colours:* Blue shirts, white shorts, blue stockings.
Telephone: 00965 2555851 or 2555822; *Cable:* FOOTKUWAIT; *Telex:* FOOTKUW 22600 KT; *Fax:* 00965 2563737 or 2549955.

KYRGYZSTAN

Football Association of Kyrgyzstan, 17 Togolok Moldo Street, 720033 Bishkek, Kyrgyzstan.
Number of Players: 20,000.
Telephone: 00331 2/261752; *Fax:* 00331 2/227954; *Telex:* 251239 SALAM SU.

LAOS

Federation De Foot-Ball Lao, c/o Dir. Des Sports, Education, Physique Et Artistique, Vientiane.
Founded: 1951; *Number of Clubs:* 76; *Number of Players:* 2,060; *National Colours:* Red shirts, white shorts, blue stockings.
Telephone: 0085621 2741; *Cable:* FOOTBALL VIENTIANE.

LEBANON

Federation Libanaise De Football Association, P.O. Box 4732, Verdun Street, Bristol, Radwan Centre Building, Beirut.

Founded: 1933; *Number of Clubs:* 105; *Number of Players:* 8,125; *National Colours:* Red shirts, white shorts, red stockings.
Telephone: 009611 347157; *Cable:* FOOTBALL BEIRUT; *Telex:* 21404 LIBALL.

MACAO

Associacao De Futebol De Macau (AFM), P.O. Box 920, Macau.
Founded: 1939; *Number of Clubs:* 52; *Number of Players:* 800; *National Colours:* Green shirts, black shorts, green stockings. *Reserve Colours:* White/green or black/white.
Telephone: 00853 71996; *Fax:* 00853 260148; *Cable:* FOOTBALL MACAU.

MALDIVES REPUBLIC

Football Association of Maldives, Attn. Mr. Bandhu Ahamed Saleem, Sports Division, G. Banafsa Magu 20-04, Male.
Founded: 1986; *Number of Clubs: Number of Players: National Colours:* Green shirts, white shorts, green and white stockings.
Telephone: 0096032 5758; *Telex:* 77039 MINHOM MF; *Fax:* 0096032 4739.

MALAYSIA

Football Association of Malaysia, Wisma Fam, Tingkat 4, Jalan SS5A/9, Kelana Jaya, 47301 Petaling, Jaya Selangor.
Founded: 1933; *Number of Clubs:* 450; *Number of Players:* 11,250; *National Colours:* Black and gold shirts, white shorts, black and gold stockings.
Telephone: 00603 7763766; *Cable:* FOOTBALL PETALING JAYA SELANGO; *Telex:* FAM PJ MA 35701; *Fax:* 00603 7757984.

NEPAL

All-Nepal Football Association, Dasharath Rangashala, Tripureshwor, Kathmandu.
Founded: 1951; *Number of Clubs:* 85; *Number of Players:* 2,550; *National Colours:* Red shirts, blue shorts, blue and white stockings.
Telephone: 009771 15703; *Cable:* ANFA KATHMANDU; *Telex:* 2390 NSC NP.

OMAN

Oman Football Association, P.O. Box 6462, Ruwi-Muscat.
Founded: 1978; *Number of Clubs:* 47; *Number of Players:* 2,340; *National Colours:* White shirts, red shorts, white stockings.
Telephone: 00968 593840; *Cable:* FOOTBALL MUSCAT; *Telex:* 5320 FOOTBALL ON; *Fax:* 00968 593736.

PAKISTAN

Pakistan Football Federation, Mr. Hafiz Salman Butt, General Secretary, Punjab University Ground, Lahore 54000, Pakistan.
Founded: 1948; *Number of Clubs:* 882; *Number of Players:* 21,000; *National Colours:* Green shirts, white shorts, green stockings.
Telephone: 009242 5832786; *Cable:* FOOTBALL QUETTA; *Telex:* 47643 PFF PK; *Fax:* 009242 7281541.

PHILIPPINES

Philippine Football Federation, Room 207, Administration Building, Rizal Memorial Sports Complex, Pablo Ocampo Street, Manila.
Founded: 1907; *Number of Clubs:* 650; *Number of Players:* 45,000; *National Colours:* Blue shirts, white shorts, blue stockings.
Telephone: 00632 588317, 5233741; *Cable:* FOOTBALL MANILA; *Telex:* 65014 POC PACA PN; *Fax:* 00632 587724, 5224698.

PALESTINE

Palestinian Football Federation, P.O. Box 98, Jericho.
Fax: 00972 2922304.

QATAR

Qatar Football Association, P.O. Box 5333, Doha.
Founded: 1960; *Number of Clubs:* 8 (senior); *Number of Players:* 1,380; *National Colours:* White shirts, maroon shorts, white stockings.

Telephone: 00974 351641, 454444; *Cable:* FOOTQATAR DOHA; *Telex:* 4749 QATFOT DH; *Fax:* 00974 411660.

SAUDI ARABIA

Saudi Arabian Football Federation, Al Mather Quarter (Olympic Complex), P.O. Box 5844, Riyadh 11432.
Founded: 1959; *Number of Clubs:* 120; *Number of Players:* 9,600; *National Colours:* White shirts, white shorts, white stockings.
Telephone: 009661 4022699; *Cable:* KORA RIYADH; *Telex:* 404300 SAFOTB SJ; *Fax:* 009661 4921276.

SINGAPORE

Football Association of Singapore, Jalan Besar Stadium, Tyrwhitt Road, Singapore 0820.
Founded: 1892; *Number of Clubs:* 250; *Number of Players:* 8,000; *National Colours:* Sky blue shirts, sky blue shorts, sky blue stockings.
Telephone: 0065 2931477; *Cable:* SOCCER SINGAPORE; *Fax:* 0065 2933728; *Telex:* SINFA RS 37683.

SRI LANKA

Football Federation of Sri Lanka, No. 2, Old Grand Stand, Race Course, Reid Avenue, Colombo 7.
Founded: 1939; *Number of Clubs:* 600; *Number of Players:* 18,825; *National Colours:* Maroon shirts, white shorts, white stockings.
Telephone: 00941 696179; *Cable:* SOCCER COLOMBO; *Telex:* 21537 METALIX CE; *Fax:* 00941 580721.

SYRIA

Association Arabe Syrienne De Football, General Sport Fed. Building, October Stadium, Damascus _ Baremke.
Founded: 1936; *Number of Clubs:* 102; *Number of Players:* 30,600; *National Colours:* White shirts, white shorts, white stockings.
Telephone: 0096311 3331511, 3335866, 3117423; *Cable:* FOOTBALL DAMASCUS; *Telex:* HOTECH 411935; *Fax:* 0096311 3331511, 2128526, 2123346.

TAJIKISTAN

Football Federation of Tajikistan, 44, Rudaki Ave., PB 26, 734012 Dushanbe, Tajikistan.
Number of Clubs: 1,804; *Number of Players:* 71,400.
Telephone: 0073772 223603; *Fax:* 0073772 230996; *Telex:* 116119 SAWDO SU.

THAILAND

The Football Association of Thailand, c/o National Stadium, Rama I Road, Bangkok.
Founded: 1916; *Number of Clubs:* 168; *Number of Players:* 15,000; *National Colours:* Crimson shirts, white shorts, crimson stockings.
Telephone: 00662 2141058; *Cable:* FOOTBALL BANGKOK; *Telex:* 20211 FAT TH; *Fax:* 00662 2154494.

TURKMENISTAN

Football Federation of Turkmenistan, 44 Engels Street, 744000 Ashkabad, Turkmenistan.
Number of Players: 75,000.
Telephone: 0073632 253844; *Fax:* 0073632 290646; *Telex:* 116175 TINTO SU.

UNITED ARAB EMIRATES

United Arab Emirates Football Association, P.O. Box 916, Abu Dhabi.
Founded: 1971; *Number of Clubs:* 23 (senior); *Number of Players:* 1,787; *National Colours:* White shirts, white shorts, white stockings.
Telephone: 00971 2/445600; *Cable:* FOOTBALL EMIRATES DUBAI; *Telex:* 22121 uefa em; *Cable:* FOOTBALL EMIRATES ABU DHABI; *Fax:* 00971 2/448558.

UZBEKISTAN

Football Federation of Uzbekistan, Karl Marx Street 32, 700047 Tashkent, Uzbekistan.
Number of Clubs: 15,000; *Number of Players:* 217,000.
Telephone: 0073712 322854; *Fax:* 0073712 890046; *Telex:* 116108 PTB SU.

VIETNAM

Association De Football De La Republique Du Viet-Nam, No. 36, Boulevard Tran-Phu, Hanoi. *Founded:*

1962; *Number of Clubs:* 55 (senior); *Number of Players:* 16,000; *National Colours:* Red shirts, white shorts, red stockings. *Telephone:* 00844 4867; *Cable:* AFBVN, 36, TRAN-PHU-HANOI.

YEMEN

Yemen Football Association, P.O. Box 908, Sana'a.
Founded: 1962; *Number of Clubs:* 26; *Number of Players:* 1750; *National Colours:* Green.
Telephone: 009672 215720. *Telex:* 2710 YOUTH YE

CONCACAF

ANGUILLA

The Anguilla Football Association, P.O. Box 20, The Valley, Anguilla, West Indies.
Telephone: 001809 4972388; *Fax:* 001809 4973286.

ANTIGUA

The Antigua Football Association, P.O. Box 773, St. Johns.
Founded: 1928; *Number of Clubs:* 60; *Number of Players:* 1,008; *National Colours:* Gold shirts, black shorts, black stockings.
Telephone: 001809 4623945; *Cable:* AFA ANTIGUA; *Telex:* 2177 SIDAN AK; *Fax:* 001809 4622649.

ARUBA

Arubaanse Voetbal Bond, Schoenerstraat 2, PO Box 376, Oranjestad, Aruba.
Founded: 1932; *Number of Clubs:* 50; *Number of Players:* 1,000; *National Colours:* Yellow shirts, blue shorts, yellow stockings.
Telephone: 00297 828016; *Fax:* 00297 838438, 820624.

BAHAMAS

Bahamas Football Association, P.O. Box N 8434, Nassau, N.P.
Founded: 1967; *Number of Clubs:* 14; *Number of Players:* 700; *National Colours:* Yellow shirts, black shorts, yellow stockings.
Telephone: 001809 3233426; *Cable:* BAHSOCA NASSAU; *Fax:* 001809 3288006.

BARBADOS

Barbados Football Association, No. 7, 7th Avenue, Belleville, St. Michael, Barbados, W.I.
Founded: 1910; *Number of Clubs:* 92; *Number of Players:* 1,100; *National Colours:* Royal blue shirts, gold shorts, royal blue stockings.
Tel (General Secretary): 001246 4398848; *Fax:* 001246 2286484; *Cable:* FOOTBALL BRIDGETOWN; *Telex:* 2306 SHAMROCK WB.

BELIZE

Belize National Football Association, P.O. Box 1742, Belize City.
Founded: 1986; *National Colours:* Blue shirts, red & white trim, white shorts, blue stockings.
Telephone: 005012 44794; *Telex:* 102 FOREIGN BZ; *Fax:* 005012 35838.

BERMUDA

The Bermuda Football Association, P.O. Box HM 745, Hamilton 5 HM CX.
Founded: 1928; *Number of Clubs:* 30; *Number of Players:* 1,947; *National Colours:* Blue shirts, white shorts, white stockings.
Telephone: 001809 2952199; *Cable:* FOOTBALL BERMUDA; *Telex:* 3441 BFA BA; *Fax:* 001809 2959773.

BRITISH VIRGIN ISLANDS

The British Virgin Islands FA, P.O. Box 34, Road Town, Tortola, BVI.
Telephone: 001809 4943783 or 4943360; *Fax:* 001809 4942220.

CANADA

The Canadian Soccer Association, "Place Soccer Canada", 237 Metcalfe Street, Ottawa, Ontario K2P 1R2.

Founded: 1912; *Number of Clubs:* 1,600; *Number of Players:* 224,290; *National Colours:* Red shirts, red shorts, red stockings.
Telephone: 001613 2377678; *Cable:* SOCCANADA OTTAWA; *Telex:* 0533350; *Fax:* 001613 2371516.

CAYMAN ISLANDS

Cayman Islands Football Association, PO Box 178, Georgetown, Grand Cayman, Cayman Islands W1.
Number of Clubs: 25; *Number of Players:* 875.
Telephone: 001809 9497339. *Fax:* 001809 9492337.

COSTA RICA

Federacion Costarricense De Futbol, Apartado 670-1000, Calle 40, Avda CTL I, San Jose.
Founded: 1921; *Number of Clubs:* 431; *Number of Players:* 12,429; *National Colours:* Red shirts, blue shorts, white stockings.
Telephone: 00506 2221544; *Cable:* FEDEFUTBOL SAN JOSE; *Telex:* 3394 DIDER CR; *Fax:* 00506 2552674.

CUBA

Asociacion De Futbol De Cuba, c/o Comite Olimpico Cubano, Calle 13 No. 601, Esq. C. Vedado, La Habana, ZP4.
Founded: 1924; *Number of Clubs:* 70; *Number of Players:* 12,900; *National Colours:* White shirts, blue shorts, white stockings.
Telephone: 00537 403581; *Cable:* FOOTBALL HABANA; *Telex:* 511332 INDER CU.

DOMINICA

Dominica Football Association, P.O. Box 372, Roseau, Commonwealth of Dominica.
Number of Clubs: 30; *Number of Players:* 500.
Telephone: 00180944 87545; *Fax:* 00180944 81111.

DOMINICAN REPUBLIC

Federacion Dominicana de Futbol, Apartado De Correos No. 1953, Santo Domingo.
Founded: 1953; *Number of Clubs:* 128; *Number of Players:* 10,706; *National Colours:* Blue shirts, white shorts, red stockings.
Telephone: 001809542 6923. *Cable:* FEDOFUTBOL SANTO DOMINGO. *Fax:* 001809547 5363.

EL SALVADOR

Federacion Salvadorena De Futbol, Av. J.M. Delgado, Col. Escalon, Centro Espanol, Apartado 1029, San Salvador.
Founded: 1936; *Number of Clubs:* 944; *Number of Players:* 21,294; *National Colours:* Blue shirts, blue shorts, blue stockings.
Telephone: 00503 2637525/6, 00503 2637570/1; *Cable:* FESFUT SAN SALVADOR; *Fax:* 00503 2637583; *Telex:* 20484 FESFUT SAL.

GRENADA

Grenada Football Association, St. Juilles Street, P.O. Box 326, Grenada, West Indies.
Founded: 1924; *Number of Clubs:* 15; *Number of Players:* 200; *National Colours:* Green & yellow shirts, red shorts, green & yellow stockings.
Telephone: 001809 4401986; *Cable:* GRENBALL GRENADA; *Telex:* 3431 CW BUR; *Fax:* 001809 4401986.

GUATEMALA

Federacion Nacional De Futbol De Guatemala C.A., Avenida Reforma 1-90 Zona 9, 11 Nivel, Edificio Masval, Ciudad de Guatemala.
Founded: 1933; *Number of Clubs:* 1,611; *Number of Players:* 43,516; *National Colours:* White/blue diagonal striped shirts, blue shorts, white stockings.
Telephone: 005023 314797, 321697; *Fax:* 005023 600188; *Cable:* FEDFUTBOL GUATEMALA.

GUYANA

Guyana Football Association, P.O. Box 10727 Georgetown.
Founded: 1902; *Number of Clubs:* 103; *Number of Players:* 1,665; *National Colours:* Green & yellow shirts, black shorts, white & green stockings.
Telephone: 005922 59458/9; *Cable:* FOOTBALL GUYANA; *Telex:* 2266 RICEBRD GY; *Fax:* 005922 52169.

HAITI

Federation Haitienne De Football, P.O. Box 2258, Port-Au-Prince.
Founded: 1904; *Number of Clubs:* 40; *Number of Players:* 4,000; *National Colours:* Red shirts, black shorts, red stockings.
Telephone: 00509 46450910; *Fax:* 00509 1573001; *Cable:* FEDHAFOOB PORT-AU-PRINCE.

HONDURAS

Federacion Nacional Autonoma De Futbol De Honduras, Apartado Postal 827, Costa Oeste Del Est. Nac, Tegucigalpa, De. C.
Founded: 1951; *Number of Clubs:* 1,050; *Number of Players:* 15,300; *National Colours:* Blue shirts, blue shorts, blue stockings.
Telephone: 00504 321897; *Cable* FENAFUTH TEGUCI-GALPA; *Telex:* 1209 FENEFUTH; *Fax:* 00504 311428.

JAMAICA

Jamaica Football Federation, Attn. Anthony James, President, Room 8 INSPORTS, Independence Park, Kingston 6.
Founded: 1910; *Number of Clubs:* 266; *Number of Players:* 45,200; *National Colours:* Green shirts, black shorts, green & gold stockings.
Telephone: 001809 9290483; *Fax:* 001809 9622858; *Telex:* 2224 FEDLASCO JA; *Cable:* FOOTBALL JAMAICA KINGSTON.

MEXICO

Federacion Mexicana De Futbol Asociacion, A.C., Abraham Gonzales 74, C.P. 06600, Col. Juarez, Mexico 6, D.F.
Founded: 1927; *Number of Clubs:* 77 (senior); *Number of Players:* 1,402,270; *National Colours:* Green shirts, white shorts, green stockings.
Telephone: 00525 5662155; *Cable:* MEXFUTBOL MEXI-CO; *Telex:* 1771678 MSUTME; *Fax:* 00525 5667580.

MONSERRAT

Monserrat Football Association, P.O. Box 16, Church Road, MSR – Plymouth, Monserrat.
Telephone: 001809 4917619; *Fax:* 001809 4912264.

NETHERLANDS ANTILLES

Nederlands Antiliaanse Voetbal Unie, P.O. Box 341, Curacao, N.A.
Founded: 1921; *Number of Clubs:* 85; *Number of Players:* 4,500; *National Colours:* white shirts, white shorts, red stockings.
Telephone:Cable: NAVU CURACAO; *Telex:* 1046 ENNIA NA; *Fax:* 005999 611173.

NICARAGUA

Federacion Nicaraguense De Futbol, Inst. Nicaraguense De Deportes, Apartado Postal 976 6 383, Managua.
Founded: 1968; *Number of Clubs:* 31; *Number of Players:* 160 (senior); *National Colours:* Blue shirts, blue shorts, blue stockings.
Telephone/Fax: 005052 664134; *Cable:* FEDEFOOT MANAGUA; *Telex:* 2156 IND NK.

PANAMA

Federacion Nacional De Futbol De Panama, Apartado Postal 8-391, Zona 8, Panama.
Founded: 1937; *Number of Clubs:* 65; *Number of Players:* 4,225; *National Colours:* Red & white shirts, blue shorts, red stockings.
Telephone: 00507 2130935; *Cable:* PANAOLIMPIC PANAMA; *Telex:* 2534 INDE PG; *Fax:* 00507 2130936.

PUERTO RICO

Federacion Puertorriquena De Futbol, Coliseo Roberto Clemente, P.O. Box 4355, Hato Rey, 00919-4355.
Founded: 1940; *Number of Clubs:* 175; *Number of Players:* 4,200; *National Colours:* White & red shirts, blue shorts, white & blue stockings.
Telephone/Fax: 001809 7642025; *Cable:* BORIKENFPF; *Telex:* 3450296.

SAINT LUCIA

St Lucia National Football Union, PO Box 255, Castries, St Lucia.
Number of Clubs: 100; *Number of Players:* 4,000; *National Colours:* Blue and white striped shirts, black shorts, blue stockings.
Telephone: 001809 31519; *Fax:* 001809 4524127; *Telex:* 6394 FOR AFF LC.

SAINT KITTS AND NEVIS

St Kitts and Nevis Football Association, P.O. Box 465, Basseterre, St Kitts, West Indies.
Number of Clubs: 36; *Number of Players:* 600.
Telephone: 001809 4652521/ 4654086; *Fax:* 001809 4655501/ 4651042.

SAINT VINCENT & THE GRENADINES

St Vincent & The Grenadines Football Federation, PO Box 1278, Kingstown, St Vincent.
Number of Clubs: 500; *Number of Players:* 5,000.
Telephone: 001809 4561525; *Fax:* 001809 4571659, 4571381.

SURINAM

Surinaamse Voetbal Bond, Cultuuruinlaan 7, P.O. Box 1223, Paramaribo.
Founded: 1920; *Number of Clubs:* 168; *Number of Players:* 4,430; *National Colours:* Red shirts, white shorts, white stockings.
Telephone: 00597 473112; *Fax:* 00597 465832; *Cable:* SVB Paramaribo.

TRINIDAD AND TOBAGO

Trinidad & Tobago Football Association, Petrotrin Savannah Building 9, Queen's Park West, P.O. Box 400, Port of Spain.
Founded: 1906; *Number of Clubs:* 124; *Number of Players:* 5,050; *National Colours:* Red shirts, black shorts, red stockings.
Telephone: 001809 6271011/1013. *Cable:* TRAFA PORT OF SPAIN; *Telex:* 22652 TRAFA WG; *Fax:* 001809 6271007.

USA

United States Soccer Federation, U.S. Soccer House, 1801-1811 S. Prairie Avenue, Chicago, Illinois 60616.
Founded: 1913; *Number of Clubs:* 7,000; *Number of Players:* 1,411,500; *National Colours:* White shirts, blue shorts, red stockings.
Telephone: 001312 5784678; *Telex:* 450024 US SOCCER FED; *Fax:* 001312 5784636.

Major League Soccer
Eastern Conference

	P	W	D	L	F	A	Pts
Tampa Bay	32	19	1	12	66	51	58
Washington	32	15	1	16	62	56	46
New York/New Jersey	32	12	3	17	45	47	39
Columbus	32	11	4	17	59	60	37
New England	32	9	6	17	43	56	33

Western Conference

	P	W	D	L	F	A	Pts
Los Angeles	32	15	4	13	59	49	49
Dallas	32	12	5	15	50	48	41
Kansas City	32	12	5	15	61	63	41
San Jose	32	12	3	17	50	50	40
Colorado	32	9	2	21	44	59	29

After play-offs:
Washington beat Los Angeles 3–2

OCEANIA

AUSTRALIA

Soccer Australia, Sydney Football Stadium, Driver Avenue, P.O. Box 175, Paddington NSW 2021.
Founded: 1961; *Number of Clubs:* 6,816; *Number of Players:* 433,957; *National Colours:* Gold shirts, green shirts, white stockings.
Telephone: 0061 293806155; *Cable:* FOOTBALL SYDNEY; *Fax:* 0061 2/3806155.

COOK ISLANDS

Cook Islands Football Federation, P.O. Box 594, Avarua, Rarotonga, Cook Islands.
Number of Clubs: 9; *Number of Players:* – .
Telephone: 00682 20798; *Fax:* 00682 21798.

FIJI

Fiji Football Association, Mr. J.D. Maharaj, Hon. Secretary, Government Bldgs, P.O.Box 2514, Suva.
Founded: 1946; *Number of Clubs;* 140: *Number of Players:* 21,300; *National Colours:* White shirts, black shorts, black stockings.
Telephone: 00679 300453; *Cable:* FOOTSOCCER SUVA; *Telex:* 2366 FJ; *Fax:* 00679 304642.

GUAM

The Guam Soccer Association, P.O.Box 5093, Agana, Guam 96910.
Telephone: 00671 4725523; *Fax:* 00671 4775424.

NEW ZEALAND

Soccer New Zealand, P.O. Box 11.357, Ellerslie, Auckland.
Founded: 1891; *Number of Clubs:* 312; *Number of Players:* 52,969; *National Colours:* White shirts, black shorts, white stockings.
Telephone: 00649 5256120; *Fax:* 00649 5256123; *Telex:* NZ 63007 NZFAOFC.

PAPUA NEW GUINEA

Papua New Guinea Football (Soccer) Association Inc., c/o National Sports Institute, P.O. Box 337, Goroka, EHP.

Founded: 1962; *Number of Clubs:* 350; *Number of Players:* 8,250; *National Colours:* Red shirts, black shorts, red stockings.
Telephone: 00675 7321699, 7322043; *Telex:* TOTOTRA NE 23436; *Fax:* 00675 7321941.

SOLOMAN ISLANDS

Soloman Islands Football Federation, PO Box 532, Honiara, Soloman Islands.
Number of Players: 4,000; *National Colours:* Blue shirts, white shorts, white stockings.
Telephone: 00677 23553; *Fax:* 00677 20391; *Telex:* HQ 66349.

TAHITI

Federation Tahitienne de Football, Attn. Napoleon Spitz, B.P. 650, Papeete, Tahiti, French Polynesia.
Founded: 1938; *National Colours:* Red shirts, white shorts, white stockings.
Telephone: 00689 420410; *Fax:* 00689 421479; *Telex:* 454 FP.

TONGA

Tonga Football Association, att. General Secretary, TFA, TASA Office, P.O. Box 1278, Nuku'alofa, Kingdom of Tonga.
Number of Clubs: 23; *Number of Players:* 350.
Telephone: 00676 24127; *Fax:* 00676 21041.

VANUATU

Vanuatu Football Federation, P.O. Box 226, Port Vila, Vanuatu.
Founded: 1934; *National Colours:* Gold shirts, black shorts, gold stockings.
Telephone: 00678 22009; *Fax:* 00678 23579.

WESTERN SAMOA

Western Samoa Football (Soccer) Association, Min. of Youth, Sports Culture, Private Bag, Apia.
Founded: 1986; *National Colours:* Blue shirts, white shorts, blue and white stockings.
Telephone: 00685 21420; *Fax:* 00685 24166; *Telex:* 230 SAMGAMES SX.

AFRICA

ALGERIA

Federation Algerienne De Futbol, Route Ahmed Ouaked, Boite Postale No. 39, Alger _ Dely Ibrahim.
Founded: 1962; *Number of Clubs:* 780; *Number of Players:* 58,567; *National Colours:* Green shirts, white shorts, red stockings.
Telephone: 00213 799941; *Cable:* FAFOOT ALGER; *Telex:* 61378. *Fax:* 00213 366181.

ANGOLA

Federation Angolaise De Football, B.P. 3449, Luanda.
Founded: 1977; *Number of Clubs:* 276; *Number of Players:* 4,269; *National Colours:* Red shirts, black shorts, red stockings.
Telephone: 002442 338635/338233; *Cable:* FUTANGOLA; *Telex:* 4072 CIAM AN.

BENIN

Federation Beninoise De Football, B.P. 965, Cotonou.
Founded: 1968; *Number of Clubs:* 117; *Number of Players:* 6,700; *National Colours:* Green shirts, green shorts, green stockings.
Telephone: 00229 330537; *Cable:* FEBEFOOT COTONOU K; *Telex:* 5033 BIMEX COTONOU; *Fax:* 00229 312485.

BOTSWANA

Botswana Football Association, P.O. Box 1396, Gabarone.
Founded: 1976; *National Colours:* Sky blue shirts, white shorts, sky blue stockings.
Telephone: 00267 300279; *Cable:* BOTSBALL GABARONE; *Telex:* 2977 BD; *Fax:* 00267 372911.

BURKINA FASO

Federation Burkinabe De Foot-Ball, B.P. 57, Ouagadougou.
Founded: 1960; *Number of Clubs:* 57; *Number of Players:* 4,672; *National Colours:* Black shirts, white shorts, red stockings.
Telephone: 00226 318815; *Cable:* FEDEFOOT OUAGADOUGOU; *Fax:* 00226 318843.

BURUNDI

Federation De Football Du Burundi, B.P. 3426, Bujumbura.
Founded: 1948; *Number of Clubs:* 132; *Number of Players:* 3,930; *National Colours:* Red shirts, white shorts, green stockings.
Telephone: 00257 225160; *Fax:* 00257 212891 or 211431; *Cable:* FFB BUJA.

CAMEROON

Federation Camerounaise De Football, B.P. 1116, Yaounde.
Founded: 1960; *Number of Clubs:* 200; *Number of Players:* 9,328; *National Colours:* Green shirts, red shorts, yellow stockings.
Telephone: 00237 202538; *Fax:* 00237 222430, 234396; *Cable:* FECAFOOT YAOUNDE; *Telex:* 8568 JEUNESPO KN.

CAPE VERDE ISLANDS

Federacao Cabo-Verdiana De Futebol, P.O. Box 234, Praia.
Founded: 1986; *National Colours:* Green shirts, green shorts, green stockings.

Telephone: 00238 611362; *Fax:* 00238 611362; *Cable:* FCF-CV; *Telex:* 6005 acs cv.

CENTRAL AFRICAN REPUBLIC

Federation Centrafricaine De Football, B.P. 344, Bangui.
Founded: 1937; *Number of Clubs:* 256; *Number of Players:* 7,200; *National Colours:* Grey & blue shirts, white shorts, red stockings.
Telephone: 00236 612433 or 611917; *Fax:* 00236 611637 or 610042; *Cable:* FOOTBANGUI BANGUI.

CONGO

Federation Congolaise De Football, B.P. 4041, Brazzaville.
Founded: 1962; *Number of Clubs:* 250; *Number of Players:* 5,940; *National Colours:* Red shirts, red shorts, white stockings.
Telephone: 00242 834885, 835306, 828736, 820582; *Cable:* FECOFOOT BRAZZAVILLE; *Telex:* 5210 KG; *Fax:* 00242 820582, 836464.

DJIBOUTI

Federation Djiboutienne de Football, B.P. 1916, Djibouti.
Number of Players: 2,000.
Fax: 00253 356830.

EGYPT

Egyptian Football Association, 5, Shareh Gabalaya, Guezira, Al Borg Post Office, Cairo.
Founded: 1921; *Number of Clubs:* 247; *Number of Players:* 19,735; *National Colours:* Red shirts, white shorts, black stockings.
Telephone: 00202 3401793; *Cable:* KORA CAIRO; *Fax:* 00202 3417817; *Telex:* 93504 kora un.

ETHIOPIA

Ethiopia Football Federation, Addis Ababa Stadium, P.O. Box 1080, Addis Ababa.
Founded: 1943; *Number of Clubs:* 767; *Number of Players:* 20,594; *National Colours:* Green shirts, yellow shorts, red stockings.
Telephone: 002511 514453/514321. *Cable:* FOOTBALL ADDIS ABABA; *Fax:* 002511 513345; *Telex:* 21377 NESCO ET.

GABON

Federation Gabonaise De Football, B.P. 181, Libreville.
Founded: 1962; *Number of Clubs:* 320; *Number of Players:* 10,000; *National Colours:* Blue shirts, white shorts, white stockings.
Telephone: 00241 744747; *Cable:* FEGAFOOT LIBRE-VILLE; *Telex:* 5642 GO; *Fax:* 00241 746047.

GAMBIA

Gambia Football Association, Independence Stadium, Bakau, P.O. Box 523, Banjul.
Founded: 1952; *Number of Clubs:* 30; *Number of Players:* 860; *National Colours:* White & red shirts, white shorts, white stockings.
Telephone: 00220 95834; *Cable:* SPORTS GAMBIA BANJUL; *Fax:* 00220 29837; *Telex:* 2262 FISCO GV.

GHANA

Ghana Football Association, P.O. Box 1272, Accra.
Founded: 1957; *Number of Clubs:* 347; *Number of Players:* 11,275; *National Colours:* White shirts, white shorts, white stockings.
Telephone: 0023321 663924; *Cable:* GFA, ACCRA; *Fax:* 0023321 21662; *Telex:* 2519 SPORTS GH.

GUINEA

Federation Guineenne De Football, P.O. Box 3645, Conakry.
Founded: 1959; *Number of Clubs:* 351; *Number of Players:* 10,000; *National Colours:* Red shirts, yellow shorts, green stockings.

Telephone: 00224 445041; *Cable:* GUINEFOOT CONAKRY; *Telex:* 22302 MJ GE; *Fax:* 00224 442781.

GUINEA-BISSAU

Federacao De Football Da Guinea-Bissau, Rua4 No. 10-C, Apartado 375, 1035 Bissau Codex.
Founded: 1986; *National Colours:* Green shirts, green shorts, green stockings.
Telephone: 00245 201918; *Cable:* FUTEBOL BISSAU; *Telex:* 205 PUBLICO BI.

GUINEA, EQUATORIAL

Federacion Ecuatoguineana De Futbol, Malabo.
Founded: 1986; *National Colours:* All red.
Telephone: 00240 26523; *Telex:* 9991111 EG; *Cable:* FEGUIFUT/MALABO.

IVORY COAST

Federation Ivoirienne De Football, Stade Felix Houphouet Boigny, B.P. 1202, Abidjan.
Founded: 1960; *Number of Clubs:* 84 (senior); *Number of Players:* 3,655; *National Colours:* Orange shirts, white shorts, green stockings.
Telephone: 00225 242301; *Cable:* FIF ABIDJAN; *Telex:* 42344 FIF CI; *Fax:* 00225 244308.

KENYA

Kenya Football Federation, Nyayo National Stadium, P.O. Box 40234, Nairobi.
Founded: 1960; *Number of Clubs:* 351; *Number of Players:* 8,880; *National Colours:* Red shirts, red shorts, red stockings.
Telephone: 002542 501853; *Cable:* KEFF NAIROBI; *Fax:* 002542 501120; *Telex:* 25784 KFF.

LESOTHO

Lesotho Sports Council, P.O. Box 138, Maseru 100, Lesotho.
Founded: 1932; *Number of Clubs:* 88; *Number of Players:* 2,076; *National Colours:* Blue shirts, green shorts, white stockings.
Telephone: 00266 311291; *Cable:* LIPAPALI MASERU; *Fax:* 00266 310914; *Telex:* 4493.

LIBERIA

The Liberia Football Association, P.O. Box 1066, Monrovia 10.
Founded: 1962; *National Colours:* Blue & white shirts, white shorts, blue & white stockings.
Telephone: 00231 226284; *Cable:* LIBFOTASS MON-ROVIA; *Telex:* 44508 IFA LI. *Fax:* 00231 226101.

LIBYA

Libyan Arab Jamahiriya Football Federation, P.O. Box 5137, Tripoli.
Founded: 1963; *Number of Clubs:* 89; *Number of Players:* 2,941; *National Colours:* Green shirts, white shorts, green stockings.
Telephone: 0021821 46610; *Telex:* 20896 KURATP LY. *Fax:* 0021821 607016.

MADAGASCAR

Federation Malagasy De Football, c/o Comite Nat. De Coordination De Football, B.P. 4409, Antananarivo 101.
Founded: 1961; *Number of Clubs:* 775; *Number of Players:* 23,536; *National Colours:* Red shirts, white shorts, green stockings.
Telephone: 002612 28051; *Telex:* 22265 arosur mg; *Fax:* 00261 1/34464.

MALAWI

Football Association of Malawi, P.O. Box 865, Blantyre.
Founded: 1966; *Number of Clubs:* 465; *Number of Players:* 12,500; *National Colours:* Red shirts, red shorts, red stockings.
Telephone: 00265 636686; *Cable:* FOOTBALL BLAN-TYRE; *Telex:* 4526 SPORTS MI. *Fax:* 00265 636941.

MALI

Federation Malienne De Football, Stade Mamdou Konate, B.P. 1020, Bamako.
Founded: 1960; *Number of Clubs:* 128; *Number of Players:* 5,480; *National Colours:* Green shirts, yellow shorts, red stockings.
Telephone: 00223 224152; *Cable:* MALIFOOT BAMAKO; Telex: 1200/1202.

MAURITANIA

Federation De Foot-Ball De La Rep. Isl. De Mauritanie, B.P. 566, Nouakshott.
Founded: 1961; *Number of Clubs:* 59; *Number of Players:* 1,930; *National Colours:* Green and yellow shirts, blue shorts, green stockings.
Telephone/Fax: 00222 259057; *Telex:* 577 MTN NKTT RIM; *Cable:* FOOTRIM NOUAKSHOTT.

MAURITIUS

Mauritius Football Association, Chancery House, 14 Lislet Geoffroy Street, (2nd Floor, Nos. 303.305), Port Louis.
Founded: 1952; *Number of Clubs:* 397; *Number of Players:* 29,375; *National Colours:* Red shirts, white shorts, red stockings.
Telephone: 00230 2121418, 2125771; *Cable:* MFA PORT LOUIS; *Telex:* 4427 MSA IW; *Fax:* 00230 2084100.

MOROCCO

Federation Royale Marocaine De Football, Av. Ibn Sina, C.N.S. Bellevue, B.P. 51, Rabat.
Founded: 1955; *Number of Clubs:* 350; *Number of Players:* 19,768; *National Colours:* Red shirts, green shorts, red stockings.
Telephone: 002127 672706/08 or 67 26 07; *Cable:* FERMAFOOT RABAT; *Telex:* 32940 FERMFOOT M. *Fax:* 002127 671070

MOZAMBIQUE

Federacao Mocambicana De Futebol, Av. Samora Machel, 11-2, Caixa Postal 1467, Maputo.
Founded: 1978; *Number of Clubs:* 144; *National Colours:* Red shirts, red shorts, red stockings.
Telephone: 002581 300366; *Fax:* 002581 300367; *Cable:* MOCAMBOLA MAPUTO; *Telex:* 6575 PERCO MO.

NAMIBIA

Namibia Football Federation, PO Box 1345, Independance Avenue, Juvenis Building – First Floor Windhoek, Namibia.
Number of Clubs: 244; *Number of Players:* 7320.
Telephone: 0026461 220066; *Fax:* 0026461 221304.

NIGER

Federation Nigerienne De Football, Stade du 29 Juillet, B.P. 10299, Niamey.
Founded: 1967; *Number of Clubs:* 64; *Number of Players:* 1,525; *National Colours:* Orange shirts, white shorts, green stockings.
Telephone: 00227 734705; *Fax:* 00227 735512; *Telex:* 5527 or 5349; *Cable:* FEDERFOOT NIGER NIAMEY.

NIGERIA

Nigeria Football Association, Plot 2033, Olusegun Obasanjo Way, Wuse Zone 7, Abuja, Nigeria.
Founded: 1945; *Number of Clubs:* 326; *Number of Players:* 80,190; *National Colours:* Green shirts, white shorts, green stockings.
Telephone: 002349 5237326, 5237324, 5237325, 5237322; *Cable:* FOOTBALL LAGOS; *Telex:* 26570 NFA NG; *Fax:* 002349 5237327, 5237323.

PALESTINE

Palestinian Football Federation, P.O. Box 98, Jerico.
Telephone: 009727 829433; *Fax:* 009727 825208.

RWANDA

Federation Rwandaise De Foot-Ball Amateur, B.P. 2000, Kigali.
Founded: 1972; *Number of Clubs:* 167; *National Colours:* Red shirts, red shorts, red stockings.
Telephone: 00250 82605; *Cable:* MIJENCOOP KIGALI; *Telex:* 22504 PUBLIC RW; *Fax:* 00250 76574.

SENEGAL

Federation Senegalaise De Football, Stade De L'Amitie, Route De L'Aeroport De Yoff, B.P. 130 21, Dakar.
Founded: 1960; *Number of Clubs:* 75 (senior); *Number of Players:* 3,977; *National Colours:* Green shirts, yellow shorts, red stockings.
Telephone/Fax: 00221 273524; *Telex:* 21741; *Cable:* SENEFOOT DAKAR.

SEYCHELLES

Seychelles Football Federation, P.O. Box 843, People's Stadium, Victoria-Mahe, Seychelles.
Founded: 1986; *National Colours:* Green shirts, yellow shorts, red stockings.
Telephone: 00248 323908; *Telex:* 2240 CULSPT SZ; *Fax:* 00248 323518.

ST. THOMAS AND PRINCIPE

Federation Santomense De Fut., P.O. Box 42, Sao Tome.
Founded: 1986; *National Colours:* Green shirts, green shorts, green stockings.
Telephone: 0023912 21365; *Telex:* 213 PUBLICO STP; *Fax:* 0023912 21365, 23431.

SIERRA LEONE

Sierra Leone Amateur Football Association, Siaka Stevens Stadium, Brookfields, P.O. Box 672, Freetown.
Founded: 1967; *Number of Clubs:* 104; *Number of Players:* 8,120; *National Colours:* Green shirts, white shorts, blue stockings.
Telephone: 0023222 41872; *Cable:* SLAFA FREETOWN; *Telex:* 3210 BOOTH SL. *Fax:* 0023222 224439.

SOMALIA

Somali Football Federation, C/O CAF, 5 Gabalaya Street, 11567, El Borg, Cairo, Egypt.
Founded: 1951; *Number of Clubs:* 46 (senior); *Number of Players:* 1,150; *National Colours:* Sky blue shirts, white shorts, white stockings.
Telephone: 0020 2/3412497; *Cable:* SOMALIA FOOTBALL CAIRO; *Telex:* 93162 caf un; *Fax:* 0020 2/3420114.

SOUTH AFRICA

South African Football Association, First National Bank Stadium, Nasrec; PO Box 910, Johannesburg 2000; South Africa.
Number of Teams: 51,944; *Number of Players:* 1,039,880.
Telephone: 002711 4943522; Fax: 002711 4943447.

SUDAN

Sudan Football Association, P.O. Box 437, Khartoum.
Founded: 1936; *Number of Clubs:* 750; *Number of Players:* 42,200; *National Colours:* White shirts, white shorts, white stockings.
Telephone: 0024911 776633 or 773786; *Cable:* ALKOURA, KHARTOUM; *Fax:* 0024911 781160; *Telex:* 23007 KORA SD.

SWAZILAND

National Football Association of Swaziland, P.O. Box 641, Mbabane.
Founded: 1976; *Number of Clubs:* 136; *National Colours:* Blue and gold shirts, white shorts, blue and gold stockings.
Telephone: 00268 46852; *Telex:* 2245 EXP WD.

TANZANIA

Football Association of Tanzania, P.O. Box 1574, Dar Es Salaam.
Founded: 1930; *Number of Clubs:* 51; *National Colours:* Yellow shirts, yellow shorts, yellow stockings.

Telephone: 0025551 117931; *Telex:* 41873 TZ; *Cable:* FAT DAR ES SALAAM; *Fax:* 0025551 117930.

TOGO

Federation Togolaise De Football, C.P. 5, Lome.
Founded: 1960; *Number of Clubs:* 144; *Number of Players:* 4,346; *National Colours:* Red shirts, white shorts, red stockings.
Telephone: 00228 21412; *Cable:* TOGOFOOT LOME; *Telex:* 5015 CNOT TG. *Fax:* 00228 221413.

TUNISIA

Federation Tunisienne De Football, 2 rue Hamza Abderlmottaleb, El-Menzah VI, Tunis 1004.
Founded: 1957; *Number of Clubs:* 215; *Number of Players:* 18,300; *National Colours:* Red shirts, white shorts, red stockings.
Telephone: 002161 233303, 233544; *Cable:* FOOTBALL TUNIS; *Fax:* 002161 767929; *Telex:* 14783 FTFOOT TN.

UGANDA

Federation of Uganda Football Associations, P.O. Box 20077, Kampala, Uganda.
Founded: 1924; *Number of Clubs:* 400; *Number of Players:* 1,518; *National Colours:* Yellow shirts, black shorts, yellow stockings.
Telephone: 0025641 254477; *Cable:* FUFA KAMPALA; *Telex:* 61605; *Fax:* 0025641 258350; *Telegrams:* fufa lugogo stadium.

ZAIRE

Federation Zairoise De Football-Association, P.O. Box 1284, rue Dima No. 10, Kinshasa 1.
Founded: 1919; *Number of Clubs:* 3,800; *Number of Players:* 64,627; *National Colours:* Green shirts, yellow shorts, yellow stockings. *Cable:* FEZAFA KINSHASA; *Telex:* 63915. *Fax:* 0024312 506555.

ZAMBIA

Football Association of Zambia, P.O. Box 347 51, Lusaka.
Founded: 1929; *Number of Clubs:* 20 (senior); *Number of Players:* 4,100; *National Colours:* Green shirts, white shorts, black stockings.
Telephone: 002601 221145; *Cable:* FOOTBALL LUSAKA; *Telex:* 40204 FAZ ZA; *Fax:* 002601 225046.

ZIMBABWE

Zimbabwe Football Association, P.O. Box 8343, Causeway, Harare.
Founded: 1965; *National Colours:* White shirts, black shorts, black stockings.
Telephone: 002634 754933/6; *Cable:* SOCCER HARARE; *Telex:* 22299 SOCCER ZW; *Fax:* 00263 4/751470.

Other addition: CHAD (readmitted).

THE WORLD CUP 1930–94

Year	Winners		Runners-up		Venue	Attendance	Referee
1930	Uruguay	4	Argentina	2	Montevideo	90,000	Langenus (B)
1934	Italy	2	Czechoslovakia	1	Rome	50,000	Eklind (Se)
	(after extra time)						
1938	Italy	4	Hungary	2	Paris	45,000	Capdeville (F)
1950	Uruguay	2	Brazil	1	Rio de Janeiro	199,854	Reader (E)
1954	West Germany	3	Hungary	2	Berne	60,000	Ling (E)
1958	Brazil	5	Sweden	2	Stockholm	49,737	Guigue (F)
1962	Brazil	3	Czechoslovakia	1	Santiago	68,679	Latychev (USSR)
1966	England	4	West Germany	2	Wembley	93,802	Dienst (Sw)
	(after extra time)						
1970	Brazil	4	Italy	1	Mexico City	107,412	Glockner (EG)
1974	West Germany	2	Holland	1	Munich	77,833	Taylor (E)
1978	Argentina	3	Holland	1	Buenos Aires	77,000	Gonella (I)
	(after extra time)						
1982	Italy	3	West Germany	1	Madrid	90,080	Coelho (Br)
1986	Argentina	3	West Germany	2	Mexico City	114,580	Filho (Br)
1990	West Germany	1	Argentina	0	Rome	73,603	Codesal (Mex)
1994	Brazil	0	Italy	0	Los Angeles	94,194	Puhl (H)

(Brazil won 3-2 on penalties aet)

GOALSCORING AND ATTENDANCES IN WORLD CUP FINAL ROUNDS

Venue	Matches	Goals (av)	Attendance (av)
1930, Uruguay	18	70 (3.9)	434,500 (24,138)
1934, Italy	17	70 (4.1)	395,000 (23,235)
1938, France	18	84 (4.6)	483,000 (26,833)
1950, Brazil	22	88 (4.0)	1,337,000 (60,772)
1954, Switzerland	26	140 (5.4)	943,000 (36,270)
1958, Sweden	35	126 (3.6)	868,000 (24,800)
1962, Chile	32	89 (2.8)	776,000 (24,250)
1966, England	32	89 (2.8)	1,614,677 (50,458)
1970, Mexico	32	95 (2.9)	1,673,975 (52,311)
1974, West Germany	38	97 (2.5)	1,774,022 (46,684)
1978, Argentina	38	102 (2.7)	1,610,215 (42,374)
1982, Spain	52	146 (2.8)	2,064,364 (38,816)
1986, Mexico	52	132 (2.5)	2,441,731 (46,956)
1990, Italy	52	115 (2.2)	2,515,168 (48,368)
1994, USA	52	141 (2.7)	3,567,415 (68,604)

LEADING GOALSCORERS

Year	Player	Goals
1930	Guillermo Stabile (Argentina)	8
1934	Angelo Schiavio (Italy)	
	Oldrich Nejedly (Czechoslovakia)	
	Edmund Conen (Germany)	4
1938	Leonidas da Silva (Brazil)	8
1950	Ademir (Brazil)	9
1954	Sandor Kocsis (Hungary)	11
1958	Just Fontaine (France)	13
1962	Drazen Jerkovic (Yugoslavia)	5
1966	Eusebio (Portugal)	9
1970	Gerd Muller (West Germany)	10
1974	Grzegorz Lato (Poland)	7
1978	Mario Kempes (Argentina)	6
1982	Paolo Rossi (Italy)	6
1986	Gary Lineker (England)	6
1990	Salvatore Schillaci (Italy)	6
1994	Oleg Salenko (Russia)	
	Hristo Stoichkov (Bulgaria)	6

1998 FIFA WORLD CUP

Qualifying draw for France 1998

OCEANIA (Members 10, Entries 10)
Either one or no team qualifies

First Round (League System + 1 play-off match)
Melanesian Group: Papua New Guinea 1, Soloman
Islands 1; Soloman Islands 1, Vanuatu 1; Papua New
Guinea 2, Vanuatu 1.
Polynesian Group: Tonga 2, Cook Islands 0; Western
Samoa 1, Cook Islands 1; Tonga 1, Western Samoa 0.
Play-off: Tonga 0, Soloman Islands 4; Soloman Islands 9,
Tonga 0.

Second Round (League System)
Group 1: Australia 13, Soloman Islands 0; Australia 5,
Tahiti 0; Soloman Islands 4, Tahiti 1; Soloman Islands 2,
Australia 6; Tahiti 0, Australia 2; Tahiti 1, Soloman
Islands 1.
Group 2: Papua New Guinea 1, New Zealand 0; Fiji 0,
New Zealand 1; New Zealand 7, Papua New Guinea 0;
Fiji 3, Papua New Guinea 1; New Zealand 5, Fiji 0; Papua
New Guinea 0, Fiji 1.

Third Round (Cup System)
Winner of group 1 v winner of group 2
Third Round Winner plays team finishing fourth in Asia.
New Zealand 0, Australia 3; Australia 2, New Zealand 0.

ASIA (Members 41 +1, Entries 36)
Three or four teams qualify

First Round (League System)
Group 1: Taiwan 0, Saudi Arabia 2; Malaysia 2,
Bangladesh 0; Bangladesh 1, Taiwan 3; Malaysia 0, Saudi
Arabia 0; Bangladesh 1, Saudi Arabia 4; Malaysia 2,
Taiwan 0; Taiwan 0, Malaysia 0; Saudi Arabia 3,
Bangladesh 0; Taiwan 1, Bangladesh 2; Saudi Arabia 3,
Malaysia 0; Bangladesh 0, Malaysia 1; Saudi Arabia 6,
Taiwan 0.
Group 2: Maldives 0, Iran 17; Syria 12, Maldives 0;
Kyrgyzstan 0, Iran 7; Syria 0, Iran 1; Kyrgyzstan 3,
Maldives 0; Iran 3, Kyrgyzstan 1; Maldives 0, Syria 12;
Iran 9, Maldives 0; Kyrgyzstan 2, Syria 1; Iran 2, Syria 2;
Maldives 0, Kyrgyzstan 6.
Group 3: Jordan 0, United Arab Emirates 0; Bahrain 1,
United Arab Emirates 2; Bahrain 1, Jordan 0; Jordan 4,
Bahrain 1; United Arab Emirates 3, Bahrain 0; United
Arab Emirates 2, Jordan 0.
Group 4: Nepal 1, Macao 1; Oman 0, Japan 1; Macao 0,
Japan 10; Oman 1, Nepal 0; Nepal 0, Japan 6; Oman 4,
Macao 0; Japan 10, Macao 0; Nepal 0, Oman 6; Japan 3,
Nepal 0; Macao 0, Oman 2; Japan 1, Oman 1; Macao 2,
Nepal 1.
Group 5: Indonesia 8, Cambodia 0; Indonesia 0, Yemen
0; Cambodia 0, Yemen 1, Cambodia 1, Indonesia 1;
Yemen 0, Uzbekistan 1; Yemen 7, Cambodia 0;
Uzbekistan 6, Cambodia 0; Indonesia 1, Uzbekistan 1;
Yemen 1, Indonesia 1; Uzbekistan 3, Indonesia 0;
Cambodia 1, Uzbekistan 4.
Group 6: Hong Kong 0, Korea Republic 2; Thailand 1,
Korea Republic 3; Thailand 2, Hong Kong 0; Hong Kong
3, Thailand 2; Korea Republic 4, Hong Kong 0; Korea
Republic 0, Thailand 0.
Group 7: Lebanon 1, Singapore 1; Singapore 0, Kuwait 1;
Kuwait 2, Lebanon 0; Singapore 1, Lebanon 2; Kuwait 4,
Singapore 0; Lebanon 1, Kuwait 3.
Group 8: Tajikistan 4, Vietnam 0; Turkmenistan 1, China
4, Tajikistan 0, China 1; Turkmenistan 2, Vietnam 1;
Vietman 1, China 3; Turkmenistan 1, Tajikistan 2; China
1, Turkmenistan 0; Vietnam 0, Tajikistan 4; China 0,
Tajikistan 0; Vietnam 0, Turkmenistan 4; China 4,
Vietnam 0; Tajikistan 5, Turkmenistan 0.
Group 9: Kazakhstan 3, Pakistan 0; Pakistan 2, Iraq 6;
Iraq 1, Kazakhstan 2; Pakistan 0, Kazakhstan 7; Iraq 6,
Pakistan 1; Kazakhstan 3, Iraq 1.
Group 10: Qatar 3, Sri Lanka 0; India 2, Philippines 0;
Qatar 5, Philippines 0; Sri Lanka 1, India 1; Philippines 0,
Sri Lanka 3; Qatar 6, India 0.

Second Round (League System)
Two groups of five teams

Third Round (Cup System)
Group winners and runners-up qualify for the semi-finals.
The winners qualify for the finals, the losers compete in a
play-off , the winner qualifiying for the finals, the losing
team meets the winners of the Oceania zone.

CONCACAF (Members 30, Entries 30, including 2
late entries Bermuda and Cuba)
Three teams qualify

First Round (Cup System – Caribbean zone)
Dominican Republic 3, Aruba 2; Aruba 1, Dominican
Republic 3; Bahamas withdrew v St Kitts & Nevis w.o.;
Guyana 1, Grenada 2; Grenada 6, Guyana 0; Dominica 3,
Antigua 3; Antigua 1, Dominica 3.

Second Round (Cup System – Caribbean zone)
Bermuda withdrew v Trinidad & Tobago w.o.; Puerto
Rico 1, St Vincent & the Grenadines 2; St Vincent & the
Grenadines 7, Puerto Rico 0; Cuba 1, Cayman Islands 0;
Cayman Islands 0, Cuba 5;
St Kitts & Nevis 5, St Lucia 1; St Lucia 0, St Kitts & Nevis
1; Haiti 6, Grenada 1; Grenada 0, Haiti 1; Syrinam 0,
Jamaica 1; Jamaica 5, Syrinam 0; Dominica 0, Barbados
1; Barbados 1, Dominica 0; Dominican Republic 2,
Netherlands Antilles 1; Netherlands Antilles 0,
Dominican Republic 0.

Third Round (Cup System – Caribbean zone)
Cuba 5, Haiti 1; Haiti 1, Cuba 1; Dominican Republic 1,
Trinidad & Tobago 4; Barbados 0, Jamaica 1; Jamaica 2,
Barbados 0; St Kitts & Nevis 2, St Vincent 2; St Vincent
0, St Kitts & Nevis 0.

First Round (Cup System – Central American zone)
Nicaragua 0, Guatemala 1; Guatemala 2, Nicaragua 1;
Belize 1, Panama 2; Panama 4, Belize 1.

Semi-final Round (League System)
Group 1: Trinidad & Tobago 0, Costa Rica 1; Trinidad &
Tobago 1, Guatemala 1; USA 2, Guatemala 0; USA 2,
Trinidad & Tobago 0; Costa Rica 3, Guatemala 0;
Guatemala 1, Costa Rica 0; Trinidad & Tobago 0, USA
1; Costa Rica 2, USA 1; Guatemala 2, Trinidad &
Tobago 1; USA 2, Costa Rica 1; Costa Rica 2, Trinidad &
Tobago 1; Guatemala 2, USA 2.
Group 2: Canada 3, Panama 1; Cuba 0, El Salvador 5;
Cuba 3, Panama 0; Panama 1, El Salvador 1; Canada 2,
Cuba 0; Cuba 0, Canada 2; Panama 0, Canada 0; Canada
1, El Salvador 0; El Salvador 3, Panama 2; El Salvador 3,
Cuba 0; Panama 3, Cuba 1; El Salvador 0, Canada 2.
Group 3: Jamaica 3, Honduras 0; St Vincent & the
Genadines 0, Mexico 3; Honduras 2, Mexico 1; St
Vincent & the Grenadines 1, Jamaica 2; St Vincent & the
Grenadines 1, Honduras 4; Mexico 2, Jamaica 1;
Honduras 0, Jamaica 0; Mexico 5, St Vincent & the
Grenadines 1; Mexico 3, Honduras 1; Jamaica 5, St
Vincent & the Grenadines 0; Honduras 11, St Vincent &
the Grenadines 3; Jamaica 1, Mexico 0.

Final Round (League System)
Jamaica 0, USA 0; Mexico 4, Canada 0; Costa Rica 0,
Mexico 0; USA 3, Canada 0; Costa Rica 3, USA 2;
Canada 0, El Salvador 0; Mexico 6, Jamaica 0; USA 2,
Mexico 2; Canada 0, Jamaica 0; El Salvador 2, Costa Rica
1; Costa Rica 3, Jamaica 1; Jamaica 1, El Salvador 0;
Canada 1, Costa Rica 0; El Salvador 0, Mexico 1; El
Salvador 1, USA 1.

AFRICA (Members 51, Entries 38, Withdrawals 2)
Five teams qualify

First Round (Cup System)
Sudan 2, Zambia 0; Namibia 2, Mozambique 0; Tanzania
0, Ghana 0; Swaziland 0, Gabon 1; Uganda 0, Angola 2;
Mauritius 1, Zaire 5; Malawi 0, South Africa 1;
Madagascar 1, Zimbabwe 2; Guinea-Bissau 3, Guinea 2;
Rwanda 1,Tunisia 3; Congo 2, Ivory Coast 0; Kenya 3,
Algeria 1; Burundi 1, Sierra Leone 0; Mauritania 0,
Burkina Faso 0; Togo 2, Senegal 1; Gambia 2, Liberia 1;
Algeria 1, Kenya 0; Senegal 2, Togo 1; South Africa 3,
Malawi 1; Sierra Leone 0, Burundi 1; Angola 3, Uganda
1; Gabon 2, Swaziland 0; Guinea 3, Guinea-Bissau 1;

Ivory Coast 1, Congo 1; Mozambique 1, Namibia 1; Tunisia 2, Rwanda 0; Burkina Faso 2, Mauritania 0; Zaire 2, Mauritius 0; Zambia 3, Sudan 0; Zimbabwe 2, Madagascar 2; Ghana 2, Tanzania 1; Liberia 4, Gambia 0.

Second Round (League System)
Group 1: Nigeria 2, Burkina Faso 0; Guinea 3, Kenya 1; Kenya 1, Nigeria 1; Burkina Faso 0, Guinea 2; Nigeria 2, Guinea 1; Kenya 4, Burkina Faso 3; Kenya 1, Guinea 0; Burkina Faso 1, Nigeria 2; Nigeria 3, Kenya 0; Guinea 3, Burkina Faso 1.

Nigeria qualify for finals.
Group 2: Egypt 7, Namibia 1; Liberia 0, Tunisia 1; Namibia 0, Liberia 0; Tunisia 1, Egypt 0; Liberia 1, Egypt 0; Namibia 1, Tunisia 2; Namibia 2, Egypt 3; Tunisia 2, Liberia 0; Egypt 0, Tunisia 0; Liberia 1, Namibia 2.

Tunisia qualify for finals.
Group 3: South Africa 1, Zaire 0; Congo 1, Zambia 0; Zambia 0, South Africa 0; Zaire 1, Congo 1; Congo 2, South Africa 0; Zaire 2, Zambia 2; Zaire 1, South Africa 2; Zambia 3, Congo 0; Congo 1, Zaire 0; South Africa 3, Zambia 0.
Group 4: Angola 2, Zimbabwe 1; Togo 2, Cameroon 4; Cameroon 0, Angola 0; Zimbabwe 3, Togo 0; Angola 3, Togo 1; Cameroon 1, Zimbabwe 0; Cameroon 2, Togo 0; Zimbabwe 0, Angola 0; Angola 1, Cameroon 1; Togo 2, Zimbabwe 1.
Group 5: Morocco 4, Sierra Leone 0; Gabon 1, Ghana 1; Sierra Leone 1, Gabon 0; Ghana 2, Morocco 2; Sierra Leone 1, Ghana 1; Gabon 0, Morocco 4; Sierra Leone 0, Morocco 1; Ghana 3, Gabon 0; Morocco 1, Ghana 0.

Morocco qualify for finals.

EUROPE (Members 49 + 1, Entries 50)
Fifteen teams qualify including France as the host nation. The nine group winners and the best runner-up qualify. The eight other runners-up will be drawn in pairs, the four winners also qualifying for the final.

GROUP 1

Athens, 24 April 1996, 9000

Greece (0) 2 *(Batista 56, Nikolaidis 66)*

Slovenia (0) 0

Greece: Atmatsidis; Apostolakis, Kassapis, Ouzounidis, Kallitzakis, Kostantinidis (Alexandris 46), Zagorakis, Vrizas, Batista, Tsartas (Frantzeskos 82), Donis (Nikolaidis 61).
Slovenia: Boskovic; Galic, Englaro, Milanic, Jermanis, Ceh, Novak, Zidan (Gajser 36), Udovic (Gliha 70), Gregor, Florjancic.
Referee: Pedersen (Denmark).

Kalamata, 1 September 1996, 6000

Greece (1) 3 *(Ouzounidis 41, Apostolakis 77, Nikolaidis 83)*

Bosnia (0) 0

Greece: Atmatsidis; Apostolakis, Kassapis, Ouzounidis, Kallitzakis, Dabizas, Zagorakis, Vrizas (Batista 34), Tsartas (Frantzeskos 75), Donis (Alexandris 46), Nikolaidis.
Bosnia: Omerovic; Sabic, Katana, Glavas, Konjic, Smajic (Sasivarevic 64), Bazdarevic, Baljic, Begic (Varesanovic 67), Kodro, Bolic (Music 60).
Referee: Benko (Austria).

Ljubljana, 1 September 1996, 5000

Slovenia (0) 0

Denmark (0) 2 *(Nielsen A 78, Schjonberg 89)*

Slovenia: Boskovic; Galic, Krizan, Englaro, Binkovski, Ceh, Novak, Karic, Zahovic, Udovic (Kokol 72), Florjancic.
Denmark: Schmeichel; Helveg, Friis-Hansen, Hogh, Laursen, Bjur (Goldbaek 22), Nielsen A, Steen Nielsen (Schjonberg 61), Thomsen, Laudrup M (Andersen S 85), Laudrup B.
Referee: Meier (Switzerland).

Bologna, 8 October 1996, 1500

Bosnia (1) 1 *(Salihamidzic 25)*

Croatia (2) 4 *(Bilic 14, Vlaovic 33, Boksic 64, 83)*

Bosnia: Omerovic; Sabic (Begic 53), Geca, Konjic (Pintul 65), Katana, Besirevic, Teljigovic (Halilovic 60), Bazdarevic, Smajic, Salihamidzic, Bolic.
Croatia: Ladic; Soldo, Jerkan, Bilic (Mamic 80), Jurcevic (Simic 44), Boban, Vlaovic (Cvitanovic 85), Asanovic, Jarni, Boksic, Suker.
Referee: Ouzounov (Bulgaria).

Copenhagen, 9 October 1996, 40,226

Denmark (1) 2 *(Zagorakis 25 (og), Laudrup B 52)*

Greece (1) 1 *(Donis 35)*

Denmark: Schmeichel; Helveg, Rieper, Hogh, Laursen, Nielsen P (Goldbaek 53), Thomsen, Nielsen A, Laudrup M (Schjonberg 75), Moller (Andersen S 87), Laudrup B.
Greece: Atmatsidis; Efstratios (Niniadis 75), Ouzounidis, Kallitzakis, Zagorakis (Konstantinidis 64), Ntampizas, Nikolaidis, Tsartas (Niniadis 75), Lima (Alexandris 59), Donis.
Referee: Durkin (England).

Zagreb, 10 November 1996, 30,000

Croatia (1) 1 *(Suker 45)*

Greece (1) 1 *(Nikolaidis 9)*

Croatia: Ladic; Stimac (Soldo 52), Jerkan, Bilic, Stanic, Asanovic, Prosinecki (Vlaovic 75), Boban, Jarni, Suker, Boksic.
Greece: Atmatsidis; Apostolakis, Karataidis, Kallitzakis, Danbitzas, Kassapis, Zagorakis (Vlahos 46), Kostantinidis, Tsartas (Vrizas 83), Donis (Georgiadis 65), Nikolaidis.
Referee: Van der Ende (Holland).

Ljubljana, 10 November 1996, 4000

Slovenia (1) 1 *(Zahovic 41)*

Bosnia (2) 2 *(Bolic 6, Kodro 33)*

Slovenia: Boskovic; Englaro, Krizan, Milanic, Jermanis, Ceh, Novak, Karic (Binkovski 78), Zahovic, Simundza (Vulic 46), Udovic.
Bosnia: Dedic; Sabic (Kapetanovic 89), Besirevic, Konjic, Begic, Jasarevic, Glavas, Halilovic, Kodro, Salihamidzic (Baljic 75), Bolic (Brkic 85).
Referee: Agius (Malta).

Split, 29 March 1997, 34,000

Croatia (0) 1 *(Suker 50)*

Denmark (0) 1 *(Laudrup B 82)*

Croatia: Ladic; Kovac, Jarni, Soldo, Jerkan, Bilic, Asanovic (Pralija 84), Prosinecki, Suker, Boban, Boksic (Vlaovic 75).
Denmark: Schmeichel; Laursen, Rieper, Hogh (Schjonbjerg 14), Heintze, Helveg, Frandsen (Tomasson 70), Thomsen, Nielsen A, Beck (Pedersen P 57), Laudrup B.
Referee: Ceccarini (Italy).

Sarajevo, 2 April 1997, 40,000

Bosnia (0) 0

Greece (0) 1 *(Franzeskos 74)*

Bosnia: Dedic; Sabic (Brkic 86), Besirevic (Music 79), Ramcic, Katana, Jasarevic, Glavas (Baljic 79), Halilovic, Kodro, Salihamidzic, Bolic.
Greece: Atmatsidis; Apostolakis, Karataidis, Ouzounidis, Kalitzakis, Kursaidis, Zagorakis, Nikolaidis, Kostis (Georgatos 46), Tsartas (Franzeskos 67), Donis (Georgiadis GH 87).
Referee: Sars (France).

Split, 2 April 1997, 15,000

Croatia (2) 3 *(Prosinecki 33, Boban 43, 60)*

Slovenia (1) 3 *(Gliha 45, 65, 67)*

Croatia: Gabric (Mrmic 46); Simic, Jerkan, Bilic, Asanovic, Prosinecki, Vlaovic (Pralija 68), Boban, Boksic, Juric, Cvitanovic.
Slovenia: Boskovic; Englaro, Srebrnic, Krizan, Rudonja, Novak, Ceh (Seslar 68), Zahovic, Gajser (Karic 46), Udovic (Siljak 46), Gliha.
Referee: Durkin (England).

Copenhagen, 30 April 1997, 41,278

Denmark (2) 4 *(Nielsen A 4, 56, Pedersen P 27, Laudrup B 51)*

Slovenia (0) 0

Denmark: Schmeichel; Laursen (Bisgaard 58), Rieper, Hogh, Heintze, Helveg, Nielsen A, Thomsen (Frandsen 86), Tomasson, Pedersen P (Beck 70), Laudrup B.
Slovenia: Boskovic; Englaro, Krizan, Milanic, Rudonja (Karic 46), Jermanis, Novak, Gajser (Seslar 60), Ceh, Gliha, Siljak (Valentincic 80).
Referee: Krug (Germany).

Salonika, 30 April 1997, 35,000

Greece (0) 0

Croatia (0) 1 *(Suker 74)*

Greece: Atmatsidis; Apostolakis (Kostantinidis 46), Kassapis, Ouzounidis, Karataidis, Dabizas, Zagorakis, Nikolaidis (Mahlas 13), Poursanidis, Franzeskos, Donis.
Croatia: Ladic; Jarni, Bilic, Asanovic, Prosinecki (Vlaovic 72), Boban, Simic, Soldo (Maric 53), Juric, Suker, Boksic (Cvitanovic 67).
Referee: Nieto (Spain).

Copenhagen, 8 June 1997, 41,592

Denmark (0) 2 *(Rieper 67, Molnar 90)*

Bosnia (0) 0

Denmark: Schmeichel; Laursen, Rieper, Hogh, Heintze (Schjonberg 80), Helveg, Nielsen A, Thomsen, Tomasson (Frandsen 52), Pedersen P (Molnar 66), Laudrup B.
Bosnia: Dedic; Sabic (Music 71), Katana, Konjic (Ramcic 17), Besirevic, Hibic, Glavas, Halilovic, Baljic, Kodro (Majcin 37), Bolic.
Referee: Ihring (Slovakia).

Group 1	P	W	D	L	F	A	Pts
Denmark	5	4	1	0	11	2	13
Greece	6	3	1	2	8	4	10
Croatia	5	2	3	0	10	6	9
Bosnia	5	1	0	4	3	11	3
Slovenia	5	0	1	4	4	13	1

GROUP 2

Chisinau, 1 September 1996, 15,000

Moldova (0) 0

England (2) 3 *(Barmby 23, Gascoigne 24, Shearer 61)*

Moldova: Romanenco; Secu, Nani, Testimitanu, Gaidamasciuc, Belous (Siscin 58), Epureanu, Curtianu, Clescenco, Miterev (Rebeja 61), Popovici.
England: Seaman; Neville G, Pearce, Southgate, Pallister, Hinchcliffe, Barmby (Le Tissier 81), Ince, Shearer, Gascoigne (Batty 81), Beckham.
Referee: Koho (Finland).

Chisinau, 5 October 1996, 11,000

Moldova (1) 1 *(Curtianu 12)*

Italy (1) 3 *(Ravanelli 9, 86 (pen), Casiraghi 69)*

Moldova: Romanenco; Secu, Tolokonnikov, Culibaba, Testimitanu, Gaidamasciuc, Curtianu (Miterev 52), Epureanu, Siscin, Rebeja (Rogaciov 78), Clescenco.
Italy: Toldo; Nesta, Ferrara, Costacurta, Maldini, Conte, Di Matteo, Carboni (Zola 70), Chiesa (Di Livio 46), Casiraghi, Ravanelli.
Referee: Grabher (Austria).

Wembley, 9 October 1996, 74,663

England (2) 2 *(Shearer 24, 38)*

Poland (1) 1 *(Citko 7)*

England: Seaman; Neville G, Pearce, Southgate (Pallister 51), Ince, Hinchcliffe, McManaman, Gascoigne, Shearer, Ferdinand, Beckham.
Poland: Wozniak; Waldoch, Zielinski, Juskowiak, Hajto, Michalski, Baluszynski, Wojtala, Nowak, Citko, Warzycha (Sagamowski 75).
Referee: Krug (Germany).

Perugia, 9 October 1996, 16,146

Italy (1) 1 *(Ravanelli 43)*

Georgia (0) 0

Italy: Toldo; Pessotto, Nesta, Ferrara, Maldini, Di Livio (Panucci 82), Conte (Dino Baggio 60), Di Matteo, Carboni (Zola 17), Casiraghi, Ravanelli.
Georgia: Zoidze; Lobjanidze, Koudinov (Inalishvili 46), Tskhadadze, Shelia, Kobiashvili, Gogichaishvili, Nemsadze, Kinkladze, Ketsbaia, Gogrichiani (Aveladze R 30).
Referee: Blareau (Belgium).

Tbilisi, 9 November 1996, 48,000

Georgia (0) 0

England (2) 2 *(Sheringham 15, Ferdinand 37)*

Georgia: Zoidze; Lobjanidze, Tskhadadze, Shelia, Gogichaishvili (Gudushauri 60), Nemsadze, Kinkladze, Jamarauli, Kobiashvili, Ketsbaia, Aveladze S (Gogrichiani 52).
England: Seaman; Campbell, Hinchcliffe, Batty, Southgate, Adams, Beckham, Gascoigne, Ferdinand (Wright 81), Sheringham, Ince.
Referee: Monteiro (Portugal).

Katowice, 10 November 1996, 10,000

Poland (1) 2 *(Baluszynski 4, Warzycha 76 (pen))*

Moldova (0) 1 *(Clescenco 83 (pen))*

Poland: Szamotulski; Zielinski, Wojtala, Michalski, Juskowiak, Czerwiec (Waldoch 46), Hajto, Baluszynski (Kucharski 72), Nowak, Warzycha (Staniek 87), Citko.
Moldova: Romanenco; Secu, Tolokonnikov, Testimitanu, Culibaba, Gaidamasciuc, Curtianu, Epureanu (Cebotari 28) (Miterev 59), Siscin, Popovici (Martin 67), Clescenco.
Referee: Vorgias (Greece).

Wembley, 12 February 1997, 75,055

England (0) 0

Italy (1) 1 *(Zola 18)*

England: Walker; Neville G, Pearce, Ince, Campbell, Batty (Wright 88), McManaman (Merson 76), Le Tissier (Ferdinand 60), Shearer, Beckham, Le Saux.
Italy: Peruzzi; Ferrara, Costacurta, Cannavaro, Di Livio, Dino Baggio, Albertini, Di Matteo, Maldini, Zola (Fuser 90), Casiraghi (Ravanelli 76).
Referee: Puhl (Hungary).

Trieste, 29 March 1997, 20,767

Italy (2) 3 *(Maldini 24, Zola 44, Vieri 49)*

Moldova (0) 0

Italy: Peruzzi; Ferrara, Maldini, Costacurta, Nesta (Cannavaro 31), Albertini, Di Matteo, Di Livio (Eranio 75), Dino Baggio, Zola, Vieri (Padovano 68).
Moldova: Romanenco; Fistican, Tolokonnikov, Culibaba, Testimitanu, Gaidamasciuc (Cebotar 61), Siscin, Epureanu, Curtianu, Spinu (Suharev 61), Clescenco.
Referee: Veissiere (France).

Chorzow, 2 April 1997, 32,000

Poland (0) 0

Italy (0) 0

Poland: Wozniak; Skrzypek, Zielinski, Wojtala, Waldoch, Citko, Swierczewski P (Kowalczyk 46), Juskowiak, Nowak (Sokolowski 44), Baluszynski (Kaluzny 65), Ledwon.
Italy: Peruzzi; Ferrara, Maldini, Dino Baggio, Cannavaro, Costacurta, Di Livio, Fuser (Carboni 84), Vieri, Di Matteo, Zola.
Referee: Nielsen (Denmark).

Wembley, 30 April 1997, 71,206

England (1) 2 *(Sheringham 42, Shearer 90)*

Georgia (0) 0

England: Seaman; Neville G, Le Saux, Batty, Campbell, Adams (Southgate 87), Lee, Ince (Redknapp 77), Shearer, Sheringham, Beckham.
Georgia: Zoidze; Chikhradze, Sheqiladze, Tskhadadze, Shelia, Machavariani (Gogrichiani 30) (Arveladze A 76), Nemsadze, Jamarauli, Ketsbaia, Kinkladze (Gakhokidze 61), Arveladze S.
Referee: Harrel (France).

Naples, 30 April 1997, 37,500

Italy (2) 3 *(Di Matteo 23, Maldini 37, Roberto Baggio 66)*

Poland (0) 0

Italy: Peruzzi; Ferrara (Panucci 85), Di Livio, Costacurta, Cannavaro, Maldini, Di Matteo, Albertini, Dino Baggio (Fuser 85), Zola (Roberto Baggio 51), Ravanelli.
Poland: Wozniak; Skrzypek, Zielinski, Wojtala, Waldoch (Majak 46), Citko, Kaluzny, Baluszynski (Hajto 66), Kucharski (Warzycha K 46), Nowak, Ledwon.
Referee: Aranda (Spain).

Katowice, 31 May 1997, 35,000

Poland (0) 0
England (1) 2 *(Shearer 6, Sheringham 90)*

Poland: Wozniak; Jozwiak, Zielinski, Kaluzny, Ledwon, Bukalski (Swierczewski P 46), Nowak (Kucharski 57), Majak, Waldoch, Juskowiak (Adamczyk 51), Dembinski.
England: Seaman; Neville G, Le Saux, Southgate, Campbell, Ince, Lee, Gascoigne (Batty 16), Shearer, Sheringham, Beckham (Neville P 88).
Referee: Meier (Switzerland).

Batumi, 7 June 1997, 17,000

Georgia (1) 2 *(Aveladze S 27, Kinkladze 51 (pen))*
Moldova (0) 0

Georgia: Zoidze; Lobjanidze, Tskhadadze, Kobiashvili, Chikhradze, Gogichaishvili, Nemsadze, Jamarauli, Ketsbaia (Janashia 80), Kinkladze, Aveladze S.
Moldova: Romanenco; Fistican, Tolokonnikov, Testimitanu, Culibaba, Epureanu, Siscin (Spinu 29), Popovici, Suharev, Miterev (Rogaciov 29), Clescenco.
Referee: Agius (Malta).

Katowice, 14 June 1997, 1500

Poland (2) 4 *(Ledwon 33, Trzeciak 35, Bukalski 75 (pen), Nowak 90)*
Georgia (1) 1 *(Aveladze S 25)*

Poland: Szamotulski; Skrzypek, Kukielka, Michalski, Kaluzny, Sokolowski, Bukalski, Ledwon, Dembinski (Adamczyk 88), Nowak, Trzeciak (Kucharski 60).
Georgia: Zoidze; Lobjanidze, Tskhadadze, Kobiashvili (Kavelashvili 72), Kaladze, Gogichaishvili (Kiknadze 46), Nemsadze, Jamarauli (Aveladze A 46), Ketsbaia, Kinkladze, Aveladze S.
Referee: Benko (Austria).

Group 2

	P	W	D	L	F	A	Pts
Italy	6	5	1	0	11	1	16
England	6	5	0	1	11	2	15
Poland	6	2	1	3	7	9	7
Georgia	5	1	0	4	3	9	3
Moldova	5	0	0	5	2	13	0

GROUP 3

Oslo, 2 June 1996, 14,012

Norway (2) 5 *(Solbakken 8, 46, Solskjaer 37, 90, Strandli 60)*
Azerbaijan (0) 0

Norway: Grodas; Haaland, Berg, Johnsen R, Bjornebye, Rudi, Solbakken (Larsen 79), Rekdal, Leonhardsen (Flo T 46), Solskjaer, Strandli.
Azerbaijan: Jidkov; Gasimov, Getman, Ahmedov, Agayev (Nosenko 40), Idigov, Abusev (Asadov 79), Rzayev (Kurbanov 46), Guseynov, Lichkin, Suleimanov.
Referee: Snoddy (N Ireland).

Baku, 31 August 1996, 30,000

Azerbaijan (1) 1 *(Rzayev 28)*
Switzerland (0) 0

Azerbaijan: Jidkov; Gasimov, Asadov, Abusev, Agayev (Getman 86), Ahmedov, Rzayev (Kurbanov 69), Idigov, Lichkin (Alekperov 90), Suleimanov, Guseynov.
Switzerland: Pascolo; Hottiger, Vega, Henchoz, Quentin, Ohrel (Sesa 75), Yakin, Sforza, Comisetti (Bonvin 81), Knup (Chapuisat 67), Turkyilmaz.
Referee: Wojcik (Poland).

Budapest, 1 September 1996, 12,500

Hungary (1) 1 *(Orosz 16)*
Finland (0) 0

Hungary: Safar; Mracsko, Telek, Nagy N, Sebok, Halmai, Dombi (Plokai 18), Urban, Orosz (Balog 62), Sandor (Egressy 87), Klausz.
Finland: Niemi; Rissanen, Hyypia, Nieminen (Huhtamaki 46), Koskinen, Lindberg, Sumiala, Mahlio (Suominen 81), Jarvinen, Nyyssonen (Kolkka 65), Vanhala.
Referee: Strampe (Germany).

Helsinki, 6 October 1996, 7217

Finland (1) 2 *(Sumiala 41 (pen), Kolkka 75)*
Switzerland (2) 3 *(Lombardo 14, Sforza 34, Yakin 54)*

Finland: Niemi; Huhtamaki, Rissanen, Hyrylainen, Myyry, Lindberg (Kolkka 37), Suominen, Gronlund, Koskinen, Sumiala (Hyypia 82), Vanhala.
Switzerland: Pascolo; Haas, Vega, Henchoz, Walker, Lombardo, Yakin, Sforza, Vogel (Wicky 90), Chapuisat (Bonvin 78), Kunz (Knup 78).
Referee: Orasson (Iceland).

Oslo, 9 October 1996, 22,480

Norway (0) 3 *(Rekdal 83, 89, 90 (pen))*
Hungary (0) 0

Norway: Grodas; Haaland, Berg, Johnsen R, Bjornebye, Bohinen, Mykland, Rekdal, Leonhardsen, Solskjaer (Flo T 64), Strandli (Ostenstad 83).
Hungary: Safar; Banfi, Sebok, Mracsko, Nyilas (Illes 83), Urban, Halmai (Torma 87), Balog, Nagy N, Dombi, Klausz.
Referee: Dallas (Scotland).

Baku, 10 November 1996, 35,000

Azerbaijan (0) 0
Hungary (1) 3 *(Nyilas 42, 70 (pen), Urban 83)*

Azerbaijan: Jidkov (Koudijev 89); Kasumov, Asadov, Abusev, Agayev (Getman 85), Ahmedov, Rzayev, Idigov, Lichkin (Hasanbekov 46), Suleimanov, Kurbanov.
Hungary: Safar; Banfi, Mracsko, Kuttor, Nyilas, Urban (Szlezak 89), Illes (Sandor 75), Halmai, Nagy N, Torma (Dombi 63), Klausz.
Referee: Poljak (Croatia).

Berne, 10 November 1996, 23,000

Switzerland (0) 0
Norway (1) 1 *(Leonhardsen 32)*

Switzerland: Pascolo; Wicky, Vega, Henchoz, Walker, Lombardo (Subiat 67), Yakin (Piffaretti 88), Sforza, Vogel, Turkyilmaz, Chapuisat (Bonvin 85).
Norway: Grodas; Haaland, Berg, Johnsen R, Nilsen, Flo T (Solskjaer 75), Mykland (Solbakken 61), Rekdal, Leonhardsen, Strandli, Ostenstad (Flo H 87).
Referee: Vega (Spain).

Baku, 2 April 1997, 20,000

Azerbaijan (0) 1 *(Suleimanov 80 (pen))*
Finland (1) 2 *(Litmanen 25, Paatelainen 66)*

Azerbaijan: Jidkov; Agayev, Isayev (Kurbanov M 80), Ahmedov, Lichkin, Abusev, Guseynov, Guliyev, Kurbanov G, Suleimanov, Junuyov.
Finland: Niemi; Nuorela, Makela (Rissanen 73), Hyypia, Koskinen, Nurmela, Mahlio, Litmanen (Myyry 73), Wiss, Sumiala, Paatelainen.
Referee: Poll (England).

Oslo, 30 April 1997, 22,287

Norway (0) 1 *(Solskjaer 83)*
Finland (0) 1 *(Sumiala 60)*

Norway: Grodas; Eggen, Berg, Johnsen R (Halle 28), Bjornebye, Solskjaer, Mykland, Rekdal, Solbakken, Strandli (Flo J 62), Flo TA.
Finland: Niemi; Tuomela, Hyypia (Lehkusou 4), Nuorela, Koskinen, Mahlio, Rissanen, Nurmela (Makela 86), Sumiala, Litmanen, Johansson J (Kolkka 82).
Referee: Merk (Germany).

Zurich, 30 April 1997, 17,300

Switzerland (0) 1 *(Turkyilmaz 83)*
Hungary (0) 0

Switzerland: Lehmann; Ohrel, Walker, Vega, Wicky (Lombardo 62), Yakin, Kunz (Chassot 56), Vogel, Turkyilmaz, Sforza, Chapuisat (Grassi 73).
Hungary: Safar; Kuttor, Banfi, Nagy N (Szlezak 56), Lorincz, Kereszturi, Mracsko (Nyilas 69), Urban, Orosz (Halmai 80), Illes, Klausz.
Referee: Sundell (Sweden).

Helsinki, 8 June 1997, 13,417

Finland (0) 3 *(Vanhala 60, Litmanen 65, Sumiala 82)*
Azerbaijan (0) 0
Finland: Niemi; Nuorela, Rissanen, Hyypia, Koskinen, Nurmela (Valakari 46), Litmanen (Nyyssonen 84), Mahlio, Johansson (Kolkka 62), Sumiala, Vanhala.
Azerbaijan: Jidkov; Jabarov, Gaisumov, Ahmedov (Moussaev 65), Lichkin, Abusev, Guseynov, Agayev (Isaev 89), Guliyev, Kurbanov, Kasumov (Tagizadze 60).
Referee: Hamer (Luxembourg).

Budapest, 8 June 1997, 30,000

Hungary (1) 1 *(Kovacs Z 21)*
Norway (1) 1 *(Rudi 10)*
Hungary: Babos; Lorincz, Banfi, Kuttor, Dombi, Farkashazy, Sandor (Nyilas 79), Halmai, Nagy N (Szlezak 60), Orosz (Dragoner 86), Kovacs Z.
Norway: Grodas; Haaland, Berg, Johnsen R, Bjornebye, Rudi, Mykland (Flo J 66), Rekdal, Leonhardsen (Solbakken 76), Strandli, Flo T (Ostenstad 81).
Referee: Elleray (England).

Group 3

	P	W	D	L	F	A	Pts
Norway	5	3	2	0	11	2	11
Finland	5	2	1	2	8	6	7
Hungary	5	2	1	2	5	5	7
Switzerland	4	2	0	2	4	4	6
Azerbaijan	5	1	0	4	2	13	3

GROUP 4

Stockholm, 1 June 1996, 30,014

Sweden (2) 5 *(Andersson K 20 (pen), 62, Dahlin 30, Andersson P 77, Larsson 88)*
Belarus (0) 1 *(Belkevich 75)*
Sweden: Andersson B; Nilsson R, Andersson P, Bjorklund, Sundgren, Ingesson (Mild 85), Thern, Zetterberg, Limpar, Dahlin (Larsson 77), Andersson K.
Belarus: Satsunkhevich; Gurenko, Khatskevich, Shtanyuk, Kashentsev (Kulchi 63), Vergeichik, Belkevich, Maleyev, Romashchenko (Kachuro 57), Makovski, Baranov.
Referee: Harrel (France).

Vienna, 31 August 1996, 29,500

Austria (0) 0
Scotland (0) 0
Austria: Konsel; Schopp, Schottel, Pfeffer, Feiersinger, Marasek, Ramusch (Ogris 76), Kuhbauer, Polster (Sabitzer 68), Herzog, Heraf.
Scotland: Goram; Burley, McKinlay T, Calderwood, Hendry, Boyd, McCall, Ferguson, McCoist (Durie 75), McAllister, Collins.
Referee: Piraux (Belgium).

Minsk, 31 August 1996, 7000

Belarus (1) 1 *(Makovski 35)*
Estonia (0) 0
Belarus: Shantalosov; Gurenko, Orlovski, Shtanyuk, Yakhimovich, Oreshnikov, Kulchi, Baranov, Belkevich (Romashchenko 85), Makovski (Tchernyavski 70), Kachuro.
Estonia: Poom (Pareiko 7); Lemsalu, Rooba U, Hohlov-Simson, Lindmaa, Alonen (Kirs 57), Rooba M, Zelinski, Kristal, Reim, Oper (Arbeiter 64).
Referee: Khoussainov (Russia).

Riga, 1 September 1996, 2000

Latvia (0) 1 *(Rimkus 55)*
Sweden (2) 2 *(Dahlin 18, Andersson K 21)*
Latvia: Karavayev; Zakreshevsky (Troitsky 59), Stepanov, Shevlyakov, Bleidelis, Ivanov, Zemlinsky, Rimkus, Boulders (Babichev 74), Stradinsh (Pakhar 28), Shtolcers.
Sweden: Andersson B; Nilsson R, Andersson P, Bjorklund, Sundgren, Mild (Limpar 82), Zetterberg (Schwarz 85), Thern, Blomqvist, Dahlin (Andersson A 77), Andersson K.
Referee: Wagner (Hungary).

Tallinn, 5 October 1996, 2000

Estonia (0) 1 *(Hohlov-Simson 52)*
Belarus (0) 0
Estonia: Poom; Lemsalu, Hohlov-Simson, Rooba U, Zelinski, Alonen, Rooba M (Kallaste T 59), Lindmaa, Kristal (Arbeiter 90), Reim, Oper (Kirs 26).
Belarus: Shantalosov; Gurenko, Ostrovski, Shtanyuk, Khasskevich, Vergeichik (Baranov 43) (Tchernyavski 77), Kulchi, Maleyev, Belkevich, Makovski, Kachuro.
Referee: O'Hanlon (Rep of Ireland).

Riga, 5 October 1996, 9500

Latvia (0) 0
Scotland (1) 2 *(Collins 18, Jackson 78)*
Latvia: Karavayev; Troitsky, Astafyev, Zemlinsky, Shevlyakov, Stepanov, Ivanov, Bleidelis, Rimkus (Boulders 78), Babichev (Shtolcers 46), Pakhar.
Scotland: Goram; Burley, Boyd, McKinlay T (McNamara 65), Calderwood, Whyte, Spencer (Dodds 59), McCall (Lambert 46), Jackson, McAllister, Collins.
Referee: Ulrich (Czech Republic).

Minsk, 9 October 1996, 5000

Belarus (0) 1 *(Makovski 78)*
Latvia (1) 1 *(Zemlinksy 16)*
Belarus: Shantalosov; Gurenko, Shtanyuk, Bezmen, Ostrovski, Kulchi, Orlovski, Makovski, Tchernyavski (Vergeichik 90), Maleyev, Kachuro (Vyajevich 60).
Latvia: Karavayev; Troitsky, Zemlinsky, Shevlyakov (Zakreshevsky 64), Astafyev, Ivanov, Stepanov, Zeiberlinsh (Babichev 46), Bleidelis, Rimkus (Boulders 67), Pakhar.
Referee: Kvarastskhelia (Georgia).

Tallinn, 9 October 1996, ????

Estonia (0) 0
Scotland (0) 0
Estonia: .
Scotland: .
Game abandoned.

Stockholm, 9 October 1996, 36,859

Sweden (0) 0
Austria (1) 1 *(Herzog 11)*
Sweden: Ravelli; Nilsson R, Bjorklund, Andersson P, Schwarz, Thern, Blomqvist, Zetterberg, Ingesson (Mild 67), Dahlin (Andersson A 83), Andersson K (Larsson H 42).
Austria: Konsel; Schopp (Hatz 77), Pfeffer, Schottel, Feiersinger, Hutter A, Heraf, Herzog, Stoger (Ramusch 71), Polster, Wetl.
Referee: Krondl (Czech Republic).

Vienna, 9 November 1996, 15,700

Austria (1) 2 *(Polster 43, Herzog 73)*
Latvia (1) 1 *(Rimkus 45)*
Austria: Konsel; Schottel, Kartalija, Pfeffer, Heraf, Schopp, Stoger (Kuhbauer 60), Hutter (Ramusch 60), Herzog, Wetl, Polster.
Latvia: Karavayev; Troitsky, Stepanov, Shevlyakov, Bleidelis, Zemlinsky, Shtolcers, Astafyev, Ivanov, Rimkus, Babichev (Pakhar 65).
Referee: Mitrovic (Slovenia).

Hampden Park, 10 November 1996, 50,000

Scotland (1) 1 *(McGinlay 8)*
Sweden (0) 0
Scotland: Leighton; McNamara (Lambert 46), Boyd, Calderwood, Hendry, McKinlay T, Burley, McKinlay W, Jackson (Gallacher 78), McGinlay (McCoist 84), Collins.
Sweden: Ravelli; Nilsson R, Andersson P, Bjorklund, Sundgren, Alexandersson (Larsson 68), Thern, Zetterberg (Andersson A 76), Schwarz, Blomqvist, Dahlin (Andersson K 16).
Referee: Aranda (Spain).

Monaco, 11 February 1997, 4000

Estonia (0) 0
Scotland (0) 0

Estonia: Poom; Kirs, Hohlov-Simson, Lemsalu, Rooba U, Reim, Leetma (Oper 75), Rooba M (Pari 67), Alonen, Kristal, Zelinski.
Scotland: Goram; McNamara (McKinlay T 75), Boyd, McStay (Ferguson I 63), Hendry, Calderwood, Gallacher, McAllister, Ferguson D, McGinlay (McCoist 72), Collins.
Referee: Radoman (Yugoslavia).

Kilmarnock, 29 March 1997, 17,996

Scotland (1) 2 *(Boyd 25, Meet 52 (og))*
Estonia (0) 0

Scotland: Leighton; Burley, McKinlay T, Calderwood, Hendry (McKinlay W 65), Boyd, Gemmill, Jackson (McGinlay 83), Gallacher, McAllister, McStay.
Estonia: Poom; Kirs, Hohlov-Simson, Lemsalu, Meet, Reim, Viikmae (Leetma 72), Zelinski (Arbeiter 81), Pari (Rooba M 54), Kristal, Oper.
Referee: Heynemann (Germany).

Celtic Park, 2 April 1997, 43,295

Scotland (1) 2 *(Gallacher 24, 77)*
Austria (0) 0

Scotland: Leighton; Burley, Boyd, Lambert, Hendry, Calderwood, McKinlay T, Gallacher (McCoist 85), Jackson (McGinlay 75), McAllister (McStay 89), Collins.
Austria: Konsel; Schottel (Kogler W 46), Feiersinger, Pfeffer, Schopp, Heraf, Aigner (Ogris 81), Wetl, Stoger (Vastic 67), Herzog, Polster.
Referee: Levnikov (Russia).

Vienna, 30 April 1997, 27,500

Austria (0) 2 *(Vastic 48, Stoger 87)*
Estonia (0) 0

Austria: Konsel; Feiersinger, Schottel (Kogler W 69), Pfeffer, Cerny, Heraf, Kuhbauer, Herzog, Wetl, Vastic (Stoger 51), Polster.
Estonia: Poom; Kirs, Hohlov-Simson, Lemsalu, Meet, Viikmae (Leetma 83), Pari, Reim, Alonen (Arbeiter 80), Kristal, Oper.
Referee: Ancion (Belgium).

Riga, 30 April 1997, 3000

Latvia (1) 2 *(Shevlyakov 38, 83)*
Belarus (0) 0

Latvia: Karavayev; Troitsky, Astafyev (Strandinsh 82), Zemlinsky, Shevlyakov, Blagonadezhdin, Ivanov, Pakhar (Zakreshevsky 66), Rimkus, Babichev (Bleidelis 46), Shtolcers.
Belarus: Shantolosov; Gurenko, Shtanuk, Yakhimovich, Hackevich (Gerasimenko 46), Ostrovsky, Belkevich, Melitski, Kachuro, Antonovich (Gerasimets 46), Orlovski (Makovetsky 66).
Referee: Koho (Finland).

Gothenburg, 30 April 1997, 40,000

Sweden (1) 2 *(Andersson K 44, 64)*
Scotland (0) 1 *(Gallacher 84)*

Sweden: Ravelli; Sundgren, Andersson P, Bjorklund, Kamark, Thern, Zetterberg, Schwarz (Mild 12), Andersson A, Andersson K, Dahlin.
Scotland: Leighton; Burley, Boyd, Lambert, Hendry, Calderwood, McKinlay T (Gemmill 67), Gallacher, Jackson (Durie 66), McAllister, Collins.
Referee: Collina (Italy).

Tallinn, 18 May 1997, 3000

Estonia (1) 1 *(Zelinski 5)*
Latvia (0) 3 *(Babichev 53, Yeliseyev 80, Lemsalu 87 (og))*

Estonia: Poom; Lemsalu, Kirs, Nommik, Meet, Alonen, Viikmae (Arbeiter 81), Zelinski, Kristal, Reim, Oper (Rooba M 84).
Latvia: Karavayev; Stepanov, Astafyev, Zemlinsky, Shevlyakov, Bleidelis, Ivanov, Pakhar, Babichev (Troitsky 90), Rimkus (Boulders 73), Shtolcers (Yeliseyev 46).
Referee: Cvitkovic (Croatia).

Minsk, 8 June 1997, 12,000

Belarus (0) 0
Scotland (0) 1 *(McAllister G 49 (pen))*

Belarus: Satsunkhevich; Lavrik, Ostrovski, Yakhimovich, Gurenko, Dovnar (Belkevich 53), Romashchenko, Shtanyuk, Orlovski (Balachov 66), Khlebossolov (Makovski 61), Gerasimets.
Scotland: Leighton; Burley, Boyd, Lambert, Dailly, Hopkin (Gemmill 68), McKinlay T (McAllister B 79), Gallacher, Jackson (Dodds 87), McAllister G, Durie.
Referee: Cakar (Turkey).

Tallinn, 8 June 1997, 4000

Estonia (0) 2 *(Kristal 75, 84)*
Sweden (1) 3 *(Dahlin 13, Zetterberg 53 (pen), Andersson K 71)*

Estonia: Poom; Kirs, Lemsalu, Hohlov-Simson, Meet, Leetma (Viikmae 46), Rooba M (Pari 65), Oper, Kristal, Reim, Zelinski (Arbeiter 85).
Sweden: Hedman; Nilsson R, Andersson P, Bjorklund, Sundgren, Thern, Zetterberg, Mild (Alexandersson 76), Andersson A, Dahlin (Pettersson 72), Andersson K.
Referee: Wojcik (Poland).

Riga, 8 June 1997, 5000

Latvia (0) 1 *(Pakhar 39)*
Austria (0) 3 *(Heraf 55, Polster 79, Stoger 80)*

Latvia: Karavayev; Troitsky, Astafyev, Zemlinsky, Shevlyakov, Stepanov, Ivanov, Pakhar, Babichev (Zakreshevsky 68), Rimkus (Yeliseyev 59), Bleidelis (Shtolcers 64).
Austria: Konsel; Schottel, Pfeffer, Feiersinger, Cerny (Ramusch 85), Heraf, Kuhbauer, Herzog (Stoger 78), Wetl (Pfeifenberger 46), Vastic, Polster.
Referee: Jol (Holland).

Group 4	P	W	D	L	F	A	Pts
Scotland	8	5	2	1	9	2	17
Austria	6	4	1	1	8	4	13
Sweden	6	4	0	2	12	7	12
Latvia	7	2	1	4	9	11	7
Belarus	6	1	1	4	3	10	4
Estonia	7	1	1	5	4	11	4

GROUP 5

Tel Aviv, 1 September 1996, 25,000

Israel (1) 2 *(Harazi R 34, Banin 62 (pen))*
Bulgaria (0) 1 *(Balakov 2 (pen))*

Israel: Cohen; Halfon (Harazi A 90), Benado, Shelah, Amsalem, Banin, Hazan, Nimni, Revivo, Rosenthal (Berkovic 83), Harazi R (Klinger 77).
Bulgaria: Mikhailov; Kishishev, Hubchev, Ivanov T (Borimirov 75), Tsvetanov, Lechkov, Yankov, Balakov, Yordanov, Donkov (Iliev 62), Kostadinov.
Referee: Trentalange (Italy).

Moscow, 1 September 1996, 15,000

Russia (2) 4 *(Nikiforov 7, 50, Kolyvanov 34, Bestchastnykh 82)*
Cyprus (0) 0

Russia: Cherchesov; Radimov (Charlashev 68), Nikiforov, Mamedov, Ternavsky, Tetradze, Onopko, Kanchelskis, Bestchastnykh, Kolyvanov (Tikhonov 55), Radchenko (Kanischev 46).
Cyprus: Petrides; Larkou (Timotheou 61), Pittas, Ioannou D, Christodolou G, Andreou A, Christodolou M, Panayi, Gogic, Ioannou I (Theodotou 90), Alexandrou (Malekos 78).
Referee: Nilsson (Sweden).

Luxembourg, 8 October 1996, 3775

Luxembourg (1) 1 *(Langers 20)*
Bulgaria (2) 2 *(Balakov 14 (pen), Kostadinov 37)*

Luxembourg: Koch; Deville, Vanek, Weis, Strasser, Posing (Ganser 46), Saibene, Birsens, Hellers, Cardoni (Theis 27), Langers.
Bulgaria: Mikhailov; Kishishev, Antonov (Vassiliev 46), Ivanov T (Borimirov 62), Tsvetanov, Lechkov, Ivanov G, Yankov, Balakov, Hristov (Vidolov 46), Kostadinov.
Referee: Kollari (Albania).

Tel Aviv, 9 October 1996, 34,000

Israel (0) 1 *(Bromer G 62)*
Russia (0) 1 *(Kolyvanov 80)*

Israel: Cohen; Halfon (Benado 81), Shelah, Bromer G, Amsalem, Hazan, Nimni, Berkovic (Zohar 89), Banin, Revivo, Harazi R (Rosenthal 78).
Russia: Cherchesov; Bushmanov (Radimov 67), Tetradze, Nikiforov, Minko, Kanchelskis, Onopko, Karpin, Kolyvanov, Radchenko (Tikhonov 46), Bestchastnykh.
Referee: Batta (France).

Limassol, 10 November 1996, 15,000

Cyprus (2) 2 *(Gogic 8, 14)*
Israel (0) 0

Cyprus: Panayiotou; Aristocleous, Pittas, Ioannou D (Misos 71), Christodolou G, Stavrou, Ioannou G (Timotheou 58), Andreou, Gogic, Christodolou M, Alexandrou (Malekos 78).
Israel: Cohen; Halfon (Benado 36), Bromer G, Shelah, Amsalem (Harazi R 36), Hazan, Banin, Berkovic, Nimni, Revivo, Rosenthal (Drieks 72).
Referee: Constantin (Romania).

Luxembourg, 10 November 1996, 5650

Luxembourg (0) 0
Russia (2) 4 *(Tikhonov 34, Kanchelskis 38, Bestchatnykh 56, Karpin 79)*

Luxembourg: Koch; Vanek, Deville, Birsens, Strasser, Saibene, Ganser (Holtz 46), Weis, Thill (Amodio 82), Groff, Langers.
Russia: Cherchesov (Ovchinnikov 75); Minko, Nikiforov, Tetradze, Karpin, Onopko, Mostovoi, Tikhonov, Kanchelskis, Bestchastnykh (Radimov 80), Kolyvanov.
Referee: Hirviniemi (Finland).

Limassol, 14 December 1996, 16,000

Cyprus (1) 1 *(Pittas 29)*
Bulgaria (2) 3 *(Balakov 23, 34, Iliev 70)*

Cyprus: Panayiotou; Aristocleous (Theodotou 61), Pittas, Ioannou D, Christodoulou G, Andreou S, Christodoulou M, Stravrou (Larkou 46), Gogic, Ioannou G (Xiouroupas 81), Malekos.
Bulgaria: Mikhailov (Zdravkov 46); Kishishev (Antonov G 78), Ivanov T, Tsvetanov, Guentchev, Yordanov, Kostadinov, Nankov, Donkov (Vindolov 61), Balakov, Iliev.
Referee: Rowbotham (Scotland).

Ramatgan, 15 December 1996, 28,000

Israel (1) 1 *(Ohana 39)*
Luxembourg (0) 0

Israel: Korenfain; Amsalem, Shelah, Klinger, Hazan, Nimni, Banin, Berkovic, Abuksis, Revivo (Zohar 82), Ohana (Bromer A 90).
Luxembourg: Koch; Vanek, Weis, Strasser, Deville, Saibene, Hellers, Birsens (Holtz 28), Fanelli, Cardoni (Ganser 78), Langers.
Referee: Ashman (Wales).

Nicosia, 29 March 1997, 4000

Cyprus (1) 1 *(Gogic 29)*
Russia (1) 1 *(Simutenkov 31)*

Cyprus: Petrides; Theodotou, Pittas, Andreou A, Misos, Larkou, Papavassiliou, Malekos (Melanargitis 86), Ioannou G (Engomitis 77), Gogic (Okkas 84), Timotheou.
Russia: Cherchesov; Onopko, Tetradze, Popov, Chugainov, Kanchelskis, Karpin, Mostovoi, Tsymbalar (Gerasimenko 69), Kolyvanov, Simutenkov.
Referee: Roca (Spain).

Luxembourg, 31 March 1997, 6066

Luxembourg (0) 0
Israel (1) 3 *(Zohar 11, 80, Banin 56)*

Luxembourg: Koch; Vanek, Deville (Amodio 65), Birsens, Strasser, Saibene, Holtz (Posing 75), Thill, Langers, Cardoni, Groff.
Israel: Cohen; Halfon, Amsalem, Shelah, Benado, Rosenthal (Klinger 83), Banin, Revivo, Berkovic (Ben-Shimon 46), Zohar, Ohana (Mizrahi 46).
Referee: Temmink (Holland).

Sofia, 2 April 1997, 33,000

Bulgaria (2) 4 *(Borimirov 2, Kostadinov 36, 45, Yordanov 66)*
Cyprus (0) 1 *(Okkas 61)*

Bulgaria: Zdravkov; Kishishev, Ivanov T, Genchev, Yordanov, Yankov (Mitov 80), Kostadinov, Borimirov (Nankov 58), Donkov (Vidolov 73), Balakov, Iliev.
Cyprus: Petrides; Pittas (Melanargitis 77), Theodotou, Yiannaki, Misos, Larkou, Papavassiliou, Engomitis (Hadjilucas 46), Charalambous, Alexandrou (Okkas 46), Timotheou.
Referee: Muhmenthaler (Switzerland).

Tel Aviv, 30 April 1997, 34,000

Israel (1) 2 *(Ohana 3, 72)*
Cyprus (0) 0

Israel: Cohen; Harazi A, Glam, Hazan A, Shelah, Benado, Banin, Mizrahi (Jano 85), Berkovic, Zohar (Atar 88), Ohana.
Cyprus: Panayiotou; Theodotou, Pittas, Misos, Charalambous, Larkou (Okkas 46), Timotheou, Andreou, Gogic, Malekos (Ioannou G 46), Papavassiliou (Engomitis 88).
Referee: Melnitchuk (Ukraine).

Moscow, 30 April 1997, 10,000

Russia (1) 3 *(Kechinov 20, Grishin 58, Simutenkov 60)*
Luxembourg (0) 0

Russia: Ovchinnikov; Kovtun, Tetradze (Popov 24), Chugainov, Onopko, Radimov (Zubkov 69), Kosolapov, Alenichev, Bestchastnykh (Grishin 46), Kechinov, Simutenkov.
Luxembourg: Koch; Vanek, Strasser, Weis, Saibene (Amodio 88), Deville, Posing, Birsens, Hellers, Cardoni (Lamborelle 75), Langers (Thill 71).
Referee: Rowbotham (Scotland).

Bourgas, 8 June 1997, 20,000

Bulgaria (1) 4 *(Stoichkov 43 (pen), Kostadinov 47, Balakov 49 (pen), Lechkov 80)*
Luxembourg (0) 0

Bulgaria: Zdravkov; Nankov, Ivanov T, Yordanov, Petkov, Yankov (Lechkov 56), Balakov, Iliev (Trendafilov 84), Kostadinov, Penev (Borimirov 67), Stoichkov.
Luxembourg: Koch; Vanek, Weis, Deville, Holt (Thill 73), Birsens, Ganser (Amodio 81), Hellers, Theis, Cardoni, Langers (Posing 87).
Referee: Batista (Portugal).

Moscow, 8 June 1997, 30,000

Russia (2) 2 *(Radimov 8, Kosolapov 38)*
Israel (0) 0

Russia: Ovchinnikov; Tsveiba, Nikiforov, Onopko, Yanovski, Grishin (Tessipov 90), Kosolapov, Alenichev, Radimov, Tcherychev (Kovtun 83), Bestchastnykh (Tikhonov 60).
Israel: Cohen; Halfon, Amsalem, Hazan, Shelah, Benado, Rosenthal (Harazi A 46), Revivo (Zohar 56), Berkovic, Nimni, Ohana (Mizrahi 72).
Referee: Grabher (Austria).

Group 5

	P	W	D	L	F	A	Pts
Russia	6	4	2	0	15	2	14
Israel	7	4	1	2	9	6	13
Bulgaria	5	4	0	1	14	5	12
Cyprus	6	1	1	4	5	14	4
Luxembourg	6	0	0	6	1	17	0

GROUP 6

Belgrade, 24 April 1996, 25,000

Yugoslavia (3) 3 *(Savicevic 3, 30, Milosevic 38)*
Faeroes (0) 1 *(Petersen 54)*

Yugoslavia: Kocic; Curcic (Mirkovic 75), Djorovic, Jokanovic, Brnovic, Mihajlovic (Pantic 40), Jugovic, Savicevic, Mijatovic, Stojkovic, Milosevic (Nadj 87).
Faeroes: Knudsen; Johannesen O, Hansen J, Hansen A, Johnsson J, Morkore A, Jarnskor H, Dam, Muller, Petersen, Rasmussen JE (Jarnskor M 75).
Referee: Bec (Liechtenstein).

Belgrade, 2 June 1996, 20,000

Yugoslavia (3) 6 *(Milosevic 2, 68, Mijatovic 39, Stojkovic 45, Savicevic 71, 73)*
Malta (0) 0

Yugoslavia: Kocic; Mirkovic, Djorovic (Saveljic 85), Jokanovic, Djukic, Mihajlovic, Jugovic (Nadj 50), Savicevic, Mijatovic, Stojkovic, Milosevic (Kovacevic 79).
Malta: Cluett; Attard (Woods 46), Buhagiar, Vella S, Debono, Zammit (Camilleri 75), Busuttil, Turner, Brincat, Chetcuti, Agius.
Referee: Albrecht (Germany).

Toftir, 31 August 1996, 1445

Faeroes (0) 1 *(Muller 60)*
Slovakia (0) 2 *(Moravcik 58, Dubovsky 89)*

Faeroes: Knudsen; Morkore A, Johannesen O, Hansen J, Jarnskor H, Johnsson J, Dam, Hansen O, Petersen, Muller (Arge 75), Joensen.
Slovakia: Molnar; Kozak, Tittel, Zeman, Kinder, Juriga, Balis (Ujlaky 73), Simon (Jancula 69), Moravcik, Timko (Maixner 69), Dubovsky.
Referee: Hauge (Norway).

Toftir, 4 September 1996, 3500

Faeroes (0) 2 *(Jonsson T 47, Arge 90)*
Spain (1) 6 *(Luis Enrique 37, Alfonso 63, 83, 86, Johanessen O 70 (og), Hierro 85)*

Faeroes: Knudsen; Johannesen O, Morkore A, Joensen, Hansen J, Johnsson J, Hansen O, Petersen (Eliasen 90), Muller (Arge 74), Jarnskor H, Jonsson T.
Spain: Zubizarreta; Belsue, Alkorta (Abelardo 46), Nadal, Aranzabal (Guerrero 71), Sergi, Hierro, Guardiola, Pizzi (Alfonso 59), Kiko, Luis Enrique.
Referee: Leduc (France).

Teplice, 18 September 1996, 18,000

Czech Republic (2) 6 *(Berger 11, 62 (pen), Nedved 24, Kubik 77, Smicer 83, Frydek 87)*
Malta (0) 0

Czech Republic: Srnicek; Kubik, Hornak (Smicer 63), Suchoparek, Latal, Bejbl, Nedved (Frydek 81), Nemec, Poborsky (Verbir 86), Berger, Kuka.
Malta: Cini; Saliba, Attard, Buhagiar, Vella S, Zammit (Agius 83), Sant Fournier, Chetcuti, Debono (Said 88), Zahra, Carabott (Suda 69).
Referee: Beusen (Croatia).

Bratislava, 22 September 1996, 2236

Slovakia (3) 6 *(Tittel 13, 81, Simon 16, Zeman 36, Timko 56, Dubovsky 59)*
Malta (0) 0

Slovakia: Vencel; Zeman (Kozak 73), Karhan, Tomaschek, Kinder, Tittel, Slovak, Simon, Timko (Ujlaky 65), Dubovsky, Moravcik (Jancula 46).
Malta: Cini; Attard, Bonnici, Vella S, Chetcuti (Saliba 33), Zammit, Suda, Said, Carabott, Sant Fournier, Zahra (Agius 71).
Referee: Bikas (Greece).

Toftir, 6 October 1996, 1017

Faeroes (1) 1 *(Muller 26)*
Yugoslavia (5) 8 *(Milosevic 8, 38, 45, Jokanovic 12, 58, Mijatovic 30, Jugovic 70, Stojkovic 90 (pen))*

Faeroes: Knudsen; Johannesen, Hansen J (Hansen T 46), Hansen A, Joensen, Morkore A, Jonsson J, Dam, Jonson T, Muller (Arge 75), Petersen.
Yugoslavia: Kocic; Brnovic, Vidakovic (Djorovic 67), Djukic, Mihajlovic, Jugovic, Jokanovic, Stojkovic, Savicevic (Nadj 76), Mijatovic, Milosevic (Drobnjak 72).
Referee: Irvine (N Ireland).

Prague, 9 October 1996, 21,750

Czech Republic (0) 0
Spain (0) 0

Czech Republic: Srnicek; Hornak, Kadlec, Suchoparek, Latal, Bejbl, Nedved (Frydek 86), Poborsky (Smicer 58), Berger, Nemec, Kuka.
Spain: Zubizarreta; Alkorta, Nadal, Abelardo, Sergi, Luis Enrique, Hierro, Amor (Urzaiz 79), Guerrero (Guardiola 53), Raul, Alfonso (Rios 72).
Referee: Frisk (Sweden).

Bratislava, 23 October 1996, 5400

Slovakia (1) 3 *(Dubovsky 20, Jancula 44, Simon 57 (pen))*
Faeroes (0) 0

Slovakia: Vencel; Zeman, Karhan (Kozak 84), Tomaschek, Kinder, Tittel, Balis (Kozlej 68), Simon, Jancula, Dubovsky, Timko (Ujlaky 68).
Faeroes: Knudsen; Johannesen O, Jarnskor H, Hansen A, Hansen O, Morkore A, Johnsson J, Dam (Ennigard 63), Muller, Jonsson T (Arge 46), Petersen (Eliasen 35).
Referee: Prolic (Bosnia).

Belgrade, 10 November 1996, 50,000

Yugoslavia (1) 1 *(Mijatovic 18)*
Czech Republic (0) 0

Yugoslavia: Kocic; Jokanovic, Djukic, Djorovic, Vidakovic, Brnovic, Stojkovic, Jugovic, Mihajlovic, Mijatovic, Milosevic (Curcic 76).
Czech Republic: Srnicek; Hornak, Kadlec, Suchoparek, Latal (Poborsky 86), Nedved (Frydek 78), Berger, Bejbl, Nemec, Smicer, Kuka (Drulak 71).
Referee: Jol (Holland).

Tenerife, 13 November 1996, 15,000

Spain (1) 4 *(Pizzi 30, Amor 46, Luis Enrique 57, Hierro 61)*
Slovakia (1) 1 *(Tittel 39)*

Spain: Zubizarreta; Belsue, Alkorta, Nadal, Sergi, Luis Enrique, Hierro (Rios 80), Amor (Guardiola 59), Guerrero (Kiko 58), Raul, Pizzi.
Slovakia: Vencel; Zeman, Kozak, Tittel, Kinder, Tomaschek, Ujlaky (Kostka 65), Slovak, Simon, Jancula, Timko.
Referee: Merk (Germany).

Valencia, 14 December 1996, 40,000

Spain (2) 2 *(Guardiola 19 (pen), Raul 37)*
Yugoslavia (0) 0

Spain: Zubizarreta; Abelardo, Alkorta, Nadal, Rios, Luis Enrique, Guardiola, Alfonso (Amor 62), Sergi, Kiko (Manjarin 75), Raul (Guerrero 88).
Yugoslavia: Kocic; Saveljic, Djukic, Vidakovic (Pantic 75) (Nadj 79), Djorovic, Jokanovic, Jugovic, Stojkovic D, Brnovic, Mijatovic, Savicevic.
Referee: Muhmenthaler (Switzerland).

Ta'Qali, 18 December 1996, 2000

Malta (0) 0
Spain (3) 3 *(Guerrero 8, 25, 33)*

Malta: Cini; Chetcuti, Buhagiar, Vella, Debono, Zammit, Turner, Suda (Said 70), Brincat, Agius (Sultana 81), Zahra.
Spain: Zubizarreta; Belsue (Alvarez 70), Nadal, Abelardo, Aranzabal, Rios, Guardiola (Amor 61), Guerrero, Luis Enrique, Pizzi, Raul (Manjarin 61).
Referee: Levnikov (Russia).

Alicante, 12 February 1997, 32,000

Spain (2) 4 *(Guardiola 25, Alfonso 40, 47, Pizzi 90)*
Malta (0) 0

Spain: Zubizarreta; Armando, Nadal, Abelardo, Aranzabal, Hierro (Rios 46), Guardiola, Manjarin, Raul (Pizzi 46), Alfonso, Luis Enrique.
Malta: Cini; Brincat (Galea 85), Buhagiar, Vella, Chetcuti, Agius (Debono 60), Zammit (Camilleri 80), Sultana, Turner, Zahra, Suda.
Referee: Lodge (England).

Valletta, 31 March 1997, 5000

Malta (0) 0
Slovakia (1) 2 *(Jancula 38, Tittel 90)*

Malta: Muscat; Cauchi, Chetcuti, Attard, Debono, Saliba, Agius, Turner, Sultana (Suda 65), Brincat, Carabott.
Slovakia: Vencel; Kozak, Karhan, Zeman, Spilar, Tittel, Slovak (Zvara 57), Simon, Jancula (Majoros 50), Semenik, Moravcik.
Referee: Kowalczyk (Poland).

Prague, 2 April 1997, 19,137

Czech Republic (0) 1 *(Bejbl 75)*
Yugoslavia (1) 2 *(Mijatovic 28, Milosevic 90)*

Czech Republic: Miklosko; Latal (Berger 46), Repka, Nedved (Frydek 83), Kadlec, Hornak, Cizek, Poborsky, Kuka, Smicer (Siegl 67), Bejbl.
Yugoslavia: Kralj; Mirkovic, Govedarica, Jokanovic, Djukic, Mihajlovic (Brnovic 14), Jugovic, Savicevic (Milosevic 82), Mijatovic, Stojkovic (Drulovic 86), Nadj.
Referee: Batta (France).

Valletta, 30 April 1997, 5000

Malta (1) 1 *(Sultana 8)*
Faeroes (0) 2 *(Hansen O 60 (pen), Jonsson T 90)*

Malta: Muscat; Attard (Turner 50), Chetcuti, Vella S, Debono, Zammit, Agius, Saliba, Sultana, Brincat, Zahra.
Faeroes: Knudsen; Ennigard, Hansen K, Johannesen O, Jarnskor H, Johansen J, Thomasen, Petersen (Rasmussen JE 55), Hansen O, Morkore A, Jonsson T.
Referee: Koren (Israel).

Belgrade, 30 April 1997, 53,000

Yugoslavia (0) 1 *(Mijatovic 87 (pen))*
Spain (1) 1 *(Hierro 19 (pen))*

Yugoslavia: Kralj; Mirkovic, Djorovic, Vidakovic (Petrovic 46), Djukic, Mihajlovic (Ciric 79), Govedarica, Savicevic (Milosevic 36), Mijatovic, Stojkovic D, Drulovic.
Spain: Zubizarreta; Abelardo, Sergi, Alkorta, Nadal, Hierro, Kiko (Luis Enrique 55), Rios (Lopez 57), Guardiola, Raul, Alfonso (Amor 68).
Referee: Pedersen (Norway).

Toftir, 8 June 1997, 6400

Faeroes (2) 2 *(Arge 6, Jonsson T 41)*
Malta (0) 1 *(Agius 47 (pen))*

Faeroes: Knudsen; Johannesen O, Thorsteinsson, Hansen O, Hansen J, Morkore A, Jarnskor H, Dam, Johnsson J, Jonsson T, Arge.
Malta: Muscat; Chetcuti, Debono (Attard 33), Turner, Vella S, Zammit, Agius, Carabott, Brincat, Saliba, Sultana.
Referee: O'Hanlon (Republic of Ireland).

Valladolid, 8 June 1997, 30,000

Spain (1) 1 *(Hierro 49 (pen))*
Czech Republic (0) 0

Spain: Zubizarreta; Ferrer, Alkorta, Abelardo, Guardiola, Hierro, Amavisca (Amor 74), Manjarin (Urzaiz 55), Alfonso, Kiko (Rios 85), Raul.
Czech Republic: Srnicek; Repka, Rada, Kadlec, Hornak, Latal (Poborsky 70), Nedved, Nemec, Cizek (Frydek 69), Smicer, Wagner (Siegl 73).
Referee: Dallas (Scotland).

Belgrade, 8 June 1997, 30,000

Yugoslavia (1) 2 *(Savicevic 17, Mijatovic 78)*
Slovakia (0) 0

Yugoslavia: Kralj; Mirkovic, Djorovic, Djukic, Jokanovic, Mihajlovic, Jugovic, Stojkovic, Nadj (Drulovic 70), Savicevic (Govedarica 89), Mijatovic.
Slovakia: Molnar; Zeman, Tittel, Karhan, Kinder, Spilar, Tomaschek (Simon 46), Balis, Majoros (Nemeth 75), Moravcik, Jancula (Kozlej 83).
Referee: Mikkelsen (Denmark).

Group 6

	P	W	D	L	F	A	Pts
Spain	8	6	2	0	21	4	20
Yugoslavia	8	6	1	1	23	6	19
Slovakia	6	4	0	2	14	7	12
Faeroes	7	2	0	5	9	24	6
Czech Republic	5	1	1	3	7	4	4
Malta	8	0	0	8	2	31	0

GROUP 7

Serravalle, 2 June 1996, 1613

San Marino (0) 0
Wales (3) 5 *(Melville 20, Hughes M 32, 43, Giggs 50, Pembridge 85)*

San Marino: Muccioli S; Gasperoni L, Valentini M, Guerra, Gobbi, Manzaroli, Pasolini (Muccioli R 69), Mazza, Casadei (Peverani 74), Mularoni M (Valentini V 46), Montagna.
Wales: Southall; Bowen, Melville, Coleman, Pembridge, Browning (Goss 74), Horne (Savage 81), Robinson (Legg 80), Hughes M, Saunders, Giggs.
Referee: Lubos (Slovakia).

Brussels, 31 August 1996, 38,000

Belgium (2) 2 *(Degryse 11, Oliveira 36)*
Turkey (0) 1 *(Sergen 56)*

Belgium: De Wilde; Crasson, Medved, Renier, Claeys, Verheyen (Peiremans 59), Scifo, Degryse, Schepens (Van Kerckhoven 77), Oliveira (De Bilde 83), Nilis.
Turkey: Rustu; Recep, Ogun, Alpay, Hakan Unsal (Arif 58), Tolunay, Oguz (Sergen 53), Tayfun, Abdullah, Hakan Sukur, Saffet (Orhan 74).
Referee: Elleray (England).

Cardiff, 31 August 1996, 15,150

Wales (4) 6 *(Saunders 2, 75, Hughes M 24, 54, Melville 34, Robinson 45)*
San Marino (0) 0

Wales: Southall (Roberts 72); Bowen, Melville, Coleman (Taylor 81), Pembridge, Robinson (Speed 78), Browning, Horne, Saunders, Hughes M, Giggs.
San Marino: Muccioli S; Gasperoni L (Matteoni 67), Guerra, Gobbi, Valentini V, Mazza (Pasolini 80), Gennari, Bacciocchi (Francini 44), Gasperoni B, Manzaroli, Montagna.
Referee: Hamer (Luxemburg).

Cardiff, 5 October 1996, 37,000

Wales (1) 1 *(Saunders 17)*
Holland (0) 3 *(Van Hooijdonk 72, 75, Ronald de Boer 80)*

Wales: Southall; Bowen, Pembridge (Legg 65), Browning (Jenkins 83), Symons, Melville, Robinson, Horne, Saunders, Hughes M, Speed.
Holland: Van der Sar; Vierklau (Van Hooijdonk 71), Frank de Boer, Valckx, Bogarde, Winter, Jonk, Seedorf, Cocu, Cruyff (Makaay 46), Ronald de Boer (Van Bronckhorst 90).
Referee: Nieto (Spain).

San Marino, 9 October 1996, 1353

San Marino (0) 0
Belgium (2) 3 *(Verheyen 11, Nilis 20, 48)*

San Marino: Gasperoni F; Gobbi, Gennari, Bacciocchi, Gasperoni L, Guerra, Muccioli R (Bianchi 68), Mazza (Peverani 74), Montagna, Francini, Pasolini (Vannucci 52).
Belgium: De Wilde; Crasson, Medved, Renier, Leonard, Verheyen (Pierre 66), Staelens, Degryse, Schepens (Van Kerckhoven 63), Nilis, Oliveira (De Bilde 81).
Referee: Oganessian (Armenia).

Eindhoven, 9 November 1996, 25,000

Holland (4) 7 *(Bergkamp 22, 72, 78, Jonk 34, Ronald de Boer 33, Frank de Boer 45, Cocu 61)*

Wales (1) 1 *(Saunders 40)*

Holland: Van der Sar; Stam, Frank de Boer, Numan, Reiziger, Winter, Jonk (Van Bronckhorst 82), Cocu, Seedorf (Van Hooijdonk 69), Bergkamp, Ronald de Boer (Overmars 58).
Wales: Southall; Bowen M, Nielson, Symons, Melville, Jones, Bowen J (Robinson 58), Hartson (Taylor 67), Saunders, Pembridge, Speed.
Referee: Pereira (Portugal).

Istanbul, 10 November 1996, 35,000

Turkey (2) 7 *(Oktay 24, 38, 50, 60, Hakan Sukur 55, 65, Urtugrul 80)*

San Marino (0) 0

Turkey: Rustu; Recep, Bulent K, Celil, Alpay, Oktay (Ertugrul 87), Ogun, Tugay, Abdullah, Hami (Arif 87), Hakan Sukur.
San Marino: Gasperoni F; Valentini M, Gennari, Gasperoni L, Guerra, Manzaroli, Francini, Matteoni, Bacciocchi (Ugolini 70), Pasolini (Gatti 80), Mularoni M (Mularoni L 90).
Referee: Antonov (Moldova).

Brussels, 14 December 1996, 38,000

Belgium (0) 0

Holland (2) 3 *(Bergkamp 24, Seedorf 28, Jonk 89 (pen))*

Belgium: De Wilde; Deflandre (Jbari 77), Albert, Van Meir, Renier, Leonard (Van Kerckhoven 34), Staelens, Wilmots, Degryse (Pierre 59), Oliveira, Nilis.
Holland: Van der Sar; Reiziger, Stam, Frank de Boer, Numan, Winter, Seedorf, Jonk, Cocu, Ronald de Boer (Overmars 88), Bergkamp (Kluivert 64).
Referee: Parietto (Italy).

Cardiff, 14 December 1996, 14,200

Wales (0) 0

Turkey (0) 0

Wales: Southall; Page, Jenkins, Jones, Melville, Pembridge, Speed, Horne, Saunders (Hartson 81), Hughes M, Giggs.
Turkey: Engin; Recep, Alpay, Ogun, Bulent K, Ilker (Tolunay 88), Kemalettin (Saffet 88), Tugay, Abdullah, Arif (Oktay 70), Hakan Sukur.
Referee: Huzu (Romania).

Amsterdam, 29 March 1997, 47,000

Holland (1) 4 *(Kluivert 44, Frank De Boer 59, 90, Van Hooijdonk 82)*

San Marino (0) 0

Holland: Van der Sar; Reiziger, Stam, Frank De Boer, Numan, Seedorf (Van Hooijdonk 74), Winter (Overmars 33), Jonk, Cocu, Bergkamp, Kluivert.
San Marino: Gasperoni F; Valentini M, Gobbi L (Valentini V 54), Matteoni, Guerra, Vanucci (Gennari 78), Mazza M, Gasperoni B, Muccioli R, Francini, Montagna (Bacciocchi 81).
Referee: Klein (Israel).

Cardiff, 29 March 1997, 15,000

Wales (0) 1 *(Speed 67)*

Belgium (2) 2 *(Crasson 24, Staelens 44)*

Wales: Southall; Blackmore, Page, Symons, Pembridge, Jones, Horne, Hughes M, Saunders (Hartson 64), Speed, Giggs.
Belgium: De Wilde; De Roover, Van Meir, Smidts, Crasson, Van der Elst F, Staelens, Lemoine, Van Kerckhoven, Mpenza L (Mpenza M 64), Oliveira (Scifo 79).
Referee: Fallstrom (Sweden).

Bursa, 2 April 1997, 30,000

Turkey (0) 1 *(Hakan Sukur 53)*

Holland (0) 0

Turkey: Rustu; Ilker, Bulent K, Alpay, Ogun, Tafun, Tolunay, Tugay (Tayfur 80), Abdullah (Oguz 87), Hakan Sukur, Celil (Hakan Unsal 70).
Holland: Van der Sar; Reiziger (Overmars 80), Stam, Frank De Boer, Numan, Winter (Van Hooijdonk 67), Jonk, Seedorf, Cocu, Kluivert, Ronald De Boer.
Referee: Vega (Spain).

Serravalle, 30 April 1997, 2800

San Marino (0) 0

Holland (1) 6 *(Bergkamp 40, 90, Winter 63, Van Hooijdonk 70, Frank De Boer 74, Bosman 85)*

San Marino: Gasperoni F; Valentini M, Vanucci, Gobbi L, Guerra, Matteoni, Gasperoni B (Gasperoni L 78), Mazza M, Montagna (Bianchi 50), Francini, Muccioli R.
Holland: Van der Sar; Winter (Reiziger 73), Stam, Frank De Boer, Numan, Jonk, Van Hooijdonk, Seedorf, Zenden, Ronald De Boer (Bosman 65), Bergkamp.
Referee: Georgiou (Cyprus).

Istanbul, 30 April 1997, 29,000

Turkey (1) 1 *(Oktay 35)*

Belgium (3) 3 *(Oliveira 12, 31, 45)*

Turkey: Rustu; Recep, Bulent K, Tolunay, Hakan Unsal (Celil 46), Arif (Tayfun 46), Tayfur, Ogun, Hakan Sukur, Tugay (Hami 75), Oktay.
Belgium: De Wilde; Crasson, De Roover, Van Meir, Smidts (Doll 58), Van der Elst F, Staelens, Oliveira, Mpenza E (Lemoine 69), Scifo, Van Kerckhoven.
Referee: Heynemann (Germany).

Brussels, 7 June 1997, 22,000

Belgium (5) 6 *(Staelens 16, 85, Van Meir 26, Mpenza L 27, 45, Oliveira 33)*

San Marino (0) 0

Belgium: De Wilde; Crasson (Haagdoren 73), Van Meir, Vidovic, De Roover, Van der Elst F (Smidts 85), Staelens, Lemoine, Van Kerckhoven, Oliveira, Mpenza L (De Bilde 73).
San Marino: Gasperoni F; Valentini V, Valentini M, Gobbi L (Manzaroli 72), Vanucci, Guerra, Mazza M, Della Valle, Gasperoni B, Montagna (Gatti 55), Bacciocchi (Mularoni L 82).
Referee: Jirku (Czech Republic).

Group 7

	P	W	D	L	F	A	Pts
Holland	6	5	0	1	23	3	15
Belgium	6	5	0	1	16	6	15
Turkey	5	2	1	2	10	5	7
Wales	6	2	1	3	14	12	7
San Marino	7	0	0	7	0	37	0

GROUP 8

Skopje, 24 April 1996, 12,000

Macedonia (1) 3 *(Milosevski 5, Babunski 49 (pen), Zaharievski 80)*

Liechtenstein (0) 0

Macedonia: Celeski; Babunski, Markovski (Nikolovski 60), Jovanovski, Stojkovski, Milosevski, Milosavov, Gosev (Zaharievski 75), Ciric, Boskovski, Hristov (Naumovski 71).
Liechtenstein: Heeb; Hanselmann, Hasler, Stocker (Quaderer 46), Zech J, Frick C, Frick D, Frick M, Hilti, Oehri, Telser D (Sele 51).
Referee: Loizou (Cyprus).

Reykjavik, 1 June 1996, 5000

Iceland (0) 1 *(Gudjohnsen A 63)*

Macedonia (0) 1 *(Memed 62)*

Iceland: Kristinsson B; Sigurdsson L, Gretarsson A, Jonsson S, Adolfsson, Kristinsson R, Bergsson, Gudjohnsen A, Thordarson O (Stefansson 68), Thordur Gudjonsson (Benediktsson 81), Gunnlaugsson B (Gylfason 29).
Macedonia: Celeski; Milosavov, Markovski, Nikolovski, Stojkovski, Sedloski, Memed, Gosev, Ciric (Saciri 36), Hristov (Borov 84), Milosevski.
Referee: Luinge (Holland).

Eschen, 31 August 1996, 4000

Liechtenstein (0) 0

Republic of Ireland (4) 5 _(Townsend 5, O'Neill 9, Quinn 12, 61, Harte 20)_

Liechtenstein: Heeb; Hefti, Hasler, Stocklasa, Quaderer, Hilti, Hanselmann (Telser D 82), Zech H (Bicker 65), Schadler F (Klaunzer 78), Frick M, Schadler H.
Republic of Ireland: Given; Irwin, Kenna, McLoughlin, Breen, Staunton, Houghton, Townsend (Cascarino 83), Quinn, O'Neill (Moore 73), Harte.
Referee: Shmolik (Belarus).

Bucharest, 31 August 1996, 9000

Romania (1) 3 _(Moldovan 20, Petrescu 65, Galca 77)_

Lithuania (0) 0

Romania: Prunea (Gherasim 83); Petrescu (Popescu 80), Papura, Prodan, Selymes, Lupescu (Stinga 81), Filipescu, Galca, Munteanu, Moldovan, Ilie A.
Lithuania: Stauce; Ziukas, Vainoras, Gvildys (Zutautas 84), Miknevicius (Razanauskas 64), Baltusnikas, Maciulevicius, Tereskinas, Jankauskas, Skarbalius, Zvingilas.
Referee: Melnitchouk (Ukraine).

Vilnius, 5 October 1996, 8000

Lithuania (1) 2 _(Jankauskas 22 (pen), Slekys 71)_

Iceland (0) 0

Lithuania: Stauce; Tereskinas, Vainoras, Sukristovas, Miknevicius, Skarbalius, Zutautas, Maciulevicius (Baltusnikas 46), Slekys, Narbekovas (Zvingilas 90), Jankauskas.
Iceland: Kristinsson B; Sigurdsson L (Thordarson O 82), Thorsteinn Gudjonsson, Jonsson S, Adolfsson, Kristinsson R, Bergsson, Gudjonsson H (Gretarsson A 76), Dadason, Gudjohnsen A (Gunnlaugsson A 56), Sverrisson.
Referee: Marnix (Belgium).

Reykjavik, 9 October 1996, 3500

Iceland (0) 0

Romania (1) 4 _(Munteanu 21, Hagi 60, Popescu 75, Petrescu 81)_

Iceland: Kristinsson B; Sigurdsson L (Thordarsson O 68), Thorsteinn Gudjonsson, Jonsson S, Adolfsson, Kristinsson R, Bergsson, Gudjonsson A, Dadason (Sigurdsson H 66), Gunnlaugsson B (Gunnlaugsson A 70), Sverisson.
Romania: Stelea; Petrescu, Prodan, Dobos, Selymes, Popescu, Galca, Munteanu, Hagi (Vladoiu 82), Moldovan (Dumitrescu 82), Ilie A (Filipescu 75).
Referee: Detruche (Switzerland).

Vilnius, 9 October 1996, 5000

Lithuania (1) 2 _(Jankauskas 43, Narbekovas 55)_

Liechtenstein (0) 0

Lithuania: Stauce; Tereskinas, Vainoras, Sukristovas, Miknevicius, Slekys, Zutautas, Maciulevicius (Zvingilas 57) (Baltusnikas 82), Narbekovas, Skarbalius, Jankauskas.
Liechtenstein: Heeb; Ospelt, Hilti, Hanselmann, Telser D, Beck, Schadler S (Schadler A 75), Zech H, Hasler, Frick M, Hassler (Marxer 63).
Referee: Mamedov (Azerbaijan).

Dublin, 9 October 1996, 31,671

Republic of Ireland (1) 3 _(McAteer 8, Cascarino 46, 70)_

Macedonia (0) 0

Republic of Ireland: Kelly A; Kenna, Irwin, McAteer, Breen, Staunton, Townsend, McLoughlin (O'Brien 85), Cascarino, Harte (Moore 83), O'Neill (Aldridge 81).
Macedonia: Celeski; Sedloski, Nikolovski, Jovanovski, Milosavov, Gosev, Beganovic (Saciri 73), Micevski T, Ciric, Milosevski (Zaharievski 57), Hristov.
Referee: Fisker (Denmark).

Eschen, 9 November 1996, 2600

Liechtenstein (1) 1 _(Schadler F 34)_

Macedonia (8) 11 _(Gavevski 8, 13, 60, Hristov 23, Stojkovski 38, 44, Micevski T 45, 49, Ciric 9, 43, Micevski V 90.)_

Liechtenstein: Heeb; Ospelt, Telser D (Telser M 53), Hilti (Bicker 48), Hanselmann, Oehri, Quaderer (Marxer 73), Zech, Hasler, Hassler, Schadler F.
Macedonia: Celeski; Sedloski, Stojkovski (Milosevski 65), Markovski, Nikolovski, Zaharievski, Gosev, Micevski T (Naumoski 73), Hristov, Ciric, Gavevski (Micevski V 70).
Referee: Lipkowitz (Israel).

Dublin, 10 November 1996, 33,869

Republic of Ireland (0) 0

Iceland (0) 0

Republic of Ireland: Kelly A; Kenna (Cunningham 65), Irwin (Harte 65), Keane, Breen, Babb, McLoughlin, McAteer, Kelly D (Moore 80), Cascarino, Townsend.
Iceland: Kristinsson B; Adolfsson, Jonsson S, Sigurdsson L, Birgisson, Gudjonsson H (Thordarson O 86), Kristinsson R (Gretarsson A 71), Sverrisson, Gylfason, Thordur Gudjonsson, Sigurdsson H.
Referee: Ormandjiev (Bulgaria).

Skopje, 14 December 1996, 14,000

Macedonia (0) 0

Romania (2) 3 _(Popescu 36, 45, 90 (pen))_

Macedonia: Celeski; Sedloski, Glavevski, Nikolovski, Markovski, Zaharievski, Micevski T (Stojkovski 80), Hristov, Ciric (Milosevski 64), Glosevski, Micevski H.
Romania: Stelea; Petrescu, Prodan, Dobos, Selymes, Filipescu, Galca, Popescu, Munteanu (Stinga 83), Craioveanu (Panduru 67), Vladoiu (Viorel 88).
Referee: Filippi (Luxembourg).

Bucharest, 29 March 1997, 5000

Romania (3) 8 _(Moldovan 10, Popescu 29, 30, 67, 82, Hagi 46, Petrescu 47, Craioveanu 79)_

Liechtenstein (0) 0

Romania: Stingaciu (Prunea 62); Petrescu (Filipescu 68), Dobos, Prodan, Galca, Popescu, Selymes, Ilie A, Moldovan (Craioveanu 62), Hagi, Vladoiu.
Liechtenstein: Heeb; Stocklasa, Hefti, Zech J, Hanselmann, Hasler D, Telser D, Frick C (Ackermann 71), Schadler (Frick D 46), Klaunzer (Telser M 85), Ospelt.
Referee: Laskus (Lativa).

Vilnius, 2 April 1997, 10,000

Lithuania (0) 0

Romania (0) 1 _(Moldovan 73)_

Lithuania: Stauce; Suliauskas (Baltusnikas 75), Ziukas, Tereskinas, Vainoras, Slekys, Zutautas, Maciulevicius, Preiksaitis (Stumbrys 62), Ivanauskas, Jankauskas.
Romania: Stelea; Petrescu, Dobos, Prodan, Selymes, Galca, Popescu, Hagi, Munteanu, Vladoiu (Craioveanu 62), Moldovan (Ilie A 75).
Referee: Steinberg (Germany).

Skopje, 2 April 1997, 8000

Macedonia (2) 3 _(Stojkovski 28 (pen), 44 (pen), Hristov 59)_

Republic of Ireland (1) 2 _(McLoughlin 8, Kelly D 78)_

Macedonia: Celeski; Sedloski, Nikolovski, Markovski, Gosev, Milosavov, Sainovski (Georgioski 82), Stojkovski, Saciri, Hristov (Beganovic 78), Glavevski (Micevski V 87).
Republic of Ireland: Kelly A; McAteer, Irwin, McLoughlin, Breen, Staunton, Townsend, Keane, Cascarino (O'Neill 46) (Kelly D 76), Goodman, Phelan (Harte 57).
Referee: Trentalange (Italy).

Vaduz, 30 April 1997, 800

Liechtenstein (0) 0
Lithuania (0) 2 *(Razanauskas 65, Skarbalius 90)*
Liechtenstein: Heeb; Stocklasa, Hefti, Ospelt (Bicker 72), Hanselmann, Frick C (Ackermann 64), Telser D, Hasler D, Klaunzer (Telser M 75), Schadler, Frick D.
Lithuania: Stauce; Ziukas, Tereskinas, Suika, Vainoras, Zutautas, Maciulevicius, Ivanauskas, Stumbrys (Razanauskas 46), Jankauskas, Skarbalius.
Referee: Pregia (Albania).

Bucharest, 30 April 1997, 21,500

Romania (1) 1 *(Ilie A 32)*
Republic of Ireland (0) 0
Romania: Stelea; Petrescu, Dobos, Prodan, Hagi (Craioveanu 87), Filipescu, Georghe Popescu (Rotariu 72), Munteanu, Selymes, Moldovan, Ilie A (Gabriel Popescu 83).
Republic of Ireland: Kelly A; Kelly G, Irwin (Kenna 46), Cunningham, Staunton, Harte (Cascarino 75), Townsend, Keane, Connolly (Goodman 75), Houghton, Kennedy.
Referee: Van den Ende (Holland).

Dublin, 21 May 1997, 28,575

Republic of Ireland (3) 5 *(Connolly 29, 34, 40, Cascarino 60, 77)*
Liechtenstein (0) 0
Republic of Ireland: Given; Kenna, Cunningham, Keane, Harte, Staunton, Houghton (Cascarino 53), Kelly G, Connolly (Goodman 77), Townsend, Kennedy (Fleming 63).
Liechtenstein: Heeb; Telser D (Verling 58), Stocklasa, Hefti, Hanselmann (Ackermann 80), Frick C, Hasler D, Schadler, Frick M (Ospelt 46), Klaunzer, Frick D.
Referee: Boutenko (Russia).

Skopje, 7 June 1997, 15,000

Macedonia (0) 1 *(Hristov 53)*
Iceland (0) 0
Macedonia: Ilic; Sedloski, Markovski, Babunski, Nikolovski, Zaharievski, Gosev (Milosevic 83), Saciri (Trenevski 46), Glavevski (Sainovski 71), Hristov, Micevski T.
Iceland: Finnbogason; Sigurdsson L, Gretarsson A, Bergsson, Gislason (Dadason 85), Jonsson S, Gudjonsson B, Gudjonsson T, Gudjohnsen A (Sigurdsson H 78), Gunnlaugsson B, Sverrisson.
Referee: Tsjoek (Belarus).

Reykjavik, 11 June 1997, 4500

Iceland (0) 0
Lithuania (0) 0
Iceland: Finnbogason; Sigurdsson L, Jonsson S, Gudjonsson H (Dadason 82), Gislason (Gretarsson 79), Kristinsson R, Gudjohnsen A, Bergsson, Gunnlaugsson B, Gunnlaugsson A (Sigurdsson H 72), Sverrisson.
Lithuania: Stauce; Ziukas, Tereskinas, Vainoras, Zutautas G, Stumbrys, Zutautas R, Slekys, Skarbalius, Preitsaitis, Jankauskas.
Referee: Irvine (N Ireland).

Group 8

	P	W	D	L	F	A	Pts
Romania	6	6	0	0	20	0	18
Macedonia	7	4	1	2	19	10	13
Republic of Ireland	6	3	1	2	15	4	10
Lithuania	6	3	1	2	6	5	10
Iceland	6	0	3	3	1	8	3
Liechtenstein	7	0	0	7	2	36	0

GROUP 9

Erevan, 31 August 1996, 5000

Armenia (0) 0
Portugal (0) 0
Armenia: Berezovski; Soukiassian, Khachatrian V, Zakarian (Minassian 9), Hovsepian, Vardanian, Art Petrossian, Grigorian (Adamian 65), Mikhitarian H, Avetissian V, Avetissian A (Essayan 60).
Portugal: Vitor Baia; Secretario, Fernando Couto, Helder, Dimas, Oceano, Rui Barros, Rui Costa (Paulo Alves 80), Sa Pinto, Joao Pinto II, Folha (Cadete 46).
Referee: Ehring (Sweden).

Belfast, 31 August 1996, 9358

Northern Ireland (0) 0
Ukraine (0) 1 *(Rebrov 79)*
Northern Ireland: Fettis; Griffin (O'Neill 52), Rowland (Magilton 84), Lomas, Morrow, Hill, Gillespie, Lennon, Dowie, Gray, Hughes.
Ukraine: Shovkovskyi; Luzhnyi (Parfenov 70), Skrypnyk, Golovko, Bezhenar, Popov, Orbu, Kalitvintsev (Kriventsov 74), Luchkeyvich (Rebrov 46), Maximov, Leonenko.
Referee: Sars (France).

Belfast, 5 October 1996, 8357

Northern Ireland (1) 1 *(Lennon 29)*
Armenia (1) 1 *(Assadourian 7)*
Northern Ireland: Fettis; Nolan, Rowland, Lomas, Hunter, Hill, Gillespie (O'Neill 80), Lennon (Magilton 60), Dowie, Gray P (McMahon 60), Hughes.
Armenia: Berezovski; Soukiassian, Kachatrian V, Hovsepian, Hovhaffifyaf, Vardanian, Art Petrossian (Avetissian A 82), Tonoyan (Minassian 56), Mikhitarian H, Assadourian, Mikayelian (Ter Petrossian 70).
Referee: Danilovski (Macedonia).

Kiev, 5 October 1996, 51,300

Ukraine (1) 2 *(Popov 4, Maximov 88)*
Portugal (0) 1 *(Joao Pinto II 83)*
Ukraine: Suslov; Dmitrulin, Golovko, Vachtsjaek, Popov, Skrypnyk, Zubov (Jesin 53), Maximov, Kriventsov (Luzhnyi 66), Kosovski, Rebrov (Guseinov 75).
Portugal: Vitor Baia; Secretario, Helder, Santos, Figo, Oceano (Bento 66), Paulo Sousa, Rui Costa, Joao Pinto II, Domingos (Folha 15), Sa Pinto (Paulo Alves 64).
Referee: Nielsen (Denmark).

Tirana, 10 October 1996, 10,000

Albania (0) 0
Portugal (1) 3 *(Figo 10, Helder 75, Rui Costa 86)*
Albania: Strakosha; Dema (Kushta 46), Abazi (Malko 81), Xhumba, Vata R, Lekbello, Kacaj, Kola, Xola, Bozgo, Rraklli.
Portugal: Vitor Baia; Secretario, Fernando Couto, Helder, Santos, Oceano (Taira 83), Figo (Capucho 86), Rui Costa, Joao Pinto, Sa Pinto, Folha (Bento 67).
Referee: Sarvan (Turkey).

Erevan, 10 October 1996, 40,000

Armenia (0) 1 *(Mikayelian 85)*
Germany (3) 5 *(Hassler 20, 39, Klinsmann 26, Bobic 69, Kuntz 81)*
Armenia: Berezovski; Soukiassian, Kachatrian V, Hovsepian, Der Zakarian, Ovannessian (Ter Petrossian 46), Vardanian, Tonoyan (Avetissian A 46), Mikhitarian H, Assadourian, Mikayelian.
Germany: Kopke; Passlack, Babbel, Kohler, Reuter, Bode (Kuntz 73), Eilts, Hassler (Tarnat 76), Scholl, Klinsmann, Bierhoff (Bobic 63).
Referee: Collina (Italy).

Tirana, 9 November 1996, 5000

Albania (0) 1 *(Fraholli 58)*
Armenia (0) 1 *(Ter Petrossian 90)*
Albania: Nallbani; Vata R, Xhumba, Malko, Vila, Kola (Shulku 83), Haxhi, Paco (Alliu 46), Fraholli, Rraklli (Fortuzi 67), Vata F.
Armenia: Arm Petrossian; Soukiassian, Khachatrian V, Hovsepian, Avetissian A (Ter Petrossian 46), Vardanian (Avetissian V 72), Art Petrossian, Tonoyan (Minassian 46), Mikhitarian H, Assadourian, Mikayelian.
Referee: Stuchlik (Austria).

Nuremburg, 9 November 1996, 40,700

Germany (1) 1 *(Moller 41)*
Northern Ireland (1) 1 *(Taggart 39)*
Germany: Kopke; Strunz, Reuter, Kohler, Babbel, Tarnat, Hassler, Eilts (Passlack 62), Moller, Klinsmann, Bobic (Bierhoff 70).
Northern Ireland: Wright; Hill, Nolan, Hunter, Taggart, Horlock, Morrow, Lomas, Dowie (Gray 78), Lennon (Rogan 85), Hughes.
Referee: Cakar (Turkey).

Porto, 9 November 1996, 40,000

Portugal (0) 1 *(Fernando Couto 58)*
Ukraine (0) 0

Portugal: Vitor Baia; Joao Pinto I, Fernando Couto, Helder, Dimas, Figo, Oceano, Rui Costa (Conceicao 64), Joao Pinto II, Sa Pinto (Bento 75), Folha (Porfifio 46).
Ukraine: Suslov; Dmitrulin, Skrypnyk, Golovko, Bezhnar, Popov, Maximov, Kalitvitsev (Kriventsov 58), Orbu (Kosovski V 64), Yessine (Zubov 46), Rebrov.
Referee: Sundell (Sweden).

Belfast, 14 December 1996, 7935

Northern Ireland (2) 2 *(Dowie 12, 21)*
Albania (0) 0

Northern Ireland: Wright; Nolan, Horlock, Hunter, Hill, Taggart, Lomas, Lennon, Dowie (Quinn 89), Morrow (McMahon 72), Hughes.
Albania: Nallbani; Dede (Tole 35), Vata R, Malko, Shulku, Vata F, Fakaj, Kola, Haxhi (Fraholli 38), Rraklli, Paco.
Referee: Georgiou (Cyprus).

Lisbon, 14 December 1996, 55,000

Portugal (0) 0
Germany (0) 0

Portugal: Vitor Baia; Secretario, Dimas, Fernando Couto, Helder, Oceano, Paulinho Santos, Rui Barros (Cadete 78), Figo, Joao Pinto II, Rui Costa.
Germany: Kopke; Reuter, Sammer, Kohler, Ziege, Eilts, Basler (Kirsten 70), Moller, Babbel (Tarnat 84), Klinsmann, Bobic.
Referee: Puhl (Hungary).

Grenada, 29 March 1997, 500

Albania (0) 0
Ukraine (1) 1 *(Rebrov 39)*

Albania: Strakosha; Dema (Haxhi 46), Daja, Abazi, Vata R, Kacaj, Bozgo (Bujhaj 72), Bellai (Jphaza 82), Kola, Rraklli, Vata F.
Ukraine: Suslov; Starostyak, Golovko, Bezhenar,
Referee: McDermott (N Ireland).

Belfast, 29 March 1997, 9392

Northern Ireland (0) 0
Portugal (0) 0

Northern Ireland: Wright; Gillespie, Hill, Morrow, Taggart, Nolan, Lennon, Lomas, Quinn (McMahon 68), Dowie, Magilton.
Portugal: Vitor Baia; Paulinho Santos, Fernando Couto, Jorge Costa, Dimas (Cadete 63), Conceicao, Paulo Sousa, Rui Costa, Oceano (Martins 63), Figo, Joao Pinto II.
Referee: Cesari (Italy).

Grenada, 2 April 1997, 8000

Albania (0) 2 *(Kola 61 (pen), 90 (pen))*
Germany (0) 3 *(Kirsten 64, 80, 84)*

Albania: Strakosha; Shpuza (Bellai 61), Shulku, Vata R, Kacaj, Abazi, Haxhi, Kola, Bushi (Lance 90), Rraklli, Tare (Vata F 74).
Germany: Kopke; Reuter (Heinrich 62), Kohler, Sammer, Helmer, Ziege, Moller, Eilts (Kirsten 63), Wosz, Klinsmann, Beirhoff.
played in Spain due to civil unrest in Albania.
Referee: Piraux (Belgium).

Kiev, 2 April 1997, 70,000

Ukraine (1) 2 *(Kossovski V 2, Shevchenko 70)*
Northern Ireland (1) 1 *(Dowie 14 (pen))*

Ukraine: Kossovski O; Luzhni, Bezhenar, Golovko, Skrypnyk, Mikhailenko, Kardash, Kalitvintsev (Kriventsov 88), Kossovski V (Orbu 77), Shevchenko, Rebrov.
Northern Ireland: Wright; Gillespie (McMahon 82), Nolan, Hill, Taggart, Morrow, Lennon (Quinn 75), Lomas, Dowie, Horlock, Hughes.
Referee: Krondl (Czech Republic).

Erevan, 30 April 1997, 10,000

Armenia (0) 0
Northern Ireland (0) 0

Armenia: Berezovski; Soukiassian, Khachatrian V, Hovsepian, Ter-Zakarian, Art Petrossian (Khodgoyan 84), Mikhitarian H, Yepiskoposyan (Minassian 86), Avalian (Avetissian A 76), Mikayelian, Assadourian.
Northern Ireland: Fettis; Jenkins, Morrow, Hill, Taggart, Lomas, McCarthy (Mulryne 71), Lennon, Quinn (McMahon 59), Dowie, Horlock.
Referee: Nielsen (Sweden).

Bremen, 30 April 1997, 33,242

Germany (0) 2 *(Bierhoff 63, Basler 72)*
Ukraine (0) 0

Germany: Kopke; Helmer, Kohler, Heinrich, Eilts, Ziege, Basler, Wosz (Tarnat 83), Bobic (Novotny 13), Klinsmann, Bierhoff.
Ukraine: Shovkovskyi; Golovko, Luzhni, Skrypnyk (Orbu 70), Nagornyak (Vashchuk 70), Bezhenar, Maximov, Rebrov, Kalitvintsev (Mikhailenko 79), Kossovski V, Shevchenko.
Referee: Frisk (Sweden).

Kiev, 7 May 1997, 60,000

Ukraine (1) 1 *(Shevchenko 6)*
Armenia (0) 1 *(Art Petrossian 75)*

Ukraine: Shovkovskyi; Luzhni, Golovko, Vashchuk, Dmitrulin, Nagornyak (Orbu 66), Mikhailenko, Kalitvintsev (Kriventsov 79), Kossovski V, Rebrov (Zubov 83), Shevchenko.
Armenia: Berezovski; Soukiassian, Ter-Zakarian, Kocharyan, Oganessian, Art Petrossian, Vardanian, Mikhitarian H (Avalian 60), Sarkissian, Assadourian (Yessayan 89), Mikayelian (Avetissian A 68).
Referee: Ozonov (Russia).

Porto, 7 June 1997, 15,000

Portugal (1) 2 *(Joao Pinto 14, Figo 70)*
Albania (0) 0

Portugal: Vitor Baia; Nelson, Jorge Costa, Fernando Couto, Paulinho Santos, Conceicao, Paulo Sousa, Figo (Cadete 87), Joao Pinto (Nuno Gomes 87), Domingos (Barbosa 20), Dani.
Albania: Mallisami; Shpuza (Tole 76), Xhumba, Vata R, Shulku, Kacaj, Abazi, Bushi, Haxhi, Tare, Zela (Vila 46).
Referee: Hauge (Norway).

Kiev, 7 June 1997, 55,000

Ukraine (0) 0
Germany (0) 0

Ukraine: Shovkovskyi; Luzhnyi, Golovko, Vachtsjaek, Koval, Dmitrulin, Maximov (Zhabchenko 74), Guseinov, Nagornyak (Bezhenar 88), Rebrov (Mikhailenko 84), Shevchenko.
Germany: Kopke; Heinrich, Kohler, Sammer, Helmer, Ziege, Eilts, Wosz (Scholl 69), Basler, Klinsmann, Kirsten (Bierhoff 87).
Referee: Vagner (Hungary).

Group 9

	P	W	D	L	F	A	Pts
Ukraine	8	4	2	2	7	6	14
Germany	6	3	3	0	11	4	12
Portugal	7	3	3	1	7	2	12
Northern Ireland	7	1	4	2	5	5	7
Armenia	6	0	5	1	4	8	5
Albania	6	0	1	5	3	12	1

SOUTH AMERICA (Members 10, Entries 10)

Five teams qualify including Brazil as champions
The nine competing teams play each other twice, the first four qualifying for the finals.

Buenos Aires, 24 April 1996, 60,000

Argentina (2) 3 *(Ortega 8, 18, Batistuta 49)*
Bolivia (1) 1 *(Baldivieso 42)*
Argentina: Passet; Zanetti, Ayala, Sensini, Chamot, Simeone, Almeyda, Ortega, Morales, Caniggia (Balbo 72), Batistuta (Lopez C 87).
Bolivia: Barrero; Rimba, Pena, Paraba, Sanchez O, Ramos (Castillo I 80), Coimbra (Paniagua 77), Tufino, Baldivieso, Etcheverry (Suarez 78), Castillo R.
Referee: Sanchez (Chile).

Barranquilla, 24 April 1996, 60,000

Colombia (0) 1 *(Asprilla F 55)*
Paraguay (0) 0
Colombia: Mondragon; Perez (Estrada 69), Bermudez, Mendoza, Moreno, Alvarez, Serna, Valderrama, Rincon, Valenciano (Valencia 75), Asprilla F.
Paraguay: Chilavert; Arce, Gamarra, Ayala, Rivarola, Jara (Sarabia 80), Acuna, Sotelo, Struway, Ferreira (Benitez 64), Campos (Rojas 69).
Referee: Castrilli (Argentina).

Guayaquil, 24 April 1996, 65,000

Ecuador (0) 4 *(Hurtado E 54, 90, Tenorio 65, Gavica 77)*
Peru (0) 1 *(Palacios 62)*
Ecuador: Morales; Rivera, Montano, Hurtado I (Abregon 84), Capurro, De Souza, Tenorio, Carabali W (Carabali H 46), Aguinaga, Fernandez (Gavica 76), Hurtado E.
Peru: Miranda; Solano, Reynoso, Marengo, Ferrari (Magallanes 67), Carranza, Jayo, Del Solar, Palacios, Maestri, Guadalupe (Ramirez 68).
Referee: Matto (Uruguay).

Caracas, 24 April 1996, 12,000

Venezuela (0) 0
Uruguay (0) 2 *(Otero 54, Poyet 71)*
Venezuela: Angelucci; Filosa, Gonzalez W, Tortolero, Gonzalez L, Vallenilla, Valiente (Mackintosh 74), Hernandez, Castellin, Diaz (Rivas 55), Guerra.
Uruguay: Arbiza; Olivera, Herrera, Moas, Montero, Saralegui, Gutierrez, Bengoechea (Abeijon 90), Poyet, Otero (Cedres 87), Fonseca.
Referee: Tejada (Peru).

Quito, 2 June 1996, 55,000

Ecuador (0) 2 *(Montano 52, Hurtado E 89)*
Argentina (0) 0
Ecuador: Morales; Rivera, Hurtado I (Obregon 84), Tenorio, Capurro, Montano, Gavica (Fernandez 46), Aguinaga, Carabali H, De Souza, Hurtado E.
Argentina: Bossio; Zanetti, Caceres, Sensini, Chamot, Almeyda, Simeone, Morales (Lopez C 76), Ortega (Cardoso 71), Batistuta (Crespo 76), Caniggia.
Referee: Perez (Colombia).

Lima, 2 June 1996, 45,000

Peru (0) 1 *(Reynoso 48)*
Colombia (0) 1 *(Aristizabal 60)*
Peru: Balerio; Marengo, Reynoso, Olivares, Legario, Carranza (Guadalupe 75), Solano, Del Solar, Maestri, Palacios, Zegarra (Magallanes 79).
Colombia: Mondragon; Mendoza, Moreno, Herrera, Bermudez, Valencia (Aristizabal 46), Estrada, Valderrama (Bolano 90), Asprilla F, Rincon, Alvarez.
Referee: Rodas (Ecuador).

Montevideo, 2 June 1996, 60,000

Uruguay (0) 0
Paraguay (1) 2 *(Arce 10, Rojas 89)*
Uruguay: Arbiza; Mendez, Herrera, Moas, Montero, Saralegui (Romero 46), Gutierrez (Dorta 69), Poyet, Bengoechea, Otero, Martinez (Cedres 60).
Paraguay: Chilavert; Arce, Rivarola, Ayala, Gamarra, Struway, Enciso, Bourdier, Acuna (Suarez 90), Baez E (Gonzalez 60), Baez R (Rojas 70).
Referee: Rezende (Brazil).

Barinas, 2 June 1996, 9850

Venezuela (1) 1 *(Guerra 7)*
Chile (0) 1 *(Margas 90)*
Venezuela: Dudamel; Mackintosh, Tortolero, Gonzalez L, Diaz (Hezzel 67) (Urdaneta 85), Hernandez S, Valiente, Hernandez F, Rivas, Guerra, Castellin (Savarese 67).
Chile: Tapia; Mendoza, Ramirez, Fuentes, Margas, Vilches (Nunez 73), Estay, Vega (Rozental 46), Valencia (Musrri 46), Zamorano, Salas.
Referee: Gonzales (Paraguay).

Santiago, 6 July 1996, 75,000

Chile (1) 4 *(Zamorano 21, 85, Salas 75, Estay 83)*
Ecuador (0) 1 *(Aguinaga 74)*
Chile: Tapia; Castaneda C, Gonzalez, Margas, Miranda, Musrri, Valencia (Estay 58), Vega (Sierra 76), Castaneda V (Mora 68), Salas, Zamorano.
Ecuador: Morales; Tenorio M (Gonzalez 78), Rivera, Montano (Tenorio B 46), Capurro, Hurtado I, Obregon (Fernandez 46), Carabali, Aguinaga, De Souza, Hurtado E.
Referee: Duran (USA).

La Paz, 7 July 1996, 40,000

Bolivia (2) 6 *(Sandy 3, Etcheverry 27 (pen), Baldivieso 49, Coimbra 67, Suarez 77, Paniagua 80)*
Venezuela (0) 1 *(Tortolero 65 (pen))*
Bolivia: Trucco; Sanchez O, Quinteros, Sandy, Rimba, Pena, Cristaldo, Castillo R (Suarez 75), Baldivieso, Etcheverry (Moreno 68), Coimbra (Paniagua 78).
Venezuela: Dudamel; Filosa, Mackintosh, Tortolero, Hernandez S (Diaz 46), Vera, Gonzalez, Hernandez F, Rivas S (Urdaneta 46), Savarese (Miranda 46), Guerra.
Referee: Da Rosa (Uruguay).

Barranquilla, 7 July 1996, 40,000

Colombia (2) 3 *(Asprilla F 10, Valderrama 22, De Avila 77)*
Uruguay (0) 1 *(Cedres 55)*
Colombia: Mondragon; Cabrera, Bermudez, Mendoza, Moreno, Alvarez, Serna, Rincon, Valderrama, Asprilla F, Aristizabal (De Avila 64).
Uruguay: Arbiza; Oliveira (Bengoechea 36), Moas, Aguirregaray, Lima (Silva T 54), Pereyra, Dorta (Sosa H 71), Poyet, Saralegui, Cedres, Romero.
Referee: Ruscio (Argentina).

Lima, 7 July 1996, 45,000

Peru (0) 0
Argentina (0) 0
Peru: Balerio; Solano, Reynoso, Soto, Olivares, Jayo, Zegarra (Magallanes 68), Carranza (Farfan 83), Palacios, Julinho, Maestri.
Argentina: Burgos; Zanetti, Ayala, Sensini, Chamot, Almeyda, Simeone, Morales (Bassedas 46), Ortega (Lopez G 89), Caniggia (Paz 72), Balbo.
Referee: Souza (Brazil).

Buenos Aires, 1 September 1996, 57,886

Argentina (1) 1 *(Batistuta 26)*
Paraguay (1) 1 *(Chilavert 45)*
Argentina: Burgos; Zanetti (Albornoz 88), Caceres, Ayala, Chamot, Almeyda, Bassedas (Veron 53), Morales, Ortega,Schelotto (Lopez C 53), Batistuta.
Paraguay: Chilavert; Gamarra, Ayala, Rivarola, Suarez, Enciso, Sanabria V (Esteche 75), Acuna (Alcaraz 87), Bourdier, Baez R, Rojas.
Referee: Da Silva (Brazil).

La Paz, 1 September 1996, 45,000

Bolivia (0) 0
Peru (0) 0
Bolivia: Trucco; Rimba, Sanchez O, Pena, Sandy, Castillo I, Baldivieso, Etcheverry, Sanchez E (Paniagua 85), Castillo R, Coimbra (Moreno 65).
Peru: Balerio; Olivares, Marengo, Jose Soto, Reynoso, Serrano (Julinho 47), Jayo, Zegarra, Pereda, Palacios (Jorge Soto 81), Maestri (Carty 80).
Referee: Velasquez (Paraguay).

Barranquilla, 1 September 1996, 35,000

Colombia (3) 4 *(Asprilla F 4, 31, 47, Bermudez 43)*
Chile (0) 1 *(Zamorano 56 (pen))*
Colombia: Mondragon; Santa, Bermudez, Mendoza, Galeano, Lozano, Serna, Quinonez (Lopez 58), Valderrama, Aristizabal (De Avila 52), Asprilla F (Ramirez 85).
Chile: Tapia; Rojas (Sierra 46), Margas, Gonzalez, Mora, Estay (Castaneda V 85), Musrri, Romero, Vega (Rozental 71), Salas, Zamorano.
Referee: Marinho (Brazil).

Quito, 1 September 1996, 45,000

Ecuador (1) 1 *(Aguinaga 4)*
Venezuela (0) 0
Ecuador: Morales; Rivera, Hurtado I, Tenorio, Capurro, Diaz (Abregon 79), Carabali, Aguinaga, Garcia (Fernandez 46), De Souza, Hurtado E.
Venezuela: Dudamel; Filosa, Gonzalez W, Tortolero, Mackintosh, Hernandez S, Valiente (Urdaneta 40), Vera, Miranda, Socorro (Hernandez L 79), Garcia.
Referee: Robles (Chile).

Montevideo, 8 October 1996, 65,000

Uruguay (0) 1 *(Pena 64 (og))*
Bolivia (0) 0
Uruguay: Siboldi; Sanguinetti, Herrera, Montero, Mendez, Saralegui (Gutierrez 82), Cedres, Poyet (Romero 62), Francescoli, Otero (Bengoechea 81), Fonseca.
Bolivia: Trucco; Cristaldo, Pena, Sandy, Sanchez O, Castillo S, Soria (Tufino 34), Baldivieso (Coimbra 71), Castillo R, Melgar, Moreno.
Referee: Borgosano (Venezuela).

Quito, 9 October 1996, 45,000

Ecuador (0) 0
Colombia (0) 1 *(Asprilla F 72)*
Ecuador: Morales; Rivera, Montano, Tenorio M, Capurro, Hurtado I (Obregon 62), Carabali, De Souza (Fernandez 74), Aguinaga, Hurtado E, Delgado.
Colombia: Mondragon; Cabrera, Bermudez, Lopez, Galeano, Serna, Alvarez, Rincon (Lozano 62), Valderrama, Aristizabal (De Avila 62), Asprilla F.
Referee: Elizondo (Argentina).

Asuncion, 9 October 1996, 45,000

Paraguay (1) 2 *(Gamarra 24, Rivarola 63)*
Chile (1) 1 *(Margas 22)*
Paraguay: Chilavert; Arce, Ayala, Rivarola, Gamarra, Acuna, Struway, Enciso (Baez R 62), Caballero (Rojas 46), Benitez, Cardoso (Alcaraz 70).
Chile: Ramirez; Fuentes, Reyes, Margas (Estay 80), Castaneda, Miranda, Musrri, Cornejo, Contreras (Rozental 65), Zamorano, Vergara (Goldberg 75).
Referee: Ruiz (Colombia).

San Cristobal, 9 October 1996, 30,000

Venezuela (1) 2 *(Savarese 6, Dudamel 87)*
Argentina (1) 5 *(Ortega 35, Sorin 68, Simeone 78, Morales 86, Albornoz 90)*
Venezuela: Dudamel; Mackintosh, Gonzalez L, Gonzalez W, Hernandez S, Hernandez F (Urdaneta 42), Miranda (Garcia 70), Savarese, Vera, Moran, Guerra (Filosa 46).
Argentina: Caballero; Diaz, Ayala, Berizzo, Sorin, Simeone (Molina 88), Almeyda, Morales, Albornoz, Batistuta, Ortega (Lopez C 88).
Referee: Diuzaniewsky (Uruguay).

La Paz, 10 November 1996, 45,000

Bolivia (2) 2 *(Sandy 15, Moreno 44)*
Colombia (1) 2 *(Serna 40 (pen), Rincon 54)*
Bolivia: Trucco; Ochoaizpur, Sanchez O, Pena, Sandy, Cristaldo, Castillo, Melgar (Soria 70), Etcheverry, Ramallo (Coimbra 75), Moreno.
Colombia: Mondragon; Cabrera, Mendoza, Bermudez, Galeano, Alvarez, Serna, Valderrama, Rincon (Estrada 75), Asprilla F (Quinonez 75), De Avila (Angel 87).
Referee: Serna (Peru).

Asuncion, 10 November 1996, 37,000

Paraguay (1) 1 *(Benitez 24)*
Ecuador (0) 0
Paraguay: Chilavert; Ayala, Rivarola, Gamarra, Arce, Caniza (Enciso 46), Struway, Acuna, Benitez, Baez R (Cardoso 77), Rojas (Gonzalez G).

Ecuador: Morales; Hurtado I, Rivera, Tenorio, Montano, Quinonez, De Souza, Aguinaga, De la Cruz, Hurtado E, Smith.
Referee: Gimenez (Argentina).

Lima, 10 November 1996, 31,000

Peru (2) 4 *(Reynoso 5, Julinho 22, Palacios 49, 82)*
Venezuela (0) 1 *(Vera 77)*
Peru: Balero; Solano, Jose Soto, Reynoso, Olivares, Lejario, Serrano (Maldonado 64), Palacios, Zegarra, Maestri (Carty 64), Julinho (Saenz 76).
Venezuela: Dudamel; Gonzalez, Tortolero, Mackintosh, Echenausi, Filosa, Hernandez (Diaz 46), Miranda (Vera 62), Valiente, Savarese (Moran 46), Garcia.
Referee: Betancourt (Bolivia).

Santiago, 12 November 1996, 70,000

Chile (0) 1 *(Salas 60)*
Uruguay (0) 0
Chile: Tapia; Fuentes, Castaneda C, Reyes, Margas, Perez (Basay 46), Cornejo, Chavarria, Castaneda V (Contreras 69), Salas, Rozental (Mora 77).
Uruguay: Siboldi; Sanguinetti, Montero, Herrera, Mendez, Saralegui (Bengoechea 57), Gutierrez, Cedres (Recoba 72), Poyet, Otero, Francescoli (Romero 46).
Referee: Guevara (Ecuador).

Buenos Aires, 15 December 1996, 60,000

Argentina (0) 1 *(Bastistuta 70 (pen))*
Chile (0) 1 *(Cornejo 51)*
Argentina: Cavallero; Vivas (Lopez G 46), Ayala, Berizzo, Sorin, Almeyda, Zanetti, Morales (Camps 66), Albornoz (Balbo 36), Ortega, Bastistuta.
Chile: Tapia; Castaneda C, Fuentes, Margas, Reyes, Mora, Chavarria, Cornejo, Castaneda V (Contreras 65), Rozental (Miranda 46), Salas (Zamorano 75).
Referee: Aquino (Paraguay).

La Paz, 15 December 1996, 45,000

Bolivia (0) 0
Paraguay (0) 0
Bolivia: Trucco; Rimba, Sandy, Pena, Castillo I, Ochaizpur, Tufino (Soria 46), Castillo R, Etcheverry, Moreno (Suarez B 60), Ramallo (Suarez R 46).
Paraguay: Chilavert; Acuna (Mesa 85), Villamayor, Ayala, Alcaraz, Caniza, Struway, Enciso, Benitez (Bourdier 46), Baez R (Cohener 75), Rojas.
Referee: Nieves (Uruguay).

Montevideo, 15 December 1996, 55,000

Uruguay (2) 2 *(Montero 2, Bengoechea 38)*
Peru (0) 0
Uruguay: Siboldi; Tais, Herrera, Montero, Sanguinetti, Abeijon (Saralegui 85), Moas (De los Santos G 77), Bengoechea, Francescoli, Otero, Fonseca (O'Neill 59).
Peru: Balerio; Marengo (Dulanto 46), Reynoso, Jose Soto, Olivares, Serrano, Jayo, Palacios, Zegarra (Carty 80), Maestri, Julinho (Saenz 84).
Referee: Russi (Colombia).

San Cristobal, 15 December 1996, 25,000

Venezuela (0) 0
Colombia (1) 2 *(Bermudez 7, Valenciano 50)*
Venezuela: Dudamel; Filosa, Tortolero, Gonzalez W, Martinez, Hernandez F (Urdaneta 78), Hernandez S, Ramos, Paez, Savarese (Diaz 74), Castellin (Sanabria 82).
Colombia: Mondragon; Cabrera, Bermudez, Lopez O (Valencia M 68), Moreno, Serna, Lozano, Valderrama, Rincon, Valenciano (Ricard 65), De Avila (Aristizabal 65).
Referee: Gamboa (Peru).

La Paz, 12 January 1997, 37,000

Bolivia (2) 2 *(Moreno 7, Etcheverry 12)*
Ecuador (0) 0
Bolivia: Trucco; Ochaizpur, Pena, Sandy, Sanchez O, Cristaldo, Baldivieso (Melgar 70), Soria, Castillo R (Gutierrez 65), Etcheverry, Moreno (Ramallo 75).
Ecuador: Morales; Rivera, Montano, Tenorio, Quinones, Carabali, Hurtado I, Aguinaga, De la Cruz (Gilson 46), Chala (Delgado 70), Fernandez (Hurtado E 46).
Referee: Acosta (Colombia).

Lima, 12 January 1997, 45,000

Peru (2) 2 *(Maestri 15, Palacios 35)*

Chile (0) 1 *(Zamorano 89)*

Peru: Miranda; Solano, Reynoso, Jose Soto, Olivarez, Jayo, Serrano, Palacios, Maldonado (Pereda 46), Julinho (Carty 70), Maestri (Jorge Soto 82).
Chile: Tapia; Castaneda C, Reyes, Gonzalez J, Miranda, Mora, Cornejo, Musrri (Riveros 58), Rozental (Contreras 83), Vergara (Gonzalez P 63), Zamorano.
Referee: Varela (Uruguay).

Montevideo, 12 January 1997, 70,000

Uruguay (0) 0

Argentina (0) 0

Uruguay: Siboldi; Tais, Herrera, Montero, Mendez, Moas, Abeijon, Cedres, Bengoechea, Francescoli (Recoba 73), Fonseca (Abreu 63).
Argentina: Gonzalez; Vivas, Sensini, Paz, Chamot, Almeyda, Simeone, Bassedas, Gorosito (Crespo 60), Ortega, Batistuta.
Referee: Rezende (Brazil).

Merida, 12 January 1997, 16,000

Venezuela (0) 0

Paraguay (1) 2 *(Benitez 5, Enciso 62)*

Venezuela: Dudamel; Mackintosh, Medina, Echenique, Vallenilla, Ramos, Castellano (Tizamo 46), Nabollin (Valiente 68), Urdaneta, Savarese, Paez.
Paraguay: Diaz; Arce, Sarabia, Gamarra, Alcaraz, Enciso, Benitez (Mesa 73), Struway, Acuna, Rojas (Baez R 73), Cohener (Ferreira 78).
Referee: Sanchez (Argentina).

La Paz, 12 February 1997, 45,000

Bolivia (1) 1 *(Soria 28)*

Chile (1) 1 *(Gonzalez P 45)*

Bolivia: Trucco; Sanchez O, Pena, Ochaizpur (Gutierrez 46), Sandy, Tufino, Soria, Castillo R (Castillo S 46), Cristaldo, Moreno, Etcheverry.
Chile: Tapia; Castaneda C, Reyes, Fuentes, Miranda, Chavarria, Castaneda V (Flores 56), Riveros (Contreras 76), Gonzalez P, Salas, Zamorano (Lee Chong 89).
Referee: Tejada (Peru).

Barranquilla, 12 February 1997, 60,000

Colombia (0) 0

Argentina (1) 1 *(Claudio Lopez 9)*

Colombia: Mondragon; Cabrera, Bermudez, Mendoza, Galeano (De Avila 58), Alvarez (Pacheco 46), Serna, Valderrama, Rincon, Valenciano, Asprilla F.
Argentina: Gonzalez; Diaz, Sensini, Berizzo, Paz, Simeone, Zapata, Veron, Ortega, Crespo (Vivas 46), Claudio Lopez (Sorin 83).
Referee: Pereira (Brazil).

Quito, 12 February 1997, 25,000

Ecuador (1) 4 *(Aguinaga 6, Delgado 69, 77, Chala 88)*

Uruguay (0) 0

Ecuador: Ibarra; Rivera, Montano, Hurtado I, Capurro, Ruiz, Blandon, De la Cruz (Chala 81), Gilson (Fernandez 81), Aguinaga, Delgado.
Uruguay: Siboldi; Tais, Montero, Herrera, Mendez, Moas, Abeijon, O'Neill, Cedres (Silva D 54), Francescoli (Saralegui 64), Abreu (Fonseca 54).
Referee: Castrilli (Argentina).

Asuncion, 12 February 1997, 35,000

Paraguay (2) 2 *(Rivarola 12, Rojas 40)*

Peru (1) 1 *(Pereda 33)*

Paraguay: Chilavert; Ayala, Rivarola, Gamarra, Arce, Struway, Acuna (Bourdier 72), Enciso, Benitez, Soto (Cardozo 81), Rojas (Campos 71).
Peru: Balerio; Reynoso, Jose Soto (Carty 53), Solano, Olivares, Jayo, Serrano, Pereda, Palacios (Saenz 72), Zegarra (Magallanes 67), Maestri.
Referee: Sanchez (Chile).

La Paz, 2 April 1997, 45,000

Bolivia (1) 2 *(Sandy 7, Ochaizpur 48)*

Argentina (1) 1 *(Gorosito 43)*

Bolivia: Trucco; Castillo S, Rimba, Sandy, Sanchez O, Castillo I, Ochaizpur (Melgar 89), Soria, Castillo R, Gutierrez (Blanco 51), Moreno (Angola 70).
Argentina: Gonzalez; Sensini, Vivas, Paz, Sorin, Diaz, Zapata, Cagna (Ortega 50), Gorosito (Veron 46), Delgado (Calderon 71), Cruz.
Referee: Marinho (Brazil).

Bogota, 2 April 1997, 42,000

Colombia (1) 1 *(Serna 37 (pen))*

Paraguay (1) 2 *(Gamarra 37, Soto 85)*

Colombia: Mondragon; Santa, Mendoza, Lopez, Galeano, Serna, Lozano (Pacheco 59), Alvarez (De Avila 89), Valderrama, Asprilla F, Aristizabal (Hamilton 76).
Paraguay: Chilavert; Ayala, Rivarola, Gamarra, Arce, Bourdier, Acuna, Enciso (Ruiz Diaz 77), Soto, Rojas, Yegros (Sarabia 66).
Referee: Souza (Brazil).

Lima, 2 April 1997, 47,000

Peru (0) 1 *(Palacios 58)*

Ecuador (0) 1 *(Aguinaga 78 (pen))*

Peru: Balerio; Solano, Reynoso, Jose Soto, Olivares, Carranza, Carazas, Zegarra (Carty 82), Palacios, Maestri, Julinho (Saenz 63).
Ecuador: Ibarra; Rivera, Montano, Hurtado I, Capurro, Ruiz (Chala 63), Carabali, Blandon, Aguinaga, Delgado, Graziani (Hurtado E 46).
Referee: Toro (Colombia).

Montevideo, 2 April 1997, 45,000

Uruguay (1) 3 *(De los Santos G 30, Montero 47, Otero 60)*

Venezuela (0) 1 *(Castellin 57)*

Uruguay: Siboldi; Tais, Moas, Montero, De los Santos J, Saralegui, De los Santos G, Bengoechea, Francescoli (Martinez 70), Otero (Hernandez 76), Abreu (Romero 42).
Venezuela: Dudamel; Gonzalez W, Tortolero, Echenique, Martinez, Rodriguez (Paez 73), Ramos, Hernandez F, Gerson, Guerra, Castellin.
Referee: Ortube (Bolivia).

Santiago, 29 April 1997, 42,000

Chile (3) 6 *(Zamorano 19, 26, 31, 47, 85, Reyes 66)*

Venezuela (0) 0

Chile: Tapia; Mora, Reyes, Gonzalez J, Ponce, Musrri, Acuna, Vega (Villarroel 81), Sierra (Castaneda V 68), Nunez (Goldberg 68), Zamorano.
Venezuela: Dudamel; Gonzalez W, Echenique, Tortolero, Martinez, Ramos, Rodriguez (Paez 46), Hernandez F, Gerson, Savarese, Guerra (Castellin 55).
Referee: Carter (Mexico).

Buenos Aires, 30 April 1997, 65,000

Argentina (2) 2 *(Ortega 17, Crespo 32)*

Ecuador (0) 1 *(Aguinaga 67)*

Argentina: Roa; Ayala, Paz, Chamot, Almeyda, Simeone, Veron, Berti (Morales 80), Ortega, Lopez C (Berizzo 76), Crespo.
Ecuador: Ibarra; Rivera (Urbano 79), Noriega, Montano, Mendez, Blandon, Carabali, Gilson, Chala (De la Cruz 64), Aguinaga, Hurtado E.
Referee: Benegas (Paraguay).

Barranquilla, 30 April 1997, 30,000

Colombia (0) 0

Peru (0) 1 *(Pereda 61)*

Colombia: Mondragon; Cabrera, Bermudez, Lopez (Palacios 44), Galeano, Gaviria (Lozano 46), Alvarez, Rincon, Valderrama, Valencia, De Avila (Ricard 57).
Peru: Balerio; Solano, Jose Soto, Reynoso, Olivares, Serrano (Bazalar 80), Jayo, Pereda, Palacios, Carazas (Jorge Soto 63), Carty (Julinho 84).
Referee: Rezende (Brazil).

Asuncion, 30 April 1997, 45,000

Paraguay (1) 3 *(Rojas 37, Cardozo 73 (pen), Soto 83)*

Uruguay (0) 1 *(Dario Silva 87)*

Paraguay: Ruiz Diaz; Gamarra, Rivarola, Ayala, Villamayor, Enciso (Soto 33), Acuna, Struway, Benitez (Ferreira 57), Rojas (Brizuela 76), Cardozo.
Uruguay: Siboldi; Mendez, Herrera, Moas, Ramos, Gutierrez, De los Santos G, Poyet, Francescoli, Otero (Dario Silva 65), Martinez (Bengoechea 46).
Referee: Pereira (Brazil).

Buenos Aires, 8 June 1997, 77,000

Argentina (1) 2 *(Crespo 45, Simeone 46)*
Peru (0) 0

Argentina: Roa; Ayala, Sensini, Chamot, Diaz, Almeyda, Simeone, Berti (Borelli 65), Ortega (Bassedas 53), Crespo (Calderon 86), Lopez C.
Peru: Balerio; Solano, Reynoso, Jose Soto, Olivares, Jorge Soto, Serrano (Carranza 76), Jayo, Palacios, Saenz (Julinho 46), Maestri (Carty 62).
Referee: Cerdeira (Brazil).

Quito, 8 June 1997, 42,000

Ecuador (1) 1 *(Graziani 43)*
Chile (0) 1 *(Salas 53)*

Ecuador: Ibarra; Hurtado I, De la Cruz U, Montano, Mendez, Constante, Blandon, De la Cruz O (Hurtado E 60), Delgado (Gilson 60), Aguinaga, Graziani (Fernandez 65).
Chile: Ramirez; Castaneda, Margas, Gonzalez C, Miranda, Musrri (Cornejo 57), Acuna, Reyes, Sierra (Rivero 71), Gonzalez P (Nunez 52), Salas.
Referee: Tellez (Mexico).

Montevideo, 8 June 1997, 50,000

Uruguay (1) 1 *(Dario Silva 7)*
Colombia (0) 1 *(Ricard 51)*

Uruguay: Alvez; Mendez, Moas, Montero, Ramos, Abeijon (Ruben da Silva 60), De los Santos, O'Neill (Romero 83), Bengoechea, Dario Silva, Recoba (Martinez 60).
Colombia: Mondragon; Santa (Estrada 86), Asprilla C, Bermudez, Moreno, Cabrera, Gaviria, Serna (Perez 11), Valderrama, Escobar (Bonilla 46), Ricard.
Referee: Dacildo (Brazil).

Valera, 8 June 1997, 7000

Venezuela (0) 1 *(Savarese 63)*
Bolivia (0) 1 *(Castillo R 73)*

Venezuela: Dudamel; Mackintosh, Rey, Vallenilla, Echenique, Gonzalez L, Gerson, Castellin, Miranda (Paez 69), Savarese, Socorro (Urdaneta 75).
Bolivia: Trucco; Pena, Sanchez O, Soria, Sandy, Castillo S (Castillo I 61), Etcheverry, Cristaldo, Baldivieso (Gutierrez 47), Moreno (Coimbra 47), Castillo R.
Referee: Zuluaga (Colombia).

Santiago, 5 July 1997, 75,000

Chile (3) 4 *(Salas 16, 27, 41, Zamorano 90 (pen))*
Colombia (0) 1 *(Ricard 53)*

Chile: Tapia; Castaneda C, Margas, Fuentes, Ponce, Vega (Valencia 75), Acuna, Musrri, Castaneda V (Cornejo 86), Zamorano, Salas.

Colombia: Mondragon; Santa, Bermudez, Mendoza, Moreno (Galeano 73), Alvarez (Morantes 46), Cabrera, Lozano, Valderrama, Angel (Ricard 46), Asprilla F.
Referee: Borgosano (Venezuela).

Asuncion, 6 July 1997, 35,000

Paraguay (0) 1 *(Acuna 60 (pen))*
Argentina (2) 2 *(Gallardo 30, Veron 40)*

Paraguay: Ruiz Diaz; Gamarra, Ayala, Struway (Ferreira 52), Esteche (Soto 46), Cardozo, Acuna, Jara, Rojas A, Rojas R, Enciso.
Argentina: Roa; Ayala, Chamot, Daiz, Almeyda, Sensini, Lopez, Simeone, Veron (Zanetti 50), Crespo (Berti 77), Gallardo (Paz 88).
Referee: Rezende (Brazil).

Maracaibo, 6 July 1997, 12,000

Venezuela (0) 1 *(Miranda 77)*
Ecuador (0) 1 *(Hurtado I 54)*

Venezuela: Dudamel; Echenique, Rey, McIntosh, Pacheco, Rodallega, Gonzalez L, Urdaneta (Martinez 89), Diaz (Miranda 55), Moran (Castellin 55), Savarese.
Ecuador: Ibarra; Burbano, Montano, Hurtado I, Mendez, Carabali (Smith 73), Blandon, Gavica (Gilson 70), Aguniga, Hurtado E, Graziani.
Referee: Angeles (USA).

Lima, 6 July 1997, 35,000

Peru (1) 2 *(Carty 9, Jorge Soto 51)*
Bolivia (0) 1 *(Cristaldo 54)*

Peru: Balerio; Jorge Soto, Reynoso, Jose Soto, Olivares, Carazas (Serrano 62), Jayo, Carranzo (Bazalar 83), Zegarra, Maestri (Rivera 68), Carty.
Bolivia: Trucco; Castillo S, Sanchez O, Pena, Sandy, Cristaldo, Soria, Baldivieso, Sanchez E, Etcheverry, Moreno (Gutierrez L 79).
Referee: Mendonca (Brazil).

South America

	P	W	D	L	F	A	Pts
Paraguay	11	7	2	2	16	8	23
Argentina	12	6	4	2	18	18	22
Colombia	12	5	3	4	17	14	18
Chile	11	4	4	3	22	14	16
Peru	12	4	4	4	13	14	16
Ecuador	12	4	3	5	16	14	15
Bolivia	11	3	5	5	16	12	14
Uruguay	11	4	2	5	11	15	14
Venezuela	12	0	3	9	8	34	3

1998 FIFA WORLD CUP – REMAINING FIXTURES

EUROPE

Group 1
20.08.97 Bosnia-Herzegovina v Denmark
06.09.97 Croatia v Bosnia-Herzegovina
06.09.97 Slovenia v Greece
10.09.97 Denmark v Croatia
10.09.97 Bosnia-Herzegovina v Slovenia
11.10.97 Greece v Denmark
11.10.97 Slovenia v Croatia

Group 2
10.09.97 England v Moldova
10.09.97 Georgia v Italy
24.09.97 Moldova v Georgia
07.10.97 Moldova v Poland
11.10.97 Italy v England
11.10.97 Georgia v Poland

Group 3
20.08.97 Finland v Norway
20.08.97 Hungary v Switzerland
06.09.97 Switzerland v Finland
06.09.97 Azerbaijan v Norway
10.09.97 Hungary v Azerbaijan
10.09.97 Norway v Switzerland
11.10.97 Finland v Hungary
11.10.97 Switzerland v Azerbaijan

Group 4
20.08.97 Estonia v Austria
20.08.97 Belarus v Sweden
06.09.97 Austria v Sweden
06.09.97 Scotland v Belarus
06.09.97 Latvia v Estonia
10.09.97 Sweden v Latvia
10.09.97 Belarus v Austria
11.10.97 Austria v Belarus

11.10.97 Scotland v Latvia
11.10.97 Sweden v Estonia

Group 5
20.08.97 Bulgaria v Israel
07.09.97 Luxembourg v Cyprus
10.09.97 Bulgaria v Russia
11.10.97 Cyprus v Luxembourg
11.10.97 Russia v Bulgaria

Group 6
20.08.97 Czech Republic v Faeroes
24.08.97 Slovakia v Czech Republic
06.09.97 Faeroes v Czech Republic
10.09.97 Slovakia v Yugoslavia
24.09.97 Malta v Czech Republic
24.09.97 Slovakia v Spain
11.10.97 Malta v Yugoslavia
11.10.97 Czech Republic v Slovakia
11.10.97 Spain v Faeroes

Group 7
20.08.97 Turkey v Wales
06.09.97 Netherlands v Belgium
10.09.97 San Marino v Turkey
11.10.97 Belgium v Wales
11.10.97 Netherlands v Turkey

Group 8
20.08.97 Liechtenstein v Iceland
20.08.97 Republic of Ireland v Lithuania
20.08.97 Romania v Macedonia
06.09.97 Iceland v Republic of Ireland
06.09.97 Liechtenstein v Romania
06.09.97 Lithuania v Macedonia
10.09.97 Romania v Iceland
10.09.97 Lithuania v Republic of Ireland

11.10.97 Iceland v Liechtenstein
11.10.97 Republic of Ireland v Romania
11.10.97 Macedonia v Lithuania

Group 9
20.08.97 Northern Ireland v Germany
20.08.97 Portugal v Armenia
20.08.97 Ukraine v Albania
06.09.97 Germany v Portugal
06.09.97 Armenia v Albania
10.09.97 Albania v Northern Ireland
10.09.97 Germany v Armenia
11.10.97 Germany v Albania
11.10.97 Portugal v Northern Ireland
11.10.97 Armenia v Ukraine

SOUTH AMERICA
20.07.97 Argentina v Venezuela
20.07.97 Bolivia v Uruguay
20.07.97 Colombia v Ecuador
20.07.97 Chile v Paraguay.
20.08.97 Uruguay v Chile
20.08.97 Colombia v Bolivia
20.08.97 Ecuador v Paraguay
20.08.97 Venezuela v Peru.
10.09.97 Chile v Argentina
10.09.97 Peru v Uruguay
10.09.97 Colombia v Venezuela
10.09.97 Paraguay v Bolivia.
12.10.97 Argentina v Uruguay
12.10.97 Chile v Peru
12.10.97 Paraguay v Venezuela
12.10.97 Ecuador v Bolivia.
16.11.97 Argentina v Colombia
16.11.97 Uruguay v Ecuador
16.11.97 Peru v Paraguay
16.11.97 Chile v Bolivia.

EUROPEAN FOOTBALL CHAMPIONSHIP
(formerly EUROPEAN NATIONS' CUP)

Year	Winners		Runners-up		Venue	Attendance
1960	USSR	2	Yugoslavia	1	Paris	17,966
1964	Spain	2	USSR	1	Madrid	120,000
1968	Italy	2	Yugoslavia	0	Rome	60,000
	After 1-1 draw					75,000
1972	West Germany	3	USSR	0	Brussels	43,437
1976	Czechoslovakia	2	West Germany	2	Belgrade	45,000
	(Czechoslovakia won on penalties)					
1980	West Germany	2	Belgium	1	Rome	47,864
1984	France	2	Spain	0	Paris	48,000
1988	Holland	2	USSR	0	Munich	72,308
1992	Denmark	2	Germany	0	Gothenburg	37,800
1996	Germany	2	Czech Republic	1	Wembley	73,611

EURO 96 – the penalties

England v Spain
Shearer 1-0; Hierro hit bar 1-0; Platt 2-0; Amor 2-1; Pearce 3-1; Belsue 3-2; Gascoigne 4-2; Nadal saved 4–2

England v Germany
Shearer 1-0; Hassler 1-1; Platt 2-1; Strunz 2-2; Pearce 3-2; Reuter 3-3; Gascoigne 4-3; Ziege 4-4; Sheringham 5-4; Kuntz 5-5; Southgate saved 5-5; Moller 5-6

Holland v France
De Kock 1-0; Zidane 1-1; Ronald de Boer 2-1; Djorkaeff 2-2; Kluivert 3-2; Lizarazu 3-3; Seedorf saved 3-3; Guerin 3-4; Blind 4-4; Blanc 4-5

France v Czech Republic
Zidane 1-0; Kubik 1-1; Djorkaeff 2-1; Nedved 2-2; Lizarazu 3-2; Berger 3-3; Guerin 4-3; Poborsky 4-4; Blanc 5-4; Rada 5-5; Pedros saved; Kadlec 5-6

EURO 96 – the cards

Red
Bulgaria 1, Croatia 1, Czech Republic 1, Germany 1, Italy 1, Russia 1, Spain 1

Yellow
Czech Republic 18, Germany 16, Portugal 12, Spain 12, Switzerland 12, France 11, Croatia 10, England 9, Holland 9, Russia 9, Scotland 8, Turkey 8, Bulgaria 7, Romania 7, Italy 5, Denmark 4

EURO 96 – the top scorers

Shearer (England)	**5**	Klinsmann (Germany)	3
Stoichkov (Bulgaria)	3	Suker (Croatia)	3
Brian Laudrup (Denmark)	3		

EURO 96 – the awards

Mastercard Man of the Match
Shearer, England v Switzerland
Stoichkov, Bulgaria v Spain
Sammer, Germany v Czech Republic
Schmeichel, Denmark v Portugal
McAllister, Scotland v Holland
Djorkaeff, France v Romania
Casiraghi, Italy v Russia
Prosinecki, Croatia v Turkey
Stoichkov, Bulgaria v Romania
Bergkamp, Holland v Switzerland
Couto, Portugal v Turkey
Bejbl, Czech Republic v Italy
Seaman, England v Scotland
Caminero, Spain v France
Klinsmann, Germany v Russia
Suker, Croatia v Denmark
Blanc, France v Bulgaria
Sergi, Romania v Spain

Sheringham, England v Holland
McCall, Scotland v Switzerland
Joao Pinto, Portugal v Croatia
Brian Laudrup, Denmark v Turkey
Kopke, Germany v Italy
Poborsky, Czech Republic v Russia
Seaman, England v Spain
Lama, France v Holland
Sammer, Germany v Croatia
Poborsky, Czech Republic v Portugal
Kadlec, Czech Republic v France
Eilts, Germany v England
Poborsky, Czech Republic v Germany

Fair Play Award
England

Crowd Assessment
Holland

EURO 96 – the crowds

1,268,201 for an average of 40,916

EURO 96 – in perspective

		Games	Crowds	Average	Goals
1960	France	4	78,958	19,739	17
1964	Spain	4	156,253	39,063	13
1968	Italy	5	260,936	52,187	7
1972	Belgium	4	107,326	26,831	10
1976	Yugoslavia	4	106,087	26,521	19
1980	Italy	14	350,655	25,046	27
1984	France	15	599,655	39,977	41
1988	Germany	15	809,844	53,989	34
1992	Sweden	15	906,946	37,789	32
1996	England	31	1,268,201	40,916	64

BRITISH AND IRISH INTERNATIONAL RESULTS 1872–1997

Note: In the results that follow, wc=World Cup, ec=European Championship, ui=Umbro International Trophy. tf = Tournoi de France. For Ireland, read Northern Ireland from 1921.

ENGLAND v SCOTLAND

Played: 107; England won 43, Scotland won 40, Drawn 24. *Goals:* England 188, Scotland 168.

			E	S				E	S
1872	30 Nov	Glasgow	0	0	1931	28 Mar	Glasgow	0	2
1873	8 Mar	Kennington Oval	4	2	1932	9 Apr	Wembley	3	0
1874	7 Mar	Glasgow	1	2	1933	1 Apr	Glasgow	1	2
1875	6 Mar	Kennington Oval	2	2	1934	14 Apr	Wembley	3	0
1876	4 Mar	Glasgow	0	3	1935	6 Apr	Glasgow	0	2
1877	3 Mar	Kennington Oval	1	3	1936	4 Apr	Wembley	1	1
1878	2 Mar	Glasgow	2	7	1937	17 Apr	Glasgow	1	3
1879	5 Apr	Kennington Oval	5	4	1938	9 Apr	Wembley	0	1
1880	13 Mar	Glasgow	4	5	1939	15 Apr	Glasgow	2	1
1881	12 Mar	Kennington Oval	1	6	1947	12 Apr	Wembley	1	1
1882	11 Mar	Glasgow	1	5	1948	10 Apr	Glasgow	2	0
1883	10 Mar	Sheffield	2	3	1949	9 Apr	Wembley	1	3
1884	15 Mar	Glasgow	0	1	wc1950	15 Apr	Glasgow	1	0
1885	21 Mar	Kennington Oval	1	1	1951	14 Apr	Wembley	2	3
1886	31 Mar	Glasgow	1	1	1952	5 Apr	Glasgow	2	1
1887	19 Mar	Blackburn	2	3	1953	18 Apr	Wembley	2	2
1888	17 Mar	Glasgow	5	0	wc1954	3 Apr	Glasgow	4	2
1889	13 Apr	Kennington Oval	2	3	1955	2 Apr	Wembley	7	2
1890	5 Apr	Glasgow	1	1	1956	14 Apr	Glasgow	1	1
1891	6 Apr	Blackburn	2	1	1957	6 Apr	Wembley	2	1
1892	2 Apr	Glasgow	4	1	1958	19 Apr	Glasgow	4	0
1893	1 Apr	Richmond	5	2	1959	11 Apr	Wembley	1	0
1894	7 Apr	Glasgow	2	2	1960	19 Apr	Glasgow	1	1
1895	6 Apr	Everton	3	0	1961	15 Apr	Wembley	9	3
1896	4 Apr	Glasgow	1	2	1962	14 Apr	Glasgow	0	2
1897	3 Apr	Crystal Palace	1	2	1963	6 Apr	Wembley	1	2
1898	2 Apr	Glasgow	3	1	1964	11 Apr	Glasgow	0	1
1899	8 Apr	Birmingham	2	1	1965	10 Apr	Wembley	2	2
1900	7 Apr	Glasgow	1	4	1966	2 Apr	Glasgow	4	3
1901	30 Mar	Crystal Palace	2	2	ec1967	15 Apr	Wembley	2	3
1902	3 Mar	Birmingham	2	2	ec1968	24 Jan	Glasgow	1	1
1903	4 Apr	Sheffield	1	2	1969	10 May	Wembley	4	1
1904	9 Apr	Glasgow	1	0	1970	25 Apr	Glasgow	0	0
1905	1 Apr	Crystal Palace	1	0	1971	22 May	Wembley	3	1
1906	7 Apr	Glasgow	1	2	1972	27 May	Glasgow	1	0
1907	6 Apr	Newcastle	1	1	1973	14 Feb	Glasgow	5	0
1908	4 Apr	Glasgow	1	1	1973	19 May	Wembley	1	0
1909	3 Apr	Crystal Palace	2	0	1974	18 May	Glasgow	0	2
1910	2 Apr	Glasgow	0	2	1975	24 May	Wembley	5	1
1911	1 Apr	Everton	1	1	1976	15 May	Glasgow	1	2
1912	23 Mar	Glasgow	1	1	1977	4 June	Wembley	1	2
1913	5 Apr	Chelsea	1	0	1978	20 May	Glasgow	1	0
1914	14 Apr	Glasgow	1	3	1979	26 May	Wembley	3	1
1920	10 Apr	Sheffield	5	4	1980	24 May	Glasgow	2	0
1921	9 Apr	Glasgow	0	3	1981	23 May	Wembley	0	1
1922	8 Apr	Aston Villa	0	1	1982	29 May	Glasgow	1	0
1923	14 Apr	Glasgow	2	2	1983	1 June	Wembley	2	0
1924	12 Apr	Wembley	1	1	1984	26 May	Glasgow	1	1
1925	4 Apr	Glasgow	0	2	1985	25 May	Glasgow	0	1
1926	17 Apr	Manchester	0	1	1986	23 Apr	Wembley	2	1
1927	2 Apr	Glasgow	2	1	1987	23 May	Glasgow	0	0
1928	31 Mar	Wembley	1	5	1988	21 May	Wembley	1	0
1929	13 Apr	Glasgow	0	1	1989	27 May	Glasgow	2	0
1930	5 Apr	Wembley	5	2	ec1996	15 June	Wembley	2	0

ENGLAND v WALES

Played: 97; England won 62, Wales won 14, Drawn 21. *Goals:* England 239, Wales 90.

			E	W				E	W
1879	18 Jan	Kennington Oval	2	1	1882	13 Mar	Wrexham	3	5
1880	15 Mar	Wrexham	3	2	1883	3 Feb	Kennington Oval	5	0
1881	26 Feb	Blackburn	0	1	1884	17 Mar	Wrexham	4	0

			E	W
1885	14 Mar	Blackburn	1	1
1886	29 Mar	Wrexham	3	1
1887	26 Feb	Kennington Oval	4	0
1888	4 Feb	Crewe	5	1
1889	23 Feb	Stoke	4	1
1890	15 Mar	Wrexham	3	1
1891	7 May	Sunderland	4	1
1892	5 Mar	Wrexham	2	0
1893	13 Mar	Stoke	6	0
1894	12 Mar	Wrexham	5	1
1895	18 Mar	Queen's Club, Kensington	1	1
1896	16 Mar	Cardiff	9	1
1897	29 Mar	Sheffield	4	0
1898	28 Mar	Wrexham	3	0
1899	20 Mar	Bristol	4	0
1900	26 Mar	Cardiff	1	1
1901	18 Mar	Newcastle	6	0
1902	3 Mar	Wrexham	0	0
1903	2 Mar	Portsmouth	2	1
1904	29 Feb	Wrexham	2	2
1905	27 Mar	Liverpool	3	1
1906	19 Mar	Cardiff	1	0
1907	18 Mar	Fulham	1	1
1908	16 Mar	Wrexham	7	1
1909	15 Mar	Nottingham	2	0
1910	14 Mar	Cardiff	1	0
1911	13 Mar	Millwall	3	0
1912	11 Mar	Wrexham	2	0
1913	17 Mar	Bristol	4	3
1914	16 Mar	Cardiff	2	0
1920	15 Mar	Highbury	1	2
1921	14 Mar	Cardiff	0	0
1922	13 Mar	Liverpool	1	0
1923	5 Mar	Cardiff	2	2
1924	3 Mar	Blackburn	1	2
1925	28 Feb	Swansea	2	1
1926	1 Mar	Crystal Palace	1	3
1927	12 Feb	Wrexham	3	3
1927	28 Nov	Burnley	1	2
1928	17 Nov	Swansea	3	2
1929	20 Nov	Chelsea	6	0
1930	22 Nov	Wrexham	4	0
1931	18 Nov	Liverpool	3	1
1932	16 Nov	Wrexham	0	0
1933	15 Nov	Newcastle	1	2
1934	29 Sept	Cardiff	4	0
1936	5 Feb	Wolverhampton	1	2
1936	17 Oct	Cardiff	1	2
1937	17 Nov	Middlesbrough	2	1
1938	22 Oct	Cardiff	2	4
1946	13 Nov	Manchester	3	0
1947	18 Oct	Cardiff	3	0
1948	10 Nov	Aston Villa	1	0
wc1949	15 Oct	Cardiff	4	1
1950	15 Nov	Sunderland	4	2
1951	20 Oct	Cardiff	1	1
1952	12 Nov	Wembley	5	2
wc1953	10 Oct	Cardiff	4	1
1954	10 Nov	Wembley	3	2
1955	27 Oct	Cardiff	1	2
1956	14 Nov	Wembley	3	1
1957	19 Oct	Cardiff	4	0
1958	26 Nov	Aston Villa	2	2
1959	17 Oct	Cardiff	1	1
1960	23 Nov	Wembley	5	1
1961	14 Oct	Cardiff	1	1
1962	21 Oct	Wembley	4	0
1963	12 Oct	Cardiff	4	0
1964	18 Nov	Wembley	2	1
1965	2 Oct	Cardiff	0	0
EC1966	16 Nov	Wembley	5	1
EC1967	21 Oct	Cardiff	3	0
1969	7 May	Wembley	2	1
1970	18 Apr	Cardiff	1	1
1971	19 May	Wembley	0	0
1972	20 May	Cardiff	3	0
wc1972	15 Nov	Cardiff	1	0
wc1973	24 Jan	Wembley	1	1
1973	15 May	Wembley	3	0
1974	11 May	Cardiff	2	0
1975	21 May	Wembley	2	2
1976	24 Mar	Wrexham	2	1
1976	8 May	Cardiff	1	0
1977	31 May	Wembley	0	1
1978	3 May	Cardiff	3	1
1979	23 May	Wembley	0	0
1980	17 May	Wrexham	1	4
1981	20 May	Wembley	0	0
1982	27 Apr	Cardiff	1	0
1983	23 Feb	Wembley	2	1
1984	2 May	Wrexham	0	1

ENGLAND v IRELAND

Played: 96; England won 74, Ireland won 6, Drawn 16. *Goals:* England 319, Ireland 80.

			E	I
1882	18 Feb	Belfast	13	0
1883	24 Feb	Liverpool	7	0
1884	23 Feb	Belfast	8	1
1885	28 Feb	Manchester	4	0
1886	13 Mar	Belfast	6	1
1887	5 Feb	Sheffield	7	0
1888	31 Mar	Belfast	5	1
1889	2 Mar	Everton	6	1
1890	15 Mar	Belfast	9	1
1891	7 Mar	Wolverhampton	6	1
1892	5 Mar	Belfast	2	0
1893	25 Feb	Birmingham	6	1
1894	3 Mar	Belfast	2	2
1895	9 Mar	Derby	9	0
1896	7 Mar	Belfast	2	0
1897	20 Feb	Nottingham	6	0
1898	5 Mar	Belfast	3	2
1899	18 Feb	Sunderland	13	2
1900	17 Mar	Dublin	2	0
1901	9 Mar	Southampton	3	0
1902	22 Mar	Belfast	1	0
1903	14 Feb	Wolverhampton	4	0
1904	12 Mar	Belfast	3	1
1905	25 Feb	Middlesbrough	1	1
1906	17 Feb	Belfast	5	0
1907	16 Feb	Everton	1	0
1908	15 Feb	Belfast	3	1
1909	13 Feb	Bradford	4	0
1910	12 Feb	Belfast	1	1
1911	11 Feb	Derby	2	1
1912	10 Feb	Dublin	6	1
1913	15 Feb	Belfast	1	2
1914	14 Feb	Middlesbrough	0	3
1919	25 Oct	Belfast	1	1
1920	23 Oct	Sunderland	2	0
1921	22 Oct	Belfast	1	1
1922	21 Oct	West Bromwich	2	0
1923	20 Oct	Belfast	1	2
1924	22 Oct	Everton	3	1
1925	24 Oct	Belfast	0	0
1926	20 Oct	Liverpool	3	3
1927	22 Oct	Belfast	0	2

			E	I
1928	22 Oct	Everton	2	1
1929	19 Oct	Belfast	3	0
1930	20 Oct	Sheffield	5	1
1931	17 Oct	Belfast	6	2
1932	17 Oct	Blackpool	1	0
1933	14 Oct	Belfast	3	0
1935	6 Feb	Everton	2	1
1935	19 Oct	Belfast	3	1
1936	18 Nov	Stoke	3	1
1937	23 Oct	Belfast	5	1
1938	16 Nov	Manchester	7	0
1946	28 Sept	Belfast	7	2
1947	5 Nov	Everton	2	2
1948	9 Oct	Belfast	6	2
wc1949	16 Nov	Manchester	9	2
1950	7 Oct	Belfast	4	1
1951	14 Nov	Aston Villa	2	0
1952	4 Oct	Belfast	2	2
wc1953	11 Nov	Everton	3	1
1954	2 Oct	Belfast	2	0
1955	2 Nov	Wembley	3	0
1956	10 Oct	Belfast	1	1
1957	6 Nov	Wembley	2	3
1958	4 Oct	Belfast	3	3
1959	18 Nov	Wembley	2	1
1960	8 Oct	Belfast	5	2
1961	22 Nov	Wembley	1	1
1962	20 Oct	Belfast	3	1
1963	20 Nov	Wembley	8	3
1964	3 Oct	Belfast	4	3
1965	10 Nov	Wembley	2	1
EC1966	20 Oct	Belfast	2	0
EC1967	22 Nov	Wembley	2	0
1969	3 May	Belfast	3	1
1970	21 Apr	Wembley	3	1
1971	15 May	Belfast	1	0
1972	23 May	Wembley	0	1
1973	12 May	Everton	2	1
1974	15 May	Wembley	1	0
1975	17 May	Belfast	0	0
1976	11 May	Wembley	4	0
1977	28 May	Belfast	2	1
1978	16 May	Wembley	1	0
EC1979	7 Feb	Wembley	4	0
1979	19 May	Belfast	2	0
EC1979	17 Oct	Belfast	5	1
1980	20 May	Wembley	1	1
1982	23 Feb	Wembley	4	0
1983	28 May	Belfast	0	0
1984	24 Apr	Wembley	1	0
wc1985	27 Feb	Belfast	1	0
wc1985	13 Nov	Wembley	0	0
EC1986	15 Oct	Wembley	3	0
EC1987	1 Apr	Belfast	2	0

SCOTLAND v WALES

Played: 102; Scotland won 60, Wales won 19, Drawn 23. *Goals:* Scotland 238, Wales 112.

			S	W
1876	25 Mar	Glasgow	4	0
1877	5 Mar	Wrexham	2	0
1878	23 Mar	Glasgow	9	0
1879	7 Apr	Wrexham	3	0
1880	3 Apr	Glasgow	5	1
1881	14 Mar	Wrexham	5	1
1882	25 Mar	Glasgow	5	0
1883	12 Mar	Wrexham	4	1
1884	29 Mar	Glasgow	4	1
1885	23 Mar	Wrexham	8	1
1886	10 Apr	Glasgow	4	1
1887	21 Mar	Wrexham	2	0
1888	10 Mar	Edinburgh	5	1
1889	15 Apr	Wrexham	0	0
1890	22 Mar	Paisley	5	0
1891	21 Mar	Wrexham	4	3
1892	26 Mar	Edinburgh	6	1
1893	18 Mar	Wrexham	8	0
1894	24 Mar	Kilmarnock	5	2
1895	23 Mar	Wrexham	2	2
1896	21 Mar	Dundee	4	0
1897	20 Mar	Wrexham	2	2
1898	19 Mar	Motherwell	5	2
1899	18 Mar	Wrexham	6	0
1900	3 Feb	Aberdeen	5	2
1901	2 Mar	Wrexham	1	1
1902	15 Mar	Greenock	5	1
1903	9 Mar	Cardiff	1	0
1904	12 Mar	Dundee	1	1
1905	6 Mar	Wrexham	1	3
1906	3 Mar	Edinburgh	0	2
1907	4 Mar	Wrexham	0	1
1908	7 Mar	Dundee	2	1
1909	1 Mar	Wrexham	2	3
1910	5 Mar	Kilmarnock	1	0
1911	6 Mar	Cardiff	2	2
1912	2 Mar	Tynecastle	1	0
1913	3 Mar	Wrexham	0	0
1914	28 Feb	Glasgow	0	0
1920	26 Feb	Cardiff	1	1
1921	12 Feb	Aberdeen	2	1
1922	4 Feb	Wrexham	1	2
1923	17 Mar	Paisley	2	0
1924	16 Feb	Cardiff	0	2
1925	14 Feb	Tynecastle	3	1
1925	31 Oct	Cardiff	3	0
1926	30 Oct	Glasgow	3	0
1927	29 Oct	Wrexham	2	2
1928	27 Oct	Glasgow	4	2
1929	26 Oct	Cardiff	4	2
1930	25 Oct	Glasgow	1	1
1931	31 Oct	Wrexham	3	2
1932	26 Oct	Edinburgh	2	5
1933	4 Oct	Cardiff	2	3
1934	21 Nov	Aberdeen	3	2
1935	5 Oct	Cardiff	1	1
1936	2 Dec	Dundee	1	2
1937	30 Oct	Cardiff	1	2
1938	9 Nov	Edinburgh	3	2
1946	19 Oct	Wrexham	1	3
1947	12 Nov	Glasgow	1	2
wc1948	23 Oct	Cardiff	3	1
1949	9 Nov	Glasgow	2	0
1950	21 Oct	Cardiff	3	1
1951	14 Nov	Glasgow	0	1
wc1952	18 Oct	Cardiff	2	1
1953	4 Nov	Glasgow	3	3
1954	16 Oct	Cardiff	1	0
1955	9 Nov	Glasgow	2	0
1956	20 Oct	Cardiff	2	2
1957	13 Nov	Glasgow	1	1
1958	18 Oct	Cardiff	3	0
1959	4 Nov	Glasgow	1	1
1960	20 Oct	Cardiff	0	2
1961	8 Nov	Glasgow	2	0
1962	20 Oct	Cardiff	3	2
1963	20 Nov	Glasgow	2	1
1964	3 Oct	Cardiff	2	3
EC1965	24 Nov	Glasgow	4	1
EC1966	22 Oct	Cardiff	1	1

			S	W					S	W
1967	22 Nov	Glasgow	3	2	wc1977	12 Oct	Liverpool		2	0
1969	3 May	Wrexham	5	3	1978	17 May	Glasgow		1	1
1970	22 Apr	Glasgow	0	0	1979	19 May	Cardiff		0	3
1971	15 May	Cardiff	0	0	1980	21 May	Glasgow		1	0
1972	24 May	Glasgow	1	0	1981	16 May	Swansea		0	2
1973	12 May	Wrexham	2	0	1982	24 May	Glasgow		1	0
1974	14 May	Glasgow	2	0	1983	28 May	Cardiff		2	0
1975	17 May	Cardiff	2	2	1984	28 Feb	Glasgow		2	1
1976	6 May	Glasgow	3	1	wc1985	27 Mar	Glasgow		0	1
wc1976	17 Nov	Glasgow	1	0	wc1985	10 Sept	Cardiff		1	1
1977	28 May	Wrexham	0	0	1997	27 May	Kilmarnock		0	1

SCOTLAND v IRELAND

Played: 91; Scotland won 60, Ireland won 15, Drawn 16. *Goals:* Scotland 253, Ireland 81.

			S	I				S	I
1884	26 Jan	Belfast	5	0	1934	20 Oct	Belfast	1	2
1885	14 Mar	Glasgow	8	2	1935	13 Nov	Edinburgh	2	1
1886	20 Mar	Belfast	7	2	1936	31 Oct	Belfast	3	1
1887	19 Feb	Glasgow	4	1	1937	10 Nov	Aberdeen	1	1
1888	24 Mar	Belfast	10	2	1938	8 Oct	Belfast	2	0
1889	9 Mar	Glasgow	7	0	1946	27 Nov	Glasgow	0	0
1890	29 Mar	Belfast	4	1	1947	4 Oct	Belfast	0	2
1891	28 Mar	Glasgow	2	1	1948	17 Nov	Glasgow	3	2
1892	19 Mar	Belfast	3	2	1949	1 Oct	Belfast	8	2
1893	25 Mar	Glasgow	6	1	1950	1 Nov	Glasgow	6	1
1894	31 Mar	Belfast	2	1	1951	6 Oct	Belfast	3	0
1895	30 Mar	Glasgow	3	1	1952	5 Nov	Glasgow	1	1
1896	28 Mar	Belfast	3	3	1953	3 Oct	Belfast	3	1
1897	27 Mar	Glasgow	5	1	1954	3 Nov	Glasgow	2	2
1898	26 Mar	Belfast	3	0	1955	8 Oct	Belfast	1	2
1899	25 Mar	Glasgow	9	1	1956	7 Nov	Glasgow	1	0
1900	3 Mar	Belfast	3	0	1957	5 Oct	Belfast	1	1
1901	23 Feb	Glasgow	11	0	1958	5 Nov	Glasgow	2	2
1902	1 Mar	Belfast	5	1	1959	3 Oct	Belfast	4	0
1903	21 Mar	Glasgow	0	2	1960	9 Nov	Glasgow	5	2
1904	26 Mar	Dublin	1	1	1961	7 Oct	Belfast	6	1
1905	18 Mar	Glasgow	4	0	1962	7 Nov	Glasgow	5	1
1906	17 Mar	Dublin	1	0	1963	12 Oct	Belfast	1	2
1907	16 Mar	Glasgow	3	0	1964	25 Nov	Glasgow	3	2
1908	14 Mar	Dublin	5	0	1965	2 Oct	Belfast	2	3
1909	15 Mar	Glasgow	5	0	1966	16 Nov	Glasgow	2	1
1910	19 Mar	Belfast	0	1	1967	21 Oct	Belfast	0	1
1911	18 Mar	Glasgow	2	0	1969	6 May	Glasgow	1	1
1912	16 Mar	Belfast	4	1	1970	18 Apr	Belfast	1	0
1913	15 Mar	Dublin	2	1	1971	18 May	Glasgow	0	1
1914	14 Mar	Belfast	1	1	1972	20 May	Glasgow	2	0
1920	13 Mar	Glasgow	3	0	1973	16 May	Glasgow	1	2
1921	26 Feb	Belfast	2	0	1974	11 May	Glasgow	0	1
1922	4 Mar	Glasgow	2	1	1975	20 May	Glasgow	3	0
1923	3 Mar	Belfast	1	0	1976	8 May	Glasgow	3	0
1924	1 Mar	Glasgow	2	0	1977	1 June	Glasgow	3	0
1925	28 Feb	Belfast	3	0	1978	13 May	Glasgow	1	1
1926	27 Feb	Glasgow	4	0	1979	22 May	Glasgow	1	0
1927	26 Feb	Belfast	2	0	1980	17 May	Belfast	0	1
1928	25 Feb	Glasgow	0	1	wc1981	25 Mar	Glasgow	1	1
1929	23 Feb	Belfast	7	3	1981	19 May	Glasgow	2	0
1930	22 Feb	Glasgow	3	1	wc1981	14 Oct	Belfast	0	0
1931	21 Feb	Belfast	0	0	1982	28 Apr	Belfast	1	1
1931	19 Sept	Glasgow	3	1	1983	24 May	Glasgow	0	0
1932	12 Sept	Belfast	4	0	1983	13 Dec	Belfast	0	2
1933	16 Sept	Glasgow	1	2	1992	19 Feb	Glasgow	1	0

WALES v IRELAND

Played: 90; Wales won 42, Ireland won 27, Drawn 21. *Goals:* Wales 181, Ireland 126.

			W	I				W	I
1882	25 Feb	Wrexham	7	1	1886	27 Feb	Wrexham	5	0
1883	17 Mar	Belfast	1	1	1887	12 Mar	Belfast	1	4
1884	9 Feb	Wrexham	6	0	1888	3 Mar	Wrexham	11	0
1885	11 Apr	Belfast	8	2	1889	27 Apr	Belfast	3	1

			W	I					W	I
1890	8 Feb	Shrewsbury	5	2		1936	11 Mar	Belfast	2	3
1891	7 Feb	Belfast	2	7		1937	17 Mar	Wrexham	4	1
1892	27 Feb	Bangor	1	1		1938	16 Mar	Belfast	0	1
1893	8 Apr	Belfast	3	4		1939	15 Mar	Wrexham	3	1
1894	24 Feb	Swansea	4	1		1947	16 Apr	Belfast	1	2
1895	16 Mar	Belfast	2	2		1948	10 Mar	Wrexham	2	0
1896	29 Feb	Wrexham	6	1		1949	9 Mar	Belfast	2	0
1897	6 Mar	Belfast	3	4	wc1950	8 Mar	Wrexham	0	0
1898	19 Feb	Llandudno	0	1		1951	7 Mar	Belfast	2	1
1899	4 Mar	Belfast	0	1		1952	19 Mar	Swansea	3	0
1900	24 Feb	Llandudno	2	0		1953	15 Apr	Belfast	3	2
1901	23 Mar	Belfast	1	0	wc1954	31 Mar	Wrexham	1	2
1902	22 Mar	Cardiff	0	3		1955	20 Apr	Belfast	3	2
1903	28 Mar	Belfast	0	2		1956	11 Apr	Cardiff	1	1
1904	21 Mar	Bangor	0	1		1957	10 Apr	Belfast	0	0
1905	18 Apr	Belfast	2	2		1958	16 Apr	Cardiff	1	1
1906	2 Apr	Wrexham	4	4		1959	22 Apr	Belfast	1	4
1907	23 Feb	Belfast	3	2		1960	6 Apr	Wrexham	3	2
1908	11 Apr	Aberdare	0	1		1961	12 Apr	Belfast	5	1
1909	20 Mar	Belfast	3	2		1962	11 Apr	Cardiff	4	0
1910	11 Apr	Wrexham	4	1		1963	3 Apr	Belfast	4	1
1911	28 Jan	Belfast	2	1		1964	15 Apr	Cardiff	2	3
1912	13 Apr	Cardiff	2	3		1965	31 Mar	Belfast	5	0
1913	18 Jan	Belfast	1	0		1966	30 Mar	Cardiff	1	4
1914	19 Jan	Wrexham	1	2	EC1967	12 Apr	Belfast	0	0
1920	14 Feb	Belfast	2	2	EC1968	28 Feb	Wrexham	2	0
1921	9 Apr	Swansea	2	1		1969	10 May	Belfast	0	0
1922	4 Apr	Belfast	1	1		1970	25 Apr	Swansea	1	0
1923	14 Apr	Wrexham	0	3		1971	22 May	Belfast	0	1
1924	15 Mar	Belfast	1	0		1972	27 May	Wrexham	0	0
1925	18 Apr	Wrexham	0	0		1973	19 May	Everton	0	1
1926	13 Feb	Belfast	0	3		1974	18 May	Wrexham	1	0
1927	9 Apr	Cardiff	2	2		1975	23 May	Belfast	0	1
1928	4 Feb	Belfast	2	1		1976	14 May	Swansea	1	0
1929	2 Feb	Wrexham	2	2		1977	3 June	Belfast	1	1
1930	1 Feb	Belfast	0	7		1978	19 May	Wrexham	1	0
1931	22 Apr	Wrexham	3	2		1979	25 May	Belfast	1	1
1931	5 Dec	Belfast	0	4		1980	23 May	Cardiff	0	1
1932	7 Dec	Wrexham	4	1		1982	27 May	Wrexham	3	0
1933	4 Nov	Belfast	1	1		1983	31 May	Belfast	1	0
1935	27 Mar	Wrexham	3	1		1984	22 May	Swansea	1	1

OTHER BRITISH INTERNATIONAL RESULTS 1908–1997

ENGLAND

		v ALBANIA	E	A					E	A
wc1989	8 Mar	Tirana	2	0		1909	1 June	Vienna	8	1
wc1989	26 Apr	Wembley	5	0		1930	14 May	Vienna	0	0
						1932	7 Dec	Chelsea	4	3
		v ARGENTINA	E	A		1936	6 May	Vienna	1	2
1951	9 May	Wembley	2	1		1951	28 Nov	Wembley	2	2
1953	17 May	Buenos Aires	0	0		1952	25 May	Vienna	3	2
(*abandoned after 21 mins*)					wc1958	15 June	Boras	2	2
wc1962	2 June	Rancagua	3	1		1961	27 May	Vienna	1	3
1964	6 June	Rio de Janeiro	0	1		1962	4 Apr	Wembley	3	1
wc1966	23 July	Wembley	1	0		1965	20 Oct	Wembley	2	3
1974	22 May	Wembley	2	2		1967	27 May	Vienna	1	0
1977	12 June	Buenos Aires	1	1		1973	26 Sept	Wembley	7	0
1980	13 May	Wembley	3	1		1979	13 June	Vienna	3	4
wc1986	22 June	Mexico City	1	2						
1991	25 May	Wembley	2	2				**v BELGIUM**	E	B
						1921	21 May	Brussels	2	0
		v AUSTRALIA	E	A		1923	19 Mar	Highbury	6	1
1980	31 May	Sydney	2	1		1923	1 Nov	Antwerp	2	2
1983	11 June	Sydney	0	0		1924	8 Dec	West Bromwich	4	0
1983	15 June	Brisbane	1	0		1926	24 May	Antwerp	5	3
1983	18 June	Melbourne	1	1		1927	11 May	Brussels	9	1
1991	1 June	Sydney	1	0		1928	19 May	Antwerp	3	1
						1929	11 May	Brussels	5	1
		v AUSTRIA	E	A		1931	16 May	Brussels	4	1
1908	6 June	Vienna	6	1		1936	9 May	Brussels	2	3
1908	8 June	Vienna	11	1		1947	21 Sept	Brussels	5	2

			E	B
1950	18 May	Brussels	4	1
1952	26 Nov	Wembley	5	0
wc1954	17 June	Basle	4	4*
1964	21 Oct	Wembley	2	2
1970	25 Feb	Brussels	3	1
EC1980	12 June	Turin	1	1
wc1990	27 June	Bologna	1	0*
*After extra time				

v BOHEMIA			E	B
1908	13 June	Prague	4	0

v BRAZIL			E	B
1956	9 May	Wembley	4	2
wc1958	11 June	Gothenburg	0	0
1959	13 May	Rio de Janeiro	0	2
wc1962	10 June	Vina del Mar	1	3
1963	8 May	Wembley	1	1
1964	30 May	Rio de Janeiro	1	5
1969	12 June	Rio de Janeiro	1	2
wc1970	7 June	Guadalajara	0	1
1976	23 May	Los Angeles	0	1
1977	8 June	Rio de Janeiro	0	0
1978	19 Apr	Wembley	1	1
1981	12 May	Wembley	0	1
1984	10 June	Rio de Janeiro	2	0
1987	19 May	Wembley	1	1
1990	28 Mar	Wembley	1	0
1992	17 May	Wembley	1	1
1993	13 June	Washington	1	1
UI1995	11 June	Wembley	1	3
TF1997	10 June	Paris	0	1

v BULGARIA			E	B
wc1962	7 June	Rancagua	0	0
1968	11 Dec	Wembley	1	1
1974	1 June	Sofia	1	0
EC1979	6 June	Sofia	3	0
EC1979	22 Nov	Wembley	2	0
1996	27 Mar	Wembley	1	0

v CAMEROON			E	C
wc1990	1 July	Naples	3	2*
1991	6 Feb	Wembley	2	0

v CANADA			E	C
1986	24 May	Burnaby	1	0

v CHILE			E	C
wc1950	25 June	Rio de Janeiro	2	0
1953	24 May	Santiago	2	1
1984	17 June	Santiago	0	0
1989	23 May	Wembley	0	0

v CHINA			E	C
1996	23 May	Beijing	3	0

v CIS			E	C
1992	29 Apr	Moscow	2	2

v COLOMBIA			E	C
1970	20 May	Bogota	4	0
1988	24 May	Wembley	1	1
1995	6 Sept	Wembley	0	0

v CROATIA			E	C
1996	24 Apr	Wembley	0	0

v CYPRUS			E	C
EC1975	16 Apr	Wembley	5	0
EC1975	11 May	Limassol	1	0

v CZECHOSLOVAKIA			E	C
1934	16 May	Prague	1	2
1937	1 Dec	Tottenham	5	4
1963	29 May	Bratislava	4	2
1966	2 Nov	Wembley	0	0
wc1970	11 June	Guadalajara	1	0
1973	27 May	Prague	1	1
EC1974	30 Oct	Wembley	3	0
EC1975	30 Oct	Bratislava	1	2
1978	29 Nov	Wembley	1	0
wc1982	20 June	Bilbao	2	0
1990	25 Apr	Wembley	4	2
1992	25 Mar	Prague	2	2

v DENMARK			E	D
1948	26 Sept	Copenhagen	0	0
1955	2 Oct	Copenhagen	5	1
wc1956	5 Dec	Wolverhampton	5	2
wc1957	15 May	Copenhagen	4	1
1966	3 July	Copenhagen	2	0
EC1978	20 Sept	Copenhagen	4	3
EC1979	12 Sept	Wembley	1	0
EC1982	22 Sept	Copenhagen	2	2
EC1983	21 Sept	Wembley	0	1
1988	14 Sept	Wembley	1	0
1989	7 June	Copenhagen	1	1
1990	15 May	Wembley	1	0
EC1992	11 June	Malmo	0	0
1994	9 Mar	Wembley	1	0

v ECUADOR			E	Ec
1970	24 May	Quito	2	0

v EGYPT			E	Eg
1986	29 Jan	Cairo	4	0
wc1990	21 June	Cagliari	1	0

v FIFA			E	FIFA
1938	26 Oct	Highbury	3	0
1953	21 Oct	Wembley	4	4
1963	23 Oct	Wembley	2	1

v FINLAND			E	F
1937	20 May	Helsinki	8	0
1956	20 May	Helsinki	5	1
1966	26 June	Helsinki	3	0
wc1976	13 June	Helsinki	4	1
wc1976	13 Oct	Wembley	2	1
1982	3 June	Helsinki	4	1
wc1984	17 Oct	Wembley	5	0
wc1985	22 May	Helsinki	1	1
1992	3 June	Helsinki	2	1

v FRANCE			E	F
1923	10 May	Paris	4	1
1924	17 May	Paris	3	1
1925	21 May	Paris	3	2
1927	26 May	Paris	6	0
1928	17 May	Paris	5	1
1929	9 May	Paris	4	1
1931	14 May	Paris	2	5
1933	6 Dec	Tottenham	4	1
1938	26 May	Paris	4	2
1947	3 May	Highbury	3	0
1949	22 May	Paris	3	1
1951	3 Oct	Highbury	2	2
1955	15 May	Paris	0	1
1957	27 Nov	Wembley	4	0
EC1962	3 Oct	Sheffield	1	1
EC1963	27 Feb	Paris	2	5
wc1966	20 July	Wembley	2	0
1969	12 Mar	Wembley	5	0
wc1982	16 June	Bilbao	3	1

			E	F
1984	29 Feb	Paris	0	2
1992	19 Feb	Wembley	2	0
EC1992	14 June	Malmo	0	0
TF1997	7 June	Montpellier	1	0

v GEORGIA			E	G
wc1996	9 Nov	Tbilisi	2	0
wc1997	30 Apr	Wembley	2	0

v GERMANY			E	G
1930	10 May	Berlin	3	3
1935	4 Dec	Tottenham	3	0
1938	14 May	Berlin	6	3
1991	11 Sept	Wembley	0	1
1993	19 June	Detroit	1	2
EC1996	26 June	Wembley	1	1

v EAST GERMANY			E	EG
1963	2 June	Leipzig	2	1
1970	25 Nov	Wembley	3	1
1974	29 May	Leipzig	1	1
1984	12 Sept	Wembley	1	0

v WEST GERMANY			E	WG
1954	1 Dec	Wembley	3	1
1956	26 May	Berlin	3	1
1965	12 May	Nuremberg	1	0
1966	23 Feb	Wembley	1	0
wc1966	30 July	Wembley	4	2*
1968	1 June	Hanover	0	1
wc1970	14 June	Leon	2	3*
EC1972	29 Apr	Wembley	1	3
EC1972	13 May	Berlin	0	0
1975	12 Mar	Wembley	2	0
1978	22 Feb	Munich	1	2
wc1982	29 June	Madrid	0	0
1982	13 Oct	Wembley	1	2
1985	12 June	Mexico City	3	0
1987	9 Sept	Dusseldorf	1	3
wc1990	4 July	Turin	1	1*

*After extra time

v GREECE			E	G
EC1971	21 Apr	Wembley	3	0
EC1971	1 Dec	Athens	2	0
EC1982	17 Nov	Athens	3	0
EC1983	30 Mar	Wembley	0	0
1989	8 Feb	Athens	2	1
1994	17 May	Wembley	5	0

v HOLLAND			E	H
1935	18 May	Amsterdam	1	0
1946	27 Nov	Huddersfield	8	2
1964	9 Dec	Amsterdam	1	1
1969	5 Nov	Amsterdam	1	0
1970	14 Jun	Wembley	0	0
1977	9 Feb	Wembley	0	2
1982	25 May	Wembley	2	0
1988	23 Mar	Wembley	2	2
EC1988	15 June	Dusseldorf	1	3
wc1990	16 June	Cagliari	0	0
wc1993	28 Apr	Wembley	2	2
wc1993	13 Oct	Rotterdam	0	2
EC1996	18 June	Wembley	4	1

v HUNGARY			E	H
1908	10 June	Budapest	7	0
1909	29 May	Budapest	4	2
1909	31 May	Budapest	8	2
1934	10 May	Budapest	1	2
1936	2 Dec	Highbury	6	2
1953	25 Nov	Wembley	3	6
1954	23 May	Budapest	1	7
1960	22 May	Budapest	0	2

			E	H
wc1962	31 May	Rancagua	1	2
1965	5 May	Wembley	1	0
1978	24 May	Wembley	4	1
wc1981	6 June	Budapest	3	1
wc1982	18 Nov	Wembley	1	0
EC1983	27 Apr	Wembley	2	0
EC1983	12 Oct	Budapest	3	0
1988	27 Apr	Budapest	0	0
1990	12 Sept	Wembley	1	0
1992	12 May	Budapest	1	0
1996	18 May	Wembley	3	0

v ICELAND			E	I
1982	2 June	Reykjavik	1	1

v REPUBLIC OF IRELAND			E	RI
1946	30 Sept	Dublin	1	0
1949	21 Sept	Everton	0	2
wc1957	8 May	Wembley	5	1
wc1957	19 May	Dublin	1	1
1964	24 May	Dublin	3	1
1976	8 Sept	Wembley	1	1
EC1978	25 Oct	Dublin	1	1
EC1980	6 Feb	Wembley	2	0
1985	26 Mar	Wembley	2	1
EC1988	12 June	Stuttgart	0	1
wc1990	11 June	Cagliari	1	1
EC1990	14 Nov	Dublin	1	1
EC1991	27 Mar	Wembley	1	1
1995	15 Feb	Dublin	0	1

(abandoned after 27 mins)

v ISRAEL			E	I
1986	26 Feb	Ramat Gan	2	1
1988	17 Feb	Tel Aviv	0	0

v ITALY			E	I
1933	13 May	Rome	1	1
1934	14 Nov	Highbury	3	2
1939	13 May	Milan	2	2
1948	16 May	Turin	4	0
1949	30 Nov	Tottenham	2	0
1952	18 May	Florence	1	1
1959	6 May	Wembley	2	2
1961	24 May	Rome	3	2
1973	14 June	Turin	0	2
1973	14 Nov	Wembley	0	1
1976	28 May	New York	3	2
wc1976	17 Nov	Rome	0	2
wc1977	16 Nov	Wembley	2	0
EC1980	15 June	Turin	0	1
1985	6 June	Mexico City	1	2
1989	15 Nov	Wembley	0	0
wc1990	7 July	Bari	1	2
wc1997	12 Feb	Wembley	0	1
TF1997	4 June	Nantes	2	0

v JAPAN			E	J
UI1995	3 June	Wembley	2	1

v KUWAIT			E	K
wc1982	25 June	Bilbao	1	0

v LUXEMBOURG			E	L
1927	21 May	Luxembourg	5	2
wc1960	19 Oct	Luxembourg	9	0
wc1961	28 Sept	Highbury	4	1
wc1977	30 Mar	Wembley	5	0
wc1977	12 Oct	Luxembourg	2	0
EC1982	15 Dec	Wembley	9	0
EC1983	16 Nov	Luxembourg	4	0

v MALAYSIA			E	M
1991	12 June	Kuala Lumpur	4	2

		v MALTA	E	M
EC1971	3 Feb	Valletta	1	0
EC1971	12 May	Wembley	5	0

		v MEXICO	E	M
1959	24 May	Mexico City	1	2
1961	10 May	Wembley	8	0
wc1966	16 July	Wembley	2	0
1969	1 June	Mexico City	0	0
1985	9 June	Mexico City	0	1
1986	17 May	Los Angeles	3	0
1997	29 Mar	Wembley	2	0

		v MOLDOVA	E	M
wc1996	1 Sept	Chisinau	3	0

		v MOROCCO	E	M
wc1986	6 June	Monterrey	0	0

		v NEW ZEALAND	E	NZ
1991	3 June	Auckland	1	0
1991	8 June	Wellington	2	0

		v NIGERIA	E	N
1994	16 Nov	Wembley	1	0

		v NORWAY	E	N
1937	14 May	Oslo	6	0
1938	9 Nov	Newcastle	4	0
1949	18 May	Oslo	4	1
1966	29 June	Oslo	6	1
wc1980	10 Sept	Wembley	4	0
wc1981	9 Sept	Oslo	1	2
wc1992	14 Oct	Wembley	1	1
wc1993	2 June	Oslo	0	2
1994	22 May	Wembley	0	0
1995	11 Oct	Oslo	0	0

		v PARAGUAY	E	P
wc1986	18 June	Mexico City	3	0

		v PERU	E	P
1959	17 May	Lima	1	4
1962	20 May	Lima	4	0

		v POLAND	E	P
1966	5 Jan	Everton	1	1
1966	5 July	Chorzow	1	0
wc1973	6 June	Chorzow	0	2
wc1973	17 Oct	Wembley	1	1
wc1986	11 June	Monterrey	3	0
wc1989	3 June	Wembley	3	0
wc1989	11 Oct	Katowice	0	0
EC1990	17 Oct	Wembley	2	0
EC1991	13 Nov	Poznan	1	1
wc1993	29 May	Katowice	1	1
wc1993	8 Sept	Wembley	3	0
wc1996	9 Oct	Wembley	2	0
wc1997	31 May	Katowice	2	0

		v PORTUGAL	E	P
1947	25 May	Lisbon	10	0
1950	14 May	Lisbon	5	3
1951	19 May	Everton	5	2
1955	22 May	Oporto	1	3
1958	7 May	Wembley	2	1
wc1961	21 May	Lisbon	1	1
wc1961	25 Oct	Wembley	2	0
1964	17 May	Lisbon	4	3
1964	4 June	São Paulo	1	1
wc1966	26 July	Wembley	2	1
1969	10 Dec	Wembley	1	0
1974	3 Apr	Lisbon	0	0
EC1974	20 Nov	Wembley	0	0
EC1975	19 Nov	Lisbon	1	1
wc1986	3 June	Monterrey	0	1
1995	12 Dec	Wembley	1	1

		v ROMANIA	E	R
1939	24 May	Bucharest	2	0
1968	6 Nov	Bucharest	0	0
1969	15 Jan	Wembley	1	1
wc1970	2 June	Guadalajara	1	0
wc1980	15 Oct	Bucharest	1	2
wc1981	29 April	Wembley	0	0
wc1985	1 May	Bucharest	0	0
wc1985	11 Sept	Wembley	1	1
1994	12 Oct	Wembley	1	1

		v SAN MARINO	E	SM
wc1992	17 Feb	Wembley	6	0
wc1993	17 Nov	Bologna	7	1

		v SAUDI ARABIA	E	SA
1988	16 Nov	Riyadh	1	1

		v SOUTH AFRICA	E	SA
1997	24 May	Old Trafford	2	1

		v SPAIN	E	S
1929	15 May	Madrid	3	4
1931	9 Dec	Highbury	7	1
wc1950	2 July	Rio de Janeiro	0	1
1955	18 May	Madrid	1	1
1955	30 Nov	Wembley	4	1
1960	15 May	Madrid	0	3
1960	26 Oct	Wembley	4	2
1965	8 Dec	Madrid	2	0
1967	24 May	Wembley	2	0
EC1968	3 Apr	Wembley	1	0
EC1968	8 May	Madrid	2	1
1980	26 Mar	Barcelona	2	0
EC1980	18 June	Naples	2	1
1981	25 Mar	Wembley	1	2
wc1982	5 July	Madrid	0	0
1987	18 Feb	Madrid	4	2
1992	9 Sept	Santander	0	1
EC 1996	22 June	Wembley	0	0

		v SWEDEN	E	S
1923	21 May	Stockholm	4	2
1923	24 May	Stockholm	3	1
1937	17 May	Stockholm	4	0
1947	19 Nov	Highbury	4	2
1949	13 May	Stockholm	1	3
1956	16 May	Stockholm	0	0
1959	28 Oct	Wembley	2	3
1965	16 May	Gothenburg	2	1
1968	22 May	Wembley	3	1
1979	10 June	Stockholm	0	0
1986	10 Sept	Stockholm	0	1
wc1988	19 Oct	Wembley	0	0
wc1989	6 Sept	Stockholm	0	0
EC1992	17 June	Stockholm	1	2
UI1995	8 June	Leeds	3	3

		v SWITZERLAND	E	S
1933	20 May	Berne	4	0
1938	21 May	Zurich	1	2
1947	18 May	Zurich	0	1
1948	2 Dec	Highbury	6	0
1952	28 May	Zurich	3	0
wc1954	20 June	Berne	2	0
1962	9 May	Wembley	3	1
1963	5 June	Basle	8	1
EC1971	13 Oct	Basle	3	2
EC1971	10 Nov	Wembley	1	1
1975	3 Sept	Basle	2	1
1977	7 Sept	Wembley	0	0
wc1980	19 Nov	Wembley	2	1
wc1981	30 May	Basle	1	2
1988	28 May	Lausanne	1	0
1995	15 Nov	Wembley	3	1
EC1996	8 June	Wembley	1	1

		v TUNISIA	E	T
1990	2 June	Tunis	1	1

		v TURKEY	E	T
wc1984	14 Nov	Istanbul	8	0
wc1985	16 Oct	Wembley	5	0
EC1987	29 Apr	Izmir	0	0
EC1987	14 Oct	Wembley	8	0
EC1991	1 May	Izmir	1	0
EC1991	16 Oct	Wembley	1	0
wc1992	18 Nov	Wembley	4	0
wc1993	31 Mar	Izmir	2	0

		v URUGUAY	E	U
1953	31 May	Montevideo	1	2
wc1954	26 June	Basle	2	4
1964	6 May	Wembley	2	1
wc1966	11 July	Wembley	0	0
1969	8 June	Montevideo	2	1
1977	15 June	Montevideo	0	0
1984	13 June	Montevideo	0	2
1990	22 May	Wembley	1	2
1995	29 Mar	Wembley	0	0

		v USA	E	USA
wc1950	29 June	Belo Horizonte	0	1
1953	8 June	New York	6	3
1959	28 May	Los Angeles	8	1
1964	27 May	New York	10	0
1985	16 June	Los Angeles	5	0
1993	9 June	Foxboro	0	2

			E	USA
1994	7 Sept	Wembley	2	0

		v USSR	E	USSR
1958	18 May	Moscow	1	1
wc1958	8 June	Gothenburg	2	2
wc1958	17 June	Gothenburg	0	1
1958	22 Oct	Wembley	5	0
1967	6 Dec	Wembley	2	2
EC1968	8 June	Rome	2	0
1973	10 June	Moscow	2	1
1984	2 June	Wembley	0	2
1986	26 Mar	Tbilisi	1	0
EC1988	18 June	Frankfurt	1	3
1991	21 May	Wembley	3	1

		v YUGOSLAVIA	E	Y
1939	18 May	Belgrade	1	2
1950	22 Nov	Highbury	2	2
1954	16 May	Belgrade	0	1
1956	28 Nov	Wembley	3	0
1958	11 May	Belgrade	0	5
1960	11 May	Wembley	3	3
1965	9 May	Belgrade	1	1
1966	4 May	Wembley	2	0
EC1968	5 June	Florence	0	1
1972	11 Oct	Wembley	1	1
1974	5 June	Belgrade	2	2
EC1986	12 Nov	Wembley	2	0
EC1987	11 Nov	Belgrade	4	1
1989	13 Dec	Wembley	2	1

SCOTLAND

		v ARGENTINA	S	A
1977	18 June	Buenos Aires	1	1
1979	2 June	Glasgow	1	3
1990	28 Mar	Glasgow	1	0

		v AUSTRALIA	S	A
wc1985	20 Nov	Glasgow	2	0
wc1985	4 Dec	Melbourne	0	0
1996	27 Mar	Glasgow	1	0

		v AUSTRIA	S	A
1931	16 May	Vienna	0	5
1933	29 Nov	Glasgow	2	2
1937	9 May	Vienna	1	1
1950	13 Dec	Glasgow	0	1
1951	27 May	Vienna	0	4
wc1954	16 June	Zurich	0	1
1955	19 May	Vienna	4	1
1956	2 May	Glasgow	1	1
1960	29 May	Vienna	1	4
1963	8 May	Glasgow	4	1
(abandoned after 79 mins)				
wc1968	6 Nov	Glasgow	2	1
wc1969	5 Nov	Vienna	0	2
EC1978	20 Sept	Vienna	2	3
EC1979	17 Oct	Glasgow	1	1
1994	20 Apr	Vienna	2	1
wc1996	31 Aug	Vienna	0	0
wc1997	2 Apr	Celtic Park	2	0

		v BELARUS	S	B
wc1997	8 June	Minsk	1	0

		v BELGIUM	S	B
1947	18 May	Brussels	1	2
1948	28 Apr	Glasgow	2	0
1951	20 May	Brussels	5	0
EC1971	3 Feb	Liège	0	3
EC1971	10 Nov	Aberdeen	1	0
1974	2 June	Brussels	1	2
EC1979	21 Nov	Brussels	0	2
EC1979	19 Dec	Glasgow	1	3
EC1982	15 Dec	Brussels	2	3
EC1983	12 Oct	Glasgow	1	1

			S	B
EC1987	1 Apr	Brussels	1	4
EC1987	14 Oct	Glasgow	2	0

		v BRAZIL	S	B
1966	25 June	Glasgow	1	1
1972	5 July	Rio de Janeiro	0	1
1973	30 June	Glasgow	0	1
wc1974	18 June	Frankfurt	0	0
1977	23 June	Rio de Janeiro	0	2
wc1982	18 June	Seville	1	4
1987	26 May	Glasgow	0	2
wc1990	20 June	Turin	0	1

		v BULGARIA	S	B
1978	22 Feb	Glasgow	2	1
EC1986	10 Sept	Glasgow	0	0
EC1987	11 Nov	Sofia	1	0
EC1990	14 Nov	Sofia	1	1
EC1991	27 Mar	Glasgow	1	1

		v CANADA	S	C
1983	12 June	Vancouver	2	0
1983	16 June	Edmonton	3	0
1983	20 June	Toronto	2	0
1992	21 May	Toronto	3	1

		v CHILE	S	C
1977	15 June	Santiago	4	2
1989	30 May	Glasgow	2	0

		v CIS	S	C
EC1992	18 June	Norrkoping	3	0

		v COLOMBIA	S	C
1988	17 May	Glasgow	0	0
1996	30 May	Miami	0	1

		v COSTA RICA	S	CR
wc1990	11 June	Genoa	0	1

		v CYPRUS	S	C
wc1968	17 Dec	Nicosia	5	0
wc1969	11 May	Glasgow	8	0
wc1989	8 Feb	Limassol	3	2
wc1989	26 Apr	Glasgow	2	1

v CZECHOSLOVAKIA			S	C
1937	22 May	Prague	3	1
1937	8 Dec	Glasgow	5	0
wc1961	14 May	Bratislava	0	4
wc1961	26 Sept	Glasgow	3	2
wc1961	29 Nov	Brussels	2	4*
1972	2 July	Porto Alegre	0	0
wc1973	26 Sept	Glasgow	2	1
wc1973	17 Oct	Prague	0	1
wc1976	13 Oct	Prague	0	2
wc1977	21 Sept	Glasgow	3	1
*After extra time				

v DENMARK			S	D
1951	12 May	Glasgow	3	1
1952	25 May	Copenhagen	2	1
1968	16 Oct	Copenhagen	1	0
EC1970	11 Nov	Glasgow	1	0
EC1971	9 June	Copenhagen	0	1
wc1972	18 Oct	Copenhagen	4	1
wc1972	15 Nov	Glasgow	2	0
EC1975	3 Sept	Copenhagen	1	0
EC1975	29 Oct	Glasgow	3	1
wc1986	4 June	Nezahualcayotl	0	1
1996	24 Apr	Copenhagen	0	2

v ECUADOR			S	E
1995	24 May	Toyama	2	1

v EGYPT			S	E
1990	16 May	Aberdeen	1	3

v ESTONIA			S	E
wc1993	19 May	Tallinn	3	0
wc1993	2 June	Aberdeen	3	1
wc1997	11 Feb	Monaco	0	0
wc1997	29 Mar	Kilmarnock	2	0

v FAEROES			S	F
EC1994	12 Oct	Glasgow	5	1
EC1995	7 June	Toftir	2	0

v FINLAND			S	F
1954	25 May	Helsinki	2	1
wc1964	21 Oct	Glasgow	3	1
wc1965	27 May	Helsinki	2	1
1976	8 Sept	Glasgow	6	0
1992	25 Mar	Glasgow	1	1
EC1994	7 Sept	Helsinki	2	0
EC1995	6 Sept	Glasgow	1	0

v FRANCE			S	F
1930	18 May	Paris	2	0
1932	8 May	Paris	3	1
1948	23 May	Paris	0	3
1949	27 Apr	Glasgow	2	0
1950	27 May	Paris	1	0
1951	16 May	Glasgow	1	0
wc1958	15 June	Orebro	1	2
1984	1 June	Marseilles	0	2
wc1989	8 Mar	Glasgow	2	0
wc1989	11 Oct	Paris	0	3

v GERMANY			S	G
1929	1 June	Berlin	1	1
1936	14 Oct	Glasgow	2	0
EC1992	15 June	Norrkoping	0	2
1993	24 Mar	Glasgow	0	1

v EAST GERMANY			S	EG
1974	30 Oct	Glasgow	3	0
1977	7 Sept	East Berlin	0	1
EC1982	13 Oct	Glasgow	2	0
EC1983	16 Nov	Halle	1	2
1985	16 Oct	Glasgow	0	0
1990	25 Apr	Glasgow	0	1

v WEST GERMANY			S	WG
1957	22 May	Stuttgart	3	1
1959	6 May	Glasgow	3	2
1964	12 May	Hanover	2	2
wc1969	16 Apr	Glasgow	1	1
wc1969	22 Oct	Hamburg	2	3
1973	14 Nov	Glasgow	1	1
1974	27 Mar	Frankfurt	1	2
wc1986	8 June	Queretaro	1	2

v GREECE			S	G
EC1994	18 Dec	Athens	0	1
EC1995	16 Aug	Glasgow	1	0

v HOLLAND			S	H
1929	4 June	Amsterdam	2	0
1938	21 May	Amsterdam	3	1
1959	27 May	Amsterdam	2	1
1966	11 May	Glasgow	0	3
1968	30 May	Amsterdam	0	0
1971	1 Dec	Rotterdam	1	2
wc1978	11 June	Mendoza	3	2
1982	23 Mar	Glasgow	2	1
1986	29 Apr	Eindhoven	0	0
EC1992	12 June	Gothenburg	0	1
1994	23 Mar	Glasgow	0	1
1994	27 May	Utrecht	1	3
EC1996	10 June	Birmingham	0	0

v HUNGARY			S	H
1938	7 Dec	Glasgow	3	1
1954	8 Dec	Glasgow	2	4
1955	29 May	Budapest	1	3
1958	7 May	Glasgow	1	1
1960	5 June	Budapest	3	3
1980	31 May	Budapest	1	3
1987	9 Sept	Glasgow	2	0

v ICELAND			S	I
wc1984	17 Oct	Glasgow	3	0
wc1985	28 May	Reykjavik	1	0

v IRAN			S	I
wc1978	7 June	Cordoba	1	1

v REPUBLIC OF IRELAND			S	RI
wc1961	3 May	Glasgow	4	1
wc1961	7 May	Dublin	3	0
1963	9 June	Dublin	0	1
1969	21 Sept	Dublin	1	1
EC1986	15 Oct	Dublin	0	0
EC1987	18 Feb	Glasgow	0	1

v ISRAEL			S	I
wc1981	25 Feb	Tel Aviv	1	0
wc1981	28 Apr	Glasgow	3	1
1986	28 Jan	Tel Aviv	1	0

v ITALY			S	I
1931	20 May	Rome	0	3
wc1965	9 Nov	Glasgow	1	0
wc1965	7 Dec	Naples	0	3
1988	22 Dec	Perugia	0	2
wc1992	18 Nov	Glasgow	0	0
wc1993	13 Oct	Rome	1	3

v JAPAN			S	J
1995	21 May	Hiroshima	0	0

v LATVIA			S	L
wc1996	5 Oct	Riga	2	0

v LUXEMBOURG			S	L
1947	24 May	Luxembourg	6	0
EC1986	12 Nov	Glasgow	3	0
EC1987	2 Dec	Esch	0	0

v MALTA		S	M
1988	22 Mar Valletta	1	1
1990	28 May Valletta	2	1
wc1993	17 Feb Glasgow	3	0
wc1993	17 Nov Valletta	2	0
1997	1 June Valletta	3	2

v NEW ZEALAND		S	NZ
wc1982	15 June Malaga	5	2

v NORWAY		S	N
1929	28 May Oslo	7	3
1954	5 May Glasgow	1	0
1954	19 May Oslo	1	1
1963	4 June Bergen	3	4
1963	7 Nov Glasgow	6	1
1974	6 June Oslo	2	1
EC1978	25 Oct Glasgow	3	2
EC1979	7 June Oslo	4	0
wc1988	14 Sept Oslo	2	1
wc1989	15 Nov Glasgow	1	0
1992	3 June Oslo	0	0

v PARAGUAY		S	P
wc1958	11 June Norrkoping	2	3

v PERU		S	P
1972	26 Apr Glasgow	2	0
wc1978	3 June Cordoba	1	3
1979	12 Sept Glasgow	1	1

v POLAND		S	P
1958	1 June Warsaw	2	1
1960	4 June Glasgow	2	3
wc1965	23 May Chorzow	1	1
wc1965	13 Oct Glasgow	1	2
1980	28 May Poznan	0	1
1990	19 May Glasgow	1	1

v PORTUGAL		S	P
1950	21 May Lisbon	2	2
1955	4 May Glasgow	3	0
1959	3 June Lisbon	0	1
1966	18 June Glasgow	0	1
EC1971	21 Apr Lisbon	0	2
EC1971	13 Oct Glasgow	2	1
1975	13 May Glasgow	1	0
EC1978	29 Nov Lisbon	0	1
EC1980	26 Mar Glasgow	4	1
wc1980	15 Oct Glasgow	0	0
wc1981	18 Nov Lisbon	1	2
wc1992	14 Oct Glasgow	0	0
wc1993	28 Apr Lisbon	0	5

v ROMANIA		S	R
EC1975	1 June Bucharest	1	1
EC1975	17 Dec Glasgow	1	1
1986	26 Mar Glasgow	3	0
EC1990	12 Sept Glasgow	2	1
EC1991	16 Oct Bucharest	0	1

v RUSSIA		S	R
EC1994	16 Nov Glasgow	1	1
EC1995	29 Mar Moscow	0	0

v SAN MARINO		S	SM
EC1991	1 May Serravalle	2	0
EC1991	13 Nov Glasgow	4	0
EC1995	26 Apr Serravalle	2	0
EC1995	15 Nov Glasgow	5	0

v SAUDI ARABIA		S	SA
1988	17 Feb Riyadh	2	2

v SPAIN		S	Sp
wc1957	8 May Glasgow	4	2
wc1957	26 May Madrid	1	4
1963	13 June Madrid	6	2
1965	8 May Glasgow	0	0
EC1974	20 Nov Glasgow	1	2
EC1975	5 Feb Valencia	1	1
1982	24 Feb Valencia	0	3
wc1984	14 Nov Glasgow	3	1
wc1985	27 Feb Seville	0	1
1988	27 Apr Madrid	0	0

v SWEDEN		S	Sw
1952	30 May Stockholm	1	3
1953	6 May Glasgow	1	2
1975	16 Apr Gothenburg	1	1
1977	27 Apr Glasgow	3	1
wc1980	10 Sept Stockholm	1	0
wc1981	9 Sept Glasgow	2	0
wc1990	16 June Genoa	2	1
1995	11 Oct Stockholm	0	2
wc1996	10 Nov Glasgow	1	0
wc1997	30 Apr Gothenburg	1	2

v SWITZERLAND		S	Sw
1931	24 May Geneva	3	2
1948	17 May Berne	1	2
1950	26 Apr Glasgow	3	1
wc1957	19 May Basle	2	1
wc1957	6 Nov Glasgow	3	2
1973	22 June Berne	0	1
1976	7 Apr Glasgow	1	0
EC1982	17 Nov Berne	0	2
EC1983	30 May Glasgow	2	2
EC1990	17 Oct Glasgow	2	1
EC1991	11 Sept Berne	2	2
wc1992	9 Sept Berne	1	3
wc1993	8 Sept Aberdeen	1	1
EC1996	18 June Birmingham	1	0

v TURKEY		S	T
1960	8 June Ankara	2	4

v URUGUAY		S	U
wc1954	19 June Basle	0	7
1962	2 May Glasgow	2	3
1983	21 Sept Glasgow	2	0
wc1986	13 June Nezahualcoyotl	0	0

v USA		S	USA
1952	30 Apr Glasgow	6	0
1992	17 May Denver	1	0
1996	26 May New Britain	1	2

v USSR		S	USSR
1967	10 May Glasgow	0	2
1971	14 June Moscow	0	1
wc1982	22 June Malaga	2	2
1991	6 Feb Glasgow	0	1

v YUGOSLAVIA		S	Y
1955	15 May Belgrade	2	2
1956	21 Nov Glasgow	2	0
wc1958	8 June Vasteras	1	1
1972	29 June Belo Horizonte	2	2
wc1974	22 June Frankfurt	1	1
1984	12 Sept Glasgow	6	1
wc1988	19 Oct Glasgow	1	1
wc1989	6 Sept Zagreb	1	3

v ZAIRE		S	Z
wc1974	14 June Dortmund	2	0

WALES

v ALBANIA

			W	A
Ec1994	7 Sept	Cardiff	2	0
Ec1995	15 Nov	Tirana	1	1

v ARGENTINA

			W	A
1992	3 June	Tokyo	0	1

v AUSTRIA

			W	A
1954	9 May	Vienna	0	2
Ec1955	23 Nov	Wrexham	1	2
Ec1974	4 Sept	Vienna	1	2
1975	19 Nov	Wrexham	1	0
1992	29 Apr	Vienna	1	1

v BELGIUM

			W	B
1949	22 May	Liège	1	3
1949	23 Nov	Cardiff	5	1
Ec1990	17 Oct	Cardiff	3	1
Ec1991	27 Mar	Brussels	1	1
wc1992	18 Nov	Brussels	0	2
wc1993	31 Mar	Cardiff	2	0
wc1997	29 Mar	Cardiff	1	2

v BRAZIL

			W	B
wc1958	19 June	Gothenburg	0	1
1962	12 May	Rio de Janeiro	1	3
1962	16 May	São Paulo	1	3
1966	14 May	Rio de Janeiro	1	3
1966	18 May	Belo Horizonte	0	1
1983	12 June	Cardiff	1	1
1991	11 Sept	Cardiff	1	0

v BULGARIA

			W	B
Ec1983	27 Apr	Wrexham	1	0
Ec1983	16 Nov	Sofia	0	1
Ec1994	14 Dec	Cardiff	0	3
Ec1995	29 Mar	Sofia	1	3

v CANADA

			W	C
1986	10 May	Toronto	0	2
1986	20 May	Vancouver	3	0

v CHILE

			W	C
1966	22 May	Santiago	0	2

v COSTA RICA

			W	CR
1990	20 May	Cardiff	1	0

v CYPRUS

			W	C
wc1992	14 Oct	Limassol	1	0
wc1993	13 Oct	Cardiff	2	0

v CZECHOSLOVAKIA

			W	C
wc1957	1 May	Cardiff	1	0
wc1957	26 May	Prague	0	2
Ec1971	21 Apr	Swansea	1	3
Ec1971	27 Oct	Prague	0	1
wc1977	30 Mar	Wrexham	3	0
wc1977	16 Nov	Prague	0	1
wc1980	19 Nov	Cardiff	1	0
wc1981	9 Sept	Prague	0	2
Ec1987	29 Apr	Wrexham	1	1
Ec1987	11 Nov	Prague	0	2
wc1993	28 Apr	Ostrava†	1	1
wc1993	8 Sept	Cardiff†	2	2

†Czechoslovakia played as RCS (Republic of Czechs and Slovaks).

v DENMARK

			W	D
wc1964	21 Oct	Copenhagen	0	1
wc1965	1 Dec	Wrexham	4	2
Ec1987	9 Sept	Cardiff	1	0
Ec1987	14 Oct	Copenhagen	0	1
1990	11 Sept	Copenhagen	0	1

v ESTONIA

			W	E
1994	23 May	Tallinn	2	1

v FINLAND

			W	F
Ec1971	26 May	Helsinki	1	0
Ec1971	13 Oct	Swansea	3	0
Ec1987	10 Sept	Helsinki	1	1
Ec1987	1 Apr	Wrexham	4	0
wc1988	19 Oct	Swansea	2	2
wc1989	6 Sept	Helsinki	0	1

v FAEROES

			W	F
wc1992	9 Sept	Cardiff	6	0
wc1993	6 June	Toftir	3	0

v FRANCE

			W	F
1933	25 May	Paris	1	1
1939	20 May	Paris	1	2
1953	14 May	Paris	1	6
1982	2 June	Toulouse	1	0

v GEORGIA

			W	G
Ec1994	16 Nov	Tbilisi	0	5
Ec1995	7 June	Cardiff	0	1

v GERMANY

			W	G
Ec1995	26 Apr	Dusseldorf	1	1
Ec1995	11 Oct	Cardiff	1	2

v EAST GERMANY

			W	EG
wc1957	19 May	Leipzig	1	2
wc1957	25 Sept	Cardiff	4	1
wc1969	16 Apr	Dresden	1	2
wc1969	22 Oct	Cardiff	1	3

v WEST GERMANY

			W	WG
1968	8 May	Cardiff	1	1
1969	26 Mar	Frankfurt	1	1
1976	6 Oct	Cardiff	0	2
1977	14 Dec	Dortmund	1	1
Ec1979	2 May	Wrexham	0	2
Ec1979	17 Oct	Cologne	1	5
wc1989	31 May	Cardiff	0	0
wc1989	15 Nov	Cologne	1	2
Ec1991	5 June	Cardiff	1	0
Ec1991	16 Oct	Nuremberg	1	4

v GREECE

			W	G
wc1964	9 Dec	Athens	0	2
wc1965	17 Mar	Cardiff	4	1

v HOLLAND

			W	H
wc1988	14 Sept	Amsterdam	0	1
wc1989	11 Oct	Wrexham	1	2
1992	30 May	Utrecht	0	4
wc1996	5 Oct	Cardiff	1	3
wc1996	9 Nov	Eindhoven	1	7

v HUNGARY

			W	H
wc1958	8 June	Sanviken	1	1
wc1958	17 June	Stockholm	2	1
1961	28 May	Budapest	2	3
Ec1962	7 Nov	Budapest	1	3
Ec1963	20 Mar	Cardiff	1	1
Ec1974	30 Oct	Cardiff	2	0
Ec1975	16 Apr	Budapest	2	1
1985	16 Oct	Cardiff	0	3

v ICELAND

			W	I
wc1980	2 June	Reykjavik	4	0
wc1981	14 Oct	Swansea	2	2
wc1984	12 Sept	Reykjavik	0	1
wc1984	14 Nov	Cardiff	2	1
1991	1 May	Cardiff	1	0

v IRAN

			W	I
1978	18 Apr	Teheran	1	0

v REPUBLIC OF IRELAND

			W	RI
1960	28 Sept	Dublin	3	2
1979	11 Sept	Swansea	2	1
1981	24 Feb	Dublin	3	1
1986	26 Mar	Dublin	1	0
1990	28 Mar	Dublin	0	1
1991	6 Feb	Wrexham	0	3
1992	19 Feb	Dublin	1	0
1993	17 Feb	Dublin	1	2
1997	11 Feb	Cardiff	0	0

v ISRAEL

			W	I
wc1958	15 Jan	Tel Aviv	2	0
wc1958	5 Feb	Cardiff	2	0
1984	10 June	Tel Aviv	0	0
1989	8 Feb	Tel Aviv	3	3

v ITALY

			W	I
1965	1 May	Florence	1	4
wc1968	23 Oct	Cardiff	0	1
wc1969	4 Nov	Rome	1	4
1988	4 June	Brescia	1	0
1996	24 Jan	Terni	0	3

v JAPAN

			W	J
1992	7 June	Matsuyama	1	0

v KUWAIT

			W	K
1977	6 Sept	Wrexham	0	0
1977	20 Sept	Kuwait	0	0

v LUXEMBOURG

			W	L
EC1974	20 Nov	Swansea	5	0
EC1975	1 May	Luxembourg	3	1
EC1990	14 Nov	Luxembourg	1	0
EC1991	13 Nov	Cardiff	1	0

v MALTA

			W	M
EC1978	25 Oct	Wrexham	7	0
EC1979	2 June	Valletta	2	0
1988	1 June	Valletta	3	2

v MEXICO

			W	M
wc1958	11 June	Stockholm	1	1
1962	22 May	Mexico City	1	2

v MOLDOVA

			W	M
EC1994	12 Oct	Kishinev	2	3
EC1995	6 Sept	Cardiff	1	0

v NORWAY

			W	N
EC1982	22 Sept	Swansea	1	0
EC1983	21 Sept	Oslo	0	0
1984	6 June	Trondheim	0	1
1985	26 Feb	Wrexham	1	1
1985	5 June	Bergen	2	4
1994	9 Mar	Cardiff	1	3

v POLAND

			W	P
wc1973	28 Mar	Cardiff	2	0
wc1973	26 Sept	Katowice	0	3
1991	29 May	Radom	0	0

v PORTUGAL

			W	P
1949	15 May	Lisbon	2	3
1951	12 May	Cardiff	2	1

v ROMANIA

			W	R
EC1970	11 Nov	Cardiff	0	0
EC1971	24 Nov	Bucharest	0	2
1983	12 Oct	Wrexham	5	0
wc1992	20 May	Bucharest	1	5
wc1993	17 Nov	Cardiff	1	2

v SAN MARINO

			W	SM
wc1996	2 June	Serravalle	5	0
wc1996	31 Aug	Cardiff	6	0

v SAUDI ARABIA

			W	SA
1986	25 Feb	Dahran	2	1

v SPAIN

			W	S
wc1961	19 Apr	Cardiff	1	2
wc1961	18 May	Madrid	1	1
1982	24 Mar	Valencia	1	1
wc1984	17 Oct	Seville	0	3
wc1985	30 Apr	Wrexham	3	0

v SWEDEN

			W	S
wc1958	15 June	Stockholm	0	0
1988	27 Apr	Stockholm	1	4
1989	26 Apr	Wrexham	0	2
1990	25 Apr	Stockholm	2	4
1994	20 Apr	Wrexham	0	2

v SWITZERLAND

			W	S
1949	26 May	Berne	0	4
1951	16 May	Wrexham	3	2
1996	24 Apr	Lugano	0	2

v TURKEY

			W	T
EC1978	29 Nov	Wrexham	1	0
EC1979	21 Nov	Izmir	0	1
wc1980	15 Oct	Cardiff	4	0
wc1981	25 Mar	Ankara	1	0
wc1996	14 Dec	Cardiff	0	0

v REST OF UNITED KINGDOM

			W	UK
1951	5 Dec	Cardiff	3	2
1969	28 July	Cardiff	0	1

v URUGUAY

			W	U
1986	21 Apr	Wrexham	0	0

v USSR

			W	USSR
wc1965	30 May	Moscow	1	2
wc1965	27 Oct	Cardiff	2	1
wc1981	30 May	Wrexham	0	0
wc1981	18 Nov	Tbilisi	0	3
1987	18 Feb	Swansea	0	0

v YUGOSLAVIA

			W	Y
1953	21 May	Belgrade	2	5
1954	22 Nov	Cardiff	1	3
EC1976	24 Apr	Zagreb	0	2
EC1976	22 May	Cardiff	1	1
EC1982	15 Dec	Titograd	4	4
EC1983	14 Dec	Cardiff	1	1
1988	23 Mar	Swansea	1	2

NORTHERN IRELAND

v ALBANIA

			NI	A
wc1965	7 May	Belfast	4	1
wc1965	24 Nov	Tirana	1	1
EC1982	15 Dec	Tirana	0	0
EC1983	27 Apr	Belfast	1	0
wc1992	9 Sept	Belfast	3	0
wc1993	17 Feb	Tirana	2	1
wc1996	14 Dec	Belfast	2	0

v ALGERIA

			NI	A
wc1986	3 June	Guadalajara	1	1

v ARGENTINA

			NI	A
wc1958	11 June	Halmstad	1	3

v ARMENIA

			NI	A
wc1996	5 Oct	Belfast	1	1
wc1996	30 Apr	Erevan	0	0

v AUSTRALIA

			NI	A
1980	11 June	Sydney	2	1
1980	15 June	Melbourne	1	1
1980	18 June	Adelaide	2	1

v AUSTRIA

			NI	A
wc1982	1 July	Madrid	2	2
EC1982	13 Oct	Vienna	0	2
EC1983	21 Sept	Belfast	3	1
EC1990	14 Nov	Vienna	0	0
EC1991	16 Oct	Belfast	2	1
EC1994	12 Oct	Vienna	2	1
EC1995	15 Nov	Belfast	5	3

v BELGIUM

			NI	B
wc1976	10 Nov	Liège	0	2
wc1977	16 Nov	Belfast	3	0
1997	11 Feb	Belfast	3	0

v BRAZIL

			NI	B
wc1986	12 June	Guadalajara	0	3

v BULGARIA

			NI	B
wc1972	18 Oct	Sofia	0	3
wc1973	26 Sept	Sheffield	0	0
EC1978	29 Nov	Sofia	2	0
EC1979	2 May	Belfast	2	0

v CANADA

			NI	C
1995	22 May	Edmonton	0	2

v CHILE

			NI	C
1989	26 May	Belfast	0	1
1995	25 May	Edmonton	1	2

v COLOMBIA

			NI	C
1994	4 June	Boston	0	2

v CYPRUS

			NI	C
EC1971	3 Feb	Nicosia	3	0
EC1971	21 Apr	Belfast	5	0
wc1973	14 Feb	Nicosia	0	1
wc1973	8 May	London	3	0

v CZECHOSLOVAKIA

			NI	C
wc1958	8 June	Halmstad	1	0
wc1958	17 June	Malmo	2	1*

*After extra time

v DENMARK

			NI	D
EC1978	25 Oct	Belfast	2	1
EC1979	6 June	Copenhagen	0	4
1986	26 Mar	Belfast	1	1
EC1990	17 Oct	Belfast	1	1
EC1991	13 Nov	Odense	1	2
wc1992	18 Nov	Belfast	0	1
wc1993	13 Oct	Copenhagen	0	1

v FAEROES

			NI	F
EC1991	1 May	Belfast	1	1
EC1991	11 Sept	Landskrona	5	0

v FINLAND

			NI	F
wc1984	27 May	Pori	0	1
wc1984	14 Nov	Belfast	2	1

v FRANCE

			NI	F
1951	12 May	Belfast	2	2
1952	11 Nov	Paris	1	3
wc1958	19 June	Norrkoping	0	4
1982	24 Mar	Paris	0	4
wc1982	4 July	Madrid	1	4
1986	26 Feb	Paris	0	0
1988	27 Apr	Belfast	0	0

v GERMANY

			NI	G
1992	2 June	Bremen	1	1
1996	29 May	Belfast	1	1
wc1996	9 Nov	Nuremberg	1	1

v WEST GERMANY

			NI	WG
wc1958	15 June	Malmo	2	2
wc1960	26 Oct	Belfast	3	4
wc1961	10 May	Hamburg	1	2
1966	7 May	Belfast	0	2
1977	27 Apr	Cologne	0	5
EC1982	17 Nov	Belfast	1	0
EC1983	16 Nov	Hamburg	1	0

v GREECE

			NI	G
wc1961	3 May	Athens	1	2
wc1961	17 Oct	Belfast	2	0
1988	17 Feb	Athens	2	3

v HOLLAND

			NI	H
1962	9 May	Rotterdam	0	4
wc1965	17 Mar	Belfast	2	1
wc1965	7 Apr	Rotterdam	0	0
wc1976	13 Oct	Rotterdam	2	2
wc1977	12 Oct	Belfast	0	1

v HONDURAS

			NI	H
wc1982	21 June	Zaragoza	1	1

v HUNGARY

			NI	H
wc1988	19 Oct	Budapest	0	1
wc1989	6 Sept	Belfast	1	2

v ICELAND

			NI	I
wc1977	11 June	Reykjavik	0	1
wc1977	21 Sept	Belfast	2	0

v REPUBLIC OF IRELAND

			NI	RI
EC1978	20 Sept	Dublin	0	0
EC1979	21 Nov	Belfast	1	0
wc1988	14 Sept	Belfast	0	0
wc1989	11 Oct	Dublin	0	3
wc1993	31 Mar	Dublin	0	3
wc1993	17 Nov	Belfast	1	1
EC1994	16 Nov	Belfast	0	4
EC1995	29 Mar	Dublin	1	1

v ISRAEL

			NI	I
1968	10 Sept	Jaffa	3	2
1976	3 Mar	Tel Aviv	1	1
wc1980	26 Mar	Tel Aviv	0	0
wc1981	18 Nov	Belfast	1	0
1984	16 Oct	Belfast	3	0
1987	18 Feb	Tel Aviv	1	1

v ITALY

			NI	I
wc1957	25 Apr	Rome	0	1
1957	4 Dec	Belfast	2	2
wc1958	15 Jan	Belfast	2	1
1961	25 Apr	Bologna	2	3
1997	22 Jan	Palermo	0	2

v LATVIA

			NI	L
wc1993	2 June	Riga	2	1
wc1993	8 Sept	Belfast	2	0
EC1995	26 Apr	Riga	1	0
EC1995	7 June	Belfast	1	2

v LIECHTENSTEIN

			NI	L
EC1994	20 Apr	Belfast	4	1
EC1995	11 Oct	Eschen	4	0

v LITHUANIA

			NI	L
wc1992	28 Apr	Belfast	2	2
wc1993	25 May	Vilnius	1	0

v MALTA

			NI	M
wc1988	21 May	Belfast	3	0
wc1989	26 Apr	Valletta	2	0

v MEXICO

			NI	M
1966	22 June	Belfast	4	1
1994	11 June	Miami	0	3

v MOROCCO

			NI	M
1986	23 Apr	Belfast	2	1

v NORWAY

			NI	N
EC1974	4 Sept	Oslo	1	2
EC1975	29 Oct	Belfast	3	0
1990	27 Mar	Belfast	2	3
1996	27 Mar	Belfast	0	2

v POLAND

			NI	P
EC1962	10 Oct	Katowice	2	0
EC1962	28 Nov	Belfast	2	0
1988	23 Mar	Belfast	1	1
1991	5 Feb	Belfast	3	1

v PORTUGAL

			NI	P
wc1957	16 Jan	Lisbon	1	1
wc1957	1 May	Belfast	3	0
wc1973	28 Mar	Coventry	1	1
wc1973	14 Nov	Lisbon	1	1
wc1980	19 Nov	Lisbon	0	1
wc1981	29 Apr	Belfast	1	0
EC1994	7 Sept	Belfast	1	2
EC1995	3 Sept	Lisbon	1	1
wc1997	29 Mar	Belfast	0	0

v ROMANIA

			NI	R
wc1984	12 Sept	Belfast	3	2
wc1985	16 Oct	Bucharest	1	0
1994	23 Mar	Belfast	2	0

v SPAIN

			NI	S
1958	15 Oct	Madrid	2	6
1963	30 May	Bilbao	1	1
1963	30 Oct	Belfast	0	1
EC1970	11 Nov	Seville	0	3
EC1972	16 Feb	Hull	1	1
wc1982	25 June	Valencia	1	0
1985	27 Mar	Palma	0	0
wc1986	7 June	Guadalajara	1	2
wc1988	21 Dec	Seville	0	4
wc1989	8 Feb	Belfast	0	2
wc1992	14 Oct	Belfast	0	0
wc1993	28 Apr	Seville	1	3

v SWEDEN

			NI	S
EC1974	30 Oct	Solna	2	0
EC1975	3 Sept	Belfast	1	2
wc1980	15 Oct	Belfast	3	0
wc1981	3 June	Solna	0	1
1996	24 Apr	Belfast	1	2

v SWITZERLAND

			NI	S
wc1964	14 Oct	Belfast	1	0
wc1964	14 Nov	Lausanne	1	2

v THAILAND

			NI	T
1997	21 May	Bangkok	0	0

v TURKEY

			NI	T
wc1968	23 Oct	Belfast	4	1
wc1968	11 Dec	Istanbul	3	0
EC1983	30 Mar	Belfast	2	1
EC1983	12 Oct	Ankara	0	1
wc1985	1 May	Belfast	2	0
wc1985	11 Sept	Izmir	0	0
EC1986	12 Nov	Izmir	0	0
EC1987	11 Nov	Belfast	1	0

v UKRAINE

			NI	U
wc1996	31 Aug	Belfast	0	1
wc1997	2 Apr	Kiev	1	2

v URUGUAY

			NI	U
1964	29 Apr	Belfast	3	0
1990	18 May	Belfast	1	0

v USSR

			NI	
USSR				
wc1969	19 Sept	Belfast	0	0
wc1969	22 Oct	Moscow	0	2
EC1971	22 Sept	Moscow	0	1
EC1971	13 Oct	Belfast	1	1

v YUGOSLAVIA

			NI	Y
EC1975	16 Mar	Belfast	1	0
EC1975	19 Nov	Belgrade	0	1
wc1982	17 June	Zaragoza	0	0
EC1987	29 Apr	Belfast	1	2
EC1987	14 Oct	Sarajevo	0	3
EC1990	12 Sept	Belfast	0	2
EC1991	27 Mar	Belgrade	1	4

REPUBLIC OF IRELAND

v ALBANIA

			RI	A
wc1992	26 May	Dublin	2	0
wc1993	26 May	Tirana	2	1

v ALGERIA

			RI	A
1982	28 Apr	Algiers	0	2

v ARGENTINA

			RI	A
1951	13 May	Dublin	0	1
1979	29 May	Dublin	0	0*
1980	16 May	Dublin	0	1

* Not considered a full international

v AUSTRIA

			RI	A
1952	7 May	Vienna	0	6
1953	25 Mar	Dublin	4	0
1958	14 Mar	Vienna	1	3
1962	8 Apr	Dublin	2	3
EC1963	25 Sept	Vienna	0	0
EC1963	13 Oct	Dublin	3	2
1966	22 May	Vienna	0	1
1968	10 Nov	Dublin	2	2
EC1971	30 May	Dublin	1	4
EC1971	10 Oct	Linz	0	6
EC1995	11 June	Dublin	1	3
EC1995	6 Sept	Vienna	1	3

v BELGIUM	RI	B
1928 12 Feb Liège	4	2
1929 30 Apr Dublin	4	0
	RI	B
1930 11 May Brussels	3	1
wc1934 25 Feb Dublin	4	4
1949 24 Apr Dublin	0	2
1950 10 May Brussels	1	5
1965 24 Mar Dublin	0	2
1966 25 May Liège	3	2
wc1980 15 Oct Dublin	1	1
wc1981 25 Mar Brussels	0	1
EC1986 10 Sept Brussels	2	2
EC1987 29 Apr Dublin	0	0

v BOLIVIA	RI	B
1994 24 May Dublin	1	0
1996 15 June New Jersey	3	0

v BRAZIL	RI	B
1974 5 May Rio de Janeiro	1	2
1982 27 May Uberlandia	0	7
1987 23 May Dublin	1	0

v BULGARIA	RI	B
wc1977 1 June Sofia	1	2
wc1977 12 Oct Dublin	0	0
EC1979 19 May Sofia	0	1
EC1979 17 Oct Dublin	3	0
wc1987 1 Apr Sofia	1	2
wc1987 14 Oct Dublin	2	0

v CHILE	RI	C
1960 30 Mar Dublin	2	0
1972 21 June Recife	1	2
1974 12 May Santiago	2	1
1982 22 May Santiago	0	1
1991 22 May Dublin	1	1

v CHINA	RI	C
1984 3 June Sapporo	1	0

v CROATIA	RI	C
1996 2 June Dublin	2	2

v CYPRUS	RI	C
wc1980 26 Mar Nicosia	3	2
wc1980 19 Nov Dublin	6	0

v CZECHOSLOVAKIA	RI	C
1938 18 May Prague	2	2
EC1959 5 Apr Dublin	2	0
EC1959 10 May Bratislava	0	4
wc1961 8 Oct Dublin	1	3
wc1961 29 Oct Prague	1	7
EC1967 21 May Dublin	0	2
EC1967 22 Nov Prague	2	1
wc1969 4 May Dublin	1	2
wc1969 7 Oct Prague	0	3
1979 26 Sept Prague	1	4
1981 29 Apr Dublin	3	1
1986 27 May Reykjavik	1	0

v CZECH REPUBLIC	RI	C
1994 5 June Dublin	1	3
1996 24 Apr Prague	0	2

v DENMARK	RI	D
wc1956 3 Oct Dublin	2	1
wc1957 2 Oct Copenhagen	2	0
wc1968 4 Dec Dublin	1	1
(abandoned after 51 mins)		
wc1969 27 May Copenhagen	0	2

	RI	D
wc1969 15 Oct Dublin	1	1
EC1978 24 May Copenhagen	3	3
EC1979 2 May Dublin	2	0
wc1984 14 Nov Copenhagen	0	3
wc1985 13 Nov Dublin	1	4
wc1992 14 Oct Copenhagen	0	0
wc1993 28 Apr Dublin	1	1

v ECUADOR	RI	E
1972 19 June Natal	3	2

v EGYPT	RI	E
wc1990 17 June Palermo	0	0

v ENGLAND	RI	E
1946 30 Sept Dublin	0	1
1949 21 Sept Everton	2	0
wc1957 8 May Wembley	1	5
wc1957 19 May Dublin	1	1
1964 24 May Dublin	1	3
1976 8 Sept Wembley	1	1
EC1978 25 Oct Dublin	1	1
EC1980 6 Feb Wembley	0	2
1985 26 Mar Wembley	1	2
EC1988 12 June Stuttgart	1	0
wc1990 11 June Cagliari	1	1
EC1990 14 Nov Dublin	1	1
EC1991 27 Mar Wembley	1	1
1995 15 Feb Dublin	1	0
(abandoned after 27 mins)		

v FINLAND	RI	F
wc1949 8 Sept Dublin	3	0
wc1949 9 Oct Helsinki	1	1
1990 16 May Dublin	1	1

v FRANCE	RI	F
1937 23 May Paris	2	0
1952 16 Nov Dublin	1	1
wc1953 4 Oct Dublin	3	5
wc1953 25 Nov Paris	0	1
wc1972 15 Nov Dublin	2	1
wc1973 19 May Paris	1	1
wc1976 17 Nov Paris	0	2
wc1977 30 Mar Dublin	1	0
wc1980 28 Oct Paris	0	2
wc1981 14 Oct Dublin	3	2
1989 7 Feb Dublin	0	0

v GERMANY	RI	G
1935 8 May Dortmund	1	3
1936 17 Oct Dublin	5	2
1939 23 May Bremen	1	1
1994 29 May Hanover	2	0

v WEST GERMANY	RI	WG
1951 17 Oct Dublin	3	2
1952 4 May Cologne	0	3
1955 28 May Hamburg	1	2
1956 25 Nov Dublin	3	0
1960 11 May Dusseldorf	1	0
1966 4 May Dublin	0	4
1970 9 May Berlin	1	2
1975 1 Mar Dublin	1	0†
1979 22 May Dublin	1	3
1981 21 May Bremen	0	3†
1989 6 Sept Dublin	1	1
†v West Germany 'B'		

v HOLLAND	RI	N
1932 8 May Amsterdam	2	0
1934 8 Apr Amsterdam	2	5

			RI	H
1935	8 Dec	Dublin	3	5
1955	1 May	Dublin	1	0
1956	10 May	Rotterdam	4	1
wc1980	10 Sept	Dublin	2	1
wc1981	9 Sept	Rotterdam	2	2
EC1982	22 Sept	Rotterdam	1	2
EC1983	12 Oct	Dublin	2	3
EC1988	18 June	Gelsenkirchen	0	1
wc1990	21 June	Palermo	1	1
1994	20 Apr	Tilburg	1	0
wc1994	4 July	Orlando	0	2
EC1995	13 Dec	Liverpool	0	2
1996	4 June	Rotterdam	1	3

v HUNGARY

			RI	H
1934	15 Dec	Dublin	2	4
1936	3 May	Budapest	3	3
1936	6 Dec	Dublin	2	3
1939	19 Mar	Cork	2	2
1939	18 May	Budapest	2	2
wc1969	8 June	Dublin	1	2
wc1969	5 Nov	Budapest	0	4
wc1989	8 Mar	Budapest	0	2
wc1989	4 June	Dublin	2	0
1991	11 Sept	Gyor	2	1

v ICELAND

			RI	I
EC1962	12 Aug	Dublin	4	2
EC1962	2 Sept	Reykjavik	1	1
EC1982	13 Oct	Dublin	2	0
EC1983	21 Sept	Reykjavik	3	0
1986	25 May	Reykjavik	2	1
wc1996	10 Nov	Dublin	0	0

v IRAN

			RI	I
1972	18 June	Recife	2	1

v N. IRELAND

			RI	NI
EC1978	20 Sept	Dublin	0	0
EC1979	21 Nov	Belfast	0	1
wc1988	14 Sept	Belfast	0	0
wc1989	11 Oct	Dublin	3	0
wc1993	31 Mar	Dublin	3	0
wc1993	17 Nov	Belfast	1	1
EC1994	16 Nov	Belfast	4	0
EC1995	29 Mar	Dublin	1	1

v ISRAEL

			RI	I
1984	4 Apr	Tel Aviv	0	3
1985	27 May	Tel Aviv	0	0
1987	10 Nov	Dublin	5	0

v ITALY

			RI	I
1926	21 Mar	Turin	0	3
1927	23 Apr	Dublin	1	2
EC1970	8 Dec	Rome	0	3
EC1971	10 May	Dublin	1	2
1985	5 Feb	Dublin	1	2
wc1990	30 June	Rome	0	1
1992	4 June	Foxboro	0	2
wc1994	18 June	New York	1	0

v LATVIA

			RI	L
wc1992	9 Sept	Dublin	4	0
wc1993	2 June	Riga	2	1

v LIECHTENSTEIN

			RI	L
EC1994	12 Oct	Dublin	4	0
EC1995	3 June	Eschen	0	0
wc1996	31 Aug	Eschen	5	0
wc1997	21 May	Dublin	5	0

v LITHUANIA

			RI	L
wc1993	16 June	Vilnius	1	0
wc1993	8 Sept	Dublin	2	0

v LUXEMBOURG

			RI	I
1936	9 May	Luxembourg	5	1
wc1953	28 Oct	Dublin	4	0
wc1954	7 Mar	Luxembourg	1	0
EC1987	28 May	Luxembourg	2	0
EC1987	9 Sept	Dublin	2	1

v MACEDONIA

			RI	M
wc1996	9 Oct	Dublin	3	0
wc1997	2 Apr	Skopje	2	3

v MALTA

			RI	M
EC1983	30 Mar	Valletta	1	0
EC1983	16 Nov	Dublin	8	0
wc1989	28 May	Dublin	2	0
wc1989	15 Nov	Valletta	2	0
1990	2 June	Valletta	3	0

v MEXICO

			RI	M
1984	8 Aug	Dublin	0	0
wc1994	24 June	Orlando	1	2
1996	13 June	New Jersey	2	2

v MOROCCO

			RI	M
1990	12 Sept	Dublin	1	0

v NORWAY

			RI	N
wc1937	10 Oct	Oslo	2	3
wc1937	7 Nov	Dublin	3	3
1950	26 Nov	Dublin	2	2
1951	30 May	Oslo	3	2
1954	8 Nov	Dublin	2	1
1955	25 May	Oslo	3	1
1960	6 Nov	Dublin	3	1
1964	13 May	Oslo	4	1
1973	6 June	Oslo	1	1
1976	24 Mar	Dublin	3	0
1978	21 May	Oslo	0	0
wc1984	17 Oct	Oslo	0	1
wc1985	1 May	Dublin	0	0
1988	1 June	Oslo	0	0
wc1994	28 June	New York	0	0

v POLAND

			RI	P
1938	22 May	Warsaw	0	6
1938	13 Nov	Dublin	3	2
1958	11 May	Katowice	2	2
1958	5 Oct	Dublin	2	2
1964	10 May	Kracow	1	3
1964	25 Oct	Dublin	3	2
1968	15 May	Dublin	2	2
1968	30 Oct	Katowice	0	1
1970	6 May	Dublin	1	2
1970	23 Sept	Dublin	0	2
1973	16 May	Wroclaw	0	2
1973	21 Oct	Dublin	1	0
1976	26 May	Poznan	2	0
1977	24 Apr	Dublin	0	0
1978	12 Apr	Lodz	0	3
1981	23 May	Bydgoszcz	0	3
1984	23 May	Dublin	0	0
1986	12 Nov	Warsaw	0	1
1988	22 May	Dublin	3	1
EC1991	1 May	Dublin	0	0
EC1991	16 Oct	Poznan	3	3

		v PORTUGAL	*RI*	*P*
1946	16 June	Lisbon	1	3
1947	4 May	Dublin	0	2
1948	23 May	Lisbon	0	2
1949	22 May	Dublin	1	0
1972	25 June	Recife	1	2
1992	7 June	Boston	2	0
EC1995	26 Apr	Dublin	1	0
EC1995	15 Nov	Lisbon	0	3
1996	29 May	Dublin	0	1

		v ROMANIA	*RI*	*R*
1988	23 Mar	Dublin	2	0
wc1990	25 June	Genoa	0	0*
wc1997	30 Apr	Bucharest	0	1
After extra time				

		v RUSSIA	*RI*	*R*
1994	23 Mar	Dublin	0	0
1996	27 Mar	Dublin	0	2

		v SCOTLAND	*RI*	*S*
wc1961	3 May	Glasgow	1	4
wc1961	7 May	Dublin	0	3
1963	9 June	Dublin	1	0
1969	21 Sept	Dublin	1	1
EC1986	15 Oct	Dublin	0	0
EC1987	18 Feb	Glasgow	1	0

		v SPAIN	*RI*	*S*
1931	26 Apr	Barcelona	1	1
1931	13 Dec	Dublin	0	5
1946	23 June	Madrid	1	0
1947	2 Mar	Dublin	3	2
1948	30 May	Barcelona	1	2
1949	12 June	Dublin	1	4
1952	1 June	Madrid	0	6
1955	27 Nov	Dublin	2	2
EC1964	11 Mar	Seville	1	5
EC1964	8 Apr	Dublin	0	2
wc1965	5 May	Dublin	1	0
wc1965	27 Oct	Seville	1	4
wc1965	10 Nov	Paris	0	1
EC1966	23 Oct	Dublin	0	0
EC1966	7 Dec	Valencia	0	2
1977	9 Feb	Dublin	0	1
EC1982	17 Nov	Dublin	3	3
EC1983	27 Apr	Zaragoza	0	2
1985	26 May	Cork	0	0
wc1988	16 Nov	Seville	0	2
wc1989	26 Apr	Dublin	1	0
wc1992	18 Nov	Seville	0	0
wc1993	13 Oct	Dublin	1	3

		v SWEDEN	*RI*	*S*
wc1949	2 June	Stockholm	1	3
wc1949	13 Nov	Dublin	1	3
1959	1 Nov	Dublin	3	2
1960	18 May	Malmo	1	4
EC1970	14 Oct	Dublin	1	1
EC1970	28 Oct	Malmo	0	1

		v SWITZERLAND	*RI*	*S*
1935	5 May	Basle	0	1
1936	17 Mar	Dublin	1	0
1937	17 May	Berne	1	0
1938	18 Sept	Dublin	4	0
1948	5 Dec	Dublin	0	1
EC1975	11 May	Dublin	2	1
EC1975	21 May	Berne	0	1
1980	30 Apr	Dublin	2	0
wc1985	2 June	Dublin	3	0
wc1985	11 Sept	Berne	0	0
1992	25 Mar	Dublin	2	1

		v TRINIDAD & TOBAGO	*RI*	*TT*
1982	30 May	Port of Spain	1	2

		v TUNISIA	*RI*	*T*
1988	19 Oct	Dublin	4	0

		v TURKEY	*RI*	*T*
EC1966	16 Nov	Dublin	2	1
EC1967	22 Feb	Ankara	1	2
EC1974	20 Nov	Izmir	1	1
EC1975	29 Oct	Dublin	4	0
1976	13 Oct	Ankara	3	3
1978	5 Apr	Dublin	4	2
1990	26 May	Izmir	0	0
EC1990	17 Oct	Dublin	5	0
EC1991	13 Nov	Istanbul	3	1

		v URUGUAY	*RI*	*U*
1974	8 May	Montevideo	0	2
1986	23 Apr	Dublin	1	1

		v USA	*RI*	*USA*
1979	29 Oct	Dublin	3	2
1991	1 June	Boston	1	1
1992	29 Apr	Dublin	4	1
1992	30 May	Washington	1	3
1996	9 June	Boston	1	2

		v USSR	*RI*	*USSR*
wc1972	18 Oct	Dublin	1	2
wc1973	13 May	Moscow	0	1
EC1974	30 Oct	Dublin	3	0
EC1975	18 May	Kiev	1	2
wc1984	12 Sept	Dublin	1	0
wc1985	16 Oct	Moscow	0	2
EC1988	15 June	Hanover	1	1
1990	25 Apr	Dublin	1	0

		v WALES	*RI*	*W*
1960	28 Sept	Dublin	2	3
1979	11 Sept	Swansea	1	2
1981	24 Feb	Dublin	1	3
1986	26 Mar	Dublin	0	1
1990	28 Mar	Dublin	1	0
1991	6 Feb	Wrexham	3	0
1992	19 Feb	Dublin	0	1
1993	17 Feb	Dublin	2	1
1997	11 Feb	Cardiff	0	0

		v YUGOSLAVIA	*RI*	*Y*
1955	19 Sept	Dublin	1	4
1988	27 Apr	Dublin	2	0

OTHER BRITISH AND IRISH INTERNATIONAL MATCHES 1996-97

FRIENDLIES

Palermo, 22 January 1997, 30,866
Italy (1) 2 *(Zola 8, Del Piero 88)*
Northern Ireland (0) 0
Italy: Peruzzi; Ferrara, Costacurta (Cannavaro 71), Maldini, Di Livio (Iranio 79), Dino Baggio, Albertini, Di Matteo (Fuser 57), Carboni, Zola (Del Piero 61), Casiraghi (Ravanelli 57).
Northern Ireland: Wright; Griffin, Worthington, Taggart, Hunter, Lomas, McCarthy (Dennison 83), Morrow, Quinn (O'Boyle 60), Horlock, Hughes (Rowland 69).
Referee: Frohlich (Germany).

Belfast, 11 February 1997, 7126
Northern Ireland (1) 3 *(Quinn 14, Magilton 62 (pen), Mulryne 88)*
Belgium (0) 0
Northern Ireland: Wright; Gillespie, Horlock (Whitley 85), Lomas, Taggart, Hunter (Griffin 46), Lennon (Worthington 68), Magilton, Quinn (O'Boyle 57), Morrow, McMahon (Mulryne 46).
Belgium: De Wilde; Medved, De Roover, Staelens, Albert, Van der Elst F, Verheyen (Pierre 71), Scifo (Lemoine 77), Kerckhoven (Schepens 85), Wilmots (Jbari 80), Nilis (Mpenza L 46).
Referee: Rowbotham (Scotland).

Cardiff Arms Park, 11 February 1997, 7000
Wales (0) 0
Republic of Ireland (0) 0
Wales: Crossley; Pembridge, Legg, Jones (Hughes C 74), Symons, Ready, Robinson (Bowen M 63), Horne, Hartson (Taylor 69), Hughes M (Savage 88), Speed.
Republic of Ireland: Branagan; McAteer, Phelan, Cunningham, McGrath, Harte, McLoughlin (Kelly G 53), Keane (Kelly D 75), Goodman, Cascarino, Staunton.
Referee: Young (Scotland).

Wembley, 29 March 1997, 48,076
England (1) 2 *(Sheringham 20 (pen), Fowler 55)*
Mexico (0) 0
England: James; Keown, Pearce, Batty (Redknapp 62), Southgate, Le Saux, Lee, Ince, Fowler, Sheringham (Wright I 38), McManaman (Butt 68).
Mexico: Rios (Sanchez 60); Pardo, Suarez, Davino, Ramirez R, Alfaro, Coyote (Ramirez N 67), Galindo (Bernal 56), Garcia Aspe, Hermosillo (Pelaez 46), Roberto Alvez (Hernandez 46).
Referee: Pereira (Portugal).

Old Trafford, 24 May 1997, 52,676
England (1) 2 *(Lee 20, Wright 76)*
South Africa (1) 1 *(Masinga 43)*
England: Martyn; Neville P, Pearce, Keown, Southgate, Le Saux (Beckham 68), Redknapp (Batty 56), Gascoigne, Wright, Sheringham (Scholes 64), Lee (Butt 80).
South Africa: Arendse; Fish, Tovey, Radebe, Moutaung, Tinkler, Moeti, Khumalo (Mkhalele 76), Moshoeu, Masinga (Buthelezi 85), Augustine (Sikhosana 55).
Referee: Frisk (Sweden).

Kilmarnock, 27 May 1997, 8000
Scotland (0) 0
Wales (0) 1 *(Hartson 46)*
Scotland: Sullivan (Leighton 80); Weir, Boyd, McAllister B, Dailly (McNamara 75), McKinlay T, Gallacher (Donnelly 80), Gemmill, Dodds, McAllister G, Jackson (Spencer 46).
Wales: Marriott (Jones P 46); Jenkins, Pembridge, Page, Symons, Trollope, Robinson (Browning 88), Savage, Saunders (Jones L 88), Hartson (Haworth 71), Speed.
Referee: Snoddy (Northern Ireland).

Valletta, 1 June 1997, 3500
Malta (1) 2 *(Suda 17, Sultana 57)*
Scotland (2) 3 *(Dailly 4, Jackson 44, 81)*
Malta: Muscat; Attard (Turner 66), Brincat, Debono, Chetcuti, Carabott, Vella (Giglio 75), Zammit, Saliba, Suda (Sultana 46), Agius.
Scotland: Leighton; Burley, Boyd, McAllister B (Weir 46), Dailly, McKinlay T, Hopkin (Gemmill 60), Gallacher (Durie 60), Jackson, McAllister G, Collins.
Referee: Braschi (Italy).

TOYOTA INVITATION

Bangkok, 21 May 1997, 15,000
Thailand (0) 0
Northern Ireland (0) 0
Thailand: Kampian; Tinnakorn, Krisada, Jirasirachote, Promrut, Chalermsan, Kijmongkolsak, Jaturapattarapong, Damkong-Ongtrakul, Daorung, Piyapong.
Northern Ireland: Davison (Carroll 46); Jenkins (Whitley 46), Hill, McGibbon, Griffin, McCarthy (McMahon 46), Lomas, Lennon, Horlock, Mulryne (Quinn 46), Dowie (Robinson 63).
Referee: Hanlumyaung (Thailand).

TOURNOI DE FRANCE

Lyon, 3 June 1997, 28,193
France (0) 1 *(Keller 59)*
Brazil (1) 1 *(Roberto Carlos 21)*
France: Barthez; Candela, Blanc, Desailly (Thuram 66), Karembeu (Viera 14), Ba, Zidane, Deschamps, Lizarazu, Maurice, Pires (Keller 46).
Brazil: Taffarel; Cafu, Celio Silva, Aldair (Goncalves 87), Mauro Silva, Giovanni (Djalminha 72), Dunga, Leonardo, Roberto Carlos, Ronaldo, Romario (Paolo Nunes 79).
Referee: Nielsen (Denmark).

Nantes, 4 June 1997, 25,000
Italy (0) 0
England (2) 2 *(Wright 26, Scholes 43)*
Italy: Peruzzi; Ferrara (Nesta 46), Cannavaro, Di Livio (Maini 46), Costacurta, Albertini, Dino Baggio, Di Matteo (Fuser 17), Casiraghi, Benarrivo, Zola.
England: Flowers; Neville P, Pearce, Keown, Southgate, Le Saux (Neville G 46), Scholes, Ince, Wright (Cole 76), Sheringham (Gascoigne 79), Beckham.
Referee: Renko (Austria).

Montpellier, 7 June 1997, 25,000
France (0) 0
England (0) 1 *(Shearer 86)*
France: Barthez; Thuram, Blanc, N'Gotty, Laigle (Lizarazu 81), Deschamps, Viera, Keller, Djorkaeff, Dugarry (Zidane 73), Ouedec (Loko 62).
England: Seaman; Neville G, Neville P, Batty (Ince 46), Southgate, Campbell, Beckham (Lee 73), Gascoigne, Shearer, Wright (Sheringham 78), Le Saux.
Referee: Belqola (Morocco).

Lyon, 8 June 1997, 30,000
Brazil (1) 3 *(Lombardo 35 (og), Ronaldo 71, Romario 85)*
Italy (2) 3 *(Del Piero 7, 62 (pen), Aldair 23 (og))*
Brazil: Taffarel; Cafu, Aldair, Celio Silva, Denilson, Mauro Silva (Flavio Conceicao 63), Dunga, Ronaldo, Romario, Leonardo, Roberto Carlos.
Italy: Pagliuca; Panucci, Maldini (Di Livio 90), Cannavaro, Costacurta, Albertini, Dino Baggio (Fuser 46), Di Matteo, Vieri (Inzaghi 60), Del Piero, Lombardo.
Referee: Muhmenthaler (Switzerland).

Paris, 10 June 1997, 50,000
England (0) 0
Brazil (0) 1 *(Romario 61)*
England: Seaman; Neville P, Le Saux, Keown (Neville G 19), Southgate, Campbell, Scholes (Lee 78), Gascoigne, Shearer, Sheringham (Wright 78), Ince.
Brazil: Taffarel; Cafu, Roberto Carlos, Celio Silva, Dunga, Aldair, Flavio, Denilson (Djalminha 21), Ronaldo, Leonardo (Ze Roberto 82), Romario.
Referee: Rendon (Colombia).

Paris, 11 June 1997, 30,000
France (1) 2 *(Zidane 12, Djorkaeff 73)*
Italy (0) 2 *(Casiraghi 61, Del Piero 90 (pen))*
France: Charbonnier; Thuram, Leboeuf, Desailly (N'Gotty 85), Lizarazu, Ba, Deschamps, Karembeu (Vieira 66), Zidane, Dugarry, Maurice (Djorkaeff 63).
Italy: Pagliuca; Cannavaro, Maldini, Di Livio, Costacurta (Torrisi 46), Nesta, Lombardo, Di Matteo, Casiraghi (Vieri 78), Del Piero, Zola (Panucci 56).
Referee: Nieto (Spain).

TOP TWENTY TRANSFERS

It may be the post-Bosman period, but transfer fees show no sign of either disappearing or diminishing as clubs continue the search for quality players. The proposed move of Ronaldo from Barcelona to Internazionale at a record £18 million underlined the continuing trend.

The top twenty transfers prior to this were as follows:–

Date	Player	From	To	Price in £'s
July 1996	Alan Shearer	Blackburn Rovers	Newcastle United	15 million
June 1996	Ronaldo	PSV Eindhoven	Barcelona	13.25 million
June 1992	Gianluigi Lentini	Torino	AC Milan	13 million
June 1992	Gianluca Vialli	Sampdoria	Juventus	12 million
June 1996	Enrico Chiesa	Sampdoria	Parma	11 million
June 1992	Jean-Pierre Papin	Marseille	AC Milan	10 million
June 1995	Stan Collymore	Nottingham Forest	Liverpool	8.5 million
June 1995	Roberto Baggio	Juventus	AC Milan	8.5 million
October 1993	Alen Boksic	Marseille	Lazio	8.4 million
June 1993	Dennis Bergkamp	Ajax	Internazionale	8 million
June 1996	Romario	Flamengo	Valencia	8 million
February 1997	Andrei Kanchelskis	Everton	Fiorentina	8 million
May 1990	Roberto Baggio	Fiorentina	Juventus	7.7 million
June 1995	Dennis Bergkamp	Internazionale	Arsenal	7.5 million
August 1994	Gianluca Pagliuca	Sampdoria	Internazionale	7.5 million
June 1995	Paul Ince	Manchester United	Internazionale	7 million
February 1996	Faustino Asprilla	Parma	Newcastle United	7 million
June 1992	Daniel Fonseca	Cagliari	Napoli	7 million
June 1996	Fabrizio Ravanelli	Juventus	Middlesbrough	7 million
May 1997	Stan Collymore	Liverpool	Aston Villa	7 million

SOCCER CENTURIONS

Majed Abdullah	Saudi Arabia	147	Hector Chumpitaz	Peru	106
Thomas Ravelli	Sweden	138*	Gheorghe Hagi	Romania	105*
Peter Shilton	England	125	Billy Wright	England	105
Lothar Matthaus	Germany	122	Grzegorz Lato	Poland	104
Pat Jennings	Northern Ireland	119	Torbjorn Svenssen	Norway	104
Andoni Zubizarreta	Spain	118*	Franz Beckenbauer	Germany	103
Heinz Hermann	Switzerland	117	Soon-Ho Choi	Korea Republic	102
Bjorn Nordqvist	Sweden	115	Kenny Dalglish	Scotland	102
Marcelo Balboa	USA	114*	Kazimierz Deyna	Poland	102
Dino Zoff	Italy	112	Morten Olsen	Denmark	102
Alain Geiger	Switzerland	111	Joachim Streich	East Germany	102
Wail Sulaiman Al-Habashi	Kuwait	109*	Masami Ihara	Japan	101
Oleg Blokhin	USSR	109	Joszef Bozsik	Hungary	100
Paul Caligiuri	USA	109*	Hans-Jurgen Dorner	East Germany	100
Ladislau Boloni	Romania	108	Djalma Santos	Brazil	100
Bobby Moore	England	108			
Bobby Charlton	England	106	*Still playing		

In September 1990, FIFA decreed that only games contested by the foremost national squad of each of the National Associations concerned can be classified as A Internationals with matches against club sides and other non-national teams not qualifying.

The world governing body also published the first list of players they considered eligible for the term 'centurions'.

The list above was published in the July 1997 edition of FIFA News but they do not acknowledge the figures given for either Balboa or Caligiuri.

Also it seems unlikely that Djalma Santos of Brazil made a legitimate 100 appearances. Ten of his 107 games for his country were against club sides. Then again, Bozsik of Hungary did not make the century either. One match included in his total was against a Moscow selection in May 1951, a year before the USSR restarted international fixtures.

The leader at present, Abdullah of Saudi Arabia has been confused with a number of other players with a similar name and the controversy surrounding this type of list continues.

WOMEN CENTURIONS

Heidi Stoere	Norway	148*	Gunn Nyborg	Norway	110
Pia Sundhage	Sweden	146	Elisabetta Vignotto	Italy	110
Carolina Morace	Italy	145*	Michelle Akers	USA	109*
Kristine Lilly	USA	133*	Julie Foudy	USA	108*
Mia Hamm	USA	130*	Heidi Mohr	Germany	104
Linda Medalen	Norway	120*	Joy Fawcett	USA	101*
Carin Gabarra	USA	117*	Carla Overbeck	USA	100*
Elisabeth Leidinge	Sweden	112*	Martina Voss	Germany	100*
Silvia Neid	Germany	111			
Lena Videkull	Sweden	111	*Still playing		

Oddly enough, matches in the European Championship are not included in the Women's Championship!

INTERNATIONAL APPEARANCES 1872–1997

This is a list of full international appearances by Englishmen, Irishmen, Scotsmen and Welshmen in matches against the Home Countries and against foreign nations. It does not include unofficial matches against Commonwealth and Empire countries. The year indicated refers to the season; ie 1997 is the 1996-97 season.
Explanatory code for matches played by all five countries: A represents Austria; Alb, Albania; Alg, Algeria; An, Angola; Arg, Argentina; Arm, Armenia; Aus, Australia; B, Bohemia; Bel, Belgium; Bl, Belarus; Bol, Bolivia; Br, Brazil; Bul, Bulgaria; C,CIS; Ca, Canada; Cam, Cameroon; Ch, Chile; Chn, China; Co, Colombia; Cr, Costa Rica; Cro, Croatia; Cy, Cyprus; Cz, Czechoslovakia; CzR, Czech Republic; D, Denmark; E, England; Ec, Ecuador; Ei, Republic of Ireland; EG, East Germany; Eg, Egypt; Es, Estonia; F, France; Fa, Faeroes; Fi, Finland; G, Germany; Ge, Georgia; Gr, Greece; H, Hungary; Ho, Holland; Hon, Honduras; I, Italy; Ic, Iceland; Ir, Iran; Is, Israel; J,Japan; K, Kuwait; L, Luxembourg; La, Latvia; Li, Lithuania; Lie, Liechtenstein; M, Mexico; Ma, Malta; Mac, Macedonia; Mal, Moldavia; Mor, Morocco; N, Norway; Ni, Ng, Nigeria; Northern Ireland; Nz, New Zealand; P, Portugal; Para, Paraguay; Pe, Peru; Pol, Poland; R, Romania; RCS, Republic of Czechs and Slovaks; R of E, Rest of Europe; R of W, Rest of World; Ru, Russia; S.Af, South Africa; S.Ar, Saudi Arabia; S, Scotland; Se, Sweden; Sm, San Marino; Sp, Spain; Sw, Switzerland; T, Turkey; Th, Thailand; Tr, Trinidad & Tobago; Tun, Tunisia; U, Uruguay; Uk, Ukraine; US, United States of America; USSR, Soviet Union; W, Wales; WG, West Germany; Y, Yugoslavia; Z, Zaire.
As at June 1997.

ENGLAND

Abbott, W. (Everton), 1902 v W (1)
A'Court, A. (Liverpool), 1958 v Ni, Br, A, USSR; 1959 v W (5)
Adams, T. A. (Arsenal), 1987 v Sp, T, Br; 1988 v WG, T, Y, Ho, H, S, Co, Sw, Ei, Ho, USSR; 1989 v D, Se, S.Ar.; 1991 v Ei (2); 1993 v N, T, Sm, T, Ho, Pol, N; 1994 v Pol, Ho, D, Gr, N; 1995 v US, R, Ei, U; 1996 v Co, N, Sw, P, Chn, Sw, S, Ho, Sp, G; 1997 v Ge (2) (47)
Adcock, H. (Leicester C), 1929 v F, Bel, Sp; 1930 v Ni, W (5)
Alcock, C. W. (Wanderers), 1875 v S (1)
Alderson, J. T. (C Palace), 1923 v F (1)
Aldridge, A. (WBA), 1888 v Ni; (with Walsall Town Swifts), 1889 v Ni (2)
Allen, A. (Stoke C) 1960 v Se, W, Ni (3)
Allen, A. (Aston Villa), 1888 v Ni (1)
Allen, C. (QPR), 1984 v Br (sub), U, Ch; (with Tottenham H), 1987 v T; 1988 v Is (5)
Allen, H. (Wolverhampton W), 1888 v S, W, Ni; 1889 v S; 1890 v S (5)
Allen, J. P. (Portsmouth), 1934 v Ni, W (2)
Allen, R. (WBA), 1952 v Sw; 1954 v S; 1955 v WG, W (5)
Alsford, W. J. (Tottenham H), 1935 v S (1)
Amos, A. (Old Carthusians), 1885 v S; 1886 v W (2)
Anderson, R. D. (Old Etonians), 1879 v W (1)
Anderson, S. (Sunderland), 1962 v A, S (2)
Anderson, V. (Nottingham F), 1979 v Cz, Se; 1980 v Bul, Sp; 1981 v N, R, W, S; 1982 v Ni, Ic; 1984 v Ni; (with Arsenal), 1985 v T, Ni, Ei, R, Fi, S, M, US; 1986 v USSR, M; 1987 v Se, Ni (2), Y, Sp, T; (with Manchester U), 1988 v WG, H, Co (30)
Anderton, D. R. (Tottenham H), 1994 v D, Gr, N; 1995 v US, Ei, U, J, Se, Br; 1996 v H, Chn, Sw, S, Ho, Sp, G (16)
Angus, J. (Burnley), 1961 v A (1)
Armfield, J. C. (Blackpool), 1959 v Br, Pe, M, US; 1960 v Y, Sp, H, S; 1961 v L, P, Sp, M, I, A, W, Ni, S; 1962 v A, Sw, Pe, W, Ni, S, L, P, H, A, Bul, Br; 1963 v F (2), Br, EG, Sw, Ni, W, S; 1964 v R of W, W, Ni, S; 1966 v Y, Fi (43)
Armitage, G. H. (Charlton Ath), 1926 v Ni (1)
Armstrong, D. (Middlesbrough), 1980 v Aus; (with Southampton), 1983 v WG; 1984 v W (3)
Armstrong, K. (Chelsea), 1955 v S (1)
Arnold, J. (Fulham), 1933 v S (1)
Arthur, J. W. H. (Blackburn R), 1885 v S, W, Ni; 1886 v S, W; 1887 v W, Ni (7)
Ashcroft, J. (Woolwich Arsenal), 1906 v Ni, W, S (3)
Ashmore, G. S. (WBA), 1926 v Bel (1)
Ashton, C. T. (Corinthians), 1926 v Ni (1)
Ashurst, W. (Notts Co), 1923 v Se (2); 1925 v S, W, Bel (5)
Astall, G. (Birmingham C), 1956 v Fi, WG (2)
Astle, J. (WBA), 1969 v W; 1970 v S, P, Br (sub), Cz (5)
Aston, J. (Manchester U), 1949 v S, W, D, Sw, Se, N, F; 1950 v S, W, Ni, Ei, I, P, Bel, Ch, US; 1951 v Ni (17)
Athersmith, W. C. (Aston Villa), 1892 v Ni, 1897 v S, W, Ni; 1898 v S, W, Ni; 1899 v S, W, Ni; 1900 v S, W (12)
Atyeo, P. J. W. (Bristol C), 1956 v Br, Se, Sp; 1957 v D, Ei (2) (6)
Austin, S. W. (Manchester C), 1926 v Ni (1)

Bach, P. (Sunderland), 1899 v Ni (1)
Bache, J. W. (Aston Villa), 1903 v W; 1904 v W, Ni; 1905 v S; 1907 v Ni; 1910 v Ni; 1911 v S (7)
Baddeley, T. (Wolverhampton W), 1903 v S, Ni; 1904 v S, W, Ni (5)
Bagshaw, J. J. (Derby Co), 1920 v Ni (1)
Bailey, G. R. (Manchester U), 1985 v Ei, M (2)
Bailey, H. P. (Leicester Fosse), 1908 v W, A (2), H, B (5)
Bailey, M. A. (Charlton Ath), 1964 v US; 1965 v W (2)

Bailey, N. C. (Clapham Rovers), 1878 v S; 1879 v S, W; 1880 v S; 1881 v S; 1882 v S, W; 1883 v S, W; 1884 v S, W, Ni; 1885 v S, W, Ni; 1886 v S, W; 1887 v S, W (19)
Baily, E. F. (Tottenham H), 1950 v Sp; 1951 v Y, Ni, W; 1952 v A (2), Sw, W; 1953 v Ni (9)
Bain, J. (Oxford University), 1887 v S (1)
Baker, A. (Arsenal), 1928 v W (1)
Baker, B. H. (Everton), 1921 v Bel; (with Chelsea), 1926 v Ni (2)
Baker, J. H. (Hibernian), 1960 v Y, Sp, H, Ni, S; (with Arsenal) 1966 v Sp, Pol, Ni (8)
Ball, A. J. (Blackpool), 1965 v Y, WG, Se; 1966 v S, Sp, Fi, D, U, Arg, P, WG (2), Pol (2); (with Everton), 1967 v W, S, Ni, A, Cz, Sp; 1968 v W, S, USSR, Sp (2), Y, WG; 1969 v Ni, W, S, R (2), M, Br, U; 1970 v P, Co, Ec, R, Br, Cz (sub), WG, W, S, Bel; 1971 v Ma, EG, Gr, Ma (sub), Ni, S; 1972 v Sw, Gr; (with Arsenal) WG (2), S; 1973 v W (3), Y, S (2), Cz, Ni, Pol; 1974 v P (sub); 1975 v WG, Cy (2), Ni, W, S (72)
Ball, J. (Bury), 1928 v Ni (1)
Balmer, W. (Everton), 1905 v Ni (1)
Bamber, J. (Liverpool), 1921 v W (1)
Bambridge, A. L. (Swifts), 1881 v W; 1883 v W; 1884 v Ni (3)
Bambridge, E. C. (Swifts), 1879 v S; 1880 v S; 1881 v S; 1882 v S, W, Ni; 1883 v W; 1884 v S, W, Ni; 1885 v S, W, Ni; 1886 v S, W; 1887 v S, W, Ni (18)
Bambridge, E. H. (Swifts), 1876 v S (1)
Banks, G. (Leicester C), 1963 v S, Br, Cz, EG; 1964 v W, Ni, S, R of W, U, P (2), US, Arg; 1965 v Ni, S, H, Y, WG, Se; 1966 v Ni, S, Sp, Pol (2), WG (2), Y, Fi, U, M, F, Arg, P; 1967 v Ni, W, S, Cz; (with Stoke C), 1968 v W, Ni, S, USSR (2), Sp, WG, Y; 1969 v Ni, S, R (2), F, U, Br; 1970 v W, Ni, S, Ho, Bel, Co, Ec, R, Br, Cz; 1971 v Gr, Ma (2), Ni, S; 1972 v Sw, Gr, WG (2), W, S (73)
Banks, H. E. (Millwall), 1901 v Ni (1)
Banks, T. (Bolton W), 1958 v USSR (3), Br, A; 1959 v Ni (6)
Bannister, W. (Burnley), 1901 v W; (with Bolton W), 1902 v Ni (2)
Barclay, R. (Sheffield U), 1932 v S; 1933 v Ni; 1936 v S (3)
Bardsley, D. J. (QPR), 1993 v Sp (sub), Pol (2)
Barham, M. (Norwich C), 1983 v Aus (2) (2)
Barkas, S. (Manchester C), 1936 v Bel; 1937 v S; 1938 v W, Ni, Cz (5)
Barker, J. (Derby Co), 1935 v I, Ho, S, W, Ni; 1936 v G, A, S, W, Ni; 1937 v W (11)
Barker, R. (Herts Rangers), 1872 v S (1)
Barker, R. R. (Casuals), 1895 v W (1)
Barlow, R. J. (WBA), 1955 v Ni (1)
Barmby, N.J. (Tottenham H), 1995 v U (sub), Se (sub); (with Middlesbrough), 1996 v Co, N, P, Chn, Sw (sub), Ho (sub), Sp (sub); 1997 v Mol (11)
Barnes, J. (Watford), 1983 v Ni (sub), Aus (sub), Aus (2); 1984 v D, L (sub), F (sub), S, USSR, Br, U, Ch; 1985 v EG, Fi, T, Ni, R, Fi, S, I (sub), M, WG (sub), US (sub); 1986 v R (sub), Is (sub), M (sub), Ca (sub), Arg (sub); 1987 v Se, T (sub), Br; (with Liverpool), 1988 v WG, T, Y, Is, Ho, S, Co, Sw, Ei, Ho, USSR; 1989 v Se, Gr, Alb, Pol, D; 1990 v Se, I, Br, D, U, Tun, Ei, Ho, Eg, Bel, Cam; 1991 v H, Pol, Cam, Ei, T, USSR, Arg; 1992 v Cz, Fi; 1993 v Sm, T, Ho, Pol, US, G; 1995 v US, R, Ng, U, Se; 1996 v Co (sub) (79)
Barnes, P. S. (Manchester C), 1978 v I, WG, Br, W, S, H; 1979 v D, Ei, Cz, Ni (2), S, Bul, A; (with WBA), 1980 v D, W; 1981 v Sp (sub), Br, W, Sw (sub); (with Leeds U), 1982 v N (sub), Ho (sub) (22)
Barnet, H. H. (Royal Engineers), 1882 v Ni (1)
Barrass, M. W. (Bolton W), 1952 v W, Ni; 1953 v S (3)

Burton, F. E. (Nottingham F), 1889 v Ni (1)

Bury, L. (Cambridge University), 1877 v S; (with Old Etonians), 1879 v W (2)

Butcher, T. (Ipswich T), 1980 v Aus; 1981 v Sp; 1982 v W, S, F, Cz, WG, Sp; 1983 v D, WG, L, W, Gr, H, Ni, S, Aus (3); 1984 v D, H, L, F, Ni; 1985 v EG, Fi, T, Ni, Ei, R, Fi, S, I, WG, US; 1986 v Is, USSR, S, M, Ca, P, Mor, Pol, Para, Arg; (with Rangers), 1987 v Se, Ni (2), Y, Sp, Br, S; 1988 v T, Y; 1989 v D, Se, Gr, Alb (2), Ch, S, Pol, D; 1990 v Se, Pol, I, Y, Br, Cz, D, U, Tun, Ei, Ho, Bel, Cam, WG (77)

Butler, J. D. (Arsenal), 1925 v Bel (1)

Butler, W. (Bolton W), 1924 v S (1)

Butt, N. (Manchester U), 1997 v M (sub), S.Af (sub) (2)

Byrne, G. (Liverpool), 1963 v S; 1966 v N (2)

Byrne, J. J. (C Palace), 1962 v Ni; (with West Ham U), 1963 v Sw; 1964 v S, U, P (2), Ei, Br, Arg; 1965 v W, S (11)

Byrne, R. W. (Manchester U), 1954 v S, H, Y, Bel, Sw, U; 1955 v S, W, Ni, WG, F, Sp, P; 1956 v S, W, Ni, Br, Se, Fi, WG, D, Sp; 1957 v S, W, Ni, Y, D (2), Ei (2); 1958 v W, Ni, F (33)

Callaghan, I. R. (Liverpool), 1966 v Fi, F; 1978 v Sw, L (4)

Calvey, J. (Nottingham F), 1902 v Ni (1)

Campbell, A. F. (Blackburn R), 1929 v W, Ni; (with Huddersfield T), 1931 v W, S, Ni; 1932 v W, Ni, Sp (8)

Campbell, S. (Tottenham H), 1996 v H (sub), S (sub); 1997 v Ge, I, Ge, Pol, F, Br (8)

Camsell, G. H. (Middlesbrough), 1929 v F, Bel; 1930 v Ni, W; 1934 v F; 1936 v S, G, A, Bel (9)

Capes, A. J. (Stoke C), 1903 v S (1)

Carr, J. (Middlesbrough), 1920 v Ni; 1923 v W (2)

Carr, J. (Newcastle U), 1905 v Ni; 1907 v Ni (2)

Carr, W. H. (Owlerton, Sheffield), 1875 v S (1)

Carter, H. S. (Sunderland), 1934 v S, H; 1936 v G; 1937 v S, Ni, H; (with Derby Co), 1947 v S, W, Ni, Ei, Ho, F, Sw (13)

Carter, J. H. (WBA), 1926 v Bel; 1929 v Bel, Sp (3)

Catlin, A. E. (Sheffield W), 1937 v W, Ni, H, N, Se (5)

Chadwick, A. (Southampton), 1900 v S, W (2)

Chadwick, E. (Everton), 1891 v S, W; 1892 v S; 1893 v S; 1894 v S; 1896 v Ni; 1897 v S (7)

Chamberlain, M (Stoke C), 1983 v L (sub); 1984 v D (sub), S, USSR, Br, U, Ch; 1985 v Fi (sub) (8)

Chambers, H. (Liverpool), 1921 v S, W, Bel; 1923 v S, W, Ni, Bel; 1924 v Ni (8)

Channon, M. R. (Southampton), 1973 v Y, S (2), Ni, W, Cz, USSR, I; 1974 v A, Pol, I, P, W, Ni, S, Arg, EG, Bul, Y; 1975 v Cz, P, WG, Cy (2), Ni (sub), W, S; 1976 v Sw, Cz, P, W, Ni, S, Br, I, Fi; 1977 v Fi, I, L, Ni, W, S, Br (sub), Arg, U; (with Manchester C), 1978 v Sw (46)

Charles, G. A. (Nottingham F), 1991 v Nz, Mal (2)

Charlton, J. (Leeds U), 1965 v S, H, Y, WG, Se; 1966 v W, Ni, S, A, Sp, Pol (2), WG (2), Y, Fi, D, U, M, F, Arg, P; 1967 v W, S, Ni, Cz; 1968 v W, Sp; 1969 v W, R, F; 1970 v Ho (2), P, Cz (35)

Charlton, R. (Manchester U), 1958 v S, P, Y; 1959 v S, W, Ni, USSR, I, Br, Pe, M, US; 1960 v W, S, Se, Y, Sp, H; 1961 v Ni, W, S, L, P, Sp, M, I, A; 1962 v W, Ni, S, A, Sw, Pe, L, P, H, Arg, Bul, Br; 1963 v S, F, Br, Cz, EG, Sw; 1964 v S, W, Ni, R of W, U, P, Ei, Br, Arg, US (sub); 1965 v Ni, S, Ho; 1966 v W, Ni, S, A, Sp, WG (2), Y, Fi, N, Pol, U, M, F, Arg, P; 1967 v Ni, W, S, Cz; 1968 v W, Ni, S, USSR (2), Sp (2), Se, Y; 1969 v S, W, Ni, R (2), Bul, M, Br; 1970 v W, Ni, Ho (2), P, Co, Ec, Cz, Br, WG (106)

Charnley, R. O. (Blackpool), 1963 v F (1)

Charsley, C. C. (Small Heath), 1893 v Ni (1)

Chedgzoy, S. (Everton), 1920 v W; 1921 v W, S, Ni; 1922 v Ni; 1923 v S; 1924 v W; 1925 v Ni (8)

Chenery, C. J. (C Palace), 1872 v S; 1873 v S; 1874 v S (3)

Cherry, T. J. (Leeds U), 1976 v W, S (sub), Br, Fi; 1977 v Ei, I, L, Ni, S (sub), Br, Arg, U; 1978 v Sw, L, I, Br, W; 1979 v Cz, W, Se; 1980 v Ei, Arg (sub), W, Ni, S, Aus, Sp (sub) (27)

Chilton, A. (Manchester U), 1951 v Ni; 1952 v F (2)

Chippendale, H. (Blackburn R), 1894 v Ni (1)

Chivers, M. (Tottenham H), 1971 v Ma (2), Gr, Ni, S; 1972 v Sw (1+1 sub), Gr, WG (2), Ni (sub), S; 1973 v W (3), S (2), Ni, Cz, Pol, USSR, I; 1974 v A, Pol (24)

Christian, E. (Old Etonians), 1879 v S (1)

Clamp, E. (Wolverhampton W), 1958 v USSR (2), Br, A (4)

Clapton, D. R. (Arsenal), 1959 v W (1)

Clare, T. (Stoke C), 1889 v Ni; 1892 v Ni; 1893 v W; 1894 v S (4)

Clarke, A. J. (Leeds U), 1970 v Cz; 1971 v EG, Ma, Ni, W (sub), S (sub); 1973 v S (2), W, Cz, Pol, USSR, I; 1974 v A, Pol, I; 1975 v P; 1976 v Cz, P (sub) (19)

Clarke, H. A. (Tottenham H), 1954 v S (1)

Clay, T. (Tottenham H), 1920 v W; 1922 v W, S, Ni (4)

Clayton, R. (Blackburn R), 1956 v Ni, Br, Se, Fi, WG, Sp; 1957 v S, W, Ni, Y, D (2), Ei (2); 1958 v S, W, Ni, F, P, Y, USSR; 1959 v S, W, Ni, USSR, I, Br, Pe, M, US; 1960 v W, Ni, S, Se, Y (35)

Clegg, J. C. (Sheffield W), 1872 v S (1)

Clegg, W. E. (Sheffield W), 1873 v S; (with Sheffield Albion), 1879 v W (2)

Clemence, R. N. (Liverpool), 1973 v W (2); 1974 v EG, Bul, Y; 1975 v Cz, P, WG, Cy, Ni, W, S; 1976 v Sw, Cz, P, W (2), Ni, S, Br, Fi; 1977 v Ei, Fi, I, Ho, L, S, Br, Arg, U; 1978 v Sw, L, I, WG, Ni, S; 1979 v D, Ei, Ni (2), S, Bul, A (sub); 1980 v D, Bul, Ei, Arg, W, S, Bel, Sp; 1981 v R, Sp, Br, Sw, H; (with Tottenham H), 1982 v N, Ni, Fi; 1983 v L; 1984 v U (61)

Clement, D. T. (QPR), 1976 v W (sub+1), I; 1977 v I, Ho (5)

Clough, B. H. (Middlesbrough), 1960 v W, Se (2)

Clough, N. H. (Nottingham F), 1989 v Ch; 1991 v Arg (sub), Aus, Mal; 1992 v F, Cz, C; 1993 v Sp, T (sub), Pol (sub), N (sub), US, Br, G (14)

Coates, R. (Burnley), 1970 v Ni; 1971 v Gr (sub); (with Tottenham H), Ma, W (4)

Cobbold, W. N. (Cambridge University), 1883 v S, Ni; 1885 v S, Ni; 1886 v S, W; (with Old Carthusians), 1887 v S, W, Ni (9)

Cock, J. G. (Huddersfield T), 1920 v Ni; (with Chelsea), v S (2)

Cockburn, H. (Manchester U), 1947 v W, Ni, Ei; 1948 v S, I; 1949 v S, Ni, D, Sw, Se; 1951 v Arg, P; 1952 v F (13)

Cohen, G. R. (Fulham), 1964 v U, P, Ei, US, Br; 1965 v W, S, Ni, Bel, H, Ho, Y, WG, Se; 1966 v W, S, Ni, A, Sp, Pol (2), WG (2), N, D, U, M, F, Arg, P; 1967 v W, S, Ni, Cz, Sp; 1968 v W, Ni (37)

Cole, A. (Manchester U), 1995 v U (sub); 1997 v I (sub) (2)

Coleclough, H. (C Palace), 1914 v W (1)

Coleman, E. H. (Dulwich Hamlet), 1921 v W (1)

Coleman, J. (Woolwich Arsenal), 1907 v Ni (1)

Collymore, S. V. (Nottingham F), 1995 v J, Br (sub) (2)

Common, A. (Sheffield U), 1904 v W, Ni; (with Middlesbrough), 1906 v W (3)

Compton, L. H. (Arsenal), 1951 v W, Y (2)

Conlin, J. (Bradford C), 1906 v S (1)

Connelly, J. M. (Burnley), 1960 v W, N, S, Se; 1962 v W, A, Sw, P; 1963 v W, F; (with Manchester U), 1965 v H, Y, Se; 1966 v W, Ni, S, A, N, D, U (20)

Cook, T. E. R. (Brighton), 1925 v W (1)

Cooper, C. T. (Nottingham F), 1995 v Se, Br (2)

Cooper, N. C. (Cambridge University), 1893 v Ni (1)

Cooper, T. (Derby Co), 1928 v Ni; 1929 v W, Ni, S, F, Bel, Sp; 1931 v F; 1932 v W, Sp; 1933 v S; 1934 v S, H, Cz; 1935 v W (15)

Cooper, T. (Leeds U), 1969 v W, S, F, M; 1970 v Ho, Bel, Co, Ec, R, Cz, Br, WG; 1971 v EG, Ma, Ni, W, S; 1972 v Sw (2); 1975 v P (20)

Coppell, S. J. (Manchester U), 1978 v I, WG, Br, W, Ni, S, H; 1979 v D, Ei, Cz, Ni (2), W (sub), S, Bul, A; 1980 v D, Ni, Ei (sub), Sp, Arg, W, S, Bel, I; 1981 v R (sub), Sw, R, Br, W, S, Sw, H; 1982 v H, S, Fi, F, Cz, K, WG; 1983 v L, Gr (42)

Copping, W. (Leeds U), 1933 v I, Sw; 1934 v S, Ni, W, F; (with Arsenal), 1935 v Ni, I; 1936 v A, Bel; 1937 v N, Se, Fi; 1938 v S, W, Ni, Cz; 1939 v W, R of E; (with Leeds U), R (20)

Corbett, B. O. (Corinthians), 1901 v W (1)

Corbett, R. (Old Malvernians), 1903 v W (1)

Corbett, W. S. (Birmingham), 1908 v A, H, B (3)

Corrigan, J. T. (Manchester C), 1978 v I (sub); Br; 1979 v W; 1980 v Ni, Aus; 1981 v W, S; 1982 v W, Ic (9)

Cottee, A. R. (West Ham U), 1987 v Se (sub), Ni (sub); 1988 v H (sub); (with Everton) 1989 v D (sub), Se (sub), Ch (sub), S (7)

Cotterill, G. H. (Cambridge University), 1891 v Ni; (with Old Brightonians), 1892 v W; 1893 v S, Ni (4)

Cottle, J. R. (Bristol C), 1909 v Ni (1)

Cowan, S. (Manchester U), 1926 v Bel; 1930 v A; 1931 v Bel (3)

Cowans, G. (Aston Villa), 1983 v W, H, Ni, S, Aus (3); (with Bari), 1986 v Eg, USSR; (with Aston Villa), 1991 v Ei (10)

Cowell, A. (Blackburn R), 1910 v Ni (1)

Cox, J. (Liverpool), 1901 v Ni; 1902 v S; 1903 v S (3)

Cox, J. D. (Derby Co), 1892 v Ni (1)

Crabtree, J. W. (Burnley), 1894 v Ni; 1895 v Ni, S; (with Aston Villa), 1896 v W, S, Ni; 1899 v S, W, Ni; 1900 v S, W, Ni; 1901 v W; 1902 v W (14)

Crawford, J. F. (Chelsea), 1931 v S (1)

Crawford, R. (Ipswich T), 1962 v Ni, A (2)

Crawshaw, T. H. (Sheffield W), 1895 v Ni; 1896 v S, W, Ni; 1897 v S, W, Ni; 1901 v Ni; 1904 v W, Ni (10)

Crayston, W. J. (Arsenal), 1936 v S, W, G, A, Bel; 1938 v W, Ni, Cz (8)

Creek, F. N. S. (Corinthians), 1923 v F (1)
Cresswell, W. (South Shields), 1921 v W; (with Sunderland), 1923 v F; 1924 v Bel; 1925 v Ni; 1926 v W; 1927 v Ni; (with Everton), 1930 v Ni (7)
Crompton, R. (Blackburn R), 1902 v S, W, Ni; 1903 v S, W; 1904 v S, W, Ni; 1906 v S, W, Ni; 1907 v S, W, Ni; 1908 v S, W, Ni, A (2), H, B; 1909 v S, W, Ni, H (2), A; 1910 v S, W; 1911 v S, W, Ni; 1912 v S, W, Ni; 1913 v S, W, Ni; 1914 v S, W, Ni (41)
Crooks, S. D. (Derby Co), 1930 v S, G, A; 1931 v S, W, Ni, F, Bel; 1932 v S, W, Ni, Sp; 1933 v Ni, W, A; 1934 v S, Ni, W, F, H, Cz; 1935 v Ni; 1936 v S, W; 1937 v W, H (26)
Crowe, C. (Wolverhampton W), 1963 v F (1)
Cuggy, F. (Sunderland), 1913 v Ni; 1914 v Ni (2)
Cullis, S. (Wolverhampton W), 1938 v S, W, Ni, F, Cz; 1939 v S, Ni, R of E, N, I, R, Y (12)
Cunliffe, A. (Blackburn R), 1933 v Ni, W (2)
Cunliffe, D. (Portsmouth), 1900 v Ni (1)
Cunliffe, J. N. (Everton), 1936 v Bel (1)
Cunningham, L. (WBA), 1979 v W, Se, A (sub); (with Real Madrid), 1980 v Ei, Sp (sub); 1981 v R (sub) (6)
Curle, K. (Manchester C), 1992 v C (sub), H, D (3)
Currey, E. S. (Oxford University), 1890 v S, W (2)
Currie, A. W. (Sheffield U), 1972 v Ni; 1973 v USSR, I; 1974 v A, Pol, I; 1976 v Sw; (with Leeds U), 1978 v Br, W (sub), Ni, S, H (sub); 1979 v Cz, Ni (2), W, Se (17)
Cursham, A. W. (Notts Co), 1876 v S; 1877 v S; 1878 v S; 1879 v W; 1883 v S, W (6)
Cursham, H. A. (Notts Co), 1880 v W; 1882 v S, W, Ni; 1883 v S, W, Ni; 1884 v Ni (8)

Daft, H. B. (Notts Co), 1889 v Ni; 1890 v S, W; 1891 v Ni; 1892 v Ni (5)
Daley, A. M. (Aston Villa), 1992 v Pol (sub), C, H, Br, Fi (sub), D (sub), Se (7)
Danks, T. (Nottingham F), 1885 v S (1)
Davenport, P. (Nottingham F), 1985 v Ei (sub) (1)
Davenport, J. K. (Bolton W), 1885 v W; 1890 v Ni (2)
Davis, G. (Derby Co), 1904 v W, Ni (2)
Davis, H. (Sheffield W), 1903 v S, W, Ni (3)
Davison, J. E. (Sheffield W), 1922 v W (1)
Dawson, J. (Burnley), 1922 v S, Ni (2)
Day, S. H. (Old Malvernians), 1906 v Ni, W, S (3)
Dean, W. R. (Everton), 1927 v S, W, F, Bel, L; 1928 v S, W, Ni, F, Bel; 1929 v S, W, Ni; 1931 v S; 1932 v Sp; 1933 v Ni (16)
Deane, B. C. (Sheffield U), 1991 v Nz (sub + 1); 1993 v Sp (sub) (3)
Deeley, N. V. (Wolverhampton W), 1959 v Br, Pe (2)
Devey, J. H. G. (Aston Villa), 1892 v Ni; 1894 v Ni (2)
Devonshire, A. (West Ham U), 1980 v Aus (sub), Ni; 1982 v Ho, Ic; 1983 v WG, W, Gr; 1984 v L (8)
Dewhurst, F. (Preston NE), 1886 v W, Ni; 1887 v S, W, Ni; 1888 v S, W, Ni; 1889 v W (9)
Dewhurst, G. P. (Liverpool Ramblers), 1895 v W (1)
Dickinson, J. W. (Portsmouth), 1949 v N, F; 1950 v S, W, Ei, P, Bel, Ch, US, Sp; 1951 v Ni, W, Y; 1952 v W, Ni, S, A (2), I, Sw; 1953 v W, Ni, S, Bel, Arg, Ch, U, US; 1954 v W, Ni, S, R of E, H (2), Y, Bel, Sw, U; 1955 v Sp, P; 1956 v W, Ni, S, D, Sp; 1957 v W, Y, D (48)
Dimmock, J. H. (Tottenham H), 1921 v S; 1926 v W, Bel (3)
Ditchburn, E. G. (Tottenham H), 1949 v Sw, Se; 1953 v US; 1957 v W, Y, D (6)
Dix, R. W. (Derby Co), 1939 v N (1)
Dixon, J. A. (Notts Co), 1885 v W (1)
Dixon, K. M. (Chelsea), 1985 v M (sub), WG, US; 1986 v Ni, Is, M (sub), Pol (sub); 1987 v Se (8)
Dixon, L. M. (Arsenal), 1990 v Cz; 1991 v H, Pol, Ei (2), Cam, T, Arg; 1992 v G, T, Pol, Cz (sub); 1993 v Sp, N, T, Sm, T, Ho, N, US; 1994 v Sm (21)
Dobson, A. T. C. (Notts Co), 1882 v Ni; 1884 v S, W, Ni (4)
Dobson, C. F. (Notts Co), 1886 v Ni (1)
Dobson, J. M. (Burnley), 1974 v P, EG, Bul, Y; (with Everton), 1975 v Cz (5)
Doggart, A. G. (Corinthians), 1924 v Bel (1)
Dorigo, A. R. (Chelsea), 1990 v Y (sub), Cz (sub), D (sub), I; 1991 v H (sub), USSR; (with Leeds U), 1992 v G, Cz (sub), H, Br; 1993 v Sm, Pol, US, Br; 1994 v H (15)
Dorrell, A. R. (Aston Villa), 1925 v W, Bel, F; 1926 v Ni (4)
Douglas, B. (Blackburn R), 1958 v S, W, Ni, F, P, Y, USSR (2), Br, A; 1959 v S, USSR; 1960 v Y, H; 1961 v Ni, W, S, L, P, Sp, M, I, A; 1962 v W, Ni, S, A, Sw, Pe, L, P, H, Arg, Bul, Br; 1963 v S, Br, Sw (36)
Downs, R. W. (Everton), 1921 v Ni (1)
Doyle, M. (Manchester C), 1976 v W, S (sub), Br, I; 1977 v Ho (5)
Drake, E. J. (Arsenal), 1935 v Ni, I; 1936 v W; 1937 v H; 1938 v F (5)

Ducat, A. (Woolwich Arsenal), 1910 v S, W, Ni; (with Aston Villa), 1920 v S, W; 1921 v Ni (6)
Dunn, A. T. B. (Cambridge University), 1883 v Ni; 1884 v Ni; (with Old Etonians), 1892 v S, W (4)
Duxbury, M. (Manchester U), 1984 v L, F, W, S, USSR, Br, U, Ch; 1985 v EG, Fi (10)

Earle, S. G. J. (Clapton), 1924 v F; (with West Ham U), 1928 v Ni (2)
Eastham, G. (Arsenal), 1963 v Br, Cz, EG; 1964 v W, Ni, S, R of W, U, P, Ei, US, Br, Arg; 1965 v H, WG, Se; 1966 v Sp, Pol, D (19)
Eastham, G. R. (Bolton W), 1935 v Ho (1)
Eckersley, W. (Blackburn R), 1950 v Sp; 1951 v S, Y, Arg, P; 1952 v A (2), Sw; 1953 v Ni, Arg, Ch, U, US; 1954 v W, Ni, R of E, H (17)
Edwards, D. (Manchester U), 1955 v S, F, Sp, P; 1956 v S, Br, Se, Fi, WG; 1957 v S, Ni, Ei (2), D (2); 1958 v W, Ni, F (18)
Edwards, J. H. (Shropshire Wanderers), 1874 v S (1)
Edwards, J. (Leeds U), 1926 v S, W; 1927 v W, Ni, S, F, Bel, L; 1928 v S, F, Bel; 1929 v S, W, Ni; 1930 v W, Ni (16)
Ehiogu, U. (Aston Villa), 1996 v Chn (sub) (1)
Ellerington, W. (Southampton), 1949 v N, F (2)
Elliott, G. W. (Middlesbrough), 1913 v Ni; 1914 v Ni; 1920 v W (3)
Elliott, W. H. (Burnley), 1952 v I, A; 1953 v Ni, W, Bel (5)
Evans, R. E. (Sheffield U), 1911 v S, W, Ni; 1912 v W (4)
Ewer, F. H. (Casuals), 1924 v F; 1925 v Bel (2)

Fairclough, P. (Old Foresters), 1878 v S (1)
Fairhurst, D. (Newcastle U), 1934 v F (1)
Fantham, J. (Sheffield W), 1962 v L (1)
Fashanu, J. (Wimbledon), 1989 v Ch, S (2)
Felton, W. (Sheffield W), 1925 v F (1)
Fenton, M. (Middlesbrough), 1938 v S (1)
Fenwick, T. (QPR), 1984 v W (sub), S, USSR, Br, U, Ch; 1985 v Fi, S, R, M, US; 1986 v R, T, Ni, Eg, M, P, Mor, Pol, Arg; (with Tottenham H), 1988 v Is (sub) (20)
Ferdinand, L. (QPR), 1993 v Sm, Ho, N, US; 1994 v Pol, Sm; 1995 v US (sub); (with Newcastle U), 1996 v P, Bul, H; 1997 v Pol, Ge, I (sub) (13)
Field, E. (Clapham Rovers), 1876 v S; 1881 v S (2)
Finney, T. (Preston NE), 1947 v W, Ni, Ei, Ho, F, P; 1948 v S, W, Ni, Bel, Se, I; 1949 v S, W, Ni, Se, N, F; 1950 v S, W, Ni, Ei, I, P, Bel, Ch, US, Sp; 1951 v S, Arg, P; 1952 v W, Ni, S, F, I, Sw, A; 1953 v W, Ni, S, Bel, Arg, Ch, U, US; 1954 v W, S, Bel, Sw, U, H, Y; 1955 v WG; 1956 v S, W, Ni, D, Sp; 1957 v S, W, Y, D (2), Ei (2); 1958 v W, S, F, P, Y, USSR (2); 1959 v Ni, USSR (76)
Fleming, H. J. (Swindon T), 1909 v S, H (2); 1910 v W, Ni; 1911 v W, Ni; 1912 v Ni; 1913 v S, W; 1914 v S (11)
Fletcher, A. (Wolverhampton W), 1889 v W; 1890 v W (2)
Flowers, R. (Wolverhampton W), 1955 v F; 1959 v S, W, I, Br, Pe, US, M (sub); 1960 v W, Ni, S, Se, Y, Sp, H; 1961 v Ni, W, S, L, P, Sp, M, I, A; 1962 v W, Ni, S, A, Sw, Pe, L, P, H, Arg, Bul, Br; 1963 v Ni, W, S, F (2), Sw; 1964 v Ei, US, P; 1965 v W, Ho, WG; 1966 v N (49)
Flowers, T. D. (Southampton), 1993 v Br; (with Blackburn R), 1994 v Gr; 1995 v Ng, U, J, Se, Br; 1996 v Chn; 1997 v I (9)
Forman, Frank (Nottingham F), 1898 v S, Ni; 1899 v S, W, Ni; 1901 v S; 1902 v S, Ni; 1903 v W (9)
Forman, F. R. (Nottingham F), 1899 v S, W, Ni (3)
Forrest, J. H. (Blackburn R), 1884 v W; 1885 v S, W, Ni; 1886 v S, W; 1887 v S, W, Ni; 1889 v S; 1890 v Ni (11)
Fort, J. (Millwall), 1921 v Bel (1)
Foster, R. E. (Oxford University), 1900 v W; (with Corinthians), 1901 v W, Ni, S; 1902 v W (5)
Foster, S. (Brighton & HA), 1982 v Ni, Ho, K (3)
Foulke, W. J. (Sheffield U), 1897 v W (1)
Foulkes, W. A. (Manchester U), 1955 v Ni (1)
Fowler, R. B. (Liverpool), 1996 v Bul (sub), Cro, Chn (sub), Ho (sub), Sp (sub); 1997 v M (6)
Fox, F. S. (Millwall), 1925 v F (1)
Francis, G. C. J. (QPR), 1975 v Cz, P, W, S; 1976 v Sw, Cz, P, W, Ni, S, Br, Fi (12)
Francis, T. (Birmingham C), 1977 v Ho, L, S, Br; 1978 v Sw, L, I (sub), WG (sub), Br, W, S, H; (with Nottingham F), 1979 v Bul (sub), Se, A (sub); 1980 v Ni, Bul, Sp; 1981 v Sp, R, S (sub), Sw; (with Manchester C), 1982 v N, Ni, W, S (sub), Fi (sub), F, Cz, K, WG, Sp; (with Sampdoria), 1983 v D, Gr, H, Ni, S, Aus (3); 1984 v Ni, USSR; 1985 v EG (sub), T (sub), Ni, Ni, R, Fi, S, I, M; 1986 v S (52)
Franklin, C. F. (Stoke C), 1947 v S, W, Ni, Ei, Ho, F, Sw, P; 1948 v S, W, Ni, Bel, Se, I; 1949 v S, W, Ni, D, Sw, N, F, Se; 1950 v W, S, Ni, Ei, I (27)
Freeman, B. C. (Everton), 1909 v S, W; (with Burnley), 1912 v S, W, Ni (5)

Hodge, S. B. (Aston Villa), 1986 v USSR (sub), S, Ca, P (sub), Mor (sub), Pol, Para, Arg; 1987 v Se, Ni, Y; (with Tottenham H), Sp. Ni, T, S; (with Nottingham F), 1989 v D; 1990 v I (sub), Y (sub), Cz, D, U, Tun; 1991 v Cam (sub), T (sub) (24)

Hodgetts, D. (Aston Villa), 1888 v S, W, Ni; 1892 v S, Ni; 1894 v Ni (6)

Hodgkinson, A. (Sheffield U), 1957 v S, Ei (2), D; 1961 v W (5)

Hodgson, G. (Liverpool), 1931 v S, Ni, W (3)

Hodkinson, J. (Blackburn R), 1913 v W, S; 1920 v Ni (3)

Hogg, W. (Sunderland), 1902 v S, W, Ni (3)

Holdcroft, G. H. (Preston NE), 1937 v W, Ni (2)

Holden, A. D. (Bolton W), 1959 v S, I, Br, Pe, M (5)

Holden, G. H. (Wednesbury OA), 1881 v S; 1884 v S, W, Ni (4)

Holden-White, C. (Corinthians), 1888 v W, S (2)

Holford, T. (Stoke), 1903 v W (1)

Holley, G. H. (Sunderland), 1909 v S, W, H (2), A; 1910 v W; 1912 v S, W, NI; 1913 v S (10)

Holliday, E. (Middlesbrough), 1960 v W, Ni, Se (3)

Hollins, J. W. (Chelsea), 1967 v Sp (1)

Holmes, R. (Preston NE), 1888 v Ni; 1891 v S; 1892 v S; 1893 v S, W; 1894 v Ni; 1895 v Ni (7)

Holt, J. (Everton), 1890 v W; 1891 v S, W; 1892 v S, Ni; 1893 v S; 1894 v S, Ni; 1895 v S; (with Reading), 1900 v Ni (10)

Hopkinson, E. (Bolton W), 1958 v W, Ni, S, F, P, Y; 1959 v S, I, Br, Pe, M, US; 1960 v W, Se (14)

Hossack, A. H. (Corinthians), 1892 v W; 1894 v W (2)

Houghton, W. E. (Aston Villa), 1931 v Ni, W, F, Bel; 1932 v S, Ni; 1933 v A (7)

Houlker, A. E. (Blackburn R), 1902 v S; (with Portsmouth), 1903 v S, W; (with Southampton), 1906 v W, Ni (5)

Howarth, R. H. (Preston NE), 1887 v Ni; 1888 v S, W; 1891 v S; (with Everton), 1894 v Ni (5)

Howe, D. (WBA), 1958 v S, W, Ni, F, P, Y, USSR (3), Br, A; 1959 v S, W, Ni, USSR, I, Br, Pe, M, US; 1960 v W, Ni, Se (23)

Howe, J. R. (Derby Co), 1948 v I; 1949 v S, Ni (3)

Howell, L. S. (Wanderers), 1873 v S (1)

Howell, R. (Sheffield U), 1895 v Ni; (with Liverpool) 1899 v S (2)

Howey, S. N. (Newcastle U), 1995 v Ng; 1996 v Co, P, Bul (4)

Hudson, A. A. (Stoke C), 1975 v WG, Cy (2)

Hudson, J. (Sheffield), 1883 v Ni (1)

Hudspeth, F. C. (Newcastle U), 1926 v Ni (1)

Hufton, A. E. (West Ham U), 1924 v Bel; 1928 v S, Ni; 1929 v F, Bel, Sp (6)

Hughes, E. W. (Liverpool), 1970 v W, Ni, S, Ho, P, Bel; 1971 v EG, Ma (2), Gr, W; 1972 v Sw, Gr, WG (2), W, Ni, S; 1973 v W (3), S (2), Pol, USSR, I; 1974 v A, Pol, I, W, Ni, S, Arg, EG, Bul, Y; 1975 v Cz, P, Cy (sub), Ni; 1977 v I, L, W, S, Br, Arg, U; 1978 v Sw, L, I, WG, Ni, S, H; 1979 v D, Ei, Ni, W, Se; (with Wolverhampton W), 1980 v Sp (sub), Ni, S (sub) (62)

Hughes, L. (Liverpool), 1950 v Ch, US, Sp (3)

Hulme, J. H. A. (Arsenal), 1927 v S, Bel, F; 1928 v S, Ni, W; 1929 v Ni, W; 1933 v S (9)

Humphreys, P. (Notts Co), 1903 v S (1)

Hunt, G. S. (Tottenham H), 1933 v I, Sw, S (3)

Hunt, Rev K. R. G. (Leyton), 1911 v S, W (2)

Hunt, R. (Liverpool), 1962 v A; 1963 v EG; 1964 v S, US, P; 1965 v W; 1966 v S, Sp, Pol (2), WG (2), Fi, N, U, M, F, Arg, P; 1967 v Ni, W, Cz, Sp, A; 1968 v W, Ni, USSR (2), Sp (2), Se, Y; 1969 v R (2) (34)

Hunt, S. (WBA), 1984 v S (sub), USSR (sub) (2)

Hunter, J. (Sheffield Heeley), 1878 v S; 1880 v S, W; 1881 v S, W; 1882 v S, W (7)

Hunter, N. (Leeds U), 1966 v WG, Y, Fi, Sp (sub); 1967 v A; 1968 v Sp, Se, Y, WG, USSR; 1969 v R, W; 1970 v Ho, WG (sub); 1971 v Ma; 1972 v WG (2), W, Ni, S; 1973 v W (2) USSR (sub); 1974 v A, Pol, Ni (sub), S; 1975 v Cz (28)

Hurst, G. C. (West Ham U), 1966 v S, WG (2), Y, Fi, D, Arg, P; 1967 v Ni, W, S, Cz, Sp, A; 1968 v W, Ni, S, Se (sub), WG, USSR (2); 1969 v Ni, S, R (2), Bul, F, M, U, Br; 1970 v W, Ni, S, Ho (1+1 sub), Bel, Co, Ec, R, Br, WG; 1971 v EG, Gr, W, S; 1972 v Sw (2), Gr, WG (49)

Ince, P. E. C. (Manchester U), 1993 v Sp, N, T (2), Ho, Pol, US, Br, G; 1994 v Pol, Ho, Sm, D, N; 1995 v R, Ei; (with Internazionale), 1996 v Bul, Cro, H, Sw, S, Ho, G; 1997 v Mol, Pol, Ge, I, M, Ge, Pol, I, F (sub), Br (33)

Iremonger, J. (Nottingham F), 1901 v S; 1902 v Ni (2)

Jack, D. N. B. (Bolton W), 1924 v S, W; 1928 v F, Bel; (with Arsenal), 1930 v S, G, A; 1933 v W, A (9)

Jackson, E. (Oxford University), 1891 v W (1)

James. D. B. (Liverpool), 1997 v M (1)

Jarrett, B. G. (Cambridge University), 1876 v S; 1877 v S; 1878 v S (3)

Jefferis, F. (Everton), 1912 v S, W (2)

Jezzard, B. A. G. (Fulham), 1954 v H; 1956 v Ni (2)

Johnson, D. E. (Ipswich T), 1975 v W, S; 1976 v Sw; (with Liverpool), 1980 v Ei, Arg, Ni, S, Bel (8)

Johnson, E. (Saltley College), 1880 v W; (with Stoke C), 1884 v Ni (2)

Johnson, J. A. (Stoke C), 1937 v N, Se, Fi, S, Ni (5)

Johnson, T. C. F. (Manchester C), 1926 v Bel; 1930 v W; (with Everton), 1932 v S, Sp; 1933 v Ni (5)

Johnson, W. H. (Sheffield U), 1900 v S, W, Ni; 1903 v S, W, Ni (6)

Johnston, H. (Blackpool), 1947 v S, Ho; 1951 v S; 1953 v Arg, Ch, U, US; 1954 v W, Ni, H (10)

Jones, A. (Walsall Swifts), 1882 v S, W; (with Great Lever), 1883 v S (3)

Jones, H. (Blackburn R), 1927 v S, Bel, L, F; 1928 v S, Ni (6)

Jones, H. (Nottingham F), 1923 v F (1)

Jones, M. D. (Sheffield U), 1965 v WG, Se; (with Leeds U), 1970 v Ho (3)

Jones, R. (Liverpool), 1992 v F; 1994 v Pol, Gr, N; 1995 v US, R, Ng, U (8)

Jones, W. (Bristol C), 1901 v Ni (1)

Jones, W. H. (Liverpool), 1950 v P, Bel (2)

Joy, B. (Casuals), 1936 v Bel (1)

Kail, E. I. L. (Dulwich Hamlet), 1929 v F, Bel, Sp (3)

Kay, A. H. (Everton), 1963 v Sw (1)

Kean, F. W. (Sheffield W), 1923 v S, Bel; 1924 v W; 1925 v Ni; 1926 v Ni, Bel; 1927 v L; (with Bolton W), 1929 v F, Sp (9)

Keegan, J. K. (Liverpool), 1973 v W (2); 1974 v W, Ni, Arg, EG, Bul, Y; 1975 v Cz, WG, Cy (2), Ni, S; 1976 v Sw, Cz, P, W (2), Ni, S, Br, Fi; 1977 v Ei, Fi, I, Ho, L; (with SV Hamburg), W, Br, Arg, U; 1978 v Sw, I, WG, Br, H; 1979 v D, Ei, Cz, Ni, W, S, Bul, Se, A; 1980 v D, Ni, Ei, Sp (2), Arg, Bel, I; (with Southampton), 1981 v Sp, Sw, H; 1982 v N, H, Ni, S, Fi, Sp (sub) (63)

Keen, E. R. L. (Derby Co), 1933 v A; 1937 v W, Ni, H (4)

Kelly, R. (Burnley), 1920 v S; 1921 v S, W, Ni; 1922 v S, W; 1923 v S; 1924 v Ni; 1925 v W, Ni, S; (with Sunderland), 1926 v W; (with Huddersfield T), 1927 v L; 1928 v S (14)

Kennedy, A. (Liverpool), 1984 v Ni, W (2)

Kennedy, R. (Liverpool), 1976 v W (2), Ni, S; 1977 v L, W, S, Br (sub), Arg (sub); 1978 v Sw, L; 1980 v Bul, Sp, Arg, W, Bel (sub), I (17)

Kenyon-Slaney, W. S. (Wanderers), 1873 v S (1)

Keown, M. R. (Everton), 1992 v F, Cz, C, H, Br, Fi, D, Fe, Se; (with Arsenal), 1993 v Ho, G (sub); 1997 v M, S.Af, I, Br (15)

Kevan, D. T. (WBA), 1957 v S; 1958 v W, Ni, S, P, Y, USSR (3), Br, A; 1959 v M, US; 1961 v M (14)

Kidd, B. (Manchester U), 1970 v Ni, Ec (sub) (2)

King, R. S. (Oxford University), 1882 v Ni (1)

Kingsford, R. K. (Wanderers), 1874 v S (1)

Kingsley, M. (Newcastle U), 1901 v W (1)

Kinsey, G. (Wolverhampton W), 1892 v W; 1893 v S; (with Derby Co), 1896 v W, Ni (4)

Kirchen, A. J. (Arsenal), 1937 v N, Se, Fi (3)

Kirton, W. J. (Aston Villa), 1922 v Ni (1)

Knight, A. E. (Portsmouth), 1920 v Ni (1)

Knowles, C. (Tottenham H), 1968 v USSR, Sp, Se, WG (4)

Labone, B. L. (Everton), 1963 v Ni, W, F; 1967 v Sp, A; 1968 v S, Sp, Se, Y, USSR, WG; 1969 v Ni, S, R, Bul, M, U, Br; 1970 v S, W, Bel, Co, Ec, R, Br, WG (26)

Lampard, F. R. G. (West Ham U), 1973 v Y; 1980 v Aus (2)

Langley, E. J. (Fulham), 1958 v S, P, Y (3)

Langton, R. (Blackburn R), 1947 v W, Ni, Ei, Ho, F, Sw; 1948 v Se; (with Preston NE), 1949 v D, Se; (with Bolton W), 1950 v S; 1951 v Ni (11)

Latchford, R. D. (Everton), 1978 v I, Br, W; 1979 v D, Ei, Cz (sub), Ni (2), W, S, Bul, A (12)

Latheron, E. G. (Blackburn R), 1913 v W; 1914 v Ni (2)

Lawler, C. (Liverpool), 1971 v Ma, W, S; 1972 v Sw (4)

Lawton, T. (Everton), 1939 v S, W, Ni, R of E, N, I, R, Y; (with Chelsea), 1947 v S, W, Ni, Ei, Ho, F, Sw, P; 1948 v W, Ni, Bel; (with Notts Co), 1948 v S, Se, I; 1949 v D (23)

Leach, T. (Sheffield W), 1931 v W, Ni (2)

Leake, A. (Aston Villa), 1904 v S, Ni; 1905 v S, W, Ni (5)

Lee, E. A. (Southampton), 1904 v W (1)

Lee, F. H. (Manchester C), 1969 v Ni, W, S, Bul, F, M, U; 1970 v W, Ho (2), P, Bel, Co, Ec, R, Br, WG; 1971 v EG, Gr, Ma, Ni, W, S; 1972 v Sw (2), Gr, WG (27)

Lee, J. (Derby Co), 1951 v Ni (1)

Lee, R. M. (Newcastle U), 1995 v R, Ng; 1996 v Co (sub), N, Sw, Bul (sub), H; 1997 v M, Ge, S.Af, Pol, F (sub), Br (sub) (13)

Lee, S. (Liverpool), 1983 v Gr, L, W, Gr, H, S, Aus; 1984 v D, H, L, F, Ni, W, Ch (sub) (14)

Leighton, J. E. (Nottingham F), 1886 v Ni (1)

Le Saux, G. P. (Blackburn R), 1994 v D, Gr, N; 1995 v US, R, Ng, Ei, U, Se, Br; 1996 v Co, P (sub); 1997 v I, M, Ge, S.Af, Pol, I, F, Br (20)

Le Tissier, M. P. (Southampton), 1994 v D (sub), Gr (sub), N (sub); 1995 v R, Ng (sub), Ei; 1997 v Mol (sub), I (8)

Lilley, H. E. (Sheffield U), 1892 v W (1)

Linacre, H. J. (Nottingham F), 1905 v W, S (2)

Lindley, T. (Cambridge University), 1886 v S, W, Ni; 1887 v S, W, Ni; 1888 v S, W, Ni; (with Nottingham F), 1889 v S; 1890 v S, W; 1891 v Ni (13)

Lindsay, A. (Liverpool), 1974 v Arg, EG, Bul, Y (4)

Lindsay, W. (Wanderers), 1877 v S (1)

Lineker, G. (Leicester C), 1984 v S (sub); 1985 v Ei, R (sub), S (sub), I (sub), WG, US; (with Everton), 1986 v R, T, Ni, Eg, USSR, Ca, P, Mor, Pol, Para, Arg; (with Barcelona), 1987 v Ni (2), Y, Sp, T, Br; 1988 v WG, T, Y, Ho, H, S, Co, Sw, Ei, Ho, USSR; 1989 v Se, S.Ar, Gr, Alb (2), Pol, D; (with Tottenham H) 1990 v Se, Pol, I, Y, Br, Cz, D, U, Tun, Ei, Ho, Eg, Bel, Cam, WG, I; 1991 v H, Pol, Ei (2), Cam, T, Arg, Aus, Nz, Mal; 1992 v G, T, Pol, F (sub), Cz (sub), C, H, Br, Fi, D, F, Se (80)

Lintott, E. H. (QPR), 1908 v S, W, Ni; (with Bradford C), 1909 v S, Ni, H (2) (7)

Lipsham, H. B. (Sheffield U), 1902 v W (1)

Little, B. (Aston Villa), 1975 v W (sub) (1)

Lloyd, L. V. (Liverpool), 1971 v W; 1972 v Sw, Ni; (with Nottingham F), 1980 v W (4)

Lockett, A. (Stoke C), 1903 v Ni (1)

Lodge, L. V. (Cambridge University), 1894 v W; 1895 v S, W; (with Corinthians), 1896 v S, Ni (5)

Lofthouse, J. M. (Blackburn R), 1885 v S, W, Ni; 1887 v S, W; (with Accrington), 1889 v Ni; (with Blackburn R), 1890 v Ni (7)

Lofthouse, N. (Bolton W), 1951 v Y; 1952 v W, Ni, S, A (2), I, Sw; 1953 v W, Ni, S, Bel, Arg, Ch, U, US; 1954 v W, Ni, R of E, Bel, U; 1955 v Ni, S, F, Sp, P; 1956 v W, S, Sp, D, Fi (sub); 1959 v W, USSR (33)

Longworth, E. (Liverpool), 1920 v S; 1921 v Bel; 1923 v S, W, Bel (5)

Lowder, A. (Wolverhampton W), 1889 v W (1)

Lowe, E. (Aston Villa), 1947 v F, Sw, P (3)

Lucas, T. (Liverpool), 1922 v Ni; 1924 v F; 1926 v Bel (3)

Luntley, E. (Nottingham F), 1880 v S, W (2)

Lyttelton, Hon. A. (Cambridge University), 1877 v S (1)

Lyttelton, Hon. E. (Cambridge University), 1878 v S (1)

McCall, J. (Preston NE), 1913 v S, W; 1914 v S; 1920 v S; 1921 v Ni (5)

McDermott, T. (Liverpool), 1978 v Sw, L; 1979 v Ni, W, Se; 1980 v D, Ni (sub), Ei, Ni, S, Bel (sub), Sp; 1981 v N, R, Sw, R (sub), Br, Sw (sub), H; 1982 v N, H, W (sub), Ho, S (sub), Ic (25)

McDonald, C. A. (Burnley), 1958 v USSR (3), Br, A; 1959 v W, Ni, USSR (8)

McFarland, R. L. (Derby Co), 1971 v Gr, Ma (2), Ni, S; 1972 v Sw, Gr, WG, W, S; 1973 v W (3), Ni, S, Cz, Pol, USSR, I; 1974 v A, Pol, I, W, Ni; 1976 v Cz, S; 1977 v Ei, I (28)

McGarry, W. H. (Huddersfield T), 1954 v Sw, U; 1956 v W, D (4)

McGuinness, W. (Manchester U), 1959 v Ni, M (2)

McInroy, A. (Sunderland), 1927 v Ni (1)

McMahon, S. (Liverpool), 1988 v Is, H, Co, USSR; 1989 v D (sub); 1990 v Se, Pol, I, Y (sub), Br, Cz (sub), D, Ei (sub), Eg, Bel, I; 1991 v Ei (17)

McManaman, S. (Liverpool), 1995 v Ng (sub), U (sub), J (sub); 1996 v Co, N, Sw, P (sub), Bul, Cro, Chn, Sw, S, Ho, Sp, G; 1997 v Pol, I, M (18)

McNab, R. (Arsenal), 1969 v Ni, Bul, R (1+1 sub) (4)

McNeal, R. (WBA), 1914 v S, W (2)

McNeil, M. (Middlesbrough), 1961 v W, Ni, S, L, P, Sp, M, I; 1962 v L (9)

Mabbutt, G. (Tottenham H), 1983 v WG, Gr, L, W, Gr, H, Ni, S (sub); 1984 v H; 1987 v Y, Ni, T; 1988 v WG; 1992 v T, Pol, Cz (16)

Macaulay, R. H. (Cambridge University), 1881 v S (1)

Macdonald, M. (Newcastle U), 1972 v W, Ni, S (sub); 1973 v USSR (sub); 1974 v P, S (sub), Y (sub); 1975 v WG, Cy (2), Ni; 1976 v Sw (sub), Cz, P (14)

Macrae, S. (Notts Co), 1883 v S, W, Ni; 1884 v S, W, Ni (6)

Maddison, F. B. (Oxford University), 1872 v S (1)

Madeley, P. E. (Leeds U), 1971 v Ni; 1972 v Sw (2), Gr, WG (2), W, S; 1973 v S, Cz, Pol, USSR, I; 1974 v A, Pol, I; 1975 v Cz, P, Cy; 1976 v Cz, P, Fi; 1977 v Ei, Ho (24)

Magee, T. P. (WBA), 1923 v W, Se; 1925 v S, Bel, F (5)

Makepeace, H. (Everton), 1906 v S; 1910 v S; 1912 v S, W (4)

Male, C. G. (Arsenal), 1935 v S, Ni, I, Ho; 1936 v S, W, Ni, G, A, Bel; 1937 v S, Ni, H, N, Se, Fi; 1939 v I, R, Y (19)

Mannion, W. J. (Middlesbrough), 1947 v S, W, Ni, Ei, Ho, F, Sw, P; 1948 v W, Ni, Bel, Se, I; 1949 v N, F; 1950 v S, Ei, P, Bel, Ch, US; 1951 v A, W, Ni, W, S, Y; 1952 v F (26)

Mariner, P. (Ipswich T), 1977 v L (sub), Ni; 1978 v L, W (sub), S; 1980 v W, Ni (sub), S, Aus, I (sub), Sp (sub); 1981 v N, Sw, Sp, Sw, H; 1982 v N, H, Ho, S, Fi, F, Cz, K, WG, Sp; 1983 v D, WG, Gr, W; 1984 v D, H, L; (with Arsenal), 1985 v EG, R (35)

Marsden, J. T. (Darwen), 1891 v Ni (1)

Marsden, W. (Sheffield W), 1930 v W, S, G (3)

Marsh, R. W. (QPR), 1972 v Sw (sub); (with Manchester C), WG (sub+1), W, Ni, S; 1973 v W (2), Y (9)

Marshall, T. (Darwen), 1880 v W; 1881 v W (2)

Martin, A. (West Ham U), 1981 v Br, S (sub); 1982 v H, Fi; 1983 v Gr, L, W, Gr, H; 1984 v H, L, W; 1985 v Ni; 1986 v Is, Ca, Para; 1987 v Se (17)

Martin, H. (Sunderland), 1914 v Ni (1)

Martyn, A. N. (C Palace), 1992 v C (sub), H; 1993 v G; (with Leeds U), 1997 v S.Af (4)

Marwood, B. (Arsenal), 1989 v S.Ar (sub) (1)

Maskrey, H. M. (Derby Co), 1908 v Ni (1)

Mason, C. (Wolverhampton W), 1887 v Ni; 1888 v W; 1890 v Ni (3)

Matthews, R. D. (Coventry C), 1956 v S, Br, Se, WG; 1957 v Ni (5)

Matthews, S. (Stoke C), 1935 v W, I; 1936 v G; 1937 v S; 1938 v S, W, Cz, G, Sw, F; 1939 v S, W, Ni, R of E, N, I, Y; 1947 v S; (with Blackpool), 1947 v Sw, P; 1948 v S, W, Ni, Bel, I; 1949 v S, W, Ni, D, Sw; 1950 v Sp; 1951 v Ni, S; 1954 v Ni, R of E, H, Bel, U; 1955 v Ni, W, S, F, WG, Sp, P; 1956 v W, Br; 1957 v S, W, Ni, Y, D (2), Ei (54)

Matthews, V. (Sheffield U), 1928 v F, Bel (2)

Maynard, W. J. (1st Surrey Rifles), 1872 v S; 1876 v S (2)

Meadows, J. (Manchester C), 1955 v S (1)

Medley, L. D. (Tottenham H), 1951 v Y, W; 1952 v F, A, W, Ni (6)

Meehan, T. (Chelsea), 1924 v Ni (1)

Melia, J. (Liverpool), 1963 v S, Sw (2)

Mercer, D. W. (Sheffield U), 1923 v Ni, Bel (2)

Mercer, J. (Everton), 1939 v S, Ni, I, R, Y (5)

Merrick, G. H. (Birmingham C), 1952 v Ni, S, A (2), I, Sw; 1953 v W, S, Bel, Arg, Ch, U; 1954 v W, Ni, S, R of E, H (2), Y, Bel, Sw, U (23)

Merson, P. C. (Arsenal), 1992 v G (sub), Cz, H, Br (sub), Fi (sub), D, Se (sub); 1993 v Sp (sub), N (sub), Ho (sub), Br (sub), G; 1994 v Ho, Gr; 1997 v I (sub) (15)

Metcalfe, V. (Huddersfield T), 1951 v Arg, P (2)

Mew, J. W. (Manchester U), 1921 v Ni (1)

Middleditch, B. (Corinthians), 1897 v Ni (1)

Milburn, J. E. T. (Newcastle U), 1949 v S, W, Ni, Sw; 1950 v W, P, Bel, Sp; 1951 v W, Arg, P; 1952 v F; 1956 v D (13)

Miller, B. G. (Burnley), 1961 v A (1)

Miller, H. S. (Charlton Ath), 1923 v Se (1)

Mills, G. R. (Chelsea), 1938 v W, Ni, Cz (3)

Mills, M. D. (Ipswich T), 1973 v Y; 1976 v W (2), Ni, S, Br, I (sub), Fi; 1977 v Fi (sub), I, Ni, W, S; 1978 v WG, Br, W, Ni, S, H; 1979 v D, Ei, Ni (2), S, Bul, A; 1980 v D, Ni, Sp (2); 1981 v Sw (2), H; 1982 v N, H, S, Fi, F, Cz, K, WG, Sp (42)

Milne, G. (Liverpool), 1963 v Br, Cz, EG; 1964 v W, Ni, S, R of W, U, P, Ei, Br, Arg; 1965 v Ni, Bel (14)

Milton, C. A. (Arsenal), 1952 v A (1)

Milward, A. (Everton), 1891 v S, W; 1897 v S, W (4)

Mitchell, C. (Upton Park), 1880 v W; 1881 v S; 1883 v S, W; 1885 v W (5)

Mitchell, J. F. (Manchester C), 1925 v Ni (1)

Moffat, H. (Oldham Ath), 1913 v W (1)

Molyneux, G. (Southampton), 1902 v S; 1903 v S, W, Ni (4)

Moon, W. R. (Old Westminsters), 1888 v S, W; 1889 v S, W; 1890 v S, W; 1891 v S (7)

Moore, H. T. (Notts Co), 1883 v Ni; 1885 v W (2)

Moore, J. (Derby Co), 1923 v Se (1)

Moore, R. F. (West Ham U), 1962 v Pe, H, Arg, Bul, Br; 1963 v W, Ni, S, F (2), Br, Cz, EG, Sw; 1964 v W, Ni, S, R of W, U, P (2), Ei, Br, Arg; 1965 v Ni, S, Bel, H, Y, WG, Se; 1966 v W, Ni, S, A, Sp, Pol (2), WG (2), N, D, U, M, F, Arg, P; 1967 v W, Ni, S, Cz, Sp, A; 1968 v W, Ni, S, USSR (2), Sp (2), Se, Y, WG; 1969 v Ni, W, S, R, Bul, F, M, U, Br; 1970 v W, Ni, S, Ho, P, Bel, Co, Ec, R, Br, Cz, WG; 1971 v EG, Gr, Ma, Ni, S; 1972 v Sw (2), Gr, WG (2), W, S; 1973 v W (3), Y, S (2), Ni, Cz, Pol, USSR, I; 1974 v I (108)

Moore, W. G. B. (West Ham U), 1923 v Se (1)

Mordue, J. (Sunderland), 1912 v Ni; 1913 v Ni (2)

Morice, C. J. (Barnes), 1872 v S (1)

Morley, A. (Aston Villa), 1982 v H (sub), Ni, W, Ic; 1983 v D, Gr (6)

Morley, H. (Notts Co), 1910 v Ni (1)
Morren, T. (Sheffield U), 1898 v Ni (1)
Morris, F. (WBA), 1920 v S; 1921 v Ni (2)
Morris, J. (Derby Co), 1949 v N, F; 1950 v Ei (3)
Morris, W. W. (Wolverhampton W), 1939 v S, Ni, R (3)
Morse, H. (Notts Co), 1879 v S (1)
Mort, T. (Aston Villa), 1924 v W, F; 1926 v S (3)
Morten, A. (C Palace), 1873 v S (1)
Mortensen, S. H. (Blackpool), 1947 v P; 1948 v W, S, Ni, Bel, Se, I; 1949 v S, W, Ni, Se, N; 1950 v S, W, Ni, I, P, Bel, Ch, US, Sp; 1951 v S, Arg; 1954 v R of E, H (25)
Morton, J. R. (West Ham U), 1938 v Cz (1)
Mosforth, W. (Sheffield W), 1877 v S; (with Sheffield Albion), 1878 v S; 1879 v S, W; 1880 v S, W; (with Sheffield W), 1881 v W; 1882 v S, W (9)
Moss, F. (Arsenal), 1934 v S, H, Cz; 1935 v I (4)
Moss, F. (Aston Villa), 1922 v S, Ni; 1923 v Ni; 1924 v S, Bel (5)
Mosscrop, E. (Burnley), 1914 v S, W (2)
Mozley, B. (Derby Co), 1950 v W, Ni, Ei (3)
Mullen, J. (Wolverhampton W), 1947 v S; 1949 v N, F; 1950 v Bel (sub), Ch, US; 1954 v W, Ni, S, R of E, Y, Sw (12)
Mullery, A. P. (Tottenham H), 1965 v Ho; 1967 v Sp, A; 1968 v W, Ni, S, USSR, Sp (2), Se, Y; 1969 v Ni, S, R, Bul, F, M, U, Br; 1970 v W, Ni, S (sub), Ho (sub), Bel, P, Co, Ec, R, Cz, WG, Br; 1971 v Ma, EG, Gr; 1972 v Sw (35)

Neal, P. G. (Liverpool), 1976 v W, I; 1977 v W, S, Br, Arg, U; 1978 v Sw, I, WG, Ni, S, H; 1979 v D, Ei, Ni (2), S, Bul, A; 1980 v D, Ni, Sp, Arg, W, Bel, I; 1981 v R, Sw, Sp, Br, H; 1982 v N, H, W, Ho, Ic, F (sub); K; 1983 v D, Gr, L, W, Gr, H, Ni, S, Aus (2); 1984 v D (50)
Needham, E. (Sheffield U), 1894 v S; 1895 v S; 1897 v S, W, Ni; 1898 v S, W; 1899 v S, W, Ni; 1900 v S, Ni; 1901 v S, W, Ni; 1902 v W (16)
Neville, G. A. (Manchester U), 1995 v J, Br; 1996 v Co, N, Sw, P, Bul, Cro, H, Chn, Sw, S, Ho, Sp; 1997 v Mol, Pol, I, Ge, Pol, I (sub), F, Br (sub) (22)
Neville, P. J. (Manchester U), 1996 v Chn; 1997 v S.Af, Pol (sub), I, F, Br (6)
Newton, K. R. (Blackburn R), 1966 v S, WG; 1967 v Sp, A; 1968 v W, S, Sp, Se, Y, WG; 1969 v Ni, W, S, R, Bul, M, U, Br, F; (with Everton), 1970 v Ni, S, Ho, Co, Ec, R, Cz, WG (27)
Nicholls, J. (WBA), 1954 v S, Y (2)
Nicholson, W. E. (Tottenham H), 1951 v P (1)
Nish, D. J. (Derby Co), 1973 v Ni; 1974 v P, W, Ni, S (5)
Norman, M. (Tottenham H), 1962 v Pe, H, Arg, Bul, Br; 1963 v S, F, Br, Cz, EG; 1964 v W, Ni, S, R of W, U, P (2), US, Br, Arg; 1965 v Ni, Bel, Ho (23)
Nuttall, H. (Bolton W), 1928 v W, Ni; 1929 v S (3)

Oakley, W. J. (Oxford University), 1895 v W; 1896 v S, W, Ni; (with Corinthians), 1897 v S, W, Ni; 1898 v S, W, Ni; 1900 v S, W, Ni; 1901 v S, W, Ni (16)
O'Dowd, J. P. (Chelsea), 1932 v S; 1933 v Ni, Sw (3)
O'Grady, M. (Huddersfield T), 1963 v Ni; (with Leeds U), 1969 v F (2)
Ogilvie, R. A. M. M. (Clapham R), 1874 v S (1)
Oliver, L. F. (Fulham), 1929 v Bel (1)
Olney, B. A. (Aston Villa), 1928 v F, Bel (2)
Osborne, F. R. (Fulham), 1923 v Ni, F; (with Tottenham H), 1925 v Bel; 1926 v Bel (4)
Osborne, R. (Leicester C), 1928 v W (1)
Osgood, P. L. (Chelsea), 1970 v Bel, R (sub), Cz (sub); 1974 v I (4)
Osman, R. (Ipswich T), 1980 v Aus; 1981 v Sp, R, Sw; 1982 v N, Ic; 1983 v D, Aus (3); 1984 v D (11)
Ottaway, C. J. (Oxford University), 1872 v S; 1874 v S (2)
Owen, J. R. B. (Sheffield), 1874 v S (1)
Owen, S. W. (Luton T), 1954 v H, Y, Bel (3)

Page, L. A. (Burnley), 1927 v S, W, Bel, L, F; 1928 v W, Ni (7)
Paine, T. L. (Southampton), 1963 v Cz, EG; 1964 v W, Ni, S, R of W, U, US, P; 1965 v Ni, H, Y, WG, Se; 1966 v W, A, Y, N, M (19)
Pallister, G. A. (Middlesbrough), 1988 v H; 1989 v S.Ar; (with Manchester U), 1991 v Cam (sub), T; 1992 v G; 1993 v N, US, Br, G; 1994 v Pol, Ho, Sm, D; 1995 v US, R, Ei, U, Se; 1996 v N, Sw; 1997 v Mol, Pol (sub) (22)
Palmer, C. L. (Sheffield W), 1992 v C, H, Br, Fi (sub), D, F, Se; 1993 v Sp (sub), N (sub), T, Sm, T, Ho, Pol, N, SB (sub); 1994 v Ho (18)
Pantling, H. H. (Sheffield U), 1924 v Ni (1)
Paravacini, P. J. de (Cambridge University), 1883 v S, W, Ni (3)

Parker, P. A. (QPR), 1989 v Alb (sub), Ch, D; 1990 v Y, U, Ho, Eg, Bel, Cam, WG, I; 1991 v H, Pol, USSR, Aus, Nz; (with Manchester U), 1992 v G; 1994 v Ho, D (19)
Parker, T. R. (Southampton), 1925 v F (1)
Parkes, P. B. (QPR), 1974 v P (1)
Parkinson, J. (Liverpool), 1910 v S, W (2)
Parr, P. C. (Oxford University), 1882 v W (1)
Parry, E. H. (Old Carthusians), 1879 v W; 1882 v W, S (3)
Parry, R. A. (Bolton W), 1960 v Ni, S (2)
Patchitt, B. C. A. (Corinthians), 1923 v Se (2) (2)
Pawson, F. W. (Cambridge University), 1883 v Ni; (with Swifts), 1885 v Ni (2)
Payne, J. (Luton T), 1937 v Fi (1)
Peacock, A. (Middlesbrough), 1962 v Arg, Bul; 1963 v Ni, W; (with Leeds U), 1966 v W, N (6)
Peacock, J. (Middlesbrough), 1929 v F, Bel, Sp (3)
Pearce, S. (Nottingham F), 1987 v Br, S; 1988 v WG (sub), Is, H; 1989 v D, Se, S.Ar, Gr, Alb (2), Ch, S, Pol, D; 1990 v Pol, I, Y, Br, Cz, D, U, Tun, Ei, Ho, Eg, Bel, Cam, WG; 1991 v H, Pol, Ei (2), Cam, T, Arg, Aus, Nz (2), Mal; 1992 v T, Pol, F, Cz, Br (sub), Fi, D, F, Se; 1993 v Sp, N, T; 1994 v Pol, Sm, Gr (sub); 1995 v R (sub), J, Br; 1996 v N, Sw, P, Bul, Cro, H, Sw, S, Ho, Sp, G; 1997 v Mol, Pol, I, M, S.Af, I (76)
Pearson, H. F. (WBA), 1932 v S (1)
Pearson, J. H. (Crewe Alex), 1892 v Ni (1)
Pearson, J. S. (Manchester U), 1976 v W, Ni, S, Br, Fi; 1977 v Ei, Ho (sub), W, S, Br, Arg, U; 1978 v I (sub), WG, Ni (15)
Pearson, S. C. (Manchester U), 1948 v S; 1949 v S, Ni; 1950 v Ni, I; 1951 v P; 1952 v S, I (8)
Pease, W. H. (Middlesbrough), 1927 v W (1)
Pegg, D. (Manchester U), 1957 v Ei (1)
Pejic, M. (Stoke C), 1974 v P, W, Ni, S (4)
Pelly, F. R. (Old Foresters), 1893 v Ni; 1894 v S, W (3)
Pennington, J. (WBA), 1907 v S, W; 1908 v S, W, Ni, A; 1909 v S, W, H (2), A; 1910 v S, W; 1911 v S, W, Ni; 1912 v S, W, Ni; 1913 v S, W; 1914 v S, Ni; 1920 v S, W (25)
Pentland, F. B. (Middlesbrough), 1909 v S, W, H (2), A (5)
Perry, C. (WBA), 1890 v Ni; 1891 v Ni; 1893 v W (3)
Perry, T. (WBA), 1898 v W (1)
Perry, W. (Blackpool), 1956 v Ni, S, Sp (3)
Perryman, S. (Tottenham H), 1982 v Ic (sub) (1)
Peters, M. (West Ham U), 1966 v Y, Fi, Pol, M, F, Arg, P, WG; 1967 v Ni, W, S, Cz; 1968 v W, Ni, S, USSR (2), Sp (2), Se, Y; 1969 v Ni, S, R, Bul, F, M, U, Br; 1970 v Ho (2), P (sub), Bel; (with Tottenham H), Ni, S, Co, Ec, R, Br, Cz, WG; 1971 v EG, Gr, Ma (2), Ni, W, S; 1972 v Sw, Gr, WG (1+1 sub), Ni (sub); 1973 v S (2), Ni, W, Cz, Pol, USSR, I; 1974 v A, Pol, I, P, S (67)
Phelan, M. C. (Manchester U), 1990 v I (sub) (1)
Phillips, L. H. (Portsmouth), 1952 v Ni; 1955 v W, WG (3)
Pickering, F. (Everton), 1964 v US; 1965 v Ni, Bel (3)
Pickering, J. (Sheffield U), 1933 v S (1)
Pickering, N. (Sunderland), 1983 v Aus (1)
Pike, T. M. (Cambridge University), 1886 v Ni (1)
Pilkington, B. (Burnley), 1955 v Ni (1)
Plant, J. (Bury), 1900 v S (1)
Platt, D. (Aston Villa), 1990 v I (sub), Y (sub), Br, D (sub), Tun (sub), Ho (sub), Eg (sub), Bel (sub), Cam, WG, I; 1991 v H, Pol, Ei (2), T, USSR, Arg, Aus, Nz (2), Mal; (with Bari), 1992 v G, T, Pol, Cz, C, Br, Fi, D, F, Se; (with Juventus), 1993 v Sp, N, T, Sm, T, Ho, Pol, N, Br (sub), G; (with Sampdoria), 1994 v Pol, Ho, Sm, D, Gr, N; 1995 v US, Ng, Ei, U, J, Se, Br; (with Arsenal), 1996 v Bul (sub), Cro, H, Sw (sub), Ho (sub), Sp, G (62)
Plum, S. L. (Charlton Ath), 1923 v F (1)
Pointer, R. (Burnley), 1962 v W, L, P (3)
Porteous, T. S. (Sunderland), 1891 v W (1)
Priest, A. E. (Sheffield U), 1900 v Ni (1)
Prinsep, J. F. M. (Clapham Rovers), 1879 v S (1)
Puddefoot, S. C. (Blackburn R), 1926 v S, Ni (2)
Pye, J. (Wolverhampton W), 1950 v Ei (1)
Pym, R. H. (Bolton W), 1925 v S, W; 1926 v W (3)

Quantrill, A. (Derby Co), 1920 v S, W; 1921 v W, Ni (4)
Quixall, A. (Sheffield W), 1954 v W, Ni, R of E; 1955 v Sp, P (sub) (5)

Radford, J. (Arsenal), 1969 v R; 1972 v Sw (sub) (2)
Raikes, G. B. (Oxford University), 1895 v W; 1896 v W, Ni, S (4)
Ramsey, A. E. (Southampton), 1949 v Sw; (with Tottenham H), 1950 v S, I, P, Bel, Ch, US, Sp; 1951 v S, Ni, W, Y, Arg, P; 1952 v S, W, Ni, F, A (2), I, Sw; 1953 v Ni, S, Bel, Arg, Ch, U, US; 1954 v R of E, H (32)
Rawlings, A. (Preston NE), 1921 v Bel (1)
Rawlings, W. E. (Southampton), 1922 v S, W (2)
Rawlinson, J. F. P. (Cambridge University), 1882 v Ni (1)

Smith, C. E. (C Palace), 1876 v S (1)
Smith, G. O. (Oxford University), 1893 v Ni; 1894 v W, S; 1895 v W; 1896 v Ni, W, S; (with Old Carthusians), 1897 v Ni, W, S; 1898 v Ni, W, S; (with Corinthians), 1899 v Ni, W, S; 1899 v Ni, W, S; 1901 v S (20)
Smith, H. (Reading), 1905 v W, S; 1906 v W, Ni (4)
Smith, J. (WBA), 1920 v Ni; 1923 v Ni (2)
Smith, Joe (Bolton W), 1913 v Ni; 1914 v S, W; 1920 v W, Ni (5)
Smith, J. C. R. (Millwall), 1939 v Ni, N (2)
Smith, J. W. (Portsmouth), 1932 v Ni, W, Sp (3)
Smith, Leslie (Brentford), 1939 v R (1)
Smith, Lionel (Arsenal), 1951 v W; 1952 v W, Ni; 1953 v W, S, Bel (6)
Smith, R. A. (Tottenham H), 1961 v Ni, W, S, L, P, Sp; 1962 v S; 1963 v S, F, Br, Cz, EG; 1964 v W, Ni, R of W (15)
Smith, S. (Aston Villa), 1895 v S (1)
Smith, S. C. (Leicester C), 1936 v Ni (1)
Smith, T. (Birmingham C), 1960 v W, Se (2)
Smith, T. (Liverpool), 1971 v W (1)
Smith, W. H. (Huddersfield T), 1922 v W, S; 1928 v S (3)
Sorby, T. H. (Thursday Wanderers, Sheffield), 1879 v W (1)
Southgate, G. (Aston Villa), 1996 v P (sub), Bul, H (sub), Chn, Sw, S, Ho, Sp, G; 1997 v Mol, Pol, Ge, M, Ge (sub), S,Af, Pol, I, F, Br (19)
Southworth, J. (Blackburn R), 1889 v W; 1891 v W; 1892 v S (3)
Sparks, F. J. (Herts Rangers), 1879 v S; (with Clapham Rovers), 1880 v S, W (3)
Spence, J. W. (Manchester U), 1926 v Bel; 1927 v Ni (2)
Spence, R. (Chelsea), 1936 v A, Bel (2)
Spencer, C. W. (Newcastle U), 1924 v S; 1925 v W (2)
Spencer, H. (Aston Villa), 1897 v S, W; 1900 v W; 1903 v Ni; 1905 v W, S (6)
Spiksley, F. (Sheffield W), 1893 v S, W; 1894 v S, Ni; 1896 v Ni; 1898 v S, W (7)
Spilsbury, B. W. (Cambridge University), 1885 v Ni; 1886 v Ni, S (3)
Spink, N. (Aston Villa), 1983 v Aus (sub) (1)
Spouncer, W. A. (Nottingham F), 1900 v W (1)
Springett, R. D. G. (Sheffield W), 1960 v Ni, S, Y, Sp, H; 1961 v Ni, S, L, P, Sp, M, I, A; 1962 v W, Ni, S, A, Sw, Pe, L, P, H, Arg, Bul, Br; 1963 v Ni, W, F (2), Sw; 1966 v W, A, N (33)
Sproston, B. (Leeds U), 1937 v W; 1938 v S, W, Ni, Cz, G, Sw, F; (with Tottenham H), 1939 v W, R of E; (with Manchester C), N (11)
Squire, R. T. (Cambridge University), 1886 v S, W, Ni (3)
Stanbrough, M. H. (Old Carthusians), 1895 v W (1)
Staniforth, R. (Huddersfield T), 1954 v S, H, Y, Bel, Sw, U; 1955 v W, WG (8)
Starling, R. W. (Sheffield W), 1933 v S; (with Aston Villa), 1937 v S (2)
Statham, D. (WBA), 1983 v W, Aus (2) (3)
Steele, F. C. (Stoke C), 1937 v S, W, Ni, N, Se, Fi (6)
Stein, B. (Luton T), 1984 v F (1)
Stephenson, C. (Huddersfield T), 1924 v W (1)
Stephenson, G. T. (Derby Co), 1928 v F, Bel; (with Sheffield W), 1931 v F (3)
Stephenson, J. E. (Leeds U), 1938 v S; 1939 v Ni (2)
Stepney, A. C. (Manchester U), 1968 v Se (1)
Sterland, M. (Sheffield W), 1989 v S.Ar (1)
Steven, T. M. (Everton), 1985 v Ni, Ei, R, Fi, I, US (sub); 1986 v T (sub), Eg, USSR, Mal (sub), Pol, Para, Arg; 1987 v Se, Y (sub), Sp (sub); 1988 v T, Y, Ho, H, S, Sw, Ho, USSR; 1989 v S; (with Rangers), 1990 v Cz, Cam (sub), WG (sub), I; 1991 v Cam; (with Marseille), 1992 v G, C, Br, Fi, D (36)
Stevens, G. A. (Tottenham H), 1985 v Fi (sub), T (sub), Ni; 1986 v S (sub), M (sub), Mor (sub), Para (sub) (7)
Stevens, M. G. (Everton), 1985 v I, WG; 1986 v R, T, Ni, Eg, Is, S, Ca, P, Mor, Pol, Para, Arg; 1987 v Br, S; 1988 v T, Y, Is, Ho, H (sub), S, Sw, Ei, Ho, USSR; (with Rangers), 1989 v D, Se, Gr, Alb (2), S, Pol; 1990 v Se, Pol, I, Br, D, Tun, Ei, I; 1991 v USSR; 1992 v C, H, Br, Fi (46)
Stewart, J. (Sheffield W), 1907 v S, W; (with Newcastle U), 1911 v S (3)
Stewart, P. A. (Tottenham H), 1992 v G (sub), Cz (sub), C (sub) (3)
Stiles, N. P. (Manchester U), 1965 v S, H, Y, Se; 1966 v W, Ni, S, A, Sp, Pol (2), WG (2), N, D, U, M, F, Arg, P; 1967 v Ni, W, S, Cz; 1968 v USSR; 1969 v R; 1970 v Ni, S (28)
Stoker, J. (Birmingham), 1933 v W; 1934 v S, H (3)
Stone, S. B. (Nottingham F), 1996 v N (sub), Sw (sub), P, Bul, Cro, Chn (sub), Sw (sub), S (sub), Sp (sub) (9)
Storer, H. (Derby Co), 1924 v F; 1928 v Ni (2)
Storey, P. E. (Arsenal), 1971 v Gr, Ni, S; 1972 v Sw, WG, W, Ni, S; 1973 v W (3), Y, S (2), Ni, Cz, Pol, USSR, I (19)

Storey-Moore, I. (Nottingham F), 1970 v Ho (1)
Strange, A. H. (Sheffield W), 1930 v S, A, G; 1931 v S, W, Ni, F, Bel; 1932 v S, W, Ni, Sp; 1933 v S, Ni, A, I, Sw; 1934 v Ni, W, F (20)
Stratford, A. H. (Wanderers), 1874 v S (1)
Streten, B. (Luton T), 1950 v Ni (1)
Sturgess, A. (Sheffield U), 1911 v Ni; 1914 v S (2)
Summerbee, M. G. (Manchester C), 1968 v S, Sp, WG; 1972 v Sw, WG (sub), W, Ni; 1973 v USSR (sub) (8)
Sunderland, A. (Arsenal), 1980 v Aus (1)
Sutcliffe, J. W. (Bolton W), 1893 v W; 1895 v S, Ni; 1901 v S; (with Millwall), 1903 v W (5)
Swan, P. (Sheffield W), 1960 v Y, Sp, H; 1961 v Ni, W, S, L, P, Sp, M, I, A; 1962 v W, Ni, S, A, Sw, L, P (19)
Swepstone, H. A. (Pilgrims), 1880 v S; 1882 v S, W; 1883 v S, W, Ni (6)
Swift, F. V. (Manchester C), 1947 v S, W, Ni, Ei, Ho, F, Sw, P; 1948 v S, W, Ni, Bel, Se, I; 1949 v S, W, Ni, D, N (19)

Tait, G. (Birmingham Excelsior), 1881 v W (1)
Talbot, B. (Ipswich T), 1977 v Ni (sub), S, Br, Arg, U; (with Arsenal), 1980 v Aus (6)
Tambling, R. V. (Chelsea), 1963 v W, F; 1966 v Y (3)
Tate, J. T. (Aston Villa), 1931 v F, Bel; 1933 v W (3)
Taylor, E. (Blackpool), 1954 v H (1)
Taylor, E. H. (Huddersfield T), 1923 v S, W, Ni, Bel; 1924 v S, Ni, F; 1926 v S (8)
Taylor, J. G. (Fulham), 1951 v Arg, P (2)
Taylor, P. H. (Liverpool), 1948 v W, Ni, Se (3)
Taylor, P. J. (C Palace), 1976 v W (sub+1), Ni, S (4)
Taylor, T. (Manchester U), 1953 v Arg, Ch, U; 1954 v Bel, Sw; 1956 v S, Br, Se, Fi, WG; 1957 v Ni, Y (sub), D (2), Ei (2); 1958 v W, Ni, F (19)
Temple, D. W. (Everton), 1965 v WG (1)
Thickett, H. (Sheffield U), 1899 v S, W (2)
Thomas, D. (Coventry C), 1983 v Aus (1+1 sub) (2)
Thomas, D. (QPR), 1975 v Cz (sub), P, Cy (sub+1), W, S (sub); 1976 v Cz (sub), P (sub) (8)
Thomas, G. R. (C Palace), 1991 v T, USSR, Arg, Aus, Nz (2), Mal; 1992 v Pol, F (9)
Thomas, M. L. (Arsenal), 1989 v S.Ar; 1990 v Y (2)
Thompson, P. (Liverpool), 1964 v P (2), Ei, US, Br, Arg; 1965 v W, S, Bel, Ho; 1966 v Ni; 1968 v Ni, WG; 1970 v S, Ho (sub) (16)
Thompson, P. B. (Liverpool), 1976 v W (2), Ni, S, Br, I, Fi; 1977 v Fi; 1979 v Ei (sub), Cz, Ni, S, Bul, Se (sub), A; 1980 v D, Ni, Bul, Ei, Sp (2), Arg, W, S, Bel, I; 1981 v N, R, H; 1982 v N, H, W, Ho, S, Fi, F, Cz, K, WG, Sp; 1983 v WG, Gr (42)
Thompson T. (Aston Villa), 1952 v W; (with Preston NE), 1957 v S (2)
Thomson, R. A. (Wolverhampton W), 1964 v Ni, US, P, Arg; 1965 v Bel, Ho, Ni, W (8)
Thornewell, G. (Derby Co), 1923 v Se (2); 1924 v F; 1925 v F (4)
Thornley, I. (Manchester C), 1907 v W (1)
Tilson, S. F. (Manchester C), 1934 v H, Cz; 1935 v W; 1936 v Ni (4)
Titmuss, F. (Southampton), 1922 v W; 1923 v W (2)
Todd, C. (Derby Co), 1972 v Ni; 1974 v P, W, Ni, S, Arg, EG, Bul, Y; 1975 v P (sub), WG, Cy (2), Ni, W, S; 1976 v Sw, Cz, P, Ni, S, Br, Fi; 1977 v Ei, Fi, Ho (sub), Ni (27)
Toone, G. (Notts Co), 1892 v S, W (2)
Topham, A. G. (Casuals), 1894 v W (1)
Topham, R. (Wolverhampton W), 1893 v Ni; (with Casuals) 1894 v W (2)
Towers, M. A. (Sunderland), 1976 v W, Ni (sub), I (3)
Townley, W. J. (Blackburn R), 1889 v W; 1890 v Ni (2)
Townrow, J. E. (Clapton Orient), 1925 v S; 1926 v W (2)
Tremelling, D. R. (Birmingham), 1928 v W (1)
Tresadern, J. (West Ham U), 1923 v S, Se (2)
Tueart, D. (Manchester C), 1975 v Cy (sub), Ni; 1977 v Fi, Ni, W (sub), S (sub) (6)
Tunstall, F. E. (Sheffield U), 1923 v S; 1924 v S, W, Ni, F; 1925 v Ni, S (7)
Turnbull, R. J. (Bradford), 1920 v Ni (1)
Turner, A. (Southampton), 1900 v Ni; 1901 v Ni (2)
Turner, H. (Huddersfield T), 1931 v F, Bel (2)
Turner, J. A. (Bolton W), 1893 v W; (with Stoke C) 1895 v Ni; (with Derby Co) 1898 v Ni (3)
Tweedy, G. J. (Grimsby T), 1937 v H (1)

Ufton, D. G. (Charlton Ath), 1954 v R of E (1)
Underwood, A. (Stoke C), 1891 v Ni; 1892 v Ni (2)
Unsworth, D. G. (Everton), 1995 v J (1)
Urwin, T. (Middlesbrough), 1923 v Se (2); 1924 v Bel; (with Newcastle U), 1926 v W (4)
Utley, G. (Barnsley), 1913 v Ni (1)

Vaughton, O. H. (Aston Villa), 1882 v S, W, Ni; 1884 v S, W (5)
Veitch, C. C. M. (Newcastle U), 1906 v S, W, Ni; 1907 v S, W; 1909 v W (6)
Veitch, J. G. (Old Westminsters), 1894 v W (1)
Venables, T. F. (Chelsea), 1965 v Ho, Bel (2)
Venison, B. (Newcastle U), 1995 v US, U (2)
Vidal, R. W. S. (Oxford University), 1873 v S (1)
Viljoen, C. (Ipswich T), 1975 v Ni, W (2)
Viollet, D. S. (Manchester U), 1960 v H; 1962 v L (2)
Von Donop (Royal Engineers), 1873 v S; 1875 v S (2)

Wace, H. (Wanderers), 1878 v S; 1879 v S, W (2)
Waddle, C. R. (Newcastle U), 1985 v Ei, R (sub), Fi (sub), S (sub), I, M (sub); (with Tottenham H), 1986 v R, T, Ni, Is, USSR, S, M, Ca, P, Mor, Pol (sub), Arg (sub); 1987 v Se (sub), Ni (2), Y, Sp, T, Br, S; 1988 v WG, Is, H, S (sub), Co, Sw (sub), Ei, Ho (sub); 1989 v Se, S.Ar, Alb (2), Ch, S, Pol, D (sub); (with Marseille), 1990 v Se, Pol, I, Y, Br, D, U, Tun, Ei, Ho, Eg, Bel, Cam, WG, I (sub); 1991 v H (sub), Pol (sub); 1992 v T (62)
Wadsworth, S. J. (Huddersfield T), 1922 v S; 1923 v S, Bel; 1924 v S, Ni; 1925 v S, Ni; 1926 v W; 1927 v Ni (9)
Wainscoat, W. R. (Leeds U), 1929 v S (1)
Waiters, A. K. (Blackpool), 1964 v Ei, Br; 1965 v W, Bel, Ho (5)
Walker, D. S. (Nottingham F), 1989 v D (sub), Se (sub), Gr, Alb (2), Ch, S, Pol, D; 1990 v Se, Pol, I, Y, Br, Cz, D, U, Tun, Ei, Ho, Eg, Bel, Cam, WG, I; 1991 v H, Pol, Ei (2), Cam, T, Arg, Aus, Nz (2), Mal; 1992 v T, Pol, F, Cz, C H, Br, Fi, D, F, Se; (with Sampdoria), 1993 v Sp, N, T, Sm, T, Ho, Pol, N, US (sub), Br, G; (with Sheffield W), 1994 v Sm (59)
Walker, I. M. (Tottenham H), 1996 v H (sub), Chn (sub); 1997 v I (3)
Walden, F. I. (Tottenham H), 1914 v S; 1922 v W (2)
Walker, W. H. (Aston Villa), 1921 v Ni; 1922 v Ni, W, S; 1923 v Se (2); 1924 v S; 1925 v Ni, W, S, Bel, F; 1926 v Ni, W, S; 1927 v Ni, W; 1933 v A (18)
Wall, G. (Manchester U), 1907 v W; 1908 v Ni; 1909 v S; 1910 v W, S; 1912 v S; 1913 v Ni (7)
Wallace, C. W. (Aston Villa), 1913 v W; 1914 v Ni; 1920 v S (3)
Wallace, D. L. (Southampton), 1986 v Eg (1)
Walsh, P. (Luton T), 1983 v Aus (2 + 1 sub); 1984 v F, W (5)
Walters, A. M. (Cambridge University), 1885 v S, N; 1886 v S; 1887 v S, W; (with Old Carthusians), 1889 v S, W; 1890 v S, W (9)
Walters, K. M. (Rangers), 1991 v Nz (1)
Walters, P. M. (Oxford University), 1885 v S, Ni; (with Old Carthusians), 1886 v S, W, Ni; 1887 v S, W; 1888 v S, Ni; 1889 v S, W; 1890 v S, W (13)
Walton, N. (Blackburn R), 1890 v Ni (1)
Ward, J. T. (Blackburn Olympic), 1885 v W (1)
Ward, P. (Brighton & HA), 1980 v Aus (sub) (1)
Ward, T. V. (Derby Co), 1948 v Bel; 1949 v W (2)
Waring, T. (Aston Villa), 1931 v F, Bel; 1932 v S, W, Ni (5)
Warner, C. (Upton Park), 1878 v S (1)
Warren, B. (Derby Co), 1906 v S, W, Ni; 1907 v S, W, Ni; 1908 v S, W, Ni, A (2), H, B; (with Chelsea), 1909 v S, Ni, W, H (2), A; 1911 v S, Ni, W (22)
Waterfield, G. S. (Burnley), 1927 v W (1)
Watson, D. (Norwich C), 1984 v Br, U, Ch; 1985 v M, US (sub); 1986 v S; (with Everton), 1987 v Ni; 1988 v Is, Ho, S, Sw (sub), USSR (12)
Watson, D. V. (Sunderland), 1974 v P, S (sub), Arg, EG, Bul, Y; 1975 v Cz, P, WG, Cy (2), Ni, W, S; (with Manchester C), 1976 v Sw, Cz (sub), P; 1977 v Ho, L, Ni, W, S, Br, Arg, U; 1978 v Sw, L, I, WG, Br, W, Ni, S, H; 1979 v D, Ei, Cz, Ni (2), W, S, Bul, Se, A; (with Werder Bremen), 1980 v D; (with Southampton), Ni, Bul, Ei, Sp (2), Arg, Ni, S, Bel, I; 1981 v N, R, Sw, R, W, S, Sw, H; (with Stoke C), 1982 v Ni, Ic (65)
Watson, V. M. (West Ham U), 1923 v W, S; 1930 v S, G, A (5)
Watson, W. (Burnley), 1913 v S; 1914 v Ni; 1920 v Ni (3)
Watson, W. (Sunderland), 1950 v Ni, I; 1951 v W, Y (4)
Weaver, S. (Newcastle U), 1932 v S, 1933 v S, Ni (3)
Webb, G. W. (West Ham U), 1911 v S, W (2)
Webb, N. J. (Nottingham F), 1988 v WG (sub), T, Y, Is, Ho, S, Sw, Ei, USSR (sub); 1989 v D, Se, Gr, Alb (2), Ch, S, Pol, D; (with Manchester U), 1990 v Se, I (sub); 1992 v F, H, Br (sub), Fi, D (sub), Se (26)
Webster, M. (Middlesbrough), 1930 v S, A, G (3)
Wedlock, W. J. (Bristol C), 1907 v S, Ni, W; 1908 v S, Ni, W, A (2), H, B; 1909 v S, W, Ni, H (2), A; 1910 v S, W, Ni; 1911 v S, W, Ni; 1912 v S, W, Ni; 1914 v W (26)
Weir, D. (Bolton W), 1889 v S, Ni (2)

Welch, R. de C. (Wanderers), 1872 v S; (with Harrow Chequers), 1874 v S (2)
Weller, K. (Leicester C), 1974 v W, Ni, S, Arg (4)
Welsh, D. (Charlton Ath), 1938 v G, Sw; 1939 v R (3)
West, G. (Everton), 1969 v W, Bul, M (3)
Westwood, R. W. (Bolton W), 1935 v S, W, Ho; 1936 v Ni, G; 1937 v W (6)
Whateley, O. (Aston Villa), 1883 v S, Ni (2)
Wheeler, J. E. (Bolton W), 1955 v Ni (1)
Wheldon, G. F. (Aston Villa), 1897 v Ni; 1898 v S, W, Ni (4)
White, D. (Manchester C), 1993 v Sp (1)
White, T. A. (Everton), 1933 v I (1)
Whitehead, J. (Accrington), 1893 v W; (with Blackburn R), 1894 v Ni (2)
Whitfeld, H. (Old Etonians), 1879 v W (1)
Whitham, M. (Sheffield U), 1892 v Ni (1)
Whitworth, S. (Leicester C), 1975 v WG, Cy, Ni, W, S; 1976 v Sw, P (7)
Whymark, T. J. (Ipswich T), 1978 v L (sub) (1)
Widdowson, S. W. (Nottingham F), 1880 v S (1)
Wignall, F. (Nottingham F), 1965 v W, Ho (2)
Wilcox, J. M. (Blackburn R), 1996 v H (1)
Wilkes, A. (Aston Villa), 1901 v S, W; 1902 v S, W, Ni (5)
Wilkins, R. G. (Chelsea), 1976 v I; 1977 v Ei, Fi, Ni, Br, Arg, U; 1978 v Sw (sub), L, I, WG, W, Ni, S, H; 1979 v D, Ei, Cz, Ni, W, S, Bul, Se (sub), A; (with Manchester U), 1980 v D, Ni, Bul, Sp (2), Arg, W (sub), Ni, S, Bel, I; 1981 v Sp (sub), R, Br, W, S, Sw, H (sub); 1982 v Ni, W, Ho, S, Fi, F, Cz, K, WG, Sp; 1983 v D, WG; 1984 v D, Ni, W, S, USSR, Br, U, Ch; (with AC Milan), 1985 v EG, Fi, T, Ni, Ei, R, Fi, S, I, M; 1986 v T, Ni, Is, Eg, USSR, S, M, Ca, P, Mor; 1987 v Se, Y (sub) (84)
Wilkinson, B. (Sheffield U), 1904 v S (1)
Wilkinson, L. R. (Oxford University), 1891 v W (1)
Williams, B. F. (Wolverhampton W), 1949 v F; 1950 v S, W, Ei, I, P, Bel, Ch, US, Sp; 1951 v Ni, W, S, Y, Arg, P; 1952 v W, F; 1955 v S, WG, F, Sp, P; 1956 v W (24)
Williams, O. (Clapton Orient), 1923 v W, Ni (2)
Williams, S. (Southampton), 1983 v Aus (1+1 sub); 1984 v F; 1985 v EG, Fi, T (6)
Williams, W. (WBA), 1897 v Ni; 1898 v W, Ni, S; 1899 v W, Ni (6)
Williamson, E. C. (Arsenal), 1923 v Se (2) (2)
Williamson, R. G. (Middlesbrough), 1905 v Ni; 1911 v Ni, S, W; 1912 v S, W; 1913 v Ni (7)
Willingham, C. K. (Huddersfield T), 1937 v Fi; 1938 v S, G, Sw, F; 1939 v S, W, Ni, R of E, N, I, Y (12)
Willis, A. (Tottenham H), 1952 v F (1)
Wilshaw, D. J. (Wolverhampton W), 1954 v W, Sw, U; 1955 v S, F, Sp, P; 1956 v W, Ni, Fi, WG; 1957 v Ni (12)
Wilson, C. P. (Hendon), 1884 v S, W (2)
Wilson, C. W. (Oxford University), 1879 v W; 1881 v S (2)
Wilson, G. (Sheffield W), 1921 v S, W, Bel; 1922 v S, Ni; 1923 v S, W, Ni, Bel; 1924 v W, Ni, F (12)
Wilson, G. P. (Corinthians), 1900 v S, W (2)
Wilson, R. (Huddersfield T), 1960 v S, Y, Sp, H; 1962 v W, Ni, S, A, Sw, Pe, P, H, Arg, Bul, Br; 1963 v Ni, F, Br, Cz, EG, Sw; 1964 v W, S, R of W, U, P (2), Ei, Br, Arg; (with Everton), 1965 v S, H, Y, WG, Se; 1966 v WG (sub), W, Ni, A, Sp, Pol (2), Y, Fi, D, U, M, F, Arg, P, WG; 1967 v Ni, W, S, Cz, A; 1968 v Ni, S, USSR (2), Sp (2), Y (63)
Wilson, T. (Huddersfield T), 1928 v S (1)
Winckworth, W. N. (Old Westminsters), 1892 v W; 1893 v Ni (2)
Windridge, J. E. (Chelsea), 1908 v S, W, Ni, A (2), H, B; 1909 v Ni (8)
Wingfield-Stratford, C. V. (Royal Engineers), 1877 v S (1)
Winterburn, N. (Arsenal), 1990 v I (sub); 1993 v G (sub) (2)
Wise, D. F. (Chelsea), 1991 v T, USSR, Aus (sub), Nz (2); 1994 v N; 1995 v R (sub), Ng; 1996 v Co, N, P, H (sub) (12)
Withe, P. (Aston Villa), 1981 v Br, S; 1982 v N (sub), W, Ic; 1983 v H, Ni, S; 1984 v H (sub); 1985 v T (11)
Wollaston, C. H. R. (Wanderers), 1874 v S; 1875 v S; 1877 v S; 1880 v S (4)
Wolstenholme, S. (Everton), 1904 v S; (with Blackburn R), 1905 v W, Ni (3)
Wood, H. (Wolverhampton W), 1890 v S, W; 1896 v S (3)
Wood, R. E. (Manchester U), 1955 v Ni, W; 1956 v Fi (3)
Woodcock, A. S. (Nottingham F), 1978 v Ni; 1979 v Ei (sub), Cz, Bul (sub), Se; 1980 v Ni; (with Cologne), Bul, Ei, Sp (2), Arg, Bel, I; 1981 v N, R, Sw, R, W (sub), S; 1982 v Ni (sub), Ho, Fi (sub), WG (sub), Sp; (with Arsenal), 1983 v WG (sub), Gr, L, Gr; 1984 v L, F (sub), Ni, W, S, Br, U (sub); 1985 v EG, Fi, T, Ni; 1986 v R (sub), T (sub), Is (sub) (42)
Woodger, G. (Oldham Ath), 1911 v Ni (1)
Woodhall, G. (WBA), 1888 v S, W (2)

Woodley, V. R. (Chelsea), 1937 v S, N, Se, Fi; 1938 v S, W, Ni, Cz, G, Sw, F; 1939 v S, W, Ni, R of E, N, I, R, Y (19)
Woods, C. C. E. (Norwich C), 1985 v US; 1986 v Eg (sub), Is (sub), Ca (sub); (with Rangers), 1987 v Y, Sp (sub), Ni (sub), T, S; 1988 v Is, H, Sw (sub), USSR; 1989 v D (sub); 1990 v Br (sub), D (sub); 1991 v H, Pol, Ei, USSR, Aus, Nz (2), Mal; (with Sheffield W), 1992 v G, T, Pol, F, C, Br, Fi, D, F, Se; 1993 v Sp, N, T, Sm, T, Ho, Pol, N, US (43)
Woodward, V. J. (Tottenham H), 1903 v S, W, Ni; 1904 v S, Ni; 1905 v S, W, Ni; 1907 v S; 1908 v S, W, Ni, A (2), H, B; 1909 v W, Ni, H (2), A; (with Chelsea), 1910 v Ni; 1911 v W (23)
Woosnam, M. (Manchester C), 1922 v W (1)
Worrall, F. (Portsmouth), 1935 v Ho; 1937 v Ni (2)
Worthington, F. S. (Leicester C), 1974 v Ni (sub), S, Arg, EG, Bul, Y; 1975 v Cz, P (sub) (8)
Wreford-Brown, C. (Oxford University), 1889 v Ni; (with Old Carthusians), 1894 v W; 1895 v W; 1898 v S (4)
Wright, E, G. D. (Cambridge University), 1906 v W (1)
Wright, I. E. (C Palace), 1991 v Cam, Ei (sub), USSR, Nz; (with Arsenal), 1992 v H (sub); 1993 v N, T (2), Pol (sub), N (sub), US (sub), Br, G (sub); 1994 v Pol, Ho (sub), Sm, Gr (sub); 1995 v US (sub), R; 1997 v Ge (sub), I (sub), M (sub), S.Af, I, F, Br (sub) (27)
Wright, J. D. (Newcastle U), 1939 v N (1)
Wright, M. (Southampton), 1984 v W; 1985 v EG, Fi, T, Ei, R, I, WG; 1986 v R, T, Ni, Eg, USSR; 1987 v Y, Ni, S;

(with Derby Co), 1988 v Is, Ho (sub), Co, Sw, Ei, Ho; 1990 v Cz (sub), Tun (sub), Ho, Eg, Bel, Cam, WG, I; 1991 v H, Pol, Ei (2), Cam, USSR, Arg, Aus, Nz, Mal; (with Liverpool), 1992 v F, Fi; 1993 v Sp; 1996 v Cro, H (45)
Wright, T. J. (Everton), 1968 v USSR; 1969 v R (2), M (sub), U, Br; 1970 v W, Ho, Bel, R (sub), Br (11)
Wright, W. A. (Wolverhampton W), 1947 v S, W, Ni, Ei, Ho, F, Sw, P; 1948 v S, W, Ni, Bel, Se, I; 1949 v S, W, Ni, D, Sw, Se, N, F; 1950 v S, W, Ni, Ei, I, P, Bel, Ch, US, Sp; 1951 v Ni, S, Arg; 1952 v W, Ni, S, F, A (2), I, Sw; 1953 v Ni, W, S, Bel, Arg, Ch, U, US; 1954 v W, Ni, S, R of E, H (2), Y, Bel, Sw, U; 1955 v W, Ni, S, WG, F, Sp, P; 1956 v Ni, W, S, Br, Se, Fi, WG, D, Sp; 1957 v S, W, Ni, Y, D (2), Ei (2); 1958 v W, Ni, S, P, Y, USSR (3), Br, A, F; 1959 v W, Ni, S, USSR, I, Br, Pe, M, US (105)
Wylie, J. G. (Wanderers), 1878 v S (1)

Yates, J. (Burnley), 1889 v Ni (1)
York, R. E. (Aston Villa), 1922 v S; 1926 v S (2)
Young, A. (Huddersfield T), 1933 v W; 1937 v S, H, N, Se; 1938 v G, Sw, F; 1939 v W (9)
Young, G. M. (Sheffield W), 1965 v W (1)

R. E. Evans also played for Wales against E, Ni, S; J. Reynolds also played for Ireland against E, W, S.

NORTHERN IRELAND

Aherne, T. (Belfast C), 1947 v E; 1948 v S; 1949 v W; (with Luton T), 1950 v W (4)
Alexander, A. (Cliftonville), 1895 v S (1)
Allen, C. A. (Cliftonville), 1936 v E (1)
Allen, J. (Limavady), 1887 v E (1)
Anderson, T. (Manchester U), 1973 v Cy, E, S, W; 1974 v Bul, P; (with Swindon T), 1975 v S (sub); 1976 v Is; 1977 v Ho, Bel, WG, E, S, W, Ic; 1978 v Ic, Ho, Bel; (with Peterborough U), S, E, W; 1979 v D (sub) (22)
Anderson, W. (Linfield), 1898 v W, E, S; 1899 v S (4)
Andrews, W. (Glentoran), 1908 v S; (with Grimsby T), 1913 v E, S (3)
Armstrong, G. (Tottenham H), 1977 v WG, E, W (sub), Ic (sub); 1978 v Bel, S, E, W; 1979 v Ei, D, Bul, E, Bul, E, S, W, D; 1980 v E, Ei, Is, S, E, W, Aus (3); 1981 v Se; (with Watford), P, S, P, S, Se; 1982 v Is, E, F, W, Y, Hon, Sp, A, F; 1983 v A, T, Alb, S, E, W; (with Real Mallorca), 1984 v A, WG, E, W, Fi; 1985 v R, Fi, E, Sp; (with WBA), 1986 v T, R (sub), E (sub), F (sub); (with Chesterfield), D (sub), Br (sub) (63)

Baird, G. (Distillery), 1896 v S, E, W (3)
Baird, H. (Huddersfield T), 1939 v E (1)
Balfe, J. (Shelbourne), 1909 v E; 1910 v W (2)
Bambrick, J. (Linfield), 1929 v W, S, E; 1930 v W, S, E; 1932 v W; (with Chelsea), 1935 v W; 1936 v E, S; 1938 v W (11)
Banks, S. J. (Cliftonville), 1937 v W (1)
Barr, H. H. (Linfield), 1962 v E; (with Coventry C), 1963 v E, Pol (3)
Barron, H. (Cliftonville), 1894 v E, W, S; 1895 v S; 1896 v S; 1897 v E, W (7)
Barry, H. (Bohemians), 1900 v S (1)
Baxter, R. A. (Cliftonville), 1887 v S, W (2)
Bennett, L. V. (Dublin University), 1889 v W (1)
Berry, J. (Cliftonville), 1888 v S, W; 1889 v E (3)
Best, G. (Manchester U), 1964 v W, U; 1965 v E, Ho (2), S, Sw (2), Alb; 1966 v S, E, Alb; 1967 v E; 1968 v S; 1969 v E, S, W, T; 1970 v S, E, W, USSR; 1971 v Cy (2), Sp, E, S, W; 1972 v USSR, Sp; 1973 v Bul; 1974 v P; (with Fulham), 1977 v Ho, Bel, WG; 1978 v Ic, Ho (37)
Bingham, W. L. (Sunderland), 1951 v F; 1952 v E, S, W; 1953 v E, S, F, W; 1954 v E, S, W; 1955 v E, S, W; 1956 v E, S, W; 1957 v E, S, W, P (2), I; 1958 v S, E, W, I (2), Arg, Cz (2), WG, F; (with Luton T), 1959 v E, S, W, Sp; 1960 v S, E, W; (with Everton), 1961 v E, S, WG (2), Gr, I; 1962 v E, Gr; 1963 v E, S, Pol (2), Sp; (with Port Vale), 1964 v S, E, Sp (56)
Black, J. (Glentoran), 1901 v E (1)
Black, K. (Luton T), 1988 v Fr (sub), Ma (sub); 1989 v Ei, H, Sp (2), Ch (sub); 1990 v H, N, U; 1991 v Y (2), D, A, Pol, Fa; (with Nottingham F), 1992 v Fa, A, D, S, Li, G; 1993 v Sp, D (sub), Alb, Ei (sub), Sp; 1994 v D (sub), Ei (sub), R (sub) (30)
Blair, H. (Portadown), 1931 v S; 1932 v S; (with Swansea), 1934 v S (3)
Blair, J. (Cliftonville), 1907 v W, E, S; 1908 v E, S (5)
Blair, R. V. (Oldham Ath), 1975 v Se (sub), S (sub), W; 1976 v Se, Is (5)

Blanchflower, R. D. (Barnsley), 1950 v S, W; 1951 v E, S; (with Aston Villa), F; 1952 v W; 1953 v E, S, W, F; 1954 v E, S, W; 1955 v E, S (with Tottenham H), W; 1956 v E, S, W; 1957 v E, S, W, I, P (2); 1958 v E, S, W, I (2), Cz (2), Arg, F, WG; 1959 v E, S, W, Sp; 1960 v E, S, W; 1961 v E, S, W, WG (2); 1962 v E, S, W, Gr, Ho; 1963 v E, S, Pol (2) (56)
Blanchflower, J. (Manchester U), 1954 v W; 1955 v E, S; 1956 v S, W; 1957 v S, E, P; 1958 v S, E, I (2) (12)
Bookman, L. O. (Bradford C), 1914 v W; (with Luton T), 1921 v S, W; 1922 v E (4)
Bothwell, A. W. (Ards), 1926 v S, E, W; 1927 v E, W (5)
Bowler, G. C. (Hull C), 1950 v E, S, W (3)
Boyle, P. (Sheffield U), 1901 v E; 1902 v E; 1903 v S, W; 1904 v E (5)
Braithwaite, R. S. (Linfield), 1962 v W; 1963 v P, Sp; (with Middlesbrough), 1964 v W, U; 1965 v E, S, Sw (2), Ho (10)
Breen, T. (Belfast C), 1935 v E, W; 1937 v E, S; (with Manchester U), 1937 v W; 1938 v E, S; 1939 v W, S (9)
Brennan, B. (Bohemians), 1912 v W (1)
Brennan, R. A. (Luton T), 1949 v W; (with Birmingham C), 1950 v E, S, W; (with Fulham), 1951 v E (5)
Briggs, W. R. (Manchester U), 1962 v W; (with Swansea T), 1965 v Ho (2)
Brisby, D. (Distillery), 1891 v S (1)
Brolly, T. (Millwall), 1937 v W; 1938 v W; 1939 v E, W (4)
Brookes, E. A. (Shelbourne), 1920 v S (1)
Brotherston, N. (Blackburn R), 1980 v S, E, W, Aus (3); 1981 v Se, P; 1982 v S, Is, E, F, S, W, Hon (sub), A (sub); 1983 v A (sub), WG, Alb, T, Alb, S (sub), E (sub), W; 1984 v T; 1985 v Is (sub), T (27)
Brown, J. (Glenavon), 1921 v W; (with Tranmere R), 1924 v E, W (3)
Brown, J. (Wolverhampton W), 1935 v E, W; 1936 v E; (with Coventry C), 1937 v E, W; 1938 v S, W; (with Birmingham C), 1939 v E, S, W (10)
Brown, W. G. (Glenavon), 1926 v W (1)
Brown, W. M. (Limavady), 1887 v E (1)
Browne, F. (Cliftonville), 1887 v E, S, W; 1888 v E, S (5)
Browne, R. J. (Leeds U), 1936 v E, W; 1938 v E, W; 1939 v E, S (6)
Bruce, W. (Glentoran), 1961 v S; 1967 v W (2)
Buckle, H. (Cliftonville), 1882 v E (1)
Buckle, H. R. (Sunderland), 1904 v E; (with Bristol R), 1908 v W (2)
Burnett, J. (Distillery), 1894 v E, W, S; (with Glentoran), 1895 v E, W (5)
Burnison, J. (Distillery), 1901 v E, W (2)
Burnison, S. (Distillery), 1908 v E; 1910 v E, S; (with Bradford), 1911 v E, S, W; (with Distillery), 1912 v E; 1913 v W (8)
Burns, J. (Glenavon), 1923 v E (1)
Butler, M. P. (Blackpool), 1939 v W (1)

Campbell, A. C. (Crusaders), 1963 v W; 1965 v Sw (2)
Campbell, D. A. (Nottingham F), 1986 v Mor (sub), Br; 1987 v E (2), T, Y; (with Charlton Ath), 1988 v Y, T (sub), Gr (sub), Pol (sub) (10)

Campbell, J. (Cliftonville), 1896 v W; 1897 v E, S, W; (with Distillery), 1898 v E, S, W; (with Cliftonville), 1899 v E; 1900 v E, S; 1901 v S, W; 1902 v S; 1903 v E; 1904 v S (15)

Campbell, J. P. (Fulham), 1951 v E, S (2)

Campbell, R. (Bradford C), 1982 v S, W (sub) (2)

Campbell, W. G. (Dundee), 1968 v S, E; 1969 v T; 1970 v S, W, USSR (6)

Carey, J. J. (Manchester U), 1947 v E, S, W; 1948 v E; 1949 v E, S, W (7)

Carroll, E. (Glenavon), 1925 v S (1)

Carroll, R. E. (Wigan Ath), 1997 v Th (sub) (1)

Casey, T. (Newcastle U), 1955 v W; 1956 v W; 1957 v E, S, W, I, P (2); 1958 v WG, F; (with Portsmouth), 1959 v E, Sp (12)

Cashin, M. (Cliftonville), 1898 v S (1)

Caskey, B. (Derby Co), 1979 v Bul, E, Bul, E, D (sub); 1980 v E (sub); (with Tulsa R), 1982 v F (sub) (7)

Cassidy, T. (Newcastle U), 1971 v E (sub); 1972 v USSR (sub); 1974 v Bul (sub), S, E, W; 1975 v N; 1976 v S, E, W; 1977 v WG (sub); 1980 v E, Ei (sub), Is, S, E, W, Aus (3); (with Burnley), 1981 v Se, P; 1982 v Is, Sp (sub) (24)

Caughey, M. (Linfield), 1986 v F (sub), D (sub) (2)

Chambers, J. (Distillery), 1921 v W; (with Bury), 1928 v E, S, W; 1929 v E, S, W; 1930 v S, W; (with Nottingham F), 1932 v E, S, W (12)

Chatton, H. A. (Partick T), 1925 v E, S; 1926 v E (3)

Christian, J. (Linfield), 1889 v S (1)

Clarke, C. J. (Bournemouth), 1986 v F, D, Mor, Alg (sub), Sp, Br; (with Southampton), 1987 v E, T, Y; 1988 v Y, T, Gr, Pol, F, Ma; 1989 v Ei, H, Sp (1+1 sub); (with QPR), Ma, Ch; 1990 v H, Ei, N; (with Portsmouth), 1991 v Y (sub), D, A, Pol, Y (sub), Fa; 1992 v Fa, D, S, G; 1993 v Alb, Sp, D (38)

Clarke, R. (Belfast C), 1901 v E, S (2)

Cleary, J. (Glentoran), 1982 v S, W; 1983 v W (sub); 1984 v T (sub); 1985 v Is (5)

Clements, D. (Coventry C), 1965 v W, Ho; 1966 v M; 1967 v S, W; 1968 v S, E; 1969 v T (2), S, W; 1970 v S, E, W, USSR (2); 1971 v Sp, E, S, W, Cy; (with Sheffield W), 1972 v USSR (2), Sp, E, S, W; 1973 v Bul, Cy (2), P, E, S, W; (with Everton), 1974 v Bul, P, S, E, W; 1975 v N, Y, E, S, W; 1976 v Se, Y; (with New York Cosmos), E, W (48)

Clugston, J. (Cliftonville), 1888 v W; 1889 v W, S, E; 1890 v E, S; 1891 v E, W; 1892 v E, S, W; 1893 v E, S, W (14)

Cochrane, D. (Leeds U), 1939 v E, W; 1947 v E, S, W; 1948 v E, S, W; 1949 v S, W; 1950 v S, E (12)

Cochrane, M. (Distillery), 1898 v S, W, E; 1899 v E; 1900 v E, S, W; (with Leicester Fosse), 1901 v S (8)

Cochrane, T. (Coleraine), 1976 v N (sub); (with Burnley), 1978 v S (sub), E (sub), W (sub); 1979 v Ei (sub); (with Middlesbrough), D, Bul, E, Bul, E; 1980 v Is, E (sub), W (sub), Aus (1+2 sub); 1981 v Se (sub), P (sub), S, P, S, Se; 1982 v E (sub), F; (with Gillingham), 1984 v S, Fi (sub) (26)

Collins, F. (Celtic), 1922 v S (1)

Condy, J. (Distillery), 1882 v W; 1886 v E, S (3)

Connell, T. (Coleraine), 1978 v W (sub) (1)

Connor, J. (Glentoran), 1901 v S, E; (with Belfast C), 1905 v E, S, W; 1907 v E, S; 1908 v E, S; 1909 v W; 1911 v S, E, W (13)

Connor, M. J. (Brentford), 1903 v S, W; (with Fulham), 1904 v E (3)

Cook, W. (Celtic), 1933 v E, W, S; (with Everton), 1935 v E; 1936 v S, W; 1937 v E, S, W; 1938 v E, S, W; 1939 v E, S, W (15)

Cooke, S. (Belfast YMCA), 1889 v E; (with Cliftonville), 1890 v E, S (3)

Coulter, J. (Belfast C), 1934 v E, S, W; (with Everton), 1935 v E, S, W; 1937 v S, W; (with Grimsby T), 1938 v S, W; (with Chelmsford C), 1939 v S (11)

Cowan, J. (Newcastle U), 1970 v E (sub) (1)

Cowan, T. S. (Queen's Island), 1925 v W (1)

Coyle, L. (Derry C), 1989 v Ch (sub) (1)

Coyle, R. (Coleraine), 1956 v E, S; 1957 v P; (with Nottingham F), 1958 v Arg (4)

Coyle, L. (Derry C), 1989 v Ch (sub) (1)

Coyle, R. I. (Sheffield W), 1973 v P, Cy (sub), W (sub); 1974 v Bul (sub), P (sub) (5)

Craig, A. B. (Rangers), 1908 v E, S, W; 1909 v S; (with Morton), 1912 v S, W; 1914 v E, S, W (9)

Craig, D. J. (Newcastle U), 1967 v W; 1968 v W; 1969 v T (2), E, S, W; 1970 v E, S, W, USSR; 1971 v Cy (2), Sp, S (sub); 1972 v USSR, S (sub); 1973 v Cy (2), E, S, W; 1974 v Bul, P; 1975 v N (25)

Crawford, S. (Distillery), 1889 v E, W; (with Cliftonville), 1891 v E, S, W; 1893 v E, W (7)

Croft, T. (Queen's Island), 1924 v E (1)

Crone, R. (Distillery), 1889 v S; 1890 v E, S, W (4)

Crone, W. (Distillery), 1882 v W; 1884 v E, S, W; 1886 v E, S, W; 1887 v E; 1888 v E, W; 1889 v S; 1890 v W (12)

Crooks, W. (Manchester U), 1922 v W (1)

Crossan, E. (Blackburn R), 1950 v S; 1951 v E; 1955 v W (3)

Crossan, J. A. (Sparta-Rotterdam), 1960 v E; (with Sunderland), 1963 v W, P, Sp; 1964 v E, S, W, U, Sp; 1965 v E, S, Sw (2); (with Manchester C), W, Ho (2), Alb; 1966 v S, E, Alb, WG; 1967 v E, S; (with Middlesbrough), 1968 v S (24)

Crothers, C. (Distillery), 1907 v W (1)

Cumming, L. (Huddersfield T), 1929 v W, S; (with Oldham Ath), 1930 v E (3)

Cunningham, R. (Ulster), 1892 v S, E, W; 1893 v E (4)

Cunningham, W. E. (St Mirren), 1951 v W; 1953 v E; 1954 v S; 1955 v S; (with Leicester C), 1956 v E, S, W; 1957 v E, S, W, I, P (2); 1958 v S, W, I, Cz (2), Arg, WG, F; 1959 v E, S, W; 1960 v E, S, W; (with Dunfermline Ath), 1961 v W; 1962 v W, Ho (30)

Curran, S. (Belfast C), 1926 v S, W; 1928 v S (3)

Curran, J. J. (Glenavon), 1922 v W; (with Pontypridd), 1923 v E, S; (with Glenavon), 1924 v E (4)

Cush, W. W. (Glenavon), 1951 v E, S; 1954 v S, E; 1957 v W, I, P (2); (with Leeds U), 1958 v I (2), W, Cz (2), Arg, WG, F; 1959 v S, W, Sp; 1960 v E, S, W; (with Portadown), 1961 v WG, Gr; 1962 v Gr (26)

Dalton, W. (YMCA), 1888 v S; (with Linfield), 1890 v S, W; 1891 v S, W; 1892 v E, S, W; 1894 v E, S, W (11)

D'Arcy, S. D. (Chelsea), 1952 v W; 1953 v E; (with Brentford), 1953 v S, W, F (5)

Darling, J. (Linfield), 1897 v E, S; 1900 v S; 1902 v E, S, W; 1903 v E, S, W; 1905 v E, S, W; 1906 v E, S, W; 1908 v W; 1909 v E; 1910 v E, S, W; 1912 v S (21)

Davey, H. H. (Reading), 1926 v E; 1927 v E, S; 1928 v E; (with Portsmouth), 1928 v W (5)

Davis, T. L. (Oldham Ath), 1937 v E (1)

Davison, A. J. (Bolton W), 1996 v Se; (with Bradford C), 1997 v Th (2)

Davison, J. R. (Cliftonville), 1882 v E, W; 1883 v E, W; 1884 v E, W, S; 1885 v E (8)

Dennison, R. (Wolverhampton W), 1988 v F, Ma; 1989 v H, Sp Ch (sub); 1990 v Ei, U; 1991 v Y (2), A, Pol, Fa (sub); 1992 v Fa, A, D (sub); 1993 v Sp (sub); 1994 v Co (sub); 1997 v I (sub) (18)

Devine, J. (Glentoran), 1990 v U (sub) (1)

Devine, W. (Limavady), 1886 v E, W; 1887 v W; 1888 v W (4)

Dickson, D. (Coleraine), 1970 v S (sub), W; 1973 v Cy, P (4)

Dickson, T. A. (Linfield), 1957 v S (1)

Dickson, W. (Chelsea), 1951 v W, F; 1952 v E, S, W; 1953 v E, S, W, F; (with Arsenal), 1954 v E, W; 1955 v E (12)

Diffin, W. (Belfast C), 1931 v W (1)

Dill, A. H. (Knock and Down Ath), 1882 v E, W; (with Cliftonville), 1883 v W; 1884 v E, S, W; 1885 v E, S, W (9)

Doherty, I. (Belfast C), 1901 v E (1)

Doherty, J. (Cliftonville), 1933 v E, W (2)

Doherty, L. (Linfield), 1985 v Is; 1988 v T (sub) (2)

Doherty, M. (Derry C), 1938 v S (1)

Doherty, P. D. (Blackpool), 1935 v E, W; 1936 v E, S; (with Manchester C), 1937 v E, W; 1938 v E, S; 1939 v E, W; (with Derby Co), 1947 v E; (with Huddersfield T), 1947 v W; 1948 v E, W; 1949 v S; (with Doncaster R), 1951 v S (16)

Donaghy, M. (Luton T), 1980 v S, E, W; 1981 v Se, P, S (sub); 1982 v Is, E, F, S, W, Y, Hon, Sp, F; 1983 v A, WG, Alb, T, Alb, S, E, W; 1984 v A, T, WG, S, E, W, Fi; 1985 v R, Fi, E, Sp, T; 1986 v T, R, E, F, D, Mor, Alg, Sp, Br; 1987 v E (2), T, Is, Y; 1988 v Y, T, Gr, Pol, F, Ma; 1989 v Ei, H; (with Manchester U), Sp (2), Ma, Ch; 1990 v Ei, N; 1991 v Y (2), D, A, Pol, Fa; 1992 v Fa, A, D, S, Li, G; (with Chelsea), 1993 v Alb, Sp, D, Alb, Ei, Sp, Li, La; 1994 v La, D, Ei, R, Lie, Co, M (91)

Donnelly, L. (Distillery), 1913 v W (1)

Doran, J. F. (Brighton), 1921 v E; 1922 v E, W (3)

Dougan, A. D. (Portsmouth), 1958 v Cz; (with Blackburn R), 1960 v S; 1961 v E, W, I, Gr; (with Aston Villa), 1963 v S, Pol (2); (with Leicester C), 1966 v S, E, W, M, Alb, WG; 1967 v S, E; (with Wolverhampton W), 1967 v W; 1968 v S, W, Is; 1969 v T (2), E, S, W; 1970 v S, E, USSR (2); 1971 v Cy (2), Sp, E, S, W; 1972 v USSR (2), E, S, W; 1973 v Bul, Cy (43)

Douglas, J. P. (Belfast C), 1947 v E (1)

Dowd, H. O. (Glenavon), 1974 v W; (with Sheffield W), 1975 v N (sub), Se (3)

Dowie, I. (Luton T), 1990 v N (sub), U; 1991 v Y, D, A (sub), (with West Ham U), Y, Fa; (with Southampton) 1992 v Fa, A, D (sub), S (sub), Li; 1993 v Alb (2), Ei, Sp (sub), Li, La; La, D, Ei (sub), R (sub), Lie, Co, M (sub); 1995 v A, Ei; (with C Palace) Ei, La, Ca, Ch, La; 1996 v P; (with West Ham U), A, N, G; 1997 v Uk, Arm, G, Alb, P, Uk, Arm, Th (44)

Horlock, K. (Swindon T), 1995 v La, Ca; 1997 v G, Alb, I; (with Manchester C), v Bel, Uk, Arm, Th (9)

Houston, J. (Linfield), 1912 v S, W; 1913 v W; (with Everton), 1913 v E, S; 1914 v S (6)

Houston, W. (Linfield), 1933 v W (1)

Houston, W. G. (Moyola Park), 1885 v E, S (2)

Hughes, M. E. (Manchester C), 1992 v D, S, Li, G; (with Strasbourg), 1993 v Alb, Sp, D, Ei, Sp, Li, La; 1994 v La, D, Ei, R, Lie, Co, M; 1995 v P, A, Ei (2) La, Ca, La; 1996 v P, Lie, A, N, G; (with West Ham U), 1997 v Uk, Arm, G, Alb, I, Uk (37)

Hughes, P. (Bury), 1987 v E, T, Is (3)

Hughes, W. (Bolton W), 1951 v W (1)

Humphries, W. (Ards), 1962 v W; (with Coventry C), 1962 v Ho; 1963 v E, S, W, Pol, Sp; 1964 v S, E, Sp; 1965 v S; (with Swansea T), 1965 v W, Ho, Alb (14)

Hunter, A. (Distillery), 1905 v W; 1906 v W, E, S; (with Belfast C), 1908 v W; 1909 v W, E, S (8)

Hunter, A. (Blackburn R), 1970 v USSR; 1971 v Cy (2), E, S, W; (with Ipswich T), 1972 v USSR (2), Sp, E, S, W; 1973 v Bul, Cy (2), P, E, S, W; 1974 v Bul, S, E, W; 1975 v N, Se, Y, E, S, W; 1976 v Se, N, Y, Is, S, E, W; 1977 v Ho, Bel, WG, E, S, W, Ic; 1978 v Ic, Ho, Bel; 1979 v Ei, D, S, W, D; 1980 v E, Ei (53)

Hunter, B.V. (Wrexham), 1995 v La; 1996 v P, Lie, A, Se, G; (with Reading), 1997 v Arm, G, Alb, I, Bel (11)

Hunter, R. J. (Cliftonville), 1884 v E, S, W (3)

Hunter, V. (Coleraine), 1962 v E; 1964 v Sp (2)

Irvine, R. J. (Linfield), 1962 v Ho; 1963 v E, S, W, Pol (2), Sp; (with Stoke C), 1965 v W (8)

Irvine, R. W. (Everton), 1922 v S; 1923 v E, W; 1924 v E, S; 1925 v E; 1926 v E; 1927 v E, W; 1928 v E, S; (with Portsmouth), 1929 v E; 1930 v S; (with Connah's Quay), 1931 v E; (with Derry C), 1932 v W (15)

Irvine, W. J. (Burnley), 1963 v W, Sp; 1965 v S, W, Sw, Ho (2), Alb; 1966 v S, E, W, M, Alb; 1967 v E, S; 1968 v E, W; (with Preston NE), 1969 v Is, T, E; (with Brighton), 1972 v E, S, W (23)

Irving, S, J. (Dundee), 1923 v S, W; 1924 v S, E, W; 1925 v S, E, W; 1926 v S, W; (with Cardiff C), 1927 v S, E, W; 1928 v S, E, W; (with Chelsea), 1929 v E; 1931 v W (18)

Jackson, T. (Everton), 1969 v Is, E, S, W; 1970 v USSR (1+1 sub); (with Nottingham F), 1971 v Sp; 1972 v E, S, W; 1973 v Cy, E, S, W; 1974 v Bul, P, S (sub), E (sub), W (sub); 1975 v N (sub), Se, Y, E, S, W; (with Manchester U); 1976 v Se, N, Y; 1977 v Ho, Bel, WG, E, S, W, Ic (35)

Jamison, J. (Glentoran), 1976 v N (1)

Jenkins, I. (Chester C), 1997 v Arm, Th (2)

Jennings, P. A. (Watford), 1964 v W, U; (with Tottenham H), 1965 v S, Sw (2), Ho, Alb; 1966 v S, E, W, Alb, WG; 1967 v E, S; 1968 v S, E, W; 1969 v Is, T (2), E, S, W; 1970 v S, E, USSR (2); 1971 v Cy (2), E, S, W; 1972 v USSR, Sp, S, E, W; 1973 v Bul, Cy, P, E, S, W; 1974 v P, S, E, W; 1975 v N, Se, Y, E, S, W; 1976 v Se, N, Y, Is, S, E, W; 1977 v Ho, Bel, WG, E, S, W, Ic; (with Arsenal), 1978 v Ic, Ho, Bel; 1979 v Ei, D, Bul, E, Bul, E, S, W, D; 1980 v E, Ei, Is; 1981 v S, P, S, Se; 1982 v S, Is, E, W, Y, Hon, Sp, F; 1983 v Alb, S, E, W; 1984 v A, T, WG, S, W, Fi; 1985 v R, Fi, E, Sp, T; (with Tottenham H), 1986 v T, R, E, F, D, Mor, Alg, Sp, Br (119)

Johnston, H. (Portadown), 1927 v W (1)

Johnston, R. (Old Park), 1885 v S, W (2)

Johnston, S. (Distillery), 1882 v W; 1884 v E; 1886 v E, S (4)

Johnston, S. (Linfield), 1890 v W; 1893 v S, W; 1894 v E (4)

Johnston, S. (Distillery), 1905 v W (1)

Johnston, W. C. (Glenavon), 1962 v W; (with Oldham Ath), 1966 v M (sub) (2)

Jones, J. (Linfield), 1930 v S, W; 1931 v S, W, E; 1932 v S, E; 1933 v S, E, W; 1934 v S, E, W; 1935 v S, E, W; 1936 v E, S; (with Hibernian), 1936 v W; 1937 v E, W, S; (with Glenavon), 1938 v E (23)

Jones, J. (Glenavon), 1956 v W; 1957 v E, W (3)

Jones, S. (Distillery), 1934 v E; (with Blackpool), 1934 v W (2)

Jordan, T. (Linfield), 1895 v E, W (2)

Kavanagh, P. J. (Celtic), 1930 v E (1)

Keane, T. R. (Swansea T), 1949 v S (1)

Kearns, A. (Distillery), 1900 v E, S, W; 1902 v E, S, W (6)

Kee, P. V. (Oxford U), 1990 v N; 1991 v Y (2), D, A, Pol, Fa; (with Ards), 1995 v A, Ei (9)

Keith, R. M. (Newcastle U), 1958 v E, W, Cz (2), Arg, I, WG, F; 1959 v E, S, W, Sp; 1960 v S, E; 1961 v S, E, W, I, WG (2), Gr; 1962 v W, Ho (23)

Kelly, H. R. (Fulham), 1950 v E, W; (with Southampton), 1951 v E, S (4)

Kelly, J. (Glentoran), 1896 v E (1)

Kelly, J. (Derry C), 1932 v E, W; 1933 v E, W, S; 1934 v W; 1936 v E, S, W; 1937 v S, E (11)

Kelly, P. (Manchester C), 1921 v E (1)

Kelly, P. M. (Barnsley), 1950 v S (1)

Kennedy, A. L. (Arsenal), 1923 v W; 1925 v E (2)

Kernaghan, N. (Belfast C), 1936 v W; 1937 v S; 1938 v E (3)

Kirkwood, H. (Cliftonville), 1904 v W (1)

Kirwan, J. (Tottenham H), 1900 v W; 1902 v E, W; 1903 v E, S, W; 1904 v S, W; 1905 v E, S, W; (with Chelsea), 1906 v E, S, W; 1907 v W; (with Clyde), 1909 v S (17)

Lacey, W. (Everton), 1909 v E, S, W; 1910 v E, S, W; 1911 v E, S, W; 1912 v E; (with Liverpool), 1913 v W; 1914 v E, S, W; 1920 v E, S, W; 1921 v E, S, W; 1922 v E, S; (with New Brighton), 1925 v E (23)

Lawther, W. I. (Sunderland), 1960 v W; 1961 v I; (with Blackburn R), 1962 v S, Ho (4)

Leatham, J. (Belfast C), 1939 v W (1)

Ledwidge, J. J. (Shelbourne), 1906 v S, W (2)

Lemon, J. (Glentoran), 1886 v W; 1888 v S; (with Belfast YMCA), 1889 v W (3)

Lennon, N. F. (Crewe Alex), 1994 v M (sub); 1995 v Ch; 1996 v P, Lie, A; (with Leicester C), v N; 1997 v Uk, Arm, G, Alb, Bel, P, Uk, Arm, Th (15)

Leslie, W. (YMCA), 1887 v E (1)

Lewis, J. (Glentoran), 1899 v S, E, W; (with Distillery), 1900 v S (4)

Little, J. (Glentoran), 1898 v W (1)

Lockhart, H. (Rossall School), 1884 v W (1)

Lockhart, N. (Linfield), 1947 v E; (with Coventry C), 1950 v W; 1951 v W; 1952 v W; (with Aston Villa), 1954 v S, E; 1955 v W; 1956 v W (8)

Lomas, S. M. (Manchester C), 1994 v R, Lie, Co (sub), M (sub); 1995 v P, A; 1996 v P, Lie, A, N, Se, G; 1997 v Uk, Arm, G, Alb, I, Bel; (with West Ham U), P, Uk, Arm, Th (22)

Lowther, R. (Glentoran), 1888 v E, S (2)

Loyal, J. (Clarence), 1891 v S (1)

Lutton, R. J. (Wolverhampton W), 1970 v S, E; (with West Ham U), 1973 v Cy (sub), S (sub), W (sub); 1974 v P (6)

Lyner, D. (Glentoran), 1920 v E, W; 1922 v S, W; (with Manchester U), 1923 v E; (with Kilmarnock), 1923 v W (6)

McAdams, W. J. (Manchester C), 1954 v W; 1955 v S; 1957 v E; 1958 v S, I; (with Bolton W), 1961 v E, S, W, I, WG (2), Gr; 1962 v E, Gr; (with Leeds U), Ho (15)

McAlery, J. M. (Cliftonville), 1882 v E, W (2)

McAlinden, J. (Belfast C), 1938 v S; 1939 v S; (with Portsmouth), 1947 v E; (with Southend U), 1949 v E (4)

McAllen, J. (Linfield), 1898 v E; 1899 v E, S, W; 1900 v E, S, W; 1901 v W; 1902 v S (9)

McAlpine, W. J. (Cliftonville), 1901 v S (1)

McArthur, A. (Distillery), 1886 v W (1)

McAuley, J. L. (Huddersfield T), 1911 v E, W; 1912 v E, S; 1913 v E, S (6)

McAuley, P. (Belfast C), 1900 v S (1)

McBride, S. (Glenavon), 1991 v D (sub), Pol (sub); 1992 v Fa (sub), D (4)

McCabe, J. (Leeds U), 1949 v S, W; 1950 v E; 1951 v W; 1953 v W; 1954 v S (6)

McCabe, W. (Ulster), 1891 v E (1)

McCambridge, J. (Ballymena), 1930 v S, W; (with Cardiff C), 1931 v W; 1932 v E (4)

McCandless, J. (Bradford), 1912 v W; 1913 v W; 1920 v W, S; 1921 v E (5)

McCandless, W. (Linfield), 1920 v E, W; 1921 v E; (with Rangers), 1921 v W; 1922 v S; 1924 v W, S; 1925 v S; 1929 v W (9)

McCann, P. (Belfast C), 1910 v E, S, W; 1911 v E; (with Glentoran), 1911 v S; 1912 v E; 1913 v W (7)

McCarthy, J. D. (Port Vale), 1996 v Se; 1997 v I, Arm, Th (4)

McCashin, J. (Cliftonville), 1896 v W; 1898 v S, W; 1899 v S (4)

McCavana, W. T. (Coleraine), 1955 v S; 1956 v E, S (3)

McCaw, D. (Distillery), 1882 v E (1)

McCaw, J. H. (Linfield), 1927 v W; 1930 v S; 1931 v E, S, W (5)

McClatchey, J. (Distillery), 1886 v E, S, W (3)

McClatchey, R. (Distillery), 1895 v S (1)

McCleary, J. W. (Cliftonville), 1955 v W (1)

McCleery, W. (Linfield), 1930 v E, W; 1931 v E, S, W; 1932 v S, W; 1933 v E, W (9)

McClelland, J. (Arsenal), 1961 v W, I, WG (2), Gr; (with Fulham), 1966 v M (6)

McClelland, J. (Mansfield T), 1980 v S (sub), Aus (3); 1981 v Se, S; (with Rangers), S, Se (sub); 1982 v S, W, Y, Hon, Sp, A, F; 1983 v A, WG, Alb, T, Alb, S, E, W; 1984 v A,

Mercer, J. T. (Distillery), 1898 v E, S, W; 1899 v E; (with Linfield), 1902 v E, W; (with Distillery), 1903 v S, W; (with Derby Co), 1904 v E, W; 1905 v S (11)
Millar, W. (Barrow), 1932 v W; 1933 v S (2)
Miller, J. (Middlesbrough), 1929 v W, S; 1930 v E (3)
Milligan, D. (Chesterfield), 1939 v W (1)
Milne, R. G. (Linfield), 1894 v E, S, W; 1895 v E, W; 1896 v E, S, W; 1897 v E, S; 1898 v S, W; 1899 v E, W; 1901 v W; 1902 v E, S, W; 1903 v E, S; 1904 v E, S, W; 1906 v E, S, W (27)
Mitchell, E. J. (Cliftonville), 1933 v S; (with Glentoran), 1934 v W (2)
Mitchell, W. (Distillery), 1932 v E, W; 1933 v E, W; (with Chelsea), 1934 v W, S; 1935 v S, E; 1936 v S, E; 1937 v E, S, W; 1938 v E, S (15)
Molyneux, T. B. (Ligoniel), 1883 v E, W; (with Cliftonville), 1884 v E, W, S; 1885 v E, W; 1886 v E, W, S; 1888 v S (11)
Montgomery, F. J. (Coleraine), 1955 v E (1)
Moore, C. (Glentoran), 1949 v W (1)
Moore, J. (Linfield Ath), 1891 v E, S, W (3)
Moore, P. (Aberdeen), 1933 v E (1)
Moore, T. (Ulster), 1887 v S, W (2)
Moore, W. (Falkirk), 1923 v S (1)
Moorhead, F. W. (Dublin University), 1885 v E (1)
Moorhead, G. (Linfield), 1923 v S; 1928 v S; 1929 v S (3)
Moran, J. (Leeds C), 1912 v S (1)
Moreland, V. (Derby Co), 1979 v Bul (2 sub), E, S; 1980 v E, Ei (6)
Morgan, F. G. (Linfield), 1923 v E; (with Nottingham F), 1924 v S; 1927 v E; 1928 v E, S, W; 1929 v E (7)
Morgan, S. (Port Vale), 1972 v Sp; 1973 v Bul (sub), P, Cy, E, S, W; (with Aston Villa), 1974 v Bul, P, S, E; 1975 v Se; 1976 v Se (sub), N, Y; (with Brighton & HA), S, W (sub); (with Sparta Rotterdam), 1979 v D (18)
Morrison, J. (Linfield Ath), 1891 v E, W (2)
Morrison, T. (Glentoran), 1895 v E, S, W; (with Burnley), 1899 v W; 1900 v W; 1902 v E, S (7)
Morrogh, E. (Bohemians), 1896 v S (1)
Morrow, S. J. (Arsenal), 1990 v U (sub); 1991 v A (sub), Pol, Y; 1992 v Fa, S (sub), G (sub); 1993 v Sp (sub), Alb, Ei; 1994 v R, Co, M (sub); 1995 v P, Ei (2), La; 1996 v P, Se; 1997 v Uk, G, Alb, I, Bel; (with QPR), P, Uk, Arm (27)
Morrow, W. J. (Moyola Park), 1883 v E, W; 1884 v S (3)
Muir, R. (Oldpark), 1885 v S, W (2)
Mullan, G. (Glentoran), 1983 v S, E, W, Alb (sub) (4)
Mulholland, S. (Celtic), 1906 v S, E (2)
Mulligan, J. (Manchester C), 1921 v S (1)
Mulryne, P. P. (Manchester U), 1997 v Bel (sub), Arm (sub), Th (3)

Murphy, J. (Bradford C), 1910 v E, S, W (3)
Murphy, N. (QPR), 1905 v E, S, W (3)
Murray, J. M. (Motherwell), 1910 v E, S; (with Sheffield W), 1910 v W (3)

Napier, R. J. (Bolton W), 1966 v WG (1)
Neill, W. J. T. (Arsenal), 1961 v I, Gr, WG; 1962 v E, S, W, Gr; 1963 v E, W, Pol, Sp; 1964 v S, E, W, U, Sp; 1965 v E, S, W, Sw, Ho (2); 1966 v S, E, W, Alb, WG, M; 1967 v S, W; 1968 v S, E; 1969 v E, S, W, Is, T (2); 1970 v S, E, W, USSR (2); (with Hull C), 1971 v Cy, Sp; 1972 v USSR (2), Sp, S, E, W; 1973 v Bul, Cy (2), P, E, S, W (59)
Nelis, P. (Nottingham F), 1923 v E (1)
Nelson, S. (Arsenal), 1970 v W, E (sub); 1971 v Cy, Sp, E, S, W; 1972 v USSR (2), Sp, E, S, W; 1973 v Bul, Cy, P; 1974 v S, E; 1975 v Se, Y; 1976 v Se, N, Is, E; 1977 v Bel (sub), WG, W, Ic; 1978 v Ic, Ho, Bel; 1979 v Ei, D, Bul, E, Bul, E, S, W, D; 1980 v Ei, Is; 1981 v S, P, S, Se; (with Brighton & HA), 1982 v S, Sp (sub), A (51)
Nicholl, C. J. (Aston Villa), 1975 v Se, Y, E, S, W; 1976 v Se, N, Y, S, E, W; 1977 v W; (with Southampton), 1978 v Bel (sub), S, E, W; 1979 v Ei, Bul, E, Bul, E, W; 1980 v Ei, Is, S, E, W, Aus (3); 1981 v Se, P, S, P, S, Se; 1982 v S, Is, E, F, W, Y, Hon, Sp, A, F; 1983 v S (sub), E, W; (with Grimsby T), 1984 v A, T (51)
Nicholl, H. (Belfast C), 1902 v E, W; 1905 v E (3)
Nicholl, J. M. (Manchester U), 1976 v Is, W (sub); 1977 v Ho, Bel, E, S, W, Ic; 1978 v Ic, Ho, Bel, S, E, W; 1979 v Ei, D, Bul, E, Bul, E, S, W, D; 1980 v Ei, Is, S, E, W, Aus (3); 1981 v Se, P, S, P, S, Se; 1982 v S, Is, E; (with Toronto B), F, W, Y, Hon, Sp, A, F; (with Sunderland), 1983 v A, WG, Alb, T, Alb; (with Toronto B), S, E, W; 1984 v T; (with Rangers), WG, S, E; (with Toronto B), Fi; 1985 v R; (with WBA), Fi, E, Sp, T; 1986 v T, R, E, F, Alg, Sp, Br (73)
Nicholson, J. J. (Manchester U), 1961 v S, W; 1962 v E, W, Gr, Ho; 1963 v S, Pol (2); (with Huddersfield T), 1965 v W, Ho (2), Alb; 1966 v S, E, W, Alb, M; 1967 v S, W; 1968 v S, E, W; 1969 v S, E, W, T (2); 1970 v S, E, W, USSR (2); 1971 v Cy (2), E, S, W; 1972 v USSR (2) (41)

Nixon, R. (Linfield), 1914 v S (1)
Nolan, I.R. (Sheffield W), 1997 v Arm, G, Alb, P, Uk (5)
Nolan-Whelan, J. V. (Dublin Freebooters), 1901 v E, W; 1902 v S, W (4)

O'Boyle, G. (Dunfermline Ath), 1994 v Co (sub), M; (with St Johnstone), 1995 v P (sub), La (sub), Ca (sub), Ch (sub); 1996 v Se (sub), G (sub); 1997 v I (sub), Bel (sub) (10)
O'Brien, M. T. (QPR), 1921 v S; (with Leicester C), 1922 v S, W; 1924 v S, W; (with Hull C), 1925 v S, E, W; 1926 v W; (with Derby Co), 1927 v W (10)
O'Connell, P. (Sheffield W), 1912 v E, S; (with Hull C), 1914 v E, S, W (5)
O'Doherty, A. (Coleraine), 1970 v E, W (sub) (2)
O'Driscoll, J. F. (Swansea T), 1949 v E, S, W (3)
O'Hagan, C. (Tottenham H), 1905 v S, W; 1906 v S, W, E; (with Aberdeen), 1907 v E, S, W; 1908 v S, W; 1909 v E (11)
O'Hagan, W. (St Mirren), 1920 v E, W (2)
O'Kane, W. J. (Nottingham F), 1970 v E, W, S (sub); 1971 v Sp, E, S, W; 1972 v USSR (2); 1973 v P, Cy; 1974 v Bul, P, S, E, W; 1975 v N, Se, E, S (20)
O'Mahoney, M. T. (Bristol R), 1939 v S (1)
O'Neill, C. (Motherwell), 1989 v Ch (sub); 1990 v Ei (sub); 1991 v D (3)
O'Neill, J. (Leicester C), 1980 v Is, S, E, W, Aus (3); 1981 v P, S, P, S, Se; 1982 v S, Is, E, F, S, F (sub); 1983 v A, WG, Alb, T, Alb, S; 1984 v S (sub); 1985 v Is, Fi, E, Sp, T; 1986 v T, R, E, F, D, Mor, Alg, Sp, Br (39)
O'Neill, J. (Sunderland), 1962 v W (1)
O'Neill, M. A. (Newcastle U), 1988 v Gr, Pol, F, Ma; 1989 v Ei, H, Sp (sub), Ma (sub), Ch; (with Dundee U), 1990 v H (sub), Ei; 1991 v Pol; 1992 v Fa (sub), S (sub), G (sub); 1993 v Alb (sub + 1), Ei, Sp, Li, La; (with Hibernian), 1994 v Lie (sub); 1995 v A (sub), Ei; 1996 v Lie, A, N, Se; (with Coventry C), 1997 v Uk (sub), Arm (sub) (31)
O'Neill, M. H. (Distillery), 1972 v USSR (sub), (with Nottingham F), Sp (sub), W (sub); 1973 v P, Cy, E, S, W; 1974 v Bul, P, E (sub); W; 1975 v Se, Y, E, S; 1976 v Y (sub); 1977 v E (sub), S; 1978 v Ic, Ho, S, E, W; 1979 v Ei, D, Bul, E, Bul, D; 1980 v Ei, Is, Aus (3); 1981 v Se, P; (with Norwich C), P, S, Se; (with Manchester C), 1982 v S; (with Norwich C), E, F, S, Y, Hon, Sp, A, F; 1983 v A, WG, Alb, T, Alb, S, E; (with Notts Co), 1984 v A, T, WG, E, W, Fi; 1985 v R, Fi (64)
O'Reilly, H. (Dublin Freebooters), 1901 v S, W; 1904 v S (3)

Parke, J. (Linfield), 1964 v S; (with Hibernian), 1964 v E, Sp; (with Sunderland), 1965 v Sw, S, W, Ho (2), Alb; 1966 v WG; 1967 v E, S; 1968 v S, E (14)
Patterson, D. J. (C Palace), 1994 v Co (sub), M (sub); 1995 v Ei (sub+1), La, Ca, Ch (sub), La (sub); (with Luton T), 1996 v N (sub), Se (10)
Peacock, R. (Celtic), 1952 v S; 1953 v F; 1954 v W; 1955 v E, S; 1956 v E, S; 1957 v W, I, P; 1958 v S, E, W, I (2), Arg, Cz (2), WG; 1959 v E, S, W; 1960 v S, E; 1961 v E, S, I, WG (2), Gr; (with Coleraine), 1962 v S (31)
Peden, J. (Linfield), 1887 v S, W; 1888 v W, E; 1889 v S, E; 1890 v W, S; 1891 v W, E; 1892 v W, E; 1893 v E, S, W; (with Distillery), 1896 v W, E, S; 1897 v W, S; 1898 v W, E, S; (with Linfield), 1899 v W (24)
Penney, S. (Brighton & HA), 1985 v Is; 1986 v T, R, E, F, D, Mor, Alg, Sp; 1987 v E, T, Is; 1988 v Pol, F, Ma; 1989 v Ei, Sp (17)
Percy, J. C. (Belfast YMCA), 1889 v W (1)
Platt, J. A. (Middlesbrough), 1976 v Is (sub); 1978 v S, E, W; 1980 v S, E, W, Aus (3); 1981 v Se, P; 1982 v F, S, W (sub), A; 1983 v A, WG, Alb, T; (with Ballymena U), 1984 v E, W (sub); (with Coleraine), 1986 v Mor (sub) (23)
Ponsonby, J. (Distillery), 1895 v S; 1896 v E, S, W; 1897 v E, S, W; 1899 v E (8)
Potts, R. M. C. (Cliftonville), 1883 v E, W (2)
Priestley, T. J. (Coleraine), 1933 v S; (with Chelsea), 1934 v E (2)
Pyper, Jas. (Cliftonville), 1897 v S, W; 1898 v S, E, W; 1899 v S; 1900 v E (7)
Pyper, John (Cliftonville), 1897 v E, S, W; 1899 v E, W; 1900 v E, W, S; 1902 v S (9)
Pyper, M. (Linfield), 1932 v W (1)

Quinn, J. M. (Blackburn R), 1985 v Is, Fi, E, Sp, T; 1986 v T, R, E, F, D (sub), Mor (sub); 1987 v E (sub), T; (with Swindon T), 1988 v Y (sub), T, Gr, Pol, F (sub), Ma; (with Leicester C), 1989 v Ei, H (sub), Sp (sub+1); (with Bradford C), Ma, Ch; 1990 v H, (with West Ham U), N; 1991 v Y (sub); (with Bournemouth), 1992 v Li; (with Reading), 1993 v Sp, D, Alb (sub), Ei (sub), La (sub);

Walker, J. (Doncaster R), 1955 v W (1)
Walker, T. (Bury), 1911 v S (1)
Walsh, D. J. (WBA), 1947 v S, W; 1948 v E, S, W; 1949 v E, S, W; 1950 v W (9)
Walsh, W. (Manchester C), 1948 v E, S, W; 1949 v E, S (5)
Waring, R. (Distillery), 1899 v E (1)
Warren, P. (Shelbourne), 1913 v E, S (2)
Watson, J. (Ulster), 1883 v E, W; 1886 v E, S, W; 1887 v S, W; 1889 v E, W (9)
Watson, P. (Distillery), 1971 v Cy (sub) (1)
Watson, T. (Cardiff C), 1926 v S (1)
Wattle, J. (Distillery), 1899 v E (1)
Webb, C. G. (Brighton), 1909 v S, W; 1911 v S (3)
Weir, E. (Clyde), 1939 v W (1)
Welsh, E. (Carlisle U), 1966 v W, WG, M; 1967 v W (4)
Whiteside, N. (Manchester U), 1982 v Y, Hon, Sp, A, F; 1983 v WG, Alb, T; 1984 v A, T, WG, S, E, W, Fi; 1985 v R, Fi, Is, E, Sp, T; 1986 v R, E, F, D, Mor, Alg, Sp, Br; 1987 v E (2), Is, Y; 1988 v T, Pol, F; (with Everton), 1990 v H, Ei (38)
Whiteside, T. (Distillery), 1891 v E (1)
Whitfield, E. R. (Dublin University), 1886 v W (1)
Whitley, J. (Manchester C), 1997 v Bel (sub), Th (sub) (2)
Williams, J. R. (Ulster), 1886 v E, S (2)
Williams, P. A. (WBA), 1991 v Fa (sub) (1)
Williamson, J. (Cliftonville), 1890 v E; 1892 v S; 1893 v S (3)
Willigham, T. (Burnley), 1933 v W; 1934 v S (2)
Willis, G. (Linfield), 1906 v S, W; 1907 v S; 1912 v S (4)
Wilson, D. J. (Brighton & HA), 1987 v T, Is, E (sub); (with Luton T), 1988 v Y, T, Gr, Pol, F, Ma; 1989 v Ei, H, Sp, Ma, Ch; 1990 v H, Ei, N, U; (with Sheffield W), 1991 v Y, D, A, Fa; 1992 v A (sub), S (24)
Wilson, H. (Linfield), 1925 v W (1)

Wilson, K. J. (Ipswich T), 1987 v Is, E, Y; (with Chelsea), 1988 v Y, T, Gr (sub), Pol (sub), F (sub); 1989 v H (sub), Sp (2), Ma, Ch; 1990 v Ei (sub), N, U; 1991 v Y (2), A, Pol, Fa; 1992 v Fa, A, D, S; (with Notts Co), Li, G; 1993 v Alb, Sp, D, Ei, Sp, Li, D, Ei, R, Lie, Co, M; (with Walsall), 1995 v Ei (sub), La (42)
Wilson, M. (Distillery), 1884 v E, S, W (3)
Wilson, R. (Cliftonville), 1888 v S (1)
Wilson, S. J. (Glenavon), 1962 v S; 1964 v S; (with Falkirk), 1964 v E, W, U, Sp; 1965 v E, Sw; (with Dundee), 1966 v W, WG; 1967 v S; 1968 v E (12)
Wilton, J. M. (St Columb's Court), 1888 v E, W; 1889 v S, E; (with Cliftonville), 1890 v E; (with St Columb's Court), 1892 v W; 1893 v S (7)
Wood, T. J. (Walsall), 1996 v Lie (sub) (1)
Worthington, N. (Sheffield W), 1984 v W, Fi (sub); 1985 v Is, Sp (sub); 1986 v T, R (sub), E (sub), D, Alg, Sp; 1987 v E (2), T, Is, Y; 1988 v Y, T, Gr, Pol, F, Ma; 1989 v Ei, H, Sp, Ma; 1990 v H, Ei, U; 1991 v Y, D, A, Fa; 1992 v A, D, S, Li, G; 1993 v Alb, Sp, D, Ei, Sp, Li, La; 1994 v La, D, Ei, Lie, Co, M; (with Leeds U), 1995 v P, A, Ei (2), La, Ca (sub), Ch, La; 1996 v P, Lie, A, N, Se, G; (with Stoke C), 1997 v I, Bel (sub) (66)
Wright, J. (Cliftonville), 1906 v E, S, W; 1907 v E, S, W (6)
Wright, T. J. (Newcastle U), 1989 v Ma, Ch; 1990 v H, U; 1992 v Fa, A, S, G; 1993 v Alb, Sp, Alb, Ei, Sp, Li, La; 1994 v La; (with Nottingham F), D, Ei, R, Lie, Co, M (sub); 1997 v G, Alb, I, Bel; (with Manchester C), P, Uk (28)

Young, S. (Linfield), 1907 v E, S; 1908 v E, S; (with Airdrie), 1909 v E; 1912 v S; (with Linfield), 1914 v E, S, W (9)

SCOTLAND

Adams, J. (Hearts), 1889 v Ni; 1892 v W; 1893 v Ni (3)
Agnew, W. B. (Kilmarnock), 1907 v Ni; 1908 v W, Ni (3)
Aird, J. (Burnley), 1954 v N (2), A, U (4)
Aitken, A. (Newcastle U), 1901 v E; 1902 v E; 1903 v E, W; 1904 v E; 1905 v E, W; 1906 v E; (with Middlesbrough), 1907 v E, W; 1908 v E; (with Leicester Fosse), 1910 v E; 1911 v E, Ni (14)
Aitken, G. G. (East Fife), 1949 v E, F; 1950 v W, Ni, Sw; (with Sunderland), 1953 v W, Ni; 1954 v E (8)
Aitken, R. (Dumbarton), 1886 v E; 1888 v Ni (2)
Aitken, R. (Celtic), 1980 v Pe (sub), Bel, W (sub), E, Pol; 1983 v Bel, Ca (1+1 sub); 1984 v Bel (sub), Ni, W (sub); 1985 v E, Ic; 1986 v W, EG, Aus (2), Is, R, E, D, WG, U; 1987 v Bul, Ei (2), L, Bel, E, Br; 1988 v H, Bel, Bul, L, S.Ar, Ma, Sp, Co, E; 1989 v N, Y, I, Cy, F, Cy, E, Ch; 1990 v Y, F, N; (with Newcastle U), Arg (sub), Pol, Ma, Cr, Se, Br; (with St Mirren), 1992 v R (sub) (57)
Aitkenhead, W. A. C. (Blackburn R), 1912 v Ni (1)
Albiston, A. (Manchester U), 1982 v Ni; 1984 v U, Bel, EG, W, E; 1985 v Y, Ic, Sp (2), W; 1986 v EG, Ho, U (14)
Alexander, D. (East Stirlingshire), 1894 v W, Ni (2)
Allan, D. S. (Queen's Park), 1885 v E, W; 1886 v W (3)
Allan, H. (Hearts), 1902 v W (1)
Allan, J. (Liverpool), 1897 v E (1)
Allan, J. (Queen's Park), 1887 v E, W (2)
Allan, T. (Dundee), 1974 v WG, N (2)
Ancell, R. F. D. (Newcastle U), 1937 v W, Ni (2)
Anderson, A. (Hearts), 1933 v E; 1934 v A, E, W, Ni; 1935 v E, W, Ni; 1936 v E, W, Ni; 1937 v G, E, W, Ni, A; 1938 v E, W, Ni, Cz, Ho; 1939 v W, H (23)
Anderson, F. (Clydesdale), 1874 v E (1)
Anderson, G. (Kilmarnock), 1901 v Ni (1)
Anderson, H. A. (Raith R), 1914 v W (1)
Anderson, J. (Leicester C), 1954 v Fi (1)
Anderson, K. (Queen's Park), 1896 v Ni; 1898 v E, Ni (3)
Anderson, W. (Queen's Park), 1882 v E; 1883 v E, W; 1884 v E; 1885 v E, W (6)
Andrews, P. (Eastern), 1875 v E (1)
Archibald, A. (Rangers), 1921 v W; 1922 v W, E; 1923 v Ni; 1924 v E, W; 1931 v E; 1932 v E (8)
Archibald, S. (Aberdeen), 1980 v P (sub); (with Tottenham H), Ni, Pol, H; 1981 v Se (sub), Is, Ni, Is, Ni, E; 1982 v Ni, P, Sp (sub), Ho, Nz (sub), Br, USSR; 1983 v EG, Sw (sub), Bel; 1984 v EG, E, F; (with Barcelona), 1985 v Sp, E, Ic (sub); 1986 v W (27)
Armstrong, M. W. (Aberdeen), 1936 v W, Ni; 1937 v G (3)
Arnott, W. (Queen's Park), 1883 v W; 1884 v E, Ni; 1885 v E, W; 1886 v E; 1887 v E, W; 1888 v E; 1889 v E; 1890 v E; 1891 v E; 1892 v E; 1893 v E (14)
Auld, J. R. (Third Lanark), 1887 v E, W; 1889 v W (3)
Auld, R. (Celtic), 1959 v H, P; 1960 v W (3)

Baird, A. (Queen's Park), 1892 v Ni; 1894 v W (2)
Baird, D. (Hearts), 1890 v Ni; 1891 v E; 1892 v W (3)
Baird, H. (Airdrieonians), 1956 v A (1)
Baird, J. C. (Vale of Leven), 1876 v E; 1878 v W; 1880 v E (3)
Baird, S. (Rangers), 1957 v Y, Sp (2), Sw, WG; 1958 v F, Ni (7)
Baird, W. U. (St Bernard), 1897 v Ni (1)
Bannon, E. (Dundee U), 1980 v Bel; 1983 v Ni, W, E, Ca; 1984 v EG; 1986 v Is, R, E, D (sub), WG (11)
Barbour, A. (Renton), 1885 v Ni (1)
Barker, J. B. (Rangers), 1893 v W; 1894 v W (2)
Barrett, F. (Dundee), 1894 v Ni; 1895 v W (2)
Battles, B. (Celtic), 1901 v E, W, Ni (3)
Battles, B. jun. (Hearts), 1931 v W (1)
Bauld, W. (Hearts), 1950 v E, Sw, P (3)
Baxter, J. C. (Rangers), 1961 v Ni, Ei (2), Cz; 1962 v Ni, W, E, Cz (2), U; 1963 v W, Ni, E, A, N, Sp; 1964 v W, E, N, WG; 1965 v W, Ni, Fi; (with Sunderland), 1966 v P, Br, Ni, W, E, I; 1967 v W, E, USSR; 1968 v W (34)
Baxter, R. D. (Middlesbrough), 1939 v E, W, H (3)
Beattie, A. (Preston NE), 1937 v E, A, Cz; 1938 v E; 1939 v W, Ni, H (7)
Beattie, R. (Preston NE), 1939 v W (1)
Begbie, I. (Hearts), 1890 v Ni; 1891 v E; 1892 v W; 1894 v E (4)
Bell, A. (Manchester U), 1912 v Ni (1)
Bell, J. (Dumbarton), 1890 v Ni; 1892 v E; (with Everton), 1896 v E; 1897 v E; 1898 v E; (with Celtic), 1899 v E, W, Ni; 1900 v E, W (10)
Bell, M. (Hearts), 1901 v W (1)
Bell, W. J. (Leeds U), 1966 v P, Br (2)
Bennett, A. (Celtic), 1904 v W; 1907 v Ni; 1908 v W; (with Rangers), 1909 v W, Ni, E; 1910 v E, W; 1911 v E, W; 1913 v Ni (11)
Bennie, R. (Airdrieonians), 1925 v W, Ni; 1926 v Ni (3)
Bernard, P. R. J. (Oldham Ath), 1995 v J (sub), Ec (2)
Berry, D. (Queen's Park), 1894 v W; 1899 v W, Ni (3)
Berry, W. H. (Queen's Park), 1888 v E; 1889 v E; 1890 v E; 1891 v E (4)
Bett, J. (Rangers), 1982 v Ho; 1983 v Bel; (with Lokeren), 1984 v Bel, W, E, F; 1985 v Y, Ic, Sp (2), W, E, Ic; (with Aberdeen), 1986 v W, Is, Ho; 1987 v Bel; 1988 v H (sub); 1989 v Y; 1990 v F (sub), N, Arg, Eg, Ma, Cr (25)
Beveridge, W. W. (Glasgow University), 1879 v E, W; 1880 v W (3)
Black, A. (Hearts), 1938 v Cz, Ho; 1939 v H (3)
Black, D. (Hurlford), 1889 v Ni (1)
Black, E. (Metz), 1988 v H (sub), L (sub) (2)
Black, I. H. (Southampton), 1948 v E (1)
Blackburn, J. E. (Royal Engineers), 1873 v E (1)

Connachan, E. D. (Dunfermline Ath), 1962 v Cz, U (2)
Connelly, G. (Celtic), 1974 v Cz, WG (2)
Connolly, J. (Everton), 1973 v Sw (1)
Connor, J. (Airdrieonians), 1886 v Ni (1)
Connor, J. (Sunderland), 1930 v F; 1932 v Ni; 1934 v E; 1935 v Ni (4)
Connor, R. (Dundee), 1986 v Ho; (with Aberdeen), 1988 v S.Ar (sub); 1989 v E; 1991 v R (4)
Cook, W. L. (Bolton W), 1934 v E; 1935 v W, Ni (3)
Cooke, C. (Dundee), 1966 v W, I; (with Chelsea), P, Br; 1968 v E, Ho; 1969 v W, Ni, A, WG (sub), Cy (2); 1970 v A; 1971 v Bel; 1975 v Sp, P (16)
Cooper, D. (Rangers), 1980 v Pe, A (sub); 1984 v W, E; 1985 v Y, Ic, Sp (2), W; 1986 v W (sub), EG, Aus (2), Ho, WG (sub), N, Eg (22)
Cormack, P. B. (Hibernian), 1966 v Br; 1969 v D (sub); 1970 v Ei, WG; (with Nottingham F), 1971 v D (sub), W, P, E; 1972 v Ho (sub) (9)
Cowan, J. (Aston Villa), 1896 v E; 1897 v E; 1898 v E (3)
Cowan, J. (Morton), 1948 v Bel, Sw; F; 1949 v E, W, F; 1950 v E, W, Ni, Sw, P, F; 1951 v E, W, Ni, A (2), D, F, Bel; 1952 v Ni, W, USA, D, Se (25)
Cowan, W. D. (Newcastle U), 1924 v E (1)
Cowie, D. (Dundee), 1953 v E, Se; 1954 v Ni, W, Fi, N, A, U; 1955 v W, Ni, A, H; 1956 v W, A; 1957 v Ni, W; 1958 v H, Pol, Y, Par (20)
Cox, C. J. (Hearts), 1948 v F (1)
Cox, S. (Rangers), 1949 v E, F; 1950 v E, F, W, Ni, Sw, P; 1951 v E, D, F, Bel, A; 1952 v Ni, W, USA, D, Se; 1953 v W, Ni, E; 1954 v W, Ni, E (24)
Craig, A. (Motherwell), 1929 v N, Ho; 1932 v E (3)
Craig, J. (Celtic), 1977 v Se (sub) (1)
Craig, J. P. (Celtic), 1968 v W (1)
Craig, T. (Rangers), 1927 v Ni; 1928 v Ni; 1929 v N, G, Ho; 1930 v Ni, E, W (8)
Craig, T. B. (Newcastle U), 1976 v Sw (1)
Crapnell, J. (Airdrieonians), 1929 v E, N, G; 1930 v F; 1931 v Ni, Sw; 1932 v E, F; 1933 v N (9)
Crawford, D. (St Mirren), 1894 v W, Ni; 1900 v W (3)
Crawford, J. (Queen's Park), 1932 v F, Ni; 1933 v E, W, Ni (5)
Crawford, S. (Raith R), 1995 v Ec (sub) (1)
Crerand, P. T. (Celtic), 1961 v Ei (2), Cz; 1962 v Ni, W, E, Cz (2), U; 1963 v W, Ni; (with Manchester U), 1964 v Ni; 1965 v E, Pol, Fi; 1966 v Pol (16)
Cringan, W. (Celtic), 1920 v W; 1922 v E, Ni; 1923 v W, E (5)
Crosbie, J. A. (Ayr U), 1920 v W; (with Birmingham), 1922 v E (2)
Croal, J. A. (Falkirk), 1913 v Ni; 1914 v E, W (3)
Cropley, A. J. (Hibernian), 1972 v P, Bel (2)
Cross, J. H. (Third Lanark), 1903 v Ni (1)
Cruickshank, J. (Hearts), 1964 v WG; 1970 v W, E; 1971 v D, Bel; 1976 v R (6)
Crum, J. (Celtic), 1936 v E; 1939 v Ni (2)
Cullen, M. J. (Luton T), 1956 v A (1)
Cumming, D. S. (Middlesbrough), 1938 v E (1)
Cumming, J. (Hearts), 1955 v E, H, P, Y; 1960 v E, Pol, A, H, T (9)
Cummings, G. (Partick T), 1935 v E; 1936 v W, Ni; (with Aston Villa), E; 1937 v G; 1938 v W, Ni, Cz; 1939 v E (9)
Cunningham, A. N. (Rangers), 1920 v W; 1921 v W, E; 1922 v Ni; 1923 v E, W; 1924 v E, Ni; 1926 v E, Ni; 1927 v E, W (12)
Cunningham, W. C. (Preston NE), 1954 v N (2), U, Fi, A; 1955 v W, E, H (8)
Curran, H. P. (Wolverhampton W), 1970 v A; 1971 v Ni, E, D, USSR (sub) (5)

Dailly, C. (Derby Co), 1997 v W, Ma, Bl (3)
Dalglish, K. (Celtic), 1972 v Bel (sub), Ho; 1973 v D (1+1 sub), E (2), W, Ni, Sw, Br; 1974 v Cz (2), WG (2), Ni, W, E, Bel, N (sub), Z, Br, Y; 1975 v EG, Sp (sub+1), Se, P, W, Ni, E, R; 1976 v D (2), R, Sw, Ni, E; 1977 v Fi, Cz, W (2), Se, Ni, E, Ch, Arg, Br; (with Liverpool), 1978 v EG, Cz, W, Bul, Ni (sub), W, E, Pe, Ir, Ho; 1979 v A, N, P, W, Ni, E, Arg, N; 1980 v Pe, A, Bel (2), P, Ni, W, E, Pol, H; 1981 v Se, P, Is; 1982 v Ni, P (sub), Sp, Ho, Ni, W, E, Nz, Br (sub); 1983 v Bel, Sw; 1984 v U, Bel, EG; 1985 v Y, Ic, Sp, W; 1986 v EG, Aus, R; 1987 v Bul (sub), L (102)
Davidson, D. (Queen's Park), 1878 v W; 1879 v W; 1880 v W; 1881 v E, W (5)
Davidson, J. A. (Partick T), 1954 v N (2), A, U; 1955 v W, Ni, E, H (8)
Davidson, S. (Middlesbrough), 1921 v E (1)
Dawson, A. (Rangers), 1980 v Pol (sub), H; 1983 v Ni, Ca (2) (5)

Dawson, J. (Rangers), 1935 v Ni; 1936 v E; 1937 v G, E, W, Ni, A, Cz; 1938 v W, Ho, Ni; 1939 v E, Ni, H (14)
Deans, J. (Celtic), 1975 v EG, Sp (2)
Delaney, J. (Celtic), 1936 v W, Ni; 1937 v G, E, A, Cz; 1938 v Ni; 1939 v W, Ni; (with Manchester U), 1947 v E; 1948 v E, W, Ni (13)
Devine, A. (Falkirk), 1910 v W (1)
Dewar, G. (Dumbarton), 1888 v Ni; 1889 v E (2)
Dewar, N. (Third Lanark), 1932 v E, F; 1933 v W (3)
Dick, J. (West Ham U), 1959 v E (1)
Dickie, M. (Rangers), 1897 v Ni; 1899 v Ni; 1900 v W (3)
Dickson, W. (Dumbarton), 1888 v Ni (1)
Dickson, W. (Kilmarnock), 1970 v Ni, W, E; 1971 v D, USSR (5)
Divers, J. (Celtic), 1895 v W (1)
Divers, J. (Celtic), 1939 v Ni (1)
Docherty, T. H, (Preston NE), 1952 v W; 1953 v E, Se; 1954 v N (2), A, U; 1955 v W, E, H (2), A; 1957 v E, Y, Sp (2), Sw, WG; 1958 v Ni, W, E, Sw; (with Arsenal), 1959 v W, E, Ni (25)
Dodds, D. (Dundee U), 1984 v U (sub), Ni (2)
Dodds, J. (Celtic), 1914 v E, W, Ni (3)
Dodds, W. (Aberdeen), 1997 v La (sub), W, Bl (sub) (3)
Doig, J. E. (Arbroath), 1887 v Ni; 1889 v Ni; (with Sunderland), 1896 v E; 1899 v E; 1903 v E (5)
Donachie, W. (Manchester C), 1972 v Pe, Ni, E, Y, Cz, Br; 1973 v D, E, W, Ni; 1974 v Ni; 1976 v R, Ni, W, E; 1977 v Fi, Cz, W (2), Se, Ni, E, Ch, Arg, Br; 1978 v EG, Bul, W, E, Ir, Ho; 1979 v A, N, P (sub) (35)
Donaldson, A. (Bolton W), 1914 v E, Ni, W; 1920 v E, Ni; 1922 v Ni (6)
Donnachie, J. (Oldham Ath), 1913 v E; 1914 v E, Ni (3)
Donnelly, S. (Celtic), 1997 v W (sub) (1)
Dougall, C. (Birmingham C), 1947 v W (1)
Dougall, J. (Preston NE), 1939 v E (1)
Dougan, R. (Hearts), 1950 v Sw (1)
Douglas, A. (Chelsea), 1911 v Ni (1)
Douglas, J. (Renfrew), 1880 v W (1)
Dowds, P. (Celtic), 1892 v Ni (1)
Downie, R. (Third Lanark), 1892 v W (1)
Doyle, D. (Celtic), 1892 v E; 1893 v W; 1894 v E; 1895 v E, Ni; 1897 v E; 1898 v E, Ni (8)
Doyle, J. (Ayr U), 1976 v R (1)
Drummond, J. (Falkirk), 1892 v Ni; (with Rangers), 1894 v Ni; 1895 v Ni, E; 1896 v E, Ni; 1897 v Ni; 1898 v E; 1900 v E; 1901 v E; 1902 v E, W, Ni; 1903 v Ni (14)
Dunbar, M. (Cartvale), 1886 v Ni (1)
Duncan, A. (Hibernian), 1975 v P (sub), W, Ni, E, R; 1976 v D (sub) (6)
Duncan, D. (Derby Co), 1933 v E, W; 1934 v A, W; 1935 v E, W; 1936 v E, W, Ni; 1937 v G, E, W, Ni; 1938 v W (14)
Duncan, D. M. (East Fife), 1948 v Bel, Sw, F (3)
Duncan, J. (Alexandra Ath), 1878 v W; 1882 v W (2)
Duncan, J. (Leicester C), 1926 v W (1)
Duncanson, J. (Rangers), 1947 v Ni (1)
Dunlop, J. (St Mirren), 1890 v W (1)
Dunlop, W. (Liverpool), 1906 v E (1)
Dunn, J. (Hibernian), 1925 v W, Ni; 1927 v Ni; 1928 v Ni, E; (with Everton), 1929 v W (6)
Durie, G. S. (Chelsea), 1988 v Bul (sub); 1989 v I (sub), Cy; 1990 v Y, EG, Eg, Se; 1991 v Sw (sub), Bul (2), USSR (sub), Sm; (with Tottenham H), 1992 v Sw, R, Sm, Ni (sub), Fi, Ca, N (sub), Ho, G; 1993 v Sw, I; 1994 v Sw, I; (with Rangers), Ho (2); 1996 v US, Ho, E, Sw; 1997 v A (sub), Se (sub), Ma (sub), Bl (35)
Durrant, I. (Rangers), 1988 v H, Bel, Ma, Sp; 1989 v N (sub); 1993 v Sw (sub), P (sub), I, P (sub); 1994 v I (sub), Ma (11)
Dykes, J. (Hearts), 1938 v Ho; 1939 v Ni (2)

Easson, J. F. (Portsmouth), 1931 v A, Sw; 1934 v W (3)
Ellis, J. (Mossend Swifts), 1892 v Ni (1)
Evans, A. (Aston Villa), 1982 v Ho, Ni, E, Nz (4)
Evans, R. (Celtic), 1949 v E, W, Ni, F; 1950 v W, Ni, Sw, P; 1951 v E, A; 1952 v Ni; 1953 v Se; 1954 v Ni, W, E, N, Fi; 1955 v Ni, P, Y, A, H; 1956 v E, Ni, W, A; 1957 v WG, Sp; 1958 v Ni, W, E, Sw, H, Pol, Y, Par, F; 1959 v E, WG, Ho, P; 1960 v E, Ni, W, Pol; (with Chelsea), 1960 v A, H, T (48)
Ewart, J. (Bradford C), 1921 v E (1)
Ewing, T. (Partick T), 1958 v W, E (2)

Farm, G. N. (Blackpool), 1953 v W, Ni, E, Se; 1954 v Ni, W, E; 1959 v WG, Ho, P (10)
Ferguson, D. (Rangers), 1988 v Ma, Co (sub) (2)
Ferguson, D. (Dundee U), 1992 v US (sub), Ca, Ho (sub); 1993 v G; (with Everton) 1995 v Gr; 1997 v A, Es (7)

Ferguson, I. (Rangers), 1989 v I, Cy (sub), F; 1993 v Ma (sub), Es; 1994 v Ma, A (sub), Ho (sub); 1997 v Es (sub) (9)

Ferguson, J. (Vale of Leven), 1874 v E; 1876 v E, W; 1877 v E, W; 1878 v W (6)

Ferguson, R. (Kilmarnock), 1966 v W, E, Ho, P, Br; 1967 v W, Ni (7)

Fernie, W. (Celtic), 1954 v Fi, A, U; 1955 v W, Ni; 1957 v E, Ni, W, Y; 1958 v W, Sw, Par (12)

Findlay, R. (Kilmarnock), 1898 v W (1)

Fitchie, T. T. (Woolwich Arsenal), 1905 v W; 1906 v W, Ni; (with Queen's Park), 1907 v W (4)

Flavell, R. (Airdrieonians), 1947 v Bel, L (2)

Fleck, R. (Norwich C), 1990 v Arg, Se, Br (sub); 1991 v USSR (4)

Fleming, C. (East Fife), 1954 v Ni (1)

Fleming, J. W. (Rangers), 1929 v G, Ho; 1930 v E (3)

Fleming, R. (Morton), 1886 v Ni (1)

Forbes, A. R. (Sheffield U), 1947 v Bel, L, E; 1948 v W, Ni; (with Arsenal), 1950 v E, P, F; 1951 v W, Ni, A; 1952 v W, D, Se (14)

Forbes, J. (Vale of Leven), 1884 v E, W, Ni; 1887 v W, E (5)

Ford, D. (Hearts), 1974 v Cz (sub), WG (sub), W (3)

Forrest, J. (Rangers), 1966 v W, I; (with Aberdeen), 1971 v Bel (sub), D, USSR (5)

Forrest, J. (Motherwell), 1958 v E (1)

Forsyth, A. (Partick T), 1972 v Y, Cz, Br; 1973 v D; (with Manchester U), E; 1975 v Sp, Ni (sub), R, EG; 1976 v D (10)

Forsyth, C. (Kilmarnock), 1964 v E; 1965 v W, Ni, Fi (4)

Forsyth, T. (Motherwell), 1971 v D; (with Rangers), 1974 v Cz; 1976 v Sw, Ni, W, E; 1977 v Fi, Se, Ni, E, Ch, Arg, Br; 1978 v Cz, W, Ni, W (sub), E, Pe, Ir (sub), Ho (22)

Foyers, R. (St Bernards), 1893 v W; 1894 v W (2)

Fraser, D. M. (WBA), 1968 v Ho; 1969 v Cy (2)

Fraser, J. (Moffat), 1891 v Ni (1)

Fraser, M. J. E. (Queen's Park), 1880 v W; 1882 v W, E; 1883 v W, E (5)

Fraser, J. (Dundee), 1907 v Ni (1)

Fraser, W. (Sunderland), 1955 v W, Ni (2)

Fulton, W. (Abercorn), 1884 v Ni (1)

Fyfe, J. H. (Third Lanark), 1895 v W (1)

Gabriel, J. (Everton), 1961 v W; 1964 v N (sub) (2)

Gallacher, H. K. (Airdrieonians), 1924 v Ni; 1925 v E, W, Ni; 1926 v W; (with Newcastle U), 1926 v E, Ni; 1927 v E, W, Ni; 1928 v E, W; 1929 v E, Ni; 1930 v W, Ni, F; (with Chelsea), 1934 v E; (with Derby C), 1935 v E (20)

Gallacher, K. W. (Dundee U), 1988 v Co, E (sub); 1989 v N, I; (with Coventry C), 1991 v Sm; 1992 v R (sub), Sm (sub), Ni (sub), N (sub), Ho (sub), G (sub), C; 1993 v Sw (sub), P; (with Blackburn R), P, Es (2); 1994 v I, Ma; 1996 v Aus (sub), D, Co (sub), Ho; 1997 v Se (sub), Es (2), A, Se, W, Ma, Bl (31)

Gallacher, P. (Sunderland), 1935 v Ni (1)

Galloway, M. (Celtic), 1992 v R (1)

Galt, J. H. (Rangers), 1908 v W, Ni (2)

Gardiner, I. (Motherwell), 1958 v W (1)

Gardner, D. R. (Third Lanark), 1897 v W (1)

Gardner, R. (Queen's Park), 1872 v E; 1873 v E; (with Clydesdale), 1874 v E; 1875 v E; 1878 v E (5)

Gemmell, T. (St Mirren), 1955 v P, Y (2)

Gemmell, T. (Celtic), 1966 v E; 1967 v W, Ni, E, USSR; 1968 v Ni, E; 1969 v W, Ni, E, D, A, WG, Cy; 1970 v E, Ei, WG; 1971 v Bel (18)

Gemmill, A. (Derby Co), 1971 v Bel; 1972 v P, Ho, Pe, Ni, W, E; 1976 v D, R, Ni, W, E; 1977 v Fi, Cz, W (2), Ni (sub), E (sub), Ch (sub), Arg, Br; 1978 v EG (sub); (with Nottingham), Bul, Ni, W, E (sub), Pe (sub), Ir, Ho; 1979 v A, N, P, N; (with Birmingham C), 1980 v A, P, Ni, W, E, H; 1981 v Se, P, Is, Ni (43)

Gemmill, S. (Nottingham F), 1995 v J, Ec, Fa (sub); 1996 v Sm, D (sub), US; 1997 v Es, Se (sub), W, Ma (sub), Bl (sub) (11)

Gibb, W. (Clydesdale), 1873 v E (1)

Gibson, D. W. (Leicester C), 1963 v A, N, Ei, Sp; 1964 v Ni; 1965 v W, Fi (7)

Gibson, J. D. (Partick T), 1926 v E; 1927 v E, W, Ni; (with Aston Villa), 1928 v E, W; 1930 v W, Ni (8)

Gibson, N. (Rangers), 1895 v E, Ni; 1896 v E, Ni; 1897 v E, Ni; 1898 v E; 1899 v E, W, Ni; 1900 v E, W, Ni; 1901 v W; (with Partick T), 1905 v Ni (14)

Gilchrist, J. E. (Celtic), 1922 v E (1)

Gilhooley, M. (Hull C), 1922 v W (1)

Gillespie, G. (Rangers), 1880 v W; 1881 v E, W; 1882 v E; (with Queen's Park), 1886 v W; 1890 v W; 1891 v Ni (7)

Gillespie, G. T. (Liverpool), 1988 v Bel, Bul, Sp; 1989 v N, F, Ch; 1990 v Y, EG, Eg, Pol, Ma, Br (sub); 1991 v Bul (13)

Gillespie, Jas (Third Lanark), 1898 v W (1)

Gillespie, John (Queen's Park), 1896 v W (1)

Gillespie, R. (Queen's Park), 1927 v W; 1931 v W; 1932 v F; 1933 v E (4)

Gillick, T. (Everton), 1937 v A, Cz; 1939 v W, Ni, H (5)

Gilmour, J. (Dundee), 1931 v W (1)

Gilzean, A. J. (Dundee), 1964 v W, E, N, WG; 1965 v Ni, (with Tottenham H), Sp; 1966 v Ni, W, Pol, I; 1968 v W; 1969 v W, E, WG, Cy (2), A (sub); 1970 v Ni, E (sub), WG, A; 1971 v P (22)

Glavin, R. (Celtic), 1977 v Se (1)

Glen, A. (Aberdeen), 1956 v E, Ni (2)

Glen, R. (Renton), 1895 v W; 1896 v W; (with Hibernian), 1900 v Ni (3)

Goram, A. L. (Oldham Ath), 1986 v EG (sub), R, Ho; 1987 v Br; (with Hibernian) 1989 v Y, I; 1990 v EG, Pol, Ma; 1991 v R, Sw, Bul (2), USSR, Sm; (with Rangers), 1992 v Sw, R, Sm, Fi, N, Ho, G, C; 1993 v Sw, P, I, Ma, P; 1994 v Ho; 1995 v Fi, Fa, Ru, Gr; 1996 v Se (sub), D (sub), Co, Ho, E, Sw; 1997 v A, La, Es (42)

Gordon, J. E. (Rangers), 1912 v E, Ni; 1913 v E, Ni, W; 1914 v E, Ni; 1920 v W, E, Ni (10)

Gossland, J. (Rangers), 1884 v Ni (1)

Goudie, J. (Abercorn), 1884 v Ni (1)

Gough, C. R. (Dundee U), 1983 v Sw, Ni, W, E, Ca (3); 1984 v U, Bel, EG, Ni, W, E, F; 1985 v Sp, E, Ic; 1986 v W, EG, Aus, Is, R, E, D, WG, U; (with Tottenham H), 1987 v Bul, L, Ei (2), Bel, E, Br; 1988 v H; (with Rangers), S.Ar, Sp, Co, E; 1989 v Y, I, Cy, F, Cy; 1990 v F, Arg, EG, Eg, Pol, Ma, Cr; 1991 v USSR, Bul; 1992 v Sm, Ni, Ca, N, Ho, G, C; 1993 v Sw, P (61)

Gourlay, J. (Cambuslang), 1886 v Ni; 1888 v W (2)

Govan, J. (Hibernian), 1948 v E, W, Bel, Sw, F; 1949 v Ni (6)

Gow, D. R. (Rangers), 1888 v E (1)

Gow, J. J. (Queen's Park), 1885 v E (1)

Gow, J. R. (Rangers), 1888 v Ni (1)

Graham, A. (Leeds U), 1978 v EG (sub); 1979 v A (sub), N, W, Ni, E, Arg, N; 1980 v A; 1981 v W (10)

Graham, G. (Arsenal), 1972 v P, Ho, Ni, Y, Cz, Br; 1973 v D (2); (with Manchester U), E, W, Ni, Br (sub) (12)

Graham, J. (Annbank), 1884 v Ni (1)

Graham, J. A. (Arsenal), 1921 v Ni (1)

Grant, J. (Hibernian), 1959 v W, Ni (2)

Grant, P. (Celtic), 1989 v E (sub), Ch (2)

Gray, A. (Hibernian), 1903 v Ni (1)

Gray, A. M. (Aston Villa), 1976 v R, Sw; 1977 v Fi, Cz; 1979 v A, N; (with Wolverhampton W), 1980 v P, E (sub); 1981 v Se, P, Is (sub), Ni; 1982 v Se (sub), Ni (sub); 1983 v Ni, W, E, Ca (1+1 sub); (with Everton), 1985 v Ic (20)

Gray, D. (Rangers), 1929 v W, Ni, G, Ho; 1930 v W, E, Ni; 1931 v W; 1933 v W, Ni (10)

Gray, E. (Leeds U), 1969 v E, Cy; 1970 v WG, A; 1971 v W, Ni; 1972 v Bel, Ho; 1976 v W, E; 1977 v Fi, W (12)

Gray, F. T. (Leeds U), 1976 v Sw; 1979 v N, P, W, Ni, E, Arg (sub); (with Nottingham F), 1980 v Bel (sub); 1981 v Se, P, Is, Ni, Is, W; (with Leeds U), Ni, E; 1982 v Se, Ni, P, Sp, Ho, W, Nz, Br, USSR; 1983 v EG, Sw, Bel, Sw, W, E, Ca (32)

Gray, W. (Pollokshields Ath), 1886 v E (1)

Green, A. (Blackpool), 1971 v Bel (sub), P (sub), Ni, E; (with Newcastle U), 1972 v W, E (sub) (6)

Greig, J. (Rangers), 1964 v E, WG; 1965 v W, Ni, E, Fi (2), Sp, Pol; 1966 v Ni, W, E, Pol, I (2), P, Ho, Br; 1967 v W, Ni, E; 1968 v Ni, W, E, Ho; 1969 v W, Ni, E, D, A, WG, Cy (2); 1970 v W, E, Ei, WG, A; 1971 v D, Bel, W (sub), Ni, E; 1976 v D (44)

Groves, W. (Hibernian), 1888 v W; (with Celtic), 1889 v Ni; 1890 v E (3)

Guilliland, W. (Queen's Park), 1891 v W; 1892 v Ni; 1894 v E; 1895 v E (4)

Gunn, B. (Norwich C), 1990 v Eg; 1993 v Es (2); 1994 v Sw, I, Ho (sub) (6)

Haddock, H. (Clyde), 1955 v E, H (2), P, Y; 1958 v E (6)

Haddow, D. (Rangers), 1894 v E (1)

Haffey, F. (Celtic), 1960 v E; 1961 v E (2)

Hamilton, A. (Queen's Park), 1885 v E, W; 1886 v E; 1888 v E (4)

Hamilton, A. W. (Dundee), 1962 v Cz, U, W, E; 1963 v W, Ni, E, A, N, Ei; 1964 v Ni, W, E, N, WG; 1965 v Ni, W, E, Fi (2), Pol, Sp; 1966 v Pol, Ni (24)

Hamilton, G. (Aberdeen), 1947 v Ni; 1951 v Bel, A; 1954 v N (2) (5)

Hamilton, G. (Port Glasgow Ath), 1906 v Ni (1)

Hamilton, J. (Queen's Park), 1892 v W; 1893 v E, Ni (3)

Hamilton, J. (St Mirren), 1924 v Ni (1)

Hamilton, R. C. (Rangers), 1899 v E, W, Ni; 1900 v W; 1901 v E, Ni; 1902 v W, Ni; 1903 v E; 1904 v Ni; (with Dundee), 1911 v W (11)

Hamilton, T. (Hurlford), 1891 v Ni (1)

Hamilton, T. (Rangers), 1932 v E (1)
Hamilton, W. M. (Hibernian), 1965 v Fi (1)
Hannah, A. B. (Renton), 1888 v W (1)
Hannah, J. (Third Lanark), 1889 v W (1)
Hansen, A. D. (Liverpool), 1979 v W, Arg; 1980 v Bel, P; 1981 v Se, P, Is; 1982 v Se, Ni, P, Sp, Ni (sub), W, E, Nz, Br, USSR; 1983 v EG, Sw, Bel, Sw; 1985 v W (sub); 1986 v R (sub); 1987 v Ei (2), L (26)
Hansen, J. (Partick T), 1972 v Bel (sub), Y (sub) (2)
Harkness, J. D. (Queen's Park), 1927 v E, Ni; 1928 v E; (with Hearts), 1929 v W, E, Ni; 1930 v E, W; 1932 v W, F; 1934 v Ni, W (12)
Harper, J. M. (Aberdeen), 1973 v D (1+1 sub); (with Hibernian), 1976 v D; (with Aberdeen), 1978 v Ir (sub) (4)
Harper, W. (Hibernian), 1923 v E, Ni, W; 1924 v E, Ni, W; 1925 v E, Ni, W; (with Arsenal), 1926 v E, Ni (11)
Harris, J. (Partick T), 1921 v W, Ni (2)
Harris, N. (Newcastle U), 1924 v E (1)
Harrower, W. (Queen's Park), 1882 v E; 1884 v Ni; 1886 v W (3)
Hartford, R. A. (WBA), 1972 v Pe, W (sub), E, Y, Cz, Br; (with Manchester C), 1976 v D, R, Ni (sub); 1977 v Cz (sub), W (sub), Se, W, Ni, E, Ch, Arg, Br; 1978 v EG, Cz, W, Bul, W, E, Pe, Ir, Ho; 1979 v A, N, P, W, Ni, E, Arg, N; (with Everton), 1980 v Pe, Bel; 1981 v Ni (sub), Is, W, Ni, E; 1982 v Se; (with Manchester C), Ni, P, Sp, Ni, W, E, Br (50)
Harvey, D. (Leeds U), 1973 v D; 1974 v Cz, WG, Ni, W, E, Bel, Z, Br, Y; 1975 v EG, Sp (2); 1976 v D (2); 1977 v Fi (sub) (16)
Hastings, A. C. (Sunderland), 1936 v Ni; 1938 v Ni (2)
Haughney, M. (Celtic), 1954 v E (1)
Hay, D. (Celtic), 1970 v Ni, W, E; 1971 v D, Bel, W, P, Ni; 1972 v P, Bel, Ho; 1973 v W, Ni, E, Sw, Br; 1974 v Cz (2), WG, Ni, W, E, Bel, N, Z, Br, Y (27)
Hay, J. (Celtic), 1905 v Ni; 1909 v Ni; 1910 v W, Ni, E; 1911 v Ni, E; (with Newcastle U), 1912 v E, W; 1914 v E, Ni (11)
Hegarty, P. (Dundee U), 1979 v W, Ni, E, Arg, N (sub); 1980 v W, E; 1983 v Ni (8)
Heggie, C. (Rangers), 1886 v Ni (1)
Henderson, G. H. (Rangers), 1904 v Ni (1)
Henderson, J. G. (Portsmouth), 1953 v Se; 1954 v Ni, E, N; 1956 v W; (with Arsenal), 1959 v W, Ni (7)
Henderson, W. (Rangers), 1963 v W, Ni, E, A, N, Ei, Sp; 1964 v Ni, E, N, WG; 1965 v Fi, Pol, E, Sp; 1966 v Ni, W, Pol, I, Ho; 1967 v W, Ni; 1968 v Ho; 1969 v Ni, E, Cy; 1970 v Ei; 1971 v P (29)
Hendry, E. C. J. (Blackburn R), 1993 v Es (2); 1994 v Ma, Ho, A, Ho; 1995 v Fi, Fa, Gr, Ru, Sm; 1996 v Fi, Se, Sm, Aus, D, US, Co, Ho, E, Sw; 1997 v A, Se, Es (2), A, Se (27)
Hepburn, J. (Alloa Ath), 1891 v W (1)
Hepburn, R. (Ayr U), 1932 v Ni (1)
Herd, A. C. (Hearts), 1935 v Ni (1)
Herd, D. G. (Arsenal), 1959 v E, W, Ni; 1961 v E, Cz (5)
Herd, G. (Clyde), 1958 v E; 1960 v H, T; 1961 v W, Ni (5)
Herriot, J. (Birmingham C), 1969 v Ni, E, D, Cy (2), W (sub); 1970 v Ei (sub), WG (8)
Hewie, J. D. (Charlton Ath), 1956 v E, A; 1957 v E, Ni, W, Y, Sp (2), Sw, WG; 1958 v H, Pol, Y, F; 1959 v Ho, P; 1960 v Ni, W, Pol (19)
Higgins, A. (Kilmarnock), 1885 v Ni (1)
Higgins, A. (Newcastle U), 1910 v E, Ni; 1911 v E, Ni (4)
Highet, T. C. (Queen's Park), 1875 v E; 1876 v E, W; 1878 v E (4)
Hill, D. (Rangers), 1881 v E, W; 1882 v W (3)
Hill, D. A. (Third Lanark), 1906 v Ni (1)
Hill, F. R. (Aberdeen), 1930 v F; 1931 v W, Ni (3)
Hill, J. (Hearts), 1891 v E; 1892 v W (2)
Hogg, G (Hearts), 1896 v E, Ni (2)
Hogg, J. (Ayr U), 1922 v Ni (1)
Hogg, R. M. (Celtic), 1937 v Cz (1)
Holm, A. H. (Queen's Park), 1882 v W; 1883 v E, W (3)
Holt, D. D. (Hearts), 1963 v A, N, Ei, Sp; 1964 v WG (sub) (5)
Holton, J. A. (Manchester U), 1973 v W, Ni, E, Sw, Br; 1974 v Cz, WG, Ni, W, E, N, Z, Br, Y; 1975 v EG (15)
Hope, R. (WBA), 1968 v Ho; 1969 v D (2)
Hopkin, D. (Crystal Palace), 1997 v Ma, Bl (2)
Houliston, W. (Queen of the South), 1949 v E, Ni, F (3)
Houston, S. M. (Manchester U), 1976 v D (1)
Howden, W. (Partick T), 1905 v Ni (1)
Howe, R. (Hamilton A), 1929 v N, Ho (2)
Howie, J. (Newcastle U), 1905 v E; 1906 v E; 1908 v E (3)
Howie, H. (Hibernian), 1949 v W (1)
Howieson, J. (St Mirren), 1927 v Ni (1)
Hughes, J. (Celtic), 1965 v Pol, Sp; 1966 v Ni, I (2); 1968 v E; 1969 v A; 1970 v Ei (8)

Hughes, W. (Sunderland), 1975 v Se (sub) (1)
Humphries, W. (Motherwell), 1952 v Se (1)
Hunter, A. (Kilmarnock), 1972 v Pe, Y; (with Celtic), 1973 v E; 1974 v Cz (4)
Hunter, J. (Dundee), 1909 v W (1)
Hunter, J. (Third Lanark), 1874 v E; (with Eastern), 1875 v E; (with Third Lanark), 1876 v E; 1877 v W (4)
Hunter, R. (St Mirren), 1890 v Ni (1)
Hunter, W. (Motherwell), 1960 v H, T; 1961 v W (3)
Husband, J. (Partick T), 1947 v W (1)
Hutchison, T. (Coventry C), 1974 v Cz (2), WG (2), Ni, W, Bel (sub), N, Z (sub), Y (sub); 1975 v EG, Sp (2), P, E (sub), R (sub); 1976 v D (17)
Hutton, J. (Aberdeen), 1923 v E, W, Ni; 1924 v Ni; 1926 v W, E, Ni; (with Blackburn R), 1927 v Ni; 1928 v W, Ni (10)
Hutton, J. (St Bernards), 1887 v Ni (1)
Hyslop, T. (Stoke C), 1896 v E; (with Rangers), 1897 v E (2)

Imlach, J. J. S. (Nottingham F), 1958 v H, Pol, Y, F (4)
Imrie, W. N. (St Johnstone), 1929 v N, G (2)
Inglis, J. (Kilmarnock Ath), 1884 v Ni (1)
Inglis, J. (Rangers), 1883 v E, W (2)
Irons, J. H. (Queen's Park), 1900 v W (1)
Irvine, B. (Aberdeen), 1991 v R; 1993 v G, Es (2); 1994 v Sw, I, Ma, A, Ho (9)

Jackson, A. (Cambuslang), 1886 v W; 1888 v Ni (2)
Jackson, A. (Aberdeen), 1925 v E, W, Ni; (with Huddersfield T), 1926 v E, W, Ni; 1927 v W, Ni; 1928 v E, W; 1929 v E, W, Ni; 1930 v E, W, Ni, F (17)
Jackson, C. (Rangers), 1975 v Se, P (sub), W; 1976 v D, R, Ni, W, E (8)
Jackson, D. (Hibernian), 1995 v Ru, Sm, J, Ec, Fa; 1996 v Gr, Fi (sub), Se (sub), Sm (sub), Aus (sub), D (sub), US; 1997 v La, Se, Es, A, Se, W, Ma, Bl (20)
Jackson, J. (Partick T), 1931 v A, I, Sw; 1933 v E; (with Chelsea), 1934 v E; 1935 v E; 1936 v W, Ni (8)
Jackson, T. A. (St Mirren), 1904 v W, E, Ni; 1905 v W; 1907 v W, Ni (6)
James, A. W. (Preston NE), 1926 v W; 1928 v E; 1929 v E, Ni; (with Arsenal), 1930 v E, W, Ni; 1933 v W (8)
Jardine, A. (Rangers), 1971 v D (sub); 1972 v P, Bel, Ho; 1973 v E, Sw, Br; 1974 v Cz (2), WG (2), Ni, W, E, Bel, N, Z, Br, Y; 1975 v EG, Sp (2), Se, P, W, Ni, E; 1977 v Se (sub), Ch (sub), Br (sub); 1978 v Cz, W, Ni, Ir; 1980 v Pe, A, Bel (2) (38)
Jarvie, A. (Airdrieonians), 1971 v P (sub), Ni (sub), E (sub) (3)
Jenkinson, T. (Hearts), 1887 v Ni (1)
Jess, E. (Aberdeen), 1993 v I (sub), Ma; 1994 v Sw (sub), I, Ho (sub), A, Ho (sub); 1995 v Fi (sub); 1996 v Se (sub), Sm, US, Co (sub), E (sub) (13)
Johnston, L. H. (Clyde), 1948 v Bel, Sw (2)
Johnston, M. (Watford), 1984 v W (sub), E (sub), F; 1985 v Y; (with Celtic), Ic, Sp (2), W; 1986 v EG; 1987 v Bul, Ei (2), L; (with Nantes), 1988 v H, Bel, L, S.Ar, Sp, Co, E; 1989 v N, Y, I, Cy, F, Cy, E, Ch (sub); (with Rangers), 1990 v F, N, EG, Pol, Ma, Cr, Se, Br; 1992 v Sw, Sm (sub) (38)
Johnston, R. (Sunderland), 1938 v Cz (1)
Johnston, W. (Rangers), 1966 v W, E, Pol, Ho; 1968 v W, E; 1969 v Ni (sub); 1970 v Ni; 1971 v D; (with WBA), 1977 v Se, W (sub), Ni, E, Ch, Arg, Br; 1978 v EG, Cz, W (2), E, Pe (22)
Johnstone, D. (Rangers), 1973 v W, Ni, E, Sw, Br; 1975 v EG (sub), Se (sub); 1976 v Sw, Ni (sub), E (sub); 1978 v Bul (sub), Ni, W; 1980 v Bel (14)
Johnstone, J. (Abercorn), 1888 v W (1)
Johnstone, J. (Celtic), 1965 v W, Fi; 1966 v E; 1967 v W, USSR; 1968 v W; 1969 v A, WG; 1970 v E, WG; 1971 v D, E; 1972 v P, Bel, Ho, Ni, E (sub); 1974 v W, E, Bel, N; 1975 v EG, Sp (23)
Johnstone, Jas (Kilmarnock), 1894 v W (1)
Johnstone, J. A. (Hearts), 1930 v W; 1933 v W, Ni (3)
Johnstone, R. (Hibernian), 1951 v E, D, F; 1952 v Ni, E; 1953 v E, Se; 1954 v W, E, N, Fi; 1955 v Ni, H; (with Manchester C), 1955 v E; 1956 v E, Ni, W (17)
Johnstone, W. (Third Lanark), 1887 v Ni; 1889 v W; 1890 v E (3)
Jordan, J. (Leeds U), 1973 v E (sub), Sw (sub), Br; 1974 v Cz (sub+1), WG (sub), Ni (sub), W, E, Bel, N, Z, Br, Y; 1975 v EG, Sp (2); 1976 v W, E; 1977 v Cz, W, Ni, E; 1978 v EG, Cz, W; (with Manchester U), Bul, Ni, E, Pe, Ir, Ho; 1979 v A, P, W (sub), Ni, E, N; 1980 v Bel, Ni (sub), W, E, Pol; 1981 v Is, W, E; (with AC Milan), 1982 v Se, Ho, W, E, USSR (52)

Kay, J. L. (Queen's Park), 1880 v E; 1882 v E, W; 1883 v E, W; 1884 v W (6)
Keillor, A. (Montrose), 1891 v W; 1892 v Ni; (with Dundee), 1894 v Ni; 1895 v W; 1896 v W; 1897 v W (6)
Keir, L. (Dumbarton), 1885 v W; 1886 v Ni; 1887 v E, W; 1888 v E (5)
Kelly, H. T. (Blackpool), 1952 v USA (1)
Kelly, J. (Renton), 1888 v E; (with Celtic), 1889 v E; 1890 v E; 1892 v E; 1893 v E, Ni; 1894 v W; 1896 v Ni (8)
Kelly, J. C. (Barnsley), 1949 v W, Ni (2)
Kelso, R. (Renton), 1885 v W, Ni; 1886 v W; 1887 v E, W; 1888 v E, Ni; (with Dundee), 1898 v Ni (8)
Kelso, T. (Dundee), 1914 v W (1)
Kennaway, J. (Celtic), 1934 v A (1)
Kennedy, A. (Eastern), 1875 v E; 1876 v E, W; (with Third Lanark), 1878 v E; 1882 v W; 1884 v W (6)
Kennedy, J. (Celtic), 1964 v W, E, WG; 1965 v W, Ni, Fi (5)
Kennedy, J. (Hibernian), 1897 v W (1)
Kennedy, S. (Aberdeen), 1978 v Bul, W, E, Pe, Ho; 1979 v A, P; 1982 v P (sub) (8)
Kennedy, S. (Partick T), 1905 v W (1)
Kennedy, S. (Rangers), 1975 v Se, P, W, Ni, E (5)
Ker, G. (Queen's Park), 1880 v E; 1881 v E, W; 1882 v W, E (5)
Ker, W. (Granville), 1872 v E; (with Queen's Park), 1873 v E (2)
Kerr, A. (Partick T), 1955 v A, H (2)
Kerr, P. (Hibernian), 1924 v Ni (1)
Key, G. (Hearts), 1902 v Ni (1)
Key, W. (Queen's Park), 1907 v Ni (1)
King, A. (Hearts), 1896 v E, W; (with Celtic), 1897 v Ni; 1898 v Ni; 1899 v Ni, W (6)
King, J. (Hamilton A), 1933 v Ni; 1934 v Ni (2)
King, W. S. (Queen's Park), 1929 v W (1)
Kinloch, J. D. (Partick T), 1922 v Ni (1)
Kinnaird, A. F. (Wanderers), 1873 v E (1)
Kinnear, D. (Rangers), 1938 v Cz (1)

Lambert, P. (Motherwell), 1995 v J, Ec (sub); (with Borussia Dortmund), 1997 v La (sub), Se (sub), A, Se, Bl (7)
Lambie, J. A. (Queen's Park), 1886 v Ni; 1887 v Ni; 1888 v E (3)
Lambie, W. A. (Queen's Park), 1892 v Ni; 1893 v W; 1894 v E; 1895 v E, Ni; 1896 v E, Ni; 1897 v E, Ni (9)
Lamont, D. (Pilgrims), 1885 v Ni (1)
Lang, A. (Dumbarton), 1880 v W (1)
Lang, J. J. (Clydesdale), 1876 v W; (with Third Lanark), 1878 v W (2)
Latta, A. (Dumbarton), 1888 v W; 1889 v E (2)
Law, D. (Huddersfield T), 1959 v W, Ni, Ho, P; 1960 v Ni, W; (with Manchester C), 1960 v E, Pol, A; 1961 v E, Ni; (with Torino), 1962 v Cz (2), E; (with Manchester U), 1963 v W, Ni, E, A, N, Ei, Sp; 1964 v W, E, N, WG; 1965 v W, Ni, E, Fi (2), Pol, Sp; 1966 v Ni, E, Pol; 1967 v E, USSR; 1968 v Ni; 1969 v Ni, A, WG; 1972 v Pe, Ni, W, E, Y, Cz, Br; (with Manchester C), 1974 v Cz (2), WG (2), Ni, Z (55)
Law, G. (Rangers), 1910 v E, Ni, W (3)
Law, T. (Chelsea), 1928 v E; 1930 v E (2)
Lawrence, J. (Newcastle U), 1911 v E (1)
Lawrence, T. (Liverpool), 1963 v Ei; 1969 v W, WG (3)
Lawson, D. (St Mirren), 1923 v E (1)
Leckie, R. (Queen's Park), 1872 v E (1)
Leggat, G. (Aberdeen), 1956 v E; 1957 v W; 1958 v Ni, H, Pol, Y, Par; (with Fulham), 1959 v E, W, Ni, WG, Ho; 1960 v E, Ni, W, Pol, A, H (18)
Leighton, J. (Aberdeen), 1983 v EG, Sw, Bel, Sw, W, E, Ca (2); 1984 v U, Bel, Ni, W, E, F; 1985 v Y, Ic, Sp (2), W, E, Ic; 1986 v W, EG, Aus (2), Is, D, WG, U; 1987 v Bul, Ei (2), L, Bel, E; 1988 v H, Bel, Bul, L, S.Ar, Ma, Sp; (with Manchester U), Co, E; 1989 v N, Cy, F, Cy, E, Ch; 1990 v Y, F, N, Arg, Ma (sub, Cr, Se, Br; (with Hibernian), 1994 v Ma, A, Ho; 1995 v Gr (sub), Ru, Sm, J, Ec, Fa; 1996 v Gr, Fi, Se, Sm, Aus, D, US; 1997 v Se, Es, A, Se, W (sub), Ma, Bl (81)
Lennie, W. (Aberdeen), 1908 v W, Ni (2)
Lennox, R. (Celtic), 1967 v Ni, E, USSR; 1968 v W, L; 1969 v D, A, WG, Cy (sub); 1970 v W (sub) (10)
Leslie, L. G. (Airdrieonians), 1961 v W, Ni, Ei (2), Cz (5)
Levein, C. (Hearts), 1990 v Arg, EG, Eg (sub), Pol, Ma (sub), Se; 1992 v R, Sm; 1993 v P, G, P; 1994 v Sw, Ho; 1995 v Fi, Fa, Ru (16)
Liddell, W. (Liverpool), 1947 v W, Ni; 1948 v E, W, Ni; 1950 v E, W, P, F; 1951 v W, Ni, E, A; 1952 v W, Ni, E, USA, D, Se; 1953 v W, Ni, E; 1954 v W; 1955 v P, Y, A, H; 1956 v Ni (28)
Liddle, D. (East Fife), 1931 v A, I, Sw (3)
Lindsay, D. (St Mirren), 1903 v Ni (1)

Lindsay, J. (Dumbarton), 1880 v W; 1881 v W, E; 1884 v W, E; 1885 v W, E; 1886 v E (8)
Lindsay, J. (Renton), 1888 v E; 1893 v E, Ni (3)
Linwood, A. B. (Clyde), 1950 v W (1)
Little, R. J. (Rangers), 1953 v Se (1)
Livingstone, G. T. (Manchester C), 1906 v E; (with Rangers), 1907 v W (2)
Lochhead, A. (Third Lanark), 1889 v W (1)
Logan, J. (Ayr U), 1891 v W (1)
Logan, T. (Falkirk), 1913 v Ni (1)
Logie, J. T. (Arsenal), 1953 v Ni (1)
Loney, W. (Celtic), 1910 v W, Ni (2)
Long, H. (Clyde), 1947 v Ni (1)
Longair, W. (Dundee), 1894 v Ni (1)
Lorimer, P. (Leeds U), 1970 v A (sub); 1971 v W, Ni; 1972 v Ni (sub), W, E; 1973 v D (2), E (2); 1974 v WG (sub), E, Bel, N, Z, Br, Y; 1975 v Sp (sub); 1976 v D (2), R (sub) (21)
Love, A. (Aberdeen), 1931 v A, I, Sw (3)
Low, A. (Falkirk), 1934 v Ni (1)
Low, T. P. (Rangers), 1897 v Ni (1)
Low, W. L. (Newcastle U), 1911 v E, W; 1912 v Ni; 1920 v E, Ni (5)
Lowe, J. (Cambuslang), 1891 v Ni (1)
Lowe, J. (St Bernards), 1887 v Ni (1)
Lundie, J. (Hibernian), 1886 v W (1)
Lyall, J. (Sheffield W), 1905 v E (1)

McAdam, J. (Third Lanark), 1880 v W (1)
McAllister, B. (Wimbledon), 1997 v W, Ma, Bl (sub) (3)
McAllister, G. (Leicester C), 1990 v EG, Ma (sub); (with Leeds U), 1991 v R, Sw, Bul, USSR (sub), Sm; 1992 v Sw (sub), Sm, Ni, Fi (sub), US, Ca, N, Ho, G, C; 1993 v Sw, P, I, Ma; 1994 v Sw, I, Ma, Ho, A, Ho; 1995 v Fi, Ru, Gr, Ru, Sm; 1996 v Gr, Fi, Se, Sm, Aus, D, US (sub), Co, Ho, E, Sw; (with Coventry C), 1997 v A, La, Es (2), A, Se, W, Ma, Bl (53)
McArthur, D. (Celtic), 1895 v E, Ni; 1899 v W (3)
McAtee, A. (Celtic), 1913 v W (1)
McAulay, J. (Dumbarton), 1882 v W; (with Arthurlie), 1884 v Ni (2)
McAulay, J. (Dumbarton), 1883 v E, W; 1884 v E; 1885 v E, W; 1886 v E; 1887 v E, W (8)
McAuley, R. (Rangers), 1932 v Ni, W (2)
McAvennie, F. (West Ham U), 1986 v Aus (2), D (sub), WG (sub); (with Celtic), 1988 v S.Ar (5)
McBain, E. (St Mirren), 1894 v W (1)
McBain, N. (Manchester U), 1922 v E; (with Everton), 1923 v Ni; 1924 v W (3)
McBride, J. (Celtic), 1967 v W, Ni (2)
McBride, P. (Preston NE), 1904 v E; 1906 v E; 1907 v E, W; 1908 v E; 1909 v W (6)
McCall, J. (Renton), 1886 v W; 1887 v E, W; 1888 v E; 1890 v E (5)
McCall, S. M. (Everton), 1990 v Arg, EG, Eg (sub), Pol, Ma, Cr, Se, Br; 1991 v Sw, USSR, Sm; (with Rangers), 1992 v Sw, R, Sm, US, Ca, N, Ho, G, C; 1993 v Sw, P (2); 1994 v I, Ho, A (sub), Ho; 1995 v Fi (sub), Ru, Gr; 1996 v Gr, D, US (sub), Co, Ho, E, Sw; 1997 v A, La (39)
McCalliog, J. (Sheffield W), 1967 v E, USSR; 1968 v Ni; 1969 v D; (with Wolverhampton W), 1971 v P (5)
McCallum, N. (Renton), 1888 v Ni (1)
McCann, R. J. (Motherwell), 1959 v WG; 1960 v E, Ni, W; 1961 v E (5)
McCartney, W. (Hibernian), 1902 v Ni (1)
McClair, B. (Celtic), 1987 v L, Ei, E, Br (sub); (with Manchester U), 1988 v Bul, Ma (sub), Sp (sub); 1989 v N, Y, I (sub), Cy, F (sub); 1990 v N (sub), Arg (sub); 1991 v Bul (2), Sm; 1992 v Sw (sub), Ni, US, Ca (sub), N, Ho, G, C; 1993 v Sw, P (sub), Es (2) (30)
McClory, A. (Motherwell), 1927 v W; 1928 v Ni; 1935 v W (3)
McCloy, P. (Ayr U), 1924 v E; 1925 v E (2)
McCloy, P. (Rangers), 1973 v W, Ni, Sw, Br (4)
McCoist, A. (Rangers), 1986 v Ho; 1987 v L (sub), Ei (sub), Bel, E, Br; 1988 v H, Bel, Ma, Sp, Co, E; 1989 v Y (sub), F, Cy, E; 1990 v Y, F, N, EG (sub), Eg, Pol, Ma (sub), Cr (sub), Se (sub); Br; 1991 v R, Sw, Bul (2), USSR; 1992 v Sw, Sm, Ni, Fi (sub), US, Ca, N, Ho, G, C; 1993 v Sw, P, I, Ma, P; 1996 v Gr (sub), Fi (sub), Sm (sub), Aus, D (sub), Co, E (sub), Sw; 1997 v A, Se (sub), Es (sub), A (sub) (58)
McColl, A. (Renton), 1888 v Ni (1)
McColl, I. M. (Rangers), 1950 v E, F; 1951 v W, Ni, Bel; 1957 v W, Ni, W, Y, Sp, Sw, WG; 1958 v Ni, E (14)
McColl, R. S. (Queen's Park), 1896 v W, Ni; 1897 v Ni; 1898 v Ni; 1899 v Ni, E, W; 1900 v E, W; 1901 v E, W; (with Newcastle U), 1902 v E; (with Queen's Park), 1908 v Ni (13)
McColl, W. (Renton), 1895 v W (1)

McCombie, A. (Sunderland), 1903 v E, W; (with Newcastle U), 1905 v E, W (4)

McCorkindale, J. (Partick T), 1891 v W (1)

McCormick, R. (Abercorn), 1886 v W (1)

McCrae, D. (St Mirren), 1929 v N, G (2)

McCreadie, A. (Rangers), 1893 v W; 1894 v E (2)

McCreadie, E. G. (Chelsea), 1965 v E, Sp, Fi, Pol; 1966 v P, Ni, W, Pol, I; 1967 v E, USSR; 1968 v Ni, W, E, Ho; 1969 v W, Ni, E, D, A, WG, Cy (2) (23)

McCulloch, D. (Hearts), 1935 v W; (with Brentford), 1936 v E; 1937 v W, Ni; 1938 v Cz; (with Derby Co), 1939 v H, W (7)

MacDonald, A. (Rangers), 1976 v Sw (1)

McDonald, J. (Edinburgh University), 1886 v E (1)

McDonald, J. (Sunderland), 1956 v W, Ni (2)

MacDougall, E. J. (Norwich C) 1975 v Se, P, W, Ni, E; 1976 v D, R (sub) (7)

McDougall, J. (Liverpool), 1931 v I, A (2)

McDougall, J. (Airdrieonians), 1926 v Ni (1)

McDougall, J. (Vale of Leven), 1877 v E, W; 1878 v E; 1879 v E, W (5)

McFadyen, W. (Motherwell), 1934 v A, W (2)

Macfarlane, A. (Dundee), 1904 v W; 1906 v W; 1908 v W; 1909 v Ni; 1911 v W (5)

McFarlane, R. (Greenock Morton), 1896 v W (1)

Macfarlane, W. (Hearts), 1947 v L (1)

McGarr, E. (Aberdeen), 1970 v Ei, A (2)

McGarvey, F. P. (Liverpool), 1979 v Ni (sub), Arg; (with Celtic), 1984 v U, Bel (sub), EG (sub), Ni, W (7)

McGeoch, A. (Dumbreck), 1876 v E, W; 1877 v E, W (4)

McGhee, J. (Hibernian), 1886 v W (1)

McGhee, M. (Aberdeen), 1983 v Ca (1+1 sub); 1984 v Ni (sub), E (4)

McGinlay, J. (Bolton W), 1994 v A, Ho; 1995 v Fa, Ru, Gr, Ru, Sm, Fa; 1996 v Se; 1997 v Se, Es (1 + sub), A (sub) (13)

McGonagle, W. (Celtic), 1933 v E; 1934 v A, E, Ni; 1935 v Ni, W (6)

McGrain, D. (Celtic), 1973 v W, Ni, E, Sw, Br; 1974 v Cz (2), WG, W (sub), E, Bel, N, Z, Br, Y; 1975 v Sp, Se, P, W, Ni, E, R; 1976 v D (2), Sw, Ni, W, E; 1977 v Fi, Cz, W (2), Se, Ni, E, Ch, Arg, Br; 1978 v EG, Cz; 1980 v Bel, P, Ni, W, E, Pol, H; 1981 v Se, P, Is, Ni, Is, W (sub), Ni, E; 1982 v Se, Sp, Ho, Ni, E, Nz, USSR (sub) (62)

McGregor, J. C. (Vale of Leven), 1877 v E, W; 1878 v E; 1880 v E (4)

McGrory, J. E. (Kilmarnock), 1965 v Ni, Fi; 1966 v P (3)

McGrory, J. (Celtic), 1928 v Ni; 1931 v E; 1932 v Ni, W; 1933 v E, Ni; 1934 v Ni (7)

McGuire, W. (Beith), 1881 v E, W (2)

McGurk, F. (Birmingham), 1934 v W (1)

McHardy, H. (Rangers), 1885 v Ni (1)

McInally, A. (Aston Villa), 1989 v Cy (sub), Ch; (with Bayern Munich), 1990 v Y (sub), F (sub), Arg, Pol (sub), Ma, Cr (8)

McInally, J. (Dundee U), 1987 v Bel, Br; 1988 v Ma (sub); 1991 v Bul (2); 1992 v US (sub), N (sub), C (sub); 1993 v G, P (10)

McInally, T. B. (Celtic), 1926 v Ni; 1927 v W (2)

McInnes, T. (Cowlairs), 1889 v Ni (1)

McIntosh, W. (Third Lanark), 1905 v Ni (1)

McIntyre, A. (Vale of Leven), 1878 v E; 1882 v E (2)

McIntyre, H. (Rangers), 1880 v W (1)

McIntyre, J. (Rangers), 1884 v W (1)

McKay, D. (Celtic), 1959 v E, WG, Ho, P; 1960 v E, Pol, A, H, T; 1961 v W, Ni; 1962 v Ni, Cz, U (sub) (14)

Mackay, D. C. (Hearts), 1957 v Sp; 1958 v F; 1959 v W, Ni; (with Tottenham H), 1959 v WG, E; 1960 v W, Ni, A, Pol, H, T; 1961 v W, Ni, E; 1963 v E, A, N; 1964 v Ni, W, N; 1966 v W (22)

Mackay, G. (Hearts), 1988 v Bul (sub), L (sub), S.Ar (sub), Ma (4)

McKay, J. (Blackburn R), 1924 v W (1)

McKay, R. (Newcastle U), 1928 v W (1)

McKean, R. (Rangers), 1976 v Sw (sub) (1)

McKenzie, D. (Brentford), 1938 v Ni (1)

Mackenzie, J. A. (Partick T), 1954 v W, E, N, Fi, A, U; 1955 v E, H; 1956 v A (9)

McKeown, M. (Celtic), 1889 v Ni; 1890 v E (2)

McKie, J. (East Stirling), 1898 v W (1)

McKillop, T. R. (Rangers), 1938 v Ho (1)

McKimmie, S. (Aberdeen), 1989 v E, Ch; 1990 v Arg, Eg, Cr (sub), Br; 1991 v R, Sw, Bul, Sm; 1992 v Sw, R, Ni, F, US, Ca (sub), N (sub), Ho, G, C; 1993 v P, Es (sub); 1994 v Sw, I, Ho, A, Ho; 1995 v Fi, Fa, Ru, Gr, Ru, Fa; 1996 v Gr, Fi, Se, D, Co (sub), Ho, E (40)

McKinlay, D. (Liverpool), 1922 v W, Ni (2)

McKinlay, T. (Celtic), 1996 v Gr, Fi, D, Co, E, Sw; 1997 v A, La, Se, Es (sub + 1), A, Se, W, Ma, Bl (16)

McKinlay, W. (Dundee U), 1994 v Ma, Ho (sub), A, Ho; 1995 v Fa (sub), Ru, Gr, Ru (sub), Sm (sub), J, Ec, Fa; 1996 v Fi (sub), Se (sub); (with Blackburn R), Sm (sub), Aus, D (sub), Ho (sub); 1997 v Se, Es (sub) (20)

McKinnon, A. (Queen's Park), 1874 v E (1)

McKinnon, R. (Rangers), 1966 v W, E, I (2), Ho, Br; 1967 v W, Ni, E; 1968 v W, E, Ho; 1969 v D, A, WG, Cy; 1970 v Ni, W, E, Ei, WG, A; 1971 v D, Bel, P, USSR, D (28)

McKinnon, R. (Motherwell), 1994 v Ma; 1995 v J, Fa (3)

MacKinnon, W. (Dumbarton), 1883 v E, W; 1884 v E, W (4)

McKinnon, W. W. (Queen's Park), 1872 v E; 1873 v E; 1874 v E; 1875 v E; 1876 v E, W; 1877 v E; 1878 v E; 1879 v E (9)

McLaren, A. (St Johnstone), 1929 v N, G, Ho; 1933 v W, Ni (5)

McLaren, A. (Preston NE), 1947 v E, Bel, L; 1948 v W (4)

McLaren, A. (Hearts), 1992 v US, Ca, N; 1993 v I, Ma, G, Es (sub + 1); 1994 v I, Ma, Ho, A; 1995 v Fi, Fa; (with Rangers), Ru, Gr, Ru, Sm, J, Ec, Fa; 1996 v Fi, Se, Sm (24)

McLaren, J. (Hibernian), 1888 v W; (with Celtic), 1889 v E; 1890 v E (3)

McLean, A. (Celtic), 1926 v W, Ni; 1927 v W, E (4)

McLean, D. (St Bernards), 1896 v W; 1897 v Ni (2)

McLean, D. (Sheffield W), 1912 v E (1)

McLean, G. (Dundee), 1968 v Ho (1)

McLean, T. (Kilmarnock), 1969 v D, Cy, W; 1970 v Ni, W; 1971 v D (6)

McLeish, A. (Aberdeen), 1980 v F, Ni, W, E, Pol, H; 1981 v Se, Is, Ni, Is, Ni, E; 1982 v Se, Sp, Ni, Br (sub); 1983 v Bel, Sw (sub), W, E, Ca (3); 1984 v U, Bel, EG, Ni, W, E, F; 1985 v Y, Ic, Sp (2), W, E, Ic; 1986 v W, EG, Aus (2), E, Ho, D; 1987 v Bel, E, Br; 1988 v Bel, Bul, L, S.Ar (sub), Ma, Sp, Co, E; 1989 v N, Y, I, Cy, F, Cy, E, Ch; 1990 v Y, F, N, Arg, EG, Eg, Cr, Se, Br; 1991 v R, Sw, USSR, Bul; 1993 v Ma (77)

McLeod, D. (Celtic), 1905 v Ni; 1906 v E, W, Ni (4)

McLeod, J. (Dumbarton), 1888 v Ni; 1889 v W; 1890 v Ni; 1892 v E; 1893 v W (5)

MacLeod, J. M. (Hibernian), 1961 v E, Ei (2), Cz (4)

MacLeod, M. (Celtic), 1985 v E (sub); 1987 v Ei, L, E, Br; (with Borussia Dortmund), 1988 v Co, E; 1989 v I, Ch; 1990 v Y, F, N (sub), Arg, EG, Pol, Se Br; (with Hibernian), 1991 v R, Sw, USSR (sub) (20)

McLeod, W. (Cowlairs), 1886 v Ni (1)

McLintock, A. (Vale of Leven), 1875 v E; 1876 v E; 1880 v E (3)

McLintock, F. (Leicester C), 1963 v N (sub), Ei, Sp; (with Arsenal), 1965 v Ni; 1967 v USSR; 1970 v Ni; 1971 v W, Ni, E (9)

McLuckie, J. S. (Manchester C), 1934 v W (1)

McMahon, A. (Celtic), 1892 v E; 1893 v E, Ni; 1894 v E; 1901 v Ni; 1902 v W (6)

McMenemy, J. (Celtic), 1905 v Ni; 1909 v Ni; 1910 v E, W; 1911 v Ni, W, E; 1912 v W; 1914 v W, Ni, E; 1920 v Ni (12)

McMenemy, J. (Motherwell), 1934 v W (1)

McMillan, J. (St Bernards), 1897 v W (1)

McMillan, I. L. (Airdrieonians), 1952 v E, USA, D; 1955 v E; 1956 v E; (with Rangers), 1961 v Cz (6)

McMillan, T. (Dumbarton), 1887 v Ni (1)

McMullan, J. (Partick T), 1920 v W; 1921 v W, Ni, E; 1924 v E, Ni; 1925 v E; 1926 v W; (with Manchester C), 1926 v E; 1927 v E, W; 1928 v E, W; 1929 v W, E, Ni (16)

McNab, A. (Morton), 1921 v E, Ni (2)

McNab, A. (Sunderland), 1937 v A; (with WBA), 1939 v E (2)

McNab, C. D. (Dundee), 1931 v E, W, A, I, Sw; 1932 v E (6)

McNab, S. (Liverpool), 1923 v W (1)

McNair, A. (Celtic), 1906 v W; 1907 v Ni; 1908 v E, W; 1909 v E; 1910 v W; 1912 v E, W, Ni; 1913 v E; 1914 v E, Ni; 1920 v E, W, Ni (15)

McNamara, J. (Celtic), 1997 v La (sub), Se, Es, W (sub) (4)

McNaught, W. (Raith R), 1951 v A, W, Ni; 1952 v E; 1955 v Ni (5)

McNeil, H. (Queen's Park), 1874 v E; 1875 v E; 1876 v E, W; 1877 v W; 1878 v E; 1879 v E, W; 1881 v E, W (10)

McNeil, M. (Rangers), 1876 v W; 1880 v E (2)

McNeill, W. (Celtic), 1961 v E, Ei (2), Cz; 1962 v Ni, E, Cz, U; 1963 v Ei, Sp; 1964 v W, E, WG; 1965 v E, Fi, Pol, Sp; 1966 v Ni, Pol; 1967 v USSR; 1968 v E; 1969 v Cy, W, E, Cy (sub); 1970 v WG; 1972 v Ni, W, E (29)

McPhail, J. (Celtic), 1950 v W; 1951 v W, Ni, A; 1954 v Ni (5)

McPhail, R. (Airdrieonians), 1927 v E; (with Rangers), 1929 v W; 1931 v E, Ni; 1932 v W, Ni, F; 1933 v E, Ni; 1934 v A, Ni; 1935 v E; 1937 v G, E, Cz; 1938 v W, Ni (17)

McPherson, D. (Kilmarnock), 1892 v Ni (1)

McPherson, D. (Hearts), 1989 v Cy, E; 1990 v N, Ma, Cr, Se, Br; 1991 v Sw, Bul (2), USSR (sub), Sm; 1992 v Sw, R,

O'Donnell, F. (Preston NE), 1937 v E, A, Cz; 1938 v W; (with Blackpool), E, Ho (6)
O'Donnell, P. (Motherwell), 1994 v Sw (sub) (1)
Ogilvie, D. H. (Motherwell), 1934 v A (1)
O'Hare, J. (Derby Co), 1970 v W, Ni, E; 1971 v D, Bel, W, Ni; 1972 v P, Bel, Ho (sub), Pe, Ni, W (13)
O'Neil, B. (Celtic), 1996 v Aus (1)
Ormond, W. E. (Hibernian), 1954 v E, N, Fi, A, U; 1959 v E (6)
O'Rourke, F. (Airdrieonians), 1907 v Ni (1)
Orr, J. (Kilmarnock), 1892 v W (1)
Orr, R. (Newcastle U), 1902 v E; 1904 v E (2)
Orr, T. (Morton), 1952 v Ni, W (2)
Orr, W. (Celtic), 1900 v Ni; 1903 v Ni; 1904 v W (3)
Orrock, R. (Falkirk), 1913 v W (1)
Oswald, J. (Third Lanark), 1889 v E; (with St Bernards), 1895 v E; (with Rangers), 1897 v W (3)

Parker, A. H. (Falkirk), 1955 v P, Y, A; 1956 v E, Ni, W, A; 1957 v Ni, W, Y; 1958 v Ni, W, E, Sw; (with Everton), Par (15)
Parlane, D. (Rangers), 1973 v W, Sw, Br; 1975 v Sp (sub), Se, P, W, Ni, E, R; 1976 v D (sub); 1977 v W (12)
Parlane, R. (Vale of Leven), 1878 v W; 1879 v E, W (3)
Paterson, G. D. (Celtic), 1939 v Ni (1)
Paterson, J. (Leicester C), 1920 v E (1)
Paterson, J. (Cowdenbeath), 1931 v A, I, Sw (3)
Paton, A. (Motherwell), 1952 v D, Se (2)
Paton, D. (St Bernards), 1896 v W (1)
Paton, M. (Dumbarton), 1883 v E; 1884 v W; 1885 v W, E; 1886 v E (5)
Paton, R. (Vale of Leven), 1879 v E, W (2)
Patrick, J. (St Mirren), 1897 v E, W (2)
Paul, H. McD. (Queen's Park), 1909 v E, W, Ni (3)
Paul, J. (Partick T), 1888 v W; 1889 v W; 1890 v W (3)
Paul, W. (Dykebar), 1891 v Ni (1)
Pearson, T. (Newcastle U), 1947 v E, Bel (2)
Penman, A. (Dundee), 1966 v Ho (1)
Pettigrew, W. (Motherwell), 1976 v Sw, Ni, W; 1977 v W (sub), Se (5)
Phillips, J. (Queen's Park), 1877 v E, W; 1878 v W (3)
Plenderleith, J. B. (Manchester C), 1961 v Ni (1)
Porteous, W. (Hearts), 1903 v Ni (1)
Pringle, C. (St Mirren), 1921 v W (1)
Provan, D. (Rangers), 1964 v Ni, N; 1966 v I (2), Ho (5)
Provan, D. (Celtic), 1980 v Bel (2 sub), P (sub), Ni (sub); 1981 v Is, W, E; 1982 v Se, P, Ni (10)
Pursell, P. (Queen's Park), 1914 v W (1)

Quinn, J. (Celtic), 1905 v Ni; 1906 v Ni, W; 1908 v Ni, E; 1909 v E; 1910 v E, Ni, W; 1912 v E, W (11)
Quinn, P. (Motherwell), 1961 v E, Ei (2); 1962 v U (4)

Rae, J. (Third Lanark), 1889 v W; 1890 v Ni (2)
Raeside, J. S. (Third Lanark), 1906 v W (1)
Raisbeck, A. G. (Liverpool), 1900 v E; 1901 v E; 1902 v E; 1903 v E, W; 1904 v E; 1906 v E; 1907 v E (8)
Rankin, G. (Vale of Leven), 1890 v Ni; 1891 v E (2)
Rankin, R. (St Mirren), 1929 v N, G, Ho (3)
Redpath, W. (Motherwell), 1949 v W, Ni; 1951 v E, D, F, Bel, A; 1952 v Ni, E (9)
Reid, J. G. (Airdrieonians), 1914 v W; 1920 v W; 1924 v Ni (3)
Reid, R. (Brentford), 1938 v E, Ni (2)
Reid, W. (Rangers), 1911 v E, W, Ni; 1912 v Ni; 1913 v E, W, Ni; 1914 v E, Ni (9)
Reilly, L. (Hibernian), 1949 v E, W, F; 1950 v W, Ni, Sw, F; 1951 v W, E, D, F, Bel, A; 1952 v Ni, W, E, USA, D, Se; 1953 v Ni, W, E, Se; 1954 v W; 1955 v H (2), P, Y, A, E; 1956 v E, W, Ni, A; 1957 v E, Ni, W, Y (38)
Rennie, H. G. (Hearts), 1900 v E, Ni; (with Hibernian), 1901 v E; 1902 v E, Ni, W; 1903 v Ni, W; 1904 v Ni; 1905 v W; 1906 v Ni; 1908 v Ni, W (13)
Renny-Tailyour, H. W. (Royal Engineers), 1873 v E (1)
Rhind, A. (Queen's Park), 1872 v E (1)
Richmond, A. (Queen's Park), 1906 v W (1)
Richmond, J. T. (Clydesdale), 1877 v E; (with Queen's Park), 1878 v E; 1882 v W (3)
Ring, T. (Clyde), 1953 v Se; 1955 v W, Ni, E, H; 1957 v E, Sp (2), Sw, WG; 1958 v Ni, Sw (12)
Rioch, B. D. (Derby Co), 1975 v P, W, Ni, E, R; 1976 v D (2), R, Ni, W, E; 1977 v Fi, Cz, W; (with Everton), W, Ni, E, Ch, Br; 1978 v Cz; (with Derby Co), Ni, E, Pe, Ho (24)
Ritchie, A. (East Stirlingshire), 1891 v W (1)
Ritchie, H. (Hibernian), 1923 v W; 1928 v Ni (2)
Ritchie, J. (Queen's Park), 1897 v E (1)
Ritchie, W. (Rangers), 1962 v U (sub) (1)
Robb, D. T. (Aberdeen), 1971 v W, E, P, D (sub), USSR (5)

Robb, W. (Rangers), 1926 v W; (with Hibernian), 1928 v W (2)
Robertson, A. (Clyde), 1955 v P, A, H; 1958 v Sw, Par (5)
Robertson, D. (Rangers), 1992 v Ni; 1994 v Sw, Ho (3)
Robertson, G. (Motherwell), 1910 v W; (with Sheffield W), 1912 v W; 1913 v E, Ni (4)
Robertson, G. (Kilmarnock), 1938 v Cz (1)
Robertson, H. (Dundee), 1962 v Cz (1)
Robertson, J. (Dundee), 1931 v A, I (2)
Robertson, J. (Hearts), 1991 v R, Sw, Bul (sub), Sm (sub); 1992 v Sm, Ni (sub), Fi; 1993 v I (sub), Ma (sub), G, Es; 1995 v J (sub), Ec, Fa (sub); 1996 v Gr (sub), Se (16)
Robertson, J. N. (Nottingham F), 1978 v Ni, W (sub), Ir; 1979 v P, N; 1980 v Pe, A, Bel (2), P; 1981 v Se, P, Is, Ni, Is, Ni, E; 1982 v Se, Ni (2), E (sub), Nz, Br, USSR; 1983 v EG, Sw; (with Derby Co), 1984 v U, Bel (28)
Robertson, J. G. (Tottenham H), 1965 v W (1)
Robertson, J. T. (Everton), 1898 v E; (with Southampton), 1899 v E; (with Rangers), 1900 v E, W; 1901 v W, Ni, E; 1902 v W, Ni, E; 1903 v E, W; 1904 v E, W, Ni; 1905 v W (16)
Robertson, P. (Dundee), 1903 v Ni (1)
Robertson, T. (Queen's Park), 1889 v Ni; 1890 v E; 1891 v W; 1892 v Ni (4)
Robertson, T. (Hearts), 1898 v Ni (1)
Robertson, W. (Dumbarton), 1887 v E, W (2)
Robinson, R. (Dundee), 1974 v WG (sub); 1975 v Se, Ni, R (sub) (4)
Rough, A. (Partick T), 1976 v Sw, Ni, W, E; 1977 v Fi, Cz, W (2), Se, Ni, E, Ch, Arg, Br; 1978 v Cz, W, Ni, E, Pe, Ir, Ho; 1979 v A, P, W, Arg, N; 1980 v Pe, A, Bel (2), P, W, E, Pol, H; 1981 v Se, P, Is, Ni, Is, W, E; 1982 v Se, Ni, Sp, Ho, W, E, Nz, Br, USSR; (with Hibernian), 1986 v W (sub), E (53)
Rougvie, D. (Aberdeen), 1984 v Ni (1)
Rowan, A. (Caledonian), 1880 v E; (with Queen's Park), 1882 v W (2)
Russell, D. (Hearts), 1895 v E, Ni; (with Celtic), 1897 v W; 1898 v Ni; 1901 v W, Ni (6)
Russell, J. (Cambuslang), 1890 v Ni (1)
Russell, W. F. (Airdrieonians), 1924 v W; 1925 v E (2)
Rutherford, E. (Rangers), 1948 v F (1)

St John, I. (Motherwell), 1959 v WG; 1960 v E, Ni, W, Pol, A; 1961 v E; (with Liverpool), 1962 v Ni, W, E, Cz (2), U; 1963 v W, Ni, E, N, Ei (sub), Sp; 1964 v Ni; 1965 v E (21)
Sawers, W. (Dundee), 1895 v W (1)
Scarff, P. (Celtic), 1931 v Ni (1)
Schaedler, E. (Hibernian), 1974 v WG (1)
Scott, A. S. (Rangers), 1957 v Ni, Y, WG; 1958 v W, Sw; 1959 v P; 1962 v Ni, W, E, Cz, U; (with Everton), 1964 v W, N; 1965 v Fi; 1966 v P, Br (16)
Scott, J. (Hibernian), 1966 v Ho (1)
Scott, J. (Dundee), 1971 v D (sub), USSR (2)
Scott, M. (Airdrieonians), 1898 v W (1)
Scott, R. (Airdrieonians), 1894 v Ni (1)
Scoular, J. (Portsmouth), 1951 v D, F, A; 1952 v E, USA, D, Se; 1953 v W, Ni (9)
Sellar, W. (Battlefield), 1885 v E; 1886 v E; 1887 v E, W; 1888 v E; (with Queen's Park), 1891 v E; 1892 v E; 1893 v E, Ni (9)
Semple, W. (Cambuslang), 1886 v W (1)
Shankly, W. (Preston NE), 1938 v E; 1939 v E, W, Ni, H (5)
Sharp, G. M. (Everton), 1985 v Ic; 1986 v W, Aus (2 sub), Is, R, U; 1987 v Ei; 1988 v Bel (sub), Bul, L, Ma (12)
Sharp, J. (Dundee), 1904 v W; (with Woolwich Arsenal), 1907 v W, E; 1908 v E; (with Fulham), 1909 v W (5)
Shaw, D. (Hibernian), 1947 v W, Ni; 1948 v E, Bel, Sw, F; 1949 v W, Ni (8)
Shaw, F. W. (Pollokshields Ath), 1884 v E, W (2)
Shaw, J. (Rangers), 1947 v E, Bel, L; 1948 v Ni (4)
Shearer, D. (Aberdeen), 1994 v A (sub), Ho (sub); 1995 v Fi, Ru (sub), Sm, Fa; 1996 v Gr (7)
Shearer, R. (Rangers), 1961 v E, Ei (2), Cz (4)
Sillars, D. C. (Queen's Park), 1891 v Ni; 1892 v E; 1893 v W; 1894 v E; 1895 v W (5)
Simpson, J. (Third Lanark), 1895 v E, W, Ni (3)
Simpson, J. (Rangers), 1935 v E, W, Ni; 1936 v E, W, Ni; 1937 v G, E, W, Ni, A, Cz; 1938 v W, Ni (14)
Simpson, N. (Aberdeen), 1983 v Ni; 1984 v F (sub); 1987 v E; 1988 v E (4)
Simpson, R. C. (Celtic), 1967 v E, USSR; 1968 v Ni; 1969 v A (5)
Sinclair, G. L. (Hearts), 1910 v Ni; 1912 v W, Ni (3)
Sinclair, J. W. E. (Leicester C), 1966 v P (1)
Skene, L. H. (Queen's Park), 1904 v W (1)
Sloan, T. (Third Lanark), 1904 v W (1)
Smellie, R. (Queen's Park), 1887 v Ni; 1888 v W; 1889 v E; 1891 v E; 1893 v E, Ni (6)

Smith, A. (Rangers), 1898 v E; 1900 v E, Ni, W; 1901 v E, Ni, W; 1902 v E, Ni, W; 1903 v E, Ni, W; 1904 v Ni; 1905 v W; 1906 v E, Ni; 1907 v W; 1911 v E, Ni (20)
Smith, D. (Aberdeen), 1966 v Ho; (with Rangers), 1968 v Ho (2)
Smith, G. (Hibernian), 1947 v E, Ni; 1948 v W, Bel, Sw, F; 1952 v E, USA; 1955 v P, Y, A, H; 1956 v E, Ni, W; 1957 v Sp (2), Sw (18)
Smith, H. G. (Hearts), 1988 v S.Ar (sub); 1992 v Ni, Ca (3)
Smith, J. (Rangers), 1935 v Ni; 1938 v Ni (2)
Smith, J. (Ayr U), 1924 v E (1)
Smith, J. (Aberdeen), 1968 v Ho (sub); (with Newcastle U), 1974 v WG, Ni (sub), W (sub) (4)
Smith, J. E. (Celtic), 1959 v H, P (2)
Smith, Jas (Queen's Park), 1872 v E (1)
Smith, John (Mauchline), 1877 v E, W; 1879 v E, W; (with Edinburgh University), 1880 v E; (with Queen's Park), 1881 v W, E; 1883 v E, W; 1884 v E (10)
Smith, N. (Rangers), 1897 v E; 1898 v W; 1899 v E, W, Ni; 1900 v E, W, Ni; 1901 v Ni, W; 1902 v E, Ni (12)
Smith, R. (Queen's Park), 1872 v E; 1873 v E (2)
Smith, T. M. (Kilmarnock), 1934 v E; (with Preston NE), 1938 v E (2)
Somers, P. (Celtic), 1905 v E, Ni; 1907 v Ni; 1909 v W (4)
Somers, W. S. (Third Lanark), 1879 v E, W; (with Queen's Park), 1880 v W (3)
Somerville, G. (Queen's Park), 1886 v E (1)
Souness, G. J. (Middlesbrough), 1975 v EG, Sp, Se; (with Liverpool), 1978 v Bul, W, E (sub), Ho; 1979 v A, N, W, Ni, E; 1980 v Pe, A, Bel, P, Ni; 1981 v P, Is (2); 1982 v Ni, P, Sp, W, E, Nz, Br, USSR; 1983 v EG, Sw, Bel, Sw, W, E, Ca (2 + 1 sub); 1984 v U, Ni, W; (with Sampdoria), 1985 v Y, Ic, Sp (2), W, E, Ic; 1986 v EG, Aus (2), R, E, D, WG (54)
Speedie, D. R. (Chelsea), 1985 v E; 1986 v W, EG (sub), Aus, E; (with Coventry C), 1989 v Y (sub), I (sub), Cy (1+1 sub), Ch (10)
Speedie, F. (Rangers), 1903 v E, W, Ni (3)
Speirs, J. H. (Rangers), 1908 v W (1)
Spencer, J. (Chelsea), 1995 v Ru (sub), Gr (sub), Sm (sub), J; 1996 v Fi, Aus, D, US (sub), Co, Ho (sub), E, Sw (sub); 1997 v La; (with QPR), W (sub) (14)
Stanton, P. (Hibernian), 1966 v Ho; 1969 v Ni; 1970 v Ei, A; 1971 v D, Bel, P, USSR, D; 1972 v P, Bel, Ho, W; 1973 v W, Ni; 1974 v WG (16)
Stark, J. (Rangers), 1909 v E, Ni (2)
Steel, W. (Morton), 1947 v E, Bel, L; (with Derby Co), 1948 v F, E, W, Ni; 1949 v E, W, Ni, F; 1950 v E, W, Sw, P, F; (with Dundee), 1951 v W, Ni, E, A (2), D, F, Bel; 1952 v W; 1953 v W, E, Ni, Se (30)
Steele, D. M. (Huddersfield), 1923 v E, W, Ni (3)
Stein, C. (Rangers), 1969 v W, Ni, D, E, Cy (2); 1970 v A (sub), Ni (sub), W, E, Ei, WG; 1971 v D, USSR, Bel, D; 1972 v Cz (sub); (with Coventry C), 1973 v E (2 sub), W (sub), Ni (21)
Stephen, J. F. (Bradford), 1947 v W; 1948 v W (2)
Stevenson, G. (Motherwell), 1928 v W, Ni; 1930 v Ni, E, F; 1931 v E, W; 1932 v W, Ni; 1933 v Ni; 1934 v E; 1935 v Ni (12)
Stewart, A. (Queen's Park), 1888 v Ni; 1889 v W (2)
Stewart, A. (Third Lanark), 1894 v W (1)
Stewart, D. (Dumbarton), 1888 v Ni (1)
Stewart, D. (Queen's Park), 1893 v W; 1894 v Ni; 1897 v Ni (3)
Stewart, D. S. (Leeds U), 1978 v EG (1)
Stewart, G. (Hibernian), 1906 v W, E; (with Manchester C), 1907 v E, W (4)
Stewart, J. (Kilmarnock), 1977 v Ch (sub); (with Middlesbrough), 1979 v N (2)
Stewart, R. (West Ham U), 1981 v W, Ni, E; 1982 v Ni, P, W; 1984 v F; 1987 v Ei (2), L (10)
Stewart, W. E. (Queen's Park), 1898 v Ni; 1900 v Ni (2)
Storrier, D. (Celtic), 1899 v E, W, Ni (3)
Strachan, G. (Aberdeen), 1980 v Ni, W, E, Pol, H (sub); 1981 v Se, P; 1982 v Ni, P, Sp, Ho (sub), Nz, Br, USSR; 1983 v EG, Sw, Bel, Sw, Ni (sub), W, E, Ca (2 + 1 sub); 1984 v EG, Ni, E, F; (with Manchester U), 1985 v Sp (sub), E, Ic; 1986 v W, Aus, R, D, WG, U; 1987 v Bul, Ei (2); 1988 v H; 1989 v F (sub); (with Leeds U), 1990 v F; 1991 v USSR, Bul, Sm; 1992 v Sw, R, Ni, Fi (50)
Sturrock, P. (Dundee U), 1981 v W (sub), Ni, E (sub); 1982 v P, Ni (sub), W (sub), E (sub); 1983 v EG (sub), Sw, Bel (sub), Ca (3); 1984 v W; 1985 v Y (sub); 1986 v Is (sub), Ho, D, U; 1987 v Bel (20)
Sullivan, N. (Wimbledon), 1997 v W (1)
Summers, W. (St Mirren), 1926 v E (1)
Symon, J. S. (Rangers), 1939 v H (1)

Tait, T. S. (Sunderland), 1911 v W (1)

Taylor, J. (Queen's Park), 1872 v E; 1873 v E; 1874 v E; 1875 v E; 1876 v E, W (6)
Taylor, J. D. (Dumbarton), 1892 v W; 1893 v W; 1894 v Ni; (with St Mirren), 1895 v Ni (4)
Taylor, W. (Hearts), 1892 v E (1)
Telfer, W. (Motherwell), 1933 v Ni; 1934 v Ni (2)
Telfer, W. D. (St Mirren), 1954 v W (1)
Templeton, R. (Aston Villa), 1902 v E; (with Newcastle U), 1903 v W; 1904 v E; (with Woolwich Arsenal), 1905 v W; (with Kilmarnock), 1908 v Ni; 1910 v E, Ni; 1912 v E, Ni; 1913 v W (11)
Thomson, A. (Arthurlie), 1886 v Ni (1)
Thomson, A. (Third Lanark), 1889 v W (1)
Thomson, A. (Airdrieonians), 1909 v Ni (1)
Thomson, A. (Celtic), 1926 v E; 1932 v F; 1933 v W (3)
Thomson, C. (Hearts), 1904 v Ni; 1905 v E, Ni, W; 1906 v W, Ni; 1907 v E, W, Ni; 1908 v E, W, Ni; (with Sunderland), 1909 v W; 1910 v E; 1911 v Ni; 1912 v E, W; 1913 v E, W; 1914 v E, Ni (21)
Thomson, C. (Sunderland), 1937 v Cz (1)
Thomson, D. (Dundee), 1920 v W (1)
Thomson, J. (Celtic), 1930 v F; 1931 v E, W, Ni (4)
Thomson, J. J. (Queen's Park), 1872 v E; 1873 v E; 1874 v E (3)
Thomson, J. R. (Everton), 1933 v W (1)
Thomson, R. (Celtic), 1932 v W (1)
Thomson, R. W. (Falkirk), 1927 v E (1)
Thomson, S. (Rangers), 1884 v W, Ni (2)
Thomson, W. (Dumbarton), 1892 v W; 1893 v W; 1898 v Ni, W (4)
Thomson, W. (Dundee), 1896 v W (1)
Thornton, W. (Rangers), 1947 v W, Ni; 1948 v E, Ni; 1949 v F; 1952 v D, Se (7)
Thomson, W. (St Mirren), 1980 v Ni; 1981 v Ni (sub+1) 1982 v P; 1983 v Ni, Ca; 1984 v EG (7)
Toner, W. (Kilmarnock), 1959 v W, Ni (2)
Townsley, T. (Falkirk), 1926 v W (1)
Troup, A. (Dundee), 1920 v E; 1921 v W, Ni; 1922 v Ni; (with Everton), 1926 v E (5)
Turnbull, E. (Hibernian), 1948 v Bel, Sw; 1951 v A; 1958 v H, Pol, Y, Par, F (8)
Turner, T. (Arthurlie), 1884 v W (1)
Turner, W. (Pollokshields Ath), 1885 v Ni; 1886 v Ni (2)

Ure, J. F. (Dundee), 1962 v W, Cz; 1963 v W, Ni, E, A, N, Sp; (with Arsenal), 1964 v Ni, N; 1968 v Ni (11)
Urquhart, D. (Hibernian), 1934 v W (1)

Vallance, T. (Rangers), 1877 v E, W; 1878 v E; 1879 v E, W; 1881 v E, W (7)
Venters, A. (Cowdenbeath), 1934 v Ni; (with Rangers), 1936 v E; 1939 v E (3)

Waddell, T. S. (Queen's Park), 1891 v Ni; 1892 v E; 1893 v E, Ni; 1895 v E, Ni (6)
Waddell, W. (Rangers), 1947 v W; 1949 v E, W, Ni, F; 1950 v E, Ni; 1951 v E, D, F, Bel, A; 1952 v Ni, W; 1954 v Ni; 1955 v W, Ni (17)
Wales, H. M. (Motherwell), 1933 v W (1)
Walker, A. (Celtic), 1988 v Co (sub); 1995 v Fi, Fa (sub) (3)
Walker, F. (Third Lanark), 1922 v W (1)
Walker, G. (St Mirren), 1930 v F; 1931 v Ni, A, Sw (4)
Walker, J. (Hearts), 1895 v Ni; 1897 v W; 1898 v Ni; (with Rangers), 1904 v W, Ni (5)
Walker, J. (Swindon T), 1911 v E, W, Ni; 1912 v E, W, Ni; 1913 v E, W, Ni (9)
Walker, J. N. (Hearts), 1993 v G; (with Partick T), 1996 v US (sub) (2)
Walker, R. (Hearts), 1900 v E, Ni; 1901 v E, Ni; 1902 v E, W, Ni; 1903 v E, W, Ni; 1904 v E, W, Ni; 1905 v E, W, Ni; 1906 v Ni; 1907 v E, Ni; 1908 v E, W, Ni; 1909 v E, W; 1912 v E, W, Ni; 1913 v E, W (29)
Walker, T. (Hearts), 1935 v E, W; 1936 v E, W, Ni; 1937 v G, E, W, Ni, A, Cz; 1938 v E, W, Ni, Cz, Ho; 1939 v E, W, Ni, H (20)
Walker, W. (Clyde), 1909 v Ni; 1910 v Ni (2)
Wallace, I. A. (Coventry C), 1978 v Bul (sub); 1979 v P (sub), W (3)
Wallace, W. S. B. (Hearts), 1965 v Ni; 1966 v E, Ho; (with Celtic), 1967 v E, USSR (sub); 1968 v Ni; 1969 v E (sub) (7)
Wardhaugh, J. (Hearts), 1955 v H; 1957 v Ni (2)
Wark, J. (Ipswich T), 1979 v W, Ni, E, Arg, N (sub); 1980 v Pe, A, Bel (2); 1981 v Ni; 1982 v Se, Sp, Ho, Ni, Nz, Br, USSR; 1983 v EG, Sw (2), Ni, E (sub); 1984 v U, Bel, EG; (with Liverpool), 1985 v F (sub); 1987 v Is (sub), Y (29)
Watson, A. (Queen's Park), 1881 v E, W; 1882 v E (3)
Watson, J. (Sunderland), 1903 v E, W; 1904 v E; 1905 v E; (with Middlesbrough), 1909 v E, Ni (6)

Watson, J. (Motherwell), 1948 v Ni; (with Huddersfield T), 1954 v Ni (2)
Watson, J. A. K. (Rangers), 1878 v W (1)
Watson, P. R. (Blackpool), 1934 v A (1)
Watson, R. (Motherwell), 1971 v USSR (1)
Watson, W. (Falkirk), 1898 v W (1)
Watt, F. (Kilbirnie), 1889 v W, Ni; 1890 v W; 1891 v E (4)
Watt, W. W. (Queen's Park), 1887 v Ni (1)
Waugh, W. (Hearts), 1938 v Cz (1)
Weir, A. (Motherwell), 1959 v WG; 1960 v E, P, A, H, T (6)
Weir, D. G. (Hearts), 1997 v W, Ma (sub) (2)
Weir, J. (Third Lanark), 1887 v Ni (1)
Weir, J. B. (Queen's Park), 1872 v E; 1874 v E; 1875 v E; 1878 v W (4)
Weir, P. (St Mirren), 1980 v Ni, W, Pol (sub), H; (with Aberdeen), 1983 v Sw; 1984 v Ni (6)
White, John (Albion R), 1922 v W; (with Hearts), 1923 v Ni (2)
White, J. A. (Falkirk), 1959 v WG, Ho, P; 1960 v Ni; (with Tottenham H), 1960 v W, Pol, A, T; 1961 v W; 1962 v Ni, W, E, Cz (2); 1963 v W, Ni, E; 1964 v Ni, W, E, N, WG (22)
White, W. (Bolton W), 1907 v E; 1908 v E (2)
Whitelaw, A. (Vale of Leven), 1887 v Ni; 1890 v W (2)
Whyte, D. (Celtic), 1988 v Bel (sub), L; 1989 v Ch (sub); 1992 v US (sub); (with Middlesbrough), 1993 v P, I; 1995 v J (sub), Ec; 1996 v US; 1997 v La (10)
Wilson, A. (Sheffield W), 1907 v E; 1908 v E; 1912 v E; 1913 v E, W; 1914 v Ni (6)
Wilson, A. (Portsmouth), 1954 v Fi (1)
Wilson, A. N. (Dunfermline), 1920 v E, W, Ni; 1921 v E, W, Ni; (with Middlesbrough), 1922 v E, W, Ni; 1923 v E, W, Ni (12)
Wilson, D. (Queen's Park), 1900 v W (1)
Wilson, D. (Oldham Ath), 1913 v E (1)
Wilson, D. (Rangers), 1961 v E, W, Ni, Ei (2), Cz; 1962 v Ni, W, E, Cz, U; 1963 v W, E, A, N, Ei, Sp; 1964 v E, WG; 1965 v Ni, E, Fi (22)

Wilson, G. W. (Hearts), 1904 v W; 1905 v E, Ni; 1906 v W; (with Everton), 1907 v E; (with Newcastle U), 1909 v E (6)
Wilson, Hugh, (Newmilns), 1890 v W; (with Sunderland), 1897 v E; (with Third Lanark), 1902 v W; 1904 v Ni (4)
Wilson, I. A. (Leicester C), 1987 v E, Br; (with Everton), 1988 v Bel, Bul, L (5)
Wilson, J. (Vale of Leven), 1888 v W; 1889 v E; 1890 v E; 1891 v E (4)
Wilson, P. (Celtic), 1926 v Ni; 1930 v F; 1931 v Ni; 1933 v E (4)
Wilson, P. (Celtic), 1975 v Sp (sub) (1)
Wilson, R. P. (Arsenal), 1972 v P, Ho (2)
Wiseman, W. (Queen's Park), 1927 v W; 1930 v Ni (2)
Wood, G. (Everton), 1979 v Ni, E, Arg (sub); (with Arsenal), 1982 v Ni (4)
Woodburn, W. A. (Rangers), 1947 v E, Bel, L; 1948 v W, Ni; 1949 v E; 1950 v E, W, Ni, P, F; 1951 v E, W, Ni, A (2), D, F, Bel; 1952 v E, W, Ni, USA (24)
Wotherspoon, D. N. (Queen's Park), 1872 v E; 1873 v E (2)
Wright, K. (Hibernian), 1992 v Ni (1)
Wright, S. (Aberdeen), 1993 v G, Es (2)
Wright, T. (Sunderland), 1953 v W, Ni, E (3)
Wylie, T. G. (Rangers), 1890 v Ni (1)

Yeats, R. (Liverpool), 1965 v W; 1966 v I (2)
Yorston, B. C. (Aberdeen), 1931 v Ni (1)
Yorston, H. (Aberdeen), 1955 v W (1)
Young, A. (Hearts), 1960 v E, A (sub), H, T; 1961 v W, Ni; (with Everton), Ei; 1966 v P (8)
Young, A. (Everton), 1905 v E; 1907 v W (2)
Young, G. L. (Rangers), 1947 v E, Ni, Bel, L; 1948 v E, Ni, Bel, Sw, F; 1949 v E, W, Ni, F; 1950 v E, W, Ni, Sw, P, F; 1951 v E, W, Ni, A (2), D, F, Bel; 1952 v E, W, Ni, USA, D, Se; 1953 v W, E, Ni, Se; 1954 v Ni, W; 1955 v W, Ni, P, Y; 1956 v Ni, W, E, A; 1957 v E, Ni, W, Y, Sp, Sw (53)
Young, J. (Celtic), 1906 v Ni (1)
Younger, T. (Hibernian), 1955 v P, Y, A, H; 1956 v E, Ni, W, A; (with Liverpool), 1957 v E, Ni, W, Y, Sp (2), Sw, WG; 1958 v Ni, W, E, Sw, H, Pol, Y, Par (24)

WALES

Adams, H. (Berwyn R), 1882 v Ni, E; (with Druids), 1883 v Ni, E (4)
Aizlewood, M. (Charlton Ath), 1986 v S.Ar, Ca (2); 1987 v Fi; (with Leeds U), USSR, Fi (sub); 1988 v D (sub), Se, Ma, I; 1989 v Ho, Se (sub), WG; (with Bradford C), 1990 v Fi, WG, Ei, Cr; (with Bristol C), 1991 v D, Bel (2), L, Ei, Ic, Pol, WG; 1992 v Br, L, Ei, A, R, Ho, Arg, J; 1993 v Ei, Bel, Fa; 1994 v RCS, Cy; (with Cardiff C) 1995v Bul (39)
Allchurch, I. J. (Swansea T), 1951 v E, Ni, P, Sw; 1952 v E, S, Ni, R of UK; 1953 v S, E, Ni, F, Y; 1954 v S, E, Ni, A; 1955 v S, E, Ni, Y; 1956 v E, S, Ni, A; 1957 v E, S; 1958 v Ni, Is (2), H (2), M, Sw, Br; (with Newcastle U), 1959 v E, S, Ni; 1960 v S; 1961 v Ni, H, Sp (2); 1962 v E, S, Br (2), M; (with Cardiff C), 1963 v S, E, Ni, H (2); 1964 v E; 1965 v S, E, Ni, Gr, I, USSR; (with Swansea T), 1966 v USSR, E, S, D, Br (2), Ch (68)
Allchurch, L. (Swansea T), 1955 v Ni; 1956 v A; 1958 v S, Ni, EG, Is; 1959 v S; (with Sheffield U), 1962 v S, Ni, Br; 1964 v E (11)
Allen, B. W. (Coventry C), 1951 v S, E (2)
Allen, M. (Watford), 1986 v S.Ar (sub), Ca (1 + 1 sub); (with Norwich C), 1989 v Is (sub); 1990 v Ho, WG; (with Millwall), Ei, Se, Cr (sub); 1991 v L (sub), Ei (sub); 1992 v A; 1993 v Ei (sub); (with Newcastle U), 1994 v R (sub) (14)
Arridge, S. (Bootle), 1892 v S, Ni; (with Everton), 1894 v Ni; 1895 v Ni; 1896 v E; (with New Brighton Tower), 1898 v E, Ni; 1899 v E (8)
Astley, D. J. (Charlton Ath), 1931 v Ni; (with Aston Villa), 1932 v E; 1933 v E, S, Ni; 1934 v E, S; 1935 v S; 1936 v E, Ni; (with Derby Co), 1939 v E, S; (with Blackpool), F (13)
Atherton, R. W. (Hibernian), 1899 v E, Ni; 1903 v E, S, Ni; (with Middlesbrough), 1904 v E, S, Ni; 1905 v Ni (9)

Bailiff, W. E. (Llanelly), 1913 v E, S, Ni; 1920 v Ni (4)
Baker, C. W. (Cardiff C), 1958 v M; 1960 v S, Ni; 1961 v S, E, Ei; 1962 v S (7)
Baker, W. G. (Cardiff C), 1948 v Ni (1)
Bamford, T. (Wrexham), 1931 v E, S, Ni; 1932 v Ni; 1933 v F (5)
Barnes, W. (Arsenal), 1948 v E, S, Ni; 1949 v E, S, Ni; 1950 v E, S, Ni, Bel; 1951 v E, S, Ni, P; 1952 v E, S, Ni, R of UK; 1954 v E, S; 1955 v S, Y (22)
Bartley, T. (Glossop NE), 1898 v E (1)
Bastock, A. M. (Shrewsbury), 1892 v Ni (1)
Beadles, G. H. (Cardiff C), 1925 v E, S (2)

Bell, W. S. (Shrewsbury Engineers), 1881 v E, S; (with Crewe Alex), 1886 v E, S, Ni (5)
Bennion, S. R. (Manchester U), 1926 v S; 1927 v S; 1928 v S, E, Ni; 1929 v S, E, Ni; 1930 v S; 1932 v Ni (10)
Berry, G. F. (Wolverhampton W), 1979 v WG; 1980 v Ei, WG (sub); T; (with Stoke C), 1983 v E (sub) (5)
Blackmore, C. G. (Manchester U), 1985 v N (sub); 1986 v S (sub), H (sub), S.Ar, Ei, U; 1987 v Fi (2), USSR, Cz; 1988 v D (2), Cz, Y, Se, Ma, I; 1989 v Ho, Fi, Is, WG; 1990 v F; Ho, WG, Cr; 1991 v Bel, L; 1992 v Ei (sub), A, R (sub), Ho, Arg, J; 1993 v Fa, Cy, Bel, RCS; 1994 v Se (sub); (with Middlesbrough), 1997 v Bel (39)
Blake, N. A. (Sheffield U), 1994 v N, Se (sub); 1995 v Alb, Mol; 1996 v G (with Bolton W), I (sub) (6)
Blew, H. (Wrexham), 1899 v E, S, Ni; 1902 v S, Ni; 1903 v E, S; 1904 v E, S, Ni; 1905 v S, Ni; 1906 v E, S, Ni; 1907 v S; 1908 v E, S, Ni; 1909 v E, S; 1910 v E (22)
Boden, T. (Wrexham), 1880 v E (1)
Bodin, P. J. (Swindon T), 1990 v Cr; 1991 v D, Bel, L, Ei; (with C Palace), Bel, Ic, Pol, WG; 1992 v Br, G, L (sub); (with Swindon T), Ei (sub), Ho, Arg; 1993 v Ei, Bel, RCS, Fa; 1994 v R, Se, Es (sub); 1995 v Alb (23)
Boulter, L. M. (Brentford), 1939 v Ni (1)
Bowdler, H. E. (Shrewsbury), 1893 v S (1)
Bowdler, J. C. H. (Shrewsbury), 1890 v Ni; (with Wolverhampton W), 1891 v S; 1892 v Ni; (with Shrewsbury), 1894 v E (4)
Bowen, D. L. (Arsenal), 1955 v S, Y; 1957 v Ni, Cz, EG; 1958 v S, Ni, EG, Is (2), H (2), M, Se, Br; 1959 v E, S, Ni (19)
Bowen, E. (Druids), 1880 v S; 1883 v S (2)
Bowen, J. P. (Swansea C), 1994 v Es; (with Birmingham C), 1997 v Ho (2)
Bowen, M. R. (Tottenham H), 1986 v Ca (2 sub); (with Norwich C), 1988 v Y (sub); 1989 v Fi (sub), Is, Se, WG (sub); 1990 v Fi (sub), Ho, WG, Se; 1992 v Br (sub), G, L, Ei, A, R, Ho (sub); J; 1993 v Fa, Cy, Bel (1 + sub), RCS (sub); 1994 v RCS, Se; 1995 v Mol, Ge, Bul (2), G, Ge; 1996 v Mol, G, Alb, Sw, Sm; (with West Ham U), 1997 v Sm, Ho, Ei (sub) (41)
Bowsher, S. J. (Burnley), 1929 v Ni (1)
Boyle, T. (C Palace), 1981 v Ei, S (sub) (2)
Britten, T. J. (Parkgrove), 1878 v S; (with Presteigne), 1880 v S (2)
Brookes, S. J. (Llandudno), 1900 v E, Ni (2)
Brown, A. I. (Aberdare Ath), 1926 v Ni (1)

Browning, M. T. (Bristol R), 1996 v I (sub), Sm; 1997 v Sm, Ho, S (sub) (5)
Bryan, T. (Oswestry), 1886 v E, Ni (2)
Buckland, T. (Bangor), 1899 v E (1)
Burgess, W. A. R. (Tottenham H), 1947 v E, S, Ni; 1948 v E, S; 1949 v E, S, Ni, P, Bel, Sw; 1950 v E, S, Ni, Bel; 1951 v S, Ni, P, Sw; 1952 v E, S, Ni, R of UK; 1953 v S, E, Ni, F, Y; 1954 v S, E, Ni, A (32)
Burke, T. (Wrexham), 1883 v E; 1884 v S; 1885 v E, S, Ni; (with Newton Heath), 1887 v E, S; 1888 v S (8)
Burnett, T. B. (Ruabon), 1877 v S (1)
Burton, A. D. (Norwich C), 1963 v Ni, H; (with Newcastle U), 1964 v E; 1969 v S, E, Ni, I, EG; 1972 v Cz (9)
Butler, J. (Chirk), 1893 v E, S, Ni (3)
Butler, W. T. (Druids), 1900 v S, Ni (2)

Cartwright, L. (Coventry C), 1974 v E (sub), S, Ni; 1976 v S (sub); 1977 v WG (sub); (with Wrexham), 1978 v Ir (sub); 1979 v Ma (7)
Carty, T. [s] See McCarthy [s] (Wrexham).
Challen, J. B. (Corinthians), 1887 v E, S; 1888 v E; (with Wellingborough GS), 1890 v E (4)
Chapman, T. (Newtown), 1894 v E, S, Ni; 1895 v S, Ni; (with Manchester C), 1896 v E; 1897 v E (7)
Charles, J. M. (Swansea C), 1981 v Cz, T (sub), S (sub), USSR (sub); 1982 v Ic; 1983 v N (sub), Y (sub), Bul (sub), S, Ni, Br; 1984 v Bul (sub); (with QPR), Y (sub), S; (with Oxford U), 1985 v Ic (sub), Sp, Ic; 1986 v Ei; 1987 v Fi (19)
Charles, M. (Swansea T), 1955 v Ni; 1956 v E, S, A; 1957 v E, Ni, Cz (2), EG; 1958 v E, S, EG, Is (2), H (2), M, Se, Br; 1959 v E, S; (with Arsenal), 1961 v Ni, H, Sp (2); 1962 v E, S; (with Cardiff C), 1962 v Br, Ni; 1963 v S, H (31)
Charles, W. J. (Leeds U), 1950 v Ni; 1951 v Sw; 1953 v Ni, F, Y; 1954 v E, S, Ni, A; 1955 v S, E, Ni, Y; 1956 v E, S, A, Ni; 1957 v E, S, Ni, Cz (2), EG; (with Juventus), 1958 v Is (2), H (2), M, Se; 1960 v S; 1962 v E, Br (2), M; (with Leeds U), 1963 v S; (with Cardiff C), 1964 v S; 1965 v S, USSR (38)
Clarke, R. J. (Manchester C), 1949 v E; 1950 v S, Ni, Bel; 1951 v E, S, Ni, P, Sw; 1952 v S, E, Ni, R of UK; 1953 v S, E; 1954 v E, S, Ni; 1955 v Y, S, E; 1956 v Ni (22)
Coleman, C. (C Palace), 1992 v A (sub); 1993 v Ei (sub); 1994 v N, Es; 1995 v Alb, Mol, Ge, Bul (2), G; 1996 v Mol; (with Blackburn R), I, Sw, Sm; 1997 v Sm (15)
Collier, D. J. (Grimsby T), 1994 v S (1)
Collins, W. S. (Llanelly), 1931 v S (1)
Conde, C. (Chirk), 1884 v E, S, Ni (3)
Cook, F. C. (Newport Co), 1925 v E, S; (with Portsmouth), 1928 v E, S; 1930 v E, S, Ni; 1932 v E (8)
Cornforth, J.M. (Swansea C), 1995 v Bul (sub), Ge (2)
Coyne, D. (Tranmere R), 1996 v Sw (1)
Crompton, W. (Wrexham), 1931 v E, S, Ni (3)
Cross, E. A. (Wrexham), 1876 v S; 1877 v S (2)
Cross, K. (Druids), 1879 v S; 1881 v E, S (3)
Crossley, M. G. (Nottingham F), 1997 v Ei (1)
Crowe, V. H. (Aston Villa), 1959 v E, Ni; 1960 v E, Ni; 1961 v S E, Ni, Ei, H, Sp (2); 1962 v E, S, Br, M; 1963 v H (16)
Cumner, R. H. (Arsenal), 1939 v E, S, Ni (3)
Curtis, A. (Swansea C), 1976 v E, Y (sub), S, Ni, Y (sub), E; 1977 v WG, S (sub), Ni (sub); 1978 v WG, E, S; 1979 v WG, S; (with Leeds U), E, Ni, Ma; 1980 v Ei, WG, T; (with Swansea C), 1982 v Cz, Ic, USSR, Sp, E, S, Ni; 1983 v N; 1984 v R (sub); (with Southampton), S; 1985 v Sp, N (1 + 1 sub); 1986 v H; (with Cardiff C), 1987 v USSR (35)
Curtis, E. R. (Cardiff C), 1928 v S; (with Birmingham), 1932 v S; 1934 v Ni (3)

Daniel, R. W. (Arsenal), 1951 v E, Ni, P; 1952 v E, S, Ni, R of UK; 1953 v S, E, Ni, F, Y; (with Sunderland), 1954 v E, S, Ni; 1955 v E, Ni; 1957 v S, E, Ni, Cz (21)
Darvell, S. (Oxford University), 1897 v S, Ni (2)
Davies, A. (Manchester U), 1983 v Ni, Br; 1984 v E, Ni; 1985 v Ic; (with Newcastle U), 1986 v H; (with Swansea C), 1988 v Ma, I; 1989 v Ho; (with Bradford C), 1990 v Fi, Ei (11)
Davies, A. (Wrexham), 1876 v S; 1877 v S (2)
Davies, A. (Druids), 1904 v S; (with Middlesbrough), 1905 v S (2)
Davies, A. O. (Barmouth), 1885 v Ni; 1886 v E, S; (with Swifts), 1887 v E, S; 1888 v E, Ni; (with Wrexham), 1889 v S; (with Crewe Alex), 1890 v E (9)
Davies, A. T. (Shrewsbury), 1891 v Ni (1)
Davies, C. (Brecon), 1899 v Ni; (with Hereford), 1900 v Ni (2)
Davies, C. (Charlton Ath), 1972 v R (sub) (1)
Davies, D. (Bolton W), 1904 v S, Ni; 1908 v E (sub) (3)
Davies, D. C. (Brecon), 1899 v Ni; (with Hereford); 1900 v Ni (2)

Davies, D. W. (Treharris), 1912 v Ni; (with Oldham Ath), 1913 v Ni (2)
Davies, E. Lloyd (Stoke C), 1904 v E; 1907 v E, S, Ni; (with Northampton T), 1908 v S; 1909 v Ni; 1910 v Ni; 1911 v E, S; 1912 v E, S; 1913 v E, S; 1914 v Ni, E, S (16)
Davies, E. R. (Newcastle U), 1953 v S, E; 1954 v E, S; 1958 v E, EG (6)
Davies, G. (Fulham), 1980 v T, Ic; 1982 v Sp (sub), F (sub); 1983 v E, Bul, S, Ni, Br; 1984 v R (sub), S (sub), E, Ni; 1985 v Ic; (with Manchester C), 1986 v S.Ar, Ei (16)
Davies, Rev. H. (Wrexham), 1928 v Ni (1)
Davies, Idwal (Liverpool Marine), 1923 v S (1)
Davies, J. E. (Oswestry), 1885 v E (1)
Davies, Jas (Wrexham), 1878 v S (1)
Davies, John (Wrexham), 1879 v S (1)
Davies, Jos (Newton Heath), 1888 v E, S, Ni; 1889 v S; 1890 v E; (with Wolverhampton W), 1892 v E; 1893 v E (7)
Davies, Jos (Everton), 1889 v S, Ni; (with Chirk), 1891 v Ni; (with Ardwick), v E, S; (with Sheffield U), 1895 v E, S, Ni; (with Manchester C), 1896 v E; (with Millwall), 1897 v E; (with Reading), 1900 v E (11)
Davies, J. P. (Druids), 1883 v E, Ni (2)
Davies, Ll. (Wrexham), 1907 v Ni; 1910 v Ni, S, E; (with Everton), 1911 v S, Ni; (with Wrexham), 1912 v Ni, S, E; 1913 v Ni, S, E; 1914 v Ni (13)
Davies, L. S. (Cardiff C), 1922 v E, S, Ni; 1923 v E, S, Ni; 1924 v E, S, Ni; 1925 v S, Ni; 1926 v E, Ni; 1927 v E, Ni; 1928 v S, Ni, E; 1929 v S, Ni, E; 1930 v E, S (23)
Davies, O. (Wrexham), 1890 v S (1)
Davies, R. (Wrexham), 1883 v Ni; 1884 v Ni; 1885 v Ni (3)
Davies, R. (Druids), 1885 v E (1)
Davies, R. O. (Wrexham), 1892 v Ni, E (2)
Davies, R. T. (Norwich C), 1964 v Ni; 1965 v E; 1966 v Br (2), Ch; (with Southampton), 1967 v S, E, Ni; 1968 v S, Ni, WG; 1969 v S, E, Ni, I, WG, R of UK; 1970 v S, Ni; 1971 v Cz, S, E, Ni; 1972 v R, E, S, N; (with Portsmouth), 1974 v E (29)
Davies, R. W. (Bolton W), 1964 v E; 1965 v E, S, Ni, D, Gr, USSR; 1966 v E, S, Ni, USSR, D, Br (2), Ch (sub); 1967 v S; (with Newcastle U), E; 1968 v S, Ni, WG; 1969 v S, E, Ni, I; 1970 v EG; 1971 v R, Cz; (with Manchester C), 1972 v E, S, Ni; (with Manchester U), 1973 v E, S (sub), Ni; (with Blackpool), 1974 v Pol (34)
Davies, S. I. (Manchester U), 1996 v Sw (sub) (1)
Davies, Stanley (Preston NE), 1920 v E, S, Ni; (with Everton), 1921 v E, S, Ni; (with WBA), 1922 v E, S, Ni; 1923 v S; 1925 v S, Ni; 1926 v S, E, Ni; 1927 v S; 1928 v S; (with Rotherham U), 1930 v Ni (18)
Davies, T. (Oswestry), 1886 v E (1)
Davies, T. (Druids), 1903 v E, Ni, S; 1904 v S (4)
Davies, W. (Wrexham), 1884 v Ni (1)
Davies, W. (Swansea C), 1924 v E, S, Ni; (with Cardiff C), 1925 v E, S, Ni; 1926 v E, S, Ni; 1927 v S; 1928 v Ni; (with Notts Co), 1929 v E, S, Ni; 1930 v E, S, Ni (17)
Davies, William (Wrexham), 1903 v Ni; 1905 v Ni; (with Blackburn R), 1908 v E, S; 1909 v E, S, Ni; 1911 v E, S, Ni; 1912 v Ni (11)
Davies, W. C. (C Palace), 1908 v S; (with WBA), 1909 v E; 1910 v S; (with C Palace), 1914 v E (4)
Davies, W. D. (Everton), 1975 v H, L, S, E, Ni; 1976 v Y (2), E, Ni; 1977 v WG, S (2), Cz, E, Ni; 1978 v K; (with Wrexham), S, Cz, WG, Ir, E, S, Ni; 1979 v Ma, T, WG, S, E, Ni, Ma; 1980 v Ei, WG, T, E, S, Ni, Ic; 1981 v T, Cz, Ei, T, S, E, USSR; (with Swansea C), 1982 v Cz, Ic, USSR, Sp, E, S, F; 1983 v Y (52)
Davies, W. H. (Oswestry), 1876 v S; 1877 v S; 1879 v E; 1880 v E (4)
Davies, W. O. (Millwall Ath), 1913 v E, S, Ni; 1914 v S, Ni (5)
Davis, G. (Wrexham), 1978 v Ir, E (sub), Ni (3)
Day, A. (Tottenham H), 1934 v Ni (1)
Deacy, N. (PSV Eindhoven), 1977 v Cz, S, E, Ni; 1978 v K (sub), S (sub), Cz (sub), WG, Ir, S (sub), Ni; (with Beringen), 1979 v T (12)
Dearson, D. J. (Birmingham), 1939 v S, Ni, F (3)
Derrett, S. C. (Cardiff C), 1969 v S, WG; 1970 v I; 1971 v Fi (4)
Dewey, F. T. (Cardiff Corinthians), 1931 v E, S (2)
Dibble, A. (Luton T), 1986 v Ca (1+1 sub); (with Manchester C), 1989 v Is (3)
Doughty, J. (Druids), 1886 v S; (with Newton Heath), 1887 v S, Ni; 1888 v E, S, Ni; 1889 v S; 1890 v E (8)
Doughty, R. (Newton Heath and Druids), 1888 v S, Ni (2)
Durban, A. (Derby Co), 1966 v Br (sub); 1967 v Ni; 1968 v E, S, Ni; 1969 v EG, S, E, Ni, WG; 1970 v E, S, Ni, EG, I; 1971 v R, S, E, Ni, Cz, Fi; 1972 v Fi, Cz, E, S, Ni (27)
Dwyer, P. (Cardiff C), 1978 v Ir, E, S, Ni; 1979 v T, S, E, Ni, Ma (sub); 1980 v WG (10)

Edwards, C. (Wrexham), 1878 v S (1)
Edwards, C. N. H. (Swansea C), 1996 v Sw (sub) (1)
Edwards, G. (Birmingham C), 1947 v E, S, Ni; 1948 v E, S, Ni; (with Cardiff C), 1949 v Ni, P, Bel, Sw; 1950 v E, S (12)
Edwards, H. (Wrexham Civil Service), 1878 v S; 1880 v E; 1882 v E, S; 1883 v S; 1884 v Ni; 1887 v Ni (7)
Edwards, J. H. (Wanderers), 1876 v S (1)
Edwards, J. H. (Oswestry), 1895 v Ni; 1897 v E, Ni (3)
Edwards, J. H. (Aberystwyth), 1898 v Ni (1)
Edwards, L. T. (Charlton Ath), 1957 v Ni, EG (2)
Edwards, R. I. (Chester), 1978 v K (sub); 1979 v Ma, WG; (with Wrexham), 1980 v T (sub) (4)
Edwards, T. (Linfield), 1932 v S (1)
Egan, W. (Chirk), 1892 v S (1)
Ellis, B. (Motherwell), 1932 v E; 1933 v E, S; 1934 v S; 1936 v E; 1937 v S (6)
Ellis, E. (Nunhead), 1931 v S; (with Oswestry), E; 1932 v Ni (3)
Emanuel, W. J. (Bristol C), 1973 v E (sub), Ni (sub) (2)
England, H. M. (Blackburn R), 1962 v Ni, Br, W; 1963 v Ni, H; 1964 v E, S, Ni; 1965 v E, D, Gr (2), USSR, Ni, I; 1966 v E, S, Ni, USSR, D; (with Tottenham H), 1967 v S, E; 1968 v E, Ni, WG; 1969 v EG; 1970 v R of UK, EG, E, S, Ni, I; 1971 v R; 1972 v Fi, E, S, Ni; 1973 v E (3), S; 1974 v Pol; 1975 v H, L (44)
Evans, B. C. (Swansea C), 1972 v Fi, Cz; 1973 v E (2), Pol, S; (with Hereford U), 1974 v Pol (7)
Evans, D. G. (Reading), 1926 v Ni; 1927 v Ni, E; (with Huddersfield T), 1929 v S (4)
Evans, H. P. (Cardiff C), 1922 v E, S, Ni; 1924 v E, S, Ni (6)
Evans, I. (C Palace), 1976 v A, E, Y (2), E, Ni; 1977 v WG, S (2), Cz, Ni; 1978 v K (13)
Evans, J. (Oswestry), 1893 v Ni; 1894 v E, Ni (3)
Evans, J. (Cardiff C), 1912 v Ni; 1913 v Ni; 1914 v S; 1920 v S, Ni; 1922 v Ni; 1923 v E, Ni (8)
Evans, J. H. (Southend U), 1922 v E, S, Ni; 1923 v S (4)
Evans, Len (Aberdare Ath), 1927 v Ni; (with Cardiff C), 1931 v E, S; (with Birmingham), 1934 v Ni (4)
Evans, M. (Oswestry), 1884 v E (1)
Evans, R. (Clapton), 1902 v Ni (1)
Evans, R. E. (Wrexham), 1906 v E, S; (with Aston Villa), Ni; 1907 v E; 1908 v E, S; (with Sheffield U), 1909 v S; 1910 v E, S, Ni (10)
Evans, R. O. (Wrexham), 1902 v Ni; 1903 v E, S, Ni; (with Blackburn R), 1908 v Ni; (with Coventry C), 1911 v E, Ni; 1912 v E, S, Ni (10)
Evans, R. S. (Swansea T), 1964 v Ni (1)
Evans, T. J. (Clapton Orient), 1927 v S; 1928 v E, S; (with Newcastle U), Ni (4)
Evans, W. (Tottenham H), 1933 v Ni; 1934 v E, S; 1935 v E; 1936 v E, Ni (6)
Evans, W. A. W. (Oxford University), 1876 v S; 1877 v S (2)
Evans, W. G. (Bootle), 1890 v E; 1891 v E; (with Aston Villa), 1892 v E (3)
Evelyn, E. C. (Crusaders), 1887 v E (1)
Eyton-Jones, J. A. (Wrexham), 1883 v Ni, E, S (4)

Farmer, G. (Oswestry), 1885 v E, S (2)
Felgate, D. (Lincoln C), 1984 v R (sub) (1)
Finnigan, R. J. (Wrexham), 1930 v Ni (1)
Flynn, B. (Burnley), 1975 v L (2 sub), H (sub), S, E, Ni; 1976 v A, E, Y (2), E, Ni; 1977 v WG (sub), S (2), Cz, E, Ni; 1978 v K (2), S; (with Leeds U), Cz, WG, Ir (sub), E, S, Ni; 1979 v Ma, T, S, E, Ni, Ma; 1980 v Ei, WG, E, S, Ni, Ic; 1981 v T, Cz, Ei, T, S, E, USSR; 1982 v Cz, USSR, E, S, Ni, F; 1983 v N; (with Burnley), Y, E, Bul, S, Ni, Br; 1984 v N, R, Bul, Y, S, N, Is (66)
Ford, T. (Swansea T), 1947 v S; (with Aston Villa), 1947 v Ni; 1948 v Ni; 1949 v E, S, Ni, P, Bel, Sw; 1950 v E, S, Ni, Bel; 1951 v S; (with Sunderland), 1951 v Ni, P, Sw; 1952 v E, S, Ni, R of UK; 1953 v S, E, Ni, F, Y; (with Cardiff C), 1954 v A; 1955 v S, E, Ni, Y; 1956 v S, Ni, E, A; 1957 v S (38)
Foulkes, H. E. (WBA), 1932 v Ni (1)
Foulkes, W. I. (Newcastle U), 1952 v E, S, Ni, R of UK; 1953 v E, S, F, Y; 1954 v E, S, Ni (11)
Foulkes, W. T. (Oswestry), 1884 v Ni; 1885 v S (2)
Fowler, J. (Swansea T), 1925 v E; 1926 v E, Ni; 1927 v S; 1928 v S; 1929 v E (6)

Garner, J. (Aberystwyth), 1896 v S (1)
Giggs, R. J. (Manchester U), 1992 v G (sub), L (sub), R (sub); 1993 v Fa (sub), Bel (sub + 1), RCS, Fa; 1994 v RCS, Cy, R; 1995 v Alb, Bul; 1996 v G, Alb, Sm; 1997 v Sm, T, Bel (19)
Giles, D. (Swansea T), 1980 v E, S, Ni, Ic; 1981 v T, Cz, T (sub), E (sub), USSR (sub); (with C Palace), 1982 v Sp (sub); 1983 v Ni (sub), Br (12)

Gillam, S. G. (Wrexham), 1889 v S (sub), Ni; (with Shrewsbury), 1890 v E, Ni; (with Clapton), 1894 v S (5)
Glascodine, G. (Wrexham), 1879 v E (1)
Glover, E. M. (Grimsby T), 1932 v S; 1934 v Ni; 1936 v S; 1937 v E, S, Ni; 1939 v Ni (7)
Godding, G. (Wrexham), 1923 v S, Ni (2)
Godfrey, B. C. (Preston NE), 1964 v Ni; 1965 v D, I (3)
Goodwin, U. (Ruthin), 1881 v E (1)
Goss, J. (Norwich C), 1991 v Ic, Pol (sub); 1992 v A; 1994 v Cy (sub), R (sub), Se; 1995 v Alb; 1996 v Sw (sub), Sm (sub) (9)
Gough, R. T. (Oswestry White Star), 1883 v S (1)
Gray, A. (Oldham Ath), 1924 v E, S, Ni; 1925 v E, S, Ni; 1926 v E, S; 1927 v S; (with Manchester C), 1928 v E, S; 1929 v E, S, Ni; (with Manchester Central), 1930 v S; (with Tranmere R), 1932 v E, S, Ni; (with Chester), 1937 v E, S, Ni; 1938 v E, S, Ni (24)
Green, A. W. (Aston Villa), 1901 v Ni; (with Notts Co), 1903 v E; 1904 v S, Ni; 1906 v Ni, E; (with Nottingham F), 1907 v E; 1908 v S (8)
Green, C. R. (Birmingham C), 1965 v USSR, I; 1966 v E, S, USSR, Br (2); 1967 v E; 1968 v E, S, Ni, WG; 1969 v S, I, Ni (sub) (15)
Green, G. H. (Charlton Ath), 1938 v Ni; 1939 v E, Ni, F (4)
Grey, Dr W. (Druids), 1876 v S; 1878 v S (2)
Griffiths, A. T. (Wrexham), 1971 v Cz (sub); 1975 v A, H (2), L (2), E, Ni; 1976 v A, E, S, E (sub), Ni, Y (2); 1977 v WG, S (17)
Griffiths, F. J. (Blackpool), 1900 v E, S (2)
Griffiths, G. (Chirk), 1887 v Ni (1)
Griffiths, J. H. (Swansea T), 1953 v Ni (1)
Griffiths, L. (Wrexham), 1902 v S (1)
Griffiths, M. W. (Leicester C), 1947 v Ni; 1949 v P, Bel; 1950 v E, S, Bel; 1951 v E, Ni, P, Sw; 1954 v A (11)
Griffiths, P. (Chirk), 1884 v E, Ni; 1888 v E; 1890 v S, Ni; 1891 v Ni (6)
Griffiths, P. H. (Everton), 1932 v S (1)
Griffiths, S. (Wrexham), 1902 v S (1)
Griffiths, T. P. (Everton), 1927 v E, Ni; 1929 v E; 1930 v E; 1931 v Ni; 1932 v Ni, S, E; (with Bolton W), 1933 v E, S, Ni; (with Middlesbrough), F; 1934 v E, S; 1935 v E, Ni; 1936 v S; (with Aston Villa), Ni; 1937 v E, S, Ni (21)

Hall, G. D. (Chelsea), 1988 v Y (sub), Ma, I; 1989 v Ho, Fi, Is; 1990 v Ei; 1991 v Ei; 1992 v A (sub) (9)
Hallam, J. (Oswestry), 1889 v E (1)
Hanford, H. (Swansea T), 1934 v Ni; 1935 v S; 1936 v E; (with Sheffield W), 1938 v E, S; 1939 v F (7)
Harrington, A. C. (Cardiff C), 1956 v Ni; 1957 v E, S; 1958 v S, Ni, Is (2); 1961 v S, E; 1962 v E, S (11)
Harris, C. S. (Leeds U), 1976 v E, S; 1978 v WG, Ir, E, S, Ni; 1979 v Ma, T, WG, E (sub), Ma; 1980 v Ni (sub), Ic (sub); 1981 v T, Cz (sub), Ei, T, S, E, USSR; 1982 v Cz, Ic, E (sub) (24)
Harris, W. C. (Middlesbrough), 1954 v A; 1957 v EG, Cz; 1958 v E, S, EG (6)
Harrison, W. C. (Wrexham), 1899 v E; 1900 v E, S, Ni; 1901 v Ni (5)
Hartson, J. (Arsenal), 1995 v Bul, G (sub), Ge (sub); 1996 v Mol (sub), Sw; 1997 v Ho, T (sub), Ei; (with West Ham U), Bel (sub), S (10)
Haworth, S. O. (Cardiff C), 1997 v S (sub) (1)
Hayes, A. (Wrexham), 1890 v Ni; 1894 v Ni (2)
Hennessey, W. T. (Birmingham C), 1962 v Ni, Br (2); 1963 v S, E, H (2); 1964 v E, S; 1965 v S, E, D, Gr, USSR; 1966 v E, USSR; (with Nottingham F), 1966 v S, Ni, D, Br (2), Ch; 1967 v S, E; 1968 v E, S, Ni; 1969 v WG, EG, R of UK; 1970 v EG; (with Derby Co), E, S, Ni; 1972 v Fi, Cz, E, S; 1973 v E (39)
Hersee, A. M. (Bangor), 1886 v S, Ni (2)
Hersee, R. (Llandudno), 1886 v Ni (1)
Hewitt, R. (Cardiff C), 1958 v Ni, Is, Se, H, Br (5)
Hewitt, T. J. (Wrexham), 1911 v E, S, Ni; (with Chelsea), 1913 v E, S, Ni; (with South Liverpool), 1914 v E, S (8)
Heywood, D. (Druids), 1879 v E (1)
Hibbott, H. (Newtown Excelsior), 1880 v E, S; (with Newtown), 1885 v S (3)
Higham, G. G. (Oswestry), 1878 v S; 1879 v E (2)
Hill, M. R. (Ipswich T), 1972 v Cz, R (2)
Hockey, T. (Sheffield U), 1972 v Fi, R; 1973 v E (2); (with Norwich C), Pol, S, E, Ni; (with Aston Villa), 1974 v Pol (9)
Hoddinott, T. F. (Watford), 1921 v E, S (2)
Hodges, G. (Wimbledon), 1984 v N (sub), Is (sub); 1987 v USSR, Fi, Cz; (with Newcastle U), 1988 v D; (with Watford), D (sub), Cz (sub), Se, Ma (sub), I (sub); 1990 v Se, Cr; (with Sheffield U), 1992 v Br (sub), Ei (sub), A; 1996 v G (sub), I (18)
Hodgkinson, A. V. (Southampton), 1908 v Ni (1)

Jones, R. (Bangor), 1887 v S; 1889 v E; (with Crewe Alex), 1890 v E (3)
Jones, R. (Leicester Fosse), 1898 v S (1)
Jones, R. (Druids), 1899 v S (1)
Jones, R. (Bangor), 1900 v S, Ni (2)
Jones, R. (Millwall), 1906 v S, Ni (2)
Jones, R. A. (Druids), 1884 v E, Ni, S; 1885 v S (4)
Jones, R. A. (Sheffield W), 1994 v Es (1)
Jones, R. S. (Everton), 1894 v Ni (1)
Jones, S. (Wrexham), 1887 v Ni; (with Chester), 1890 v S (2)
Jones, S. (Wrexham), 1893 v S, Ni; (with Burton Swifts), 1895 v S; 1896 v E, Ni; (with Druids), 1899 v E (6)
Jones, T. (Manchester U), 1926 v Ni; 1927 v E, Ni; 1930 v Ni (4)
Jones, T. D. (Aberdare), 1908 v Ni (1)
Jones, T. G. (Everton), 1938 v Ni; 1939 v E, S, Ni; 1947 v E, S; 1948 v E, S, Ni; 1949 v E, Ni, P, Bel, Sw; 1950 v E, S, Bel (17)
Jones, T. J. (Sheffield W), 1932 v Ni; 1933 v F (2)
Jones, T. J. (Wimbledon), 1995 v Bul (2), G, Ge; 1996 v Sw; 1997 v Ho, T, Ei, Bel (9)
Jones, W. E. A. (Swansea T), 1947 v E, S; (with Tottenham H), 1949 v E, S (4)
Jones, W. J. (Aberdare), 1901 v E, S; (with West Ham U), 1902 v E, S (4)
Jones, W. Lot (Manchester C), 1905 v E, Ni; 1906 v E, S, Ni; 1907 v E, S, Ni; 1908 v S; 1909 v E, S, Ni; 1910 v E; 1911 v E; 1913 v E, S; 1914 v S, Ni; (with Southend U), 1920 v E, Ni (20)
Jones, W. P. (Druids), 1889 v E, Ni; (with Wynstay), 1890 v S, Ni (4)
Jones, W. R. (Aberystwyth), 1897 v S (1)

Keenor, F. C. (Cardiff C), 1920 v E, Ni; 1921 v E, Ni, S; 1922 v Ni; 1923 v E, Ni, S; 1924 v E, Ni, S; 1925 v E, Ni, S; 1926 v S; 1927 v E, Ni, S; 1928 v E, Ni, S; 1929 v E, Ni, S; 1930 v E, Ni, S; 1931 v E, Ni, S; (with Crewe Alex), 1933 v S (32)
Kelly, F. C. (Wrexham), 1899 v S, Ni; (with Druids), 1902 v Ni (3)
Kelsey, A. J. (Arsenal), 1954 v Ni, A; 1955 v S, Ni, Y; 1956 v E, Ni, S, A; 1957 v E, Ni, S, Cz (2), EG; 1958 v E, S, Ni, Is (2), H (2), M, Se, Br; 1959 v E, S; 1960 v E, Ni, S; 1961 v E, Ni, S, H, Sp (2); 1962 v E, S, Ni, Br (2) (41)
Kenrick, S. L. (Druids), 1876 v S; 1877 v S; (with Oswestry), 1879 v E, S; (with Shropshire Wanderers), 1881 v E (5)
Ketley, C. F. (Druids), 1882 v Ni (1)
King, J. (Swansea T), 1955 v E (1)
Kinsey, N. (Norwich C), 1951 v Ni, P, Sw; 1952 v E; (with Birmingham C), 1954 v Ni; 1956 v E, S (7)
Knill, A. R. (Swansea C), 1989 v Ho (1)
Krzywicki, R. L. (WBA), 1970 v EG, I; (with Huddersfield T), Ni, E, S; 1971 v R, Fi; 1972 v Cz (sub) (8)

Lambert, R. (Liverpool), 1947 v S; 1948 v E; 1949 v P, Bel, Sw (5)
Latham, G. (Liverpool), 1905 v E, S; 1906 v S; 1907 v E, S, Ni; 1908 v E; 1909 v Ni; (with Southport Central), 1910 v E; (with Cardiff C), 1913 v Ni (10)
Law, B. J. (QPR), 1990 v Se (1)
Lawrence, E. (Clapton Orient), 1930 v Ni; (with Notts Co), 1932 v S (2)
Lawrence, S. (Swansea T), 1932 v Ni; 1933 v F; 1934 v S, E, Ni; 1935 v E, S; 1936 v S (8)
Lea, A. (Wrexham), 1889 v E; 1891 v S, Ni; 1893 v Ni (4)
Lea, C. (Ipswich T), 1965 v Ni, I (2)
Leary, P. (Bangor), 1889 v Ni (1)
Leek, K. (Leicester C), 1961 v S, E, Ni, H, Sp (2); (with Newcastle U), 1962 v S; (with Birmingham C), v Br (sub), M; 1963 v E; 1965 v S, Gr; (with Northampton T), 1965 v Gr (13)
Legg, A. (Birmingham C), 1996 v Sw, Sm (sub); 1997 v Ho (sub), Ei (4)
Lever, A. R. (Leicester C), 1953 v S (1)
Lewis, B. (Chester), 1891 v Ni; (with Wrexham), 1892 v S, E, Ni; (with Middlesbrough), 1893 v S, E; (with Wrexham), 1894 v S, E, Ni; 1895 v S (10)
Lewis, D. (Arsenal), 1927 v E; 1928 v Ni; 1930 v E (3)
Lewis, D. (Swansea C), 1983 v Br (sub) (1)
Lewis, D. J. (Swansea T), 1933 v E, S (2)
Lewis, D. M. (Bangor), 1890 v Ni, S (2)
Lewis, J. (Bristol R), 1906 v E (1)
Lewis, J. (Cardiff C), 1926 v S (1)
Lewis, T. (Wrexham), 1881 v E, S (2)
Lewis, W. (Bangor), 1885 v E; 1886 v E, S; 1887 v E, S; 1888 v E; 1889 v E, Ni, S; (with Crewe Alex), 1890 v E; 1891 v E, S; 1892 v E, S, Ni; 1894 v E, S, Ni; (with Chester), 1895 v S, Ni, E; 1896 v E, S, Ni; (with Manchester C), 1897 v E, S; (with Chester), 1898 v Ni (27)

Lewis, W. L. (Swansea T), 1927 v E, Ni; 1928 v E, Ni; 1929 v S; (with Huddersfield T), 1930 v E (6)
Lloyd, B. W. (Wrexham), 1976 v A, E, S (3)
Lloyd, J. W. (Wrexham), 1879 v S; (with Newtown), 1885 v S (2)
Lloyd, R. A. (Ruthin), 1891 v Ni; 1895 v S (2)
Lockley, A. (Chirk), 1898 v Ni (1)
Lovell, S. (C Palace), 1982 v USSR (sub); (with Millwall), 1985 v N; 1986 v S (sub), H (sub), Ca (1+1 sub) (6)
Lowrie, G. (Coventry C), 1948 v E, S, Ni; (with Newcastle U), 1949 v P (4)
Lowndes, S. (Newport Co), 1983 v S (sub), Br (sub); (with Millwall), 1985 v N (sub); 1986 v S.Ar (sub), Ei, U, Ca (2); (with Barnsley), 1987 v Fi (sub); 1988 v Se (sub) (10)
Lucas, P. M. (Leyton Orient), 1962 v Ni, M; 1963 v S, E (4)
Lucas, W. H. (Swansea T), 1949 v S, Ni, P, Bel, Sw; 1950 v E; 1951 v E (7)
Lumberg, A. (Wrexham), 1929 v Ni; 1930 v E, S; (with Wolverhampton W), 1932 v S (4)

McCarthy, T. P. (Wrexham), 1899 v Ni (1)
McMillan, R. (Shrewsbury Engineers), 1881 v E, S (2)
Maguire, G. T. (Portsmouth), 1990 v Fi (sub), Ho, WG, Ei, Se; 1992 v Br (sub), G (7)
Mahoney, J. F. (Stoke C), 1968 v E; 1969 v EG; 1971 v Cz; 1973 v E (3), Pol, S, Ni; 1974 v Pol, E, S, Ni; 1975 v A, H (2), L (2), S, E, Ni; 1976 v A, Y (2), E, Ni; 1977 v WG, Cz, S, E, Ni; (with Middlesbrough), 1978 v K (2), S, Cz, Ir, E (sub), S, Ni; 1979 v WG, S, E, Ni, Ma; (with Swansea C), 1980 v Ei, WG, T (sub); 1982 v Ic, USSR; 1983 v Y, E (51)
Mardon, P. J. (WBA), 1996 v G (sub) (1)
Marriott, A. (Wrexham), 1996 v Sw (sub); 1997 v S (2)
Martin, T. J. (Newport Co), 1930 v Ni (1)
Marustik, C. (Swansea C), 1982 v Sp, E, S, Ni, F; 1983 v N (6)
Mates, J. (Chirk), 1891 v Ni; 1897 v E, S (3)
Mathews, R. W. (Liverpool), 1921 v Ni; (with Bristol C), 1923 v E; (with Bradford), 1926 v Ni (3)
Matthews, W. (Chester), 1905 v Ni; 1908 v E (2)
Matthias, J. S. (Brymbo), 1896 v S, Ni; (with Shrewsbury), 1897 v E, S; (with Wolverhampton W), 1899 v S (5)
Matthias, T. J. (Wrexham), 1914 v S, E; 1920 v Ni, S, E; 1921 v S, E, Ni; 1922 v S, E, Ni; 1923 v S (12)
Mays, A. W. (Wrexham), 1929 v Ni (1)
Medwin, T. C. (Swansea T), 1953 v Ni, F, Y; (with Tottenham H), 1957 v E, S, Ni, Cz (2), EG; 1958 v E, S, Ni, Is (2), H (2), M, Br; 1959 v E, S, Ni; 1960 v E, S, Ni; 1961 v S, Ei, E, Sp; 1963 v E, H (30)
Melville, A. K. (Swansea C), 1990 v WG, Ei, Se, Cr (sub); (with Oxford U), 1991 v Ic, Pol, WG; 1992 v Br, G, L, R, Ho, J (sub); 1993 v RCS, Fa (sub); (with Sunderland), 1994 v RCS (sub), R, N, Se, Es; 1995 v Alb, Mol (sub), Ge, Bul; 1996 v G, Alb, Sm; 1997 v Sm, Ho (2), T (31)
Meredith, S. (Chirk), 1900 v S; 1901 v S, E, Ni; (with Stoke C), 1902 v E; 1903 v Ni; 1904 v E; (with Leyton), 1907 v E (8)
Meredith, W. H. (Manchester C), 1895 v E, Ni; 1896 v E, Ni; 1897 v E, Ni, S; 1898 v E, Ni; 1899 v E; 1900 v E, Ni; 1901 v E, Ni; 1902 v E, S; 1903 v E, S, Ni; 1904 v E; 1905 v E, S; (with Manchester U), 1907 v E, S, Ni; 1908 v E, Ni; 1909 v E, S, Ni; 1910 v E, S, Ni; 1911 v E, S, Ni; 1912 v E, S, Ni; 1913 v E, S, Ni; 1914 v E, S, Ni; 1920 v E, S, Ni (48)
Mielczarek, R. (Rotherham U), 1971 v Fi (1)
Millership, H. (Rotherham Co), 1920 v E, S, Ni; 1921 v E, S, Ni (6)
Millington, A. H. (WBA), 1963 v S, E, H; (with C Palace), 1965 v E, USSR; (with Peterborough U), 1966 v Ch, Br; 1967 v E, Ni; 1968 v Ni, WG; 1969 v I, EG; (with Swansea T), 1970 v E, S, Ni; 1971 v Cz, Fi; 1972 v Fi (sub), Cz, R (21)
Mills, T. J. (Clapton Orient), 1934 v E, Ni; (with Leicester C), 1935 v E, S (4)
Mills-Roberts, R. H. (St Thomas' Hospital), 1885 v E, S, Ni; 1886 v E; 1887 v E, S; (with Preston NE), 1888 v E, Ni; (with Llanberis), 1892 v E (8)
Moore, G. (Cardiff C), 1960 v E, S, Ni; 1961 v Ei, Sp; (with Chelsea), 1962 v Br; 1963 v Ni, H; (with Manchester U), 1964 v S, Ni; (with Northampton T), 1966 v Ni, Ch; (with Charlton Ath), 1969 v S, E, Ni, R of UK; 1970 v E, S, Ni, I; 1971 v P (21)
Morgan, J. R. (Cambridge University), 1877 v S; (with Swansea T), 1879 v S; (with Derby School Staff), 1880 v E, S; 1881 v E, S; 1882 v E, S, Ni; (with Swansea T), 1883 v E (10)
Morgan, J. T. (Wrexham), 1905 v Ni (1)
Morgan-Owen, H. (Oxford University), 1901 v E; 1902 v S; 1906 v E, Ni; (with Welshpool), 1907 v S (5)

Morgan-Owen, M. M. (Oxford University), 1897 v S, Ni; 1898 v E, S; 1899 v S; 1900 v E, S; (with Corinthians), 1903 v S; 1906 v S, E, Ni; 1907 v E (12)

Morley, E. J. (Swansea T), 1925 v E; (with Clapton Orient), 1929 v E, S, Ni (4)

Morris, A. G. (Aberystwyth), 1896 v E, Ni, S; (with Swindon T), 1897 v E; 1898 v S; (with Nottingham F), 1899 v E, S; 1903 v S; 1905 v E, S; 1907 v E, S; 1908 v E; 1910 v E, S, Ni; 1911 v E, S, Ni; 1912 v E (21)

Morris, C. (Chirk), 1900 v E, S, Ni; (with Derby Co), 1901 v E, S, Ni; 1902 v E, S; 1903 v E, S, Ni; 1904 v Ni; 1905 v E, S, Ni; 1906 v S; 1907 v S; 1908 v E, S; 1909 v E, S, Ni; 1910 v E, S, Ni; (with Huddersfield T), 1911 v E, S, Ni (28)

Morris, E. (Chirk), 1893 v E, S, Ni (3)

Morris, H. (Sheffield U), 1894 v S; (with Manchester C), 1896 v E; (with Grimsby T), 1897 v E (3)

Morris, J. (Oswestry), 1887 v S (1)

Morris, J. (Chirk), 1898 v Ni (1)

Morris, R. (Chirk), 1900 v E, Ni; 1901 v Ni; 1902 v S; (with Shrewsbury T), 1903 v E, Ni (6)

Morris, R. (Druids), 1902 v E, S; (with Newtown); Ni; (with Liverpool), 1903 v S, Ni; 1904 v E, S, Ni; (with Leeds C), 1906 v S; (with Grimsby T), 1907 v Ni; (with Plymouth Arg), 1908 v Ni (11)

Morris, S. (Birmingham), 1937 v E, S; 1938 v E, S; 1939 v F (5)

Morris, W. (Burnley), 1947 v Ni; 1949 v E; 1952 v S, Ni, R of UK (5)

Moulsdale, J. R. B. (Corinthians), 1925 v Ni (1)

Murphy, J. P. (WBA), 1933 v F, E, Ni; 1934 v E, S; 1935 v E, S, Ni; 1936 v E, S, Ni; 1937 v S, Ni; 1938 v E, S (15)

Nardiello, D. (Coventry C), 1978 v Cz, WG (sub) (2)

Neal, J. E. (Colwyn Bay), 1931 v E, S (2)

Neilson, A. B. (Newcastle U), 1992 v Ei; 1994 v Se, Es; 1995 v Ge; (with Southampton), 1997 v Ho (5)

Newnes, J. (Nelson), 1926 v Ni (1)

Newton, L. F. (Cardiff Corinthians), 1912 v Ni (1)

Nicholas, D. S. (Stoke C), 1923 v S; (with Swansea T), 1927 v E, Ni (3)

Nicholas, P. (C Palace), 1979 v S (sub), Ni (sub), Ma; 1980 v Ei, WG, T, E, S, Ni, Ic; 1981 v T, Cz, E; (with Arsenal), T, S, E, USSR; 1982 v Cz, Ic, USSR, Sp, E, S, Ni, F; 1983 v Y, Bul, S, Ni; 1984 v N, Bul, N, Is; (with C Palace), 1985 v Sp; (with Luton T), N, S, Sp, N; 1986 v S, H, S.Ar, Ei, U, Ca (2); 1987 v Fi (2) USSR, Cz; (with Aberdeen), 1988 v D (2), Cz, Y, Se; (with Chelsea), 1989 v Ho, Fi, Is, Se, WG; 1990 v Fi, Ho, WG, Ei, Se, Cr; 1991 v D (sub), Bel, L, Ei; (with Watford), Bel, Pol, WG; 1992 v L (73)

Nicholls, J. (Newport Co), 1924 v E, Ni; (with Cardiff C), 1925 v E, S (4)

Niedzwiecki, E. A. (Chelsea), 1985 v N (sub); 1988 v D (2)

Nock, W. (Newtown), 1897 v Ni (1)

Nogan, L. M. (Watford), 1992 v A (sub); (with Reading), 1996 v Mol (2)

Norman, A. J. (Hull C), 1986 v Ei (sub), U, Ca; 1988 v Ma, I (5)

Nurse, M. T. G. (Swansea T), 1960 v E, Ni; 1961 v S, E, H, Ni, Ei, Sp (2); (with Middlesbrough), 1963 v E, H; 1964 v S (12)

O'Callaghan, E. (Tottenham H), 1929 v Ni; 1930 v S; 1932 v S, E; 1933 v Ni, S, E; 1934 v Ni, S, E; 1935 v E (11)

Oliver, A. (Blackburn R), 1905 v E; (with Bangor), S (2)

O'Sullivan, P. A. (Brighton), 1973 v S (sub); 1976 v S; 1979 v Ma (sub) (3)

Owen, D. (Oswestry), 1879 v E (1)

Owen, E. (Ruthin Grammar School), 1884 v E, Ni, S (3)

Owen, G. (Chirk), 1888 v S; (with Newton Heath), 1889 v S, Ni; 1893 v Ni (4)

Owen, J. (Newton Heath), 1892 v E (1)

Owen, Trevor (Crewe Alex), 1899 v E, S (2)

Owen, T. (Oswestry), 1879 v E (1)

Owen, W. (Chirk), 1884 v E; 1885 v Ni; 1887 v E; 1888 v E; 1889 v E, Ni, S; 1890 v S, Ni; 1891 v E, S, Ni; 1892 v E, S; 1893 v S, Ni (16)

Owen, W. P. (Ruthin), 1880 v E, S; 1881 v E, S; 1882 v E, S, Ni; 1883 v E, S; 1884 v E, S, Ni (12)

Owens, J. (Wrexham), 1902 v S (1)

Page, M. E. (Birmingham C), 1971 v Fi; 1972 v S, Ni; 1973 v E (1+1 sub), Ni; 1974 v S, Ni; 1975 v H, L, S, E, Ni; 1976 v E, Y (2), E, Ni; 1977 v WG, S; 1978 v K (sub+1), WG, Ir, E, S; 1979 v Ma, WG (28)

Page, R. J. (Watford), 1997 v T, Bel, S (3)

Palmer, D. (Swansea T), 1957 v Cz; 1958 v E, EG (3)

Parris, J. E. (Bradford), 1932 v Ni (1)

Parry, B. J. (Swansea T), 1951 v S (1)

Parry, C. (Everton), 1891 v E, S; 1893 v E; 1894 v E; 1895 v E, S; (with Newtown), 1896 v E, S, Ni; 1897 v Ni; 1898 v E, S, Ni (13)

Parry, E. (Liverpool), 1922 v S; 1923 v E, Ni; 1925 v Ni; 1926 v Ni (5)

Parry, M. (Liverpool), 1901 v E, S, Ni; 1902 v E, S, Ni; 1903 v E, S; 1904 v E, Ni; 1906 v E; 1908 v E, S, Ni; 1909 v E, S (16)

Parry, T. D. (Oswestry), 1900 v E, S, Ni; 1901 v E, S, Ni; 1902 v E (7)

Parry, W. (Newtown), 1895 v Ni (1)

Pascoe, C. (Swansea C), 1984 v N, Is; (with Sunderland), 1989 v Fi, Is, WG (sub); 1990 v Ho (sub), WG (sub); 1991 v Ei, Ic (sub); 1992 v Br (10)

Paul, R. (Swansea T), 1949 v E, S, Ni, P, Sw; 1950 v E, S, Ni, Bel; (with Manchester C), 1951 v S, E, Ni, P, Sw; 1952 v E, S, Ni, R of UK; 1953 v S, E, Ni, F, Y; 1954 v E, S, Ni; 1955 v S, E, Y; 1956 v E, Ni, S, A (33)

Peake, E. (Aberystwyth), 1908 v Ni; (with Liverpool), 1909 v Ni, S, E; 1910 v S, Ni; 1911 v Ni; 1912 v E; 1913 v E, Ni; 1914 v Ni (11)

Peers, E. J. (Wolverhampton W), 1914 v Ni, S, E; 1920 v E, S; 1921 v S, Ni, E; (with Port Vale), 1922 v E, S, Ni; 1923 v E (12)

Pembridge, M. A. (Luton T), 1992 v Br, Ei, R (with Derby Co), Ho, J (sub); 1993 v Bel (sub), Ei; 1994 v N (sub); 1995 v Alb (sub), Mol, Ge (sub); (with Sheffield W), 1996 v Mol, G, Alb, Sw, Sm; 1997 v Sm, Ho (2), T, Ei, Bel, S (23)

Perry, E. (Doncaster R), 1938 v E, S, Ni (3)

Perry, J. (Cardiff C), 1994 v N (1)

Phennah, E. (Civil Service), 1878 v S (1)

Phillips, C. (Wolverhampton W), 1931 v Ni; 1932 v E; 1933 v S; 1934 v E, S, Ni; 1935 v E, S, Ni; 1936 v S; (with Aston Villa), 1936 v E, Ni; 1938 v S (13)

Phillips, D. (Plymouth Arg), 1984 v E, Ni, N; (with Manchester C), 1985 v Sp, Ic, S, Sp, N; 1986 v S, H, S.Ar, Ei, U; (with Coventry C), 1987 v Fi, Cz; 1988 v D (2), Cz, Y, Se; 1989 v Se, WG; (with Norwich C), 1990 v Fi, Ho, WG, Ei, Se; 1991 v D, Bel, Ic, Pol, WG; 1992 v L, Ei, A, R, Ho (sub), Arg, J; 1993 v Fa, Cy, Bel, Ei, Bel, RCS, Fa; (with Nottingham F), 1994 v RCS, Cy, R, N, Se, Es; 1995 v Alb, Mol, Ge, Bul (2), G, Ge; 1996 v Mol (sub), Alb, I (62)

Phillips, L. (Cardiff C), 1971 v Cz, S, E, Ni; 1972 v Cz, R, S, Ni; 1973 v E; 1974 v Pol (sub), Ni; 1975 v A; (with Aston Villa), H (2), L (2), S, E, Ni; 1976 v A, E, Y (2), E, Ni; 1977 v WG, S (2), Cz, E; 1978 v K (2), S, Cz, WG, S, E; 1979 v Ma; (with Swansea C), T, WG, S, E, Ni, Ma; 1980 v Ei, WG, T, S (sub), Ni, Ic; 1981 v T, Cz, T, S, E, USSR; (with Charlton Ath), 1982 v Cz, USSR (58)

Phillips, T. J. S. (Chelsea), 1973 v E; 1974 v E; 1975 v H (sub); 1978 v K (4)

Phoenix, H. (Wrexham), 1882 v S (1)

Poland, G. (Wrexham), 1939 v Ni, F (2)

Pontin, K. (Cardiff C), 1980 v E (sub), S (2)

Powell, A. (Leeds U), 1947 v E, S; 1948 v E, S, Ni; (with Everton), 1949 v E; 1950 v Bel; (with Birmingham C), 1951 v S (8)

Powell, D. (Wrexham), 1968 v WG; (with Sheffield U), 1969 v S, E, Ni, I, WG; 1970 v E, S, Ni, EG; 1971 v R (11)

Powell, I. V. (QPR), 1947 v E; 1948 v E, S, Ni; (with Aston Villa), 1949 v Bel; 1950 v S, Bel; 1951 v S (8)

Powell, J. (Druids), 1878 v S; 1880 v E, S; 1882 v E, S, Ni; 1883 v E, S, Ni; (with Bolton W), 1884 v E; (with Newton Heath), 1887 v E, S; 1888 v E, S, Ni (15)

Powell, Seth (WBA), 1885 v S; 1886 v E, Ni; 1891 v E, S; 1892 v E, S (7)

Price, H. (Aston Villa), 1907 v S; (with Burton U), 1908 v Ni; (with Wrexham), 1909 v S, E, Ni (5)

Price, J. (Wrexham), 1877 v S; 1878 v S; 1879 v E; 1880 v E, S; 1881 v E, S; (with Druids), 1882 v S, E, Ni; 1883 v S, Ni (12)

Price, P. (Luton T), 1980 v E, S, Ni, Ic; 1981 v T, Cz, Ei, T, S, E, USSR; (with Tottenham H), 1982 v USSR, Sp, F; 1983 v N, Y, E, Bul, S, Ni; 1984 v N, R, Bul, Y, S (sub) (25)

Pring, K. D. (Rotherham U), 1966 v Ch, D; 1967 v Ni (3)

Pritchard, H. K. (Bristol C), 1985 v N (sub) (1)

Pryce-Jones, A. W. (Newtown), 1895 v Ei (1)

Pryce-Jones, W. E. (Cambridge University), 1887 v S; 1888 v S, E, Ni; 1890 v Ni (5)

Pugh, A. (Rhostyllen), 1889 v S (1)

Pugh, D. H. (Wrexham), 1896 v S, Ni; 1897 v S, Ni; (with Lincoln C), 1900 v S; 1901 v S, E (7)

Pugsley, J. (Charlton Ath), 1930 v Ni (1)

Pullen, W. J. (Plymouth Arg), 1926 v E (1)

Rankmore, F. E. J. (Peterborough), 1966 v Ch (sub) (1)

Ratcliffe, K. (Everton), 1981 v Cz, Ei, T, S, E, USSR; 1982 v Cz, Ic, USSR, Sp, E; 1983 v Y, E, Bul, S, Ni, Br; 1984 v N, R, Bul, Y, S, E, Ni, N, Is; 1985 v Ic, Sp, Ic, N, S, Sp; 1986 v S, H, S.Ar, U; 1987 v Fi (2), USSR, Cz; 1988 v D (2), Cz; 1989 v Fi, Is, Se, WG; 1990 v Fi; 1991 v D, Bel (2), L, Ei, Ic, Pol, WG; 1992 v Br, G; (with Cardiff C), 1993 v Bel (59)

Rea, J. C. (Aberystwyth), 1894 v Ni, S, E; 1895 v S; 1896 v S, Ni; 1897 v S, Ni; 1898 v Ni (9)

Ready, K. (QPR), 1997 v Ei (1)

Reece, G. I. (Sheffield U), 1966 v E, S, Ni, USSR; 1967 v S; 1969 v R of UK (sub); 1970 v I (sub); 1971 v S, E, Ni, Fi; 1972 v Fi, R, E (sub), S, Ni; (with Cardiff C), 1973 v E (sub), Ni; 1974 v Pol (sub), E, S, Ni; 1975 v A, H (2), L (2), S, Ni (29)

Reed, W. G. (Ipswich T), 1955 v S, Y (2)

Rees, A. (Birmingham C), 1984 v N (sub) (1)

Rees, J. M. (Luton T), 1992 v A (sub) (1)

Rees, R. R. (Coventry C), 1965 v S, E, Ni, D, Gr (2), I, R; 1966 v E, S, Ni, R, D, Br (2), Ch; 1967 v E, Ni; 1968 v E, S, Ni; (with WBA), WG; 1969 v I; (with Nottingham F), 1969 v WG, EG, S (sub), R of UK; 1970 v E, S, Ni, EG, I; 1971 v Cz, R, E (sub), Ni (sub), Fi; 1972 v Cz (sub), R (39)

Rees, W. (Cardiff C), 1949 v Ni, Bel, Sw; (with Tottenham H), 1950 v Ni (4)

Richards, A. (Barnsley), 1932 v S (1)

Richards, D. (Wolverhampton W), 1931 v Ni; 1933 v E, S, Ni; 1934 v E, S, Ni; 1935 v E, S, Ni; 1936 v S; (with Brentford), 1936 v E, Ni; 1937 v S, E; (with Birmingham), Ni; 1938 v E, S, Ni; 1939 v E, S (21)

Richards, G. (Druids), 1899 v E, S, Ni; (with Oswestry), 1903 v Ni; (with Shrewsbury), 1904 v S; 1905 v Ni (6)

Richards, R. W. (Wolverhampton W), 1920 v E, S; 1921 v Ni; 1922 v E, S; (with West Ham U), 1924 v E, S, Ni; (with Mold), 1926 v S (9)

Richards, S. V. (Cardiff C), 1947 v E (1)

Richards, W. E. (Fulham), 1933 v Ni (1)

Roach, J. (Oswestry), 1885 v Ni (1)

Robbins, W. W. (Cardiff C), 1931 v E, S; 1932 v Ni, E, S; (with WBA), 1933 v F, E, S, Ni; 1934 v S; 1936 v S (11)

Roberts, A. M. (QPR), 1993 v Ei (sub); 1997 v Sm (sub) (2)

Roberts, D. F. (Oxford U), 1973 v Pol, E (sub), Ni; 1974 v E, S; 1975 v A; (with Hull C), L, Ni; 1976 v S, Ni, Y; 1977 v E (sub), Ni; 1978 v K (1+1 sub), S, Ni (17)

Roberts, I. W. (Watford), 1990 v Ho; (with Huddersfield T), 1992 v A, Arg, J; (with Leicester C), 1994 v Se; 1995 v Alb (sub), Mol (7)

Roberts, Jas (Chirk), 1898 v S (1)

Roberts, J. (Wrexham), 1913 v S, Ni (2)

Roberts, J. (Corwen), 1879 v S; 1880 v E, S; 1882 v E, S, Ni; (with Berwyn R), 1883 v E (7)

Roberts, J. (Ruthin), 1881 v S; 1882 v S (2)

Roberts, J. (Bradford C), 1906 v Ni; 1907 v Ni (2)

Roberts, J. G. (Arsenal), 1971 v S, E, Ni, Fi; 1972 v Fi, E, Ni; (with Birmingham C), 1973 v E (2), Pol, S, Ni; 1974 v Pol, E, S, Ni; 1975 v A, H, S, E; 1976 v E, S (22)

Roberts, J. H. (Bolton), 1949 v Bel (1)

Roberts, P. S. (Portsmouth), 1974 v E; 1975 v A, H, L (4)

Roberts, R. (Druids), 1884 v S; (with Bolton W), 1887 v S; 1888 v S, E; 1889 v S, E; 1890 v S; 1892 v Ni; (with Preston NE), S (9)

Roberts, R. (Wrexham), 1886 v Ni; 1887 v Ni (2)

Roberts, R. (Rhos), 1891 v Ni; (with Crewe Alex), 1893 v E (2)

Roberts, W. (Llangollen), 1879 v E, S; 1880 v E, S; (with Berwyn R), 1881 v S; 1883 v S (6)

Roberts, W. (Wrexham), 1886 v E, S, Ni; 1887 v Ni (4)

Roberts, W. H. (Ruthin), 1882 v E, S; 1883 v E, S, Ni; (with Rhyl), 1884 v S (6)

Robinson, J. R. C. (Charlton Ath), 1996 v Alb (sub), Sw, Sm; 1997 v Sm, Ho (1 + sub), Ei, S (8)

Rodrigues, P. J. (Cardiff C), 1965 v Ni, Gr (2); 1966 v USSR, E, S, D; (with Leicester C), Ni, Br (2), Ch; 1967 v S; 1968 v E, S, Ni; 1969 v E, Ni, EG, R of UK; 1970 v E, S, Ni, EG; (with Sheffield W), 1971 v R, E, S, Cz, Ni; 1972 v Fi, Cz, R, E, Ni (sub); 1973 v E (3), Pol, S, Ni; 1974 v Pol (40)

Rogers, J. P. (Wrexham), 1896 v E, S, Ni (3)

Rogers, W. (Wrexham), 1931 v E, S (2)

Roose, L. R. (Aberystwyth), 1900 v Ni; (with London Welsh), 1901 v E, S, Ni; (with Stoke C), 1902 v E, S; 1904 v E; (with Everton), 1905 v S, E; (with Stoke C), 1906 v E, S, Ni; 1907 v E, S, Ni; (with Sunderland), 1908 v E, S; 1909 v E, S, Ni; 1910 v E, S, Ni; 1911 v S (24)

Rouse, R. V. (C Palace), 1959 v Ni (1)

Rowlands, A. C. (Tranmere R), 1914 v E (1)

Rowley, T. (Tranmere R), 1959 v Ni (1)

Rush, I. (Liverpool), 1980 v S (sub), Ni; 1981 v E (sub); 1982 v Ic (sub), USSR, E, S, Ni, F; 1983 v N, Y, E, Bul; 1984 v N, R, Bul, Y, S, E, Ni; 1985 v Ic, N, S, Sp; 1986 v S, S.Ar,

Ei, U; 1987 v Fi (2), USSR, Cz; (with Juventus), 1988 v D, Cz, Y, Se, Ma, I; (with Liverpool), 1989 v Ho, Fi, Se, WG; 1990 v Fi, Ei; 1991 v D, Bel (2), L, Ei, Pol, WG; 1992 v G, L, R; 1993 v Fa, Cy, Bel (2), RCS, Fa; 1994 v RCS, Cy, R, N, Se, Es; 1995 v Alb, Ge, Bul, G, Ge; 1996 v Mol, I (73)

Russell, M. R. (Merthyr T), 1912 v S, Ni; 1914 v E; (with Plymouth Arg), 1920 v E, S, Ni; 1921 v E, S, Ni; 1922 v E, Ni; 1923 v E, S, Ni; 1924 v E, S, Ni; 1925 v E, S; 1926 v E, S; 1928 v S; 1929 v E (23)

Sabine, H. W. (Oswestry), 1887 v Ni (1)

Saunders, D. (Brighton & HA), 1986 v Ei (sub), Ca (2); 1987 v Fi, USSR (sub); (with Oxford U), 1988 v Y, Se, Ma, I (sub); 1989 v Ho (sub), Fi; (with Derby Co), Is, Se, WG; 1990 v Fi, Ho, WG, Se, Cr; 1991 v D, Bel (2), L, Ei, Ic, Pol, WG; (with Liverpool), 1992 v Br, G, Ei, R, Ho, Arg, J; 1993 v Fa; (with Aston Villa), Cy, Bel (2), RCS, Fa; 1994 v RCS, Cy, R, N (sub); 1995 v Ge, Bul (2), G, Ge; (with Galatasaray), 1996 v G, Alb, Sm; (with Nottingham F), 1997 v Sm, Ho (2), T, Bel, S (58)

Savage, R. W. (Crewe Alex), 1996 v Alb (sub), Sw (sub), Sm (sub); 1997 v Ei (sub), S (5)

Savin, G. (Oswestry), 1878 v S (1)

Sayer, P. (Cardiff C), 1977 v Cz, S, E, Ni; 1978 v K (2), S (7)

Scrine, F. H. (Swansea T), 1950 v E, Ni (2)

Sear, C. R. (Manchester C), 1963 v E (1)

Shaw, E. G. (Oswestry), 1882 v Ni; 1884 v S, Ni (3)

Sherwood, A. T. (Cardiff C), 1947 v E, Ni; 1948 v S, Ni; 1949 v E, S, Ni, P, Sw; 1950 v E, S, Ni, Bel; 1951 v E, S, Ni, P, Sw; 1952 v E, S, Ni, R of UK; 1953 v S, E, Ni, F, Y; 1954 v E, S, Ni, A; 1955 v S, E, Y, Ni; 1956 v E, S, Ni, A; (with Newport Co), 1957 v E, S (41)

Shone, W. W. (Oswestry), 1879 v E (1)

Shortt, W. W. (Plymouth Arg), 1947 v Ni; 1950 v Ni, Bel; 1952 v E, S, Ni, R of UK; 1953 v S, E, Ni, F, Y (12)

Showers, D. (Cardiff C), 1975 v E (sub), Ni (2)

Sidlow, C. (Liverpool), 1947 v E, S; 1948 v E, S, Ni; 1949 v S; 1950 v E (7)

Sisson, H. (Wrexham Olympic), 1885 v Ni; 1886 v S, Ni (3)

Slatter, N. (Bristol R), 1983 v S; 1984 v N (sub), Is; 1985 v Ic, Sp, Ic, N, S, Sp, N; (with Oxford U), 1986 v H (sub), S.Ar, Ca (2); 1987 v Fi (sub), Cz; 1988 v D (2), Cz, Ma, I; 1989 v Is (sub) (22)

Smallman, D. P. (Wrexham), 1974 v E (sub), S (sub), Ni; (with Everton), 1975 v H (sub), E, Ni (sub); 1976 v A (7)

Southall, N. (Everton), 1982 v Ni; 1983 v N, E, Bul, S, Ni, Br; 1984 v N, R, Bul, Y, S, E, Ni, N, Is; 1985 v Ic, Sp, Ic, N, S, Sp, N; 1986 v S, H, S.Ar, Ei; 1987 v USSR, Fi, Cz; 1988 v D, Cz, Y, Se; 1989 v Ho, Fi, Se, WG; 1990 v Fi, Ho, WG, Ei, Se, Cr; 1991 v D, Bel (2), L, Ei, Ic, Pol, WG; 1992 v Br, G, L, Ei, A, R, Ho, Arg, J; 1993 v Fa, Cy, Bel, Ei, Bel, RCS, Fa; 1994 v RCS, Cy, R, N, Se, Es; 1995 v Alb, Mol, Ge, Bul (2), G, Ge; 1996 v Mol, G, I, Sw (sub); (with Everton), 1997 v Sm (sub), Ho (2), T, Ei, Bel, S (92)

Speed, G. A. (Leeds U), 1990 v Cr (sub); 1991 v D, L (sub), Ei (sub), Ic, WG (sub); 1992 v Br, G (sub), L, Ei, R, Ho,Arg,J; 1993 v Fa, Cy, Bel, Ei, Bel, Fa (sub); 1994 v RCS (sub), Cy, R, N, Se; 1995 v Alb, Mol, Ge, Bul (2), G; 1996 v Mol, G, I, Sw (sub); (with Everton), 1997 v Sm (sub), Ho (2), T, Ei, Bel, S (42)

Sprake, G. (Leeds U), 1964 v S, Ni; 1965 v S, D, Gr; 1966 v E, Ni, USSR; 1967 v S; 1968 v E, S; 1969 v S, E, Ni, WG, R of UK; 1970 v EG, I; 1971 v R, S, E, Ni; 1972 v Fi, E, S, Ni; 1973 v E (2), Pol, S, Ni; 1974 v Pol; (with Birmingham C), S, Ni; 1975 v A, H, L (37)

Stansfield, F. (Cardiff C), 1949 v S (1)

Stevenson, B. (Leeds U), 1978 v Ni; 1979 v Ma, T, S, E, Ni, Ma; 1980 v WG, T, Ic (sub); 1982 v Cz; (with Birmingham C), Sp, S, Ni, F (15)

Stevenson, N. (Swansea C), 1982 v E, S, Ni; 1983 v N (4)

Stitfall, R. F. (Cardiff C), 1953 v E; 1957 v Cz (2)

Sullivan, D. (Cardiff C), 1953 v Ni, F, Y; 1954 v Ni; 1955 v E, Ni; 1957 v E, S; 1958 v Ni, H (2), Se, Br; 1959 v S, Ni; 1960 v E, S (17)

Symons, C. J. (Portsmouth), 1992 v Ei, Ho, Arg, J; 1993 v Fa, Cy, Bel, Ei, RCS, Fa; 1994 v RCS, Cy, R; 1995 v Mol, Ge (sub), Bul, G, Ge; (with Manchester C), 1996 v Mol, G, I, Sw; 1997 v Ho (2), Ei, Bel, S (27)

Tapscott, D. R. (Arsenal), 1954 v A; 1955 v S, E, Ni, Y; 1956 v E, Ni, S, A; 1957 v Ni, Cz, EG; (with Cardiff C), 1959 v E, Ni (14)

Taylor, G. K. (C Palace), 1996 v Alb, I (sub); (with Sheffield U), Sw; 1997 v Sm (sub), Ho (sub), Ei (sub) (6)

Taylor, J. (Wrexham), 1898 v E (1)

Taylor, O. D. S. (Newtown), 1893 v S, Ni; 1894 v S, Ni (4)

Thomas, C. (Druids), 1899 v Ni; 1900 v S (2)

Thomas, D. A. (Swansea T), 1957 v Cz; 1958 v EG (2)

Thomas, D. S. (Fulham), 1948 v E, S, Ni; 1949 v S (4)

Thomas, E. (Cardiff Corinthians), 1925 v E (1)
Thomas, G. (Wrexham), 1885 v E, S (2)
Thomas, H. (Manchester U), 1927 v E (1)
Thomas, M. (Wrexham), 1977 v WG, S (1+1 sub), Ni (sub); 1978 v K (sub), S, Cz, Ir, E, Ni (sub); 1979 v Ma; (with Manchester U), T, WG, Ma (sub); 1980 v Ei, WG (sub), T, E, S, Ni; 1981 v Cz, S, E, USSR; (with Everton), 1982 v Cz; (with Brighton & HA), USSR (sub), Sp, E, S (sub), Ni (sub); 1983 (with Stoke C), v N, Y, E, Bul, S, Ni, Br; 1984 v R, Bul, Y; (with Chelsea), S, E; 1985 v Ic, Sp, Ic, S, Sp, N; 1986 v S; (with WBA), H, S.Ar (sub) (51)
Thomas, M. R. (Newcastle U), 1987 v Fi (1)
Thomas, R. J. (Swindon T), 1967 v Ni; 1968 v WG; 1969 v E, Ni, I, WG, R of UK; 1970 v E, S, Ni, EG, I; 1971 v S, E, Ni, R, Cz; 1972 v Fi, Cz, R, E, S, Ni; 1973 v E (3), Pol, S, Ni; 1974 v Pol; (with Derby Co), E, S, Ni; 1975 v H (2), L (2), S, E, Ni; 1976 v A, Y, E; 1977 v Cz, S, E, Ni; 1978 v K, S; (with Cardiff C), Cz (50)
Thomas, T. (Bangor), 1898 v S, Ni (2)
Thomas, W. R. (Newport Co), 1931 v E, S (2)
Thomson, D. (Druids), 1876 v S (1)
Thomson, G. F. (Druids), 1876 v S; 1877 v S (2)
Toshack, J. B. (Cardiff C), 1969 v S, E, Ni, WG, EG, R of UK; 1970 v EG, I; (with Liverpool), 1971 v S, E, Ni, Fi; 1972 v Fi, E; 1973 v E (3), Pol, S; 1975 v A, H (2), L (2), S, E; 1976 v Y (2), E; 1977 v S; 1978 v K (2), Cz; (with Swansea C), 1979 v WG (sub), S, E, Ni, Ma; 1980 v WG (40)
Townsend, W. (Newtown), 1893 v Ni (2)
Trainer, H. (Wrexham), 1895 v E, S, Ni (3)
Trainer, J. (Bolton W), 1887 v S; (with Preston NE), 1888 v S; 1889 v E; 1890 v S; 1891 v S; 1892 v Ni, S; 1893 v E; 1894 v Ni, E; 1895 v Ni, E; 1896 v S; 1897 v Ni, S, E; 1898 v S, E; 1899 v Ni, S (20)
Trollope, P. J. (Derby Co), 1997 v S (1)
Turner, H. G. (Charlton Ath), 1937 v E, S, Ni; 1938 v E, S, Ni; 1939 v Ni, F (8)
Turner, J. (Wrexham), 1892 v E (1)
Turner, R. E. (Wrexham), 1891 v E, Ni (2)
Turner, W. H. (Wrexham), 1887 v E, Ni; 1890 v S; 1891 v E, S (5)

Van Den Hauwe, P. W. R. (Everton), 1985 v Sp; 1986 v S, H; 1987 v USSR, Fi, Cz; 1988 v D (2), Cz, Y, I; 1989 v Fi, Se (13)
Vaughan, Jas (Druids), 1893 v E, S, Ni; 1899 v E (4)
Vaughan, John (Oswestry), 1879 v S; 1880 v S; 1881 v E, S; 1882 v E, S, Ni; 1883 v E, S, Ni; (with Bolton W), 1884 v E (11)
Vaughan, J. O. (Rhyl), 1885 v Ni; 1886 v Ni, E, S (4)
Vaughan, N. (Newport Co), 1983 v Y (sub), Br; 1984 v N; (with Cardiff C), R, Bul, Y, Ni (sub), N, Is; 1985 v Sp (sub) (10)
Vaughan, T. (Rhyl), 1885 v E (1)
Vearncombe, G. (Cardiff C), 1958 v EG; 1961 v Ei (2)
Vernon, T. R. (Blackburn R), 1957 v Ni, Cz (2), EG; 1958 v E, S, EG, Se; 1959 v S; (with Everton), 1960 v Ni; 1961 v S, E, Ei; 1962 v Ni, Br (2), M; 1963 v S, E, H; 1964 v E, S; (with Stoke C), 1965 v Ni, Gr, I; 1966 v E, S, Ni, USSR, D; 1967 v Ni; 1968 v E (32)
Villars, A. K. (Cardiff C), 1974 v E, S, Ni (sub) (3)
Vizard, E. T. (Bolton W), 1911 v E, S, Ni; 1912 v E, S; 1913 v S; 1914 v E, Ni; 1920 v E; 1921 v E, S, Ni; 1922 v E, S; 1923 v E, Ni; 1924 v E, S, Ni; 1926 v E, S; 1927 v S (22)

Walley, J. T. (Watford), 1971 v Cz (1)
Walsh, I. (C Palace), 1980 v Ei, T, E, S, Ic; 1981 v T, Cz, Ei, T, S, E, USSR; 1982 v Cz (sub), Ic; (with Swansea C), Sp, S (sub), Ni (sub), F (18)
Ward, D. (Bristol R), 1959 v E; (with Cardiff C), 1962 v E (2)
Warner, J. (Swansea T), 1937 v E; (with Manchester U), 1939 v F (2)
Warren, F. W. (Cardiff C), 1929 v Ni; (with Middlesbrough), 1931 v Ni; 1933 v F, E; (with Hearts), 1937 v Ni; 1938 v Ni (6)
Watkins, A. E. (Leicester Fosse), 1898 v E, S; (with Aston Villa), 1900 v E, S; (with Millwall), 1904 v Ni (5)

Watkins, W. M. (Stoke C), 1902 v E; 1903 v E, S; (with Aston Villa); 1904 v E, S, Ni; (with Sunderland), 1905 v E, S, Ni; (with Stoke C), 1908 v Ni (10)
Webster, C (Manchester U), 1957 v Cz; 1958 v H, M, Br (4)
Whatley, W. J. (Tottenham H), 1939 v E, S (2)
White, P. F. (London Welsh), 1896 v Ni (1)
Wilcocks, A. R. (Oswestry), 1890 v Ni (1)
Wilding, J. (Wrexham Olympians), 1885 v E, S, Ni; 1886 v E, Ni; (with Bootle), 1887 v E; 1888 v S, Ni; (with Wrexham), 1892 v S (9)
Williams, A. (Reading), 1994 v Es; 1995 v Alb, Mol, G (sub), Ge; 1996 v Mol, I (7)
Williams, A. L. (Wrexham), 1931 v E (1)
Williams, B. (Bristol C), 1930 v Ni (1)
Williams, B. D. (Swansea T), 1928 v Ni, E; 1930 v E, S; (with Everton), 1931 v Ni; 1932 v E; 1933 v E, S, Ni; 1935 v Ni (10)
Williams, D. G. (Derby Co), 1988 v Cz, Y, Se, Ma, I; 1989 v Ho, Is, Se, WG; 1990 v Fi, Ho; (with Ipswich T), 1993 v Ei; 1996 v G (sub) (13)
Williams, D. M. (Norwich C), 1986 v S.Ar (sub), U, Ca (2); 1987 v Fi (3)
Williams, D. R. (Merthyr T), 1921 v E, S; (with Sheffield W), 1923 v S; 1926 v S; 1927 v E, Ni; (with Manchester U), 1929 v E, S (8)
Williams, E. (Crewe Alex), 1893 v E, S (2)
Williams, E. (Druids), 1901 v E, Ni, S; 1902 v E, Ni (5)
Williams, G. (Chirk), 1893 v S; 1894 v S; 1895 v E, S, Ni; 1898 v Ni (6)
Williams, G. E. (WBA), 1960 v Ni; 1961 v S, E, Ei; 1963 v Ni, H; 1964 v E, S, Ni; 1965 v S, E, Ni, D, Gr (2), USSR, I; 1966 v Ni, Br (2), Ch; 1967 v S, E, Ni; 1968 v Ni; 1969 v I (26)
Williams, G. G. (Swansea T), 1961 v Ni, H, Sp (2); 1962 v E (5)
Williams, G. J. J. (Cardiff C), 1951 v Sw (1)
Williams, G. O. (Wrexham), 1907 v Ni (1)
Williams, H. J. (Swansea), 1965 v Gr (2); 1972 v R (3)
Williams, H. T. (Newport Co), 1949 v Ni, Sw; (with Leeds U), 1950 v Ni; 1951 v S (4)
Williams, J. H. (Oswestry), 1884 v E (1)
Williams, J. J. (Wrexham), 1939 v F (1)
Williams, J. T. (Middlesbrough), 1925 v Ni (1)
Williams, J. W. (C Palace), 1912 v S, Ni (2)
Williams, R. (Newcastle U), 1935 v S, E (2)
Williams, R. P. (Caernarvon), 1886 v S (1)
Williams, S. G. (WBA), 1954 v A; 1955 v E, Ni; 1956 v E, S, A; 1958 v E, S, Ni, Is (2), H (2), M, Se, Br; 1959 v E, S, Ni; 1960 v Ni; 1961 v Ni, Ei, H, Sp (2); 1962 v E, S, Ni, Br (2), M; (with Southampton), 1963 v S, E, H (2); 1964 v E, S; 1965 v S, E, D; 1966 v D (43)
Williams, W. (Druids), 1876 v S; 1878 v S; (with Oswestry), 1879 v S; (with Druids), 1880 v E; 1881 v E, S; 1882 v E, S, Ni; 1883 v Ni (11)
Williams, W. (Northampton T), 1925 v S (1)
Witcomb, D. F. (WBA), 1947 v E, S; (with Sheffield W), 1947 v Ni (3)
Woosnam, A. P. (Leyton Orient), 1959 v S; (with West Ham U), E; 1960 v E, S, Ni; 1961 v S, E, Ni, Ei, Sp, H; 1962 v E, S, Ni, Br; (with Aston Villa), 1963 v Ni, H (17)
Woosnam, G. (Newton White Star), 1879 v S (1)
Worthington, F. (Newtown), 1894 v S (1)
Wynn, G. A. (Wrexham), 1909 v E, S, Ni; (with Manchester C), 1910 v E; 1911 v Ni; 1912 v E, S; 1913 v E, S; 1914 v E, S (11)
Wynn, W. (Chirk), 1903 v Ni (1)

Yorath, T. C. (Leeds U), 1970 v I; 1971 v S, E, Ni; 1972 v Cz, E, S, Ni; 1973 v E, Pol, S; 1974 v Pol, E, S, Ni; 1975 v A, H (2), L (2), S; 1976 v A, E, S, Y (2), E, Ni; (with Coventry C), 1977 v WG, S (2), Cz, E, Ni; 1978 v K (2), S, Cz, WG, Ir, E, S, Ni; 1979 v T, WG, S, E, Ni; (with Tottenham H), 1980 v Ei, T, E, S, Ni, Ic; 1981 v T, Cz; (with Vancouver W), Ei, T, USSR (59)
Young, E. (Wimbledon), 1990 v Cr; (with C Palace), 1991 v D, Bel (2), L, Ei; 1992 v G, L, Ei, A; 1993 v Fa, Cy, Bel, Ei, Bel, Fa; 1994 v RCS, Cy, R, N; (with Wolverhampton W), 1996 v Alb (21)

REPUBLIC OF IRELAND

Aherne, T. (Belfast C), 1946 v P, Sp; (with Luton T), 1950 v Fi, E, Fi, Se, Bel; 1951 v N, Arg, N; 1952 v WG (2), A, Sp; 1953 v F; 1954 v F (16)
Aldridge, J. W. (Oxford U), 1986 v W, U, Ic, Cz; 1987 v Bel, S, Pol; (with Liverpool), S, Bul, Bel, Br, L; 1988 v Bul, Pol, N, E, USSR, Ho; 1989 v Ni, Tun, Sp, F (sub), H, Ma (sub), H; 1990 v WG; (with Real Sociedad), Ni, Ma, Fi (sub), T, E, Eg, Ho, R, I; 1991 v T, E (2), Pol; (with Tranmere R), 1992 v H (sub), T, W (sub), Sw (sub), US

(sub), Alb, I, P (sub); 1993 v La, D, Sp, D, Alb, La, Li; 1994 v Li, Ni, CzR, I (sub), M (sub), N; 1995 v La, Ni, P, Lie; 1996 v La, P, Ho, Ru; 1997 v Mac (sub) (69)
Ambrose, P. (Shamrock R), 1955 v N, Ho; 1964 v Pol, N, E (5)
Anderson, J. (Preston NE), 1980 v Cz, US (sub); 1982 v Ch, Br, Tr; (with Newcastle U), 1984 v Chn; 1986 v W, Ic, Cz; 1987 v Bul, Bel, Br, L; 1988 v R (sub), Y (sub); 1989 v Tun (16)

Andrews, P. (Bohemians), 1936 v Ho (1)
Arrigan, T. (Waterford), 1938 v N (1)

Babb, P. A. (Coventry C), 1994 v Ru, Ho, Bol, G, CzR (sub), I, M, N, Ho; (with Liverpool), 1995 v La, Lie, Ni (2), P, Lie, A; 1996 v La, P, Ho, CzR; 1997 v Ic (21)
Bailham, E. (Shamrock R), 1964 v E (1)
Barber, E. (Shelbourne), 1966 v Sp; (with Birmingham C), 1966 v Bel (2)
Barry, P. (Fordsons), 1928 v Bel; 1929 v Bel (2)
Beglin, J. (Liverpool), 1984 v Chn; 1985 v M, D, I, Is, E, N, Sw; 1986 v Sw, USSR, D, W; 1987 v Bel (sub), S, Pol (15)
Bermingham, J. (Bohemians), 1929 v Bel (1)
Bermingham, P. (St James' Gate), 1935 v H (1)
Braddish, S. (Dundalk), 1978 v T (sub), Pol (2)
Bonner, P. (Celtic), 1981 v Pol; 1982 v Alg; 1984 v Ma, Is, Chn; 1985 v I, Is, E, N; 1986 v U, Ic; 1987 v Bel (2), S (2), Pol, Bul, Br, L; 1988 v Bul, R, Y, N, E, USSR; 1989 v Sp, F, H, Sp, Ma, H; 1990 v WG, Ni, Ma, W, Fi, T, E, Eg, Ho, R, I; 1991 v Mor, T, E (2), W, Pol, US; 1992 v H, Pol, T, W, Sw, Alb, I; 1993 v La, D, Sp, W, Ni, D, Alb, La, Li; 1994 v Li, Sp, Ni, Ru, Ho, Bol, CzR, I, M, N, Ho; 1995 v Lie; 1996 v M, Bol (sub) (80)
Bradshaw, P. (St James' Gate), 1939 v Sw, Pol, H (2), G (5)
Brady, F. (Fordsons), 1926 v I; 1927 v I (2)
Brady, T. R. (QPR), 1964 v A (2), Sp (2), Pol, N (6)
Brady, W. L. (Arsenal), 1975 v USSR, T, Sw, USSR, Sw, WG; 1976 v T, N, Pol; 1977 v E, T, F (2), Sp, Bul; 1978 v Bul, N; 1979 v Ni, E, D, Bul, WG; 1980 v W, Bul, E, Cy; (with Juventus), 1981 v Ho, Bel, F, Cy, Bel; 1982 v Ho, F, Ch, Br, Tr; (with Sampdoria), 1983 v Ho, Sp, Ic, Ma; 1984 v Ic, Ho, Ma, Pol, Is; (with Internazionale), 1985 v USSR, N, D, I, E, N, Sp, Sw; 1986 v Sw, USSR, D, W; (with Ascoli), 1987 v Bel, S (2), Pol; (with West Ham U), Bul, Bel, Br, L; 1988 v L, Bul; 1989 v F, H (sub), H (sub); 1990 v WG, Fi (72)
Branagan, K. G. (Bolton W), 1997 v W (1)
Breen, G. (Birmingham C), 1996 v P (sub), Cro, Ho, US, M, Bol (sub); 1997 v Lie, Mac, Ic; (with Coventry C), v Mac (10)
Breen, T. (Manchester U), 1937 v Sw, F; (with Shamrock R), 1947 v E, Sp, P (5)
Brennan, F. (Drumcondra), 1965 v Bel (1)
Brennan, S. A. (Manchester U), 1965 v Sp; 1966 v Sp, A, Bel; 1967 v Sp, T, Sp; 1969 v Cz, D, H; 1970 v S, Cz, D, H, Pol (sub), WG; (with Waterford), 1971 v Pol, Se, I (19)
Brown, J. (Coventry C), 1937 v Sw, F (2)
Browne, W. (Bohemians), 1964 v A, Sp, E (3)
Buckley, L. (Shamrock R), 1984 v Pol (sub); (with Waregem), 1985 v M (2)
Burke, F. (Cork Ath), 1952 v WG (1)
Burke, J. (Cork), 1934 v Bel (1)
Burke, J. (Shamrock R), 1929 v Bel (1)
Byrne, A. B. (Southampton), 1970 v D, Pol, WG; 1971 v Pol, Se (2), I (2), A; 1973 v F, USSR (sub), F, N; 1974 v Pol (14)
Byrne, D. (Shelbourne), 1929 v Bel; (with Shamrock R), 1932 v Sp; (with Coleraine), 1934 v Bel (3)
Byrne, J. (Bray Unknowns), 1928 v Bel (1)
Byrne, J. (QPR), 1985 v I, Is (sub), E (sub), Sp (sub); 1987 v S (sub), Bel (sub), Br, L (sub); 1988 v L, Bul (sub), Is, R, Y (sub), Pol (sub); (with Le Havre), 1990 v WG (sub), W, Fi, T (sub), Ma; (with Brighton & HA), 1991 v W; (with Sunderland), 1992 v T, W; (with Millwall), 1993 v W (23)
Byrne, P. (Shamrock R), 1984 v Pol, Chn; 1985 v M; 1986 v D (sub), W (sub), U (sub), Ic (sub), Cz (8)
Byrne, P. (Dolphin), 1931 v Sp; 1932 v Ho; (with Drumcondra), 1934 v Ho (3)
Byrne, S. (Bohemians), 1931 v Sp (1)

Campbell, A. (Santander), 1985 v I (sub), Is, Sp (3)
Campbell, N. (St Patrick's Ath), 1971 v A (sub); (with Fortuna, Cologne), 1972 v Ir, Ec, Ch, P; 1973 v USSR, F (sub); 1975 v WG; 1976 v N; 1977 v Sp, Bul (sub) (11)
Cannon, H. (Bohemians), 1926 v I; 1928 v Bel (2)
Cantwell, N. (West Ham U), 1954 v L; 1956 v Sp, Ho; 1957 v D, WG, E (2); 1958 v D, Pol, A; 1959 v Pol, Cz (2); 1960 v Se, Ch, Se; 1961 v N; (with Manchester U), S (2); 1962 v Cz (2), A; 1963 v Ic (2), S; 1964 v A, Sp, E; 1965 v Pol, Sp; 1966 v Sp (2), A, Bel; 1967 v Sp, T (36)
Carey, B. P. (Manchester U), 1992 v US (sub); 1993 v W; (with Leicester C), 1994 v Ru (3)
Carey, J. J. (Manchester U), 1938 v N, Cz, Pol; 1939 v Sw, Pol, H (2), G; 1946 v P, Sp; 1947 v E, Sp, P; 1948 v P, Sp; 1949 v Sw, Bel, P, Se, Sp; 1950 v Fi, E, Fi, Se; 1951 v N, Arg, N; 1953 v F, A (29)
Carolan, J. (Manchester U), 1960 v Se, Ch (2)
Carroll, B. (Shelbourne), 1949 v Bel; 1950 v Fi (2)

Carroll, T. R. (Ipswich T), 1968 v Pol; 1969 v Pol, A, D; 1970 v Cz, Pol, WG; 1971 v Se; (with Birmingham C), 1972 v Ir, Ec, Ch, P; 1973 v USSR (2), Pol, F, N (17)
Cascarino, A. G. (Gillingham), 1986 v Sw, USSR, D; (with Millwall), 1988 v Pol, N (sub), USSR (sub), Ho (sub); 1989 v Ni, Ho, F, H, Sp, Ma, H; 1990 v WG (sub), Ni, Ma; (with Aston Villa), W, Fi, T, E, Eg, Ho (sub), R (sub), I (sub); 1991 v Mor (sub),T(sub), E (2 sub), Pol (sub), Ch (sub), US; (with Celtic), 1992 v Pol, T; (with Chelsea), W, Sw, US (sub); 1993 v W, Ni (sub), D (sub), Alb (sub), La (sub); 1994 v Li (sub), Sp (sub), Ni (sub), Ru, Bol (sub), G, CzR, Ho (sub); (with Marseille), 1995 v La (sub), Ni (sub), P (sub), Lie (sub), A (sub); 1996 v A (sub), P (sub), Ho, Ru (sub), P, Cro (sub), Ho; 1997 v Lie (sub), Mac, Ic; (with Nancy), v W, Mac, R (sub), Lie (sub) (70)
Chandler, J. (Leeds U), 1980 v Cz (sub), US (2)
Chatton, H. A. (Shelbourne), 1931 v Sp; (with Dumbarton), 1932 v Sp; (with Cork), 1934 v Ho (3)
Clarke, J. (Drogheda U), 1978 v Pol (sub) (1)
Clarke, K. (Drumcondra), 1948 v P, Sp (2)
Clarke, M. (Shamrock R), 1950 v Bel (1)
Clinton, T. J. (Everton), 1951 v N; 1954 v F, L (3)
Coad, P. (Shamrock R), 1947 v E, Sp, P; 1948 v P, Sp; 1949 v Sw, Bel, P, Se; 1951 v N (sub); 1952 v Sp (11)
Coffey, T. (Drumcondra), 1950 v Fi (1)
Colfer, M. D. (Shelbourne), 1950 v Bel; 1951 v N (2)
Collins, F. (Jacobs), 1927 v I (1)
Conmy, O. M. (Peterborough U), 1965 v Bel; 1967 v Cz; 1968 v Cz, Pol; 1970 v Cz (5)
Connolly, D. J. (Watford), 1996 v P, Ho, US, M; 1997 v R, Lie (6)
Connolly, H. (Cork), 1937 v G (1)
Connolly, J. (Fordsons), 1926 v I (1)
Conroy, G. A. (Stoke C), 1970 v Cz, D, H, Pol, WG; 1971 v Pol, Se (2), I; 1973 v USSR, F, USSR, N; 1974 v Pol, Br, U, Ch; 1975 v T, Sw, USSR, Sw, WG (sub); 1976 v T (sub); 1977 v E, T, Pol (27)
Conway, J. P. (Fulham), 1967 v Sp, T; 1968 v Cz; 1969 v A (sub), H; 1970 v S, Cz, D, H, Pol, WG; 1971 v I, A; 1974 v U, Ch; 1975 v WG (sub); 1976 v N, Pol; (with Manchester C), 1977 v Pol (20)
Corr, P. J. (Everton), 1949 v P, Sp; 1950 v E, Se (4)
Courtney, E. (Cork U), 1946 v P (1)
Coyle, O. C. (Bolton W), 1994 v Ho (sub) (1)
Coyne, T. (Celtic), 1992 v Sw, US, Alb (sub), US (sub), I (sub), P (sub); 1993 v W (sub), La (sub); (with Tranmere R), Ni; (with Motherwell), 1994 v Ru (sub), Ho, Bol, G (sub), CzR (sub), I, M, Ho; 1995 v Lie, Ni (sub), A; 1996 v Ru (sub) (21)\
Cummins, G. P. (Luton T), 1954 v L (2); 1955 v N (2), WG; 1956 v Y, Sp; 1958 v D, Pol, A; 1959 v Pol, Cz (2); 1960 v Se, Ch, WG, Se; 1961 v S (2) (19)
Cuneen, T. (Limerick), 1951 v N (1)
Cunningham, K. (Wimbledon), 1996 v CzR, P, Cro, Ho (sub), US, Bol; 1997 v Ic (sub), W, R, Lie (10)
Curtis, D. P. (Shelbourne), 1957 v D, WG; (with Bristol C), 1957 v E (2); 1958 v D, Pol, A; (with Ipswich T), 1959 v Pol; 1960 v Se, Ch, WG, Se; 1961 v N, S; 1962 v A; 1963 v Ic; (with Exeter C), 1964 v A (17)
Cusack, S. (Limerick), 1953 v F (1)

Daish, L. S. (Cambridge U), 1992 v W, Sw (sub); (with Coventry C), 1996 v CzR (sub), Cro, M (5)
Daly, G. A. (Manchester U), 1973 v Pol (sub), N; 1974 v Br (sub), U (sub); 1975 v Sw (sub), WG; 1977 v E, T, F; (with Derby Co), F, Bul; 1978 v Bul, T, D; 1979 v Ni, E, D, Bul; 1980 v Ni, E, Cy, Sw, Arg; (with Coventry C), 1981 v WG'B', Ho, Bel, Cy, W, Bel, Cz, Pol (sub); 1982 v Alg, Ch, Br, Tr; 1983 v Ho, Sp (sub); 1984 v Is (sub), Ma; (with Birmingham C), 1985 v M (sub), N, Sp, Sw; 1986 v Sw; (with Shrewsbury T), U, Ic (sub), Cz (sub); 1987 v S (sub) (48)
Daly, J. (Shamrock R), 1932 v Ho; 1935 v Sw (2)
Daly, M. (Wolverhampton W), 1978 v T, Pol (2)
Daly, P. (Shamrock R), 1950 v Fi (sub) (1)
Davis, T. L. (Oldham Ath), 1937 v G, H; (with Tranmere R), 1938 v Cz, Pol (4)
Deacy, E. (Aston Villa), 1982 v Alg (sub), Ch, Br, Tr (4)
De Mange, K. J. P. P. (Liverpool), 1987 v Br (sub); (with Hull C), 1989 v Tun (sub) (2)
Dempsey, J. T. (Fulham), 1967 v Sp, Cz; 1968 v Cz, Pol; 1969 v Pol, A, D; (with Chelsea), 1969 v Cz, D; 1970 v H, WG; 1971 v Pol, Se (2), I; 1972 v Ir, Ec, Ch, P (19)
Dennehy, J. (Cork Hibernians), 1972 v Ec; Ch; (with Nottingham F), 1973 v USSR (sub), Pol, F, N; 1974 v Pol (sub); 1975 v T (sub), WG (sub); (with Walsall), 1976 v Pol (sub); 1977 v Pol (sub) (11)
Desmond, P. (Middlesbrough), 1950 v Fi, E, Fi, Se (4)

Harrington, W. (Cork), 1936 v Ho, Sw, H, L; 1938 v Pol (sub) (5)
Harte, I.P. (Leeds U), 1996 v Cro (sub), Ho, M, Bol; 1997 v Lie, Mac, Ic (sub), W, Mac (sub), R, Lie (11)
Hartnett, J. B. (Middlesbrough), 1949 v Sp; 1954 v L (2)
Haverty, J. (Arsenal), 1956 v Ho; 1957 v D, WG, E (2); 1958 v D, Pol, A; 1959 v Pol; 1960 v Se, Ch; 1961 v W, N, S (2); (with Blackburn R), 1962 v Cz (2); (with Millwall), 1963 v S; 1964 v A, Sp, Pol, N, E; (with Celtic), 1965 v Pol; (with Bristol R), 1965 v Sp; (with Shelbourne), 1966 v Sp (2), WG, A, Bel; 1967 v T, Sp (32)
Hayes, A. W. P. (Southampton), 1979 v D (1)
Hayes, W. E. (Huddersfield T), 1947 v E, P (2)
Hayes, W. J. (Limerick), 1949 v Bel (1)
Healey, R. (Cardiff C), 1977 v Pol; 1980 v E (sub) (2)
Heighway, S. D. (Liverpool), 1971 v Pol, Se (2), I, A; 1973 v USSR; 1975 v USSR, T, USSR, WG; 1976 v T, N; 1977 v E, F (2), Sp, Bul; 1978 v Bul, N, D; 1979 v Ni, Bul; 1980 v Bul, US, Ni, E, Cy, Arg; 1981 v Bel, F, Cy, W, Bel; (with Minnesota K), 1982 v Ho (34)
Henderson, B. (Drumcondra), 1948 v P, Sp (2)
Hennessy, J. (Shelbourne), 1965 v Pol, Bel, Sp; 1966 v WG; (with St Patrick's Ath), 1969 v A (5)
Herrick, J. (Cork Hibernians), 1972 v A, Ch (sub); (with Shamrock R), 1973 v F (sub) (3)
Higgins, J. (Birmingham), 1951 v Arg (1)
Holmes, J. (Coventry C), 1971 v A (sub); 1973 v F, USSR, Pol, F, N; 1974 v Pol, Br; 1975 v USSR, Sw; 1976 v T, N, Pol; 1977 v E, T, F, Sp; (with Tottenham H), F, Pol, Bul; 1978 v Bul, T, Pol, N, D; 1979 v Ni, E, D, Bul; (with Vancouver W), 1981 v W (30)
Horlacher, A. F. (Bohemians), 1930 v Bel; 1932 v Sp, Ho; 1934 v Ho (sub); 1935 v H;1936 v Ho, Sw (7)
Houghton, R. J. (Oxford U), 1986 v W, U, Ic, Cz; 1987 v Bel (2), S (2), Pol, L; 1988 v L, Bul; (with Liverpool), Is, Y, N, E, USSR, Ho; 1989 v Ni, Tun, Sp, F, H, Sp, Ma, H; 1990 v Ni, Ma, Fi, E, Eg, Ho, R, I; 1991 v Mor, T, E (2), Pol, Ch, US; 1992 v H, Alb, US, I, P; (with Aston Villa), 1993 v D, Sp, Ni, D, Alb, La, Li; 1994 v Li, Sp, Ni, Bol, G (sub), I, M, N, Ho; (with C Palace), 1995 v P, A; 1996 v A, CzR; 1997 v Lie, R, Lie (69)
Howlett, G. (Brighton & HA), 1984 v Chn (sub) (1)
Hoy, M. (Dundalk), 1939 v N; 1939 v Sw, Pol, H (2), G (6)
Hughton, C. (Tottenham H), 1980 v US, E, Sw, Arg; 1981 v Ho, Bel, F, Cy, W, Bel, Pol; 1982 v F; 1983 v Ho, Sp, Ma, Sp; 1984 v Ic, Ho, Ma; 1985 v M (sub), USSR, N, I, Is, E, Sp; 1986 v Sw, USSR, U, Ic; 1987 v Bel, Bul; 1988 v Is, Y, Pol, N, E, USSR, Ho; 1989 v Ni, F, H, Sp, Ma, H; 1990 v W (sub), USSR (sub), Fi, T (sub), Ma; 1991 v T; (with West Ham U), Ch; 1992 v T (53)
Hurley, C. J. (Millwall), 1957 v E; (with Sunderland), 1958 v D, Pol, A; 1959 v Cz (2); 1960 v Se, Ch, WG, Se; 1961 v W, N, S (2); 1962 v Cz (2), A; 1963 v Ic (2), S; 1964 v A (2), Sp (2), Pol, N; 1965 v Sp; 1966 v WG, A, Bel; 1967 v T, Sp, T, Cz; 1968 v Cz, Pol; 1969 v Pol, D, Cz, (with Bolton W), H (40)
Hutchinson, F. (Drumcondra), 1935 v Sw, G (2)

Irwin, D. J. (Manchester U), 1991 v Mor, T, W, E, Pol, US; 1992 v H, Pol, W, US, Alb, US (sub), I; 1993 v La, D, Sp, Ni, D, Alb, La, Li; 1994 v Li, Sp, Ni, Bol, G, I, M; 1995 v La, Lie, Ni, E, Ni, P, Lie, A; 1996 v A, P, Ho, CzR; 1997 v Lie, Mac, Ic, Mac, R (45)

Jordan, D. (Wolverhampton W), 1937 v Sw, F (2)
Jordan, W. (Bohemians), 1934 v Ho; 1938 v N (2)

Kavanagh, P. J. (Celtic), 1931 v Sp; 1932 v Sp (2)
Keane, R. M. (Nottingham F), 1991 v Ch; 1992 v H, Pol, W, Sw, Alb, US; 1993 v La, D, Sp, W, Ni, D, Alb, La, Li; (with Manchester U), 1994 v Li, Sp, Ni, Bol, G, CzR (sub), I, M, N, Ho; 1995 v Ni (2); 1996 v A, Ru; 1997 v Ic, W, Mac, R, Lie (35)
Keane, T. R. (Swansea T), 1949 v Sw, P, Se, Sp (4)
Kearin, M. (Shamrock R), 1972 v A (1)
Kearns, F. T. (West Ham U), 1954 v L (1)
Kearns, M. (Oxford U), 1971 v Pol (sub); (with Walsall), 1974 v Pol (sub), U, Ch; 1976 v N, Pol; 1977 v E, T, F (2), Sp, Bul; 1978 v N, D; 1979 v Ni, E; (with Wolverhampton W), 1980 v US, Ni (18)
Kelly, A. T. (Sheffield U), 1993 v W (sub); 1994 v Ru (sub), G; 1995 v La, Ni, E, Ni, P, Lie, A; 1996 v A, La, P, Ho; 1997 v Mac, Ic, Mac, R (18)
Kelly, D. T. (Walsall), 1988 v Is, R, Y; (with West Ham U), 1989 v Tun (sub); (with Leicester C), 1990 v USSR, Ma; 1991 v Mor, W (sub), Ch, US; 1992 v H; (with Newcastle U), I (sub), P; 1993 v Sp (sub), Ni; (with Wolverhampton W), 1994 v Ru, N (sub); 1995 v E, Ni; (with Sunderland), 1996 v La (sub); 1997 v Ic, W (sub), Mac (sub) (23)

Kelly, G. (Leeds U), 1994 v Ru, Ho, Bol (sub), G (sub), CzR, N, Ho; 1995 v La, Lie, Ni (2), P, Lie, A; 1996 v A, La, P, Ho; 1997 v W (sub), R, Lie (21)
Kelly, J. (Derry C), 1932 v Ho; 1934 v Bel; 1936 v Sw, L (4)
Kelly, J. A. (Drumcondra), 1957 v WG, E; (with Preston NE), 1962 v A; 1963 v Ic (2), S; 1964 v A (2), Sp (2), Pol; 1965 v Bel; 1966 v A, Bel; 1967 v Sp (2), T, Cz; 1968 v Pol, Cz; 1969 v Pol, A, D, Cz, D, H; 1970 v S, D, H, Pol, WG; 1971 v Pol, Se (2) I (2), A; 1972 v Ir, Ec, Ch, P; 1973 v USSR, F, USSR, Pol, F, N (47)
Kelly, J. P. V. (Wolverhampton W), 1961 v W, N, S; 1962 v Cz (2) (5)
Kelly, M. J. (Portsmouth), 1988 v Y, Pol (sub); 1989 v Tun; 1991 v Mor (4)
Kelly, N. (Nottingham F), 1954 v L (1)
Kendrick, J. (Everton), 1927 v I; (with Dolphin) 1934 v Bel, Ho; 1936 v Ho (4)
Kenna, J. J. (Blackburn R), 1995 v P (sub), Lie (sub), A (sub); 1996 v La, P, Ho, Ru (sub), CzR, P, Cro, Ho, US; 1997 v Lie, Mac, Ic, R (sub), Lie (17)
Kennedy, M. (Liverpool), 1996 v A, La (sub), P, Ru, CzR, Cro, Ho (sub), US (sub), M, Bol (sub); 1997 v R, Lie (12)
Kennedy, M. F. (Portsmouth), 1986 v Ic, Cz (sub) (2)
Kennedy, W. (St James' Gate), 1932 v Ho; 1934 v Bel, Ho (3)
Keogh, J. (Shamrock R), 1966 v WG (sub) (1)
Keogh, S. (Shamrock R), 1959 v Pol (1)
Kernaghan, A. N. (Middlesbrough), 1993 v La, D (2), Alb, La, Li; 1994 v Li; (with Manchester C), Sp, Ni, Bol (sub), CzR; 1995 v Lie, E; 1996 v A, P (sub), Ho (sub), Ru, P, Cro (sub), Ho, US, Bol (22)
Kiernan, F. W. (Shamrock R), 1951 v Arg, N; (with Southampton), 1952 v WG (2), A (5)
Kinnear, J. P. (Tottenham H), 1967 v T; 1968 v Cz, Pol; 1969 v A; 1970 v Cz, D, H, Pol; 1971 v Se (sub), I; 1972 v Ir, Ec, Ch, P; 1973 v USSR, F; 1974 v Pol, Br, U, Ch; 1975 v USSR, T, Sw, USSR, WG; (with Brighton & HA), 1976 v T (sub) (26)
Kinsella, J. (Shelbourne), 1928 v Bel (1)
Kinsella, O. (Shamrock R), 1932 v Ho; 1938 v N (2)
Kirkland, A. (Shamrock R), 1927 v I (1)

Lacey, W. (Shelbourne), 1927 v I; 1928 v Bel; 1930 v Bel (3)
Langan, D. (Derby Co), 1978 v T, N; 1980 v Sw, Arg; (with Birmingham C), 1981 v WG`B', Ho, Bel, F, Cy, W, Bel, Cz, Pol; 1982 v Ho, F; (with Oxford U), 1985 v N, Sp, Sw; 1986 v W, U; 1987 v Bel, S, Pol, Br (sub), L (sub); 1988 v L (26)
Lawler, J. F. (Fulham), 1953 v A; 1954 v L, F; 1955 v N, H, N, WG; 1956 v Y (8)
Lawlor, J. C. (Drumcondra), 1949 v Bel; (with Doncaster R), 1951 v N, Arg (3)
Lawlor, M. (Shamrock R), 1971 v Pol, Se (2), I (sub); 1973 v Pol (5)
Lawrenson, M. (Preston NE), 1977 v Pol; (with Brighton), 1978 v Bul, Pol, N (sub); 1979 v Ni, E; 1980 v E, Cy, Sw; 1981 v Ho, Bel, F, Cy, Pol; (with Liverpool), 1982 v Ho, F; 1983 v Ho, Sp, Ic, Ma, Sp; 1984 v Ic, Ho, Ma, Is; 1985 v USSR, N, D, I, E, Ni; 1986 v Sw, USSR, D; 1987 v Bel, S; 1988 v Bul, Is (38)
Leech, M. (Shamrock R), 1969 v Cz, D, H; 1972 v A, Ir, Ec, P; 1973 v USSR (sub) (8)
Lennon, C. (St James' Gate), 1935 v H, Sw, G (3)
Lennox, G. (Dolphin), 1931 v Sp; 1932 v Sp (2)
Lowry, D. (St Patrick's Ath), 1962 v A (sub) (1)
Lunn, R. (Dundalk), 1939 v Sw, Pol (2)
Lynch, J. (Cork Bohemians), 1934 v Bel (1)

McAlinden, J. (Portsmouth), 1946 v P, Sp (2)
McAteer, J. W. (Bolton W), 1994 v Ru, Ho (sub), Bol (sub), G, CzR (sub), I (sub), M (sub), N, Ho (sub); 1995 v La, Lie, Ni (2 sub), Lie; (with Liverpool), 1996 v La, P, Ho (sub), Ru; 1997 v Mac, Ic, W, Mac (22)
McCann, J. (Shamrock R), 1957 v WG (1)
McCarthy, J. (Bohemians), 1926 v I; 1928 v Bel; 1930 v Bel (3)
McCarthy, M. (Manchester C), 1984 v Pol, Chn; 1985 v M, D, I, Is, E, Sp, Sw; 1986 v Sw, USSR, W (sub), U, Ic, Cz; 1987 v S (2), Pol, Bul, Bel (with Celtic), Br, L; 1988 v Bul, Is, R, Y, N, E, USSR, Ho; 1989 v Ni, Tun, Sp, F, H, Sp; (with Lyon), 1990 v WG, Ni (with Millwall), W, USSR, Fi, T, E, Eg, Ho, R, I; 1991 v Mor, T, E, US; 1992 v H, T, Alb (sub), US, I, P (57)
McCarthy, M. (Shamrock R), 1932 v Ho (1)
McConville, T. (Dundalk), 1972 v A; (with Waterford), 1973 v USSR, F, USSR, Pol, F (6)
McDonagh, Jacko (Shamrock R), 1984 v Pol (sub), Ma (sub); 1985 v M (sub) (3)

McDonagh, J. (Everton), 1981 v WG`B`, W, Bel, Cz; (with Bolton W), 1982 v Ho, F, Ch, Br; 1983 v Ho, Sp, Ic, Ma, Sp; (with Notts Co), 1984 v Ic, Ho, Pol; 1985 v M, USSR, N, D, Sp, Sw; 1986 v Sw, USSR (with Wichita Wings) D (25)

McEvoy, M. A. (Blackburn R), 1961 v S (2); 1963 v S; 1964 v A, Sp (2), Pol, N, E; 1965 v Pol, Bel, Sp; 1966 v Sp (2); 1967 v Sp, T, Cz (17)

McGee, P. (QPR), 1978 v T, N (sub), D (sub); 1979 v Ni, E, D (sub), Bul (sub); 1980 v Cz, Bul; (with Preston NE), US, Ni, Cy, Sw, Arg; 1981 v Bel (sub) (15)

McGoldrick, E. J. (C Palace), 1992 v Sw, US, I, P (sub); 1993 v D, W, Ni (sub), D; (with Arsenal), 1994 v Ni, Ru, Ho, CzR; 1995 v La (sub), Lie, E (15)

McGowan, D. (West Ham U), 1949 v P, Se, Sp (3)

McGowan, J. (Cork U), 1947 v Sp (1)

McGrath, M. (Blackburn R), 1958 v A; 1959 v Pol, Cz (2); 1960 v Se, WG, Se; 1961 v W; 1962 v Cz (2); 1963 v S; 1964 v A (2), E; 1965 v Pol, Bel, Sp; 1966 v Sp; (with Bradford), 1966 v WG, A, Bel; 1967 v T (22)

McGrath, P. (Manchester U), 1985 v I (sub), Is, E, N (sub), Sw (sub); 1986 v Sw (sub), D, W, Ic, Cz; 1987 v Bel (2), S (2), Pol, Bul, Br, L; 1988 v L, Bul, Y, Pol, N, E, Ho; 1989 v Ni, F, H, Sp, Ma, H; (with Aston Villa), 1990 v WG, Ma, USSR, Fi, T, E, Eg, Ho, R, I; 1991 v E, Pol, Ch (sub), US; 1992 v Pol, T, Sw, US, Alb, US, I, P; 1993 v La, Sp, Ni, D, La, Li; 1994 v Sp, Ni, G, CzR, I, M, N, Ho; 1995 v La, Ni, E, Ni, P, Lie, A; 1996 v A, La, P, Ho, Ru, CzR; (with Derby Co), 1997 v W (83)

McGuire, W. (Bohemians), 1936 v Ho (1)

McKenzie, G. (Southend U), 1938 v N (2), Cz, Pol; 1939 v Sw, Pol, H (2), G (9)

Mackey, G. (Shamrock R), 1957 v D, WG, E (3)

McLoughlin, A. F. (Swindon T), 1990 v Ma, E (sub), Eg (sub); 1991 v Mor (sub), E (sub); (with Southampton), W, Ch (sub); 1992 v H (sub), W (sub); (with Portsmouth), US, I (sub), P; 1993 v W; 1994 v Ni (sub), Ru, Ho (sub); 1995 v Lie (sub); 1996 v P, Cro, Ho, US, M, Bol (sub); 1997 v Lie, Mac, Ic, W, Mac (28)

McLoughlin, F. (Fordsons), 1930 v Bel; (with Cork), 1932 v Sp (2)

McMillan, W. (Belfast Celtic), 1946 v P, Sp (2)

McNally, J. B. (Luton T), 1959 v Cz; 1961 v S; 1963 v Ic (3)

Macken, A. (Derby Co), 1977 v Sp (1)

Madden, O. (Cork), 1936 v H (1)

Maguire, J. (Shamrock R), 1929 v Bel (1)

Malone, G. (Shelbourne), 1949 v Bel (1)

Mancini, T. J. (QPR), 1974 v Pol, Br, U, Ch; (with Arsenal), 1975 v USSR (5)

Martin, C. (Bo'ness), 1927 v I (1)

Martin, C. J. (Glentoran), 1946 v P (sub), Sp; 1947 v E; (with Leeds U), 1947 v Sp; 1948 v P, Sp; (with Aston Villa), 1949 v Sw, Bel, P, Se, Sp; 1950 v Fi, E, Fi, Se, Bel; 1951 v Arg; 1952 v WG, A, Sp; 1954 v F (2), L; 1955 v N, Ho, N, WG; 1956 v Y, Sp, Ho (30)

Martin, M. P. (Bohemians), 1972 v A, Ir, Ec, Ch, P; 1973 v USSR; (with Manchester U), 1973 v USSR, Pol, F, N; 1974 v Pol, Br, U, Ch; 1975 v USSR, T, Sw, USSR, Sw, WG; (with WBA), 1976 v T, N, Pol; 1977 v E, T, F (2), Sp, Pol, Bul; (with Newcastle U), 1979 v D, Bul, WG; 1980 v W, Cz, Bul, US, Ni; 1981 v WG`B`, F, Bel, Cz; 1982 v Ho, F, Alg, Ch, Br, Tr; 1983 v Ho, Sp, Ma, Sp (52)

Meagan, M. K. (Everton), 1961 v S; 1962 v A; 1963 v Ic; 1964 v Sp; (with Huddersfield T), 1965 v Bel; 1966 v Sp (2), A, Bel; 1967 v Sp, T, Sp, T, Cz; 1968 v Cz, Pol; (with Drogheda), 1970 v S (17)

Meehan, P. (Drumcondra), 1934 v Ho (1)

Milligan, M. J. (Oldham Ath), 1992 v US (sub) (1)

Monahan, P. (Sligo R), 1935 v Sw, G (2)

Mooney, J. (Shamrock R), 1965 v Pol, Bel (2)

Moore, A. (Middlesbrough), 1996 v CzR, Cro (sub), Ho, M, Bol; 1997 v Lie (sub), Mac (sub), Ic (sub) (8)

Moore, P. (Shamrock R), 1931 v Sp; 1932 v Ho; (with Aberdeen), 1934 v Bel, Ho; 1935 v H, G; (with Shamrock R), 1936 v Ho; 1937 v G, H (9)

Moran, K. (Manchester U), 1980 v Sw, Arg; 1981 v WG`B`, Bel, F, Cy, W (sub), Bel, Cz, Pol; 1982 v F, Alg; 1983 v Ic; 1984 v Ic, Ho, Ma, Is; 1985 v M; 1986 v D, Ic, Cz; 1987 v Bel (2), S (2), Pol, Bul, Br, L; 1988 v L, Bul, Is, R, Y, Pol, N, E, USSR, Ho; (with Sporting Gijon), 1989 v Ni, Sp, H, Sp, Ma, H; 1990 v Ni, Ma; (with Blackburn R), W, USSR (sub), Ma, E, Eg, Ho, R, I; 1991 v T (sub), W, E, Pol, Ch, US; 1992 v Pol, US; 1993 v D, Sp, Ni, Alb; 1994 v Li, Sp, Ho, Bol (71)

Moroney, T. (West Ham U), 1948 v Sp; 1949 v P, Se, Sp; 1950 v Fi, E, Fi, Bel; 1951 v N (2); 1952 v WG; (with Evergreen U), 1954 v F (12)

Morris, C. B. (Celtic), 1988 v Is, R, Y, Pol, N, E, USSR, Ho; 1989 v Ni, Tun, Sp, F, H (1+1 sub); 1990 v WG, Ni, Ma (sub), W, USSR, Fi (sub), T, E, Eg, Ho, R, I; 1991 v E; 1992 v H (sub), Pol, W, Sw, US (2), P; (with Middlesbrough), 1993 v W (35)

Moulson, C. (Lincoln C), 1936 v H, L; (with Notts Co), 1937 v H, Sw, F (5)

Moulson, G. B. (Lincoln C), 1948 v P, Sp; 1949 v Sw (3)

Mucklan, C. (Drogheda U), 1978 v Pol (1)

Muldoon, T. (Aston Villa), 1927 v I (1)

Mulligan, P. M. (Shamrock R), 1969 v Cz, D, H; 1970 v S, Cz, D; (with Chelsea), 1970 v H, Pol, WG; 1971 v Pol, Se, I; 1972 v A, Ir, Ec, Ch, P; (with C Palace), 1973 v F, USSR, Pol, F, N; 1974 v Pol, Br, U, Ch; 1975 v USSR, T, Sw, USSR, Sw; (with WBA), 1976 v T, Pol; 1977 v E, T, F (2), Pol, Bul; 1978 v Bul, N, D; 1979 v E, D, Bul (sub), WG; (with Shamrock R), 1980 v W, Cz, Bul, US (sub) (50)

Munroe, L. (Shamrock R), 1954 v L (1)

Murphy, A. (Clyde), 1956 v Y (1)

Murphy, B. (Bohemians), 1986 v U (1)

Murphy, J. (C Palace), 1980 v W, US, Cy (3)

Murray, T. (Dundalk), 1950 v Bel (1)

Newman, W. (Shelbourne), 1969 v D (1)

Nolan, R. (Shamrock R), 1957 v D, WG, E; 1958 v Pol; 1960 v Ch, WG, Se; 1962 v Cz (2); 1963 v Ic (10)

O'Brien, F. (Philadelphia F), 1980 v Cz, E, Cy (sub) (3)

O'Brien, L. (Shamrock R), 1986 v U; (with Manchester U), 1987 v Br; 1988 v Is (sub), R (sub), Y (sub), Pol (sub); 1989 v Tun; (with Newcastle U), Sp (sub); 1992 v Sw (sub); 1993 v W; (with Tranmere U), 1994 v Ru; 1996 v Cro, Ho, US, Bol; 1997 v Mac (sub) (16)

O'Brien, M. T. (Derby Co), 1927 v I; (with Walsall), 1929 v Bel; (with Norwich C), 1930 v Bel; (with Watford), 1932 v Ho (4)

O'Brien, R. (Notts Co), 1976 v N, Pol; 1977 v Sp, Pol; 1980 v Arg (sub) (5)

O'Byrne, L. B. (Shamrock R), 1949 v Bel (1)

O'Callaghan, B. R. (Stoke C), 1979 v WG (sub); 1980 v W, US; 1981 v W; 1982 v Br, Tr (6)

O'Callaghan, K. (Ipswich T), 1981 v WG`B`, Cz, Pol; 1982 v Alg, Ch, Br, Tr (sub); 1983 v Sp, Ic (sub), Ma (sub), Sp (sub); 1984 v Ic, Ho, Ma; 1985 v M (sub), N (sub), D (sub), (with Portsmouth) E (sub); 1986 v Sw (sub), USSR (sub); 1987 v Br (21)

O'Connell, A. (Dundalk), 1967 v Sp; (with Bohemians), 1971 v Pol (sub) (2)

O'Connor, T. (Shamrock R), 1950 v Fi, E, Fi, Se (4)

O'Connor, T. (Fulham), 1968 v Cz; (with Dundalk), 1972 v A, Ir (sub), Ec (sub), Ch; (with Bohemians), 1973 v F (sub), Pol (sub) (7)

O'Driscoll, J. F. (Swansea T), 1949 v Sw, Bel, Se (3)

O'Driscoll, S. (Fulham), 1982 v Ch, Br, Tr (sub) (3)

O'Farrell, F. (West Ham U), 1952 v A; 1953 v A; 1954 v F; 1955 v Ho, N; 1956 v Y, Ho; (with Preston NE), 1958 v D; 1959 v Cz (9)

O'Flanagan, K. P. (Bohemians), 1938 v N, Cz, Pol; 1939 v Pol, H (2), G; (with Arsenal), 1947 v Sp, P (10)

O'Flanagan, M. (Bohemians), 1947 v E (1)

O'Hanlon, K. G. (Rotherham U), 1988 v Is (1)

O'Kane, P. (Bohemians), 1935 v H, Sw, G (3)

O'Keefe, E. (Everton), 1981 v W; (with Port Vale), 1984 v Chn; 1985 v M, USSR (sub), E (5)

O'Keefe, T. (Cork), 1934 v Bel; (with Waterford), 1938 v Cz, Pol (3)

O'Leary, D. (Arsenal), 1977 v E, F (2), Sp, Bul; 1978 v Bul, N, D; 1979 v E, Bul, WG; 1980 v W, Bul, Ni, E, Cy; 1981 v WG`B`,Ho, Cz, Pol; 1982 v Ho, F; 1983 v Ho, Ic, Sp; 1984 v Pol, Is, Chn; 1985 v USSR, N, D, Is, E (sub), N, Sp, Sw; 1986 v Sw, USSR, D, W; 1989 v Sp, Ma, H; 1990 v WG, Ni (sub), Ma, W (sub), USSR, Fi, T, Ma, R (sub); 1991 v Mor, T, E (2), Pol, Ch; 1992 v H, Pol, T, W, Sw, US, Alb, I, P; 1993 v W (68)

O'Leary, P. (Shamrock R), 1980 v Bul, US, Ni, E (sub), Cz, Arg; 1981 v Ho (7)

O'Mahoney, M. T. (Bristol R), 1938 v Cz, Pol; 1939 v Sw, Pol, H, G (6)

O'Neill, F. S. (Shamrock R), 1962 v Cz (2); 1965 v Pol, Bel, Sp; 1966 v Sp (2), WG, A; 1967 v Sp, T, Sp, T; 1969 v Pol, A, D, Cz D (sub), H (sub); 1972 v A (20)

O'Neill, J. (Everton), 1952 v Sp; 1953 v F, A; 1954 v F, L, F; 1955 v N, Ho, N, WG; 1956 v Y, Sp; 1957 v D; 1958 v A; 1959 v Pol, Cz (2) (17)

O'Neill, J. (Preston NE), 1961 v W (1)

O'Neill, K. P. (Norwich C), 1996 v P (sub), Cro, Ho (sub), US (sub), Bol; 1997 v Lie, Mac (1 + sub) (9)

O'Neill, W. (Dundalk), 1936 v Ho, Sw, H, L; 1937 v G, H, Sw, F; 1938 v N; 1939 v H, G (11)

O'Regan, K. (Brighton & HA), 1984 v Ma, Pol; 1985 v M, Sp (sub) (4)
O'Reilly, J. (Brideville), 1932 v Ho; (with Aberdeen) 1934 v Bel, Ho; (with Brideville), 1936 v Ho; Sw, H, L; (with St James' Gate), 1937 v G, H, Sw, F; 1938 v N (2), Cz, Pol; 1939 v Sw, Pol, H (2), G (20)
O'Reilly, J. (Cork U), 1946 v P, Sp (2)

Peyton, G. (Fulham), 1977 v Sp (sub); 1978 v Bul, T, Pol; 1979 v D, Bul, WG; 1980 v W, Cz, Bul, E, Cy, Sw, Arg; 1981 v Ho, Bel, F, Cy; 1982 v Tr; 1985 v M (sub); 1986 v W, Cz; (with Bournemouth), 1988 v L, Pol; 1989 v Ni, Tun; 1990 v USSR, Ma; 1991 v Ch; (with Everton) 1992 v US (2), I (sub), P (33)
Peyton, N. (Shamrock R), 1957 v WG; (with Leeds U), 1960 v WG, Se (sub); 1961 v W; 1963 v Ic, S (6)
Phelan, T. (Wimbledon), 1992 v H, Pol (sub), T, W, Sw, US, I (sub), P; (with Manchester C), 1993 v La (sub), D, Sp, Ni, Alb, La, Li; 1994 v Li, Sp, Ni, Ho, Bol, G, CzR, I, M, Ho; 1995 v E; 1996 v La; (with Chelsea), Ho, Ru, P, Cro, Ho, US, M (sub), Bol; (with Everton), 1997 v W, Mac (37)

Quinn, N. J. (Arsenal), 1986 v Ic (sub), Cz; 1987 v Bul (sub), Br (sub); 1988 v L (sub), Bul (sub), Is, R (sub), Pol (sub), E (sub); 1989 v Tun (sub), Sp (sub), H (sub); (with Manchester C), 1990 v USSR, Ma, Eg (sub), Ho, R, I; 1991 v Mor, T, E(2) W, Pol; 1992 v H, W (sub), US, Alb, US, I (sub), P; 1993 v La, D, Sp, Ni, D, Alb, La, Li; 1994 v Li, Sp, Ni; 1995 v La, Lie, Ni, E, Ni, P, Lie, A; 1996 v A, La, P, Ru, CzR, P (sub), Cro, Ho (sub), US; (with Sunderland), 1997 v Lie (61)

Reid, C. (Brideville), 1931 v Sp (1)
Richardson, D. J. (Shamrock R), 1972 v A (sub); (with Gillingham), 1973 v N (sub); 1980 v Cz (3)
Rigby, A. (St James' Gate), 1935 v H, Sw, G (3)
Ringstead, A. (Sheffield U), 1951 v Arg, N; 1952 v WG (2), A, Sp; 1953 v A; 1954 v F; 1955 v N; 1956 v Y, Sp, Ho; 1957 v E (2); 1958 v D, Pol, A; 1959 v Pol, Cz (2) (20)
Robinson, J. (Bohemians), 1928 v Bel; (with Dolphin), 1931 v Sp (2)
Robinson, M. (Brighton & HA), 1981 v WG'B', F, Cy, Bel, Pol; 1982 v Ho, F, Alg, Ch; 1983 v Ho, Sp, Ic, Ma; (with Liverpool), 1984 v Ic, Ho, Is; 1985 v USSR, N; (with QPR), N, Sp, Sw; 1986 v D (sub), W, Cz (24)
Roche, P. J. (Shelbourne), 1972 v A; (with Manchester U), 1975 v USSR, T, Sw, USSR, Sw, WG; 1976 v T (8)
Rogers, E. (Blackburn R), 1968 v Cz, Pol; 1969 v Pol, A, D, Cz, D, H; 1970 v S, D, H; 1971 v I (2), A; (with Charlton Ath), 1972 v Ir, Ec, Ch, P; 1973 v USSR (19)
Ryan, G. (Derby Co), 1978 v T; (with Brighton & HA), 1979 v E, WG; 1980 v W, Cy (sub), Sw, Arg (sub); 1981 v WG'B' (sub), F (sub), Pol (sub); 1982 v Br (sub), Ho (sub), Alg (sub), Ch (sub), Tr; 1984 v Pol, Chn; 1985 v M (18)
Ryan, R. A. (WBA), 1950 v Se, Bel; 1951 v N, Arg, N; 1952 v WG (2), A, Sp; 1953 v F, A; 1954 v F, L, F; 1955 v N; (with Derby Co), 1956 v Sp (16)

Savage, D. P. T. (Millwall), 1996 v P (sub), Cro (sub), US (sub), M, Bol (5)
Saward, P. (Millwall), 1954 v L; (with Aston Villa), 1957 v E (2); 1958 v D, Pol, A; 1959 v Pol, Cz; 1960 v Se, Ch, WG, Se; 1961 v W, N; (with Huddersfield T), 1961 v S; 1962 v A; 1963 v Ic (2) (18)
Scannell, T. (Southend U), 1954 v L (1)
Scully, P. J. (Arsenal), 1989 v Tun (sub) (1)
Sheedy, K. (Everton), 1984 v Ho (sub), Ma; 1985 v D, I, Is, Sw; 1986 v Sw, D; 1987 v S, Pol; 1988 v Is, R, Pol, E (sub), USSR; 1989 v Ni, Tun, H, Sp, Ma, H; 1990 v Ni, Ma, W (sub), USSR, Fi (sub), T, E, Eg, Ho, R, I; 1991 v W, E, Pol, Ch, US; 1992 v H, Pol, T, W; (with Newcastle U), Sw (sub), Alb; 1993 v La, W (sub) (45)
Sheridan, J. J. (Leeds U), 1988 v R, Y, Pol, N (sub); 1989 v Sp; (with Sheffield W), 1990 v W, T (sub), Ma, I (sub); 1991 v Mor (sub), T, Ch, US (sub); 1992 v H; 1993 v La; 1994 v Sp (sub), Ho, Bol, G, CzR, I, M, N, Ho; 1995 v La, Lie, Ni, E, Ni, P, Lie, A; 1996 v A, Ho (34)
Slaven, B. (Middlesbrough), 1990 v W, Fi, T (sub), Ma; 1991 v W, Pol (sub); 1993 v W (7)
Sloan, J. W. (Arsenal), 1946 v P, Sp (2)
Smyth, M. (Shamrock R), 1969 v Pol (sub) (1)
Squires, J. (Shelbourne), 1934 v Ho (1)
Stapleton, F. (Arsenal), 1977 v T, F, Sp, Bul; 1978 v Bul, N, D; 1979 v Ni, E (sub), D, WG; 1980 v W, Bul, Ni, E, Cy;

1981 v WG'B', Ho, Bel, F, Cy, Bel, Cz, Pol; (with Manchester U), 1982 v Ho, F, Alg; 1983 v Ho, Sp, Ic, Ma, Sp; 1984 v Ic, Ho, Ma, Pol, Is, Chn; 1985 v N, D, I, Is, E, N, Sw; 1986 v Sw, USSR, D, U, Ic, Cz (sub); 1987 v Bel (2), S (2), Pol, Bul, L; (with Ajax), 1988 v L, Bul, R, Y, N, E, USSR, Ho; (with Le Havre), 1989 v F, Sp, Ma; (with Blackburn R), 1990 v WG, Ma (sub) (71)
Staunton, S. (Liverpool), 1989 v Tun, Sp (2), Ma, H; 1990 v WG, Ni, Ma, W, USSR, Fi, T, Ma, E, Eg, Ho, R, I; 1991 v Mor, T, E (2), W, Pol, Ch, US; (with Aston Villa), 1992 v Pol, T, Sw, US, Alb, US, I, P; 1993 v La, Sp, Ni, D, Alb, La, Li; 1994 v Li, Sp, Ho, Bol, G, CzR, I, M, N, Ho; 1995 v La, Lie, Ni, E, Ni, P, Lie, A; 1996 v La, P, Ru; 1997 v Lie, Mac (2), W, R, Lie (68)
Stevenson, A. E. (Dolphin), 1932 v Ho; (with Everton), 1947 v E, Sp, P; 1948 v P, Sp; 1949 v Sw (7)
Strahan, F. (Shelbourne), 1964 v Pol, N, E; 1965 v Pol; 1966 v WG (5)
Sullivan, J. (Fordsons), 1928 v Bel (1)
Swan, M. M. G. (Drumcondra), 1960 v Se (sub) (1)
Synnott, N. (Shamrock R), 1978 v T, Pol; 1979 v Ni (3)

Taylor, T. (Waterford), 1959 v Pol (sub) (1)
Thomas, P. (Waterford), 1974 v Pol, Br (2)
Townsend, A. D. (Norwich C), 1989 v F, Sp (sub), Ma (sub), H; 1990 v WG (sub), Ni, Ma, W, USSR, Fi (sub), T, Ma (sub), E, Eg, Ho, R, I; (with Chelsea), 1991 v Mor, T, E (2), W, Pol, Ch, US; 1992 v Pol, W, US, Alb, US, I; 1993 v La, D, Sp, Ni, D, Alb, La, Li; (with Aston Villa), 1994 v Li, Ni, Ho, Bol, G, CzR, I, M, N, Ho; 1995 v La, Ni, E, Ni, P; 1996 v A, La, Ho, Ru, CzR, P; 1997 v Lie, Mac (2), Ic, R, Lie (66)
Traynor, T. J. (Southampton), 1954 v L; 1962 v A; 1963 v Ic (2), S; 1964 v A (2), Sp (8)
Treacy, R. C. P. (WBA), 1966 v WG; 1967 v Sp, Cz; 1968 v Cz; (with Charlton Ath), 1968 v Pol; 1969 v Pol, Cz, D; 1970 v S, D, H (sub), Pol (sub), WG (sub); 1971 v Pol, Se (sub+1), I, A; (with Swindon T), 1972 v Ir, Ec, Ch, P; 1973 v USSR, F, USSR, Pol, F, N; 1974 v Pol; (with Preston NE), Br; 1975 v USSR, Sw (2), WG; 1976 v T, N (sub), Pol (sub); (with WBA), 1977 v F, Pol; (with Shamrock R), 1978 v T, Pol; 1980 v Cz (sub) (42)
Tuohy, L. (Shamrock R), 1956 v Y; 1959 v Cz (2); (with Newcastle U), 1962 v A; 1963 v Ic (2); (with Shamrock R), 1964 v A; 1965 v Bel (8)
Turner, C. J. (Southend U), 1936 v Sw; 1937 v G, H, Sw, F; 1938 v N (2), (with West Ham U) Cz, Pol; 1939 v H (10)
Turner, P. (Celtic), 1963 v S; 1964 v Sp (2)

Vernon, J. (Belfast C), 1946 v P, Sp (2)

Waddock, G. (QPR), 1980 v Sw, Arg; 1981 v W, Pol (sub); 1982 v Alg; 1983 v Ic, Ma, Sp, Ho (sub); 1984 v Ma (sub), Ic, Ho, Is; 1985 v I, Is, E, N, Sp; 1986 v USSR; (with Millwall), 1990 v USSR, T (21)
Walsh, D. J. (Linfield), 1946 v P, Sp; (with WBA), 1947 v Sp, P; 1948 v P, Sp; 1949 v Sw, P, Se, Sp; 1950 v E, Fi, Se; 1951 v N; (with Aston Villa), Arg, N; 1952 v Sp; 1953 v A; 1954 v F (2) (20)
Walsh, J. (Limerick), 1982 v Tr (1)
Walsh, M. (Blackpool), 1976 v N, Pol; 1977 v F (sub), Pol; (with Everton), 1979 v Ni (sub); (with QPR), D (sub), Bul, WG (sub); (with Porto), 1981 v Bel (sub), Cz; 1982 v Alg (sub); 1983 v Sp, Ho (sub), Sp (sub); 1984 v Ic (sub), Ma, Pol, Chn; 1985 v USSR, N (sub), D (21)
Walsh, M. (Everton), 1982 v Ch, Br, Tr; 1983 v Ic (4)
Walsh, W. (Manchester C), 1947 v E, Sp, P; 1948 v P, Sp; 1949 v Bel; 1950 v E, Se, Bel (9)
Waters, J. (Grimsby T), 1977 v T; 1980 v Ni (sub) (2)
Watters, F. (Shelbourne), 1926 v I (1)
Weir, E. (Clyde), 1939 v H (2), G (3)
Whelan, R. (St Patrick's Ath), 1964 v A, E (sub) (2)
Whelan, R. (Liverpool), 1981 v Cz (sub); 1982 v Ho (sub), F; 1983 v Ic, Ma, Sp; 1984 v Is; 1985 v USSR, N, I (sub), Is, E, N (sub), Sw (sub); 1986 v USSR (sub), W; 1987 v Bel (sub), S, Bul, Bel, Br, L; 1988 v L, Bul, Pol, N, E, USSR, Ho; 1989 v Ni, F, H, Sp, Ma; 1990 v WG, Ni, Ma, W, Ho (sub); 1991 v Mor, E; 1992 v Sw; 1993 v La, W (sub), Li (sub); 1994 v Li (sub), Sp, Ru, Ho, G (sub), N (sub); (with Southend U), 1995 v Lie, A (53)
Whelan, W. (Manchester U), 1956 v Ho; 1957 v D, E (2) (4)
White, J. J. (Bohemians), 1928 v Bel (1)
Whittaker, R. (Chelsea), 1959 v Cz (1)
Williams, J. (Shamrock R), 1938 v N (1)

BRITISH AND IRISH INTERNATIONAL GOALSCORERS SINCE 1872

Where two players with the same surname and initials have appeared for the same country, and one or both have scored, they have been distinguished by reference to the club which appears *first* against their name in the international appearances section (pages 796–836). Unfortunately, four of the scorers in Scotland's 10-2 victory v Ireland in 1888 are unknown, as is the scorer of one of their nine goals v Wales in March 1878.

ENGLAND

Name	Goals	Name	Goals	Name	Goals	Name	Goals
A'Court, A.	1	Carter, H. S.	7	Goulden, L. A.	4	Lofthouse, N.	30
Adams, T. A.	4	Carter, J. H.	4	Grainger, C.	3	Hon. A. Lyttelton	1
Adcock, H.	1	Chadwick, E.	3	Greaves, J.	44		
Alcock, C. W.	1	Chamberlain, M.	1	Grovesnor, A. T.	2	Mabbutt, G.	1
Allen, A.	3	Chambers, H.	5	Gunn, W.	1	Macdonald, M.	6
Allen, R.	2	Channon, M. R.	21			Mannion, W. J.	11
Anderson, V.	2	Charlton, J.	6	Haines, J. T. W.	2	Mariner, P.	13
Anderton, D. R.	5	Charlton, R.	49	Hall, G. W.	9	Marsh, R. W.	1
Astall, G.	1	Chenery, C. J.	1	Halse, H. J.	2	Matthews, S.	11
Athersmith, W. C.	3	Chivers, M.	13	Hampson, J.	5	Matthews, V.	1
Atyeo, P. J. W.	5	Clarke, A. J.	10	Hampton, H.	2	McCall, J.	1
		Cobbold, W. N.	7	Hancocks, J.	2	McDermott, T.	3
Bache, J. W.	4	Cock, J. G.	2	Hardman, H. P.	1	Medley, L. D.	1
Bailey, N. C.	2	Common, A.	2	Harris, S. S.	2	Melia, J.	1
Baily, E. F.	5	Connelly, J. M.	7	Hassall, H. W.	4	Mercer, D. W.	1
Baker, J. H.	3	Coppell, S. J.	7	Hateley, M.	9	Merson, P. C.	1
Ball, A. J.	8	Cotterill, G. H.	2	Haynes, J. N.	18	Milburn, J. E. T.	10
Bambridge, A. L.	1	Cowans, G.	2	Hegan, K. E.	4	Miller, H. S.	1
Bambridge, E. C.	12	Crawford, R.	1	Henfrey, A. G.	2	Mills, G. R.	3
Barclay, R.	2	Crawshaw, T. H.	1	Hilsdon, G. R.	14	Milward, A.	3
Barmby, N. J.	3	Crayston, W. J.	1	Hine, E. W.	4	Mitchell, C.	5
Barnes, J.	11	Creek, F. N. S.	1	Hirst, D. E.	1	Moore, J.	1
Barnes, P. S.	4	Crooks, S. D.	7	Hitchens, G. A.	5	Moore, R. F.	2
Barton, J.	1	Currey, E. S.	2	Hobbis, H. H. F.	1	Moore, W. G. B.	2
Bassett, W. I.	7	Currie, A. W.	3	Hoddle, G.	8	Morren, T.	1
Bastin, C. S.	12	Cursham, A. W.	2	Hodgetts, D.	1	Morris, F.	1
Beardsley, P. A.	9	Cursham, H. A.	5	Hodgson, G.	1	Morris, J.	3
Beasley, A.	1			Holley, G. H.	8	Mortensen, S. H.	23
Beattie, T. K.	1	Daft, H. B.	3	Houghton, W. E.	5	Morton, J. R.	1
Becton, F.	2	Davenport, J. K.	2	Howell, R.	1	Mosforth, W.	3
Bedford, H.	1	Davis, G.	1	Hughes, E. W.	1	Mullen, J.	6
Bell, C.	9	Davis, H.	1	Hulme, J. H. A.	4	Mullery, A. P.	1
Bentley, R. T. F.	9	Day, S. H.	2	Hunt, G. S.	1		
Bishop, S. M.	1	Dean, W. R.	18	Hunt, R.	18	Neal, P. G.	5
Blackburn, F.	1	Devey, J. H. G.	1	Hunter, N.	2	Needham, E.	3
Blissett, L.	3	Dewhurst, F.	11	Hurst, G. C.	24	Nicholls, J.	1
Bloomer, S.	28	Dix, W. R.	1			Nicholson, W. E.	1
Bond, R.	2	Dixon, K. M.	4	Ince, P. E. C.	2		
Bonsor, A. G.	1	Dixon, L. M.	1			O'Grady, M.	3
Bowden, E. R.	1	Douglas, B.	11	Jack, D. N. B.	3	Osborne, F. R.	3
Bowers, J. W.	2	Drake, E. J.	6	Johnson, D. E.	6	Own goals	23
Bowles, S.	1	Ducat, A.	1	Johnson, E.	2		
Bradford, G. R. W.	1	Dunn, A. T. B.	2	Johnson, J. A.	2	Page, L. A.	1
Bradford, J.	7			Johnson, T. C. F.	5	Paine, T. L.	7
Bradley, W.	2	Eastham, G.	2	Johnson, W. H.	1	Palmer, C. L.	1
Bradshaw, F.	3	Edwards, D.	5			Parry, E. H.	1
Bridges, B. J.	1	Elliott, W. H.	3	Kail, E. I. L.	2	Parry, R. A.	1
Bridgett, A.	3	Evans, R. E.	1	Kay, A. H.	1	Pawson, F. W.	1
Brindle, T.	1			Keegan, J. K.	21	Payne, J.	2
Britton, C. S.	1	Ferdinand, L.	5	Kelly, R.	8	Peacock, A.	3
Broadbent, P. F.	2	Finney, T.	30	Kennedy, R.	3	Pearce, S.	4
Broadis, I. A.	8	Fleming, H. J.	9	Kenyon-Slaney, W. S.	2	Pearson, J. S.	5
Brodie, J. B.	1	Flowers, R.	10	Keown, M. R.	3	Pearson, S. C.	5
Bromley-Davenport, W.	2	Forman, Frank	1	Kevan, D. T.	8	Perry, W.	2
Brook, E. F.	10	Forman, Fred	3	Kidd, B.	1	Peters, M.	20
Brooking, T. D.	5	Foster, R. E.	3	Kingsford, R. K.	1	Pickering, F.	5
Brooks, J.	2	Fowler, R. B.	1	Kirchen, A. J.	2	Platt, D.	27
Broome, F. H.	3	Francis, G. C. J.	3	Kirton, W. J.	1	Pointer, R.	2
Brown, A.	4	Francis, T.	12				
Brown, A. S.	1	Freeman, B. C.	3	Langton, R.	1	Quantrill, A.	1
Brown, G.	5	Froggatt, J.	2	Latchford, R. D.	5		
Brown, J.	3	Froggatt, R.	2	Latherton, E. G.	1	Ramsay, A. E.	3
Brown, W.	1			Lawler, C.	1	Revie, D. G.	4
Buchan, C. M.	4	Galley, T.	1	Lawton, T.	22	Reynolds, J.	3
Bull, S. G.	4	Gascoigne, P. J.	9	Lee, F.	10	Richardson, J. R.	2
Bullock, N.	2	Geary, F.	3	Lee, J.	1	Rigby, A.	3
Burgess, H.	4	Gibbins, W. V. T.	3	Lee, R. M.	2	Rimmer, E. J.	2
Butcher, T.	3	Gilliatt, W. E.	3	Lee, S.	2	Roberts, H.	1
Byrne, J. J.	8	Goddard, P.	1	Le Saux, G. P.	1	Roberts, W. T.	4
		Goodall, J.	12	Lindley, T.	15	Robinson, J.	3
Camsell, G. H.	18	Goodyer, A. C.	1	Lineker, G.	48	Robson, B.	26
		Gosling, R. C.	2	Lofthouse, J. M.	3	Robson, R.	4

Rowley, J. F.	6
Royle, J.	2
Rutherford, J.	3
Sagar, C.	1
Sandilands, R. R.	2
Sansom, K.	1
Schofield, J.	1
Scholes, P.	1
Seed, J. M.	1
Settle, J.	6
Sewell, J.	3
Shackleton, L. F.	1
Sharp, J.	1
Shearer, A.	16
Shepherd, A.	2
Sheringham, E. P.	8
Simpson, J.	1
Smith, A. M.	2
Smith, G. O.	12
Smith, Joe	1
Smith, J. R.	2
Smith, J. W.	4
Smith, R.	13
Smith, S.	1
Sorby, T. H.	1
Southworth, J.	3
Sparks, F. J.	3
Spence, J. W.	1
Spiksley, F.	5
Spilsbury, B. W.	5
Steele, F. C.	8
Stephenson, G. T.	2
Steven, T. M.	4
Stewart, J.	2
Stiles, N. P.	1
Storer, H.	1
Stone, S. B.	2
Summerbee, M. G.	1
Tambling, R. V.	1
Taylor, P. J.	2
Taylor, T.	16
Thompson, P. B.	1
Thornewell, G.	1
Tilson, S. F.	6
Townley, W. J.	2
Tueart, D.	2
Vaughton, O. H.	6
Veitch, J. G.	3
Violett, D. S.	1
Waddle, C. R.	6
Walker, W. H.	9
Wall, G.	2
Wallace, D.	1
Walsh, P.	1
Waring, T.	4
Warren, B.	2
Watson, D. V.	4
Watson, V. M.	4
Webb, G. W.	1
Webb, N.	4
Wedlock, W. J.	2
Weir, D.	2
Weller, K.	1
Welsh, D.	1
Whateley, O.	2
Wheldon, G. F.	6
Whitfield, H.	1
Wignall, F.	2
Wilkes, A.	1
Wilkins, R. G.	3
Willingham, C. K.	1
Wilshaw, D. J.	10
Wilson, D.	1
Wilson, G. P.	1
Winckworth, W. N.	1
Windridge, J. E.	7
Wise, D. F.	1
Withe, P.	1
Wollaston, C. H. R.	1
Wood, H.	1
Woodcock, T.	16
Woodhall, G.	1
Woodward, V. J.	29
Worrall, F.	2
Worthington, F. S.	2
Wright, I. E.	7
Wright, M.	1
Wright, W. A.	3
Wylie, J. G.	1
Yates, J.	3

NORTHERN IRELAND

Anderson, T.	4
Armstrong, G.	12
Bambrick, J.	12
Barr, H. H.	1
Barron, H.	3
Best, G.	9
Bingham, W. L.	10
Black, K.	1
Blanchflower, D.	2
Blanchflower, J.	1
Brennan, B.	1
Brennan, R. A.	1
Brotherston, N.	3
Brown, J.	1
Browne, F.	2
Campbell, J.	1
Campbell, W. G.	1
Casey, T.	2
Caskey, W.	1
Cassidy, T.	1
Chambers, J.	3
Clarke, C. J.	13
Clements, D.	2
Cochrane, T.	1
Condy, J.	1
Connor, M. J.	1
Coulter, J.	1
Croft, T.	1
Crone, W.	1
Crossan, E.	1
Crossan, J. A.	10
Curran, S.	2
Cush, W. W.	5
Dalton, W.	6
D'Arcy, S. D.	1
Darling, J.	1
Davey, H. H.	1
Davis, T. L.	1
Dill, A. H.	1
Doherty, L.	1
Doherty, P. D.	3
Dougan, A. D.	8
Dowie, I.	11
Dunne, J.	4
Elder, A. R.	1
Emerson, W.	1
English, S.	1
Ferguson, W.	1
Ferris, J.	1
Ferris, R. O.	1
Finney, T.	2
Gaffkin, J.	5
Gara, A.	3
Gawkrodger, G.	1
Gibb, J. T.	2
Gibb, T. J.	1
Gibson, W. K.	1
Gillespie, K. R.	1
Gillespie, W.	12
Goodall, A. L.	2
Gray, P.	5
Halligan, W.	1
Hamill, M.	1
Hamilton, B.	4
Hamilton, W.	5
Hannon, D. J.	1
Harkin, J. T.	2
Harvey, M.	3
Hill, C. F.	1
Hughes, M.	2
Humphries, W.	1
Hunter, A. (*Distillery*)	1
Hunter, A. (*Blackburn R*)	1
Hunter, B. V.	1
Irvine, R. W.	3
Irvine, W. J.	8
Johnston, H.	2
Johnston, S.	2
Johnston, W. C.	1
Jones, S.	1
Jones, J.	1
Kelly, J.	4
Kernaghan, N.	2
Kirwan, J.	2
Lacey, W.	3
Lemon, J.	2
Lennon, N. F.	1
Lockhart, N.	3
Lomas, S. M.	1
Magilton, J.	5
Mahood, J.	2
Martin, D. K.	3
Maxwell, J.	7
McAdams, W. J.	7
McAllen, J.	1
McAuley, J. L.	1
McCandless, J.	3
McCaw, J. H.	1
McClelland, J.	1
McCluggage, A.	2
McCracken, W.	1
McCrory, S.	1
McCurdy, C.	1
McDonald, A.	3
McGarry, J. K.	1
McGrath, R. C.	4
McIlroy, J.	10
McIlroy, S. B.	5
McKnight, J.	2
McLaughlin, J. C.	6
McMahon, G. J.	2
McMordie, A. S.	3
McMorran, E. J.	4
McParland, P. J.	10
McWha, W. B. R.	1
Meldon, J.	1
Mercar, J.	1
Mercer, J. T.	1
Millar, W.	1
Milligan, D.	1
Milne, R. G.	2
Molyneux, T. B.	1
Moreland, V.	1
Morgan, S.	3
Morrow, S. J.	1
Morrow, W. J.	1
Mulryne, P. P.	1
Murphy, N.	1
Neill, W. J. T.	2
Nelson, S.	1
Nicholl, C. J.	3
Nicholl, J. M.	2
Nicholson, J. J.	6
O'Boyle, G.	1
O'Hagan, C.	2
O'Kane, W. J.	1
O'Neill, J.	1
O'Neill, M. A.	4
O'Neill, M. H.	8
Own goals	5
Peacock, R.	2
Peden, J.	7
Penney, S.	2
Pyper, James	2
Pyper, John	1
Quinn, J. M.	12
Quinn, S. J.	1
Reynolds, J.	1
Rowley, R. W. M.	2
Sheridan, J.	2
Sherrard, J.	1
Simpson, W. J.	5
Sloan, H. A. de B.	4
Smyth, S.	5
Spence, D. W.	3
Stanfield, O. M.	9
Stevenson, A. E.	5
Stewart, I.	2
Taggart, G. P.	6
Thompson, F. W.	2
Tully, C. P.	3
Turner, E.	1
Walker, J.	1
Walsh, D. J.	5
Welsh, E.	1
Whiteside, N.	9
Whiteside, T.	1
Williams, J. R.	1
Williamson, J.	1
Wilson, D. J.	1
Wilson, K. J.	6
Wilson, S. J.	7
Wilton, J. M.	2
Young, S.	2

SCOTLAND

Aitken, R.	1
Aitkenhead, W. A. C.	2
Alexander, D.	1
Allan, D. S.	4
Allan, J.	2
Anderson, F.	1
Anderson, W.	4
Andrews, P.	1
Archibald, A.	1
Archibald, S.	4
Baird, D.	2
Baird, J. C.	2
Baird, S.	2
Bannon, E.	1
Barbour, A.	1
Barker, J. B.	4
Battles, B. Jr	1
Bauld, W.	2
Baxter, J. C.	3
Bell, J.	5
Bennett, A.	2
Berry, D.	1
Bett, J.	1
Beveridge, W. W.	1
Black, A.	3
Black, D.	1
Bone, J.	1
Booth, S.	5
Boyd, R.	2
Boyd, T.	1
Boyd, W. G.	1
Brackenridge, T.	1
Brand, R.	8
Brazil, A.	1
Bremner, W. J.	3
Brown, A. D.	6
Buchanan, P. S.	1
Buchanan, R.	1
Buckley, P.	1
Buick, A.	2
Burns, K.	1
Cairns, T.	1
Calderwood, C.	1
Calderwood, R.	2
Caldow, E.	4
Campbell, C.	1
Campbell, John (*Celtic*)	5

Campbell, John (*Rangers*)	4
Campbell, P.	2
Campbell, R.	1
Cassidy, J.	1
Chalmers, S.	3
Chambers, T.	1
Cheyne, A. G.	4
Christie, A. J.	1
Clunas, W. L.	1
Collins, J.	9
Collins, R. Y.	10
Combe, J. R.	1
Conn, A.	1
Cooper, D.	6
Craig, J.	1
Craig, T.	1
Crawford, S.	1
Cunningham, A. N.	5
Curran, H. P.	1
Dailly, C.	1
Dalglish, K.	30
Davidson, D.	1
Davidson, J. A.	1
Delaney, J.	3
Devine, A.	1
Dewar, G.	1
Dewar, N.	4
Dickson, W.	4
Divers, J.	1
Docherty, T. H.	1
Dodds, D.	1
Donaldson, A.	1
Donnachie, J.	1
Dougall, J.	1
Drummond, J.	2
Dunbar, M.	1
Duncan, D.	7
Duncan, D. M.	1
Duncan, J.	1
Dunn, J.	2
Durie, G. S.	1
Easson, J. F.	1
Ellis, J.	1
Ferguson, J.	6
Fernie, W.	1
Fitchie, T. T.	1
Flavell, R.	2
Fleming, C.	2
Fleming, J. W.	3
Fraser, M. J. E.	4
Gallacher, H. K.	23
Gallacher, K. W.	5
Gallacher, P.	1
Galt, J. H.	1
Gemmell, T. (*St Mirren*)	1
Gemmell, T. (*Celtic*)	1
Gemmill, A.	8
Gibb, W.	1
Gibson, D. W.	3
Gibson, J. D.	2
Gibson, N.	1
Gillespie, Jas.	3
Gillick, T.	3
Gilzean, A. J.	12
Gossland, J.	2
Goudie, J.	1
Gough, C. R.	6
Gourlay, J.	1
Graham, A.	2
Graham, G.	3
Gray, A.	7
Gray, E.	3
Gray, F.	1
Greig, J.	3
Groves, W.	5
Hamilton, G.	4
Hamilton, J. (*Queen's Park*)	3
Hamilton, R. C.	14
Harper, J. M.	2

Harrower, W.	5
Hartford, R. A.	4
Heggie, C.	5
Henderson, J. G.	1
Henderson, W.	5
Hendry, E. C. J.	1
Herd, D. G.	4
Hewie, J. D.	2
Higgins, A. (*Newcastle U*)	1
Higgins, A. (*Kilmarnock*)	4
Highet, T. C.	1
Holton, J. A.	2
Houliston, W.	2
Howie, H.	1
Howie, J.	2
Hughes, J.	1
Hunter, W.	1
Hutchison, T.	1
Hutton, J.	1
Hyslop, T.	1
Imrie, W. N.	1
Jackson, A.	8
Jackson, C.	1
Jackson, D.	3
James, A. W.	3
Jardine, A.	1
Jenkinson, T.	1
Jess, E.	1
Johnston, L. H.	1
Johnston, M.	14
Johnstone, D.	2
Johnstone, J.	4
Johnstone, Jas.	1
Johnstone, R.	9
Johnstone, W.	1
Jordan, J.	11
Kay, J. L.	5
Keillor, A.	3
Kelly, J.	1
Kelso, J.	1
Ker, G.	10
King, A.	1
King, J.	1
Kinnear, D.	1
Lambie, W. A.	5
Lang, J. J.	1
Law, D.	30
Leggat, G.	8
Lennie, W.	1
Lennox, R.	3
Liddell, W.	6
Lindsay, J.	6
Linwood, A. B.	1
Logan, J.	1
Lorimer, P.	4
Love, A.	1
Lowe, J. (*Cambuslang*)	1
Lowe, J. (*St Bernards*)	1
Macari, L.	5
MacDougall, E. J.	3
MacLeod, M.	1
Mackay, D. C.	4
Mackay, J.	1
MacKenzie, J. A.	1
Madden, J.	5
Marshall, H.	1
Marshall, J.	1
Mason, J.	4
Massie, A.	1
Masson, D. S.	5
McAdam, J.	1
McAllister, G.	5
McAulay, J.	1
McAvennie, F.	1
McCall, J.	1
McCall, S. M.	1
McCalliog, J.	1
McCallum, N.	1
McClair, B. J.	2
McCoist, A.	19

McColl, R. S.	13
McCulloch, D.	3
McDougall, J.	4
McFarlane, A.	1
McFadyen, W.	2
McGhee, M.	2
McGinlay, J.	4
McGregor, J. C.	1
McGrory, J.	6
McGuire, W.	1
McInally, A.	3
McInnes, T.	2
McKie, J.	2
McKimmie, S.	1
McKinlay, W.	4
McKinnon, A.	1
McKinnon, R.	1
McKinnon, W. W.	5
McLaren, A.	4
McLaren, J.	1
McLean, A.	1
McLean, T.	1
McLintock, F.	1
McMahon, A.	6
McMenemy, J.	5
McMillan, I. L.	2
McNeil, H.	5
McNeil, W.	3
McPhail, J.	3
McPhail, R.	7
McPherson, J.	8
McPherson, R.	1
McQueen, G.	5
McStay, P.	9
Meiklejohn, D. D.	3
Millar, J.	2
Miller, T.	2
Miller, W.	1
Mitchell, R. C.	1
Morgan, W.	1
Morris, D.	1
Morris, H.	3
Morton, A. L.	5
Mudie, J. K.	9
Mulhall, G.	1
Munro, A. D.	1
Munro, N.	1
Murdoch, R.	5
Murphy, F.	1
Murray, J.	1
Napier, C. E.	3
Narey, D.	1
Neil, R. G.	2
Nevin, P. K. F.	5
Nicholas, C.	5
Nisbet, J.	2
O'Donnell, F.	2
O'Hare, J.	5
Ormond, W. E.	1
O'Rourke, F.	1
Orr, R.	1
Orr, T.	1
Oswald, J.	1
Own goals	15
Parlane, D.	1
Paul, H. McD.	2
Paul, W.	6
Pettigrew, W.	2
Provan, D.	1
Quinn, J.	7
Quinn, P.	1
Rankin, G.	2
Rankin, R.	2
Reid, W.	4
Reilly, L.	22
Renny-Tailyour, H. W.	1
Richmond, J. T.	1
Ring, T.	2
Rioch, B. D.	6
Ritchie, J.	1
Robertson, A.	2

Robertson, J.	2
Robertson, J. N.	9
Robertson, J. T.	2
Robertson, T.	1
Robertson, W.	1
Russell, D.	1
Scott, A. S.	5
Sellar, W.	4
Sharp, G.	1
Shaw, F. W.	1
Shearer, D.	2
Simpson, J.	2
Smith, A.	5
Smith, G.	4
Smith, J.	1
Smith, John	12
Somerville, G.	1
Souness, G. J.	3
Speedie, F.	2
St John, I.	9
Steel, W.	12
Stein, C.	10
Stevenson, G.	4
Stewart, R.	1
Stewart, W. E.	1
Strachan, G.	5
Sturrock, P.	3
Taylor, J. D.	1
Templeton, R.	1
Thomson, A.	1
Thomson, C.	4
Thomson, R.	1
Thomson, W.	1
Thornton, W.	1
Waddell, T. S.	1
Waddell, W.	6
Walker, J.	2
Walker, R.	7
Walker, T.	9
Wallace, I. A.	1
Wark, J.	7
Watson, J. A. K.	1
Watt, F.	2
Watt, W. W.	1
Weir, A.	1
Weir, J. B.	2
White, J. A.	3
Wilson, A.	2
Wilson, A. N.	13
Wilson, D. (*Queen's Park*)	2
Wilson, D. (*Rangers*)	9
Wilson, H.	1
Wylie, T. G.	1
Young, A.	5

WALES

Allchurch, I. J.	23
Allen, M.	3
Astley, D. J.	12
Atherton, R. W.	2
Bamford, T.	1
Barnes, W.	1
Blackmore, C. G.	1
Blake, N. A.	1
Bodin, P. J.	3
Boulter, L. M.	1
Bowdler, J. C. H.	3
Bowen, D. L.	1
Bowen, M.	3
Boyle, T.	1
Bryan, T.	1
Burgess, W. A. R.	1
Burke, T.	1
Butler, A.	1
Chapman, T.	2
Charles, J.	1
Charles, M.	6
Charles, W. J.	15

Clarke, R. J.	5
Coleman, C.	3
Collier, D. J.	1
Cross, K.	1
Cumner, R. H.	1
Curtis, A.	6
Curtis, E. R.	3
Davies, D. W.	1
Davies, E. Lloyd	1
Davies, G.	2
Davies, L. S.	6
Davies, R. T.	8
Davies, R. W.	7
Davies, S.	5
Davies, W.	6
Davies, W. H.	1
Davies, William	5
Davies, W. O.	1
Deacy, N.	4
Doughty, J.	6
Doughty, R.	2
Durban, A.	2
Dwyer, P.	2
Edwards, G.	2
Edwards, R. I.	4
England, H. M.	3
Evans, I.	1
Evans, J.	1
Evans, R. E.	2
Evans, W.	1
Eyton-Jones, J. A.	1
Flynn, B.	7
Ford, T.	23
Foulkes, W. I.	1
Fowler, J.	3
Giles, D.	2
Giggs, R. J.	4
Glover, E. M.	7
Godfrey, B. C.	2
Green, A. W.	3
Griffiths, A. T.	6
Griffiths, M. W.	2
Griffiths, T. P.	3
Harris, C. S.	1
Hartson, J.	1
Hersee, R.	1
Hewitt, R.	1
Hockey, T.	1
Hodges, G.	2
Hole, W. J.	1
Hopkins, I. J.	2
Horne, B.	2
Howell, E. G.	3
Hughes, L. M.	16
James, E.	2
James, L.	10
James, R.	8
Jarrett, R. H.	3
Jenkyns, C. A.	1
Jones, A.	1
Jones, Bryn	6
Jones, B. S.	2
Jones, Cliff	15
Jones, C. W.	1
Jones, D. E.	1
Jones, Evan	1
Jones, H.	1
Jones, I.	1
Jones, J. O.	1
Jones, J. P.	1
Jones, Leslie J.	1
Jones, R. A.	2
Jones, W. L.	6

Keenor, F. C.	2
Krzywicki, R. L.	1
Leek, K.	5
Lewis, B.	3
Lewis, J.	1
Lewis, W.	10
Lewis, W. L.	2
Lovell, S.	1
Lowrie, G.	2
Mahoney, J. F.	1
Mays, A. W.	1
Medwin, T. C.	6
Melville, A. K	2
Meredith, W. H.	11
Mills, T. J.	1
Moore, G.	1
Morgan, J. R.	2
Morgan-Owen, H.	1
Morgan-Owen, M. M.	2
Morris, A. G.	9
Morris, H.	2
Morris, R.	1
Nicholas, P.	2
O'Callaghan, E.	3
O'Sullivan, P. A.	1
Owen, G.	2
Owen, W.	4
Owen, W. P.	6
Own goals	12
Palmer, D.	3
Parry, T. D.	3
Paul, R.	1
Peake, E.	1
Pembridge, M.	3
Perry, E.	1
Phillips, C.	5
Phillips, D.	2
Powell, A.	1
Powell, D.	1
Price, J.	4
Price, P.	1
Pryce-Jones, W. E.	3
Pugh, D. H.	2
Reece, G. I.	2
Rees, R. R.	3
Richards, R. W.	1
Roach, J.	2
Robbins, W. W.	4
Roberts, J. (*Corwen*)	1
Roberts, Jas.	1
Roberts, P. S.	1
Roberts, R. (*Druids*)	1
Roberts, W. (*Llangollen*)	2
Roberts, W. (*Wrexham*)	1
Roberts, W. H.	1
Robinson, J. R. C.	1
Rush, I.	28
Russell, M. R.	1
Sabine, H. W.	1
Saunders, D.	20
Shaw, E. G.	2
Sisson, H.	4
Slatter, N.	2
Smallman, D. P.	1
Speed, G. A.	3
Symons, C. J.	1
Tapscott, D. R.	4
Thomas, M.	4
Thomas, T.	1
Toshack, J. B.	13
Trainer, H.	2

Vaughan, John	2
Vernon, T. R.	8
Vizard, E. T.	1
Walsh, I.	7
Warren, F. W.	3
Watkins, W. M.	4
Wilding, J.	4
Williams, G. E.	1
Williams, G. G.	1
Williams, W.	1
Woosnam, A. P.	4
Wynn, G. A.	1
Yorath, T. C.	2
Young, E.	1

EIRE

Aldridge, J.	19
Ambrose, P.	1
Anderson, J.	1
Bermingham, P.	1
Bradshaw, P.	4
Brady, L.	9
Breen, G.	1
Brown, D.	1
Byrne, J. (*Bray*)	1
Byrne, J. (*QPR*)	4
Cantwell, J.	14
Carey, J.	3
Carroll, T.	1
Cascarino, A.	16
Coad, P.	5
Connolly, D. J.	3
Conroy, T.	2
Conway, J.	3
Coyne, T.	6
Cummings, G.	5
Curtis, D.	8
Daly, G.	13
Davis, T.	4
Dempsey, J.	1
Dennehy, M.	2
Donnelly, J.	3
Donnelly, T.	1
Duffy, B.	1
Duggan, H.	1
Dunne, J.	12
Dunne, L.	1
Eglington, T.	2
Ellis, P.	1
Fagan, F.	5
Fallon, S.	2
Fallon, W.	2
Farrell, P.	3
Fitzgerald, P.	2
Fitzgerald, J.	1
Fitzsimmons, A.	7
Flood, J. J.	4
Fogarty, A.	3
Fullam, J.	1
Fullam, R.	1
Galvin, A.	1
Gavin, J.	2
Geoghegan, M.	2
Giles, J.	5
Givens, D.	19
Glynn, D.	1
Grealish, T.	8
Grimes, A. A.	1
Hale, A.	2
Hand, E.	2

Harte, I. P.	2
Haverty, J.	3
Holmes, J.	1
Horlacher, A.	2
Houghton, R.	5
Hughton, C.	1
Hurley, C.	2
Irwin, D.	1
Jordan, D.	1
Keane, R. M.	1
Kelly, D.	9
Kelly, G.	1
Kelly, J.	2
Kernaghan, A. N.	1
Lacey, W.	1
Lawrenson, M.	5
Leech, M.	2
McAteer, J. W.	1
McCann, J.	1
McCarthy, M.	2
McEvoy, A.	6
McGee, P.	4
McGrath, P.	8
McLoughlin, A. F.	2
Madden, O.	1
Mancini, T.	1
Martin, C.	6
Martin, M.	4
Mooney, J.	1
Moore, P.	7
Moran, K.	6
Moroney, T.	1
Mulligan, P.	1
O'Callaghan, K.	1
O'Connor, T.	2
O'Farrell, F.	2
O'Flanagan, K.	3
O'Keefe, E.	1
O'Leary, D. A.	1
O'Neill, F.	1
O'Neill, K. P.	2
O'Reilly, J. (*Brideville*)	4
O'Reilly, J. (*Cork*)	1
Own goals	7
Quinn, N.	16
Ringstead, A.	7
Robinson, M.	4
Rogers, E.	5
Ryan, G.	1
Ryan, R.	3
Sheedy, K.	9
Sheridan, J.	5
Slaven, B.	1
Sloan, W.	1
Squires, J.	1
Stapleton, F.	20
Staunton, S.	5
Strahan, J.	1
Sullivan, J.	1
Townsend, A. D.	7
Treacy, R.	5
Touhy, L.	4
Waddock, G.	3
Walsh, D.	5
Walsh, M.	3
Waters, J.	1
White, J. J.	2
Whelan, R.	3

OTHER INTERNATIONAL RESULTS

(where both teams are shown playing away, the match was played on neutral ground)

SOUTH AMERICA

International matches 1996

Argentina
Bolivia (h) 3-1, Ecuador (a) 0-2, Poland (h) 2-0, Peru (h) 0-0, Paraguay (h) 1-1, Venezuela (a) 5-2, Chile (h) 1-1, Yugoslavia (h) 2-3.

Bolivia
Slovakia (h) 2-0, Chile (h) 1-1, Peru (a) 3-1, Paraguay (h) 4-1, Peru (h) 2-0, Colombia (a) 1-4, Argentina (a) 1-3, El Salvador (h) 1-1, Chile (a) 0-2, Mexico (a) 0-1, USA (a) 2-0, Republic of Ireland (a) 0-3, Venezuela (h) 6-1, Paraguay (a) 0-2, Peru (h) 0-0, Uruguay (a) 0-1, Colombia (h) 2-2, Paraguay (h) 0-0.

Brazil
Bulgaria (h) 2-0, Ukraine (h) 1-0, Ghana (h) 8-2, South Africa (a) 3-2, Croatia (h) 1-1, Poland (h) 3-1, Denmark (h) 5-1, Russia (a) 2-2, Holland (a) 2-2, Lithuania (h) 3-1, Bosnia (h) 1-0, Cameroon (h) 2-0, Canada (h) 4-1, Honduras (a) 5-0, Mexico (a) 0-2, USA (a) 1-0.

Chile
Bolivia (a) 1-1, Mexico (h) 2-1, Peru (h) 4-0, Australia (h) 3-0, Bolivia (h) 2-0, Venezuela (a) 1-1, Ecuador (h) 4-1, Costa Rica (a) 1-1, Colombia (a) 1-4, Paraguay (a) 1-2, Uruguay (h) 1-0, Argentina (a) 1-1.

Colombia
Honduras (h) 2-1, Trinidad & Tobago (h) 3-0, Bolivia (h) 4-1, Paraguay (h) 1-0, Scotland (h) 1-0, Peru (a) 1-1, Uruguay (h) 3-1, Chile (h) 4-1, Ecuador (a) 1-0, Bolivia (a) 2-2, Venezuela (a) 2-0.

Ecuador
Venezuela (a) 1-0, Libya (a) 0-1, Oman (a) 2-0, Qatar (a) 1-1, Kuwait (a) 3-0, Qatar (a) 2-1, Japan (a) 1-0, Peru (h) 4-1, Argentina (h) 2-0, Armenia (h) 3-0, Chile (a) 1-4, Costa Rica (h) 1-1, Venezuela (h) 1-0, Jamaica (h) 2-1, Colombia (h) 0-1, Mexico (a) 1-0, Paraguay (a) 0-1.

Paraguay
Bolivia (a) 1-4, Bosnia (h) 3-0, Colombia (a) 0-1, Uruguay (a) 2-0, Armenia (h) 1-2, Bolivia (h) 2-0, China (a) 2-0, Argentina (a) 1-1, Chile (h) 2-1, Ecuador (h) 1-0, Bolivia (a) 0-0.

Peru
Bolivia (h) 1-3, Chile (a) 0-4, Bolivia (a) 0-2, Ecuador (a) 1-4, Colombia (h) 1-1, Armenia (h) 4-0, Argentina (h) 0-0, Costa Rica (h) 3-0, Bolivia (a) 0-0, USA (h) 4-1, Venezuela (h) 4-1, Uruguay (a) 0-2.

Uruguay
Venezuela (a) 2-0, Paraguay (h) 0-2, Colombia (a) 1-3, China (a) 1-1, Japan (a) 3-5, Bolivia (h) 1-0, Chile (a) 0-1, Peru (h) 2-0.

Venezuela
Trinidad & Tobago (a) 0-0, Ecuador (h) 0-1, Guatemala (a) 0-3, Uruguay (h) 0-2, Chile (h) 1-1, Honduras (a) 0-1, Bolivia (a) 1-6, Panama (a) 2-0, Ecuador (a) 0-1, El Salvador (a) 1-0, Costa Rica (h) 2-0, Argentina (h) 2-5, Peru (a) 1-4, Colombia (h) 0-2.

AFRICA

Algeria
Mozambique (a) 0-1, Zambia (a) 0-0, Sierra Leone (h) 2-0, Burkina Faso (h) 2-1, South Africa (a) 1-2, Oman (a) 1-0, Kenya (a) 1-3, Kenya (h) 1-0, Ivory Coast (h) 4-1.

Angola
Egypt (h) 2-1, South Africa (a) 0-1, Cameroon (h) 3-3, Uganda (a) 2-0, Uganda (h) 3-1, Ghana (a) 1-2, Zimbabwe (h) 2-1.

Benin
Togo (a) 0-2, Mauritania (h) 4-1, Mauritania (a) 0-0, Mali (h) 1-2, Gabon (h) 3-3, Ghana (h) 1-1, Burkina Faso (h) 1-1, Burkina Faso (h) 0-0.

Botswana
Namibia (h) 0-0, Namibia (a) 0-6.

Burkina Faso
Sierra Leone (h) 1-2, Zambia (h) 1-5, Algeria (a) 1-2, Niger (h) 0-0, Mauritania (a) 0-0, Ivory Coast (a) 1-1, Mauritania (h) 2-0, Gabon (a) 0-2, Nigeria (a) 0-2, Mali (a) 0-2, Gabon (a) 1-1, Ghana (a) 2-1, Benin (a) 1-1, Benin (a) 0-0.

Cameroon
South Africa (a) 0-3, Egypt (h) 2-1, Angola (a) 3-3, Gabon (a) 0-0, Togo (a) 4-2, Brazil (a) 0-2.

Central Africa
Guinea (h) 2-3.

Congo
Zaire (h) 2-1, Zaire (a) 1-3, Ivory Coast (h) 2-0, Ivory Coast (a) 1-1, Togo (h) 0-0, Togo (a) 0-1, Zambia (h) 1-0.

Egypt
Tunisia (h) 2-1, Angola (a) 1-2, Cameroon (a) 1-2, South Africa (a) 1-0, Zambia (h) 1-3, Morocco (a) 0-2, UAE (a) 0-0, South Korea (a) 1-1, Ghana (a) 2-0, Morocco (h) 1-1, Mali (h) 0-0, Namibia (h) 7-1.

Ethiopia
Ghana (h) 2-0, Uganda (a) 1-1, Uganda (h) 1-1, Senegal (h) 1-2.

Gabon
Zimbabwe (a) 2-1, Mozambique (a) 0-1, Liberia (a) 1-2, Zaire (a) 2-0, Tunisia (a) 1-1, Ivory Coast (h) 0-1, Swaziland (a) 1-0, Swaziland (h) 3-0, Guinea (a) 1-0, Mali (h) 1-1, Cameroon (h) 0-0, Burkina Faso (h) 2-0, Togo (a) 1-0, Ghana (h) 1-1, Burkina Faso (a) 1-1, Benin (a) 3-3, Ghana (a) 1-1, Zambia (a) 4-2.

Gambia
Senegal (h) 1-2, Guinea (h) 1-1, Guinea (h) 1-1, Liberia (h) 2-1, Liberia (a) 0-4.

Ghana
Saudi Arabia (a) 1-1, Zimbabwe (a) 1-1, Ivory Coast (h) 2-0, Tunisia (a) 2-1, Mozambique (a) 2-0, Zaire (h) 1-0, South Africa (a) 0-3, Zambia (a) 0-1, Brazil (a) 2-8, Ethiopia (a) 0-2, Egypt (h) 0-2, Denmark (a) 0-1, Tanzania (a) 0-0, Tanzania (h) 2-1, Australia (h) 0-2, Kenya (a) 1-0, South Africa (h) 0-0, Angola (a) 2-1, Gabon (h) 1-1, Burkina Faso (a) 1-2, Benin (a) 1-1, Gabon (a) 1-1.

Guinea
Gambia (a) 1-1, Gambia (a) 1-1, Guinea-Bissau (a) 3-2, Guinea-Bissau (h) 3-1, Gabon (h) 0-1, Central Africa (a) 3-2, Kenya (h) 3-1.

Guinea-Bissau
Guinea (a) 2-3, Guinea (a) 1-3.

Ivory Coast
Ghana (a) 0-2, Mozambique (a) 1-0, Tunisia (a) 1-3, Gabon (a) 1-0, Congo (a) 0-2, Burkina Faso (h) 1-1, Congo (h) 1-1, Algeria (a) 1-4.

Kenya
Uganda (a) 1-1, Uganda (a) 2-1, Algeria (h) 3-1, Algeria (a) 0-1, South Africa (a) 0-1, Ghana (a) 0-1, Australia (h) 0-4, Namibia (a) 0-1, Guinea (a) 1-3, Rwanda (a) 2-1, Uganda (a) 0-2, Sudan (a) 1-1.

Liberia
Sierra Leone (h) 2-1, Gabon (a) 2-1, Zaire (a) 0-2, Gambia (a) 1-2, Gambia (h) 4-0, Zaire (a) 0-0, Tunisia (h) 0-1.

Madagascar
Mauritius (a) 0-0, Zimbabwe (h) 1-2, Zimbabwe (a) 2-2.

Malawi
Zambia (h) 0-1, Zambia (h) 1-1, Mozambique (h) 1-0, South Africa (h) 0-1, South Africa (a) 0-3, Tanzania (h) 3-2, Tanzania (h) 1-0, Mauritius (a) 2-1.

Mali
Oman (a) 0-1, Oman (a) 1-1, Senegal (a) 0-1, Gabon (a) 1-1, Benin (a) 2-1, Egypt (a) 0-0, Saudi Arabia (a) 3-1, Kuwait (a) 2-4, Burkina Faso (h) 2-0.

Mauritania
Senegal (h) 0-0, Burkina Faso (h) 0-0, Burkina Faso (a) 0-2, Benin (a) 1-4, Benin (h) 0-0.

Mauritius
Madagascar (h) 0-0, Zaire (h) 1-5, Zaire (a) 0-2, Seychelles (h) 1-0, Seychelles (a) 1-1, Malawi (h) 1-2.

Morocco
Tunisia (h) 3-1, Armenia (a) 6-0, Luxembourg (h) 2-0, Egypt (a) 2-0, South Korea (a) 2-2, UAE (a) 0-1, Egypt (a) 1-1, Sierra Leone (h) 4-0, Croatia (h) 2-2, Nigeria (h) 2-0.

Mozambique
Algeria (h) 1-0, Gabon (h) 1-0, Tunisia (a) 1-1, Ivory Coast (a) 0-1, Ghana (a) 0-2, Swaziland (a) 1-0, Malawi (a) 0-1, Namibia (a) 0-2, Namibia (h) 1-1, Oman (a) 2-0, Zambia (a) 0-1.

Namibia
Mozambique (h) 2-0, Mozambique (a) 1-1, Botswana (a) 0-0, Botswana (h) 6-0, Kenya (h) 1-0, Egypt (a) 1-7.

Niger
Burkina Faso (a) 0-0.

Nigeria
Burkina Faso (h) 2-0, Czech Republic (h) 1-2, Morocco (a) 0-2.

Rwanda
Tunisia (h) 1-3, Tunisia (a) 0-2, Uganda (h) 0-0, Uganda (a) 2-3, Uganda (a) 1-1, Kenya (a) 1-2.

Senegal
Gambia (a) 2-1, Mauritania (a) 0-0, Tunisia (a) 0-2, Togo (a) 1-2, Togo (h) 1-1, Mali (h) 1-0, Ethiopia (a) 2-1.

Seychelles
Mauritius (a) 0-1, Mauritius (h) 1-1.

Sierra Leone
Liberia (a) 1-2, Burkina Faso (a) 2-1, Algeria (a) 0-2, Zambia (a) 0-4, Burundi (a) 0-1, Burundi (h) 0-1, Tunisia (a) 0-2, Morocco (a) 0-4.

South Africa
Cameroon (h) 3-0, Angola (h) 1-0, Egypt (h) 0-1, Algeria (h) 2-1, Ghana (h) 3-0, Tunisia (h) 2-0, Brazil (h) 2-3, Malawi (a) 1-0, Malawi (h) 3-0, Kenya (h) 1-0, Australia (h) 2-0, Ghana (h) 0-0, Zaire (h) 1-0.

Canada
Honduras (a) 3-1, Brazil (a) 1-4, Costa Rica (h) 0-1, Panama (h) 3-1, Cuba (h) 2-0, Cuba (a) 2-0, Panama (a) 0-0, El Salvador (h) 1-0, El Salvador (a) 2-0.

Costa Rica
Canada (a) 1-0, Honduras (h) 1-1, Honduras (a) 0-0, Peru (a) 0-3, Ecuador (a) 1-1, Chile (h) 1-1, Trinidad & Tobago (a) 1-0, Venezuela (a) 0-2, Jamaica (h) 0-0, Panama (h) 2-0, Guatemala (h) 3-0, Guatemala (a) 0-1, USA (h) 2-1, USA (a) 1-2, Trinidad & Tobago (a) 2-1.

El Salvador
Trinidad & Tobago (a) 3-2, USA (a) 0-2, Bolivia (a) 1-1, Honduras (a) 1-2, Honduras (h) 1-2, USA (a) 1-3, Cuba (h) 5-0, Venezuela (h) 0-1, Guatemala (a) 2-1, Panama (a) 1-1, Honduras (a) 1-1, Canada (a) 0-1, Panama (h) 3-2, Mexico (a) 1-3, Cuba (h) 3-0, Canada (h) 0-2.

Guatemala
Mexico (a) 0-1, St Vincent & the Grenadines (h) 3-0, Mexico (a) 0-1, USA (a) 0-3, Jamaica (a) 0-2, Venezuela (h) 3-0, Nicaragua (a) 1-0, Nicaragua (h) 2-1, Panama (h) 1-0, Panama (a) 0-1, Honduras (a) 1-1, Jamaica (h) 2-1, Cuba (h) 1-1, El Salvador (h) 1-2, Trinidad & Tobago (a) 1-1, USA (a) 0-2, Costa Rica (a) 0-3, Costa Rica (h) 1-0, Trinidad & Tobago (h) 2-1, USA (h) 2-2.

Honduras
Canada (a) 1-3, Brazil (h) 0-5, Colombia (a) 1-2, Nicaragua (a) 1-0, Panama (h) 1-1, Trinidad & Tobago (h) 0-0, Panama (a) 1-2, Costa Rica (h) 0-0, El Salvador (h) 2-1, Guatemala (a) 1-1, El Salvador (a) 2-1, Cuba (h) 4-0, Jamaica (a) 0-3, Mexico (h) 2-1, St Vincent & the Grenadines (a) 4-1, El Salvador (h) 1-1, Jamaica (h) 0-0, Mexico (a) 1-3, St Vincent & the Grenadines (h) 11-3, Venezuela (h) 1-0. Costa Rica (a) 1-1.

Jamaica
Guatemala (h) 2-0, Surinam (a) 1-0, Surinam (h) 1-0, Barbados (h) 2-0, Barbados (a) 0-2, Trinidad & Tobago (a) 0-1, St Kitts & Nevis (h) 4-1, Surinam (h) 1-3, Barbados (a)

Sudan
Zambia (h) 2-0, Tanzania (a) 0-0, Zambia (a) 0-3, Syria (a) 2-1, Syria (a) 0-1, Zimbabwe (h) 0-3, Uganda (h) 1-1, Tanzania (h) 3-2, Kenya (h) 1-1.

Swaziland
Mozambique (h) 0-1, Gabon (h) 0-1, Gabon (a) 0-3.

Tanzania
Zambia (a) 0-1, Ghana (h) 0-0, Sudan (h) 0-0, Ghana (a) 1-2, Malawi (a) 2-3, Malawi (a) 0-1, Zimbabwe (a) 0-1, Togo (a) 1-2, Uganda (a) 0-1, Sudan (a) 2-3.

Togo
Senegal (h) 2-1, Senegal (a) 1-1, Congo (a) 0-0, Benin (a) 2-0, Congo (h) 1-0, Tanzania (h) 2-1, Gabon (h) 0-1, Cameroon (h) 2-4.

Tunisia
Morocco (a) 1-3, Mozambique (a) 1-1, Ghana (a) 1-2, Ivory Coast (a) 3-1, Gabon (a) 1-1, Zambia (h) 4-2, South Africa (a) 0-2, Senegal (h) 2-0, Rwanda (a) 3-1, Rwanda (h) 2-0, Sierra Leone (h) 2-0, Japan (a) 0-1, Liberia (a) 1-0, Egypt (a) 1-2.

Uganda
Kenya (h) 1-1, Kenya (h) 1-2, Angola (h) 0-2, Angola (a) 1-3, Ethiopia (h) 1-1, Rwanda (a) 0-0, Ethiopia (a) 1-1, Sudan (a) 1-1, Tanzania (h) 1-0, Kenya (a) 2-0, Rwanda (h) 3-2, Rwanda (h) 1-1.

Zaire
Gabon (a) 0-2, Liberia (h) 2-0, Ghana (a) 0-1, Congo (a) 1-2, Congo (h) 3-1, Mauritius (a) 5-1, Mauritius (h) 2-0, Liberia (h) 0-0, South Africa (a) 0-1.

Zambia
Algeria (a) 0-0, Burkina Faso (a) 5-1, Sierra Leone (a) 4-0, Egypt (h) 3-1, Gabon (h) 2-4, Ghana (h) 1-0, Malawi (a) 1-0, Malawi (a) 1-1, Tanzania (h) 1-0, Sudan (a) 0-2, Sudan (h) 3-0, Oman (a) 0-0, Saudi Arabia (a) 1-2, Saudi Arabia (a) 3-1, Mozambique (h) 1-0, Congo (a) 0-1, Tunisia (a) 2-4.

Zimbabwe
Gabon (h) 1-2, Ghana (h) 1-1, Madagascar (a) 2-1, Madagascar (h) 2-2, Tanzania (h) 1-0, Sudan (a) 3-0, Angola (a) 1-2.

CONCACAF

1-0, Barbados (h) 2-0, Panama (h) 0-0, Panama (a) 0-2, Guatemala (a) 1-2, Honduras (h) 3-0, St Vincent & the Grenadines (a) 2-1, Ecuador (a) 1-2, Costa Rica (a) 0-0, Mexico (a) 1-2, Honduras (a) 0-0, St Vincent & the Grenadines (h) 5-0, Mexico (h) 1-0.

Mexico
St Vincent & the Grenadines (h) 5-0, Guatemala (a) 1-0, Guatemala (a) 1-0, Brazil (h) 2-0, Chile (a) 1-2, Yugoslavia (h) 0-0, Japan (a) 2-3, Bolivia (h) 1-0, Republic of Ireland (h) 2-2, USA (a) 2-2, St Vincent & the Grenadines (a) 3-0, Honduras (a) 1-2, Jamaica (h) 2-1, Ecuador (a) 0-1, St Vincent & the Grenadines (h) 5-1, Honduras (h) 3-1, Jamaica (a) 0-1, El Salvador (h) 3-1.

Panama
Belize (a) 2-1, Belize (h) 4-1, Venezuela (h) 0-2, Honduras (h) 1-1, Jamaica (a) 0-0, Trinidad & Tobago (h) 1-0, Guatemala (a) 0-1, Honduras (h) 2-1, Guatemala (h) 1-0, Jamaica (h) 2-0, Canada (a) 1-3, Cuba (h) 3-1, El Salvador (h) 1-1, Canada (h) 0-0, Costa Rica (a) 0-2, El Salvador (a) 2-3, Cuba (h) 3-1.

Trinidad & Tobago
Venezuela (h) 0-0, El Salvador (h) 2-3, USA (a) 2-3, Colombia (a) 0-3, Jamaica (h) 1-0, Surinam (h) 3-0, St Kitts & Nevis (h) 5-1, Martinique (h) 2-1, Cuba (h) 2-0, Dominican Republic (a) 4-1, Dominican Republic (h) 8-0, Honduras (a) 0-0, Panama (a) 0-1, Costa Rica (h) 0-1, Guatemala (a) 1-1, USA (a) 0-2, USA (h) 0-1, Guatemala (a) 1-2, Costa Rica (a) 1-2.

USA
Trinidad & Tobago (h) 3-2, El Salvador (h) 2-0, Brazil (h) 0-1, Guatemala (h) 3-0, Scotland (h) 2-1, Republic of Ireland (h) 2-1, Bolivia (h) 0-2, Mexico (h) 2-2, El Salvador (h) 3-1, Peru (a) 1-4, Guatemala (h) 2-0, Trinidad & Tobago (h) 2-0, Trinidad & Tobago (a) 1-0, Costa Rica (a) 1-2, Costa Rica (h) 2-1, Guatemala (a) 2-2.

SOUTH AMERICA

COPA LIBERTADORES 1997

First Round

Group 1

	P	W	D	L	F	A	Pts
Bolivar	6	3	1	2	15	10	10
Oriente Petrolero	6	2	2	2	9	10	8
Guarani	6	2	2	2	8	11	8
Cerro Porteno	6	2	1	3	7	8	7

Group 2

	P	W	D	L	F	A	Pts
Velez Sarsfield	6	4	1	1	10	5	13
Nacional	6	3	0	3	5	7	9
Racing	6	2	1	3	7	7	7
Emelec	6	1	1	4	7	10	4

Group 3

	P	W	D	L	F	A	Pts
Colo Colo	6	5	1	0	12	4	16
Univ Catolica	6	2	2	2	15	6	8
Minerven	6	2	1	3	3	9	7
Mineros	6	0	2	4	2	13	2

Group 4

	P	W	D	L	F	A	Pts
Gremio	6	4	0	2	10	3	12
Cruzeiro	6	3	0	3	6	5	9
Sporting Cristal	6	2	2	2	4	5	8
Alianza	6	1	2	3	2	9	5

Group 5

	P	W	D	L	F	A	Pts
Penarol	6	4	0	2	12	10	12
Millonarios	6	3	1	2	10	8	10
Nacional	6	2	1	3	6	9	7
Dep Cali	6	1	2	3	9	10	5

Second Round, First Leg
Racing 3, River Plate 3
Sporting Cristal 0, Velez Sarsfield 0
Millonarios 2, Penarol 0
Minerven 1, Bolivar 1
Guarani 2, Gremio 1
Univ Catolica 4, Oriente Petrolero 0
Nacional (Uru) 1, Colo Colo 3
Nacional (Ecu) 1, Cruzeiro 0

Second Round, Second Leg
Penarol 3, Millonarios 1
(Penarol won 3-2 on penalties)
Gremio 2, Guarani 1
(Gremio won 2-1 on penalties)
Bolivar 7, Minerven 0
River Plate 1, Racing 1
(Racing won 5-3 on penalties)
Velez Sarsfield 0, Sporting Cristal 1

Colo Colo 1, Nacional (Uru) 2
Oriente Petrolero 1, Univ Catolica 5
Cruzeiro 2, Nacional (Ecu) 1
(Cruzeiro won 5-3 on penalties)

Quarter-Finals, First Leg
Univ Catolica 2, Colo Colo 1
Bolivar 2, Sporting Cristal 1
Penarol 1, Racing 0
Cruzeiro 2, Gremio 0

Quarter-Finals, Second Leg
Sporting Cristal 3, Bolivar 0
Colo Colo 3, Univ Catolica 1
Racing 1, Penarol 0
(Racing won 3-2 on penalties)
Gremio 2, Cruzeiro 1

Competition still being played.

SOUTH AMERICAN SUPER CUP

FIRST ROUND GROUP
Argentinos Juniors 0, Boca Juniors 2
Argentinos Juniors 0, Racing 1
Boca Juniors 1, Racing 1
Boca Juniors 3, Argentinos Juniors 0
Racing 0, Boca Juniors 0
Racing 1, Argentinos Juniors 0

FIRST ROUND, FIRST LEG
River Plate 2, Nacional (Col) 2
Independiente 0, Flamengo 0
Penarol 1, Santos 2
Olimpia 2, Sao Paulo 1
Estudiantes 2, Colo Colo 4
Nacional (Uru) 1, Cruzeiro 1
Gremio 3, Velez Sarsfield 3

FIRST ROUND, SECOND LEG
Nacional (Col) 2, River Plate 1
Flamengo 1, Independiente 0
Santos 3, Penarol 0
Sao Paulo 2, Olimpia 1
Colo Colo 2, Estudiantes 1
Cruzeiro 3, Nacional (Uru) 1
Velez Sarsfield 1, Gremio 0

SECOND ROUND, FIRST LEG
Santos 2, Nacional (Col) 0
Velez Sarsfield 3, Olimpia 0
Boca Juniors 0, Cruzeiro 0
Flamengo 1, Colo Colo 1

SECOND ROUND, SECOND LEG
Nacional (Col) 3, Santos 1
(Santos won 7-6 on penalties).
Olimpia 0, Velez Sarsfield 1
Cruzeiro 1, Boca Juniors 1
(Cruzeiro won 7-6 on penalties).
Colo Colo 1, Flamengo 0

SEMI-FINALS, FIRST LEG
Cruzeiro 3, Colo Colo 2
Santos 1, Velez Sarsfield 2

SEMI-FINALS, SECOND LEG
Colo Colo 0, Cruzeiro 4
Velez Sarsfield 1, Santos 1

FINAL FIRST LEG
Cruzeiro 0, Velez Sarsfield 1

FINAL SECOND LEG
Velez Sarsfield 2, Cruzeiro 0

CONMEBOL CUP

FIRST ROUND, FIRST LEG
Cobreloa 3, Rosario Central 2
Porongos 2, River Plate 2
Bragantino 5, Palmeiras 1
Dep Tolima 1, Vasco da Gama 0
Tachira 2, Independiente Santa Fe 2
Bolivar 1, Lanus 0
Alianza 2, Emelec 1
Guarani 3, Fluminense 1

FIRST ROUND, SECOND LEG
Vasco da Gama 4, Dep Tolima 0
Emelec 2, Alianza 1
(Emelec won 4-3 on penalties).
Independiente Santa Fe 3, Tachira 0
Lanus 4, Bolivar 1
Rosario Central 4, Cobreloa 1
River Plate 6, Porongos 0
Fluminense 2, Guarani 2
Palmeiras 3, Bragantino 0

SECOND ROUND, FIRST LEG
Rosario Central 4, River Plate 0
Guarani 0, Lanus 2
Emelec 0, Vasco da Gama 2
Independiente Santa Fe 1, Bragantino 0

SECOND ROUND, SECOND LEG
River Plate 0, Rosario Central 0
Vasco da Gama 0, Emelec 1
Lanus 6, Guarani 2
Bragantino 0, Independiente Santa Fe 0

SEMI-FINALS, FIRST LEG
Lanus 3, Rosario Central 0
Vasco da Gama 2, Independiente Santa Fe 1

SEMI-FINALS, SECOND LEG
Rosario Central 1, Lanus 3
Independiente Santa Fe 1, Vasco da Gama 0
(Independiente Santa Fe won 7-6 on penalties).

FINAL, FIRST LEG
Lanus 2, Independiente Santa Fe 0

FINAL, SECOND LEG
Independiente Santa Fe 1, Lanus 0

COPA AMERICA 1997 (IN BOLIVIA)

GROUP A
Chile 0, Paraguay 1
Argentina 0, Ecuador 0
Paraguay 0, Ecuador 2
Argentina 2, Chile 0
Chile 1, Ecuador 2
Argentina 1, Paraguay 1

GROUP B
Peru 1, Uruguay 0
Bolivia 1, Venezuela 0
Bolivia 2, Peru 0
Uruguay 2, Venezuela 0
Venezuela 0, Peru 2
Bolivia 1, Uruguay 0

GROUP C
Mexico 2, Colombia 1
Brazil 5, Costa Rica 0
Colombia 4, Costa Rica 1

Brazil 3, Mexico 2
Mexico 1, Costa Rica 1
Brazil 2, Colombia 0

QUARTER-FINALS
Peru 2, Argentina 1
Bolivia 2, Colombia 1
Ecuador 1, Mexico 1
(Mexico won 5-4 on penalties)
Brazil 2, Paraguay 0

SEMI-FINALS
Bolivia 3, Mexico 1
Brazil 7, Peru 0

THIRD PLACE
Mexico 1, Peru 0

FINAL
Brazil 3, Bolivia 1

AFRICA

AFRICAN NATIONS' CUP 1998

GROUP 1
Ghana 2, Angola 1
Sudan 0, Zimbabwe 3
Zimbabwe 0, Ghana 0
Zimbabwe 1, Angola 0

GROUP 2
Algeria 4, Ivory Coast 1
Benin 1, Mali 2
Ivory Coast 1, Benin 0
Mali 1, Algeria 0
Benin 1, Algeria 1
Mali 1, Ivory Coast 2

GROUP 3
Egypt 1, Morocco 1
Ethiopia 1, Senegal 2
Senegal 2, Egypt 0
Senegal 0, Morocco 0
Ethiopia 1, Egypt 1

GROUP 4
Tunisia 2, Sierra Leone 0
Central Africa 2, Guinea 3
Guinea 1, Tunisia 0
Guinea 1, Sierra Leone 0

GROUP 5
Namibia 1, Kenya 0
Gabon 0, Cameroon 0
Kenya 1, Gabon 0
Cameroon 4, Namibia 0
Kenya 0, Cameroon 0
Namibia 1, Gabon 1

GROUP 6
Togo 2, Tanzania 1
Zaire 0, Liberia 0
Tanzania 1, Zaire 2
Liberia 1, Togo 2
Tanzania 1, Liberia 1
Togo 1, Zaire 1

GROUP 7
Mauritius 1, Malawi 2
Zambia 1, Mozambique 0
Malawi 0, Zambia 0
Mozambique 3, Mauritius 0
Malawi 2, Mozambique 0
Mauritius 0, Zambia 0

OLYMPIC FOOTBALL

Previous medallists

1896 Athens*	1 Denmark	1932 Los Angeles			1968 Mexico City	1 Hungary
	2 Greece		no tournament			2 Bulgaria
1900 Paris*	1 Great Britain	1936 Berlin	1 Italy			3 Japan
	2 France		2 Austria		1972 Munich	1 Poland
1904 St Louis**	1 Canada		3 Norway			2 Hungary
	2 USA	1948 London	1 Sweden			3 E Germany/USSR
1908 London	1 Great Britain		2 Yugoslavia		1976 Montreal	1 East Germany
	2 Denmark		3 Denmark			2 Poland
	3 Holland	1952 Helsinki	1 Hungary			3 USSR
1912 Stockholm	1 England		2 Yugoslavia		1980 Moscow	1 Czechoslovakia
	2 Denmark		3 Sweden			2 East Germany
	3 Holland	1956 Melbourne	1 USSR			3 USSR
1920 Antwerp	1 Belgium		2 Yugoslavia		1984 Los Angeles	1 France
	2 Spain		3 Bulgaria			2 Brazil
	3 Holland	1960 Rome	1 Yugoslavia			3 Yugoslavia
1924 Paris	1 Uruguay		2 Denmark		1988 Seoul	1 USSR
	2 Switzerland		3 Hungary			2 Brazil
	3 Sweden	1964 Tokyo	1 Hungary			3 West Germany
1928 Amsterdam	1 Uruguay		2 Czechoslovakia	1992 Barcelona	1 Spain
	2 Argentina		3 East Germany			2 Poland
	3 Italy					3 Ghana

* No official tournament
** No official tournament but gold medal later awarded by IOC

1996 OLYMPIC FOOTBALL TOURNAMENT

South America

GROUP A
Brazil 4, Peru 1
Bolivia 0, Uruguay 2
Brazil 3, Paraguay 1
Peru 2, Uruguay 4
Bolivia 1, Brazil 4
Paraguay 4, Peru 2
Peru 2, Bolivia 1
Uruguay 3, Paraguay 2
Paraguay 1, Bolivia 4
Uruguay 0, Brazil 0

GROUP B
Argentina 6, Ecuador 0
Venezuela 1, Colombia 0
Argentina 2, Chile 0
Ecuador 3, Colombia 3
Chile 4, Ecuador 0
Venezuela 0, Argentina 3
Colombia 3, Chile 3
Ecuador 2, Venezuela 5
Chile 0, Venezuela 0
Colombia 0, Argentina 4

FINAL ROUND
Argentina 2, Uruguay 0
Brazil 5, Venezuela 0
Argentina 2, Venezuela 0
Brazil 3, Uruguay 1
Brazil 2, Argentina 2
Uruguay 3, Venezuela 1
(Brazil and Argentina qualified)

Asia

GROUP A
Singapore 2, Malaysia 0
China 4, Singapore 0
China 2, Malaysia 1
Malaysia 0, Singapore 0
Malaysia 0, China 2
Singapore 1, China 3

GROUP B
Thailand 0, Japan 5
Japan 4, Taiwan 1
Thailand 7, Taiwan 0
Thailand 5, Taiwan 0
Japan 6, Taiwan 0
Japan 1, Thailand 0

GROUP C
Hong Kong 0, Korea Republic 5
Indonesia 1, Korea Republic 2
Indonesia 1, Hong Kong 0
Korea Republic 7, Hong Kong 0

Korea Republic 1, Indonesia 0
Hong Kong 1, Indonesia 4

GROUP D
Pakistan 0, Oman 2
Pakistan 1, India 2
Oman 3, India 2
India 3, Pakistan 1
Oman 6, Pakistan 0
India 1, Oman 2

GROUP E
Kyrgyzstan 1, Uzbekistan 5
Tajikistan 0, Kazakhstan 3
Kyrgyzstan 2, Kazakhstan 2
Uzbekistan 2, Tajikistan 0
Uzbekistan 1, Kazakhstan 2
Tajikistan 3, Kyrgyzstan 0
Kyrgyzstan 5, Tajikistan 4
Kazakhstan 3, Uzbekistan 1

GROUP F
Saudi Arabia 2, Syria 0
Kuwait 0, Saudi Arabia 1
Syria 0, Kuwait 1
Syria 0, Saudi Arabia 1
Saudi Arabia 0, Kuwait 0
Kuwait 2, Syria 2

GROUP G
Turkmenistan 2, Iran 4
UAE 2, Turkmenistan 1
Iran 1, UAE 1
Iran 4, Turkmenistan 0
Turkmenistan 1, UAE 1
UAE 1, Iran 0

GROUP H
Jordan 1, Qatar 2
Qatar 0, Iraq 0
Jordan 0, Iraq 4
Qatar 4, Jordan 2
Iraq 3, Qatar 2
Iraq 1, Jordan 1

SECOND ROUND

GROUP A
Iraq 1, Japan 1
UAE 1, Oman 3
Iraq 3, UAE 1
Japan 4, Oman 1
Iraq 1, Oman 0
Japan 1, UAE 0

GROUP B
Korea Republic 1, Saudi Arabia 1
Kazakhstan 2, China 4

China 1, Saudi Arabia 1
Kazakhstan 1, Korea Republic 2
China 0, Korea Republic 3
Kazakhstan 0, Saudi Arabia 4

SEMI-FINALS
Japan 2, Saudi Arabia 1
Korea Republic 2, Iraq 1

3RD/4TH PLACE
Saudi Arabia 1, Iraq 0

FINAL
Japan 1, Korea Republic 2
(Japan, Korea Republic and Saudi Arabia qualified)

Africa

PRELIMINARY ROUND
Lesotho 1, Namibia 0
Namibia 3, Lesotho 0
Burundi v Djibouti; Burkina Faso v Guinea Bissau; Guinea Bissau v Burkina Faso and Djibouti v Burundi abandoned.

FIRST ROUND

GROUP 1
Nigeria 0, Kenya 0
Egypt 1, Mauritius 0
Zambia 2, Botswana 0
Zimbabwe 4, Malawi 0
Kenya 0, Nigeria 3
Malawi 0, Zimbabwe 0
Botswana 1, Zambia 4
Mauritius 0, Egypt 1

GROUP 2
Algeria 1, Guinea 1
Mali 1, Togo 2
Morocco 0, Senegal 0
Tunisia 4, Burkina Faso 1
Senegal 1, Morocco 0
Guinea 2, Algeria 0
Togo 1, Mali 0
Burkina Faso 1, Tunisia 0

GROUP 3
South Africa 1, Burundi 1
Cameroon 0, Namibia 0
Gabon 1, Angola 3
Namibia 0, Cameroon 1
Angola 2, Gabon 0
Burundi 4, South Africa 1
Congo withdrew v Ghana w.o.

SECOND ROUND
Nigeria 3, Egypt 2
Senegal 2, Guinea 3
Tunisia 1, Togo 1
Burundi 1, Cameroon 0
Ghana 3, Angola 1
Zimbabwe 1, Zambia 1
Egypt 1, Nigeria 1
Angola 1, Ghana 0
Cameroon 2, Burundi 0
Guinea 2, Senegal 0
Togo 2, Tunisia 1
(Togo suspended due to fielding over aged players).
Zambia 1, Zimbabwe 2

THIRD ROUND
Ghana 3, Cameroon 0
Tunisia 5, Guinea 2
Zimbabwe 0, Nigeria 1
Cameroon 0, Ghana 0
Guinea 2, Tunisia 0

Nigeria 1, Zimbabwe 0
(Ghana, Nigeria and Tunisia qualified).

Concacaf

PRELIMINARY ROUND
Guatemala 4, Belize 0
Belize 2, Guatemala 2

FIRST ROUND
Guatemala 0, El Salvador 1
El Salvador 1, Guatemala 1
Bermuda 0, Costa Rica 2
Costa Rica 5, Bermuda 0
Panama 0, Mexico 5
Mexico 4, Panama 0

GROUP 1
Antigua 1, Cayman 2
Jamaica 6, St Lucia 0
Antigua 1, Jamaica 6
Cayman 0, St Lucia 4
Jamaica 7, Cayman 0
St Lucia 3, Antigua 0

GROUP 2
Guyana 1, St Vincent & the Grenadines 2
Trinidad & Tobago 5, Guyana 0
Trinidad & Tobago 2, St Vincent & the Grenadines 1

FINAL ROUND
Canada 3, Jamaica 0
Costa Rica 4, Trinidad & Tobago 2
Mexico 3, El Salvador 0
Canada 0, Trinidad & Tobago 0
Mexico 4, Costa Rica 0
El Salvador 3, Jamaica 1
Canada 4, El Salvador 2
Jamaica 2, Costa Rica 1
Mexico 2, Trinidad & Tobago 0
Canada 0, Costa Rica 0
Mexico 2, Jamaica 1
El Salvador 1, Trinidad & Tobago 2
Canada 0, Mexico 1
Jamaica 3, Trinidad & Tobago 2
El Salvador 1, Costa Rica 4

OCEANIA
Australia 9, Vanuatu 1
Fiji 4, Solomon Islands 0
New Zealand 1, Fiji 2
Solomon Islands 2, Vanuatu 1
Solomon Islands 0, Australia 4
Vanuatu 0, New Zealand 10
Australia 10, Fiji 0
New Zealand 2, Solomon Islands 0
Fiji 4, Vanuatu 0
New Zealand 0, Australia 5
Fiji 1, New Zealand 3
Vanuatu 1, Solomon Islands 1
Solomon Islands 1, Fiji 1
Vanuatu 0, Australia 12
Australia 7, Solomon Islands 0
New Zealand 5, Vanuatu 1
Fiji 0, Australia 5
Solomon Islands 0, New Zealand 6
Australia 0, New Zealand 1
Vanuatu 1, Fiji 0

Play-Off

CONCACAF/OCEANIA
Canada 2, Australia 2
Australia 5, Canada 0
(Australia qualified).

FINAL TOURNAMENT IN ATLANTA

GROUP A
Portugal 2, Tunisia 0
USA 1, Argentina 3
USA 2, Tunisia 0
Argentina 1, Portugal 1
Argentina 1, Tunisia 0
USA 1, Portugal 1

GROUP B
Spain 1, Saudi Arabia 0
France 2, Australia 0
Spain 1, France 1
Saudi Arabia 1, Australia 2
Spain 3, Australia 2
Saudi Arabia 1, France 2

GROUP C
Italy 0, Mexico 1
Ghana 0, Korea Republic 1
Korea Republic 0, Mexico 0
Ghana 3, Italy 2
Korea Republic 1, Italy 2
Ghana 1, Mexico 1

GROUP D
Hungary 0, Nigeria 1
Brazil 0, Japan 1
Japan 0, Nigeria 2
Brazil 3, Hungary 1
Japan 3, Hungary 2
Brazil 1, Nigeria 0

QUARTER-FINALS
Argentina 4, Spain 0
France 1, Portugal 1
(Portugal won on sudden death).
Mexico 0, Nigeria 2
Brazil 4, Ghana 2

SEMI-FINALS
Argentina 2, Portugal 0
Nigeria 3, Brazil 3
(Nigeria won on sudden death).

3RD/4TH PLACE
Portugal 0, Brazil 5

FINAL
Argentina 2, Nigeria 3

UEFA UNDER-21 CHAMPIONSHIP 1996–98

GROUP 1
Greece 0, Slovenia 2
Greece 3, Bosnia 0
Slovenia 0, Denmark 3
Denmark 1, Greece 3
Slovenia 2, Bosnia 0
Bosnia 3, Croatia 1
Croatia 0, Greece 1
Croatia 2, Denmark 0
Bosnia 0, Greece 0
Croatia 2, Slovenia 0
Denmark 2, Slovenia 1
Greece 2, Croatia 0
Denmark 5, Bosnia 0

GROUP 2
Moldova 0, England 2
Moldova 0, Italy 3
England 0, Poland 0
Georgia 0, England 1
Italy 6, Georgia 0
Poland 1, Moldova 3
England 1, Italy 0
Italy 6, Moldova 0
Poland 1, Italy 1
England 0, Georgia 0
Italy 1, Poland 1
Poland 1, England 1
Georgia 1, Moldova 0
Poland 2, Georgia 2

GROUP 3
France 1, Switzerland 0
Finland 1, Switzerland 1
France 2, Hungary 0
Switzerland 3, Norway 7
Norway 4, Hungary 1
Norway 1, France 1
Hungary 0, Finland 1
Norway 3, Finland 0
Switzerland 4, Hungary 1
France 2, Finland 1
Finland 1, France 1
Hungary 2, Norway 0

GROUP 4
Austria 4, Scotland 0
Estonia 1, Belarus 1
Latvia 0, Scotland 0
Belarus 2, Latvia 0

Sweden 1, Belarus 3
Belarus 3, Estonia 1
Sweden 4, Austria 1
Estonia 0, Scotland 1
Latvia 0, Sweden 2
Austria 0, Latvia 0
Scotland 1, Sweden 4
Scotland 4, Estonia 0
Scotland 1, Austria 2
Austria 7, Estonia 1
Sweden 2, Scotland 1
Latvia 0, Belarus 3
Estonia 0, Sweden 2
Latvia 1, Austria 3
Belarus 1, Scotland 0
Estonia 0, Latvia 1

GROUP 5
Israel 2, Bulgaria 0
Russia 2, Cyprus 1
Cyprus 1, Israel 1
Luxembourg 0, Bulgaria 4
Israel 1, Russia 0
Luxembourg 1, Russia 7
Cyprus 3, Bulgaria 0
Israel 2, Luxembourg 1
Cyprus 0, Russia 4
Luxembourg 0, Israel 5
Bulgaria 3, Cyprus 1
Russia 8, Luxembourg 0
Israel 4, Cyprus 3
Bulgaria 3, Luxembourg 0
Russia 1, Israel 1

GROUP 6
Czech Repblic 4, Malta 0
Yugoslavia 1, Malta 0
Slovakia 3, Malta 0
Czech Republic 1, Spain 2
Yugoslavia 3, Czech Republic 0
Spain 1, Slovakia 1
Spain 1, Yugoslavia 0
Malta 0, Spain 3
Spain 1, Malta 0
Malta 0, Slovakia 6
Czech Republic 0, Yugoslavia 1
Yugoslavia 1, Spain 2
Spain 4, Czech Republic 0
Yugoslavia 1, Slovakia 0

GROUP 7
Wales 4, San Marino 0
Wales 0, Holland 2
San Marino 0, Wales 3
Belgium 1, Turkey 2
San Marino 1, Belgium 5
Turkey 3, San Marino 0
Holland 0, Wales 1
Turkey 0, Holland 1
Holland 6, San Marino 0
Wales 0, Turkey 3
Belgium 2, Holland 2
Wales 1, Belgium 0
Turkey 1, Belgium 2
San Marino 0, Holland 7
Belgium 3, San Marino 0

GROUP 8
Republic of Ireland 0, Iceland 1
Lithuania 0, Iceland 3
Iceland 2, Macedonia 0
Romania 2, Lithuania 1
Republic of Ireland 4, Macedonia 0
Iceland 2, Romania 3
Macedonia 0, Romania 1
Lithuania 1, Romania 2
Macedonia 0, Republic of Ireland 4
Romania 1, Republic of Ireland 0
Macedonia 1, Iceland 1
Iceland 0, Lithuania 2

GROUP 9
Albania 3, Armenia 2
Ukraine 1, Portugal 0
Armenia 3, Portugal 4
Portugal 1, Ukraine 0
Albania 2, Portugal 4
Armenia 0, Germany 1
Portugal 1, Germany 2
Albania 0, Ukraine 3
Albania 0, Germany 4
Ukraine 7, Armenia 0
Germany 2, Ukraine 0
Portugal 1, Albania 1
Ukraine 1, Germany 1

13th EUROPEAN UNDER-18 YOUTH CHAMPIONSHIP

(Finals in France)

GROUP A
France 2, Hungary 1
Belgium 2, Portugal 2
France 1, Portugal 0
Belgium 2, Hungary 1
France 1, Belgium 1
Portugal 3, Hungary 0

GROUP B
England 0, Spain 0
Italy 1, Republic of Ireland 1
Italy 1, England 1
Republic of Ireland 0, Spain 0
England 1, Republic of Ireland 0
Spain 3, Italy 0

3RD/4TH PLACE
England 2, Belgium 2
(England won on sudden death).

FINAL
France 1, Spain 0

WORLD YOUTH UNDER-20 CHAMPIONSHIP

UEFA (as Under-18's)

GROUP A
Belgium 2, Portugal 2
Hungary 1, France 2
Belgium 2, Hungary 1
Portugal 0, France 1
France 1, Belgium 1
Portugal 0, Hungary 3

GROUP B
England 0, Spain 0
Italy 1, Republic of Ireland 1
Republic of Ireland 0, Spain 0
Italy 1, England 1
Republic of Ireland 0, England 1
Spain 3, Italy 0

3RD/4TH PLACE
Belgium 2, England 2
(England won on sudden death).

FINAL
France 1, Spain 0

Africa

GROUP A
Morocco 0, Egypt 0
Sudan 0, Ghana 4
Egypt 0, Ghana 1
Morocco 2, Sudan 0
Egypt 2, Sudan 1
Ghana 1, Morocco 0

GROUP B
Mali 2, Zambia 2
South Africa 0, Ivory Coast 1
Mali 1, South Africa 2
Zambia 1, Ivory Coast 1
Ivory Coast 4, Mali 1
South Africa 2, Zambia 1

SEMI-FINALS
Ghana 1, South Africa 1
(South Africa won 4-3 on penalties).
Ivory Coast 1, Morocco 2

3RD/4TH PLACE
Ghana 0, Ivory Coast 2

FINAL
Morocco 1, South Africa 0

South America

GROUP A
Chile 3, Peru 1
Venezuela 2, Brazil 10
Chile 3, Venezuela 4
Ecuador 1, Brazil 2
Brazil 2, Peru 0

Venezuela 1, Ecuador 0
Chile 1, Ecuador 0
Peru 2, Venezuela 2
Chile 1, Brazil 3
Peru 0, Ecuador 0

GROUP B
Argentina 5, Paraguay 2
Bolivia 3, Colombia 4
Argentina 1, Colombia 1
Uruguay 3, Paraguay 1
Argentina 2, Bolivia 1
Uruguay 1, Colombia 1
Colombia 0, Paraguay 3
Uruguay 2, Bolivia 1
Argentina 0, Uruguay 1
Paraguay 2, Bolivia 0

FINAL
Brazil 3, Paraguay 0
Uruguay 2, Chile 2
Venezuela 0, Argentina 3
Brazil 4, Chile 2
Uruguay 1, Argentina 1
Venezuela 1, Paraguay 2
Brazil 0, Argentina 2
Chile 0, Paraguay 0
Uruguay 3, Venezuela 0
Argentina 3, Chile 0
Brazil 2, Venezuela 2
Uruguay 1, Paraguay 2
Argentina 1, Paraguay 1
Brazil 0, Uruguay 0
Venezuela 4, Chile 1

Asia

GROUP A
Bangladesh 1, UAE 6
Korea Republic 4, Thailand 0
Iran 0, Thailand 0
Korea Republic 3, UAE 0
Iran 0, Bangladesh 0
Thailand 2, UAE 3
Iran 0, UAE 0
Korea Republic 5, Bangladesh 2
Iran 1, Korea Republic 2
Thailand 1, Bangladesh 0

GROUP B
India 1, Qatar 1
Syria 1, Japan 3
China 2, Japan 1
Syria 2, Qatar 0
China 2, India 1
Japan 4, Qatar 0
China 5, Qatar 2
Syria 1, India 0
China 2, Syria 1
Japan 2, India 0

SEMI-FINALS
Korea Republic 1, Japan 0
China 5, UAE 1

3RD/4TH PLACE
Japan 2, UAE 2
(UAE won 4-3 on penalty kicks).

FINAL
Korea Republic 3, China 0

Oceania

Australia 10, Fiji 0
Tahiti 0, New Zealand 5
Australia 3, New Zealand 0
Tahiti 2, Fiji 4
New Zealand 3, Fiji 1
Tahiti 0, Australia 10

3RD/4TH PLACE
Tahiti 1, Fiji 1
(Fiji won 5-4 on penalties).

FINAL
Australia 2, New Zealand 1

Concacaf

GROUP 1
Mexico 4, Netherlands Antilles 0
El Salvador 2, Guatemala 3
Mexico 1, Guatemala 0
Netherlands Antilles 1, El Salvador 1
Guatemala 0, Netherlands Antilles 0
Mexico 2, El Salvador 0

GROUP 2
Honduras 3, Martinique 0
USA 4, Jamaica 1
Jamaica 1, Honduras 0
Martinique 0, USA 2
USA 0, Honduras 0
Martinique 0, Jamaica 3

GROUP 3
Costa Rica 3, Nicaragua 0
Trinidad & Tobago 0, Canada 1
Costa Rica 5, Trinidad & Tobago 0
Nicaragua 0, Canada 3
Canada 2, Costa Rica 0
Trinidad & Tobago 6, Nicaragua 1

CHAMPIONSHIP ROUND
Mexico 2, Canada 2
USA 0, Canada 2
Mexico 2, USA 1

QUALIFICATION ROUND
Guatemala 1, Costa Rica 2
Jamaica 1, Costa Rica 2
Guatemala 0, Jamaica 0

FINALS

GROUP A
Malaysia 1, Morocco 3
Uruguay 3, Belgium 0
Malaysia 1, Uruguay 3
Morocco 1, Belgium 1
Malaysia 0, Belgium 3
Morocco 0, Uruguay 0

GROUP B
Korea Republic 0, South Africa 0
Brazil 3, France 0
France 4, Korea Republic 2
Brazil 2, South Africa 0
Brazil 10, Korea Republic 3
France 4, South Africa 2

GROUP C
Ghana 2, Republic of Ireland 1
USA 1, China 0
Ghana 1, China 1
Republic of Ireland 2, USA 1
Ghana 1, USA 0
Republic of Ireland 1, China 1

GROUP D
Spain 3, Japan 1
Costa Rica 1, Paraguay 1
Japan 6, Costa Rica 2
Spain 2, Paraguay 1
Japan 3, Paraguay 3
Spain 4, Costa Rica 0

GROUP E
Argentina 3, Hungary 0
Australia 0, Canada 0
Australia 1, Hungary 0
Argentina 2, Canada 1
Canada 2, Hungary 1
Australia 4, Argentina 3

GROUP F
Mexico 5, UAE 0
England 2, Ivory Coast 1
Mexico 1, Ivory Coast 1
England 5, UAE 0
England 1, Mexico 0
UAE 2, Ivory Coast 0

SECOND ROUND
Uruguay 3, USA 0
Republic of Ireland 2, Morocco 1
Brazil 10, Belgium 0
France 1, Mexico 0
Ghana 3, UAE 0
Spain 2, Canada 0
Japan 1, Australia 0
Argentina 2, England 1

QUARTER-FINALS
Uruguay 1, France 1
(Uruguay won 7-6 on penalties)
Republic of Ireland 1, Spain 0
Argentina 2, Brazil 0
Ghana 2, Japan 1

SEMI-FINALS
Uruguay 2, Ghana 2
(Uruguay won on sudden death)
Argentina 1, Republic of Ireland 0

THIRD PLACE
Republic of Ireland 2, Ghana 1

FINAL
Argentina 2, Uruguay 1

7th WORLD UNDER-17 CHAMPIONSHIP

South America

GROUP A
Paraguay 1, Peru 0
Venezuela 2, Ecuador 0
Argentina 6, Venezuela 0
Paraguay 1, Ecuador 2
Ecuador 2, Argentina 3
Peru 0, Venezuela 1
Argentina 2, Peru 0
Paraguay 3, Venezuela 0
Ecuador 2, Peru 2
Paraguay 2, Argentina 0

GROUP B
Bolivia 0, Colombia 2
Brazil 1, Chile 1
Brazil 4, Bolivia 0
Uruguay 1, Chile 0
Bolivia 1, Chile 7
Uruguay 0, Colombia 2
Brazil 1, Colombia 1
Uruguay 2, Bolivia 0
Brazil 2, Uruguay 1
Chile 1, Colombia 0

FINAL ROUND
Argentina 3, Chile 0
Brazil 5, Paraguay 0
Argentina 0, Paraguay 0
Brazil 5, Chile 3
Argentina 1, Brazil 2
Paraguay 1, Chile 2

Oceania

GROUP 1
Australia 14, Cook Islands 0
Tahiti 1, Fiji 2
Australia 7, Tahiti 0
Fiji 3, Cook Islands 0
Fiji 0, Australia 5
Cook Islands 0, Tahiti 9

GROUP 2
New Zealand 8, Vanuatu 1
Solomon Islands 4, Western Samoa 0
New Zealand 3, Solomon Islands 0
Western Samoa 0, Vanuatu 6
Western Samoa 0, New Zealand 1
Vanuatu 1, Solomon Islands 2

SEMI-FINALS
Australia 4, Solomon Islands 0
New Zealand 2, Fiji 0

3RD/4TH PLACE
Fiji 0, Solomon Islands 3

FINAL
New Zealand 1, Australia 0

Asia

GROUP A
Japan 2, Oman 2
Kuwait 1, Korea Republic 3
Japan 3, Korea Republic 2
Uzbekistan 1, Oman 6
Oman 3, Korea Republic 1
Uzbekistan 0, Kuwait 2
Japan 5, Kuwait 2
Uzbekistan 1, Korea Republic 1
Oman 1, Kuwait 0
Uzbekistan 0, Japan 3

GROUP B
China 2, Iran 0
Thailand 7, India 0
Bahrain 3, India 2
Thailand 3, Iran 0
Bahrain 6, China 0
India 1, Iran 4
Bahrain 2, Thailand 4
India 3, China 2
Bahrain 2, Iran 1
Thailand 1, China 1

SEMI-FINALS
Oman 1, Bahrain 0
Thailand 1, Japan 0

3RD/4TH PLACE
Bahrain 0, Japan 0
(Bahrain won 4-1 on penalties).

FINAL
Oman 1, Thailand 0

Concacaf

GROUP 1
Bermuda 0, USA 5
Dominican Republic 1, Costa Rica 2
Bermuda 1, Costa Rica 8
USA 3, Dominican Republic 0
USA 2, Costa Rica 3
Bermuda v Dominican Republic not played.

GROUP 2
Guatemala 3, Martinique 0
Mexico 3, Honduras 0
Guatemala 1, Honduras 0
Mexico 7, Martinique 0
Mexico 5, Guatemala 1
Honduras v Martinique not played.

GROUP 3
Netherlands Antilles 0, Trinidad & Tobago 5
El Salvador 0, Canada 2
Canada 3, Netherlands Antilles 1
Trinidad & Tobago 1, El Salvador 1
El Salvador 5, Ntherlands Antilles 1
Trinidad & Tobago 1, Canada 1

FINAL ROUND
Canada 1, Costa Rica 3
Mexico 3, USA 1
Costa Rica 0, Mexico 4
USA 2, Canada 0
Canada 0, Mexico 1
USA 1, Costa Rica 1

15th UEFA UNDER-16 CHAMPIONSHIP

(in Germany)

GROUP A
Germany 3, Israel 0
Switzerland 2, Northern Ireland 1
Germany 2, Switzerland 0
Israel 1, Northern Ireland 2
Germany 1, Northern Ireland 0
Israel 2, Switzerland 3

GROUP B
Poland 0, Austria 4
Spain 6, Ukraine 1
Poland 1, Spain 2
Austria 0, Ukraine 2
Ukraine 2, Poland 3
Austria 0, Spain 2

GROUP C
Hungary 6, Georgia 3

Belgium 1, Italy 0
Hungary 0, Belgium 1
Georgia 3, Italy 5
Italy 1, Hungary 2
Georgia 1, Belgium 5

GROUP D
Turkey 2, Slovenia 0
Slovakia 1, Iceland 0
Turkey 1, Slovakia 0
Slovenia 0, Iceland 2
Iceland 0, Turkey 4
Slovenia 2, Slovakia 2

QUARTER FINALS
Germany 3, Hungary 1
Belgium 0, Switzerland 0

(Switzerland won 5-4 on penalties).
Spain 3, Slovakia 1
Turkey 0, Austria 3

SEMI FINALS
Germany 1, Spain 2
Switzerland 0, Austria 0
(Austria won 6-5 on penalties).

3RD/4TH PLACE
Germany 3, Switzerland 1

FINAL
Spain 0, Austria 0
(Spain won 5-4 on penalties)

ENGLAND UNDER-21 RESULTS 1976–97

EC UEFA Competition for Under-21 Teams

v ALBANIA

Year	Date		Venue	Eng	Alb
EC1989	Mar	7	Shkroda	2	1
EC1989	April	25	Ipswich	2	0

v ANGOLA

Year	Date		Venue	Eng	Ang
1995	June	10	Toulon	1	0
1996	May	28	Toulon	0	2

v AUSTRIA

Year	Date		Venue	Eng	Aus
1994	Oct	11	Kapfenberg	3	1
1995	Nov	14	Middlesbrough	2	1

v BELGIUM

Year	Date		Venue	Eng	Bel
1994	June	5	Marseille	2	1
1996	May	24	Toulon	1	0

v BRAZIL

Year	Date		Venue	Eng	B
1993	June	11	Toulon	0	0
1995	June	6	Toulon	0	2
1996	June	1	Toulon	1	2

v BULGARIA

Year	Date		Venue	Eng	Bul
EC1979	June	5	Pernik	3	1
EC1979	Nov	20	Leicester	5	0
1989	June	5	Toulon	2	3

v CROATIA

Year	Date		Venue	Eng	Cro
1996	Apr	23	Sunderland	0	1

v CZECHOSLOVAKIA

Year	Date		Venue	Eng	Cz
1990	May	28	Toulon	2	1
1992	May	26	Toulon	1	2
1993	June	9	Toulon	1	1

v DENMARK

Year	Date		Venue	Eng	Den
EC1978	Sept	19	Hvidovre	2	1
EC1979	Sept	11	Watford	1	0
EC1982	Sept	21	Hvidovre	4	1
EC1983	Sept	20	Norwich	4	1
EC1986	Mar	12	Copenhagen	1	0
EC1986	Mar	26	Manchester	1	1
1988	Sept	13	Watford	0	0
1994	Mar	8	Brentford	1	0

v EAST GERMANY

Year	Date		Venue	Eng	EG
EC1980	April	16	Sheffield	1	2
EC1980	April	23	Jena	0	1

v FINLAND

Year	Date		Venue	Eng	Fin
EC1977	May	26	Helsinki	1	0
EC1977	Oct	12	Hull	8	1
EC1984	Oct	16	Southampton	2	0
EC1985	May	21	Mikkeli	1	3

v FRANCE

Year	Date		Venue	Eng	Fra
EC1984	Feb	28	Sheffield	6	1
EC1984	Mar	28	Rouen	1	0
1987	June	11	Toulon	0	2
EC1988	April	13	Besancon	2	4
EC1988	April	27	Highbury	2	2
1988	June	12	Toulon	2	4
1990	May	23	Toulon	7	3
1991	June	3	Toulon	1	0
1992	May	28	Toulon	0	0
1993	June	15	Toulon	1	0
1994	May	31	Aubagne	0	3
1994	Sept	6	Leicester	0	0
1995	June	10	Toulon	0	2

v GEORGIA

Year	Date		Venue	Eng	Geo
EC1996	Nov	8	Batumi	1	0
EC1997	April	29	Charlton	0	0

v GERMANY

Year	Date		Venue	Eng	Ger
1991	Sept	10	Scunthorpe	2	1

v GREECE

Year	Date		Venue	Eng	Gre
EC1982	Nov	16	Piraeus	0	1
EC1983	Mar	29	Portsmouth	2	1
1989	Feb	7	Patras	0	1

v HOLLAND

Year	Date		Venue	Eng	H
EC1993	April	27	Portsmouth	3	0
EC1993	Oct	12	Utrecht	1	1

v HUNGARY

Year	Date		Venue	Eng	Hun
EC1981	June	5	Keszthely	2	1
EC1981	Nov	17	Nottingham	2	0
EC1983	April	26	Newcastle	1	0
EC1983	Oct	11	Nyiregyhaza	2	0
1990	Sept	11	Southampton	3	1
1992	May	12	Budapest	2	2

v ITALY

Year	Date		Venue	Eng	Italy
EC1978	Mar	8	Manchester	2	1
EC1978	April	5	Rome	0	0
EC1984	April	18	Manchester	3	1
EC1984	May	2	Florence	0	1
EC1986	April	9	Pisa	0	2
EC1986	April	23	Swindon	1	1
EC1997	Feb	12	Bristol	1	0

v ISRAEL

Year	Date		Venue	Eng	Isr
1985	Feb	27	Tel Aviv	2	1

v LATVIA

Year	Date		Venue	Eng	Lat
1995	April	25	Riga	1	0
1995	June	7	Burnley	4	0

v MALAYSIA

Year	Date		Venue	Eng	Mal
1995	June	8	Toulon	2	0

v MEXICO

Year	Date		Venue	Eng	Mex
1988	June	5	Toulon	2	1
1991	May	29	Toulon	6	0
1992	May	25	Toulon	1	1

v MOLDOVA

Year	Date		Venue	Eng	Mol
EC1996	Aug	31	Chisinau	2	0

v MOROCCO

Year	Date		Venue	Eng	Mor
1987	June	7	Toulon	2	0
1988	June	9	Toulon	1	0

v NORWAY

Year	Date		Venue	Eng	Nor
EC1977	June	1	Bergen	2	1
EC1977	Sept	6	Brighton	6	0
1980	Sept	9	Southampton	3	0
1981	Sept	8	Drammen	0	0
EC1992	Oct	13	Peterborough	0	2
EC1993	June	1	Stavanger	1	1
1995	Oct	10	Stavanger	2	2

v POLAND

Year	Date		Venue	Eng	Pol
EC1982	Mar	17	Warsaw	2	1
EC1982	April	7	West Ham	2	2
EC1989	June	2	Plymouth	2	1
EC1989	Oct	10	Jastrzebie	3	1
EC1990	Oct	16	Tottenham	0	1
EC1993	May	28	Zdroj	4	1
EC1993	Sept	7	Millwall	1	2
EC1996	Oct	8	Wolverhampton	0	0
EC1997	May	30	Katowice	1	1

v PORTUGAL

Year	Date		Venue	Eng	Por
1987	June	13	Toulon	0	0
1990	May	21	Toulon	0	1
1993	June	7	Toulon	2	0
1994	June	7	Toulon	2	0
1995	Sept	2	Lisbon	0	2
1996	May	30	Toulon	1	3

v REPUBLIC OF IRELAND

Year	Date		Venue	Eng	RoI
1981	Feb	25	Liverpool	1	0
1985	Mar	25	Portsmouth	3	2
1989	June	9	Toulon	0	0
EC1990	Nov	13	Cork	3	0
EC1991	Mar	26	Brentford	3	0
1994	Nov	15	Newcastle	1	0
1995	Mar	27	Dublin	2	0

v ROMANIA

Year	Date		Venue	Eng	Rom
EC1980	Oct	14	Ploesti	0	4
EC1981	April	28	Swindon	3	0
EC1985	April	30	Brasov	0	0
EC1985	Sept	10	Ipswich	3	0

v RUSSIA

Year	Date		Venue	Eng	Rus
1994	May	30	Bandol	2	0

v SAN MARINO

Year	Date		Venue	Eng	SM
EC1993	Feb	16	Luton	6	0
EC1993	Nov	17	San Marino	4	0

v SENEGAL

Year	Date		Venue	Eng	Sen
1989	June	7	Toulon	6	1
1991	May	27	Toulon	2	1

			v SCOTLAND	Eng	Sco
1977	April	27	Sheffield	1	0
EC1980	Feb	12	Coventry	2	1
EC1980	Mar	4	Aberdeen	0	0
EC1982	April	19	Glasgow	1	0
EC1982	April	28	Manchester	1	1
				Eng	Sco
EC1988	Feb	16	Aberdeen	1	0
EC1988	Mar	22	Nottingham	1	0
1993	June	13	Toulon	1	0

			v SPAIN	Eng	Spa
EC1984	May	17	Seville	1	0
EC1984	May	24	Sheffield	2	0
1987	Feb	18	Burgos	2	1
1992	Sept	8	Burgos	1	0

			v SWEDEN	Eng	Swe
1979	June	9	Vasteras	2	1
1986	Sept	9	Ostersund	1	1
EC1988	Oct	18	Coventry	1	1
EC1989	Sept	5	Uppsala	0	1

			v SWITZERLAND	Eng	Swit
EC1980	Nov	18	Ipswich	5	0
EC1981	May	31	Neuenburg	0	0
1988	May	28	Lausanne	1	1
1996	April	1	Swindon	0	0

			v USA	Eng	USA
1989	June	11	Toulon	0	2
1994	June	2	Toulon	3	0

			v TURKEY	Eng	Tur
EC1984	Nov	13	Bursa	0	0
EC1985	Oct	15	Bristol	3	0
				Eng	Tur
EC1987	April	28	Izmir	0	0
EC1987	Oct	13	Sheffield	1	1
EC1991	April	30	Izmir	2	2
1991	Oct	15	Reading	2	0
EC1992	Nov	17	Orient	0	1
EC1993	Mar	30	Izmir	0	0

			v USSR	Eng	USSR
1987	June	9	Toulon	0	0
1988	June	7	Toulon	1	0
1990	May	25	Toulon	2	1
1991	May	31	Toulon	2	1

			v WALES	Eng	Wales
1976	Dec	15	Wolverhampton	0	0
1979	Feb	6	Swansea	1	0
1990	Dec	5	Tranmere	0	0

			v WEST GERMANY	Eng	WG
EC1982	Sept	21	Sheffield	3	1
EC1982	Oct	12	Bremen	2	3
1987	Sept	8	Ludenscheid	0	2

			v YUGOSLAVIA	Eng	Yugo
EC1978	April	19	Novi Sad	1	2
EC1978	May	2	Manchester	1	1
EC1986	Nov	11	Peterborough	1	1
EC1987	Nov	10	Zemun	5	1

ENGLAND B RESULTS 1949–97

Year	Date		Venue		
			v ALGERIA	Eng	Alg
1990	Dec	11	Algiers	0	0
			v AUSTRALIA	Eng	Aust
1980	Nov	17	Birmingham	1	0
			v AUSTRIA	Eng	Aus
1979†	June	12	Klagenfurt	1	0

†Abandoned 60 mins; waterlogged pitch.

			v CIS	Eng	CIS
1992	April	28	Moscow	1	1
			v CZECHOSLOVAKIA	Eng	Cz
1978	Nov	28	Prague	1	0
1990	April	24	Sunderland	2	0
1992	Mar	24	Budejovice	1	0
			v FINLAND	Eng	Fin
1949	May	15	Helsinki	4	0
			v FRANCE	Eng	Fra
1952	May	22	Le Havre	1	7
1992	Feb	18	Loftus Road	3	0
			v WEST GERMANY	Eng	WG
1954	Mar	24	Gelsenkirchen	4	0
1955	Mar	23	Sheffield	1	1
1978	Feb	21	Augsburg	2	1
			v HOLLAND	Eng	Hol
1949	May	18	Amsterdam	4	0
1950	Feb	22	Newcastle	1	0
1952	Mar	26	Amsterdam	1	0
			v ICELAND	Eng	Ice
1989	May	19	Reykjavik	2	0
1991	April	27	Watford	1	0
			v ITALY	Eng	Italy
1950	May	11	Milan	0	5
1989	Nov	14	Brighton	1	1
			v LUXEMBOURG	Eng	Lux
1950	May	21	Luxembourg	2	1
			v MALAYSIA	Eng	Mal
1978	May	30	Kuala Lumpur	1	1
			v MALTA	Eng	Mal
1987	Oct	14	Ta'Qali	2	0

			v NEW ZEALAND	Eng	NZ
1978	June	7	Christchurch	4	0
1978	June	11	Wellington	3	1
1978	June	14	Auckland	4	0
1979	Oct	15	Leyton	4	1
1984	Nov	13	Nottingham	2	0
			v NORTHERN IRELAND	Eng	NI
1994	May	10	Sheffield	4	2
			v NORWAY	Eng	Nor
1989	May	22	Stavanger	1	0
			v REPUBLIC OF IRELAND	Eng	RoI
1990	Mar	27	Cork	1	4
1994	Dec	13	Liverpool	2	0
			v SCOTLAND	Eng	Sco
1953	Mar	11	Edinburgh	2	2
1954	Mar	3	Sunderland	1	1
1956	Feb	29	Dundee	2	2
1957	Feb	6	Birmingham	4	1
			v SINGAPORE	Eng	Sin
1978	June	18	Singapore	8	0
			v SPAIN	Eng	Sp
1980	Mar	26	Sunderland	1	0
1981	Mar	25	Granada	2	3
1991*	Dec	18	Castellon	1	0

*Spanish Olympic XI

			v SWITZERLAND	Eng	Swit
1950	Jan	18	Sheffield	5	0
1954	May	22	Basle	0	2
1956	Mar	21	Southampton	4	1
1989	May	16	Winterthur	2	0
1991	May	20	Walsall	2	1
			v USA	Eng	USA
1980	Oct	14	Manchester	1	0
			v WALES	Eng	Wales
1991	Feb	5	Swansea	1	0
			v YUGOSLAVIA	Eng	Yugo
1954	May	16	Ljubljana	1	2
1955	Oct	19	Manchester	5	1
1989	Dec	12	Millwall	2	1

BRITISH AND IRISH UNDER-21 TEAMS
1996–97

ENGLAND UNDER-21 INTERNATIONALS

31 Aug
Moldova (0) 0
England (1) 2 *(Dyer 39, Eadie 53)*   850
England: Day; Scimeca, Thatcher, Duberry, Potter, Newton, Ford, Holland, Dyer, Eadie (Moore 70), Bowyer.

8 Oct
England (0) 0
Poland (0) 0   3183
England: Marshall; Scimeca, Thatcher, Duberry, Hall, Holland (Morris 72), Butt, Scowcroft, Humphreys (Thompson 46), Newton, Heskey (Branch 72).

8 Nov
Georgia (0) 0
England (0) 1 *(Duberry 81)*   4000
England: Day; Scimeca, Neville P, Duberry, Thompson, Butt, Scowcroft, Dyer, Newton (Rose 69), Eadie (Humphreys 87).

12 Feb
England (0) 1 *(Eadie 50)*
Italy (0) 0   13,850
England: Marshall; Scimeca, Hall, Rose, Rufus, Carbon, Murray, Hughes, Heskey (Scowcroft 89), Eadie (Huckerby 60), Bowyer (Carragher 16).

1 Apr
England (0) 0
Switzerland (0) 0   10,167
England: Day (Roberts 62); Broomes, Hall, Ferdinand (Morris 55), Carbon (Briscoe 46), Holland, Carragher, Hughes, Huckerby (Moore 84), Humphreys (Bridges 67), Bowyer.

29 Apr
England (0) 0
Georgia (0) 0   12,714
England: Wright; Oakley, Hall, Broomes (Granville 46), Ferdinand, Carragher, Scowcroft, Hughes, Heskey (Huckerby 46), Eadie (Morris 68), Bowyer.

30 May
Poland (0) 1 *(Dubicki 66)*
England (1) 1 *(Heskey 35)*   2000
England: Wright; Hamilton, Granville, Moses, Hall, Carragher, Murray, Quashie, Heskey (Huckerby 67), Hughes, Bradbury.

SCOTLAND UNDER-21 INTERNATIONALS

30 Aug
Austria (3) 4 *(Brenner 5, Stieglmair 42, Brunmayr 43, 56)*
Scotland (0) 0   800
Scotland: Meldrum; Browne, McConnell (McMillan 46), Ritchie, Shields, Miller, Glass, Bonar, Thomas (Hartley 46), Hamilton (Gillies 58), Harper.

6 Oct
Latvia (0) 0
Scotland (0) 0   500
Scotland: Meldrum; Shields, Dods, Rowson, Naysmith, Ritchie, Harper (Teale 78), Miller, Gillies (McCulloch 67), Hamilton, Bonar (Anthony 46).

8 Oct
Estonia (0) 0
Scotland (1) 1 *(Hamilton 31)*   500
Scotland: Meldrum; McCluskey, Dods, Ritchie, Naysmith, Miller (Bonar 39), Rowson, Gillies (Hetherston 78), Teale, Hamilton (Anthony 51), McCulloch.

9 Nov
Scotland (1) 1 *(Johannesson 40 (og))*
Sweden (0) 4 *(Pettersson 49, Lantz 55, 69, Ljungberg 77)*
                                                           3878
Scotland: Meldrum; Jupp, Dods, Ritchie, Naysmith, Gillies, Boyack, Rowson, Bonar (McCulloch 61), Hamilton, Harper.

28 Mar
Scotland (2) 4 *(Harper 23, Glass 35, Hamilton 47, Anderson R 70)*
Estonia (0) 0   3223
Scotland: McKenzie; McCluskey, Locke, Ritchie, Anderson R, Bagan (McCulloch 67), Gillies, Burke, Glass (Naysmith 76), Harper (Young 58), Hamilton.

1 Apr
Scotland (0) 1 *(Hamilton 64)*
Austria (2) 2 *(Aukhauser 32, McCluskey 41 (og))*   4079
Scotland: Meldrum; Anderson R, McCluskey, Ritchie (Bagan 79), Naysmith, Gillies, Locke, Glass, Harper (McCulloch 46), Hamilton, Burke (McMillan 46).

29 Apr
Sweden (1) 2 *(Mellberg 38, Jonsson 86)*
Scotland (1) 1 *(Hamilton 18)*   2200
Scotland: Germaine; Anderson R, Davidson, Buchan, Dods, McCluskey, Young (Bagan 57), McCulloch (O'Neill 67), Hamilton, Rowson, McMillan.

25 May
Colombia (0) 2 *(Quinones, Victoria)*
Scotland (0) 0
Scotland: Mathieson; McEwan (Anderson I), McCluskey, Buchan, Naysmith, Young (Ferguson), Brebner, Easton, Paterson, McFarlane (McCulloch), Anthony.

27 May
Scotland (1) 1 *(McGarry)*
USA (1) 1 *(Wolff)*
Scotland: Scrimgour; Whiteford (McEwan 50), McCluskey, Horn, Naysmith, Anderson I, Ferguson, Easton, Paterson (Brebner 87), McGarry, Thompson (McFarlane 70).

29 May
Scotland (0) 0
Czech Republic (0) 0
Scotland: Scrimgour; McCluskey (McEwan 50), Horn, Buchan, Naysmith, Anderson I (Young 89), Ferguson, Easton, Paterson (Brebner 82), McGarry, Thompson.

31 May
Scotland (0) 1 *(Brebner)*
Portugal (0) 1 *(Ramos)*
Scotland: Alexander; McEwan, Buchan, Horn, Naysmith, Young, Brebner, Ferguson, Anderson I (McGarry), Easton, Thompson (McFarlane).

7 June

Belarus (0) 1 *(Ryndiouk 70)*
Scotland (0) 0   1000
Scotland: McKenzie; Renicks (O'Neill 63), Davidson, Locke, James, Dods, Bagan, Rowson, Peacock (Teale 62), Gillies (Burke 38), McMillan.

WALES UNDER-21 INTERNATIONALS

30 Aug

Wales (2) 4 *(Hartson 12, 56, 83, Young 24)*
San Marino (0) 0   1800
Wales: Williams A; Blaney, Brace, Young (Oster 61), Jarman (Hughes 78), Edwards, Bellamy, Robinson, Hartson, Thomas, Rowlands.

4 Oct

Wales (0) 0
Holland (0) 2 *(Bruggnik 52, Fuchs 83 (pen))*   767
Wales: Williams A; Brace, Coates, Hughes, Jarman, Edwards, Young (Oster 53), Robinson, Thomas, Hartson (Roberts P 69), Rowlands.

8 Nov

Holland (0) 0
Wales (1) 1 *(Haworth 7)*   8809
Wales: Mountain; Blaney, Roberts G, Hughes, Edwards, Jarman, Young, Robinson, Thomas, Haworth (Williams E 63), Ramasut (Rowlands 79).

13 Dec

Wales (0) 0
Turkey (1) 3 *(Aykut 29, 80, Topraktepe 73)*   700
Wales: Mountain; Blaney (Rowlands 63), Roberts G, Hughes, Edwards, Partridge, Bellamy, Robinson (Coates 57), Thomas (Williams E 79), Haworth, Oster.

28 Mar

Wales (1) 1 *(Haworth 20)*
Belgium (0) 0   1025
Wales: Williams A; Jarman, Bellamy, Hughes, Edwards, Robinson, Thomas, Roberts G, Ramasut (Young), Haworth, Oster.

REPUBLIC OF IRELAND UNDER-21 INTERNATIONALS

8 Oct

Republic of Ireland (2) 4 *(Foley 32, Carr 72, Kennedy 86, 88)*
Macedonia (0) 0   2300
Republic of Ireland: Murphy; Carr, Kennedy, Worrell, Coll, Darcy, O'Toole, O'Halloran, Farrelly (Mahon 89), Finnan, Foley (Crowe 46).

9 Nov

Republic of Ireland (0) 0
Iceland (0) 1 *(Gudjonsson 61)*   1975
Republic of Ireland: Murphy; Carr, Kennedy, Worrell, O'Toole, Darcy, O'Halloran (Mahon 58), Finnan, Foley, Boland (Scully 58), Farrelly.

1 Apr

Macedonia (0) 0
Republic of Ireland (2) 4 *(Kennedy 10, 34, Delap 64, Farrelly 73)*   3750
Republic of Ireland: Murphy; Worrell, Quinn, Maher, Carr, Finnan, Boland, Farrelly, Kilbane, Foley (Delap 54), Kennedy.

29 Apr

Romania (1) 1 *(Frasineanu 15)*
Republic of Ireland (0) 0   7820
Republic of Ireland: Murphy; Quinn, Coll (Foley 80), Maher (Inman 46), Worrell, Finnan, Boland, Farrelly, Kilbane, Delap, Fenn.

BRITISH UNDER-21 APPEARANCES 1976–1997

ENGLAND

Ablett, G. (Liverpool), 1988 v F (1)

Adams, A. (Arsenal). 1985 v Ei, Fi; 1986 v D; 1987 v Se, Y (5)

Adams, N. (Everton), 1987 v Se (1)

Allen, B. (QPR), 1992 v H, M, Cz, F; 1993 v N (sub), T, P, Cz (sub) (8)

Allen, C. A. (Oxford U), 1995 v Br (sub), F (sub) (2)

Allen, C. (QPR), 1980 v EG (sub); (with C Palace), 1981 v N, R (3)

Allen, M. (QPR), 1987 v Se (sub); 1988 v Y (sub) (2)

Allen, P. (West Ham U), 1985 v Ei, R; (with Tottenham H, 1986 v R (3)

Anderson, V. A. (Nottingham F), 1978 v I (1)

Anderton, D. R. (Tottenham H), 1993 v Sp, Sm, Ho, Pol, N, P, Cz, Br, S, F; 1994 v Pol, Sm (12)

Andrews, I. (Leicester C), 1987 v Se (1)

Ardley, N. C. (Wimbledon), 1993 v Pol, N, P, Cz, Br, S, F, 1994 v Pol (sub), Ho, Sm (10)

Ashcroft, L. (Preston NE), 1992 v H (sub) (1)

Atherton, P. (Coventry C), 1992 v T (1)

Atkinson, B. (Sunderland), 1991 v W (sub), Sen, M, USSR (sub); F; 1992 v Pol (sub) (6)

Awford, A. T. (Portsmouth), 1993 v Sp, N, T, P, Cz, Br, S, F; 1994 v Ho (9)

Bailey, G. R. (Manchester U), 1979 v W, Bul; 1980 v D, S (2), EG; 1982 v N; 1983 v D, Gr; 1984 v H, F (2), I, Sp (14)

Baker, G. E. (Southampton), 1981 v N, R (2)

Barker, S. (Blackburn R), 1985 v Is (sub), Ei, R; 1986 v I (4)

Barmby, N. J. (Tottenham H), 1994 v D; 1995 v P, A (sub) (3)

Bannister, G. (Sheffield W), 1982 v Pol (1)

Barnes, J. (Watford), 1983 v D, Gr (2)

Barnes, P. S. (Manchester C), 1977 v W (sub), S, Fi, N; 1978 v N, Fi, I (2), Y (9)

Barrett, E. D. (Oldham Ath), 1990 v P, F, USSR, Cz (4)

Bart-Williams, C. G. (Sheffield W), 1993 v Sp, N, T; 1994 v D, Ru, F, Bel, P; 1995 v P, A, Ei (2), La (2); (with Nottingham F) 1996 v P (sub), A (16)

Batty, D. (Leeds U), 1988 v Sw (sub); 1989 v Gr (sub), Bul, Sen, Ei, US; 1990 v Pol (7)

Bazeley, D. S. (Watford), 1992 v H (sub) (1)

Beagrie, P. (Sheffield U), 1988 v WG, T (2)

Beardsmore, R. (Manchester U), 1989 v Gr, Alb (sub), Pol, Bul, USA (5)

Beckham, D. R. J. (Manchester U), 1995 v Br, Mal, An, F; 1996 v P, A (sub), Bel, An, P (9)

Beeston, C (Stoke C), 1988 v USSR (1)

Bertschin, K. E. (Birmingham C), 1977 v S; 1978 v Y (2) (3)

Birtles, G. (Nottingham F), 1980 v Bul, EG (sub) (2)

Blackwell, D. R. (Wimbledon), 1991 v W, T, Sen (sub), M, USSR, F (6)

Blake, M. A. (Aston Villa), 1990 v F (sub), Cz (sub); 1991 v H, Pol, Ei (2), W; 1992 v Pol (8)

Blissett, L. L. (Watford), 1979 v W, Bul (sub), Se; 1980 v D (4)

Booth, A. D. (Huddersfield T), 1995 v La (2 subs); 1996 v N (3)

Bowyer, L. D. (Charlton Ath), 1996 v N (sub), Bel, P, Br; (with Leeds U), 1997 v Mol, I, Sw, Ge (8)

Bracewell, P. (Stoke C), 1983 v D, Gr (1 + 1 sub), H; 1984 v D, H, F (2), I (2), Sp (2); 1985 v T (13)

Bradbury, L. M. (Portsmouth), 1997 v Pol (1)

Branch, P. M. (Everton), 1997 v Pol (sub) (1)

Bradshaw, P. W. (Wolverhampton W), 1977 v W, S; 1978 v Fi, Y (4)

Breacker, T. (Luton T), 1986 v I (2) (2)

Brennan, M. (Ipswich T), 1987 v Y, Sp, T, Mor, F (5)

Bridges, M. (Sunderland), 1997 v Sw (sub) (1)

Brightwell, I. (Manchester C), 1989 v D, Alb; 1990 v Se (sub), Pol (4)

Briscoe, L. S. (Sheffield W), 1996 v Cro, Bel (sub), An, Br; 1997 v Sw (sub) (5)

Brock, K. (Oxford U), 1984 v I, Sp (2); 1986 v I (4)

Broomes, M. C. (Blackburn R), 1997 v Sw, Ge (2)

Brown, M. R. (Manchester U), 1996 v Cro, Bel, An, P (4)

Bull, S. G. (Wolverhampton W), 1989 v Alb (2) Pol; 1990 v Se, Pol (5)

Burrows, D. (WBA), 1989 v Se (sub); (with Liverpool), Gr, Alb (2), Pol; 1990 v Se, Pol (7)

Butcher, T. I. (Ipswich T), 1979 v Se; 1980 v D, Bul, S (2), EG (2) (7)

Butt, N. (Manchester U), 1995 v Ei (2), La; 1996 v P, A; 1997 v Ge, Pol (7)

Butters, G. (Tottenham H), 1989 v Bul, Sen (sub), Ei (sub) (3)

Butterworth, I. (Coventry C), 1985 v T, R; (with Nottingham F), 1986 v R, T, D (2), I (2) (8)

Caesar, G. (Arsenal), 1987 v Mor, USSR (sub), F (3)

Callaghan, N. (Watford), 1983 v D, Gr (sub), H (sub); 1984 v D, H, F (2), I, Sp (9)

Campbell, K. J. (Arsenal), 1991 v H, T (sub); 1992 v G, T (4)

Campbell, S. (Tottenham), 1994 v D, Ru, F, US, Bel, P; 1995 v P, A, Ei; 1996 v N, A (11)

Carbon, M. P. (Derby Co), 1996 v Cro (sub); 1997 v Ge, I, Sw (4)

Carr, C. (Fulham), 1985 v Ei (sub) (1)

Carr, F. (Nottingham F), 1987 v Se, Y, Sp (sub), Mor, USSR; 1988 v WG (sub), T, Y, F (9)

Carragher, J. L. (Liverpool), 1997 v I (sub), Sw, Ge, Pol (4)

Casper, C. M. (Manchester U), 1995 v Mal (1)

Caton, T. (Manchester C), 1982 v N, H (sub), Pol (2), S; 1983 v WG (2), Gr; 1984 v D, H, F (2), I (2) (14)

Challis, T. M. (QPR), 1996 v An, P (2)

Chamberlain, M. (Stoke C), 1983 v Gr; 1984 v F (sub), I, Sp (4)

Chapman, L. (Stoke C), 1981 v Ei (1)

Charles, G. A. (Nottingham F), 1991 v H, W (sub), Ei; 1992 v T (4)

Chettle, S. (Nottingham F), 1988 v M, USSR, Mor, F; 1989 v D, Se, Gr, Alb (2), Bul; 1990 v Se, Pol (12)

Clark, L. R. (Newcastle U), 1992 v Cz, F; 1993 v Sp, N, T, Ho (sub), Pol (sub), Cz, Br, S; 1994 v Ho (11)

Clough, N. (Nottingham F), 1986 v D (sub); 1987 v Se, Y, T, USSR, F (sub), P; 1988 v WG, T, Y, S (2), M, Mor, F (15)

Cole, A. A. (Arsenal), 1992 v H, Cz (sub), F (sub); (with Bristol C), 1993 v Sm; (with Newcastle U), Pol, N; 1994 v Pol, Ho (8)

Coney, D. (Fulham), 1985 v T (sub); 1986 v R; 1988 v T, WG (4)

Connor, T. (Brighton & HA), 1987 v Y (1)

Cooke, R. (Tottenham H), 1986 v D (sub) (1)

Cooke, T. J. (Manchester U), 1996 v Cro, Bel, An (sub), P (4)

Cooper, C. (Middlesbrough), 1988 v F (2), M, USSR, Mor; 1989 v D, Se, Gr (8)

Corrigan, J. T. (Manchester C), 1978 v I (2), Y (3)

Cottee, A. (West Ham U), 1985 v Fi (sub), Is (sub), Ei, R, Fi; 1987 v Sp, P; 1988 v WG (8)

Couzens, A. J. (Leeds U), 1995 v Mal (sub), An, F (sub) (3)

Cowans, G. S. (Aston Villa), 1979 v W, Se; 1980 v Bul, EG; 1981 v R (5)

Cox, N. J. (Aston Villa), 1993 v T, Ho, Pol, N; 1994 v Pol, Sm (6)

Cranson, I. (Ipswich T), 1985 v Fi, Is, R; 1986 v R, I (5)

Croft, G. (Grimsby T), 1995 v Br, Mal, An, F (4)

Crooks, S. (Stoke C), 1980 v Bul, S (2), EG (sub) (4)

Crossley, M. G. (Nottingham F), 1990 v P, USSR, Cz (3)

Cundy, J. V. (Chelsea), 1991 v Ei (2); 1992 v Pol (3)

Cunningham, L. (WBA), 1977 v S, Fi, N (sub); 1978 v N, Fi, I (6)

Curbishley, L. C. (Birmingham C), 1981 v Sw (1)

Daniel, P. W. (Hull C), 1977 v S, Fi, N; 1978 v Fi, I, Y (2) (7)

Davis, K. G. (Luton T), 1995 v An; 1996 v Cro (sub), P (3)

Davis, P. (Arsenal), 1982 v Pol, S; 1983 v D, Gr (1 + 1 sub), H (sub); 1987 v T; 1988 v WG, T, Y, Fr (11)

Day, C. N. (Tottenham H), 1996 v Cro, Bel, Br; (with Crystal Palace), 1997 v Mol, Ge, Sw (6)

D'Avray, M. (Ipswich T), 1984 v I, Sp (sub) (2)

Deehan, J. M. (Aston Villa), 1977 v N; 1978 v N, Fi, I; 1979 v Bul, Se (sub); 1980 v D (7)

Dennis, M. E. (Birmingham C), 1980 v Bul; 1981 v N, R (3)

Dichio, D. S. E. (QPR), 1996 v N (sub) (1)

Dickens, A. (West Ham U), 1985 v Fi (sub) (1)

Dicks, J. (West Ham U), 1988 v Sw (sub), M, Mor, F (4)

Digby, F. (Swindon T), 1987 v Sp (sub), USSR, P; 1988 v T; 1990 v Pol (5)
Dillon, K. P. (Birmingham C), 1981 v R (1)
Dixon, K. (Chelsea), 1985 v Fi (1)
Dobson, A. (Coventry C), 1989 v Bul, Sen, Ei, US (4)
Dodd, J. R. (Southampton), 1991 v Pol, Ei, T, Sen, M, F; 1992 v G, Pol (8)
Donowa, L. (Norwich C), 1985 v Is, R (sub), Fi (sub) (3)
Dorigo, A. (Aston Villa), 1987 v Se, Sp, T, Mor, USSR, F, P; 1988 v WG, Y, S (2) (11)
Dozzell, J. (Ipswich T), 1987 v Se, Y (sub), Sp, USSR, F, P; 1989 v Se, Gr (sub); 1990 v Se (sub) (9)
Draper, M. A. (Notts Co), 1991 v Ei (sub); 1992 v G, Pol (3)
Duberry, M. W. (Chelsea), 1997 v Mol, Pol, Ge (3)
Duxbury, M. (Manchester U), 1981 v Sw (sub), Ei (sub), R (sub), Sw; 1982 v N; 1983 v WG (2) (7)
Dyer, B. A. (Crystal Palace), 1994 v Ru, F, US, Bel, P; 1995 v P (sub); 1996 v Cro; 1997 v Mol, Ge (9)
Dyson, P. I. (Coventry C), 1981 v N, R, Sw, Ei (4)

Eadie, D. M. (Norwich C), 1994 v F (sub), US; 1997 v Mol, Ge (2), I (6)
Ebbrell, J. (Everton), 1989 v Sen, Ei, US (sub); 1990 v P, F, USSR, Cz; 1991 v H, Pol, Ei, W, T; 1992 v G, T (14)
Edghill, R. A. (Manchester C), 1994 v D, Ru; 1995 v A (3)
Ehiogu, U. (Aston Villa), 1992 v H, M, Cz, F; 1993 v Sp, N, T, Sm, T, Ho, Pol, N; 1994 v Pol, Ho, Sm (15)
Elliott, J. (Luton T), 1985 v Fi; 1986 v T, D (3)
Elliott, R. J. (Newcastle U), 1996 v P, A (2)

Fairclough, C. (Nottingham F), 1985 v T, Is, Ei; 1987 v Sp, T; (with Tottenham H), 1988 v Y, F (7)
Fairclough, D. (Liverpool), 1977 v W (1)
Fashanu, J. (Norwich C), 1980 v EG; 1981 v N (sub), R, Sw, Ei (sub), H; (with Nottingham F), 1982 v N, H, Pol, S; 1983 v WG (sub) (11)
Fear, P. (Wimbledon), 1994 v Ru, F, US (sub) (3)
Fenton, G. A. (Aston Villa), 1995 v Ei (1)
Fenwick, T. W. (C Palace), 1981 v N, R, Sw, Ei; (with QPR), R; 1982 v N, H, S (2); 1983 v WG (2) (11)
Ferdinand, R. G. (West Ham U), 1997 v Sw, Ge (2)
Fereday, W. (QPR), 1985 v T, Ei (sub). Fi; 1986 v T (sub), I (5)
Flitcroft, G. W. (Manchester C), 1993 v Sm, Hol, N, P, Cz, Br, S, F; 1994 v Pol, Ho (10)
Flowers, T. (Southampton), 1987 v Mor, F; 1988 v WG (sub) (3)
Ford, M. (Leeds U), 1996 v Cro; 1997 v Mol (2)
Forster, N. M. (Brentford), 1995 v Br, Mal, An, F (4)
Forsyth, M. (Derby Co), 1988 v Sw (1)
Foster, S. (Brighton & HA), 1980 v EG (sub) (1)
Fowler, R. B. (Liverpool), 1994 v Sm, Ru (sub), F, US; 1995 v P, A (8)
Froggatt, S. J. (Aston Villa), 1993 v Sp, Sm (sub) (2)
Futcher, P. (Luton T), 1977 v W, S, Fi, N; (with Manchester C), 1978 v N, Fi, I (2), Y (2); 1979 v D (11)

Gabbiadini, M. (Sunderland), 1989 v Bul, USA (2)
Gale, A. (Fulham), 1982 v Pol (1)
Gallen, K. A. (QPR), 1995 v Ei, La (2); 1996 v Cro (4)
Gascoigne, P. (Newcastle U), 1987 v Mo, USSR, P; 1988 v WG, Y, S (2), F (2), Sw, M, USSR (sub), Mor (13)
Gayle, H. (Birmingham C), 1984 v I, Sp (2) (3)
Gernon, T. (Ipswich T), 1983 v Gr (1)
Gerrard, P. W. (Oldham Ath), 1993 v T, Ho, Pol, N, P, Cz, Br, S, F; 1994 v D, Ru; 1995 v P, A, Ei (2), La (2); 1996 v P (18)
Gibbs, N. (Watford), 1987 v Mor, USSR, F, P; 1988 v T (5)
Gibson, C. (Aston Villa), 1982 v N (1)
Gilbert, W. A. (C Palace), 1979 v W, Bul; 1980 v Bul; 1981 v N, R, Sw, R, Sw, H; 1982 v N (sub), H (11)
Goddard, P. (West Ham U), 1981 v N, Sw, Ei (sub); 1982 v N (sub), Pol, S; 1983 v WG (2) (8)
Gordon, D. (Norwich C), 1987 v T (sub), Mor (sub), F, P (4)
Gordon, D. D. (Crystal Palace), 1994 v Ru, F, US, Bel, P; 1995 v P, A, Ei (2), La (2); 1996 v P, N (13)
Grant, A. J. (Everton), 1996 v An (sub) (1)
Granville, D. P. (Chelsea), 1997 v Ge (sub), Pol (2)
Gray, A. (Aston Villa), 1988 v S, F (2)

Haigh, P. (Hull C), 1977 v N (sub) (1)
Hall, M. T. J. (Coventry C), 1997 v Pol (2), I, Sw, Ge (5)
Hall, R. A. (Southampton), 1992 v H (sub), F; 1993 v Sm, T, Ho, Pol, P, Cz, Br, S, F (11)
Hamilton, D. V. (Newcastle U), 1997 v Pol (1)

Hardyman, P. (Portsmouth), 1985 v Ei; 1986 v D (2)
Hateley, M. (Coventry C), 1982 v Pol, S; 1983 v Gr (2), H; (with Portsmouth), 1984 v F (2), I, Sp (2) (10)
Hayes, M. (Arsenal), 1987 v Sp, T; 1988 v F (sub) (3)
Hazell, R. J. (Wolverhampton W), 1979 v D (1)
Heaney, N. A. (Arsenal), 1992 v H, M, Cz, F; 1993 v N, T (6)
Heath, A. (Stoke C), 1981 v R, Sw, H; 1982 v N, H; (with Everton), Pol, S; 1983 v WG (8)
Hendon, I. M. (Tottenham H), 1992 v H, M, Cz, F; 1993 v Sp, N, T (7)
Hendrie, L. A. (Aston Villa), 1996 v Cro (sub) (1)
Hesford, I. (Blackpool), 1981 v Ei (sub), Pol (2), S (2); 1983 v WG (2) (7)
Heskey, E. W. I. (Leicester C), 1997 v I, Ge, Pol (2) (4)
Hilaire, V. (C Palace), 1980 v Bul, S (1+1 sub), EG (2); 1981 v N, R, Sw (sub); 1982 v Pol (sub) (9)
Hill, D. R. L. (Tottenham H), 1995 v Br, Mal, An, F (4)
Hillier, D. (Arsenal), 1991 v T (1)
Hinchcliffe, A. (Manchester C), 1989 v D (1)
Hinshelwood, P. A. (C Palace), 1978 v N; 1980 v EG (2)
Hirst, D. (Sheffield W), 1988 v USSR, F; 1989 v D, Bul (sub), Sen, Ei, US (7)
Hoddle, G. (Tottenham H), 1977 v W (sub); 1978 v Fi (sub), I (2), Y; 1979 v D, W, Bul; 1980 v S (2), EG (2) (12)
Hodge, S. (Nottingham F), 1983 v Gr (sub); 1984 v D, F, I, Sp (2); (with Aston Villa), 1986 v R, T (8)
Hodgson, D. J. (Middlesbrough), 1981 v N, R (sub), Sw, Ei; 1982 v Pol; 1983 v WG (6)
Holdsworth, D. (Watford), 1989 v Gr (sub) (1)
Holland, C. J. (Newcastle U), 1995 v La; 1996 v N (sub), A (sub), Cro, Bel, An, Br; 1997 v Mol, Pol, Sw (10)
Holland, P. (Mansfield T), 1995 v Br, Mal, An, F (4)
Horne, B. (Millwall), 1989 v Gr (sub), Pol, Bul, Ei, US (5)
Hucker, P. (QPR), 1984 v I, Sp (2)
Huckerby, D. (Coventry C), 1997 v I (sub), Sw, Ge (sub), Pol (sub) (4)
Hughes, S. J. (Arsenal), 1997 v I, Sw, Ge, Pol (4)
Humphreys, R. J. (Sheffield W), 1997 v Pol, Ge (sub), Sw (3)

Impey, A. R. (QPR), 1993 v T (1)
Ince, P. (West Ham U), 1989 v USSR; 1990 v Alb; 1990 v Se (2)

Jackson, M. A. (Everton), 1992 v H, M, Cz, F; 1993 v Sm (sub), T, Ho, Pol, N; 1994 v Pol (10)
James, D. (Watford), 1991 v Ei (2), T, Sen, M, USSR, F; 1992 v G, T, Pol (10)
James, J. C. (Luton T), 1990 v F, USSR (2)
Jemson, N. B. (Nottingham F), 1991 v W (1)
Joachim, J. K. (Leicester C), 1994 v D (sub); 1995 v P, A, Ei, Br, Mal, An, F; 1996 v N (9)
Johnson, T. (Notts Co), 1991 v H (sub), Ei (sub); 1992 v G, T, Pol; (with Derby Co), M, Cz (sub) (7)
Johnston, C. P. (Middlesbrough), 1981 v N, Ei (2)
Jones, D. R. (Everton), 1977 v W (1)
Jones, C. H. (Tottenham H), 1978 v Y (sub) (1)
Jones, R. (Liverpool), 1993 v Sm, Ho (2)

Keegan, G. A. (Manchester C), 1977 v W (1)
Kenny, J. (Everton), 1993 v T (1)
Keown, M. (Aston Villa), 1987 v Sp, Mor, USSR, P; 1988 v T, S, F (2) (8)
Kerslake, D. (QPR), 1986 v T (1)
Kilcline, B. (Notts C), 1983 v D, Gr (2)
King, A. E. (Everton), 1977 v W; 1978 v Y (2)
Kitson, P. (Leicester C), 1991 v Sen (sub), M, F; 1992 v Pol; (with Derby Co), M, Cz, F (7)
Knight, A. (Portsmouth), 1983 v Gr, H (2)
Knight, I. (Sheffield W), 1987 v Se (sub), Y (2)

Lake, P. (Manchester C), 1989 v D, Alb (2), Pol; 1990 v Pol (5)
Langley, T. W. (Chelsea), 1978 v I (sub) (1)
Lee, D. J. (Chelsea), 1990 v F; 1991 v H, Pol, Ei (2), T, Sen, USSR, F; 1992 v Pol (10)
Lee, R. (Charlton Ath), 1986 v I (sub); 1987 v Se (sub) (2)
Lee, S. (Liverpool), 1981 v R, Sw, H; 1982 v S; 1983 v WG (2) (6)
Le Saux, G. (Chelsea), 1990 v P, F, USSR, Cz (4)
Lowe, D. (Ipswich T), 1988 v F, Sw (sub) (2)
Lukic, J. (Leeds U), 1981 v N, R, Ei, R, Sw, H; 1982 v H (7)
Lund, G. (Grimsby T), 1985 v T; 1986 v R, T (3)

McCall, S. H. (Ipswich T), 1981 v Sw, H; 1982 v H, S; 1983 v WG (2) (6)

McDonald, N. (Newcastle U), 1987 v Se (sub), Sp, T; 1988 v WG, Y (sub) (5)

McGrath, L. (Coventry C), 1986 v D (1)

MacKenzie, S. (WBA), 1982 v N, S (2) (3)

McLeary, A. (Millwall), 1988 v Sw (1)

McMahon, S. (Everton), 1981 v Ei; 1982 v Pol; 1983 v D, Gr (2); (with Aston Villa), 1984 v H (6)

McManaman, S. (Liverpool), 1991 v W, M (sub); 1993 v N, T, Sm, T; 1994 v Pol (7)

Mabbutt, G. (Bristol R), 1982 v Pol (2), S; (with Tottenham H), 1983 v D; 1984 v F; 1986 v D, I (7)

Makin, C. (Oldham Ath), 1994 v Ru (sub), F, US, Bel, P (5)

Marriott, A. (Nottingham F), 1992 v M (1)

Marshall, A. J. (Norwich C), 1995 v Mal, An; 1997 v Pol, I (4)

Martin, L. (Manchester U), 1989 v Gr (sub), Alb (sub) (2)

Martyn, N. (Bristol R), 1988 v S (sub), M, USSR, Mor, F; 1989 v D, Se, Gr, Alb (2); 1990 v Se (11)

Matteo, D. (Liverpool), 1994 v F (sub), Bel, P (3)

Matthew, D. (Chelsea), 1990 v P, USSR (sub), Cz; 1991 v Ei, M, USSR, F; 1992 v G (sub), T (9)

May, A. (Manchester C), 1986 v I (sub) (1)

Merson, P. (Arsenal), 1989 v D, Gr, Pol (sub); 1990 v Pol (4)

Middleton, J. (Nottingham F), 1977 v Fi, N; (with Derby Co), 1978 v N (3)

Miller, A. (Arsenal), 1988 v Mor (sub); 1989 v Sen; 1991 v H, Pol (4)

Mills, G. R. (Nottingham F), 1981 v R; 1982 v N (2)

Mimms, R. (Rotherham U), 1985 v Is (sub), Ei (sub); (with Everton), 1986 v I (3)

Minto, S. C. (Charlton Ath), 1991 v W; 1992 v H, M, Cz; 1993 v T; 1994 v Ho (6)

Moore, I. (Tranmere R), 1996 v Cro (sub), Bel (sub), An, P, Br; 1997 v Mol (sub); (with Nottingham F), Sw (sub) (7)

Moran, S. (Southampton), 1982 v N (sub); 1984 v F (2)

Morgan, S. (Leicester C), 1987 v Se, Y (2)

Morris, J. (Chelsea), 1997 v Pol (sub), Sw (sub), Ge (sub) (3)

Mortimer, P. (Charlton Ath), 1989 v Sen, Ei (2)

Moses, A. P. (Barnsley), 1997 v Pol (1)

Moses, R. M. (WBA), 1981 v N (sub), Sw, Ei, R, Sw, H; 1982 v N (sub); (with Manchester U), H (8)

Mountfield, D. (Everton), 1984 v Sp (1)

Muggleton, C. D. (Leicester C), 1990 v F (1)

Murray, P. (QPR), 1997 v I, Pol (2)

Mutch, A. (Wolverhampton W), 1989 v Pol (1)

Myers, A. (Chelsea), 1995 v Br, Mal, An (sub), F (4)

Nethercott, S. (Tottenham), 1994 v D, Ru, F, US, Bel, P; 1995 v La (2) (8)

Neville, P. J. (Manchester U), 1995 v Br, Mal, An, F; 1996 v P, N (sub); 1997 v Ge (7)

Newell, M. (Luton T), 1986 v D (1 + 1 sub), I (1 + 1 sub) (4)

Newton, E. J. I. (Chelsea), 1993 v T (sub); 1994 v Sm (2)

Newton, S. O. (Charlton Ath), 1997 v Mol, Pol, Ge (3)

Nicholls, A. (Plymouth Arg), 1994 v F (1)

Oakes, M. C. (Aston Villa), 1994 v D (sub), F (sub), US, Bel, P; 1996 v A (6)

Oakes, S. J. (Luton T), 1993 v Br (sub) (1)

Oakley, M. (Southampton), 1997 v Ge (1)

O'Connor, J. (Everton), 1996 v Cro, An, Br (3)

Oldfield, D. (Luton T), 1989 v Se (1)

Olney, I. A. (Aston Villa), 1990 v P, F, USSR, Cz; 1991 v H, Pol, Ei (2), T; 1992 v Pol (sub) (10)

Ord, R. J. (Sunderland), 1991 v W, M, USSR (3)

Osman, R. C. (Ipswich T), 1979 v W (sub), Se; 1980 v D, S (2), EG (2) (7)

Owen, G. A. (Manchester C), 1977 v S, Fi, N; 1978 v N, Fi, I (2), Y; 1979 v D, W; (with WBA), Bul, Se (sub); 1980 v D, S (2), EG; 1981 v Sw, R; 1982 v N (sub), H; 1983 v WG (2) (22)

Painter, I. (Stoke C), 1986 v I (1)

Palmer, C. (Sheffield W), 1989 v Bul, Sen, Ei, US (4)

Parker, G. (Hull C), 1986 v I (2); (with Nottingham F), F; 1987 v Se, Y (sub), Sp (6)

Parker, P. (Fulham), 1985 v Fi, T, Is (sub), Ei, R, Fi; 1986 v T, D (8)

Parkes, P. B. F. (QPR), 1979 v D (1)

Parkin, S. (Stoke C), 1987 v Sp (sub); 1988 v WG (sub), T, S (sub), F (5)

Parlour, R. (Arsenal), 1992 v H, M, Cz, F; 1993 v Sp, N, T; 1994 v D, Ru, Bel, P; 1995 v A (12)

Peach, D. S. (Southampton), 1977 v S, Fi, N; 1978 v N, I (2) (6)

Peake, A. (Leicester C), 1982 v Pol (1)

Pearce, I. A. (Blackburn R), 1995 v Ei, La; 1996 v N (3)

Pearce, S. (Nottingham F), 1987 v Y (1)

Pickering, N. (Sunderland), 1983 v D (sub), Gr, H; 1984 v F (sub + 1), I (2), Sp; 1985 v Is, R, Fi; 1986 v R, T; (with Coventry C), D, I (15)

Platt, D. (Aston Villa), 1988 v M, Mor, F (3)

Plummer, C. S. (QPR), 1996 v Cro (sub), Bel, An, P (sub), Br (5)

Pollock, J. (Middlesbrough), 1995 v Ei (sub); 1996 v N, A (3)

Porter, G. (Watford), 1987 v Sp (sub), T, Mor, USSR, F, P (sub); 1988 v T (sub), Y, S (2), F, Sw (12)

Potter, G. S. (Southampton), 1997 v Mol (1)

Pressman, K. (Sheffield W), 1989 v D (sub) (1)

Proctor, M. (Middlesbrough), 1981 v Ei (sub), Sw; (with Nottingham F) 1982 v N, Pol (4)

Quashie, N. F. (QPR), 1997 v Pol (1)

Ramage, C. D. (Derby Co), 1991 v Pol (sub), W; 1992 v Fr (sub) (3)

Ranson, R. (Manchester C), 1980 v Bul, EG; 1981 v R (sub), R, Sw (1 + 1 sub), H, Pol (2), S (10)

Redknapp, J. F. (Liverpool), 1993 v Sm, Pol, N, P, Cz, Br, S, F; 1994 v Pol, Ho (sub), D, Ru, F, US, Bel, P; 1995 v P, A (18)

Redmond, S. (Manchester C), 1988 v F (2), M, USSR, Mor, F; 1989 v D, Se, Gr, Alb (2), Pol; 1990 v Se, Pol (14)

Reeves, K. P. (Norwich C), 1978 v I, Y (2); 1979 v N, W, Bul, Sw; 1980 v D, S; (with Manchester C), EG (10)

Regis, C. (WBA), 1979 v D, Bul, Se; 1980 v S, EG; 1983 v D (6)

Reid, N. S. (Manchester C), 1980 v H (sub); 1982 v H, Pol (2), S (2) (6)

Reid, P. (Bolton W), 1977 v S, Fi, N; 1978 v Fi, I, Y (6)

Richards, D. I. (Wolverhampton W), 1995 v Br, Mal, An, F (4)

Richards, J. P. (Wolverhampton W), 1977 v Fi, N (2)

Rideout, P. (Aston Villa), 1985 v Fi, Is, Ei (sub), R; (with Bari), 1986 v D (5)

Ripley, S. (Middlesbrough), 1988 v USSR, F (sub); 1989 v D (sub), Se, Gr, Alb (2); 1990 v Se (8)

Ritchie, A. (Brighton & HA), 1982 v Pol (1)

Rix, G. (Arsenal), 1978 v Fi (sub), Y; 1979 v D, Se; 1980 v D (sub), Bul, S (7)

Roberts, A. J. (Millwall), 1995 v Ei, La (2); (with C Palace), 1996 v N, A (5)

Roberts, B. J. (Middlesbrough), 1997 v Sw (sub) (1)

Robins, M. G. (Manchester U), 1990 v P, F, USSR, Cz; 1991 v H (sub), Pol (6)

Robson, B. (WBA), 1979 v W, Bul (sub), Se; 1980 v D, Bul, S (2) (7)

Robson, S. (Arsenal), 1984 v I; 1985 v Fi, Is, Fi; 1986 v R, I (with West Ham U); 1988 v S, Sw (8)

Rocastle, D. (Arsenal), 1987 v Se, Y, Sp, T; 1988 v WG, T, Y, S (2), F (2 subs), M, USSR, Mor (14)

Rodger, G. (Coventry C), 1987 v USSR, F, P; 1988 v WG (4)

Rosario, R. (Norwich C), 1987 v T (sub), Mor, F, P (sub) (4)

Rose, M. (Arsenal), 1997 v Ge (sub), I (2)

Rowell, G. (Sunderland), 1977 v Fi (1)

Ruddock, N. (Southampton), 1989 v Bul (sub), Sen, Ei, US (4)

Rufus, R. R. (Charlton Ath), 1996 v Cro, Bel, An, P, Br; 1997 v I (6)

Ryan, J. (Oldham Ath), 1983 v H (1)

Ryder, S.H. (Walsall), 1995 v Br, An, F (3)

Samways, V. (Tottenham H), 1988 v Sw (sub), USSR, F; 1989 v D, Se (5)

Sansom, K. G. (C Palace), 1979 v D, W, Bul, Se; 1980 v S (2), EG (2) (8)

Scimeca, R. (Aston Villa), 1996 v P; 1997 v Mol, Pol, Ge, I (5)

Scowcroft, J. B. (Ipswich T), 1997 v Pol, Ge (2), I (sub) (4)

Seaman, D. (Birmingham C), 1985 v Fi, T, Is, Ei, R, Fi; 1986 v R, F, D, I (10)

Sedgley, S. (Coventry C), 1987 v USSR, F (sub), P; 1988 v F; 1989 v D (sub), Se, Gr, Alb (2), Pol; (with Tottenham H), 1990 v Se (11)

Sellars, S. (Blackburn R), 1988 v S, F, Sw (3)

Selley, I. (Arsenal), 1994 v Ru (sub), F (sub), US (3)

Sharpe, L. (Manchester U), 1989 v Gr; 1990 v P (sub), F, USSR, Cz; 1991 v H, Pol (sub), Ei (8)

Shaw, G. R. (Aston Villa), 1981 v Ei, Sw, H; 1982 v H, S; 1983 v WG (2) (7)

Shearer, A. (Southampton), 1991 v Ei (2), W, T, Sen, M, USSR, F; 1992 v G, T, Pol (11)
Shelton, G. (Sheffield W), 1987 v Fi (1)
Sheringham, T. (Millwall), 1988 v Sw (1)
Sheron, M. N. (Manchester C), 1992 v H, F; 1993 v N (sub), T (sub), Sm, Ho, Pol, N, P, Cz, Br, S, F; 1994 v Pol (sub), Ho, Sm (16)
Sherwood, T. A. (Norwich C), 1990 v P, F, USSR, Cz (4)
Shipperley, N. J. (Chelsea), 1994 v Sm (sub); (with Southampton) 1995 v Ei, La (2); 1996 v P, N, A (7)
Simpson, P. (Manchester C), 1986 v D (sub); 1987 v Y, Mor, F, P (5)
Sims, S. (Leicester C), 1977 v W, S, Fi, N; 1978 v N, Fi, I (2), Y (2) (10)
Sinclair, F. M. (Chelsea), 1994 v Ho, Sm, D, Ru, F, US, Bel, P (8)
Sinclair, T. (QPR), 1995 v P, Ei (2), La; 1996 v P (5)
Sinnott, L. (Watford), 1985 v Is (sub) (1)
Slade, S. A. (Tottenham H), 1996 v Bel, An, P, Br (4)
Slater, S. I. (West Ham U), 1990 v P, USSR (sub), Cz (sub) (3)
Small, B. (Aston Villa), 1993 v Sm, T, Ho, Pol, N, P, Cz, Br, S, F; 1994 v Pol, Sm (12)
Smith, D. (Coventry C), 1988 v M, USSR (sub), Mor; 1989 v D, Se, Alb (2), Pol; 1990 v Se, Pol (9)
Smith, M. (Sheffield W), 1981 v Ei, R, Sw, H; 1982 v Pol (sub) (5)
Smith, M. (Sunderland), 1995 v Ei (sub) (1)
Snodin, I. (Doncaster R), 1985 v T, Is, R, Fi (4)
Statham, B. (Tottenham H), 1988 v Sw; 1989 v D (sub), Se (3)
Statham, D. J. (WBA), 1978 v Fi, 1979 v W, Bul, Se; 1980 v D; 1983 v D (6)
Stein, B. (Luton T), 1984 v D, H, I (3)
Sterland, M. (Sheffield W), 1984 v D, H, F (2), I, Sp (2) (7)
Steven, T. (Everton), 1985 v Fi, T (2)
Stevens, G. (Brighton & HA), 1983 v H; (with Tottenham H), 1984 v H, F (1+1 sub), I (sub), Sp (1+1 sub); 1986 v I (8)
Stewart, P. (Manchester C), 1988 v F (1)
Stuart, G. C. (Chelsea), 1990 v P (sub), F, USSR, Cz; 1991 v T (sub) (5)
Stuart, J. C. (Charlton Ath), 1996 v Bel, An, P, Br (4)
Suckling, P. (Coventry C), 1986 v D; (with Manchester C), 1987 v Se (sub), Y, Sp, T; (with C Palace), 1988 v S (2), F (2), Sw (10)
Summerbee, N.J. (Swindon T), 1993 v P (sub), S (sub), F (3)
Sunderland, A. (Wolverhampton W), 1977 v W (1)
Sutton, C. R. (Norwich), 1993 v Sp (sub), T (sub + 1), Ho, P (sub), Cz, Br, S, F; 1994 v Pol, Ho, Sm, D (13)
Swindlehurst, D. (C Palace), 1977 v W (1)
Sutch, D. (Norwich C), 1992 v H, M, Cz; 1993 v T (4)

Talbot, B. (Ipswich T), 1977 v W (1)
Thatcher, B. D. (Millwall), 1996 v Cro; (with Wimbledon), 1997 v Mol, Pol (3)
Thomas, D. (Coventry C), 1981 v Ei; 1983 v WG (2), Gr, H; (with Tottenham H), I, Sp (7)
Thomas, M. (Luton T), 1986 v T, D, I (3)
Thomas, M. (Arsenal), 1988 v Y, S, F (2), M, USSR, Mor; 1989 v Gr, Alb (2), Pol; 1990 v Se (12)
Thomas, R. E. (Watford), 1990 v P (1)
Thompson, A. (Bolton W), 1995 v La; 1996 v P (2)
Thompson, D. A. (Liverpool), 1997 v Pol (sub), Ge (2)
Thompson, G. L. (Coventry C), 1981 v R, Sw, H; 1982 v N, H, S (6)
Thorn, A. (Wimbledon), 1988 v WG (sub). Y, S, F, Sw (5)
Thornley, B. L. (Manchester U), 1996 v Bel, P, Br (3)
Tiler, C. (Barnsley), 1990 v P, USSR, Cz; 1991 v H, Pol, Ei (2), T, Sen, USSR, F; (with Nottingham F), 1992 v G, T (13)

Unsworth, D. G. (Everton), 1995 v A, Ei (2), La; 1996 v N, A (6)

Venison, B. (Sunderland), 1983 v D, Gr; 1985 v Fi, T, Is, Fi; 1986 v R, T, D (2) (10)
Vinnicombe, C. (Rangers), 1991 v H (sub), Pol, Ei (2), T, Sen, M, USSR (sub), F; 1992 v G, T, Pol (12)

Waddle, C. (Newcastle U), 1985 v Fi (1)
Wallace, D. (Southampton), 1983 v Gr, H; 1984 v D, H, F (2), I, Sp (sub); 1985 v Fi, T, Is; 1986 v R, D, I (14)
Wallace, Ray (Southampton), 1989 v Bul, Sen (sub), Ei; 1990 v Se (4)

Wallace, Rod (Southampton), 1989 v Bul, Ei (sub), US; 1991 v H, Pol, Ei, T, Sen, M, USSR, F (11)
Walker, D. (Nottingham F), 1985 v Fi; 1987 v Se, T; 1988 v WG, T, S (2) (7)
Walker, I. M. (Tottenham H), 1991 v W; 1992 v H, Cz, F; 1993 v Sp, N, T, Sm; 1994 v Pol (9)
Walsh, G. (Manchester U), 1988 v WG, Y (2)
Walsh, P. M. (Luton T), 1983 v D (sub), Gr (2), H (4)
Walters, K. (Aston Villa), 1984 v D (sub), H (sub); 1985 v Is, Ei, R; 1986 v R, T, D, I (sub) (9)
Ward, P. D. (Brighton & HA), 1978 v N; 1980 v EG (2)
Warhurst, P. (Oldham Ath), 1991 v H, Pol, W, Sen, M (sub), USSR, F (sub); (with Sheffield W), 1992 v G (8)
Watson, D. (Norwich C), 1984 v D, F (2), I (2), Sp (2) (7)
Watson, D. N. (Barnsley), 1994 v Ho, Sm; 1995 v Br, F; 1996 v N (5)
Watson, G. (Sheffield W), 1991 v Sen, USSR (2)
Watson, S. C. (Newcastle U), 1993 v Sp (sub), N; 1994 v Sm (sub), D; 1995 v P, A, Ei (2), La (2); 1996 v N, A (12)
Webb, N. (Portsmouth), 1985 v Ei; (with Nottingham F), 1986 v D (2) (3)
Whelan, P. J. (Ipswich T), 1993 v Sp, T (sub), P (3)
Whelan, N. (Leeds U), 1995 v A (sub), Ei (2)
White, D. (Manchester C), 1988 v S (2), F, USSR; 1989 v Se; 1990 v Pol (6)
Whyte, C. (Arsenal), 1982 v S (1+1 sub); 1983 v D, Gr (4)
Wicks, S. (QPR), 1982 v S (1)
Wilkins, R. C. (Chelsea), 1977 v W (1)
Wilkinson, P. (Grimsby T), 1985 v Ei, R (sub); (with Everton), 1986 v R (sub), I (4)
Williams, P. (Charlton Ath), 1989 v Bul, Sen, Ei, US (sub) (4)
Williams, P. D. (Derby Co), 1991 v Sen, M, USSR; 1992 v G, T, Pol (6)
Williams, S. C. (Southampton), 1977 v S, Fi, N; 1978 v N, I (1 + 1 sub), Y (2); 1979 v D, Bul, Se (sub); 1980 v D, EG (2) (14)
Winterburn, N. (Wimbledon), 1986 v I (1)
Wise, D. (Wimbledon), 1988 v Sw (1)
Woodcock, A. S. (Nottingham F), 1978 v Fi, I (2)
Woods, C. C. E. (Nottingham F), 1979 v W (sub), Se; (with QPR), 1980 v Bul, EG; 1981 v Sw; (with Norwich C), 1984 v D (6)
Wright, A. G. (Blackburn), 1993 v Sp, N (2)
Wright, M. (Southampton), 1983 v Gr, H; 1984 v D, H (4)
Wright, R. I. (Ipswich T), 1997 v Ge, Pol (2)
Wright, W. (Everton), 1979 v D, W, Bul; 1980 v D, S (2) (6)

Yates, D. (Notts Co), 1989 v D (sub), Bul, Sen, Ei, US (5)

SCOTLAND

Aitken, R. (Celtic), 1977 v Cz, W, Sw; 1978 v Cz, W; 1979 v P, N (2); 1980 v Bel, E; 1984 v EG, Y (2); 1985 v WG, Ic, Sp (16)
Albiston, A. (Manchester U), 1977 v Cz, W, Sw; 1978 v Sw, Cz (5)
Alexander, N. (Stenhousemuir), 1997 v P (1)
Anderson, I. (Dundee), 1997 v Co (sub), US, CzR, P (4)
Anderson, R. (Aberdeen), 1997 v Es, A, Se (3)
Anthony, M. (Celtic), 1997 v La (sub), Es (sub), Co (3)
Archdeacon, O. (Celtic), 1987 v WG (sub) (1)
Archibald, S. (Aberdeen), 1980 v B, E (2), WG; (with Tottenham H), 1981 v D (5)

Bagen, D. (Kilmarnock), 1997 v Es, A (sub), Se (sub), Bl (4)
Bain, K. (Dundee), 1993 v P, I, Ma, P (4)
Baker, M. (St. Mirren), 1993 v F, M, E; 1994 v Ma, A; 1995 v Gr, M, F (sub), Sk (sub); 1996 v H (sub) (10)
Bannon, E. J. P. (Hearts), 1979 v US; (with Chelsea), P, N (2); (with Dundee U), 1980 v Bel, WG, E (7)
Beattie, J. (St Mirren), 1992 v D, US, P, Y (4)
Beaumont, D. (Dundee U), 1985 v Ic (1)
Bell, D. (Aberdeen), 1981 v D; 1984 v Y (2)
Bernard, P. R. J. (Oldham Ath), 1992 v R (sub), D, Se (sub); 1993 v Sw, P, I, Ma, P, F, Bul, M, E; 1994 v I, Ma (15)
Bett, J. (Rangers), 1981 v Se, D; 1982 v Se, D, I, E (2) (7)
Black, A. (Aberdeen), 1983 v EG, Sw (2), Bel; 1985 v Ic, Sp (2), Ic (8)
Blair, A. (Coventry C), 1980 v E; 1981 v Se; (with Aston Villa), 1982 v Se, D, I (5)
Bollan, G. (Dundee U), 1992 v D, G (sub), US, P, Y; 1993 v Sw, P, I, P, F, Bul, M, E; 1994 v Sw; 1995 v Gr; (with Rangers) v Ru, Sm (17)
Bonar, P. (Raith R), 1997 v A, La, Es (sub), Se (4)

Booth, S. (Aberdeen), 1991 v R (sub), Bul (sub + 1), Pol, F (sub); 1992 v Sw, R, D, Se, US, P, Y; 1993 v Ma, P (14)

Bowes, M. J. (Dunfermline Ath), 1992 v D (sub) (1)

Bowman, D. (Hearts), 1985 v WG (sub) (1)

Boyack, S. (Rangers), 1997 v Se (1)

Boyd, T. (Motherwell), 1987 v WG, Ei (2), Bel; 1988 v Bel (5)

Brazil, A. (Hibernian), 1978 v W (1)

Brazil, A. (Ipswich T), 1979 v N; 1980 v Bel (2), E (2), WG; 1981 v Se; 1982 v Se (8)

Brebner, G. I. (Manchester U), 1997 v Co, CzR (sub), US (sub), P (4)

Brough, J. (Hearts), 1981 v D (1)

Browne, P. (Raith R), 1997 v A (1)

Buchan, J. (Aberdeen), 1997 v Se, Co, CzR, P (4)

Burke, A. (Kilmarnock), 1997 v Es, A, Bl (sub) (3)

Burley, G. E. (Ipswich T), 1977 v Cz, W, Sw; 1978 v Sw, Cz (5)

Burley, C. (Chelsea), 1992 v D; 1993 v Sw, P, I, P; 1994 v Sw, I (sub) (7)

Burns, H. (Rangers), 1985 v Sp, Ic (sub) (2)

Burns, T. (Celtic), 1977 v Cz, W, E; 1978 v Sw; 1982 v E (5)

Campbell, S. (Dundee), 1989 v N (sub), Y, F (3)

Casey, J. (Celtic), 1978 v W (1)

Christie, M. (Dundee), 1992 v D, P (sub), Y (3)

Clark, R. (Aberdeen), 1977 v Cz, W, Sw (3)

Clarke, S. (St Mirren), 1984 v Bel, EG, Y; 1985 v WG, Ic, Sp (2), Ic (8)

Cleland, A. (Dundee U), 1990 v F, N (2); 1991 v R, Sw, Bul; 1992 v Sw, R, G, Se (2) (11)

Collins, J. (Hibernian), 1988 v Bel, E; 1989 v N, Y, F; 1990 v Y, F, N (8)

Connolly, P. (Dundee U), 1991 v R (sub), Sw, Bul (3)

Connor, R. (Ayr U), 1981 v Se; 1982 v Se (2)

Cooper, D. (Clydebank), 1977 v Cz, W, Sw, E; (with Rangers), 1978 v Sw, Cz (6)

Cooper, N. (Aberdeen), 1982 v D, E (2); 1983 v Bel, EG, Sw (2); 1984 v Bel, EG, Y; 1985 v Ic, Sp, Ic (13)

Crabbe, S. (Hearts), 1990 v Y (sub), F (2)

Craig, T. (Newcastle U), 1977 v E (1)

Crainie, D. (Celtic), 1983 v Sw (sub) (1)

Crawford, S. (Raith R), 1994 v A, Eg, P, Bel; 1995 v Fi, Ru,Gr, Ru, Sm, M, F (sub), Sk (sub), Br (sub); 1996 v Gr, Fi (sub), H (1 + sub), Sp (sub), F (sub) (19)

Creaney, G. (Celtic), 1991 v Sw, Bul (2), Pol, F; 1992 v Sw, R, G (2), Se (2) (11)

Dailly, C. (Dundee U), 1991 v R; 1992 v US, R; 1993 v Sw, P, I, Ic, P, F, Bul, M, E; 1994 v Sw, I, Ma, A, Eg, P, Bel; 1995 v Fi, Ru, Gr, Ru, Sm, M, F, Sk, Br; 1996 v Sm, H (2), Sp, F (34)

Davidson, C. (St Johnstone), 1997 v Se, Bl (2)

Dawson, A. (Rangers), 1979 v P, N (2); 1980 v B (2), E (2), WG (8)

Deas, P. A. (St Johnstone), 1992 v D (sub); 1993 v Ma (2)

Dennis, S. (Raith R), 1992 v Sw (1)

Dickov, P. (Arsenal), 1992 v Y; 1993 v F, M, E (4)

Dodds, D. (Dundee U), 1978 v W (1)

Dods, D. (Hibernian), 1997 v La, Es, Se (2), Bl (5)

Donald, G. S. (Hibernian), 1992 v US (sub), P, Y (sub) (3)

Donnelly, S. (Celtic), 1994 v Eg, P, Bel; 1995 v Fi, Gr (sub); 1996 v Gr (sub), Sm, H (2), Sp, F (11)

Dow, A. (Dundee), 1993 v Ma (sub), Ic; (with Chelsea) 1994 v I (3)

Duffy, J. (Dundee), 1987 v Ei (1)

Durie, G. S. (Chelsea), 1987 v WG, Ei, Bel; 1988 v Bel (4)

Durrant, I. (Rangers), 1987 v WG, Ei, Bel; 1988 v E (4)

Doyle, J. (Partick Th), 1981 v D, I (sub) (2)

Easton, C. (Dundee U), 1997 v Co, US, CzR, P (4)

Ferguson, B. (Rangers), 1997 v Co (sub), US, CzR, P (4)

Ferguson, D. (Rangers), 1987 v WG, Ei, Bel; 1988 v E; 1990 v Y (5)

Ferguson, D. (Dundee U), 1992 v D, G, Se (2); 1993 v Sw, I, Ma (7)

Ferguson, D. (Manchester U), 1992 v US, P (sub), Y; 1993 v Sw, Ma (5)

Ferguson, I. (Dundee), 1983 v EG (sub), Sw (sub); 1984 v Bel (sub), EG (4)

Ferguson, I. (Clyde), 1987 v WG (sub), Ei; (with St Mirren), Ei, Bel; 1988 v Bel; (with Rangers), E (sub) (6)

Ferguson, R. (Hamilton A), 1977 v E (1)

Findlay, W. (Hibernian), 1991 v R, Pol, Bul (2), Pol (5)

Fitzpatrick, A. (St Mirren), 1977 v W (sub), Sw (sub), E; 1978 v Sw, Cz (5)

Flannigan, C. (Clydebank), 1993 v Ic (sub) (1)

Fleck, R. (Rangers), 1987 v WG (sub), Ei, Bel; (with Norwich C), 1988 v E (2); 1989 v Y (6)

Freedman, D. A. (Barnet), 1995 v Ru (sub + 1), Sm, M, F, Sk, Br; (with C Palace) 1996 v Sm (sub) (8)

Fridge, L. (St Mirren), 1989 v F; 1990 v Y (2)

Fullarton, J. (St. Mirren), 1993 v F, Bul; 1994 v Ma, A, Eg, P, Bel; 1995 v M, F, Sk, Br; 1996 v Gr, Fi, H (sub + 1), Sp (sub), F (17)

Fulton, M. (St Mirren), 1980 v Bel, WG, E; 1981 v Se, D (sub) (5)

Fulton, S. (Celtic), 1991 v R, Sw, Bul, Pol, F; 1992 v G (2) (7)

Gallacher, K. (Dundee U), 1987 v WG, Ei (2), Bel (sub); 1988 v E (2); 1990 v Y (7)

Galloway, M. (Hearts), 1989 v F; (with Celtic), 1990 v N (2)

Gardiner, J. (Hibernian), 1993 v F (1)

Geddes, R. (Dundee), 1982 v Se, D, E (2); 1988 v E (5)

Gemmill, S. (Nottingham F), 1992 v Sw, R (sub), G (sub), Se (sub) (4)

Germaine, G. (WBA), 1997 v Se (1)

Gilles, R. (St Mirren), 1997 v A (1 + sub), La, Es (2), Se, Bl (7)

Gillespie, G. (Coventry C), 1979 v US; 1980 v E; 1981 v D; 1982 v Se, D, I (2), E (8)

Glass, S. (Aberdeen), 1995 v M, F, Sk, Br; 1996 v Gr, Fi, H, Sp; 1997 v A (2), Es (11)

Glover, L. (Nottingham F), 1988 v Bel (sub); 1989 v N; 1990 v Y (3)

Goram, A. (Oldham Ath), 1987 v Ei (1)

Gough, C. R. (Dundee U), 1983 v EG, Sw, Bel; 1984 v Y (2) (5)

Grant, P. (Celtic), 1985 v WG, Ic, Sp; 1987 v WG, Ei (2), Bel; 1988 v Bel, E (2) (10)

Gray, S. (Celtic), 1995 v F, Sk, Br; 1996 v Gr, H, Sp, F (7)

Gray, S. (Aberdeen), 1987 v WG (1)

Gunn, B. (Aberdeen), 1984 v EG, Y (2); 1985 v WG, Ic, Sp (2), Ic; 1990 v F (9)

Hagen, D. (Rangers), 1992 v D (sub), US (sub), P, Y; 1993 v Sw (sub), P, Ic, P (8)

Hamilton, B. (St Mirren), 1989 v Y, F (sub); 1990 v F, N (4)

Hamilton, J. (Dundee) 1995 v Sm (sub), Br; 1996 v Fi (sub), Sm, H (sub), Sp (sub), F; 1997 v A, La, Es, Se; (with Hearts), Es, A, Se (14)

Handyside, P. (Grimsby T), 1993 v Ic (sub), Bul, M, E; 1995 v Ru; 1996 v Fi, Sm (7)

Hannah, D. (Dundee U), 1993 v F (sub), Bul, M; 1994 v A, Eg, P, Bel; 1995 v Fi, Ru (sub), Gr, Ru, M, F, Sk, Br; 1996 v Gr (16)

Harper, K. (Hibernian), 1995 v Ru (sub); 1996 v Fi; 1997 v A (2), La, Es, Se (7)

Hartford, R. A. (Manchester C), 1977 v Sw (1)

Hartley, P. (Millwall), 1997 v A (sub) (1)

Hegarty, P. (Dundee U), 1987 v WG, Bel; 1988 v E (2); 1990 v F, N (6)

Hendry, J. (Tottenham H), 1992 v D (sub) (1)

Hetherston, B. (St Mirren), 1997 v Es (sub) (1)

Hewitt, J. (Aberdeen), 1982 v I; 1983 v EG, Sw (2); 1984 v Bel (sub) (6)

Hogg, G. (Manchester U), 1984 v Y; 1985 v WG, Ic, Sp (4)

Hood, G. (Ayr U), 1993 v F, E (sub); 1994 v A (3)

Horn, R. (Hearts), 1997 v US, CzR, P (3)

Howie, S. (Cowdenbeath), 1993 v Ma, Ic, P; 1994 v Sw, I (5)

Hunter, G. (Hibernian), 1987 v Ei (sub); 1988 v Bel, E (3)

Hunter, P. (East Fife), 1989 v N (sub), F (sub); 1990 v F (sub) (3)

James, K. F. (Falkirk), 1997 v Bl (1)

Jardine, I. (Kilmarnock), 1979 v US (1)

Jess, E. (Aberdeen), 1990 v F (sub), N (sub); 1991 v R, Sw, Bul (2), Pol, F; 1992 v Sw, R, G (2), Se (1 + 1 sub) (14)

Johnson, G. I. (Dundee U), 1992 v US, P, Y; 1993 v Sw, P, Ma (6)

Johnston, A. (Hearts), 1994 v Bel; 1995 v Ru, 1996 v Sp (3)

Johnston, F. (Falkirk), 1993 v Ic (1)

Johnston, M. (Partick Th), 1984 v EG (sub); (with Watford), Y (2) (3)

Jupp, D. A. (Fulham), 1995 v Fi, Ru (2), Sm, M, F, Sk, Br; 1997 v Se (9)

Kirkwood, D. (Hearts), 1990 v Y (1)
Kerr, S. (Celtic), 1993 v Bul, M, E; 1994 v Ma, A, Eg, P, Bel; 1995 v Fi, Gr (10)

Lambert, P. (St Mirren), 1991 v R, Sw, Bul (2), Pol, F; 1992 v Sw, R, G (2), Se (11)
Lavety, B. (St. Mirren), 1993 v Ic, Bul (sub), M (sub), E; 1994 v Ma, A (sub), Eg (sub), Bel (sub); 1995 v Fi (sub) (9)
Lavin, G. (Watford), 1993 v F, Bul, M; 1994 v Ma, Eg, P, Bel (7)
Leighton, J. (Aberdeen), 1982 v I (1)
Levein, C. (Hearts), 1985 v Sp, Ic (2)
Liddell, A. M. (Barnsley), 1994 v Ma (sub); 1995 v Sm (sub), M (sub), F, Sk; 1996 v Gr, Fi, Sm, H (2), Sp, F (sub) (12)
Lindsey, J. (Motherwell), 1979 v US (1)
Locke, G. (Hearts), 1994 v Ma, A, Eg, P; 1995 v Fi; 1996 v Fi, H; 1997 v Es, A, Bl (10)
Love, G. (Hibernian), 1995 v Ru (1)

McAllister, G. (Leicester C), 1990 v N (1)
McAlpine, H. (Dundee U), 1983 v EG, Sw (2), Bel; 1984 v Bel (5)
McAuley, S. (St. Johnstone), 1993 v P (sub) (1)
McAvennie, F. (St Mirren), 1982 v I, E; 1985 v Is, Ei, R (5)
McBride, J. (Everton), 1981 v D (1)
McCall, S. (Bradford C), 1988 v E; (with Everton), 1990 v F (2)
McCann, N. (Dundee), 1994 v A, Eg, P, Bel; 1995 v Fi, Gr (sub), Sm; 1996 v Fi, Sm (9)

McClair, B. (Celtic), 1984 v Bel (sub), EG, Y (1 + 1 sub); 1985 v WG, Ic, Sp, Ic (8)
McCluskey, G. (Celtic), 1979 v US, P; 1980 v Bel (2); 1982 v D, I (6)
McCluskey, S. (St Johnstone), 1997 v Es (2), A, Se, Co, US, CzR (7)
McCoist, A. (Rangers), 1984 v Bel (1)
McConnell, I. (Clyde), 1997 v A (1)
McCulloch, A. (Kilmarnock); 1981 v Se (1)
McCulloch, I. (Notts Co), 1982 v E (2)
McCulloch, L. (Motherwell), 1997 v La (sub), Es (1 + sub), Se (sub + 1), A (sub), Co (sub) (7)
MacDonald, J. (Rangers), 1980 v WG (sub); 1981 v Se; 1982 v Se (sub), L, I (2), E (2 sub) (8)
McDonald, C. (Falkirk), 1995 v Fi (sub), Ru, M (sub), F (sub), Br (sub) (5)
McEwan, C. (Clyde), 1997 v Co, US (sub), CzR (sub), P (4)
McFarlane, D. (Hamilton A), 1997 v Co, US (sub), P (sub) (3)
McGarry, S. (St Mirren), 1997 v US, CzR, P (sub) (3)
McGarvey, F. (St Mirren), 1977 v E; 1978 v Cz; (with Celtic), 1982 v D (3)
McGarvey, S. (Manchester U), 1982 v E (sub); 1983 v Bel, Sw; 1984 v Bel (4)
McGhee, M. (Aberdeen), 1981 v D (1)
McGinnis, G. (Dundee U), 1985 v Sp (1)
McGrillen, P. (Motherwell), 1994 v Sw (sub), I (2)
McInally, J. (Dundee U), 1989 v F (1)
McKenzie, R. (Hearts), 1997 v Es, Bl (2)
McKimmie, S. (Aberdeen), 1985 v WG, Ic (2) (3)
McKinlay, T. (Dundee), 1984 v EG (sub); 1985 v WG, Ic, Sp (2), Ic (6)
McKinlay, W. (Dundee U), 1989 v N, Y (sub), F; 1990 v Y, F, N (6)
McKinnon, R. (Dundee U), 1991 v R, Pol (sub); 1992 v G (2), Se (2) (6)
McLaren, A. (Hearts), 1989 v F; 1990 v Y, N; 1991 v Sw, Bul, Pol, F; 1992 v R, G, Se (2) (11)
McLaren, A. (Dundee U), 1993 v I, Ma (sub); 1994 v Sw, I (sub) (4)
McLaughlin, B. (Celtic), 1995 v Ru, Sm, M, Sk (sub), Br (sub); 1996 v Gr (sub), Sm (sub), H (8)
McLaughlin, J. (Morton), 1981 v D; 1982 v Se, D, I, E (2); 1983 v EG, Sw (2), Bel (10)
McLeish, A. (Aberdeen), 1978 v W; 1979 v US; 1980 v Bel, E (2); 1987 v Ei (6)
MacLeod, A. (Hibernian), 1979 v P, N (2) (3)
McLeod, J. (Dundee U), 1989 v N; 1990 v F (2)
MacLeod, M. (Dumbarton), 1979 v US; (with Celtic), P (sub), N (2); 1980 v Bel (5)
McMillan, S. (Motherwell), 1997 v A (sub + sub), Se, Bl (4)

McNab, N. (Tottenham H), 1978 v W (1)
McNally, M. (Celtic), 1991 v Bul; 1993 v Ic (2)
McNamara, J. (Dunfermline Ath), 1994 v A, Bel; 1995 v Gr, Ru, Sm; 1996 v Gr, Fi; (with Celtic), Sm, H (2), Sp, F (12)
McNichol, J. (Brentford), 1979 v P, N (2); 1980 v Bel (2), WG, E (7)
McNiven, D. (Leeds U), 1977 v Cz, W (sub), Sw (sub) (3)
McNiven, S. A. (Oldham Ath), 1996 v Sm (sub) (1)
McPherson, D. (Rangers), 1984 v Bel; 1985 v Sp; (with Hearts), 1989 v N, Y (4)
McQuilken, J. (Celtic), 1993 v Bul, E (2)
McStay, P. (Celtic), 1983 v EG, Sw (2); 1984 v Y (2) (5)
McWhirter, N. (St Mirren), 1991 v Bul (sub) (1)
Main, A. (Dundee U), 1988 v E; 1989 v Y; 1990 v N (3)
Malpas, M. (Dundee U), 1983 v Bel, Sw (1+1 sub); 1984 v Bel, EG, Y (2); 1985 v Sp (8)
Marshall, S. R. (Arsenal), 1995 v Ru, Gr; 1996 v H, Sp, F (5)
Mathieson, D. (Queen of the South), 1997 v Co (1)
May, E. (Hibernian), 1989 v Y (sub), F (2)
Meldrum, C. (Kilmarnock), 1996 v F (sub); 1997 v A (2), La, Es, Se (6)
Melrose, J. (Partick Th), 1977 v Sw; 1979 v US, P, N (2); 1980 v Bel (sub), WG, E (8)
Miller, C. (Rangers), 1995 v Gr, Ru; 1996 v Gr, Sp, F; 1997 v A, La, Es (8)
Miller, J. (Aberdeen), 1987 v Ei (sub); 1988 v Bel; (with Celtic); E; 1989 v N, Y; 1990 v F, N (7)
Miller, W. (Aberdeen), 1978 v Sw, Cz (2)
Miller, W. (Hibernian), 1991 v R, Sw, Bul, Pol, F; 1992 v R, G (sub) (7)
Milne, R. (Dundee U), 1982 v Se (sub); 1984 v Bel, EG (3)
Money, I. C. (St Mirren), 1987 v Ei; 1988 v Bel; 1989 v N (3)
Muir, L. (Hibernian), 1977 v Cz (sub) (1)
Murray, N. (Rangers), 1993 v P (sub), Ma, Ic, P; 1994 v Sw, I; 1995 v Fi, Ru, Gr, Sm; 1996 v Gr (sub), Fi, Sm, H (2), F (16)
Murray, R. (Bournemouth), 1993 v Ic (sub) (1)

Narey, D. (Dundee U), 1977 v Cz, Sw; 1978 v Sw, Cz (4)
Naysmith, G. (Hearts), 1997 v La, Es (1 + sub), Se, A, Co, US, CzR, P (9)
Nevin, P. (Chelsea), 1985 v WG, Ic, Sp (2), Ic (5)
Nicholas, C. (Celtic), 1981 v Se; 1982 v Se; 1983 v EG, Sw, Bel; (with Arsenal), 1984 v Y (6)
Nicol, S. (Ayr U), 1981 v Se; 1982 v Se, D; (with Liverpool), I (2), E (2); 1983 v EG, Sw (2), Bel; 1984 v Bel, EG, Y (14)
Nisbet, S. (Rangers), 1989 v N, Y, F; 1990 v Y, F (5)

O'Donnell, P. (Motherwell), 1992 v Sw (sub), R, D, G (2), Se (1 + 1 sub); 1993 v P (8)
O'Neil, B. (Celtic), 1992 v D, G, Se (2); 1993 v Sw, P, I (7)
O'Neil, J. (Dundee U), 1991 v Bul (sub) (1)
O'Neill, M. (Clyde), 1995 v Ru (sub), F, Sk, Br; 1997 v Se (sub), Bl (sub) (6)
Orr, N. (Morton), 1978 v W (sub); 1979 v US, P, N (2); 1980 v Bel, E (7)

Parlane, D. (Rangers), 1977 v W (1)
Paterson, C. (Hibernian), 1981 v Se; 1982 v I (2)
Paterson, J. (Dundee U), 1997 v Co, US, CzR (3)
Payne, G. (Dundee U), 1978 v Sw, Cz, W (3)
Peacock, L. A. (Carlisle U), 1997 v Bl (1)
Pressley, S. (Rangers), 1993 v Ic, F, Bul, M, E; 1994 v Sw, I, M, A, Eg, P, Bel; 1995 v Fi; (with Coventry C), Ru (2), Sm, M, F, Sk, Br; (with Dundee U), 1996 v Gr, Sm, H (2), Sp, F (26)
Provan, D. (Kilmarnock), 1977 v Cz (sub) (1)

Rae, A. (Millwall), 1991 v Bul (sub + 1), F (sub); 1992 v Sw, R, G (sub), Se (2) (8)
Redford, I. (Rangers), 1981 v Se (sub); 1982 v Se, D, I (2), E (6)
Reid, B. (Rangers), 1991 v F; 1992 v D, US, P (4)
Reid, C. (Hibernian), 1993 v Sw, P, I (3)
Reid, M. (Celtic), 1982 v E; 1984 v Y (2)
Reid, R. (St Mirren), 1977 v W, Sw, E (3)
Renicks, S. (Hamilton A), 1997 v Bl (1)
Rice, B. (Hibernian), 1985 v WG (1)
Richardson, L. (St Mirren), 1980 v WG, E (sub) (2)
Ritchie, A. (Morton), 1980 v Bel (1)
Ritchie, P. R. (Hearts), 1996 v H; 1997 v A (2), La, Es (2), Se (7)
Robertson, A. (Rangers) 1991 v F (1)

Robertson, C. (Rangers), 1977 v E (sub) (1)
Robertson, D. (Aberdeen), 1987 v Ei (sub); 1988 v E (2); 1989 v N, Y; 1990 v Y, N (7)
Robertson, H. (Aberdeen), 1994 v Eg; 1995 v Fi (2)
Robertson, J. (Hearts), 1985 v WG, Ic (sub) (2)
Robertson, L. (Rangers), 1993 v F, M (sub), E (sub) (3)
Roddie, A. (Aberdeen), 1992 v US, P; 1993 v Sw (sub), P, Ic (5)
Ross, T. W. (Arsenal), 1977 v W (1)
Rowson, D. (Aberdeen), 1997 v La, Es, Se (2), Bl (5)
Russell, R. (Rangers), 1978 v W; 1980 v Bel; 1984 v Y (3)

Salton, D. B. (Luton T), 1992 v D, US, P, Y; 1993 v Sw, I (6)
Scott, P. (St Johnstone), 1994 v A (sub), Eg (sub), P, Bel (4)
Scrimgour, D. (St Mirren), 1997 v US, CzR (2)
Shannon, R. (Dundee), 1987 v WG, Ei (2), Bel; 1988 v Bel, E (2) (7)
Sharp, G. (Everton), 1982 v E (1)
Sharp, R. (Dunfermline Ath), 1990 v N (sub); 1991 v R, Sw, Bul (4)
Sheerin, P. (Southampton), 1996 v Sm (1)
Shields, G. (Rangers), 1997 v A, La (2)
Simpson, N. (Aberdeen), 1982 v I (2), E; 1983 v EG, Sw (2), Bel; 1984 v Bel, EG, Y; 1985 v Sp (11)
Sinclair, G. (Dumbarton), 1977 v E (1)
Skilling, M. (Kilmarnock), 1993 v Ic (sub); 1994 v I (2)
Smith, B. M. (Celtic), 1992 v G (2), US, P, Y (5)
Smith, G. (Rangers), 1978 v W (1)
Smith, H. G. (Hearts), 1987 v WG, Bel (2)
Sneddon, A. (Celtic), 1979 v US (1)
Speedie, D. (Chelsea), 1985 v Sp (1)
Spencer, J. (Rangers), 1991 v Sw (sub), F; 1992 v Sw (3)
Stanton, P. (Hibernian), 1977 v Cz (1)
Stark, W. (Aberdeen), 1985 v Ic (1)
Stephen, R. (Dundee), 1983 v Bel (sub) (1)
Stevens, G. (Motherwell), 1977 v E (1)
Stewart, J. (Kilmarnock), 1978 v Sw, Cz; (with Middlesbrough), 1979 v P (3)
Stewart, R. (Dundee U), 1979 v P, N (2); (with West Ham U), 1980 v Bel (2), E (2), WG; 1981 v D; 1982 v I (2), E (12)
Stillie, D. (Aberdeen), 1995 v Ru (2), Sm, M, F, Sk, Br; 1996 v Gr, Fi, Sm, H (2), Sp, F (14)
Strachan, G. (Aberdeen), 1980 v Bel (1)
Sturrock, P. (Dundee U), 1977 v Cz, W, Sw, E; 1978 v Sw, Cz; 1982 v Se, I, E (9)
Sweeney, S. (Clydebank), 1991 v R, Sw (sub), Bul (2), Pol; 1992 v Sw, R (7)

Teale, G. (Clydebank), 1997 v La (sub), Es, Bl (3)
Telfer, P. (Luton T), 1993 v Ma, P; 1994 v Sw (3)
Thomas, K. (Hearts), 1993 v F (sub), Bul, M, E; 1994 v Sw, Ma; 1995 v Gr; 1997 v A (8)
Thompson, S. (Dundee U), 1997 v US, CzR, P (3)
Thomson, W. (Partick Th), 1977 v E (sub); 1978 v W; (with St Mirren), 1979 v US, N (2); 1980 v Bel (2), E (2), WG (10)
Tolmie, J. (Morton), 1980 v Bel (sub) (1)
Tortolano, J. (Hibernian), 1987 v WG, Ei (2)
Tweed, S. (Hibernian), 1993 v Ic; 1994 v Sw, I (3)

Walker, A. (Celtic), 1988 v Bel (1)
Wallace, I. (Coventry C), 1978 v Sw (1)
Walsh, C. (Nottingham F), 1984 v EG, Sw (2), Bel; 1984 v EG (5)
Wark, J. (Ipswich T), 1977 v Cz, W, Sw; 1978 v W; 1979 v P; 1980 v E (2), WG (8)
Watson, A. (Aberdeen), 1981 v Se, D; 1982 v D, I (sub) (4)
Watson, K. (Rangers), 1977 v E; 1978 v Sw (sub) (2)
Watt, M. (Aberdeen), 1991 v R, Sw, Bul (2), Pol, F; 1992 v Sw, R, G (2), Se (2) (12)
Whiteford, A. (St Johnstone), 1997 v US (1)
Whyte, D. (Celtic), 1987 v Ei (2), Bel; 1988 v E (2); 1989 v N, Y; 1990 v Y, N (9)
Will, J. A. (Arsenal), 1992 v D (sub), Y; 1993 v Ic (sub) (3)
Wilson, T. (St Mirren), 1983 v Sw (sub) (1)
Wilson, T. (Nottingham F), 1988 v E; 1989 v N, Y; 1990 v F (4)
Winnie, D. (St Mirren), 1988 v Bel (1)
Wright, P. (Aberdeen), 1989 v Y, F; (with QPR), 1990 v Y (sub) (3)
Wright, S. (Aberdeen), 1991 v Bul, Pol, F; 1992 v Sw, G (2), Se (2); 1993 v Sw, P, I, Ma; 1994 v I, Ma (14)
Wright, T. (Oldham Ath), 1987 v Bel (1)

Young, D. (Aberdeen), 1997 v Es (sub), Se, Co, CzR (sub), P (5)

WALES

Aizlewood, M. (Luton T), 1979 v E; 1981 v Ho (2)

Baddeley, L. M. (Cardiff C), 1996 v Mol (sub), G (sub) (2)
Balcombe, S. (Leeds U), 1982 v F (sub) (1)
Barnhouse, D. J. (Swansea), 1995 v Mol; 1996 v Mol, Sm (3)
Bater, P. T. (Bristol R), 1977 v E, S (2)
Bellamy, C. D. (Norwich C), 1996 v Sm (sub); 1997 v Sm, T, Bel (4)
Bird, A. (Cardiff C), 1993 v Cy (sub); 1994 v Cy (sub); 1995 v Mol, Ge (sub), Bul; 1996 v G (sub) (6)
Blackmore, C. (Manchester U), 1984 v N, Bul, Y (3)
Blake, N. (Cardiff C), 1991 v Pol (sub); 1993 v Cy, Bel, RCS; 1994 v RCS (5)
Blaney, S. D. (West Ham U), 1997 v Sm, Ho, T (3)
Bodin, P. (Cardiff C), 1983 v Y (1)
Bowen, J. P. (Swansea C), 1993 v Cy, Bel (2); 1994 v RCS, R (sub) (5)
Bowen, M. (Tottenham H), 1983 v N; 1984 v Bul, Y (3)
Boyle, T. (C Palace), 1982 v F (1)
Brace, D. P. (Wrexham), 1995 v Ge, Bul (2); 1997 v Sm, Ho (5)

Cegielski, W. (Wrexham), 1977 v E (sub), S (2)
Chapple, S. R. (Swansea C), 1992 v R; 1993 v Cy, Bel (2), RCS; 1994 v RCS; Bul (2) (8)
Charles, J. M. (Swansea C), 1979 v E; 1981 v Ho (2)
Clark, J. (Manchester U), 1978 v S; (with Derby Co), 1979 v E (2)
Coates, J. S. (Swansea C), 1996 v Mol, G; 1997 v Ho, T (sub) (4)
Coleman, C. (Swansea C), 1990 v Pol; 1991 v E, Pol (3)
Coyne, D. (Tranmere R), 1992 v R; 1994 v Cy (sub), R; 1995 v Mol, Ge, Bul (2) (7)
Curtis, A. T. (Swansea C), 1977 v E (1)

Davies, A. (Manchester U), 1982 v F (2), Ho; 1983 v N, Y, Bul (6)
Davies, G. M. (Hereford U), 1993 v Bel, RCS; 1995 v Mol (sub), Ge, Bul (2); (with C Palace) 1996 v Mol (7)
Davies, I. C. (Norwich C), 1978 v S (sub) (1)
Deacy, N. (PSV Eindhoven), 1977 v S (1)
Dibble, A. (Cardiff C), 1983 v Bul; 1984 v N, Bul (sub) (3)
Doyle, S. C. (Preston NE), 1979 v E (sub); (with Huddersfield T), 1984 v N (2)
Dwyer, P. J. (Cardiff C), 1979 v E (1)

Ebdon, M. (Everton), 1990 v Pol; 1991 v E (2)
Edwards, C. N. H. (Swansea C), 1996 v G; 1997 v Sm, Ho (2), T, Bel (6)
Edwards, R. I. (Chester), 1977 v S; 1978 v W (2)
Edwards, R. W. (Bristol C), 1991 v Pol; 1992 v R; 1993 v Cy, Bel (2), RCS; 1994 v RCS, Cy, R; 1995 v Ge, Bul; 1996 v Mol, G (13)
Evans, A. (Bristol R), 1977 v E (1)
Evans, P. S. (Shrewsbury T), 1996 v G (1)
Evans, T. (Cardiff C), 1995 v Bul (sub); 1996 v Mol, G (3)

Foster, M. G. (Tranmere R), 1993 v RCS (1)
Freestone, R. (Chelsea), 1990 v Pol (1)

Gale, D. (Swansea C), 1983 v Bul; 1984 v N (sub) (2)
Giggs, R. (Manchester U), 1991 v Pol (1)
Giles, D. C. (Cardiff C), 1977 v S; 1978 v S; (with Swansea C), 1981 v Ho; (with C Palace), 1983 v Y (4)
Giles, P. (Cardiff C), 1982 v F (2), Ho (3)
Graham, D. (Manchester U), 1991 v E (1)
Griffith, C. (Cardiff C), 1990 v Pol (1)
Griffiths, C. (Shrewsbury T), 1991 v Pol (sub) (1)

Hall, G. D. (Chelsea), 1990 v Pol (1)
Hartson, J. (Luton T), 1994 v Cy, R; 1995 v Mol, Ge, Bul; (with Arsenal), 1996 v G, Sm; 1997 v Sm, Ho (9)
Haworth, S. O. (Cardiff C), 1997 v Ho, T, Bel (3)
Hodges, G. (Wimbledon), 1983 v Y (sub), Bul (sub); 1984 v N, Bul, Y (5)
Holden, A. (Chester C), 1984 v Y (sub) (1)
Hopkins, J. (Fulham), 1982 v F (sub), Ho; 1983 v N, Y, Bul (5)
Huggins, D. S. (Bristol C), 1996 v Sm (1)
Hughes, D. R. (Southampton), 1994 v R (1)
Hughes, R. D. (Aston Villa), 1996 v Sm; 1997 v Sm (sub), Ho (2), T, Bel (6)
Hughes, I. (Bury), 1992 v R; 1993 v Cy, Bel (sub), RCS; 1994 v Cy, R; 1995 v Mol, Ge, Bul; 1996 v Mol (sub), G (11)

Hughes, L. M. (Manchester U), 1983 v N, Y; 1984 v N, Bul, Y (5)
Hughes, W. (WBA), 1977 v E, S; 1978 v S (3)

Jackett, K. (Watford), 1981 v Ho; 1982 v F (2)
James, R. M. (Swansea C), 1977 v E, S; 1978 v S (3)
Jarman, L. (Cardiff C), 1996 v Sm; 1997 v Sm, Ho (2), Bel (5)
Jenkins, S. R. (Swansea C), 1993 v Cy (sub), Bel (2)
Jones, F. (Wrexham), 1981 v Ho (1)
Jones, L. (Cardiff C), 1982 v F (2), Ho (3)
Jones, P. L. (Liverpool), 1992 v R; 1993 v Cy, Bel (2), RCS; 1994 v RCS (sub), Cy, R; 1995 v Mol, Ge; 1996 v Mol, G (12)
Jones, R. (Sheffield W), 1994 v N; 1995 v Bul (2) (3)
Jones, V. (Bristol R), 1979 v E; 1981 v Ho (2)

Kendall, M. (Tottenham H), 1978 v S (1)
Kenworthy, J. R. (Tranmere R), 1994 v Cy; 1995 v Mol, Bul (3)
Knott, G. R. (Tottenham H), 1996 v Sm (1)

Law, B. J. (QPR), 1990 v Pol; 1991 v E (2)
Letheran, G. (Leeds U), 1977 v E, S (2)
Lewis, D. (Swansea C), 1982 v F (2), Ho; 1983 v N, Y, Bul; 1984 v N, Bu1, Y (9)
Lewis, J. (Cardiff C), 1983 v N (1)
Loveridge, J. (Swansea C), 1982 v Ho; 1983 v N, Bul (3)
Lowndes, S. R. (Newport Co), 1979 v E; 1981 v Ho; (with Millwall), 1984 v Bul, Y (4)

McCarthy, A. J. (QPR), 1994 v RCS, Cy, R (3)
Maddy, P. (Cardiff C), 1982 v Ho; 1983 v N (sub) (2)
Margetson, M. W. (Manchester C), 1992 v R; 1993 v Cy, Bel (2), RCS; 1994 v RCS, Cy (7)
Marustik, C. (Swansea C), 1982 v F (2); 1983 v Y, Bul; 1984 v N, Bul, Y (7)
Meaker, M. J. (QPR), 1994 v RCS (sub), R (sub) (2)
Melville, A. K. (Swansea C), 1990 v Pol; (with Oxford U), 1991 v E (2)
Micallef, C. (Cardiff C), 1982 v F, Ho; 1983 v N (3)
Morgan, A. M. (Tranmere R), 1995 v Mol, Bul; 1996 v Mol, G (4)
Mountain, P. D. (Cardiff C), 1997 v Ho, T (2)

Nardiello, D. (Coventry C), 1978 v S (1)
Neilson, A. B. (Newcastle U), 1993 v Cy, Bel (2), RCS; 1994 v RCS, Cy, R (7)
Nicholas, P. (C Palace), 1978 v S; 1979 v E; (with Arsenal), 1982 v F (3)
Nogan, K. (Luton T), 1990 v Pol; 1991 v E (2)
Nogan, L. (Oxford U) 1991 v E (1)

Oster, J. M. (Grimsby T), 1997 v Sm (sub), Ho (sub), T, Bel (4)
Owen, G. (Wrexham), 1991 v E (sub), Pol; 1992 v R; 1993 v Cy, Bel (2); 1994 v Cy, R (8)

Page, R. J. (Watford), 1995 v Mol, Ge, Bul; 1996 v Mol (4)
Partridge, D. W. (West Ham U), 1997 v T (1)
Pascoe, C. (Swansea C), 1983 v Bul (sub); 1984 v N (sub), Bul, Y (4)
Pembridge, M. (Luton T), 1991 v Pol (1)
Perry, J. (Cardiff C), 1994 v Pol; 1991 v E, Pol (3)
Peters, M. (Manchester C), 1992 v R; (with Norwich C), 1993 v Cy, RCS (3)
Phillips, D. (Plymouth Arg), 1984 v N, Bul, Y (3)
Phillips, L. (Swansea C), 1979 v E; (with Charlton Ath), 1983 v N (2)

Pontin, K. (Cardiff C), 1978 v S (1)
Powell, A. (Southampton), 1991 v Pol (sub); 1992 v R (sub); 1993 v Bel (sub); 1994 v RCS (4)
Price, P. (Luton T), 1981 v Ho (1)
Pugh, D. (Doncaster R), 1982 v F (2) (2)
Pugh, S. (Wrexham), 1993 v Bel (2 subs) (2)

Ramasut, M. W. T. (Bristol R), 1997 v Ho, Bel (2)
Ratcliffe, K. (Everton), 1981 v Ho; 1982 v F (2)
Ready, K. (QPR), 1992 v R; 1993 v Bel (2); 1994 v RCS, Cy (5)
Rees, A. (Birmingham C), 1984 v N (1)
Rees, J. (Luton T), 1990 v Pol; 1991 v E, Pol (3)
Roberts, A. (QPR), 1991 v E, Pol (2)
Roberts, G. (Hull C), 1983 v Bul (1)
Roberts, G. W. (Liverpool), 1997 v Ho, T, Bel (3)
Roberts, J. G. (Wrexham), 1977 v E (1)
Roberts, P. (Porthmadog), 1997 v Ho (sub) (1)
Robinson, C. P. (Wolverhampton W), 1996 v Sm; 1997 v Sm, Ho (2), T, Bel (6)
Robinson, J. (Brighton & HA), 1992 v R; (with Charlton Ath), 1993 v Bel; 1994 v RCS, Cy, R (5)
Rowlands, A. J. R. (Manchester C), 1996 v Sm; 1997 v Sm, Ho (1 + sub), T (sub) (5)
Rush, I. (Liverpool), 1981 v Ho; 1982 v F (2)

Savage, R. W. (Crewe Alex), 1995 v Bul; 1996 v Mol, G (3)
Sayer, P. A. (Cardiff C), 1977 v E, S (2)
Searle, D. (Cardiff C), 1991 v Pol (sub); 1992 v R; 1993 v Cy, Bel (2), RCS; 1994 v RCS (6)
Slatter, N. (Bristol R), 1983 v N, Y, Bul; 1984 v N, Bul, Y (6)
Speed, G. A. (Leeds U), 1990 v Pol; 1991 v E, Pol (3)
Stevenson, N. (Swansea C), 1982 v F, Ho (2)
Stevenson, W. B. (Leeds U), 1977 v E, S; 1978 v S (3)
Symons, K. (Portsmouth), 1991 v E, Pol (2)

Taylor, G. K. (Bristol R), 1995 v Ge, Bul (2); 1996 v Mol (4)
Thomas, J. A. (Blackburn R), 1996 v Sm; 1997 v Sm, Ho (2), T, Bel (6)
Thomas, Martin R. (Bristol R), 1979 v E; 1981 v Ho (2)
Thomas, Mickey R. (Wrexham), 1977 v E; 1978 v S (2)
Thomas, D. G. (Leeds U), 1977 v E; 1979 v E; 1984 v N (3)
Tibbott, L. (Ipswich T), 1977 v E, S (2)
Twiddy, C. (Plymouth Arg), 1995 v Mol, Ge; 1996 v G (sub) (3)

Vaughan, N. (Newport Co), 1982 v F, Ho (2)

Walsh, I. P. (C Palace), 1979 v E; (with Swansea C), 1983 v Bul (2)
Walton, M. (Norwich C.), 1991 v Pol (sub) (1)
Ward, D. (Notts Co), 1996 v Mol, G (2)
Williams, A. S. (Blackburn R), 1996 v Sm; 1997 v Sm, Ho, Bel (4)
Williams, D. (Bristol R), 1983 v Y (1)
Williams, E. (Caernarfon C), 1997 v Ho (sub), T (sub) (2)
Williams, G. (Bristol R), 1983 v Y, Bul (2)
Williams, S. J. (Wrexham), 1995 v Mol, Ge, Bul (2) (4)
Wilmot, R. (Arsenal), 1982 v F (2), Ho; 1983 v N, Y; 1984 v Y (6)

Young, S. (Cardiff C), 1996 v Sm; 1997 v Sm, Ho (2), Bel (sub) (5)

REPRESENTATIVE MATCHES

Italian Second Division (1) 1 *(Pirri 35)*
Football League (0) 1 *(Newton 62)*   500
in Genoa.

Italian Second Division: Gianello; Brioschi (Mercuri 69), Baccin, Mezzano, Zancetta, Rutzittu, Zanetti, Tedesco (Amoroso 74), Lanna, Pirri (Chanese 61), Campolonghi.
Football League: Marshall (Norwich C); Moses (Barnsley), Mills (Norwich C), Serrant (Oldham Ath), Hamilton (Bradford C), Hughes (Wrexham), Holland (Birmingham C), Bullock (Barnsley), Rogers (Tranmere Rovers) [Newton (Charlton Ath) 60], Dyer (Crystal Palace), Bradbury (Portsmouth) [Taylor (Bolton W) 60].

Europe (1) 1 *(Guerin 43)*
Africa (1) 2 *(Pele 14, Hadji 78)*   8000
in Lisbon.

Europe: Van der Sar (Cherchesov 60); Sammer (Henchoz 46), Paulinho Santos (Nedved 46), Kohler, Frank De Boer, Boban, Ronald De Boer, Guerin, Rui Costa (Casiraghi 46), Joao Pinto (Moller 46), Klinsmann (Domingos 46).
Africa: Arense (Baruwa 46); Fish, Awankwah, West, Radwan (Sane 65), Oliseh, Saib (Quinizinho 58), Pele, Babangida (Hadji 58), Paulao (Conde 64), Ouattara.

INTERNATIONAL RECORDS

MOST GOALS IN AN INTERNATIONAL

Record	Sofus Nielsen (Denmark) 10 goals v France, at White City (Olympics)	22.10.1908
	Gottfried Fuchs (Germany) 10 goals v Russia, in Stockholm (Olympics)	1.7.1912
World Cup	Gary Cole (Australia) 7 goals v Fiji, in Melbourne	14.8.1981
	Karim Bagheri (Iran) 7 goals v Maldives, in Damascus	2.6.1997
England	Malcolm Macdonald (Newcastle U) 5 goals v Cyprus, at Wembley	16.4.1975
	Willie Hall (Tottenham H) 5 goals v Ireland, at Old Trafford	16.11.1938
	G. O. Smith (Corinthians) 5 goals v Ireland, at Sunderland	18.2.1899
	Steve Bloomer (Derby Co) 5 goals* v Wales, at Cardiff	16.3.1896
	Oliver Vaughton (Aston Villa) 5 goals v Ireland, at Belfast	18.2.1882
Scotland	Charles Heggie (Rangers) 5 goals v Ireland, at Belfast	20.3.1886
Ireland	Joe Bambrick (Linfield) 6 goals v Wales, at Belfast	1.2.1930
Wales	James Price (Wrexham) 4 goals v Ireland, at Wrexham	25.2.1882
	Mel Charles (Cardiff C) 4 goals v Ireland, at Cardiff	11.4.1962
	Ian Edwards (Chester) 4 goals v Malta, at Wrexham	25.10.1978

There are conflicting reports which make it uncertain whether Bloomer scored four or five goals in this game.

MOST GOALS IN AN INTERNATIONAL CAREER

		Goals	Games
England	Bobby Charlton (Manchester U)	49	106
Scotland	Denis Law (Huddersfield T, Manchester C, Torino, Manchester U)	30	55
	Kenny Dalglish (Celtic, Liverpool)	30	102
Ireland	Colin Clarke (Bournemouth, Southampton, QPR, Portsmouth)	13	38
Wales	Ian Rush (Liverpool, Juventus)	28	73
	Ivor Allchurch (Swansea T, Newcastle U, Cardiff C)	23	68
Republic of Ireland	Frank Stapleton (Arsenal, Manchester U, Ajax, Derby Co, Le Havre, Blackburn R)	20	70

HIGHEST SCORES

World Cup Match	Iran	17	Maldives	0	1997
European Championship	Spain	12	Malta	1	1983
Olympic Games	Denmark	17	France	1	1908
	Germany	16	USSR	0	1912
International Match	Germany	13	Finland	0	1940
	Spain	13	Bulgaria	0	1933
European Cup	Feyenoord	12	K R Reykjavik	2	1969
European Cup-Winners' Cup	Sporting Lisbon	16	Apoel Nicosia	1	1963
Fairs & UEFA Cups	Ajax	14	Red Boys	0	1984

GOALSCORING RECORDS

World Cup Final	Geoff Hurst (England) 3 goals v West Germany	1966
World Cup Final tournament	Just Fontaine (France) 13 goals	1958
Major European Cup game	Lothar Emmerich (Borussia Dortmund) v Floriana in Cup-Winners' Cup – 6 goals	1965
Career	Artur Friedenreich (Brazil) 1329 goals	1910–30
	Pelè (Brazil) 1281 goals	*1956–78
	Franz 'Bimbo' Binder (Austria, Germany) 1006 goals	1930–50

Pelé subsequently scored two goals in Testimonial matches making his total 1283.

MOST CAPPED INTERNATIONALS IN BRITISH ISLES

England	Peter Shilton	125 appearances	1970–90
Northern Ireland	Pat Jennings	119 appearances	1964–86
Scotland	Kenny Dalglish	102 appearances	1971–86
Wales	Neville Southall	91 appearances	1982–97
Republic of Ireland	Paul McGrath	83 appearances	1984–97

BRITISH & IRISH INTERNATIONAL MANAGERS

England
Walter Winterbottom 1946–1962 (after period as coach); Alf Ramsey 1963–1974; Joe Mercer (caretaker) 1974; Don Revie 1974–1977; Ron Greenwood 1977–1982; Bobby Robson 1982–1990; Graham Taylor 1990–1993; Terry Venables (coach) 1994–1996; Glenn Hoddle from May 1996.

Northern Ireland
Billy Bingham 1967–1971; Terry Neill 1971–1975; Dave Clements (player-manager)1975–76; Danny Blanchflower 1976–1979; Billy Bingham 1980–1993; Bryan Hamilton from February 1994.

Scotland
Bobby Brown 1967–1971; Tommy Docherty 1971–1972; Willie Ormond 1973–1977; Ally MacLeod 1977–1978; Jock Stein 1978–1985; Alex Ferguson (caretaker) 1985–1986 Andy Roxburgh (coach) 1986–1993; Craig Brown from September 1993.

Wales
Mike Smith 1974–1979; Mike England 1980–1988; David Williams (caretaker) 1988; Terry Yorath 1988–1993; John Toshack 1994 for one match; Mike Smith 1994–1995; Bobby Gould from August 1995.

Republic of Ireland
Liam Tuohy 1971–1972; Johnny Giles 1973–1980 (after period as player-manager); Eoin Hand 1980–1985; Jack Charlton 1986–1996; Mick McCarthy from February 1996.

FA SCHOOLS AND YOUTH GAMES 1996–97

ENGLAND UNDER-16

28 Sept
England 0
France 1
England: Ghent (Aston Villa); Canoville (Millwall), Nicholson (Sheffield W), Allman (Charlton Ath) [Wheatcroft (Manchester U) 50], King (Tottenham H) [Weston (Arsenal) 57], Maley (Sunderland) [Gough (Coventry C) 67], Parker (Charlton Ath), Holmes (Sheffield W) [Bullock (Stoke C) 40], Fitzpatrick (Manchester U), Jeffers (Everton), Higgins (Sheffield W).

28 Oct
England 2 *(Jeffers 31, Parker 42)*
Czech Republic 2
England: Ghent (Aston Villa); Canoville (Millwall), Nicholson (Sheffield W), Maley (Sunderland), King (Tottenham H), Parker (Charlton Ath), Wheatcroft (Manchester U) [Gough (Coventry C) 61], Higgins (Sheffield W), Fitzpatrick (Manchester U) [Taylor (Tranmere R) 75], Jeffers (Everton), Holmes (Shefffield W).

30 Oct
Spain 5
England 1 *(Fitzpatrick 6)*
England: Bywater (Rochdale); Canoville (Millwall), Nicholson (Sheffield W), Maley (Sunderland) [Gough (Coventry C) 50], King (Tottenham H), Wheatcroft (Manchester U) [Taylor (Tranmere R) 65], Higgins (Sheffield W) [Allman (Charlton Ath) 75], Fitzpatrick (Manchester U), Jeffers (Everton), Bullock (Stoke C).

17 Feb
England 2 *(Nicholson, Wheatcroft)*
Sweden 2
England: Ghent (Aston Villa) [Taylor S (Arsenal)]; Canoville (Millwall), Nicholson (Sheffield W), Weston (Arsenal [Allman (Charlton Ath)], Holmes (Sheffield W) [Dixon (Leeds U)], Thomas (Nottingham F), Gough (Coventry C), Lyons (Derby Co), Parker (Charlton Ath), Jeffers (Everton), Wheatcroft (Manchester U).

19 Feb
England 0
Sweden 0
England: Green (Norwich C) [Bywater (Rochdale)]; Murphy (Liverpool), Evans (Leeds U) [Joynson (Norwich C)], Woodgate (Leeds U), King (Tottenham H), Dixon (Leeds U) [Bullock (Stoke C)], Gerrard (Liverpool), Wellens (Manchester U), Smith (Leeds U), Woodcock (Newcastle U), Demietriou (Chelsea) [Konchosky (Charlton Ath)].

6 Mar
Scotland 5
England 1 *(Smith 10)*
England: Taylor S (Arsenal) [Ghent (Aston Villa)]; Canoville (Millwall), Nicholson (Sheffield W), Gough (Coventry C), Allman (Charlton Ath), Higgins (Sheffield W) [Lyons (Derby Co)], Jeffers (Everton), Parker (Charlton Ath) [Thomas (Nottingham F)], Smith (Leeds U) [Holmes (Sheffield W)], Wheatcroft (Manchester U), Joynson (Norwich C).

ENGLAND UNDER-18

11 Oct
England 1 *(Perry 67)*
Finland 0
England: Weaver (Leyton Orient); Dickman (Sunderland), Crowe (Arsenal) [Wicks (Arsenal) 75], Ferdinand (West Ham U), Ball (Everton) [Platts (Sheffield W) 25], Clement (Chelsea), Curtis (Manchester U), Gower (Tottenham H), Perry (QPR), Owen (Liverpool), Williams R (Mansfield T) [Lisbie (Charlton Ath) 71].

13 Oct
Northern Ireland 0
England 4 *(Owen 36, 38, 52, 77)*
England: Weaver (Leyton Orient) [Stewart (Blackburn R) 77]; Brightwell (Manchester U), Ferdinand (West Ham U), Platts (Sheffield W), Clement (Chelsea) [Ball (Everton) 34], Curtis (Manchester U), Gower (Tottenham H) [Williams R (Mansfield T) 65], Perry (QPR), Owen (Liverpool), Lisbie (Charlton Ath).

29 Apr
England 2 *(Owen 6, Lisbie 85)*
Portugal 1
England: Simonsen (Tranmere R); Perry (QPR), Griffin (Stoke C), Dyer (Ipswich T) [Forbes (Norwich C 89], Curtis (Manchester U), Ball (Everton), Nicholls (Charlton Ath), Gower (Tottenham H), Noel-Williams (Watford), Owen (Liverpool), Bridges (Sunderland) [Lisbie (Charlton Ath) 84].

13 May
Portugal 3
England 0
England: Simonsen (Tranmere R); Perry (QPR), Griffin (Stoke C) [Upson (Arsenal) 57], Forbes (Norwich C), Curtis (Manchester U), Ball (Everton), Nicholls (Charlton Ath), Gower (Tottenham H) [Lisbie (Charlton Ath) 65], Noel-Williams (Watford), Owen (Liverpool), Bridges (Sunderland).

ENGLAND UNDER-20
(In Malaysia)

18 June
England 2 *(Owen 5, Shepherd 69)*
Ivory Coast 1
England: Lucas (Preston NE); Shepherd (Leeds U), Wallwork (Manchester U), Curtis (Manchester U), Broomes (Blackburn R), Dyer (Ipswich T), Morris (Chelsea), Carragher (Liverpool), Easton (Watford) [Jackson (Leeds U) 46], Owen (Liverpool), Murphy (Crewe Alex) [Humphreys (Sheffield W) 68].

20 June
England 5 *(Murphy 7, 34, 49 (pen), Owen 52, Al Yarees 59 (og))*
UAE 0
England: Lucas (Preston NE); Crowe (Arsenal), Wallwork (Manchester U), Curtis (Manchester U), Dyer (Ipswich T), Shepherd (Leeds U), Morris (Chelsea), Carragher (Liverpool), Murphy (Crewe Alex) [Macken (Manchester U) 64], Easton (Watford) [Jackson (Leeds U) 56)], Owen (Liverpool) [Euell (Wimbledon) 64].

23 June
England 1 *(Owen 65)*
Mexico 0
England: Lucas (Preston NE); Wallwork (Manchester U), Curtis (Manchester U), Broomes (Blackburn R), Shepherd (Leeds U) [Crowe (Arsenal) 87], Morris (Chelsea), Carragher (Liverpool), Jackson (Leeds U), Dyer (Ipswich T), Murphy (Crewe Alex), Owen (Liverpool).

26 June
England 1 *(Carragher 48)*
Argentina 2
England: Lucas (Preston NE); Dyer (Ipswich T), Wallwork (Manchester U), Curtis (Manchester U), Crowe (Arsenal), Murphy (Crewe Alex), Jackson (Leeds U), Carragher (Liverpool), Morris (Chelsea), Owen (Liverpool), Humphreys (Sheffield W) [Euell (Wimbledon) 81].

WOMEN'S FOOTBALL

In recent years there has been, and will continue to be, an expansion in women's football through the aegis of FIFA. The English FA are themselves very intent in promoting the 'Ladies game' which although amateur in the British Isles has professionals playing it in other parts of Europe. There are plans to develop not only in the playing sphere but also in coaching and refereeing.

The first recorded women's match was in England in 1895 between Northern and Southern teams with the 'Northerners' winning 7-1. The first international match was between an English side and a French side in April 1920; and later in that year 53,000 people, the largest ever crowd recorded for a domestic women's game, turned out to see Dick Kerr's Ladies beat their closest rivals St Helens 4-0 at Goodison Park.

In 1969 the Women's Football Association (WFA) was formed and three years later the WFA was recognised when it was confirmed that all affiliated clubs must be controlled by the National Association. In 1983 the English FA invited the WFA into affiliation on a basis equal to that of a County FA.

In 1991 the WFA launched the National League with twenty-four clubs divided into Premier, Northern and Southern divisions, primarily with eight clubs in each. The format currently is the same except that when the English FA assumed responsibility for the organisation and administration of the National League, it changed its name to the FA Women's Premier League (FAWPL) and raised the number of teams to ten in each division.

The most successful club since the organisation of cups and leagues is Arsenal FC. Since season 1992/93 they have won the National League three times, the National Cup twice and the League Cup twice and included therein are two 'doubles' of League and WFA Cup and one treble of League, League Cup and WFA Cup. Their manager throughout all of this time has been Vic Akers.

National League Winners		Women's FA Cup Winners		League Cup	
1992/93	Arsenal	1992/93	Arsenal (WFA Competition)	1992/93	Arsenal (WFA Competition)
1993/94	Doncaster Belles	1993/94	Doncaster Belles	1993/94	Arsenal (WFA Competition)
1994/95	Arsenal	1994/95	Arsenal	1994/95	Wimbledon
1995/96	Croydon	1995/96	Croydon	1995/96	Wembley
1996/97	Arsenal	1996/97	Millwall Lionesses	1996/97	Millwall Lionesses

The current administrative structure for women at the FA consists of a Football Co-ordinator, Kelly Simmons and three Assistant Regional Directors who cover the North, Midlands and Southern Divisions.

The England Women's Football Manager is Ted Copeland.

Anyone interested in learning more about women's football should contact the Football Association whose headquarters for women is at 9 Wyllyotts Place, Potters Bar, Hertfordshire, EN6 2JD telephone no. 01707 6518 40; fax no. 01707 6441 90.

KEN GOLDMAN

FA WOMEN'S PREMIER LEAGUE 1996–97

National Division

	P	W	D	L	F	A	GD	Pts
Arsenal	18	16	1	1	65	9	+56	49
Doncaster Belles	18	13	2	3	44	15	+29	41
Croydon	18	9	4	5	39	26	+13	31
Liverpool	18	9	3	6	30	16	+14	30
Millwall Lionesses	18	7	6	5	25	19	+1	27
Everton	18	8	3	7	36	36	0	27
Wembley	18	6	4	8	26	27	−1	22
Tranmere Rovers	18	3	3	12	23	48	−25	12
Southampton Saints	18	3	0	15	16	61	−45	9
Ilkeston Town	18	1	4	13	14	56	−42	7

Northern Division

	P	W	D	L	F	A	GD	Pts
Bradford City	16	15	0	1	56	13	+43	45
Aston Villa	16	12	1	3	50	15	+35	37
Blyth Spartans Kestrels	16	9	2	5	40	25	+15	29
Huddersfield Town	16	8	3	5	37	32	+5	27
Wolverhampton Wanderers	16	7	1	8	30	29	+1	22
Sheffield Wednesday	16	4	4	8	25	36	−11	16
Garswood Saints	16	3	5	8	26	29	−3	14
Stourport Swifts	16	3	2	11	22	60	−38	11
Notts County	16	0	4	12	21	68	−47	4

Bronte withdrawn – all results expunged

Southern Division

	P	W	D	L	F	A	GD	Pts
Berkhamsted Town	18	14	2	2	57	16	+41	44
Brighton & Hove Albion	18	13	2	3	59	33	+26	41
Whitehawk	18	12	1	5	39	17	+22	37
Wimbledon	18	10	2	6	66	28	+38	32
Three Bridges	18	7	5	6	36	28	+8	26
Langford	18	7	5	6	28	33	−5	26
Ipswich Town	18	5	4	9	24	26	−2	19
Leyton Orient	18	3	4	11	27	50	−23	13
Town & County	18	2	3	13	18	65	−47	9
Oxford United	18	2	2	14	17	75	−58	8

Play-off Winners

Northern Division	Coventry City
Southern Division	Barry Town

Winners, Promotion and Relegation Movements
National Division
Champions   Arsenal
Relegated   Ilkeston Town (to Nth Div)
               Southampton Saints (to Sth Div)

Northern Division
Champions   Bradford City (to Nat Div)
Relegated   No clubs relegated

Southern Division
Champions   Berkhamsted Town (to Nat Div)
Relegated   Oxford United

UK LIVING WOMEN'S FA CUP 1996–97

Preliminary Round

Bedford Bells v Cambridge United	1-0
Truro City v Barry Town	1-7

Swindon Town Spitfires v Clevedon AFC	10-0
Cinderford Town v Swindon Town	0-10
Elmore Eagles v Cabletel	0-4

First Round

Sunderland v Chesterfield	3-4
Newcastle v Chester-le-Street	0-1
Chester City v Brighouse	6-0
Trafford v Liverpool Feds	1-3
Newsham PH v Manchester United	1-2
Sheffield Hallam United v Warrington Town	1-2
Darlington v Runcorn	4-2
Doncaster Rovers v Winsford United	8-1
Kirklees v Leeds United	1-3
Bangor City Girls v Stockport County	5-1
Radcliffe Borough v Wrexham	6-0
Haslingden v Oldham Athletic	0-7
Wakefield v York City	7-0
Rochdale v Deans	10-0
Manchester Belle Vue v Middlesbrough	0-1
Wigan v Hull City	2-1
Blackburn Rovers v Barnsley	6-1
Preston Rangers v Whalley Rangers	9-0
Scunthorpe Ironesses v Stockport	2-3
Lowestoft Town v Rea Valley Rovers	12-0
Canary Racers v Calverton MW	1-2
Nettleham v Birmingham City	1-2
Leek Town v Highfield Rangers	1-2
Milton Keynes Athletic v Coventry City	0-3
Belper Town v Tamworth	1-7
Colchester v Newcastle Town	0-3
Pye v Colchester United	1-3
Leicester City v Norwich United	1-0
Cambridge City v Clacton	3-5
Derby County v Bedford Bells	3-4
Haverhill Rovers v Shrewsbury Town	2-3
Abbey Rangers v Camberwell Old Fallopians	8-0
Denham United v Camberley Town	6-1
Barnet v Winchester & Ealing	3-1
Charlton v Farnborough Town	4-1
Sawbridgeworth Town v Stanway	4-1
Surbiton Town v Crowborough Athletic	2-1
Hastings Town v Harlequins	1-6
Dunstable withdrew v Chelsea w.o.	
Romford withdrew v Slough Town w.o.	
London v Queens Park Rangers LSA	9-1
Teynham Gunners v St George's (Eltham)	2-8
Chelmsford v Leatherhead	2-1
Hassocks v Harlow Town	1-2
Collier Row v Chipstead	5-1
Clapton v Enfield	3-2
Newham v Redbridge Wanderers	5-0
Hackney v Aylesbury Stocklake	4-1
(Tie awarded to Hackney; match abandoned 76 minutes	
due to injury to Aylesbury player)	
Watford & Evergreen v Chesham United	3-2
Dulwich Hamlet v Gillingham Girls	3-2
Tottenham Hotspur v Stevenage Borough	11-0
West Ham v Fulham	1-2
Brentford & Hampton v Luton	5-0
Mill Hill United v Great Wakering Rovers	11-0
Cardiff County v Thame United	1-0
Bath City v Wokingham Town	6-2
Clevedon United v Portsmouth	0-6
Bracknell Town v Yate Town	1-9
Binfield w.o. v Freeway withdrew	
Worcester City v Newton Abbot	8-3
Exeter Rangers v Bristol City	3-7
Okeford United v Bridgwater Town	3-2
Sherborne v Barnstaple Town	3-1
Reading Royals v Frome	7-0
Barry Town v Plymouth Pilgrims	3-1

Second Round

Garswood Saints v Manchester United	2-1
Sheffield Wednesday v Darlington	8-1
Wakefield v Wigan	8-0
Oldham Athletic v Warrington Town	11-3
Blackburn Rovers w.o v Bronte withdrew	
Stockport v Liverpool Feds	3-0
Middlesbrough w.o. v Chester-le-Street withdrew	
Doncaster Rovers v Huddersfield Town	2-4
Bradford City v Blyth Spartans Kestrels	1-2
Rochdale v Leeds United	0-7
Radcliffe Borough v Preston Rangers	2-3
Chesterfield v Bangor City Girls	1-3
Wolverhampton Wanderers v Aston Villa	0-5
Coventry City v Leicester City	3-1
Town & County Diamonds v Birmingham City	0-2
Tamworth v Calverton MW	1-5
Notts County v Newcastle Town	0-5
Highfield Rangers v Chester City	4-2
Stourport Swifts v Shrewsbury Town	3-1
Tottenham Hotspur v Wimbledon	2-1
Abbey Rangers v Chelmsford	4-5
Brentford & Hampton v Whitehawk	1-3
Harlequins v Clacton	3-1
Berkhamsted Town v Lowestoft Town	8-0
St George's (Eltham) v Leyton Orient	2-5
Langford v Chelsea	0-1
London v Sawbridgeworth Town	2-2, 2-0
Brighton & Hove Albion v Newham	5-0
Bedford Bells v Three Bridges	0-1
Charlton v Dulwich Hamlet	0-4
Harlow Town v Mill Hill United	0-4
Colchester United v Collier Row	1-4
Ipswich Town v Surbiton Town	3-0
Watford & Evergreen v Barnet	1-3
Fulham v Clapton	2-3
Hackney v Denham United	3-4
Worcester City v Binfield	0-2
Portsmouth v Oxford United	0-1
Reading Royals v Swindon Town	5-0
Bath City v Okeford United	2-2, 1-2
Barry Town v Bristol City	18-0
Slough Town v Swindon Town Spitfires	0-6
Sherborne v Yate Town	5-2
Cardiff County v Cabletel	1-3

Third Round

Sheffield Wednesday v Wakefield	3-2
Blackburn Rovers v Preston Rangers	0-3
Leeds United v Aston Villa	2-5
Blyth Spartans Kestrels v Garswood Saints	1-4
Highfield Rangers v Oldham Athletic	1-0
Calverton MW v Stockport	1-2
Coventry City v Huddersfield Town	2-3
Middlesbrough v Stourport Swifts	3-2
Bangor City Girls v Newcastle Town	2-2, 1-1
(Bangor City Girls won 5-3 on penalties.)	
Dulwich Hamlet v Berkhamsted Town	1-6
Whitehawk v Binfield	2-1
London v Sherborne	0-5
Oxford United v Reading Royals	1-4
Harlequins v Tottenham Hotspur	0-12
Swindon Town Spitfires v Chelsea	0-1
Three Bridges v Leyton Orient	1-2
Collier Row v Birmingham City	3-1
Chelmsford v Barnet	1-1, 2-2
(Chelmsford won 5-3 on penalties.)	

Okeford United v Denham United	1-2
Mill Hill United v Ipswich Town	0-1
Brighton & Hove Albion v Cabletel	7-2
Clapton v Barry Town	1-5

Fourth Round

Croydon v Liverpool	2-1
Highfield Rangers v Berkhamsted Town	2-3
Chelmsford v Huddersfield Town	2-5
Preston Rangers v Denham United	12-0
Southampton Saints v Whitehawk	4-0
Reading Royals v Leyton Orient	2-1
Doncaster Belles v Sheffield Wednesday	10-1
Ipswich Town v Middlesbrough	0-8
Garswood Saints v Ilkeston Town	3-4
Arsenal v Barry Town	6-0
Tottenham Hotspur v Collier Row	7-2
Sherborne v Everton	0-7
Stockport v Bangor City Girls	2-6
Aston Villa v Brighton & Hove Albion	1-0
Chelsea v Millwall Lionesses	0-3
Tranmere Rovers v Wembley	1-2

Fifth Round

Wembley v Preston Rangers	1-0
Southampton Saints v Berkhamsted Town	1-1, 2-3
Middlesbrough v Ilkeston Town	0-3
Millwall Lionesses v Doncaster Belles	3-0
Bangor City Girls v Everton	0-2
Tottenham Hotspur v Croydon	0-4

Reading Royals v Aston Villa	2-4
Arsenal v Huddersfield Town	9-0

Sixth Round

Croydon v Everton	1-0
Berkhamsted Town v Wembley	0-0, 1-3
Millwall Lionesses v Aston Villa	4-1
Ilkeston Town v Arsenal	2-4

Semi-finals

Wembley v Arsenal	1-0
Millwall Lionesses v Croydon	1-1
(Millwall Lionesses won 3-1 on penalties.)	

Final at (Upton Park)

4 MAY

Millwall Lionesses (0) 1 *(Waller)*

Wembley (0) 0   3015

Millwall Lionesses: Cope; Walsh, Chapman (Fletcher), Phillip, Osborn, Waller, Murphy, Lorton, Lindsay, Ede (Bedzrah), Buckley.
Wembley: Higgs; Hewitson, Frampton, Melia, Harwood, Darby, Calinan (Liran), Burns, Lee (Jones), Ball, Coch.
Referee: C. Wilkes (Glos).

FA WOMEN'S LEAGUE CUP

First Round

Blyth Spartans Kestrels v Aston Villa	3-5
Town & County Diamonds v Three Bridges	1-4
Wolverhampton Wanderers w.o. v Bronte withdrew	
Liverpool v Arsenal	1-2
Garswood Saints v Huddersfield Town	0-1
Brighton & Hove Albion v Tranmere Rovers	2-1
Ilkeston Town v Bradford City	3-1
Notts County v Wimbledon	0-5
Oxford United v Stourport Swifts	1-4
Southampton Saints v Everton	0-5
Whitehawk v Croydon	0-2
Leyton Orient v Langford	3-1
Berkhamsted Town v Ipswich Town	1-2
Millwall Lionesses v Sheffield Wednesday	3-2

Second Round

Stourport Swifts v Leyton Orient	3-1
Brighton & Hove Albion v Everton	1-6
Three Bridges v Ilkeston Town	0-1
Ipswich Town v Wimbledon	1-4

Wolverhampton Wanderers v Wembley	1-8
Huddersfield Town v Millwall Lionesses	0-5
Croydon v Aston Villa	1-1
(Aston Villa won on penalties.)	
Doncaster Belles v Arsenal	2-1

Third Round

Wembley v Everton	2-3
Aston Villa v Ilkeston Town	5-2
Wimbledon v Doncaster Belles	1-8
Millwall Lionesses v Stourport Swifts	4-0

Semi-finals

Everton v Aston Villa	5-2
Doncaster Belles v Millwall Lionesses	1-1
(aet; Millwall Lionesses won 4-2 on penalties.)	

Final (at Barnet)

Millwall Lionesses v Everton	2-1

WOMEN'S OLYMPICS FINAL

GROUP E
USA 3, Denmark 0
Sweden 0, China 2
USA 2, Sweden 1
Denmark 1, China 5
Denmark 1, Sweden 3
USA 0, China 0

GROUP F
Germany 3, Japan 2
Norway 2, Brazil 2
Brazil 2, Japan 0
Norway 3, Germany 2
Brazil 1, Germany 1
Norway 4, Japan 0

SEMI-FINALS
China 3, Brazil 2
Norway 1, USA 1
(USA won on sudden death)

3RD/4TH PLACE
Brazil 0, Norway 2

FINAL
China 1, USA 2

VAUXHALL CONFERENCE 1996–97

VAUXHALL CONFERENCE TABLE 1996–97

	P	W	D	L	F	A	W	D	L	F	A	Pts
			Home		Goals			Away			Goals	
Macclesfield Town	42	15	4	2	41	11	12	5	4	39	19	90
Kidderminster Harriers	42	14	4	3	48	18	12	3	6	36	24	85
Stevenage Borough	42	15	4	2	53	23	9	6	6	34	30	82
Morecambe	42	10	5	6	34	23	9	4	8	35	33	66
Woking	42	10	5	6	41	29	8	5	8	30	34	64
Northwich Victoria	42	11	5	5	31	20	6	7	8	30	34	63
Farnborough Town	42	9	6	6	35	29	7	7	7	23	24	61
Hednesford Town	42	10	7	4	28	17	6	5	10	24	33	60
Telford United	42	6	7	8	21	30	10	3	8	25	26	58
Gateshead	42	8	6	7	32	27	7	5	9	27	36	56
Southport	42	8	5	8	27	28	7	5	9	24	33	55
Rushden & Diamonds	42	8	8	5	30	25	6	3	12	31	38	53
Stalybridge Celtic	42	9	5	7	35	29	5	5	11	18	29	52
Kettering Town	42	9	4	8	30	28	5	5	11	23	34	51
Hayes	42	7	7	7	27	21	5	7	9	27	34	50
Slough Town	42	7	7	7	42	32	5	7	9	20	33	50
Dover Athletic	42	7	9	5	32	30	5	5	11	25	38	50
Welling United	42	9	2	10	24	26	4	7	10	26	34	48
Halifax Town	42	9	5	7	39	37	3	7	11	16	37	48
Bath City	42	9	5	7	27	28	3	6	12	26	52	47
Bromsgrove Rovers	42	8	4	9	29	30	4	1	16	12	37	41
Altrincham	42	6	3	12	25	34	3	9	9	24	39	39

ATTENDANCES BY CLUB 1996–97

	Aggregate Attendance 1996–97	Average Attendance 1996–97	Average Attendance 1995–96	% Change
Altrincham	17,271	822	852	–3.5
Bath City	14,483	690	526	+31.2
Bromsgrove Rovers	17,778	847	1,071	–20.9
Dover Athletic	22,474	1,070	1,002	+6.8
Farnborough Town	16,921	806	811	–0.6
Gateshead	12,353	588	623	–5.6
Halifax Town	17,668	841	838	+0.4
Hayes	13,931	663	480	+38.1
Hednesford Town	27,582	1,313	1,310	+0.2
Kettering Town	35,896	1,709	1,427	+19.8
Kidderminster Harriers	55,858	2,660	2,020	+31.7
Macclesfield Town	29,551	1,407	1,264	+11.3
Morecambe	21,213	1,010	1,130	–10.6
Northwich Victoria	20,316	967	814	+18.8
Rushden & Damonds	52,800	2,514	2,169	+15.9
Slough Town	22,443	1,069	923	+15.8
Southport	20,362	970	944	+2.8
Stalybridge Celtic	13,598	648	613	+5.7
Stevenage Borough	60,496	2,881	1,897	+51.9
Telford United	18,591	885	817	+8.3
Welling United	14,997	714	615	+16.1
Woking	54,504	2,595	2,384	+8.9

HIGHEST ATTENDANCES 1996–97

6,489	Stevenage Borough 2-2 Kidderminster H	25.1.97	3,305	Kidderminster Harriers 6-0 Bath City	28.12.96
6,081	Kidderminster H 1-2 Bromsgrove R	26.12.96	3,288	Rushden & Diamonds 0-1 Stevenage Boro	24.9.96
5,760	Stevenage Borough 2-3 Macclesfield Town	29.3.97	3,208	Woking 2-0 Slough Town	28.12.96
5,170	Rushden & Diamonds 1-0 Kettering Town	18.3.97	3,139	Kidderminster Harriers 3-0 Southport	26.4.97
4,628	Kettering Town 1-5 Rushden & Diamonds	8.3.97	3,134	Rushden & Diamonds 2-2 Hayes	31.3.97
4,352	Stevenage Borough 0-3 Woking	2.11.96	3,091	Woking 3-1 Northwich Victoria	9.11.96
3,461	Kettering Town 1-4 Macclesfield Town	3.5.97	3,009	Kidderminster Harriers 2-2 Morecambe	29.3.97
3,420	Woking 2-1 Kidderminster Harriers	31.3.97	3,004	Macclesfield Town 4-0 Bromsgrove Rovers	26.4.97
3,352	Woking 1-2 Hayes	25.3.97			

VAUXHALL CONFERENCE LEADING GOALSCORERS 1996–97

Conf.			FAC	SCC	FAT
30	Lee Hughes *(Kidderminster Harriers)*	+	1	1	2
21	Lennie Dennis *(Welling United)*	+	1	2	1
19	Andy Whittaker *(Southport)*	+	6	–	2
18	Gary Abbott *(Slough Town)*	+	–	–	–
17	Justin Jackson *(Woking)*	+	4	–	2
16	Barry Hayles *(Stevenage Borough)*	+	3	–	2
	David Leworthy *(Rushden & Diamonds)*	+	4	–	–
	Lee Steele *(Northwich Victoria)*	+	–	–	–
15	Joe O'Connor *(Hednesford Town)*	+	9	–	–
	Paul Thompson *(Gateshead)*	+	6	1	1
	Clive Walker *(Woking)*	+	3	–	1
	Steve Wood *(Macclesfield Town)*	+	–	1	–
14	Mike Davis *(Bath City)*	+	7	–	–
	Neil Doherty *(Kidderminster Harriers)*	+	1	–	1
	Niell Hardy *(Altrincham)*	+	3	–	1
	Mick Norbury *(Halifax Town)*	+	–	–	–
13	Carl Alford *(Rushden & Diamonds)*	+	2	–	–
	Ian Arnold *(Stalybridge Celtic)*	+	–	–	–
	Chris Boothe *(Farnborough Town)*	+	9	3	–
	Martin Randall *(Hayes)*	+	–	–	4
	Phil Wingfield *(Farnborough Town)*	+	2	–	1

FAC: FA Cup; SCC: Spalding Challenge Cup; FAT: FA Trophy.

CLUB REVIEW

	VC	FAT	SCC	FAC
Altrincham	22	3	2	1
1995–96	12	2	2	1
Bath City	20	1	1	4q
	18	QF	1	4q
Bromsgrove Rovers	21	2	QF	4q
	11	QF	W	1
Dover Athletic	17	1	1	3q
	20	2	QF	1q
Farnborough Town	7	2	SF	1
	10	1	2	1
Gateshead	10	1	2	4q
	5	QF	QF	2q
Halifax Town	19	2	1	2q
	15	2	2	4q
Hayes	15	2	1	1
	–	2	–	1
Hednesford Town	8	1	2	4
	3	1	1	4q
Kettering Town	14	1	2	3q
	16	2	SF	4q
Kidderminster H.	2	3	W	1
	7	1	2	1
Macclesfield Town	1	1	F	1
	4	F	F	4q
Morecambe	4	3	SF	1
	9	1	QF	4q
Northwich Victoria	6	2	1	1
	8	F	1	1
Rushden & Diamonds	12	1	QF	1
	–	1	–	1
Slough Town	16	1	1	4q
	17	2	QF	1
Southport	11	2	2	1
	6	1	SF	4q
Stalybridge Celtic	13	1	QF	1
	14	1	1	4q
Stevenage Borough	3	SF	2	3
	1	QF	2	1
Telford United	9	1	1	4q
	13	1	2	2
Welling United	18	2	QF	1
	19	2	1	2q
Woking	5	W	2	3
	2	1	2	3

VC: Vauxhall Conference; FAT: FA Trophy; SCC: Spalding Challenge Cup; FAC: FA Cup.

HIGHEST AGGREGATE SCORES

Halifax Town 4-5 Bath City 15.2.97
Woking 7-1 Altrincham 30.11.96
Slough Town 1-6 Stevenage Borough 1.1.96
Slough Town 5-2 Bath City 3.9.96

LARGEST HOME MARGINS

Woking 7-1 Altrincham 30.11.96
Kidderminster Harriers 6-0 Bath City 28.12.96
Stevenage Borough 6-0 Halifax Town 17.8.96
Slough Town 6-0 Telford United 19.10.96

LARGEST AWAY MARGINS

Slough Town 1-6 Stevenage Borough 1.1.97
Bromsgrove Rovers 0-5 Northwich Victoria 1.3.97
Dover Athletic 0-5 Kidderminster Harriers 24.8.96
Telford United 0-5 Rushden & Diamonds 7.12.96

MATCHES WITHOUT DEFEAT

12 Morecambe
11 Kidderminster Harriers

9   Farnborough Town, Macclesfield Town, Rushden & Diamonds, Stevenage Borough, Telford United, Woking

MATCHES WITHOUT SUCCESS

15 Altrincham
13 Slough Town
11 Dover Athletic

CONSECUTIVE CONFERENCE VICTORIES

8 Macclesfield Town
7 Kidderminster Harriers
6 Stevenage Borough, Kidderminster Harriers

CONSECUTIVE CONFERENCE DEFEATS

7 Bromsgrove Rovers
6 Altrincham, Bromsgrove Rovers
5 Welling United

VAUXHALL CONFERENCE 1996–97

APPEARANCES AND GOALSCORERS

Altrincham
Vauxhall Appearances: Ayorinde, S. 6; Beckford, J. 3; Brown, A. 10(2), Brown, R. 7; Butler, B. 9; Byrne, P. 5; Cain, P. 2(9); Carmoody, M. 20(1); Carroll, S. 3(16); Croft, B. 1; Daws, A. 6: Dickins, M. 42; Doherty, N. 39; France, P. 30(2); Hardy, N. 30(3); Harris, R. 30(3); Harris, S. 1(1); Heesom, D. 36; Horrigan, I. 19(6); Jardine, J. 3; Johnson, D. 5(2); Limbert, M. 14; McGoona, D. 15(3); Maddox, M. 23; Moore, M. 0(8); Morgan, A. 3; Pritchard, D. 9(2); Pybus, D. 1(3); Reid, A. 0(3); Rimmer, N. 5; Royle, D. 0(1); Ryan, T. 5; Sharratt, C. 11(3); Shepherd, D. 20(1); Terry, S. 40; Williams, M. 2(1); Williams, P. 5(2).
Goals (49): Ayorinde 2, Cain 1, Doherty 5, France 2, Hardy 14, Harris R. 3, Johnson 2, McGoona 3, Pritchard 2, Pybus 1, Sharratt 1, Terry 12, og 1.

Bath City
Vauxhall Appearances: Adcock, P. 3; Brooks, M, 16; Brooks, N. 20; Cann, D. 2; Cleverley, J. 5; Colbourne, G. 12; Cross, S. 7; Crowley, R. 16; Davey, J. 18; Davis, M. 39; Dicks, G. 21; Fraser, J. 2; French, J. 9; Gill, T. 4; Harte, S. 5; Harrington, M. 39; Harvey, I. 15; Hazlehurst, D. 15; Hedges, I. 27; Hervin, M. 26; Hirons, P. 11; Honor, C. 10; James, S. 36; Laight, E. 4; Lucas, J. 8; Madge, M. 9; Mehew, D. 9; Micciche, M. 1; Mogg, D. 19; Murray, E. 1; Nicholl, J. 1; Paul, M. 17; Penny, S. 25; Rollo, J. 4; Scott, A. 12; Tovey, P. 15; Towler, C. 17; Walker, M. 17; Withey, G. 18; Wyatt, M. 39.
Goals (53): Adcock 1, Brooks 1, Colbourne 6, Cross 1, Davis 14, Harrington 3, Hedges 1, Hirons 2, James 1, Laight 1, Mehew 3, Paul 3, Penny 5, Towler 2, Walker 1, Withey 2, Wyatt 5, og 1.

Bromsgrove Rovers
Vauxhall Appearances: Amos, N. 19; Brighton, S. 27; Burgher, S. 3; Clarke, N. 23; Clarke, S. 2; Crisp, M. 37; Dunphy, N. 9; Elmes, R. 3; Gardner, R. 26; Grocutt, D. 26; Hunt, J. 25; Knight, R. 14; Lewis, C. 6; Mainwaring, A. 30; Marlowe, A. 8; Meyrick, D. 2; Nesbitt, J. 5; Peters, M. 27; Petty, J. 1; Powell, R. 2; Richardson, K. 5; Simpson, B. 2; Skelding, J. 36; Smith, A. 37; Smith, C. 17; Sutton, P. 1; Taylor, C. 39; Taylor, S. 20; Talbot, N. 2; Trowman, W. 5; Wardle, P. 29; White, C. 6; Whitehead, M. 3; Willgrass, A. 10.
Goals (41): Brighton 1, Amos 1, Burgher 3, Clarke 1, Crisp 7, Dunphy 2, Gardner 3, Grocutt 1, Hunt 2, Mainwaring 9, Smith A. 1, Smith C. 1, Skelding 2, Taylor 5, Wardle 1, og 1.

Dover Athletic
Vauxhall Appearances: Adams, D. 12(1); Barber, P. 26(10); Brown, S. 3; Budden, J. 28(9); Daniels, S. 33; Dobbs, G. 29(4); Fearon, R. 15; Guiver, L. 0(1); Haag, K. 2; Hanlon, R. 6; Horne, B. 27; Jones, S. 0(10); Leworthy, D. 21; Lindsey, S. 24(13); McCabe, R. 3(11); Milton, R. 30(2); Mitten, C. 0(3); Morish, L. 7(10); Munday, S. 29(1); O'Connell, I. 26(9); Onwere, U. 0(3); Palmer, L. 14; Pilkington, P. 3(6); Reina, R. 28; Shepherd, I. 0(5); Sowerby, C. 4(7); Stebbing, G. 40; Strouts, J. 35(3); Sykes, P. 0(2); Theodosiou, A. 17(8); Wilson, P. 0(8).
Goals (57): Adams 5, Brown 2, Budden 1, Dobbs 5, Haag 1, Hanlon 2, Leworthy 8, Lindsey 1, Milton 4, Munday 2, O'Connell 1, Reina 7, Stebbing 2, Strouts 11, Theodosiou 4, Wilson 1.

Farnborough Town
Vauxhall Appearances: Baker, N. 13; Baker, S. 32(2); Boothe, C. 37(2); Coney, D. 21; Day, K. 21(3); Denny, R. 8(5); Dobson, R. 0(1); Gavin, P. 30(8); Harford, P. 20(1); Harlow, D. 42; Hayward, D. 0(2); Jansen, N. 2(2); MacKenzie, S. 42; McAvoy, G. 0(3); Mintram, S. 26(4); Robson, D. 37(1); Rowe, A. 0(1); Rowlands, K. 3(2); Stedman, C. 1(2); Stemp, W. 40; Underwood, J. 37(1); Williams, R. 12(2); Wingfield, P. 38.
Goals (58): Baker 2, Boothe 13, Coney 1, Day 1, Gavin 8, Harlow 5, Jansen 1, Mintram 2, Robson 5, Underwood 4, Williams 1, Wingfield 13, og 2.

Gateshead
Vauxhall Appearances: Bos, G. 10; Bowey, S. 8; Brady, I. 7(2); Byrne, W. 5(2); Conlon, P. 4; Connelly, S. 1(3); Cuggy, S. 2(3); Dia, A. 5(3); Dixon, A. 5(1); Dowson, A. 7(3); Edgcumbe, W. 3(1); Foreman, D. 7(2); Hauge, P. 13(6); Harkus, S. 6(6); Harper, S. 12; Houston, J. 0(6); Howarth, A. 2(4); Innes, G. 8; Johnson, F. 8; Key, D. 4(4); Kitchen, S. 40; Lagaville, T. 0(1); Lowe, K. 23(7); Ord, D. 34(2); Pearson, G. 18(12); Proudlock, P. 22(4); Robson, G. 27(2); Robson, J. 19(8); Rowe, B. 35; Sherwood, S. 22; Skedd, T. 5(5); Smith, M. 1; Thompson, P. 38(2); Thornton, M. 1(1); Watson, J. 34(4); Wrightson, J. 27(1).
Goals (59): Bos 8, Conlon 2, Cuggy 1, Dia 2, Edgcumbe 1, Foreman 2, Harkus 5, Innes 1, Lowe 1, Ord 2, Pearson 2, Proudlock 7, Robson G. 1, Robson J. 2, Skedd 1, Thompson 15, Watson 3, Wrightson 1, og 2.

Halifax Town
Vauxhall Appearances: Beckford, J. 3; Brook, G. 34(4); Brown, Jim 7(2); Brown, Jon 31(2); Cameron, M. 0(2); Cochrane, K. 2(2); Cox, P. 22(2); Davison, B. 11(13); Ellison, L. 1(1); Francis, J. 2; Gibson, P. 3; Goulding, D. 8(2); Harold, I. 4; Hendrick, J. 8(3); Heyes, D. 1; Horner, N. 27(10); Horsfield, G. 19(5); Hulme, K. 21; Kelly, T. 0(1); Lee, A. 8; Lyons, D. 14(3); Martin, D. 17; McInerney, I. 12(12); Midwood, M. 2(4); Mudd, P. 36(1); Murphy, J. 10; Norbury, M. 30(1); O'Regan, K. 39; Place, D. 0(2); Stoneman, P. 26(2); Trotter, M. 8(1); Woods, A. 38; Worthington, G. 19(8).
Goals (55): Brook 8, Brown Jim 1, Davison 1, Ellison 1, Horner 3, Horsfield 9, Hulme 2, Lyons 4, Martin 2, McInerney 1, Midwood 1, Murphy 2, Norbury 14, Stoneman 3, Trotter 1, Worthington 1, og 1.

Hayes
Vauxhall Appearances: Adams, K. 7(2); Ansah, A. 3; Baker, S. 1; Bartley, C. 2(8); Brady, J. 39(2); Bunce, N. 24(3); Cox, A. 26(1); Duncan, I. 17(4); Donoghue, C. 1; Flynn, L. 7(1); Francis, J. 11(3); Goodliffe, J. 37(2); Hall, M. 25(3); Haynes, J. 19(11); Hedge, A. 0(1); Heyrettin, H. 5(1); Hooper, D. 3; Hyatt, F. 10(9); Kelly, W. 18; Lewis, J. 5(1); Lillington, W. 5; Meara, R. 41; Mee, E. 0(2); Mettioui, A. 0(1); O'Brien, A. 0(1); Odetoyinbo, K. 1; Pickett, R. 2(1); Randall, M. 26(6); Roberts, J. 18(9); Roberts, O. 0(1); Roddis, N. 18(5); Scott, P. 2(1); Sugrue, J. 6(4); Ulasi, O. 5; Williams, G. 26(6); Wilkinson, D. 38(2); Wise, G. 2(1); Wotton, G. 7(4);
Goals (54): Cox 4, Flynn 2, Francis 2, Goodliffe 6, Hall 4, Haynes 9, Lillington 1, Randall 13, Roberts 6, Williams 6, og 1.

Hednesford Town
Vauxhall Appearances: Braut, G. 1; Broadhurst, N. 2(1); Carty, P. 27; Collins, K. 35(2); Comyn, A. 39; Cooksey, S. 41; Cotterill, J. 4(4); Dandy, R. 0(2); Derry, L. 0(1); Devine, S. 19(2); Ecclestone, T. 3; Edwards, P. 4; Essex, S. 25(5); Fitzpatrick, G. 32(1); Francis, D. 8(2); Harnett, D. 1(1); Hemmings, T. 16(2); Holmes, D. 2(1); Lake, S. 20(1); Lambert, C. 29; Lawrence, G. 2(2); McKenzie, C. 3(4); McNally, R. 18(1); Mason, R. 8(2); O'Conner, J. 37; Russell, K. 19; Rowlands, S. 0(2); Simpson, W. 34(2); Street, T. 23(6); Sykes, R. 4(1); Yates, L. 0(1);
Goals (52): Carty 3, Comyn 2, Cotterill 1, Devine 1, Fitzpatrick 3, Francis 3, Harnett 1, Lake 3, Lambert 6, Lawrence 1, McNally 2, Mason 2, O'Conner 15, Russell 5, Street 4.

Kettering Town
Vauxhall Appearances: Berry, S. 41; Carter, R. 8; Cherry, S. 3; De Vito, C. 1(6); Dowling, L. 0(1); Dudfield, L. 1(24); Flatts, M. 2; Gaunt, C. 36; Harding, P. 4(4); Harmon, D. 24(9); Holliday, D. 0(1); Judge, A. 17(10); King, E. 0(1); Lynch, T. 24(6); Lyne, N. 19; March, J. 24(14); Marshall, R. 37(2); May, L. 10(1); McMahon, S. 4; Miles, P. 1(9); Mustafa, T. 19(11); Norman, C. 38; Nugent, R. 27; Nyamah, K. 17; Pearson, C. 13(2); Pope, N. 14(2); Shoemake, K. 13(5); Slawson, S. 15(1); Smith, S. 4(2); Stock, R. 13(14); Tallentire, D. 2; Turley, B. 9; Venables, D. 10; Wilkes, T. 9(1); Woodsford, J. 3.
Goals (53): Berry 2, Gaunt 2, Harmon 2, Lynch 7, Lyne 3, May 2, Mustafa 6, Norman 10, Nugent 3, Nyamah 2, Pearson 4, Pope 2, Slawson 1, Stock 3, Venables 1, Wilkes 2, Woodsford 1.

Kidderminster Harriers

Vauxhall Appearances: Barber, F. 18; Bignot, M. 39; Brindley, C. 36; Cartwright, N. 2(4); Casey, K. 6(11); Davies, P. 9(4); Deakin, J. 13(6); Dearlove, M. 1(1); Doherty, N. 39(1); Hodson, S. 1; Hughes, L. 37(1); McCue, J. 10(7); Olney, I. 28(5); Prindiville, S. 41; Shepherd, M. 1; Steadman, D. 24; Webb, P. 35(1); Weir, M. 41; Willetts, K. 40; Yates, M. 41.

Goals (84): Bignot 1, Brindley 2, Casey 3, Davies 4, Doherty 14, Hughes 30, McCue 1, Olney 7, Prindiville 1, Webb 6, Weir 3, Willetts 4, Yates 7, og 1.

Macclesfield Town

Vauxhall Appearances: Askey, J. 34(3); Bradshaw, M. 12(9); Byrne, C. 18; Circuit, S. 6(5); Coates, M. 4(4); Davenport, P. 13(2); Edey, C. 26(3); Gardiner, M. 14(3); Gee, D. 0(1); Hemmings, T. 16(1); Howarth, N. 39; Hulme, K. 0(1); Landon, R. 6; Mitchell, N. 19(7); Morgan, P. 5; Mottram, F. 5(6); O'Reilly, J. 3; Ohandjianian, D. 1; Payne, S. 44; Peel, N. 0(2); Power, P. 33(3); Price, R. 37; Sorvel, N. 42; Tinson, D. 36; Williams, C. 12(15); Wood, S. 40(1).

Goals (80): Askey 7, Bradshaw 1, Byrne 10, Circuit 1, Coates 1, Davenport 6, Gardiner 1, Hemmings 2, Howarth 1, Landon 3, Mitchell 4, Mottram 2, Payne 2, Power 11, Sorvel 4, Tinson 1, Williams 6, Wood 15.

Morecambe

Vauxhall Appearances: Annan, R. 18(1); Banks, A. 7; Bignall M. 12; Burns, P. 27(1); Cain, I. 9(4); Ceraolo, M. 2(8); Drummond, S. 1(2); Grimshaw, A. 22(4); Healy, R. 15(1); Hodgson, S. 11(1); Hughes, T. 23; Knowles, M. 34(4); Jackson, J. 22(1); Lavelle, B. 17(3); Leaver, D. 19(2); McCluskie, J. 3(25); McIlhargy, S. 35; McKearney, D. 37(1); Miller, D. 1(2); Monk, I. 34(4); Norman, J. 41(1); Rushton, P. 16(4); Shirley, M. 17(2); Sang, N. 4(3); Udall, J. 2; West, P. 15(6); Williams, G. 3(7).

Goals (69): Bignall 6, Burns 7, Cain 2, Ceraolo 3, Grimshaw 3, Healy 3, Hodgson 1, Knowles 1, Jackson 15, McCluskie 6, McKearney 3, Miller 1, Monk 6, Norman 7, Shirley 1, Udall 1, og 3.

Northwich Victoria

Vauxhall Appearances: Bishop, E. 30; Burgess, D. 6(2); Cooke, I. 28(4); Crookes, D. 38(3); Davies, S. 0(1); Duffy, C. 33(5); Fairclough, W. 26(4); Greygoose, D. 37; Hughes, J. 0(2); Hughes, R. 4; Humphreys, D. 19(10); Hutchinson, S. 2; Lewis, C. 2; Page, D. 0(4); Reddish, S. 35(3); Simpson, W. 38; Stannard, J. 7(9); Steele, L. 33(8); Tait, P. 24(9); Vicary, D. 36(3); Walters, S. 34(1); Ward, D. 31(9); Woods, P. 1.

Goals (61): Bishop 3, Cooke 6, Crookes 3, Duffy 2, Humphreys 3, Simpson 1, Stannard 3, Steele 16, Tait 10, Vicary 5, Walters 6, og 3.

Rushden & Diamonds

Vauxhall Appearances: Alford, C. 32(4); Allardyce, C. 0(1); Ashby, N. 20; Ayorinde, S. 2; Bailey, R. 5(1); Benstead, G. 6; Butterworth, G. 41; Capone, J. 11; Cherry, S. 10; Collins, D. 32(2); Cramman, K. 37(2); Davies, M. 27; Furnell, A. 2(6); Hackett, B. 24(7); Hannigan, A-J. 2; Hodson, S. 22; Holden, S. 7; King, I. 11(11); Kirkup, A. 0(7); Leworthy, D. 18; Lilwall, S. 4; Morrison, D. 2(3); Peaks, A. 19(2); Rodwell, J. 41; Smith, N. 7(2); Stapleton, S. 3(3); Stott, S. 31; Tucker, M. 6; Wilson, T. 6; Wilkin, K. 14(8); Wooding, T. 16(1).

Goals (61): Alford 13, Bailey 1, Butterworth 2, Capone 3, Collins 6, Cramman 6, Hackett 3, King 2, Leworthy 8, Rodwell 4, Stapleton 2, Stott 2, Wilkin 4, Wilson 1, og 2.

Slough Town

Vauxhall Appearances: Abbott, G. 37(1); Barclay, D. 1(2); Bateman, S. 37; Blackford, G. 34(1); Bolt, D. 18(8); Brazil, G. 12; Cash, S. 4; Clement, A. 20(2); Eaton, G. 2(3); Fiore, M. 24(9); Hardyman, P. 10; Hercules, C. 30; Imber, N. 5; McGinnis, G. 30(2); McMinn, T. 9; Mernagh, G. 1(6); Micklewhite, G. 15; Miles, R. 16; Murphy, M. 6(4); Nolan, T. 2; Owusu, L. 6(9); Paris, R. 0(2); Pye, M. 7(4); Simpson, D. 10(4); Smart, G. 39; Smith, R. 22(1); Stapleton, S. 22(2); Walton, B. 6(7); West, M. 16(1); Wilkerson, P. 21.

Goals (62): Abbott 18, Barclay 1, Bateman 2, Blackford 3, Bolt 3, Brazil 3, Clement 1, Fiore 2, Hardyman 1, Hercules 5, Mernagh 1, Murphy 1, Owusu 5, Smart 1, Smith 1, Stapleton 3, Walton 1, West 9, og 1.

Southport

Vauxhall Appearances: Anderson, L. 14(3); Blakeman, C. 8(4); Borwick, C. 0(1); Butler, B. 31; Carroll, D. 8(2); Clark, M. 34; Davenport, P. 15(4); Dove, L. 13(4); Duerden, I. 11; Ellison, K. 2(2); Eyre, S. 2(1); Farley, A. 32(4); Gamble, D. 33(8); Griffiths, B. 1(5); Haw, S. 7(6); Horner, P. 38(1); Horner, R. 17; Jones, A. 17; Kenworthy, J. 2; McDonald, R. 12; Mayers, K. 4; Mitten, P. 2; Moran, S. 13(1); Morgan, J. 1(5); Powell, F. 0(1); Preece, R. 9; Rogers, D. 22(1); Sharratt, C. 25(2); Stewart, B. 42; Turner, M. 5(3); Vickers, I. 1(7); Whittaker, A. 41.

Goals (51): Anderson 1, Butler 4, Clark 1, Davenport 5, Dove 1, Duerden 1, Farley 1, Gamble 9, Haw 1, Horner 2, Jones 3, Rogers 1, Sharratt 1, Whittaker 19, og 1.

Stalybridge Celtic

Vauxhall Appearances: Arnold, I. 33(4); Bates, J. 29(2); Boardman, C. 41(4); Burke, B. 35(3); Challender, G. 24(3); Charles, S. 38(4); Coathup, L. 37(3); Crane, T. 11; Ellis, D. 1; Frain, D. 7; Goldbourne, R. 7; Goodacre, S. 1; Hall, D. 37(4); Heaton, S. 5(1); Hine, M. 38(4); Howard, S. 1; Jackson, R. 3; Jones, S. 34(4); O'Shaughnessy, S. 8; Powell, C. 9(2); Powell, M. 38(4); Thomas, G. 21(2); Thomas, K. 9(1); Todd, M. 7(1); Trott, D. 30(3); Vine, D. 23(2); Westhead, M. 8; Willetts, H. 12; Williams, D. 20(3).

Goals (53): Arnold 13, Burke 11, Charles 10, Crane 1, Goldbourne 1, Goodacre 1, Hall 3, Jones 5, Trott 6, Vine 1, og 1.

Stevenage Borough

Vauxhall Appearances: Adams, C. 7(6); Barrowcliff, P. 36(2); Bates, M. 1; Beevor, S. 28(7); Bignall, M. 8(2); Browne, C. 23(12); Catlin, N. 21(2); Crawshaw, G. 22(9); Cretton, S. 5(1); Endersby, L. 2; Gallagher, D. 31; Gentle, D. 8(2); Grime, D. 2; Hayles, B. 24(6); Hooper, D. 21; Kirby, R. 27; Mison, M. 9; Mutchell, R. 32(3); Paris, A. 11(2); Smith, M. 40; Sodje, E. 39; Soloman, J. 10; Stevens, S. 0(1); Trebble, N. 10(17); Ugbah, J. 8(5); Venables, D. 9(4); Webster, K. 17; Wilmot, R. 11(1).

Goals (87): Adams 4, Barrowcliff 5, Bates 1, Beevor 3, Bignall 4, Browne 10, Catlin 7, Crawshaw 12, Hayles 16, Hooper 1, Kirby 2, Mison 5, Sodje 4, Soloman 3, Trebble 5, Ugbah 1, Venables 1, Webster 2, og 1.

Telford United

Vauxhall Appearances: Ashley, K. 22(11); Challinor, P. 15; Croft, B. 0(2); Dudley, D. 4(2); Ecclestone, S. 21(21); Foster, S. 15; Fowler, L. 36; Gray, B. 37; Hughes, K. 7(3); Jones, M. 34(3); Joseph, A. 4(4); Kearney, M. 35(5); Langford, T. 15(5); Martin, L. 1(5); Naylor, M. 15(9); Niblett, N. 39(2); Page, D. 11(2); Robinson, L. 29(1); Rodosthenous, M. 4; Preece, R. 8; Rose, G. 0(2); Purdie, J. 29(8); Russell, D. 7(15); Simkin, D. 3(5); Todd, M. 1; Turner, M. 28(8); Wilcox, B. 23(3); Wilding, P. 13; Williams, M. 2(4); Woods, R. 12(3).

Goals (46): Ashley 2, Foster 1, Fowler 5, Gray 12, Langford 4, Niblett 3, Preece 1, Purdie 4, Robinson 1, Rodosthenous 2, Russell 3, Turner 3, Wilding 3, Woods 1, og 1.

Welling United

Vauxhall Appearances: Appiah, S. 0(4); Brown, D. 41; Brown, W. 7(1); Cooper, G. 30; Copley, P. 40(1); Corbyn, R. 1; Dennis, L. 34(1); Dimmock, R. 2(11); Evans, D. 0(1); Farley, J. 19(2); Hales, K. 1; Horton, D. 38; Jones, M. 4; King, T. 0(3); Knight, G. 39; Lakin, B. 28(4); Lewington, C. 2; Morah, O. 39; Rattray, K. 7; Rutherford, M. 39; Smith, D. 10(15); Tierling, L. 5; Trott, R. 41; Wastell, J. 1; Watts, L. 33(1); Watts, S. 0(6); Zorichich, C. 1.

Goals (50): Brown W. 1, Cooper 1, Copley 1, Dennis 21, Farley 1, Lakin 5, Morah 9, Rutherford 4, Smith 1, Trott 3, Watts 1, og 2.

Woking

Vauxhall Appearances: Batty, L. 32; Betsy, K. 1(1); Brooks, S. 1; Brown, K. 40; Ellis, A. 26(7); Fielder, C. 9(1); Foster, S. 28; Garner, S. 0(5); Grazioli, G. 5; Gregory, J. 9(1); Hay, D. 18(9); Howard, T. 28(1); Hunter, J. 13(10); Hyde, P. 1; Jackson, J. 14(2); Jones, T. 30(3); Kamara, B. 2(3); Kilner, A. 2(3); Palmer, L. 7; Payne, G. 3; Sailsman, S. 1; Steele, S. 28(5); Taylor, R. 27(10); Thompson, S. 36; Timothy, D. 13(3); Walker, C. 36(1); Wood, S. 7; Wye, L. 20(5); Wye, S. 25.

Goals (71): Batty 1, Ellis 1, Foster 3, Grazioli 6, Hay 10, Howard 1, Hunter 3, Jackson 2, Jones 1, Kilner 1, Payne 1, Steele 12, Taylor 4, Thompson 5, Timothy 1, Walker 15, S Wye 1, og 3.

VAUXHALL CONFERENCE: MEMBERS CLUBS SEASON 1997–98

Club: CHELTENHAM TOWN
Colours: Red and white shirts, white shorts
Ground: Whaddon Road, Cheltenham, Glos,
GL52 5NA
Tel: 01242 573558
Year Formed: 1892
Record Gate: 8236 (1956 v Reading)
Nickname: The Robins
Manager: Steve Cotterill
Secretary: Reg Woodward

Club: DOVER ATHLETIC
Colours: White shirts, black shorts
Ground: Crabble Athletic Ground, Lewisham
Road, River, Dover, Kent CT17 0PB
Tel: 01304 822373
Year Formed: 1983
Record Gate: 4035 (1992 v Bromsgrove Rovers)
Nickname: The Lillywhites
Manager: Bill Williams
Secretary: John Durrant

Club: FARNBOROUGH TOWN
Colours: Yellow and royal blue shirts, blue shorts
Ground: Cherrywood Road, Farnborough,
Hampshire GU14 8UD
Tel: 01252 541469
Year Formed: 1967
Record Gate: 3069 (1991 v Colchester U)
Nickname: Boro
Manager: Alan Taylor
Secretary: Terry Parr

Club: GATESHEAD
Colours: Black and white halved shirts, black
shorts
Ground: International Stadium, Neilson Road,
Gateshead NE10 0EF
Tel: 0191-478 3883
Year Formed: 1977 (Reformed)
Record Gate: 20,752 (1937 v Lincoln C)
Nickname: Tynesiders
Manager: Jim Platt
Secretary: Mark Donnelly

Club: HALIFAX TOWN
Colours: Blue shirts white trim, blue shorts white
trim
Ground: Shay Ground, Halifax HX1 2YS
Tel: 01422 345543 (330383 Match Days Only)
Year Formed: 1911
Record Gate: 36,885 (1953 v Tottenham
Hotspur)
Nickname: The Shaymen
Manager: George Mulhall/Kieren O'Regan
Secretary: Derek Newiss

Club: HAYES
Colours: Red and white striped shirts, black
shorts
Ground: Townfield House, Church Road, Hayes,
Middlesex UB3
Tel: 0181 573 2075
Year formed: 1909
Record Gate: 15,370 (1951 v Bromley)
Nickname: Missioners
Manager: Terry Brown
Secretary: John Price

Club: HEDNESFORD TOWN
Colours: White and red shirts black trim, white
shorts
Ground: Keys Park, Hill Street, Hednesford,
Staffordshire
Tel: 01543 422870
Year Formed: 1880
Record Gate: 10,000 (1927 v Walsall)
Nickname: The Pitmen
Manager: John Baldwin
Secretary: Richard Murning

Club: HEREFORD UNITED
Colours: White shirts black trim, black shorts
white trim
Ground: Edgar Street, Hereford, HR4 9JU
Tel: 01432 276666
Year Formed: 1924
Record Gate: 18,114 (1958 v Sheffield
Wednesday)
Nickname: United
Manager: Graham Turner
Secretary: Joan Fennessy

Club: KETTERING TOWN
Colours: Red shirts, red shorts
Ground: Rockingham Road, Kettering,
Northants NN16 9AW
Tel: 01536 483028
Year Formed: 1875
Record Gate: 11,536 (1947 v Peterborough)
Nickname: The Poppies
Manager: Steve Berry
Secretary: Gerry Knowles

Club: KIDDERMINSTER HARRIERS
Colours: Red shirts black trim, red shorts
Ground: Aggborough, Hoo Road, Kidderminster
DY10 1NB
Tel: 01562 823931
Year Formed: 1886
Record Gate: 9155 (1948 v Hereford)
Nickname: The Harriers
Manager: Graham Allner
Secretary: Roger Barlow

Club: LEEK TOWN
Colours: Royal blue shirts old gold trim, royal
blue shorts old gold trim
Ground: Harrison Park, Macclesfield Road,
Leek, Staffs ST13 8LD
Tel: 01538 399378
Year Formed: 1947
Record Gate: 5312 (1973 v Macclesfield Town)
Nickname: The Blues
Manager: Peter Ward
Secretary: Michael Rowley

Club: MORECAMBE
Colours: Red shirts, black shorts
Ground: Christie Park, Lancaster Road,
Morecambe, Lancashire LA4 5TJ
Tel: 01524 411797
Year Formed: 1920
Record Gate: 9326 (1962 FA Cup Third Round
Proper v Weymouth)
Nickname: The Shrimps
Manager: Jim Harvey
Secretary: Neil Marsdin

Club: NORTHWICH VICTORIA
Colours: Green shirts, white shorts
Ground: The Drill Field, Northwich, Cheshire
   CW9 5HN
Tel: 01606 41450
Year Formed: 1874
Record Gate: 11,290 (1949 v Witton A) 12,000
   (1977 v Watford FAC4)
Nickname: The Vics
Manager: Phil Wilson
Secretary: Derek Nuttall

Club: RUSHDEN & DIAMONDS
Colours: White shirts (red and blue trim), blue
   shorts
Ground: Nene Park, Station Road,
   Irthlingborough, Northants NN9 5QF
Tel: 01933 652000
Year Formed: 1992
Record Gate: 5170 (1997 v Kettering Town)
Nickname: Diamonds
Manager: Brian Talbot
Secretary: David Joyce

Club: SLOUGH TOWN
Colours: Amber shirts, navy blue shorts
Ground: Wexham Park Stadium, Wexham Road,
   Slough, Berkshire SL2 5QR
Tel: 01753 523358
Year Formed: 1980
Record Gate: 5000 (1982 v Millwall)
Nickname: The Rebels
Manager: Brian McDermott
Secretary: Trevor Gorman

Club: SOUTHPORT
Colours: Old gold and black shirts, black and old
   gold shorts
Ground: Haig Avenue, Southport PR8 6JZ
Tel: 01704 533422
Year Formed: 1881
Record Gate: 20,010 (1932 v Newcastle United)
Nickname: The Sandgrounders
Manager: Paul Futcher
Secretary: Ken Hilton

Club: STALYBRIDGE CELTIC
Colours: Blue shirts, blue shorts
Ground: Bower Fold, Mottram Road,
   Stalybridge, Cheshire SK15 2RT
Tel: 0161-338 2828
Year Formed: 1911
Record Gate: 9753 (1922–23 v West Bromwich
   Albion)
Nickname: Celtic
Manager: Brian Kettle
Secretary: Martyn Torr

Club: STEVENAGE BOROUGH
Colours: White shirts with red stripe, white
   shorts with red trim
Ground: Broadhall Way, Stevenage, Herts
   SG2 8RH
Tel: 01438 743322
Year Formed: 1976
Record Gate: 15,365 (1997 v Birmingham City at
   St Andrews)
Nickname: The Boro
Manager: Paul Fairclough
Secretary: Janice Hutchings

Club: TELFORD UNITED
Colours: White shirts, black shorts
Ground: Bucks Head, Watling Street, Telford
   TF1 2NJ
Tel: 01952 270767
Year Formed: 1877
Record Gate: 13,000 (1935 v Shrewsbury)
Nickname: The Lillywhites
Manager: Steve Daley
Secretary: Mike Ferriday

Club: WELLING UNITED
Colours: Red shirts, red shorts
Ground: Park View Road Ground, Welling, Kent
   DA16 1SY
Tel: 0181-301 1196
Year Formed: 1963
Record Gate: 4020 (1989 v Gillingham)
Nickname: The Wings
Manager: Kevin Hales
Secretary: Barrie Hobbins

Club: WOKING
Colours: Red and white halved shirts, black
   shorts
Ground: Kingfield Sports Ground, Kingfield,
   Woking, Surrey GU22 9AA
Tel: 01483 772470
Year Formed: 1889
Record Gate: 6084 (1997 v Coventry City)
Nickname: The Cardinals
Manager: John McGovern
Secretary: Phil Ledger, JP

Club: YEOVIL TOWN
Colours: Green and white shirts, white shorts
Ground: Huish Park
Tel: 01935 423662
Year Formed: 1896
Record Gate: 8612 (1993 v Arsenal)
Nickname: The Glovers
Manager: Graham Roberts
Secretary: Jean Cotton

VAUXHALL CONFERENCE RESULTS 1996-97

	Altrincham	Bath City	Bromsgrove Rovers	Dover Athletic	Farnborough Town	Gateshead	Halifax Town	Hayes	Hednesford Town	Kettering Town	Kidderminster H.	Macclesfield Town	Morecambe	Northwich Victoria	Rushden & Diamonds	Slough Town	Southport	Stalybridge Celtic	Stevenage Borough	Telford United	Welling United	Woking
Altrincham	—	1-3	3-1	1-2	0-3	1-1	1-1	3-1	2-2	4-3	1-1	0-1	2-1	2-3	3-2	0-1	1-3	1-0	1-2	2-3	1-1	1-1
Bath City	1-3	—	1-0	2-1	1-1	3-0	4-5	3-1	2-1	0-2	6-0	2-1	3-0	3-2	3-2	0-0	0-2	0-1	0-0	2-3	3-1	1-1
Bromsgrove Rovers	4-0	2-0	—	3-1	1-1	2-0	1-0	3-1	1-0	1-2	6-0	1-2	4-0	0-5	0-1	4-1	1-1	0-1	1-1	2-1	1-0	0-3
Dover Athletic	2-2	2-2	2-0	—	0-0	0-1	2-2	1-0	2-2	0-1	2-1	3-0	3-0	2-2	1-1	0-0	0-1	2-1	3-3	1-4	2-1	5-1
Farnborough Town	1-1	4-1	2-1	2-3	—	1-2	3-0	1-1	1-0	0-2	2-3	2-2	0-3	5-1	1-0	0-0	3-3	1-0	3-1	0-2	2-1	1-2
Gateshead	1-0	5-0	1-0	1-3	1-0	—	0-0	2-2	1-0	1-1	3-3	0-3	0-3	5-1	1-3	4-1	2-2	4-1	4-2	2-3	1-2	3-2
Halifax Town	4-5	0-1	1-0	1-3	3-0	1-0	—	2-2	4-0	2-1	1-0	3-3	1-1	0-3	1-3	4-1	2-0	4-1	4-2	0-3	1-1	0-4
Hayes	3-1	3-1	3-1	0-1	1-0	2-2	0-0	—	4-0	0-0	0-1	0-2	2-3	1-1	1-1	5-0	1-1	0-2	1-3	0-1	1-1	3-2
Hednesford Town	3-1	3-1	1-0	3-0	4-0	1-0	4-0	2-0	—	0-0	0-2	4-1	2-3	3-0	1-0	5-0	1-1	2-1	0-0	0-1	1-1	2-0
Kettering Town	4-3	0-2	1-2	0-2	0-2	1-1	2-1	0-0	0-0	—	1-0	5-2	2-0	1-0	1-0	1-1	3-3	2-2	3-1	0-1	2-1	4-3
Kidderminster H.	1-1	6-0	1-2	4-1	3-0	3-1	1-0	2-4	4-0	1-0	—	0-0	2-2	1-0	1-0	1-2	3-0	1-1	3-0	1-0	3-2	1-0
Macclesfield Town	0-1	2-1	3-0	1-0	3-1	2-2	3-0	1-0	2-1	4-0	0-0	—	0-3	0-1	2-0	2-0	3-2	0-0	2-2	0-2	0-0	1-1
Morecambe	2-1	2-2	4-0	3-1	2-2	0-3	1-0	2-4	2-0	5-2	1-0	1-0	—	2-0	2-0	0-0	2-1	0-0	1-2	0-1	1-2	1-2
Northwich Victoria	2-2	0-0	0-1	2-2	2-2	4-0	1-0	2-0	2-2	2-1	1-1	1-1	2-0	—	1-2	1-2	0-1	1-1	0-1	1-0	0-0	1-2
Rushden & Diamonds	3-2	4-1	1-0	0-2	1-1	0-4	1-3	2-2	2-1	1-0	1-5	1-3	2-0	3-4	—	5-0	3-0	4-1	0-1	6-0	3-3	3-0
Slough Town	0-1	5-2	2-0	0-1	1-1	0-0	1-0	0-2	1-1	2-2	0-2	0-0	1-2	0-0	—	2-2	0-1	3-0	0-1	6-0	3-2	4-1
Southport	1-3	3-1	0-0	0-1	2-0	1-0	2-1	0-2	2-2	3-1	1-5	3-1	3-1	0-0	2-1	0-1	—	3-0	0-0	0-0	0-0	0-2
Stalybridge Celtic	1-0	2-2	3-0	4-2	2-0	2-3	2-3	3-1	1-2	3-1	2-3	2-3	4-2	0-1	2-0	2-2	2-1	—	2-3	3-0	2-1	0-3
Stevenage Borough	2-1	2-1	2-0	4-1	2-1	0-0	6-0	0-0	1-0	0-0	0-3	0-3	2-3	2-2	0-5	1-0	2-1	1-1	—	3-0	2-0	1-2
Telford United	1-0	1-1	3-1	0-3	2-0	0-1	0-1	1-0	1-2	1-2	0-3	0-3	1-4	1-1	0-1	3-2	2-3	1-1	2-0	—	2-0	1-2
Welling United	1-0	2-0	1-2	1-0	0-2	0-1	0-1	1-0	1-2	1-2	2-0	0-3	1-1	3-1	1-2	3-2	2-3	2-1	2-0	2-0	—	1-1
Woking	7-1	2-2	1-3	1-1	2-1	3-1	2-2	1-2	2-0	2-1	3-1	2-3	1-2	4-2	4-2	2-0	0-1	3-2	3-1	0-0	2-1	—

SPALDING CHALLENGE CUP 1996–97

FIRST ROUND
Bath City 0
Welling United 2 *(Dennis, Rutherford)* — 237

Dover Athletic 2 *(Lindsey, Reina)*
Rushden & Diamonds 3 *(Cramman, Wilkin 2)* — 723

Farnborough Town 3 *(Gavin 3)*
Hayes 2 *(Hyatt, Bunce)* — 317

Halifax Town 0
Altrincham 1 *(Terry)* aet — 379

Kettering Town 1 *(May)*
Slough Town 0 — 702

Stalybridge Celtic 3 *(Burke 2, Hall)*
Telford United 1 *(Turner)* aet — 278

SECOND ROUND
Altrincham 0
Macclesfield Town 1 *(Sorvel)* — 903

Bromsgrove Rovers 3 *(Grocutt 2 Amos)*
Northwich Victoria 1 *(Tait)* — 271

Gateshead 1 *(Thompson)*
Morecambe 3 *(Ceraolo, Knowles, Leaver)* — 166

Hednesford Town 1 *(Dandy)*
Kidderminster Harriers 6 *(Olney, Davies 2, Cartwright 2, Casey)* — 333

Kettering Town 0
Farnborough Town 2 *(Harford, Boothe)* — 503

Rushden & Diamonds 1 *(Collins)*
Stevenage Borough 0 — 1073

Stalybridge Celtic 2 *(Jones, Burke)*
Southport 1 *(Clark)* — 224

Woking 0
Welling United 2 *(Dennis, Lakin)* — 597

QUARTER-FINALS
Kidderminster Harriers 1 *(Hughes)*
Rushden & Diamonds 0 — 811

Macclesfield Town 1 *(Coates)*
Bromsgrove Rovers 0 — 347

Morecambe 3 *(Grimshaw 2, Norman)*
Stalybridge Celtic 3 *(Trott, Hall 2)* aet — 407

Stalybridge Celtic 0
Morecambe 1 *(Shirley)* — 335

Welling United 1 *(Morah)*
Farnborough Town 2 *(Harlow 2)* aet — 312

SEMI-FINALS (two legs)
Farnborough Town 2 *(Boothe 2)*
Kidderminster Harriers 2 *(Cartwright, Casey)* — 370

Kidderminster Harriers 1 *(Davies)*
Farnborough Town 1 *(Underwood)* aet — 927
Kidderminster Harriers won on away goals rule

Morecambe 0
Macclesfield Town 2 *(Ohandjanian, Byrne)* — 513

Macclesfield Town 4 *(Wood, Sorvel 3)*
Morecambe 1 *(Healy)* — 826

FINAL (two legs)
Macclesfield Town 1 *(Davenport)*
Kidderminster Harriers 1 *(Prindiville)* — 1320

Kidderminster Harriers 0
Macclesfield Town 0 — 2218
Kidderminster Harriers won on away goals rule

THE MAIL ON SUNDAY
Monthly Awards

Goalscorer Of The Month	Team Performance Of The Month	Manager Of The Month
AUGUST		
Gary Abbott *Slough Town*	*Kidderminster Harriers* (5-0 v Dover Athletic (A) 24/8)	Steve Joel *Southport*
Barry Hayles *Stevenage Borough*		
Lee Hughes *Kidderminster Harriers*		
SEPTEMBER		
Lennie Dennis *Welling United*	*Dover Athletic* (5-1 v Woking (H) 3/9)	Graham Allner *Kidderminster Harriers*
		Alan Taylor *Farnborough Town*
OCTOBER		
Jim McCluskie *Morecambe*	*Slough Town* (6-0 v Telford United (H) 19/10)	Graham Allner *Kidderminster Harriers*
NOVEMBER		
Neil Doherty *Kidderminster Harriers*	*Woking* (7-1 v Altrincham (H) 30/11)	Geoff Chapple *Woking*
DECEMBER		
Lee Hughes *Kidderminster Harriers*	*Hayes* (4-2 v Morecambe (A) 7/12)	Sammy McIlroy *Macclesfield Town*
JANUARY		
Corey Browne *Stevenage Borough*	*Bath City* (2-1 v Morecambe (A) 11/1)	John Baldwin *Hednesford Town*
Martin Randall *Hayes*		
FEBRUARY		
Mike Davis *Bath City*	*Welling United* (2-0 v Stevenage Borough (H) 1/2)	Jake King *Telford United*
Steve Wood *Macclesfield Town*		
MARCH		
Gijsbert Bos *Gateshead*	*Stalybridge Celtic* (4-1 v Kidderminster Harriers (H) 22/3)	Sammy McIlroy *Macclesfield Town*
APRIL		
Barry Hayles *Stevenage Borough*	*Bromsgrove Rovers* (3-1 v Woking (A) 8/4)	Graham Allner *Kidderminster Harriers*
		Steve Millard *Bath City*

UNIBOND LEAGUE

Premier Division

	P	W	D	L	F	A	Pts
Leek Town	44	28	9	7	71	35	93
Bishop Auckland	44	23	14	7	88	43	83
Hyde United	44	22	16	6	93	46	82
Emley	44	23	12	9	89	54	81
Barrow	44	23	11	10	71	45	80
Boston United	44	22	13	9	74	47	79
Blyth Spartans	44	22	11	11	74	49	77
Marine	44	20	15	9	53	37	75
Guiseley	44	20	11	13	63	54	71
Gainsborough Trinity	44	18	12	14	65	46	66
Accrington Stanley	44	18	12	14	77	70	66
Runcorn	44	15	15	14	63	62	60
Chorley	44	16	9	19	69	66	57
Winsford United	44	13	14	17	50	56	53
Knowsley United*	44	12	14	18	58	79	49
Colwyn Bay	44	11	13	20	60	76	46
Lancaster City	44	12	9	23	48	75	45
Frickley Athletic	44	12	8	24	62	91	44
Spennymoor United	44	10	10	24	52	68	40
Bamber Bridge	44	11	7	26	59	99	40
Alfreton Town	44	8	13	23	45	83	37
Witton Albion	44	5	14	25	41	91	29
Buxton	44	5	12	27	33	86	27

*1pt deducted; breach of rule

LEADING GOALSCORERS

(In order of League Goals)

Premier Division

Lge	Cup	Tot	
28	12	40	Nick Peverill (Bishop Auckland)
22	4	26	Neil Morton (Barrow)
20	2	22	Steve Soley (Leek Town)
19	6	25	Neil Matthews (Guiseley)
18	11	29	Deiniol Graham (Emley)
18	5	23	Jock Russell (Winsford United)
17	7	24	Phil Brown (Boston United)
17	5	22	Tony Carroll (Hyde United)
17	5	22	Ged Kimmins (Hyde United)
16	4	20	Jason Maxwell (Gainsborough Trinity)
16	3	19	Damien Henderson (Blyth Spartans)
16	2	18	Brian Ross (Chorley)
15	13	28	Brett Ormerod (Accrington Stanley)
15	6	21	Dave Nolan (Hyde United)
15	5	20	Stuart Young (Blyth Spartans)
15	4	19	Joey Dunn (Runcorn)
15	-	15	Andy Green (Barrow)

UNIBOND CLUB OF THE MONTHS AWARDS

Aug/Sept	Leek Town
October	Winsford United
November	Hyde United
December	Gainsborough Trinity
January	Bamber Bridge
February	Leek Town
March	Emley
April	Bishop Auckland

First Division

	P	W	D	L	F	A	Pts
Radcliffe Borough	42	26	7	9	77	33	85
Leigh RMI	42	24	11	7	65	33	83
Lincoln United	42	25	8	9	78	47	83
Farsley Celtic	42	23	8	11	75	48	77
Worksop Town*	42	20	12	10	68	38	69
Stocksbridge Park Steels	42	19	11	12	66	54	68
Bradford Park Avenue	42	20	8	14	58	50	68
Ashton United	42	17	14	11	73	52	65
Great Harwood Town	42	16	12	14	56	46	60
Droylsden	42	15	14	13	69	67	59
Matlock Town	42	16	10	16	61	69	58
Whitley Bay	42	14	12	16	47	54	54
Flixton	42	15	7	20	57	72	52
Netherfield	42	12	14	16	54	56	50
Eastwood Town	42	12	14	16	42	50	50
Gretna	42	10	18	14	55	68	48
Harrogate Town	42	13	8	21	55	76	47
Congleton Town	42	12	9	21	47	64	45
Workington	42	10	12	20	45	63	42
Curzon Ashton	42	8	10	24	48	79	34
Warrington Town	42	5	18	19	42	79	33
Atherton LR	42	7	9	26	45	85	30

*3pts deducted; breach of rules

LEADING GOALSCORERS

(In order of League Goals)

First Division

Lge	Cup	Tot	
30	5	35	Billy O'Callaghan (Droylsden)
26	8	34	Robbie Whellans (Farsley Celtic)
26	5	31	Ian Lunt (Radcliffe Borough)
23	18	41	Paddy Wilson (Ashton United)
22	3	25	Tony Simmons (Lincoln United)
20	8	28	Chris Shaw (Leigh)
17	12	29	Gary Hurlstone (Stocksbridge Park Steels)
17	5	22	Kenny Clark (Matlock T–3 + 3 for Worksop Town)
16	3	19	Darren Washington (Congleton Town)
15	6	21	Keith Evans (Leigh)
14	8	22	Lee Cryer (Atherton LR)
14	4	18	Rick Ranshaw (Lincoln United)
13	18	31	John Coleman (Ashton Uinted–7 + 14 for Lancaster City)
13	5	18	Darren Emmett (Netherfield)
13	4	17	Ricardo Gabbiadini (Bradford Park Avenue)
13	2	15	Paul Baker (Great Harwood Town)
12	5	17	Jamie Close (Gretna–5 + 4 for Netherfield)
11	11	22	Linden Whitehead (Worksop Town)
11	6	17	Trefor Jones (Stocksbridge Park Steels)
11	5	16	Terry Harris (Worksop Town)
11	4	15	Paul Renwick (Netherfield)

UNIBOND CLUB OF THE MONTHS AWARDS

Aug/Sept	Lincoln United
October	Whitley Bay
November	Leigh
December	Bradford Park Avenue
January	Stocksbridge Park Steels
February	Farsley Celtic
March	Leigh
April	Lincoln United

UNIBOND LEAGUE—PREMIER DIVISION RESULTS 1996–97

	Accrington Stanley	Alfreton Town	Bamber Bridge	Barrow	Bishop Auckland	Blyth Spartans	Boston United	Buxton	Chorley	Colwyn Bay	Emley	Frickley Athletic	Gainsborough Trinity	Guiseley	Hyde United	Knowsley United	Lancaster City	Leek Town	Marine	Runcorn	Spennymoor United	Winsford United	Witton Albion
Accrington Stanley	—	4-2	4-1	1-2	1-4	2-3	3-1	5-3	0-3	3-1	1-1	4-0	0-4	1-2	3-2	1-1	2-1	1-2	1-0	2-2	2-0	0-0	4-1
Alfreton Town	1-3	—	2-1	2-3	3-0	1-2	1-2	1-2	0-3	2-1	0-0	1-0	0-1	4-5	0-3	2-0	1-0	1-1	0-1	1-1	2-1	1-1	2-1
Bamber Bridge	1-1	2-2	—	1-3	1-1	0-1	0-2	2-2	0-2	2-3	0-3	5-1	1-1	6-4	1-4	1-2	0-2	0-4	1-0	0-5	1-3	1-2	4-2
Barrow	4-3	3-0	1-1	—	0-1	2-2	3-0	0-0	3-0	1-0	3-0	2-0	2-2	1-1	1-4	1-1	3-0	3-0	0-1	1-1	1-0	2-1	3-1
Bishop Auckland	1-1	2-2	2-0	0-1	—	1-3	1-0	5-0	1-3	3-1	0-1	2-2	3-3	1-0	3-0	4-1	4-2	1-1	2-2	2-0	4-1	2-0	3-1
Blyth Spartans	1-1	2-1	2-1	1-0	0-0	—	1-2	5-0	1-3	0-0	1-1	6-3	1-1	1-0	2-1	6-0	3-1	0-2	1-1	3-2	2-0	1-2	5-0
Boston United	3-1	1-1	1-1	3-5	1-1	2-1	—	3-0	3-0	3-2	4-1	2-3	1-1	1-1	0-0	1-0	4-2	0-2	2-0	2-2	2-0	2-0	0-0
Buxton	1-3	0-1	0-1	0-1	1-1	1-2	0-2	—	0-1	4-0	0-3	1-3	2-1	0-1	0-3	0-0	1-0	0-0	2-1	0-2	1-0	1-2	1-1
Chorley	1-1	2-1	1-3	1-3	1-1	1-3	3-4	2-2	—	4-0	1-2	0-1	3-4	1-0	3-3	2-2	0-2	3-1	0-0	4-0	1-0	0-1	1-1
Colwyn Bay	0-2	1-1	5-2	1-2	1-2	3-0	1-5	3-4	1-1	—	3-2	5-0	0-2	1-1	1-3	5-0	1-1	3-1	0-0	3-3	1-1	0-1	6-1
Emley	3-1	4-0	1-2	3-0	2-0	3-2	1-1	3-0	1-0	0-1	—	3-3	3-3	4-0	2-4	2-4	1-1	2-3	5-1	2-1	3-0	1-1	0-0
Frickley Athletic	0-1	7-2	1-0	0-2	2-2	2-2	2-2	3-1	2-1	3-4	1-2	—	2-2	0-1	0-3	0-2	3-1	2-3	0-1	1-1	5-2	3-2	4-1
Gainsborough Trinity	2-2	3-0	0-2	3-0	3-0	0-1	1-1	1-1	3-0	2-0	3-0	2-0	—	1-0	0-1	2-0	1-1	0-1	0-1	4-1	1-0	2-0	3-0
Guiseley	1-0	1-1	5-0	1-3	0-0	2-1	1-0	2-0	1-4	0-1	2-0	1-0	1-0	—	2-3	1-0	1-1	2-0	0-1	0-1	2-1	1-1	3-0
Hyde United	7-2	5-0	2-2	1-0	1-1	0-1	3-2	2-0	3-2	1-1	5-1	5-1	2-1	2-2	—	4-0	3-3	1-1	1-1	2-0	4-0	0-0	1-0
Knowsley United	1-1	1-1	0-1	0-3	0-5	0-0	0-0	4-1	4-1	3-0	1-2	0-0	2-1	4-0	3-3	—	3-1	3-2	3-1	1-1	2-2	0-3	2-1
Lancaster City	1-2	1-0	2-3	1-0	2-1	2-1	0-1	1-0	1-1	2-2	1-3	1-3	0-2	2-2	0-4	2-2	—	0-3	0-2	0-2	1-0	1-2	1-1
Leek Town	2-1	4-0	4-1	2-1	1-0	0-2	1-0	1-1	4-1	2-1	3-0	1-3	1-0	1-0	0-4	2-0	2-1	—	0-1	0-3	1-0	0-1	0-0
Marine	2-1	1-1	2-0	1-1	2-3	0-3	1-1	3-0	1-0	5-0	3-1	0-0	3-1	1-2	1-1	2-2	2-1	5-1	—	1-0	1-1	0-0	0-1
Runcorn	1-3	1-0	1-2	0-0	1-3	1-0	1-1	1-1	1-0	3-3	2-1	1-1	4-1	0-1	1-1	2-0	4-0	1-0	1-0	—	1-0	4-3	2-1
Spennymoor United	0-0	3-2	2-1	1-2	1-5	0-2	1-3	1-1	0-0	1-2	2-3	3-1	1-2	4-1	5-0	2-2	1-0	5-0	1-1	1-0	—	2-0	1-0
Winsford United	1-1	1-0	4-2	1-2	1-2	0-2	0-1	1-1	0-1	3-0	2-2	1-0	1-1	1-1	2-1	3-1	0-1	0-1	0-0	0-0	1-1	—	1-1
Witton Albion	0-1	1-1	1-3	2-2	1-1	1-1	1-0	2-2	1-1	2-2	1-4	0-2	2-1	2-1	0-0	1-3	1-2	1-2	2-2	1-5	1-2	1-3	—

UNIBOND LEAGUE—FIRST DIVISION RESULTS 1996-97

	Ashton United	Atherton LR	Bradford Park Avenue	Congleton Town	Curzon Ashton	Droylsden	Eastwood Town	Farsley Celtic	Flixton	Great Harwood Town	Gretna	Harrogate Town	Leigh	Lincoln United	Matlock Town	Netherfield	Radcliffe Borough	Stocksbridge Park Steels	Warrington Town	Whitley Bay	Workington	Worksop Town
Ashton United	—	4-1	0-0	0-1	4-0	1-1	1-2	1-2	1-0	4-2	1-1	2-2	2-1	1-2	2-0	2-2	1-3	1-2	2-2	1-1	1-1	2-2
Atherton LR	0-2	—	1-3	1-2	3-3	0-5	0-2	0-0	0-2	1-0	2-2	4-1	1-0	3-1	4-1	2-2	0-1	0-1	2-3	2-0	1-0	1-2
Bradford Park Avenue	0-1	4-2	—	3-0	1-2	0-1	1-1	1-0	2-1	2-1	3-1	1-0	3-2	2-1	1-1	2-0	0-0	2-0	2-0	1-3	1-1	1-1
Congleton Town	2-7	4-1	0-1	—	1-1	0-1	2-0	0-1	0-1	5-1	2-0	5-1	1-0	0-3	1-1	2-0	0-3	2-0	3-0	1-3	1-1	3-0
Curzon Ashton	0-0	0-1	0-1	1-1	—	3-3	2-2	3-1	2-0	1-2	1-2	1-3	0-1	2-2	1-2	1-3	3-1	3-1	3-0	1-3	3-1	0-2
Droylsden	3-3	3-1	2-2	0-0	0-0	—	0-0	3-1	2-3	0-0	2-2	3-1	3-2	1-2	0-1	1-0	3-1	2-2	2-3	1-1	3-1	2-3
Eastwood Town	2-1	0-0	1-1	0-0	3-2	0-0	—	3-0	2-0	2-0	0-2	2-0	0-0	0-1	1-2	2-2	1-0	2-1	1-0	1-2	0-1	1-1
Farsley Celtic	2-3	0-2	1-0	3-0	1-2	3-0	3-1	—	1-1	3-0	1-1	3-0	0-0	2-0	1-1	2-1	0-1	2-1	1-1	1-1	1-2	1-0
Flixton	0-0	1-0	2-1	0-1	2-1	1-3	3-1	2-2	—	0-2	2-3	5-0	0-1	1-1	0-0	1-0	1-3	1-2	1-2	2-2	1-2	1-2
Great Harwood Town	0-2	4-1	2-1	2-1	0-0	4-4	2-0	2-3	4-1	—	0-0	1-0	1-1	2-3	2-0	0-0	2-0	1-0	6-0	2-0	1-0	0-0
Gretna	1-1	2-2	3-1	1-1	1-1	3-0	0-5	3-0	4-1	2-2	—	1-2	0-2	0-3	3-3	1-3	1-0	1-2	3-3	3-1	2-1	1-0
Harrogate Town	2-2	4-1	1-2	1-2	4-2	4-4	2-0	3-0	5-0	1-0	0-0	—	1-2	2-0	1-1	1-1	2-2	1-0	1-0	1-0	1-0	0-2
Leigh	2-0	1-0	2-1	3-2	2-0	1-3	0-0	0-0	0-1	1-1	0-0	1-2	—	2-1	4-1	0-2	2-1	1-2	1-0	1-0	2-1	0-1
Lincoln United	1-2	3-1	0-2	1-0	0-1	0-1	0-1	2-0	1-1	2-3	4-1	4-1	1-2	—	1-4	2-1	2-1	2-1	2-2	1-0	1-0	1-0
Matlock Town	2-2	4-1	0-3	2-0	1-4	0-2	1-2	3-0	0-0	2-0	2-1	0-2	2-1	1-4	—	3-3	0-2	2-1	2-2	3-0	1-0	0-4
Netherfield	1-0	2-2	2-0	1-0	2-0	1-0	2-2	1-0	1-1	1-1	0-1	0-1	0-3	1-4	5-1	—	1-1	0-1	0-0	5-0	1-1	1-5
Radcliffe Borough	2-0	2-0	3-2	3-2	3-1	4-0	2-0	3-0	3-2	2-1	5-2	2-0	0-1	0-1	3-1	1-1	—	0-1	3-0	1-2	5-1	1-1
Stocksbridge Park Steels	2-2	0-1	0-0	2-0	2-2	3-0	2-4	3-4	3-2	1-0	2-2	1-1	0-0	2-1	0-2	1-0	0-2	—	5-0	2-0	3-0	2-1
Warrington Town	0-4	2-3	0-0	2-2	3-1	0-0	1-1	1-1	1-2	0-4	3-1	0-4	1-1	0-1	1-1	0-0	0-3	1-2	—	0-1	1-1	1-1
Whitley Bay	3-2	2-0	3-4	0-0	1-0	4-0	1-1	0-2	0-2	4-1	0-1	0-2	1-2	1-0	1-0	1-2	1-1	1-0	5-1	—	0-0	2-2
Workington	2-1	1-1	0-0	4-0	3-0	4-0	4-1	1-1	1-1	4-1	1-1	0-2	0-4	2-4	3-4	0-3	1-1	2-2	0-0	2-1	—	2-0
Worksop Town	1-0	2-2	1-2	1-0	5-0	1-1	2-0	1-0	2-0	0-0	1-1	2-1	2-0	2-0	2-0	4-0	1-0	0-1	2-0	2-0	4-0	—

UNIBOND CHALLENGE CUP

FIRST ROUND
Ashton United 4, Bradford Park Avenue 2 *(after 0-0 draw)*
Congleton Town 0, Flixton 2
Curzon Ashton 3, Atherton LR 2
Droylsden 1, Warrington Town 2
Frickley Athletic 1, Farsley Celtic 0
Great Harwood Town 2, Workington 1
Harrogate Town 3, Stocksbridge Park Steels 2
Lincoln United 3, Alfreton Town 1
Matlock Town 4, Buxton 1
Netherfield 2, Lancaster City 3 *(after 2-2 draw)*
Radcliffe Borough 3, Leigh 1 *(after 0-0 draw)*
Whitley Bay 0, Gretna 2
Worksop Town 5, Eastwood Town 2 *(after 1-1 draw and extra time)*

SECOND ROUND
Ashton United 0, Guiseley 2
Bamber Bridge 1, Radcliffe Borough 5
Barrow 1, Gretna 0
Blyth Spartans 1, Emley 2
Boston United 3, Lincoln United 0 *(after 1-1 draw)*
Flixton 2, Warrington Town 0
Frickley Athletic 1, Bishop Auckland 0
Gainsborough Trinity 1, Leek Town 0 *(after 0-0 draw)*
Great Harwood Town 2, Chorley 1
Hyde United 3, Curzon Ashton 0
Lancaster City 0, Accrington Stanley 2
Marine 1, Knowsley United 3
Matlock Town 3, Worksop Town 1
Spennymoor United 4, Harrogate Town 3
Winsford United 3, Runcorn 1
Witton Albion 0, Colwyn Bay 5

THIRD ROUND
Accrington Stanley 4, Flixton 1
Boston United 3, Hyde United 2 *(after 1-1 draw)*
Colwyn Bay 3, Winsford United 2
Emley 1, Spennymoor United 0
Gainsborough Trinity 3, Frickley Athletic 0
Great Harwood Town 0, Knowsley United 1 *(after 2-2 draw)*
Matlock Town 1, Guiseley 4
Radcliffe Borough 2, Barrow 1

FOURTH ROUND
Boston United 2, Emley 1
Gainsborough Trinity 2, Knowsley United 1
Guiseley 0, Colwyn Bay 2 *(after 2-2 draw)*
Radcliffe Borough 0, Accrington Stanley 3 *(after 0-0 draw)*

SEMI-FINALS (TWO LEGS)
Accrington Stanley 1, Gainsborough Trinity 0
Gainsborough Trinity 3, Accrington Stanley 1
Gainsborough Trinity won 3-2 on aggregate.
Boston United 1, Colwyn Bay 0
Colwyn Bay 1, Boston United 3
Boston United won 4-1 on aggregate.

FINAL
Boston United 0, Gainsborough Trinity 1 *(aet; at Lincoln City)*

UNIBOND LEAGUE PRESIDENT'S CUP

FIRST ROUND
Bamber Bridge 2, Runcorn 3
Barrow 5, Accrington Stanley 4
Blyth Spartans 2, Spennymoor United 1 *(after 2-2 draw)*
Boston United 5, Gainsborough Trinity 2
Curzon Ashton 0, Alfreton Town 3 *(after 0-0 draw)*
Emley 0, Radcliffe Borough 1
Farsley Celtic 2, Guiseley 0 *(after 1-1 draw)*
Worksop Town 3, Lincoln United 0

SECOND ROUND
Farsley Celtic 2, Boston United 1 *(aet and 1-1 draw)*
Radcliffe Borough 3, Alfreton Town 1
Runcorn 3, Barrow 1
Worksop Town 1, Blyth Spartans 2 *(after 2-2 draw)*

SEMI-FINAL (TWO LEGS)
Radcliffe Borough 0, Blyth Spartans 0
Blyth Spartans 1, Radcliffe Borough 0
(Blyth Spartans won 1-0 on aggregate)
Runcorn 0, Farsley Celtic 0
Farsley Celtic 1, Runcorn 2
(Runcorn won 2-1 on aggregate)

FINAL (TWO LEGS)
Runcorn 0, Blyth Spartans 1
Blyth Spartans 3, Runcorn 2
(Blyth Spartans won 4-2 on aggregate)

UNIFILLA FIRST DIVISION CUP

FIRST ROUND
Droylsden 4, Flixton 0 *(after 0-0 draw)*
Eastwood Town 0, Harrogate Town 1
Leigh 1, Ashton United 1
(after 3-3 draw aet, Ashton United won 6-5 on penalties)
Netherfield 2, Gretna 1
Stocksbridge Park Steels 2, Matlock Town 1
Workington 1, Whitley Bay 0

SECOND ROUND
Atherton LR 1, Workington 0
Bradford Park Avenue 0, Harrogate Town 2
Droylsden 4, Ashton United 4
(after 1-1 draw aet, Ashton United won 4-1 on penalties)
Farsley Celtic 1, Stocksbridge Park Steels 2
Great Harwood Town 2, Netherfield 3 *(after 1-1 draw)*
Lincoln United 2, Workington Town 1 *(after 2-2 draw)*
Radcliffe Borough 1, Curzon Ashton 0
Warrington Town 0, Congleton Town 8

THIRD ROUND
Harrogate Town 2, Atherton LR 1
Netherfield 0, Ashton United 3 *(after 4-4 draw)*
Radcliffe Borough 5, Lincoln United 1
Stocksbridge Park Steels 1, Congleton Town 0

SEMI-FINALS (TWO LEGS)
Ashton United 2, Harrogate Town 1
Harrogate Town 2, Ashton United 2
(aet, Ashton United won 4-3 on aggregate)
Radcliffe Borough 1, Stocksbridge Park Steels 1
Stocksbridge Park Steels 1, Radcliffe Borough 0
(aet, Stocksbridge Park Steels won on away goals)

FINAL (TWO LEGS)
Stocksbridge Park Steels 0, Ashton United 3
Ashton United 5, Stocksbridge Park Steels 4
(Ashton United won 8-4 on aggregate)

DR MARTENS LEAGUE 1996–97

Premier Division

	P	W	D	L	F	A	Pts
Gresley Rovers	42	25	10	7	75	40	85
Cheltenham Town	42	21	11	10	76	44	74
Gloucester City	42	21	10	11	81	56	73
Halesowen Town	42	21	10	11	77	54	73
King's Lynn	42	20	8	14	65	61	68
Burton Albion	42	18	12	12	70	53	66
Nuneaton Borough	42	19	9	14	61	52	66
Sittingbourne	42	19	7	16	76	65	64
Merthyr Tydfil	42	17	9	16	69	61	60
Worcester City	42	15	14	13	52	50	59
Atherstone United	42	15	13	14	46	47	58
Salisbury City	42	15	13	14	57	66	58
Sudbury Town	42	16	7	19	72	72	55
Gravesend & Northfleet	42	16	7	19	63	73	55
Dorchester Town	42	14	9	19	62	66	51
Hastings Town	42	12	15	15	49	60	51
Crawley Town	42	13	8	21	49	67	47
Cambridge City	42	11	13	18	57	65	46
Ashford Town	42	9	18	15	53	79	45
Baldock Town	42	11	8	23	52	90	41
Newport AFC	42	9	13	20	40	60	40
Chelmsford City	42	6	14	22	49	70	32

Midland Division

	P	W	D	L	F	A	Pts
Tamworth	40	30	7	3	90	28	97
Rothwell Town	40	20	11	9	82	54	71
Ilkeston Town	40	19	13	8	76	50	70
Grantham Town	40	22	4	14	65	46	70
Bedworth United	40	18	11	11	77	41	65
Solihull Borough	40	19	8	13	84	62	65
Bilston Town	40	18	10	12	74	57	64
Moor Green	40	18	7	15	88	68	61
Stafford Rangers	40	17	9	14	68	62	60
Raunds Town	40	16	11	13	61	66	59
Racing Club Warwick	40	16	10	14	70	72	58
Shepshed Dynamo	40	14	12	14	64	65	54
Redditch United	40	15	8	17	56	59	53
Paget Rangers	40	13	9	18	42	55	48
Dudley Town	40	12	10	18	70	89	46
Hinckley Town	40	11	11	18	39	63	44
Stourbridge	40	10	9	21	61	81	39
Evesham United	40	9	12	19	55	77	39
VS Rugby	40	9	9	22	49	81	36
Corby Town	40	8	8	24	49	88	32
Sutton Coldfield Town	40	7	9	24	29	85	30

(Leicester United folded after 2 games – record expunged)

Southern Division

	P	W	D	L	F	A	Pts
Forest Green Rovers	42	27	10	5	87	40	91
St Leonards Stamcroft	42	26	9	7	95	48	87
Havant Town	42	23	10	9	81	49	79
Weston-super-Mare	42	21	13	8	82	43	76
Margate	42	21	9	12	70	47	72
Witney Town	42	20	11	11	71	42	71
Weymouth	42	20	10	12	82	51	70
Tonbridge Angels	42	17	15	10	56	44	66
Newport IOW	42	15	15	12	73	58	60
Fisher Athletic London	42	18	6	18	77	77	60
Clevedon Town	42	17	9	16	75	76	60
Fareham Town	42	14	12	16	53	70	54
Bashley	42	15	8	19	73	84	53
Dartford	42	14	10	18	59	64	52
Waterlooville	42	14	9	19	58	67	51
Cirencester Town	42	12	12	18	50	68	48
Cinderford Town	42	13	7	22	64	76	46
Trowbridge Town	42	11	11	20	50	61	44
Yate Town	42	12	8	22	55	87	44
Fleet Town	42	12	6	24	47	91	42
Erith & Belvedere	42	9	10	23	60	95	37
Buckingham Town	42	2	8	32	27	107	14

LEADING GOALSCORERS
(League and Cup)

Premier Division

R. Straw (Nuneaton Borough)	28
E. Wright (Halesowen Town)	28
O. Pickard (Dorchester Town)	26
I. Brown (Sudbury Town)	25
D. Watkins (Gloucester City)	25
D. Arter (Gravesend & Northfleet)	20
I. Stringfellow (King's Lynn)	19
D. Fenton (Baldock Town)	17
C. McLean (Sudbury Town)	17
S. Restarick (Crawley Town)	17
C. Summers (Merthyr Tydfil)	17
A. Walker (Sittingbourne)	15
M. Cotter (Burton Albion)	15
M. Nuttell (Burton Albion)	15
P. Evans (Merthyr Tydfil)	14
A. Garner (Gresley Rovers)	14
T. Marsden (Gresley Rovers)	14
B. McNamara (King's Lynn)	14
L. Webb (Salisbury City)	14
S. Cuggy (Hastings Town)	13
M. Boyle (Cheltenham Town)	12
N. Dent (Ashford Town)	12
R. Harbut (Salisbury City)	12
A. Mings (Gloucester City)	12
A. Thomas (Worcester City)	12
D. Webb (Gloucester City)	12

Midland Division

H. Wright (Bilston Town)	28
D. Christopher (Redditch United)	25
K. McGuire (Rothwell Town)	25
B. Agar (Racing Club Warwick)	22
I. Bennett (Tamworth)	22
D. King (Grantham Town)	22
G. Piggott (Dudley Town)	22
P. Hunter (Tamworth)	19
R. Mitchell (Stafford Rangers)	19
L. Dixon (Evesham United)	18
J. Dowling (Solihull Borough)	18
S. Keeble (Raunds Town)	18
T. Burroughs (Paget Rangers)	17
K. Johnstone (Evesham United)	17
D. Beazeley (Rothwell Town)	16
A. Johnson (Stourbridge)	16
M. Moore (Moor Green)	16
G. Smith (Tamworth)	16
A. Warner (Rothwell Town)	16
M. Coppin (Solihull Borough)	15
P. Eshelby (Ilkeston Town)	15
S. Clifford (Stafford Rangers)	14
J. Kabia (Ilkeston Town)	13
P. McBean (Bedworth United)	13

Southern Division

M. Buglione (Margate)	26
P. Hunt (Forest Green Rovers)	26
D. Laws (Weymouth)	22
C. Wilkins (Tonbridge Angels)	22
S. Tate (Waterlooville)	22
E. Fearon (Newport IOW)	21
J. Magee (St Leonards Stamcroft)	21
D. Tilley (Weston-super-Mare)	20
K. Bayliss (Forest Green Rovers)	19
P. Sykes (Margate)	19
J. Caffel (Witney Town)	19
P. Gorman (Fisher Athletic London)	18
P. Sales (Bashley)	18
C. Soares (Newport IOW)	18
S. Leigh (Havant Town)	17
K. Miles (St Leonards Stamcroft)	17
S. Portway (Erith & Belvedere)	17
T. White (St Leonards Stamford)	17
D. Clarke (Yate Town)	16
S. Tapp (Witney Town)	15
K. Haag (Fisher Athletic London)	14
C. Hoult (Weymouth)	14
R. Semark (Fareham Town)	14
A. Sykes (Forest Green Rovers)	14
D. Bright (Clevedon Town)	13
P. McLoughlin (Weston-super-Mare)	13
G. Payne (Dartford)	13
D. Puckett (Newport IOW)	13

DR MARTENS CUP

PRELIMINARY ROUND, FIRST LEG
King's Lynn 0, Rothwell Town 0
Dorchester Town 1, Newport (IOW) 1

PRELIMINARY ROUND, SECOND LEG
Newport (IOW) 2, Dorchester Town 1
Rothwell Town 1, King's Lynn 3

FIRST ROUND, FIRST LEG
Corby Town 2, Grantham Town 1
Stourbridge 1, Worcester City 1
Tamworth 3, Bedworth United 0
Buckingham Town 0, Cambridge City 3
Gloucester City 5, Cinderford Town 0
Witney Town 1, Clevedon Town 1
Dartford 1, Crawley Town 1
Evesham United 6, Dudley Town 2
Ilkeston Town 1, Gresley Rovers 1
Erith & Belvedere 1, Margate 2
Yate Town 2, Merthyr Tydfil 2
Sutton Coldfield 2, Moor Green 2
Hinckley Town 1, Nuneaton Borough 2
Shepshed Dynamo 2, Racing Club Warwick 2
Ashford Town 3, Tonbridge Angels 2
Chelmsford City 0, Baldock Town 1
Bashley 2, Salisbury City 3
Gravesend & Northfleet 2, Sittingbourne 3
Paget Rangers 3, Solihull Borough 2
Atherstone United 0, VS Rugby 2
Weymouth 4, Fareham Town 1
Newport (IOW) 3, Havant Town 2
Hastings Town 1, St Leonards Stamcroft 2
Cirencester Town 3, Forest Green Rovers 3
Halesowen Town 1, Stafford Rangers 0
Redditch United 1, Bilston Town 1
Sudbury Town 2, Fisher 1
Waterlooville 0, Fleet Town 1
Weston-Super-Mare 0, Trowbridge Town 2
Newport AFC 2, Cheltenham Town 1
Raunds Town 0, King's Lynn 1
Leicester United withdrew; Burton Albion w.o.

FIRST ROUND, SECOND LEG
Worcester City 3, Stourbridge 1
Bedworth United 1, Tamworth 4
Cambridge City 4, Buckingham Town 0
Cinderford Town 2, Gloucester City 1
Clevedon Town 2, Witney Town 2
(aet; Witney Town won 4-2 on penalties)
Crawley Town 2, Dartford 0
Dudley Town 1, Evesham United 2
Grantham Town 1, Corby Town 3
Gresley Rovers 2, Ilkeston Town 2
(Ilkeston Town won on away goals)
Margate 2, Erith & Belvedere 0
Merthyr Tydfil 5, Yate Town 0
Moor Green 0, Sutton Coldfield 0
(Moor Green won on away goals)
Nuneaton Borough 2, Hinckley Town 2
Racing Club Warwick 1, Shepshed Dynamo 1
(Racing Club Warwick won on away goals)
Tonbridge Angels 3, Ashford Town 0
Baldock Town 2, Chelmsford City 1 *(aet)*
Salisbury City 3, Bashley 0
Sittingbourne 1, Gravesend & Northfleet 2
(Sittingbourne won on away goals)
Solihull Borough 1, Paget Rangers 2
VS Rugby 1, Atherstone United 4

Fareham Town 3, Weymouth 3
Havant Town 3, Newport (IOW) 4
St Leonards Stamcroft 3, Hastings Town 0
King's Lynn 1, Raunds Town 2
Stafford Rangers 0, Halesowen Town 2
Bilston Town 0, Redditch United 3
Fisher 5, Sudbury Town 4
Fleet Town 1, Waterlooville 2
Cheltenham Town 5, Newport AFC 0
Trowbridge Town 0, Weston-Super-Mare 0
Forest Green Rovers 3, Cirencester Town 1

SECOND ROUND
Worcester City 1, Racing Club Warwick 1
replay: Racing Club Warwick 2, Worcester City 1
Atherstone United 0, Tamworth 3
Cambridge City 1, Sudbury Town 4
Merthyr Tydfil 2, Witney Town 2
replay: Witney Town 1, Merthyr Tydfil 2
Cheltenham Town 1, Gloucester City 0
Crawley Town 1, Tonbridge Angels 2
Trowbridge Town 1, Forest Green Rovers 1
replay: Forest Green Rovers 4, Trowbridge Town 2
Waterlooville 0, Weymouth 1
Corby Town 0, Raunds Town 2
Evesham United 0, Moor Green 3
Salisbury City 3, Newport (IOW) 1
Sittingbourne 0, Baldock Town 2
St Leonards Stamcroft 3, Margate 2
Nuneaton Borough 1, Burton Albion 2
Redditch United 0, Halesowen Town 3
Paget Rangers 0, Ilkeston Town 3

THIRD ROUND
Raunds Town 2, Tamworth 1
Baldock Town 3, Tonbridge Angels 4
Salisbury City 1, Weymouth 3
Merthyr Tydfil 0, Racing Club Warwick 2
(after 1-1 abandoned 50 mins; frozen pitch)
Sudbury Town 1, St Leonards Stamcroft 0
Burton Albion 1, Halesowen Town 0
Cheltenham Town 0, Forest Green Rovers 1
Ilkeston Town 2, Moor Green 1

FOURTH ROUND
Weymouth 2, Forest Green Rovers 0
Raunds Town 0, Burton Albion 2
Racing Club Warwick 1, Ilkeston Town 0
Sudbury Town 3, Tonbridge Angels 2

SEMI-FINAL, FIRST LEG
Racing Club Warwick 1, Burton Albion 4
Sudbury Town 1, Weymouth 0

SEMI-FINAL, SECOND LEG
Burton Albion 4, Racing Club Warwick 1
Weymouth 0, Sudbury Town 3

FINAL, FIRST LEG
Burton Albion 2, Sudbury Town 1

FINAL, SECOND LEG
Sudbury Town 0, Burton Albion 1

DR MARTENS LEAGUE—PREMIER LEAGUE RESULTS 1996-97

	Ashford Town	Atherstone United	Baldock Town	Burton Albion	Cambridge City	Chelmsford City	Cheltenham Town	Crawley Town	Dorchester Town	Gloucester City	Gravesend & Northfleet	Gresley Rovers	Halesowen Town	Hastings Town	King's Lynn	Merthyr Tydfil	Newport AFC	Nuneaton Borough	Salisbury City	Sittingbourne	Sudbury Town	Worcester City
Ashford Town	—	0-3	1-1	1-0	4-0	1-0	1-1	3-3	2-1	0-3	1-1	1-3	1-1	3-3	4-0	0-1	1-1	2-0	0-1	1-1	2-2	0-0
Atherstone United	1-1	—	1-3	1-2	1-2	0-1	2-0	2-0	2-1	0-0	0-0	0-1	0-5	0-0	1-1	3-4	1-0	0-0	4-0	2-1	1-0	2-2
Baldock Town	1-1	0-2	—	1-3	1-1	4-1	1-0	1-2	2-1	2-3	0-5	0-3	0-1	2-0	1-1	2-2	1-0	1-2	1-1	1-5	3-2	0-3
Burton Albion	1-0	1-2	1-3	—	3-3	4-2	0-0	2-0	4-1	3-1	1-3	2-3	0-0	0-0	4-1	0-1	3-0	2-0	1-1	1-0	2-1	2-2
Cambridge City	4-0	1-2	1-1	3-3	—	1-0	1-4	4-0	2-2	0-1	4-2	2-3	1-4	1-3	0-2	2-2	0-0	2-2	1-2	1-3	1-3	1-2
Chelmsford City	1-1	0-1	2-3	4-2	1-0	—	2-4	1-0	1-1	1-3	4-0	2-2	3-0	2-2	0-2	0-0	1-1	3-1	0-2	1-4	1-3	1-2
Cheltenham Town	6-0	2-0	3-2	1-0	1-4	2-4	—	1-2	1-1	1-1	0-1	0-0	2-1	1-0	1-2	2-0	0-0	2-0	2-2	2-0	0-2	2-0
Crawley Town	2-3	2-0	2-0	2-0	4-0	1-0	1-2	—	2-0	1-1	0-2	2-2	0-3	0-2	0-0	1-0	1-3	1-0	4-2	2-2	1-2	2-1
Dorchester Town	0-2	1-0	3-2	5-0	1-0	0-2	3-3	2-5	—	1-1	2-2	1-3	1-1	0-2	1-2	2-0	1-3	2-0	3-2	2-0	0-2	2-0
Gloucester City	6-1	0-0	3-1	2-4	0-2	2-2	1-3	2-1	3-1	—	3-1	1-2	0-3	1-1	0-0	6-3	2-1	1-0	1-3	1-1	3-3	1-1
Gravesend & Northfleet	1-3	1-1	1-2	0-1	2-0	2-0	2-1	2-0	2-0	2-2	—	2-1	1-1	2-0	3-0	3-1	3-0	1-1	5-0	3-0	4-2	2-0
Gresley Rovers	2-2	1-1	3-0	1-0	0-2	1-0	1-3	0-0	0-0	2-1	2-1	—	2-3	3-0	1-0	0-2	1-0	1-4	0-4	2-0	1-1	3-0
Halesowen Town	3-1	0-2	6-0	2-1	1-4	1-0	1-5	2-2	3-1	5-4	2-0	1-1	—	1-2	0-2	1-2	2-0	2-0	3-2	2-2	1-0	0-0
Hastings Town	2-2	0-0	1-0	0-0	1-3	1-2	1-2	1-0	1-0	0-2	2-1	1-2	1-4	—	2-2	2-2	2-2	0-0	5-0	3-2	4-3	0-1
King's Lynn	2-0	2-1	4-2	4-1	0-2	0-2	0-2	0-1	0-4	2-1	5-1	0-2	0-1	2-2	—	2-1	0-1	4-0	2-3	1-4	2-1	0-1
Merthyr Tydfil	3-0	3-2	4-1	0-1	2-2	2-0	2-2	3-1	3-2	1-0	5-0	0-1	0-1	4-1	1-2	—	2-0	5-1	1-1	2-3	1-3	2-0
Newport AFC	3-0	2-0	2-2	3-0	0-0	2-2	1-5	0-1	3-0	2-1	1-3	1-0	0-2	0-2	0-2	3-1	—	0-0	3-1	4-0	3-1	1-1
Nuneaton Borough	3-0	3-2	0-3	2-1	2-2	3-1	1-0	1-2	3-0	2-0	3-0	1-0	1-2	2-1	2-4	1-1	1-0	—	4-0	1-1	1-1	2-1
Salisbury City	0-1	3-2	2-3	2-0	1-1	1-1	1-2	1-0	0-0	0-4	4-1	1-1	4-2	2-0	2-0	1-3	0-0	1-1	—	0-1	2-1	1-1
Sittingbourne	4-1	1-1	1-0	1-0	2-1	2-1	1-0	3-5	1-3	1-1	1-3	2-0	4-2	3-0	0-2	3-1	3-0	2-2	0-1	—	4-5	0-1
Sudbury Town	2-2	0-1	4-0	0-3	4-0	1-1	1-4	2-0	2-4	2-1	2-0	0-3	2-1	3-0	5-1	1-0	1-1	0-2	2-1	4-5	—	3-2
Worcester City	0-2	3-0	3-0	2-1	2-2	1-1	2-2	2-1	1-0	0-0	4-2	1-2	1-1	3-0	2-1	2-1	1-1	0-1	0-2	0-2	2-1	—

DR MARTENS LEAGUE—MIDLAND DIVISION RESULTS 1996-97

Home \ Away	Bedworth United	Bilston Town	Corby Town	Dudley Town	Evesham United	Grantham Town	Hinckley Town	Ilkeston Town	Leicester United	Moor Green	Paget Rangers	Racing Club Warwick	Raunds Town	Redditch United	Rothwell Town	Shepshed Dynamo	Solihull Borough	Stafford Rangers	Stourbridge	Sutton Coldfield Town	Tamworth	VS Rugby
Bedworth United	—	0-2	1-2	1-1	2-0	4-1	1-0	2-0	—	1-0	3-0	1-3	2-2	1-1	1-1	2-0	2-0	1-1	7-0	6-0	0-1	3-1
Bilston Town	2-1	—	7-1	2-4	1-2	2-3	4-1	4-1	—	1-5	4-0	1-1	2-2	2-0	0-4	4-1	1-0	0-1	3-2	5-0	0-0	4-3
Corby Town	1-2	1-3	—	2-4	2-2	0-5	0-1	0-0	—	1-6	2-3	1-0	4-2	5-4	1-2	0-0	0-1	1-2	1-2	2-0	0-3	3-1
Dudley Town	1-1	3-2	1-3	—	1-1	3-2	0-1	0-0	—	2-1	2-2	3-0	1-5	1-2	1-1	0-0	3-2	3-3	3-3	0-0	0-4	1-4
Evesham United	0-0	2-2	0-0	3-1	—	0-2	1-2	3-2	2-3	1-2	4-0	2-2	1-2	1-0	2-0	0-0	2-1	1-0	1-3	0-1	2-3	2-2
Grantham Town	0-3	1-2	1-0	1-0	3-2	—	3-0	0-2	2-3	3-1	2-0	2-4	3-0	1-2	0-0	2-0	3-2	1-0	3-2	2-0	0-1	1-0
Hinckley Town	0-0	0-0	1-1	1-0	2-1	3-0	—	0-2	—	1-5	0-2	2-1	0-0	1-2	3-1	3-4	2-2	0-6	3-3	1-1	0-1	4-0
Ilkeston Town	1-1	2-1	1-2	2-2	3-4	3-1	4-0	—	—	2-0	1-1	3-0	2-0	1-0	3-4	4-0	1-4	—	4-2	2-0	1-0	1-0
Leicester United	—	—	—	—	—	2-3	—	—	—	—	—	—	—	—	—	—	—	—	—	—	—	—
Moor Green	1-0	1-5	—	—	1-2	3-1	1-5	2-0	—	—	1-2	2-4	4-1	2-3	1-3	2-4	5-2	2-2	2-2	0-3	3-1	1-2
Paget Rangers	1-4	2-3	—	5-3	0-2	0-1	3-1	4-1	—	1-2	—	0-0	0-1	1-2	1-3	3-0	3-1	0-2	2-1	0-1	0-3	2-2
Racing Club Warwick	0-4	4-1	3-2	3-1	2-1	0-1	5-2	1-1	—	1-6	2-3	—	1-1	1-2	1-1	0-0	3-3	3-3	0-1	3-0	0-3	1-0
Raunds Town	2-1	1-4	0-0	1-3	2-1	1-0	0-0	3-2	—	2-1	2-2	1-0	—	1-0	0-4	0-0	1-1	1-3	0-3	2-2	0-2	3-0
Redditch United	1-0	2-0	2-0	2-3	0-0	1-0	0-1	1-1	—	2-3	4-0	1-3	1-0	—	5-2	0-5	2-2	0-2	1-2	1-2	2-3	1-2
Rothwell Town	1-2	1-0	3-1	2-1	3-0	3-1	0-0	3-4	—	3-1	5-2	1-1	5-2	1-2	—	3-4	1-2	3-1	4-2	2-1	2-2	2-2
Shepshed Dynamo	1-0	2-0	3-0	1-0	6-1	1-0	0-0	3-5	—	2-4	4-1	0-0	3-2	4-0	3-4	—	1-4	3-2	1-0	0-0	0-3	3-2
Solihull Borough	3-2	2-1	2-0	5-1	0-1	3-1	0-1	0-0	—	5-2	3-1	1-2	1-1	2-2	1-2	3-0	—	4-1	1-3	2-0	2-0	1-1
Stafford Rangers	3-1	1-1	2-0	4-3	1-2	3-1	0-1	2-2	—	2-2	3-1	1-2	0-2	2-1	2-1	2-1	3-1	—	2-0	3-0	0-5	2-0
Stourbridge	2-2	0-3	2-2	1-4	2-2	0-4	2-2	1-2	—	2-2	2-1	3-3	1-3	2-4	2-3	0-5	2-4	2-2	—	3-0	1-2	1-2
Sutton Coldfield Town	1-1	1-1	1-0	1-4	2-2	2-0	1-0	1-0	—	0-3	0-4	1-1	2-4	0-2	3-0	4-0	0-1	0-4	1-4	—	1-2	2-2
Tamworth	2-1	4-2	2-0	1-1	2-0	0-0	1-0	2-0	—	3-1	1-0	6-0	5-2	1-0	3-0	4-0	2-4	1-0	1-0	1-0	—	0-0
VS Rugby	2-2	0-2	2-1	2-4	2-2	1-2	1-0	2-0	—	1-2	1-1	2-1	1-2	1-1	0-2	0-4	1-4	2-2	2-1	0-2	2-6	—

Leicester United withdrew after 2 matches

DR MARTENS LEAGUE—SOUTHERN DIVISION RESULTS 1996–97

	Bashley	Buckingham Town	Cinderford Town	Cirencester Town	Clevedon Town	Dartford	Erith & Belvedere	Fareham Town	Fisher 93	Fleet Town	Forest Green Rovers	Havant Town	Margate	Newport IOW	St Leonards Stamcroft	Tonbridge Angels	Trowbridge Town	Waterlooville	Weston-super-Mare	Weymouth	Witney Town	Yate Town
Bashley	—	3-1	2-2	1-1	0-1	1-4	2-3	2-2	0-2	1-2	1-5	0-3	0-1	0-0	0-0	0-2	2-1	2-2	3-1	4-1	2-0	3-1
Buckingham Town	0-9	—	0-2	1-3	1-2	1-1	3-0	1-1	0-2	1-2	0-2	0-2	1-2	0-0	0-0	0-1	1-3	2-1	0-1	0-5	1-2	1-3
Cinderford Town	2-4	7-0	—	7-2	2-3	3-0	2-1	1-3	0-0	2-1	1-3	2-0	0-3	1-2	1-2	0-0	1-3	3-1	2-2	0-5	2-1	1-1
Cirencester Town	1-2	2-0	1-4	—	1-5	2-4	1-1	1-1	1-0	2-0	0-1	1-1	0-0	0-1	1-2	2-0	2-0	1-4	1-2	0-0	1-0	2-0
Clevedon Town	5-2	2-2	4-1	4-2	—	0-6	5-0	0-1	2-0	5-2	3-0	2-3	1-1	4-3	2-2	2-0	2-0	2-2	0-0	2-2	2-0	3-1
Dartford	2-1	1-0	2-0	0-0	3-1	—	1-0	1-2	1-4	1-0	0-0	0-0	0-3	4-4	3-2	3-2	0-3	1-2	1-1	3-5	1-2	0-0
Erith & Belvedere	1-3	3-0	2-0	0-0	1-0	3-0	—	4-1	2-0	0-2	0-0	2-3	1-1	4-4	1-2	3-2	1-1	0-0	1-5	1-1	1-2	0-3
Fareham Town	1-1	3-1	3-0	1-3	1-0	2-0	3-0	—	4-1	1-3	0-1	2-1	0-3	2-1	2-2	1-1	1-1	2-2	0-3	2-0	1-3	1-2
Fisher 93	3-1	4-2	3-3	1-1	2-0	1-0	3-2	5-3	—	2-3	3-3	2-4	2-3	0-1	4-3	1-2	0-3	0-6	1-3	1-2	0-0	0-1
Fleet Town	1-2	1-1	2-0	1-1	0-1	0-4	1-4	2-0	3-1	—	1-2	0-1	0-6	0-4	0-2	1-2	0-3	3-2	2-1	1-1	0-0	4-3
Forest Green Rovers	4-0	2-0	2-1	3-1	4-1	2-1	5-2	8-0	2-0	1-2	—	3-2	2-1	2-1	0-2	3-3	1-1	1-1	3-1	2-0	3-0	4-0
Havant Town	1-1	4-1	4-1	0-1	2-1	0-0	4-0	1-0	1-2	5-1	0-0	—	1-2	2-0	2-1	1-2	2-0	2-2	1-1	2-1	3-0	1-0
Margate	3-5	2-0	3-2	3-2	0-1	1-1	2-0	2-0	1-3	3-0	0-0	0-2	—	0-0	1-2	2-3	2-0	2-2	1-0	1-2	0-4	4-1
Newport IOW	3-1	2-0	1-3	3-2	0-1	1-1	3-3	2-4	1-3	1-1	2-0	0-2	1-1	—	1-2	2-3	4-3	3-2	2-2	2-1	2-1	7-0
St Leonards Stamcroft	4-3	4-1	1-3	5-0	4-1	3-1	3-3	5-0	2-1	2-1	1-1	4-2	2-2	1-2	—	1-0	3-0	1-0	2-2	1-2	1-2	3-0
Tonbridge Angels	3-1	1-0	2-0	3-1	2-1	1-0	2-0	2-0	0-1	2-0	1-1	4-2	0-0	1-2	2-2	—	1-1	2-0	1-3	4-1	1-1	3-1
Trowbridge Town	2-3	1-0	2-0	1-1	0-0	1-1	2-2	1-2	0-1	1-3	1-1	1-3	0-0	0-1	1-4	2-0	—	1-0	0-4	1-2	1-2	1-0
Waterlooville	1-0	5-3	2-1	3-0	3-0	2-3	2-1	1-0	1-3	2-0	1-2	1-2	0-1	0-3	0-1	0-0	1-4	—	1-2	2-2	2-2	0-4
Weston-super-Mare	6-0	1-1	1-0	0-0	2-3	2-0	2-0	5-1	2-2	3-1	0-0	3-3	2-0	1-0	0-2	3-1	2-0	2-0	—	1-2	2-0	0-1
Weymouth	0-1	5-0	2-3	3-1	5-1	2-1	5-0	1-1	6-2	5-0	1-3	2-0	2-0	1-0	0-0	0-0	2-0	5-0	2-0	—	0-2	0-1
Witney Town	0-1	9-0	2-1	2-1	0-0	5-1	2-2	1-0	1-3	4-0	2-3	1-2	3-1	1-1	3-1	0-1	2-1	0-1	1-1	1-1	—	4-1
Yate Town	6-3	3-1	2-1	1-1	2-1	3-2	4-1	2-2	1-1	1-5	0-1	1-5	1-3	1-5	0-1	1-1	0-3	1-2	1-1	0-2	4-1	—

ICIS FOOTBALL LEAGUE 1996–97

Premier Division

	P	W	D	L	W	D	L	W	D	L	F	A	Pts
		Home			*Away*			*Total*			*Goals*		
Yeovil Town	42	17	3	1	14	5	2	31	8	3	83	34	101
Enfield	42	14	4	3	14	7	0	28	11	3	91	29	95
Sutton United	42	10	7	4	8	6	7	18	13	11	87	70	67
Dagenham & Redbridge	42	11	3	7	7	8	6	18	11	13	57	43	65
Yeading	42	10	6	5	7	8	6	17	14	11	58	47	65
St Albans City	42	7	7	7	11	4	6	18	11	13	65	55	65
Aylesbury United	42	11	5	5	7	6	8	18	11	13	64	54	65
Purfleet	42	8	9	4	9	2	10	17	11	14	67	63	62
Heybridge Swifts	42	9	7	5	7	7	7	16	14	12	62	62	62
Boreham Wood	42	9	7	5	6	6	9	15	13	14	56	52	58
Kingstonian	42	10	4	7	6	4	11	16	8	18	79	79	56
Dulwich Hamlet	42	9	3	9	5	10	6	14	13	15	57	57	55
Carshalton Athletic	42	10	5	6	4	6	11	14	11	17	51	56	53
Hitchin Town	42	10	3	8	5	4	12	15	7	20	67	73	52
Oxford City	42	8	5	8	6	5	10	14	10	18	67	83	52
Hendon	42	8	5	8	5	7	9	13	12	17	53	59	51
Harrow Borough	42	8	7	6	4	7	10	12	14	16	58	62	50
Bromley	42	10	5	6	3	4	14	13	9	20	67	72	48
Bishop's Stortford	42	7	7	7	3	6	12	10	13	19	43	64	43
Staines Town	42	6	6	9	4	2	15	10	8	24	46	71	38
Grays Athletic	42	3	6	12	5	3	13	8	9	25	43	78	33
Chertsey Town	42	4	5	12	4	2	15	8	7	27	40	98	31

Division One

	P	W	D	L	W	D	L	W	D	L	F	A	Pts
		Home			*Away*			*Total*			*Goals*		
Chesham United	42	16	2	3	11	4	6	27	6	9	80	46	87
Basingstoke Town	42	13	5	3	9	8	4	22	13	7	81	38	79
Walton & Hersham	42	14	1	6	7	12	2	21	13	8	67	41	76
Hampton	42	13	5	3	8	7	6	21	12	9	62	39	75
Billericay Town	42	12	6	3	9	6	6	21	12	9	69	49	75
Bognor Regis Town	42	12	5	4	9	4	8	21	9	12	63	44	72
Aldershot Town	42	10	7	4	9	7	5	19	14	9	67	45	71
Uxbridge	42	7	12	2	8	5	8	15	17	10	65	48	62
Whyteleafe	42	8	3	10	10	4	7	18	7	17	71	68	61
Molesey	42	4	6	11	13	3	5	17	9	16	50	53	60
Abingdon Town	42	10	6	5	5	5	11	15	11	16	44	42	56
Leyton Pennant	42	8	8	5	6	4	11	14	12	16	71	72	54
Maidenhead United*	42	9	5	7	6	5	10	15	10	17	57	57	52
Wokingham Town	42	6	5	10	8	5	8	14	10	18	41	45	52
Thame United	42	9	5	7	4	5	12	13	10	19	57	69	49
Worthing	42	6	5	10	5	6	10	11	11	20	58	77	44
Barton Rovers	42	7	7	7	4	4	13	11	11	20	31	58	44
Croydon	42	7	4	10	4	6	11	11	10	21	40	57	43
Berkhamsted Town	42	8	4	9	3	5	13	11	9	22	47	66	42
Canvey Island	42	5	8	8	4	6	11	9	14	19	52	71	41
Marlow	42	7	4	10	4	2	15	11	6	25	41	84	39
Tooting & Mitcham United	42	4	4	13	4	4	13	8	8	26	40	85	32

*Maidenhead United had 3 points deducted—ineligible player

Division Two

	P	W	D	L	W	D	L	W	D	L	F	A	Pts
		Home			*Away*			*Total*			*Goals*		
Collier Row & Romford	42	16	3	2	12	9	0	28	12	2	93	33	96
Leatherhead	42	15	3	3	15	2	4	30	5	7	116	45	95
Wembley	42	12	5	4	11	6	4	23	11	8	92	45	80
Barking	42	13	5	3	9	8	4	22	13	7	69	40	79
Horsham	42	14	2	5	8	9	4	22	11	9	78	48	77
Edgware Town	42	9	8	4	11	6	4	20	14	8	74	50	74
Bedford Town	42	10	3	8	11	5	5	21	8	13	77	43	71
Banstead Athletic	42	9	3	9	12	2	7	21	5	16	75	52	68
Windsor & Eton	42	8	9	4	9	4	8	17	13	12	65	62	64
Leighton Town	42	12	6	3	5	6	10	17	12	13	64	52	63
Bracknell Town	42	9	8	4	8	1	12	17	9	16	78	71	60
Wivenhoe Town	42	7	6	8	10	3	8	17	9	16	69	62	60
Chalfont St Peter	42	9	7	5	5	6	10	14	13	15	53	61	55
Hungerford Town	42	8	9	4	6	4	11	14	13	15	68	77	55
Metropolitan Police	42	9	2	10	5	5	11	14	7	21	72	75	49
Tilbury	42	4	6	11	10	1	10	14	7	21	68	77	49
Witham Town	42	4	6	11	7	4	10	11	10	21	39	67	43
Egham Town	42	7	3	11	3	6	12	10	9	23	47	86	39
Cheshunt	42	4	2	15	5	1	15	9	3	30	37	101	30
Ware	42	5	3	13	2	5	14	7	8	27	44	80	29
Dorking	42	5	1	15	2	5	14	7	6	29	40	100	27
Hemel Hempstead	42	1	2	18	4	4	13	5	6	31	34	125	21

Division Three

	P	Home W	D	L	Away W	D	L	Total W	D	L	Goals F	A	Pts
Wealdstone	32	14	0	2	10	3	3	24	3	5	72	24	75
Braintree Town	32	13	2	1	10	3	3	23	5	4	99	29	74
Northwood	32	11	4	1	7	6	3	18	10	4	60	31	64
Harlow Town	32	10	1	5	9	3	4	19	4	9	60	41	61
Aveley	32	8	4	4	9	2	5	17	6	9	64	39	57
East Thurrock United	32	10	3	3	6	3	7	16	6	10	58	51	54
Camberley Town	32	8	2	6	7	4	5	15	6	11	55	44	51
Wingate & Finchley	32	7	4	5	4	3	9	11	7	14	52	63	40
Hornchurch	32	5	4	7	6	2	8	11	6	15	35	51	39
Clapton	32	3	4	9	8	2	6	11	6	15	31	49	39
Lewes	32	6	6	4	4	2	10	10	8	14	45	53	38
Kingsbury Town	32	6	2	8	5	2	9	11	4	17	41	54	37
Hertford Town	32	6	3	7	4	3	9	10	6	16	55	65	36
Epsom & Ewell	32	4	2	10	4	3	9	8	5	19	62	78	29
Flackwell Heath	32	6	3	7	2	2	12	8	5	19	36	71	29
Tring Town	32	3	1	12	4	2	10	7	3	22	33	74	24
Southall	32	3	2	11	3	2	11	6	4	22	28	69	22

LEADING GOALSCORERS

Premier Division		Lge	GIC	FMC
38	Howard Forinton (Yeovil Town)	37	1	–
	(includes 14 league and 1 GIC goal for Oxford City)			
35	Paul Cobb (Purfleet)	29	5	1
27	Steve Clark (St Albans City)	21	6	–
26	Mark Hynes (Sutton United)	20	4	2
25	Eddie Akaumoah (Kingstonian)	20	4	1
24	Steve Darlington (Kingstonian)	22	1	1

Division One				
22	Neil Pearson (Whyteleafe)	22	–	–
21	Paul Coombs (Basingstoke Town)	21	–	–
20	Ansil Bushay (Walton & Hersham)	20	–	–
	John Lawford (Chesham United)	18	2	–
	Andy Jones (Canvey Island)	18	–	2
	Leon Gutzmore (Billericay Town)	17	3	–

Division Two				AMT
44	Steve Lunn (Leatherhead)	41	1	2
37	Jason Reed (Bedford Town)	30	5	2
32	Simon Liddle (Banstead Athletic)	31	1	–
27	Nigel Webb (Leatherhead)	23	1	3

Division Three				
31	Wade Falana (Braintree Town)	29	2	–
25	Gary Bennett (Braintree Town)	14	8	3
23	Paul Halbert (Northwood)	22	–	1
22	Andy Boxhall (Epsom & Ewell)	21	1	–

Lge: ICIS League; GIC: Guardian Insurance Cup; FMC: Full Members Cup; AMT: Associate Members Trophy

ATTENDANCES

Premier Divison
Aggregate: 229,996
Highest Individual crowd: 8007 Yeovil Town v Enfield

Division One
Aggregate: 139,584
Highest Individual crowd: 2262 Aldershot Town v Basingstoke Town

Division Two
Aggregate: 62,058
Highest Individual crowd: 702 Bedford Town v Leighton Town

Division Three
Aggregate: 30,306
Highest Individual crowd: 630 Wealdstone v Epsom & Ewell

PREVIOUS SEASONS

SEASON	CLUBS	GAMES	AGG	AVE
1988–1989	86	1764	323,197	183
1989–1990	87	1806	387,441	215
1990–1991	88	1848	404,703	219
1991–1992	86	1764	397,553	225
1992–1993	85	1724	430,518	247
1993–1994	87	1806	423,306	234
1994–1995	87	1806	433,703	240
1995–1996	86	1764	440,285	250
1996–1997	83	1658	461,944	278

ICIS FOOTBALL LEAGUE—PREMIER DIVISION RESULTS 1996-97

	Aylesbury United	Bishop's Stortford	Boreham Wood	Bromley	Carshalton Athletic	Chertsey Town	Dagenham & Redbridge	Dulwich Hamlet	Enfield	Grays Athletic	Harrow Borough	Hendon	Heybridge Swifts	Hitchin Town	Kingstonian	Oxford City	Purfleet	St Albans City	Staines Town	Sutton United	Yeading	Yeovil Town
Aylesbury United	—	2-2	2-0	1-1	3-1	2-1	0-1	2-0	1-3	3-0	2-0	1-2	1-0	2-1	2-5	6-1	0-2	2-1	2-1	3-3	2-2	0-0
Bishop's Stortford	2-0	—	0-0	4-3	2-1	3-1	2-0	0-1	1-3	0-0	0-1	2-1	0-0	1-2	2-2	2-2	2-3	1-1	1-0	2-5	1-1	0-1
Boreham Wood	1-1	4-1	—	2-2	3-0	1-2	3-1	2-2	1-1	2-1	2-0	1-2	0-0	4-0	0-0	3-2	0-1	0-2	3-0	1-0	1-1	0-3
Bromley	0-2	2-1	2-0	—	2-0	5-1	1-0	0-0	0-2	1-2	1-2	2-2	1-1	3-2	2-2	3-0	2-1	1-1	1-2	2-1	5-1	1-2
Carshalton Athletic	3-1	1-0	1-2	3-2	—	2-0	0-0	0-0	0-1	6-0	2-1	0-2	4-1	1-2	1-3	1-1	2-1	2-0	2-0	3-3	0-0	0-1
Chertsey Town	0-0	0-3	1-1	3-1	2-3	—	0-3	0-2	1-1	0-6	2-2	1-0	3-5	0-5	0-3	2-4	0-1	0-5	3-2	1-1	2-1	0-2
Dagenham & Redbridge	0-2	3-0	2-1	0-2	0-1	2-1	—	1-1	0-1	2-1	3-1	1-1	3-0	1-1	1-0	4-2	2-0	1-2	3-0	2-1	1-2	0-1
Dulwich Hamlet	1-1	2-0	2-1	2-1	4-1	3-0	0-2	—	2-3	3-0	0-0	1-1	1-3	2-2	1-2	0-1	2-1	1-2	4-0	0-1	0-1	4-1
Enfield	3-0	1-1	3-0	4-3	2-0	5-0	0-1	2-3	—	4-0	1-0	2-2	1-2	1-0	3-0	3-3	3-0	1-0	1-2	3-1	0-1	3-0
Grays Athletic	2-0	0-1	2-4	1-0	0-1	0-2	0-3	1-1	0-2	—	3-2	0-0	0-1	2-2	1-1	1-1	0-1	1-2	0-2	1-2	1-1	2-3
Harrow Borough	0-0	1-1	2-0	2-0	1-1	1-0	1-1	2-1	1-1	1-0	—	2-2	3-3	3-1	1-2	2-3	3-1	0-1	1-1	2-1	1-2	2-3
Hendon	0-3	3-1	1-2	4-1	2-2	1-0	2-1	2-2	0-3	0-1	2-1	—	1-1	1-0	2-1	2-0	2-3	0-2	2-1	3-3	0-1	1-3
Heybridge Swifts	1-3	0-0	0-2	4-3	0-2	4-1	4-1	1-1	0-0	3-0	0-0	1-1	—	2-1	2-1	2-1	1-3	2-1	2-1	2-5	1-1	0-0
Hitchin Town	2-1	3-0	1-2	5-2	3-2	2-1	0-0	0-0	0-3	0-2	2-4	1-2	2-1	—	4-1	4-2	2-0	1-1	3-3	2-3	0-5	0-1
Kingstonian	0-1	0-1	5-1	1-1	1-1	2-0	2-3	4-2	0-1	5-2	4-4	1-2	1-0	3-1	—	4-1	3-2	0-1	1-0	1-3	3-1	0-3
Oxford City	3-2	4-1	0-0	2-3	1-1	0-2	2-2	1-1	1-4	1-1	2-1	2-0	1-2	5-1	3-1	—	1-2	3-2	2-0	3-2	4-2	0-2
Purfleet	0-1	3-0	1-1	2-0	2-0	4-5	2-2	1-4	1-3	2-4	2-0	0-0	3-3	1-1	3-2	2-2	—	2-2	2-0	1-1	0-1	1-1
St Albans City	0-0	1-1	0-2	0-3	0-0	0-0	0-2	1-3	1-4	4-2	2-2	1-0	4-2	2-1	2-0	0-1	2-1	—	3-0	2-3	2-2	1-1
Staines Town	3-1	0-0	2-1	3-0	2-0	4-2	2-1	2-1	0-2	3-1	1-1	0-3	2-2	1-2	5-2	1-2	1-3	3-0	—	2-3	0-0	0-3
Sutton United	3-3	2-1	1-1	2-2	2-0	1-1	1-1	2-0	2-0	1-1	3-3	2-1	1-0	4-3	5-1	1-2	0-0	1-2	2-0	—	2-3	1-2
Yeading	0-1	3-0	2-1	1-0	0-0	0-0	1-1	3-0	1-1	3-0	1-2	2-1	1-0	0-1	2-3	4-1	1-1	0-3	1-0	3-2	—	2-0
Yeovil Town	3-2	1-0	0-0	1-0	3-0	4-0	0-0	6-1	2-2	2-0	2-1	2-0	1-0	1-0	1-0	4-1	4-3	3-1	3-1	3-2	2-0	—

ICIS FOOTBALL LEAGUE—DIVISION ONE RESULTS 1996–97

	Abingdon Town	Aldershot Town	Barton Rovers	Basingstoke Town	Berkhamsted Town	Billericay Town	Bognor Regis Town	Canvey Island	Chesham United	Croydon	Hampton	Leyton Pennant	Maidenhead United	Marlow	Molesey	Thame United	Tooting & Mitcham United	Uxbridge	Walton & Hersham	Whyteleafe	Wokingham Town	Worthing
Abingdon Town	—	0-0	2-0	1-1	3-1	2-1	0-3	2-2	0-1	1-0	0-1	1-0	0-0	2-1	0-1	1-0	1-0	6-0	0-0	0-1	2-1	4-1
Aldershot Town	3-1	—	3-1	1-0	0-0	1-1	1-0	1-2	2-2	1-0	1-1	2-2	3-0	0-1	1-3	0-0	2-2	2-0	1-1	5-2	1-0	0-2
Barton Rovers	0-0	0-0	—	1-4	1-0	0-0	0-3	2-0	0-1	0-1	3-1	1-0	2-0	0-1	1-1	3-0	3-1	2-1	0-1	0-1	0-0	1-1
Basingstoke Town	3-0	2-0	3-0	—	2-0	2-2	2-2	2-1	4-0	2-1	0-2	6-1	2-0	1-0	2-2	3-0	1-0	0-2	0-0	4-1	0-2	1-1
Berkhamsted Town	1-1	0-3	1-0	1-3	—	2-0	2-0	1-4	2-2	0-2	0-4	2-3	0-3	1-0	2-1	2-0	0-1	4-1	1-1	1-1	1-0	0-2
Billericay Town	2-1	2-2	1-1	1-1	3-0	—	4-1	2-0	1-2	2-0	0-0	2-0	1-0	0-2	0-1	2-2	4-1	2-1	2-1	2-1	3-1	4-0
Bognor Regis Town	2-2	0-5	0-1	0-2	3-0	4-1	—	1-0	4-1	1-0	1-1	4-3	1-0	3-0	0-1	2-2	3-0	2-1	0-0	2-2	3-0	2-1
Canvey Island	1-0	0-1	1-2	0-2	1-0	1-3	1-0	—	0-3	3-0	1-0	2-0	4-2	2-2	0-1	3-3	2-1	0-0	0-0	1-4	0-1	2-2
Chesham United	2-1	1-3	4-0	2-1	5-2	1-2	4-1	4-0	—	2-2	1-0	1-2	2-1	3-0	4-0	3-2	4-0	1-0	1-1	0-1	2-0	2-1
Croydon	2-0	1-1	1-0	0-2	1-0	2-2	1-0	3-0	2-2	—	0-2	2-2	0-2	2-1	0-1	3-0	3-1	0-3	3-3	1-2	1-2	0-1
Hampton	2-1	1-1	3-2	1-0	1-1	1-1	3-0	1-0	1-0	2-1	—	4-3	3-4	1-0	1-0	2-1	0-2	2-2	0-0	1-0	2-0	2-0
Leyton Pennant	1-0	4-2	4-0	1-1	0-5	4-2	4-3	2-1	1-2	1-2	0-0	—	1-1	5-0	2-3	2-4	4-1	1-0	1-1	2-1	1-1	1-3
Maidenhead United	0-1	1-1	1-0	1-0	2-0	2-2	3-0	3-0	2-1	1-0	1-2	2-0	—	2-0	0-2	1-0	1-1	1-0	1-1	4-3	4-0	3-1
Marlow	0-1	3-1	1-1	1-0	2-0	0-2	0-2	2-2	3-0	2-1	2-1	0-1	2-0	—	0-2	2-2	1-1	1-7	0-2	1-2	0-2	3-1
Molesey	0-1	0-2	1-1	1-2	2-1	2-1	0-1	1-2	4-0	0-1	1-1	1-1	1-2	4-2	—	3-2	0-2	1-1	1-4	1-1	0-0	1-1
Thame United	0-3	0-2	2-0	3-2	3-2	0-4	1-1	3-2	3-0	2-1	1-2	2-1	1-0	6-1	0-2	—	1-0	0-3	1-1	0-3	1-1	1-1
Tooting & Mitcham United	1-1	0-1	4-0	1-0	4-1	0-0	1-0	2-1	4-0	3-1	0-1	1-2	1-5	0-0	0-1	1-3	—	0-2	2-3	0-5	1-1	2-1
Uxbridge	0-0	3-3	1-1	2-2	1-0	2-2	1-0	0-0	1-0	0-0	1-1	2-2	2-0	4-0	2-2	4-2	5-0	—	2-1	1-3	0-2	1-1
Walton & Hersham	2-0	3-1	5-0	0-4	2-1	3-1	3-0	0-0	1-1	2-1	1-0	1-2	2-2	2-1	1-0	0-2	4-0	0-3	—	2-1	0-3	4-0
Whyteleafe	0-2	1-0	0-0	0-2	0-1	2-1	0-3	2-1	0-1	1-2	1-0	2-3	1-2	3-1	2-0	2-0	2-5	1-3	1-2	—	1-2	3-4
Wokingham Town	3-0	0-1	0-1	2-2	0-0	3-1	3-0	0-1	2-0	1-2	1-0	2-0	0-0	2-0	1-2	1-0	1-0	0-1	0-2	1-1	—	2-0
Worthing	1-0	2-5	1-0	1-1	1-2	2-3	2-3	3-3	2-1	1-2	0-3	2-0	4-0	3-1	1-0	1-4	2-2	0-0	1-2	4-5	1-2	—

ICIS FOOTBALL LEAGUE—DIVISION TWO RESULTS 1996-97

	Banstead Athletic	Barking	Bedford Town	Bracknell Town	Chalfont St Peter	Cheshunt	Collier Row & Romford	Dorking	Edgware Town	Egham Town	Hemel Hempstead	Horsham	Hungerford Town	Leatherhead	Leighton Town	Metropolitan Police	Tilbury	Ware	Wembley	Windsor & Eton	Witham Town	Wivenhoe Town
Banstead Athletic	—	0-1	1-2	0-3	3-1	4-2	2-2	3-0	1-2	2-0	3-0	1-1	5-2	1-2	0-0	1-2	2-3	2-0	1-0	3-0	1-2	1-2
Barking	1-1	—	0-0	2-1	1-2	4-0	0-1	4-2	1-1	2-0	2-1	1-0	4-0	2-1	3-1	1-0	2-2	4-1	2-2	1-3	1-0	3-0
Bedford Town	2-3	0-0	—	5-4	1-3	6-0	0-1	1-1	0-3	2-1	1-0	0-1	2-0	3-0	2-1	0-0	1-0	4-1	1-3	1-2	3-0	1-3
Bracknell Town	1-0	2-2	2-1	—	1-1	0-0	0-0	3-2	1-2	6-1	7-1	0-0	3-3	2-4	0-3	4-4	5-1	4-3	1-2	2-0	5-1	0-3
Chalfont St Peter	0-2	0-1	2-1	1-1	—	4-0	2-2	1-1	1-3	2-0	0-0	0-1	1-3	0-3	1-0	3-0	2-1	3-2	0-0	1-1	2-0	2-1
Cheshunt	0-2	1-1	0-4	1-1	1-0	—	0-1	4-2	2-3	0-1	0-1	0-2	3-5	2-5	5-1	1-0	2-5	3-2	1-4	1-2	1-0	1-2
Collier Row & Romford	2-0	1-1	1-1	1-0	3-0	1-0	—	3-1	1-6	3-0	9-2	1-1	3-0	2-1	1-0	2-1	4-2	2-2	1-0	2-0	0-0	4-0
Dorking	0-3	2-4	0-3	2-1	0-3	3-1	0-2	—	1-6	0-2	2-3	3-3	0-3	0-3	5-2	2-0	0-2	3-0	1-2	0-2	0-3	2-1
Edgware Town	4-1	4-1	3-0	0-1	1-1	4-2	0-2	1-6	—	1-1	9-2	2-1	6-4	4-0	2-1	2-1	1-1	0-2	1-0	2-0	1-1	2-2
Egham Town	0-4	0-4	0-3	3-2	1-0	2-3	1-0	3-0	1-1	—	4-0	1-0	2-0	0-4	0-0	2-0	1-1	3-1	1-1	1-0	2-2	2-2
Hemel Hempstead	0-2	1-1	0-6	0-4	4-2	0-0	1-1	2-3	2-2	4-0	—	5-1	3-0	3-0	5-0	1-4	2-4	1-1	1-1	2-0	1-3	5-2
Horsham	3-2	0-6	0-2	4-1	2-1	2-3	1-2	4-0	2-1	1-0	5-1	—	3-1	0-4	2-3	1-1	0-1	1-0	4-2	3-1	6-3	0-2
Hungerford Town	1-3	3-1	2-3	1-0	1-3	3-5	1-1	5-0	6-4	2-0	3-1	1-2	—	0-4	3-1	3-0	4-2	2-2	1-1	0-0	6-3	1-1
Leatherhead	3-1	0-1	0-2	4-1	0-3	2-5	2-2	4-0	4-0	0-4	9-0	0-4	2-0	—	4-1	3-0	5-2	2-1	1-1	1-4	2-0	1-4
Leighton Town	2-1	0-3	1-1	2-0	1-0	5-1	1-0	4-0	2-1	2-1	5-0	2-3	2-0	4-1	—	2-0	2-3	3-1	1-2	4-2	2-0	2-1
Metropolitan Police	0-1	0-3	0-0	0-1	3-0	1-0	2-1	2-0	2-1	2-0	10-4	1-3	2-3	2-4	0-1	—	2-1	4-1	3-2	3-1	2-3	0-2
Tilbury	0-0	1-1	1-0	2-2	2-2	2-2	0-4	0-1	1-1	0-1	1-1	2-1	2-4	0-1	1-3	2-1	—	0-0	0-4	1-2	2-3	2-4
Ware	0-1	0-0	2-1	0-2	0-4	3-2	0-4	3-0	0-2	3-1	1-1	0-0	3-2	3-1	3-1	0-0	1-3	—	0-4	0-1	1-1	3-1
Wembley	4-3	1-2	3-1	4-0	2-0	1-4	1-0	4-0	1-0	1-1	4-2	4-2	1-1	1-1	1-2	3-2	0-1	0-4	—	3-0	0-3	0-2
Windsor & Eton	0-2	2-0	0-4	1-2	2-2	2-0	2-0	1-0	2-2	1-4	2-0	1-4	2-1	1-4	2-2	2-2	4-3	3-1	3-0	—	2-1	1-1
Witham Town	0-1	2-0	0-4	0-1	2-1	1-0	0-3	2-0	0-3	0-3	1-1	0-3	2-0	2-1	1-1	1-0	1-0	1-1	1-1	2-3	—	0-0
Wivenhoe Town	2-5	2-2	0-2	6-1	2-1	1-2	1-3	2-2	2-2	2-2	5-2	0-2	3-2	1-1	5-2	1-1	0-1	3-1	0-2	1-0	3-0	—

ICIS FOOTBALL LEAGUE—DIVISION THREE RESULTS 1996–97

	Aveley	Braintree Town	Camberley Town	Clapton	East Thurrock United	Epsom & Ewell	Flackwell Heath	Harlow Town	Hertford Town	Hornchurch	Kingsbury Town	Lewes	Northwood	Southall	Tring Town	Wealdstone	Wingate & Finchley
Aveley	—	1-2	1-2	1-2	0-4	4-1	1-1	3-1	3-1	5-0	2-0	1-0	2-2	4-1	2-0	1-1	1-1
Braintree Town	3-2	—	0-0	6-0	7-1	4-1	6-0	0-0	6-1	4-0	5-3	6-1	1-0	3-0	0-1	2-0	6-0
Camberley Town	0-2	0-1	—	1-0	8-3	2-2	3-1	0-1	3-0	2-1	2-0	0-1	3-1	1-1	0-2	0-3	4-2
Clapton	0-2	1-11	0-1	—	0-1	0-1	3-1	0-2	0-2	0-0	0-0	2-0	1-1	1-2	5-1	0-1	0-0
East Thurrock United	0-0	3-2	2-0	3-0	—	3-2	4-0	1-3	4-2	0-1	4-2	3-0	0-0	3-0	2-2	0-1	2-0
Epsom & Ewell	3-5	2-5	2-3	1-2	1-3	—	5-0	1-3	3-1	0-3	1-1	1-1	2-3	2-0	4-3	2-3	4-7
Flackwell Heath	0-7	0-3	2-5	0-2	0-0	2-1	—	3-1	1-1	0-3	0-1	2-0	1-1	0-1	5-0	4-0	1-0
Harlow Town	3-0	1-1	3-1	1-3	3-2	3-1	3-0	—	2-3	2-1	2-1	0-2	1-3	2-0	1-2	2-1	5-3
Hertford Town	0-1	0-1	3-0	1-2	5-1	2-1	2-2	0-2	—	3-1	0-1	4-0	0-1	1-1	4-2	0-2	3-3
Hornchurch	0-1	1-5	2-2	0-1	1-1	2-2	2-1	0-2	3-1	—	1-0	2-2	1-0	0-1	1-4	0-3	0-1
Kingsbury Town	1-3	1-0	1-2	3-1	3-0	1-3	0-2	3-0	3-1	1-1	—	2-1	1-1	3-1	1-1	0-0	3-0
Lewes	6-2	1-1	1-1	0-1	2-3	2-5	0-1	2-2	0-0	1-0	4-1	—	1-1	4-0	4-1	0-1	2-0
Northwood	2-0	2-2	1-1	0-0	0-0	2-1	4-1	1-0	7-3	4-0	4-1	4-1	—	3-2	4-0	1-3	1-0
Southall	0-4	0-3	2-1	2-2	0-2	2-3	3-1	0-3	1-5	2-3	0-2	0-1	0-1	—	4-0	1-1	0-2
Tring Town	0-2	0-2	0-1	0-2	0-2	2-1	2-1	2-3	2-2	0-1	1-2	1-3	1-2	2-0	—	0-3	0-3
Wealdstone	1-0	6-0	3-1	2-0	4-1	2-1	3-0	0-2	5-1	2-0	5-0	2-1	0-2	1-0	7-0	—	3-2
Wingate & Finchley	1-1	0-1	0-5	2-0	2-0	2-2	4-3	1-1	2-1	2-3	1-4	3-1	1-1	5-1	2-1	0-3	—

GUARDIAN INSURANCE CUP 1996–97

Preliminary Round
Banstead Athletic 1, Camberley Town 0
Chalfont St Peter 0, Leighton Town 1
Cheshunt 1, Horsham 3
East Thurrock United 1, Clapton 0 *aet*
Egham Town 0, Collier Row & Romford 2
Epsom & Ewell 1, Wivenhoe Town 2
Flackwell Heath 1, Bedford Town 4
Hemel Hempstead 5, Barking 2
Hertford Town 1, Edgware Town 2
Hungerford Town 2, Metropolitan Police 1
Leatherhead 2, Harlow Town 2 *aet*
Lewes 0, Dorking 2
Northwood 2, Windsor & Eton 1
Southall 0, Tilbury 1
Tring Town 1, Braintree Town 6
Ware 0, Aveley 2
Wealdstone 1, Kingsbury Town 0
Wembley 1, Bracknell Town 0
Witham Town 0, Wingate & Finchley 1

Replay
Harlow Town 2, Leatherhead 3 *aet*

First Round
Aldershot Town 0, Enfield 3
Aveley 5, Leatherhead 1
Aylesbury United 1, Braintree Town 4
Banstead Athletic 3, Northwood 1
Barton Rovers 0, Bedford Town 1
Berkhamsted Town 5, Harrow Borough 6
Billericay Town 2, Basingstoke Town 1
Bognor Regis Town 6, East Thurrock United 2 *aet*
Boreham Wood 3, Edgware Town 2 *aet*
Canvey Island 1, Sutton United 2
Carshalton Athletic 6, Whyteleafe 0
Chesham United 3, Epsom & Ewell 3 *aet*
Collier Row & Romford 4, Bromley 3 *aet*
Croydon 0, Leighton Town 1
Dagenham & Redbridge 3, Marlow 0
Dorking 1, Hitchin Town 0
Dulwich Hamlet 0, Yeading 1
Grays Athletic 1, Hornchurch 0
Hemel Hempstead 1, Abingdon Town 0
Hendon 1, Wembley 0 *aet*
Hungerford Town 0, Walton & Hersham 1
Kingstonian 2, Tilbury 1
Leyton Pennant 1, Purfleet 4
Maidenhead United 1, Heybridge Swifts 2
Oxford City 2, Chertsey Town 3 *aet*
Staines Town 1, Uxbridge 0
Thame United 4, Hampton 1
Wealdstone 4, Horsham 2 *aet*
Wingate & Finchley 1, St Albans City 6
Wokingham Town 2, Bishop's Stortford 1
Worthing 0, Tooting & Mitcham United 3
Yeovil Town 6, Molesey 1

Replay
Epsom & Ewell 1, Chesham United 2

Second Round
Banstead Athletic 6, Wealdstone 0
Bedford Town 1, Chertsey Town 0
Billericay Town 1, Collier Row & Romford 1 *aet*
Bognor Regis Town 2, Staines Town 1
Boreham Wood 1, Dagenham & Redbridge 0
Carshalton Athletic 1, Braintree Town 2
Chesham United 3, Thame United 2 *aet*
Dorking 0, Heybridge Swifts 4
(Match ordered to be replayed)
Harrow Borough 3, Enfield 2
Kingstonian 3, Hemel Hempstead 2 *aet*
Leighton Town 1, Hendon 0
Purfleet 3, Sutton United 6
St Albans City 3, Aveley 1
Walton & Hersham 0, Grays Athletic 3
Wokingham Town 3, Tooting & Mitcham United 0
Yeading 1, Yeovil Town 1 *aet*

Replays
Collier Row & Romford 4, Billericay Town 3 *aet*
(Collier Row & Romford were removed from the competition)
Heybridge Swifts 8, Dorking 0
Yeovil Town 0, Yeading 1

Third Round
Bedford Town 2, Heybridge Swifts 1 *aet*
Braintree Town 3, Billericay Town 1
Grays Athletic 1 Chesham United 2
Kingstonian 2, Banstead Athletic 1 *aet*
Leighton Town 0, Boreham Wood 2
St Albans City 2, Harrow Borough 4
Sutton United 3, Yeading 2
Wokingham Town 1, Bognor Regis Town 2
(Bognor Regis Town were removed from the competition)

Fourth Round
Braintree Town 2, Bedford Town 1 *aet*
Chesham United 2, Sutton United 1
(Chesham United were removed from the competition)
Harrow Borough 1, Boreham Wood 3
Kingstonian 2, Wokingham Town 0

Semi-finals First Leg
Braintree Town 1, Sutton United 0
Kingstonian 1, Boreham Wood 1

Semi-finals Second Leg
Boreham Wood 3, Kingstonian 2 *aet*
(Boreham Wood won 4-3 on aggregate)
Sutton United 1, Braintree Town 2
(Braintree Town won 3-1 on aggregate)

Final
Boreham Wood 1, Braintree Town 0 *aet*

FULL MEMBERS CUP

First Round
Aylesbury United 1, Boreham Wood 0
Barton Rovers 0, Canvey Island 3
Chertsey Town 3, Wokingham Town 1
Croydon 1, Carshalton Athletic 4 *aet*
Grays Athletic 1, Leyton Pennant 0
Hampton 2, Bromley 1
Hendon 3, Berkhamsted Town 1
Marlow 2, Staines Town 1
Molesey 3, Worthing 1
Oxford City 2, Aldershot Town 1 *aet*
St Albans City 0, Hitchin Town 4
Thame United 0, Yeading 1

Second Round
Aylesbury United 2, Canvey Island 1
Basingstoke Town 2, Tooting & Mitcham United 1
Billericay Town 2, Harrow Borough 1

Bognor Regis Town 1, Dulwich Hamlet 0 *aet*
Chertsey Town 0, Abingdon Town 3
Dagenham & Redbridge 2, Hendon 2 *aet*
(Dagenham & Redbridge won 5-4 on penalties)
Grays Athletic 0, Chesham United 0 *aet*
(Chesham United won 7-6 on penalties)
Heybridge Swifts 0, Enfield 1
Kingstonian 4, Walton & Hersham 4 *aet*
(Walton & Hersham won 5-3 on penalties)
Molesey 0, Maidenhead United 2
Oxford City 2, Whyteleafe 3
Purfleet 3, Hitchin Town 2
Sutton United 2, Hampton 2 aet
(Sutton United won 5-3 on penalties)
Uxbridge 0, Bishop's Stortford 3
Yeading 4, Marlow 0
Yeovil Town 2, Carshalton Athletic 0

Third Round
Aylesbury United 3, Billericay Town 0
Basingstoke Town 1, Abingdon Town 0
Bishop's Stortford 1, Yeading 2
Chesham United 3, Enfield 3 *aet*
  (Chesham United won 3-1 on penalties)
Dagenham & Redbridge 0, Purfleet 1
Sutton United 4, Whyteleafe 0
Walton & Hersham 0, Maidenhead United 1
Yeovil Town 3, Bognor Regis Town 2

Fourth Round
Aylesbury United 2, Chesham United 0
Purfleet 0, Yeading 2

Sutton United 5, Basingstoke Town 3
Yeovil Town 0, Maidenhead United 1

Semi-finals
Maidenhead United 3, Sutton United 1
Yeading 2, Aylesbury United 2 *aet*

Replay
Aylesbury United 1, Yeading 0

Final
Maidenhead United 3, Aylesbury United 0

ASSOCIATE MEMBERS TROPHY

First Round
Aveley 2, Barking 2 *aet*
  (Barking won 4-2 on penalties)
Chalfont St Peter 0, Banstead Athletic 2
Cheshunt 0, Ware 3
Dorking 0, Wealdstone 7
Epsom & Ewell 2, Lewes 0
Leatherhead 5, Northwood 3
Wembley 4, Hertford Town 1

Second Round
Barking 2, Harlow Town 0
Camberley Town 0, Horsham 3
Clapton 1, Braintree Town 6 *aet*
Collier Row & Romford 3, Ware 1
East Thurrock United 2, Witham Town 3
Flackwell Heath 0, Egham Town 1
Hemel Hempstead 0, Leighton Town 1
Hornchurch 1, Bedford Town 2 *aet*
Kingsbury Town 1, Wingate & Finchley 1
Leatherhead 3, Banstead Athletic 1 *aet*
Metropolitan Police 1, Epsom & Ewell 0
Tring Town 4, Southall 4 *aet*
  (Southall won 4-2 on penalties)
Wealdstone 3, Bracknell Town 1
Wembley 4, Tilbury 1
Windsor & Eton 1, Hungerford Town 2
Wivenhoe Town 2, Edgware Town 0

Replay
Wingate & Finchley 3, Kingsbury Town 0

Third Round
Barking 2, Bedford Town 2 *aet*
  (Bedford Town won 5-4 on penalties)
Collier Row & Romford 3, Wivenhoe Town 4
Horsham 2, Egham Town 3
Hungerford Town 4, Southall 2 *aet*
Leatherhead 1, Wembley 0
Leighton Town 2, Braintree Town 1 *aet*
Wealdstone 4, Metropolitan Police 2
Witham Town 1, Wingate & Finchley 2

Fourth Round
Egham Town 1, Wealdstone 2
Leatherhead 6, Hungerford Town 2
Leighton Town 1, Bedford Town 1 *aet*
  (Leighton Town won 4-3 on penalties)
Wivenhoe Town 2, Wingate & Finchley 1

Semi-finals
Leatherhead 0, Wealdstone 0 *aet*
Wivenhoe Town 0, Leighton Town 2

Replay
Wealdstone 3, Leatherhead 0

Final
Leighton Town 1, Wealdstone 0

FA UMBRO TROPHY 1996–97

First Qualifying Round

Atherstone United v Whitley Bay	0-2
Atherton LR v Moor Green	1-1, 1-6
Stafford Rangers v Curzon Ashton	1-2
Droylsden v Leigh RMI	1-1, 3-1
Nuneaton Borough v Congleton Town	0-3
Alfreton Town v Bilston Town	4-4, 1-4
Warrington Town v Lancaster City	0-2
Bedworth United v Gretna	0-0, 4-1
Hinckley Town v Worksop Town	0-2
Harrogate Town v Knowsley United	2-3
Grantham Town v Leek Town	1-0
Racing Club Warwick v Frickley Athletic	1-2
Tamworth v Great Harwood Town	2-2, 0-1
Paget Rangers v Eastwood Town	0-1
Buxton v VS Rugby	2-1
Matlock Town v Winsford United	1-4
Stocksbridge Park Steels v Sutton Coldfield Town	1-0
Solihull Borough w.o. v Leicester United withdrew	
Witton Albion v Workington	3-3, 0-1
Netherfield v Farsley Celtic	2-3
Cirencester Town v Cambridge City	2-2, 5-6
Wokingham Town v Erith & Belvedere	1-0
Ashford Town v Hitchin Town	4-1
Tonbridge v Aylesbury United	0-2
Fareham Town v Weymouth	2-2, 0-7
Whyteleafe v Yeading	0-1
Baldock Town v Stourbridge	3-2
Margate v Aldershot Town	1-2
Buckingham Town v Forest Green Rovers	0-1
Hendon v Thame United	1-1, 1-1, 3-0
Chesham United v Walton & Hersham	1-1, 3-1
Bishops Stortford v Croydon	3-0
Hampton v Trowbridge Town	4-1
Raunds Town v Barton Rovers	4-1
Canvey Island v Heybridge Swifts	0-1
Gravesend & Northfleet v St Leonards Stamcroft	2-2, 3-4
Yate Town v King's Lynn	1-3
Sittingbourne v Fleet Town	3-2
Weston-Super-Mare v Worthing	2-0
Newport (IOW) v Leyton Pennant	3-3, 1-2
Abingdon Town v Evesham United	0-2
Maidenhead United v Corby Town	4-2
Bromley v Uxbridge	1-0
Cinderford Town v Havant Town	2-3
Grays Athletic v Bashley	2-1
Billericay Town v Berkhamsted Town	3-0
Fisher Athletic v Molesey	2-2, 2-1
Marlow v Witney Town	1-1, 1-2
Dorchester Town v Waterlooville	1-0

Second Qualifying Round

Moor Green v Ilkeston Town	2-1
Workington v Redditch United	1-0
Farsley Celtic v Worksop Town	1-1, 1-2
Stocksbridge Park Steels v Shepshed Dynamo	2-2, 1-0
Buxton v Eastwood Town	1-0
Congleton Town v Solihull Borough	1-3
Whitley Bay v Bradford (Park Avenue)	0-1
Bilston Town v Great Harwood Town	4-0
Lancaster City v Droylsden	2-0
Lincoln United v Frickley Athletic	3-4
Grantham Town v Winsford United	2-1
Curzon Ashton v Bedworth United	0-2
Knowsley United v Flixton	3-2
Heybridge Swifts v Grays Athletic	2-1
Oxford City v Basingstoke Town	1-6
Weymouth v Clevedon Town	4-1
Aylesbury United v Sittingbourne	1-1, 1-2
Salisbury City v Witney Town	1-0
Weston-Super-Mare v Raunds Town	1-3
Forest Green Rovers v Cambridge City	1-2
Maidenhead United v Bromley	1-3
Aldershot Town v Chesham United	3-0
Hendon v Sutton United	1-3
Hampton v St Leonards Stamcroft	0-1
Chertsey Town v Yeading	1-1, 1-3
Fisher Athletic v Havant Town	3-2
Dartford v Tooting & Mitcham United	1-1, 3-2

Wokingham Town v Leyton Pennant	2-0
Billericay Town v Dorchester Town	0-4
Staines Town v King's Lynn	0-1
Ashford Town v Bishops Stortford	6-1
Baldock Town v Evesham United	0-1

Third Qualifying Round

Bradford (Park Avenue) v Barrow	1-1, 1-0
Marine v Gainsborough Trinity	0-1
Buxton v Grantham Town	1-1, 1-2
Runcorn v Solihull Borough	2-1
Moor Green v Dudley Town	6-1
Ashton United v Burton Albion	1-0
Colwyn Bay v Frickley Athletic	1-0
Blyth Spartans v Bilston Town	7-3
Worksop Town v Lancaster City	0-0, 2-4
Bishop Auckland v Stocksbridge Park Steels	2-1
Spennymoor United v Radcliffe Borough	1-0
Bedworth United v Accrington Stanley	2-0
Rothwell Town v Workington	1-7
Knowsley United v Emley	2-2, 2-5
Dartford v Dulwich Hamlet	0-0, 1-3
Bromley v Worcester City	1-1, 0-2
Sutton United v Dorchester Town	0-2
Aldershot Town v Chelmsford City	1-3
Crawley Town v Chelmsford City	0-2
Yeovil Town v Evesham United	2-0
Carshalton Athletic v Heybridge Swifts	0-3
St Leonards Stamcroft v Purfleet	6-0
Weymouth v Ashford Town	2-0
Raunds Town v Bognor Regis Town	4-2
Harrow Borough v Salisbury City	2-2, 1-2
Sudbury Town v Cheltenham Town	2-3
Cambridge City v Newport AFC	1-1, 1-4
Sittingbourne v Yeading	0-0, 1-3
Basingstoke Town v Hastings Town	0-1
St Albans City v King's Lynn	3-1
Gloucester City v Kingstonian	3-1
Fisher Athletic v Wokingham Town	1-2

First Round

Gresley Rovers v Altrincham	3-3, 0-1
Morecambe v Chorley	3-1
Workington v Bamber Bridge	2-5
Colwyn Bay v Lancaster City	6-0
Gainsborough Trinity v Bradford (Park Avenue)	1-3
Emley v Boston United	2-1
Spennymoor United v Bishop Auckland	0-2
Northwich Victoria v Hednesford Town	3-1
Blyth Spartans v Grantham Town	1-1, 1-1, 1-3
Southport v Halesowen Town	0-0, 2-0
Hyde United v Bedworth United	4-2
Guiseley v Telford United	2-1
Kidderminster Harriers v Macclesfield Town	3-0
Gateshead v Runcorn	1-2
Ashton United v Moor Green	5-3
Stalybridge Celtic v Halifax Town	0-1
Bath City v Stevenage Borough	1-1, 1-6
Slough Town v Dorchester Town	2-2, 2-2, 1-2
Cheltenham Town v Dulwich Hamlet	1-2
St Leonards Stamcroft v Newport AFC	1-0
St Albans City v Weymouth	2-0
Rushden & Diamonds v Farnborough Town	1-2
Enfield v Boreham Wood	1-3
Hastings Town v Salisbury City	1-3
Wokingham Town v Woking	0-1
Kettering Town v Chelmsford City	0-1
Raunds Town v Welling United	0-1
Yeovil Town v Hayes	2-2, 2-2, 1-2
Bromsgrove Rovers v Merthyr Tydfil	2-1
Yeading v Gloucester City	0-3
Worcester City v Heybridge Swifts	1-2
Dover Athletic v Dagenham & Redbridge	0-2

Second Round

Bishop Auckland v Northwich Victoria	3-2
Grantham Town v Heybridge Swifts	0-1

Dagenham & Redbridge v Chelmsford City	2-1
St Albans City v Woking	1-1, 1-3
Gloucester City v Halifax Town	3-0
Ashton United v Bamber Bridge	3-1
Boreham Wood v Stevenage Borough	0-1
Bradford (Park Avenue) v Morecambe	0-1
Bromsgrove Rovers v Hyde United	1-1, 2-2, 0-2
Welling United v Guiseley	1-1, 0-1
Farnborough Town v Altrincham	0-2
Colwyn Bay v Southport	2-0
Hayes v Runcorn	1-2
Kidderminster Harriers v Emley	0-0, 5-1
Salisbury City v Dorchester Town	1-1, 2-3
St Leonards Stamcroft v Dulwich Hamlet	2-1

Third Round

Colwyn Bay v St Leonards Stamcroft	2-2, 0-0, 2-1
Ashton United v Hyde United	2-0
Stevenage Borough v Guiseley	1-0
Gloucester City v Runcorn	3-1
Dorchester Town v Woking	2-3
Altrincham v Bishop Auckland	0-1
Morecambe v Dagenham & Redbridge	0-0, 1-2
Heybridge Swifts v Kidderminster Harriers	3-0

Fourth Round

Dagenham & Redbridge v Ashton United	1-0
Heybridge Swifts v Woking	0-1
Bishop Auckland v Gloucester City	0-0, 3-4
Stevenage Borough v Colwyn Bay	2-0

Semi-finals (two legs)

Dagenham & Redbridge v Gloucester City	0-0, 2-2, 2-1
Woking v Stevenage Borough	1-0, 1-2, 2-1

FINAL (AT WEMBLEY)

18 MAY

Dagenham & Redbridge (0) 0

Woking (0) 1 *(Hay)* 24,376

Dagenham & Redbridge: Gothard; Culverhouse, Conner, Creaser, Jacques (Double), Davidson, Pratt (Naylor), Parratt, Broom, Rogers, Stimson (John).
Woking: Batty; Brown, Howard, Foster, Taylor, Wye S, Thompson (Jones), Ellis, Steele (Wye L), Walker, Jackson (Hay).
Referee: J. Winter (North Riding).

SEMI-PROFESSIONAL INTERNATIONALS

25 Feb

FAI National League 2

England 0 1500

England: Cooksey (Hednesford T) [Gothard (Dagenham & Redbridge)]; Gill (Yeovil T), Gardiner (Macclesfield T), Webb (Kidderminster H) [Harlow (Farnborough T)], Howarth (Macclesfield T), Brown (Woking), Doherty (Kidderminster H) [O'Connor (Hednesford T)], Cramman (Rushden & Diamonds), Leworthy (Rushden & Diamonds), Butterworth (Rushden & Diamonds), Hughes (Kidderminster H) [Kimmins (Hyde U)].

8 Apr

The Netherlands 0

England 0 1500

England: Price (Macclesfield T); Bignot (Kidderminster H), Cramman (Rushden & Diamonds), Harlow (Farnborough T) [Prindiville (Kidderminster H)], Payne (Macclesfield T), Butterworth (Rushden & Diamonds), Webb (Kidderminster H), Walters (Northwich Vic), Leworthy (Rushden & Diamonds), Byrne (Macclesfield T), Hughes (Kidderminster H) [O'Connor (Hednesford T)].

FA CARLSBERG VASE 1996–97

First Qualifying Round

Penrith v Darwen	2-0
Ashington v Tadcaster Albion	2-3
Billingham Town v Blackpool (Wren) Rovers	1-2
Evenwood Town v Morpeth Town	0-2
Stockton v Newcastle Benfield Park	6-4
Horden CW v Harrogate Railway	0-3
West Allotment Celtic v Holker Old Boys	0-2
Rossendale United v Nelson	0-2
Cheadle Town v Merseyside Police	1-2
Heanor Town v Hall Road Rangers	1-2
Vauxhall GM v Castleton Gabriels	3-0
Abbey Hey v Shirebrook Town	1-2
Staveley MW v Hallam	0-2
Ramsbottom United v Tetley Walker	0-1
Harworth CI v Pontefract Collieries	1-0
Liversedge v Formby	1-4
Salford City v Bacup Borough	0-2
St Helens Town v Haslingden	3-4
South Normanton Athletic v Kimberley Town	0-1
Burscough v Heswall	3-2
Brodsworth v Borrowash Victoria	0-2
Denaby United v Atherton Collieries	2-0
Glapwell v Glasshoughton Welfare	2-1
Long Eaton United v Skelmersdale United	0-4
Parkgate v Rainworth MW	3-2
Holwell Sports v Birstall United	2-2, 1-1, 1-2
Kings Heath v Halesowen Harriers	1-0
Wellingborough Town v Gedling Town	2-4
Northampton Spencer v Chasetown	0-3
Dunkirk v Cradley Town	6-4
Stratford Town v Oldbury United	3-2
Meir KA v Newport Pagnell Town	2-0
Northfield Town removed v Wednesfield w.o.	
Friar Lane OB v Coleshill Town	5-2
March Town United v Brightlingsea United	1-2
Downham Town v Saffron Walden Town	1-2
Thetford Town v Haverhill Rovers	0-4
Wotton United v Whitton United	0-3
Great Wakering Rovers v Mildenhall Town	6-0
Great Yarmouth Town v Southend Manor	0-2
Basildon United v Soham Town Rangers	1-3
Somersham Town v Braintree Town	1-2
Clacton Town v Sudbury Wanderers	1-4
New Bradwell St Peter v Stansted	0-3
Hanwell Town v East Ham United	5-0
Milton Keynes v Viking Sports	2-2, 1-6
Totternhoe v Flackwell Heath	3-5
Brimsdown Rovers v Bedford United	1-2
Hertford Town v Ford United	1-4
Southall v Potters Bar Town	1-2
Feltham v Biggleswade Town	5-1
Tring Town v Wingate & Finchley	2-1
St Margaretsbury v East Thurrock United	1-7
London Colney v Tottenham Omada	5-0
Clapton v Kingsbury Town	2-0
Wealdstone v Kempstone Rovers	4-0
Harringey Borough v Amersham Town	0-3
Deal Town v Horsham YMCA	6-3
Broadbridge Heath v Leatherhead	3-9
Sheppey United v Folkestone Invicta	2-0
Epsom & Ewell v Tonbridge Wells	3-1
Walton Casuals v Pagham	1-3
East Preston v Sidley United	2-1
Netherne v Eastbourne Town	0-2
Lewes v Woolwich Town	4-0
Newhaven v Cray Wanderers	1-2
Langney Sports v Canterbury City	3-2
Selsey v Faversham Town	3-0
Ashford Town (Middlesex) v Saltdean United	4-0
Cobham v Egham Town	0-4
Chipstead v Ash United	2-1
Redhill v Croydon Athletic	2-1
Hailsham Town v East Grinstead	7-0
Three Bridges v Beckenham Town	2-5
Steyning Town v Bedfont	0-4
Corinthian Casuals v Crowborough Athletic	3-2
Lambourn Sports v Bournemouth	0-1
Portsmouth Royal Navy v Kintbury Rangers	0-3
Cove v Swindon Supermarine	0-3
Abingdon United v Sherbourne Town	5-0
North Leigh v Ryde	1-0
Andover v Downton	2-4
Petersfield Town v Reading Town	2-4
Westbury United v Sandhurst Town	1-4
Barnstaple Town v Melksham Town	0-1
Liskeard Athletic v Larkhall Athletic	2-0
St Blazey v Dawlish Town	1-2
Odd Down v Hallen	3-2
Old Georgians v Tuffley Rovers	4-0
Shortwood United v Exmouth Town	4-0
Brislington v Portleven	1-3
Endsleigh v Bristol Manor Farm	2-1
St Austell v Bridgwater Town	1-2

Second Qualifying Round

Nelson v Easington Colliery	2-4
Washington v Shotton Comrades	2-2, 1-3
Blackpool (Wren) Rovers v Ryhope CA	4-2
Tadcaster Albion v Brandon United	2-6
Bedlington Terriers v Stockton	5-0
Seaton Delaval Amateurs v Thackley	0-1
Alnwick Town v Willington	2-1
Anfield Plain v Pickering Town	6-3
Whickham v Marske United	2-1
Norton & Stockton Ancients v Ferryhill Athletic	3-4
Armthorpe Welfare v Ossett Albion	1-2
Esh Winning v Ponteland United	1-2
Crook Town v Jarrow Roofing Boldon CA	4-1
Holker Old Boys v Yorkshire Amateur	2-1
Penrith v South Shields	2-2, 3-4
Harrogate Railway v Morpeth Town	1-3
Selby Town v Denaby United	0-1
Eccleshill United v Bootle	1-1, 2-0
Merseyside Police v Newcastle Town	1-4
Garforth Town v Hucknall Town	0-4
Ashfield United v Sandiacre Town	1-1, 1-0
Maltby Main v Arnold Town	0-2
Bacup Borough v Vauxhall GM	1-5
Worsbro Bridge MW v Radford	4-0
Parkgate v Hall Road Rangers	1-0
Borrowash Victoria v Blidworth MW	2-0
Glapwell v Maghull	3-2
Sheffield v Rossington Main	4-2
Douglas High School OB v Nantwich Town	0-3
Formby v Shirebrook Town	8-1
Burscough v Glossop North End	0-0, 3-0
Haslingden v Daisy Hill	4-0
Chadderton v Poulton Victoria	0-1
Kidsgrove Athletic v Grove United	0-1
Hallam v Nettleham	5-1
Maine Road v Tetley Walker	0-1
Harworth CI v Ossett Town	1-7
Nuthall v Skelmersdale United	4-5
Oldham Town v Kimberley Town	7-0
Louth United v Wivenshawe Amateur	3-1
Blakenall v Boldmere St Michaels	1-2
Stourport Swifts v Wednesfield	3-2
Brierley Hill Town v Stewarts & Lloyds	1-4
West Midlands Police v Sandwell Borough	3-6
Knowle v Shifnal Town	0-1
Gedling Town v Westfields	7-1
Pershore Town v Highgate United	2-1
Malvern Town v St Andrews	0-3
Banbury United v Cogenhoe United	0-1
Knypersley Victoria v Desborough Town	2-3
Walsall Wood v Chasetown	1-2
Worcester Athletico v Long Buckby	1-3
Rushall Olympic v Stratford Town	0-2
Friar Lane OB v Meir KA	2-1
Gornal Athletic v Bloxwich Town	1-5
Stapenhill v Pegasus Juniors	3-1
Kings Heath v Oadby Town	0-3
Darlaston v Brackley Town	1-2
Dunkirk v Rocester	0-0, 2-2, 2-0
Tivedale v Barrow Town	1-2
Birstall United v Bolehill Swifts	0-1
Witham Town v Mirfleas Blackstone	1-1, 3-3, 5-1
Bourne Town v Saffron Walden Town	1-2
Great Wakering Rovers v Newmarket Town	3-0
Stamford AFC v St Neots Town	0-0, 4-3
Haverhill Rovers v Fakenham Town	1-3
Felixstowe Port & Town v Stowmarket Town	2-1
Ipswich Wanderers v Wroxham	1-0

Histon v Norwich United	7-0
Whitton United v Worboys Town	2-1
Eynesbury Rovers v Burnham Ramblers	3-2
Sawbridgeworth Town v Southend Manor	1-2
Brightlingsea United v Swaffham Town	1-2
Soham Town Rangers v Harwich & Parkeston	0-4
Cornard United v Braintree Town	2-9
Spalding United v Sudbury Wanderers	4-1
Lowestoft Town v Chatteris Town	6-1
Maldon Town v Hullbridge Sports	4-1
Stanway Rovers v Tiptree United	1-1, 0-2
Holbech United v Boston Town	0-3
Woodbridge Town v Ely City	2-1
Chalfont St Peter v Amersham Town	4-1
Harefield United v Leverstock Green	1-5
Stansted v Cheshunt	1-0
Letchworth v Edgware Town	0-5
Waltham Abbey v Cockfosters	1-2
Brache Sparta v Hillingdon Borough	3-2
Tring Town v Viking Sports	1-3
Royston Town v Bowers United	4-0
Brentwood v Hanwell Town	2-1
Wealdstone v Hoddesdon Town	1-0
Aveley v Harpenden Town	2-0
Barkingside v Ruislip Manor	3-0
Wootton Blue Cross w.o.v Shillington withdrew	
Feltham v Flackwell Heath	5-2
Clapton v Brook House	1-1, 3-2
East Thurrock United v Hemel Hempstead	1-0
Stotfold v Hornchurch	3-2
Concord Rangers v Welwyn Garden City	5-3
Bedford United v Leighton Town	2-0
Tilbury v Ford United	0-2
Potters Bar Town v Ware	0-2
Harlow Town v Bedford Town	1-0
Langford v London Colney	1-1, 0-2
Potton United v Beconsfield Sycob	3-1
Hythe United v Windsor & Eton	1-2
Bracknell Town v Camberley Town	2-1
Epsom & Ewell v Eastbourne Town	4-1
Eastbourne United v Ringmer	2-4
Lewes v Chatham Town	1-3
Godalming & Guildford v Deal Town	3-1
Mile Oak v Southwick	0-0, 0-2
Chichester City v Selsey	0-2
Langney Sports v Egham Town	2-1
Oakwood v Wick	0-3
Cray Wanderers v Merstham	4-0
Bedfont v Slade Green	0-1
Chipstead v Redhill	1-2
Beckenham Town v Corinthian	2-1
East Preston v Hassocks	2-5
Sheppey United v Cranleigh	3-2
Shoreham v Herne Bay	0-0, 0-4
Arundel v Corinthian-Casuals	2-1
Greenwich Borough v Portfield	3-1
Worthing United v Leatherhead	1-6
Littlehampton Town v Hailsham Town	0-1
Farnham Town v Horsham	1-3
Pagham v Raynes Park Vale	3-1
Lancing v Whitstable Town	0-4
Ashford Town (Middlesex) v Crockenhill	4-0
North Leigh v Bournemouth	2-0
Amesbury Town v Sandhurst Town	2-1
Downton v Bicester Town	3-2
Bemerton Heath Harlequins v Swindon Supermarine	1-0
Totton AFC v Reading Town	1-4
Kintbury Rangers v Brockenhurst	3-5
Christchurch v Cowes Sports	3-1
First Tower United v Hungerford Town	3-0
Milton United v Wantage Town	1-4
Carterton Town v Holmer Green	2-0
BAT Sports v Didcot Town	3-1
Gosport Borough v Eastleigh	2-0
Calne Town v Abingdon United	1-3
Backwell United v Warminster Town	5-1
Crediton United v Minehead	0-4
Fairford Town v Porthleven	0-2
Old Georgians v Ilfracombe Town	2-3
Cadbury Heath v Frome Town	1-1, 0-0, 2-1
Glastonbury v Almondsbury Town	1-2
Chard Town v Bridport	2-3
Chippenham Town v Bishop Sutton	3-1
Endsleigh v Welton Rovers	2-1
Bridgwater Town v Liskeard Athletic	6-0
Bideford v Harrow Hill	3-2
Dawlish Town v Elmore	1-0
Shortwood United v Wellington Town	3-2

Torrington v DRG AFC	3-1
Keynsham Town v Devizes Town	2-3
Melksham Town v Saltash United	1-3
Odd Down v Newquay	2-0

First Round

Burscough v Trafford	1-2
Skelmersdale United v Formby	0-2
Poulton Victoria v Ferry Hill Athletic	7-0
Whitby Town v Crook Town	2-1
Blackpool (Wren) Rovers v Consett	1-0
Shildon v Bedlington Terriers	0-7
Annfield Plain v Vauxhall GM	0-2
Haslingden v Alnwick Town	7-0
Peterlee Newtown v Tetley Walker	0-2
Brandon United v Oldham Town	5-1
Easington Colliery v Whickham	3-0
Ossett Town v Holker Old Boys	1-3
Sheffield v RTM Newcastle	3-4
North Ferriby United v Parkgate	3-1
Shotton Comrades v Tow Law Town	1-2
South Shields v Northallerton	1-0
Grove United v Thackley	0-2
Ossett Albion v Ponteland United	4-1
Eccleshill United v Morpeth Town	0-3
Denaby United v Worsbro Bridge MW	2-0
Hallam v Hatfield Main	3-1
Long Buckby v Oadby Town	1-1, 0-4
Barrow Town v Sandwell Borough	1-6
Borrowash Victoria v Arnold Town	1-3
Stewarts & Lloyds v Anstey Nomads	5-3
Stratford Town v Brackley Town	0-1
Glapwell v Pelsall Villa	3-1
Boldmere St Michaels v Ashfield United	3-2
Newcastle Town v Lye Town	4-0
Stapenhill v Friar Lane OB	4-2
Bloxwich Town v Hucknall Town	1-1, 0-2
Stourport Swifts v Hinckley Athletic	1-2
Coggenhoe United v Chasetown	1-0
St Andrews v Desborough Town	4-2
Gedling Town v Shifnal Town	2-0
Dunkirk v Bolehall Swifts	2-1
Nantwich Town v Willenhall Town	3-1
Pershore Town v Louth United	2-3
London Colney v Harlow Town	0-1
Braintree Town v Great Wakering Rovers	3-1
Concord Rangers v Witham Town	3-1
Clapton v Southend Manor	1-2
Hadleigh United v Swaffham Town	0-2
Chalfont St Peter v Leverstock Green	2-1
Cockfosters v Boston Town	1-2
Spalding United v Wealdstone	1-1, 2-1
Fakenham Town v Woodbridge Town	1-2
Viking Sports v Brache Sparta	1-3
Gorleston v Ipswich Wanderers	3-5
Stotfold v Feltham	2-2, 1-3
Ford United v Aveley	0-1
Saffron Walden Town v Harwich & Parkston	1-0
Wootton Blue Cross v Northwood	1-4
Royston Town v Wisbech Town	0-1
Ware v Felixstowe Port & Town	4-0
Histon v Stansted	5-0
East Thurrock United v Lowestoft Town	1-2
Tiptree United v Barkingside	4-1
Brentwood v Maldon Town	2-0
Stamford v Edgware Town	3-1
Potton United v Whitton United	3-0
Bedford United v Eynesbury Rovers	0-4
Whitehawk v BAT Sports	2-1
Wantage Town v Bracknell Town	2-4
Langney Sports v Chatham Town	2-3
Ringmer v Burnham	1-3
Arundel v Greenwich Borough	0-6
Dorking v Reading Town	0-2
Ashford Town (Middlesex) v Horsham	1-0
Carterton Town v North Leigh	1-3
Abingdon United v Epsom & Ewell	1-0
Southwick v Whitstable Town	1-3
Slade Green v Thamesmead Town	2-0
Burgess Hill Town v Leatherhead	1-0
Windsor & Eton v Thatcham Town	0-3
Beckingham Town v Redhill	2-1
Wick v Cray Wanderers	1-0
Hassocks v Herne Bay	1-3
Sheppey United v Pagham	3-1
Hailsham Town v Furness	3-1
First Tower United v Godalming & Guildford	6-2
Selsey v Gosport Borough	0-3

Torpoint Athletic v Chippenham Town	2-3
Torrington v Odd Down	1-2
Shortwood United v Tiverton Town	0-2
Bideford v Endsleigh	3-1
Porthleven v Bemerton Heath Harlequins	2-3
Bridgwater Town v Downton	2-0
Minehead v Amesbury Town	3-4
Devizes Town v Christchurch	0-1
Backwell United v Ilfracombe Town	2-0
Almondsbury Town v Poulton Rovers	1-3
Saltash United v Cadbury Heath	4-2
Brockenhurst v Dawlish Town	5-2
Truro City v Bridport	4-0
Lymington AFC v Wimborne Town	0-2

Second Round

Haslingden v Trafford	1-2
North Ferriby United v Hebburn	4-0
Blackpool (Wren) Rovers v South Shields	1-1, 1-3
Brandon United v Brigg Town	0-3
Chester-Le-Street Town v Dunston FB	1-3
Tow Law Town v Murton	5-2
Guisborough Town v Prudhoe Town	2-0
Whitby Town v Billingham Synthonia	1-0
Poulton Victoria v RTM Newcastle	3-1
Seaham Red Star v Ossett Albion	0-4
Mossley v Morpeth Town	2-1
Formby v Tetley Walker	0-5
Durham City v Easington Colliery	2-1
Cammell Laird v Bedlington Terriers	0-2
West Auckland Town v Holker Old Boys	2-3
Vauxhall GM v Clitheroe	3-1
Stewarts & Lloyds v Glapwell	3-2
Boldmere St Michaels v Belper Town	3-1
Dunkirk v Cogenhoe United	0-5
Hallam v Sandwell Borough	1-1, 1-0
Oadby Town v Arnold Town	3-1
Hinckley Athletic v Eastwood Hanley	2-0
Denaby United v Newcastle Town	2-4
Bridnorth Town v Stapenhill	2-2, 2-1
Brackley Town v Hucknall Town	2-4
Gedling Town v Barwell	2-1
Thackley v Louth United	0-0, 1-2
Nantwich Town v St Andrews	2-1
Bury Town v Collier Row & Romford	1-2
Histon v Ware	3-2
Wivenhoe Town v Harlow Town	3-4
Woodbridge Town v Brentwood	2-0
Northwood v Chalfont St Peter	3-1
Wembley v Spalding United	0-1
Swaffham Town v Saffron Walden Town	1-1, 0-3
Feltham v Braintree Town	2-4
Boston Town v Barking	1-3
Eynesbury Rovers v Concord Rangers	1-2
Stamford AFC v Lowestoft Town	2-0
Diss Town v Potton United	2-1
Halstead Town v Gorleston	2-1
Tiptree United v Southend Manor	0-3
Aveley v Arlesey Town	2-2, 2-3
Brache Sparta v Wisbech Town	1-3
Ashford Town (Middlesex) v Burnham	0-1
Burgess Hill Town v North Leigh	3-0
Sheppey United v Metropolitan Police	0-1
Wick v Thatcham Town	2-4
Banstead Athletic v Bracknell Town	2-0
Abingdon United v Herne Bay	0-3
Reading Town v Chatham Town	2-1
Whitstable Town v Slade Green	1-0
Beckenham Town v Peacehaven & Telscombe	2-5
First Tower United v Hailsham Town	4-2
Whitehawk v Greenwich Borough	2-3
Gosport Borough v Saltash United	0-2
Chippenham Town v Amesbury Town	6-0
Tiverton Town v Bideford	3-0
Paulton Rovers v Truro City	0-0, 1-2
Odd Down v Bemerton Heath Harlequins	0-1
Falmouth Town v Truro City	1-2
Christchurch v Mangotsfield United	0-2
Bridgwater Town v Brockenhurst	2-1
Wimborne Town v Backwell United	1-2
(Abandoned after 71 minutes; floodlight failure)	5-1

Third Round

Brigg Town v Tow Law Town	1-3
South Shields v Bedlington Terriers	1-3
Louth United v Whitby Town	2-4
Dunston FB v Holker Old Boys	5-0
Tetley Walker v Trafford	1-0

Hallam v North Ferriby United	1-3
Guisborough Town v Poulton Victoria	4-3
Ossett Albion v Nantwich Town	0-1
Vauxhall GM v Mossley	1-3
Gedling Town v Durham City	0-1
Hucknall Town v Newcastle Town	
(Abandoned after 33 minutes at 1-0 due to injury to a match official)	2-1
Woodbridge Town v Halstead Town	3-1
Hinckley Athletic v Stamford AFC	0-1
Oadby Town v Cogenhoe United	1-3
Spalding United v Bridgnorth Town	1-1, 2-1
Barking v Saffron Walden Town	1-1, 3-1
Northwood v Harlow Town	2-1
Histon v Metropolitan Police	2-1
Stewarts & Lloyds v Southend Manor	0-1
Collier Row & Romford v Braintree Town	2-2
(abandoned after 112 minutes: floodlight failure)	1-1, 3-1
Wisbech Town v Diss Town	3-0
Concord Rangers v Greenwich Borough	1-1, 3-1
Arlesey Town v Boldmere St Michaels	3-0
Burgess Hill Town v Bemerton Heath Harlequins	0-1
Bridgwater Town v Taunton Town	1-3
Mangotsfield United v Chippenham Town	2-1
Tiverton Town v Peacehaven & Telscombe	8-0
First Tower United v Reading Town	1-5
Burnham v Whitstable Town	1-2
Herne Bay v Saltash United	3-0
Banstead Athletic v Truro City	3-1
Thatcham Town v Wimborne Town	4-1

Fourth Round

Stamford AFC v North Ferriby United	1-1, 0-1
Guisborough Town v Tow Law Town	4-2
Mossley v Cogenhoe United	3-2
Bedlington Terriers v Dunston FB	4-1
Tetley Walker v Durham City	0-1
Hucknall Town v Spalding United	2-5
Whitby Town v Nantwich Town	3-1
Barking v Woodbridge Town	1-0
Arlesey Town v Herne Bay	2-3
Southend Manor v Wisbech Town	0-1
Mangotsfield United v Taunton Town	2-3
Thatcham Town v Tiverton Town	0-1
Concord Rangers v Whitstable Town	0-0, 1-2
Bemerton Heath Harlequins v Collier Row & Romford	0-1
Histon v Northwood	0-2
Reading Town v Banstead Athletic	0-2

Fifth Round

Guisborough Town v Wisbech Town	2-0
Taunton Town v Spalding United	3-0
North Ferriby United v Whitstable Town	1-0
Durham City v Northwood	0-2
Mossley v Barking	1-0
Whitby Town v Tiverton Town	1-0
Banstead Athletic v Herne Bay	2-0
Collier Row & Romford v Bedlington Terriers	2-2, 1-2

Sixth Round

Northwood v Banstead Athletic	0-1
Guisborough Town v Taunton Town	3-0
Whitby Town v Mossley	5-1
North Ferriby United v Bedlington Terriers	2-0

Semi-finals (two legs)

Guisborough Town v North Ferriby United	0-2, 1-1
Banstead Athletic v Whitby Town	0-1, 1-1

FINAL (AT WEMBLEY)

10 MAY

North Ferriby United (0) 0
Whitby Town (3) 1 *(Logan, Williams, Toman)*   11,098

North Ferriby United: Sharp; Deacey, Walmsley, Brentano, Smith A, Harrison (Horne), Smith M, Phillips (Milner), Tennison, France (Newman), Flounders.
Whitby Town: Campbell; Goodchild, Pearson, Cook, Williams, Hodgson, Goodrick (Borthwick), Toman (Pyle), Logan, Robinson, Pitman (Hall).
Referee: G. Poll (Herts).

FA YOUTH CHALLENGE CUP 1996–97

Extra Preliminary Round

Darlington v Hartlepool United	1-5
Harrogate Town v Shotton Comrades	5-2
Hull City v Mansfield Town	0-1
Southport v Lincoln City	1-1, 0-2
Bury v Stockport County	0-0, 1-0
Wigan Athletic v Rochdale	2-0
Leigh RMI v Cheadle Town	2-3
Bootle v Port Vale	0-1
Stalybridge Celtic v Willenhall Town	3-3, 1-0
Nuneaton Borough v Banbury United	3-0
Stratford Town v Hinckley Athletic	1-5
Bedworth United v Kidderminster Harriers	1-4
Bromsgrove Rovers v Pelsall Villa	2-1
Newport Pagnell Town v Gornal Athletic	2-2
(tie awarded to Gornal Athletic, Newport Pagnell Town withdrew)	
Lye Town v Stourbridge	1-0
Basildon United v Wivenhoe Town	2-2, 0-3
Cambridge United v Bishops Stortford	5-0
Cambridge City v Gorleston	8-2
Ipswich Wanderers v Great Wakering Rovers	3-2
Sudbury Town v Hitchin Town	4-0
Barnet v Potters Bar Town	4-0
Harefield United v Northwood	2-1
Uxbridge v Hillingdon Borough	4-6
Royston Town v Kingsbury Town	9-2
Wingate & Finchley v Clapton	2-2, 3-1
Marlow v Hampton	2-2, 0-7
Viking Sports w.o. v Slough Town withdrew	
Staines Town v Tooting & Mitcham United	3-0
Carshalton Atheltic v Redhill	2-0
Hastings Town v Dartford	1-0
Sittingbourne v Dover Athletic	2-1
Thamesmead Town v Herne Bay	2-2, 0-1
Ashford Town v Faversham Town	0-1
Shoreham v Leatherhead	7-3
Crawley Town v Oakwood	0-3
Windsor & Eton v Bedfont	3-1
Bracknell Town v Horsham YMCA	8-0
Bognor Regis Town v Eastbourne Town	4-2
Egham Town v Ashford Town (Middlesex)	1-4
Langney Sports v Basingstoke Town	1-0
Maidenhead United v Eastleigh	1-2
Oxford City v Waterlooville	2-0
Forest Green Rovers v Worcester City	0-1
Gloucester City v Cheltenham Town	2-1
Bristol Rovers v Paulton Rovers	5-0

Preliminary Round

Guisborough Town v Hartlepool United	1-2
Scarborough v Harrogate Town	5-0
Lancaster City v Barnsley	0-4
Carlisle United v Barrow	4-0
Bolton Wanderers v Mansfield Town	3-0
Frickley Athletic v Lincoln City	1-3
Chorley v Hallam	1-2
Scunthorpe United v Farsley Celtic	1-1, 0-0
(Farsley Celtic won 7-6 on penalties.)	
Worksop Town v Bury	0-2
Chadderton v Wigan Athletic	1-5
Chesterfield v Chester City	0-5
Marine v Warrington Town	3-1
Northwich Victoria v Cheadle Town	3-1
Nantwich Town v Port Vale	1-2
Louth United v Shifnal Town	4-2
Stalybridge Celtic v Walsall Wood	1-2
Bilston Town v Nuneaton Borough	0-2
Redditch United v Hinckley Athletic	6-1
Birstall United v Burton Albion	0-5
Kidderminster Harriers v Chasetown	5-2
Lutterworth Town v Bromsgrove Rovers	1-1, 0-7
Cradley Town v Gornal Athletic	1-3
Bolehall Swifts v Northampton Spencer	0-6
Lye Town v Rothwell Town	2-0
Braintree Town v Wivenhoe Town	0-5
Billericay Town v Cambridge United	0-2
Wisbech Town v Southend Manor	0-0, 4-3
Cambridge City v Eynesbury Rovers	11-0

Thetford Town v Ipswich Wanderers	1-4
Stevenage Borough v Sudbury Town	1-0
St Albans City v Waltham Abbey	3-1
Maldon Town v Hornchurch	2-3
Cheshunt v Barnet	1-4
Beaconsfield SYCOB v Harefield United	2-1
Wembley v Collier Row & Romford	1-0
Hillingdon Borough v Hemel Hempstead	8-1
Bedford Town v Royston Town	3-5
Chesham United v Wingate & Finchley	5-0
Aveley v Welwyn Garden City	4-1
Ruislip Manor v Flackwell Heath	1-0
Sutton United v Hampton	8-2
Banstead Athletic v Viking Sports	1-3
Hayes v Farnborough Town	1-3
Staines Town v Kingstonian	2-2, 2-2
(Staines won 4-2 on penalties.)	
Bromley v Carshalton Athletic	2-3
Whitstable Town v Hastings Town	1-1, 0-2
Tonbridge v Chatham Town	2-1
Sittingbourne v Croydon	3-0
Chipstead v Herne Bay	1-6
Gravesend & Northfleet v Faversham Town	1-1, 2-0
Folkestone Invicta v Margate	0-1
Three Bridges v Erith & Belvedere	2-4
Merstham v Shoreham	1-2
Walton & Hersham v Oakwood	3-0
Ringmer v Corinthian	2-8
Southwick v Raynes Park Vale	3-2
St Leonards Stamcroft v Windsor & Eton	5-2
Lewes v Bracknell Town	0-3
Camberley Town v Whitehawk	6-1
Bognor Regis Town v Burgess Hill Town	3-0
Portfield v Ashford Town (Middlesex)	0-5
Aldershot Town v Langney Sports	3-2
Thatcham Town v Wokingham Town	1-7
Horsham v Thame United	3-2
Romsey Town v Eastleigh	1-3
Witney Town v Oxford City	3-1
Fareham Town v Yeovil Town	3-5
Weymouth v Havant Town	0-3
Mangotsfield United v Worcester City	2-2, 0-1
Yate Town v Gloucester City	2-4
Chippenham Town v Cirencester Town	0-3
Bristol Rovers v Odd Down	8-0

First Qualifying Round

Barnsley v Scarborough	2-0
Carlisle United v Hartlepool United	0-0, 1-2
Hallam v Lincoln City	3-3, 1-5
Farsley Celtic v Bolton Wanderers	1-4
Chester City v Wigan Athletic	3-0
Marine v Bury	0-1
Louth United v Port Vale	0-5
Walsall Wood v Northwich Victoria	1-1, 1-0
Burton Albion v Redditch United	3-1
Kidderminster Harriers v Nuneaton Borough	0-4
Northampton Spencer v Gornal Athletic	0-1
Lye Town v Bromsgrove Rovers	1-1, 0-4
Wisbech Town v Cambridge United	1-5
Cambridge City v Wivenhoe Town	1-3
St Albans City v Stevenage Borough	0-2
Hornchurch v Ipswich Wanderers	1-1, 1-0
Wembley v Beconsfield Sycob	3-0
Hillingdon Borough v Barnet	3-1
Aveley v Chesham United	2-2, 3-2
Ruislip Manor v Royston Town	2-3
Farnborough Town v Viking Sports	1-1, 0-4
Staines Town v Sutton United	1-1, 2-9
Tonbridge v Hastings Town	2-0
Sittingbourne v Carshalton Athletic	3-1
Margate v Gravesend & Northfleet	1-6
Erith & Belvedere v Herne Bay	1-3
Corinthian v Walton & Hersham	3-1
Southwick v Shoreham	2-0
Camberley Town v Bracknell Town	4-3
Bognor Regis Town v St Leonards Stamcroft	6-1
Wokingham Town v Aldershot Town	2-1
Horsham v Ashford Town (Middlesex)	2-4

Yeovil Town v Witney Town 5-0
Havant Town v Eastleigh 2-3
Cirencester Town v Gloucester City 1-1, 2-2
(Cirencester Town won 5-3 on penalties.)
Bristol Rovers v Worcester City 6-0

Second Qualifying Round
Barnsley v Hartlepool United 3-0
Lincoln City v Bolton Wanderers 0-0, 0-2
Chester City v Bury 0-2
Port Vale v Walsall Wood 7-0
Burton Albion v Nuneaton Borough 0-1
Gornal Athletic v Bromsgrove Rovers 1-2
Cambridge United v Wivenhoe Town 3-1
Stevenage Borough v Hornchurch 7-1
Wembley v Hillingdon Borough 2-3
Aveley v Royston Town 3-0
Viking Sports v Sutton United 1-1, 2-1
Tonbridge v Sittingbourne 1-1, 0-1
Gravesend & Northfleet v Herne Bay 6-3
Corinthian v Southwick 3-2
Camberley Town v Bognor Regis Town 0-2
Wokingham Town v Ashford Town (Middlesex) 8-1
Yeovil Town v Eastleigh 4-1
Cirencester Town v Bristol Rovers 1-1, 1-2

First Round
Rotherham United v Barnsley 3-1
Notts County v Bury 0-0, 0-2
Huddersfield Town v Leicester City 0-0, 1-0
Preston North End v Port Vale 0-1
Shrewsbury Town v Wrexham 0-5
Grimsby Town v Bradford City 5-0
Leeds United v Sheffield Wednesday 2-2, 4-0
Blackburn Rovers v Blackpool 3-1
Newcastle United v Burnley 1-2
Everton v Nuneaton Borough 3-0
Bolton Wanderers v Derby County 5-0
Walsall v Bromsgrove Rovers 3-0
Peterborough United v Stevenage Borough 2-1
Hereford United v Luton Town 1-3
Rushden & Diamonds v Hillingdon Borough 6-1
Welling United v Wolverhampton Wanderers 0-1
Enfield v Boreham Wood 0-0, 2-1
Leighton Town v Watford 0-3
Birmingham City v Boldmere St Michaels 3-0
Northampton Town v Chelsea 0-5
Charlton Athletic v Aveley 6-1
Cambridge United v Colchester United 2-4
Bognor Regis Town v Viking Sports 1-4
Reading v Dulwich Hamlet 2-1
Plymouth Argyle v Brighton & Hove Albion 3-0
Exeter City v Torquay United 0-7
Bristol Rovers v Woking 4-1
Oxford United v Cardiff City 2-1
Croydon Athletic v Gravesend & Northfleet 1-5
Wycombe Wanderers v Corinthian 5-0
Fulham v Gillingham 0-3
Yeovil Town v AFC Bournemouth 3-3, 0-4
Southampton v Sittingbourne 1-0
Wokingham Town v Swansea City 1-4

Second Round
Tranmere Rovers v Grimsby Town 2-0
Oldham Athletic v York City 3-0
Blackburn Rovers v Port Vale 2-0
Bury v Huddersfield Town 1-0
Bolton Wanderers v Sheffield United 1-1, 5-4
Coventry City v Aston Villa 2-1
Liverpool v Burnley 5-2
Manchester City v Walsall 2-2, 4-2
Manchester United v Wrexham 7-0
Rotherham United v Stoke City 2-1
Nottingham Forest v Middlesbrough 3-1
Leeds United v Crewe Alexandra 2-0
Sunderland v Birmingham City 1-0
West Bromwich Albion v Everton 1-2
Oxford United v Luton Town 1-1, 2-3
Enfield v Gravesend & Northfleet 1-1, 0-2
Ipswich Town v Arsenal 1-0
Chelsea v Crystal Palace 2-3
AFC Bournemouth v Portsmouth 2-1
Swansea City v Norwich City 0-6
Charlton Athletic v Brentford 2-1

Millwall v Gillingham 1-0
Viking Sports v Wimbledon 0-2
Wolverhampton Wanderers v Wycombe Wanderers 2-3
Leyton Orient v Bristol City 1-2
Colchester United v West Ham United 1-3
Rushden & Diamonds v Southend United 2-2, 0-4
Bristol Rovers v Queens Park Rangers 0-0, 0-1
Southampton v Tottenham Hotspur 1-3
Torquay United v Swindon Town 1-1, 2-0
Plymouth Argyle v Peterborough United 1-2
Watford v Reading 8-0

Third Round
Nottingham Forest v Rotherham United 1-0
Manchester City v Leeds United 1-2
Oldham Athletic v Sunderland 1-2
Bury v Blackburn Rovers 0-0, 2-3
Bolton Wanderers v Everton 1-2
Liverpool v Manchester United 1-2
Coventry City v Tranmere Rovers 0-1
Southend United v Watford 0-0
(Abandoned at half-time; frozen pitch) 2-3r
Norwich City v Wycombe Wanderers 5-1
Torquay United v Luton Town 0-2
Crystal Palace v West Ham United 2-1
Bristol City v AFC Bournemouth 2-3
Queens Park Rangers v Wimbledon 3-2
Tottenham Hotspur v Gravesend & Northfleet 2-5
Peterborough United v Millwall 3-0
Charlton Athletic v Ipswich Town 5-4

Fourth Round
Leeds United v Queens Park Rangers 2-0
Norwich City v Everton 1-1, 2-0
Nottingham Forest v Blackburn Rovers 0-3
Charlton Athletic v Tottenham Hotspur 0-2
Sunderland v Luton Town 2-5
Manchester United v Watford 1-1, 2-3
AFC Bournemouth v Tranmere Rovers 0-3
Peterborough United v Crystal Palace 1-3

Fifth Round
Luton Town v Watford 0-0, 1-1
(Luton Town won 5-3 on penalties.)
Leeds United v Tranmere Rovers 0-0, 1-0
Blackburn Rovers v Norwich City 2-1
Crystal Palace v Tottenham Hotspur 1-0

Semi-finals (two legs)
Luton Town v Leeds United 1-2, 0-1
Crystal Palace v Blackburn Rovers 2-1, 2-2

FINAL FIRST LEG

24 APR

Leeds United (2) 2 *(Boyle, Jones)*
Crystal Palace (0) 1 *(Harris)* 6649
Leeds United: Robinson; Maybury, Woodgate, Lynch, Kewell, Dixon, Knarvik, McPhail, Boyle, Jones, Matthews.
Crystal Palace: Ormshaw; Hibbert, Mullins, Woozley, Folan, Carlisle, Kennedy, Stevens, Graham, Martin, Morrison (Harris).
Referee: G. Barber (Warwick).

FINAL SECOND LEG

15 MAY

Crystal Palace (0) 0
Leeds United (0) 1 *(Matthews)* 4759
Crystal Palace: Ormshaw; Hibbert, Mullins, Woozley, Folan, Carlisle (Harris); Kennedy, Stevens, Graham, Martin, Morrison (Sears).
Leeds United: Robinson; Maybury, Woodgate, Lynch, Kewell, Dixon, Knarvik, McPhail, Boyle, Jones (Wright), Matthews.
Referee: G. Barber (Warwick).

FA SUNDAY CUP 1996–97

First Round

Bolton Woods v Britannia	4-2
Dudley & Weetslade v A3	5-5, 2-4
Caldway v East Bowling Unity	2-1
Shankhouse United v Andy J Leisure (Walford)	0-3
Crown v Dock	1-2
Fidlers v BRNESC	3-0
Hartlepool Staincliffe Hotel v Lobster	3-4
Oakenshaw v Boulevard Mode Force	0-1
Newfield v Seaton Sluice SC	4-0
Stanley Road v Clubmoor Nalgo	2-1
Littlewoods Athletic v Northwood	2-3
Sandon v Humbledon Plains Farm	2-5
Seymour v Stockton Roseworth Social	4-3
The Tiger v Manfast	1-3
Almithak v Albion Sports	1-1, 0-3
Boundary v Eden Vale	1-3
Park Inn v Bayldon Junction Athletic	2-0
Caversham Park v Marston Sports	1-5
Romulus v BRSC Aidan	0-1
Reading Borough v Rovers Sports	0-1
Sandwell v Golden Bottle	2-1
Courage v Luton Old Boys	1-3
Slade Celtic v Broad Plain House (Sunday)	4-3
Clifton Albion v Gamlingay Eagles	5-1
Heathfield v Brookvale Athletic	4-2
Dulwich v Fownhope	2-1
Melton Youth Old Boys v Ashwell Globe	0-6
Hobbies United v Leicester City Bus	4-3
Watford Labour v Grosvenor Park	0-2
Sawston Keys v New Inn Keynsham	4-2
Duke of York v Bedmond Only	2-1
Olympic Star v Theale (Sunday)	1-0
Warriors v Hanham (Sunday)	3-1
Continental v Kendal Albion	1-2
St Joseph's (Bristol) v Bournemouth Electric	2-3
Cavaliers v Pitsea	3-3, 2-3
St Joseph's (South Oxhey) v Bournemouth	3-4
Ouzavich v Roofwork	3-0
Levesden Sports & Social v Belstone	2-2, 3-2
Oakwood Sports v Italia Wasteels	3-2
Cherry Tree (Warley) v Chequers	1-2
Winter Royals v Peckham Rye	5-0
Ford Basildon v Berner United	5-1
Celtic SC (Luton) v Oxford Road Social	2-0
Forest Athletic v Coach & Horses	1-0

Second Round

Saltbox v Dock	3-3, 2-3
Seymour v A3	0-2
Andy J Leisure (Walford) v Caldway	2-0
Nelson Victoria v Bolton Woods	2-1
Boulevard Mode Force v Stanley Road	0-3
Eden Vale v Lobster	5-1
Croxteth & Gilmoss RBL v Humbledon Plains Farm	2-0
Northwood v Newfield	4-2
Hartlepool Lion Hotel v Fiddlers	4-0
Nicosia v Queens Park AFC	4-3
Albion Sports v Allerton	3-4
Park Inn v Manfast	2-1
Salerno v Marston Sports	2-4
BRSC Aidan v Sandwell	1-2
Rovers Sports v Luton Old Boys	2-3

Heathfield v Slade Celtic	1-3
Dulwich Hamlet v Clifton Albion	1-1, 2-4
Hobbies United v Ashwell Globe	0-3
Grosvenor Park v Duke of York	2-1
Sawston Keys v Lebeq Tavern	3-0
Kendall Albion v Olympic Star	0-3
Greenacres Tavern v Warriors	0-3
Morden Nomads v Capel Plough	0-1
Bournemouth Electric v St Josephs (Luton)	5-2
Pitsea v Hammer	0-1
Leavesden Sports & Social v Bournemouth	5-4
Oakwood Sports v Ouzavich	2-1
Holderness United v Hundred Acre	2-0
Park Royals v Forest Athletic	1-2
Old Oak v Winter Royals	1-3
Celtic SC (Luton) v Ford Basildon	3-1
Lodge Cottrell v Chequers	5-4

Third Round

Allerton v A3	0-2
Park Inn v Slade Celtic	2-1
Dock v Clifton Albion	0-1
Northwood v Olympic Star	2-0
Hartlepool Lion Hotel v Nelson Victoria	3-0
Croxteth & Gilmoss RBL v Marston Sports	0-3
Nicosia v Stanley Road	2-5
Eden Vale v Andy J Leisure (Walford)	2-1
Winter Royals v Warriors	3-5
Sandwell v Oakwood Sports	0-4
Ashwell Globe v Lodge Cottrell	2-1
Bournemouth Electric v Holderness United	4-1
Leavesden Sports & Social v Capel Plough	1-3
Forest Athletic v Luton Old Boys	1-1, 1-0
Celtic SC (Luton) v Grosvenor Park	3-1
Sawston Keys v Hammer	2-5

Fourth Round

Hartlepool Lion Hotel v Marston Sports	1-2
Northwood v Clifton Albion	6-0
Stanley Road v A3	0-3
Eden Vale v Park Inn	3-1
Capel Plough v Forest Athletic	1-3
Bournemouth Electric v Ashwell Globe	0-2
Celtic SC (Luton) v Oakwood Sports	7-0
Hammer v Warriors	2-3

Fifth Round

Eden Vale v Ashwell Globe	3-0
Northwood v Celtic SC (Luton)	2-1
Marston Sports v Forest Athletic	4-1
A3 v Warriors	3-0

Semi-finals

Eden Vale v Northwood	0-2
Marston Sports v A3	1-0

Final

Marston Sports v Northwood	1-0

FA COUNTY YOUTH CHALLENGE CUP
1996–97

First Round

North Riding v Cumberland	3-4
Northumberland v East Riding	3-2
West Riding v Cheshire	1-0
Shropshire v Liverpool	1-4
Staffordshire v Herefordshire	3-1
Worcestershire v Derbyshire	3-2
Suffolk v Berks & Bucks	4-2
Oxfordshire v Essex	1-9
Sussex v Cambridgeshire	1-4
Middlesex v Bedfordshire	4-0
Somerset v Army	7-0
Wiltshire v Cornwall	0-2

Second Round

Durham v Westmoreland	7-0
Cumberland v Lancashire	1-4
Northumberland v Manchester	3-2
West Riding v Nottinghamshire	0-1
Liverpool v Sheffield & Hallamshire	3-2
Staffordshire v Huntingdonshire	3-1
Worcestershire v Lincolnshire	2-0
Birmingham v Norfolk	0-1
Devon v Gloucestershire	2-1
Suffolk v Northamptonshire	2-4
Essex v Hampshire	4-3
Hertfordshire v Surrey	0-0, 0-4
Cambridgeshire v London	4-1
Middlesex v Leicestershire & Rutland	4-3

Somerset v Kent	1-3
Cornwall v Dorset	4-1

Third Round

Northumberland v Staffordshire	2-4
Lancashire v Nottinghamshire	3-1
Durham v Liverpool	2-0
Cornwall v Devon	0-1
Worcestershire v Essex	2-1
Norfolk v Surrey	0-2
Kent v Middlesex	4-2
Cambridgeshire v Northamptonshire	9-2

Fourth Round

Devon v Lancashire	0-1
Durham v Surrey	0-1
Kent v Cambridgeshire	0-1
Worcestershire v Staffordshire	1-2

Semi-finals

Surrey v Lancashire	1-2
Staffordshire v Cambridgeshire	2-3

Final

Cambridgeshire v Lancashire	1-0

FA XI REPRESENTATIVE MATCHES

5 Nov

FA XI 3 *(Walters 2, own goal)*

Northern Premier League 0   402

FA XI: Price (Macclesfield T) [Stuart (Southport)]; Simpson (Hednesford T), Prindiville (Kidderminster H) [Mason (Boston U)], Walters (Northwich Vic), Howarth (Macclesfield T), Payne (Macclesfield T), Terry (Altrincham) [Bates (Stalybridge C)], Sorvel (Macclesfield T), Norbury (Halifax T) [Power (Macclesfield T)], Cooke (Northwich Vic), Vicary (Northwich Vic).

10 Dec

FA XI 0

Isthmian League 1   307

FA XI: Batty (Woking) [Gallagher (Stevenage B)]; Smart (Slough T), Wingfield (Farnborough T) [Hyatt (Hayes)], Smith (Stevenage B) [Stemp (Farnborough T)], Munday (Dover Ath) [Brown (Woking)], Foster (Woking), Harlow (Farnborough T), Barrowcliff (Stevenage B), Boothe (Farnborough T), Browne (Stevenage B) [Taylor (Woking)], Walker (Woking).

14 Jan

FA XI 5 *(Hughes 3, Forinton, Hercules)*

Combined Services 0   205

FA XI: Gothard (Dagenham & Redbridge) [Steadman (Kidderminster H)]; Gill (Yeovil T), Mason (Boston U), Butterworth (Rushden & Diamonds) [Appleby (Boston U)], Hercules (Slough T), Cousins (Yeovil T) [Tucker (Rushden & Diamonds)], Doherty (Kidderminster H), Cramman (Rushden & Diamonds), Forinton (Oxford C) [Collins (Rushden & Diamonds)], Webb (Kidderminster H), Hughes (Kidderminster H) [Coombs (Basingstoke T)].

10 May

Highland League 1

FA XI 5 *(O'Connor, Hughes, Hayles, Harlow 2)*   500

FA XI: Stewart (Southport) [MacKenzie (Farnborough T)]; Bignot (Kidderminster H), Prindiville (Kidderminster H), Cousins (Yeovil T) [Cramman (Rushden & Diamonds)], Smith (Stevenage B), Ellender (Gainsborough T), Terry (Altrincham), Butterworth (Rushden & Diamonds), Hughes (Kidderminster H) [Harlow (Farnborough T)], Bignall (Morecambe) [Hayles (Stevenage B)], O'Connor (Hednesford T).

UNIVERSITY FOOTBALL 1996–97

113th UNIVERSITY MATCH
(at Craven Cottage, Fulham, att 1504)
Oxford 0, Cambridge 0 (h-t 0-0)

Oxford: Rutter; Dutton, Lea, O'Brien, Parker, Loebinger (Buckley), Jennings, Loosemore, Worthington (Bissell), Goff, (Duncan), Kintish.
Cambridge: Lloyd; Clarance, Watson (Lewis), White, Budd, Ball, Jolley, Pett, Millar, Williamson (Thompson), Echeverria (Howe).
Referee: E. Green.
Cambridge have not won the fixture for nine years, but still lead Oxford by 45 wins to 42 with 26 drawn.

LONDON UNIVERSITY XI REPRESENTATIVE MATCH RESULTS

Old Boys' League	Lost	0–2
Ulysses	Won	3–2
Southern Amateur League	Won	2–1
Arthurian League	Won	3–1
SE Region BUSA	Lost	0–4
Metropolitan Police	Lost	1–3
Army Crusaders	Won	5–4
Southern Olympian League	Won	4–2
Oxford University	Drawn	0–0
Amateur Football Alliance	Lost	2–3

West London Institute, Chelsea XI (twice), Lloyds of London, Cambridge University, London Legal League all lost to bad weather.

UNIVERSITY OF LONDON INTER-COLLEGIATE LEAGUE

PREMIER DIVISION	P	W	D	L	F	A	Pts
Royal Holloway College	14	9	3	2	35	11	30
Queen Mary Westfield C.	14	8	4	2	37	17	28
Imperial College	14	8	2	4	38	28	26
Goldsmiths' College	14	6	6	2	41	14	24
London School of Econ.	14	6	3	5	34	19	21
King's College	14	3	3	8	25	46	12
University College	14	3	1	10	22	53	10
Univ. Coll. & Middx.	14	2	0	12	8	52	6

DIVISION ONE	P	W	D	L	F	A	Pts
Royal Holloway Coll. Res.	18	13	3	2	55	11	42
London Sch. of Econ. Res.	18	10	4	4	47	29	34

Royal Holloway Coll. 3rd	18	10	4	4	35	30	34
U.M.D.S.	18	9	4	5	53	31	31
Qn. Mary Westfield Coll.	18	9	2	7	44	31	29
University College Res.	18	7	4	7	28	39	25
Ch. Cross & W'min. Hosp	18	7	1	10	34	45	22
King's College Hosp. MS	18	5	3	10	32	43	18
R. Lon'n & St. Bart's Hos.	18	3	2	13	12	53	11
St George's Hospital MS	18	1	5	12	15	43	8

DIVISION TWO–10 Teams–Won by RSM, Imperial College.
DIVISION THREE–10 Teams–Won by Q. Mary & Westfield College 3rd.
DIVISION FOUR–10 Teams–Won by Imperial College 4th.
DIVISION FIVE–10 Teams–Won by Wye College, Kent
DIVISION SIX–7 Teams–R. Holloway College 6th.

Challenge Cup–Goldsmiths' College 1, London School of Economics 0
Upper Reserves Cup:–R. Holloway College Res. 5, London School of Economics Res. 0
Lower Reserves Cup–R. Holloway College 5th. 1, Q. Mary & Westfield College 4th. 3

United Hospitals:
Senior Cup–University College Hospital Medical School 3, Charing Cross & Westminster Hospital Medical School 4

Junior Cup–United Medical & Dental Schs. of Guy's & St. Thomas's Hospitals Res. 4, United Medical & Dental Schs. of Guy's & St. Thomas's Hospitals 3rd. 1

BRITISH UNIVERSITIES SPORTS ASSOCIATION CHAMPIONSHIP

Nottingham achieved its first success since 1958 beating Crewe & Alsager on penalties after a 1–1 draw. O'Connor scored for Nottingham, Barrett for Crewe & Alsager in the final played at Walsall.

Finals (Men)

First XI
Nottingham 1, Crewe & Alsager 1 aet
(Nottingham won 5–3 on penalties)

Second XI
Loughborough 1, Birmingham 1 aet
(Loughborough won 5–3 on penalties)

Third XI
Luton 1, Crewe & Alsager 2

Fourth XI
Wolverhampton 1, Crewe & Alsager 2

Women's
Crewe & Alsager 4, Brighton 2

Shield (Men)
Univ. of Wales, Swansea 1, Newcastle 2

Second XI
Durham 0, Liverpool Hope 1

Third XI
Chester 1, Warwick 2

Fourth XI
Warwick 3, Salford 1

Women's
Glasgow 3, Warwick 2

BUSA Games (Edinburgh)
Wales 2, N. Ireland 2
England 2, Scotland 2
England 0, Wales 0
Scotland 2, N. Ireland 1
Scotland 1, Wales 0
England 1, N. Ireland 1

Positions:
1. Scotland
2= England, Wales
4. N. Ireland

UNIVERSITY OF LONDON INTER-COLLEGIATE WOMENS' LEAGUE

FIRST DIVISION–8 Teams–Won by University College.
SECOND DIVISION–7 Teams–Won by Royal Free Hospital Res.

Womens' Challenge Cup–University College 2, London School of Economics 0

SCHOOLS FOOTBALL 1996–97

ESFA FUJI FILM TROPHY
FINAL: 1ST LEG
Liverpool 0, Islington & Camden 2
Played at Everton FC 6 May

FINAL: 2ND LEG
Islington & Camden 1, Liverpool 5
Played at Arsenal FC 10 May
Liverpool won 5–3 on aggregate

ESFA SNICKERS U.19 SCHOOLS AND COLLEGES COMPETITION
FINAL:
Colchester Sixth Form College 0, Cardinal Newman College (Preston) 1
Played at West Bromwich Albion FC 28 April

ESFA SNICKERS U.19 INDIVIDUAL SCHOOLS COMPETITION
FINAL:
Monkseaton High School (Whitley Bay) 0, Parmiters School (Watford) 0
Trophy shared
Played at West Bromwich Albion FC 28 April

ESFA GOODYEAR U.16 COMPETION
(with Channel 4)
FINAL:
City School (Sheffield) 0, William Parker School (Hastings) 0
Trophy shared
Played at Wolverhampton Wanderers FC 5 May

ESFA PREMIER LEAGUE U.16 INTER COUNTY COMPETITION
FINAL:
Oxfordshire 2, Northumberland 3
Played at Oxford United FC 21 April

ESFA PREMIER LEAGUE U.19 INTER COUNTY COMPETITION
FINAL:
West Midlands 3, Hampshire 2
Played at Aston Villa FC 1 May

ESFA VIMTO GIRLS U.16 COMPETITION
FINAL:
Montgomery High School (Blackpool) 2, Archbishop Grimshaw School (Birmingham) 1
Played at Blackpool FC 23 April

ESFA WAGON WHEELS 5-A-SIDE COMPETITION
GIRLS FINAL:
ADT College (South London) 3, Archbishop Beck (Liverpool) 2

BOYS FINAL:
Audenshaw High School (Tameside) 2, Eastbrook School (Dagenham) 1
Staged at Aston Villa Sports Centre 26 April

ESFA PREDATOR PREMIER 7-A-SIDE TROPHY
SEMI-FINALS:
Swindon 0, Barnsley 1
Newham 0, Nottingham 1

THIRD PLACE:
Swindon 1, Newham 1

FINAL:
Barnsley 0, Nottingham 0
Trophy shared
Played at Old Trafford, Manchester 19 April

ESFA PREDATOR 6-A-SIDE TROPHY
SEMI-FINALS:
Loudwater School, High Wycombe 2, Downsway School, Tilehurst 1
Kingmoor School, Carlisle 1, High Oakham School, Mansfield 4
THIRD PLACE:
Downsway School 0, Kingmoor School 6
FINAL:
Loudwater School 0, High Oakham School 0
Trophy shared
Played at Wembley Stadium 7 June

ESFA SMALL PRIMARY SCHOOLS 6-A-SIDE COMPETITION
FINAL:
Kilworth School (Leics) 1, Kimberley School (Notts) 2
Played at Leicester City FC 14 April

PANINI U.11 6-A-SIDE COMPETITION
(ESFA/PFA Community Scheme activity)
FINAL:
High Oakham Middle School *(Mansfield Town FC)* 1, Cherry Orchard Primary School *(Kidderminster Harriers FC)* 0
Played at Wembley Stadium 20 April

AUTO WINDSCREENS U.13 6-A-SIDE COMPETITION
(ESFA/FL Community Scheme activity)
FINAL: Division 1 Play-Off: 26 May
Wright Robinson High School *(Manchester City FC)* 1, Bradon Forest High School *(Swindon Town FC)* 0
FINAL: Division 2 Play-Off: 25 May
St Theodores High School *(Burnley FC)* 1, ADT College *(Millwall FC)* 0
FINAL: Division 3 Play-Off: 24 May
Exmouth Community College *(Exeter City FC)* 5, North Cumbria Technology College *(Carlisle United FC)* 0

BOODLE & DUNTHORNE INDEPENDENT SCHOOLS FA CUP 1996–97

PRELIMINARY ROUND
Kimbolton 3, City of London 1
Shrewsbury 9, Oswestry 0
Repton 4, John Lyon 0

FIRST ROUND
Aldenham 1, Hampton 4
Manchester GS 2, Ardingly 1 *(aet)*
Highgate 3, Alleyn's 4
Bolton 6, Brentwood 0
King's School, Chester 4, Kimbolton 0
St Bede's 4, Repton 3 *(aet)*
Charterhouse 2, Malvern 1
Haileybury 3, Batley GS 0
Chigwell 0, Bradfield 2
Wolverhampton GS 2, Shrewsbury 4
KES Witley 2, Forest 1
Eton 2, Winchester 0
Welling Borough 2, Latymer Upper 1
Bury GS 4, St Edmund's Canterbury 0
Westminster 1, Lancing 3
Hulme GS 0, QEGS, Blackburn 2

SECOND ROUND
Bolton 3, KES Witley 1
Hampton 1, Bury GS 2
Eton 0, Shrewsbury 2
Welling Borough 0, Bradfield 0 *(aet)*
(Bradfield won 4–1 on penalties).
Alleyns 0, Manchester GS 4
QEGS, Blackburn 2, St Bede's 1
King's Chester 4, Haileybury 0
Lancing 3, Charterhouse 0

THIRD ROUND
Shrewsbury 1, Manchester GS 1 *(aet)*
(Manchester GS won 5–4 on penalties).
Bury GS 0, Lancing 1
QEGS, Blackburn 0, King's Chester 1
Bolton 2, Bradford 0

SEMI-FINALS
Lancing 2, King's Chester 1
Manchester GS 2, Bolton 3

FINAL (AT CRAVEN COTTAGE)
Lancing 2 *(Bird, Rum)*
Bolton 1 *(Coleman)* 1400
Lancing: G Campbell; T Maberley, T Coulter, S Revill, D
Wiltshire, L Taylor, W Rum, A Frampton, M Russell, S
Bird (M Stewart), G Allen.
Bolton: R Sellers; R Thompson, D Williams, C Jolley, S
Charles (D Prestage), T Entwistle, C Waith, A Price, A
Coleman, T Whittaker, M Dewhurst.
Referee: D. Elleray (Harrow).

INTERNATIONAL PROGRAMME
1996–97

UNDER 15
England 3, Wales 2–Cardiff, 13 February
England 3, N. Ireland 0–Belfast, 13 March
England 0, France 0–Old Trafford, 19 April
England 1, Scotland 1–Nottingham, 24 April
England 1, Switzerland 1–Ebikon, 30 April
England 3, Eire 2–Blackburn, 13 May
England 2, Germany 1–Wembley, 7 June
Overall Record ... Played 7, Won 4, Drew 3, Lost 0,
Goals For 13, Goals Against 7
Goals: Armstrong (3), Mike (3), Osman (2), Taylor (2),
Cole, Standing, own goal

MONTAIGU TOURNAMENT – FRANCE

England 1, Lithuania 1; England 2, Greece 0; England 3,
Israel 0; England 2, Sweden 1
England 0, Holland 2 (Quarter-final – England 8th)

UNDER 18
England 0, Eire 2–Waterford, 21 February
England 1, Holland 1–Zwolle, 4 March
England 2, Wales 0–Rushden, 11 March

England 0, France 1–Norwich, 8 May
England* 1, Switzerland 1–Sheffield, 28 May
* *Won on penalties*
Overall Record ... Played 5, Won 2, Drew 1, Lost 2,
Goals For 4, Goals Against 5
Goals: Leonard, Phelps, Robinson, Sedgemoor

ADIDAS VICTORY SHIELD SEASON
1996–97

Wales 2, England 3–Cardiff, 13 February
N. Ireland 0, England 3–Belfast, 13 March
Scotland 2, Wales 1–Inverness, 20 March
Scotland 1, N. Ireland 0–Stirling, 10 April
England 1, Scotland 1–Nottingham, 24 April
Scotland 1, England 1–Kilmarnock, 28 March

	P	W	D	L	F	A	Pts
England	3	2	1	0	7	3	5
Scotland	3	2	1	0	2	5	5
Wales	3	0	1	2	3	5	1
N. Ireland	3	0	1	2	0	4	1

HEINZ CENTENARY SHIELD SEASON
1996–97

GROUP A
Wales 0, Holland 1–Afan Lido, 18 February
Holland 1, England 1–Zwolle, 4 March
England 2, Wales 0–Rushden, 11 March

	P	W	D	L	F	A	Pts
England	2	1	1	0	3	1	4
Holland	2	1	1	0	2	1	4
Wales	2	0	0	2	0	3	0

GROUP B
Switzerland 2, N. Ireland 1–Austria, 14 April
Austria 3, N. Ireland 2–Austria, 16 April
Austria 1, Switzerland 2–Austria, 22 April

	P	W	D	L	F	A	Pts
Switzerland	2	2	0	0	4	2	6
Austria	2	1	0	1	4	4	3
N. Ireland	2	0	0	2	3	5	0

FINAL
England* 1, Switzerland 1–Sheffield, 28 May
* *England won 5–4 on penalties*

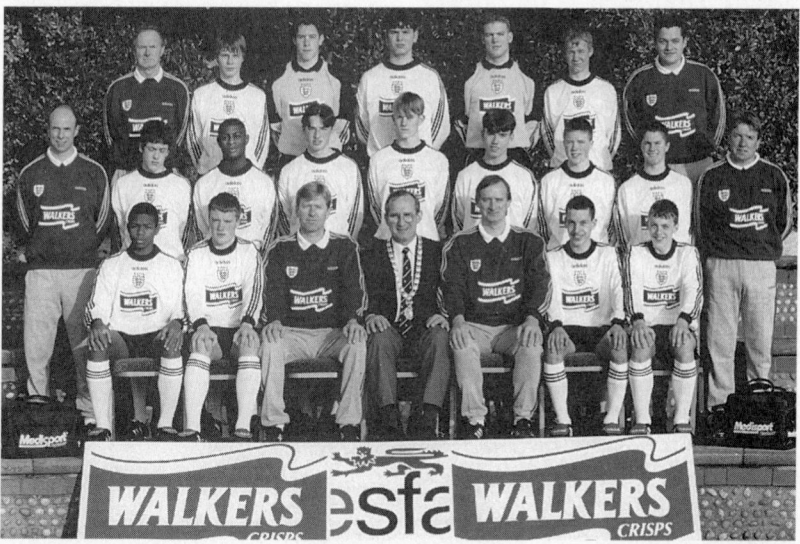

ENGLAND BOYS: *Back Row:* Arthur Tabor, Steven Flitcroft, Rhys Evans, Perry Taylor, Michael Bingham,
Gareth Strange, Mark Eales
Middle Row: Ian Shead, Joe Cole, Paul Burke, Chris McCready, Christian Hanson, Michael Standing,
Chris O'Brien, Ian Armstrong, Alex Gibson
Front Row: Leon Mike, Mark Maley, Dave Parnaby, John Morton, John Owens, Leon Osman, Stephen Warnock

AVON INSURANCE COMBINATION 1996–97

Wimbledon achieved the Avon Insurance Combination Championship for the first time in their history, taking the title by a three-point margin over their nearest challengers, Portsmouth, and the Dons narrowly failed to win the first Combination League and Cup double since Arsenal's in 1970 when they were narrowly beaten by three goals to two by Tottenham Hotspur after extra time in the final of the Avon Insurance Combination League Cup.

Ably managed by Lawrie Sanchez, Wimbledon's team comprised a successful blend of experienced professionals such as Scott Fitzgerald and Alan Reeves and exciting young talent like Jason Euell, Carl Cort, Brendan Murphy and Richard O'Connor.

Portsmouth, too, deserved praise for their efforts with David Waterman, Aaron Flahavan and Martin Allen excelling.

Tottenham Hotspur and Ipswich Town were also challenging at the top of the League, and much credit should also go to Brighton & Hove Albion, who put their troubles at first team level behind them to finish a creditable seventh in the table. Arsenal, too, in a transitional year with a much younger team being introduced to the Combination, did well to finish sixth.

The main purpose of the Avon Insurance Combination is to encourage the development of young talent and names to watch out for in the near future include Arsenal's Nicolas Anelka, Luton Town's Matthew Upson (since signed by Arsenal), Tottenham's Neale Fenn, the top scorer in the Avon Insurance Combination with 21 goals, Ipswich's Kieron Dyer and Norwich City's Adrian Forbes.

Stars who graced the Avon Insurance Combination throughout the season included Matthew Le Tissier, Ian Wright and Ruud Gullit.

Ipswich Town won the Avon Insurance Enterprise Award for their Family Night Football scheme which saw gates rise dramatically for Reserve matches at Portman Road.

Avon Insurance have renewed their sponsorship until the end of the 2002–03 season and their efforts were rewarded when they won the First Time Sponsor category in the prestigious Hollis Sponsorship Awards.

1996–97 SEASON SUMMARY
Champions – Wimbledon
League Cup Winners – Tottenham Hotspur
Top Scorer – Neale Fenn (Tottenham Hotspur) 21 goals
Fair Play Award – Tottenham Hotspur
Avon Insurance Enterprise Award – Ipswich Town
Avon Insurance Programme Award – QPR

Wimbledon Avon Insurance Combination Champions
League Appearances: Castledine 10; Clarke 2; Cort 17 + 1; Elkins 1; Euell 11; Fitzgerald 9; Francis 8 + 4; Futcher 10; Gardner 4 + 3; Goodman 4; Harford 2; Hawkins 14; Heald 4; Hinds +2; Hodges 17; Holdsworth 1; Jennings 1; Jupp 6; Laidlaw 15 + 2; McAllister 1; Murphy 13; Newhouse 18; O'Connor 19 + 1; Odlum 6; Owusu +1; O'Sullivan 1 + 1; Payne 11 + 1; Pearce 10; Petrovic 3 + 1; Reeves 9; Renner 4 + 7; Reynolds 4 + 2; Rothon 1; Searle 3; Thompson +1; Ulla 1; Vella +1; Williamson 2.
Goals: Cort 10, Euell 7, Payne 5, Castledine 4, Newhouse 4, O'Connor 4, Goodman 3, Elkins 1, Francis 1, Hawkins 1, Hinds 1, Holdsworth 1, Laidlaw 1, own goal 1.
Cup Appearances: Castledine 5; Clarke 1; Cort 2 + 3; Elkins 1; Euell 5 + 1; Fear 3; Fitzgerald 4; Francis 2 + 1; Futcher 2 + 1; Gardner +2; Harford 2; Hawkins 3 + 1; Heald 2; Hodges 5; Jupp 3; Kimble 1; Laidlaw 4; Leonhardsen 1; McAllister 1; Murphy 5; Newhouse 6; O'Connor 5; Owusu +1; Payne 4 + 1; Pearce 6; Reeves 3; Renner 1; Reynolds +1.
Goals: Euell 3, Kimble 2, Cort 1, Hawkins 1, Laidlaw 1, Leonhardsen 1, Newhouse 1, O'Connor 1, Payne 1, Pearce 1, own goal 1.

Division One

	P	W	D	L	F	A	Pts
Wimbledon	22	14	5	3	44	25	47
Portsmouth	22	14	2	6	40	23	44
Tottenham Hotspur	22	13	4	5	50	26	43
Ipswich Town	22	12	5	5	41	18	41
Crystal Palace	22	10	6	6	37	32	36
Arsenal	22	10	5	7	49	30	35
Brighton & Hove Albion	22	9	8	5	40	31	35
Luton Town	22	10	5	7	32	24	35
Swindon Town	22	9	5	8	37	35	32
Chelsea	22	9	5	8	31	35	32
Queens Park Rangers	22	9	4	9	37	37	31
Watford	22	7	8	7	28	32	29
Swansea City	22	7	7	8	24	33	28
Charlton Athletic	22	7	6	9	30	38	27
Southampton	22	7	5	10	34	40	26
AFC Bournemouth	22	7	5	10	34	43	26
Millwall	22	7	4	11	30	38	25
Bristol City	22	6	5	11	38	37	23
Oxford United	22	6	5	11	37	40	23
West Ham United	22	6	4	12	29	45	22
Bristol Rovers	22	6	4	12	22	42	22
Cardiff City	22	4	7	11	17	42	19
Norwich City	22	4	6	12	32	47	18

LEAGUE CUP

GROUP 1
QPR 3, Charlton Ath 0
Millwall 2, Watford 0
Watford 2, QPR 2
Millwall 1, Tottenham H 2
QPR 0, Millwall 0
Watford 1, Charlton Ath 1
Charlton Ath 8, Millwall 0
Tottenham H 1, Watford 2
Charlton Ath 2, Tottenham H 2
Tottenham H 1, QPR 0

GROUP 2
Wimbledon 1, Bournemouth 1
Brighton & HA 0, Portsmouth 1
Crystal Palace 2, Wimbledon 3
Bournemouth 0, Southampton 4
Brighton & HA 0, Bournemouth 0
Crystal Palace 0, Southampton 0
Bournemouth 4, Crystal Palace 3
Southampton 3, Portsmouth 1
Wimbledon 6, Brighton & HA 1
Crystal Palace 3, Brighton & HA 2
Southampton 0, Wimbledon 1
Wimbledon 1, Portsmouth 1
Southampton 4, Brighton & HA 3
Portsmouth 1, Bournemouth 2
Portsmouth v Crystal Palace not played.

GROUP 3
Ipswich T 0, Arsenal 2
Norwich C 1, Ipswich T 0
Norwich C 0, West Ham U 1
Luton T 3, Norwich C 0
Luton T 0, West Ham U 3
West Ham U 3, Ipswich T 1
Arsenal 0, Luton T 1
West Ham U 0, Arsenal 2
Arsenal 1, Norwich C 3
Ipswich T 2, Luton T 0

GROUP 4
Bristol R 6, Cardiff C 0
Oxford U 2, Swindon T 1
Oxford U 1, Cardiff C 0
Swindon T 0, Bristol R 0
Swansea C 1, Swindon T 2
Bristol C 2, Oxford U 2
Bristol C 3, Bristol R 1
Cardiff C 1, Swansea C 1
Bristol R 1, Swansea C 2
Swansea C 0, Bristol C 0
Swindon T 1, Cardiff C 0
Oxford U 2, Bristol R 0
Swansea C 1, Oxford U 1
Cardiff C 0, Bristol C 3
Bristol C 1, Swindon T 2

SEMI-FINALS
West Ham U 2, Tottenham H 5
Wimbledon 2, Oxford U 1

FINAL
Tottenham H 3, Wimbledon 2

PONTIN'S LEAGUE 1996–97

Manchester United retained their Pontin's League title having made a fine start to the season by winning their first four matches. After a 4–0 success away to Nottingham Forest on November 9, they stayed unbeaten for a dozen games and lost just once more.

United called upon the services of 40 different players using a mixture of senior professionals and younger members of the staff. This success was mirrored throughout the club by the first team taking the Premiership, of course, and the A and B teams winning their respective divisions of the Lancashire League to record a splendid quartet of trophies.

Next season the Pontin's League welcomes back the reserve side of Newcastle United. The club left the competition during Kevin Keegan's reign as manager, but Kenny Dalglish has reinstated a team in it.

The histroy of the Central League – as it began its life – dates back to the 1911–12 season. The inaugural composition of the League comprised 17 clubs: the first teams of Burslem Port Vale, Crewe Alexandra, Lincoln City and Southport; and the reserve teams of Blackburn Rovers, Blackpool, Bolton Wanderers, Burnley, Bury, Everton, Glossop North End, Liverpool, Manchester City, Manchester United, Oldham Athletic, Preston North End and Stockport County.

The following season Lincoln were elected to the Football League, but the Central League was extended to 20 clubs by the election of the first teams of Rochdale and Stalybridge Celtic and the reserves of Barnsley and Bradford City.

In 1913–14 Huddersfield Town reserves replaces Glossop North End reserves and after the First World War the League was extended to 22 clubs. Barnsley reserves did not compete again for a time but the first teams of Nelson and Tranmere Rovers plus the reserve team of Aston Villa were elected. During the season Port Vale took over Leeds City's fixtures in the Football League and Vale's reserves completed the Central League programme.

However in 1921–22 Crewe Alexandra, Nelson, Rochdale, Southport, Stalybridge Celtic and Tranmere Rovers were elected to the Football League and from this season only reserve teams competed in the Central League. Stockport did not carry on and the teams filling the vacancies were Birmingham, Derby County, Leeds United, Sheffield United, Stoke, West Bromwich Albion and Wolverhampton Wanderers.

In more recent years the trend has been to reduce the number of matches but increase the complement of teams.

PONTIN'S LEAGUE CUP

GROUP 1
Burnley 4, Carlisle U 1
Wigan Ath 3, Oldham Ath 3
Wigan Ath 1, Burnley 2
Burnley 2, Oldham Ath 1

GROUP 2
Barnsley 1, Huddersfield T 0
Barnsley 2, Scarborough 0
Bradford 2, Huddersfield T 4
York C 3, Barnsley 0
Huddersfield T 1, Scarborough 1
York C 3, Bradford C 2
Bradford C 4, Barnsley 2
Scarborough 1, York C 1
York C 1, Huddersfield T 3

GROUP 3
Stockport Co 1, Stoke C 2
Manchester C 1, Tranmere R 0
Stoke C 3, Wrexham 2
Tranmere R 5, Wrexham 3
Manchester C 0, Stockport Co 1
Stoke C 0, Manchester C 1
Tranmere R 0, Stoke C 1
Wrexham 2, Manchester C 1
Wrexham 4, Stockport Co 0
Stockport Co 1, Tranmere R 1

GROUP 4
Doncaster R 6, Scunthorpe U 3
Grimsby T 1, Chesterfield 1
Grimsby T 4, Lincoln C 0
Lincoln C 2, Doncaster R 2
Chesterfield 1, Scunthorpe U 3
Doncaster R 1, Grimsby T 2
Lincoln C 1, Chesterfield 0
Chesterfield 2, Doncaster R 2
Scunthorpe U 0, Grimsby T 2
Scunthorpe U 1, Lincoln C 1

GROUP 5
Notts Co 1, Leicester C 0
Derby Co 0, Walsall 1
Derby Co 2, Leicester C 0
Notts Co 1, Derby Co 1
Walsall 3, Notts Co 0
Leicester C 2, Walsall 0

QUARTER-FINALS
Doncaster R 0, Burnley 2
Huddersfield T 1, Walsall 3
York C 2, Wrexham 1
Stoke C 4, Grimsby T 2

SEMI-FINALS
York C 2, Burnley 1
Stoke C 3, Walsall 2

FINAL
Stoke C 3, York C 1

Manchester United Pontin's League Appearances:
Appleton 15; Brebner 5+2; Brown D. 1+1; Casper 18; Clegg 17; Cole 9; Cooke 17; Cruyff 5; Culkin 1; Curtis 11; Davies 16+1; Duncan 5+3; Ford 0+𝔦; Gibson 3; Giggs 1; Hilton 0+1; Keane 1; Macken 7+5; May 2; McClair 12; McGibbon 2; Mulryne 10; Murdock 4; Neville P 1; Nevland 1; Notman 2+1; O'Kane 15; Pilkington 8; Poborsky 1; Scholes 9; Solskjaer 1; Teather 7+2; Thornley 16; Tomlinson 5; Twiss 5+4; Van der Gouw 12; Wallwork 18+1; Wellens 0+1; Wilson 1+1; Wood 0+1.
Goals: Cole 10, Scholes 5, Tomlinson 5, Cruyff 4, Notman 4, Thornley 4, Cooke 3, Nevland 3, Brebner 2, Macken 2, Solskjaer 2, Appleton 1, Clegg 1, Davies 1, McClair 1, Mulryne 1, Neville P 1, O'Kane 1, Poborsky 1, Twiss 1, Wallwork 1, Wilson 1.

Premier Division

	P	W	D	L	F	A	Pts
Manchester United	24	15	6	3	55	24	51
Blackburn Rovers	24	13	4	7	28	23	43
Sheffield Wednesday	24	12	4	8	42	32	40
Stoke City	24	11	2	11	34	37	35
Leeds United	24	10	4	10	29	34	34
Derby County	24	9	6	9	41	32	33
Birmingham City	24	8	7	9	34	31	31
Nottingham Forest	24	9	4	11	33	45	31
Tranmere Rovers	24	9	3	12	48	48	30
Everton	24	8	6	10	31	42	30
Liverpool	24	8	5	11	32	39	29
Bolton Wanderers	24	7	5	12	31	38	26
Oldham Athletic	24	5	8	11	27	40	23

Division One

	P	W	D	L	F	A	Pts
Preston North End	24	16	6	2	42	14	54
Aston Villa	24	16	4	4	62	25	52
Notts County	24	12	5	7	38	35	41
Middlesbrough	24	10	8	6	42	36	38
Wolverhampton W	24	11	5	8	37	32	38
Leicester City	24	11	3	10	37	42	36
Sunderland	24	9	8	7	47	37	35
Huddersfield Town	24	8	5	11	32	39	29
Port Vale	24	7	6	11	30	37	27
Coventry City	24	6	8	10	22	25	26
West Bromwich Albion	24	6	6	12	21	36	24
Sheffield United	24	7	3	14	26	44	24
Blackpool	24	1	5	18	12	46	8

Division Two

	P	W	D	L	F	A	Pts
Grimsby Town	24	15	5	4	54	29	50
Manchester City	24	14	6	4	43	26	48
York City	24	13	6	5	41	30	45
Wrexham	24	13	5	6	51	30	44
Barnsley	24	12	5	7	53	39	41
Shrewsbury Town	24	10	5	9	42	38	35
Rotherham United	24	10	4	10	29	30	34
Burnley	24	9	5	10	46	41	32
Carlisle United	24	10	2	12	37	38	32
Stockport County	24	7	5	12	34	43	26
Bradford City	24	7	5	12	36	47	26
Hull City	24	7	4	13	27	45	25
Mansfield Town	24	0	1	23	29	86	1

Division Three

	P	W	D	L	F	A	Pts
Rochdale	20	14	4	2	39	20	46
Lincoln City	20	11	7	2	35	20	40
Walsall	20	9	8	3	35	16	35
Doncaster Rovers	20	7	5	8	37	35	26
Bury	20	6	7	7	20	25	25
Chesterfield	20	7	4	9	25	31	25
Wigan Athletic	20	6	5	9	24	33	23
Chester City	20	6	4	10	26	30	22
Scunthorpe United	20	6	4	10	29	35	22
Darlington	20	4	7	9	25	37	19
Scarborough	20	5	3	12	22	35	18

NON-LEAGUE TABLES 1996–97

ENDSLEIGH INSURANCE MIDLAND FOOTBALL COMBINATION

Premier Division

	P	W	D	L	F	A	Pts
Richmond Swifts	38	30	5	3	92	29	95
Meir KA	38	26	6	6	91	39	84
Coleshill Town	38	22	10	6	69	30	76
Studley BKL	38	22	6	10	100	49	72
Knowle	38	22	4	12	83	47	70
Worcester Athletico	38	20	7	11	85	60	67
Kings Heath	38	16	8	14	66	50	56
Massey Ferguson	38	15	11	12	62	61	56
David Lloyd AFC	38	14	11	13	54	57	53
Handrahan Timbers	38	15	6	17	46	54	51
Coventry Sphinx	38	14	8	16	51	74	50
Bilston Community College	38	14	7	17	83	71	49
Bolehall Swifts	38	11	14	13	62	59	47
Southam United	38	13	8	17	53	62	47
Wellesbourne	38	12	5	21	62	89	41
Kenilworth Town	38	11	8	19	49	80	41
Highgate United	38	11	3	24	55	77	36
Alvechurch	38	9	5	24	46	82	32
Shirley Town	38	7	8	23	51	94	29
West Midlands Fire Service	38	4	4	30	26	122	16

COURAGE COMBINED COUNTIES FOOTBALL LEAGUE

Premier Division

	P	W	D	L	F	A	Pts
Ashford Town (Middx)	38	27	6	5	107	39	87
Corinthian-Casuals	38	25	8	5	86	36	83
Bedfont	38	23	4	11	94	56	73
Feltham	38	21	3	14	88	67	66
Farnham Town	38	19	7	12	80	42	64
Reading Town	38	17	13	8	62	60	64
Chipstead	38	18	8	12	67	55	62
Sandhurst Town	38	17	10	11	61	63	61
Godalming & Guildford	38	17	8	13	69	47	59
Netherne	38	14	6	18	55	62	48
Viking Sports	38	14	6	18	59	67	48
Hartley Wintney	38	12	11	15	65	78	47
Cove	38	12	11	15	43	59	47
Cobham	38	11	9	18	62	72	42
Westfield	38	10	12	16	34	46	42
Ash United	38	10	8	20	45	64	38
Raynes Park Vale	38	10	6	22	53	90	36
Cranleigh	38	9	6	23	52	88	33
Merstham	38	9	6	23	39	87	33
Walton Casuals	38	9	4	25	47	90	31

UNIJET SUSSEX COUNTY LEAGUE

Divison One

	P	W	D	L	F	A	Pts
Burgess Hill Town	38	28	4	6	105	46	88
Wick	38	23	7	8	102	44	76
Peacehaven & Telscombe	38	22	8	8	75	41	74
Saltdean United	38	20	6	12	66	42	66
Ringmer	38	19	5	14	62	53	62
Langney Sports	38	16	10	12	72	56	58
Eastbourne Town	38	17	6	15	59	51	57
Horsham YMCA	38	14	9	15	58	53	51
Hassocks	38	14	8	16	47	53	50
Pagham	38	14	7	17	59	67	49
Shoreham	38	14	6	18	62	66	48
Arundel	38	12	11	15	66	78	47
Hailsham Town	38	11	13	14	66	67	46
Portfield	38	13	6	19	61	81	45
Selsey	38	13	6	19	49	70	45
Mile Oak	38	12	9	17	47	74	45
Whitehawk	38	14	3	21	46	80	45
Three Bridges	38	12	8	18	53	69	44
Oakwood	38	11	9	18	48	69	42
Southwick	38	7	7	24	44	87	28

Division Two

	P	W	D	L	F	A	Pts
Littlehampton Town	34	24	4	6	95	31	76
Chichester City	34	22	3	9	69	35	69
Redhill	34	20	7	7	88	42	67
Sidley United	34	18	10	6	80	38	64
Eastbourne United	34	18	9	7	75	43	63
East Preston	34	18	5	11	79	48	59
Withdean	34	17	8	9	70	46	59
Worthing United	34	16	10	8	83	51	58
East Grinstead	34	16	2	16	49	56	50
Crawley Down Village	34	14	7	13	63	63	49
Bexhill Town	34	14	5	15	65	72	47
Newhaven	34	13	7	14	67	62	46
Midhurst & Easebourne	34	10	6	18	57	91	36
Crowborough Athletic	34	10	5	19	46	81	35
Lancing	34	8	6	20	45	73	30
Broadbridge Heath	34	8	3	23	46	98	27
Bosham	34	6	2	26	46	107	20
Steyning Town	34	3	3	28	32	118	12

HIGHLAND LEAGUE

	P	W	D	L	F	A	Pts	GD
Huntly	30	23	4	3	86	26	73	+60
Keith	30	21	3	6	76	36	66	+40
Peterhead	30	17	7	6	77	30	58	+47
Lossiemouth	30	18	4	8	66	31	58	+35
Clachnacuddin	30	16	5	9	59	46	53	+13
Fraserburgh	30	15	7	8	56	38	52	+18
Cove Rangers	30	15	5	10	84	47	50	+37
Deveronvale	30	16	2	12	55	54	50	+1
Elgin City	30	13	4	13	64	66	43	–2
Wick Academy	30	9	8	13	41	46	35	–5
Rothes	30	9	8	13	44	52	35	–8
Forres Mechanics	30	8	5	17	40	60	29	–20
Buckie Thistle	30	8	4	18	41	55	28	–14
Brora Rangers	30	5	10	15	43	88	25	–45
Nairn County	30	4	3	23	21	93	15	–72
Fort William	30	2	3	25	31	116	9	–85

LANCASHIRE FOOTBALL LEAGUE

Divison One

	P	W	D	L	F	A	Pts
Manchester United A	28	22	4	2	108	30	70
Stoke City A	28	18	5	5	57	24	59
Crewe Alexandra Reserves	28	17	4	7	64	34	55
Everton A	28	13	7	8	58	46	46
Liverpool A	28	14	4	10	46	36	46
Oldham Athletic A	28	13	5	10	41	42	44
Tranmere Rovers A	28	13	4	11	40	48	43
Wrexham A	28	13	3	12	49	45	42
Burnley A	28	12	3	13	44	49	39
Bury A	28	10	4	14	26	47	34
Blackburn Rovers A	28	9	6	13	44	40	33
Bolton Wanderers A	28	6	4	18	38	52	22
Marine Reserves	28	5	7	16	28	68	22
Preston North End A	28	6	3	19	26	65	21
Morecambe Reserves	28	6	3	19	31	74	21

Divison Two

	P	W	D	L	F	A	Pts
Manchester United B	32	20	4	8	89	53	64
Manchester City A	32	19	7	6	56	29	64
Liverpool B	32	19	3	10	67	39	60
Crewe Alexandra A	32	17	6	9	72	63	57
Chester City A	32	15	7	10	49	44	52
Everton B	32	14	7	11	74	58	49
Burnley B	32	15	3	14	55	51	48
Oldham Athletic B	32	12	10	10	54	46	46
Blackburn Rovers B	32	12	9	11	53	40	45
Stockport County A	32	12	6	14	52	62	42
Blackpool A	32	11	7	14	50	49	40
Tranmere Rovers B	32	11	7	14	60	62	40
Carlisle United A	32	11	7	14	50	60	40
Wigan Athletic A	32	10	9	13	49	58	39
Rochdale A	32	10	5	17	43	64	35
Bury B	32	8	5	19	40	69	29
Marine Youth	32	2	6	24	29	95	12

NORTH WEST COUNTIES LEAGUE

Divison One

	P	W	D	L	F	A	Pts
Trafford	42	29	7	6	99	38	94
Newcastle Town	42	27	7	8	71	31	88
Clitheroe	42	23	14	5	75	36	83
Penrith	42	23	10	9	75	49	79
Burscough	42	22	9	11	68	48	75
Eastwood Hanley	42	20	10	12	64	51	70
Mossley	42	20	8	14	79	58	68
Blackpool Rovers	42	17	19	9	70	47	67
Prescot Cables	42	17	11	14	68	60	62
Vauxhall GM	42	14	15	13	70	69	57
Nantwich Town	42	14	11	17	75	74	53
Glossop North End	42	14	11	17	56	67	53
Bootle	42	15	8	19	61	73	53
St Helens Town	42	14	6	22	65	79	48
Atherton Collieries	42	12	9	21	63	85	45
Kidsgrove Athletic	42	10	14	18	53	73	44
Rossendale United	42	11	9	22	51	77	42
Chadderton	42	10	11	21	49	80	41
Holker Old Boys	42	10	9	23	60	80	39
Maine Road	42	9	11	22	49	85	38
Darwen	42	9	10	23	49	81	37
Salford City	42	8	12	22	53	82	36

Divison Two

	P	W	D	L	F	A	Pts
Ramsbottom United	38	27	6	5	100	34	87
Haslingden	38	27	6	5	90	32	87
Garswood United	38	26	5	7	90	38	83
Tetley Walker	38	24	5	9	105	58	77
Castleton Gabriels	38	22	8	8	78	39	74
Leek CSOB	38	22	7	9	67	49	73
Formby	38	21	6	11	86	57	69
Maghull	38	17	7	14	52	50	58
Cheadle Town	38	15	8	15	59	63	53
Skelmersdale United	38	14	10	14	72	66	52
Nelson	38	14	10	14	64	72	52
Stantondale	38	11	12	15	69	69	45
Middlewich Athletic	38	13	6	19	54	65	45
Squires Gate	38	12	4	22	44	79	40
Daisy Hill	38	10	5	23	47	76	35
Bacup Borough	38	9	6	23	48	83	33
Ashton Town	38	6	14	18	53	77	32
Blackpool Mechanics	38	7	5	26	48	88	26
Oldham Town	38	6	7	25	48	113	25
Colne	38	6	5	27	35	91	23

VAUX WEARSIDE LEAGUE

Divison One

	P	W	D	L	F	A	Pts
Boldon CA	34	25	6	3	105	33	81
Marske United	34	25	5	4	97	24	80
Birtley Town	34	21	9	4	74	33	72
Annfield Plain	34	19	8	7	83	52	62
Nissan	34	17	10	7	63	41	61
Windscale	34	17	8	9	65	40	59
South Tyneside	34	17	7	10	69	37	58
Kennek Roker	34	15	6	13	66	53	51
Wolviston	34	12	5	17	59	65	41
Harton & Westoe	34	11	5	18	63	66	38
Whitehaven Ams	34	10	8	16	50	81	38
Stanley United	34	10	6	18	58	88	36
Cleadon SC	34	9	6	19	47	72	33
North Shields	34	8	9	17	44	70	33
Hartlepool BWOB	34	10	2	22	46	97	32
Ryhope CW	34	9	3	22	35	68	30
South Bank	34	5	9	20	34	90	24
Jarrow	34	6	8	20	36	84	23

Washington Glebe; record expunged

THE JEWSON SOUTH-WESTERN FOOTBALL LEAGUE

	P	W	D	L	F	A	Pts
Falmouth Town	30	24	0	6	90	27	72
Truro City	30	22	6	2	68	25	72
Portleven	30	20	6	4	70	28	66
Bodmin Town	30	16	6	8	60	34	54
Saltash United	30	15	8	7	63	42	53
Penzance	30	14	7	9	62	37	49
Liskeard Athletic	30	13	7	10	39	31	46
Torpoint Athletic	30	11	9	10	52	49	42
Tavistock	30	11	4	15	48	71	37
Newquay	30	10	6	14	44	63	36
Holsworthy	30	8	8	14	28	43	32
St Blazey	30	9	5	16	51	70	32
St Austell	30	8	4	18	38	59	28
Millbrook	30	5	7	18	32	70	22
Wadebridge Town	30	4	6	20	21	49	18
Launceston	30	4	3	23	26	94	15

NORTHERN ALLIANCE LEAGUE

Premier Division

	P	W	D	L	F	A	Pts
Lemington United	32	25	4	3	84	25	79
Ponteland United	32	25	3	4	109	30	78
Middlesbrough A	32	21	6	5	89	44	69
West Allotment	32	21	3	8	78	44	66
Carlisle City*	32	19	5	8	71	41	59
St Columbas	32	14	4	14	60	59	46
Hartlepool	32	13	6	13	56	56	45
Walker Ledwood	32	12	6	14	47	71	42
Seaton Delaval	32	11	8	13	43	51	41
Spittal Rovers	32	11	7	14	36	53	40
Gillford Park	32	10	5	17	57	65	35
Benfield Park	32	10	5	17	52	63	35
Winlaton	32	8	9	15	44	59	33
Walker Central*	32	10	3	19	44	67	30
Haltwhistle CP	32	8	6	18	40	76	30
Amble Town	32	5	6	21	40	76	21
Bohemians	32	3	6	23	32	102	15

*3 pts deducted

Divison One

	P	W	D	L	F	A	Pts
Ryton	26	21	1	4	84	27	64
Hebburn Reyrolle	26	19	3	4	65	23	60
Newbiggin CW	26	17	4	5	68	26	55
Shankhouse	26	16	3	7	65	38	51
Heddon Institute	26	14	4	8	72	49	46
Walbottle*	26	14	4	8	77	53	43
Percy Main Amateurs	26	12	5	9	60	40	41
Hexham Swinton	26	10	3	13	38	61	33
Longbenton	26	6	3	17	46	75	21
Heaton Stannington**	26	8	3	15	42	79	21
Swalwell	26	4	7	15	45	68	19
Procter & Gamble	26	4	6	16	33	61	18
Ashington Hirst P	26	4	6	16	45	86	18
Orwin	26	4	6	16	32	86	18

Forest Hall resigned; record expunged
*3 points deducted; **6 pts deducted

CARLSBERG WEST CHESHIRE LEAGUE

Divison One

	P	W	D	L	F	A	Pts
Poulton Victoria	30	23	4	3	84	23	50
Heswall	30	21	4	5	79	28	46
Bromborough Pool*	30	22	1	7	58	26	43
Merseyside Police	30	16	4	10	57	39	36
Mond Rangers	30	15	6	9	55	54	36
Mersey Royal	30	13	7	10	51	42	33
Christleton	30	12	9	9	53	52	33
Cammell Laird	30	12	8	10	54	45	32
Vauxhall Motors	30	12	6	12	58	54	30
Newton	30	8	9	13	48	56	25
Stork	30	8	7	15	44	66	23
Ashville	30	7	8	15	40	50	22
Capenhurst	30	9	3	18	44	62	21
Moreton	30	8	3	19	35	70	19
Shell	30	6	4	20	37	77	16
General Chemicals	30	4	5	21	29	82	13

*2 points deducted

NOTTS FOOTBALL ALLIANCE

Senior Division

	P	W	D	L	F	A	Pts
Rainworth MW	30	22	5	3	88	32	71
Welbeck CW	30	18	7	5	75	39	61
Hucknall Rolls Royce	30	16	10	4	53	37	58
Ruddington United	30	17	5	8	64	44	56
Boots Athletic	30	17	4	9	58	37	55
Pelican	30	13	9	8	61	51	48
Greenwood Meadow	30	11	11	8	49	43	44
John Player	30	11	7	12	50	46	40
Notts Police	30	11	7	12	37	38	40
Wollaton	30	9	7	14	35	51	34
Cotgrave CW	30	8	8	14	37	55	32
Southwell City	30	7	7	16	33	61	28
Keyworth United	30	8	3	19	30	59	27
Ollerton Town	30	4	11	15	28	52	23
Awsworth Villa	30	5	8	17	46	77	23
Thoresby CW	30	4	9	17	33	55	21

INTERLINK EXPRESS MIDLAND FOOTBALL ALLIANCE

	P	W	D	L	F	A	Pts
Blakenall	38	23	11	4	85	39	80
Hinckley Athletic	38	22	10	6	77	44	76
Boldmere St Michaels	38	22	7	9	69	41	73
Willenhall Town	38	20	9	9	77	45	69
Barwell	38	17	10	11	65	51	61
Bridgnorth Town	38	18	4	16	76	67	58
Rocester	38	16	9	13	62	53	57
Stratford Town	38	15	10	13	53	48	55
Bloxwich Town	38	16	6	16	63	53	54
Oldbury United	38	14	11	13	50	43	53
Pelsall Villa	38	13	9	16	52	70	48
Knypersley Vics	38	11	12	15	42	53	45
Stapenhill	38	10	14	14	45	58	44
Shifnal Town	38	11	10	17	45	50	43
West Midlands Police	38	10	11	17	37	60	41
Rushall Olympic	38	10	10	18	40	59	40
Sandwell Borough	38	9	13	16	48	69	40
Chasetown	38	9	12	17	44	65	39
Halesowen Harriers	38	8	12	18	44	67	36
Pershore Town	38	8	6	24	41	80	30

MANCHESTER LEAGUE

Premier Division

	P	W	D	L	F	A	Pts
Highfield United	30	23	5	2	70	23	74
Abbey Hey	30	18	6	6	76	41	60
East Manchester	30	19	3	8	62	39	60
Little Hulton United	30	16	7	7	63	41	55
Dukinfield Town	30	15	8	7	48	40	53
Wythenshawe Amateurs	30	13	3	14	42	44	42
Woodley SC	30	10	7	13	43	45	37
Stand Athletic	30	11	4	15	46	61	37
Atherton Town	30	9	9	12	36	45	36
Mitchell Shackleton	30	10	6	14	45	56	36
Monton	30	10	4	16	43	43	34
Springhead	30	10	4	16	46	57	34
Elton Fold	30	8	10	12	43	55	34
Stockport Georgians	30	8	6	16	40	60	30
BICC	30	8	6	16	41	67	30
Wythenshawe Town	30	6	4	20	32	59	22

Division One

	P	W	D	L	F	A	Pts
Prestwich Heys	30	27	2	1	87	17	83
Tottington United	30	23	2	5	89	42	71
Gamesley	30	20	7	3	84	36	67
Willows	30	14	6	10	73	56	48
Sacred Heart	30	13	7	10	61	47	46
Old Alts	30	13	5	12	77	71	44
New Mills	30	13	3	14	70	62	42
Hollinwood	30	11	7	12	64	69	40
Milton	30	10	4	16	55	73	34
Whitworth Valley	30	9	7	14	58	84	34
Pennington	30	7	10	13	51	57	31
Breightmet United	30	8	7	15	50	69	31
GMP	30	9	4	17	35	78	31
Manchester Royal	30	8	3	19	57	85	27
Ashton Athletic	30	8	3	19	31	68	27
Whalley Range	30	7	3	20	53	81	24

WINSTONLEAD KENT LEAGUE

Division One

	P	W	D	L	F	A	Pts
Herne Bay	40	23	11	6	73	35	80
Ramsgate	40	24	5	11	82	47	77
Furness	40	23	8	9	66	38	77
Sheppey United	40	22	7	11	74	47	73
Deal Town	40	20	5	15	80	56	65
Folkestone Invicta	40	19	7	14	66	57	64
Whitstable Town	40	17	12	11	61	44	63
Chatham Town	40	16	11	13	60	52	59
Greenwich Borough	40	16	10	14	71	62	58
Faversham Town	40	16	9	15	58	73	57
Beckenham Town	40	15	10	15	49	47	55
Canterbury City	40	15	10	15	47	55	55
Hythe United	40	15	8	17	70	76	53
Thamesmead Town	40	15	8	17	53	61	53
Lordswood	40	14	8	18	57	72	50
Slade Green	40	12	9	19	45	50	45
Woolwich Town	40	10	13	17	40	62	43
Cray Wanderers	40	11	6	23	43	66	39
Crockenhill	40	9	11	20	51	80	38
Tunbridge Wells	40	8	10	22	44	76	34
Corinthian	40	8	6	26	37	71	30

SCREWFIX DIRECT LEAGUE

Premier Division

	P	W	D	L	F	A	Pts
Tiverton Town	34	31	1	2	103	20	94
Taunton Town	34	24	6	4	99	28	78
Mangotsfield United	34	19	8	7	75	44	65
Paulton Rovers	34	17	10	7	86	42	61
Chippenham Town	34	12	12	10	58	52	48
Brislington	34	12	9	13	53	48	45
Calne Town	34	13	6	15	55	52	45
Torrington	34	11	11	12	54	54	44
Bridgwater Town	34	12	8	14	53	55	44
Bridport	34	11	10	13	41	50	43
Odd Down*	34	11	15	8	42	46	39
Bideford	34	11	6	17	51	84	39
Barnstaple Town	34	10	8	16	54	62	38
Bristol Manor Farm	34	9	10	15	40	60	37
Backwell United	34	9	9	16	42	55	36
Chard Town	34	9	7	18	45	67	34
Westbury United	34	8	6	20	40	70	30
Elmore	34	4	4	26	30	132	16

*9 pts deducted

Division One

	P	W	D	L	F	A	Pts
Melksham Town	38	27	8	3	82	20	89
Keynsham Town	38	27	7	4	77	21	88
Exmouth Town	38	23	7	7	77	42	76
Clyst Rovers	38	23	6	9	92	48	75
Bishop Sutton	38	21	7	10	96	52	70
Wellington	38	21	5	12	82	62	68
Devizes Town	38	18	11	9	75	39	65
Dawlish Town	38	18	9	11	66	36	63
Ilfracombe Town	38	15	12	11	62	44	57
Welton Rovers	38	15	7	16	68	59	52
Minehead	38	16	4	18	61	56	52
Frome Town	38	12	11	15	45	60	47
Yeovil Town	38	12	8	18	66	77	44
Glastonbury	38	12	7	19	54	72	43
Crediton United	38	12	4	22	58	91	40
Warminster Town	38	9	8	21	44	75	35
Larkhall Athletic	38	7	13	18	51	92	34
Heavitree United	38	7	11	21	44	95	32
Pewsey Vale	38	5	4	29	26	105	19
Amesbury Town	38	1	9	31	27	107	12

ESSEX SENIOR LEAGUE

Premier Division

	P	W	D	L	F	A	Pts
Ford United	28	21	6	1	91	24	69
Great Wakering Rovers	28	20	6	2	67	19	66
Concord Rangers	28	19	5	4	106	31	62
Stansted	28	19	2	7	53	37	59
Burnham Ramblers	28	13	6	9	62	40	45
Brentwood	28	11	10	7	46	34	43
Hullbridge Sports	28	13	4	11	52	42	43
Ilford	28	11	3	14	36	40	36
Basildon United*	28	11	5	12	39	52	35
Saffron Walden Town	28	8	8	12	40	39	32
Southend Manor	28	8	5	15	32	42	29
Bowers United	28	8	4	16	32	77	28
East Ham United	28	7	3	18	29	61	24
Sawbridgeworth Town	28	3	3	22	17	69	12
Eton Manor	28	1	4	23	13	108	7

*3 pts deducted

JEWSON (EAST COUNTIES) LEAGUE

Premier Division

	P	W	D	L	F	A	Pts
Wroxham	44	34	7	3	122	25	109
Wisbech Town	44	32	8	4	141	37	104
Harwich & Parkeston	44	32	8	4	133	34	104
Diss Town	44	29	4	11	81	41	91
Great Yarmouth Town	44	26	7	11	87	51	85
Gorleston	44	26	5	13	86	54	83
Bury Town	44	23	10	11	101	54	79
Newmarket Town	44	23	8	13	97	75	77
Lowestoft Town	44	22	9	13	84	56	75
Stowmarket Town	44	22	4	18	74	62	70
Tiptree United	44	19	8	17	64	59	65
Halstead Town	44	19	6	19	87	79	63
Soham Town Rangers	44	17	7	20	82	87	58
Fakenham Town	44	15	11	18	78	80	56
Warboys Town	44	15	10	19	62	72	55
Woodbridge Town	44	12	12	20	51	63	48
Sudbury Wanderers	44	13	5	26	61	100	44
Felixstowe Port & Town	44	11	6	27	56	103	39
Watton United	44	10	6	28	49	106	36
Sudbury Town Reserves	44	7	7	30	46	96	28
Clacton Town	44	7	5	32	43	156	26
Hadleigh United	44	5	8	31	41	128	23
March Town United	44	5	3	36	25	133	18

Divison One

	P	W	D	L	F	A	Pts
Ely City	34	27	5	2	93	36	86
Histon	34	22	7	5	85	31	73
Maldon Town	34	21	6	7	89	44	69
Needham Market	34	19	11	4	67	24	68
Ipswich Wanderers	34	20	6	8	80	35	66
Brightlingsea United	34	14	14	6	50	33	56
Swaffham Town	34	13	13	8	62	48	52
Haverhill Rovers	34	15	7	12	54	46	52
Stanway Rovers	34	15	7	12	55	49	52
Whitton United	34	10	9	15	45	58	39
Norwich United	34	10	8	16	48	61	38
Cambridge City Reserves	34	10	7	17	51	68	37
Downham Town	34	9	4	21	45	88	31
Thetford Town	34	7	9	18	34	66	30
Mildenhall Town	34	7	8	19	35	61	29
Cornard United	34	6	8	20	40	70	26
Somersham Town	34	5	10	19	23	69	25
Chatteris Town	34	2	9	23	27	96	15

REDFERNS INTERNATIONAL REMOVERS CENTRAL MIDLANDS LEAGUE

Supreme Division

	P	W	D	L	F	A	Pts
Heanor Town	30	24	2	4	72	26	74
Dunkirk	30	17	6	7	66	35	57
Staveley Miners Welfare	30	16	7	7	45	32	55
Gedling Town	30	16	6	8	59	44	54
Graham Street Prims	30	16	5	9	61	34	53
Mickleover Sports	30	12	12	6	62	40	48
Thorne Colliery	30	13	4	13	35	44	43
Nettleham	30	11	9	10	42	48	42
Nuthall	30	10	6	14	55	52	36
Long Eaton United	30	9	7	14	41	49	34
Shirebrook Town	30	8	9	13	32	51	33
Case Sports	30	7	10	13	38	62	31
Kimberley Town	30	8	6	16	45	53	30
South Normanton Athletic	30	7	9	14	32	51	30
Harworth Colliery Institute	30	5	7	18	28	57	22
Sandiacre Town	30	5	7	18	35	70	22

Premier Division

	P	W	D	L	F	A	Pts
Clipstone Welfare	34	25	6	3	110	28	81
Grimethorpe MW	34	23	7	4	104	26	76
Rossington	34	22	3	9	92	51	69
Collingham	34	20	7	7	73	37	67
Killamarsh Juniors	34	19	6	9	89	51	63
Sheffield Hallam University	34	18	6	10	72	53	60
Sneinton	34	17	6	11	60	38	57
Askern Welfare	34	17	4	13	76	57	55
Shardlow St James	34	15	4	15	72	63	49

LONDON SPARTAN FOOTBALL LEAGUE

Premier Division

	P	W	D	L	F	A	Pts
Barkingside	30	20	6	4	60	23	66
Hillingdon Borough	30	19	8	3	65	31	65
Croydon Athletic	30	18	6	6	56	30	60
St Margaretsbury	30	17	4	9	51	49	55
Beaconsfield SYCOB	30	13	10	7	52	28	49
Ruislip Manor	30	14	6	10	74	44	48
Woodford Town	30	13	6	11	42	39	45
Brimsdown Rovers	30	13	5	12	54	52	44
Islington St Mary's	30	9	10	11	38	38	37
Waltham Abbey	30	11	4	15	39	45	37
Amersham Town	30	9	6	15	34	51	33
Hanwell Town	30	8	8	14	49	49	32
Brook House	30	9	5	16	31	55	32
Cockfosters	30	6	6	18	35	57	24
Haringey Borough	30	5	6	19	24	58	21
Harefield United	30	5	6	19	32	87	21

Tottenham Omada withdrew; record expunged

Divison One

	P	W	D	L	F	A	Pts
Leyton County	14	10	2	2	34	14	32
Catford Wanderers*	14	9	1	4	33	16	25
Old Roan	14	7	4	3	28	19	25
Trojan	14	7	3	4	25	18	24
Craven	14	6	3	5	39	25	21
Cray Valley	14	4	3	7	25	35	15
Bridon Ropes	14	2	3	9	15	29	9
Classic Inter	14	1	1	12	18	61	4

*3 pts deducted
AC Milla FC failed to complete 90% of its fixtures and as per Rule 12(b) all points obtained by or against them have been expunged.

Derby Rolls Royce etc. (continuation of top-right table)

	P	W	D	L	F	A	Pts
Derby Rolls Royce	34	13	5	16	68	61	44
Sheepbridge	34	12	5	17	64	69	41
Hemsworth Town*	34	13	5	16	52	63	41
Radford	34	12	5	17	50	70	41
Stanton Ilkeston	34	9	9	16	53	75	36
Mexborough Athletic	34	8	7	19	48	102	31
Holbrook	34	8	4	22	46	98	28
Blackwell MW	34	3	5	26	25	130	14
Mickleover RBL	34	3	4	27	22	104	13

*3pts deducted

NORTHERN COUNTIES (EAST) LEAGUE

Premier Division

	P	W	D	L	F	A	Pts
Denaby United	38	25	10	3	82	33	85
Belper Town	38	24	7	7	78	41	79
Brigg Town	38	23	8	7	80	43	77
North Ferriby United	38	21	9	8	86	36	72
Ossett Albion	38	21	8	9	73	36	71
Hucknall Town	38	19	8	11	84	48	65
Hallam	38	17	7	14	56	69	58
Ossett Town	38	14	11	13	52	53	53
Arnold Town	38	12	15	11	48	43	51
Glasshoughton Welfare	38	13	12	13	58	58	51
Selby Town	38	14	9	15	63	69	51
Armthorpe Welfare	38	12	9	17	42	48	45
Thackley	38	12	9	17	43	58	45
Maltby Main	38	12	8	18	58	81	44
Pickering Town	38	11	8	19	45	72	41
Pontefract Collieries	38	8	11	19	44	73	35
Hatfield Main	38	8	10	20	40	75	34
Sheffield	38	7	11	20	50	70	32
Ashfield United	38	7	11	20	51	80	32
Liversedge	38	5	9	24	40	87	24

Divison One

	P	W	D	L	F	A	Pts
Eccleshill United	28	21	4	3	81	30	67
Garforth Town	28	20	4	4	57	22	64
Harrogate Railway Ath.	28	15	7	6	54	32	52
Yorkshire Amateur	28	15	4	9	52	52	49
Glapwell	28	14	4	10	52	41	46
Borrowash Victoria	28	12	6	10	47	39	42
Hall Road Rangers	28	12	5	11	48	46	41
Louth United	28	9	9	10	47	37	36
Rossington Main	28	10	6	12	44	46	36
Worsbrough Bridge MW	28	9	8	11	41	49	35
Parkgate	28	8	7	13	38	46	31
Winterton Rangers	28	7	9	12	39	51	30
Tadcaster Albion	28	4	10	14	20	51	22
Brodsworth MW	28	4	5	19	22	58	17
Blidworth Welfare	28	4	4	20	31	73	16

BANKS'S BREWERY WEST MIDLANDS LEAGUE

Premier Division

	P	W	D	L	F	A	Pts
Wednesfield	34	26	5	3	103	25	83
Stourport Swifts	34	24	5	5	103	34	77
Bloxwich Strollers	34	23	7	4	84	29	76
Lye Town	34	20	6	8	82	40	66
Brierley Hill Town	34	20	5	9	83	44	65
Stafford Town	34	17	9	8	57	40	60
W'pton Casuals	34	17	7	10	72	69	58
Gornal Athletic	34	15	8	11	55	48	53
Ludlow Town	34	15	7	12	63	57	52
Westfields	34	13	8	13	50	53	47
Tividale	34	12	8	14	53	78	44
Darlaston Town	34	10	9	15	49	60	39
Ettingshall HT	34	8	7	19	42	81	31
Cradley Town	34	7	6	21	51	83	27
Malvern Town	34	6	8	20	47	70	26
Walsall Wood	34	6	6	22	35	72	24
W'pton United	34	5	7	22	34	102	22
Hill Top Rangers	34	2	2	30	27	105	8

SOUTH EAST COUNTIES LEAGUE

Divison One

	P	W	D	L	F	A	Pts
Norwich City	30	20	6	4	66	26	46
Chelsea	30	19	4	7	61	41	42
West Ham United	30	16	7	7	74	31	39
Arsenal	30	14	7	9	51	38	35
Tottenham Hotspur	30	14	6	10	46	31	34
Watford	30	16	2	12	60	50	34
Queens Park Rangers	30	14	5	11	53	44	33
Gillingham	30	12	9	9	50	47	33
Ipswich Town	30	11	8	11	57	62	30
Portsmouth	30	11	4	15	45	54	26
Millwall	30	10	6	14	47	64	26
Cambridge United	30	7	8	15	34	55	22
Charlton Athletic	30	6	9	15	46	66	21
Southend United	30	7	7	16	38	62	21
Fulham	30	8	5	17	36	65	21
Leyton Orient	30	3	11	16	35	63	17

Divison Two

	P	W	D	L	F	A	Pts
Luton Town	30	22	5	3	70	30	49
Crystal Palace	30	19	7	4	69	27	45
Southampton	30	20	2	8	59	25	42
Oxford United	30	14	11	5	54	37	39
Tottenham Hotspur	30	12	9	9	48	33	33
Colchester United	30	12	8	10	51	40	32
Swindon Town	30	12	8	10	54	46	32
Wimbledon	30	11	8	11	40	27	30
Brighton & Hove Albion	30	12	6	12	41	51	30
Wycombe Wanderers	30	11	7	12	32	33	29
AFC Bournemouth	30	10	7	13	44	59	27
Bristol City	30	9	7	14	46	63	25
Bristol Rovers	30	9	5	16	44	56	23
Brentford	30	5	7	18	37	65	17
Reading	30	7	3	20	35	86	17
Barnet	30	2	6	22	27	73	10

HELLENIC LEAGUE

Premier Division

	P	W	D	L	F	A	Pts
Brackley Town	34	25	6	3	79	20	81
Abingdon United	34	22	5	7	57	32	71
Burnham	34	20	9	5	67	34	69
Swindon Supermarine	34	21	5	8	72	40	68
North Leigh	34	17	7	10	56	39	58
Tuffley Rovers	34	16	8	10	62	43	56
Endsleigh	34	13	11	10	49	50	50
Banbury United	34	14	5	15	51	46	47
Didcot Town	34	13	7	14	42	52	46
Carterton Town	34	12	5	17	57	57	41
Shortwood United	34	11	6	17	53	60	39
Lambourn Sports	34	10	8	16	44	53	38
Bicester Town	34	10	7	17	31	53	37
Wantage Town	34	11	4	19	36	69	37
Almondsbury Town	34	8	10	16	44	52	34
Kintbury Rangers	34	9	5	20	41	67	32
Highworth Town	34	8	5	21	40	73	29
Fairford Town	34	7	5	22	32	73	26

MINERVA FOOTBALLS SOUTH MIDLANDS LEAGUE

Premier Division

	P	W	D	L	F	A	Pts
Potters Bar Town	28	18	8	2	53	18	62
Brache Sparta	28	19	5	4	54	20	62
Arlesey Town	28	16	7	5	49	20	55
Toddington Rovers	28	14	4	10	45	29	46
Buckingham Athletic	28	14	3	11	52	34	45
Royston Town	28	13	6	9	47	42	45
London Colney	28	12	8	8	47	41	44
Bedford United	28	10	8	10	44	49	38
Welwyn Garden City	28	9	9	10	45	44	36
Harpenden Town	28	9	7	12	32	33	34
Milton Keynes	28	7	10	11	25	36	31
Letchworth	28	7	7	14	35	50	28
Langford	28	6	6	16	22	56	24
Hoddesdon Town	28	5	7	16	30	55	22
Biggleswade Town	28	2	3	23	21	74	9

Senior Division

	P	W	D	L	F	A	Pts
Leverstock Green	26	19	3	4	54	19	60
Holmer Green	26	18	1	7	71	21	55
Tring Athletic	26	17	3	6	62	29	54
Stony Stratford Town	26	16	2	8	60	46	50
New Bradwell St Peter	26	13	7	6	49	30	46
Houghton Town	26	10	8	8	31	32	38
Mercedes Benz	26	10	7	9	48	38	37
Risborough Rangers	26	11	4	11	35	50	37
Winslow United	26	10	5	11	40	51	35
Kent Athletic	26	9	5	12	46	57	32
Ampthill Town	26	6	5	15	33	57	23
ACD Tridon	26	5	6	15	33	57	21
Totternhoe	26	2	9	15	27	62	15
The 61 FC (Luton)	26	2	3	21	26	67	9

Divison One

	P	W	D	L	F	A	Pts
Biggleswade United	34	26	4	4	116	35	82
Caddington**	34	22	7	5	89	45	72
De Havilland	34	22	5	7	88	52	71
Crawley Green S&S	34	19	7	8	77	51	64
Old Bradwell United	34	19	6	9	69	49	63
Emberton	34	19	5	10	67	46	62
Bedford Eagles*	34	18	6	10	79	48	57
Scot	34	16	4	14	49	57	52
Walden Rangers	34	14	6	14	70	46	48
Buckingham United	34	13	6	15	66	75	45
Bridger Packaging	34	13	4	17	61	74	43
Luton Old Boys	34	10	7	17	43	53	37
Old Dunstablians	34	10	6	18	62	85	36
Leighton Athletic	34	9	5	20	50	75	32
Flamstead	34	8	6	20	44	80	30
Abbey National (MK)	34	5	9	20	39	92	24
Mursley United*	34	6	8	20	58	91	23
Pitstone & Ivinghoe	34	5	3	26	26	94	18

*3 pts deducted; **1 pt deducted

EVERARDS BREWERY LEICESTERSHIRE SENIOR LEAGUE

Premier Division

	P	W	D	L	F	A	Pts
Oadby Town	32	27	4	1	85	21	85
Friar Lane OB	32	19	6	7	79	34	83
St Andrews SC	32	19	6	7	82	39	63
Cottesmore Amateurs	32	19	4	9	73	50	61
Birstall United	32	16	8	8	65	41	56
Downes Sports	32	14	7	11	58	50	49
Anstey Nomads	32	14	5	13	83	69	47
Ibstock Welfare	32	12	11	9	55	43	47
Kirby Muxloe SC	32	13	3	16	50	63	42
Holwell Sports	32	12	4	16	55	58	40
Barrow Town	32	10	8	14	49	67	38
Highfield Rangers	32	11	4	17	50	69	37
Quorn	32	10	6	16	42	50	36
Newfoundpool	32	9	8	15	42	86	35
Aylestone Park OB	32	8	7	17	52	78	31
Asfordby Amateurs	32	6	5	21	28	59	23
Thringstone MW	32	3	4	25	38	109	13

JEWSON WESSEX FOOTBALL LEAGUE

First Division

	P	W	D	L	F	A	Pts
AFC Lymington	40	35	5	0	112	22	110
Wimborne Town	40	26	7	7	97	42	85
Ryde Sports	40	25	4	11	77	50	79
Bemerton Hth Har.	40	23	9	8	69	45	78
Thatcham Town**	40	25	6	9	91	47	77
Andover	40	19	12	9	80	42	69
Eastleigh	40	19	8	13	71	56	65
Downton	40	18	7	15	72	70	61
Cowes Sports	40	15	14	11	65	55	59
Portsmouth RN*	40	16	4	20	65	79	51
Gosport Borough	40	15	5	20	56	66	50
Aerostructures	40	13	9	18	45	66	48
Bournemouth	40	14	5	21	50	72	47
Brockenhurst	40	13	7	20	54	73	46
Whitchurch United	40	12	8	20	60	81	44
Christchurch	40	13	4	23	49	72	43
East Cowes Vics	40	10	7	23	53	72	37
Romsey Town	40	10	7	23	52	94	37
BAT Sports	40	8	9	23	43	74	33
AFC Totton	40	8	8	24	54	87	32
Petersfield Town	40	8	5	27	42	92	29

**4 pts deducted; *1 pt deducted

FEDERATION BREWERY NORTHERN LEAGUE

Divison One

	P	W	D	L	F	A	Pts
Whitby Town	38	32	3	3	131	37	99
Billingham Synthonia	38	28	6	4	109	46	90
Bedlington Town*	38	28	5	5	113	37	86
Durham City	38	19	11	8	69	50	68
Crook Town	38	19	9	10	88	56	66
Morpeth Town	38	20	6	12	73	56	66
Guisborough Town	38	17	9	12	68	54	60
Tow Law Town	38	14	11	13	76	70	53
South Shields	38	13	11	14	52	63	50
Murton	38	15	5	18	58	80	50
Consett	38	12	11	15	65	59	47
Dunston Feds	38	12	10	16	64	70	46
Shildon	38	13	7	18	72	86	46
Easington Colliery	38	12	8	18	56	72	44
RTM Newcastle	38	13	3	22	66	87	42
Seaham Red Star	38	7	14	17	50	83	35
Stockton	38	8	10	20	70	105	34
Chester-le-Street Town	38	7	12	19	53	86	33
Whickham	38	5	6	27	38	98	21
West Auckland Town	38	6	3	29	41	117	18

Divison Two

	P	W	D	L	F	A	Pts
Northallerton	36	25	6	5	98	41	81
Billingham Town*	36	24	6	6	111	39	75
Jarrow Roofing	36	23	6	7	88	34	75
Ashington	36	22	5	9	71	38	71
Evenwood Town	36	21	4	11	84	46	67
Horden CW*	36	20	7	9	67	37	64
Prudhoe Town	36	18	10	8	73	48	64
Shotton Comrades*	36	20	6	10	91	43	63
Willington	36	18	7	11	78	54	61
Peterlee Newtown	36	16	8	12	56	56	56
Hebburn	36	16	3	17	66	61	51
Ryhope CA	36	12	5	19	50	70	41
Norton & SA*	36	11	7	18	47	58	37
Brandon United	36	10	7	19	64	76	37
Alnwick Town*	36	11	4	21	55	79	34
Eppleton CW	36	6	7	23	44	110	25
Washington*	36	6	7	23	43	79	22
Esh Winning*	36	7	3	26	44	100	21
Ferryhill Athletic	36	1	2	33	16	177	5

*3 pts deducted

UNITED COUNTIES FOOTBALL LEAGUE

Premier Division

	P	W	D	L	F	A	Pts
Stamford	38	26	3	9	79	51	81
Spalding United	38	23	7	8	78	37	76
Long Buckby	38	21	10	7	63	39	73
Boston Town	38	21	9	8	88	39	72
S & L Corby	38	21	8	9	84	64	71
Stotfold	37	21	7	9	87	46	70
Cogenhoe United	38	20	6	12	90	62	66
Potton United	38	18	8	12	57	49	62
Desborough Town	38	17	9	12	63	49	60
St Neots Town	36	16	10	10	75	51	58
Mirrlees Blackstone	38	16	5	17	68	65	53
Ford Sports Daventry	38	14	7	17	64	64	49
Eynesbury Rovers	38	12	11	15	52	56	47
Northampton Spen	36	13	6	17	63	64	45
Wellingborough Town	38	10	6	22	52	72	36
Wootton Blue Cross	38	9	8	21	40	60	35
Kempston Rovers	37	9	5	23	39	87	32
Bourne Town	38	8	7	23	49	100	31
Holbeach United	38	7	6	25	43	101	27
Newport Pagnell Town	38	3	6	29	37	115	15

Divison One

	P	W	D	L	F	A	Pts
Yaxley	34	23	5	6	81	25	74
Well. Whitworths	34	19	12	3	78	28	69
Bugbrooke St M.	34	20	8	6	60	30	68
Higham Town	33	18	10	5	59	40	64
Huntingdon United	34	19	2	13	87	57	59
Rothwell Corinthians	34	16	7	11	61	40	55
St Ives Town	34	16	7	11	52	34	55
Cottingham	33	16	3	14	54	59	51
Thrapston Town	34	14	7	13	51	51	49
Northampton Vanaid	34	13	6	15	56	55	45
Olney Town	34	13	6	15	42	47	45
Harrowby United	34	12	6	16	62	68	42
Daventry Town	34	10	6	18	46	78	36
ON Chenecks	34	10	5	19	46	54	35
Burton Park Wanderers	34	9	7	18	50	64	34
Sharnbrook	34	10	4	20	34	83	34
Irchester United	34	7	7	20	34	70	28
Blisworth	34	5	2	27	28	92	17

AMATEUR FOOTBALL ALLIANCE 1996–97

AFA SENIOR CUP

1st Round Proper
Nottsborough 4*:5, 4*:2 Old Addeyans
Bank of England 1, 0 Old Parkonians
Old Meadonians 2, 3 Old Lyonian
Ulysses 2, 4 Cardinal Manning Old Boys
Parkfield 1, 3 Civil Service
Old Suttonians 6, 1 Broomfield
Old Wilsonians 3*, 2* Old Cholmeleans
John Fisher Old Boys 1, 2 Wake Green
Old Aloysians 5, 1 Old Manorians
Old Latymerians 1, 0 New Scotland Yard Comets
Hampstead Heathens 1, 3 Old Tiffinian
Carshalton 9, 2 Old Malvernian
Latymer Old Boys 4, 2 Old Owens
Norsemen 1, 3 Enfield Old Grammarians
Old Tollingtonians 0, 5 West Wickham
Lancing Old Boys 2:3, 2:0 Lloyds Bank
Southgate Olympic 3, 0 Old Elizabethans
Crouch End Vampires 3, 0 Cuaco
Shene Old Grammarians 1, 3 Old Tenisonians
Polytechnic 3, 2 Old Bromleians
Mill Hill Village 2, 5 Old Buckwellians
St. Mary's College 1, 3 Old Minchendenians
Cardinal Pole Old Boys 1, 2 Merton
Midland Bank 9, 2 Old Salesians
Lensbury 3, 1 Old Actonians Association
Old Sinjuns 5, 0 Mill Hill County Old Boys
East Barnet Old Grammarians 6, 1 Derbyshire Amateurs
Barclays Bank 4, 1 Old Ignatians
Old Hamptonians 1*:0*, 1*:2* Glyn Old Boys
Southgate County 2, 0 Kew Association
Fulham Compton Old Boys 0, 3 Old Vaughanians
Brentham 0*, 4* Witan

2nd Round Proper
Nottsborough 3, 0 Bank of England

Old Lyonian 1*:3*, 1*:4* Cardinal Manning Old Boys
Civil Service 4, 1 Old Suttonians
Old Wilsonians 3, 2 Wake Green
Old Aloysians 2, 1 Old Latymerians
Old Tiffinian 1, 2 Carshalton
Latymer Old Boys 4:0, 4:1 Enfield Old Grammarians
West Wickham 6*, 2* Lancing Old Boys
Southgate Olympic 2, 3 Crouch End Vampires
Old Tenisonians 3, 1 Polytechnic
Old Buckwellians 0, 2 Old Minchendenians
Merton 4, 0 Midland Bank
Lensbury 4, 1 Old Sinjuns
East Barnet Old Grammarians 3, 4 Barclays Bank
Glyn Old Boys 3, 1 Southgate County
Old Vaughanians 1, 2 Witan

3rd Round Proper
Nottsborough 4*:5, 4*:0 Cardinal Manning Old Boys
Civil Service 2, 1 Old Wilsonians
Old Aloysians 1, 0 Carshalton
Enfield Old Grammarians 0, 4 West Wickham
Crouch End Vampires 1*, 0* Old Tenisonians
Old Minchendenians 3, 2 Merton
Lensbury 3*:4, 3*:2 Barclays Bank
Glyn Old Boys 2, 3 Witan

4th Round Proper
Nottsborough 2, 3 Civil Service
Old Aloysians 1*:1, 1*:2 West Wickham
Crouch End Vampires 1, 0 Old Minchendenians
Lensbury 3, 1 Witan

Semi-Finals
Civil Service 4, 2 Old Aloysians
Crouch End Vampires 2, 4 Lensbury
(*after extra time*)

OTHER AFA CUP RESULTS 1996–97

Intermediate
Lloyds Bank Res. 4, Civil Service Res. 1
Junior
Old Finchleians 3rd. 4*, Old Bealonians 2*
Minor
Norsemen 4th 1, Hampstead Heathens 4th. 0
Senior Novets
Old Actonians Association 5th. 2, Polytechnic 5th. 0
Intermediate Novets
Old Parmiterians 6th. 2, Old Camdenians 6th. 0
Junior Novets
Old Parmiterians 8th. 2, National Westminster Bank 7th. 0
Veterans
Old Parmiterians Vets. 2, Old Chigwellians Vets. 1
Open Veterans
Snaresbrook Vets. 3, Belstone Vets. 1
Youth
Old Salesians 2, Old Actonians Association 1
Essex Divisional Senior
Old Foresters 1, Old Brentwoods 0

Middlesex Divisional Senior
Cardinal Manning Old Boys 1*:5, Old Ignatians 1*:1
Surrey Divisional Senior
Carshalton 1*:0, Lloyds Bank 1*:2
Essex Divisional Intermediate
Leyton County Old Boys Res. 3*:2, Hale End Athletic Res. 3*:0
Kent Divisional Intermediate
West Wickham Res. 0, Lloyds Bank Res. 1
Middlesex Divisional Intermediate
Old Actonians Ass'n Res. 2*:4, Crouch End Vampires Res. 2*:1
Surrey Divisional Intermediate
Old Thorntonians Res. 2, South Bank Res. 1
W E Greenland Memorial
Sun Alliance 3, Gray's Inn 0
(*after extra time*)

LONDON OLD BOYS' CUPS

Senior:
Old Chigwellians 2, 1 Old Manorians
Intermediate:
Latymer Old Boys Res. 4*, 1* Old Thorntonians
Junior:
Latymer Old Boys 3rd. 1, 4 Old Tenisonians 3rd.
Minor:
Old Actonians Ass'n 4th. 1, 0 Old Aloysians 4th.
Novets:
Old Actonians Ass'n 5th. 4*, 3* Old Vaughanians 5th.
Drummond:
Withheld
Nemean:
Old Actonians Ass'n 9th. 2*, 1 Old Addeyans 7th.
Veterans':
Old Meadonians Vets. 4, 2 Old Salvatorians Vets.
(*after exta time*)

OLD BOYS' INVITATION CUPS
Senior:
Old Tenisonians 2, 0 Old Parkonians
Junior:
Old Owens Res. 1*:6p, 1*:5p Old Tenisonians Res.
Minor:
Old Tenisonians 3rd. 2, 1 Glyn Old Boys 3rd.
4th XI:
Old Owens 4th. 1, 0 Old Finchleians 4th.
5th XI:
Old Stationers 5th. 7, 3 Old Suttonians 5th.
6th XI:
Old Tenisonians 6th. 3, 4 Old Finchleians 6th.
7th XI:
Old Suttonians 7th. 5, 1 East Barnet Old Grammarians 7th.
Veterans' XI:
Old Tenisonians "A" Vets. 1*:5p, 1*:4p Old Tenisonians "B" Vets.
(*after exta time*)

OLD BOYS' LEAGUE

PREMIER DIVISION	P	W	D	L	F	A	Pts
Old Ignatians	20	15	4	1	53	13	34
Old Aloysians	20	15	4	1	40	18	34
Old Tenisonians	20	11	5	4	25	16	27
Glyn Old Boys	20	8	6	6	37	27	22
Old Hamptonians	20	8	3	9	41	35	19
Cardinal Manning Old Boys	20	7	4	9	32	36	18
Latymer Old Boys	20	5	8	7	25	37	18
Old Vaughanians	20	8	1	11	34	30	17
Old Meadonians	20	5	5	10	32	45	15
Old Kingsburians	20	2	5	13	16	44	9
Clapham Old Xaverians	20	2	3	15	17	51	7

SENIOR DIVISION ONE							
Enfield Old Grammarians	20	13	5	2	68	19	31
Old Suttonians	20	11	7	2	44	20	29
Phoenix Old Boys	20	10	7	3	51	26	27
Old Manorians	20	12	3	5	38	23	27
Old Tiffinians	20	9	3	8	39	46	21
Old Salvatorians	20	6	8	6	31	35	20
Old Wilsonians	20	5	4	11	35	41	14
Old Isleworthians	20	5	3	12	25	39	13
Chertsey Old Salesians	20	5	2	13	25	55	10*
Old Danes	20	4	2	14	23	57	10
Old Westhamians	20	6	4	10	34	52	8*

SENIOR DIVISION TWO							
Old Buckwellians	20	12	3	5	54	33	27
Old Reigatians	20	10	6	4	35	21	26
Old Tollingtonians	20	11	3	6	53	31	25
Old Camdenians	20	9	3	8	36	36	21
Old Minchendenians	20	9	1	10	44	41	19
Shene Old Grammarians	20	8	3	9	39	43	19
Latymer Old Boys Res.	20	7	5	8	29	35	19
Old Tenisonians Res.	20	7	4	9	39	39	18
Old Meadonians Res.	20	6	4	10	33	43	16
Mill Hill County Old Boys	20	6	4	10	25	50	16
Old Wokingians	20	4	6	10	21	36	14

SENIOR DIVISION THREE							
Old Dorkinians	20	12	5	3	48	19	29
Old Sinjuns	20	10	7	3	51	26	27
Phoenix Old Boys Res.	20	10	5	5	55	35	25
Old Addeyans	20	12	1	7	42	30	25
Old Hamptonians Res.	20	8	6	6	41	37	22
Old Southallians	20	6	8	6	32	34	20
Old Aloysians Res.	20	7	4	9	42	43	18
Old Vaughanians Res.	20	6	3	11	30	46	15
Old Salvatorians Res.	20	6	2	12	34	39	14
Wood Green Old Boys	20	4	4	12	22	58	12
Glyn Old Boys Res.	20	2	9	9	20	50	11*

* – points deducted for breach of rule

Intermediate Division North–12 Teams–Won by Enfield O. Grammarians Res.
Intermediate Division South–12 Teams–Won by John Fisher Old Boys
Division One North–10 Teams–Won by Old Kingsburians Res.
Division One South–11 Teams–Won by Old Josephians
Division One West–10 Teams–Won by Old Alpertonians Res.
Division Two North–11 Teams–Won by Leyton County Old Boys Res.
Division Two South–11 Teams–Won by Old Wilsonians 3rd.
Division Two West–10 Teams–Won by Old Alpertonians 3rd.
Division Three North–11 Teams–Won by Old Aloysians 5th.
Division Three South–12 Teams–Won by Old Suttonians 5th.
Division Three West–10 Teams–Won by Old Southallians 3rd.
Division Four North–9 Teams–Won by Old Camdenians 5th.
Division Four South–12 Teams–Won by Fitzwilliam Old Boys
Division Four West–10 Teams–Won by Phoenix Old Boys 4th.
Division Five North–10 Teams–Won by Old Camdenians 6th.
Division Five South–10 Teams–Won by John Fisher Old Boys 3rd.
Division Five West–10 Teams–Won by Old Meadonians 6th.
Division Six North–8 Teams–Won by Old Egbertians 4th.
Division Six South–10 Teams–Won by Old Sinjuns 3rd.
Division Six West–10 Teams–Won by Holland Park Old Boys 3rd.
Division Seven North–8 Teams–Won by Old Ignatians 6th.
Division Seven South–11 Teams–Won by Old Tiffinian 6th.
Division Seven West–9 Teams–Won by Holland Park Old Boys 4th.
Division Eight South–10 Teams–Won by Chertsey Old Salesians 6th.
Division Eight West–9 Teams–Won by Old Salvatorians 10th.
Division Nine South–8 Teams–Won by Old Tiffinian 7th.

ARTHUR DUNN CUP FINAL TIE

Old Foresters (2) 3 *(Francis 27, Elliot 43, Gray 55)*
Old Salopians (1) 1 *(Cooke R 4)*   (at Motspur Park)

Old Foresters: M. Butler; J. Banks, C. Hossain, N. Francis, M. Kendall, J. Gray, L. Douris, R. Harnack, P. Risby (A Heyes), C. Elliot, M. Robinson (S. Yankson).
Old Salopians: P. Hollands; H. Raven, M. Lascelles, T. Cooke, R. Cooke, P. Deans, D. Cookson (M. Bailey), T. Onions (D. Saunders), P. Dyke, S. Ellis, D. Honychurch.
Referee: P. Burrowes.

ARTHURIAN LEAGUE

PREMIER DIVISION	P	W	D	L	F	A	Pts
Old Foresters	16	8	5	3	32	15	21
Lancing Old Boys	16	10	1	5	39	23	21
Old Brentwoods	16	8	4	4	47	24	20
Old Carthusians	16	8	4	4	39	33	20
Old Etonians	16	7	3	6	27	28	17
Old Chigwellians	16	6	4	6	31	23	16
Old Cholmeleians	16	7	1	8	27	39	15
Old Reptonians	16	4	2	10	28	53	10
Old Witleians	16	2	0	14	18	50	4

DIVISION 1	P	W	D	L	F	A	Pts
Old Haberdashers	16	14	0	2	62	17	28
Old Salopians	16	10	5	1	48	26	25
Old Bradfieldians	16	10	2	4	46	27	22
Old Aldenhamians	16	8	1	7	44	28	17
Old Harrovians	16	6	3	7	39	37	15
Old Malvernians	16	6	1	9	35	55	13
Old Haileyburians	16	4	2	10	28	49	10
Old Wykehamists	16	4	0	12	33	67	8
Old Wellingburians	16	2	2	12	27	56	6

DIVISION 2	P	W	D	L	F	A	Pts
Old Chigwellians Res.	16	13	2	1	49	13	28
Old Cholmeleians Res.	16	12	2	2	49	15	26
Old Etonians Res.	16	9	2	5	40	22	20
Old Carthusians Res.	16	8	1	7	27	26	17
Old Etonians 3rd.	16	8	1	7	29	37	17
Old Foresters Res.	16	5	2	9	17	30	12
Old Cholmeleians 3rd.	16	5	1	10	24	36	11
Lancing Old Boys Res.	16	5	1	10	20	39	11
Old Harrovians Res.	16	1	0	15	16	53	2

DIVISION 3	P	W	D	L	F	A	Pts
Old Chigwellians 3rd.	18	11	6	1	40	15	28
Old Brentwoods Res.	18	11	3	4	50	27	25
Old Salopians Res.	18	9	3	6	46	38	21
Old Cholmeleians 4th.	18	8	5	5	33	29	21
Old Aldenhamians Res.	18	7	6	5	46	47	20
Old Westminsters	18	7	4	7	44	35	18
Old Eastbournians	18	8	2	8	38	39	18
Old Ardinians	18	7	3	8	41	42	17
Old Foresters 3rd.	18	3	2	13	26	43	8
Old Haberdashers Res.	18	1	2	15	22	71	2#

DIVISION 4	P	W	D	L	F	A	Pts
Old Millhillians	16	11	2	3	55	23	24
Old Brentwoods 3rd.	16	9	3	4	57	28	21
Old Haileyburians Res.	16	9	3	4	46	32	21
Old Carthusians 3rd.	16	7	3	6	32	45	17
Old Reptonians Res.	16	7	1	8	50	45	15
Old Malvernians Res.	16	5	3	8	24	31	13
Old Bradfieldians Res.	16	4	5	7	33	39	11#
Old Cholmeleians 5th.	16	3	4	9	23	44	10
Old Salopians 3rd.	16	4	2	10	21	54	10

DIVISION 5	P	W	D	L	F	A	Pts
Old Foresters 4th.	12	8	4	0	30	12	20
Old Brentwoods 4th.	12	3	6	3	26	21	12
Old Chigwellians 4th.	12	2	6	4	14	17	10
Old Chigwellians 5th.	12	3	3	6	27	37	9
Old Brentwoods 5th.	12	2	5	5	25	35	7#

(#*Points deducted – breach of rule*)

Junior League Cup–Old Chigwellians Res. 3, Old Etonians Res. 1
Derrik Moore Veterans Cup–Old Cholmeleians Vets 0, Old Etonians Vets 2

LONDON FINANCIAL FA

DIVISION ONE	P	W	D	L	F	A	Pts
Churchill Insurance	16	10	4	2	37	23	24
Morgan Guaranty	16	10	3	3	44	24	23
Royal Bank of Scotland	16	8	3	5	55	42	19
Morgan Stanley Int.	16	8	2	6	51	39	18
Bank America	16	6	4	6	20	23	16
Kleinwort Benson	16	5	5	6	36	31	15
Sun Alliance	16	6	2	8	36	44	14
Coutts	16	2	4	10	28	50	8
Citibank	16	2	3	11	22	53	7

DIVISION TWO	P	W	D	L	F	A	Pts
Allied Irish Bank	16	14	1	1	54	9	29
Bowring	16	10	4	2	47	20	24
Eagle Star	16	8	3	5	39	30	19
Temple Bar	16	7	4	5	54	47	18
Granby	16	4	7	5	24	28	15
Chase Manhattan Bank	16	5	4	7	25	30	14
Salomon Brothers	16	5	2	9	27	58	12
Liverpool Victoria	16	3	3	10	26	48	9
Royal Bank of Scot. Res.	16	2	0	14	26	52	4

DIVISION THREE	P	W	D	L	F	A	Pts
Vantage	12	10	2	0	36	13	22
Union Bank of Switzerland	12	8	1	3	32	18	17
Bankers Trust	12	5	2	5	31	25	12
Century Life	12	4	3	5	21	17	11
ANZ Banking Group	12	4	2	6	23	30	10
Sedgwick Noble Lowndes	12	3	3	6	23	32	9
Coutts Res.	12	0	3	9	12	43	3

DIVISION FOUR	P	W	D	L	F	A	Pts
Lincoln National	16	13	3	0	53	10	29
Credit Suisse Finan'l P.	16	12	2	2	44	18	26
Bank America Res.	16	10	1	5	61	31	21
Sun Alliance Res.	16	7	4	5	40	32	18
Churchill Res.	16	5	1	10	35	45	11
Granby Res.	16	5	1	10	22	39	11
Bank of Ireland	16	4	2	10	26	62	10
Royal Bank of Scot. 3rd.	16	2	5	9	24	45	9
Citibank Res.	16	2	5	9	30	53	9

Division Five–8 Teams–Won by Standard Chartered Bank
Division Six–7 Teams–Won by St. Paul International
Challenge Cup–Lensbury 1, Barclays Bank 2
Senior Cup–Sun Alliance 2, Morgan Guaranty 3
Senior Plate–Kleinwort Benson 2, Churchill Insurance 1
Junior Cup–Century Life 0, Union Bank of Switzerland 4
Junior Plate–Bank America Res. 5, Granby Res. 2
Minor Cup–Temple Bar Res. 1, Standard Chartered Bank 3
Minor Plate–Eagle Star Res. 3, Sun Alliance 3rd. 1
Veterans' Cup–Lensbury 5, Temple Bar 0
Veterans' Plate–Citibank 3, Royal Bank of Scotland 2
W A Jewell Memorial–Morgan Guaranty 5-a-Side
Saunders Shield–Salomon Brothers 5-a-Side
Sportsmanship Shield–C. Hoare & Co.

Representative Matches

v Southern Olympian League	Lost	2-4
v Royal Marines	Won	2-1
v Southern Amateur League "B"	Lost	3-4
v Old Boys' League	Lost	0-1
v Stock Exchange F.A.	Drawn	1-1
v Bristol Insurance Institute	Drawn	2-2

LONDON LEGAL LEAGUE

DIVISION ONE	P	W	D	L	F	A	Pts
Gray's Inn	18	14	2	2	64	15	30
Nabarro Nathanson	18	10	4	4	44	36	24
Herbert Smith	18	9	4	5	45	35	22
Lovell White Durrant	18	9	3	6	34	26	21
Linklaters & Paines	18	8	3	7	31	31	19
Pegasus (Inner Temple)	18	6	5	7	38	44	17
Cameron Markby Hewitt	18	7	1	10	18	39	15
Wilde Sapte	18	6	2	10	31	33	14
Clifford Chance	18	6	0	12	35	70	1
Gouldens	18	3	0	15	16	27	6

DIVISION TWO	P	W	D	L	F	A	Pts
Slaughter & May	18	13	3	2	70	14	29
Taylor Joynson Garrett	18	13	3	2	53	19	29
Rosling King	18	11	2	5	50	35	24
Norton Rose	18	8	3	7	43	34	19
Freshfields	18	8	3	7	41	34	19
Macfarlanes	18	7	2	9	53	41	16
S.J. Berwin	18	6	2	10	32	32	14
Allen & Overy	18	5	3	10	26	62	13
D.J. Freeman & Co.	18	5	1	12	21	43	11
Baker & McKenzie	18	2	2	14	14	89	6

DIVISION THREE	P	W	D	L	F	A	Pts
Kennedy's	16	10	3	3	41	25	23
Stephenson Harwood	16	10	2	4	41	13	22
Simmons & Simmons	16	7	5	4	32	22	19
K.P.M.G.	16	6	5	5	24	18	17
McKenna & Co.	16	6	4	6	19	20	16
Barlow Lyde & Gilbert	16	5	4	7	23	36	14
Denton Hall	16	4	3	9	20	27	11
Titmus Sainer Dechert	16	5	1	10	12	29	11
Richards Butler	16	4	3	9	14	36	11

League Challenge Cup–Gray's Inn 1:2p, Linklaters & Paine's 1:4p
Weavers Arms Cup–Wilde Sapte 5, Nabarro Nathanson 2
Invitation Cup–Clifford Chance 5, McKenna's 4

SOUTHERN AMATEUR LEAGUE 1996-97

SENIOR SECTION:

FIRST DIVISION	P	W	D	L	F	A	Pts
Old Parmiterians	22	15	5	2	51	30	35
Crouch End Vampires	22	10	10	2	33	22	30
Old Actonians Association	22	11	5	6	35	20	27
Polytechnic	22	8	8	6	39	34	24
Carshalton	22	7	9	6	29	34	23
Norsemen	22	7	7	8	21	26	21
East Barnet Old Gram.	22	7	4	11	28	28	18
South Bank Polytechnic	22	5	8	9	35	36	18
West Wickham	22	7	4	11	30	36	18
Civil Service	22	4	10	8	33	44	18
Old Esthameians	22	6	5	11	29	38	17
National West. Bnk	22	5	5	12	26	41	15

SECOND DIVISION	P	W	D	L	F	A	Pts
Lloyds Bank	22	12	8	2	48	20	32
Lensbury	22	14	2	6	68	31	30
Barclays Bank	22	13	4	5	58	21	30
Alexandra Park	22	12	4	6	45	30	28
Old Latymerians	22	8	7	7	46	38	23
Old Lyonians	22	8	6	8	29	42	22
Old Salesians	22	7	6	9	33	34	20
Old Parkonians	22	7	6	9	33	42	20
Cuaco	22	7	5	10	35	36	19
Winchmore Hill	22	8	3	11	41	51	19
Kew Association	22	4	7	11	32	50	15
Old Stationers	22	1	4	17	14	87	6

THIRD DIVISION	P	W	D	L	F	A	Pts
Midland Bank	22	15	3	4	54	29	33
Old Owens	22	14	4	4	62	28	32
Bank of England	22	12	5	5	41	25	29
Southgate Olympic	22	12	5	5	37	23	29
Broomfield	22	11	4	7	54	41	26
Ibis	22	11	3	8	58	41	25
Merton	22	11	3	8	53	36	25
Old Bromleians	22	9	3	10	63	60	21
Alleyn Old Boys	22	5	4	13	39	53	14
Old Westminster Citizens	22	4	4	14	44	72	12
Reigate Priory	22	3	4	15	20	67	10
Brentham	22	3	2	17	27	77	8

Reserve Teams Section:
First Division–12 Teams–Won by Barclays Bank Res.
Second Division–12 Teams–Won by Lloyds Bank Res.
Third Division:–12 Teams–Won by Broomfield Res.

3rd. Teams Section:
First Division–12 Teams–Won by Old Stationers 3rd.
Second Division:–12 Teams–Won by Old Actonians Association 3rd.
Third Division–12 Teams–Won by Southgate Olympic 3rd.

4th. Teams Section:
First Division–12 Teams–Won by Old Actonians Association 4th.
Second Division–12 Teams–Won by Midland Bank 4th.
Third Division:–11 Teams–Won by Old Owens 4th.

5th. Teams Section:
First Division–10 Teams–Won by Old Actonians Association 5th.
Second Division:–11 Teams–Won by Norsemen 5th.
Third Division–11 Teams–Won by Old Westminster Citizens 5th.

6th. Teams Section:
First Division–10 Teams–Won by Old Stationers 6th.
Second Division–9 Teams–Won by Crouch End Vampires 6th.
Third Division–7 Teams–Won by East Barnet O. Grammarians 6th.

Minor Section:
First Division–10 Teams–Won by National Westminster Bank 7th.
Second Division–10 Teams–Won by Old Parmiterians 8th.
Third Division–11 Teams–Won by Old Actonians Association 9th.
Fourth Division–11 Teams–Won by Old Parmiterians 10th.

Challenge Cups:
Junior–Crouch End Vampires 3rd. 5, Norsemen 3rd. 1
Minor–Midland Bank 4th. 4, Norsemen 4th. 1
Senior Novets–Norsemen 5th. 2, Lloyds Bank 5th. 1
Intermediate Novets–O. Parmiterians 6th. 2, Polytechnic 6th. 0
Junior Novets–O. Parmiterians 8th. 4, Norsemen 8th. 1

SOUTHERN OLYMPIAN LEAGUE

SENIOR SECTION:

DIVISION ONE	P	W	D	L	F	A	Pts
Nottsborough	18	12	2	4	53	24	26
Old Finchleians	18	12	1	5	57	34	25
Hale End Athletic	18	9	4	5	48	32	21*
Southgate County	18	8	3	7	34	39	19
Parkfield	18	5	6	7	30	36	16
Witan	18	6	4	8	28	39	16
St. Mary's College	18	5	5	8	25	34	15
Ulysses	18	6	3	9	26	38	15
Wandsworth Borough	18	5	3	10	32	43	13
Albanian	18	5	3	10	29	43	13

DIVISION TWO	P	W	D	L	F	A	Pts
Hon. Artillery Co'y	18	11	5	2	30	11	27
City of London	18	12	2	4	54	25	26
Old Simmarobians	18	8	5	5	34	21	21
Old Grammarians	18	7	5	6	22	20	19
Westerns	18	8	4	6	34	35	17*
UCL Academicals	18	6	4	8	30	33	16
Old Woodhouseians	18	5	5	8	32	35	15
Mill Hill Village	18	7	1	10	29	42	15
Ealing Association	18	4	5	9	23	38	13
Hadley	18	4	0	14	25	52	8

DIVISION THREE	P	W	D	L	F	A	Pts
Fulham Compton Old Boys	16	12	1	3	52	26	24*
Hampstead Heathens	16	10	2	4	44	30	22
B.B.C.	16	10	0	6	51	33	20
Pegasus (Inner Temple)	16	8	2	6	42	21	18
Duncombe Sports	16	7	3	6	37	27	17
Old Bealonians	16	7	1	8	27	24	15
Old Colfeians	16	6	1	9	22	35	13
London Welsh	16	6	0	10	27	51	12
Birkbeck College	16	0	2	14	18	73	2

DIVISION FOUR	P	W	D	L	F	A	Pts
The Cheshunt Club	18	14	2	2	65	27	30
Inland Revenue	18	12	2	4	58	33	26
Mayfield Athletic	18	10	1	7	37	30	21
New Scotland Yard Comets	18	9	2	7	40	34	20
Centymca	18	6	6	6	27	32	18
Cardinal Pole Old Boys	18	9	0	9	41	50	18
Economicals	18	6	4	8	30	38	15*
London Airways	18	5	2	11	30	44	12
Tansley	18	4	2	12	32	51	10
Brent	18	4	1	13	24	45	9

(*points deducted - breach of rule*)

Intermediate Section:
Division One–10 Teams–Won by Nottsborough Res.
Division Two–10 Teams–Won by Hale End Athletic Res.
Division Three–10 Teams–Won by Wandsworth Borough Res.
Division Four–10 Teams–Won by Old Bealonians 3rd.

Junior Section:
Division One–Does not exist
Division Two N–10 Teams–Won by Albanian 4th..
Division Two S&W–10 Teams–Won by Old Colfeians Res.
Division Three N–10 Teams–Won by Parkfield 5th.
Division Three S&W–10 Teams–Won by Old Colfeians 3rd.

Minor Section:
Division "A" N–10 Teams–Won by Albanian 6th
Division "A" S&W–10 Teams–Won by Witan 4th.
Division "B" N–11 Teams–Won by Old Fairlopians Res.
Division "B" S&W–10 Teams–Won by Inland Revenue 4th.

Senior Challenge Bowl–Won by Wandsworth Borough
Senior Challenge Shield–Won by The Cheshunt Club
Intermediate Challenge Cup–Won by Nottsborough Res.
Intermediate Challenge Shield–Won by Ealing Association Res.
Junior Challenge Cup–Won by Old Bealonians 3rd.
Junior Challenge Shield–Won by Old Finchleians 3rd.
Mander Cup–Won by Old Finchleians 4th.
Mander Shield–Won by Ealing Associaion 4th.
Burntwood Trophy–Won by Albanian 5th.
Burntwood Shield–Won by Ealing Association 5th.
Thomas Parmiter Cup–Won by Parkfield 6th.
Thomas Parmiter Shield–Won by Old Finchleians 6th.
Veterans' Challenge Cup–Won by Old Finchleians Vets.
Veterans' Challenge Shield–Won by Centymca Vets.

MIDLAND AMATEUR ALLIANCE
(Following a merger with Nottingham Spartan & 3 pts for a win)

PREMIER DIVISION	P	W	D	L	F	A	Pts
Old Elizabethans	20	14	5	1	71	28	47
Lady Bay	20	14	3	3	88	31	45
Bassingfield	20	11	3	6	57	47	36
Caribbean Cavaliers	20	11	1	8	60	37	34
Kirton Brown 'A'	20	10	2	8	41	42	32
Kirton B. W.	20	10	2	8	43	27	32
Derbyshire Amateurs	20	8	5	7	35	36	29
Old Bemrosians	20	6	2	12	42	62	20
Racing Toton	20	5	3	12	49	60	18
Magdala Amateurs 'A'	20	4	2	14	28	72	14
County Nalgo	20	3	0	17	26	98	9

DIVISION ONE	P	W	D	L	F	A	Pts
Rylands Athletic	24	16	6	2	67	28	54
Old Elizabethans Res.	24	16	5	3	69	29	53
Beeston Old Boys Assn.	24	16	3	5	81	36	51
Nottingham Univ. Postgraduates	24	15	5	4	75	31	50
Dynamo Baptist	24	10	9	5	59	47	39
Tibshelf Old Boys	24	8	6	10	69	72	30
Woodborough United	24	8	6	10	53	53	30
Nottinghamshire	24	7	7	10	41	60	28
Lady Bay Res.	24	6	8	10	48	68	26
Cadland Chilwell	24	6	1	17	29	67	19
Edwinstowe J G	24	4	6	14	34	59	18
Ilkeston Rangers	24	4	5	15	39	72	17
Thistle 'S'	24	4	5	15	37	75	17

DIVISION TWO	P	W	D	L	F	A	Pts
Parkhead Academicals	24	18	1	5	88	26	55
Bassingfield Res.	24	16	4	4	77	36	52
Radcliffe Olympic Res.	24	15	2	7	75	41	47
Southwell Amateurs	24	15	1	8	69	39	46
Arnold & Carlton College	24	11	4	9	64	44	37
Old Elizabethans 3rd.	24	12	2	10	42	33	37
Brunts Old Boys	24	9	5	10	47	54	32
Nottinghamshire Res.	24	7	8	9	42	49	29
West-Clif	24	8	4	12	43	61	28
Magdala Amateurs Res.	24	8	2	14	48	74	26
Derbyshire Amateurs Res.	24	5	8	11	54	71	23
Ilkeston Rangers Res.	24	7	1	16	39	115	22
Beeston Old Boys Res.	24	3	4	17	28	73	13

Division Three–11 Teams–Won by Hucknall Sports Y C
League Cups
Senior
Lady Bay 3, Southwell Amateurs 1
Intermediate
Radcliffe Olympic Res. 4, Old Elizabethans Res. 1
Minor
Hucknall Sports Y C 5, A S C Dayncourt 1
H. B. Poole Trophy
Lady Bay 2, Old Elizabethans 1

RECORDS

Major British Records

HIGHEST WINS

First-Class Match	Arbroath *(Scottish Cup 1st Round)*	36	Bon Accord	0	12 Sept 1885
International Match	England	13	Ireland	0	18 Feb 1882
FA Cup	Preston NE *(1st Round)*	26	Hyde U	0	15 Oct 1887
League Cup	West Ham U *(2nd Round, 2nd Leg)*	10	Bury	0	25 Oct 1983
	Liverpool *(2nd Round, 1st Leg)*	10	Fulham	0	23 Sept 1986

FA PREMIER LEAGUE

	(Home)	Manchester U	9	Ipswich T	0	4 March 1995
	(Away)	Sheffield W	1	Nottingham F	7	1 April 1995

FOOTBALL LEAGUE

Division 1	*(Home)*	WBA	12	Darwen	0	4 April 1892
		Nottingham F	12	Leicester Fosse	0	21 April 1909
	(Away)	Newcastle U	1	Sunderland	9	5 Dec 1908
		Cardiff C	1	Wolverhampton W	9	3 Sept 1955
Division 2	*(Home)*	Newcastle U	13	Newport Co	0	5 Oct 1946
	(Away)	Burslem PV	0	Sheffield U	10	10 Dec 1892
Division 3	*(Home)*	Gillingham	10	Chesterfield	0	5 Sept 1987
	(Away)	Halifax T	0	Fulham	8	16 Sept 1969
Division 3(S)	*(Home)*	Luton T	12	Bristol R	0	13 April 1936
	(Away)	Northampton T	0	Walsall	8	2 Feb 1947
Division 3(N)	*(Home)*	Stockport Co	13	Halifax T	0	6 Jan 1934
	(Away)	Accrington S	0	Barnsley	9	3 Feb 1934
Division 4	*(Home)*	Oldham Ath	11	Southport	0	26 Dec 1962
	(Away)	Crewe Alex	1	Rotherham U	8	8 Sept 1973
Aggregate Division 3(N)		Tranmere R	13	Oldham Ath	4	26 Dec 1935

SCOTTISH LEAGUE

Premier Division	*(Home)*	Aberdeen	8	Motherwell	0	26 March 1979
	(Away)	Hamilton A	0	Celtic	8	5 Nov 1988
Division 1	*(Home)*	Celtic	11	Dundee	0	26 Oct 1895
	(Away)	Airdrieonians	1	Hibernian	11	24 Oct 1950
Division 2	*(Home)*	Airdrieonians	15	Dundee Wanderers	1	1 Dec 1894
	(Away)	Alloa Ath	0	Dundee	10	8 March 1947

LEAGUE CHAMPIONSHIP HAT-TRICKS

Huddersfield T	1923–24 to 1925–26
Arsenal	1932–33 to 1934–35
Liverpool	1981–82 to 1983–84

MOST GOALS FOR IN A SEASON

FA PREMIER LEAGUE		Goals	Games	Season
	Newcastle U	82	42	1993–94
FOOTBALL LEAGUE				
Division 1	Aston V	128	42	1930–31
Division 2	Middlesbrough	122	42	1926–27
Division 3(S)	Millwall	127	42	1927–28
Division 3(N)	Bradford C	128	42	1928–29
Division 3	QPR	111	46	1961–62
Division 4	Peterborough U	134	46	1960–61
SCOTTISH LEAGUE				
Premier Division	Rangers	101	44	1991–92
	Dundee U	90	36	1982–83
	Celtic	90	36	1982–83
	Celtic	90	44	1986–87
Division 1	Hearts	132	34	1957–58
Division 2	Raith R	142	34	1937–38
New Division 1	Dunfermline Ath	93	44	1993–94
	Motherwell	92	39	1981–82
New Division 2	Ayr U	95	39	1987–88
New Division 3	Forfar Ath	74	36	1996–97

FEWEST GOALS FOR IN A SEASON

FA PREMIER LEAGUE		*Goals*	*Games*	*Season*
	Leeds U	28	38	1996–97
FOOTBALL LEAGUE	(minimum 42 games)			
Division 1	Stoke C	24	42	1984–85
Division 2	Watford	24	42	1971–72
	Leyton Orient	30	46	1994–95
Division 3(S)	Crystal Palace	33	42	1950–51
Division 3(N)	Crewe Alex	32	42	1923–24
Division 3	Stockport Co	27	46	1969–70
Division 4	Crewe Alex	29	46	1981–82
SCOTTISH LEAGUE	(minimum 30 games)			
Premier Division	Hamilton A	19	36	1988–89
	Dunfermline Ath	22	44	1991–92
Division 1	Brechin C	30	44	1993–94
	Ayr U	20	34	1966–67
Division 2	Lochgelly U	20	38	1923–24
New Division 1	Stirling Alb	18	39	1980–81
	Dumbarton	23	36	1995–96
New Division 2	Berwick R	22	36	1994–95
New Division 3	Alloa	26	36	1995–96

MOST GOALS AGAINST IN A SEASON

FA PREMIER LEAGUE		*Goals*	*Games*	*Season*
	Swindon T	100	42	1993–94
FOOTBALL LEAGUE				
Division 1	Blackpool	125	42	1930–31
Division 2	Darwen	141	34	1898–99
Division 3(S)	Merthyr T	135	42	1929–30
Division 3(N)	Nelson	136	42	1927–28
Division 3	Accrington S	123	46	1959–60
Division 4	Hartlepools U	109	46	1959–60
SCOTTISH LEAGUE				
Premier Division	Morton	100	36	1984–85
	Morton	100	44	1987–88
Division 1	Leith Ath	137	38	1931–32
Division 2	Edinburgh C	146	38	1931–32
New Division 1	Queen of the S	99	39	1988–89
	Cowdenbeath	109	44	1992–93
New Division 2	Meadowbank T	89	39	1977–78
New Division 3	Albion R	82	36	1994–95

FEWEST GOALS AGAINST IN A SEASON

FA PREMIER LEAGUE		*Goals*	*Games*	*Season*
	Arsenal	28	42	1993–94
	Manchester U	28	42	1994–95
FOOTBALL LEAGUE	(minimum 42 games)			
Division 1	Liverpool	16	42	1978–79
Division 2	Manchester U	23	42	1924–25
	West Ham U	34	46	1990–91
Division 3(S)	Southampton	21	42	1921–22
Division 3(N)	Port Vale	21	46	1953–54
Division 3	Gillingham	20	46	1995–96
Division 4	Lincoln C	25	46	1980–81
SCOTTISH LEAGUE	(minimum 30 games)			
Premier Division	Rangers	19	36	1989–90
	Rangers	23	44	1986–87
	Celtic	23	44	1987–88
Division 1	Celtic	14	38	1913–14
Division 2	Morton	20	38	1966–67
New Division 1	St Johnstone	23	36	1996–97
	Hibernian	24	39	1980–81
	Falkirk	32	44	1993–94
New Division 2	St Johnstone	24	39	1987–88
	Stirling Alb	24	39	1990–91
New Division 3	Brechin C	21	36	1995–96

MOST POINTS IN A SEASON

FOOTBALL LEAGUE	(under old system of two points for a win)	Points	Games	Season
Division 1	Liverpool	68	42	1978–79
Division 2	Tottenham H	70	42	1919–20
Division 3	Aston V	70	46	1971–72
Division 3(S)	Nottingham F	70	46	1950–51
	Bristol C	70	46	1954–55
Division 3(N)	Doncaster R	72	42	1946–47
Division 4	Lincoln C	74	46	1975–76
SCOTTISH LEAGUE				
Premier Division	Aberdeen	59	36	1984–85
	Rangers	73	44	1992–93
Division 1	Rangers	76	42	1920–21
Division 2	Morton	69	38	1966–67
New Division 1	St Mirren	62	39	1976–77
	Falkirk	66	44	1993–94
New Division 2	Forfar Ath	63	39	1983–84
FA PREMIER LEAGUE	(three points for a win)			
	Manchester U	92	42	1993–94
FOOTBALL LEAGUE				
Division 1	Bolton W	98	46	1996–97
	Everton	90	42	1984–85
	Liverpool	90	40	1987–88
Division 2	Chelsea	99	46	1988–89
Division 3	Bournemouth	97	46	1986–87
Division 4	Swindon T	102	46	1985–86
SCOTTISH LEAGUE				
Premier Division	Rangers	87	36	1995–96
New Division 1	St Johnstone	80	36	1996–97
New Division 2	Stirling Alb	81	36	1995–96
New Division 3	Forfar Ath	80	36	1994–95

FEWEST POINTS IN A SEASON

FA PREMIER LEAGUE		Points	Games	Season
	Ipswich T	27	42	1994–95
FOOTBALL LEAGUE	(minimum 34 games)			
Division 1	Stoke C	17	42	1984–85
Division 2	Doncaster R	8	34	1904–05
	Loughborough T	8	34	1899–1900
	Walsall	31	46	1988–89
Division 3	Rochdale	21	46	1973–74
	Cambridge U	21	46	1984–85
Division 3(S)	Merthyr T	21	42	1924–25 & 1929–30
	QPR	21	42	1925–26
Division 3(N)	Rochdale	11	40	1931–32
Division 4	Workington	19	46	1976–77
SCOTTISH LEAGUE	(minimum 30 games)			
Premier Division	St Johnstone	11	36	1975–76
	Morton	16	44	1987–88
Division 1	Stirling Alb	6	30	1954–55
Division 2	Edinburgh C	7	34	1936–37
New Division 1	Queen of the S	10	39	1988–89
	Cowdenbeath	13	44	1992–93
New Division 2	Berwick R	16	39	1987–88
	Stranraer	16	39	1987–88
New Division 3	Albion R	18	36	1994–95

MOST WINS IN A SEASON

FA PREMIER LEAGUE		Wins	Games	Season
	Manchester U	27	42	1993–94
	Blackburn R	27	42	1994–95
FOOTBALL LEAGUE				
Division 1	Tottenham H	31	42	1960–61
Division 2	Tottenham H	32	42	1919–20
Division 3(S)	Millwall	30	42	1927–28
	Plymouth Arg	30	42	1929–30
	Cardiff C	30	42	1946–47
	Nottingham F	30	46	1950–51
	Bristol C	30	46	1954–55

Division 3(N)	Doncaster R	33	42	1946–47
Division 3	Aston V	32	46	1971–72
Division 4	Lincoln C	32	46	1975–76
	Swindon T	32	46	1985–86

SCOTTISH LEAGUE

Premier Division	Rangers	27	36	1995–96
	Aberdeen	27	36	1984–85
	Rangers	33	44	1991–92
	Rangers	33	44	1992–93
Division 1	Rangers	35	42	1920–21
Division 2	Morton	33	38	1966–67
New Division 1	Motherwell	26	39	1981–82
New Division 2	Forfar Ath	27	39	1983–84
	Ayr U	27	39	1987–88
New Division 3	Forfar Ath	25	36	1994–95

RECORD HOME WINS IN A SEASON

Brentford won all 21 games
in Division 3(S), 1929–30

UNDEFEATED AT HOME

Liverpool 85 games (63
League, 9 League Cup, 7
European, 6 FA Cup), Jan
1978–Jan 1981

RECORD AWAY WINS IN A SEASON

Doncaster R won 18
of 21 games in Division 3(N),
1946–47

FEWEST WINS IN A SEASON

FA PREMIER LEAGUE		*Wins*	*Games*	*Season*
	Swindon T	5	42	1993–94
FOOTBALL LEAGUE				
Division 1	Stoke C	3	22	1889–90
	Woolwich Arsenal	3	38	1912–13
	Stoke C	3	42	1984–85
Division 2	Loughborough T	1	34	1899–1900
	Walsall	5	46	1988–89
Division 3(S)	Merthyr T	6	42	1929–30
	QPR	6	42	1925–26
Division 3(N)	Rochdale	4	40	1931–32
Division 3	Rochdale	2	46	1973–74
Division 4	Southport	3	46	1976–77
SCOTTISH LEAGUE				
Premier Division	St Johnstone	3	36	1975–76
	Kilmarnock	3	36	1982–83
	Morton	3	44	1987–88
Division 1	Vale of Leven	0	22	1891–92
Division 2	East Stirlingshire	1	22	1905–06
	Forfar Ath	1	38	1974–75
New Division 1	Queen of the S	2	39	1988–89
	Cowdenbeath	3	44	1992–93
New Division 2	Forfar Ath	4	26	1975–76
	Stranraer	4	39	1987–88
New Division 3	Albion R	5	36	1994–95

MOST DEFEATS IN A SEASON

FA PREMIER LEAGUE		*Defeats*	*Games*	*Season*
	Ipswich T	29	42	1994–95
FOOTBALL LEAGUE				
Division 1	Stoke C	31	42	1984–85
Division 2	Tranmere R	31	42	1938–39
	Chester C	33	46	1992–93
Division 3	Cambridge U	33	46	1984–85
Division 3(S)	Merthyr T	29	42	1924–25
	Walsall	29	46	1952–53
	Walsall	29	46	1953–54

Division 3(N)	Rochdale	33	40	1931–32
Division 4	Newport Co	33	46	1987–88
SCOTTISH LEAGUE				
Premier Division	Morton	29	36	1984–85
Division 1	St Mirren	31	42	1920–21
Division 2	Brechin C	30	36	1962–63
	Lochgelly	30	38	1923–24
New Division 1	Queen of the S	29	39	1988–89
	Dumbarton	31	36	1995–96
	Cowdenbeath	34	44	1992–93
New Division 2	Berwick R	29	39	1987–88
New Division 3	Albion R	28	36	1994–95

HAT-TRICKS

Career 34 Dixie Dean (Tranmere R, Everton, Notts Co, England)
Division 1 (one season post-war) 6 Jimmy Greaves (Chelsea), 1960–61
Three for one team one match
West, Spouncer, Hooper, Nottingham F v Leicester Fosse, Division 1, 21 April 1909
Barnes, Ambler, Davies, Wrexham v Hartlepools U, Division 4, 3 March 1962
Adcock, Stewart, White, Manchester C v Huddersfield T, Division 2, 7 Nov 1987
Loasby, Smith, Wells, Northampton T v Walsall, Division 3S, 5 Nov 1927
Bowater, Hoyland, Readman, Mansfield T v Rotherham U, Division 3N, 27 Dec 1932

FEWEST DEFEATS IN A SEASON
(Minimum 20 games)

		Defeats	*Games*	*Season*
FA PREMIER LEAGUE				
	Manchester U	4	42	1993–94
FOOTBALL LEAGUE				
Division 1	Preston NE	0	22	1888–89
	Arsenal	1	38	1990–91
	Liverpool	2	40	1987–88
	Leeds U	2	42	1968–69
Division 2	Liverpool	0	28	1893–94
	Burnley	2	30	1897–98
	Bristol C	2	38	1905–06
	Leeds U	3	42	1963–64
	Chelsea	5	46	1988–89
Division 3	QPR	5	46	1966–67
	Bristol R	5	46	1989–90
Division 3(S)	Southampton	4	42	1921–22
	Plymouth Arg	4	42	1929–30
Division 3(N)	Port Vale	3	46	1953–54
	Doncaster R	3	42	1946–47
	Wolverhampton W	3	42	1923–24
Division 4	Lincoln C	4	46	1975–76
	Sheffield U	4	46	1981–82
	Bournemouth	4	46	1981–82
SCOTTISH LEAGUE				
Premier Division	Rangers	3	36	1995–96
	Celtic	3	44	1987–88
Division 1	Rangers	0	18	1898–99
	Rangers	1	42	1920–21
Division 2	Clyde	1	36	1956–57
	Morton	1	36	1962–63
	St Mirren	1	36	1967–68
New Division 1	Partick T	2	26	1975–76
	St Mirren	2	39	1976–77
	Raith R	4	44	1992–93
	Falkirk	4	44	1993–94
New Division 2	Raith R	1	26	1975–76
	Clydebank	3	26	1975–76
	Forfar Ath	3	39	1983–84
	Raith R	3	39	1986–87
	Livingston	6	36	1995–96
New Division 3	Forfar Ath	6	36	1994–95
	Inverness T	6	36	1996–97

MOST DRAWN GAMES IN A SEASON

		Draws	*Games*	*Season*
FA PREMIER LEAGUE				
	Manchester C	18	42	1993–94
	Sheffield U	18	42	1993–94
	Southampton	18	42	1994–95
FOOTBALL LEAGUE				
Division 1	Norwich C	23	42	1978–79
Division 4	Exeter C	23	46	1986–87
SCOTTISH LEAGUE				
Premier Division	Aberdeen	21	44	1993–94
New Division 1	East Fife	21	44	1986–87

MOST GOALS IN A GAME

FA PREMIER LEAGUE	Andy Cole (Manchester U) 5 goals v Ipswich T	4 Mar 1995
FOOTBALL LEAGUE		
Division 1	Ted Drake (Arsenal) 7 goals v Aston V	14 Dec 1935
	James Ross (Preston NE) 7 goals v Stoke	6 Oct 1888
Division 2	Tommy Briggs (Blackburn R) 7 goals v Bristol R	5 Feb 1955
	Neville Coleman (Stoke C) 7 goals v Lincoln C (away)	23 Feb 1957
Division 3(S)	Joe Payne (Luton T) 10 goals v Bristol R	13 April 1936
Division 3(N)	Bunny Bell (Tranmere R) 9 goals v Oldham Ath	26 Dec 1935
Division 3	Steve Earle (Fulham) 5 goals v Halifax T	16 Sept 1969
	Barrie Thomas (Scunthorpe U) 5 goals v Luton T	24 April 1965
	Keith East (Swindon T) 5 goals v Mansfield T	20 Nov 1965
	Alf Wood (Shrewsbury T) 5 goals v Blackburn R	2 Oct 1971
	Tony Caldwell (Bolton W) 5 goals v Walsall	10 Sept 1983
	Andy Jones (Port Vale) 5 goals v Newport Co	4 May 1987
	Steve Wilkinson (Mansfield T) 5 goals v Birmingham C	3 April 1990
Division 4	Bert Lister (Oldham Ath) 6 goals v Southport	26 Dec 1962
FA CUP	Ted MacDougall (Bournemouth) 9 goals v Margate (*1st Round*)	20 Nov 1971
LEAGUE CUP	Frankie Bunn (Oldham Ath) 6 goals v Scarborough	25 Oct 1989
SCOTTISH LEAGUE		
Premier Division	Paul Sturrock (Dundee U) 5 goals v Morton	17 Nov 1984
Division 1	Jimmy McGrory (Celtic) 8 goals v Dunfermline Ath	14 Sept 1928
Division 2	Owen McNally (Arthurlie) 8 goals v Armadale	1 Oct 1927
	Jim Dyet (King's Park) 8 goals v Forfar Ath	2 Jan 1930
	John Calder (Morton) 8 goals v Raith R	18 April 1936
	Norman Hayward (Raith R) 8 goals v Brechin C	20 Aug 1937
SCOTTISH CUP	John Petrie (Arbroath) 13 goals v Bon Accord (*1st Round*)	12 Sept 1885

MOST LEAGUE GOALS IN A SEASON

		Goals	*Games*	*Season*
FA PREMIER LEAGUE	Andy Cole (Newcastle U)	34	40	1993–94
	Alan Shearer (Blackburn R)	34	42	1994–95
Division 1	Dixie Dean (Everton)	60	39	1927–28
Division 2	George Camsell (Middlesbrough)	59	37	1926–27
Division 3(S)	Joe Payne (Luton T)	55	39	1936–37
Division 3(N)	Ted Harston (Mansfield T)	55	41	1936–37
Division 3	Derek Reeves (Southampton)	39	46	1959–60
Division 4	Terry Bly (Peterborough U)	52	46	1960–61
FA CUP	Sandy Brown (Tottenham H)	15	8	1900–01
LEAGUE CUP	Clive Allen (Tottenham H)	12	9	1986–87
SCOTTISH LEAGUE				
Division 1	William McFadyen (Motherwell)	52	34	1931–32
Division 2	Jim Smith (Ayr U)	66	38	1927–28

MOST LEAGUE GOALS IN A CAREER

		Goals	*Games*	*Season*
FOOTBALL LEAGUE				
Arthur Rowley	WBA	4	24	1946–48
	Fulham	27	56	1948–50
	Leicester C	251	303	1950–58
	Shrewsbury T	152	236	1958–65
		434	619	
SCOTTISH LEAGUE				
Jimmy McGrory	Celtic	1	3	1922–23
	Clydebank	13	30	1923–24
	Celtic	396	375	1924–38
		410	408	

MOST CUP GOALS IN A CAREER

FA CUP (post-war)

Ian Rush 42 (Chester, Liverpool)
Pre-war: Henry Cursham 48 (Notts Co)

A CENTURY OF LEAGUE AND CUP GOALS IN CONSECUTIVE SEASONS

George Camsell	Middlesbrough	59 Lge	5 Cup	1926–27
(101 goals)		33	4	1927–28
Steve Bull	Wolverhampton W	34 Lge	18 Cup	1987–88
(102 goals)		37	13	1988–89

(Camsell's cup goals were all scored in the FA Cup; Bull had 12 in the Sherpa Van Trophy, 3 Littlewoods Cup, 3 FA Cup in 1987–88; 11 Sherpa Van Trophy, 2 Littlewoods Cup in 1988–89.)

LONGEST SEQUENCE OF CONSECUTIVE SCORING (Individual)

FA PREMIER LEAGUE
Mark Stein (Chelsea)   9 in 7 games   1993–94
FOOTBALL LEAGUE
RECORD
Dixie Dean (Everton)   23 in 12 games   1930–31

LONGEST WINNING SEQUENCE

FOOTBALL LEAGUE		*Games*	*Season*
Division 1	Tottenham H	13	1959–60 (2)
			and 1960–61 (11)
	Preston NE	13	1891–92
	Sunderland	13	1891–92
Division 2	Manchester U	14	1904–05
	Bristol C	14	1905–06
	Preston NE	14	1950–51
Division 3	Reading	13	1985–86
From Season's start			
Division 1	Tottenham H	11	1960–61
Division 3	Reading	13	1985–86

LONGEST WINNING SEQUENCE IN A SEASON

FOOTBALL LEAGUE		*Games*	*Season*
Division 1	Tottenham H	11	1960–61
Division 2	Manchester U	14	1904–05
Division 2	Bristol C	14	1905–06
Division 2	Preston NE	14	1950–51
SCOTTISH LEAGUE			
Division 2	Morton	23	1963–64

LONGEST UNBEATEN SEQUENCE

FOOTBALL LEAGUE		*Games*	*Seasons*
Division 1	Nottingham F	42	Nov 1977–Dec 1978

LONGEST UNBEATEN CUP SEQUENCE

Liverpool   25 rounds   League/Milk Cup   1980–84

LONGEST UNBEATEN SEQUENCE IN A SEASON

FOOTBALL LEAGUE		*Games*	*Season*
Division 1	Burnley	30	1920–21

LONGEST UNBEATEN START TO A SEASON

FOOTBALL LEAGUE		*Games*	*Season*
Division 1	Leeds U	29	1973–74
Division 1	Liverpool	29	1987–88

LONGEST SEQUENCE WITHOUT A WIN IN A SEASON

FOOTBALL LEAGUE		*Games*	*Season*
Division 2	Cambridge U	31	1983–84

LONGEST SEQUENCE WITHOUT A WIN FROM SEASON'S START

Division 1	Sheffield U	16	1990–91

LONGEST SEQUENCE OF CONSECUTIVE DEFEATS

FOOTBALL LEAGUE		*Games*	*Season*
Division 2	Darwen	18	1898–99

GOALKEEPING RECORDS (WITHOUT CONCEDING A GOAL)

British record (all competitive games)
Chris Woods, Rangers, in 1196 minutes from 26 November 1986 to 31 January 1987.

Football League
Steve Death, Reading, 1103 minutes from 24 March to 18 August 1979.

PENALTIES

		Goals	Season
Most in a Season (individual)			
Division 1	Francis Lee (Manchester C)	13	1971–72
Most awarded in one game			
Five	Crystal Palace (4 – 1 scored, 3 missed) v Brighton & HA (1 scored), Div 2		1988–89
Most saved in a Season			
Division 1	Paul Cooper (Ipswich T)	8 (of 10)	1979–80

MOST LEAGUE APPEARANCES (750+ matches)

1005 Peter Shilton (286 Leicester City, 110 Stoke City, 202 Nottingham Forest, 188 Southampton, 175 Derby County, 34 Plymouth Argyle, 1 Bolton Wanderers, 9 Leyton Orient)1966–97
863 Tommy Hutchison (165 Blackpool, 314 Coventry City, 46 Manchester City, 92 Burnley 178 Swansea City, 68 Alloa) 1965–91
824 Terry Paine (713 Southampton, 111 Hereford United) 1957–77
782 Robbie James (484 Swansea C, 48 Stoke C, 87 QPR, 23 Leicester C, 89 Bradford C, 51 Cardiff C)
777 Alan Oakes (565 Manchester C, 211 Chester C, 1 Port Vale) 1959–84
771 John Burridge (27 Workington, 134 Blackpool, 65 Aston Villa, 6 Southend U (loan), 88 Crystal Palace, 39 QPR, 74 Wolverhampton W, 6 Derby Co (loan), 109 Sheffield U, 62 Southampton, 67 Newcastle U, 65 Hibernian, 3 Scarborough, 4 Lincoln C, 3 Aberdeen, 3 Dumbarton, 3 Falkirk, 4 Manchester C, 3 Darlington, 6 Queen of the South) 1968–96
770 John Trollope (all for Swindon Town) 1960–80†
764 Jimmy Dickinson (all for Portsmouth) 1946–65
761 Roy Sproson (all for Port Vale) 1950–72
758 Ray Clemence (48 Scunthorpe United, 470 Liverpool, 240 Tottenham Hotspur) 1966–87
758 Billy Bonds (95 Charlton Ath, 663 West Ham U)
757 Pat Jennings (48 Watford, 472 Tottenham Hotspur, 237 Arsenal) 1963–86
757 Frank Worthington (171 Huddersfield T, 210 Leicester C, 84 Bolton W, 75 Birmingham C, 32 Leeds U, 195 Sunderland, 34 Southampton, 31 Brighton & HA, 59 Tranmere R, 23 Preston NE, 19 Stockport Co) 1966–88
† record for one club

Consecutive
401 Harold Bell (401 Tranmere R; 459 in all games) 1946–55

FA CUP
88 Ian Callaghan (79 Liverpool, 7 Swansea C, 2 Crewe Alex)

Most Senior Matches
1390 Peter Shilton (1005 League, 86 FA Cup, 102 League Cup, 125 Internationals, 13 Under-23, 4 Football League XI, 20 European Cup, 7 Texaco Cup, 5 Simod Cup, 4 European Super Cup, 4 UEFA Cup, 3 Screen Sport Super Cup, 3 Zenith Data Systems Cup, 2 Autoglass Trophy, 2 Charity Shield, 2 Full Members Cup, 1 Anglo-Italian Cup, 1 Football League play-offs, 1 World Club Championship)

MOST FA CUP FINAL GOALS

Ian Rush (Liverpool) 5: 1986(2), 1989(2), 1992(1)

MOST LEAGUE MEDALS

Phil Neal (Liverpool) 8: 1976, 1977, 1979, 1980, 1982, 1983, 1984, 1986

OTHER RECORDS

YOUNGEST PLAYERS
FA Premier League   Neil Finn, 17 years 3 days, West Ham v Manchester C 1.1.96.
FA Premier League scorer   Andy Turner, 17 years 166 days, Tottenham H v Everton, 5.9.92.
Football League   Albert Geldard, 15 years 158 days, Bradford Park Avenue v Millwall, Division 2, 16.9.29; and Ken Roberts, 15 years 158 days, Wrexham v Bradford Park Avenue, Division 3N, 1.9.51
Football League scorer
   Ronnie Dix, 15 years 180 days, Bristol Rovers v Norwich City, Division 3S, 3.3.28.
Division 1
   Derek Forster, 15 years 185 days, Sunderland v Leicester City, 22.8.84.
Division 1 scorer
   Jason Dozzell, 16 years 57 days as substitute Ipswich Town v Coventry City, 4.2.84
Division 1 hat-tricks
   Alan Shearer, 17 years 240 days, Southampton v Arsenal, 9.4.88
   Jimmy Greaves, 17 years 10 months, Chelsea v Portsmouth, 25.12.57
FA Cup (any round)
   Andy Awford, 15 years 88 days as substitute Worcester City v Boreham Wood, 3rd Qual. rd, 10.10.87
FA Cup proper
   Scott Endersby, 15 years 288 days, Kettering v Tilbury, 1st rd, 26.11.77
FA Cup Final
   James Prinsep, 17 years 245 days, Clapham Rovers v Old Etonians, 1879

FA Cup Final scorer
 Norman Whiteside, 18 years 18 days, Manchester United v Brighton & Hove Albion, 1983
FA Cup Final captain
 David Nish, 21 years 212 days, Leicester City v Manchester City, 1969
League Cup Final scorer
 Norman Whiteside, 17 years 324 days, Manchester United v Liverpool, 1983
League Cup Final captain
 Barry Venison, 20 years 7 months 8 days, Sunderland v Norwich City, 1985
OLDEST PLAYERS
Football League
 Neil McBain, 52 years 4 months, New Brighton v Hartlepools United, Div 3N, 15.3.47 (McBain was New Brighton's manager and had to play in an emergency)
Division 1
 Stanley Matthews, 50 years 5 days, Stoke City v Fulham, 6.2.65
FA Cup Final
 Walter Hampson, 41 years 8 months, Newcastle United v Aston Villa, 1924
FA Cup
 Billy Meredith, 49 years 8 months, Manchester City v Newcastle United, 29.3.24
International debutant
 Leslie Compton, 38 years 2 months, England v Wales, 15.11.50
International
 Billy Meredith, 45 years 229 days, Wales v England, 15.3 20

SENDINGS-OFF

Season	314 (League alone)	1994–95
Day	15 (3 League, 12 FA Cup*)	20 Nov 1982
	worst overall FA Cup total	
League	13	14 Dec 1985
Weekend	15	22/23 Dec 1990
FA Cup Final	Kevin Moran, Manchester U v Everton	1985
Other Wembley	Boris Stankovic, Yugoslavia v Sweden (Olympics)	1948
	Antonio Rattin, Argentina v England (World Cup)	1966
	Billy Bremner (Leeds U) and Kevin Keegan (Liverpool), Charity Shield	1974
	Gilbert Dresch, Luxembourg v England (World Cup)	1977
	Mike Henry, Sudbury T v Tamworth (FA Vase)	1989
	Jason Cook, Colchester U v Witton Alb (FA Vase)	1992
	Lee Dixon, Arsenal v Tottenham H (FA Cup semi-final)	1993
	Peter Swan, Port Vale v WBA (play-offs)	1993
	Andrei Kanchelskis, Manchester U v Aston Villa (Coca-Cola Cup Final)	1994
	Michael Wallace and Chris Beaumont (both Stockport Co) v Burnley (play-offs)	1994
	Tetsuji Hashiratani, Japan v England (Umbro Cup)	1995
	Derek Ward, Northwich Vic v Macclesfield T (FA Trophy)	1996
	Tony Rogers, Dagenham & Redbridge v Woking (FA Trophy)	1997
	Brian Statham, Brentford v Crewe Alex (play-offs)	1997
Quickest	Mark Smith, Crewe Alex v Darlington (away) Div 3: 19 secs	12 March 1994
Division 1	Liam O'Brien, Manchester U v Southampton (away): 85 secs	3 Jan 1987
World Cup	Jose Batista, Uruguay v Scotland, Neza, Mexico (World Cup): 55 secs	13 June 1986
Most one game	Four: Northampton T (0) v Hereford U (4) Div 3	11 Nov 1992
	Four: Crewe Alex (2) v Bradford PA (2) Div 3N	8 Jan 1955
	Four: Sheffield U (1) v Portsmouth (3) Div 2	13 Dec 1986
	Four: Port Vale (2) v Northampton T (2) Littlewoods Cup	18 Aug 1987
	Four: Brentford (2) v Mansfield T (2) Div 3	12 Dec 1987

RECORD ATTENDANCES

FA Premier League	55,269	Manchester U v Southampton	1.2.97
Football League	83,260	Manchester U v Arsenal, Maine Road	17.1.1948
Scottish League	118,567	Rangers v Celtic, Ibrox Stadium	2.1.1939
FA Cup Final	126,047*	Bolton W v West Ham U, Wembley	28.4.1923
European Cup	135,826	Celtic v Leeds U, semi-final at Hampden Park	15.4.1970
Scottish Cup	146,433	Celtic v Aberdeen, Hampden Park	24.4.37
World Cup	199,854†	Brazil v Uruguay, Maracana, Rio	16.7.50

* It has been estimated that as many as 70,000 more broke in without paying.
† 173,830 paid.

IMPORTANT ADDRESSES

The Football Association: R. H. G. Kelly, F.C.I.S., 16 Lancaster Gate, London W2 3LW. *0171 262 4542*

Scotland: J. Farry, 6 Park Gardens, Glasgow G3 7YE. *0141-332 6372*

Northern Ireland (Irish FA): D. I. Bowen, 20 Windsor Avenue, Belfast BT9 6EG. *01232 669458*

Wales: A. Evans, 3 Westgate Street, Cardiff, South Glamorgan CF1 1JF. *01222 372325*

Republic of Ireland (FA of Ireland): 80 Merrion Square South, Dublin 2. *00353 16766864*

International Federation (FIFA): S. Blatter, P. O. Box 85 8030 Zurich, Switzerland. *00 411 384 9595. Fax: 00 411 384 9696*

Union of European Football Associations: G. Aigner, Chemin de la Redoute 54, Case Postale 303 CH-1260 Nyon, Switzerland. *01041 22 994 44 44. Fax: 0041 22 994 44 88*

THE LEAGUES

The Premier League: P. Leaver, 16 Lancaster Gate, London W2 3LW. *0171-262 4542*

The Football League: J. D. Dent, F.C.I.S., The Football League, Lytham St Annes, Lancs FY8 1JG. *01253-729421. Telex 67675*

The Scottish League: P. Donald, 188 West Regent Street, Glasgow G2 4RY. *0141-248 3844*

The Irish League: H. Wallace, 87 University Street, Belfast BT7 1HP. *01232 242888*

Football League of Ireland: E. Morris, 80 Merrion Square South, Dublin 2. *003531 765120*

Vauxhall Conference: J. A. Moules, Collingwood House, Schooner Court, Crossways, Dartford DA2 6QQ. *01322 303120*

Central League: A. Williamson, The Football League, Lytham St Annes, Lancs FY8 1JG. *01253 729421*

North West Counties League: M. Darby, 87 Hillary Road, Hyde, Cheshire SK14 4EB.

Eastern Counties League: C. Lamb, 26 Dunthorpe Road, Clacton, Essex CO12 8UJ. *01255 436398*

Football Combination: N. Chamberlain, 2 Vicarage Close, Old Costessey, Norwich NR8 5DL. *10603 743998*

Hellenic League: B. King, 83 Queens Road, Carterton, Oxon OX18 3YF. *01793 493502*

Kent League: R. Vinter, The Thatched Barn, Lower Hardres, Canterbury, Kent CT4 5PG

Lancashire Amateur League: R. G. Bowker, 13 Shores Green Drive, Wincham, Northwich, Cheshire CW9 6EE. *0161-480 7723*

Lancashire Football League: J. W. Howarth, 465 Whalley Road, Clapton-le-Moors, Accrington, Lancs BB5 5RP. *01254 398957*

Leicestershire Senior League: R. J. Holmes, 8 Huntsman Close, Markfield, Leics LE67 9EX. *01530 243093*

London Spartan: D. Cordell, 44 Greenleas, Waltham Abbey, Essex EN9 1SZ. *01992 712428*

Manchester League: J. A. Warrington, 17 Broadacre, Mottram Rise, Stalybridge, Cheshire SK15 2TX. *01457 764427*

Midland Combination: N. Harvey, 115 Millfield Road, Handsworth Wood, Birmingham B20 1ED. *0121 357 4172*

Mid-Week Football League: N. A. S. Matthews, Cedar Court, Steeple Aston, Oxford. *01869 40347*

Northern Premier: R. D. Bayley, 22 Woburn Drive, Hale, Altrincham, Cheshire WA15 8LZ. *0161-980 7007*

Northern Intermediate League: G. Thompson, Clegg House, 253 Pitsmoor Road, Sheffield S3 9AQ. *01742 27817*

Northern League: J. H. McLackland, 92 Appletree Gardens, Walkerville NE6 4SX

North Midlands League: G. Thompson, 7 Wren Park Close, Ridgway, Sheffield.

Peterborough and District League: M. J. Croson, 44 Storrington Way, Werrington, Peterborough, Cambs PE4 6QP.

Isthmian League: N. Robinson, 226 Rye Lane, Peckham SE15 4NL. *0181 409 1978. Fax: 0181 409 1979*

Southern Amateur League: S. J. Lucas, 23 Beaufort Close, North Weald Bassett, Epping, Essex CM16 6JZ. *0137882 3932*

South-East Counties League: A. Leather, 66 Green Acres, Chichester Road, Croydon, Surrey CR0 5UX. *0181-681 7100*

Southern League: D. J. Strudwick, 11 Welland Close, Durrington, Worthing, West Sussex BN13 3NR. *01903 267788*

South Midlands League: M. Mitchell, 26 Leighton Court, Dunstable, Beds LU6 1EW. *01582 667291*

South Western League: M. Goodenough, Rose Cottage, Horrelsford, Milton Damerel, Holsworthy, Devon EX22 7NJ. *01409 261402*

United Counties League: R. Gamble, 8 Bostock Avenue, Northampton. *01604 37766*

Wearside League: B. Robson, 12 Deneside, Howden-le-Wear, Crook, Co. Durham DL15 8JR. *01388 762034*

Western League: M. E. Washer, 16 Heathfield Road, Nailsea, Bristol BS19 1EB.

The Welsh League: K. J. Tucker, 16 The Parade, Merthyr Tydfil, Mid Glamorgan CF47 0ET. *01685 723884*

West Midlands Regional League: N. R. Juggins, 14 Badger Way, Blackwell, Bromsgrove, Worcs B60 1EX.

West Yorkshire League: W. Keyworth, 2 Hill Court Grove, Bramley, Yorks L13 2AP. *0113 74465*

Northern Counties (East): B. Wood, 6 Restmore Avenue, Guiseley, Nr Leeds LS20 9DG. *01943 874558*

COUNTY FOOTBALL ASSOCIATIONS

Bedfordshire: P. D. Brown, Century House, Skimpot Road, Dunstable, Beds LU5 4JU. *01582 565111*

Berks and Bucks: B. G. Moore, 15a London Street, Faringdon, Oxon SN7 7HD. *01367 242099*

Birmingham County: M. Pennick, County FA Offices, Rayhall Lane, Great Barr, Birmingham B43 6JF. *0121 357 4278*

Cambridgeshire: A. K. Pawley, 3 Signet Court, Swanns Road, Cambridge CB5 8LA. *01223 576770*

Cheshire: A. Collins, The Cottage, Hartford Moss Rec Centre, Winnington, Northwich CW8 4BG.

Cornwall: B. Cudmore, 14 High Cross Street, St. Austell, Cornwall PL25 4AB. *01726 74080*

Cumberland: J. A. Murphy, 17 Oxford Street, Workington, Cumbria CA14 2AL. *01900 872310*

Derbyshire: K. Compton, The Grandstand, Moorways Stadium, Moor Lane, Derby DE2 8FB. *01332 361422*

Devon County: C. Squirrel, County HQ, Coach Road, Newton Abbot, Devon TQ12 1EJ. *01626 332077*

Dorset County: P. Hough, County Ground, Blandford Close, Hamsworthy, Poole, Dorset BH15 4BF. *01202 682375*

Durham: J. Topping, 'Codeslaw', Ferens Park, Durham DH1 1JZ. *0191 3848653*

East Riding County: D. R. Johnson, 52 Bethune Ave, Hull HU4 7EJ. *01482 641458*

Essex County: P. Sammons, 31 Mildmay Road, Chelmsford, Essex CM2 0DN. *01245 357727*

Gloucestershire: P. Britton, Oaklands Park, Almondsbury, Bristol BS12 4AG. *01454 615888*

Guernsey: D. Dorey, Haut Regard, St. Clair Hill, St. Sampson's, Guernsey, GY2 4DT, CI. *01481 46231*

Hampshire: R. G. Barnes, 8 Ashwood Gardens, off Winchester Road, Southampton SO16 7PW. *01703 791110*

Herefordshire: J. S. Lambert, Muirfield Close, Holmer, Hereford HR1 1QB. *01432 270308*

Hertfordshire: R. G. Kibble, Marquis House, 68 Great North Road, Hatfield, Herts AL9 5ER. *01707 256891*

Huntingdonshire: M. M. Armstrong, 1 Chapel End, Great Giddings, Huntingdon, Cambs PE17 5NP. *01832 293262*

Isle of Man: Mrs A. Garrett, P.O. Box 53, The Bowl, Douglas IOM IM99 1GY. *01624 615576*

Jersey: S. Monks, Rocqueberg View, La Rue De Samares, St. Clement, Jersey JE2 6LS

Kent County: K. T. Masters, 69 Maidstone Road, Chatham, Kent ME4 6DT. *01634 843824*

Lancashire: J. Kenyon, 31a Wellington St, St John's, Blackburn, Lancs BB1 8AU. *01254 264333*

Leicestershire and Rutland: R. E. Barston, Holmes Park, Dog and Gun Lane, Whetstone, Leicester LE8 3LJ. *0116 2867828*

Lincolnshire: J. Griffin, PO Box 26, 12 Dean Road, Lincoln LN2 4DP. *01522 524917*

Liverpool County: F. L. J. Hunter, 23 Greenfield Road, Old Swann, Liverpool L13 3BN. *0151-220 6089*

London: D. Fowkes, Aldworth Grove, London SE13 6HY. *0181 690 9626*

Manchester County: P. Smith, Brantingham Road, Chorlton, Manchester M21 0TT. *0161-881 0299*

Middlesex County: P. J. Clayton, 39 Roxborough Road, Harrow, Middx HA1 1NS. *0181 424 8524*

Norfolk County: R. J. Howlett, 153 Middleton Lane, Hellesdon, Norwich, Norfolk NR6 5SF. *01603 488222*

Northamptonshire: B. Walden, 2 Duncan Close, Moulton Park, Northampton NN3 6WL. *01604 670741*

North Riding County: M. Jarvis, 284 Linthorpe Road, Middlesbrough TS1 3QU. *01642 224585*

Northumberland: R. E. Maughan, Seymour House, 10 Brenkley Way, Blezard Bus Park, Seaton Burn, Newcastle upon Tyne NE13 6DT. *0191 236 8020*

Nottinghamshire: W. T. Annable, 7 Clarendon Street, Nottingham NG1 5HS. *0115 9418954*

Oxfordshire: P. J. Ladbrook, 3 Wilkins Road, Cowley, Oxford OX4 2HY. *01865 775432*

Sheffield and Hallamshire: G. Thompson, Clegg House, 5 Onslow Road, Sheffield S11 7AF. *011422 670068*

Shropshire: A. W. Brett, 5 Ebnal Road, Shrewsbury SY2 6PW. *01743 236145*

Somerset & Avon (South): Mrs H. Marchment, 30 North Road, Midsomer Norton, Bath BA3 2QD. *01761 410280*

Staffordshire: B. J. Adshead, County Showground, Weston Road, Stafford ST18 0DB. *01785 256994*

Suffolk County: W. M. Steward, 2 Millfields, Haughley, Stowmarket, Suffolk IP14 3PU. *01449 673481*

Surrey County: A. P. Adams, 321 Kingston Road, Leatherhead, Surrey KT22 7TU. *01372 373543*

Sussex County: D. M. Worsfold, County Office, Culver Road, Lancing, Sussex BN15 9AX. *01903 753547*

Westmorland: P. G. Ducksbury, 1 Dalton Road, Kendal LA9 6AG. *01539 730946*

West Riding County: R. Carter, Fleet Lane, Woodlesford, Leeds LS26 8NX. *0113 2821222*

Wiltshire: E. M. Parry, 44 Kennet Avenue, Swindon SN2 3LG. *01793 529036*

Worcestershire: M. R. Leggett Fermain, 12 Worcester Road, Evesham, Worcs WR11 4JU. *01905 612336*

OTHER USEFUL ADDRESSES

Amateur Football Alliance: W. P. Goss, 55 Islington Park Street, London N1 1QB. *0171-359 3493*

English Schools FA: M. R. Berry, 1/2 Eastgate Street, Stafford ST16 2NN. *01785 51142*

Oxford University: M. H. Matthews, University College, Oxford OX1 4BH.

Cambridge University: Dr J. A. Little, St Catherine's College, Cambridge CB2 1RL.

Army: Major T. C. Knight ASCB (MOD), Clayton Barracks, Aldershot, Hants GU11 2BG. *01252 348571/4*

Royal Air Force: WG CDR W. E. Mahon, BA, RAF, SM 88 (RAF) Palmer Pavilion, Room V028, P. O. Box 69, RAF Wyton, Huntingdon, Cambs PE17 2DL. *01480 52451 Ex 4628*

Royal Navy: Lt-Cdr J. Danks, R.N. Sports Office, H.M.S. Temeraire, Portsmouth, Hants PO1 2HB. *01705 722671*

British Universities Sports Association: G. Gregory-Jones, Chief Executive: BUSA, 8 Union Street, London SE1 1SZ. *0171-357 8555*

Central Council of Physical Recreation: General Secretary, 70 Brompton Road, London SW3 1HE. *0171-584 6651*

British Olympic Association: 6 John Prince's Street, London W1M 0DH. *0171-408 2029*

National Federation of Football Supporters' Clubs: Chairman: Tony Kershaw, 87 Brookfield Avenue, Loughborough, Leicestershire LE11 3LN. *01509 267643 (and fax)*. National Secretary: Mark Agate, "The Stadium", 14 Coombe Close, Lordswood, Chatham, Kent ME5 8NU. *01634 319461 (and fax)*

National Playing Fields Association: Col R. Satterthwaite, O.B.E., 578b Catherine Place, London, SW1.

The Scottish Football Commercial Managers Association: J. E. Hillier (Chairman), c/o Keith FC Promotions Office, 60 Union Street, Keith, Banffshire, Scotland.

Professional Footballers' Association: G. Taylor, 2 Oxford Court, Bishopsgate, Off Lower Mosley Street, Manchester M2 3WQ. *0161-236 0575*

Referees' Association: A. Smith, 1 Westhill Road, Coundon, Coventry CV6 2AD *01203 601701*

Women's Football Alliance: Miss K. Simmons, 9 Wyllyotts Place, Potters Bar, Herts EN6 2JD. *01707 651840*

Institute of Football Management and Administration: Olaf Dixon, 1^ Chapel Court, Holly Walk, Leamington Spa, Warwickshire CV32 4YS. *01926 882313. Fax: 01926 886829*

Football Administrators Association: as above.

Commercial and Marketing Managers Association: as above.

Management Statts Association: as above.

League Managers Association: as above.

The Association of Football Statisticians: R. J. Spiller, 22 Bretons, Basildon, Essex SS15 5BY. *01268 416020*

The Football Programme Directory: David Stacey, 'The Beeches', 66 Southend Road, Wickford, Essex SS11 8EN. *01268 732041 (and fax)*

England Football Supporters Association: Publicity Officer, David Stacey, 'The Beeches', 66 Southend Road, Wickford, Essex SS11 8EN. *01268 732041 (and fax)*

The Football League Executive Staffs Association: PO Box 52, Leamington Spa, Warwickshire.

The Ninety-Two Club: 104 Gilda Crescent, Whitchurch, Bristol BS14 9LD.

Scottish 38 Club: Mark Byatt, 6 Greenfields Close, Loughton, Essex IG10 3HG. *0181-508 6088*

The Football Trust: Second Floor, Walkden House, 10 Melton Street, London NW1 2EJ. *0171-388 4504*

The Football Supporters' Association: PO Box 11, Liverpool L26 1XP. *0151-709 2594*

Association of Provincial Football Supporters' Clubs in London: Ian D. Todd, 8 Wyke Close, Isleworth, Middx TW7 5PE. *0181-847 2905 (and fax)*

World Association of Friends of English Football: PO Box 2221, D-30022 Hannover, Germany. *0049 511 885616*

Football Postcard Collectors Club: PRO: Bryan Horsnell, 275 Overdown Road, Tilehurst, Reading RG3 6NX. *01734 424448*

UK Programme Collectors Club: Secretary, John Litster, 46 Milton Road, Kirkcaldy, Fife KY1 1TL. *01592 268718. Fax: 01592 595069*

Programme Monthly: as above.

Scottish Football Historians Association: as above.

FOOTBALL AWARDS 1996–97

FOOTBALLER OF THE YEAR

The Football Writers' Association Award for the Footballer of the Year went to Gianfranco Zola of Chelsea and Italy.

Past Winners
1947–48 Stanley Matthews (Blackpool); 1948–49 Johnny Carey (Manchester U); 1949–50 Joe Mercer (Arsenal); 1950–51 Harry Johnston (Blackpool); 1951–52 Billy Wright (Wolverhampton W); 1952–53 Nat Lofthouse (Bolton W); 1953–54 Tom Finney (Preston NE); 1954–55 Don Revie (Manchester C); 1955–56 Bert Trautmann (Manchester C); 1956–57 Tom Finney (Preston NE); 1957–58 Danny Blanchflower (Tottenham H); 1958–59 Syd Owen (Luton T); 1959–60 Bill Slater (Wolverhampton W); 1960–61 Danny Blanchflower (Tottenham H); 1961–62 Jimmy Adamson (Burnley); 1962–63 Stanley Matthews (Stoke C); 1963–64 Bobby Moore (West Ham U); 1964–65 Bobby Collins (Leeds U); 1965–66 Bobby Charlton (Manchester U); 1966–67 Jackie Charlton (Leeds U); 1967–68 George Best (Manchester U); 1968–69 Dave Mackay (Derby Co) shared with Tony Book (Manchester C); 1969–70 Billy Bremner (Leeds U); 1970–71 Frank McLintock (Arsenal); 1971–72 Gordon Banks (Stoke C); 1972–73 Pat Jennings (Tottenham H); 1973–74 Ian Callaghan (Liverpool); 1974–75 Alan Mullery (Fulham); 1975–76 Kevin Keegan (Liverpool); 1976–77 Emlyn Hughes (Liverpool); 1977–78 Kenny Burns (Nottingham F); 1978–79 Kenny Dalglish (Liverpool); 1979–80 Terry McDermott (Liverpool); 1980–81 Frans Thijssen (Ipswich T); 1981–82 Steve Perryman (Tottenham H); 1982–83 Kenny Dalglish (Liverpool); 1983–84 Ian Rush (Liverpool); 1984–85 Neville Southall (Everton); 1985–86 Gary Lineker (Everton); 1986–87 Clive Allen (Tottenham H); 1987–88 John Barnes (Liverpool); 1988–89 Steve Nicol (Liverpool); 1989–90 John Barnes (Liverpool); 1990–91 Gordon Strachan (Leeds U); 1991–92 Gary Lineker (Tottenham H); 1992–93 Chris Waddle (Sheffield W); 1993–94 Alan Shearer (Blackburn R); 1994–95 Jurgen Klinsmann (Tottenham H); 1995–96 Eric Cantona (Manchester U).

THE PFA AWARDS 1997

Player of the Year: Alan Shearer (Newcastle U).
Previous Winners: 1974 Norman Hunter (Leeds U); 1975 Colin Todd (Derby Co); 1976 Pat Jennings (Tottenham H); 1977 Andy Gray (Aston Villa); 1978 Peter Shilton (Nottingham F); 1979 Liam Brady (Arsenal); 1980 Terry McDermott (Liverpool); 1981 John Wark (Ipswich T); 1982 Kevin Keegan (Southampton); 1983 Kenny Dalglish (Liverpool); 1984 Ian Rush (Liverpool); 1985 Peter Reid (Everton); 1986 Gary Lineker (Everton); 1987 Clive Allen (Tottenham H); 1988 John Barnes (Liverpool); 1989 Mark Hughes (Manchester U); 1990 David Platt (Aston Villa); 1991 Mark Hughes (Manchester U); 1992 Gary Pallister (Manchester U); 1993 Paul McGrath (Aston Villa); 1994 Eric Cantona (Manchester U); 1995 Alan Shearer (Blackburn R); 1996 Les Ferdinand (Newcastle U).

Young Player of the Year: David Beckham (Manchester U).
Previous Winners: 1974 Kevin Beattie (Ipswich T); 1975 Mervyn Day (West Ham U); 1976 Peter Barnes (Manchester C); 1977 Andy Gray (Aston Villa); 1978 Tony Woodcock (Nottingham F); 1979 Cyrille Regis (WBA); 1980 Glenn Hoddle (Tottenham H); 1981 Gary Shaw (Aston Villa); 1982 Steve Moran (Southampton); 1983 Ian Rush (Liverpool); 1984 Paul Walsh (Luton T); 1985 Mark Hughes (Manchester U); 1986 Tony Cottee (West Ham U); 1987 Tony Adams (Arsenal); 1988 Paul Gascoigne (Tottenham H); 1989 Paul Merson (Arsenal); 1990 Matthew Le Tissier (Southampton); 1991 Lee Sharpe (Manchester U); 1992 Ryan Giggs (Manchester U); 1993 Ryan Giggs (Manchester U); 1994 Andy Cole (Newcastle U); 1995 Robbie Fowler (Liverpool); 1996 Robbie Fowler (Liverpool).

Merit Award: Peter Beardsley (Newcastle U).
Previous Winners: 1974 Bobby Charlton CBE, Cliff Lloyd OBE; 1975 Denis Law; 1976 George Eastham OBE; 1977 Jack Taylor OBE; 1978 Bill Shankly OBE; 1979 Tom Finney OBE; 1980 Sir Matt Busby CBE; 1981 John Trollope MBE; 1982 Joe Mercer OBE; 1983 Bob Paisley OBE; 1984 Bill Nicholson; 1985 Ron Greenwood; 1986 The 1966 England World Cup team, Sir Alf Ramsey, Harold Shepherdson; 1987 Sir Stanley Matthews; 1988 Billy Bonds MBE; 1989 Nat Lofthouse; 1990 Peter Shilton; 1991 Tommy Hutchison; 1992 Brian Clough; 1993 the 1968 Manchester United team; 1994 Billy Bingham; 1995 Gordon Strachan; 1996 Pelé.

THE SCOTTISH PFA AWARDS 1997

Player of the Year: Paolo Di Canio (Celtic).
Previous Winners: 1978 Derek Johnstone (Rangers); 1979 Paul Hegarty (Dundee U); 1980 Davie Provan (Celtic); 1981 Sandy Clark (Airdrieonians); 1982 Mark McGhee (Aberdeen); 1983 Charlie Nicholas (Celtic); 1984 Willie Miller (Aberdeen); 1985 Jim Duffy (Morton); 1986 Richard Gough (Dundee U); 1987 Brian McClair (Celtic); 1988 Paul McStay (Celtic); 1989 Theo Snelders (Aberdeen); 1990 Jim Bett (Aberdeen); 1991 Paul Elliott (Celtic); 1993 Ally McCoist (Rangers); 1993 Andy Goram (Rangers); 1994 Mark Hateley (Rangers); 1995 Brian Laudrup (Rangers); 1996 Paul Gascoigne (Rangers).
Young Player of the Year: Alex Burke (Kilmarnock).
Previous Winners: 1978 Graeme Payne (Dundee U); 1979 Graham Stewart (Dundee U); 1980 John MacDonald (Rangers); 1981 Francis McAvennie (St Mirren); 1982 Charlie Nicholas (Celtic); 1983 Pat Nevin (Clyde); 1984 John Robertson (Hearts); 1985 Craig Levein (Hearts); 1986 Craig Levein (Hearts); 1987 Robert Fleck (Rangers); 1988 John Collins (Hibernian); 1989 Bill McKinlay (Dundee U); 1990 Scott Crabbe (Hearts); 1991 Eoin Jess (Aberdeen); 1992 Phil O'Donnell (Motherwell); 1993 Eoin Jess (Aberdeen); 1994 Phil O'Donnell (Motherwell); 1995 Charlie Miller (Rangers); 1996 Jackie McNamara (Celtic).

SCOTTISH FOOTBALL WRITERS' ASSOCIATION

Player of the Year 1997 – Brian Laudrup (Rangers)

1965	Billy McNeill (Celtic)	1981	Alan Rough (Partick Th)
1966	John Greig (Rangers)	1982	Paul Sturrock (Dundee U)
1967	Ronnie Simpson (Celtic)	1983	Charlie Nicholas (Celtic)
1968	Gordon Wallace (Raith R)	1984	Willie Miller (Aberdeen)
1969	Bobby Murdoch (Celtic)	1985	Hamish McAlpine (Dundee U)
1970	Pat Stanton (Hibernian)	1986	Sandy Jardine (Hearts)
1971	Martin Buchan (Aberdeen)	1987	Brian McClair (Celtic)
1972	Dave Smith (Rangers)	1988	Paul McStay (Celtic)
1973	George Connelly (Celtic)	1989	Richard Gough (Rangers)
1974	Scotland's World Cup Squad	1990	Alex McLeish (Aberdeen)
1975	Sandy Jardine (Rangers)	1991	Maurice Malpas (Dundee U)
1976	John Greig (Rangers)	1992	Ally McCoist (Rangers)
1977	Danny McGrain (Celtic)	1993	Andy Goram (Rangers)
1978	Derek Johnstone (Rangers)	1994	Mark Hateley (Rangers)
1979	Andy Ritchie (Morton)	1995	Brian Laudrup (Rangers)
1980	Gordon Strachan (Aberdeen)	1996	Paul Gascoigne (Rangers)

EUROPEAN FOOTBALLER OF THE YEAR 1996

Matthias Sammer (Borussia Dortmund), captain of the 1997 European Cup winners, was originally capped by the now non-existent East Germany, before being honoured at full level by Germany, whom he led to the 1996 European Championship.
Past winners

1956	**Stanley Matthews** (Blackpool)	1977	**Allan Simonsen** (Borussia Moenchengladbach)
1957	**Alfredo Di Stefano** (Real Madrid)		
1958	**Raymond Kopa** (Real Madrid)	1978	**Kevin Keegan** (SV Hamburg)
1959	**Alfredo Di Stefano** (Real Madrid)	1979	**Kevin Keegan** (SV Hamburg)
1960	**Luis Suarez** (Barcelona)	1980	**Karl-Heinz Rummenigge** (Bayern Munich)
1961	**Omar Sivori** (Juventus)		
1962	**Josef Masopust** (Dukla Prague)	1981	**Karl-Heinz Rummenigge** (Bayern Munich)
1963	**Lev Yashin** (Moscow Dynamo)		
1964	**Denis Law** (Manchester United)	1982	**Paolo Rossi** (Juventus)
1965	**Eusebio** (Benfica)	1983	**Michel Platini** (Juventus)
1966	**Bobby Charlton** (Manchester United)	1984	**Michel Platini** (Juventus)
1967	**Florian Albert** (Ferencvaros)	1985	**Michel Platini** (Juventus)
1968	**George Best** (Manchester United)	1986	**Igor Belanov** (Dynamo Kiev)
1969	**Gianni Rivera** (AC Milan)	1987	**Ruud Gullit** (AC Milan)
1970	**Gerd Muller** (Bayern Munich)	1988	**Marco Van Basten** (AC Milan)
1971	**Johan Cruyff** (Ajax)	1989	**Marco Van Basten** (AC Milan)
1972	**Franz Beckenbauer** (Bayern Munich)	1990	**Lothar Matthaus** (Inter-Milan)
1973	**Johan Cruyff** (Barcelona)	1991	**Jean-Pierre Papin** (Marseille)
1974	**Johan Cruyff** (Barcelona)	1992	**Marco Van Basten** (AC Milan)
1975	**Oleg Blokhin** (Dynamo Kiev)	1993	**Roberto Baggio** (Juventus)
1976	**Franz Beckenbauer** (Bayern Munich)	1994	**Hristo Stoichkov** (Barcelona)
		1995	**George Weah** (AC Milan)

WORLD PLAYER OF THE YEAR

Ronaldo (Barcelona) the Brazilian international striker was overwhelmingly voted FIFA world player of the year for 1996 with 329 points. The runner-up was Liberian international **George Weah** (AC Milan) with 140, whilst Newcastle United's England international **Alan Shearer** came third with 123.

THE CARLING AWARDS WINNERS 1996–97

The Carling No. 1 Awards

The month-by-month guide to the Carling Premiership's top performing players and managers.

Carling Manager of the Month

August	David Pleat	Sheffield Wednesday
September	Joe Kinnear	Wimbledon
October	Graeme Souness	Southampton
November	Jim Smith	Derby County
December	Gordon Strachan	Coventry City
January	Stuart Pearce	Nottingham Forest
February	Alex Ferguson	Manchester United
March	Bryan Robson	Middlesbrough
April	Graeme Souness	Southampton
Carling Manager of the Season	**Alex Ferguson**	**Manchester United**

Carling Player of the Month

August	David Beckham	Manchester United
September	Patrik Berger	Liverpool
October	Matt Le Tissier	Southampton
November	Ian Wright	Arsenal
December	Gianfranco Zola	Chelsea
January	Tim Flowers	Blackburn Rovers
February	Robbie Earle	Wimbledon
March	Juninho	Middlesbrough
April	Mickey Evans	Southampton
Carling Player of the Season	**Juninho**	**Middlesbrough**

(Carling Sponsors of the Football Writers Association)

Carling No. 1 Awards
Awarded for outstanding contributions to the national game.

Peter Shilton, for achieving a record of 1000 League appearances during his distinguished career.
John Motson, in recognition for his 25 years as a BBC TV commentator.
Tony Parkes, for his work as caretaker/manager of Blackburn Rovers.

NATIONAL FEDERATION OF FOOTBALL SUPPORTERS' CLUBS

Supporters' concerns about varying interpretations of their responsibilities by local police commanders are reflected in the adoption of a motion at the Federation's conference to ensure the provisions of the House of Commons 1990–91 report on Policing Football Hooliganism are followed through. Discussions will take place with the Association of Chief Police Officers and the Football Licensing Authority *"with the aim of preparing a national statement of good practice for police to follow when dealing with supporters"*.

Clubs also unanimously decided to recommend an independent panel, to include supporter representatives, be formed to investigate breaches of Football League Regulation 25(b) *"no club should charge higher admission prices for visiting supporters for accommodation comparable with that used by supporters of the home club"*. Also that monetary punishment is allowed when the Regulation is breached.

Not surprisingly, Sunderland and Newcastle supporters clubs were in the forefront of a motion calling for appropriate stewarding and policing arrangements to ensure no competitive match takes place without a reasonable proportion of away fans being present. ACPO say that police do not have the power to ban away fans; it appears the Ground Safety Officer can bow under pressure from local Police Commanders.

As well as the depth of atmosphere lacking with no away fans (singing, chanting, banter, visual etc), civil liberties of travelling fans come into the equation, the proliferation of CCTV should surely help control any problems, some away fans will always find a way to see the game and clubs could lose out financially.

The Federation actually negotiated with the Premier League to allocate accommodation of 10% or 3000 (whichever is the fewer) for away fans; the Football League recommend a reasonable proportion.

Other formal motions adopted at the conference concerned an appeal to enforce more strictly the provision of the Football Offences Act in respect of fans on the pitch and a decision to investigate the Internet for the Federation's benefit and an urgent call for a larger national stadium, possibly away from London.

Various other discussions included the Coca-Cola Cup, future structure of the Football League, player behaviour, attitudes of costumed mascots, the admission of drums and trumpets but not umbrellas, the League Managers Association and Pay-per-View television.

It was felt that the Coca-Cola Cup should not overlap the FA Cup by being completed before Christmas, starting earlier and on a straight knock-out basis. With more European involvement, one school of thought felt Premier League clubs could be exempted and replaced by an equivalent number from the Vauxhall Conference. There were more Conference teams in the FA Cup Third Round last season than those from Division Three of the Football League.

As far as Pay-per-View television was concerned, it was generally felt to be a real threat in the next eighteen months to two years. As one delegate put it *"couch potatoes will run football"*. Arising from this is the inevitable consensus that money should be spread more evenly within the game; noted that the Football Trust has now committed a total of £50 million to Divisions Two, Three and Vauxhall Conference to make grounds safer.

Chairman Tony Kershaw announced a three year sponsorship deal with Bass Breweries at £2000 a year as the new sponsor for the Football Quiz.

REFEREEING AND THE REFEREES

There are again a number of Law changes implemented by the International Board, some cosmetic and some quite profound for the start of this season.

The major changes are to Law 8 being "The start and re-start of play"—where for the first time a player may score directly from the kick-off. From time immemorial the ball has never been in play until touched by another player of either side. This change may now lead to numerous efforts to score from the centre spot.

In Law 12 "Fouls and Misconduct" it will now be an offence for the goalkeeper to handle the ball when receiving it from a throw-in by his *own team*. The punishment for this offence is an indirect free-kick from the point at which the goalkeeper catches the ball. Obviously this further restricts the goalkeeper's ability to handle the ball but is not as draconian as prohibiting all forms of playing the ball to the goalkeeper as was feared might happen.

Law 14 "The Penalty Kick" has seen a triumph for the Law-breakers in that goalkeepers who were almost never punished when moving at penalties are now *officially* allowed to do so. They will in fact be permitted to move their feet. The new text refers to the deletion of the phrase "without moving his feet" but there is no indication as to the direction. However since the 'keeper is still required to remain on his goal-line, it would appear that only lateral movement will be tolerated. Referees need no longer caution any player encroaching into the penalty area at the taking of a penalty.

Although in Law 16 another revolutionary change has been made, it is considered to be of little consequence because of the physical aspects involved. The change involves the permission now for a player to score direct from a goal kick.

The changing times have led to a new definition in Law 12. The old Public School concept prevalent in the last century where the term "ungentlemanly conduct" was coined, has no longer any real significance because firstly behaviour patterns have changed and secondly with so many women playing the game, it has become anachronistic. Accordingly the wording of the Law has been changed to reflect modern times and the words "unsporting behaviour" have replaced those of "ungentlemanly conduct" as a cautionable offence. Similarly "using offensive, insulting or abusive language" have replaced "foul or abusive language" as a sending-off offence.

There are additions to the cautionable offences categories, these being failure to retreat the required distance at free kicks or delaying the restart of play.

Other minor changes include referees requiring players bleeding from wounds to leave the field; thermal shorts to be the same main colour as the player's shorts; and the ball being placed *inside* the arc at a corner.

Not in the Laws but in the mandatory instructions to referees, comes the requirement to clamp down on goalkeepers taking more than four steps whilst holding the ball and if they do hold it for more than 5/6 seconds, the referee must treat it as time-wasting and award an indirect free kick against him.

KEN GOLDMAN

The full list of Referees and Assistant Referees on the National List is set out below and those Referees on the Premier List of whom there are nineteen are marked with an asterisk. There are two new Referees on that Premier List namely Neale Barry and Uriah Rennie. Six new Assistant Referees have been appointed to the Premier League, namely Messrs Brand, French, Gagen, Webster, Wing and the first ever woman Wendy Toms. Last season's most senior referee David Allison has now retired.

NATIONAL LIST OF REFEREES FOR SEASON 1997–98

* Alcock, P.E. (Redhill, Surrey)
* Ashby, G.R. (Worcester)
  Bailey, M.C. (Impington, Cambridge)
  Baines, S.J. (Chesterfield)
* Barber, G.P. (Pyrford, Surrey)
* Barry, N.S. (Scunthorpe)
  Bates, A. (Stoke-on-Trent)
  Bennett, S.G. (Redhill, Surrey)
* Bodenham, M.J. (East Looe, Cornwall)
  Brandwood, M.J. (Lichfield, Staffs)
* Burge, K.W. (Tonypandy)
  Burns, W.C. (Scarborough)
  Butler, A.N. (Sutton-in-Ashfield)
  Cain, G. (Bootle)
  Coddington, B. (Sheffield)
– Crick, D.R. (Worcester Park, Surrey)
  Danson, P.S. (Leicester)
– Dean, M.L. (Eastham, Wirral)
* Dunn, S.W. (Bristol)
* Durkin, P.A. (Portland, Dorset)
  D'Urso, A.P. (Billericay, Essex)
* Elleray, D.R. (Harrow-on-the-Hill)
  Finch, C.T. (Bury St Edmunds)

Fletcher, M. (Warley, West Midlands)
Foy, C.J. (St Helens)
Frankland, G.B. (Middlesbrough)
Furnandiz, R.D. (Doncaster)
* Gallagher, D.J. (Banbury, Oxon)
– Hall, A.R. (Birmingham)
  Halsey, M.R. (Welwyn Garden City, Herts)
  Harris, R.J. (Oxford)
  Heilbron, T. (Newton Aycliffe)
– Jones, M.J. (Chester)
* Jones, P. (Loughborough)
  Jones, T. (Barrow-in-Furness)
  Kirkby, J.A. (Sheffield)
  Knight, B. (Orpington)
  Laws, D. (Whitley Bay)
  Laws, G. (Whitley Bay)
  Leach, K.A. (Wolverhampton)
  Leake, A.R. (Darwen, Lancashire)
* Lodge, S.J. (Barnsley)
  Lomas, E. (Manchester)
  Lynch, K.M. (Knaresborough)
  Mathieson, S.W. (Stockport)
– Messias, M.D. (York)
  Orr, D. (Iver, Bucks)
  Pearson, R. (Peterlee, Durham)

Pierce, M.E. (Portsmouth)
– Pike, M.S. (Barrow-in-Furness)
* Poll, G. (Tring, Hertfordshire)
  Pugh, D. (Wirral)
* Reed, M.D. (Birmingham)
  Rejer, P. (Tipton, West Midlands)
* Rennie, U.D. (Sheffield)
  Richards, P.R. (Preston)
* Riley, M.A. (Leeds)
  Robinson, J.P. (Hull)
  Singh, G. (Wolverhampton)
  Stretton, F.G. (Nottingham)
  Styles, R. (Waterlooville, Hants)
  Taylor, P. (Cheshunt, Hertfordshire)
  Wiley, A.G. (Burntwood, Staffs)
  Wilkes, C.R. (Gloucester)
* Wilkie, A.B. (Chester-le-Street)
* Willard, G.S. (Worthing, W. Sussex)
* Winter, J.T. (Stockton-on-Tees)
  Wolstenholme, E.K. (Blackburn)

* *Denotes Premiership Referee.*
– *Denotes promotion to list for first time.*

ASSISTANT REFEREES

Adcock, D.J. (Long Eaton, Notts)
Armstrong, P. (Thatcham, Berks)
* Atkins, G. (Bradford)
* Babski, D.S. (Scunthorpe)
Baker, B.L. (Warminster, Wilts)
Baker, L. (Watchet, Somerset)
Barnes, P.W. (Peterborough)
Barston, P.S. (Loughborough)
* Bassindale, C. (Doncaster)
Beale, G.A. (Taunton)
Beeby, R.J. (Northampton)
Bello, B. (Manchester)
* Blanchard, I. (Hull)
Bone, R. (Orpington, Kent)
* Booth, D.A. (Barnsley)
Boulton, J.T. (Birmingham)
Boyeson, C. (Hull)
Brammer, D.S. (Weston-super-Mare)
* Brand, S.R. (Wirral)
– Brayne, R.E. (Harlow, Essex)
Brown, A.R. (Preston)
* Bryan, D.S. (Stamford)
Buller, K.R. (Bridgwater)
* Burton, R. (Burton-on-Trent)
* Butler, A.N. (Wigan)
* Cable, L.E. (Woking)
Cairns, M.J. (Coventry)
Canadine, P. (Rotherham)
* Carrington, M. (Loughborough)
– Carter, J.E. (Sunderland)
Castle, S. (Wolverhampton)
– Chittenden, S. (St Albans)
Clingo, S.G. (Wisbech, Cambs)
Clyde, A.L. (Doncaster)
Cockwill, N.R. (Barnstaple, North Devon)
Cooper, M.A. (Walsall)
Cooper, R.J. (Tynemouth)
Cowburn, M.G. (Blackpool)
Coxhead, R. (Huntingdon, Cambs)
Curson, B. (Hinckley, Leics)
* Dearing, M.D. (Northolt, Middlesex)
– Desmond, R.P. (Swindon)
* Devine, J.P. (Middlesbrough)
Dexter, M.C. (Thurmaston, Leics)
* Dowd, P. (Stoke-on-Trent)
Downs, D.G. (Hook, Hants)
Drysdale, D. (Lincoln)
Dyce, O. (Manchester)
Eastwood, P. (Manchester)
– Ebbage, M. (High Wycombe)
Edwards, C.D. (Oldham)
Ellicott, B.P. (Redditch)
Elwick, P.A. (Friskney, Lincs)
Evans, E.M. (Manchester)
Evans, R.J. (Beckenham, Kent)
– Foulkes, G.W. (Liverpool)
Francis, C.J. (Ely, Cambs)
* French, S.J. (Wolverhampton)
* Gagen, S.L. (New Malden, Surrey)
– Garratt, A.M. (Willenhall, West Midlands)
– Gosling, I.J. (Broomfield, Kent)
* Gould, R. (Swadlincote, Derbyshire)
Gowers, W.G. (Shipston-on-Stour, Warks)
* Green, A.J. (Hinckley, Leics)
* Green, E.W. (Slough)
* Green, N.E. (Stourport-on-Severn, Worcs)
Griffin, P.J. (Hornchurch, Essex)
Griffiths, J.H. (Chippenham)
Griffiths, S.J. (Macclesfield)
Habgood, S. (Swindon)
Hall, G.A. (Hixon, Nr Stafford)
* Hall, M. (Whitley Bay)
* Hancox, N. (Walsall Wood, West Midlands)

Harding, P.D. (Crewe)
– Harris, I.R. (Torpoint, Cornwall)
Harris, P.I. (Warrington)
Harteveld, A.C. (York)
Harvey, A.C. (Croxley Green, Herts)
* Hawkes, K.J. (Quedgley, Glos)
– Hawken, M. (St Austell)
Haxby, M.D. (New Brighton, Wirral)
Head, S. (Stokenchurch, Bucks)
Hegley, G.K. (Bishops Stortford)
* Hill, K.D. (Royston, Herts)
Hills, C.J. (Ely, Cambs)
Hine, D.J. (Worcester)
* Hogg, A.S. (Dronfield, Derbys)
* Holbrook, J.H. (Telford)
* Horlick, D.M. (Liverpool)
Horton, A.J. (Wolverhampton)
Howells, A.C. (Port Talbot)
Howes, T.P. (Norwich)
Hubbard, J.R. (Leicester)
Ingram, K.R. (Kingswinford)
– Ives, G.L. (Hornchurch)
– James, R.G. (Milton Keynes)
Jones, C. (Pontypridd)
Jones, L.C. (Bournemouth)
– Jones, N.L. (Plymouth)
* Jordan, W.M. (Pinner, Middlesex)
* Joslin, P.J. (Newark)
Joy, M.J. (Bristol)
* Kaye, A. (Bradford)
– Kasey, J.R. (Epsom)
Kellett, D.G. (Bradford)
– King, E.A. (Newmarket)
Lee, R.S. (Brentwood, Essex)
Leech, J. (Wigan)
Legg, A.R. (East Grinstead, West Sussex)
Lilley, S.J. (Bury St Edmunds)
Lockhart, R. (Newcastle-upon-Tyne)
* Lowe, B. (Doncaster)
McGee, A. (Prescot)
– McGirl, P.J. (Bedford)
McGregor, R.E. (Grimsby)
March, P. (Ramsgate)
* Martin, A.J. (Stafford)
Martin, E.A.C. (Williton, Somerset)
– Martin, R.W. (Sheffield)
– Massey, T. (Stockport)
– Maynard, M. (Hertford)
– Maynard, R. (Bristol)
– Meads, C.J. (Wetherby)
– Melinn, R.J. (Bridgwater, Somerset)
Mellor, G.S. (Rotherham)
Millership, B.T. (Atherstone, Warks)
* Morrall, D.A. (Sheffield)
Morrison, D.P. (Littleover, Derbys)
– Nicholson, P.W. (Durham)
Nind, K.J. (Bromsgrove)
Norman, P.V. (Sherborne, Dorset)
North, M.J. (Wimborne)
Oldham, A.B. (Poulton-le-Fylde, Lancs)
Oliver, D.S. (Darlington)
* Olivier, R.J. (Sutton Coldfield, West Midlands)
Parish, G.B. (Harlow)
– Parker, K.E. (Hartlepool)
Parkes, T.A. (Birmingham)
Pashley, R.A. (Chesterfield)
Pawson, P.M. (Sheffield)
Payne, R.G. (Flitwick, Beds)
Peacock, D. (Redcar, Cleveland)
Pearce, J.E. (Dagenham)
Peeks, S. (Northfleet, Kent)

Penn, A.M. (Kingswinford)
– Penton, C. (Brighton)
Perkin, N.F. (Gravesend)
Perlejewski, A.J. (Yeovil)
Perry, M.J. (Wimborne, Dorset)
* Pettitt, J.W. (Welling, Kent)
Philips, D.C. (Bracknell, Berks)
* Pike, K. (Gillingham, Dorset)
Polkey, B.L. (Nottingham)
Pollard, T.J. (Bury St Edmunds)
Pollock, R.M. (Liverpool)
Postles, M.D. (Coneyhurst Common, West Sussex)
Powell, K. (Hartlepool)
Prosser, P.J. (Albrighton, West Midlands)
– Rawcliffe, A. (Manchester)
Reynolds, K.S. (East Barnet)
* Richards, D.C. (Llanelli, Carmarthen)
* Roberts, P.M. (Northampton)
Robinson, M.G. (Darlington)
Rogers, C.J. (Swindon)
* Ross, J.J. (London)
* Ryan, M. (Preston)
– Salisbury, G. (Penwortham, Preston)
* Sharp, P.R. (St Albans)
Shaw, G. (Ashton-under-Lyne)
Shaw, I.D. (Crewe)
* Sheffield, J.A. (Burntwood, Staffs)
* Short, M.L. (Grantham, Lincs)
* Sims, M.R. (Bristol)
Smith, A.N. (Castleford, West Yorks)
Smith, J.P. (Hyde, Cheshire)
Smith, R.A. (Loughborough)
Spicer, D.R. (Totten, Hants)
* Stobbart, M. (Guildford)
– Stott, G.T. (Manchester)
Swift, M. (Sheffield)
Tarry, E.J. (Manchester)
– Taylor, J.T. (Blackburn)
Thiarra, S.S. (Bedford)
Thornewill, C. (Chaddesden, Derby)
Thorpe, M. (Woodbridge, Suffolk)
Tiffin, R. (Houghton-le-Spring)
* Tingey, M. (High Wycombe)
* Tomlin, S.G. (Lewes, East Sussex)
* Toms, Mrs W. (Poole)
Torrance, K.R. (Camberley, Surrey)
– Townsend, K.N. (Stourbridge)
– Turner, G.B. (Chesterfield)
Unsworth, D. (Bolton)
* Vosper, P.A. (London)
* Wade, B. (Isle of Wight)
* Walsh, E.J. (Rubery, Worcs)
* Walton, P. (West Haddon, Northants)
Ward, J. (Ferryhill, Co Durham)
Ward, R.B. (Milton Keynes)
Wardle, K. (Houghton-le-Spring)
* Warren, M.R. (Walsall)
Webb, A.J. (Winnersh, Berks)
Webb, H.M. (Rotherham)
* Webster, C.H. (Chester-le-Street)
– Whitby, D. (Merseyside)
Whitehouse, I. (Calne, Wiltshire)
– Wilkins, A.M. (Longfield, Kent)
* Williams, M.A. (Hereford)
* Wing, P.B. (Peterborough)
Wood, A.R. (Birkenhead)
Wood, D. (Harrogate)
Wood, D.R. (Liverpool)
Woodhall, D.J. (Shipley)
Woolmer, K.A. (Northampton)
– Yates, N.A. (Blackburn)
Zipfel, R.J. (Thetford, Norfolk)

FOOTBALL AND THE LAW

The law's involvement all the year round reflects the game's development as a never-ending saga. Thus the criminal, civil and administrative issues which surfaced during the 1996-97 season will still be unsolved at the time of going to press.

Winchester Crown Court's jury box for the second time within twelve months will reflect a grandstand looking down on a dramatic conflict between barristers, witnesses and the fate and integrity of three professional footballers and a Malaysian business man, refereed on this occasion by a full-time professional judge. For many with a sense of history and/or the memory to look back down the years, it will recall the events of a quarter-of-a-century earlier and convictions for conspiracy by international professional footballers at Nottingham Assizes in 1964. In addition to their inevitable custodial sentences, the bans then on their future involvement with the game were no different from the consequences of criminality on any practising professional, doctor, dentist, lawyer, surveyor and any others similarly qualified. R *v* Grobbelaar, Fashanu, Segers, and Heng Lim will be studied beyond the narrow touchlines of the football fraternity. The outcome can never be prophesied.

Correspondingly, litigation which has been commenced between two Nationwide League clubs and their players for injuries suffered during the course of play, must await a judgement which could occur during the currency of the new season; but in principle, it will follow on the type of claim for a broken leg suffered by Brian McCord of Stockport County against a Swansea City opponent for which a £250,000 damages award resulted.

At a different level, but no less legally binding and effective, watchers from the touchlines, in the boardroom and in legal chambers will be closely monitoring the fall-out from the landmark Jean-Marc Bosman European Court of Justice decision, which rumbles on with threats to the abolition of the transfer system within the UK, based upon its four separate footballing nation states in the eyes of football law, as it has dented the transfer system within the European Union generally.

At present, negotiations between the Professional Footballers Association and the governing football authorities are still unresolved; and because of the separate constitutional levels of existence between the four home countries, the most serious threat to a negotiated settlement and a resulting threat to the UK football structure is looming from Scotland.

There, a reference to the Edinburgh Court of Session equivalent to London's High Court (prior to a reference to the European Court of Justice on the lines of the Bosman case) is on the cards from Airdrie and its discontented Chris Honor backed by the Scottish PFA.

Honour of a different kind was publicised when Middlesbrough pulled out of their pre-Christmas fixture with Blackburn Rovers on the basis of inability to field a fit team. They were charged by the FA Premier League with breach of its Section B, Rule 19: "No club shall without just cause fail to fulfil its fixture obligations in respect of any League match on the appointed date or dates."

The well-publicised three points deduction, ultimately causing relegation, was appealed unsuccessfully to a Commission which confirmed that "Middlesbrough was quite capable of fielding a team and that the club did not have just cause in cancelling the fixture".

Indeed, more than one commentator pointed out that even if it had played its youth or reserve team and lost, the points would not have been deducted and its Premier League status preserved. Who or whatever legal and/or medical (if any) source considered this position resulted in unfortunate consequences for Middlesbrough and its supporters.

That the law of the land does not stop at the touchline or boundary is as true for the board and committee room as it is for the playing field. While the game becomes ever more part of a world-wide global village, the need for observance of the rules of play on and off the field is as essential as it is for the rule of law in society generally. For without its existence, anarchy and chaos will exist at every level and whilst sport holds a mirror up to reflect society generally, the law within sport and football in particular becomes more essential with every passing day.

EDWARD GRAYSON

DISCIPLINE

And then there was one. In the first crowded month of the season, there were 73 dismissals in first class matches covering England and Scotland. Comparing this with the previous season, it was a decrease of 13. With a variance in the number of matches played during this period, no conclusions could be drawn.

As the season progressed, there were the usual peculiarities which the two-tiered system of redress allows, i.e. matches televised can often be presented as evidence of wrongful dismissal where those without the cameras may not be as fortunate. However, there are other mitigating circumstances.

Chesterfield's Chris Perkins had his red card torn up when referee Mike Reed changed his mind two days after sending the player off in the game against Millwall. Sunderland, who had two players sent off at Arsenal towards the end of September, later discovered that referee Paul Danson admitted he had been wrong in showing Paul Stewart a second yellow card.

Scott McGleish escaped the ultimate sanction when the red card he had been given for Leyton Orient against Fulham on 14 December, faded in colour following a subsequent change of heart. And the Christmas spirit might have been the reason why Andy Bernal of Reading had his red card squashed after referee Richard Poulain admitted his mistake for the match with West Bromwich Albion on Boxing Day. Yet it took the official until 8 January to retract his decision.

It was not all one-way traffic, of course. Take the example of Terry Fleming at Lincoln City, who temporarily forgot his own name and gave that of his nearest colleague, when a second booking was about to be made. He did not escape the wrath of officialdom . . .

March was a pretty dreadful month for discipline, or rather a good one for blossoming shades of red. English clubs found themselves having to do without services of many players, as 51 red cards were shown, almost twice the figure of the previous year for the same period.

As the last weeks of the season passed and tensions mounted around promotion and relegation struggles, so the number of clubs who had been spared the ignominy of being sent to the proverbial early bath diminished. Noel Blake (Exeter) and Andy Cooke (Burnley) on 26 April, Tim Sherwood (Blackburn Rovers) a week later, became their respective clubs' first dismissals of the season. On the same day, Peter Whiston of Shrewsbury Town was sent off against Gillingham. It gave him an unwanted hat-trick – his third red card of the League campaign.

On 11 May, Matt Clarke, the Sheffield Wednesday goalkeeper, was sent off late in the match against Liverpool. Later he, too, was reprieved by an admission from referee David Elleray.

Play-offs done and dusted and a quick recap of the defaulters among 92 English League and 40 Scottish League clubs revealed that only one of their number had remained relatively squeaky clean. That was West Bromwich Albion.

This is but one side of the story. What of the defeats and loss of points which can be attributed to refereeing errors? No more, one suspects than the mistakes made by players in presenting the opposition with goals.

BOOKINGS AND DISMISSALS

Premier League	1192	44
Division One	1395	84
Division Two	1282	82
Division Three	1450	97
Scottish Premier	548	43
Division One	554	46
Division Two	482	28
Division Three	507	39

FROM THE CHAPLAIN

The football chaplains held their now annual conference last autumn, again, thanks to the kindness of the Premier League who sponsored the event, in the well-appointed surroundings of the National Sports Centre at Lilleshall. Organised by SCORE – Sports Chaplaincy Offering Resources and Encouragement – some fifty men and one lady attended the gathering, coming from some thirty of the Premier and Football League outfits who now benefit from the services of a chaplain, with five clubs represented for the first time. A new aspect of such get-togethers was the strong contingent of a dozen or so who came from the ranks of clubs further down the pyramid.

These clerical personnel were delighted to take in the much delayed England Under-21 international against Poland at Molineux and took encouragement from England's bright display which effectively mirrored the progress that has been made within football towards an understanding and acceptance of the involvement of chaplains within the sport and at clubs large and small. Warmly welcomed among the speakers was Wolves' manager Mark McGhee and the conference focused around the theme of 'Serving with Integrity'.

A new dimension to football chaplaincy was reported at the Lilleshall Conference – the involvement of chaplains in Euro '96. This is, as far as we are aware, the first time that a major international football tournament has had an officially recognised chaplaincy programme as an integrated part of it, although, as some of our older readers will know, there were football chaplains at a few Football League clubs even before England's 1966 World Cup success.

However, whilst there was a 1st Division fixture last season where the two watching chaplains totalled nearly sixty years' service to their respective clubs, some readers who have more recently begun to follow our sport may not be aware of the work of the football chaplains, for these men are, of choice, low profile, do not seek and seldom receive publicity. So, it may therefore be helpful here just briefly to point out that the employees and supporters of football clubs are not immune to the pressures, problems, responsibilities and sorrows which beset all of us in life, and, just as many major stores, theatres and business houses for example have found it worthwhile to have a chaplain, so the role is becoming ever more widely accepted and utilised within football.

Indeed, it is the considered judgement of the chaplains that there is not a single club listed below where there has not at some time or another been a player who has performed better, a member of the ground or office staff enabled to cope with a personal problem, or a fan who felt himself to be supported at a difficult time as a result of the chaplain's availability and involvement, for 'The Rev's' specialist skills, training and in some cases many years of experience, make him an invaluable asset to the club he serves.

THE REV

OFFICIAL CHAPLAINS TO FA PREMIERSHIP AND FOOTBALL LEAGUE CLUBS

Rev John Bingham—Chesterfield
Rev Richard Chewter—Exeter C
Rev Michael Lowe—AFC Bournemouth
Rev Andrew Taggart—Torquay U
Rev David Jeans—Sheffield W
Rev Nigel Sands—Crystal Palace
Rev Graham Spencer—Leicester C
Rev Phillip Miller—Ipswich T
Rev Allen Bagshawe—Hull C
Rev David Tully—Newcastle U
Rev Derek Cleave—Bristol C
Rev Brian Rice—Hartlepool U
Revs Andy Cowley and John Graham—Watford
Rev Michael Chantry—Oxford U
Rev Michael Futens—Derby C
Very Rev Brandon Jackson—Lincoln C
Rev Ken Hawkins—Birmingham C
Rev Simon Stevenette—Bristol R
Rev Canon Michael Hunter—Grimsby T
Rev Dick Syms—York C
Rev Stephen Cooper—Middlesbrough
Rev Tony Porter—Manchester C
Fr Joe Jordan—Cardiff C
Fr Andrew McMahon—Southampton

Rev Mervyn Terrett—Luton T
Rev Peter Bye—Carlisle U
Rev Robert de Berry—QPR
Rev Gary Piper—Fulham
Rev Peter Amos—Barnsley
Rev Barry Kirk—Reading
Rev Martin Short—Bradford C
Rev John Boyers—Manchester U
Rev Martin Butt—Walsall
Rev Steve Riley and Capt Andrew Vertigan—Leeds U
Rev Alan Poulter and Fr Gerald Courell—Tranmere R
Rev Mark Kichenside—Charlton Ath
Rev Owen Beament—Millwall
Rev Elwin Cockett—West Ham U
Rev Mick Woodhead—Sheffield U
Rev Alan Comfort—Leyton Orient
Rev John Hall-Matthews—Wolverhampton W
Rev Mark Cockayne—Doncaster R
Rev Peter Naylor—Northampton T
Rev Steve Halliwell—Barnet
Rev Richard Hayton—Gillingham
Rev Clive Andrews—Notts Co
Rev Chris Nelson—Preston North End
Rev Paul Brown—Wrexham

The chaplains hope that those who read this page will see the value and benefit of chaplaincy work in football and will take appropriate steps to spread the word where this is possible. They would also like to thank the editors of the Rothmans Yearbook *for their continued support for this specialist and growing area of work.*

The following addresses may be helpful: SCORE (Sports Chaplaincy Offering Resources and Encouragement), PO Box 123, Sale, Manchester M33 4ZA and Christians in Sport, PO Box 93, Oxford OX2 7YP.

OBITUARIES

Ken Allcock (b. Kirkby-in-Ashfield 24.4.21; d. 9.96). Joined Mansfield Town in April, 1947, having previously played for Notts County as an amateur, but made only one League appearance for the Stags at centre-forward.

Chris Anderson (b. East Wemyss 28.11.28; d. 20.7.96). An outside-right who started his League career with Blackburn Rovers in August, 1950 and went on to make 13 League appearances (1 goal) before joining Stockport County in June, 1953. Chris spent a season at Edgeley Park, playing 34 League games. The following summer, he signed for Southport, where he had 28 League outings.

Robert Anderson (b. Portsmouth 23.2.36; d. 11.96). Son of Jock Anderson who scored one of Pompey's four goals in their 1939 FA Cup final win over Wolves. Bobby was a winger who joined Mansfield Town in September, 1956, and stayed until the end of the 1959–60 season. He played 41 League games for the Stags, scoring three times, before seeing out his career with Halesowen Town and Wellington Town.

Wilf Armory (b. 1912; d. 21.12.96). A wing-half with Ayr United, Aldershot and Nuneaton Borough, Wilf will be fondly remembered by all at Folkestone, where he served as a player, manager and, latterly, as president. He was a key member of the Folkestone side that won the Southern League and Cup double in the 1934–35 season, before turning to management in the forties. He went on to become president and his death brought about the end of a 62-year association with the club.

Joe 'Billy' Arnison (b. South Africa 27.6.24; d. 8.96). A goalscoring centre-forward who was snapped up by Rangers in 1945, having played representative matches for Eastern Transvaal. Played in the first ever Scottish League Cup final for Rangers against Aberdeen in the 1946–47 season before moving south to Luton Town in August, 1948. He hit 19 goals in 44 League outings for the Hatters, but injury curtailed his career, and he returned to South Africa.

Peter Beckers (b. Dundee 3.10.47; d. 6.6.96). Joined Grimsby Town from Craigmore Thistle in November, 1964 but, in three seasons, he only made one League appearance. Joined Skegness in 1967 and later became manager at the club.

John Bell (b. Morpeth 29.8.19; d. 3.6.96). A left-back who played 50 League matches for Gateshead between 1946 and 1949.

Alf Bentley (b. Aylesham 28.10.31; d. 15.10.96). Goalkeeper Alf joined Coventry City in October, 1955, but during his short stay at Highfield Road he only made 29 League appearances due to the outstanding form of Reg Matthews. He moved on to Chelsea the following year, but could not break into the side and was allowed to join Margate. Alf did have further Football League involvement, however, when he signed for Gillingham in August, 1958, and there he had 13 League outings.

Cliff Birkett (b. Newton-le-Willows 17.9.33; d. 1.97). An outside-right, Cliff signed professional forms for Manchester United in 1950 after representing England Schoolboys. He made nine League appearances during the 1950–51 season, scoring two goals, but then had to be content with reserve team football until he left for Southport in June, 1956. At Haig Avenue, he scored four times in 14 League outings.

Les Blizzard (b. Acton 13.3.23; d. 12.96). Les began with Queens Park Rangers during the war, but after hostilities he made only four League appearances at half-back before joining Bournemouth in May, 1947. But after just one League outing, he left for Southern League Yeovil, where he starred in the famous FA Cup victory over First Division Sunderland. In July, 1950, he returned to the Football League with Leyton Orient and went on to amass 221 League appearances, scoring 12 times. He completed his career with Headington United in 1957.

Vince Blore (b. Uttoxeter 1908; d. 1.97). A goalkeeper who started out with Aston Villa in 1932, then moved to Derby County the following year, where he had 15 League outings. Vince was transferred to West Ham in 1935, where he made a further nine League appearances before moving across London to Crystal Palace. Following 38 League games, he joined Exeter City in 1938, but was only able to make four appearances before the onset of the Second World War.

Albert Bloxham (b. Solihull 22.11.05; d. 29.8.96). A tricky winger who served Torquay United, Birmingham City and Chesterfield in the twenties. He also had spells with Raith Rovers and Yeovil before joining Millwall in the early thirties, where he made 70 League appearances and scored 11 goals.

Frank Bokas (b. Bellshill 13.5.14; d. 29.10.96). A half-back who began his Football League career with Blackpool in the mid-thirties before moving on to Barnsley having had six League outings. He remained at Oakwell up to the outbreak of the war, then continued to play for the Yorkshire club during hostilities, as well as guesting for Chesterfield, Leeds United, Huddersfield Town and Bradford City. His final League club was Carlisle United, whom he joined in 1945.

Billy Bostock (b. Inverkeithing 1944; d. 7.7.96). Cowdenbeath's leading scorer in 1968–69 with 23 goals and was a member of the side that won promotion to the top flight in 1970, finishing runners-up behind

Falkirk. In that season he finished third highest scorer with 10 goals as 'Beath amassed an impressive 81 for the season.

Frank Brennan (b. Annathill 23.4.24; d. Newcastle 5.3.97). A centre-half, Frank started out with Airdrie, then signed for Newcastle United in May, 1946. He made 318 League appearances for his one and only League club in a ten year period, during which time he helped the Magpies win the FA Cup in 1951 and 1952. He also won seven caps for Scotland.

Fred Butcher (b. 1914; d. 1996). Fred made two League appearances in defence for Aston Villa during the early thirties, before moving to Reading in 1935. He completed his career with Blackpool.

Syd Cann (b. Torquay 30.10.11; d. 1.12.96). A full-back who started out in the late twenties with his local club Torquay United and made 44 League appearances before moving to Manchester City in 1930. Syd played for City in the 1933 FA Cup final, then in 1935, he left to join Charlton, where he remained until the early forties. He managed Southampton between 1949 and 1951.

Len Carney (b. Liverpool 30.5.15; d. 3.96). Len played for his local club as an amateur during the war and then resumed his career after hostilities in 1946 when League football returned. He had the distinction of hitting Liverpool's opening goal in the 1946–47 season, when the club won the title, but unfortunately, he only made a further five League appearances.

Sam Chessell (b. Shirebrook 9.7.21; d. 14.3.96). Sam made his debut during the Second World War for Mansfield Town before going on to play 257 League matches for the Stags between 1946 and 1954. Converted from a winger to a full-back, he found the net on six occasions.

Allenby Chilton (b. South Hylton 16.9.18; d. 16.6.96). A centre-half who played 352 League games for Manchester United between 1946 and 1955, when he left Old Trafford to become player-manager of Grimsby Town. Allenby also made two appearances for England, against Northern Ireland in 1950 in Belfast, and against France a year later, at Highbury.

Wilf Chitty (b. Walton-on-Thames 10.7.12; d. 2.2.97). Generally an outside-left, Wilf could also play at full-back. He saw service with Chelsea and Plymouth Argyle in the thirties, but the war interrupted a promising career. Throughout hostilities he guested for Reading, then joined them full-time in the mid-forties. In the 1946–47 season he had 23 League outings for the Elm Park side, scoring seven goals.

Frank Christie (b. Scone 17.2.27; d. 12.9.96). Started his League career with Forfar before joining Liverpool in March, 1949. However, after only four League appearances, Frank returned to Scotland to join East Fife and became a hero when he scored the winning goal in the 1953–54 Scottish League Cup final – a 3–2 victory over Partick Thistle. He went on to make 244 League appearances for the club. After retiring, he filled posts as a trainer with Forfar and St Johnstone, before returning to the Fifers as manager.

Bobby Clark (b. 1929; d. 14.6.96). A right-back who played for Arbroath in the mid-fifties, before seeing out his playing career with Nairn County and Keith.

Denis Compton (b. Hendon 23.5.18; d. 23.4.97). The legendary Middlesex and England cricketer was no mean footballer. An outside-left, Denis joined Arsenal from Hampstead Town, and between 1946 and 1950 he had 32 League outings, finding the back of the net on ten occasions. Was a member of the Arsenal side that won the FA Cup in 1950.

Bobby Cook (b. Letchworth 13.6.24; d. 6.3.97). Bobby signed for Reading in March, 1948, but after failing to break into the first team, he left to join Tottenham in July, 1949. At White Hart Lane, he only had three League outings and so two years later he moved on to Watford. Generally a winger, Bobby had greater success with the Hornets, making 54 League appearances and scoring eight times.

John Craven (b. St Annes 15.5.47; d. 14.12.96). Signed for Blackpool in January, 1965 and went on to make 163 League appearances, scoring 24 times. In the seventies the bustling striker plied his trade with Crystal Palace (63 League games, 14 goals), Coventry City (89 League appearances, 8 goals) and Plymouth Argyle (45 League outings and 3 goals). At the time of his death, John was living in California.

Robert Dennison (b. Ambleside 6.3.12; d. 19.6.96). Bob began as an inside-forward and played for Newcastle United, Nottingham Forest and Fulham before the Second World War. After hostilities, he played as a centre-half for Northampton Town, for whom he had guested during the war. Became manager of Middlesbrough in the mid-fifties and stayed until 1963 when he took over the helm at Hereford.

Don Dorman (b. Birmingham 18.9.22; d. 12.1.97). Signed for Birmingham City in May, 1946 and went on to make 60 League appearances for the Blues, scoring four times. He was transferred in September, 1951 to Coventry City and hit 29 goals in 91 League games, having made the transition from wing-half to inside-forward with considerable success. He completed his League career with Walsall, whom he joined in October, 1954. There, he had 115 League outings and found the net on 33 occasions.

Denis Compton

Tommy Lawton

Jimmy Duncanson (b. Glasgow 13.10.19; d. 1.9.96). Joined Rangers in 1939, but had to wait until after the war to realise his enormous potential as a forward. At Ibrox he won countless honours – three Championships in 1947, 1949 and 1950, Cup winners' medals in 1948, 1949 and 1950 and had League Cup success in 1947 and 1949. After leaving Rangers in the early fifties, he served St Mirren and Stranraer.

Roger Frude (b. Plymouth 19.11.46; d. 14.6.96). An England youth international who made 41 League appearances for Bristol Rovers, scoring 8 times, following his debut in 1964. After three years at Eastville, Roger moved to Mansfield Town, where he had 16 League outings, scoring once. He completed his League career at Brentford in the 1969–70 season, with two League appearances for the Bees.

John Eric Garbutt (b. Scarborough 27.3.20; d. 6.1.97). Known as 'Eric', he joined Newcastle United before the outbreak of war, but did not make his League debut until after hostilities. When League football resumed he made 51 League appearances for United and, in October, 1946, he played in the club's recording-breaking 13–0 victory over Newport County.

Tommy Godwin (b. Dublin 20.8.27; d. 8.96). Tommy was with Shamrock Rovers when he won the first of 13 caps in goal for the Republic of Ireland. In October, 1949, he moved to Leicester City, but after 45 League games, he was on his way south to Bournemouth. At Dean Court he became a legend, making 357 League appearances. Highlights of a memorable career came in September, 1949, when he helped Ireland to become the first ever team from outside the United Kingdom to beat England on home soil and, in the 1956–57 season, he was in the Bournemouth side that recorded historic FA Cup victories over Wolves and Tottenham.

Jimmy Gordon (b. Fauldhouse 23.10.15; d. 8.96). A half-back, Jimmy made his name with Newcastle United before the outbreak of war, making 132 League appearances, before joining Middlesbrough in 1945. At Ayresome he had a further 231 League outings between 1946 and 1954. When Brian Clough and Peter Taylor enjoyed their successful period at Derby County, Jimmy was an important part of the management staff and he was also a great influence behind the scenes when Forest won the Championship and lifted the European Cup in 1979 and 1980. As a tribute to his work behind the scenes, he led the Forest out at Wembley before the 1980 League Cup final.

Reg Gore (b. Chesterfield 1.8.13; d. 1.97). Reg was a forward who had spells with Chesterfield and Birmingham in the early thirties, without making any League appearances. In 1934, he moved to Southport, where he had 16 League outings and scored twice. He then had a three-year spell outside the League, before returning to serve West Ham in the 1938–39 season.

Tom Grice (b. Sutton, Nottinghamshire 17.3.08; d. 12.11.96). A centre-half, Tom began with Worksop Town in 1927, before moving on to Mansfield Town. He had an additional spell with Worksop, then served Birmingham City, Torquay United and Walsall.

Walter Grimsditch (b. Farnworth 8.10.20; d. 19.6.96). A goalkeeper with Southport, who played ten League matches immediately after the war.

Jimmy Grummett (Snr) (b. Barnsley 31.7.18; d. 11.5.96). Jimmy, a wing-half, became a Lincoln City player during the war before helping the club win the Third Division North Championship in 1948. In September, 1952, after 165 League appearances and 12 goals, he left to join Accrington Stanley, where he made 40 appearances, scoring once, during his one and only season at Peel Park.

Harry Hanford (b. Swansea 9.10.07; d. 26.11.96). A centre-half who started out with his local club, Swansea Town in 1926 and won seven international caps for Wales. Ten years later he signed for Sheffield Wednesday, where the war interrupted his League career. After hostilities, Harry joined Exeter City where he had 37 League outings.

Dennis Hellings (b. Lincoln 9.12.23; d. 19.5.96). Known as 'Danny', he was an inside-forward who joined Lincoln City in 1945. Unfortunately, his career at Sincil Bank was short – he made just three League appearances during the 1946–47 season, before moving to Grantham in 1949.

Roy Henderson (b. Wishaw 1923; d. 11.1.97). A great goalkeeping servant to Queen of the South between 1946 and 1958.

Doug Hillard (b. Bristol 10.8.35; d. 6.1.97). A loyal one-club man who served Bristol Rovers between May, 1957 and 1968. During that period, the popular defender made 317 League appearances and scored 13 goals.

Eric Houghton (b. Billingborough 29.6.10; d. 1.5.96). Served Aston Villa with distinction for over 50 years as a player, manager and director. Eric was originally an amateur at Villa Park, having joined the club in 1927. He scored 160 League goals in 361 appearances and was an expert from the penalty spot – successful on 72 occasions out of 79. He was also a free-kick specialist and made seven appearances for the full England side, scoring five times. After the war, the left-winger had four outings for Villa before moving to Notts County. At Meadow Lane he made 51 League appearances and found the net on seven occasions. In 1949 he retired and stepped into management, taking over the helm at Notts County. Four years later, he became boss at Villa Park and was in charge when the club won the FA Cup in 1957. Also a talented cricketer, he represented Warwickshire. Eric continued his association with Villa in the 1970s, first becoming a director, then a vice president in 1983.

George Hunt (b. Barnsley 22.2.10; d. 19.9.96). A centre-forward who started out with Chesterfield in January, 1930 and scored on his debut. In the summer of that year, George moved to Tottenham and during his seven year stay at White Hart Lane he played three times for England and scored on his debut. His goalscoring record with Spurs was remarkable – 125 in 185 League matches, which persuaded Arsenal to sign him in 1937. After only six months, he was off to Bolton Wanderers, but there the war interrupted his career, although 110 goals in a grand total of 228 matches (including 177 wartime games) shows what he would have been capable of had normal competition been possible. George left Burnden Park in 1946 to join Sheffield Wednesday and hit a further eight goals in 32 League games before retiring in 1948. He became a trainer at Bolton Wanderers, where he remained until the late sixties.

George Hutchinson (b. Castleford 31.10.29; d. 30.7.96). Signed for Huddersfield Town in January, 1947, but following just one League outing, the fleet-of-foot forward joined Sheffield United the following year. At Bramall Lane he made 73 League appearances and found the net on ten occasions before moving to Tottenham. At White Hart Lane, he made just five League appearances (1 goal), then left League soccer before returning to the professional game with Leeds United in 1955. Five goals in 11 games helped secure promotion to the First Division, but a year later he was on the move once more – this time to Halifax – where he hit 12 goals in 44 League outings. He completed his League career with Bradford City, before drifting into non-League football.

Ralph Jones (b. Maesteg 19.5.21; d. 18.1.97). Ralph joined Newport County from Leicester City in May, 1946, and made 19 League appearances before moving to Bristol Rovers in December, 1947. At Eastville, the full-back had a further 12 League outings and scored once.

John Kerr (b. 1922; d. 24.12.96). Played for Dundee United in the late forties and also served Glentoran.

Vic Lambden (b. Bristol 24.10.25; d. 3.7.96). A one-club man with his local club, Bristol Rovers, Vic served the club as a player from 1945 until 1955, during which time he amassed 271 League appearances and scored 116 goals. An outstanding forward who was Rovers' leading marksman for four seasons, Vic hit the fastest goal in the club's history – after only eight seconds, against Aldershot in the FA Cup during the 1950–51 season.

Tom Lawrenson (b. Preston 24.5.29; d. 7.5.96). Father of Preston, Brighton and Liverpool defender, Mark, Tom signed for his local club in April, 1949, but after just one League match, he joined Southport. At Haig Avenue he made 37 League appearances between 1955 and 1957.

Tommy Lawton (b. Bolton 6.10.19; d. 6.11.96). One of the absolute greats with a phenomenal goal-scoring record. Even as a schoolboy, Tommy had great goalscoring aptitude, hitting in excess of 500 goals during his schooldays in Bolton. He started out at Burnley, signing as an amateur in 1935, then achieving professional status on 6 October, 1936, his 17th birthday, and followed that up by hitting a hat-trick against Tottenham. On 1 January, 1937, he moved to Everton for £6,500 and eventually replaced the legendary Dixie Dean. A prolific marksman in World War Two with 212 goals for

Everton, Aldershot, Chelsea and Tranmere Rovers, he also won 23 wartime and victory international caps for England. After the war years he joined Chelsea and scored 30 goals in 42 League games. In November, 1947, he became the first £20,000 footballer by virtue of a shock move to Notts County. Between 1947 and 1952 he played 151 League games for County which reaped an astonishing 90 goals. He then had an 18 month spell at Brentford, bagging 17 goals in 50 League outings, until finishing at Arsenal in 1956 with 35 games and 13 goals to his credit. At international level, he made 23 appearances for England between September, 1946 and September, 1948, scoring 16 times in the process.

Steve Leavy (b. Longford 18.6.25; d. 26.1.97). A defender who made 36 League appearances (one goal) for Swansea Town between 1950 and 1958.

Terry Lee (b. Stepney 20.9.52; d. 22.6.96). A goalkeeper who made his debut for Tottenham in 1974, but following loan periods at Cardiff and Gillingham, he was transferred to Torquay United the following summer. He played 106 League games for the Plainmoor side before injury curtailed his League career while he was with Newport County in the late seventies.

Colin Liddell (b. 1926; d. 24.2.97). Colin played for Morton in the 1948 Scottish Cup final and the subsequent replay and was an outstanding winger. In 1949, he moved to Hearts for £10,000, then a record, but his stay at Tynecastle was brief. The following year, he was snapped up by Rangers, but in six years at Ibrox he only made 35 League appearances, scoring eight times.

Phil McCarthy (b. Liverpool 19.4.44; d. 12.96). A wing-half who played just three times for Oldham in 1965, before moving on to Halifax Town in January, 1966. At the Shay, Phil made 181 League appearances and found the net 14 times.

Roger McDonald (b. Glasgow 2.2.33; d. 22.10.96). Began with St Mirren, then came south to join Mansfield Town where, as a full-back, he made 14 League appearances. He was transferred to Crystal Palace in January, 1958, but he failed to make a League appearance.

Archie McFeat (b. Kincardine 23.1.24; d. 1.4.96). A goalkeeper for Morton, who joined Torquay United in May, 1948, but only made nine League appearances, before returning to Scotland, where he served Falkirk and Stenhousemuir.

George McKnight (b. Belfast 17.11.23; d. 28.9.96). Signed by Blackpool from Linfield in 1946, but only made 41 appearances, scoring nine times in eight years for the Seasiders. Incredibly he still holds the record for the fastest hat-trick ever scored. Deputizing for Stan Mortensen against Fulham in 1950, he found the net on three occasions in three-and-a-half minutes! After he left Bloomfield Road, he had spells with Chesterfield and Southport.

Andy McLaren (b. Larkhall 24.1.22; d. 12.96). A Scottish international inside-forward who won four caps and scored four times for his country. He played for Preston North End immediately after the Second World War and was the club's top scorer in the 1947–48 season, forming a lethal left-wing partnership with Tom Finney. In December, 1948, he began his travels, starting at Burnley, before taking in Sheffield United, Barrow (155 League outings, 52 goals), Bradford Park Avenue, Southport and Rochdale, where his League career terminated in 1957.

Len Millard (b. Coseley 7.3.19; d. 3.3.97). Joined West Bromwich Albion as an amateur in 1939, signing professionally in 1942, Len was originally a forward, but became a thoroughly accomplished full-back. He skippered the Baggies to FA Cup victory over Preston North End in the 1954 final and made 436 League appearances between 1946 and 1958 for his one and only club, scoring seven times.

Ian Mitchell (b. Falkirk 9.5.46; d. 2.4.96). A forward who began with Dundee United, before signing for Newcastle United in July, 1970. At St James' Park, the former Scotland Under-23 and schools international only made three League appearances, then served Falkirk and Brechin City.

Harry Noon (b. Sutton-in-Ashfield 6.10.37; d. 9.96). Harry made 122 League appearances for Notts County between 1957 and 1962, having signed for the Meadow Lane club in May, 1955. In July, 1962, the full-back moved to Bradford City, but had only one League outing. He emigrated to Australia after a spell in non-League football.

Stan Pearson (b. Salford 11.1.19; d. 20.2.97). A Manchester United favourite of the late forties and early fifties, he will be fondly remembered at Old Trafford for his winning goal in the 1948 FA Cup final, when United beat Blackpool 4–3. A gifted inside-forward, Stan scored five times in eight appearances for England between 1948 and 1952, including a brace in a two-one victory over Scotland in Glasgow. After 124 goals in 292 League matches for United, he moved on to Bury in February, 1954, where he continued to find the net regularly. In 122 League outings for the Gigg Lane club, Stan scored 56 times. In October, 1957, he was transferred to Chester where he hit a further 16 goals in 56 League matches.

Cliff Pinchbeck (b. Cleethorpes 20.1.25; d. 2.11.96). Cliff, a centre-forward, began with Scunthorpe United, then moved to Everton in December, 1947, where he made just three League appearances before departing to Brighton and Hove Albion in August, 1949. At the Goldstone, he hit five goals in 14 League outings, then was snapped up by Port Vale where he had great success in two-and-a-half

Roy Sproson

George Young

seasons, finding the net 34 times in 69 League games. In December, 1951, Cliff signed for Northampton, but broke his ankle after only three matches, which unfortunately terminated his League career.

Vic Potts (b. Birmingham 20.8.15; d. 22.10.96). Vic made his first League appearances as a full-back for Doncaster Rovers before the Second World War. During hostilities he guested for Aston Villa, which was a prelude to him joining the club full-time. After the war he had 62 League outings, but injury brought a premature end to his career.

William Rees (b. Blaengarw 10.2.24; d. 27.7.96). A goalscoring inside-forward who won three caps for Wales, against Northern Ireland, Belgium and Switzerland, while he was with Cardiff City (101 League appearances, 33 goals). In June, 1949, he moved to Spurs, won another cap against Northern Ireland, and scored three times in 11 League games before leaving for Leyton Orient. At Brisbane Road, between 1950 and 1955, his strike rate was 55 goals in 184 League games.

Robert Robinson (b. Edinburgh 10.11.50; d. 24.12.96). Played for both Dundee and Dundee United, after beginning his League career with Falkirk. While he was at Dens Park in the mid-seventies, he won four caps for Scotland, against West Germany, Sweden, Northern Ireland and Romania. A determined midfielder, he moved to Tannadice in 1977, then two years later returned to his home city to play for Hearts, before seeing out his League career with Raith Rovers.

Jimmy Rogers (b. Wednesbury 31.12.29; d. 3.97). A battling centre-forward, Jimmy started with Wolves in May, 1948, but after failing to get first team action, he moved to Bristol City two years later. At Ashton Gate he poached 32 goals in 153 League games before a highly productive period at Coventry came in December, 1956. In a two year period with the Highfield Road club, he struck 27 goals in 76 League matches, including three hat-tricks – all against Aldershot. Jimmy completed his League career at Bristol City, where he returned in December, 1958, to score a further 28 times in 115 League outings.

Alfred Rowland (b. Stokesley 2.9.20; d. 1.97). A centre-half who served Aldershot and Cardiff City in the late forties. At the Shots, Alf amassed 93 League games, before moving to Ninian Park in 1949. There, he had a further three League outings.

Reg Ryan (b. Dublin 30.10.25; d. 2.97). Reg won 16 caps for Ireland as an inside-forward between the late forties and mid-fifties and enjoyed a highly successful career with West Bromwich Albion, Derby County and Coventry City. He joined the Baggies in 1945 and went on to make a formidable 234 League appearances (28 goals), winning an FA Cup medal in 1954. He was transferred to Derby County in July, 1955 and became skipper at The Baseball Ground. The club won the Third Division (North) in 1957 and Reg was top scorer at the end of the following campaign. In September, 1958, he took his inspirational qualities to Coventry and helped the club win promotion to Division Three.

Ron Spence (b. Tudhoe 7.1.24; d. 24.4.96). Ron was a one-club man who gave sterling service to York City between March, 1948 and 1960. During that period the dependable wing-half made 281 League appearances and scored 25 goals for the Minstermen.

Roy Sproson (b. Stoke-on-Trent 23.9.30; d. 1.97). Known as 'Mr Loyalty' at Port Vale where he amassed a phenomenal 761 League appearances between July, 1949 and 1971. In 1954 he was part of a great Vale side that won the Third Division (North) title and reached the semi-finals of the FA Cup. On top of that he won a Fourth Division Championship medal in 1959. In the mid-seventies he became manager at Vale Park, following periods as a coach and a scout.

Sid Tickridge (b. Stepney 10.4.23; d. 6.1.97). A full-back who won England schoolboy honours in the thirties. He made his League debut for Tottenham in 1946 and made 95 League appearances before moving across London to Chelsea in March, 1951. At Stamford Bridge he made 61 League appearances, then joined Brentford in 1955. Following 62 League outings, injury forced his retirement in 1957.

Gary Thompson (b. Glasgow 11.6.56; d. 3.11.96). A combative midfielder who played for Morton, Falkirk, Alloa, Dunfermline, St Johnstone and Forfar in a career that spanned the late seventies to 1990.

Ray Thompson (b. Bishop Auckland 21.10.25; d. 1996). A full-back who began at Sunderland after the war, but did not make a League appearance during two years at Roker. Ray moved to Hartlepools in January, 1947, and gave sterling service, making 374 League appearances and scoring 12 times.

Cammy Thomson (b. 1948; d. 1996). Centre-half and skipper of Queens Park in the seventies, he made nearly 200 appearances for the Glasgow club. In December, 1973, he was called upon to take over in goal during a Scottish Cup first round match against Edinburgh University, when goalkeeper Lowrie was sent off. Cammy not only saved a penalty, he remained unbeaten during a remarkable one-nil win. Queens Park went on to beat Hawick Royal Albert in the second round, before losing in round three to Rangers.

Geoff Walker (b. Bradford 29.9.26; d. 13.3.97). Geoff began at Bradford Park Avenue during the war years, but his left-wing exploits were spotted by Middlesbrough after hostilities and he joined the Ayresome Park club in June, 1946. 239 League games and 51 goals followed until, in December, 1954, he signed for Doncaster Rovers. He made 84 League appearances and scored 15 goals at Rovers before seeing out his League career with Bradford City in the 1957–58 season.

Jock Wallace (b. Wallyford; d. 24.7.96). John Martin Bokas Wallace started out at Workington and followed in his father's footsteps as a goalkeeper. He made five League appearances for the club and then saw army service before resuming his football career with Berwick Rangers and Airdrie in the mid-fifties. In October, 1959, he came south to join West Bromwich Albion. A return to Scotland was always on the cards and he became manager of Berwick Rangers in 1966. One of his early successes was masterminding a one-nil win over Rangers in the Scottish Cup in 1967. Two years later he went to Hearts as coach and assistant manager. In 1970, he accepted the position of coach at Rangers and became manager in 1972. With Jock at the helm Rangers won the Championship in 1975, the treble the following year, and again in 1978. He then left to join Leicester City and guided the Filberts to the Second Division title in 1980. He left two years later to take over at Motherwell, but after only a year returned to Rangers where he had Scottish League Cup success in 1984 and 1985. Twelve months later he was appointed coach at Seville, but returned in 1987, and saw out his managerial career with Colchester United in 1989.

George Warburton (b. Netherlands 1916; d. 26.10.96). Played non-League football for Morecambe and had spells at Aston Villa and Preston, without making a League appearance. In the 1938–39 season he was transferred to Chester, where he played 10 matches and scored once. During the war he guested for Chester, Notts County, Leeds United, Middlesbrough and Darlington.

Dickie Whitehead (b. 1928; d. 4.8.96). A wing-half with Hearts in the late forties and early fifties, Dickie went on to play for Stirling Albion and Queen of the South.

Gordon Williams (b. Swindon 19.6.25; d. 23.6.96). A one-club man who played at wing-half for his local club and made 127 League appearances (13 goals) between 1946 and 1956.

Kilburn Wilmot (b. Nuneaton 3.4.11; d. 4.96). A well-known character in the midlands who served Nuneaton Town, Hinckley United, Coventry City, Walsall and Dudley Town. He also played cricket for Warwickshire during the thirties.

George Young (b. Grangemouth 27.10.22; d. 10.1.97). George captained Scotland 48 times in 53 appearances between 1948 and 1957. He was a superbly talented defender who starred for Rangers during six Championship victories, four Scottish Cup successes and two League Cup triumphs. He could play either at full-back or centre-half and is one of the few players never to have been cautioned or sent off.

THE FA CARLING PREMIERSHIP
and NATIONWIDE FOOTBALL LEAGUE
FIXTURES 1997–98

Saturday 9 August 1997
FA Carling Premiership
Barnsley v West Ham U
Blackburn R v Derby Co
Coventry C v Chelsea
Everton v Crystal Palace
Leeds U v Arsenal
Leicester C v Aston Villa
Newcastle U v Sheffield W
Southampton v Bolton W
Wimbledon v Liverpool

Nationwide Football League Division 1
Birmingham C v Stoke C
Bradford C v Stockport Co
Bury v Reading
Manchester C v Portsmouth
Middlesbrough v Charlton Ath
Norwich C v Wolverhampton W
Oxford U v Huddersfield T
Port Vale v Nottingham F
QPR v Ipswich T
Swindon T v Crewe Alex
WBA v Tranmere R

Nationwide Football League Division 2
Blackpool v Luton T
Bristol R v Plymouth Arg
Chesterfield v Walsall
Fulham v Wrexham
Gillingham v Preston NE
Grimsby T v Bristol C
Millwall v Brentford
Northampton T v AFC Bournemouth
Oldham Ath v York C
Southend U v Carlisle U
Watford v Burnley
Wigan Ath v Wycombe W

Nationwide Football League Division 3
Chester C v Lincoln C
Colchester U v Darlington
Exeter C v Hartlepool U
Leyton Orient v Cardiff C
Macclesfield T v Torquay U
Mansfield T v Hull C
Notts Co v Rochdale
Peterborough U v Scunthorpe U
Rotherham U v Barnet
Scarborough v Cambridge U
Shrewsbury T v Doncaster R
Swansea C v Brighton & HA

Sunday 10 August 1997
FA Carling Premiership
Tottenham H v Manchester U (4:00)

Nationwide Football League Division 1
Sheffield U v Sunderland (1:00)

Monday 11 August 1997
FA Carling Premiership
Arsenal v Coventry C (8:00)

Tuesday 12 August 1997
FA Carling Premiership
Crystal Palace v Barnsley

Wednesday 13 August 1997
FA Carling Premiership
Aston Villa v Blackburn R
Derby Co v Wimbledon
Liverpool v Leicester C
Manchester U v Southampton (8:00)
Sheffield W v Leeds U
West Ham U v Tottenham H

Friday 15 August 1997
Nationwide Football League Division 1
Bradford C v Stoke C
Nottingham F v Norwich C

Saturday 16 August 1997
Nationwide Football League Division 1
Charlton Ath v Oxford U
Crewe Alex v WBA
Huddersfield T v Birmingham C
Portsmouth v Port Vale
Reading v Swindon T
Stockport Co v Bury
Sunderland v Manchester C
Tranmere R v QPR
Wolverhampton W v Sheffield U

Nationwide Football League Division 2
AFC Bournemouth v Wigan Ath
Brentford v Chesterfield
Bristol C v Blackpool
Burnley v Gillingham
Carlisle U v Watford
Plymouth Arg v Grimsby T
Preston NE v Millwall
Walsall v Fulham
Wrexham v Oldham Ath
Wycombe W v Northampton T
York C v Bristol R

Nationwide Football League Division 3
Barnet v Exeter C
Brighton & HA v Macclesfield T
Cambridge U v Rotherham U
Cardiff C v Chester C
Darlington v Swansea C
Doncaster R v Peterborough U
Hartlepool U v Colchester U
Hull C v Notts Co
Lincoln C v Shrewsbury T
Rochdale v Mansfield T
Scunthorpe U v Leyton Orient
Torquay U v Scarborough

Sunday 17 August 1997
Nationwide Football League Division 1
Ipswich T v Middlesbrough (1:00)

Monday 18 August 1997
Nationwide Football League Division 2
Luton T v Southend U

Friday 22 August 1997
Nationwide Football League Division 1
Manchester C v Tranmere R

Nationwide Football League Division 3
Colchester U v Barnet
Scarborough v Brighton & HA (7:30)

Saturday 23 August 1997
FA Carling Premiership
Blackburn R v Liverpool
Coventry C v Bolton W
Everton v West Ham U
Leeds U v Crystal Palace
Leicester C v Manchester U
Newcastle U v Aston Villa
Southampton v Arsenal
Tottenham H v Derby Co
Wimbledon v Sheffield W

Nationwide Football League Division 1
Birmingham C v Reading
Bradford C v Ipswich T
Bury v Charlton Ath
Middlesbrough v Stoke C
Norwich C v Crewe Alex
Oxford U v Nottingham F
Port Vale v Sunderland
QPR v Stockport Co
Sheffield U v Portsmouth
Swindon T v Huddersfield T

Nationwide Football League Division 2
Blackpool v Wycombe W
Bristol R v Carlisle U
Chesterfield v Preston NE
Fulham v Luton T
Gillingham v Walsall
Grimsby T v Wrexham
Millwall v York C
Northampton T v Bristol C
Oldham Ath v AFC Bournemouth
Southend U v Burnley
Watford v Brentford
Wigan Ath v Plymouth Arg

Nationwide Football League Division 3
Chester C v Cambridge U
Exeter C v Darlington
Leyton Orient v Rochdale
Macclesfield T v Doncaster R
Mansfield T v Cardiff C
Notts Co v Lincoln C
Peterborough U v Hull C
Rotherham U v Hartlepool U
Shrewsbury T v Torquay U
Swansea C v Scunthorpe U

Sunday 24 August 1997
FA Carling Premiership
Barnsley v Chelsea (4:00)

Nationwide Football League Division 1
WBA v Wolverhampton W (1:00)

Monday 25 August 1997
FA Carling Premiership
Blackburn R v Sheffield W (8:00)

Tuesday 26 August 1997
FA Carling Premiership
Leeds U v Liverpool

Wednesday 27 August 1997
FA Carling Premiership
Barnsley v Bolton W
Coventry C v West Ham U
Everton v Manchester U (8:00)

Leicester C v Arsenal
Southampton v Crystal Palace (7:30)
Tottenham H v Aston Villa
Wimbledon v Chelsea

Friday 29 August 1997
Nationwide Football League Division 1
Stockport Co v Birmingham C

Saturday 30 August 1997
FA Carling Premiership
Arsenal v Tottenham H
Aston Villa v Leeds U
Chelsea v Southampton
Crystal Palace v Blackburn R
Derby Co v Barnsley
Manchester U v Coventry C
Sheffield W v Leicester C
West Ham U v Wimbledon

Nationwide Football League Division 1
Charlton Ath v Manchester C
Huddersfield T v Sheffield U
Ipswich T v WBA
Nottingham F v QPR
Portsmouth v Oxford U
Reading v Bradford C
Stoke C v Swindon T
Sunderland v Norwich C
Tranmere R v Middlesbrough
Wolverhampton W v Bury

Nationwide Football League Division 2
AFC Bournemouth v Blackpool
Brentford v Grimsby T
Bristol C v Wigan Ath
Burnley v Bristol R
Carlisle U v Northampton T
Luton T v Oldham Ath
Plymouth Arg v Chesterfield
Preston NE v Watford
Walsall v Southend U
Wycombe W v Fulham
York C v Gillingham

Nationwide Football League Division 3
Barnet v Chester C
Brighton & HA v Leyton Orient
Cambridge U v Shrewsbury T
Cardiff C v Notts Co
Darlington v Rotherham U
Doncaster R v Exeter C
Hartlepool U v Macclesfield T
Hull C v Swansea C
Lincoln C v Scarborough
Rochdale v Peterborough U
Scunthorpe U v Mansfield T
Torquay U v Colchester U

Sunday 31 August 1997
FA Carling Premiership
Liverpool v Newcastle U (4:00)

Nationwide Football League Division 1
Crewe Alex v Port Vale (1:00)

Monday 1 September 1997
FA Carling Premiership
Bolton W v Everton (8:00)

Tuesday 2 September 1997
Nationwide Football League Division 1
Charlton Ath v Sheffield U
Crewe Alex v Bury
Huddersfield T v Bradford C
Ipswich T v Swindon T
Portsmouth v Norwich C
Reading v QPR
Stockport Co v Middlesbrough (7:30)
Sunderland v Oxford U
Tranmere R v Birmingham C

Nationwide Football League Division 2
AFC Bournemouth v Bristol R

Brentford v Gillingham
Bristol C v Fulham
Burnley v Oldham Ath
Carlisle U v Wigan Ath
Luton T v Millwall
Plymouth Arg v Watford
Preston NE v Grimsby T
Walsall v Northampton T
Wrexham v Blackpool (7:30)
Wycombe W v Southend U
York C v Chesterfield

Nationwide Football League Division 3
Barnet v Swansea C
Cambridge U v Colchester U
Cardiff C v Shrewsbury T (7:30)
Darlington v Scarborough (7:30)
Doncaster R v Leyton Orient (7:30)
Hartlepool U v Notts Co (7:30)
Hull C v Rotherham U (7:30)
Lincoln C v Mansfield T
Rochdale v Macclesfield T
Scunthorpe U v Chester C (7:30)
Torquay U v Exeter C (7:30)

Wednesday 3 September 1997
Nationwide Football League Division 1
Nottingham F v Manchester C
Stoke C v WBA
Wolverhampton W v Port Vale

Nationwide Football League Division 3
Brighton & HA v Peterborough U

Friday 5 September 1997
Nationwide Football League Division 1
Bradford C v Sunderland

Saturday 6 September 1997
Nationwide Football League Division 1
Birmingham C v Ipswich T
Bury v Tranmere R
Manchester C v Crewe Alex
Norwich C v Charlton Ath
Port Vale v Stockport Co
QPR v Portsmouth
Sheffield U v Stoke C
Swindon T v Nottingham F
WBA v Reading

Nationwide Football League Division 2
Blackpool v Carlisle U
Bristol R v Walsall
Chesterfield v Burnley
Fulham v Plymouth Arg
Gillingham v AFC Bournemouth
Grimsby T v York C
Millwall v Bristol C
Northampton T v Luton T
Oldham Ath v Preston NE
Southend U v Brentford
Watford v Wycombe W

Nationwide Football League Division 3
Chester C v Hull C
Colchester U v Brighton & HA
Exeter C v Cardiff C
Leyton Orient v Cambridge U
Macclesfield T v Darlington
Mansfield T v Doncaster R
Notts Co v Scunthorpe U
Peterborough U v Barnet
Rotherham U v Lincoln C
Scarborough v Hartlepool U
Shrewsbury T v Rochdale
Swansea C v Torquay U

Sunday 7 September 1997
Nationwide Football League Division 1
Oxford U v Wolverhampton W (1:00)

Monday 8 September 1997
Nationwide Football League Division 2
Wigan Ath v Wrexham

Tuesday 9 September 1997
Nationwide Football League Division 1
Middlesbrough v Huddersfield T

Friday 12 September 1997
Nationwide Football League Division 1
Bury v Manchester C

Nationwide Football League Division 3
Colchester U v Scarborough

Saturday 13 September 1997
FA Carling Premiership
Arsenal v Bolton W
Barnsley v Aston Villa
Coventry C v Southampton
Crystal Palace v Chelsea
Derby Co v Everton
Leicester C v Tottenham H
Liverpool v Sheffield W
Manchester U v West Ham U
Newcastle U v Wimbledon

Nationwide Football League Division 1
Bradford C v Middlesbrough
Huddersfield T v Ipswich T
Norwich C v Port Vale
Portsmouth v Crewe Alex
QPR v WBA
Reading v Oxford U
Sheffield U v Nottingham F
Stoke C v Stockport Co
Swindon T v Tranmere R
Wolverhampton W v Charlton Ath

Nationwide Football League Division 2
AFC Bournemouth v Luton T
Bristol R v Gillingham
Fulham v Grimsby T
Millwall v Southend U
Oldham Ath v Northampton T
Plymouth Arg v Brentford
Preston NE v Walsall
Watford v Chesterfield
Wigan Ath v Blackpool
Wrexham v Bristol C
Wycombe W v Carlisle U
York C v Burnley

Nationwide Football League Division 3
Brighton & HA v Darlington
Cambridge U v Barnet
Cardiff C v Rochdale
Chester C v Shrewsbury T
Hartlepool U v Torquay U
Hull C v Lincoln C
Leyton Orient v Exeter C
Macclesfield T v Swansea C
Notts Co v Mansfield T
Rotherham U v Peterborough U
Scunthorpe U v Doncaster R

Sunday 14 September 1997
FA Carling Premiership
Blackburn R v Leeds U (4:00)

Nationwide Football League Division 1
Birmingham C v Sunderland (1:00)

Friday 19 September 1997
Nationwide Football League Division 2
Brentford v Wycombe W

Saturday 20 September 1997
FA Carling Premiership
Aston Villa v Derby Co
Bolton W v Manchester U
Everton v Barnsley
Leeds U v Leicester C
Sheffield W v Coventry C
Southampton v Liverpool
Tottenham H v Blackburn R
West Ham U v Newcastle U
Wimbledon v Crystal Palace

Nationwide Football League Division 1
Crewe Alex v QPR
Ipswich T v Stoke C
Manchester C v Norwich C
Middlesbrough v Birmingham C
Nottingham F v Portsmouth
Oxford U v Sheffield U
Port Vale v Bury
Stockport Co v Huddersfield T
Sunderland v Wolverhampton W
Tranmere R v Reading
WBA v Swindon T

Nationwide Football League Division 2
Blackpool v Oldham Ath
Bristol C v AFC Bournemouth
Burnley v Preston NE
Carlisle U v Plymouth Arg
Chesterfield v Bristol R
Gillingham v Watford
Grimsby T v Millwall
Luton T v Wrexham
Northampton T v Wigan Ath
Southend U v Fulham
Walsall v York C

Nationwide Football League Division 3
Barnet v Scunthorpe U
Doncaster R v Cambridge U
Exeter C v Rotherham U
Lincoln C v Cardiff C
Mansfield T v Chester C
Peterborough U v Leyton Orient
Rochdale v Hull C
Scarborough v Macclesfield T
Shrewsbury T v Notts Co
Swansea C v Colchester U
Torquay U v Brighton & HA

Sunday 21 September 1997

FA Carling Premiership
Chelsea v Arsenal (4:00)

Nationwide Football League Division 1
Charlton Ath v Bradford C (1:00)

Nationwide Football League Division 3
Darlington v Hartlepool U

Monday 22 September 1997

FA Carling Premiership
Liverpool v Aston Villa (8:00)

Tuesday 23 September 1997

FA Carling Premiership
Bolton W v Tottenham H
Wimbledon v Barnsley

Wednesday 24 September 1997

FA Carling Premiership
Arsenal v West Ham U (8:00)
Coventry C v Crystal Palace
Leicester C v Blackburn R
Manchester U v Chelsea (8:00)
Newcastle U v Everton
Sheffield W v Derby Co
Southampton v Leeds U (7:30)

Friday 26 September 1997

Nationwide Football League Division 1
Norwich C v Ipswich T

Saturday 27 September 1997

FA Carling Premiership
Aston Villa v Sheffield W
Barnsley v Leicester C
Chelsea v Newcastle U
Crystal Palace v Bolton W
Derby Co v Southampton
Everton v Arsenal
Leeds U v Manchester U
Tottenham H v Wimbledon
West Ham U v Liverpool

Nationwide Football League Division 1
Bury v WBA
Charlton Ath v Stockport Co
Crewe Alex v Tranmere R
Manchester C v Swindon T
Nottingham F v Stoke C
Oxford U v Bradford C
Port Vale v QPR
Portsmouth v Reading
Sheffield U v Birmingham C
Wolverhampton W v Huddersfield T

Nationwide Football League Division 2
AFC Bournemouth v Grimsby T
Blackpool v Southend U
Brentford v Burnley
Bristol C v Luton T
Carlisle U v Gillingham
Northampton T v Millwall
Oldham Ath v Bristol R
Plymouth Arg v Walsall
Watford v York C
Wigan Ath v Fulham
Wrexham v Chesterfield
Wycombe W v Preston NE

Nationwide Football League Division 3
Barnet v Lincoln C
Brighton & HA v Rochdale
Cambridge U v Cardiff C
Colchester U v Exeter C
Darlington v Mansfield T
Hartlepool U v Shrewsbury T
Macclesfield T v Peterborough U
Rotherham U v Chester C
Scarborough v Notts Co
Scunthorpe U v Hull C
Swansea C v Leyton Orient
Torquay U v Doncaster R

Sunday 28 September 1997

FA Carling Premiership
Blackburn R v Coventry C (4:00)

Nationwide Football League Division 1
Sunderland v Middlesbrough (1:00)

Tuesday 30 September 1997

Nationwide Football League Division 2
Wrexham v Millwall (7:30)

Friday 3 October 1997

Nationwide Football League Division 1
Huddersfield T v Nottingham F

Saturday 4 October 1997

FA Carling Premiership
Arsenal v Barnsley
Bolton W v Aston Villa
Coventry C v Leeds U
Manchester U v Crystal Palace
Newcastle U v Tottenham H
Sheffield W v Everton
Southampton v West Ham U
Wimbledon v Blackburn R

Nationwide Football League Division 1
Birmingham C v Crewe Alex
Bradford C v Wolverhampton W
Ipswich T v Manchester C
QPR v Charlton Ath
Reading v Sunderland
Stockport Co v Portsmouth
Stoke C v Bury
Swindon T v Port Vale
Tranmere R v Norwich C
WBA v Oxford U

Nationwide Football League Division 2
Bristol R v Wrexham
Burnley v Wycombe W
Chesterfield v AFC Bournemouth
Fulham v Oldham Ath
Gillingham v Bristol C

Grimsby T v Wigan Ath
Luton T v Watford
Millwall v Blackpool
Preston NE v Brentford
Southend U v Northampton T
Walsall v Carlisle U
York C v Plymouth Arg

Nationwide Football League Division 3
Cardiff C v Barnet
Chester C v Hartlepool U
Doncaster R v Brighton & HA
Exeter C v Scarborough
Hull C v Torquay U
Leyton Orient v Macclesfield T
Lincoln C v Cambridge U
Mansfield T v Colchester U
Notts Co v Darlington
Peterborough U v Swansea C
Rochdale v Scunthorpe U
Shrewsbury T v Rotherham U

Sunday 5 October 1997

FA Carling Premiership
Liverpool v Chelsea (4:00)

Nationwide Football League Division 1
Middlesbrough v Sheffield U (1:00)

Monday 6 October 1997

FA Carling Premiership
Leicester C v Derby Co (8:00)

Saturday 11 October 1997

Nationwide Football League Division 1
Bradford C v Sheffield U
Huddersfield T v Charlton Ath
Ipswich T v Sunderland
Middlesbrough v Nottingham F
QPR v Norwich C
Reading v Crewe Alex
Stockport Co v Oxford U
Swindon T v Bury
Tranmere R v Portsmouth
WBA v Manchester C

Nationwide Football League Division 2
Bristol R v Watford
Burnley v Carlisle U
Chesterfield v Wigan Ath
Fulham v Blackpool
Gillingham v Wycombe W
Grimsby T v Northampton T
Luton T v Plymouth Arg
Millwall v Oldham Ath
Preston NE v AFC Bournemouth
Southend U v Bristol C
Walsall v Wrexham
York C v Brentford

Nationwide Football League Division 3
Cardiff C v Scunthorpe U
Chester C v Brighton & HA
Doncaster R v Hartlepool U
Exeter C v Swansea C
Hull C v Scarborough
Leyton Orient v Rotherham U
Lincoln C v Torquay U
Mansfield T v Cambridge U
Notts Co v Macclesfield T
Peterborough U v Colchester U
Rochdale v Darlington
Shrewsbury T v Barnet

Sunday 12 October 1997

Nationwide Football League Division 1
Birmingham C v Wolverhampton W (4:00)
Stoke C v Port Vale (1:00)

Friday 17 October 1997

Nationwide Football League Division 2
Bristol C v York C
Carlisle U v Preston NE

Saturday 18 October 1997

FA Carling Premiership
Aston Villa v Wimbledon
Blackburn R v Southampton
Chelsea v Leicester C
Crystal Palace v Arsenal
Derby Co v Manchester U
Everton v Liverpool
Leeds U v Newcastle U
West Ham U v Bolton W

Nationwide Football League Division 1
Bury v Birmingham C
Crewe Alex v Middlesbrough
Manchester C v Reading
Norwich C v Stockport Co
Nottingham F v Tranmere R
Oxford U v Ipswich T
Port Vale v Bradford C
Portsmouth v WBA
Sheffield U v QPR
Sunderland v Huddersfield T
Wolverhampton W v Swindon T

Nationwide Football League Division 2
AFC Bournemouth v Fulham
Blackpool v Grimsby T
Brentford v Walsall
Northampton T v Gillingham
Oldham Ath v Chesterfield
Plymouth Arg v Southend U
Watford v Millwall
Wigan Ath v Luton T
Wrexham v Burnley
Wycombe W v Bristol R

Nationwide Football League Division 3
Barnet v Hull C
Brighton & HA v Exeter C
Cambridge U v Rochdale
Colchester U v Shrewsbury T
Darlington v Doncaster R
Hartlepool U v Leyton Orient
Macclesfield T v Mansfield T
Rotherham U v Cardiff C
Scarborough v Peterborough U
Scunthorpe U v Lincoln C
Swansea C v Notts Co
Torquay U v Chester C

Sunday 19 October 1997

FA Carling Premiership
Tottenham H v Sheffield W (4:00)

Nationwide Football League Division 1
Charlton Ath v Stoke C (1:00)

Monday 20 October 1997

FA Carling Premiership
Barnsley v Coventry C (8:00)

Tuesday 21 October 1997

Nationwide Football League Division 1
Bury v QPR
Crewe Alex v Ipswich T
Oxford U v Middlesbrough
Port Vale v Huddersfield T
Portsmouth v Bradford C
Sheffield U v Stockport Co
Sunderland v Swindon T

Nationwide Football League Division 2
AFC Bournemouth v Millwall
Blackpool v Chesterfield (7:30)
Brentford v Bristol R
Bristol C v Preston NE
Carlisle U v Luton T
Northampton T v York C
Oldham Ath v Grimsby T
Plymouth Arg v Burnley
Watford v Fulham
Wigan Ath v Gillingham
Wrexham v Southend U (7:30)
Wycombe W v Walsall

Nationwide Football League Division 3
Barnet v Rochdale
Cambridge U v Hull C
Colchester U v Doncaster R
Darlington v Cardiff C (7:30)
Hartlepool U v Peterborough U (7:30)
Macclesfield T v Exeter C
Rotherham U v Notts Co
Scarborough v Chester C (7:30)
Scunthorpe U v Shrewsbury T (7:30)
Swansea C v Mansfield T (7:30)
Torquay U v Leyton Orient (7:30)

Wednesday 22 October 1997

Nationwide Football League Division 1
Charlton Ath v Birmingham C
Manchester C v Stoke C
Norwich C v Reading
Nottingham F v WBA
Wolverhampton W v Tranmere R

Nationwide Football League Division 3
Brighton & HA v Lincoln C

Friday 24 October 1997

Nationwide Football League Division 1
Reading v Nottingham F

Nationwide Football League Division 3
Doncaster R v Swansea C (7:30)

Saturday 25 October 1997

FA Carling Premiership
Coventry C v Everton
Liverpool v Derby Co
Manchester U v Barnsley
Newcastle U v Blackburn R
Sheffield W v Crystal Palace
Southampton v Tottenham H
Wimbledon v Leeds U

Nationwide Football League Division 1
Birmingham C v Oxford U
Bradford C v Crewe Alex
Huddersfield T v Portsmouth
Ipswich T v Bury
Middlesbrough v Port Vale
Stockport Co v Wolverhampton W
Stoke C v Sunderland
Swindon T v Norwich C
Tranmere R v Charlton Ath
WBA v Sheffield U

Nationwide Football League Division 2
Bristol R v Blackpool
Burnley v AFC Bournemouth
Chesterfield v Wycombe W
Fulham v Northampton T
Gillingham v Plymouth Arg
Grimsby T v Watford
Luton T v Brentford
Millwall v Wigan Ath
Preston NE v Wrexham
Southend U v Oldham Ath
Walsall v Bristol C
York C v Carlisle U

Nationwide Football League Division 3
Cardiff C v Hartlepool U
Chester C v Macclesfield T
Exeter C v Scunthorpe U
Hull C v Brighton & HA
Leyton Orient v Colchester U
Lincoln C v Darlington
Mansfield T v Barnet
Notts Co v Cambridge U
Peterborough U v Torquay U
Rochdale v Rotherham U
Shrewsbury T v Scarborough

Sunday 26 October 1997

FA Carling Premiership
Arsenal v Aston Villa (4:00)
Bolton W v Chelsea (3:00)

Nationwide Football League Division 1
QPR v Manchester C (1:00)

Monday 27 October 1997

FA Carling Premiership
Leicester C v West Ham U (8:00)

Friday 31 October 1997

Nationwide Football League Division 1
Portsmouth v Swindon T

Nationwide Football League Division 3
Colchester U v Scunthorpe U

Saturday 1 November 1997

FA Carling Premiership
Aston Villa v Chelsea
Barnsley v Blackburn R
Bolton W v Liverpool
Derby Co v Arsenal
Manchester U v Sheffield W
Newcastle U v Leicester C
Tottenham H v Leeds U
Wimbledon v Coventry C

Nationwide Football League Division 1
Bradford C v WBA
Charlton Ath v Ipswich T
Huddersfield T v Stoke C
Norwich C v Bury
Nottingham F v Crewe Alex
Oxford U v Manchester C
Port Vale v Reading
QPR v Birmingham C
Sheffield U v Tranmere R
Stockport Co v Sunderland
Wolverhampton W v Middlesbrough

Nationwide Football League Division 2
AFC Bournemouth v Brentford
Bristol C v Oldham Ath
Burnley v Walsall
Carlisle U v Wrexham
Fulham v Chesterfield
Gillingham v Millwall
Grimsby T v Southend U
Northampton T v Bristol R
Preston NE v Plymouth Arg
Watford v Blackpool
Wigan Ath v York C
Wycombe W v Luton T

Nationwide Football League Division 3
Barnet v Notts Co
Cambridge U v Torquay U
Chester C v Rochdale
Darlington v Hull C
Exeter C v Peterborough U
Hartlepool U v Brighton & HA
Lincoln C v Leyton Orient
Rotherham U v Macclesfield T
Scarborough v Doncaster R
Shrewsbury T v Mansfield T

Sunday 2 November 1997

FA Carling Premiership
Everton v Southampton (4:00)

Nationwide Football League Division 3
Cardiff C v Swansea C (12:00)

Monday 3 November 1997

FA Carling Premiership
West Ham U v Crystal Palace (8:00)

Tuesday 4 November 1997

Nationwide Football League Division 1
Birmingham C v Bradford C
Bury v Nottingham F
Crewe Alex v Wolverhampton W
Ipswich T v Stockport Co
Manchester C v Port Vale
Reading v Sheffield U
Sunderland v Charlton Ath

Tranmere R v Huddersfield T
WBA v Norwich C

Nationwide Football League Division 2
Blackpool v Northampton T (7:30)
Brentford v Carlisle U
Bristol R v Bristol C
Chesterfield v Gillingham
Luton T v Burnley
Oldham Ath v Wigan Ath
Plymouth Arg v Wycombe W
Southend U v Watford
Walsall v Grimsby T
Wrexham v AFC Bournemouth (7:30)
York C v Preston NE

Nationwide Football League Division 3
Doncaster R v Cardiff C (7:30)
Hull C v Exeter C (7:30)
Leyton Orient v Scarborough
Macclesfield T v Colchester U
Mansfield T v Rotherham U
Notts Co v Chester C
Peterborough U v Shrewsbury T
Rochdale v Lincoln C
Scunthorpe U v Cambridge U (7:30)
Swansea C v Hartlepool U (7:30)
Torquay U v Darlington

Wednesday 5 November 1997
Nationwide Football League Division 1
Middlesbrough v Portsmouth
Stoke C v Oxford U
Swindon T v QPR

Nationwide Football League Division 2
Millwall v Fulham

Nationwide Football League Division 3
Brighton & HA v Barnet

Friday 7 November 1997
Nationwide Football League Division 1
Manchester C v Huddersfield T

Saturday 8 November 1997
FA Carling Premiership
Blackburn R v Everton
Coventry C v Newcastle U
Crystal Palace v Aston Villa
Leeds U v Derby Co
Liverpool v Tottenham H
Sheffield W v Bolton W
Southampton v Barnsley

Nationwide Football League Division 1
Birmingham C v Norwich C
Bury v Portsmouth
Crewe Alex v Oxford U
Middlesbrough v QPR
Reading v Stockport Co
Stoke C v Wolverhampton W
Sunderland v Nottingham F
Swindon T v Bradford C
Tranmere R v Port Vale
WBA v Charlton Ath

Nationwide Football League Division 2
Blackpool v Burnley
Brentford v Bristol C
Bristol R v Fulham
Chesterfield v Grimsby T
Luton T v Preston NE
Millwall v Carlisle U
Oldham Ath v Gillingham
Plymouth Arg v AFC Bournemouth
Southend U v Wigan Ath
Walsall v Watford
Wrexham v Northampton T
York C v Wycombe W

Nationwide Football League Division 3
Barnet v Doncaster R
Brighton & HA v Rotherham U
Cardiff C v Torquay U

Hull C v Shrewsbury T
Leyton Orient v Chester C
Macclesfield T v Cambridge U
Mansfield T v Scarborough
Notts Co v Exeter C
Peterborough U v Darlington
Rochdale v Colchester U
Scunthorpe U v Hartlepool U
Swansea C v Lincoln C

Sunday 9 November 1997
FA Carling Premiership
Arsenal v Manchester U (4:00)
Chelsea v West Ham U (3:00)

Nationwide Football League Division 1
Ipswich T v Sheffield U (1:00)

Monday 10 November 1997
FA Carling Premiership
Leicester C v Wimbledon (8:00)

Saturday 15 November 1997
Nationwide Football League Division 1
Bradford C v Tranmere R
Charlton Ath v Crewe Alex
Huddersfield T v Reading
Norwich C v Middlesbrough
Nottingham F v Birmingham C
Oxford U v Bury
Port Vale v WBA
Portsmouth v Sunderland
QPR v Stoke C
Sheffield U v Manchester C
Stockport Co v Swindon T
Wolverhampton W v Ipswich T

Tuesday 18 November 1997
Nationwide Football League Division 2
AFC Bournemouth v Southend U
Bristol C v Plymouth Arg
Burnley v Millwall
Carlisle U v Chesterfield
Fulham v York C
Gillingham v Blackpool
Grimsby T v Luton T
Northampton T v Brentford
Preston NE v Bristol R
Watford v Oldham Ath
Wigan Ath v Walsall
Wycombe W v Wrexham

Nationwide Football League Division 3
Barnet v Torquay U
Cambridge U v Brighton & HA
Cardiff C v Hull C (7:30)
Chester C v Peterborough U (7:30)
Colchester U v Notts Co
Darlington v Leyton Orient (7:30)
Exeter C v Mansfield T
Hartlepool U v Rochdale (7:30)
Lincoln C v Doncaster R
Rotherham U v Scunthorpe U
Scarborough v Swansea C (7:30)
Shrewsbury T v Macclesfield T

Friday 21 November 1997
Nationwide Football League Division 2
Fulham v Gillingham

Saturday 22 November 1997
FA Carling Premiership
Aston Villa v Everton
Blackburn R v Chelsea
Derby Co v Coventry C
Leicester C v Bolton W
Liverpool v Barnsley
Newcastle U v Southampton
Sheffield W v Arsenal
Wimbledon v Manchester U

Nationwide Football League Division 1
Bury v Sunderland
Crewe Alex v Stockport Co

Manchester C v Bradford C
Norwich C v Oxford U
Nottingham F v Charlton Ath
Port Vale v Sheffield U
Portsmouth v Wolverhampton W
QPR v Huddersfield T
Reading v Ipswich T
Swindon T v Middlesbrough
Tranmere R v Stoke C

Nationwide Football League Division 2
AFC Bournemouth v Carlisle U
Blackpool v York C
Bristol C v Wycombe W
Grimsby T v Burnley
Luton T v Walsall
Millwall v Chesterfield
Northampton T v Watford
Oldham Ath v Brentford
Southend U v Bristol R
Wigan Ath v Preston NE
Wrexham v Plymouth Arg

Nationwide Football League Division 3
Brighton & HA v Cardiff C
Colchester U v Lincoln C
Darlington v Cambridge U
Doncaster R v Rochdale
Exeter C v Shrewsbury T
Hartlepool U v Barnet
Leyton Orient v Notts Co
Macclesfield T v Hull C
Peterborough U v Mansfield T
Scarborough v Rotherham U
Swansea C v Chester C
Torquay U v Scunthorpe U

Sunday 23 November 1997
FA Carling Premiership
Leeds U v West Ham U (4:00)

Nationwide Football League Division 1
WBA v Birmingham C (1:00)

Monday 24 November 1997
FA Carling Premiership
Tottenham H v Crystal Palace (8:00)

Wednesday 26 November 1997
FA Carling Premiership
Chelsea v Everton

Friday 28 November 1997
Nationwide Football League Division 1
Charlton Ath v Swindon T

Saturday 29 November 1997
FA Carling Premiership
Barnsley v Leeds U
Bolton W v Wimbledon
Chelsea v Derby Co
Coventry C v Leicester C
Crystal Palace v Newcastle U
Everton v Tottenham H
Manchester U v Blackburn R
Southampton v Sheffield W
West Ham U v Aston Villa

Nationwide Football League Division 1
Birmingham C v Portsmouth
Bradford C v Norwich C
Huddersfield T v Bury
Ipswich T v Nottingham F
Middlesbrough v WBA
Oxford U v Port Vale
Sheffield U v Crewe Alex
Stockport Co v Manchester C
Stoke C v Reading
Sunderland v Tranmere R
Wolverhampton W v QPR

Nationwide Football League Division 2
Brentford v Wrexham
Bristol R v Millwall
Burnley v Northampton T

Carlisle U v Bristol C
Chesterfield v Southend U
Gillingham v Grimsby T
Plymouth Arg v Oldham Ath
Preston NE v Fulham
Walsall v Blackpool
Watford v Wigan Ath
Wycombe W v AFC Bournemouth
York C v Luton T

Nationwide Football League Division 3
Barnet v Darlington
Cambridge U v Hartlepool U
Cardiff C v Scarborough
Chester C v Exeter C
Hull C v Doncaster R
Lincoln C v Macclesfield T
Mansfield T v Leyton Orient
Notts Co v Peterborough U
Rochdale v Torquay U
Rotherham U v Colchester U
Scunthorpe U v Brighton & HA
Shrewsbury T v Swansea C

Sunday 30 November 1997
FA Carling Premiership
Arsenal v Liverpool (4:00)

Monday 1 December 1997
FA Carling Premiership
Bolton W v Newcastle U (8:00)

Tuesday 2 December 1997
Nationwide Football League Division 2
AFC Bournemouth v York C
Blackpool v Plymouth Arg (7:30)
Bristol C v Burnley
Fulham v Brentford
Grimsby T v Wycombe W
Luton T v Gillingham
Northampton T v Chesterfield
Oldham Ath v Carlisle U
Southend U v Preston NE
Wigan Ath v Bristol R
Wrexham v Watford (7:30)

Nationwide Football League Division 3
Colchester U v Cardiff C
Darlington v Shrewsbury T (7:30)
Doncaster R v Chester C (7:30)
Exeter C v Lincoln C
Hartlepool U v Hull C (7:30)
Leyton Orient v Barnet
Macclesfield T v Scunthorpe U
Peterborough U v Cambridge U
Scarborough v Rochdale (7:30)
Swansea C v Rotherham U (7:30)
Torquay U v Mansfield T (7:30)

Wednesday 3 December 1997
Nationwide Football League Division 2
Millwall v Walsall

Nationwide Football League Division 3
Brighton & HA v Notts Co

Saturday 6 December 1997
FA Carling Premiership
Aston Villa v Coventry C
Blackburn R v Bolton W
Derby Co v West Ham U
Leeds U v Everton
Leicester C v Crystal Palace
Liverpool v Manchester U (11:15)
Newcastle U v Arsenal
Tottenham H v Chelsea

Nationwide Football League Division 1
Bury v Middlesbrough
Crewe Alex v Huddersfield T
Manchester C v Wolverhampton W
Norwich C v Sheffield U
Nottingham F v Bradford C
Port Vale v Birmingham C

Portsmouth v Stoke C
QPR v Sunderland
Reading v Charlton Ath
Swindon T v Oxford U
Tranmere R v Ipswich T
WBA v Stockport Co

Sunday 7 December 1997
FA Carling Premiership
Wimbledon v Southampton (4:00)

Monday 8 December 1997
FA Carling Premiership
Sheffield W v Barnsley (8:00)

Friday 12 December 1997
Nationwide Football League Division 1
Oxford U v QPR

Nationwide Football League Division 2
Bristol R v Grimsby T

Nationwide Football League Division 3
Cambridge U v Exeter C

Saturday 13 December 1997
FA Carling Premiership
Arsenal v Blackburn R
Barnsley v Newcastle U
Chelsea v Leeds U
Coventry C v Tottenham H
Crystal Palace v Liverpool
Everton v Wimbledon
Southampton v Leicester C
West Ham U v Sheffield W

Nationwide Football League Division 1
Birmingham C v Manchester C
Bradford C v Bury
Charlton Ath v Port Vale
Huddersfield T v Norwich C
Ipswich T v Portsmouth
Middlesbrough v Reading
Sheffield U v Swindon T
Stockport Co v Tranmere R
Stoke C v Crewe Alex
Sunderland v WBA

Nationwide Football League Division 2
Brentford v Blackpool
Burnley v Wigan Ath
Carlisle U v Fulham
Chesterfield v Luton T
Gillingham v Southend U
Plymouth Arg v Millwall
Preston NE v Northampton T
Walsall v AFC Bournemouth
Watford v Bristol C
Wycombe W v Oldham Ath
York C v Wrexham

Nationwide Football League Division 3
Barnet v Macclesfield T
Cardiff C v Peterborough U
Chester C v Darlington
Hull C v Colchester U
Lincoln C v Hartlepool U
Mansfield T v Brighton & HA
Notts Co v Doncaster R
Rochdale v Swansea C
Rotherham U v Torquay U
Scunthorpe U v Scarborough
Shrewsbury T v Leyton Orient

Sunday 14 December 1997
FA Carling Premiership
Bolton W v Derby Co (4:00)

Nationwide Football League Division 1
Wolverhampton W v Nottingham F
(1:00)

Monday 15 December 1997
FA Carling Premiership
Manchester U v Aston Villa (8:00)

Wednesday 17 December 1997
FA Carling Premiership
Newcastle U v Derby Co

Friday 19 December 1997
Nationwide Football League Division 2
Oldham Ath v Walsall
Southend U v York C

Nationwide Football League Division 3
Colchester U v Chester C
Doncaster R v Rotherham U (7:30)
Scarborough v Barnet (7:30)

Saturday 20 December 1997
FA Carling Premiership
Aston Villa v Southampton
Blackburn R v West Ham U
Derby Co v Crystal Palace
Leeds U v Bolton W
Leicester C v Everton
Liverpool v Coventry C
Sheffield W v Chelsea
Tottenham H v Barnsley

Nationwide Football League Division 1
Bury v Sheffield U
Crewe Alex v Sunderland
Manchester C v Middlesbrough
Norwich C v Stoke C
Nottingham F v Stockport Co
Port Vale v Ipswich T
Portsmouth v Charlton Ath
QPR v Bradford C
Reading v Wolverhampton W
Swindon T v Birmingham C
Tranmere R v Oxford U
WBA v Huddersfield T

Nationwide Football League Division 2
AFC Bournemouth v Watford
Blackpool v Preston NE
Bristol C v Chesterfield
Fulham v Burnley
Grimsby T v Carlisle U
Luton T v Bristol R
Millwall v Wycombe W
Northampton T v Plymouth Arg
Wigan Ath v Brentford
Wrexham v Gillingham

Nationwide Football League Division 3
Brighton & HA v Shrewsbury T
Darlington v Scunthorpe U
Exeter C v Rochdale
Hartlepool U v Mansfield T
Leyton Orient v Hull C
Macclesfield T v Cardiff C
Peterborough U v Lincoln C
Swansea C v Cambridge U
Torquay U v Notts Co

Sunday 21 December 1997
FA Carling Premiership
Newcastle U v Manchester U (4:00)

Monday 22 December 1997
FA Carling Premiership
Wimbledon v Arsenal (8:00)

Friday 26 December 1997
FA Carling Premiership
Arsenal v Leicester C (12:00)
Aston Villa v Tottenham H (5:00)
Bolton W v Barnsley
Chelsea v Wimbledon (12:00)
Crystal Palace v Southampton (12:00)
Derby Co v Newcastle U
Liverpool v Leeds U

Manchester U v Everton
Sheffield W v Blackburn R
West Ham U v Coventry C (12:00)

Nationwide Football League Division 1
Charlton Ath v Norwich C (12:00)
Crewe Alex v Manchester C
Huddersfield T v Middlesbrough
Ipswich T v Birmingham C
Nottingham F v Swindon T
Portsmouth v QPR
Reading v WBA (12:00)
Stockport Co v Port Vale
Stoke C v Sheffield U
Sunderland v Bradford C
Tranmere R v Bury
Wolverhampton W v Oxford U

Nationwide Football League Division 2
AFC Bournemouth v Gillingham (12:00)
Brentford v Southend U (12:00)
Bristol C v Millwall (12:00)
Burnley v Chesterfield
Carlisle U v Blackpool
Luton T v Northampton T
Plymouth Arg v Fulham
Preston NE v Oldham Ath
Walsall v Bristol R
Wrexham v Wigan Ath
Wycombe W v Watford
York C v Grimsby T

Nationwide Football League Division 3
Barnet v Peterborough U (12:00)
Brighton & HA v Colchester U
Cambridge U v Leyton Orient
Cardiff C v Exeter C
Darlington v Macclesfield T
Doncaster R v Mansfield T
Hartlepool U v Scarborough
Hull C v Chester C
Lincoln C v Rotherham U
Rochdale v Shrewsbury T
Scunthorpe U v Notts Co
Torquay U v Swansea C (12:15)

Sunday 28 December 1997
FA Carling Premiership
Barnsley v Derby Co
Blackburn R v Crystal Palace
Coventry C v Manchester U
Everton v Bolton W
Leeds U v Aston Villa
Leicester C v Sheffield W
Newcastle U v Liverpool (5:00)
Tottenham H v Arsenal
Wimbledon v West Ham U

Nationwide Football League Division 1
Birmingham C v Tranmere R
Bradford C v Huddersfield T
Bury v Crewe Alex
Manchester C v Nottingham F
Middlesbrough v Stockport Co
Oxford U v Sunderland
Port Vale v Wolverhampton W (1:00)
QPR v Reading
Sheffield U v Charlton Ath
Swindon T v Ipswich T
WBA v Stoke C

Nationwide Football League Division 2
Blackpool v Wrexham
Bristol R v AFC Bournemouth
Chesterfield v York C
Fulham v Bristol C (12:00)
Gillingham v Brentford
Grimsby T v Preston NE
Millwall v Luton T
Northampton T v Walsall (12:00)
Oldham Ath v Burnley (1:00)
Southend U v Wycombe W
Watford v Plymouth Arg
Wigan Ath v Carlisle U

Nationwide Football League Division 3
Chester C v Scunthorpe U
Exeter C v Torquay U (11:00)
Leyton Orient v Doncaster R
Macclesfield T v Rochdale
Mansfield T v Lincoln C
Notts Co v Hartlepool U
Peterborough U v Brighton & HA
Rotherham U v Hull C
Scarborough v Darlington
Shrewsbury T v Cardiff C (12:00)
Swansea C v Barnet

Monday 29 December 1997
FA Carling Premiership
Southampton v Chelsea (8:00)

Nationwide Football League Division 3
Colchester U v Cambridge U

Tuesday 30 December 1997
Nationwide Football League Division 1
Norwich C v Portsmouth

Saturday 3 January 1998
Nationwide Football League Division 2
Blackpool v Bristol C
Bristol R v York C
Chesterfield v Brentford
Fulham v Walsall
Gillingham v Burnley
Grimsby T v Plymouth Arg
Millwall v Preston NE
Northampton T v Wycombe W
Oldham Ath v Wrexham
Southend U v Luton T
Watford v Carlisle U
Wigan Ath v AFC Bournemouth

Nationwide Football League Division 3
Chester C v Cardiff C
Colchester U v Hartlepool U
Exeter C v Barnet
Leyton Orient v Scunthorpe U
Macclesfield T v Brighton & HA
Mansfield T v Rochdale
Notts Co v Hull C
Peterborough U v Doncaster R
Rotherham U v Cambridge U
Scarborough v Torquay U
Shrewsbury T v Lincoln C
Swansea C v Darlington

Saturday 10 January 1998
FA Carling Premiership
Arsenal v Leeds U
Aston Villa v Leicester C
Bolton W v Southampton
Chelsea v Coventry C
Crystal Palace v Everton
Derby Co v Blackburn R
Liverpool v Wimbledon
Manchester U v Tottenham H
Sheffield W v Newcastle U
West Ham U v Barnsley

Nationwide Football League Division 1
Charlton Ath v Middlesbrough
Crewe Alex v Swindon T
Huddersfield T v Oxford U
Ipswich T v QPR
Nottingham F v Port Vale
Portsmouth v Manchester C
Reading v Bury
Stockport Co v Bradford C
Stoke C v Birmingham C
Sunderland v Sheffield U
Tranmere R v WBA
Wolverhampton W v Norwich C

Nationwide Football League Division 2
AFC Bournemouth v Northampton T
Brentford v Millwall
Bristol C v Grimsby T

Burnley v Watford
Carlisle U v Southend U
Luton T v Blackpool
Plymouth Arg v Bristol R
Preston NE v Gillingham
Walsall v Chesterfield
Wrexham v Fulham
Wycombe W v Wigan Ath
York C v Oldham Ath

Nationwide Football League Division 3
Barnet v Rotherham U
Brighton & HA v Swansea C
Cambridge U v Scarborough
Cardiff C v Leyton Orient
Darlington v Colchester U
Doncaster R v Shrewsbury T
Hartlepool U v Exeter C
Hull C v Mansfield T
Lincoln C v Chester C
Rochdale v Notts Co
Scunthorpe U v Peterborough U
Torquay U v Macclesfield T

Friday 16 January 1998
Nationwide Football League Division 1
Stoke C v Bradford C

Nationwide Football League Division 3
Colchester U v Torquay U

Saturday 17 January 1998
FA Carling Premiership
Barnsley v Crystal Palace
Blackburn R v Aston Villa
Coventry C v Arsenal
Everton v Chelsea
Leeds U v Sheffield W
Leicester C v Liverpool
Newcastle U v Bolton W
Southampton v Manchester U
Tottenham H v West Ham U
Wimbledon v Derby Co

Nationwide Football League Division 1
Birmingham C v Huddersfield T
Bury v Stockport Co
Manchester C v Sunderland
Middlesbrough v Ipswich T
Norwich C v Nottingham F
Oxford U v Charlton Ath
Port Vale v Portsmouth
QPR v Tranmere R
Sheffield U v Wolverhampton W
Swindon T v Reading
WBA v Crewe Alex

Nationwide Football League Division 2
Blackpool v AFC Bournemouth
Bristol R v Burnley (12:00)
Chesterfield v Plymouth Arg
Fulham v Wycombe W
Gillingham v York C
Grimsby T v Brentford
Millwall v Wrexham
Northampton T v Carlisle U
Oldham Ath v Luton T
Southend U v Walsall
Watford v Preston NE
Wigan Ath v Bristol C

Nationwide Football League Division 3
Chester C v Barnet
Exeter C v Doncaster R
Leyton Orient v Brighton & HA
Macclesfield T v Hartlepool U
Mansfield T v Scunthorpe U
Notts Co v Cardiff C
Peterborough U v Rochdale
Rotherham U v Darlington
Scarborough v Lincoln C
Shrewsbury T v Cambridge U
Swansea C v Hull C

Saturday 24 January 1998

Nationwide Football League Division 2
AFC Bournemouth v Oldham Ath
Brentford v Watford
Bristol C v Northampton T
Burnley v Southend U
Carlisle U v Bristol R
Luton T v Fulham
Plymouth Arg v Wigan Ath
Preston NE v Chesterfield
Walsall v Gillingham
Wrexham v Grimsby T
Wycombe W v Blackpool
York C v Millwall

Nationwide Football League Division 3
Barnet v Colchester U
Brighton & HA v Scarborough
Cambridge U v Chester C
Cardiff C v Mansfield T
Darlington v Exeter C
Doncaster R v Macclesfield T
Hartlepool U v Rotherham U
Hull C v Peterborough U
Lincoln C v Notts Co
Rochdale v Leyton Orient
Scunthorpe U v Swansea C
Torquay U v Shrewsbury T

Tuesday 27 January 1998

Nationwide Football League Division 1
Birmingham C v Stockport Co
Bradford C v Reading
Bury v Wolverhampton W
Oxford U v Portsmouth
Port Vale v Crewe Alex
Sheffield U v Huddersfield T
WBA v Ipswich T

Wednesday 28 January 1998

Nationwide Football League Division 1
Manchester C v Charlton Ath
Middlesbrough v Tranmere R
Norwich C v Sunderland
QPR v Nottingham F
Swindon T v Stoke C

Friday 30 January 1998

Nationwide Football League Division 3
Doncaster R v Scunthorpe U (7:30)

Saturday 31 January 1998

FA Carling Premiership
Arsenal v Southampton
Aston Villa v Newcastle U
Bolton W v Coventry C
Chelsea v Barnsley
Crystal Palace v Leeds U
Derby Co v Tottenham H
Liverpool v Blackburn R
Manchester U v Leicester C
Sheffield W v Wimbledon
West Ham U v Everton

Nationwide Football League Division 1
Charlton Ath v Bury
Crewe Alex v Norwich C
Huddersfield T v Swindon T
Ipswich T v Bradford C
Nottingham F v Oxford U
Portsmouth v Sheffield U
Reading v Birmingham C
Stockport Co v QPR
Stoke C v Middlesbrough
Sunderland v Port Vale
Tranmere R v Manchester C
Wolverhampton W v WBA

Nationwide Football League Division 2
Blackpool v Wigan Ath
Brentford v Plymouth Arg
Bristol C v Wrexham
Burnley v York C
Carlisle U v Wycombe W

Chesterfield v Watford
Gillingham v Bristol R
Grimsby T v Fulham
Luton T v AFC Bournemouth
Northampton T v Oldham Ath
Southend U v Millwall
Walsall v Preston NE

Nationwide Football League Division 3
Barnet v Cambridge U
Darlington v Brighton & HA
Exeter C v Leyton Orient
Lincoln C v Hull C
Mansfield T v Notts Co
Peterborough U v Rotherham U
Rochdale v Cardiff C
Scarborough v Colchester U
Shrewsbury T v Chester C
Swansea C v Macclesfield T
Torquay U v Hartlepool U

Friday 6 February 1998

Nationwide Football League Division 3
Colchester U v Swansea C

Saturday 7 February 1998

FA Carling Premiership
Arsenal v Chelsea
Barnsley v Everton
Blackburn R v Tottenham H
Coventry C v Sheffield W
Crystal Palace v Wimbledon
Derby Co v Aston Villa
Leicester C v Leeds U
Liverpool v Southampton
Manchester U v Bolton W
Newcastle U v West Ham U

Nationwide Football League Division 1
Birmingham C v Middlesbrough
Bradford C v Charlton Ath
Bury v Port Vale
Huddersfield T v Stockport Co
Norwich C v Manchester C
Portsmouth v Nottingham F
QPR v Crewe Alex
Reading v Tranmere R
Sheffield U v Oxford U
Stoke C v Ipswich T
Swindon T v WBA
Wolverhampton W v Sunderland

Nationwide Football League Division 2
AFC Bournemouth v Bristol C
Bristol R v Chesterfield
Fulham v Southend U
Millwall v Grimsby T
Oldham Ath v Blackpool
Plymouth Arg v Carlisle U
Preston NE v Burnley
Watford v Gillingham
Wigan Ath v Northampton T
Wrexham v Luton T
Wycombe W v Brentford
York C v Walsall

Nationwide Football League Division 3
Brighton & HA v Torquay U
Cambridge U v Doncaster R
Cardiff C v Lincoln C
Chester C v Mansfield T
Hartlepool U v Darlington
Hull C v Rochdale
Leyton Orient v Peterborough U
Macclesfield T v Scarborough
Notts Co v Shrewsbury T
Rotherham U v Exeter C
Scunthorpe U v Barnet

Friday 13 February 1998

Nationwide Football League Division 3
Colchester U v Mansfield T

Saturday 14 February 1998

FA Carling Premiership
Aston Villa v Barnsley
Bolton W v Arsenal
Chelsea v Crystal Palace
Everton v Derby Co
Leeds U v Blackburn R
Sheffield W v Liverpool
Southampton v Coventry C
Tottenham H v Leicester C
West Ham U v Manchester U
Wimbledon v Newcastle U

Nationwide Football League Division 1
Charlton Ath v Wolverhampton W
Crewe Alex v Portsmouth
Ipswich T v Huddersfield T
Manchester C v Bury
Middlesbrough v Bradford C
Nottingham F v Sheffield U
Oxford U v Reading
Port Vale v Norwich C
Stockport Co v Stoke C
Sunderland v Birmingham C
Tranmere R v Swindon T
WBA v QPR

Nationwide Football League Division 2
AFC Bournemouth v Chesterfield
Blackpool v Millwall
Brentford v Preston NE
Bristol C v Gillingham
Carlisle U v Walsall
Northampton T v Southend U
Oldham Ath v Fulham
Plymouth Arg v York C
Watford v Luton T (12:00)
Wigan Ath v Grimsby T
Wrexham v Bristol R
Wycombe W v Burnley

Nationwide Football League Division 3
Barnet v Cardiff C
Brighton & HA v Doncaster R
Cambridge U v Lincoln C
Darlington v Notts Co
Hartlepool U v Chester C
Macclesfield T v Leyton Orient
Rotherham U v Shrewsbury T
Scarborough v Exeter C
Scunthorpe U v Rochdale
Swansea C v Peterborough U
Torquay U v Hull C

Tuesday 17 February 1998

Nationwide Football League Division 1
Bury v Stoke C
Charlton Ath v QPR
Crewe Alex v Birmingham C
Oxford U v WBA
Port Vale v Swindon T
Portsmouth v Stockport Co
Sheffield U v Middlesbrough
Sunderland v Reading

Wednesday 18 February 1998

Nationwide Football League Division 1
Manchester C v Ipswich T
Norwich C v Tranmere R
Nottingham F v Huddersfield T
Wolverhampton W v Bradford C

Saturday 21 February 1998

FA Carling Premiership
Arsenal v Crystal Palace
Bolton W v West Ham U
Coventry C v Barnsley
Leicester C v Chelsea
Liverpool v Everton
Manchester U v Derby Co
Newcastle U v Leeds U
Sheffield W v Tottenham H
Southampton v Blackburn R
Wimbledon v Aston Villa

Nationwide Football League Division 1
Birmingham C v Sheffield U
Bradford C v Oxford U
Huddersfield T v Wolverhampton W
Ipswich T v Norwich C
Middlesbrough v Sunderland
QPR v Port Vale
Reading v Portsmouth
Stockport Co v Charlton Ath
Stoke C v Nottingham F
Swindon T v Manchester C
Tranmere R v Crewe Alex
WBA v Bury

Nationwide Football League Division 2
Bristol R v Oldham Ath
Burnley v Brentford
Chesterfield v Wrexham
Fulham v Wigan Ath
Gillingham v Carlisle U
Grimsby T v AFC Bournemouth
Luton T v Bristol C
Millwall v Northampton T
Preston NE v Wycombe W
Southend U v Blackpool
Walsall v Plymouth Arg
York C v Watford

Nationwide Football League Division 3
Cardiff C v Cambridge U
Chester C v Rotherham U
Doncaster R v Torquay U
Exeter C v Colchester U
Hull C v Scunthorpe U
Leyton Orient v Swansea C
Lincoln C v Barnet
Mansfield T v Darlington
Notts Co v Scarborough
Peterborough U v Macclesfield T
Rochdale v Brighton & HA
Shrewsbury T v Hartlepool U

Tuesday 24 February 1998
Nationwide Football League Division 1
Birmingham C v Bury
Bradford C v Port Vale
Huddersfield T v Sunderland
Ipswich T v Oxford U
Reading v Manchester C
Stockport Co v Norwich C (7:30)
Tranmere R v Nottingham F
WBA v Portsmouth

Nationwide Football League Division 2
Bristol R v Wycombe W
Burnley v Wrexham
Chesterfield v Oldham Ath
Fulham v AFC Bournemouth
Gillingham v Northampton T
Grimsby T v Blackpool
Luton T v Wigan Ath
Preston NE v Carlisle U
Southend U v Plymouth Arg
Walsall v Brentford
York C v Bristol C

Nationwide Football League Division 3
Cardiff C v Rotherham U (7:30)
Chester C v Torquay U (7:30)
Doncaster R v Darlington (7:30)
Exeter C v Brighton & HA
Hull C v Barnet (7:30)
Leyton Orient v Hartlepool U
Lincoln C v Scunthorpe U
Mansfield T v Macclesfield T
Notts Co v Swansea C
Peterborough U v Scarborough
Rochdale v Cambridge U
Shrewsbury T v Colchester U

Wednesday 25 February 1998
Nationwide Football League Division 1
Middlesbrough v Crewe Alex
QPR v Sheffield U
Stoke C v Charlton Ath
Swindon T v Wolverhampton W

Nationwide Football League Division 2
Millwall v Watford

Friday 27 February 1998
Nationwide Football League Division 3
Colchester U v Peterborough U

Saturday 28 February 1998
FA Carling Premiership
Aston Villa v Liverpool
Barnsley v Wimbledon
Blackburn R v Leicester C
Chelsea v Manchester U
Crystal Palace v Coventry C
Derby Co v Sheffield W
Everton v Newcastle U
Leeds U v Southampton
Tottenham H v Bolton W
West Ham U v Arsenal

Nationwide Football League Division 1
Bury v Swindon T
Charlton Ath v Huddersfield T
Crewe Alex v Reading
Manchester C v WBA
Norwich C v QPR
Nottingham F v Middlesbrough
Oxford U v Stockport Co
Portsmouth v Tranmere R
Sheffield U v Bradford C
Sunderland v Ipswich T
Wolverhampton W v Birmingham C

Nationwide Football League Division 2
AFC Bournemouth v Preston NE
Blackpool v Fulham
Brentford v York C
Bristol C v Southend U
Carlisle U v Burnley
Northampton T v Grimsby T
Oldham Ath v Millwall
Plymouth Arg v Luton T
Watford v Bristol R
Wigan Ath v Chesterfield
Wrexham v Walsall
Wycombe W v Gillingham

Nationwide Football League Division 3
Barnet v Shrewsbury T
Brighton & HA v Chester C
Cambridge U v Mansfield T
Darlington v Rochdale
Hartlepool U v Doncaster R
Macclesfield T v Notts Co
Rotherham U v Leyton Orient
Scarborough v Hull C
Scunthorpe U v Cardiff C
Swansea C v Exeter C
Torquay U v Lincoln C

Sunday 1 March 1998
Nationwide Football League Division 1
Port Vale v Stoke C (1:00)

Tuesday 3 March 1998
Nationwide Football League Division 1
Bradford C v Swindon T
Charlton Ath v WBA
Huddersfield T v Manchester C
Oxford U v Crewe Alex
Port Vale v Tranmere R
Portsmouth v Bury
Sheffield U v Ipswich T
Stockport Co v Reading (7:30)

Nationwide Football League Division 2
AFC Bournemouth v Plymouth Arg
Bristol C v Brentford
Burnley v Blackpool
Carlisle U v Millwall
Fulham v Bristol R
Gillingham v Oldham Ath
Grimsby T v Chesterfield
Northampton T v Wrexham

Preston NE v Luton T
Watford v Walsall
Wigan Ath v Southend U
Wycombe W v York C

Nationwide Football League Division 3
Cambridge U v Macclesfield T
Chester C v Leyton Orient (7:30)
Colchester U v Rochdale
Darlington v Peterborough U (7:30)
Doncaster R v Barnet(7:30)
Exeter C v Notts Co
Hartlepool U v Scunthorpe U (7:30)
Lincoln C v Swansea C
Rotherham U v Brighton & HA
Scarborough v Mansfield T (7:30)
Shrewsbury T v Hull C (7:30)
Torquay U v Cardiff C

Wednesday 4 March 1998
Nationwide Football League Division 1
Norwich C v Birmingham C
Nottingham F v Sunderland
QPR v Middlesbrough
Wolverhampton W v Stoke C

Friday 6 March 1998
Nationwide Football League Division 3
Doncaster R v Scarborough (7:30)

Saturday 7 March 1998
FA Carling Premiership
Arsenal v Derby Co
Blackburn R v Barnsley
Chelsea v Aston Villa
Coventry C v Wimbledon
Crystal Palace v West Ham U
Leeds U v Tottenham H
Leicester C v Newcastle U
Liverpool v Bolton W
Sheffield W v Manchester U
Southampton v Everton

Nationwide Football League Division 1
Birmingham C v QPR
Bury v Norwich C
Crewe Alex v Nottingham F
Ipswich T v Charlton Ath
Manchester C v Oxford U
Middlesbrough v Wolverhampton W
Reading v Port Vale
Stoke C v Huddersfield T
Sunderland v Stockport Co
Swindon T v Portsmouth
Tranmere R v Sheffield U
WBA v Bradford C

Nationwide Football League Division 2
Blackpool v Watford
Brentford v AFC Bournemouth
Bristol R v Northampton T
Chesterfield v Fulham
Luton T v Wycombe W
Millwall v Gillingham
Oldham Ath v Bristol C
Plymouth Arg v Preston NE
Southend U v Grimsby T
Walsall v Burnley
Wrexham v Carlisle U
York C v Wigan Ath

Nationwide Football League Division 3
Brighton & HA v Hartlepool U
Hull C v Darlington
Leyton Orient v Lincoln C
Macclesfield T v Rotherham U
Mansfield T v Shrewsbury T
Notts Co v Barnet
Peterborough U v Exeter C
Rochdale v Chester C
Scunthorpe U v Colchester U
Swansea C v Cardiff C
Torquay U v Cambridge U

Saturday 14 March 1998
FA Carling Premiership
Aston Villa v Crystal Palace
Barnsley v Southampton
Bolton W v Sheffield W
Derby Co v Leeds U
Everton v Blackburn R
Manchester U v Arsenal
Newcastle U v Coventry C
Tottenham H v Liverpool
West Ham U v Chelsea
Wimbledon v Leicester C

Nationwide Football League Division 1
Bradford C v Birmingham C
Charlton Ath v Sunderland
Huddersfield T v Tranmere R
Norwich C v WBA
Nottingham F v Bury
Oxford U v Stoke C
Port Vale v Manchester C
Portsmouth v Middlesbrough
QPR v Swindon T
Sheffield U v Reading
Stockport Co v Ipswich T
Wolverhampton W v Crewe Alex

Nationwide Football League Division 2
AFC Bournemouth v Wrexham
Bristol C v Bristol R
Burnley v Luton T
Carlisle U v Brentford
Fulham v Millwall
Gillingham v Chesterfield
Grimsby T v Walsall
Northampton T v Blackpool
Preston NE v York C
Watford v Southend U
Wigan Ath v Oldham Ath
Wycombe W v Plymouth Arg

Nationwide Football League Division 3
Barnet v Brighton & HA
Cambridge U v Scunthorpe U
Cardiff C v Doncaster R
Chester C v Notts Co
Colchester U v Macclesfield T
Darlington v Torquay U
Exeter C v Hull C
Hartlepool U v Swansea C
Lincoln C v Rochdale
Rotherham U v Mansfield T
Scarborough v Leyton Orient
Shrewsbury T v Peterborough U

Saturday 21 March 1998
Nationwide Football League Division 1
Birmingham C v Nottingham F
Bury v Oxford U
Crewe Alex v Charlton Ath
Ipswich T v Wolverhampton W
Manchester C v Sheffield U
Middlesbrough v Norwich C
Reading v Huddersfield T
Stoke C v QPR
Sunderland v Portsmouth
Swindon T v Stockport Co
Tranmere R v Bradford C
WBA v Port Vale

Nationwide Football League Division 2
Blackpool v Gillingham
Brentford v Northampton T
Bristol R v Preston NE
Chesterfield v Carlisle U
Luton T v Grimsby Tow n
Millwall v Burnley
Oldham Ath v Watford
Plymouth Arg v Bristol C
Southend U v AFC Bournemouth
Walsall v Wigan Ath
Wrexham v Wycombe W
York C v Fulham

Nationwide Football League Division 3
Brighton & HA v Cambridge U

Doncaster R v Lincoln C
Hull C v Cardiff C
Leyton Orient v Darlington
Macclesfield T v Shrewsbury T
Mansfield T v Exeter C
Notts Co v Colchester U
Peterborough U v Chester C
Rochdale v Hartlepool U
Scunthorpe U v Rotherham U
Swansea C v Scarborough
Torquay U v Barnet

Friday 27 March 1998
Nationwide Football League Division 2
Bristol R v Southend U

Saturday 28 March 1998
FA Carling Premiership
Arsenal v Sheffield W
Barnsley v Liverpool
Bolton W v Leicester C
Chelsea v Blackburn R
Coventry C v Derby Co
Crystal Palace v Tottenham H
Everton v Aston Villa
Manchester U v Wimbledon
Southampton v Newcastle U
West Ham U v Leeds U

Nationwide Football League Division 1
Birmingham C v WBA
Bradford C v Manchester C
Charlton Ath v Nottingham F
Huddersfield T v QPR
Ipswich T v Reading
Middlesbrough v Swindon T
Oxford U v Norwich C
Sheffield U v Port Vale
Stockport Co v Crewe Alex
Stoke C v Tranmere R
Sunderland v Bury
Wolverhampton W v Portsmouth

Nationwide Football League Division 2
Brentford v Oldham Ath
Burnley v Grimsby T
Carlisle U v AFC Bournemouth
Chesterfield v Millwall
Gillingham v Fulham
Plymouth Arg v Wrexham
Preston NE v Wigan Ath
Walsall v Luton T
Watford v Northampton T
Wycombe W v Bristol C
York C v Blackpool

Nationwide Football League Division 3
Barnet v Hartlepool U
Cambridge U v Darlington
Cardiff C v Brighton & HA
Chester C v Swansea C
Hull C v Macclesfield T
Lincoln C v Colchester U
Mansfield T v Peterborough U
Notts Co v Leyton Orient
Rochdale v Doncaster R
Rotherham U v Scarborough
Scunthorpe U v Torquay U
Shrewsbury T v Exeter C

Friday 3 April 1998
Nationwide Football League Division 2
Southend U v Chesterfield

Nationwide Football League Division 3
Colchester U v Rotherham U (7:30)
Scarborough v Cardiff C (7:30)

Saturday 4 April 1998
FA Carling Premiership
Aston Villa v West Ham U
Blackburn R v Manchester U
Derby Co v Chelsea
Leeds U v Barnsley
Leicester C v Coventry C

Liverpool v Arsenal
Newcastle U v Crystal Palace
Sheffield W v Southampton
Tottenham H v Everton
Wimbledon v Bolton W

Nationwide Football League Division 1
Bury v Huddersfield T
Crewe Alex v Sheffield U
Manchester C v Stockport Co
Norwich C v Bradford C
Nottingham F v Ipswich T
Port Vale v Oxford U
Portsmouth v Birmingham C
QPR v Wolverhampton W
Reading v Stoke C
Swindon T v Charlton Ath
Tranmere R v Sunderland
WBA v Middlesbrough

Nationwide Football League Division 2
AFC Bournemouth v Wycombe W
Blackpool v Walsall
Bristol C v Carlisle U
Fulham v Preston NE
Grimsby T v Gillingham
Luton T v York C
Millwall v Bristol R
Northampton T v Burnley
Oldham Ath v Plymouth Arg
Wigan Ath v Watford
Wrexham v Brentford

Nationwide Football League Division 3
Brighton & HA v Scunthorpe U
Darlington v Barnet
Doncaster R v Hull C
Exeter C v Chester C
Hartlepool U v Cambridge U
Leyton Orient v Mansfield T
Macclesfield T v Lincoln C
Peterborough U v Notts Co
Swansea C v Shrewsbury T
Torquay U v Rochdale

Friday 10 April 1998
Nationwide Football League Division 2
Wycombe W v Grimsby T (3:00)

Saturday 11 April 1998
FA Carling Premiership
Arsenal v Newcastle U
Barnsley v Sheffield W
Bolton W v Blackburn R
Chelsea v Tottenham H
Coventry C v Aston Villa
Crystal Palace v Leicester C
Everton v Leeds U
Manchester U v Liverpool
Southampton v Wimbledon
West Ham U v Derby Co

Nationwide Football League Division 1
Birmingham C v Port Vale
Bradford C v Nottingham F
Charlton Ath v Reading
Huddersfield T v Crewe Alex
Ipswich T v Tranmere R
Middlesbrough v Bury
Oxford U v Swindon T
Sheffield U v Norwich C
Stockport Co v WBA
Stoke C v Portsmouth
Sunderland v QPR
Wolverhampton W v Manchester C

Nationwide Football League Division 2
Brentford v Fulham
Bristol R v Wigan Ath
Burnley v Bristol C
Carlisle U v Oldham Ath
Chesterfield v Northampton T
Gillingham v Luton T
Plymouth Arg v Blackpool
Preston NE v Southend U
Walsall v Millwall

Watford v Wrexham
York C v AFC Bournemouth

Nationwide Football League Division 3
Barnet v Leyton Orient
Cambridge U v Peterborough U
Cardiff C v Colchester U
Chester C v Doncaster R
Hull C v Hartlepool U
Lincoln C v Exeter C
Mansfield T v Torquay U
Notts Co v Brighton & HA
Rochdale v Scarborough
Rotherham U v Swansea C
Scunthorpe U v Macclesfield T
Shrewsbury T v Darlington

Monday 13 April 1998

FA Carling Premiership
Aston Villa v Manchester U
Blackburn R v Arsenal
Derby Co v Bolton W
Leeds U v Chelsea
Liverpool v Crystal Palace
Newcastle U v Barnsley
Sheffield W v West Ham U
Tottenham H v Coventry C
Wimbledon v Everton

Nationwide Football League Division 1
Bury v Bradford C
Crewe Alex v Stoke C
Manchester C v Birmingham C
Norwich C v Huddersfield T
Nottingham F v Wolverhampton W
Port Vale v Charlton Ath
Portsmouth v Ipswich T
Reading v Middlesbrough
Swindon T v Sheffield U
Tranmere R v Stockport Co
WBA v Sunderland

Nationwide Football League Division 2
Blackpool v Brentford
Bristol C v Watford
Fulham v Carlisle U
Grimsby T v Bristol R
Millwall v Plymouth Arg
Northampton T v Preston NE
Oldham Ath v Wycombe W
Southend U v Gillingham
Wigan Ath v Burnley
Wrexham v York C

Nationwide Football League Division 3
Brighton & HA v Mansfield T
Colchester U v Hull C
Darlington v Chester C
Doncaster R v Notts Co
Exeter C v Cambridge U
Hartlepool U v Lincoln C
Leyton Orient v Shrewsbury T
Macclesfield T v Barnet
Peterborough U v Cardiff C
Scarborough v Scunthorpe U
Swansea C v Rochdale
Torquay U v Rotherham U

Tuesday 14 April 1998

FA Carling Premiership
Leicester C v Southampton

Nationwide Football League Division 1
QPR v Oxford U

Nationwide Football League Division 2
AFC Bournemouth v Walsall
Luton T v Chesterfield

Saturday 18 April 1998

FA Carling Premiership
Arsenal v Wimbledon
Barnsley v Tottenham H
Bolton W v Leeds U
Chelsea v Sheffield W
Coventry C v Liverpool

Crystal Palace v Derby Co
Everton v Leicester C
Manchester U v Newcastle U
Southampton v Aston Villa
West Ham U v Blackburn R

Nationwide Football League Division 1
Birmingham C v Swindon T
Bradford C v QPR
Charlton Ath v Portsmouth
Huddersfield T v WBA
Ipswich T v Port Vale
Middlesbrough v Manchester C
Oxford U v Tranmere R
Sheffield U v Bury
Stockport Co v Nottingham F
Stoke C v Norwich C
Sunderland v Crewe Alex
Wolverhampton W v Reading

Nationwide Football League Division 2
Brentford v Wigan Ath
Bristol R v Luton T
Burnley v Fulham
Carlisle U v Grimsby T
Chesterfield v Bristol C
Gillingham v Wrexham
Plymouth Arg v Northampton T
Preston NE v Blackpool
Walsall v Oldham Ath
Watford v AFC Bournemouth
Wycombe W v Millwall
York C v Southend U

Nationwide Football League Division 3
Barnet v Scarborough
Cambridge U v Swansea C
Cardiff C v Macclesfield T
Chester C v Colchester U
Hull C v Leyton Orient
Lincoln C v Peterborough U
Mansfield T v Hartlepool U
Notts Co v Torquay U
Rochdale v Exeter C
Rotherham U v Doncaster R
Scunthorpe U v Darlington
Shrewsbury T v Brighton & HA

Saturday 25 April 1998

FA Carling Premiership
Aston Villa v Bolton W
Barnsley v Arsenal
Blackburn R v Wimbledon
Chelsea v Liverpool
Crystal Palace v Manchester U
Derby Co v Leicester C
Everton v Sheffield W
Leeds U v Coventry C
Tottenham H v Newcastle U
West Ham U v Southampton

Nationwide Football League Division 1
Bury v Ipswich T
Charlton Ath v Tranmere R
Crewe Alex v Bradford C
Manchester C v QPR
Norwich C v Swindon T
Nottingham F v Reading
Oxford U v Birmingham C
Port Vale v Middlesbrough
Portsmouth v Huddersfield T
Sheffield U v WBA
Sunderland v Stoke C
Wolverhampton W v Stockport Co

Nationwide Football League Division 2
AFC Bournemouth v Burnley
Blackpool v Bristol R
Brentford v Luton T
Bristol C v Walsall
Carlisle U v York C
Northampton T v Fulham
Oldham Ath v Southend U
Plymouth Arg v Gillingham
Watford v Grimsby T

Wigan Ath v Millwall
Wrexham v Preston NE
Wycombe W v Chesterfield

Nationwide Football League Division 3
Barnet v Mansfield T
Brighton & HA v Hull C
Cambridge U v Notts Co
Colchester U v Leyton Orient
Darlington v Lincoln C
Hartlepool U v Cardiff C
Macclesfield T v Chester C
Rotherham U v Rochdale
Scarborough v Shrewsbury T
Scunthorpe U v Exeter C
Swansea C v Doncaster R
Torquay U v Peterborough U

Saturday 2 May 1998

FA Carling Premiership
Arsenal v Everton
Bolton W v Crystal Palace
Coventry C v Blackburn R
Leicester C v Barnsley
Liverpool v West Ham U
Manchester U v Leeds U
Newcastle U v Chelsea
Sheffield W v Aston Villa
Southampton v Derby Co
Wimbledon v Tottenham H

Nationwide Football League Division 2
Bristol R v Brentford
Burnley v Plymouth Arg
Chesterfield v Blackpool
Fulham v Watford
Gillingham v Wigan Ath
Grimsby T v Oldham Ath
Luton T v Carlisle U
Millwall v AFC Bournemouth
Preston NE v Bristol C
Southend U v Wrexham
Walsall v Wycombe W
York C v Northampton T

Nationwide Football League Division 3
Cardiff C v Darlington
Chester C v Scarborough
Doncaster R v Colchester U
Exeter C v Macclesfield T
Hull C v Cambridge U
Leyton Orient v Torquay U
Lincoln C v Brighton & HA
Mansfield T v Swansea C
Notts Co v Rotherham U
Peterborough U v Hartlepool U
Rochdale v Barnet
Shrewsbury T v Scunthorpe U

Sunday 3 May 1998

Nationwide Football League Division 1
Birmingham C v Charlton Ath
Bradford C v Portsmouth
Huddersfield T v Port Vale
Ipswich T v Crewe Alex
Middlesbrough v Oxford U
QPR v Bury
Reading v Norwich C
Stockport Co v Sheffield U
Stoke C v Manchester C
Swindon T v Sunderland
Tranmere R v Wolverhampton W
WBA v Nottingham F

Sunday 10 May 1998

FA Carling Premiership
Aston Villa v Arsenal (4:00)
Barnsley v Manchester U (4:00)
Blackburn R v Newcastle U (4:00)
Chelsea v Bolton W (4:00)
Crystal Palace v Sheffield W (4:00)
Derby Co v Liverpool (4:00)
Everton v Coventry C (4:00)
Leeds U v Wimbledon (4:00)
Tottenham H v Southampton (4:00)
West Ham U v Leicester C (4:00)

FA CARLING PREMIERSHIP FIXTURES 1997–98

Copyright © The FA Premier League Ltd 1997. Copyright Licence No. NCH 10497. Compiled in association with SEMA Group.

	Arsenal	Aston Villa	Barnsley	Blackburn R	Bolton W	Chelsea	Coventry C	Crystal Palace	Derby Co	Everton	Leeds U	Leicester C	Liverpool	Manchester U	Newcastle U	Sheffield W	Southampton	Tottenham H	West Ham U	Wimbledon
Arsenal	—	26.10	4.10	13.12	13.9	7.2	11.8	21.2	7.3	2.5	10.1	26.12	30.11	9.11	11.4	28.3	31.1	30.8	24.9	18.4
Aston Villa	10.5	—	14.2	13.8	25.4	1.11	6.12	14.3	20.9	22.11	30.8	10.1	28.2	13.4	31.1	27.9	20.12	26.12	4.4	18.10
Barnsley	25.4	13.9	—	1.11	27.8	24.8	20.10	17.1	28.12	7.2	29.11	27.9	28.3	10.5	13.12	11.4	14.3	18.4	9.8	28.2
Blackburn R	13.4	17.1	7.3	—	6.12	22.11	28.9	28.12	9.8	8.11	14.9	28.2	23.8	4.4	10.5	25.8	18.10	7.2	20.12	25.4
Bolton W	14.2	4.10	26.12	11.4	—	26.10	10.1	2.5	14.12	1.9	18.4	28.3	1.11	20.9	1.12	14.3	10.1	23.9	21.2	29.11
Chelsea	21.9	7.3	31.1	28.3	10.5	—	10.1	14.2	29.11	26.11	13.12	18.10	25.4	28.2	27.9	18.4	30.8	11.4	9.11	26.12
Coventry C	17.1	11.4	21.2	2.5	23.8	9.8	—	24.9	28.3	25.10	4.10	29.11	18.4	28.12	29.11	7.2	13.9	13.12	27.8	7.3
Crystal Palace	18.10	8.11	12.8	30.8	27.9	13.9	20.12	—	18.4	10.1	31.1	11.4	13.12	25.4	29.11	10.5	26.12	28.3	7.3	7.2
Derby Co	1.11	7.2	30.8	10.1	13.4	4.4	18.4	20.12	—	13.9	14.3	25.4	10.5	18.10	26.12	28.2	27.9	31.1	23.8	13.8
Everton	27.9	28.3	20.9	14.3	20.12	13.4	22.11	20.12	14.2	—	11.4	20.9	26.8	27.9	28.2	25.4	2.11	7.3	23.11	13.12
Leeds U	9.8	28.12	4.4	14.2	20.12	13.4	4.4	6.12	8.11	6.12	—	20.9	26.8	23.8	18.10	17.1	28.2	7.3	23.11	10.5
Leicester C	27.8	9.8	2.5	28.3	9.8	18.10	29.11	11.4	20.9	20.9	7.2	—	17.1	23.8	27.9	17.1	14.4	13.9	27.10	10.11
Liverpool	4.4	22.9	22.11	24.9	7.3	5.10	20.12	13.4	25.10	21.2	26.12	13.8	—	6.12	31.8	13.9	7.2	8.11	2.5	10.1
Manchester U	14.3	15.2	22.11	25.10	7.2	24.9	30.8	4.10	21.2	26.12	2.5	31.1	6.12	—	18.4	1.11	22.11	10.1	13.9	28.3
Newcastle U	6.12	23.8	13.4	25.10	17.1	2.5	14.3	4.4	17.12	24.9	13.8	1.11	28.12	21.12	—	9.8	22.11	4.10	7.2	13.9
Sheffield W	22.11	2.5	8.12	26.12	8.11	20.12	14.2	25.10	24.9	4.10	13.8	30.8	14.2	7.3	10.1	—	4.4	21.2	13.4	31.1
Southampton	23.8	18.4	8.11	21.2	9.8	20.12	14.2	27.8	2.5	7.3	24.9	13.12	20.9	17.1	28.3	29.11	—	25.10	4.10	11.4
Tottenham H	28.12	27.8	20.12	20.9	9.8	6.12	27.8	24.11	23.8	4.4	1.11	14.2	14.3	10.8	25.4	19.10	10.5	—	17.1	27.9
West Ham U	28.2	29.11	10.1	18.4	18.10	14.3	3.11	11.4	31.1	28.3	10.5	27.9	14.2	20.9	13.2	25.4	13.8	17.1	—	30.8
Wimbledon	22.12	21.2	23.9	4.10	4.4	27.8	1.11	20.9	17.1	13.4	25.10	14.3	9.8	22.11	14.2	23.8	7.12	2.5	28.12	—

NATIONWIDE FOOTBALL LEAGUE FIXTURES 1997-98

Copyright © The Football League Ltd 1997. Copyright Licence No. NCH 10497. Compiled in association with SEMA Group.

DIVISION ONE

	Birmingham C	Bradford C	Bury	Charlton Ath	Crewe Alex	Huddersfield T	Ipswich T	Manchester C	Middlesbrough	Norwich C	Nottingham F	Oxford U	Port Vale	Portsmouth	QPR	Reading	Sheffield U	Stockport Co	Stoke C	Sunderland	Swindon T	Tranmere R	WBA	Wolverhampton W
Birmingham C	—	4.11	24.2	3.5	4.10	17.1	6.9	13.12	7.2	8.11	21.3	25.10	11.4	29.11	7.3	23.8	21.2	27.1	9.8	14.9	18.4	28.12	28.3	12.10
Bradford C	14.3	—	13.12	7.2	25.10	28.12	31.1	28.3	13.9	29.11	11.4	21.2	24.2	3.5	18.4	27.1	11.10	9.8	15.8	5.9	3.3	15.11	1.11	4.10
Bury	18.10	13.4	—	23.8	28.12	4.4	25.10	12.9	6.12	1.11	6.12	21.3	7.2	8.11	21.10	9.8	20.12	17.1	17.2	22.11	28.2	6.9	27.9	27.1
Charlton Ath	22.10	21.9	31.1	—	15.11	28.2	1.11	30.8	10.1	26.12	28.3	16.8	13.12	18.4	17.2	11.4	28.2	27.9	19.10	14.3	28.11	25.4	3.3	14.2
Crewe Alex	17.2	25.4	2.9	21.3	—	6.12	13.9	26.12	18.10	31.1	7.3	8.11	31.8	14.2	20.9	28.2	4.4	27.9	13.4	20.12	10.1	27.9	16.8	4.11
Huddersfield T	16.8	2.9	29.11	11.10	11.4	—	13.9	3.3	26.12	31.1	3.10	8.11	3.5	14.2	28.3	30.8	9.11	7.2	1.11	24.2	2.9	11.4	18.4	21.2
Ipswich T	26.12	31.1	25.10	7.3	3.5	14.2	—	4.10	17.8	21.2	29.11	24.2	18.4	25.10	10.1	28.3	30.8	9.11	20.9	11.10	2.9	11.4	30.8	21.3
Manchester C	13.4	28.2	28.1	9.8	6.9	7.11	17.8	—	20.12	20.9	28.12	7.3	4.11	9.8	25.4	18.10	21.3	4.4	22.10	23.8	27.9	22.8	28.2	6.12
Middlesbrough	20.9	14.2	11.4	9.8	25.2	9.9	17.8	4.11	—	21.3	11.10	3.5	25.10	5.11	8.11	13.12	5.10	28.12	23.8	21.2	28.3	28.1	29.11	7.3
Norwich C	4.3	4.4	1.11	6.9	23.8	13.4	18.2	18.4	20.12	—	17.1	22.11	13.9	30.12	28.2	22.10	6.12	18.10	20.12	28.1	25.4	18.2	14.3	9.8
Nottingham F	15.11	6.12	14.3	22.11	1.11	18.2	17.1	28.3	15.11	15.8	—	31.1	13.9	14.4	30.8	25.4	14.2	27.9	3.9	28.12	26.12	18.10	22.10	13.4
Oxford U	25.4	27.9	20.9	22.11	3.3	9.8	20.12	1.11	25.4	14.2	28.3	—	29.11	17.1	12.12	14.2	20.9	28.2	14.3	28.12	17.2	18.4	17.2	7.9
Port Vale	6.12	18.10	20.9	30.12	27.1	21.10	10.12	9.8	2.9	2.9	9.8	30.8	—	17.1	27.9	1.11	26.12	17.2	1.3	15.11	31.10	3.3	18.10	28.12
Portsmouth	4.4	20.12	3.3	7.2	7.2	18.2	4.3	10.1	30.8	11.10	28.1	14.4	16.8	—	26.12	28.12	25.2	23.8	15.11	6.12	14.3	17.1	13.9	4.4
QPR	7.3	18.4	21.10	17.2	20.9	30.8	25.4	28.3	5.11	28.2	30.8	12.12	27.9	17.1	—	14.2	31.1	21.3	11.4	18.10	15.11	17.1	13.9	29.11
Reading	31.1	30.8	10.1	6.12	11.10	18.2	3.5	24.10	13.4	3.5	24.10	13.9	7.3	28.3	18.10	—	4.11	8.11	4.4	10.8	13.12	7.2	26.12	20.12
Sheffield U	27.9	28.2	18.4	28.12	29.11	27.1	17.2	15.11	17.2	11.4	24.2	7.2	28.3	23.8	18.10	14.3	—	3.5	6.9	10.8	13.12	1.11	25.4	17.1
Stockport Co	29.8	10.1	16.8	21.2	28.3	20.9	14.3	29.11	2.9	24.2	18.4	11.10	26.12	4.10	31.1	3.3	3.5	—	14.2	1.11	15.11	13.9	11.4	25.10
Stoke C	10.1	16.1	4.10	25.2	13.12	7.3	7.2	3.5	31.1	18.4	30.8	5.11	12.10	11.4	21.3	29.11	26.12	13.9	—	25.10	30.8	28.3	3.9	8.11
Sunderland	14.2	26.12	28.3	4.11	18.4	18.10	28.2	16.8	28.9	30.8	8.11	2.9	31.1	21.3	11.4	17.2	10.1	13.4	25.4	—	21.10	29.11	13.12	20.9
Swindon T	20.12	8.11	11.10	4.4	9.8	23.8	28.12	21.2	22.11	4.10	6.12	8.11	4.10	21.3	5.11	21.10	16.8	20.9	7.3	3.5	—	14.2	13.9	25.2
Tranmere R	2.9	21.3	26.12	25.10	21.2	4.11	6.9	30.8	4.10	24.2	6.9	20.12	8.11	11.10	5.11	13.4	22.11	13.4	28.1	22.11	14.2	—	10.1	3.5
WBA	23.11	7.3	21.2	8.11	17.1	20.12	7.2	25.10	4.10	4.11	3.5	4.10	21.3	24.2	14.2	6.9	25.10	6.12	28.12	13.4	20.9	9.8	—	24.8
Wolverhampton W	28.2	18.2	30.8	13.9	14.3	27.9	10.1	11.4	1.11	10.1	14.12	26.12	3.9	28.3	29.11	18.4	16.8	25.4	4.3	7.2	18.10	22.10	31.1	—

NATIONWIDE FOOTBALL LEAGUE FIXTURES 1997–98

Copyright © The Football League Ltd 1997. Copyright Licence No. NCH 10497. Compiled in association with SEMA Group.

DIVISION TWO

Home \ Away	Blackpool	AFC Bournemouth	Brentford	Bristol C	Bristol R	Burnley	Carlisle U	Chesterfield	Fulham	Gillingham	Grimsby T	Luton T	Millwall	Northampton T	Oldham Ath	Plymouth Arg	Preston N E	Southend U	Walsall	Watford	Wigan Ath	Wrexham	Wycombe W	York C
Blackpool	—	17.1	13.4	3.1	25.4	8.11	6.9	21.10	28.2	21.3	18.10	9.8	14.2	4.11	20.9	2.12	20.12	27.9	4.4	7.3	31.1	28.12	23.8	22.11
AFC Bournemouth	30.8	—	1.11	7.2	2.9	25.4	22.11	14.2	18.10	26.12	27.9	13.9	21.10	10.1	24.1	3.3	28.2	18.11	14.4	20.12	16.8	14.3	4.4	2.12
Brentford	13.12	7.3	—	8.11	21.10	27.9	4.11	16.8	11.4	2.9	30.8	25.4	10.1	21.3	28.3	31.1	14.2	26.12	18.10	24.1	18.4	29.11	19.9	28.2
Bristol C	16.8	20.9	3.3	—	14.3	2.12	4.4	20.12	2.9	14.2	10.1	27.9	26.12	24.1	1.11	31.1	21.10	28.2	25.4	13.4	30.8	31.1	22.11	17.10
Bristol R	25.10	28.12	2.5	4.11	—	17.1	11.10	7.2	8.11	13.9	12.12	18.4	9.8	7.3	1.11	18.11	21.3	27.3	6.9	11.10	11.4	31.1	4.10	3.1
Burnley	3.3	25.10	21.2	11.4	30.8	—	11.10	26.12	18.4	16.8	28.3	14.1	18.11	30.8	2.9	9.8	20.9	24.1	1.11	16.8	13.12	24.2	4.10	31.1
Carlisle U	26.12	28.3	14.3	29.11	24.1	28.2	—	18.11	13.12	26.8	18.4	14.10	18.11	30.8	11.4	20.9	17.10	10.1	14.2	16.8	2.9	24.2	4.10	25.4
Chesterfield	2.5	4.10	3.1	18.4	9.8	6.9	21.3	—	7.3	4.1	8.11	13.12	3.3	11.4	24.2	17.1	23.8	10.1	9.8	31.1	21.2	1.11	31.1	28.12
Fulham	11.10	24.2	2.12	28.12	1.11	21.2	13.4	1.11	—	21.11	13.9	23.8	14.3	25.10	4.10	6.9	23.8	29.11	9.8	2.5	21.2	9.8	17.1	18.11
Gillingham	18.11	6.9	28.12	4.10	18.11	3.1	21.2	14.3	28.3	—	29.11	11.4	20.9	24.2	3.3	25.10	4.4	13.12	23.8	20.9	2.5	18.4	2.12	17.1
Grimsby T	24.2	21.2	17.1	9.8	21.2	22.11	20.12	3.3	31.1	4.4	—	18.11	2.9	11.10	2.5	3.1	9.8	1.11	3.12	25.10	4.10	23.8	7.3	6.9
Luton T	10.1	31.1	25.10	21.2	20.12	4.11	2.5	14.4	24.1	2.12	21.3	—	28.12	26.12	30.8	3.1	28.12	18.8	3.12	7.2	24.2	20.9	7.3	4.4
Millwall	4.10	2.5	9.8	6.9	4.4	17.1	8.11	22.11	5.11	2.12	21.3	28.12	—	21.2	11.10	13.4	8.11	13.9	3.12	25.2	25.10	17.1	20.12	23.8
Northampton T	14.3	9.8	18.11	23.8	4.4	1.11	17.1	2.12	25.4	18.10	7.2	6.9	27.9	—	31.1	20.12	13.4	14.2	28.12	21.3	20.9	3.3	3.1	21.10
Oldham Ath	7.2	23.8	22.11	7.3	27.9	28.12	2.12	18.10	14.2	8.11	7.2	17.1	28.2	13.9	—	4.4	6.9	25.4	19.12	21.3	4.11	3.1	13.4	9.8
Plymouth Arg	11.4	8.11	13.9	21.3	10.1	21.10	7.2	30.8	26.12	25.4	2.9	28.2	13.12	18.4	29.11	—	7.3	18.10	27.9	2.9	24.1	28.3	4.11	14.2
Preston N E	18.4	11.10	4.10	2.5	18.11	7.2	24.2	24.1	29.11	10.1	2.9	3.3	16.8	13.12	26.12	1.11	—	11.4	13.9	30.8	28.3	25.10	21.2	14.3
Southend U	21.2	21.3	6.9	11.10	22.11	23.8	9.8	3.4	29.11	13.4	7.3	3.1	31.1	4.10	25.10	24.2	2.12	—	17.1	4.11	8.11	2.5	28.12	19.12
Walsall	29.11	13.12	24.2	25.10	26.12	7.3	4.10	10.1	16.8	24.1	7.2	28.3	11.4	2.9	18.4	21.2	31.1	30.8	—	8.11	21.3	11.10	2.5	20.9
Watford	1.11	18.4	20.12	13.12	2.12	9.8	3.1	13.9	13.12	7.2	25.4	14.2	28.12	28.3	18.11	28.12	17.1	14.3	3.3	—	29.11	11.4	6.9	27.9
Wigan Ath	13.9	4.11	17.1	17.1	14.2	9.8	28.12	28.2	27.9	20.12	24.1	18.10	25.4	7.2	14.3	22.11	25.4	21.10	18.11	4.4	—	8.9	9.8	13.4
Wrexham	2.9	4.11	4.4	13.9	14.2	18.10	7.3	27.9	10.1	20.12	24.1	7.2	30.9	8.11	16.8	22.11	25.4	2.9	28.2	2.12	26.12	—	21.3	3.3
Wycombe W	24.1	29.11	7.2	28.3	18.10	14.2	13.9	25.4	30.8	28.2	10.4	1.11	18.4	16.8	13.12	22.11	27.9	2.9	21.10	26.12	10.1	18.11	—	8.11
York C	28.3	11.4	11.10	24.2	16.8	13.9	25.10	2.9	21.3	30.8	26.12	29.11	24.1	2.5	10.1	4.10	4.11	18.4	7.2	21.2	7.3	13.12	8.11	—

NATIONWIDE FOOTBALL LEAGUE FIXTURES 1997–98

DIVISION THREE

	Barnet	Brighton & H A	Cambridge U	Cardiff C	Chester C	Colchester U	Darlington	Doncaster R	Exeter C	Hartlepool U	Hull C	Leyton O	Lincoln C	Macclesfield T	Mansfield T	Notts Co	Peterborough U	Rochdale	Rotherham U	Scarborough	Scunthorpe U	Shrewsbury T	Swansea C	Torquay U
Barnet	—	14.3	31.1	14.2	30.8	24.1	29.11	8.11	16.8	28.3	18.10	11.4	27.9	13.12	25.4	1.11	26.12	21.10	10.1	18.4	20.9	28.2	2.9	18.11
Brighton & H A	5.11	—	21.3	22.11	28.2	26.12	13.9	14.2	18.10	7.3	25.4	30.8	22.10	16.8	13.4	3.12	3.9	27.9	8.11	24.1	4.4	20.12	10.1	7.2
Cambridge U	13.9	18.11	—	27.9	24.1	2.9	28.3	7.2	12.12	29.11	21.10	26.12	14.2	3.3	28.2	25.4	11.4	18.10	16.8	10.1	14.3	30.8	18.4	1.11
Cardiff C	4.10	28.3	21.2	—	16.8	11.4	2.5	7.2	14.3	25.10	26.12	10.1	7.2	18.4	24.1	30.8	13.12	18.10	13.9	24.2	11.10	2.9	2.11	8.11
Chester C	17.1	11.10	23.8	3.1	—	18.4	13.12	11.4	29.11	25.10	18.11	6.9	9.8	25.10	7.2	14.3	18.11	1.11	21.2	2.5	28.12	13.9	28.3	24.2
Colchester U	22.8	6.9	29.12	2.12	18.4	—	9.8	21.10	27.9	3.1	6.9	20.12	22.11	14.3	13.2	14.2	27.2	3.3	3.4	12.9	31.10	13.9	6.2	16.1
Darlington	4.4	31.1	22.11	21.10	10.1	9.8	—	18.10	3.1	21.9	1.11	18.11	22.11	26.12	27.9	14.2	3.3	28.2	30.8	2.9	20.12	18.10	16.8	14.3
Doncaster R	3.3	4.10	20.9	4.11	13.4	2.5	11.10	—	30.8	11.10	4.4	2.9	21.3	24.1	27.9	13.4	16.8	22.11	19.12	6.3	30.1	3.3	24.10	21.2
Exeter C	3.1	24.2	13.4	6.9	14.2	30.8	10.1	30.8	—	9.8	2.12	18.10	10.1	28.12	18.11	24.1	27.9	14.3	18.4	26.12	3.3	27.9	14.3	2.9
Hartlepool U	22.11	1.11	4.4	5.4	14.2	16.8	9.8	17.1	30.8	—	2.12	18.10	13.4	30.8	20.12	2.9	21.10	18.11	24.1	26.12	3.3	27.9	14.3	13.9
Hull C	24.2	25.10	2.5	21.3	26.12	13.12	11.10	28.2	10.1	2.12	—	18.4	13.9	28.3	10.1	16.8	24.1	7.2	23.8	11.10	21.2	8.11	30.8	4.10
Leyton O	2.12	2.5	6.9	9.8	8.11	25.10	21.3	13.9	11.4	21.10	20.12	—	7.3	4.10	4.4	22.11	7.2	23.8	14.3	28.12	3.1	9.8	13.9	2.5
Lincoln C	21.2	2.5	4.10	20.9	10.1	28.3	4.4	18.11	14.2	11.4	31.1	7.3	—	29.11	2.9	24.1	18.4	27.9	7.3	30.8	24.2	4.10	13.9	11.10
Macclesfield T	13.4	3.1	8.11	23.8	11.10	4.11	13.12	17.1	11.4	14.2	22.11	9.8	4.4	—	18.10	28.2	27.9	28.12	4.11	7.2	2.12	21.3	13.9	9.8
Mansfield T	25.10	13.12	11.10	23.8	25.10	4.11	18.4	13.12	17.1	11.4	9.8	3.1	29.11	24.2	—	31.1	28.3	3.1	2.5	8.11	17.1	7.3	24.2	18.4
Notts Co	7.3	11.4	25.10	17.1	7.3	21.3	24.1	23.8	9.8	14.2	9.8	22.11	24.1	28.2	18.10	—	31.1	9.8	4.4	8.11	6.9	7.2	24.2	18.4
Peterborough U	6.9	28.12	2.12	23.8	20.9	3.3	3.3	6.9	27.9	28.3	3.1	24.2	11.10	24.2	18.10	31.1	—	29.11	31.1	11.4	17.1	9.8	4.10	25.10
Rochdale	2.5	21.2	24.2	13.4	3.1	13.2	28.2	21.3	23.8	2.5	23.8	20.9	24.1	4.11	11.10	4.4	—	17.1	25.10	11.4	4.10	4.11	4.10	25.10
Rotherham U	9.8	3.3	3.1	31.1	27.9	3.4	21.3	28.3	18.4	6.9	28.2	24.1	4.11	2.9	16.8	10.1	30.8	25.4	—	25.10	18.11	21.10	11.4	13.12
Scarborough	19.12	12.8	9.8	3.4	7.3	12.9	23.8	3.1	18.4	9.8	28.2	14.3	17.1	2.9	16.8	10.1	13.9	2.12	22.11	—	28.3	25.4	18.11	3.1
Scunthorpe U	7.2	29.11	4.11	28.2	2.9	31.10	21.2	13.9	9.8	8.11	27.9	16.8	18.10	11.4	30.8	26.12	10.1	14.2	21.3	13.4	—	21.10	24.1	28.3
Shrewsbury T	11.10	18.4	17.1	28.12	24.2	25.10	11.4	21.2	28.3	3.3	3.3	6.9	18.11	18.11	1.11	20.9	14.3	6.9	4.10	25.10	2.5	—	29.11	23.8
Swansea C	28.12	9.8	20.12	7.3	31.1	28.12	9.8	25.4	28.2	27.9	3.3	13.4	8.11	31.1	21.10	18.10	14.2	13.4	2.12	21.3	23.8	4.4	—	6.9
Torquay U	21.3	20.9	7.3	3.3	18.10	30.8	31.1	27.9	2.9	13.9	14.2	21.10	18.10	10.1	2.12	20.12	25.4	4.4	13.4	16.8	22.11	24.1	26.12	—

OTHER FIXTURES – SEASON 1997–98

August

3 Sun   Littlewoods FA Charity Shield
9 Sat   Commencement of FA Premier League and Football League
13 Wed   Euro Comps Prel (1)
         FL Coca-Cola Cup 1st Rd (1)
20 Wed   Northern Ireland v Germany (WC)
         Republic of Ireland v Lithuania (WC)
         Turkey v Wales (WC)
27 Wed   Euro Comps Prel (2)
         FL Coca-Cola Cup 1st Rd (2)
30 Sat   FA Cup Sponsored by Littlewoods Prel Rd

September

6 Sat   Iceland v Republic of Ireland
         Scotland v Belarus
         FA Carlsberg Vase 1st Rd Qual
         FA Youth Cup Extra Prel Rd*
7 Sun   UK Living FA Women's FA Cup Prel Rd
10 Wed   Albania v Northern Ireland (WC)
         England v Moldova (WC)
         Lithuania v Republic of Ireland (WC)
13 Sat   FA Cup Sponsored by Littlewoods 1st Rd Qual
17 Wed   Euro Comps 1st Rd (1)
         FL Coca-Cola Cup 2nd Rd (1)
20 Sat   FA Youth Cup Prel Rd*
24 Wed   FL Coca-Cola Cup 2nd Rd (2)
27 Sat   FA Cup Sponsored by Littlewoods 2nd Rd Qual
28 Sun   UK Living FA Women's Cup 1st Rd

October

1 Wed   Euro Comps 1st Rd (2)
4 Sat   FA Carlsberg Vase 2nd Rd Qual
11 Sat   FA Cup Sponsored by Littlewoods 3rd Rd Qual
         FA Youth Cup 1st Rd Qual Rd*
         FA County Youth Cup 1st Rd*
         Belgium v Wales (WC)
         Italy v England (WC)
         Portugal v Northern Ireland (WC)
         Republic of Ireland v Romania (WC)
         Scotland v Latvia (WC)
15 Wed   FL Coca-Cola Cup 3rd Rd
18 Sat   FA Umbro Trophy 1st Rd Qual
22 Wed   Euro Comps 2nd Rd (1)
25 Sat   FA Cup Sponsored by Littlewoods 4th Rd Qual
26 Sun   FA Sunday Cup 1st Rd
29 Wed   FL Coca-Cola Cup 3rd Rd (Replays)
         Possible World Cup Play-Off

November

1 Sat   FA Carlsberg Vase 1st Rd Proper
         FA Youth Cup 2nd Rd Qual*
2 Sun   UK Living Women's FA Cup 2nd Rd
5 Wed   Euro Comps 2nd Rd (2)

8 Sat   FA Umbro Trophy 2nd Rd Qual
15 Sat   FA Cup Sponsored by Littlewoods 1st Rd Proper
         Possible World Cup Play-Off
19 Wed   International
         FL Coca-Cola Cup 4th Rd
22 Sat   FA Carlsberg Vase 2nd Rd Proper
         FA Youth Cup 1st Rd Proper*
         FA County Youth Cup 2nd Rd*
23 Sun   FA Sunday Cup 2nd Rd
26 Wed   FA Cup Sponsored by Littlewoods 1st Rd Proper Replays
         Euro Comps 3rd Rd (1)
29 Sat   FA Umbro Trophy 3rd Rd Qual
30 Sun   UK Living Women's FA Cup 3rd Rd

December

3 Wed   FL Coca-Cola Cup 4th Rd (Replay)
6 Sat   FA Cup Sponsored by Littlewoods 2nd Rd Proper
10 Wed   Euro Comps 3rd Rd (2)
13 Sat   FA Carlsberg Vase 3rd Rd Proper
         FA Youth Cup 2nd Rd Proper*
14 Sun   FA Sunday Cup 3rd Rd
17 Wed   FA Cup Sponsored by Littlewoods 2nd Rd Proper Replays
         International

January 1998

3 Sat   FA Cup Sponsored by Littlewoods 3rd Rd Proper
4 Sun   UK Living Women's FA Cup 4th Rd
7 Wed   FL Coca-Cola Cup 5th Rd
         Auto Windscreens Shield (2)
10 Sat   FA Umbro Trophy 1st Rd Proper
         FA Youth Cup 3rd Rd Proper*
         FA County Youth Cup 3rd Rd*
11 Sun   FA Sunday Cup 4th Rd
14 Wed   FA Cup Sponsored by Littlewoods 3rd Rd Proper Replays
         International
17 Sat   FA Carlsberg Vase 4th Rd Proper
21 Wed   FL Coca-Cola Cup 5th Rd Replays
24 Sat   FA Cup Sponsored by Littlewoods 4th Rd Proper
31 Sat   FA Umbro Trophy 2nd Rd Proper

February

1 Sun   UK Living Women's FA Cup 5th Rd
4 Wed   FA Cup Sponsored by Littlewoods 4th Rd Proper Replays
7 Sat   FA Carlsberg Vase 5th Rd Proper
8 Sun   FA Sunday Cup 5th Rd
11 Wed   International
14 Sat   FA Cup Sponsored by Littlewoods 5th Rd Proper
         FA Youth Cup 4th Rd Proper*
         FA County Youth Cup 4th Rd*
18 Wed   FL Coca-Cola Cup Semi-Finals (1)
21 Sat   FA Umbro Trophy 3rd Rd Proper
22 Sun   FL Coca-Cola Cup Semi-Finals (2)

| 25 Wed | FA Cup Sponsored by Littlewoods 5th Rd Proper Replays |
| 28 Sat | FA Carlsberg Vase 6th Rd Proper |

March

1 Sun	UK Living Women's FA Cup 6th Rd
4 Wed	Euro Comps Quarter-Finals (1)
7 Sat	FA Cup Sponsored by Littlewoods 6th Rd Proper
	FA Youth Cup 5th Rd Proper*
14 Sat	FA Umbro Trophy 4th Rd Proper
	FA Carlsberg Vase Semi-Finals (1)
	FA County Youth Cup Semi-Finals*
15 Sun	FA Sunday Cup Semi-Final
18 Wed	Euro Comps Quarter-Finals (2)
	FA Cup Sponsored by Littlewoods 6th Rd Proper Replays
21 Sat	FA Carlsberg Vase Semi-Finals (2)
25 Wed	INTERNATIONAL
28 Sat	FA Umbro Trophy Semi-Finals (1)
29 Sun	UK Living Women's FA Cup Semi-Finals
	FL Coca-Cola Cup Final

April

1 Wed	Euro Comps Semi-Finals (1)
4 Sat	FA Umbro Trophy Semi-Finals (2)
	FA Youth Cup Semi-Finals*
5 Sun	FA Cup Sponsored by Littlewoods Semi-Finals
8 Wed	FA Cup Sponsored by Littlewoods Semi-Final Replay (prov)
15 Wed	Euro Comps Semi-Finals (2)
	FA Cup Sponsored by Littlewoods Semi-Final Replay (prov)

19 Sun	Auto Windscreens Shield Final
22 Wed	International
25 Sat	FA County Youth Final (fixed date)
26 Sun	FA Sunday Cup Final
29 Wed	UEFA Cup Final (1)

May

2 Sat	Final matches in Football League
3 Sun	UK Living Women's FA Cup Final
6 Wed	UEFA Cup Winners Cup Final
9 Sat	Final matches in FA Premier League
	FA Carlsberg Vase Final – Wembley Stadium
	FA Youth Cup Final*
10 Sun	FA Umbro Trophy Final – Wembley Stadium
	FL Play-off Semi-Finals (1)
13 Wed	UEFA Cup Final (2)
	FL Play-off Semi-Finals (2)
16 Sat	FA Cup Sponsored by Littlewoods Final – Wembley Stadium
20 Wed	UEFA Champions Cup Final
21 Thu	FA Cup Sponsored by Littlewoods Final replay – Wembley Stadium
23 Sat	FL Play-off Final Division 3
24 Sun	FL Play-off Final Division 2
25 Mon	FL Play-off Final Division 1

June

| 10 Wed | Commencement of World Cup Final |

July

| 12 Sun | World Cup Final |

*closing date of rounds

STOP PRESS

Brighton rocked by League expulsion threat ... FIFA complicate the Ronaldo move ... FA School of Excellence gates may close in two years ... Red/yellow monopoly hit by 'Get out of Jail' cards for good behaviour ... Seaside incursion: Alvin Martin becomes Southend manager ... Germany beat Italy 2-0 in Women's Euro Final ... Manchester United hope £4m Brazilian Celio Silva of Corinthians will be no casual signing ... Premier League aim for only two down ... Sheffield United not keen on Howard's way, take legal action over Everton and ex-boss Kendall ... Tennis supremo David Lloyd bids to trawl Hull into his net ... Ian Wright fined £15,000 by the FA for poor discipline ... Liverpool's £4.2m Paul Ince pinch ... Stuart Pearce joins Newcastle ... Welsh legend Ivor Allchurch dies at 67 ... World Cup: Bolivia 1, Uruguay 0; Argentina 2, Venezuela 0; Colombia 1, Ecuador 0; Chile 2, Paraguay 1 ... Juninho back in Brazilian squad after £12m Atletico Madrid move.

Transfers:– Paul Merson, Arsenal to Middlesbrough £5m; Marc Overmars, Ajax to Arsenal £5m; Emmanuel Petit and Gilles Grimandi, both Monaco to Arsenal £5m; Lorenzo Amoruso, Fiorentina to Rangers £3.9m; Marco Negri, Perugia to Rangers £3.7m; Oyvind Leonhardsen, Wimbledon to Liverpool £3.5m; Teddy Sheringham, Tottenham H to Manchester U £3.5m; David Hopkin, Crystal Palace to Leeds U £3.25m; Sergio Porrini, Juventus to Rangers £3m.

Other moves completed and pending:– Anders Andersson, Malmo to Blackburn R; Andy Arnott, Leyton Orient to Fulham; Andre Arendse, Cape Town to Fulham; Celestine Babayaro, Anderlecht to Chelsea; Patrick Blondeau, Monaco to Sheffield W; Steve Blatherwick, Nottingham F to Burnley; Luis Boamorte, Sporting Lisbon to Arsenal; Eyal Berkovic, Southampton to West Ham U; Vassilis Borbokis, AEK Athens to Sheffield U; Chris Byrne, Macclesfield T to Sunderland; Tony Battersby, Notts Co to Bury; Ian Bryson, Preston NE to Rochdale; Thierry Bonalair, Neuchatel Xamax to Nottingham F; Scott Booth, Aberdeen to Borussia Dortmund; David Connolly, Watford to Feyenoord; Iyseden Christie, Coventry C to Mansfield T; Lee Clark, Newcastle U to Sunderland; Andy Couzens, Leeds U to Carlisle U; Ian Crook, Norwich C to Hiroshima; Simon Clark, Peterborough U to Leyton Orient; Ed de Goey, Feyenoord to Chelsea; Julian Darby, WBA to Preston NE; Martin Dahlin, Roma to Blackburn R; Sean Dyche, Chesterfield to Bristol C; Chris Day, Crystal Palace to Watford; Stefan Eranio, AC Milan to Derby Co; Robbie Elliott, Newcastle U to Bolton W; Scott Fitzgerald, Wimbledon to Millwall; Craig Forrest, Ipswich T to West Ham U; Craig Fleming, Oldham Ath to Norwich C; Tore Andre Flo, Brann to Chelsea; Mark Ford, Leeds U to Burnley; Gareth Farrelly, Aston Villa to Everton; Shaun Gale, Barnet to Exeter C; Shay Given, Blackburn R to Newcastle U; Scott Green, Bolton W to Wigan Ath; Simon Grayson, Leicester C to Aston Villa; David Ginola, Newcastle U to Tottenham H; Paul Groves, WBA to Grimsby T; Arnar Gunnlaugsson, Akranes to Bolton W; Jimmy Floyd Hasselbaink, Boavista to Leeds U; Gary Hanmer, WBA to Shrewsbury T; Simon Haworth, Cardiff C to Coventry C; Steve Hayward, Carlisle U to Fulham; Ceri Hughes, Luton T to Wimbledon; Magnus Hedman, AIK to Coventry C; Matt Holmes, Blackburn R to Charlton Ath; Georgi Hristov, Partizan Belgrade to Barnsley; Tony Hey, Fortuna Cologne to Birmingham C; Jonathan Hunt, Birmingham C to Derby Co; Barry Hayles, Stevenage to Bristol R; Mark Hottiger, Everton to Lausanne; Alf-Inge Haaland, Nottingham F to Leeds U; Richard Hughes, Atalanta to Arsenal; Lee Harper, Arsenal to QPR; Ian Hathaway, Torquay U to Colchester U; Mike Harle, Millwall to Barnet; Hermann Hreidarsson, IBV to Crystal Palace; Andrew Impey, QPR to West Ham U; Martin Johansen, FC Copenhagen to Coventry C; Eoin Jess, Coventry C to Aberdeen; Paul Jones, Stockport Co to Southampton; Darren Jackson, Hibs to Celtic; Andy Johnson, Norwich C to Nottingham F; Lee Jones, Liverpool to Tranmere Rovers; Peter Kennedy, Notts Co to Watford; George Koch, Fortuna Dusseldorf to Rangers; Ales Krizan, Branik Maribor to Barnsley; Temuri Ketsbaia, AEK Athens to Newcastle U; Kevin Kilbane, Preston NE to WBA; Bernard Lambourde, Bordeaux to Chelsea; Kyle Lightbourne, Walsall to Coventry C; Lars Lees, Leverkusen to Barnsley; Jason Lee, Nottingham F to Watford; Neil Lewis, Leicester C to Peterborough U; David Lee, Bolton W to Wigan Ath; Jamie Lawrence, Leicester C to Bradford C; Jim Leighton, Hibernian to Aberdeen; Jehad Muntasser, Atalanta to Arsenal; Chris Marsh, Walsall to Chesterfield; Darren Moore, Doncaster R to Bradford C; Kevin Miller, Watford to Crystal Palace; Paul Moody, Oxford U to Fulham; Ian McGuckin, Hartlepool U to Fulham; Jim McInally, Dundee U to Dundee; Alberto Mendez, Feucht to Arsenal; Scott Minto, Chelsea to Benfica; Alex Manninger, Salzburg to Arsenal; Neil Moss, Southampton to Stockport Co; Danny Murphy, Crewe Alex to Liverpool; Antti Niemi, FC Copenhagen to Rangers; Eric Nevland, Viking Stavanger to Manchester U; Peter Ndlovu, Coventry C to Birmingham C; Aidan Newhouse, Wimbledon to Fulham; Mike Newell, Birmingham C to Aberdeen; Lee Nogan, Reading to Grimsby T; Kevin Nugent, Bristol C to Cardiff C; John Oster, Grimsby T to Everton; Mark Patterson, Sheffield U to Burnley; Gary Parkinson, Burnley to Preston NE; Jason Perry, Cardiff C to Bristol R; Marco Pascolo, Cagliari to Nottingham F; Kevin Phillips, Watford to Sunderland; Mark Prudhoe, Stoke C to Bradford C; Gustavo Poyet, Zaragoza to Chelsea; Gary Porter, Watford to Walsall; Jimmy Quinn, Reading to Peterborough U; Mark Robson, Charlton Ath to Notts Co; Alan Rogers, Tranmere R to Nottingham F; Bruno Riberio, Vitoria Setubal to Leeds U; Iwan Roberts, Wolverhampton W to Norwich C; David Robertson, Rangers to Leeds U; Staale Stensaas, Rosenborg to Rangers; Steve Sedgley, Ipswich T to Wolverhampton W; Paul Stewart, Sunderland to Stoke C; Dick Schreuder, RKC to Stoke C; Mike Sheron, Stoke C to QPR; Lee Sinnott, Huddersfield T to Oldham Ath; David Seal, Bristol C to Northampton T; Trond Egil Soltvedt, Rosenborg to Coventry C; Robert Steiner, Norrkoping to Bradford C; Dean Smith, Hereford U to Leyton Orient; Aaron Skelton, Luton T to Colchester U; Jon Dahl Tomasson, Heerenveen to Newcastle U; Eric Tinkler, Cagliari to Barnsley; Lee Todd, Stockport Co to Southampton; Geoff Thomas, Wolverhampton W to Nottingham F; David Thomas, Swansea C to Watford; Andy Thompson, Wolverhampton W to Tranmere R; David Terrier, Metz to West Ham U; Tony Vaughan, Ipswich T to Manchester C; Patrick Valery, Bastia to Blackburn R; Mark Venus, Wolverhampton W to Ipswich T; Michael Williams, Sheffield W to Burnley; Phil Whelan, Middlesbrough to Oxford U; Gerard Welkens, Veendam to Manchester C; Chris Woods, Sunderland to Burnley; Peter Wilding, Telford U to Shrewsbury T; Edwin Zoetebier, Volendam to Sunderland.

Coaching moves:– Ray Houghton Crystal Palace to Reading as player-coach; Phil Bater replaces Geoff Twentyman as first team coach at Bristol R.

Bolton's new ground:– Reebok Stadium, Burnden Way, Lostock, Bolton BL6 6JW.